1233 - 1268

W9-BUE-793

WEST ACADEMIC PUBLISHING'S LAW SCHOOL ADVISORY BOARD

JESSE H. CHOPER
Professor of Law and Dean Emeritus,
University of California, Berkeley

JOSHUA DRESSLER
Professor of Law, Michael E. Moritz College of Law,
The Ohio State University

YALE KAMISAR
Professor of Law Emeritus, University of San Diego
Professor of Law Emeritus, University of Michigan

MARY KAY KANE
Professor of Law, Chancellor and Dean Emeritus,
University of California,
Hastings College of the Law

LARRY D. KRAMER
President, William and Flora Hewlett Foundation

JONATHAN R. MACEY
Professor of Law, Yale Law School

ARTHUR R. MILLER
University Professor, New York University
Formerly Bruce Bromley Professor of Law, Harvard University

GRANT S. NELSON
Professor of Law, Pepperdine University
Professor of Law Emeritus, University of California, Los Angeles

A. BENJAMIN SPENCER
Professor of Law,
Washington & Lee University School of Law

JAMES J. WHITE
Professor of Law, University of Michigan

LAW AND THE MENTAL HEALTH SYSTEM

CIVIL AND CRIMINAL ASPECTS

Sixth Edition

■ ■ ■

By

Christopher Slobogin
Milton Underwood Professor of Law
Vanderbilt University

Thomas L. Hafemeister
Independent

Douglas Mossman
Department of Psychiatry and Behavioral Neuroscience
University of Cincinnati College of Medicine

Ralph Reisner
Professor of Law, Emeritus
University of Illinois–Champaign

AMERICAN CASEBOOK SERIES®

Mat #41059397

The publisher is not engaged in rendering legal or other professional advice, and this publication is not a substitute for the advice of an attorney. If you require legal or other expert advice, you should seek the services of a competent attorney or other professional.

American Casebook Series is a trademark registered in the U.S. Patent and Trademark Office.

COPYRIGHT © 1985, 1990 WEST PUBLISHING CO.
© West, a Thomson business, 1999, 2004, 2009
© 2014 LEG, Inc. d/b/a West Academic Publishing
  444 Cedar Street, Suite 700
  St. Paul, MN 55101
  1-877-888-1330

West, West Academic Publishing, and West Academic are trademarks of West Publishing Corporation, used under license.

Printed in the United States of America

ISBN: 978–0–314–26729–0

To Cindy

   —Christopher Slobogin

To Shelly, Jackson, & Katriana

   —Thomas L. Hafemeister

*For the students who will become more
capable and compassionate attorneys
through the materials contained
in this book*
   —Douglas Mossman

To Danute

   —Ralph Reisner

PREFACE

This sixth edition of Law and the Mental Health System continues to pursue the objectives of the first five editions. First, we want to provide students with a clear picture of past, present, and possible future legal doctrine, along with examples of the clinical and empirical literature, in three major topic areas: the delivery of mental health services, the regulation of the mental health professions, and the relationship between society and people with mental disorders.* Second, in each of these areas, we provide insights into how and to what degree the legal system can implement desired social objectives. Third, we aim to sensitize readers not only to the views of courts, legislatures, regulatory agencies, and lawyers on these issues, but also to the (often-competing) perspectives of both mental health professionals and the persons they serve.**

The book retains its three-part organization, which has been updated extensively with new legal, empirical, and critical material through 2013. Part I, "Mental Health Treatment and the Therapeutic Relationship," examines the role of the legal system in promoting the quality of mental health treatment services and in protecting the autonomy, privacy and well-being of those who seek such treatment. Chapter One provides background information about mental disorders, the diagnostic process, the types of mental health treatment, mental health professionals, and the economics of mental health care. This chapter thus serves as a backdrop not only to the chapters in Part I but to the other chapters of the book. The remaining chapters in Part I explore administrative licensing and regulation of the mental health professions (Chapter Two), the application of malpractice law (Chapter Three), informed consent doctrine (Chapter Four), and confidentiality (Chapter Five).

---

* Courts, legislatures and scholars refer to the mental conditions of the individuals who are the primary topic of this book by many names: "mental disorder," "mental disability," and "mental illness" are the most common. As Chapter One suggests, each of these terms can be stigmatizing in its own way. They are used interchangeably throughout the book, depending on the context and the laws being discussed, although the preference is for "mental disorder," the broader and arguably more neutral term. Additionally, to emphasize that a mental condition is just one aspect of a person, we use phrases such as "persons with a mental disorder" rather than "the mentally disordered."

** Most statutes and cases refer to the individuals who receive mental health treatment as "patients." So do most medical providers (in this book's context, psychiatric physicians and nurses), who believe the term acknowledges the vulnerability of the persons they treat and their duty to look out for the welfare of persons under their care. However, some persons who receive mental health treatment and many treatment providers, especially those outside the medical profession, prefer the term "client," which they view as less paternalistic and stigmatizing or more appropriate for individuals outside a hospital setting. In the past couple of decades, many recipients of treatment and their advocates have also used the word "consumer" to emphasize the idea that the treatment recipient is (or should be) in control of the treatment process. This book uses these terms, particularly the first two, interchangeably.

Part II, "Deprivations of Liberty and Property," switches the focus to state intervention into the lives of people with mental disorders. Chapter Six examines the preliminary issue of how well mental health professionals can identify mental disorders and their consequences. The next three chapters provide materials on laws affecting individuals with mental disorders who are charged with or convicted of crimes (Chapter Seven), who are thought to be in need of hospitalization (Chapter Eight), and who are believed to be incompetent to exercise control over their own persons or property (Chapter Nine). Chapter Ten ends Part II with an exploration of issues that arise in treating persons with mental disorders who have been the subject of state intervention.

Part III, "Benefits Eligibility and Legal Protection Against Discrimination," examines a number of laws meant to benefit all people with mental disorders, whether or not the state has acted to deprive them of liberty or property. Chapter Eleven looks at federal benefit programs connected with education and Social Security. Chapter Twelve discusses laws that attempt to prevent discrimination against people with mental disorders, including the Americans with Disabilities Act and the Federal Housing Act.

With this edition, two new authors join the book. Professor Thomas Hafemeister, who has degrees in both law and social psychology, has taught at the University of Virginia, Chicago-Kent, William & Mary and the University of Nebraska law schools. Dr. Douglas Mossman, teaches at the University of Cincinnati College of Medicine as a member of the Department of Psychiatry and Behavioral Neuroscience. They join Christopher Slobogin, who occupies the Milton Underwood chair at Vanderbilt University, where he is also an Affiliate Professor of Psychiatry, and Ralph Reisner, who co-authored earlier editions of the book.

The authors wish to acknowledge the help of several individuals in producing this book or its earlier editions: Frank Bloch, Vanderbilt University Law School; Shaun Boedicker, University of Virginia law student; Professor Richard Bonnie, University of Virginia Law School; Professor Nancy Ehrenreich, Denver Law School; Alex Hurder, Vanderbilt University Law School; Professor John Monahan, University of Virginia Law School; Professor Stephen Morse, University of Pennsylvania Law School; Patrick Mulligan, University of Virginia law student; Professor Michael Perlin, New York Law School; John Petrila, University of South Florida; Professor Elyn Saks, University of Southern California; Professor Elizabeth Scott, Columbia University Law School; and Professor David Wexler, University of Puerto Rico and Arizona Law Schools.

CHRISTOPHER SLOBOGIN, J.D., LL.M.

THOMAS L. HAFEMEISTER, J.D., PH.D.

DOUGLAS MOSSMAN, M.D.

October 1, 2013

ACKNOWLEDGMENTS

The authors wish to acknowledge, with gratitude, permission to reprint the following copyrighted materials.

From DIAGNOSTIC AND STATISTICAL MANUAL OF MENTAL DISORDERS, 5TH EDITION. Reprinted with permission from the Diagnostic and Statistical Manual of Mental Disorders, 5th Edition. Washington, DC, American Psychiatric Association, 2013.

The Politics of Hysteria, by Joan Acocella, from THE NEW YORKER, April 6, 1998, p. 64, 66. Copyright © 1998. Reprinted by permission of Joan Acocella.

From MANAGEMENT OF MENTAL HEALTH AND SUBSTANCE ABUSE SERVICES: STATE OF THE ART AND EARLY RESULTS, by David Mechanic, Mark Schlesinger, and Donna D. McAlpine, 3/22/95. Reprinted by permission of Blackwell Publishers.

Managed Care and the Evolving Role of the Clinical Social Worker in Mental Health, by Jeffrey Cohen, 48 SOCIAL WORK 34 (2003). Copyright © 2003, National Association of Social Workers, Inc. Reprinted by permission of the National Association of Social Workers.

All Illnesses are (Not) Created Equal: Reforming Federal Mental Health Insurance Law, by Stacey A. Tovino, 49 HARVARD JOURNAL OF LEGLISATION 1 (2012). Reprinted with permission. Licensing Mental Therapists, by D. Hogan, from The New York Times, July 18, 1979. Copyright © 1979 by The New York Times Company. Reprinted by permission of the New York Times, Inc.

Occupational Licensing: A Framework for Analysis, by Jonathon Rose, 1979 ARIZONA STATE LAW JOURNAL 189 (1979). Copyright © 1979 by Arizona State University College of Law. Reprinted by permission of the Arizona State Law Journal and the author.

Professional Liability and Quality of Health Care, by Richard Bonnie, 16 LAW MEDICINE & HEALTH CARE, p. 229 (1988). Copyright © 1988. Reprinted by permission.

The Tarasoff Decisions: Suing Psychotherapists to Safeguard Society, by Gerald Stone, 90 HARVARD LAW REVIEW, 375–376. Copyright © 1976. Reprinted with permission of the Harvard Law Review Association.

The Psychiatric Patient's Right to Effective Treatment: Implications of Osheroff vs. Chestnut Lodge, by Gerald Klerman, 147 AMERICAN JOURNAL OF PSYCHIATRY, 409, 410–411 (April 1990). Copyright

© 1990 by The American Psychiatric Association. Reprinted by permission.

Drug Free Research in Schizophrenia: An Overview of the Controversy, by Paul Appelbaum, M.D., 18 IRB; A REVIEW OF HUMAN SUBJECTS RESEARCH (Jan.–Feb. 1996). Copyright © 1996 by the Hastings Center. Reprinted by permission.

HIPAA Preemption Implications for Covered Entities Under State Law, by Adam Butera, 37 TORT & INSURANCE LAW JOURNAL NO. 4, Summer 2003. Copyright © 2003 ABA Publishing. Reprinted by permission of The American Bar Association.

Federal Health Privacy Comes to Maryland: What's the Big Deal?, by Frederick Ryland, 36 MARYLAND BAR JOURNAL 26, Jan.–Feb. 2003. Copyright © Maryland State Bar Association, Inc., 2003. Reprinted by permission of the Maryland Bar Journal, published by the Maryland State Bar Association, Inc.

From LAW, PSYCHIATRY AND MORALITY, by Alan Stone. Copyright © 1984, the American Psychiatric Association. Reprinted by permission of the American Psychiatric Association and the author.

Crazy Behavior, Morals, and Science: An Analysis of Mental Health Law, by Stephen Morse, from 51 SOUTHERN CALIFORNIA LAW REVIEW 527 (1978). Reprinted with permission of the Southern California Law Review and the author.

The Role of Mental Health Professionals in the Criminal Process: The Case for Informed Speculation, by Richard Bonnie and Christopher Slobogin, from 66 VIRGINIA LAW REVIEW, 427 (1980). Reprinted with permission from the Virginia Law Review Association.

To Have and Have Not: Assessing the Value of Social Science to the Law as Science and Policy, by David Faigman, from 38 EMORY LAW JOURNAL 1005 (1989). Reprinted with permission.

Myself Alone: Individualizing Justice Through Psychological Character Evidence, by Andrew Taslitz, from 52 MARYLAND LAW REVIEW 1 (1993). Reprinted with permission.

Sex Offender Civil Commitments: Scientists Or Psychics?, by Donna Cropp Bechman, from 16 CRIMINAL JUSTICE MAGAZINE 24 (2001). Reprinted with permission from the American Bar Association.

From COMPETENCY TO STAND TRIAL, by Ronald Roesch and Stephen Golding (1980). Reprinted with permission from Ronald Roesch.

From PSYCHOLOGICAL EVALUATIONS FOR THE COURTS: A HANDBOOK FOR MENTAL HEALTH PROFESSIONALS AND LAWYERS, by Gary Melton, John Petrila, Norman Poythress,

Christopher Slobogin (second edition, 1997). Reprinted with permission granted by Guilford Press.

Psychiatry and the Dangerous Criminal, by Norval Morris, from 41 SOUTHERN CALIFORNIA LAW REVIEW 514 (1968). Reprinted with the permission of the Southern California Law Review.

Book review of Abraham Goldstein's THE INSANITY DEFENSE, by Lady Wooton (1968). Reprinted by permission of the Yale Law Journal Company and Fred B. Rothman & Company, Vol. 77, pp. 1019–1051.*

From THE INSANITY DEFENSE, by David Hermann (1983). Courtesy of Charles C. Thomas, Publisher, Springfield, Illinois.

Dangerousness as a Criterion in the Criminal Process, by Christopher Slobogin, from Bruce Sales & Daniel Shuman, eds., LAW, MENTAL HEALTH & MENTAL DISORDER (1996). Reprinted with permission.

The Constitutionality and Morality of Civilly Committing Violent Sexual Predators, by Alexander Brooks, from 15 U. PUGET SOUND LAW REVIEW 709 (1992). Reprinted with permission.

Washington's Sexually Violent Predator Law: A Deliberate Misuse of the Therapeutic State for Social Control, by John LaFond, from 15 U. PUGET SOUND LAW REVIEW 655 (1992). Reprinted with permission.

Acute Psychiatric Hospitalization of the Mentally Ill in the Metropolis: An Empirical Study, by George Dix, from 1968 WASHINGTON UNIVERSITY LAW QUARTERLY 485 (1968). Reprinted with permission from the Washington University Law Quarterly.

Developments in the Law—Civil Commitment of the Mentally Ill, from 87 HARVARD LAW REVIEW 1190 (1974). Reprinted with permission from the Harvard Law Review.

A Preference for Liberty: The Case Against Involuntary Commitment of The Mentally Disordered, by Stephen Morse, from 70 CALIFORNIA LAW REVIEW 54 (1982). Copyright © 1982 by California Law Review, Inc. Reprinted by permission of California Law Review, Inc. and the author.

Assessing and Predicting Violence: Research, Law, and Applications, by T. Litwack and L. Schlesinger, in HANDBOOK OF FORENSIC PSYCHOLOGY 205 (Weiner, Hess, eds. 1987). Copyright © 1987 by John Wiley & Sons, Inc.

Dangerousness Defined, from LAW, PSYCHIATRY & MENTAL HEALTH SYSTEMS, by Alexander Brooks. Copyright © 1974 by Little, Brown. Reprinted with permission of Little, Brown and author.

Dangerousness as a Criterion for Confinement, by Alan Dershowitz, from 11 BULLETIN OF AMERICAN ACADEMY OF PSYCHIATRY AND LAW 172 (1974). Copyright © 1974 by American Academy of Psychiatry and Law. Reprinted by permission.

Where Involuntary Commitment, Civil Liberties, and the Right to Mental Health Care Collide: An Overview of California's Mental Illness System, by Meredith Karasch, from 54 HASTINGS L.J. 493 (2003). Reprinted with permission.

From OFFENSE TO OTHERS, by Joel Feinberg (1985). Reprinted by permission of Oxford University Press.

From MENTAL HEALTH LAW, by David Wexler. Copyright © 1981. Reprinted with permission granted by Plenum Publishing Corporation and the author.

Least Restrictive Treatment of the Mentally Ill: A Doctrine in Search of Its Senses, by Browning Hoffman and Larry Foust, from 14 SAN DIEGO LAW REVIEW 1100 (1977). Reprinted with permission from the San Diego Law Review.

Guidelines for Involuntary Civil Commitment, by the National Center for State Courts, from 10 MENTAL DISABILITY LAW REPORTER 409 (1986). Reprint permission granted by Ingo Keilitz, Director, Institute of Mental Disability and Law, National Center for State Courts.

Institutionalization, Deinstitutionalization, and the Adversary Process, by Judge David Bazelon, from 75 COLUMBIA LAW REVIEW 897 (1975). Copyright © 1975 by the Directors of the Columbia Law Review Association, Inc. All rights reserved. Reprinted by permission.

Of Rights Lost and Rights Found: The Coming Restoration of the Right to a Jury Trial in Minnesota Civil Commitment Proceedings, by C. Peter Erlinder, from 29 WILLIAM. MITCHELL LAW REVIEW 1269 (2003). Reprinted with permission.

Litigiousness as a Resistance to Therapy, by Robert Miller et al., from David Wexler, ed., THERAPEUTIC JURISPRUDENCE: THE LAW AS THERAPEUTIC AGENT (1991). Reprinted with permission.

A Model State Law on Civil Commitment of the Mentally Ill, by Clifford Stromberg and Alan Stone, from 20 HARVARD JOURNAL OF LEGISLATION 274 (1983). Copyright © 1983 by the President and Fellows of Harvard College. Reprinted by permission of the Harvard Journal of Legislation.

The Waivability of Recommitment Hearings, by David Wexler, from 20 ARIZONA LAW REVIEW 175 (1978). Copyright © 1978 by the

Arizona Board of Regents. Reprinted by permission of the Arizona Law Review and the author.

Voluntary Hospitalization of the Mentally Ill, by Janet Gilboy and John Schmidt, from 66 NORTHWESTERN LAW REVIEW 429 (1971). Reprinted with permission.

The Negotiation of Voluntary Admission in Chicago State Mental Hospitals, by Susan Reed & Dan Lewis, from 18 JOURNAL OF PSYCHIATRY & LAW 137 (1990). Reprinted with permission.

The Consequences of the Insanity Defense: Proposals to Reform Post-Acquittal Commitment Law, by James Ellis, from 35 CATHOLIC UNIVERSITY LAW REVIEW 961 (1986). Reprinted by permission of Catholic University Law Review.

REINVENTING JUSTICE: THE AMERICAN DRUG COURT MOVEMENT, by James L. Nolan, Jr. Copyright © 2001. Reprinted by permission of Princeton University Press.

Distributive and Paternalist Motives in Contract and Tort Law, with Special Reference to Compulsory Terms and Unequal Bargaining Power, by Duncan Kennedy, from 41 MARYLAND LAW REVIEW 563 (1982). Reprinted with permission from the Maryland Law Review.

Competency to Consent to Research: A Psychiatric Overview, by Paul Appelbaum and Loren Roth, from 39 ARCHIVES OF GENERAL PSYCHIATRY 951 (1982). Copyright © 1982 by American Medical Association. Reprinted by permission.

The Side Effects of Incompetency Labeling and the Implications for Mental Health Law, by Bruce Winick, from 1 PSYCHOLOGY, PUBLIC POLICY & LAW 6 (1995). Reprinted with permission.

Competency to Refuse Treatment, by Elyn Saks, from 69 NORTH CAROLINA LAW REVIEW 945 (1991). Reprinted with permission of the North Carolina Law Review.

Sterilization of Mentally Retarded Persons: Reproductive Rights and Family Privacy, by Elizabeth Scott, from 1986 DUKE LAW JOURNAL 806 (1986). Reprinted with permission from the Duke Law Journal.

The Right to Refuse Antipsychotic Medications: Law and Policy, by Alexander Brooks, from 39 RUTGERS LAW REVIEW 339 (1987). Reprinted with permission of the author.

Unbuckling the "Chemical Straitjacket:" The Legal Significance of Recent Advances in the Pharmacological Treatment of Psychosis, by Douglas Mossman, from 39 SAN DIEGO LAW REVIEW 1033 (2002). Reprinted with the permission of the San Diego Law Review.

Awakenings with the New Antipsychotics, by Kenneth Duckworth, from PSYCHIATRIC TIMES, May, 1998. Reprinted with permission.

Legal Regulation of Applied Behavior Analysis in Mental Institutions and Prisons, by Paul Friedman, from 17 ARIZONA LAW REVIEW 61 (1975). Copyright © 1975 by Arizona Board of Regents. Reprinted by permission.

The Role of the Criminal Defense Lawyer in Representing the Mentally Impaired Defendant: Zealous Advocate or Office of the Court?, by Rodney Uphoff, from 1988 WISCONSIN LAW REVIEW 65. Copyright © by Wisconsin Law Review. Reprinted by permission.

Incompetency to Stand Trial: As Assessment of Costs and Benefits, and a Proposal for Reform, by Bruce Winick, from 39 RUTGERS LAW REVIEW 243 (1987). Reprinted with permission of Rutgers Law Review and the author.

Insight into Schizophrenia: Anosognosia, Competency, and Civil Liberties, by Xavier F. Amador & Andrew A. Shiva, from 11 GEORGE MASON CIVIL RIGHTS LAW JOURNAL 24 (2000). Reprinted with permission.

Voluntariness, Free Will and the Law of Confessions, by Joseph Grano, from 65 VIRGINIA LAW REVIEW 859 (1979). Reprinted with permission from the Virginia Law Review Association and Fred B. Rothman & Co.

Words Without Meaning: The Constitution, Confessions, and Mentally Retarded Suspects, by Morgan Cloud et al., from 69 UNIVERSITY OF CHICAGO LAW REVIEW 495 (2002). Reprinted with permission.

The Long Lonesome Road, by Joseph Nocera, from THE TEXAS MONTHLY, November, 1986. Copyright © 1987 by Texas Monthly. Reprinted with permission.

Note: The Supreme Court: 1981 Term, from 96 HARVARD LAW REVIEW 62 (1982). Copyright © 1982 by the Harvard Law Review Association. Reprinted with permission.

Leaving Civil Rights to the "Experts": From Defense to Abdication Under the Professional Judgment Standard, by Susan Stefan, from 102 YALE LAW JOURNAL 639 (1992). Reprinted by permission of the Yale Law Journal Company and Fred B. Rothman & Company.

Mental Hospitals and the Civil Liberties Dilemma, by H. Davidson, from 31 MENTAL HYGIENE 371 (1967). Reprinted with permission of the National Mental Health Association, Alexandria, Va.

Note: The Wyatt Case: Implementation of a Judicial Decree Ordering Institutional Change, from 84 YALE LAW JOURNAL 1338 (1975).

Reprinted by permission of The Yale Law Journal Company and Fred B. Rothman & Company.

Beyond Least Restrictive Alternative Doctrine: A Constitutional Right to Treatment for Mentally Disabled Persons in the Community, by Jan Costello and James Preis, from 20 LOYOLA LOS ANGELES LAW REVIEW 1527 (1987). Reprinted with permission of the Loyola L.A. Law Review.

My Week in the Psych Ward, by Laurie Kramer, http://lauriekramer.com/psychward. Reprinted with permission.

The Changing Role of the State Psychiatric Hospital, by William Fisher, Jeffrey L. Geller and John A. Pandini, from 23 HEALTH AFFAIRS 676 (2009).

Federal Power, Segregation, and Mental Disability, by John V. Jacobi, from 39 HOUSTON LAW REVIEW 1231 (2003). Reprinted with permission.

Treatment of the Mentally Disabled: Rethinking the Community–First Idea, from 69 UNIVERSITY NEBRASKA LAW REVIEW 413 (1990). Reprinted with permission.

The Role of Cost in Educational Decisionmaking for the Handicapped Child, by Katharine T. Bartlett, from 48 LAW & CONTEMPORARY PROBLEMS 7 (1985). Reprinted with permission.

Peter David Blanck et al., Implementing Reasonable Accommodation Using ADR Under the ADA: The Case of a White-collar Employee with Bipolar Mental Illness, 18 MEN. & PHYS. DIS. L. REP. 458 (1994).

SUMMARY OF CONTENTS

PART 2. DEPRIVATIONS OF LIBERTY AND PROPERTY

PART 3. BENEFITS ELIGIBILITY AND LEGAL PROTECTION AGAINST DISCRIMINATION

TABLE OF CONTENTS

PART 2. DEPRIVATIONS OF LIBERTY AND PROPERTY

TABLE OF CASES

The principal cases are in bold type.

LAW AND THE MENTAL HEALTH SYSTEM

CIVIL AND CRIMINAL ASPECTS

Sixth Edition

PART 1

MENTAL HEALTH TREATMENT AND THE PATIENT-THERAPIST RELATIONSHIP

■ ■ ■

CHAPTER 1

MENTAL DISORDERS AND THEIR TREATMENT, THE MENTAL HEALTH PROFESSIONS, AND THE FINANCING OF MENTAL HEALTH CARE

■ ■ ■

Table of Sections

I. INTRODUCTION

This book is about law and the "mental health system"—the constellation of services, institutions, and personnel involved in the diagnosis, assessment, and treatment of emotional, behavioral, and mental disorders. The mental health system includes both public and private diagnostic and treatment services carried out not only in hospitals, community mental health centers, and private offices, but in other institutions such as schools, prisons, and drug rehabilitation centers. The law affects every aspect of this system, structuring the mechanisms that finance mental health care, regulating mental health professionals' practice, evaluations, and testimony, establishing criteria governing when individuals can be forced to use the system, and governing when the system must accommodate people's treatment needs.

Before examining these laws, some understanding of the mental health system is crucial. Over the last half-century, the U.S. mental health system has undergone profound changes. Among the most prominent changes are the following four:

- The proportion of the population utilizing the mental health system has increased substantially, due to greater awareness of mental disorders and their impact, improvements in and enhanced availability of mental health treatment, the decreased stigma associated with such treatment, federal and state statutes that provide an entitlement to care, and an expanding view of what constitutes a mental disorder.

- Pharmacological advances have fundamentally altered the treatment of serious mental illnesses by dramatically expanding the use of medications in treatment, reducing the importance and duration of hospitalization, and fueling debates over how much control patients, clients, or consumers[a] should have over their treatment.

- Where pharmacological treatment is not needed or desired, non-medical personnel, most prominently psychologists and social workers, have replaced psychiatrists as the primary providers of psychotherapy, driven in large part by economic concerns.

- Managed care and the expansion of insurance for mental health care has greatly influenced the nature and duration of mental health treatment, along with the types of professionals who supply mental health care and the settings where this care is provided.

This chapter discusses several key matters related to these developments and forms the backdrop for the rest of this book. The first issue the chapter addresses is the definition of mental disorder, a matter that is crucial to many of the laws and regulations discussed in the following chapters. Then follows a description of current knowledge about the treatment of mental disorders, a subject with significant implications both for determining the degree to which a mental health professional can be held liable for the nature of the care provided and for assessing whether coerced treatment is warranted. Next is a description of the mental health professions, with a focus on psychiatrists, psychologists, and social workers, all of whom play key roles in the legal system as experts, litigants, and, occasionally, legal decisionmakers. Finally, the chapter examines how mental health care is financed, because economic factors often exert significant influence on the law and policy pertaining to the mental health system.

II.   PERSPECTIVES ON MENTAL DISORDERS

A. THE INTERFACE OF LAW AND MENTAL DISORDERS

Most of the issues examined in this book flow from an assertion or a finding regarding the presence of a "mental disorder." For example, a diagnosis of a mental disorder is almost always required to obtain coverage for mental health treatment (see Part V of this chapter). Similarly, some knowledge about the nature of mental disorders is important in determining the scope of mental health professionals' authority and liability when providing diagnoses and treatment (Chapters Two through Four). A mental disorder finding is often crucial in many types of criminal and civil litigation, such as when seeking to establish an excuse or mitigation for a crime (Chapter Seven), forming the predicate for involuntary civil commitment (Chapter Eight), or

---

[a] For a comment on this terminology, see note ** in the Preface.

establishing a basis for a finding of incompetency (Chapter Nine). A diagnosis of a mental disorder is also generally required to qualify for various entitlements (e.g., disability payments) and receive protections from discrimination (Chapters Eleven and Twelve). Typically, as detailed in Chapter Six, these and numerous other issues involving the mental status of a party are resolved at least in part through the testimony of mental health providers.

In all of these contexts, the expectations and requirements of the legal system are often in tension with the diagnostic paradigms of mental health professionals. This is so for at least two reasons. The first reason is that mental disorders are not susceptible to precise definition. As is the case with medical problems generally, diagnoses rely significantly on the subjective impressions and judgment of the health care provider. Additionally, the "symptoms" associated with a mental disorder often overlap with the "normal" difficulties experienced by many. Moreover, the symptoms of a specific mental disorder may vary from day to day and frequently overlap with the symptoms of other mental disorders. Finally, unlike most medical illnesses, mental disorders usually do not have physiologically detectible symptoms (for example, a fever or an elevated blood sugar level) that are susceptible to clinical measurement. Yet fair and just adjudication requires legal standards that are relatively clear and unambiguous.

The second reason the mental health professions' diagnostic enterprise is in some tension with the law is that, even if diagnostic precision can be achieved, the assignment of a clinical diagnosis is not sufficient for legal purposes to establish that a person has a mental disability, disorder, or impairment.[b] By and large, U.S. mental health professionals employ the diagnostic scheme contained in the American Psychiatric Association's Diagnostic and Statistical Manual (DSM). In the words of the latest edition of the DSM (labeled DSM–5, because it is the fifth edition of this publication):

> When DSM–5 categories, criteria, and textual descriptions are employed for forensic purposes, there is a risk that diagnostic information will be misused or misunderstood. These dangers arise because of the imperfect fit between the questions of ultimate concern to the law and the information contained in a clinical diagnosis. In most situations, the clinical diagnosis of a DSM–5 mental disorder . . . does not imply that an individual with such a condition meets *legal criteria* for the presence of a mental disorder or a specific legal standard (e.g., for competence, criminal responsibility, or disability). It is precisely because impairments, abilities, and disabilities vary widely within each diagnostic category that

---

[b]   For a comment on terminology regarding mental condition, see note * in the Preface.

assignment of a particular diagnosis does not imply a specific level of impairment or disability.

. . . Nonclinical decision makers should also be cautioned that a diagnosis does not carry any necessary implications regarding the etiology or causes of the individual's mental disorder or the individual's degree of control over behaviors that may be associated with the disorder.

DSM–5 at 25 [emphasis added].

In short, legal standards usually do not have direct counterparts in the diagnostic paradigm employed for mental disorders. The interface of law and the mental health system is also complicated by limitations in how well mental health experts can explain and predict behavior and address the legal system's needs for determinative or guiding judgments. For example, the laws governing criminal sentencing and civil commitment require judgments about the future actions of a given individual. Yet, as discussed in Chapter Six, the accuracy of predictions by mental health experts in these matters is far from perfect.

The discrepancy between what the legal system seeks and what mental health professionals can deliver reflects both the limitations on what mental health professionals can do and a lack of understanding by courts, attorneys, and legislators about what information they can reasonably hope to obtain from mental health experts. The result often is an uneasy alliance between the law and the mental health professions, particularly in adjudicative contexts. Most of the chapters in this book highlight these interface challenges.

B. WHAT IS A MENTAL DISORDER?

DSM–5 states:

A mental disorder is a syndrome characterized by clinically significant disturbance in an individual's cognition, emotion regulation, or behavior that reflects a dysfunction in the psychological, biological, or developmental processes underlying mental functioning. Mental disorders are usually associated with significant distress or disability in social, occupational, or other important activities.

DSM–5, at 20. DSM–5 draws a distinction between a mental disorder and behavior that is "[a]n expectable or culturally approved response to a common stressor or loss, such as the death of a loved one." Moreover, "socially deviant behavior . . . and conflicts that are primarily between the individual and society are not [by themselves] mental disorders unless the deviance or conflict" stem from "a dysfunction in the individual" as previously defined. Id.

Although such language imposes limits on the diagnoses of mental disorders, terms like "distress," "disability," and "expectable or culturally approved" are value-laden and permit wide interpretation when diagnosing specific disorders. The absence of physical correlates and the ambiguous boundaries of mental disorders have even caused a few commentators to question whether the mental disorder concept makes sense. For more than half a century, the prominent "radical psychiatrist" Thomas Szasz argued that most mental disorder diagnoses did not reflect biological conditions (as was the case for the rest of medicine); instead, he argued, psychiatric diagnoses are tools for controlling unacceptable or unpopular behavior. As Szasz put it shortly before his death in 2012, so-called mental disorders merely "provide medical, legal and ethical justification for physicians to diagnose and treat [and for] judges to incarcerate and excuse . . ." James Phillips et al., *The Six Most Essential Questions in Psychiatric Diagnosis: A Pluralogue Part 1: Conceptual and Definitional Issues in Psychiatric Diagnosis*, 7 Philo. Ethics Humanities Med. 3, 12–13 (2012).

Szasz's positions had numerous followers when he first asserted them in the 1960s, and similar criticisms of psychiatric diagnoses persist. For example, Dr. Marcia Angell, former editor of *The New England Journal of Medicine*, wrote in 2011:

> [T]he boundaries of mental illness are being stretched for a variety of reasons—to increase drug company sales, to enhance the income and status of the psychiatry profession, and to get insurance coverage or disability benefits for troubled families.
>
> * * *
>
> [M]ental illness is diagnosed on the basis of symptoms (medically defined as subjective manifestations of disease, such as pain) and behaviors, not signs (defined as objective manifestations, such as swelling of a joint). Most diseases in other specialties produce physical signs and abnormal lab tests or radiologic findings, in addition to symptoms.
>
> Moreover, even if the underlying causes of [nonpsychiatric medical] diseases are unknown, the mechanisms by which they produce illness usually are, and the treatments usually target those mechanisms . . . [O]ther medical specialists, unlike psychiatrists, would be very reluctant to offer long-term symptomatic treatment without knowing what lies behind the symptoms.

'The Illusions of Psychiatry': An Exchange; Marcia Angell Replies, New York Rev. Books (Aug. 18, 2011).

Critics of this position counter that scientific advances in brain imaging, genetics, and psychopharmacology show that abnormal mental state arise from physiological or chemical perturbations within the nervous system. They also contend that biological abnormalities have been correlated with a substantial proportion of mental disorders. The following examples make the point:

- Studies have found irregularities in the ratios of brain tissue to brain fluid among individuals with schizophrenia, which reflects loss of tissue in those portions of the brain responsible for memory, attention, emotional expression, and information integration; deficiencies also appear in those brain areas associated with self-awareness. See Douglas Mossman, *Unbuckling the 'Chemical Straightjacket': The Legal Significance of Recent Advances in the Pharmacological Treatment of Psychosis*, 39 San Diego L. Rev. 1033, 1049–56 (2002).

- Researchers have discovered changes in brain volume, neuronal atrophy, and a disruption of brain circuits among individuals with bipolar disorder. See Danilo Armone, *Magnetic Resonance Imaging Studies in Bipolar Disorder and Schizophrenia: Meta-analysis*, 195 Brit. J. Psychiatry 194 (2009); Ronald S. Duman & George K. Aghajanian, *Synaptic Dysfunction in Depression: Potential Therapeutic Targets*, 338 Science 68 (2012).

- Even mental disorders defined primarily in terms of unacceptable behavior and a failure to conform to social norms—such as antisocial personality disorder (ASPD) and conduct disorder— may reflect underlying brain problems. ASPD has been linked with frontal lobe dysfunction, and conduct disorder is associated with various neurochemical abnormalities. See M. Catherine Cappadocia et al., *Contextualizing the Neurobiology of Conduct Disorder in an Emotion Dysregulation Framework*, 29 Clinical Psychol. Rev. 506 (2009); Yaling Yanga & Adrian Raine, *Prefrontal Structural and Functional Brain Imaging Findings in Antisocial, Violent, and Psychopathic Individuals: A Meta–Analysis*, 174 Psychiatry Res. 81 (2009).

Biological abnormalities are not the usual bases for making diagnoses of mental disorder, however. Researchers and mental health professionals use several other conceptual perspectives to describe psychological functioning and to understand mental disorders. Among the nonbiological perspectives are those that focus on developmental, environmental, and social factors, including what are referred to as *psychodynamic* and various *cognitive-behavioral* models. Moreover, current versions of the biological model incorporate the importance of nonbiological factors. For example, Eric Kandel, a prominent Nobel prize-winning, psychoanalytically-trained psychiatrist whose research explores nervous system mechanisms underlying behavior, explains that environmental factors produce significant alterations in the expression of relevant genes and hence in the functioning of nerve cells. Thus, when psychotherapy is effective, it is because, at the neuronal level, it alters gene expression and promotes new neuronal interconnections. In addition, adverse experiences (e.g., undergoing a severe emotional trauma) can produce disadvantageous changes in gene expression. Thus, the Surgeon General's 1999 report on Mental Health recognized that "mental illness appears to result from the interaction of multiple genes that confer risk, and this risk is converted into illness by the interaction of genes with environmental factors." Mental Health: Report of the Surgeon General 53 (1999). Indeed, as the American Psychiatric Association explained in its 2000 diagnostic manual, the term mental disorder "implies a distinction between 'mental' disorders and 'physical' disorders that is a reductionistic anachronism of mind/body dualism. A compelling literature documents that there is much 'physical' in mental disorders and much 'mental' in 'physical' disorders." See DSM–IV–TR, at 1497.

The materials that follow explore the biological, psychodynamic, and cognitive-behavioral models in more detail.

1.   The Biological Model

The following statement of principles, taken from an article by Dr. Kandel, is representative of current approaches to the biological model.

As a result of advances in neural science in the last several years, both psychiatry and neural science are in a new and better position for a rapprochement, a rapprochement that would allow the insights of the psychoanalytic perspective to inform the search for a proper understanding of the biological basis of behavior. As a first step towards such a rapprochement, I here outline an intellectual framework designed to align current psychiatric thinking and the training of future practitioners with modern biology.

This framework can be summarized in five principles, that constitute, in simplified form, the current thinking of biologists about the relationship of mind to brain.

Principle 1. All mental processes, even the most complex psychological processes, derive from operations of the brain. The central tenet of this view is that what we commonly call mind is a range of functions carried out by the brain. The actions of the brain underlie not only relatively simple motor behaviors, such as walking and eating, but all of the complex cognitive actions, conscious and unconscious, that we associate with specifically human behavior, such as thinking, speaking, and creating works of literature, music, and art. As a corollary, behavioral disorders that characterize psychiatric illness are disturbances of the brain function, even in those cases where the causes of the disturbances are clearly environmental in origin.

Principle 2. Genes and their protein products are important determinants of the pattern of interconnections between neurons in the brain and the details of their functioning. Genes, specifically combinations of genes, therefore exert a significant control over behavior. As a corollary, one component contributing to the development of major mental illnesses is genetic.

Principle 3. Altered genes do not, by themselves, explain all the variance of a given major mental illness. Social or developmental factors also contribute very importantly to behavior, including social behavior, so behavior and social factors can exert actions on the brain by feeding back upon it to modify the expression of genes and thus the function of nerve cells. Learning, including learning that results in dysfunctional behavior, produces alterations in gene expression. Thus all of "nurture" is ultimately expressed as "nature".

Principle 4. Alterations in gene expression induced by learning give rise to changes in patterns of neuronal connections These changes not only contribute to the biological basis of individuality but presumably are responsible for initiating and maintaining abnormalities of behavior that are induced by social contingencies.

Principle 5. Insofar as psychotherapy or counseling is effective and produces long-term changes in behavior, it presumably does so through learning, by producing changes in gene expression that alter the strength of synaptic connections and structural changes that alter the anatomical pattern of interconnections between nerve cells of the brain. As the resolution of brain imaging increases, it should eventually permit quantitative evaluation of the outcome of psychotherapy.

Eric R. Kandel, *A New Intellectual Framework for Psychiatry*, 155 Am. J. Psychiatry 457, 460 (1998); but see Thomas R. Insel, *Translating Scientific Opportunity into Public Health Impact: A Strategic Plan for Research on Mental Illness*, 66 Archives Gen. Psychiatry 128, 128 (2009) (discussing efforts to close "the gap between the surge in basic biological knowledge and the state of mental health care" but noting that "[d]espite high expectations, neither genomics nor imaging has yet impacted the diagnosis or treatment [of mental illness]").

2. The Psychodynamic Model

The psychodynamic model asserts that mental problems are the product of underlying conflicts of which people often have scant awareness. Sigmund Freud (1856–1939) was a towering proponent of psychoanalytic theory, the first of many 20th–century psychodynamic approaches to understanding mental problems. In general, modern psychodynamic explanations of human functioning retain two fundamental tenets that originated with Freud: (1) much of mental life is unconscious (i.e., outside awareness), and (2) past experiences, especially in early childhood, shape how a person feels and behaves throughout life.

Freud's final "structural" model of the mind divided the human personality into three parts: the id, the ego, and the superego. The largely unconscious id is the source of relatively raw "drives," such as those that underlie sexual desires or aggression; the ego, which has conscious and unconscious elements, guides interactions between the individual and the outside world and mediates between conflicting aspirations and desires; and the superego acts much like a conscience, imposing on a person's behavior social constraints learned from parents, teachers, and others.

Freud believed that mental health problems arise out of the ego's failure to mediate successfully the unconscious conflicts between the urges of the id and the demands of the superego. The symptoms associated with mental disorders are (in Freud's view) the expression of these underlying conflicts, and treatment—psychoanalysis—aims to help the individual understand and manage these conflicts more successfully.

In the 21st century, very few mental health professionals accept Freud's original formulations of psychological functioning and mental problems. Those clinicians who still trace their intellectual lineage back to Freud use psychodynamic constructs and therapeutic approaches that place less emphasis on underlying conflict as the central component of mental problems. Psychodynamic therapists (most of whom, nowadays, are *not* psychiatrists) help patients identify maladaptive responses and behaviors using a therapeutic alliance that fosters self-analysis. If successful, psychodynamic therapy promotes understanding of the sources of repetitive, dysfunctional patterns in interpersonal relationships. During treatment, the patient identifies and talks through painful memories and uncomfortable feelings, and, with the help of the therapist, recreates and examines situations and psychological defenses with which the patient struggles, with the aim of developing strategies to deal with them.

3.   The Cognitive–Behavioral Model

Cognitive-behavioral therapy (CBT) applies principles drawn from research on behavioral patterns and thinking to produce psychotherapeutic approaches to many mental disorders. The theory and practice of 21st–century CBT reflects the work of researchers and practitioners who trace their efforts primarily to social learning theorist Albert Bandura and psychiatrist Aaron T. Beck. The social learning model asserts that people's cognitions—their views, perceptions, and expectations of their environment—affect who they are and what they do. People do not respond passively to the conditions of their environments, but instead take active roles in deciding who and what they will be.

Beck first articulated his therapeutic approach in the 1960s. Although he started his career as a psychoanalyst, Beck noticed that his patients often reported what he eventually termed *automatic thoughts*—beliefs about themselves ("nothing will ever work out for me") of which they were not always aware but which had a significant impact on their emotions, behavior, and self-perception ("I'm a failure"). Beck noted that his patients structured their world according to certain core beliefs or *schemas* ("I have to do everything superbly; otherwise, I'm a failure") that they had developed from earlier experiences and through which they interpreted what happened to them. Beck found, however, that patients could identify these thoughts and beliefs if questioned closely. Patients could then consciously evaluate and challenge the veracity of these thoughts, which proved very useful in helping them overcome their difficulties. Aaron T. Beck et al., Cognitive Therapy of Depression 3–7 (1979).

CBT differs from psychodynamic treatment in its shorter duration (typically 12–20 sessions) and by having the patient engage in several flexibly developed but structured activities as part of treatment. At the outset, the patient and therapist identify specific problems and goals for their work together; subsequently, they use these to plan sessions and structure treatment activities. Sessions often begin with a mutual setting of an agenda for what will be addressed that day, allotting time for evaluating conclusions reached and "homework" assignments developed during a previous session. Early in the course of treatment, homework might involve keeping track of troublesome events and writing down associated thoughts and feelings for examination at the next session. Later, homework assignments may include exercises that the therapist and the patient have designed to help the patient cope better with problems that may arise. The CBT approach highly values patients' functioning independently (rather than feeling dependent on the therapist), and this ethos gets expressed through the therapist's frequent soliciting of the patient's opinion about how things are going and by promoting the patient's active collaboration in structuring the treatment employed. Jesse H. Wright et al., Learning Cognitive–Behavior Therapy: An Illustrated Guide 19, 40–42, 76–79 (2006).

CBT is probably the best tested psychotherapeutic modality, and innumerable scientific studies have demonstrated its effectiveness in treating a broad variety of mental disorders. For example, CBT is an effective treatment for depression, and its benefits (especially for mild and moderate depression) probably are greater than those conferred by antidepressant medications. Andrew C. Butler et al., *The Empirical Status of Cognitive–Behavioral Therapy: A Review of Meta–Analyses*, 26 Clinical Psychol. Rev. 17, 20–23 (2006). CBT is also effective for treating many anxiety disorders (described in more detail later in this chapter), including panic disorder, specific phobias, social phobias, obsessive-compulsive disorder, posttraumatic stress disorder, and generalized anxiety disorder. Bunmi O. Olatunji et al., *Efficacy of Cognitive Behavioral Therapy for Anxiety Disorders: A Review of Meta–Analytic Findings*, 33 Psychiatric Clinics N. Am. 557 (2010). As the editors of a 2010 volume on CBT explain, "recent clinical and research efforts have begun to develop CBT for an increasingly wider range of problems," including attention-deficit hyperactivity disorder, substance abuse disorders, psychoses, eating disorders, sleep problems, and personality disorders. Bunmi O. Olatunji & Steven D. Hollon, *The Current Status of Cognitive Behavioral Therapy for Psychiatric Disorders*, 33 Psychiatric Clinics N. Am. xiii, xviii (2010) (summarizing studies).

QUESTIONS AND COMMENTS

1.   *The relationship between society and mental disorders.* The models described above can help us understand the sources, nature, and boundaries of mental disorders. However, they do not necessarily tell us <u>what</u> we as a society should consider to be a mental disorder. Social considerations necessarily influence both what we call a mental disorder and its parameters. For example, absolute (or "perfect") musical pitch is correlated with a leftward asymmetry of a part of the brain called the planum temporale. Julian Paul Keenan et al., *Absolute Pitch and Planum Temporale*, 14 Neuroimage 1402 (2001). Should this unusual ability be considered a mental disorder? Unless it is somehow maladaptive, most would say no. But what constitutes "maladaptive" behavior or thinking and thus a mental disorder is obviously influenced to some extent by the requirements and expectations of the society in which one lives.

Two attempts to "objectify" the definition of mental disorder in a way that minimizes the influence of societal expectations and mollifies the criticisms of people like Szasz come from Robert Kendell and Michael Moore. Kendell argued that mental illness should be defined with reference to whether "the abnormality place[s] the individual at a 'biological disadvantage,'" by which he meant "increased mortality and reduced fertility." Robert Evan Kendell, *The Concept of Disease and Its Implications for Psychiatry*, 127 Brit. J. Psychiat. 305 (1975). Moore, in contrast, focused on whether the person can be said to be "irrational." He stated, "Unless we can perceive another being as acting for intelligible ends in light of rational beliefs, we cannot understand that being in the same fundamental way that we understand each other's actions in daily life." Michael Moore, *Some Myths about Mental Illness*, 18 Inquiry 233 (1975).

2.   *The relative contributions of heredity and environment.* Some of the most interesting work regarding mental disorders has attempted to track the relative contributions of heredity and environment. For example, the heritability of bipolar disorder, according to a rigorous twin study, is about 59%. Twin studies indicate that schizophrenia also has a high rate of heritability. Mental Health: Report of the Surgeon General 54 (1999). Genetic factors have also been found to contribute to personality disorders (PDs).

Kenneth S. Kendler et al., *The Structure of Genetic and Environmental Risk Factors for DSM–IV Personality Disorders: A Multivariate Twin Study*, 65 Archives Gen. Psychiatry 1438 (2008) (20–41%); Svenn Torgersen et al., *The Heritability of Cluster B Personality Disorders Assessed Both by Personal Interview and Questionnaire*, 26 J. Personality Disorders 848, 848 (2012) (the heritability of antisocial, borderline, narcissistic, and histrionic personality characteristics "appears to be in the upper range of previous findings for mental disorders"). However, genetic factors do not account for all occurrences of PDs. See 2 Psychiatry 1293, 1299–1300 (Allan Tasman et al. eds., 1997) (there is "considerable" evidence "from twin, family, and adoption studies for a genetic contribution to the etiology of the criminal, delinquent tendencies of persons with ASPD [anti-social personality disorder]," yet environmental influences, including "[m]odeling by parental figures and peers; excessively harsh, lenient, or erratic discipline; and a tough, harsh environment in which feelings of empathy and warmth are discouraged (if not punished) and tough-mindedness, aggressiveness, and exploitation are encouraged (if not rewarded) have [also] all been associated with the development of ASPD").

3. *Legal implications of etiology.* The law has tended to prefer the biological model of mental disorders over the psychodynamic and cognitive-behavioral models. To some extent, this preference is probably an accident of history. The biological model preceded the other two (for example, Hippocrates theorized that depression was caused by black bile and hence could be cured by purgatives) and thus was the first one encountered by the law.

But the law's affinity for the biological model has a pragmatic and philosophical justification as well, particularly in the context of the criminal justice and civil commitment systems discussed in Part II of this casebook. The other models tend to explain individual behavior as a function of environmental factors, which would undercut the legal principles of individual causation and responsibility for one's actions. By and large, psychodynamic and behavioral models explain the symptoms of mental disorders and related behavior as products of one's surroundings—e.g., the result of being rewarded for aggressive behavior, being raised by certain types of parents, or being driven and shaped by poverty. Were the legal system to endorse these models of explanation, it could broaden enormously the availability of defenses based on a lack of criminal responsibility. See, e.g., David Bazelon, *The Morality of the Criminal Law*, 49 S. Cal. L. Rev. 385, 396 (1976) (arguing that social background, including poverty, should be considered in evaluating criminal responsibility). Similarly, to the extent that the law authorizes coercive treatment to ameliorate a mental disorder associated with dangerousness or incompetency, embracing these exogenous models might permit state intervention into the lives of other persons who are contributors to the disorder (such as the parents of delinquent juveniles). See Heather J. Davies and Howard A. Davidson, Parental Involvement Practices of Juvenile Courts: Report to the Office of Juvenile Justice and Delinquency Prevention 103 (2001) (asserting that the laws in every state provide "ways through which parents may be held accountable by the courts for the actions of their children"). It bears noting, however, that to the extent the biological model expands to show that biology and genetics influence a wider range of criminal behavior (cf. the research on antisocial personality disorder discussed in note 2) and to incorporate the importance of environmental factors (cf. the Kandel excerpt on pp. 10–11, the biological model may similarly expand, for example, the availability of criminal defenses and the scope of coercive treatment regimes.

Etiology can be relevant to other areas of the law as well. As discussed in Part V of this chapter, the increasingly blurred distinction between mental and physical disorders becomes particularly salient in the context of health care coverage because coverage by third-party payors for a "mental illness" has traditionally been much less generous than coverage for a "physical illness." Plaintiffs who have been denied coverage on the grounds that they have exhausted their mental health benefits have brought suits arguing that their illness (for example, bipolar disorder) is actually a physical disorder of the brain.

4.   *The Surgeon General's discussion of mental disorders.* In 1999, the Surgeon General of the United States issued an informative report on mental health and treatment that discussed the science of mental disorders. The drafters of the Report focused on three types of "mental disorder"—anxiety, psychosis, and mood disorders—that they considered the most serious and most prevalent. These three conditions figure in many of the legal issues discussed in this book.

> **Anxiety:** [T]he mechanisms that regulate anxiety may break down in a wide variety of circumstances, leading to excessive or inappropriate expression of anxiety. Specific examples include phobias, panic attacks, and generalized anxiety. In phobias, high-level anxiety is aroused by specific situations or objects that may range from concrete entities such as snakes, to complex circumstances such as social interactions or public speaking. Panic attacks are brief and very intense episodes of anxiety that often occur without a precipitating event or stimulus. Generalized anxiety represents a more diffuse and nonspecific kind of anxiety that is most often experienced as excessive worrying, restlessness, and tension occurring with a chronic and sustained pattern. In each case, an anxiety disorder may be said to exist if the anxiety experienced is disproportionate to the circumstance, is difficult for the individual to control, or interferes with normal functioning.

> In addition to these common manifestations of anxiety, obsessive-compulsive disorder and post-traumatic stress disorder are generally believed to be related to the anxiety disorders.... In the case of obsessive-compulsive disorder, individuals experience a high level of anxiety that drives their obsessional thinking or compulsive behaviors. When such an individual fails to carry out a repetitive behavior such as hand washing or checking, there is an experience of severe anxiety.... Post-traumatic stress disorder is produced by an intense and

overwhelmingly fearful event that is often life-threatening in nature. The characteristic symptoms that result from such a traumatic event include the persistent reexperience of the event in dreams and memories, persistent avoidance of stimuli associated with the event, and increased arousal.

Psychosis: Disturbances of perception and thought process fall into a broad category of symptoms referred to as psychosis. . . . One of the most common groups of symptoms that result from disordered processing and interpretation of sensory information are the hallucinations . . . A more complex group of symptoms resulting from disordered interpretation of information consists of delusions. A delusion is a false belief that an individual holds despite evidence to the contrary. A common example is paranoia, in which a person has delusional beliefs that others are trying to harm him or her. Attempts to persuade the person that these beliefs are unfounded typically fail and may even result in the further entrenchment of the beliefs.

. . . In addition to hallucinations and delusions, patients with psychotic disorders such as schizophrenia frequently have marked disturbances in the logical process of their thoughts. Specifically, psychotic thought processes are characteristically loose, disorganized, illogical, or bizarre. . . .

However, in addition to positive symptoms, patients with schizophrenia and other psychoses have been noted to exhibit major deficits in motivation and spontaneity that are referred to as negative symptoms. . . . Positive symptoms such as hallucinations are responsible for much of the acute distress associated with schizophrenia, but negative symptoms appear to be responsible for much of the chronic and long-term disability associated with the disorder.

* * *

Disturbances of Mood: Disturbances of mood characteristically manifest themselves as a sustained feeling of sadness or sustained elevation of mood. As with anxiety and psychosis, disturbances of mood may occur in a variety of patterns associated with different mental disorders. The disorder most closely associated with persistent sadness is major depression, while that associated with sustained elevation or fluctuation of mood is bipolar disorder. . . . Along with the prevailing feelings of sadness or elation, disorders of mood are associated with a host of related symptoms that include disturbances in appetite, sleep patterns, energy level, concentration, and memory.

Mental Health: A Report of the Surgeon General 39–43 (1999).

5.   *Epidemiology of mental disorders.* The Surgeon General's Report estimates that 28 to 30% of the American population suffers from a mental or addictive disorder. About 9% of the population suffers *significant* impairment from these disorders. The Report also summarizes the available data about

the prevalence of mental disorders among various ethnic and cultural groups. According to the Report, socioeconomic differences account for a higher prevalence of mental disorders among African Americans than among whites. Moreover, even accounting for higher prevalence rates, African Americans are overrepresented in inpatient psychiatric facilities. The Report suggests that poverty, a disinclination to seek help, and a lack of appropriate outpatient services may lead African Americans to delay seeking treatment until symptoms become sufficiently severe to warrant inpatient care. As for Hispanic Americans, those born in the U.S. appear to have rates of mental disorders similar to U.S. whites. The prevalence of mental illness among Asian Americans (and among different groups of Asian Americans) has not been studied thoroughly, but one study suggests that Asian Americans are only a quarter as likely as whites, and half as likely as African Americans and Hispanic Americans to seek outpatient treatment. Like studies on Asian Americans, studies on Native Americans are limited. Depression and suicide appear to be significant problems. Alcohol abuse and dependence is particularly problematic, with rates of occurrence twice that found in any other population group. Among Native American military veterans, post-traumatic stress disorder is more prevalent than in white veterans. Native Americans are also overrepresented in public psychiatric facilities compared to whites. Id. at 83–86.

6. *Public perception of mental disorders*. The Surgeon General's Report observes that, by the 1990s, Americans had achieved a greater scientific understanding of mental illness. While distinguishing mental illness from ordinary worry and unhappiness, the public also expanded its definition of mental illness to encompass anxiety, depression, and other mental disorders. The public attributed mental illness to a mix of biological abnormalities and vulnerabilities to social and psychological stress. On the other hand, the public's perception of mental illness today more frequently incorporates violent behavior than it did fifty years ago. Thirty-one percent of the group that associated mental illness with psychosis (i.e., a disturbance of perception and thought process) mentioned violence in its descriptions of mental illness, in comparison to 13% in the 1950s. Id. at 7–8.

7. *Case studies*. In the following eight cases, do the people exhibit signs or symptoms of a "mental disorder"? Why or why not? In answering this question, consider (1) the DSM's definition of mental disorders (as well as specific diagnostic categories, found in Appendix A); (2) the different etiological approaches to mental disorders; (3) Szasz's and Angell's critique of the mental disorder concept and Kendell's and Moore's responses; and (4) the descriptions of mental disorders in the Surgeon General's Report on Mental Health. Are there other variables that should be considered as well?

Case 1. John works at a convenience store. He is very quiet. One of his co-workers discovers that, each day after work, John spends several hours in a closet. When questioned about this, John says, "I've been doing it for three or four months, you know; it's where my mother used to put me." When asked what he does there, he explains, "I'm talking with Martians. They left me here to teach Earthlings about Mars. I'm also a rock star you know, but I'm *yes PTSD* getting smaller every day and pretty soon you won't be able to see me."

Case 2. Sam wants to set the world record for number of days on top of a flag pole. At the present time, he has been on a platform on top of a pole for 33 days. Although he is malnourished and dizzy from lack of food and sleep, he says he will not come down until he has stayed on the pole for 73 days, which will be a new world record. *no*

Case 3. Alyson, 55, lives in the country. She has been drinking heavily for years. Recently she has become convinced that the crop dusters flying over her house are government airplanes bombarding her house with electronic particles. As evidence of this, she points to several places where the foundations of her house are weakened and notes the fact that recently, her dog mysteriously died. She also believes her house is being bugged by the government. *yes*

Case 4. Cecelia goes to all-night worship services at her fundamentalist church. During these services, she claims to hear voices talking to her, often speaks in tongues, and occasionally behaves in a wild way so that others have to restrain her. The monthly meetings are the only times she acts like this. *yes*

Case 5. Jimmy is a member of an ashram, a commune centered around Eastern religious beliefs. Since joining the ashram, Jimmy has been required to participate every day in strenuous series of classes, meditation, and prayer sessions, as well as engage in street solicitations. He is constantly fatigued, has lost all sexual desire and sense of humor, and goes into trances quite frequently. He says, however, that he has found the true answer to "Life's Questions" and wants to continue at the ashram. *?*

Case 6. Mary, a lawyer, says she feels hopeless and worthless. When asked why, she says she is single, has no good friends or family, and thinks her work is meaningless. She is barely able to go to the office in the morning and in the evening she goes straight home, watches TV and falls asleep by 8 p.m. She cries frequently and sometimes wishes she were dead. She resists any efforts to "cheer her up" or get her involved socially. *—depression*

Case 7. Sarah is 21 and lives with her parents. She says she has no idea what she wants to do with her life. She has been put on probation for shoplifting. She holes up in her room with piles of junk food for days. When her mother or father tries to talk to her, Sarah often explodes with anger and usually retreats to her room. Recently, she has taken to sticking safety pins in her skin and letting them hang. *yes*

Case 8. As a child, Donald would torture small animals. He was always getting in fights with other children. By the time he was 25, he had been charged with several crimes, and convicted of burglary, two assaults, and arson. When asked about these events, he merely states that they seemed like the thing to do at the time; he is only sorry that he got caught.

Now consider the eight cases "contextually." If the people described sought treatment, should their health care plan cover the treatment? Assume *prob not 8, 5?*

instead that (1) none of these people wants treatment; (2) that the relevant civil commitment law permits forcible treatment if a person suffers from a mental disorder that causes dangerousness to self or others; (3) that the requisite dangerousness has been proven; and (4) that effective treatment is available. Is there enough evidence of a mental disorder to justify intervention? More is said about insurance and civil commitment law elsewhere in this casebook. The effort here is to stimulate some initial thinking about the contextual nature of mental disorders. They may be defined differently depending on whether a mental health professional, an insurance company, or a judge is making the decision.

C. DIAGNOSING A MENTAL DISORDER

DSM–5 includes in its listing of mental disorders an enormous number of syndromes and psychological patterns organized into twenty categories, examples of which appear below:

- Neurodevelopmental disorders that usually appear and are first diagnosed in childhood, including intellectual disabilities (formerly known as mental retardation), autism and related conditions, learning disabilities, and attention-deficit/ hyperactivity disorder;

- Psychotic disorders (e.g., schizophrenia, a chronic disorder that often involves episodes of thought disorganization, hallucinations, and delusions);

- Mood disorders, including depression and bipolar disorder (an illness manifested by intermittent periods of severe depression and mania);

- Anxiety disorders, including panic disorder and agoraphobia;

- Trauma-related disorders, including posttraumatic stress disorder;

- Dissociative disorders, including dissociative identity disorder, which was formerly known as multiple personality disorder;

- Disorders affecting aspects of sexual identity, behavior, and functioning;

- Neurocognitive disorders such as dementias, which involve significant impairments of instrumental functioning and memory;

- Personality disorders, a large category of syndromes defined as "an enduring pattern of inner experience and behavior that deviates markedly from the expectations of the individual's culture, is pervasive and inflexible, . . . and leads to distress or impairment," DSM–5 at 645, and includes paranoid personality disorder, schizoid personality disorder (detachment from social relationships and a restricted range of emotional expression), schizotypal personality disorder (odd beliefs or magical thinking, unusual perceptual experiences including cognitive or perceptual distortions, and excessive social anxiety); antisocial personality disorder (disregard for and violation of the rights of others), borderline personality disorder (impulsiveness, unstable relationships, overly intense emotional responses); histrionic personality disorder (excessive emotionality and attention seeking); narcissistic personality disorder (grandiosity, need for admiration, and lack of empathy); avoidant personality disorder (feelings of inadequacy and hypersensitivity to negative evaluation); dependent personality disorder (submissive and clinging behavior related to an excessive need to be take care of); and obsessive-compulsive personality disorder (preoccupation with orderliness, perfectionism, and control);

- Eating and sleeping disorders, and other disorders that feature exaggerated physical symptoms (somatoform and factitious disorders);

- Substance use disorders, including not just alcohol and drug-related disorders but caffeine and nicotine-related disorders as well.

Appendix A to this book contains DSM–5 diagnostic criteria for several commonly diagnosed mental disorders (e.g., various psychotic, mood, and anxiety disorders).

As noted earlier, the American Psychiatric Association's Diagnostic and Statistical Manual is the best known taxonomy of mental disorders and is now in its fifth edition. The first edition of the DSM appeared in 1952. This edition and the second edition (DSM–II), which was published in 1958, were dominated by psychoanalytic thinking (as was organized psychiatry at the time). Because of the nature of psychoanalytic practice, in which a small number of individuals are treated intensively over a period of years, DSM–I and DSM–II did not draw from a large data set in devising diagnoses. As a result, the probability that two clinicians examining the same client would arrive at the same diagnosis was low. DSM–II's lack of reliability led to criticism from a number of different quarters: from researchers who were interested in the nature, causes, and consequences of mental illness and thus needed to conduct their research on comparable populations of individuals with a given mental disorder; from legal scholars, who were concerned about presenting and addressing information pertaining to mental disorders in court where reliable evidence is required; and from insurance providers who were concerned about providing coverage for disorders that were vaguely defined. See Robert D. Miller, *History of Psychiatric Diagnosis: A Guidebook for Nonclinicians*, 23 Colo. Law. 39, 40 (1994).

In response to these criticisms, a task force was appointed in 1974 to revise DSM–II. From 1975 through 1979, successive task force drafts of DSM–III were considered at the annual meeting of the American Psychiatric Association, as well as at a special meeting in 1976 that focused entirely on DSM–III. Throughout that period, critiques were solicited from psychiatrists, psychoanalysts, psychologists, and social workers.

DSM–III, published in 1980, replaced the unstructured approach of DSM–I and DSM–II with a more descriptive and objective approach. DSM–III also contained a significant expansion in the diagnoses listed: while DSM–II was only about 150 pages long, DSM–III was more than 500 pages in length. Between 1977 and 1980, the DSM–III diagnostic scheme underwent field trials to determine the extent to which different clinicians arrived at the same diagnosis using DSM–III categories. These trials revealed that interrater agreement for the major diagnostic categories (e.g., schizophrenia, manic-depressive psychosis) was quite high (between 69% and 85%). For other diagnostic categories, the rate of agreement was lower (often below 50%), though markedly better than diagnostic reliability using DSM–II. With DSM–IV, the research process became even more exhaustive. In addition to the clinical experience of task force members, literature searches were incorporated into the reviews. Published in 1994, DSM–IV was over 900 pages long and contained more than 300 diagnoses organized into 16 diagnostic categories. DSM–IV–TR (published in 2000) was somewhat longer but held the same number of diagnoses as DSM–IV.

In DSM–III and DSM–IV, which figure prominently in some of the cases reported in this book, clinicians were to describe patients' conditions using a "multi-axial system" of diagnosis. Axis I was for reporting all the major diagnostic classes of mental disorders, except for personality disorders and mental retardation (which were reported on Axis II). Axis III was for reporting general medical conditions that might bear upon an individual's mental disorder or treatment. Axis IV was for reporting psychosocial and environmental problems that affected the individual's diagnosis and treatment. These problems might have included difficulties associated with the individual's primary support group, challenges in the social environment, educational problems, or economic impediments. Finally, Axis V was for summarizing the clinician's global assessment of the individual's functioning (GAF), which was reported on a scale of 1 to 100. The following is an example of how a diagnosis reported under this multi-axial system might appear in a given case (the numbers in Axes I and II are the DSM–IV diagnostic codes):

Axis 1   296.23   Major Depressive Disorder, Single Episode, Severe Without Psychotic Features

           305.00   Alcohol Abuse

Axis II   301.6   Dependent Personality Disorder
Axis III   None
Axis IV   Problems related to primary support
Axis V   GAF=35 (current)

As a result of the multi-axial scheme, mental health professionals often speak in terms of an "Axis I" or "Axis II" diagnosis, with the latter usually designating a personality disorder. Again, we mention this usage here because it occasionally appears elsewhere in this book.

In May 2013, the American Psychiatric Association released the fifth edition of its diagnostic manual, DSM–5. Publication of this manual was the culmination of a fourteen-year effort involving hundreds of clinicians. In the first decade of the 21st century, workgroups (on nomenclature, neuroscience and genetics, developmental issues and diagnosis, personality and relational disorders, mental disorders and disability, and cross-cultural issues), white papers (concerning gender issues, geriatrics, and infants and young children), and a series of research conferences laid the groundwork for creation of DSM–5, which began formally in July 2007 with the announcement of a revision task force. The APA required that potential task force members disclose any competing interests or potentially conflicting relationships that might influence the shaping, inclusion, or exclusion of psychiatric diagnoses, and several nominees were ruled ineligible because of their competing interests. Field trials of DSM–5 that began in 2010 included a process in which different clinicians conducted independent evaluations of the same patients to evaluate "test-retest" consistency of diagnoses, which resulted in removal of some diagnostic categories that proved insufficiently reliable.

DSM–5 continues the practice of requiring clinicians to apply specified criteria in making diagnoses. In this respect, and in most other respects, DSM–5 is similar to DSM–III and DSM–IV. A major overall difference, however, was the elimination of the multi-axial diagnostic scheme, to remove what many mental health professionals had come to view as artificial distinctions between various mental disorders. Additionally, the mental disorder diagnoses were recategorized and reordered to reflect updated views about their interrelationships, and criteria for many diagnoses were modified in light of scientific advances and changed clinical opinion over the previous 20 years. Some diagnoses that appear in DSM–IV were dropped from DSM–5. For example, DSM–5 no longer lists Asperger syndrome as a distinct classification (incorporating it, along with autism, into the "autism spectrum" of disorders), and it no longer contains subtype classifications of schizophrenia (e.g., "paranoid" and "disorganized") because research evidence for these long-time clinical distinctions had ultimately proved lacking. In contrast, binge eating disorder, premenstrual dysphoric disorder, and a new gambling disorder became official diagnoses in DSM–

5, and hoarding disorder was recognized as a condition distinct from obsessive-compulsive disorder. Additionally, some conditions were renamed. For example, instead of referring to "mental retardation" and "hypochondriasis," DSM–5 speaks of "intellectual disabilities" and "illness anxiety disorder," terms that are less pejorative and that reflect practices in related disciplines.

Because the development and evaluation process was largely open to public view, DSM–5 received criticism from a wide range of sources well before its publication. These criticisms included concerns that its changes did not have adequate scientific support, that many members of the development task force had financial ties to outside interests (e.g., received payments from pharmaceutical companies for research or lecturing), and that some of the diagnoses unduly pathologized normal human experiences as mental illnesses (some examples of which are given below). Asserting that distinctions were being made that were insufficiently supported by good evidence, critics voiced concerns about how DSM–5 would change the delivery of treatment, drug prescription practices, and the availability of health insurance coverage for care.

QUESTIONS AND COMMENTS

1.   *Social and political influences on the DSM.* Political and social forces have strongly influenced the DSM system. Probably the most prominent example is the APA's treatment of homosexuality. Prior to the 1960s, homosexual activity was a crime in most states. Most psychiatrists regarded homosexuality as a "disorder," and it was classified as such in the DSM system. Beginning in the early 1960s, many states either repealed such laws or stopped enforcing them as society's attitudes toward homosexuality changed. In 1973, in response to widespread criticism by various lobbying groups, the APA "delisted" homosexuality as a diagnostic classification. For a detailed discussion of the events surrounding the delisting of homosexuality, see Herb Kutchins & Stuart Kirk, Making Us Crazy 55–99 (1997).

Other illustrations of diagnostic definitions that reflect political influence abound. For example, in 1980, in response to pressure from Vietnam veterans groups, the APA added a posttraumatic stress disorder to the DSM. That same year, DSM added the condition popularly known as multiple personality disorder ("MPD"). According to proponents of the diagnosis, MPD is closely associated with childhood sexual abuse that is generally not remembered until adulthood. While MPD had been diagnosed in a small number of cases before 1980, after its inclusion in the DSM–III, it took on a life of its own. According to one estimate, almost 40,000 new cases of MPD were diagnosed between 1985 and 1995. See Joan Acocella, *The Politics of Hysteria*, The New Yorker, Apr. 6, 1998, at 66. The MPD diagnosis was endorsed not only by some feminist writers and child protection advocates but also by a variety of culturally conservative organizations. By the early 1990s, however, there had been a significant backlash: individuals who had been diagnosed with MPD were suing therapists and winning multi-million dollar awards for being misdiagnosed. Id. at 71–72. DSM–IV and DSM–5 do not include MPD; "dissociative identity disorder" appears in its stead and encompasses some of the same symptoms (see Appendix A). The litigation engendered by MPD is discussed more fully in Chapter Three.

Controversy about the listing and nomenclature of disorders related to sexual behavior provides a recent example of how the APA was cognizant of the political and legal implications of its diagnostic manual. In the run-up to publication of DSM–5, many mental health professionals voiced concerns about how certain proposed diagnoses might be used to facilitate detention under state systems for civilly committing sex offenders. As Chapter Eight explains in detail, statutes governing sex offender commitments typically require only a finding that the respondent has a "mental abnormality" that creates a predisposition to commit sex offenses and an inability to control behavior that makes it likely that the respondent will commit sex offenses if not confined. See, e.g., N.Y. Mental Hygiene Law Art. 10, § 10.07(f). When DSM–5 was undergoing development, prominent mental health professionals wrote that the paraphilia diagnoses in DSM–IV–TR were already being misused by forensic clinicians and that the proposed expansion of pedophilia (sexual attraction to children) to include early adolescents ("pedohebephilia") would "make the current bad situation very much worse." Allen Frances & Michael B. First, *Hebephilia Is Not a Mental Disorder in DSM–IV–TR and Should Not Become One in DSM–5*, 39 J. Amer. Acad. Psychiatry & Law 78 (2011). As a result, pedohebephilia was not included in DSM–5. Driven by similar concerns, the developers of DSM–5 consulted forensic clinicians (colleagues with special expertise in applying psychiatric considerations to legal determinations) on a number of other disorders "with high potential for influencing civil and criminal judgments in courtroom settings." DSM–5 at 9.

2.   *Criticism of modern versions of the DSM.* Perhaps the most persistent and widespread criticism of the third, fourth, and fifth editions of the DSM is that the diagnostic criteria are often still too broad and/or vague, making their application by mental health professionals a self-serving "pathologizing" of everyday behavior. As a group of British psychologists stated in their pre-publication comments on DSM–5:

> [C]lients and the general public are negatively affected by the continued and continuous medicalisation of responses to their experiences; responses which undoubtedly have distressing consequences which demand helping responses, but which do not reflect illnesses so much as normal individual variation. . . . The putative diagnoses presented in DSM–[5] are clearly based largely on social norms, with 'symptoms' that all rely on subjective judgements, with little confirmatory physical 'signs' or evidence of biological causation. The criteria are not value-free, but rather reflect current normative social expectations.

British Psychological Society, Response to the American Psychiatric Association: DSM–5 Development (June 2011) (available at http://apps.bps. org.uk/_publicationfiles/consultation-responses/DSM-5%202011%20-%20BPS

%20response.pdf). Among the critics' targets in DSM–5 are the inclusion of: "disruptive mood dysregulation disorder" (which applies to "severe recurrent temper outbursts, by children and others, "grossly out of proportion . . . to the situation" at least three times a week); "mild neurocognitive disorder" (which applies to "modest cognitive decline" from aging that does *not* "interfere with capacity for independence in everyday activities" such as paying bills or taking medication, other than requiring "greater effort, compensatory strategies, or accommodation"); "somatic symptom disorder" (which refers to "excessive thoughts, feelings or behaviors" about one's health and symptoms, including pain), "binge eating disorder" (diagnosable when serious overeating is accompanied by "a sense of lack of control" and occurs at least once a week for three months), and, within the diagnosis of "major depressive disorder," the extreme sadness, weight loss, fatigue and trouble sleeping that might be experienced after a loved one's death, financial ruin or losses from a natural disaster. See Associated Press, *New Psychiatric Manual, DSM–5, Faces Criticism for Turning "Normal" Human Problems into Mental Illness* (May 13, 2013).

Critics of the earlier versions of the DSM have also pointed to studies showing that, in representative samples of adults, 50% of respondents reported at least one lifetime mental disorder and about 30% reported at least one disorder in the past 12 months as defined by the DSM. See Ronald C. Kessler et al., *Lifetime and 12–month Prevalence of DSM–III–R Psychiatric Disorders in the United States*, 51 Archives Gen. Psychiatry 8 (1994). The Surgeon General's estimate of a 28%–30% prevalence of mental disorder noted previously was also based on DSM criteria. Criticisms about overly broad or easily misapplied diagnostic criteria have been particularly pointed in the case of diagnoses that apply to children and adolescents. One such diagnosis is attention-deficit/hyperactivity disorder (ADHD), which now is said to affect 9% of U.S. children and adolescents and has led to 2.7 million children receiving ADHD pharmacotherapy. Christopher J. Kratochvil, *ADHD Pharmacotherapy: Rates of Stimulant Use and Cardiovascular Risk*, 169 Amer. J. Psychiatry 112 (2012). Professor Diller catalogued some of the results of the changes in ADHD diagnostic criteria that followed the revisions to DSM–III and DSM–IV:

> The increasing numbers of children and adults who meet the broader ADHD criteria are beginning to have an impact in the classroom and workplace. Parents find the only way to get extra help for their children is to have them labeled with a disorder. The Individuals with Disabilities Education Act of 1990 and recent interpretations of Section 504 of the 1973 Rehabilitation Act [discussed in Chapters 11 and 12] have become broad and potent legal tools for families of children with ADHD seeking special services from their school districts. . . . In the workplace more and more employers are being asked to make changes for their workers who are affected with ADHD. . . . Attention–Deficit Hyperactivity Disorder has contributed to a crisis in the disability insurance industry. Claims have soared for a host of ill-defined conditions. Insurers have fled the business of providing disability insurance, making it prohibitively

expensive or impossible to obtain. As more people meet diagnostic criteria, many will attempt to gain services. It remains to be seen whether broadly defined disabilities ultimately trivialize suffering or make it more difficult for the more severely impaired person to obtain urgently needed recognition and service.

Lawrence Diller, *The Run of Ritalin: Attention Deficit Disorder and Stimulant Treatment in the 1990s*, Hastings Center Report, Mar. 1996.

Others critics have claimed that DSM covers so many conditions that it may lead to situations in which the diagnosis, not the patient, is treated. Clinicians, it is said, may "grind out" patients based on which DSM criteria they meet, rather than fashioning treatment based on the individual's constellation of symptoms, which often vary from what is found in the DSM. Gary Tucker, *Putting DSM–IV in Perspective*, 155 Am. J. Psychiatry 159 (1998).

— no individual care

Finally, the earlier DSMs received criticism for failing to recognize how mental disorders might express themselves in members of non-Western and minority cultures. Before DSM–IV appeared, only a few descriptions of the various mental disorders included cultural information. In DSM–IV, however, 14 of the 16 major diagnostic classes included some discussion of cultural issues, and an appendix entitled "Outline for Cultural Formulation and Glossary of Culture–Bound Syndromes" described "recurrent, locality-specific patterns of aberrant behavior and troubling experience that may or may not be linked to a particular DSM–IV diagnostic category." Thus, for instance, clinicians were alerted to the phenomena known as *amok* (a period of brooding followed by violent outbursts, observed in Malaysia, Laos, the Philippines and other Pacific nations), *ataque de nervios* (a syndrome of "uncontrollable shouting, crying, trembling, and aggression typically triggered by a stressful event involving family" observed in Latino groups), and *ghost sickness* (anxiety, hallucinations, loss of consciousness and other symptoms associated with a preoccupation with death, observed in Native American cultures). DSM–IV–TR, at 898–903.

— cultural

DSM–5 takes further steps to address cultural features of clinical presentations. Rather than including a mere listing of culture-bound syndromes, the diagnostic criteria in DSM–5 now reflect awareness of cross-cultural variations and include detailed information about cultural expressions of distress. For example, DSM–5 notes that the expression, interpretation, and attribution of panic symptoms often reflect cultural expectations. DSM–5 also contains a 11–page chapter describing the "Cultural Formulation," which begins by stating, "Understanding the cultural context of illness experience is essential for effective diagnostic assessment and clinical management." DSM–5 at p. 749. The chapter provides a detailed "Cultural Formulation Interview," a structured guide for eliciting information about culture that is relevant to understanding why individuals seek treatment or come to the attention of mental health professionals.

III.   TREATMENT OF A MENTAL DISORDER

A. INTRODUCTION

Since ancient times, "deranged states" that might be diagnosed today as psychoses have been recognized as conditions that required some sort of response. Societal reactions to afflicted individuals ranged from banishment to punishment. In both Greece and Rome, seriously ill persons were often kept under restraint by their families, imprisoned, or exiled. In medieval times and during the Renaissance, mental illness was often thought to result from possession by demons or witchcraft that could only be expunged by torture or exorcism.

As early as the 14th century, institutions referred to as asylums began to take the place of prisons for confining individuals with a mental illness. The regimen in asylums was generally harsh, with an emphasis on restraint. Early in the 19th century, reformers, starting with Philippe Pinel (the author of the influential Medico–Philosophical Treatise on Mental Alienation or Mania published in 1801) began to advocate for the "humane treatment" of these individuals. Since effective treatments for mental illness did not yet exist, this goal typically simply meant that asylums should be operated in a more humane manner. Not until the end of the 19th century did a search for means to treat mental illness commence. Through the mid–20th century, treatment approaches were highly experimental and focused mainly on patients who had been committed to asylums. These therapies—including malarial fever therapy (inducing, then curing, malaria to treat syphilis-induced general paresis of the insane), lobotomies (cutting neuronal connections to the frontal lobes), insulin coma therapy, and electro-convulsive therapy (ECT)—achieved only marginal beneficial results. Among these treatment, only ECT is still employed today, though its administration has undergone dramatic change.

Psychotropic medications (which include anti-psychotic medications, anti-depressants and a host of other drugs) were first introduced in the late 1940s and have since revolutionized the treatment of serious mental disorders. The first breakthrough came in 1949, with the discovery that lithium could be used to treat bipolar disorder (then often called manic-depression). The success of lithium hastened the development of many other drugs. In the 1950s, two types of antidepressant drugs—monoamine oxidase inhibitor (MAOIs) and tricyclics/heterocyclics—were released for use in the U.S., as was the antipsychotic chlorpromazine, which ultimately contributed to a major reduction of the populations of state-operated psychiatric facilities. During the 1970s and 1980s, many pharmacologic agents were produced to address anxiety, while in the late 1980s and early 1990s the selective serotonin reuptake inhibitors (SSRIs) fluoxetine (Prozac®) and sertraline (Zoloft®) emerged to treat depression.

Today, care of most persons with mental illnesses relies on biological interventions (primarily psychopharmacology), psychotherapy, or the two in combination. Psychopharmacology is now widely used to treat disabling psychotic conditions and many other less serious disorders, with primary care physicians (i.e., not psychiatrists) generating most psychotropic prescriptions. See Mark Olfson et al., National Trends in the Outpatient Treatment of Depression, 287 JAMA 203 (2002) (determining that family practitioners and internists account for three-fourths of the psychotropic medications prescribed annually for depression). Alternative biological treatments include electroconvulsive therapy (ECT), repetitive transcranial magnetic stimulation (rTMS), and light therapy. ECT or rTMS are generally used when an individual is unresponsive to or cannot tolerate pharmacological treatment for depression, while light therapy (a.k.a. phototherapy or heliotherapy) is used to treat seasonal affective disorders.

Non-biological treatment methods include a range of what are often referred to as "psychosocial" or "talk" therapies. These therapies encompass a variety of techniques, all of which rely basically on verbal communications between the therapist and the client. The progenitors for many of these approaches were the psychodynamically oriented therapies developed during the 20th century, but today, as noted earlier, cognitive-behavioral therapy is more prevalent.

The decision to use either a biological treatment or psychotherapy is generally determined by the nature of the disorder, its severity, patient and clinician preferences, and the availability of reimbursement. Mental health providers typically believe that the most severe disorders (such as depression with psychotic features and schizophrenia) require pharmacological therapy to address associated symptoms, although they often supplement medication with some form of psychosocial therapy. Less severe disorders, on the other hand, are often amenable to some form of psychotherapy, although psychotropic medication is sometimes employed as an adjunct.

The general trend has been toward decreased use of psychotherapy and increased use of psychotropic medication. For instance, for 1987 to 1997, while the percentage of the population receiving psychotherapy increased only slightly (3.2% in 1987 versus 3.6% in 1997), the percentage of individuals receiving psychotherapy who also received psychotropic medication increased dramatically—from 31.5% in 1987 to 61.5% in 1997. Mark Olfson et al., *National Trends in the Use of Outpatient Psychotherapy*, 159 Am. J. Psychiatry 1914 (2002). A more recent study concluded that "[p]rescription rates among adults were 73 percent higher in 2006 than in 1996, and more than one in ten adults reported a mental health prescription." Sherry A. Glied & Richard G. Frank, *Better but Not Best: Recent Trends in the Well–Being of the Mentally Ill*, 28 Health Aff.

637, 643 (2009). The latter study also found that the rate at which mental health problems were diagnosed by primary care physicians had increased by 30% from 1996 to 2006, with slightly over 10% of primary care physician visits including a mental health diagnosis in 2006. Id. at 639–40. However, the authors also concluded that this rate was still well below the estimated prevalence of mental illness, with underdiagnosis (and thus undertreatment) remaining a problem. Id. at 639. Furthermore, "[f]or adults impaired by a mental illness, rates of treatment remained essentially constant [from 1996] through 2006." Id. at 646. The authors also expressed concern that while the treatment of individuals with less limiting mental health conditions had expanded in recent years, the ability of the most impaired individuals to obtain treatment had declined. Id. at 641.

The following materials briefly summarize the principal characteristics of the various biological and non-biological therapies that are currently employed. The attention given to the biological therapies and their associated side effects is driven by the following considerations:

- As noted in Chapter Two, the complexities involved in the selection of specific medications and the sometimes serious side effects associated with their use has been a key issue in the debate over whether physicians/psychiatrists should have exclusive authority to prescribe psychotropic medication, an authority currently being challenged by non-physician mental health professionals such as psychologists.

- As detailed in Chapter Three, the growing use of psychotropic medication in the treatment of mental disorders coupled with the potential for adverse side effects raises complex issues with regard to the application of malpractice law.

- As discussed in Chapter Four, application of the doctrine of informed consent presupposes that basic, but nonetheless sometimes complex, information concerning a proposed treatment will be communicated to a client, including information about treatment alternatives and possible side effects associated with psychotropic medications.

- As addressed in Chapter Nine, an understanding of psychotropic medication, particularly the subcategory of drugs known as antipsychotic medication, is an important predicate to analyzing the scope of the constitutional right to refuse treatment, which has occasioned a significant amount of litigation in the past several decades.

B. BIOLOGICAL THERAPIES

Advances in psychopharmacology have provided powerful tools to treat a range of mental disorders. Yet most of these drugs have potential side effects that can be unpleasant, impair normal functioning, or cause significant and sometimes permanent damage. Given the significance of these negative outcomes in various legal contexts, the following materials not only describe the most commonly used psychopharmacological drugs, but also highlight side effects that sometimes occur during their use. The discussion examines the most frequent treatments for depression, biopolar illness, schizophrenia, ADHD, and anxiety and phobias.

1. Treatment of Depression

a. *Pharmacological Therapy*

Antidepressant drugs can be roughly divided into four major categories:

- selective serotonin reuptake inhibitors (SSRIs), including fluoxetine (Prozac®), sertraline (Zoloft®), paroxetine (Paxil®), fluovoxamine (Luvox®), citalopram (Celexa®), and escitalopram (Lexapro®);

- monoamine oxidase inhibitors (MAOIs);

- tricyclic antidepressants; and

- antidepressants with other chemical actions, including bupropion (Wellbutrin®), venlafaxine (Effexor®), duloxetine (Cymbalta®), mirtazepine (Remeron®), trazodone (Desyrel®), and vilazodone (Viibryd®).

Scientists are not sure how antidepressants work, but all the currently available drugs alter levels of one or more of three *neurotransmitters*—serotonin, norepinephrine, and dopamine—that play key roles in modifying signaling between the brain's nerve cells. The four categories of antidepressant drugs listed above have fairly similar overall effectiveness in treating depression, but they differ in their modes of actions and side effects. Some of these drugs are infrequently used today, but they are described here because they figure in some of the discussion in this book.

- The SSRIs were developed in a search for antidepressants with lower levels of toxicity and fewer side effects than the older medications such as the MAOIs and tricyclics. The first and most famous of these, Prozac (introduced in 1987), is effective in treating depressive conditions and many other disorders (e.g., panic disorder and obsessive-compulsive disorder), as are many of the subsequently introduced SSRIs. SSRIs and other, newer antidepressants (e.g., venlafaxine and duloxetine) have become very popular, with recent reports suggesting that one-ninth of the U.S. population over the age of 12 take them. Laura A. Pratt et al., *Antidepressant Use in Persons Aged 12 and Over: United States, 2005–2008*, NCHS Data Brief no. 76 (Oct. 2011). SSRIs do not require lab monitoring, they are easy to take (usually once-a-day dosing), and they are relatively free of serious side effects. Nevertheless, commonly experienced side effects include sexual dysfunction (particularly decreased libido and anorgasmia in both men and women). A significant proportion (10–15%) of individuals who take these drugs experience anxiety, nervousness, and insomnia. Available evidence suggests that during the first few weeks of treatment with antidepressants of all kinds (including SSRIs), suicidality—suicidal thoughts, preparatory acts, nonfatal attempts—may increase among patients under age 25 years (but not among middle-aged or older adults). Richard A. Friedman & Andrew C. Leon, *Expanding the Black Box—Depression, Antidepressants, and the Risk of Suicide*, 356 New Eng. J. Med. 2343 (2007).

- The side effects of MAOIs have always limited their use, and now that many other antidepressants are available, they are typically not prescribed. These medications can be highly effective, however, and they are occasionally used when other treatments have not worked. Older literature suggests that MAOIs may be particularly helpful in the treatment of "atypical depression," which involves oversleeping, overeating, fatigue, and intense sensitivity to interpersonal rejection. Common side effects of MAOIs include sleepiness or insomnia, lightheadedness, nervousness, and weight gain. Concern about the risks of severe elevations of blood pressure, which may occur with the consumption of foods containing large amounts of tyramine or with the concurrent administration of several other medications (including some over-the-counter medications), have limited the use of MAOIs, although some argue unnecessarily. Meghan M. Grady & Stephen M. Stahl, *Practical Guide for Prescribing MAOIs: Debunking Myths and Removing Barriers*, 17 CNS Spectrums 17 (2012).

- Before 1990, tricyclic antidepressants such as amitriptyline (Elavil®), imiprimine (Tofranil®) and nortryptiline (Pamelor®) were the agents most commonly used to treat major depression. The side effects of tricyclics include dry mouth, blurred vision, weight gain, constipation, dizziness and fainting (from lower blood pressure), sedation, and decreased sexual energy. Most individuals experienced at least some side effects, which they tolerated if the medications were otherwise helpful. Tricyclics, however, require careful dose adjustment, and overdoses with tricyclics have a substantial likelihood of being fatal. By contrast, SSRIs are once-a-day drugs that are comparatively safe even if an overdose occurs. This accounts for the current unpopularity of tricyclics unless other drugs have proven unhelpful.

- The remaining antidepressant drugs have a variety of properties and side effects:

  - Bupropion differs from most other antidepressants in that it primarily influences levels of the neurotransmitters dopamine and norepinephrine rather than serotonin. Bupropion is therefore more prone than the SSRIs to increase anxiety and insomnia, but it is less prone to cause sexual problems.

  - Venlafaxine and duloxetine appear to work by blocking uptake of serotonin (as do the SSRIs), but they also block reuptake of norepinephrine. This feature may explain why these drugs, which are sometimes called "serotonin-norepinephrine reuptake inhibitors ("SNRIs"), are more likely than the SSRIs to cause gastrointestinal side effects (e.g., nausea or diarrhea).

  - The therapeutic effects of mirtazapine appear related to its interaction with specific subtypes of noradrenergic and serotonin receptors in the brain, thereby enhancing levels of norepinephrine and serotonergic transmission. Its more common side effects are dry mouth, sedation, increased appetite, and weight gain.

b. *Electroconvulsive Therapy ("ECT")*

Electroconvulsive therapy, or ECT (colloquially called "shock therapy"), is used to treat severe depression, particularly when immediate relief is needed or a patient has not responded to antidepressant medication. ECT involves the application of electric impulses to the brain to induce a seizure, which, for unknown reasons, is very effective in alleviating depression. ECT is typically administered in a series of 8–12 treatments over two to four weeks. Unlike medication, ECT can produce beneficial results fairly rapidly, which is an advantage when an individual is suicidal or cannot, because of side effects, tolerate antidepressant medication. See 9 Mental Health Disorders Sourcebook 469–70 (Karen Bellenir ed., 1996). ECT is considered by many to be the most effective treatment for severe depression. ECT was fairly widely used (and, some claimed, abused) in earlier years, particularly in psychiatric hospitals. It is used far less frequently used today, primarily because of its relative expense, its negative reputation, and the development of newer antidepressant medications.

Formerly, ECT was associated with two major problems: the discomfort and fear caused by the procedure, and bone fractures associated with the induced seizures. Today, these side effects have been largely eliminated with the conjunctive use of general anesthetics and pharmacological muscle relaxants. When properly administered, the primary side effect of ECT is impaired memory formation during the time that an individual is receiving treatment. However, studies indicate that the individual's ability to store memories in the future and to recall memories predating the treatment is unaffected. Hence, individuals receiving this treatment typically can recall pre-treatment memories, and experience no change in their ability to learn and remember things in the future. However, they may never clearly recall what occurred during the period in which they were receiving ECT. Annual use of ECT in the U.S. has declined substantially in the last two decades—from 12.6 to 7.2/100,000 adult hospital patients in 1993 to 2009, primarily because of a declining use of this treatment for elderly persons. See Brady G. Case, *Declining Use of Electroconvulsive Therapy in United States General Hospitals*, 73 Biological Psychiatry 119 (2013).

2.   Treatment of Bipolar Disorders

Bipolar disorders are characterized by episodes of depression and episodes of euphoria (extreme elation) or very irritable mood, with the latter episodes corresponding to what is termed the "manic" phase. People with bipolar disorder are susceptible to manic or hypomanic episodes if they take antidepressants, and because of this reaction, doctors often prescribe mood stabilizers rather than antidepressants for the depressive phase of bipolar disorder. When prescribing for the manic phase, doctors select from among several mood stabilizing medications based on the urgency of treatment, their patient's past experience with particular drugs, their patient's preferences, and possible side effects.

The FDA approved lithium for the treatment of bipolar disorder more than four decades ago. Lithium, an oral medication, is particularly effective for treating depression and "classic" bipolar disorder (in which individuals experience euphoria during manic periods). Lithium significantly diminishes severe manic symptoms in five to fourteen days, although if used alone, it often takes weeks until the manic phase fully abates. For this reason, lithium is usually supplemented with a second-generation antipsychotic medication (described later in this chapter), particularly during the first several days of treatment.

The common side effects of lithium include upset stomach and nausea, fatigue, hand tremors, and frequent urination. Further, blood levels of lithium just a bit above the therapeutic range can harm kidney and nervous system functioning. Because high lithium levels can be life-threatening, use of this drug requires regular blood tests throughout the course of treatment. 9 Mental Health Disorders Sourcebook 422–23 (Karen Bellenir ed., 1996).

Several drugs originally developed to treat other conditions are also effective for either the depressive or manic phases of bipolar disorder. These include sodium divalproex (Depakote®), carbamazepine (Tegretol®), lamotrigine (Lamictal®), olanzapine (Zyprexa®), risperidone (Risperdal®), quetiapine (Seroquel®), and lurasidone (Latuda®). Divalproex is particularly effective in treating the irritable forms of mania and is often tolerated better than lithium. Lamotrigine, quetiapine, and lurasidone have received express FDA approval for the treatment of the depressive phase of bipolar disorder, but the strongest data for the long-term reduction of the risk of suicide is associated with the use of lithium. Many of these drugs are used not only for the treatment of acute mania but also for prophylactic purposes. They are not without side effects, however. For example, divalproex may induce weight gain and liver dysfunction, while lamotrigine can cause a serious skin reaction.

3.   Treatment of Schizophrenia

Schizophrenia is a chronic, severe mental disorder characterized by psychotic symptoms, which may include disordered thinking, hallucinations, and delusions such as paranoia. Schizophrenia affects about 1.1% or 2.4 million American adults and is associated with significant functional impairments that impede the ability to work and social interactions. The primary medications used to treat this disorder are called antipsychotic medications. Although these medications do not cure schizophrenia, they are generally effective in alleviating or reducing its symptoms. Psychiatrists regard antipsychotic drugs as a mainstay of treatment efforts.

Chlorpromazine (Thorazine®), the first medication of this kind, became available for use in the United States in the 1950s. See William T. Carpenter & James I. Koenig, *The Evolution of Drug Development in Schizophrenia: Past Issues and Future Opportunities*, 33 Neuropsychopharmacology 2061 (2008). The success of chlorpromazine led, within a few years, to the development of other medications with similar chemical structures, as well as compounds with different chemical structures but very similar abilities to control psychotic symptoms. At this point, around twenty antipsychotic medications have received FDA approval for the treatment of schizophrenia. Most of these drugs are taken orally, but several are available in injectable forms that act more quickly or last longer.

Although researchers have demonstrated convincingly that these drugs can be effective, exactly why remains a puzzle. In the early 1960s, what came to be termed the "dopamine hypothesis" of schizophrenia emerged; in its most basic form, this theory suggests that schizophrenia results from an excess of the neurotransmitter dopamine in the brain. The dopamine hypothesis drew upon observations that hallucinations and delusions could be induced by drugs that increase levels of dopamine and from the finding that the potency of all then-available antipsychotic drugs was directly proportional to their ability to block the dopamine D_2 receptor. Blocking D_2 receptors remains the key means by which all currently FDA-approved antipsychotic drugs exert their main therapeutic effects.

Yet for several decades, neuroscientists and clinicians have known that the excess-dopamine hypothesis does not fully explain the causes and nature of schizophrenia. For example, compounds that do not affect dopamine activity (e.g., the anesthetic ketamine) can cause florid psychoses. Also, although all antipsychotic drugs can reduce the "positive" symptoms of schizophrenia—i.e., hallucinations and delusional thinking—they often have little impact on these individuals' functioning. Rather, the "negative" symptoms of schizophrenia—disruptions to normal emotions and behavior, such as deficits in their interest in their surroundings, the volume of their communications, and the extent of their social relationships—are more predictive of long-term functional problems, and these symptoms seem closely related to a *dearth* of dopaminergic activity in certain areas of the brain. Recent efforts at treatment development are therefore looking at influencing neurotransmitters other than dopamine (particularly glutamate) and the impact of drugs on related gene expression.

Prior to the arrival of neuroleptics, persons with schizophrenia often spent years hospitalized in a terrible state. The "first generation" antipsychotic drugs (FGAs) that became available between 1960 and 1990 were a key force in shortening the length of hospitalizations to months or weeks and in allowing many individuals to live outside a hospital setting. Yet these medications also had serious limitations and drawbacks. Although FGAs reduced many individuals' psychotic symptoms, they did not help all persons who suffered from psychotic disorders. One-half to three-fourths of patients had "a moderate to excellent response and up to 90 percent of patients showed some response." See Daniel P. Van Kammen & Stephen R. Marder, Dopamine Receptor Antagonists, 2 Comprehensive Textbook of Psychiatry 1987 (6th ed. 1995). However, this meant that up to half of patients show no response or only a partial one. Further, many patients who experienced a reduction in their positive symptoms showed little improvement in their cognitive impairments and negative symptoms.

FGAs also consistently cause a constellation of side effects known as extrapyramidal symptoms (EPS), including stiffness, diminished facial expression, tremors, and restlessness. Indeed, the pronounced effects of these drugs on many aspects of the nervous system led to their being termed "neuroleptics," a combination of the Greek words for nerve and seizing. These side effects—tremors, shuffling gait, stiffness, restlessness, and looking "drugged"—are esthetically unappealing, can be intensely unpleasant to experience, and often led patients to stop taking their medication. In addition, many patients who take FGAs develop permanent and sometimes disabling neuromotor syndromes such as tardive dyskinesia (TD). TD rarely occurs in individuals who have been exposed to neuroleptics for fewer than three months, but individuals with schizophrenia must take medication for years to stay symptom free. One study estimated the risk of developing TD to be approximately 5% per year of exposure. See John M. Kane et al., *Integrating Evidence and Prevalence of Tardive Dyskinesia*, 22 Psychopharmacological Bull. 254 (1986). A small fraction of patients (0.02%–2.4% of persons receiving FGAs) develop a severe and sometimes fatal reaction to these drugs called "neuroleptic malignant syndrome," in which they suffer fever, muscle rigidity, autonomic instability, altered consciousness, elevated cardiac enzymes and white blood cell count, and (if left untreated) a significant risk of death. Herbert Y. Meltzer & S. Hossein Fatemi, Treatment of Schizophrenia, American Psychiatric Press Textbook of Psychopharmacology 747, 760–61 (2d ed. 1998).

Though clinicians can reduce these side effects and monitor for the emergence of TD, these problems are all-too-common occurrences during treatment with FGAs. TD usually is mild and not disabling, and it often remits when medication is stopped or the dosage reduced. But in severe cases, the nervous system damage can be grossly disabling, and more recent evidence suggests that even when overt side effects are minimal, FGAs may subtly damage the brain. The potential side effects of FGAs figured prominently in several legal decisions (discussed in later chapters) about forcible medications and the right to refuse treatment.

Over the past two decades, the availability of so-called second-generation antipsychotic drugs (SGAs) has drastically altered prescribing patterns among clinicians who treat psychoses, such that only a minority of patients with psychoses undergo long-term exposure to FGAs. In 1989, the FDA approved the use of clozapine to treat refractory psychosis. Clozapine was the first really new antipsychotic medication to become available in 35 years. It often works better than FGAs—30% to 60% of individuals with schizophrenia who do not respond to the older drugs improve when they take it—and it has a much lower risk of causing EPS and TD. However, taking clozapine creates a small risk that an individual's bone marrow will stop making certain the white blood cells responsible for fighting bacterial infections, a condition called agranulocytosis. Accordingly, patients who take clozapine must be monitored with frequent blood tests, which greatly increases the cost and annoyance of taking the drug.

Since 1994, the FDA has approved several other SGAs for the treatment of schizophrenia and other conditions. SGAs available in the U.S. as of 2013 include risperidone (Risperdal®), olanzepine (Zyprexa®), quetiapine (Seroquel®), ziprasadone (Geodon®), aripiprazole (Abilify®), asenapine (Saphris®), iloperidone (Fanapt®), lurasidone (Latuda®), and paliperidone (Invega®). These newer SGAs are not associated with a substantial risk of agranulocytosis, and thus the recipients of these drugs do not require frequent blood counts, though other blood tests are recommended to check for elevated blood sugar and lipids. The features and possible advantages of SGAs include:

- The ability to treat positive symptoms at least as effectively as FGAs, often with a lower frequency and intensity of EPS.

- The risk of developing TD appears to be lower as well, with a 2004 study suggesting that the risk with SGAs is one-seventh the risk with FGAs.

- Individuals who need antipsychotic medication often prefer these agents, in part because they may leave patients less burdened with negative symptoms such as motor slowing.

- Their use may lead to less cortical tissue loss (which is associated with schizophrenia) and higher levels of brain growth factors, which may contribute to greater clinical stability.

Peter F. Buckley et al., *Brain Derived Neurotropic Factor in First–Episode Psychosis*, 91 Schizophrenia Res. 1 (2007); Christoph U. Correll et al., *Lower Risk for Tardive Dyskinesia Associated with Second–Generation Antipsychotics: A Systematic Review of 1–Year Studies*, 161 Am. J. Psychiatry 414 (2004); Christine Rummel–Kluge et al., *Second–Generation Antipsychotic Drugs and Extrapyramidal Side Effects: A Systematic Review and Meta-analysis of Head-to-Head Comparisons*, 38 Schizophr Bulletin 167 (2012).

A few recent studies have expressed doubts about some of these matters. See Michael J. Peluso, *Extrapyramidal Motor Side–Effects of First- and Second–Generation Antipsychotic Drugs*, 200 Brit. J. Psychiatry 387 (2012) (concluding that the expected improvement in EPS profiles for participants randomly assigned to SGAs rather than FGAs was not found, though patients taking FGAs received more medication to *prevent* EPS); Scott W. Woods et al., *Incidence of Tardive Dyskinesia with Atypical and Conventional Antipsychotics: Prospective Cohort Study*, 71 J. Clinical Psychiatry 463 (2010) (concluding that, in this cohoert, SGAs and FGAs posed similar risks of TD). Furthermore, while the SGAs may have fewer neuromotor side effects, they create risks of their own. To varying degrees, SGAs increase the likelihood that patients will become obese and develop high blood pressure, diabetes, or elevated blood lipids—all significant risk factors for strokes, heart attacks, and early death (see note 1 in "Questions and Comments" section, *infra*).

4. Treatment of Attention Deficit Hyperactivity Disorder (ADHD)

Methylphenidate and amphetamine-based stimulants have been used to treat ADHD since the 1960s. Stimulants are the treatments of first choice for ADHD. Older stimulants (e.g., Ritalin® and dextro-amphetamine) persist in the body for just a few hours after ingestion, so their benefits wane quickly; also, stimulants are classified as Schedule II drugs by the federal government because of concerns about potential abuse. The recent recognition that ADHD is both more common in childhood than was once thought and that it often persists into adulthood has coincided with the introduction and marketing of several newer stimulant drugs. Some of these compounds are extended-release formulations (e.g., Concerta®, Metadate®, and Adderall XR®) of older stimulants, and some are molecular variations fashioned to improve tolerability (e.g., dexmethylphenidate [Focalin®]) or to reduce abuse (e.g., lisdexamfetamine [Vyvanse®]). Various stimulants have received FDA approval for children as young as three or six years of age, as well as adolescents and adults. In addition, non-stimulant drugs (e.g., the antidepressant bupropion and the anti-hypertensive drugs clonidine and guanfacine) are used if other treatments are ineffective or poorly tolerated (i.e., as second- or third-line pharmacotherapy). A non-stimulant, atomoxetine (Strattera®) was developed expressly as an ADHD treatment that would have low abuse potential.

Prescriptions of ADHD medications are often combined with other remedial measures (e.g., attention-improving and behavior management strategies) when administered by mental health professionals. But much ADHD pharmacotherapy is prescribed by pediatricians and family practitioners who use medication alone as the initial therapy. Stimulants are well tested and relatively free of severe adverse effects, but they require careful monitoring because approximately 15%–30% of children who take these drugs develop minor motor tics in their facial, neck, or shoulder muscles. Common side effects also include appetite suppression, weight loss, and sleep disturbances. Less common problems include increased heart rate or blood pressure, headaches, and emotional changes (social withdrawal, nervousness, and moodiness). In susceptible individuals, stimulants can occasionally precipitate or aggravate other psychiatric problems, including psychoses, mania, depression, and anxiety.

5. Treatment of Anxiety, Panic Disorders, and Phobias

Various medications are available for the treatment of severe anxiety and panic disorders. In the 1970s and 1980s, benzodiazepine "tranquilizers"—e.g., diazepam (Valium®) and lorazepam (Ativan®)—were often the preferred medications for treating anxiety disorders. Now, however, psychiatrists recommend taking these drugs briefly, if at all, because of potential tolerance to their effects and their abuse potential. Borwin Bandelow et al., *World Federation of Societies of Biological Psychiatry (WFSBP) Guidelines for the Pharmacological Treatment of Anxiety, Obsessive–Compulsive and Posttraumatic Stress Disorders*, 3 World J. Biological Psychiatry 171 (2002). Instead, SSRI or SNRI antidepressants are often preferred, and several of these drugs now have FDA approval for use in treating conditions such as panic disorder, generalized anxiety disorder, social phobia, and PTSD.

Benzodiazepines have few side effects when taken over brief periods. They may cause drowsiness and some loss of coordination, and these can be problems for persons who operate motor vehicles or other machinery. Also, benzodiazepines, when taken in combination with other nervous system depressants such as alcohol, have effects that can be more than just additive and can lead to severe problems such as memory impairment, pronounced intoxication, and respiratory depression. The risks of tolerance and addiction are most likely with extended use (several weeks) at higher dosages.

QUESTIONS AND COMMENTS

1. *Risks associated with second-generation antipsychotic drugs.* Individuals with psychotic disorders such as schizophrenia are at increased risk for respiratory problems, metabolic disturbances, and cardiovascular disease. One reason is that the onset of severe mental illness is correlated with other behaviors that increase the risk for such ailments, including smoking, poor dietary choices, and sedentary life style, which in turn aggravate other conditions—e.g., obesity, hypertension, diabetes, hyperlipidemia, and cancer. Both FGAs and SGAs increase the risk of these problems, particularly cardiovascular disease and diabetes. Lars Vedel Kessing, *Treatment with Antipsychotics and the Risk of Diabetes in Clinical Practice*, 197 Br. J. Psychiat. 266 (2010). Growing evidence indicates SGAs create a greater risk of cardiovascular disease and diabetes than do FGAs, though SGAs cause fewer neurological problems. A. H. Barnett et al., *Minimising Metabolic and Cardiovascular Risk in Schizophrenia: Diabetes, Obesity and Dyslipidaemia*, 21 J. Psychopharmacology 357 (2007). Because of these risks, prescriptions of SGAs should be accompanied by periodic monitoring of patients' weight, blood pressure, abdominal circumference, blood sugar, and blood lipids, and patients should take steps to avoid weight gain. American Diabetes Association et al., *Consensus Development Conference on Antipsychotic Drugs and Obesity and Diabetes*, 65 J. Clinical Psychiatry 267 (2004).

2. *Incidence of prescription of SGAs.* More than 15 million prescriptions were written in 2002 for two of the leading SGAs, olanzapine

and risperidone. Erica Goode, *Three Schizophrenia Drugs May Raise Diabetes Risk*, N.Y. Times, Aug. 25, 2003, at A–8. By 2007, more than 85% of people with schizophrenia were prescribed SGAs rather than FGAs. Robert A. Rosenheck & Michael J. Sernyak, *Developing a Policy for Second–Generation Antipsychotic Drugs*, 28 Health Aff. 782 (2009).

3. *Fiscal factors influencing choice of psychopharmacology.* Current trends favoring biological treatment over psychotherapy are partly due to advances in psychopharmacology and partly because of effective marketing campaigns by pharmaceutical companies. Differential third-party reimbursement also pays a large role. See Ramin Mojtabai & Mark Olfson, *National Trends in Psychotherapy by Office–Based Psychiatrists*, 65 Archives Gen. Psychiatry 962, 968–69 (2008) (noting that much of the reduction in the use of psychotherapy versus medication "can be explained by shifts in [the] financing of outpatient mental health care," illustrated by findings "that third-party reimbursement for one 45 to 50–minute outpatient psycho-therapy session is 40.9% less than reimbursement for three 15–minute medication management visits"). A choice of one drug over another may also be influenced by cost factors, particularly when the third-party payor is a state or federal agency or a managed care organization. See Rosenheck & Sernyak, supra, at 785 (citing studies showing increased annual per patient health care costs of $3,000–$10,000 with olanzapine and $2,400–$6,000 per year with SGAs in general that have no clinical advantages over FGAs).

4. *Questions about over-prescribing.* Stimulants such as methyl-phenidate help *most people* concentrate and focus better—not just people with ADHD. This has raised concerns about college students' misuse of stimulants as study aids. See Amelia M. Arria et al., *Nonmedical Use of Prescription Stimulants Among College Students: Associations with Attention–Deficit–Hyperactivity Disorder and Polydrug Use*, 28 Pharmaco-therapy 156 (2008). In addition, rates of diagnosing ADHD have shown "a marked rise over the last decade and could fuel growing concern among many doctors that the A.D.H.D. diagnosis and its medication are overused in American children." Alan Schwarz & Sarah Cohen, *A.D.H.D. Seen in 11% of U.S. Children as Diagnoses Rise*, N.Y. Times, Apr. 1, 2013, at A1. This phenomenon has raised concerns that these drugs are being prescribed not just for kids who really have a disorder, but for kids who are merely immature or misbehaving. See Helga Zoëga et al., *Age, Academic Performance, and Stimulant Prescribing for ADHD: A Nationwide Cohort Study*, 130 Pediatrics 1012 (2012) (showing that compared to older children in the same grade, younger children were 50% more likely to be prescribed stimulants).

5. *Psychosurgery.* Psychosurgery is another biological therapy, although it is not widely used today and is generally limited to hospitalized patients with serious mental disorders that have not responded to other forms of treatment. Generally referred to as "stereotactic" procedures, including subcaudate tractotomy, anterior cingulotomy, limbic leucotomy, and anterior capsulotomy, these surgeries create very small lesions in specific

areas of the brain or involve a placement of electrodes to allow for focused stimulation of brain tissue. Nonetheless, given their intrusiveness, these procedures are reserved for persons with seriously disabling psychotic disorders, mood disorders, or obsessive-compulsive disorder who have not benefited from other forms of treatment. A recent review of pertinent studies showed that these types of psychosurgery produce symptom-free outcomes or significant improvement for many of those treated. James W. Leiphart & Frank H. Valone, *Stereotactic Lesions for the Treatment of Psychiatric Disorders: A Review*, 113 J. Neurosurgery 1204 (2010). As now performed, severe long-term adverse effects from these procedures tend to be limited, and these effects are perceived by some to be relatively "modest" in their impact on overall functioning, with little evidence of resulting impaired neurocognitive functioning. David Christmas et al., *Long Term Outcome of Thermal Anterior Capsulotomy for Chronic, Treatment Refractory Depression*, 82 J. Neurology, Neurosurgery & Psychiatry 594 (2011). However, a prominent medical textbook notes, "The history of psychosurgery in the early twentieth century must incite us to prudence when we consider surgical intervention in psychiatric patients. In fact, only after strong ethical consideration [can we] decide to perform neurosurgery for psychiatric disorders." L. Gabriëls et al., *DBS for OCD*, in Textbook of Stereotactic and Functional Neurosurgery 2897, 2901–02 (Andres M. Lozano et al. eds., 2d ed. 2009) ("Recent data suggest that between 30 and 40% of OCD patients experience significant symptom relief and a further proportion shows some improvement after stereotactic neurosurgery. Although the target symptoms, compulsions and anxiety, are successfully reduced, side effects remain a major concern. These include weight gain, memory problems, attentional slowing, lower performance intelligence quotient, loss of initiative/psychasthenia, diminution of inhibition, elevated mood occasionally with an overshoot toward carelessness, emotional shallowness, and in some cases severe alcoholism, aggressive tendencies, poor impulse control, sexual assaults, and even suicide.").

C. INTERACTIVE TREATMENTS (PSYCHOTHERAPY)

Although psychotherapy is treated here separately from biological therapies, both pharmacotherapy and psychotherapy are biological therapies in the sense that both help patients by facilitating changes in how neurons signal and connect to each other. Whereas medications seek to accomplish this through a pharmaceutical interaction with neurons, psychotherapy uses verbal interactions and communication to alter neuronal activity. As noted earlier, interactive therapy comes in many varieties, including psychodynamic psychotherapy and cognitive-behavioral therapy, as well as many other approaches such as educational counseling and what some clinicians call "plain old therapy"—empathic, attentive listening. The following excerpt addresses some of the commonly used psychotherapies.

MENTAL HEALTH: REPORT OF THE SURGEON GENERAL
65–67 (1999).

. . . Participants in psychotherapy can vary in age from the very young to the very old, and problems can vary from mental health problems to disabling and catastrophic mental disorders. Although people often are seen individually, psychotherapy also can be done with couples, families, and groups. . . . Estimates of the number of orientations to psychotherapy vary from a very small number to well over 400. The larger estimate generally refers to all the variations of the three major orientations, that is, psychodynamic, behavioral, and humanistic. Each orientation falls under the more general conceptual category of either action or reflection.

Psychodynamic orientations are the oldest. They place a premium on self-understanding, with the implicit (or sometimes explicit) assumption that increased self-understanding will produce salutary changes in the participant. Behavioral orientations are geared toward action, with a clear attempt to mobilize the resources of the patient in the direction of change, whether or not there is any understanding of the etiology of the problem. Humanistic orientations aim toward increased self-understanding, often in the direction of personal growth, but use treatment techniques that often are much more active than are likely to be employed by the psychodynamic clinician. While the following paragraphs focus on psychodynamic, behavioral, and humanistic orientations, they also discuss interpersonal therapy and cognitive-behavioral therapy as outgrowths of psychodynamic and behavioral therapy, respectively. . . .

1. Psychodynamic Therapy — past behavior

The first major approach to psychotherapy was developed by Sigmund Freud and is called psychoanalysis. Since its origin more than a century ago, psychoanalysis has undergone many changes. Today, Freudian (or classical) psychoanalysis is still practiced, but other variations have been developed—ego psychology, object relations theory, interpersonal psychology, and self-psychology, each of which can be grouped under the general term "psychodynamic". The psychodynamic therapies, even though they differ somewhat in theory and approach, all have some concepts in common. With each, the role of the past in shaping the present is emphasized, so it is important, in understanding behavior, to understand its origins and how people come to act and feel as they do. A second critical concept common to all psychodynamic approaches is the belief in the unconscious, so that there is much that influences our behavior of which we are not aware. This makes the process of understanding more difficult, as we often act for reasons that we cannot state, and these reasons often are linked to previous experiences. Thus, an important part of psychodynamic psychotherapy is to make the unconscious conscious or to help the patient understand the origin of actions that are troubling so that they can be corrected.

For some psychodynamic approaches, such as the classical Freudian approach, the focus is on the individual and the experiences the person had in the early years that give shape to current behavior, even beyond the awareness of the patient. For other, more contemporary approaches, such as *interpersonal therapy*, the focus is on the relationship between the person and others. First developed as a time-limited treatment for midlife depression, interpersonal therapy focuses on grief, role disputes, role transitions, and interpersonal deficits. The goal of interpersonal therapy is to improve current interpersonal skills. The therapist takes an active role in teaching patients to evaluate their interactions with others and to become aware of self-isolation and interpersonal difficulties. The therapist also offers advice and helps the patient to make decisions.

2.   Behavior Therapy — Current behavior

A second major approach to psychotherapy is known as behavior modification or behavior therapy. It focuses on current behavior rather than on early patterns of the patient. In its earlier form, behavior therapy dealt exclusively with what people did rather than what they thought or felt. The general principles of learning were applied to the learning of maladaptive as well as adaptive behaviors. Thus, if a person could be conditioned to act in a functional way, there was no reason why the same principles of conditioning could not be employed to help the person unlearn dysfunctional behavior and learn to replace it with more functional behavior. The role of the environment was very important for behavior therapists, because it provided the positive and negative reinforcements that sustained or eliminated various behaviors. Therefore, ways of shaping that environment to make it more responsive to the needs of the individual were important in behavior therapy.

More recently, there has been a significant addition to the interests and activities of behavior therapists. Although behavior continued to be important in relation to reinforcements, cognitions—what the person thought about, perceived, or interpreted what was transpiring—were also seen as important. This combined emphasis led to a therapeutic variant known as cognitive-behavioral therapy, an approach that incorporates cognition with behavior in understanding and altering the problems that patients present.

Cognitive-behavioral therapy draws on behaviorism as well as cognitive psychology, a field devoted to the scientific study of mental processes, such as perceiving, remembering, reasoning, decision making, and problem solving. The use of cognition in cognitive-behavioral therapy varies from attending to the role of the environment in providing a model for behavior, to the close study of irrational beliefs, to the importance of individual thought processes in constructing a vision of the surrounding world. In each case, it is critical to study what the individual in therapy thinks and does and less important to understand the past events that led to that pattern of thinking and doing. Cognitive-behavioral therapy strives to alter faulty cognitions and replace them with thoughts and self-statements that promote adaptive behavior. For instance, cognitive-behavioral therapy tries to replace self-defeatist expectations ("I can't do anything right") with positive expectations ("I can do this right"). Cognitive-behavioral therapy has gained such ascendancy as a means of integrating cognitive and behavioral views of human functioning that the field is more frequently referred to as cognitive-behavioral therapy rather than behavior therapy.

3. Humanistic Therapy

The third wave of psychotherapy is referred to variously as humanistic, existential, experiential, or Gestalt therapy. It owes its origins as a treatment to the client-centered therapy that was originated by Carl Rogers, and the theory can be traced to philosophical roots beginning with the 19th century philosopher, Soren Kierkegaard. The central focus of humanistic therapy is the immediate experience of the client. The emphasis is on the present and the potential for future development rather than on the past, and on immediate feelings rather than on thoughts or behaviors. It is rooted in the everyday subjective experience of the person seeking assistance and is much less concerned with mental illness than it is with human growth.

One critical aspect of humanistic treatment is the relationship that is forged between the therapist, who in some ways serves as a guide in an exploration of self-discovery, and the client, who is seeking greater knowledge of the self and an expansion of inherent human potential. The focus on the self and the search for self-awareness is akin to psychodynamic psychotherapy, while the emphasis on the present is more similar to behavior therapy.

Although it is possible to describe distinctive orientations to psychotherapy, as has been done above, most psychotherapists describe themselves as eclectic in their practice, rather than as adherents to any single approach to treatment. As a result, there is a growing development referred to as "psychotherapy integration". It strives to capture what is best about each of the individual approaches.

QUESTIONS AND COMMENTS

1.   *Duration of therapy and managed care.* Talk therapies vary in their intensity and duration. Classical psychoanalysis typically involves "free association"—the reporting of all that comes to one's mind, including

dreams—while in the presence of the analyst, who then interprets this information to promote a "regressive transference neurosis" in which the early years of childhood are re-created within the therapist-client relationship. American Psychiatric Association, The Psychiatric Therapies 834 (Toksoz B. Karasu ed., 1984). As practiced by Freud, this process involved daily sessions of one hour each over several months to a few years, and even today, anything less than three sessions a week "would not entitle the procedure to be called analysis." Id. Psychodynamic psychotherapy, which represents a less time-intensive application of Freud's approach, typically involves one or two 45– or 50–minute sessions a week, often for periods of months or years. Id. The average "dosage" of "brief" psychotherapies (which de-emphasize free association in favor of more direct questioning) and of interpersonal, behavioral, and cognitive therapies is not as long, but these treatments can still last anywhere from several weeks to over a year, depending on the problem being treated.

For individuals with a mental disorder who rely on third-party payor benefits that limit reimbursement to a certain number of sessions, long-term therapies are not feasible. The cost implications of long-term therapies has led "[m]anaged care companies [to] focus on resolving patients' acute symptoms, rather than ridding them of their mental health conditions[,] . . . [leading] to the gradual disappearance of the use of the psychodynamic model as the dominant framework in the treatment of individuals suffering from mental illness." Jeffrey Cohen, *Managed Care and the Evolving Role of the Clinical Social Worker in Mental Health*, 48 Social Work 34 (2003).

2.   *Educational background and choice of treatment by the therapist.* For some diagnostic categories such as schizophrenia and bipolar disorder, mental health professionals generally agree that treatment should include medication to control and reduce active symptoms. For many disorders, however, including moderate depression and anxiety conditions, studies show that psychotherapy, alone or in combination with medication, can be effective. To a great extent, the type of treatment patients receive reflects where they seek care. Most treatment for depression and general anxiety is provided not by mental health professionals, but by primary care clinicians (that is, physicians and nurse practitioners working in internal medicine, family practice, pediatrics, and gynecology), who usually prescribe medications to alleviate patients' problems.

When individuals seek treatment from mental health professionals, they tend to do so with an eye toward the kind of treatment they prefer. Nowadays, the training of most psychiatrists emphasizes developing expertise in pharmacotherapy, and individuals who want a medication-based treatment from a mental health specialist will typically seek it from a psychiatrist. Other mental health professionals (e.g., psychologists, social workers, and counselors) generally are not licensed to prescribe medication (although a few jurisdictions allow psychologists to do so if they receive additional special training; see Chapter Two). Individuals who want psychotherapeutic treatment therefore tend to seek it from these clinicians, whose training emphasizes this approach. For individuals who desire both medication and psychotherapy, a now-common arrangement is for a psychiatrist to provide and monitor medication in brief appointments occurring at several-week intervals (often called "med checks"), while a non-physician therapist conducts more frequent psychotherapy sessions.

D. TREATMENT OUTCOMES

Treatment efficacy and safety are obviously critical matters for both the people who receive the treatment and society in general. The efficacy of some therapies has been subject to considerable testing. The FDA initially reviews all medications, including psychotropic drugs, for their safety and efficacy for a given condition, so pharmaceutical companies must conduct studies on their potential products that satisfy the FDA's requirements. These studies evaluate a drug's effectiveness for a specific purpose (an "indication"), not all possible uses. If the drug receives FDA approval, its manufacturer can legally market it, but only for the approved indication. The FDA is not authorized to direct or restrict how physicians prescribe an approved drug, however, and physicians may prescribe medications for other than their approved indications. This practice, known as "off-label" prescribing, is common and not inherently inappropriate. Many drugs are more often prescribed off-label than on-label, although ideally, off-label prescribing should be based on a firm scientific rationale and sound medical evidence. Barry R. Furrow et al., Liability and Quality Issues in Health Care 80, 359–60 (2008). According to one report looking at all medication prescriptions (psychiatric and non-psychiatric), "[t]he greatest disparity between supported and unsupported off-label uses was found among prescriptions for psychiatric uses (4% strong support vs 96% limited or no support)." Tracy Hampton, *Experts Weigh In on Promotion, Prescription of Off–Label Drugs*, 297 JAMA 683, 683 (2007). Psychotherapies, in contrast, are not subject to FDA review, and clinicians who develop a psychotherapy typically have neither the financial incentive nor the economic wherewithal to mount efficacy studies. Such studies may be funded by a research grant, but these generally occur well after the treatment has been promulgated.

The section that follows summarizes a series of studies on the efficacy of various modalities used to treat the most common mental disorders. Before looking at these studies, a few words about study methods are in order. The investigation of a treatment for a particular disorder would ideally employ a "double-blind" experimental design, which randomly divides research participants who have the disorder into two separate groups. In double-blind studies, one group receives the treatment being tested (the "experimental" group), and the other receives a placebo (the "control" group, although this group may receive an alternative well-established treatment). However, neither the research participants nor the investigators know who is receiving the treatment being tested—hence the use of the term "double-blind." This approach is employed to reduce the chances that outcomes or interpretations of outcomes will be biased, a well-documented psychological tendency that regularly occurs when participants or investigators know who is in which group.

At the conclusion of the test period, the "blind" is removed and the groups are compared with respect to their positive and negative reactions to the intervention. This design can only be employed reliably when (1) both groups of test participants have roughly similar symptoms at the start of the study; (2) the therapies being studied are standardized so they can be consistently applied within the study groups; and (3) comparisons of results obtained from the treatment and placebo groups are based on clear, unambiguous, and consistently applied outcome measures—such as mortality levels, white cell counts, or symptom ratings.

Implementing such studies is far from easy, even when evaluating medications, which are the interventions most amenable to double-blind research paradigms. For example, experts often do not agree fully on diagnoses, with the range of symptoms exhibited by an individual making it difficult to assign a particular diagnosis. As a result, the cohorts being tested frequently lack the precise common characteristics needed for an ideal double-blind study. Although this is true for medical studies generally, it is a problem with which mental health investigators regularly struggle. The contours of the various mental disorders are often ill-defined—most individuals with a mental disorder have signs and symptoms that vary from the "classic" manifestation of a particular disorder. Also, many such individuals have more than one problem—for example, they may have a coexisting substance use disorder, another mental disorder, a nonpsychiatric illness, or personality characteristics that affect them separate from the mental disorder being studied.

In addition, the second requirement—uniformity of the treatment modality—is difficult to achieve in the case of psychotherapies (as compared to a medication study, where the control group can receive an identical looking pill containing no active ingredients). For example, therapists may vary quite a bit in the way they employ a particular therapeutic technique, as well as in their personal warmth (which is an important component of psychotherapy). If it is difficult to attribute a particular outcome to the specific therapeutic approach, the evaluation of a particularly type of psychotherapy will suffer as a result. Also, research participants in psychotherapy studies are more likely to figure out whether they really are in treatment or not, and this may influence how they report symptoms and benefits. Further, a research participant may simply benefit from having someone to talk to regularly rather than the specific "ingredients" of the particular type of psychotherapy being evaluated.

Finally, any evaluation of the effect of a particular intervention on a mental disorder is likely to encounter problems in measuring outcomes (e.g., no effect, improvement, or deterioration). With few exceptions, mental disorders have no physiologically quantifiable signs. An assessment of treatment effects must therefore depend on research participants' reports of their symptoms and on observations of behavioral signs by the researcher or a third party. However, these are inherently subjective interpretations, which will limit the reliability of any study findings. Mental health researchers have developed rating scales of observable behavior that have relatively good reliability, but such scales are of limited value for certain outcomes, such as assessing the mood or anxiety a research participant experiences at a given time.

In spite of these challenges, as indicated by the materials that follow, researchers have sought over the years to evaluate both specific therapies and competing therapies. As might be expected given the just-described problems and limitations, the studies do not always generate consistent results. Yet as a group, they may provide general guidance about the value of various therapeutic approaches for treating particular mental disorders.

1.   Psychotropic Medications

A significant amount of data is available with respect to two major classes of psychotropic drugs, the antidepressants and the antipsychotics. When effectiveness is defined as a greater than 50% decrease in scores on the Hamilton Rating Scale for Depression, studies indicate that antidepressant medications are effective for about two-thirds of patients. Depending on the specific antidepressant used, tricyclics have an effectiveness rate of 60% to 68% and SSRIs of 45% to 79%. MAOIs have an effectiveness rate of about 65%. In addition, certain subtypes of depression (e.g., severe depression) may respond better to some classes of drugs than others. See Jan Fawcett & Robert Barkin, *Efficacy Issues with Antidepressants*, 58(6) J. Clinical Psychiatry Supp. 32 (1997); see also Ralitza Gueorguieva et al., *Trajectories of Depression Severity in Clinical Trials of Duloxetine: Insights Into Antidepressant and Placebo*, 68 Archives Gen. Psychiatry 1227, 1233 (2011) (finding three-quarters of individuals who received active drug in placebo-controlled trials of duloxetine and SSRIs responded positively). However, compliance with these drug regimens is important: 65% of patients who stop treatment relapse within a year compared to 15% of those who continue the treatment. See Somitra Pathare & Carol Paton, *Psychotropic Drug Treatment*, 315 Brit. Med. J. 661 (1997).

As noted earlier, antipsychotic medications produce a response in about 75% of individuals with schizophrenia. About one-quarter of individuals with this disorder do not respond, however. Of these nonresponders, some (one-third to one-half) may respond to another antipsychotic drug, particularly clozapine. Nevertheless, placebo-controlled studies show that despite taking maintenance medication after recovering from an acute psychotic episode, about one-fourth of individuals with schizophrenia experience a relapse in any given year, compared to about two-thirds of those who received a placebo. Stefan Leucht et al., *Antipsychotic Drugs Versus Placebo for Relapse Prevention in Schizophrenia: A Systematic Review and Meta–Analysis*, 379 Lancet 2063 (2012).

Pharmacological treatment is effective for treating panic disorder as well. In placebo-controlled studies, approximately three-fourths of individuals with panic disorder respond to either SSRI or SNRI antidepressants. Mark H. Pollack et al., *A Double–Blind Study of the Efficacy of Venlafaxine Extended–Release, Paroxetine, and Placebo in the Treatment of Panic Disorder*, 24 Depression & Anxiety 1, 10 (2007) (citing other studies as well). As for bipolar disorder, a recent meta-analysis showed that several SGAs—carbamazepine, haloperidol, lithium, and valproate—were more effective than placebo treatments, with response rates averaging 48% in two to three weeks. Ayşegül Yildiz et al., *Efficacy of Antimanic Treatments: Meta-analysis of Randomized, Controlled Trials*, 36 Neuropsychopharmacology 375 (2011). Finally, stimulant drugs used as a treatment for ADHD produce a response rate of about 70%, with parents, teachers, and researchers observing statistically significant declines in hyperactivity and increases in attention. Larry Goldman et al., *Diagnosis and Treatment of Attention–Deficit/Hyperactivity Disorder in Children and Adolescents*, 279 JAMA 1100 (1998). Individuals with ADHD are at elevated risk of being convicted of crimes, and a recent study from Sweden showed that criminal behavior in this population dropped sharply during periods when they took such medication. Paul Lichtenstein et al., *Medication for Attention Deficit–Hyperactivity Disorder and Criminality*, 367 New Eng. J. Med. 2006 (2012).

2. Non–Biological Treatments

As noted earlier, attempts to evaluate the efficacy of psychotherapies encounter nettlesome methodological problems. Yet researchers have nonetheless found ways to evaluate the effectiveness of psychotherapies, and hundreds of such studies have now been published. Most of the first studies examined cognitive-behavioral therapies, while more recent studies have looked at psychodynamic therapies as they have been practiced over the past quarter century. The following excerpt (with citations deleted) appeared in a leading psychology journal and summarizes results from numerous studies.

JONATHAN SHEDLER, THE EFFICACY OF PSYCHODYNAMIC PSYCHOTHERAPY

65 Amer. Psychologist 98, 100–07 (2010).

How Effective Is Psychotherapy in General?

In psychology and in medicine more generally, meta-analysis is a widely accepted method for summarizing and synthesizing the findings of independent studies. Meta-analysis makes the results of different studies comparable by converting findings into a common metric, allowing findings to be aggregated or pooled across studies. A widely used metric is effect size. . . . An effect size of 0.8 is considered a large effect in psychological and medical research, an effect size of 0.5 is considered a moderate effect, and an effect size of 0.2 is considered a small effect.

The first major meta-analysis of psychotherapy outcome studies included 475 studies and yielded an overall effect size (various diagnoses and treatments) of 0.85 for patients who received psychotherapy compared with untreated controls. . . . The influential review by Lipsey and Wilson [in 1993] tabulated results for 18 meta-analyses concerned with general psychotherapy outcomes, which had a median effect size of 0.75. It also tabulated results for 23 metaanalyses concerned with outcomes in CBT [cognitive-behavioral therapy] and behavior modification, which had a median effect size of 0.62. A meta-analysis by Robinson, Berman, and Neimeyer [in 1990] summarized the findings of 37 psychotherapy studies concerned specifically with outcomes in the treatment of depression, which had an overall effect size of 0.73. These are relatively large effects.

To provide some points of reference, it is instructive to consider effect sizes for antidepressant medications. An analysis of U.S. Food and Drug Administration (FDA) databases (published and unpublished studies) reported in the *New England Journal of Medicine* found effect sizes of 0.26 for fluoxetine (Prozac), 0.26 for sertraline (Zoloft), 0.24 for citalopram (Celexa), 0.31 for escitalopram (Lexapro), and 0.30 for duloxetine (Cymbalta). The overall mean effect size for antidepressant medications approved by the FDA between 1987 and 2004 was 0.31. A meta-analysis reported in the prestigious Cochrane Library found an effect size of 0.17 for tricyclic antidepressants compared with active placebo (an active placebo mimics the side effects of an antidepressant drug but is not itself an antidepressant). These are relatively small effects. Methodological differences between medication trials and psychotherapy trials are sufficiently great that effect sizes may not be directly comparable, and the findings should not be interpreted as conclusive evidence that psychotherapy is more effective. Effect sizes for antidepressant medications are reported to provide reference points that will be familiar to many readers.

How Effective Is Psychodynamic Therapy?

A [2006] metaanalysis of psychodynamic therapy ... compared patients with a range of common mental disorders who received short-term (≤40 hours) psychodynamic therapy with controls (wait list, minimal treatment, or "treatment as usual") and yielded an overall effect size of 0.97 for general symptom improvement. The effect size increased to 1.51 when the patients were assessed at long-term follow-up ((9 months posttreatment). In addition to change in general symptoms, the meta-analysis reported an effect size of 0.81 for change in somatic symptoms, which increased to 2.21 at long-term follow-up; an effect size of 1.08 for change in anxiety ratings, which increased to 1.35 at follow-up; and an effect size of 0.59 for change in depressive symptoms, which increased to 0.98 at follow-up. The consistent trend toward larger effect sizes at follow-up suggests that psychodynamic therapy sets in motion psychological processes that lead to ongoing change, even after therapy has ended.

A meta-analysis published in *Archives of General Psychiatry* included 17 high-quality randomized controlled trials of short-term (average of 21 sessions) psychodynamic therapy and reported an effect size of 1.17 for psychodynamic therapy compared with controls. The pretreatment to posttreatment effect size was 1.39, which increased to 1.57 at long-term follow-up, which occurred an average of 13 months posttreatment. Translating these effect sizes into percentage terms, the authors noted that patients treated with psychodynamic therapy were "better off with regard to their target problems than 92% of the patients before therapy."

A [2009] meta-analysis examined the efficacy of short-term psychodynamic therapy for somatic disorders ... Among studies that reported data on health care utilization, 77.8% reported reductions in health care utilization that were due to psychodynamic therapy—a finding with potentially enormous implications for health care reform.

A [2003] meta-analysis reported in the *American Journal of Psychiatry* examined the efficacy of both psychodynamic psychotherapy (14 studies) and CBT (11 studies) for personality disorders. The metaanalysis reported pretreatment to posttreatment effect sizes using the longest term follow-up available. For psychodynamic therapy (mean length of treatment was 37 weeks), the mean follow-up period was 1.5 years and the pretreatment to posttreatment effect size was 1.46. For CBT (mean length of treatment was 16 weeks), the mean follow-up period was 13 weeks and the effect size was 1.0. The authors concluded that both treatments demonstrated effectiveness.

* * *

The "active ingredients" of therapy are not necessarily those presumed by the theory or treatment model. For this reason, randomized controlled trials that evaluate a therapy as a "package" do not necessarily provide support for its theoretical premises or the specific interventions that derive from them. For example, the available evidence indicates that the mechanisms of change in cognitive therapy (CT) are not those presumed by the theory. Kazdin, reviewing the empirical literature on mediators and mechanisms of change in psychotherapy, concluded, "Perhaps we can state more confidently now than before that whatever may be the basis of changes with CT, it does not seem to be the cognitions as originally proposed" (p. 8).

There are also profound differences in the way therapists practice, even therapists ostensibly providing the same treatment. What takes place in the clinical consulting room reflects the qualities and style of the individual therapist, the individual patient, and the unique patterns of interaction that develop between them. Even in controlled studies designed to compare manualized treatments, therapists interact with patients in different ways, implement interventions differently, and introduce processes not specified by the treatment manuals.

*   *   *

After reviewing the psychotherapy outcome literatures of the time, Rosenzweig [in 1936] and subsequently Luborsky, Singer, and Luborsky [in 1975], reached the conclusion of the Dodo bird in *Alice in Wonderland*: "Everybody has won, and all must have prizes." Outcomes for different therapies were surprisingly equivalent, and no form of psychotherapy proved superior to any other. . . .

Subsequent research has done little to alter the Dodo bird verdict. For example, studies that have directly compared CBT with short-term psychodynamic therapy for depression have failed to show greater efficacy for CBT over psychodynamic therapy or vice versa. . . . [B]oth treatments appeared to qualify as empirically supported therapies according to the criteria specified by the American Psychological Association. . . .

*   *   *

In light of the accumulation of empirical findings, blanket assertions that psychodynamic approaches lack scientific support are no longer defensible. Presentations that equate psychoanalysis with dated concepts that last held currency in the psychoanalytic community in the early 20th century are similarly misleading; they are at best uninformed and at worst disingenuous.

QUESTIONS AND COMMENTS

1. *Comparing the efficacy of psychotherapy and medication.* A number of studies have attempted to quantify the efficacy of the non-biological therapies and compare them to medication-based treatment. In 1989, the National Institute of Mental Health conducted the first comprehensive

federally funded effort to investigate the efficacy of various mental health treatment modalities for depression. The study, which randomly assigned research participants with a diagnosis of depression to short-term psychotherapy (both behavior therapy and more traditional interpersonal psychotherapy), pharmacotherapy, and a control group, found that participants who saw a trained psychotherapist were better off 18 months later than those who did not receive psychotherapy. The group treated with psychotherapy did not, however, do as well as the group given standard antidepressant drug treatment. Jerry E. Bishop, *Psychotherapy Has Measurable Effect on Depression in Closely Watched Test*, Wall St. J., Nov. 13, 1989, at B4. Later studies, however, have found that psychotherapies of several types are at least as effective in treating depression as medication. For example, in a recent meta-analytic study:

> The authors first reviewed data from Food and Drug Administration Summary Basis of Approval reports of 62 pivotal antidepressant trials consisting of data from 13,802 depressed patients. This was followed by a systematic review of data from 115 published trials evaluating efficacy of psychotherapies and alternative therapies for depression. The published depression trials consisted of 10,310 depressed patients. . . . Overall, antidepressants led to greater symptom reduction compared to placebo. . . . [T]he combination of antidepressants and psychotherapy provided a slight advantage over antidepressants ($p = 0.027$) and psychotherapy ($p = 0.022$) alone. The magnitude of symptom reduction was greater with psychotherapies compared to placebo ($p = 0.019$), treatment-as-usual ($p = 0.012$) and waiting-list ($p < 0.001$). Differences were not seen with psychotherapy compared to antidepressants, alternative therapies or active intervention controls. . . . [T]he combination of psychotherapy and antidepressants for depression may provide a slight advantage, whereas antidepressants alone and psychotherapy alone are not significantly different from alternative therapies or active intervention controls. These data suggest that type of treatment offered is less important than getting depressed patients involved in an active therapeutic program.

Arik Khan et al., *A Systematic Review of Comparative Efficacy of Treatments and Controls for Depression*, PLoS ONE 7(7): e41778. doi:10.1371/journal.pone.0041778 (2012).

2.   *Efforts to reconcile the biological and psychodynamic models.* In the 1960s, psychoanalysts often were vocal critics of psychopharmacology. Though the practice of psychotherapy has decreased substantially among psychiatrists, psychoanalytically oriented psychiatrists frequently treat their patients with a combination of medication and psychoanalytically oriented therapy. According to one survey from the 1990s, 89% of responding psychoanalysts stated that they prescribed psychotropics. Steven P. Roose & Robin H. Stern, *Medication Use in Training Cases: A Survey*, 43 J. Am. Psychoanalytic Assoc. 163 (1995). At the same time, psychoanalysts are uncertain about how to conceptually integrate pharmacotherapy and

psychoanalysis (they still regard the latter as the primary treatment modality). Consider this brief description of "neuropsychoanalysis," an effort that tries to integrate psychoanalytic insights and brain research:

> Neuropsychoanalysts . . . are not trying to demonstrate that all (or even most) of Freud's ideas were right. A dream doesn't necessarily represent a repressed wish, and no one thinks brain imaging will find evidence for penis envy or even the existence of an ego, id, and superego locked in an unending tug-of-war. But neuropsychoanalysts contend that Freud's view of the mind, despite its many flaws, remains the richest one yet developed. And even as they welcome advances in neuroscience, they are also wary of the field's impact. Like psychotherapists of all stripes, [neuropsychoanalysts] worry that brain research is encouraging a biological reductionism in which psychiatrists focus exclusively on neurotransmitters and drugs. "The structure of the human personality has not traditionally been on the agenda of most neuroscientists," says [one neuropsychoanalyst].

Joshua Kendall, *Managed Care Tried to Kill Off Freud: Can Tony Soprano Help Revive Him?*, Boston Globe, Feb. 9, 2003, at D1.

IV. THE MENTAL HEALTH PROFESSIONS

A. OVERVIEW

The specialized purveyors of mental health treatment can be classified into three primary groups—psychiatrists, psychologists, and clinical social workers. Other emerging groups of mental health practitioners include advanced practice psychiatric nurses, licensed professional counselors, and marriage and family therapists. See Alan R. Ellis et al., *County–Level Estimates of Mental Health Professional Supply in the United States*, 60 Psychiatric Services 1315 (2009) (estimating that there are over 350,000 clinically active providers in the six professions). Until the 1970s, psychiatrists were the dominant providers of mental health care, delivering both psychosocial therapy and psychopharmacology. However, clinical social workers may now account for as much as 65% of all mental health services, see Cohen, infra, with the role of psychiatrists increasingly becoming one of supervision and management of psychopharmacological treatment.

The reasons for these changes in the respective roles of the various professions are complex. In part, they are a product of economics, representing the preferences of third-party payors and self-paying consumers for lower-cost service providers. Richard M. Scheffler & Paul B. Kirby, *The Occupational Transformation of the Mental Health System*, 22 Health Aff. 177 (2003). As detailed in Chapter Two, these changes also have been affected by court decisions and legislation that have reduced the medical profession's control over the delivery of mental health services. Additionally, national studies have identified widespread shortages of psychiatrists and a maldistribution of other mental health professionals, especially in rural areas. Kathleen Thomas et al., *County–Level Estimates of Mental Health Professional Shortage in the United States*, 60 Psychiatric Services 1323 (2009).

The materials that follow describe the education, training, and general functions of the three primary categories of mental health professionals. It then recounts recent trends that have brought about significant changes in the roles of these professions.

B. PSYCHIATRISTS

1. Development of the Profession

The origins of psychiatry lie in the practice of medicine within asylums for the insane where, during the 19th century, physicians attributed their patients' bizarre statements and behavior to diseases of the mind. Following World War II, however:

> psychiatry became an accepted part of the American scene and even achieved a certain fashionableness. Since this development owes so much to the impact upon psychiatry of Freudian psychoanalysis—one is tempted to credit Freud with both the birth of psychoanalysis and the rebirth of psychiatry—it is conceivable that psychiatry without psychoanalysis would have taken quite a different direction, perhaps back toward the mental hospital from which it emerged more than a century ago, or toward an easier synthesis with other behavioral sciences.

Arnold A. Rogow, The Psychiatrists 31–32 (1970). As noted earlier, the latter move has now occurred; both the practice of psychiatry and psychiatrists' conceptualization of mental disorders have become much more biological during the past half-century and, to a significant extent, psychiatrists have returned to the disease model embraced by their predecessors a century ago.

As a result, in current mainstream psychiatric publications, citations to early–20th–century psychiatrists such as Bleuler and Kraepelin are much more common than citations to Freud or Jung. This development reflects several forces: the adoption of a diagnostic system (DSM–III and its successors) that attempts to emulate medical systems that employ diagnosis-based treatments and assessments of prognosis; the use of explicit, observable criteria rather than psychodynamically based concepts for determining the presence of disorders; the availability of effective pharmacotherapeutic treatments; third-party health care coverage systems that favor pharmacotherapy; and pharmaceutical promotions that influence psychiatrists' views about their patients' problems and how to treat them.

2. Education and Training

The definition of who is a psychiatrist or, more important, who is qualified to practice psychiatry is determined—at least on a formal level—by state law. States generally make it lawful for *any licensed physician* to practice and render *any* form of medical care, including psychiatric treatment. As a practical matter, however, norms imposed by the medical profession itself and constraints on reimbursement imposed by third-party payors ensure that the practice of psychiatry is restricted to those physicians who have completed a psychiatric residency program approved by the American College of Graduate Medical Education (ACGME). These non-statutory methods of control are normally exercised both locally and nationally. Thus, only physicians who have completed the requisite residency program are likely to receive referrals from other health care practitioners in the community. Similarly, most hospitals give psychiatric treatment privileges (i.e., permission to treat patients at their facilities) only to physicians who have completed an accredited psychiatric residency.

In the U.S., training to become a "general" psychiatrist has three phases: obtaining an undergraduate degree, completing medical school, and finishing a post-graduate education program in a psychiatric residency of at least four years' duration. The first year of residency includes substantial work in a psychiatric treatment setting, but residents also spend at least four months providing primary care medicine (usually, in conjunction with a hospital's internal medicine department) and two months assigned to a neurological services program. The next three years of psychiatric residency are devoted solely to assessment and treatment of patients with psychiatric disorders, either in hospitals or in outpatient settings.

All psychiatric residency programs must meet certain requirements governing the subject matter covered and the minimum amounts of time spent on particular types of clinical activities. Yet this does leave room for residencies to differ somewhat in their emphases. Nowadays, most programs are oriented primarily toward providing trainees with a sound grounding in biological treatment (principally psychopharmacology) and the kinds of assessment techniques needed to administer such treatments competently. All such programs have residents conduct supervised psychotherapeutic treatment, but the training in this modality is modest—perhaps fewer than a dozen cases seen over one or two years. A few psychiatry residency programs still provide trainees with the sort of deep grounding in psychotherapy that was characteristic of the 1960s and 1970s, when psychodynamic theory held sway. In current programs that emphasize psychotherapeutic skills, residents learn about and conduct treatment under several models, including CBT and interpersonal psychotherapy. Knowledge of psychodynamic principles that are applicable to *all* treatment remains an important educational component even at biologically oriented programs. Thus, for instance, knowledge of psychological defense mechanisms, such as denial of illness, and of the transference phenomenon (where the patient attributes unconscious feelings and emotions, usually developed during childhood, to the therapist) is still considered relevant in all types of psychiatric training.

Psychiatrists-in-training learn largely by doing—that is, by treating patients under graded supervision by faculty members. One or two half-days a week, residents participate in didactic sessions focused on a host of topics, including the principles and techniques of psychotherapy, somatic therapies (psychotropic medications), diagnosis, interviewing skills and techniques, personality development, child psychiatry, substance use disorders and their treatment, legal issues, neuroanatomical correlates of psychiatric disorders, and research problems.

As is true of other medical specialties, psychiatry is subject to accreditation procedures established under the auspices of a relevant medical professional group. In the case of psychiatry, these are provided by the American Board of Psychiatry and Neurology. Certification in general psychiatry is available to any candidate who passes a rigorous examination and has completed a psychiatric residency. Most practicing psychiatrists attain board certification within a few years after completing their residency. Over the last two decades, certification has become much more important for psychiatrists because many third-party payors use it as a criterion for deciding whether to admit specialists to their panels of clinicians authorized to receive reimbursement for their services. Since the 1990s, board certification has been time-limited. Newly certified psychiatrists now must take recertification board exams every ten years, and between exams they must complete "performance in practice" and "maintenance of certification" activities to retain their board certification status.

The past two decades have witnessed a growing trend toward subspecialization training throughout medicine, and psychiatry is no exception. As of 2013, the ACGME has recognized programs in eight psychiatric subspecialties—addiction psychiatry, child and adolescent psychiatry, forensic psychiatry, geriatric psychiatry, hospice and palliative medicine, pain medicine, psychosomatic medicine, and sleep medicine—graduates of which are eligible to take additional board certification exams. Usually, psychiatrists enter these programs upon completion of their general psychiatry training, but psychiatrists can use the first year of a two-year child psychiatry fellowship to "count" as their final year of general psychiatry training.

Of all these fellowships, forensic psychiatry is perhaps of greatest interest to readers of this volume. The ACGME first certified forensic psychiatry training programs in 1997, and about 50 of these exist in the

U.S. and Canada. At this point, only psychiatrists who have completed forensic fellowships are eligible to become board-certified in forensic psychiatry. Forensic fellowships last one year and offer psychiatrists special teaching and experiences in civil and criminal law, including death penalty issues; legal systems and regulations; special assessment issues, including violence risk assessment; the administration of treatment in correctional settings; special consultations; and providing expert testimony—matters that usually are covered only briefly in general psychiatry training.

3. Function

The roles and functions of psychiatrists vary substantially depending on the practice setting. About half of psychiatrists work in multiple places and perform somewhat different functions depending on the workplace context. Settings range from a private office practice (although this is becoming less and less common) to a public or private hospital. Psychiatric practice may also involve employment at a community mental health center focusing solely on psychiatric problems, or a general medical group practice (or managed care organization) that offers specialized psychiatric care in addition to other medical services.

Psychiatrists in a private office setting most commonly use a combination of treatment methods, varying with the severity and nature of the disorder. Moreover, these psychiatrists are increasingly affiliating with nonmedical professionals, such as psychologists and psychiatric social workers. In these group practice situations, treatment often is divided between psychiatrists and non-physician psychotherapists, with the former responsible for initial diagnosis and management of the medication regime, and the latter primarily providing needed psychotherapy. Recent studies indicate that only 29% of psychiatrists still do psychotherapy and only 11% of visits to psychiatrists involve psychotherapy. Mojtabai & Olfson, supra, p. 962. Psychiatrists who work as staff members in a psychiatric hospital tend to principally provide diagnostic services and medication management.

Few psychiatrists now espouse a narrow theoretical orientation—e.g., biological or psychoanalytic—toward mental disorders. Instead, the vast majority of them embrace what is called the *biopsychosocial model*. This approach recognizes that biological, psychological, and social factors all influence the experience and manifestations of mental disorders. George L. Engel, *The Need for a New Medical Model: A Challenge for Biomedicine*, 196 Science 129 (1977). In current practice, however, most psychiatrists apply primarily what they perceive to be a biological approach, as they regard all psychiatric treatments—including psychotherapy—as biological in nature.

C. PSYCHOLOGISTS

1. Development of the Profession

William James (1842–1910), an American, is generally viewed as the founder of psychology, although he was trained as a physician and is most noted for his work as a philosopher. During his early adulthood, he suffered from a series of physical and mental ailments, including depression, which led to thoughts of suicide. While attending medical school, he was drawn to the scientific study of the human mind. Widely credited as the originator of the fields of pragmatism, radical empiricism, and functionalism, he established the first laboratory of experimental psychology in 1875 and taught courses in scientific psychology at Harvard.

The emergence of clinical psychology as a treatment-oriented profession is a relatively recent phenomenon. In fact, from the mid-nineteenth century to the middle 1940s, the field was essentially an academic discipline. The following excerpt traces the developments leading to the profession's eventual emergence as a major presence in the practice of psychotherapy:

> [Pre–1940, t]he bulk of psychologists were employed in institutions of higher learning where they engaged in teaching and conducting research in animal learning behavior and brain behavior relations. It was in the mid–1940s that the psychologist practitioner role within the health field began to emerge in a significant manner. The large-scale employment of clinical and counseling psychologists by the Veterans Administration during the World War II era is widely accepted as providing a significant impetus to the emergence of psychologists as practitioners in the health area. In the mental health area, the initial functioning of the psychologist was within the framework of the mental health team. This was particularly the case within health service delivery systems such as hospitals and mental health clinics. Such teams usually were comprised of a psychiatrist (who was frequently the team leader), a social worker, a nurse (whose special interest and training were in psychiatric nursing), and usually a clinical psychologist.

Francis R. J. Fields & Rudy J. Horwitz, Psychology and Professional Practice: The Interface of Psychology and the Law xi (1982).

Since 1950, clinical psychology has become a major force in U.S. mental health treatment, and the majority of individuals who now undertake graduate psychology training do so with the eventual aim of providing related assessments and treatment. In some states, the practice of psychology is open to both those who hold a master's degree in psychology and those who have obtained a doctorate degree, but most states now require that licensees in clinical psychology hold a doctoral degree. A recent estimate suggests that doctoral-level clinical psychologists (Ph.D. and Psy.D.) outnumber practicing psychiatrists by more than 2 to 1. See Ronald W. Manderscheid & Joyce T. Berry, Mental Health, United States, 2004, 259 (Center for Mental Health Services, 2004) (reporting 41,000 practicing psychiatrists and 88,500 clinical psychologists with a Ph.D. or Psy.D. degree).

2. Education and Training

There are several different types of psychologists, including clinical psychologists, counseling psychologists, industrial psychologists, social psychologists, and experimental/research psychologists. The category of most relevance to this book is clinical psychology, which is the largest specialty and is the one most directly involved in helping people with mental disorders.

To practice psychology, an individual must hold a license and be registered as a psychologist in accordance with the laws and regulations of the jurisdiction(s) where he or she practices. Though the specific criteria vary from state to state, obtaining a license to practice as a clinical psychologist generally involves satisfying basic educational requirements, passing one or more examinations, and having had supervised experience. As noted earlier, a doctoral degree in psychology is a requirement for licensure for the independent practice of psychology in most states. Some states also have a licensing category under which holders of a master's degree may practice psychology under the supervision of a licensed doctoral-level psychologist.

Almost all states require licensure applicants to pass the Examination for Professional Practice in Psychology. This examination, administered and prepared by the Association of State and Provincial Psychology Boards (ASPPB), assesses whether examinees possess the knowledge of psychology needed to practice competently as an entry-level psychologist. Many states also require that licensees pass a written examination on their knowledge of the state's laws and rules governing the practice of psychology and an oral examination as well. Prior to licensure, psychologists also must undertake supervised practice experiences. In most states, these experiences include a one-year internship during the doctoral program and a second, "post-doc" year after having received the doctoral degree. Most states require that these supervised experiences meet specific criteria laid out in the *Handbook of Licensing and Certification Requirements for Psychologists in the U.S. and Canada* (published by the ASPPB).

Until 1950, an academic background and a Ph.D. in psychology were the primary educational criteria for entry into clinical practice. In response to charges that the traditional Ph.D. programs in psychology were too research-oriented, universities began in the 1970s to establish separate Doctorate in Psychology (Psy.D.) programs or tracts within their Ph.D. programs that emphasize the development of clinical practice skills. Although both Ph.D. and Psy.D. programs generally take five to seven years to complete, the Psy.D. programs focus primarily on clinical training while Ph.D. programs retain an emphasis on research skills. Clinical psychology training typically includes classes that explore the bases of behavior, types of personalities, human development, psychopathology, diagnostics, assessment methods, psychotherapy, psychopharmacology, statistics, and research design. Throughout their graduate training, psychologists-to-be also participate in various "clinical practica" where they work with clients under faculty supervision. As noted earlier, psychologists complete a supervised internship and supervised post-doctoral practice after they have finished their classwork. Finally, they usually author a doctoral dissertation, a lengthy document that describes an original research project they have undertaken in which they collect and analyze empirical data using sophisticated statistical methods.

States agencies that regulate the practice of psychology traditionally did not mandate that degree programs meet accreditation standards. However, professional organizations such as the American Psychological Association have developed an accreditation process with specific requirements. This accreditation, while not always binding for purposes of obtaining clinical licensure, does influence a clinical psychologist's job prospects. For instance, the Veterans Administration, which is the largest employer of psychologists in the United States, will only employ psychologists who have earned a Ph.D. or Psy.D. from a program accredited by the American Psychological Association. Further, state licensing boards today typically require a minimum of a doctoral degree in psychology from a regionally accredited or government-chartered institution, while some states require applicants to have a doctoral degree in psychology from a program accredited by the American Psychological Association. Candidates who did not attend an accredited program may have their program's curriculum scrutinized by the licensing board from which they seek licensure. American Psychological Association, *What You Need to Know to Get Licensed* (2013), http://www.apa.org/gradpsych/2004/01/get-licensed.aspx. The U.S. has more than 350 accredited psychology doctoral programs, and the number of enrolled graduate students has risen from under 15,000 in the mid–1980s to more than 25,000. See Manderscheid & Berry, supra, at 270.

3.   Function

While the primary function of psychologists in earlier years was psychological assessment and diagnosis, clinical psychologists today are increasingly engaged in psychotherapy, either by maintaining a private practice, working as part of a larger treatment team, or delivering services through a clinic at a university or some other setting. Differences in training and theoretical orientations lead to contrasting styles among psychologists in their treatment approaches. For instance, psychologists trained in psychoanalytic theory and techniques are more prone to provide psychodynamic psychotherapy than psychologists trained in behavioral methods, who more frequently employ behavioral or cognitive approaches in their practices. Behaviorally oriented treatment is especially appropriate for certain conditions (for example, phobias and obsessive-compulsive disorder), where unlearning one's abnormal behavioral responses is very helpful in alleviating emotional distress and overall dysfunction. While some clinical psychologists routinely employ a very specific treatment modality, most use an "eclectic" approach, drawing on different theoretical models to implement the best treatment plan for each client, and, if necessary, later revise it.

At the same time, psychological assessment remains an important part of the work of many clinical psychologists. Unlike most psychiatrists and social workers, clinical psychologists receive detailed, specialized training in the administration and interpretation of standardized tests such as the Minnesota Multiphasic Personality Inventory (MMPI) and intelligence (IQ) tests. Psychological testing is not limited to treatment contexts. For instance, personality assessments, intelligence tests, risk and malingering instruments, and other tests administered by psychologists provide screening tools for employment decisions, aids to courts resolving child custody disputes, guidance for determinations of competence, responsibility, and future risk in criminal proceedings, and assistance with a range of other legal questions.

D. CLINICAL SOCIAL WORKERS

1. Development of the Profession

The roots of clinical social work are generally traced back to the social and economic upheavals associated with the Industrial Revolution and the resulting concentrated pockets of poverty and hardship. In the U.S., the origins of clinical social work are usually associated with the waves of immigrants that arrived in this country during the latter portions of the 19th century and the beginning of the 20th century. Attempts to respond to the challenges faced by these immigrants led to a recognition of the mental health problems of the poor and individuals in transition, as well as an appreciation of the pervasive nature of mental disorders in the community.

Jane Addams (1860–1935)—who was active in working for women's rights, a founder of the American Civil Liberties Union and the NAACP, and a recipient of the Nobel Peace Prize in 1931—is generally viewed as the "mother of social work." In 1889, with Ellen Gates Starr, she co-founded Hull House in Chicago, one of the first settlement houses in the

United States, which attempted to assist immigrants and the poor. Influenced by Toynbee Hall in the East End of London, settlement houses like Hull House were a type of welfare center for the neighborhood poor and a focal point for social reform. The Hull House, which served about 2,000 people a week, provided facilities for a night school for adults, kindergarten classes, clubs for older children and a girls club, a public kitchen and a coffeehouse, a gymnasium and swimming pool, a book bindery, and a library.

The first official social work class was offered by Columbia University in the summer of 1898. This enabled individuals interested in charitable work to become trained professionals addressing the ills of poverty, including the mental health problems of the poor. With the rise of clinical social workers, a clearer understanding of mental disorders and their consequences in the community began to emerge, with clinical social workers quickly coming to play a significant role in the asylums being established across the country (see Chapter Ten). In 1968, the New York State legislature legally recognized social work as a profession by passing a title certification law (see Chapter Two, Part I), which created the title of "certified social worker (CSW)." However, compliance with this law was voluntary, and as many as one-third of the clinical social workers in the state chose not to obtain this certification. Furthermore, the description of the functions of social workers was so vague it made the law difficult to enforce. In 2004, however, New York passed a law establishing that the only psychotherapists who could practice autonomously without physician consultation, referral, or supervision (excluding psychiatrists) were licensed clinical social workers and licensed clinical psychologists. Marsha Wineburgh, We Are Clinical Social Work Psychotherapists (2013). Social work as a profession celebrated its centennial in 1998.

2.   Education and Training

Clinical social work is a subspeciality of social work and generally developed later than either psychiatry or clinical psychology. A clinical social worker typically will have a Masters of Social Work (M.S.W.) degree from an accredited school of social work. The degree requires a minimum of two years graduate study after college, including a field placement in the community. The focus of study tends to include individual development and behavior, the dynamics of families, the techniques of individual, group and family therapy, and the use of community resources for individuals with a mental disorder. More advanced degrees in clinical social work are becoming increasingly available, including a Doctorate of Social Work. Licensure varies from state-to-state.

3. Function

Clinical social workers often focus on people's relationships to their family and community. Social workers also can be heavily involved in the evaluation, treatment, and monitoring of people with mental disorders, as well as in addressing substance abuse and domestic conflict. They often operate as part of a treatment team, which may be based in a hospital or another treatment facility, although increasingly they function independently in private practice, with over 20% of clinical social workers now engaged in such practice.

The primary reason for the latter development has been states' willingness to license social workers. Licensure gave social workers credibility and entitlement to third-party reimbursement. A second reason social workers have become more independent is explored in the next section.

E. THE INTERACTION OF THE PROFESSIONS IN AN ERA OF MANAGED CARE

Managed care, which is discussed in detail in the next section of this chapter, is the provision of health services paid for by a third party (either the government or an insurance company) and ultimately directed by the third party rather than mental health professionals delivering the care or the persons who receive care. The following excerpt explores some of the effects managed care has had on the three mental health professions just described.

JEFFREY COHEN, MANAGED CARE AND THE EVOLVING ROLE OF THE CLINICAL SOCIAL WORKER IN MENTAL HEALTH
48 Social Work 34 (2003).

. . . As recently as 1960, before the onset of managed mental health care, the roles of psychiatrists, psychologists, and clinical social workers tended to be distinct. Psychiatrists had the overall responsibility of patient care, conducted psychotherapy, prescribed medication, and supervised hospital care. Clinical psychologists conducted testing and provided group therapy and other therapeutic modalities in institutions and hospitals. Clinical social workers performed comprehensive psychosocial assessments, counseled regarding family issues, and created discharge plans for patients in social services agencies. At that time, the mental health field was far from overcrowded.

By the mid–1970s the number of clinical social workers providing mental health treatment in the United States had grown, almost equaling the number of psychiatrists. Both professions had almost twice the number of clinical psychologists. In the subsequent 15 years, clinical social workers and clinical psychologists tripled their numbers, while the number of psychiatrists grew by less than 40 percent. With the increased number of nonpsychiatric practitioners, along with the introduction of psychotropic medication, the role of the psychiatrist shifted. As psychopharmacology, biology, genetics, and hard science influenced psychiatry, psychiatrists began to withdraw from psychotherapy. Psychiatric practice instead shifted its primary focus to patients in need of psychopharmacological agents, with psychiatrists prescribing and monitoring medication use and administering medical procedures such as electroconvulsive therapy (ECT).

With psychiatrists' shift in emphasis, clinical social workers and clinical psychologists assumed more responsibility in mental health treatment, and psychotherapy, in particular. The proliferation of managed care companies during the 1980s furthered the increased involvement of clinical social workers and clinical psychologists. Because of improved training and the less-expensive nature of their services, clinical social workers and clinical psychologists were more involved in providing psychotherapy to patients suffering from mental illness. . . . For some time, clinical social workers have performed the largest portion of psychotherapeutic work done in the United States. Clinical social workers provide as much as 65 percent of all psychotherapy and mental health services.

. . . With managed care's influence, psychiatrists are being replaced by nonmedical practitioners in many domains of mental health treatment in which they once predominated. Psychiatrists are being forced into new practice arrangements and roles, such as consultants for multidisciplinary groups. Psychiatrists are also increasingly being limited to dealing with patients with the most severe mental disorders, which tend to involve the use of medication and need for prescription privilege. Past responsibilities of long-term therapy and treatment aimed at overcoming problems that diminish patients' quality of life have given way to treatment of such cases as serious psychotic disorders, with threat to life and risk of decompensation deemed the main reasons for their involvement.

The new trend of using clinical social workers in place of clinical psychologists and psychiatrists by managed care companies has touched off territorial disputes among practitioners in the mental health field. As the mental health professions compete for the same health care dollars, each profession guards its turf, protecting itself by defining responsibilities it is uniquely qualified to perform, and, at the same time, vying for the right to expand services. For example, as the number of clinical social workers has grown in the area of psychotherapeutic treatment, clinical psychologists have lobbied for prescription and full hospital privileges, which historically have been reserved for psychiatrists. Clinical psychologists reason that they could serve as a less-expensive replacement for psychiatrists, or even provide both psychotherapeutic and psychopharmacological treatment to patients [prescription privileges for psychologists is discussed in detail in Chapter Two]. As managed care companies pass psychologists over for less-expensive clinical social workers, the lack of differentiation among mental health professionals by managed care companies undoubtedly frustrates clinical psychologists.

. . . As managed care companies continue to reduce reimbursement dollars, changes in multidisciplinary team structures are inevitable, with even more reliance on master's-level service providers. Practitioner distinctions already have begun to diminish in favor of more team-oriented models, with the boundaries between the uniqueness of the individual disciplines beginning to blur. Psychiatrists often head the team, coordinating services in conjunction with psychotherapists and other mental health care providers on the treatment team. However, it is not unusual for a clinical psychologist or even a clinical social worker to lead the team, with the psychiatrist relegated to the role of psychopharmacology consultant rather than an active team member.

. . . In the future, indicators suggest that nonpsychiatric practitioners will emerge as the dominant providers of treatment. . . . [M]anaged care companies will expect nonmedical practitioners, such as clinical social workers to provide the bulk of outpatient care in the mental health care field. . . . Distinctions between master's-level and doctoral-level providers will become more evident as master's-level practitioners assume primary responsibility for direct mental health services, and doctoral-level providers assume more administrative, supervisory, and research-oriented roles. The rapid increase in managed care's influence, accompanied by the reduction of referrals to more expensive specialists, suggests that demand for clinical psychologists will continue to diminish. As managed health care organizations restrict consumer choice of providers, many mental health professionals, such as clinical psychologists, may have difficulty joining reimbursement plans.

Despite the shift away from doctoral-level providers and the narrowing role of the medical practitioner in the treatment regime of managed care companies, psychiatrists will likely have an essential and continuing role in the mental health care system. [M]anaged mental health care still needs medical practitioners for their knowledge of psychopharmacology and experience in prescribing medications. . . . The distance between the domains of psychotherapists and psychopharmacologists will continue to widen, however, as psychiatrists undoubtedly will continue to be the most-expensive mental health professionals. Psychotherapy has already become a predominantly nonmedical activity, and there is every indication that this trend will continue until the medically trained therapist becomes rare. Some practitioners (for example, psychiatric nurses) who are not psychiatrists can circumvent the barrier to their prescribing drugs through an alliance with a psychiatrist. This practice is likely to increase in frequency, further narrowing the role of the psychiatrist and widening the gap between the medical and nonmedical mental health practitioner. . . .

QUESTIONS AND COMMENTS

1. *Pay scales.* The excerpt notes that psychiatrists are the most expensive type of mental health care provider. According to the 2013 edition of the U.S. Labor Department's Occupational Outlook Handbook, the median annual earnings of psychiatrists in 2010 was $166,400, the median for psychologists was $68,640, and the median for social workers was $42,480.

2. *Other clinical disciplines.* Mental health services are also provided to a limited extent by psychiatric nurses. Under the law of many states, advanced-practice psychiatric clinical nurse specialists have limited prescription privileges.

The mental health system also includes various counselors, such as clergy, school counselors, and marriage and family counselors, who provide counseling that can constitute mental health treatment. As far back as 1985, one commentator suggested that marriage and family counselors were challenging social workers in their field of specialty, noting that in California there were already 16,000 marriage and family counselors. See *Social Workers Vault into a Leading Role in Psychotherapy*, N.Y. Times, Apr. 30, 1985, at 20, col. 4. According to a 2004 official government tally, more than 100,000 counselors and more than 50,000 marriage and family counselors practice in the U.S. Manderscheid & Berry, supra, at 259–260.

3. *Choosing a mental health provider.* The discussion in the preceding section suggests that the mental health field is made up of different professional categories and that consumers need only elect the one that best fits their needs. In reality, however, individuals may have their choice circumscribed by economic or other factors. For instance, state licensing laws have a significant influence on the public's use of one rather than another category of professional, and excluded professions have increasingly sought relief through legislative or judicial channels. The nature of these efforts is considered in Chapter Two, Part II. In addition, as discussed in the following section, if an individual is enrolled in a managed care organization ("MCO"), the MCO may dictate the professional category of therapists for which reimbursement is available. For example, MCOs sometimes authorize treatment by high-cost psychiatrists only for biological therapies.

Aside from insurance considerations, the choice of a therapist will also be influenced by the overall economic circumstances of the individuals seeking services. Even if they have coverage under an insurance or governmental program, the associated co-payments and deductibles means that persons of limited means are likely to be more sensitive to differences in the fee structure of the respective professions and consequently, rather than seek treatment from psychiatrists or psychologists in private practice, they will be more inclined to seek low-cost services at public mental health centers or help from less costly mental health professionals. Moreover, persons who do not have coverage under an insurance or governmental program and who do not have the necessary private resources must generally rely on the subsidized services provided by community mental health centers. Here, their opportunity to select a particular professional category to provide treatment may be restricted by staff availability or by the assignment practices of the center.

Recall the eight individuals described on pp. 18–19. Assuming they seek treatment and have no financial restrictions on their ability to choose, what type of mental health professional might each choose as a therapist?

V.   FINANCING MENTAL HEALTH CARE: COST AND COVERAGE ISSUES

The financing of mental health treatment is a complex and important aspect of mental health law. Financing arrangements affect how and where treatment takes place; as noted below, for instance, the advent of managed care has had a significant impact on who is involuntarily hospitalized and for how long. More importantly, public and private insurance programs determine who will receive assistance in paying for treatment, and thus often whether a person obtains treatment at all. Of all persons with diagnosable mental disorders, only about 40% of adults and 30% of children receive specialized treatment in the mental health treatment system. Perceived cost is by far the most frequent reason given for failing to seek this specialized care, followed by a belief that care is not needed and confusion about how to obtain it. Rachel Garfield, Mental Health Financing in the United States 4 (Kaiser Foundation, 2011).

After an overview of the public and private financing mechanisms for mental health care that have developed over the past several decades, this part examines the "parity" issue—whether and to what extent mental and physical illnesses ought to be governed by identical insurance schemes—and the effect of the managed care movement on mental health treatment.

A. AN OVERVIEW OF PUBLIC AND PRIVATE FINANCING OPTIONS

One reason for the complexity of mental health care financing is the tremendous variety of institutions, both public and private, that provide care. These institutions include psychiatric hospitals (both public and private), general hospitals, community-based supported living arrangements, private office-based practices, nursing homes, correctional facilities, and school-based counseling services. Treatment received through this system is funded through a combination of public and private financing, which is described in the following two sections.

1. Public Sources of Financing

One notable feature of U.S. mental health care financing is the predominance of the public sector—that is, federal, state, and local government funding—particularly for individuals with serious mental illness. About 62% of the funding for mental health treatment comes from governmental sources, with the rest paid by private insurance or out-of-pocket expenditures. Garfield, supra, at 5. The centrality of the public sector is unsurprising, since many individuals with serious mental illness often incur high treatment costs yet frequently cannot secure private sector health insurance through a full-time job.

As Chapter Eight discusses in detail, through much of the 20th century individuals with a serious mental illness were institutionalized in public hospitals, financed largely by state governments. But beginning in the early 1960s, a process of deinstitutionalization began in which patients were moved from large state mental hospitals to other types of treatment programs. This process—which accelerated in the last three decades of the twentieth century—occurred for a number of reasons, including constricted state budgets, changing legal standards, federal funding for community treatment, and new medications. But the creation of Medicaid and Medicare in 1965 may have played the most significant role.

Because Medicaid and Medicare cover people who cannot work or otherwise impoverished (Medicaid) or who are elderly (Medicare), these two programs provide assistance to a large percentage of those with a serious mental illness. Yet from the outset, both Medicaid and Medicare imposed significant restrictions on their coverage of services at so-called "institutions for mental disease" (IMDs)—that is, hospitals or nursing facilities of more than 16 beds that are "primarily engaged in providing diagnosis, treatment, or care of persons with mental diseases . . . ." Even today, Medicaid will cover inpatient services at IMDs only if the recipient is under 21 or over 65 years of age, 42 U.S.C. § 1396d(a)(xi)(1), 4(A), (14), (16), and Medicare has a 190–day lifetime maximum limitation on inpatient coverage in an IMD. 42 U.S.C. § 1395d(b)(3). The legislative history of the Medicaid statute shows that Congress considered inpatient psychiatric care to be a state, not a federal, function. More importantly, Congress was suspicious of the efficacy of large, state-funded psychiatric hospitals. *Schweiker v. Wilson*, 450 U.S. 221, 241–42, 101 S. Ct. 1074, 67 L. Ed.2d 186 (1981) (Powell, J., dissenting).

Medicaid's and Medicar'es coverage restrictions quickly transformed how mental health care was delivered. By having patients who formerly would have been placed at state hospitals get care at other types of facilities (e.g., group homes and general hospitals), states rapidly transferred much of the fiscal burden of treating persons with mental impairments to the federal government. From 1970 to 1975, state hospital populations fell at a rate of 11% a year. See Joanmarie Davoli, *No Room at the Inn: How the Federal Medicaid Program Created Inequities in Psychiatric Hospital Access for the Indigent Mentally Ill*, 29 Am. J.L. & Med. 159, 170 (2003). In contrast, the advent of effective antipsychotic medicines in the decade between 1955 and 1965 had only reduced state hospital populations by about 1.75% annually. Id. Many commentators also argue that civil libertarian concerns—specifically, elevated legal requirements for civil commitment of the type discussed in Chapter Eight—were less important in reducing state hospital populations than was the monetary incentive. See, e.g., Clifford J. Levy, *Ingredients of a Failing System: A Lack of State Money, a Group Without a Voice*, N.Y. Times, Apr. 28, 2002, at A32; E. Fuller Torrey, Out of the Shadows 91–140 (1997). Currently, fewer than 40,000 patients remain in state psychiatric hospitals.

Thus today, individuals with a serious mental illness typically receive treatment not in large mental hospital but in nursing homes, general hospitals with psychiatric beds, or community-based facilities, with a significant number of them covered by Medicare or Medicaid. As recounted in detail in Chapter Eleven, federal law provides that persons with disabilities who have the appropriate work history are eligible for Social Security Disability Insurance ("SSDI") and therefore for Medicare. Individuals with a qualifying disability who do not have the requisite work history may be eligible for Supplemental Security Income (SSI) and thus for Medicaid. By the late 2000s, nearly 30% of individuals who qualified for SSDI did so based on a mental disorder and over 40% of SSI recipients under age 65 (and about half of the eligible children) qualified for SSI on the basis of a mental illness. See Garfield, supra, at 6, 9. Together, Medicare and Medicaid fund about 34% of total U.S. mental health expenditures. Id. at 5. Under the Patient Protection and Affordable Care Act (ACA, popularly termed "Obamacare"), passed in 2010, Medicaid was expanded to include nearly all individuals with incomes up to 133% of the poverty level. According to one prediction made in 2011, the ACA will result in nearly 2 million new Medicaid enrollees with a probable diagnosis of depression or serious psychological distress, while more than a million new enrollees without these disorders will also use some mental health services. Rachel Garfield et al., The Impact of National Health Reform on Adults with Mental Disorders, 168 Am. J. Psychiatry 486 (2011). However, the Supreme Court's decision in *National Federation of Independent Business v. Sebellius*, 132 S.Ct. 2566 (2012), allowing states to opt out of that provision of the ACA, should probably reduce that estimate.

Even if state and local governments do not fully participate in the Medicaid program and thus have reduced matching obligations, they still will bear significant financial responsibility for supporting people with mental disability. In the first decade of the twenty-first century, they provided approximately 21% of all mental health care funding. Garfield, supra, at 5. State and local sources may also end up paying for mental health services for people who are not covered by any specific government program because, when public funds are unavailable, individuals with serious mental illness are often incarcerated through the criminal justice system. According to one study, the odds of a person with serious mental illness ending up in jail or prison rather than a mental hospital is 3.2 to 1.0. E. Fuller Torrey et al., Treatment Advocacy Center & National Sheriffs' Association, More Mentally Ill Persons Are in Jails and Prisons Than Hospitals: A Survey of the States 8 (2010). While incarcerated, people with mental disability cost state and local governments roughly $12,000 more a year than inmates without mental disability. Catlin T. Harrington, *Breaking the Cycle and Stepping Out of the "Revolving Door,"* 2013 Ill. L. Rev. 319, 325.

2.   Private Sources of Financing

The private sector pays for 38% of all mental health care costs. Notably, however, private *insurance* pays for only 24% of such costs. The remainder (14%) is largely paid for through patients' out-of-pocket expenditures. Garfield, supra, at 5. Historically, many private insurers have placed strict limits on mental health care coverage, and some insurers did not cover mental health care at all. Although by the 1960s, over 90% of employers did provide such coverage, most restricted it to a greater extent than they did for physical illnesses, by limiting annual inpatient hospital days and outpatient mental health visits (e.g., to 25 or 30 days) or by imposing annual or lifetime caps on mental health expenditures that were much more stringent than those applied to nonpsychiatric conditions. *See* 142 Cong. Rec. S3589 (daily ed. Apr. 18, 1996) (statement of Sen. Paul Wellstone).

Starting in the 1970s, several states attempted to address this differential through "parity laws" that required insurers to cover behavioral health treatment on the same terms as medical treatment in general. In 1996, Congress joined this effort by passing the Mental Health Parity Act (MHPA), 20 U.S.C. § 1885a & 42 U.S.C. §§ 300gg–26. The MHPA provided that insurance plans offering both mental health benefits and medical/surgical benefits could not impose annual or lifetime limits on mental health benefits that were lower than comparable limits on medical/surgical benefits. The MHPA had many limitations, however. It did not apply to employers with fewer than 50 employees. It did not place any limitations on the co-payments or deductibles a plan can charge for mental health services, nor did it forbid plans from restricting the number of visits or inpatient days they covered. Indeed, under the MHPA, plans were not required to offer *any* mental health benefits. In addition, a plan was exempted from the MHPA's requirements if it could prove that compliance would lead to an increase of at least 1% in the cost of the plan (although this provision was rarely invoked). Finally, treatment for substance abuse or chemical dependency was not covered by the MHPA's provisions.

In an attempt to expand parity coverage, in 2008 Congress passed the Paul Wellstone and Pete Domenici Mental Health Parity and Addiction Equity Act of 2008 ("MHPAEA"). Unlike the MHPA, the MHPAEA protected individuals with substance use disorders as well, and imposed comprehensive parity requirements (in connection with deductibles, copayments, coinsurance and other out-of-pocket expenses) and treatment limitations (including inpatient day and outpatient visit limitations). However, the MHPAEA (like the MHPA) did not apply to small businesses, nor to small group health and individual health plans, Medicare, Medicaid that was not part of a managed care plan, or any self-funded plan that chose to opt out of the MHPAEA. Further, like the MHPA, nothing in the MHPAEA required a covered group health plan to offer or provide any mental health benefits and, like the MHPA, it contained an "increased cost" exemption.

The passage of the ACA in 2010 dramatically changed the regulation of the private insurance market. First, the ACA expanded the application of MHPA and MHPAEA to all qualified group health plans (large and small) that are offered through one of the new ACA-created state or regional health insurance exchanges, as well as to individual health insurance coverage. Second, the ACA prevented group health plans and health insurance issuers offering group or individual health insurance coverage from establishing lifetime limits and most types of annual limits on "essential health benefits," and defined "essential health benefits" to include mental health and substance use disorder services, including behavioral health treatment. § 1302. Thus, for the first time, federal law mandated mental health and substance use disorder benefits in numerous plan settings, including exchange-offered qualified health plans, non-exchange individual and small group health plans, and certain Medicaid plans.

However, under regulations issued by the Departments of Treasury, Labor, and Health and Human Services, this essential health benefit requirement does not apply to grandfathered health plans (plans in effect at the time the ACA was signed into law), which the federal government estimates currently cover over 100 million people. Interim Final Rules, 75 Fed.Reg. 34538, 34559 (June 17, 2010). Thus, grandfathered health plans are regulated only by the MHPA and the MHPAEA, neither of which contains a mandated mental health or substance use disorder benefit, as well as by state law, which may or may not contain a mandated mental health or substance use disorder benefit. Furthermore, the ACA exempts from the essential health benefits requirement large group health plans not offered on a health insurance exchange, as well as plans governed by the federal Employee Retirement Income Security Act of 1974 ("ERISA"), which regulates insurance plans set up by private employers that provide life, health or disability benefits. While state parity laws would normally still apply to these private employer plans, ERISA preempts any state statutory or common law that "relates to" an ERISA governed plan, 29 U.S.C.A. § 1144(a), including self-insured employee benefits plans. 29 U.S.C.A. § 1144(b)(2)(B). Because many large companies are self-insured, about 40% of Americans who receive insurance coverage through a private employer may not be covered by either the ACA or state parity laws.

B. PARITY AND THE LINE BETWEEN MENTAL AND PHYSICAL DISABILITY

As the previous section explained, while state and federal statutory mandates have vastly increased the scope of third-party financing for behavioral health treatment since the 1960s, a substantial percentage of people still do not have any federal or state-mandated coverage for mental health and substance use disorder benefits and scores of millions who do have such benefits are not in plans that require parity. The key disparities in the latter plans are related to annual and lifetime overage limits, deductibles, and co-payments, with behavioral treatment coverage likely to be subject to more limits and higher deductibles and co-payments.

The reasons for this differential treatment are several. One is the "moral hazard" problem, which in this context refers to a belief that helping people pay for mental healthcare will induce them to ("immorally") overuse mental health care. Though this problem might arise during treatment for non-mental ("physical") problems as well, mental health care (so the argument goes) is especially prone to moral hazard effects because the definition of mental disorder and the scope of treatment is more ambiguous. One response to this problem, discussed further below, is "managed care," in which the third-party payor tries to carefully supervise (and limit) the amount of treatment delivered. A second reason sometimes given to justify disparity between coverage for mental and physical illness is referred to as "adverse selection." Here the fear is that people will flock to plans that offer better behavioral health coverage, leading to higher costs and premiums for those insurers. To the extent all plans are required to provide the same essential coverage, this problem is reduced, but, as noted above, even the ACA has numerous exceptions. A third reason for the lack of parity is that insurance companies can get away with it (and thereby keep their costs down) because people with mental health problems have historically been reluctant or unable to campaign for comprehensive coverage in the way that individuals with (say) cancer have lobbied to have their treatment paid for. A final possible reason for the lack of parity is simply discrimination against people with mental disorder. Such people might be viewed as more responsible for their symptoms, or in some other way less deserving of support for their health problems.

Over the last two decades, researchers have conducted studies that relevant to all of these concerns. A summary of their findings states:

> Notwithstanding insurers' concerns regarding moral hazard in the context of mental health care, . . . recent studies demonstrate that the demand for mental health services is less price elastic than the demand for physical health services and that the current demand for mental health services is less price elastic than the demand for mental health services was twenty-five to thirty years ago. Recent studies also suggest that deductibles (in both the traditional indemnity and managed care settings) and coinsurance amounts (in the managed care setting) have no impact and very little impact, respectively, on the demand for mental health care. Additional studies that analyze the impact of managed health care and behavioral health carve-out plans on demand for mental health care suggest that the implementation of managed behavioral health care undermines . . . an efficiency argument against parity. As a result, economists now suggest that the imposition of higher deductibles, copayments, and coinsurance amounts on mental health care may no longer be justified on efficiency grounds and that the traditional practice of unequal health insurance benefit sets may need to be revisited.

> * * *

> [A] number of studies show that mental health benefit restrictions [lead to] untreated mental illness. Studies also show that untreated mental illness can increase total health care costs over and above the cost of treating the mental illness, perhaps because individuals who have a mental illness are more likely to have a physical illness and because untreated mental illness can worsen the prognosis of, prolong the period of recovery from, and increase the risk of mortality associated with physical illness. Finally, a number of studies suggest that treating mental illness can decrease total health care costs. . . .

> * * *

> Reports indicate that states with mental health parity legislation have had similar experiences. By several reports, California, Maine, Maryland, Minnesota, North Carolina, Pennsylvania, Rhode Island,

South Carolina, and Vermont implemented mental health parity and subsequently experienced either lower costs or extremely modest cost increases (e.g., nineteen cents per member per month) in the first year of implementation. Additional studies report that Maryland and North Carolina experienced decreased costs following the implementation of mental health parity when such parity coincided with the introduction of managed behavioral health care. . . .

[Finally, research shows that] untreated mental illness is associated with decreased rates of work productivity as well as increased rates of disability, homelessness, welfare, and crime. Although [they] do not show that mental illness causes these problems, the studies do suggest the possibility of significant returns on initial mental health treatment investments from employer and public health and social service programs.

Stacey A. Tovino, *All Illnesses are (Not) Created Equal: Reforming Federal Mental Health Insurance Law*, 49 Harv. J. Legis. 1, 10–11, 14–15, 26–27, 31 (2012).

Despite this evidence, disparity in coverage is still significant for large numbers of people who need mental health treatment, whether they are in public or private insurance plans. The following case illustrates one possible legal response to this disparity—characterizing a mental condition as a physical one. The notes that follow examine possible challenges to lack of parity under the Americans with Disabilities Act, as well as the issue of whether managed care does in fact, as claimed above, successfully address the moral hazard issue.

RINGWALD V. PRUDENTIAL INSURANCE CO. OF AMERICA

United States District Court, E.D. Missouri, 2010.
754 F.Supp.2d 1047.

DONALD J. STOHR, DISTRICT JUDGE.

Plaintiff Eric S. Ringwald challenges the discontinuation of his long-term disability benefits under a group insurance plan ("the Plan") in which he participated through his employer, Harrah's Casino. The Plan, identified as "Harrah's Operating Company, Inc. Short Term Disability–Grade 17 and below/Long Term Disability–Grade 22 and below," is governed by the Employee Retirement Income Security Act of 1974 ("ERISA"), 29 U.S.C. § 1001. Now before the Court is defendant The Prudential Insurance Company of America's motion for summary judgment.

* * *

Facts

The following facts are undisputed for purposes of the instant motion. In April 2004, plaintiff was a Table Game Dealer at Harrah's. At that time, plaintiff was a participant in the Plan within the meaning of ERISA § 3(7). The Plan, which was issued to Harrah's by defendant, is an employee welfare benefit plan within the meaning of ERISA § 3(1). In relevant part, the long-term disability coverage provides as follows:

BENEFIT INFORMATION

How Does Prudential Define Disability?

You are disabled when Prudential determines that:

- you are unable to perform the material and substantial duties of your regular occupation due to your sickness or injury; and

- you have a 20% or more loss in your indexed monthly earnings due to that sickness or injury.

After 24 months of payments you are disabled when Prudential determines that due to the same sickness or injury, you are unable to perform the duties of any gainful occupation for which you are reasonably fitted by education, training or experience.

* * *

What Disabilities Have a Limited Pay Period Under Your Plan?

Disabilities, which, as determined by Prudential, are due in whole or part to mental illness have a limited pay period during your lifetime.

The limited pay period for mental illness is 24 months during your lifetime.

* * *

Mental illness means a psychiatric or psychological condition regardless of cause. Mental illness includes but is not limited to schizophrenia, depression, manic depressive or bipolar illness, anxiety, somatization, substance related disorders and/or adjustment disorders or other conditions. These conditions are usually treated by a mental health provider or other qualified provider using psychotherapy, psychotropic drugs, or other similar methods of treatment as standardly accepted in the practice of medicine.

In October 2005, plaintiff submitted a claim to defendant for long-term disability benefits, claiming he had been disabled since April 16, 2004. He claimed to be unable to work because of depression and HIV. Defendant initially denied the claim, but after reconsidering it through the established appeals process, concluded that plaintiff was disabled by his mental illness. Defendant then paid plaintiff long-term disability benefits for 24 months from July 17, 2004 through July 16, 2006. Defendant denied long-term benefits beyond 24 months, citing the limitation on benefits for disabilities caused in whole or part by mental illness. Plaintiff was regularly treated by a psychiatrist, Dr. Kevin Miller, and a psychologist, Dr. Alice Vliestra, and since 2004, plaintiff has been diagnosed by numerous doctors with depression and bipolar disorder, and prescribed Lamictal, Zoloft, and Lexapro for these illnesses.

Administrative Record

The administrative record in this case consists of nearly 500 pages of medical reports, medical records, and correspondence. The Court chronologically summarizes the relevant portions of the record below.

In 2005, plaintiff was examined by Dr. Kenneth Bohm, a clinical psychologist, as part of a custody proceeding in state court to determine whether plaintiff was fit to serve as a parent to his child. Dr. Bohm noted that plaintiff was prescribed Zoloft as an antidepressant. He suggested that plaintiff be prescribed mood stabilizing or antipsychotic medication. Dr. Bohm's diagnosis of plaintiff included schizoaffective disorder and personality disorder.

On May 5, 2006, Dr. Morton Singer, one of plaintiff's treating physicians, wrote to defendant's claim representative "to appeal the denial of Mr. Ringwald's disability claim." He stated that:

> This patient was experiencing progressively symptomatic HIV disease from December 2003 through July 2004 when he resumed antiretroviral therapy. He was not receiving medication for his HIV infection due to adverse effects he had experienced in the past. In addition to the HIV related thrombocytopenia which developed in 2002 and persisted until resuming treatment in July 2004, he was also experiencing HIV related wasting syndrome. He sustained a 20 pound weight loss or greater than 10% loss body weight in the preceding 12 months. His weight declined from 171 pounds to 151 pounds in March 2004 which is documented in his medical records. This meets criteria for CDC defined HIV Wasting Syndrome.

> During this same time period off of antiretroviral therapy, his CD4 lymphocyte count declined from 520 to 280 and his HIV viral load increased from 22000 to 60000. The HIV infection had become more active with increased viral burden, immunodeficiency, wasting and weight loss as well as progressive fatigue. This was responsible for Mr. Ringwald's disability.

> He may also have a sleep disorder for which he was taking Valium at that time, but I do not believe his use of Valium at bedtime was causing his fatigue, weight loss, wasting, and progressive immunodeficiency. In fact, when Mr. Ringwald restarted antiretroviral therapy in July 2004, his CD4 lymphocyte count

increased to 490 and HIV viral load declined to undetectable levels. His weight increased to 172 pounds within six months and his fatigue improved.

His disability in March 2004 was due to his HIV disease and improved with treatment starting in July 2004. Please reconsider your denial of his claim.

On May 23, 2006, Dr. Vliestra wrote a letter on plaintiff's behalf concerning his treatment. The letter was addressed "To Whom It May Concern" and appears to be written in regards to plaintiff's parenting abilities. Dr. Vliestra noted that their "counseling sessions focused on assessing his depression, parenting capacities, and family support, and then focused on a treatment plan for establishing healthier relationships." Her letter concluded:

He currently is on medication which has improved his ability to focus and concentrate. His original depression has improved significantly. He informs me that he is fully cooperating and complying with all court requests in order to be a parent for [his minor child]. I believe he is capable of parenting a child,

On May 30, 2006, defendant's claims representative responded to Dr. Singer regarding his May 5, 2006, assessment of plaintiff's condition. Defendant's representative noted that Dr. Singer's assessment indicated that "with treatment, Mr. Ringwald's CD4 count increased, his viral load decreased, his weight increased to 172 within 6 months, and his fatigue improved." Defendant's representative asked Dr. Singer to "[p]lease advise our office if, given these improvements, you believe that Mr. Ringwald remained unable to work after July, 2004. If so, please advise for what period(s) he remained disabled and how he was impaired."

In June 2006, Dr. Singer responded to defendant's representative's request for additional information concerning plaintiff's disability claim. He stated that plaintiff:

has remained disabled since 2004 despite improvement in his immune function. He has had persistent depression since 2004 causing impairment in his cognitive function and his ability to work. His ability to concentrate has been severely compromised as well as his ability to function socially. He has been seen by several psychiatrists and neurologist [sic] in the past two years and most recently has been started on Lexapro and Risperdal. His disability remains ongoing.

At the end of July, 2006, Dr. Vliestra wrote a letter to plaintiff responding to his request for a statement concerning their counseling. Dr. Vliestra stated that plaintiff "has been in counseling with me since May 2005 to the present. He has suffered from depression and anxiety as a result of his medication for HIV as well as the stress in his life."

In a report dated December 1, 2006, Dr. Stephen Gerson offered an evaluation of plaintiff's disability claim with respect to his mental illness. Having only reviewed his medical records, Dr. Gerson opined that the records did not support a disability based on mental illness. In a second report dated December 12, 2006, Dr. Gerson changed his opinion. After issuing his first report, Dr. Gerson received a telephone call from Dr. Miller, plaintiff's treating psychiatrist, and they discussed Dr. Miller's treatment of plaintiff. Dr. Gerson's second report states that "the information from Dr. Miller, who was a reliable informant, radically changed my opinion from the file review of 12/1/06." Having spoken with Dr. Miller, Dr. Gerson believed that plaintiff was indeed disabled by bipolar psychosis through July 2006. Based on this new report, defendant paid plaintiff long-term disability benefits through July 2006.

On January 18, 2007, Dr. Singer wrote to defendant's claim representative. He stated that, "Eric Ringwald has been disabled due to his HIV disease since April 2004. He remains totally disabled at this present time."

On June 14, 2007, plaintiff's attorney wrote defendant regarding plaintiff's appeal of defendant's decision to discontinue his benefits after July 2006. Plaintiff's attorney acknowledged that plaintiff was receiving long-term disability benefits due to bipolar disorder and wrote that "[w]hile we maintain that Bi Polar Disorder is a physical disorder and not mental, we also contend that Mr. Ringwald has several physical disabilities which prevent him from performing any gainful occupation." The letter continued: "The new medical documentation will show that Mr. Ringwald is unable to work due to HIV. While his condition is controlled, the side effects of the many medications prevents him from performing any work. We ask that you give controlling weight to the opinions of Mr. Ringwald's treating physician, Dr. Morton Singer."

On June 27, 2007, in response to defendant's request, Dr. Michael Silverman submitted his "independent peer review" of the medical evidence. Dr. Silverman concluded that plaintiff was not functionally impaired as of July 2006. He summarized his conclusion as follows:

> Upon review of the medical records, the claimant has a diagnosis of HIV, which is managed by [an] excellent regimen of therapy. There is no evidence that the claimant is functionally impaired due to this condition specifically as of 7/16/06, forward. The claimant also has a prolonged history of psychiatric condition of which clearly can have a role into [sic] medical condition with respect to his physical condition, although there is no evidence that this is affecting his physical condition, specifically a diagnosis of HIV. The diagnosis of fatigue is reportedly improved according to psychiatry and neurology notes with respect to adjustment of psychiatric medications. Specifically in relation to his infectious disease diagnosis of HIV, as of the time

period in question, there is no evidence of impairment. This is well controlled with the current treatment regimen. His status with excellent CD4 count and viral load are maintained with Mr. Ringwald's continuing treatment regimen. Although Mr. Ringwald had musculoskeletal complaints, which are being followed by chiropractic services, this falls outside the scope of this review. Solely in relation to his infectious disease diagnosis of HIV, as described above . . . Mr. Ringwald has no evidence of impairment as of the time period in question that would limit or restrict his ability to function.

In September 2007, Dr. Singer wrote a letter for plaintiff describing plaintiff's inability to work. He stated that plaintiff:

> remains unable to work due to a variety of disabling symptoms that have persisted since 2005. These symptoms include, fatigue, anxiety, poor concentration and attention, disorganized thoughts, dyspepsia, gastroesophageal reflux, intermittent diarrhea, chronic rhinitis, headaches, dermatitis, chest pain, and sleep disturbance.
>
> His symptoms do not fit into a single clinical syndrome but are likely related to a variety of conditions including his HIV disease, Bipolar disease, allergic rhinitis, gastroesophageal reflux disease, allergic rhinitis [sic], atopic dermatitis, Helicobacter gastritis, chronic insomnia, as well as adverse effects from his antiretrovirals.
>
> Having observed this patient since his diagnosis with HIV disease, his ability to function in a work situation, his ability to focus mentally, perform high level cognitive functions, and even live independently have progressively deteriorated. This loss of function has occurred despite adequately suppressing his HIV infection, treating his bipolar disease, and attempting to manage his other complex of symptoms.
>
> The cause of his disability remains unclear but I have no uncertainty that Mr. Ringwald is incapable of employment at this time. His level of functioning has not improved despite aggressive treatment of his medical conditions. I disagree with Dr. Silverman's conclusions that Mr. Ringwald's functional impairment is unrelated to his HIV disease. He was fully functional, living independently, working 2 jobs prior to his diagnosis of HIV. Clearly other factors have contributed to his impairment but Dr. Clifford did not rule out HIV as a possible factor.

On January 11, 2008, plaintiff's attorney wrote to defendant regarding plaintiff's appeal. He asked "that [defendant] take into account the co-morbidity of Mr. Ringwald's symptoms." He further stated that "[a]s Dr. Singer points out, Mr. Ringwald's symptoms do not fit into one clinical syndrome."

In a letter dated January 25, 2008, Dr. Silverman reevaluated plaintiff's claim, at defendant's request, taking into account plaintiff's new supporting information, namely the September 2007 letter from Dr. Singer and the July 2007 letter from plaintiff's attorney. Dr. Silverman concluded that these documents did not change his opinion that plaintiff was not disabled by his physical ailments. With respect to the mental illnesses, Dr. Silverman did not express an opinion and deferred to a specialist in that field.

ERISA Standards

Under ERISA, plan beneficiaries are entitled to judicial review of benefits determinations. The Court reviews defendant's decision to discontinue plaintiff's long-term disability benefits after 24 months under a de novo standard of review. . . . To the extent the Court's review requires it to interpret the language of the ERISA plan, the Supreme Court refers the Court to the law of trusts, in which the terms of written trusts are "determined by the provisions of the instrument as interpreted in light of all the circumstances and such other evidence of the intention of the settlor with respect to the trust as is not inadmissible." The intent of the settlor is first determined by careful examination of the provision in question, giving plainly stated terms their ordinary meanings. If a provision is unambiguous, the Court need not refer to other plan provisions or extrinsic evidence to determine the settlor's intent. . . . Only if an ambiguity remains after giving the language its ordinary meaning, considering the context of the ambiguous provision within the plan as a whole, and admitting extrinsic evidence, will a court construe an ambiguity against the drafter under federal common law concerning construction of ERISA plans. . . .

Discussion

Suit under ERISA is authorized by 29 U.S.C. § 1132(a)(1)(B), which allows a plan participant "to recover benefits due to him under the terms of his plan." The ERISA plan in this case is disability insurance, in which defendant agrees to pay a Plan participant if he becomes unable to work due to a disability. At first, defendant will pay the participant if he is unable to perform his regular occupation. After 24 months, the Plan requires the participant to obtain other gainful employment for which he is reasonably suited given his background. Only if the participant is unable to perform the duties of any gainful employment will defendant continue to pay benefits after 24 months.

At the 24–month mark, the Plan also distinguishes between physical and mental illnesses. If a physical illness prevents a participant from performing any gainful employment, then he can receive benefits until he reaches retirement age. If a mental illness, in whole or part, causes a participant to be unable to perform any gainful employment, then he will not receive any further benefits beyond the 24 months of benefits he has already received. Thus, if a mental illness, in combination with a physical illness, causes a participant to be unable to perform any gainful employment, then benefits are limited to 24 months.

Issue in Dispute

As an initial matter, the Court notes that plaintiff argues that defendant "failed to consider an abundance of doctor's reports that provide objective evidence of the basis of Ringwald's impairment." Plaintiff argues that defendant "cherry-picked" from the medical evidence, discounting the reports of Dr. Singer and relying on the reports of Drs. Vliestra and Miller. Plaintiff further argues that Dr. Singer's appraisals should carry more weight because he has been treating plaintiff for more than 10 years and since before he was diagnosed with HIV. . . . Plaintiff concludes that "Prudential abused its discretion acted [sic] solely in its own interests."

With this argument, plaintiff loses sight of the standard of review. The Court is applying a de novo standard in this case, not abuse of discretion. [See *Firestone Tire & Rubber Company v. Bruch*, 489 U.S. 101, 115, 109 S.Ct. 948, 956, 103 L.Ed.2d 80 (1989).] Given the de novo standard, the Court is not concerned with defendant's decision-making process. Rather, the Court is only concerned with whether the ultimate decision was correct, giving no deference to defendant's decision. Accordingly, defendant's alleged failure to accord proper weight to plaintiff's treating physician's opinion and defendant's alleged improper reliance on its reviewing doctor's reports are irrelevant because the Court gives de novo consideration to the medical evidence in the record and makes an independent determination.

In this case, it is undisputed that defendant paid plaintiff benefits for 24 months. Because he has already received 24 months of benefits, in order to receive any additional benefits, he must be disabled from any gainful employment and his disability must not be due in whole or part to a mental illness. . . . Plaintiff argues that . . . "the burden was on Prudential to establish that Mr. Ringwald was disabled exclusively due to a mental illness." [He also] he argues that the mental illness limitation is ambiguous and not applicable. . . .

Burden of Proof

The parties raise the issue of who has the burden of proof regarding the mental illness limitation. Plaintiff argues that the mental illness limitation is an exclusion upon which defendant has the burden of proving that his disability is due to a mental illness in order to deny benefits. Defendant argues that it is a condition precedent, which plaintiff must prove that he has satisfied in order to obtain benefits.

When a requirement is "a prerequisite for entitlement to a benefit under an ERISA plan, the burden of proof will generally be on the plan participant." When a requirement "is set forth in the 'exclusions' section of the plan, the burden is usually on the plan sponsor, who must prove that the exclusion applies." Thus, when a question arises as to the burden of proof, the Court must determine whether the language at issue is tied to the benefits section of the policy or the exclusions section.

Examining the language of the Plan, it does not have clearly labeled benefits and exclusions sections. Instead, it begins by defining disability and describing the benefits provided. The Plan indicates that some disabilities have a limited benefits period, namely partial disabilities and mental illnesses. In a later section, the Plan states which disabilities are not covered under the Plan, such as intentionally self-inflicted injuries. The Plan states that the participant must submit proof of his claim and that the proof must show documentation of the disabling disorder, the extent of the disability, and the names and address of any doctors, hospitals, and institutions with which the participant treated. The Plan further provides that defendant may request proof of continuing disability.

The Court finds that the Plan is ambiguous as to whether the mental illness limitation is a condition precedent or an exclusion because it is reasonably susceptible to the two interpretations proposed by the parties. The Court finds that the ambiguity can be resolved by examining the language of the mental illness limitation in the context of the structure of the Plan and without reference to extrinsic evidence. The Court finds that the mental illness limitation is tied to the benefits section of the policy, not the exclusions. The Plan places the burden on plaintiff to provide proof of his disability and its extent. After 24 months of benefits have been paid, the burden rests with the Plan participant to establish entitlement to continued benefits by proving both that he is unable to perform the duties of any gainful employment and that his disability is not due in whole or part to mental illness. Thus, the burden of proof is on plaintiff to establish that his alleged disability is not due in whole or part to mental illness. . . .

Construction of the Mental Illness Limitation

Plaintiff has never denied that his disability was due in part to depression. Plaintiff's case is based on the argument that his depression has a physical, rather than a purely mental, etiology. He alleges that this entitles him to benefits because the term "mental illness" in the Plan is ambiguous, the ambiguity must be resolved against defendant, and must be resolved to exclude depression with a physical basis from the definition. Specifically, he states that "[t]he term 'mental illness' is ambiguous because it fails to set forth whether sicknesses, illnesses, or diseases should be classified based on etiology or physical manifestation." Plaintiff cites numerous cases in which courts were required to interpret whether certain brain-related illnesses fell within the definition of the term "mental illness" or some other similar term. These cases turn to distinctions between illnesses with an organic, physical basis and illnesses with no demonstrable organic or physical basis. Plaintiff attempts to categorize his illness as one with an organic or physical basis. He argues that it, accordingly, is not considered a mental illness under the Plan and that the mental illness limitation does not apply.

The cases upon which plaintiff relies were interpreting plans in which terms like "mental illness" were not defined. The courts in these cases found that, when undefined, terms like "mental illness" were ambiguous. The courts turned to principles of plan interpretation in order to resolve the ambiguities. Plaintiff cites only two cases in which "mental illness" or "mental disorder" were defined within the policy, Lang v. Long–Term Disability Plan of Sponsor Applied Remote Technology, Inc., 125 F.3d 794 (9th Cir.1997), and Dorsk v. UNUM Life Insurance Cos. of America, 8 F.Supp.2d 19 (D.Me.1998). In Lang, the term "mental disorder" was defined as a "mental, emotional, behavioral, or stress-related disorder." The court found this general definition of the term to be ambiguous and resolved the ambiguity by finding that the term " 'mental disorder' does not include 'mental' conditions resulting from 'physical disorders.' In Dorsk, the plan defined the term "mental illness" as "mental, nervous or emotional diseases or disorders of any type." The court found the use of the term "mental disorder" within the definition of "mental illness" to be ambiguous and construed the term "mental disorder" to exclude disorders with organic causes.

The present case is distinguishable from all of the cases cited by plaintiff because the term "mental illness" is clearly defined by the Plan. The Plan's definition of "mental illness," quoted in full above, explicitly includes depression and bipolar illness, regardless of cause. For purposes of this case, as defined, the term "mental illness" is not reasonably susceptible to more than one interpretation. Thus, the Court finds that, having been clearly defined by the Plan to include depression and bipolar disorder regardless of cause, the term "mental illness" is not ambiguous when applied to the facts of this case and whether plaintiff's depression and bipolar disorder have physical or non-physical bases is not controlling.

Thus, with regard to the construction of the mental illness limitation, the Court notes the following: (1) the Plan specifically includes both depression and bipolar disorder in its definition of mental illness; (2) the Plan specifically states that these illnesses are mental illnesses regardless of their causes; (3) the Plan further clarifies that mental illnesses, as defined by the Plan, are usually treated by mental health providers using psychotherapy or psychotropic drugs; and (4) the Plan indicates that the mental illness limitation applies if the disability is due in whole or part to depression or bipolar disease.

Merits Analysis

In his June 2006 letter to defendant, Dr. Singer, upon whom plaintiff relies to oppose summary judgment, attributed plaintiff's disability to his "persistent depression." In his September 2007 letter to defendant, Dr. Singer attributed plaintiff's disability, in part, to his bipolar disorder. In his January 2008 letter, plaintiff's attorney admitted that plaintiff suffered from bipolar disorder. Plaintiff's attorney did not deny that plaintiff was disabled by the bipolar disorder but instead insisted that the condition was physical, not mental, and implored defendant to consider the "co-morbidity" of his symptoms. Plaintiff's opposition to the motion for summary judgment admits that he was disabled because of depression. Defendant's reviewing expert, Dr. Gerson, provides plaintiff with the only evidence in the record indicating his mental illness did not contribute to his inability to work in his December 1, 2006, letter. Yet, Dr. Gerson immediately changed his opinion after speaking with plaintiff's treating psychiatrist and recommended in his December 12, 2006, letter that plaintiff was disabled by his mental illness. For his depression and bipolar disorder, plaintiff was treated by mental health providers, including both a psychiatrist and a psychologist, and he was treated with psychotropic drugs.

Taking into account the overwhelming evidence that plaintiff's inability to work was caused by depression and bipolar disease, including his admission of that fact, combined with the Court's review of plaintiff's medical records, the reports of plaintiff's treating physicians, and the reports of defendant's reviewing physicians, the Court finds that it is beyond dispute that plaintiff's alleged inability to perform the duties of any gainful employment was due at least in part to mental illness as defined by the Plan. Because plaintiff's inability to work was due in part to mental illness, defendant did not breach the terms of the Plan by limiting plaintiff's benefits to 24 months, and defendant is entitled to judgment as a matter of law.[3]

For the above stated reasons, IT IS HEREBY ORDERED that defendant Prudential Insurance Company of America's motion for summary judgment is granted, and a corresponding judgment will issue this day.

QUESTIONS AND COMMENTS

1.   *The court's analysis.* Judge Stohr makes two noteworthy evidentiary decisions in granting summary judgment for Prudential. First, he states that, because ERISA claims are decided *de novo*, he need not address whether Dr.

---

[3]   . . . Upon this record, the Court finds that it would reach the same result even if the mental illness constituted an exclusion upon which the defendant had the burden of proof because defendant has affirmatively established that plaintiff's disability was due at least in part to mental illness

Singer's opinion deserved extra weight. Second, Judge Stohr decides that the burden of proof on the issue of whether Ringwald's disability is caused "in whole or part" by mental illness is on Ringwald. Do you agree with these two rulings? Should the reports prepared in connection with the custody issue be relevant? Should the reports of Drs. Gerson and Silverman, who were hired by Prudential, be given the same weight as Dr. Singer's? Was the language in Ringwald's insurance contract governing receipt of benefits for disability due to mental health treatment a "benefit" or an "exclusion?"

On the merits, the court does not address the issue of whether Ringwald is disabled but rather only addresses the cause of the disability. Dr. Singer states in two of his reports that Ringwald's disability was "due to his HIV disease" and in a third report states that Ringwald was "fully functional" before contacting HIV. Assume that to be the case. Could Prudential still argue that Ringwald's coverage should be terminated after 24 months if the HIV resulted in depression that contributed to his disability? Alternatively, assume that Ringwald's bipolar illness was at least "in part" an initial cause of his disability. Should that mean he loses coverage, regardless of how small a role the bipolar illness played in causing his disability? What if he clearly established that bipolar illness is a "physical" illness? Cf. *Arkansas Blue Cross v. Doe*, 733 S.W.2d 429, 431–32 (Ark.Ct.App. 1987) (deferring to a trial court finding that bipolar disorder is a "physical illness"). Finally, assume that Ringwald was disabled solely because of the "sleeping disorder" and "fatigue" mentioned in the reports, and that these symptoms stemmed from his HIV infection. Should he receive long-term disability? Should any of this analysis be affected by the fact that people with serious mental illness are much more likely to have chronic medical conditions as well? See Institute of Medicine, Improving the Quality of Health Care for Mental and Substance–Use Conditions: Quality Chasm Series (Washington, DC: Institute of Medecine of the National Academies of Sciences, 2006).

2.   *Definitions of mental illness.* The court mentions several cases in which mental illness was not defined in the relevant insurance contract. In such cases, courts have resorted to a number of methods for determining whether an asserted condition is "mental" or "physical," all of which are profitably compared to the definitions of "mental disorder" canvassed earlier in this chapter. Courts have asked: (1) whether a mental health professional—i.e., a psychiatrist, psychologist, social worker or mental health counselor—carried out the treatment; (2) whether the treatment is "traditional" mental health treatment, such as individual or group mental health counseling, psychoanalysis, electroconvulsive shock therapy, or psychotropic medication; (3) whether the condition has an organic or biological cause; and (4) whether the symptoms are "mental"—e.g., mood swings, delusions, hallucinations, aberrant behavior, lying—rather than physical. See Tovino, supra, at 31–36. Professor Tovino points out that all these definitions can run into application problems or create perverse incentives. For instance, roughly two-thirds of the psychotropic medication administered in the United States is prescribed by primary care physicians and other non-psychiatrists, so under the first definition beneficiaries would

have a financial incentive to seek treatment from non-specialists. Id. at 32. The second test might encourage waiting until a mental problem becomes a physical one (e.g., waiting until a person with depression overdoses on drugs). Id. at 33. With respect to the third test, previous materials in this chapter explored the complex relationship between biology and mental disorder. And diseases like Alzheimer's are difficult to classify under the fourth test. Id. at 35.

Because of these problems, most insurance companies today use language like that found in the contract involved in *Ringwald*. Given that language, why did Judge Stohr feel the need to discuss the types of factors mentioned in the previous paragraph? Of course, another approach would be to avoid differentiating between mental illness and "physical" conditions in such contracts. In long-term disability cases like *Ringwald*, the question would then become whether a person is "disabled" because of mental illness. That determination can be difficult, but the Social Security Administration has developed protocols for making this determination. See Chapter 11, Part II.

3.   *Anti-discrimination challenges.* As described in detail in Chapter 12, the Rehabilitation Act of 1973 and the Americans with Disabilities Act of 1990 ("ADA") are parallel federal statutes that respectively bar discrimination against disabled persons in federally funded programs and various non-federally funded programs. Plaintiffs have been particularly aggressive in using the ADA as means of addressing the parity issue, because that statute extends protection against discrimination "on the basis of disability," toward those who are "otherwise qualified," in three settings: private employment (Title I), public services and programs provided by state and local governments (Title II), and "public accommodations" (Title III), the latter a broadly defined category that includes insurance offices.

To date, these ADA challenges have been largely unsuccessful. In the context of a typical health insurance plan, the Equal Employment Opportunity Commission ("EEOC"), which has authority to promulgate regulations under Title I, has taken the position that insurance coverage restrictions that specifically target mental illness do not necessarily represent distinctions based on disability as that term is defined under the ADA (which provides that a disability is a condition that "substantially limits one or more life activities"). According to the EEOC, restrictions on mental health coverage that apply to a broader category of people with mental disability are not the type of discrimination barred by the ADA. See generally EEOC Interim Guidance on Application of ADA to Health Insurance, Daily Lab. Rep. (BNA) No. 109, at E1–E3 (June 9, 1993). Under the EEOC position, for a restriction in an ordinary health insurance plan to be disability-based, it would have to target a particular disability or set of disabilities (e.g., schizophrenia, mood disorders). Id. at E–2.

Because of the EEOC position, most lawsuits that have challenged an insurance plan's unfavorable treatment of mental illness under the ADA have arisen in the context of long-term disability insurance of the type involved in

Ringwald, where the individuals involved are clearly mentally disabled under the ADA's definition and receive different benefits from those who are physically disabled. In this setting, the EEOC itself brought one of the first and most influential challenges to such laws, under Title I of the ADA. The disability plan at issue in *EEOC v. CNA Insurance*, 96 F.3d 1039 (7th Cir. 1996) provided a maximum of two years of benefit for those with mental disabilities, but had no such restriction for those with physical disabilities. The Seventh Circuit rejected the EEOC's discrimination argument, stating that under CNA's policy:

> [a]ll employees—the perfectly healthy, the physically disabled, and the mentally disabled—had a plan that promised them long-term benefits from the onset of disability until age 65 if their problem was physical, and long-term benefits for two years if the problem was mental or nervous. This may or may not be an enlightened way to do things, but it was not discriminatory in the usual sense of the term.

In reaching this conclusion, the Seventh Circuit relied on a Supreme Court case interpreting the Rehabilitation Act, *Alexander v. Choate*, 469 U.S. 287, 105 S. Ct. 712, 83 L. Ed.2d 661 (1985). In that case, the Court had held that so long as a facially neutral limitation on insurance coverage (in this instance, 14 days of coverage for inpatient hospital care) provided "meaningful access" to individuals with mental disabilities, the fact that the limitation had a disparate impact on such people (because people with mental disability need longer hospital care) did not create a Rehabilitation Act violation. But does *Choate* apply when, as in *Ringwald*, the insurance contract specifically singles out mental health care for different coverage?

Most other circuit courts that have addressed challenges to restrictions on mental health coverage in long-term disability policies have followed the Seventh Circuit. Some have held that since Title I of the ADA requires that a person with a disability be "otherwise qualified" to carry out the job, people who are already in need of long-term disability cannot, by definition, bring suit under the Act. See, e.g., *Weyer v. Twentieth Century Fox Film Corp.*, 198 F.3d 1104 (9th Cir. 2000); *Gonzales v. Garner Food Services, Inc.*, 89 F.3d 1523 (11th Cir. 1996). Other courts have rejected this position as defeating the anti-discriminatory intent of the ADA. See, e.g., *Ford v. Schering Plough Corp.*, 145 F.3d 601, 607–08 (3d Cir. 1998); *Castellano v. City of New York*, 142 F.3d 58 (2d Cir. 1998). But even the latter courts have usually gone on to adopt the Seventh Circuit's reasoning, with some adding that Congress would not have passed the various parity acts if it meant for the ADA to mandate equal insurance treatment of mental and physical disabilities. See *Ford*, supra; *Parker v. Metro. Life Ins. Co.*, 121 F.3d 1006, 1017–18 (6th Cir. 1997) (rejecting the parity claim under both Title I and Title III of the ADA). Does the latter argument hold water? That is, might not dissatisfaction and disagreement with the results in these cases been what motivated Congress to pass additional parity laws?

Finally, all ADA-based discrimination claims brought against insurance plans are vulnerable to defenses based on the ADA's "safe harbor" provision.

Under this provision, if a defendant insurance company can demonstrate that its coverage restrictions are based on sound actuarial principles, then the company cannot be held liable for discrimination. 42 U.S.C. § 12201(c). The safe-harbor defense is subject to the caveat that the coverage restrictions cannot be used as a "subterfuge" to evade the purposes of Title I or Title III. Courts have, however, interpreted the subterfuge language narrowly, to hold that unless the employer intended to discriminate in a non-fringe benefit related aspect of the employment relation, the coverage restriction cannot be a subterfuge. *Krauel v. Iowa Methodist Med. Ctr.*, 95 F.3d 674 (8th Cir. 1996). Can Prudential's plan in *Ringwald* be called a "subterfuge," given its extremely broad exemption for long-term mental disability and the data reported earlier about the minimal cost increases associated with insuring people with a mental disability?

4. *Managed care.* As noted above, some research indicates that managed care, which now governs the health care of a majority of people under age 65, can reduce the moral hazard problem. Defined broadly, managed care is any system of health care payment or delivery that attempts to contain costs by influencing or controlling enrollees' use of healthcare services. *See* Physician Payment Review Commission, Annual Report (1996). Managed care organizations (MCOs) control costs through a variety of mechanisms. One arrangement is capitation, under which the clinician receives a fixed amount of money for all services provided to the enrollee. In contrast to a fee-for-service payment approach, which gives providers a financial incentive to deliver as much care as they can, capitation discourages provision of services. Another cost-control mechanism is prospective utilization review or case management. Under this arrangement, before a clinician commences an intervention the utilization reviewer or case manager for the managed care plan determines whether the plan will pay for the intervention. In addition, MCO contracts often limit explicitly the scope and duration of coverage. For example, MCOs not subject to parity laws impose limits on how many inpatient psychiatric hospital days or outpatient visits they will pay for in a given year. (By contrast, fee-for-service plans typically impose annual or lifetime caps on mental health care expenditures.) Finally, MCOs often cut costs by directing or incentivizing enrollees to see social workers (and other relatively inexpensive personnel) rather than psychiatrists or psychologists for psychotherapy services.

These cost-control techniques are typically applied not by the MCO that covers the enrollees' nonpsychiatric health care but, rather, by specialized, for-profit "behavioral health" MCOs (the "carve-outs" referred to in Professor Tovino's excerpt above). In most cases, the behavioral health MCO contracts directly with the employer or state, and either assumes the insurance risk by agreeing to provide care for a predetermined price per enrollee or administers the plan without assuming the insurance risk. The variety of different contractual arrangements is large, and these arrangements are often quite complex. Further, the penetration of managed care in the private sector is significantly higher than in the public sector. While approximately 72% of all individuals with private insurance are enrolled in some type of managed behavioral health care, only about 55% of Medicaid recipients are enrolled in managed mental health care and only a very small percentage of Medicare recipients is in managed care of any sort. Garfield, supra, at 12.

There is no doubt that the rise of managed mental health care has enhanced cost control efforts. Indeed, according to one estimate, behavioral health benefits as a portion of the total private employer health care costs fell from 6.1% in 1988 to 3.1% in 1998. See Health Care Plan Design and Cost Trends—1988 through 1997 (Washington: Hay Group, 1998). The important question is whether this cost saving is achieved only by sacrificing quality of care.

One large study of private sector managed care involving 50,000 enrollees found that managed care cost-cutting often works by strictly limiting hospital stays. A number of other studies have reached similar findings. See David Mechanic & Donna McAlpine, *Mission Unfulfilled: Potholes on the Road to Mental Health Parity*, 18(5) Health Affairs 7 (Sept./Oct. 1999) (summarizing studies). As Mechanic and McAlpine point out, if managed care functions properly, reductions in inpatient care should be accompanied by increases in claims for substitute services, such as outpatient treatment. Some studies show a substitution effect, but other studies find little evidence of it. Id. In addition, a study by Wickizer and Lessler indicates that the reduced length of stay resulting from utilization management makes it more likely that patients will be readmitted to the hospital within 60 days. See Thomas M. Wickizer & Daniel Lessler, *Effects of Utilization Management on Patterns of Hospital Care Among Privately Insured Patients*, 36(11) Medical Care 1545 (1998). Another study found that patients were more likely to deteriorate under a capitation, prepaid care regime than a fee-for-service arrangement. See David Mechanic, Mark Schlesinger, & Donna D. McAlpine, *Management of Mental Health and Substance Abuse Services: State of the Art and Early Results*, 73 Milbank Q. 19 (1995).

Public sector experimentation with capitation and other forms of managed care has also been studied. Here, too, prepaid care reduces admissions and the number of days of hospitalization. However, in some states a corresponding rise in outpatient services occurred, and a few studies found that states' decision to adopt prepaid services did not significantly affect the quality of care. Id. See also U.S. Gen. Acct. Off., Medicaid: States Turn to Managed Care to Improve Access and Control (1993); Jaclyn W. Hausman et al., *Managed Mental Health Experience in Colorado*, in Managed Behavioral Health Care (David Mechanic ed., 1998); Richard G. Frank & Thomas G. McGuire, *Savings from a Medicaid Carve–Out for Mental Health and Substance Abuse Services in Massachusetts*, 48 Psychiatric Services 1147 (1997).

Nonetheless, according to one commentator, capitation plans are antithetical to the type of continuous long-range planning that is needed for good mental health care:

One of the characteristics of many managed care plans is that treatment on both an inpatient and outpatient basis is focused on stabilization and resolution of the presenting problem. Treatment is conceptualized as episodic in nature rather than continuous. This acute care model is conceptually, philosophically, and financially at odds with the long-term engagement strategy which appears to be most successful in treating people with the most disabling mental disorders. If the treatment provider operating in the capitated setting cannot afford financially to follow an engagement strategy, or sustain the person over a long period of time, coercion may become a short-cut. This provides the treatment provider with the means to get the person into treatment or shift care to another provider if the provider operating within a managed care setting is not responsible for hospitalization occurring as a result of civil commitment.

John Petrila, *Ethics, Money, and the Problem of Coercion in Managed Behavioral Health Care*, 40 St. Louis U. L.J. 359, 395–96 (1996).

5. *Criteria for Allocating Care*. One way to allocate a limited pool of societal resources for mental health services would be to give priority to coverage for the most serious mental illnesses. The argument in favor of this allocation method is that serious illnesses interfere much more profoundly with an individual's life. In addition, focusing resources on serious illness would address the worry that expansive DSM diagnostic criteria have resulted in money and attention being diverted towards relatively ordinary behavior. See pp. 25–27. For a famous argument that societal resources should be preferentially allocated towards the least well-off, see John Rawls, A Theory of Justice 302–03 (1971); for an application of this argument in the health care arena, see Norman Daniels, Just Health Care 35 (1985). Other mechanisms for allocating mental health resources might focus on those interventions that are most cost-effective—in other words, those interventions that have proven, relative to their cost, to have the most impact in treating mental illness. The effectiveness of any given intervention could be measured in terms of the percentage of individuals who had their symptoms alleviated. Alternatively, it could be measured in terms of the average amount by which the intervention improved individuals' quality-of-life. For a discussion of cost-effectiveness as an allocation criterion, see Arti K. Rai, *Rationing Through Choice: A New Approach to Cost–Effectiveness Analysis in Health Care*, 72 Ind. L.J. 1015 (1997).

What advantages or disadvantages can you see to each of these approaches? Are there alternative approaches to allocation/rationing that might be preferable? To what extent, if any, does our current system of mental health care financing follow a systematic approach to allocation? Imagine that you are a policy assistant to a recently elected senator from your state. She asks you to review the current system of mental health coverage, both public and private, and to come up with a proposal that will improve the current system. What would your proposal envision? What would be the respective roles of the federal and state governments? Would your proposal provide recipients with any judicially enforceable rights? Would you advocate parity in both public and private programs? Which interest groups do you expect to be most supportive of, or opposed to, your proposal? Are the members of these groups major contributors to your Senator's campaign fund?

CHAPTER 2

REGULATION OF THE MENTAL HEALTH PROFESSIONS

■ ■ ■

Table of Sections

I. ADMINISTRATIVE REGULATION

A. INTRODUCTION

The state uses two types of approaches to promote its long-recognized interest in assuring the quality of professional healthcare services.

One is the torts system, which subjects professionals who fail to meet standards of care to monetary liability for resulting injuries. This approach, discussed in Chapter Three, provides compensation to injured parties, seeks to deter future improper conduct, and relies on the judicial system to resolve related cases.

The other approach—and the focus of this chapter—involves administrative regulation, which can be either preventive or remedial in its focus. To achieve the former, states impose direct or indirect "entry" criteria to ensure that persons who provide health care services have the requisite qualifications. Administrative regulation can also be remedial, where the emphasis is on imposing administrative sanctions if there has been a departure from accepted professional standards. These sanctions may range from a reprimand to a fine to the loss of one's license to practice. The following materials describe the administrative regulation systems typically employed to maintain and promote the quality of care in the delivery of mental health services.

B. LICENSURE AND CERTIFICATION

1. Perspectives on Occupational Licensing

The regulation of a profession, whatever its form, must promote some legitimate governmental purpose. The following excerpts summarize the rationale for occupational regulation, while also exploring the debate over its use in the field of health care:

> Consumer protection is the rationale most commonly advanced as a justification for occupational licensing. In particular it is believed that control of entry and regulation of the practice are necessary to protect consumers from incompetent, dishonest, financially irresponsible, unsafe, and unsanitary provision of various services.
>
> Such a broad consumer protection rationale is incomplete and deficient. First and foremost, government intervention to protect consumers is only necessary when the market fails to perform that function. A market solution is preferable to an administrative solution unless the latter facilitates the transaction more efficiently than the market. While the market may fail to produce competitive results because the firms engage in anticompetitive conduct or because an industry is not competitively structured, the type of market failure that is particularly relevant here involves that caused by transaction costs. . . . [T]he question is whether consumers of a particular service are able to make informed and intelligent selections of various service providers, free from undue exploitation by the latter. If the market failure is significant, [e.g., because of a failure by the industry to provide adequate information or an inability of the consumer to comprehend available information], consumers will not be able to make such a selection. Consequently they will have difficulty determining their needs, evaluating the quality of the alternatives or the services rendered, and judging the price and other characteristics of the transaction. Thus the market will not permit consumers quickly to detect and avoid incompetent, fraudulent, or financially irresponsible providers. On the other hand,

if there is no significant market failure, a consumer will be able to choose those service providers who, in the mind of the consumer, represent the best combination of high quality service and cost. . . .

Thus in examining occupational licensing the critical question is which types of service transactions are likely to be characterized by sufficient market failure to warrant governmental intervention. In many situations an administrative solution seems unnecessary. For example, in the case of barbers, cosmetologists, funeral homes, taxidermists, driver training schools, private investigators, and probably contractors, architects, and engineers, to name a few, a priori reasoning suggests that the market functions adequately. In fact in such areas it is doubtful that consumers of the services know or care whether the provider is licensed. . . . In some areas it is difficult to generalize, particularly since the nature and sophistication of all consumers are not equivalent. The health field, and perhaps lawyers, present the most difficult questions. Market failure may be more likely in these areas. . . . Moreover one may be influenced by the fact that the potential for serious harm from an incorrect decision is greater in these areas, and by a fear that consumers of these services may be insufficiently risk-adverse. In any event, some licensing seems warranted with doctors, dentists, other providers of health services, and lawyers.

Jonathan Rose, *Occupational Licensing: A Framework for Analysis*, 1979 Ariz. St. L.J. 189, 190–91 (1979).

The following provides another perspective that incorporates the recent emphasis on how best to enhance the quality of health care services while controlling their costs:

Licensure may be an efficient response to several potential types of market failure. First, when there are information asymmetries between professionals and consumers and quality information is costly, professionals may be insulated against the competitive disadvantages of offering lower quality services, and at the same time unable to capture the gains associated with higher quality services. . . . Second, licensure may address some quality and consumption problems in markets where externalities are striking— where providers or consumers are not likely to take into account the effects of services on third-parties [and] the public health consequences of substandard care or under-treatment. Third, licensure may help to address problems associated with professionals who play the dual roles of diagnostician and treatment provider. In such cases . . . there may be a bias toward overconsumption: providers may tend to offer more services than necessary to consumers, who often are poorly equipped to evaluate the marginal value of additional services and, in any case, may be insulated from some of the costs of overconsumption.

Licensure is not always, however, an efficient response to these types of market failure. Moreover, licensure may be associated with certain competitive problems. Most generally, licensure may be used by incumbent professionals to insulate themselves from competition. . . . By restricting the entry of competing professionals, licensure can restrict supply, which can increase the income of incumbents (at consumer expense) or decrease the pressure on incumbents to improve non-price aspects of their services, such as quality or convenience.

Daniel J. Gilman, *Physician Licensure and Telemedicine: Some Competitive Issues Raised by the Prospect of Practicing Globally While Regulating Locally*, 14 J. Health Care L. & Pol'y 87, 96–97 (2011).

While licensing is an established part of the regulatory landscape, some contend that licensing is contrary to the public interest. Consider the merits of the arguments advanced by one commentator concerning the provision of psychotherapy services:

Invariably, the rationale advanced for restricting the right to practice is protection of the public. But a strong case can be made that the only ones really being protected are the professionals themselves. First, psychotherapy is nearly incapable of definition, and regulations invariably encroach on such related fields as education. Second, academic credentials and written examinations are worthless as measures of therapeutic effectiveness. . . . [One researcher] has concluded that neither criteria predicts anything but future grades and test scores, no matter what the profession. . . .

* * *

. . . Moreover, there are so many negative side effects to licensing that it is hard to imagine when it would be a useful means of regulation: Evidence is accumulating that licensing significantly increases the cost of professional services, decreases the supply of practitioners, inhibits improvements in the organization and delivery of services, stifles innovative training programs, and is discriminatory.

* * *

The question is whether alternatives exist. . . . [S]tatutes might only restrict the right to use certain titles while basing the requirements for licensing on competency, not credentials. Such changes, however, don't go far enough. Since we know so little about therapeutic effectiveness, we need regulations that encourage responsible experimentation and diversity, but also protect the public from incompetence and unethical conduct.

All practitioners should be required to register with the state but not to make academic or other credentials a prerequisite to practice. Laws should, however, require therapists to disclose their training and techniques to all clients. An active, powerful and well-financed disciplinary board, a variety of nongovernment certification organizations, and a comprehensive campaign to educate the public are necessary, if this system is to work properly. There are certainly risks involved in this approach, but I believe they are fewer than if we continue on our current path. The fact is that the only sure losers in today's continuing war among the mental-health professions will ultimately be their patients.

Daniel B. Hogan, *Licensing Mental Therapists*, N.Y. Times, July 18, 1979, at A23. See also Daniel B. Hogan, *The Effectiveness of Licensing: History, Evidence, and Recommendations*, 7 Law & Hum. Behav. 117, 121 (1983):

In the first place, licensing has not accomplished its state[d] purposes. Little evidence suggests that the quality of professional services has improved as a result of licensing laws, disciplinary actions are woefully inadequate, and the prevention of illegal practice is generally spotty, often being aimed at eliminating competition, rather than incompetence.

In the second place, even if licensing laws do assure competent practitioners, the price may not be worth it. The increased cost of services, the creation of shortages of supply, and the development of maldistributions of professionals resulting from licensing laws lead to direct harm to the public through the inability of the poor and other disadvantaged groups to afford or find any practitioner at all. . . . Quite apart from these more obvious costs, the entry requirements of licensing laws have a tendency to discriminate against the poor, the aged, women, and minorities, as well as inhibiting important innovations in the methods of organizing and delivering professional services.

In the third place, even if the net benefits of licensing outweigh the costs, equally beneficial but less expensive alternatives may be available. In addition, other factors than licensing may be far more influential in determining the quality of service ultimately received by the public; and it is these factors that should be looked to if sound regulation is desired.

2. Entry into the Profession

a. Licensing of Psychiatrists

As is true for professional licensing generally, the licensing of psychiatrists is a state rather than a federal function. Thus, psychiatrists, like other physicians, must obtain licenses in states where they wish to practice—and, as we explain below in discussing telemedicine, where their patients are. The licensing requirements applicable to physicians generally include graduation from an accredited medical school, satisfactory completion of a series of standardized examinations, and at least one year of postgraduate medical education in the form of residency training. More specifically, the licensing of physicians and thus psychiatrists entails the following:

> Each state has its own board of medical examiners and each individual board of medical examiners selects the criteria it will require for licensure of physicians in its state. The individual states rely on the approval of various national organizations with specialized expertise to satisfy certain state licensure criteria. For example, the Liaison Committee of Medical Education (LCME) of the American Medical Association accredits medical schools, guaranteeing that they provide the recognized four-year medical school curriculum containing the required academic and clinical elements. Generally, boards of medical examiners across the nation will accept candidates with medical degrees from schools accredited by the LCME, thus avoiding the need of each state to independently develop criteria for medical education.

> In order to obtain initial licensure, states generally require candidates to present evidence of graduation from an accredited medical school having successfully received an M.D. (doctor of medicine) or D.O. (doctor of osteopathy) in a four-year program. The candidate also must have passed a proficiency examination; currently, that is the United States Medical Licensing Exam (USMLE), or other combination of older tests, such as that formerly given by the National Board of Medical Examiners (NBME).

> The Federation of State Medical Boards (FSMB) and the NBME have collaborated in establishing a single, three-step examination for medical licensure. Step 1 of the exam process tests the examinee's knowledge of basic biomedical sciences, with an emphasis on principles and mechanisms of health, disease, and modes of therapy. Step 2 assesses whether an examinee can apply the medical knowledge and understanding of clinical science considered essential for the provision of patient care. Step 3 assesses the physician's ability to apply biomedical and clinical sciences, emphasizing patient management in ambulatory settings. Most state licensing authorities require completion of Steps 1, 2 and 3 within a seven-year period. Licensing boards also set a limit on the number of attempts allowed to pass each step and have established, as an eligibility requirement for Step 3, the completion or near completion of at least one postgraduate training year.

Physicians seeking initial licensure must have successfully completed 'postgraduate' medical education in the form of residency training. . . . All state licensing authorities require at least one year of postgraduate training; . . .

Kenneth R. Wing, Michael S. Jacobs, & Patricia C. Kuszler, The Law and American Health Care 462–63 (1998). See also Nadia N. Sawicki, *Character, Competence, and the Principles of Medical Discipline*, 13 J. Health Care L. & Pol'y 285, 291–92 (2010) ("Beyond imposing educational and training requirements, many medical practice acts also require that applicants for medical licensure demonstrate good moral character. Some states also impose additional requirements, such as proof of malpractice insurance coverage; a clear criminal background check; or age, citizenship, or residency requirements.").

While the practice of psychiatry requires a medical license, completion of a psychiatric residency is not legally mandated. Nevertheless, a psychiatric residency is likely to be a practical necessity for any physician who wishes to function primarily as a psychiatrist. For instance, most hospitals accord admissions privileges to their psychiatric units only to those physicians who have completed a psychiatric residency and may permit only such physicians to evaluate, diagnose, and treat patients who suffer from mental disorders. In the community, completion of residency training is often a prerequisite for reimbursement from third-party payors for referrals received from general practitioners when specialized mental health care is needed.

b. *Licensing of Psychologists*

The regulation of psychologists usually takes one of two basic forms—licensing or certification. A license entitles the holder to engage in activities otherwise proscribed by law. Licensing statutes have two essential features: (1) they limit the performance of certain activities or services to a designated class of persons, typically the holders of a particular professional license; and (2) they restrict the acquisition of this license to those who meet specified educational requirements (usually, having received a doctoral degree, although in some states a master's degree will still suffice), have successfully completed a state-administered examination, and employ certain authorized procedures.

In contrast, certification, or "title licensing" as it is sometimes called, does not seek to reserve certain functions or activities to a specific class of individuals (i.e., those holding a license), but rather limits the use of a designated *title* to those who meet specified training and experience requirements. A certification or title licensing statute may provide, for example, that only those who have obtained a doctoral degree in psychology may refer to themselves as "certified psychologists," "psychologists," or any other title incorporating the term "psychology" or similar terms. Although many jurisdictions initially adopted a certification approach, most now use licensing in lieu of or in addition to certification. Randolph P. Reaves, The History of Licensure of Psychologists in the United States and Canada, in Psychology Licensure and Certification: What Students Need to Know 17, 21 (Thomas J. Vaughn ed., 2006).

i.   Licensing Approach to Regulation

In states that use a licensing scheme, anyone not licensed is prohibited from practicing or performing the services normally rendered by or assigned to psychologists, with the violation of this prohibition being a potential criminal offense. The effectiveness of this approach, however, depends on whether the functions and activities that require a license are clearly defined.

California employs fairly typical language, limiting the "practice of psychology" (as well as the ability to "represent" oneself as a psychologist) to license holders. The key phrase, "practice of psychology," is defined as the

> rendering or offering to render for a fee to individuals, groups, organizations or the public any psychological service involving the application of psychological principles, methods, and procedures of understanding, predicting, and influencing behavior, such as the principles pertaining to learning, perception, motivation, emotions, and interpersonal relationships; and the methods and procedures of interviewing, counseling, psychotherapy, behavior modification, and hypnosis; and of constructing, administering, and interpreting tests of mental abilities, aptitudes, interests, attitudes, personality characteristics, emotions, and motivations.

Cal. Bus. & Prof. Code § 2903 (2013). At the same time, persons "doing work of a psychological nature" (such as providing verbal therapy) are exempted so long as the services they provide are "consistent with the laws governing their respective professions [and] they do not hold themselves out to the public by any title or description of services incorporating the words 'psychological,' 'psychologist,' 'psychology,' 'psychometrist,' 'psychometrics,' or 'psychometry,' or [ ] they do not state or imply that they are licensed to practice psychology." Cal. Bus. & Prof. Code § 2908 (2013).

ii.   Certification or Title Licensing Approach to Regulation

States that use a certification or title licensing approach typically provide for the issuance of a license to persons who meet specified educational requirements and have successfully completed a state administered examination. In this respect, the certification model is not substantially different from a straight licensing scheme. However, title licensing generally makes it a criminal offense for anyone not licensed to use various titles such as "psychologist," "psychotherapist," or "mental health counselor." Nevertheless, unlicensed individuals may perform the functions of a psychologist (for example, by providing psychotherapy) so long as they do not hold themselves out or advertise themselves as being a psychologist.

The certification form of licensing avoids the need to define the precise functions that only those who hold a license can perform. However, it may be challenged on other grounds. For instance, one appellate court held that a title licensing statute that made it a criminal offense for unlicensed psychologists to hold themselves out or use the title of "psychologist" was a violation of the petitioners' commercial speech rights under the First Amendment. In *Abramson v. Gonzalez*, 949 F.2d 1567 (11th Cir. 1992), the majority concluded that the State's interest in protecting its citizens from incompetent health professionals could be achieved by means less restrictive than the blanket prohibition on unlicensed practitioners' advertising themselves as "psychologists." The dissenting opinion, in contrast, would have sustained the Florida statute as an appropriate exercise of the State's police power to protect the health and safety of its citizens. Except for the decision in *Gonzalez*, this issue has received little attention, probably because few states now solely employ this model.

As suggested by the above materials, professional licensing, in contrast to the certification approach, enables a state to exercise greater control over identified professional functions, with most states today using some combination of a licensing (restricting the practice of psychology to licensed individuals) and certification (preventing unlicensed individuals from holding themselves out as psychologists) approach. Frank M. Dattilio et al., *An Empirical Survey on Psychological Testing and the Use of the Term Psychological: Turf Battles or Clinical Necessity?*, 38 Prof. Psychol.: Res. & Prac. 682, 687 (2007).

c.   *Clinical Social Workers*

As noted in Chapter One, clinical social workers have emerged as one of the major providers of psychotherapy. In fact, some estimates indicate they now deliver more mental health care than any other profession. As the importance of clinical social workers has grown, so has regulation of the field. In 1972, only eleven states and Puerto Rico had licensing or certification requirements for clinical social workers. Today, every state recognizes clinical social workers with their own licensure and title. Am. Bd. of Exam'rs in Clinical Soc. Work, Clinical Social Workers, http://www.abecsw.org/csw-marketplace.html (last visited May 26, 2013). Although licensure laws differ from state to state, in most states clinical social workers can practice autonomously (i.e., without clinical supervision) only after obtaining a Master's Degree in Social Work (M.S.W.) and completing at least two years of full-time supervised clinical practice. Am. Bd. of Exam's in Clinical Soc. Work, Professional Development and Practice Competencies in Clinical Social Work 7 (2002).

In 2004, New York amended its licensure statute (N.Y. Educ. Law § 7701 (McKinney)) and created a very broad and inclusive scope of practice for clinical social workers. In 2005, a New York court upheld this expansion and said that "as a matter of law, . . . in terms of clinical functions, the scope of practice of psychology and the scope of practice of licensed clinical social work, although described using some different words at times, do not vary in substance and are wholly equal and the same." *People v. R.R.*, 807 N.Y.S.2d 516, 528 (N.Y. Sup. Ct. 2005).

QUESTIONS AND COMMENTS

1. *Questions.* What are the possible advantages and disadvantages of licensing models in contrast to certification or title licensing? What are possible reasons why one or the other would be more likely to enhance the quality of the care provided? Which form of regulation provides better information to potential users of mental health care? Which system better provides for ease of enforcement?

2. *Administration of licensing laws.* While licensing laws are products of state legislative action, the rules established are typically fairly general and delegate to administrative bodies the task of developing the specific standards pertaining to licensure. The appointees to these bodies are frequently representatives of the various professional groups and organizations that represent the profession within the state. Thus, professional organizations may have a considerable influence on the standards adopted by the various regulatory boards. This has led some commentators to express concern that licensure may be "captured" by the profession and become relatively lax in protecting the public, and to assert that licensing boards should include non-professional or "public" members. Thomas Tso, *Mediation's Boundaries:* In re Licensure of Penny v. State ex rel. Wyoming, 11 Harv. Negot. L. Rev. 453, 459–60 (2006).

3. *Enforcement of licensing laws.* Even though states generally insist that individuals practicing psychology have a license, with a violation of the licensing act usually deemed a misdemeanor, very few criminal cases charging the unauthorized practice of psychology occurred are ever brought. Why do you think this is?

4. *Indirect effects of licensing.* State licensing serves not only to provide an imprimatur of competency but may be a pre-condition for reimbursement for the delivery of professional services under either private health insurance plans or publicly financed health care plans such as Medicare or Medicaid. See Daniel Goleman, *Social Workers Vault Into a Leading Role in Psychotherapy*, N.Y. Times, Apr. 30, 1985, at 17.

5. *Application of licensing laws to "unconventional" therapy providers.* What obstacles, if any, exist to using licensing laws to regulate the provision of counseling or treatment services by ostensibly religiously affiliated or other unlicensed entities? Consider the following excerpt from the obituary of L. Ron Hubbard, founder of the Church of Scientology:

> Clients paid Scientology up to $300 an hour for a one-on-one counseling process, known as auditing. To monitor a client's responses to questions, church staff members use an electrical instrument on the client's skin.

> The goal of "auditing," which can go on for years and cost clients hundreds of thousands of dollars, is to increase control over thought processes in a portion of the mind where, Scientologists assert, emotional problems and psychosomatic illnesses are born.

Robert Lindsey, *L. Ron Hubbard Dies of Stroke; Founder of Church of Scientology*, N.Y. Times, Jan. 29, 1986, at A–21. Could licensing laws be applied to prevent the rendering of counseling services by the Church of Scientology where the auditor has not been licensed by the state as a mental health professional? Would there be any First Amendment problems with such a regulation? For another unconventional therapy asserted to induce dramatic results, see Phil Mollon, *Thought Field Therapy and Its Derivatives: Rapid Relief of Mental Health Problems Through Tapping on the Body*, 12(3–4) Primary Care & Community Psychiatry 123 (2007) (addressing rhythmic tapping on a client's body to relieve anxiety, emotional distress).

6. *Retroactive effect of regulation.* Can newly enacted state licensing and certification statutes operate to exclude established therapists from continuing to provide mental health services? Such statutes and regulations often include "grandfather clauses," under which persons who do not meet the newly imposed criteria but who were practitioners before the restriction took effect may nonetheless be licensed. If grandfather clauses are not provided, does the practitioner have any legal remedies? In *Berger v. Bd. of Psychologist Exam'rs,* 521 F.2d 1056 (D.C. Cir. 1975), the court found a relatively restrictive grandfather clause to be unconstitutional. The clause in question permitted a practitioner to substitute seven years practice and a master's degree (or twenty-four credit hours of psychology courses completed subsequent to obtaining a bachelor's degree) for a doctorate degree and passage of an examination. Berger, a practicing psychologist for fourteen years, received his training through apprenticeships with several psychiatrists. The court found that the statute's irrebuttable presumption of his incompetence to practice psychology violated the Due Process Clause of the Fifth Amendment. The court remanded the case to the licensing board to determine whether Berger's experience was commensurate with that of licensed psychologists. But see *Gersch v. Ill. Dep't of Prof'l Regulation*, 720 N.E.2d 672, 680 (Ill. App. Ct. 1999) (absence of a grandfather clause in legislature's revision of licensing statute for social workers did not violate plaintiff's substantive due process rights when this was not the first time the legislature regulated the profession).

7.   *License mobility.* Due to the cost and difficulty of obtaining state licensure, as well as a lack of services in some border communities, there has been a push for increased mobility for psychologists wanting to practice in another state. The Association of State and Provincial Psychology Boards (ASPPB) has begun to implement and test programs to remove barriers to cross-state practice, such as a Credentials Bank, a Disciplinary Data System, Certificates of Professional Qualification, and a Uniform Application for Psychology Licensure. Pat DeLeon, *Licensure Mobility* (June 11, 2011), http:// pathdeleon.blogspot.com/2011/06/licensure-mobility.html. Another option is to issue licenses at the national level. What are the likely advantages and disadvantages of such an approach? What legal and political challenges would a Congressional law implementing national licensing likely face?

8.   *Telepractice.* Increasing demands for telepractice (also referred to as e-therapy, telehealth, or telemedicine)—the use of electronic media such as video conferencing to deliver mental health services—is also associated with efforts to remove barriers to cross-state practice and to assist clients in remote, underserved areas. See Jeffrey E. Barnett, *Utilizing Technological Innovations to Enhance Psychotherapy Supervision, Training, and Outcomes*, 48 Psychotherapy 103 (2011); Randall Stross, *The Therapist Will See You Now, Via the Web*, N.Y. Times, July 10, 2011, at BU3. One largely unanswered question is: "If the patient is in state A, and the provider in state B, does the provider need a license in both states A and B, or does he or she need a license only in state A or state B?" Generally, physicians (and therefore, psychiatrists) who practice telemedicine must hold licenses in the states where their patients are located. See Federation of State Medical Boards, *Telemedicine Overview: Board-by-Board Approach* (August 2012), available at http://www.fsmb.org/pdf/grpol_telemedicine_licensure.pdf (listing applicable statutes and administrative codes). In general, what are the pros and cons of telepractice involving mental health services? For a related discussion, see Helen M. Farrell and Douglas Mossman, *Practicing Psychiatry via Skype: Medicolegal Considerations*, 10(12) Current Psychiatry 30 (2011). How would you advise a state licensing board that was considering creation of a special license for practitioners who want to engage solely in telepractice within the state? What legal challenges might arise? How would you feel about getting mental health treatment via your computer or other electronic devices (rather than going to a practitioner's office)?

The federal government's Medicaid website states:

Telemedicine is viewed as a cost-effective alternative to the more traditional face-to-face way of providing medical care (e.g., face-to-face consultations or examinations between provider and patient). As such, states have the option/ flexibility to determine whether (or not) to cover telemedicine; what types of telemedicine to cover; where in the state it can be covered; how it is provided/covered; what types of telemedicine practitioners/ providers may be covered/reimbursed . . .

Telemedicine, http://www.medicaid.gov/Medicaid-CHIP-Program-Information/ By-Topics/Delivery-Systems/Telemedicine.html. Assuming this statement is true, and assuming that lack of state licensure is a barrier to cross-state provision of mental health services, should states consider changing their licensing regulations or developing reciprocity arrangements to promote greater access to care?

C. ADMINISTRATIVE REGULATION OF PROFESSIONAL ACTIVITY

A recurrent component of state regulation of the professions is a disciplinary system designed to ensure adherence to a professional code of conduct. This function is usually undertaken by an administrative body with the authority to both promulgate rules of conduct and conduct disciplinary proceedings when there has been a breach of professional conduct. The governing boards of such administrative bodies tend to largely be composed of members of the regulated profession. They are generally responsible for developing practice standards for the profession and supervising the disciplinary system. The latter involves investigating complaints of professional misconduct and imposing sanctions on wrongdoers. Permissible sanctions include a verbal or written reprimand, mandated completion of a program intended to rehabilitate the professional, imposition of a fine, and license suspension or revocation.

The practitioner is entitled to a hearing on a claim of professional misconduct. The primary purpose of the hearing is to provide the practitioner an opportunity to be heard, to present evidence, and to challenge the testimony of adverse witnesses. The hearing need not be a formal trial before a judge or jury; rather, it is often relatively informal and conducted by a member of a panel or by the full board of the regulatory agency. The practitioner has various procedural rights, including the right to receive prior notice of and to be present at the hearing. While the assistance of legal counsel is usually permitted, it has not been viewed as a constitutional right of the professional facing a disciplinary action. Witnesses generally may present testimony in an informal narrative fashion, rather than in accordance with the rules of evidence employed at trials.

Despite its informal nature, a disciplinary hearing must, as a matter of constitutional doctrine, comport with basic notions of fairness. The tribunal must reach its decision on the basis of probative evidence, and not rely on unsupported allegations or prejudice. Normally, a practitioner may obtain judicial review of an adverse agency decision. The scope of review, however, tends to be limited. Typically, a court will confine its inquiry to determining whether the practitioner received a fair hearing, as well as whether the tribunal based its decision upon substantial probative evidence and not upon speculation, bias, or other arbitrary factors.

The case below illustrates both the legal issues that may be raised in these types of proceedings and the role of the courts in reviewing the administrative decisions.

MISSISSIPPI STATE BOARD OF PSYCHOLOGICAL EXAMINERS V. HOSFORD

Supreme Court of Mississippi, 1987.
508 So. 2d 1049.

ROBERTSON, JUSTICE, for the Court:

I.

This case presents sensitive questions regarding the authority of a state-created board, charged with the governance of a learned profession, to interpret the canons of ethics of that profession and in accordance therewith to discipline a member of that profession. The case also presents questions regarding the scope of appellate judicial review of such disciplinary action.

Substantially, the case involves a charge that a psychologist disclosed patient confidences without the patient's consent and in violation of his profession's confidentiality principles. The state board found that the violation had occurred and suspended the psychologist's license for ninety days. The Chancery Court reversed. As we regard the action taken [to be] within the authority and discretion of the Board, we reverse and reinstate the order of suspension.

II.

A.

Robert L. Hosford, Ph.D., holds a license issued by the Mississippi State Board of Psychological Examiners to engage in the professional practice of psychology in this state. Dr. Hosford maintains his offices in Jackson, Mississippi, and exercises his license by practicing in the field of clinical psychology. . . .

*   *   *

This case has its genesis in the psychologist-patient relationship between Dr. Hosford and Patricia F. Lindsey and her former husband, Jimmy G. Lindsey. That relationship came into being on December 31, 1981, when the Lindseys, then husband and wife, consulted Dr. Hosford in his professional capacity and sought counseling and advice regarding difficulties they were experiencing in their marital relationship. These consultations continued for a little over two months. During their course, from time to time Patricia Lindsey would meet with Dr. Hosford privately, at other times Jimmy Lindsey would meet with Dr. Hosford privately, and on still other occasions the Lindseys would jointly consult with Dr. Hosford.

In March of 1982 the Lindseys' marriage was clearly on the rocks as Patricia filed in the Chancery Court of Madison County, Mississippi, an action for divorce. Of immediate concern was the temporary custody of the parties' six-year-old son, Jon D. Lindsey. A temporary custody hearing was scheduled in Chancery Court for March 19, 1982. At that hearing Jimmy [Lindsey] submitted an affidavit made by Dr. Hosford, dated March 18, 1982, setting forth the background of his professional relationship with the Lindseys and giving his opinion that temporary custody of the child should be placed with his father, Jimmy G. Lindsey. The giving of this affidavit has given rise to the present proceedings.

At some time prior to the temporary hearing Dr. Hosford talked with the attorney representing Jimmy G. Lindsey and furnished certain information to the attorney who then prepared a draft of the proposed affidavit. Dr. Hosford then reviewed the affidavit and made editing changes and corrections. The affidavit was then retyped in final form and was executed by Dr. Hosford on March 18, 1982, in the presence of a notary public.

In relevant part the affidavit states that Dr. Hosford counseled with Patricia Lindsey and Jimmy Lindsey both together and separately concerning their personal relationship as well as their respective relationships with their son; that during the course of these consultations Dr. Hosford reached conclusions regarding the "psychological traits of the parties including those which have a bearing on or relate to their respective concepts of parenthood in general and their respective responsibilities and roles as parents to their child in particular." The affidavit continued, making clear that the opinion to be given was "based upon his [Dr. Hosford's] counseling with the parties, his observations of them. . . . " In the affidavit Dr. Hosford then gave rather specific opinions regarding the parenting skills of the two parties, the details of which need not be recounted, except to say that the opinion of Patricia F. Lindsey was quite unfavorable. In the final analysis, Dr. Hosford gave his "professional opinion that the interest and welfare of the child will be best served and promoted by placing his care, custody and control with Jimmy G. Lindsey. . . . "

Patricia Lindsey did not consent to the giving of this affidavit. . . . If we understand the record correctly, Dr. Hosford stipulated before the Board that he "did not receive a signed waiver of the psychologist-patient privilege."

B.

On March 9, 1983, Patricia F. Lindsey filed with the Mississippi State Board of Psychological Examiners a complaint against Dr. Robert L. Hosford wherein she charged Dr. Hosford with unauthorized, unprofessional and illegal disclosure of matters communicated to him and protected from disclosure by the psychologist-patient privilege. The matter came on for hearing before the Board on November 30, 1984. At that hearing Patricia and Dr. Hosford appeared personally and testified. Patricia established her prima facie case as recited above. Dr. Hosford defended on the alternative grounds that he disclosed no matters the confidentiality of which was protected or, in the alternative, that there was a "clear danger" to the child which created an exception to his profession's confidentiality principle and necessitated disclosure.

In due course on January 22, 1985, the Board rendered its final decision finding that Dr. Hosford had violated Principle 5 of the American Psychological Association's Ethical Principles of Psychologists[2] and further that this violation could not be excused under the clear danger principle, the Board finding "that the clear danger exception to Principle 5 pertains to only life and death situations." The Board exonerated Dr. Hosford from violation of the Mississippi statutory psychologist-patient privilege. Miss. Code Ann. § 73–31–29 (1972). By reason of Dr. Hosford's violation of Principle 5, the Board ordered Dr. Hosford's license to practice psychology in the State of Mississippi suspended for a period of ninety days.

Thereafter Dr. Hosford perfected his appeal to the Chancery Court of the First Judicial District of Hinds County, Mississippi. . . . [The Chancery Court reversed the Board's decision] and ordered Dr. Hosford's license reinstated and all proceedings pertaining to the matter expunged.

The Board now appeals to this Court and asks reinstatement of its order of suspension.

* * *

IV.

. . . Proceedings seeking suspension or termination of the license of a professional are serious matters. Quite literally one's ability to earn a living is at stake. Balanced against the professional's legitimate self-interest is the interest of the profession and the consumers of its services in honesty, competency and the observance of reasonable ethical principles.

---

[2] Principle 5, considered by the Board under the authority of Miss. Code Ann. § 73–31–21(a)(1) (1972), reads as follows:

CONFIDENTIALITY

Psychologists have a primary obligation to respect the confidentiality of information obtained from persons in the course of their work as psychologists. They reveal such information to others only with the consent of the person or the person's legal representative, except in those unusual circumstances in which not to do so would result in clear danger to the person or to others. Where appropriate, psychologists inform their clients of the legal limits of confidentiality.

* * *

See *Ethical Principles of Psychologists*, as printed in American Psychologist, Vol. 36, No. 6, pp. 633, 635–36 (June 1981).

In a variety of contexts we have held that disciplinary charges against a professional must be proved by clear and convincing evidence. [T]his burden of proof rule applies as well to disciplinary proceedings before the State Board of Psychological Examiners.

Board decisions affecting the license of a psychologist are appealable. In such case the Chancery Court sits as an appellate court, as do we. The Chancery Court has no authority to proceed de novo. . . . Put otherwise, only where the decision is arbitrary and capricious may a court on appeal intervene.

The Chancery Court violated this premise with regard to the issue of consent. The record before the Board reflects that Patricia Lindsey gave no consent or otherwise waived her right to confidentiality. . . .

We emphasize further the role of the Board. It consisted at the time of six members, five of whom were licensed psychologists. One Board member was a person not a psychologist but who has expressed a continuing interest in the field of psychology. Its members are selected by the governor from a list of nominees submitted by the Mississippi Psychological Association. Ordained by statute, the Board is the keeper of the conscience of those who engage in the professional practice of psychology in this state. From this it follows that the Board [is] the primary interpreter of the ethical principles to which psychologists in this state are subject.

V.

At all times relevant hereto, the Board had authority to suspend the license of one subject to its jurisdiction where that individual "has violated the current code of ethics of the American Psychological Association." One provision of that code regards patient confidences. Principle 5 of the Ethical Principles of Psychologists requires respect for "the confidentiality of information obtained from persons in the course of their work as psychologists." Only two exceptions to the principle of confidentiality are found. The first, of course, is where the patient consents to the disclosure. In the second, even though no consent be given, the psychologist may disclose otherwise confidential information where "not to do so would result in clear danger to the person or to others."

Having well in mind our limited scope of review in matters such as this, there can be little doubt but that the matters disclosed in Dr. Hosford's affidavit[5] were protected from disclosure by the confidentiality

---

[5]   The record is not clear whether the Board considered Dr. Hosford's transgression to have been at the point of disclosure of the affidavit to the Chancery Court or at the earlier point of disclosure to Jimmy Lindsey's attorney of the information necessary for preparation of the affidavit. We will proceed here on the assumption that the violation of Principle 5 occurred when the affidavit was filed with the court. Because Dr. Hosford also had a professional relationship with Jimmy Lindsey, he was to some extent empowered to communicate otherwise confidential

strictures of Principle 5. Indeed, we perceive nothing in this appeal which turns upon disputed facts. All agree what happened. At issue is the Board's authority and the propriety of the sanction it has imposed.

* * *

VI.

. . . The Board does not have carte blanche authority to say that Principle 5 means anything it wishes. Yet we do not consider it appropriate that we interject ourselves between the Board and Dr. Hosford regarding its interpretation of the clear danger exception. The Board construes the exception narrowly to apply only to cases where "life and limb" were in danger. Dr. Hosford would have us read it more broadly, to cover situations where the best interest[s] of the child are at stake. In the context of this case, the danger at issue is that without the disclosure temporary custody of the child may not be placed with the parent better suited to exercise such custody in the child's best interest. The Board has considered this danger as one not within the scope of the ethical principle.

While today's opinion should not be read as suggesting that we will sanction any reading the Board may give to the language of the Ethical Principles, the reading the Board has given these principles in the case at bar is not one that is so arbitrary or unreasonable that we should intervene. It may be true that placement of temporary custody within the wrong parent may result in some emotional or psychological damage to the child. And, indeed, where that issue is presented to a Chancery Court and the issue and facts fully fleshed out, we are by no means prepared to say that the psychologist's lips will be forever sealed by the privilege (although we do not decide that point today as the matter is not before us).[6]

In the context of this record we recognize the Board's authority, in the construction of the clear danger exception to Principle 5, to determine that the requirement of confidentiality is paramount to the danger that temporary custody of the child might be placed with the wrong parent. Put otherwise, it is within the Board's authority, as the keeper of the conscience of the psychologists of this state, to consider the requirement of confidentiality of sufficient strength and importance that the clear danger exception should be read narrowly and limited to cases involving imminent danger to life and limb.

REVERSED AND RENDERED

---

information to Jimmy's attorney. The ultimate dimensions of this "some extent" need not be addressed as the point was not directly presented below nor is it before us this day.

[6] We are aware that there is authority in other jurisdictions that the best interest of the child does override the psychologist-patient privilege in a child custody proceeding. [citations omitted]

QUESTIONS AND COMMENTS

1. *Questions.* How explicit must ethical standards be before sanctions can be applied? Was the ethical principle that the Board found Dr. Hosford violated drawn clearly enough for Dr. Hosford to know whether he could disclose the information he obtained from Mrs. Lindsey? Did he have adequate notice that "the clear danger exception . . . pertains to only life and death situations" and does not encompass a custodial placement that could adversely affect a child? Should a Board have an obligation to provide a mechanism whereby a professional can obtain advice on whether a contemplated action violates professional standards?

2. *Hypothetical.* How would you, as an attorney, advise your client, a psychologist, who informs you that one of his patients, while not an abusive parent, fantasizes about abusing her child because she does not like the child and does not like parenthood? Would disclosure in the course of a custody proceeding violate Principle 5 of the Ethical Principles of Psychologists? Could such information be subpoenaed by a court in a child custody proceeding under most state laws? For further discussion of confidentiality between patient and therapist, see infra Chapter Five.

3. *Effectiveness of administrative remediation.* How effective are disciplinary hearings as a remedial device? Is the public interest likely to be adequately protected by hearings conducted and controlled by members of the same profession as the professional brought before the disciplinary tribunal? Is there a significant risk that leaving the control of discipline to representatives of the profession will lead to policies that are overly protective of the profession and individual practitioners? What are the risks of having disciplinary hearings controlled by individuals who lack formal education regarding what members of a profession do?

A recent study reported that medical boards took only 3.06 serious actions per 1,000 physicians, a level down 18% from its peak in 2004. *Most States Do Not Protect Patients from Substandard Physicians*, Public Citizen's Annual State Medical Board Ranking Finds (May 17, 2012), http://www.citizen.org/pressroom/pressroomredirect.cfm?ID=3612. This study concluded: "Most states . . . are not living up to their obligations to protect patients from doctors who are practicing substandard medicine, in part because of budget cuts." Id. Another report found that 55% of the 10,672 physicians whose names were placed in the National Practitioner Data Bank (NPDB) from 1990–2009 following revocation or restriction of their clinical privileges by a hospital faced no subsequent action by their state medical licensing board, including 220 disciplined because they were an "Immediate Threat to Health or Safety" of patients. Alan Levine et al., *State Medical Boards Fail to Discipline Doctors with Hospital Actions Against Them*, Pub. Citizen (Mar. 2011), http://www.citizen.org/hrg1937. The NPDB is "a national clearinghouse of doctor disciplinary and medical malpractice information operated by the Department of Health and Human Services [DHHS] and available to only health care organizations and State medical boards." Id. This report led one of the co-authors, a physician and Director of the Health

Research Group of the organization that sponsored the research, to write a letter to the Secretary of the DHHS calling for "investigations concerning the dangerously lax disciplinary actions by so many state medical boards." Letter from Sidney Wolfe to Kathleen Sebelius (Mar. 15, 2011), http://www.citizen.org/documents/1937A.pdf.

An exploration of disciplinary action taken by state psychology boards reached similar results, determining that "few complaints are filed, many of those complaints are not investigated, informal actions . . . are few, and even fewer formal actions are taken against psychologists' licenses." Barbara A. Van Horne, *Psychology Licensing Board Disciplinary Actions: The Realities*, 35 Prof. Psychol.: Res. and Prac. 170, 175 (2004). However, another study of physicians disciplined by the California Medical Board found that psychiatrists were far more likely to be disciplined by the Board than other physicians. James Morrison & Theodore Morrison, *Psychiatrists Disciplined by a State Medical Board*, 158 Am. J. Psychiatry 474, 475 (2001). Inappropriate sexual contact was a common reason for Board action, and psychiatrists were also over-represented with regard to drug and alcohol problems, fraud, and theft. Id. at 476.

Another report determined that "a substantial fraction of sanctioned physicians are subsequently sanctioned again, at rates far higher than those of unsanctioned physicians." Darren Grant & Kelly C. Alfred, *Sanctions and Recidivism: An Evaluation of Physician Discipline by State Medical Boards*, 32 J. Health Pol., Pol'y & L. 867, 881 (2007). The authors contend that high recidivism does not mean that the boards' actions are generally ineffective, but rather are ineffective with regard to "low-quality physicians who are the least responsive to regulatory incentives." Id. at 882. Another commentator has argued that criticism focusing on the rate of disciplinary actions alone is misguided. She contends that licensing boards need to focus "less on character-related misconduct and more on misconduct that is arguably more likely to harm patients and the public—for example, gross incompetence, sexual assault of patients, and repeated violations of the standard of the care." Nadia N. Sawicki, *Character, Competence, and the Principles of Medical Discipline*, 13 J. Health Care L. & Pol'y 285, 321 (2010).

Do these findings suggest that disciplinary boards should adopt a different approach with regard to health care providers? In general, the goal of these Boards is to rehabilitate the provider involved. Should they instead devote more resources to identifying high-risk providers and then subjecting them to on-going monitoring or exclusion? Does the malpractice system, addressed in Chapter Three, provide a better way of responding to such providers? Or is this evidence that malpractice litigation is ineffective, too? What kind of empirical evidence might support your position?

4.   *Self-regulation by the professions.* In addition to state regulation, the national organizations of each of the major mental health professional groups have adopted standards of conduct that govern their members, with local chapters employing an internal regulatory system to monitor the behavior of their members. Further, these codes of ethics frequently

influence, at least indirectly, the development of standards applicable to the entire profession. For instance, while psychiatrists, as physicians, must adhere to the state-mandated ethical standards governing the practice of medicine in that jurisdiction, the American Psychiatric Association has also adopted *The Principles of Medical Ethics: With Annotations Especially Applicable to Psychiatry*, which it periodically revises. The annotations are intended to assist psychiatrists in dealing with the "special ethical problems in psychiatric practice that differ in coloring and degree from ethical problems in other branches of medical practice, even though the basic principles are the same." Am. Psychiatric Ass'n, The Principles of Medical Ethics with Annotations Especially Applicable to Psychiatry 1–2 (2013 ed.), available at http://www.psychiatry.org/practice/ethics/resources-standards. Similarly, ethical standards for psychologists and social workers are provided, respectively, by the American Psychological Association's *Ethical Principles of Psychologists and Code of Ethics* and the National Association of Social Workers' *Code of Ethics*.

As noted, the professional organizations also perform a policing function in that they may investigate allegations of a member's misconduct. An organization may censure a member or even withdraw membership upon a finding of misconduct. In addition to imposing disciplinary sanctions on individual members, these organizations have attempted to take more pervasive steps to solve profession-wide problems. For example, in the face of growing evidence of sexual exploitation of patients by therapists during the 1980s, the American Psychological Association, the American Psychiatric Association, and the National Association of Social Workers directly addressed the problem by declaring that sexual contact between therapists and their patients was unethical. Linda Jorgenson et al., *The Furor over Psychotherapist–Patient Sexual Contact: New Solutions to an Old Problem*, 32 Wm. & Mary L. Rev. 645, 647 (1991).

5. *Regulation of sexual misconduct.* Mental health professionals agree that sexual relations between a psychotherapist and a client are likely to harm the client. In the early 1990s, a national study of nearly 1000 patients who had been sexually involved with a therapist found that 90% of patients were harmed when sex with the therapist occurred during treatment, and 80% were harmed when the sex began after therapy had ended. About 11% of the patients needed hospitalization, 14% had attempted suicide, and 1% committed suicide. About 5% of the patients had been minors when sex with the therapist occurred. Of those harmed, only 17% fully recovered. Kenneth S. Pope & Valerie A. Vetter, *Prior Therapist–Patient Sexual Involvement Among Patients Seen by Psychologists*, 28 Psychotherapy 429 (1991). Discussing the kinds of problems that patients may experience, Hankins and colleagues explained:

> Harm to the patient may result directly from substandard care, the stress of the seduction process, and/or the psychic trauma associated with overt sexual contact. Psychic trauma may be present clinically as aggravation of underlying psychopathology, stress-related psychosomatic

disorders, posttraumatic stress disorder, suicide and homicide attempts, sexual dysfunction, disruption of support network, and vocational and educational impairment.

Gary C. Hankins et al., *Patient–Therapist Sexual Involvement: A Review of Clinical and Research Data*, 22 Bull. Am. Acad. Psychiatry L. 109, 120 (1994)

As noted above, professional recognition of the harms flowing from these sexual encounters finds expression in the ethical guidelines of the various national associations of mental health professionals, which proscribe this behavior. Nevertheless, various studies suggest that sexual misconduct by mental health professionals remains a problem. A 1986 report found that 7% of male and 3% of female psychiatrists reported having sexual contact with patients. Nanette Gartrell et al., *Psychiatrist–Patient Sexual Contact: Results of a National Survey, I: Prevalence*, 143 Am. J. Psychiatry 1126 (1986). A 2001 report of the California Medical Board found that psychiatrists accounted for 34% of all physicians disciplined for sexual relations or inappropriate contact with patients, despite making up only 13% of the disciplined physician population. James Morrison & Theodore Morrison, *Psychiatrists Disciplined by a State Medical Board*, 158 Am. J. Psychiatry 474, 475 (2001).

A variety of legal mechanisms are intended to discourage such sexual relations. Licensing agencies have typically adopted professional standards prohibiting this behavior and impose sanctions if these standards are violated. Approaches vary substantially. In addition to prohibiting sexual relationships with current clients, many states will revoke the licenses of psychologists if they have sex with a former client, with this ban ranging from one to five years after treatment has ended. S. Wesley Gorman, *Sex Outside of the Therapy Hour: Practical and Constitutional Limits on Therapist Sexual Misconduct Regulations*, 56 UCLA L. Rev. 983, 984 (2009). The effectiveness of this regulatory approach, however, depends on the extent to which state licensing agencies are willing to vigorously investigate complaints and impose meaningful sanctions. There are seemingly significant differences in their capacity or willingness to deal with this particular problem. Jorgenson et al., supra, at 727.

Therapists who engage in sexual relations with clients may also face criminal sanctions. Matt J. O'Laughlin, *Dr. Strangelove: Therapist–Client Dual Relationship Bans and Freedom of Association, or How I Learned to Stop Worrying and Love My Clients*, 69 UMKC L. Rev. 697, 700 (2001). See Cal. Bus. & Prof. Code §§ 2960(o), 2970 (West 2013), which make sexual relations between a psychologist and "a patient or former patient within two years following termination of therapy" a criminal offense punishable by imprisonment for up to six months and a fine not exceeding $2,000; see also Colo. Rev. Stat. Ann. § 18–3–405.5 (West 2013) (sexual assault of a client by a psychotherapist); Fla. Stat. Ann. § 491.0112(1) (West 2013) ("Any psychotherapist who commits sexual misconduct with a client, or former client when the professional relationship was terminated primarily for the purpose of engaging in sexual contact, commits a felony of the third degree.").

As discussed in Chapter Three, the tort system may also be used to sanction and deter sexual relations in the course of therapy by exposing the therapist to civil liability for resulting damages. Several states have enacted statutes that create a cause of action for clients if sexual relations occur during or after treatment. *O'Laughlin*, supra, at 700. See Cal. Civ. Code § 43.93 (West 2013); Minn. Stat. Ann. § 604.201 (2013); 740 Ill. Comp. Stat. Ch. Ann. § 140/2 (West 2013); Wis. Stat. Ann. § 895.441 (West 2013); Tex. Civ. Prac. & Rem. Code Ann. § 81.002 (West 2013).

As noted, sexual misconduct at one point accounted for 17% of the malpractice actions brought by clients. A number of obstacles, however, limit the effectiveness of the tort system as a deterrent of this behavior. For one thing, clients may fear the publicity and exposure of confidential matters that accompanies such a law suit as they must be prepared to disclose not only the details of the sexual relations but also the fact that they had been receiving mental health treatment. In addition, the costs of pursuing a law suit may be prohibitive, particularly in light of the uncertainty regarding whether they will prevail and significant monetary damages be awarded. The deterrent potential of the tort system may also be limited by the ability of therapists to obtain malpractice insurance, which tends to shield them from direct economic loss. However, some insurance programs have restricted coverage of sexual misconduct, thereby presumably enhancing the deterrent effect of the tort system. David M. Lang, *Sexual Malpractice and Professional Liability: Some Things They Don't Teach in Medical School—A Critical Examination of the Formative Case Law*, 6 Conn. Ins. L.J. 151, 159–60 (2000).

Having sexual relations with a trainee or a student may also constitute professional misconduct. See Am. Psychiatric Ass'n, The Principles of Medical Ethics: With Annotations Especially Applicable to Psychiatry 7 (2010 ed.) ("14. Sexual involvement between a faculty member or supervisor and a trainee or student, in those situations in which an abuse of power can occur, often takes advantage of inequalities in the working relationship and may be unethical because: a. Any treatment of a patient being supervised may be deleteriously affected. b. It may damage the trust relationship between teacher and student. c. Teachers are important professional role models for their trainees and affect their trainees' future professional behavior.").

6. *Administrative remediation versus the tort system.* What are the advantages, if any, of administratively conducted disciplinary hearings over other remedial actions such as private suits for malpractice or criminal prosecution? To what extent will the monetary costs and other burdens of litigation discourage an injured or aggrieved client from pursuing his or her private remedies? Are administrative disciplinary proceedings a good substitute? Does the client obtain relief in this system, even if the disciplinary proceeding results in a sanction against the practitioner? In general, the administrative approach is designed to sanction professionals who have engaged in professional misconduct rather than compensate injured patients.

However, note that one of the possible advantages of disciplinary proceedings is that clients and witnesses can frequently avoid the publicity that is typically associated with court proceedings that are open to the public. Under the laws of some states, a disciplinary hearing may be closed to the public and the press. Could this be a significant advantage to complainants? Are practitioners prejudiced by a closed hearing if they are represented by counsel? Further, in many states, administrative proceedings may benefit clients by the lesser burden of proof employed, less stringent rules of evidence, or longer statute of limitations than associated with a malpractice claim or criminal prosecution. Jorgenson et al., supra, at 718–23; Van Horne, supra, at 170–71.

7. *Right to counsel and other procedural safeguards.* State law typically allows professionals facing disciplinary proceedings before a regulatory agency to have legal representation. In contrast, the right to have the assistance of counsel may be discretionary where the disciplinary hearings are conducted through the self-regulation mechanism of a professional organization. However, the American Psychiatric Association, for example, has adopted *Procedures for Handling Complaints of Unethical Conduct*, which provides for notice of the complaint; confidentiality; a right to request a hearing; a right to legal representation; a right to have a record made of the proceedings; a right to call, examine, and cross-examine witnesses; and a right to receive a written decision and appeal any adverse decision to the Ethics Committee of the American Psychiatric Association. Am. Psychiatric Ass'n, The Principles of Medical Ethics: With Annotations Especially Applicable to Psychiatry 11–21 (2013 ed.). See also David S. Wahl, *Introduction: Role of the APA in Developing and Enforcing Psychiatric Ethics*, in Ethics Primer of the American Psychiatric Association ix, xi (2008) (these procedures are meant to ensure "full and fair hearings" in which "complainants and accused members are treated with dignity and respect").

8. *Violations under federal law.* A mental health professional's misconduct may also violate a federal law or regulation. In a somewhat unusual case, a psychiatrist was convicted of securities fraud and mail fraud after he used non-public information acquired from a patient to make a profitable purchase and sale of BankAmerica stock. The District Court found that he "fraudulently induced his patient to confide in him in connection with his purchase and sale of securities." *United States v. Willis*, 737 F. Supp. 269, 274 (S.D.N.Y. 1990). See also *SEC v Cooper, Litigation Rel. No. 14754*, 60 S.E.C. Docket 2430 (1995) (social worker was fined after making investments based on insider information, acquired during a therapy session, about the 1994 Lockheed–Martin Marietta merger).

Additionally, mental health professionals can face federal charges and sanctions for submitting false claims for services to federally-funded healthcare programs such as Medicaid and Medicare. See Brooks Baehr, *Indicted Hawaii Psychiatrist Arrested in Argentina*, Hawaii News Now, May 25, 2011 (indicting psychiatrist "for allegedly pocketing more than $500,000 in fraudulent insurance claims"); Michael Laforgia, *Jailed Juveniles' Doctors*

Draw Medicaid Inquiry, Palm Beach Post, May 25, 2011 (reporting an investigation of state-hired psychiatrists who prescribed high doses of anti-psychotics and billed Medicaid for these prescriptions while receiving speaker fees and gifts totaling more than $250,000 over two years from drug firms that made the drugs); *Mental Health Clinic Worker Pleads Guilty to Role in $171.5 Million Medicare Fraud*, White Collar Crime Rep., May 24, 2013 (discussing liability of counselor stemming from charges he billed for medically unnecessary partial hospitalization services). One study found psychiatrists to be the most over-represented physician specialty sanctioned for fraud and abuse against Medicare and Medicaid, although it was noted this might be because the most common type of fraud was inflating the amounts of time spent with patients, which is easier to detect than the types of fraud committed by other physician specialties. Henry Pontell, *A Demographic Portrait of Physicians Sanctioned by the Federal Government for Fraud and Abuse Against Medicare and Medicaid*, 23 Med. Care 1028, 1031 (1985). A more recent study suggests that psychiatrists continue to be overrepresented among physicians convicted of Medicare and Medicaid fraud. Vivek Pande & Will Maas, *Physician Medicare Fraud: Characteristics and Consequences*, 7 Intern. J. Pharmaceutical Healthcare Marketing 8 (2013). See also Kristin Madison, *Rethinking Fraud Regulation by Rethinking the Health Care System*, 32 Hamline J. Pub. L. & Pol'y 411 (2011).

9. *Ethical prohibitions on participation in executions and torture.* States that permit capital punishment now rely almost exclusively on lethal injection as the means of execution. However, an inmate cannot be executed if he is incompetent at the time of execution. Debate has arisen over whether mental health professionals' participation in these executions or in treatment to restore the competence of inmates so they may be executed violates their ethical code. The American Psychiatric Association has stated that a psychiatrist "should not be a participant in a legally authorized execution." Am. Psychiatric Ass'n, The Principles of Medical Ethics: With Annotations Especially Applicable to Psychiatrists 4 (2013). While the American Psychological Association's *Ethical Principles of Psychologists and Code of Conduct* does not contain a similar statement, the organization has issued a resolution calling for jurisdictions to halt capital punishment until a number of concerns can be resolved. Am. Psychological Ass'n, The Death Penalty in the United States (2001). These issues are discussed further in Chapter Nine, Part V.C.

There is also a debate over whether mental health professionals should assist intrusive efforts to extract information from individuals detained by the government for national security purposes. *The Principles of Medical Ethics* states that psychiatrists "shall not participate in torture." Principles of Medical Ethics, supra, at 9. See also Am. Psychological Ass'n, APA Ethics Committee Statement—No Defense to Torture (2009). Relatedly, see Kristina Fiore, *Breaching Medical Ethics to Catch bin Laden?*, MedPage Today, July 14, 2011, http://www.medpagetoday.com/Blogs/InOtherWords/27538.

10. *Is self-regulation too costly?* Some members of the American Psychiatric Association have argued that the financial support for ethics enforcement should be cut as a way to lower costs. Critics argue that the program is too expensive, enforcement is inconsistent, and psychiatrists are ill-suited to play the role of prosecutor. Supporters respond that the program is "important for the stature of APA as a self-regulating organization," and that its elimination would lead to greater medical board involvement. Lea Defrancisci Lis & Wade Myers, *Should APA Continue Involvement in Ethics Enforcement?*, 45 Psychiatric News 21 (2010).

11. *Drugs, alcohol, and the mental health of mental health providers.* Several studies have shown that psychiatrists have the highest rates of drug and alcohol misuse among physician specialties, and that they have higher rates of depression, burn-out, and suicide. See Jenny Firth–Cozens, *Improving the Health of Psychiatrists*, 13 Advances Psychiatric Treatment 161, 162–63 (2007); Patrick H. Hughes et al., *Resident Physician Substance Use, by Specialty*, 149 Am. J. Psychiatry 1348, 1350 (1992). What might explain these findings? Might psychiatrists just be more willing to talk about their issues than other physicians? Firth–Cozens, supra, at 163. Or is it a more emotionally draining discipline, compounded by threats of violence and typically having to work in isolation? Id. at 164. Many state licensing boards allow impaired physicians to enter drug and alcohol abuse rehabilitation programs; a physician who enters such a program and successfully completes it may be shielded from disciplinary action, while failure to timely enroll in or complete such a program can result in disciplinary action or criminal prosecution. Timothy J. Aspinwall, *Representing Healthcare Professionals in Disciplinary Actions: Containing the Collateral Damage*, 20 Health L. 1, 3 (2008). Does this approach adequately protect patient safety? Should this information be available to the public, to hospitals issuing privileges or managed care plans selecting approved providers, or in related legal proceedings? Should a prior history of such problems preclude licensure?

II. ALLOCATION OF RESPONSIBILITIES AMONG THE MENTAL HEALTH PROFESSIONS

Before the 1940s, the treatment of mental disorders was primarily the domain of psychiatrists and, perhaps to a lesser extent, "general practice" physicians. Only since then have psychologists, who previously had focused on academic research, provided mental health services to clients. Ultimately, clinical psychologists, along with clinical social workers, have become a dominant force in mental health treatment and counseling.

This changed allocation of functions stems from several factors, but particularly the changing economics of health care, coupled with structural changes in the way that health services are delivered. In the 1990s, the increasing influence of managed care systems heightened an already-present trend towards the utilization of less costly, non-medical professionals such as clinical psychologists and clinical social workers. Previously, however, legislation and court decisions had removed legal barriers that previously solidified the dominant position of the medical profession in the delivery of mental health services. The materials that follow examine the role of the legal system in reallocating functions among the professions. A concluding section will focus on a key emerging issue: legislative efforts by psychologists to gain authority to prescribe medications for the treatment of mental disorders.

A. INDEPENDENT BILLING AUTHORITY

VIRGINIA ACADEMY OF CLINICAL PSYCHOLOGISTS V. BLUE SHIELD OF VIRGINIA

United States Court of Appeals, Fourth Circuit, 1980.
624 F.2d 476.

K.K. HALL, CIRCUIT JUDGE:

This controversy arises over the refusal by defendants Blue Shield of Virginia and Blue Shield of Southwestern Virginia to pay for services rendered by clinical psychologists unless such services are billed through a physician. Plaintiffs Virginia Academy of Clinical Psychologists and Dr. Robert J. Resnick, a practicing clinical psychologist, claim that this policy violates Section 1 of the Sherman Act. 15 U.S.C. § 1. The district court found no violation.

We affirm in part and reverse in part.

Since 1962, Blue Shield of Virginia [BSV or the Richmond Plan] and Blue Shield of Southwestern Virginia [BSSV or the Roanoke Plan] have included outpatient coverage for mental and nervous disorders and for psychotherapy as a method of treating those disorders. Between 1962 and 1972, Richmond Plan coverage included direct payment to psychologists for psychotherapy rendered to subscribers. In 1972, this policy was revised to allow payment only when the services were billed through a physician.

The revised policy of the Richmond Plan was announced after consultation with various provider groups, including the American Psychological Association and the defendant Neuropsychiatric Society of Virginia [NSV]. Contact between the Richmond Plan and NSV, however, was particularly close.

Beginning in 1971, Dr. Levi Hulley, M.D., the head of the Plan's professional relations committee, met several times with NSV's president, Dr. Terrell Wingfield, M.D., over the question of payment for psychotherapy. Cooperation between the two groups followed: NSV, at the Plan's request, conducted a survey of Virginia psychiatrists on various aspects of psychiatric practice and later passed a resolution recommending, inter alia, that the Richmond Plan terminate direct payment to clinical psychologists. Immediately prior to adopting its policy, Richmond Plan officials met with a special NSV committee to discuss the scope of mental health coverage. The Plan adopted some of NSV's recommendations, including that of refusing to cover services rendered by psychologists unless billed by a physician.

* * *

[The court first reversed the district court's holding that the challenged activity was entitled to First Amendment protection. It then rejected the district court's alternative holding that the defendant's agreement was protected by the McCarran–Ferguson Act, which exempts from antitrust liability all state regulated "business of insurance." 15 U.S.C. § 1913(b) (1976).]

The final, critical issue is whether these combinations were "in restraint of trade." 15 U.S.C. § 1. The district court held that under the rule of reason, no violation was established. We disagree.

The district court began: "[t]he starting point in deciding the proper factual context for this case is deciding what sector of the economy is affected. . . . In other words, the court looks to see who is competing with whom." 469 F. Supp. at 560. The court found that clinical psychologists are not equal providers of therapy with psychiatrists because they do not render medical treatment and are not qualified to diagnose nervous and mental disorders or ascertain their source. The court further found that medical necessity in most, if not all cases requires regular contact between the psychologist's patient and a medical doctor.

The district court concluded that the clinical psychologist is not competitive with the psychiatrist unless the clinical psychologist is working under the "supervision" of a medical doctor. A psychologist working with a physician, the court continued, is paid by the Plans on an equal basis with a psychiatrist, except that the psychologist must bill through a physician.

> The court can well understand that plaintiffs do not like to bill through a physician as a matter of professional pride. The evidence shows that billing through a medical doctor is a requirement of the Blue Shield plan as a means of ascertaining that the treatment given and billed for was medically necessary. This procedure also tends to promote contact between the clinical psychologists and the physicians at all stages of treatment, and thus enhances the supervisory process.

469 F. Supp. at 561.

Appellants assert that the evidence establishes a boycott and therefore their exclusion from direct Blue Shield coverage is illegal *per se*.

We agree that the challenged policy closely resembles that alleged in *Ballard v. Blue Shield of Southern West Virginia*, 543 F.2d 1075 (4th Cir. 1976), which we found to be a boycott. Nor does the comparison necessarily fail because the concerted refusal to deal is conditional, rather than absolute.

The "boycott" characterization, however, avails us little in determining whether an agreement such as this is *per se* illegal. Because of the special considerations involved in the delivery of health services, we are not prepared to apply a *per se* rule of illegality to medical plans which refuse or condition payments to competing or potentially competing providers.

While we agree with the district court's rejection of a *per se* rule in this case, we think the court's analysis was misdirected. The rule of reason looks to the impact of the challenged practice upon competitive conditions. The district court's finding that "the clinical psychologist is not competitive with the psychiatrist in treating nervous and mental disorders unless the clinical psychologist is working under the supervision of a medical doctor" reflects a value judgment, rather than an evaluation of anticompetitive effects.

The record demonstrates that psychologists and psychiatrists do compete; indeed it is susceptible to judicial notice. Both provide psychotherapy, and are licensed to do so by State law. Competition in the health care market between psychologist and M.D. providers of psychotherapy is encouraged by the legislature, and its existence is well documented.

The Blue Shield Plans are a dominant source of health care coverage in Virginia. Their decisions as to who will be paid for psychotherapy necessarily dictate, to some extent, which practitioners will be chosen from among those competent under the law to provide such services.

Whether the "medical necessity" of referral and close contact between the therapist and a physician satisfies the rule of reason, as a cost control measure, is a matter not before us. The Plan's requirement that the psychologists' fee be billed through a physician, however, cannot stand.

The issue is more than one of professional pride. State law recognizes the psychologist as an independent economic entity as it does the physician. The Blue Shield policy forces the two independent economic entities to act as one, with the necessary result of diminished competition in the health care field. The subscriber who has a need for psychotherapy must choose a psychologist who will work as an employee of a physician; a psychologist who maintains his economic independence may well lose his patient. In either case, the psychologist ceases to be a competitor.

. . . [W]e are not inclined to condone anticompetitive conduct upon an incantation of "good medical practice." Moreover, we fail to see how the policy in question fulfills that goal. Any assertion that a physician must actually *supervise* the psychologist to assure the quality of the psychotherapy treatment administered is refuted by the policy itself. The Blue Shield policy provides for payment to psychologists for psychotherapy if billed through *any* physician—not just those who regularly treat mental and nervous disorders. It defies logic to assume that the average family practitioner can supervise a licensed psychologist in psychotherapy, and there is no basis in the record for such an assumption.

There are, of course, procompetitive reasons for requiring examination and consultation by a physician in order to assure that psychotherapy is not needlessly performed to treat a problem with physical etiology, but such safeguards must be accomplished in ways which do not sacrifice the economic independence of the psychologist.

The elimination of the bill-through provision does not preclude a variety of other cost control and quality control measures by Blue Shield. It does, however, expand consumer and provider alternatives. In addition, competition from licensed non-M.D. providers is likely to result in lower costs and the elimination of needless duplication of administrative costs created by the bill-through requirement.

Affirmed in Part, Vacated and Remanded in Part.

QUESTIONS AND COMMENTS

1. *Antitrust laws.* The *Blue Shield of Virginia* case illustrates the use of federal antitrust laws to prevent insurance companies from limiting coverage and reimbursement for psychotherapy to services rendered under the aegis of a licensed physician. However, because the rule applied in this case stems from these antitrust laws, a violation occurs only when the insurance carrier's policy is the product of an agreement by the carrier with another entity. Thus, the decision would not preclude an individual company from unilaterally adopting a policy limiting reimbursement for clinical services to when they were performed under the supervision of a physician (unless such limitations have independently been prohibited by state law; see Note 2, infra). A unilateral action "lacks the requisite agreement between two or more separate entities" needed for the Sherman Act to become applicable. See Jacqueline A. Rypma, *The Physician Cartel—Potential Hospital Federal Antitrust Liability in Class–Based Denial of Staff Privileges to Clinical Psychologists*, 39 Drake L. Rev. 509, 518 (1990). A single company is generally unable to "conspire" with itself, but an organization made up of competing independent entities could satisfy the joint action requirement. Id. In *Blue Shield of Virginia*, the court found that the Blue Shield Plans are actually "combinations of physicians, operating under the direction and control of their physician members." *Blue Shield of Virginia*, supra, at 479. As such, their actions could provide a "sufficient basis for the conspiratorial requirement under section 1 of the Sherman Act." Rypma, supra, at 519. In a

similar case, the Tenth Circuit found that a large health maintenance organization (HMO) was not acting anti-competitively by including ophthalmologists in its network of providers while excluding optometrists. The plaintiffs (optometrists and their professional groups) failed to prove the existence of a conspiracy between the defendant ophthalmologists (and their professional groups) and the HMO. *Abraham v. Intermountain Health Care Inc.*, 461 F.3d 1249, 1269 (10th Cir. 2006).

Why would a carrier impose such a limitation on access to mental health services? Concerns have been expressed that there are insufficient checks on the use of mental health services and related expenditures. What other steps might an insurance carrier take to ensure that mental health expenditures are limited to those that are appropriate? What steps might be taken to ensure that coverage is available when needed? See Chapter One, Part V.

2. *Any-willing-provider and freedom-of-choice laws.* A number of states have adopted what are known as any-willing-provider [AWP] and freedom-of-choice [FOC] laws.

> AWP laws require managed care plans to accept any qualified provider who is willing to accept the terms and conditions of a managed care plan. These laws do not require managed care plans to contract with all providers. However, they do require managed care plans to explicitly state evaluation criteria and ensure "due process" for providers wishing to contract with the plan.
>
> FOC laws permit an enrollee to obtain reimbursable health care services from any qualified provider even if the provider has not signed a contract with the managed care plan. These laws often compel managed care plans to pay the same amount to a nonnetwork provider chosen by an enrollee as they pay to a network provider. Yet this does not guarantee that an enrollee will incur the same out-of-pocket costs[, as copayments and deductibles may be higher for an out-of-network provider].

Fred J. Hellinger, *Any–Willing–Provider and Freedom-of-Choice Laws: An Economic Assessment*, 14 Health Aff. 297, 297 (1995). A 1985 report summarized the trend over the prior twenty years:

> 40 states now have "freedom of choice" laws that require insurance companies to reimburse psychologists for therapy if patients prefer them to psychiatrists. . . .
>
> Social workers are following in the psychologists' footsteps, but are meeting with more opposition, both from insurance companies and psychiatrists. Social work associations . . . have persuaded only 14 [states] to pass laws requiring insurers to reimburse social workers for psychotherapy.

Daniel Goleman, *Social Workers Vault Into a Leading Role in Psychotherapy*, N.Y. Times, Apr. 30, 1985, at 17, col. 5. These laws have been criticized for increasing healthcare costs, as managed care organizations (MCOs) lose the ability to establish a limited network of cheaper approved providers. William

J. Bahr, *Although Offering More Freedom to Choose, "Any Willing Provider" Legislation Is the Wrong Choice*, 45 U. Kan. L. Rev. 557, 570 (1997). The Supreme Court, however, has ruled that AWP laws are not preempted by the Employee Retirement Income Security Act of 1974 (ERISA), a federal law that preempts many state laws that attempt to govern health plans. *Kentucky Ass'n of Health Plans, Inc. v. Miller*, 538 U.S. 329, 342 (2003).

3.   *Damages*. Anti-trust cases in healthcare are often thrown out for plaintiff's failure to show compensable injury.

> To prevail on an antitrust claim, the plaintiff must establish an injury to competition. This typically requires the defendant to be large enough to possess some level of market power and the conduct in question to be substantial enough to have an adverse impact on the market. If these conditions are not satisfied, then the case can be dismissed at a relatively early stage of the proceedings. Our data suggest that this is happening in a large number of medical antitrust cases and that staff privileges and exclusive contracting cases are particularly vulnerable to this type of attack.

Peter J. Hammer & William M. Sage, *Antitrust, Health Care Quality, and the Courts*, 102 Colum. L. Rev. 545, 583 (2002).

4.   *Growth of managed care and the decreased power of providers*. As managed care has grown, so has the power of health plans to negotiate reduced reimbursement rates with health care providers. One study found that anti-trust cases involving insurance issues have decreased over time, possibly because "managed care has increased the power of insurers and allowed them to dictate terms to physicians rather than vice versa." Id. at 570.

5.   *Federal mental health parity legislation*. As discussed in Chapter One, Part V, federal law requires parity between mental and substance abuse services, on the one hand, and physical health services on the other in a number of situations, including self-funded group health plans covering more than fifty employees, plans which state parity laws previously could not reach under the provisions of [the] Employee Retirement Income Security Act of 1974 (ERISA). State provisions must conform to or expand upon the federal mandates.

B. AUTHORITY WITHIN A PSYCHIATRIC FACILITY

CALIFORNIA ASSOCIATION OF PSYCHOLOGY PROVIDERS V. RANK

Supreme Court of California, 1990.
51 Cal. 3d 1, 270 Cal. Rptr. 796, 793 P.2d 2.

BROUSSARD, JUSTICE.

The issue before us is whether a hospital may permit clinical psychologists to take primary responsibility for the diagnosis and treatment of their hospitalized patients. Prior to 1978, regulations of the Department of Health Services (hereafter Department) declared that a psychiatrist must take charge of the diagnosis and treatment of all patients admitted to psychiatric wards or hospitals. In 1978, however, the Legislature enacted Health and Safety Code section 1316.5, which after confirming that hospitals could admit psychologists to their staffs, provided that such psychologists may, subject to the rules of the hospital, "carry professional responsibilities consistent with the scope of their licensure and competence." In 1980 the Legislature added language declaring that if such a hospital offered services that both physicians and psychologists could perform, "such service may be performed by either, without discrimination."

When the Department in 1983 reissued its 1975 regulations prohibiting hospitals from permitting a psychologist to carry primary responsibility for the diagnosis and treatment of patients, plaintiffs sued for declaratory relief. The trial court granted their motion for summary judgment, declared the regulations invalid, and directed the Department to issue new regulations permitting psychologists to take primary responsibility for the diagnosis and treatment of hospitalized patients. After a complex procedural history, . . . the Court of Appeal reversed the trial court.

* * *

[The Court of Appeal] held that the Legislature intended clinical psychologists to have the right to diagnose and treat their hospitalized patients without supervision from a physician "only in those instances where a physician has initially ruled out a medical basis for the patient's mental disorder and determined that it is not subject to medical treatment, and where the patient's mental disorder does not subsequently become susceptible to medical treatment after admission to the *health* facility." The statutory prohibition against discrimination, it said, prohibits requiring supervision by a psychiatrist, but only "after a medical diagnosis and medical treatment have been ruled out. . . ." [We granted review, and now uphold the ruling of the trial court, which we believe conforms to the language and carries out the purpose of the 1978 and 1980 legislation.]

III. Diagnosis and treatment of hospitalized patients

The Department's 1983 regulations, by providing that a psychiatrist must be responsible for diagnosis and treatment of all mental patients, prohibited a hospital from permitting a clinical psychologist to take responsibility for diagnosis and treatment of his own patients. The Court of Appeal opinion went halfway, permitting the psychologist to exercise that responsibility only after a physician has ruled out a medical cause for the patient's condition or medical treatment of that condition. We explain that neither the Department's regulations nor the limitations in the Court of Appeal opinion conforms to the language of section 1316.5.

(a) The Scope of Review

*   *   *

"[W]hile the construction of a statute by officials charged with its administration . . . is entitled to great weight, nevertheless, '[w]hatever the force of administrative construction . . . final responsibility for the interpretation of the law rests with the courts.' Administrative regulations that alter or amend the statute or enlarge or impair its scope are void and courts not only may, but it is their obligation to strike down such regulations."

(b) The Plain Meaning of Section 1316.5.

[The majority opinion reached the following conclusions. First, it determined that the clear intent of § 1316.5 was to *equalize* the authority of psychiatrists and psychologists to diagnose and treat patients who had been *admitted into a hospital* on psychiatric grounds. The majority opinion relied primarily on an analysis of a related provision pertaining generally to the practice of psychology.

Second, the court found that § 2903 of the Business and Professions Code antedated enactment of § 1316.5 and authorized psychologists to diagnose and treat mental disorders *without* the involvement of any other professionals. While acknowledging that § 2903 pertained to the authority of psychologists in the outpatient context, the majority nevertheless found § 2903 to be relevant to the interpretation of the key phrase of § 1316.5 that gives equal authority to physicians, psychiatrists, and clinical psychologists as to those functions that each profession is "authorized by law to perform." Finally, concluding that it would be anomalous to construe § 1316.5 to give psychologists in hospital and institutions *less* authority than they would have in outpatient settings, the majority held that the legislature intended that "psychologists may [like psychiatrists] carry the responsibility of diagnosing and treating the psychological problems of patients in hospitals" without the involvement or supervision of another professional.]

We conclude that section 1316.5 means what the trial court said it meant: that a hospital may permit clinical psychologists or its staff to "provide psychological services within the legal scope of their licensure, without physician supervision and without discriminatory restrictions."

*   *   *

We perceive no statutory basis for [a] distinction between hospital practice and outpatient practice. . . .

Appellants contend that hospital practice is different because hospitalized patients generally have more serious disorders. It is up to the Legislature, however, to decide whether and how to distinguish between outpatient and hospital practice, and whether any restrictions on the psychologist's hospital practice should take the form of law, administrative regulation, or hospital rule. The Legislature here has chosen to leave the matter to the discretion of each hospital. By authorizing hospitals to permit psychologists to carry responsibilities consistent with their licensure, it has given hospitals discretion to allow psychologists to assume the same responsibilities vis-a-vis their hospitalized patients as in an outpatient setting. Under section 1316.5, hospitals may also adopt nondiscriminatory rules that may restrict the psychologist's scope of practice. Section 1316.5 does not permit the courts, or the Department, to enact such restrictions themselves.

Moreover, the first condition laid down by the Court of Appeal opinion—that before a psychologist may take responsibility for a hospitalized patient it must be determined the patient's disorder has no "medical basis"—appears to mistake the distinction between psychology and medicine. That distinction turns on the nature of the treatment each can provide, not the origin of the condition treated. Medical methods, especially medication, are commonly used to treat mental conditions of no known organic origin. Conversely, psychological methods, including testing, counseling, and psychotherapy, are commonly used to treat organic disorders. Psychological tests, for example, are frequently used to diagnose the existence and extent of brain damage resulting from physical injury or disease and, depending on the nature of the damage, psychological methods may be the best or only way to treat the condition.

There is no bright line distinguishing conditions of physical from those of psychological origin. The ultimate cause of a patient's condition may be uncertain or unknown, and in some cases it may be unnecessary to determine that cause to treat him. Indeed, depending on one's view of theories concerning the possible genetic or chemical origin of various disorders, it may be impossible for a physician ever to "rule out" the possibility of an organic basis of the patient's condition. Thus, the authority of the psychologist cannot hinge upon a requirement that the patient's condition derive from a nonorganic cause.

* * *

IV. Conclusion

* * *

We conclude that under California law a hospital that admits clinical psychologists to its staff may permit such psychologists to take primary responsibility for the admission, diagnosis, treatment, and discharge of their patients. The 1983 Department regulations requiring a psychiatrist to supervise diagnosis and treatment of all admitted mental patients are therefore invalid. The judgment of the Court of Appeal is reversed, and the case is remanded for further proceedings consistent with this opinion.

MOSK and EAGLESON, JJ., STEVEN J. STONE, J. PRO TEM, concurring.

KENNARD, JUSTICE, dissenting.

In granting plaintiff psychologists primary responsibility for the admission, diagnosis, treatment and discharge of hospitalized patients, the majority grants by litigation what could not be achieved by legislation. In doing so, the majority fails to adhere to established standards of judicial review; disregards an eminently reasonable interpretation of the governing statute by the agency charged with its enforcement; and, through a strained interpretation of legislative history, converts legislative rejection into implied legislative acceptance.

* * *

The standard governing our review of the Department's regulations in this case is unambiguous. The regulations are not alleged to be arbitrary, capricious or wholly lacking in evidentiary support; the only question before this court is whether the regulations "transgress statutory power." . . .

The majority invokes this legal standard but ignores its application. The majority accords no deference whatsoever to the Department's interpretation of the statutes it is charged with implementing and enforcing. Disregarding the Department's reasonable interpretation of the law, the majority substitutes its judgment for that of the rule making agency—in violation of Government Code section 11340.1

* * *

B.   Statutory Analysis

* * *

The statute contains no express language granting clinical psychologists primary responsibility for hospitalized patients. The majority, however, insists that such a grant is implied in the statute's references to (1) the performance of services by clinical psychologists within "the scope of their licensure" and "without discrimination," and (2) their eligibility for membership on a hospital's medical staff. I disagree.

1.   Scope of Licensure

* * *

Patients do not necessarily enter hospitals with psychological conditions neatly divorced from biological, neurological, physiological or genetic disorders. The nature of an illness cannot be ascertained prior to diagnosis by a legally authorized professional. Physicians are legally qualified to provide comprehensive diagnosis and treatment; psychologists are not.

Unlike psychologists, physicians possess the legal authority to consider all possible causes of an illness. The State Medical Practice Act, which governs physicians, defines diagnosis as including "any undertaking by any method, device, or procedure whatsoever . . . to ascertain or establish whether a person is suffering from any physical or mental disorder. In contrast, the diagnostic authority granted psychologists is severely limited. The scope of their licensure limits psychologists to the diagnosis of *psychological* problems." Unlike physicians, psychologists are not allowed to "use any method, device, or procedure" or determine whether a person is suffering from "any physical or mental disorder." Psychologists are limited to the application of psychological principles to psychological disorders. Thus, they may not diagnose an illness caused or complicated by nonpsychological factors.

Unlike psychologists, physicians are authorized to use "any and all . . . methods," including drugs and devices, in the treatment of physical and mental conditions. Psychologists, on the other hand, are statutorily prohibited from prescribing drugs, performing surgery, or administering electro-convulsive therapy. Nor may they use biofeedback instruments that pierce or cut the skin; the law restricts them to the use of psychological principles. Thus, psychologists may not provide treatment that would require more than the application of psychological principles.

*   *   *

As demonstrated above, the authority of a physician to diagnose and treat is different and much broader than that granted psychologists. Because the concept of primary responsibility includes the ability to evaluate a hospitalized patient's *overall* condition and to select the most appropriate methods of treatment, the Legislature's grant of limited authority to psychologists cannot be equated with *primary* responsibility. Nothing in the statutory scheme suggests otherwise.

*   *   *

2.   Prohibition Against Discrimination

Section 1316.5 prohibits discrimination between physicians and clinical psychologists with respect to the health services *both* are authorized to perform. As shown above, the health services psychologists are authorized to provide and the health services physicians are authorized to provide are not coextensive.

The antidiscrimination clause does not address the issue of who has primary responsibility for a patient. It simply requires that when psychologists and physicians are *both authorized* to provide the health service, one may not be preferred over the other. Thus, if *psychological* services are required as part of the treatment of a patient, a physician may not be selected to perform the services over a psychologist. The clause neither says nor implies that psychologists are to be given overall primary responsibility for the admission, diagnosis, treatment, and discharge of hospitalized patients. . . .

C.   Legislative History

[A review of the legislative-history of section 1316.5 indicates that the] Legislature specifically considered and *rejected* giving clinical psychologists the very expansion of authority that the majority grants them. . . .

Conclusion

Section 1316.5 does not expressly give clinical psychologists authority to assume primary responsibility for hospitalized patients. The statute is, at best, ambiguous and its legislative history strongly suggests that the Legislature had no intention to confer such authority. The regulations the Department enacted were within the scope of its statutory authority and consistent with the language and legislative history of section 1316.5. In disregarding the reasonable interpretation of the administrative agency charged with responsibility for enforcing the statute, and possessed of the expertise necessary to assess the practical impact of alternative interpretations, the majority has succumbed to the temptation to substitute its judgment for that of the Legislature and the Department.

LUCAS, C.J., and PANNELLI, J., concur.

QUESTIONS AND COMMENTS

1.   *The role of legislatures and courts in regulating therapy.* Was California Health and Safety Code section 1316.5 unambiguous? Is the dissent correct that it was inherently ambiguous as to whether the legislature intended to give psychologists equal responsibility for intake diagnoses? If the dissent is correct, is it possible that the proponents of the legislation, which broadened the rights of psychologists, intentionally supported a bill that was ambiguous as to its scope? That might be the case if the proponents of the legislation felt that clarity in the bill (particularly a clear expansion making the rights of psychologists co-existent with those of psychiatrists) would prevent its adoption, with the proponents of the legislation having foreseen the courts as a more favorable battle ground. In light of the issues posed below, are courts really the appropriate forum for resolving these issues?

2.   *Primary responsibility for treatment.* The majority opinion characterizes the Court of Appeal's decision as having conferred "primary responsibility for treatment" on psychiatrists. The dissent claims that the Court of Appeal's decision did not allocate primary responsibility for *treatment* to psychiatrists, but rather only *initial diagnostic* responsibility. Is it, in fact, possible to bifurcate diagnoses from subsequent treatment, with psychiatrists having primary diagnostic responsibility but co-equal treatment responsibility? Or are the two so intertwined that they are virtually inseparable? As noted in Chapter One, diagnoses of mental illness are often

imprecise and must be modified over time and during the course of treatment.

3. *Implications of a decision on choice of treatment modality.* Is the majority's decision to strike down the Department of Health Services regulation likely to affect the kind of treatment that psychiatric patients will receive? As will be discussed later in this chapter, consider that generally psychologists are not authorized by law to prescribe psychotropic medications. Because the court's ruling will permit psychologists to have primary treatment responsibility, including formulating diagnoses and charting treatment plans, is this likely to have an impact on the choice of treatment selected? If a psychologist is the attending or admitting clinician, is the patient more likely to be offered psychotherapy than more medically-oriented therapies, such as psychotropic medication? Conversely, would the allocation of primary responsibility exclusively to psychiatrists result in far greater use of psychotropic medication? What implications do these allocations of responsibility have for the patients involved? See Jacqueline A. Rypma, *The Physician Cartel—Potential Hospital Federal Antitrust Liability in Class–Based Denial of Staff Privileges to Clinical Psychologists*, 39 Drake L. Rev. 509, 535–36 (1990) ("The intense physician resistance to full medical staff privileges for clinical psychologists as a group cannot be globally justified on the basis of quality of care. . . . The denial of [staff] privileges to [psychologists] . . . has the anticompetitive effect of maintaining higher consumer prices, because physicians generally charge more. . . . ").

4. *Non-extension of special privileges of psychiatrists to psychologists.* While the court in *Rank* concluded that California law indicates a legislative intent to equalize the status of psychiatrists and psychologists with respect to providing services in psychiatric facilities, courts in other contexts have been unwilling to imply a similar legislative intent. For instance, another California court refused to interpret a California law granting immunity to institutional psychiatrists who erroneously order the release of a dangerous patient as also covering institutional psychologists. See *Ford v. Norton*, 107 Cal. Rptr. 2d 776 (Cal. Ct. App. 2001). Is there a justification for this distinction other than a different interpretation of statutory language? In 2003, the law was amended to also grant psychologists immunity for these releases. See Cal. Welf. & Inst. Code § 5154 (West 2013).

5. *Restrictive practices in education.* Challenges to the dominance of the medically trained therapist have also been pressed in the field of education. For instance, psychoanalytic institutes, which are the primary training base for psychoanalysts, had traditionally excluded non-medically trained applicants. In 1985, a group of mental health professionals who were not physicians brought suit against the American Psychoanalytic Association, challenging their exclusion from affiliated training institutes on antitrust grounds. While denying the motions by both plaintiffs and defendants for summary judgment, the court rejected the argument that defendant's actions were protected by the First Amendment. *Welch v. Am. Psychoanalytic Ass'n*, No. 85 Civ. 1651, 1986 WL 4537 (S.D.N.Y. Apr. 4, 1986). The case was

subsequently settled under an agreement reached by the parties in which the American Psychoanalytic Association agreed to admit non-physicians into its training institutes. As noted in the commentary which follows, the result in *Welch* was applauded not only by psychologists but also by other non-medical mental health professionals.

> To the Editor:
>
> Millions of Americans have undergone, or will undergo, psychoanalysis. All of us, therefore, should applaud the legal settlement of a lawsuit brought by four psychologists against the American Psychoanalytic Association and the International Psychoanalytical Association to get them to open the doors of their major training institutes to therapists who do not hold medical degrees (Health pages, Oct. 20).
>
> Before this case, the American Psychoanalytic Association and the International Psychoanalytical Association restricted admission to their training institutes to psychiatrists, barring clinical social workers, psychologists and other mental-health professionals who are not psychiatrists. This policy disregarded the basic reality that nonmedical therapists now perform most of this country's therapy.
>
> That this is so was documented in a May 1, 1985 article, according to which the number of social workers offering psychotherapy in the United States more than doubled between 1975 and 1985, rising from 25,000 to 60,000. During the same period, the number of clinical psychologists doubled from 15,000 to slightly more than 30,000. In comparison, the total number of psychiatrists increased by only one-third, from 26,000 to 38,000.
>
> In addition, as your report on the successful suit noted, competent provision of psychotherapy and psychoanalysis does not require medical training. In the event that a client needs drug therapy or other medical care, he or she can be referred to a psychiatrist or other physician for treatment.
>
> That clinical social workers and psychologists can now attend American Psychoanalytic and International Psychoanalytical Association institutes is not a crucial victory. They have long studied side by side with psychiatrists in the many psychoanalytical institutes that are not affiliated with those organizations. It is, however, a gain for simple fairness. The majority of this country's therapists will no longer be subject to arbitrary restrictions on their training.

ROBERT J. EVANS

[President, New York State Society of Clinical Social Work Psychotherapists]

Robert J. Evans, *Opening of Therapy Institute Is Only Fair*, N.Y. Times, Nov. 12, 1988, at 26.

6. *Perspectives on the allocation of responsibility among the professions.* As noted, a significant reallocation of functions among the

primary mental health professions has occurred. The perspectives of the respective professions to these changes are captured by the two commentaries set out below:

To the Editor:

The growth of lay psychotherapy in the United States (*Social Workers Vault Into a Leading Role in Psychotherapy* by Daniel Goleman, Science Times, April 30) threatens to denude the country of its only wholly qualified line of defense against mental and emotional illness: the physician trained both in biological and psychodynamic psychiatry. Behind this growth are historical, economic and social reasons.

For decades, social workers, psychologists, nurses and others were brought into the herculean task of dealing with mental illness in hospitals and outpatient clinics. All originally had other tasks, but were permitted, under supervision, to assume some treatment with certain patients. They were essentially "barefoot doctors" in this struggle.

The development of Medicaid and Medicare furthered the process. It became very profitable for hospitals and clinics to use salaried nonmedical personnel to treat patients, since the hourly rates for reimbursement were identical whether treatment was by physician-psychiatrists or others.

Many of these barefoot doctors jumped to the erroneous conclusion that they were fully competent to do what they had been encouraged to do in an emergency, and now present themselves as independent practitioners capable of treating all patients for all conditions. They left salaried positions, where there was at least a semblance of medical and psychiatric supervision, for the marketplace.

They are often either unaware, or will deny, that they lack the essential medical and psychiatric training that is the only basis for diagnosis and treatment. The result is malpractice.

Depression, for instance, is not diagnosed or is misdiagnosed, and the wrong kind of treatment is then prescribed; a patient is given psychotherapy for a type of phobia that responds well to other treatment; physical symptoms are misinterpreted as "psychosomatic." Since patients rarely complain or sue, this has not caught the public attention.

A preliminary physical examination by a physician; getting a psychiatrist or general physician who will agree to "cover" by prescribing antianxiety or antidepressant medication; "supervision" of cases by a psychiatrist—none of these suffice to prevent serious errors of diagnosis and treatment by a lay therapist in independent private practice. Every patient is, in effect, unwittingly playing Russian roulette. And fees by all who entered the market have risen quickly to a common level.

Psychiatrists are not blameless. Heads of department are reluctant to antagonize professional blocs within their administrations. . . . Absence of criticism has emboldened lay therapists.

The extent to which they are emboldened is indicated by lawsuits entered or pending against the American Psychoanalytic Association and the American Academy of Psychoanalysis, major educational bodies that train physician-psychiatrists. The suits seek to force these organizations to train nonphysicians. The suits will not be won because these organizations have the right to set the standards they consider proper for the public health, but the suits will affect public opinion and serve to harass those organizations.

Will the barefoot doctors drive out the doctors? Will treatment of mental and emotional illness sink to the lowest common denominator? Since anyone can claim competence, is it likely, by a Gresham's Law, that there will be no truly competent medical specialists to treat mental or emotional illness? The implication for the public health is not good.

SEYMOUR C. POST, M.D.

ASSOC. CLINICAL PROFESSOR OF PSYCHIATRY

COLLEGE OF PHYSICIANS AND SURGEONS OF COLUMBIA UNIVERSITY

NEW YORK, MAY 15, 1985

Seymour C. Post, *And Now the Age of the Barefoot Psychotherapist*, N.Y. Times, May 19, 1985, at 20, col. 3.

The following was provided in response to Dr. Post's letter-to-the-editor:

To the Editor:

Dr. Seymour C. Post's letter ("And Now the Age of the Barefoot Psychotherapist," May 19), in response to Daniel Goleman's article on the growing psychotherapeutic role of social workers (Science Times, April 30) was, sadly, further evidence of the elitist attitude American psychiatry has toward the treatment of mental illness. One need only look at the shrinking therapy dollar in terms of third-party unwillingness to underwrite lengthy treatment to understand American Psychiatric Association rationalizations for its "closed-shop" attitude.

Dr. Post's choice of the "barefoot doctor" metaphor is interesting in light of differences in medical versus graduate training within psychology. While most medical schools offer a four-to six-week course in behavioral science in addition to several weeks' rotation through a psychiatric unit, graduate programs in clinical and service-oriented psychology provide four years of academic and specialized training in psychopathology and its treatment in addition to a year's internship, usually in a hospital or an outpatient setting.

While a newly graduated physician entering a psychiatric residency knows little about psychopathology, a newly graduated psychologist already possesses specialized graduate training. It is common practice in many medical centers for psychologists to participate in the training of psychiatry residents.

Dr. Post does, however, have a valid point in emphasizing that a medical background is necessary in dealing with specific psychiatric disorders. Most psychologists would agree that there are subgroups of psychiatric disorders that require medication. Despite this, there are psychological disorders that do not require medication and that respond favorably to drug-free psychotherapy. Since most hospital-based staff psychiatrists rarely carry regular therapy cases within the hospital, a task usually relegated to psychologists, it is difficult not to wonder who the most experienced and specialized individual is.

Let us propose a truce, with medication issues and medically oriented diagnoses within the purview of psychiatry and behavioral psychodiagnostics and psychotherapy as the domain of psychologists and others licensed to practice. "The implication for the public health," of which Dr. Post speaks, is certainly "not good," given the unfortunate animosity these fields have toward one another, and taking potshots at each other is not conducive to the cooperation necessary to provide quality mental-health care.

PAUL MICHAEL RAMIREZ

CLINICAL NEUROPSYCHOLOGIST

BRONX PSYCHIATRIC CENTER

BRONX, MAY 21, 1985

Paul Michael Ramirez, *Psychotherapy Should Not Be a Closed Shop*, N.Y. Times, May 29, 1985, at 20, col. 3.

C. PRESCRIPTION PRIVILEGES

1. Overview

As noted in Chapter One, advances in neuroscience coupled with the development of a range of psychotropic medications that can be used to treat a variety of mental disorders have fundamentally transformed the nature of mental health services. Treatment increasingly involves psychopharmacology, either by itself, or in conjunction with psychotherapy.

While federal law regulates the distribution and dispensing of pharmaceuticals, state legislatures assign prescription privileges to designated classes of professionals. The legal authority to write prescriptions has, with limited exceptions, been the exclusive province of those holding a medical license. Thus, the use of psychopharmacology to treat mental disorders has generally been restricted to medical practitioners (i.e., physicians and advanced practice nurses). Because legal authority to prescribe has largely been confined to the medical profession, psychologists and other mental health professionals may not legally prescribe psychopharmacologic agents and are largely limited to using psychotherapy to treat their clients.

The economic implications for clinical psychologists, which are likely to continue with future advances in psychopharmacology, led the American Psychological Association to adopt a resolution in 1995 making "the pursuit of prescription privileges an official objective of the organization." William N. Robiner et al., *Prescription Authority for Psychologists: A Looming Health Hazard?*, 9 Clinical Psychol.: Sci. & Prac. 231, 232 (2002). As a result, the American Psychological Association and its local affiliates have pressed for changes in state laws to extend to psychologists who have undergone additional training in psychopharmacology the authority to write prescriptions for psychotropic medications.

Four arguments have been advanced to support efforts to obtain prescription privileges for psychologists. First, costs limit access to mental health care, and this problem would be mitigated if psychologists, whose hourly rates are generally less than psychiatrists, were allowed to prescribe. Second, the scarcity of psychiatrists to serve some rural areas and populations such as active duty military and veterans and prison inmates means that the mental health treatment needs of these communities are not being met. Extending prescription privileges to psychologists would, it is argued, address this shortfall. See Robert K. Ax et al., *Prescriptive Authority for Psychologists and the Public Sector: Serving Underserved Health Care Consumers*, 5 Psychol. Services 184 (2008).

Third, the bulk of psychotropic medications are not prescribed by psychiatrists, but rather by "internists and family practitioners . . . who [do] not possess significant training in the mental health field." Patrick H. DeLeon & Jack G. Wiggins, Jr., *Prescription Privileges for Psychologists*, 51 Am. Psychologist 225, 228 (1996). Finally, advocates point to the fact that other non-physician health care professionals currently have full or partial prescription privileges. For instance, dentists, podiatrists, nurse practitioners, and physicians' assistants have partial or complete prescription privileges in all fifty states. See Ronald E. Fox et al., *Prescriptive Authority and Psychology: A Status Report*, 64 Amer. Psychologist 257 (2009); see also Patrick H. DeLeon et al., *Prescription Privileges: Psychology's Next Frontier?*, 46 Amer. Psychologist 384, 387 (1991).

Organizations that represent physicians, including the American Psychiatric Association and the American Medical Association, vigorously oppose extending prescription privileges to psychologists. They dispute the purported shortage of mental health care in rural areas, responding that primary care physicians, and not psychiatrists, are responsible for at least 50% of all psychotropic prescriptions written throughout the country, and they are available in these areas. Robiner et al., supra, at 241. With regard to the prescription privileges already held by non-physician health care professionals, they contend that the "training models [of these non-physician health care professionals] are much closer to that of physicians than to that of psychologists, and their clinical practice is more focused on physical functioning, including medication effects." Id. at 235. Relatedly, they assert that understanding the risks and possible complications associated with the use of prescription drugs require education and training that psychologists do not generally receive. Specifically, they argue that while these medications have potential significant benefits, they also pose substantial risks of side effects and adverse interactions with other medications, and that someone prescribing them must be able to balance their potential beneficial impact against their possible risks, a balancing that requires a thorough knowledge of their biological effects. Phyllis Coleman & Ronald A. Shellow, *Prescribing Privileges for Psychologists: Should Only "Medicine Men" Control the Medicine Cabinet?*, Fall–Winter 1990 J. Psychiatry & L. 269, 276 (1990). The exercise by psychologists of independent prescription privilege will, it is claimed, "undermine patient care and contribute to medication errors." Robiner et al., supra, at 243.

2. Legislative Initiatives and Developments

The model state legislation for prescription privileges endorsed by the American Psychological Association would grant privileges to psychologists who meet specific requirements, including the holding of a doctorate level psychology degree, completion of a specialized psychopharmacology training program, and passage of a certifying exam. These requirements would be in addition to those needed to qualify for a license to practice psychology.

Since 1995, bills patterned on the American Psychological Association's model legislation have been introduced in a number of states, but have generally not been enacted. New Mexico became the first state in 2002 to enact legislation enabling psychologists who meet specified requirements to qualify for a prescription license. N.M. Stat. § 61–9–17 (2013). In 2004, Louisiana added the category of "medical psychologists," who upon meeting various qualifications are permitted to prescribe pharmaceutical medications for the treatment of mental or emotional disorders. La. Rev. Stat. Ann. § 37:1360.61 (2013).

The New Mexico legislation establishes a three-stage procedure whereby psychologists who fulfill various conditions may be licensed to prescribe psychotropic medications. An initial stage leading to a *conditional* license requires an applicant to satisfy various steps, including (1) completion of a doctorate program in psychology from an accredited institution of higher learning; (2) the holding of a license to practice as a psychologist in New Mexico; (3) successful completion of 450 classroom hours from an approved "organized program of education" pertaining to psychopharmacology; (4) completion of an approved eighty-hour supervised practicum in clinical assessment and pathophysiology; (5) completion of at least 400 hours treating no fewer than 100 patients with mental disorders under the supervision of a psychiatrist or other appropriately trained physician; and (6) passage of an approved national certification examination that tests the applicant's knowledge of pharmacology in the diagnosis, care, and treatment of mental disorders.

Upon satisfactorily completing these requirements, an applicant is eligible to apply for a phase two conditional prescription certificate. Those holding this certificate, which is valid for two years, may prescribe psychotropic medication "under the supervision of a licensed physician." At the end of the two-year supervised prescription period, an applicant may apply for a phase three certificate. This certificate will be issued if the applicant provides evidence that he or she (1) has successfully completed a two-year period of prescribing psychotropic medication as certified by a supervising licensed physician; (2) has successfully completed a process of independent peer review; (3) holds a valid psychologist license; and (4) has adequate malpractice insurance coverage. The issuance of this certificate permits psychologists to prescribe psychotropic medications, provided they annually satisfy established continuing education requirements for prescribing psychologists, which must be no fewer than twenty hours per year.

The Louisiana legislation is somewhat more restrictive than New Mexico's. Persons licensed as medical psychologists may only prescribe in consultation and collaboration with the patient's primary or attending physician. Also, medical psychologists must re-consult with the patient's physician prior to making a change in the patient's medication regime.

3. Educational Requirements for Competency to Prescribe

A key issue in the debate over prescription privileges for psychologists is the education and training needed to properly exercise prescription authority. Such prerequisites are designed to instill basic knowledge about underlying diagnostic complexities, the benefits and risks of these medications, including their interactions with other treatments, and the potential for error.

a. Risk Factors Associated with the Prescription Function

As detailed in Chapter One, various classes of psychotropic drugs pose serious risks of side effects that in some instances can be life threatening. For instance, some can lead to or exacerbate kidney disease or result in permanent neurological damage. Antidepressants can cause cardiac arrhythmias. Moreover, "[a]lthough newer psychoactive medications, such as the SSRIs, have more favorable side effect profiles than previous generations of medications, they are still powerful drugs that can yield serious adverse effects and drug interactions." Robiner et al., supra, at 242. These possibilities can require close monitoring and continuous evaluation of a recipient's blood chemistry or anatomical functions, including, in particular, neurological responses.

A further complication is the potential for adverse effects due to drug interactions. Psychotropic drugs interact not only with each other but with drugs prescribed for other medical conditions. In fact, "[p]sychoactive medications have been described as presenting more complex drug interactions and adverse effects than any other class of drug." Id. Indeed, many individuals who take these medications also take other medications. For example, more than 70% of those prescribed an antidepressant also take another drug, with a third taking at least three other drugs. Id. Practitioners often overlook harmful interactions between drugs, which are "responsible for considerable patient morbidity and mortality." Neil B. Sandson et al., *An Overview of Psychotropic Drug–Drug Interactions*, 46 Psychosomatics 464, 464 (2005).

The complexities associated with the prescription of psychotropic medications are compounded by the continuing expansion of medication options. For instance, in 2012 the Food and Drug Administration approved 39 "New Molecular Entities," drugs that include an active ingredient that has not previously been approved for marketing in the United States. U.S. Food & Drug Admin., New Molecular Entity Approvals for 2012 (Jan. 28, 2013). From 2001–2010, the FDA issued 229 such approvals. U.S. Food & Drug Admin., New Molecular Entity Approvals for 2010 (Feb. 17, 2011). The increasing number of drugs on the market increases the need for those prescribing mediations to have a working knowledge of the full pharmaceutical spectrum and a sufficient science background to manage potential drug interactions. Robiner et al., supra, at 242.

b. Educational Requirements

As might be expected, very different views are held regarding the educational background needed to prescribe these medications in an effective and safe manner. The model legislation endorsed by the American Psychological Association would require, in addition to a doctorate degree in psychology, a post-doctorate training program of psychopharmacology-related instruction with a minimum of 300 contact hours of didactic instruction taken either full or part-time, although the subject matter to be covered is not further specified. Additionally, supervised practice involving at least 100 patients would be required, although the amount of time that must be devoted to it is not delineated.

As described earlier, the New Mexico educational requirements exceed those proposed by the American Psychological Association. New Mexico mandates 450 rather than 300 hours of psychopharmacology-related instruction, as well as an additional 80–hour supervised practicum in clinical assessment and psychophysiology. While also requiring the supervised treatment of 100 patients, New Mexico further establishes that a minimum of 400 hours be devoted to this treatment. New Mexico additionally imposes a subsequent two-year period during which the psychologist must be supervised by a licensed physician.

Professional organizations representing physicians have not articulated what might—in lieu of a medical education—qualify psychologists to exercise a prescription function short of becoming advanced practice nurses in addition to psychologists. However, physicians' organizations reject the model backed by the American Psychological Association as inadequate for achieving competence to prescribe medications. Moreover, the underlying differences seem fundamental and unlikely to be bridged by nuanced changes in the basic requirements.

Essentially, opponents take the view that the overall educational experience of doctoral graduates in psychology, particularly its lack of focus on the biological sciences and related course work, does not provide an adequate basis for prescribing medications safely. It is asserted:

> The training of physicians and other doctoral providers (e.g., dentists) entails coursework in anatomy, biochemistry, cell biology, immunology, microbiology, pathology, pharmacology, physiology, as well as laboratory experiences in the biological and physical sciences and physical, clinical training. . . . [By comparison, doctoral-level p]rograms vary in how much training is provided in the biological and physical sciences, but it is generally quite limited. . . . [Further, i]f anything, the training of psychologists is moving away from the 'scientist-practitioner' model to other models that de-emphasize scientific background and activities.

Robiner et al., supra, at 237.

The American Psychological Association model, as well as that adopted by New Mexico, assumes that any deficiencies in basic science and biology of psychologists can be rectified by *post-doctoral* education and training. Clearly, a key dividing issue is the adequacy of this education and training. From the standpoint of the medical profession, these deficiencies cannot be remedied with a relatively concentrated post-doctoral educational experience. For example, the number of contact hours of classroom instruction required of psychologists is viewed as an inadequate substitute for the instruction in clinical and biological subjects received in medical school. John W. Bush, *Commentary, Prescription Privileges: Comments on Robiner et al.*, 9 Clinical Psychol.: Sci. & Prac.

443, 445 (2002). Similarly, the supervised clinical training is deemed a poor alternative to medical students' devoting two years of medical school to biologically focused classroom studies, and two years of medical school and a one-year internship following medical school of supervised clinical work with patients. However, these training years include experiences other than prescribing medications, and thus the basic medical school paradigm may not provide an appropriate gauge of the efforts needed to gain competency in prescribing medications.

As suggested by the following section, resolution of the educational requirements issue is unlikely to be decided by legislatures based solely on what is the *optimal* level needed for mental health treatment. While public health considerations are likely to be a primary consideration, other factors—including financial ones—will undoubtedly influence the outcome.

4. Economic Dimension of the Debate

Legislatures faced with having to decide whether to authorize prescription privileges for psychologists will have to weigh the *economic* implications, as well as health and safety issues. For example, assume a legislative finding that the extension of the privilege to psychologists will lead to a 30% increase in errors (i.e., prescriptions that are either contra-indicated because of the client's condition or because they will interact adversely with other medications the client is taking) compared to that of either primary care physicians or psychiatrists. At the same time, assume the current billing rates for psychiatrists average $200 per session, compared to $100 per session for prescribing psychologists. Under this scenario, although more errors would occur, extending prescription privileges to psychologists might make services available to individuals who might otherwise be unable to afford them. Alternatively, it might lead to a significant cost savings for a traditionally underfunded mental health system. Relatedly, it may increase the number of sessions covered by third-party payors. Given these decision variables, the way the issue is legislatively resolved will affect the interests of not only the respective mental health professions, but also the consumers of their services, including insurers and governmental entities funding mental health services.

QUESTIONS AND COMMENTS

1. *Review of Chapter One materials on psychopharmacology.* The range of psychopharmacological medications currently being utilized is described in Chapter One. As indicated by these materials, these medications have very serious potential side effects and sometimes interact adversely with other medications being taken for non-psychiatric disorders. Would you feel comfortable prescribing these medications after receiving the amount of training required by New Mexico?

2. *Alternative educational models.* The American Psychological Association's emphasis on post-doctoral training rather than modifying psychologists' undergraduate and graduate educational requirements undoubtedly reflects in part the need of the organization to accommodate the interests of psychologists who are already established in their careers but want to be allowed to prescribe medications. Notwithstanding this consideration, what educational requirements at these levels should be imposed as a minimum condition for qualifying as a prescribing psychologist? Because these medications can have a profound effect on not only the nervous system but also other biological functions, some background in physiology and the biological sciences would seem to be indicated. Should legislatures considering prescription privileges for psychologists therefore stipulate a set of undergraduate and graduate requirements in the biological sciences, at least for those who have not yet completed their training in psychology? If such requirements were established, is it likely that institutions of higher learning would in turn modify their programs in psychology to incorporate the required courses?

3. *Hypothetical.* Henry Helper is a clinical psychologist in Dry Gulch, New Mexico. Two years ago, Dr. Helper completed all requirements stipulated by New Mexico for being licensed as a prescribing psychologist. As a result, he is seeing a number of new clients who have problems treatable with psychotropic medication. Ten months ago, a new client, Jane Doe, came to see him with a variety of complaints, including a feeling of depression accompanied by constant fatigue, low energy, and forgetfulness. During their initial session, Dr. Helper diagnosed Ms. Doe's condition—based on her symptoms and the disclosure that six months earlier she had been briefly hospitalized for a severe depressive episode—as depression, and Dr. Helper prescribed sertraline (Zoloft®), an antidepressant. Over the next two months, Ms. Loop's condition did not improve, and she continued to suffer from the original symptoms, which if anything had become more pronounced. Because she was not responding to the sertraline, Dr. Helper changed her medication to bupropion (Wellbutrin®), another antidepressant.

Five months after she had started seeing Dr. Helper, Ms. Loop was involved in a motor vehicle accident that resulted from momentary confusion on her part, during which she stepped on the accelerator rather than the brake. Following the accident, she was taken to the local emergency room where she was found to have fractures of the femur and the collarbone. Additionally, blood tests disclosed that she had a severe thyroid hormone deficiency. In the view of the attending physician, her thyroid condition had developed to the point that she was suffering from mental symptoms because of it. Moreover, the physician informed her that her thyroid condition, which can have symptoms similar to those of depression, was probably responsible for the symptoms that led her to consult Dr. Helper, and that this condition could easily have been diagnosed with a simple blood test and readily treated with medication.

In view of her substantial medical bills and claims for damages by the driver of the other vehicle, Ms. Doe consults Sam Bailey, a personal injury lawyer. Upon reviewing the case, Lawyer Bailey advises Ms. Doe to file a malpractice action against Dr. Helper on the basis that he both failed to properly diagnose her condition and prescribed the wrong medication, which in combination worsened her condition and ultimately led to the accident.

At trial, the defense did not attempt to refute any of the facts. However, the defense asserted, as a matter of law, that Dr. Helper's actions had not deviated from the "degree of skill and care ordinarily employed under similar circumstances by members of the psychology profession in good standing." Lawyer Bailey, however, argued that the standard of care should be based on the skill and care ordinarily exercised by *psychiatrists* or, alternatively, "all classes of health practitioners legally authorized to prescribe medication." Which standard of care should be applied? See James E. Long, *Power to Prescribe: The Debate Over Prescription Privileges for Psychologists and the Legal Issues Implicated*, 29 Law & Psychol. Rev. 243, 256 (2005); see also Chapter Three.

4. *Contrary positions.* Not all psychologists and organizations representing psychologists concur that properly-qualified psychologists should be able to obtain prescription privileges. For instance, the American Association of Applied and Preventive Psychology opposes prescription privileges for psychologists. See Kenneth M. Adams & Linas A. Bieliauskas, *On Perhaps Becoming What You Had Previously Despised: Psychologists as Prescribers of Medication*, 1 J. Clin. Psychol. Med. Settings 189 (1994); Diane M. Moyer, *An Opposing View on Prescription Privileges for Psychologists*, 26 Prof. Psychol.: Res. & Prac. 586 (1995); Stephen Diamond, *Drug Wars: The Siren Call of Prescription Privilege*, Psychol. Today (Apr. 8, 2010), http://www.psychologytoday.com/blog/evil-deeds/201004/drug-wars-the-siren-call-prescription-privilege?page=2. On the other hand, not all psychiatrists are opposed to granting prescription privileges to psychologists. See Daniel Carlat, *Psychiatry Benefits When Psychologists Prescribe Drugs*, KevinMD.com (Apr. 7, 2010), http://www.kevinmd.com/blog/2010/04/psychiatry-benefits-psychologists-prescribe-drugs.html (permitting psychologists to prescribe will enhance the practice of psychiatry).

5. *The Patient Protection and Affordable Care Act (PPACA).* The health care reform bill signed by President Barack Obama on March 30, 2010, brings significant changes to the health care system in the United States. All major stakeholders in the health care industry, including the professional organizations representing psychiatrists, psychologists, and clinical social workers, invested considerable resources to protect their interests throughout the legislative process.

This can be seen in the continuing development of regulations concerning accountable care organizations (ACOs). ACOs attempt to lower the cost of providing for Medicare patients by "[creating] incentives for health care providers to work together to treat an individual patient across care settings—including doctor's offices, hospitals, and long-term care facilities."

U.S. Dep't of Health & Human Servs., News Release, Affordable Care Act to Improve Quality of Care for People with Medicare (Mar. 31, 2011). Both the American Psychological Association (APA) and the National Association of Social Workers (NASW) sent comment letters to the U.S. Department of Health and Human Services (DHHS) calling for their professions to be included as eligible providers for ACOs. See Letter from Norman B. Anderson & Katherine C. Nordal, APA, to Kathleen Sebelius, Secretary, DHHS (June 3, 2011); Letter from Elizabeth J. Clark, Executive Director, NASW, to Donald Berwick, Administrator, Centers for Medicare & Medicaid Services, DHHS (June 6, 2011).

Many more PPACA-related regulations are expected to be generated in the next few years, and representatives of mental health professionals will surely continue to work to maintain and expand their interests. In addition, payment issues and efforts to limits the costs associated with Medicare and Medicaid, in particular the fees paid to participating health care providers, are similarly likely to be closely scrutinized by these professionals and their organizations.

CHAPTER 3

PROFESSIONAL LIABILITY FOR MALPRACTICE

■ ■ ■

Table of Sections

I. INTRODUCTION

As noted in Chapter Two, society's interest in protecting the consumers of mental health services has resulted in a system of state regulation of mental health professionals, which seeks to ensure the quality of these services, in part, by mandating that those who desire to be a mental health professional possess and maintain basic qualifications. This approach is *prospective* in the sense that its main objective is to prevent injury by unqualified providers. In contrast, a malpractice cause of action is *remedial* in nature. Its emphasis is on compensating individuals for the harm they incurred from substandard professional care. Both approaches, however, seek to enhance adherence to professional standards in the delivery of treatment services.

The term "malpractice" is something of a catchall and encompasses all lawsuits asserting that substandard professional care was provided, regardless of the specific doctrinal foundation underlying the claim. A private suit asserting malpractice may be based on any of several legal grounds. Most actions are grounded in negligence doctrine, but some rest on the tort doctrines of assault and battery, invasion of privacy, or breach of confidentiality. Malpractice suits also occasionally draw upon principles of contract law.

While malpractice claims are asserted to have reached critically high levels for some medical specialties, mental health professionals to date have generally not experienced extensive malpractice liability exposure. For example, data from the insurance industry show psychiatry is one of the least frequently sued physician specialty groups. Anupam B. Jena et al., *Malpractice Risk According to Physician Specialty*, 365 New Eng. J. Med. 629 (2011); Jonathan Klick & Thomas Stratmann, *Medical Malpractice Reform and Physicians in High–Risk Specialties*, 36 J. Legal Stud. S121, S142 (2007); Carol I. Tsao & Joseph B. Layde, *A Basic Review of Psychiatric Medical Malpractice Law in the United States*, 48 Comprehensive Psychiatry 309 (2007).

A number of factors may account for the relative paucity of malpractice actions against mental health professionals. One factor is probably the nature of the therapeutic interventions often employed. Many treatment modalities, such as psychotherapy, do not involve a biological intervention (as opposed to psychopharmacology and ECT). Even if improperly employed, psychotherapy will generally not result in demonstrable *physical* harm, which is often required for a suit to be successful and is the most common basis for a large award. Additionally, it may be difficult for a plaintiff to establish that the alleged injury, such as an adverse psychological reaction, was the result of malpractice and not merely a symptom of the disorder for which the individual was being treated.

Also, the diverse range of psychotherapeutic treatment modalities employed, coupled with a lack of consensus among mental health professionals as to the most appropriate approach to be employed in a given case, makes it difficult for a plaintiff to establish what should have been done instead. Finally, many recipients of mental health services may find it difficult or lack the resources to pursue a lawsuit or they may avoid litigation rather than publically disclose that they have undergone treatment for a mental disorder.

While these factors appear to have deterred lawsuits in the past, there are indications that the relative immunity enjoyed by mental health professionals may be diminishing. For example, the incidence of malpractice claims targeting psychiatrists has been increasing. While in 1980 there were 0.6 claims per 100 psychiatrists, this rate rose to approximately 4 claims per 100 psychiatrists in 1990, and 10–12 claims per 100 psychiatrists in the late 1990s. Thomas G. Gutheil & Paul S. Appelbaum, *Clinical Handbook of Psychiatry and the Law* 141 (3d ed. 2000).

Changes in the methods of treatment, particularly the increased use of psychopharmacology, have contributed to a substantial rise in malpractice actions against psychiatrists. Today, claims based on improper psychopharmacological treatment constitute the largest category of malpractice claims in the mental health field. Other changes eroding the immunity of mental health providers from liability "include a clearer delineation of the standard of care, a willingness to award damages for psychological harm, . . . a surge in the number of governmental actions brought against mental health providers[,]. . . . [a] greater number of advocates willing to assist individuals pursuing these suits[,] . . . [and] the empowerment of the recipients of mental health care." Thomas L. Hafemeister, Leah G. McLaughlin, & Jessica Smith, *Parity at a Price: The Emerging Professional Liability of Mental Health Providers*, 50 San Diego L. Rev. 29, 32–33 (2013).

In addition, while most malpractice suits in the past involved psychiatrists, increasingly other mental health professionals may be the target of such lawsuits. This development is in part attributable to changes in the law expanding malpractice liability to a variety of circumstances where physical injury is not necessarily present. For instance, courts and juries are increasingly willing to assign liability when therapists engage in sexual intimacies with clients. See infra Part

II.B.3. Courts have also become more receptive to claims focusing on unorthodox treatment techniques, such as those involving the use of recovered memories. See infra Part II.B.1.

Finally, another doctrinal change that has increased the exposure of mental health professionals to malpractice actions is the expansion of the class of persons to whom a therapist owes a duty of care, such as third parties harmed by a client. The nature of this change and its impact on mental health professionals will be explored more fully in Part II.C.

The materials that follow will first address the elements of a negligence claim, particularly as they apply to cases involving mental health services. Thereafter, three issues at the forefront of this litigation will be explored in greater detail. A final section will examine alternative remedies available to plaintiffs who have been injured in conjunction with mental health treatment. In addition, malpractice cases alleging invasion of privacy or breach of confidentiality are addressed in Chapter Five, while the doctrine of informed consent, which has developed as a separate theory of recovery, is covered in Chapter Four.

QUESTIONS AND COMMENTS

1. *Effect of tort law on professional standards.* The extent to which malpractice law actually induces adherence to professional standards of care has been the subject of considerable debate. Its impact on health care professionals is the subject of the following excerpts:

> For law-and-economics scholars, deterrence is the primary rationale for torts, easily outstripping corrective justice and compensation. The costs of litigation create an incentive to take safety precautions. Yet deterrence theory has its skeptics. . . . Some have argued that while morality itself should provide a sufficient reason for avoidance of dangerous activities, the tort system fails as a vehicle for expressing moral judgment. Other critics of deterrence theory accept the general assumptions of the law-and-economics school, but suggest that insurance tends to insulate reasonable economic actors from taking appropriate precautionary steps. This point is quite applicable in health care, where liability insurance is nearly universal. . . . There is little evidence of true error deterrence stemming from medical malpractice liability.

Michelle M. Mello & Troyen A. Brennan, *Deterrence of Medical Errors: Theory and Evidence for Malpractice Reform*, 80 Tex. L. Rev. 1595, 1603, 1607 (2002).

> Most mental health professionals are eclectic in their approach to treating patients. Rather than relying on a single approach for all patients, most mental health professionals vary their techniques based upon what works with a particular patient. The lesson to be learned from their collective experience is that no single psychiatric or psychological approach incorporated within the tort system is likely to

deter unsafe behavior across the board. Thus, adoption of any single psychiatric or psychological model by the tort system is unlikely to serve the goal of deterrence adequately. Because it is a practical necessity that the tort system choose a theory of human behavior to inform its structure without knowing the identity or psyche of each of the actors it should address, it is unlikely to be successful in deterring unsafe behavior.

Daniel W. Shuman, *The Psychology of Deterrence in Tort Law*, 42 U. Kan. L. Rev. 115, 166 (1993).

The standard of care for health care providers has traditionally been determined by what members of their profession would customarily do, rather than the reasonable and prudent person standard generally applied in negligence cases. . . . This approach means health care providers tend to be subject to liability only if they provide care that is out of step with what members of their profession are currently delivering, even if the customary approach could be expected to result in a poor outcome for a given client.

However, there are indications that this manner of establishing the standard of care may be eroding. "In more than half the states, either through an explicit statutory change or through case law, malpractice law has moved away from a customary-practice standard, and toward a reasonably-prudent-physician standard." This approach undercuts a "safety-in-numbers" approach that encouraged the status quo, and it has coincided with the rise of "evidence-based medicine," with testifying experts referring to such evidence when articulating the standard of care. To the extent mental health providers can cite empirical support for the steps they have taken, they are far more likely to be shielded from liability. At the same time, an evidence-based approach may increasingly be viewed as necessary to satisfy the standard of care.

Hafemeister et al., supra, at 38–39. See also Richard J. Bonnie, *Professional Liability and the Quality of Mental Health Care*, 16 Law, Med. & Health Care 229, 234–35 (1988); Kirk Heilbrun et al., *Standards of Practice and Care in Forensic Mental Health Assessment: Legal Professional, and Principles–Based Considerations*, 14(1) Psychol., Pub. Pol'y & L. 1 (2008).

2. *Caps on damages for medical malpractice.* Periodic dramatic increases in the cost of medical malpractice insurance, which some have attributed to increases in the size and number of medical malpractice awards, have led some states, such as California and Texas, to place caps on the non-economic damages for pain and suffering available in medical malpractice suits, as well as restrict awards for punitive damages. In addition, there have been calls for federal legislation to mandate such limits nationally. In the spring of 2003, separate bills were introduced in both the House of Representatives and the Senate to cap medical malpractice damages for pain and suffering. These bills had different provisions, though both would have placed limits on non-economic damages. The House passed its

version by a vote of 229–196. In the Senate, on a procedural vote, a majority voted to block its bill by a vote of 49–48. This issue has been revisited by Congress on a regular basis, but as of September 2013 no such law has been enacted.

3. *Health Care Reform of 2010 and malpractice.* The Patient Protection and Affordable Care Act (PPACA), enacted on March 23, 2010, brought substantial changes to the American health care system. However, although the PPACA authorized studies regarding medical malpractice liability reform, it did not include any provisions that directly affected the malpractice system. Thomas L. Hafemeister & Joshua Hinckley Porter, *The Health Care Reform Act of 2010 and Medical Malpractice Liability: Worlds in Collision or Ships Passing in the Night?*, 64 SMU L. Rev. 735 (2011).

II.   CLAIMS OF NEGLIGENT CARE

A. THE DOCTRINE: AN OVERVIEW

The unique characteristics of a therapist's work pose a particular challenge for legal institutions judging the quality of the services rendered. For one thing, mental health treatment has been described as both a science and an art. While technical skills are clearly required, the course of treatment is also highly dependent on the oftentimes idiosyncratic nature of the client's therapeutic needs, as well as the personal relationship between the therapist and the client, involves a certain amount of trial and error, and relies heavily on the therapist's intuition and subjective impressions. It is frequently difficult to assess both prospectively and retroactively the impact of a given course of therapy. Changes may be relatively unpredictable or so subtle as to be imperceptible. Moreover, it can be difficult to attribute a particular outcome to the therapeutic intervention as opposed to the underlying mental health problem or other factors present in the client's life.

Nevertheless, determinations as to the quality of the care provided in a particular instance cannot be avoided. The doctrinal framework governing most malpractice claims is the jurisprudence of negligence. In general terms, a professional who renders services has a legal duty to perform them in a manner comporting with the skill and technical proficiency normally exercised by other professionals in the same field under similar circumstances. A failure to meet this standard is a key element in a claim of negligence. But to prevail, a plaintiff must prove more than just that the services were of substandard quality. A negligence claim typically has four distinct elements, each of which must be established by the plaintiff. These elements have been described as:

1.   A duty, or obligation, recognized by the law, requiring the person to conform to a certain standard of conduct, for the protection of others against unreasonable risks.

2.   A failure . . . to conform to the standard required: a breach of the duty. . . .

3.   A reasonably close causal connection between the conduct and the resulting injury. . . .

4.   Actual loss or damage resulting to the interests of another.

Dan B. Dobbs et al., *Prosser and Keeton on the Law of Torts* § 30 (5th ed. 1984). The third element is often divided into two parts, with the resulting required elements generally stated as: (1) the defendant owed the plaintiff a duty of care (*duty*), (2) the defendant breached that duty (*breach*), (3) the defendant's conduct in fact caused harm to the plaintiff (*causation in fact*), (4) the defendant's conduct was not only a cause in fact of the plaintiff's harm but also a proximate cause, meaning that the defendant's conduct had a significant relationship to the harm suffered by the plaintiff and the harm was not the result of some other intervening variable (*proximate cause*), and (5) harm of a legally recognized kind occurred (*damages*). Dan B. Dobbs, *The Law of Torts* § 114 (2000). Historically, damages were limited to when physical injury to a person or property occurred. Id. Either an act or a failure to act (i.e., an omission) can constitute breach of a duty. Richard A. Epstein et al., *Cases & Materials on Torts* 170 (9th ed. 2008).

Applying these elements to actual cases in a technologically evolving society is one of the major challenges faced by the legal system. Changes in the methods of treatment, particularly the growing emphasis on the use of psychotropic medications, and structural changes in the delivery of health services (e.g., the impact of managed care systems), complicate the development of coherent and consistent legal standards. Nevertheless, it is in this context that courts are called upon to identify and apply standards governing professional liability. The following materials explore the special problems raised in the adjudication of malpractice claims against mental health providers.

QUESTIONS AND COMMENTS

1.   *Predominant claims.* The most common claims in psychiatric malpractice suits involve mistakes in diagnosis, improper treatment, failure to prevent an attempted or completed suicide, inadequate supervision, and medication errors or adverse drug reactions. Robert I. Simon, *The Law and Psychiatry*, 1 Focus 349, 350 (2003); see also Carol I. Tsao & Joseph B. Layde, *A Basic Review of Psychiatric Medical Malpractice Law in the United States*, 48 Comprehensive Psychiatry 309 (2007).

2.   *Drugs and psychiatric malpractice.* The increasing use of drugs to treat mental disorders increases the likelihood of adverse drug reactions and associated malpractice suits. The serious side effects associated with the use of some psychotropic medications are described in Chapter One. The dilemma confronting health care professionals with prescribing privileges is that for

some disorders, such as schizophrenia, there may be few viable treatment alternatives for obtaining immediate relief from symptoms. Thus, the choice may be between prescribing a medication that carries the risk of significant side-effects or doing nothing. Perhaps in recognition of this dilemma, the cases that impose liability on the prescribing professional generally involve a failure to monitor the medication regime and terminate it or substitute an alternative when adverse side effects appear. The other major category of claims is based on the improper choice of a particular medication (particularly if there was a negligent diagnosis) when another medication might have been more effective or carry fewer side effects.

Should a professional be less subject to liability if there are no or few viable treatment alternatives? Should the standard vary depending on the urgency of the client's condition? What if it was the professional's perception that without medication the client was likely to harm himself or others, be involuntarily hospitalized, or be arrested? On the other hand, it has been asserted that for various reasons professionals with prescribing privileges tend to overlook treatment alternatives that do not involve medications. How much consideration must professionals give to treatment alternatives that they personally rarely, if ever, employ?

Should a professional be less subject to liability if it was the client who initially requested the medication? What if the client insisted on the medication? What if the client insisted on the medication after watching an infomercial or receiving other direct-to-consumer advertising? What if the client was fully informed of the possible benefits and risks of the medication and agreed to take it after due deliberation? Does the professional have a responsibility to determine the reasons for the request or agreement to take the medication? Do the reasons have to be rational? What if both rational and irrational reasons are given? What if a family member insisted on or agreed to the medication? An authorized substitute decision maker? See Thomas L. Hafemeister & Richard M. Gulbrandsen, Jr., *The Fiduciary Obligation of Physicians to "Just Say No" if an "Informed" Patient Demands Services That Are Not Medically Indicated*, 39 Seton Hall L. Rev. 335 (2009).

3.   *Relationships creating a duty of care.* A threshold question in any case alleging professional negligence is whether the injured party is a member of the class of persons legally protected under the law of negligence. Traditionally, the answer to this question was relatively clear cut. No duty of care was owed except to those individuals with whom the professional had established a contractual relationship (express or implied) pursuant to which services were to be provided. In other words, unless the health care provider affirmatively agreed to such a relationship or by his or her actions indicated that such a relationship had been established (e.g., by meeting with and examining the person), a relationship was not deemed to be established. However, the existence of a professional relationship—establishing privity between a client and a therapist—is no longer always a dispositive factor in professional negligence cases. An increasing number of jurisdictions have modified or repudiated the privity doctrine. For example, a relationship may

be established if a professional responds to an e-mail inquiry and provides professional advice, notwithstanding that the professional has not met with the individual, has not made an appointment to see the individual, nor has otherwise indicated that a professional relationship has been established. The Vermont Supreme Court held that a duty of care was established between a psychiatrist and a child when the psychiatrist engaged in a 90 minute telepsychiatry study with the child. *White v. Harris*, 36 A.3d 203 (Vt. 2011).

Is a professional relationship established when a professional is interacting with someone in a social setting (e.g., at a party) and casually offers some professional advice? What if someone calls the professional's office and speaks with a member of the professional's administrative staff who provides advice (e.g., take two aspirins and call back in the morning)?

As noted, the circumstances under which a therapist may be held liable to third parties are elaborated in Part II.C., infra.

4. *Liability for services carried out at the request of a third party.* A related question concerns the liability of a therapist for negligence when performing a diagnostic service at the request of a third party. This situation may arise when an employer requires an employee or an applicant for employment to submit to a psychological evaluation by a mental health provider hired by the employer or when a mental health professional performs an independent examination in the course of litigation. Here the individual being evaluated, who neither requested nor paid for the service, is not technically a client of the therapist and thus is not in contractual privity with the therapist, but may rely upon the information provided in the course of the evaluation. May a therapist who is negligent in carrying out the diagnostic evaluation and consequently misdiagnoses the individual's condition be held liable to the individual for malpractice? There is a recent trend among state courts to find that at least a limited professional relationship is established in these situations. Liza H. Gold & John E. Davidson, *Do You Understand Your Risk? Liability and Third–Party Evaluations in Civil Litigation*, 35 J. Am. Acad. Psychiatry L. 200, 202 (2007). See, e.g., *Todd v. Angelloz*, 844 So. 2d 316 (La. Ct. App. 2003); *Lambley v. Kameny*, 682 N.E.2d 907 (Mass. App. Ct. 1997).

1. The "Standard of Care" Element

a. Introduction

As noted, a key requirement for the imposition of liability is a failure to meet the requisite "standard of care" in the particular circumstances under which treatment was rendered. A departure from the applicable standard of care can arise from either the selection of an inappropriate therapy or the improper *implementation* of the therapy. The improper use of a treatment modality might involve either its use when no beneficial result should have been expected or when one should have anticipated that its use would adversely exacerbate the condition or generate some other side effect. For example, a physician might be liable for the wrongful death of a patient after prescribing Serentil at a dosage five times higher than that recommended by its manufacturer. *Georgia Dep't of Human Res. v. Phillips*, 486 S.E.2d 851, 858 (1997). See also *Brandt v. Grubin*, 329 A.2d 82 (N.J. Super. Ct. 1974). An example of improper implementation of a therapeutic modality would be the administration of ECT without employing an adequate muscle relaxant. It might also include the uninterrupted and prolonged administration of a psychotropic medication coupled with a failure to terminate treatment upon the appearance of symptoms of Tardive Dyskinesia. See, e.g., *Clites v. State*, 322 N.W.2d 917 (Iowa App.1982).

A departure from the standard of due care may also occur if a therapist fails to take actions that could have averted injury. Claims of this nature can arise where the therapist is alleged to have failed to prevent a client's suicide by failing to initiate civil commitment. In *Foster v. Charter Medical Corp.*, the court allowed a claim to be brought against a psychiatrist for negligently causing a patient's suicide when the psychiatrist allowed the patient to leave a hospital unsupervised. 601 So. 2d 435 (Ala. 1992). See also *Williams v. Shelby Cnty. Health Care Corp.*, 803 F. Supp. 1306 (W.D. Tenn. 1992); *Mulhern v. Catholic Health Initiatives*, 799 N.W.2d 104 (Iowa 2011).

Application of the standard of care element in the mental health treatment context is complicated by a number of factors. As noted in Chapter One, conceptual differences among professionals have resulted in a lack of consensus as to both the etiology of psychiatric disorders and the appropriate method of treatment.

Additionally, the diagnostic process is frequently confounded by the lack of clear, *physical* symptoms and other biological markers. With regard to health care in general, the diagnostic process relies heavily on the presentation of physical symptoms and laboratory tests such as x-rays, ultrasounds, blood chemistry analyses, and CAT scans. The diagnosis of mental disorders, on the other hand, depends primarily on somewhat subjective observations of behavioral traits and the symptoms reported by the client or others. The lack of objectively verifiable symptomatology in the case of most mental disorders means that there is likely to be far less agreement among mental health professionals as to a particular diagnosis. The uncertainty that permeates the diagnostic process in turn impacts psychiatric malpractice litigation where diagnostic error has been alleged as it can subject the therapist to second-guessing and possible hindsight bias. Although, the general lack of diagnostic certainty can ultimately work to the benefit of a therapist who may be seen as free of fault in not reaching a different diagnosis, the accuracy of the diagnosis can be critical as an inaccurate diagnosis can adversely influence subsequent treatment decisions.

Finally, studies have shown that exceptional behaviors such as suicide or extreme violence towards others are extremely difficult to predict with any degree of certainty, even by trained behavioral specialists such as psychologists and psychiatrists. Martin Blinder, *Suicide, Psychiatric Malpractice, and the Bell Curve*, 32 J. Am. Acad. Psychiatry L. 319 (2004); Maggie Murray, Note, *Determining a Psychiatrist's Liability When a Patient Commits Suicide:* Haar v. Ulwelling, 39 N.M. L. Rev. 641 (2009). Nevertheless, the failure to prevent such occurrences is a common basis for malpractice claims against mental health professionals, an unsurprising result in light of the consequences. See Part II.B.2, infra.

The materials that follow address the challenges that confront the legal system when applying the doctrine of negligence in a variety of mental health treatment contexts. As an initial matter, the materials focus on the legal criteria pertaining to the standard of care element.

b.   *Defining the Standard*

STEPAKOFF V. KANTAR

Supreme Judicial Court of Massachusetts, 1985.
393 Mass. 836, 473 N.E.2d 1131.

O'CONNOR, JUSTICE.

Helen J. Stepakoff, widow of Gerald Stepakoff (Stepakoff) and executrix of his estate, brought this action . . . against William G. Kantar, Stepakoff's psychiatrist. The plaintiff alleged that, although the defendant either knew or reasonably should have known that Stepakoff was suicidal, he negligently failed to inform her of that fact or to make appropriate arrangements for Stepakoff's protection, as a result of which Stepakoff committed suicide. The plaintiff seeks damages for Stepakoff's . . . wrongful death.

The case was tried to a jury. The . . . jury found for the defendant on the claim for wrongful death. Judgment was entered, and the plaintiff appealed. We transferred the appeal to this court on our own motion.

The plaintiff argues that the judge erred by refusing to instruct the jury that a psychiatrist who knows or reasonably should know that his patient is likely to harm himself has a duty to take reasonable precautions to prevent such harm, and by refusing to instruct the jury regarding a psychiatrist's statutory authority to hospitalize a patient involuntarily. . . . We conclude that the judge did not commit reversible error, and we affirm the judgment for the defendant.

The jury could have found the following facts. Stepakoff began to see the defendant in November of 1973, and the two established a relationship as psychiatrist and patient that lasted until Stepakoff's death on or about February 16, 1975. The defendant diagnosed Stepakoff as a manic-depressive psychotic, and he formed the opinion that Stepakoff was "potentially suicidal." The defendant thought, however, that Stepakoff had a defense mechanism that rendered him less able to take decisive action as his predicament worsened. Furthermore, the defendant thought that he had a "solid pact" with Stepakoff that Stepakoff would contact him if Stepakoff felt suicidal.

During 1974 and early 1975, the plaintiff and Stepakoff had marital difficulties. On February 13, 1975, the plaintiff went to Florida. Before going, she told Stepakoff to be out of the house when she returned. She telephoned the defendant to express her concern about the situation, but he assured her that she should feel free to go.

The defendant planned to spend the weekend that began on Saturday, February 15, in Maine. Before his departure, he prepared Stepakoff for his absence. He gave Stepakoff the name and telephone number of another psychiatrist who had agreed to cover for him. He developed with Stepakoff a plan for the weekend, and he told Stepakoff that he would call him each night that he remained away. On Friday, February 14, the defendant and Stepakoff had an "emergency" meeting. During that meeting, the defendant considered involuntarily hospitalizing Stepakoff, but decided against it. After the meeting, he dictated a note for his files that included the following sentence: "There is a question of whether he will make it over the weekend."[1] The defendant also called the covering psychiatrist and described Stepakoff's situation.

On Saturday, February 15, Stepakoff called the covering psychiatrist, and the two met. Stepakoff reassured the doctor that he did not intend to commit suicide. That night, as planned, the defendant called Stepakoff. Based on that conversation, the defendant formed a favorable diagnostic impression of Stepakoff's condition. The defendant hung up after agreeing with Stepakoff that they would talk again the next night, but on Sunday, February 16, the police found Stepakoff in his garage, dead from carbon monoxide inhalation.

The jury heard the testimony of two psychiatrists. One of them expressed the opinion that the defendant's treatment of Stepakoff did not conform to good medical practice. He testified that the defendant should have involuntarily hospitalized Stepakoff. The other disagreed. In his opinion, Stepakoff did not meet the requirements for involuntary hospitalization set forth in G.L. c. 123, § 12. Over the plaintiff's objection,

---

[1] At trial, the defendant testified that when he used those words he meant: "Whether he would be able to carry out the activities that he and I outlined, or whether the type of thing that happened to him just preceding his psychiatric admission to Newton–Wellesley [in 1974] would occur, in which he seemed to be paralyzed in his capacities to function, to—at that time, he couldn't get up out of the chair in my office and drive his car home. And it was that type of regression and inability to function that I was questioning."

the judge allowed the witness to testify as to what those requirements were.

1.   *Instructions as to the Defendant's Duty.*

The plaintiff argues that the trial judge committed reversible error by failing to give the jury her requested instructions, numbered 10, 11, and 12, regarding a psychiatrist's duty to his patient. We reprint those requested instructions in the margin.[2] . . .

*   *   *

The plaintiff concedes that the judge correctly instructed the jury concerning the defendant's "general medical malpractice duty . . . ," but she contends that the judge should *also* have instructed the jury that if, under that general malpractice standard, the defendant knew or should have known that Stepakoff presented a serious danger to himself, the defendant owed Stepakoff a specific legal duty to safeguard him from that danger, or at least to use reasonable care to do so. We will assume that requests 10, 11, and 12 fairly presented that instruction to the judge, but we conclude that the judge correctly refused to give it.

"Negligence, without qualification and in its ordinary sense, is the failure of a responsible person, either by omission or by action, to exercise that degree of care, vigilance and forethought which, in the discharge of the duty then resting on him, the person of ordinary caution and prudence ought to exercise under the particular circumstances." [ ] Negligence of a physician who practices a specialty consists of a failure to exercise the degree of care and skill of the average qualified physician practicing that specialty, taking into account the advances in the profession and the resources available to the physician. [ ] The rule with respect to the physician-patient relationship is an adaption of the broader negligence principle. In the context of that relationship, the law views the care and skill commonly exercised by the average qualified physician as the equivalent of the "care, vigilance and forethought which . . . the person of ordinary caution and prudence ought to exercise under the particular circumstances." [ ]

The judge instructed the jury: "[I]f you find that the care and treatment given by Dr. Kantar to Gerald Stepakoff from December of 1973 to February of 1975 was not in accordance with good medical practice and in violation or breach of the standard of care and skill of the

---

2   "10. A treating psychiatrist owes to his patient a duty to safeguard the patient from danger due to mental incapacity where that incapacity is known, or ought to have been known, to the psychiatrist through the exercise of ordinary care. . . .

"11. If Dr. Kantar knew of facts from which he could have reasonably thought that the patient was likely to harm himself in the absence of protective measures, then Dr. Kantar had a duty to use reasonable care under the circumstances to prevent such harm and to safeguard the patient from self-inflicted injury or death. . . .

"12. This duty is proportionate to the patient's needs, that is, such reasonable care and attention as the patient's known mental condition requires. . . . " (Citations omitted.)

average member of the medical profession practicing his specialty of psychiatry between December '73 and February of 1975, and that, if as a direct and proximate result of that negligence, Gerald Stepakoff died, the plaintiff, Helen Stepakoff, would be entitled to recover. . . . " That instruction fully and accurately stated the law. The plaintiff was not entitled to further instructions relative to the reasonableness of the defendant's acts or failures to act. The plaintiff has not directed our attention to any case in which a court has bifurcated the duty owed by a psychiatrist to a suicidal patient by declaring that, when diagnosing a patient, the psychiatrist must exercise the care and skill customarily exercised by an average qualified psychiatrist, while, after diagnosing a patient as suicidal, the psychiatrist's duty to take preventive measures becomes one of "reasonableness." We are unwilling to disturb our longstanding rule that a physician, practicing a specialty, owes to his or her patient a duty to comply in all respects with the standard set by the average physician practicing that specialty.

We are not moved to a different conclusion . . . by cases from other jurisdictions cited by the plaintiff in support of the proposition that a hospital and its staff must exercise reasonable care for the safety of confined patients likely to harm themselves. Even if those cases support the proposition that hospitals must meet an ordinary negligence standard, as distinguished from a good medical practice standard, they do not persuade us that the duty owed by a psychiatrist to a suicidal outpatient should differ from that imposed by this court on physicians to other patients.

* * *

Judgment affirmed.

QUESTIONS AND COMMENTS

1. *The ordinary negligence standard compared to the medical malpractice standard.* Often referred to as the *customary* or *accepted practice standard*, the actions of health care providers facing a malpractice claim are typically measured against the standard of their profession, not merely the standard of a reasonable and prudent person. This means that the profession itself sets the standards of practice, not the judge or jury, with heavy reliance placed on "expert testimony describing the actual pattern of medical practice, without any reference to the effectiveness of that practice." Barry R. Furrow et al., *Health Law* 265 (2d ed. 2000). In *Stepakoff,* the plaintiff unsuccessfully sought instructions that would have the jury measure liability in terms of the "reasonableness" of the psychiatrist's suicide prevention measures. Would the standards sought by the plaintiff result in elevating the standard of care ordinarily applicable to physicians and other health professionals? Would a jury find such a standard easier or more difficult to apply?

2.   *Malpractice vs. an error of judgment.* A widely cited medical malpractice case stated: "Medical malpractice is legal fault by a physician or surgeon. It arises from the failure of a physician to provide the quality of care required by law. . . . A competent physician is not liable *per se* for a mere error of judgment, mistaken diagnosis or the occurrence of an undesirable result." *Hall v. Hilbun*, 466 So. 2d 856, 866 (Miss. 1985). When does an error become malpractice? This ruling added: "Each physician [is] expected to possess or have reasonable access to such medical knowledge as is commonly possessed or reasonably available to minimally competent physicians in the same specialty or general field of practice throughout the United States, to have a realistic understanding of the limitations on his or her knowledge or competence, and, in general, to exercise minimally adequate medical judgment." Id. at 871. What does this require a health care professional to do in conjunction with a given patient? Is the health care provider required to do a literature or internet search before giving any opinions or advice or commencing treatment? As noted above, diagnosing and treating a mental disorder can be particularly tricky and challenging. Does the above suggest that physicians without specialized training in psychiatry should routinely refer patients with mental health problems to a mental health professional? That mental health providers without medical training should insist that their clients first see a physician? Would such rules delay needed treatment? Increase the costs of mental health services?

3.   *Standards generated by the professions.* Professional organizations, such as the American Psychiatric Association, the American Psychological Association, and consortiums of medical centers, sometimes formulate practice guidelines that set out protocols for the treatment of various disorders. Such guidelines can be introduced by litigants to establish either adherence to or a lack of due care. Thus, such guidelines are likely to be highly influential in establishing professional standards and influencing the outcomes of litigation. However, a recent study of six different major guidelines for the treatment of patients with schizophrenia found that clinicians generally treated the guidelines as only recommendations. Troy Moore, *Schizophrenia Treatment Guidelines in the United States*, 5 Clinical Schizophrenia & Related Psychoses 40 (2011). For a call for the development of standards of care applicable to the field of forensic mental health assessment, see Kirk Heilbrun et al., *Standards of Practice and Care in Forensic Mental Health Assessment: Legal, Professional, and Principles–Based Considerations*, 14(1) Psychol., Pub. Pol'y & L. 1, 1 (2008). Why might a professional organization be reluctant to issue such standards?

4.   *Which standard applies?* The liability of a therapist for negligence may turn on the expertise and knowledge of fellow members of the therapist's profession. Thus, a psychologist, unlike a medically trained psychiatrist, may not be liable for a failure to diagnose an *organic* disorder presented by a client, at least if its manifestation would not be relatively obvious to members of that profession. On the other hand, therapists who hold themselves out as having the expertise of another profession may be held to the standards applicable to that profession and be expected to have the same level of

knowledge and expertise. As discussed in Chapter Two, some psychologists have pushed to obtain prescribing privileges, with two states having granted these privileges. Are these efforts likely to have an impact upon the standard of care applicable to clinical psychologists in general? For a discussion of the legal issues psychologists might face if granted prescription power, see Julia Johnson, *Whether States Should Create Prescription Power for Psychologists*, 33 Law & Psychol. Rev. 167 (2009).

5. *Should the standard vary with the nature of the problem?* It has been reported that adults with a serious mental illness treated in the public mental health system live about twenty-five years less than Americans in general, a gap that has widened since the early 1990s. Marilyn Elias, *Mentally Ill Die 25 Years Earlier, on Average*, USA Today, May 3, 2007. It has also been reported that 90% of people who die by suicide have risk factors that include depression and other mental disorders or a substance-abuse disorder. Nat'l Inst. of Mental Health, *Suicide in the U.S.: Statistics and Prevention* (2010). Are there certain groups of clients or situations for whom the standard of care should be greater to ensure professionals take special care in treating these clients? *Stepakoff* seems to reject this possibility. Do you agree?

2.   Defenses and Limitations

a. *Professional Judgment Rule*

SCHREMPF V. STATE
Court of Appeals of New York, 1985.
66 N.Y.2d 289, 496 N.Y.S.2d 973, 487 N.E.2d 883.

OPINION OF THE COURT

WACHTLER, CHIEF JUDGE.

Claimant's husband was stabbed and killed by Joseph Evans, a mental patient who had been released from a State institution and was still receiving outpatient care from that facility. In a suit for wrongful death the Court of Claims found the State liable for negligently failing to have the assailant committed as an inpatient sometime prior to the assault. The Appellate Division affirmed, with one justice dissenting.

On this appeal, the State of New York urges that the claim be dismissed. . . . [I]t is urged that the decisions of the State psychiatrist fell within the area of professional medical judgment and thus cannot serve as a basis for a negligence or malpractice award. For the reasons that follow, we agree with the State's . . . contention and reverse the Appellate Division's order.

In December 1981 claimant's husband, Albert Schrempf, was employed at Consolidated Industries of Greater Syracuse, Inc., a private nonprofit organization which provides vocational rehabilitation for outpatients from mental institutions. On December 9, 1981 he was stabbed to death at his place of employment by Joseph Evans, a 27–year–old outpatient from Hutchings Psychiatric Institute, a State mental facility.

Evans had been admitted for treatment at Hutchings on six occasions beginning in May 1979. The admissions usually followed violent altercations with members of his family and involved some property damage and attempted assaults, but not the infliction of personal injury. On these occasions he claimed that he was prompted by inner voices commanding him to act. He was generally diagnosed as a manic depressive hypomanic type or, more rarely, as a paranoid schizophrenic, which were described at trial as degrees of the same general condition. . . . Several of the admissions were voluntary. Evans generally resented the involuntary commitments and sometimes responded with threats against staff members or resorted to violent resistance. On one occasion, he broke the jaw of another patient.

Evans' condition was generally improved or stabilized by psychotherapy and medication which could be provided on an outpatient basis. However, he was a difficult outpatient because he had an erratic attendance record and did not regularly take prescribed medications. He was sensitive to, and had an adverse reaction to, certain drugs and sometimes stated that he would not take his medication because it was against his religion.

Evans' last involuntary commitment as an inpatient ended in January of 1981. In the summer of that year, he broke windows in his mother's house and subsequently pleaded guilty to criminal mischief. He was sentenced to probation and his probation officer suggested that he seek psychiatric treatment.

On September 28, 1981 he returned to Hutchings and was voluntarily admitted. He was examined on that occasion by the psychiatrist who had first admitted him in 1979 and who had also treated him on most of his subsequent admissions. She found that he was experiencing "persecutory delusions" that he was possessed and might be changing into a homosexual. However, she noted that he was calm and remained cooperative. Based on the examination and her knowledge of his psychiatric history, she determined that he was again suffering from manic depression and that at that time he did not pose a risk to himself or others. She placed him on outpatient status but assigned him to a special clinic for recalcitrant outpatients so that his use of the medication could be monitored.

In October Evans worked at a part-time job, without apparent incident. In November he was referred by his probation officer to Consolidated Industries for vocational rehabilitation. He participated in that program on a trial basis for approximately 10 days over the next three or four weeks.

Throughout this period his participation in the outpatient program diminished. In October he said he did not want to come any more because he had a job. He rarely met with his psychiatrist in October and did not see her after November 1. He did not regularly go to the clinic for his medication in October, and in November only appeared on two dates, November 9 and November 30.

His psychiatrist encouraged him to continue in the outpatient program and to take his medication. When he complained that the drugs made him drowsy at work, she reduced the dosage and directed him to take the medicine at night. On November 17 she informed his probation officer that he was not taking his medication. She also monitored his behavior through the probation officer and others and found no evidence that his condition was deteriorating. On the contrary, she was informed that he appeared to be polite and cooperative by all who observed him at the clinic, the probation office and Consolidated Industries. Indeed he was being considered for permanent membership at Consolidated at the time of the assault on December 9, 1981.

At the trial, the claimant urged that the State had been negligent in the care and treatment of Evans by releasing him and permitting him to remain on outpatient status in 1981, particularly after his psychiatrist had reason to believe he was not taking his medication as prescribed. The Court of Claims held that the decision to release Evans in January 1981 involved a medical judgment for which the State could not be held liable. However, the court concluded that the State was negligent in admitting Evans to outpatient care, instead of confining him as an inpatient in September 1981. The court also held that the State psychiatrist should have done "something more" when it became evident that the patient was not taking his prescribed medication.

The Appellate Division affirmed, without opinion. . . .

*   *   *

A physician's duty is to provide the level of care acceptable in the professional community in which he practices. He is not required to achieve success in every case and cannot be held liable for mere errors of professional judgment. The "line between medical judgment and deviation from good medical practice is not easy to draw" particularly in cases involving psychiatric treatment.

Although in the past, the care of those suffering from mental infirmities was generally limited to confinement, the modern and more humane policy of the medical profession and the law contemplates returning the mental patient to society, if he does not pose an immediate risk of harm to himself or others. This, we have noted, requires a sensitive appraisal of competing interests: "(1) the State's duty to treat and care for its mental defective wards, with an eye toward returning them to society more useful citizens, and (2) the State's concern that the inmates in its institutions cause no injury or damage to the property of those in the vicinity." Because psychiatry is not an exact science, decisions with respect to the proper course of treatment often involve a calculated risk and disagreement among experts as to whether the risk was warranted or in accord with accepted procedures. These circumstances necessarily broaden the area of professional judgment to include treatments tailored to the particular case, where the "accepted procedure" does not take into account factors which the treating physician could reasonably consider significant. . . .

The only remaining question is whether the treating physician was negligent in failing to intervene in some manner once she had reason to believe that Evans was not taking his medication as prescribed. In view of the fact that Evans was a voluntary outpatient, the State's control over him, and consequent duty to prevent him from harming others, is more limited than in cases involving persons confined to mental institutions. Even the claimant's experts did not agree as to what should and could be done with such a patient. They variously proposed compelling or coercing him to resume medication, changing the medication to a drug with longer lasting effects, conducting a full reexamination of him, initiating involuntary commitment proceedings or threatening him with commitment if he did not cooperate. The court held that the treating psychiatrist should have done "something more", and suggested that "at the very least, an in-depth psychiatric evaluation should have been conducted to determine Evans' level of functioning." The court did not indicate what should have been done had Evans refused to cooperate.

One point on which all the experts agreed was that the patient's failure to take his medication did not necessarily mean that his condition was deteriorating or that he would become dangerous. That would largely depend on his behavior and, again, there was agreement that his outward appearance and behavior did not show any "warning signs" indicative of this kind of change. Although claimant's experts ignored or discounted these factors, they played a significant role in the attending physician's assessment. They indicated to her that there was a chance that his condition was improving as it appeared to be, and suggested a corresponding risk that intervention by resort to aggressive measures might disrupt the process. As noted, she knew from past experience that he resented involuntary treatment and often responded violently in that setting. Thus, there were risks either way. The treating physician, as she testified at trial, simply attached greater significance to those factors which seemed most promising and chose the course which appeared to offer the best opportunity for long-term rehabilitation. We know with hindsight that it was a mistaken impression. However, under the circumstances, it must be recognized as an exercise of professional judgment for which the State cannot be held responsible.

Accordingly, the order of the Appellate Division should be reversed and the claim dismissed.

JASEN, MEYER, KAYE, ALEXANDER and TITONE, JJ., concur.

SIMONS, J., taking no part.

Order reversed, with costs, and claim dismissed.

QUESTIONS AND COMMENTS

1.   *Significance of the professional judgment defense.* Another ruling applying New York law determined that the professional judgment rule means that "physicians cannot be held liable for mistakes made in the course of treatment when the treatment has a proper medical foundation." *Rivera v. New York City Health & Hosps. Corp.*, 191 F. Supp. 2d 412, 418 (S.D.N.Y. 2002). The likelihood that a professional will be held liable for malpractice is obviously influenced by the governing standard employed. The professional judgment defense recognized in *Schrempf* should at least in theory carry with it a reduced risk of liability when compared to a standard formulated simply in terms of whether the mental health provider's actions conformed to the "care and skill of the average qualified physician [or other health care professional] practicing that specialty," as set forth in *Stepakoff*. The latter tends to shift the inquiry away from the perceptions of the professional being charged with malpractice to what members of that profession would do in general under the circumstances that arose.

2.   *Absence of liability as a matter of law.* Note that the high court of New York in *Schrempf* holds that in spite of a finding of negligence by the trial court, the professional judgment rule requires a judgment for the defendant as a matter of law. On what basis does the court reach the conclusion that the circumstances were such that the decision taken by the physician of necessity involved a significant element of guesswork and thus fell within the professional judgment rule? Is the rule, as applied, simply a way of trumping the imposition of liability at the trial level because of the court's conclusion that liability is not justified because of the uncertainties of predicting suicide or other extraordinary behaviors?

3.   *Recognition of the doctrine in other jurisdictions.* The professional judgment rule—which calls for appropriate instructions to the jury when applicable—has not been universally adopted. In fact, it has been expressly recognized by only a minority of jurisdictions and many have stated that "only non-negligent judgments should be protected from liability." Joseph King, *Reconciling the Exercise of Judgment and the Objective Standard of Care in Medical Malpractice*, 52 Okla. L. Rev. 49, 62 (1999). See *Morlino v. Medical Ctr.*, 706 A.2d 721 (N.J. 1998). The rule seems to have had its origins in New York where it has been applied to all phases of malpractice, including psychiatry. See *Littleton v. Good Samaritan Hosp.*, 529 N.E.2d 449 (Ohio

1988). The "best judgment rule" shields a physician from liability "for mere errors of judgment provided he does what he thinks best after careful examination." Id. at 457.

In the mental health context, the rule—adopted expressly or *sub silentio*—has most commonly been applied to exculpate mental health professionals for their decision to not seek involuntary hospitalization. As explained by the Supreme Court of Ohio:

> "Under such a 'psychotherapist judgment rule,' the court would not allow liability to be imposed on therapists for simple errors in judgment. Instead, the court would examine the 'good faith, independence and thoroughness' of a psychotherapist's decision not to commit a patient. . . . Factors in reviewing such good faith include the competence and training of the reviewing psychotherapists, whether the relevant documents and evidence were adequately, promptly and independently reviewed, whether the advice or opinion of another therapist was obtained, whether the evaluation was made in light of the proper legal standards for commitment, and whether other evidence of good faith exists."

Id. at 458 (quoting *Currie v. United States*, 644 F. Supp. 1074, 1083 (M.D.N.C. 1986)). See also *Soutear v. United States*, 646 F. Supp. 524, 536 (E.D. Mich. 1986) (" 'Psychiatry . . . is not an exact science. Medical doctors cannot predict with perfect accuracy whether or not an individual will do violence to himself or to someone else. . . . The concept of 'due care' in appraising psychiatric problems, assuming proper procedures are followed, must take account of the difficulty often inevitable in definitive diagnosis.' [ ] *Thus, a psychiatrist will not be held liable for his patient's violent behavior simply because he failed to predict it accurately*.") (emphasis in the original).

4. *Limitations on the professional judgment rule*. Note that the professional judgment rule only applies where the decision taken has been preceded by a "careful examination" of the individual. *Littleton*, 529 N.E.2d at 457.

5. *Implications of the professional judgment rule*. What issues may arise if a court adopts the professional judgment rule? How should courts view mental health providers who receive kickbacks for utilizing certain medications or forms of treatment? Should providers be required to inform their patients if the course of treatment deviates from the standard of care? For a discussion of these issues, see Richard Bourne, *Medical Malpractice: Should Courts Force Doctors to Confess Their Own Negligence to Their Patients?*, 61 Ark. L. Rev. 621 (2009); see also Tracy Weber & Charles Ornstein, *This Won't Hurt a Bit*, Wash. Post, Sept. 18, 2011, at G01.

b. *Respectable Minority Doctrine*

A client who received treatment involving a particular technique may, if the outcome is unsatisfactory, claim that the practitioner was negligent in not utilizing a more appropriate treatment modality. Such a claim may be advanced, moreover, even when the practitioner obtained the informed consent of the client prior to commencing treatment. (The doctrine of informed consent is treated in Chapter Four).

Traditionally, claims that practitioners utilized the wrong therapeutic technique or failed to use the most effective one will be measured by what members of that profession would customarily do under such circumstances. While a finding that the therapeutic approach used was not "customary" does not necessarily lead to liability, proof of conformity to professional custom generally precludes a finding of liability.

Proof that a particular procedure is customary does not, however, require that it be used by a majority of practitioners (or as is often said, it is not determined by a "plebiscite"). In a number of jurisdictions, a defense can be established by showing that the treatment is employed by a "respectable minority" of those in the field. In other words, "where two or more schools of thought exist among competent members of the medical profession concerning proper medical treatment for a given ailment, each of which is supported by responsible medical authority, it is not malpractice to be among the minority . . . who follow one of the accepted schools." *Chumbler v. McClure,* 505 F.2d 489, 492 (6th Cir. 1974).

However, some unresolved questions remain. For instance, does this doctrine immunize a practitioner from liability upon a showing that the treatment is used by a "respectable minority," even though it is on average less likely to be effective than an alternative treatment modality or its use is declining? In the treatment of mental disorders, these questions can particularly arise as newer treatment techniques based on biological precepts compete with more traditional forms of psychotherapy. The case that follows is illustrative of the context in which cases of this type are likely to arise.

Osheroff v. Chestnut Lodge, Inc.

[No official report of this case exists as the action was initially brought in 1982 as an arbitration proceeding before the Maryland Health Care Arbitration Panel. The facts set out below are based on several secondary sources and the decision of the Maryland Court of Special Appeals, 490 A.2d 720 (1985), which affirmed the arbitration award on procedural grounds.]

Summary of the Legal Proceedings

In 1982, Dr. Rafael Osheroff initiated a lawsuit against Chestnut Lodge, Inc., claiming that Chestnut Lodge negligently misdiagnosed his condition and negligently failed to utilize psychopharmacological treatment. This, he alleged, prevented him from returning promptly to normal functioning, with the consequential loss of a lucrative medical practice and his standing in the medical community.

As required under Maryland law, Osheroff's suit was initially submitted to the Maryland Health Care Arbitration Panel (HCAP), which held extended hearings during which numerous experts were called to testify. The panel found in Osheroff's favor and ultimately a determination of damages in the amount of $250,000 was issued. *Osheroff v. Chestnut Lodge*, 62 Md. App. 519, 521–22 (Md. Ct. Spec. App. 1985). In his review of the case, Professor Gerald L. Klerman summarized the events leading up to the settlement:

> Under Maryland statute, once an arbitration process is concluded, any party to the proceedings may reject the panel's arbitration and call for court review. Both sides appealed. The claimant, Dr. Osheroff, requested a jury trial, which was to have taken place in October, 1987. However, before any action was taken by the court, a settlement was agreed upon by both parties.

Gerald L. Klerman, *The Psychiatric Patient's Right to Effective Treatment: Implications of Osheroff vs. Chestnut Lodge*, 147 Am. J. Psychiatry 409, 410–11 (Apr. 1990).

Factual Background

Osheroff's medical history prior to his hospitalization has been summarized as follows:

> The patient, Dr. Rafael Osheroff, a 42–year–old, white male physician, was admitted to Chestnut Lodge in Maryland . . . on Jan. 2, 1979. His history included brief periods of depressive and anxious symptoms as an adult; these had been treated on an outpatient basis. He had completed medical school and residency training, was certified as an internist and became a sub-specialist in nephrology. . . .

> Before his 1979 hospitalization, Dr. Osheroff had been suffering from anxious and depressive symptoms for approximately two years and had been treated as an outpatient with individual psychotherapy and tricyclic antidepressant medications. Dr. Nathan Kline, a prominent psychopharmacologist in New York, had initiated outpatient treatment with tricyclic medication, which, according to Dr. Kline's notes, produced moderate improvement. The patient, however, did not maintain the recommended dose, his clinical condition gradually worsened and hospitalization was recommended.

Id. at 410.

In January 1979, Osheroff admitted himself into Chestnut Lodge, which for over forty years had been one of the major centers devoted to "a clinical practice in intensive individual psychotherapy based on psychoanalytic and interpersonal paradigms." Id. at 411. A number of prominent American psychiatrists had been trained at Chestnut Lodge, many of whom subsequently became leaders in psychoanalytically oriented clinical psychiatry.

Upon admission, Osheroff was diagnosed as suffering from "psychotic reaction, agitated type and narcissistic personality disorder." John G. Malcolm, *Treatment Choices and Informed Consent in Psychiatry: Implications of the Osheroff Case for the Profession*, 14 J. Psychiatry & L. 9, 16 (1986). Both following his admission and throughout his stay in Chestnut Lodge, Osheroff's treatment program consisted of four sessions of individual psychotherapy per week and group therapy. Id. at 17–18. At no time was he given antidepressive medication because of the facility's decision to "attempt a 'more ambitious treatment goal' of dealing with the long range difficulties of the underlying personality disorder." Id. at 17.

Although the hospital records indicate that at various times the staff felt that Osheroff was making progress, it seems evident that he did not noticeably improve during his seven-month stay at Chestnut Lodge. In fact, he "lost 40 pounds, experienced severe insomnia, and had marked psychomotor agitation. His agitation, manifested by incessant pacing, was so extreme that his feet became swollen and blistered, requiring medical attention." Klerman, supra, at 410.

The circumstances leading to Osheroff's release and admission into another facility are also described by Prof. Klerman:

> The patient's family became distressed by the length of the hospitalization and by his lack of improvement. They consulted a psychiatrist in the Washington, D.C., area, who spoke to the hospital leadership on the patient's behalf. In response, the staff at Chestnut Lodge held a clinical case conference to review the patient's treatment. They decided not to make any major changes—specifically not to institute any medication regimen but to continue the intensive individual psychotherapy. Dr. Osheroff's clinical condition continued to worsen. At the end of 7 months, his family had him discharged from Chestnut Lodge and admitted to Silver Hill Foundation in Connecticut.

> On admission to Silver Hill Foundation, Dr. Osheroff was diagnosed as having a psychotic depressive reaction. His treating physician began treatment with a combination of phenothiazines and tricyclic antidepressants. Dr. Osheroff showed improvement within 3 weeks and was discharged from Silver Hill Foundation within 3 months.

* * *

Following his discharge from Silver Hill Foundation in the summer of 1979, the patient resumed his medical practice. He has been in outpatient treatment, receiving psychotherapy and medication. He has not been hospitalized and has not experienced any episodes of depressive symptoms severe enough to interfere with his professional or social functioning. He has resumed contact with his children and has also become active socially.

Id. at 410.

Impact of Practitioner Orientation on Diagnosis and Treatment

Prof. Klerman's observations on the theoretical divisions that characterize psychiatry in this country serve as a useful starting point in considering the diagnostic and treatment issues raised by the Osheroff case.

> Resolution of both the clinical and scientific issues is made difficult by the divisions within psychiatry in the United States, where psychiatry is divided theoretically and clinically into different schools—biological, psychoanalytic, and behavioral. . . . Various terms have been used to describe these divisions and split—schools, movements, ideologies, and paradigms. Whatever term is used, there is agreement that these differences in theory and practice involve controversies over the nature of mental illness [and] the appropriateness of different forms of treatment. . . .

Id. at 411.

Chestnut Lodge—where Osheroff was initially admitted—was, as noted, one of the leading psychoanalytically oriented in-patient treatment centers in the country (it functioned as a psychiatric facility from 1910 to 2001). There is a general consensus that the theoretical orientation of the treating therapist is likely to significantly influence both the diagnostic process and the choice of treatment. In Osheroff's case, the admitting psychiatrist at Chestnut Lodge made a *primary* diagnosis of "major narcissistic personality disorder."[a] A diagnosis of "manic-depressive illness, depressed type" was entered as a secondary diagnosis. Malcolm, supra, at 16. While the existence of "personality disorder" as a diagnostic category is not necessarily rejected by biologically oriented psychiatrists, it is far more central to the psychoanalytic paradigm. As in the case of other similar psychopathologies, a "narcissistic personality disorder" is seen as a derivative of an early childhood developmental crisis. Id. at 17–18. Thus, under one prevalent hypothesis at the time, the disorder results

---

[a] "The essential feature is a Personality Disorder in which there are a grandiose sense of self-importance or uniqueness; preoccupation with fantasies of unlimited success; exhibitionistic need for constant attention and admiration; characteristic responses to threats to self-esteem; and characteristic disturbances in interpersonal relationships, such as feelings of entitlement, interpersonal exploitativeness, relationships that alternate between the extremes of overidealization and devaluation, and lack of empathy. The exaggerated sense of self-importance may be manifested as extreme self-centeredness and self-absorption. Abilities and achievements tend to be unrealistically overestimated. Frequently the sense of self-importance alternates with feelings of special unworthiness. . . . " Am. Psychiatric Ass'n, *Diagnostic and Statistical Manual of Mental Disorders* 315–16 (3d ed. 1980).

because during childhood the affected individual "failed to internalize an idealized parental image because he either lost or was traumatically disappointed in idealized objects. This idealized image is a forerunner of the superego. Because this idealized image is missing, certain superego functions are missing." Id. at 17.

Not only is the diagnostic approach likely to be influenced by the theoretical orientation of the therapist, but so is the choice of treatment. Adherence to the psychoanalytic model is likely to influence the therapeutic approach in three ways. First, there is a general consensus on the part of those adhering to the psychoanalytic model that many disorders can only be treated through long term psychoanalysis. Second, and of equal significance, certain forms of depression are perceived as being derived from, and associated with a psychopathology the origin of which is in early childhood development. Klerman, supra, at 412. As a consequence, whatever treatment program is undertaken must address the underlying root causes of the disorder rather than the surface symptomatology. In Osheroff's case, this meant that the staff of Chestnut Lodge placed emphasis on the treatment of the narcissistic personality disorder rather than the depression, which was seen as a derivative symptom. Finally, a psychoanalytic orientation leads many therapists to avoid the use of psychotropic medication during the course of therapy "because of the possible adverse effects of the pharmacotherapy." Id. at 413.

The Silver Hill Foundation, where Osheroff was admitted following his release from Chestnut Lodge, entered a diagnosis of severe depressive reaction. In this respect, the diagnosis of the two institutions were in accord. However, unlike Chestnut Lodge, the psychiatrist at Silver Hill did not diagnose the patient as suffering from a narcissistic personality disorder.[b]

Silver Hill's diagnosis of "psychotic depression" led to a treatment program of psychotropic medication combined with "supportive therapy" rather than analytical therapy. This choice of treatment would be regarded as standard by those in the biologically oriented schools of psychiatry. Id. at 412.

The Efficacy of Alternate Treatment Modalities

A court hearing on an Osheroff-type claim could be expected to admit evidence relevant to the efficacy of the treatment modalities that were used or could have been used. The state of evidence relevant to this issue has been summarized by Prof. Klerman:

---

[b]   In subsequent testimony, the admitting psychiatrist at Silver Hill stated that while she considered a diagnosis of personality disorder, she did not enter the diagnosis because it was "not preeminent" at the time. Malcolm, supra, at 22.

With regard to all kinds of therapeutics—pharmacotherapy, surgery, radiation, psychotherapy—the most scientifically valid evidence as to the safety and efficacy of a treatment comes from randomized controlled trials when these are available. Although there may be other methods of generating evidence, such as naturalistic and follow-up studies, the most convincing evidence comes from randomized controlled trials.

There have been many controlled clinical trials of psychiatric treatments; most have been conducted to evaluate psychopharmacological agents.

* * *

Research on the efficacy of psychotherapy has lagged behind that of psychopharmacology, but has, nevertheless, been extensive. . . . Specific reviews of the evidence have appeared with regard to psychotherapy of . . . schizophrenia, depression, and obsessive-compulsive disorders.

* * *

With regard to the treatment of the patient's diagnosis of *narcissistic personality* [emphasis added] disorder, there were no reports of controlled trials of any pharmacological or psychotherapeutic treatment for this condition at the time of his hospitalization. The doctors at Chestnut Lodge decided to treat Dr. Osheroff's personality disorder with intensive individual psychotherapy based on psychodynamic theory.

With regard to the treatment of the patient's DSM–II diagnosis of psychotic depressive reaction, there was very good evidence at the time of his hospitalization for the efficacy of two biological treatments—ECT and the combination of phenothiazines and tricyclic antidepressants. The combination pharmacotherapy was the treatment later prescribed at Silver Hill Foundation.

There are no reports of controlled trials supporting the claims for efficacy of psychoanlytically-oriented intensive individual psychotherapy of the type advocated and practiced at Chestnut Lodge and administered to Dr. Osheroff.

* * *

It should not be concluded there is no evidence for the value of any psychotherapy in the treatment of depressive states. Depressive states are heterogeneous and there are many forms of psychotherapy. There is very good evidence from controlled clinical trials for the value of a number of brief psychotherapies for nonpsychotic and nonbipolar forms of depression in ambulatory patients. The psychotherapies for which there is evidence include cognitive-behavioral therapy, interpersonal psychotherapy, and behavioral therapy. However, no clinical trials have been reported to support the claims for efficacy of psychoanalysis of intensive individual psychotherapy based on psychoanalytic theory for any form of depression.

* * *

Even if we assume that the personality disorder was correctly diagnosed in Dr. Osheroff's case, there is no evidence to support the premise that the presence of a narcissistic personality disorder militates against the use of antidepressant medication.

* * *

A related therapeutic issue raised by the case has to do with the possible negative interactions between psychotherapy and pharmacotherapy for depression. Many psychoanalytically oriented psychotherapists have argued against the use of medication in patients receiving psychotherapy because of the possible adverse effects of the pharmacotherapy on the conduct of the psychotherapy, although there is evidence that the combination of drugs and psychotherapy does not interfere with the psychotherapy of depression. Moreover, findings from controlled trials suggest the combination of drugs and psychotherapy may have beneficial additive effects in the treatment of depression.

Id. at 412–13.

QUESTIONS AND COMMENTS

1.   *The relationship of diagnosis to treatment.* What was the ostensible negligence in Osheroff's case? Was it an erroneous diagnosis, inadequate treatment, or both? What should the defendants have done differently? In his complaint, Osheroff alleged negligence both as to the diagnosis (i.e., the diagnosis of narcissistic personality disorder), and as to the choice of treatment. To what extent is a decision of the second issue dependent on the resolution of the first?

2.   *Relevance of theoretical orientation.* Is the theoretical orientation of the therapist relevant to the question of liability in the sense that the diagnosis is to some extent influenced by the particular school to which the therapist adheres? For instance, the diagnosis of narcissistic personality disorder is closely associated with psychoanalytic concepts pertaining to ego formation. For those who adhere to the psychoanalytic model, the diagnosis made at Chestnut Lodge may not have been far afield.

3.   *Relevance of emerging trends.* Some commentators speculate that such a respectable minority defense is losing currency with recent developments in and the increasing use of psychopharmacology, which can provide a fairly rapid cessation of symptoms for some disorders. See Douglas

Mossman, *Unbuckling the 'Chemical Straitjacket': The Legal Significance of Recent Advances in the Pharmacological Treatment of Psychosis*, 39 San Diego L. Rev. 1033, 1093 (2002). Other commentators take a more skeptical view of the value and efficacy of these medications. See Irving Kirsch, *The Emperor's New Drugs: Exploding the Antidepressant Myth* (2010); Robert Whitaker, *Anatomy of an Epidemic: Magic Bullets, Psychiatric Drugs, and the Astonishing Rise of Mental Illness in America* (2010).

As Chapter One indicated, a raging debate continues over the relative efficacy and appropriateness of psychotherapy and psychopharmacology across a range of disorders, with both camps citing research that ostensibly documents the value of their treatment approach. Compare Marcia Angell, *The Epidemic of Mental Illness: Why?*, 58(11) N.Y. Rev. Books, June 23, 2011; Marcia Angell, *The Illusions of Psychiatry*, 58(12) N.Y. Rev. Books, July 14, 2011; with Peter D. Kramer, *In Defense of Antidepressants*, N.Y. Times, July 10, 2011, at SR1. Some, however, have asserted that psychotherapy and psychopharmacology should be viewed as alternative or complementary approaches rather than antithetical to one another. See Ripu D. Jindal & Michael E. Thase, *Integration of Care: Integrating Psychotherapy and Pharmacotherapy to Improve Outcomes Among Patients with Mood Disorders*, 54 Psychiatric Serv. 1484 (2003); Sandro Pampallona, *Combined Pharmacotherapy and Psychological Treatment for Depression*, 61 Archives Gen. Psychiatry 714 (2004); but see Jacqueline A. Sparks et al., *Integrating Psychotherapy and Pharmacotherapy: Myths and the Missing Link*, 17 J. Fam. Psychotherapy 83 (2006).

When should an emerging or declining trend be taken into account in determining the standard of care, particularly in conjunction with a respectable minority defense? Should the fact that the relative use of a given therapy is driven by cost factors be taken into account in determining the standard of care and the availability of the respectable minority doctrine? One of the reasons for the decline in the use of a psychoanalytical approach is the considerable expense associated with its application as it typically involves numerous therapeutic sessions extending across a lengthy period of time.

4. *Application of the respectable minority doctrine.* A fundamental question, of course, is what constitutes a "respectable minority"? How many proponents are needed for a therapeutic approach to constitute a "respectable minority"? Is this judged on a national basis or by the number of proponents within the local community? For example, if only one practitioner in the community uses a technique, will she be entitled to the defense if she can identify other practitioners in the nation that use it? What if these practitioners are only found in other countries? How is it to be determined whether the technique "is supported by responsible medical authority," particularly with regard to mental health problems where there is so much uncertainty over diagnosis and treatment? Should disposition of an *Osheroff*-type case take into account that traditional psychoanalytically oriented

therapists tend to avoid psychotropic medication on the grounds it interferes with the classical analytic course of treatment?

Are these questions that should be decided as a matter of law (i.e., by the presiding judge) or as a matter of fact (i.e., by the factfinder)? Should they be based on a review of research studies that claim to have directly compared the different therapeutic approaches? Should such reviews be limited to randomized controlled trials or may they include naturalistic, follow-up, or anecdotal studies? Are surveys of practitioners or recipients of the treatments relevant or required? Should the purported scientific foundations of the approaches be explored? Should the positions of relevant professional organizations be considered? Should the novelty or the history of the approach be taken into account, including its potential promise or past abuses? Should the intransigence or the urgency of the condition or lack of alternatives be considered?

5. *Effect of informed consent.* Should it be relevant in assessing liability whether the patient was informed of the relative length and potential advantages and disadvantages of the various available treatments? Should cost be a part of this discussion? If so, does this suggest that the doctrine of informed consent, which will be treated in Chapter Four, may have some relevance in assessing liability for alleged negligence in the selection of a course of treatment? In other words, why should a client who has made an informed choice after being presented with all the relevant facts be allowed to pursue a claim for negligence if the outcome is disappointing? Should such a pre-treatment discussion provide stronger grounds for absolving the practitioner of liability when a mental disorder is being treated because of the vagaries of diagnosis and treatment? But does the presence of a mental disorder limit the ability of the client to understand and appreciate this information?

Can a client, at the outset, contractually exempt the therapist from liability? Can the clinician demand such a contractual agreement as a condition for commencing treatment? Does it matter how many other treatment options the client has? The enforceability of covenants not to sue in the context of medical treatment is questionable. In some instances, particularly as to relatively standardized treatments, such contractual limitations on liability have been held to violate public policy. However, where the procedure is experimental and the patient has been informed of the alternatives and risks, such provisions may be enforced. See *Schneider v. Revici,* 817 F.2d 987 (2d Cir. 1987).

6. *Questioning the Effectiveness of a Treatment.* Could it be argued that staff at the Chestnut Lodge facility was not necessarily negligent in their initial use of intensive individual psychotherapy but that it became negligent when they persisted in its use after the patient's condition did not improve and, in fact, deteriorated over the period of several months?

If a clinician is not satisfied with a client's response, then it might be appropriate to change the treatment being employed. When switching from one psychopharamaceutical regimen to another, a general rule is to "change only one medication at a time, in order to distinguish among efficacy, side effects, and worsening of the illness itself." Ahsan Khan, *Challenging the Established Diagnosis in Psychiatric Practice: Is It Worth It?*, 14 J. Psychiatric Prac. 67, 68 (2008). Others have expressed concerns about the widespread use of polypharmacy in general, in part because of concerns about interactive effects and the ability to make needed modifications in treatment on a timely basis. See Kirsch, supra; Whitaker, supra.

During the 1990s, the FDA approved a number of new anti-psychotic drugs. Mossman, supra, at 1039. These new drugs (known as "novel" or "atypical" drugs) were initially believed to be at least as effective as conventional anti-psychotic drugs with a much reduced risk of negative side effects (such as tardive dyskinesia). Id. at 1040. The advent of these drugs caused much concern about potential malpractice liability for clinicians who continued to prescribe the conventional drugs. Id. at 1093. Subsequent studies have questioned the safety and enhanced effectiveness of this newer generation of drugs, with some calling for greater reliance on the older medications and others asserting that medications should be used less in general. See Kirsch, supra; Whitaker, supra. What impact should these shifting and diverse perspectives play in establishing the standard of care for treating a mental disorder?

7.   *Effect on the development of new treatment modalities.* Is there a danger that diversity in treatment will be stifled if the immunity normally provided by the respectable minority rule can be overridden by evidence that the challenged treatment is demonstratively less effective or safe on average than an alternative? What nature of evidence and degree of proof as to superiority in safety or efficacy should be required? Would this standard have been met in the *Osheroff* case?

8.   *Duty to refer.* What would be the implications for mental health professionals who are not physicians of a holding that the staff of Chestnut Lodge was negligent in not using antidepressants to treat Osheroff. Recall that non-physicians in almost all states do not have the legal authority to prescribe psychotropic medications. Would a finding that staff at Chestnut Lodge was negligent in not using psychotropic medication suggest that a non-physician dealing with a depressed client has a duty to refer the client to a physician so that the client may receive psychopharmacological treatment? Should this duty arise notwithstanding the fact that clinical depression covers a wide spectrum of impairment and its manifestations may vary over time? Would a physician who is not a psychiatrist have a duty to refer a patient who is not responding to a prescribed treatment to a mental health professional to take advantage of the greater mental health expertise of such professionals? Is the cost of the treatment or the individual's ability or willingness to pay for an alternative treatment provider relevant?

9.   *Treatment "beyond the pale".* Treatment techniques may be used that do not reach the level of a "respectable minority." This may occur either where the treatment is explicitly innovative in general, or where it is simply

the product of an idiosyncratic approach to addressing the problems of the client. Sometimes it may be a combination of the two. There are two earlier reported cases imposing liability on mental health professionals who used non-biologically based "innovative" therapy.

One such case was *Hammer v. Rosen*, 165 N.E.2d 756 (N.Y. 1960), where a psychiatrist, Dr. John Nathaniel Rosen, developed shortly after World War II a reputation for dramatic successes in the treatment of patients with schizophrenia. At the time, few treatment options were available for this population. To bridge the communication gap often faced with such patients, Dr. Rosen attempted to project himself in a manner that he asserted was necessary to establish mental contact and eventually rapport and trust, namely, as a "substitute protective parental figure." H. Newcomb Morse, *The Tort Liability of the Psychiatrist*, 18 Syracuse L. Rev. 691, 704 (1967). "In executing this technique, which of course was highly personalized, but which was consented to by the spouse, next of kin, or legal guardian of each patient, . . . Dr. Rosen might touch certain patients from time to time with differing degrees of force, depending upon the mental condition and needs of the patient." Id. at 704–07. In reversing the trial court's dismissal of the plaintiff's claim for malpractice, the appellate court held that in view of the "fantastic" (i.e., abnormal) nature of the treatment (the court found that Dr. Rosen "had beaten [the plaintiff] on a number of occasions"), the plaintiff's case could be submitted to the jury without any expert testimony that the treatment constituted malpractice. *Hammer*, 165 N.E.2d at 757. Significantly, no evidence was introduced at trial as to the reasonableness of this approach or its acceptance within the psychiatric profession. It is unclear how the case might ultimately have been decided had Dr. Rosen introduced such testimony or evidence that the therapy was viewed as promising by some segment of the psychiatric profession.

The use of "innovative" therapy also led to a finding of liability in *Abraham v. Zaslow* (San Francisco, Cnty. Sup. Ct. 1972) as reported in *The New York Times* and the *APA Monitor* (March 1973). See *$170,000 Damages Won for a Therapy Session*, N.Y. Times, July 5, 1972, at 27. The therapy in question was called "Rage Reduction Therapy or Z–Process." This involved breaking down the patient's resistance by applying extensive physical stimulation to an immobilized patient to reduce what had been diagnosed as a repressed compulsion to escape. The process was originally developed for autistic children, but Dr. Zaslow expanded its use to adults. At trial the plaintiff testified, "I was tortured, including choking, beating, holding and tying me down and sticking fingers in my mouth." Ralph Slovenko, *Psychiatry and Law* 428, n.39 (1973). The use of aversive conditioning with autistic children continues to be debated. See *Parents Seek Shock Treatment for Son*, CNN.com, Mar. 28, 2007. For an account of another "innovative" technique that was highly controversial and became the focus of litigation, see Myrna Oliver & E. Paul Bindram, *Father of Nude Psychotherapy*, L.A. Times, Jan. 8, 1998.

10. *Criminal liability for therapy "Beyond the Pale"*. The treatment provided by two unlicensed psychotherapists to a ten-year-old child who died in the course of their treatment resulted in a conviction for reckless child abuse in a 2001 Colorado case. The child was being treated for "reactive detachment disorder," which presumably involved a diagnosed inability to form loving relationships because of early trauma. As part of the treatment, the child was "wrapped in a sheet to simulate a womb while four adults pushed against her with pillows." The aim of the treatment was to have her "emerge 'reborn'" and able to bond with her adoptive mother. The child died of asphyxiation, leading to the charges and subsequent conviction. Publicity concerning the case resulted in the adoption by the Colorado legislature of a law outlawing "rebirthing" therapy. *Therapists Convicted of Abuse in Girl's Death During Treatment*, N.Y. Times, Apr. 21, 2001, at A–7.

Similarly, James Arthur Ray, a "self-help guru," was convicted of three counts of negligent homicide after a two-hour sweat lodge ceremony intended to be a rebirthing experience resulted in the deaths of three people and the hospitalization of eighteen others in 2009. The sweat lodge session, which was "intended to push people to conquer their limitations," was the culmination of a five day seminar for which participants paid as much as $10,000 and that offered "a menu of services like soul retrieval, vortex healing and dolphin energy healing." All of the participants had signed waivers warning that death was among the associated risks. At trial, the prosecution played a recording of Ray saying during the ceremony that "You will have to get to a point . . . where you surrender and it's O.K. to die." John Dougherty, *For Some Seeking Rebirth, Sweat Lodge Was End*, N.Y. Times, Oct. 22, 2009, at A1; Marc Lacey, *New Age Guru Guilty in Sweat Lodge Deaths*, N.Y. Times, June 23, 2011, at A16.

11. *Evolving standards governing innovative therapy*. Innovations play a significant role in health care as practitioners adapt standard protocols to match the treatment needs of their clients. Innovations are particularly likely to be viewed favorably when conventional treatments are largely ineffective and the need for care is great. At the same time, the development of a successful innovation can be highly rewarding for practitioners, creating the potential for a conflict-of-interests between their own interests and those of their clients.

Among mental health professionals with prescribing privileges, innovation is perhaps most likely to occur in conjunction with the off-label use of a medication. While initial approval for a specified use (after the medication has been tested for safety and efficacy) by the federal Food and Drug Administration (FDA) is necessary before such medications can be made available to the public, health care professionals with prescribing privileges—in recognition of their need and ability to innovate when treating patients—are not required to limit the use of a medication to the tested and approved usage. Indeed, medications are frequently employed for "off-label" purposes (i.e., uses extending beyond the FDA-approved drug label that supplies information regarding the safe and effective use of the drug as tested). While expected to take this information into account, these professionals are not exposed to liability for an off-label use as long as they have adhered to the applicable standard of care.

Off-label prescriptions are now an integral part of the modern practice of medicine, with estimates that as many as 40% to 60% of prescriptions are for off-label use, a usage that is also frequent in conjunction with mental health care. Nevertheless, the prescribing of medications for off-label uses, particularly for psychiatric uses, has generated considerable controversy and raises questions of possible exposure to liability should an adverse outcome result. Tracy Hampton, *Experts Weigh In on Promotion, Prescription of Off–Label Drugs*, 297 JAMA 683, 684 (2007) (finding that there was strong support for off-label uses of prescriptions for psychiatric purposes 4% of the time and limited or no support 96% of the time); David C. Radley et al., *Off–Label Prescribing Among Office–Based Physicians*, 166 Archives Internal Med. 1021 (2006); M. Maglione et al., *Off–Label Use of Atypical Antipsychotics: An Update* (Sept. 2011). This controversy has been especially pronounced with regard to the treatment of children and adolescents with psychiatric problems, where only a few psychotropic medications have been approved for use among individuals under the age of eighteen. See A. Rachel Camp, *A Mistreated Epidemic: State and Federal Failure to Adequately Regulate Psychotropic Medications Prescribed to Children in Foster Care*, 83 Temp. L. Rev. 369 (2011); Douglas Mossman & Jill L. Steinberg, *Promoting, Prescribing, and Pushing Pills: Understanding the Lessons of Antipsychotic Drug Litigation*, 13 Mich. St. U. J. Med. & L. 263 (2009); Judith G. Edersheim, *Off–Label Prescribing*, 26(4) Psychiatric Times (Apr. 14, 2009).

Should innovation be viewed more or less favorably when assessing the liability of a practitioner treating a mental health problem? What should be the key factors when assessing these liability claims? Should obtaining informed consent to an off-label use enhance or reduce liability when a mental health service is being provided? Should the off-label uses of medications for the treatment of psychiatric problems be more or less subject to liability? Should possible conflicts-of-interests be weighed more or less heavily in determining liability for off-label uses addressing mental disorders?

12. *Controversial psychotherapy.* Perhaps no form of psychotherapy in recent years has been as controversial as the technique known as Recovered Memory therapy (RM) (although considerable attention of late has also been given to "conversion" or "reparative" therapy, an effort to change the sexual orientation of gay clients; see Cheryl Wetzstein, *Gay 'Conversion' Treatment Faces Novel Court Challenge: Gay Clients Sue in N.J. Citing 'Consumer Fraud'*, Wash. Times (July 18, 2013)). Over an eight year span, starting in 1990, the use of RM led to 105 malpractice suits by former clients against their therapists. Of nine cases that went to trial, all resulted in a verdict for the plaintiff, while one settlement led to the payment of $10.2 million to the client and her family. Elizabeth F. Loftus, *The Price of Bad Memories*, 22 Skeptical Inquirer 22, 24 (1998) [hereinafter Loftus, *Price of Bad Memories*];

see also Allison Garton, *Reconciling the Incongruous Demands of Therapist–Patient Confidentiality and Falsely Accused Third–Parties*, 37 Cumb. L. Rev. 77 (2006–07). In all of these cases, the plaintiff alleged that the use of RM was not a legitimate form of therapy. The defense, on the other hand, generally took the position that RM was an innovative and state-of-the-art treatment for Multiple Personality Disorder. The section that follows provides a more detailed discussion of these cases and the issues they raised.

B. SELECTED MALPRACTICE ISSUES

1. Recovered Memory Therapy

a. *Prologue*

The idea that troubling childhood events may be repressed from consciousness and recalled through therapy has been a fundamental tenet of Freudian psychoanalytic theory. However, until the mid–1970s, the notion that childhood memories could be repressed served more as a theoretical abstraction than the central focus of a treatment regime. Its acceptance as a treatment technique by a committed minority of therapists is closely associated with diagnostic developments that gave special prominence to a disorder initially known as "Multiple Personality Disorder" (MPD), and later referred to as "Dissociative Identity Disorder." August Piper & Harold Merskey, *The Persistence of Folly: A Critical Examination of Dissociative Identity Disorder. Part I. The Excesses of an Improbable Concept*, 49 Can. J. Psychiatry 592–600 (2004).

Even before the mid–1970s there was some recognition within the psychiatric community that individuals might develop distinct multiple personalities, although this disorder was generally regarded as being fairly esoteric and rare. Nevertheless, it gained a certain prominence among the public as the result of a best-selling book, *The Three Faces of Eve*, which was followed by an award-winning movie of the same title. The disorder gained additional prominence with the 1973 publication of the highly publicized book, *Sybil*, which subsequently became a TV movie. Like Eve, Sybil would spontaneously lapse into multiple personalities, or "alters" (alternate personalities). Notwithstanding these popular depictions, the disorder was generally viewed by the psychiatric profession as extremely rare. A 1964 study of the medical literature up to that time yielded only six reported cases of the disorder.

However, by 1990 MPD had become a commonly diagnosed disorder. One estimate is that an MPD diagnosis was ascribed to 40,000 patients from 1985 to 1995. The factors leading to the increased use of this diagnosis have been outlined by one commentator:

> Until about 1975, there had been no M.P.D. specialty. Multiple-personality disorder had no separate listing in the American Psychiatric Association's "Diagnostic and Statistical Manual of

Mental Disorder," or D.S.M., the guidebook to diagnosis. But in 1980, after vigorous lobbying by interested therapists, the new edition of D.S.M. gave M.P.D. a primary-level listing among the dissociative disorders—conditions in which some part of mental functioning splits off from consciousness. In 1984, the new M.P.D. enthusiasts founded an organization of their own, the International Society for the Study of Multiple Personality and Dissociation . . . , and began holding annual conferences, co-sponsored by Rush–Presbyterian–St. Luke's Medical Center, in Chicago. That hospital subsequently set up the country's first dissociative-disorders unit, under the M.P.D. expert Bennett Braun. Other units followed. Between 1970 and 1990, the average annual output of publications on M.P.D. increased six thousand per cent.

Among those publications were two 1989 textbooks: "Diagnosis and Treatment of Multiple Personality Disorder," by Frank Putnam, and "Multiple Personality Disorder," by Colin Ross. Both offered treatment plans focusing on presumed childhood abuse. Using hypnosis, the therapist was instructed to flush out the alters and get them to divulge their secrets, a process that often involved protracted reenactments called "abreactions."

Joan Acocella, *The Politics of Hysteria*, The New Yorker, Apr. 6, 1998, at 66. MPD also gained prominence as a consequence of media attention.

[Throughout the 1980s] magazines and newspapers were retailing utterly credulous stories about M.P.D. And then there was television. Phil Donahue was apparently the first talk-show host to present a program on M.P.D.; he was followed by Sally Jessy Raphael, Larry King, Leeza Gibbons, and Oprah Winfrey. Meanwhile, celebrities were coming forward with tales of childhood abuse: Roseanne, La Toya Jackson, Oprah herself. Some claimed to be multiples. Roseanne, for example, had unearthed 21 personalities in herself, including Piggy, Bambi, and Fucker. M.P.D. experts also went on TV. Bennett Braun appeared on the Chicago evening news with his star patient, who switched personalities on camera. Again and again, on the talk shows it was stressed that M.P.D. was not rare, it was common.

Id. at 68.

MPD rests on the following set of fundamental assumptions: "[t]hat people routinely banish traumatic experiences from consciousness because they are too horrifying to contemplate; that these forgotten experiences cannot be recalled by any normal process but only by special techniques; that these techniques produce reliable recovery of memory; that before such recovery, these forgotten experiences cause miserable symptoms; that healing is possible only by digging out and reliving the forgotten experiences." See Elizabeth F. Loftus, *Memory Distortions and*

False Memory Creation, 24 Bull. Am. Acad. Psychiatry & L. 281, 283 (1996) [hereinafter, Loftus, *Memory Distortions*].

The recovery of early childhood memories, which is a central feature of MPD treatment, relies on a variety of techniques, such as "age regression and guided visualization"—where a client is talked through an imagined scene to awaken repressed memories. Repressed Memory (RM) therapy also frequently utilizes hypnosis and sodium amytal (truth serum) for the ostensible purpose of removing barriers to the recovery of forgotten or repressed experiences. The primary purpose of such therapeutic sessions is presumably to uncover traumatic childhood events, particularly those involving sexual abuse by an adult. Not infrequently, the offending adult is identified as a member of the client's family, most often a parent. Other less common "discovered" traumatic experiences include satanism, torture, ritual murder, and cannibalism.

The number of individuals who underwent RM therapy in the 1980s and 1990s cannot be estimated with any degree of certainty. It is clear, however, that a relatively small but energetic group of mental health professionals, including psychiatrists and psychologists, at one point subscribed to MPD and RM therapy. Moreover, the proposition that memories elicited under hypnosis are more accurate than non-hypnotic recall had fairly widespread support among mental health professionals.

For many individuals and their families, the effects of MPD therapy were devastating. Charges of sexual abuse by parents and other relatives were a common outcome of therapy. Litigation to recover damages caused by the sexual abuse that had been uncovered in the course of RM therapy became a fairly common phenomenon.

The tide changed, however, in the early 1990s as cases of false recall (and their devastating impact on parents and families) were publicized in professional journals and the media. A 1993 issue of the *Harvard Mental Health Letter* subsequently called for an immediate end to MPD treatment. The popular press followed suit with articles in magazines such as *Time* and exposés on television questioning the reliability of RM therapy. The controversy surrounding MPD soon made its way to the legal system with lawsuits filed by numerous former clients who asserted that their memories of sexual abuse had been falsely implanted by their therapists. By December of 1997, at least 105 former clients had filed malpractice suits against their therapists. See Loftus, *Price of Bad Memories*, supra, at 23–24. Overall, the plaintiffs in these cases prevailed; a verdict in favor of the plaintiffs was obtained in all of the nine cases that had come to trial by December of 1997, with forty-two resulting in settlements involving some payment of damages, and fifty-three still pending. Id. at 24. See also Lynn Neary, *Real 'Sybil' Admits Multiple Personalities Were Fake*, npr Books, Oct. 20, 2011.

b. Anatomy of a Recovered Memory Malpractice Law Suit

[The Facts set out below have been abstracted from various secondary sources and the plaintiffs' complaints in *Burgus v. Rush Presbyterian St. Luke's Med. Ctr. et al.* (Cir. Ct. Cook County, Ill., Nos. 91L8394 & 93L14050.)]

In early spring of 1986, Patricia Burgus was referred to the psychiatric trauma section of Rush–Presbyterian–St. Luke's Hospital in Chicago [hereinafter "St. Luke's"]. The basis for the referral was severe, postpartum depression. At the time, St. Luke's had established a dissociative-disorders unit headed by Dr. Bennett Braun.

Following her admission as a voluntary patient on March 5, 1986, Ms. Burgus—who was diagnosed as suffering from mental illness, including MPD—remained hospitalized for the next 27 months as a patient in the hospital's dissociative disorders program. According to her complaint, throughout her hospital stay, and in the three years she was treated as an outpatient following discharge in June of 1988, she received RM therapy in addition to various medications, including sedatives, hypnotics, and psychotropic drugs such as Inderal, Halcion, and Xanax.

The RM treatment regime that Burgus underwent involved the use of techniques intended to bring to the surface "repressed memories." Aided by hypnosis, she developed numerous "alters" (alternate personalities), which led her to uncover supposedly "repressed memories," including membership in a satanic cult, abuse by numerous men during childhood, abuse of her children, and cannibalism.

Approximately one week following Ms. Burgus' hospitalization, she and her husband were asked to agree to the psychiatric hospitalization (also at St. Luke's) of their two children, John and Mikey, who at the time of their admission were four and five years old, respectively. In the course of their hospitalization, which lasted approximately three years, the children were subjected to various therapies, including extensive psychotropic medication and psychotherapy that relied in part on RM techniques. The complaint alleged that in some sessions the children were "encouraged" to develop "alter" personalities and were exposed to suggestive techniques, such as being shown handguns and handcuffs.

During her treatment, Ms. Burgus apparently accepted various recovered memories of traumatic events as true. But she eventually concluded that the memories were false and had been implanted by her psychiatrist in the course of treatment, which on occasion involved hypnosis. She subsequently filed a lawsuit against St. Luke's, Dr. Braun, and another psychiatrist who had treated her and her two sons. Her complaint alleged misdiagnosis and lack of due care in the selection and application of treatment. She also alleged a lack of informed consent to the treatment, namely, that she had not been informed of the risks and the psychiatric trauma associated with RM therapy.

A separate complaint on behalf of the children alleged that while both children were diagnosed as suffering from MPD, neither child was in fact afflicted with this disorder. The complaint further alleged that neither child suffered from any kind of disorder for which psychiatric hospitalization for three years was medically justified.

The plaintiffs' claims for damages included medical expenses in excess of $2.8 million, lost earnings resulting from a permanent disability caused by the failed therapy, and unspecified damages for mental suffering.

In defending against Ms. Burgus' lawsuit, Dr. Braun asserted that the memories had not been implanted but were generated by the patient herself. He stated: "She just spit it out . . . all of the cult stuff that she was talking about I learned from her. The idea to bring the meat in was hers. I merely said if he [her husband] does bring it in, I will try to get it analyzed for human protein [for the purpose of establishing whether it was human flesh]. Yes, the kids did see the handcuffs. They did see a gun. But it was for therapeutic reasons." See Pam Belluck, *'Memory' Therapy Leads to a Lawsuit and Big Settlement*, N.Y. Times, Nov. 6, 1997, at A1.

The Burgus case was settled shortly before it was scheduled to go to trial. Under the terms of the settlement, Patricia Burgus and her two children received $10.6 million from the insurance companies of the two psychiatrists and St. Luke's hospital. After the settlement, which Dr. Braun opposed, both psychiatrists denied any malpractice. Dr. Elva Poznanski, the section chief of child and adolescent psychiatry, was quoted as saying: "On the basis of the knowledge available at that time, I would not change the treatment of these boys." Id. Dr. Braun called the settlement "a travesty" and contended: "A patient comes into the hospital doing so bad that she belongs in the hospital, and after several serious events in the hospital which I can't disclose because of patient confidentiality, she was discharged and is doing much better. . . . Where's the damage?" Id.

c.   *Legal Issues Raised by MPD Litigation Cases*

i.   *MPD as a Diagnostic Category*

A threshold question relates to the validity of MPD as a diagnostic category. Arguably, if the diagnostic category is flawed—in the sense that the primary characteristics ascribed to the disorder are unfounded—its use in diagnosis may not be warranted and constitutes a deviation from the standard of care. There appears to be some consensus among the psychiatric profession that in rare cases an individual may suffer from a disorder characterized by the manifestation of distinct alternate personalities, although it has been said that "it rarely occurs spontaneously and therefore does not deserve to be a primary-level diagnosis." Acocella, supra, at 71. Instead, "[l]ike the majority of psychiatric patients, people diagnosed with M.P.D. tend to be 'co-morbid'; that is, they meet the diagnostic criteria for more than one disorder." Id. at 72. Some have therefore questioned whether therapists are justified in labeling a patient as suffering from MPD when the dominant symptomology is chronic depression or a borderline personality disorder.

The primary significance of mislabeling a diagnosis is that it is likely to trigger the selection of an inappropriate therapy, which either harms the client or fails to improve the client's condition. For instance, assigning an MPD diagnosis to a client whose major symptomology is depression may constitute a departure from the standard of care, particularly if the subsequent treatment is inappropriate for a person suffering from depression.

ii. Methods of Treatment

Even more controversial than the diagnosis of MPD are the methods advocated for treating it, such as flushing out "alters" for the purpose of having them reveal their secrets. As noted, RM treatment rests on several assumptions, which include (1) a client's psychopathology, and specifically MPD, is caused by trauma and in most cases sexual abuse during childhood; (2) traumatic events are frequently repressed; (3) repressed trauma can be brought to the surface by the use of various techniques, including "abreaction" (a process involving a reenactment of prior events), regressed memory processes, and hypnosis; (4) memories elicited by hypnosis or the application of sodium amytal have a high likelihood of being accurate; and (5) the recovery of forgotten traumatic experiences can provide relief from the symptoms associated with MPD.

Successful plaintiffs in malpractice actions against therapists for the use of RM therapy have been able to establish a lack of due care through expert testimony that challenges the scientific validity of several of the assumptions underlying RM. For instance, one leading expert has written, "there is no cogent scientific support for this repression folklore, and an ample reason to believe that extraordinarily suggestive prolonged searches for hidden memories can be harmful. . . . This is not to say that people cannot forget horrible things that have happened to them; most certainly they can. But there is virtually no extensive histories of abuse of which they are completely unaware. Yet an unfounded faith in the repressed memory ideology has led some clinicians to engage in practices that are risky if not dangerous in terms of their potential for creating false beliefs and memories." Loftus, *Memory Distortions*, at 282–83. See also Elizabeth F. Loftus, *Creating False Memories*, Sci. Am., Sept. 1997, at 71.

Successful cases have also challenged the reliability of memories elicited through hypnosis. In this regard, plaintiffs have relied on a body of research indicating that post-event information often becomes incorporated into memory, supplementing or altering a person's recollection. Wendy J. Kisch, *From the Couch to the Bench: How Should the Legal System Respond to Recovered Memories of Childhood Sexual Abuse?*, 5 Am. U. J. Gender & L. 207, 222 (1996). Evidence that hypnotically induced recall is not necessarily reliable has in turn allowed plaintiffs to argue that the therapist's misrepresentations to the client concerning the accuracy of recalled memories constitutes a departure from the standard of care.

Additionally, plaintiffs in various cases have been able to establish that the recalled memories are not only inherently unreliable, but moreover they were distorted by suggestions planted by the therapists. Again, evidence to this effect has allowed plaintiffs to assert that the therapist's misrepresentation of the accuracy of these recalled memories constituted malpractice. It has been asserted that a "great majority" of the courts that have addressed the issue "have refused to acknowledge the validity of repressed and recovered memory." August Piper et al., *Custer's Last Stand: Brown, Scheflin' and Whitfield's Latest Attempt to Salvage "Dissociative Amnesia"*, 28 J. Psychiatry & L. 149 (2000).

QUESTIONS AND COMMENTS

1. *Other RM cases.* Cases involving RM malpractice claims continue to reach the courts. See, e.g., Doug Erickson, *Parents Awarded $1 Million in Suit Claiming Therapists Created False Memories of Abuse*, Wis. State J., Jan. 23, 2011 (lawsuit claimed therapists created false memories in plaintiffs' daughter during therapy in the early 1990s, with the couple accused of being Satanists and incest perpetrators; the defense argued the therapists did not implant the daughter's memories and merely sought to get to the bottom of her problems and probably saved her life as a result; the daughter has not had contact with her parents since 1993 and opposed the lawsuit).

2. *Application of the respectable minority rule.* Would the respectable minority rule discussed above in Part II.A.2.b. be available to a therapist defending a malpractice action involving the use of RM therapy? Does RM therapy have a sufficient scientific foundation to qualify for the respectable minority rule? Is the rule—in those jurisdictions where it is applied—limited to where the therapist considers several possible therapies and where the one selected has the potential to effectively treat the disorder? Is RM therapy sufficiently effective to qualify for this defense?

3. *Impact of RM litigation.* The series of successful lawsuits against therapists employing RM therapy had a number of consequences. In 1993, the American Psychiatric Association issued a circular to its members in which it cautioned that memories obtained through RM techniques are often not true and that memories obtained under hypnosis may be unreliable. In

1998, *Dissociation*, a journal dedicated to work written about dissociative disorders, ceased publication. Piper & Merskey, supra, at 592. Also, a number of specialized psychiatric units established to treat Dissociative Disorders closed, including Dr. Braun's unit at St. Luke's. Id. Further, the MPD diagnosis was removed from the DSM in 1994 with the publication of the *DSM–IV* and replaced with the diagnosis of "Dissociative Identity Disorder," although it has been asserted that there is considerable overlap between the two. According to one commentator, this change reflects the desire of the psychiatric profession to "shake off the scandal" associated with MPD. Acocella, supra, at 76. Moreover, criticism of the diagnosis has continued with assertions made that many psychiatrists question this diagnosis. Piper et al., supra, at 149; see also Piper & Merskey, supra, at 592.

4.   *Changes in malpractice insurance coverage.* The legal liability associated with RM therapy has caused some insurance malpractice carriers to exclude or otherwise limit coverage of therapy involving the use of hypnosis. Such exclusions have the effect of limiting a client's choices regarding therapy. Are such exclusions appropriate and, if so, under what circumstances?

5.   *Legislative proposals.* At one point, efforts to curb abuses resulting from therapies such as RM led to some legislative initiatives. One proposal called for the adoption by state legislatures and Congress of a "Truth and Responsibility in Mental Health Practices Act." The proposed text read: "No tax or tax exempt monies may be used for any form of health care treatment, including any form of psychotherapy, that has not been proven safe and effective by rigorous, valid and reliable scientific investigations and accepted as safe and effective by a substantial majority of the relevant scientific community." Acocella, supra, at 78. If such a proposal were adopted, how would the legislation be implemented and which entity would be empowered to determine whether a particular psychotherapy is "safe and effective?" Is the effectiveness of psychotherapy amenable to being validated by reliable scientific investigation? See also *N.J. State Assembly Passes Ban on 'Conversion Therapy' for Gay Youth*, CBS New York News (June 24, 2013).

6.   *Rights of third parties to maintain a legal action.* The rights of *third* parties falsely accused of abuse during RM therapy to bring a cause of action against the therapist involved is treated infra Part II.C.2. That section focuses on the case *Ramona v. Ramona*, No. Civ. 61898 (Sup. Ct. Napa Cnty., Cal. 1994), which is one of the first successful lawsuits brought by a third party (the father of the client) against a therapist who employed RM treatment.

7.   *Risk of immediate harm versus long-term benefit.* As indicated in the introduction to this chapter, most malpractice lawsuits against mental health professionals have targeted the use of biological therapies such as medication and ECT. Only rarely (see, e.g., *Osheroff v. Chestnut Lodge Inc.*, discussed infra Part II.A.2.) have therapists faced malpractice claims where *psychotherapy* was the treatment of choice. What then explains the volume of litigation focused on RM therapy (105 malpractice actions initiated between

1988 and 1998)? Is it because, unlike psychotherapy generally, RM treatment can be very distressing not only for the client but also for those linked to the repressed memories and this distress is due to the actions of the therapist? At what point should a psychotherapist refrain from exploring an underlying problem with a client for fear that it may cause more harm than good? Does it matter that the harm is likely to be relatively immediate, while any benefit is uncertain and likely only to occur in the future? It should be noted that a mental health professional employing a biological therapy may similarly have to weigh the risk of immediate harm from side effects against the more long-term and oftentimes uncertain beneficial effects of treatment.

8. *Client law suits against "discovered" abusers.* RM therapy has led some clients to initiate lawsuits against parents, relatives, and neighbors, alleging sexual abuse during their childhood. Typically, the events upon which such suits are based were repressed or disassociated until therapeutic intervention brought the repressed memories to the surface. In some instances, such suits have been based on events that occurred many years earlier, which can preclude their pursuit under a jurisdiction's statute of limitations. See Loftus, *Memory Distortions*. Some legislatures have facilitated the bringing of such suits by changing their statute of limitations so that the statute does not begin to run until a plaintiff has discovered the facts essential to the cause of action. Id. at 282. As a result, "[h]undreds of civil plaintiffs have now taken advantage of [the modified statute of limitations] . . . and brought suits in which they claim that their memories surfaced in therapy." Id. at 282. According to one report, however, "[a]s the suits against therapists multiplied, suits against the alleged abusers receded and those that were filed did not fare well." Acocella, supra, at 76.

Nevertheless, cases continue to be pursued based on the asserted validity of RM. See *Doe v. Archdiocese of St. Paul & Minneapolis*, 801 N.W.2d 203 (Minn. Ct. App. 2011) (holding plaintiff should have been allowed to present expert testimony describing memory repression and the characteristics present in an individual suffering from repressed memory in his recovered memory lawsuit against the Archiodiocese for personal injury and fraud); Sean O'Sullivan, *Jury Faults Delaware Parish in Sex Abuse: Ex–Priest, St. Elizabeth Must Pay $30 Million*, The News J., Dec. 2, 2010 ("The jury found evidence, under a 'repressed memory' theory, that [the plaintiff] only became aware of much of the sexual abuse he suffered as a child in 2007 after reading an article in The News Journal about a different priest sex abuse case . . . , meaning his case fell within the standard statute of limitations for such civil claims.").

9. *Criminal prosecution of "discovered" abusers.* The questionable validity and reliability of recovered memories has caused particular concern when identified abusive individuals face related criminal charges, in part because of the heightened standard of proof associated with criminal cases. The Second Circuit issued an opinion in which it provided a lengthy discourse, with extensive citations, expressing its concerns about these cases.

While the law may require us to deny relief in this case, it does not compel us to do so without voicing some concern regarding the process by which the petitioner's conviction was obtained. The magnitude of the allegations against petitioner must be viewed in the context of the late–1980's and early–1990's, a period in which allegations of outrageously bizarre and often ritualistic child abuse spread like wildfire across the country and garnered world-wide media attention. . . .

Vast moral panic fueled a series of highly-questionable child sex abuse prosecutions. [ ] By 1991, for example, 25 percent of prosecutors had handled at least one case involving satanic abuse. [ ] Although many of these cases included "fantastical accusations," such as those of satanic abuse—a strand of accusations which has been discredited entirely—others involved allegations of real and serious crimes committed in an impossible manner. . . .

Overall, at least seventy-two individuals were convicted in nearly a dozen major child sex abuse and satanic ritual prosecutions between 1984 and 1995, although almost all the convictions have since been reversed. [ ] Some defendants, fearing trial, pled guilty or "no contest" to impossible acts of ritualistic abuse, and in some cases they provided detailed confessions in exchange for immunity or generous plea bargains. [ ] Many have described these widespread prosecutions as a modern-day "witch hunt." [ ]

These prosecutions were largely based on memories that alleged victims "recovered" through suggestive memory recovery tactics, including those petitioner claims were used in this case. Indeed, the dramatic increase in conspiratorial charges of child sexual abuse has been traced to a relatively small group of clinical psychologists who supported the psychoanalytic notion of "repressed memories" and encouraged patients to employ extensive "memory recovery procedures" to "break through the barrier of repression and bring memories into conscious awareness." [ ] Popular memory recovery procedures included hypnosis, age regression, dream interpretation, guided abuse-related imagery, use of photographs to trigger memories, journaling, and interpretation of symptoms as implicit memories. [ ] These procedures and others commonly employed have great potential to induce false memories. [ ] . . . The prevailing view is that the vast majority of traumatic memories that are recovered through the use of suggestive recovery procedures are false, and that almost all—if not all—of the recovered memories of horrific abuse from the late–1980's and early–1990's were false.

Moreover, many highly-publicized and large-scale investigations into alleged child abuse conspiracies were also accompanied by a variety of interviewing techniques designed to assist children in recalling abuse—techniques which an extensive body of research suggests can induce false reports. [ ] . . . Scholars have suggested that each interviewing technique can induce false reports on its own. . . . But the techniques have their greatest impact in combination. . . .

Finally, once individuals "recovered" memories of abuse or otherwise labeled themselves victims of abuse, they were generally encouraged to participate in various activities on an individual and community level to reinforce and develop existing memories of abuse. [ ] There, proponents of recovered memories advised alleged victims to expand on existing memories through suggestive memory recovery procedures (both in and out of therapy), participation in survivor groups, and solicitation of consistent information from others, "all with significant potential both to bias construction of historical narratives and to lead to confabulation of false memories." [ ] When allegations of abuse span an entire community, these activities can provide an outlet for community reinforcement—an outlet which can . . . foster the collective growth of increasingly inaccurate memories.

Friedman v. Rehal, 618 F.3d 142, 155–57 (2d Cir. 2010).

10. *Criminal prosecutions of RM therapists.* Although relatively rare, litigation involving RM therapists has not been confined to the civil courts. In 1998, federal authorities in Houston obtained a sixty-count criminal indictment against the administrator and four mental health professionals of the former Spring Shadows Glen Hospital. See *United States v. Peterson et al.*, No. Civ. H97–237 (S.D. Tex. 1998). The professionals named in the indictment—including two psychiatrists, a doctoral-level psychologist, and a psychiatric social worker—were charged with "exaggerating diagnosis" and overstating the need for expensive treatment to unjustly collect insurance payments. According to the indictment, the defendants were part of a conspiracy that "did fraudulently treat the insured patients for MPD caused by unsubstantiated and unrealistic allegations and abuses, including satanic ritual abuse and cult activity, while at the same time creating medical records to substantiate such treatment." Additionally, the indictment alleged that the defendants "did fraudulently elicit statements of satanic ritual abuse and cult activities from the admitted patients, through nontraditional treatment modalities, including the use of leading or suggestive questions during therapy sessions while the patients were: under hypnosis; under the influence of a drug or combination of drugs; isolated from their families, friends, and the outside world . . . " See Mark Smith, *Mental Health Workers Fear Indictments' Impact*, Hous. Chron., Oct. 30, 1997, at 1.

Following the indictments, the International Society for the Study of Dissociative Disorders issued a news release that asserted the indictments would have a "chilling effect" on health care delivery and indicate the federal government's willingness to set standards for diagnosis and treatment and to decide which patient memories are "accurate." Id.

The jury trial began on September 8, 1998, and continued for five months until February 9, 1999, when the judge declared a mistrial due to an insufficient number of remaining jurors to continue the trial without the agreement of all the parties. On March 1, 1999, the prosecutor moved to dismiss the indictment, a motion that was granted. *United States v. Peterson*, 71 F. Supp. 2d 695 (S.D. Tex. 1999).

2.   Liability for the Suicide of a Client

One of the more vexing issues concerns the liability of a therapist when a client commits suicide. Suicidal impulses may have been one of the prime reasons why the client was in therapy. When a client receiving treatment commits suicide, the next-of-kin may file a lawsuit in which it is asserted that the therapist's actions constituted malpractice. For instance, it may be argued that the therapy employed was an improper response to the client's therapeutic needs. Thus, it may be asserted that the client entered therapy professing suicidal impulses, which was coupled with depression, and the therapist failed to prescribe antidepressant medication. Liability might also arise from a failure to take appropriate precautions, such as properly monitoring the patient's condition or instituting civil commitment.

In general, a therapist's "inaction" is the most problematic in terms of assigning liability. One reason is that suicide prediction is notoriously unreliable. Various studies have shown that suicide tends to be grossly overpredicted, resulting in numerous "false positives," i.e., predictions that individuals will attempt to commit suicide, when in fact they do not. But there is also often a lack of warning signs associated with individuals who do commit suicide. See Martin Blinder, *Suicide, Psychiatric Malpractice, and the Bell Curve*, 32 J. Am. Acad. Psychiatry L. 319 (2004). Additionally, the invocation of civil commitment or other interventions by a therapist after a client has disclosed suicidal ideas can rupture the client-therapist relationship, which relies on trust, making it less likely that the therapist will be in a position thereafter to provide effective treatment.

These considerations have made courts hesitant to assign liability in those instances when it is contended that a client's suicide resulted from the therapist's failure to take some affirmative action, such as initiating commitment. *Weathers v. Pilkinton*, which follows, illustrates this trend, although the specific rule used by the court to limit liability—that suicide is, as a matter of law, an independent intervening event—is not universally accepted.

WEATHERS V. PILKINTON
Court of Appeals of Tennessee, 1988.
754 S.W.2d 75.

Opinion

CANTRELL, JUDGE.

In this action for wrongful death against a doctor who allegedly failed to take the proper steps to prevent his patient from taking his own life, the trial judge held that the suicide of the [decedent] was an independent intervening cause and directed a verdict for the defendant. We affirm, on a related, although slightly different, ground.

*   *   *

[The decedent, Michael Weathers, was married in 1982 at the age of 27. His wife gave birth to a son a year later. He made the first overt reference to his death during an argument with his wife on Christmas day of 1983, when he pulled a gun from a drawer and asked her to shoot him. Three months later, after another argument with his wife, he entered a psychiatric hospital as a voluntary patient, and remained in treatment there for two months. Four months later, in August 1984, the decedent and his wife separated. Two weeks later, he took an overdose of codeine, which did not prove fatal. Some weeks later, he again had an argument with his wife, and again, asked her to kill him. This episode was followed by a two-week psychiatric hospitalization coupled with medication.

On September 14, the decedent took an overdose of Elavil and was again admitted to a regional hospital under the care of Dr. Pilkinton, a general physician. He was discharged eight days later, but was readmitted on November 10, 1984, after taking another overdose of drugs and leaving a suicide note. He was taken unconscious to the hospital, but upon his insistence he was released the next morning. Upon his release, he was urged by Dr. Pilkinton to enter outpatient therapy at a local community mental health clinic. For the next three weeks, the decedent seemed in a reasonably good mood, and was able to resume his employment. However, on November 28, after coming home from work, he called his wife and informed her that he intended to shoot himself. He carried out his threat before the arrival of the police, who had been summoned by his wife.]

*   *   *

The plaintiff, Ellen Weathers, brought this action against Dr. Pilkinton. The complaint contains two counts. The first count is for the wrongful death [of her husband]. . . . The second count is for the tort of outrageous conduct and is brought on behalf of Mrs. Weathers personally. Under the first count the plaintiff alleged that the negligence of Dr. Pilkinton was the proximate cause of Mr. Weathers' death.

At the trial the plaintiff presented two expert witnesses. They testified that to fulfill the standard of care in effect in the Nashville area, Dr. Pilkinton should have committed Mr. Weathers involuntarily on November 11, 1984 and should have ordered a psychiatric evaluation of Mr. Weathers after the three recent suicide attempts. In addition the experts testified that it was a mistake for Dr. Pilkinton to order Mr. Weathers to return to Luton Mental Health Center for outpatient care since his previous experience there had proved unsuccessful. Finally, each expert testified that in his opinion Dr. Pilkinton's negligence was the proximate cause of Mr. Weathers' death.

At the close of the plaintiff's proof the trial judge directed a verdict in favor of Dr. Pilkinton on both counts. On the negligence count the trial judge held that Mr. Weathers' suicide was an intervening intentional act that proximately caused his death. (Therefore, assuming that Dr. Pilkinton deviated from the standard of care, his negligence could not constitute the proximate cause of the death of Mr. Weathers.) On the second count, the trial judge held that there was simply no evidence of an intentional infliction of emotional distress on Mrs. Weathers which is a necessary element of the tort of outrageous conduct.

The Outrageous Conduct Action

We affirm the directed verdict on the outrageous conduct count. . . .

The facts of this case simply do not warrant a finding that Dr. Pilkinton's conduct was outrageous nor a finding that as a result of his conduct Mrs. Weathers suffered the type of severe emotional distress that is a necessary element of the tort.

The Wrongful Death Action

* * *

There is evidence in the record from which the jury might find that Dr. Pilkinton was negligent in treating Mr. Weathers. . . .

If there is evidence from which the jury could have concluded that Dr. Pilkinton was negligent, the sole remaining question is whether there is evidence from which the jury could have concluded that the alleged negligence of Dr. Pilkinton was the proximate cause of the death of the decedent. As our Supreme Court said in *Lancaster v. Montesi* (1965), the cases in this jurisdiction and elsewhere have generally held that an act of suicide breaks the chain of causation unless the decedent's reason and memory were so far obscured that he did not know and understand what he was doing and was not therefore a responsible human agency. . . .

The court quoted the following excerpt from *Daniels v. New York, N.H. & H.R. Co.* (1903): "An act of suicide resulting from a moderately intelligent power of choice, even though the choice is determined by a disordered mind, should be deemed a new and independent, efficient cause of the death that immediately ensues."

From this line of cases we conclude that where a defendant injures another either wilfully or negligently and as a result of the injury, the injured person commits suicide the act of suicide is, as a matter of law, an intervening independent cause if the decedent knew and understood the nature of his or her act or the act resulted from a moderately intelligent power of choice.

The appellant does not contest the rule established in . . . *Lancaster,* but instead argues that there is a different rule where the decedent is under the care of a health care provider and consequently the health care provider has a specific duty of care to the patient. We acknowledge that there is a difference and—since proximate cause is based on forseeability—that the fact that mentally ill persons might take their lives if adequate precautions are not taken to protect them from themselves is more forseeable than the fact that a person injured by an ordinary act of negligence might become so depressed that suicide would result.

However, we must recognize that this is still an action for wrongful death and the right that survives to the widow is the same cause of action the decedent would have had had he survived. Thus, if the decedent could not have sued no right survives.

*   *   *

The rule is otherwise, of course, where the decedent did not know the nature or consequences of his act, or his reason and memory [were], at the time, so far obscured that he did not know and understand what he was doing and was therefore not a responsible human agency. Under those circumstances the act of suicide would not be a wilful, calculated, deliberate act that would defeat an action for wrongful death.

Therefore, we are of the opinion that the result in this case turns on the question of whether there is evidence in the record from which the jury might conclude that on the date of his death Mr. Weathers did not know and understand the nature of his suicidal act and, therefore, did not have a wilful and intelligent purpose to accomplish it. The only evidence in the record tending to show that Mr. Weathers did not know and understand the nature of his acts on November 28, 1984 is the circumstantial evidence of his history of depression, his treatment, and his prior suicide attempts. Neither of the medical experts who testified on behalf of the plaintiff testified that Mr. Weathers was bereft of reason or that he did not know and understand what he was doing.

On the other hand, the overwhelming evidence shows that from November 11 until November 28, 1984, Mr. Weathers functioned normally and lived an unremarkable life. Viewing the evidence in the light most favorable to the plaintiff, we are of the opinion that there is no evidence from which the jury could conclude that Mr. Weathers was, on November 28, 1984, in such a state of anxiety or depression that he did not know what he was doing. Therefore, the trial judge was correct in directing a verdict for the defendant.

The judgment of the court below is affirmed.

TATUM, SPECIAL JUDGE, dissenting:

I agree with the majority in the dismissal of the outrageous conduct action, but must respectfully dissent from the majority opinion affirming the action of the Trial Court in directing a verdict for the defendant in the negligence action. In my view, a jury question was presented.

I agree with the majority that there was evidence of negligence on the part of the defendant. I disagree that such negligence could not be found by a jury to be the proximate cause of the death of the decedent. . . .

The history of the previous attempts of the decedent to commit suicide is strong evidence that he was afflicted with a mental illness that caused suicidal compulsions. It was for this reason that the decedent was placed in the care of the defendant, a health provider. It was the duty of the defendant to attempt to prevent the decedent from committing suicide.

In *Adams v. Carter County Memorial Hospital* (Tenn.1977), our Supreme Court cited, with apparent approval, a treatise in 24 Vanderbilt Law Review, 217 (1971) entitled "Civil Liability for Causing Suicide: A Synthesis of Law and Psychiatry." I quote from this treatise:

> Hospitals and psychiatrists with an affirmative duty to prevent their patients from committing suicide. . . .

> First, it seems clear that liability could be imposed upon a psychiatrist for a gross error in judgment with respect to whether a patient should be confined. Giving full ambit to psychological justifications for not confining patients unless absolutely necessary, suicidal symptoms may be so apparent that confinement would be ordered by a psychiatrist of ordinary skill. For example, if an individual has made serious suicidal attempts, has been deeply depressed, has suffered loss of sleep, appetite, and in effect is almost unable to function in society, but his psychiatrist has declined to have him placed in a hospital, the psychiatrist might be held liable for the individual's subsequent suicide.

* * *

I also agree with the New Jersey Superior Court in *Cowan v. Doering* (1987). In that case, a physician admitted a depressed patient to intensive care, who had taken an overdose of sleeping pills. The physician failed to take suicidal precautions. The patient subsequently attempted suicide by jumping from the hospital window. At trial, the physician took the position that the patient understood and appreciated the consequences of her acts and therefore her suicidal attempt was an independent intervening cause. In rejecting this defense and upholding a jury verdict, the New Jersey court stated:

Observation has particular efficacy where, as here, the duty of the physician and the hospital encompasses the responsibility to safeguard the patient from the reasonably foreseeable risk of self-inflicted harm.

We find no sound reason to adopt the sterile and unrealistic approach that if a disabled plaintiff is not totally incompetent, he is fully legally accountable for his own negligence. In view of the present state of medical knowledge, it is possible and practical to evaluate the degrees of mental acuity and correlate them with legal responsibility. In our view, a patient known to harbor suicidal tendencies whose judgment has been blunted by a mental disability should not have his conduct measured by external standards applicable to a normal adult. Where it is reasonably foreseeable that a patient by reason of his mental or emotional illness may attempt to injure himself, those in charge of his care owe a duty to safeguard him from his self-damaging potential. This duty contemplates the reasonably forseeable occurrence of self-inflicted injury regardless of whether it is the product of the patient's volitional or negligent act.

*   *   *

In my view, suicide is not an intervening independent cause that will relieve a physician of liability or negligence when the patient had no power of choice. There was evidence in this case that the decedent acted with compulsion and not through a power of choice. . . . As stated, the history of the decedent's previous attempts to commit suicide is circumstantial evidence sufficient to make a jury question as to whether the suicide was committed by "intelligent power of choice" or by compulsion due to mental illness. I repeat that this suicidal tendency or compulsion was specifically the ailment which the defendant was entrusted to treat.

*   *   *

I have a high respect for the opinions of my colleagues. However, I would reverse the judgment of the trial court and remand the case for trial on the negligence issue.

QUESTIONS AND COMMENTS

1. *Suicide as an independent intervening cause.* The majority in *Weathers* held that suicide is an independent intervening cause unless the patient "did not know and understand the nature of his suicidal act and, therefore, did not have willful and intelligent purpose to accomplish this." Would this include or exclude an individual suffering from a Major Depressive Disorder with Psychotic Features whose basic motivation for suicide is a feeling of worthlessness and a pessimistic attitude about the future? If such an individual is held to "understand the nature of his suicidal

act," would it not preclude liability even when the individual is being treated specifically to minimize the risk of suicide?

2. *Liability for the suicide of outpatients.* The common law rule adopted in part by the court in *Weathers* (limiting a therapist's liability for a patient's suicide on the basis that suicide is an independent intervening event) may be losing favor. An emerging view is illustrated by *Kockelman v. Segal*, 71 Cal. Rptr. 2d 552 (Cal. Ct. App. 1998). In reversing the granting of defendant's motion for summary judgment by the trial court, the appellate court explained the contemporary approach to the liability of a treating therapist in the following terms:

> Defendants' summary judgment was based upon the single claim that as a matter of law a psychiatrist owes no duty of care to an outpatient who may be suicidal. . . . Under traditional tort law principles, a person is not ordinarily liable for the actions of another and is under no duty to protect another person from harm. An affirmative duty to protect another from harm may arise, however, where a "special relationship" exists. Such a special relationship is typically where the plaintiff is particularly vulnerable and dependent upon the defendant who, correspondingly, has some control over the plaintiff's welfare. "[T]he relationship between a therapist and his patient satisfies this requirement . . . " (*Tarasoff v. Regents of University of California* (1976)).

> . . . Existing case law provides that a psychotherapist or other mental health care provider has a duty to use a reasonable degree of skill, knowledge and care in treating a patient, commensurate with that possessed and exercised by others practicing within that specialty in the professional community. "If those who are caring for and treating mentally disturbed patients know of facts from which they could reasonably conclude that the patient would be likely to self-inflict harm in the absence of preventative measures, then those caretakers must use reasonable care under the circumstances to prevent such harm from occurring."

This emerging view can also be seen in *Winger v. Franciscan Med. Ctr.*, 701 N.E.2d 813, 819 (Ill. App. Ct. 1998):

> We disagree with *Weathers*. Despite the fact that a patient is not bereft of reason and may appreciate the consequences of his actions, we recognize the fact that there are varying degrees of mental affectation. Although a patient may be in full understanding of his actions, an illness may still exist for which treatment has been requested and admission sought. . . . Rather than absolve the physician of liability when self-destructive conduct is reasonably foreseeable, the better approach is to require reasonable precautions in light of the special relationship between the physician and his patient.

See also *Stepakoff v. Kantar* (1985), which is set out above, holding the psychiatrist liable for the suicide of a client who was being treated on an outpatient basis. See also Murray, supra, at 641 ("failure to prevent suicide is one of the leading causes for malpractice suits against mental health care providers. . . . While many jurisdictions have found that a psychiatrist does owe a duty of care to his patient, they have not been consistent in deciding whether the partial defenses of contributory negligence or comparative fault can be applied. . . . [T]he duty should be imposed in limited situations. . . . [B]ecause of the inability of many mentally ill patients to appreciate the significance of their actions, the court should adopt . . . a reduced capacity standard for determining the fault of mentally ill patients."); Judy Regan et al., *Liability for Outpatient Suicide in Tennessee*, Tenn. Med. 40, 40 (May 2006) ("The law is clearly evolving toward imposing liability on physicians for their negligent acts or omissions in treating outpatients who present a foreseeable risk of suicide or other self-harm.").

3. *Liability for the suicide of hospitalized patients.* In the case of individuals who are hospitalized because of suicidal tendencies and who subsequently commit suicide while in the facility, courts have generally rejected the proximate cause limitation that some jurisdictions apply when the patient was being treated as an outpatient, because of the greater level of control and supervision available to the therapist. In the case of institutionalized individuals, courts have generally held that both proximate cause and contributory or comparative negligence are issues to be decided by the jury. Thus, the key issue in these cases is whether the risk of suicide was reasonably foreseeable and whether the care and treatment by the institution and treating staff conformed to the standard of care. The legal principles applicable to cases of this type were expounded by the court in *Winger v. Franciscan Med. Ctr.*, 701 N.E.2d 813 (Ill. App. Ct. 1998). In explaining why the proximate cause limitation is not applicable when the individual was institutionalized, the court noted:

> This is an action asserting psychiatric malpractice and the failure to properly supervise; it is different from general medical malpractice actions because the negligence is not in the diagnosis or treatment but, rather, it is in the failure to carefully protect a patient from inflicting self-harm. "There is a substantial difference between holding one liable to foresee the suicide of a person sane . . . who later commits suicide, and holding a hospital liable where it admits a psychiatric patient with known suicidal tendencies."

Id. at 818.

In the above excerpt, is the court's rationale persuasive in distinguishing between the liability of therapists who are treating a client on an outpatient basis from the care of patients who are institutionalized? Is the failure to properly supervise a hospitalized patient materially different from the failure of a mental health professional to exercise due care and, if necessary, initiate commitment proceedings where a potentially suicidal client is being treated on an outpatient basis? If a significant indicator of a suicide risk is the individual telling the therapist that she is considering suicide and has formulated a plan to do so, does it matter whether the individual is being seen on an inpatient or an outpatient basis? If a client is being seen pursuant to an outpatient civil commitment order (discussed infra Chapter Eight, Part III.), which entails enhanced monitoring and control of the individual, should the same standard of liability be imposed on a therapist as in an inpatient setting? A recent article noted that around 6% of all suicides in the country are inpatient suicides, and that around half of those will result in a legal claim, as opposed to one in four suicides committed by outpatients. James Knoll, *Inpatient Suicide: Identifying Vulnerability in the Hospital Setting*, Psychiatric Times (May 22, 2012).

4. *Liability for the suicide of college students.* A discussion of the liability of Institutions of Higher Learning for failing to adequately address the mental health needs of their students is addressed infra Part II.D.3. A recurring issue is whether college counseling centers and their staff should be held liable following the suicide of a student.

Numerous lawsuits have been filed against universities for allegedly failing to provide adequate treatment for students who subsequently committed suicide. One article discussed highly publicized cases involving MIT and Ferrum College, a small Methodist-affiliated school in Virginia, and suggested that the standard of care is not changing so much as the amount of attention and scrutiny these cases are being given. The article also asserted that "these events illustrate the increased pressures experienced by counseling centers as colleges are admitting students with serious mental disorders who, in the past, would not be admitted to or [be] able to stay in college." It also noted a survey that "showed a substantial increase in the number of students with complex mental health problems, including a three-fold increase in suicidal students from 1989 to 2001." Samuel Knapp, *Suicides Prompt Suits in College Counseling Centers: Is the Standard of Care Changing?*, Penn. Psychol. 4 (Oct. 2003).

See also Robert P. Gallagher, *Suicide Trial Highlights Current Legal Standards for Mental Health Professionals*, Penn. Psychol. 3, 5 (July/Aug. 2008) (describing trial that followed suicide of a junior at Allegheny College in which it was claimed that a college counselor and a consulting psychiatrist were negligent in their treatment of the student and in failing to notify his parents of his suicidal ideation; jury found in favor of the defendants); Heather E. Moore, Note: *University Liability When Students Commit Suicide: Expanding the Scope of the Special Relationship*, 40 Ind. L. Rev. 423, 423 (2007) ("In recent years there has been a significant increase in the number of suicides occurring on college campuses. Statistics reveal that more than one thousand suicides occur on campus every year, and media reports indicate that no institution is exempt. As depression and suicide become more prevalent on college campuses, it is expected that suicide will replace binge drinking as the 'number-one student risk factor in the minds of most college administrators.' The legal significance of the issue is evidenced by the dramatic rise in lawsuits directed at universities. As universities have become more vulnerable to liability in general, student suicide liability is one of the areas that universities have watched closely. Recent decisions have further created uncertainty regarding the legal responsibility of universities and have compounded the concern regarding suicide liability.").

5. *Proximate cause in other contexts.* The issue of proximate cause has also arisen in a related context. For instance, hospitalized psychiatric patients will sometimes wander away from the facility and suffer injuries or die. While it may not have been negligence to permit the patient to be on the grounds of the facility unaccompanied, the question that may need to be resolved is whether the death could have been prevented by an earlier or more diligent search of the surrounding grounds. This was the basic fact situation in *Lando v. State,* 366 N.Y.S.2d 679 (N.Y. App. Div. 1975), modified, 351 N.E.2d 426 (N.Y. 1976), involving a suit against a state psychiatric hospital by the administrator of the estate of a deceased patient. The suit alleged negligence for a failure on the part of the hospital to promptly conduct a search for the patient after she disappeared from the hospital grounds. The body was not found until eleven days after her disappearance. At the trial, the extent and thoroughness of the search were seriously questioned, and the testimony as to the measures taken by the hospital was sharply disputed. Reversing an award for the plaintiff administrator, the court concluded that the element of proximate cause had not been adequately proven:

> Even if we assume the existence of a duty and assume but do not concede its breach, the claim here must fail because of a lack of proof that the breach was the proximate cause of the result. Without this connection between the duty and the result, there can be no recovery. The deceased may have been the victim of foul play or she may have died from natural causes and the time of death is uncertain. There is no proof as to when [she] fell or was placed or thrown into the obscuring foliage. Hence, several possibilities as to what occurred exist and, since the State would not be responsible for one or more of these possibilities, the claimant cannot recover without proving that the death was sustained wholly or in part by a cause for which the State was responsible. To conclude here that the failure to make an adequate search was the proximate cause requires speculation of the rankest sort.

Id. at 680. On review by New York's highest court, this decision denying the claim for decedent's wrongful death was affirmed. However, the father's claim for damages for mental anguish resulting from his being "denied access and control over the body of his deceased daughter for a period of 11 days" was reinstated. 351 N.E.2d 426 (N.Y. 1976). See also *Wilson by Wilson v. Formigoni,* 832 F. Supp. 1152 (N.D. Ill. 1993) (ruling that a patient at a state mental health facility stated a negligence cause of action under Illinois law against the facility director, a psychiatrist, and a social worker, alleging that officials owed her a duty of reasonable care and their conduct resulted in the patient wandering from the facility and becoming severely injured).

6. *Mental health providers not liable for "mere error."* In some jurisdictions, the professional judgment rule, discussed supra Part II.A.2.a., can serve as a defense in cases of patient suicide. One court stated that:

Should a psychiatrist fail to predict that a patient will harm himself or herself if released, the psychiatrist cannot be held liable for a mere error in professional judgment. Even if other psychiatrists disagree with a decision to release a patient, such "disagreement represents, at most, a difference of opinion among physicians, which is not sufficient to sustain a prima facie case of malpractice." Were this not the rule, every judgment made by a psychiatrist would be subjected to the second guess of a jury, few releases would ever be made, and the hope of recovery and rehabilitation of a vast number of patients would be impeded and frustrated. However, a psychiatrist may be held liable if a decision to release a patient was less than a professional medical determination.

Seibert v. Fink, 720 N.Y.S.2d 564, 565 (N.Y. App. Div. 2001). See also *Betty v. City of New York*, 884 N.Y.S.2d 439, 441 (N.Y. App. Div. 2009).

3.   Sexual Misconduct as a Basis for Liability

CORGAN V. MUEHLING
Appellate Court of Illinois, First District, 1988.
167 Ill. App. 3d 1093, 118 Ill. Dec. 698, 522 N.E.2d 153.

JUSTICE SCARIANO delivered the opinion of the court:

In March of 1979, Penelope Corgan came under the psychological care of Conrad Muehling. She alleges in count I of her complaint that he conducted her treatment negligently, was negligent in having sexual relations with her during this treatment, and "negligently failed either to recognize the evolution of the psychotherapeutic phenomenon of transference and countertransference or deal appropriately with such evolving phenomenon," all of which caused her emotional trauma.

* * *

This appeal is taken from those orders of the trial court which dismissed counts II and IV of the plaintiff's third amended complaint. [In addition,] the trial judge certified the related questions of whether *Rickey v. Chicago Transit Authority* (1983), bars Corgan from recovering for emotional damages under counts I and III. . . .

Counts I, III

A.   Introduction.

In count I, Corgan charges Muehling with malpractice. Malpractice is a form of negligence thus the first count is in essence for negligence. . . . Furthermore, the parties agree that count III, wherein Corgan alleges willful and wanton misconduct, also is basically an action for negligence, since this court has held that willful and wanton misconduct is an aggravated form of negligence. Count III is *not* for the intentional infliction of emotional distress; indeed, Corgan does not contend otherwise. While we must accept all well-pleaded facts as true, Corgan does not plead the elements that constitute intentional infliction of emotional distress. She does not allege that Muehling's actions were calculated to cause severe emotional distress; rather, among other allegations, she claims that he was acting solely for his own sexual gratification. . . .

B.   The Rickey Case.

Simply and briefly, the questions certified by the circuit court in this case are whether counts I and III of Corgan's third amended complaint are barred by *Rickey v. Chicago Transit Authority* (1983). In *Rickey,* the plaintiff was attempting to recover damages for the emotional distress he allegedly suffered as a result of the CTA's negligence when he saw his brother being injured on an escalator. The Illinois supreme court, in a unanimous opinion, framed the issue in the following manner: "The underlying question is, of course, whether any person who suffers emotional distress can recover, but the question here specifically is whether a bystander at the injury of another who, generally under the decisions, is a close relative of the bystander can recover." *Rickey.*

The court then discussed the "impact rule," the governing law in Illinois at that time, which required physical impact or injury in order for a plaintiff to recover in an action for the negligent infliction of emotional distress. The *Rickey* court noted that this requirement had been frequently satisfied by trivial contacts, and that consequently the impact rule had fallen into disfavor. The court also recognized that although recovery for emotional distress should not be determined solely on the basis of whether there was any physical impact visited upon the plaintiff, the appellate court went too far in adopting a standard which "would permit recovery for emotional disturbance alone." Our supreme court acknowledged that courts were hesitant in allowing recovery for purely emotional injuries and explained such unwillingness as follows: "courts have given as reasons for this reluctance apprehensions that the door would be opened for fraudulent claims, that damages would be difficult to ascertain and measure, that emotional injuries are hardly foreseeable and that frivolous litigation would be encouraged."

The court then proceeded to announce its holding:

> The standard that we substitute for the one requiring contemporaneous injury or impact is the standard which has been adopted in the majority of jurisdictions where this question of *recovery by a bystander* for emotional distress has been examined. [ ] That standard has been described as the zone-of-physical-danger rule. Basically, under it a *bystander who is in a zone of physical danger* and who, because of the defendant's negligence, has reasonable fear for his own safety is given a right of action for physical injury or illness resulting from emotional distress. *The*

bystander, as stated, must show physical injury or illness as a result of the emotional distress caused by the defendant's negligence. [ ].

Accordingly, the supreme court remanded the case because the complaint did allege physical manifestations, and it was unclear whether the plaintiff was endangered by the alleged negligence and had a reasonable fear for his own safety.

C. Therapist–Patient Sexual Contact.

We have long been aware that plaintiffs in other states have successfully maintained malpractice actions against their psychologist, psychiatrist, or social worker, predicated primarily on the therapist's alleged sexual contact with his patient. The leading case is from the State of New York, wherein the plaintiff alleged that she "was induced to have sexual intercourse with the defendant as part of her prescribed therapy," and was as a result "so emotionally and mentally injured that she was required to seek hospitalization on two occasions during 1971." (*Roy v. Hartogs* (1976).) The court in *Roy* upheld the trial court's award of damages to the plaintiff, justifying its holding as follows: "By alleging his client's mental and emotional status was adversely affected by this deceptive and damaging treatment, plaintiff's counsel asserted a viable cause of action." [ ].

The court of appeals in our sister state of Michigan, relying on *Roy,* held that allegations analogous to those in *Roy* were sufficient to state a cause of action for psychiatrist malpractice. (*Cotton v. Kambly* (1980)) . . .

The United States court of appeals has upheld an award for a plaintiff who alleged that the individual treating her psychiatric problems had committed malpractice by having sexual intercourse with her. (*Simmons v. United States* (9th Cir. 1986).) The plaintiff contended that her therapist, employed by the United States as a social worker in the Indian Health Service, was guilty of malpractice which had caused her to attempt suicide. A doctor who gave psychiatric counseling to Simmons subsequent to her having terminated consultation with the social worker "stated that her counselor's misconduct was the cause of her psychological problems and that her problems were due essentially to his inappropriate response to the normal 'transference phenomenon' in therapy." [ ].

The court, in a unanimous opinion, proceeded to analyze the plaintiff's malpractice claim. It said that "[t]ransference is the term used by psychiatrists and psychologists to denote a patient's emotional reaction to a therapist." [ ]. The court went on to explain that transference is crucial to the therapeutic process and that "[t]he proper therapeutic response is countertransference, a reaction which avoids emotional involvement and assists the patient in overcoming problems." The court described as follows the legal consequences of a counselor's failure to properly manage the transference phenomenon: "When the therapist mishandles transference and becomes sexually involved with a patient, medical authorities are nearly unanimous in considering such conduct to be malpractice." Moreover, it recognized that "[c]ourts have uniformly regarded mishandling of transference as malpractice or gross negligence."

In a malpractice action in the State of Washington, the plaintiff alleged that she had a sexual relationship with her psychiatrist which "was the direct and proximate cause of damages to the plaintiff, including humiliation, mental anguish, shock, outrage, depression, inconvenience, medical expenses, loss of wages, marital difficulties and general deterioration of emotional well being." (*Omer v. Edgren* (1984).) The trial court granted summary judgment to the therapist, but the appellate court reversed, holding that there was sufficient evidence for a finder of fact to determine that the defendant had committed malpractice.

The court concluded by addressing the doctor's contention that his patient had not been damaged. It noted that the plaintiff "testified in her deposition she suffered no loss with respect to medical expenses, lost earnings, or marital difficulties," but that she "claimed general as well as special damages." [ ]. The court, although cognizant of the difficulty articulated in *Rickey* of proving damages of this nature, nevertheless held that this problem in itself was not enough to bar the plaintiff from recovery because "[i]njury flowing from the alleged relationship, though difficult to prove, may be as real as that type of injury which can be proven with mathematical certainty." [ ].

D.   The Application of Rickey

. . . [T]here is considerable controversy and confusion over whether the zone of danger test should be used in cases involving direct victims of negligence. It is clear, however, that *Rickey* does not become inapplicable solely because a case involves a malpractice claim.

*   *   *

We believe that the application of the *Rickey* test in cases involving direct victims of malpractice is inappropriate. Our conclusion is supported by the decisions of courts in other jurisdictions which have awarded damages to plaintiffs who have had sexual relations with their therapists, although these plaintiffs have not alleged that they were physically injured. As we have seen, the Washington court in *Omer* directly addressed this concern, concluding that the plaintiff nevertheless deserved compensation. Moreover, were we to hold to the contrary, it would be hopelessly difficult for individuals to plead an action for psychologist malpractice which results only in emotional distress, for it seems incongruous to the point of absurdity that in cases involving malpractice by psychologists a victim should be required to demonstrate that he or she was put in fear of *physical* injury. Nor can there be any rational justification for our courts to mandate that in order to qualify for damages in a psychologist or social worker malpractice case a patient exhibit physical manifestations of his or her emotional trauma suffered at the hand of therapists who are qualified to minister to their needs only in cases of mental or emotional malaise, especially since, as the *Omer* court points out, such an injury, "though difficult to prove, may be as real as that type of injury which can be proven with mathematical certainty." [ ]. We do not glean from *Rickey* any overarching unitary theory that would apply to the case at bar.

Therefore, in the absence of a decision by our supreme court which mandates a clearly different result, and supported by the law of our own appellate court and other jurisdictions, we hold that the zone of danger rule enunciated in *Rickey* has no application in this case, which involves a direct victim of negligence.

* * *

In conclusion, we hold that counts I, III, and IV of the complaint state valid causes of action.

HARTMAN, P.J., and BILANDIC, J., concur.

QUESTIONS AND COMMENTS

1. *Historical perspective.* Until the 1970s, litigation claiming malpractice for sexual misconduct was rarely successful. In fact, a fringe element of the psychiatric profession had, at one point, openly advocated sexual relations between a client and a therapist as a legitimate form of therapy. Jeffrey D. Robertson, *Psychiatric Malpractice: Liability of Mental Health Professionals* 325–26 (1988). The case of *Roy v. Hartogs*, 381 N.Y.S.2d 587 (N.Y. App. Div. 1976), signaled a decided turn of attitude on the part of the courts and the psychiatric profession. In *Hartogs*, the defendant was charged with having "induced" the plaintiff "to have sexual intercourse as a part of her prescribed therapy." The plaintiff alleged that as a result of the improper treatment, she had become "so emotionally and mentally injured that she was required to seek hospitalization on two occasions." Id. at 588. *Hartogs,* which resulted in a judgment for the plaintiff, received considerable publicity, particularly as the result of a subsequent 1976 book, *Betrayal,* co-authored by the plaintiff, Julie Roy.

2. *Requirement of intentional infliction or physical impact.* Some jurisdictions continue to adhere to the rule that recovery for mental suffering will not be allowed unless: (a) the distress was inflicted intentionally, or (b) the mental suffering is accompanied by a physical manifestation of the injury. Dan B. Dobbs et al., *Prosser and Keeton on the Law of Torts* § 12 (5th ed. 1984). Because the emotional harm resulting from the sexual misconduct of a therapist cannot generally be said to have been *intentionally* inflicted, the plaintiff has at least a theoretical barrier to overcome in these jurisdictions. *Corgan v. Muehling* is illustrative of the approach taken by courts in these jurisdictions. On what basis was the court able to hold that

the plaintiff had a cause of action in spite of the fact that there was neither an intentional harm nor a physical impact or injury? What might a court recognize as satisfying the physical injury requirement in this type of case? An anxiety-induced rash? Weight loss or gain? Bags under the eyes due to a lack of sleep? Do these provide sufficiently reliable indicators of actual physical harm?

3. *Per se rule of liability.* Courts appear to be moving toward a *per se* rule in therapist sexual misconduct cases. There is an increasing tendency to permit recovery even in the absence of proof of actual damages. Does it make sense for courts to adopt a *per se* rule that sexual misconduct is actionable as negligence even in the absence of proof of actual damages? Some cases have suggested that difficulties of proof in cases of sexual misconduct should not bar a recovery. In *Omer v. Edgren,* 685 P.2d 635 (Wash. Ct. App. 1984), a psychiatrist defended his lawsuit on the grounds that the patient had not been damaged by the affair. In rejecting this defense, the court noted prior courts had determined:

> The most elementary conceptions of justice and public policy require that the wrongdoer shall bear the risk of the uncertainty [of actual damages] which his own wrong has created. . . .

> 'The constant tendency of the courts is to find some way in which damages can be awarded where a wrong has been done. Difficulty of ascertainment is no longer confused with right of recovery' for a proven invasion of the plaintiff's rights.

Id. at 638.

A number of states, including California, Illinois, and Texas, have recognized causes of action making sexual relations between a psychotherapist and a client negligence per se. Matt J. O'Laughlin, *Dr. Strangelove: Therapist–Client Dual Relationship Bans and Freedom of Association, or How I Learned to Stop Worrying and Love My Clients*, 69 UMKC L. Rev. 697, 700 (2001). Minnesota was one of the first states to do so, and their statute has provided a framework for other states:

> A cause of action against a psychotherapist for sexual exploitation exists for a patient or former patient for injury caused by sexual contact with the psychotherapist, if the sexual contact occurred:

> > (1) during the period the patient was receiving psychotherapy from the psychotherapist; or

> > (2) after the period the patient received psychotherapy from the psychotherapist if (a) the former patient was emotionally dependent on the psychotherapist; or (b) the sexual contact occurred by means of therapeutic deception.

> The patient or former patient may recover damages from a psychotherapist who is found liable for sexual exploitation. It is not a defense to the action that sexual contact with a patient occurred outside

a therapy or treatment session or that it occurred off the premises regularly used by the psychotherapist for therapy or treatment sessions.

Minn. Stat. § 604.201 (2012). Minnesota also makes the employer of the psychotherapist potentially liable and limits discovery and admission into evidence of the plaintiff's sexual history. Minn. Stat. § 604.202–.204 (2012).

4. *Other theories for recovery.* In jurisdictions that do not recognize a cause of action for negligence per se or limit the availability of a *negligent* infliction of emotional distress claim, a client who has been sexually involved with a therapist may be able to rely on other theories to recover damages. An Ohio state court for instance, has allowed an action for assault against the offending therapist, even if the client admitted to consenting to the act of intercourse. *Bunce v. Parkside Lodge of Columbus*, 596 N.E.2d 1106, 1107 (Ohio Ct. App. 1991). Additionally, courts have found that the relationship between a therapist and a client is fiduciary in nature, and sexual contact between the two parties constitutes a breach of the fiduciary duty. See *Horak v. Biris*, 474 N.E.2d 13 (Ill. App. Ct. 1985); *Omer v. Edgren*, 685 P.2d 635 (Wash. Ct. App. 1984). Most courts, however, have found that sexual contact with a client constitutes negligence based on the "therapist's mishandling of the so-called 'transference phenomenon.'" See *Am. Home Assur. Co. v. Cohen*, 881 P.2d 1001, 1005 (1994). What other theories might be used to obtain a recovery from a therapist who becomes sexually involved with a client during the course of treatment?

5. *Punitive damages.* Punitive damages may be awarded for conduct that is "outrageous, because of the defendant's evil motive or his reckless indifference to the rights of others." Restatement (Second) of Torts § 908 (1979). Somewhat surprisingly, cases of sexual misconduct have historically generally not been awarded punitive damages. For instance, in *Roy v. Hartogs,* discussed in note 1, supra, the trial judge had allowed $100,000 in punitive damages on the grounds that a "patient must not be fair game for a lecherous doctor." However, on appeal, while sustaining general damages, the court eliminated punitive damages altogether on the basis that actions constituting malpractice were not "wanton or reckless." Punitive damages have, however, been sustained in a few sexual misconduct cases and attitudes towards these awards may be changing, particularly in light of evolving professional and criminal standards, discussed supra Chapter Two, Part I.C., that prohibit this behavior. See *Miranda v. Newman*, No. 02–CV–000812, 2003 WL 24096742 (Wis. Cir. Ct. Oct. 20, 2003) (awarding $40,000 in compensatory damages and $10,000 in punitive damages for sexual contact during an ongoing therapeutic relationship as the result of which plaintiff suffered and continues to suffer mental or emotional injuries).

6. *Non-client claims.* Does a client have a cause of action when the therapist has sexual relations with the client's spouse? A recovery has been allowed to a non-participating party where both spouses were patients of the offending psychiatrist. *Mazza v. Huffaker,* 300 S.E.2d 833 (N.C. Ct. App. 1983). In sustaining a judgment in favor of a patient who discovered the psychiatrist and the plaintiff's wife (who was also a patient) together in bed,

the court relied on the theory of *de facto* abandonment. In its conventional form a cause of action for abandonment lies for the "failure by a physician to continue to provide services to a patient when it is needed in a case for which the physician has assumed responsibility and from which he has not been properly relieved." *Brandt v. Grubin,* 329 A.2d 82 (N.J. Super. Ct. 1974) (finding no abandonment of a psychiatric patient). Aside from abandonment, could it be argued that the psychiatrist's relations with the patient's wife also constituted negligence in the treatment of the husband?

C. LIABILITY TO THIRD PARTIES

1. The Dangerous Client and the Duty of Care to Third Persons

a. *Introduction*

As mentioned earlier, a traditional requirement for a professional liability claim was the existence of an explicit or implicit contractual relationship between the professional and her client at the time of the purported malpractice (usually called privity of contract). See supra Part II.A. Thus, the threshold question in these suits was always whether the plaintiff had been the defendant's client. Unless a professional relationship had existed between the two parties, the court would usually dismiss the plaintiff's suit. As noted, the privity doctrine is no longer always a dispositive factor in these cases. An increasing number of jurisdictions have modified or repudiated this doctrine, concluding that while the privity requirement provides certainty, it may not promote justice or deter misconduct. A related move away from traditional limitations on professionals' liability to third parties with whom no contractual relationship existed is traceable to a 1928 decision rendered by one of the most influential state courts of the time.

In the landmark case of *Palsgraf v. Long Island R.R.,* 162 N.E. 99 (N.Y. 1928), the New York Court of Appeals established a test of foreseeability to determine whether the defendant owed a duty of care to the injured party.[c] Under this test, the court asked whether the defendant's actor reasonably should have foreseen that his actions would injure the plaintiff. If that question is answered affirmatively, the

---

[c] In *Palsgraf,* a passenger was attempting to board one of the defendant's trains while carrying a bulky and apparently fragile package. The railroad company's employees, while attempting to help the passenger board the train, jostled him, and the package fell to the ground. The unmarked package contained fireworks, which exploded upon impact. The force of the explosion knocked over a platform scale thirty feet away, which in turn fell upon and injured another passenger, the plaintiff in the case. At trial, the jury found the defendant's employees negligent and entered an award for the plaintiff. New York's highest court, however, reversed that decision, concluding that although the trainmen might have acted in a negligent manner with regard to the passenger boarding the train, those trainmen could not have foreseen that their negligent actions would injure the plaintiff, who had been standing thirty feet away. The foreseeability of the harm, Chief Judge Benjamin Cardozo said, would determine whether the defendant's actions constituted negligence toward the plaintiff.

defendant can be found liable. The court added: "The risk reasonably to be perceived defines the duty to be obeyed . . . ; it is risk to another or to others within the range of apprehension." 162 N.E. at 100.

A foreseeable injury to a third person, therefore, may constitute an alternative basis of professional malpractice liability, imposing liability even though the therapist had no contractual or any other direct relationship with the injured party. This foreseeability criterion, although a widely-accepted benchmark in determining liability, is a decidedly imprecise standard that nevertheless extends professional liability beyond the limits set by the privity doctrine.

While foreseeability became a basis for tort liability in general under *Palsgraf*, malpractice cases against physicians continued to be governed mostly by the privity requirement. However, the extension of physicians' liability to third parties began in the early 1920s with cases involving contagious diseases. In 1919, the Supreme Court of Minnesota upheld a cause of action targeting a physician treating a patient for scarlet fever for failing to advise her parents that the disease was infectious. The physician incorrectly advised them that it was safe to visit and even to take her home without risk of the disease being communicated. *Skillings v. Allen*, 173 N.W. 663 (Minn. 1919). The court found that the physician owed a duty of care to those who were "naturally exposed to infection to a greater degree than anyone else." Id. at 664.

In 1928, the Ohio Supreme Court held that a physician has a duty to warn persons in dangerous proximity to a smallpox patient of the infectiousness of the disease. *Jones v. Stanko*, 160 N.E. 456 (Ohio 1928). The court upheld an award for the wrongful death of a man who visited the doctor's patient after being assured that the patient was not contagious. The patient died of smallpox, as did the decedent in the case. The following materials trace the development of the third-person liability doctrine in the context of mental health treatment.

b.   Foundations for Tarasoff: Institutional Liability

MERCHANTS NATIONAL BANK & TRUST CO. OF FARGO V. UNITED STATES

United States District Court, District of North Dakota, 1967.
272 F. Supp. 409.

RONALD N. DAVIES, DISTRICT JUDGE.

[This case involved an action against the United States under the Federal Torts Claim Act by the administrator of the Estate of Eloise A. Newgard for negligence in the treatment of Newgard's husband, who killed her shortly after being released by a Veterans Administration hospital.]

Early in the morning of January 17, 1965, Dr. Mack V. Traynor, a Fargo physician, was called to the Newgard apartment in Fargo, North Dakota, by Newgard's wife, Eloise. She was frantic-voiced and said she needed help. The doctor, promptly responding to the call, found Newgard glassy-eyed and making senseless talk about horses, cattle "and God most of the time." Dr. Traynor felt Newgard was completely psychotic. . . .

Dr. Albert C. Kohlmeyer, a well qualified psychiatrist, saw Newgard the same day in the Neuropsychiatric Institute section of the hospital. He found him very agitated, "carrying on" about religious ideas and testified that Newgard thought "he was Christ or some representative of Christ." Because of his delusional ideas, the psychiatrist thought Newgard was psychotic and although he saw Newgard only a couple of days, it was his belief that Newgard's illness had been coming on for a long time. Dr. Kohlmeyer felt Newgard was a schizophrenic, chronic, with acute exacerbation, paranoid type.

On January 19, 1965, the Cass County, North Dakota, Mental Health Board after a hearing, ordered Newgard committed to the State Hospital at Jamestown, North Dakota. Later because he was a veteran, an amended order was issued by the board, making the commitment a dual one so that Newgard could eventually be transferred to the Veterans Administration Hospital at Fort Meade, South Dakota. Effective March 23, 1965, Newgard was transferred to Meade where he was admitted to a ward and placed under the direct supervision of Dr. Leonard S. Linnell, a medical doctor and psychiatrist. . . .

For a number of weeks Newgard was treated with tranquilizers and saw a clinical psychologist, Dr. Jesse H. Craft, weekly, for psychotherapy and examinations. During the course of Newgard's treatment and care he was interviewed by Dr. Linnell about once a week. The psychiatrist also sent Newgard to Dr. Truman M. Cheney, a vocational psychologist, for testing and reporting his job aptitudes. Newgard was given various jobs around the hospital, a procedure followed by Meade in the treatment of hospital patients and which is followed in hospitals of a similar nature. . . .

Sometime before July 18, 1965, Dr. Truman M. Cheney, Counseling Psychologist at Meade, had made arrangements to put Newgard on leave at the ranch owned by Mr. and Mrs. Clarence A. Davis located some ten miles north of Belle Fourche, South Dakota. Dr. Cheney told Mr. Davis that Newgard had had "a mental disturbance, a nervous breakdown" and that Newgard wanted hard work to forget some of his troubles and for rehabilitation purposes. Mr. Davis had never before had a Meade patient working on his ranch.

On July 18, 1865, Newgard was released by Dr. Linnell on work leave to rancher Davis. . . .

It develops that on July 24, 1965, Newgard left the ranch for the weekend. He was to have returned Monday, July 26th, but Newgard went to his parents' home at Mayville, North Dakota. His wife Eloise had no idea he was in Mayville and was there herself only for a brief visit. Newgard wanted his wife to return with him to Fargo but she declined. Newgard got possession of a car and ultimately drove to his mother-in-law's home in Detroit Lakes, Minnesota, where on July 31, 1965, he first attempted to run Eloise Newgard down with the car and failing that, got out of the vehicle, shot and killed her.

* * *

[The court reviewed evidence that showed that in arranging for Newgard's placement on the ranch, the Meade staff made no attempt to inform Rancher Davis of Newgard's condition or the conditions governing his release. It was also shown that no member of the Meade staff attempted to monitor Newgard after he was placed on the ranch.]

Dr. Linnell ignored and rejected every warning signal that Newgard was delusional at Meade and every warning signal that Eloise A. Newgard had every reason to be in mortal fear of her husband because of his prior conduct and the nature of some of the letters he wrote her while a patient at Meade. . . .

The plaintiff alleges that the Government, acting through its duly authorized agents employed by the Veterans Administration, undertook the custody, care and treatment of Newgard, knowing him to be an insane and incompetent person with homicidal tendencies, and that the Government's inexcusable negligence was the proximate cause of Eloise A. Newgard's death on July 31, 1965, at the hands of her husband.

* * *

Considering the circumstances under which Newgard was placed on leave of absence at the Davis ranch, as disclosed by the credible evidence, the Government's agents and employees not only did not exercise due care; in the view of this Court they exercised no care at all. . . .

This Court is of the opinion that in the case of Newgard the defendant's agents were tortiously negligent both in the matter of substandard professional conduct on the part of Dr. Linnell, and because of gross negligence on the part of Dr. Linnell and Dr. Cheney in the careless custodial care of Newgard. . . .

The Court concludes that plaintiff is entitled to recover the sum of Two Hundred Thousand Dollars ($200,000.00) from the defendant, as compensatory damages, arising out of and from the gross negligence of the defendant, acting by and through its agents and employees, which was the sole and proximate cause of the death of Eloise A. Newgard.

QUESTIONS AND COMMENTS

1.   *Restatement of Torts.* While the court in *Merchants National Bank* did not rely on the Second Restatement of Torts, § 319 of the Restatement does provide a basis for the imposition of liability on institutions:

> One who takes charge of a third person whom he knows or should know to be likely to cause bodily harm to others if not controlled is under a duty to exercise reasonable care to control the third person to prevent him from doing such harm.

The commentary accompanying this section of the Restatement makes it clear that an institution may be liable to a third party who is injured by an institution's patient if:

1.   A patient is released when the facility knew or had reason to know of the patient's dangerous proclivities;

2.   The institution fails to conduct an adequate pre-discharge examination of a patient with a history of violent behavior; or

3.   The institution's failure to take adequate precautions allows a patient to escape.

2.   *Liability for release or escape of a dangerous patient.* A number of cases have imposed liability on psychiatric facilities for the release of patients the institution knew or should have known to be dangerous. See *Semler v. Psychiatric Inst. of Washington, D.C.*, 538 F.2d 121 (4th Cir. 1976); *Estate of Mathes v. Ireland*, 419 N.E.2d 782 (Ind. Ct. App. 1981). In *Semler*, the psychiatric facility had custody of a convicted felon who, without court authorization, was placed on outpatient status. The patient killed an individual, and in a subsequent wrongful death suit brought by the victim's parents, the institution was found liable for this death. But see *Jones v. Gaines*, 978 So. 2d 522 (La. Ct. App. 2008) (no duty to victim to take steps to prevent patient with schizophrenia from driving after release); *Griffin v. Twin Valley Psychiatric Sys.*, No. 02AP–744, 2003 WL 22999355 (Ohio Ct. App. Dec. 23, 2003) (psychiatric hospital not liable for harm done by discharged involuntarily committed patient who committed multiple murders).

Liability may also attach when the psychiatric institution due to negligence permits a foreseeably dangerous patient to escape. For instance, in *Tamsen v. Weber*, 802 P.2d 1063 (Ariz. Ct. App. 1990), the court held that a cause of action was stated where the psychiatric facility had given the escaped patient, who subsequently injured a third person, unsupervised ground privileges. See also *Davis v. Puryear*, 673 So. 2d 1298 (La. Ct. App. 1996).

3.   *Voluntary patients.* For purposes of assigning liability, should it matter that the patient was voluntarily admitted, rather than involuntarily committed? As discussed in Chapter Eight, Part IV.E., voluntary patients generally have the right to be released upon their request unless civilly committed. Some courts have adopted the position that a different standard

applies when the patient who causes the injury was in the institution on a voluntary status. See, e.g., *Sellers v. United States,* 870 F.2d 1098, 1104 (6th Cir. 1989), in which the court stated:

> [T]here are additional reasons why Sellers cannot succeed on his claim of negligent discharge. . . . Firestine was admitted to the VAH voluntarily. A review of the case law will demonstrate that this fact is central to a determination of the VAH's duty. . . . An analysis of this issue centers on the question of whether a "special relationship" exists between the patient and the hospital.
>
> In *Hinkelman v. Borgess Medical Center* [ ] (Mich. Ct. App. 1987), the court specifically addressed the issue of when a special relationship should be found to exist. The court explained that the existence of a special relationship, such as that between a physician and patient, is premised on the notion of control over the patient. [ ] In *Hinkelman,* the court found that there was no special relationship between the patient and the hospital when the patient had been admitted voluntarily, had not stayed more than a few days, and had left before he could be treated. [ ] The court placed great weight on the fact that the duty imposed on mental hospitals is "based on the control vested by *involuntary* commitment." [ ] "In contrast, where a patient's hospitalization was voluntary, no duty has been imposed due to the facility's inability to compel patient confinement."

But see *Williams v. State,* 924 N.Y.S.2d 23, 23 (App. Div. 2011) (reversing the dismissal of a claim notwithstanding that the voluntary patient had left the mental health facility without consent two years earlier; noting that a voluntary patient is not simply free to walk away from the facility and, if properly discharged, should receive several kinds of needed support; also noted that the patient had eloped from the facility for the eighth time in a 29–month period and that the patient, who required an escort on the facility's grounds, eloped when his escort permitted him to use a bathroom out of her sight, in violation of proper procedure for an escorted patient).

4. *Statutory immunity.* Some states have enacted laws that specifically grant immunity to institutions that improvidently release a patient who subsequently injures a third party. For instance, California's civil commitment statute (the Lanterman–Petris–Short Act) grants immunity from all criminal and civil liability to any psychiatrist responsible for evaluating an involuntarily committed patient during an initial 72–hour treatment and evaluation period. If the treating psychiatrist, based on his or her personal observation, authorizes the release of the patient within the initial 72–hour period, the psychiatrist is immune from all liability even if the patient later causes harm to a third person or him or herself. Such immunity reflects "the legislature's determination that the goal of ending indefinite confinement outweighs the early release potential for harm." *Ford v. Norton,* 107 Cal. Rptr. 2d 776 (Ct. App. 2001).

c. *The* Tarasoff *Doctrine*

TARASOFF V. REGENTS OF UNIVERSITY OF CALIFORNIA

Supreme Court of California, 1976.
17 Cal. 3d 425, 131 Cal. Rptr. 14, 551 P.2d 334.

TOBRINER, JUSTICE.

On October 27, 1969, Prosenjit Poddar killed Tatiana Tarasoff. Plaintiffs, Tatiana's parents, allege that two months earlier Poddar confided his intention to kill Tatiana to Dr. Lawrence Moore, a psychologist employed by the Cowell Memorial Hospital at the University of California at Berkeley. They allege that on Moore's request, the campus police briefly detained Poddar, but released him when he appeared rational. They further claim that Dr. Harvey Powelson, Moore's superior, then directed that no further action be taken to detain Poddar. No one warned plaintiffs of Tatiana's peril.

Concluding that these facts set forth causes of action against neither therapists and policemen involved, nor against the Regents of the University of California as their employer, the superior court sustained defendants' demurrers to plaintiffs' second amended complaints without leave to amend.[2] This appeal ensued.

Plaintiffs' complaints predicate liability on two grounds: defendants' failure to warn plaintiffs of the impending danger and their failure to bring about Poddar's confinement pursuant to the Lanterman–Petris–Short Act. Defendants, in turn, assert that they owed no duty of reasonable care to Tatiana. . . .

We shall explain that defendant therapists cannot escape liability merely because Tatiana herself was not their patient. When a therapist determines, or pursuant to the standards of his profession should determine, that his patient presents a serious danger of violence to another, he incurs an obligation to use reasonable care to protect the intended victim against such danger. The discharge of this duty may require the therapist to take one or more of various steps, depending upon the nature of the case. Thus it may call for him to warn the intended victim or others likely to apprise the victim of the danger, to notify the police, or to take whatever other steps are reasonably necessary under the circumstances.

In the case at bar, plaintiffs admit that defendant therapists notified the police, but argue on appeal that the therapists failed to exercise

---

[2] The therapist defendants include Dr. Moore, the psychologist who examined Poddar and decided that Poddar should be committed; Dr. Gold and Dr. Yandell, psychiatrists at Cowell Memorial Hospital who concurred in Moore's decision; and Dr. Powelson, chief of the department of psychiatry, who countermanded Moore's decision and directed that the staff take no action to confine Poddar.

reasonable care to protect Tatiana in that they did not confine Poddar and did not warn Tatiana or others likely to apprise her of the danger.

* * *

1.   Plaintiffs' Complaints

Plaintiffs, Tatiana's mother and father, filed separate but virtually identical second amended complaints. The issue before us on this appeal is whether those complaints now state, or can be amended to state, causes of action against defendants. We therefore begin by setting forth the pertinent allegations of the complaints.

Plaintiffs' first cause of action, entitled "Failure to Detain a Dangerous Patient," alleges that on August 20, 1969, Poddar was a voluntary outpatient receiving therapy at Cowell Memorial Hospital. Poddar informed Moore, his therapist, that he was going to kill an unnamed girl, readily identifiable as Tatiana, when she returned home from spending the summer in Brazil. Moore, with the concurrence of Dr. Gold, who had initially examined Poddar, and Dr. Yandell, assistant to the director of the department of psychiatry, decided that Poddar should be committed for observation in a mental hospital. Moore orally notified Officers Atkinson and Teel of the campus police that he would request commitment. He then sent a letter to Police Chief William Beall requesting the assistance of the police department in securing Poddar's confinement.

Officers Atkinson, Brownrigg, and Halleran took Poddar into custody, but, satisfied that Poddar was rational, released him on his promise to stay away from Tatiana. Powelson, director of the department of psychiatry at Cowell Memorial Hospital, then asked the police to return Moore's letter, directed that all copies of the letter and notes that Moore had taken as therapist be destroyed, and "ordered no action to place Prosenjit Poddar in 72–hour treatment and evaluation facility."

Plaintiffs' second cause of action, entitled "Failure to Warn Of a Dangerous Patient," incorporates the allegations of the first cause of action, but adds the assertion that defendants negligently permitted Poddar to be released from police custody without "notifying the parents of Tatiana Tarasoff that their daughter was in grave danger from Posenjit Poddar." Poddar persuaded Tatiana's brother to share an apartment with him near Tatiana's residence; shortly after her return from Brazil, Poddar went to her residence and killed her. . . .

2.   Plaintiffs Can State a Cause of Action Against Defendant Therapists for Negligent Failure to Protect Tatiana

The second cause of action can be amended to allege that Tatiana's death proximately resulted from defendants' negligent failure to warn Tatiana or others likely to apprise her of her danger. Plaintiffs contend that as amended, such allegations of negligence and proximate causation, with resulting damages, establish a cause of action. Defendants, however, contend that in the circumstances of the present case they owed no duty of care to Tatiana or her parents and that, in the absence of such duty, they were free to act in careless disregard of Tatiana's life and safety.

In analyzing this issue, we bear in mind that legal duties are not discoverable facts of nature, but merely conclusory expressions that, in cases of a particular type, liability should be imposed for damage done.

* * *

. . . [Duty] is not sacrosanct in itself, but only an expression of the sum total of those considerations of policy which lead the law to say that the particular plaintiff is entitled to protection.

* * *

We depart from "this fundamental principle" only upon the "balancing of a number of considerations"; major ones "are the foreseeability of harm to the plaintiff, the degree of certainty that the plaintiff suffered injury, the closeness of the connection between the defendant's conduct and the injury suffered, the moral blame attached to the defendant's conduct, the policy of preventing future harm, the extent of the burden to the defendant and consequences to the community of imposing a duty to exercise care with resulting liability for breach, and the availability, cost and prevalence of insurance for the risk involved."

The most important of these considerations in establishing duty is foreseeability. As a general principle, a "defendant owes a duty of care to all persons who are foreseeably endangered by his conduct, with respect to all risks which make the conduct unreasonably dangerous." As we shall explain, however, when the avoidance of foreseeable harm requires a defendant to control the conduct of another person, or to warn of such conduct, the common law has traditionally imposed liability only if the defendant bears some special relationship to the dangerous person or to the potential victim. Since the relationship between a therapist and his patient satisfies this requirement, we need not here decide whether foreseeability alone is sufficient to create a duty to exercise reasonable care to protect a potential victim of another's conduct.

Although, as we have stated above, under the common law, as a general rule, one person owed no duty to control the conduct of another nor to warn those endangered by such conduct, the courts have carved out an exception to this rule in cases in which the defendant stands in some special relationship to either the person whose conduct needs to be controlled or in a relationship to the foreseeable victim of that conduct (see Rest. 2d Torts §§ 315–320). Applying this exception to the present case, we note that a relationship of defendant therapists to either Tatiana or Poddar will suffice to establish a duty of care; as explained in section

315 of the Restatement Second of Torts, a duty of care may arise from either "(a) a special relation between the actor and the third person which imposes a duty upon the actor to control the third person's conduct, or (b) a special relation between the actor and the other which gives to the other a right of protection."

Although plaintiffs' pleadings assert no special relation between Tatiana and defendant therapists, they establish as between Poddar and defendant therapists the special relation that arises between a patient and his doctor or psychotherapist. Such a relationship may support affirmative duties for the benefit of third persons. Thus, for example, a hospital must exercise reasonable care to control the behavior of a patient which may endanger other persons. A doctor must also warn a patient if the patient's condition or medication renders certain conduct, such as driving a car, dangerous to others.

Although the California decisions that recognize this duty have involved cases in which the defendant stood in a special relationship *both* to the victim and to the person whose conduct created the danger, we do not think that the duty should logically be constricted to such situations. Decisions of other jurisdictions hold that the single relationship of a doctor to his patient is sufficient to support the duty to exercise reasonable care to protect others against dangers emanating from the patient's illness. The courts hold that a doctor is liable to persons infected by his patient if he negligently fails to diagnose a contagious disease or, having diagnosed the illness, fails to warn members of the patient's family.

Since it involved a dangerous mental patient, the decision in *Merchants Nat. Bank & Trust Co. of Fargo v. United States* comes closer to the issue. The Veterans Administration arranged for the patient to work on a local farm, but did not inform the farmer of the man's background. The farmer consequently permitted the patient to come and go freely during nonworking hours; the patient borrowed a car, drove to his wife's residence and killed her. Notwithstanding the lack of any "special relationship" between the Veterans Administration and the wife, the court found the Veterans Administration liable for the wrongful death of the wife.

* * *

Defendants contend, however, that imposition of a duty to exercise reasonable care to protect third persons is unworkable because therapists cannot accurately predict whether or not a patient will resort to violence. In support of this argument amicus representing the American Psychiatric Association and other professional societies cites numerous articles which indicate that therapists, in the present state of the art, are unable reliably to predict violent acts; their forecasts, amicus claims, tend consistently to overpredict violence, and indeed are more often wrong than right. Since predictions of violence are often erroneous, amicus concludes, the courts should not render rulings that predicate the liability of therapists upon the validity of such predictions.

The role of the psychiatrist, who is indeed a practitioner of medicine, and that of the psychologist who performs an allied function, are like that of the physician who must conform to the standards of the profession and who must often make diagnoses and predictions based upon such evaluations. Thus the judgment of the therapist in diagnosing emotional disorders and in predicting whether a patient presents a serious danger of violence is comparable to the judgment which doctors and professionals must regularly render under accepted rules of responsibility.

We recognize the difficulty that a therapist encounters in attempting to forecast whether a patient presents a serious danger of violence. Obviously we do not require that the therapist, in making that determination, render a perfect performance; the therapist need only exercise "that reasonable degree of skill, knowledge, and care ordinarily possessed and exercised by members of [that professional specialty] under similar circumstances." Within the broad range of reasonable practice and treatment in which professional opinion and judgment may differ the therapist is free to exercise his or her own best judgment without liability; proof, aided by hindsight, that he or she judged wrongly is insufficient to establish negligence.

In the instant case, however, the pleadings do not raise any question as to failure of defendant therapists to predict that Poddar presented a serious danger of violence. On the contrary, the present complaints allege that defendant therapists did in fact predict that Poddar would kill, but were negligent in failing to warn.

Amicus contends, however, that even when a therapist does in fact predict that a patient poses a serious danger of violence to others, the therapist should be absolved of any responsibility for failing to act to protect the potential victim. In our view, however, once a therapist does in fact determine, or under applicable professional standards reasonably should have determined that a patient poses a serious danger of violence to others, he bears a duty to exercise reasonable care to protect the foreseeable victim of that danger. While the discharge of this duty of due care will necessarily vary with the facts of each case, in each instance the adequacy of the therapist's conduct must be measured against the traditional negligence standard of the rendition of reasonable care under the circumstances.

. . . In sum, the therapist owes a legal duty not only to his patient, but also to his patient's would-be victim and is subject in both respects to scrutiny by judge and jury. . . .

The risk that unnecessary warnings may be given is a reasonable price to pay for the lives of possible victims that may be saved. We would hesitate to hold that the therapist who is aware that his patient expects to attempt to assassinate the President of the United States would not be obligated to warn the authorities because the therapist cannot predict with accuracy that his patient will commit the crime.

Defendants further argue that free and open communication is essential to psychotherapy that "Unless a patient is assured that information [revealed by him] can and will be held in utmost confidence, he will be reluctant to make the full disclosure upon which diagnosis and treatment depends." The giving of a warning, defendants contend, constitutes a breach of trust which entails the revelation of confidential communications.

We recognize the public interest in supporting effective treatment of mental illness and in protecting the rights of patients to privacy and the consequent public importance of safeguarding the confidential character of psychotherapeutic communication. Against this interest, however, we must weigh the public interest in safety from violent assault. The Legislature has undertaken the difficult task of balancing the countervailing concerns. In [California] Evidence Code section 1014, it established a broad rule of privilege to protect confidential communications between patient and psychotherapist. In Evidence Code section 1024, the Legislature created a specific and limited exception to the psychotherapist-patient privilege: "There is no privilege if the psychotherapist has reasonable cause to believe that the patient is in such mental or emotional condition as to be dangerous to himself or to the person or property of another and that disclosure of the communication is necessary to prevent the threatened danger."

We realize that the open and confidential character of psychotherapeutic dialogue encourages patients to express threats of violence, few of which are ever executed. Certainly a therapist should not be encouraged routinely to reveal such threats; such disclosures could seriously disrupt the patient's relationship with his therapist and with the persons threatened. To the contrary, the therapist's obligations to his patient require that he not disclose a confidence unless such disclosure is necessary to avert danger to others, and even then that he do so discreetly, and in a fashion that would preserve the privacy of his patient to the fullest extent compatible with the prevention of the threatened danger.

The revelation of a communication under the above circumstances is not a breach of trust or a violation of professional ethics; as stated in the Principles of Medical Ethics of the American Medical Association (1957), section 9: "A physician may not reveal the confidence entrusted to him in the course of medical attendance . . . *unless he is required to do so by law or unless it becomes necessary in order to protect the welfare of the individual or of the community.*" (Emphasis added.) We conclude that the public policy favoring protection of the confidential character of patient-psychotherapist communications must yield to the extent to which disclosure is essential to avert danger to others. The protective privilege ends where the public peril begins.

Our current crowded and computerized society compels the interdependence of its members. In this risk-infested society we can hardly tolerate the further exposure to danger that would result from a concealed knowledge of the therapist that his patient was lethal. If the exercise of reasonable care to protect the threatened victim requires the therapist to warn the endangered party or those who can reasonably be expected to notify him, we see no sufficient societal interest that would protect and justify concealment. The containment of such risks lies in the public interest. For the foregoing reasons, we find that plaintiffs' complaints can be amended to state a cause of action against defendants Moore, Powelson, Gold, and Yandell, and against the Regents as their employer, for breach of a duty to exercise reasonable care to protect Tatiana.

[The court went on to reject a claim by the defendants that release of information obtained from Poddar would violate a state statute governing the disclosure of confidential information in the possession of state officials. The court also held that the plaintiffs' claim was not barred by the state's governmental immunity statute in so far as it related to the psychiatrist's failure to warn third persons.]

WRIGHT, C.J., and SULLIVAN and RICHARDSON, JJ., concur.

MOSK, JUSTICE (concurring and dissenting).

I concur in the result in this instance only because the complaints allege that defendant therapists did in fact predict that Poddar would kill and were therefore negligent in failing to warn of that danger. Thus the issue here is very narrow: we are not concerned with whether the therapists, pursuant to the standards of their profession, "should have" predicted potential violence; they allegedly did so in actuality. Under these limited circumstances I agree that a cause of action can be stated.

*   *   *

I would restructure the rule designed by the majority to eliminate all reference to conformity to standards of the profession in predicting violence. If a psychiatrist does in fact predict violence, then a duty to warn arises. The majority's expansion of that rule will take us from the world of reality into the wonderland of clairvoyance.

CLARK, JUSTICE (dissenting).

Until today's majority opinion, both legal and medical authorities have agreed that confidentiality is essential to effectively treat the mentally ill, and that imposing a duty on doctors to disclose patient threats to potential victims would greatly impair treatment. Further, recognizing that effective treatment and society's safety are necessarily intertwined, the Legislature has already decided effective and confidential treatment is preferred over imposition of a duty to warn.

The issue whether effective treatment for the mentally ill should be sacrificed to a system of warnings is, in my opinion, properly one for the Legislature, and we are bound by its judgment. Moreover, even in the absence of clear legislative direction, we must reach the same conclusion because imposing the majority's new duty is certain to result in a net increase in violence.

The majority rejects the balance achieved by the Legislature's Lanterman–Petris–Short Act. ([Calif.] Welf. & Inst. Code, § 5000 et seq., hereafter the act.) In addition, the majority fails to recognize that, even absent the act, overwhelming policy considerations mandate against sacrificing fundamental patient interests without gaining a corresponding increase in public benefit.

* * *

Common Law Analysis

Entirely apart from the statutory provisions, the same result must be reached upon considering both general tort principles and the public policies favoring effective treatment, reduction of violence, and justified commitment.

Generally, a person owes no duty to control the conduct of another. Exceptions are recognized only in limited situations where (1) a special relationship exists between the defendant and injured party, or (2) a special relationship exists between defendant and the active wrongdoer, imposing a duty on defendant to control the wrongdoer's conduct. The majority does not contend the first exception is appropriate to this case.

* * *

Overwhelming policy considerations weigh against imposing a duty on psychotherapists to warn a potential victim against harm. While offering virtually no benefit to society, such a duty will frustrate psychiatric treatment, invade fundamental patient rights and increase violence.

The importance of psychiatric treatment and its need for confidentiality have been recognized by this court. "It is clearly recognized that the very practice of psychiatry vitally depends upon the reputation in the community that the psychiatrist will not tell."

Assurance of confidentiality is important for three reasons.

Deterrence from Treatment

First, without substantial assurance of confidentiality, those requiring treatment will be deterred from seeking assistance. It remains an unfortunate fact in our society that people seeking psychiatric guidance tend to become stigmatized. Apprehension of such stigma—apparently increased by the propensity of people considering treatment to see themselves in the worst possible light—creates a well-recognized reluctance to seek aid. This reluctance is alleviated by the psychiatrist's assurance of confidentiality.

Full Disclosure

Second, the guarantee of confidentiality is essential in eliciting the full disclosure necessary for effective treatment. The psychiatric patient approaches treatment with conscious and unconscious inhibitions against revealing his innermost thoughts. "Every person, however well-motivated, has to overcome resistances to therapeutic exploration. These resistances seek support from every possible source and the possibility of disclosure would easily be employed in the service of resistance."

Until a patient can trust his psychiatrist not to violate their confidential relationship, "the unconscious psychological control mechanism of repression will prevent the recall of past experiences."

Successful Treatment

Third, even if the patient fully discloses his thoughts, assurance that the confidential relationship will not be breached is necessary to maintain his trust in his psychiatrist—the very means by which treatment is effected.

. . . All authorities appear to agree that if the trust relationship cannot be developed because of collusive communication between the psychiatrist and others, treatment will be frustrated.

Given the importance of confidentiality to the practice of psychiatry, it becomes clear the duty to warn imposed by the majority will cripple the use and effectiveness of psychiatry. Many people, potentially violent—yet susceptible to treatment—will be deterred from seeking it; those seeking it will be inhibited from making revelations necessary to effective treatment; and, forcing the psychiatrist to violate the patient's trust will destroy the interpersonal relationship by which treatment is effected.

Violence and Civil Commitment

By imposing a duty to warn the majority contributes to the danger to society of violence by the mentally ill and greatly increases the risk of civil commitment—the total deprivation of liberty—of those who should not be confined. The impairment of treatment and risk of improper commitment resulting from the new duty to warn will not be limited to a few patients but will extend to a large number of the mentally ill. Although under existing psychiatric procedures only a relatively few receiving treatment will ever present a risk of violence, the number making threats is huge, and it is the latter group—not just the former—whose treatment will be impaired and whose risk of commitment will be increased.

Both the legal and psychiatric communities recognize that the process of determining potential violence in a patient is far from exact, being fraught with complexity and uncertainty. In fact precision has not even been attained in predicting who of those having already committed violent acts will again become violent, a task recognized to be of much simpler proportions.

This predictive uncertainty means that the number of disclosures will necessarily be large. As noted above, psychiatric patients are encouraged to discuss all thoughts of violence, and they often express such thoughts. However, unlike this court, the psychiatrist does not enjoy the benefit of overwhelming hindsight in seeing which few, if any, of his patients will ultimately become violent. Now, confronted by the majority's new duty, the psychiatrist must instantaneously calculate potential violence from each patient on each visit. The difficulties researchers have encountered in accurately predicting violence will be heightened for the practicing psychiatrist dealing for brief periods in his office with heretofore nonviolent patients. And, given the decision not to warn or commit must always be made at the psychiatrist's civil peril, one can expect most doubts will be resolved in favor of the psychiatrist protecting himself.

Neither alternative open to the psychiatrist seeking to protect himself is in the public interest. The warning itself is an impairment of the psychiatrist's ability to treat, depriving many patients of adequate treatment. It is to be expected that after disclosing their threats, a significant number of patients, who would not become violent if treated according to existing practices, will engage in violent conduct as a result of unsuccessful treatment. In short, the majority's duty to warn will not only impair treatment of many who would never become violent but worse, will result in a net increase in violence.

The second alternative open to the psychiatrist is to commit his patient rather than to warn. Even in the absence of threat of civil liability, the doubts of psychiatrists as to the seriousness of patient threats have led psychiatrists to overcommit to mental institutions. This overcommitment has been authoritatively documented in both legal and psychiatric studies.

Given the incentive to commit created by the majority's duty, this already serious situation will be worsened, contrary to Chief Justice

Wright's admonition "that liberty is no less precious because forfeited in a civil proceeding than when taken as a consequence of a criminal conviction."

Conclusion

* * *

The tragedy of Tatiana Tarasoff has led the majority to disregard the clear legislative mandate of the Lanterman–Petris–Short Act. Worse, the majority impedes medical treatment, resulting in increased violence from—and deprivation of liberty to—the mentally ill.

We should accept legislative and medical judgment, relying upon effective treatment rather than on indiscriminate warning.

The judgment should be affirmed.

McCOMB, J., concurs.

QUESTIONS AND COMMENTS

1.   *Scope of the holding.* Note that the *Tarasoff* opinion does not decide whether Dr. Moore or the University of California outpatient clinic was negligent. The case merely holds that the plaintiff has stated a cause of action that, if proven at trial, would entitle the plaintiff to relief. On remand to the lower court, the trier of fact would have had to decide whether Dr. Moore's failure to notify the victim or her family did in fact constitute a breach of his duty to the third-party victim. A jury might also have found that by notifying the police Dr. Moore had exercised due care and thus was not negligent. (The case was settled by the parties out of court prior to retrial.)

2.   *The* Tarasoff *analysis.* The majority decision in *Tarasoff* strives to make the formulation of new doctrine appear as a natural and logical extension of existing doctrine. In reaching its conclusion that therapists may have a duty to third parties, the majority pursues three lines of analysis.

First, it cites earlier cases from other jurisdictions that imposed a duty on physicians to notify third parties who are likely to come into contact with a patient suffering from a contagious disease. However, is there a difference between a situation where there is a readily diagnosable and invariably contagious disease and where a therapist is dealing with a condition that is difficult to diagnose and has an uncertain impact on future conduct?

Second, the majority opinion looks to § 315 of the Restatement of Torts Second, which provides:

> There is no duty . . . to control the conduct of a third person as to prevent him from causing physical harm to another unless
>
>> (a) a special relation exists between the actor and the third person which imposes a duty upon the actor to control the third person's conduct, or

(b) a special relation exists between the actor and the other which gives to the other a right to protection.

Although the wording of § 315 seems compatible with the majority's holding in *Tarasoff,* the commentary accompanying this section should not be overlooked. It emphasizes that the duty attaches only to certain enumerated "special relations," for example, when the defendant is an innkeeper, common carrier, or landowner. Arguably, therefore, the drafters of the Restatement Second did not encompass the psychiatrist-patient relationship within § 315.

The third part of the court's opinion was a policy analysis. Here the court addressed the competing interests of protecting the integrity of the therapist-client relationship and promoting the safety of persons who may be endangered by these clients. The court concluded as a matter of policy that the need to protect persons from serious harm outweighed the possibly destructive effects on the client-therapist relationship that might be caused by a rule requiring disclosure to third parties. Do you agree?

3.   Tarasoff *and the ability to predict.* To what extent are the divergent conclusions of Justice Tobriner's opinion for the majority and Justice Clark's dissenting opinion founded on different perceptions as to the ability of clinicians to predict dangerous or abnormal behavior? Do any policy considerations support the imposition of a duty to protect if, in fact, the ability of the therapist to predict future dangerous behavior is very limited? See Chapter Six, Part II.C., discussing the challenges of accurately predicting dangerous behavior.

Regarding clinicians' abilities to predict dangerousness, consider Daniel J. Givelber et al., *Tarasoff, Myth and Reality: An Empirical Study of Private Law in Action*, 1984 Wis. L. Rev. 443 (1984). The authors asked a group of psychiatrists, psychologists, and social workers to gauge their ability to predict dangerous behavior. Over 75% of the clinicians responded that they could make firm predictions ranging from probable violence to certain violence. Only 5% suggested that violence is impossible to predict. Research studies, however, have long questioned the ability of clinicians to make these predictions. As one commentator has noted:

> Recent literature on violence prediction contrasts two broad types of assessment methods—those that rely on "clinical judgment," and those that rely on "actuarial methods." In risk assessments made using clinical judgment alone, mental health professionals use traditional interviewing and history-taking techniques similar to those used in the common practice of outpatient medicine and psychotherapy. . . . By contrast, actuarial methods feature algorithms, formulae, or some other mechanical combination of information for classification purposes, and the resulting probability assessment is derived from relationships between risk factors and outcomes that have been established empirically. The term "actuarial" is applied to this type of assessment because the process resembles what insurance companies do when judging the risk of some future event. When professionals perform

actuarial risk assessments for dangerousness, they look for information about prespecified items concerning their evaluees, then plug this information into a formula or other predetermined scoring system. The result is a numerical value or category that summarizes the evaluee's violence risk. . . .

[E]mpirically based, statistical prediction methods probably provide more accurate assessments of dangerousness than does the unaided clinical judgment of mental health professionals. In support of this position are numerous studies of various prediction tasks comparing actuarial techniques with predictions by unaided clinicians, and finding that the former were better (more accurate) than the latter.

Douglas Mossman, *The Imperfection of Protection Through Detection and Intervention Lessons from Three Decades of Research on the Psychiatric Assessment of Violence Risk*, 30 J. Legal Med. 109, 127 (2009). How can clinicians utilize actuarial methods when deciding whether a client is dangerous?

4.   *An alternative approach.* Justice Mosk in his concurring opinion would limit the duty to warn to those cases in which the "psychiatrist does in fact predict violence." Presumably, this means liability cannot be imposed unless the clinician has actually concluded that the client is likely to be violent. One commentator has praised this approach:

Making the legal duty dependent on the therapist's subjective determination of the patient's dangerousness would of course extremely limit the number of instances in which suit could successfully be brought. In the usual case, once the therapist has convinced himself that a patient is certainly dangerous, he will take some action. Only where he has reached this conclusion—and made it clear in records or consultation—and then failed to act would liability be imposed. Unlike the *Tarasoff* standard, then, this formulation would provide no incentive to the therapist to overpredict dangerousness early in the treatment process and to act to warn potential victims who might or might not be in serious danger. It seems to me quite clear that both the public interest and the patient's needs are better served by a legal standard which does not serve to discourage or undermine the effective treatment of potentially dangerous individuals. Moreover, the safety of the potential victims may well be more successfully promoted by such a standard, since premature action by the therapist is likely to terminate the therapeutic relationship, with the result that patients whose illnesses might have been successfully treated would remain a source of danger to those they originally threatened.

Alan Stone, *The Tarasoff Decisions: Suing Psychotherapists to Safeguard Society*, 90 Harv. L. Rev. 358, 375–76 (1976).

How practical is Justice Mosk's standard? Are the arguments in favor of it convincing? What evidence would a plaintiff have to introduce to establish the existence of a duty? Would this approach in effect permit clinicians to insulate themselves from liability? In other words, would they be able to avoid liability for a failure to protect a third-party by merely refusing to formulate predictions of violence? Would they avoid related discussions with a client, even when therapeutically needed, to avoid generating any such prediction? Following an unexpected violent act by a client, are they likely to selectively remember only those aspects of their therapy sessions that would discount their ability to make such a prediction? Or simply not recall one of many conversations with this and other clients.

5. *Source of the threat.* A relatively recent California ruling that has caused considerable concern among mental health providers determined that the communication of the client's threat triggering the duty to protect could come from someone other than the client. In *Ewing v. Goldstein*, 15 Cal. Rptr. 3d 864 (Ct. App. 2004), a patient's father had informed his son's therapist that his son had threatened to harm his ex-girlfriend's new boyfriend. The patient subsequently killed the boyfriend, and the court ruled that this indirect communication of the patient's threat could suffice to impose on the therapist the duty to protect. The court stated that "[a] communication from a patient's family member to the patient's therapist, made for the purpose of advancing the patient's therapy, is a 'patient communication.'" Id. at 868. See Hafemeister et al., supra, at 83.

6. *Influence of* Tarasoff. The *Tarasoff* duty to warn foreseeable victims has been widely adopted by courts in numerous other jurisdictions. However, the doctrine has been explicitly rejected by courts in at least three states. See *Boynton v. Burglass*, 590 So. 2d 446 (Fla. Dist. Ct. App. 1991); *Thapar v. Zezulka*, 994 S.W.2d 635 (Tex. 1999); *Nasser v. Parker*, 455 S.E.2d 502 (Va. 1995).

7. *Hypothetical.* Assume the same basic fact situation as in *Tarasoff*, except that the psychiatrist, Dr. Kareful, upon learning of the patient's intent to murder his supervisor at his place of work, immediately initiates emergency commitment proceedings [emergency commitments are considered in Chapter Eight, Part IV.B.]. However, he does not notify the patient's supervisor. The patient is hospitalized but a week later is released, at which point he goes to the place where he previously worked and murders his supervisor. Under these circumstances could Dr. Kareful be held liable under California law in an action by the victim's next of kin? What legal standard should be applied to determine liability in this situation?

8. *Statutory limitations on* Tarasoff. At least thirty-seven states have enacted statutes that limit or clarify psychotherapists' liability to third parties. Colorado has restricted the duty to protect to when the client has communicated "a serious threat of imminent physical violence against a specific person or persons." Colo. Rev. Stat. 13–21–117. Louisiana has limited the duty to when the client "has communicated a threat of physical violence, which is deemed to be significant in the clinical judgment of the treating [clinician], against a clearly identified victim or victims, coupled with the apparent intent and ability to carry out such threat." La. Rev. Stat. Ann. § 9:2800.2. In some states, a duty to protect is established (and limited) by

exceptions to their confidentiality requirements. See, e.g., Fla. Stat. Ann. § 456.059 (clinician may disclose client communications "to the extent necessary" if a client "has made an actual threat to physically harm an identifiable victim or victims; and [the clinician] makes a clinical judgment that the patient has the apparent capability to commit such an act and that it is more likely than not that in the near future the [client] will carry out that threat").

California now exempts psychiatrists from liability under certain involuntary treatment situations. For example, psychiatrists cannot be held liable for "any action by a person released" from a facility offering "72–hour [detention of inebriates for] treatment and evaluation" at or before the end of 72 hours. Cal. Welf. & Inst. Code § 5173. Other statutes address facilities specifically treating suicidal patients (§ 5267), facilities offering 90–day involuntary treatments of "imminently dangerous persons" (§ 5306), and facilities and professionals responsible for the detention of a person pursuant to the Lanterman–Petris–Short Act (§ 5113).

California modified the *Tarasoff* duty in 1985 by adopting § 43.92 of its Civil Code (West's Ann. Cal. Civ. Code § 43.92). Section 43.92 immunizes therapists from liability except where the client "has communicated to the psychotherapist a serious threat of physical violence against a reasonably identifiable victim or victims." Governor Deukemejian had vetoed a similar measure in 1984, claiming that the bill increased the danger to the public by limiting the *Tarasoff* duty. Does § 43.92 embrace a standard even narrower than that advocated by Justice Mosk? Suppose that in *Tarasoff*, Poddar, during therapy sessions, made numerous statements exhibiting extreme hostility toward Tatiana but never explicitly threatened to kill her. If the defendants nevertheless concluded that Poddar evinced a threat to Tatiana, would the *Tarasoff* majority find a duty to protect? Would there be a duty under Justice Mosk's formulation? Under § 43.92? How explicit must the communication be before liability will be found under § 43.92?

9.   *Criminal liability after* Tarasoff. Assume a psychotherapist fails to take steps to prevent a client from killing another after the client has specified the victim during therapy, in contravention of the California law described above. Could the psychotherapist be found liable not only in tort, but criminally as well? Under the Model Penal Code, an individual who purposely fails to perform a duty and is aware of a substantial risk that the failure to perform this duty will lead to the death of another can be convicted of manslaughter. See Model Penal Code § 2.06(3), (4). Furthermore, a breach of a duty toward another that causes a reasonably foreseeable death can amount to negligent or reckless homicide. Model Penal Code §§ 2.01(3), 210.3, 210.4. If, as under California law, the duty is triggered merely by hearing an individual threaten to harm a specified individual and a breach of duty is established by failing to take steps to protect the specified individual, could *anyone* (a teacher, lawyer, or lay person) be liable, civilly or criminally, for a subsequent death caused by the person who threatened the harm? What special expertise is needed under such a legal regime? See generally

Christopher Slobogin, *Tarasoff as a Duty to Treat: Insights from Criminal Law*, 75 U. Cin. L. Rev. 645 (2006). The liability of various defendants under *Tarasoff* is considered again below.

10. *Use of patient disclosures in criminal prosecutions.* Essentially, the *Tarasoff* doctrine and its later permutations represent a decision by the courts that the protection of the public outweighs the benefits of maintaining the traditional confidentiality associated with client-psychotherapist communications. While confidentiality is deemed overridden when the psychotherapist is expected to either warn potential victims or take other actions to protect them such as notifying the police, the use of these communications may have limits in conjunction with a criminal prosecution focused on the client's actions.

In *United States v. Glass*, 133 F.3d 1356 (10th Cir. 1998), the defendant, while hospitalized, disclosed to the psychotherapist his intent to shoot President Clinton because "he wanted to get into the history books like Hinckley." Several days later, upon agreeing to participate in outpatient treatment and reside in his father's home, he was released. Ten days later, upon discovering that the defendant had left his father's home, a hospital staff member notified the police, which referred the matter to the Secret Service. Secret Service agents then interviewed the psychotherapist who had been treating the defendant at the hospital and were told of the threat made by the defendant. The defendant was subsequently indicted for knowingly and willfully making a "threat to take the life of, to kidnap, or to inflict bodily harm against the President of the United States." In reversing the trial court's admission into evidence of the otherwise privileged communications between the defendant and the psychotherapist, the appellate court remanded the case to the trial court to "determine whether, in [the] context of this case, the threat was serious when it was uttered and whether its disclosure was the only means of averting harm to the President when the disclosure was made." While the court, thus, did not hold that the privileged information was inadmissible, it did place limits on its admission into evidence by requiring the prosecution to show that the disclosure at the time it was made to the police "was the only means of averting harm to the President." In *United States v. Hayes*, 227 F.3d 578 (6th Cir. 2000), the Sixth Circuit took a more restrictive view of the admissibility of client disclosures as a basis for criminal prosecution. The opinion of the court in *Hayes* and a contra opinion by the Florida Supreme Court are treated infra Chapter Five, Part II.D.4.b.

d. Later Applications of Tarasoff

Brady v. Hopper

United States District Court, District of Colorado, 1983.
570 F. Supp. 1333.

I.

Allegations of the Complaint

Plaintiffs James Scott Brady, Timothy John McCarthy, and Thomas K. Delahanty were all shot and seriously injured by John W. Hinckley, Jr. ("Hinckley") in his attempt to assassinate President Reagan on March 30, 1981, in Washington, D.C. The defendant, Dr. John J. Hopper, Jr., is the psychiatrist who had been treating Hinckley from late October, 1980, until March, 1981.

Plaintiffs' complaint alleges that Dr. Hopper was negligent in examining, diagnosing, and treating Hinckley in conformity with reasonable standards of psychiatric care. According to the complaint, Hinckley was brought to Dr. Hopper in late October, 1980, by Hinckley's parents because the parents were concerned about their son's behavior, including a purported suicide attempt by drug overdose. Plaintiffs allege [that] despite Hinckley's attempted suicide on at least one if not several occasions, Dr. Hopper negligently formed the opinion that Hinckley was not seriously ill. Dr. Hopper proceeded to treat Hinckley and prescribed valium and biofeedback therapy. Dr. Hopper also recommended to Hinckley's parents that Hinckley be on his own by the end of March, 1981. Plaintiffs assert that Dr. Hopper's treatment was not only ineffective, but that it actually aggravated Hinckley's mental condition, and made him more aggressive and dangerous, thereby creating an unreasonable risk of harm to others.

The complaint alleges that Dr. Hopper knew or should have known that Hinckley was a danger to himself or others, and that Dr. Hopper either possessed or had access to, information which would have indicated that Hinckley identified with the assassin in the movie "Taxi Driver"; that he was collecting books and articles on political assassination; and that Hinckley possessed guns and ammunition. According to the complaint, Hinckley's parents were aware of and concerned about their son's worsening condition, and contacted Dr. Hopper and recommended that their son be hospitalized. Despite the possibility Hinckley might have been amenable to that idea, Dr. Hopper recommended that Hinckley not be hospitalized, and that treatment continue on an outpatient basis.

The rest of Hinckley's strange story is well known. In March, 1981, Hinckley left Denver and traveled across the country to Washington, D.C. On March 30, 1981, he attempted to assassinate President Reagan, and, in the process, shot and injured plaintiffs. Hinckley was subsequently tried for these crimes and found not guilty by reason of insanity. He is currently confined to St. Elizabeth's Hospital where he is receiving medical and psychiatric care.

The gravamen of plaintiffs' complaint is that if Dr. Hopper had properly performed his professional duties, he would have controlled Hinckley's behavior; therefore, Hinckley would not have made the presidential assassination attempt. Specifically, plaintiffs assert that the prescription of valium and biofeedback therapy, coupled with the advice that Hinckley's parents "cut him off", aggravated Hinckley's condition and actually contributed to his dangerous propensity. Further, plaintiffs assert that Dr. Hopper should have consulted with another psychiatrist regarding his form of treatment, and that Dr. Hopper should have taken steps to have Hinckley confined. Finally, plaintiffs allege that Dr. Hopper should have warned Hinckley's parents of their son's extremely dangerous condition, and that he should have warned law enforcement officials of Hinckley's potential for political assassination.

II.

Summary of the Arguments

The primary issue raised by defendant's motion is whether the relationship between therapist and patient gives rise to a legal duty such that Dr. Hopper can be held liable for the injuries caused to plaintiffs by Hinckley. The Restatement (Second) of Torts § 315 states as follows:

> There is no duty so to control the conduct of a third person as to prevent him from causing physical harm to another unless
>
> (a) a special relation exists between the actor and the third person which imposes a duty upon the actor to control the third person's conduct, or
>
> (b) a special relation exists between the actor and the other which gives to the other a right to protection.

The thrust of defendant's argument is that the relationship between Dr. Hopper and Hinckley, that of a therapist and outpatient, is not a "special relationship" which gives rise to a duty on the part of the therapist to control the actions of the patient. In other words, defendant asserts that the therapist-outpatient relationship lacks sufficient elements of control required to bring the therapist within the language of § 315.

* * *

Defendant next argues that the duty to control the violent acts of another does not arise absent specific threats directed to a reasonably identifiable victim. The leading case on a therapist's liability for the violent actions of a patient is *Tarasoff.*

*   *   *

In *Thompson v. County of Alameda* (1980), the California Supreme Court again faced the question of the extent of liability to a third party for the dangerous acts of another. In *Thompson*, a juvenile offender known to have dangerous propensities was confined in a county institution. This patient had made generalized threats regarding his intention to kill, but had made no specific threats regarding any identifiable person. The county institution released the patient on temporary leave, and, within a day, the patient killed a young boy in his neighborhood. The court refused to extend *Tarasoff* to a setting where there was no identifiable victim. Instead, it took a more limited approach to the duty to warn, and concluded that even in the case of a person with a history of violence, no duty existed when the person had made only nonspecific threats of harm directed at nonspecific victims. *Id.* [ ]

*   *   *

III.

Discussion

In my opinion, the main issue raised by the pleadings and briefs is not simply whether the therapist-outpatient relationship is a "special relationship" which gives rise to a legal duty on the part of the therapist; rather the key issue is to what extent was Dr. Hopper obligated to protect these particular plaintiffs from this particular harm?[8] It is implicit in the majority of cases in this area that the therapist-patient relationship is one which under certain circumstances will give rise to a duty on the part of the therapist to protect third persons from harm. *Tarasoff* [ ]. However, the existence of a special relationship does not necessarily mean that the duties created by that relationship are owed to the world at large. It is fundamental that the duty owed be measured by the foreseeability of the risk and whether the danger created is sufficiently large to embrace the specific harm. *Palsgraf* [ ].

It is this requirement of foreseeability which has led numerous courts to conclude that a therapist or others cannot be held liable for injuries inflicted upon third persons absent specific threats to a readily identifiable victim. [ ] Unless a patient makes specific threats, the possibility that he may inflict injury on another is vague, speculative, and a matter of conjecture. However, once the patient verbalizes his intentions and directs his threats to identifiable victims, then the possibility of harm to third persons becomes foreseeable, and the therapist has a duty to protect those third persons from the threatened harm.

---

[8]   Definition of the scope of the defendant's duty is a question of law for the court. [ ]

For purposes of this motion only, it must be assumed that Dr. Hopper's treatment and diagnosis of Hinckley fell below the applicable standard of care. Moreover, the doctor-patient relationship between Dr. Hopper and Hinckley was one which gave rise to certain duties on the part of Dr. Hopper. The real question, however, is whether that duty encompasses the injuries of which plaintiffs complain. In other words, was there a foreseeable risk that Hinckley would inflict the harm that he did?

Accepting as true the facts alleged in the complaint and viewing them in a light most favorable to plaintiffs, it is my conclusion that plaintiffs' injuries were not foreseeable; therefore, the plaintiffs fall outside of the scope of defendant's duty. Nowhere in the complaint are there allegations that Hinckley made any threats regarding President Reagan, or indeed that he ever threatened anyone. At most, the complaint states that if Dr. Hopper had interviewed Hinckley more carefully, he would have discovered that Hinckley was obsessed with Jodie Foster and the movie "Taxi Driver", that he collected books on Ronald Reagan and political assassination, and that he practiced with guns. According to plaintiffs, if Dr. Hopper had properly performed his professional duties, he would have learned that Hinckley suffered from delusions and severe mental illness, as opposed to being merely maladjusted. Even assuming all of these facts and many of plaintiffs' conclusions to be true, the allegations are still insufficient to create a legal duty on the part of Dr. Hopper to protect these plaintiffs from the specific harm.

The parties have for the most part cast their arguments in terms of whether the relationship between Dr. Hopper and *Hinckley* gave rise to a particular duty on the part of Dr. Hopper. However, the legal obstacle to the maintenance of this suit is that there is no relationship between Dr. Hopper and *plaintiffs* which creates any legal obligation from Dr. Hopper to these plaintiffs. As explained by Justice Cardozo, negligence is a matter of relation between the parties, and must be founded upon the foreseeability of harm to the person in fact injured. *Palsgraf* [ ].

In essence, defendant argues that the instant case presents an even clearer basis than *Thompson* for a finding of no duty. It is argued that even according to the allegations in the complaint, Hinckley had no history of violence directed to persons other than himself; he had no history of arrests; no previous hospitalizations arising from any violent episodes; and in fact, he did not appear to be a danger to others. Thus, defendant asserts, this case involves, and plaintiffs have pled, none of the "warning signs" by which Hinckley's conduct or mental state would give rise to a duty on the part of Dr. Hopper.

The question of whether a legal duty should be imposed necessarily involves social policy considerations. See *Prosser, Law of Torts* § 43, 257 (4th ed. 1971). In the present case, there are cogent policy reasons for limiting the scope of the therapist's liability. To impose upon those in the counseling professions an ill-defined "duty to control" would require therapists to be ultimately responsible for the actions of their patients. Such a rule would closely approximate a strict liability standard of care, and therapists would be potentially liable for all harm inflicted by persons presently or formerly under psychiatric treatment. Human behavior is simply too unpredictable, and the field of psychotherapy presently too inexact, to so greatly expand the scope of therapists' liability. In my opinion, the "specific threats to specific victims" rule states a workable, reasonable, and fair boundary upon the sphere of a therapist's liability to third persons for the acts of their patients.

The present case is one which makes application of the previously stated rules and policy considerations particularly difficult. Plaintiffs' injuries are severe and their damages extensive. Their plight as innocent bystanders to a bizarre and sensational assassination attempt is tragic and evokes great sympathy. Nevertheless, the question before the Court is whether Dr. Hopper can be subjected to liability as a matter of law for the injuries inflicted upon plaintiffs by Hinckley. I conclude that under the facts pleaded in the complaint, the question must be answered in the negative. Accordingly, it is ORDERED that defendant's motion to dismiss is granted.

QUESTIONS AND COMMENTS

1. *The readily identifiable victim standard.* The *Brady* court requirement of a readily identifiable victim, affirmed on appeal at *Brady v Hopper*, 751 F.2d 329 (10th Cir. 1984), tracks the standard established by the California Supreme Court. The requirement has also been followed by most jurisdictions, at least with respect to the duty to protect a potential victim (as opposed to a duty to take more general preventive steps).

2. *Application of the standard.* Three years after *Tarasoff, Thompson v. Cnty. of Alameda*, 614 P.2d 728 (Cal. 1980), held that a general threat that the client would kill some child in his neighborhood precluded the imposition of liability for failure to warn because of the lack of a clearly identifiable victim. However, as illustrated in the case that follows, the absence of a readily identifiable victim does not necessarily relieve the therapist of liability to third parties who are injured by a predictably dangerous client.

HAMMAN v. COUNTY OF MARICOPA
Supreme Court of Arizona, 1989.
161 Ariz. 58, 775 P.2d 1122.

HOLOHAN, JUSTICE (Retired).

We granted the plaintiffs' petition for review to determine the nature and extent of a psychiatrist's duty to third parties injured by the psychiatrist's patient. The plaintiffs filed a tort action against the defendants for injuries inflicted on Robert Hamman by John Carter, a patient of the defendant, Dr. Manuel Suguitan. The superior court granted the defendants' motion for summary judgment, and the Court of Appeals affirmed the judgment of the lower court in part and reversed in part.

* * *

John Carter is the son of plaintiff Alice Hamman, and stepson of plaintiff Robert Hamman. On January 5, 1982, the Hammans brought Carter to the Maricopa County Hospital emergency psychiatric center because Carter had been exhibiting strange behavior. Dr. Suguitan, a psychiatrist who had previously admitted Carter to the hospital in August, 1981, interviewed Carter for about five minutes and noted the following symptoms: (1) anxious but cooperative, (2) fear and apprehension about a place to live, (3) loose associations and blocking,[1] (4) inappropriate affect,[2] (5) tries to conceal depression by grimacing, and (6) employs denial[3] and projection.[4] Dr. Suguitan did not review the medical records of Carter's 1981 hospitalization.

After interviewing Carter, Dr. Suguitan had a discussion with Mrs. Hamman, the specifics of which are disputed by the parties. Mrs. Hamman stated in her deposition that she told Dr. Suguitan the details of Carter's abnormal behavior since his hospitalization in August 1981. She described various incidents of strange behavior, a few instances of violent conduct, and a recent incident in which Carter was discovered to be carrying photos of animals with their heads cut off. Mrs. Hamman also testified in her deposition that she told Dr. Suguitan that she and Mr. Hamman feared that Carter would either be killed or kill somebody and that they never turned their backs on Carter. Mrs. Hamman further testified that Dr. Suguitan told her that Carter was schizophrenic and psychotic, but that he was "harmless." Dr. Suguitan denied in his deposition that Mrs. Hamman told him about the specific details of the patient's conduct, and he denied that he ever told her that Carter was "harmless."

Dr. Suguitan did not refer to Carter's medical records from his previous hospitalization at Maricopa County. Those records would have shown among other things that Carter expressed jealousy of his

---

[1] " 'Loose associations' occur when a person starts talking on one subject and going on a tangent and continues on another subject unrelated to the first topic. . . . "

" 'Blocking' is when a person starts to say something and in midsentence he stops and he is unable to proceed to complete that sentence or statement that he intended to make."

[2] "Affect" is "a freudian term for the feeling of pleasantness or unpleasantness evoked by a stimulus; also the emotional complex associated with a mental state. . . . "

[3] " 'Denial' is manifestations when the patient does not want to talk about what is bothering them."

[4] "Projection" is "a mental mechanism by which a repressed complex is disguised by being regarded as belonging to the external world or to someone else."

stepfather and that the treatment plan had been to "seclude and restrain" the patient from agitation, assaultive, or dangerous behavior. Carter had also been examined and treated in the past at Desert Samaritan Hospital. Dr. Suguitan did not review the patient's medical records from that hospital. Those records would have revealed that Carter had a history of drug abuse and violent behavior, and he had made statements that he wanted to punish someone.

On January 5, 1982, as Mrs. Hamman discussed Carter's behavior and the Hammans' fear of him, she repeatedly begged Dr. Suguitan to admit Carter to the hospital. Dr. Suguitan refused to admit Carter. Instead, he wrote a prescription for Navane, gave it to Mrs. Hamman, and instructed her to give Carter 10 milligrams of Navane each morning and night. Dr. Suguitan admits he ordered this treatment knowing that Carter had not been taking the Navane which had been previously prescribed for him in August, 1981. Mrs. Hamman stated that Dr. Suguitan then told her to call him again in one week. Dr. Suguitan states that he advised Mrs. Hamman to take Carter to Tri–City Medical Center for follow-up care.

Upon being denied admission, Carter fled down the street brushing his teeth. The Hammans eventually persuaded him to get in their truck and go home. They gave him the medication as prescribed that night and again the following morning and night on January 6.

Although Mrs. Hamman tried to give Carter his medication on the morning of January 7, Carter refused to take it. At approximately 11:00 a.m. that day, Mr. Hamman while working on a home project with an electric drill, was attacked without warning by Carter. He repeatedly beat Hamman over the head with wooden dowels. Mr. Hamman suffered a heart attack during the beating as well as severe brain damage from the blows to his head. Carter later stated he believed Mr. Hamman was going to physically attack Mrs. Hamman with the drill, and that he (Carter) reacted as he did to protect his mother. Carter was later criminally charged for the beating, but found not guilty by reason of insanity.

The Hammans subsequently filed this civil action. The complaint contained three counts charging medical malpractice by Dr. Suguitan while employed by Maricopa County, general negligence, and a claim against Maricopa County for negligent training and supervision of psychiatric personnel.

The defendants filed a motion for summary judgment, essentially contending Dr. Suguitan owed no duty to the Hammans because Carter had never communicated to Suguitan any specific threat against the Hammans. The trial court granted the defendants' motion, and entered judgment against the plaintiffs dismissing all their claims for relief.

On appeal, the Court of Appeals divided the plaintiffs' claims into two separate theories of liability: (1) that Dr. Suguitan owed them a duty not to negligently diagnose and treat Carter's condition, and (2) that they reasonably relied upon Dr. Suguitan's advice that Carter was harmless. Regarding the first theory, the majority of the Court of Appeals followed the "specific threats to specific victims" approach. *See Brady v. Hopper.* Under this view, a psychiatrist incurs no duty to any third party unless his patient communicates to the psychiatrist a specific threat against a specific person.

*   *   *

We approve of the ruling of the Court of Appeals that the alleged negligent representation by Dr. Suguitan that Carter was "harmless" stated a valid claim. The issue taken for review is whether Dr. Suguitan and Maricopa County owed a duty to the Hammans, absent a specific threat by the patient against them, properly to diagnose, treat or control the patient.

Analysis

A negligence action may be maintained only if there is a duty or obligation, recognized by law, which requires the defendant to conform to a particular standard of conduct in order to protect others from unreasonable risks of harm. The issue of duty is usually one for the court as a matter of law. The danger reasonably to be perceived defines the duty to be obeyed.

*   *   *

Tarasoff and its progeny

The landmark case regarding the duty of a psychiatrist to protect others against the conduct of a patient is *Tarasoff.* . . . The *Tarasoff* court held that the psychiatrist-patient relationship was sufficient under [Restatement of Torts, Second] § 315 to support the imposition of an affirmative duty on the defendant for the benefit of third persons. The court ruled that when a psychiatrist determines or, pursuant to the standards of the profession, should determine that a patient presents a serious danger of violence to another, the psychiatrist incurs an obligation to use reasonable care to protect the intended victim against such danger. According to the *Tarasoff* court, discharge of that duty may require the psychiatrist to warn the intended victim or others reasonably likely to notify the victim, to notify the police, *"or to take whatever other steps are reasonably necessary under the circumstances."* (Emphasis added).

Although the *Tarasoff* decision did not state that a psychiatrist's duty to third parties arises only when his patient communicates a specific threat concerning a specific individual, numerous subsequent decisions [so] interpret *Tarasoff.* For example, in *Brady*, John W. Hinckley, Jr. injured the plaintiffs in his attempt to assassinate President Reagan. The suit alleged, in part, that Hinckley's psychiatrist had negligently diagnosed and treated him. The *Brady* court held that the psychiatrist owed no duty to the plaintiffs because Hinckley had not made specific threats against a readily identifiable victim.

Similarly, in *Thompson v. County of Alameda* (1980), the parents of a young child sued the county for the wrongful death of their son. The juvenile offender, James F., killed the child within 24 hours of his release from confinement into the temporary custody of his mother. James stated he would kill a child in the community at random, and the county knew it. Nonetheless, county officials released him without warning local police, parents, or James' mother. Distinguishing *Thompson* from *Tarasoff*, the majority of the California Supreme Court refused to impose "blanket liability." The court stated that liability may be imposed only in those instances in which the released offender posed a predictable threat of harm to a named or readily identifiable victim. James made a generalized threat to a segment of the population. Consequently, the majority refused to impose upon the psychiatrist a duty to protect such a large group in the community.

Other courts, however, have not required a specific threat as a prerequisite for liability. Instead, they require that the psychiatrist reasonably foresee that the risk engendered by the patient's condition would endanger others. For example, in *Petersen v. State* (Wash. 1983), a patient was hospitalized for several weeks and treated with Navane after his psychiatrist diagnosed him as having schizophrenic and hallucinogenic symptoms. The hospital allowed the patient to go home for Mother's Day, but required him to return that night. Upon his return, hospital personnel observed the patient driving recklessly and spinning his car in circles on hospital grounds. The psychiatrist nevertheless released the patient the following morning and continued to prescribe Navane even though he knew of the patient's reluctance to take such medication. Five days later, the patient drove through a red light at 50–60 miles per hour, striking plaintiff's car and injuring her. The *Petersen* court emphasized the importance of foreseeability in defining the scope of a person's duty to exercise due care. In affirming plaintiff's claim based on negligent treatment of the patient, the court ruled that the psychiatrist had a duty to protect any person foreseeably endangered by the patient.

*   *   *

In the present case, the Court of Appeals would limit a psychiatrist's duty and liability to cases in which there are specific threats against third parties, *i.e.*, the *Brady* approach. The plaintiffs concede that Carter never made any specific threats against Mr. Hamman.

Standard

We believe the *Brady* approach is too narrow. *Tarasoff* envisioned a broader scope of a psychiatrist's duty when the court stated: "[O]nce a therapist does in fact determine, or under applicable professional standards reasonably should have determined, that a patient poses a serious danger of violence to others, he bears a duty to exercise reasonable care to protect the foreseeable victim of that danger." Additionally, we agree with those cases interpreting *Tarasoff* which state that a psychiatrist should not be relieved of this duty merely because his patient never verbalized any specific threat. We recognize the concern about adopting a rule which would be too inclusive, subjecting psychiatrists to an unreasonably wide range of potential liability. However, we believe that the approach used by the Ninth Circuit in *Jablonski* allays such fears and represents a sound analytical foundation for the facts before us. In holding that Jablonski's girlfriend (Kimball) was a foreseeable victim, the court stated:

> Unlike the killer in *Tarasoff*, Jablonski made no specific threats concerning any specific individuals. Nevertheless, Jablonski's previous history indicated that he would likely direct his violence against Kimball. He had raped and committed other acts of violence against his wife. His psychological profile indicated that his violence was likely to be directed against women very close to him. This, in turn, was borne out by his attack on Pahls. Thus, Kimball was specifically identified or "targeted" to a much greater extent than were the neighborhood children in *Thompson*. [ ]

Dr. Suguitan was aware that schizophrenic-psychotic patients such as Carter are prone to unexpected episodes of violence. He knew that Carter was living with and being cared for by the Hammans. Dr. Suguitan, in denying Carter's admission to the hospital, released the patient into the care of the Hammans. If indeed Dr. Suguitan negligently diagnosed Carter as harmless, the most likely affected victims would be the Hammans. Their constant physical proximity to Carter placed them in an obvious zone of danger. The Hammans were readily identifiable persons who might suffer harm if the psychiatrist was negligent in the diagnosis or treatment of the patient. The fact that Carter never verbalized any specific threats against the Hammans does not change the circumstances that, even without such threats, the most likely victims of the patient's violent reaction would be the Hammans. We reject the notion that the psychiatrist's duty to third persons is limited to those against whom a specific threat has been made. We hold that the standard originally suggested in *Tarasoff* is properly applicable to psychiatrists. When a psychiatrist determines, or under applicable professional standards reasonably should have determined, that a patient poses a serious danger of violence to others, the psychiatrist has a duty to exercise reasonable care to protect the *foreseeable victim* of that danger. The foreseeable victim is one who is said to be within the zone of danger, that is, subject to probable risk of the patient's violent conduct.

Control

The defendants contend that Dr. Suguitan did not fail in any obligation to protect the Hammans. They point out that any duty by the psychiatrist to control his patient is limited by statute. Unless a patient meets the statutory criteria, the psychiatrist cannot involuntarily admit a patient into the hospital.

The defendants argue if the patient was not dangerous, there could be no involuntary commitment. Dr. Suguitan found Carter not dangerous, therefore, he could not be committed and the defendant could not control him.

The plaintiffs, however, submitted evidence from two psychiatrists in opposition to the defendants' motion for summary judgment. The plaintiffs' psychiatrists, in their affidavits, stated that a competent examination and proper diagnosis would have disclosed that Carter was a person suffering from a mental illness which made him dangerous to others. He was, therefore, admittable to the hospital on an involuntary basis under the statutes. They further stated that the defendant's examination of the patient fell below the acceptable standard for psychiatrists. The issue of ability to control is one which must be decided at trial.

The plaintiffs' experts in their affidavits also stated that even if Carter was not admittable as an emergency patient, there were numerous other acceptable medical procedures and precautions which Dr. Suguitan should have taken to lessen the danger posed to the Hammans. Some of these other steps include not only warning the Hammans of Carter's potential for danger, but also providing detailed instructions to follow should Carter's condition deteriorate. The doctor should have provided for outpatient follow-up care which would take into consideration the risk inherent in Carter's medical condition. Thus, the discharge of the defendant psychiatrist's duty is not limited to instances when the psychiatrist can control a patient by commitment to a hospital. The psychiatrist to fulfill his duty to those within the zone of risk must take the action reasonable under the circumstances.

Conclusion

The rule which we adopt does not impose upon psychiatrists a duty to protect the public from all harm caused by their patients. We do not, however, limit the duty of the psychiatrist to third parties only in those instances in which a specific threat is made against them. We hold that the duty extends to third persons whose circumstances place them within the reasonably foreseeable area of danger where the violent conduct of the patient is a threat.

. . . The judgment of the trial court is reversed, and the case is remanded for further proceedings consistent with this opinion.

QUESTIONS AND COMMENTS

1. *Scope of the holding.* Note that the *Hamman* decision does not establish liability, but simply holds that the trial court improperly granted the defendant's motion for summary judgment. The plaintiffs' suit had asserted that the defendant's psychiatrist was negligent in not anticipating that the patient was dangerous. Under their theory, once dangerousness is determined, the psychiatrist was under a duty to protect potential victims. This duty could presumably be discharged *either* by warning the family with whom the patient was living (ultimately the victims of the assault) or by initiating commitment proceedings.

2. *Courts v. the legislature.* In response to the Arizona Supreme Court's holding in the *Hamman* case, the Arizona legislature enacted Ariz. Rev. Stat. § 36–517.02, which provided that "There shall be no cause of action" nor any "legal liability" against a mental health provider unless "[t]he patient has communicated to the mental health provider an explicit threat of imminent serious physical harm or death to a clearly identified or identifiable victim." However, the Arizona Court of Appeals in *Little v. All Phoenix South Community Mental Health Center*, 919 P.2d 1368 (Ariz. Ct. App. 1995), subsequently held that the legislature's enactment violated a provision of the state's constitution that bars the abrogation of the "right of action to recover damages for injuries." Id. at 1375. According to the court, the *Hamman* decision created a common law cause of action that, once established, could not be legislatively restricted. Thus, the reach of *Hamman* could only be restrained by an amendment to the state's constitution.

The expansion of third party liability, which eliminates the need for an identified or clearly identifiable victim, obviously has significant financial implications for health care providers as it significantly enlarges their potential liability. Are courts or legislatures better equipped to determine the allocation of responsibility for damages resulting from injuries caused by clients who harm others? What information is available to a court to make the economic judgments implicit in a decision that significantly expands the liability of health care providers? What resources are generally available to legislatures? What factors are likely to drive the respective determinations of courts and legislatures?

3. *Construction of the "identifiable victim" standard.* The identifiable victim requirement has been broadly construed in a number of jurisdictions. For instance, in *Jablonski v. United States*, 712 F.2d 391 (9th Cir. 1983), a patient who had served a five-year prison term for raping his wife subsequently killed his girlfriend after attempting to rape her mother. In holding the treating psychiatrist liable, the court ruled that although the

patient had not made a *specific* threat, "[h]is psychological profile indicated that his violence was likely to be directed against women very close to him." Id. at 398. See also *Lipari v. Sears, Roebuck & Co.*, 497 F. Supp. 185, 195 (D. Neb. 1980) (permitting a suit if the mental health provider "could have reasonably foreseen an unreasonable risk of harm to the [victims] or a class of persons of which the [victims] were members").

4.   *Non-professionals and the duty to warn.* Should the duty to warn apply to a non-professional? In *Rozycki v. Peley*, 489 A.2d 1272 (N.J. Super. Ct. 1984), a group of neighborhood children were sexually assaulted by Arthur Peley in 1981. Their parents sued on the children's behalf, naming Peley's wife, Catherine, as a co-defendant. Peley had been previously arrested in 1977 on a morals charge involving a minor. At that time he was placed in a diversion program in which he, accompanied by Catherine, received psychiatric treatment. The plaintiffs alleged that Catherine knew of her husband's pedophilia and thus had a duty to warn the children of the potential danger. The court declined to extend a duty to warn to non-professionals, reasoning that lay persons are not experts and could not be expected to assess another person's dangerousness. The court added that in this particular case the public interest in protecting the marital relationship also counseled against imposing such a duty on the defendant. The *Tarasoff* doctrine had previously been adopted in New Jersey in *McIntosh v. Milano*, 403 A.2d 500 (N.J. Super. Ct. 1979).

However, *Rozycki* was ultimately overruled by the Appellate Division of the New Jersey Superior Court in a similar case. In *J.S. v. R.T.H.*, 693 A.2d 1191 (N.J. Super. Ct. App. Div. 1997), the court determined that New Jersey's "strong public policy favoring protection of children" trumped "the privacy of an offending adult" and "preserving the defendants' marital relationship." The court agreed that the wife did not necessarily have a duty to warn all of their neighbors about her husband, but rather "to take reasonable steps to prevent foreseeable harm under the circumstances." Thus if plaintiffs could establish that the wife was aware of her husband's conduct or history and that it was foreseeable that he posed a danger to the young girls involved, then it was "fair" to hold her to a duty to take reasonable steps to protect them from this danger. The court added that its conclusion was derived "from the continuity and nature of the social relationship between these next-door neighbors and the girls' habitual and repeated visits of which [the wife] was clearly aware" and that a similar duty had been found by courts in Texas and California.

If liability is limited only to psychotherapists, which professions should fall into the category of "therapists"? A licensed marriage counselor? An unlicensed marriage counselor? A marriage counselor in a state that does not require a license? In *Taggart v. State*, 822 P.2d 243 (Wash. 1992), the court found that "parole officers have a duty to protect others from reasonably foreseeable dangers engendered by parolees' dangerous propensities." One commentator has cautioned "biofeedback" practitioners who provide mental health care and related services that they may be subject to such a duty. Sebastian Striefel, *Duty to Protect or Warn*, 36(3) Biofeedback 86 (2008).

5. *Contributory negligence.* Should liability attach to the psychotherapist when the victim was aware of the danger posed by the client? Several courts have held that knowledge by the victim of the risk posed by a client forecloses liability on the part of the psychotherapist. In *Matter of Votteler's Estate*, 327 N.W.2d 759 (Iowa 1982), a psychiatric patient seriously injured the plaintiff by intentionally running over her with a car. Although the patient had attempted to run her down twice before, the plaintiff nevertheless argued that the defendant psychiatrist had a duty to warn her about his patient's violent nature. Plaintiff insisted that she would have appreciated the seriousness of the danger only if warned by a professional. Without deciding whether it would embrace the *Tarasoff* doctrine, the Iowa Supreme Court held that in any case the duty would not extend to situations where the foreseeable victim knew of the danger. See also *Weitz v. Lovelace Health Sys., Inc.*, 214 F.3d 1175 (10th Cir. 2000); *Jacobs v. Taylor*, 379 S.E.2d 563 (Ga. Ct. App. 1989); Howard v. Parsons' Child & Family Ctr., 761 N.Y.S.2d 381 (N.Y. App. Div. 2003); Leonard v. Latrobe Area Hosp., 625 A.2d 1228 (Pa. Super. Ct. 1993); Brian Ginsberg, Tarasoff *at Thirty: Victim's Knowledge Shrinks the Psychotherapist's Duty to Warn and Protect*, 21 J. Contemp. Health L. & Pol'y 1, 25 (2004) (addressing when the victim learned of the potential for violence and the specificity of her knowledge of this propensity).

6. *Liability in the absence of a "foreseeable victim".* While most jurisdictions have adhered to the clearly identifiable victim standard, a minority of courts have held that a cause of action can be pursued even when the injured third party was not a particularized potential victim. For instance, in *Currie v. United States,* 644 F. Supp. 1074 (M.D. N.C. 1986), the patient, who was being seen on an outpatient basis for "post-traumatic stress disorder," had originally sought psychiatric help from the VA staff for "rage attacks," which caused him to fear "losing control" due to anger directed at fellow employees. The treating psychiatrist was aware that the patient, at times, carried a gun and had "thoughts of hurting anyone who would take his property." The disclosure by the patient that he had feelings of hostility about IBM, his former employer that had recently discharged him, led the psychiatrist to call representatives at IBM to notify them of the possibility of violent action by the patient. Additionally, both the police and FBI were informed by VA staff of the patient's condition and potential for harm. At the same time, the VA treating staff concluded that while the patient was probably dangerous, they did not believe him to be "mentally ill," which was a necessary condition for involuntary commitment under state law.

While granting the defendant's motion to dismiss, the court nevertheless opined that a treating psychiatrist could be held liable even in the absence of a clearly foreseeable victim. In these circumstances, the basis for an action would be the failure to initiate commitment proceedings or to take some other action such as notifying the police. In holding that a cause of action does not require the identification of a foreseeable victim, the court tempered the scope of liability by imposing a "good faith" test under which liability would attach only if the psychiatrist's decision lacked "good faith, independence, and thoroughness." Thus, simple errors of judgment would not, as a matter of law, lead to liability. In applying this standard to the uncontested facts of this case, the court concluded that the psychiatrist's decision to not initiate commitment proceedings showed good faith and therefore warranted summary judgment.

7. *Liability for unintentional injuries.* The Wisconsin Supreme Court has extended the duty of care to non-foreseeable victims for the *unintentional* acts of a client that caused injury to third persons. In *Schuster v. Altenberg*, 424 N.W.2d 159 (Wis. 1988), the plaintiffs were the relatives of a patient who was being treated for manic depression on an outpatient basis by the defendant psychiatrist and were injured in a car accident while being driven by the patient. The cause of action was based on the defendant's failure to properly diagnose and treat the patient or, alternatively, on the failure to either warn the victims of the risk posed by the patient driving or to take steps to have the patient voluntarily or involuntarily committed. In holding that the pleadings stated a legally cognizable claim, the court concluded that there is no "legitimate policy reason which could operate to support a distinction between a psychotherapist's duty to warn on the basis of whether the patient particularizes potential victims of his or her violent tendencies or makes generalized statements of dangerous intent." Discharge of the duty, according to the majority, did not necessarily require the notification of a potential victim, but, depending on the circumstances, could be satisfied by taking other steps such as contacting the police or initiating commitment proceedings. The court also ruled that the failure to commit a patient can lead to liability, despite noting that some jurisdictions would not hold psychiatrists liable if the patient was being treated on an outpatient basis.

Do you agree with the conclusion of the court's majority that there is no significant policy reason to distinguish between the imposition of liability when a psychotherapist treats a client on an outpatient basis and fails to initiate commitment, from the liability that may attach to the decision to release someone who has been hospitalized and who subsequently injures a third person? Are the predictive capacities of mental health professionals likely to be the same in these two circumstances?

Is it significant that patients who have been involuntarily committed may have been found to be both mentally ill and dangerous to themselves or others? Once such a finding has been made in a judicial or administrative proceeding, should it have any continuing evidentiary weight so that a decision to release requires an affirmative determination by the clinician that the individual is no longer mentally ill or dangerous or both to avoid liability for harm to third persons caused by the individual? Should a therapist who is treating a client on an outpatient basis be under the same duty to affirmatively establish the dangerousness or non-dangerousness of the client?

What impact might this have on release decisions? These issues are discussed further in Chapter Eight.

8.   *Liability for the acts of institutionalized patients.* As noted earlier, the tendency, even before *Tarasoff,* had been to hold institutions and key associated personnel liable to third persons if a psychiatric facility negligently released a dangerous patient. Liability in these cases, however, was not based on a failure to warn a particular foreseeable victim, but rather a general duty to protect the public from the release of dangerous patients.

9.   *Liability for the acts of outpatients.* Ostensibly, harm to third parties by an individual seen by a mental health provider on an outpatient basis (i.e., the individual comes to the provider for a brief visit pursuant to a scheduled appointment or on an as-needed basis) would not subject the provider to the same level of liability as for an institutionalized patient because of a reduced ability to monitor and control the individual. See *Adams v. Bd. of Sedgwick Cnty. Comm'rs*, 214 P.3d 1173 (Kan. 2009) (finding outpatient mental health facility and associated mental health professionals did not take charge of the patient in a manner that gave rise to a duty to control the patient's conduct); *Santana v. Rainbow Cleaners*, 969 A.2d 653 (R.I. 2009) (holding, in a case of first impression, that mental health center's provision of treatment to outpatient did not create an affirmative duty to exercise control over the outpatient by initiating civil commitment to prevent subsequent violent assault).

But see *Rivera v. New York City Health & Hosps. Corp.*, 191 F. Supp. 2d 412 (S.D. N.Y. 2002), where the plaintiff was injured after being pushed into the path of a subway by an outpatient who was mentally ill and homeless. The outpatient was receiving medical care or other assistance from three medical facilities and two homeless shelters and was determined by the court to be "a diagnosed paranoid schizophrenic who showed violent tendencies, had a known history of violence, and did not take his medications." The plaintiff sued the health care providers, alleging they were negligent in failing to protect the public from the outpatient.

Relying on the Second Restatement of Torts, § 319, the court determined that in general "[t]he duty owed to third parties by a psychiatrist or mental health practitioner is somewhat different than that owed by a physician. . . . [in that] in certain circumstances [the duty of care] is owed not only to patients and the narrow category of individuals the physician could expect to be affected by the treatment, but to the outside public as well." With regard to the patient's status:

> Where the individual involved is a voluntary psychiatric outpatient, the institution's control over the patient, and thus its duty to prevent the patient from harming others, is more limited [than for an inpatient]. . . . However, *the duty does not disappear,* and the institution may be held liable if the failure to place the patient on inpatient status resulted from something other than an exercise of professional judgment.

Id. at 420–21. The court rejected the defendants' contention "that a bright-line rule exists protecting mental health providers from liability for treating outpatients who later harm third parties" and ruled that "in certain limited circumstances, a mental health provider may be liable for failing to control or commit a voluntary outpatient who later harms a member of the public."

In rejecting the mental health providers' motion to dismiss, the court noted that the plaintiff alleged more than just an error in the exercise of professional judgment, but that the providers failed to conduct careful examinations and make considered decisions, knew that the outpatient "presented 'a danger and risk of harm to the general public,'" treated the outpatient "immediately before the incident," and knew or should have known, that being homeless, he would "be returning to the street where . . . he would present a threat."

The plaintiff also sued the homeless shelters where the outpatient resided. The court did grant the shelters' motions for summary judgment, finding that the plaintiff failed to prove "any facts that would suggest that the shelters had any ability to control [the outpatient]."

See also *Dawe v. Bar–Levav*, 808 N.W.2d 240, 248 (Mich. Ct. App. 2010) (determining that liability may ensue from a failure to protect a participant in a group therapy session from another member of this group, noting that "because [the plaintiff] was among the class of persons who could foreseeably be harmed by defendants' decision to place [the assailant] into group therapy, defendants owed [the plaintiff] a duty to take reasonable precautions to ensure that the patients assigned to the group were sufficiently healthy to participate in group therapy").

e. Perspectives on Tarasoff: Ability to Predict Dangerousness

From the dissenting opinion of Justice Mosk in *Hedlund v. Superior Court of Orange Cnty.*, 669 P.2d 41 (Cal. 1983):

> The majority opinion unfortunately perpetuates the myth that psychiatrists and psychologists inherently possess powers of clairvoyance to predict violence. There is no evidence to support this remarkable belief, and, indeed, all the credible literature in the field discounts the existence of any such mystical attribute in those who practice the mind-care professions.

> The serious flaw in the majority opinion is its acceptance of the claim that a failure to diagnose "dangerousness" may be a basis for liability. In its text, the opinion employs such terms as failure to "predict" behavior, and flatly declares that a negligent act occurs "when the therapist has, or *should have* diagnosed dangerousness" (italics added), as if that subjective characteristic would be revealed through a stethoscope or by an X-ray.

In *People v. Burnick* (1975), we discussed at considerable length the virtually unanimous authorities in the field of psychiatry who concede their inability to predict violence. "In light of recent studies it is no longer heresy to question the reliability of psychiatric predictions. Psychiatrists themselves would be the first to admit that however desirable an infallible crystal ball might be, it is not among the tools of their profession. It must be conceded that psychiatrists still experience considerable difficulty in confidently and accurately *diagnosing* mental illness." Yet those difficulties are multiplied manyfold when psychiatrists venture from diagnosis to prognosis and undertake to predict the consequences of such illness: "A diagnosis of mental illness tells us nothing about whether the person so diagnosed is or is not dangerous. Some mental patients are dangerous, some are not. Perhaps the psychiatrist is an expert at deciding whether a person is mentally ill, but is he an expert at predicting which of the persons so diagnosed are dangerous? Sane people, too, are dangerous, and it may legitimately be inquired whether there is anything in the education, training or experience of psychiatrists which renders them particularly adept at predicting dangerous behavior. Predictions of dangerous behavior, no matter who makes them, are incredibly inaccurate, and there is a growing consensus that psychiatrists are not uniquely qualified to predict dangerous behavior and are, in fact, less accurate in their predictions than other professionals."

During the past several years further empirical studies have transformed the earlier trend of opinion into an impressive unanimity: "The evidence, as well as the consensus of opinion by responsible scientific authorities, is now unequivocal." In the words of spokesmen for the psychiatric profession itself, "Unfortunately, this is the state of the art. Neither psychiatrists nor anyone else have reliably demonstrated an ability to predict future violence or "dangerousness." Neither has any special psychiatric "expertise" in this area been established." And the same studies which proved the inaccuracy of psychiatric predictions have demonstrated beyond dispute the no less disturbing manner in which such prophecies consistently err: they predict acts of violence which will not in fact take place ('false positives'), thus branding as 'dangerous' many persons who are in reality totally harmless.

Because of the inherent undependability of such predictions, we adopted in *Burnick* the beyond-a-reasonable-doubt standard for commitment to mental facilities.

Unfortunately a year later in *Tarasoff v. Regents of University of California* a thin majority of this court employed a loose and ill-conceived dictum that encourages a dilution of *Burnick*. Although the case involved *actual* knowledge of planned violence, the four-to-three majority spoke expansively in terms of what the doctor "knew or should have known." My separate opinion pointed out that there are no professional standards for forecasting violence and concluded that any rule should "eliminate all reference to conformity to standards of the profession in predicting violence. If a psychiatrist does in fact predict violence, then a duty to warn arises. The majority's expansion of that rule will take us from the world of reality into the wonderland of clairvoyance."

Id. at 48–49.

Compare the following:

H]ospitals and individual practitioners might respond to the perceived threat of litigation by taking steps to reduce the risk of liability. But the impact on clinical practice may not necessarily be favorable. Indeed, it is possible that the threat of liability, however remote, actually has had an adverse effect in recent years on the costs of medical services and perhaps on the quality of care as well.

The argument runs something like this: Because many practitioners actually exaggerate the relatively low risk of liability, they will be led to take "defensive" measures that either make no real contribution to the patient's care or are not cost-effective from a purely clinical standpoint. These so-called "defensive" practices increase the cost of care and . . . have a regressive effect on the quality of care by diverting professional energies from their best clinical use. In economic terms, it is said that the practitioner, by overreacting to the threat of malpractice liability, increases the preventive costs without a corresponding reduction in injury costs.

Examples of purely defensive practices, with little clinical utility, are often said to include unnecessary diagnostic tests.

*   *   *

I am not inclined to believe that mental health practitioners are led to engage in what they believe to be clinically useless practices solely to reduce the risk of liability. . . . [For example,] good record keeping in mental health has considerable clinical utility, and any additional documentation that is provided "purely" for legal purposes exacts no significant incremental cost.

Another feature of the defensive medicine argument should be taken more seriously, however. Exaggerated fear of malpractice liability may generate disincentives for adopting practices that, while clinically preferable, entail a higher risk of bad outcomes. . . . Hypothetically, practitioners may avoid procedures thought to be associated with high legal risks even though they may be in the patients' best interests. Even worse, defensive practices induced by the threat of liability may actually reduce the quality of care available to patients.

. . . Because treatment of the potentially violent patient in the community is perceived to be a high-risk endeavor, one response to the prospect of *Tarasoff* liability . . . has been a lowered threshold for hospitalizing these patients and a tendency to prolong the period of hospitalization. There is also some evidence that senior clinicians in hierarchical practice settings avoid treating potentially violent patients, leaving the care of such patients in the hands of junior, less adequately trained colleagues.

Similarly, one empirical investigation of clinical practice in the wake of the *Tarasoff* decision found that almost one-fifth of the responding clinicians reported having decided to avoid asking their patients questions that could yield information bearing on the likelihood of violent behavior. Even more reported that they had changed their record-keeping practices in an effort to reduce the risk of liability—some by keeping more detailed records, . . . but others by refraining from keeping detailed records. Obviously the failure to inquire about, or to record, clinically relevant material could seriously compromise the quality of care in this clinical context.

Richard Bonnie, *Professional Liability and the Quality of Mental Health Care*, 16 L., Med., & Health Care 229, 233–34 (1988).

The *Tarasoff* court did nothing new. Once it determined that therapists owe a duty to third parties, it acted according to accepted legal norms for formulating how that duty must be carried out. The court did so in a way that sought to maximize the benefits for the population at large and minimize needless liability to therapists. In fact, the court merely codified what had been required for some time by the ethical standards of the therapeutic profession itself. In some sense, the debate that rages in academia and irritates therapists has little consequence. Twenty years after *Tarasoff*, plaintiffs win few court battles against psychotherapists. Therapists themselves pay little heed to *Tarasoff*, and the practice of psychotherapy thrives. In the long run, *Tarasoff* is less a threat than a misplaced fear in our collective mind.

Vikram S. Mangalmurti, *Psychotherapists' Fear of Tarasoff: All in the Mind?*, 22 J. Psychiatry & L. 379, 404–05 (1994).

With its seemingly broad mandate to protect third parties, encountering a *Tarasoff*-like scenario has tended to strike fear in the hearts of mental health providers. . . .

It is, however, now widely acknowledged that for a number of reasons, *Tarasoff*-like rules were not ruinous to clinical practice.

Among the reasons given are that (1) mental health providers should be dedicated to assisting all who are in need, including the potential victims of client threats, with most therapists having already embraced such a duty; (2) these duties resulted in a needed closer examination of clients' potential for such behavior, which can enhance their treatment and rehabilitation and help them avoid criminal and civil sanctions that might otherwise ensue; (3) taking protective steps can actually "further the therapeutic alliance and contribute[] to a [client's therapeutic] progress; and (4) the scope of the duty was not as broad as commonly believed.

It has even been asserted that the *Tarasoff* duty "has [now] become a central aspect of patient care," with "practitioners . . . view[ing] the duty . . . as they would other essential elements of care."

* * *

In addition, "[b]y the late 1990s, . . . mental health professionals had developed new views about the accuracy of violence predictions, which led [some] to conclude that, contrary to what had [been asserted previously], 'clinicians are able to distinguish violent from nonviolent patients with a modest, better-than-chance level of accuracy." These predictions were further enhanced as "[t]he 1990s also witnessed the beginnings and dissemination of a new approach to, or 'technology,' for, making violence risk assessments." Although significant concerns remain about a clinician's ability to adequately assess risk and prevent harm in a given case, these developments suggest that more may be expected of clinicians in preventing harm to third parties threatened by their clients and that they will be expected to be aware of and proficient in utilizing this new knowledge and these tools. . . .

Finally, more may be expected of mental health providers following widely publicized tragedies such as the recent mass shootings in Connecticut, Colorado, Arizona, and Virginia. In each of the postmortems following these events, considerable attention has been given to indications that the individuals responsible for these shootings suffered from a mental illness and had previously received at least some mental health services, with questions raised whether more effective mental health interventions or additional steps taken by involved mental health providers could have prevented these events. For example, subsequent to the [December 14, 2012,] shootings in Newtown, Connecticut, a law was passed in New York that "require[es] physicians, social workers and other therapists to report potentially dangerous patients to local health officials."

Hafemeister et al., supra, at 79–87.

2.   Third Party Recovery under Alternate Theories: Negligent Infliction of Emotional Distress

As noted in the preface to this section, liability to third persons in the event of health care provider malpractice has traditionally been confined to a very limited number of circumstances. For instance, *Tarasoff* and its progeny limited liability to clients who were foreseeably dangerous to identified (or identifiable) individuals. However, an alternative basis for third party liability emerged in litigation brought before a California state trial court. That case, *Ramona v. Ramona,* No. Civ. 61898 (Sup. Ct. Napa Cnty. 1994), which involved repressed memory therapy, led to a $500,000 judgment against the therapist (a licensed marriage and family counselor), a consulting psychiatrist, and the facility where the treatment took place.

In August, 1989, Holly Ramona disclosed to her mother, Stephanie, that she had an eating disorder and that she felt she needed professional help. Mrs. Ramona put Holly in touch with Dr. Barry Grundlin, the Ramona family psychiatrist. Dr. Grundlin diagnosed Holly as suffering from bulimia.

Through a referral, Mrs. Ramona obtained the name of Marche Isabella, a licensed Marriage Family and Child Counselor (MFCC), whose practice concentrated on the treatment of eating disorders. Holly, then a student at the University of California at Irvine, began individual psychotherapy sessions with Isabella in September of 1989 and which lasted through the fall semester. According to Isabella, Holly, on her own, began to vaguely recall having been sexually abused by her father, Gary, when she was between five and eight years old. Subsequent sessions dealt with these "nascent memories." At some point, these recollections were communicated to Holly's mother (Stephanie). Having reached the tentative conclusion that Holly's condition was attributable to having been sexually abused as a child, Isabella arranged to have Holly seen by a psychiatrist, Dr. Richard Rose, for the purpose of administering sodium amytal, which Isabella believed would lead to the recovery of Holly's repressed memories. During the sodium amytal treatment, Holly purportedly recalled episodes of sexual abuse by her father during childhood.

Subsequently, Isabella arranged for a meeting of the family, which included Holly, Holly's father (Gary), and her father's wife (Stephanie). At the March 21, 1990, meeting, Gary was for the first time told of the diagnosis of childhood sexual abuse and of Holly's recollections that he had abused her. At the same time, those present were informed that the diagnosis of sexual abuse had been verified during the sodium amytal session. They were also told that sodium amytal acts like a truth serum and that someone under the influence of sodium amytal cannot lie unless trained to do so.

After hearing these revelations, Stephanie filed for divorce from Gary. Information pertaining to the purported sexual abuse also reached Gary's employer, who initially placed him on leave of absence and sometime thereafter terminated his employment.

Gary subsequently filed suit in state court against Isabella, Dr. Rose, and Western Medical Center, where the sodium amytal therapy was administered. The suit sought damages for negligent infliction of emotional distress (NIED). This cause of action was based on a California Supreme Court precedent, *Molien v. Kaiser Foundation Hospitals*, 616 P.2d 813 (Cal. 1980). In *Molien*, a physician misdiagnosed a married female patient as having a sexually transmitted disease (STD). She was then advised by the physician to inform her husband so he could receive testing and, if necessary, treatment. It later turned out the diagnosis was incorrect and the patient did not have a STD. The husband subsequently sued the physician under a third-party NIED theory. In ruling the husband had a viable claim, the California Supreme Court noted:

> In the case at bar the risk of harm to plaintiff was reasonably foreseeable to defendants. It is easily predictable that an erroneous diagnosis of syphilis and its probable source would produce marital discord and resultant emotional distress to a married patient's spouse; Dr. Kilbridge's advice to Mrs. Molien to have her husband examined for the disease confirms that plaintiff was a foreseeable victim of the negligent diagnosis. Because the disease is normally transmitted only by sexual relations, it is rational to anticipate that both husband and wife would experience anxiety, suspicion, and hostility when confronted with what they had every reason to believe was reliable medical evidence of a particularly noxious infidelity.

> We thus agree with plaintiff that the alleged tortious conduct of defendant was directed to him as well as to his wife. Because the risk of harm to him was reasonably foreseeable we hold, in negligence parlance, that under these circumstances defendants owed plaintiff a duty to exercise due care in diagnosing the physical condition of his wife.

Id. at 835.

The basic principle underlying *Molien* was reaffirmed by the California Supreme Court in *Burgess v. Superior Court,* 831 P.2d 1197 (Cal. 1992). In *Burgess,* the plaintiff was a pregnant woman who went into labor, and because of the physician's malpractice, delivered a child born with brain damage. She subsequently filed suit in her own behalf against the physician on a theory of NIED. In affirming a judgment in favor of the plaintiff, the court reviewed the dimensions of the doctrine:

> The law of negligent infliction of emotional distress in California is typically analyzed . . . by reference to two "theories" of recovery: the

"bystander" theory and the "direct victim" theory. In cases involving family relationships and medical treatment, confusion has reigned as to whether and under which "theory" plaintiffs may seek damages for negligently inflicted emotional distress.

Because the use of the "direct victim" designation has tended to obscure rather than illuminate the relevant inquiry in cases such as the one at hand, we briefly turn our attention to the present state of the law in this area before proceeding to apply this law to the facts that confront us.

We have repeatedly recognized that "[t]he negligent causing of emotional distress is not an independent tort, but the tort of negligence. The traditional elements of duty, breach of duty, causation, and damages apply. Whether a defendant owes a duty of care is a question of law. Its existence depends upon the foreseeability of the risk and a weighing of policy considerations for and against imposition of liability."

The distinction between the "bystander" and "direct victim" cases is found in the source of the duty owed by the defendant to the plaintiff. The "bystander" cases . . . culminating in *Thing v. La Chusa* (1989), address "the question of duty in circumstances in which a plaintiff seeks to recover damages as a percipient witness to the injury of another." These cases "all arise in the context of physical injury or emotional distress caused by the negligent conduct of a defendant with whom the plaintiff *had no* preexisting relationship, and to whom the defendant *had not* previously assumed a duty of care *beyond that* owed to the public in general." (emphasis added). In other words, bystander liability is premised upon a defendant's violation of a duty not to negligently cause emotional distress to people who observe conduct which causes harm to another.

Because in such cases the class of potential plaintiffs could be limitless, resulting in the imposition of liability out of all proportion to the culpability of the defendant, this court has circumscribed the class of bystanders to whom a defendant owes a duty to avoid negligently inflicting emotional distress. These limits are set forth in *Thing* as follows: "In the absence of physical injury or impact to the plaintiff himself, damages for emotional distress should be recoverable only if the plaintiff: (1) is closely related to the injury victim, (2) is present at the scene of the injury-producing event at the time it occurs and is then aware that it is causing injury to the victim and, (3) as a result suffers emotional distress beyond that which would be anticipated in a disinterested witness."

In contrast, the label "direct victim" arose to distinguish cases in which damages for serious emotional distress are sought as a result of a breach of duty owed the plaintiff that is "assumed by the defendant or imposed on the defendant as a matter of law, or that arises out of a relationship between the two." In these cases, the limits set forth in *Thing* have no direct application. Rather, well-settled principles of negligence are invoked to determine whether all elements of a cause of action, including a duty of care, are present in a given case.

Much of the confusion in applying rules for bystander and direct victim recovery to the facts of specific cases can be traced to this court's decision in *Molien,* which first used the "direct victim" label. In that case, we answered in the affirmative the question of whether, in the context of a negligence action, damages may be recovered for serious emotional distress unaccompanied by physical injury.

In so holding, we found that a hospital and a doctor owed a duty directly to the husband of a patient, who had been diagnosed incorrectly by the doctor as having syphilis and had been told to so advise her husband in order that he could receive testing and, if necessary, treatment. We reasoned that the risk of harm to the husband was reasonably foreseeable and that the "alleged tortious conduct of the defendant was directed to him as well as to his wife." Under such circumstances we deemed the husband to be a "direct victim" and found the criteria for bystander recovery not to be controlling.

The broad language of the *Molien* decision coupled with its perceived failure to establish criteria for characterizing a plaintiff as a "direct victim" rather than a "bystander," has subjected *Molien* to criticism from various sources, including this court. (E.g., *Thing*). The great weight of this criticism has centered upon the perception that *Molien* introduced a new method for determining the existence of a duty, limited only by the concept of foreseeability. To the extent that *Molien* stands for this proposition, it should not be relied upon and its discussion of duty is limited to its facts. As recognized in *Thing*, "[It] is clear that foreseeability of the injury alone is not a useful 'guideline' or a meaningful restriction on the scope of [an action for damages for negligently inflicted emotional distress.]"

Nevertheless, other principles derived from *Molien* are sound: (1) damages for negligently inflicted emotional distress may be recovered in the absence of physical injury or impact, and (2) a cause of action to recover damages for negligently inflicted emotional distress will lie, notwithstanding the criteria imposed upon recovery by bystanders, in cases where a duty arising from a preexisting relationship is negligently breached. In fact, it is this later principle which defines the phrase "direct victim." That label signifies nothing more.

Id. at 617–19.

In *Ramona,* the plaintiff introduced compelling evidence that the therapist had committed malpractice by erroneously representing to the patient, to her mother, and to him that sodium amytal was, in effect, a truth serum, and that recollections made under the influence of sodium amytal therapy were completely reliable. The plaintiff also introduced evidence that repressed memory therapy coupled with the use of sodium amytal to enhance recall was not an appropriate therapy for the treatment of bulimia.

The existence of malpractice alone, however, would not allow the plaintiff to recover because an action for malpractice is ordinarily only maintainable by a patient or client. As a third party, the plaintiff had to predicate his suit on another ground. In the case at hand, the selected cause of action was NIED. Under *Molien* and *Burgess,* such third party actions could be maintained as long as the plaintiff was a "direct victim." Throughout the proceeding, the defendants took the position that *Burgess* had limited the reach of *Molien* and the plaintiff in *Ramona* did not have the status of a direct victim.

In denying a motion for non-suit at the close of the plaintiff's case in *Ramona,* the trial judge addressed the policy questions involved as follows:

> The third issue that was raised, . . . is frankly the most . . . compelling and difficult one in this case. And it's the most interesting one because it . . . brings in to conflict with one another several really important policies in the law. And this is the question of whether a father may maintain a lawsuit against the therapists or other health care providers of his daughter alleging that he was damaged by their negligent treatment of her.

> Through counsel he diligently tried to argue again and again that he was a patient and I have found that no duty arose. I found that he was not a patient for purposes of the assessment of whether a duty existed. And that's a legal determination that the Court makes, whether a duty existed. I have found that a duty did not exist to him by reason of the circumstances of the case under Supreme Court law that has been existent for some time and which I have found still exists.

> What's going on in a lawsuit of this sort, as I say, is the conflict of policies. And on the one hand, the defendants argue if you allow nonpatients to sue health care providers, it will have a terrible, chilling effect upon the ability of any health care provider to do what his or her patient needs. . . .

> How, they ask, is a health care provider to know what to do when presented with a patient who recalls or thinks he or she is recalling

the sorts of things that are presented by this lawsuit. . . . That's an argument that has significant social implications attendant to it.

Of equal significance, however, and with equal social implications, is the question of what is somebody who, for the sake of this point we will presume to be factually innocent of having engaged in misconduct with respect to his daughter, to do if confronted with the unfounded and incorrect accusation of having molested her which results in his loss of everything?

It's as unpalatable to some to have health care providers put in the impossible situation of dealing with a patient presenting real problems but knowing that the health care providers might be subjected to liability as it is to others to have a falsely accused parent lose everything and have no recourse in court.

Those are the kinds of policy issues that the courts are called upon to resolve, because in the area of tort law, and this is a tort action, there's very little statutory law. There's very little law created by the legislature that creates norms. Probably because the situations giving rise to tort actions are so fluid and so changing and so we have generalized concepts of law that are handed down through cases and through traditions, through precedents, according to which we regulate ourselves as a society.

And the purposes of tort law are twofold; to provide redress for people who are injured in some way or another; and to mediate, to control, to direct the conduct of other people. And these are the kinds of difficult conflicts that the court [sic] are called upon to resolve.

Ramona v. Ramona, No. Civ. 61898 (Sup. Ct. Napa Cnty. 1994).

Ultimately, the trial court held that the plaintiff had met the legal standards of *Molien* and *Burgess,* and permitted the case to go to a jury, which found for the plaintiff and awarded him $500,000. No appeal was taken from this judgment.

QUESTIONS AND COMMENTS

1. *"Direct victim".* As the excerpts from *Molien* and *Burgess* indicate, a mere "bystander" cannot generally recover for NIED. However, according to *Burgess,* one who is a "direct victim" of the negligent act can recover so long as there is a "duty arising from a pre-existing relationship [that] is negligently breached." *Burgess v. Superior Court*, 831 P.2d 1197 (Cal. 1992). It is not clear from *Burgess* whether the pre-existing relationship must be between the victim and the defendant or simply between any two parties, such as the therapist and the client. However, the trial court in *Ramona* apparently took the view that the pre-existing relationship need not be between the plaintiff and the therapist, but could be satisfied by the

relationship between the therapist and the client, Holly. Is this an appropriate reading of the rule announced by *Burgess*?

2. *Must falsity be proven?* To prevail in a *Ramona*-type case, must the plaintiff prove that the recalled memory of abuse is false? Note that in *Ramona* the jury specifically found that the defendants had implanted or reinforced "false memories that plaintiff had molested [Holly] as a child." What is the doctrinal connection between the falsity of the recall and the NIED claim? Is the reason falsity must be proven simply that it is a common sense predicate to recovery?

3. *Scope of disclosure needed to maintain action.* What would have been the result in *Ramona* if the only communication the father had as to the false recall was from his daughter, Holly? In other words, if there had been no communication between the father and the therapist, would recovery have been possible? Would the answer be the same if Holly instead disclosed this information to a friend, who then informed the father's employer?

4. *Definition of who is a client.* The plaintiff originally pleaded his case on the theory that he could maintain the action as a client of the therapist because he had participated in the meeting of the family members with the therapist. However, the trial court dismissed this theory of recovery, ruling this meeting did not make him the therapist's client.

5. *Plaintiff's election of cause of action.* The plaintiff could theoretically have elected to sue on a defamation theory. Why didn't he? Under California Civil Code § 47 there is a conditional privilege granted to therapists that protects them from defamation suits. Thus, the only individual whom the father could successfully sue under this approach was his daughter and other nonprofessionals who communicated the allegations concerning abuse.

6. *Legitimacy of recovered memory therapy.* As recounted supra in Part II.B.1, there exists a significant difference of opinion among professionals as to the effectiveness and appropriateness of recovered memory therapy. Various authorities have criticized it as unreliable and without therapeutic value. See Elke Geraerts, *Recovered Memories of Childhood Sexual Abuse: Current Findings and Their Legal Implications*, 13 Legal & Criminological Psychol. 165 (2008); Elizabeth F. Loftus & Deborah Davis, *Recovered Memories*, 2 Ann. Rev. Clinical Psychol. 469 (2006); Richard J. Ofshe & Margaret Thaler Singer, *Recovered–Memory Therapy and Robust Repression–Influence and Pseudomemories*, 42 Int'l J. Clinical & Experimental Hypnosis 391 (1994); Yacov Rofe, *Does Repression Exist? Memory, Pathogenic, Unconscious and Clinical Evidence*, 12 Rev. Gen. Psychol. 63 (2008). As discussed, this type of therapy has generated numerous successful lawsuits brought by former clients against their therapists.

7. *NIED recovery by a patient or a client.* In a recent case from Georgia, a patient was allowed to sue his psychiatrist for NIED after he killed his own mother following the discontinuation of his medication, which allegedly caused the patient to revert to a psychotic, homicidal state. *O'Brien v. Bruscato*, 715 S.E.2d 120 (Ga. 2011). While acknowledging that the general

rule is that one who knowingly commits a wrongful act cannot profit from that act, the court concluded that because the patient had been found incompetent to stand trial, he had not knowingly committed a wrongful act. Furthermore, he was not seeking to profit from the murder of his mother, but rather was seeking damages for the suffering the alleged malpractice caused him. The court also ruled that the impact rule and its physical injury requirement was not applicable to an emotional distress claim linked to medical malpractice. For a general discussion of NIED claims, see Dan B. Dobbs, *Undertakings and Special Relationships in Claims for Negligent Infliction of Emotional Distress*, 50 Ariz. L. Rev. 49 (2008).

8. *Therapists' concerns.* After the *Ramona* decision, "mental health professionals expressed concern that the expansion of a therapist's duty to include third parties would become unlimited in scope and would have a chilling effect on the profession." Sheila F. Rock, *A Claim for Third Party Standing in Malpractice Cases Involving Repressed Memory Syndrome*, 37 Wm. & Mary L. Rev. 337, 374 (1995).

D. LIABILITY OF OTHER PARTIES

1. Liability of Non–Licensed Therapists

NALLY V. GRACE COMMUNITY CHURCH OF THE VALLEY

Supreme Court of California, 1988.
47 Cal. 3d 278, 253 Cal. Rptr. 97, 763 P.2d 948.

LUCAS, CHIEF JUSTICE.

I. Introduction

On April 1, 1979, 24–year–old Kenneth Nally (hereafter Nally) committed suicide by shooting himself in the head with a shotgun. His parents (hereafter plaintiffs) filed a wrongful death action against Grace Community Church of the Valley (hereafter Church), a Protestant Christian congregation located in Sun Valley, California, and four Church pastors: MacArthur, Thomson, Cory and Rea (hereafter collectively referred to as defendants), alleging "clergyman malpractice," i.e., negligence and outrageous conduct in failing to prevent the suicide. (See Code Civ. Proc., § 377.) Nally, a member of the Church since 1974, had participated in defendants' pastoral counseling programs prior to his death. . . .

II. Facts

A. *Background*

In 1973, while attending University of California at Los Angeles (hereafter UCLA), Nally became depressed after breaking up with his girlfriend. He often talked about the absurdity of life, the problems he had with women and his family, and he occasionally mentioned suicide to his friends. Though Nally had been raised in a Roman Catholic household, he converted to Protestantism while he was a student at UCLA, and in 1974 he began attending the Church, the largest Protestant church in Los Angeles County. Nally's conversion became a source of controversy between him and his family. During this time, Nally developed a close friendship with defendant Pastor Cory, who was responsible for overseeing the ministry to the collegians attending the Church. On occasion, Nally discussed his problems with Cory, but the two never established a formal counseling relationship. Between 1974 and 1979, Nally was active in defendants' various Church programs and ministries.

Defendants offered pastoral counseling to church members in matters of faith, doctrine and the application of Christian principles. During 1979, defendant Church had approximately 30 counselors on its staff, serving a congregation of more than 10,000 persons. Defendants taught that the Bible is the fundamental Word of God containing truths that must govern Christians in their relationship with God and the world at large, and in their own personal lives. Defendant Church had no professional or clinical counseling ministry, and its pastoral counseling was essentially religious in nature. Such counseling was often received through instruction, study, prayer and guidance, and through mentoring relationships called "discipleships."

* * *

In essence, defendants held themselves out as *pastoral* counselors able to deal with a variety of problems—not as professional, medical or psychiatric counselors.

In 1975, Nally was seeing a secular psychologist to discuss problems he was having with his girlfriend. After graduating from UCLA in 1976, he spent one semester at Biola College in La Mirada and was enrolled in the Talbot Theological Seminary's extension on defendants' church grounds. During this time, Nally became involved in a relationship with a girlfriend who was a fellow Bible student. In January 1978, he established a "discipling relationship" with Pastor Rea with whom he often discussed girlfriend and family problems. They met five times in early 1978, but when Nally lost interest in "discipling," the meetings were discontinued.

Following the breakup with his girlfriend in December 1978, Nally became increasingly despondent. Pastor Cory encouraged him to seek the counsel of either Pastor Thomson or Rea. The friendship with Cory and the five discipling sessions with Rea in early 1978, constituted the full extent of the "counseling" Nally received from defendants before the spring of 1979.

In February 1979, Nally told his mother he could not "cope." She arranged for him to see Dr. Milestone, a general practitioner, who prescribed Elavil, a strong anti-depressant drug, to relieve his depression.

* * *

B.   The Events Preceding Nally's Suicide

On March 11, 1979, Nally took an overdose of the antidepressant prescribed by Dr. Milestone. Plaintiffs found him the following day and rushed him to a hospital. At the hospital, Dr. Evelyn, Nally's attending physician, advised plaintiffs that because their son "was actually suicidal," she could not authorize his release from the hospital until he had seen a psychiatrist. The record indicates that plaintiffs, concerned about their friends' reactions to their son's suicide attempt, asked Dr. Evelyn to inform other persons that Nally had been hospitalized only for the aspiration pneumonia he suffered after the drug overdose rendered him unconscious.

On the afternoon of March 12, Pastors MacArthur and Rea visited Nally at the hospital. Nally, who was still drowsy from the drug overdose, separately told both pastors that he was sorry he did not succeed in committing suicide. Apparently, MacArthur and Rea assumed the entire hospital staff was aware of Nally's unstable mental condition, and they did not discuss Nally's death-wish comment with anyone else.

Four days later, Dr. Hall, a staff psychiatrist at the hospital, examined Nally and recommended he commit himself to a psychiatric hospital. When both Nally and his father expressed reluctance at the thought of formal commitment, Hall agreed to release Nally for outpatient treatment, but warned Nally's father that it would not be unusual for a suicidal patient to repeat his suicide attempt. Nally was released from the hospital by Drs. Hall and Evelyn the next day.

On his release from the hospital on March 17, 1979, Nally arranged to stay with Pastor MacArthur, because he did not want to return home. MacArthur encouraged Nally to keep his appointments with Dr. Hall, and arranged for him to see Dr. John Parker, a physician and Church deacon, for a physical examination.

* * *

Eleven days before his suicide, Nally met with Pastor Thomson for spiritual counseling. According to the record, Nally asked Thomson whether Christians who commit suicide would nonetheless be "saved." Thomson referred Nally to his training as a seminary student and acknowledged "a person who is once saved is always saved," but told Nally that "it would be wrong to be thinking in such terms." Following their discussion, Thomson made an appointment for Nally to see Dr. Bullock for a physical examination but did not refer Nally to a psychiatrist.

* * *

The day after his visit with Bullock, Nally encountered Pastor Thomson in the Church parking lot. Nally told Thomson that he was thinking of seeing a psychologist. Thomson recommended Nally contact Dr. Mohline, Director of the Rosemead Graduate School of Professional Psychology. The following day, Nally spent approximately 90 minutes with Mohline, who in turn referred him to the Fullerton Psychological Clinic. Nally and his father went to the clinic the next day, and Nally discussed possible therapy with Mr. Raup, a registered psychologist's assistant. Raup testified he believed that Nally was "shopping for a therapist or counselor or psychologist" and that he was not going to return to the clinic. At the end of the week, Nally met with a former girlfriend. She turned down an apparent marriage proposal by telling Nally, "I can't marry you when you are like this. You have got to pull yourself together. You have got to put God first in your life." The next day, Nally left plaintiffs' home following a family disagreement. Two days later, he was found in a friend's apartment, dead of a self-inflicted gunshot wound.

III. Procedural Background

A. *Allegations of the Complaint*

. . . In the first two counts of the complaint, alleging wrongful death based on "clergyman malpractice" and negligence, plaintiffs asserted that defendant Church was negligent in the training, selection and hiring of its spiritual counselors. Plaintiffs also claimed that following Nally's suicide attempt by drug overdose, defendants failed to make themselves available to Nally for counseling and "actively and affirmatively dissuaded and discouraged [Nally] from seeking further professional psychological and/or psychiatric care."

* * *

In ruling [affirmatively] on the nonsuit motion, the trial court noted that Nally voluntarily sought defendants' counsel and that the court had no compelling reason to interfere in defendants' pastoral activities. . . .

The Court of Appeal . . . reversed, holding that although the "clergyman malpractice" count failed to state a cause of action separate from the "negligence" count, both could be construed as stating a cause of action for the "negligent failure to prevent suicide" by "nontherapist counselors." In this context, the Court of Appeal held that nontherapist counselors—*both religious and secular*—have a duty to refer suicidal persons to psychiatrists or psychotherapists qualified to prevent suicides. Moreover, the court held, imposition of a negligence standard of care on pastoral counselors does not impinge on the free exercise of religion guaranteed by the First Amendment, because the state's compelling interest in the preservation of life justifies the narrowly tailored burden on religious expression imposed by such tort liability.

*   *   *

Our review of the record reveals the trial court correctly granted a nonsuit as to plaintiffs' causes of action. Neither the evidence adduced at trial nor well-established principles of tort law support the Court of Appeal's reversal of nonsuit in this case. As we explain below, we need not address the constitutional issues posed by defendants.

IV. Discussion

*   *   *

B.   Cause of Action for Negligent Failure to Prevent Suicide

*   *   *

1.   Legal Requirements for Imposing a Duty of Care

a) Creation of a Duty of Care

"A tort, whether intentional or negligent, involves a violation of a *legal duty,* imposed by statute, contract or otherwise, owed by the defendant to the person injured. Without such a duty, any injury is 'damnum absque injuria'—injury without wrong." Thus, in order to prove facts sufficient to support a finding of negligence, a plaintiff must show that defendant had a duty to use due care, that he breached that duty, and that the breach was the proximate or legal cause of the resulting injury.

*   *   *

b) Special Relationship

Although we have not previously addressed the issue presently before us, we have imposed a duty to prevent a foreseeable suicide only when a special relationship existed between the suicidal individual and the defendant or its agents. For example, two cases imposed such a duty in wrongful death actions after plaintiffs proved that the deceased committed suicide in a hospital or other in-patient facility that had accepted the responsibility to care for and attend to the needs of the suicidal patient. In *Meier,* a cause of action for negligence was held to exist against both the treating psychiatrist and the hospital, and in *Vistica,* liability was imposed on the hospital alone, the only named defendant in the case.

The Court of Appeal here would extend the previously carefully limited precedent, relying initially for the creation of a duty of care (on defendants and other nontherapist counselors) in the foregoing *Meier* and *Vistica* cases. Indeed, the Court of Appeal specifically stated that "Logic and policy both dictate the duty announced in those cases applies to non-therapist counselors as well." We disagree. As defendants and amici curiae point out, *Meier* and *Vistica* are readily distinguishable from the facts of the present case and, as we explain, severely circumscribe the duty they create.

Both *Meier* and *Vistica* address the issue of a special relationship, giving rise to a duty to take precautions to prevent suicide, in the limited context of hospital-patient relationships where the suicidal person died while under the care and custody of hospital physicians who were aware of the patient's unstable mental condition. In both cases, the patient committed suicide while confined in a hospital psychiatric ward. Liability was imposed because defendants failed to take precautions to prevent the patient's suicide even though the medical staff in charge of the patient's care knew that the patient was likely to attempt to take his own life.

Neither case suggested extending the duty of care to personal or religious counseling relationships in which one person provided nonprofessional guidance to another seeking advice and the counselor had no control over the environment of the individual being counseled. In sharp contrast, Nally was not involved in a supervised medical relationship with defendants, and he committed suicide well over two weeks after he was released from the hospital against the advice of his attending psychiatrist and physician.

* * *

Thus, contrary to the Court of Appeal's interpretation, none of these cases supports the finding of a special relationship between Nally and defendants, or the imposition of a duty to refer a suicidal person to a professional therapist as urged in the present case. Indeed, on their limited facts, *Bellah, Vistica* and *Meier* weigh against creating such a duty. With the foregoing in mind, we now turn to other considerations and explain further why we should not impose a duty to prevent suicide on defendants and other nontherapist counselors.

c) The Connection Between Defendants' Conduct and Nally's Suicide and the Foreseeability of Harm

Other factors to consider in determining whether to impose a duty of care on defendants include the closeness of the causal connection between defendants' conduct and the injury suffered, and the foreseeability of the particular harm to the injured party. . . .

Plaintiffs argue that Nally's statement to Pastors Rea and MacArthur (while he was recovering from his suicide attempt at the hospital), "that he was sorry he wasn't successful and that he would attempt suicide after his release from the hospital," were "hidden dangers" that would have affected his prognosis and treatment. Accordingly, plaintiffs reason that Rea and MacArthur should have warned the hospital staff and plaintiffs that Nally was still contemplating suicide after his initial attempt. We disagree.

The closeness of [the] connection between defendants['] conduct and Nally's suicide was tenuous at best. As defendants observe, Nally was examined by five physicians and a psychiatrist during the weeks following his suicide attempt. Defendants correctly assert that they "arranged or encouraged many of these visits and encouraged Nally to continue to cooperate with all doctors." In addition, as stated above, following Nally's overdose attempt Dr. Evelyn warned plaintiffs that Nally remained suicidal and that they should encourage him to see a psychiatrist on his release from the hospital. Plaintiffs also rejected both Dr. Hall's and Dr. Parker's suggestion that Nally be institutionalized because, according to plaintiffs, their son was "not crazy."

Nevertheless, we are urged that mere knowledge on the part of the defendants that Nally may have been suicidal at various stages in his life should give rise to a duty to refer. Imposition of a duty to refer Nally necessarily would imply a general duty on all nontherapists to refer all potentially suicidal persons to licensed medical practitioners.

One can argue that it is foreseeable that if a nontherapist counselor fails to refer a potentially suicidal individual to professional, licensed therapeutic care, the individual may commit suicide. While under some circumstances counselors may conclude that referring a client to a psychiatrist is prudent and necessary, our past decisions teach that it is inappropriate to impose a duty to refer—which may stifle all gratuitous or religious counseling—based on foreseeability alone. Mere foreseeability of the harm or knowledge of the danger, is insufficient to create a legally cognizable special relationship giving rise to a legal duty to prevent harm.

d) Public Policy Considerations

Imposing a duty on defendants or other nontherapist counselors to, in the Court of Appeal's words, "insure their counselees [are also] under the care of psychotherapists, psychiatric facilities, or others authorized and equipped to forestall imminent suicide," could have a deleterious effect on counseling in general. Although both plaintiffs and the present Court of Appeal, in dictum, exempt services such as "teen hotlines" which offer only "band aid counseling," from a newly formulated standard of care that would impose a "duty to refer," the indeterminate nature of liability the Court of Appeal imposes on nontherapist counselors could deter those most in need of help from seeking treatment out of fear that their private disclosures could subject them to involuntary commitment to psychiatric facilities.

As defendants, amici curiae, and the Court of Appeal dissenter observe, neither the Legislature nor the courts have ever imposed a legal obligation on persons to take affirmative steps to prevent the suicide of one who is not under the care of a physician in a hospital. . . . Indeed, for all practical purposes, a doctor to whom a nontherapist counselor refers a suicidal person may refuse to take the patient. Furthermore, under the

Lanterman–Petris–Short Act (Welf. & Inst. Code, §§ 5200, 5201), "[a]ny individual may" but is not required to institute involuntary commitment proceedings.

We also note that the Legislature has exempted the clergy from the licensing requirements applicable to marriage, family, child and domestic counselors (Bus. & Prof. Code, § 4980 et seq.) and from the operation of statutes regulating psychologists (id., § 2908 et seq.). In so doing, the Legislature has recognized that access to the clergy for counseling should be free from state imposed counseling standards, and that "the secular state is not equipped to ascertain the competence of counseling when performed by those affiliated with religious organizations."

Furthermore, extending liability to voluntary, noncommercial and noncustodial relationships is contrary to the trend in the Legislature to encourage private assistance efforts. This public policy goal is expressed in the acts of the Legislature abrogating the "Good Samaritan" rule. Statutes barring the imposition of ordinary negligence liability on one who aids another now embrace numerous scenarios. (See, e.g., Gov. Code, § 50086 [exempting from liability first aid volunteers summoned by authorities to assist in search or rescue operations]; Health & Saf. Code, §§ 1799.100, 1799.102 [exempting from liability nonprofessional persons giving cardiopulmonary resuscitation].)

*　*　*

Even assuming that workable standards of care could be established in the present case, an additional difficulty arises in attempting to identify with precision those to whom the duty should apply. Because of the differing theological views espoused by the myriad of religions in our state and practiced by church members, it would certainly be impractical, and quite possibly unconstitutional, to impose a duty of care on pastoral counselors. Such a duty would necessarily be intertwined with the religious philosophy of the particular denomination or ecclesiastical teachings of the religious entity. We have previously refused to impose a duty when to do so would involve complex policy decisions, and we are unpersuaded by plaintiffs that we should depart from this policy in the present case. . . .

e) Availability of Insurance

As several commentators observe, although lawsuits stemming from spiritual counseling are few, a new type of "clergyman malpractice" insurance has been offered to religious organizations to protect against potential liability for spiritual counseling that causes injury. Apparently, such insurance provides coverage to religious congregations and their pastors for damages caused by the counseling activities of the pastors while acting within the scope of their duties. The value of such insurance, however, is unknown and difficult to determine because few cases have been filed against the clergy.

f) Conclusion

For the foregoing reasons, we conclude that plaintiffs have not met the threshold requirements for imposing on defendants a duty to prevent suicide. Plaintiffs failed to persuade us that the duty to prevent suicide (heretofore imposed only on psychiatrists and hospitals while caring for a suicidal patient) or the general professional duty of care (heretofore imposed only on psychiatrists when treating a mentally disturbed patient) should be extended to a nontherapist counselor who offers counseling to a potentially suicidal person on secular or spiritual matters.

. . . Accordingly, we conclude the trial court correctly granted defendants' nonsuit motion as to the "clergyman malpractice" or negligence causes of action.

*   *   *

The judgment of the Court of Appeal is reversed and the Court of Appeal is directed to enter judgment affirming the judgment of nonsuit and dismissing the action.

KAUFMAN, JUSTICE, concurring.

I concur in the judgment that nonsuit was properly granted, but disagree with the majority's holding that defendants owed no duty of care to the plaintiffs.

The majority appears to reject the proposition that defendants in this matter, or "nontherapist counselors in general," have a duty to advise potentially suicidal counselees to seek competent medical care. Yet the majority does not purport to "foreclose imposing liability on nontherapist counselors, who hold themselves out as professionals, for injuries related to their counseling activities."

In view of the majority's suggestion that a nontherapist counselor who holds himself out as competent to treat a suicidal person owes a duty of care to that person, I am baffled as to the basis or the *necessity* of the majority's broad conclusion that "nontherapist counselors in general" do *not* owe such a duty. The evidence in the record, viewed—as the law requires—in *plaintiffs'* favor, demonstrates that defendants (1) expressly held themselves out as fully competent to deal with the most severe psychological disorders, including major depression with suicidal symptoms, (2) developed a close counseling relationship with Kenneth Nally for that very purpose, and (3) realized that Nally's suicide was at least a possibility. Thus, the evidence was more than sufficient, in my view, to trigger a minimal duty of care to Nally. What was fatally *absent* from plaintiffs' case was not evidence of duty, but proof that defendants breached that duty, and that such breach constituted a proximate cause of Nally's suicide. Therefore, while I concur in the decision to reverse the judgment of the Court of Appeal and to reinstate the judgment of nonsuit and dismissal of the action, I strongly disagree with the conclusion that defendants owed no duty of care in this matter.

QUESTIONS AND COMMENTS

1. *Competing views.* Which view is more compelling, that of the majority or that of Justice Kaufman, who would not foreclose imposing liability on non-therapist counselors if they "hold themselves out as professionals, for injuries related to their counseling activities"? What might be the consequences of adopting the latter position? Would it cut down on the availability of religious counseling or simply encourage religious counselors to make referrals when they are in doubt as to the condition or prognosis of the person they are counseling?

Regarding recent trends, one commentator asserts:

[I]t appears there has been an increase in the number of tort actions against clerics and religious establishments for professional or clergy misconduct since 1980. According to one writer, a reason for this apparent escalation may be the fact that fundamentalist churches are providing more personal, spiritual, and psychological counseling to parishioners and others. This movement by fundamentalist churches toward greater involvement in the field of psychological counseling, as well as the litigious nature of society, indicates a possible increase in future clergy malpractice litigation. Churches in general appear to be providing more counseling services to their congregants. Consequently, many pastor-counselee relationships have resulted in negligent pastoral and/or professional counseling, thereby engendering a number of lawsuits. These lawsuits involving negligent counseling and other significant tort claims include: assertions of negligent counseling by a protestant minister resulting in a parishioner's suicide; negligent marital counseling resulting in a sexual relationship between a Roman Catholic priest and a parishioner; disclosure of confidential communications by an ordained Baptist minister to church officials and parishioners; defamation of a parishioner-counselee by a pastor after the parishioner terminated their marital counseling relationship; invasion of privacy by a pastor who agreed to provide family counseling to a husband and wife and their children; and various other tort actions.

Constance Frisby Fain, *Minimizing Liability for Church–Related Counseling Services: Clergy Malpractice and First Amendment Religion Clauses*, 44 Akron L. Rev. 221, 224–25 (2011).

If liability is imposed on religious counselors who purport to deal with mentally distressed parishioners, is there any way of distinguishing "teen hotlines" or other telephone hotlines that offer only "band aid counseling"? Does the majority opinion speak to this?

2. *Liability of clergymen counselors for sexual misconduct.* The tendency to shield clergy-counselors from malpractice liability has also been extended to claims based on sexual misconduct, where, for instance, a clergyman who acted as a marriage counselor had sexual relations with the advisee's wife. In *Bladen v. First Presbyterian Church of Sallisaw*, 857 P.2d 789 (Okla. 1993), the Oklahoma Supreme Court refused to apply malpractice liability concepts to clergy-counselors because unlike psychologists and psychiatrists, they "do not use the transference mechanism" in carrying out their counseling functions. Id. at 794.

However, this exemption from liability may be receding. In 1998, the Fifth Circuit sustained a jury award of $100,000 against a minister who, while rendering marital and mental health counseling, engaged in sexual relations with the women he was counseling. *Mullanix v. Baucum*, 134 F.3d 331 (5th Cir.1998). In rejecting the defendant's constitutional defense, the court held that the Free Exercise clause of the First Amendment does not categorically insulate religious relationships from judicial scrutiny. In evaluating constitutional defenses, "[c]ourts have noted that the Free Exercise Clause insures 'the protection of two concepts, 'freedom to believe and freedom to act.' ' 'Freedom to believe' is said to be absolute while 'freedom to act' or 'religious conduct' is said to be subject to regulation in order to safeguard the public." Fain, supra, at 247–48.

3. *Liability of unlicensed therapists.* Persons who hold themselves out as mental health professionals, even though they are not licensed under state law, will generally be held to the standard of care of the profession they are purporting to practice. For instance, in *Horak v. Biris,* the defendant, a certified social worker who operated a "center for psychotherapy," was charged with malpractice (after he engaged in sexual relations with a client) and defended on the grounds that he should not be held to the standard of care governing psychologists. In rejecting this defense, the court made the following observation:

> The field of practice engaged in by defendant here more closely resembles the practice of psychology rather than social work, as those two practices are currently defined in the Illinois Revised Statutes. Because of the apparent overlapping of these two fields, we think the proofs may well reveal that defendant possessed or should have possessed a basic knowledge of fundamental psychological principles which routinely come into play during marriage and family counseling. The "transference phenomenon" is apparently one such principle, and has been defined in psychiatric practice as "a phenomenon . . . by which the patient transfers feelings towards everyone else to the doctor, who then must react with a proper response, the counter transference, in order to avoid emotional involvement and assist the patient in overcoming problems." The mishandling of this phenomenon, which generally results in sexual relations or involvement between the psychiatrist or therapist and the patient, has uniformly been considered as malpractice or gross negligence in other jurisdictions, whether the

sexual relations were prescribed by the doctor as part of the therapy, or occurred outside the scope of treatment.

Horak v. Biris, 474 N.E.2d 13, 18 (Ill. 1985). See also *Corgan v. Muehling*, 574 N.E.2d 602 (Ill. 1991) (non-licensed psychologist held to standard of care of licensed psychologists).

2.   Liability of Health Care Institutions

As noted in Chapter One, Part IV, health care institutions may play a pivotal role in mental health treatment decisions. As a consequence, they are often named as defendants in malpractice suits. These actions seek to hold the institution directly or vicariously liable for negligent treatment or release decisions. The oft-cited case that follows is illustrative of claims of this type involving a patient who was allegedly discharged prematurely from a hospital.

MUSE V. CHARTER HOSPITAL OF WINSTON–SALEM, INC.
Court of Appeals of North Carolina, 1995.
117 N.C. App. 468, 452 S.E.2d 589.

LEWIS, JUDGE.

This appeal arises from a judgment in favor of plaintiffs in an action for the wrongful death of Delbert Joseph Muse, III (hereinafter "Joe"). Joe was the son of Delbert Joseph Jr., (hereinafter "Mr. Muse") and Jane K. Muse (hereinafter "Mrs. Muse"), plaintiffs. The jury found that defendant Charter Hospital of Winston–Salem, Inc. (hereinafter "Charter Hospital" or "the hospital") was negligent in that, *inter alia*, it had a policy or practice which required physicians to discharge patients when their insurance expired and that this policy interfered with the medical judgment of Joe's treating physician, Dr. L. Jarrett Barnhill, Jr. The jury awarded plaintiffs compensatory damages of approximately $1,000,000. The jury found that Mr. and Mrs. Muse were contributorily negligent, but that Charter Hospital's conduct was willful or wanton, and awarded punitive damages of $2,000,000 against Charter Hospital. Further, the jury found that Charter hospital was an instrumentality of defendant Charter Medical Corporation (hereinafter "Charter Medical") and awarded punitive damages of $4,000,000 against healthcare Charter Medical.

The facts on which this case arose may be summarized as follows. Joe, who was sixteen years old at the time, was admitted to Charter Hospital for treatment related to his depression and suicidal thoughts. On 12 June 1986, Joe's treatment team consisted of Dr. Barnhill, as treating physician, Fernando Garzon, as nursing therapist, and Betsey Willard, as social worker. During his hospitalization, Joe experienced auditory hallucinations, suicidal and homicidal thoughts, and major depression. Joe's insurance coverage was set to expire on 12 July 1986. As that date neared, Dr. Barnhill decided that a blood test was needed to determine the proper dosage of a drug he was administering to Joe. The blood test was scheduled for 13 July, the day after Joe's insurance was to expire. Dr. Barnhill requested that the hospital administrator allow Joe to stay at Charter Hospital two more days, until 14 July, with Mr. and Mrs. Muse signing a promissory note to pay for the two extra days. The test results did not come back from the lab until 15 July. Nevertheless, Joe was discharged on 14 July and was referred by Dr. Barnhill to the Guilford County Area Mental Health, Mental Retardation and Substance Abuse Authority (hereinafter "Mental Health Authority") for outpatient treatment. Plaintiffs' evidence tended to show that Joe's condition upon discharge was worse than when he entered the hospital. Defendants' evidence, however, tended to show that while his prognosis remained guarded, Joe's condition at discharge was improved. Upon his discharge, Joe went on a one-week family vacation. On 22 July he began outpatient treatment at the Mental Health Authority, where he was seen by Dr. David Slonaker, a clinical psychologist. Two days later, Joe again met with Dr. Slonaker. Joe failed to show up at his 30 July appointment, and the next day he took a fatal overdose of Desipramine, one of his prescribed drugs.

On appeal, defendants present numerous assignments of error. We find merit in one of defendants' arguments.

I.

[The court agreed that it had been improper to assign separate awards of punitive damages to Charter Hospital and Charter Medical because the one was a mere instrumentality of the other and thus they were jointly and severally liable.]

II.

Defendants next argue that the trial court submitted the case to the jury on an erroneous theory of hospital liability that does not exist under the law of North Carolina. As to the theory in question, the trial court instructed: "[A] hospital is under a duty not to have policies or practices which operate in a way that interferes with the ability of a physician to exercise his medical judgment. A violation of this duty would be negligence." The jury found that there existed "a policy or practice which required physicians to discharge patients when their insurance benefits expire and which interfered with the exercise of Dr. Barnhill's medical judgment." Defendants contend that this theory of liability does not fall within any theories previously accepted by our courts.

* * *

Our Supreme Court has recognized that hospitals in this state owe a duty of care to their patients. In *Burns v. Forsyth County Hospital Authority, Inc.*, this Court held that a hospital has a duty to the patient to obey the instructions of a doctor, absent the instructions being obviously negligent or dangerous. Another recognized duty is the duty to make a reasonable effort to monitor and oversee the treatment prescribed and administered by doctors practicing at the hospital. In light of these holdings, it seems axiomatic that the hospital has the duty not to institute policies or practices which interfere with the doctor's medical judgment. We hold that pursuant to the reasonable person standard, Charter Hospital had a duty not to institute a policy or practice which required that patients be discharged when their insurance expired and which interfered with the medical judgment of Dr. Barnhill.

III.

Defendants next argue that even if the theory of negligence submitted to the jury was proper, the jury's finding that Charter Hospital had such a practice was not supported by sufficient evidence. . . . We conclude that in the case at hand, the evidence was sufficient to go to the jury.

Plaintiffs' evidence included the testimony of Charter Hospital employees and outside experts. Fernando Garzon, Joe's nursing therapist at Charter Hospital, testified that the hospital had a policy of discharging patients when their insurance expired. Specifically, when the issue of insurance came up in treatment team meetings, plans were made to discharge the patient. When Dr. Barnhill and the other psychiatrists and therapists spoke of insurance, they seemed to lack autonomy. For example, Garzon testified, they would state, "So and so is to be discharged. We must do this." Finally, Garzon testified that when he returned from a vacation, and Joe was no longer at the hospital, he asked several employees why Joe had been discharged [and] they all responded that he was discharged because his insurance had expired. Jane Sims, a former staff member at the hospital, testified that several employees expressed alarm about Joe's impending discharge, and that a therapist explained that Joe could no longer stay at the hospital because his insurance had expired. Sims also testified that Dr. Barnhill had misgivings about discharging Joe, and that Dr. Barnhill's frustration was apparent to everyone. One of plaintiff's experts testified that based on a study regarding the length of patient stays at Charter Hospital it was his opinion that patients were discharged based on insurance, regardless of their medical condition. Other experts testified that based on Joe's serious condition on the date of discharge, the expiration of insurance coverage must have caused Dr. Barnhill to discharge Joe. The experts further testified as to the relevant standard of care, and concluded that Charter Hospital's practices were below the standard of care and caused Joe's death. We hold that this evidence was sufficient to go to the jury.

Defendants further argue that the evidence was insufficient to support the jury's finding that Charter Hospital engaged in conduct that was willful or wanton. An act is willful when it is done purposely and deliberately in violation of the law, or when it is done knowingly and of set purpose, or when the mere will has free play, without yielding to reason. . . . We conclude that the jury could have reasonably found from the above-stated evidence that Charter Hospital acted knowingly and of set purpose, and with reckless indifference to the rights of others. Therefore, we hold that the finding of willful or wanton conduct on the part of Charter Hospital was supported by sufficient evidence.

IV.

Defendants' next argument is that the trial court erred in not granting their motion for judgment notwithstanding the verdict, on the ground that the negligent acts of the Muses and Dr. Barnhill were superseding causes of Joe's death. . . .

. . . In order for an intervening cause to relieve the original wrongdoer of liability, the intervening cause must be a new cause, which intervenes between the original negligent act and the injury ultimately suffered, and which breaks the chain of causation set in motion by the original wrongdoer and becomes itself solely responsible for the injury. . . .

The evidence . . . tended to show that the hospital had a policy of requiring the discharge of patients when their insurance expired and that this policy interfered with Dr. Barnhill's medical judgment regarding Joe's discharge. Dr. Barnhill was thereby put in a position such that he could not disclose the severity of Joe's condition to the Muses. . . . Any negligence of Dr. Barnhill in discharging Joe and in not warning the Muses, or of the Muses, in not properly supervising Joe after discharge, did not turn aside the natural sequence of events set in motion by the hospital's misconduct.

*   *   *

Defendants next contend that Joe's suicide was a superseding cause of his death. . . . This question is apparently one of first impression in this state. However, we cannot agree with defendants' contention. The rule must be that where a psychiatric hospital has assumed the care of a suicidal patient, and as a result of its negligence, the patient commits suicide, the hospital cannot claim that the suicide was a superseding cause, insulating the hospital from liability. Were the rule otherwise, the wrongdoer "could become indifferent to the performance of his duty [to care for the suicidal patient] knowing that the very eventuality that he was under a duty to prevent would, upon its occurrence, relieve him from responsibility."

*   *   *

For the reasons stated, we find no error in the judgment of the trial court, except for that part of the judgment awarding punitive damages, which is reversed and remanded for proceedings consistent with this opinion.

No error in part, reversed in part and remanded.

ORR, J., dissents.

* * *

While the jury found that defendant was negligent, I find insufficient evidence to raise the defendant's conduct to the level required to submit the issue of willful and wanton conduct to the jury. A policy to terminate a patient's hospitalization based upon insurance benefits ending in and of itself is not wilful or wanton conduct. To sustain plaintiff's contention there must be, according to our law, a deliberate purpose not to discharge a duty necessary for a person's safety. If the hospital had simply discharged the patient with no referral to another physician or medical facility, then a cognizable claim for wilful or wanton conduct would have been established. Such was not the case here, as I read the record, and although Dr. Barnhill's care in discharging the patient may well have been negligent, there is nothing to suggest that the hospital's policy or its implementation by Dr. Barnhill was done with reckless or deliberate disregard for the patient's safety. Therefore, I conclude that the trial court erred in submitting the issue of wilful and wanton conduct to the jury and would accordingly vote to reverse.

QUESTIONS AND COMMENTS

1. *Law in other jurisdictions.* The *Muse* case is the first reported appellate decision imposing liability on a hospital under similar circumstances. Historically, hospitals, which traditionally operated as a charitable institute for the poor (the wealthy would receive services in their home), were immune from liability. This changed as the practice of medicine became more of a science and a business largely available to and demanded by everyone, became both more complex and profitable, and became more likely to be delivered through large institutions where patients were highly dependent on the expertise, skills, and judgment of the hospital's health care staff. As a result, during the latter half of the twentieth century, hospitals generally became directly liable for the negligence of their staff and vicariously liable (through the doctrine of apparent or ostensible agency) for the negligence of community physicians who had been granted privileges by the hospitals to deliver services to their patients on site (with the assistance of hospital staff and while employing the technology and medical devices provided by the hospital).

In recent years, the scope of potential liability of hospitals has expanded even further, as they are increasingly directly liable for a range of activities. See *Thompson v. Nason Hosp.*, 591 A.2d 703 (Pa. 1991) (hospitals have a duty to maintain safe and adequate facilities and equipment, select and retain only competent physicians, oversee all persons who practice medicine within its walls as to patient care, and formulate, adopt, and enforce adequate rules and policies to ensure quality care for their patients); *Shannon v. McNulty*, 718 A.2d 828 (Pa. Super. Ct. 1998). For a discussion of the expanding liability of hospitals, including their fiduciary duties and a duty of care owed to discharged patients, see Thomas L. Hafemeister & Joshua Hinckley Porter, *Don't Let Go of the Rope: Reducing Readmissions by Recognizing Hospitals' Fiduciary Duties to Their Discharged Patients*, 62 Am. U. L. Rev. 513 (2013).

Even more recently, however, the delivery of health care services has decentralized somewhat, with many services now delivered in the community through free-standing or hospital-affiliated centers or institutes. In addition, community-based physicians, who had predominantly worked as solo practitioners, have increasingly joined together for practical and business reasons in practice groups where staff and often patients are shared. These entities may also be the focus of liability suits for the negligence of their practitioners.

The delivery of mental health services has also evolved in recent years. Historically, jails and almshouses were filled with individuals with a mental illness. From 1830–1865, society began to recognize that these were poor places to care for these individuals and state psychiatric facilities began to be established across the country. From 1865–1890, the quality of care in these facilities declined, in part because of states' inability or unwillingness to adequately fund these facilities and pressures on them to house more residents. During the 1960s and 1970s in particular, but continuing today as well, many of these facilities have closed and the ones that remain open have been downsized, driven in part by a series of exposés regarding the deplorable conditions within these facilities, lawsuits challenging conditions within these facilities, fiscal constraints, and treatment developments that ostensibly make community care more viable. See Paul S. Appelbaum, *History of Civil Commitment and Related Reforms: Lessons for Today*, 25(1) Dev. Mental Health L. 13 (Jan. 2006); see also Chapter Ten, infra.

In their place, many private facilities, including a number that were part of national chains, as in *Muse*, were established across the country. However, these facilities have also come under financial pressure and today most mental health services are decentralized and delivered in the community. Further paralleling the general health care system, community-based mental health providers have also increasingly joined practice groups or free-standing or hospital-affiliated community mental health centers. As a result, many of the developments regarding the liability of health care facilities in general also apply to the delivery of mental health services. A primary difference is that many of the mental health centers are funded by governmental agencies, which raises issues of governmental immunity. See Part II.D.4, infra.

2. *Implications of the Muse decision.* Can the *Muse* decision be read as holding that—contractual limitations notwithstanding—a hospital may not discharge a patient where the discharge holds the potential of serious injury? If this is the holding, it can have very substantial implications for hospitals

and health care organizations. If gratuitous services must be provided on any extended basis, the provider could confront serious financial difficulties, including insolvency. Are courts in a better position than legislatures to make basic policy decisions that have very significant financial implications for industries such as the health care system? Will legislatures be sensitive to the risks and challenges associated with a discharge decision? What kinds of fact-gathering should be the basis of these kinds of economic decisions that reallocate financial burdens outside the private ordering process, including contracts between parties?

3. *Physicians' duty to contest reimbursement limits.* In the *Muse* case, the decedent's treating physician, Dr. Barnhill, did make some efforts to get him extra time in the hospital. Ultimately, however, he did not contest the reimbursement limit. Some courts have held that physicians have a duty to contest reimbursement limits and may be held liable for violations of that duty. In *Wickline v. State*, 239 Cal. Rptr. 810 (Ct. App. 1986), the court, in *dicta,* indicated that a physician could be held liable in negligence for not contesting vigorously a reimbursement decision made by Medi–Cal (California's version of Medicaid). As a result of the reimbursement decision, the plaintiff was discharged prematurely after an operation; her leg subsequently became gangrenous and had to be amputated.

4. *Managed care organizations as defendants.* Managed care organizations (MCOs), which have come to dominate the financing of health care services and thereby wield enormous influence over health care decisions (both private and government-funded services), have also been sued under various theories. They have been held vicariously liable for the negligent behavior of the physicians with whom they directly contract. See, e.g., *Boyd v. Albert Einstein Med. Ctr.*, 547 A.2d 1229 (Pa. Super. Ct. 1988); *Petrovich v. Share Health Plan of Ill., Inc.*, 719 N.E.2d 756 (Ill. 1999). MCOs may also be held directly liable for negligence in setting up a financial incentive scheme that encourages physicians to refrain from providing care. See *Bush v. Dake*, File No. 86–25767 NM–2 (Mich. Cir. Ct. Apr. 27, 1989); but see *Brannan v. Northwest Permanente, P.C.*, 2006 WL 2794881 (W.D. Wash. 2006) (physician's employment compensation contract with HMO found irrelevant in plaintiff's malpractice case).

In addition, the California Supreme Court has held that utilization reviewers, who determine whether a given medical service is eligible for payment by a MCO, can be held liable for "tortious inducement of breach of contract." *Wilson v. Blue Cross of S. Cal.*, 271 Cal. Rptr. 876 (Cal. Ct. App. 1990) (premature discharge of patient who subsequently committed suicide; insurance coverage covered 30 days of hospitalization, though patient was discharged after 10 days). Finally, in the largest and most significant number of cases, plaintiffs have challenged the MCO utilization review process, arguing that the MCO owed the plaintiff a duty of care and was negligent in prospectively denying coverage for a particular intervention. See, e.g., *Andrews–Clarke v. Travelers Ins. Co.*, 984 F. Supp. 49 (D. Mass. 1997) (suit against insurance company and utilization reviewer, where defendants denied coverage for admission to 30–day private detoxification program and plaintiff's husband subsequently committed suicide). As discussed in note 5, infra, however, suits that allege wrongdoing by MCOs have had limited success when brought against employer-sponsored health plans, primarily because of the preemptive role of the federal Employee Retirement Income Security Act ("ERISA").

5.   *The role of ERISA.* ERISA governs the vast majority of *employer-sponsored* health plans, which continues to be the predominant vehicle for the financing of health care services in this country. Due to its broad preemption clauses, ERISA plays an important role in negligence-based challenges to insurers' denials of coverage. ERISA's preemption clauses displace any state statute or common law that implicates the administration or structure of the plan benefit. ERISA beneficiaries who want to contest benefits determinations are required to utilize the remedial scheme provided by ERISA and must pursue their claims in federal court; this scheme limits recovery to the value of the benefits denied. Compensatory and consequential damages are not available under ERISA's remedial scheme. As a result, many courts held that because negligence-based challenges to coverage denials are really benefits determination disputes, they are preempted by ERISA. See, e.g., *Andrews–Clarke v. Travelers Ins. Co.*, 984 F. Supp. 49 (D. Mass. 1997); *Jass v. Prudential Health Care Plan*, 88 F.3d 1482 (7th Cir. 1996).

In an attempt to bypass these rulings, a number of states passed laws explicitly authorizing patients to sue their health plans directly in the state's court system. Texas was the first to enact such "right-to-sue" legislation. Under the Texas law, which was passed in 1997, a MCO could be sued for failure to exercise ordinary care in making a "health care treatment decision." The law made health plans directly liable for coverage decisions and also vicariously liable for the negligence of their employees or agents in making coverage decisions. Tex. Civ. Prac. & Rem. §§ 88.001–88.003 (1997). Similarly, the Third Circuit tried to draw a distinction between negligence suits that involve the "quantity" of the care made available and those that target the "quality" of the care, arguing that only the former was preempted by ERISA. *Dukes v. U.S. Healthcare, Inc.*, 57 F.3d 350 (3d Cir. 1995). In *Pegram v. Herdrich*, 530 U.S. 211 (2000), the U.S. Supreme Court appeared to support the Third Circuit's position to some extent by indicating that, given the states' historic obligation to regulate health care quality, state law-based challenges to coverage decisions that raise *both* eligibility and treatment quality questions may not be preempted by ERISA. The Pennsylvania Supreme Court immediately applied *Pegram* when it held that an MCO's denial of permission to use a hospital outside its network was a mixed eligibility and treatment decision and hence subject to challenge under state law. The state court focused on the fact that the utilization reviewer, a physician employed by the MCO, "rejected another medical doctor's opinion based on his clinical judgment." *Pappas v. Asbel*, 768 A.2d 1089, 1096 (Pa. 2001).

However, in *Aetna Health Inc. v. Davila*, 542 U.S. 200 (2004), the Supreme Court struck down two challenges brought by individuals under the Texas statute discussed above and asserted that MCOs had failed to exercise ordinary care in the handling of their coverage decisions. The Court unanimously concluded that these were challenges to benefits' denials and hence entirely preempted by ERISA. In essence, the Supreme Court said that unless Congress modified ERISA, states cannot independently authorize employer health plan subscribers to sue MCOs for the damages caused by their wrongful denial of benefits.

Do you see any problems with a preemption analysis that turns on whether a particular decision regarding health care plan benefits can be characterized as "purely" involving eligibility questions? The 2004 Supreme Court decision in *Aetna Health* narrows the scope of *Pegram* by emphasizing that, even when determinations regarding benefits made by ERISA plan administrators are based on medical judgments, challenges to such determinations are generally preempted. According to *Aetna Health*, the defendants in liability suits for negligent health care are largely limited to suing their treating health care providers or the providers' employers.

6. *Independent Review Provisions and ERISA*. In addition to passing right-to-sue laws, some states have passed laws requiring MCOs to provide an independent review of coverage disputes. These statutes were also challenged as preempted by ERISA. In *Rush Prudential HMO v. Moran*, 536 U.S. 355 (2002), however, the Supreme Court determined that although such statutes did "relate to" the administration and structure of ERISA-governed plans, they were nonetheless not preempted because they fell within an ERISA "savings clause" that exempts from preemption those laws that regulate the "business of insurance."

7. *Federal legislative proposals to impose liability on MCOs*. As various observers have pointed out, the liability gap created by ERISA preemption was probably not intended by the framers of ERISA. In the early 1970s, when ERISA was enacted (primarily as a means of protecting employee pension plans and ensuring that national employers were relieved of the administrative burden of complying with multiple state laws in designing their benefits plans), insurers typically did not play a role in determining whether a particular treatment could be provided (i.e., prospective review). At most, insurers contested their responsibility to provide payment after treatment had been delivered (i.e., retrospective review).

In 2001, the 107th Congress took its last significant step to date towards amending health care liability claims under ERISA. The Senate passed a bill that authorized liability against MCOs that are part of ERISA plans if they failed to exercise "ordinary care" in making decisions about eligibility or coverage. The bill also eliminated ERISA preemption of state law causes of action challenging coverage determination based on clinical criteria. S. 1052, 107th Cong., § 402 (2001) (amending § 502 of ERISA). A bill passed by the House created a cause of action for ERISA plan beneficiaries similar to that provided in the Senate bill. Unlike the Senate bill, however, the House bill prohibited courts from classifying coverage disputes as challenges to the quality of medical care under state tort law. H.R. 2563, 107th Cong., § 402 (2001). The differences between the Senate and House bills were not resolved, and the bill was not enacted.

Why do you think Congress has not acted to extend the liability of MCOs who have inappropriately denied requests for health care benefits? If you were a national employer, which approach would you favor? What if you were a health care provider? An MCO? What would be the likely impact of such an extension of liability?

8. *Managed care limitations on types of medication.* Medical utilization review by MCOs extends to the type of medication that will be paid for under an insurance plan. Such review can sometimes lead to an MCO requiring that a different medication be substituted for the one prescribed by the physician. Generally, the substitution replaces the prescribed drug with a less expensive one. In one reported case, the patient had been taking Risperdal, a new anti-psychotic drug with a retail cost of $5.75 per day. The MCO to which he belonged, however, ordered that Navane (with a retail cost of 42 cents per day) be substituted. The patient's condition deteriorated and he ultimately committed suicide. Milt Freudenheim, *Drug Substitutions Add to Discord Over Managed Care*, N.Y. Times, Oct. 8, 1996. Additionally, after a drug goes "off-patent," generic substitutes may become available with the MCO mandating the use of the generic substitute, notwithstanding that the recipient of the generic version finds it less effective.

3. Liability of Institutions of Higher Learning

a. Introduction

Public attention has been drawn in recent years to the violent acts of students on campuses, including mass shootings. While these events remain rare, they can have catastrophic consequences. For instance, the April 2007 shootings at Virginia Tech resulted in the deaths of thirty-two students and staff.

In some instances, these events have resulted in legal action against the educational institution where the shooting took place. Such suits have been based on the alleged failure of the mental health providers employed by the institution to exercise due care in the protection of students and staff.[d] In states that adhere to the *Tarasoff* doctrine, these institutions may be liable if a therapist associated with the institution fails to take appropriate actions to forestall the forseeably dangerous acts of a client, such as notification of law enforcement officials, civil commitment, or a warning to third persons at risk (the latter duty often limited to

---

[d] Federal civil rights laws may provide an alternate theory of liability when the defendant is a public university. An action for damages can theoretically be brought under 42 U.S.C. § 1983.

"identifiable" potential victims). See *Eckhardt v. Kirts*, 534 N.E.2d 1339 (Ill. App. Ct. 1989) (collecting cases).

Even when a student has not been receiving treatment from an institution-operated facility, the institution may be charged with having failed to take appropriate action to prevent a student suicide or to protect students and staff from the violent acts of a student. The legal standard that applies under these circumstances is still developing. Where a student commits suicide, a threshold issue is whether the institution has a "special relationship" with the student. Under § 314A of the Restatement of Torts (Second), examples of a special relationship include "the relationship between a common carrier and its passengers, an innkeeper and his guests, a possessor of land and his invitees, and one who takes custody of another thereby depriving him of other assistance," but is not limited to these scenarios. In at least two cases involving student suicides, the trial court ruled that the allegation of a student's "special relationship" with the university involved was sufficient to avoid dismissal. See *Schieszler v. Ferrum Coll.*, 236 F. Supp. 2d 602 (W.D. Va. 2002); *Shin v. Mass. Inst. of Tech.*, 19 Mass. L. Rptr. 570, 2005 WL 1869101 (Mass. Super. Ct. 2005). Implicit in both cases was the perception that universities have some control of the actions of students (particularly if they reside in university residence halls). Also, there may be the lingering notion that a university stands in *loco parentis* to underage students. But see *Jain v. State*, 617 N.W.2d 293 (Iowa 2000) (rejecting the notion that university-student relations establish a special relationship). For a general discussion of institutional duty and how educational institutions can better protect themselves and their students in the future, see Helen DeHaven, *The Academy and the Public Peril: Mental Illness, Student Rampage, and Institutional Duty*, 37 J.C. & U.L. 267 (2011).

The liability of institutions of higher education for the violent acts of students who harm third persons is more problematic. Here § 315 of the Restatement is apposite and provides:

> There is no duty so to control the conduct of a third person as to prevent him from causing physical harm to another unless
>
> (a) a special relation exists between the actor and the third person which imposes a duty upon the actor to control the third person's conduct, or
>
> (b) a special relation exists between the actor and the other which gives the other a right to protection.

This provision *explicitly* requires a finding that a college or university had a duty to control the conduct of a third person. Given the limited control that these institutions have over student conduct that does not violate either the criminal law or institutional regulations, victims of student violence may have difficulty sustaining this burden. It also requires a "special" relationship between the institution and the injured party which, in cases that do not involve institution-affiliated mental health providers or arise in non-*Tarasoff* jurisdictions, can also be difficult to show. The Virginia Tech incident, which involved a student with a mental disorder, illustrates the complexity of the issues raised in cases of this type.

b.   Case Study—The Virginia Tech Shootings of April 2007

Most of the following material is taken from the monograph, *Mass Shootings at Virginia Tech, Report of the Review Panel*, presented to then-Governor Timothy Kaine and the Commonwealth of Virginia (Aug. 2007) (hereafter *Review Panel Report*) and the Timeline therein, available at http://www.governor.virginia.gov/tempcontent/techpanelreport.cfm.

Prologue

Virginia Polytechnic Institute and State University (Virginia Tech) is a sprawling campus with 131 buildings on 2,600 acres in Southwest Virginia. In 2007, it had an enrollment of approximately 26,000 students. The university has its own police department, with thirty-five officers on April 16, 2007. The campus police operate in close cooperation with the police department of the adjacent city of Blacksburg. There are no guards at any of the entrance roads leading to the campus nor are guards stationed at any university buildings.

On April 16, 2007, a senior student, Seung Hui Cho, shot to death thirty-two students and faculty and wounded seventeen others before killing himself. These shootings were committed in two separate episodes. First, in the early hours of April 16, Cho murdered two students in a dormitory room in West Ambler Johnston Hall. Approximately two and a half hours later, Cho entered Norris Hall, an engineering building, systematically went from classroom to classroom, and fatally shot thirty students and staff members using automatic pistols.

An investigation following these events found that Cho had a history of mental health problems, beginning in early childhood. For instance, immediately prior to entering high school, Cho was diagnosed by a psychiatrist as suffering from "selective mutism" and "major depression, single episode." During the nearly four years that Cho attended Virginia Tech, he also exhibited behaviors that were symptomatic of a mental disorder. Key events and Cho's behavioral history while enrolled at Virginia Tech are summarized below.

Timeline of Events During Cho's Enrollment at Virginia Tech

August 2003: Cho entered Virginia Tech as a business information systems major. He attracted little attention during his freshman year. He had a difficult time with his roommate over neatness issues and changed rooms. His parents made weekly trips to visit him. His grades were good. He did not see a counselor at school or at home. He was purportedly excited about college.

Fall 2004: During his sophomore year, Cho moved off campus to room with a senior who was rarely at home. Cho complained that mites in the apartment were affecting his skin, but doctors told him that his facial blemishes were acne and prescribed minocycline. He became interested in writing and decided to switch his major to English beginning his junior year, submitting the necessary paperwork late in his sophomore year. His sister noted a growing passion for writing over the summer break, although he was secretive about its content. Cho submitted a book idea to a publishing house.

Spring 2005: The book proposal was rejected, an event that depressed him, according to his family. He still saw no counselor at school or home, and exhibited no behavioral problems other than extreme quietness.

Fall 2005: Cho started his junior year and moved back into the dorms. Serious problems began to surface. His sister noted that he was writing less, and wondered if the publisher's rejection letter curbed his enthusiasm for writing and reversed his improving attitude. At school, Cho was taken to some parties by his suitemates at the start of the fall semester. At one of these parties, he stabbed at the carpet in a girl's room with a knife. Prof. Nikki Giovanni, Cho's poetry professor, was concerned about the violence expressed in his writings. She also asked him to stop taking pictures of classmates from a camera held under the desk. She offered to get him into another class and wrote a letter to English Department Chair Lucinda Roy to accelerate that process. Dr. Roy agreed to remove Cho from the class and tutored him one-on-one with assistance from Prof. Frederick D'Aguiar. When Cho refused to go to counseling, Dr. Roy notified the Division of Student Affairs, the University's Cook Counseling Center, the Schiffert Health Center, the Virginia Tech police, and the College of Liberal Arts and Human Sciences. Cho's problems were also discussed with the university's Care Team, a unit that reviews students with problems, but no direct action was taken.

Nov. 27, 2005: A female resident filed a report with the Virginia Tech Police Department (VTPD), indicating that Cho had made "annoying" contact with her on the Internet, by phone, and in person. The VTPD interviewed Cho, but the female student declined to press charges. The investigating officer referred Cho to the school's disciplinary system, the Office of Judicial Affairs.

Nov. 30, 2005: Following his interaction with VTPD police, Cho called Cook Counseling Center and was triaged (i.e., given a preliminary screening) by phone.

Dec. 6, 2005: E-mails among resident advisors (RAs) reflected complaints by a female resident in Cochrane residence hall regarding instant messages (IMs) from Cho sent under various strange aliases. E-mails from an R.A. also reported that Cho went in disguise to a female student's room (i.e., the event of Nov. 27).

Dec. 12, 2005: A female student from Campbell Hall filed a report with the VTPD complaining of "disturbing" IMs from Cho. She requested that Cho have no further contact with her. Cho did not keep a 2:00 p.m. appointment at Cook Counseling Center but was triaged by the Center again by phone that afternoon.

Dec. 13, 2005: VTPD notified Cho that he was to have no further contact with the second female student who had filed a complaint. After the campus police left, Cho's suitemate received an IM from Cho stating, "I might as well kill myself now." The suitemate alerted the VTPD, who arranged for a prescreener, a licensed clinical social worker from the New River Valley Community Services Board (the regional outpatient mental health center), to evaluate him. The prescreener concluded that Cho was "an imminent danger to self or others." She also noted that Cho was "mentally ill and was not willing to be treated voluntarily." A magistrate issued a temporary detention order, and Cho was transported to Carilion St. Albans Psychiatric Hospital for an overnight stay and evaluation to determine if civil commitment was appropriate.

Dec. 14, 2005:

7 a.m. The person assigned as an independent evaluator pursuant to state law, psychologist Roy Crouse, evaluated Cho and concluded that he did *not* present an imminent danger to himself, a requirement for civil commitment in Virginia.

Before 11 a.m. During the overnight stay at Carilion, Cho received one milligram of Ativa, which was administered to treat anxiety. A staff psychiatrist at Carilion evaluated Cho, concluding he was not a danger to himself or others, and recommended outpatient counseling. He gathered no collateral information.

11–11:30 a.m. Special Justice Paul M. Barnett conducted Cho's commitment hearing. Cho was represented by an attorney. After hearing evidence on Cho, the Special Justice ruled, contrary to the Carilion evaluators, that "Cho presents an imminent danger to self or others as a result of mental illness" and ordered outpatient treatment.

Noon. Following the hearing, the Carilion staff psychiatrist dictated in his evaluation summary that "there is no indication of psychosis, delusions, suicidal or homicidal ideation." The psychiatrist found that "his insight and judgment are normal. . . . Followup and aftercare to be arranged with the counseling center at Virginia Tech; medications, none." Cho was released.

No information was available concerning the interactions between Carilion's staff and the university's Cook Center before and after Cho's psychiatric hospitalization. But shortly before Cho's discharge from Carilion on December 14, a clinical support representative affiliated with the New River Valley Community Services Board established contact with Cook Center to make an appointment for Cho. The Review Panel's Report elaborated on the events immediately prior to and following Cho's discharge.

The clinical support representative (CSR) contacted Cook Counseling Center at Virginia Tech to make an appointment for Cho. The Cook Counseling Center required that Cho be put on the phone (a practice begun shortly before this hearing according to the CSR) to make the appointment, which he did. The appointment was scheduled for 3:00 p.m. that afternoon, December 14. The CSR does not recall whether this phone call was made prior to or following the hearing. . . .

Due to the rapidly approaching outpatient appointment for Cho, the CSR urged the treating psychiatrist to expedite the dictation and transcription of his discharge summary. It was transcribed shortly before noon and the physical evaluation findings and recommendation about an hour later. The [CSR] recalls faxing the records to Cook Counseling Center, but he did not place a copy of the transmittal confirmation in the hospital records. Cook Counseling Center, however, has no record of having received any hospital records until January 2006. The physical evaluation report indicated that Cho was to be treated by the psychiatrist at [Carilion] "and hopefully have some intervention in therapy for treatment of his mood disorder." The discharge summary, which was not part of the records received by the panel from Cook Counseling Center, indicated "followup and aftercare to be arranged with counseling center at Virginia Tech. Medications none."

Cho was discharged from [Carilion] at 2:00 p.m. on December 14. [No person that was interviewed by the Review Panel] could say how Cho got back to campus. However, the electronic scheduling program at the Cook Counseling Center indicates that Cho kept his appointment that day at 3:00 p.m. He was triaged again, this time face-to-face, but no diagnosis was given. The triage report is missing (as well as those from his two prior phone triages), and the counselor who performed the triage has no independent recollection of Cho. It is her standard practice to complete appropriate forms and write a note to document critical information, recommendations, and plans for follow-up.

It is unclear why Cho would have been triaged for a third time rather than receiving a treatment session at his afternoon appointment following release from [Carilion]. The *Collegiate Times* had run an article at the beginning of the fall semester expressing "concern about the diminished services provided by the counseling center" and the temporary loss of its only psychiatrist. It was the policy of the Cook Counseling Center to allow patients to decide whether to make a followup appointment. According to the existing Cook Counseling Center records, none was ever scheduled by Cho. Because Cook Counseling Center had accepted Cho as a voluntary patient, no notice was given to the CSB, the court, [Carilion], or Virginia Tech officials that Cho never returned to Cook Counseling Center."

Review Panel Report, at 48–49.

Jan. 2006. The Cook Counseling Center received a psychiatric summary from Carilion. No action was taken by Cook Counseling Center or the Care Team to follow up on Cho.

Apr. 17, 2006. Cho's technical writing professor, Carl Bean, suggested that Cho drop his class after repeated efforts to address his shortcomings and Cho's inappropriate choice of writing assignments. Cho followed the professor to his office, raised his voice angrily, and was asked to leave. Prof. Bean did not report this incident to university officials.

Spring 2006. Cho wrote a paper for Prof. Hicok's creative writing class concerning a young man who hated the students at his school and planned to kill them and himself. The writing contained a number of parallels to the events of April 16, 2007 and the recorded messages later sent to NBC (which were released after Cho's death).

Sept. 6–12, 2006. Prof. Lisa Norris, another of Cho's writing professors, alerted the Associate Dean of Liberal Arts and Human Sciences, Mary Ann Lewis, about disturbing behavior by Cho, but the dean's notes made "no mention of mental health issues or police reports" on Cho. Prof. Norris encouraged Cho to go to counseling with her, but he declined.

Fall 2006. Prof. Falco, another of Cho's writing instructors, conferred with Profs. Roy and Norris, who told him that Prof. Roy in Fall 2005 and Prof. Norris in 2006 alerted the Associate Dean of Students, Mary Ann Lewis, about Cho.

Feb. 2, 2007. Cho ordered a .22 caliber Walther P22 handgun online from TGSCOM, Inc.

Feb. 9, 2007. Cho picked up the handgun from J–N–D Pawnbrokers in Blacksburg, across the street from the university.

Mar. 12, 2007. Cho rented a van from Enterprise Rent–A–Car at the Roanoke Regional Airport, which he kept for almost a month. (Cho videotaped some of his subsequently released diatribe in the van).

Mar. 13–Apr. 7, 2007. On March 13, having waited the thirty days between gun purchases required by Virginia law, Cho purchased a 9mm Glock 19 handgun and a box of fifty 9mm full metal jacket practice rounds at Roanoke Firearms. The store initiated the required background check by police, who found no record of mental health issues. Nine days later, Cho went to PSS Range and Training, an indoor pistol range, and spent an hour practicing. In the following weeks he purchased additional ammunition magazines, ammunition, and a hunting knife from eBay, Wal–Mart, and Dick's Sporting Goods, and chains from Home Depot.

Apr. 8, 2007. Cho spent the night at the Hampton Inn in Christiansburg, Virginia, videotaping segments for his manifesto-like diatribe against his fellow students and society at large (which he later sent to NBC). He also bought more ammunition.

Apr. 13, 2007. Bomb threats were made to Torgersen, Durham, and Whittemore halls, in the form of an anonymous note. The threats were assessed by the VTPD and the buildings evacuated. There was no lockdown or cancellation of classes elsewhere on campus. Handwriting analysis failed to link these threats to Cho.

Apr. 14, 2007. An Asian male wearing a hooded garment was seen by a faculty member in Norris Hall. The faculty member later (after Apr. 16) told police that one of her students had told her the doors were chained. Cho may thus have been practicing his assault. He also bought more ammunition.

Apr. 15, 2007. Cho placed his weekly Sunday night call to his family in Fairfax County. They reported the conversation as normal and that Cho said nothing that caused them concern.

Apr. 16, 2007. Cho went on his shooting rampage, resulting in the murder of two students in West Ambler Johnston residence hall and thirty students two-and-a-half hours later in Norris Hall.

Selected Legal/Policy Issues

The Virginia Tech shootings raised multiple policy issues, which the *Review Panel Report* divided into three categories. One set of issues pertained to the institutional capacity of universities to identify at-risk students who have "problems" and take appropriate action to channel such students into treatment. The Report included the following findings:

> Residence Life [an administrative unit having responsibility over the resident halls] knew through their staff (two resident advisors and their supervisor) that there were multiple reports and concerns expressed over Cho's behavior in the dorm, but this was not brought before the Care Team. The academic component of the university spoke up loudly about a sullen, foreboding male student who refused to talk, frightened classmate and faculty with macabre writings, and refused faculty exhortations to get counseling. However, after Judicial Affairs and the Cook Counseling Center opined that Cho's writings were not actionable threats, the Care Team's one review of

Cho [in 2005] resulted in their being satisfied that private tutoring would resolve the problem. No one sought to revisit Cho's progress the following semester or inquire into whether he had come to the attention of other stakeholders on campus.

Review Panel Report, at 52.

The *Review Panel Report* also noted a lack of coordination between psychiatric facilities to which people have been committed and after-care outpatient clinics. In particular, the panel found a lack of follow up on the part of Carilion and insufficient or non-existent communications between that facility and the university's Cook Counseling Center.

Finally, the review panel found that communications between campus units and outside agencies such as Carilion were hampered both by misinterpretations of state and federal law requirements and by defects in state and federal regulations governing when disclosures pertaining to students evidencing signs of mental abnormality and dangerousness may be made. In the words of the report:

> The Care Team was hampered by overly strict interpretations of federal and state privacy laws (acknowledged as being overly complex), a decentralized corporate university structure, and the absence of someone on the team who was experienced in threat assessment and knew to investigate the situation more broadly, checking for collateral information that would help determine if this individual truly posed a risk or not.

Review Panel Report, at 52.

Issues associated with the protection of student privacy when students are either dangerous to themselves or to third persons are treated in Chapter Five, infra.

QUESTIONS AND COMMENTS

1. *The university's options.* As noted in the excerpt from the Review Panel's Timeline of Events, Cho's behavior and his threat to commit suicide led the university police to initiate commitment proceedings on December 13, 2005, well over a year before the shootings. Was there any other event during the nearly four years that Cho was a student at Virginia Tech that would have justified involuntary commitment? Assuming there was not, what options were open to the Virginia Tech administration? Could the university have conditioned enrollment on Cho's agreement to undergo outpatient therapy?

2. *The university's response to the shootings.* There was a lapse of two-and-a-half hours between the time of the original two shootings and Cho's rampage in Norris Hall. Some have questioned why, during this period, the university did not lock down the campus or make any effort to inform

students of a potential danger either by text messaging, email, or phone communications.

3. *Gun control.* The federal Gun Control Act, originally enacted in 1968, prohibits gun purchases by anyone who has been adjudicated as a "mental defective" or has been committed to a mental institution. 18 U.S.C. § 922(g)(4). In spite of this prohibition, Cho was able to purchase two automatic weapons in the months preceding his rampage.

Administration of the federal law relies on a federal registry of persons barred from purchasing guns. Gun sellers are legally required, before making a sale, to access the federal registry to ascertain that the purchaser is not a person prohibited from making a purchase. The federal data base in turn relies on reports from state agencies that under state law are charged with gathering and reporting data pertaining to psychiatric hospitalizations. The *Review Panel Report* found that while Virginia law authorized state agencies to report involuntary hospitalization to the federal registry, no report on Cho's *outpatient* commitment on December 2005 had been filed, which allowed him to purchase two automatic pistols and ammunition without hindrance. As a result, the Review Panel called for an amendment of Virginia law to "clarify . . . the appropriate recipients of certified copies of [involuntary outpatient] orders . . . [and] the party responsible for reporting non-compliance with outpatient orders and to whom noncompliance is ordered." Review Panel Report, supra, at 61. The Virginia Tech and similar episodes spurred Congress to enact the NICS (National Instant Criminal Background Check System) Improvement Amendments Act of 2007. This legislation, signed into law on January 8, 2008, provides grants to states to upgrade information and identification technologies for firearms eligibility determination. The adequacy of this law and associated requirements was called into question again following the 2011 shootings at a political rally in Tucson, Arizona, during which six individuals were killed and Congresswoman Gabrielle Giffords was gravely wounded, by 22–year–old Jared Lee Loughner, a suspended community college student who, after a series of run-ins with campus police, had been told he would need "mental health clearance" before he could resume taking classes. Janet Novack, *Giffords Shooting Points Up Mental Health, Gun Control Gaps*, Forbes, Jan. 10, 2011.

4. *Immunity.* State operated institutions of higher learning, unlike their private counterparts, are generally covered by state sovereign immunity law. See infra Part II.D.4. Indeed, Virginia Tech University and its staff were protected from liability for the Cho shootings by Virginia's governmental immunity legislation. In general, such legislation limits suits against public institutions and their staff for non-intentional torts. Additionally, they impose various procedural requirements that restrict the filing of a lawsuit. Although in a number of such cases the relevant state legislature has nonetheless provided compensation for victims.

5. *Settlement in the Virginia Tech case.* An $11 million settlement with the families of twenty-four of the victims of the Virginia Tech shootings was

judicially approved on June 17, 2008, thus avoiding "a court battle over whether anyone but the gunman was to blame." *Settlement in Virginia Tech Shootings*, N.Y. Times, June 18, 2008, at A15. Of the remaining eight families involved, four agreed to the settlement but were not prepared to go before the judge and four did not participate. The settlement also covers the claims of seventeen persons who were injured in the mayhem. Id. Of the four non-participating families, two elected not to sue and two successfully sued on grounds of negligence, asserting that their daughters would have survived if the university had alerted the campus following the first two shootings. After an eight-day trial, a jury awarded $4 million to each family, an amount that was reduced to $100,000 by a county circuit judge, who ruled that this was the highest amount allowed under a cap on damages in actions against the state. Steve Szkotak, *Negligence Verdict from Va. Tech Killings Stands*, Associated Press, June 20, 2012. Virginia has appealed the verdict to the Virginia Supreme Court. Tonia Moxley, *State Appeals Virginia Tech Negligence Verdict in Shootings*, Roanoke Times, Apr. 7, 2013,

6. *Addendum to the* Review Panel Report. In July 2009, Cho's missing mental health records were discovered at the home of Robert C. Miller, the former director of the Cook Counseling Center who retired more than a year before the April 16, 2007, shootings, and had accidentally taken Cho's records home with him. Ian Urbina, *New Inquiry Is Sought in Virginia Tech Massacre*, N.Y. Times, July 29, 2009, at A14. A group of over thirty parents and relatives of the victims issued a statement calling for the state's investigation to be reopened, due to "grave errors, misinformation, and glaring omissions" in the Report. Id. In November 2009, an addendum to the *Review Panel Report* was released, reporting on this discovery and other findings made subsequent to the original Report (available at http://www.governor.virginia.gov/tempcontent/techPanelReport-docs/VT_Ad dendum_12–2–2009.pdf).

4. Public Officials and Governmental Units

a. *Introduction*

As the preceding sections make clear, a mental health professional who provides substandard care or fails to conform to legal requirements such as obtaining informed consent may be liable for damages. The mental health professional's employer also may be liable for these damages. However, when the employer is a governmental agency, special rules often apply to limit liability. These rules stem from the doctrines of sovereign and official immunity.

The doctrine of sovereign immunity has a lengthy history. When the United States was formed from the former colonies of England, the new government maintained the sovereign immunity that had been enjoyed by the English monarch. The doctrine was based on a semi-religious tenet that "the king can do no wrong," and its effect was to prevent the government from being sued without its consent. Justice Holmes stated the proposition in a more pragmatic way when he wrote in *Kawananakoa v. Polyblank*, 205 U.S. 349 (1907):

> A sovereign is exempt from suit, not because of any formal conception or obsolete theory, but on the logical and practical ground that there can be no legal right as against the authority that makes the law on which the right depends.

Sovereign immunity is rooted in social policy as well. It is seen as preserving the government's control over its resources. Without immunity, it is argued, the government would lack the funds to conduct its essential functions. Some argue that a democratic society needs sovereign immunity to prevent individuals bringing lawsuits from depleting the treasury at the expense of the remainder of the population.

The immunity doctrine has come under increasing criticism, however, as government has become larger and more pervasive. It is argued that injuries caused by the government should be borne by the entire society as a cost of government rather than by the individual who has been wronged and injured.

b.   *Immunity under Federal Law*

Originally, the federal government alleviated this burden upon individuals on a case-by-case basis, allowing certain individuals to sue the government. In 1946, however, Congress passed the Federal Tort Claims Act [FTCA], which waived the federal government's immunity from suit in a broad range of circumstances. Through the FTCA, Congress intended to generally compensate victims for the negligent conduct of governmental activities under the circumstances in which a victim could collect damages from a private tortfeasor.

The FTCA, however, excludes some torts from coverage, and thus the immunity doctrine continues to bar those causes of action. For example, the federal government remains immune from suits for damages resulting from combat activities in time of war. A section of the FTCA also provides that the United States will not be liable for "[a]ny claim arising out of assault, battery, false imprisonment, false arrest, malicious prosecution, abuse of process, libel, slander, misrepresentation, deceit, or interference with contract rights," with the exception of "acts or omissions of investigative or law enforcement officers of the United States Government" for which claims may arise "out of assault, battery, false imprisonment, false arrest, abuse of process, or malicious prosecution." 28 U.S.C. § 2680(h). The FTCA has also sometimes been broadly construed to preclude recovery from the government for medical malpractice. Thus, a claim of battery for an operation on the wrong leg of the plaintiff performed in a Veterans Administration hospital was denied in *Moos v. United States*, 118 F. Supp. 275 (D. Minn. 1954), *affirmed*, 225 F.2d 705 (8th Cir. 1955). See also *Witt ex rel. Estate of Witt v. U.S.*, 379 Fed. Appx.

559 (9th Cir. 2010), *cert. denied*, Jan. 10, 2011 (No. 10–885) (dismissing spouse's claim for malpractice after a serviceman was admitted to an Air Force hospital for a routine appendectomy and was left in a vegetative state after doctors made repeated mistakes during the operation).

The FTCA also excludes from liability acts or omissions that are within the "discretionary function or duty" of any federal agency or employee. 28 U.S.C. § 2680(a). The distinction between discretionary and non-discretionary duties is often difficult to discern as almost every act performed by a governmental official includes some discretion in the way it is performed. As a result, the discretionary function exclusion has been construed by courts to involve a distinction between planning and operational functions. *Dalehite v. United States,* 346 U.S. 15 (1953). Under this test, the federal government has been held to be immune from claims of negligence in the making of top-level planning decisions. Id. In contrast, the federal government may be held liable for the negligence of federal employees at the "operational" level of government. Thus, the government can be liable when employees negligently carry out the plans made by others, even though such actions may involve a certain amount of discretion. For example, the Supreme Court in *Indian Towing Co. v. United States,* 350 U.S. 61 (1955), found that checking the electrical system of a lighthouse was at the "operational level" and did not involve "discretion" within the meaning of the FTCA. The government was therefore not immune from a suit to recover damages suffered by a barge that ran aground while a Coast Guard lighthouse was not operating.

The FTCA additionally imposes various procedural requirements on persons with claims against the government. The most important is the requirement that administrative remedies first be exhausted. The injured party must have been denied relief from the agency from which recovery is sought before suit may be brought in court. Congress thereby sought to encourage compromise and to minimize the burden on the courts otherwise associated with these suits.

c. *Immunity under State Law*

The principle that the sovereign cannot be sued without its consent also applies to state governments. Absent waiver, states, state agencies, and state officers in their official capacities are generally immune from suit. However, the general immunity of states from law suits is problematic where Congress has enacted legislation providing a private cause of action against private or public actors for the violation of a federally protected right. In this situation, though, the Eleventh Amendment is likely to bar the award of damages against a state, although other forms of relief—including injunctions—may be available even when the state has not consented to be sued. The jurisprudence pertaining to the reach of the Eleventh Amendment as a bar to lawsuits against the states is discussed below. Further, every state has, at least to some extent, consented to being sued by adopting legislation waiving sovereign immunity in some circumstances. These statutes, although generally not as comprehensive as the FTCA, serve much the same purpose. Immunity is waived only for those circumstances explicitly set forth in the statute and only if the prescribed procedures are followed. There are some circumstances, however, in which a state or state agency may be sued even though it has not waived its immunity. Such a circumstance arises when the state is acting not in its governmental capacity, but in a "proprietary" capacity, as when the state creates an agency to engage in a primarily commercial venture.

There is no uniform rule declaring whether state and municipal hospitals exist under the proprietary or governmental function of the state. The maintenance of a hospital for the service of the public health and the treatment of indigent patients is generally held to be a governmental function, making such hospitals immune from suit absent a waiver of immunity. In contrast, the operation of a hospital for the purpose of obtaining a pecuniary profit is generally considered to be a proprietary function not immune from suit. Unfortunately, the majority of state hospitals fall within a middle category for which generalizations are impossible. See generally E. H. Schopler, *Immunity from Liability for Damages in Tort of State or Governmental Unit or Agency in Operating Hospital*, 25 A.L.R.2d 203, 228 (1952, Supp. 1981).

Some cases arise in which the governmental agency is immune from suit, but the employees who actually committed the wrong are subject to suit in their individual capacity. Additionally, a plaintiff may wish to seek recovery from the individual employee as well as the government agency. However, in any suit against a government employee one must consider the doctrine of official immunity.

Government employees are not, of course, absolved from their private and personal tort liabilities merely because of their employment. When, however, a person is injured as a result of a governmental (federal, state, or local) action, the employee causing the injury may be immune from liability under the doctrine of official immunity.

Official immunity has been recognized by the courts as a means of relieving the burden that would otherwise fall upon government officials if they could readily be held liable in a private tort suit for actions taken or decisions made. Immunity permits government employees to execute their duties without unreasonable fear of liability and keeps qualified persons from being deterred from entering government employment out of such fear. Courts have, however, recognized that not every government employee requires the same type of protection. The scope of the immunity therefore varies among government employees.

In essence there are two types of immunity: absolute and qualified. Judges have long been granted *absolute immunity* for their judicial acts, even when their conduct is corrupt or malicious. This immunity was recognized to preserve an independent judiciary by eliminating the possibility of vexatious suits. Because the immunity extends to all members of the judicial branch, mental health professionals such as hearing officers in commitment proceedings and court-appointed evaluators benefit from this doctrine. Mental health professionals who sign papers in a commitment process or testify at a commitment hearing or a child custody proceeding also have "absolute immunity" from liability for actions taken in their capacity as an officer of the court. See *Duzynski v. Nosal,* 324 F.2d 924 (7th Cir. 1963); *Morstad v. Dep't of Corr. & Rehab.,* 147 F.3d 741 (8th Cir. 1998); *Muzingo v. St. Luke's Hosp.,* 518 N.W.2d 776 (Iowa 1994); *Diehl v. Daniloff,* 618 N.W.2d 83 (Mich. Ct. App. 2000); *Parker v. Dodgion,* 971 P.2d 496 (Utah 1998).

For example, generally when a defamatory statement is made during the course of a judicial proceeding it is absolutely privileged, even if made maliciously and with knowledge that it was false. So long as the statement was required or permitted by law, the privilege bars a civil cause of action for libel or slander. In some jurisdictions, the privilege exists during preliminary proceedings involving pleadings, affidavits, or other papers, whereas in other jurisdictions the privilege exists only after the trial or hearing has begun. The privilege also extends to post-trial motions and final judgment enforcement proceedings. However, for such immunity to attach, the statement must be made with the honest belief that it was relevant or material to the litigation. Slanderous statements are not protected if they were plainly irrelevant, were voluntarily made, and the declarant could not reasonably have believed they were relevant.

Outside the hearing context, decisions relating to diagnosis, care, and treatment require the exercise of both judgment and choice. These decisions are therefore considered discretionary and entitled only to *qualified immunity.* Specifically, a decision outside the court process to detain an individual believed to be in need of hospitalization or to release a patient on either a temporary or permanent basis is protected only by qualified immunity. See *Coburn v. Sievert,* 35 Cal. Rptr. 3d 596 (Ct. App. 2005); *Porter v. Maunnangi,* 764 S.W.2d 699 (Mo. Ct. App. 1988). Similarly, an evaluation of the suitability of an individual to participate in an outpatient versus an inpatient program is considered to be discretionary. See *Canon v. Thumudo,* 422 N.W.2d 688 (Mich. 1988).

If qualified immunity applies, officers cannot be held liable for any act within their governmental duties that was performed in good faith. Thus, for example, a psychiatrist employed by a state psychiatric facility who negligently but in good faith determines that a civilly committed patient remains mentally ill and denies the patient release would be immune from liability for false imprisonment. If, however, the psychiatrist generates a report in bad faith knowing that the patient is qualified for release, qualified immunity will not protect the psychiatrist from liability. See, e.g., *Bragg v. Valdez*, 3 Cal. Rptr. 3d 804 (Ct. App. 2003); *Mierop v. State,* 201 N.Y.S.2d 2 (Ct. Cl. 1960); *Hoffman v. Halden*, 268 F.2d 280 (9th Cir. 1959).

Actions that are wholly outside the authority of the official (*ultra vires*) are not protected by either absolute or qualified immunity. However, courts will often extend immunity to an officer if it is determined that the scope of his or her authority would have required the determination of legal questions that could perplex a court. Thus, if an officer acted under the authority of a statute that is later determined to be unconstitutional, the officer is protected by the same immunity available if the statute had been constitutional. The immunity of public officials in actions brought under the federal Civil Rights Acts is discussed in the following section.

The various types of immunity recognized for governments and government employees have come under increasing attack as the role of government has increased in this country. Many have argued that liability should be borne by all as a cost of government, and that government employees should not enjoy more privileges than they would have if employed in a similar function in the private sector. See Margaret Z. Johns, *A Black Robe Is Not a Big Tent: The Improper Expansion of Absolute Judicial Immunity to Non–Judges in Civil–Rights Cases*, 59 SMU L. Rev. 265 (2006). Certainly many of the original justifications for these immunities have changed. Courts and legislatures have waived or eroded immunity in some areas and extended it into others to address these changes. That process continues today. Whatever the ultimate outcome, government and official immunity will undoubtedly continue to have an important role in litigation involving mental health providers.

III.   RECOVERY AND DAMAGES UNDER ALTERNATIVE THEORIES

A. MISCELLANEOUS NON–NEGLIGENCE THEORIES

A deviation from professional standards may give rise to a cause of action based on theories other than negligence. Some of these special theories, such as an action for failure to obtain the patient's informed consent or for a breach of confidentiality, are treated in Chapters Four and Five, infra, respectively. Depending on the circumstances, clients may also be able to resort to various intentional tort theories to vindicate their rights (e.g., an action for assault where the therapist has engaged in sexual relations with a client, particularly if the client lacks effective capacity to give consent). See *McCracken v. Walls–Kaufman*, 717 A.2d 346 (D.C. 1998); *Omer v. Edgren*, 685 P.2d 635 (Wash. Ct. App. 1984). As also noted, a therapist might be held liable for negligent infliction of emotional distress. See Parts II.B.3, II.C.2, supra.

A therapist's failure to meet professional standards may also lead to an action for breach of contract. The reasons to ground a client's claim in contract will vary. It may be to take advantage of a longer statute of limitations. Alternatively, the plaintiff may use a contract theory to avoid problems in proving negligence. For instance, as noted, in some jurisdictions recovery under a negligence theory for mental distress will only be allowed when the mental suffering was accompanied by physical harm or injury. In these jurisdictions, a plaintiff may be more successful under a breach of contract theory that will allow at least a recovery of all fees paid to the therapist. See *Anclote Manor Foundation v. Wilkinson*, 263 So. 2d 256 (Fla. Ct. App. 1972); *Spiess v. Johnson*, 748 P.2d 1020 (Or. Ct. App. 1988), *aff'd*, 765 P.2d 811 (Or. 1988).

Some courts have, however, imposed limits on a client's freedom to select a contractual theory of recovery over a negligence suit. In *Dennis v. Allison*, 698 S.W.2d 94 (Tex. 1985), for instance, the Texas Supreme Court, in holding that the plaintiff—who had been sexually assaulted by her therapist—could not maintain an action for breach of implied warranty, stated: "It is not necessary to impose an implied warranty theory as a matter of public policy because the plaintiff/patient has adequate remedies [in tort] to redress wrongs committed during treatment." Id. at 96.

B. CLAIMS BASED ON FEDERAL CIVIL RIGHTS LAWS

Certain federal statutes, collectively known as the Civil Rights Statutes, allow clients to sue mental health professionals for deprivations of their civil rights. The most widely used of these statutes provides that:

> Every person who, under color of any statute, ordinance, regulation, custom, or usage, of any State or Territory, subjects, or causes to be subjected, any citizen of the United States or other person within the jurisdiction thereof to the deprivation of any rights, privileges, or immunities secured by the Constitution and laws, shall be liable to the party injured in an action at law, suit in equity, or other proper proceeding for redress.

42 U.S.C. § 1983.

Although these statutes were originally passed after the Civil War to assure the rights of the newly emancipated slaves, since the civil rights movements of the 1960s and 70s the scope of their application has expanded beyond racial discrimination. Accordingly, the number of civil rights actions filed each year has increased from 296 in 1961 to 18,793 in 1990 to 33,761 in 2009. James C. Duff, *Judicial Facts and Figures, Administrative Office of the United States Courts* (May 2010); Michael

Kao, *Calculating Lawyers' Fees: Theory and Reality,* 51 UCLA L. Rev. 825, 847 (2004). Today, a mental health client can bring a civil rights action against a mental health professional under the following circumstances: (1) the conduct complained of was committed by a person acting under color of state law; (2) this conduct deprived the person of rights, privileges, or immunities secured by the Constitution or laws of the United States; and (3) the conduct complained of was not protected by the professional's qualified immunity.

While meeting these three requirements will often be somewhat burdensome, the advantages of a civil rights action over the traditional state tort action will often justify this effort. The most obvious advantage in seeking a federal forum, where such a claim will be heard, is that plaintiffs are able to remove their case from a state court, which may have subtle political ties to an involved state or local agency. Additionally, a successful plaintiff may qualify for attorney's fees under 42 U.S.C. § 1988. Also, actions under the Civil Rights statutes allows a plaintiff to avoid a state's exhaustion of remedies requirement. The federal forum may also be necessary to avoid state created limitations on liability, whether they be a fixed ceiling on recoverable damages or a bar on punitive damages. However, certain governmental immunities may still operate to bar recovery of damages (although not necessarily injunctive relief). Further, if the client seeks only relief that is equally available under state tort law, the advantages of a federal action may be outweighed by the additional elements of proof that confront a plaintiff in a federal civil rights action.

A major hurdle in every claim based on § 1983 is the requirement that the conduct forming the basis of the suit occurred under color of state law. The case that follows highlights the difficult issues involved in the application of this criterion.

SPENCER V. LEE

United States Court of Appeals, Seventh Circuit, 1989.
864 F.2d 1376.

POSNER, CIRCUIT JUDGE.

Do a private physician and a private hospital act under color of state law, and therefore lay themselves open to suit under 42 U.S.C. § 1983, when they commit a mentally disturbed person? Adhering to *Byrne v. Kysar* (7th Cir. 1965), and *Duzynski v. Nosal* (7th Cir. 1963), we hold they do not.

* * *

The plaintiff, William Spencer, appeals from the dismissal of his complaint for failure to state a claim, so we must proceed on the assumption that the facts alleged in the complaint are true. In 1982 and

1984, Spencer's physician, defendant Bumyong Lee, authorized Spencer to be involuntarily committed to St. Elizabeth Hospital. On the second of these occasions the police were called in to take Spencer to the hospital against his will, and on the fourth day of his five days of hospitalization Dr. Lee directed a nurse to inject Spencer with a drug. Spencer protested that he was allergic to the drug, but he was injected anyway and sustained bodily injury. Spencer seeks damages under 42 U.S.C. § 1983 for the deprivation of his liberty without due process of law and for the reckless infliction of injury during his second confinement. Pendent counts seek damages under the common law of Illinois for false imprisonment and malpractice. Spencer had no lawyer in the district court, and his complaint is barely coherent. The district court ordered him to furnish a more definite statement of his claim. In response, Spencer submitted medical records. . . . These documents depict Spencer as a schizophrenic with suicidal tendencies who has been in and out of mental institutions many times. Among his delusions are that "all winter he was sick until this time when the police starting a kind of prostitution operation also near motel where he is staying, they have been running a chain saw, the chain saw produced hormones in his testes and he couldn't sit still." . . . However, the district judge did not rely on any of the medical records—which Spencer did not vouch for (he just produced them in response to the judge's order) and has had no chance to explain (away)—and we won't rely on them either.

The casting of this lawsuit as one for the redress of a violation of the Fourteenth Amendment's due process clause, which forbids *states* to deprive persons of life, liberty, or property without due process of law, would certainly strike the innocent eye as puzzling. The due process clause is directed to action by state government; 42 U.S.C. § 1983 creates a remedy against persons acting under color of state law, such as police officers. The defendants in this case are not public employees. They provide no services under contract to the state government or any of its subdivisions. They do not participate (so far as is relevant to this case) in any state or other governmental programs. A purely private physician and a purely private hospital are alleged to have confined the plaintiff against his will and to have injured him by improper medical treatment. These are classic allegations of false imprisonment and malpractice—torts for which the common law of Illinois provides remedies that the plaintiff does not suggest are inadequate.

In arguing that the defendants are nonetheless state actors for purposes of the Fourteenth Amendment and section 1983, the plaintiff relies on the Illinois Mental Health and Developmental Disabilities Code, which provides that "when a person is asserted to be subject to involuntary admission and in such a condition that immediate hospitalization is necessary for the protection of such person or others from physical harm, any person 18 years of age or older may present a [commitment] petition to the facility director of a mental health facility in the county where the respondent resides or is present." ILL. REV. STAT. ch. 91 ½, § 3–601(a). The petition must include much factual detail and be accompanied by a certificate, signed by a physician or other qualified professional, stating that the respondent requires immediate hospitalization and that the physician has examined the respondent within the previous 72 hours, and setting forth the factual basis for the physician's opinion that immediate hospitalization is required. §§ 3–601(b), 3–602. Within 24 hours of the respondent's admission to the mental health facility, the facility must forward the relevant papers to the local state court, which must in turn hold a hearing within 5 days (exclusive of weekends and holidays—so the longest possible prehearing commitment is 8 days) on whether there are grounds for continuing to hold the respondent. § 3–611.

This complex of provisions, Spencer argues, operates to "deputize" private physicians such as Dr. Lee and private hospitals such as St. Elizabeth to carry out the exclusive state function of committing the mentally ill. For a maximum of eight days these ostensibly private actors are empowered by the Mental Health Code to hold and treat people against their will. This power, Spencer concludes, is a state power that does not cease to be such merely because delegated to private persons.

If the State of Illinois ordered or encouraged private persons to commit the mentally ill, they would indeed be state actors, for they would be doing the state's business. It would make no difference that they were not technically employees of the state. Or if the state decided to contract out the provision of state highway police or the administration of state prisons to private entrepreneurs of security and correctional services, the entrepreneurs and their employees would (we may assume) be state actors. The details of the contractual relationship between state agencies and the persons who actually implement state policy—whether those persons are state employees or independent contractors or the employees of independent contractors—are of no moment. In accordance with *Marsh v. Alabama* (U.S. 1946), we may further assume that if the state allowed a residential subdivision or high-rise apartment building to form its own de facto municipal government, that government would be an arm of the state for purposes of the Fourteenth Amendment, just as de jure municipal governments are; again the technicality of governmental employment would not control the case. Who does the state's business is the state's actor.

At the opposite extreme is the situation where the state decides to reduce the scope of government. Suppose the state owned a railroad, and decided to sell it to a private person. Would the new owner be deemed a state actor under the Constitution, on the ground that the state had "deputized" him to operate "its" railroad? He would not. The scope of government is not fixed; deregulation does not create a host of state actors in the private sector, like the moraine that marks the farthest advance of a glacier. Certain powers, however, are "traditionally the exclusive prerogative of the State," and their exercise by private persons is state action. *Marsh* can be understood in this light—as a case not of deregulation, but of the delegation of public powers to private actors.

We have to situate the present case in this grid. It is not a case of governmental encouragement or direction of private persons; and "a State normally can be held responsible for a private decision only when it has exercised coercive power or has provided such significant encouragement, either overt or covert, that the choice must in law be deemed to be that of the State." *Blum v. Yaretsky*. [The plaintiff's] argument is that the commitment of the mentally ill, like the arrest of criminal suspects, is so central and traditional a function of government that the state cannot limit its responsibility for performing the function. Any private individual who is empowered to commit a person to an institution against the person's will *is* government, just as the "company town" in *Marsh* was a part of the government of Alabama, although a part that had been handed over to a private entity to administer.

Spencer is thus appealing—with support in the language of cases like *Blum* and in the outcome of *Marsh*—to the idea that governmental functions that have traditionally been the *exclusive* prerogative of government, usually because they involved a high degree of coercion, can be delegated but not abandoned. The treatment of the mentally disabled, however, as of the sick and infirm generally, is not such a function. The issue here, it is true, is involuntary commitment rather than treatment. But the analogy that Spencer seeks to draw to arrest is inapt, since a citizen's arrest is not subject to challenge under section 1983. There have been citizen arrests for as long as there have been public police—indeed much longer. In ancient Greece and Rome, and in England until the nineteenth century, most arrests and prosecutions were by private individuals. (Some crimes, e.g., shoplifting, are still privately prosecuted in England.) Arrest has never been an exclusively governmental function. Not all state-authorized coercion is government action. . . .

The question we are trying to answer is whether a private person is doing the state's business and should be treated as an employee or other formal agent of the state. So we ask, is there a tradition of treating civil commitment of the mentally disturbed as a governmental function and, if so, how well established is it? . . .

The specific provisions of the Mental Health Code dealing with emergency commitment by private physicians to private hospitals are not 200 years old; they are less than 50 years old. But commitment has long been a private remedy, albeit one subject (like repossession, self-defense, citizen's arrest, and other infringements on rights of liberty or property) to rigorous safeguards. Even public commitment in Illinois is private in a sense, because the state requires relatives of voluntarily and involuntarily committed mental patients alike to pay the cost of their upkeep in the state's institutions, and it allows the involuntarily committed to be placed in private homes as well as public and private hospitals. And long before the passage of the 1945 statute, the law of Illinois authorized the confinement of an insane person by private persons, for up to ten days, if he was a danger to himself or others.

Private commitment was not novel in 1893; nor was it invented in Illinois. According to Blackstone, writing in 1765, "On the first attack of lunacy, or other occasional insanity, while there may be hope of a speedy restitution of reason, it is usual to confine the unhappy objects in private custody under the direction of their nearest friends and relations." Histories of the treatment of the insane focus on public institutions, but involuntary extrajudicial commitment to private institutions has long been commonplace. London's notorious lunatic asylum, nicknamed "Bedlam," was originally private; it was representative of private medieval institutions to which the insane were committed to have their demons exorcised. . . .

The reasons for private commitment, as for self-defense, citizen's arrests, and other private remedies, are intensely practical. If a person displays symptoms of acute and violent mental illness, his family or physician—in an appropriate case a passerby or other stranger—may have to act immediately to restrain him from harming himself or others, and there may be no public institution at hand. That is why the Illinois Mental Health Code allows private persons to commit to private (as well as to public) institutions. We do not know the circumstances in which Mr. Spencer was committed, but it appears that the first commitment was because he had tried to commit suicide, and let us assume this was indeed the reason. If his father and Dr. Lee and St. Elizabeth had had to initiate a judicial proceeding before committing him, he might have killed himself before they could obtain the necessary order. When family members commit a person who has just tried to kill himself, they do not, by virtue of this action, become state actors subject to suit under section 1983.

To allow family members, physicians, and other private persons to exercise the commitment power without safeguards, however, including a provision for a hearing eventually—and sooner rather than later—would be monstrous. If Spencer thinks the eight days allowed by Illinois law for confinement prior to hearing is too much, he can challenge the constitutionality of the statute. He has not done so. Indeed, he relies on the statute to make the defendants state actors. But a private commitment is no more state action than a citizen's arrest, the repossession of chattels, or the ejection of trespassers is. The statutes authorizing or constraining these private activities may or may not be constitutional; the activities themselves remain private. . . .

We are given some pause by the allegation in Spencer's complaint of involvement by the local police. . . . It is possible that the police were called in to assist with one of Spencer's commitments, though this does not seem to be what he is alleging. At all events, police assistance in the lawful exercise of self-help does not create a conspiracy with the private person exercising that self-help. The citizen who makes a citizen's arrest is not transformed into a state actor by handing over the arrested person to the police—indeed, if he fails to do so, the arrest is invalid and he is liable for false imprisonment.

The pressure to transform state common law torts into federal constitutional torts comes from the immunities and the damage ceilings that states frequently impose on suits against their public officials, from a sense that state judges are sometimes unsympathetic to suits against the state, and from the availability of attorney's fee awards in civil rights suits under 42 U.S.C. § 1988. Only the last of these considerations is present in a case such as this where the only defendants are private persons (or private institutions) not acting pursuant to formal judicial order. There is neither practical nor legal basis for this suit.

Affirmed.

CUMMINGS, CIRCUIT JUDGE, with whom CUDAHY, CIRCUIT JUDGE, joins, dissenting.

Disagreeing with the majority's conclusion that the actions of the defendants in committing Spencer to St. Elizabeth Hospital necessarily cannot constitute state action, I respectfully dissent from the majority's holding.

* * *

Spencer has clearly articulated a sufficient liberty interest in his allegations of involuntary commitment and treatment during his detention at St. Elizabeth Hospital. The only issue remaining is whether the actions of Dr. Lee and St. Elizabeth Hospital implicate state action.

I.   Involuntary Commitment

A.   *Function of the State*

The involuntary commitment of an individual believed to be a danger to himself or others without a judicial hearing is no doubt one of the most severe infringements of personal liberty. However, the state has power to cause such a deprivation acting pursuant to its *parens patriae* power to protect and provide care for the mentally ill. *Addington v. Texas* [ ]. Although neither Dr. Lee nor St. Elizabeth Hospital is a state employee, the state action component may be fulfilled if their actions may be "fairly attributable to the state." *Lugar* [ ]. The test of "fair attribution" involves two elements where a private party is alleged to be a state actor:

> First, the deprivation must be caused by the exercise of some right or privilege created by the State or by a rule of conduct imposed by the State or by a person for whom the State is responsible. . . . Second, the party charged with the deprivation must be a person who may fairly be said to be a state actor.

Lugar [ ]. The Supreme Court explained further that mere action by a private party pursuant to a statute without "something more" will not transform the private party into a state actor. The "something more" necessary to convert the private activity into state action varies with the factual circumstances, resulting in correspondingly varied tests: the "public function" test, the "state compulsion" test, the "nexus" test, and the "joint action" test. *Lugar* [ ].

* * *

As support for its decision, the majority traces the historical roots of involuntary commitment, concluding that since the commitment of the mentally ill has never been the exclusive prerogative or traditional function of the state, it is not state action when performed by a private entity. However interesting this history lesson may be, the more relevant question for determining whether state action exists is not whether private citizens were capable of unilaterally committing the mentally ill in the days when Bedlam existed in England, but whether under the present law private citizens are capable of depriving individuals of their liberty to the same extent as may the state or whether the state has a superior, unique authority to deprive individuals of liberty in this manner, an authority not inured in the general citizenry. Indeed, as the majority readily concedes, every public function has an analogous private function in history. The majority's opinion, nonetheless, assumes as a premise of its argument that what constitutes a public function is relatively stagnant over time. It may have been the case that in the time of Bedlam the rights of the mentally ill were not recognized and protected to the same extent they are today, as were the rights of minorities prior to the Thirteenth and Fourteenth Amendments. Illinois has altered the course of history by affirmatively recognizing the rights of the mentally ill through its enactment of Chapter II of the Illinois Mental Health and Developmental Disabilities Code.

* * *

It is clear from the statutory framework that no private individual may commit a patient to a mental health institution for treatment on an emergency basis without a prior determination by a qualified physician or mental health facility that the patient warrants confinement. In the commitment procedure, the physician's certificate serves a quasi-judicial function correlative to an arrest warrant issued by a judge authorizing the seizure of a suspect. This Court recognized the nature of the physician's function in the commitment process in *Byrne,* where doctors, who were members of a court-appointed committee, were held to have performed a quasi-judicial function in examining and recommending commitment of the patient. Under the Illinois mental health code, the state has delegated its adjudicatory determination in the emergency context to the physician, empowering the physician to use the force of state law enforcement agencies to confine any individual the physician determines to be in need of emergency commitment.

* * *

B.   *Participation of State Officials*

* * *

In his *pro se* complaint, as indicated by the majority opinion, Spencer does not specifically allege a "conspiracy" with police officers in his emergency involuntary commitment at St. Elizabeth Hospital. Indeed, it would be surprising if a *pro se* plaintiff with a history of mental illness had sufficient working knowledge of the law to plead the legal phrases which compose the elements of a Section 1983 action. The Court should not penalize Spencer for his inartfully pleaded complaints and subsequent motions. Nonetheless, the majority summarily disposes of this claim due to Spencer's inability to name police officers as defendants or mention the involvement of the police with sufficient frequency. Given the Court's obligation to construe Spencer's complaint liberally and dismiss the complaint only if he can prove no set of facts which would entitle him to relief, Spencer has sufficiently alleged the involvement of the Danville Police Department to sustain defendants' motion to dismiss.

* * *

[T]he mere presence of the police while Spencer was detained at St. Elizabeth Hospital is sufficient participation to constitute state action.

* * *

In my opinion, the judgment should be reversed and the cause remanded for further proceedings.

QUESTIONS AND COMMENTS

1.   *Other decisions. Spencer v. Lee* has been followed by the Sixth and Eleventh Circuits, both of which rejected a finding of state action in the context of an involuntary commitment to a private psychiatric facility. *Ellison v. Garbarino,* 48 F.3d 192 (6th Cir. 1995); *Harvey v. Harvey,* 949 F.2d 1127 (11th Cir. 1992).

However, a district court ruling from the Second Circuit, *Rubenstein v. Benedictine Hosp.,* 790 F. Supp. 396 (N.D. N.Y. 1992), held that the actions by a private hospital emergency room physician who involuntarily hospitalized the plaintiff constituted state action and, therefore, § 1983 could be invoked as a basis for relief. In reaching this conclusion, the court noted that the emergency room physician was a "designee" of the county director of community services and that as a "designee" the physician was empowered to take custody, detain, and transport individuals after signing an application for involuntary commitment, as well as direct peace officers to take them into custody and transport them. Other courts have reached the same conclusion the *Rubenstein* court did. See generally *Jensen v. Lane County*, 222 F.3d 570 (9th Cir. 2000); *Schorr v. Borough of Lemoyne*, 265 F. Supp. 2d 488 (M.D. Pa. 2003); *Moore v. Wyoming Med. Ctr.*, 825 F. Supp. 1531 (D. Wyo. 1993).

In *Ruhlmann v. Ulster County Dep't of Social Services*, 234 F. Supp. 2d 140 (N.D.N.Y. 2002), the court, in denying the defendants' motion for summary judgment, held that the determination of whether a private physician should be characterized as a "state actor" is a fact specific inquiry. The court added that in making this determination, courts "typically look to such factors as the public function of the party's conduct, whether the party acted under state compulsion and whether the party's action was jointly taken with the state." Id. at 160.

2. *State funding of private facilities.* Would the "under color of law" requirement be met if the mental health professional who is the object of a § 1983 action was employed by a private non-profit mental health center that receives 85% of its funding from state agencies and the rest from fees? See *Rendell–Baker v. Kohn,* 457 U.S. 830 (1982) (dismissing a § 1983 claim brought by former teachers against a private school).

3. *The deprivation of federal rights requirement.* Section 1983 is intended to protect an individual from "the deprivation of any rights, privileges, or immunities secured by the Constitution and laws." 42 U.S.C. § 1983. The statute covers only violations of rights guaranteed by the federal Constitution and federal laws and not those guaranteed by state law.

Two kinds of constitutional rights are protected by the Civil Rights statutes: substantive rights and procedural rights. Substantive rights include those rights guaranteed by the Bill of Rights. Procedural rights are those protected by the due process clause of the Fourteenth Amendment. As might be expected, one of the most common procedurally grounded claims in the mental health treatment context involves irregularities in civil commitment. In fact, a violation may occur even when the psychiatric admission was ostensibly voluntary. For instance, in *Zinermon v. Burch*, 494 U.S. 113 (1990), the Supreme Court held that a valid § 1983 claim was stated when the claimant contended that state officials knew or should have known that he was incompetent to give informed consent to his psychiatric admission. His admission under these circumstances, according to the Court, denied him his constitutionally guaranteed procedural rights. See Chapter Eight, infra.

The imposition or the withholding of treatment may also provide grounds for an action under § 1983. In *Wade v. Castillo*, 658 F. Supp. 2d 906

(W.D. Wisc. 2009), a district court allowed a claim under § 1983 to go to a jury where the defendant psychiatrist had stopped giving the inmate-plaintiff some of his medications. The court held that a reasonable jury could conclude that not medicating a prisoner in need of treatment could be construed as deliberate indifference to the inmate's medical needs, and thus a violation of the inmate's Eighth Amendment right to be free of cruel and unusual punishment. In *Philipp v. Carey*, 517 F. Supp. 513 (N.D.N.Y. 1981), the plaintiffs had an intellectual disability (formerly mental retardation) and were voluntary residents of a state mental health facility. They complained that they were being given debilitating psychotropic drugs as a substitute for treatment and rehabilitation. The court found a § 1983 cause of action based on a violation of § 504 of the Rehabilitation Act, a federal law prohibiting the denial of benefits to persons with a disability by a facility receiving federal funding. 29 U.S.C. § 794. See also *Knecht v. Gillman*, 488 F.2d 1136 (8th Cir. 1973) (set out in Chapter Nine, infra).

Individuals with a mental disability may also attack the conditions of their confinement through a civil rights action. In *Jobson v. Henne*, 355 F.2d 129 (2d Cir. 1966), the resident of a facility for individuals with intellectual disabilities was assigned uncompensated work for up to sixteen hours a day. The work was not part of a therapy program, nor was it related to the resident's housekeeping needs. The court held that this stated a possible cause of action as a violation of the resident's Thirteenth Amendment rights (freedom from involuntary servitude). See also *Gerrard v. Blackman*, 401 F. Supp. 1189 (N.D. Ill. 1975); *Jones v. Superintendent*, 370 F. Supp. 488 (W.D. Va. 1974). *Jobson v. Henne* and related Thirteenth Amendment issues are discussed in greater detail in Chapter Ten, Part III, infra. In recent years, such claims are particularly likely to be brought by inmates with a mental disorder confined in a correctional facility, with special emphasis being given to the confinement of these inmates in prolonged solitary confinement. See *Brown v. Plata*, 131 S. Ct. 1910 (2010); Thomas L. Hafemeister & Jeff George, *The Ninth Circle of Hell: An Eighth Amendment Analysis of Imposing Prolonged Supermax Solitary Confinement on Inmates with a Mental Illness*, 90 Denv. U. L. Rev. 1 (2012).

4. *Negligent deprivation of rights*. Whether negligent deprivations of a federal right are actionable under § 1983 is not entirely clear. The U.S. Supreme Court has generally avoided establishing a specific state of mind requirement for § 1983 claims. In *Daniels v. Williams*, 474 U.S. 327 (1986), however, the Court held that a lack of due care by a state official could not "deprive" a person of life, liberty, or property under the Fourteenth Amendment. Thus, after *Daniels,* it is clear that a § 1983 action is not available where the plaintiff alleges only that he was negligently deprived of liberty or property without due process. However, *Daniels* leaves open the question of whether a state of mind short of intent, such as recklessness or gross negligence, is a sufficient basis for a § 1983 claim.

5. *Immunity under § 1983*. The need to give decision makers relative freedom to exercise discretionary judgment has caused the Supreme Court to

interpret § 1983 as to provide officials sued under the Act with qualified immunity similar to that described supra in Part II.A.d. As a result, a plaintiff will not prevail in a § 1983 action unless the defendant's conduct violated "clearly established statutory or constitutional rights which a reasonable person would have known." *Harlow v. Fitzgerald,* 457 U.S. 800, 818 (1982).

6. *Other civil rights statutes.* Although most psychiatric civil rights actions are brought under § 1983, two other sections should be noted. 42 U.S.C. § 1985 is very similar to § 1983, but provides a remedy for a conspiracy to violate civil rights. Second, 18 U.S.C. § 242 provides criminal sanctions for a violation of civil rights by one acting under color of state law. The major difference between the civil and criminal statutes is intent. Criminal sanctions are typically premised on a finding that the wrongdoer acted knowingly and intentionally (i.e., understood that he or she was doing something wrong). Civil law, on the other hand, is primarily a method of allocating losses. The intent requirement, therefore, in a criminal civil rights action is more stringent, and, indeed, the statute itself declares that the deprivation must be "willful." The Supreme Court has interpreted this to mean that the act must be done knowingly and with the specific intent to deprive the victim of a constitutional right. *Screws v. United States*, 325 U.S. 91 (1945). If, for example, the supervising psychiatrist of a psychiatric facility knew that a patient was sane and not dangerous, yet refused to authorize the patient's discharge, the psychiatrist could be found guilty of a § 242 violation of the patient's rights.

CHAPTER 4

INFORMED CONSENT

■ ■ ■

Table of Sections

I.   INTRODUCTION: THE ORIGINS OF THE DOCTRINE OF INFORMED CONSENT

The principle that individuals should decide the course of their treatment has a surprisingly short history. The following passage describes the evolution of the doctrine of informed consent for health care.

Historically, the doctor-patient relationship has been founded upon the principle of beneficence, played out through the doctrine of medical paternalism. Medical paternalism eventually gave way to notions of patient autonomy during the twentieth century when it was determined that patients have the right to make their own treatment decisions. . . .

A. Paternalism

Medical paternalism can be defined as "an action taken by one person in the best interests of another without their consent." Since the days of Hippocrates, doctors have been empowered to make decisions *for* their patients. Jay Katz, in his landmark work on the physician-patient relationship, observed that giving patients the liberty to make their own treatment decisions "was never part of the ethos of medicine." Another scholar has written that "[t]he doctor decided what was best for the patient, and the patient accepted the decision, usually without questioning, [without] understanding, or perhaps even [without] a real choice."

Ancient Greeks, including Plato and Hippocrates, taught that patients should not play a part in the decision-making process. They viewed such participation as unnecessary and counterproductive because the doctor and the patient presumably had the same objective: to heal the sick. The physician alone possessed the knowledge and experience needed to make a medical decision, so a patient's input was viewed as unnecessary. In addition, ancient physicians believed that a patient's psychological well-being was critical to the healing process. They thought it would be therapeutically counterproductive for a patient to truly understand their compromised state of health and the risks that they faced, knowledge which in turn would jeopardize, limit, and slow recovery.

The *Corpus Hippocraticum* went so far as to recognize a duty of deceit, which encouraged physicians to conceal the patient's true condition—especially from the patient. Ancient healers justified manipulation of the patient by noting, as Socrates did, "the healing effects of fair words." Ancient doctors believed optimism and confidence were essential to the healing process. According to Hippocrates, the therapeutic effect of encouraging words was so important that a good doctor should always "promise to cure what is curable and to cure what is incurable." Needless to say, the patient had little role to play in deciding the course of treatment.

This belief in the therapeutic importance of "fair words," even when these "words" did not accurately reflect the patient's condition, and the limited involvement of patients in treatment decisions, continued to pervade medical ethics centuries later. In the words of ninth-century Jewish physician Isaac Israeli: "Reassure the patient and declare his safety even though you may not be certain of it, for by this you will strengthen his Nature." The importance of optimism and the value of deceit continued to justify physicians' paternalistic treatment of their patients.

In addition to the therapeutic impact of limited disclosures and optimism, physicians also insisted that there was an intimate relationship between God and doctors. During the middle ages, Jewish, Arabic, and Christian physicians asserted that God anointed doctors; therefore, any attempt to question the physician would be questioning God, which would be blasphemous. As a result, the paternalistic model for physician-patient interactions was, if anything, stronger during medieval times than its more recent manifestations.

Paternalism continued to pervade the physician-patient relationship throughout the seventeenth, eighteenth, and nineteenth centuries. Until the middle of the twentieth century, doctors—and society—viewed physicians as having an obligation to act in their patients' best interests, with no duty to inform patients of their treatment options.

A particularly striking judicial recognition of paternalism occurred in *John F. Kennedy Memorial Hospital v. Heston*, [279 A.2d 670 (N.J. 1971),] where the New Jersey Supreme Court found that a physician was justified in ordering a blood transfusion even when a patient's objections were based on a religious belief that this treatment would result in the eternal damnation of the patient's soul. The court stated, "When the [interests of a] hospital and staff are . . . pitted against the belief of the patient, we think it reasonable to resolve the problem by permitting the hospital and its staff to pursue their functions according to their professional standards."

B. Patient Autonomy

In 1914, in *Schloendorff v. Society of New York Hospital*, [105 N.E. 92 (N.Y. 1914),] Justice Benjamin Cardozo wrote, "Every human being of adult years and sound mind has a right to determine what shall be done with his own body; and a surgeon who performs an operation without his patient's consent commits an assault." To assert that a physician dedicated to healing the sick could assault a patient in the course of providing care that was neither negligent nor willfully deficient was nothing short of remarkable at that time (a view shared by many physicians now as well) and marked a radical shift toward recognizing patients' rights in the physician-patient relationship.

The notion that patients should have the legal right to make their own decisions—and that doctors should obtain consent before performing invasive procedures—originated in contract law. Indeed, it has been widely noted that the consent Justice Cardozo called for in *Schloendorff* "had its basis in the prominent and ancient legal principle of consent in contract law."

Analyzing the physician-patient relationship as merely a contractual arrangement, however, ultimately proved to be inadequate. Under a traditional contractual approach, the physician merely had to show that the patient gave his or her general consent for the treatment provided, even though the patient had not been told about potential treatment alternatives; only a "minimalist expression of autonomy" was required. General consent may be sufficient for contractual parties with equal bargaining power who possess similar insights into and information about a proposed contractual agreement, but the knowledge disparity between a doctor and a patient can result in an enormous asymmetry between the two. Analyzing the formation and implications of a physician-patient relationship under a contractual framework proved insufficient because of this asymmetry, particularly when physicians' potential conflicts of interest began to be recognized [e.g., more treatment or more expensive treatment meant more income for the physician]. In addition, patients are typically sick, injured, or worried about their state of health and in no position to engage in a traditional bargaining process. In other words, the physician and patient are not conducting an arms-length transaction in the traditional sense. Contract law provided insufficient protection for the under-informed, vulnerable, distracted, or anxious patient.

[One of the reasons, among many, that modern informed consent law developed was the civil rights movement, because it created] a social atmosphere in which Americans placed increased value on the rights of individuals, including those of medical patients. . . . In the political and social climate of the 1950s and 1960s, the patient autonomy movement was born. One scholar has gone so far as to describe the resulting rise in patient autonomy as " 'the greatest revolution of twentieth century American society.' " During this time, "Patients began to voice the ethical proposition, founded on the autonomy principle, that they, rather than the doctors, should have the ultimate authority to decide the course of their medical treatment." In an attempt to secure this newfound "ultimate authority," patients turned to the American court system.

The courts ultimately endorsed the position espoused by the patients, finding doctors liable if they failed to properly disclose significant risks and obtain "informed consent" before initiating medical treatment. A California court first used the phrase "informed consent" in 1957 in a case where a physician admitted that he failed to disclose the dangers of a surgical procedure to his patient, and the patient awoke from surgery paralyzed. [*Salgo v. Leland Stanford Jr. Univ. Bd. of Trs.*, 317 P.2d 170, 181 (Cal. Ct. App. 1957).] The doctrine was affirmed and further explicated in the seminal case of *Canterbury v. Spence*[, 464 F.2d 772 (D.C. Cir. 1972)], where the court ruled that a physician has a duty to disclose to a patient the material risks associated with a proposed procedure that a reasonable patient would need to hear to make an informed decision. The informed consent requirement marked the culmination of the shift in the nature of the physician-patient relationship from a paternalistic approach to one that emphasizes patient autonomy.

Under the patient-autonomy model, patients make the ultimate decisions concerning their healthcare, although these decisions are "based on the physician's description of the relative risks, benefits, and alternatives available." To determine which procedures are in their best interest, patients are entitled to know their viable options and the material risks and benefits associated with each option. The doctor is responsible for dispensing information; the patient is responsible for making the decisions.

On its face, alarmists could view this shift as resulting in highly trained professionals being reduced to mere information conduits with little decision-making authority, their extensive knowledge and expertise utilized only to the extent desired by the patient. In practice, however, patients usually seek and follow their doctors' treatment recommendations, and the recognition of patient autonomy did not revolutionize the physician-patient relationship, nor did it dramatically change the nature of the interaction between physicians and patients. For example, although advance directives were and continue to be highly heralded as a means of preserving the decision-making rights of patients, they have been found to have had a limited impact on medical decisions, notwithstanding that the Patient Self–Determination Act of 1991 mandates that patients must be notified of their right to execute such a document prior to every hospital admission.

Nevertheless, the respect afforded patient autonomy in the latter half of the twentieth century did represent an important landmark: society and the courts emphasized that patients have the *right* to make their own medical decisions, even if they do not necessarily exercise it. As one scholar has indicated, "Informed consent has become the legal and philosophical cornerstone of physician-patient relationships." From a doctrinal perspective, the pendulum of power in the physician-patient relationship may appear to have swung almost entirely to the side of the patients, even if it is a right of patients that is infrequently exercised and even more rarely enforced.

C.   Shared Duty Between Doctor and Patient

Some scholars argue that the pendulum has appropriately swung back to a more moderate position and that a shared decision-making model governs today's physician-patient relationship. The terms used more recently to describe physician-patient relationships are "negotiation" and "concordance." Such concepts signify a decision-making process where both parties are actively involved. . . .

Indeed, "[i]n its purest form, there is a two way exchange of information, [with] both doctor and patient reveal[ing] treatment preferences, and both agree[ing] on the decision to implement." When making decisions, both the physician and the patient have access to important and relevant information, but each also lacks vital information. On the one hand, physicians understand the medical implications, consequences, and risks of various treatment options. Patients, however, know what is important to their lives, what they hope to accomplish, and which risks they are willing to take.

. . . Under the shared decision-making model, physicians explain alternative treatment options and offer their opinion as to which option is superior, while patients describe their individual circumstances and desires and, in light of the available options, express their view on which option is best. Such a dialogue is believed to enhance the likelihood of a successful and mutually embraced treatment. At the end of the day, they hopefully can and generally do agree on the proper course of treatment.

Thomas L. Hafemeister & Richard M. Gulbrandsen, Jr., *The Fiduciary Obligation of Physicians to "Just Say No" if an "Informed" Patient Demands Services That Are Not Medically Indicated*, 39 Seton Hall L. Rev. 335 (2009).

From a legal standpoint, the meaningful application of the doctrine of informed consent stems from two cases decided in 1960, *Natanson v. Kline*, 350 P.2d 1093 (Kan. 1960), *clarified*, 354 P.2d 670 (Kan. 1960), and *Mitchell v. Robinson*, 334 S.W.2d 11 (Mo. 1960) (addressing a failure to disclose the risk of bone fractures during insulin and electro-shock therapy). The doctrine was solidified and enhanced by the highly influential 1972 ruling, *Canterbury v. Spence*, 464 F.2d 772 (D.C. Cir. 1972), reproduced below.

Initially, courts typically treated problems of consent as interlocked with the tort of battery, which insulated a physician from liability if the patient assented to a particular medical procedure, regardless of the adequacy of the information provided the patient about the proposed treatment. Since 1960, however, courts have recognized that a patient's consent cannot be meaningful or binding unless it is based upon information concerning the risks and benefits of the treatment and available alternatives. Courts have held that consent based on inaccurate or incomplete information deprived individuals of the right to charter their own course of treatment. It is now well settled that healthcare professionals have a duty to provide recipients of care with sufficient information to make an informed decision, unless one of the exceptions described below in Part II.A.2. applies.

The doctrine of informed consent in its present form comprises two separate elements. One involves a duty to *disclose* relevant information, while the other is a duty to obtain *consent* for the proposed therapy. Disclosure refers to the transmission of needed information to the client, while the latter addresses the patient's understanding of this information. Traditionally, the doctrine of informed consent addressed medical treatment and, until recently, its application was limited to physically intrusive treatment modalities such as ECT or psychopharmacology. Its extension to psychotherapy and other non-biological treatments is a relatively recent phenomenon, driven in part by the recognition that they can also have adverse effects, as discussed in conjunction with recovered memory therapy (see Chapter Three, supra).

Two other reasons may explain why the doctrine has until very recently been limited to biological therapies. One relates to historical bounds associated with the law of damages. In some jurisdictions, recovery of monetary damages in a tort action requires that the injured party suffered physical injury. Such injury is more likely to be associated with surgery or psychopharmacology than conventional psychotherapy. In recent years, however, courts have expanded compensation for non-physical injuries in tort law, which exposes psychotherapists to an increased risk of liability under the doctrine of informed consent.

Second, a cause of action predicated on a lack of informed consent requires that the patient's injury be the direct and proximate cause of the treatment, which may be difficult to establish in an informed consent claim focusing on a non-biological therapy. This point is illustrated by the following hypothetical.

A client receiving psychotherapy thinks that she is not advancing in her job due to excessive passivity and an inability to direct subordinates. On the therapist's recommendation, the client agrees to undergo assertiveness training, but is not informed that such training may also alter her personal relationships. The training is successful in that the client becomes more assertive and can better carry out her job-related responsibilities; however, her assertiveness alters how she and her husband interact and leads to a divorce. The client could assert that she would have not consented to the therapy had she been informed of the risks it posed to her personal relationships. However, the client faces the significant difficulty of proving both that the therapy in fact led to a personality change and that this (rather than the client's independent decisions about how she should interact with her spouse or her spouse's unwillingness to accept these decisions) was the proximate cause of the failure of her marriage. While this burden of proof might not be impossible to meet, it presents problems far more formidable than demonstrating that a particular physical injury was the direct and proximate cause of a surgical procedure or that an administered medication produced an adverse effect. Nevertheless, the informed consent doctrine is increasingly being applied to non-biological treatments.

As a result, mental health professionals' ability to avoid civil liability no longer hinges exclusively on whether they provided therapy in a customary manner or exercised the skill of a reasonable practitioner in providing treatment. Rather, professionals can face liability for damages even when the treatment was delivered flawlessly, as recovery can be predicated solely on a failure to obtain informed consent.

QUESTIONS AND COMMENTS

1.   *Battery as a basis for recovery.* Numerous cases, some decided as early as the beginning of the twentieth century, used the tort of battery to impose liability on physicians who performed medical procedures without the patient's authorization. Typically, these cases involved one of two basic scenarios. In one, the physician performed a medical or surgical procedure different from the one authorized by the patient. For instance, in *Hively v. Higgs*, 253 P. 363 (Or. 1927), during an operation on a patient's nose, a surgeon also removed a patient's tonsils, and was held liable for battery. Similarly, a dentist was held liable for battery after he removed eight teeth from an unconscious patient when the prior agreement was that he would extract only two. *Moore v. Webb*, 345 S.W.2d 239 (Mo. Ct. App. 1961).

The second scenario involved the performance of a procedure to which the patient consented, but on a different part of the body than authorized. For instance, in *Mohr v. Williams*, 104 N.W. 12 (Minn. 1905), the physician initially diagnosed the patient's right ear as requiring surgery. The patient consented to the recommended procedure, but during the operation the surgeon discovered a more serious defect in the patient's left ear and operated on that ear instead. The court found that these facts established a basis for liability under a theory of battery. In these early cases, liability was not predicated on the physician's failure to disclose information about collateral risks inherent in the treatment. Thus, a physician could establish a complete defense by showing that the patient had authorized the treatment performed.

2.   *Alternate theories.* The modern doctrine of informed consent is generally no longer based on the tort of battery, but rather sounds in negligence. A foundation in negligence rather than battery is of more than theoretical interest. Conceptually, it means the focus is on the standard of care rather than simply the right to be free from unconsented-to-touching.

This change can also have important practical implications for related litigation. First, to proceed with a negligence claim in general, expert testimony must typically be produced that the physician deviated from the standard of care, whereas expert testimony is usually not required for a battery claim (where the focus is essentially whether the patient consented to the "touching"). A full explanation of this point is provided in the notes following *Canterbury v. Spence*, which appears in the next section.

In addition, causation is a required element for a negligence action, and thus claimants must establish that they would have refused the procedure if they had known all the details and risks. Under a battery approach, claimants need only show that an unconsented-to-touching occurred. Furthermore, under the applicable statute of limitations, a plaintiff may have a different length of time in which to file a claim based on negligence than one asserting battery. Many states have also enacted "tort reforms" that may make pursuing negligence claims more difficult or limit the damages available. At the same time, under the terms of malpractice insurance policies, the defendant may be covered if the suit alleged negligence, as intentional torts are specifically excluded from coverage in some policies.

Finally, the measure of damages may vary with the theory utilized. Because battery is an intentional tort, under this doctrine a plaintiff may be able to recover punitive damages, especially if the element of malice can be established, whereas punitive damages are typically not available in conjunction with a claim of negligence. Also, with a battery claim, even though no actual injury can be established, nominal damages may still be available, while in negligence actions, damages are ordinarily awarded only for injuries actually suffered, as well as limited to physical injuries in some jurisdictions.

II.   ELEMENTS OF THE DOCTRINE OF INFORMED CONSENT

A. THE DISCLOSURE REQUIREMENT

1.   Standards Governing the Scope of Disclosure

As indicated in the preceding section, the doctrine of informed consent requires that a therapist disclose the collateral risks of a proposed treatment. However, a rule framed in these general terms leaves two issues unanswered. First, must there be a disclosure of every risk, or is it sufficient if the therapist informs the client of only the more significant and probable potential adverse consequences? Second, is the adequacy of disclosure to be judged by what the mental health provider regards as appropriate in the particular circumstances or by some other standard? The cases that follow represent two divergent approaches to these questions.

AIKEN V. CLARY
Supreme Court of Missouri, 1965.
396 S.W.2d 668.

FINCH, JUDGE.

Plaintiff went to trial on Count III of a malpractice action wherein he alleged negligence of [the] defendant in failing sufficiently to advise [the] plaintiff of the hazards and risks involved in insulin shock therapy [a treatment, developed before effective psychotropic medications were available, in which patients received injections of insulin large enough to induce a coma] to enable plaintiff to give an informed consent for the treatment. Plaintiff alleged that as a result of such therapy administered by defendant he was caused to lapse into a coma and to suffer organic brain damage, resulting in total disability. He sought recovery of $150,000. The jury returned a verdict for defendant. After an unavailing motion for new trial, plaintiff appealed to this court.

* * *

We proceed . . . to examine the evidence, which, insofar as pertinent to this assignment and viewed most favorably to plaintiff, was as follows:

After military service from 1941 to 1945 plaintiff entered employment of the Frisco Railroad, ultimately serving as an electrician in the diesel engine department. Early in 1961 plaintiff became irritable and "changed almost his entire personality." He was cross with the children, particularly a teen-age daughter, spent money on things for which he had never spent money before, and had trouble sleeping so that he lost a great amount of sleep and rest. His wife discussed with him the matter of seeing a doctor, but he maintained that his wife needed a doctor as much as he did, and that it was she who was "way out in left field." He agreed to see a doctor if she would, and they then consulted Dr. Lewis E. Jorel of Springfield, who previously had treated their daughter.

Following conferences by the doctor with both plaintiff and his wife, plaintiff entered St. John's Hospital at Springfield, Missouri, on June 3, 1961, for a complete physical examination.

[Following the administration of various tests and procedures, the plaintiff was found to have no physical disorder. Plaintiff was referred to Dr. Clary for a psychiatric examination. Dr. Clary diagnosed plaintiff as suffering from paranoid schizophrenia, and recommended both electric and insulin shock therapy. After consulting both his wife and his family physician, plaintiff gave his consent to ECT and insulin therapy.]

With respect to the information given by Dr. Clary to plaintiff in these conversations as to the nature of the treatment and the risks involved, plaintiff offered in evidence certain statements of the defendant given in an earlier deposition. That testimony was as follows:

"Q. When you talked to him previous to the moving down to psychiatry and signing the release, did you tell him what the possible effects of insulin shock therapy might be?

"A. I told him it would put him to sleep, I told him there [were] risks involved, I told him the same thing about electric shock therapy. I didn't belabor the point, I told him it was risky because this guy was real shook, but I told him it was risky, and he had no questions.

"Q. Did you tell him it might possibly result in his death?

"A. I implied it. In talking about the anesthetic, I said people take anesthetic, and there are hazards. Some people over-react to anesthetics, and insulin, I told him, it is like being put to sleep, there are risks involved. In terms of specifically telling him, 'This can kill you,' no, sir, I didn't.

"Q. Did you tell him it might possibly result in a delayed awakening, possible brain damage?

"A. No, I didn't tell him that."

Dr. Clary testified that he thought the plaintiff had the mental capacity at least to understand the ordinary affairs of life, understand what the treatment really was and what it might do to him. He again related what he had told plaintiff and stated that he tried to explain it to him on a level he would understand, and he thought plaintiff knew exactly what he was getting into. At the second conference between Dr. Clary and plaintiff, the latter agreed to take whatever treatment Dr. Clary recommended.

Accordingly, on June 9, 1961, a nurse in the psychiatric ward presented to plaintiff a form of "Consent to Shock Therapy." It read as follows: "I (We) hereby request and authorize Dr. Clary and whomever he may designate to assist him, to administer insulin and/or electroshock therapy to Mr. Aiken; and to continue to administer such therapy and such other supplemental treatment as he may deem advisable from time to time. The effect and nature of shock and/or insulin treatment have been fully explained to me (us), as well as the hazards involved. Notwithstanding the fact that there are risks to the patient inherent in this treatment, I (we) voluntarily accept the risks involved. No assurance has been made by anyone with respect to the results that may be obtained. I have been given a copy of the pamphlet 'Information to Relatives.'" The nurse testified that she did not explain anything about the dangers involved in the therapy when she presented the consent for signature. The plaintiff read the consent in her presence and she asked him if he had any questions, but he had none and he signed the consent.

Beginning on June 12, 1961, and continuing through June 22, 1961, plaintiff was given a series of shock treatments which involved insulin in increasing amounts of from 40 to 260 units. On June 22, 1961, plaintiff went into a deep coma. He suffered a delayed awakening from the insulin and did not respond to the procedures used for the purpose of bringing the patient out of the coma. A specialist in internal medicine was called in and plaintiff was transferred to the intensive care unit but the coma was prolonged and as a result plaintiff suffered brain damage.

Dr. Robert L. Lam, M.D., a specialist in neurology and psychiatry, testified for plaintiff that from an examination made by him at the Veterans Hospital in Little Rock, Arkansas, on January 16, 1964, his opinion was that plaintiff had severe organic brain damage, that he was totally incapacitated in terms of employment and that his condition was permanent as a result of the prolonged insulin coma. Plaintiff was still in the Veterans Hospital at the time of trial.

Dr. Lam was interrogated as to dangers in insulin shock therapy and he testified that the possible dangers or complications thereof are coma and death or prolonged coma resulting in various degrees of brain damage, or that there might be the production of epilepsy or localized paralysis, or there might be a vascular disturbance. In addition, he said that with convulsions that may occur one could have fractures of certain types, either of the vertebrae or the extremities. The doctor was not asked and did not undertake to testify as to the frequency of occurrence of such events, or any of them, and said that no doctor could predict which patient would be the one to have trouble, saying, "So that the only thing one can say is that, when one has a patient getting deep coma insulin, that there is a possibility that this could occur." Dr. Lam also testified that there was nothing improper in the administration of the insulin shock therapy and that the administration thereof was according to good medical practice. Dr. Lam was not asked about the adequacy of defendant's disclosures to plaintiff.

*   *   *

Defendant first asserts that plaintiff failed to make a submissible case because he failed to offer any expert medical evidence as to what a reasonably careful and prudent physician engaged in similar practice would do under the same or similar circumstances with respect to disclosure of risks involved in the proposed therapy. There is no dispute but that plaintiff did not offer any expert testimony on this matter of what a reasonably prudent practitioner would disclose. We must determine, therefore, whether plaintiff is required to offer such proof in order to make a submissible case.

The basic philosophy in malpractice cases is that the doctor is negligent by reason of the fact that he has failed to adhere to a standard of reasonable medical care, and that consequently the service rendered was substandard and negligent. In our judgment, this is true whether the alleged malpractice consists of improper care and treatment (the usual malpractice case) or whether it is based, as here, on an alleged failure to inform the patient sufficiently to enable him to make a judgment and give an informed consent if he concludes to accept the recommended treatment.

How, then, is a jury to determine whether a physician has been negligent in failing to inform his patient adequately to enable him to make an informed decision whether to consent to recommended treatment? What proof must a plaintiff offer? Obviously, in addition to evidence as to plaintiff's condition and the treatment proposed and administered, there must be testimony as to what risks are involved and what disclosures were made by the doctor. These necessarily are a part of plaintiff's case. Such evidence was offered by plaintiff in this case. The real issue here is whether plaintiff is required to go further and as a part of his case offer evidence as to a standard of medical conduct with reference to disclosures by the physician to his patient or whether this is a matter which the jury may decide without such expert testimony. There are cases from some states which hold that such expert testimony is necessary as a part of plaintiff's case and cases from other states holding that such evidence is not required. Plaintiff asserts that Missouri is in this latter group because this court, in the case of *Mitchell v. Robinson, Mo.*, 334 S.W.2d 11, 79 A.L.R.2d 1017, held that expert medical testimony was not necessary for the jury to pass upon the alleged failure of the doctor to warn of the hazards of shock therapy. Counsel says that he relied thereon in not offering any expert testimony on the standard for disclosure by a physician. The factual situation in the Mitchell case was different from that here, plaintiff there contending that the doctors made *no* disclosure of risks and the doctors testifying that they did make *full* disclosure to the patient. . . .

We have reexamined this question and have concluded that the question of what disclosure of risks incident to proposed treatment should be made in a particular situation involves medical judgment and that expert testimony thereon should be required in malpractice cases involving that issue. The question to be determined by the jury is whether defendant doctor in that particular situation failed to adhere to a standard of reasonable care. These are not matters of common knowledge or within the experience of laymen. Expert medical evidence thereon is just as necessary as is such testimony on the correctness of the handling in cases involving surgery or treatment. . . . [Expert testimony as to the appropriate level of disclosure required in a particular case would need to take into account such factors as] the state of the patient's health, the condition of his heart and nervous system, his mental state, and . . . among other things, whether the risks involved were mere remote possibilities or something which occurred with some sort of frequency or regularity. This determination involves medical judgment as to whether disclosure of possible risks may have such an adverse effect on the patient as to jeopardize success of the proposed therapy, no matter how expertly performed. (Defendant in this case testified that plaintiff was "real shook.") After a consideration of these and other proper factors, a reasonable medical practitioner, under some circumstances, would make full disclosure of all risks which had any reasonable likelihood of occurring, but in others the facts and circumstances would dictate a guarded or limited disclosure. In some cases the judgment would be less difficult than in others, but, in any event, it would be a medical judgment. . . . Accordingly, we hold that plaintiff, in order to sustain his burden of proof, is required to offer expert testimony to show what disclosures a reasonable medical practitioner, under the same or similar circumstances, would have made, or, stated another way, that the disclosures as made by the defendant do not meet the standard of what a reasonable medical practitioner would have disclosed under the same or similar circumstances. To whatever extent *Mitchell v. Robinson* is inconsistent with the views herein expressed, it is disapproved.

Once plaintiff has offered sufficient proof to make a submissible case, including the required expert testimony which we have discussed, then the ultimate determination of whether defendant did or did not fail to disclose to plaintiff in accordance with the standard of what a reasonable medical practitioner would have done is a jury question under proper instructions from the court. . . .

In view of the fact that plaintiff made no offering of any expert testimony relative to the extent of disclosure a reasonable medical practitioner would have made under the same or similar circumstances, he failed to make a submissible case for the jury. However, we will not affirm this case on that basis for the reason that counsel for plaintiff asserted in the presentation of the case that in the case of *Mitchell v. Robinson*, supra, this court had stated that expert testimony is not necessary in cases involving extent of duty to warn, and that he relied thereon in offering no proof of that character. In the light of language used in the opinion of *Mitchell v. Robinson*, supra, it was reasonable for counsel to assume the lack of a requirement of such testimony in this case. Under those circumstances, we feel compelled to reverse and remand for a new trial in order to afford plaintiff an opportunity to offer expert testimony on the standard of disclosure required.

* * *

The judgment is reversed and the cause remanded for a new trial.

All of the Judges concur.

QUESTIONS AND COMMENTS

1. *Comment on* Aiken. Note that although the *Aiken* court sustained the defendant's legal argument, it reversed the judgment in defendant's favor

and remanded the case for retrial. The court ordered this unusual outcome on the basis that the plaintiff's lawyer had reasonably relied on the *Mitchell v. Robinson* opinion, which did not signal that a plaintiff must present expert testimony to establish that medical practitioners make such disclosures in similar circumstances. Normally when an attorney errs in this way, appellate courts are less forgiving and the client is precluded from a second opportunity to litigate the case. Why do you suppose that was not the case here?

2.   *Scope of disclosure.* Under *Aiken,* a medical practitioner is only required to disclose those risks that "a reasonable medical practitioner would have made under the same or similar circumstances" when obtaining consent for treatment. Thus, in those jurisdictions that have adopted the reasonable-practitioner standard (as opposed to the customary-practice standard) for their medical malpractice test, the scope of the mandated disclosure is to be judged by the same standard as would be used for a malpractice claim. The critical issue in such cases is whether the disclosure deviated from the applicable standard of care.

Does this standard reflect an appropriate compromise between the patient's interests in receiving sufficient information upon which to base the decision to accept or reject treatment and the interest of healthcare providers in being able to carry out their functions without undue risk of liability? If the jurisdiction applies the customary-practice standard as its test for assessing the adequacy of the informed consent disclosure, what impact is this likely have on the required scope of disclosures? See Thomas L. Hafemeister, Leah G. McLaughlin, & Jessica Smith, *Parity at a Price: The Emerging Professional Liability of Mental Health Providers,* 50 San Diego L. Rev. 29, 38–39 (2013) (" 'In more than half the states, either through an explicit statutory change or through case law, malpractice law has moved away from a customary-practice standard, and toward a reasonably-prudent-physician standard.' " This approach undercuts a "safety-in-numbers" approach that encouraged the status quo, and it has coincided with the rise of 'evidence-based medicine,' with testifying experts referring to such evidence when articulating the standard of care.).

3.   *Need for expert testimony.* Under the *Aiken* formulation, liability will attach only when a deviation from the prevailing professional standard has occurred. Therefore, to succeed, a plaintiff must introduce expert testimony on the question of whether practitioners generally would disclose a particular risk in the same or similar circumstances. See also *Wilkerson v. Mid–Am. Cardiology,* 908 S.W.2d 691, 697 (Mo. Ct. App. 1995). Who would qualify as an expert witness in such a case? If the defendant is a mental health professional, should it only be someone who is an authority on therapist-client interactions? On decision-making theory? Someone from the same profession as the defendant?

4.   *Exceptions permitting withholding of information.* Can an individual's fragile mental state be a legally sufficient basis for withholding information pertaining to a risk and, if so, under what circumstances? The scope of such an exception is addressed in Part II.A.2, infra.

5. *Alternative to the reasonable practitioner standard.* The case of *Canterbury v. Spence*, which follows, established an alternate test, which limits the ability of the practitioner to define the boundaries of what risks must be disclosed.

CANTERBURY V. SPENCE

United States Court of Appeals, District of Columbia Circuit, 1972.
464 F.2d 772.

SPOTTSWOOD W. ROBINSON, III, CIRCUIT JUDGE:

This appeal is from a judgment entered in the District Court on verdicts directed for the two appellees at the conclusion of plaintiff-appellant Canterbury's case in chief. His action sought damages for personal injuries allegedly sustained as a result of an operation negligently performed by appellee Spence, a negligent failure by Dr. Spence to disclose a risk of serious disability inherent in the operation, and negligent post-operative care by appellee Washington Hospital Center. On close examination of the record, we find evidence which required submission of these issues to the jury. We accordingly reverse the judgment as to each appellee and remand the case to the District Court for a new trial.

[In 1958, appellant, nineteen years old at the time, sought medical attention for severe pain between his shoulder blades. After tests revealed a "filling defect" in appellant's spine, Dr. Spence told the appellant that he required surgery to repair what Dr. Spence suspected was a ruptured disc. The surgery revealed a swollen spinal cord, dilated veins, and an absence of fat surrounding the spine. Dr. Spence attempted to relieve the pressure by surgically enlarging the outer wall of the spinal cord.

The day after surgery, the appellant, unassisted by hospital personnel, fell off of his bed while voiding. Several hours later he was virtually paralyzed from the waist down. Dr. Spence reopened the surgical wound "to allow the spinal cord greater room in which to pulsate." At the time of his 1968 trial, the appellant required crutches to walk, and still suffered from urine incontinence and paralysis of the bowels.

The damages claimed by appellant included pain and suffering, medical expenses, and loss of earnings.]

* * *

II

Appellant filed suit in the District Court on March 7, 1963, four years after the laminectomy and approximately two years after he attained his majority. The complaint stated several causes of action against each defendant. Against Dr. Spence it alleged, among other things, negligence in the performance of the laminectomy and failure to inform him beforehand of the risk involved. . . . The answers denied the allegations of negligence. . . .

. . . Appellant introduced no evidence to show medical and hospital practices, if any, customarily pursued in regard to the critical aspects of the case, and only Dr. Spence, called as an adverse witness, testified on the issue of causality. Dr. Spence described the surgical procedures he utilized in the two operations and expressed his opinion that appellant's disabilities stemmed from his pre-operative condition as symptomized by the swollen, non-pulsating spinal cord. . . . Dr. Spence further testified that[,] even without trauma[,] paralysis can be anticipated "somewhere in the nature of one percent" of the laminectomies performed, a risk he termed "a very slight possibility." He felt that communication of that risk to the patient is not good medical practice because it might deter patients from undergoing needed surgery and might produce adverse psychological reactions which could preclude the success of the operation.

At the close of appellant's case in chief, each defendant moved for a directed verdict and the trial judge granted both motions. The basis of the ruling, he explained, was that appellant had failed to produce any medical evidence indicating negligence on Dr. Spence's part in diagnosing appellant's malady or in performing the laminectomy; that there was no proof that Dr. Spence's treatment was responsible for appellant's disabilities; . . . The judge did not allude specifically to the alleged breach of duty by Dr. Spence to divulge the possible consequences of the laminectomy.

We reverse. The testimony of appellant and his mother that Dr. Spence did not reveal the risk of paralysis from the laminectomy made out a prima facie case of violation of the physician's duty to disclose which Dr. Spence's explanation did not negate as a matter of law. There was also testimony from which the jury could have found that the laminectomy was negligently performed by Dr. Spence. . . . These considerations entitled appellant to a new trial.

* * *

III

Suits charging failure by a physician adequately to disclose the risks and alternatives of proposed treatment are not innovations in American law. They date back a good half-century, and in the last decade they have multiplied rapidly. There is, nonetheless, disagreement among the courts and the commentators on many major questions, and there is no precedent of our own directly in point. For the tools enabling resolution of the issues on this appeal, we are forced to begin at first principles.

The root premise is the concept, fundamental in American jurisprudence, that "[e]very human being of adult years and sound mind has a right to determine what shall be done with his own body. . . . " True consent to what happens to one's self is the informed exercise of a choice, and that entails an opportunity to evaluate knowledgeably the options available and the risks attendant upon each. The average patient has little or no understanding of the medical arts, and ordinarily has only his physician to whom he can look for enlightenment with which to reach an intelligent decision. From these almost axiomatic considerations springs the need, and in turn the requirement, of a reasonable divulgence by physician to patient to make such a decision possible.

A physician is under a duty to treat his patient skillfully but proficiency in diagnosis and therapy is not the full measure of his responsibility. The cases demonstrate that the physician is under an obligation to communicate specific information to the patient when the exigencies of reasonable care call for it. . . .

The context in which the duty of risk-disclosure arises is invariably the occasion for decision as to whether a particular treatment procedure is to be undertaken. To the physician, whose training enables a self-satisfying evaluation, the answer may seem clear, but it is the prerogative of the patient, not the physician, to determine for himself the direction in which his interests seem to lie. To enable the patient to chart his course understandably, some familiarity with the therapeutic alternatives and their hazards becomes essential.

A reasonable revelation in these respects is not only a necessity but, as we see it, is as much a matter of the physician's duty. It is a duty to warn of the dangers lurking in the proposed treatment, . . . It is, too, a duty to impart information which the patient has every right to expect.[27] The patient's reliance upon the physician is a trust of the kind which traditionally has exacted obligations beyond those associated with arms-length transactions. His dependence upon the physician for information affecting his well-being, in terms of contemplated treatment, is well-nigh abject. As earlier noted, long before the instant litigation arose, courts had recognized that the physician had the responsibility of satisfying the vital informational needs of the patient. More recently, we ourselves have found "in the fiducial qualities of [the physician-patient] relationship the

---

[27] Some doubt has been expressed as to [the] ability of physicians to suitably communicate their evaluations of risks and the advantages of optional treatment, and as to the lay patient's ability to understand what the physician tells him. We do not share these apprehensions. The discussion need not be a disquisition, and surely the physician is not compelled to give his patient a short medical education; the disclosure rule summons the physician only to a reasonable explanation. That means generally informing the patient in non-technical terms as to what is at stake: the therapy alternatives open to him, the goals expectably to be achieved, and the risks that may ensue from particular treatment and no treatment. So informing the patient hardly taxes the physician, and it must be the exceptional patient who cannot comprehend such an explanation at least in a rough way.

physician's duty to reveal to the patient that which in his best interests it is important that he should know." We now find, as a part of the physician's overall obligation to the patient, a similar duty of reasonable disclosure of the choices with respect to proposed therapy and the dangers inherently and potentially involved.

This disclosure requirement, on analysis, reflects much more of a change in doctrinal emphasis than a substantive addition to malpractice law. . . .

IV

Duty to disclose has gained recognition in a large number of American jurisdictions, but more largely on a different rationale. The majority of courts dealing with the problem have made the duty depend on whether it was the custom of physicians practicing in the community to make the particular disclosure to the patient. If so, the physician may be held liable for an unreasonable and injurious failure to divulge, but there can be no recovery unless the omission forsakes a practice prevalent in the profession. We agree that the physician's noncompliance with a professional custom to reveal, like any other departure from prevailing medical practice, may give rise to liability to the patient. We do not agree that the patient's cause of action is dependent upon the existence and nonperformance of a relevant professional tradition.

There are, in our view, formidable obstacles to acceptance of the notion that the physician's obligation to disclose is either germinated or limited by medical practice. To begin with, the reality of any discernible custom reflecting a professional consensus on communication of option and risk information to patients is open to serious doubt. We sense the danger that what in fact is no custom at all may be taken as an affirmative custom to maintain silence, and that physician-witnesses to the so-called custom may state merely their personal opinions as to what they or others would do under given conditions. We cannot gloss over the inconsistency between reliance on a general practice respecting divulgence and, on the other hand, realization that the myriad of variables among patients makes each case so different that its omission can rationally be justified only by the effect of its individual circumstances. Nor can we ignore the fact that to bind the disclosure obligation to medical usage is to arrogate the decision on revelation to the physician alone. Respect for the patient's right of self-determination on particular therapy demands a standard set by law for physicians rather than one which physicians may or may not impose upon themselves.

*   *   *

V

Once the circumstances give rise to a duty on the physician's part to inform his patient, the next inquiry is the scope of the disclosure the physician is legally obliged to make. The courts have frequently confronted this problem but no uniform standard defining the adequacy of the divulgence emerges from the decisions. Some have said "full" disclosure, a norm we are unwilling to adopt literally. It seems obviously prohibitive and unrealistic to expect physicians to discuss with their patients every risk of proposed treatment—no matter how small or remote—and generally unnecessary from the patient's viewpoint as well. Indeed, the cases speaking in terms of "full" disclosure appear to envision something less than total disclosure, leaving unanswered the question of just how much.

The larger number of courts, as might be expected, have applied tests framed with reference to prevailing fashion within the medical profession. Some have measured the disclosure by "good medical practice," others by what a reasonable practitioner would have bared under the circumstances, and still others by what medical custom in the community would demand. We have explored this rather considerable body of law but are unprepared to follow it. The duty to disclose, we have reasoned, arises from phenomena apart from medical custom and practice. The latter, we think, should no more establish the scope of the duty than its existence. Any definition of scope in terms purely of a professional standard is at odds with the patient's prerogative to decide on projected therapy himself. That prerogative, we have said, is at the very foundation of the duty to disclose, and both the patient's right to know and the physician's correlative obligation to tell him are diluted to the extent that its compass is dictated by the medical profession.

In our view, the patient's right of self-decision shapes the boundaries of the duty to reveal. That right can be effectively exercised only if the patient possesses enough information to enable an intelligent choice. The scope of the physician's communications to the patient, then, must be measured by the patient's need, and that need is the information material to the decision. Thus the test for determining whether a particular peril must be divulged is its materiality to the patient's decision: all risks potentially affecting the decision must be unmasked. And to safeguard the patient's interest in achieving his own determination on treatment, the law must itself set the standard for adequate disclosure.

Optimally for the patient, exposure of a risk would be mandatory whenever the patient would deem it significant to his decision, either singly or in combination with other risks. Such a requirement, however, would summon the physician to second-guess the patient, whose ideas on materiality could hardly be known to the physician. That would make an undue demand upon medical practitioners, whose conduct, like that of others, is to be measured in terms of reasonableness. Consonantly with orthodox negligence doctrine, the physician's liability for nondisclosure is to be determined on the basis of foresight, not hindsight; no less than any other aspect of negligence, the issue on nondisclosure must be approached from the viewpoint of the reasonableness of the physician's divulgence in terms of what he knows or should know to be the patient's informational needs. If, but only if, the fact-finder can say that the physician's communication was unreasonably inadequate is an imposition of liability legally or morally justified.

Of necessity, the content of the disclosure rests in the first instance with the physician. Ordinarily it is only he who is in position to identify particular dangers; always he must make a judgment, in terms of materiality, as to whether and to what extent revelation to the patient is called for. He cannot know with complete exactitude what the patient would consider important to his decision, but on the basis of his medical training and experience he can sense how the average, reasonable patient expectably would react. Indeed, with knowledge of, or ability to learn, his patient's background and current condition, he is in a position superior to that of most others—attorneys, for example—who are called upon to make judgments on pain of liability in damages for unreasonable miscalculation.

From these considerations we derive the breadth of the disclosure of risks legally to be required. The scope of the standard is not subjective as to either the physician or the patient; it remains objective with due regard for the patient's informational needs and with suitable leeway for the physician's situation. In broad outline, we agree that "[a] risk is thus material when a reasonable person, in what the physician knows or should know to be the patient's position, would be likely to attach significance to the risk or cluster of risks in deciding whether or not to forego the proposed therapy."

The topics importantly demanding a communication of information are the inherent and potential hazards of the proposed treatment, the alternatives to that treatment, if any, and the results likely if the patient remains untreated. The factors contributing significance to the dangerousness of a medical technique are, of course, the incidence of injury and the degree of the harm threatened. A very small chance of death or serious disablement may well be significant; a potential disability which dramatically outweighs the potential benefit of the therapy or the detriments of the existing malady may summons discussion with the patient.

There is no bright line separating the significant from the insignificant; the answer in any case must abide a rule of reason. Some dangers—infection, for example—are inherent in any operation; there is no obligation to communicate those of which persons of average sophistication are aware. Even more clearly, the physician bears no responsibility for discussion of hazards the patient has already discovered, or those having no apparent materiality to patients' decision on therapy. The disclosure doctrine, like others marking lines between permissible and impermissible behavior in medical practice, is in essence a requirement of conduct prudent under the circumstances. Whenever nondisclosure of particular risk information is open to debate by reasonable-minded men, the issue is for the finder of the facts.

* * *

VIII.

* * *

The guiding consideration our decisions distill, however, is that medical facts are for medical experts and other facts are for any witnesses—expert or not—having sufficient knowledge and capacity to testify to them. It is evident that many of the issues typically involved in nondisclosure cases do not reside peculiarly within the medical domain. Lay witness testimony can competently establish a physician's failure to disclose particular risk information, the patient's lack of knowledge of the risk, and the adverse consequences following the treatment. Experts are unnecessary to a showing of the materiality of a risk to a patient's decision on treatment, or to the reasonably, expectable effect of risk disclosure on the decision. These conspicuous examples of permissible uses of nonexpert testimony illustrate the relative freedom of broad areas of the legal problem of risk nondisclosure from the demands for expert testimony that shackle plaintiffs' other types of medical malpractice litigation.

IX.

[The court next determined whether the appellant's suit was barred by the statute of limitations and ruled that it was not.]

X

This brings us to the remaining question, common to all three causes of action: whether appellant's evidence was of such caliber as to require a submission to the jury. On the first, the evidence was clearly sufficient to raise an issue as to whether Dr. Spence's obligation to disclose information on risks was reasonably met or was excused by the surrounding circumstances. Appellant testified that Dr. Spence revealed to him nothing suggesting a hazard associated with the laminectomy. His mother testified that, in response to her specific inquiry, Dr. Spence informed her that the laminectomy was no more serious than any other operation. When, at trial, it developed from Dr. Spence's testimony that paralysis can be expected in one percent of laminectomies, it became the jury's responsibility to decide whether that peril was of sufficient magnitude to bring the disclosure duty into play.

[The court next addressed the issues of whether there was sufficient evidence to reach the jury on whether the defendant, Dr. Spence, had performed the laminectomy negligently and whether the hospital was negligent in the aftercare provided. The court ruled that there was sufficient evidence for this purpose.]

Reversed and remanded for a new trial.

QUESTIONS AND COMMENTS

1. *Materiality as a criterion for liability.* Canterbury defines the breadth of required disclosure to include any risk that would be deemed significant by "a reasonable person, in what the physician knows or should know to be the patient's position." The court adds that

> the scope of the physician's communications to the patient . . . must be measured by the patient's need, and that need is the information material to the decision. Thus the test for determining whether a particular peril must be divulged is its materiality to the patient's decision: all risks potentially affecting the decision must be unmasked.

The shorthand expression of this principle is that the health care provider must disclose all "material" risks associated with a given treatment to a client.

But what constitutes a "material" risk? The *Canterbury* court suggests that the threshold for disclosure will vary with the product of the probability and the severity of the risk. Thus, a low-probability (e.g., 1%) risk may be material if the severity of the harm that might occur is very great (e.g., death or permanent disability). Alternatively, if the probability of the event occurring is very high, even the risk of a relatively minor harm (for example, sedation from a psychotropic drug) may have to be disclosed. But what if the probability of the risk falls within a relatively broad range (e.g., 1% to 10%), and the severity of the possible harm that might occur relies on a number of factors (e.g., the promptness of detection and response)? Does it matter that it is a temporary or short-term risk rather than a risk of long-term or permanent harm? What if the risk depends on a number of post-treatment factors largely beyond the health care provider's control (e.g., a client's compliance with post-treatment directions—such as not consuming alcohol or maintaining medication—or the availability of auxiliary health care providers or services, or the avoidance of post-treatment injury or trauma)? How clairvoyant must the health care provider be? Must the provider always assume the worst?

2. *Rules in other jurisdictions.* Although the *Aiken* and *Canterbury* courts both anchor the duty of disclosure to the doctrine of negligence, the operational standard for assessing liability under these two approaches is quite different. Potentially, there are four different standards available: the subjective patient standard (i.e., what the patient receiving treatment believes is a material risk), the objective patient standard (i.e., what a reasonable patient under similar circumstances would believe is a material risk), the subjective health care provider standard (i.e., what the health care provider giving treatment believes is a material risk), and the objective

health care provider standard (i.e., what a reasonable health care provider giving such treatment under similar circumstances would believe is a reasonable risk). What are the strengths and weaknesses of each approach? Which would a plaintiff find most favorable? A defendant?

There is a split among jurisdictions as to the appropriate standard. As of 2006, twenty-four jurisdictions had adopted a patient-based standard similar to the *Canterbury* rule. Jaime Staples King & Benjamin W. Moulton, *Rethinking Informed Consent: The Case for Shared Medical Decision–Making*, 32 Am. J.L. & Med. 429, 493 (2006). Twenty-five jurisdictions followed a professional standards rule similar to the more traditional *Aiken* approach. Id.

Jurisdictions that have rejected the professional standards rule have tended to do so on the basis that under this approach disclosure "is totally subject to the whim of the physicians in the particular community" and vests the physician "with virtually unlimited discretion in establishing the proper scope of disclosure" and is "inconsistent with the patient's right to self-determination." *Largey v. Rothman*, 540 A.2d 504 (N.J. 1988).

Jurisdictions that adhere to the professional standards rule give the following justifications: only physicians can determine the effect that a risk might have on a particular patient; the physician does not have enough time to give all the information patients may request; negligence normally evaluates the conduct of a reasonable actor, not the expectations of a reasonable victim; and the physician should not be subject to the hindsight of the disgruntled client and the second guessing of a jury. See Barry R. Furrow et al., Health Law 313–14 (2000).

3.   *Characteristics of the health care provider.* Usually a discussion of the material risks of treatment focuses on the benefits and risks of a proposed treatment, various alternative treatments, and the option of no treatment at all. But the likelihood that a given treatment will be successful may vary with the characteristics of the treatment provider. For example, particularly for treatments that are more complex or require greater expertise (e.g., surgery), inexperienced providers have lower success or greater complication rates. Pursuant to informed consent doctrine, do treatment providers have an obligation to disclose their level of experience with a given treatment? See *Johnson v. Kokemoor*, 545 N.W.2d 495 (Wis. 1996) (holding that the trial court did not err in admitting evidence regarding physician's lack of experience and the difficulty of the proposed procedure); *Goldberg v. Booner*, 912 A.2d 698 (Md. Ct. App. 2006). On the other hand, if disclosing one's inexperience dissuades patients and clients from employing inexperienced health care providers, how can a treatment provider obtain the experience needed to become proficient?

What about other characteristics that might compromise treatment? For example, the health care provider is in the midst of a messy divorce? Recently lost a loved one or been diagnosed with a terminal illness? Has a possible conflict of interests? Believes in witchcraft? Is a chronic alcoholic? Was previously an alcoholic? Has been diagnosed as having a psychiatric disorder? Was recently hospitalized for a psychiatric condition? Is currently receiving mental health treatment? Received mental health treatment in the recent past? Received licensure sanction for any of the above in the past? Must each of these matters be disclosed? If so, to what extent? See Marc D. Ginsberg, *Informed Consent: No Longer Just What the Doctor Ordered—The Contributions of Medical Associations and Courts to a More Patient Friendly Doctrine*, 15 Mich. St. U.J. Med. & L. 17 (2010).

4. *Characteristics of the client.* Does it matter that the client is highly risk-averse? Is untroubled by risks, does not take them seriously, or is a risk-taker? Demands a given treatment? Wants a treatment that is unlikely to be effective? Is told about possible risks but clearly does not take them seriously? Is highly pessimistic and believes that no treatment will be effective or overvalues the risks? Is unlikely to understand the risks and benefits no matter how fully they are explained? Asks not to be told about the risks and benefits? Has a very limited understanding of the language spoken by the health care provider? Has an intellectual disability? Has some other mental disorder? Has a serious mental illness? Is psychotic but believes he is not mentally ill? Is currently being treated for a mental illness? Is currently being treated for a mental illness but denies the existence of this condition? Is just beginning treatment for a mental illness? What steps must a health care provider taken to ascertain whether the client comprehends the disclosure? Elyn R. Saks & Shahrokh Golshan, *Informed Consent to Psychoanalysis: The Law, the Theory, and the Data* (2013); Thomas L. Hafemeister & Richard M. Gulbrandsen, Jr., *The Fiduciary Obligation of Physicians to "Just Say No" if an "Informed" Patient Demands Services That Are Not Medically Indicated*, 39 Seton Hall L. Rev. 335 (2009).

5. *Need for expert testimony.* In contrast to the rule in *Aiken*, the *Canterbury* court would allow a plaintiff to prevail notwithstanding the absence of expert testimony as to the medical standard regarding the disclosure of a particular risk (or benefit or an alternate mode of treatment). However, expert testimony would still be necessary to establish that a particular procedure or treatment is associated with a specific degree of risk. At the same time, under the *Canterbury* formulation, a plaintiff would not need to introduce expert testimony to establish that the non-disclosed risk was material, i.e., that it was the kind of risk or cluster of risks that "a reasonable person, in . . . the patient's position, would be likely to attach significance . . . in deciding whether or not to forego the proposed therapy." The determination of whether a risk that was not disclosed was material would then be a question to be decided by the trier of fact.

6. *Disclosure of alternatives.* To what extent does either standard require disclosure of alternative therapies? Could a therapist be held liable if he has disclosed all collateral risks of the proposed therapy but has failed to point out alternatives? Does either case speak to this point? Is there a threshold of likely success that the alternative must reach before it must be disclosed? Note that the success rates of mental health treatments vary

substantially depending on individual patient and client characteristics and are therefore hard to specify.

What if the undisclosed alternative involves even greater risk than the actual procedure? Consider *Logan v. Greenwich Hospital Association*, 465 A.2d 294 (Conn. 1983). Plaintiff had undergone a procedure to obtain a specimen of kidney tissue. The procedure involved inserting a surgical needle into the plaintiff's back, under a local anesthetic, to extract the sample (and took place before currently-available technology was developed to localize needle biopsies). Plaintiff's gall bladder was punctured during the biopsy, and abdominal surgery was required to remove it. At the time she gave her consent, the plaintiff was unaware of an alternate procedure, an open biopsy, which required an incision under general anesthetic. The defendants testified that the plaintiff was not informed about this alternative because the risk of complications associated with it was greater than for a needle biopsy. The trial court instructed the jury that doctors have a duty to warn of feasible alternatives but that "an alternative that is more hazardous is not a viable alternative." The jury returned a verdict for the defendants. On appeal, the Connecticut Supreme Court reversed. The court reasoned the instruction was inconsistent with the view that patients must be provided with sufficient information to make an intelligent choice for themselves. Connecticut follows the *Canterbury* standard. Would the result be different under the *Aiken* rule?

7.   *Scope of the duty to communicate.* What is a therapist's liability for non-disclosure of risk data not known by the therapist? In the instance of established therapies, the therapist has a duty to disclose only those risks known to the therapist or that are generally known by a reasonably proficient practitioner. The *Canterbury* court defined this rule in the following terms:

> The category of risks which the physician should communicate is, of course, no broader than the complement [of risk] he could communicate. The duty to divulge may extend to any risk he actually knows, but he obviously cannot divulge any of which he may be unaware.

464 F.2d 772, 787 n.84 (D.C. Cir. 1972).

However, if the therapist is unaware of risks that are generally known by practitioners in the field, non-disclosure could give rise to a claim based on negligence. As noted in *Canterbury*:

> Nondisclosure of an unknown risk does not, strictly speaking, present a problem in terms of the duty to disclose although it very well might pose problems in terms of the physician's duties to have known of it and to have acted accordingly.

Id.

8.   *Disclosure of costs.* Are the costs of a given treatment a "material risk"? Should health care providers be required to disclose whether an individual's health insurance plan will cover a certain procedure or alternative? Entities such as managed care organizations decide whether a given procedure is covered and, if so, to what extent. Whatever cost is not

covered is the responsibility of the consumer. Costs may significantly affect whether a client decides to undergo a certain procedure. For a further discussion of this problem as it relates to psychotherapists, see Geoffrey Marczyk & Ellen Wertheimer, *The Bitter Pill of Empiricism: Health Maintenance Organizations, Informed Consent and the Reasonable Psychotherapist Standard of Care,* 46 Villanova L. Rev. 33 (2001). Does a health care provider have a duty to help a client negotiate and challenge a coverage refusal? See *Wickline v. State*, 239 Cal. Rptr. 810 (Ct. App. 1986).

9. *Evidentiary problems.* When the parties agree on what was communicated, all that must be adjudicated is whether this quantum of information was sufficient. Often, however, the extent of disclosure will be disputed by the parties. In this situation, the trier of fact must decide what the therapist in fact disclosed by weighing the credibility of the evidence provided. Once the factual questions have been resolved, application of the governing legal standard will produce the verdict. This initial stage of fact determination, however, can be challenging. Unless the disclosure has been reduced to writing, typically the only evidence available is the parties' conflicting testimony. In addition to the risk of intentional distortion, inadvertent distortion may also occur when witnesses attempt to recollect the substance of a verbal communication that took place several years earlier, with their recollection shaped by various intervening factors, including their interest in the outcome of the litigation.

Can therapists protect themselves from claims based on faulty client recollection of what was disclosed? Is it feasible to make audio recordings of risk disclosure sessions? Will this shape future interactions with the client? How long should the recordings be kept? Alternatively, is it feasible to reduce to writing a complete description of the benefits and risks of the contemplated therapy and the various alternatives and to require the client to read, understand, and sign this document? At what point is a client likely to experience "information overload"? To resent what may be an onerous task? Furthermore, today, informed consent documents are so ubiquitous as to potentially become a formality to which a client pays little attention. In addition, to keep these forms to a length that the client will actually read, only a partial description of the proposed treatment, its risks and benefits, and alternatives can usually be provided. It is also unlikely that all of the questions of a given client can be anticipated in advance and reduced to a standardized form. Finally, because of the technical language typically used in these forms, the information provided is unlikely to be fully understood by most clients. This may particularly be the case for a client with a mental disorder. As a result, such documents are unlikely to fully resolve an informed consent claim and may create more liability exposure. See Lawrence H. Brenner et al., *Beyond Informed Consent: Educating the Patient*, 467 Clinical Orthopedics & Related Res. 348 (2009). These issues are considered in greater detail in Part II.C., infra.

10. *Informed consent to psychotherapy.* The imposition of liability on psychotherapists for failure to obtain informed consent has been relatively

rare. But see *Osheroff v. Chestnut Lodge* and *Burgus v. Rush Presbyterian St. Luke's Medical Center*, discussed supra in Chapter Three, Parts II.A.2.b. and II.B.1.b, respectively, where a lack of informed consent was alleged. This result is undoubtedly explained in large part by the evidentiary problems that generally confront the client-plaintiff in the proof of causation and damages. Putting aside these practical difficulties, are there not numerous situations in everyday practice that at least technically violate the rights of a client to give informed consent? To what extent would the doctrine of informed consent require disclosure in the following situations?

(a) There is a substantial body of expert opinion that long-term outpatient psychotherapy involves a significant risk of "negative" effects. See Susan A. Nolan, *Negative Treatment Effects in Dyadic Psychotherapy: A Focus on Prevention and Intervention Strategies*, 34 J. Contemp. Psychotherapy 311, 311–12 (2004). Is there an obligation on the part of the therapist to always disclose the risk of these effects prior to the commencement of a prolonged course of treatment? Recall that it is very difficult to anticipate all such effects and predict the likelihood of their occurrence.

(b) In some instances a client who is close to decompensation may not tolerate intense psychoanalysis or fully understand the mechanisms involved. See Saks & Golshan, supra. One of the risks in these cases is that the analysis will in fact trigger decompensation. Must this risk always be communicated when, in the analyst's view, there is a possibility that the analysis will result in decompensation?

(c) An established novelist has for some time suffered from intermittent bouts of anxiety and occasional episodes of depression. The novelist consults a therapist to explore the possibilities of treatment. At the initial interview, the novelist expresses some fear that successful treatment might detract from or at least reduce his creative abilities. In response to a direct question as to the risks of the proposed treatment, the therapist answers, "To the extent that your creativity is the result of some pathology, there may be some loss, but your true creativity will be enhanced by the removal of blocks, inhibitions, and distortions associated with your anxiety and depression." Would this reply constitute a sufficient disclosure of the risks inherent in the therapy?

2. Exceptions to the Duty to Disclose

CANTERBURY V. SPENCE

United States Court of Appeals, District of Columbia Circuit, 1972.
464 F.2d 772.

[The main body of the opinion is set out in the preceding Section.]

VI

Two exceptions to the general rule of disclosure have been noted by the courts. Each is in the nature of a physician's privilege not to disclose, and the reasoning underlying them is appealing. Each, indeed, is but a recognition that, as important as is the patient's right to know, it is greatly outweighed by the magnitudinous circumstances giving rise to the privilege. The first comes into play when the patient is unconscious or otherwise incapable of consenting, and harm from a failure to treat is imminent and outweighs any harm threatened by the proposed treatment. When a genuine emergency of that sort arises, it is settled that the impracticality of conferring with the patient dispenses with need for it. Even in situations of that character the physician should, as current law requires, attempt to secure a relative's consent if possible. But if time is too short to accommodate discussion, obviously the physician should proceed with the treatment.

The second exception obtains when risk-disclosure poses such a threat of detriment to the patient as to become unfeasible or contraindicated from a medical point of view. It is recognized that patients occasionally become so ill or emotionally distraught on disclosure as to foreclose a rational decision, or complicate or hinder the treatment, or perhaps even pose psychological damage to the patient. Where that is so, the cases have generally held that the physician is armed with a privilege to keep the information from the patient, and we think it clear that portents of that type may justify the physician in action he deems medically warranted. The critical inquiry is whether the physician responded to a sound medical judgment that communication of the risk information would present a threat to the patient's well-being.

The physician's privilege to withhold information for therapeutic reasons must be carefully circumscribed, however, for otherwise it might devour the disclosure rule itself. The privilege does not accept the paternalistic notion that the physician may remain silent simply because divulgence might prompt the patient to forego therapy the physician feels the patient really needs. That attitude presumes instability or perversity for even the normal patient, and runs counter to the foundation principle that the patient should and ordinarily can make the choice for himself. Nor does the privilege contemplate operation save where the patient's reaction to risk information, as reasonably foreseen by the physician, is menacing. And even in a situation of that kind, disclosure to a close relative with a view to securing consent to the proposed treatment may be the only alternative open to the physician.

QUESTIONS AND COMMENTS

1. *Scope of the exception.* Non-disclosure, under the *Canterbury v. Spence* formulation, is justified in two instances: first, when the patient is unconscious or otherwise incapacitated and a medical emergency exists; and, second, when disclosure is likely to cause the patient to become so "ill or emotionally distraught" as to "foreclose a rational decision," "complicate or hinder the treatment," or perhaps "pose psychological damage to the patient."

The second exception raises several problems of interpretation. What is the requisite nature and level of illness or emotional distress that can invoke this exception? Because this is a prediction on the part of the health care provider, how certain must the provider be and on what can or should this prediction be based? Should the exception be construed to preclude only those situations where the disclosure itself is expected to cause the client to become emotionally distraught, or does it include those clients who, because of their mental disorder, already have an irrational fear of the treatment (i.e., the irrationality is an underlying feature or symptom of the mental disorder)? See Ben A. Rich, *Prognostication in Clinical Medicine*, 23 J. Legal Med. 297, 329 (2002).

Also, what constitutes a "rational" decision? Because decisions often reflect both rational judgments and less-than-rational thinking, to what degree must rational decision-making be precluded? Must it be totally absent? To what degree must the treatment be complicated or hindered? To just some degree or fully? Does this include the delivery of the treatment, or is limited to the impact of the treatment? Can the two be separated when psychotherapy is involved? What is the degree and type of "psychological damage" that must be shown to justify non-disclosure? Would the risk of depression be a sufficient justification? Must the possible depression be at least of a moderate or severe nature? A risk of anxiety? Would anticipation of a severe but transient anxiety reaction justify non-disclosure?

2. *Rules in other jurisdictions.* The California Supreme Court has articulated the disclosure exception in somewhat different terms. This court has observed:

A disclosure need not be made beyond that required within the medical community when a doctor can prove by a preponderance of the evidence he relied upon facts which would demonstrate to a reasonable man the disclosure would have so seriously upset the patient that the patient would not have been able to dispassionately weigh the risks of refusing to undergo the recommended treatment.

Cobbs v. Grant, 502 P.2d 1 (Cal. 1972).

Other courts have allowed the privilege of nondisclosure "where an explanation of every risk attendant upon a treatment procedure may well result in alarming a patient who is already apprehensive and who may, as a result, refuse to undertake surgery or treatment in which there is minimal risk." *Woods v. Brumlop*, 377 P.2d 520, 525 (N.M. 1962). See also *Arato v. Avedon*, 858 P.2d 598, 610 (1993) (recognizing a "therapeutic exception" and permitting expert testimony to the effect that "the standard of medical practice cautioned against disclosing to pancreatic cancer patients specific life expectancy data unless the patient directly requested such information"). Can an exception framed in these terms be applied without devouring the disclosure rule itself? Given the current widespread expectation of informed consent, do you think a twenty–first–century court would rule this way?

3.   *Waiver of the right.* May a client waive the right to be informed (e.g., the client tells the therapist to "do whatever you think is best" or says "I don't care"), and can the therapist rely on such a waiver? This issue has not been conclusively resolved; however, the California Supreme Court has stated in *dicta*: "[A] medical doctor need not make disclosure of risks when the patient requests that he not be informed." *Cobbs v. Grant,* 502 P.2d 1, 12 (Cal. 1972). Must a client be competent to make such a waiver and, if so, how does the therapist determine and establish that the client is indeed competent? What information must be provided to the client and what steps must be taken to ensure that the client makes an informed decision regarding this waiver? Should a therapist treating a client with a mental disorder assume that such a statement is an indication of a lack of decision-making capacity? Why should a client with a mental disorder be less able to waive the right to informed consent when many individuals prefer to defer to their health care provider in general?

4.   *Hypotheticals.* The exceptions permitting non-disclosure of risks may have particular relevance when the patient is mentally ill. Assume the following: a hospitalized psychiatric patient, suffering from a number of phobias and delusions, believes that death will inevitably follow any prolonged period of impotence. In addition to the psychiatric disorder, the patient also suffers from high blood pressure. The best drug to treat his high blood pressure sometimes causes erectile dysfunction. Would the treating physician be justified in prescribing the drug without disclosing to the patient the risk of impotence? Does it matter that the warnings accompanying the drug state, "Do not stop using this drug without first consulting your doctor. Your condition may become worse if the medication is suddenly stopped." Does your opinion change if the individual is being seen on an outpatient basis?

Assume now that a person with a psychotic disorder who is not informed of the risk of tardive dyskinesia, a condition marked by involuntary muscle movements that can occur in a small percentage of cases (see Chapter One). The physician had determined that disclosing this side effect to the patient was not "medically feasible" because had he known of the risk of this side effect, he probably would have refused the treatment "no matter how minimal the risk and how great the need for the medication." Is nondisclosure justifiable under these circumstances? See *Barclay v. Campbell*, 704 S.W.2d 8 (Tex. 1986) (reversing a lower court opinion dismissing the informed consent claim of a person who developed tardive dyskinesia, because "[t]he issue is not whether [the patient] could have been influenced in making a decision whether to give or withhold consent to the procedure had he known of the risk [but] whether a 'reasonable person' could have been influenced in making a decision whether to give or withhold consent to the procedure had he known of the risk.")

5. *Misrepresentation compared to nondisclosure.* Does the privilege to withhold information also allow a therapist to misrepresent the nature of the treatment or diagnosis to a client with a mental disorder to induce the client to undergo needed therapy? In the somewhat unusual case of *Kraus v. Spielberg*, 236 N.Y.S.2d 143 (Sup. Ct. 1962), the plaintiff, who had a tuberculosis phobia, consulted a physician because of acute stomach pains. To induce the patient to agree to needed chemotherapy, the plaintiff was led to believe that the tuberculosis had spread to her stomach. In fact, however, the doctor had not verified the exact location of the tubercular condition. The plaintiff consented to the therapy and later suffered unpleasant side effects. Finding that the misrepresentation was necessary to induce the plaintiff to undergo the treatment, the court held for the defendant. Is it likely that such a case would be decided the same way today in light of the evolution of the doctrine of informed consent?

6. *Informed consent and psychotherapy.* Full disclosure of the benefits and risks of psychotherapy can be detrimental to client outcomes in some circumstances. Two psychiatrists assert:

> An overly detailed informed consent presentation can stifle the establishment of initial rapport with a suffering individual in crisis, who needs but is already fearful of therapeutic support. Furthermore, too much emphasis on the pitfalls of psychotherapy could be negatively suggestive, or experienced by the patient as discouraging, thereby leading to more entangled negative therapeutic issues than necessary or desirable. Thus, misapplied informed consent can paradoxically undermine the tenets of good psychotherapy.

John O. Beahrs & Thomas G. Gutheil, *Informed Consent in Psychotherapy*, 158 Am. J. Psychotherapy 4, 6 (2001). See also Rebecca Erwin Wells & Ted J. Kaptchuk, *To Tell the Truth, the Whole Truth, May Do Patients Harm: The Problem of the Nocebo Effect for Informed Consent*, 12(3) Amer. J. Bioethics 22 (2012) (asserting that providing a detailed enumeration of every possible adverse effect, especially subjective self-appraised symptoms, can itself induce adverse effects through an expectancy mechanism known as the "nocebo effect" and to minimize this response "contextualized informed consent" should be employed). However, it can also be argued that building the client's trust in the therapist is one of the keys to successful psychotherapy, and deception or nondisclosure may undercut this trust, miss an opportunity to gain an enhanced understanding of the client's fears and concerns, and reflect a tendency to underestimate the competence of individuals with a mental disorder.

B. OTHER ELEMENTS NECESSARY TO ESTABLISH A CLAIM

1. Causation

Mere non-disclosure of a risk is not sufficient to impose liability on the therapist. Liability results only if an *injury* occurs that would not have occurred *but for* the non-disclosure. Thus, a client must prove that if the risk of injury had been disclosed, he would not have consented to the therapy that resulted in the injury. "Causation" is the shorthand legal term used to describe the relationship that must exist between the breach of a duty (e.g., non-disclosure of a material fact) and the resulting injury.

In determining causation, the trier of fact can either focus on the likely decision the particular plaintiff would have made (a subjective test) or on what clients similarly situated would ordinarily decide (an objective test) had the requisite disclosure been made. The following excerpt from *Canterbury v. Spence* establishes the majority rule.

CANTERBURY V. SPENCE
United States Court of Appeals, District of Columbia Circuit, 1972.
464 F.2d 772.

[The main body of the opinion is set forth supra].

VII

*   *   *

A causal connection exists when, but only when, disclosure of significant risks incidental to treatment would have resulted in a decision against it. The patient obviously has no complaint if he would have submitted to the therapy notwithstanding awareness that the risk was one of its perils. On the other hand, the very purpose of the disclosure rule is to protect the patient against consequences which, if known, he would have avoided by foregoing the treatment. The more difficult question is whether the factual issue on causality calls for an objective or a subjective determination.

It has been assumed that the issue is to be resolved according to whether the factfinder believes the patient's testimony that he would not have agreed to the treatment if he had known of the danger which later ripened into injury. We think a technique which ties the factual conclusion on causation simply to the assessment of the patient's credibility is unsatisfactory. . . . [W]hen causality is explored at a post-injury trial with a professedly uninformed patient, the question whether he actually would have turned the treatment down if he had known the risks is purely hypothetical: "Viewed from the point at which he had to decide, would the patient have decided differently had he known something he did not know?" And the answer which the patient supplies hardly represents more than a guess, perhaps tinged by the circumstance that the uncommunicated hazard has in fact materialized.

In our view, this method of dealing with the issue on causation comes in second-best. It places the physician in jeopardy of the patient's hindsight and bitterness. It places the factfinder in the position of deciding whether a speculative answer to a hypothetical question is to be credited. It calls for a subjective determination solely on testimony of a patient-witness shadowed by the occurrence of the undisclosed risk.

Better it is, we believe, to resolve the causality issue on an objective basis: in terms of what a prudent person in the patient's position would have decided if suitably informed of all perils bearing significance. If adequate disclosure could reasonably be expected to have caused that person to decline the treatment because of the revelation of the kind of risk or danger that resulted in harm, causation is shown, but otherwise not. The patient's testimony is relevant on that score of course but it would not threaten to dominate the findings.

QUESTIONS AND COMMENTS

1. *Causation vs. materiality.* Causation must be distinguished from the element of materiality. Material risks under *Canterbury*, as discussed previously, are those to which a reasonable person is "likely to attach significance . . . in deciding whether or not to forego the proposed therapy." *Canterbury v. Spence,* 464 F.2d 772, 787 (D.C. Cir. 1972). Not all material risks, of course, would prompt a reasonable person to refuse therapy and, in such a case, disclosure would be irrelevant to the reasonable person's final decision. As an example of this distinction: "[I]t would be reasonable to conclude that a patient who required brain surgery to survive would not have refused it even had he known of an undisclosed risk of speech impediment. At the same time the risk of a speech impediment could well be deemed to constitute nondisclosure of a material fact." Jon R. Waltz & Thomas W. Scheuneman, *Informed Consent to Therapy,* 64 Nw. U. L. Rev. 628, 648 (1970).

2. *Objective and subjective tests of causation.* Basically, two approaches—either an objective or a subjective test—can be used to determine the element of causation. Whichever test is applied, the determination is a question for the trier of fact. However, the choice of either the objective or subjective test will determine the standard by which the trier of fact makes its determination. Under the objective test adopted by the court in *Canterbury v. Spence,* the fact-finder will be called upon to determine causation in terms of the effect that non-disclosure of a material risk would have for a hypothetical reasonable person in the plaintiff's position. This test has been adopted by most jurisdictions.

Under the subjective test, fact-finders focus on the plaintiff before them to determine whether that individual would have foregone the therapy if the risk had been disclosed. Thus, the "subjective" approach is likely to focus on the plaintiff's testimony. Here, the key is the plaintiff's credibility as judged by the fact-finder. Only a minority of courts have adopted this approach. See *Zalazar v. Vercimak*, 633 N.E.2d 1223 (Ill. App. Ct. 1993); *Scott v. Bradford*, 606 P.2d 554 (Okla.1979); *Arena v. Gingrich*, 733 P.2d 75 (Or. Ct. App. 1987).

2. Damages

As has been pointed out, generally a successful plaintiff will establish that a material risk of the therapy was not disclosed and that a reasonable person in the plaintiff's position would not have consented to the therapy had the risk been disclosed. What remains to be considered is the measure of damages applicable to this type of case. While few cases have addressed this question, it has generally been assumed that a successful plaintiff is entitled to damages to compensate for the loss or injury resulting from the risk that materialized. Thus, the measure of damages is generally the same as in a malpractice case. It has been argued that this rule is unduly harsh from the perspective of a therapist where the treatment provided did not deviate from the standard of care, and that the recovery should be reduced by an amount attributable to the benefit received from this treatment. Further, if the plaintiff inevitably would have suffered physical deterioration had he received no therapy whatsoever, that factor would reduce the amount of damages that can be recovered.

In addition, as noted earlier, in the few jurisdictions that treat the doctrine of informed consent as a variant of an action in battery, because the basis of the claim is an "unauthorized touching," the therapist can be liable for at least nominal monetary damages even if the plaintiff suffered no actual injury. Also, because battery is viewed as an intentional tort, the defendant can be assessed punitive or exemplary damages. However, most courts will not impose exemplary damages unless the health care provider was guilty of actual malice.

Prevailing rules on damages in some jurisdictions also significantly limit the impact of the informed consent doctrine. Unless some *physical injury* results from the failure to obtain informed consent, it is unlikely that a client can recover anything more than nominal damages. In a number of states, mental distress, fright, shock, humiliation, or similar violations of psychological integrity do not ordinarily constitute compensable injury unless accompanied by physical impact. As a result, conventional psychotherapists in such jurisdictions, unless they also use treatment modalities such as drugs that can cause physical harm, are relatively immune from liability. Undoubtedly, this explains in part the relative absence of reported cases against non-medically trained psychotherapists for a failure to secure the client's informed consent. It also explains why behavioral science researchers, as discussed below in Part III, despite numerous reported violations of the requirements of informed consent, have escaped liability. However, the trend is clearly toward recognizing psychological harm as a sufficient basis for the recovery of monetary damages even when not associated with a physical injury. With these considerations in mind consider the following hypothetical fact situation:

> A client consults a psychotherapist to overcome his flying phobia, which in view of his occupational need to travel is proving to be an increasing handicap to his professional advancement. The therapist agrees to treat the client, and over the next three months gives him a series of desensitization procedures coupled with hypnotherapy.
>
> The client is informed that he has made material progress and that the next step is to take a short flight. The client is not alerted to the possibility that he will feel great anxiety during the flight. In fact, the therapist assures him that he is entirely ready to take the next step. Pursuant to the therapist's recommendations, the client secures a ticket and boards an airline flight to the next city. Shortly after takeoff, in spite of the client's use of an app designed to facilitate self-hypnosis, the client experiences a severe anxiety attack. By the time the airplane lands thirty minutes later, the client is in a state of total collapse. He is taken by ambulance to the nearest hospital and is placed under sedation. Upon release a week later, the client remains in a highly agitated and anxious state, which is accompanied by insomnia. As a result of this condition he is absent from work for the next three weeks. Upon his return to work, he learns that during his absence he was considered but rejected for a promotion, on the grounds that his records indicate that he has health problems. Badly shaken by the experience and somewhat angry at the therapist for having encouraged him to take the flight, he consults an attorney to inquire whether he has any basis to sue the therapist and what damages he can recover.

What is the attorney likely to advise? Would the result be different in a jurisdiction that requires physical injury for an award of damages?

Because of these limitations on damages, some commentators have proposed that an informed consent remedy should be recognized for the resulting deprivation of choice, either through the imposition of dignitary tort damages or damages for the anguish of choice deprivation. See Margaret A. Berger & Aaron D. Twerski, *Uncertainty and Informed Choice: Unmasking Daubert*, 104 Mich. L. Rev. 257, 280 (2005).

C. ISSUES PERTAINING TO CLIENT UNDERSTANDING AND ASSENT

1. Introduction

In its original form, a health care provider needed nothing more than a patient's assent to the proposed treatment, with a failure to obtain this assent subjecting the therapist to liability for a claim sounding in battery. The modern doctrine, on the other hand, requires that the assent be an *informed* one.

The elements of informed consent are thus twofold. First, the therapist must disclose information pertaining to the material benefits and risks of the proposed therapy and possible alternative treatments. Second, as under the original doctrine, the client must agree to undergo the therapy.

Two types of problems arise in connection with the element of assent. One, what actions or expressions on the part of the client will suffice to establish assent? Must assent be in writing? Must it be witnessed by a third party or notarized? Will a nod of the head, a hand gesture suffice? Does silence constitute agreement? Generally, the legal system will accept relatively informal expressions of assent, provided the intent is clear.

A second and more complex problem relates to the level of client understanding that must accompany the assent. More specifically, does the legal system require that the client understand all aspects of the nature and degree of risk that was disclosed, the related benefits, and the relevant alternatives? On a related point, can the requisite level of understanding be presumed from the client's expression of assent, or must the therapist establish its existence? These interrelated issues are explored in the materials that follow.

Both judicial rulings and the writings of legal commentators have advanced the view that the needed understanding is established when a practitioner provides the client with "relevant and material information regarding the physician's proposed treatment" that "enables the [client] to knowingly consent to—or to reject—the treatment that the health care provider is proposing." William G. Cobb, *Defending the Informed Consent Case*, 72 Def. Couns. J. 330 (2005). What this leaves unanswered, however, is whether the client must have actual rather than imputed knowledge. Consider for a moment the legal efficacy of an assent given by a client who has been fully informed of all relevant risks, benefits, and alternatives but who, unknown to the health care provider, fails to adequately understand the information received. Two different approaches can be employed in dealing with this problem.

One alternative focuses on the therapist's disclosure. If that disclosure is deemed adequate, in the sense that an ordinary (i.e., reasonable) client would comprehend the information transmitted, awareness will be imputed without regard to the client's *actual level of comprehension*. This is the approach that the *Canterbury* court advocated. In a footnote, the court observed that "the physician discharges the duty when he makes a reasonable effort to convey sufficient information *although the patient, without fault of the physician, may not fully grasp it*." 464 F.2d 772, 780 n.15 (D.C. Cir. 1972) [emphasis added]. Thus, under this approach, the therapist has discharged his duty when he has made full disclosure in terms that would be comprehensible to the average (i.e., reasonable) client.

Under the other approach, a client's assent would not be effective unless she had *actual* knowledge and understanding of the therapist's disclosure. In the event of litigation, then, the fact-finder would be required to determine whether this client had understood what the therapist had told her. One commentator has explained the rationale for this approach:

> Even when the information presented is adequate, the consenting process may be nothing more than a "ritual" if the patient-subject remains "uneducated and uncomprehending." To avoid this result, the physician could be held responsible for taking reasonable steps to ascertain whether the information presented has been understood, so that if it has not he may supplement it as needed or may convey the same information in a manner more comprehensible to the particular patient.

Alexander Morgan Capron, *Informed Consent in Catastrophic Disease Research and Treatment*, 123 U. Pa. L. Rev. 340, 414 (1974).

The weight of legal opinion has, however, rejected this "subjective" approach on a variety of grounds. It has been noted:

> There is no question that testing patients' understanding of the knowledge conveyed to them about their condition and treatment alternatives is time consuming, and therefore costly. Testing raises the cost of physicians' services to individual patients, and it reduces the number of patients the physicians can see, thereby denying or delaying physicians' services to other patients.

Cathy J. Jones, *Autonomy and Informed Consent in Medical Decisionmaking: Toward a New Self–Fulfilling Prophecy*, 47 Wash. & Lee L. Rev. 379, 414 (1990).

COMMENTS AND QUESTIONS

As a practical matter, the question of whether a client's awareness should be measured objectively or subjectively has rarely arisen in modern informed consent cases. The reasons for this are twofold. First, modern cases have emphasized the element of disclosure. To the extent that the therapist fails to inform the client adequately, the question of client understanding is typically never reached as the case can be disposed of on the failure-to-disclose ground. Thus, the scope of the client's awareness is only an issue if the fact-finder determines or the client acknowledges that the therapist had indeed provided an adequate disclosure, and the client contends that he did not understand its content. Cases of this type are, however, very hard to win and thus rarely pursued, in part because the burden of proof to establish a lack of understanding falls on the client-plaintiff, and in part because it can be difficult to prove a lack of understanding retrospectively, especially as the client typically indicated originally that he understood this information in assenting to the commencement of treatment.

Moreover, a client's case will be be weakened by the dual contentions that there was insufficient disclosure and that the client did not understand what was disclosed. While these are not necessarily inconsistent positions, the plaintiff's lawyer will be concerned that emphasizing the client's lack of comprehension may buttress the defendant's contentions that there was full disclosure and that the client, through no fault of the therapist, failed to adequately attend to, explore, or question what was said. Would you pursue such a case?

2. The Determination of Client Assent: Evidentiary Problems

As has been noted, consent consists of the dual elements of understanding and assent. To establish informed consent, it must be shown that the client understood the benefits and risks of a proposed treatment and alternatives and assented to the treatment provided. Thus, in the event of litigation, the fact-finder must determine whether the client's expressions of assent in their totality (both verbal and nonverbal) support a conclusion that the client consented to the treatment. The test for client assent is an objective therapist standard. Under this test, the question is whether a reasonable therapist under similar circumstances would have concluded from the client's statements and behavior that the client understood the communicated benefits, risks, and alternatives and manifested a willingness to undergo the therapeutic procedure. Any other approach would subject the therapist to the unfair risk that a client who would have appeared to manifest assent to a reasonable practitioner was, nevertheless, also subtly signaling unrecognized or unexpressed reservations about the treatment.

When divorced from the question of knowledge, however, the element of assent is generally not likely to be an issue. The mere fact that the client continues to interact with the therapist typically indicates assent to at least some form of treatment. The crucial question for the fact-finder is usually not whether the client assented in the narrow sense, but whether the assent was coupled with sufficient knowledge and awareness. The client will contend that because of inadequate disclosure, he was not made aware of the risks of the treatment, while the therapist may have a substantially different recollection of what was disclosed. To lower the risk of erroneous recollection, a therapist would be wise to keep a written summary of the information communicated to the client and a written or otherwise memorialized record of the client's assent.

The primary instance when the element of assent may be an issue is when language or cultural barriers exist that cloud communication or the client asserts that she was pressured or coerced into assenting to treatment by the therapist. As is discussed generally in Chapter Nine, Part IV, infra, a client may feel a need to assent to treatment to escape an onerous situation (e.g., to obtain discharge from or avoid admission to a psychiatric facility, to avoid sanctions pursuant to an outpatient commitment order or as part of a plea bargain to avoid more serious criminal charges, or to obtain privileges within a correctional institution or some other facility). Additionally, family members or other involved individuals may push hard for assent. Alternatively, if non-written assent was obtained, the meaning of an ambiguous indication of assent may later be disputed.

QUESTIONS AND COMMENTS

1. *Empirical data on information recall.* What are the implications of various studies showing that within a relatively short period of time, patients frequently cannot recall much of what they are told during the disclosure process? One review article noted, "Data repeatedly show that patients remember little of the information disclosed during the informed consent process and that their level of comprehension is often overestimated." Daniel E. Hall et al., *Informed Consent for Clinical Treatment*, 184 CMAJ 533, 534 (2012). For instance, one often-cited study that involved 200 cancer patients found that one day after receiving relevant information on the risks of chemotherapy, "[o]nly 60 per cent understood the purpose and the nature of the procedure, and only 55 per cent correctly listed even one major risk or complication." Barry R. Cassileth et al., *Informed Consent—Why Are Its Goals Imperfectly Realized?*, 302 New Eng. J. Med. 896 (1980). See also Alan R. Tait, *Parental Recall of Anesthesia Information: Informing the Practice of Informed Consent*, 112 Anesthesia & Analgesia 918 (2011) (in a survey of 263 parents, 50% had no recall of the risks of administering anesthesia to their child).

Do such studies call into question the practical utility of the informed consent doctrine? Should these types of findings cause courts to modify the doctrine? Or do these findings call into question the adequacy of current means used to obtain informed consent (which may involve a nurse or even an administrative assistant providing the patient with a form containing a brief summary of the proposed procedure and possible risks while awaiting the arrival of the physician), with the process often a cursory, pro forma event that fails to engage and educate the patient? What distractions are likely to be present at the time at which informed consent is obtained that undercut a patient's attention, understanding, and ability to retain the information conveyed? Should practitioners be required to question their clients both initially and after the passage of a given period of time regarding their level of understanding?

2. *Statutory requirements.* A number of states have enacted statutes that spell out the evidentiary requirements for obtaining informed consent to medical or surgical procedures. Typically, these statutes require that the attending physician provide the patient with a document that sets forth the procedures of the treatment to be undertaken and the major risks. At the same time, they require that patients sign a document acknowledging that the disclosure of information occurred and that all their questions pertaining to the treatment were answered. In turn, the fulfillment of these documentary requirements constitutes either *prima facie* or conclusive evidence that informed consent to treatment was given. The Iowa statute illustrates this approach:

> A consent in writing to any medical or surgical procedure or course of procedures in patient care which meets the requirements of this section shall create a presumption that informed consent was given. A consent in writing meets the requirements of this section if it:
>
> 1. Sets forth in general terms the nature and purpose of the procedure or procedures, together with the known risks, if any, of death, brain damage, quadriplegia, paraplegia, the loss or loss of function of any organ or limb, or disfiguring scars associated with such procedure or procedures, with the probability of each such risk if reasonably determinable.
>
> 2. Acknowledges that the disclosure of that information has been made and that all questions asked about the procedure or procedures have been answered in a satisfactory manner.
>
> 3. Is signed by the patient for whom the procedure is to be performed, or if the patient for any reason lacks legal capacity to consent, is signed by a person who has legal authority to consent on behalf of that patient in those circumstances.

Iowa Code Ann. § 147.137.

Note that the Iowa statute only requires disclosure of certain itemized major risks. Also, note that the statute does not require any information on alternative treatments. What application, if any, would this statute have to practitioners of psychotherapy? How would you respond to the argument that the passage of such laws shows that lawyers have turned the "doctor-patient" relationship into a "doctor-litigant" relationship?

In those states with a statute regulating informed consent, the question of legislative preemption may arise. A judge may have to determine whether the legislature has preempted the field or whether there is room for judicially developed approaches and remedies to supplement the statutory provisions.

3. *Effect of a signed informed consent document.* Clients who have signed a form that exhaustively lists the risks and hazards of a given therapy might say (legitimately) that although they signed the form, they did not, in fact, understand its content. Should courts allow plaintiffs to make such an argument in support of their case? The answer to this question would presumably turn on whether, under the law of the state controlling the disposition of the case, the signing of such a statement is *conclusive* evidence of informed consent. If it is only *prima facie* evidence, the client's signature would not preclude a contention that the client was not, in fact, adequately informed. This suggests that for maximum protection, the therapist should do more than obtain the client's written consent on a form that recites the significant risks. The therapist should also verbally explain the risks and alternatives, ask for and answer any questions that the client may have, and then enter a notation in the client's file recounting the nature of the conversation.

In *Hondroulis v. Schuhmacher*, 553 So. 2d 398 (La. 1988), the court held that the Louisiana informed consent statute, which mandated that patients be provided with a written listing of all potential complications that might result from any medical procedure, and which must be signed by the patient, merely created a presumption of disclosure, which may be rebutted by proof that material facts were not adequately disclosed via the consent form.

4. *Standardized forms.* Note that standardized consent forms that merely recite that the client has been informed of "all risks" are likely to be of little legal protection. Valid consent requires disclosure of the specific risks and available alternative therapies.

Therefore, a summary consent form merely attesting that "all risks" have been communicated will not foreclose the admission of evidence that there was not, in fact, a sufficient disclosure. Not surprisingly, fairly detailed standardized consent forms are now widely used. Illustrative of the standardized forms that have been developed is the one set out below for obtaining consent to electroshock therapy (ECT). How adequate is this disclosure?

CONSENT TO ELECTRIC SHOCK THERAPY

A.M.

Date _____ Time _____ P.M.

1. I authorize Dr. _____, and assistants of his choice, to administer electric shock treatment, and relaxant drugs and other medication, to *(name of patient)* and to continue such treatment at such intervals as he and his assistants may deem advisable.

2. I understand that this treatment consists of passing a controlled electric current between two electrodes applied to the patient's temples. In some instances, the patient may be given medication prior to

treatment to reduce tension and produce muscular relaxation. I understand that the patient will not feel the electric current and will feel no pain. When the electric current is administered, the patient becomes unconscious and has strong convulsive muscular contractions which may last from 35 to 50 seconds. The patient gradually regains consciousness and his confusion clears within 15 to 60 minutes. The patient may experience headache and nausea.

3.   I understand that the treatments may cause temporary confusion and memory impairment. I also understand that certain risks and complications are involved in the treatment. The most common risk is fracture and dislocation of the limbs and vertebrae. I acknowledge that these and other risks and complications of this procedure have been explained to me.

4.   In addition to the foregoing, the strict care which will be required immediately following treatment and during convalescence has been fully explained to me.

5.   The alternative methods of treatment have been explained and no guarantee or assurance has been given by anyone as to the results that may be obtained.

SIGNED _____

WITNESS _____

5.   *Revocation of consent.* The right to consent implies the right to revoke any consent that has been given. Thus, clients may withdraw their consent at any time before the treatment commences or has been concluded. However, under the law of most states this principle does not apply to the consent given by a patient entering a psychiatric institution through a voluntary admission procedure. Typically, laws governing admission to psychiatric facilities stipulate that voluntary patients may be forcibly detained for a few days even after they have withdrawn their voluntary admission consent. See Chapter Eight, Part IV.E., *infra.*

3.   Psychiatric Client Consent

Recall that the doctrine of informed consent incorporates two elements: (1) the communication of relevant information and (2) assent predicated upon an adequate understanding of the communicated information. The application of this model in the mental health treatment context, however, raises particular problems. Clients with a mental illness and those with an intellectual disability may have impairments that diminish or interfere with the requisite comprehension. Persons with an intellectual disability typically have trouble understanding and processing complex information. Some mental illnesses also impair information reception and processing, cause the person to distort the information received, or impair the person's ability to communicate her choice of treatment. One commentator has provided an example of how mental illness can interfere with the giving of informed consent:

> [H]ow does one obtain consent from a severely ill catatonic schizophrenic who sits and stares at a blank wall all day, refusing to speak to anyone? Certainly if a patient is psychotic or hallucinating and cannot assimilate information about a proposed procedure, he does not have the capacity to reach a decision about the matter in question. Some mental patients are incapable of evaluating information in what most people would call a rational manner. A treatment decision might ordinarily be based on considerations of perceived personal objectives, or long-term versus short-term risks and benefits. But there are patients whose acceptance or rejection of a treatment is not made in relation to any "factual" information. To add to this dilemma, while a mental patient may refuse to give his consent to a procedure, his refusal may only be a manifestation of his illness, having little resemblance to his actual desires.

George J. Annas et al., *Informed Consent to Human Experimentation: The Subject's Dilemma* 152 (1977).

When it is clear that the client's condition precludes the giving of informed consent, non-emergency treatment cannot be administered without a judicial determination that the client is legally incompetent, with consent provided by an appointed guardian or other substitute decision maker. (The competency adjudication process and the mechanism for giving substituted consent are discussed in Chapter Nine.) Thus, unless the client has already been adjudicated to be incompetent, any substantial doubt as to the client's capacity to provide consent should call for the initiation of a substitute decision-making procedure by the mental health provider.

In some instances, however, the capacity of a particular client to give informed consent will not be altogether clear. Assessments are frequently complicated by the fact that "competency is not necessarily a fixed state that can be assessed with equivalent results at any one of a number of times. Like the patient's mental status as a whole, a patient's competency may fluctuate as a function of the natural course of his or her illness, response to treatment, psychodynamic factors[,] ... metabolic status, intercurrent illnesses, or the effects of medication." Paul S. Appelbaum & Loren H. Roth, *Clinical Issues in the Assessment of Competency*, 138 Am. J. Psychiatry 1462 (1981).

The clinician's assessment may be further clouded by the lack of clear legal guidelines as to what constitutes capacity to consent. See Chapter Nine, infra. Except for highly generalized judicial prescriptions, there are at the present time no detailed uniform standards governing the determination of decision-making *capacity* in the treatment context. The distinction between *competency* and *capacity* has been explained as follows:

> *Competence* is a legal construct: in most jurisdictions only a court can decide if a person is incompetent. Assessments of *capacity*, on the other hand, are relegated to medical or mental health professionals. Legislatures, in drafting competence statutes, may determine what type and degree of clinically assessed incapacity will allow a judge to declare an individual legally "incompetent." Theories of competence to make medical decisions focus on various criteria, the most common of which, and the ones adopted by the law, are cognitive. Although the law focuses on cognitive impairments, there are no uniform standards among the jurisdictions to identify the relevant abilities that, when impaired, constitute incompetence.

Jessica Wilen Berg et al., *Constructing Competence: Formulating Standards of Legal Competence to Make Medical Decisions*, 48 Rutgers L. Rev. 345, 348–49 (1996).

Whatever the governing legal standard, the determination of capacity to consent will, as a practical matter, need to be decided in most instances by the treating clinician or by an institutional review board or other body set up for such a purpose.

Exposure to liability under such circumstances is minimized, however, by the judicially announced rule that a "physician discharges the duty when he makes a reasonable effort to convey sufficient information although the patient, without fault of the physician, may not fully grasp it." *Canterbury v. Spence*, 464 F.2d 772, 780 n.15 (D.C. Cir. 1972). Thus if the clinical determination of decision-making capacity at the time of the giving of consent reflects an exercise of due care, those providing treatment will generally be insulated from liability even if the assessment is subsequently deemed to have been erroneous.

QUESTIONS AND COMMENTS

1. *Judicial criteria for substituted consent.* Some courts have refused to authorize treatment for an incompetent individual when the individual, during a prior lucid phase, objected to the particular form of treatment being considered. In *Conservatorship of Waltz*, 27 Cal. Rptr. 436 (Ct. App. 1986), an inpatient was found to be incompetent to give informed consent because of a psychotic fear reaction to even a discussion of the proposed ECT treatment. However, during periods when he was rational, the patient expressed what would be considered a normal fear of ECT. The opposition to treatment previously manifested while competent governed. The court held that "even though he has a mental illness which causes him to be paranoid about ECT and many other things, this fact alone cannot be used to negate the presence of a rational fear of ECT which causes him to refuse treatment even during nonpsychotic moments."

The issue in *Waltz* concerned an individual's capacity to give informed consent. As elaborated in Chapter Nine, different approaches have been adopted to deal with this problem. In some states there are proceedings to determine the individual's overall decision-making competency. In the absence of this competency, plenary power to consent to treatment can be delegated to a guardian or other substitute decision maker. Other states have adopted a *limited* guardianship approach, where the inquiry focuses on the individual's decision-making capacity with regard to a particular activity, and any subsequent decision-making authority assigned to a guardian is limited to related decisions. In some states, such as California, special statutory provisions govern the giving of consent to intrusive psychiatric treatment modalities. Finally, New York uses non-judicial Surrogate Decision Making Committees, composed of both professionals and interested lay people, to determine patients' capacity to give informed consent and to determine whether treatment is in their best interests by considering their values and preferences. N.Y. Mental Hyg. Law § 80.03–80.13.

Different procedures also have been adopted by the states to manage the administration of antipsychotic medications to prisoners. The procedures established by the state of Washington were sustained by the U.S. Supreme Court in *Washington v. Harper*, 494 U.S. 210 (1990), set out in Chapter Nine. Similarly, states have different approaches to and varying views on the administration of antipsychotic medication to involuntarily committed psychiatric patients. In Alaska, even if the patient is incompetent, the decision to refuse certain medications will be upheld unless a court finds that the drugs are in a patient's best interest and the treating physician has no less intrusive alternative treatment to offer. *Myers v. Alaska Psychiatric Inst.*, 138 P.3d 238, 240 (Alaska 2006).

2. *The capacity of individuals with a mental disorder to consent.* A few empirical studies have attempted to ascertain how well individuals with a mental disorder can understand treatment information. See Paul S. Appelbaum & Thomas Grisso, *The MacArthur Treatment Competence Study: I. Mental Illness and Competence to Consent to Treatment*, 19 Law & Hum. Behav. 105 (1995); Thomas Grisso & Paul S. Appelbaum, *The MacArthur Treatment Competence Study: III. Abilities of Patients to Consent to Psychiatric and Medical Treatment*, 19 Law & Hum. Behav. 149 (1995). Among the key findings from these studies are the following:

- Individuals undergoing hospitalization for the treatment of schizophrenia or depression displayed more deficits in their decision-making capacity than individuals hospitalized for nonpsychiatric medical problems.

- Nevertheless, about half of all patients with schizophrenia did well on standardized measures of decision-making capacity.

- Patients with schizophrenia did especially poorly when they were suffering from disturbances of thought and perception (e.g., disorganized thinking and delusions). Demographic factors (e.g., age, gender, race) and the presence of other psychiatric symptoms (e.g., anxiety) did not influence decision-making capacity.

- When patients with schizophrenia were retested after two weeks of treatment, those whose psychiatric symptoms had abated also experienced substantial improvement in their decision-making capacities.

- About three-fourths of patients hospitalized with depression performed well on standardized measures of decision-making.

- Medical patients hospitalized with potentially life-threatening conditions (ischemic heart disease) did about as well on standardized decision-making measures as did healthy persons living in the community; just a small fraction of these hospitalized patients had decision-making deficits.

3.   *Standardized measurements of capacity to consent.* The preceding note mentions "standardized measures of decision-making." This is a reference to efforts by mental health professionals to develop instruments to measure individuals' capacity to consent to treatment. Several instruments exist, but the findings summarized above used the MacArthur Treatment Competence Research Instruments, which were later refined to make them better suited for routine use by clinicians and resulted in the MacArthur Assessment Competence Assessment Tool-Treatment (MacCAT–T). A comprehensive summary of this work can be found in Thomas Grisso & Paul S. Appelbaum, Assessing Competence to Consent to Treatment: A Guide for Physicians and Other Health Professionals (1998).

III.   INFORMED CONSENT TO PARTICIPATE IN RESEARCH

A.   INTRODUCTION

The preceding section considered the doctrine of informed consent in the context of treatment. However, informed consent is typically also required in conjunction with research involving human participants. Unlike treatment, which is focused on enhancing the well-being of a patient, research studies involving human participants are primarily or wholly designed to develop or contribute to generalizable scientific or medical knowledge. Because the interests of the researcher and the research participant are thus potentially in conflict, special regulations have been developed to protect the rights of human study participants.

The evolution of professional and legal standards to control research involving human participants largely parallels the development of the doctrine of informed consent in the therapeutic treatment context. In the not-too-distant past, informed consent was not always obtained, or it was obtained in a deceptive manner. Researchers often assumed that harm was unlikely to result, particularly when psychological research was involved; that the benefits of these studies outweighed the risks to the participants, with the benefits based on the value of the research to human beings in general, not necessarily the research participants; and that if the nature of a study was explained to the research participants, it would bias and invalidate the results obtained.

It was not until the early 1960s that courts, legislatures, and professional organizations began to seriously search for methods to protect research participants. Much of the impetus for this activity came from the disclosure of abuses in various research studies. Between 1932 and 1972, for example, the U.S. Public Health Service conducted a study at the Tuskegee Institute in Alabama of the natural progression of untreated syphilis to learn more about its long-term effects. The participants in the study were poor black sharecroppers who had been previously infected with syphilis. They received free medical care, food, and burial insurance for their participation, a substantial inducement for them. The researchers neither told the men about their infections (they were told they were being treated for "bad blood") nor treated them for syphilis, even after a simple, very effective treatment—penicillin—became available in the 1940s. When this conduct was revealed, the researchers and the study were heavily criticized. In the social sciences, Stanley Milgram's obedience experiments, in which participants were expected to administer what they thought were painful electric shocks to other persons, also drew considerable criticism.

Although these experiments were not typical of biomedical and behavioral research in general, fear of such overzealousness in the cause of science has been a primary motive for the regulation of human-participant research. Today, consent must typically be obtained from individuals prior to their participation in a research study. See Barry Rosenfeld, *The Psychology of Competence and Informed Consent: Understanding Decision–Making with Regard to Clinical Research*, 30 Fordham Urb. L.J. 173 (2002).

The materials in this section will examine the legal regulation of both biomedical and behavioral research involving human participants. Because the risk to participants is ordinarily greater in biomedical research, most current regulations were promulgated with that type of research in mind. Nevertheless, under 45 C.F.R. § 46.102(d), *"[r]esearch* means a systematic investigation, including research development, testing and evaluation, designed to develop or contribute to generalizable knowledge." This definition encompasses both biomedical research—studies that attempt to find the biological causes of and best treatments for diseases and other physiological disorders, including (for example) the effects and effectiveness of psychotropic drugs—and behavioral research—studies that examine human attitudes, thought processes, and behavior, including (for example) how best to employ psychotherapy to modify dysfunctional human behavior.

B. OVERVIEW OF STATUTORY AND ADMINISTRATIVE REGULATION

Congress and several state legislatures have responded to the public concern over the propriety of experiments involving human participants by enacting related legislation. Congress has created two regulatory mechanisms, both under the aegis of the Department of Health and Human Services (HHS), to insure the proper conduct of human-participant research. Both the Food and Drug Act of 1938 (21 U.S.C. § 355) and the National Research Act of 1974 (42 U.S.C. §§ 2891–2892) empower the Secretary of HHS to promulgate regulations affecting research involving human participants.

Two principal checks on biomedical and behavioral research are created by the HHS regulations. First, researchers must submit detailed protocols describing their proposed research to an Institutional Review Board (IRB) made up of representatives drawn from different academic disciplines. Each institution receiving HHS funding for research must establish an IRB to oversee the conduct of all research involving human participants, empowered to prohibit or modify the research being proposed. 45 C.F.R. § 46.113. In reviewing proposals, the IRBs are under a mandate to insure that risks to human participants are minimized. Moreover, each proposal must reasonably balance the risk to human participants against the anticipated benefit of the research. 45 C.F.R. § 46.111(a)(1), (2). Where the proposed research involves participants who "are likely to be vulnerable to coercion or undue influence, such as children, prisoners, pregnant women, mentally disabled persons, or economically or educationally disadvantaged persons," additional safeguards must be included in the study to protect their rights and welfare. 45 C.F.R. § 46.111(b).

A second feature of the regulations is the requirement that researchers obtain informed consent from all human participants. 45 C.F.R. § 46.116. Much like therapists, researchers must disclose "any reasonably foreseeable risks or discomforts" and "appropriate alternative procedures or courses of treatment, if any, that might be advantageous" to the prospective research participant. Researchers must also inform participants that they may withdraw at any time. The list of associated requirements in obtaining informed consent is quite extensive.

The Food and Drug Act of 1938 creates a second area of federal regulation of human-participant research. The act empowers the Secretary of HHS to approve the use of investigational drugs and medical devices. All researchers administering investigational drugs and devices must certify that the informed consent of either the human participant or their proxies will be obtained. Regulations require consent by research participants or their legal representative except when four specific conditions are met, including "a life-threatening situation necessitating the use of the test article." 21 C.F.R. § 50.23.

A number of states, such as California and New York, have enacted legislation similar to the HHS regulations. See Cal. Penal Code §§ 2670–2678 (West 2012); N.Y. Pub. Health Law §§ 2440–2446 (McKinney 2013). Like the HHS regulations, both New York and California require participant's informed consent. Unlike the HHS regulations, both the California and New York statutes cover all medical research conducted within the state, not just research in institutions receiving state funding. Neither the California nor the New York statutes explicitly cover behavioral research (unlike the HHS regulations, which cover all human-participant research but do explicitly exempt several categories of behavioral research including surveys, educational testing, and observation of public behavior. 45 C.F.R. § 46.101(b)).

Neither federal nor most state regulations provide specific remedies for individuals injured while participating in research. HHS does deny funding to institutions with whom an offending researcher is affiliated, while California imposes criminal penalties and fines on medical researchers who fail to obtain participants' informed consent. Cal. Health & Safety Code § 24176 (West 2012). A private legal remedy may nevertheless be available to an injured participant under state tort law or conceivably under one of the federal civil rights statutes. See *Grimes v. Kennedy Krieger Inst., Inc.*, 782 A.2d 807 (Md. Ct. App. 2001). The scope of the Federal Civil Rights laws and their impact on the mental health treatment field is discussed in Chapter Three, supra.

QUESTIONS AND COMMENTS

1.   *Disclosure under HIPAA of PHI obtained in a research context.* A research institution is only subject to the Health Insurance Portability and Accountability Act (HIPAA) privacy rules if it is a covered entity. (HIPAA privacy provisions and the definition of "covered entity" are discussed in detail in Chapter Five, infra.) However, if the research facility is also involved in treatment and meets HIPAA's covered entity criteria it must comply with these privacy rules. This means that it can transfer personal health information (PHI) to another covered entity without a patient's authorization, but transfer of PHI to a non-covered entity requires the research participant's authorization. As a practical matter, however, such authorization will generally be obtained before admitting an individual into the research program. Such pre-admission authorization is permitted by HIPAA privacy rules (45 CFR § 164.508(b)(4)(i)), discussed in greater detail in Chapter Five, infra.

2.   *International standards.* An important contributing factor to the movement for reform—both in the U.S. and in other countries—was the

disclosure of human rights abuses carried out under the guise of scientific and medical experimentation by Nazi scientists and physicians during World War II. See Marian F. Ratnoff & Justin C. Smith, *Human Laboratory Animals: Martyrs for Medicine*, 36 Ford. L. Rev. 673, 679 (1968). The World Medical Association has been at the forefront of efforts to develop international standards for the control of human experimentation. One result of these efforts is the Helsinki Declaration, the sixth revision of which was issued in 2008, which sets out ethical principles regarding human experimentation. See Jon R. Waltz & Fred E. Inbau, *Medical Jurisprudence* 381–83 (1971); Edmund Pellegrino, *The Nazi Doctors and Nuremberg: Some Moral Lessons Revisited*, 127 Annals Internal Med. 307 (1997); Joseph E. Persico, *Nuremberg: Infamy on Trial* (1994).

The Tuskegee study and other abuses that stimulated the movement towards greater regulation of research involving human participants are discussed in Nathan Hershey and Robert D. Miller, *Human Experimentation and the Law* 153–56 (1976); see also Giselle Corbie–Smith, *The Continuing Legacy of the Tuskegee Syphilis Study: Considerations for Clinical Investigation*, 317 Am. J. Med. Sci. 5 (1999).

3. *HHS regulations.* The HHS regulations under the National Research Act delegate to each institution's IRB the power to prospectively review all consent forms and procedures. But the regulations do not indicate to what degree IRB representatives should monitor or intervene in the consent process to insure that research participants are truly informed. Some commentators have argued IRBs concentrate too heavily on the review and revision of consent forms, suggesting that participants might receive better protection if IRB representatives more frequently intervened in the consent process itself. See John A. Robertson, *Taking Consent Seriously: IRB Intervention in the Consent Process*, 4 IRB: A Rev. of Hum. Subject Res. 1 (1982) (citing a study by Gray (1975) in which 40% of participants signing consent forms did not know they were involved in research). See also James Flory & Ezekiel Emanuel, *Interventions to Improve Research Participants' Understanding in Informed Consent for Research: A Systematic Review*, 292 JAMA 1593 (2004) (concluding "investing additional effort in forms is . . . unlikely to have a large effect on understanding" and that "adding an extra meeting with a qualified person is the most reliable approach to improving understanding," while noting "lower educational attainment, mental illness, and perhaps advanced age are associated with lower understanding").

4. *Definition of "risk of harm."* Under the HHS regulations, determinations of the likely risks to human participants should have a significant impact on whether the IRB will approve proposed research. Accordingly, the definition of risk of harm will be pertinent to a court's determination of whether a researcher acted negligently. Neither state nor federal regulations, however, adequately define risk of harm. Under the HHS regulations "minimal risk" means "that the probability and magnitude of harm or discomfort anticipated in the research are not greater . . . than those ordinarily encountered in daily life or during the performance of routine

physical or psychological examinations or tests." 45 C.F.R. § 46.102(i). But such definitions provide little guidance to IRBs. Risk of harm would certainly include physical harm, but what kinds of psychological harm are included?

Some IRBs have sought to eliminate this uncertainty by providing a definition of "risk of harm." For example, the University of Illinois IRB provides researchers with lists of examples. One list identifies research involving minimal risk, while a second list covers research involving greater than minimal risk (e.g., studies of the effects of prescribed anti-anxiety medications on driving skills).

5. *Self-regulation.* To a certain degree, researchers police their own activities through a process of self-examination, which is normally a part of any legitimate scientific inquiry. That scientists are encouraged and often expected to publish the results of their studies also affects the procedures utilized in research (although it may also add pressures to "bend" ethical norms). With increasing frequency, medical and scientific journals will not publish the results of studies involving human participants if the studies were not conducted in conformance with ethical guidelines and did not receive prior IRB approval. Also, publication itself means that both the results and the research methods become available to the research community at large, which can then offer its own critique. The ethical codes and policy statements of professional organizations have also played a part in the process of self-regulation, particularly with regard to biomedical research. A recent concern is the publishing of research from other countries where standards for ethical research are limited or ignored. See Robert M. Sade, *Publication of Unethical Research Studies: The Importance of Informed Consent*, 75 Annals Thoracic Surgery 325 (2003) (noting that medical journal editors have debated this issue for years, with many editors ignoring the Declaration of Helsinki,statement that reports of research studies not in accordance with the Helsinki principles should not be accepted for publication).

C. PEOPLE WITH A MENTAL DISORDER AS RESEARCH PARTICIPANTS

1. Introduction

Few issues in the mental health field are as difficult to sort out as the standards that should regulate research involving persons who have a severe mental health problem. Often, such research is designed to develop new approaches to the treatment of mental disorders but may not provide any benefit to some participants and in fact may cause deterioration of some participants' mental status. The dilemma posed by this type of research has been described by a leading authority in the following terms:

Research into the etiology and treatment of severe mental disorders must often confront a difficult conundrum: persons suffering from these disorders—usually the only appropriate subjects for study—

may lack the capacity to consent to research. Thus the very illnesses from which they suffer appear to throw a roadblock in the path of developing better treatments. A recent court decision in New York suggests that it may not be easy to find ways around this problem.

Most persons with mental illness retain the capacity to make decisions, even during acute exacerbations. Patients in this group can choose for themselves whether to participate in research. However, some of the most severely affected patients—including those with treatment-resistant schizophrenia, psychotic depression, and Alzheimer's disease—lack sufficient decision-making capacity to understand, appreciate, or reason about joining a research project, or they may be unable to indicate their decision. In legal terms, they are incompetent to decide about participating in research, and they would be precluded from consenting to enter a research project.

Researchers in New York and elsewhere have often felt frustrated by the exclusion of this group of potential subjects. Their frustration grows when the research involves innovative approaches to treatment-resistant disorders, which might not otherwise be available to patients.

Paul S. Appelbaum, *Psychiatric Research and the Incompetent Subject*, 48 Psychiatric Services 873, 873 (1997) [hereinafter Appelbaum, *Psychiatric Research and the Incompetent Subject*]; see also K. W. M. Fulford & K. Howse, *Ethics of Research with Psychiatric Patients: Principles, Problems and the Primary Responsibilities of Researchers*, 19 J. Med. Ethics 85 (1993).

Under current law and regulation, research involving persons with a mental disorder may proceed so long as various standards are met, including the obtaining of informed consent, either from the research participant or the participant's surrogate. The exposition that follows explores the issues that must be addressed when the research participant has the capacity to consent or, in the absence of decision-making capacity, when alternative methods of obtaining consent from a surrogate or a court must be followed.

2.   Obtaining Consent

When consent for participation in research is being sought, the initial issue to be addressed is the same as when a patient is being asked to consent to treatment—does the prospective participant have sufficient decision-making capacity to provide consent? This issue tends to be decided pursuant to the same criteria discussed previously with regard to treatment decisions. Particularly important in the research context is full disclosure of the possible short- and long-term harm that a research participant may suffer. A case illustrating the issues that may arise in this context was the subject of the following commentary:

In May 1994, the federal Office of Protection from Research Risks (OPRR) issued a report on its investigation of complaints against a leading group of schizophrenia researchers at the University of California at Los Angeles (UCLA) Medical School. The subjects on whose behalf complaints were filed had participated in a series of studies using Prolixin decanoate, a long-lasting, injectable form of a standard antipsychotic agent.

Subjects in the UCLA studies initially went through a one-year, fixed-dose study in which they received injections every two weeks. On the successful completion of the first study, subjects who were willing to continue in the research were enrolled in a second, more controversial protocol. Each subject was assigned, in a randomized, double-blind fashion, to continue the same dose of Prolixin or to receive a placebo injection. After twelve weeks, the groups crossed-over, with those subjects who had received active medication now getting a placebo, and vice versa. Subjects who were still stable after an additional twelve weeks were then assigned to a withdrawal protocol. The medications were stopped and subjects were followed for at least one year, or until a serious exacerbation or psychotic relapse occurred. The goal of the study was to identify predictors of successful functioning without antipsychotic medication.

Two subjects who had been enrolled in the withdrawal protocol ran into trouble. One subject committed suicide after completion of the formal one-year drug withdrawal study, while continuing to be followed by the research team in a drug-free state. A second person, a young college student, experienced a severe psychotic relapse that began not long after the medication was discontinued. During this period, he left school, began to hallucinate, and threatened to kill his parents when he became convinced that they were possessed by the devil. He and his parents alleged that, despite repeated appeals to the research team, it took nine months before he was put back on medication.

In the wake of these episodes, allegations were made to OPRR that the drug withdrawal protocols in which the subjects had been enrolled were unethical because they virtually guaranteed that subjects would relapse; that proper informed consent had not been obtained from the subjects; and that the investigators, who were also the subjects' clinicians, had not monitored their conditions closely enough and had been too slow about pulling them off the protocol and restarting medications.

OPRR's investigation concluded that the design of the research was not unethical, since it comported with current clinical and scientific standards. However, the agency determined that the informed consent obtained from subjects was inadequate, because the consent documents failed to describe clearly the differences between being in the research project and receiving ordinary clinical care. Although UCLA's monitoring of subjects' clinical status was deemed to be acceptable, OPRR also found that subjects should have been informed that their clinicians simultaneously were acting as investigators in the study.

Far from settling the controversy regarding drug-free research in schizophrenia, the OPRR report stimulated renewed consideration of the issues. The controversy was widely covered in the popular media, congressional hearings were held, and a lawsuit was filed against UCLA by the family of one of the subjects.

Paul S. Appelbaum, *Drug–Free Research in Schizophrenia: An Overview of the Controversy*, 18 IRB: A Rev. of Hum. Subjects Res. 1 (1996); see also Siow Ann Chong et al., *Authorizing Psychiatric Research: Principles, Practices and Problems*, 25 Bioethics 27 (2011); Umesh Chandra Gupta & Saifuddin Kharawala, *Informed Consent in Psychiatry Clinical Research: A Conceptual Review of Issues, Challenges, and Recommendations*, 3 Persp. Clinical Res. 8 (2012); Scott Y. H. Kim, *When Does Decisional Impairment Become Decisional Incompetence? Ethical and Methodological Issues in Capacity Research in Schizophrenia*, 32 Schizophrenia Bull. 92 (2006).

QUESTIONS AND COMMENTS

1.   *Media attention.* The issue of research participant consent has received considerable attention from the media. Some reports suggest research involving participants with a mental illness is not insubstantial. According to a New York Times report, "Federal ethics officials estimate that there have been 100 to 300 experiments in which patients were taken off their medicines when no new medicine was being tried; rather, they were taken off their medicines to observe the patients as they relapsed in order to study the illnesses." Philip J. Hilts, *Psychiatric Researchers Under Fire*, N.Y. Times, May 19, 1998.

Additionally, a veteran's hospital in Los Angeles was criticized after doctors in the cardiology unit conducted various experiments on patients who suffered from a variety of mental illnesses. Terrence Monmaney, *VA Hospital's Ethical Nightmare; Morality and Medicine Collide at West L.A. Facility, Where Probe About Informed Consent Clouds Research*, L.A. Times, Mar. 25, 1999. In some cases consent was not given at all, and in others consent was given by people who later argued that they did not know or understand to what they were consenting. Id. The problem is also an international one, as some drug companies have come under fire for testing psychiatric medications in other countries after misleading participants as to the nature and effects of the medications before obtaining their consent. Sharon LaFraniere et al., *The Dilemma: Submit or Suffer, 'Uninformed Consent' Is Rising Ethic of the Drug Test Boom*, Wash. Post, Dec. 19, 2000.

2.   *Questions about the scope of federal regulation.* Are there alternatives to using research participants with a mental disorder when the research pertains specifically to the development of new and improved related treatments? If individuals who suffer from a mental disorder are denied an opportunity to participate in research, does that constitute illegal discrimination? Because decision-making capacity is likely to vary among such participants, should their continuing capacity to consent be monitored and, if so, how? What requirements should be imposed beyond obtaining informed consent for research participants who, while mentally ill, may be legally competent? Under what circumstances, if any, should a surrogate be able to authorize the participation of an incompetent individual—for example, someone who suffers from Alzheimer's disease—in a research study (see discussion regarding state law below)? What if the study involves an experimental drug that may provide immediate benefit to the participant but may also have substantial adverse side effects? Under what circumstances should a participant with a mental disorder be withdrawn from a study? What if the participant wants to continue? What treatment obligations does a researcher owe to a participant with a mental disorder?

3.   *Adequacy of disclosure.* As the materials in the earlier part of this chapter suggest, consent cannot be effective unless the person from whom consent is sought is provided with sufficient information to make an informed decision. A problem with psychiatric research is that many participants may not be capable of providing informed consent because they cannot fully comprehend what they are told. For instance, one study found that participants with schizophrenia did not fully understand a procedure to which they had consented as well as a control group given the same information. William T. Carpenter et al., *Decisional Capacity for Informed Consent in Schizophrenia Research*, 57 Archives Gen. Psychiatry 533, 534 (2000). The study also found, however, that if participants with schizophrenia received an educational intervention designed to improve their ability to provide consent, they could achieve a similar level of understanding. Id. at 538.

Due to the importance of research in psychiatry, as well as the highly sensitive nature of informed consent in this setting, some commentators have argued for stricter federal guidelines concerning what constitutes informed consent in this domain. See Dorothy Derrickson, *Informed Consent to Human Subject Research: Improving the Process of Obtaining Informed Consent from Mentally Ill Persons*, 25 Fordham Urban L.J. 143 (1997); Stephen Hjelt, *Informed Consent and Psychotherapy: Apples and Oranges in the Garden of Doctrine*, 22 J. Nat'l Ass'n Admin. L.J. 1 (2002). These articles both cite the inability of researchers and other practitioners to accurately tell when individuals with a mental disorder fully understand to what they are consenting.

4.   *Participants in institutions.* At one time, persons who had been institutionalized, particularly prison inmates, frequently served as research participants in clinical tests conducted by pharmaceutical companies. In

some instances, those who participated had a condition that pertained to the drug being tested. In other cases, they did not, which means that participating had no therapeutic value for them. Typically, when inmates serve as research participants, they do so because of some inducement they received. An example appears in *Bailey v. Lally*, 481 F. Supp. 203 (D. Md. 1979), where prison inmates who had volunteered to participate in a research project involving the testing of a drug to counter malaria and other disorders brought suit asserting that a violation of their constitutional rights had occurred. They had given their consent and received compensation for participating in the clinical trial. However, they asserted that the conditions of incarceration were "so bad and the inducements to participate so great" that their participation had in fact not been voluntary. In rejecting their claim, the court held that the conditions of imprisonment were not so oppressive as to invalidate the consent that had been given.

3.   Consent in the Absence of Capacity

Current regulations at both the federal and state level do not altogether preclude the use of persons who lack the capacity to consent to research. However, the process for obtaining consent when the research will not directly provide a treatment benefit to research participants requires a formal approval process with governing standards that differ from state to state. As noted:

> Legal proceedings for purposes of assigning guardianship for such patients may offer a way out in some cases, but such efforts usually depend on the presence of involved family members who are willing to spend the money required for legal representation and court fees associated with the proceedings. Even then, the power of a guardian to consent to research participation is not always clear. In practice, guardianship is rarely a viable option; incompetent patients usually end up excluded from research studies.

Appelbaum, *Psychiatric Research and the Incompetent Subject*, supra, at 873.

QUESTIONS AND COMMENTS

1.   *State regulation of surrogate consent.* Some states, such as New York, have sought to deal with the problem of obtaining valid consent from research participants with a mental illness by issuing detailed regulations governing research in psychiatric facilities owned or licensed by the state. Some of the requirements typically imposed have been described as follows:

> Before subjects lacking decision-making capacity could be recruited for a research project, an institutional review board was required to determine that the research could not be done without including this group. Moreover, the study had to be judged "likely to produce knowledge of overriding therapeutic importance for the understanding or treatment of a condition that is presented by the patient." Subjects could

also be included when the study offered the prospect of direct benefit to them that would not be obtainable otherwise.

If patients meeting these criteria had not appointed a surrogate decision maker through a durable power of attorney—which most patients have not—the regulations offered a list of persons from whom consent for their participation in research could be obtained. These persons included the patient's spouse, parent, adult child, adult sibling, or guardian, or, in the absence of any of these, a "close friend," as defined in the regulations or by an appropriate court. Even if one of these persons consented on a patient's behalf, an objection by the patient would block his or her entry into the study, unless a court ruled that it offered the only option for direct benefit to the patient.

Appelbaum, *Psychiatric Research and the Incompetent Subject*, supra, at 873.

Notwithstanding the fact that these regulations were drafted through a process that involved patient advocates and other concerned parties, the regulations were challenged by plaintiffs who were concerned that patients might be forced into research without their consent. While not reaching the sufficiency of the regulations themselves, the New York appellate court hearing the case struck them down, finding that the Office of Mental Health lacked authority to issue the regulations. At the same time, the court suggested that the rules could be reissued in a technically correct fashion, which would then open the way for a substantive review. See *T.D. v. New York State Office of Mental Health*, 650 N.Y.S.2d 173 (App. Div. 1996). For an example of a current state regulation of such research, including the definition of and process for obtaining informed consent, see 12 Va. Admin. Code §§ 35–180–10 to 35–180–150 (2013).

D. SPECIAL PROBLEMS ASSOCIATED WITH BEHAVIORAL RESEARCH

In biomedical research, the participant's knowledge regarding the research usually has little or no effect on the outcome of the research. In contrast, behavioral research frequently requires some deception of the participant as to the nature and purpose of the experiment. Consequently, strict imposition of the informed consent requirement would severely limit the behavioral research that could be conducted.

As a result, it has been argued that some adjustment in the informed consent doctrine developed for biomedical research is called for with regard to behavioral research. Moreover, it has been suggested that the need for strict informed consent standards is somewhat reduced by the nature of the risks posed by behavioral research, which rarely poses a risk of physical harm. Some types of behavioral research, however, may expose participants to a risk of legally compensable psychological harm. Because the magnitude of these risks depends on the type of research conducted, it may be useful in evaluating current and proposed standards of informed consent to consider the legal implications associated with different types of behavioral research.

1.   Passive Observation Studies

Passive observation of individuals in public places, without any modification of their environment, normally poses no risk of psychological harm. For example, in an experiment conducted by Bryan and Test (1967), the researchers measured the effect that the employment of black or white Santas as Salvation Army bell ringers had on the frequency of donation. The mere act of giving or not giving constituted an experience of ordinary life that the researchers did not alter. These individuals were completely unaware of ever having participated in the experiment.

In some instances, however, passive observation studies can subject researchers to legal liability. For instance, in one controversial experiment by Humphreys (1970), the researcher stationed himself in public restrooms and posed as a "lookout" for gay men engaging in sex acts. By pretending to stand watch, the researcher witnessed hundreds of sexual acts. The researcher sometimes followed up on these observations with interviews in which the purpose of the experiment was disclosed.

In this instance, even though the acts were committed in a public place, the nature of the activities plus the reasonable expectations of the parties would presumably give rise to protected privacy interests. Thus, by failing to inform the individuals he was observing the true reason for his presence, the researcher could in some jurisdictions be held liable for invasion of privacy. See Fried, *Problems of Consent in Sex Research: Legal and Ethical Considerations in Ethical Issues*, in Sex Therapy and Research 31 (Masters et al. eds., 1980).

An action for invasion of privacy can also occur when an individual publishes a matter concerning the private life of another that is highly offensive and not of legitimate concern to the public. Restatement (Second) of Torts § 652D (1977). Thus, if an acquaintance of one of the participants in the Humphreys experiment had been able to identify the participant from the information presented in the published findings, the research might again constitute an invasion of privacy.

The HHS regulations promulgated under the National Research Act take into account participants' right to privacy in research involving passive observation. They generally exempt passive observation from coverage. Researchers lose the exemption, however, if (1) they keep records that identify participants, and (2) any disclosure of "human subjects' responses outside the research could reasonably place the subjects at risk of criminal or civil liability or be damaging to the subjects financial standing, employability, or reputation." 45 C.F.R. § 46.101(b)(2)(i).

2. Surveys and Manipulation Studies Without Overt Deception

A second type of behavioral research involves some manipulation of the participant's environment, but without any significant deception of the participant. One famous experiment by Meritz and Fowler (1944) involved the use of a "lost letter" technique to test the honesty of persons in various cities. Two different kinds of addressed envelopes were distributed, one containing a letter and the other containing a coin-shaped slug. The difference in the percentage of returns between the two kinds of letters was expected to indicate the honesty of the general population. The experiment would have been impossible to perform if informed consent had been required. The researchers, however, had no duty to inform because participation posed no risk to the participants greater than that encountered in ordinary life.

Similarly, survey interviews normally create little risk of harm to research participants. But if the questions deal with sensitive or personal matters, the researcher should take steps to insure the anonymity of the participant. If the participant must be identified in the researcher's records, the researcher may need to take special precautions to insure that the participant's responses remain confidential. HHS regulations also exempt interviews and surveys from coverage, provided that the researcher maintains the participants' anonymity and any disclosure does not reasonably place them at risk of criminal or civil liability nor is damaging to their financial standing, employability, or reputation. 45 C.F.R. § 46.101(b)(2)(i).

3. Studies Involving Deception

A third type of behavioral research combines manipulation of the participant's environment with some form of deception. Several years ago, a study found that as much as 44% of the research in social psychology involved deception of the participants. Ed Diener & Rick Crandall, *Ethics in Social and Behavioral Research* 74 (1978). The American Psychological Association's *Code of Ethics* § 8.07, "Deception in Research," states in part:

> Psychologists do not conduct a study involving deception unless they have determined that the use of deceptive techniques is justified by the study's significant prospective scientific, educational, or applied value and that effective nondeceptive alternative procedures are not feasible.

> * * *

> Psychologists explain any deception that is an integral feature of the design and conduct of an experiment to participants as early as is feasible, preferably at the conclusion of their participation, but no

later than at the conclusion of the data collection, and permit participants to withdraw their data.

As the above paragraphs acknowledge, deceit is a necessity in some types of behavioral research. The research participant's knowledge of the goal of the study would in many situations compromise the validity of the research outcome. Imposing traditional standards of informed consent on researchers would obviously preclude the conduct of such research. The HHS regulations recognize this problem by allowing an IRB to completely waive the informed consent requirement if the research poses "no more than minimal risk of harm to subjects and involves no procedures for which consent is normally required." 45 C.F.R. § 46.117(c)(2).

The nature and degree of risk of psychological harm varies with the type of deception employed. Psychological harm may arise from a participant's misapprehension, intended by the researcher, of what appears to be an emergency situation. For example, in an experiment conducted by the United States Army, military recruits were placed in an aircraft and flown to an altitude of 5,000 feet. The researcher then instructed the pilot to turn off the plane's propellers. The recruits were allowed to overhear communications designed to convince them that the pilot would be forced to crash land the plane. The behavior of the recruits under these artificial stress conditions was monitored by researchers who were also aboard the aircraft.

The threat of psychological harm also may arise from a deception that causes participants to misapprehend the nature of their own personalities. In a study by Bergin (1965) on dissonance theory, researchers falsely told male participants that personality tests had revealed that they had latent homosexual tendencies. Eventually, researchers "dehoaxed" the participants, but not before many of the participants suffered psychological distress.

Either of these experiments could have exposed the researchers to liability for failure to obtain informed consent or for the tort of intentional infliction of emotional distress. To establish an intentional infliction of emotional distress claim, a plaintiff must show that the defendant's action amounted to conduct "so outrageous in character, and so extreme in degree, as to go beyond all possible bounds of decency." Restatement (Second) of Torts § 46 cmt. d (1965). Some states, however, have the added requirement that the emotional distress cause some physical manifestation of illness or injury. Thus, under current standards, except in those states that require a physical manifestation of the injury, the subjects in both the Army and the Bergin studies could conceivably prevail in an action for intentional infliction of mental distress.

QUESTIONS AND COMMENTS

1. *Behavioral research and the requirement of informed consent.* When IRBs were initially introduced, some commentators contended that the low risk of injury from participation in behavioral research called into question the necessity of applying the HHS regulations to behavioral research. See E.L. Pattullo, *Who Risks What in Social Research?*, 2 IRB: A Rev. of Hum. Subject Res. 1, 3 (1980). Cumbersome IRB procedures may indeed discourage some researchers from engaging in valuable scientific inquiry. See Morton Hunt, *Research Through Deception*, N.Y. Times, Sept. 12, 1982, § 6. After years of experience with IRBs, however, the overwhelming consensus both within and outside the social sciences is that some regulation and institutional control of researchers is necessary and only rarely onerous.

2. *Debriefing.* Researchers employing deception have developed several safeguards to decrease the risk that research participants will become emotionally upset as a result of the deception. Note that the psychologists' ethics code above requires researchers to debrief participants at the experiment's conclusion. In debriefing sessions, researchers meet with participants and fully disclose the hoax. Disturbed participants are comforted and reassured. If you were a member of an IRB, how would you decide whether a debriefing would adequately protect participants from the psychological trauma that may accompany an experiment?

3. *Incomplete disclosure.* Behavioral and biomedical researchers have also developed several forms of "consent" that fall short of giving the research participant all the information necessary to satisfy legal standards of informed consent, but do provide some disclosure. For example, researchers have asked participants to consent to not being informed of the real purposes of the experiment. Robert J. Levine, *Consent to Incomplete Disclosure as an Alternative to Deception*, 4 IRB: A Rev. of Hum. Subject Res. 9, 10 (1982). Another technique consists of asking prospective participants to waive their right to disclosure without forewarning the participant that the research involves deception. Still another approach, used primarily in biomedical research, is to inform an incompetent participant's proxy of the experiment, but to not initially obtain consent from the proxy. Within a specific period after the beginning of the experiment, however, the researcher obtains the proxy's consent. The theory behind this technique, called "deferred consent," is that by delaying the consent decision, the proxy will have more time to consider the matter and come to a "correct" decision. The HHS regulations under the National Research Act appear to authorize such techniques, but only if the research poses no more than minimal risk to the participant and other conditions are met. 45 C.F.R. § 46.116(d). See Norman Fost & John Robertson, *Deferring Consent with Incompetent Patients in an Intensive Care Unit*, 2 IRB: A Rev. of Hum. Subject Res. 5 (1980). Cf. Tom L. Beauchamp, *The Ambiguities of 'Deferred Consent'*, 2 IRB: A Rev. of Hum. Subject Res. 6 (1980) (criticizing the deferred consent technique). Should the use of any of these techniques constitute a defense in an action based on a failure to obtain informed consent?

CHAPTER 5

CONFIDENTIALITY AND ACCESS TO RECORDS

■ ■ ■

Table of Sections

I.   PROTECTION OF PRIVACY AND CONFIDENTIALITY

A. THE DEVELOPMENT OF PRIVACY AND CONFIDENTIALITY IN MENTAL HEALTH CARE

The right of individuals to control the disclosure and distribution of information contained in their health care records is closely tied to the concept of personal privacy that first gained recognition as a legal concept close to the end of the nineteenth century. As initially conceived by Justice Brandeis, the right of privacy is "[t]he right to be left alone." Samuel D. Warren & Louis D. Brandeis, *The Right to Privacy*, 4 Harv. L. Rev. 193 (1890).

The Supreme Court has not deemed personal privacy to be a stand-alone right entitled to constitutional protection. Over time, however, numerous Supreme Court decisions have given constitutional protection to privacy interests under the First Amendment and the search and seizure clause of the Fourth Amendment. The protection of privacy interests has also served as the bedrock for various decisions under the due process clause of the Fourteenth Amendment recognizing freedom of choice in a variety of personal activities including procreation and sexual expression. Yet in *Paul v. Davis*, 424 U.S. 693, 713, 96 S. Ct. 1155, 47 L. Ed. 2d 405 (1976), the Court noted that the privacy rights afforded protection from state actions had to do only with "matters relating to marriage, procreation, contraception, family relationship, and child rearing and education."

The degree to which the privacy of health care records might merit constitutional protection came before the Supreme Court in *Whalen v. Roe*, 429 U.S. 589 (1977). *Whalen* examined "whether the state of New York may record, in a centralized computer file, the names and addresses of all persons who have obtained, pursuant to a doctor's prescription, certain drugs for which there is both a lawful and an unlawful market." Id. at 591. While upholding the statute authorizing this action, the Court also announced that "in some circumstances" the State may be under a constitutional duty to avoid "unwarranted disclosures." These words have led some to speculate that the *Whalen* decision "created a framework by which future courts would develop the right to privacy in medical records." Joel Grover & Erin Toll, *The Right to Privacy of Medical Records: Balancing Competing Perspectives*, 79 Denv. U. L. Rev. 540 (2002).

The protection of personal privacy from intrusions by private actors gained increasing recognition in the last half of the twentieth century. However, this development was the product of either state legislation or common law development. As a result, privacy protections were very uneven, and the degree of protection varied from state to state. For instance, the tort of public disclosure of a private fact is an actionable tort in some states but not others. The same is true of medical privacy, which is protected to varying degrees in some states but not others. See *Biddle v. Warren General Hospital*, 715 N.E.2d 518 (Ohio 1999). In some states, the physician's duty to not disclose information obtained in the course of treatment is embedded in a specific statute. In others, a physician's duty to preserve the confidentially of patient records is either inferred from cognate statutory provisions (such as laws giving patients the right to exclude their doctor's testimony in civil litigation) or derived from medical licensing statutes or professional codes of conduct. See *Humphers v. First Interstate Bank of Oregon*, 696 P.2d 527 (Or. 1985).

While medical privacy laws cover psychiatrists, who are by definition licensed physicians, they do not necessarily cover psychologists or other non-physician professionals involved in mental health treatment. At the same time there is also a growing recognition that the privacy interest of persons receiving treatment for mental disorders is just as compelling, if not more so, than the privacy interest of persons being treated for general medical conditions. As noted by the Supreme Court,

> a psychiatrist's ability to help her patients "is completely dependent upon [the patients'] willingness and ability to talk freely. This makes it difficult if not impossible for [a psychiatrist] to function without being able to assure . . . patients of confidentiality and, indeed, privileged communication. Where there may be exceptions to this general rule . . . , there is wide agreement that confidentiality is a *sine qua non* for successful psychiatric treatment."

Jaffee v. Redmond, 518 U.S. 1, 10, 116 S. Ct. 1923, 135 L. Ed. 2d 337 (1996). This may be something of an overstatement as mental health care may proceed satisfactorily in less-than-confidential circumstances (a matter discussed further infra). Yet the Court's overall point is valid. People usually enter treatment with an expectation of confidentiality. Moreover, optimal mental health care can occur only when persons make full and frank disclosure of private facts, and assurances of confidentiality can help people get past the embarrassment or shame that might otherwise limit interpersonal disclosure.

The critical role of privacy and confidentiality in mental health treatment has led various states over the past fifty years to enact specific psychotherapy statutes that bar the disclosure of records and communications between care providers and treatment recipients. Significantly, these laws generally apply not only to psychiatrists but also to all mental health professionals, including psychologists and clinical social workers. Even when a state has not enacted legislation protecting the confidentiality of mental health treatment records or failed to provide remedies for litigants seeking compensation for a breach of confidentiality, courts in some instances adapted established doctrines of general application—such as defamation or intentional infliction of emotional distress—to provide redress for patients and clients whose privacy had been compromised. The doctrinal approaches courts have used to provide these remedies are detailed in Part I.D.2, infra.

B.   FEDERAL PROTECTION OF HEALTH CARE PRIVACY

1.   Overview of HIPAA Legislation

Federal protection of health care privacy derives from Congress's enactment of the Health Insurance Portability and Accountability Act of 1996 (HIPAA). Prior to HIPAA, federal law only protected the medical information of specific groups such as Medicare participants and individuals with AIDS. See Adam Butera, *HIPAA Preemption Implications for Covered Entities Under State Law*, 37 Tort & Insurance L.J. 1181 (2002).

The primary purpose of HIPAA was to enable persons covered by group health plans to transfer their coverage when changing employers. The health benefit portability provisions are set out in what is known as Title I. In support of the benefits portability provisions, Title II of the Act established a regulatory regime for what are termed "administrative simplification provisions" designed to promote the replacement of paper-based transactions with more efficient electronic communications. Included within Title II are three major components: (1) transactions and code sets, (2) privacy, and (3) security and electronic signatures. In brief, the transactions and code sets provisions require that certain information transfers pertaining to health care, when conducted electronically, follow standards prescribed by the Secretary of the Department of Health and Human Services (DHHS).

The privacy provisions that are discussed in greater detail in Part I.B.3., infra, establish rules for the use and disclosure of personal health information in the hands of (1) health care providers (both individuals and institutions), (2) health plan sponsors (e.g., employer sponsored group health plans, Medicare, etc.), and (3) health maintenance organizations (HMOs) and Health Care Clearinghouses. These three categories are termed "covered entities." Under the terms of HIPAA, covered entities have a duty to prevent unwarranted disclosure, destruction, or corruption of personal health information. Title II also authorizes DHHS to issue regulations establishing enforcement mechanisms to ensure compliance with the mandated terms of the Act.

In enacting Title II, Congress charged the DHHS with the task of filling in the gaps in the law, including the ground rules governing how HIPAA privacy protections are to be implemented. Given the multiplicity of issues, and the complexity and fragmentation of the health care industry, this has proven to be a massive undertaking. The results of this multi-year effort are rules that take up hundreds of pages in the federal register implementing the privacy provisions. 45 C.F.R. pts. 160, 164. DHHS issued final standards for the privacy of individual identifiable health information ("privacy rule") in 2000. 65 Fed. Reg. 82,462. The privacy rules are supplemented by the Security Rule, which was issued in final form in 2003.

2.   Rationale for Federal Regulation of Health Care Privacy

DEPARTMENT OF HEALTH AND HUMAN SERVICES
Office of the Secretary.
65 Fed. Reg. 82462. 45 C.F.R. Parts 160 & 164. December 28, 2000.

In enacting HIPAA, Congress recognized the fact that administrative simplification cannot succeed if we do not also protect the privacy and confidentiality of personal health information. The provision of high-quality health care requires the exchange of personal, often-sensitive information between an individual and a skilled practitioner. Vital to that interaction is the patient's ability to trust that the information shared will be protected and kept confidential. Yet many patients are concerned that their information is not protected. Among the factors adding to this concern are the growth of the number of organizations involved in the provision of care and the processing of claims, the growing use of electronic information technology, increased efforts to market health care and other products to consumers, and the increasing ability to collect highly sensitive information about a person's current and future health status as a result of advances in scientific research.

*   *   *

INCREASING USE OF INTERCONNECTED ELECTRONIC INFORMATION SYSTEMS

Until recently, health information was recorded and maintained on paper and stored in the offices of community-based physicians, nurses, hospitals, and other health care professionals and institutions. In some ways, this imperfect system of record keeping created a false sense of privacy among patients, providers, and others. Patients' health information has never remained completely confidential. Until recently, however, a breach of confidentiality involved a physical exchange of paper records or a verbal exchange of information. Today, however, more and more health care providers, plans, and others are utilizing electronic means of storing and transmitting health information. In 1996, the health care industry invested an estimated $10 billion to $15 billion on information technology. The electronic information revolution is transforming the recording of health information so that the disclosure of information may require only a push of a button. In a matter of seconds, a person's most profoundly private information can be shared with hundreds, thousands, even millions of individuals and organizations at a time. While the majority of medical records still are in paper form, information from those records is often copied and transmitted through electronic means.

This ease of information collection, organization, retention, and exchange made possible by the advances in computer and other electronic technology affords many benefits to individuals and to the health care industry. Use of electronic information has helped to speed the delivery of effective care and the processing of billions of dollars worth of health care claims. Greater use of electronic data has also increased our ability to identify and treat those who are at risk for disease, conduct vital research, detect fraud and abuse, and measure and improve the quality of care delivered in the U.S.

At the same time, these advances have reduced or eliminated many of the financial and logistical obstacles that previously served to protect the confidentiality of health information and the privacy interests of individuals. And they have made our information available to many more people. The shift from paper to electronic records, with the accompanying greater flows of sensitive health information, thus strengthens the arguments for giving legal protection to the right to privacy in health information. In an earlier period where it was far more expensive to access and use medical records, the risk of harm to individuals was relatively low. In the potential near future, when technology makes it almost free to send lifetime medical records over the Internet, the risks may grow rapidly. It may become cost-effective, for instance, for companies to offer services that allow purchasers to obtain details of a person's physical and mental treatments. In addition to legitimate possible uses for such services, malicious or inquisitive persons may download medical records for purposes ranging from identity theft to embarrassment to prurient interest in the life of a celebrity or neighbor.

*   *   *

Moreover, electronic health data is becoming increasingly "national"; as more information becomes available in electronic form, it can have value far beyond the immediate community where the patient resides. Neither private action nor state laws provide a sufficiently comprehensive and rigorous legal structure to allay public concerns, protect the right to privacy, and correct the market failures caused by the absence of privacy protections. Hence, a national policy with consistent rules is necessary to encourage the increased and proper use of electronic information while also protecting the very real needs of patients to safeguard their privacy.

* * *

THE CHANGING HEALTH CARE SYSTEM

The number of entities who are maintaining and transmitting individually identifiable health information has increased significantly over the last 10 years. In addition, the rapid growth of integrated health care delivery systems requires greater use of integrated health information systems. The health care industry has been transformed from one that relied primarily on one-on-one interactions between patients and clinicians to a system of integrated health care delivery networks and managed care providers. Such a system requires the processing and collection of information about patients and plan enrollees (for example, in claims files or enrollment records), resulting in the creation of databases that can be easily transmitted. This dramatic change in the practice of medicine brings with it important prospects for the improvement of the quality of care and reducing the cost of that care. It also, however, means that increasing numbers of people have access to health information. And, as health plan functions are increasingly outsourced, a growing number of organizations not affiliated with our physicians or health plans also have access to health information.

According to the American Health Information Management Association (AHIMA), an average of 150 people "from nursing staff to x-ray technicians, to billing clerks" have access to a patient's medical records during the course of a typical hospitalization. While many of these individuals have a legitimate need to see all or part of a patient's records, no laws govern who those people are, what information they are able to see, and what they are and are not allowed to do with that information once they have access to it. According to the National Research Council, individually identifiable health information frequently is shared with:

Consulting physicians;

Managed care organizations;

Health insurance companies;

Life insurance companies;

Self-insured employers;

Pharmacies;

Pharmacy benefit managers;

Clinical laboratories;

Accrediting organizations;

State and Federal statistical agencies; and

Medical information bureaus.

Much of this sharing of information is done without the knowledge of the patient involved. While many of these functions are important for smooth functioning of the health care system, there are no rules governing how that information is used by secondary and tertiary users. For example, a pharmacy benefit manager could receive information to determine whether an insurance plan or HMO should cover a prescription, but then use the information to market other products to the same patient. Similarly, many of us obtain health insurance coverage through our employer and, in some instances, the employer itself acts as the insurer. In these cases, the employer will obtain identifiable health information about its employees as part of the legitimate health insurance functions such as claims processing, quality improvement, and fraud detection activities. At the same time, there is no comprehensive protection prohibiting the employer from using that information to make decisions about promotions or job retention.

* * *

Congress recognized the importance of protecting the privacy of health information by enacting the Health Insurance Portability and Accountability Act of 1996. The Act called on Congress to enact a medical privacy statute and asked the Secretary of Health and Human Services to provide Congress with recommendations for protecting the confidentiality of health care information. The Congress further recognized the importance of such standards by providing the Secretary with authority to promulgate regulations on health care privacy in the event that lawmakers were unable to act within the allotted three years.

3. Regulatory Implementation of HIPAA Privacy Provisions

When Congress failed to act within the allotted time, responsibility for issuing regulations regarding health care privacy fell to the DHHS. The promulgated HIPAA privacy rules for the first time established national standards governing patient and client privacy rights in all health treatment situations, including mental health. The length and complexity of the privacy regulations preclude our discussing them in detail here. Nevertheless, given their impact, an examination of the key provisions is necessary. For one thing, the key features set out below will serve as a backdrop for a consideration of many of the issues addressed later in this chapter, which in some instances are now governed by the HIPAA rules. HIPAA's privacy rules extend to not only health care providers but also to other participants in the health care system, such as health plans and health care clearinghouses. While the privacy rules are basically the same for the different entities, some provisions may apply only to one of the entities listed above because of its distinct functions within the health care system. Given the focus of this and prior chapters on the treatment role of mental health professionals, the materials that follow will only consider the HIPAA privacy rules as they pertain to health care providers.

a.   Covered Health Care Providers

HIPAA regulations apply only to "covered entities." An entity is deemed to be covered if it is (1) a "health plan" (interpreted to be a program that provides or pays the cost of health care services, which includes employer-sponsored group health insurance and health plans, health insurance sold to individuals, Medicare, Medicaid, and other public protection programs); (2) a "health care clearinghouse" (interpreted to be a public or private entity that processes received data into standard or nonstandard formats, which includes billing services and community health information systems); or (3) "a health care provider who transmits any health information in electronic form in connection with a transaction covered [by HIPAA regulations]." 45 C.F.R. § 160.102. Thus, only health care professionals who transmit health information in electronic form are subject to HIPAA's privacy protection regime.

A health care *provider* is defined to include any "provider of medical or health services . . . and any other person or organization who furnishes, bills, or is paid for health care in the normal course of business." 45 C.F.R. § 160.103. The other operative term "health care" is broadly defined to include:

> (1) Preventive, diagnostic, therapeutic, rehabilitative, maintenance, or palliative care, and counseling, service, assessment, or procedure with respect to the physical or mental condition, or functional status, of an individual or that affects the structure or function of the body; and

> (2) Sale or dispensing of a drug, device, equipment, or other item in accordance with a prescription.

Id. The breadth of the definition of "provider" thus includes non-medical professionals who furnish or are paid for mental health treatment services, such as psychologists and clinical social workers.

Since only health care providers that use electronic means to transmit health information (for the definition of "Protected Health Information," see Part I.B.3.b., infra) are subject to HIPAA's privacy provisions, the definition of both "electronic means" and "health information" becomes relevant for determining coverage. While "electronic" is not defined by the regulations, the DHHS has taken the position that the term includes any hard wire or wireless electronic communications of health information, including e-mail. As a result, "a nursing home that transmits health plan participants' information electronically to an auditor triggers HIPAA, whereas one that submits only paper copies does not." Butera, supra. In general, voice, telephone, and paper transmissions are not covered, but coverage is triggered even if the electronic communication is only internal. Moreover, as one commentator notes, "[d]espite a less-than-transparent statutory mandate, . . . HHS decided that once an organization constitutes a [covered entity] under HIPAA, [having once used an electronic communication,] all [future] individually identifiable health information maintained or transmitted in any medium—electronic, paper, or oral—are protected." Id.

The result of this somewhat catch-all definition of electronic transmission means that any provider who seeks reimbursement for services from Medicare or a defined health plan automatically becomes a covered entity, as HIPAA mandates that applications for reimbursement under these programs must be submitted electronically using standardized claim forms. 63 Fed. Reg. 25,272 (1998), 45 C.F.R. pt. 142.

b. Protected Health Information

The fundamental purpose of the privacy rule "is to enable the individual who receives health care treatment to control the manner in which the information is used and to whom it is disclosed." *2002 HIPAA Desk Reference—A Physician's Guide to Understanding the Administration Simplification Provisions*, at 73 (2001) [hereinafter 2002 HIPAA Desk Reference]. Accordingly, HIPAA establishes rules governing both disclosures to third parties and internal use of "protected health information," or "PHI." In the HIPAA context, PHI includes:

[A]ny information, whether oral or recorded in any form or medium, that:

(1) Is created or received by a health care provider, health plan, employer, or health care clearinghouse; and

(2) Relates to the past, present, or future physical or mental health or condition of an individual; the provision of health care to an individual; or the past, present, or future payment for the provision of health care to an individual; and (i) [t]hat identifies the individual; or (ii) [w]ith respect to which there is a reasonable basis to believe the information can be used to identify the individual.

45 C.F.R. § 160.103.

As a result, the prohibition on unauthorized disclosure covers virtually any information pertaining to past, current, or future health care, including the payment for such care. Also, coverage extends to information in any form, including electronic, written, or oral transmissions. Id. HIPAA presumably covers oral information to ensure that information retains protection when discussed or read aloud from a computer screen or a written document or when communicated in the course of a treatment session. However, because the definition of health care is restricted to information that can be used to identify an individual, removal of personal identifiers renders the information exempt from HIPAA restrictions. The specific identifiers that must be removed to achieve de-identification are listed at 45 C.F.R. § 164.514. This makes it possible for treatment providers to provide third-party aggregate or statistical data without the consent of a patient/client so long as the data do not identify any individual. 2002 HIPAA Desk Reference, supra, at 73.

c. Regulation of Disclosure

The rules governing disclosure of PHI vary depending on (1) the relationship of the provider to the third person or entity that is to be the recipient of information or (2) the purpose of the disclosure. If the person or entity to whom disclosure is to be made is involved in providing "indirect treatment" (i.e., providing treatment or diagnostic services at the direction of the primary provider), PHI may be disclosed to the indirect provider without the consent of the patient.

Similarly, disclosure of PHI may be made without the consent of the patient to a "business associate," which includes, among others, consultants, lawyers, and accountants. Both in the case of indirect health care providers and business associates the regulations require that the disclosure be limited to the "minimum necessary" to accomplish the specific purpose. Moreover, when the third party is a business associate, the provider must establish a "business associate contract" as a condition for the disclosure of any PHI. Such contracts must specify (1) "the protected health information to be disclosed and the uses that may be made of the information and, (2) impose security, inspection and reporting requirements on the business associate." 2002 HIPAA Desk Reference, supra, at 56. However, because under current law simply being a business associate is not classified under HIPAA as a covered entity, such entities are not directly subject to DHHS regulation (although if business associates are health plans, health care clearing houses, or health care providers, they may on that basis be covered entities).

The rules governing disclosure are also relaxed when the disclosure is to a third-party covered entity and the disclosure pertains to "treatment, payment or health care operations." 45 C.F.R. § 164.501. For these purposes, the provider has the option of disclosing PHI either with or without the consent of the patient. In any event, the disclosure must be the "minimum necessary" to accomplish the intended purpose. 45 C.F.R. § 164.502. This limitation does not apply to disclosures made to a covered entity for the purpose of treatment. Id. While the regulations permit disclosure in connection with treatment, payment, or health care operations without the consent or authorization of the patient, the risk of unauthorized use or disclosure by the recipients of the PHI is minimized by the fact that the recipient entity must be a covered entity such as an insurance company or HMO and is therefore also subject to HIPAA's privacy rules. 45 C.F.R. § 164.506.

In all cases except the above, PHI may not be disclosed to a third party without the patient's express authorization or where the disclosure is permitted under one of the exceptions discussed below in Part I.B.3.d. If the patient is an unemancipated minor or a person under guardianship, the individual's personal representative is—with limited exceptions that pertain to health care that under state law can be obtained by unemancipated minors without their parents' or guardians' consent—authorized to act on the patient's behalf in authorizing disclosure of PHI. 45 C.F.R. § 164.500(g)(2). The designation of a personal representative is determined by "applicable [state] law." 45 C.F.R. § 164.500(g)(2). Because the death of a patient does not terminate HIPAA privacy protections, a personal representative is authorized to consent to the disclosure of a decedent's PHI.

While for the most part mental health treatment is subject to the same privacy protection provisions as apply to other classes of treatment, "psychotherapy notes" constitute a separate class of protected health information. 45 C.F.R. § 164.501. In particular, this class of data is treated as distinct from the rest of the individual's health record and is subject to more stringent rules. Moreover, authorization can only be sought by a provider in connection with "treatment, payment or health operations." However, authorization is not required for the following:

(A) Use by the originator of the psychotherapy notes for treatment;

(B) Use or disclosure by the covered entity for its own training programs in which students, trainees, or practitioners in mental health learn under supervision to practice or improve their skills in group, joint, family, or individual counseling; or

(C) Use or disclosure by the covered entity to defend itself in a legal action or other proceeding brought by the individual.

45 C.F.R. § 164.508(a)(2)(i). Also, providers may disclose to covered entities PHI pertaining to medication prescription and monitoring, counseling sessions, and start and stop times. 45 C.F.R. § 164.501.

d. *Exceptions to the Authorization Requirement*

The Regulations do permit the disclosure of PHI to specified persons and entities without the patient's authorization in a variety of special circumstances, which include: (1) to public health authorities for the purpose of controlling or preventing disease; (2) to a coroner or medical examiner "for the purpose of identifying a deceased person, determining a cause of death, or other duties as authorized by law"; (3) where authorized by state law to report child abuse or neglect, or domestic violence; (4) where needed for various law enforcement purposes including the apprehension of an individual who has admitted participating in a violent crime; (5) where necessary to prevent or lessen a serious and imminent threat to the health or safety of a person or the public; (6) in any judicial or administrative proceeding in response to an express order, subpoena, or discovery request; or (7) where disclosure is required by law and the use or disclosure complies with and is limited to the relevant requirements of the law. 45 C.F.R. § 164.512. A number of these exceptions only apply where the disclosure is specifically authorized by state law. The conditions governing disclosure in response to a subpoena or discovery motion are discussed in Part II.D., infra.

e. *Miscellaneous Requirements*

The regulations impose various notification requirements, including posting and/or distributing to all present or prospective clients a notice that spells out the provider's privacy policies. Such notice must include: (1) the provider's policies and procedures concerning the use and disclosure of PHI; (2) the individual's rights under HIPAA; and (3) the covered entity's legal obligation under HIPAA with respect to PHI. 45 C.F.R. § 164.520. The privacy rules also provide that "[a] covered entity must have in place appropriate administrative, technical, and physical safeguards to protect the privacy of protected health information." 45 C.F.R. § 164.530.

These provisions, commonly referred to as the "mini-security rules," are embedded in HIPAA's security and privacy regulations. A separate set of regulations that expands on these provisions became effective in 2005. 45 C.F.R. pt 164(C). These security rules are less a series of check lists and more a description of principles to be used by covered entities and their business associates to evaluate and apply specific security protections based on an entity's particular situation. Among its mandates is the adoption of intensive management of processes that will enable the covered entity to detect intrusions into its data systems and to respond with appropriate counter measures.

Finally, HIPAA grants clients a qualified right of access to their health information and a right to seek amendment of the health information. The scope of this right is discussed more fully in Part III.B., infra. Clients also have the right to revoke authorization granting the release of their information at any time. 45 C.F.R. § 164.508.

f.   Enforcement

The Office for Civil Rights (OCR) of DHHS administers and enforces HIPAA and conducts complaint investigations and compliance reviews. Covered entities must cooperate with any compliance investigation, which includes providing broad access to administrative records. Butera, supra.

However, DHHS has declared that "OCR will seek the cooperation of covered entities and may provide technical assistance to help them comply voluntarily with the Privacy Rule." U.S. Department of Health & Human Services, *Summary of HIPAA Privacy Rule*, http://www.hhs. gov/ocr/privacy/hipaa/understanding/summary/ (last visited July 28, 2013) [hereinafter DHHS, *Summary*]. Further, a penalty will not be imposed if "the failure to comply was not due to willful neglect, and was corrected during a 30–day period after the entity knew or should have known the failure to comply had occurred (unless the period is extended at the discretion of OCR)." Id. "In addition, OCR may choose to reduce a penalty if the failure to comply was due to reasonable cause and the penalty would be excessive given the nature and extent of the noncompliance." Id.

Nevertheless, violation of HIPAA regulations may lead to civil or criminal penalties. For violations occurring on or after February 18, 2009, the following civil penalties are available. If the covered entity did not know and, by exercising reasonable diligence, would not have known, that HIPAA was violated, the minimum civil penalty is $100 per violation. If the violation was known but was due to reasonable cause and not due to willful neglect, the minimum penalty is $1,000 per violation. If the violation was due to willful neglect but the violation was corrected within a thirty-day window, the minimum penalty is $10,000 per violation. For all three of these categories, the maximum is $50,000 per violation, with different annual maximums. If the violation was due to willful neglect and not corrected within the thirty-day window, the minimum fine is $50,000 per violation, with an annual maximum of $1.5 million. 45 C.F.R. § 160.404.

In addition, DHHS has noted:

A person who knowingly obtains or discloses individually identifiable health information in violation of the Privacy Rule may face a criminal penalty of up to $50,000 and up to one-year imprisonment. The criminal penalties increase to $100,000 and up to five years imprisonment if the wrongful conduct involves false pretenses, and to $250,000 and up to 10 years imprisonment if the wrongful conduct involves the intent to sell, transfer, or use identifiable health information for commercial advantage, personal gain or malicious harm. The Department of Justice is responsible for criminal prosecutions under the Privacy Rule.

DHHS, *Summary*, supra.

Before penalties are imposed, however, OCR

will notify the covered entity and provide the covered entity with an opportunity to provide written evidence of those circumstances that would reduce or bar a penalty. This evidence must be submitted to OCR within 30 days of receipt of the notice. In addition, if OCR states that it intends to impose a penalty, a covered entity has the right to request an administrative hearing to appeal the proposed penalty.

Id.

Finally, "[n]either HIPAA nor the Privacy Rule explicitly grants a private cause of action, including qui tam actions. Still, covered entities and business associates fear that the plaintiffs' bar, in state and federal tort actions, will use a Privacy Rule violation as evidence that the duty of care was ignored." Butera, supra. See also Joshua D. W. Collins, *Toothless HIPAA: Searching for a Private Right of Action to Remedy Privacy Rule Actions*, 60 Vand. L. Rev. 199 (2007).

g.   *Relationship to State Laws*

HIPAA's privacy provisions interact with state law in three ways. First, federal preemption in this context means that HIPAA potentially displaces any state law that conflicts with the national standards established by HIPAA. At the same time, HIPAA defers to state law to the extent that state law more restrictively limits disclosure of PHI without a patient's consent. Third, HIPAA relies on state law to establish and define some of the imposed responsibilities and exceptions. For instance, as discussed previously, HIPAA privacy regulations authorize disclosure of PHI without the patient's consent in a variety of circumstances, such as disclosures in connection with litigation, or disclosures pertaining to a patient's dangerousness when permitted or required by state law. Thus, state law can, in certain instances, serve to define HIPAA's disclosure rules. Part II, infra, discusses several of the state law exceptions permitting disclosure of PHI without a patient's consent.

HIPAA's preemption aspects are express but selective. The excerpt below summarizes the scope and operation of the preemption provisions:

Congress adopted a general rule that any HIPAA medical privacy statute, standard or implementation specification "shall supersede any contrary provision of State law, including a provision of state law that requires medical or health plan records . . . to be maintained in written rather than electronic form." [42 USC § 1320d–7(a)(1).] However, conflict between state and federal law is not presumed, and whenever possible, state and federal provisions should be construed in a manner that makes them compatible. In practice, HIPAA preemption does not represent a wholesale federal preemption of the field of privacy law, but rather a national floor of medical privacy protection.

Congress created three protected areas of state law, or statutory carve-outs, where federal HIPAA does not trump or override state law by preemption. Certain portions of state public health law are protected, with Congress stating that "[n]othing in this part shall be construed to invalidate or limit" the authority, power or procedures established under any law providing for the reporting of disease, injury, child abuse, birth or death; public health surveillance; public health investigation; and (public health) intervention.

Certain, other, mandatory state regulatory reporting and state licensure investigatory activities are also expressly saved by statute from federal preemption. These include requiring a health plan to report or provide access to information for management audits, financial audits, program monitoring and evaluation, facility licensure or certification, or individual licensure or certification. Thus, the statute gives state health departments and licensing boards broad access for the uninterrupted conducting of traditional state public health licensure and programmatic financial review activities. The HIPAA statute contains another savings provision which was designed to go into effect only if HIPAA privacy was promulgated by Department of Health and Human Services (DHHS) rulemaking, rather than by Congressional passage. Since Congress itself did not pass comprehensive medical privacy law, but instead, by inaction, delegated it to DHHS, an uncodified statutory provision states that the federal regulations "shall not supersede a contrary provision of State law, if the provision of State law imposes requirements, standards, or implementation specifications that are 'more stringent' than" the comparable federal DHHS standard.

By definition, DHHS has clarified several aspects of this savings clause. First, DHHS sets the bar quite high when it finds a conflict, defining "contrary" to mean either, 1) that an entity would find it impossible to comply with both the state and federal provisions ("impossibility test"), or 2) that the provision of the state law stands as an obstacle to the full purposes and objectives of HIPAA ("obstacle test"). Similarly, the term "more stringent" means that the state law restricts a disclosure permitted under HIPAA, grants greater access to a person's own health information, more severely restricts the scope or duration of authorized access by another, requires greater record-keeping or generally provides greater privacy protection to the individual who is the subject of the record.

Frederick Ryland, *Federal Health Privacy Comes to Maryland: What's the Big Deal?*, 36(1) Md. Bar J. (Jan./Feb. 2003).

QUESTIONS AND COMMENTS

1.   *Non-covered health providers.* Not all professionals who provide mental health care or psychology-related services are covered entities under HIPAA. Mental health professionals are exempt from HIPAA rules if they do not use electronic modes of communication to transmit personal health information in their practice, including, for instance, billing for services. Thus, a therapist who only has clients who themselves pay for their treatment and who are billed by mail would not be subject to HIPAA, nor would a psychologist who bills electronically for services but whose practice is restricted to providing court-related evaluations. However, a therapist who bills a third-party private insurer or a public insurance plan such as Medicare or Medicaid must, by law, submit the billing electronically. In doing so, the therapist becomes a covered entity and is subject to HIPAA privacy regulations.

2.   *Success of HIPAA?* Is the privacy rule created by HIPAA sufficient to ensure the privacy of health records controlled by covered entities? A news report issued two years after HIPAA's implementation suggested that doctors had a difficult time understanding the regulations, and therefore might unknowingly or unwillingly violate HIPAA regulations. Virgina A. Smith & Dawn Fallik, *Doctors, Patients Grapple with Specifics of Privacy Rule*, Phil. Enq., Mar. 8, 2005, at A01. Additionally, one commentator has noted that DHHS' emphasis on voluntary compliance undercuts efforts to ensure the protection of client privacy. Kendra Gray, *The Privacy Rule: Are We Being Deceived?*, 11 DePaul J. Health Care L. 89, 91 (2007).

Additionally, some commentators have argued that the complexity of HIPAA may lead to substandard care, especially in the mental health field, as providers are so fearful of violating a provision within the law that it compromises their treatment. Bryan Touchet et al., *Brief Reports: The Impact of Fear of HIPAA Violation on Patient Care*, 55 Psychiatric Services 575, 576 (2004). These commentators discuss the multiple parties often involved in the same persons' mental health care and the importance of sharing relevant information. The commentators contend that psychiatrists should not be "hiding" behind HIPAA and using it as an excuse for failing to take steps needed to care for their clients, including proper, appropriate disclosures of information. Id. at 578.

3.   *Disclosures authorized by state law.* Numerous states also authorize mental health providers to disclose confidential information when a person's condition makes it necessary to set in motion commitment proceedings. For instance, in Illinois records and communications may be disclosed when it is "necessary to the provision of emergency medical care to a recipient" or in "commitment proceedings." 740 Ill. Comp. Stat. Ill. 110/11 (Mental Health and Development Disability Confidentiality Act, 1979). HIPAA does not expressly authorize disclosure in connection with civil commitment, but it

does permit disclosure when "necessary to prevent or lessen a serious and imminent threat to the health or safety of a person or the public." 45 C.F.R. § 164.512. Because civil commitment generally requires a similar showing (see Chapter Eight, infra), this exception can be read to permit disclosure in conjunction with a civil commitment proceeding.

4. *Continuing importance of state confidentiality laws.* State confidentiality laws that do not conflict with HIPAA retain their vitality. Such laws may provide protections that exceed those called for by HIPAA and moreover, may provide private rights of action to persons whose privacy rights have been infringed. This stands in contrast to HIPAA, which only assigns remedies and provides for enforcement by DHHS. See *Smith v. Am. Home Products Corp. Wyeth–Ayerst Pharm.*, 855 A.2d 608 (N.J. 2003) (holding that a New Jersey law providing broader protection of health records than HIPAA controlled).

5. *Hypothetical.* Rick Rocker, a famous rock star, had come to Metro City for a rock concert in which he was the featured performer. In the early morning hours of January 1, 2005, friends of Rick's called 9–1–1 to report that Rick, who was in a hotel penthouse suite, was unconscious and turning blue. The 9–1–1 operator immediately relayed the call to the Metro City Emergency Response Office, which in turn dispatched an ambulance owned and operated by a local hospital. By coincidence, Brenda Star, ace reporter with the Metro Sentinel, a local newspaper, happened to be interviewing a doctor at the Metro City Emergency Response Office when the call came in. Having overhead the call on a speakerphone, Brenda thought that this might make an interesting story and decided to follow the ambulance in her own vehicle to Rocker's hotel. A short time later, two ambulance paramedics emerged from the hotel wheeling Rocker out on a stretcher. Just as the ambulance was ready to leave for the hospital, Brenda asked one of the paramedics what had caused Rocker's collapse and "Will he be okay?" In response, the paramedic replied, "It looks like he overdid the partying bit— we gave him a shot of Narcan to help bring him out of it." Knowing that Narcan is used to reverse the effects of opiate drugs, Brenda concluded that Rocker's condition was the result of an overdose of Percocet or another opiate.

Ten days later, Rocker recovered. Upon being released from the hospital he was told by his manager that the press report on his overdose will probably hurt his career and that he has already been dropped by one TV sponsor, who was planning to use a video he had previously made. Unhappy at this turn of events, Rocker asks his legal representative to file a complaint with the DHHS Office of Civil Rights (OCR) asserting a violation of his HIPAA privacy rights. Does the OCR have any grounds for bringing charges against any of the parties involved in this case? If so, which party or parties, and on what basis?

6. *Review of HIPAA constitutionality.* HIPAA regulations have withstood constitutional challenges asserting they violate the non-delegation of legislative power doctrine. See *South Carolina Med. Ass'n v. Thompson*, 327 F.3d 346 (4th Cir. 2003), *cert den.*, 540 U.S. 981 (2003). See also Abigail

English & Carol A. Ford, *The HIPAA Privacy Rule and Adolescents: Legal Questions and Clinical Challenges*, 36(2) Persp. Sexual & Reproductive Health 80 (2004); Andrew S. Krulwich & Bruce L. McDonald, *The Vulnerability of HIPAA Regulations to First and Fourth Amendment Attack*, 56 Food & Drug L.J. 281 (2001).

7.   *Application to state facilities.* While the HIPAA legislation does not expressly purport to cover public sector entities, it has been assumed that the regulations concerning privacy protection are not limited to the private sector. Apparently state agencies and institutions are complying with the HIPAA rules. However, at some point, some provisions of HIPAA could be challenged by a state on the basis that HIPAA may not constitutionally be applied to the states because of the Eleventh Amendment. The doctrinal basis for a challenge to the application of HIPAA to the states and the relevant cases that have addressed this issue are discussed in Chapter Twelve, infra.

C. PROTECTION OF EDUCATIONAL RECORDS UNDER FERPA

The Family Educational Rights and Privacy Act of 1974 (FERPA) protects the confidentiality of school records maintained by any educational institution that accepts federal funding (which, as a practical matter, includes virtually all institutions of higher learning, as well as public elementary and secondary schools). In general, FERPA bars the disclosure of personally identifiable information drawn from a student's education records to a third party without the written consent of a parent if the student is under 18, and the written consent of the student if he or she is 18 years or older. Under FERPA, the term "educational records" is defined as "[t]hose records, files, documents and other materials which (i) contain information directly related to a student; and (ii) are maintained by an educational agency or institution or by a person acting for such agency or institution." 20 U.S.C. § 1232g(a)(4)(A); 34 C.F.R. § 99.3. However, FERPA excludes from the definition of educational records:

> records of a student who is eighteen years of age or older, or is attending an institution of postsecondary education, which are made or maintained by a physician, psychiatrist, psychologist, or other recognized professional or paraprofessional acting in his professional or paraprofessional capacity, or assisting in that capacity, and which are made, maintained, or used only in connection with the provision of treatment to the student.

20 U.S.C. § 1232g(a)(4)(B)(iv); 34 C.F.R. § 99.3.

It is not clear whether HIPAA covers these records. Compare 45 C.F.R. § 160.103 and Memorandum, *Sharing Information About Potentially Dangerous Students*, Office of the General Counsel, University of Texas System, July 10, 2007, with U.S. Department of Education

Guidance Letter of Nov. 29, 2004, to M. Baise, Associated University Counsel, University of New Mexico. In any event, even if HIPAA applies, HIPAA regulations permit disclosure when "necessary to prevent or lessen a serious and imminent threat to the health or safety of a person or the public, . . . to a person or persons reasonably able to prevent or lessen the threat, including the target of the threat." 45 C.F.R. § 164.512(j). As a practical matter, the generality with which the FERPA and HIPAA exceptions are phrased makes it likely that a university would have wide discretion to disclose information drawn from treatment records if the university believed in good faith that a student presented a serious danger to herself or third persons.

Aside from the possibility that health treatment records maintained by a university may be covered by FERPA or HIPAA Privacy Rules, state law could also come into play in determining whether non-consensual disclosure may be made in a particular circumstance. The exceptions for non-consensual disclosure under both HIPAA and FERPA do not displace state laws that are more protective of health record privacy. Thus, even where disclosure is permitted under one of the HIPAA or FERPA exceptions, state law could prevent disclosure or at least limit disclosure to specific persons and entities.

QUESTIONS AND COMMENTS

1.   *Contrasting scope of HIPAA and FERPA.* Differences in the scope of HIPAA's and HIPAA's privacy rules are summarized in the report of the Virginia Tech Review Panel, which was assembled in the aftermath of the mass shootings that occurred at the school in 2007 (see Chapter Three):

> FERPA was drafted to apply to educational records, not medical records [and therefore does not enumerate the different types of disclosures that are authorized]. . . . FERPA also has a different scope than HIPAA. Medical privacy laws such as HIPAA apply to all information—written or oral—gained in the course of treatment. FERPA applies only to information in student *records*. Personal observations and conversations with a student fall outside FERPA. Thus, for example, teachers or administrators who witness students acting strangely are not restricted by FERPA from telling anyone—school officials, law enforcement, parents or any other person or organization.

Review Panel Report, supra, at 66.

2.   *Transfer of health information from a medical unit to university administration.* While the treatment records of a university health facility are not subject to FERPA, a record that originates as a university medical record but is shared with another university official for a legitimate educational purpose becomes an education record subject to FERPA. For example, if a medical record is provided at a student's request to a faculty member or the dean of students in support of the student's request to be

granted a medical leave of absence, that record would become part of the student's education record and would be subject to FERPA.

D. LEGAL REMEDIES FOR BREACH OF CONFIDENTIALITY UNDER STATE LAW

State remedies for breach of confidentiality in the context of mental health treatment remain available despite the enactment of HIPAA and the promulgation of the related privacy regulations. HIPAA authorizes enforcement action only by the Department of Health and Human Services' Office of Civil Rights and does not provide the client/patient whose privacy interests have been compromised with any private cause of action. Thus, the client/patient whose privacy rights have been violated would need to seek redress against an offending health care provider under state law. At the same time, it is likely that HIPAA's privacy protection standards will influence the development and application of state remedial laws. This is likely to happen when state laws are drafted in general terms, with HIPAA standards incorporated by courts when applying these state laws.

1. General Remedies

a. *Actions Based on Breach of Privacy*

Essentially four distinct types of privacy actions have been identified. In one, the privacy refers to a physical intrusion into a person's private affairs, such as wiretapping someone's telephone. A second type involves appropriation, i.e., the use of another person's photograph or likeness for commercial gain or advantage (e.g., for advertising purposes) without permission. A third entails publication of incomplete or misleading information, which places another person in a "false light" in the public eye. For instance, using a person's photograph to illustrate a story about drug addicts when the person is neither a drug addict nor has any relationship to the story may violate that person's privacy rights. A fourth type, and the one that most concerns mental health professionals, is the revelation of confidential information about a person. This action is founded on the premise that if information that a person (e.g., someone in treatment) could reasonably expect to remain private is disclosed, a cause of action may arise based on that disclosure. This cause of action is most often referred to as the public disclosure of private facts and covers the disclosure of those matters that would be embarrassing to the average individual. The following case, which arose from the efforts of a noted producer of documentary films to expose abuses in a state psychiatric facility, illustrates the application of this doctrine.

COMMONWEALTH V. WISEMAN

Supreme Judicial Court of Massachusetts, 1969.
356 Mass. 251, 249 N.E.2d 610.

CUTTER, JUSTICE.

This bill seeks, among other relief, to enjoin all showings of a film entitled "Titicut Follies," containing scenes at Massachusetts Correctional Institution at Bridgewater (Bridgewater), to which insane persons charged with crime and defective delinquents may be committed. The film was made between April 22, and June 29, 1966. Mr. Wiseman and Bridgewater Film Company, Inc. (BFC) appeal from an interlocutory decree, an order for a decree, and the final decree which enjoins showing the film "to any audience" and requires Mr. Wiseman and BFC to deliver up to the Attorney General for destruction specified films, negatives, and sound tapes. The plaintiffs appeal from the final decree because it did not order sums realized by various defendants from showing the film to be held for distribution as the court might direct.

The trial judge made a report of material facts. The evidence (2,556 pages of proceedings on eighteen trial days and sixty-four exhibits) is reported. The facts, except as otherwise indicated, are stated on the basis of the trial judge's findings and certain exhibits. The film has been shown to the Justices participating in this decision.

In 1965, Mr. Wiseman first requested permission from the Superintendent and from the Commissioner to make an educational documentary film concerning Bridgewater. His first request was denied. On January 28, 1966, permission was granted, subject to the receipt of a favorable opinion from the Attorney General (that the officials could grant permission) and to the conditions (a) that "the rights of the inmates and patients . . . [would be] fully protected," (b) that there would be used only "photographs of inmates and patients . . . legally competent to sign releases," (c) that a written release would be obtained "from each patient whose photograph is used in the film," and (d) that the film would not be released "without first having been . . . approved by the Commissioner and Superintendent." The existence of the final condition was the subject of conflicting evidence but there was oral testimony upon which the trial judge could reasonably conclude that it had been imposed.

* * *

In April, 1966, Mr. Wiseman and his film crew started work at Bridgewater. They were given free access to all departments except the treatment center for the sexually dangerous, whose director made "strong objections" in writing to any photography there without compliance with explicit written conditions. In three months, 80,000 feet of film were exposed. Pictures were made "of mentally incompetent patients . . . in the nude . . . [and] in the most personal and private situations."

In approaching the Commissioner and the Superintendent, Mr. Wiseman had indicated that he planned a documentary film about three people: an adult inmate, a youthful offender, and a correctional officer. It was to be an effort "to illustrate the various services performed—custodial, punitive, rehabilitative, and medical." The judge concluded (a) that the "plain import of [Mr.] Wiseman's representations was that his film was to be . . . non-commercial and non-sensational," whereas, in the judge's opinion, it was "crass . . . commercialism"; (b) that, in fact, the film "constitutes a most flagrant abuse[2] of the privilege . . . [Mr. Wiseman] was given"; and (c) that, instead of "a public service project," the film, as made, is "to be shown to the general public in movie houses."

* * *

In September, 1967, Mr. Wiseman made an agreement with Grove for distribution of the film for "showing to the general public . . . throughout the United States and Canada," with Mr. Wiseman to receive "50% of the theatrical gross receipts, and 75% from any television sale." Grove, for promotion of the film, was to have "complete control of the manner and means of distribution." The film was shown privately, and to the public for profit, in New York City in the autumn of 1967.

The trial judge ruled, inter alia, (a) that such "releases as may have been obtained [from inmates] are a nullity"; (b) "that the film is an unwarranted . . . intrusion . . . into the . . . right to privacy of each inmate" pictured, degrading "these persons in a manner clearly not warranted by any legitimate public concern"; (c) that the "right of the public to know" does not justify the unauthorized use of pictures showing identifiable persons "in such a manner as to . . . cause . . . humiliation"; (d) that "it is the responsibility of the State to protect" the inmates "against any such . . . exploitation"; and (e) that the Commonwealth is under "obligation . . . to protect the right of privacy of those . . . committed to its . . . custody."

Reactions to the film set out in the record vary from the adversely critical conclusions of the trial judge to those expressed by witnesses who regarded it as fine journalistic reporting, as education, and as art.[5] The

---

[2]   Among the findings are the following: The film "is a hodge-podge of sequences . . . depicting mentally ill patients engaged in repetitive, incoherent, and obscene rantings. . . . The film is excessively preoccupied with nudity. . . . [N]aked inmates are shown desperately attempting to hide . . . their privates with their hands. . . . There is a scene of . . . [a priest] administering the last rites of the church to a dying patient [and] the preparation of corpse for burial. . . . A . . . patient, grossly deformed by . . . congenital brain damage, is paraded before the camera."

[5]   For example the *Life* review said, in part, "The Bridgewater atmosphere is one of aimless hopelessness. . . . A psychiatrist turns an interview with an inmate into a sadistic baiting, or, with malicious cheerfulness, force-feeds a dying old man, while we wonder whether the ash from the doctor's carelessly dangling cigarette is really going to fall into the glop being funneled into the convulsively shuddering throat. A society's treatment of the least of its citizens . . . is perhaps the best measure of its civilization. The repulsive reality . . . forces us to contemplate our

Attorney General (Mr. Richardson) testified that the film "was impressive in many ways . . . powerful in impact." He, however, expressed concern about the problem of obtaining valid releases, even from those "conceivably competent," since the releases would have been given before the inmates "could have any idea how they would be depicted." There was testimony from experts about the value of the film for instruction of medical and law students, and "exposure of conditions in a public institution."

1. [As an initial matter, the Court held that because the film constituted documentary evidence, the appellate court could undertake its appraisal without regard to the findings of the trial court.]

2. The Commissioner and the Superintendent would have acted wisely if they had reduced any agreement to writing rather than to have risked the misunderstandings possible in oral discussions. They also might have avoided dispute if they had supervised the filming itself much more closely. . . .

Early in the negotiations, Mr. Wiseman represented in writing that only pictures of inmates "legally competent to sign releases" would be used and that the "question of competency would . . . be determined by the Superintendent and his staff." In the 1966 request for the Attorney General's opinion, Mr. Wiseman was quoted as giving assurance that a written release would be obtained "from each . . . patient whose photograph is used." The latter assurance was quoted in the opinion (March 21, 1966) stating that the Superintendent had power to permit the film to be made. In the circumstances, the judge reasonably could conclude that these representations were a part of the arrangement.

The judge was also clearly justified in deciding on the basis of expert testimony, that some of sixty-two inmates identified as shown in the film were incompetent to understand a release and, on the basis of a stipulation, that releases were obtained only from eleven or twelve of the numerous inmates depicted. There was ample basis for concluding that Mr. Wiseman had not fulfilled important undertakings clearly designed to assure that the film would show only those consenting in writing to their appearance in the film and competent to understand and to give such consent.

3. The film shows many inmates in situations which would be degrading to a person of normal mentality and sensitivity. Although to a casual observer most of the inmates portrayed make little or no specific individual impression, others are shown in close-up pictures. These inmates are sufficiently clearly exhibited (in some instances naked) to enable acquaintances to identify them. Many display distressing mental

---

capacity for callousness. No one seeing this film can but believe that reform of the conditions it reports is urgent business."

symptoms. There is a collective, indecent intrusion into the most private aspects of the lives of these unfortunate persons in the Commonwealth's custody.

We need not discuss to what extent in Massachusetts violation of privacy will give rise to tort liability to individuals. We think, in any event, that Mr. Wiseman's massive, unrestrained invasion of the intimate lives of these State patients may be prevented by properly framed injunctive relief. The Commonwealth has standing and a duty to protect reasonably, and in a manner consistent with other public interests, the inmates from any invasions of their privacy substantially greater than those inevitably arising from the very fact of confinement.

There is a "general power of the Legislature, in its capacity as parens patriae, to make suitable provision for incompetent persons." A "comprehensive system for their care and custody" is contained in [Massachusetts statutory provisions]. The Legislature has exercised that power with specific reference to Bridgewater, among other institutions. These general provisions import all reasonable power, and the duty, to exercise proper controls over the persons confined and the conditions of their custody and to afford the inmates protection and kindness consistent with the terms and rehabilitative purposes of their commitments.

The Commissioner and Superintendent, under reasonable standards of custodial conduct, could hardly permit merely curious members of the public access to Bridgewater to view directly many activities of the type shown in the film. We think it equally inconsistent with their custodial duties to permit the general public (as opposed to members of groups with a legitimate, significant, interest) to view films showing inmates naked or exhibiting painful aspects of mental disease.

These considerations, taken with the failure of Mr. Wiseman to comply with the contractual condition that he obtain valid releases from all persons portrayed in the film, amply justify granting injunctive relief to the Commonwealth. The impracticability of affording relief to the inmates individually also supports granting this collective relief to the Commonwealth as parens patriae, in the interest of all the affected inmates. We give no weight to any direct interest of the Commonwealth itself in suppressing the film.

4.   The defendants contend that no asserted interest of privacy may be protected from the publication of this film because the conditions at Bridgewater are matters of continuing public concern, as this court has recognized. Indeed, it was concern over conditions at Bridgewater which led various public officials in 1965 and 1966 to consider a documentary film, in the hope that, if suitable, it might arouse public interest and lead to improvement.

Even an adequate presentation to the public of conditions at Bridgewater, however, would not necessitate the inclusion of some episodes shown in the film, nor would it justify the depiction of identifiable inmates, who had not given valid written consents and releases, naked or in other embarrassing situations. We agree with the trial judge that Mr. Wiseman's wide ranging photography amounted to "abuse of the privilege he was given to make a film" and a serious failure to comply with conditions reasonably imposed upon him. Mr. Wiseman could hardly have fairly believed that officials, solicitous about obtaining consent and releases from all inmates portrayed, could have been expected to approve this type of film for general distribution.

The record does not indicate to us that any inmate shown in the film, by reason of past conduct, had any special news interest as an individual. Each inmate's importance to the film was that he was an inmate of Bridgewater, that he suffered from some form of mental disease, and that he was undergoing in the Bridgewater facilities particular types of custody and treatment. Recognizable pictures of individuals, although perhaps resulting in more effective photography, were not essential. In the circumstances, there will be no unreasonable interference with any publication of matters of public concern if showing the film to the general public is prevented (a) to protect interests of the inmates in privacy, and (b) because Mr. Wiseman went unreasonably beyond the scope of the conditional permission to enter, and take pictures upon, State owned premises properly not generally open for public inspection and photography.

The case is distinguishable from decisions which have permitted publication of newsworthy events where the public interest in reasonable dissemination of news has been treated as more significant than the private interests in privacy. We need not now consider to what extent Mr. Wiseman could have been wholly excluded from making a film at Bridgewater. In this aspect of the case, we hold merely that he violated the permission given to him, reasonably interpreted, and did not comply with valid conditions that he obtain written releases.

* * *

5.   That injunctive relief may be granted against showing the film to the general public on a commercial basis does not mean that all showings of the film must be prevented. As already indicated, the film gives a striking picture of life at Bridgewater and of the problems affecting treatment at that or any similar institution. It is a film which would be instructive to legislators, judges, lawyers, sociologists, social workers, doctors, psychiatrists, students in these or related fields, and organizations dealing with the social problems of custodial care and mental infirmity. The public interest in having such persons informed about Bridgewater, in our opinion, outweighs any countervailing interests

of the inmates and of the Commonwealth (as parens patriae) in anonymity and privacy.

The effect upon inmates of showing the film to persons with a serious interest in rehabilitation, and with potential capacity to be helpful, is likely to be very different from the effect of its exhibition merely to satisfy general public curiosity. There is possibility that showings to specialized audiences may be of benefit to the public interest, to the inmates themselves, and to the conduct of an important State institution. Because of the character of such audiences, the likelihood of humiliation, even of identifiable inmates, is greatly reduced. In any event the likelihood of harm seems to us less than the probability of benefits.

6. . . . The decree is to be modified to permit (according to standards to be defined in the decree) the showing of the film to audiences of the specialized or professional character already mentioned.

* * *

[The Court held that individual inmates who had been filmed were not entitled to damages.]

QUESTIONS AND COMMENTS

1. *Impact of HIPAA.* What might have happened had HIPAA been in effect at the time that Mr. Wiseman filmed the documentary? HIPAA privacy rules apply to any psychiatric hospital that is "a covered entity." If the Bridgewater institution was a covered entity (possible challenges on Eleventh Amendment grounds to the application of HIPAA to state institutions are discussed in Part I.B.3.g., supra), would it be a violation of HIPAA for Bridgewater to allow a documentary filmmaker to film the inmates? Would HIPAA limitations also cover the documentary filmmaker?

2. *"Titicut Follies" revisited.* As indicated by the following news report, the film *"Titicut Follies"* continued to be the subject of judicial proceedings twenty years after the court rendered the above decision.

> BOSTON, Sept. 29—A judge has said that a 22–year–old ban on the public showing of a film that depicts brutality in a state prison hospital for the mentally ill may be lifted if the faces of many of the inmates are blurred.
>
> But the filmmaker, Frederick Wiseman, says that blurring faces is not technically feasible. Even if it were, he said, such an action would violate his right to free speech as a journalist and the public's right to know how state-supported institutions are run.
>
> "The film would lose its meaning," said Mr. Wiseman, an award-winning director known for his unflinchingly realistic portrayal of the police, schools, hospitals and other institutions that bring people in contact with the state. "The whole point is that these are not faceless people. Their faces reflect the lives they've lived and how they've been treated."

Judge Proposes Compromise on Banned Film, N.Y. Times, Sept. 30, 1989, at 8, col. 6.

   3.   *Basis for standing to bring action.* The action, brought by the state of Massachusetts to enjoin the showing of the film, relied on the *parens patriae* power of the state to protect persons unable to care for themselves. The dimensions of this power will be explored in greater detail in Chapter Nine.

   4.   *Capacity to consent.* Some patients were sufficiently mentally ill as to lack capacity to consent to the filming. Could state authorities acting under the *parens patriae* power consent on behalf of these patients? If not, under what circumstances, if any, could they be filmed? Issues relating to this question are also taken up in Chapter Nine.

   5.   *Privacy vs. the public's interest to know.* In some circumstances, the general public may have a legitimate interest in the proper conduct of incompetency or involuntary commitment hearings. As the court noted in *Commonwealth v. Wiseman*, a public interest in the treatment of individuals with a mental illness may sufficiently outweigh patients' countervailing interest in privacy. To what extent should public concerns override privacy rights? Should disclosure be limited to cases where it is hoped that public attention will lead to improved conditions for patients, as in *Commonwealth v. Wiseman?*

   Consider In re *New York News, Inc.*, 494 N.E.2d 1379 (N.Y. 1986). The New York Court of Appeals described the facts as follows:

> During the evening rush hour on October 22, 1985, at the Times Square subway station in Manhattan, appellant Mary Ventura, in what the police termed "an unprovoked assault", pushed a young woman into the path of an oncoming train, causing serious injury. . . .

> In the ensuing days, the newspapers reported that in July 1985 Ventura had been a psychiatric patient in Kings County Hospital, and that she had been released on September 27, 1985—only weeks before the assault—following a judicial proceeding under the Mental Hygiene Law. Her name and photograph, the details of the incident, her hospitalization and her background were widely publicized. Ventura's mother and her neighbors made public statements about her hospitalization, her release and her past erratic, even violent behavior. Within two days of the incident, a spokesman for appellant Health and Hospitals Corporation (HHC) announced that the Judge who had presided at Ventura's retention hearing ordered release over the objection of psychiatrists, and the Judge and his law clerk responded that the psychiatric recommendation had been followed. Controversy immediately erupted over whether procedures for the release of mental patients, designed for the protection of both the patients and the public, were being properly applied—and if not where the fault lay.

> After HHC's disclosure, New York News, Inc., petitioned for release of the retention hearing transcript, redacted to include only counsel's

arguments, the psychiatrist's recommendation, and the court's determination. Although New York law limited disclosure to a party or to "someone properly interested" in such proceedings, the paper argued that the press was "properly interested" because of the surrounding controversy. In holding that release was justified, the court noted that Ventura's assault and statements made by her mother and neighbors focused attention on her identity and condition, and that public apprehension concerning the proceeding which resulted in her release naturally resulted. The court concluded that blindly maintaining secrecy "even where a patient's identity is known . . . sacrifices a legitimate public interest in information regarding procedures for the release of mental patients." 494 N.E.2d at 1381.

b. Defamation

Defamation is the tort of making a statement to a third person that tends to injure the reputation of another, that is, which tends to diminish the person's esteem and respect in the eyes of the community, or to excite adverse or unpleasant opinions about the person. When the statement is oral, the tort is called slander; when it is written, the tort is called libel. Sometimes courts require that the statement be made with malice or ill will toward the plaintiff. Even when the statement was made without actual malice, however, the speaker may be held liable for resulting injury to the plaintiff. In such cases the malice is said to be implied.

Generally, two defenses are available in an action for defamation. One is truth; the second is privilege. The privilege associated with the law of defamation is not coextensive with the testimonial privilege to be discussed later in this chapter. Privilege here means that certain statements that might otherwise be considered defamatory are immune from attack given the context in which they were spoken. For example, statements made by a therapist during the course of judicial or quasi-judicial proceedings are absolutely immune from legal challenge. This would apply to a therapist's testimony in civil commitment hearings or malpractice trials.

It is also a general rule that defamatory statements, if made in good faith to discharge a legitimate duty with which the speaker is charged, or to advance a valid and important interest of the speaker, are privileged if the statements are made to another person having a corresponding interest or responsibility. This interest need not necessarily be of a legal nature, but may arise from a moral or social imperative.

While a detailed analysis of the law of defamation is beyond the scope of these materials, we consider next a case that illustrates its application in the context of treatment.

HUGHLEY V. MCDERMOTT

Court of Special Appeals of Maryland, 1987.
72 Md. App. 391, 530 A.2d 13.

KARWACKI, JUDGE.

David E. Hughley appeals from a summary judgment rendered against him by the Circuit Court of Prince George's County in the defamation action he filed against Michael T. McDermott, the appellee. We disagree with the hearing judge's conclusion that the pleadings, depositions, answers to interrogatories, admissions and affidavits filed in the proceeding showed that there was no genuine dispute between the parties as to any material fact and that the appellee was entitled to judgment as a matter of law. Consequently, under Rule 2–501, summary judgment was not appropriate, and we shall vacate that judgment and remand the case for trial.

We restate the questions presented by the parties as follows:

1.   Did the appellee enjoy an absolute privilege in publishing the allegedly defamatory matter because of appellant's actual or implied consent to its publication?

2.   Was the content of the publications actionable as defamation?

3.   Did the appellee abuse the qualified privilege he enjoyed to publish the defamatory matter concerning the appellant?

*   *   *

The record before the hearing judge discloses the following "facts."

The appellant applied to the Maryland–National Capital Park and Planning Commission (MNCPPC) for the position of a Park Police Officer in October of 1981. He was accepted as a Park Police candidate on August 9, 1982. At that time he was advised that he would have to complete candidate training school, as well as a 12 month probationary period before final acceptance as a Park Police Officer. He worked as a police dispatcher through November of 1982 and then entered the Police Academy in Prince George's County. After completing his training at the Academy in April of 1983, he began field patrol training. When the appellant learned that he might be transferred to the horse mounted training unit, he wrote to Captain George Klotz, who was the commanding officer of that unit. He advised Captain Klotz that he had "no love of horses," and would be uncomfortable in mounted training. Captain Klotz met with the appellant, and the appellant explained his reservations about working with horses, relating his limited personal experiences with horses which included vivid childhood recollections of falling off a pony and of a disfiguring injury suffered by his uncle who was kicked in the face by a horse. Nevertheless, Captain Klotz informed the appellant that he was a "natural" for mounted training because he "was bowlegged and skinny," and convinced the appellant to "try" the mounted unit. He began training with the mounted unit on August 15, 1983.

The appellant's first contact with horses precipitated the onset of nausea which plagued the appellant whenever he rode a horse or was in a stall with one. His symptoms progressed from "mild stomach problems" to vomiting. At first the appellant was determined to overcome his fear which he felt produced the physical discomfort he experienced. At the conclusion of the first week of training the appellant informed Captain Klotz that he was "uncomfortable." On the morning of Monday, August 22, 1983, the appellant had stomach cramps and diarrhea, and called in sick. On the following Tuesday and Wednesday he participated in the program but advised his supervisors of his condition. The appellant was absent from work from August 25 until September 6 because he was experiencing leg, back and hip pain from riding horses. The appellant sought medical treatment from Dr. Gary Jones at his group health association for this problem.

When he returned to work on September 6, 1983, the appellant again spoke with Captain Klotz who insisted that the appellant complete mounted training, notwithstanding appellant's pleas that his illnesses were related to contact with horses. Later that day the appellant went to see Dr. Ann L.B. Williams, another physician at his group health association. On September 7, 1983, Dr. Williams, after consulting a psychiatrist, wrote a letter to MNCPPC on the appellant's behalf which recommended that the appellant be excused from mounted training because of his "extreme anxiety with associated physical symptoms" when around horses.

On September 12, 1983, appellant was summoned to appear before Lieutenant Robert Fox of the mounted unit. After they discussed the problems which appellant had experienced with horse mounted training, Lieutenant Fox told appellant that he would have to see the appellee [a psychologist]. Two days later appellant received a telephone call from Lieutenant Fox advising him to report for an appointment with appellee that evening.

The appellee, a psychologist, had contracted with MNCPPC to act as its consultant and to provide counseling and referral services for its employees who needed help in resolving emotional problems which affected their work. The appellee met with the appellant for approximately 30 minutes on September 14, 1983.

At that meeting the appellant described his above mentioned unhappy childhood experiences with horses, and his observations as a Park Police candidate that several mounted officers had injured their knees as a result of horseback riding accidents. He chronicled his physical reactions to horseback riding and to being in a stall with a horse. He told the appellee that Captain Klotz insisted that he ride, and that other

officers referred to the captain's methods of training as "Gestapo tactics."
... [During the interview, according to the plaintiff's complaint, the appellee stated:] "They told me you had an authority problem but I don't think you have one, I don't think you are abnormal." Finally, the appellee agreed to provide a copy of his diagnosis to the appellant.

On September 29, 1983, the appellant was ordered to appear before Major Richard Belt of MNCPPC, Larry Brownlee of the Fraternal Order of Police, and the appellee. The appellee opened the meeting by stating that he had advised Major Belt that appellant's phobia of horses was real. Appellee next stated that he and appellant had agreed that appellant would submit to hypnosis to treat his phobia. At that point appellant interrupted and advised those present that he had not agreed to hypnosis. That contradiction precipitated an argument between appellant and appellee, and the meeting deteriorated. The appellee told the appellant to sign a "release" for his lawyers before leaving the meeting. The appellant complied. That document, preprinted with blanks which were completed in handwriting, is entitled "Consent for Release of Confidential Information." As completed and signed on September 29, 1983, it provided:

> I do hereby authorize Michael T. McDermott, Ph.D. to disclose to Major Belt the following information: Diagnosis and Recommendations for the purpose of suitability for mounted training.

... On October 4, 1983, the appellee wrote to Major Belt:

> At the request of Lt. Fox, I conducted an evaluation of POC David Hughley on September 22, 1983.[1] As an outcome of this evaluation, a meeting was scheduled with you and Mr. Hughley on September 29, 1983. The purpose of these meetings was to determine if POC Hughley suffers a phobic reaction to horses which prevents him from receiving training in the Mounted Unit.

> It is my opinion based on the session with Officer Hughley and conversation with other officers that no such phobic reaction exists and the symptoms of anxiety (stomach cramps) are presentations of false and grossly exaggerated symptoms. The symptoms appear to be produced to avoid working in the Mounted Unit and specifically to avoid working under the command of Captain Klotz. In a word, this is termed "malingering." Most notable in the process of arriving at this diagnosis was POC Hughley's lack of cooperation with the evaluation and prescribed treatment regimen.

> I will supply you with a full detailed explanation of these findings in the near future. . . .

---

[1]   Both the appellant and the appellee in their deposition testimony stated that the date of this interview was September 14, 1983.

As he had promised, the appellee supplemented that correspondence on October 22, 1983. On that date he related to Major Belt:

> This report will elaborate on my letter of October 4, 1983 regarding POC Hughley in which I reported my findings that he was "malingering" in regard to work on the Mounted Unit.

* * *

[After detailing appellant's rejection of appellee's hypnotherapy recommendation, the appellee's report concluded:]

> Based on his irascible mood, refusal to cooperate in any way to alleviate this situation at the Mounted Unit other than to be removed, the [fact that his] symptom[s] occur[ed] only when given an order, and his stated dislike of the Unit commander, I was forced to conclude that this was not a bona fide phobia but a manipulation to get out of a work assignment he did not like.

> Beyond the issues in this incident, one must speculate on the viability of such an officer to be relied upon in the future to follow orders and deal with your organization in a forthright and honest manner. I would also question his ability to deal with authority in an orderly way and become a contributing member of the force. To date his actions have been a severe drain on all involved from supervisory personnel to fellow officers. The manipulations he demonstrated indicate there may be more pathological character issues involved here than just contempt for superiors. Other than with criminal elements, I have not seen an individual lie so boldly or so vehemently when to cooperate or to be truthful would only be in his best interest. In sum, one must wonder about his ability to be a police officer and carry out that task responsibly and honestly.

> In summary I find that POC Hughley does not suffer from a phobia to horses which prevents his working in the Mounted Unit. I did find that he was trying to avoid working in the Unit and specifically avoiding the command of Capt. Klotz. His exaggerated symptoms are false presentations aimed at reassignment.

> If I can be more detailed or of further assistance in this matter, please call me.

The appellant was notified on October 18, 1983 of MNCPPC's intention to fire him, and he was officially terminated on December 2, 1983.

I.

Appellee contends that his publication of any defamatory matter in his letters of October 4 and 22, 1983, was absolutely privileged because the appellant consented to such publication. He posits that the record before the hearing judge indisputably showed that, (1) the appellant, at the time of his appointment with the appellee on September 14, 1983, was aware of the fact that the appellee would be reporting his diagnosis and recommendations with regard to the appellant's suspected phobia to the officials at MNCPPC, (2) the appellant implicitly consented to a lack of confidentiality in connection with that meeting by participating in the interview, and (3) the appellant expressly consented to the contents of appellee's reports to his employer by requesting a copy of the appellee's reports and by execution of the "Consent for Release of Confidential Information" on September 29, 1983. The hearing judge rejected the appellee's defense based upon absolute privilege as do we.

* * *

Appellant did not volunteer to see the appellee; he was ordered to that interview by one of his supervisors, Lieutenant Fox. Moreover, at the conclusion of the interview, appellant was advised by appellee that his phobia to horses was real and that the appellee would recommend to MNCPPC that appellant be transferred from the mounted unit. Finally, at the beginning of the meeting on September 29, 1983, appellee reported to those present that appellant's phobia was not feigned. Given these "facts," appellant could not reasonably be charged with knowledge either of the language of appellee's reports, or that appellee's reports would be defamatory when he consented to their publication.

II.

Appellee argues that the summary judgment of the court should be affirmed because his letters of October 4 and 22, 1983 contained only expressions of his opinions following his professional evaluation of the appellant. We are not persuaded.

Accepting, as we must, appellant's version of what occurred on September 14, 1983, the appellee diagnosed the appellant's condition as a genuine phobia to horses and advised him that he would recommend his transfer from the mounted unit. Appellee repeated his diagnosis at the commencement of the meeting on September 29, 1983. After appellant contradicted appellee's report at the meeting that appellant was willing to undergo hypnosis as a treatment for his phobia, they argued, and the meeting abruptly ended. Appellee in his letters which followed that disagreement knowingly falsified his earlier diagnosis. That knowing falsehood is the basis of the appellant's cause of action. . . .

* * *

. . . In the case *sub judice* the record before the hearing judge would support a finding by the trier of fact that the statements of the appellee, although couched as expressions of opinion, were calculated untruths which adversely affected the appellant's employment and were therefore defamatory.

III.

In granting the appellee's motion for summary judgment the hearing judge rested his decision on the ground that appellee enjoyed a qualified privilege for the defamatory statements he made in his letters of October 4 and 22, 1983 and that there was no evidence of an abuse of that privilege. We hold that he erred in his second conclusion.

The appellee, as a consultant retained by the appellant's employer to examine the appellant, enjoyed a qualified privilege to communicate defamatory information derived from that examination to the employer. . . .

It is well settled, however, that the qualified privilege accorded to a defamatory communication published within the employer-employee relationship is defeasible where the publication is made with knowledge of its falsity or with reckless disregard for its truth. Furthermore, where there is any evidence of such knowing falsity or reckless disregard for truth, the issue of whether the qualified privilege has been lost by its abuse must be resolved by the trier of fact and not as a matter of law by the court. Since there was disputed evidence before the hearing judge in the instant case as to whether the appellee defamed the appellant in his letters of October 4 and 22, 1983, with knowledge that the information contained in those communications was false, the issue of appellee's forfeiture of his privilege by abuse was not one which could be resolved by summary judgment.

Judgment vacated; case remanded to the Circuit Court . . . for further proceedings consistent with this Opinion.

QUESTIONS AND COMMENTS

1. *Proof of knowledge of falsity.* Psychologists are frequently retained by employers to evaluate job applicants and employees. What are the risks that a psychologist who provides a negative evaluation will be sued for defamation? Is the test for potential liability whether the psychologist/defendant had *knowledge* of the falsity of the conclusions contained in the evaluation? If knowledge is a requirement, what was the plaintiff's offer of proof in this regard in the *Hughley v. McDermott* case? Assume that McDermott knew the diagnosis was false. Was he or should he have been immune from liability by virtue of his employment with the department?

2. *HIPAA.* Would HIPAA privacy regulations cover the evaluation by McDermott? If so, was the right type of "release" obtained? Under HIPAA, client "consent" and client "authorization" are different concepts. A provider has the option but is not required to use the *consent* format where the purpose of the disclosure of PHI is restricted to treatment, payment, or health care operations. 45 C.F.R. § 164.506. Where the provider chooses to obtain consent for this purpose, it can be drafted to permit multiple

disclosures. For instance, patient consent at the outset of treatment will permit a health care provider to disclose PHI in connection with future payment requests by an insurance carrier. An *authorization*, on the other hand, refers to a specific permission to use or disclose PHI for any purpose other than treatment, payment, or health care operations. An authorization will only be valid if it provides the client with detailed information including: the precise PHI to be disclosed, the identity of the person(s) to whom it is to be disclosed, an expiration date for the proposed disclosure, and the right of the client to revoke the authorization at any time. 45 C.F.R. § 164.508.

2. Remedies Arising from a Breach During a Treatment Relationship

DOE V. ROE
Supreme Court, New York County, 1977.
93 Misc.2d 201, 400 N.Y.S.2d 668.

MARTIN B. STECHER, JUSTICE:

This action for an injunction and for damages for breach of privacy is a matter of first impression in this State, and so far as I am able to ascertain, a matter of first impression in the United States. It arises out of the publication, verbatim, by a psychiatrist of a patient's disclosures during the course of a lengthy psychoanalysis. I have made and filed detailed findings of fact which are briefly summarized here.

Dr. Joan Roe is a physician who has practiced psychiatry for more than fifty years. Her husband, Peter Poe, has been a psychologist for some 25 years. The plaintiff and her late, former husband were each patients of Dr. Roe for many years. The defendants, eight years after the termination of treatment, published a book which reported verbatim and extensively the patients' thoughts, feelings, and emotions, their sexual and other fantasies and biographies, their most intimate personal relationships and the disintegration of their marriage. Interspersed among the footnotes are Roe's diagnoses of what purport to be the illnesses suffered by the patients and one of their children.

The defendants allege that the plaintiff consented to this publication. This defense is without substance. Consent was sought while the plaintiff was in therapy. It was never obtained in writing. In Dr. Roe's own words consent "was there one day and not there another day. That was the nature of the illness I was treating, unreliable." I need not deal with the value of an oral waiver of confidentiality given by a patient to a psychiatrist during the course of treatment. It is sufficient to conclude that not only did the defendants fail to obtain the plaintiff's consent to publication, they were well aware that they had none.

[The plaintiff contended that in the absence of a statutory provision expressly recognizing a cause of action against a therapist who wrongfully discloses confidential information, an action is impliedly authorized by various state laws including sections of the New York Civil Practice Law and Rules (Sec. 4504(a)) and provisions of the New York Licensing and Disciplinary Statutes (Ed. L. 6509 et seq.). Following a review of the text and history of these statutory provisions the court concluded that these sections standing by themselves did not authorize a private cause of action. The court next addressed the plaintiff's contention that other theories including the right to privacy and rights flowing from the contract between the therapist and patient grant a cause of action for wrongful disclosure.]

* * *

As hereafter indicated there are theories on which liability may be predicated other than violation of the CPLR [4504(a)], the licensing and disciplinary statutes [Ed. L. 6509 et seq.] and what I perceive as this State's public policy. In two of the very few cases which have come to grips with the issue of wrongful disclosure by physicians of patients' secrets the courts predicated their holdings on the numerous sources of obligation which arise out of the physician-patient relationship. . . .

* * *

I too find that a physician, who enters into an agreement with a patient to provide medical attention, impliedly covenants to keep in confidence all disclosures made by the patient concerning the patient's physical or mental condition as well as all matters discovered by the physician in the course of examination or treatment. This is particularly and necessarily true of the psychiatric relationship, for in the dynamics of psychotherapy "(t)he patient is called upon to discuss in a candid and frank manner personal material of the most intimate and disturbing nature . . . He is expected to bring up all manner of socially unacceptable instincts and urges, immature wishes, perverse sexual thoughts—in short the unspeakable, the unthinkable, the repressed. To speak of such things to another human being requires an atmosphere of unusual trust, confidence and tolerance. . . . "

There can be little doubt that under the law of the State of New York and in a proper case, the contract of private parties to retain in confidence matter which should be kept in confidence will be enforced by injunction and compensated in damages.

The contract between the plaintiff and Dr. Roe is such a contract. . . .

* * *

Every patient, and particularly every patient undergoing psychoanalysis, has such a right of privacy [emanating from the plaintiff's contract right to confidentiality and other state laws including the licensing and disciplinary statute and the New York civil practice law]. Under what circumstances can a person be expected to reveal sexual fantasies, infantile memories, passions of hate and love, one's most intimate relationship with one's spouse and others except upon the inferential agreement that such confessions will be forever entombed in the psychiatrist's memory, never to be revealed during the psychiatrist's lifetime or thereafter? The very needs of the profession itself require that confidentiality exist *and be enforced.* As pointed out in *Matter of Lifschutz* [(Cal. 1970),] "a large segment of the psychiatric profession concurs in Dr. Lifschutz's strongly held belief that an absolute privilege of confidentiality is essential to the effective practice of psychotherapy" (cf. Ann., 20 A.L.R.3d, 1109–1112). Despite the fact that in no New York case has such a wrong been remedied due, most likely, to the fact that so few physicians violate this fundamental obligation, it is time that the obligation not only be recognized but that the right of redress be recognized as well.

What label we affix to this wrong is unimportant (although the category of wrong could, under certain circumstances—such as determining the applicable statute of limitations—be significant). It is generally accepted that "There is no necessity whatever that a tort must have a name. New and nameless torts are being recognized constantly". (Prosser, Torts [2d ed.], p. 3.) What is important is that there must be the infliction of intentional harm, resulting in damage, without legal excuses or justification.

The defendants contend that the physician's obligation of confidentiality is not absolute and must give way to the general public interest. The interest, as they see it in this case, is the scientific value of the publication.

It is not disputed that under our public policy the right of confidentiality is less than absolute. . . . Despite the duty of confidentiality courts have recognized the duty of a psychiatrist to give warning where a patient clearly presents a danger to others [*Tarasoff*], to disclose the existence of a contagious disease, to report the use of "controlled substances" in certain situations and to report gunshot and other wounds. In no case, however, has the curiosity or education of the medical profession superseded the duty of confidentiality. I do not reach the question of a psychiatrist's right to publish case histories where the identities are fully concealed for that is not our problem here, nor do I find it necessary to reach the issue of whether or not an important scientific discovery would take precedence over a patient's privilege of non-disclosure. I do not consider myself qualified to determine the contribution which this book may have made to the science or art of psychiatry. I do conclude, however, that if such contribution was the defendants' defense they have utterly failed in their proof that this volume represented a major contribution to scientific knowledge. The evidence is to the contrary and this defense must necessarily fail.

Nor is the argument available that by enjoining the further distribution of this book the court will be engaging in a "prior restraint" on publication. . . .

There is no prior restraint in the case at bar. The book has been published and it does offend against the plaintiff's right of privacy, contractual and otherwise, not to have her innermost thoughts offered to all for the price of this book. There is no prior restraint and, therefore, no censorship within constitutional meaning.

* * *

The liability of Dr. Roe to respond in damages is clear, and Mr. Poe's liability is equally clear. True, he and the plaintiff were not involved in a physician-patient relationship and he certainly had no contractual relationship to her. But, the conclusion is unassailable that Poe, like anyone else with access to the book, knew that its source was the patient's production in psychoanalysis. He knew as well as, and perhaps better than Roe, of the absence of consent, of the failure to disguise. If anyone was the actor in seeing to it that the work was written, that it was manufactured, advertised and circulated, it was Poe. He is a co-author and a willing, indeed avid, co-violator of the patient's rights and is therefore equally liable.

The plaintiff seeks punitive damages and suggests that a proper measure of those damages, in addition to compensatory damage, is approximately $50,000, the sum plaintiff has thus far expended on and incurred for attorneys' fees. . . .

In order to warrant an award of punitive damages, it must have been affirmatively demonstrated that the wrong committed was willful and malicious, that the act complained of was "morally culpable or . . . actuated by evil and reprehensible motives, not only to punish the defendant but to deter him, as well as others". Where the act complained of is willful, malicious and wanton, punitive damages are sometimes available to "express indignation at the defendants' wrong rather than a value set on plaintiff's loss." Certainly, the acts of the defendants here are such as to warrant an expression of indignation and punishment for the purpose of deterring similar acts by these defendants or others. The difficulty, however, is that the defendants' acts were not willful, malicious or wanton—they were merely stupid. I have no doubt that the defendants were of the opinion that they had sufficiently concealed the identity of the plaintiff and her family. I have no doubt that in addition to the commercial success they hoped to have, they believed that they were rendering a public service in publishing what they considered an in-depth description of the plaintiff's family. But there was no motive to harm. Under these circumstances, punitive damages are not available.

On turning to compensatory damages, . . .

* * *

The plaintiff has suffered damage as a consequence of this publication. She suffered acute embarrassment on learning the extent to which friends, colleagues, employer, students and others, had read or read of the book. Her livelihood, as indicated in the findings, was threatened; but fortunately, the actual cash loss was only some $1,500. Medical attention, principally treatment with Dr. Lowenfeld, cost an additional $1,400. But beyond these sums the plaintiff suffered in health. She had insomnia and nightmares. She became reclusive as a consequence of the shame and humiliation induced by the book's publication and her well-being and emotional health were significantly impaired for three years. In my opinion the fair and reasonable value of the injury she sustained—to the extent it can be compensated in damages—is $20,000.

Damages, of course, do not provide an adequate remedy; for should the book circulate further, beyond the 220 copies already sold, the damage must accrue anew. The plaintiff is entitled to a judgment permanently enjoining the defendants, their heirs, successors and assigns from further violating the plaintiff's right to privacy whether by circulating this book or by otherwise disclosing any of the matters revealed by the plaintiff to Dr. Roe in the course of psychotherapy.

QUESTIONS AND COMMENTS

1. *Health evaluations at the request of third parties.* Insurance companies frequently require an applicant to supply their medical background and may also request that applicants undergo a physical or other health examination. Similarly, employers may sometimes require a current or prospective employee to undergo a medical or psychological evaluation. Frequently, these evaluations are arranged and paid for by the third party. Under the laws of some states, a practitioner's duty of confidentiality does not apply where the encounter occurred at the request of a third party. However, under HIPAA, persons retain their privacy rights even where the evaluation was performed at the request of a third party. However, a third party such as an employer or insurer may gain access to the evaluation, or PHI in general, by obtaining the evaluee's authorization prior to the referral for the evaluation. See, for example, *Estate of Turnbow v. Ogden City*, 254 F.R.D. 434, 437–38 (D. Utah 2008) (in an evaluation undertaken as part of an application for employment as a police officer, "the psychotherapist-patient privilege [did] not apply" because the applicant "knew that his evaluation would be disclosed as part of the application process[;] he could not have had a reasonable expectation that the communications would be kept private.").

2. *HIPAA and the disclosure of PHI in conjunction with research.* A researcher or research institution is only subject to HIPAA privacy rules if the researcher or the institution is a covered entity. However, if the research facility is also involved in treatment and meets HIPAA's covered entity

criteria, it must comply with the privacy rules. This means that it can transfer PHI to another covered entity without the person's authorization. On the other hand, transfer of PHI to a non-covered entity requires the research participant's authorization. However, as a practical matter, such authorization will generally have been obtained before an individual is admitted into the research program. Such pre-admission authorization is permitted by HIPAA privacy rules. 45 C.F.R. § 164.508(b)(4)(i).

3. *Confidentiality rights following the death of a client.* May a therapist disclose confidential information following the death of a client? This issue has arisen in the context of several celebrated cases where the therapist, following the death of a client, either wrote a book concerning the client or made public disclosures on television or to other media of information obtained from the client in the course of providing treatment.

Anne Sexton, a noted poet who committed suicide in 1974, had been treated for a number of years by Dr. Martin T. Orne, a psychiatrist. In 1991, Dr. Orne, with co-author Diane Wood Middlebrook, published a biography of Sexton. The book relied in part on material taken from Sexton's private therapy sessions and covered her revelations that chronicled "harrowing detail [of] Sexton's madness, alcoholism and sexual abuse of her daughter, along with her many extramarital affairs, including one with a woman and another with the second of her many therapists." Alessandra Stanley, *Poet Told All; Therapist Provides the Record*, N.Y. Times, Jul. 15, 1991, at 1.

More recently, following the 1994 murder of Nicole Simpson, the ex-wife of O.J. Simpson, Susan Forward (a licensed clinical social worker) disclosed to the media in various interviews that she had counseled Nicole Simpson on two occasions and that Ms. Simpson told her that she had been battered and threatened by O.J. Simpson. Shari Roan & Maura Dolan, *Therapist May Face Discipline for Discussing Case*, L.A. Times, June 16, 1994, at A13.

What are the legal rights, if any, of the next of kin or heirs of a deceased client to prevent the disclosure of information obtained by a therapist in the course of treatment? Leading legal commentators have in the past subscribed to the view that a client's rights of privacy terminate at death and that the heirs or next of kin do not have any cause of action for unauthorized disclosures. Fowler V. Harper & Fleming James, *The Law of Torts* § 9.6, at 645 (2d ed. 1986). The Supreme Court, in a different context, held that the attorney-client privilege does not survive the death of the client. *Swidler & Berlin v. United States*, 524 U.S. 399 (1998).

4. Post mortem *privacy of PHI under HIPAA.* Unlike many state health privacy laws, under HIPAA, PHI in the hands of a covered entity retains its protection after a patient's death, and disclosure to non-covered third parties may not be made without the authorization of the decedent's personal representative. The designation of a personal representative is a matter of state law. What factors justify protecting health information *post mortem* when other privacy interests are not generally protected under the laws of most states? Also, an action for defamation cannot be brought where

the alleged defamation occurred after the death of the defamed party. Is there not, in some instances, a public interest in the disclosure of health information of individuals after their death? For instance, does the public have a right to know if a senior government official such as a president was suffering from various disorders and taking heavy doses of medication during his or her term as president? Presumably health providers would not be permitted to disclose such information after the death of the senior official without getting authorization from the official's personal representative who, if a family member, might well prefer to not have such information disclosed. What public interest might be served by the *post mortem* disclosure of health information of this kind? For a discussion of the impact of HIPAA privacy regulations on historical research, see Julie Bell, *Privacy of Dead Perplexes Living*, Baltimore Sun, Nov. 13, 2003, at 1A.

MacDonald v. Clinger

Supreme Court, Appellate Division, Fourth Department, 1982.
84 A.D.2d 482, 446 N.Y.S.2d 801.

Denman, Justice.

We here consider whether a psychiatrist must respond in damages to his former patient for disclosure of personal information learned during the course of treatment and, if he must, on what theory of recovery the action may be maintained. We hold that such wrongful disclosure is a breach of the fiduciary duty of confidentiality and gives rise to a cause of action sounding in tort.

The complaint alleges that during two extended courses of treatment with defendant, a psychiatrist, plaintiff revealed intimate details about himself which defendant later divulged to plaintiff's wife without justification and without consent. As a consequence of such disclosure, plaintiff alleges that his marriage deteriorated, that he lost his job, that he suffered financial difficulty and that he was caused such severe emotional distress that he required further psychiatric treatment. The complaint set forth three causes of action: breach of an implied contract; breach of confidence in violation of public policy; and breach of the right of privacy guaranteed by article 5 of the [N.Y.] Civil Rights Law. Defendant moved to dismiss for failure to state a cause of action, asserting that there was in reality only one theory of recovery, that of breach of confidence, and that such action could not be maintained against him because his disclosure to plaintiff's wife was justified. The court dismissed the third cause of action but denied the motion with respect to the first two causes of action and this appeal ensued.

Research reveals few cases in American jurisprudence which treat the doctor-patient privilege in this context. That is undoubtedly due to the fact that the confidentiality of the relationship is a cardinal rule of the medical profession, faithfully adhered to in most instances, and thus has come to be justifiably relied upon by patients seeking advice and treatment. This physician-patient relationship is contractual in nature, whereby the physician, in agreeing to administer to the patient, impliedly covenants that the disclosures necessary to diagnosis and treatment of the patient's mental or physical condition will be kept in confidence.

Examination of cases which have addressed this problem makes it apparent that courts have immediately recognized a legally compensable injury in such wrongful disclosure based on a variety of grounds for recovery: public policy; right to privacy; breach of contract; breach of fiduciary duty. As the Supreme Court of Washington stated in *Smith v. Driscoll* [(Wash. 1917)]:

> Neither is it necessary to pursue at length the inquiry of whether a cause of action lies in favor of a patient against a physician for wrongfully divulging confidential communications. For the purposes of what we shall say it will be assumed that, for so palpable a wrong, the law provides a remedy.

An excellent and carefully researched opinion exploring the legal ramifications of this confidentiality is *Doe v. Roe* [(N.Y. Sup. Ct. 1977)], a decision after a non-jury trial in which plaintiff sought injunctive relief and damages because of the verbatim publication by her former psychiatrist of extremely personal details of her life revealed during years of psychoanalysis. The court considered several proposed theories of recovery, including violation of public policy and breach of privacy rights. We agree with the court's observation that the several statutes and regulations requiring physicians to protect the confidentiality of information gained during treatment are clear evidence of the public policy of New York, but that there is a more appropriate theory of recovery than one rooted in public policy.

Neither do we believe that an action for breach of the right of privacy may be maintained despite some current predictions to the contrary.

*   *   *

[The] position [that from the contractual relationship of a physician and a patient arises a fiduciary obligation that confidences communicated by a patient should be held as a trust] was generally adopted by the court in *Doe v. Roe*, thus:

> I too find that a physician, who enters into an agreement with a patient to provide medical attention, impliedly covenants to keep in confidence all disclosures made by the patient concerning the patient's physical or mental condition as well as all matters discovered by the physician in the course of examination or treatment. This is particularly and necessarily true of the psychiatric relationship, for in the dynamics of psychotherapy "[t]he patient is called upon to discuss in a candid and frank manner personal

material of the most intimate and disturbing nature ... He is expected to bring up all manner of socially unacceptable instincts and urges, immature wishes, perverse sexual thoughts—in short, the unspeakable, the unthinkable, the repressed. To speak of such things to another human requires an atmosphere of unusual trust, confidence and tolerance. . . . Patients will be helped only if they can form a trusting relationship with the psychiatrist."

* * *

It is obvious then that this relationship gives rise to an implied covenant which, when breached, is actionable. If plaintiff's recovery were limited to an action for breach of contract, however, he would generally be limited to economic loss flowing directly from the breach and would thus be precluded from recovering for mental distress, loss of his employment and the deterioration of his marriage. We believe that the relationship contemplates an additional duty springing from but extraneous to the contract and that the breach of such duty is actionable as a tort. Indeed, an action in tort for a breach of a duty of confidentiality and trust has long been acknowledged in the courts of this State. . . . "When such duty grows out of relations of trust and confidence, as that of the agent to his principal or the lawyer to his client, the ground of the duty is apparent, and the tort is, in general, easily separable from the mere breach of contract".

* * *

Such duty, however, is not absolute, and its breach is actionable only if it is wrongful, that is to say, without justification or excuse. Although public policy favors the confidentiality described herein, there is a countervailing public interest to which it must yield in appropriate circumstances. Thus where a patient may be a danger to himself or others [*Tarasoff*], a physician is required to disclose to the extent necessary to protect a threatened interest. "The protective privilege ends where the public peril begins" [*Tarasoff*].

* * *

Although the disclosure of medical information to a spouse may be justified under some circumstances, a more stringent standard should apply with respect to psychiatric information. One spouse often seeks counseling concerning personal problems that may affect the marital relationship. To permit disclosure to the other spouse in the absence of an overriding concern would deter the one in need from obtaining the help required. Disclosure of confidential information by a psychiatrist to a spouse will be justified whenever there is a danger to the patient, the spouse or another person; otherwise information should not be disclosed without authorization. Justification or excuse will depend upon a showing of circumstances and competing interests which support the need to disclose. Because such showing is a matter of affirmative defense, defendant is not entitled to dismissal of the action.

The order should be modified to dismiss the cause of action for breach of contract and as modified should be affirmed.

Order modified on the law and as modified affirmed with costs to defendant.

SIMONS, J.P., concurs in a separate opinion.

QUESTIONS AND COMMENTS

1.   *Implications of HIPAA.* If a case involving a similar fact situation were to arise post-HIPAA, would a breach of confidentiality, such as occurred in *MacDonald v. Clinger*, be the basis for administrative sanctions by the DHHS Office of Civil Rights under HIPAA? What additional facts would need to be known to answer this question?

2.   *Disciplinary proceedings for breach of confidentiality.* Wrongful disclosure can also lead to discipline by a regulatory authority. For instance, in *Mississippi State Board of Psychological Examiners v. Hosford*, 508 So. 2d 1049 (Miss. 1987), the psychologist had provided family counseling to a husband and wife. Later, during the couple's divorce proceeding, he submitted an authorized affidavit to the court recommending the award of custody to the husband. This recommendation was based in part on disclosures made by the wife during counseling. These facts were deemed sufficient to justify disciplinary action against the psychologist for his violation of the ethical principles of psychologists. See Chapter Two, supra.

3.   *Claim under contract theory.* A violation of a client's right to confidentiality could be the basis for an action based on breach of contract involving an implied covenant on the part of the therapist to maintain confidentiality. This theory was the basis of a claim in *Allen v. Smith*, 368 S.E.2d 924 (W. Va. 1988). While the court found a breach, it was unwilling to award damages for emotional distress alone.

4.   *Defenses.* In a proceeding brought under state law alleging breach of confidentiality by a therapist, the defendant is generally entitled to raise certain defenses, the merits of which can determine the outcome of the case. These defenses include client consent, absolute privilege, and qualified privilege.

As discussed further in the following note, if a client consents to having his or her information released, the right to confidentiality is considered waived. Under these circumstances, the therapist can disclose to third parties information that otherwise must be kept confidential and successfully raise this waiver as a defense to a breach of confidentiality claim.

A privilege permits disclosure without client consent and attaches when the public has a strong interest in the disclosure. Absolute privilege (sometimes referred to as absolute immunity) is associated with a range of disclosures in which this interest is particularly high. For example, judicial proceedings and statements made in the course of them, as long as they have some reasonable relation or reference to the subject of inquiry, are entitled to absolute immunity. In addition, some disclosures are compelled by law and an absolute privilege is attached to them. Examples of compelled disclosures, which are treated in greater detail in Part II of this chapter, include reports of child or elder abuse, drug dependency, gunshot wounds, or illnesses that pose a threat to the public safety, such as hepatitis, tuberculosis, sexually transmitted diseases, and other serious contagious diseases. Disclosure may also be compelled by courts or legislative and administrative agencies.

When disclosure of confidential information is not unequivocally mandated by law, a therapist's disclosures may nevertheless be immune under the doctrine of "qualified privilege," which allows disclosure only if certain conditions are met. The first condition is that the therapist's purpose in disclosing the confidential information is to achieve some societal purpose of importance comparable to the client's interest in preserving confidentiality. Such interests may include, for example, protection of the safety of a third party endangered by a violent client or disclosures made in good faith in proceedings for the civil commitment of a client. A second condition is that the disclosure be no greater than reasonably necessary to achieve the purpose sought. Third, the disclosure must be by a method that is appropriate under the circumstances to achieve the purpose sought. A therapist usually will not be liable, for example, for entrusting a confidential report to an office secretary for filing. The therapist may incur liability, on the other hand, for submitting the report to the client's employer when such action is neither authorized nor necessary to achieve any legitimate purpose outweighing the client's interest in confidentiality.

It remains to be seen whether in light of HIPAA, these traditional defenses will continue to be recognized in proceedings applying state law. HIPAA's exceptions permitting disclosure of PHI may, depending on the state law in question, be narrower. Thus, in a proceeding brought by the DHHS's Office of Civil Rights for violation of HIPAA privacy rules, some of the defenses discussed above may not be available to a defendant. However, this would not necessarily bind state courts applying state law in determining whether a breach of confidentiality occurred. Nevertheless, HIPAA standards could possibly influence the development of related state law, leading to a curtailment of some of the traditional defenses.

5.   *The defense of consent or authorization.* If a client has authorized disclosure of PHI, the therapist cannot be held liable under either HIPAA or under state law. While HIPAA establishes very clear criteria for the requirements for a valid authorization, state laws frequently do not. Thus, it may not always be clear whether under state law a client has consented to disclosure. Nevertheless, the client's consent constitutes a third possible defense in an action for wrongful disclosure.

The issue of consent is not as simple as it may appear at first. First, it is not always clear whether a patient has consented to disclosure. Even if the patient's express consent is obtained, the scope of disclosure permitted by the consent or state law is not always clear. Suppose, for example, that a client consented to a therapist's telling his prospective employer that he has received therapy. Would such consent authorize disclosure of the nature of the client's problem? The nature or length of treatment? Specific facts about the client relating to his suitability for employment?

II.   EXCEPTIONS TO THE DUTY OF CONFIDENTIALITY

A. INTRODUCTION

The preceding materials have explored doctrines that prevent health care professionals from making unauthorized disclosures about persons with whom they have a treatment relationship. The client's rights of privacy, however, are not absolute, and in some circumstances a therapist may be under a legal duty to make disclosures to either agencies of the state or private citizens.

Three principal situations *require* disclosure of information by the therapist. One situation is created by compulsory reporting statutes, which cover matters such as child and elder abuse. The second category is the duty of a therapist in many jurisdictions to communicate to endangered parties the known risk of a client's doing harm.

A third category of compelled disclosure is the duty to give testimony in a judicial proceeding. However, this duty is not applied universally, and in fact the legal system has carved out special exceptions for health care providers, including physicians and psychotherapists. These exceptions fall within the ambit of what is known as the testimonial privilege, are fairly technical in nature, and do not apply with equal force in all jurisdictions. While any comprehensive treatment of the testimonial privilege is beyond the purview of these materials, subsection D below explains the general legal framework governing the application of the privilege.

Significantly, in all of the situations noted above, HIPAA regulations defer to state law where such law authorizes disclosure without a patient's or client's consent.

B. MANDATORY REPORTING REQUIREMENTS

Nearly all states have enacted laws that require physicians and mental health professionals to disclose to designated authorities certain types of treatment-related information, even if the information would otherwise be confidential. Most states, for instance, require reporting to health authorities the fact that a patient is suffering from certain communicable diseases. Deborah A. Adams et al., *Summary of Notifiable Diseases—United States, 2011*, 60 Morbidity and Mortality Weekly Report

1 (July 5, 2013). Nearly all states also impose a duty on physicians or hospital administrators to report to police authorities any case where a patient appears for treatment of gunshot injuries. Jon R. Waltz & Fred E. Inbau, *Medical Jurisprudence* 364 (1971). Some states also require attending or consulting physicians to report the name of any person known to be a "habitual user of a narcotic drug." Adams et al., supra. Finally, states typically require any physician or mental health professional who has reasonable cause to suspect an incidence of child or elder abuse to file a related report with a designated agency. Id. at 320–22. In some jurisdictions psychiatrists are subject to various provisions whereas other mental health professionals are not.

There is an interplay between these reporting statutes and the testimonial privilege. It has been argued that mandatory reporting statutes destroy the privilege of confidentiality granted by testimonial privilege statutes. The case set forth below addresses the question of whether the legislature, by requiring reporting, also intends to abrogate confidentiality rights.

DAYMUDE V. STATE
Court of Appeals of Indiana, First District, 1989.
540 N.E.2d 1263.

BAKER, JUDGE.

Statement of the Facts

The Greene County Division of the Indiana State Department of Public Welfare (Department) filed a petition in the Greene Circuit Court, Juvenile Docket, alleging that Daymude's 13–year–old daughter was a "child in need of services" as defined by IND. CODE 31–6–4–3. As provided by the CHINS [Child in Need of Services] statute, the Department, pursuant to court order, provided services to the child and her family. The daughter was admitted as an in-patient at Charter Hospital of Terre Haute (the hospital). In addition, the juvenile court ordered Daymude, the alleged victim, and her mother to undergo family counseling.

The hospital's clinical director referred the daughter's case to James Walker (Walker), a certified clinical mental health counselor working as an independent contractor for the hospital. Walker worked under the supervision of Dr. Mary Anne Johnson, the hospital's chief psychiatrist for the child and adolescent division. Walker developed and scheduled a treatment program in which the alleged victim and her family were to participate in a series of individual and group therapy sessions. During the course of a counseling session, Daymude disclosed information relating to alleged instances of sexual abuse.

On July 8, 1989, the State formally charged Daymude with child molesting and criminal deviate conduct in violation of IND. CODE 35–42–4–2 and 35–42–4–3, and with the offense of incest in violation of IND. CODE 35–26–1–3. Thereafter, the State sought to depose Walker regarding the content of communications between Walker and Daymude disclosed in the course of the family therapy. Daymude objected to the State's inquiry, insofar as it related to privileged and confidential communications between himself and Walker or any other member of the hospital's treatment team. The question was certified to the trial court and on January 31, 1989, the trial court overruled the defendant's objection and ordered Walker to answer such questions as were asked by the State pertaining to his communication with Daymude during the course of counseling. It is from this order that the instant interlocutory appeal is taken.

Issue

Whether the trial court erred in finding that Daymude's right to privileged communication with his health care provider was abrogated by IND. CODE 31–6–11–8 when that communication was undertaken subsequent to the State's involvement in allegations of child sexual abuse against Daymude, and when that communication was undertaken in the course of treatment and rehabilitation recommended by the State through its Department of Public Welfare.

Discussion and Decision

Communications between a physician and a patient, of a confidential nature, are privileged and may not be disclosed by the physician without a waiver of that privilege by the patient. . . . This physician-patient privilege is codified in IND. CODE 34–1–14–5 which provides, in pertinent part:

The following persons shall not be competent witnesses:

. . . .☐4th. Physicians, as to matter communicated to them, as such, by patients, in the course of their professional business, or advice given in such cases, except as provided in IND. CODE 9–4–4.5–7.[1]

The privilege applies to those communications undertaken in the course of, and necessary to treatment.

However, in Indiana "*any individual* who has reason to believe that a child is a victim of child abuse or neglect shall make a report" as required by statute (emphasis added). IND. CODE 31–6–11–3. Thus, this language and the physician-patient privilege place conflicting duties upon a physician who learns of child abuse during the course

---

1   IND. CODE 9–11–4–6, formerly 9–4–4.5–7, provides for the abrogation of the physician-patient privilege in certain cases involving chemical tests for purposes of Title 9, Criminal Investigations.

of a physician-patient relationship. Consequently, the Indiana legislature adopted IND. CODE 31–6–11–8 which abrogates the physician-patient privilege when reporting child abuse. The abrogation statute states:

> The privileged communication between a husband and wife, between a health care provider and that health care provider's patient, or between a school counselor and a student is not a ground for:
>
> > (1) excluding evidence in any judicial proceeding resulting from a report of a child who may be a victim of child abuse or neglect, or relating to the subject matter of such a report; or (2) failing to report as required by this chapter.

Id.

Daymude acknowledges that Walker, as a mental health professional had a duty under IND. CODE 31–6–11–3 to report suspected or known instances of child abuse or neglect even though such information is received in the course of confidential communications. *See* IND. CODE 31–6–11–3 (Duty to Report); IND. CODE 34–1–14–5 (Physician–Patient Privilege); IND. CODE 31–6–11–8 (Abrogation of Privilege). However, Daymude argues that the privilege is abrogated only in reporting child abuse, and that the abrogation does not extend to communications made during counseling ordered by the court as a result of CHINS proceedings.

Because of the special circumstances of this case, this appeal presents an issue of first impression for this court. However, we believe that the purpose of the reporting statutes and decisions from courts facing similar issues clearly support Daymude's contentions here.

The purpose of the Indiana reporting statute is:

> [T]o encourage effective reporting of suspected or known incidents of child abuse or neglect, to provide in each county an effective child protection service to quickly investigate reports of child abuse or neglect, to provide protection for such a child from further abuse or neglect, and to provide rehabilitative services for such a child and his parent, guardian, or custodian.

IND. CODE 31–6–11–1. Thus, the reporting statute attempts to promote the reporting of child abuse cases, and thereafter, to provide a mechanism for the investigation of the abuse in order to protect the child and provide rehabilitative services for the child and parents, guardian, or custodian. The abrogation statute as set forth in IND. CODE 31–6–11–8 must be read in light of the purpose of the entire act.

Clearly, confidential communications between a health care provider and his patient are abrogated to the extent that the health care provider must report all suspected or known instances of child abuse. However, to extend the abrogation statute to information disclosed during Daymude's court ordered counseling goes beyond the purpose of the statute. The statute makes no mention of prosecuting alleged abusers, and instead only discusses means to facilitate the identification of the children who need the immediate attention of child welfare professionals.

* * *

In the present case, the reporting of child abuse is not an issue. The alleged abuse was reported long before Daymude made confidential statements to Walker. In fact the confidential communications arose only after the CHINS proceedings during which the court ordered Daymude to attend and participate in individual and family counseling sessions. Thus, because the alleged abuse already had been reported, the reporting statute's purpose had been served and the physician-patient privilege need not be abrogated further.

There is no question that the family therapy sessions are an integral and necessary part of the patient's diagnosis and treatment. If the physician-patient privilege is denied to those family members involved in CHINS counseling, then the alleged child abusers will be discouraged from openly and honestly communicating with their counselors. Without open and honest communications between the physician and the family members, the rehabilitative process will fail. Consequently, the child, whom the statute is designed to help and protect, is denied an opportunity for complete rehabilitation. As the *Andring* court stated:

> Once the abuse is discovered, however, the statute should not be construed, nor can the legislature have intended it to be construed, to permit total elimination of this important privilege. The central purpose of the child abuse reporting statute is the protection of children, not punishment of those who mistreat them.

Id.

* * *

In the present case, the physician-patient privilege arose as a direct result of therapy ordered by the court during a CHINS proceeding. The privileged communications were made long after the report of the child abuse. Since the abuse already had been reported, the purpose of the reporting statute had been fulfilled. To allow the abrogation of the privileged communication under these specific facts goes beyond the purpose of the statute. Thus, because of the specific facts of the present case, we hold that the physician-patient privilege is not abrogated with regard to confidential communications disclosed by a defendant while participating in counseling sessions ordered by a trial court pursuant to a report of child molesting.

For the above reasons, we reverse the trial court's ruling.

Judgment reversed.

RATLIFF, C.J., and ROBERTSON, J., concur.

QUESTIONS AND COMMENTS

1. *Constitutional limits on state disclosure requirements.* Recent cases suggest that there are constitutional limits on the power of legislatures to impose health care provider reporting requirements. For instance, a majority of the justices of the Supreme Court have found broad state law requirements for notifying the parents of minors seeking an abortion to be constitutionally defective. *Bellotti v. Baird*, 443 U.S. 622, 99 S.Ct. 3035, 61 L.Ed.2d 797 (1979). But see *H. L. v. Matheson*, 450 U.S. 398, 101 S.Ct. 1164, 67 L.Ed.2d 388 (1981). In the mental health care context, a California appellate court has held that a state law provision that required institutions to notify a "responsible relative" of a patient prior to the administration of ECT or psychosurgery violated the patient's right to privacy. *Aden v. Younger*, 129 Cal. Rptr. 535 (Ct. App. 1976) (see Chapter Nine, Part IV.B.).

2. *Rule for covered entities under HIPAA.* HIPAA authorizes disclosure of PHI without the patient's authorization when mandated by state law or regulation when it relates to child abuse or neglect or where the covered entity believes the individual is the victim of domestic violence. Additionally, disclosure may be made in a number of other situations including the following: (1) where necessary to prevent serious harm to the individual or other potential victims; (2) when requested by a public health authority for the purpose of preventing or controlling disease; (3) to a coroner or medical examiner for the purpose of identifying a deceased person or determining a cause of death, or PHI about a deceased person to a law enforcement official for the purpose of alerting law enforcement of the death of the individual if the covered entity suspects the death may have resulted from criminal conduct; (4) where disclosure is needed for protective services for the President and other senior government officials; (5) to federal officials in connection with lawful intelligence activities; (6) to military authorities regarding Armed Forces personnel when necessary to ensure proper execution of the military mission; or (7) to prevent or lessen a serious and imminent threat to the health or safety of a person or the public. 45 C.F.R. § 164.512.

With the exception of (3) and perhaps (6), all of these permissible disclosure situations aim at preventing some sort of harm. What is the scope of permitted disclosure of past crimes under HIPAA? § 164.512(f)(6)(i) of HIPAA reads as follows:

> A covered health care provider providing emergency health care in response to a medical emergency, other than such emergency on the premises of the covered health care provider, may disclose protected health information to a law enforcement official if such disclosure appears necessary to alert law enforcement to:

> (A) The commission and nature of a crime;

(B) The location of such crime or of the victim(s) of such crime; and

(C) The identity, description and location of the perpetrator of such crime.

See also discussion of *Menendez v. Superior Court*, Part II.D.4.b., infra. Would disclosure of this information, if discovered by a criminal defense attorney through his or her client, be permissible under the ethical rules or laws governing lawyers? Should the rule here be any different?

3.   *The admissibility of facts disclosed under reporting statutes.* *Daymude* appears to hold that facts that are disclosed by a therapist as required by a reporting statute are typically not admissible in evidence. A number of federal courts are in substantial agreement. See, e.g., *United States v. Glass*, 133 F.3d 1356 (1998) (patient's statement to therapist that "he wanted to get in the history books like Hinkley [sic] and wanted to shoot Bill Clinton and Hilary [sic]" could not be used in a prosecution for knowingly and willfully threatening to kill the President because the government had not shown a "significant evidentiary need"); *United States v. Hayes*, 227 F.3d 578 (6th Cir. 2000) (statements outlining "in great detail" patient's plan to kill his supervisor were excluded because "compliance with the professional duty to protect does not imply a duty to testify against a patient in criminal proceedings or in civil proceedings other than directly related to the patient's involuntary hospitalization, and such testimony is privileged and inadmissible if a patient properly asserts the psychotherapist/patient privilege."). In contrast, a number of states abrogate the privilege when the confidential information is "essential to the court proceeding" or when "disclosure is necessary to a proper administration of justice," language that is often interpreted loosely, particularly in child custody and termination of parental rights proceedings. See Deborah Paruch, *The Psychotherapist–Patient Privilege in the Family Court: An Exemplar of Disharmony Between Social Policy Goals, Professional Ethics, and the Current State of the Law*, 29 N. Ill. U. L. Rev. 499, 537–548 (2009). Which is the better approach? What if the reports of abuse are from the victim? One commentator has suggested that the potential for disclosing such information in lawsuits discourages claims by sexual abuse victims. Jennifer L. Herbert, *Mental Health Records in Sexual Assault Cases: Striking a Balance to Ensure a Fair Trial for Victims and Defendants*, 83 Tex. L. Rev. 1453, 1460 (2005).

4.   *Derivative evidence and the privilege.* Even in jurisdictions where the privilege protects against revelation of statements made to a therapist, evidence derived from those statements may be admissible. In *State v. Beatty*, 770 S.W.2d 387 (Mo. App. 1989), the court held that, although it did not "condone" the disclosure, a therapist's anonymous report that the patient had been involved in a robbery, which resulted in a search of the patient's apartment that discovered incriminating evidence, did not bar a subsequent robbery prosecution. Although the court reaffirmed that the privilege prohibits the introduction of testimony that falls within its scope, neither oral nor written testimony from the therapist was proffered in the case. The court did suggest, however, that the patient had a private cause of action against

the therapist for a breach of confidentiality. What would be the extent of damages the patient could obtain? Should the term of imprisonment that resulted from the conviction be compensable? More fundamentally, should the government be able to introduce at trial evidence derived from a breach of therapist-client confidentiality?

5. *The relevance of state reporting statutes to the duty to warn.* Consider the following excerpt from *Peck v. Counseling Service of Addison County*, 499 A.2d 422, 426 (Vt. 1985):

> Defendant . . . argues that the therapist could not lawfully have warned the plaintiffs . . . because of the physician-patient privilege against disclosure of confidential information. 12 V.S.A. § 1612(a). . . . Defendant points out that the legislature has specified certain "public policy" exceptions to the physician-patient privilege, see, e.g., 33 V.S.A. §§ 683–684 (Supp.1984) (report of child abuse), 13 V.S.A. § 4012 (disclosure of gunshot wounds), 18 V.S.A. §§ 1152–1153 (report of abuse of the elderly), and that a therapist's duty to disclose the risk of harm posed by his or her patient to a foreseeable victim is not a recognized legislative exception. Given this, defendant argues that this Court is preempted from finding a duty-to-warn exception to the physician-patient privilege. The statutory exceptions to the physician-patient privilege indicate to this Court, however, that the privilege is not sacrosanct and can properly be waived in the interest of public policy under appropriate circumstances. A mental patient's threat of serious harm to an identified victim is an appropriate circumstance under which the physician-patient privilege may be waived.

Do you agree? Does this holding mean that a therapist's disclosure to authorities or victims under the duty-to-warn exception is admissible in court? Is the court confusing the privilege with confidentiality?

C. DISCLOSURES OF INFORMATION INDICATIVE OF A MENTAL DISORDER AND/OR DANGEROUSNESS

1. Disclosure by Entities Covered by HIPAA

As discussed, HIPAA regulations permit disclosure "necessary to prevent or lessen a serious and imminent threat to the health or safety of a person or the public . . . to a person or persons reasonably able to prevent or lessen the threat, including the target of the threat." 45 C.F.R. § 164.512. HIPAA does not provide any further guidance about who may qualify as a "person or persons" reasonably able to prevent or lessen the threat. In any event, where an imminent threat to the health and safety of a person or the public is concerned, HIPAA gives health care providers significant leeway to disclose that information to appropriate third parties.

Moreover, the law in most states provides similar exceptions. The primary difference among state laws pertains to the authorized scope of disclosure. In some states, the disclosure of imminent harm may be made not only to other health care providers and law enforcement personnel but also to identifiable third persons who are at risk. Rules regarding such disclosures may result from legislative actions or judicial interpretations. For instance, as noted above, in *Peck v. Counseling Service of Addison County*, 499 A.2d 422, 426 (Vt. 1985), the Vermont Supreme Court held that even though legislation only authorized disclosure of protected medical information in the case of child abuse or gunshot wounds, public policy requires that when a patient poses a threat of serious harm to an identifiable victim, disclosure may be made to the potential victim. Other states, such as Texas, authorize the disclosure of a mental health patient's imminent dangerousness only to law enforcement personnel or other health care providers. Thus, in states that follow the Texas model, disclosure of protected health information cannot be made to persons at risk of imminent harm without incurring potential tort liability for breach of privacy.

2. Disclosure by Institutions Covered by FERPA (Institutions of Higher Learning)

As noted in Chapter Three, recent student suicides and mass shootings on campuses have focused attention on the responsibility of universities to identify students' mental health problems and to take preventive action when a student poses a significant threat to self or others. How well institutions of higher learning can detect mental illness in students depends in part on an exchange of information between relevant units of the university. Such exchanges might involve faculty, administrators, residence hall advisors, university health center personnel, campus law enforcement units, and special university units with responsibility to assess threats. As detailed below, the disclosure of student records or exchanging information between university staff are subject to both federal and state law, the most significant of which is the Federal Educational Rights and Privacy Act (FERPA). In some instances, these laws may inhibit aggregation of the kinds of information needed to consistently identify students with serious mental health problems who are potentially dangerous to themselves or others. As noted in the report on the Virginia Tech shootings, which involved the murder of 32 students and staff on campus:

> Information privacy laws governing mental health, law enforcement, and educational records and information revealed widespread lack of understanding, conflicting practice, and laws that were poorly designed to accomplish their goals. Information privacy laws are intended to strike a balance between protecting privacy and allowing information sharing that is necessary or desirable. Because of this difficult balance, the laws are often complex and hard to understand.

Mass Shootings at Virginia Tech, Report of the Review Panel (Aug. 2007), at 63, available at http://www.governor.virginia.gov/tempcontent/tech panelreport.cfm [hereinafter Review Panel Report].

Earlier, this chapter noted that HIPAA privacy rules may exempt from coverage the records of health maintenance entities operated by institutions of higher learning and that FERPA exempts from its coverage "records . . . which are made or maintained by a physician, psychiatrist, psychologist, or other recognized professional or paraprofessional acting in his professional or paraprofessional capacity, or assisting in that capacity, and which are made, maintained, or used only in connection with the provision of treatment to the student, and are not available to anyone other than persons providing such treatment." 20 U.S.C. § 1232g(a)(4)(B)(iv). Thus, the records of a university-operated health care facility may not be subject to either HIPAA or FERPA privacy rules and their disclosure may only be governed by state law.

In some states, mental health treatment records are subject to the same rules as general medical records. In other states, records associated with mental health treatment are subject to special and more restricted disclosure rules. Under Virginia law in effect when the Virginia Tech shootings occurred, the disclosure of health information held by health providers was authorized only under the following circumstances: (1) with the consent of "the person who is the subject of the records"; (2) to other health care providers where the sharing of information is necessary for treatment; and (3) in selected other situations, including where a person "presents an imminent threat to the health and safety of individuals and the public." Review Panel Report, at 65. Similar laws have been adopted by other states. Also, state laws vary concerning the class of persons to whom information about dangerousness can be communicated. Under Texas law, for instance, disclosures about the imminent danger of an individual undergoing treatment may only be disclosed to law enforcement offices and other health providers, but not to university officials. Office of General Counsel, University of Texas System, *Sharing Information About Potentially Dangerous Students* (July 10, 2007), at 4 [hereinafter Memo, University of Texas General Counsel].

FERPA does govern the disclosure of student "educational records." While this phrase does not encompass university records maintained by university health units, it does include most other records kept by the university. FERPA rules about disclosure of educational records also apply to *communications* between and among campus personnel, as well as to disclosures to persons outside of the community. *Within* the university, student records covered by FERPA may only be disclosed to anyone who has a "legitimate educational interest" in these records. 34 C.F.R. § 99.31(a)(1). Disclosure of student record information to external persons or agencies is in general limited to disclosures to which the student has consented. However, FERPA permits nonconsensual disclosure in some limited circumstances. An analysis of the FERPA exceptions reached the following conclusion:

> If the university determines that individuals outside of the university should be informed about student conduct, other FERPA exceptions permit student education records to be shared with third parties. Notably, disclosure of information in education records is always permitted in connection with a health or safety emergency under certain conditions. FERPA permits disclosure to appropriate parties in connection with an emergency if knowledge of the information is necessary to protect the health or safety of the student or other individuals. This exception allows university officials to act quickly in emergencies to contact outside parties such as law enforcement or health authorities for assistance in arresting or detaining a student without regard to whether the information about the student is contained in the student's education record.

> Release under the health or safety emergency exception must be limited to "appropriate parties." FERPA does not define "appropriate parties," and thus it would be a matter for the university to determine who is an "appropriate party" based on the particular circumstances. So, for example, the emergency exception would permit university officials to share necessary information with local broadcast media as needed to alert the public to a threat posed by a student during an emergency situation, but it would not justify the university's sharing of information from a student's education record with a reporter for a news feature about the incident. In addition, once the threat of harm has dissipated, the exception is no longer available to the university. Even in the absence of an emergency, FERPA permits an institution to contact its own law enforcement unit to investigate possible violations of and to enforce any local, state, or federal law.

Memo, University of Texas General Counsel, at 3.

QUESTIONS AND COMMENTS

1. *Scope of FERPA and HIPAA exemptions.* Assume that a university establishes a unit to assess campus safety and security. The unit is not part of a university's mental health treatment center. The unit gathers information from residence dorm advisors and academic units about student behavior that is indicative of mental illness and potential dangerousness either to self or others. Assuming that no student has violated any law, what course of action is open to a university to deal with such findings? For instance, could a university require a troubled student whose actions suggest a risk of future violence to undergo treatment as a condition for continued enrollment? In the event that a student declines to voluntarily undergo

treatment and is suspended, should anyone be contacted? Should the university assume that the suspension has removed the threat?

2. *FERPA regulations amendment.* Largely in reaction to the Virginia Tech shootings, the United States Department of Education amended the regulations governing federal educational rights and privacy under FERPA. Under the rules, when "an articulable and significant threat to the health or safety of a student or other individuals" arises, disclosure may be made to "any person whose knowledge of the information is necessary to protect the health or safety of the student or other individuals." 34 C.F.R. 99.36(c). Further, "[i]n making a determination . . . , an educational agency or institution may take into account the totality of the circumstances pertaining to a threat to the health or safety of a student or other individuals." Id. Moreover, "[i]f, based on the information available at the time of the determination, there is a rational basis for the determination, [DHHS] will not substitute its judgment for that of the educational agency or institution in evaluating the circumstances and making its determination." Id. Based on this rule, would a covered educational institution that makes an appropriate finding as to dangerousness be authorized to notify the parents of a student who is deemed to present a danger to self or others? Would the rule also authorize an institution to notify a student's roommates?

3. *Disclosures by university health care facilities.* If a student has received treatment in a university-operated health facility, the facility might be a good source of information concerning the mental health and behavioral propensities of the student. Yet the law of some states, such as Texas, restricts the disclosure of health information by mental health treatment providers to law enforcement agencies and other health care providers. At the same time, universities can be liable for failing to take appropriate action to avert student suicides. How might one modify the rules governing communications between a university health center and the administration to offer reasonable protection to student privacy while also letting the university access information needed to determine whether a student should be suspended academically so that he or she may be moved into a different environment?

4. *Disclosing limits of confidentiality to clients.* The normal rules pertaining to confidentiality are, of course, partially waived in those jurisdictions that follow *Tarasoff*, as therapists in such jurisdictions have not only a legal right but a duty to take steps to prevent third parties from being harmed by their clients. See Chapter Three, supra. In those jurisdictions that recognize *Tarasoff*-type duties to protect, should a therapist have an obligation to inform potential clients that confidentiality may be broken if the therapist later perceives the client to be a threat to a third person? For psychologists who belong to the American Psychological Association, Section 4.02 of the Association's *Ethics Code* answers, "Yes":

4.02 Discussing the Limits of Confidentiality

(a) Psychologists discuss with persons . . . with whom they establish a scientific or professional relationship (1) the relevant limits of confidentiality and (2) the foreseeable uses of the information generated through their psychological activities . . .

(b) Unless it is not feasible or is contraindicated, the discussion of confidentiality occurs at the outset of the relationship and thereafter as new circumstances may warrant.

American Psychological Association, *Ethical Principles of Psychologists and Code of Conduct, with 2010 Amendments* (available at http://www.apa. org/ethics/code/index.aspx, site visited August 3, 2013). See also Mary Alice Fisher, *Protecting Confidentiality Rights: The Need for an Ethical Practice Model*, 63 Am. Psychologist 1, 3 (2008) ("if confidentiality will be conditional, clients have a right to be informed about the 'conditions' before they consent to confide, regardless of the clinical consequences of that conversation"). Under these rules, should the therapist also have to inform the client that any reports of past crimes might be revealed to authorities and could be used to prosecute (see notes 2 through 4 in the previous section)? In answering these questions, is it relevant that such warnings might inhibit disclosure? See Daniel O. Taube & Amiram Elwork, *Researching the Effects of Confidentiality Law on Patients' Self–Disclosures*, 21 Prof. Psychol.: Res. & Prac. 72–75 (1990) (study finding that laws requiring the disclosure by therapists of certain patient "confessions," when described to patients, discourage disclosure and may hinder treatment, thus ultimately failing in the intended objective of protecting society).

5.   *Hypothetical.* Dr. I is a noted psychiatrist and a clinical professor at New York Medical College. He is also President of the Academy of Psychoanalysis and editor of the American Journal of Psychoanalysis. As part of his faculty duties, he acts as a teaching analyst for psychiatric residents who plan to become psychoanalysts. (Note: full membership in a psychoanalytic institute, the qualifying emblem of a psychoanalyst, requires a period of specialized training including personal analysis by a training analyst).

Dr. D is a third-year resident in psychiatry at New York Medical College. As part of his psychoanalytic training, he is being analyzed by Dr. I. In the course of an analytic session, he tells Dr. I that he had recently gone to South America to see the night sky in the southern hemisphere. He also confesses that another reason for his trip was to "meet a nice child." Following the disclosure, Dr. I continues his regular bi-weekly analysis of Dr. D. Concluding that Dr. D is both intelligent and very professionally focused and is therefore able to control his impulses, Dr. I does nothing to have him removed from the residency program. He also concludes that his completion of the analysis is likely either to reorient Dr. D's sexual preferences or, at a minimum, to enhance his impulse controls. Four months after his confession during analysis, Dr. D, who at the time was working as a psychiatric resident at

Danbury Hospital in Connecticut, is charged with molesting a ten-year-old boy, who was a patient in the hospital. The boy and his family subsequently filed a lawsuit against Dr. I and New York Medical College alleging that he should have taken steps to prevent Dr. D from working with children. (Additional details concerning the case, which was filed in the Federal District Court in Connecticut in the spring of 1998, are reported in Frank Bruni, *A Child Psychiatrist and Pedophile; His Therapist Knew But Didn't Tell Victim*, N.Y. Times, Apr. 19, 1998, at Sec. 1, 35).

Would HIPAA permit the disclosure of the information pertaining to Dr. D's pedophilia?

D. JUDICIAL PROCEEDINGS AND THE TESTIMONIAL PRIVILEGE

1. Introduction

a. *Perspectives on the Judicial Process*

In many situations, society, through an arm of government, needs information known only to a few. In these situations, according to an old maxim, the public has a right to every man's evidence. That is, each person has a responsibility to disclose information of vital importance to society. This responsibility arises when society's need to ascertain the truth outweighs the individual's interest in concealing the information. The public, through the coercive forces of government, may then compel disclosure. The usual contexts in which the need for information arises include civil and criminal trials, as well as hearings and investigations by legislatures and administrative agencies. In each of these contexts, ascertaining the truth is essential to promote an important societal interest.

The cases that follow illustrate the potential tension between a governmental interest in ascertaining the truth in the legal process and protecting the privacy of health care records. In these cases, the contours of the testimonial privilege reflect a balancing of government and individual privacy interests. Whatever rule governing the scope of the testimonial privilege emerges from a legislative or judicial decision, its application is not impeded by HIPAA. As noted previously, HIPAA's privacy rules do not protect a patient's health records—including those pertaining to mental health treatment—when they are obtained in response to an order or subpoena by either a state or federal court or administrative tribunal. 45 C.F.R. § 164.512(e) (1)(ii). See generally Vani Singhal et al., *Recent Developments in Medicine and Law*, 37 Insur. Tort J. 601 (2002). Moreover, in discovery proceedings, the PHI must be disclosed to either the court or an opposing party even in the absence of a court-issued subpoena so long as the individual about whom health care information is being sought is provided with adequate notice and has a reasonable opportunity to challenge the subpoena or discovery request.

b. Role and Function of the Testimonial Privilege

Governmental authority to compel disclosure is not unlimited. It extends only as far as necessary to achieve the governmental purpose at hand. Thus, no witness may be compelled to testify concerning matters irrelevant to the case before the court or other tribunal.

Governmental authority is also limited when mandatory disclosure conflicts with fundamental rights or interests. To preserve important rights and interests, courts and other tribunals may recognize a "privilege" on the part of a witness to decline to answer certain questions. For example, no person may be compelled to make statements that might incriminate her. The privilege against self-incrimination is inherent in the American concept of liberty. Long recognized under the English common law, the privilege was incorporated by the Fifth Amendment to the federal Constitution and is made applicable to the states through the Fourteenth Amendment. Similarly, under the First Amendment's guarantees of free speech and religion, no person may be compelled to state his political or religious beliefs under oath. Of course, a witness may waive the privilege and volunteer this information. The privilege merely protects against compulsory disclosure.

In addition to privileges articulated in the Constitution, legislatures may create testimonial privileges by statute. In the absence of a statute or constitutional mandate, courts may also recognize a privilege because of the importance of the interests thereby protected.

A testimonial privilege may protect certain *topics*, such as the witness's political or religious beliefs, or information tending to incriminate the witness. Another form of privilege protects confidential communications in the context of certain relationships that society seeks to foster. When such a privilege is asserted, *neither* party to such a relationship may be compelled to disclose information exchanged in confidence. Relationships that traditionally have given rise to privileges of this sort include those between attorney and client, physician and patient, husband and wife, and priest and penitent. In recent years, this privilege for confidential communications has been extended by statute or by the courts in various states to such diverse professional groups as journalists, accountants, and psychotherapists.*

---

* The reader may recall that the term "privilege" arises in many contexts. The term can refer to an exemption from liability for an action that would ordinarily give rise to liability. See, for example, the earlier discussion of privilege as a defense to defamation in this chapter. In the present context, the action that would ordinarily give rise to liability is the withholding of subpoenaed testimony or information. Although the ordinary penalty for withholding subpoenaed information may be a fine or imprisonment, the valid assertion of a recognized testimonial privilege exempts a witness from liability.

Traditionally, a privilege involving confidential communications is justified when four conditions are met. First, the relationship must be one that society seeks to foster. Second, the communications must originate in a confidence that they will not be disclosed. Third, the element of confidentiality must be essential to achieve the purpose of the relationship. Finally, injury to the relationship resulting from compelled disclosure must be greater than the benefit gained by the correct disposal of litigation. John Henry Wigmore, 4 Treatise on the System of Evidence in Trials at Common Law § 2285 (1905).

The availability and scope of the testimonial privilege depend upon the profession of the psychotherapist and upon the law of the particular jurisdiction. Confidential communications between a psychiatrist and a patient can be protected by physician-patient privilege statutes, which have been enacted by about two-thirds of the states. In addition, in most states, statutes licensing psychologists provide a privilege for communications between a psychologist and a client. Finally, some states provide a privilege for other mental health professionals who provide psychotherapy, such as marriage counselors and social workers. Privilege statutes, however, are frequently ambiguous, and the availability and scope of the privilege in various contexts may be difficult to predict. The case that follows establishes the dimensions of the privilege in all federal civil cases where it is being asserted by the defendant.

JAFFEE v. REDMOND
Supreme Court of the United States, 1996.
518 U.S. 1, 116 S. Ct. 1923, 135 L. Ed. 2d 337.

JUSTICE STEVENS delivered the opinion of the Court.

[Plaintiff, the administrator of the estate of Ricky Allen, brought a civil suit against the defendant, Mary Lu Redmond, a police officer who shot and killed Mr. Allen in the line of duty, for allegedly violating the constitutional rights of the deceased. Following the shooting, the defendant officer received extensive counseling from Karen Beyer, a licensed clinical social worker. Plaintiff petitioned the trial court for access to the records of the counseling session.]

. . . The question we address is whether statements the officer made to her therapist during the counseling sessions are protected from compelled disclosure in a federal civil action brought by the family of the deceased. Stated otherwise, the question is whether it is appropriate for federal courts to recognize a "psychotherapist privilege" under Rule 501 of the Federal Rules of Evidence.

*　*　*

The Court of Appeals for the Seventh Circuit . . . concluded that "reason and experience," the touchstones for acceptance of a privilege under Rule 501 of the Federal Rules of Evidence, compelled recognition of a psychotherapist-patient privilege. "Reason tells us that psychotherapists and patients share a unique relationship, in which the ability to communicate freely without the fear of public disclosure is the key to successful treatment." As to experience, the court observed that all 50 States have adopted some form of the psychotherapist-patient privilege. The court attached particular significance to the fact that Illinois law expressly extends such a privilege to social workers like Karen Beyer. The court also noted that, with one exception, the federal decisions rejecting the privilege were more than five years old and that the "need and demand for counseling services has skyrocketed during the past several years."

The Court of Appeals qualified its recognition of the privilege by stating that it would not apply if "in the interests of justice, the evidentiary need for the disclosure of the contents of a patient's counseling sessions outweighs that patient's privacy interests." Balancing those conflicting interests, the court observed, on the one hand, that the evidentiary need for the contents of the confidential conversations was diminished in this case because there were numerous eyewitnesses to the shooting, and, on the other hand, that Officer Redmond's privacy interests were substantial. Based on this assessment, the court concluded that the trial court had erred by refusing to afford protection to the confidential communications between Redmond and Beyer.

The United States Courts of Appeals do not uniformly agree that the federal courts should recognize a psychotherapist privilege under Rule 501. Because of the conflict among the Courts of Appeals and the importance of the question, we granted certiorari. We affirm.

* * *

III

Like the spousal and attorney-client privileges, the psychotherapist-patient privilege is "rooted in the imperative need for confidence and trust." Treatment by a physician for physical ailments can often proceed successfully on the basis of a physical examination, objective information supplied by the patient, and the results of diagnostic tests. Effective psychotherapy, by contrast, depends upon an atmosphere of confidence and trust in which the patient is willing to make a frank and complete disclosure of facts, emotions, memories, and fears. Because of the sensitive nature of the problems for which individuals consult psychotherapists, disclosure of confidential communications made during counseling sessions may cause embarrassment or disgrace. For this reason, the mere possibility of disclosure may impede development of the confidential relationship necessary for successful treatment. As the Judicial Conference Advisory Committee observed in 1972 when it recommended that Congress recognize a psychotherapist privilege as part of the Proposed Federal Rules of Evidence, a psychiatrist's ability to help her patients

> "is completely dependent upon [the patients'] willingness and ability to talk freely. This makes it difficult if not impossible for [a psychiatrist] to function without being able to assure . . . patients of confidentiality and, indeed, privileged communication. Where there may be exceptions to this general rule, there is wide agreement that confidentiality is a *sine qua non* for successful psychiatric treatment."

By protecting confidential communications between a psychotherapist and her patient from involuntary disclosure, the proposed privilege thus serves important private interests.

Our cases make clear that an asserted privilege must also "serve public ends." Thus, the purpose of the attorney-client privilege is to "encourage full and frank communication between attorneys and their clients and thereby promote broader public interests in the observance of law and administration of justice." And the spousal privilege, . . . is justified because it "furthers the important public interest in marital harmony." The psychotherapist privilege serves the public interest by facilitating the provision of appropriate treatment for individuals suffering the effects of a mental or emotional problem. The mental health of our citizenry, no less than its physical health, is a public good of transcendent importance.[10]

In contrast to the significant public and private interests supporting recognition of the privilege, the likely evidentiary benefit that would result from the denial of the privilege is modest. If the privilege were rejected, confidential conversations between psychotherapists and their patients would surely be chilled, particularly when it is obvious that the circumstances that give rise to the need for treatment will probably result in litigation. Without a privilege, much of the desirable evidence to which litigants such as petitioner seek access—for example, admissions against interest by a party—is unlikely to come into being. This unspoken "evidence" will therefore serve no greater truth-seeking function than if it had been spoken and privileged.

*   *   *

IV

All agree that a psychotherapist privilege covers confidential communications made to licensed psychiatrists and psychologists. We

---

[10] This case amply demonstrates the importance of allowing individuals to receive confidential counseling. Police officers engaged in the dangerous and difficult tasks associated with protecting the safety of our communities not only confront the risk of physical harm but also face stressful circumstances that may give rise to anxiety, depression, fear, or anger. The entire community may suffer if police officers are not able to receive effective counseling and treatment after traumatic incidents, either because trained officers leave the profession prematurely or because those in need of treatment remain on the job.

have no hesitation in concluding in this case that the federal privilege should also extend to confidential communications made to licensed social workers in the course of psychotherapy. The reasons for recognizing a privilege for treatment by psychiatrists and psychologists apply with equal force to treatment by a clinical social worker such as Karen Beyer. Today, social workers provide a significant amount of mental health treatment. Their clients often include the poor and those of modest means who could not afford the assistance of a psychiatrist or psychologist, but whose counseling sessions serve the same public goals. Perhaps in recognition of these circumstances, the vast majority of States explicitly extend a testimonial privilege to licensed social workers. We therefore agree with the Court of Appeals that "[d]rawing a distinction between the counseling provided by costly psychotherapists and the counseling provided by more readily accessible social workers serves no discernible public purpose."

We part company with the Court of Appeals on a separate point. We reject the balancing component of the privilege implemented by that court and a small number of States. Making the promise of confidentiality contingent upon a trial judge's later evaluation of the relative importance of the patient's interest in privacy and the evidentiary need for disclosure would eviscerate the effectiveness of the privilege. [I]f the purpose of the privilege is to be served, the participants in the confidential conversation "must be able to predict with some degree of certainty whether particular discussions will be protected. An uncertain privilege, or one which purports to be certain but results in widely varying applications by the courts, is little better than no privilege at all."

These considerations are all that is necessary for decision of this case. A rule that authorizes the recognition of new privileges on a case-by-case basis makes it appropriate to define the details of new privileges in a like manner. Because this is the first case in which we have recognized a psychotherapist privilege, it is neither necessary nor feasible to delineate its full contours in a way that would "govern all conceivable future questions in this area."

V

The conversations between Officer Redmond and Karen Beyer and the notes taken during their counseling sessions are protected from compelled disclosure under Rule 501 of the Federal Rules of Evidence. The judgment of the Court of Appeals is affirmed.

It is so ordered.

JUSTICE SCALIA, with whom the CHIEF JUSTICE joins as to Part III, dissenting.

*   *   *

. . . Effective psychotherapy undoubtedly is beneficial to individuals with mental problems, and surely serves some larger social interest in maintaining a mentally stable society. But merely mentioning these values does not answer the critical question: are they of such importance, and is the contribution of psychotherapy to them so distinctive, and is the application of normal evidentiary rules so destructive to psychotherapy, as to justify making our federal courts occasional instruments of injustice? On that central question I find the Court's analysis insufficiently convincing to satisfy the high standard we have set for rules that "are in derogation of the search for truth."

When is it, one must wonder, that *the psychotherapist* came to play such an indispensable role in the maintenance of the citizenry's mental health? For most of history, men and women have worked out their difficulties by talking to, *inter alios,* parents, siblings, best friends and bartenders—none of whom was awarded a privilege against testifying in court. Ask the average citizen: Would your mental health be more significantly impaired by preventing you from seeing a psychotherapist, or by preventing you from getting advice from your mom? I have little doubt what the answer would be. Yet there is no mother-child privilege.

How likely is it that a person will be deterred from seeking psychological counseling, or from being completely truthful in the course of such counseling, because of fear of later disclosure in litigation? And even more pertinent to today's decision, to what extent will the evidentiary privilege reduce that deterrent? The Court does not try to answer the first of these questions; and it *cannot possibly have any notion* of what the answer is to the second, since that depends entirely upon the scope of the privilege, which the Court amazingly finds it "neither necessary nor feasible to delineate." If, for example, the psychotherapist can give the patient no more assurance than "A court will not be able to make me disclose what you tell me, unless you tell me about a harmful act," I doubt whether there would be much benefit from the privilege at all. That is not a fanciful example, at least with respect to extension of the psychotherapist privilege to social workers.

Even where it is certain that absence of the psychotherapist privilege will inhibit disclosure of the information, it is not clear to me that that is an unacceptable state of affairs. Let us assume the very worst in the circumstances of the present case: that to be truthful about what was troubling her, the police officer who sought counseling would have to confess that she shot without reason, and wounded an innocent man. If (again to assume the worst) such an act constituted the crime of negligent wounding under Illinois law, the officer would of course have the absolute right not to admit that she shot without reason in criminal court. But I see no reason why she should be enabled *both* not to admit it in criminal court (as a good citizen should), *and* to get the benefits of psychotherapy by admitting it to a therapist who cannot tell anyone else. And even less reason why she should be enabled to *deny* her guilt in the criminal trial—or in a civil trial for negligence—while yet obtaining the benefits of psychotherapy by confessing guilt to a social worker who cannot testify. It seems to me entirely fair to say that if she wishes the benefits of telling the truth she must also accept the adverse consequences. To be sure, in most cases the statements to the psychotherapist will be only marginally relevant, and one of the purposes of the privilege (though not one relied upon by the Court) may be simply to spare patients needless intrusion upon their privacy, and to spare psychotherapists needless expenditure of their time in deposition and trial. But surely this can be achieved by means short of excluding even evidence that is of the most direct and conclusive effect.

The Court confidently asserts that not much truth-finding capacity would be destroyed by the privilege anyway, since "[w]ithout a privilege, much of the desirable evidence to which litigants such as petitioner seek access . . . is unlikely to come into being." If that is so, how come psychotherapy got to be a thriving practice before the "psychotherapist privilege" was invented? Were the patients paying money to lie to their analysts all those years? Of course the evidence-generating effect of the privilege (if any) depends entirely upon its scope, which the Court steadfastly declines to consider. And even if one assumes that scope to be the broadest possible, is it really true that most, or even many, of those who seek psychological counseling have the worry of litigation in the back of their minds? I doubt that, and the Court provides no evidence to support it.

* * *

III

Turning from the general question that was not involved in this case to the specific one that is: The Court's conclusion that a social-worker psychotherapeutic privilege deserves recognition is even less persuasive. In approaching this question, the fact that five of the state legislatures that have seen fit to enact "some form" of psychotherapist privilege have elected not to extend *any form* of privilege to social workers ought to give one pause. The Court, however, has "no hesitation in concluding . . . that the federal privilege should also extend" to social workers, and goes on to prove that by polishing off the reasoned analysis with a topic sentence and two sentences of discussion:

> "The reasons for recognizing a privilege for treatment by psychiatrists and psychologists apply with equal force to treatment by a clinical social worker such as Karen Beyer. Today, social workers provide a significant amount of mental health treatment. Their clients often include the poor and those of modest means who

could not afford the assistance of a psychiatrist or psychologist, but whose counseling sessions serve the same public goals."

So much for the rule that privileges are to be narrowly construed.

Of course this brief analysis—like the earlier, more extensive, discussion of the general psychotherapist privilege—contains no explanation of why the psychotherapy provided by social workers is a public good of such transcendent importance as to be purchased at the price of occasional injustice. Moreover it considers only the respects in which social workers providing therapeutic services are *similar* to licensed psychiatrists and psychologists; not a word about the respects in which they are different. A licensed psychiatrist or psychologist is an expert in psychotherapy—and that may suffice (though I think it not so clear that this Court should make the judgment) to justify the use of extraordinary means to encourage counseling with him as opposed to counseling with one's rabbi, minister, family or friends. One must presume that a social worker does *not* bring this greatly heightened degree of skill to bear, which is alone a reason for not encouraging that consultation as generously. Does a social worker bring to bear at least a significantly heightened degree of skill—more than a minister or rabbi, for example? I have no idea, and neither does the Court. The social worker in the present case, Karen Beyer, was a "licensed clinical social worker" in Illinois, a job title whose training requirements consist of a "master's degree in social work from an approved program," and "3,000 hours of satisfactory, supervised clinical professional experience." It is not clear that the degree in social work requires any training in psychotherapy. The "clinical professional experience" apparently will impart some such training, but only of the vaguest sort. . . .

Another critical distinction between psychiatrists and psychologists, on the one hand, and social workers, on the other, is that the former professionals, in their consultations with patients, *do nothing but psychotherapy*. Social workers, on the other hand, interview people for a multitude of reasons. The Illinois definition of "[l]icensed social worker," for example, is as follows:

> 'Licensed social worker' means a person who holds a license authorizing the practice of social work, which includes social services to individuals, groups or communities in any one or more of the fields of social casework, social group work, community organization for social welfare, social work research, social welfare administration or social work education.

Thus, in applying the "social worker" variant of the "psychotherapist" privilege, it will be necessary to determine whether the information provided to the social worker was provided to him *in his capacity as a psychotherapist*, or in his capacity as an administrator of social welfare, a community organizer, etc. Worse still, if the privilege is to have its desired effect (and is not to mislead the client), it will presumably be necessary for the social caseworker to advise, as the conversation with his welfare client proceeds, which portions are privileged and which are not.

QUESTIONS AND COMMENTS

1. *The empirical basis for the* Jaffee *holding.* The facts of the *Jaffee* case starkly present the potential conflict between society's interest in ascertaining the truth in the judicial process versus the facilitation of mental health treatment. In giving preference to the latter, the majority assumes that without the protection of confidentiality associated with the testimonial privilege, people would be less likely to seek treatment, or that the treatment provided would be less effective because persons getting treatment would limit their disclosures to their therapists. Is this conclusion based on empirical fact or, as the dissent suggests, merely speculation? In this connection, consider a 1982 study that concluded that "patients are probably not deterred [by the lack of privilege] from seeking psychiatric help to any significant degree." In surveying a group of lay people, the study found that "93% of those surveyed 'would have sought help for serious emotional problems' without the privilege and 74% 'did not know whether there was a privilege statute or guessed incorrectly that there was (no privilege statute).'" Daniel Shuman & Myron S. Weiner, *The Privilege Study: An Empirical Examination of the Psychotherapist–Patient Privilege*, 60 N. Car. L. Rev. 893, 924–25 (1982). However, a number of other laboratory studies, which compare the reactions of people who are told about the privilege to those who are not, conclude that the privilege is conducive to more communication about psychological problems. See, e.g., Jennifer Evans Marsh, *Empirical Support for the United States Supreme Court's Protection of the Psychotherapist–Patient Privilege*, 13 Ethics & Behav. 385 (2003); David Nowell & Jean Spruill, *If It's Not Absolutely Confidential, Will Information Be Disclosed?*, 24 Prof. Psychol.: Res. & Prac. 367, 368–69 (1993). These differing conclusions may result largely from the differing levels of knowledge the study participants had about the existence and scope of the privilege.

Taken as a whole, the research suggests that, even without the privilege, people would seek help from mental health professionals, but that the degree of disclosure might depend on the extent to which confidentiality is promised. In light of this empirical evidence, what can be said about the advantages and disadvantages of the majority's rule?

2. *The doctrinal basis for* Jaffee. Is the majority decision recognizing the privilege based on a constitutional right of privacy or on more general policy grounds? In *United States v. Glass*, 133 F.3d 1356 (1998), the 10th Circuit found that the privilege in *Jaffee* "is not rooted in any constitutional right of privacy, but in a public good, which overrides the quest for relevant evidence." Further, Justice Scalia and the Chief Justice dissented in *Jaffee* primarily on public policy grounds. If the majority's approach was based on public policy rather than a constitutional right, which opinion is the more persuasive, given the interests at stake?

3.   *Who is covered by privilege statutes?* It is sometimes difficult to determine whether a specific professional group, particularly in the mental health field, is covered by a particular privilege statute and, if so, the extent of the exemption. States have commonly enacted separate privilege statutes for various professional groups such as physicians, psychologists, marriage counselors, and social workers. Various problems are raised by the existence of multiple privilege statutes. For instance, in the absence of explicit legislative direction, should psychiatrists be entitled to the special privilege of psychologists, which is normally broader and more comprehensive than that for physicians? In one jurisdiction, the court held that the psychologist privilege did *not* cover psychiatrists. See *Ritt v. Ritt*, 238 A.2d 196 (N.J. Super. Ct. 1967). In another state, the court held that the psychologist privilege did cover psychiatrists. See *Day v. State*, 378 So. 2d 1156 (Ala. Cr. App. 1979), *reversed sub nom.*, *Ex parte* Day, 378 So. 2d 1159 (Ala. 1979).

As noted by the court in *Jaffee*, a number of states have enacted privilege statutes specifically covering clinical social workers. However, the privilege is generally limited to clinical social workers who are registered with the state. See *In re Westland*, 362 N.E.2d 1153, 1157 (Ill. Ct. App. 1977). If a privilege is available for social workers, should it also apply to communications with other types of counselors (e.g., school counselors, pastoral counselors, marriage counselors)? Rape counselors were held to be covered by the privilege in *United States v. Lowe*, 948 F. Supp. 97 (D. Mass. 1996).

Similar problems occur where the coverage of the privilege for psychologists and marriage counselors differ. For instance, in New Jersey the privilege for marriage counselors is virtually absolute, and confidential communications are not admissible in a divorce proceeding. However, under the Practicing Psychology Licensing Act the psychologist's privilege would not necessarily bar the admission of confidential information in a divorce proceeding. Nevertheless, in *Wichansky v. Wichansky*, 313 A.2d 222 (N.J. Super. 1973), the court held that a psychologist who engages in marriage counseling is covered by the broader marriage counselor's privilege, even though he was not a licensed marriage counselor.

In some divorce proceedings, a court-ordered psychologist may be called upon to evaluate a parent during a custody battle. One court recently ruled that the notes of such a psychologist, as opposed to psychologists in general, were not subject to disclosure absent a showing of bias or another basis for questioning the credibility of the report issued by the psychologist. The court noted its concern that providing routine access to the notes of court-ordered psychologists in such proceedings would increase the emotional and financial costs to the parties, including the children, and the psychologists would be less willing to state the impressions they form during their interviews. *Ochs v. Ochs*, 749 N.Y.S.2d 650 (N.Y. Sup. Ct. 2002).

5.   *What is covered by the privilege?* Another consideration for mental health professionals is what portions of their work is covered by the privilege. For example, one ruling held that while certain client communications might

be exempt from the privilege, a psychologist's "personal notes" about those communications were protected from disclosure under Illinois law. *Millman v. Captain Harris Guest House*, 2007 WL 951928 (N.D. Ill 2007) (citing 740 ILCS 110/3(b)).

2.   Conditions Giving Rise to the Privilege

a.   *The Course of Treatment Requirement*

STATE V. COLE
Supreme Court of Iowa, 1980.
295 N.W.2d 29.

LARSON, JUSTICE.

This defendant appeals her conviction, in a jury-waived trial, of first-degree murder in violation of section 690.2, The Code 1977. She challenges the trial court's rulings in regard to psychiatric evidence secured by depositions and in-trial testimony. . . . We affirm the trial court.

It is undisputed that on September 15, 1977, the defendant shot and killed Dr. Alan Tyler, her ex-husband, in his office at Wilden Clinic. Immediately after the shooting, she proceeded to the reception area and announced that she had "shot her husband." She then called the police and waited for them at the clinic. She was brought before a magistrate for an initial appearance where she was represented by Lawrence Scalise and Thomas Levis. At that time an order was signed by the magistrate to take the defendant to Iowa Lutheran Hospital "to undergo psychiatric and physical examination and evaluation." It is this order and the related evidence concerning the mental condition of the defendant which give rise to the most troublesome issues.

I.   The Psychiatric Evidence

A.   *Effect of the commitment order.* Pursuant to the court's order, the defendant was first examined by Dr. Michael Taylor, a psychiatrist who had been treating her on a private basis since before the shooting. He ceased his examination of her on September 30, 1977, at which time he was replaced by Dr. Vernon Varner. The defendant filed notice, . . . that she intended to rely upon the defense of diminished capacity. The State then sought to obtain psychiatric evidence through these doctors' depositions and in-trial testimony.

Upon application of the State, and over defendant's objections, pretrial depositions of Doctors Taylor and Varner were ordered by the court. Dr. Varner complied, and his deposition was taken. . . . Again over objection, the trial court permitted Dr. Taylor to testify at trial in the State's case in chief.

Defendant argues the trial court's rulings on the admissibility of the psychiatric evidence was erroneous because they violated her doctor-patient privilege, set out in section 622.10, The Code, as follows:

> No practicing attorney, counselor, physician, surgeon, or the stenographer or confidential clerk of any such person, who obtains such information by reason of his employment, . . . shall be allowed, in giving testimony, to disclose any confidential communication properly entrusted to him in his professional capacity, and necessary and proper to enable him to discharge the functions of his office according to the usual course of practice or discipline. Such prohibition shall not apply to cases where the person in whose favor the same is made waives the rights conferred. . . .

[N]ot every doctor-patient relationship provides a basis for exclusion of the doctor's testimony. In some cases the privilege never arises; in others it exists but is held to be waived by the patient. The privilege did not exist at common law, and its embodiment by statute has been criticized by at least one writer.

While our cases have evidenced no hostility to the rule itself, they have uniformly required three elements to be established: (1) the relationship of doctor-patient; (2) acquisition of the information or knowledge during this relationship; and (3) the necessity of the information to enable the doctor to treat the patient skillfully.

The order signed by the magistrate was as follows:

Order for Psychiatric Evaluation and Report

Now, on this 15th day of September, 1977, this matter having been brought to the attention of the court, and the court being fully advised of the charges against the defendant in the above captioned cause, and the present condition of the defendant; it is the considered opinion of this court that before further proceedings may be had an evaluation of the above-named defendant's physical and psychological state should be made by competent professionals in the fields of medicine and psychology in order that the court may be more fully advised and that the best interests of the parties and of justice may be realized.

* * *

The effect of [the Court's] order, and of the medical relationship which followed it, are determinative on the issue of whether or not the defendant could assert the doctor-patient privilege. In court-ordered evaluations, the third requirement of the privilege is lacking; the communication is not for the purpose of treatment but to determine the existence of a fact or condition for the benefit of the court. Therefore, "[t]he physician-patient privilege does not arise where on order of the court a defendant is examined to determine his mental or physical condition."

. . . The order clearly provided for evaluation and report to the court and made no provision for diagnosis or treatment.

The defendant, while acknowledging that the order appears to be for evaluation and report, argues it was really only intended to provide for her safekeeping in order to avoid a possible suicide. We do not believe the intentions of the parties can be properly used to countermand the unambiguous provisions of a court order.

* * *

Even if we were to consider the intentions of the parties, as appellant suggests, we do not believe the record supports her contention that "[t]he record unquestionably shows that Kathleen Cole was sent to Lutheran Hospital for the primary, if not the sole purpose, of obtaining diagnosis and treatment." Even under her own evidence, the commitment was for her protection; no one testified she was committed for treatment.

* * *

We find no reversible error; we therefore affirm the trial court.

Affirmed.

All Justices concur except HARRIS, J., who dissents, joined by REES and ALLBEE, JJ.

QUESTIONS AND COMMENTS

1.   *Court ordered examinations.* The *Cole* case affirms the basic rule that under state law, a privilege only attaches where the client's relationship to the psychologist or psychiatrist arose in the course of treatment. Problems may arise in the application of this rule when the professional relationship involves both diagnosis undertaken as a result of a court order and treatment carried out at the initiative of the examining facility.

2.   *Disclosure requirement.* Where the psychiatrist or psychologist examines a person on behalf of the court or an adverse party, does the examiner have an obligation to inform the evaluee that any disclosures will not be privileged? This question has only been addressed in the context of criminal cases, where it has generally been held that, unless the person being examined is specifically informed that the purpose of the examination is not for treatment, any disclosures that may be made are not admissible in a subsequent criminal trial. See *State v. Shaw*, 471 P.2d 715 (Ariz. 1970), and *State v. Cole*, 295 N.W.2d 29, 34 (Iowa 1980).

3.   *Scope of privilege.* In those jurisdictions where a privilege attaches to information or disclosures communicated in the course of psychotherapy, the scope of the privilege may require judicial interpretation. An issue that has arisen is whether confidential information as used in statutes setting

forth a privilege includes observations or any other information about the client that came from sources other than what the client himself told the mental health professional. For example, in *People v. Doe*, 430 N.E.2d 696 (Ill. Ct. App. 1981), the psychiatrist was subpoenaed to appear before the grand jury and was presented with a drawing purporting to be a composite sketch of a person suspected of an ax murder. Claiming statutory privilege, the psychiatrist refused to state whether she had seen anyone resembling the drawing even though there was independent evidence indicating that the person depicted by the composite drawing had been admitted to the psychiatric unit where the psychiatrist was working at the time. In finding the psychiatrist-patient privilege inapplicable, the court construed "communications" as used by the privilege statute to include only information obtained from conversations with the patient and not observations. Courts of other jurisdictions, however, have given a different interpretation to similar language. The American Psychiatric Association's *Model Law of Confidentiality of Health and Social Service Records* would specifically extend the privilege to all "confidential information," which is defined to include "the fact that a person is or has been a patient/client." See Judy Beckner Sloan & Betsy Hall, *Confidentiality of Psychotherapeutic Records*, 5 J. Legal Med. 435, 463 (1984).

4. *Hospital admissions.* In some jurisdictions, the client-psychotherapist privilege does not cover the fact that someone was admitted to a hospital, the dates of hospitalization, or the purpose of the admission, so long as the inquiry does not implicate a client-psychotherapist communication. In *Commonwealth v. Clancy*, 524 N.E.2d 395 (Mass. 1988), the court held that defense counsel was allowed this limited access to a witness's record without any showing of need as this was not privileged information.

5. *Records covered.* When privilege protects confidential communications with a psychotherapist, the privilege extends as well to the treatment records that the psychotherapist maintains. Generally, such records are protected to the same extent as the communications they describe. When treatment records are maintained at a hospital, school, or other public agency, however, the status of privilege is unclear. Similarly, when a person is committed for treatment to a psychiatric hospital, a variety of personnel may have access to her records. Courts, therefore, may regard the records as non-confidential and hence not privileged. On the other hand, other courts view nurses and ward staff as agents of the patient's psychiatrist and, accordingly, extend any applicable psychiatrist-patient or physician-patient privilege to hospital records.

Records at publicly funded hospitals pose additional problems. A few courts have found no confidential relationship between a patient and psychiatrists employed at a state hospital, and hence no privilege applicable to psychiatric records of state hospital patients. Additionally, courts sometimes treat state hospital records as public documents and therefore not privileged, or that the privilege is subject to waiver by the government, without the consent of the patient. (See, for example, the dissent in *Taylor v. United States*, 222 F.2d 398, 404 (D.C. Cir. 1955) and New York cases cited therein.)

6.   *Hypothetical*. A distraught person telephones a state psychiatric hospital and reaches the hospital's receptionist. He informs the receptionist that he has just "strangled a kid." The receptionist contacts the psychiatrist on duty, who without the knowledge of the caller, asks her to keep the caller on the line so that the sheriff's office can trace the call. The psychiatrist then gets on the line and speaks to the caller for ten to fifteen minutes, "asking him for background information similar to what the psychiatrist usually obtains from a patient in a psychiatric interview." During the conversation with the psychiatrist, the caller makes a number of incriminating statements about his homosexual encounters with the victim and his role in the victim's death.

While the caller is on the line with the psychiatrist, the police, who have in the meantime been notified by the hospital, trace the call and arrest the caller in a hotel room, where they also discover the deceased victim's body. The caller is charged with murder and brought to trial. At the trial, the prosecution seeks to obtain the testimony of both the hospital psychiatrist and the receptionist to whom the defendant had made incriminating statements.

Under the law of the state where the case is being tried, a testimonial privilege is available for statements made in the course of examination and treatment. The statutory provisions also extend to "persons *present* [emphasis added] to further the interests of the patient in the consultation, examination, or interview." If the privilege is applicable, would it preclude the testimony of either the psychiatrist or the receptionist? The prosecution asserts that the privilege is inapplicable because the psychiatrist was not diagnosing or treating the defendant, but rather was keeping him on the line to assist police apprehension. Also, the prosecution contends that the privilege does not apply to the receptionist because she was not "present" at the examination or interview. How should the privilege issue be resolved by the court? See *State v. Miller*, 709 P.2d 225 (Or. 1985).

b.   *Scope of the Privilege: Communications Made in the Presence of Others*

STATE V. ANDRING
Supreme Court of Minnesota, 1984.
342 N.W.2d 128.

WAHL, JUSTICE.

Defendant David Gerald Andring is charged with three counts of criminal sexual conduct in the second degree in violation of Minn. Stat. § 609.343 (1982). The two complaints setting out these counts allege that defendant had sexual contact with his 10–year–old stepdaughter and his

11–year–old niece. A hearing was held to consider a probable cause challenge to the complaints. Probable cause was found. Defendant was released on bond, pending trial, on condition that he have no contact with the alleged victims.

Defendant voluntarily entered the Crisis Intervention Unit at Bethesda Lutheran Medical Center (crisis unit) after the probable cause hearing but before trial. A social history of defendant was taken by a registered nurse; the admitting diagnosis was acute alcoholism and depression. During his stay, defendant received one-on-one counseling with staff physicians and other medical personnel. He also participated in a daily 2–hour group therapy session with other patients in the crisis unit, sessions which were supervised by physicians and registered nurses. Those present at the group therapy sessions were informed that such sessions were confidential and that only the staff would have access to information disclosed in the sessions. Defendant related his experience of sexual conduct with young girls (1) during one-on-one counseling sessions with registered nurses and a medical student, (2) during the taking of his social history with a registered nurse, and (3) during group therapy sessions.[1]

The state, in the course of its investigation of the case, learned of inculpatory disclosures made by defendant at the crisis unit. The state then moved for discovery and disclosure of defendant's medical records and statements made to crisis unit personnel. No request for disclosure from non-staff participants in the group therapy sessions was made. The trial court, after an extensive inquiry into the ramifications of the state's motion, denied the state's motion for discovery of statements made by defendant during the taking of his social history and during one-on-one therapy but granted the motion for discovery of defendant's disclosures made during group therapy sessions.

Considering the issue of confidentiality of group therapy disclosures as both important and doubtful, the trial court certified the following question to this court:

> Whether the scope of the physician-patient and/or registered nurse-patient privilege is to be extended to prevent disclosures of communications concerning Defendant's sexual conduct with minor children during group therapy sessions, a crime for which he has already been charged, where such group therapy sessions are an integral and necessary part of Defendant's diagnosis and treatment and consist of physicians and/or registered nurses and other patients, who participate in said group therapy sessions and are an aid to Defendant's diagnosis and treatment as well as their own, i.e., are

---

[1] The trial court found no reason to believe that any minor children other than defendant's stepdaughter and niece were involved in any of defendant's disclosures to the crisis unit's personnel.

such patients to be considered as agents of the physicians and/or registered nurses and/or do such patients come within the meaning of "being reasonably necessary for the accomplishment of the purpose of such a communication" so as to render the relationship confidential?

* * *

We [now] reach the question . . . as to whether confidential group therapy sessions which are an integral and necessary part of a patient's diagnosis and treatment are to be included within the scope of the medical privilege. The troublesome aspect of this question lies in the fact that third parties, other patients and participants in the therapy, are present at the time the information is disclosed. Does their presence destroy the privilege?

McCormick, in discussing the issue of whether the presence of third parties renders a statement to a physician nonprivileged, argues that the court should analyze the problem in terms of whether the third persons are necessary and customary participants in the consultation or treatment and whether the communications were confidential for the purpose of aiding in diagnosis and treatment. McCormick's Handbook of the Law of Evidence, § 101 (E. Cleary 2d ed. 1972). Under this approach, we conclude that the medical privilege must be construed to encompass statements made in group psychotherapy. The participants in group psychotherapy sessions are not casual third persons who are strangers to the psychiatrist/psychologist/nurse-patient relationship. Rather, every participant has such a relationship with the attending professional, and, in the group therapy setting, the participants actually become part of the diagnostic and therapeutic process for co-participants.

This point is more fully developed in Cross, *Privileged Communications Between Participants in Group Psychotherapy*, 1970 L. & Soc. Order 191, 196–98, 200–01 (1970):

> [T]he chief characteristic of group therapy that distinguishes it from individual analysis is that each patient becomes the therapeutic agent of the others. . . . Effective social interaction within the group is therefore a crucial prerequisite to group therapy. The type of interaction required can only be achieved, however, when group members respond to each other spontaneously, both in their speech and their actions. . . . No group participant would make himself vulnerable to community scorn and loss of spouse, job, or freedom by placing his most secret thoughts before the group, unless he could be assured of confidentiality. . . . [S]ociety should certainly foster a relationship that has an important prophylactic effect and thus shields both society and the patient from the consequences of antisocial behavior. . . . [A]lthough there may be occasional losses [of relevant important information] such sporadic occurrences are

overshadowed by the potential destruction of the therapeutic relationship.

An interpretation which excluded group therapy from the scope of the psychotherapist-patient privilege would seriously limit the effectiveness of group psychotherapy as a therapeutic device. This would be particularly unfortunate because group therapy is a cost-effective method of psychotherapy in that it allows the therapist to treat a number of patients at the same time. It is also more effective with some patients, who, upon hearing other people reveal their innermost thoughts, are less reluctant to reveal their own. Many commentators agree that the psychotherapist-patient privilege should be extended to include group therapy. Because the confidentiality of communications made during group therapy is essential in maintaining its effectiveness as a therapeutic tool, we answer the certified question in the affirmative. We hold that the scope of the physician-patient/medical privilege extends to include confidential group psychotherapy sessions where such sessions are an integral and necessary part of a patient's diagnosis and treatment. We reverse the order of the trial court allowing disclosure of defendant's statements made during group therapy.

Certified question answered in the affirmative.

Reversed.

QUESTIONS AND COMMENTS

1. *Conjoint therapy.* Mental health treatment frequently involves the presence and participation of individuals other than the "identified patient" or client who is the focus of treatment. Joint participation in therapy session is standard practice in couples therapy. Such treatments can raise questions about confidentiality, particularly if the parties later engage in litigation against each other (e.g., a divorce proceeding). To what extent, for instance, are decisions made during a therapy session in the presence of a spouse privileged? Under the traditional test, no privilege would attach to prevent a spouse from testifying as to the communications made during such a therapy session. But several states (including Colorado, Kentucky, and Wisconsin) have enacted legislation or developed evidence rules that extended the privilege to individuals who have participated in psychotherapeutic treatment. For example, Colorado prohibits the questioning of any persons who have participated in group therapy sessions "concerning any knowledge gained during the course of such therapy without the consent of the person to whom the testimony sought relates." Colo. Rev. Stat. Ann. § 13–90–107 (West 1998). See also Wis. § 905.04(2) (privilege covers "persons, including members of the patient's family, who are participating in the diagnosis or treatment"); Ky. Evid. R. 506(b) (client in counseling may prevent "any other person from disclosing confidential communications made for the purpose of counseling the client, between himself, his counselor, and persons present at the direction of the counselor").

2.   *Casual third party rule.* It is unclear to what extent multiple-person interactions are protected by the rules of privileged communication. If a "casual third party" is present during communications between a client and a therapist, then such communications usually are not privileged. There is a presumption that the client did not intend that the information remain confidential under such circumstances.

3.   Express or Implied Waiver of the Privilege

A common element of psychotherapist-client privilege is that its purpose is to protect the *client's* interest in confidentiality. It is the client, not the therapist, who is injured by compulsory public disclosure, for the client is thereby deterred either from seeking needed treatment or from confiding fully during therapy. Privilege, therefore, belongs to the client, not to the therapist, and a client's assertion or waiver of privilege is binding upon the therapist. That is, if a client asserts privilege, the therapist may not be compelled to testify, nor may she voluntarily testify concerning confidential communications. Similarly, if a client waives privilege, the therapist may not invoke the privilege to refuse to testify.

A client must assert or waive privilege when a party to litigation seeks to compel disclosure of confidential information. A litigant may compel testimony from the client or from the psychotherapist by obtaining a subpoena issued by the court, and she may compel production of a psychotherapist's records by obtaining a subpoena *duces tecum.* The client need not be a party to the litigation to assert the privilege.

A client may waive privilege in two ways. First, she may simply fail to assert privilege when confidential information is sought by a party in litigation. That is, the client may provide the information himself, or she may consent to its acquisition from the therapist. The therapist, however, has an affirmative duty to assert the privilege on behalf of the client if the client is not present or otherwise cannot assert the privilege.

Second, a client may waive privilege by making her mental or emotional condition an element of a claim or defense. In some jurisdictions, for example, a criminal defendant who raises an insanity defense may not invoke privilege to bar testimony concerning the results of a psychiatric interview to evaluate his sanity. See, e.g., *People v. Edney*, infra. Similarly, a client who initiates a malpractice suit against her therapist may not invoke the privilege to preclude testimony concerning the conduct of the therapy. Finally, a client makes her mental condition an element of a claim, and thereby waives privilege, when she seeks to recover damages for mental or emotional distress allegedly caused by another person's actions. But see *Ireland v. Francis*, 945 So. 2d 524 (Fla. Ct. App. 2006) (holding that notwithstanding that plaintiff initially put her mental condition in issue when she sought damages for "mental anguish" following a car accident, her psychotherapist-patient privilege was not waived as she withdrew this claim prior to trial).

Generally, courts attempt to limit compulsory disclosures to those elements of the communications that are essential to the issues of a case. The practice recognizes the sensitive nature of the information and accords with a general policy to protect witnesses and litigants from harassment.

A communication remains privileged despite the termination of therapy and continues even after the client's death. Although usually only a client may waive privilege, in some circumstances a client's personal representative, acting on behalf of the client, may waive the privilege. Persons who may be granted this authority include the guardian of an individual who is mentally incompetent and the heirs or persons appointed to manage the estate of a deceased client. Waiver of privilege after the death of a client occurs most often in disputes concerning the client's mental capacity at the time of making a will.

State law rules governing waivers of the privilege are not curtailed by HIPAA. The regulations permit disclosure of PHI without a patient's authorization in any judicial or administrative proceeding in response to an express order, a subpoena, or a discovery request. 45 C.F.R. § 164.512(e)(1) (describing specific requirements for a qualifying subpoena or discovery request).

a.   Civil Proceedings

IN RE LIFSCHUTZ

Supreme Court of California, 1970.
2 Cal. 3d 415, 85 Cal. Rptr. 829, 467 P.2d 557.

TOBRINER, JUSTICE.

Dr. Joseph E. Lifschutz, a psychiatrist practicing in California, seeks a writ of habeas corpus to secure his release from the custody of the Sheriff of the County of San Mateo. Dr. Lifschutz was imprisoned after he was adjudged in contempt of court for refusing to obey an order of the San Mateo County Superior Court instructing him to answer questions and produce records relating to communications with a former patient. Dr. Lifschutz contends that this underlying court order was invalid as unconstitutionally infringing his personal constitutional right of privacy, his right effectively to practice his profession, and the constitutional privacy rights of his patients. He also attacks the order, or more specifically, the statutory provisions which authorize the compulsion of his testimony in these circumstances, as unconstitutionally denying him the equal protection of the laws since, under California law, clergymen could not be compelled to reveal certain confidential communications under these circumstances.

The instant proceeding arose out of a suit instituted by Joseph F. Housek against John Arabian on June 3, 1968, for damages resulting from an alleged assault. Housek's complaint alleged that the assault caused him "physical injuries, pain, suffering and severe mental and emotional distress." Defendant Arabian deposed the plaintiff and during the course of that deposition Housek stated that he had received psychiatric treatment from Dr. Lifschutz over a six-month period approximately 10 years earlier. Nothing in the record indicates that the plaintiff revealed the nature or contents of any conversation with or treatment by Dr. Lifschutz.

Arabian then subpoenaed for deposition Dr. Lifschutz and all of his medical records relating to the treatment of Housek. Although Dr. Lifschutz appeared for the deposition, he refused to produce any of his medical records and refused to answer any questions relating to his treatment of patients; the psychiatrist declined even to disclose whether or not Housek had consulted him or had been his patient. . . . [Plaintiff] Housek has neither expressly claimed a psychotherapist-patient privilege, statutory or constitutional, nor expressly waived such a privilege.

In response to the psychiatrist's refusal to cooperate, defendant Arabian moved for an order of the superior court compelling the production of the subpenaed [sic] records and the answers to questions on deposition. Relying on the patient-litigant exception of section 1016 of the Evidence Code, the superior court determined that because the plaintiff, in instituting the pending litigation, had tendered as an issue his mental and emotional condition, the statutory psychotherapist-patient (Evid. Code, § 1014) privilege did not apply. On December 20, 1968, the court therefore ordered Dr. Lifschutz to comply with the subpena and to answer questions posed during deposition. On January 15, 1969, defendant attempted to continue with the deposition of Dr. Lifschutz as ordered by the superior court, but petitioner remained resolute in his refusal to respond or produce records. . . .

*   *   *

Dr. Lifschutz presents a novel challenge, attempting to raise far-reaching questions of constitutional law. From the affidavits and correspondence included in the record we note that a large segment of the psychiatric profession concurs in Dr. Lifschutz's strongly held belief that an absolute privilege of confidentiality is essential to the effective practice of psychotherapy.

We recognize the growing importance of the psychiatric profession in our modern, ultracomplex society. The swiftness of change—economic, cultural, and moral—produces accelerated tensions in our society, and the potential for relief of such emotional disturbances offered by psychotherapy undoubtedly establishes it as a profession essential to the preservation of societal health and well-being. Furthermore, a growing consensus throughout the country, reflected in a trend of legislative enactments, acknowledges that an environment of confidentiality of treatment is vitally important to the successful operation of psychotherapy. California has embraced this view through the enactment of a broad, protective psychotherapist-patient privilege.

The nature of the actual interests involved in this case can only be properly evaluated against the California statutory background. Although petitioner, in pressing for judicial acceptance of a genuine and deeply held principle, seeks to cast the issue involved in this case in the broadest terms, we must properly address, in reality, a question of more modest dimensions. We do not face the alternatives of enshrouding the patient's communication to the psychotherapist in the black veil of absolute privilege or of exposing it to the white glare of absolute publicity. Our choice lies, rather, in the grey area.

Properly viewed, the broadest issue before our court is whether the Legislature, in attempting to accommodate the conceded need of confidentiality in the psychotherapeutic process with general societal needs of access to information for the ascertainment of truth in litigation, has unconstitutionally weighted its resolution in favor of disclosure by providing that a psychotherapist may be compelled to reveal relevant confidences of treatment when the patient tenders his mental or emotional condition in issue in litigation. For the reasons discussed below, we conclude that, under a properly limited interpretation, the litigant-patient exception to the psychotherapist-patient privilege, at issue in this case, does not unconstitutionally infringe the constitutional rights of privacy of either psychotherapists or psychotherapeutic patients. As we point out, however, because of the potential of invasion of patients' constitutional interests, trial courts should properly and carefully control compelled disclosures in this area in the light of accepted principles.

*   *   *

The primary contention of Dr. Lifschutz's attack on the judgment of contempt consists of the assertion of a constitutional right of a psychotherapist to absolute confidentiality in his communications with, and treatment of, patients. Although, as we understand it, the alleged right draws its substance primarily from the psychological needs and expectations of patients, Dr. Lifschutz claims that the Constitution grants him an absolute right to refuse to disclose such confidential communications, regardless of the wishes of a patient in a particular case.

[The court held that the privilege is that of the patient and that a psychotherapist has no constitutional right to assert the privilege in his own behalf.]

* * *

The second basis of petitioner's contention raises a more serious problem. Petitioner claims that if the state is authorized to compel disclosure of some psychotherapeutic communications, psychotherapy can no longer be practiced successfully. He asserts that the unique nature of psychotherapeutic treatment, involving a probing of the patient's subconscious thoughts and emotions, requires an environment of total confidentiality and absolute trust. Petitioner claims that unless a psychotherapist can truthfully assure his patient that all revelations will be held in strictest confidence and never disclosed, patients will be inhibited from participating fully in the psychotherapeutic process and proper treatment will be impossible. Petitioner concludes that the patient-litigation exception involved here conflicts with the preservation of an environment of absolute confidentiality and unconstitutionally constricts the field of medical practice.

Petitioner's argument, resting as it does on assertions of medical necessity, exemplifies the type of question to which the judiciary brings little expertise. Although petitioner has submitted affidavits of psychotherapists who concur in his assertion that total confidentiality is essential to the practice of their profession, we cannot blind ourselves to the fact that the practice of psychotherapy has grown, indeed flourished, in an environment of a non-absolute privilege. No state in the country recognizes as broad a privilege as petitioner claims is constitutionally compelled. Whether psychotherapy's development has progressed only because patients are ignorant of the existing legal environment can only be a matter for speculation; psychotherapists certainly have been aware of the limitations of their recognized privilege for some time.

Petitioner's broad assertion, moreover, overlooks the limited nature of the intrusion into psychotherapeutic privacy actually at issue in this case. As we explain more fully in part III infra, the patient-litigant exception of section 1016 of the Evidence Code compels disclosure of only those matters which the patient himself has chosen to reveal by tendering them in litigation. We do not know, of course, to what extent patients are deterred from seeking psychotherapeutic treatment by the knowledge that if, at some future date, they choose to place some aspect of their mental condition in issue in litigation, communications relevant to that issue may be revealed. We can only surmise that an understanding of the limits of section 1016, and the realization that the patient retains control over subsequent disclosure, may provide a measure of reassurance to the prospective patient.

* * *

... Evidence Code, section 912, subdivision (a), provides that: "... the right of any person to claim a privilege provided by Section ... 1014 (psychotherapist-patient privilege) ... is waived with respect to a communication protected by such privilege if any holder of the privilege, without coercion, has disclosed a significant part of the communication or has consented to such disclosure made by anyone. Consent to disclosure is manifested by any statement or other conduct of the holder of the privilege indicating his consent to the disclosure, including his failure to claim the privilege in any proceeding in which he has the legal standing and opportunity to claim the privilege."

Since Housek, the holder of the privilege disclosed at a prior deposition that he has consulted Dr. Lifschutz for psychiatric treatment, he has waived whatever privilege he might have had to keep such information confidential. . . .

*   *   *

Defendant contended in the superior court, however, that *any* communication between the plaintiff and Dr. Lifschutz has lost its privileged status because the plaintiff has filed a personal injury action in which he claims recovery for "mental and emotional distress." Defendant relies on section 1016 of the Evidence Code, the patient-litigant exception to the psychotherapist-patient privilege, which provides that: "[t]here is no privilege under this article as to a communication relevant to an issue concerning the mental or emotional condition of the patient if such issue has been tendered by: (a) the patient. . . ." To avoid the necessity for further contempt proceedings or delaying appellate review in the instant case, we have considered whether defendant has accurately identified the proper reach of the patient-litigant exception.

As we explain more fully below, the patient-litigant exception allows only a limited inquiry into the confidences of the psychotherapist-patient relationship, compelling disclosure of only those matters directly relevant to the nature of the specific "emotional or mental" condition which the patient has voluntarily disclosed and tendered in his pleadings or in answer to discovery inquiries. Furthermore, even when confidential information falls within this exception, trial courts, because of the intimate and potentially embarrassing nature of such communications, may utilize the protective measures at their disposal to avoid unwarranted intrusions into the confidences of the relationship.

In interpreting this exception we are necessarily mindful of the justifiable expectations of confidentiality that most individuals seeking psychotherapeutic treatment harbor. As has been aptly pointed out by Judge Edgerton in *Taylor v. United States* (1955) (quoting from Guttmacher, M., et al., Psychiatry and the Law (1952) p. 272), " 'The psychiatric patient confides more utterly than anyone else in the world. He exposes to the therapist not only what his words directly express; he lays bare his entire self, his dreams, his fantasies, his sins, and his shame. Most patients who undergo psychotherapy know that this is what will be expected of them, and that they cannot get help except on that condition. . . . It would be too much to expect them to do so if they knew that all they say—and all that the psychiatrist learns from what they say—may be revealed to the whole world from a witness stand.' "

We believe that a patient's interest in keeping such confidential revelations from public purview, in retaining this substantial privacy, has deeper roots than the California statute and draws sustenance from our constitutional heritage. . . .

* * *

. . . In previous physician-patient privilege cases the exception [to the privilege of confidentiality] has been generally applied only to compel disclosure of medical treatment and communication concerning the very injury or impairment that was the subject matter of the litigation. There is certainly nothing to suggest that in the context of the more liberal psychotherapist-patient privilege this exception should be given a broader reading.

If the provision had as broad an effect as is suggested by petitioner, it might effectively deter many psychotherapeutic patients from instituting any general claim for mental suffering and damage out of fear of opening up all past communications to discovery. This result would clearly be an intolerable and overbroad intrusion into the patient's privacy, not sufficiently limited to the legitimate state interest embodied in the provision and would create opportunities for harassment and blackmail.

In light of these considerations, the "automatic" waiver of privilege contemplated by section 1016 must be construed not as a complete waiver of the privilege but only as a limited waiver concomitant with the purposes of the exception. Under section 1016 disclosure can be compelled only with respect to *those mental conditions* the patient-litigant has "disclose[d] . . . by bringing an action in which *they* are in issue"; communications which are not directly relevant to those specific conditions do not fall within the terms of section 1016's exception and therefore remain privileged. Disclosure cannot be compelled with respect to other aspects of the patient-litigant's personality even though they may, in some sense, be "relevant" to the substantive issues of litigation. The patient thus is not obligated to sacrifice all privacy to seek redress for a specific mental or emotional injury; the scope of the inquiry permitted depends upon the nature of the injuries which the patient-litigant himself has brought before the court.

In some situations, the patient's pleadings may clearly demonstrate that his entire mental condition is being placed in issue and that records of past psychotherapy will clearly be relevant. . . .

In other cases, however, the determination of the specific "mental condition" in issue may present more complex problems. The difficulties involved in analyzing the applicability of the exception in the instant case may be illustrative. The plaintiff's complaint, containing the typical allegations of "mental and emotional distress" arising out of a physical assault, does not specifically identify the nature of the "mental or emotional condition" at issue. In incorporating this allegation in his complaint, plaintiff obviously neither disclosed his entire medical history [of] treatment for mental or emotional conditions nor realistically waived his interest in maintaining the confidentiality of that treatment. The generality of the claim, however, does create the possibility that some feature of plaintiff's psychological history will be directly relevant to the determination of whether his emotional or mental distress can be properly attributed to the alleged assault. Although we doubt that the 10–year–old therapeutic treatment sought to be discovered from Dr. Lifschutz would be sufficiently relevant to a typical claim of "mental distress" to bring it within the exception of section 1016, we cannot determine from the present state of the record whether plaintiff's "mental and emotional" distress is merely the "normal" distress experienced as a result of physical assault or whether it includes unusual or particularly serious elements upon which prior history may be directly relevant.

Because only the patient, and not the party seeking disclosure, knows both the nature of the ailments for which recovery is sought and the general content of the psychotherapeutic communications, the burden rests upon the patient initially to submit some showing that a given confidential communication is not directly related to the issue he has tendered to the court. A patient may have to delimit his claimed "mental or emotional distress" or explain, in general terms, the object of the psychotherapy in order to illustrate that it is not reasonably probable that the psychotherapeutic communications sought are directly relevant to the mental condition that he has placed in issue. In determining whether communications sufficiently relate to the mental condition at issue to require disclosure, the court should heed the basic privacy interests involved in the privilege. . . .

*   *   *

Inasmuch as plaintiff had already disclosed that he had consulted Dr. Lifschutz for psychotherapeutic treatment, petitioner could not properly have refused to answer at least that question concerning the communications; since neither plaintiff nor the psychotherapist has as yet made any claim that the subpenaed records are not directly relevant to the specific "mental and emotional" injuries for which plaintiff is claiming relief, Dr. Lifschutz had no right to refuse to produce the records. Thus the trial court's order requiring the production of records and the answering of questions was valid; the trial court properly adjudged Dr. Lifschutz in contempt of court for intentionally violating that valid court order.

The order to show cause is discharged and the petition for writ of habeas corpus is denied.

MOSK, ACTING C.J., MCCOMB, PETERS, BURKE, and SULLIVAN, JJ., and MOLINARI, J. pro tem., concur.

QUESTIONS AND COMMENTS

1.   *Critique of* Lifschutz *rule.* Lifschutz in effect requires the plaintiff-patient to "disclose at least part of the contents of protected communications to his lawyer and the trial judge as a condition to retaining the confidentiality of the communication." *Caesar v. Mountanos*, 542 F.2d 1064, 1074 (9th Cir. 1976). This result has been criticized because it forces a plaintiff who wants to preserve confidentiality to elect either to make partial disclosure or possibly forego recovery for mental distress. Some, like Judge Hufstedler of the Ninth Circuit Court of Appeals, would avoid this problem by restricting compelled disclosures in a personal injury action to "the fact of treatment, the time and length of treatment, the cost of treatment, and the ultimate diagnosis unless the party seeking disclosure establishes in the trial court a compelling need for its production." *Caesar*, 542 F.2d at 1075 (Hufstedler, J., concurring and dissenting).

2.   *Good cause limitations on waiver of privilege.* Most jurisdictions follow the rule that a plaintiff who places his or her mental state in issue potentially waives the privilege. At the same time, a defendant seeking the plaintiff's psychiatric records must show good cause in order to obtain them. The good-cause showing required varies considerably, even between federal courts. In *Doe v. Oberweis Dairy*, 456 F.3d 704, 718 (7th Cir. 2006), Judge Posner's opinion sweepingly stated, "If a plaintiff by seeking damages for emotional distress places his or her psychological state in issue, the defendant is entitled to discover any records of that state." In contrast, *Koch v. Cox*, 489 F.3d 384 (D.C. Cir. 2007), held that such holdings "*sub silento . . .* overrule" *Jaffee*; the court instead required that the defendant show the plaintiff "bas[ed] his claim upon the psychotherapist's communications with him" or " 'selectively disclosed part of a privileged communication in order to gain an advantage in litigation.' " Other courts have adopted an intermediate position, holding that the plaintiff waives the privilege if he or she alleges a "specific mental or psychiatric injury or disorder" but not if only a general claim for pain and suffering or emotional distress is made. See *EEOC v. Serramonte*, 237 F.R.D. 220, 224–25 (N.D. Cal. 2006); *Ruhlmann v. Ulster Cty.*, 194 F.R.D. 445, 450 (N.D. N.Y. 2000); *LeFave v. Symbios, Inc.*, 2000 WL 1644154 (D. Colo. 2000). For further discussion of the waiver of privilege in federal courts, see Deirdre M. Smith, *An Uncertain Privilege: Implied Waiver and the Evisceration of the Psychotherapist–Patient Privilege in Federal Courts*, 58 DePaul L. Rev. 79 (2008).

In announcing the adoption of the psychotherapist privilege in federal court, *Jaffee* emphasized the need to avoid discouraging the use of psychotherapy. If, as is usually the case (but was not the case in *Jaffee*), the psychotherapy at issue in emotional distress cases occurs *before* the allegedly stressful event (e.g., before the alleged tort, sexual harassment, or employment discrimination), should the client-litigant exception be broadly construed, as in *Doe v. Oberweis Dairy*? Is it relevant that a broad construction of the exception might deter such suits from being brought in the first instance? Is there a privacy concern, independent of the desire to encourage psychotherapy, that should be considered in developing the good cause standard?

3. *Assertion of privilege by third parties.* As noted in In re *Lifschutz,* the testimonial privilege belongs to the patient or client. Once the patient or client has waived the privilege, the psychiatrist or other mental health professional does not have standing to challenge that waiver. However, in some states, parties other than patients or clients have standing to challenge the waiver.

For instance, under New York law, anyone having official custody of psychiatric records, such as "a treating hospital, physician or other institution" may request a protective order on the grounds that disclosure of all or part of the record "may be seriously detrimental to the interest of the patient, to uninvolved third parties, or to an important program of the custodian of the record." See *Cynthia B. v. New Rochelle Hosp. Med. Ctr.*, 458 N.E.2d 363, 365 (N.Y. 1983).

Where the privilege has been waived by the plaintiff, what public policy grounds, if any, support the right of a third party that is not a party to the lawsuit to assert the privilege belonging to the plaintiff-client in the lawsuit?

b.   The Insanity Defense Context

PEOPLE V. EDNEY
Court of Appeals of New York, 1976.
39 N.Y.2d 620, 385 N.Y.S.2d 23, 350 N.E.2d 400.

GABRIELLI, JUDGE.

Defendant was charged with kidnapping and the brutal killing of the eight-year-old daughter of his former girlfriend. He interposed the defense of insanity.

The jury found defendant guilty, as charged, of manslaughter, first degree and kidnapping in the first and second degrees. He was sentenced to a term of 25 years to life on the first degree kidnapping charge and to concurrent terms of up to 25 years on the other charges. The Appellate Division unanimously affirmed.

The critical and principal issue is whether the testimony of a psychiatrist, who had examined defendant prior to trial at the request of his attorney, was admissible over objections that the physician-patient and attorney-client privilege acted to bar its admission.

At trial, the prosecution showed that late in the afternoon on July 24, 1968, defendant grabbed Lisa Washington, the victim, off the street where she was playing with friends, and forcibly pushed her into a taxicab. At approximately 8:30 p.m., Lisa's aunt, with whom she was residing, received a call from defendant who stated that "If you don't get 'C' [the nickname of Lisa's mother] on the phone in the next couple of hours, I am going to rape and kill Lisa". A barmaid testified that defendant and a young girl were in the Nu–Way Lounge at about 9:30 p.m. and that she observed defendant leave the tavern with the girl, walk around a corner toward the back of the building, and return a short while later without her. Less than an hour later, police officers, responding to a call by a woman who had reported a disturbance in her backyard which adjoined the rear of the Nu–Way Lounge, found Lisa's lifeless body. She had been stabbed 11 times. The police questioned persons in the bar and learned of defendant's presence in the bar earlier in the evening with a little girl.

Defendant was located at his father's home early the next morning and taken into custody. As he was leaving with the officers, he was asked by his father whether he had "hurt that little child", to which he replied "I'm sorry, I'm sorry". Granules of dirt taken from defendant's trousers confirmed that defendant had been in the area behind the Nu–Way Lounge.

Following his arrest, and after receiving the standard preinterrogation admonitions, defendant volunteered to a detective that he had been in the Nu–Way Lounge that evening, that he had been hearing voices which told him that God wanted Lisa, and that he might have killed Lisa but he was not sure. Taking the witness stand in his own defense, defendant testified that on the day in question, he had drunk large quantities of alcohol, had been smoking marijuana cigarettes, and that sometime after 9:00 p.m., he and Lisa had left the Nu–Way Lounge to go to his father's place; that he might have killed Lisa but he was not sure he had done so. He recalled walking to a cab across the street from the bar but could remember no more. He explained that he regained consciousness under a tree near his father's home and that he walked inside and blacked out; the next thing he was able to remember was someone pounding on him to wake up because the police were there.

A psychiatrist called by the defense testified that defendant suffered from paranoid schizophrenia of mild severity and that the condition was of long standing. It was his opinion that defendant was mentally ill to such an extent that he was unaware of the nature and quality of his act and did not know that his act was wrong.

In rebuttal, the prosecution called Dr. Daniel Schwartz, a psychiatrist, who originally examined defendant at the behest of defendant's attorney, who was not present during the examination. The defense unsuccessfully objected to his testifying on the ground that the attorney-client and physician-patient privileges barred his testimony. Dr. Schwartz described defendant as having an alcoholic psychosis, which occasionally manifested itself through hallucinations and delusions; however, he found no evidence of an underlying disease or defect. It was his opinion that at the time of the murder defendant knew and appreciated the nature of his conduct and knew that such conduct was wrong.

Another rebuttal psychiatrist, who had independently examined the defendant for the prosecution, supported the conclusions of Dr. Schwartz that defendant knew and appreciated the nature of his conduct and that such conduct was wrong.

Two other psychiatrists, produced by the defense as surrebuttal witnesses, each testified that he was unable to form an opinion as to whether defendant knew or appreciated the nature of his acts, or whether such acts were wrong, although they did agree that defendant had some form of mental disease.

People v. Al–Kanani [(N.Y., 1973)], is dispositive of the physician-patient privilege claim. There we held

> "that where insanity is asserted as a defense and . . . the defendant offers evidence tending to show his insanity in support of this plea, a complete waiver is effected, and the prosecution is then permitted to call psychiatric experts to testify regarding his sanity even though they may have treated the defendant. When the patient first fully discloses the evidence of his affliction, it is he who has given the public the full details of his case, thereby disclosing the secrets which the statute was designed to protect, thus creating a waiver removing it from the operation of the statute and once the privilege is thus waived, there is nothing left to protect against for once the revelation is made by the patient there is nothing further to disclose 'for when a secret is out it is out for all time and cannot be caught again like a bird, and put back in its cage. . . . The legislature did not intend to continue the privilege when there was no reason for its continuance and it would simply be an obstruction to public justice.'. . . . "

Our holding in the case now before us comports with this rationale and is but a logical extension of our determination in *Al–Kanani.*

Equally unavailing to defendant is the claim that the attorney-client privilege bars admission of Dr. Schwartz' testimony. Essentially, defendant relies on decisions in other jurisdictions which have excluded such testimony apparently because a psychiatrist would inevitably be required to reveal a defendant's statements to him to justify his opinion and because a contrary rule would deter attorneys from freely seeking sound professional advice as to the soundness of an insanity plea. We do not find the reasoning of these cases compelling and, accordingly, do not follow them. Rather, we think the better rationale underlies the *Al-Kanani* rule that a plea of innocence by reason of insanity constitutes a complete and effective waiver by the defendant of any claim of privilege.

A defendant who seeks to introduce psychiatric testimony in support of his insanity plea may be required to disclose prior to trial the underlying basis of his alleged affliction to a prosecution psychiatrist. Hence, where, as here, a defendant reveals to the prosecution the very facts which would be secreted by the exercise of the privilege, reason does not compel the exclusion of expert testimony based on such facts, or cross-examination concerning the grounds for opinions based thereon. It follows that no harm accrues to the defense from seeking pretrial psychiatric advice where an insanity plea is actually entered, for in such circumstances, the underlying factual basis will be revealed to the prosecution psychiatrist. Conversely, were the defendant not to enter an insanity plea, no physician-patient waiver would occur and any information divulged to the psychiatrist would remain privileged. There is, therefore, no deterrent to seeking expert psychiatric advice for, in one instance, there will be disclosure to the prosecution in any event and, in the other, disclosure will never occur. In short, no reason appears why a criminal defendant who puts his sanity in issue should be permitted to thwart the introduction of testimony from a material witness who may be called at trial by invoking the attorney-client privilege anymore than he should be able to do so by invoking the physician-patient privilege.

This is not to say, however, that an attorney cannot consult a psychiatrist in order to obtain advice concerning the efficacy of an insanity plea or, for that matter, any trial strategy, without fear of later courtroom disclosure. The product of such a consultation is protected, of course, by the work product doctrine (see CPLR 3101). However, that doctrine affords protection only to facts and observations disclosed *by the attorney*. Thus, it is the information and observations of the attorney that are conveyed to the expert which may thus be subject to trial exclusion. The work product doctrine does not operate to insulate other disclosed information from public exposure.

It is significant that the underlying purpose of the attorney-client privilege would not be diminished by the admission of the testimony of Dr. Schwartz. The privilege is grounded in the salutary policy of encouraging "persons needing professional advice to disclose freely the facts in reference to which they seek advice, without fear that such facts will be made public to their disgrace or detriment by their attorney" . . . That policy is not harmed, however, by the admission of evidence which, in any event, in these circumstances would be available to the prosecution. Indeed, with respect to the testimony of Dr. Schwartz, it is readily apparent that the traditional and statutory requirements of an attorney-client relationship were simply not established (CPLR 4503, subd. [a]). We hold, therefore, that the privilege was inapplicable.

We find no merit in defendant's other contentions.

Accordingly, the order of the Appellate Division should be affirmed.

[The dissenting opinion of Judge Fuchsberg is omitted.]

PEOPLE V. KNUCKLES
Supreme Court of Illinois, 1995.
165 Ill. 2d 125, 209 Ill. Dec. 1, 650 N.E.2d 974 (1995).

JUSTICE McMORROW delivered the opinion of the court:

The primary issue raised in this appeal is whether Illinois will permit the application of the attorney-client privilege to communications between a defendant who raises an insanity defense and the psychiatrist who examines the accused at the request of defense counsel to aid in preparation of the defense.

Defendant, Pamela J. Knuckles, was charged in the circuit court of Du Page County with the 1984 slaying of her mother, Nancy Knuckles. She pleaded guilty, but that plea was later set aside on grounds of ineffective assistance of counsel. The State reinstated murder charges in 1990, and, in preparation for trial, the State issued two subpoenas to Dr. Kyle Rossiter, a psychiatrist who had examined Knuckles at her counsel's request approximately two weeks after the killing. Defense counsel disclosed other expert witnesses expected to testify for the defendant and indicated that the defense did not plan to call Dr. Rossiter to testify at trial. Knuckles moved to quash the subpoenas served on the psychiatrist and thereby preclude the State from discovering or using the psychiatrist's notes and testimony in its case. The motion to quash was sustained. The State appealed from the trial court's order quashing the subpoenas. The appellate court affirmed, and we granted the State's petition for leave to appeal.

Background

In November 1984, Pamela Knuckles and her brother, sister, and others were charged with killing Nancy Knuckles by strangulation and suffocation. Pamela Knuckles' court-appointed public defender obtained court authorization to retain a psychiatrist to interview her. The psychiatrist, Dr. Kyle Rossiter, met with Knuckles at the Du Page County jail approximately two weeks after the murder. He took notes of her statements but did not prepare a written report, nor did he testify at any proceeding involving her. Knuckles' counsel disclosed to the State in April 1985 that the defense would not be offering evidence of physical or mental examinations or scientific tests. Following plea negotiations, Knuckles pleaded guilty and was sentenced to 33 years in prison.

New attorneys entered an appearance on Knuckles' behalf, and in January 1989, Knuckles filed a post-conviction petition challenging the validity of her guilty plea on grounds of ineffective assistance of counsel. Her petition stated that she had pleaded guilty because her appointed counsel advised her that if she went to trial she faced the death penalty. However, at the time of the killing, Knuckles was 17 years old and would have been exempted from the death penalty under Illinois law. Following an evidentiary hearing, the trial court granted Knuckles' post-conviction petition and allowed her to withdraw her plea of guilty.

Knuckles' attorneys retained several experts to evaluate Knuckles' history of physical and psychological abuse and her mental state at the time of the charged offenses. . . . [D]efense lawyers notified the prosecution that their client would rely on two defenses at trial: insanity and self-defense. At the same time, the defense disclosed the names of its five expert witnesses, the experts' reports, and test results indicating the possibility that Knuckles suffered from a brain abnormality. Dr. Rossiter was not among the experts whom the defense listed as witnesses for trial.

The State then served two subpoenas on Dr. Rossiter. One sought any written memoranda he had made of his interview with Knuckles and the other sought to compel his testimony at trial. The State also invoked its statutory right to compel Knuckles to submit to a psychiatric examination by an expert retained by the State.

On July 20, 1990, the trial court quashed the two subpoenas that had been issued to Dr. Rossiter. The court held that a psychiatrist hired by defense counsel to examine the client for purposes of trial preparation is an agent of defense counsel and therefore the communications between the defendant and the defense-retained psychiatrist are protected by the attorney-client privilege. The trial court further held that the privilege is not waived by the assertion of the insanity defense.

Analysis

This appeal highlights the tension between two competing policies: one that favors the broad discovery of relevant information and another that guards the narrow discovery exemptions, based on privilege, which are deeply rooted in the common law and the Federal and State Constitutions. The State argues that since Dr. Rossiter is the only psychiatrist who examined Pamela Knuckles near the time her mother was killed, his impressions of Knuckles' mental state are of surpassing importance in this case. If the potential relevance of the information sought were the key to determining whether the attorney-client privilege should yield to the truth-seeking process, the State's argument would be persuasive. However, the policies underlying the privilege exist apart from and run counter to the primary goals of discovery. The *raison d'être* of the privilege is to secure for the client the ability to confide freely and fully in his or her attorney, without fear that confidential information will be disseminated to others.

I. Extension of the Attorney–Client Privilege to Communications Between Defense Counsel and a Psychiatric Consultant Engaged by the Defense

Initially, this court must determine whether the attorney-client privilege should be extended to communications made to or made by an expert witness, here a psychiatrist, whose engagement by the defense is necessary to the preparation of an insanity defense. No Illinois case has decided that precise issue. [The court held that as a matter of common law, the attorney-client privilege extends to communications with and findings by a psychiatrist who has been retained by defendant's counsel to evaluate the client.]

II. Waiver of Attorney–Client Privilege by Assertion of Insanity Defense

A minority of jurisdictions have held that the attorney-client privilege is automatically waived whenever the accused puts his or her mental state in issue in the form of an insanity defense. . . .

In the case at bar, the State argues that we should follow the reasoning of those cases that employ the automatic waiver rule when a defendant puts his mental state in issue. However, we do not find those cases persuasive. In *Edney* [1976], the New York Court of Appeals held that the attorney-client privilege was waived because State law allowed prosecutors to compel a defendant to submit to an examination by a State-retained psychiatric expert, and therefore the very facts that would be secreted by the privilege necessarily would be disclosed through the compelled examination. We note that the rationale of *Edney* has been questioned. See *Miller* [(Colo. 1987)] ("[*Edney*] represents the clear minority view and has been sharply criticized by the American Bar Association as 'confused' and 'unpersuasive' ").

After carefully considering the cases from other jurisdictions, we find that the better-reasoned decisions hold that the privilege is waived only with respect to the testimony and reports of those experts who are identified by the defense as witnesses who will be called to testify on behalf of the defendant at trial, or whose notes and reports are used by other defense experts who testify. Policy reasons for recognizing the privilege in the mental health context and for limiting the waiver doctrine include the "chilling effect" disclosure of experts would have upon a client's willingness to confide in his or her attorney and consultants; inherent prejudice that occurs if the trier of fact learns that a mental health professional testifying at trial was originally retained by the defense; concern that allowing waiver would, in effect, cause the defense to assist the State in discharging its burden of proof; and recognition that the defense would be inhibited from consulting with mental health professionals for fear of creating prosecution witnesses, and might not consult them even though professional assistance might be crucial to the case.

We hold that the attorney-client privilege in Illinois protects communications between a defendant who raises an insanity defense and a psychiatrist employed by defense counsel to aid in the preparation of the defense, if the psychiatrist will not testify and the psychiatrist's notes and opinions will not be used in the formulation of the other defense experts' trial testimony. Accordingly, we hold that the attorney-client privilege has not been waived in the case at bar with respect to the testimony and notes of Dr. Rossiter.

III. Public Interest Exception

The State next argues that if we uphold the privilege and find that it was not waived by defendant's assertion of the insanity defense, we should "make an exception for the unique circumstances of this case." The State urges us to find that the privilege must yield to the public interest in the truth-finding process, because here the State's ability to rebut the insanity defense may be seriously hampered by its inability to discover the notes and opinions of the one doctor who examined defendant near the time of the alleged homicide [six years prior to the retrial following reversal of the guilty plea]. . . .

*   *   *

. . . Both sides have retained experts who presumably are prepared to render their opinions as to Knuckles' mental condition at the time of the homicide with which she is charged. Neither side will present the results of Dr. Rossiter's evaluation of Knuckles' sanity shortly after the crime was committed. Although the defense may derive a benefit from the exclusion of Dr. Rossiter's testimony, we have no way of knowing what evidence may have been presented if Knuckles had received competent assistance of counsel and received a trial, instead of entering a plea of guilty on the erroneous advice of counsel. The interests served by the preservation of the attorney-client privilege should not turn on the passage of time alone. Such a rule would be illogical and arbitrary. Although the State argues that its ability to prosecute Knuckles will be severely hampered because the prosecutors will be denied discovery and use of Dr. Rossiter's examination of her, it cites no case in which the mere passage of time and resulting loss of opportunity to discover information have been deemed to nullify the fundamental purpose of the attorney-client privilege. Indeed, to adopt the State's argument would be to eviscerate the privilege with the sword of expediency, disregarding historical policy and reasoned analysis.

*   *   *

For the reasons set out in this opinion, we hold that the attorney-client privilege applies to communications between the defense and nontestifying mental health experts retained by the defense to probe the defendant's mental condition in anticipation of relevant defenses. We further hold that the privilege is not waived merely by the assertion of defenses which place the defendant's mental condition in issue. Finally, we decline to adopt a generalized public interest exception in the case at bar to allow the State's interest in gathering evidence to overcome the attorney-client privilege. Therefore, we affirm the judgment of the appellate court.

Appellate court affirmed.

[The dissenting opinion of Justices Miller and Heiple are omitted.]

QUESTIONS AND COMMENTS

1. *Constitutional issues.* A psychiatrist may examine a criminal defendant on the issue of the defendant's sanity at the time of the offense at the request of the defendant, the prosecutor, or the court. In the last instance, the examiner is treated as an "independent" expert. Particularly complex Fifth and Sixth Amendment issues are raised when the prosecutor seeks to introduce evidence based on a psychiatric interview conducted by a court-appointed expert. The issues raised by such use are treated in Part III.C of Chapter Six.

2. *Effect of waiver on subsequent proceedings.* What effect should the defendant's privilege waiver in a criminal proceeding have in a subsequent civil suit? Compare *Novak v. Rathnam*, 478 N.E.2d 1334 (Ill. 1985), with *Simpson v. Braider*, 104 F.R.D. 512 (D. D.C. 1985). In *Novak*, the defendant, Rathnam, discharged Endicott from a mental health facility in Illinois. Endicott traveled to Florida where he shot and killed Novak's daughter. At his Florida murder trial, Endicott called four psychiatrists, including Rathnam, in successfully asserting insanity as a defense. Thereafter, Novak filed a wrongful death action in Illinois alleging that Rathnam was negligent in approving Endicott's discharge. Rathnam refused to permit Novak to depose him, arguing that any information about his treatment of Endicott was privileged by state statute. The Illinois Supreme Court rejected Rathnam's claim that he could not testify unless Endicott waived the privilege. The court held that "[i]f there is a disclosure of confidential information by the individual for whose benefit the privilege exists, or if he permits such a disclosure, the privilege is waived and cannot be reasserted." 478 N.E.2d at 1337.

In contrast, the district court in *Simpson v. Braider* focused on the context of the defendant's disclosures in the criminal proceeding. "[T]hese revelations [about the defendant's history of mental health treatment] in the Superior Court criminal case, since they were made in defense of criminal charges, cannot be truly considered voluntary. There Justin Braider was an accused, a defendant, and these revelations were made only to protect his interests in that proceeding. These were not revelations undertaken on his own initiative, where he sought advantage such as where a person seeks to use information to obtain an advantage, but then invokes the privilege to preclude the adversary from challenging a claim." The district court concluded that no waiver should be implied from "circumstances indicating there was realistically no voluntary disclosure." 104 F.R.D. at 522–23.

Which is the better view? Does the passage from *People v. Al–Kanani*, quoted in *People v. Edney*, supra, implicitly reject the rationale articulated by the court in *Simpson v. Braider*?

4.   Admissibility of Disclosures During Treatment in Criminal Prosecutions

a.   *Treatment   Information   Concerning   Prosecution Witnesses*

PENNSYLVANIA V. RITCHIE

Supreme Court of the United States, 1987.
480 U.S. 39, 107 S. Ct. 989, 94 L. Ed.2d 40.

JUSTICE POWELL announced the judgment of the Court and delivered the opinion of the Court with respect to Parts I, II, III–B, III–C, and IV, and an opinion with respect to Part III–A in which THE CHIEF JUSTICE, JUSTICE WHITE, and JUSTICE O'CONNOR join.

The question presented in this case is whether and to what extent a State's interest in the confidentiality of its investigative files concerning child abuse must yield to a criminal defendant's Sixth and Fourteenth Amendment right to discover favorable evidence.

I

As part of its efforts to combat child abuse, the Commonwealth of Pennsylvania has established Children and Youth Services (CYS), a protective service agency charged with investigating cases of suspected mistreatment and neglect. In 1979, respondent George Ritchie was charged with rape, involuntary deviate sexual intercourse, incest, and corruption of a minor. The victim of the alleged attacks was his 13–year–old daughter, who claimed that she had been assaulted by Ritchie two or three times per week during the previous four years. The girl reported the incidents to the police, and the matter then was referred to the CYS.

During pretrial discovery, Ritchie served CYS with a subpoena, seeking access to the records concerning the daughter. Ritchie requested disclosure of the file related to the immediate charges, as well as certain records that he claimed were compiled in 1978, when CYS investigated a separate report by an unidentified source that Ritchie's children were being abused. CYS refused to comply with the subpoena, claiming that the records were privileged under Pennsylvania law. The relevant statute provides that all reports and other information obtained in the course of a CYS investigation must be kept confidential, subject to 11 specific exceptions.[2] One of those exceptions is that the Agency may disclose the reports to a "court of competent jurisdiction pursuant to a court order." Pa. Stat. Ann., Title 11, § 2215(a)(5) (Purdon Supp. 1986).

Ritchie moved to have CYS sanctioned for failing to honor the subpoena, and the trial court held a hearing on the motion in chambers. Ritchie argued that he was entitled to the information because the file might contain the names of favorable witnesses, as well as other, unspecified exculpatory evidence. He also requested disclosure of a medical report that he believed was compiled during the 1978 CYS investigation. Although the trial judge acknowledged that he had not examined the entire CYS file, he accepted a CYS representative's assertion that there was no medical report in the record.[3] The judge then denied the motion and refused to order CYS to disclose the files.[4]

At trial, the main witness against Ritchie was his daughter. In an attempt to rebut her testimony, defense counsel cross-examined the girl at length, questioning her on all aspects of the alleged attacks, and her reasons for not reporting the incidents sooner. Except for routine evidentiary rulings, the trial judge placed no limitation on the scope of cross-examination. At the close of trial Ritchie was convicted by a jury on all counts, and the judge sentenced him to 3 to 10 years in prison.

On appeal to the Pennsylvania Superior Court, Ritchie claimed, *inter alia,* that the failure to disclose the contents of the CYS file violated the Confrontation Clause of the Sixth Amendment, as applied to the States through the Due Process Clause of the Fourteenth Amendment. The court agreed that there had been a constitutional violation, and accordingly vacated the conviction and remanded for further proceedings. . . .

On appeal by the Commonwealth, the Supreme Court of Pennsylvania agreed that the conviction must be vacated and the case remanded to determine if a new trial is necessary. . . . [I]t concluded that

---

[2] The statute provides in part:

(a) Except as provided in section 14 [Pa. Stat. Ann., Title 11, § 2214 (Purdon Supp. 1986)], reports made pursuant to this act including but not limited to report summaries of child abuse . . . and written reports . . . as well as any other information obtained, reports written or photographs or X-rays taken concerning alleged instances of child abuse in the possession of the department, a county children and youth social service agency or a child protective service shall be confidential and shall only be made available to:

. . . .

(5) A court of competent jurisdiction pursuant to a court order. Pa. Stat. Ann., Title 11, § 2215(a) (Purdon Supp. 1986).

At the time of trial the statute only provided five exceptions to the general rule of confidentiality, including the exception for court-ordered disclosure. . . .

[3] The trial judge stated that he did not read "50 pages or more of an extensive record." The judge had no knowledge of the case before the pretrial hearing.

[4] There is no suggestion that the Commonwealth's prosecutor was given access to the file at any point in the proceedings, or that he was aware of its contents.

Ritchie, through his lawyer, is entitled to review the entire file to search for any useful evidence. It stated: "When materials gathered become an arrow of inculpation, the person inculpated has a fundamental constitutional right to examine the provenance of the arrow and he who aims it." The Pennsylvania Court concluded that by denying access to the file, the trial court order had violated both the Confrontation Clause and the Compulsory Process Clause. The court was unpersuaded by the Commonwealth's argument that the trial judge already had examined the file and determined that it contained no relevant information. It ruled that the constitutional infirmity in this trial court's order was that Ritchie was unlawfully denied the opportunity to have the records reviewed by "the eyes and the perspective of an advocate," who may see relevance in places that a neutral judge would not.

In light of the substantial and conflicting interests held by the Commonwealth and Ritchie, we granted certiorari. 476 U.S. 1139, 106 S. Ct. 2244, 90 L. Ed. 2d 690 (1986). We now affirm in part, reverse in part, and remand for proceedings not inconsistent with this opinion.

II

[The plurality opinion rejects the defendant's contention that the Court lacked jurisdiction on the grounds that the decision below was not final.]

III

The Pennsylvania Supreme Court held that Ritchie, through his lawyer, has the right to examine the full contents of the CYS records. The court found that this right of access is required by both the Confrontation Clause and the Compulsory Process Clause. We discuss these constitutional provisions in turn.

A

The Confrontation Clause provides two types of protections for a criminal defendant: the right physically to face those who testify against him, and the right to conduct cross-examination. *Delaware v. Fensterer* ([U.S.] 1985) (*per curiam*). Ritchie does not allege a violation of the former right. . . . Instead Ritchie claims that by denying him access to the information necessary to prepare his defense, the trial court interfered with his right of cross-examination.

Ritchie argues that he could not effectively question his daughter because, without the CYS material, he did not know which types of questions would best expose the weaknesses in her testimony. Had the files been disclosed, Ritchie argues that he might have been able to show that the daughter made statements to the CYS counselor that were inconsistent with her trial statements, or perhaps to reveal that the girl acted with an improper motive. . . .

The Pennsylvania Supreme Court accepted this argument, relying in part on our decision in *Davis v. Alaska* [(U.S. 1974)]. In *Davis* the trial judge prohibited defense counsel from questioning a witness about the latter's juvenile criminal record, because a state statute made this information presumptively confidential. We found that this restriction on cross-examination violated the Confrontation Clause, despite Alaska's legitimate interest in protecting the identity of juvenile offenders. The Pennsylvania Supreme Court apparently interpreted our decision in *Davis* to mean that a statutory privilege cannot be maintained when a defendant asserts a need, prior to trial, for the protected information that might be used at trial to impeach or otherwise undermine a witness' testimony.

If we were to accept this broad interpretation of *Davis,* the effect would be to transform the Confrontation Clause into a constitutionally-compelled rule of pretrial discovery. Nothing in the case law supports such a view. The opinions of this Court show that the right of confrontation is a *trial* right, designed to prevent improper restrictions on the types of questions that defense counsel may ask during cross-examination. The ability to question adverse witnesses, however, does not include the power to require the pretrial disclosure of any and all information that might be useful in contradicting unfavorable testimony.[9] Normally the right to confront one's accusers is satisfied if defense counsel receives wide latitude at trial to question witnesses. In short, the Confrontation Clause only guarantees "an *opportunity* for effective cross-examination, not cross-examination that is effective in whatever way, and to whatever extent, the defense might wish."

* * *

The lower court's reliance on *Davis v. Alaska* therefore is misplaced. There the state court had prohibited defense counsel from questioning the witness about his criminal record, even though that evidence might have affected the witness' credibility. The constitutional error in that case was *not* that Alaska made this information confidential; it was that the defendant was denied the right "to expose to the jury the facts from which jurors . . . could appropriately draw inferences relating to the reliability of the witness." Similarly, in this case the Confrontation Clause was not violated by the withholding of the CYS file; it only would have been impermissible for the judge to have prevented Ritchie's lawyer from cross-examining the daughter. Because defense counsel was able to cross-examine all of the trial witnesses fully, we find that the Pennsylvania Supreme Court erred in holding that the failure to disclose the CYS file violated the Confrontation Clause.

---

[9] This is not to suggest, of course, that there are no protections for pretrial discovery in criminal cases. See discussion in Part III.B., infra. We simply hold that with respect to this issue, the Confrontation Clause only protects a defendant's trial rights, and does not compel the pretrial production of information that might be useful in preparing for trial.

B

The Pennsylvania Supreme Court also suggested that the failure to disclose the CYS file violated the Sixth Amendment's guarantee of compulsory process. Ritchie asserts that the trial court's ruling prevented him from learning the names of the "witnesses in his favor," as well as other evidence that might be contained in the file. Although the basis for the Pennsylvania Supreme Court's ruling on this point is unclear, it apparently concluded that the right of compulsory process includes the right to have the State's assistance in uncovering arguably useful information, without regard to the existence of a state-created restriction—here, the confidentiality of the files.

1

This Court has had little occasion to discuss the contours of the Compulsory Process Clause. . . .

. . . Instead, the Court traditionally has evaluated claims such as those raised by Ritchie under the broader protections of the Due Process Clause of the Fourteenth Amendment. Because the applicability of the Sixth Amendment to this type of case is unsettled, and because our Fourteenth Amendment precedents addressing the fundamental fairness of trials establish a clear framework for review, we adopt a due process analysis for purposes of this case. Although we conclude that compulsory process provides no *greater* protections in this area than those afforded by due process, we need not decide today whether and how the guarantees of the Compulsory Process Clause differ from those of the Fourteenth Amendment. It is enough to conclude that on these facts, Ritchie's claims more properly are considered by reference to due process.

2

It is well-settled that the Government has the obligation to turn over evidence in its possession that is both favorable to the accused and material to guilt or punishment. Although courts have used different terminologies to define "materiality," a majority of this Court has agreed, "[e]vidence is material only if there is a reasonable probability that, had the evidence been disclosed to the defense, the result of the proceeding would have been different. A 'reasonable probability' is a probability sufficient to undermine confidence in the outcome."

At this stage, of course, it is impossible to say whether any information in the CYS records may be relevant to Ritchie's claim of innocence, because neither the prosecution nor defense counsel has seen the information, and the trial judge acknowledged that he had not reviewed the full file. The Commonwealth, however, argues that no materiality inquiry is required, because a statute renders the contents of the file privileged. Requiring disclosure here, it is argued, would override the Commonwealth's compelling interest in confidentiality on the mere speculation that the file "might" have been useful to the defense.

Although we recognize that the public interest in protecting this type of sensitive information is strong, we do not agree that this interest necessarily prevents disclosure in all circumstances. This is not a case where a state statute grants CYS the absolute authority to shield its files from all eyes. Cf. 42 Pa. Cons. Stat. § 5945.1(b) (unqualified statutory privilege for communications between sexual assault counselors and victims).[14] Rather, the Pennsylvania law provides that the information shall be disclosed in certain circumstances, including when CYS is directed to do so by court order. Given that the Pennsylvania Legislature contemplated *some* use of CYS records in judicial proceedings, we cannot conclude that the statute prevents all disclosure in criminal prosecutions. In the absence of any apparent state policy to the contrary, we therefore have no reason to believe that relevant information would not be disclosed when a court of competent jurisdiction determines that the information is "material" to the defense of the accused.

We therefore affirm the decision of the Pennsylvania Supreme Court to the extent it orders a remand for further proceedings. Ritchie is entitled to have the CYS file reviewed by the trial court to determine whether it contains information that probably would have changed the outcome of his trial. If it does, he must be given a new trial. If the records maintained by CYS contain no such information, or if the nondisclosure was harmless beyond a reasonable doubt, the lower court will be free to reinstate the prior conviction.

C

This ruling does not end our analysis, because the Pennsylvania Supreme Court did more than simply remand. It also held that defense counsel must be allowed to examine all of the confidential information, both relevant and irrelevant, and present arguments in favor of disclosure. The court apparently concluded that whenever a defendant alleges that protected evidence might be material, the appropriate method of assessing this claim is to grant full access to the disputed information, regardless of the State's interest in confidentiality. We cannot agree.

A defendant's right to discover exculpatory evidence does not include the unsupervised authority to search through the Commonwealth's files. Although the eye of an advocate may be helpful to a defendant in ferreting out information, this Court has never held—even in the absence of a statute restricting disclosure—that a defendant alone may make the determination as to the materiality of the information. Settled practice is

---

[14] We express no opinion on whether the result in this case would have been different if the statute had protected the CYS files from disclosure to *anyone,* including law-enforcement and judicial personnel.

to the contrary. In the typical case where a defendant makes only a general request for exculpatory material . . . , it is the State that decides which information must be disclosed. Unless defense counsel becomes aware that other exculpatory evidence was withheld and brings it to the court's attention, the prosecutor's decision on disclosure is final. Defense counsel has no constitutional right to conduct his own search of the State's files to argue relevance.

We find that Ritchie's interest (as well as that of the Commonwealth) in ensuring a fair trial can be protected fully by requiring that the CYS files be submitted only to the trial court for *in camera* review. Although this rule denies Ritchie the benefits of an "advocate's eye," we note that the trial court's discretion is not unbounded. If a defendant is aware of specific information contained in the file (*e.g.*, the medical report), he is free to request it directly from the court, and argue in favor of its materiality. Moreover, the duty to disclose is ongoing; information that may be deemed immaterial upon original examination may become important as the proceedings progress, and the court would be obligated to release information material to the fairness of the trial.

To allow full disclosure to defense counsel in this type of case would sacrifice unnecessarily the Commonwealth's compelling interest in protecting its child abuse information. If the CYS records were made available to defendants, even through counsel, it could have a seriously adverse effect on Pennsylvania's efforts to uncover and treat abuse. Child abuse is one of the most difficult crimes to detect and prosecute, in large part because there often are no witnesses except the victim. A child's feelings of vulnerability and guilt, and his or her unwillingness to come forward are particularly acute when the abuser is a parent. It therefore is essential that the child have a state-designated person to whom he may turn, and to do so with the assurance of confidentiality. Relatives and neighbors who suspect abuse also will be more willing to come forward if they know that their identities will be protected. Recognizing this, the Commonwealth—like all other States—has made a commendable effort to assure victims and witnesses that they may speak to the CYS counselors without fear of general disclosure. The Commonwealth's purpose would be frustrated if this confidential material had to be disclosed upon demand to a defendant charged with criminal child abuse, simply because a trial court may not recognize exculpatory evidence. Neither precedent nor common sense requires such a result.

IV

We agree that Ritchie is entitled to know whether the CYS file contains information that may have changed the outcome of his trial had it been disclosed. Thus we agree that a remand is necessary. We disagree with the decision of the Pennsylvania Supreme Court to the extent that it allows defense counsel access to the CYS file. An *in camera* review by the trial court will serve Ritchie's interest without destroying the Commonwealth's need to protect the confidentiality of those involved in child-abuse investigations. The decision of the Pennsylvania Supreme Court is affirmed in part, reversed in part, and remanded for further proceedings not inconsistent with this opinion.

It is so ordered.

JUSTICE BLACKMUN, concurring in part and concurring in the judgment.

I join Parts I, II, III–B, III–C, and IV of the Court's opinion. I write separately, however, because I do not accept the plurality's conclusion, as expressed in Part III–A of Justice Powell's opinion, that the Confrontation Clause protects only a defendant's trial rights and has no relevance to pretrial discovery. In this, I am in substantial agreement with much of what Justice Brennan says, *post,* in dissent. In my view, there might well be a confrontation violation if, as here, a defendant is denied pretrial access to information that would make possible effective cross-examination of a crucial prosecution witness.

* * *

Despite my disagreement with the plurality's reading of the Confrontation Clause, I am able to concur in the Court's judgment because, in my view, the procedure the Court has set out for the lower court to follow on remand is adequate to address any confrontation problem. Here I part company with Justice Brennan. Under the Court's prescribed procedure, the trial judge is directed to review the CYS file for "material" information. This information would certainly include such evidence as statements of the witness that might have been used to impeach her testimony by demonstrating any bias towards respondent or by revealing inconsistencies in her prior statements. . . .

JUSTICE BRENNAN, with whom JUSTICE MARSHALL joins, dissenting.

I join Justice Stevens' dissenting opinion regarding the lack of finality in this case. I write separately to challenge the Court's narrow reading of the Confrontation Clause as applicable only to events that occur at trial. That interpretation ignores the fact that the right of cross-examination also may be significantly infringed by events occurring outside the trial itself, such as the wholesale denial of access to material that would serve as the basis for a significant line of inquiry at trial. In this case, the trial court properly viewed Ritchie's vague speculations that the agency file might contain something useful as an insufficient basis for permitting general access to the file. However, in denying access to the prior statements of the victim the court deprived Ritchie of material crucial to any effort to impeach the victim at trial. I view this deprivation as a violation of the Confrontation Clause.

* * *

The right of a defendant to confront an accuser is intended fundamentally to provide an opportunity to subject *accusations* to critical scrutiny. Essential to testing a witness' account of events is the ability to compare that version with other versions the witness has earlier recounted. Denial of access to a witness' prior statements thus imposes a handicap that strikes at the heart of cross-examination.

* * *

The Court today adopts an interpretation of the Confrontation Clause unwarranted by previous case law and inconsistent with the underlying values of that constitutional provision. I therefore dissent.

JUSTICE STEVENS, with whom JUSTICE BRENNAN, JUSTICE MARSHALL, and JUSTICE SCALIA join, dissenting.

[Justice Stevens dissented on the grounds that the Court did not have jurisdiction to consider the case because in its present posture it lacked finality.]

QUESTIONS AND COMMENTS

1. *Constitutional basis for decision.* The plurality's opinion holds that the defendant has a constitutional right in appropriate circumstances to have the CYS's files, including communications with the counselor, subject to *in camera* review by the trial judge. Does the plurality's opinion indicate the specific provision of the Constitution this right is based on?

2. *Effect of absolute privilege.* As noted by Justice Powell in footnote 14 of *Ritchie*, the plurality opinion does not purport to decide whether the same result would be reached where there is an absolute privilege under state law. For instance, Pennsylvania law (42 Pa. Cons. Stat. Ann. § 5945.1) provides that a sexual assault counselor has "a privilege not to be examined as a witness in any civil or criminal proceedings without the prior written consent of the victim being counseled by the counselor as to any confidential communication." The effect of absolute privilege laws on a defendant's rights to access data has not been conclusively adjudicated by the Supreme Court. However, state courts have divided on the right of access where state law provides an absolute privilege. Compare *Commonwealth v. Two Juveniles*, 491 N.E.2d 234, 238 (Mass. 1986), with *Commonwealth v. Kyle*, 533 A.2d 120 (Pa. Super. 1987).

3. *Pre-trial discovery of privileged records.* Left open by *Ritchie* is whether the right to have privileged records reviewed *in camera* by a trial judge extends to the pre-trial discovery phase. A number of courts have drawn a distinction between a defendant's right to *in camera* review at the pre-trial stage and during the trial. For instance, in *People v. Hammon*, 938 P.2d 986 (Cal. 1997), the court, in refusing to extend the defendant's right to an *in camera* review at the pre-trial stage, noted, "[I]t is not at all clear 'whether and to what extent the confrontation or compulsory process clause of the sixth amendment grant pre-trial discovery rights to the accused . . . For

the reasons stated, therefore, we decline to extend the defendant's Sixth Amendment rights of confrontation and cross-examination to authorize *pretrial* [emphasis added] disclosure of privileged information.'"

4. *A proposal.* In answering the questions posed in the foregoing notes, consider this analysis, from Clifford S. Fishman, *Defense Access to a Prosecution Witness's Psychotherapy or Counseling Records*, 86 Or. L. Rev. 1, 62–63 (2007):

> Whether a defense attorney should have access to a prosecution witness's psychotherapy or counseling records presents a conflict between three highly held values: a prosecutor's right and duty to bring a suspect to trial, the witness's right to privacy and to avoid exposure that might interfere with his or her recovery, and a defendant's right to obtain exculpatory evidence. A procedure has developed that requires the trial judge to conduct an in camera inspection of such records to determine whether they contain exculpatory information, but only if the defendant first makes an adequate preliminary showing that such information will be found. The law governing this procedure, however, is ridden with vagueness and uncertainties. [T]hese uncertainties are best resolved as follows:

> (1) Just as a defendant has a right pursuant to the Due Process Clause of the Sixth Amendment to seek such in camera review when records are in possession of the State, so too a defendant must be allowed to seek in camera review of records that are possessed by a private entity, pursuant to the Compulsory Process Clause of the Sixth Amendment.

> (2) In camera review of such records must be available whether the privilege on its face is conditional or absolute.

> (3) A judge must conduct an in camera inspection of such records if, but only if defense counsel can offer specific evidence that establishes probable cause to believe that the records in question contain information that casts serious doubts on the truthfulness or accuracy of the witness's testimony, and such information is not available from less intrusive sources. As a rule, the judge should not conduct such an inspection until the witness has testified at trial but may conduct the inspection prior to trial where it appears that postponing the review until after the witness testifies may require a lengthy adjournment.

> (4) The judge must release portions of the records to defense counsel only if they contain information that raises a significant question about the credibility of a witness or the accuracy of testimony that is important to resolving important issues in the case.

> The solution I propose has its costs. The possibility that a judge might review a witness's therapy or counseling records may undermine the witness's ability to cope with whatever experiences or difficulties led the witness to therapy or counseling in the first place. The far-more-upsetting possibility is that the fear that such information will be provided to the defense may diminish the witness's willingness to engage

in therapy or counseling at all. Each of these results is lamentable. The alternative, however, is to increase the risk that an innocent person will be convicted of a serious crime and deprived of his or her liberty or, in an extreme case, his or her life. I believe the latter is the greater evil, and a more liberal approach toward judicial in camera review of such records, coupled with the flexible disclosure standard for evidence that may raise a serious question about the truthfulness or accuracy of the witness's testimony regarding important issues of the case, strikes the best balance.

5. *Scope of* Ritchie *as applied to information held by third parties.* Another issue left open by *Ritchie* is the defendant's rights under *Ritchie* to require *in-camera* examination of data that is not in the hands of the prosecutor. As noted by the authors of a leading criminal procedure treatise:

> Another related issue left open in *Ritchie* was the proper scope of the due process right of access when the material sought by defense subpoena was privileged under state law such that, unlike the records in *Ritchie*, the information was never available to court or prosecutor. Some courts have rejected claims by defendants that the Constitution entitled them to even in camera review in these circumstances, reasoning that the due process holding in *Ritchie* applies only to information possessed by the government.

4 Wayne LaFave, Jerold Israel, & Nancy King, Criminal Procedure § 24.3(f) (2d ed. 1999).

b. *Defendant Disclosures During Treatment*

UNITED STATES V. HAYES
United States Court of Appeals, Sixth Circuit, 2000.
227 F.3d 578.

RYAN, CIRCUIT JUDGE.

In this appeal, we are required to decide whether there is a "dangerous patient" exception to the federal psychotherapist/patient testimonial privilege under Fed. R. Evid. 501. We hold there is not.

The United States seeks to prosecute the defendant Roy Lee Hayes under 18 U.S.C. § 115 for making threats, during several psychotherapy sessions, to murder his supervisor at the United States Postal Service. Shortly after being indicted, Hayes filed a motion to suppress medical records prepared by his psychotherapists, and to exclude his therapist's expected testimony, on the ground that the medical records and testimony were privileged. The district court granted Hayes's motion to suppress and, soon thereafter, dismissed the indictment. We will affirm.

Aside from a period of military service, Hayes has worked for the United States Postal Service his entire adult life. In July 1996, Veda Odle assumed the position of postmaster in Marion, Virginia, and, consequently, interacted regularly with Hayes, who was the union steward for that post office branch.

Beginning in 1997, Hayes began to behave erratically at work, at times becoming inconsolably depressed and unable to function. On February 9, 1998, after several episodes of irregular behavior, Hayes sought professional help at the Veterans Administration Mountain Home Hospital (MHH), Johnson City, Tennessee. The admitting diagnosis for Hayes was major depression accompanied by severe psychotic features. During treatment, Hayes informed Dr. Dianne Hansen of a desire to kill Odle, a desire Hayes claimed he could resist only because he "recognized" that such action could jeopardize his continued employment. Dr. Hansen released Hayes on February 18, instructing him to contact a local health care provider and to return to work on February 23. Although records at MHH indicate plans to warn Odle of the potential threat Hayes posed, it is undisputed that Odle never received any warning from the staff at MHH.

On February 22, Hayes returned to MHH, admitting himself as an in-patient for several days. During this stay, Hayes reiterated his homicidal inclinations, but MHH doctors concluded that he was capable of controlling himself and understanding the consequences of his actions. Consequently, on February 26, MHH again released Hayes with a prescription for various psychotropic drugs.

* * *

On March 24, 1998, because Hayes was experiencing certain undesirable side effects from the drugs he was taking, Dr. Hansen discontinued Hayes's prescriptions. Soon thereafter, apparently due to the termination of his prescriptions, the death of his uncle, and sleep deprivation prior to undergoing an EEG on March 31, Hayes began to experience increased anxiety and some unraveling of his previous self restraint.

On the evening of March 31, Hayes attended a session with Van Dyke at the Veterans Center. At that time, Hayes outlined in great detail his plan to kill Odle, describing the layout of Odle's home and explaining that he knew when she would be home alone. According to Van Dyke, during this visit, he again advised Hayes that his serious threats toward Odle could not be kept confidential. When the session concluded, however, Van Dyke allowed Hayes to leave for a therapy appointment at MHH. Van Dyke took no further action that evening.

The next day, Van Dyke spoke with a supervisor about Hayes's statements and the supervisor advised contacting the Veterans Center's legal counsel for advice on how to handle this potentially dangerous situation. Counsel for the Veterans Center informed Van Dyke that he had a legal obligation to warn Odle of the threat that Hayes posed, and a short time later Van Dyke did so.

Upon receipt of Van Dyke's warning, Odle understandably became frightened and immediately contacted Postal Inspector Terrance Vlug, who requested all of Hayes's medical records from Van Dyke. Van Dyke provided the records which disclosed Hayes's repeated homicidal statements. Vlug then filed a criminal complaint on April 3, 1998, charging Hayes with threatening to murder a federal official in violation of 18 U.S.C. § 115.

A grand jury issued a three-count indictment against Hayes, charging that, on three occasions, Hayes's murderous remarks to psychotherapists constituted criminal wrongdoing under 18 U.S.C. § 115(a)(1), which provides, in pertinent part:

> Whoever . . . threatens to assault, kidnap, or murder, a United States official . . . with intent to impede, intimidate, or interfere with such official . . . while engaged in the performance of official duties, or with intent to retaliate against such official . . . on account of the performance of official duties, shall be punished[.]

After a judicial determination that Hayes was competent to stand trial and discussion on various preliminary motions, Hayes filed a motion to dismiss the indictment and to suppress his medical records and any testimony from his psychotherapists, asserting the psychotherapist/patient privilege.

* * *

The district court ordered suppression of any testimony by Van Dyke. Citing *United States v. Glass*, 133 F.3d 1356 (10th Cir.1998), the district court held that a psychotherapist may testify as to otherwise privileged statements of threats allegedly made by a patient only where such "disclosure was the only means of averting harm to the [federal official] when the disclosure was made." The district court held that any communications made to psychotherapists at MHH remained privileged because those doctors had never disclosed to third parties the substance of their therapy sessions with Hayes. Based on Van Dyke's admissions that he considered no option other than disclosure to protect Odle and, in fact, disclosed Hayes's statements only because of an order from a supervisor, the district court held that Van Dyke could not testify since his disclosure was not "the only means of averting harm." Accordingly, the court granted Hayes's motion to exclude the testimony of his psychotherapists whose information formed the basis of the indictment. Soon thereafter, the district court dismissed the case, an order which the government timely appealed.

II.

The Federal Rules of Evidence leave the establishment of testimonial privileges to the federal courts. . . .

* * *

A psychotherapist/patient evidentiary privilege has been well-established in the Sixth Circuit for some time. The Supreme Court recently recognized the privilege in *Jaffee,* holding that "confidential communications between a licensed psychotherapist and her patients in the course of diagnosis or treatment are protected from compelled disclosure under Rule 501 of the Federal Rules of Evidence." The Court observed that recognizing as privileged psychotherapist/patient discussions in the course of therapy would likely facilitate "an atmosphere of confidence and trust" conducive to meaningful treatment. The Court also reasoned that a federal psychotherapist/patient privilege would "serv[e] public ends" as "[t]he mental health of [the American citizen] . . . is a public good of transcendent importance." The Court observed that all 50 States and the District of Columbia had "enacted into law some form of psychotherapist privilege." The Court rejected a "balancing component . . . [m]aking the promise of confidentiality contingent upon a trial judge's later evaluation of the relative importance of the patient's interest in privacy and the evidentiary need for disclosure." The Court wisely declined to identify all situations where the privilege would and would not apply, but observed in a footnote: "[W]e do not doubt that there are situations in which the privilege must give way, *for example,* if a serious threat of harm to the patient or to others can be averted only by means of a disclosure by the therapist."

Among the courts of appeals, only the Tenth Circuit has decided whether there exists a "dangerous patient" exception to the federal psychotherapist/patient privilege. In *Glass,* the defendant told his psychotherapist that he intended to kill the President. Although, initially, the defendant's threats were not taken seriously, after the defendant could not be located for 10 days, a nurse reported the threat to local law enforcement. Eventually, the Secret Service became involved and the defendant's psychotherapist revealed the defendant's threatening statements. After the government charged the defendant under 18 U.S.C. § 871, the defendant moved to exclude his psychotherapist's testimony as privileged. The district court denied the motion.

On appeal, the Tenth Circuit reversed and held that the alleged "exception" to the *Jaffee* privilege, described in footnote 19, is applicable only where the threat was serious *when made* and disclosure was literally the only means of averting harm. The court concluded that, given that the psychotherapist had initially released the defendant, his threat could not be classified as serious. Moreover, the court ruled, the government failed to show that disclosure was the only means of protecting the President from harm and, therefore, the privilege applied to the psychotherapist's testimony.

Before *Jaffee* was handed down, this court decided *United States v. Snelenberger* (6th Cir. 1994), in which Snelenberger, attempting to establish an entitlement to social security benefits, informed his psychotherapist that he intended to kill an administrative law judge who had ruled against him on a previous claim to benefits. After hearing this and other similarly disturbing statements, the psychotherapist decided that involuntary hospitalization was appropriate and directed Snelenberger to the hospital staff for transportation to an institution. While in the custody of the hospital staff, Snelenberger repeated several times his plan to kill the ALJ. Eventually, Snelenberger was indicted on three counts of threatening to murder an ALJ, in violation of 18 U.S.C. § 115(a)(1)(B). Over Snelenberger's objection, the psychotherapist testified against him at his trial. This court ruled that such testimony was proper because the Michigan legislature had enacted a statute requiring a psychotherapist to take steps to protect those "seriously threatened." In the alternative, this court ruled that Snelenberger had waived the privilege by disclosing his intentions toward the ALJ to various parties after speaking with the psychotherapist.

The government argues that the purported exception to the psychotherapist/patient privilege, set forth in the *Jaffee* footnote, applies here and that Van Dyke's testimony is admissible, an argument which relies heavily on *Snelenberger,* and is structured as follows: (1) Tennessee law placed an affirmative obligation on Van Dyke to protect Odle after he learned of the serious threat Hayes posed, Tenn. Code Ann. § 33–10–302(a); (2) Van Dyke complied with this duty; and (3) after Van Dyke made this disclosure, the psychotherapist/patient privilege became inapplicable for all future court proceedings. Moreover, the government contends, once Hayes's statements to Van Dyke ceased to be privileged, Hayes could no longer claim that statements made during therapy sessions with psychotherapists other than Van Dyke were privileged.

* * *

III.

Before turning to the question whether it is advisable to graft a "dangerous patient" exception for criminal proceedings onto the federal psychotherapist/patient privilege, we will first clarify a misperception held by Hayes, the government, and, to some extent, the Tenth Circuit that the standard of care exercised by a treating psychotherapist prior to complying with (or, for that matter, failing to comply with) a state's "duty to protect" requirement is somehow pertinent to the applicability of the psychotherapist/patient privilege in criminal proceedings. We think there is little correlation between those two inquiries.

The "duty to protect" now imposed on psychotherapists throughout the country began with *Tarasoff v. Regents of the University of California* (Cal. 1976). In that case, the California Supreme Court held that "once a therapist does in fact determine, or under applicable professional standards reasonably should have determined, that a patient poses a serious danger of violence to others, he bears a duty to exercise reasonable care to protect the foreseeable victim of that danger." The obvious rationale behind this rule is that the preservation and protection of the health and safety of innocent third parties outweighs the good achieved by maintaining the confidentiality of life-threatening communications. After that decision, Tennessee, like most other states, codified the psychotherapist's "duty to protect" third parties from serious threats. *See, e.g.,* Tenn. Code Ann. § 33–10–302.

We see only a marginal connection, if any at all, between a psychotherapist's action in notifying a third party (for his own safety) of a patient's threat to kill or injure him and a court's refusal to permit the therapist to testify about such threat (in the interest of protecting the psychotherapist/patient relationship) in a later prosecution of the patient for making it. State law requirements that psychotherapists take action to prevent serious and credible threats from being carried out serve a far more immediate function than the proposed "dangerous patient" exception. Unlike the situation presented in *Tarasoff,* the threat articulated by a defendant such as Hayes is rather unlikely to be carried out once court proceedings have begun against him.

Moreover, we think that conditioning the applicability of the proposed "dangerous patient" exception on the standard of care exercised by a treating psychotherapist is unsound in theory and in practice. Were we to adopt the analytical methodology proposed by Hayes and the government, future cases of this sort will devolve into a battle of experts testifying whether a psychotherapist behaved "reasonably" before disclosing what was believed to be a serious threat. Such an inquiry would, at a minimum, be highly speculative and very likely lead to erratic results. More fundamentally, we think it would be rather perverse and unjust to condition the freedom of individuals on the competency of a treating psychotherapist. Moreover, it cannot be the case that the scope of a federal testimonial privilege should vary depending upon state determinations of what constitutes "reasonable" professional conduct. Thus, we reject the purported relevance of the degree of care exercised by Van Dyke or the psychotherapists at MHH on the issue of Hayes's right to assert the psychotherapist/patient privilege. Given that the "dangerous patient" exception crafted by the Tenth Circuit in *Glass* is linked to the standard of care exercised by the psychotherapist, we respectfully decline to follow that court's treatment of the privilege.

IV.

At the threshold, we note the paradoxical nature of this case. On the one hand, Hayes should be applauded for seeking professional help for the mental and emotional difficulties he was suffering. Yet, because the psychotic delusions for which he sought treatment took the form of homicidal intentions toward an employee of the federal government, Hayes now finds himself facing a felony conviction and incarceration because his professional care givers are prepared to testify against him.

* * *

First, recognition of a "dangerous patient" exception surely would have a deleterious effect on the "atmosphere of confidence and trust" in the psychotherapist/patient relationship. While early advice to the patient that, in the event of the disclosure of a serious threat of harm to an identifiable victim, the therapist will have a duty to protect the intended victim, may have a marginal effect on a patient's candor in therapy sessions, an additional warning that the patient's statements may be used against him in a subsequent criminal prosecution would certainly chill and very likely terminate open dialogue. Thus, if our Nation's mental health is indeed as valuable as the Supreme Court has indicated, and we think it is, the chilling effect that would result from the recognition of a "dangerous patient" exception and its logical consequences is the first reason to reject it.

Second, we think that allowing a psychotherapist to testify against his or her patient in a criminal prosecution about statements made to the therapist by the patient for the purposes of treatment arguably "serv[es] [a] public end," but it is an end that does not justify the means. The *Jaffee* footnote recognizes that in cases such as this, there are at least two interests at stake: the improvement of our citizens' mental health achieved, in part, by open dialogue in psychotherapy, on the one hand, and the protection of innocent third parties, on the other. Both are "public ends" which the federal common law should foster . . . [P]sychotherapists will sometimes need to testify in court proceedings, such as those for the involuntary commitment of a patient, to comply with their "duty to protect" the patient or identifiable third parties. After involuntary hospitalization, for example, the patient would no longer pose a "serious threat of harm" to anyone and, hopefully, the psychotherapist/patient relationship can continue during the patient's hospitalization. While that patient, by definition, will initially reject the prospect of hospitalization, it may ultimately improve his mental state and should not leave a stigma after the stay concludes. In such a case, therefore, both "public ends" will likely be served.

On the other hand, a psychotherapist's testimony used to prosecute and incarcerate a patient who came to him or her for professional help cannot be similarly justified. Once in prison, even partly as a consequence of the testimony of a therapist to whom the patient came for help, the probability of the patient's mental health improving diminishes significantly and a stigma certainly attaches after the patient's sentence is served. While, as with involuntary hospitalization, incarceration would serve the "public end" of neutralizing the threat posed by a patient, the price paid in achieving that neutralization may often be that many patients will not seek the professional help they need to regain their mental and emotional health. Thus, we conclude that the proposed "dangerous patient" exception is unnecessary to allow a psychotherapist to comply with his or her professional responsibilities and would seriously disserve the "public end" of improving the mental health of our Nation's citizens.

Third, we are persuaded that adoption of a "dangerous patient" exception as part of the federal common law is ill-advised. The majority of states have no such exception as part of their evidence jurisprudence; California, alone, has enacted a "dangerous patient" exception as part of its evidence code which would arguably apply in a criminal case. West's Ann. CAL. EVID. CODE § 1024. We note, too, that the Proposed Rules of Evidence on the subject of privileges submitted by the Supreme Court in 1972 recognized a psychotherapist patient privilege with three exceptions, none of which approximated what is proposed here. *See* Rules of Evidence for United States Courts and Magistrates, 56 F.R.D. 183, 241 (1972). To conclude, "reason and experience" teach us that a "dangerous patient" exception which would allow a psychotherapist to testify against a patient in criminal proceedings should not become part of the federal common law.

We hold, therefore, that the federal psychotherapist/patient privilege does not impede a psychotherapist's compliance with his professional and ethical duty to protect innocent third parties, a duty which may require, among other things, disclosure to third parties or testimony at an involuntary hospitalization proceeding. Conversely, compliance with the professional duty to protect does not imply a duty to testify against a patient in criminal proceedings or in civil proceedings other than directly related to the patient's involuntary hospitalization, and such testimony is privileged and inadmissible if a patient properly asserts the psychotherapist/patient privilege.

Finally, our holding today and the Supreme Court's discussion of the psychotherapist/patient privilege in *Jaffee* require a revisitation of *Snelenberger,* a case which preceded *Jaffee.* We conclude that, to the extent that this court held that once the Michigan "duty to protect" attached, the federal psychotherapist/patient privilege ceased to apply in any further court proceedings, *Jaffee* requires the conclusion that *Snelenberger* is no longer good law.

* * *

For the foregoing reasons, the district court orders suppressing the testimony of Hayes's psychotherapists and dismissing the indictment against Hayes are AFFIRMED.

BOGGS, CIRCUIT JUDGE, dissenting.

The court's opinion quite properly distinguishes the questions of whether a mental health professional (apparently including, in this case, a social worker) can inform the intended victim of a threat, from the question of whether that person can testify in court. I agree with the court's analysis of the former question. With respect to the latter question, I believe that when the social worker has specifically informed the patient that the social worker will not keep the communications confidential, there is no barrier to that person testifying, and I therefore respectfully dissent from the court's holding to the contrary.

*   *   *

In my opinion, the court's view of this case may be somewhat muddled by the fact that the "crime" at issue here is what some would consider the purely victimless one of making a threat that is not made to the subject of the threat. It is true that, on one view, simply making a threat that is not intended to be conveyed to the potential victim is not a traditional *malum in se* crime. However, it is important to recognize that, if the proffered evidence is believed, what occurred here was a crime, no different in nature than making similar threats against Odle to fellow drinkers at a bar, or to a policeman in casual conversation, or to one's lawyer. In addition, the court's rule would apparently be the same even if the victim of the threat ended up dead, in a fashion exactly paralleling the material revealed to the mental health professional, after a warning of non-confidentiality. I simply do not see that such tender concern for criminal evidence is required by the common law, or by reason and experience, when the patient has been put on notice.

. . . Dr. Radford told Hayes in February, as Hayes himself testified, that his threats to kill Odle would have to be reported. Van Dyke warned Hayes twice that his threats would not and could not be kept in confidence. . . .

This constituted more than ample notice that such discussion was outside the bounds of any promised or assumed confidentiality. . . .

*   *   *

All of the court's concerns in support of encouraging persons to confide in mental health professionals would be satisfied by a more limited rule that such recipients of information could not testify about anything said up to the point at which notice is given that the actual or threatened criminal conduct being discussed is no longer covered by confidentiality. Otherwise, we have the odd spectacle that a criminal can perpetrate his crimes (the threats) simply by either purchasing, or being provided at public expense, a particular type of listener, with no opportunity for the listener to avoid facilitating the crime.

If the real problem is that we don't think that this type of threat, alone, is a very serious matter, then that is for Congress. I object to creating a barrier that prevents competent testimony as to the commission of a crime by a fully warned patient from coming into court, and I therefore DISSENT.

QUESTIONS AND COMMENTS

1. *An alternative approach to the dangerous patient situation.* Hayes held that, under the Federal Rules of Evidence, being a "dangerous patient" does not vitiate the testimonial privilege. State courts may confront similar issues when interpreting their privilege statutes. In *Guerrier v. State*, 811 So. 2d 852 (Fla. App. 5 Dist. 2002), the defendant was arrested for stalking his girlfriend; while being evaluated by the prison psychiatrist he stated that upon his release he intended to kill her. Following this threat, a nurse who was working with the psychiatrist called and warned the potential victim. The defendant was subsequently charged with aggravated stalking. The prosecution sought to introduce the testimony of the psychiatrist and the nurse concerning the death threat made by the defendant. The Florida Evidence Code recognizes a psychotherapist-patient privilege similar to that of the Federal Rules of Evidence. However, Florida law authorizes psychotherapists to disclose to a potential victim threats posed by a patient. In the view of the court, by enacting a law that permits psychotherapists to warn foreseeable victims, the legislature made clear that the protection of potential victims is of paramount importance. Barring the admission of the same information in a later prosecution would, according to the court, "thwart the intent of the Legislature."

If a therapist will or must disclose certain information a client tells him, such as the threat in *Guerrier*, should the therapist inform the client of this possibility? If so, when? Prior to the commencement of therapy? After the threatening information is disclosed by the client? For a further discussion of this issue, as well the impact disclosure has had at the federal level and in criminal proceedings, see Elisia Klinka, *It's Been a Privilege: Advising Patients of the Tarasoff Duty and It's Legal Consequences for the Federal Psychotherapist–Patient Privilege*, 78 Fordham L. Rev. 863 (2009).

2. *Impact of the evidentiary privilege on the willingness of patients to seek counseling.* The *Hayes* opinion emphasizes the deterrent effect the admission of the incriminating statements by a client will have on the "atmosphere of confidence and trust" and the willingness of persons suffering from mental disorders to seek treatment. However, as noted earlier, various studies suggest that the existence of the psychotherapist-client evidentiary privilege has an ambiguous effect on individuals considering counseling. Consistent with our earlier description of these studies, one commentator concluded:

It is certainly dangerous to extrapolate from the available data, because there have been only a few handfuls of studies. However, the findings in the studies are relatively uniform. The researchers have fairly consistently found that: Even absent a privilege, only a small minority of lay persons would be deterred from consulting the professional; without a privilege, perhaps a significant minority of the lay-persons would be somewhat more guarded in their communications, particularly written communications, with the confidant; but the vast majority of laypersons would still consult and communicate with their confidants to roughly the same extent.

Edward Imwinkelried, *The Historical Cycle in the Law of Evidentiary Privileges: Will Instrumentalism Come into Conflict with the Modern Humanistic Theories?*, 55 Ark L. Rev. 251, 255–56 (2002).

3.   *Disclosure of confessions of past crimes.* Earlier in this chapter, we briefly discussed the admissibility of statements about crimes made to a therapist. Consider here a case widely reported by the media, *Menendez v. Superior Court*, which raised the question of whether confessions made to a treating clinical psychotherapist by two brothers accused of murdering their parents could be introduced in a later homicide prosecution. The prosecutor in *Menendez* sought to introduce certain notes and three audiotape cassettes in the custody of Dr. Jerome Oziel, a clinical psychotherapist who had counseled the Menendez brothers following the death of their parents. The notes and audiotapes included confessions by the Menendez brothers that they had carried out the homicides. Dr. Oziel and the defendants contested the introduction of the notes and tapes. The trial court admitted some of the notes and tapes based on a provision of the California Evidence Code, which creates an exception to the usual rule of confidential communications between patient and psychotherapist (Cal. Evid. Code § 1014). In admitting the evidence, the court relied primarily on § 1024 of the Evidence Code, which provides:

> There is no privilege . . . if the psychotherapist has reasonable cause to believe that the patient is in such mental or emotional condition as to be dangerous to himself or to the person or property of another and that disclosure of the communication is necessary to prevent the threatened danger.

In its effort to have the incriminating evidence introduced, the prosecution showed that Dr. Oziel had disclosed the confession of the Menendez brothers and their threats to harm him (Dr. Oziel) to his wife, Laurel Oziel, and his lover, Judalyn Smyth. The recordings and notes made by Dr. Oziel, as well as the disclosures to his wife and confidant concerning the Menendez brothers' threats, were intended to deter the Menendez brothers from harming him. According to the testimony introduced at the hearing on the admission of the evidence, "he told the brothers the audiotape recordings would be revealed if 'something happened to him', i.e., he was killed or disappeared mysteriously." *Menendez v. Superior Court*, 834 P.2d 786 (Cal. 1992).

The Menendez brothers brought an interlocutory appeal challenging the admission of the evidence. In the interim, while the admissibility of the notes and tapes was being adjudicated in separate proceedings, the criminal trial was suspended. The case challenging the admissibility of the evidence ultimately reached the California Supreme Court, which found the key notes and audiotapes admissible based on the exception under § 1024 of the Evidence Code. Id. In finding certain of the evidence admissible, the Court construed the § 1024 exception as including threats aimed at the therapist, rather than only third persons. Id. Under this rationale, the privilege was immediately lost when the Menendez brothers threatened the therapist. The notes and recordings pertaining to the threats, coupled with the admissions of culpability for the parents' deaths, then became admissible. The subsequent criminal trial against the brothers ended in a hung jury. However, in 1996, at a second trial in which the therapist, Dr. Oziel, did not testify, the brothers were convicted of the homicide of their parents.

Assume that Dr. Oziel was a covered entity under HIPAA. Recall that, under HIPAA a health provider may disclose information to prevent various harms as well as past crimes by a client where "such disclosure appears necessary to alert law enforcement to: (A) The commission and nature of a crime; (B) The location of such crime or of the victim(s) of such crime; and (C) The identity, description, and location of the perpetrator of such crime." 45 C.F.R. § 164.512(f)(6). Aside from this provision, a psychotherapist is authorized to make a disclosure of PHI in the course of any judicial or administrative proceeding in response to an express order of the court or administrative tribunal, or generally in response to a subpoena, discovery request, or other lawful process. 45 C.F.R. § 164.512(e)(1). Would the disclosure by the therapist of the Menendez confessions have been authorized under HIPAA? Assuming so, should it have been admissible at the Menendez trial? Do you think the omission of the therapist's testimony at the second trial made a difference in the outcome?

4. *Testimonial privilege in civil commitment proceedings.* Most jurisdictions allow an exception to the testimonial privilege rules to allow care-givers to testify about clients' statements in treatment to support civil commitment. Presumably, state laws governing the disclosure of personal health information (PHI) in commitment proceedings would not be impacted by HIPAA, as the regulations permit disclosure of PHI in judicial and administrative proceedings in response to an express order, subpoena, or discovery request. 45 C.F.R. § 164.512(e)(1).

III. INSURANCE MANDATED DISCLOSURES AND CLIENT ACCESS ISSUES

A. COMMUNICATIONS INVOLVING INSURERS AND MANAGED CARE ENTITIES

The public's access to the mental health system has substantially expanded in recent years. In part, this trend reflects increases in the number of employees covered by insurance, coupled with the expansion of mental health care benefits (e.g., The Mental Health Parity Act of 1996, which enhances equivalency in mental health benefits, and the passage of the Patient Protection and Affordable Care Act of 2010, which curtails exclusions based on pre-existing conditions and further promotes parity in physical and mental health benefits; see Chapter 1, supra).

At the same time, employer-sponsored health insurance programs are relying increasingly on managed care systems to administer these programs. In fact, most workers insured through their work are enrolled in some form of managed care. T. Lewin, *Questions of Privacy Roil Arena of Psychotherapy*, N.Y. Times, May 22, 1998, at 1 [hereinafter *Privacy*, N.Y. Times].

By all accounts, the increased reliance on managed care programs has had a very substantial impact on patient privacy interests. Typically, managed companies require patients, as a condition for coverage, to sign broad releases authorizing therapists to submit to the insurer or managed care contractor extensive data pertaining to any proposed or completed treatment. Such data will generally include the therapist's diagnosis together with presenting symptoms, a treatment plan, and an itemization of the treatment contemplated or provided (including dates and treatment modalities). In some instances, particularly when the employer is self-insured, the managed care organization that manages the employer plan may at some point transmit the treatment data to the human resources department of the employer.

From the standpoint of insurers and their managed care contractors, the availability of such data is essential to effective utilization review, which will normally include a determination of whether the particular disorder is one that is covered under the terms of the policy (for instance, pre-existing conditions were traditionally often excluded from coverage) and whether the proposed treatment is "medically necessary." Clearly, one purpose of managed care is the standardization of care (and the diminishment of the cost of care) by increased use of "protocols outlining what treatment will be allowed for what conditions." *Privacy*, N.Y. Times.

From the standpoint of mental health professionals and mental health advocacy groups, managed care is an unnecessary intrusion into the professional prerogatives of therapists and the privacy interests of clients. Overall, mental health professionals believe that the care provider is better equipped than the utilization reviewers of a managed care organization to determine the health needs of a client. In response to this claim, the insurance industry notes that there is very little consensus concerning the most effective mode of treatment for many mental health problems, and that care providers benefit financially in opting for the most time-consuming method of treating mental disorders.

The breach of confidentiality that results from the submission of treatment data to insurers and managed care contractors is an especially onerous consequence of managed care. This is particularly the case when the managed care organization transmits the data to the patient's employer, which is a distinct possibility when the employer is self-insured. The client may fear that her employer's knowledge of her disorder and treatment will have an adverse effect on her prospects for retention and promotion. As a consequence, employees may choose to forego treatment altogether or pursue treatment "off-plan" and pay for treatment themselves without seeking reimbursement under their health care plan. The extent to which confidentiality concerns actually deter the utilization of mental health services is difficult to gauge. However, some people pay for the services themselves to avoid disclosure of treatment information to insurers and managed care contractors. See *Psychotherapy Patients Pay a Price for Privacy*, Wall St. J., Jan. 22, 1998, at B2.

Many of the risks associated with the maintenance of records by managed care entities have been substantially reduced by the enactment of HIPAA. While health care providers may still disclose protected health care information (PHI) to the client's insurer or managed care contractor, the amount of information that can be provided is severely restricted by HIPAA (see Regulatory Implementation of HIPAA Privacy Provisions at I.B.3., supra). Moreover, HIPAA regulations mandate that any information received by the covered entity not be disclosed to any non-covered entity and further, that any information maintained by the insurer or managed care contractor be retained in a secure manner.

B. PATIENTS' ACCESS TO RECORDS

There was no common law right of patients to their medical records. Recipients of health care were not seen as having a property interest in their health care records nor an implied contractual right. However, after World War II, various states enacted legislation giving patients limited access rights to their health care information, and in some instances, the right to amend such information. Whatever considerations justify patients' access to health records for general medical treatment, they are more compelling when the treatment involves a mental disorder. A patient without access confronting either civil commitment (see Chapter Eight) or the imposition of involuntary treatment (see Chapter Nine) will find it difficult to challenge the basis for the proposed action. Paradoxically, patients who allegedly were a subject of malpractice, either because the treatment was inappropriate or hospitalization was not legally justified, can be stymied in pursuing a legal action against their health care provider because of a lack of access to their treatment records. For instance, in *Gotkin v. Miller*, 514 F.2d 125 (2d Cir. 1975), the Court of Appeals for the Second Circuit held that persons who were suing for wrongful commitment did not have a legal right to their psychiatric records that had been the basis for their involuntary hospitalization.

Cases such as *Miller* brought to the surface the paradox of imposing involuntary treatment while denying plaintiffs the opportunity to challenge in a subsequent lawsuit the correctness of the diagnosis and the appropriateness of the treatment selected by the provider. Partially as a result of cases of this kind, a number of states enacted legislation giving individuals who had undergone mental health treatment a right of access to their health care records. A typical statute enacted by Illinois provided that any recipient of mental health and developmental disabilities services "shall be entitled, upon request, to inspect and copy [his/her] record or any part thereof." Ill.—S.H.A. ch. 91 1/2, ¶ 804. Significantly, the Illinois statute, like that of other states with similar legislation, distinguished between a "patient's record" and the therapist's "personal notes." Other states, such as California, granted patients' access to their records unless, in the view of the physician or administrative officer in question, the release of such records to the patient would not "serve his best interest." West's Ann. Cal. Code § 5328.9. Statutes such as those enacted by Illinois and California became wide spread by the end of the twentieth century and, as a result, most states currently have legislation providing the recipients of mental health services special access rights to their records. However, these state laws tend to vary in terms of the scope of access and the limitations that may be imposed by the health care provider.

Existing state laws are also now supplemented by HIPAA, which grants individuals a qualified but substantial right of access to their health care information. The access rights under HIPAA do not include "psychotherapy notes," however. Under HIPAA, individuals have the right to inspect and obtain copies of their PHI held by covered entities. Also, individuals have the right to amend information that is not "accurate and complete." 45 C.F.R. § 164.526.

The right of access is not absolute, however, and various exceptions are set out in the regulations that enable a provider to deny access. 45 C.F.R. § 164.524. For example, exceptions include the right to deny access where (1) "[a] licensed health care professional has determined, in the exercise of professional judgment, that the access requested is reasonably likely to endanger the life or physical safety of the individual or another person" (45 C.F.R. § 164.524(a)(3)(i)), and (2) "[t]he protected health information makes reference to another person (unless such other person is a health provider) and a licensed health care professional has determined, in the exercise of professional judgment, that the access requested is reasonably likely to cause substantial harm to such other person" (45 C.F.R. § 164.524(a)(3)(ii)).

QUESTIONS AND COMMENTS

1. *Justification for access.* What policy reasons support clients' access to the records of their mental health services? Are statutes that provide access merely protecting an abstract interest in the client's right to know, or are there more practical reasons for giving clients access to their records? Might access enable a client to bring to the attention of the therapist previously undisclosed information that might lead to a more accurate diagnosis or more appropriate treatment? Should clients have a right to insist that therapists supplement their records to include the clients' views regarding related mistakes or omissions?

2. *Negative consequences of access.* Are there any negative consequences to individuals gaining access to their mental health treatment records? For instance, if a psychiatrist were to enter a diagnosis of "unspecified psychosis," how might learning about this diagnosis affect a patient? Might learning about this diagnosis alarm or offend the patient and perhaps disrupt the treatment relationship? Might learning about the diagnosis help the patient develop insight into his condition, for example, by encouraging him to consider whether some of his beliefs were delusional? In this connection, recall that HIPAA gives patients the right to access their PHI (which would include their diagnosis), but this right does not extend to psychotherapy notes. At the same time, HIPAA does not preclude state laws that provide greater access rights. Thus, state law could authorize access to psychotherapy notes, although this degree of disclosure could, as noted above, have both positive and negative effects.

PART 2

DEPRIVATIONS OF LIBERTY AND PROPERTY

■ ■ ■

CHAPTER 6

MENTAL HEALTH PROFESSIONALS AND EXPERTISE

■ ■ ■

I.   INTRODUCTION

The government acts to deprive its citizens of liberty or property in a number of contexts. These interventions may be subdivided into three types. Under a *punishment* system, the goal of the government is punishment for past acts. The principal example of this type of intervention is the criminal justice process, which penalizes through incarceration or fines those who violate certain norms. Under a *prevention* system, the government deprives individuals of their liberty for the purpose of preventing future harm to others or themselves. The post-sentence detention of so-called "sexual predators" and the civil commitment process (at least that aspect of it which results in involuntary hospitalization of the "dangerous mentally ill") are exemplars of this model. Finally, under a *protection* system, the government acts to prevent "incompetent" choices and ensure that individuals capably exercise rights and privileges. One illustration of this type of intervention is the involuntary hospitalization of those found incompetent to stand trial for the purpose of restoring them to competency. Another is the coerced relinquishment of control over property or person that may occur pursuant to guardianship proceedings.

Under current law, mental disability assumes a significant role in the application of all three intervention models. For instance, under the punishment model as applied in this country, the law has been unwilling to punish those who are considered "insane." With a few exceptions, application of the prevention model is predicated on a finding of mental disorder. Similarly, a finding of incompetency usually requires evidence of diagnosable mental disability.

Part II of this book—composed of Chapters Six through Ten—examines the impact of these three models of state intervention on people who have a mental disability. The punishment model is explored in Chapter Seven, the prevention model in Chapter Eight and the protection model in Chapter Nine. Chapter Ten looks at legal issues connected with post-intervention treatment and habilitation, issues that concern all three models. Finally, this chapter—Chapter Six—deals with an important preliminary matter that also cuts across the three models: our ability to identify who, if anyone, is "mentally disabled" and our ability to assess what the consequences of such disability are. Can we distinguish people with mental illness from those who are not mentally ill, the sane from the insane, the dangerous from the nondangerous, and the incompetent from the competent? The extent to which we can answer such questions may determine the extent to which we ask them, and obviously has practical consequences for the operation of the different models.

Traditionally, laypersons provided the evidence necessary to decide whether a person was insane, committable, or incompetent. But with the growth and acceptance of the mental health professions in the past century and a half (detailed in Chapter One), psychiatrists, and to a lesser extent psychologists and social workers, have all but taken over the evidence-production role and have even assumed the judicial role in some contexts. Such a development is not surprising, since these individuals were, and are, thought to know more about mental disorder and its effects than other groups.

Over the last several decades, however, several writers have questioned the wisdom of this development. Relying on an impressive array of research, these commentators have suggested that opinions reached by behavioral scientists lack sufficient reliability for legal purposes and may not even be relevant to the law's needs. Many conclude that the role of mental health professionals in their evidence-production role should be substantially circumscribed or even eliminated altogether.[a]

---

[a] For a well-reasoned (although by now somewhat outdated) example, see David Faust & Jay Ziskin, *The Expert Witness in Psychology and Psychiatry*, 241 Science 31 (1988). For a denunciation of forensic mental health expertise written for the popular press, see Margaret Hagen, Whores of the Court: The Fraud of Psychiatric Testimony and the Rape of American Justice (1997).

The first section of this chapter focuses on the debate about the appropriate scope of this role.[b] It looks at the core issue of when, if ever, testimony by mental health professionals should be prohibited or substantially limited. On the assumption that mental health professionals should be permitted to testify as experts in some or all of these contexts, the second section examines the types of professionals who should qualify as experts, the proper bases for expert opinions, and the form that those opinions should take.

II.   ADMISSIBILITY OF CLINICAL OPINION TESTIMONY

To evaluate the admissibility issue, further knowledge of the topics the law requires mental health professionals to address is necessary. Also essential is some understanding of the law's framework for deciding when evidence is admissible.

Legally Relevant Behavior. As noted in the introduction, one can think of government-sponsored deprivations of liberty under three rubrics: the punishment model, the prevention model, and the protection model. The differences between these models are developed in detail in following chapters. Here only enough will be said to make clear the types of issues that need to be addressed under each system when people with mental disability are involved.

The punishment model, epitomized by the criminal justice system, is primarily concerned with gauging one's culpability. Only if a person is considered sufficiently culpable will he or she be sanctioned. Mental disorder is usually considered relevant under this model because it is thought to diminish or eliminate one's culpability. An individual's responsibility for his or her acts is reduced, it is believed, to the extent mental disorder blunts perception and awareness or makes it difficult to control behavior.

A prevention system, exemplified by commitment, is not interested in culpability for past acts but in preventing future harm. Intervention is authorized if it is predicted that harm may occur. Mental disorder is considered relevant here because it may be related to a propensity toward harmful behavior directed at others or oneself. Its presence also allows the law to hypothesize that a person's dangerousness can be "treated," a hypothesis which, again, can only be proven by making a prediction (as to the person's responsiveness to treatment).

The protection model focuses neither on culpability for one's acts nor on one's propensities but rather on one's ability to perform certain functions. Mental disorder is relevant here because it may make someone

---

[b]   The extent to which clinicians should be allowed to function as legal decision-makers is an issue left for later chapters.

dysfunctional in legally relevant ways. It is thought to render a person unable to exercise his or her prerogatives in a capable manner.

In short, laws that contemplate depriving the people with mental disorder of liberty pose four issues: (1) the mental disorder predicate; and whether mental disorder is connected with (2) one's responsibility for one's past actions (as with the insanity defense); or (3) one's future behavior (as with civil commitment); or (4) one's ability to function (as with competency to stand trial). Put functionally, the questions posed by the legal system focus on a person's: (1) normality; (2) responsibility; (3) propensity; and (4) competency.

Evidence Law: The Framework of Analysis. All four of these issues are difficult ones. Crucial to determining how they should be addressed is the law of evidence, since it regulates the types of information courts may consider. In this chapter, we will rely on the federal rules of evidence as the guiding source of evidence law, since they reflect the consensus view on the issues we are examining. A brief foray into these rules is necessary as an introduction.

All evidence, whether lay or expert, must clear what could be called "the relevance/prejudice hurdle." Under the federal rules of evidence, evidence is relevant if it has "any tendency to make the existence of any fact that is of consequence to the determination of the action more probable or less probable than it would be without the evidence." Fed.R.Evid. 401. If evidence is found to be relevant, then it is generally admissible unless "its probative value is substantially outweighed by the danger of unfair prejudice, confusion of the issues, or misleading the jury, or by considerations of undue delay, waste of time, or needless presentation of cumulative evidence." Fed.R.Evid. 403. In short, the admissibility of testimony depends initially upon how one balances its probative value against its potential for misleading or confusing the factfinder.

When a witness wishes to go beyond a description of "facts" which he or she has observed or has knowledge of, and instead wants to offer an "opinion" about those facts, additional considerations come into play. Generally, only if the witness is qualified as an "expert" is opinion testimony permissible. Of course, any testimony is inferential to some extent. According to federal rule 701, even the lay witness may recite "opinions or inferences which are rationally based on the perception of the witness and helpful to a clear understanding of his testimony or the determination of a fact in issue." This rule recognizes that the difference between "facts" and "inferences" is difficult to discern at best, but that the lay witness generally must avoid conclusory language unless common everyday usage requires it to make the testimony understandable and helpful. On the other hand, the expert witness is not so limited. According to Rule 702, "[i]f scientific, technical, or other specialized knowledge will assist the trier of fact to understand the evidence or to determine a fact in issue, a witness qualified as an expert by knowledge, skill, experience, training, or education, may testify thereto in the form of an opinion or otherwise, if (1) the testimony is based upon sufficient facts or data, (2) the testimony is the product of reliable principles and methods, and (3) the witness has applied the principles and methods reliably to the facts of the case." Put another way, a witness with the appropriate qualifications may offer testimony in the form of an opinion when it is based on sufficient facts, relies on reliable, specialized knowledge and will add to what the factfinder could discern for itself. Of course, the factual basis for the opinion can be and usually is brought out on direct or cross-examination.

Whereas lay witnesses who provide evidence on normality, responsibility, propensity, or competency will normally be confined to giving descriptions of actions and speech that they observed and that are relevant to the issue at hand, mental health professionals are usually asked to offer an interpretation of such behavior. Thus, assuming appropriate education and training on the part of the proffered clinician witness (a topic discussed in section III of this chapter), determining the admissibility of his or her testimony must involve three related inquiries: (1) whether its probative value outweighs its potential prejudicial impact; (2) whether it is based on reliable scientific, technical or other specialized knowledge; and (3) whether it will add to what the factfinder can determine for itself. In practice, these three issues can often be lumped together under the query: will the testimony assist the factfinder? But keeping them distinct may be helpful in the following discussion, which looks at the admissibility issue with respect to each of the topics identified above: normality, responsibility, propensity, and competency.

A. NORMALITY

Traditionally, the principal way mental health professionals have provided information about whether someone is mentally disordered (i.e., abnormal or "crazy") is by indicating whether the person has a diagnosis and what that diagnosis is. For example, in insanity cases, testimony as to whether the defendant was suffering from a "mental disease or defect" which rendered him or her insane at the time of the offense is usually framed in terms of diagnostic categories. The following excerpt from the trial of John Hinckley, who shot President Ronald Reagan and three others, captures the flavor of this type of testimony. The selections that follow argue that this type of testimony should be prohibited.

TESTIMONY IN THE HINCKLEY CASE

John Hinckley's attempted assassination of President Reagan took place on March 30, 1981 in the District of Columbia as the president and his entourage were entering the Washington Hilton. Apparently one reason Hinckley shot the president was to impress the actress Jodie Foster. His actions on the day of the offense were allegedly meant to mimic the actions of a character who tried to shoot the president in the film Taxi Driver, in which Foster played a major role. Hinckley's lawyers indicated that he would plead insanity; under the District of Columbia's test for insanity—the American Law Institute, or ALI test—the jury would thus have to decide whether, at the time of the offense, Hinckley was "substantially unable to appreciate the wrongfulness of his act or conform his behavior to the requirements of the law" as a result of "mental disease or defect." Over the seven month period between the assassination attempt and the trial, various mental health professionals for the defense and the prosecution interviewed Hinckley and collected information about his life in an effort to answer this question. The testimony of two of these clinicians on the preliminary issue of whether Hinckley had a "mental disease or defect"—the normality issue—is set out below. William Carpenter was one of the defense's psychiatrists and Park Dietz was one of the prosecution's psychiatrists.

a.) Direct Examination of William T. Carpenter, M.D.

Q. Doctor, yesterday, before we started the chronological development of your exhaustive interview process, I asked you whether you had an opinion as to whether Mr. Hinckley had suffered from a mental disease on March 30, 1981. Do you recall that question?

A. Yes.

Q. And your answer was?

A. Yes, that I had formed an opinion.

Q. Now, would you tell us how you diagnose the defendant's mental illness, mental disease?

A. Yes.

* * *

THE WITNESS: * * * I concluded then that on March 30th, and before, that he did have the following manifestations of mental illness, that he had blunted affect or restricted affect.

This process where he has an incapacity to have an ordinary emotional arousal that should be associated with events in life. Blunt affect is of critical importance because from the beginning of the descriptions of the major psychotic or major psychiatric illnesses the blunted affect has been one of the prime distinctions of the process of one of the psychotic illnesses, so that I concluded that he did have blunted affect and as a symptomatic expression of an illness process.

He also had what technically we would call an "autistic retreat from reality." The autistic refers to the process of pulling into your own inner mind and away from the outer realty * * *.

The third major symptom status that he had is the depression and the associated features, including the suicidal features that were present in Mr. Hinckley.

And the fourth—* * * [t]here was important illness derived manifestations of dysfunction and his ability to work and his ability to establish social bonds. And these were of a severe magnitude and help measure the impact of illness.

The diagnostic labels that I want to mention, as you say in psychiatry, in approaching diagnoses, there are two somewhat overlapping approaches and it may be important to mention both to you.

The American Psychiatric Association has recently accepted a revision in its diagnostic manual and this is called the Diagnostic and Statistical Manual. It is the third volume.

But it has the listing of the different categories of illness and the descriptions and criteria that go with these different categories and there are many different categories of illness.

This manual notices the fact that we cannot draw emphatically clear distinctions between different types of illnesses, that the manifestations of illnesses may overlap so we don't know exactly where to draw the dividing line.

We are better at drawing the dividing line as to whether illness is present or absent than precisely how to define each illness category. For that reason in this diagnostic manual that is used now in this psychiatrists are encouraged to make multiple diagnoses; that is, if a person meets criteria for a number of diagnoses.

So that Mr. Hinckley does meet either full or partial criteria for a large number of diagnoses listed in that manual. It is only useful to—for me to present in my diagnostic findings the way he fits into a couple of major categories.

The first category that I want to mention, it draws from a concept of schizophrenia, which is one of the major psychotic illnesses which was identified at the turn of the century and has usually lifetime implications in terms of the pattern of illness and the outcome of illness.

And conceptually linked to this are personality dysfunctions, that the term "schizotypal and schizoid personality" mean. To define these labels, "schizoid" refers to someone who is withdrawn from social contacts, aloof from them, a sense of the kind of tender feelings that are associated with tender feelings, usually implying a life-long pattern and may be used for a pattern of socialization and alienation.

The schizotypal personality is a very similar personality formation with the difference being that the person has either something eccentric or bizarre or their use of language gets—but some more severe symptoms than otherwise are similar.

And psychiatrists are directed if schizotypal features are there, to use that instead of the diagnosis of schizoid personality.

Mr. Hinckley did meet criteria for both schizotypal and schizoid. He also met criteria for schizophrenia. This is generally thought of as a more severe form of illness, but that has many of the same kinds of personality features, the development of illness is shown through the personality function that schizotypal and schizoid have.

And I would make, using the criteria of the Diagnostic and Statistical Manual, then from the American Psychiatric Association, a diagnosis of Mr. Hinckley of schizophrenia and would not use the label schizotypal and schizoid, because it is the same symptoms. If they are explained by schizophrenia, you would not resort to those.

Mr. Hinckley at this—to some extent on the point of view he had illness manifestation symptoms that meet the criteria for what is called a major affective disorder. For many years the two major severe psychiatric disorders were the schizophrenia and relating conditions and the manic depressive and related conditions.

Mr. Hinckley in his depression reached the criteria for major depressive disorder and, using DSM–III as a guide, one would make—I would make that diagnosis. The only reason to argue against making that diagnosis is if the presence of schizophrenia can potentially explain the disorder mood that he had, the depression that he had, one could account for the depressive components within the single diagnostic framework.

Those are the diagnoses that I would use in terms of DSM–III.

A more broadly used concept in the world for schizophrenia involves a concept which is called "process schizophrenia" and this term is the primary term that I have used in diagnosing Mr. Hinckley. This term is important because it implies a certain form of development of the illness, an illness that usually begins during adolescence or early adulthood. It has usually a slow development so that the first years in the illness will be the illness manifestation, begin with fairly subtle disorders and social functioning and in personality functioning, and it progresses to a more severe psychiatric disorder and psychotic disorder, and that is where the presence of the delusion and ideas of reference, this type of symptom comes in.

And in this concept people who have developed this disorder, in most instances they are persevering impairments in their health. It runs chronic on long-standing courses. So it is typically slow and gradual in development and once reaching the psychotic state, as the person continues to have continued dysfunction and a broad range of social and psychological measures.

Process schizophrenia, which is the diagnostic conclusion I have reached, is related both in concept and related in a genetic basis to the schizotypal and schizophrenic reference as well as overlapping with schizophrenia as defined in DSM–III so that the clinical diagnosis—that I concluded that the illness Mr. Hinckley had on and before March 30th is process schizophrenia.

[Excerpted from page 3295 through page 3304 of the trial transcript.]

* * *

b.) Cross–Examination

Q.   Now you testified Friday Mr. Hinckley had been suffering from what you called "process schizophrenia" from 1976, all the way back to 1976.

A.   Well, expressing all the difficulties and pinpointing a beginning date for an illness, it began slowly and developed over time.

Q.   But as best you can recall that is when he began to have—

A.   I refer to '76 as when it began to reach the proportions that one could begin to consider schizophrenic illness present.

Q.   In other words, you would have diagnosed him as process schizophrenic if you had seen him in 1976, from your testimony?

A.   I don't know. That I would have if I had seen him. I don't know what I would have found out if I had seen him in 1976. Putting the development of the illness into a picture, you are always helped by subsequent developments. That is part of the very nature.

Q.   All right.

A.   And so when you find out that when symptoms have reached their greatest intensity in any illness, it helps you to interpret things that would be compatible with that illness as they developed earlier. It is like you went back to the earliest stages now that you know somebody had tuberculosis, if you had seen him when he had the first cough, you would have diagnosed it.

* * *

Q.   Friday * * * [you testified that] * * * "his process schizophrenia did not become psychotic until 1976, right?" And you answered: "I think that would be the case." You still stick to that now?

A.   Yes.

Q. And * * * your answer on the previous page to the same point, [was] "I don't think it was until about then," 1976, "that it developed to an intensity that it reached psychotic proportions." Right?

A. Right.

Q. Are you aware that Mr. Hinckley in the period of 1976 through 1980, was a student at Texas Tech University from time to time?

A. From time to time.

Q. Were you aware, then, as it comes to your attention, that during that period, '76 to '79, when he was there in certain courses he received As; did you learn that?

A. Yes.

Q. And he got some Bs.

A. Yes.

Q. And generally he kept a pretty good grade point average, right?

A. He had a lot of academic difficulty. He dropped a lot of courses because he was having difficulty with them. He had success in some courses.

Q. Well, Doctor, he got an A in writing, didn't he?

A. Yes.

Q. And he got this A in writing during this period you said he was suffering from process schizophrenia; right?

A. Yes.

Q. And you are aware, are you not, that in early 1977, he held a job at a place called Taylor's Supper Club in the Lakewood, Colorado area?

A. Yes, for about five months.

Q. Five months. And I take it you learned that he worked everyday at a busboy job there; right?

A. He didn't come to work quite everyday, but he did work fairly regularly during that period of time. Some absences.

Q. Right. And this is during a period of time when you say he suffered from process schizophrenia; right?

A. Yes.

Q. And you are also aware that in 1976, Mr. Hinckley traveled all by himself to California for several months; right?

A. Yes.

Q. And while he was there, he went trying to sell his songs; right?

A. Yes.

* * *

Q. And this is during a period of time when you say that Mr. Hinckley was a process schizophrenic; right?

A. Well, this is a time when I think it is beginning to develop its magnitude and it is this information from this very period of time that I would fit into that picture, yes.

Q. And then Mr. Hinckley got back from California all by himself in 1976; are you aware of that?

A. Oh, yes.

Q. I mean his parents didn't have to come out and bring him home in their car, did they?

A. Oh, certainly no.

Q. And this is during the time you said he was suffering from process schizophrenia; right?

A. Yes.

Q. You are aware in 1977, he spent a few weeks in California as well; right?

A. Yes.

Q. And again, he went out there by himself, did he not?

* * *

A. Yes.

Q. He didn't have any trouble getting out there. He didn't get lost in Arizona or run into the Grand Canyon, did he?

A. No.

Q. And while he was there he functioned pretty well, did he not?

A. Oh, no. He had impairments—you see, you may want to define "functioning" for me.

Q. He didn't get arrested by the police, he wasn't found walking around with no clothes on or anything of that sort while he was in California to 1977?

A. That's right and he never walked around without clothes.

[Excerpted from page 3517 through page 3524 of the trial transcript.]

c.) Prosecution Rebuttal Testimony (Park Elliott Dietz, M.D.)

Q. All right. Now, let me ask you formally, if you determined whether at the time of the criminal conduct on March 30, 1981 the defendant Hinckley, as a result of mental disease or defect, lacked substantial capacity to conform his conduct to the requirements of the law?

A.   I did make such a determination.

Q.   What determination did you make?

A.   That on March 30, 1981, as a result of mental disease or defect, Mr. Hinckley did not lack substantial capacity to conform his conduct to the requirements of the law.

*   *   *

Q.   All right. Now, I take it you have some reasons for those conclusions?

A.   Yes, I do.

Q.   . . . [Y]ou have announced diagnosis of four mental disorders in Mr. Hinckley as of March 30, 1981. And you gave them certain labels, did you not?

A.   Yes.

Q.   Where did those labels come from?

A.   Well, like other labels in medicine, these are derived from Greek and Latin words. These specific labels of mental disorder come from the official diagnostic system, the DSM–III.

Q.   In each of the four instances that you mentioned were the diagnoses you announced from DSM–III?

A.   Yes.

Q.   All right. Now, in connection with DSM–III, can you tell us whether this book is designed for medical purposes or for legal purposes?

A.   For medical purposes.

Q.   And what do you mean by that?

A.   I mean that this volume DSM–III is designed to allow physicians to make reliable diagnoses, to exchange information and know what they are talking about with one another, to be able to speak a common language. But that the diagnoses there do not automatically translate into anything legal and certain not into determination of criminal responsibility.

Q.   And criminal responsibility to repeat has how many parts?

A.   Depending on how one counts it, it would.

Q.   As we have counted it, how many does it have?

A. Two [(1) mental disease or defect which causes (2) substantial inability to appreciate the wrongfulness of actions or to control behavior].

Q. DSM–III deals with how many of those two parts?

A. One.

Q. Now, can you tell us, Doctor, with respect to the matter of mental disorders whether there is a range of mental disorders in DSM–III?

A. Yes, there is.

Q. Can you explain the range of mental disorders to the jury?

A. Well, DSM–III covers every conceivable sort of mental disorder from extremely serious to quite minor ones.

The types of disorders within the volume included such things as organic brain syndromes with psychosis, serious depressions with psychosis. Other serious disturbances of mood with psychosis.

It includes neuroses or what are now called anxiety disorders. It includes sorts of personality disorders that I've mentioned and will be talking more about. And it includes what we call situational stress disorders, when in a certain situation a person develops symptoms. For example, after a serious stressful incident.

It includes addictions of various kinds. It even includes tobacco dependence disorder. It ranges from minor to serious. From long-standing to brief. It includes a whole host of conditions.

Q. Can you compare that range in some way to the range that we all might be familiar with in functional medicine?

A. Well, for just about any system of the body there is a range of disorders that can occur. People may, for example, have the sniffles or a cold which is an infection of the respiratory system. They may have more serious infection of the respiratory system like pneumonia and can have life threatening disorders of the respiratory system like pneumonia in a very old person or lung cancer or serious injuries to the lungs.

Q. Does that same range exist in mental disorders?

A. A similar range does.

Q. A similar range. Now, you have already mentioned, actually, certain psychotic disorders, correct?

A. Yes.

Q. And can you briefly describe those in terms of the range of mental disorders?

A. Well, the psychotic disorders, I think, all would agree, are the most serious of the mental disorders. There are many different ways to look at seriousness. I think it is fair to say that the disorders associated with psychoses at least while an individual is psychotic are the most serious.

Q.   Going down the range, if you will, can you tell us the next general category of disorders?

A.   Well, again, it depends on how one classifies it but there is a group of nonpsychotic mental disorders and, generally speaking, the nonpsychotic disorders are considerably less serious than psychotic. Nonpsychotic disorders that are less serious, for example, include the anxiety disorders and the personality disorders. There are other examples.

Q.   All right. You mentioned personality disorders. Where do they fit on this spectrum?

A.   On the nonpsychotic, less serious side.

Q.   And further down or further along are there any other set of disorders that you would care to comment on?

A.   Farther down.

Q.   Along the range, along the spectrum?

A.   Well, the organic mental disorders one associates with psychoses are further up toward the serious end.

Q.   All right.

A.   Many of the anxiety disorders are toward the less serious end.

Q.   In Mr. Hinckley's case, did you find and determine that he had a psychotic disorder?

A.   No.

Q.   Did you find and determine that Mr. Hinckley had any organic disorder?

A.   No.

Q.   Now, where in the range do the disorders that you found in Mr. Hinckley, that is to say, the dysthymic disorder, the narcissistic and the schizoid disorder and mixed personality disorders, fall?

A.   These are all within them, the dysthymic is an affective disorder and this is on the less serious side.

*   *   *

Q.   Before I go any further, you are aware of a category in DSM–III called Schizophrenia; is that right?

A.   Yes.

Q. Is Schizoid Personality the same as Schizophrenia?

A. No, it is not.

Q. All right, and briefly at this point could you explain your answer?

A. Schizophrenia is a serious mental disorder in which a patient will at least sometimes and frequently for long times be psychotic.

Schizoid Personality Disorder is a personality disorder. It is not a functional psychotic disorder, as we refer to Schizophrenia.

An individual whose problem is Schizoid Personality Disorder does not become psychotic as a result of it, and does not develop some of the symptoms so characteristic of Schizophrenia such as delusions and hallucinations.

Q. Dr. Dietz, in DSM–III, are Schizoid Personality and Schizophrenia in the same categories or in different categories?

A. They are in different chapters altogether.

Q. Now could you tell us a little bit about the nature of the Schizoid Personality Disorder?

A. Yes, I can. As I have mentioned, this, this is the lonely personality disorder. As a consequence of that, people who have the features of Schizoid Personality Disorder tend to do loner sorts of things. Many of these people, for example, will engage in occupations that don't require much interaction with other people.

For example, cowboys frequently don't have to interact much with others and that's the kind of thing that can appeal to someone who is Schizoid.

Computer operators may not have to interact too much with other people. Even librarians, forest rangers. Now, this is not to say that there is any problem with people who engage in these occupations. It's to say that these are occupations that one can do without having to interact much with others. And people perform beautifully at those kinds of professions if, even if they have this disorder. It's a way to, to be able to function well without having to run into the problem that individuals with these disorders run into when they try to interact with others.

Q. Would people with this Schizoid Personality Disorder function in everyday life without any difficulty?

A. I wouldn't say without any difficulty, but I would say they certainly function in everyday life in many ways. The one way that they are not likely to function, and this is part of the definition, is that they don't have friends.

Q. Can they hold jobs?

A.   Yes.

Q.   Can they go to school?

A.   Yes.

Q.   Can they travel?

A.   Yes.

Q.   Now Schizoid Personality, does that mean a person is out of contact with reality or psychotic?

A.   No, it does not.

Q.   Could you explain to the jury what you saw in Mr. Hinckley on March 30th, 1981, to indicate that he suffered from a Schizoid Personality Disorder on that day?

A.   Well, I think there are really only two features that are known to have been present on that date in Mr. Hinckley, and the first of those is what we describe as emotional coldness and aloofness. That is, being, being cruel and unemotional, not becoming involved emotionally with other people.

Q.   Does that mean a person is out of contact with reality?

A.   No, no, but it may mean that they have trouble making friends.

Q.   All right. What are the other characteristics?

A.   Well, another one that I think was observable that day was indifference to the feelings of others. There are, one of the things we use to diagnose many of these mental disorders is to, to say that if there is, there are certain things that must not be present, if it's present, then we can't make this diagnosis, and one of those in Mr. Hinckley's case that was not present on March 30, and which we have to make sure wasn't present was no eccentricities of speech, behavior or thought, and there was nothing eccentric about his speech, behavior or his thought that day, and there were many observers I have interviewed to determine that.

*   *   *

[Excerpted from page 6388 through page 6411 of the trial transcript.]

d.) Cross–Examination

Q.   Before we get into the substance of your testimony, I would like to extract an agreement I think we can reach, and that is that you share the view of other defense psychiatrists that Mr. Hinckley on March 30, 1981 was suffering from a mental disease? You do agree with that statement, do you not?

A.   No, I do not.

Q. All right. Was it not your testimony on direct examination that Mr. Hinckley suffered a mental disease of dysthymic mental disorder?

A. No. I testified that Mr. Hinckley suffered in the past and indeed on March 30 from a mental disorder.

Q. Are you distinguishing between a mental disease and mental disorder?

A. Yes.

Q. I see.

Would you agree that on March 30, 1981 Mr. Hinckley had a mental illness in a broad sense?

A. I testified about a mental disorder, and I would have some difficulty agreeing with your statement that he suffered from a mental illness.

Q. All right, taking your term as a mental disorder, how do you distinguish that, sir, from a mental disease?

A. Well, a mental disorder is any of the diagnostic categories listed in DSM–III, the guide book for mental disorders, and for the diagnosis of mental disorders. When one switches to the term mental disease or mental illness, one is suggesting that this is a sickness, that it has some kind of biological basis.

That is quite a difference.

Q. So it is your testimony that all of the descriptions of mental conditions in DSM–III constitute mental disorders as compared or contrasted to mental diseases?

A. Yes, sir.

Q. Accepting your qualification, then, you will agree that on March 30, 1981 Mr. Hinckley suffered from a mental disorder?

A. Yes.

Q. And that the question before this Court and this jury would become as to the question of the severity of that disorder?

A. No, sir. The question before the jury is about his criminal responsibility.

*   *   *

[Excerpted from page 6388 through page 6411 of the trial transcript.]

*   *   *

QUESTIONS AND COMMENTS

1. *Use of DSM–III.* The witness' heavy reliance on the diagnostic categories found in the American Psychiatric Association's Diagnostic and Statistical Manual (now in its fifth edition) is typical. You may want to check the criteria for each diagnosis used by the experts by referring to Appendix A. Note, however, that the diagnostic categories and criteria used in the current manual, DSM–5, differ from those that appeared in DSM–III. As Chapter One made clear, the categorization of mental disorder is an ongoing process. On this point, consider the following commentary on the Hinckley trial from Professor Alan Stone, past president of the APA:

A Suggested Diagnosis for John Hinckley

Based on my own reading of the testimony of all the psychiatrists, I believe that before DSM–III, I would have diagnosed John Hinckley as a case of erotomania, and Freud's classic paper written in 1911 would have helped me to clarify Hinckley's psychopathology. Most clinicians have seen patients with delusions of love—a condition that is not that uncommon. There is even a French name for such delusions— Clerambault's syndrome. * * * But erotomania per se no longer appears in DSM–III, and one could debate whether it is or is not a psychosis. It is my own clinical and theoretical opinion that a delusion of love may protect the person against ego decompensation into florid psychosis, and this may have been the case with Hinckley. His pathological attachment to Jodie Foster is in my view crucial not only to his diagnosis but also to his prognosis. It is interesting, however, that delusions of love seem to have disappeared from DSM–III. Such delusions do not make up a separate diagnosis and are not listed as a specific symptom in any of the diagnostic categories of the paranoid spectrum. Perhaps the Hinckley case may also lead us to reconsider this gap in DSM–III.[c]

Evaluating the Psychiatric Diagnoses

* * * In evaluating [the testimony of the experts who testified in the Hinckley case], several things should be kept in mind. First, the preparation and the quality of the psychiatric testimony in the Hinckley case was far superior to what one usually finds. Second, these experts appear to have genuinely and honestly come to their various conclusions. The Hinckley testimony is not an example of what happens when lawyers buy psychiatric experts for a price. The testimony may have been rehearsed, the experts may have been carefully sorted and selected by the lawyers, but these experts believed what they said. If Hinckley did not fall readily into any DSM–III category, if his disorder is in the gray area between psychosis and personality disorder, then we can see that there was room for honest disagreement. Third, * * * [i]f there was

---

[c] Erotomania appeared in the 1987 revision of the DSM as a type of delusional disorder, and it retains this status in DSM–5. See "Delusional Disorders", pp. 1580–1581 of this book. Many psychiatrists who have studied John Hinckley's behavior have subsequently agreed with Dr. Stone's diagnosis. [footnote by eds.]

something flawed about the psychiatric testimony, it is in the sense one gets of the psychiatrists getting caught up in and succumbing to the adversarial process. There is a kind of overstatement in their testimony as though they had taken on the responsibility of convincing the jury and outwitting the opposition. Clinical working hypotheses became scientific truths. Clinical possibilities became certainties. And as these truths and certainties from one side meet contradictory truths and certainties from the other side, one has the feeling that psychiatry's credibility hangs in the balance.

Alan Stone, Law, Psychiatry and Morality 92–93 (1984).

2.   *The purpose of diagnosis in an insanity trial.* The witnesses obviously agree that Hinckley had *some* diagnosable mental disorder. But, given the wide array of behavior that can be called disordered and that is found in DSM, that finding alone is insufficient as a predicate for the insanity defense. The mental disorder must be a "serious" one. Recall also from Chapter One the DSM's admonition against equating any given diagnosis with legal constructs. Why did Dietz insist on the term "mental disorder" as opposed to "mental disease"? Using the language of the Federal Rules of Evidence, is the diagnostic testimony "relevant" to deciding whether Hinckley's mental disorder was serious? Reliable? Does it "assist" the factfinder? Consider the following excerpt.

STEPHEN MORSE, CRAZY BEHAVIOR, MORALS & SCIENCE: AN ANALYSIS OF MENTAL HEALTH LAW

51 S.Cal.L.Rev. 527, 604–613 (1978).

*   *   *

The crucial question for the law is not, or at least should not be, whether the actor allegedly fits one of the mental health diagnostic categories, but whether the actor behaves crazily enough to warrant special legal treatment on moral and social grounds. The law must therefore decide on legal grounds and for legal purposes which cases fit this criterion of sufficient craziness. These decisions should not and cannot be totally dependent on scientific categories that may serve other purposes, and experts should not testify about whether an actor suffers from a mental disorder or even about whether the actor is normal. Conclusions about mental disorder or psychiatric normality are not particularly and precisely relevant to *legal* decisions about normality. Rather, for various reasons, experts should be limited to describing behavior to the factfinder that laypersons may not notice but that may be relevant to legal decisionmaking.

The first reason for limiting experts to descriptions of behavior is that their conclusions are based, in part, on mental health diagnostic categories that are generally overinclusive. These categories are much broader than the crazy behaviors that seem to compel special legal treatment. The various disorder categories delineated by both the present and proposed diagnostic manuals of the American Psychiatric Association may be ranged along a quantitative and qualitative continuum of craziness. Some categories seem to describe behavior that would be considered quite crazy, at least in its extreme forms, by anyone. Others describe behavior that would not be considered crazy and, at worst, would be considered normally quirky.

Thus, present definitions of mental disorder cover such a wide range of behavior that vast percentages of the population may be considered disordered, including most persons whom the legal system would not consider crazy or different enough to warrant special treatment. A large proportion of the diagnostic categories simply do not describe behavior that seems very crazy and the inexorable product of a deranged mind. If no conclusions about diagnosis, illness, disease, or abnormality are drawn by experts, the law will avoid the confusion engendered by the metaphysical complexities of the mental health debate about which behaviors ought to be labeled and considered illnesses. Further, whether behavior is considered disordered for clinical or research purposes should not be dispositive of legal decision-making where narrower moral and social definitions of craziness are appropriate.

The second reason for limiting experts to descriptions of behavior is that particular diagnoses do not *accurately* convey legally relevant information concerning the person's behavior. A diagnosis will not inform the law whether, how, or to what degree an actor behaves crazily. The major related reasons for this fact are that present psychiatric diagnoses are not highly reliable or descriptively precise.

In behavioral science, reliability is a complex construct, but for the purposes of legal decisionmaking about abnormality it can be defined as the accuracy of a diagnosis. The preeminent "measuring tool" used to make diagnoses is a human observer applying the present diagnostic categories to behavior. Unlike much physical disorder that often can be verified by various tests that measure pathology (whether or not the cause of the symptom, syndrome, or condition is known), there is no objective, empirical referent of *mental* disorder other than crazy behavior itself. Indeed, the only possible verification of the presence of mental disorder is by a consensus of those who have observed the actor's behavior. There is no postmortem pathological examination or other diagnostic procedure to verify conclusively whether or not a person suffered from a particular disorder or any disorder at all. Even if objectively verifiable referents other than behavior itself are present, an actor is not considered mentally disordered unless he behaves crazily.

In a sense, there is no such thing as an independently "correct" or "incorrect" mental health diagnosis; there are only agreed on and disagreed on diagnoses. The crucial issue, then, is the extent of agreement achieved by professional diagnosticians when they apply their categories of disorder to behavior itself. The best evidence of the reliability of present diagnostic categories indicates that if two professionals independently diagnose a person on the basis of the same or similar data, it is rare for them to agree on the diagnosis in more than half the cases. The large amount of disagreement is not narrowed appreciably by limiting the possible diagnoses to broad diagnostic categories. Thus, mental health diagnoses are not terribly reliable; people who do not have mental disorder or a specific disorder will be diagnosed as having it, and vice versa. Of course, in clear cases everyone will agree the actor is crazy, but such cases are few.

*   *   *

The major cause of diagnostic unreliability—criterion variance— further explains why particular diagnoses do not convey legally relevant information. Criterion variance is both a general cause of unreliability and a bar in specific cases to the ability of a diagnosis to convey precise information, even when observers agree on the diagnosis. The diagnostic categories of mental disorders are descriptions of allegedly recurring clusters of behaviors, that is, of recurring patterns of thoughts, feelings, and actions. It is hypothesized that each category describes a more or less distinguishable disorder. The present and proposed diagnostic categories, however, are vague and overlap; each includes a quite heterogeneous range of behavior. Some persons who receive the most severe diagnoses that seem to map legal craziness, such as "schizophrenia," may not be crazy enough to warrant special legal treatment. Vastly different behavior, ranging from only mildly to wildly crazy, may properly fit into the same and most serious diagnostic categories. Thus, even if two psychiatrists do agree on a diagnosis, it is impossible to know whether social and moral purposes will be served by special legal treatment unless the behavior itself is described to the factfinder.

*   *   *

* * * There is still a role, however, for expert assistance and expert testimony in deciding whether an actor is crazy.

Because experts interact with all types of crazy persons far more often than laypersons, they may be especially sensitive to or inquire about behavior that would go unnoticed by laypersons. Laypersons may not know to ask, for example, if a person hears voices, entertains crazy beliefs, or has trouble sleeping or staying awake. Because the expert is attuned to crazy behavior, he may help the factfinder attend to a fuller range of the actor's behavior. Nonetheless, the expert need not and should not report conclusions about mental disorder, abnormality, or even craziness; these are legal determinations for the judge or jury. It is far more precise and useful to the judge or jury if the expert simply describes his observations of behavior. For the legal question of normality, then, the relevant expertise of mental health professionals is not their ability to draw inferences from data or to form opinions. Rather, their special skill is observational—to perceive behaviors that nonexperts may fail to notice. The expert should describe, in as much precise but commonsense detail as possible, his observations of how the person thinks, feels, and acts. The test of relevance for the testimony of experts and laypersons alike should be whether their observations of the actor's behavior shed light on the question of whether the actor is crazy.

For example, experts should not testify that an actor is "hallucinatory and probably schizophrenic." Instead, the expert should testify that the actor told the expert that on some (specified) occasions, the actor heard or hears voices despite the fact that no one was or is talking to him and the voices told or tell him the following (specified) things. For another example, experts should not testify that an actor "suffers from loose associations when questioned on an ego-threatening topic and is therefore probably schizophrenic." Rather, the expert should testify that when the expert asked the actor certain (specified) questions about topics that seem to mean a lot to the actor, the actor responded in the following way (specified by examples). Of course, if laypersons such as family, friends, coworkers, or neighbors are aware of such behavior, they too can testify about it.

Using lay as well as expert testimony about the actor's behavior, the decisionmaker can then decide if the person is sufficiently crazy to be an appropriate candidate for the application of mental health laws. If the factfinder's response to the behavioral data it hears is "so what," then the actor probably does not meet the legal criterion of mental disorder; if the response is "that's crazy" or "he's crazy," then the criterion of mental abnormality may be met.

*   *   *

QUESTIONS AND COMMENTS

1. *The nature of Morse's argument about diagnoses.* Is Morse arguing that diagnostic testimony is irrelevant (i.e., has no tendency to make the fact at issue—craziness—more or less probable)? That it is relevant, but unduly misleading or confusing? Or that it is not based on reliable specialized knowledge that adds to what the factfinder can determine for itself?

Note that present practice usually requires witnesses to give the basis of their opinions. Federal Rule 705 states that "[t]he expert may testify in terms of opinion or inference and give his reasons therefore without prior disclosure of the underlying facts or data, unless the judge requires otherwise." But the Rule also states "[t]he expert may in any event be required to disclose the underlying facts or data on cross-examination." Thus, in part of the Hinckley trial testimony that is not included in the previous excerpt, the factual bases for the diagnoses given by the witnesses were brought out on direct and cross-examination. For instance, to bolster his diagnosis of process schizophrenia, Dr. Carpenter described Hinckley's beliefs that a "union with Jodie Foster was in some sense ordained," that they "could become an extraordinary couple," and that by killing President Reagan he would gain Foster's "respect and love." Carpenter labeled these beliefs "delusions"— which psychiatrists define as false beliefs that are not typical for someone from the individual's culture and that are maintained despite overwhelming evidence to the contrary. Carpenter also described Hinckley's feeling that, as Reagan went into the Hilton and waved at the crowd, the President's attention was aimed at him in particular, a phenomenon Carpenter termed an "idea of reference," or a tendency to "interpret in a highly personal and idiosyncratic way—that is, a personal and unusual way—what may be common-place events." Dr. Dietz, on the other hand, testified that Hinckley was not delusional about Jodie Foster, but "recognized throughout that the relationship was one-sided;" at most he had "unrealistic hopes" that a relationship would materialize and that his assassination of Reagan would "impress upon her who he is and cause her to remember him." He also testified that, with respect to Reagan's waving at the crowd, Hinckley himself stated only that Reagan had looked "right at me, and I waved back. I was kind of startled but maybe it was just my imagination." According to Dietz, at most Hinckley thought that "the President couldn't see anybody else [because most of the people had cameras] and didn't intend to communicate anything other than 'hello.' "

If this and other descriptive data are provided, are diagnoses helpful or, as Morse argues, merely superfluous? In *Washington v. United States*, 390 F.2d 444 (D.C.Cir.1967), Judge Bazelon, one of the country's most influential judges on mental health law matters, wrote that a trial judge should limit "use of medical labels [like] schizophrenia" and require experts to explain them, but should not bar them altogether, because "they sometimes provide a convenient and meaningful method of communication." Consider also the expert testimony in *Clark v. Arizona*, 548 U.S. 735, 126 S.Ct. 2709, 165 L.Ed.2d 842 (2006), reprinted in full at p. 675. There the defendant killed a police officer who came to his car to tell him to turn down his radio; the prosecution argued that Clark had intentionally played his radio loudly to lure the officer to the car. The defendant asserted an insanity defense, based on a diagnosis of schizophrenia; he claimed he thought the officer was a space alien. The expert testified that people with schizophrenia often use loud music to drown out their hallucinatory voices and also often perceive people to be aliens. Is this diagnosis-based testimony helpful within the meaning of the rules of evidence?

2.   *The reliability of diagnoses.* Morse notes that, because diagnoses are constructs rather than "facts," there is no independent method of determining whether a diagnosis is correct or not correct (or "valid" or "invalid," to use behavioral science terminology). Rather validity can only be indirectly determined through an assessment of the extent to which different raters agree that a given diagnosis is correct (i.e., a "reliability" assessment). As

Morse states, the reliability of most diagnoses is far from perfect. But Morse authored his article before mental health professionals began using the new diagnostic scheme introduced by DSM–III. Field tests conducted in two phases between 1977 and 1980, indicated for some major diagnostic categories the inter-rater agreement was quite high or at least above the one out of two ratio Morse cites: organic disorders (79% in the first phase, 76% in the second phase); schizophrenia (81% in both phases), paranoid disorders (66% and 75%); mood disorders (69% and 83%); impulse disorders (28% and 80%); personality disorders (56% and 65%). This improved diagnostic reliability presumably resulted from the more precise diagnostic criteria found in DSM–III. In other words, the results of the field tests suggested that DSM–III reduced the criterion variance of which Morse writes.

Some have questioned the methodology of the DSM–III field tests, Herb Kutchins & Stuart A. Kirk, *The Reliability of DSM–III: A Critical Review*, 1986 Social Work Res. & Abstr. 3 (1986), and others have had difficulty replicating their results, at least in the emergency context. Ahmed Aboraya et al., *The Reliability of Psychiatric Diagnosis Revisited: The Clinician's Guide to Improve the Reliability of Psychiatric Diagnosis*, 3(1) Psychiatry 41 (2006) (reliability using DSM–IV is poor in clinical settings unless evaluators have two to three hours to devote to diagnosis); Samuel Fennig et al., *Comparison of Facility and Research Diagnoses in First–Admission Psychotic Patients*, 151 Am. J. Psychiat. 1423, 1426 (1994) (57.1% agreement on schizophrenia); Paul Lieberman & Frances Baker, *The Reliability of Psychiatric Diagnosis in the Emergency Room*, 36 Hosp. & Comm. Psychiat. 291 (1985) (41% agreement on schizophrenia, 50% agreement on mood disorders; 37% on organic disorder). But field research using more recent DSM–IV criteria have achieved better results. See Enrique Baca–Garcia et al., *Diagnostic Stability of Psychiatric Disorders in Clinical Practice*, 210 British J. Psychiatry 214 (2007) (79.2% for schizophrenia, 81.1% for bipolar affective disorder, and 62.5% for dysthymia). The diagnoses in DSM–5, which underwent two years of field-trial tests, also produced fairly good results. Of the 23 diagnoses for which sample sizes were sufficient to develop and apply precise statistical criteria, reliability was in the "very good" range for five diagnoses, in the "good" range for nine diagnoses, in the "questionable" range for six diagnoses, and "unacceptable" for three. Darrel A. Regier, et al., *DSM–5 Field Trials in the United States and Canada, Part II: Test–Retest Reliability of Selected Categorical Diagnoses*, 170 Am. J. Psychiatr. 59, 63–65 (2013). Psychiatrists remain acutely aware of their profession's limited diagnostic success and the need for continuous improvement in classification strategies and diagnostic methods. Robert Freedman, et al., *The Initial Field Trials of DSM–5: New Blooms and Old Thorns*, 170 Am. J. Psychiat. 1, 4 (2013) ("these field trials will be used to make further improvements . . . Like its predecessors, DSM–5 does not accomplish all that it intended, but it marks continued progress").

3.   *Other causes of unreliability.* Although, as Morse indicates, criterion variance is the major cause of diagnostic unreliability, there are other causes as well, which are worth noting not only because they may infect diagnostic

assessments but also because they can influence assessments of responsibility, propensity, and competency as well. The following excerpt provides a good summary of the issue.

AHMED ABORAYA, ERIC RANKIN, AHMED EL–MISSIRY & COLLIN JOHN, THE RELIABILITY OF PSYCHIATRIC DIAGNOSIS REVISITED: THE CLINICIAN'S GUIDE TO IMPROVE THE RELIABILITY OF PSYCHIATRIC DIAGNOSIS

3 Psychiatry 41 (2006).

. . . Ward, et al., conducted a study to pinpoint the reasons for diagnostic disagreement among psychiatrists. . . . The three main reasons for diagnostic disagreement were: inconstancy of the patient (5%), inconstancy of the clinician (32.5%), and inadequacy of the nomenclature (62.5%).

Patient factors—Patient's psychological state. Some patients are in a state that enables them to provide useful and reliable information to the clinician. Some patients may forget important information due to anxiety, poor concentration, or poor memory. Other patients with disorganized thoughts are unable to provide any useful information due to psychosis. Others may omit information due to shame, denial, fear of legal consequences, to obtain or avoid particular treatments, or for a host of other reasons. Patients with personality disorders may make an effort to manipulate the clinician. Such factors related to the patient are usually not under the control of the clinician, whose role is to elicit the information from the patient, assess the information, and make a rational judgment in the form of psychiatric diagnosis.

Patient factors—The use of proxy information. For patients who are unable or unwilling to provide reliable information, the clinician must, when possible, resort to proxy information, which can be either incomplete or distorted. The individual providing the proxy information may have a vested interest in minimizing or exaggerating elements of the history. Perhaps the most extreme example of a problem with reliance on proxy information would be Munchausen Syndrome by Proxy (MSP). MSP is a label for a pattern of behavior in which caretakers deliberately exaggerate and/or fabricate and/or induce physical and/or psychological-behavioral-mental health problems in others. In such instances it would be anticipated that information by the proxy would only obfuscate a reliable diagnosis. Another example is the inclusion of family input in making a diagnosis of early dementia, which is often essential. [C]linical reports by concerned family can vary widely depending upon whether they have a primary or secondary role in the patient care. Whether the family member resides with the patient, has contact during day and evening times, or is limited to patient reports (e.g., telephone conversations) rather than direct observation will all influence the quality of their information and its reliability. Therefore, when soliciting proxy information, it is important that the clinician be able to assess its quality in order to determine its relative utility.

Patient factors—Atypical presentations of psychiatric disorders. . . . It is important to remember that the majority of patients do not fit the classic psychiatric diagnoses. For most patients, forcing the diagnostician to choose among the categories requires an arbitrary decision that may contribute to the unreliability of psychiatric diagnoses. . . . [A] patient with a major depressive episode should have a two-week period of depressed mood or anhedonia and four of the following symptoms: weight loss, insomnia or hypersomnia, fatigue, feeling of worthlessness or guilt, poor concentration, or suicidal thoughts. [But many patients] with serious depressive symptoms that require clinical treatment do not fit the criteria described in the textbooks. In other instances, the physiologic changes associated with normal age often influence the presentation of psychiatric disorders in later life. For example, current DSM–IV diagnosis for alcohol dependency requires the presence of tolerance and withdrawal. However, it has been noted for elders, dependency upon alcohol may not result in either clinical symptom due to a decline in their ability to clear the substance. This, in turn, is likely to cause diagnostic unreliability in this age group. Such patients with atypical presentations pose a challenge even to experienced clinicians and cause diagnostic unreliability.

Clinician Factors—The clinician interview. . . . Most clinicians use an open-form type of interview in routine psychiatric evaluation. The reliability of psychiatric diagnoses using this type of routine clinical psychiatric evaluation has been found to be low. There are three main reasons for this. First, clinicians typically focus on the most pressing presenting symptoms that have brought the patient to clinical attention to the detriment of other symptoms, which are present, but less acute. For example, the same patient might present with mainly depressive symptoms at one time and with nightmares and flashbacks of past abuse at another time. If only focusing on the present prominent symptoms, the clinician may diagnose major depression at one visit and posttraumatic stress disorder at the next. However, without further exploration, it is unclear if the patient has both diagnoses or has only one with some overlapping symptoms of a second. The workload and time constraints of clinicians create a disincentive to perform a comprehensive assessment and assign multiple diagnoses. Second, clinicians are pressured by institutional requirements and financial incentives to make diagnoses that reimburse at a higher rate. Patients, their families, or the clinician's desire to be helpful to the patient may lead him or her to make a diagnosis that will facilitate receiving governmental assistance or insurance coverage. Third, use of an unstructured interview increases the risk of overlooking important areas of inquiry. Some even question whether free-form interview is adequate for good clinical practice.

Clinician Factors—Clinician training, experience, and school of thoughts. Clinician background and training may influence interpretation of symptoms. One clinician with developmental training might explain the hallucinatory experience of the patient as part of posttraumatic experience of past abuse. Another clinician with a biomedical orientation might explain the same hallucinations as part of a schizophrenic process. This explains the tendency of some clinicians to overuse or underuse a particular diagnosis. The reliance on the patient's subjective symptoms, the clinician's interpretation of the symptoms, and the absence of objective measure (such as blood test) implant the seeds of diagnostic unreliability of psychiatric disorders.

Clinician factors—Reliance on observation. Use of clinical data derived from direct observation is a core component in any mental status examination. Nevertheless, there remains the potential that the standard methods employed by clinicians to solicit information may in fact bias patient data. One clinical area where data collection methods may unduly influence clinical findings is in the diagnostic assessment of dementia. Current diagnostic criteria require documentation of a drop in functional status as well as decline in two or more cognitive domains. Collateral data has often been used to satisfy this requirement; however, it too may be biased by various caregiver variables. . . . .

Clinician factors—Psychiatric nomenclature. As mentioned previously, Ward, et al., found that inadequacy of the psychiatric nomenclature is the main reason for diagnostic unreliability (62.5%). The dissatisfaction with the DSM–I and –II . . . sparked major efforts by prominent psychiatrists and researchers and eventually led to the publication of the DSM–III in 1980. . . . The development of the DSM–III and its subsequent versions has been a major accomplishment in the history of psychiatric nomenclature. . . . . However, the widespread use of diagnostic criteria does not mean by any measure that the status of psychiatric nomenclature is perfect or void of problems. In fact, the critics of current psychiatric nomenclature are extensive.

QUESTIONS AND COMMENTS

1.   *Rosenhan Study: Labelling and normality.* Older but still valuable research confirms that inter-rater disagreement can occur because of orientation and training, the context of an evaluation, changes in a patient over time, class and cultural differences between the evaluator and the patient, and personal biases. For instance, research indicates that "being a mental health professional may constitute a set to perceive mental illness," that "[a patient's] lower socio-economic history biases diagnosis toward greater illness and poorer prognosis," and that negative attitudes toward criminals, patient endorsement of "radical" political ideas, and patient criticisms of the mental health professions can influence diagnosis. See Bruce

Ennis & Thomas Litwack, *Psychiatry and the Presumption of Expertise: Flipping Coins in the Courtroom*, 62 Cal. L. Rev. 693, 719–729 (1974).

Probably the most controversial of all the research addressing the problem of diagnostic reliability is a study conducted by Daniel Rosenhan. In that study, eight "normal" individuals showed up at various mental hospitals with feigned symptoms (specifically, they all reported having an auditory hallucination). Otherwise they acted normally. All but one were diagnosed with schizophrenia and all were admitted to the hospital. Their behavior after admission was normal; they never again reported hearing unusual sounds or voices. Although all were eventually discharged (with a diagnosis of schizophrenia in remission), they spent an average of 19 days in the hospital, with the range from 7 to 52 days. David L. Rosenhan, *On Being Sane in Insane Places*, 179 Science 250 (1973).

Some have argued that it would have been much more disturbing if the pseudopatients had *not* been admitted for further investigation, since auditory hallucinations are considered indicative of schizophrenia. Kety commented: "If I were to drink a quart of blood and, concealing what I had done, come to the emergency room of any hospital vomiting blood, the behavior of the staff would be quite predictable. If they labeled and treated me as having a bleeding ulcer, I doubt that I could argue convincingly that medical science does not know how to diagnose that condition." Seymour Kety, *From Rationalization to Reason*, 131 Am.J.Psychiat. 957 (1974). Consider also that good medical practice requires that patients believe their doctors will listen to them and take their reports seriously. Does the Rosenhan study prove anything more than liars can fool doctors? Spitzer has suggested that, to some extent at least, the study reflects staffing and resource problems rather than deficiencies in psychiatric judgment. Robert Spitzer, *More on Pseudoscience in Science and the Case for Psychiatric Diagnosis*, 33 Arch.Gen.Psychiat. 459 (1976).

2. *Implications of variance.* Ways of trying to minimize the effect of the distorting influences are for the most part self-evident, although not always successful. For example multiple interviews by independent interviewers might alleviate the effects of training, context, time and bias. Probably the best minimization technique, already alluded to, is to improve the criteria for decision-making. For instance, the authors of the above excerpt propose that reliability can be enhanced through: (1) improved diagnostic criteria; (2) improved definitions of symptoms, because "[i]f clinicians cannot agree on the presence or absence of symptoms, due to multiple definitions of a symptom, the diagnostic criteria are of little use;" (3) use of rating scales such as the Positive and Negative Syndrome Scale (PANSS), Brief Psychiatric Rating Scale (BPRS), and Hamilton Rating Scale for Depression (Ham–D); and (4) since these scales "produce clusters of symptoms that do not necessarily take the entire clinical picture into account and have not been shown to have the same predictive utility as diagnoses," use of a structured format that involves initially asking 24 screening questions that cover different areas of psychopathology (e.g., anxiety, depression, psychosis, alcohol, and drug

problems) and then poses questions focused on seven "disease-specific modules" (anxiety and panic disorders, mood disorders, psychotic disorders, alcohol and psychoactive drugs disorders, somatoform disorders, eating disorders, and adjustment disorders). Aboraya, supra, at 47–48.

Nonetheless, it is probable that diagnostic and other criteria will always carry some ambiguity; greater precision is unlikely to remove entirely the effects of the influences described in the excerpt (such as time pressure, insurance-driven incentives, and patient volatility). Does this fact make all or most psychiatric judgments so suspect that they should be barred in legal proceedings? Does replacing diagnoses with "descriptive" information solve the problem? Or are "descriptions of facts" just as susceptible to the influences described above?

3.   *The admissibility of other types of expert testimony.* Psychiatry is not the only medical specialty in which doctors disagree about diagnoses. A study of pathologists' examination of tissue from malignant mesothelioma showed that "most indexes of agreement between pathologists ranged from poor (needle biopsy) to moderate (necropsy/surgery)." A. Andrion et al., *Malignant Mesothelioma of the Pleura: Interobserver Variability*, 48 J.Clin.Pathol. 856, 856 (1995). Another study involving examination of breast cells showed that pathologists often disagreed with each other *and with their own previous conclusions* about whether cells were precancerous or malignant. Kala Visvanathan et al., *The Importance of Cytologic Intrarater and Interrater Reproducibility: the Case of Ductal Lavage*, 15 Cancer Epidemiol. Biomarkers Prev. 2553 (2006). In a study of 160 expert neurological diagnoses of ischemic stroke, agreement was only "fair to good" for most types of ischemic stroke. C. J. Johnson et al., *Interrater Reliability of an Etiologic Classification of Ischemic Stroke*, 26 Stroke 46 (1995). After describing the "impressively high" inter-rater reliability for four common psychiatric diagnoses (depression, bipolar disorder, panic disorder, and alcohol dependence), psychiatrist Ronald Pies concluded recently that diagnostic agreement "for these major psychiatric disorders compares favorably with [agreement statistics] in several other medical specialties." Ronald Pies, *How "Objective" Are Psychiatric Diagnoses? (Guess Again)*, 4 Psychiatry (Edgmont) 18, 20–21 (October, 2007) (better reliability for psychiatric diagnoses than for diagnoses of stroke, colorectal cancer, renal stenosis, knee osteoarthritis, and breast cancer).

Other types of expert testimony have significant validity and reliability problems as well. For instance, one study found that police crime labs misidentify paint samples 51 percent of the time, drug samples 18 percent of the time, blood samples 71 percent of the time, and firearms 28 percent of the time. Joseph Peterson et al., Crime Laboratory Proficiency Testing Research Program: Final Report (1978). Error rates in identifying handwriting and voices may also be over 50% under certain circumstances. David L. Faigman et al., 4 Science in the Law: Forensic Science Issues 346 (2005) (studies in 1980s indicate that handwriting experts correct only 57% of time); 538 (talker identification accuracy ranges from 40 to 80%). Yet courts often allow experts to testify about these matters. Id. 231–38; 298–304; 504–05.

The testimony of economists in antitrust cases is another interesting example of expertise in action. Battles of the experts in such cases are much more common than in insanity cases. As Younger noted:

> Unlike any other country, we submit many issues to the courts that don't turn on factual determinations at all. Should I.B.M. be broken up? Is it good for America to break up A.T. & T.? We pretend those are factual questions and call economists to testify, but they're simply a matter of opinion. And in virtually every case in this country in which experts end up on the witness stand there are vast possibilities for honest differences of opinion. In a case where opinions can reasonably differ on a question, each lawyer simply scouts around until he finds an expert who has an opinion that comports with his client's interest. Experts can testify in good faith and still be testifying to opposites.

Reported in John Jenkins, *Expert's Day in Court*, New York Times Magazine, Dec. 11, 1983, p. 98, col. 4. Despite the lack of precision in economic science, courts have allowed experts to offer opinions about market conditions, the opportunities for collusion, market behavior and whether industries conspired to form a cartel. See, e.g., *In re Japanese Electronic Products Antitrust Litigation*, 723 F.2d 238, 280 (3d Cir.1983); reversed on other grounds, 475 U.S. 574, 106 S.Ct. 1348, 89 L.Ed.2d 538 (1986).

Do these examples from other legal arenas support retaining diagnostic and other psychiatric opinion testimony? A revamping of *all* expert testimony? Or are they different from psychiatric testimony in significant ways? Consider these questions again after reviewing the materials on responsibility assessments.

B. RESPONSIBILITY

The relationship between mental disorder and responsibility is most obviously raised by the insanity defense, but is also implicated by other criminal law doctrines. Generally, the criminal law assumes that the effect of mental disorder is either "cognitive" or "volitional." In the first instance, the focus is on one's awareness and perceptions about one's actions at the time of the offense; in the second, the emphasis is on one's ability to control one's behavior at the time of the offense. The following case deals with the mental health profession's expertise on the latter issue.

UNITED STATES V. LEWELLYN

United States Court of Appeals, Eighth Circuit, 1983.
723 F.2d 615.

FAGG, CIRCUIT JUDGE.

[Gary Lewellyn, a Des Moines stockbroker, was indicted on fifteen counts of embezzlement, making false statements, and mail fraud for converting over $17 million in money and securities from two Iowa banks. In response to the government's pretrial motion, the district court ruled that Lewellyn could not rely on a defense of insanity "by reason of pathological gambling" and excluded evidence related to that defense. Lewellyn was convicted on all counts. On appeal, he contended that the district court erred in precluding his insanity defense. The test for insanity was the ALI test, which recognizes a defense, *inter alia*, when "mental disease or defect" causes a person to lack "substantial capacity . . . to conform his conduct to the requirements of the law."]

We have recognized that in order to raise the issue of insanity a defendant must make a minimum showing. A defendant is presumed sane, but the introduction of evidence of insanity dispels the presumption and subjects the prosecution to the burden of proving sanity beyond a reasonable doubt. *United States v. Dresser*, 542 F.2d 737, 742 (8th Cir.1976), citing *Davis v. United States*, 160 U.S. 469, 486–88, 16 S.Ct. 353, 357–58, 40 L.Ed. 499 (1895). In *Dresser* we referred to this threshold showing as a "prima facie case of insanity." 542 F.2d at 742 n. 7.

[I]n the present case we need not decide whether pathological gambling may never be grounds for an insanity defense. In the particular circumstances of this case we are concerned with the connection between pathological gambling and collateral criminal activity. To make the required minimum showing of insanity Lewellyn had to show that at least some pathological gamblers lack substantial capacity to conform their conduct to the requirements of laws prohibiting criminal activities like embezzlement. We now turn to the record to determine whether Lewellyn made a showing which would have allowed him to rely on an insanity defense at trial.

DSM–III [i.e., Diagnostic and Statistical Manual of Mental Disorders (3d ed.1980)] contains the following description of pathological gambling:

> The essential features are a chronic and progressive failure to resist impulses to gamble and gambling behavior that compromises, disrupts, or damages personal, family, or vocational pursuits. The gambling preoccupation, urge, and activity increase during periods of stress. Problems that arise as a result of the gambling lead to an intensification of the gambling behavior. Characteristic problems include loss of work due to absences in order to gamble, defaulting on debts and other financial responsibilities, disrupted family

relationships, borrowing money from illegal sources, forgery, fraud, embezzlement, and income tax evasion.

Commonly these individuals have the attitude that money causes and is also the solution to all their problems. As the gambling increases, the individual is usually forced to lie in order to obtain money and to continue gambling, but hides the extent of the gambling. There is no serious attempt to budget or save money. When borrowing resources are strained, antisocial behavior in order to obtain money for more gambling is likely. Any criminal behavior— e.g., forgery, embezzlement, or fraud—is typically nonviolent. There is a conscious intent to return or repay the money.

Id. at 291. The diagnostic criteria for pathological gambling included in DSM–III are:

A.   The individual is chronically and progressively unable to resist impulses to gamble.

B.   Gambling compromises, disrupts, or damages family, personal, and vocational pursuits, as indicated by at least three of the following:

(1) arrest for forgery, fraud, embezzlement, or income tax evasion due to attempts to obtain money for gambling

* * *

C.   The gambling is not due to Antisocial Personality Disorder.

Id. at 292–93.

The language of DSM–III does not establish that pathological gamblers may lack substantial capacity to refrain from engaging in embezzlement and similar criminal activities. Portions of DSM–III no doubt indicate that criminal activity is often associated with pathological gambling. DSM–III does not state, however, that pathological gamblers who engage in criminal conduct do so because they lack substantial capacity to conform their conduct to the requirements of law, nor does it state anything of equivalent meaning. It is not remarkable, though, that the language of DSM–III does not conform to the legal principles embodied in the ALI insanity rule.

The purpose of DSM–III is to provide clear descriptions of diagnostic categories in order to enable clinicians and investigators to diagnose, communicate about, study, and treat various mental disorders. The use of this manual for nonclinical purposes, such as determination of legal responsibility, competency or insanity * * * must be critically examined in each instance within the appropriate institutional context.

Id. at 12. When we examine DSM–III carefully within the context of the criminal law we conclude that its language does not establish a relationship between pathological gambling and criminal activity sufficient to constitute insanity under the ALI standard. As a consequence, DSM–III does not alone supply the minimum showing Lewellyn was required to make before he could rely on an insanity defense.

Expert testimony adduced by Lewellyn, couched in terms more like those of the ALI insanity rule, does suggest the requisite connection between pathological gambling and criminal activity because it supports the proposition that some pathological gamblers lack substantial capacity to resist engaging in embezzlement and similar offenses. Dr. Julian Taber, a psychologist, testified that in some instances pathological gamblers are incapable of conforming their conduct to the requirements of law, and are unable to avoid behavior such as forgery, fraud, and embezzlement. Dr. Robert Custer, a psychiatrist, testified that in the late stage of pathological gambling individuals are unable to resist activities like embezzlement or fraud because they have to gamble and they have to obtain money in order to gamble.

Lewellyn is dependent on this scientific expert testimony to sustain his burden of making the required minimum showing that would permit him to rely on an insanity defense at trial. The expert testimony is essential because it supports a proposition not established in DSM–III: that some pathological gamblers lack substantial capacity to refrain from committing embezzlement and similar offenses. We note, however, that established principles control admissibility of scientific evidence. "[W]hile courts will go a long way in admitting expert testimony deduced from a well-recognized scientific principle or discovery, the thing from which the deduction is made must be sufficiently established to have gained general acceptance in the particular field in which it belongs." *Frye v. United States,* 293 F. 1013, 1014 (D.C.Cir.1923). In deciding whether a scientific principle meets the *Frye* standard we have recognized reliability as "one of the most important factors" that should be considered. United States v. Alexander, 526 F.2d 161, 163 (8th Cir.1975). Because our analysis of the *Frye* rule would govern the admission at trial of expert testimony similar to that given at the pretrial hearing, this analysis is equally applicable in determining whether expert testimony adduced by Lewellyn is sufficient to constitute the required minimum showing of insanity.

Pathological gambling has received relatively little scientific attention. Dr. Custer testified that pathological gambling has only recently been recognized as a disease. Both Dr. Taber and Dr. Custer cited the inclusion of pathological gambling in DSM–III, published in 1980, as evidence that the condition is generally accepted as a mental disease by mental health professionals. Pathological gambling was not listed, however, in DSM–II, published in 1968.

From the testimony at the pretrial hearing it is apparent that few psychologists or psychiatrists have had much experience dealing with pathological gamblers. Dr. Taber estimated that there may be perhaps 20 psychologists with some in-depth experience working with pathological gamblers, but he said that to his knowledge he was the only psychologist devoted full-time to their treatment. Dr. Taber knew of no psychiatrist who would work full-time with pathological gamblers. Dr. Custer stated that probably not more than 20 or 25 doctors have had experience with pathological gambling.

There is accordingly little knowledge about pathological gambling within the community of mental health professionals. Dr. Taber testified that in talking with physicians, social workers, and psychologists, he had "found very prevalent ignorance or just lack of concern with the problem." Dr. Custer indicated that it is necessary to spend a significant amount of time working with pathological gamblers in order to understand the problem "because it is so new and there is so very little that has been known about it." Dr. Custer said he does not think many doctors know about pathological gambling, and that as a result they do not recognize it as a disease.

In order to make the necessary minimum showing of insanity Lewellyn was required to demonstrate that there is general acceptance in the fields of psychiatry and psychology of the principle that some pathological gamblers lack substantial capacity to conform their conduct to the requirements of laws prohibiting embezzlement and similar offenses. There is no evidence in the record, however, either in DSM–III or the expert testimony, that this principle is generally accepted in the mental health professions. Indeed, the record shows that the pathological gambling disorder itself has only recently been recognized in DSM–III, and that there is scant experience and limited knowledge concerning this problem. In our view, Lewellyn has failed to show that the opinions espoused by his expert witnesses possess the requisite indicia of scientific reliability.

Because we find that Lewellyn did not make the required minimum showing of insanity, we affirm the district court's exclusion of evidence pertaining to a defense of insanity by reason of pathological gambling.

QUESTIONS AND COMMENTS

1. *Presumptions and expert testimony.* The court in *Lewellyn* decided that the evidence presented by the defendant did not overcome the presumption of sanity and thus upheld its exclusion by the trial court. In most jurisdictions, the presumption of sanity functions only as a requirement that the defendant produce *some* evidence of insanity in order to get the issue

to the jury; the usual approach is to hold that a "scintilla" of evidence satisfactorily rebuts the presumption. Abraham Goldstein, The Insanity Defense 113 (1967); 17 A.L.R.3d 146 § 5 (2012). However, the *Lewellyn* court, relying on precedent, stated that the presumption can be overcome only if a *prima facie* case of insanity is made out by the defendant, thus raising the threshold for admission. Put another way, in most jurisdictions, the defendant overcomes the presumption of sanity if relevant rebuttal evidence (i.e., evidence having any tendency to prove insanity) is presented. But here the court requires the defendant to "establish" insanity to the satisfaction of the court before the jury may hear the evidence.

Relying on the prima facie test for overcoming the presumption of sanity, the *Lewellyn* court found that the language in the DSM about pathological gambling, by itself, was insufficient. Do you agree? If the court were to adopt the more typical "scintilla" or relevance rule in determining whether the presumption is met, would a diagnosis of pathological gambling be enough? Should a diagnosis, if believed, ever be sufficient by itself to overcome the presumption?

2. *Screening tests*: Frye, *the relevancy rule, and* Daubert. The defendant in *Lewellyn* also relied on the testimony of Drs. Custer and Taber in support of his insanity defense. The court implies that had this testimony been admissible, the defendant would have overcome the presumption of sanity and could have asserted an insanity defense at trial. But it found the testimony inadmissible, relying on a second evidentiary doctrine, announced in *Frye v. United States,* 293 Fed. 1013 (App.D.C.1923). As the court states, the "*Frye* rule" holds that "the thing" from which scientific evidence is deduced "must be sufficiently established to have gained general acceptance in the particular field in which it belongs." Some have criticized the *Frye* rule on the ground that the "general acceptance" standard is confusing and difficult to apply consistently. One commentator has noted that, under the rule, "courts must decide *who* must find the procedure acceptable, they must define exactly *what* must be accepted, and they must determine what methods will be used to establish general acceptance." Paul Gianelli, *The Admissibility of Novel Scientific Evidence: Frye v. United States, A Half-Century Later*, 80 Colum.L.Rev. 1197, 1208 (1980). Did the *Lewellyn* court properly address these issues?

A separate criticism of the *Frye* test has to do with its conceptual underpinning. Many commentators reject the *Frye* rule as a means of determining the admissibility of scientific testimony because they feel that the traditional relevance/prejudice inquiry is a more sensitive tool for this purpose. See, e.g., Charles McCormick, Handbook of the Law of Evidence § 203 (6th ed. 2006). Implicit in the relevance inquiry is an accuracy assessment: evidence that is inaccurate has no tendency to make a proposition more or less probable. But if it is not known whether evidence in a particular case is inaccurate, as is often the case with scientific evidence, then exclusion should only occur if the jury is likely to accept it unquestioningly. If, on the other hand, problems with the evidence can be made clear to the jury, it should be admitted and the jury allowed to make up its mind. In other words, questions about the inaccuracy of expert testimony should go to the weight of the evidence and not its admissibility. *Frye* held the opposite. In response to this criticism, it could be argued that the *Frye* rule is merely an application of the relevance/prejudice inquiry in the scientific evidence context. That is, the courts that apply it have decided that scientific evidence is, by its nature, so likely to persuade a jury that it must be "screened" for accuracy before it is admitted. Does this reasoning apply to psychiatric testimony? See Neil J. Vidmar & Regina A. Schuller, *Juries and Expert Evidence: Social Framework Testimony*, 1989 Law & Contemp. Probs. 133, 173 (reporting research indicating that jurors do not treat expert behavioral science testimony offered by the defense with an unwarranted aura of accuracy).

The *Frye* and "relevancy" doctrines were the two most prominent screening tests for expert testimony until 1993. In that year, the U.S. Supreme Court decided *Daubert v. Merrell Dow Pharmaceuticals*, 509 U.S. 579, 113 S.Ct. 2786, 125 L.Ed.2d 469 (1993), which held that, in federal courts, neither the relevancy test or the *Frye* test pose the proper question. According to the Court, *Frye* was superseded by the adoption of the federal rules of evidence, particularly Rule 702. At the time, the latter rule stated that "if scientific, technical, or other specialized knowledge will assist the trier of fact to understand the evidence or to determine a fact in issue, a witness qualified as an expert . . . may testify thereto in the form of an opinion or otherwise." Justice Blackmun's opinion concluded that "a rigid 'general acceptance' requirement would be at odds with the 'liberal thrust' of the Federal rules." Rather the test for admitting scientific evidence should be a "flexible" one and can rely on a number of factors other than general acceptance, including the "falsifiability" of the underlying theory, the extent to which it has been subject to peer review, and its known or potential "error rates."

This language sounded as if the Court was adopting a relaxed version of *Frye*. The *Daubert* opinion also stated, however, that even under Rule 702 the basis of scientific testimony "must be derived by the scientific method," meaning that the underlying hypothesis "can be (and has been) tested." Further, in *Kumho Tire Co. v. Carmichael*, 526 U.S. 137, 119 S.Ct. 1167, 143 L.Ed.2d 238 (1999), the Court made clear that *Daubert* applies not just to "scientific" expertise, but also to "technical" and "specialized knowledge" (the other two types of expertise mentioned in Rule 702).[d] One year later Congress ratified this relatively rigorous approach to expertise by amending Rule 702 to state that scientific, technical or specialized knowledge is admissible only if "(1) the testimony is based upon sufficient facts or data, (2) the testimony is the product of reliable principles and methods, and (3) the witness has applied the principles and methods reliably to the facts of the case." Thus, in

---

[d] A third Supreme Court decision, *General Electric Co. v. Joiner*, 522 U.S. 136, 118 S.Ct. 512, 139 L.Ed.2d 508 (1997), stressed that the trial judge is to play a "gatekeeper" role in determining admissibility of expert testimony, and that the trial judge's decision, whether to exclude or admit, is to be given great deference on appeal.

federal courts and in those twenty-five to thirty states that follow *Daubert* (see David Faigman et al., Modern Scientific Evidence: The Law and Science of Expert Testimony 20–21 (2008) for a survey of state law), psychiatric expertise must be based on facts, theory and methodology that are "reliable" (i.e., valid or accurate), not simply "generally accepted."

One commentator, noting the relatively unscientific nature of most behavioral science expertise, has stated that *Daubert*, "read literally would dictate the end of the receipt of psychiatric and psychological testimony in federal courts." Michael J. Gottesman, *Admissibility of Expert Testimony After Daubert: The "Prestige" Factor*, 43 Emory L.J. 867, 875–76 (1994). Another stated that "the testability or falsifiability and potential error rate factors for appraising [social science evidence] will rarely be sufficiently present to meet the *Daubert* standard." Michael H. Graham, Daubert v. Merrell Dow Pharmaceuticals, Inc.: *No* Frye, *Now What?*, 30 Crim. L. Bull. 153, 162 (1994). In practice, however, these dire predictions have not come to pass. One study of the caselaw addressing the admissibility of psychological "syndrome" evidence between 1993, when *Daubert* was handed down, and 1998 found that "[c]ourts are not generally engaging in scientific reviews of the proffered syndrome[; m]ost typically, the focus is on general acceptance and the qualifications of the expert, and even then the judicial review tends to be cursory." Shirley Dobbin & James Richardson, *A Case Law Survey of Social and Behavioral Science Evidence After* Daubert, unpublished manuscript presented at 1998 American–Psychology Law Association Annual Meeting. According to one commentator, as of 2001, there had been "no reported *Daubert* challenges to retrospective psychiatric assessments of criminal responsibility." Daniel W. Shuman, *Expertise in Law, Medicine and Health Care*, 26 J. Health Policy & L. 267, 282 (2001). The few exclusions of psychiatric testimony that occur in such cases appear to be on the ground the testimony is irrelevant, rather than unreliable. See Henry F. Fradella et al., *The Impact of* Daubert *on the Admissibility of Behavioral Science Testimony*, 30 Pepperdine L. Rev. 403, 421–23, 431–34 (2003). Can you think of any reason why lawyers and courts are handling psychiatric testimony regarding responsibility issues with kid gloves?

How, if at all, would a *Daubert* analysis have affected the analysis in *Lewellyn*? Consider also whether the outcome in the following cases would differ depending upon whether *Frye*, relevancy, or *Daubert* is the applicable test:

A.   Dr. Dietz's testimony in the Hinckley case that Hinckley had a schizoid personality disorder (see pp. 503–508). Recall that the DSM field tests showed that inter-rater agreement on diagnoses of personality disorders was between 56 and 65% (and one study found that inter-rater reliability of schizoid personality disorder in everyday clinical settings was 1%!). Does *Daubert* prohibit testimony associated with high error rates? Does *Frye*? Should testimony be admissible as long as the associated error rates, however high, are known?

Consider now that the broad, general diagnosis of a psychotic disorder (such as schizophrenia) has high inter-rater reliability, which means that psychiatrists tend to agree about the *absence* of psychosis, too. Should courts consider Dr. Dietz's testimony to be adequately reliable type because he is testifying about the absence of a psychotic disorder? Suppose you learned that most psychiatrists subsequently agreed with Dr. Stone and believed Hinckley most likely had a delusional disorder—which is a diagnosis that was not available to either Dr. Dietz or Dr. Carpenter (see n. c, on p. 510). In retrospect, should the court in that case not have accepted any diagnostic testimony?

B.   "Rape trauma syndrome" testimony, offered by the prosecution in a case in which the defendant admits intercourse with the alleged victim but claims it was consensual. The testimony asserts that women who have been raped are "consistently more likely" than women who have not been raped to experience discomfort or fear of men, an inability to sleep, nightmares about rape, and constant anxiety, all of which the alleged victim experiences. The studies on which the testimony is based found that rape victims are more likely than those who have not been raped to experience such symptoms, but also found that victims' reactions to rape vary from individual to individual, that the symptoms experienced by victims of rape are no different from those experienced by victims of other traumatic events (such as war), and that there is little distinction between the reactions of a victim of rape and the reactions of the victim of any other sort of stressful sexual event. The syndrome is not found in DSM–5, but since the fourth edition of the DSM the diagnostic manual has explicitly said that post-traumatic stress disorder (PTSD) can result not only from wartime and "major catastrophes" but also from traumatic events involving "a threat to the physical integrity of self" that "involved intense fear, helpless, or horror" (and DSM–5 does explicitly include for the first time "sexual violence" as a triggering trauma). The manual also states that PTSD is associated with nightmares, anxiety, and attempts to avoid situations associated with the trauma. Assuming the alleged victim in the case suffers from these types of symptoms, should the expert testimony about "rape trauma syndrome" be admissible? Should admissibility analysis under *Daubert* or *Frye* vary depending on whether the prosecution or defense is the initial proponent of psychiatric testimony?

3.   *Novel defenses and substantive law.* The pathological gambling defense was of recent vintage at the time it was raised in *Lewellyn*. To the extent they should be relied upon at all, use of the *Frye* rule, *Daubert* and other screening rules is most easily justified in just such a situation, when novel and relatively untested scientific evidence is at issue. But in some cases involving novel defense arguments reliance on these rules may serve another goal, one that is substantive rather than evidentiary. That is, they might be used to exclude evidence not because of its inaccuracy but because of its effect on accepted legal doctrine. Is it possible that the real concern of the *Lewellyn*

court was not that the testimony would be inaccurate or misleading, but that it might lead to an improper expansion of the insanity defense?

In any event, as noted above, the types of evidentiary issues raised in *Lewellyn* are seldom raised in more "routine" insanity cases, even post-*Daubert* and *Kumho Tire*. The next excerpt takes exception to this practice.

STEPHEN MORSE CRAZY BEHAVIOR, MORALS & SCIENCE: AN ANALYSIS OF MENTAL HEALTH LAW
51 S.Cal.L.Rev. 527, 582–88, 618–19 (1978).

[I]

[T]he law is concerned with specific cases where an actor may be clearly crazy and where the craziness is clearly related to legally relevant behavior. . . . In terms of responsibility, . . . [i]ndividual cases of clear relationship may be separated into two types: *crazy urges* and *crazy reasons*. In each case, this section considers the particular factors that help one decide whether the actor could have behaved otherwise. Even assuming that the craziness was a causal variable, the critical question remains: Was the crazy urge uncontrollable or was the crazy reason and the legally relevant behavior based on it the inexorable result of a disturbed mind?

a. *Crazy urges:* The case of crazy urges refers to what is usually termed an "irresistible impulse." The actor may be perfectly rational cognitively, but he *feels* as if he must carry out a particular behavior and that he cannot prevent himself from doing so. He may be quite aware that the action he feels compelled to perform is weird, deviant, immoral, maladaptive, or the like. Still, he feels incapable of behaving otherwise. If the behavior felt to be compelled is weird, deviant, or immoral, we are inclined to believe that the urge is crazy, because no one would desire to behave in those ways when he comprehends how those behaviors were assessed. The prototypical case of a crazy urge is the sexual deviant, *e.g.,* a child molester, who knows that his actions are viewed as sick or evil (or both) by most persons, and yet who feels an overwhelming desire to molest children.

Is the child molester's behavior the irresistible effect of his crazy urge? To analyze this question we must first ask the threshold question of whether the actor's crazy urge is related to mental illness. This case is a clear example of the situation where craziness is diagnosed because the legally relevant behavior seems crazy itself and where no other significant evidence of mental disorder may exist. We assume that there must be some underlying abnormality because no rational person would choose to molest children unless he was "forced to" by circumstances beyond his control. [T]here is no evidence of underlying abnormality in such cases, but let us accept arguments that it is reasonable to call this person crazy because he experiences a perhaps inexplicable and crazy urge.

Is the urge irresistible? For at least two reasons, most persons would assume that the urge must be very strong. First, the molester reports that the urge is overwhelming. Second, it seems intuitively obvious that most persons would not "give in" to such an urge unless it was overpowering. Let us assume that, indeed, the urge is powerful and perhaps even tormenting to our molester. But could it have been resisted, albeit at the cost of frustration and discomfort? Do all persons who feel such urges give in to them, or are there some who resist?

Although there exists little systematic epidemiological study of such questions, it is clear from clinical practice that many persons report extremely strong "deviant" urges that are often a source of misery to them. Yet most persons do not engage in the urged behavior; indeed, many seek assistance from clergymen, doctors, counselors, and psychotherapists in order to defeat the urge. Holding that the urge is not overwhelming in such cases, but that it is overwhelming in the cases of those who give in, is tautological reasoning: the urge must be overwhelming because the person gave in. In terms more familiar to lawyers, we are faced with the difficulty of distinguishing between the irresistible impulse and the impulse not resisted.

There is no scientific measure of the strength of urges. Nor is there evidence of what percentage of people who experience various urges of various strengths act on those urges. Even if such measures and data were available, as they may be someday, the measured strength of the urge would not answer the question of whether the urge was irresistible. Such data may help us to identify how predisposing, in a statistical sense, the urge might be, but they would not answer the question of moral and legal responsibility. Where to draw the cutting point would clearly be a moral and legal determination. In the future, behavioral science may provide more precise information to help draw the line, but science alone cannot draw the line of legal responsibility.

At present, then, the determination of the irresistibility of crazy urges must rest on commonsense assessments of the craziness and strength of the urge. The data to be evaluated would be first, the report of the urged actor, and second, the craziness of the urged action. Whether certain urges are crazy is not a scientific question that needs expert answers. And whether the urge is sufficiently strong or crazy is a question that is answered by assessing the reported feelings of the actor and the sincerity of his report. There is simply no test for knowing when an urge is irresistible, and indeed, there is no reason to believe that there is any urge that is not, to some degree, resistible. Deciding whether an urge is irresistible is not a scientific decision.

b.   *Crazy reasons:* It may also be believed that an actor had no free choice about whether to engage in certain behavior if the actor reports crazy reasons for his behavior. If an actor kills someone because he sincerely believes the victim was a hostile agent, we believe that the killing not only is related to the crazy belief as was seen above, but that it is the compelled result of the crazy belief. After all, no one would hold and act on such beliefs unless there were something uncontrollably wrong with him that caused him to have those beliefs.

Before we can determine whether an actor had control over his crazy reasons and consequent actions, we must first analyze the nature of a crazy reason. Following from our definition of craziness itself, we may define a crazy reason as one that is irrational and inexplicable. Of course, the degree of craziness of a reason varies along a lengthy continuum.

* * *

It may be very hard for a person to think straight; in some cases, crazy beliefs may powerfully compel the crazy person to act on them. But there is no certainty that an actor cannot control his crazy beliefs or, at least, control actions based on them. Indeed, even the craziest persons seem to behave quite normally or rationally a great deal of the time, especially if there is good reason to do so. On at least some occasions, including some instances when they are behaving crazily, crazy persons are clearly capable of playing by the usual rules. Nor do they always act on the basis of their crazy reasons. Moreover, the defects and disordered thinking that supposedly distinguish crazy persons from normal ones are very prevalent in the general population. * * * Even if it is found that the person typically seems out of touch with reality, reasons crazily, and gives mostly crazy reasons for his behavior, scientific evidence cannot demonstrate that such behavior is the result of mental disorder and that related legally relevant behavior is sufficiently unfree to ascribe nonresponsibility to the actor. At most it can be urged that a person who typically does not think "straight" is more or less predisposed to give crazy reasons and to act on them.

* * *

[II]

Whether an actor could have behaved otherwise and is legally and morally responsible for his legally relevant behavior cannot be determined scientifically. No diagnosis gives the answer to these questions, and there are no scientific tests to measure the strength of crazy urges or the strength of the actor's self-control. Nor are there tests to distinguish the person who *cannot* think straight or control himself from the person who *will not* think straight or control himself. Whether a person cannot or will not think straight or control himself is a moral and commonsense judgment that should be made by the legal decisionmaker.

Let us take an example to examine how experts might help or hinder legal decisions about responsibility. In a famous homicide case,[194] clinicians testified that the defendant killed the victim in order to avoid psychic disintegration and insanity. If this formulation is correct, the defendant was faced with a very hard choice indeed—kill or psychically disintegrate—and the defendant would hardly seem as responsible as most criminal homicide defendants, or perhaps, responsible at all. Some clarifying questions, however, should be asked: (1) Are there hard data behind the theorizing that the killing was the inexorable or nearly inexorable result of threatened ego-disintegration?; and (2) What percentage of persons with such fears kill? The answer to question (1) is "no," and the answer to question (2) is that the data are unavailable although the actual percentage is probably quite low. Such fears are not a proven necessary or sufficient cause of homicidal behavior. In this case, as in all cases, the expert's assertion that the person could not have acted otherwise is really a moral guess and not a scientific fact. Justice would be better served if the expert drew no conclusions and simply described in ordinary language the cognitive and affective state of the defendant without intruding terms and theories of unproven accuracy and usefulness.[195]

* * *

RICHARD BONNIE & CHRISTOPHER SLOBOGIN, THE ROLE OF MENTAL HEALTH PROFESSIONALS IN THE CRIMINAL PROCESS: THE CASE FOR INFORMED SPECULATION
66 Va.L.Rev. 427, 461–64, 486–93 (1980).

* * *

We concede that the central etiological theories and conceptual categories of the clinical behavioral disciplines have not been scientifically validated, and that few clinical opinions can be stated with a high degree of certainty. At best, opinions about psychological processes—beyond merely descriptive observations—are clinical probability judgments rooted in theoretical constructs that are more or less widely shared among mental health professionals.

According to the weight of authority, however, the fact that opinion testimony is uncertain does not by itself justify exclusion, as long as the

---

[194] People v. Gorshen, 51 Cal.2d 716, 336 P.2d 492 (1959).

[195] Of course, an expert who tries to describe the person's past mental state faces grave difficulties. This probably cannot be done with substantial accuracy unless the expert had occasion to know or examine the actor at the past time in question. Thus, experts probably should never testify about an actor's mental state at a time when the expert had no direct knowledge of it. Still, descriptions of a present mental state may help a factfinder draw inferences about a past mental state provided that the time in question is not too remote and that there is some direct evidence of the actor's behavior at the past time.

evidence rises above mere conjecture or speculation. If it has any tendency to prove a fact, and is otherwise qualified as expert opinion, the evidence is admissible unless some overriding reason requires exclusion. The rationale for this position is that many observations, both scientific and lay, can be expressed only in terms of "probabilities" or "possibilities"; to deny the factfinder such evidence on this ground alone might deplete seriously the amount of information available.

Although Professor Morse acknowledges this general evidentiary principle, he asserts that "an exception should be made for mental health professionals, primarily because their expertise is limited on most issues and their unrestricted testimony tends to obscure the moral and social nature of the questions being asked." We do not think the case for an exception can be made. Particularly when the defendant determines whether expert testimony by mental health professionals will be introduced—typically the case in the reconstructive inquiries of the criminal law—the opinions of qualified witnesses within their sphere of specialized knowledge should be freely admitted.

A defendant's past psychological functioning cannot be reconstructed with scientific precision. The truth will remain very much in the shadows whether or not mental health professionals are permitted to offer their opinions. In formulating an evidentiary test, then, we should begin by comparing the knowledge of mental health professionals not with the knowledge of physicists about the laws of motion, but with that of laymen about psychological aberration and criminal behavior. We should ask whether the observations, intuitions, and hypotheses of clinicians offer a useful and acceptable supplement to those of Everyman.

Morse insists that inferences concerning the nature, extent, and consequences of mental dysfunction are within the range of lay experience and common sense. To some extent this is correct; the factfinder is competent to draw such inferences in the absence of expert testimony, and need not yield to such testimony even when undisputed.[118] Moreover, lay witnesses sometimes may express opinions on a defendant's mental condition. Nevertheless, we stress the incremental nature of the modern test: we must ask whether "specialized knowledge will assist the trier of fact," not whether the fact finder can manage when left to his own devices.

*   *   *

---

[118] It is generally accepted that an opinion of an expert, even if uncontradicted, need not be accepted by the jury as long as there is some evidence to support a contrary conclusion. This same concept has also been expressed as a requirement that a "jury may not arbitrarily disregard expert testimony. . . ." Of course, in jurisdictions where the government bears the burden of proving the defendant's "sanity" beyond a reasonable doubt, a jury cannot find the defendant sane, even if they find the defendant's expert unbelievable, unless the government has presented some evidence from which sanity can be inferred.

[In the responsibility assessment] setting the "factual" inquiry concerns the relationship, if any, between a defendant's aberrational psychological functioning and his behavior. We agree that categorizing the strength of that relationship, and evaluating it according to some externally derived moral gradient, is the responsibility of the judge or jury and not an appropriate subject for expert opinion. Professor Morse's exclusionary approach to expert testimony, however, also would preclude an expert from expressing any opinion regarding why a relationship may or may not exist between the defendant's psychological functioning and his criminal behavior. We think this would unnecessarily deprive the factfinder of helpful insights and would unfairly hamper the defendant's effort to present a case-in-exculpation or-mitigation.

Morse refers to the famous *Gorshen* case to illustrate his rationale. Gorshen shot his supervisor after a fight at work. A psychiatric witness testified that Gorshen was a chronic paranoid schizophrenic who for twenty years had experienced trances accompanied by auditory and visual hallucinations. He claimed to see and hear devils in disguise committing abnormal sexual acts, sometimes upon Gorshen himself. These experiences had intensified during the months before the crime.

On the day of the shooting, Gorshen had been drinking at work. His supervisor told him to go home, and a fight ensued. He then went home, obtained a pistol, returned, and shot the victim. According to the psychiatrist, Gorshen said, "All I was thinking about all of this time is to shoot O'Leary. I forgot about my family, I forgot about God's laws and human's laws and everything else. The only thing was to get that guy, get that guy, get that guy, like a hammer in the head."

The expert witness explained that during the period of the offense Gorshen was driven by an obsessive murderous rage aroused by the stress of the beating and by what he perceived as challenges to his manhood. Psychologically, this rage reflected a desperate attempt to ward off imminent and total disintegration of his personality:

> The strength of the obsession is proportioned not to the reality of danger but to the danger of the insanity. . . . [F]or this man to go insane means to be permanently in the world of these visions and under the influence of the devil. . . . [A]n individual in this state of crisis will do anything to avoid the threatened insanity. . . .

Professor Morse questions the highly speculative quality of this formulation, pointing out that no "hard data" support the hypothesis "that the killing was the inexorable or nearly inexorable result of threatened ego-disintegration," and that probably very few persons with such fears kill, although there are no data available. Of course, both of these points could have been made very effectively by skillful cross-examination. Skillful redirect examination in response might have brought out the psychodynamic concepts from which this formulation was derived, perhaps with descriptions from the clinical literature of the characteristics of violent behavior committed by individuals with comparable paranoid thought patterns.

Morse characterizes the *Gorshen* expert's testimony as "really a moral guess and not a scientific fact." Although explanatory clinical formulations by careful forensic specialists are hardly "scientific facts," they do represent something more than idiosyncratic "guesses." Such witnesses offer "informed speculation," essentially in the following form:

> I cannot assure you that this is what happened, and I cannot measure for you the impact that these intrapsychic variables had on the defendant's behavior under the circumstances which existed at the time of the offense. Nonetheless, based on our operating theories of psychology, which we employ in our everyday clinical practice, and on my own study of the relevant literature concerning this type of psychological functioning and this type of criminal behavior, I think the following explanation(s) are possible (or probable).

These explanatory formulations can assist the factfinder, who must speculate in any event, by identifying "clinically reasonable" possibilities that otherwise may not occur to him. Appropriately instructed, the jury will know that these explanations are only possibilities and will not be misled.[192]

* * *

[Indeed] in the context of the reconstructive inquiries of the criminal law, the risk that a jury will give undue weight to such an expert opinion, notwithstanding any cautionary instructions, has been grossly exaggerated. If only the defense has offered psychiatric testimony, the natural skepticism of the jurors, and the corrective value of cross-examination, virtually eliminate the risk that the jury will abdicate its factfinding function to the experts. If each side has its own witness, expert "dominance" is not the problem, and the risk of confusion can be minimized by adequate preparation by counsel and by ordinary judicial supervision. In short, we see little disadvantage in admitting appropriately restricted opinion testimony by qualified mental health professionals.

Most important, the wholesale exclusion of such testimony would unduly restrict the defendant's opportunity to present relevant evidence in his defense, and would enhance the natural advantage enjoyed by the prosecution on reconstructive issues. In particular, a defendant's opportunity to carry his de facto burden of proving that he did not perceive, believe, expect, or intend what a normal person would have

---

[192] The *Gorshen* trial judge stated that "up till the time that [the defense expert] testified in this case, there was no explanation of why this crime was committed. . . . [He is] the first person that has any reasonable explanation. Whether it's correct or not, I don't know."

under the same circumstances—and that he therefore lacked the mens rea required for the offense—is undermined by rules which altogether exclude qualified opinion testimony or which allow such testimony only if the expert finds that the defendant's abnormal functioning was attributable to a mental disease or defect. Similarly, a defendant's opportunity to offer a plausible explanation for his behavior—and thereby to establish a meaningful case in exculpation or mitigation under the applicable responsibility doctrines—would be restricted severely and unjustifiably by rules that exclude explanatory formulations by qualified mental health professionals.

* * *

QUESTIONS AND COMMENTS

1.   *Levels of inference.* To make clearer the nature of the debate between Morse on the one hand and Bonnie & Slobogin on the other it might be helpful to conceptualize expert testimony as consisting of ascending levels of inference. For instance, in the Hinckley insanity case, the progressive levels of inference might be as follows:

1.   Application of meaning to an observation of behavior (e.g., "When Hinckley saw President Reagan wave, he believed Reagan was waving at him.")

2.   Categorization of the behavioral manifestation as a symptom (e.g., Hinckley was experiencing an "idea of reference.")

3.   "Formulation" of the perception of general mental state to fit into theoretical constructs or the research literature and/or to synthesize observations (e.g., "Hinckley's interpretation of Reagan's wave is consistent with grandiose delusions of inflated worth or a special relationship to a famous person.")

4.   Diagnosis (e.g., "These symptoms, along with other evidence of delusional behavior, show that he is suffering from a psychotic disorder, either a delusional disorder or schizophrenia")

5.   Relationship of formulation or diagnosis to legally relevant behavior (e.g., "At the time of the offense, Hinckley's disorder affected his ability to understand the actual consequences of his actions.")

6.   Elements of the ultimate legal issue (e.g., "Hinckley's disorder caused him to lack substantial capacity to appreciate the wrongfulness of what he was doing."))

7.   Ultimate legal issue (e.g., "He was insane at the time of the offense.")[e]

---

[e]   This example is adapted from Gary M. Melton et al., Psychological Evaluations for the Courts 16–17 (Guilford Press, 3d ed.2007).

At what level of testimony would Morse permit mental health professionals to testify? Bonnie & Slobogin? If you were a judge deciding the admissibility of clinical testimony on the responsibility issue in the *Gorshen* case, up to which level would you allow? If you instead relied on one of the screening rules discussed previously?

2.   *Objective v. suppositional science.* The Morse/Bonnie & Slobogin debate has been carried on by Professors Faigman and Taslitz. Faigman distinguishes between "objective science"—i.e., data or opinion the validity of which has been demonstrated through the scientific method of hypothesis testing—and "suppositional" science, which is based on "social science findings advanced without pretense of having survived scientific test and social science findings advanced as having undergone scientific test but which have not actually been tested adequately." David Faigman, *To Have and Have Not: Assessing the Value of Social Science to the Law as Science and Policy*, 38 Emory L.J. 1005, 1013 (1989). He argues that suppositional science—which he analogizes to the type of story-telling engaged in by fiction writers such as Fyodor Dostoevsky in his novel *Crime and Punishment*— should generally be excluded:

> [T]he validity of suppositional science is indefinite, because it has not been subjected to adequate testing. An expert's suppositions may be accurate, or they may not be, and no way exists for the juror to discern which is the case. Presented with conflicting suppositions, the so-called battle of the experts, jurors have no well-founded basis on which to choose between them. Such battles are likely to be won by the more persuasive witness, rather than the more persuasive facts or opinion.

> Undoubtedly, cases arise in which a suppositional expert's testimony will offer insights or suggest ways of viewing the evidence that can "assist" the fact-finder's task. The difficulty comes from recognizing these cases when they arise. Without knowing the accuracy of their opinions, neither the judge nor the jury can estimate the value of their testimony. [A] Dostoevskean psychologist could sometimes provide assistance to fact-finders, perhaps as much assistance as a Freudian psychologist, but in a battle between the Dostoevskean and Freudian experts, nothing in their training or methods would necessarily enable jurors to say which expert had the more valid opinion or could provide greater assistance.

> In addition to the *potential* insights into factual questions that suppositional experts might provide juries, the only remaining potential significance of suppositional science lies in the value preferences it reflects. Perhaps, if the normative basis for nonscientific expert testimony was recognized, its discretionary allowance could be viewed as a function of legal policy formation. Thus, rather than incorporate into legal rules the factual insights and values reflected by suppositional science, suppositional experts could be allowed to testify generally, leaving to juries the task of choosing among competing suppositions. Professor Herbert Hovenkamp, for example, argues that in antitrust litigation juries should be exposed to competing economic theories and be

allowed to choose between them the way they choose among conflicting facts. Professor Hovenkamp well recognizes the political component of most economic theories, but asserts that greater stability will be achieved in the long run by leaving theory-finding to juries.

But assigning the responsibility of theory-finding to juries invests vast power in expert witnesses to define the value choices resolved by the judicial process. Because judges cannot admit all experts claiming scientific expertise, if judges do not assess the validity of proffered opinions themselves, they must defer to the professional guilds to decide what scientific evidence to admit. Admissibility of scientific evidence thus becomes a guild issue resolved not by legal principles, nor on the basis of the accuracy of the evidence, but instead by the internal dynamics of professional organizations. Hence, the Dostoevskean psychologist, for example, is barred from the courthouse not because we doubt the validity of her opinion, at least no more so than the Freudian psychologist, but because she is not represented politically in one of the two APAs.

Id. at 1085–87.

Taslitz, on the other hand, believes that there is much to be said for "art" as well as science when it comes to making determinations of criminal responsibility.

[R]ationalist critiques like that of Professor Faigman . . . seek to impose the standards of science in the courtroom. Despite its pretensions to the contrary, law is not a science but rather deals with the need for relatively quick, practical decision making in individual cases because judgments cannot be postponed while awaiting scientific confirmation. These decisions are made in a value-laden world of uncertainty. Thus, verdicts, being a practical project, do not and should not seek solely "truth," in some absolute, scientific sense of that term, but rather acceptability and stability, given the constraints and varying goals facing the decisionmaker.

Therefore, while science is not irrelevant—and, indeed, can do much to inform the legal process when truth is one of the competing goals—sometimes art can do in an acceptable fashion in the individual case what science cannot. This is especially true when there are powerful concerns other than truth, such as the political, moral, and cathartic goals of a criminal trial. We may, therefore, turn to art, in this instance, to clinical judgment with its uncertain scientific support, because the artistry serves cathartic goals or because, in our search for truth, artistry is the best means available. Indeed, the professional psychological literature recognizes both the limitations and advantages of clinical artistry.

Thus, the literature recommends a purely actuarial approach when the outcome to be predicted is objective and specific, and interest in the individual case is minimal. On the other hand, clinical judgement is recommended when (1) information is needed about areas or events for which no adequate tests are available, (2) rare, unusual events of a highly individualized nature are to be predicted or judged, or (3) the clinical judgements involve instances for which no statistical equations have been developed. These are precisely the situations likely to arise in criminal trials.

Andrew Taslitz, *Myself Alone: Individualizing Justice Through Psychological Character Evidence*, 52 Maryland L.Rev. 1, 99–100 (1993).

Reinforcing his view that "art" can usefully inform the adjudicative process, Taslitz notes the development of "storytelling theory," which suggests that, to be helpful, the story of case must be told in such a way as to satisfy a jury's need for "narrative coherence" and "narrative fidelity." Narrative coherence concerns whether the story "hangs together" in the face of competing stories and consistently depicts a person's character. Narrative fidelity concerns whether relevant facts have been omitted or distorted, whether the connections of facts to conclusions are reasonable, whether the values implied by the story are confirmed by the jurors' own experiences, and whether the story addresses the "real" issues in the cases. Taslitz argues that "suppositional science" can often provide such a story when "objective science" cannot. Id. at 94–97. How does the expert testimony in *Hinckley*, *Lewellyn*, *Gorshen* and the three hypotheticals on pp. 529–530 fare under Faigman's view? Taslitz's?

As to whether there is a meaningful difference between "objective science" and "suppositional science," consider this statement from Michael Seigel, *A Pragmatic Critique of Modern Evidence Scholarship*, 88 Nw. L.Rev. 995, 1038 (1994):

> Determining whether research results are generalizable between places and over time . . . requires the use of reasoning techniques that include analogy, imagination, common sense, experience, and induction. These are the very methods of practical reason. In other words, applied social science, though a positive endeavor, is—at least at some stages—predominately an exercise in practical reason.

3.   *The right to voice.* In *Rock v. Arkansas*, 483 U.S 44, 61, 107 S.Ct. 2704, 97 L.Ed.2d 37 (1987), the Supreme Court struck down a statute that prohibited criminal defendants from introducing hypnotically-induced testimony, on the ground that criminal defendants have a constitutional right to testify unless the type of testimony presented is "always so untrustworthy and so immune to the traditional means of evaluating credibility that it should disable a defendant from presenting her version of the events for which she is on trial." 483 U.S. at 61. Is *Rock* violated if a defendant is not permitted to present qualified expert testimony on past mental state? Is there a legally relevant difference between prohibiting the defendant from testifying about his own mental state and preventing the defendant from presenting an expert to testify about his mental state?

Twelve years after *Rock* the Court decided *United States v. Scheffer*, 523 U.S. 303, 118 S.Ct. 1261, 140 L.Ed2 1214 (1998), which held that a trial court could exclude the results of a polygraph test taken by the defendant. The Court gave three reasons for the holding: (1) despite its questionable reliability, polygraph evidence carries an "aura of infallibility"; (2) such evidence usurps the jury's role as the ultimate assessor of truth; and (3) such evidence does not advance the defendant's story but rather merely "bolsters . . . credibility." Do these reasons for excluding polygraph evidence apply to psychiatric evidence on past mental state? Or does *Rock* announce a constitutional "right to voice" that allows defendants to tell their stories with expert evidence so long as its trustworthiness can be evaluated through the adversarial process? See Christopher Slobogin, *The Right to Voice Reprised*, 40 Seton Hall L. Rev. 1647 (2010).

4.   *The importance of context.* Bonnie & Slobogin refrain from taking a position on the admissibility of clinical opinion testimony outside the "reconstructive" setting assessing mental state at the time of the offense. What are the differences between this setting and other settings in which clinical opinion testimony might be offered? In particular, what are the differences between the reconstructive context and the predictive one, to be discussed below?

C. PROPENSITY

Predictions of behavior are required in many different legal settings. Most relevant to this book are the sentencing and commitment contexts, where predictions relevant to dangerousness and treatability are often called for. The following case addresses admissibility issues in the context where such predictions have their greatest impact: death penalty proceedings.

BAREFOOT V. ESTELLE
Supreme Court of United States, 1983.
463 U.S. 880, 103 S.Ct. 3383, 77 L.Ed.2d 1090.

*   *   *

JUSTICE WHITE delivered the opinion of the Court.

*   *   *

On November 14, 1978, petitioner was convicted of the capital murder of a police officer in Bell County, Tex. A separate sentencing hearing before the same jury was then held to determine whether the death penalty should be imposed. Under Tex.Code Crim.Proc.Ann., Art. § 37.071 (Vernon 1981), two special questions were to be submitted to the jury: whether the conduct causing death was "committed deliberately and with reasonable expectation that the death of the deceased or another would result"; and whether "there is a probability that the defendant would commit criminal acts of violence that would constitute a continuing threat to society." The State introduced into evidence petitioner's prior convictions and his reputation for lawlessness. The State also called two psychiatrists, John Holbrook and James Grigson, who, in response to hypothetical questions, testified that petitioner would probably commit further acts of violence and represent a continuing threat to society. The jury answered both of the questions put to them in the affirmative, a result which required the imposition of the death penalty.

On appeal to the Texas Court of Criminal Appeals, petitioner urged, among other submissions, that the use of psychiatrists at the punishment hearing to make predictions about petitioner's future conduct was unconstitutional because psychiatrists, individually and as a class, are not competent to predict future dangerousness. Hence, their predictions are so likely to produce erroneous sentences that their use violated the Eighth and Fourteenth Amendments.

* * *

The suggestion that no psychiatrist's testimony may be presented with respect to a defendant's future dangerousness is somewhat like asking us to disinvent the wheel. In the first place, it is contrary to our cases. If the likelihood of a defendant's committing further crimes is a constitutionally acceptable criterion for imposing the death penalty, which it is, *Jurek v. Texas,* 428 U.S. 262, 96 S.Ct. 2950, 49 L.Ed.2d 929 (1976), and if it is not impossible for even a lay person sensibly to arrive at that conclusion, it makes little sense, if any, to submit that psychiatrists, out of the entire universe of persons who might have an opinion on the issue, would know so little about the subject that they should not be permitted to testify. In *Jurek,* seven Justices rejected the claim that it was impossible to predict future behavior and that dangerousness was therefore an invalid consideration in imposing the death penalty.

* * *

Although there was only lay testimony with respect to dangerousness in *Jurek,* there was no suggestion by the Court that the testimony of doctors would be inadmissible. To the contrary, the joint opinion announcing the judgment said that the jury should be presented with all of the relevant information.

* * *

Acceptance of petitioner's position that expert testimony about future dangerousness is far too unreliable to be admissible would immediately call into question those other contexts in which predictions of future behavior are constantly made. For example, in *O'Connor v. Donaldson,* 422 U.S. 563, 576, 95 S.Ct. 2486, 2494, 45 L.Ed.2d 396 (1975), we held that a nondangerous mental hospital patient could not be held in confinement against his will. Later, speaking about the requirements for civil commitments, we said:

> "There may be factual issues in a commitment proceeding, but the factual aspects represent only the beginning of the inquiry. Whether the individual is mentally ill and dangerous to either himself or others and is in need of confined therapy turns on the *meaning* of the facts which must be interpreted by expert psychiatrists and psychologists." *Addington v. Texas,* 441 U.S. 418, 429, 99 S.Ct. 1804, 1811, 60 L.Ed.2d 323 (1979).

In the second place, the rules of evidence generally extant at the federal and state levels anticipate that relevant, unprivileged evidence should be admitted and its weight left to the factfinder, who would have the benefit of cross-examination and contrary evidence by the opposing party. Psychiatric testimony predicting dangerousness may be countered not only as erroneous in a particular case but also as generally so unreliable that it should be ignored. If the jury may make up its mind about future dangerousness unaided by psychiatric testimony, jurors should not be barred from hearing the views of the State's psychiatrists along with opposing views of the defendant's doctors.[5]

Third, petitioner's view mirrors the position expressed in the *amicus* brief of the American Psychiatric Association (APA)[which argued that psychiatrists are not experts at predicting dangerousness].

* * *

[H]owever, [w]e are [not] convinced . . . that the view of the APA should be converted into a constitutional rule barring an entire category of expert testimony. We are not persuaded that such testimony is almost entirely unreliable and that the factfinder and the adversary system will not be competent to uncover, recognize, and take due account of its shortcomings.

The *amicus* does not suggest that there are not other views held by members of the Association or of the profession generally. Indeed, as this case and others indicate, there are those doctors who are quite willing to testify at the sentencing hearing, who think, and will say, that they know what they are talking about, and who expressly disagree with the Association's point of view.[7] Furthermore, their qualifications as experts

---

[5] In this case, no evidence was offered by petitioner at trial to contradict the testimony of Doctors Holbrook and Grigson. Nor is there a contention that, despite petitioner's claim of indigence, the court refused to provide an expert for petitioner. In cases of indigency, Texas law provides for the payment of $500 for "expenses incurred for purposes of investigation and expert testimony." Tex.Code Crim.Proc.Ann., Art. 26.05, § 1(d) (Vernon Supp.1982).

[7] At trial, Dr. Holbrook testified without contradiction that a psychiatrist could predict the future dangerousness of an individual, if given enough background information about the individual. Dr. Grigson obviously held a similar view. At the District Court hearing on the habeas petition, the State called two expert witnesses, Dr. George Parker, a psychologist, and

are regularly accepted by the courts. If they are so obviously wrong and should be discredited, there should be no insuperable problem in doing so by calling members of the Association who are of that view and who confidently assert that opinion in their *amicus* brief. Neither petitioner nor the Association suggests that psychiatrists are always wrong with respect to future dangerousness, only most of the time. Yet the submission is that this category of testimony should be excised entirely from all trials. We are unconvinced, however, at least as of now, that the adversary process cannot be trusted to sort out the reliable from the unreliable evidence and opinion about future dangerousness, particularly when the convicted felon has the opportunity to present his own side of the case.

* * *

JUSTICE BLACKMUN, with whom JUSTICE BRENNAN and JUSTICE MARSHALL join as to Parts I–IV, dissenting... The Court holds that psychiatric testimony about a defendant's future dangerousness is admissible, despite the fact that such testimony is wrong two times out of three. The Court reaches this result—even in a capital case—because, it is said, the testimony is subject to cross-examination and impeachment. In the present state of psychiatric knowledge, this is too much for me. One may accept this in a routine lawsuit for money damages, but when a person's life is at stake—no matter how heinous his offense—a requirement of greater reliability should prevail. In a capital case, the specious testimony of a psychiatrist, colored in the eyes of an impressionable jury by the inevitable untouchability of a medical specialist's words, equates with death itself.

Dr. Richard Koons, a psychiatrist. Both of these doctors agreed that accurate predictions of future dangerousness can be made if enough information is provided; furthermore, they both deemed it highly likely that an individual fitting the characteristics of the one in the Barefoot hypothetical would commit future acts of violence.

* * *

We are aware that many mental health professionals have questioned the usefulness of psychiatric predictions of future dangerousness in light of studies indicating that such predictions are often inaccurate.

... Dr. John Monahan, upon whom one of the State's experts relied as "the leading thinker on this issue," concluded that "the 'best' clinical research currently in existence indicates that *psychiatrists and psychologists are accurate in no more than one out of three predictions of violent behavior over a several-year period among institutionalized populations that had both committed violence in the past . . . and who were diagnosed as mentally ill.*" J. Monahan, The Clinical Prediction of Violent Behavior 47–49 (1981) (emphasis in original).

* * *

All of these professional doubts about the usefulness of psychiatric predictions can be called to the attention of the jury. Petitioner's entire argument, as well as that of Justice Blackmun's dissent, is founded on the premise that a jury will not be able to separate the wheat from the chaff. We do not share in this low evaluation of the adversary process.

I

At the sentencing hearing, the State established that Barefoot had two prior convictions for drug offenses and two prior convictions for unlawful possession of firearms. None of these convictions involved acts of violence. At the guilt stage of the trial, for the limited purpose of establishing that the crime was committed in order to evade police custody, the State had presented evidence that Barefoot had escaped from jail in New Mexico where he was being held on charges of statutory rape and unlawful restraint of a minor child with intent to commit sexual penetration against the child's will. The prosecution also called several character witnesses at the sentencing hearing, from towns in five States. Without mentioning particular examples of Barefoot's conduct, these witnesses testified that Barefoot's reputation for being a peaceable and lawabiding citizen was bad in their respective communities.

Last, the prosecution called Doctors Holbrook and Grigson, whose testimony extended over more than half the hearing. Neither had examined Barefoot or requested the opportunity to examine him. In the presence of the jury, and over defense counsel's objection, each was qualified as an expert psychiatrist witness. Doctor Holbrook detailed at length his training and experience as a psychiatrist, which included a position as chief of psychiatric services at the Texas Department of Corrections. He explained that he had previously performed many "criminal evaluations," and that he subsequently took the post at the Department of Corrections to observe the subjects of these evaluations so that he could "be certain those opinions that [he] had were accurate at the time of trial and pretrial." He then informed the jury that it was "within [his] *capacity as a doctor of psychiatry* to predict the future dangerousness of an individual within a *reasonable medical certainty*," (emphasis supplied), and that he could give "*an expert medical opinion* that would be *within reasonable psychiatric certainty* as to whether or not that individual would be dangerous to the degree that there would be a probability that that person would commit criminal acts of violence in the future that would constitute a continuing threat to society," (emphasis supplied).

Doctor Grigson also detailed his training and medical experience, which, he said, included examination of "between thirty and forty thousand individuals," including 8,000 charged with felonies, and at least 300 charged with murder. He testified that with enough information he would be able to "give *a medical opinion within reasonable psychiatric certainty* as to the psychological or psychiatric makeup of an individual," (emphasis supplied), and that this skill was "particular to the field of psychiatry and not to the average layman."

Each psychiatrist then was given an extended hypothetical question asking him to assume as true about Barefoot the four prior convictions for nonviolent offenses, the bad reputation for being law-abiding in various communities, the New Mexico escape, the events surrounding the murder for which he was on trial and, in Doctor Grigson's case, the New Mexico arrest. On the basis of the hypothetical question, Doctor Holbrook diagnosed Barefoot "within a reasonable psychiatr[ic] certainty," as a "criminal sociopath." He testified that he knew of no treatment that could change this condition, and that the condition would not change for the better but "may become accelerated" in the next few years. Finally, Doctor Holbrook testified that, "within reasonable psychiatric certainty," there was "a probability that the Thomas A. Barefoot in that hypothetical will commit criminal acts of violence in the future that would constitute a continuing threat to society," and that his opinion would not change if the "society" at issue was that within Texas prisons rather than society outside prison.

Doctor Grigson then testified that, on the basis of the hypothetical question, he could diagnose Barefoot "within reasonable psychiatric certainty" as an individual with "a fairly classical, typical, sociopathic personality disorder." He placed Barefoot in the "most severe category" of sociopaths (on a scale of one to ten, Barefoot was "above ten"), and stated that there was no known cure for the condition. Finally, Doctor Grigson testified that whether Barefoot was in society at large or in a prison society there was a *"one hundred percent and absolute"* chance that Barefoot would commit future acts of criminal violence that would constitute a continuing threat to society. (emphasis supplied).

On cross-examination, defense counsel questioned the psychiatrists about studies demonstrating that psychiatrists' predictions of future dangerousness are inherently unreliable. Doctor Holbrook indicated his familiarity with many of these studies but stated that he disagreed with their conclusions. Doctor Grigson stated that he was not familiar with most of these studies, and that their conclusions were accepted by only a "small minority group" of psychiatrists—"[i]t's not the American Psychiatric Association that believes that."

After an hour of deliberation, the jury answered "yes" to the two statutory questions, and Thomas Barefoot was sentenced to death.

II

* * *

The American Psychiatric Association (APA), participating in this case as *amicus curiae,* informs us that "[t]he unreliability of psychiatric predictions of long-term future dangerousness is by now an established fact within the profession." The APA's best estimate is that *two out of three* predictions of long-term future violence made by psychiatrists are wrong. The Court does not dispute this proposition, and indeed it could not do so; the evidence is overwhelming.

*   *   *

Neither the Court nor the State of Texas has cited a single reputable scientific source contradicting the unanimous conclusion of professionals in this field that psychiatric predictions of long-term future violence are wrong more often than they are right.[2]

The APA also concludes, as do researchers that have studied the issue, that psychiatrists simply have no expertise in predicting long-term future dangerousness. A layman with access to relevant statistics can do at least as well and possibly better; psychiatric training is not relevant to the factors that validly can be employed to make such predictions, and psychiatrists consistently err on the side of overpredicting violence. Thus, while Doctors Grigson and Holbrook were presented by the State and by self-proclamation as experts at predicting future dangerousness, the scientific literature makes crystal clear that they had no expertise whatever. Despite their claims that they were able to predict Barefoot's future behavior "within reasonable psychiatric certainty," or to a "one hundred percent and absolute" certainty, there was in fact no more than a one in three chance that they were correct.

*   *   *

III

A

Despite its recognition that the testimony at issue was probably wrong and certainly prejudicial, the Court holds this testimony admissible because the Court is "unconvinced . . . that the adversary process cannot be trusted to sort out the reliable from the unreliable evidence and opinion about future dangerousness." One can only wonder how juries are to separate valid from invalid expert opinions when the "experts" themselves are so obviously unable to do so. Indeed, the evidence suggests that juries are not effective at assessing the validity of scientific evidence. Giannelli, Scientific Evidence, 80 Colum.L.Rev., [1197], 1239–1240, and n. 319 (1980).

There can be no question that psychiatric predictions of future violence will have an undue effect on the ultimate verdict. Even judges tend to accept psychiatrists' recommendations about a defendant's dangerousness with little regard for cross-examination or other testimony. Cocozza & Steadman, *supra* n. 2, 25 Soc.Probs., at 271 (in making involuntary commitment decisions, psychiatric predictions of future dangerousness accepted in 86.7% of cases). There is every reason to believe that inexperienced jurors will be still less capable of

---

[2]   Among the many other studies reaching this conclusion are APA Task Force Report, Clinical Aspects of the Violent Individual 28 (1974) (90% error rate "[u]nfortunately . . . is the state of the art") (APA, Clinical Aspects)[.]

"separat[ing] the wheat from the chaff," despite the Court's blithe assumption to the contrary. The American Bar Association has warned repeatedly that sentencing juries are particularly incapable of dealing with information relating to "the likelihood that the defendant will commit other crimes," and similar predictive judgments. Relying on the ABA's conclusion, the joint opinion announcing the judgment in *Gregg v. Georgia,* 428 U.S., at 192, 96 S.Ct., at 2934, recognized that "[s]ince the members of a jury will have had little, if any, previous experience in sentencing, they are unlikely to be skilled in dealing with the information they are given." But the Court in this case, in its haste to praise the jury's ability to find the truth, apparently forgets this well-known and worrisome shortcoming.

As if to suggest that petitioner's position that unreliable expert testimony should be excluded is unheard of in the law, the Court relies on the proposition that the rules of evidence generally "anticipate that relevant, unprivileged evidence should be admitted and its weight left to the factfinder, who would have the benefit of cross-examination and contrary evidence by the opposing party." But the Court simply ignores hornbook law that, despite the availability of cross-examination and rebuttal witnesses, "opinion evidence is not admissible if the court believes that the state of the pertinent art or scientific knowledge does not permit a reasonable opinion to be asserted." Because it is feared that the jury will overestimate its probative value, polygraph evidence, for example, almost invariably is excluded from trials despite the fact that, at a conservative estimate, an experienced polygraph examiner can detect truth or deception correctly about 80 to 90 percent of the time. Ennis & Litwack, *supra* n. 2, at 736. In no area is purportedly "expert" testimony admitted for the jury's consideration where it cannot be demonstrated that it is correct more often than not. "It is inconceivable that a judgment could be considered an 'expert' judgment when it is less accurate than the flip of a coin." *Id.,* at 737. The risk that a jury will be incapable of separating "scientific" myth from reality is deemed unacceptably high.

B

The Constitution's mandate of reliability, with the stakes at life or death, precludes reliance on cross-examination and the opportunity to present rebuttal witnesses as an antidote for this distortion of the truth-finding process. Cross-examination is unlikely to reveal the fatuousness of psychiatric predictions because such predictions often rest, as was the case here, on psychiatric categories and intuitive clinical judgments not susceptible to cross-examination and rebuttal. Psychiatric categories have little or no demonstrated relationship to violence, and their use often obscures the unimpressive statistical or intuitive bases for prediction. The APA particularly condemns the use of the diagnosis employed by Doctors Grigson and Holbrook in this case, that of sociopathy:

"In this area confusion reigns. The psychiatrist who is not careful can mislead the judge or jury into believing that a person has a major mental disease simply on the basis of a description of prior criminal behavior. Or a psychiatrist can mislead the court into believing that an individual is devoid of conscience on the basis of a description of criminal acts alone.... The profession of psychiatry has a responsibility to avoid inflicting this confusion upon the courts and to spare the defendant the harm that may result.... Given our uncertainty about the implications of the finding, the diagnosis of sociopathy ... should not be used to justify or to support predictions of future conduct. There is no certainty in this area." Draft Report 30.

It is extremely unlikely that the adversary process will cut through the facade of superior knowledge. The Chief Justice long ago observed:

"The very nature of the adversary system ... complicates the use of scientific opinion evidence, particularly in the field of psychiatry. This system of partisan contention, of attack and counterattack, at its best is not ideally suited to developing an accurate portrait or profile of the human personality, especially in the area of abnormal behavior. Although under ideal conditions the adversary system can develop for a jury most of the necessary fact material for an adequate decision, such conditions are rarely achieved in the courtrooms in this country. These ideal conditions would include a highly skilled and experienced trial judge and highly skilled lawyers on both sides of the case, all of whom in addition to being well-trained in the law and in the techniques of advocacy would be sophisticated in matters of medicine, psychiatry, and psychology. It is far too rare that all three of the legal actors in the cast meet these standards." Burger, Psychiatrists, Lawyers, and the Courts, 28 Fed.Prob. 3, 6 (June 1964).

* * *

Nor is the presentation of psychiatric witnesses on behalf of the defense likely to remove the prejudicial taint of misleading testimony by prosecution psychiatrists. No reputable expert would be able to predict with confidence that the defendant will *not* be violent; at best, the witness will be able to give his opinion that all predictions of dangerousness are unreliable. Consequently, the jury will not be presented with the traditional battle of experts with opposing views on the ultimate question. Given a choice between an expert who says that he can predict with certainty that the defendant, whether confined in prison or free in society, will kill again, and an expert who says merely that no such prediction can be made, members of the jury charged by law with making the prediction surely will be tempted to opt for the expert who claims he can help them in performing their duty, and who predicts dire consequences if the defendant is not put to death.[13]

Moreover, even at best, the presentation of defense psychiatrists will convert the death sentence hearing into a battle of experts, with the Eighth Amendment's well-established requirement of individually focused sentencing a certain loser. The jury's attention inevitably will turn from an assessment of the propriety of sentencing to death the defendant before it to resolving a scientific dispute about the capabilities of psychiatrists to predict future violence. In such an atmosphere, there is every reason to believe that the jury may be distracted from its constitutional responsibility to consider "particularized mitigating factors," in passing on the defendant's future dangerousness.

* * *

IV

* * *

The Court . . . errs in suggesting that the exclusion of psychiatrists' predictions of future dangerousness would be contrary to the logic of *Jurek. Jurek* merely upheld Texas' substantive decision to condition the death sentence upon proof of a probability that the defendant will commit criminal acts of violence in the future. Whether the evidence offered by the prosecution to prove that probability is so unreliable as to violate a capital defendant's rights to due process is an entirely different matter, one raising only questions of fair procedure.

* * *

It makes sense to exclude psychiatric predictions of future violence while admitting lay testimony, because psychiatric predictions appear to come from trained mental health professionals, who purport to have special expertise. In view of the total scientific groundlessness of these predictions, psychiatric testimony is fatally misleading. Lay testimony, frankly based on statistical factors with demonstrated correlations to violent behavior, would not raise this substantial threat of unreliable and

[handwritten margin note: expert testimony here is misleading]

---

[13] "Although jurors may treat mitigating psychiatric evidence with skepticism, they may credit psychiatric evidence demonstrating aggravation. Especially when jurors' sensibilities are offended by a crime, they may seize upon evidence of dangerousness to justify an enhanced sentence." [George] Dix, [Expert Prediction Testimony in Capital Sentencing: Evidentiary and Constitutional Considerations, 19 Am.Crim.L.Rev. 1,] 43 n. 215 (1981). Thus, the danger of jury deference to expert opinions is particularly acute in death penalty cases. Expert testimony of this sort may permit juries to avoid the difficult and emotionally draining personal decisions concerning rational and just punishment. *Id.,* at 46. Doctor Grigson himself has noted both the superfluousness and the misleading effect of his testimony:

"'I think you could do away with the psychiatrist in these cases. Just take any man off the street, show him what the guy's done, and most of these things are so clearcut he would say the same things I do. But I think the jurors feel a little better when a psychiatrist says it— somebody that's supposed to know more than they know.'" Bloom, Killers and Shrinks, Texas Monthly 64, 68 (July 1978) (quoting Doctor Grigson).

capricious sentencing decisions, inimical to the constitutional standards established in our cases; and such predictions are as accurate as any a psychiatrist could make.

* * *

QUESTIONS AND COMMENTS

1. *Evidentiary analysis*. In arriving at their conclusions, both the majority and the dissent in *Barefoot* seem to structure their analysis primarily around the federal rules of evidence, which at the time focused on balancing relevance against prejudicial impact and on whether the expert testimony might assist the factfinder. The central arguments are over whether the jury will be able to "separate the wheat from the chaff" and whether psychiatrists can add anything to what the jury could figure out for itself. Dix, on the other hand, suggested applying the *Frye* rule in this context and concluded that, under this analysis, clinical prediction testimony should generally be excluded. George Dix, *Expert Prediction Testimony in Capital Sentencing: Evidentiary and Constitutional Considerations*, 19 Am. Crim.L.Rev. 1, 19–21 (1981). Based on practice at the time *Barefoot* was decided, do you agree with Dix that prediction testimony is not "generally accepted"? (After reading the notes below, answer this question again in light of what professionals now know about risk assessment.) What is the relevant group for determining whether violence predictions meet with general acceptance in the psychiatric field: The APA? Forensic clinicians such as Grigson and Holbrook? Does the answer depend on whether the expert merely identifies "risk factors" or instead reaches the types of conclusions that Grigson did? What would have been the outcome in *Barefoot* if *Barefoot* had been a federal case and *Daubert/Kumho Tire* had already been decided? At least one lower court has held that *Daubert* does not require re-analysis of the *Barefoot* holding, calling any objection to clinical prediction testimony "frivolous." *Johnson v. Cockrell*, 306 F.3d 249, 254 (5th Cir. 2002).

2. *Prediction testimony in other settings*. Many commentators have argued that clinical prediction testimony should be barred not just from capital sentencing proceedings but from other proceedings as well. Even before *Barefoot,* however, the courts had been reticent about adopting such a position in capital cases, much less in other types of cases. See *People v. Murtishaw,* 29 Cal.3d 733, 767–75, 175 Cal.Rptr. 738, 758–63, 631 P.2d 446, 466–71 (1981). One court did prohibit clinical prediction testimony in civil commitment proceedings. *In re Wilson,* 33 Crim.L.Rep. (BNA) 2115 (D.C.Super.Ct. Apr. 14, 1983). But it stood alone and now, presumably, is nullified by *Barefoot.*

The majority in *Barefoot* states that a different holding "would immediately call into question those other contexts in which predictions of future behavior are constantly made." Does it make sense to say, as Justice Blackmun seems to be saying in his dissent, that clinical prediction testimony is too inaccurate for capital proceedings but is permissible in other proceedings, such as civil commitments? Within a particular setting (e.g., capital sentencing), does it make sense to bar clinical prediction testimony, but allow clinical testimony on normality and responsibility issues (which also are relevant at capital sentencing[f])?

3. *The accuracy of dangerousness assessments.* The Court quotes Professor Monahan to the effect that, at best, clinical predictions of dangerousness are accurate no more than one out of three times. This statement needs to be looked at more closely from at least four different perspectives.

(a) New Research. At the time that Professor Monahan authored his monograph, much of the literature on violence prediction focused on the "false positive" rate, that is, the rate at which a person who actually turned out to be nonviolent was predicted to be violent. This terminology is used to emphasize the percentage of people who may be wrongfully sentenced to death or confined if decisions are based on dangerousness predictions. Putting Monahan's summary of the research in these terms, the "best" false positive rate obtained by clinical prediction studies has been around 66%. Some studies have found false positive rates as high as 92%. See Ernest Wenk & Robert Emrich, *Assaultive Youth: An Exploratory Study of the Assaultive Experience and Assaultive Potential of California Youth Authority Wards*, 9 J. Res. Crime & Delinq. 171 (1972).

Subsequent research on violence risk assessment has used more sophisticated predictive approaches that more accurately depict the performance of risk assessment methods in predicting violence. These statistical methods include the use of receiver operating characteristic (ROC) analysis to quantify the relative costs or evils of false positive predictions (predictions of violence that turn out to be wrong) and false negative predictions (predictions of nonviolence that turn out to be wrong). Rather than asking how often predictions are right or wrong, ROC analysis asks, "If we randomly select one person from the violent group and one person from the nonviolent group, what is the probability that the prediction method will assign a higher probability of violence to the actually violent person?" Recent studies show that the answer is "65 to 80 percent of the time." Douglas Mossman, *Evaluating Risk Assessments Using Receiver Operating Characteristic Analysis: Rationale, Advantages, Insights, and Limitations*, 31 Behav.Sci.Law 23 (2013).

In the involuntary hospitalization context, mental health professionals tend to favor false positive predictions and to minimize false negative predictions, believing that letting a patient do someone harm is far worse than treating someone who is ill but who would not have harmed anyone. The result is that if mental health professionals' judgments of high violence risk

---

f   For instance, the Model Penal Code's capital sentencing statute specifies as a mitigating circumstance the fact that, at the time of the murder, "the capacity of the defendant to appreciate the criminality [wrongfulness] of his conduct or to conform his conduct to the requirements of law was impaired as a result of mental disease or defect or intoxication." § 210.6(3)(g).

are equated with "predictions" of violence, false positive rates remain high, though not always as high as in studies discussed above. Vivenne de Vogel & Corinne de Ruiter, *Structured Professional Judgment of Violence Risk in Forensic Clinical Practice*, 12 Psychology, Crime & L. 321 (2006) (36% false positive rate for those predicted to be "high risk"); John Monahan et al., *An Actuarial Model of Violence Risk Assessment for Persons with Mental Disorders*, 56 Psychiatric Serv. 810, 814 (2005) (51%); Charles Lidz et al., The Accuracy of Predictions of Violence to Others, 269 J.Amer.Med.Ass. 1007 (1993)(47%); Jay Apperson et al., *Short–Term Clinical Prediction of Assaultive Behavior: Artifacts of Research Methods*, 150 Am. J. Psychiat. 1374 (1993)(25%); Deidre Klassen & William O'Connor, *A Prospective Study of Predictors of Violence in Adult Male Mental Patients*, 12 Law and Human Behavior 143 (1988)(40%). To be reliable under *Daubert* or generally accepted under *Frye*, should prediction testimony be based on a methodology that avoids high false positive rates? If so, what should the cut-off be: 50%, 25%, 5%? Should the answer to the latter question depend on the standard of proof that must be met (beyond a reasonable doubt, clear and convincing evidence, preponderance of the evidence)? Or should the prediction testimony always be admissible, as long as error rate information is available for the factfinder? Should the answer depend on the type of violence predicted?

(b) Methodological Problems. To some extent, false positive findings may be attributable to factors other than poor predictive capabilities. Most of the older research and some of the newer studies rely on police or hospital records to determine whether a person predicted to be violent subsequently was so. But such records notoriously underreport the amount of violent acts committed, some suggest by a factor of ten. Paul Meehl, *The Insanity Defense*, Minn. Psychol. 11, 15 (Summer, 1983). Thus, a number of the supposed "false positives" may simply be undiscovered "true positives" (i.e., individuals correctly predicted to be dangerous). As Monahan has suggested, it is possible that those who were arrested committed many of the unreported and unsolved crimes; if this is true, then the false positive rates may not be as grossly overstated as Meehl claims. John Monahan, The Clinical Prediction of Violent Behavior 52–56 (NIMH 1981). Many of the newer studies try to avoid this problem by relying on self-reports of crime or making clear that the risk assessment scheme is meant to predict only re-arrest or reconviction rates; the false positive rates in these studies are probably more accurate.

A second methodological problem with some of the research on dangerousness results from the difficulty of conducting "natural experiments" involving release of persons designated as dangerous into the community. That is, the usual response to a prediction of dangerousness, if one occurs, is to institutionalize, not release, the person thought to be violence-prone. Thus the clinical prediction that someone will be dangerous *in the community* is tested by reference to whether the person considered dangerous is assaultive *in the institution*. Because institutionalization and treatment may seriously curb the individual's assaultive behavior, the false positive rates reported in studies that use institutional violence as a criterion for violence may be significantly exaggerated. See George Dix, *Clinical Evaluation of the*

"Dangerousness" of "Normal" Criminal Defendants, 66 Va.L.Rev. 523, 544 n. 82 (1980). Even those studies that use violence in the community as the criterion variable are tainted by the fact that, once a prediction of violence is made, institutionalization and/or treatment almost always takes place before the individual returns to the community. Some of the newer studies redress this problem by following prisoners or patients after release.

(c) Base Rates. Even relatively high false positive rates do not mean that overall predictive validity is poor, given the low "base rate" for violence in most populations. The following excerpt explains why:

> [W]hen, as is usually the case, the truly violent population is quite small compared to the nonviolent population (i.e., when there is a low "base rate" for violence), even prediction methods that are highly valid will generate large numbers of false-positive errors. A brief example illustrates this phenomenon. Assume that in a population of 1,000 subjects, 15% (n = 150) will commit a violent act and 85% (n = 850) will not. Assume also that the clinician can accurately classify 90% of each group. In this example, the clinician will accurately label as violent 135 (150 × .90) truly violent individuals, whereas only 85 cases labeled "violent" (850 × .10) will be persons who on follow-up in fact will not be violent. Thus, the percent-false-positive figure will be a relatively respectable 39% (85/(135 + 85). As the incidence of violence gets smaller, however, this error rate increases. If, for instance, the incidence of violence in the 1,000–person population is only 5%, the same clinician (with the same accuracy rate of 90%) will have a false-positive rate of 68% (95/(45 + 95)).

Gary Melton et al., Psychological Evaluations for the Courts: A Handbook for Mental Health Professionals and Lawyers 302–03 (3d ed.2007).

(d) Coin-flipping and chance. Assuming psychiatric predictions of dangerousness are at best correct only one out of three times, Justice Blackmun claims that such predictions yield results that are less accurate than flipping a coin. The coin flipping analogy, first made by Bruce Ennis and Thomas Litwack in *Psychiatry and the Presumption of Expertise: Flipping Coins in the Courtroom*, 62 Calif.L.Rev. 693 (1974), is seriously misleading to the extent it suggests that clinical predictions are no better than "chance." To discover why this is so, one must first determine the "base rate" for violent behavior among the population being evaluated for dangerousness. For instance, say that the base rate for violence in the general population is roughly one out of 300, meaning that only one person out of every 300 in the general population will commit a violent act in his or her lifetime. If mental health professionals could predict accurately one-third of the time who was dangerous in the general population, their predictions would be much better than chance, specifically *100 times* better than a random selection from amongst the population. The populations involved in the research to which Monahan refers were usually institutionalized patients or criminals and tended to have a much higher base rate for violence than the general population, in the vicinity of one out of nine, rather than one out of 300. But a

predictive accuracy ratio of one out of three for such a population would still be three times better than chance. This predictive ratio would be worse than chance only for a population with a base rate for violence higher than one out of three. Thus, the coin-flipping analogy would appear to be inapt. See Christopher Slobogin, *Dangerousness and Expertise*, 133 Pa.L.Rev. 97, 110–14 (1984).

More recent research has confirmed that mental health professionals "offer predictions that are more accurate than would occur by chance, suggesting that they have some predictive power or ability," at least when the concept of "dangerousness" is "broadly conceived (i.e., threatening behavior and/or physically assaultive behavior)." Randy Otto, *Prediction of Dangerous Behavior: A Review and Analysis of 'Second–Generation' Research*, 5 Forensic Reports 103 (1992); see also, Charles Lidz et al., *The Accuracy of Predictions of Violence to Others*, 269 J.Amer.Med.Ass. 1007, 1010 (1993)("Not only did the clinicians pick out a statistically more violent group, but the violence that the predicted group committed was more serious than the acts of the comparison group"); Douglas Mossman, *Assessing Predictions of Violence: Being Accurate About Accuracy*, 62(4) J. Consulting & Clinical Psychology 783 (1994) ("This article's re-evaluation of representative data from the past two decades suggests that clinicians are able to distinguish violent from non-violent persons with a modest, better-than-chance level of accuracy."); Douglas Mossman, *Critique of Pure Risk Assessment, or Kant Meets* Tarasoff, 75 Cincinnati.L.Rev. 523, 549–567 (2006) (describing and explaining improvements in evaluating accuracy). Do these data (showing that expert predictions are far superior to chance) mean that dangerousness predictions are "reliable," as that word is used in *Daubert* and the amended version of Rule 702? Are they at least "relevant," which the Federal Rules of Evidence defines as "any tendency to make the existence of any fact that is of consequence to the determination of the action more probable or less probable than it would be without the evidence"? Rule 401. In the death penalty context, does it matter that, as Drs. Otto and Mossman note in the above-cited articles, the better-than-chance predictions focus on threatening or assaultive behavior, not homicide?

4. *Diagnosis and dangerousness*. Relevant both to predictive accuracy and to whether mental health professionals possess "specialized knowledge" about violence-proneness is the extent to which certain diagnoses can be viewed as indicative of dangerousness. The state's psychiatrists in *Barefoot* diagnosed Barefoot as a "sociopath." This diagnosis, often used interchangeably with "psychopathy," describes people who lack empathy, have shallow emotions, and feel no accountability for their actions. It is analogous to, but not congruent with, the DSM–5 diagnosis of antisocial personality disorder (see Appendix A). Forensic clinicians have often correlated all three of these diagnoses with dangerousness. For instance, Dr. Grigson, who testified for the state of Texas in scores of death penalty sentencing proceedings (and, as a result, was dubbed "Dr. Death" by the

media[g]), usually coupled his prediction that the defendant would be violent with a diagnosis of sociopathy.

There is significant research supporting such a correlation. See generally Liselotte Pedersen et al., *Psychopathy as a Risk Factor for Violent Recidivism*, 9 Int'l J. Forensic Mental Health 308 (2010) ("A robust relationship has been established between psychopathy and violence, and in the process of violence risk assessment psychopathy is considered an essential concept."). A highly studied "Psychopathy Checklist" yields ratings on 20 scales having to do with behavioral traits and historical features; a score of 30 or higher (out of 40) is probably indicative of psychopathy and considered a good indicator of risk. Robert Hare et al., *The Revised Psychopathy Checklist: Reliability and Factor Structure*, 2 Psychological Assessment: Journal of Consulting & Clinical Psychology 338 (1990). The primary author of this checklist has argued that "psychopathy is the single most important clinical construct in the criminal justice system, with particularly strong implications for the assessment of risk for recidivism and violence." Robert Hare, *The Hare PCL–R: Some Issues Concerning Its Use and Misuse*, 3 Legal & Criminol. Psychol. 99 (1998).

The evidence concerning the usefulness of other diagnoses in determining dangerousness is mixed, although it appears that serious mental illness may be correlated with a somewhat increased risk of violence. More is said about the relationship between violence and serious mental illness in Chapter Eight (see pp. 821–824).

5.   *Alternatives to clinical prediction testimony.* In his dissent in *Barefoot,* Justice Blackmun contended that "[l]ay testimony, frankly based on statistical factors with demonstrated correlations to violent behavior" could competently fill the gap created by prohibiting psychiatric testimony on dangerousness. Testimony "based on statistical factors" may have its own set of evidentiary problems, depending upon how it is implemented. Consider the following materials.

UNITED STATES V. BARNETTE

United States Court of Appeals, Fourth Circuit, 2000.
211 F.3d 803.

[Aquilia Barnette was charged with killing Donald Allen and Robin Williams. Three months before the murders, Williams had ended her relationship with Barnette and moved to the apartment of Benjamin Greene because she was scared of being alone. Two months before the murders, Barnette came to Greene's house, smashed the windows of Greene's car with a baseball bat and, when he saw Williams in the

---

g   See Time, June 1, 1981, at 64. In 1995, Dr. Grigson was expelled from the American Psychiatric Association and the Texas Society of Psychiatric Physicians for ethics violations relating to his court predictions of "future dangerousness." Jeffrey L. Kirchmeier, *Aggravating and Mitigating Factors: The Paradox of Today's Arbitrary and Mandatory Capital Punishment Scheme*, 6 Wm. & Mary Bill Rts. J. 345, 372 (1998).

window, began breaking the building's windows and threw a firebomb into the apartment. Williams and Greene escaped, although Williams was badly burned. Two months later, having evaded arrest, Barnette approached Allen (whom he apparently did not know) while Allen was in his car, aimed a shotgun at him, ordered him out, and shot him three times in the back. He then drove Allen's car to the home of Williams' mother, where he knew Williams' was staying since leaving Green's apartment. There he stated he was going to kill her and himself. When Williams ran away he shot her twice, killing her. He then escaped, but turned himself in two days later. He confessed to both crimes, was convicted of capital murder and sentenced to death. One of the aggravating factors that was considered by the jury was future dangerousness. To prove that factor, the government relied on Dr. Scott Duncan, who testified that Barnette would be "a future danger in prison" based on three factors: his high score on the Psychopathy Checklist Revised; research on predicting future dangerousness; and an actuarial analysis comparing Barnette to groups of people with characteristics similar to him. Dr. Duncan found that Barnette was likely to be violent in the future. Barnette challenged the admissibility of this testimony.]

Barnette claims as inadmissible Dr. Duncan's testimony relying on the Psychopathy Checklist Revised because it was not evaluated for reliability as required by *Daubert v. Merrell Dow Pharmaceuticals.* Barnette argues that the Psychopathy Checklist Revised is unreliable because it has not been standardized with respect to black inmates, and Dr. Duncan improperly used race, wealth, age, and sex to support his opinion that Barnette was a psychopath. . . . In *Daubert*, the Supreme Court radically changed the standard for admissibility of scientific testimony. Instead of requiring that the scientific community generally accept scientific evidence before a court could admit it, the Court set out a looser, two-step gatekeeping function that a trial court must perform when evaluating the admissibility of all expert testimony. The trial judge must ensure that the evidence is based on scientific knowledge, or is reliable, and ensure that the evidence will assist the trier of fact, or is relevant. The Court provided four factors that could be used in this evaluation, but stressed its determination that the analysis should be flexible. The Court also noted that "[v]igorous cross examination, presentation of contrary evidence and careful instruction on the burden of proof are traditional and appropriate means of attacking shaky but admissible evidence." The *Daubert* test's gatekeeping requirement is to ensure that the expert witness in question in the courtroom employs the same level of intellectual vigor that characterizes the practice of an expert in the relevant field. *Kumho Tire Co.* When making this determination, the trial judge must have considerable leeway in both his reliability determination and the means he uses to conduct it. We have consistently given the trial judge's decision on whether to admit expert testimony under *Daubert* great deference. However, we must reverse if there is a clear error in judgment on the part of the district court.

While Barnette essentially alleges that the district court made an improper initial determination that the Psychopathy Checklist Revised was reliable scientific evidence, he does not contest its relevancy. When deciding whether to admit the testimony based on the Psychopathy Checklist Revised, the court considered Barnette's objections to the test, that the list had not been standardized as to the black population (Barnette is black) or as to the post middle-age population. Barnette offered two articles written by his own expert, Dr. Cunningham, to support his position, but no other evidence. On this record, the decision to admit the evidence was not a clear error of judgment. Taking into account the discretion afforded the district court's decision, we are of opinion that its examination of the issue was sufficient and that the record does not support a determination that admitting the evidence was an abuse of discretion. . . . Here, Barnette only proffered two articles written by his expert, Dr. Cunningham, as evidence disputing the scientific validity of the Psychopathy Checklist Revised. He did not, at that time, proffer any other evidence of unreliability. In our opinion, that evidence alone is not sufficient to show unreliability when an expert in the field did rely on that type of testing. Absent evidence indicating more than such a disagreement between professionals, we do not believe the district court needed to go further to evaluate reliability.

Finally, Barnette argues that Dr. Duncan's opinion that Barnette is a psychopath rests on impermissible factors: race, age, and poverty. We find no merit in this argument. Dr. Duncan used 20 characteristics in his evaluation of Barnette under the Psychopathy Checklist Revised, in addition to the 11 characteristics he used in his future dangerousness prediction, three of which were race, age, and poverty. Barnette does not offer sufficient reasons for us to believe that Dr. Duncan's entire opinion was based only on these three factors, and not upon all the other factors combined. Additionally, Dr. Duncan utilized several other bases for his diagnosis of psychopathy and future dangerousness: the Diagnostic and Statistical Manual, Fourth Edition; his observations of Barnette's behavior; the actuarial approach; and the research on predicting future dangerousness. Under these circumstances, we do not find that Dr. Duncan based his opinion on impermissible factors. . . .

QUESTIONS AND COMMENTS

1.   Daubert *analysis and actuarial prediction.* Is the Court correct in stating that *Daubert* established "a looser analysis" than *Frye*? Is it correct in requiring Barnette to prove the unreliability of the PCL–R, rather than requiring the state to demonstrate its reliability?

In terms of determining reliability under *Daubert*, how much weight should be given to Barnette's argument that the PCL–R was not standardized with African Americans or people who are past middle age (both attributes of Barnette)? Should it matter whether the PCL–R has been normed on populations in prison? In fact, among prediction instruments, the PCL–R is one of the most heavily researched, and it has demonstrated fairly good generalizability to various populations. But consider this statement about actuarial instruments in general:

> [F]ailure to scientifically cross-validate RAIs [risk assessment instruments] can be fatal because characteristics of offender populations can vary dramatically, and an RAI constructed on one population may not generalize, or cross over, to a different population. . . . The problem presented by population demographics, or cohort characteristics, is vast and potentially insurmountable: Does an RAI derived from a study comprised of a cohort that included convicted rapists generalize to those offenders diagnosed with pedophilia? Is an instrument that excluded from its construction sample noncoercive incest offenders useful in evaluating risk in offenders with a history of noncoercive incest? Elusive as the answers to these questions may be, many scientists and professionals assert that without appropriate, scientifically scrutinized cross-validation, absolute risk predictions based upon RAI scores are meaningless.

Donna Cropp Bechman, *Sex Offender Civil Commitments: Scientists or Psychics?* 16 Crim. J. 24, 29 (2001). The same author makes additional points about the "inter-rater" reliability of risk assessments instruments.

> "[I]nter-rater reliability" is an important part of the development of any testing procedure, including RAIs, yet little is published in peer review literature that establishes whether or not these instruments have been appropriately evaluated for reliability when used by different raters in the field. Although the concept of assigning a weighted score to a risk factor, adding up the numbers, and achieving a quantification provided by mathematical calculation may sound fairly objective in nature, and, therefore, not easily the subject of inconsistencies among raters, nothing could be farther from the truth. Even the very definition of "offense" differs from instrument to instrument. Where one instrument intends by the use of the word "offense" to have the rater take into account offenses charged regardless of conviction, another instrument defines the word "offense" as only that which resulted in conviction. And is a conviction for an attempted sex offense sufficient? What if the conviction is for burglary, but the underlying intent was to commit a rape? If the conviction was later overturned on appeal due to error in the trial court, is it still a conviction? Are all raters in the field answering these questions consistently for each instrument? Are all raters aware that most instruments do not intend to include in their calculations self-reported offenses that never result in a charge or conviction?

Id. Some research confirms that experts often disagree on how to score an individual's risk level using actuarial instruments, not only when they are on different sides, but even when they are on the same side. Marcus T. Boccaccini et al., *Do PCL–R Scores from State or Defense Experts Best Predict Future Misconduct Among Civilly Committed Sex Offenders?*, 36 Law Hum.Behav. 159 (2012). In terms of admissibility analysis, should it matter that this type of information on problems with cross-validation and inter-rater reliability may be difficult for juries to understand?[h]

2. *Admissible statistical factors.* The court finds nothing wrong with relying on race, age and poverty in making predictions. Do you agree? Is the use of race to make predictions a violation of the equal protection clause? Even if it is, does the state nonetheless have a compelling interest in using race as a predictor? What if the use of race improves the accuracy of prediction by 30%?

Whatever the outcome with respect to race as a predictor, use of age or poverty clearly does not violate equal protection principles as long as they have some predictive validity. The Violence Risk Appraisal Guide (VRAG) tells evaluators to look not only at the person's PCL–R score but also at a number of age and personality-related factors, including whether the person was separated from his or her parents before 16, marital status, alcohol abuse history and diagnosis (with a personality disorder diagnosis signaling a greater likelihood of recidivism than a diagnosis of schizophrenia). Are there subconstitutional concerns associated with using factors such as these to make predictions that can result in deprivation of liberty or execution? Some commentators have argued that reliance on "fixed factors over which the individual has no control runs counter to basic traditions of criminal law that stress free will and self-determination" and that "[a] procedure that allows judgements about an individual's blameworthiness to be based on statistical correlations to anonymous prior malefactors is deeply inconsistent with the general principles undergirding our system of law." See Daniel S. Goodman, *Demographic Evidence in Capital Sentencing*, 39 Stanford L. Rev. 499, 525–27 (1987); see also Barbara Underwood, *Law and the Crystal Ball: Predicting Behavior with Statistical Inference and Individualized Judgment*, 88 Yale L.J. 1408, 1436–38 (1979). Are these concerns relevant when the context is commitment, where dangerousness rather than blameworthiness is the central issue? Are they relevant at sentencing, where incapacitation as well as retribution is considered a purpose of punishment? Adopting Goodman's view, Monahan has argued that the only risk factor that one can consider at sentencing (as opposed to civil commitment) is past acts. See John Monahan, *A Jurisprudence of Risk Assessment, Forecasting Harm among Prisoners, Predators, and Patients*, 92 Va. L. Rev. 391, 428 (2006). In practice, this limitation might seriously curtail the accuracy of predictions.

---

[h] Monahan and Walker suggest that at least some statistical information could be relayed via jury instructions. John Monahan & Laurens Walker, *Social Frameworks: A New Use of Social Science in Law*, 73 Va.L.Rev. 559, 592–98 (1987).

3.   *Structured professional judgment instruments.* A hybrid between actuarial risk assessment instruments and clinical prediction is an assessment technique known as "structured professional judgment" (SPJ). Actuarial instruments rely on empirical discovery of factors associated with recidivism, which are then weighted and combined according to an algorithm that produces recidivism probability estimates. SPJ looks at the same or similar risk categories, but delves more deeply into each factor (e.g., the duration and intensity of the person's alcohol abuse and the relevance of it to his or her particular violence potential). Although evaluators might assign scores for each factor as well as compute a combined score, neither score is usually associated with a particular probability estimate; rather based on the number of risk factors and the extent to which intervention is needed to minimize them, evaluators arrive at a conclusion as to whether risk in the absence of intervention is "high," "moderate" or "low." However, researchers have studied the relationship between composite SPJ scores and recidivism; indeed, although the PCL–R is probably best classified as a SPJ instrument, as noted above subsequent research has correlated PCL–R scores with recidivism rates. The advantage of structured professional judgment is its greater individualization of the evaluation and its usefulness as a tool for "risk management" (or treatment), not just "risk assessment" (or prediction). See Kevin S. Douglas, *Assessing Risk for Violence Using Structured Professional Judgment*, 14 AP–LS News 1 (Winter, 2009). Possible disadvantages are the ambiguity of designating a person as high, moderate or low risk rather than assigning a precise probability estimate, and a greater variability between evaluators than occurs with actuarial instruments (albeit less variability than occurs with clinical prediction). Should Dr. Duncan have been required to provide a precise probability estimate based on his PCL–R evaluation or, instead, had he offered such an estimate, should the court have barred it as irrelevant or misleading? Consider the following material.

4.   *Comparing clinical and statistical evidence.* Some actuarial instruments purport to identify small groups of individuals who have a very high rate of recidivism. See, e.g., Vernon Quinsey et al., Violent Offenders: Appraising and Managing Risk 148–151 & Fig. 1 (1998) (discussing the VRAG's ability to identify groups of offenders with a 55%, 75% and 95% likelihood of recidivism); John Monahan et al., Rethinking Risk Assessment: The MacArthur Study of Mental Disorder and Violence 127 (2001) (using an "iterative classification tree" actuarial approach, which determines on a "yes/no" basis whether a certain variable is present and then moves to the next branch of the "tree," researchers placed individuals in five risk categories representing risk levels from 1% to 76%). Furthermore, some *probabilities* developed via statistical techniques may be relatively accurate. For example, the probability of violent behavior associated with being a white male opiate user can be fairly reliably ascertained.

Some nonetheless argue that actuarial predictions are inferior to clinical prediction judgments. Consider the following comments:

As an instrument of judicial decisionmaking, [statistical or demographic] evidence is in a very palpable way substantially less 'relevant' to an individual's circumstances than is clinical psychiatric evidence. Unlike demographic studies, psychiatric evaluations are—at least in some sense—mediated through the individual. Clinical and statistical methods differ because "a clinical decisionmaker is not committed in advance of decision to the factors that will be considered and the rule for combining them. He is free to respond to individual differences whose relevance was not anticipated by any rule." Since the clinical approach recognizes the individuality of each defendant, it permits the psychiatrist or psychologist to alter in a particular case the general judgment of actuarial reckoning. . . . The fact that all assessments are to some extent relational—that is, implicitly relative or based upon some unstated empirical assumptions—does not obviate the distinction between judicial methods that focus on the individual and those that are avowedly abstract or generic. And where those generic methods rely on statistics, their potential to mislead the jury outweighs their usefulness.

Goodman, supra, at 525–27.

Goodman asserts that statistical evidence lacks relevance because it is not "individualized," and is prejudicial because it is difficult to rebut and might mislead the factfinder; that is, in attempting to rebut statistical evidence that a white male opiate user with one conviction for violent crime has, say, a one-in-five chance of committing a violent act within the next five years, such a person might find it very difficult to convince the jury that other personal characteristics he possesses place him in the group of white male opiate users who will not commit another violent act within that time period. How is clinical prediction testimony different? As Goodman admits, mental health professionals often rely on "unstated empirical assumptions" about relationships between certain traits (e.g., race, sex and opiate use) and certain behavior (e.g., violent behavior). If these assumptions are "unstated," how is it easier for the individual to rebut them?[i] Is the point that before arriving at a conclusion the clinician will observe all aspects of the individual and thus arrive at a fairer, less "stereotyped" assessment than would a jury hearing only demographic evidence and any rebuttal information the individual cares to present? To what extent do you think this is the case, given what has been discussed about the reasons for variance in clinical assessments?

Some commentators have argued for an "adjusted actuarial" approach to prediction, where the evaluator "begins with an actuarial prediction, but . . . can then adjust (or not) the actuarial prediction after considering potentially important factors that were not included in the actuarial measure." R. Karl Hanson, *What Do We Know About Sex Offender Risk Assessment?* 4

---

[i] Note that in *Barefoot,* Justice Blackmun concluded that psychiatric prediction testimony is difficult to rebut "because such predictions often rest . . . on psychiatric categories and intuitive clinical judgments . . . ; their use often obscures the unimpressive statistical or intuitive bases for prediction."

Psychology, Pub. Pol. & L. 50, 52 (1998). Apparently, this was the type of prediction methodology Dr. Duncan used in *Barnette*. Others, however, have argued that "adjusted" decisions are typically no more accurate and may be less accurate that those made through statistics alone. For instance, one commentary states that "[a]ctuarial methods are too good and clinical judgment too poor to risk contaminating the former with the latter." Quinsey et al., supra, at 171. Whether purely actuarial or SPJ judgments are superior is a matter of ongoing investigation. But suppose Quinsey and colleagues are correct. Should this make SPJ evaluations inadmissible?

Would it be best to prohibit *both* clinical and statistical prediction evidence, permit both, or rely on only one type of evidence? If the latter, which one? Courts have registered decidedly different points of view on the latter issue. Compare *State v. Kienitz*, 221 Wis.2d 275, 585 N.W.2d 609 (App. 1998) (rejecting the argument that only the actuarial method of prediction provides sufficient "precision" to make predictions) with *Massachusetts v. Reese*, 13 Mass. L.Rptr. 195 (2001), rev'd 438 Mass. 519, 781 N.E.2d 1225 (2003) ("while a factfinder may have good reason modestly to adjust a statistical probability based on idiosyncratic clinical information unique to the ... offender, there would need to be a compelling reason to justify a dramatic adjustment to the statistical probability"). Compare also *In re Valdez*, No. 99–000045CI (Fla. 2000) (rejecting actuarial prediction devices such as the VRAG because they are based on scientific principles—i.e., that a prediction can be made solely on the basis of selected items of demographic information, that a scoring system can be devised to capture the relevant information, and that the scoring scheme can apply "to any individual, anywhere, at any time" to yield a prediction—that are not "generally accepted," partly because the only professionals using these devices are the approximately 150 psychologists performing sex offender evaluations), with *State ex rel. Romley v. Fields*, 201 Ariz. 321, 35 P.3d 82 (2001) (holding that actuarial opinion testimony should be not be subject to *Frye* or any other screening test).

5. *Hypothetical questions.* In *Barefoot*, it will be remembered, both Dr. Grigson and Dr. Holbrook (the prosecution's witnesses) testified in answer to "hypothetical" questions. They did not interview Barefoot but rather were given information about his prior record and other aspects of his character and asked to formulate an opinion on that basis. Barefoot argued that use of hypotheticals is unconstitutional, both generally (because they allow testimony not based on personal examination), and in his particular case (because they allowed testimony that was based on controverted facts). The Court rejected these arguments, noting that hypothetical questions have long been in use and that, if the defendant was concerned about the accuracy of their assumptions in his particular case, he could have constructed his own questions using a different version of the facts. 463 U.S. at 903–05, 103 S.Ct. at 3399–3400, 77 L.Ed.2d at 1110–12. How is testimony based on a hypothetical question different from testimony based on statistical evidence? Should the same rule, whether it be admission or exclusion, be adopted for both?

6. *Substantive concerns.* Clearly, predicting future behavior is not easy, no matter which route is taken. Yet, as the majority in *Barefoot* noted, the Court has upheld the use of dangerousness as an aggravating factor in capital cases. *Jurek v. Texas*, 428 U.S. 262, 96 S.Ct. 2950, 49 L.Ed.2d 929 (1976). Should *Jurek* be overturned? Should dangerousness be a criterion in *any* type of legal proceeding? Would it be consistent to jettison dangerousness as a justification for legal intervention, but not abnormality or incompetency? We will revisit these questions in subsequent chapters.

D. COMPETENCY

The "competency paradigm" permeates the law. One must be "competent" to stand trial, plead guilty or make a valid confession. If one is not "competent," a guardian may be appointed to manage one's affairs, treatment may be administered involuntarily, or one's will may be declared void. Courts often asked mental health professionals to help decide competency issues under the implicit or explicit assumption that mental disorder "causes" most, if not all, incompetency; indeed, many statutes require a finding that the incompetency results from mental disorder.

The evidentiary question is whether mental health professionals possess specialized knowledge that can assist the factfinder in answering any or all of the different types of questions raised by the competency issue. This subsection will focus on the mental health profession's expertise with respect to competency to stand trial, because of the relatively greater amount of legal and empirical material on the subject. The commonly accepted legal test in this context consists of two prongs: (1) whether the person is able to assist the attorney in his or her defense; and (2) whether the person understands the nature of the charges and the trial process. In reading the sample competency to stand trial report below, taken from an old case file,[j] consider the extent to which it provides relevant reliable information that helps answer these two questions.

COMPETENCY REPORT

This [27 year old] patient was admitted on eight different occasions to the Broughton Hospital, Morgantown, North Carolina. His first hospitalization was on 28 March 1961 and he was discharged from the last, the eighth hospitalization, on 7 June 1969. His hospital records indicate that during the first few hospitalizations at Broughton it was felt that his main problem was a personality disorder, which was manifested primarily in anti-social behavior and excessive drinking. During the last few hospitalizations at Broughton, however, it has become apparent that this patient is suffering of schizophrenia, he displayed bizarre behavior

---

[j] This sample report is presented and analyzed in Ronald Roesch and Stephen Golding, "Competency to Stand Trial" 83–85 (1980).

and ideations and obviously the patient was delusional. The patient received a variety of different psychiatric treatments, his hospital course was rather unpredictable and also he has escaped a number of different occasions.

The personal past history indicates that he was born in 1942 in Shelby, North Carolina. This patient was reared mostly by his grandparents and there is very little known about his birth and early development. It should be noted that his grandmother and two maternal uncles have been in Broughton Hospital as patients. Apparently he developed properly and at the usual age began school. He stopped his education at age 18 and was in the eleventh grade. It is stated that he has stopped his education on account of earning some money. Shortly after his school he entered the United States Air Force and remained in service for approximately six months. The reason for the separation was his emotional inability to adjust to service life. This patient is described while he was in high school as a <u>fairly well adjusted individual</u> who showed considerable interest in reading. From the age of 16 he <u>began to drink</u>, at times excessively. He has shown very little interest in the opposite sex and never married. Following his short service in the United States Air Force in 1960 this patient began to show disinterest in his environment and was reluctant to assume responsibilities. In 1961 he was hospitalized the first time in Broughton. From here on until the present date this patient has been in and out of the hospital and obviously has shown evidence of a mental disturbance.

On admission the patient appeared to be alert but his affect[k] was rather fixed and at times inappropriate. He was well oriented in time, place and person.[l] He became somewhat confused and tense when he was asked about the circumstances under which he entered this Hospital. He freely admitted to paranoid ideations and pedophilia. Obviously the patient was very preoccupied and there was evidence of dissociation[m] of his thoughts. His hospital course was rather uneventful. On the ward the patient has presented no particular difficulties in his management. It is noted, that he is somewhat neglecting in his appearance and shows little interest in his environment. Generally speaking this patient appears to be tense and the psychomotor activity is somewhat increased.

During the consequent [sic] interviews the patient has expressed a great deal of his delusional system. It appears, that this patient firmly believes about his abilities to determine some individuals' future by looking in the sun. With an inappropriate affect the patient stated, that

---

[k] Emotional demeanor [eds.]

[l] This is standard psychiatric jargon implying that the patient knew the time, where he was, and who he was [eds.]

[m] Usually means distancing oneself from an idea, situation, or object. Not clear what it means here. [eds.]

"you wouldn't understand" just what those signs mean, nevertheless he does and therefore he is a different individual from us.

He gave a rather coherent and detailed account of the incidence [sic] leading to his present charges. The patient stated, that he cannot resist to these impulses although he realizes the wrongness of such. During the interview the patient has become several times confused and irrelevant. He appears to be of above average intelligence and from that standpoint he is fully aware of his present legal situation.

The physical examination on admission revealed a well developed and nourished white male with a scar on the left knee, and otherwise the findings were essentially within normal limits. The laboratory findings were within normal, including a nonreactive VDRL.[n] The skull x-ray revealed a little irregularity at the outer side of the left antral sinus and this might possibly be the result of an old fracture. Otherwise the bony structure was normal and all other findings of the skull x-ray were normal. The chest x-ray was normal. The electroencephalogram was normal.

The psychological testing revealed a full-scale I.Q. of 98, which places this patient in the average intellectual functioning level.

Diagnosis: Schizophrenic Reaction, Chronic, Undifferentiated Type. APA Code: 295–90.

Recommendations: The examination and observations reveals that this patient is subject to a mental disturbance constituting insanity. This condition is manifested primarily in delusional thinking and inability to reason or to exercise proper judgment. This patient is fully aware of the wrongness of his alleged act, however, due to his mental disturbance he was unable to adhere to right and because of his disorganized thinking he is unable to assist in his own defense. He should continue hospitalization for a minimum necessary period of time as provided in G.S. 122–91 and 122–65 as being incompetent to stand trial at this time.

QUESTIONS AND COMMENTS

1.   *The setting for competency determinations.* Adversarial hearings on competency to stand trial are rare. In many jurisdictions, the court making the competency determination usually relies entirely on a report or reports submitted by mental health professionals. Studies show that judges abide by the recommendations in such reports over 90% of the time. W. Neil Gowensmith et al., *Field Reliability of Competence to Stand Trial Opinions: How Often Do Evaluators Agree, and What Do Judges Decide when Evaluators Disagree?* 34 L. & Hum. Beh. 19, 23 (2010) (finding that judges agree with the majority of evaluators 92.7% of the time); Patricia Zapf et al., *Have the Courts Abdicated Their Responsibility for Determinations of*

---

[n]   A test for syphilis. [eds.]

Competency to Clinicians?, 4 J. Forensic Psychol. Practice 27 (2004) (finding in a sample of 328 cases in Alabama that judges agreed with clinical competency reports in all but one case). Should reports like the one above be admissible under these conditions? Are there sufficient facts about the defendant's mental state to aid the court in making a decision? How much of the report is irrelevant and/or prejudicial? Is the report internally consistent?

2.   *Diagnosis and competency.* Like the author of the report, in years past many mental health professionals often equated psychosis (e.g., schizophrenia) with incompetency to stand trial. A. Louis McGarry, *Competency for Trial and Due Process Via the State Hospital*, 122 Am.J.Psychiat. 623 (1965) (100% correlation between psychosis and incompetency finding). But many courts have held that someone who is mentally ill might well be able to meet the relatively undemanding requirements of the competency standard; that is, they might be able to exhibit an understanding of the legal process and a capacity to recount relevant facts and the names of witnesses despite mental disability. See, e.g., *Swisher v. United States,* 237 F.Supp. 921 (W.D.Mo.1965). Based on what you can glean from the above report, do you agree? In any event, is the diagnostic information relevant to the competency issue?

3.   *Competency protocols.* Since the 1960s, mental health professionals have developed structured interviews to help evaluators focus their attention on those aspects of a defendant's knowledge and thinking that are directly relevant to adjudicative competence. Some examples:

- The Georgia Court Competency Test (GCCT) contains 21 items that assess a defendant's factual knowledge about basic criminal court processes and the defendant's specific case. Patricia A. Zapf & Jodi L. Viljoen, *Issues and Considerations Regarding the Use of Assessment Instruments in the Evaluation of Competency to Stand Trial*, 21 Behav. Sci. Law 351, 356 (2003). The protocol has the defendant look at an illustration of a courtroom and point to where major personnel (judge, jury, witness, etc.), then asks about these individuals' functions (e.g., "What does a witness do?"). Subsequent questions inquire about helping the defense attorney, the alleged offense, consequences of being found guilty of the alleged crime, and appropriate courtroom behavior. The test's instructions allow the examiner to assign scores to the defendant's responses. Scores of 70 percent or higher suggest that a defendant has adequate factual knowledge, though it does not necessarily mean that the defendant is competent.

- The Competence Assessment for Standing Trial for Defendants with Mental Retardation (CAST*MR) is designed to evaluate criminal defendants with cognitive disabilities. Carol Everington, *The Competence Assessment for Standing Trial for Defendants with Mental Retardation (CAST–MR): A Validation Study*, 17 Crim Just Behav. 147, (1990). Believing that open-ended questions used in other instruments would not accurately assess the abilities of persons with limited verbal abilities, the CAST*MR developers designed a 50–item instrument that contains primarily multiple-choice questions. The questions regarding basic legal knowledge are phrased at a fourth-grade reading level. A final 10–item section asks the defendant simple questions to assess abilities to recount events leading to the charges.

- The MacArthur Competence Assessment Tool–Criminal Adjudication (MacCAT–CA™) contains 22 items that assess the defendant's *understanding* of key information, (e.g., elements of the offense, pleading guilty), *reasoning* (e.g., applying concepts such as self-defense), and *appreciation* of his specific circumstances (e.g., whether delusional beliefs influence his thoughts about being treated fairly). Randy K. Otto, et al, *Psychometric Properties of the MacArthur Competence Assessment Tool—Criminal Adjudication*, 10 Psychol. Assess. 435 (1998); Norman G. Poythress, Adjudicative Competence: The MacArthur Studies (2002). The examiner has the defendant listen to and answer questions about a hypothetical criminal case, and uses this vignette in assessing understanding and reasoning. Using the MacCAT–CA™ scoring system, the examiner can compare a specific defendant's performance to large groups of competent and incompetent defendants. The designers of MacCAT–CA™ created their instrument with the hope that it would "enhance the thoroughness and quality of clinical investigations of adjudicative competence." Poythress, supra, p. 144).

4. *Assistance to the factfinder.* Several studies have found that inter-rater agreement on competency to stand trial is quite high, usually over 90%. If mental health professionals are equating psychosis with incompetency, as recounted in note 2, this percentage may merely reflect the ability of clinicians to agree when someone is severely mentally ill. But even when clinicians understand and apply the specific competency criteria, reliability is very high, whether or not a structured interview format is used. Stephen Golding et al., supra, at 188–191 (97% agreement using IFI); Norman Poythress & Harley Stock, *Competency to Stand Trial: A Historical Review and Some New Data*, 8 J.Psychiat.L. 131 (1980) (100% agreement between raters using unstructured interview); Douglas Mossman et al., *Quantifying the Accuracy of Forensic Examiners in the Absence of a 'Gold Standard'*, 34 Law Hum. Behav. 402, 411 (2010)(ICC=0.80 for absolute agreement, ICC=0.95 for consistency). Thus, competency to stand trial determinations may be much more valid, or accurate, than normality, responsibility or propensity assessments.

Yet some research also suggests that, in the field as opposed to in controlled studies, inter-rater agreement is closer to 70% unless structured instruments like those discussed in the previous note are used. Gowensmith et al., supra. Should an expert who does not use such an instrument be allowed to testify under *Frye* or *Daubert*? For an argument that structured protocols ought to be required in every forensic area where possible, see

Christopher Slobogin, Proving the Unprovable: The Role of Law, Science, and Speculation in Adjudicating Culpability and Dangerousness 64–66 (2007). It also appears that laypersons who have received a minimal amount of training can produce reliable conclusions on the competency issue, at least when using a structured interview format. Roesch & Golding, supra, at 188–191 (90% agreement between trained laypersons and hospital evaluators using IFI). What would be the Morsian argument in the competency to stand trial context? Who should be allowed to write competency reports and testify at competency hearings, and under what limitations?

III.   IMPLEMENTATION ISSUES

Despite the arguments for eliminating or limiting expert testimony from mental health professionals, courts continue to permit such testimony on normality, responsibility, propensity and competency issues. This section addresses several topics related to how this testimony should be presented: which types of mental health professionals should be qualified to offer clinical opinions, when the state is required to provide the defendant/subject with such experts, when the state can obtain its own evaluation of the defendant/subject, what types of third party information experts may rely upon in forming their opinions, and the extent to which these opinions may embrace "ultimate" legal issues.

A.   WHO IS AN EXPERT?

Federal Rule 702 defines an expert as one who is qualified to speak on a given issue "by knowledge, skill, experience, training or education." Arguably, any mental health professional—whether a psychiatrist, psychologist, social worker or psychiatric nurse—could possess specialized knowledge, skill, experience, training and education related to mental disorder and its consequences. Courts have allowed physicians to testify about mental matters for centuries, long before physicians who specialized in mental illnesses called themselves "psychiatrists." But only in the past half-century have courts explicitly recognized the expertise of psychologists and other mental health professionals (review the materials in Part IV of Chapter One discussing the differences between psychiatrists, psychologists and social workers). The leading case in this regard is *Jenkins v. United States*, 307 F.2d 637 (D.C. Cir. 1962), which involved whether Ph.D. clinical psychologists could testify on the issue of insanity. There the court held that:

> the lack of a medical degree, and the lesser degree of responsibility for patient care which mental hospitals usually assign to psychologists, are not automatic disqualifications. Where relevant, these matters may be shown to affect the weight of their testimony, even though it be admitted in evidence. The critical factor in respect to admissibility is the actual experience of the witness and the probable probative value of his opinion. The trial judge should make

a finding in respect to the individual qualifications of each challenged expert.

Id. at 646. In dissent, Judge Bastian wrote:

> In the first place, we think it must be concluded beyond doubt that the existence of a mental disease or defect is, first and foremost, a *medical* problem. The ascertainment of such a medical illness in a given individual with reference to kind, quality, degree and influence is, except in extreme cases, a highly unverifiable process, judged by any objective standard, even when undertaken by a *medical* doctor with years of special training in the detection of medical disturbances of the mind. . . .
>
> We are not alone in our views on this precise issue. The American Psychiatric Association, an organization "comprised of those twelve thousand qualified Doctors of Medicine who specialize and practice as psychiatrists," in its amicus curiae brief, urges this court not to allow psychologists to qualify as experts to express opinions. We find in the brief this pertinent observation in regard to the proper medical ascertainment of mental disease or defect:
>
>> The diagnostic synthesis of *all data* collected is properly carried out only by an individual Doctor of Medicine with a broad training, experience, and familiarity with *all* of the areas indicated, and the diagnosis must reflect a comprehensive medical judgment in which the proper weight is given to all of the data available. Further, we know of no mental illness which does not have a biological as well as a psychological component. No facet of the data can be assumed to reflect the total diagnosis until viewed in the context of the total picture. A clinical psychologist, lacking *medical* training and the specialization required of the qualified psychiatrist, is not qualified to make this total *medical* diagnosis or to testify as a *medical* expert thereon."

Id. at 652. Consider these views in connection with the following case.

IN RE COMMITMENT OF DODSON

Court of Appeals of Texas, Beaumont, 2010.
311 S.W.3d 194.

HOLLIS HORTON, JUSTICE.

A jury determined that David Dodson is a sexually violent predator [SVP] under Texas law. The jury found that Dodson suffers from a behavioral abnormality that predisposes him to engage in a predatory act of sexual violence. . . . We reverse the judgment and remand the case for a new trial.

Background

. . . In a civil commitment proceeding under Chapter 841, the fact-finder, after a trial, decides whether the person being tried is a sexually violent predator. Because the jury is usually given a broad-form issue to answer, its determination of the issue often resolves more than one disputed issue. For example, to answer the broad-form issue submitted in Dodson's case, the jury was asked to determine whether Dodson "suffers from a behavioral abnormality that predisposes him to engage in a predatory act of sexual violence[.]" The term "behavioral abnormality"[1] has its own unique statutory definition that the trial court provided to the jury. Thus, to resolve the broad-form issue, the jury was required to resolve any dispute over whether Dodson's condition had affected him to the extent that he would, beyond a reasonable doubt, be predisposed "to engage in a predatory act of sexual violence[.]"

As is often the case, Dodson and the State both utilized experts at trial to address whether Dodson had a behavioral abnormality as defined by the Legislature. In the case before us, Dodson challenges the trial court's ruling that his expert witness, Dr. Anna Shursen, was not qualified to address whether he suffers from a "behavioral abnormality."

[At trial] Dr. Shursen testified that she holds a bachelor's degree of science, a master's degree in counseling and psychotherapy, and a doctorate in family sciences. In addition, Dr. Shursen holds Texas licenses as a professional counselor and as a sex offender treatment provider. Dr. Shursen also described that she had approximately twelve years of experience "working with juvenile and adult sex offenders." As a treatment provider, Dr. Shursen testified that she received three thousand hours of clinical training at a "psyche hospital facility" and that she had twelve years of experience providing behavioral therapy treatment to sex offenders. Dr. Shursen further explained that she had previously assessed approximately twelve to fifteen persons in cases that involved the civil commitment of sexually violent predators.

Dr. Shursen met with Dodson for approximately three hours. After briefly describing her impression of Dodson based on her interview, Dr. Shursen was asked: "Did you find Mr. Dodson to have a [behavioral] abnormality?" Dr. Shursen replied: "I did not, not at this time." Just after Dr. Shursen expressed her opinion about whether Dodson had a behavioral abnormality, Dr. Shursen noted that the term "behavioral abnormality" was a legal and not a medical term. Dr. Shursen also testified that in her opinion Dodson has stopped the behavior that previously caused him to offend. . . . Dr. Shursen provided additional

---

[1]   " 'Behavioral abnormality' means a congenital or acquired condition that, by affecting a person's emotional or volitional capacity, predisposes the person to commit a sexually violent offense, to the extent that the person becomes a menace to the health and safety of another person." Tex. Health & Safety Code Ann. § 841.002(2) (Vernon Supp. 2009).

details about her experience assessing risks of sex offenders. Dr. Shursen described that she was trained to do <u>actuarial testing</u>, and she specifically mentioned the Mn–SOST, the Hare PCL–R, and the Static 99. . . .

After Dr. Shursen had provided additional information regarding her experience, Dodson tendered Dr. Shursen as an expert witness. The . . . State's attorney argued that Dr. Shursen's "risk assessments are for treatment purposes and not related to behavioral abnormality." The trial court then ruled on the State's objection, stating that it did not hear any evidence to support her being able to make a qualified decision as to whether or not a respondent in one of these cases is likely to commit future acts of sexual violence and is, in fact, a sexually violent offender. Therefore, [the court] sustain[s] the objection." . . . [T]he trial court, . . . stated that it was "confident [Dr. Shursen's] a very excellent treatment provider. And she probably has done actuarials. But [the court] rule[s] that she is not qualified to present an opinion on [Dodson] as being a person as defined or not being a person as defined under Chapter 841 as a sexually violent predator."

[D]odson contends the trial court abused its discretion by refusing to permit Dr. Shursen, his expert witness, "to testify as to whether [Dodson] has a behavioral abnormality." . . . He also argues that Chapter 841 of the Health and Safety Code does not specify that the trial court is limited to appointing experts from particular fields to assess whether a person is a sexually violent offender, but instead contemplates that a multidisciplinary team will conduct a review of persons referred to as potential predators. According to Dodson, had the Legislature intended only for psychiatrists and psychologists to make these assessments of whether a person has a behavioral abnormality that predisposes them to reoffend, "[i]t could have so provided." Dodson further notes that the Texas Rules of Evidence do not require that an expert possess any specific type of degree, and instead, points out that Rule 702 provides: "If scientific, technical, or other specialized knowledge will assist the trier of fact to understand the evidence or to determine a fact in issue, a witness qualified as an expert by knowledge, skill, experience, training, or education may testify thereto in the form of an opinion or otherwise." . . .

In response, the State argues that . . . "[n]othing in Dr. Shursen's testimony indicated that she is qualified to determine whether someone meets [the] definition [of being a person who suffers from a 'behavioral abnormality.']"

Standard of Review

In the absence of an abuse of discretion, an appellate court will not disturb a trial court's ruling regarding whether a witness qualifies as an expert. . . . The Rules of Evidence place the burden to prove that the witness is an expert on the party seeking to offer the expert's testimony.

Analysis

. . . We have previously held: "[T]he legislature intended there be competent medical or psychiatric testimony to support an involuntary commitment under the Act, and provided for it therein." *Beasley v. Molett,* 95 S.W.3d 590, 599 (Tex.App.–Beaumont 2002, pet. denied). However, *Beasley* does not hold that in SVP commitments, the jury should only hear from psychiatrists and psychologists, or that the term "behavioral abnormality" can be addressed only by physicians and psychiatrists. Instead, in *Beasley* we reasoned that article I, section 15–a of the Texas Constitution,[7] read together with the SVP statute, required the State to produce competent medical or psychiatric testimony to support an involuntary commitment under the Act . . .

. . . Whether a person has a "behavioral abnormality," as that term is defined by statute, is not a question that is limited to determining whether the person has an underlying congenital or acquired condition. In other words, a medical opinion to demonstrate that a person suffers from a behavioral or congenital abnormality may be a precondition to commitment, as such evidence is required by the Texas Constitution, but requiring medical evidence as a part of the State's proof does not mean that medical evidence is the only admissible proof used to resolve whether a person has a "behavioral abnormality" that includes a risk assessment as a subordinate issue.

. . . An expert's opinion may assist the jury by virtue of the witness's "technical, or other specialized knowledge [.]" In *Gammill v. Jack Williams Chevrolet, Inc.,* the Texas Supreme Court used the following "beekeeper" analogy to illustrate the distinction between scientific and non-scientific expert testimony, stating:

> [I]f one wanted to explain to a jury how a bumblebee is able to fly, an aeronautical engineer might be a helpful witness. Since flight principles have some universality, the expert could apply general principles to the case of the bumblebee. Conceivably, even if he had never seen a bumblebee, he still would be qualified to testify, as long as he was familiar with its component parts.

> On the other hand, if one wanted to prove that bumblebees always take off into the wind, a beekeeper with no scientific training at all would be an acceptable expert witness if a proper foundation were laid for his conclusions. The foundation would not relate to his formal training, but to his firsthand observations. In other words, the beekeeper does not know any more about flight principles than the jurors, but he has seen a lot more bumblebees than they have.

---

[7]   "No person shall be committed as a person of unsound mind except on competent medical or psychiatric testimony." . . . Tex. Const. § 15–a.

972 S.W.2d 713, 724–25 (Tex.1998). If the ordinary person is asked to select, out of a given patient population of ill people, the patients to avoid because of concerns that those persons might commit future violent acts, we think the providers dealing with that patient-population might have valuable insight into which patients present a significant risk. In our opinion, the care-providers that have dealt with the patients and who have seen and had experience with them could provide assistance in predicting which of the specific patients represented the greatest threat.

The risk of recidivism, or whether an individual will probably reoffend, strikes us as a question that depends on both training and experience, and having insight into the recidivism risk is not a matter that is susceptible only to scientific proof. The Legislature expressly acknowledged that a risk assessment is part of determining whether a given individual is a sexual predator in the definition it provided to define the term "sexually violent predator." While Dr. Shursen was not Dodson's treatment provider, she had given him tests to assess his recidivism risk, and she had conducted a three hour interview of him to form an opinion about the threat he represented.

In a prior SVP case, we noted that the Court of Criminal Appeals referred to the field of predicting a person's future dangerousness as an area that involves a "soft" science. . . . We continue to maintain the view that predicting the risk of an individual's future recidivism is a "soft" science based largely on training and experience.

With respect to Dr. Shursen's training and experience, the record shows that in addition to her degrees and licenses, she was trained and licensed as a sex offender treatment provider. A sex offender treatment provider is, by definition:

> [A] person, licensed by the council and recognized based on training and experience to provide assessment and treatment to adult sex offenders or juveniles with sexual behavioral problems who have been convicted, adjudicated, awarded deferred adjudication, or referred by a state agency or a court, and licensed in this state to practice as a physician, psychiatrist, psychologist, psychological associate, provisionally licensed psychologist, licensed professional counselor, licensed professional counselor intern, licensed marriage and family therapist, licensed marriage and family associate, licensed clinical social worker, licensed master social worker under a clinical supervision plan approved by the Texas State Board of Social Worker Examiners, or advanced practice nurse recognized as a psychiatric clinical nurse specialist or psychiatric mental health nurse practitioner, who provides mental health or medical services for rehabilitation of sex offenders.

Tex. Occ.Code. Ann. § 110.001(7). The administrative regulations that apply to licensed sex offender treatment providers contain several standards, including one requiring a minimum of one thousand documented hours of clinical experience in the assessment and treatment of sex offenders, a reference from a qualified person who has actual knowledge of applicant's clinical work, and a minimum of forty hours of documented education in the prior three year period specific to sex offender assessment and treatment . . . The Council on Sex Offender Treatment regulates sex offender treatment licensing and is a program specifically created by the Legislature to coordinate effective assessment and treatment strategies to reduce recidivism of sex offenders and to enhance public safety.

Additionally, the Legislature did not restrict the question of risk assessment to physicians and psychologists, but instead it provided for a multidisciplinary approach for determining whether a person is a sexually violent predator. *See* Tex. Health & Safety Code Ann. § 841.022. The SVP's multidisciplinary approach implicitly recognizes that persons who are not psychiatrists or psychologists are capable of providing assistance in assessing whether an individual should be identified as a candidate for being subjected to a civil commitment proceeding under the SVP statute.

We conclude that Dr. Shursen possessed the necessary qualifications to provide an opinion related to her assessment of the risk that Dodson would commit a future act of sexual violence, a component part of the broad-form issue the jury evaluated and answered. Dr. Shursen's lack of credentials as a psychiatrist or psychologist may impact the weight the fact-finder gives her opinions about whether Dodson is predisposed to commit sexually violent acts; the lack of a medical degree does not of itself make her opinions on the issue of Dodson's risk to recidivate inadmissible.

With respect to the treatment of sex offenders and to the assessment of their risk of reoffending, the record before us reflects that Dr. Shursen possessed the knowledge and skills not possessed by the population generally, and that she was qualified to assess the risk that Dodson would commit another sexually violent offense. . . . On this record, we conclude the trial court abused its discretion by refusing to allow Dr. Shursen to further explain the basis of her conclusion that Dodson was not predisposed to engage in a predatory act of sexual violence, a component of his qualifying as a "sexually violent predator" as defined by statute . . .

QUESTIONS AND COMMENTS

1. *The relationship between qualifications and the legal issue.* What, precisely, is Dr. Shursen alleging she is qualified to do in court, and what, precisely, was Dr. Shursen's testimony addressing? In deciding whether Dr. Shursen is qualified to speak to the issues raised by the relevant statute the

court seems to draw a distinction between the underlying abnormality, on the one hand, and, on the other, the risk the abnormality poses. Can this distinction be drawn (see note 1)? If not, under Texas law is anyone other than a medically-trained expert allowed to testify on the issue (see note 7)? In supporting its position, the court notes that the legislature has "provided for a multidisciplinary approach for determining whether a person is a sexually violent predator." But does that mean Dr. Shursen can *testify*? Consider the APA's position described in *Jenkins* (excerpted in the materials before *Dodson*). This position was repeated in 1980 by the APA's president, who acknowledged that psychologists, social workers, and others can and should be members of the "treatment team," but that "it is [now] more appropriate than ever that the psychiatrist is the member of the team best equipped to perform triage, make differential diagnosis, [and to] plan and render treatment for a variety of psychological and somatic problems." Donald Langsley, *Viewpoint, A Commentary by APA's President*, Psychiatric News, Sept. 19, 1980, at 25, col. 1.

Assume that the issue is solely whether Dr. Shursen is an expert on assessing the risk of sex offenders, and thus does not involve whether Dodson has some underlying behavioral abnormality. Dr. Shursen was not a psychiatrist or psychologist, but seems to have considerable training and experience in treating sex offenders. Should that experience, alone, qualify her to address the risk issue? She also apparently has experience using "actuarials." Does the court have sufficient information to ascertain whether she is an expert in using them? Perhaps the issue is solely whether, given her experience with people like Dodson, she is qualified to assess his risk. In other words, to use the court's language, she could be seen as a "beekeeper", not an "aeronautical engineer." Should "beekeepers" be allowed to testify about risk? Does it depend on whether, as the court suggests, risk assessment is a "soft" science? *Is* risk assessment a soft science?

Finally, note that Dr. Shursen states that "behavioral abnormality" is a "legal" term, not a "medical" term. Does that help or hurt the argument that she is qualified?

2.   *Current state of the law. Dodson* is representative of a trend, triggered in part by Rule 702's broad language, toward a more expansive definition of the type of mental health professional who is qualified to testify in court. Still today, however, courts and legislatures appear to prefer psychiatrists as experts. While most states provide by statute or case law that doctoral-level clinical psychologists may offer opinions on most issues concerning people with mental disorder, see *Qualifications of Nonmedical Psychologist to Testify as to Mental Condition or Competency*, 72 A.L.R.5th 579 (1999), a few states still refuse to allow psychologists as free a rein as psychiatrists. For instance, in insanity cases, some courts still limit psychologists to interpretations of psychological tests; testimony by psychologists about degree of cognitive or volitional impairment or causes of mental deficiencies is prohibited or limited, at least when they are not licensed. *State v. Bricker*, 321 Md. 86, 581 A.2d 9 (1990); *People v. McDarrah*,

175 Ill.App.3d 284, 124 Ill.Dec. 827, 529 N.E.2d 808 (1988); *Commonwealth v. Williams,* 270 Pa.Super. 27, 410 A.2d 880 (1979). Many civil commitment provisions permit certification or testimony only by "physicians," Vernon's Ann.Tex. Const. art. 1, § 15a; N.Y.—McKinney's Mental Hygiene Law § 9.27, or, if they do allow psychologists to testify, require them to meet higher experiential standards than psychiatrists. West's Ann.Cal.Welf. & Inst.Code § 5251. In many states over 90% of guardianship reports are signed by medically-trained individuals. American Psychological Association, Assessment of Older Adults with Diminished Capacity: A Handbook for Psychologists (2008); Winsor Schmidt, *The Medicalization of the Aging: The Upside and the Downside,* 13 Marq. Elder's Advisor 55, 75–76 (2011). Even where doctoral level psychologists may testify, master's level clinical psychologists, and masters and doctoral level social workers are sometimes barred from giving opinion (as opposed to factual) testimony. See, e.g., *White v. Commonwealth,* 44 Va.App. 429, 605 S.E.2d 337, 345 (2004) (insanity defense); *State v. Zola,* 112 N.J. 384, 548 A.2d 1022, 1040 (1988) (diminished capacity defense); *State v. Baucom,* 28 Or.App. 757, 561 P.2d 641 (1977) (insanity defense). In sum, "Although less so than in years past, the cases addressing the minimum threshold qualifications for experts on questions of mental disorder still frequently favor psychiatrists' testimony and disfavor psychologists' testimony." Daniel W. Shuman, Psychiatric and Psychological Evidence 8–2 (2000).

3. *Justifications.* The limitations on and perceptions about expert qualifications of the various mental health professions can be interpreted as another illustration of the law's continued preference for the medical model of mental disorder. Such a preference clearly motivates the dissenting opinion in *Jenkins.* In its opinions that have touched on the clinical testimony issue, the United States Supreme Court has lent considerable credence to this view—whether consciously or unconsciously is hard to say—by its tendency to speak only of psychiatrists, or to mention psychologists and other mental health professions only in passing. See, e.g., *Kansas v. Hendricks,* 521 U.S. 346, 117 S.Ct. 2072, 138 L.Ed.2d 501 (referring to the "psychiatric profession's" definition of mental disorder); *Ake v. Oklahoma,* 470 U.S. 68, 105 S.Ct. 1087, 84 L.Ed.2d 53 (1985) (finding a constitutional right to "psychiatric assistance" in insanity and death penalty cases); *Barefoot v. Estelle,* 463 U.S. 880, 103 S.Ct. 3383, 77 L.Ed.2d 1090 (1983) (speaking of the validity of "psychiatric" predictions of dangerousness); *Addington v. Texas,* 441 U.S. 418, 99 S.Ct. 1804, 60 L.Ed.2d 323 (1979) (the "psychiatric diagnosis [necessary for civil commitment] is to a large extent based on medical 'impressions' "). In a more recent decision, however, *Clark v. Arizona,* 548 U.S. 735, 126 S.Ct. 2709, 165 L.Ed.2d 842 (2006), the Court referred repeatedly to psychologists and psychiatrists (in that order), perhaps a reflection of currents views about the acceptability of psychologists.

Is the apparent preference for psychiatric testimony justified? Research indicates that non-psychiatrists may be just as competent as psychiatrists in addressing many forensic issues. George Dix & Norman Poythress, *Propriety of Medical Dominance of Forensic Mental Health Practice: The Empirical*

Evidence, 23 Ariz.L.Rev. 961, 971–984 (1981). Of particular interest, one study found that psychologists and social workers tend to do more thorough forensic evaluations and more comprehensive and more relevant forensic reports than their psychiatric colleagues. Russell Petrella & Norman Poythress, *The Quality of Forensic Examinations: An Interdisciplinary Study*, 51 J. Consult. & Clinical Psychol. 76 (1983). Since the 1990s, psychologists have performed the overwhelming majority of studies on violence risk assessment and sex offense recidivism, as well as research relevant to developing evaluation instruments and interpreting their results. Psychologists have far more training than psychiatrists in the application and interpretation of statistical results, which play a key role in interpreting findings from new research. Most clinical psychologists receive training in administration of psychological tests—for example, tests of intelligence or "I.Q." Many psychiatrists understand the results of these tests, but few psychiatrists receive training or become proficient at administering them.

Morse has suggested that, under his scheme, described in section II of this chapter, "almost any person with extensive clinical experience with crazy persons should qualify as an expert." Stephen Morse, *Crazy Behavior, Morals and Science: An Analysis of Mental Health Law*, 51 S.Cal.L.Rev. 527, 623–624 (1978). On the other hand, "[p]rofessionals without extensive, recent, and relevant mental health *clinical* experience, whatever their formal training, should not be qualified as experts" on these subjects. With respect to statistical evidence, "an expert from any field [e.g., sociology as well as psychiatry] who possesses data relevant to the specific . . . issue is competent to be qualified." Id. Do you agree? Knowing that psychiatrists receive little formal training in statistics, do you think they should be prohibited from testifying about statistical matters unless they prove their qualifications beyond their medical training?

4.   *Knowledge of legal issues.* Clinical knowledge and training may not be enough to qualify a mental health professional as an expert witness. As we saw in the previous section, failure on the part of clinicians to understand the legal test for competency to stand trial can lead to virtually useless reports or testimony. In an effort to remedy this problem, psychiatrists and psychologists have established forensic distinctive board subspecialties and certification examinations for those who have achieved proficiency (and, in the case of psychiatrists, have received special training) in forensic matters. In a separate effort, several states have developed guidelines and training programs to help forensic clinicians avoid psychiatric jargon, irrelevant detail, and confusion about legal standards when they prepare reports. Kirk Heilbrun and Stephanie Brooks, *Forensic Psychology and Forensic Science: A Proposed Agenda for the Next Decade*, 16 Psychol. Public Pol'y L. 219 (2010)(describing history and current status of guidelines and training).

B. THE RIGHT TO AN EXPERT EVALUATION

AKE V. OKLAHOMA

Supreme Court of the United States, 1985.
470 U.S. 68, 105 S.Ct. 1087, 84 L.Ed.2d 53.

JUSTICE MARSHALL delivered the opinion of the Court.

The issue in this case is whether the Constitution requires that an indigent defendant have access to the psychiatric examination and assistance necessary to prepare an effective defense based on his mental condition, when his sanity at the time of the offense is seriously in question.

I

Late in 1979, Glen Burton Ake was arrested and charged with murdering a couple and wounding their two children. He was arraigned in the District Court for Canadian County, Okla., in February 1980. His behavior at arraignment, and in other prearraignment incidents at the jail, was so bizarre that the trial judge *sua sponte* ordered him to be examined by a psychiatrist "for the purpose of advising with the Court as to his impressions of whether the Defendant may need an extended period of mental observation." The examining psychiatrist reported: "At times [Ake] appears to be frankly delusional. * * * He claims to be the 'sword of vengeance' of the Lord and that he will sit at the left hand of God in heaven." He diagnosed Ake as a probable paranoid schizophrenic and recommended a prolonged psychiatric evaluation to determine whether Ake was competent to stand trial.

In March, Ake was committed to a state hospital to be examined with respect to his "present sanity," i.e., his competency to stand trial. On April 10, less than six months after the incidents for which Ake was indicted, the chief forensic psychiatrist at the state hospital informed the court that Ake was not competent to stand trial. The court then held a competency hearing, at which a psychiatrist testified:

> "[Ake] is a psychotic * * * his psychiatric diagnosis was that of paranoid schizophrenia—chronic, with exacerbation, that is with current upset, and that in addition * * * he is dangerous. * * * [B]ecause of the severity of his mental illness and because of the intensities of his rage, his poor control, his delusions, he requires a maximum security facility within—I believe—the State Psychiatric Hospital system."

The court found Ake to be a "mentally ill person in need of care and treatment" and incompetent to stand trial, and ordered him committed to the state mental hospital.

Six weeks later, the chief forensic psychiatrist informed the court that Ake had become competent to stand trial. At the time, Ake was receiving 200 milligrams of Thorazine, an antipsychotic drug, three times daily, and the psychiatrist indicated that, if Ake continued to receive that dosage, his condition would remain stable. The State then resumed proceedings against Ake.

At a pretrial conference in June, Ake's attorney informed the court that his client would raise an insanity defense. To enable him to prepare and present such a defense adequately, the attorney stated, a psychiatrist would have to examine Ake with respect to his mental condition at the time of the offense. During Ake's 3–month stay at the state hospital, no inquiry had been made into his sanity at the time of the offense, and, as an indigent, Ake could not afford to pay for a psychiatrist. Counsel asked the court either to arrange to have a psychiatrist perform the examination, or to provide funds to allow the defense to arrange one. The trial judge rejected counsel's argument that the Federal Constitution requires that an indigent defendant receive the assistance of a psychiatrist when that assistance is necessary to the defense, and he denied the motion for a psychiatric evaluation at state expense. . . .

Ake was tried for two counts of murder in the first degree, a crime punishable by death in Oklahoma, and for two counts of shooting with intent to kill. At the guilt phase of trial, his sole defense was insanity. Although defense counsel called to the stand and questioned each of the psychiatrists who had examined Ake at the state hospital, none testified about his mental state at the time of the offense because none had examined him on that point. The prosecution, in turn, asked each of these psychiatrists whether he had performed or seen the results of any examination diagnosing Ake's mental state at the time of the offense, and each doctor replied that he had not. *As a result, there was no expert testimony for either side on Ake's sanity at the time of the offense.* The jurors were then instructed that Ake could be found not guilty by reason of insanity if he did not have the ability to distinguish right from wrong at the time of the alleged offense. They were further told that Ake was to be presumed sane at the time of the crime unless *he* presented evidence sufficient to raise a reasonable doubt about his sanity at that time. If he raised such a doubt in their minds, the jurors were informed, the burden of proof shifted to the State to prove sanity beyond a reasonable doubt. The jury rejected Ake's insanity defense and returned a verdict of guilty on all counts.

At the sentencing proceeding, the State asked for the death penalty. No new evidence was presented. The prosecutor relied significantly on the testimony of the state psychiatrists who had examined Ake, and who had testified at the guilt phase that Ake was dangerous to society, to establish the likelihood of his future dangerous behavior. Ake had no expert witness to rebut this testimony or to introduce on his behalf evidence in mitigation of his punishment. The jury sentenced Ake to death on each of the two murder counts, and to 500 years' imprisonment on each of the two counts of shooting with intent to kill.

On appeal to the Oklahoma Court of Criminal Appeals, Ake argued that, as an indigent defendant, he should have been provided the services of a court-appointed psychiatrist. The court rejected this argument, observing: "We have held numerous times that, the unique nature of capital cases notwithstanding, the State does not have the responsibility of providing such services to indigents charged with capital crimes." 663 P.2d 1, 6 (1983). Finding no error in Ake's other claims, the court affirmed the convictions and sentences. We granted certiorari. 465 U.S. 1099, 104 S.Ct. 1591, 80 L.Ed.2d 123 (1984).

We hold that when a defendant has made a preliminary showing that his sanity at the time of the offense is likely to be a significant factor at trial, the Constitution requires that a State provide access to a psychiatrist's assistance on this issue, if the defendant cannot otherwise afford one. Accordingly, we reverse.

* * *

III

This Court has long recognized that when a State brings its judicial power to bear on an indigent defendant in a criminal proceeding, it must take steps to assure that the defendant has a fair opportunity to present his defense. This elementary principle, grounded in significant part on the Fourteenth Amendment's due process guarantee of fundamental fairness, derives from the belief that justice cannot be equal where, simply as a result of his poverty, a defendant is denied the opportunity to participate meaningfully in a judicial proceeding in which his liberty is at stake.

* * * We recognized long ago that mere access to the courthouse doors does not by itself assure a proper functioning of the adversary process, and that a criminal trial is fundamentally unfair if the State proceeds against an indigent defendant without making certain that he has access to the raw materials integral to the building of an effective defense. Thus, while the Court has not held that a State must purchase for the indigent defendant all the assistance that his wealthier counterpart might buy, see *Ross v. Moffitt,* 417 U.S. 600, 94 S.Ct. 2437, 41 L.Ed.2d 341 (1974), it has often reaffirmed that fundamental fairness entitles indigent defendants to "an adequate opportunity to present their claims fairly within the adversary system," *id.,* at 612, 94 S.Ct., at 2444. To implement this principle, we have focused on identifying the "basic tools of an adequate defense or appeal," *Britt v. North Carolina,* 404 U.S. 226, 227, 92 S.Ct.

431, 433, 30 L.Ed.2d 400 (1971), and we have required that such tools be provided to those defendants who cannot afford to pay for them.

To say that these basic tools must be provided is, of course, merely to begin our inquiry. In this case we must decide whether, and under what conditions, the participation of a psychiatrist is important enough to preparation of a defense to require the State to provide an indigent defendant with access to competent psychiatric assistance in preparing the defense. Three factors are relevant to this determination. The first is the private interest that will be affected by the action of the State. The second is the governmental interest that will be affected if the safeguard is to be provided. The third is the probable value of the additional or substitute procedural safeguards that are sought, and the risk of an erroneous deprivation of the affected interest if those safeguards are not provided. We turn, then, to apply this standard to the issue before us.

A

The private interest in the accuracy of a criminal proceeding that places an individual's life or liberty at risk is almost uniquely compelling. Indeed, the host of safeguards fashioned by this Court over the years to diminish the risk of erroneous conviction stands as a testament to that concern. The interest of the individual in the outcome of the State's effort to overcome the presumption of innocence is obvious and weighs heavily in our analysis.

We consider, next, the interest of the State. Oklahoma asserts that to provide Ake with psychiatric assistance on the record before us would result in a staggering burden to the State. We are unpersuaded by this assertion. Many States, as well as the Federal Government, currently make psychiatric assistance available to indigent defendants, and they have not found the financial burden so great as to preclude this assistance. This is especially so when the obligation of the State is limited to provision of one competent psychiatrist, as it is in many States, and as we limit the right we recognize today. At the same time, it is difficult to identify any interest of the State, other than that in its economy, that weighs against recognition of this right. The State's interest in prevailing at trial—unlike that of a private litigant—is necessarily tempered by its interest in the fair and accurate adjudication of criminal cases. Thus, also unlike a private litigant, a State may not legitimately assert an interest in maintenance of a strategic advantage over the defense, if the result of that advantage is to cast a pall on the accuracy of the verdict obtained. We therefore conclude that the governmental interest in denying Ake the assistance of a psychiatrist is not substantial, in light of the compelling interest of both the State and the individual in accurate dispositions.

Last, we inquire into the probable value of the psychiatric assistance sought, and the risk of error in the proceeding if such assistance is not offered. We begin by considering the pivotal role that psychiatry has come to play in criminal proceedings. More than 40 States, as well as the Federal Government, have decided either through legislation or judicial decision that indigent defendants are entitled, under certain circumstances, to the assistance of a psychiatrist's expertise. For example, in subsection (e) of the Criminal Justice Act, 18 U.S.C. § 3006A, Congress has provided that indigent defendants shall receive the assistance of all experts "necessary for an adequate defense." Numerous state statutes guarantee reimbursement for expert services under a like standard. And in many States that have not assured access to psychiatrists through the legislative process, state courts have interpreted the State or Federal Constitution to require that psychiatric assistance be provided to indigent defendants when necessary for an adequate defense, or when insanity is at issue.

These statutes and court decisions reflect a reality that we recognize today, namely, that when the State has made the defendant's mental condition relevant to his criminal culpability and to the punishment he might suffer, the assistance of a psychiatrist may well be crucial to the defendant's ability to marshal his defense. In this role, psychiatrists gather facts, both through professional examination, interviews, and elsewhere, that they will share with the judge or jury; they analyze the information gathered and from it draw plausible conclusions about the defendant's mental condition, and about the effects of any disorder on behavior; and they offer opinions about how the defendant's mental condition might have affected his behavior at the time in question. They know the probative questions to ask of the opposing party's psychiatrists and how to interpret their answers. Unlike lay witnesses, who can merely describe symptoms they believe might be relevant to the defendant's mental state, psychiatrists can identify the "elusive and often deceptive" symptoms of insanity, *Solesbee v. Balcom,* 339 U.S. 9, 12, 70 S.Ct. 457, 458, 94 L.Ed. 604 (1950), and tell the jury why their observations are relevant. Further, where permitted by evidentiary rules, psychiatrists can translate a medical diagnosis into language that will assist the trier of fact, and therefore offer evidence in a form that has meaning for the task at hand. Through this process of investigation, interpretation and testimony, psychiatrists ideally assist lay jurors, who generally have no training in psychiatric matters, to make a sensible and educated determination about the mental condition of the defendant at the time of the offense.

Psychiatry is not, however, an exact science, and psychiatrists disagree widely and frequently on what constitutes mental illness, on the appropriate diagnosis to be attached to given behavior and symptoms, on cure and treatment, and on likelihood of future dangerousness. Perhaps because there often is no single, accurate psychiatric conclusion on legal insanity in a given case, juries remain the primary factfinders on this issue, and they must resolve differences in opinion within the psychiatric profession on the basis of the evidence offered by each party. When jurors make this determination about issues that inevitably are complex and foreign, the testimony of psychiatrists can be crucial and "a virtual necessity if an insanity plea is to have any chance of success." By organizing a defendant's mental history, examination results and behavior, and other information, interpreting it in light of their expertise, and then laying out their investigative and analytic process to the jury, the psychiatrists for each party enable the jury to make its most accurate determination of the truth on the issue before them. It is for this reason that States rely on psychiatrists as examiners, consultants, and witnesses, and that private individuals do as well, when they can afford to do so. In so saying, we neither approve nor disapprove the widespread reliance on psychiatrists but instead recognize the unfairness of a contrary holding in light of the evolving practice.

The foregoing leads inexorably to the conclusion that, without the assistance of a psychiatrist to conduct a professional examination on issues relevant to the defense, to help determine whether the insanity defense is viable, to present testimony, and to assist in preparing the cross-examination of a State's psychiatric witnesses, the risk of an inaccurate resolution of sanity issues is extremely high. With such assistance, the defendant is fairly able to present at least enough information to the jury, in a meaningful manner, as to permit it to make a sensible determination.

A defendant's mental condition is not necessarily at issue in every criminal proceeding, however, and it is unlikely that psychiatric assistance of the kind we have described would be of probable value in cases where it is not. The risk of error from denial of such assistance, as well as its probable value, are most predictably at their height when the defendant's mental condition is seriously in question. When the defendant is able to make an *ex parte* threshold showing to the trial court that his sanity is likely to be a significant factor in his defense, the need for the assistance of a psychiatrist is readily apparent. It is in such cases that a defense may be devastated by the absence of a psychiatric examination and testimony; with such assistance, the defendant might have a reasonable chance of success. In such a circumstance, where the potential accuracy of the jury's determination is so dramatically enhanced, and where the interests of the individual and the State in an accurate proceeding are substantial, the State's interest in its fisc must yield. We therefore hold that when a defendant demonstrates to the trial judge that his sanity at the time of the offense is to be a significant factor at trial, the State must, at a minimum, assure the defendant access to a competent psychiatrist who will conduct an appropriate examination and assist in evaluation, preparation, and presentation of the defense. This is not to say, of course, that the indigent defendant has a constitutional right to choose a psychiatrist of his personal liking or to receive funds to hire his own. Our concern is that the indigent defendant have access to a competent psychiatrist for the purpose we have discussed, and as in the case of the provision of counsel we leave to the State the decision on how to implement this right.

B

Ake also was denied the means of presenting evidence to rebut the State's evidence of his future dangerousness. The foregoing discussion compels a similar conclusion in the context of a capital sentencing proceeding, when the State presents psychiatric evidence of the defendant's future dangerousness. We have repeatedly recognized the defendant's compelling interest in fair adjudication at the sentencing phase of a capital case. The State, too, has a profound interest in assuring that its ultimate sanction is not erroneously imposed, and we do not see why monetary considerations should be more persuasive in this context than at trial. The variable on which we must focus is, therefore, the probable value that the assistance of a psychiatrist will have in this area, and the risk attendant on its absence.

This Court has upheld the practice in many States of placing before the jury psychiatric testimony on the question of future dangerousness, see *Barefoot v. Estelle,* 463 U.S. 880, 896–905, 103 S.Ct. 3383, 3396–3400, 77 L.Ed.2d 1090 (1983), at least where the defendant has had access to an expert of his own, *id.,* n. 5. In so holding, the Court relied, in part, on the assumption that the factfinder would have before it both the views of the prosecutor's psychiatrists and the "opposing views of the defendant's doctors" and would therefore be competent to "uncover, recognize, and take due account of * * * shortcomings" in predictions on this point. Without a psychiatrist's assistance, the defendant cannot offer a well-informed expert's opposing view, and thereby loses a significant opportunity to raise in the jurors' minds questions about the State's proof of an aggravating factor. In such a circumstance, where the consequence of error is so great, the relevance of responsive psychiatric testimony so evident, and the burden on the State so slim, due process requires access to a psychiatric examination on relevant issues, to the testimony of the psychiatrist, and to assistance in preparation at the sentencing phase.

* * *

QUESTIONS AND COMMENTS

1. *Implications of* Ake. As Justice Marshall points out, almost every state provides indigent defendants the opportunity to obtain, at state expense, an evaluation on sanity. Most states also provide evaluation services on sentencing issues in capital cases. Most sanity evaluations are performed by state hospital employees, although with increasing frequency they are conducted by community mental health professionals who receive payment from the courts for their services. If an indigent defendant receives evaluative

assistance from a state employee, are the requirements of *Ake* met? Or can the defendant demand an expert who is not a regular employee of the state? Most courts hold that appointment of a state employee as the expert does not violate *Ake*. See 84 A.L.R. 19, § 17 (1991). However, at least one court has held that "the ability to subpoena a state examiner and to question that person on the stand does not amount to the expert assistance required by *Ake*." *Starr v. Lockhart*, 23 F.3d 1280, 1289 (8th Cir. 1994).

Once a "competent psychiatrist" is selected, he or she is required, under *Ake,* to "conduct an appropriate examination and assist in evaluation, preparation and presentation of the defense." Does this language merely require that the defense be able to ask questions of and elicit testimony from "a psychiatrist who acts independently of the prosecutor's office," or does it require something more? What if the expert's conclusion is that the defendant is sane or dangerous—is this expert able to "assist in evaluation, preparation and presentation of the defense?" If not, does the due process clause entitle the defendant to another expert? What if the appointed expert concludes that another expert with more specific expertise is needed? *State v. Newton*, 108 Ohio St.3d 13, 840 N.E.2d 593 (2007) (neuro-psychiatric testing request denied because no particularized showing of need made). Cf. *Vickers v. Arizona*, 497 U.S. 1033, 110 S.Ct. 3298, 111 L.Ed.2d 806 (1990) (rehearing denied). In *Vickers* both the defense experts and the state expert stated that neuropsychological testing was necessary to confirm the defendant's diagnosis but the trial court denied the motion for such testing, because another psychiatrist had made a contrary diagnosis (based on a review of the defendant's medical records and a brief interview with the defendant).

A number of states allow the defendant to seek an independent evaluation if he or she is dissatisfied with the results of the evaluation. Samuel Brakel et al., The Mentally Disabled and the Law 719 (1985). But in those states that do not, *Ake* has brought no change. Lower court decisions since *Ake* have condoned statutory procedures which permit a state-employed expert to report to the court or to the prosecution for transmittal to the defense, as well as procedures that simply give the defense access to the findings of the state's experts. See Note, *Expert Services and the Indigent Criminal Defendant: The Constitutional Mandate of Ake v. Oklahoma*, 84 Mich.L.Rev. 1326, 1348–49 nn. 150–52 (1986); see also, *Granviel v. Texas*, 495 U.S. 963, 110 S.Ct. 2577, 109 L.Ed.2d 758 (1990) (denying certiorari in a case challenging such a procedure, over a dissent by Justice Marshall). Moreover, a number of courts have held that in order to obtain an *Ake* evaluation the defendant must make a "clear showing" that mental state is a "genuine" or "real" issue, a showing that may be difficult without psychiatric assistance. Cara H. Drinan, *The Revitalization of Ake: A Capital Defendant's Right to Expert Assistance*, 60 Okla. L. Rev. 283, 290–93 (2007). See also *Ross v. Ward*, 165 F.3d 793 (10th Cir. 1999), cert. denied, 120 S.Ct. 208 (1999) (defendant failed to establish insanity would be a significant factor in his defense when expert found him competent and records revealed no other evidence of significant mental disorder).

2.   *Sixth amendment analysis*. Note that *Ake* is based on the due process clause. Some courts have held that the sixth amendment right to effective assistance of counsel entitles the defendant to an "exploratory" evaluation designed to assist the attorney in deciding what claims to make and in preparing for the case. See, e.g., *United States v. Edwards*, 488 F.2d 1154, 1163 (5th Cir.1974) (stressing the "particularly critical interrelation between expert psychiatric assistance and minimally effective representation of counsel"). See also *Wood v. Zahradnick*, 578 F.2d 980 (4th Cir.1978). Does framing the right to expert assistance in sixth amendment terms offer any advantages to the defendant? Perhaps worth noting is the Supreme Court's decision in *Wheat v. United States*, 486 U.S. 153, 108 S.Ct. 1692, 100 L.Ed.2d 140 (1988), which stated that "a defendant may not insist on representation by an attorney he cannot afford." If this is true for the right to counsel, it is likely to be true for the right to expert assistance as well.

3.   *Expert assistance in other contexts*. Besides forming the basis for an insanity defense and for rebuttal of the state's case in capital sentencing, expert assistance may be useful in raising or rebutting a number of other claims in criminal cases. Discussed in the next chapter are various other "psychiatric" defenses (e.g., diminished capacity, automatism) that might result in acquittal, and various sentencing provisions which contemplate psychiatric testimony about past mental state and future dangerousness. As noted earlier in this chapter, competency to stand trial is also often viewed as a psychiatric issue. Does anything in Justice Marshall's analysis in *Ake* foreclose a right to psychiatric assistance in these situations? Should it matter, as Marshall seems to suggest, whether a judge or a jury is the factfinder? Those courts that have considered the issue have found that *Ake* entitles the indigent to psychiatric assistance when psychiatric defenses other than insanity are raised. However, many courts have found that *Ake* does not require the state to provide expert assistance on sentencing issues other than dangerousness. Pam Casey & Ingo Keilitz, *An Evaluation of Mental Health Expert Assistance Provided to Indigent Criminal Defendants: Organization, Administration, and Fiscal Management*, 34 N.Y. L.Rev. 19, 51–55 (1989). See also *Goodwin v. Johnson*, 132 F.3d 162 (5th Cir. 1997) (*Ake* does not require appointment of a rehabilitation expert in a capital sentencing proceeding even when the state argues dangerousness). But see Drinan, supra (suggesting trend in the direction of providing expert assistance for all capital sentencing issues).

Expert assistance may also be necessary in noncriminal proceedings, such as civil commitment and guardianship hearings. Does *Ake* have implications for these types of proceedings or is it limited to criminal proceedings? The right to an independent expert in civil commitment is discussed further at pp. 949–951.

4.   *State access to results*. As noted above, in many states the results of the indigent's evaluation are immediately made available to both the defense *and* the prosecution (as well as the court). See, e.g., *Buttrum v. Black*, 721 F.Supp. 1268 (N.D. Ga. 1989), aff'd 908 F.2d 695 (11th Cir. 1990) (holding

that *Ake* does not provide indigent defendants with a right to confidential evaluation). Assuming this procedure does not compromise the expert's "independence," does state access nonetheless violate *Ake* to the extent it "chills" the exercise of the right to expert assistance by a defendant who is not sure how the evaluation will come out? Even if disclosing the results of the defense's exploratory evaluation to the prosecution does not violate *Ake,* does not state access run afoul of the attorney-client privilege and the associated right to effective assistance of counsel? An increasing number of states provide that the attorney-client privilege protects against disclosure of the results of the indigent's "exploratory" evaluation until the defendant decides to use them. See, e.g., West's Fla.S.A.R.Crim.Proc. 3.216(a).

A derivative issue arises when a *non*indigent defendant retains more than one expert, but decides to use only one or some of the experts at trial. May the prosecution call the unused expert or experts? Two leading cases on the issue, *People v. Edney*, 39 N.Y.2d 620, 385 N.Y.S.2d 23, 350 N.E.2d 400 (1976) and *People v. Knuckles,* 165 Ill.2d 125, 209 Ill.Dec. 1, 650 N.E.2d 974 (1995), are reprinted in Part II.3.b of Chapter Five; here they will only be summarized. *Edney* found that the state should have access to unused defense experts. Otherwise, the defendant would "be permitted to suppress any unfavorable psychiatric witness whom he had retained in the first instance, under the guise of the attorney-client privilege, while he endeavors to shop around for a friendly expert, and take unfriendly experts off the market." *Knuckles,* on the other hand, rejected *Edney's* approach on the ground that it would discourage defense attorneys from seeking expert assistance and disturb the rapport between the defendant and the defense-retained expert. Are the concerns evinced by either court realistic? The American Bar Association Criminal Justice Mental Health Standards adopt *Knuckles'* approach, but allow the prosecution access to unused defense experts if it can show a bad faith effort on the part of the defense to "gag" the available experts. Standard 7–3.3(b)(ii).

C. THE BASIS OF CLINICAL OPINION

Although mental health professionals increasingly rely on actuarial data, expert testimony still typically depends on the clinical evaluation process. For both criminal and civil cases, the primary source of information in this process is usually the person whose mental condition is at issue. The good evaluator also attempts to obtain as much third party information as possible to fill in gaps in the subject's story and for corroborative purposes. This section first discusses constitutional issues surrounding use of the defendant-subject as a source of clinical information; it then focuses on subconstitutional, evidentiary concerns that arise primarily in connection with use of third party information.

1. The Defendant as a Source: Constitutional Considerations

The fifth amendment states in part that "no person shall be compelled in any criminal case to be a witness against himself." The values said to underlie this right, summarized in *Murphy v. Waterfront Commission*, 378 U.S. 52, 55, 84 S.Ct. 1594, 1596, 12 L.Ed.2d 678 (1964), are manifold: the prevention of abuse by government officials, the protection of privacy, the fear that coerced statements will be unreliable, "our unwillingness to subject those suspected of crime to the cruel trilemma of self-accusation, perjury or contempt," the "preference for an accusatorial rather than an inquisitorial system of criminal justice," and "our sense of fair play which dictates 'a fair state-individual balance . . . by requiring the government in its contest with the individual to shoulder the entire load . . . '." The primary issue addressed here is whether the traditional attributes of the "accusatorial" system—which prevents the state from forcing the defendant to help it convict him or her—applies to state-requested psychiatric evaluations, or whether, instead, an "inquisitorial" approach—which relies more heavily on statements from the defendant—is permissible when the issue is the defendant's mental condition.

ESTELLE V. SMITH

Supreme Court of the United States, 1981.
451 U.S. 454, 101 S.Ct. 1866, 68 L.Ed.2d 359.

CHIEF JUSTICE BURGER, delivered the opinion of the Court.

We granted certiorari to consider whether the prosecution's use of psychiatric testimony at the sentencing phase of respondent's capital murder trial to establish his future dangerousness violated his constitutional rights.

I

A

On December 28, 1973, respondent Ernest Benjamin Smith was indicted for murder arising from his participation in the armed robbery of a grocery store during which a clerk was fatally shot, not by Smith, but by his accomplice. In accordance with Art. 1257(b)(2) of the Tex.Penal Code Ann. (Vernon 1974) concerning the punishment for murder with malice aforethought, the State of Texas announced its intention to seek the death penalty. Thereafter, a judge of the 195th Judicial District Court of Dallas County, Texas, informally ordered the State's attorney to arrange a psychiatric examination of Smith by Dr. James P. Grigson to determine Smith's competency to stand trial.[1]

---

[1] This psychiatric evaluation was ordered even though defense counsel had not put into issue Smith's competency to stand trial or his sanity at the time of the offense. The trial judge later explained: "In all cases where the State has sought the death penalty, I have ordered a mental evaluation of the defendant to determine his competency to stand trial. I have done this for my benefit because I do not intend to be a participant in a case where the defendant receives the death penalty and his mental competency remains in doubt." See Tex.Code Crim.Proc.Ann.,

Dr. Grigson, who interviewed Smith in jail for approximately 90 minutes, concluded that he was competent to stand trial. In a letter to the trial judge, Dr. Grigson reported his findings: "[I]t is my opinion that Ernest Benjamin Smith, Jr., is aware of the difference between right and wrong and is able to aid an attorney in his defense." This letter was filed with the court's papers in the case. Smith was then tried by a jury and convicted of murder.

In Texas, capital cases require bifurcated proceedings—a guilt phase and a penalty phase. If the defendant is found guilty, a separate proceeding before the same jury is held to fix the punishment. At the penalty phase, if the jury affirmatively answers three questions on which the State has the burden of proof beyond a reasonable doubt, the judge must impose the death sentence. See Tex.Code Crim.Proc.Ann., Arts. 37.071(c) and (e) (Vernon Supp.1980). One of the three critical issues to be resolved by the jury is "whether there is a probability that the defendant would commit criminal acts of violence that would constitute a continuing threat to society." Art. 37.071(b)(2). In other words, the jury must assess the defendant's future dangerousness.

At the commencement of Smith's sentencing hearing, the State rested "[s]ubject to the right to reopen." Defense counsel called three lay witnesses: Smith's stepmother, his aunt, and the man who owned the gun Smith carried during the robbery. Smith's relatives testified as to his good reputation and character. The owner of the pistol testified as to Smith's knowledge that it would not fire because of a mechanical defect. The State then called Dr. Grigson as a witness.

Defense counsel were aware from the trial court's file of the case that Dr. Grigson had submitted a psychiatric report in the form of a letter advising the court that Smith was competent to stand trial. This report termed Smith "a severe sociopath," but it contained no more specific reference to his future dangerousness. Before trial, defense counsel had obtained an order requiring the State to disclose the witnesses it planned to use both at the guilt stage, and, if known, at the penalty stage. Subsequently, the trial court had granted a defense motion to bar the testimony during the State's case in chief of any witness whose name did not appear on that list. Dr. Grigson's name was not on the witness list, and defense counsel objected when he was called to the stand at the penalty phase.

In a hearing outside the presence of the jury, Dr. Grigson stated: (a) that he had not obtained permission from Smith's attorneys to examine him; (b) that he had discussed his conclusions and diagnosis with the State's attorney; and (c) that the prosecutor had requested him to testify and had told him, approximately five days before the sentencing hearing

Art. 46.02 (Vernon 1979). No question as to the appropriateness of the trial judge's order for the examination has been raised by Smith.

began, that his testimony probably would be needed within the week. The trial judge denied a defense motion to exclude Dr. Grigson's testimony on the ground that his name was not on the State's list of witnesses. Although no continuance was requested, the court then recessed for one hour following an acknowledgment by defense counsel that an hour was "all right."

After detailing his professional qualifications by way of foundation, Dr. Grigson testified before the jury on direct examination: (a) that Smith "is a very severe sociopath"; (b) that "he will continue his previous behavior"; (c) that his sociopathic condition will "only get worse"; (d) that he has no "regard for another human being's property or for their life, regardless of who it may be"; (e) that "[t]here is no treatment, no medicine * * * that in any way at all modifies or changes this behavior"; (f) that he "is going to go ahead and commit other similar or same criminal acts if given the opportunity to do so"; and (g) that he "has no remorse or sorrow for what he has done." Dr. Grigson, whose testimony was based on information derived from his 90–minute "mental status examination" of Smith (*i.e.*, the examination ordered to determine Smith's competency to stand trial), was the State's only witness at the sentencing hearing.

The jury answered the three requisite questions in the affirmative, and, thus, under Texas law the death penalty for Smith was mandatory. The Texas Court of Criminal Appeals affirmed Smith's conviction and death sentence, *Smith v. State,* 540 S.W.2d 693 (Tex.Cr.App.1976), and we denied certiorari, 430 U.S. 922, 97 S.Ct. 1341, 51 L.Ed.2d 601 (1977).

B

After unsuccessfully seeking a writ of habeas corpus in the Texas state courts, Smith petitioned for such relief in the United States District Court for the Northern District of Texas pursuant to 28 U.S.C. § 2254. The District Court vacated Smith's death sentence because it found constitutional error in the admission of Dr. Grigson's testimony at the penalty phase. 445 F.Supp. 647 (1977). The court based its holding on the failure to advise Smith of his right to remain silent at the pretrial psychiatric examination and the failure to notify defense counsel in advance of the penalty phase that Dr. Grigson would testify. The court concluded that the death penalty had been imposed on Smith in violation of his Fifth and Fourteenth Amendment rights to due process and freedom from compelled self-incrimination, his Sixth Amendment right to the effective assistance of counsel, and his Eighth Amendment right to present complete evidence of mitigating circumstances.

The United States Court of Appeals for the Fifth Circuit affirmed. 602 F.2d 694 (1979). The court held that Smith's death sentence could not stand because the State's "surprise" use of Dr. Grigson as a witness, the consequences of which the court described as "devastating," denied Smith due process in that his attorneys were prevented from effectively challenging the psychiatric testimony. The court went on to hold that, under the Fifth and Sixth Amendments, "Texas may not use evidence based on a psychiatric examination of the defendant unless the defendant was warned, before the examination, that he had a right to remain silent; was allowed to terminate the examination when he wished; and was assisted by counsel in deciding whether to submit to the examination." Because Smith was not accorded these rights, his death sentence was set aside. While "leav[ing] to state authorities any questions that arise about the appropriate way to proceed when the state cannot legally execute a defendant whom it has sentenced to death," the court indicated that "the same testimony from Dr. Grigson, based on the same examination of Smith" could not be used against Smith at any future resentencing proceeding.

II

A

Of the several constitutional issues addressed by the District Court and the Court of Appeals, we turn first to whether the admission of Dr. Grigson's testimony at the penalty phase violated respondent's Fifth Amendment privilege against compelled self-incrimination because respondent was not advised before the pretrial psychiatric examination that he had a right to remain silent and that any statement he made could be used against him at a sentencing proceeding. Our initial inquiry must be whether the Fifth Amendment privilege is applicable in the circumstances of this case.

(1)

The State argues that respondent was not entitled to the protection of the Fifth Amendment because Dr. Grigson's testimony was used only to determine punishment after conviction, not to establish guilt. In the State's view, "incrimination is complete once guilt has been adjudicated," and, therefore, the Fifth Amendment privilege has no relevance to the penalty phase of a capital murder trial. We disagree.

The Fifth Amendment, made applicable to the states through the Fourteenth Amendment, commands that "[n]o person * * * shall be compelled in any criminal case to be a witness against himself." The essence of this basic constitutional principle is "the requirement that the State which proposes to convict *and punish* an individual produce the evidence against him by the independent labor of its officers, not by the simple, cruel expedient of forcing it from his own lips."

The Court has held that "the availability of the [Fifth Amendment] privilege does not turn upon the type of proceeding in which its protection is invoked, but upon the nature of the statement or admission and the exposure which it invites." *In re Gault,* 387 U.S. 1, 49, 87 S.Ct. 1428, 1455, 18 L.Ed.2d 527 (1967). In this case, the ultimate penalty of death was a potential consequence of what respondent told the examining psychiatrist. Just as the Fifth Amendment prevents a criminal defendant from being made " 'the deluded instrument of his own conviction,' " it protects him as well from being made the "deluded instrument" of his own execution.

We can discern no basis to distinguish between the guilt and penalty phases of respondent's capital murder trial so far as the protection of the Fifth Amendment privilege is concerned. Given the gravity of the decision to be made at the penalty phase, the State is not relieved of the obligation to observe fundamental constitutional guarantees. Any effort by the State to compel respondent to testify against his will at the sentencing hearing clearly would contravene the Fifth Amendment. Yet the State's attempt to establish respondent's future dangerousness by relying on the unwarned statements he made to Dr. Grigson similarly infringes Fifth Amendment values.

(2)

The State also urges that the Fifth Amendment privilege is inapposite here because respondent's communications to Dr. Grigson were nontestimonial in nature. The State seeks support from our cases holding that the Fifth Amendment is not violated where the evidence given by a defendant is neither related to some communicative act nor used for the testimonial content of what was said.

However, Dr. Grigson's diagnosis, as detailed in his testimony, was not based simply on his observation of respondent. Rather, Dr. Grigson drew his conclusions largely from respondent's account of the crime during their interview, and he placed particular emphasis on what he considered to be respondent's lack of remorse. Dr. Grigson's prognosis as to future dangerousness rested on statements respondent made, and remarks he omitted, in reciting the details of the crime. The Fifth Amendment privilege, therefore, is directly involved here because the State used as evidence against respondent the substance of his disclosures during the pretrial psychiatric examination.

The fact that respondent's statements were uttered in the context of a psychiatric examination does not automatically remove them from the reach of the Fifth Amendment. The state trial judge, *sua sponte,* ordered a psychiatric evaluation of respondent for the limited, neutral purpose of determining his competency to stand trial, but the results of that inquiry were used by the State for a much broader objective that was plainly adverse to respondent. Consequently, the interview with Dr. Grigson cannot be characterized as a routine competency examination restricted to ensuring that respondent understood the charges against him and was capable of assisting in his defense. Indeed, if the application of Dr. Grigson's findings had been confined to serving that function, no Fifth Amendment issue would have arisen.

Nor was the interview analogous to a sanity examination occasioned by a defendant's plea of not guilty by reason of insanity at the time of his offense. When a defendant asserts the insanity defense and introduces supporting psychiatric testimony, his silence may deprive the State of the only effective means it has of controverting his proof on an issue that he interjected into the case. Accordingly, several Courts of Appeals have held that, under such circumstances, a defendant can be required to submit to a sanity examination conducted by the prosecution's psychiatrist.[10]

Respondent, however, introduced no psychiatric evidence, nor had he indicated that he might do so. Instead, the State offered information obtained from the court-ordered competency examination as affirmative evidence to persuade the jury to return a sentence of death. Respondent's future dangerousness was a critical issue at the sentencing hearing, and one on which the State had the burden of proof beyond a reasonable doubt. See Tex.Code Crim.Proc.Ann., Arts. 37.071(b) and (c) (Vernon Supp.1980). To meet its burden, the State used respondent's own statements, unwittingly made without an awareness that he was assisting the State's efforts to obtain the death penalty. In these distinct circumstances, the Court of Appeals correctly concluded that the Fifth Amendment privilege was implicated.

(3)

In *Miranda v. Arizona,* 384 U.S. 436, 467, 86 S.Ct. 1602, 1624, 16 L.Ed.2d 694 (1966), the Court acknowledged that "the Fifth Amendment privilege is available outside of criminal court proceedings and serves to protect persons in all settings in which their freedom of action is curtailed in any significant way from being compelled to incriminate themselves." *Miranda* held that "the prosecution may not use statements, whether exculpatory or inculpatory, stemming from custodial interrogation of the defendant unless it demonstrates the use of procedural safeguards effective to secure the privilege against self-incrimination." Thus, absent other fully effective procedures, a person in custody must receive certain warnings before any official interrogation, including that he has a "right to remain silent" and that "anything said can and will be used against the individual in court." The purpose of these admonitions is to combat what the Court saw as "inherently compelling pressures" at work on the person and to provide him with an awareness of the Fifth Amendment privilege and the consequences of forgoing it, which is the prerequisite for "an intelligent decision as to its exercise."

The considerations calling for the accused to be warned prior to custodial interrogation apply with no less force to the pretrial psychiatric

---

[10] On the same theory, the Court of Appeals here carefully left open "the possibility that a defendant who wishes to use psychiatric evidence in his own behalf [on the issue of future dangerousness] can be precluded from using it unless he is [also] willing to be examined by a psychiatrist nominated by the state." 602 F.2d at 705.

examination at issue here. Respondent was in custody at the Dallas County Jail when the examination was ordered and when it was conducted. That respondent was questioned by a psychiatrist designated by the trial court to conduct a neutral competency examination, rather than by a police officer, government informant, or prosecuting attorney, is immaterial. When Dr. Grigson went beyond simply reporting to the court on the issue of competence and testified for the prosecution at the penalty phase on the crucial issue of respondent's future dangerousness, his role changed and became essentially like that of an agent of the State recounting unwarned statements made in a postarrest custodial setting. During the psychiatric evaluation, respondent assuredly was "faced with a phase of the adversary system" and was "not in the presence of [a] perso[n] acting solely in his interest."

Yet he was given no indication that the compulsory examination would be used to gather evidence necessary to decide whether, if convicted, he should be sentenced to death. He was not informed that, accordingly, he had a constitutional right not to answer the questions put to him.

The Fifth Amendment privilege is "as broad as the mischief against which it seeks to guard," *Counselman v. Hitchcock,* 142 U.S. 547, 562, 12 S.Ct. 195, 198, 35 L.Ed. 1110 (1892), and the privilege is fulfilled only when a criminal defendant is guaranteed the right "to remain silent unless he chooses to speak in the unfettered exercise of his own will, and to suffer no penalty * * * for such silence." We agree with the Court of Appeals that respondent's Fifth Amendment rights were violated by the admission of Dr. Grigson's testimony at the penalty phase.

A criminal defendant, who neither initiates a psychiatric evaluation nor attempts to introduce any psychiatric evidence, may not be compelled to respond to a psychiatrist if his statements can be used against him at a capital sentencing proceeding. Because respondent did not voluntarily consent to the pretrial psychiatric examination after being informed of his right to remain silent and the possible use of his statements, the State could not rely on what he said to Dr. Grigson to establish his future dangerousness. If, upon being adequately warned, respondent had indicated that he would not answer Dr. Grigson's questions, the validly ordered competency examination nevertheless could have proceeded upon the condition that the results would be applied solely for that purpose. In such circumstances, the proper conduct and use of competency and sanity examinations are not frustrated, but the State must make its case on future dangerousness in some other way.

"Volunteered statements * * * are not barred by the Fifth Amendment," but under *Miranda v. Arizona, supra,* we must conclude that, when faced while in custody with a court-ordered psychiatric inquiry, respondent's statements to Dr. Grigson were not "given freely and voluntarily without any compelling influences" and, as such, could be used as the State did at the penalty phase only if respondent had been apprised of his rights and had knowingly decided to waive them. These safeguards of the Fifth Amendment privilege were not afforded respondent and, thus, his death sentence cannot stand.

B

When respondent was examined by Dr. Grigson, he already had been indicted and an attorney had been appointed to represent him. The Court of Appeals concluded that he had a Sixth Amendment right to the assistance of counsel before submitting to the pretrial psychiatric interview. We agree.

The Sixth Amendment, made applicable to the states through the Fourteenth Amendment, provides that "[i]n all criminal prosecutions, the accused shall enjoy the right * * * to have the assistance of counsel for his defense." The "vital" need for a lawyer's advice and aid during the pretrial phase was recognized by the Court nearly 50 years ago in *Powell v. Alabama,* 287 U.S. 45, 57, 71, 53 S.Ct. 55, 60, 65, 77 L.Ed. 158 (1932). Since then, we have held that the right to counsel granted by the Sixth Amendment means that a person is entitled to the help of a lawyer "at or after the time that adversary judicial proceedings have been initiated against him * * * whether by way of formal charge, preliminary hearing, indictment, information, or arraignment."

*   *   *

Here, respondent's Sixth Amendment right to counsel clearly had attached when Dr. Grigson examined him at the Dallas County Jail,[14] and their interview proved to be a "critical stage" of the aggregate proceedings against respondent. Defense counsel, however, were not notified in advance that the psychiatric examination would encompass the issue of their client's future dangerousness, and respondent was denied the assistance of his attorneys in making the significant decision of whether to submit to the examination and to what end the psychiatrist's findings could be employed.

---

[14] Because psychiatric examinations of the type at issue here are conducted after adversary proceedings have been instituted, we are not concerned in this case with the limited right to the appointment and presence of counsel recognized as a Fifth Amendment safeguard in *Miranda v. Arizona,* 384 U.S. 436, 471–473, 86 S.Ct. 1602, 1626–1627, 16 L.Ed.2d 694 (1966). See *Edwards v. Arizona,* 451 U.S. 477, 101 S.Ct. 1880, 68 L.Ed.2d 378. Rather, the issue before us is whether a defendant's Sixth Amendment right to the assistance of counsel is abridged when the defendant is not given prior opportunity to consult with counsel about his participation in the psychiatric examination.

Respondent does not assert, and the Court of Appeals did not find, any constitutional right to have counsel actually present during the examination. In fact, the Court of Appeals recognized that "an attorney present during the psychiatric interview could contribute little and might seriously disrupt the examination." 602 F.2d at 708. Cf. *Thornton v. Corcoran,* 132 U.S.App.D.C. 232, 242, 248, 407 F.2d 695, 705, 711 (1969) (opinion concurring in part and dissenting in part).

Because "[a] layman may not be aware of the precise scope, the nuances, and the boundaries of his Fifth Amendment privilege," the assertion of that right "often depends upon legal advice from someone who is trained and skilled in the subject matter." As the Court of Appeals observed, the decision to be made regarding the proposed psychiatric evaluation is "literally a life or death matter" and is "difficult * * * even for an attorney" because it requires "a knowledge of what other evidence is available, of the particular psychiatrist's biases and predilections, [and] of possible alternative strategies at the sentencing hearing." It follows logically from our precedents that a defendant should not be forced to resolve such an important issue without "the guiding hand of counsel."

Therefore, in addition to Fifth Amendment considerations, the death penalty was improperly imposed on respondent because the psychiatric examination on which Dr. Grigson testified at the penalty phase proceeded in violation of respondent's Sixth Amendment right to the assistance of counsel.

C

Our holding based on the Fifth and Sixth Amendments will not prevent the State in capital cases from proving the defendant's future dangerousness as required by statute. A defendant may request or consent to a psychiatric examination concerning future dangerousness in the hope of escaping the death penalty. In addition, a different situation arises where a defendant intends to introduce psychiatric evidence at the penalty phase. See n. 10, *supra.*

Moreover, under the Texas capital sentencing procedure, the inquiry necessary for the jury's resolution of the future dangerousness issue is in no sense confined to the province of psychiatric experts.

* * * While in no sense disapproving the use of psychiatric testimony bearing on the issue of future dangerousness, the inquiry mandated by Texas law does not require resort to medical experts.

III

Respondent's Fifth and Sixth Amendment rights were abridged by the State's introduction of Dr. Grigson's testimony at the penalty phase, and, as the Court of Appeals concluded, his death sentence must be vacated. Because respondent's underlying conviction has not been challenged and remains undisturbed, the State is free to conduct further proceedings not inconsistent with this opinion. Accordingly, the judgment of the Court of Appeals is

Affirmed.

[Concurring opinions by BRENNAN, MARSHALL, STEWART and REHNQUIST, JJ., are omitted.]

QUESTIONS AND COMMENTS

1.   *State access to the defendant; the necessity of warnings. Estelle* appears to hold that had Dr. Grigson given Smith warnings, to the effect that he had the right to remain silent and that anything he said could be used against him at a subsequent capital sentencing proceeding, the prosecution could have relied on the results of the interview at that proceeding. Will the typical defendant being evaluated for competency or sanity understand such warnings? Or is the answer to this latter question irrelevant if, as *Estelle* now requires, the defendant's attorney is notified of the evaluation?

More fundamentally, in the typical state-requested evaluation, will *Miranda*-type warnings be accurate? *Estelle* speaks only of when the defendant "neither initiates a psychiatric evaluation nor attempts to introduce any psychiatric evidence." What if, as is more likely to be the case, the defendant has already obtained or is about to obtain an evaluation (either privately or as authorized by *Ake*) and plans to introduce psychiatric testimony? May such a defendant constitutionally remain silent during a state-requested evaluation? Or may the state sanction non-cooperation? Put another way, does the accusatorial paradigm continue to apply or should it give way to the inquisitorial approach? The answers to these questions depend upon the precise issue about which the state is seeking information.

Sanity Evaluations. Assume that the state is seeking evaluation of the defendant's sanity. One of the first decisions to address the implications of the fifth amendment in this context, *Pope v. United States,* 372 F.2d 710 (8th Cir.1967), held that, once the defendant gives formal notice of an intent to raise an insanity defense, the state may compel an evaluation of the defendant; in other words, the defendant has no right to remain silent during a state-requested evaluation once the defense is formally asserted. The court gave two reasons for this result. First, assertion of an insanity defense waives the fifth amendment privilege:

> [B]y raising the issue of insanity, by submitting to psychiatric and psychologic examination by his own examiners, and by presenting evidence as to mental incompetence from the lips of the defendant and these examiners, the defendant raised the issue for all purposes and . . . the government was appropriately granted leave to have the defendant examined by experts of its choice and to present their opinions in evidence.

Second, permitting the defendant to remain silent after asserting the defense would unfairly tip the "state-individual balance" in the defendant's favor:

> It would be a strange situation, indeed, if, first, the government is to be compelled to afford the defense ample psychiatric service and evidence at government expense and, second, if the government is to have the burden of proof, . . . and yet it is to be denied the opportunity to have its own corresponding and verifying examination, a step which perhaps is the most trustworthy means of attempting to meet the burden.

Both the waiver and fairness rationales have been attacked. As to the waiver rationale, one court has pointed out: "It is difficult to understand how a waiver could be characterized as either voluntary or intentional if automatically triggered by a defendant's assertion of the defense of insanity." *Commonwealth v. Pomponi,* 447 Pa. 154, 160, 284 A.2d 708, 711 (1971). In response to the fairness argument, it has been argued that the prosecution does not require access to the defendant to meet its evidentiary burden but rather can rely on lay witnesses, cross-examination of the defendant's experts, and hypothetical questions addressed to its own experts. Julia Meister, Miranda *on the Couch: An Approach to Problems of Self–Incrimination, Right to Counsel and* Miranda *Warnings in Pre–Trial Psychiatric Examinations of Criminal Defendants,* 11 Colum.J.L. & Soc.Probs. 403, 425 (1975). Compare in this regard decisions refusing to permit criminal defendants to compel evaluations of rape complainants with a history of mental problems. *Nobrega v. Commonwealth,* 271 Va. 508, 628 S.E.2d 922 (2006) (emphasizing victim's constitutional right to be treated with dignity and the discretion given trial judges to exclude expert testimony re credibility); *State v. Nelson,* 235 Neb. 15, 453 N.W.2d 454 (1990) (permitting such evaluations only when defendant demonstrates a "compelling need" and holding that conflicting accounts by an allegedly emotionally unstable complainant does not demonstrate a compelling need).

Nonetheless, most courts continue to agree with *Pope,* usually relying on the fairness rationale. The argument that the prosecution does not need its own evaluation of the defendant was forcefully rejected by Justice Scalia in an opinion he wrote while on the District of Columbia Circuit Court of Appeals:

> Appellant and *amici* would have us believe that the mere availability of cross-examination of the defendant's experts is sufficient to provide the necessary balance in the criminal process. That would perhaps be so if psychiatry were as exact a science as physics, so that, assuming the defense psychiatrist precisely described the data (consisting of his interview with the defendant), the error of his analysis could be demonstrated. It is, however, far from that. Ordinarily the only effective rebuttal of psychiatric opinion testimony is contradictory opinion testimony; and for that purpose . . . '[t]he basic tool of psychiatric study remains the personal interview, which requires rapport between the interviewer and the subject.'

> Our judgment that these practical considerations of fair but effective criminal process affect the interpretation and application of the Fifth Amendment privilege against self-incrimination is supported by the long line of Supreme Court precedent holding that the defendant in a criminal or even civil prosecution may not take the stand in his own behalf and then refuse to consent to cross-examination. The justification for this similarly 'coerced' testimony is precisely that which we apply to the present case. As said in *Brown* [*v. United States,* 356 U.S. 148, 78 S.Ct. 622, 2 L.Ed.2d 589 (1958)], a defendant cannot reasonably claim

that the Fifth Amendment gives him not only this choice [whether to testify or not] but, if he elects to testify, an immunity from cross-examination on the matters he has himself put in dispute. It would make of the Fifth Amendment not only a humane safeguard against judicially coerced self-disclosure but a positive invitation to mutilate the truth a party offers to tell. . . . The interests of the other party and regard for the function of courts of justice to ascertain the truth become relevant, and prevail in the balance of considerations determining the scope and limits of the privilege against self-incrimination.

United States v. Byers, 740 F.2d 1104 (D.C.Cir.1984).

Judge Bazelon, in a dissenting opinion in *Byers,* agreed that the fifth amendment does not necessarily bar the state from obtaining its own post-notice evaluation. But he argued that because the "state psychiatrist's aim is diagnosis, not therapy" and "[h]is primary commitment is to his institution, not to his patient," the state-referred evaluation "poses a threat of coercion similar to that in the interrogation deemed unconstitutional in *Miranda.*" Thus, he contended that the constitution requires that all such interviews be taped. This step "would quiet our concern that psychiatrists might manipulate or intimidate the defendant in an *in camera* interview" and "help inform the court's judgment regarding the voluntariness and reliability of the defendant's statement." Scalia responded that such a requirement is not imposed even on police interrogators and that, in any event, it stemmed from a concern over reliability, not compulsion; only the latter is the proper focus of fifth amendment analysis. How should the debate over the proper scope of the right to remain silent in the post-notice context be resolved? What, if anything, does *Estelle* say about this issue?

The preceding discussion has focused on state evaluations after notice of an insanity defense has been given. In many states, the prosecution may obtain such an evaluation *before* the defendant has given formal notice of an intent to raise an insanity defense. Should this practice be permitted? Why would the prosecution need such an evaluation? The American Bar Association's Criminal Justice Mental Health Standards recommend that, to guarantee the prosecution evaluation results that are "as fresh" as those obtained by the defense, the state should be notified of a defense evaluation within 48 hours and should be able to obtain its own evaluation shortly thereafter. However, the results of this pre-notice evaluation are to be disclosed to the prosecution only if and when the defense gives formal notice of its intent to raise an insanity defense. Standard 7–3.4.

Capital Sentencing Evaluations. Estelle holds that the fifth amendment applies in the capital sentencing context. Does this mean that the evaluation procedures applicable in the insanity context also apply to capital sentencing evaluations? In other words, does *Estelle* hold that the state is barred from compelling evaluation of the defendant on sentencing issues such as dangerousness if the defendant does not intend to use clinical testimony at sentencing? If the defendant *does* present clinical testimony at the sentencing proceeding, but limits it to responsibility issues having to do with culpability at the time of the offense, may the state compel an evaluation of the defendant to determine propensity, i.e., dangerousness, or is its examiner limited to addressing responsibility issues? See n.10 of *Estelle*.

Other Contexts. In a footnote, the Court in *Estelle* cautioned that it was not holding "that the same Fifth Amendment concerns are necessarily presented by all types of interviews and examinations that might be ordered or relied upon to inform a sentencing determination." 451 U.S. at 469 n. 13, 101 S.Ct. at 1876 n. 13. However, almost twenty years later, in *Mitchell v. United States*, 526 U.S. 314, 119 S.Ct. 1307, 143 L.Ed.2d 424 (1999), the Court noted that "[w]here [a noncapital] sentence has not yet been imposed a defendant may have a legitimate fear of adverse consequences from testimony" and held that the sentencing court may not use a defendant's silence against him to enhance his sentence (except, perhaps, as evidence of lack of remorse or unwillingness to accept responsibility). Thus, the defendant may also be able to refuse to cooperate with a state-requested evaluation in the typical noncapital sentencing context, at least if he or she does not plan to use expert testimony. In contrast, the Court has made clear, in *Allen v. Illinois*, 478 U.S. 364, 106 S.Ct. 2988, 92 L.Ed.2d 296 (1986), that the fifth amendment does not apply to "special" sentencing evaluations and proceedings conducted pursuant to mentally disordered sex offender (MDSO) statutes, because the primary purpose of such statutes is "treatment," not punishment. For the same reason, the fifth amendment does not apply to competency to stand trial or civil commitment evaluations and proceedings. For present purposes,[o] the importance of *Allen* is that the state may compel an evaluation of the defendant in any of these contexts, at least when, as discussed below, the results of the evaluation are used only to adjudicate the issue for which the evaluation is sought.

2. *Sanctions.* In situations where there is no right to remain silent, but the defendant still refuses to cooperate,[p] a sanction is necessary. In insanity cases, the courts have imposed four different types of sanctions. They have: (1) prohibited the defendant from presenting any evidence of insanity; (2) allowed the defendant to make the insanity claim, but prohibited use of expert testimony to support it; (3) allowed the defendant to present clinical testimony but only that which is based on facts that were revealed to the state's expert as well (in those cases where there was partial, but not complete cooperation); and (4) allowed the defendant to present unrestricted clinical testimony but also allowed the prosecution to inform the factfinder about the defendant's refusal to cooperate with the state's expert. See

---

[o]   *Allen* is reprinted at p. 999, where its implications for the civil commitment process are discussed.

[p]   Defining "non-cooperation" is a difficult issue. As one court has stated:

The fact, amply demonstrated over the years, is that a failure of a defendant who pleads insanity . . . to cooperate most often reflects an even greater degree of insanity rather than less. He is not always controllable by his lawyer, and many a psychotic defendant, who may or may not be legally insane, refuses to be represented by a lawyer. In short, non-cooperation may be evidence of insanity.

Lee v. County Ct., 27 N.Y.2d 432, 448–49, 267 N.E.2d 452, 461–62, 318 N.Y.S.2d 705, 718–19 (1971).

Christopher Slobogin, Estelle v. Smith: *The Constitutional Contours of the Forensic Evaluation*, 31 Emory L.J. 71, 103–104 (1981). Which option is fairest to both sides? See *Grattan v. Commonwealth*, 685 S.E.2d 634 (Va. 2009) (upholding trial court decision to bar defendant's expert testimony on insanity proffered because he had refused to meet with state evaluators, had met with his own experts on four separate occasions, was capable of understanding the consequences of non-cooperation and was not entitled to the "less drastic" remedy of allowing comment on his refusal to cooperate). Do any of these sanctions work when the defendant refuses to cooperate at an evaluation of competency to stand trial or on civil commitment issues? What would be an appropriate sanction in such situations?

3. *Use of evaluation results.* An issue separate from determining when the state may compel a defendant to undergo an evaluation is when, and for what purpose, the state may use the results of any evaluations that have taken place. Even when a compelled evaluation is permissible, prosecution use of its results may be limited or barred altogether. For instance, while the prosecution may compel the defendant to undergo a competency to stand trial evaluation, it may not, in most states, use the results of the evaluation for any purpose other than adjudication of competency. See, e.g., West's Fla.R.Crim.Proc. 3.211(e). Is such an approach required under *Estelle?* If not, should it be?

Most states have a similar rule with respect to the use of results from evaluations of mental state at the time of the offense. The federal rule is perhaps the most comprehensive:

> No statement made by the defendant in the course of any [psychiatric] examination ..., whether the examination be with or without the consent of the defendant, no testimony by the expert based upon such statement, and no other fruits of the statement shall be admitted in evidence against the defendant in any criminal proceeding except on an issue respecting mental condition on which the defendant has introduced testimony.

Fed.R.Crim.Pro. 12.2. This rule prohibits three things: (1) prosecution use of evaluation results when the defendant has not asserted a clinically-based defense or claim; (2) when such a claim is asserted, prosecution use of evaluation results for purposes other than rebuttal of that claim (e.g., use of an evaluator solely to establish that the defendant committed the criminal act); (3) prosecution use of evidence derived from the results of the evaluation (e.g., introduction of a murder weapon discovered as a result of leads developed solely from the psychiatric evaluation). Is there a reason other than fear of compulsion or manipulation by the expert that underlies this extensive protection?

Even this degree of protection may not satisfy the dictates of the fifth amendment. For instance, if an insanity defense is raised, expert testimony is very likely to recount in detail the defendant's actions at the time of the offense. In cases where the defendant readily admits he or she committed the criminal act, such testimony presumably does not present a problem. But what if the defendant asserts not only an insanity defense, but also a "factual" defense (e.g., self-defense or a claim that a co-defendant committed the crime)? In jurisdictions where such dual pleading is permitted, the state's expert may disclose information, highly prejudicial to the factual defense, which was obtained during a compelled evaluation. Courts have resorted to two practices in such a situation. The first is an instruction to the jury cautioning that the expert testimony is to be considered only on the issue of insanity. The second is bifurcation of the trial, with the first stage addressing the factual defense, and the second addressing, if necessary, the insanity defense. The expert testimony would be deferred until the second stage, thus avoiding revelation of disclosures that were compelled from the defendant at a psychiatric evaluation during adjudication of the factual defense.

Should the rules with respect to using evaluation results change if the results come from a *defense*-requested evaluation? In *Buchanan v. Kentucky*, 483 U.S. 402, 107 S.Ct. 2906, 97 L.Ed.2d 336 (1987), the prosecution rebutted the defendant's psychiatric defense with the results of a post-offense evaluation that was conducted to determine whether the defendant required psychiatric hospitalization and was competent to stand trial; the evaluation had been jointly requested by the prosecution and the defense. The Supreme Court found no constitutional violation because, unlike in *Estelle*, the defendant had raised a psychiatric defense and the defendant had joined in the evaluation motion. Is *Buchanan* correctly decided? What are the possible consequences of the decision? In *Penry v. Johnson*, 532 U.S. 782, 121 S.Ct. 1910, 150 L.Ed.2d 9 (2001), the state was allowed to introduce a report from a defense-requested competency evaluation in an earlier case after the defense expert, who had testified that the defendant was suffering from a mental disability and thus should not receive the death penalty, indicated he had reviewed the report in preparing his testimony. The Court strongly suggested that here too the fifth amendment was not violated, despite the absence of any warning that the original competency results might be used at a capital sentencing proceeding, because the defense had commissioned the evaluation in the earlier case, and had used an expert to address mental state in the instant case.

4.   *The right to counsel.* According to *Estelle,* the sixth amendment's guarantee of a right to counsel "in all criminal prosecutions" requires that, after the initiation of formal proceedings against the defendant, any state-requested evaluation of the defendant must be preceded by notice to counsel. Accord, *Satterwhite v. Texas*, 486 U.S. 249, 108 S.Ct. 1792, 100 L.Ed.2d 284 (1988). Presumably, this notice will permit counsel to explain the purpose of the evaluation to the defendant and to advise him or her whether to cooperate with the evaluator. However, the Supreme Court specifically avoided deciding whether there is a right to counsel's *presence* during the evaluation; if anything, it expressed some distaste for the idea. See n. 14.

Determining whether there should be a right to presence of counsel at state-requested evaluations is made difficult by the Court's somewhat muddled approach to the right to counsel generally. Under *United States v. Wade,* 388 U.S. 218, 87 S.Ct. 1926, 18 L.Ed.2d 1149 (1967), cited by *Estelle,* the right to counsel attached at any stage of the criminal prosecution which is deemed "critical"—that is, any stage where "the presence of counsel is necessary to preserve the defendant's basic right to a fair trial as affected by his right meaningfully to cross-examine the witnesses against him and to have effective assistance of counsel at the trial itself." In *Wade,* the Court found a right to counsel at post-indictment lineup identifications because (1) "the trial which might determine the accused's fate may well be not that in the courtroom but at the pretrial confrontation"; (2) "there is a serious difficulty in depicting what transpires at lineups", particularly if "the jury's choice is between the accused's unsupported version and that of the police officers present"; and (3) the "vagaries of eyewitness identification are well-known." If counsel is not present to observe, and thus enabled to reconstruct at trial, any irregularities in the identification process, these three factors create "a grave risk of erroneous conviction."

Wade's critical stage analysis was significantly modified, however, by *United States v. Ash,* 413 U.S. 300, 93 S.Ct. 2568, 37 L.Ed.2d 619 (1973), in which the Court found no right to counsel when the police show a witness photo displays for purposes of identification. Rejecting *Wade's* emphasis on whether the procedure in question might prejudice the defendant and whether counsel could alleviate the prejudice, the Court concluded that instead the key inquiry should be whether the procedure involves a "trial-like confrontation"—that is, whether it confronts the accused with the "intricacies of the law and the advocacy of the public prosecutor." *Wade's* approach, the Court stated, would give the right to counsel too broad a scope; as an example, the Court mentioned that critical stage analysis would improperly entitle the defendant to counsel at prosecutorial interviews of the victim and other witnesses.

Whether they apply the critical stage test or the trial-like confrontation test, most courts have held that defendants have no right to have counsel present during state-requested clinical evaluations. Comment, *The Right to Counsel During Court–Ordered Psychiatric Examinations of Criminal Defendants,* 26 Vill.L.Rev. 135 (1980). *United States v. Byers,* supra, is again illustrative. Then—Judge Scalia, relying on *Ash,* concluded for the majority that there is no right to counsel at a post-notice insanity evaluation. The defendant who has been advised of his or her rights by counsel prior to the evaluation "ha[s] no decisions in the nature of legal strategy or tactics to make" during the evaluation. Moreover, the "examining psychiatrist is not an adversary" or "expert in 'the intricacies of substantive and procedural criminal law.'" Scalia also registered practical objections to having counsel present during the evaluation:

> The "procedural system" of the law, which is one justification for the presence of counsel and which, by the same token, the presence of counsel brings in its train, is evidently antithetical to psychiatric examination, a process informal and unstructured by design. Even if

counsel were uncharacteristically to sit silent and interpose no procedural objections or suggestions, one can scarcely imagine a successful psychiatric examination in which the subject's eyes move back and forth between the doctor and his attorney. Nor would it help if the attorney were listening from outside the room, for the subject's attention would still wander where his eyes could not. And the attorney's presence in such a purely observational capacity, without ability to advise, suggest or object, would have no relationship to the Sixth Amendment's 'Assistance of Counsel.'

The latter observation also led Scalia to find, as he already had with respect to the fifth amendment, that the sixth amendment does not require taping of state-requested evaluations. He concluded: "It is enough, as far as the constitutional minima of the criminal process are concerned, that the defendant has the opportunity to contest the accuracy of witnesses' testimony by cross-examining them at trial, and introducing his own witnesses in rebuttal."

If *Wade* were applicable, how would you evaluate the result in *Byers*? Accepting *Ash* as the governing precedent, is Scalia's characterization of the psychiatrist as a non-adversary realistic? Is it consistent with *Estelle's* characterization of Dr. Grigson?

5.   *Summary problems on evaluation issues.* How would you rule in the following scenarios and why? What are the counterarguments to your conclusions?

A.   Assume Jones, charged with second degree murder, hires three mental health professionals to evaluate his sanity at the time of the offense. He then notifies the court and the prosecution that he intends to raise an insanity defense and that he intends to use the first two experts to support the defense. The prosecution wants to subpoena the third expert. Jones objects.

B.   Same facts as A. The prosecution also wants to compel an evaluation of Jones' sanity at the time of the offense. Jones objects.

C.   The court grants the prosecution's motion in B. Jones's attorney requests to be present during the evaluation. The state objects.

D.   At the state-requested evaluation, Jones will not talk about the day of the offense, claiming the state's expert is a CIA agent intent on "stealing my mind." The prosecution asks the court to sanction Jones.

E.   Smith, who is indigent, is charged with capital murder. He has no documented history of mental disorder, but his attorney claims that Smith is suffering from severe depression and that the depression affects his ability to communicate at the present time and affected his behavior at the time of the offense. The attorney moves for a state-paid evaluation of Smith's competency to stand trial, his sanity, and issues related to capital sentencing, including whether he was under emotional stress at the time of the offense and his treatability. He specifically requests Dr. Black as the evaluator. Dr. Black is a private psychiatrist whose rates are very high. The state argues that Smith is not entitled to an evaluation of any sort and that, even if he is, an evaluation at the state hospital would be sufficient.

F. The court orders that Smith be evaluated at the state hospital on the competency, sanity and sentencing issues. Smith moves that the results of this evaluation be sent only to him. The state objects, arguing that it is entitled to the results as well.

G. The motion in F is granted. Smith indicates he will use expert testimony only at sentencing. The state moves for an evaluation on the competency and sanity issues. In support of its motion, the state points to the defense attorney's representations in E. Smith objects.

H. The court grants the state's motion in G. Smith is found competent to stand trial, tried and convicted of capital murder. At his capital sentencing proceeding he plans to present expert testimony to the effect that he was under extreme emotional distress at the time of the offense as a result of severe depression and that, with proper care, the prognosis for his condition is good. The state wants to introduce expert testimony, based on the results of the competency evaluation it obtained, that Smith is dangerous; dangerousness is an aggravating circumstance under the state's capital punishment statute. Smith objects, noting that no warnings were given him prior to the state's evaluation and that, in any event, he "opened the door" only on mitigation issues.

2.   Hearsay and Other Evidentiary Considerations

Rarely will the testifying mental health professional have observed directly all of the behavioral or biological evidence upon which he or she relies. For instance, in evaluating a criminal accused who has asserted an insanity defense, the mental health professional will not only interview the defendant, but will interview, or obtain statements made by, family, friends and witnesses of the alleged offense. Various types of records— medical, psychological, criminal, educational, and occupational—will be acquired. Clinical reports from other mental health professionals (e.g., psychological test results, social histories) are also usually obtained.

Unless the individuals who possess or created this information are produced at trial, the evidence is "hearsay"—that is, statements from declarants who are not in court. Hearsay is generally considered inadmissible because the declarant cannot be subjected to cross-examination. Federal Rule of Evidence, Rule 802. Of course, there are several exceptions to this rule. For instance, pre-trial statements by the person who is the subject of legal proceedings are admissible, even if the person does not take the witness stand and undergo cross-examination, under the party admissions exception.[q] Documentary information may

---

[q]   Under the federal rules, if the party admission is offered *against* the party, then it is not hearsay to begin with. Rule 801(d)(2).

also be admissible under the so-called "business records" exception to the hearsay rule, if the custodian of the record or "other qualified witness" can attest to the fact that the document was kept as a regular practice of the business or profession.[r] But much of the third party information upon which mental health professionals rely is hearsay for which there is not a traditionally accepted exception. The following case addresses this problem.

PEOPLE V. GOLDSTEIN

Court of Appeals of New York, 2005.
6 N.Y.3d 119, 843 N.E.2d 727.

R.S. SMITH, JUDGE

We reverse defendant's conviction and order a new trial, because his constitutional right to be confronted with the witnesses against him was violated when a psychiatrist who testified for the prosecution recounted statements made to her by people who were not available for cross-examination.

Facts and Procedural History

On January 3, 1999, defendant killed Kendra Webdale, a woman he did not know, by throwing her into the path of an approaching subway train. He was charged with murder in the second degree; his principal defense was insanity. His first trial ended in a hung jury.

At his second trial, the two main witnesses were forensic psychiatrists, Spencer Eth, called by the defense, and Angela Hegarty, called by the prosecution. These doctors agreed that defendant was mentally ill; he had been diagnosed as schizophrenic some 10 years before the act for which he was on trial, and had been treated in a number of mental hospitals in the interim. The doctors disagreed, however, on the role that defendant's mental illness played in the killing.

In Eth's opinion, defendant pushed Kendra Webdale to her death "when he was suffering an acute exacerbation . . . of severe psychotic symptoms," perhaps resulting from a failure to take prescribed antipsychotic medications. Eth testified that the symptoms were so

---

[r]   Rule 803(6) creates an exception to the hearsay rule for records of regularly conducted activity, i.e.: "[a] memorandum, report, record, or data compilation, in any form, of acts, events, conditions, opinions, or diagnoses, made at or near the time by, or from information transmitted by, a person with knowledge, if kept in the course of a regularly conducted business activity, and if it was the regular practice of that business activity to make the memorandum, report, record, or data compilation, all as shown by the testimony of the custodian or other qualified witness, . . . unless the source of information or the method or circumstances of preparation indicate lack of trustworthiness. The term 'business' as used in this paragraph includes business, institution, association, profession, occupation, and calling of every kind, whether or not conducted for profit." Rule 803(8) creates a similar exception for "public records," except that, in light of Confrontation Clause concerns, such records are inadmissible if introduced by the government against a criminal defendant.

extreme that defendant "couldn't plan, he couldn't intend, he couldn't know as we understand what know means what he was doing or that it was wrong." Hegarty, by contrast, found that defendant had a "relatively mild" disorder "in the schizophrenic spectrum" and that his psychotic symptoms "were substantially in remission" at the time of the killing. Hegarty also testified that defendant's personality had "antisocial" features that were more relevant to his act than his schizophrenia. She testified, in substance, that defendant was a predator, driven to acts of violence against women by feelings of rejection and sexual frustration, who was using his schizophrenia as an excuse for his actions. Both doctors supported their opinions by describing their own examinations of defendant and by reviewing voluminous clinical records.

The main issue on this appeal arises because Hegarty's testimony also described another category of information—facts she had obtained in interviews of third parties. According to Hegarty, her field of expertise, "forensic psychiatry," could be distinguished from more traditional "clinical psychiatry," which "would largely . . . confine itself to what the defendant would say. And maybe the clinical record." The purpose of forensic psychiatry, Hegarty testified, is "to get to the truth," and she made clear that she believes interviews of people with firsthand knowledge are an important way of accomplishing that goal.

Over objection, Hegarty was permitted to tell the jury what she was told by six of her interviewees. The statements thus relayed from four of these people—whom we will call John P., Kimberly D., Serita G. and Isaac V.—are important to our decision.

John P. was a security guard at Waldbaum's in late 1996, about two years before the fatal attack on Kendra Webdale, when defendant assaulted a woman who was shopping there. John P. restrained defendant immediately after the assault, and he described to Hegarty, who repeated to the jury, defendant's reaction when he was seized. According to Hegarty's account of John P.'s statement, defendant said "I'm sick, I'm sick, I'm schizophrenic," kept repeating those assertions, and said that he had just got out of the hospital. Defendant made a similar statement—"I'm psychotic, take me to the hospital," or words to that effect—immediately after throwing Kendra Webdale to her death. John P.'s statement thus supported Hegarty's and the prosecution's theory that defendant had repeatedly used his schizophrenia to minimize his misconduct and avoid punishment.

Kimberly D. was the girlfriend of a man who shared an apartment with defendant in November 1998—about two months before Kendra Webdale's death—when Stephanie H., the girlfriend of another resident, visited the apartment. Hegarty testified that Kimberly D. had told Hegarty that Stephanie H., who worked in a strip club, "would tease" defendant. Hegarty also testified, apparently still recounting what

Kimberly D. said to her, that Stephanie H. "bears a rather remarkable similarity [in] appearance to Kendra Webdale." Thus, Hegarty suggested to the jury that defendant identified the woman he killed with another woman who had frustrated him sexually.

Serita G. had been defendant's landlady twice, first in 1996 and then in 1998–1999 up to the date of Kendra Webdale's death. According to Hegarty, Serita G. told her "that on one occasion . . . her maid went downstairs and the defendant was lying on his bed exposed and he didn't cover himself." This was part of the basis for Hegarty's testimony that defendant had "been sexually inappropriate with women."

Isaac V. was one of defendant's roommates in the month preceding Kendra Webdale's death. Hegarty testified to Isaac V.'s description of defendant's personality: She said that Isaac V. said that defendant was "a little weird . . . didn't act his age . . . wanted to go to college and . . . wanted to be somebody . . . was never disrespectful and never violent and very calm." This description corroborated Hegarty's overall picture of defendant as someone suffering from a relatively mild mental illness, not a hopelessly out-of-control schizophrenic.

The jury convicted defendant of second degree murder, thus rejecting his insanity defense. The Appellate Division affirmed. We now reverse.

Discussion

Defendant argues that Hegarty's testimony recounting statements of interviewees was inadmissible hearsay under New York law, because the People failed to show that the statements were information of a kind commonly relied on by members of Hegarty's profession. Defendant also argues that the admission of the interviewees' statements violated his constitutional right to confront the witnesses against him. We reject defendant's New York law argument, but we agree that his right to confrontation was violated.

I

People v. Stone, 35 N.Y.2d 69, 358 N.Y.S.2d 737, 315 N.E.2d 787 [1974] and *People v. Sugden,* 35 N.Y.2d 453, 363 N.Y.S.2d 923, 323 N.E.2d 169 [1974] govern the question of when a psychiatrist's opinion may be received in evidence, even though some of the information on which it is based is inadmissible hearsay. As we explained in *Sugden,* a psychiatrist "may rely on material, albeit of out-of-court origin, if it is of a kind accepted in the profession as reliable in forming a professional opinion," or if it "comes from a witness subject to full cross-examination on the trial." The latter ground for admissibility does not apply here; defendant had no opportunity to cross-examine the interviewees whose statements are in issue. Defendant argues that the former ground is inapplicable also, because the prosecution failed to meet its burden of showing that the interviewees' statements were "material . . . of a kind accepted in the profession as reliable."

We disagree. The proponent's burden of showing acceptance in the profession may be met through the testimony of a qualified expert, whether or not that expert is the same one who seeks to rely on the out-of-court material. Here, the People's burden was met by Hegarty's testimony. Hegarty acknowledged that "traditionally" psychiatrists did not rely on interviews with third parties, but said that "several researchers, forensic psychiatrists, past presidents of the Academy of Psychiatry and Law, Park Dietz and Philip Resnick, for example" had emphasized the need for a broader approach. While she acknowledged that "not everybody holds this view" and that "many good forensic psychiatrists might . . . disagree," she testified that interviewing of third parties is "becoming more and more the practice." She added that the seeking out of facts from sources other than defendant's own statements and the clinical record is "very, very much supported in the literature."

Any imprecision in Hegarty's description of accepted professional practice could have been explored on cross-examination; defendant's counsel was free to ask Hegarty, for example, exactly what "literature" she was referring to, and to try to show it did not support her procedure. But Hegarty's statements on this issue were neither made the subject of cross-examination nor contradicted by any other evidence. Indeed, Eth acknowledged that Hegarty's preferred approach was accepted by some reputable professionals, though he said they were a "minority." The prosecution did not have to prove that the materials in question were universally accepted; widespread acceptance by professionals of good reputation is enough. The case would be different if the procedures at issue found support only among a faction of outliers not generally respected by their colleagues. But in this case, the trial court had a sufficient basis for finding that the third-party interviews were material of a kind accepted in the profession as reliable, and that therefore Hegarty's opinion was admissible under *Stone* and *Sugden*.

II

To avoid any misinterpretation of our holding, we point out the existence of a New York law issue that the parties have not addressed and we do not reach.

We have held in section I only that Hegarty's *opinion,* although based in part on statements made out of court, was admissible because those statements met the test of acceptance in the profession. Both parties seem to assume that, if that test was met, Hegarty was free, subject to defendant's constitutional right of confrontation, not only to express her opinion but to repeat to the jury all the hearsay information on which it was based. That is a questionable assumption.

Stone and *Sugden* were concerned with the admissibility of a psychiatrist's opinion, not the facts underlying it. There is no indication in either case that the prosecution sought to elicit from the psychiatrist the content of the hearsay statements he relied on. And it can be argued that there should be at least some limit on the right of the proponent of an expert's opinion to put before the factfinder all the information, not otherwise admissible, on which the opinion is based. Otherwise, a party might effectively nullify the hearsay rule by making that party's expert a "conduit for hearsay".

The distinction between the admissibility of an expert's opinion and the admissibility of the information underlying it, when offered by the proponent, has received surprisingly little attention in this state (which perhaps accounts for the parties' failure to discuss it here). [I]n 2000, rule 703 of the Federal Rules of Evidence ("Bases of Opinion Testimony by Experts") was amended to deal with this issue. The last sentence of the rule now provides: "Facts or data that are otherwise inadmissible shall not be disclosed to the jury by the proponent of the opinion or inference unless the court determines that their probative value in assisting the jury to evaluate the expert's opinion substantially outweighs their prejudicial effect." We are not called upon to decide here, and do not decide, whether the New York rule is the same as, or less or more restrictive than, this federal rule.

III

The Sixth Amendment to the United States Constitution provides: "In all criminal prosecutions, the accused shall enjoy the right . . . to be confronted with the witnesses against him." Similarly, article I, § 6 of the New York Constitution provides: "In any trial in any court whatever the party accused shall . . . be confronted with the witnesses against him or her." The meaning of the federal Confrontation Clause was recently considered by the United States Supreme Court in *Crawford v. Washington,* 541 U.S. 36, 124 S.Ct. 1354, 158 L.Ed.2d 177 [2004], and we conclude that *Crawford* requires reversal of defendant's conviction.

Crawford, which overruled *Ohio v. Roberts,* 448 U.S. 56, 100 S.Ct. 2531, 65 L.Ed.2d 597 [1980], establishes that the Confrontation Clause generally prohibits the use of "testimonial" hearsay against a defendant in a criminal case, even if the hearsay is reliable, unless the defendant has a chance to cross-examine the out-of-court declarant. The People contend that *Crawford* does not apply here, first, because the statements by Hegarty's interviewees were not hearsay, and secondly, because they were not testimonial. We reject both arguments.

The claim that the interviewees' statements to Hegarty were not hearsay is based on the theory that they were not offered to prove the truth of what the interviewees said. Hearsay is "a statement made out of court . . . offered for the truth of the fact asserted in the statement. The

Supreme Court said in *Crawford* that the Confrontation Clause "does not bar the use of testimonial statements for purposes other than establishing the truth of the matter asserted". Here, according to the People, the interviewees' statements were not evidence in themselves, but were admitted only to help the jury in evaluating Hegarty's opinion, and thus were not offered to establish their truth.

We find the distinction the People make unconvincing. We do not see how the jury could use the statements of the interviewees to evaluate Hegarty's opinion without accepting as a premise either that the statements were true or that they were false. Since the prosecution's goal was to buttress Hegarty's opinion, the prosecution obviously wanted and expected the jury to take the statements as true. Hegarty herself said her purpose in obtaining the statements was "to get to the truth." The distinction between a statement offered for its truth and a statement offered to shed light on an expert's opinion is not meaningful in this context. We conclude that the statements of the interviewees at issue here were offered for their truth, and are hearsay.

We also conclude that the statements are testimonial, in the sense that *Crawford* used that term. *Crawford* explained that the Confrontation Clause "applies to 'witnesses' against the accused—in other words, those who 'bear testimony.'" The Court added: "'Testimony,' in turn, is typically '[a] solemn declaration or affirmation made for the purpose of establishing or proving some fact.' . . . An accuser who makes a formal statement to government officers bears testimony in a sense that a person who makes a casual remark to an acquaintance does not." The Court in *Crawford* did not adopt a definition of testimonial hearsay, but it offered some alternative definitions:

> "Various formulations of this core class of 'testimonial' statements exist: '*ex parte* in-court testimony or its functional equivalent—that is, material such as affidavits, custodial examinations, prior testimony that the defendant was unable to cross-examine, or similar pretrial statements that declarants would reasonably expect to be used prosecutorially,' . . . 'extrajudicial statements . . . contained in formalized testimonial materials, such as affidavits, depositions, prior testimony, or confessions,' . . . 'statements that were made under circumstances which would lead an objective witness reasonably to believe that the statement would be available for use at a later trial'. . . . These formulations all share a common nucleus and then define the Clause's coverage at various levels of abstraction around it."

We think the statements made to Hegarty by her interviewees were testimonial. Hegarty was an expert retained to testify for the People. The record does not specifically show that the interviewees knew this, but it would be strange if Hegarty did not tell them; we infer that they knew they were responding to questions from an agent of the State engaged in trial preparation. None of them was making "a casual remark to an acquaintance"; all of them should reasonably have expected their statements "to be used prosecutorially" or to "be available for use at a later trial."

While it is true that the Supreme Court referred, in describing testimonial hearsay, to "formal" statements made to "government officers," we do not think that these words exclude the statements at issue here. Responses to questions asked in interviews that were part of the prosecution's trial preparation are "formal" in much the same sense as "depositions" and other materials that the Supreme Court identified as testimonial. *Crawford* itself shows that the statements need not be under oath and need not be formal in their language; the statement held excludable by the *Crawford* court was unsworn and used colloquial phrasing. Nor do we think the difference between an expert retained by the State and a "government officer" is of constitutional significance here. The Confrontation Clause would offer too little protection if it could be avoided by assigning the job of interviewing witnesses to an independent contractor rather than an employee.

In short, defendant's rights under the Confrontation Clause were violated when Hegarty was allowed to tell the jury what witnesses defendant had no chance to cross-examine had said to her.

IV

[The remainder of the Court's decision concludes that the constitutional error was not harmless.]

QUESTIONS AND COMMENTS

1. *Confrontation Clause analysis.* In *Crawford v. Washington*, discussed in *Goldstein*, the U.S. Supreme Court held that the government is prohibited from introducing at a criminal trial an out-of-court statement that is "testimonial," unless the maker of the statement is unavailable at trial (i.e., dead, not accessible through subpoena, or claiming the fifth amendment) and the defendant had prior opportunity to cross-examine the declarant. As *Goldstein* indicates, a testimonial assertion is either a formalized statement to a government agent or a statement made to such an agent under circumstances "which would lead an objective witness reasonably to believe that the statement would be available for use at a later trial." In later cases, the Court clarified that to be testimonial a statement must be in response to some sort of "official interrogation," the "primary purpose" of which is to establish who did what rather than enabling the police "to meet an ongoing emergency." *Michigan v. Bryant*, ___ U.S. ___, 131 S.Ct. 2221, 279 L.Ed.2d 93 (2012) (finding that statements made to police by a shooting victim 25 minutes after the shooting were non-testimonial). Consider the statement Goldstein made to John P., the security guard, which the court does not allow

Dr. Hegarty to repeat. Is the court correct that it is testimonial? Even if it is, should the fact that Goldstein is in the courtroom nonetheless allow the government to use it?

To be testimonial the statement must also be made to a government agent. A number of lower court cases have held that statements made to relatives, friends, and emergency room doctors and nurses are not testimonial, even if they are in response to questions about the crime. In contrast, in *Melendez–Diaz v. Massachusetts*, 557 U.S. 305, 129 S.Ct. 2527, 174 L.Ed.2d 314 (2009) and *Bullcoming v. New Mexico*, ___ U.S. ___, 131 S.Ct. 2705, 180 L.Ed.2d 610 (2011), the Supreme Court held that results of tests performed by government forensic labs in an effort to determine whether physical evidence can be tied to the defendant are testimonial; thus, the individuals who perform the tests must be available to testify. The *Goldstein* court holds that Dr. Hegarty, who is a forensic psychiatrist at New York state's Creedmoor Psychiatric Center and also teaches at Columbia University, was a government agent for purposes of the Confrontation Clause, because the interviewees likely knew she was conducting an evaluation for the prosecution. Should the assumptions of the interviewees be relevant in this context? Many experts like Dr. Hegarty rely on other professionals to accumulate information. If a social worker working with Dr. Hegarty had interviewed the third party informants, could Dr. Hegarty describe those statements in the absence of corroborating testimony by the social worker?

Note that, in Section III of its opinion, the *Goldstein* court never explicitly holds that Dr. Hegarty's opinion, as opposed to its basis, is inadmissible under the Confrontation Clause and that, in Section II of the opinion, it concludes the opinion *is* admissible under state evidentiary rules. Does making a distinction between opinion and fact testimony make sense in determining admissibility? Consider the following material.

2. *Hearsay analysis.* While the *Goldstein* court holds that the Confrontation Clause precluded Dr. Hegarty from describing the hearsay statements she relied on, it also noted, in Section II of the opinion, that the same result might occur under traditional hearsay rules (in a civil case or in a criminal case with respect to non-testimonial evidence). The court states that, in contrast to the Federal Rules of Evidence, New York law is not clear as to whether hearsay relied on by a mental health professional is admissible. The full text of Federal Rule 703, briefly described in the opinion, is as follows:

> The facts or data in the particular case upon which an expert bases an opinion or inference may be those perceived by or made known to the expert at or before the hearing. If of a type reasonably relied upon by experts in the particular field in forming opinions or inferences upon the subject, the facts or data need not be admissible in evidence in order for the opinion or inference to be admitted. Facts or data that are otherwise inadmissible shall not be disclosed to the jury by the proponent of the opinion or inference unless the court determines that their probative

value in assisting the jury to evaluate the expert's opinion substantially outweighs their prejudicial effect.

The reasonable reliance test in Rule 703 is reminiscent of *Frye's* general acceptance test but applies to the facts rather than to the theory or methodology underlying an opinion. This test, now followed in most states as well, significantly modified the traditional common law rule, which excluded opinions based on inadmissible evidence. See *United States v. Sims*, 514 F.2d 147 (9th Cir. 1973) (describing and rejecting the traditional rule). The Advisory Committee's Note on this aspect of Rule 703 justified the reasonable reliance test as follows:

> [The] rule is designed . . . to bring the judicial practice into line with the practice of the experts themselves when not in court. Thus a physician in his own practice bases his diagnosis on information from numerous sources and of considerable variety, including statements by patients and relatives, reports and opinions from nurses, technicians and other doctors, hospital records, and X rays. Most of them are admissible in evidence, but only with the expenditure of substantial time in producing and examining various authenticating witnesses. The physician makes life-and-death decisions in reliance upon them. His validation, expertly performed and subject to cross-examination, ought to suffice for judicial purposes.

56 F.R.D. 183, 283.

Is the Committee's rationale persuasive when the expert testimony at issue is from mental health professionals? See Note, *Hearsay Bases of Psychiatric Opinion Testimony: A Critique of Federal Rule of Evidence 703*, 51 S.Cal.L.Rev. 129 (1977). What if, for instance, the expert opinion is based on a hearsay account of the defendant's early childhood from a litigant's parents or friends? A diagnosis given a litigant ten years ago by a psychiatrist? A description of illegal conduct given by one observer to a (non-governmental) witness? The *Goldstein* court held that the reasonable reliance test was met in that case, citing Dr. Hegarty's testimony that several well-known experts and researchers rely on hearsay in their work. Should that type of reasoning be enough to allow opinions based in whole or part on otherwise inadmissible hearsay?

In Section II of its opinion, the *Goldstein* court hastened to add that it was merely holding that its hearsay analysis would allow introduction of Dr. Hegarty's *opinion*, not necessarily the hearsay facts underlying it. Here the last sentence of Rule 703 (which, unlike the rest of the rule, many states have *not* adopted) comes into play. If you were the judge and the Confrontation Clause were not at issue, would you allow the hearsay statements in *Goldstein* into evidence?

If a court decides an expert cannot testify about hearsay facts underlying the opinion, how is the expert to explain the opinion? Is it ethical to testify in this situation? Might the answer depend on how crucial the hearsay evidence is to the opinion? Is the hearsay in *Goldstein* crucial or merely corroborative?

Another approach is to allow the expert to describe the hearsay but caution the jury that it should be considered only in evaluating the strength of the opinion, not the truth of the matters asserted. See *Sims*, supra. Does that approach make sense?

3. *Other bases for testimony*. Information that forms the basis of a clinical opinion may be inadmissible for reasons other than the hearsay rule. For instance, mental health professionals sometimes administer sodium amobarbital (a disinhibiting drug) or use hypnosis during their interview process. Although such techniques are not viewed as "truth determinants" by experienced clinicians, they may promote therapeutic recollection in cases where patients' amnesia follows traumatic experiences. Laura L. Nichols et al., *Sodium Amobarbital: Historical Perspectives and Neurorehabilitation: Clinical Caveats*, 31 NeuroRehabilitation 95, 99–100 (2012). The statements of a person who is under the influence of hypnosis or amytal are usually barred, not on hearsay grounds (because the statements are usually party admissions), but because of the unreliability of the technique used. See, e.g., *State v. Pierce*, 263 S.C. 23, 207 S.E.2d 414 (1974); *State v. Chase,* 206 Kan. 352, 480 P.2d 62 (1971). The courts that reach this result generally rely on some version of the *Frye* rule. Evidence may also be excluded for constitutional reasons. For instance, soon after the attempted assassination of President Reagan, John Hinckley's hotel room in Washington, D.C. was searched and a diary, containing a wealth of information relevant to his mental state, was discovered. The trial court held that since the police did not have a warrant or probable cause at the time of the search, the diary was inadmissible. As with hearsay, courts must decide whether an opinion based on hypnotically-induced testimony or illegally seized evidence is admissible and, if so, whether the factual basis for the opinion is also admissible.

4. *Judicial monitoring of evaluation process*. A final issue which could arise under Rule 703 is whether a clinical opinion is admissible when the facts undergirding it, although "reasonably relied upon," are so minimal that most clinicians would consider them an insufficient basis for an opinion. For example, the evaluation procedures of Dr. Grigson, the psychiatrist who testified in *Estelle v. Smith* and *Barefoot v. Estelle*, appear to fall far short of the ideal. In *Estelle,* he conducted a 90–minute interview on the basis of which he purported to be able to deliver opinions about not only the subject's dangerousness but also his competency to stand trial and sanity. *Estelle v. Smith,* 451 U.S. 454, 457, 459–60, 101 S.Ct. 1866, 1870, 1871, 68 L.Ed.2d 359 (1981). In *Barefoot,* he based his opinion about the defendant's dangerousness on a brief hypothetical question. Yet, according to Monahan's monograph published at around the same time, a comprehensive evaluation of dangerousness would include a personal interview, as well as data collection designed to investigate the person's history, future environment, reactions to stress, and base rate for violence based on actuarial factors. John Monahan, The Clinical Prediction of Violent Behavior 101–23 (NIMH, 1981). Is Rule 703 the right vehicle for challenging the adequacy of an evaluation procedure? Or is Rule 702, which requires that the expert be qualified "by knowledge, skill, experience, training, or education," the applicable rule?

5. *Differing contexts.* In some settings the hearsay rule and other exclusionary evidence rules may not apply with the same force as they do in criminal cases. For instance, some courts have held that hearsay is admissible in civil commitment proceedings. This position might have an impact on Rule 703 analysis. But see *In re Melton*, 597 A.2d 892 (D.C.1991) (holding in civil commitment context that hearsay is "reasonably relied upon" only if "the judge concludes that the information . . . is of a type for which the underlying reliability of the data can be sufficiently explored through cross-examination of the testifying expert"). The admissibility of hearsay in commitment hearings is discussed in more detail in Chapter Eight, pp. 938–939.

D. THE ULTIMATE ISSUE

One final limitation on expert testimony may exist, even if one assumes that clinical opinion testimony is generally admissible, and even if it is offered by a qualified mental health professional who has relied solely on permissible sources of information. Traditionally, a witness, whether expert or lay, was barred from addressing the "ultimate" legal issue (e.g., in this context, sanity, competency, or committability). Usually, the reason given for this rule was that such an opinion usurped the function of the factfinder. As originally promulgated, Federal Rule 704 specifically did away with the ultimate issue limitation on testimony. It stated: "Testimony in the form of an opinion or inference otherwise admissible is not objectionable because it embraces an ultimate issue to be decided by the trier of fact." The Advisory Committee justified this change for two reasons. First, it contended that the rule was impossible to enforce, because witnesses would merely paraphrase their testimony in an effort to avoid the ultimate issue language. Second, it noted that the old rule tended to deprive the factfinder of helpful testimony. "Thus . . . in cases of medical causation, witnesses were sometimes required to couch their opinions in cautious phrases of 'might or could,' rather than 'did,' though the result was to deprive many opinions of the positiveness to which they were entitled, accompanied by the hazard of a ruling of insufficiency to support a verdict." The Committee also pointed out that opinion testimony must still be helpful to the trier of fact under Rules 701 and 702, which should "afford ample assurances against the admission of opinions which would merely tell the jury what result to reach . . . [or which are] phrased in terms of inadequately explored legal criteria." 56 F.R.D. 183, 284.

However, in 1984, largely in response to the outcome of John Hinckley's trial, Congress added paragraph (b) to Rule 704. It reads: "No expert witness testifying with respect to the mental state or condition of a defendant in a criminal case may state an opinion or inference as to whether the defendant did or did not have the mental state or condition constituting an element of the crime charged or of a defense thereto. Such ultimate issues are matters for the trier of fact alone." The purpose of this amendment to Rule 704, according to the Report of the House Committee on the Judiciary, "is to eliminate the confusing spectacle of competing expert witnesses testifying to directly contradictory conclusions as to the ultimate legal issue to be found by the trier of fact." H.R.Report 98–1030, 98th cong., 2d Sess., p. 230.

In reading the following case, think about whether it makes sense for Congress to have singled out clinical testimony in this way.

UNITED STATES V. EDWARDS
United States Court of Appeals, Eleventh Circuit, 1987.
819 F.2d 262.

VANCE, CIRCUIT JUDGE:

Roland Edwards was charged with unarmed bank robbery under 18 U.S.C. § 2113(a). He pleaded not guilty by reason of insanity. After a two day trial, a jury returned a verdict of guilty. Edwards appeals, claiming that the district court allowed improper psychiatric testimony. He argues that the district court erred in permitting a government witness to give opinion testimony in violation of Fed.R.Evid. 704(b). We affirm.

* * *

At trial Edwards did not contest his role in the bank robbery, but argued that he was insane at the time that he committed the offense. Edwards' ex-wife and an old friend testified that they believed Edwards to be incapable of criminal activity. The crux of the defense case, however, was the testimony of Doctor Adolfo Vilasuso, a board-certified psychiatrist. Doctor Vilasuso examined Edwards approximately six times during October, 1985 and continued seeing Edwards once or twice a week up to the date of trial in February, 1986. Doctor Vilasuso noted that Edwards had endured a difficult past and stated that he thought Edwards was "off the wall." Doctor Vilasuso testified that he had a "very, very strong suspicion" that Edwards suffered from "manic-depressive" illness during April, 1984. The government countered with the rebuttal testimony of Doctor Albert Jaslow, another psychiatrist. Doctor Jaslow concluded from Edwards' description of events that Edwards was not in "an active manic state" at the time of the robbery because Edwards' actions were reasonably well controlled and goal directed.

The testimony at issue concerns Doctor Jaslow's analysis of Edwards' frustration with his financial problems at the time of the robbery:

Q: [by Prosecutor]:

What sort of things were going on that would have depressed him?

A: [by Doctor Jaslow]:

His inability to come to grips with his financial problems; inability to handle the relationship with the I.R.S., who were after him and who were not permitting him to, according to him, of course, to settle down sufficiently so he could gain enough monies to take care of the financial problems and so on. These were bothering him tremendously, of course.

Q: Were these feelings understandable, in your opinion?

Defense Counsel: Objection. It's improper. That's not a proper question for a doctor.

The Court: Overruled.

A: Under the circumstances of the responsibilities, the problems that he had, it was quite understandable. He would be disturbed; it was quite understandable he would be upset. It's quite understandable he would be frantically trying to find ways to modify his situation so he could get on with his life.

Edwards contends that the trial court erred in allowing this testimony because it contained a psychiatrist's opinion concerning his sanity, the ultimate issue at trial. We disagree. "In resolving the complex issue of criminal responsibility, it is of critical importance that the defendant's entire relevant symptomatology be brought before the jury and explained." It has long been the position of our court that this is the only way a jury may become sufficiently informed so as to make a determination of a defendant's legal sanity. This was also the attitude of Congress when it passed Rule 704(b):

> Psychiatrists, of course, must be permitted to testify fully about the defendant's diagnosis, mental state and motivation (in clinical and commonsense terms) at the time of the alleged act so as to permit the jury or judge to reach the ultimate conclusion about which they and only they are expert.

Congress did not enact Rule 704(b) so as to limit the flow of diagnostic and clinical information. Every actual fact concerning the defendant's mental condition is still as admissible after the enactment of Rule 704(b) as it was before. Rather, the Rule "changes the style of question and answer that can be used to establish both the offense and the defense thereto." The prohibition is directed at a narrowly and precisely defined evil:

> When, however, "ultimate issue" questions are formulated by the law and put to the expert witness who must then say "yea" or "nay," then the expert witness is required to make a leap in logic. He no longer addresses himself to medical concepts but instead must infer or intuit what is in fact unspeakable, namely, the probable relationship between medical concepts and legal or moral constructs such as free

will. These impermissible leaps in logic made by expert witnesses confuse the jury.

S.Rep. No. 225, 98th Cong., 1st Sess. 231 (quoting APA Statement on the Insanity Defense, Dec. 1982, at 18), *reprinted in* 1984 U.S.Code Cong. & Admin.News 3182, 3412–18. Accordingly, Rule 704(b) forbids only "conclusions as to the ultimate legal issue to be found by the trier of fact." *Id.* at 3412. See, e.g., *United States v. Hillsberg,* 812 F.2d 328, 331 (7th Cir.1987) (expert cannot state opinion as to whether defendant had the capacity to conform his conduct to the law); *United States v. Buchbinder,* 796 F.2d 910, 917 (7th Cir.1986) (expert could not testify as to whether defendant had the requisite mental state to defraud, but could testify as to the extent of defendant's depression over son's death).

The ultimate legal issue at Edwards' trial was whether Edwards "lack[ed] substantial capacity either to appreciate the wrongfulness of his conduct or to conform his conduct to the requirements of law." In fact, the challenged statements offer no conclusions at all about Edwards. Doctor Jaslow was simply observing that people who are not insane can nevertheless become frantic over a financial crisis.

The prosecution placed Doctor Jaslow on the stand to dispute Doctor Vilasuso's diagnosis. Using a common sense generalization, Doctor Jaslow explained why the defendant's behavior—his frantic efforts to pay bills, his manifestations of energy, his lack of sleep, and his feelings of depression—did not necessarily indicate an active manic state. We think that the doctor played exactly the kind of role which Congress contemplated for the expert witness:

> [I]t is clear that the psychiatrist's first obligation and expertise in the courtroom is to "do psychiatry," i.e., to present medical information and opinion about the defendant's mental state and motivation and to explain in detail the reason for his medical-psychiatric conclusions.

S.Rep. No. 225 supra, at 3413. We conclude that the district court committed no error in permitting this testimony.

AFFIRMED.

QUESTIONS AND COMMENTS

1. *Justification for the ultimate issue ban.* The *Edwards* court quotes the American Psychiatric Association to the effect that testimony on the ultimate issue involves the expert in a "leap of logic" from medical concepts to legal or moral ones. Isn't Dr. Jaslow's statement that Edwards's anxiety was "understandable" a leap from clinical criteria regarding mental disorder to legal criteria regarding normality and capacity to control one's behavior? If Dr. Jaslow had testified that Edwards could "appreciate the wrongfulness" of the robbery or "control his behavior" at that time, would his testimony have intruded more into moral considerations than his actual testimony? How does

one draw the line between "medical" or "clinical" concepts on the one hand, and moral concepts on the other? Does the language of Rule 704(b) help? Is Rule 704(b) necessary, given the existence of Rule 702 (requiring expert testimony to be based on specialized knowledge, skill, education, etc.)?

In answering these questions, compare *United States v. Manley*, 893 F.2d 1221 (11th Cir.1990) (defense counsel not permitted to ask expert whether a person with manic-depressive psychosis would "be able to appreciate the nature and quality or the wrongfulness of their actions") to *United States v. Salamanca*, 990 F.2d 629 (D.C.Cir. 1993) (permitting an expert to testify that "someone who had drunk as much [as the defendant] would have a diminished capacity to seek and plan"); *United States v. Davis*, 835 F.2d 274, 276 (11th Cir.1988) (approving a prosecutor's question as to whether a person diagnosed with multiple personalities was capable of understanding what he or she was doing); and *United States v. Kristiansen*, 901 F.2d 1463 (8th Cir. 1990) (permitting defense counsel to ask whether the mental disease of the type the defendant allegedly had "would affect a person's ability to appreciate their actions"). Does the following excerpt from *Kristiansen* make sense?

> [T]he defense clearly could ask whether Kristiansen was suffering from a mental disease or defect at the time of the offense. Just as clearly, the defense could not ask whether Kristiansen was unable to appreciate the nature and quality of his actions. . . . The more difficult question is whether the court erred in not permitting the defense to ask whether the mental disease or defect of the type that Kristiansen allegedly had would affect a person's ability to appreciate their actions. . . . We conclude that the defense should have been permitted to ask this question because it relates to the symptoms and qualities of the disease itself and does not call for an answer that describes Kristiansen's culpability at the time of the crime. Rule 704(b) was not meant to prohibit testimony that describes the qualities of a mental disease. "Under this proposal, expert psychiatric testimony would be limited to presenting and explaining their diagnoses, such as whether the defendant had a severe mental disease or defect and what the characteristics of such a disease or defect, if any, may have been." Comprehensive Crime Control Act of 1984, S.Rep. No. 98–225, 98th Cong., 2d Sess. 230 (1984) (Senate Report), *reprinted in* 1984 U.S.Code Cong. & Admin. News 3182, 3412. The fact that part of the wording of a question may track the legal test by asking if the disease prevents one suffering from the disease from understanding the nature and quality of an act does not violate the rule. The jury is left to ultimately decide whether the disease was so strongly present that the defendant himself suffered the effect of being unable to appreciate the quality of his act.

2. *The ABA position.* Ultimate legal language can usually be subdivided into two types. "Ultimate" conclusions directly address the dispositive legal issue, e.g., whether a person is or is not "incompetent," "insane," "committable" and so on. In contrast, a penultimate conclusion does

not reach this level of generalization but only speaks to the relevant legal test: for example, testimony that, under the American Law Institute test for insanity, a person accused of crime does or does not "as a result of mental disease or defect, lack substantial capacity to understand the wrongfulness of his act or to conform his behavior to the requirements of the law." Rule 704(b) is apparently meant to bar both types of testimony in federal court. The American Bar Association, on the other hand, distinguishes between the two. While barring testimony on the ultimate issue, the ABA would permit penultimate testimony, at least in insanity cases, because the language of the legal test (e.g., concerning a person's ability to "appreciate" the wrongfulness of his or her acts) expresses a concept which has clinical content. However, the ABA would forbid use of such language if statutory provisions or appellate decisions have given it particular legal content. American Bar Association, Criminal Justice Mental Health Standards, commentary to standard 7–6.6, at 336–338 (Little, Brown: 1987). Is the ABA claiming that penultimate testimony does not involve a moral issue, or that it combines clinical and moral issues? Whatever the answer to this question, why does further definition of the penultimate language through statute or appellate decision change the situation?

3.   *Ultimate language and the adversary process.* As noted, the reason given by Congress for adopting Rule 704(b) is the desire "to eliminate the confusing spectacle of competing expert witnesses testifying to directly contradictory conclusions as to the ultimate legal issue to be found by the trier of fact." Aren't contradictory conclusions the inevitable result of the adversary process? On the other hand, if a proceeding is *not* effectively adversarial (as is often true with competency and commitment determinations, for instance), should the expert be allowed to give *any* opinion (legal or otherwise)? See Christopher Slobogin, *The "Ultimate Issue" Issue*, 7 Behav.Sciences & Law 259 (1989).

It has been suggested that judges rely more heavily on the authority granted them under the federal rules and many state rules to appoint a "neutral" expert who would testify for the court rather than either of the parties. Stephen Golding, *Mental Health Professionals and the Courts: The Ethics of Expertise*, 13 Int'l J.L. & Psychiat. 281 (1990). Federal rule 706 provides:

> [T]he court may on its own motion or on the motion of any party enter an order to show cause why expert witnesses should not be appointed, and may request the parties to submit nominations. The court may appoint any expert witnesses agreed upon by the parties, and may appoint expert witnesses of its own selection. . . . A witness so appointed shall advise the parties of the witness' findings, if any; the witness' deposition may be taken by any party; and the witness may be called to testify by the court or any party. The witness shall be subject to cross-examination by each party, including a party calling the witness.

Will witnesses "appointed by the court" rather than retained by the parties be less likely to act in an "adversarial" manner? If so, would this be a good thing?

4. *Education of the legal profession.* To some extent, poor communication in court is the fault of mental health professionals who are ignorant of, or unwilling to call attention to, the limits of their expertise. But ultimately the blame has to fall on the legal system. Research indicates that many judges and lawyers *prefer* conclusory testimony. Gary Melton et al., Community Mental Health Centers & the Courts: An Evaluation of Community–Based Forensic Services 94–5, 99 (1985). Lawyers often are unfamiliar with the law, not to mention basic behavioral science concepts. C. Rosenberg & A. Louis McGarry, *Competency for Trial: The Making of an Expert*, 128 Am.J.Psychiat. 82 (1972) (only 10 of 28 criminal attorneys knew competency to stand trial standard). And even when they have some understanding of both, they may make little effort to use the tools of their trade in exposing spurious testimony. Norman Poythress, *Psychiatric Expertise in Civil Commitment: Training Attorneys to Cope with Expert Testimony*, 2 Law. & Hum.Behav. 1 (1978) (lawyers taught the inadequacies of clinical testimony persisted in avoiding careful cross-examination in commitment proceedings because of paternalistic attitudes). As Bonnie stated:

> The bench and bar are ultimately responsible for improving the administration of justice. If judges and juries are confused or misled by expert testimony, this usually means there has been poor lawyering. If experts give conclusory testimony, encompassing so-called ultimate issues—and fail to explain the bases for their opinions—the fault lies with the bench and bar, not with the experts. If forensic evaluators do not have access to the same information and reach different opinions for this reason, the fault lies with the legal system, not with the experts.

Richard Bonnie, *Morality, Equality, and Expertise: Renegotiating the Relationship Between Psychiatry and the Criminal Law*, 12 Bull.Am.Acad.Psychiat. & L. 5, 5–6 (1984).

CHAPTER 7

MENTAL DISORDER AND CRIMINAL LAW

■ ■ ■

Table of Sections

I. INTRODUCTION

The role of mental disability in determining whether those charged with crime should be punished and, if so, to what extent, is potentially quite broad. To understand why this is so, one must first understand the purposes of criminal punishment. Most criminal law scholars would agree that criminal punishment has at least five possible purposes: retribution, general deterrence, specific deterrence, incapacitation, and rehabilitation. Under retributive theories, punishment is imposed when a person makes a choice that deserves blame because it offends certain shared moral sensibilities; the person owes society a debt that must be paid. Deterrence theory, on the other hand, views punishment as a means of dissuading persons from committing acts that harm society, whether or not they are "blameworthy." General deterrence refers to the impact of punishment on others, while specific deterrence refers to its impact on the particular offender. Punishment is justified on incapacitative grounds when necessary to prevent an individual from committing crime again.

Similarly, punishment is justified on rehabilitation grounds if treatment would prevent a person from engaging in further criminal behavior.

This brief summary of the justifications for criminal punishment helps put in perspective the role of mental disability in the criminal law. For instance, the oldest criminal law doctrine focusing specifically on people with mental disability—the insanity defense—is often justified on the ground that certain people are so irrational, or so unable to control themselves, that they do not deserve retribution and are unlikely to understand or pay attention to criminal sanctions. As Professor Goldstein stated: "It would be widely regarded as incalculably cruel and unjust to incarcerate men who are not personally responsible in order to serve social functions. The notion of 'desert' or culpability is too deeply rooted." Further, "[u]nder the deterrent theory, . . . the insanity defense describes the man who is sufficiently different from the rest of us that he cannot be used as an effective example and who, in quite personal terms, cannot be expected to approach events mindful of the warnings sent to him by the criminal code." Abraham Goldstein, The Insanity Defense 13–14 (1967). For the same reasons, when a person's behavior is "involuntary" (as when an epileptic seizure results in death of another), criminal punishment may be inappropriate, a notion recognized by the "automatism" defense. Indeed, anyone whose mental state at the time of the offense is "abnormal" might be able to argue that his or her culpability and deterrability was diminished at that time.

At sentencing, the impact of mental disability is potentially even greater. After conviction retributive and general deterrence goals are still important, but the law also often attempts to individualize punishment through a focus on specific deterrence, incapacitation and rehabilitation. Thus, evidence of mental condition could be very useful in finetuning the punishment imposed, functioning either as a "mitigating factor" (e.g., to show diminished responsibility or to suggest amenability to treatment outside the prison setting), or as an "aggravating factor" (e.g., as proof of dangerousness).

Over the past century, the criminal law has, with some significant exceptions, moved toward full realization of the possibilities outlined above. Here these developments will only be outlined to place them in historical perspective. More detailed discussion follows in the body of this chapter.

Particularly significant has been the increasing relevance of mental disability in determining criminal liability at trial. The tendency toward expansion of the insanity defense is well known. Even more significant are developments with respect to the mental state element (mens rea) of criminal offenses. The common law usually required proof only of "objective," or inferred, intent rather than "subjective," or actual, intent. Thus, the prosecution could often secure conviction if it showed that the accused committed the criminal act under circumstances in which a "reasonable person" would intend such an act; the accused's actual intent was irrelevant. Probably the single most important trend in the substantive criminal law in the past century has been the continuing erosion of this position. The highly influential Model Penal Code, officially promulgated in 1962 by the American Law Institute, expresses a strong preference for criminal liability based solely on proof of criminal intent or awareness of the risk of harm. Following logically from this proposition, the Code permits evidence of mental abnormality to be introduced not only on the insanity issue, but also on the issue of whether the accused could form the intent associated with the alleged crime whenever that intent is subjective—sometimes called the "diminished capacity" defense. Additionally, the Model Penal Code's definitions of defensive doctrines such as mistake of fact, duress, self-defense and provocation—doctrines that were traditionally defined in "objective" terms (e.g., would a "reasonable" person be provoked to kill under the circumstances)—permit the defendant to submit evidence about his or her own feelings, desires, urges, and thoughts at the time of the offense. Theoretically, evidence of mental abnormality is relevant under any of these defenses.

The types of evidence an offender can present at sentencing—traditionally limited to pleas for mercy—have also expanded considerably over the past century. In many states, offenders may now submit virtually any mitigating information they can muster, including evidence of mental abnormality. In death penalty cases, the Supreme Court has held that offenders have a constitutional right to offer such evidence. At the same time, the state is often permitted to introduce evidence of dangerousness or untreatability at sentencing.

While mental abnormality has thus become increasingly relevant in the determination of whether and what type of punishment should be imposed, in the past few decades courts and legislatures have begun to reconsider the wisdom of this development. In the 1980's, for instance, several jurisdictions, many of them responding to John Hinckley's insanity acquittal on charges of attempting to assassinate President Ronald Reagan, either significantly reduced the scope of the insanity defense or eliminated it altogether. In a separate effort to curb the impact of the insanity defense, many states have adopted the "guilty but mentally ill" (GMBI) verdict as an intermediate option between insanity and a straight finding of guilt. Moreover, several states have rejected or severely limited the Model Penal Code's recommendation that mental abnormality be considered on the issue of intent, and many courts have demonstrated antipathy toward broadening other defenses.

Similar developments have occurred in the non-capital sentencing setting. Beginning in the 1970's, several states moved toward "determinate sentencing," or sentencing schemes that provide decisionmakers with relatively little leeway in setting punishment. In an effort to remove discretion from decision-makers, the thrust of these reforms was to base sentence lengths primarily on backward-looking culpability assessments rather than on forward-looking assessments of dangerousness, treatability and so on.

To some extent, these differing views on the role of mental disability in the criminal justice system are a function of varying perceptions about the limits of clinical expertise, a topic discussed in the previous chapter.[a] But at bottom they stem from assumptions about the fundamental purposes of the criminal sanction. The primary aim of this chapter is to examine these assumptions to provoke thought about the extent to which mental disability ought to be relevant to the doctrines of the substantive criminal law. The first section examines doctrines relevant to mental state at the time of the offense, including the defenses of insanity, "diminished capacity," and "automatism," and the GBMI verdict. The second section looks at sentencing, focusing on capital sentencing—the area in which sentencing law is most highly developed—and those special sentencing situations in which mental disability plays a significant role, such as "sexually violent predator" and other "dangerous offender" statutes.

II.   CRIMINAL RESPONSIBILITY

idea behind insanity defense

The criminal law assumes that people have the capacity to make and act upon choices and thus can be held legally (if perhaps not morally) accountable for them. But the law is also willing to assume that mental disability reduces this capacity, thus making the person less blameworthy and less able to obey the law's mandates. The assumption that people with mental disability are incapable of minimal rationality and are less deterrable than others has been called more of an "intuitive hunch" than an empirically verified fact. See Stephen Morse, *Treating Crazy People Less Specially*, 90 West.Va.L.Rev. 353, 370 (1988). Moreover, as H.L.A. Hart has pointed out, the deterrence rationale for defenses based on mental disability may be logically flawed because, even if some persons are undeterrable as a result of mental disorder, permitting such defenses may *encourage* others to commit crime in the hope that they can escape conviction through feigning mental disability. H.L.A. Hart, Punishment and Responsibility 18–20 (1968). Despite these possible problems, the central question remains the extent to which retributive or deterrence theory requires or suggests that inroads be made on the assumption that people have the capacity to choose their actions (sometimes called the "free will paradigm").

The possible impact of incapacitation and rehabilitation concerns should also be mentioned, however. For instance, as Goldstein has noted,

---

[a]   See in particular Part II.B.

one view of the insanity defense "sees the defense almost entirely as a path to treatment in a mental hospital. . . . The tacit assumption is that a paternal state can put [the acquittee] right by psychotherapy or by judicious social planning, if only the 'helping' professions are provided with the resources to do the job." Abraham Goldstein, The Insanity Defense 14 (1967). As another example, consider from the incapacitative perspective the impact of narrowing the insanity defense. Typically, persons adjudged insane are confined in a mental hospital for as long as they are considered mentally disordered and dangerous. If the insanity defense were abolished or its scope reduced significantly, individuals considered to be violent who previously might have been found insane and hospitalized indefinitely would be convicted and released from secure confinement at the end of their sentence, perhaps much earlier and with less post-release supervision than they would have experienced had they found legally insane. By changing the substantive law, the government would be deprived of a flexible dispositional device. As these examples illustrate, the extent to which policymakers want to implement rehabilitative and incapacitative goals might influence their efforts to define defenses based on mental disability.

These considerations should be kept in mind throughout the following materials.

A. THE INSANITY DEFENSE[b]

1. A Brief History

This section discusses the various formulations of the insanity defense that have been advanced through the years. A later section discusses whether the defense should be abolished, after examining its alternatives. As should become clear, the various tests set out below are the result of many variables, including changes in medical conceptualizations of mental illness, the criminal justice system, and attitudes of society toward people with mental disability.

Early Development. The idea of a defense to criminal responsibility based on mental disability goes back as far as the ancient Greek and Jewish civilizations. English case law, which heavily influenced early American courts, has long recognized the concept. At least as early as 1300, records show that English kings were pardoning murderers because their crimes were committed "while suffering from madness." Over the next several centuries, many different formulations of the defense emerged. Sir Edward Coke, a famous legal scholar of the late 16th and early 17th century, felt that "idiots" and "madmen" who "wholly loseth their memory and understanding" should be found insane. Sir Matthew

---

[b] This and the following descriptions in the text about criminal responsibility doctrines are adapted from Gary Melton et al., Psychological Evaluations for the Courts: A Handbook for Mental Health Professionals and Laywers, Chap. 8 (3d ed. 2007).

Hale, Chief Justice of the King's Bench in the 17th century, concluded in his private papers that the "best measure" for determining insanity was whether the accused had "as great understanding as ordinarily a child of fourteen hath." In 1723 Justice Tracy held that to be found insane "a man must be totally deprived of his understanding and memory so as not to know what he is doing, no more than an infant, brute or a wild beast." At about the same time, other English courts were excusing those who lacked the capacity to distinguish "good from evil" or "right from wrong."

The M'Naghten Test. It was this latter approach that, in slightly modified form, became what we now call the "M'Naghten test" of insanity. In response to controversy surrounding the insanity acquittal of Daniel M'Naghten on a charge of murdering the private secretary of Prime Minister Robert Peel, the House of Lords announced the following rule:

> To establish a defense on the ground of insanity, it must be clearly proved that, at the time of the committing of the act, the party accused was laboring under such a defect of reason, from disease of the mind, as not to know the nature and quality of the act he was doing; or, if he did know it, that he did not know he was doing what was wrong.

test

This formulation, announced in 1843, became the accepted rule in both England and the United States.

Criticism of the test was immediate, especially from the medical community. Indeed, five years before the House of Lords' pronouncement, Sir Isaac Ray, a noted American physician, had argued that the "insane mind" is often "perfectly rational, and displays the exercise of a sound and well-balanced mind." Thus, according to Ray, a defense based on mental illness that focuses merely on cognitive impairment is incomplete; the defendant's ability to control his or her acts must also be considered. Although directed at the law as it existed in 1838, Ray's comments applied with equal force to the M'Naghten test, which varied only slightly from its predecessors.

A second criticism of the rule was its rigidity. Even if one accepts the premise that cognitive dysfunction is the only appropriate focus of the insanity defense, the M'Naghten rule, some claimed, does not fairly pose the question; a literal interpretation of the M'Naghten test would seldom, if ever, lead to exculpation. In the words of one psychiatrist, "[if the test language were taken seriously,] it would excuse only those totally deteriorated, drooling hopeless psychotics of long-standing, and congenital idiots."

The Irresistible Impulse Test. In the United States, the legal response to the first criticism came in the form of a supplementary test for insanity, which eventually came to be called the "irresistible impulse" rule. Although versions of this test appeared in the first half of the nineteenth century, see *State v. Thompson*, Wright's Ohio Rep. 617 (1834); *Commonwealth v. Rogers*, 48 Mass. 500 (1844), the leading decision on the issue was handed down in 1887 and described the test as follows:

test

> [The defendant is not] legally responsible if the two following conditions concur: (1) If, by reason of the duress of . . . mental disease he had so far lost the power to choose between the right and wrong, and to avoid doing the act in question, as that his free agency was at the time destroyed; (2) and if, at the same time, the alleged crime was so connected with such mental disease, in the relation of cause and effect, as to have been the product of it solely.

Parsons v. State, 81 Ala. 577, 596, 2 So. 854, 866 (1887). The adoption of the test was usually justified on the ground that those offenders who could not control their behavior at the time of the offense were not deterrable by criminal sanctions; therefore, no legitimate moral or policy purpose was served by convicting them.

The "irresistible impulse" test met resistance from several fronts. Many in the legal community believed that impulsivity could easily be feigned, and feared that the test would lead to numerous invalid insanity acquittals. From the medical side came the criticism that a separate "control" test furthered the mistaken impression that the human psyche is compartmentalized into cognitive and volitional components. And, like M'Naghten, the test was seen as too rigid, excusing only those who were totally unable to prevent their unlawful behavior.

(3) **The Durham Rule.** In 1954, partly in response to the latter two contentions and the criticisms of M'Naghten, the federal District of Columbia Court of Appeals adopted the "product test" for insanity—a rule originally devised by Sir Isaac Ray and adopted by the New Hampshire Supreme Court in 1870, but one that had received little notice since that time. As set forth in *Durham v. United States,* 214 F.2d 862 (D.C.Cir.1954), the test stated simply that "an accused is not criminally responsible if his unlawful act was the product of mental disease or defect." Judge Bazelon, the author of the *Durham* opinion, hoped the rule would encourage mental health professionals to explain all aspects of a defendant's personality and functioning by removing legal strictures on such professionals' testimony.

test

In time, however, this lack of guidance became a problem in itself. The product test asked essentially two questions: (1) Did mental disease or defect exist at the time of the offense? (2) Was the offense the product of this disease or defect? The *Durham* court failed to define either "mental disease" or "product." Trial courts had particular difficulty dealing with the meaning of the former term, since it was no longer modified by functional criteria, as it had been in earlier tests. The problem surfaced dramatically in 1957 when staff members at St. Elizabeth Hospital,

does not define mental disease

* only vaild still in NH

which provides the District of Columbia courts with most of their experts on the insanity issue, suddenly voted to incorporate the personality disorders, including the so-called "sociopathic personality," within the definition of "mental disease" for purposes of the insanity defense. Since many criminal offenders have some type of personality disorder, this weekend change in hospital policy had a major impact in the courts.

In *McDonald v. United States,* 312 F.2d 847 (D.C.Cir.1962), the District of Columbia Court of Appeals finally conceded that trial courts required some guidelines in implementing the product test, and declared that henceforth "the jury should be told that a mental disease or defect includes any abnormal condition of the mind which substantially affects mental or emotional processes and substantially impairs behavior controls." With the judicial gloss added by *McDonald,* the difference between the product test and a test combining M'Naghten and the "irresistible impulse" rule was reduced substantially. Even so, definitional problems persisted, and *Durham* was finally overruled in 1972. New Hampshire remains the only state to follow the test.

The American Law Institute Test. In place of the product test, the District of Columbia Court of Appeals adopted still another version of the insanity test, which was first proposed a year after the *Durham* decision. This test, drafted by the American Law Institute (ALI), was an attempt to deal with most of the problems associated with previous tests by avoiding the "all-or-nothing" language of the M'Naghten and "irresistible impulse" formulations, while retaining some specific guidelines for the jury. The rule reads as follows: "A person is not responsible for criminal conduct if at the time of such conduct as a result of mental disease or defect he lacks substantial capacity either to appreciate the criminality [wrongfulness] of his conduct or to conform his conduct to the requirements of the law." This language combines the notions underlying both the M'Naghten and irresistible impulse formulations, but makes it clear that a defendant's cognitive or volitional impairment at the time of the offense need only be "substantial," rather than total, in order to merit an insanity defense.

The ALI's proposal also included a second paragraph, which, according to its drafters, was designed specifically "to exclude from the concept of 'mental disease or defect' the case of so called 'psychopathic personality.'" It states: "As used in this Article, the terms mental disease or defect do not include an abnormality manifested only by repeated criminal or otherwise anti-social conduct." Interestingly, this proposal was published two years before the St. Elizabeth's incident.

The ALI test proved to be a popular one: Over the next two decades, a majority of the country's jurisdictions adopted the first paragraph, and many of these also adopted the second.

Rejection of Medical Model. Nonetheless, the ALI test came under attack as well. One criticism was that the ALI test, as well as all of the tests that preceded it, relied too heavily on the so-called "medical model." Judge Bazelon, the author of the failed *Durham* test, was the most prominent proponent of this point of view. In a concurring opinion in *United States v. Brawner*, 471 F.2d 969 (D.C.Cir.1972), the decision that overturned *Durham*, Bazelon argued that a person should be found insane "if at the time of his unlawful conduct his mental or emotional processes or behavior controls were impaired to such an extent that he cannot justly be held responsible for his act." This test does away with the "mental disease or defect" requirement, as well as any specific requirement of functional impairment. It gives the factfinder virtually limitless discretion to decide the types of "impairment" which excuse one for one's behavior. No state has adopted the test.[c]

Several other proposed formulations also eschew the mental disease or defect predicate, but more explicitly require the jury to focus on the accused's mental state. For instance, Moore argued that the inquiry should focus on whether the accused is "so irrational as to be nonresponsible." According to Moore,

> One is a moral agent only if one is a rational agent. Only if we can see another being as one who acts to achieve some rational end in light of some rational beliefs will we understand him in the same fundamental way that we understand ourselves and our fellow persons in everyday life. We regard as moral agents only those beings we can understand in this way.

In determining whether the accused is rational, Moore explained, one should look at the intelligibility, consistency and coherency of the desires and beliefs that motivate the offense. Michael Moore, Law & Psychiatry: Rethinking the Relationship 244–45, 207 (1984). In a similar vein, Fingarette and Hasse asserted that a "lack of capacity for rational conduct" is the core of insanity. Herbert Fingarette & Ann Hasse, Mental Disabilities and Criminal Responsibility 218 (1979).[d] Although using different language, Morse tried to capture the same idea with his proposal: "A defendant is not guilty by reason of insanity if at the time of the offense the defendant was extremely crazy and the craziness affected the criminal behavior." According to Morse, "this test tracks the moral issues with greater honesty and precision, is more workable, and will not lead to the acquittal of more defendants than present tests or reformed

---

[c] Rhode Island excuses those who cannot justly be held responsible as a result of mental disease or defect. *State v. Johnson,* 121 R.I. 254, 399 A.2d 469, 476 (1979).

[d] Sendor also views irrationality as the proper test, but explains its importance somewhat differently:

> [R]ationality is not important standing alone, but rather as a condition for engaging in conduct that others can interpret. When a mentally ill person injures legally protected interests through irrational conduct, we excuse the individual because we do not interpret his conduct as expressing disrespect for those interests.

Benjamin Sendor, Crime as Communication: An Interpretive Theory of the Insanity Defense and the Mental Elements of Crime, 74 Geo.L.J. 1371, 1415 (1986).

versions of present tests." Stephen Morse, *Excusing the Crazy: The Insanity Defense Reconsidered*, 58 S.Cal.L.Rev. 780 (1985). No jurisdiction has adopted any of these tests.

Elimination of Volitional Prong. A more popular (and the most recent) trend in insanity jurisprudence was to attack the volitional prong of the defense. Soon after the 1982 insanity acquittal of John Hinckley, both the American Bar Association and the American Psychiatric Association recommended the elimination of the so-called "volitional prong" or "control" inquiry, although they continued to support the "appreciation" prong of the ALI's test, thereby indicating an unwillingness to return to the original M'Naghten formulation. The ABA's test reads as follows: "[A] person is not responsible for criminal conduct if, at the time of such conduct, and as a result of mental disease or defect, that person was unable to appreciate the wrongfulness of such conduct." American Bar Association, Criminal Justice Mental Health Standards, Standard 7–6.1 (1989). Echoing past criticism, both the ABA and the APA reasoned that if mistakes do occur in the administration of the insanity defense, they are most likely to result from utilizing a volitional test. The commentary to the ABA's standard stated: "Clinicians can be more precise and arrive at more reliable conclusions about awareness, perceptions, and understanding of an event than about the 'causes' of a person's behavior, especially when the determinants of behavior are felt to be unconscious."

In 1984, the United States Congress adopted an insanity test for the federal courts which essentially tracked the ABA proposal. The legislation, found in Title 18 of the United States Code, states:

§ 20.   Insanity Defense.

(a) Affirmative Defense.—It is an affirmative defense to a prosecution under any federal statute that, at the time of the commission of acts constituting the offense, the defendant, as a result of severe mental disease or defect, was unable to appreciate the nature and quality or the wrongfulness of his acts. Mental disease or defect does not otherwise constitute a defense.

Several states have followed this lead. Today fewer than 20 states recognize volitional impairment as a basis for an insanity defense and another four do not recognize insanity as a defense.

QUESTIONS AND COMMENTS

1. *Constitutional constraints on the scope of the insanity test.* In *Clark v. Arizona*, 548 U.S. 735, 126 S.Ct. 2709, 165 L.Ed.2d 842 (2006), the Supreme Court was asked to decide whether an insanity formulation that eliminated the first part of the *M'Naghten* test (what the Court called the "cognitive capacity" prong, given its focus on whether the defendant knows

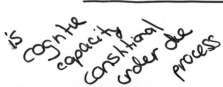

the nature and quality of the act) was constitutional under the due process clause. The Court held that the second prong of *M'Naghten* (what the Court called the "moral capacity" prong because of its focus on knowledge of wrongfulness) was constitutionally sufficient. In doing so, the Court suggested that any of the foregoing formulations would satisfy constitutional requirements:

> History shows no deference to *M'Naghten* that could elevate its formula to the level of fundamental principle, so as to limit the traditional recognition of a State's capacity to define crimes and defenses. . . . Even a cursory examination of the traditional Anglo–American approaches to insanity reveals significant differences among them, with four traditional strains variously combined to yield a diversity of American standards. The main variants are the cognitive incapacity, the moral incapacity, the volitional incapacity, and the product-of-mental-illness tests. [The Court then noted the number of states that had adopted each test].

> With this varied background, it is clear that no particular formulation has evolved into a baseline for due process, and that the insanity rule, like the conceptualization of criminal offenses, is substantially open to state choice. Indeed, the legitimacy of such choice is the more obvious when one considers the interplay of legal concepts of mental illness or deficiency required for an insanity defense, with the medical concepts of mental abnormality that influence the expert opinion testimony by psychologists and psychiatrists commonly introduced to support or contest insanity claims. For medical definitions devised to justify treatment, like legal ones devised to excuse from conventional criminal responsibility, are subject to flux and disagreement. There being such fodder for reasonable debate about what the cognate legal and medical tests should be, due process imposes no single canonical formulation of legal insanity.

*　*　*

Though Clark is correct that the application of the moral incapacity test (telling right from wrong) does not necessarily require evaluation of a defendant's cognitive capacity to appreciate the nature and quality of the acts charged against him, his argument fails to recognize that cognitive incapacity is itself enough to demonstrate moral incapacity. Cognitive incapacity, in other words, is a sufficient condition for establishing a defense of insanity, albeit not a necessary one. As a defendant can therefore make out moral incapacity by demonstrating cognitive incapacity, evidence bearing on whether the defendant knew the nature and quality of his actions is both relevant and admissible. In practical terms, if a defendant did not know what he was doing when he acted, he could not have known that he was performing the wrongful act charged as a crime.[23]

548 U.S. at 749–54, 126 S.Ct. at 2719–22.

2. *Effect of the language.* In terms of outcome, does it matter which of the various formulations described above are incorporated into jury instructions? Using a mock case based on the facts of *Durham,* Simon asked ten juries to decide the case under the *M'Naghten* standard and ten juries to decide the case under the *Durham* standard. She found a very small, although statistically significant, chance that jurors were more likely to find the defendant insane under the latter test. Rita Simon, The Jury and the Defense of Insanity 215 (1967). Professor Goldstein came to a similar conclusion after an extensive survey of the cases. Abraham Goldstein, The Insanity Defense 213–14 (1967). A more recent study used five mock cases and six different instructions: the "wild beast" test, M'Naghten, M'Naghten plus irresistible impulse, *Durham*, the ALI test and the test developed by Fingarette and Hasse. It found no overall significant differences among the six instructions, Norman Finkel et al., *Insanity Defenses: From the Jurors's Perspective*, 9 L. & Psychol.Rev. 77 (1985), a finding which has been replicated in later studies. See Norman Finkel, *The Insanity Defense: A Comparison of Verdict Schemas*, 15 L. & Hum. Beh. 533 (1991).

On the other hand, a review of studies looking at the effect of changes in the insanity standard in five states concluded that differences in acquittal rates can result when the M'Naghten test is replaced by the ALI test. Ingo Kielitz, *Researching and Reforming the Insanity Defense*, in Alexander Brooks & Bruce Winick, Current Issues in Mental Disability Law 47, 57–61 (1987). Moreover, as the American Bar Association has pointed out:

> the impact of particular language on decisions made *before* a jury retires to deliberate also must be considered—the decisions of experts whether or not to testify and, if so, the formulation of their testimony; the strategic decisions by defense counsel relating to the insanity defense, direct and cross-examination, and summation; and trial court rulings on the legal sufficiency of the evidence to raise a jury question.

ABA, Criminal Justice Mental Health Standards, Commentary to Standard 7–6.1 at 343 (1989). The ABA concluded that the difference in outcome in jurisdictions with a test that included a volitional prong and those that did not might be significant. Finally, even if the language makes no appreciable difference in terms of specific case resolutions, it may have an important effect symbolically and on the public's perception of the criminal justice system.

3. *Burden and standard of proof.* Another aspect of jury instructions in insanity cases concerns the burden and standard of proof that apply when the defense is asserted. By far the majority of the states now require the

---

[23] He might, of course, have thought delusively he was doing something just as wrongful as the act charged against him, but this is not the test: he must have understood that he was committing the act charged and that it was wrongful.

defendant to prove insanity by the preponderance of the evidence standard. About one-fourth of the states place the burden of disproving insanity on the prosecution beyond a reasonable doubt. Until 1984, federal jurisdictions followed the latter practice. After the Hinckley case, however, in the same legislation that changed the federal insanity test, the burden was switched dramatically, to require that the *defendant* show insanity by *clear and convincing evidence,* 18 U.S.C. § 20(b). Arizona has also adopted this approach. Ariz.Rev.Stat. § 13–502.

Apparently, none of these approaches is unconstitutional. In *Leland v. Oregon,* 343 U.S. 790, 72 S.Ct. 1002, 96 L.Ed. 1302 (1952) the Supreme Court held that a state rule requiring the defendant to prove insanity beyond a reasonable doubt did not deny a state defendant his federal constitutional right to due process of law. Almost two decades later, the Court held that the prosecution must prove beyond a reasonable doubt "every fact necessary to constitute proof of the crime with which [the defendant] is charged." *In re Winship,* 397 U.S. 358, 90 S.Ct. 1068, 25 L.Ed.2d 368 (1970). *Winship* suggested that *Leland* was no longer good law. But in 1976 the Court dismissed, for want of a substantial federal question, an appeal of a conviction under an instruction placing the burden of proving insanity on the defendant by a preponderance of the evidence. *Rivera v. Delaware,* 429 U.S. 877, 97 S.Ct. 226, 50 L.Ed.2d 160 (1976). Apparently the Court did not consider "sanity" a "fact necessary to constitute proof of the crime." In dissenting to the dismissal in *Rivera,* Justice Brennan wrote:

> In *Mullaney* [*v. Wilbur,* 421 U.S. 684, 95 S.Ct. 1881, 44 L.Ed.2d 508 (1975)], we considered a Maine rule that placed upon a criminal defendant charged with murder the burden of proving by a preponderance of the evidence that he had acted in the heat of passion on sudden impulse in order to reduce the homicide to manslaughter. We concluded that this rule did not comport with the due process requirement, as defined in *In re Winship* ... that the prosecution must prove beyond a reasonable doubt every fact necessary to constitute the crime charged.... Like the state rule invalidated in *Mullaney,* which implied malice unless the accused negated it, the plea of insanity, whether or not the State chooses to characterize it as an affirmative defense, relates to the accused's state of mind, an essential element of the crime. ...

429 U.S. at 878–80, 97 S.Ct. at 226–27 (Brennan, dissenting). As Brennan suggests, at least in some cases evidence of insanity is relevant to whether the defendant had the required mental state for the crime charged (such as intent or knowledge). Dix has suggested an argument in support of the Court's position in *Rivera,* however. He notes that because the insanity defense almost always relies on relatively untrustworthy or perplexing expert testimony, telling juries "that they must acquit if this evidence raises a reasonable doubt ... may [create] an unacceptably high risk of unjustified acquittals due to what are actually 'unreasonable' doubts generated simply by confusion." George Dix, *Criminal Responsibility and Mental Impairment*

in American Criminal Law, in 1 Law and Mental Health: International Perspectives 1, 24 (1984). Does this argument necessarily justify placing the burden on the defendant or does it simply support lowering the standard of proof the prosecution must meet?

The choice of a particular burden or standard of proof may be primarily of symbolic value. The data that exist suggest little or no relationship between a particular burden of proof and outcome. One informal study sampled the acquittal rates of five states, three of which used the ALI test and two of which used M'Naghten. Only one of the five placed the burden on the defendant. That state, which used the ALI test, had the second highest acquittal rate overall and the *highest* acquittal rate of the three states that used the ALI test. Melton, et al., supra note b, at 125, n. 149. However, Steadman and his colleagues found that, in Georgia and New York, switching the burden of proof from the prosecution to the defense significantly reduced both the rate at which the insanity defense was raised and its success rate. Henry Steadman et al., Before and After Hinckley: Evaluating Insanity Defense Reform 84–85 (1993).

4.   *Consequences of an insanity acquittal.* A third issue that might be addressed in instructions to the jury is the impact of an insanity acquittal. As noted earlier, most states confine insanity acquittees in mental institutions for as long as they remain mentally ill and dangerous.[e] The precise duration of post-acquittal confinement is therefore unknown at the time of trial and could be either much shorter or much longer than the sentence that would have been imposed had the person been found guilty. In most states, the jury is not informed of these facts, just as, in the typical criminal trial, they are kept in the dark about possible sentences, on the theory that dispositional information may improperly influence its decision. About a third of the states, however, authorize an instruction about the consequences of an insanity acquittal. The American Bar Association, which also adopts this position, supported its view as follows:

> [D]espite instructions cautioning them to consider only the evidence they have heard, jurors who are not informed about dispositional consequences will speculate about the practical results of a nonresponsibility verdict and, in ignorance of reality, will convict persons who are not criminally responsible in order to protect society. Jurors surely know, without being told, what happens to most convicted offenders, as well as defendants who are acquitted outright; the proposed instruction provides the same level of knowledge with respect to the fate of persons acquitted by reason of insanity.

In *Shannon v. United States*, 512 U.S. 573, 114 S.Ct. 2419, 129 L.Ed.2d 459 (1994), the Supreme Court held that such an instruction need not be given in federal court unless the prosecution suggests to the jury that an acquittal allows the defendant to "go free" or commits a similar error. In

---

[e]   The criteria and procedures for commitment of insanity acquittees are discussed in detail at Part V.A. of Chapter Eight.

addition to pointing out that jurors have traditionally not been given dispositional information, the majority opinion, by Justice Thomas, speculated that, given the publicity attending cases like Hinckley, many jurors are aware of the consequences of an acquittal. In any event, Thomas surmised, an instruction to the effect that acquittal will lead to confinement until the acquittee is no longer dangerous and mentally ill might not have the effect the defendant would want. Thomas went on to state:

> Whether the instruction works to the advantage or disadvantage of a defendant is, of course, somewhat beside the point. Our central concern here is that the inevitable result of such an instruction would be to draw the jury's attention toward the very thing—the possible consequences of its verdict—it should ignore.

Justice Stevens, in a dissent joined by Justice Blackmun, agreed with the ABA position quoted above. To the last point made by the majority, he pointed out that the instruction might help the jury focus on issues of guilt because it would no longer be worried about the practical effect of its verdict. See also, *State v. Shickles*, 760 P.2d 291, 298 (Utah 1988).

Empirical evidence as to jurors' understanding of dispositional consequences is spotty. Simon found that the overwhelming majority of jurors are aware, without being instructed, that dangerous persons are not released upon acquittal by reason of insanity, Rita Simon, The Jury and the Defense of Insanity 38 (1967), but she later admitted that her methodology may have produced inaccurate results. Harold Schwartz, *Should Juries Be Informed of the Consequences of the Insanity Verdict?*, 8 J. Psychiat. & L. 167, 173–74 (1980). Morris found that, overall, jurors have inconsistent perceptions about disposition. Grant Morris, *Whither Thou Goest?: An Inquiry into Jurors' Perceptions of the Consequences of a Successful Insanity Defense*, 14 San Diego L.Rev. 1058 (1977). If you were a defense attorney, would you want dispositional instructions? A prosecutor? Would you also want instructions on the average duration of hospitalization for insanity acquittees charged with the offense in question?

5.   *The reality of the insanity defense.* The public's position regarding the defense of insanity seems to be heavily influenced by the perception that the defense is frequently raised and widely abused. For instance, a survey taken in Wyoming revealed that the "average" resident in that state believed the defense was raised in 43% of all criminal cases in Wyoming between 1970 and 1972 and that it was successful 38% of the time. In fact, however, only 102 defendants—fewer than half of 1% of those arrested in Wyoming during the period relevant to the survey—raised the plea, and only one person out of these 102 was acquitted. Richard Pasewark et al., *Opinions About the Insanity Plea*, 8 J.Forensic Psychiatry 8 (1981). The most recent national data suggest that defendants raise the defense in less than 1% of all criminal cases and are successful in about 25% of these cases. Lisa A. Callahan et al., *The Volume And Characteristics of Insanity Defense Pleas: An Eight State Study*, 19 Bull. Am. Acad. Psychiatry & L. 331, 334 (1991); Henry Steadman et al., *Factors Associated with a Successful Insanity Defense*, 140

Am.J.Psychiat. 401 (1983). It should also be noted that in many states the overwhelming majority of acquittals by reason of insanity result from plea-bargaining or quasi-plea-bargaining with the prosecution; in these cases the prosecution agrees that the defendant should be acquitted, and there is no opportunity to "fool" a judge or jury. Jeffrey Rogers et al., *Insanity Defenses: Contested or Conceded?*, 141 Am.J.Psychiatry 885 (1984). Though trials leading to insanity verdicts (e.g., John Hinckley's trial and the second trial of Andrea Yates in 2006) sometimes receive enormous publicity, they are uncommon phenomena.

The public also seems to believe that those who successfully assert the insanity defense are released from custody quickly, thus endangering the public. In fact, although as noted above confinement time varies widely, the average duration of confinement for persons acquitted by reason of insanity roughly equals the time they would have spent in prison had they been convicted of the crime charged. See, e.g., Mark Pantle et al., *Comparing Institutionalization Periods and Subsequent Arrests of Insanity Acquittees and Convicted Felons*, 8 J.Psychiatry & L. 305 (1980). See also, Henry Steadman, et al., supra, at 98 ("insanity acquittees in New York were confined as long or longer than those found guilty"); Eric Silver, *Punishment or Treatment? Comparing the Lengths of Confinement of Successful and Unsuccessful Insanity Defendants*, 19 Law & Hum. Behav. 375 (1995) (insanity acquittees released sooner in two states and later in two other states). Moreover, more recent evidence suggests that, as a group, acquittees who are released are no more dangerous than felons who are released on parole or after serving their time. Pantle et al., supra; Stuart B. Silver et al., *Follow-up after Release of Insanity Acquittees, Mentally Disordered Offenders, and Convicted Felons*, 17 Bull. Am. Acad. Psychiatry & L. 387 (1989); Jeremy Skipworth et al., *Insanity Acquittee Outcomes in New Zealand*, 40 Aust. N. Z. J. Psychiatry 1003, 1008 (2006) (2–year violent reconviction of felons was 5 times higher than that of insanity acquittees).

6.   *The insanity defense and treatment for people with mental illness.* As noted earlier, some see the insanity defense as a means of ensuring that people with mental illness avoid the harshness of prison and receive treatment. Under present U.S. criminal justice practices, however, that is an unlikely scenario:

> Recent estimates suggest that the prevalence of serious mental illness ranges are approximately 5%–7% in the community, 6%–12% in jails, and 16%–24% in prisons. . . . There are three to five times as many persons with mental illness in prisons than in mental hospitals, and the number of prison inmates with mental illness continues to increase.

Mindy S. Bradley–Engen et al., *Trends in State Prison Admission of Offenders With Serious Mental Illness*, 61 Psychiatric Serv. 1263 (2010) (citations omitted).

2. Cognitive Impairment

THE HEADS CASE

[handwritten: brother-in-law?]

Shortly after midnight on August 22, 1977, Charles Heads shot and killed the husband of his wife's sister in Shreveport, La. Heads, a resident of Houston, had traveled to Shreveport in search of his wife, who had departed from Houston with their three children four days before in an effort to leave him. During those four days, Heads had taken a leave of absence from work and made repeated local and long distance phone calls to locate his family. He also visited his wife's parents home, again in an effort to find his wife and children. Finally he called his wife's sister. The sister's denial of knowledge about his wife's whereabouts aroused his suspicion and he drove to her home, although it was nearing midnight. No one answered his repeated knocks on the doors and windows. Heads then kicked in a door leading from the carport, entered and found his sister-in-law's husband at the end of the bedroom hall, armed with a pistol.

Though the evidence is not clear as to the precise moment when the shooting began, both the victim's wife and Heads's wife testified that Heads began firing his pistol shortly after breaking into the house. The sister-in-law's husband informed the defendant that he, too, was armed and did not want to be forced to shoot him. But Heads continued firing his pistol down the bedroom hallway until he had emptied the pistol of bullets. He then ran to his car, retrieved a rifle from the trunk, and returned, firing several blasts, one of which struck the victim in the eye, killing him.

At his first trial, despite a plea of insanity, Heads was convicted of first degree murder. See *State v. Heads,* 385 So.2d 230 (La.1980). According to Heads's attorney, "the insanity defense at this first trial never got off the ground because neither of the psychiatrists who had examined the defendant had found evidence of any recognized mental disorder." Although Heads had had a difficult tour in Vietnam and "many suspected a Vietnam connection" to the killing, "no one could articulate it. The defendant himself denied any connection in his testimony under oath." Jack Welborn, *The Vietnam Connection: Charles Heads' Verdict,* 9 Crim.Def. 7, 8 (1982).

[handwritten: —no finding of mental disorder]

Heads's conviction was overturned on unrelated grounds and his case was set for retrial. Between the two trials, the American Psychiatric Association issued the third edition of its Diagnostic and Statistical Manual (DSM) (1980), in which it included the diagnosis of Post–Traumatic Stress Disorder (PTSD), with the following criteria:

PTSD –
vietnam

A.   Existence of a recognizable stressor that would evoke significant symptoms of distress in almost everyone [such as rape or assault, military combat, earthquakes, torture and car accidents].

B.   Reexperiencing of the trauma as evidenced by at least one of the following:

     (1) recurrent and intrusive recollections of event;

     (2) recurrent dreams of the event;

↗ guns shooting

     (3) sudden acting or feeling as if the traumatic were reoccurring, because of an association with an environmental or ideational stimulus;

C.   Numbing of responsiveness to or reduced involvement with the external world, beginning some time after the trauma, as shown by at least one of the following:

     (1) markedly diminished interest in one or more significant activities;

     (2) feeling of detachment or estrangement from others;

     (3) constricted affect [emotion];

D.   At least two of the following symptoms that were not present before the trauma:

     (1) hyperalertness or exaggerated startle response;

     (2) sleep disturbance;

     (3) guilt about surviving when others have not, or about behavior required for survival;

     (4) memory impairment or trouble concentrating;

     (5) avoidance of activities that arouse recollection of the traumatic event;

     (6) intensification of symptoms by exposure to events that symbolize or resemble the traumatic event.

The DSM–III noted that, "[i]n rare instances there are dissociative states, lasting from a few seconds to several hours, or even days, during which components of the event are relived, and the person behaves as though experiencing the event at that moment." Under "Associated Features", the DSM stated: "Increased irritability may be associated with sporadic and unpredictable explosions of aggressive behavior, upon even minimal or no provocation."

At Heads's second trial, Heads again asserted an insanity defense, this time relying on a PTSD diagnosis. Under Louisiana law: "If the circumstances indicate that because of a mental disease or defect the offender was incapable of distinguishing between right and wrong with

rule of law

reference to the conduct in question, the offender shall be exempt from criminal responsibility." At trial, Heads presented three experts who testified that he had been incapable of distinguishing right from wrong at the time of the killing because of post-traumatic disorder. Reliance on the PTSD allowed the defense not only to construct a plausible theory of insanity but to introduce evidence normally not admissible: a film comparing Vietnam and World War II, extensive testimony by Vietnam veterans describing the war, and considerable testimony about Heads' childhood.

There follows a facsimile of the closing arguments for the defense and the prosecution at Heads' second trial, based in part on a description of the trial by Heads's attorney Jack Welborn, see Welborn, supra, and in part on other cases in which a PTSD defense has been raised. See, e.g., *Louisiana v. Sharp,* 418 So.2d 1344 (La.1982).

DEFENSE ARGUMENT

The evidence shows that, while he was in Vietnam, Charles Heads experienced incredible trauma. Usually he was able to deal with the stress created by his horrible sojourn there. But when the anxiety created by Vietnam combined with the stress of his family leaving him, as happened on the night of the killing, Charles was not himself. On that night, he was literally unaware of what he was doing.

Charles has not had an easy life. He grew up in a section of Houston which once called itself "The Murder Capitol of the World." When he was nine years old, his mother was killed by his father, who was sentenced to life imprisonment for this and another murder. Yet Charles managed to finish elementary and high school.

Eight months after graduation, he enlisted in the Marines, where he volunteered for the First Reconnaissance Battalion. As a Reconner, he was part of an "elite within an elite"; his mission was to collect intelligence about enemy activities deep in hostile country, staying out on lightly armed patrols for several days to a week in an attempt to locate the VietCong (VC). By his 20th birthday, Charles had his first confirmed kill. Six more followed, including a woman and an old man. The duties of a Reconner, according to the experts, were "extraordinarily stressful." As Dr. John Yost testified, it was not just the stress of combat, but the stress of waiting for something horrible to happen. No place was secure or safe. Everybody who was not an American was the enemy.

After nine months, Charles's days as a Reconner came to an abrupt end when his sixteen man patrol was ambushed one misty morning by an estimated battalion-sized VC regular unit. Charles was the point man and was hit first, twice in the gut. Eventually, those surviving the patrol were saved by an airstrike and airlifted out. Charles was considered too badly wounded to continue his tour in Vietnam. He can remember very little about his nine months in Vietnam or the ambush, although he did remember being shot in the gut.

Dr. Williams, a psychologist and a Marine Corps company commander in Vietnam, testified here at trial that this memory deficit and Charles's difficulty in talking about his Vietnam experience reflected the "psychological defense mechanism of denial." He stated that Charles had probably "used" this defense mechanism in overcoming the catastrophes of his childhood and it stood him in good stead when he returned to the United States. He became a postal employee, as did his wife. Together, they earned over $30,000 a year and, to outward appearances, Charles seemed to have put Vietnam behind him.

However, as his wife testified, Charles experienced many restless, sleepless nights. He also had many nightmares, in which he relived painful memories about the war. It was one of these nightmares, a particularly severe one, which frightened his wife so much that she took the children and went to Shreveport. Dr. John Wilson testified that Charles was on the "extreme edge of vulnerability in terms of his capacity to cope with stress." Indeed, on one occasion two years before the killing and five years after he left Vietnam, when his wife briefly left him, he vaulted onto the roof of his house with a rifle, assumed the assault position, and fired harmlessly for a few minutes into the tops of the trees in the neighborhood. This was significant evidence that Charles was a victim of the post-traumatic stress syndrome, the diagnosis given Charles by all three of our experts. Yet there were no vet centers or outreach centers, no rap groups to help him out.

When his wife left with the children shortly before the killing, Charles lost his only support system. When he went unanswered at his sister-in-law's house he felt rejected and bereft. According to the doctors, it was at this point that the post-traumatic stress triggered his violent action. As it turned out, it was shortly after midnight, the ground and foliage were wet with two inches of rain that had fallen that day, the humidity was 100% and ground fog was beginning to form. According to Charles, his attention momentarily centered on the treeline in the small field across the street. This field, according to seven other Vietnam vets who had seen it or a videotape of it, symbolized or resembled Vietnam. To Charles, "It was just like Vietnam, in a way—that last patrol when we were ambushed, the way the mist hung in the trees." Charles said he was "hit" with a "boom", and he turned back toward the house. He says he was "on automatic." From this moment until he killed, his behavior was, according to the testimony of the vets, like that of a trained Marine Reconner surviving by cleaning out a hutch. When asked whether Charles was aware of the wrongness of the killing, Dr. Williams, a vet himself, replied: "Are you kidding? They gave us ice cream for that."

When the police arrived minutes later, they found Charles wandering in a daze inside the house in the midst of frantically scurrying children, his arms hanging at his side, in one hand the barrel of his own weapon, in the other the barrel of the weapon he had secured from his brother-in-law's body. They led him quietly away. The battle was over. Ladies and gentlemen of the jury, do not let this battle be for naught. Charles was not himself on the night of the killing. He thought he was in Vietnam. He did not know that what he was doing was wrong; he thought he was fighting for his country.

PROSECUTION ARGUMENT

Ladies and gentlemen of the jury, there is no doubt that Vietnam was a stressful environment. But Vietnam is not on trial here; Mr. Charles Heads is. He did not kill because he thought he was in Vietnam. He killed because he was upset his wife had left him and because she was unwilling to take him back or respond to his entreaties. In an overreaction to the sight of a gun, he intentionally and deliberately killed a man. If Vietnam is relevant at all here, it is relevant only because it made Mr. Heads better able and more willing to use violence to achieve his ends.

The defense experts testified that Mr. Heads is suffering from something called post-traumatic stress syndrome. Even assuming there is such a thing, and that Mr. Heads meets the criteria, the defense does not explain why most veterans who experienced the same stresses do not act violently. The defense presented witnesses from the same Reconner patrol who have never committed any violent acts since leaving Vietnam. Having bad dreams is one thing; acting them out is another.

But this whole Vietnam fantasy idea—that Mr. Heads thought he was in Vietnam on the night of the killing, and that he thought his relative was an ambushing VietCong—is preposterous in any event. The prosecution's expert provided a much more plausible explanation. Mr. Heads was not crazy on the night of the murder; he was just angry. The prosecution expert testified that the defendant has an "explosive personality disorder." Mr. Heads has stored up alot of anger, starting with his father's murder of his mother. Every once in awhile, when a similar rejection occurs, this anger comes out, like the time his wife left him and he went up on the roof to let off a few rounds. This explosiveness, in fact, was one of the reasons his wife left him the final time, as she admitted.

These tantrums might have been pretty intense. But they were not signs of insanity. And they also were infrequent. Most of the time, Mr. Heads's behavior was entirely normal, even right before the murder. During the four days prior to the killing he made several calls, visited his wife's parents' home, and made personal visits to mutual friends and acquaintances. None of these people reported anything out of the ordinary. He rode his bicycle, listened to music, and studied his Vietnam photo album. This was the kind of normal behavior that he exhibited throughout the entire seven years after he left Vietnam.

So why did he act so violently on the night of the murder? By his own admission, he remembers thinking the day before the murder that he wished he were back in the service where, as he stated, "we were one big family, where you were close, where you could count on each other, where people didn't lie to you." To Mr. Heads, his wife was not acting like family, could not be counted on, and had lied to him. He was angry at her, so angry he made sure he had guns with him when he went to her sister's. When she rejected him by not answering his knocks, he exploded. Again, this is not the reaction of a diseased man. It is the reaction of a man who has alot of pent-up anger and who acts aggressively on those occasions when he can no longer hold it in. Not only did he know it was wrong to kill on the night of the murder, he probably did not feel particularly bad about it, given his experience with killing in Vietnam. It is a sad thing, but combat makes some people less sensitive to the taking of life.

The state is asking that you convict Mr. Heads of first degree murder. The evidence shows that he intentionally brought weapons with him to the house in which he thought his wife was located, intentionally brought a pistol with him when he first entered the house and then, although he had not been fired upon himself, intentionally ran back to his car to get another weapon. He then intentionally shot to kill. He acted with deliberation and without adequate provocation.[f]

QUESTIONS AND COMMENTS

1.   *Mental disease or defect and the cognitive prong.* Every insanity test currently in use requires a threshold finding of mental disease or defect. Historically, mental disease referred roughly to conditions such as schizophrenia, bipolar disorder, and psychotic depression, and "mental defect" referred to intellectual disabilities (formerly called mental retardation) and dementias. But further definition was usually imprecise. What role should the phrase "mental disease or defect"—which appears in many jurisdictions' insanity statutes—play in fixing the exculpatory scope of the insanity defense? How should it be defined?

One possible approach is to equate the law's definition of mental disease or defect with the psychiatric definition of mental disorder. In the *Heads* case, for instance, it appears that the "recognition" of the PTSD by the American Psychiatric Association had a significant impact on the legal outcome. Would the aims of the legal system be met by a simple correlation between the law's definition of mental disease or defect and the disorders found in the current DSM, assuming that the law recognized only those

---

[f]   Heads was acquitted by reason of insanity at his second trial.

disorders that have received "general acceptance" in the behavioral science community and can be reliably diagnosed?[g]

Professor LaFave, after surveying application of the various insanity tests by the courts, concluded that "any mental abnormality, be it psychosis, neurosis, organic brain disorder, or congenital intellectual deficiency . . . will suffice *if* it has caused the consequences described in the second part of the test." Wayne LaFave, Criminal Law 399 (5th ed. 2010) (emphasis in original). In other words, the mental disease or defect predicate is relatively unimportant; what is important is whether the individual was so cognitively or volitionally impaired at the time of the offense that exculpation is necessary. In a similar vein, the ALI test leaves mental disease or defect undefined except to exclude "abnormality manifested only by repeated or otherwise anti-social conduct." This approach allows an insanity defense based on any diagnosis found in the current DSM (other than perhaps anti-social personality) that the courts are willing to recognize as sufficiently trustworthy. Presumably, it also allows a defense based on conditions not found in the DSM, as was true of the post-traumatic stress disorder prior to DSM–III. (See also, *Zamora v. Florida*, 361 So.2d 776 (Fla.App.1978), in which the defendant argued he was insane, ultimately unsuccessfully, based on "involuntary subliminal television intoxication" which produced a lessened appreciation of the wrongfulness of killing).

In contrast, other formulations attempt to limit the mental disease or defect predicate by requiring that it be serious. The federal insanity statute, for example, provides that the mental condition must be "severe." According to the House Committee, this word was added "to emphasize that nonpsychotic behavior disorders or neuroses such as an 'inadequate personality,' 'immature personality,' or a pattern of 'antisocial tendencies' do not constitute the defense." H.R.Rep. No. 98–1030, 98th Cong., 2nd Sess. 229 (1984). Around the time the federal test was adopted, the American Psychiatric Association similarly concluded that an insanity defense should be limited to "those severely abnormal mental conditions that grossly and demonstrably impair a person's perception or understanding of reality and that are not attributable primarily to the voluntary ingestion of alcohol or other psychoactive substances." APA, Statement on the Insanity Defense 12 (1983).

In defining mental disease or defect, the analysis may differ depending upon whether one is applying a cognitive as opposed to a volitional test. Focusing solely on the cognitive prong of the insanity defense for present purposes, which of the various formulations described above do you prefer? Would Heads have a "mental disease or defect" under your formulation? Note that one study has found that 20 to 30 percent of all Vietnam veterans "would be formally diagnosable" as experiencing a post–traumatic stress disorder. Arthur Egendorf, *The Postwar Healing of Vietnam Veterans: Recent Research*, 33 Hosp. & Comm. Psychiat. 901 (1981). See also, James E. Helzer et al., *Post-traumatic Stress Disorder in the General Population: Findings of the*

[g] The "general acceptance" or *Frye* test of admissibility is discussed at pp. 527–530.

Epidemiologic Catchment Area Survey, 87 New Eng. J. Med. 1630 (1987) (finding lifetime prevalence of PTSD in 1% of general population, 3.5% of those who were victims of a physical attack, and in 20% in Vietnam veterans wounded in combat). Another study found that combat veterans were much more likely than controls to experience panic attacks (70%) or combat-related flashbacks (40%) when infused with a stress-inducing drug. Anthony S. Higgins, *Post-traumatic Stress Disorder and Its Role in the Defense of Vietnam Veterans*, 15 L. & Psychol. Rev. 259,273 (1991).

The prevalence of PTSD in veterans returning from the Iraq and Afghanistan wars is about the same as for Vietnam veterans (20%). Tom McGirk, *The Hell of PTSD*, TIME (Nov. 30, 2009), at 41. These individuals also appear to be disproportionately charged with homicide, rape, sexual assault and domestic violence. Deborah Sontag & Lizette Alvarez, *Wartorn*, N.Y. Times (Jan. 13, 2008), at A1 (finding an 89% increase in homicides committed by military personnel during the war period and also reporting a sharp rise in other violent crimes committed by these individuals). Several states, acting in conjunction with the U.S. Department of Veterans Affairs, have created veterans courts, meant to deal with the PTSD, substance abuse, head injuries and mental illness underlying crimes committed by veterans. However, these courts tend to handle only nonviolent crimes. Lynne Marek, *Courts for Veterans Spreading Across U.S.*, The National Law Journal (Dec. 22, 2008), at B1.

2. *Know versus Appreciate.* Whatever the definition of mental disease or defect, it must cause, under the typical formulations of the cognitive prong, either a failure to "know" (under M'Naghten) or a "substantial inability to appreciate" (under ALI) the wrongness of the act. Although the M'Naghten test seems more rigid, Professor Goldstein's study of evidence presented and instructions given in jurisdictions that use that test indicates that the language is construed liberally, when it is defined at all. Abraham Goldstein, The Insanity Defense 49–53 (1967).

With respect to the difference between the "knowledge" and "appreciation" formulations, consider some of the facts developed in United States v. Hinckley, in which John Hinckley was charged with attempting to assassinate the president of the United States in 1981. Before the attempt, Hinckley had never been charged with a criminal offense. But he seemed very interested in violent action. He read several books on famous assassinations. He joined the Nazi Party and then was expelled in November, 1979, apparently because the party was alarmed over his open advocacy of violence. He subsequently tried to organize on his own a group called The American Front, which was designed to alert white Protestants to the threat posed by minority groups.

According to evidence derived from Hinckley's diaries, his letters to his parents and interviews with Hinckley, the key aspects of his mental state at the time of the offense revolved around his obsession with the actress Jodie Foster. This preoccupation began in 1976, when Hinckley first viewed the film Taxi Driver. The film's main character, Travis Bickle, rescues Iris, a child-prostitute played by Foster, from her pimp. Hinckley identified strongly with Bickle, who, like Hinckley, was a loner and alienated from society. Over the next several years, he bought an army jacket and boots like Bickle's, acquired the same number of weapons that Bickle had possessed, and tried to develop a relationship with Foster. He left cards at her door, spoke with her over the telephone twice and tried to reach her on several other occasions. Rejected by these advances, he did what Bickle had done when rebuffed by women; he began to stalk the president of the United States, at that time Jimmy Carter. On two occasions he was near enough to Carter to attempt an assassination, but he made no move.

After Ronald Reagan became president, Hinckley continued to think about some action against the chief executive as a way of improving his relationship with Foster. He copied a skyjacking note contained in a biography of a skyjacker, intending to use it to force President Reagan to resign and to have Jodie Foster brought to him. On New Year's Eve, 1980, he recorded a monologue. He noted that, as usual, he was alone and afraid. He proclaimed Jodie Foster to be the only thing that mattered in his life and made allusions to a death pact between himself and Foster and to his own suicide. Hinckley's poetry written during the same period explored similar themes: mental deterioration, suicide, alienation, and an assassination that receives world-wide publicity. A postcard he wrote to Foster in mid-February of 1981 contained a message promising Foster that one day she and Hinckley would occupy the White House together.

On March 30, 1981, the day of the assassination attempt, Hinckley was in Washington, D.C. From the newspaper, he read of President Reagan's itinerary for the day. It was at this point that he decided to kill President Reagan. He showered, took some Valium to calm himself, and loaded his .22 caliber revolver with six Devastator bullets, ammunition that explodes on impact. (Travis Bickle had achieved a similar effect in Taxi Driver by carving crosses on the tops of bullets.) At about 12:45 p.m., Hinckley sat down to write a letter to Jodie Foster. He described how he had repeatedly tried to gain her attention and affection, but that time was running out. To win her respect and love, he was willing to give up his freedom or possibly even his life in the perpetration of what he called a "historic deed." Shortly after finishing the letter, he concealed his weapon in the pocket of his raincoat and took a cab to the Washington Hilton, where Reagan was scheduled to speak. As Reagan came out of the hotel, Hinckley drew his revolver and fired six rounds, wounding four men, including the President.

One of the defense experts testified that on the day of the assassination Hinckley was preoccupied with two things: "the termination of his own existence" and accomplishing a "union with Jodie Foster through death, after life . . .". The President and the other victims "were bit players who were there in a way to help him to accomplish the two major roles [which] . . . weighed far heavier in his emotional appreciation." The prosecution's expert emphasized the degree of planning involved in carrying out the attempt, the concealment of the weapon, Hinckley's admission that he knew the Secret

Service might try to kill an assassin, and his decision to shoot when "[t]he Secret Service and the others in the presidential entourage looked the other way." On these facts, might one reasonably arrive at different conclusions about Hinckley's insanity, depending upon whether the test focused on "knowledge" of wrongfulness rather than on "substantial inability to appreciate" wrongfulness?[h]

One commentator has suggested that the word "appreciate" as it is used in insanity cases points to the ability "to set a value, to estimate a right, perceive the full force of something, to be sensitive to delicate impressions or distinction." Douglas Mossman, "*United States v. Lyons*: Toward a New Conception of Legal Insanity," 16 Bull. Am. Acad. Psychiatry Law 49, 55 (1988). Defined this way, might the lack-of-appreciation test mean that hardened criminals could assert insanity defenses based on their lack of remorse for their criminal activity? This possibility perhaps explains the second paragraph of the ALI test excluding those whose mental illness is evidenced solely by repeated antisocial acts. The California Supreme Court offered further elaboration for the exception:

> [T]he assertion of the insanity defense by recidivists with no apparent sign of mental illness except their penchant for criminal behavior would burden the legal system, bring the insanity defense into disrepute, and imperil the ability of persons with definite mental illness to assert that defense. . . . To classify persons with "antisocial personality" as insane would put in the mental institutions persons for whom there is currently no suitable treatment, and who would be a constant danger to the staff and other inmates. Mental hospitals are not designed for this kind of person; prisons are.

People v. Fields, 35 Cal.3d 329, 370–72, 197 Cal.Rptr. 803, 830–31, 673 P.2d 680, 707–08 (1983). Consider, in response, this excerpt from *United States v. Currens,* 290 F.2d 751, 774 n. 32 (3d Cir.1961):

> Our study has . . . revealed two very persuasive reasons why this court should not hold that evidence of psychopathy is insufficient, as a matter of law, to put sanity or mental illness in issue. First, it is clear that as the majority of experts use the term, a psychopath is very distinguishable from one who merely demonstrates recurrent criminal behavior . . . [From our survey], it can be seen that in many cases the adjective "psychopathic" will be applied by experts to persons who are very ill indeed.
>
> Our second reason for not holding that psychopaths are "sane" as a matter of law is based on the vagaries of the term itself. In each individual case all the pertinent symptoms of the accused should be put before the court and jury and the accused's criminal responsibility should be developed from the totality of his symptoms. . . . The criminal

[handwritten in left margin: Appreciation]

---

[h] Hinckley was tried until the ALI test; the burden was on the prosecution to disprove insanity beyond a reasonable doubt. He was acquitted by reason of insanity, although it is unclear whether under the cognitive or volitional prong.

law is not concerned with . . . classifications but with the fundamental issue of criminal responsibility.

Are *Fields* and *Currens* necessarily inconsistent? The older term for psychopathy was "moral insanity." (The DSM–5 criteria for antisocial personality disorder, which is a related, but somewhat broader, mental condition, are found in Appendix A). Should a person who experiences no remorse for his crime or empathy for his victims and who lacks a conscience, but who knows that his criminal acts are illegal and wrong in society's eyes, be subject to punishment? Professor Arenella argues that a "threshold conception of moral agency . . . must include the following character-based attributes: the capacity to care for the interests of other human beings; the internalization of others' normative expectations, including self-identification as a participant in the community's blaming practices; the ability to engage in moral evaluation of one's character and acts, the capacity to respond to moral norms as a motivation for one's choices; and the power to control those firmly entrenched aspects of character that impair one's ability to act in accordance with one's moral judgments," because "if part of what we are communicating in our criminal culpability judgments is that the criminal deserves our moral blame and that his punishment is justified in part by a showing of his moral desert, then we need to take the concept of moral agency far more seriously than we presently do." Peter Arenella, *Convicting the Morally Blameless: Reassessing the Relationship Between Legal and Moral Accountability*, 39 UCLA L. Rev. 1511, 1525, 1622 (1992).

The Louisiana insanity law under which Heads was tried seems closer to the M'Naghten "knowledge" test than to the ALI "appreciation" language. If one accepts the defense theory of the case, is it plausible that Heads not only did not "appreciate" but did not "know" that his act was wrong? If one accepts the *prosecution's* theory of the case, does Heads have a plausible argument under either approach? Consider current research that suggests that the "hyperarousal" associated with PTSD can cause "intense threat scanning" and "an inability to discriminate genuine threats to safety . . . and exposure to danger." For instance, exposure to improvised explosive devices (IEDs) during wartime tends to make veterans drive aggressively, and has led to numerous incidents of "road rage." Mary Tramontin, *Exit Wounds: Current Issues Pertaining to Combat–Related PTSD of Relevance to the Legal System*, 29 Dev. Mental Health L. 23, 38 (2010). Combat-related PTSD can also be associated either with "sensation-seeking"—an attempt to relive a level of danger similar to combat experience—or, as the defense argued in *Heads*, with "dissociation," a condition triggered by stimuli that mimic the environment of the original stressor and that can lead to "a search-and-destroy mentality in which [the veteran's] automatic reaction is to find and kill any perceived source of danger." Daniel Burgess, Nicole Stockey & Kara Coen, *Reviving the 'Vietnam Defense': Post–Traumatic Stress Disorder and Criminal Responsibility in a Post–Iraq/Afghanistan World*, 29 Dev. Mental Health L. 59, 65–67 (2010).

3. *Criminality v. wrongfulness.* The final aspect of the cognitive tests has to do with what "wrongfulness" means. The M'Naghten decision permitted an insanity defense only if the accused did not know the act was *legally* wrong. Moreover, in cases where the delusion was "partial"—meaning, apparently, that it affects only the accused's thinking about the offense and not other aspects of his life—then he would not have an insanity defense even if he thought his act was legal, unless the delusion, if true, would justify the act. As the House of Lords stated:

> For example, if, under the influence of his delusion, he supposes another man to be in the act of attempting to take away his life, and he kills that man, as he supposes, in self-defense, he would be exempt from punishment. If his delusion was that the deceased had inflicted a serious injury to his character and fortune, and he killed him in revenge for such supposed injury, he would be liable to punishment.

Subsequently, several American courts rejected this view, at least in part. For instance, in *People v. Schmidt,* 216 N.Y. 324, 110 N.E. 945 (1915), Judge Cardozo stated that if a person has "an insane delusion that God has appeared to [him] and ordained the commission of a crime, we think it cannot be said of the offender that he knows the act to be wrong." This language would appear to permit an insanity acquittal of a person who, though knowing his act was legally wrong, felt "morally justified" in committing it because of mental illness. However, Judge Cardozo also expressed caution about this rule:

> The anarchist is not at liberty to break the law because he reasons that all government is wrong. The devotee of a religious cult that enjoins polygamy or human sacrifice as a duty is not thereby relieved from responsibility before the law.

The drafters of the ALI test did not attempt to resolve this issue. Instead they provided two options, the "legal wrong" approach encapsulated by the word "criminality" and the "moral wrong" approach represented by the word "wrongfulness." The states are divided evenly on the question. The state of Washington takes a hybrid approach. It generally follows the criminality rule. According to the Washington Supreme Court, "[i]f wrong meant moral wrong judged by the individual's own conscience, this would seriously undermine the criminal law, for it would allow one who violated the law to be excused from criminal responsibility solely because, in his own conscience, his act was not morally wrong." *State v. Crenshaw,* 98 Wash.2d 789, 659 P.2d 488 (1983). However, *Crenshaw* also created a "deific decree" exception to the general rule that "wrong" means legal wrong, thus allowing a defense in a case like the one described by Cardozo in *Schmidt.* It then found that the exception did not apply in the case before it, upholding the homicide conviction of a person who claimed he was a member of the Moscovites— apparently a religious group that believes there is a "duty to assassinate an unfaithful spouse." The defendant had killed his wife because he "knew," despite the absence of objective evidence, that she had been unfaithful. There was also evidence that the defendant had been hospitalized on several occasions with a diagnosis of paranoia. Contrast this decision to *People v. Skinner*, 39 Cal.3d 765, 217 Cal.Rptr. 685, 704 P.2d 752 (1985), where the defendant, suffering from schizophrenia, killed his wife because he delusionally believed that "the marriage vow 'till death do us part' bestows on a marital partner a God-given right to kill the other partner who has violated or was inclined to violate the marital vows, and that because the vows reflected the direct wishes of God, the killing is with complete moral and criminal impunity." The California Supreme Court reversed the defendant's conviction and directed that he be found insane, concluding on these facts that the defendant did not know that the killing was wrongful or criminal (under a version of M'Naghten).

Some commentators have argued that a deific decree defense should notbe recognized:

> A "deific decree" commanding the defendant to kill has been characterized, not as a religious belief, but as a delusional belief justifying an insanity verdict. But if a "religiousity" defense is not available to exculpate the hyperreligious from criminal liability for acts they believe are morally right, should the mentally disordered be exculpated for their religiously motivated, though illegal, acts? . . . If a mentally disordered person claims that God ordered him or her to kill, are psychiatrists competent to assess whether the defendant acted from a delusional belief, or whether he or she acted from a religious conviction? In our society in which all sincerely held religious beliefs are entitled to equal treatment, can we appropriately declare a defendant's claimed religious belief to be a false belief, the product of a mentally disordered mind?
>
> To answer these questions, [one must examine] the meaning of delusion, especially as that concept is explained in the psychiatric profession's standard diagnostic manual. Psychiatry specifically excludes religious beliefs from the definition of delusion because a religious belief cannot be declared to be a false belief. Because a person's sincerely held belief that God ordered him or her to kill qualifies as a religious belief, it should not be characterized as a delusion. Thus, the insanity defense should not be available to those who kill at God's command.

Grant H. Morris & Ansar Haroun, *"God Told Me to Kill": Religion or Delusion?*, 39 San Diego L. Rev. 973, 977 (2001). In support of this position, the authors report research suggesting the value-laden nature of distinguishing delusional and non-delusional religious sentiments.

> In a recent study, researchers developed eighteen written vignettes designed to assess clinical judgments of religious authenticity and psychopathology. A core vignette was used for each of six dimensions of religious experience. Three variations of each core vignette were written to reflect conventional, less conventional, and unconventional practices. For example, in one core vignette that focused on the dimension of what is communicated, individuals heard the voice of God telling them to: (1)

3 levels of worship practices

baptize their newborn child—a conventional religious practice, (2) prepare a worship service—a less conventional religious practice, or (3) sacrifice their child—an unconventional religious practice. The vignettes were tested on sixty-seven mental health practitioners of varying professional backgrounds, experience, and religious affiliation.

The results were not surprising. For every vignette tested, the conventional response was rated significantly more religiously authentic and significantly less pathological than the less conventional response. For every vignette tested, the less conventional response was rated significantly more religiously authentic and significantly less pathological than the unconventional response. According to the researchers: "The essential determining factor in the ratings was not the dimensions of religious experience, but the degree to which religious experience deviated from conventional religious beliefs and practices. The more unconventional the experience, the less religiously authentic and less mentally healthy it was deemed to be." The experience that was rated as least religiously authentic and most pathological of all vignettes was complying with God's request to sacrifice a child. Ironically, this experience, at least when performed by Abraham, is often considered the most religiously authentic by Jews, Christians, and Muslims; it is the supreme test of religious faith.

Id. at 1038–39.

Assuming the other criteria for insanity were met, did Heads have an insanity defense under the criminality approach? The wrongfulness approach? Had Heads sincerely believed he had been ordered by God to kill his wife for her transgressions, should he have a defense? Should it matter whether his beliefs were due to psychosis? Consider the finding, based on tests aimed at gauging people's views of fairness, that people with schizophrenia "punish unfairness at a comparable level to controls, which opposes the common view of a general lack of moral value appreciation in schizophrenia." Julie Wischniewski & Martin Brüne, *Moral Reasoning in Schizophrenia: An Explorative Study into Economic Decision–Making*, 16 Cognitive Neuropsychiatry 348 (2011).

4. *Alternative formulations.* Most people with mental illness who commit violent acts have some idea that their act might ordinarily be viewed by others as a violation of the law. Only rarely, as in the oft-used but probably unrealistic example of the man who strangles his wife thinking she is a lemon, will they have no idea they are committing a crime. Is the legal wrong approach thus too restrictive? Does the "deific decree" exception, or use of the "appreciation" language, broaden the rule sufficiently? If neither of these solutions is acceptable and the moral wrong approach must be adopted, how does one restrict that approach to avoid acquittal of anyone who has a strongly held belief that he or she is "in the right"? Does the mental disease or defect predicate handle this problem?

Several scholars reject knowledge of wrongfulness as the proper test for insanity. As noted in the introduction to this section some have suggested that insanity should be equated with "irrationality" or "craziness." Do these tests better capture the moral scope of the insanity defense?

5. *Other cases involving cognitive impairment.* Consider whether the individuals in the following cases should be found insane.

Case A. Jones, a 60 year-old retired military person, shoots at a low-flying cropduster, puncturing the fuselage and causing the plane to crash, which kills the pilot. Jones claims that the plane was sent by the government to spy on him and to bombard his house with electronic particles meant to destroy his house (he points to the cracks in the foundation as evidence) and kill his animals (one of his dogs had died a few days before). He also believes that the government has bugged his house and arranged for his neighbors to spy on him. Nothing suggests that the government has actually paid any attention to Jones. Psychiatrists say his diagnosis is delusional paranoia. (In a case similar to this, a Virginia court found the defendant insane.)

— insane

Case B: Griffin suffers from schizophrenia. He is also a very devout Catholic. He becomes convinced that he is one of the principal defenders of Catholicism against a world-wide conspiracy that is out to destroy the Church. In his mind, the conspiracy includes those who support abortion and those who work in abortion clinics. He buys automatic weapons and ammunition and proceeds to scout out one of the local abortion clinics. One day he enters the clinic with his gun, shouts "The Church says you must die!" and sprays the waiting room with bullets, killing a doctor, a clerk and two clients waiting for abortions. He is captured nearby trying to dispose of the weapons. (In a case similar to this, a Florida court found the defendant sane.)

went to go buy guns — had intent

Case C: Andrea Yates drowned all five of her children, one by one, in the bathtub. She began with Paul, age three years, then drowned two-year-old Luke, five-year-old John, six-month-old Mary, and finally Noah, age seven years. She lined up the bodies of the youngest four on her bed and covered them with a sheet, and left Noah, who had attempted to flee before she was able to overcome him, facedown in the tub. She then called 911 and requested police assistance. When officers arrived they noticed that all the doors had been locked and that the bathmat had been removed from the bath to reduce traction. During her interrogation, she said she killed her children because she had not been a "good mother." She later stated that she believed that, had she not killed her children, they would have suffered eternal damnation and have been "tormented by Satan." These beliefs could be traced back to the period after her third child was born, when Andrea and her husband Rusty began following an itinerant preacher, whose fire and brimstone sermons made her worried that she was not protecting her children from sinful influences. Four months after her fourth child was born (and after the family had moved into a bus purchased from the preacher), Yates attempted suicide and told doctors she had seen at least ten visions over a period of days. Three weeks later she tried again to commit suicide, was admitted to a hospital with a diagnosis of a postpartum depression, and was prescribed

— insane level 3 unconventional religious practice

antipsychotic and antidepressant medication. When released after 19 days in the hospital (to a new home, Rusty having moved them out of the bus), she was told that having another child could mean a severe relapse. But Yates stopped taking her medication (despite hearing voices that, she told a friend, told her to do things she was unable to describe), and gave birth to a fifth child. Within a few months she stopped eating, drinking and speaking. She was again prescribed antidepressants and antipsychotic medication, but doctors took her off the latter medication three weeks before the crime. Although her relationship with the children was strained, she was able to make their lunches and carry out other cursory tasks. To give Andrea some independence, Rusty and his mother decided Andrea would have one hour alone with the children between Rusty leaving for work and the mother arriving to help, which was the period during which the children were killed. (At her first trial, Yates was convicted and sentenced to life, failing in her claim that she was insane under a version of M'Naghten. That verdict was overturned because the prosecution's main witness had suggested that Yates, who was a fan of the Law & Order TV show, had patterned her acts after an episode on that show in which a mother had killed her children and then feigned insanity; in fact the episode had never aired. Because the first jury had rejected the death sentence, at her second trial Yates was tried in front of a jury that was not death-qualified (whereas people who expressed qualms about imposing the death penalty had been removed from her first jury). Yates was found not guilty by reason of insanity.

3. Volitional Impairment

UNITED STATES V. POLLARD[i]

Marmion Pollard, in April, 1956, had been for several years a member of the Detroit Police Department. He was an apparently well-adjusted, highly intelligent black officer on the force, of an active nature, pleasing personality, and happy disposition. His rating as a member of the Police Department was excellent, and his intelligence quotient, as appeared from the examination of the Department, was very high. He was married and had four children. He was a good husband and father and had never been in any trouble. He left a Detroit high school, where he was a good student, when he was in the twelfth grade, to enlist in the Navy, earning, after his full service there, an honorable discharge.

In April, 1956, while he was on police duty, his wife and small daughter were brutally murdered in their home by a drunken neighbor. After the murder, Pollard's three other children, all sons, continued to live with him and his mother-in-law, who cared for the children and the home. Gradually, Pollard became the victim of chronic depression or

---

[i]   The "majority" opinion in this book's version of *Pollard* is taken from the district court opinion in the *Pollard* case, 171 F.Supp. 474 (E.D.Mich.1959), and the dissenting opinion is taken from the circuit court of appeals decision reversing the district court, 282 F.2d 450 (6th Cir.1960), mandate clarified, 285 F.2d 81 (6th Cir.1960).

melancholia, appearing generally to be overcome with fatigue, bursting into tears and crying and sobbing for considerable periods, and repeatedly threatening to commit suicide with his police gun. His brother-in-law on one occasion prevented him from deliberately running onto a thru-way, where he probably would have been killed by swift-moving cars. On another occasion, his brother-in-law found him lying on the floor in his home, sobbing; his body was so limp he could hardly be lifted to the bed. After many of these incidents, Pollard seemed to recover and would become suddenly cheerful with no memory of what had happened.

His fellow officers in the Police Department noticed various changes about him after the death of his wife. They weren't abrupt changes. Sometimes a week would pass and he would seem all right; but then he would do something out of the ordinary. In the course of his duties as a policeman, on one day he would insist upon enforcing the law and issue loitering tickets for violation of ordinances, and the next day, he would express an opinion that he did not see anything wrong with such conduct. When asked a question by his fellow policemen, while driving with them in a scout car, he would sometimes be silent for about ten minutes, and then answer the question as though he had just been asked. Sometimes when he came to work with a fellow officer, they might talk to each other normally. Other times he would sit for two hours at a time and say nothing. This was a change from his prior general demeanor, when he had always been very lively and talkative. Once when he drove the scout car, he constantly beat on the steering wheel with his fist for approximately half an hour. When, on this occasion, he was asked if anything was wrong, he acted as though he didn't know he was doing it, and would continue. It should also be noted, however, that a police lieutenant of the Detroit Police Department testified that the defendant's police work, during the period with which we are now concerned, as evidenced by his efficiency rating and his written duty reports, was, if anything, more effective than his service prior to the death of his wife.

A little more than two years after the murder of his wife and daughter, Pollard remarried, on May 22, 1958. On the day before his remarriage, Pollard attempted to hold up a branch of the Detroit Bank & Trust Company about eleven o'clock in the morning. With a gun, he threatened the teller, ordering her to fill up a paper bag with money. The teller did so and handed the bag to Pollard, who ordered a bank official to accompany him to the exit. As they approached the door, the official suddenly threw his arms around Pollard, who then dropped the bag of money and ran out of the building.

About 4:00 P.M., on the same day, he entered the Chene–Medbury Branch of the Bank of the Commonwealth and walked to a railing behind which a bank employee was sitting. He pointed his gun at the man and told him to sit quietly. The employee, however, did not obey this order but instead raised an alarm, whereupon the defendant ran from the bank and again escaped.

The defendant later admitted to agents of the Federal Bureau of Investigation that after his abortive attempts to rob the two banks, he decided to rob a third bank and actually proceeded on the same day to an unnamed bank he had selected but decided not to make the attempt when he discovered that the bank was "too wide open"—had too much window area so that the possibility of apprehension was enhanced.

On June 3, at about 3:00 P.M., the defendant entered the Woodrow Wilson–Davison Branch of the Bank of the Commonwealth and went directly to an enclosure behind which a male and female employee were sitting at desks facing each other. Defendant held his gun under a jacket which he carried over his right arm. He ordered the woman employee to come out from behind the railing. In doing so, she grasped the edge of her desk. Defendant, in the belief that she may have pushed an alarm button, decided to leave but ordered the woman to accompany him out of the bank. When they reached the street, he told her to walk ahead of him, but not to attract attention. Defendant noticed a police car approaching the bank and waited until it passed him, then ran across an empty lot to his car and again escaped.

On June 11, 1958, he attempted to hold up a grocery market. He was thwarted in the attempt when the proprietor screamed and, becoming frightened, the defendant fled. In so doing, he abandoned his automobile in back of the market where he had parked it during the holdup attempt. Routinely, this car was placed under surveillance and later when the defendant, dressed in his Detroit Police Officer's uniform, attempted to get in it, he was arrested by detectives of the Detroit Police Force.

After his apprehension, the defendant confessed to eleven other robberies, or attempted robberies.

The three psychiatrists who submitted the written reports, all qualified and respected members of their profession, testified that in their opinion the defendant, at the time he committed the criminal acts, knew the difference between right and wrong and knew that the acts he committed were wrong but was suffering from a "traumatic neurosis" or "dissociative reaction", characterized by moods of depression and severe feelings of guilt, induced by the traumatic effect of the death of his wife and child and his belief that he was responsible for their deaths because by his absence from home he left them exposed to the actions of the crazed, drunken neighbor. They further stated that he had an unconscious desire to be punished by society to expiate these guilt feelings and that the governing power of his mind was so destroyed or impaired that he was unable to resist the commission of the criminal acts. In their opinion, however, the defendant was not then, nor is he now, psychotic or committable to a mental institution.

irresistible impulse

Counsel for defendant contends that since all the medical testimony was to the effect that the defendant was suffering from an irresistible impulse at the time of the commission of the offenses, this Court must accept this uncontroverted expert testimony and find him not guilty by reason of insanity.

* * *

Psychiatry and law approach the problem of human behavior from different philosophical perspectives. Psychiatry purports to be scientific and takes a deterministic position with regard to behavior. "Its view of human nature is expressed in terms of drives and dispositions which, like mechanical forces, operate in accordance with universal laws of causation." For psychiatry, what we do is determined by what we are, and there is little or no room for moral or ethical judgments. In a sense, all criminal behavior, whether it be the acts of the rapist, the forger, the embezzler, the sender of licentious literature through the mails or tax evasion by a reputable businessman, is evidence of mental disease. But the uncritical adoption of this point of view would completely do away with the concept of criminal responsibility. Criminal law is "a practical, rational, normative science which, although it draws upon theoretical science, also is concerned to pass judgment on human conduct. Its view of human nature asserts the reality of free choice and rejects the thesis that the conduct of normal adults is a mere expression of imperious psychological necessity. Given the additional purpose to evaluate conduct, some degree of autonomy is a necessary postulate."

The psychiatrists, as hereinbefore related, testified that the defendant suffered from severe feelings of depression and guilt; and that in their opinion he had an irresistible impulse to commit criminal acts, an unconscious desire to be apprehended and punished; and that he geared his behavior to the accomplishment of this end. However, his entire pattern of conduct during the period of his criminal activities militates against this conclusion. His conscious desire not to be apprehended and punished was demonstrably greater than his unconscious desire to the contrary. After his apprehension, despite searching interrogation for over five hours by Detroit Police Officers and by agents of the Federal Bureau of Investigation, he denied any participation in criminal conduct of any kind. It was only after he was positively identified by bank personnel that he finally admitted that he did attempt to perpetrate the bank robberies. The trial judge asked one of the psychiatrists to explain this apparent inconsistency. In answer, he stated that although the defendant had an unconscious desire to be apprehended and punished, when the possibility of apprehension became direct and immediate, the more dominating desire for self-preservation asserted itself. This explanation may have merit if applied to individual acts. However, the validity of a theory that attempts to explain the behavior of a person must be determined in light

guilt → wanted to be punished

of that person's entire behavioral pattern and not with reference to isolated acts which are extracted from the pattern. The defendant's pattern of behavior of May 21, 1958, discloses that the desire for self-preservation was not fleeting and momentary but continuing, consistent and dominant. What, then, becomes of the theory of irresistible impulse? Looking to the events of that day, we are asked to believe, first, that the defendant, acting pursuant to an irresistible impulse, selected a bank site to rob, entered the bank to accomplish that end, purposely failed in the attempt and when the end he sought, apprehension, was in view, escaped because of the dominance, at the moment of ultimate accomplishment, of the stronger drive for self-preservation. We must then believe that when the defendant knew he was apparently free from detection, his compulsive state reasserted itself and that he again went through the steps of planning, abortive attempt and escape. And if we acquiesce in this theory, what other psychiatric theory explains his subsequent conduct—his plan to rob a third unnamed bank and the rejection of that plan because of his subjective belief that the possibility of apprehension would be too great? If the theory remains the same, then it appears that in the latter case, the fear of apprehension and punishment tipped "the scales enough to make resistible an impulse otherwise irresistible." It is a logical inference that, in reality, the other robbery attempts were made as the result of impulses that the defendant did not choose voluntarily to resist because, to him, the possibility of success outweighed the likelihood of detection which is in essence a motivation for all criminal conduct. The impulse being resistible, the defendant is accountable for his criminal conduct.

Psychiatrists admit that the line between irresistible impulse and acts which are the result of impulses not resisted is not easy to trace. To the extent that the line may be traced, the distinguishing motivation of the action, whether the act is performed to satisfy an intrinsic need or is the result of extrinsic provocation, is a determining factor. Admittedly, motivations may be mixed. However, all the facts have clearly established that defendant's criminal activity was planned to satisfy an extrinsic need by a reasoned but anti-social method. The defendant had financial problems of varying degrees of intensity throughout his life. He had financial difficulties during his first marriage. He was now embarking upon a second marriage. He was about to undertake the responsibility of supporting not only a wife and himself, but also four children, three of them the product of his first marriage. In statements given to agents of the Federal Bureau of Investigation admitting his criminal activity, he stated: "Inasmuch as I was about to marry my second wife, I decided that I would not lead the same type of financially insecure life that I led with my first wife. I needed about $5,000 in order to buy a home. My only purpose in deciding to rob a bank was to obtain $5,000 and if I obtained the money, I did not intend to continue robbing." Defendant's entire pattern of conduct was consistent with this expressed motivation.

Life does not always proceed on an even keel. Periods of depression, feelings of guilt and inadequacy are experienced by many of us. Defendant was a devoted husband and loving father. His feelings of despondency and depression induced by the brutal killing of his wife and infant daughter were not unnatural. How else the defendant should have reacted to his tragic loss we are not told. His conduct throughout this crucial period did not cause any concern among his colleagues. All stated unequivocally that in their opinion he was sane. Significant also is the fact that his present wife married him on May 22, 1958, after a year of courtship. It is a permissible inference that defendant's conduct relative to his mental condition, as related by her, did not suggest to her that the defendant was insane.

We are satisfied beyond a reasonable doubt that the defendant committed the acts for which he is now charged and that when he committed them he was legally sane. — *Sane*

DISSENT

If the mere preponderance of evidence created a reasonable doubt as to whether appellant acted under an irresistible impulse, the government did not prove his guilt. When there has been created, by the evidence, a reasonable doubt as to whether an accused person acted under an irresistible impulse, the burden is upon the prosecution to establish, beyond a reasonable doubt, that he did not act under an irresistible impulse.

In the instant case, the psychiatric witnesses had unanimously agreed that Pollard suffered from severe feelings of depression and guilt; that, in their opinion, he had an irresistible impulse to commit criminal acts; an unconscious desire to be apprehended and punished; and that he geared his behavior to the accomplishment of this end. The court, however, states that his entire pattern of conduct during the period of his criminal activities militated against this conclusion, and that his conscious desire not to be apprehended and punished was demonstrably greater than his unconscious desire to the contrary. Without drawing any conclusions from the foregoing as to whether appellant's conscious or unconscious desires were the stronger, it can be said that acts that appear rational are not to be taken by the factfinder as evidence of sanity, where all of the other evidence in the case is proof of a defendant's mental unsoundness.

It should also be mentioned that in the Report of the Neuropsychiatric Staff Conference of the Medical Center for Federal Prisoners, it was pointed out that the attempted robberies by Pollard were bizarre and ineffectively planned and executed; that when he tried to leave one bank, he ordered a bank official to follow behind him instead of ahead of him, which resulted in his being caught from behind and barely escaping after a struggle, during which he dropped the paper bag of money he had collected; that on the various occasions of his attempted robberies, he would suddenly enter a bank that he had never seen before, without prior knowledge of the arrangement of the premises, or of the personnel. Taken in consideration with all of the other factors, such conduct, on the part of a highly intelligent police officer with a knowledge of how crimes are committed, has about it nothing of sanity.

It is emphasized by the government that Pollard was motivated to attempt the bank robberies because of his need for financial security. The claimed motivation seems pointless. Pollard, during his first marriage, had been receiving the regular salary of a policeman with promotions, of approximately $450 a month. His first wife, at that time, was receiving about $300 a month as a clerk with the Michigan Unemployment Compensation Commission. Their joint income was almost twice what a regular policeman's salary would be. His second wife, at the time of her marriage to him, had money of her own—enough to pay her own bills, and take care of her daughter with the money which was paid for support by her former husband. She had previously held a position for six years with the Michigan Bell Telephone Company. She considered herself to be relatively comfortable financially. Between the time of Pollard's arrest on June 11, 1958, and his trial, she had, herself, paid off about $700 in bills that he had owed. Pollard's financial condition could not be considered a reasonable motivation for his attempted bank robberies. As far as income went, he was much better off than most other policemen and if such a financial condition could be considered a reasonable motivation for Pollard's attempted robberies, every other policeman in the department would have had twice the motivation to commit such crimes as Pollard had.

Certain distinctions have been drawn by courts in applying the rule of irresistible impulse. While anger, greed, and passion are said, in ordinary parlance, to result in acts because of desires that have become irresistible, this is not, in law, the "irresistible impulse" that results from a mental defect or mental disease. Further, it is held that "emotional insanity," which is an unbridled passion lasting just long enough to enable the act complained of to be done, and then subsiding, does not relieve the accused of accountability, even in those jurisdictions where the doctrine of irresistible impulse, arising out of a mental defect, is recognized. Moreover, to like effect, in *Bell v. State,* 120 Ark. 530, 180 S.W. 186, 196 (1915), the court although sustaining the doctrine of irresistible impulse as a defense to crime, distinguished between such impulse and "emotional" insanity, as follows: "But it must be remembered that one who is otherwise sane will not be excused from a crime he has committed while his reason is temporarily dethroned not by disease, but by anger, jealousy, or other passion."

From all of the evidence of the lay and expert witnesses, however, it cannot be affirmatively concluded that Pollard was sane. Obviously, as a result of the murder of his wife and child while he was absent from his home, he was suffering from some grave disorder, and that disorder was, in the opinion of all the psychiatric and medical experts, a disassociative reaction resulting in Pollard's commission of the acts charged because of an irresistible impulse.

QUESTIONS AND COMMENTS

1. *Volition, causation and compulsion.* The "majority" opinion cites several commentators to the effect that the "deterministic" premise of psychiatry, if given full sway, could "do away with the concept of criminal responsibility." This concern is most often voiced when discussing application of the volitional tests for insanity, because these tests directly pose the question of whether a person could control his or her behavior. If mental health professionals answer this question honestly, the argument goes, they will always say that an individual's acts are caused by various endogenous or exogenous factors over which the individual had little or no control.

In *Pollard,* for instance, the psychiatric testimony suggested that Pollard was not aware of his true reasons for acting, and thus, in some sense, he was not "in control of" his actions. Another common type of case in which "lack-of-control" defenses are raised involves defendants diagnosed as having "impulse disorders" such as kleptomania, pyromania, or pedophilia. Other examples are legion. For example, in *People v. Yukl,* 83 Misc.2d 364, 372 N.Y.S.2d 313 (1975), the defendant raised an insanity defense relying on evidence that individuals with an extra Y (or male) chromosome are particularly aggressive, and thus less able to control their behavior (and in fact, people with an extra Y chromosome are significantly over-represented in prisons). See Note, *The XYY Chromosomal Abnormality: Use and Misuse in the Legal Process*, 9 Harv.J.Legis. 469 (1972). Several cases have involved claims that the type of posttraumatic stress syndrome raised in *Heads* not only made it difficult for the defendant to distinguish right from wrong, but also "compelled" the defendant to act violently. See, e.g., *Louisiana v. Sharp,* 418 So.2d 1344 (La.1982) (defendant had "uncontrollable 'rage reaction' " as a result of PTSD). Childhood maltreatment of individuals with low levels of monoamine oxidase-A (MAOA enzyme) appears to heighten the likelihood of developing antisocial personality and engaging in violent criminality as adults, and the presence of this genetic variation has been used in insanity defense cases. Avshalom Caspi et al., *Role of Genotype in the Cycle of Violence in Maltreated Children*, 297 Science 851 (2002); J. Kim–Cohen et al., *MAOA, Maltreatment, and Gene–Environment Interaction Predicting Children's Mental Health: New Evidence and a Meta–Analysis*, 11 Molecular Psychiatry 903 (2006); Nita A. Farahany and William Bernet, *Behavioural Genetics in Criminal Cases: Past, Present and Future*, 2 Genomics Soc'y Pol'y 72 (2006).

Other defenses have been predicated on pressures that appear to be as much "external" as "internal." In *United States v. Alexander and Murdock,* 471 F.2d 923 (D.C.Cir.1972), for instance, the evidence showed that Murdock grew up in the Watts section of Los Angeles in a large family with little love or attention and no father. He became "greatly preoccupied with the unfair treatment of negroes in this country and believe[d] that racial war is inevitable." Early one morning, Murdock and his companions became involved in an argument with a group of Marines, all of whom were white. Murdock admitted that, during the altercation, which took place in a hamburger shop, he drew his fully loaded gun and emptied it. He killed two of the Marines, even though he had not seen any weapons. As they drove from the scene, he took his companion's gun and continued firing into the restaurant. In explanation, he said that just before he began firing he had heard someone say "Get out, you black bastards." He also claimed he saw Marines advancing toward him, although the surviving Marines denied this allegation. His attorney argued that Murdock was unable to control his conduct because of a "deepseated emotional disorder that was rooted in his 'rotten social background.' " An expert witness testified that "it is probable that when the Marine called him a 'black bastard,' Murdock had an irresistible impulse to shoot." Id. at 957–59.

How should the criminal law respond to these types of claims? In *Responsibility and the Unconscious,* 53 So.Cal.L.Rev. 1563 (1980), Professor Michael Moore draws a distinction between "causation" on the one hand and "compulsion" on the other:

> Everyone is undoubtedly caused to act as they do by a myriad of environmental, physiological, or psychological factors. Yet to say that any actions are caused, for example, by an unhappy childhood, a chemical imbalance, or a belief that it is raining, is not to say the actions are compelled. One must point to something other than causation to make out the excuse of compulsion. . . .

Moore then uses the *Pollard* case to illustrate his point.

> Suppose Pollard did unconsciously feel guilty at the death of his first wife and child. He may have felt guilty because he had not been there; alternatively, he may have felt guilty because he had unconsciously wished to kill them himself. In either case, could such unconscious guilt *compel* Pollard to do an act for which he would be punished?

In answering this question, Moore compares Pollard to someone who has kleptomania (intense, irrational urges to steal). A person with kleptomania, according to Moore, feels compelled to steal and knows he is yielding to the compulsion, "yet he does not know the object of his passionate desire. . . . A few thefts readily tell him it is not the stolen objects themselves." Pollard on the other hand, "had a perfectly intelligible, conscious motive for acting. In such circumstances one is often more reluctant to accept as a factual matter that some unconscious emotion really explains his behavior."

Even accepting Moore's distinction between causation and compulsion, one may have difficulty differentiating between the two in an individual case. Do you agree with Moore that Pollard was probably not "compelled" by his unconscious guilt to commit the robberies and attempted robberies? Consider other examples based on biologically-based claims. Already noted is the research indicating that men with low levels of MAOA and a history of abuse as children are prone to engage in serious antisocial behavior as young adults. Research also shows that individuals with frontal lobe damage exhibit significant deficits in impulse control and ability to adjust behavior to changing circumstances, with one study finding that 73% of inmates with front lobe damage committed violent crimes compared to only 28% of non-injured inmates who did so. E.T. Bryant et al., *Neuropsychological Deficits, Learning Disabilities, and Violent Behavior*, 52 J. Consulting & Clin. Psychol. 323 (1984). Other studies report that people with traumatic brain injury (TBI) often become more quick-tempered and impulsive after the injury and are three times as likely as controls to exhibit aggressive behavior. Wayne Gordon et al., *Traumatic Brain Injury Rehabilitation: State of the Science*, 85 Am. J. Physical Med. & Rehab. 343, 369 (2006). See generally Richard E. Redding, *The Brain–Disordered Defendant: Neuroscience and Legal Insanity in the Twenty–First Century*, 56 Am. U. L. Rev. 51, 57–76 (2006). Finally, investigators have suggested that higher testosterone levels make persons prone to violence. Angela S. Book et al., *The Relationship Between Testosterone and Aggression: A Meta–Analysis*, 6 Aggression & Violent Behav. 579 (2001) (finding "a weak positive relationship"). Some have argued that virtually all violent crime is largely the result of such factors as genetic abnormalities, the evolutionary drive to spread one's DNA, nutrition, physiological and anatomic anomalies in offenders' brains, and environmental influences on the developing fetus. See Adrian Raine, The Anatomy of Violence: The Biological Roots of Crime (2013). Can it be said that defendants who meet these types of criteria are "compelled," or should an excuse depend upon whether they had "a perfectly intelligible, conscious motive for acting" (which will normally be the case)? Finally, using Moore's compulsion-causation distinction, how do you evaluate Murdock's claim?

2. *Reform efforts.* The previous note identified two concerns associated with the volitional prong. The first is that it could swallow up the criminal law by providing an excuse for everyone, particularly as the neurosciences elucidate more relationships between genes, experience, and behavior. The second is that, even if the volitional prong can theoretically be limited, as Moore has tried to do, difficulties associated with determining who is properly excused under the test could lead to mistake or abuse. Of the reforms advanced to address these problems, three stand out.

Elimination of Volitional Prong. The first, of course, is abolition of the volitional prong, a step the U.S. Congress took in the Insanity Defense Reform Act of 1984. Is this solution justifiable, assuming that some people knowingly commit crimes but apparently "can't help themselves?" Consider the following comment by Bonnie, an opponent of the volitional tests:

It might be argued, of course, that the risk of mistake should be tolerated if the volitional prong of the defense is morally necessary. The question may be put this way: Are there clinically identifiable cases involving defendants whose behavior controls were so pathologically impaired that they ought to be acquitted although their ability to appreciate the wrongfulness of their actions was unimpaired? I do not think so. The most clinically compelling cases of volitional impairment involve the so-called impulse disorders—pyromania, kleptomania, and the like. These disorders involve severely abnormal compulsions that ought to be taken into account in sentencing, but the exculpation of pyromaniacs would be out of touch with commonly shared moral intuitions.

Richard Bonnie, *The Moral Basis of the Insanity Defense*, 69 A.B.A.J. 194, 197 (1983). Do you agree that the conviction of pyromaniacs for arson and kleptomaniacs for theft is in "touch with commonly shared moral intuitions"?[j] Under Bonnie's approach, would Pollard be convicted and the psychiatric testimony relegated to a sentencing hearing? Or is the expert testimony in this case possibly relevant to cognitive impairment as well?

Related to this latter question and to the movement toward elimination of the volitional prong consider the effect of adopting an "irrationality" test for insanity. Would volitional impairment be irrelevant under this test? If Pollard's real reason for committing the robberies was to assuage his guilt by getting caught, was he rational? How would a kleptomaniac fare under such a test? An "XYY" defendant? Consider this excerpt from Herbert Fingarette, The Meaning of Insanity, 160–172 (1972), an advocate of the rationality test:

We may find it congenial to speak idiomatically of the insane person as one who is driven, or seized, or overwhelmed, or possessed by fear, anxiety, emotions or delusions. Yet there is one literal truth we must never lose sight of: it is the person himself who initiates and carries out the deed, it is his desire, his mood, his passion, his belief which is at issue, and it is he who acts to satisfy this desire, or to express this mood, emotion, or belief of his. Even if his motive is unconscious, it is his motive, and it is he who acts out of this motive.

From this premise, Fingarette argues that "[t]here is a crucial difference between saying a person lacks capacity to conform to law (that is, cannot conform to law) and saying that he does not control his conduct in the way a normal person does." Virtually all nonresponsible insane persons can control their conduct in the latter sense. What distinguishes them from responsible sane people "is the way in which [they come] to adopt one or another course of action"—the fact that they do so irrationally.

---

[j] One study in Maryland concluded that manic patients are often severely impaired in their capacity to control behavior, while their cognitive impairment is less striking. As a result, the authors asserted, elimination of the volitional prong could lead to conviction of "a class of psychotic patients whose illness is clearest in symptomatology, most likely biologic in origin, most eminently treatable and potentially most disruptive in penal detention." Governor's Task Force to Review the Defense of Insanity, State of Maryland (reported in Rita Simon & David Aaronson, The Insanity Defense 167 (1988)).

Tightening the Definition of Mental Disease. An alternative solution to the dangers of mistake or abuse associated with the volitional prong is to narrow the definition of mental disease or defect for purposes of the insanity defense. The traditional unstructured approach is illustrated by the "dissent" in *Pollard,* which cited several authorities for the proposition that the irresistible impulse must result from a persistent disease, rather than a "temporary," "normal" reaction. Along these lines is *United States v. Lyons,* 731 F.2d 243 (5th Cir.1984), which held that drug addiction is not a mental disease or defect for purposes of the insanity defense unless it causes "actual drug-induced or drug-aggravated psychosis, or physical damage to the brain or nervous system." Other attempts to narrow the mental disease or defect predicate have been described in the previous discussion of the cognitive prong. The most restrictive definitions are found in the federal statute, which limits the insanity defense to "severe" diseases, and in the recommendation of the American Psychiatric Association, which would only permit an insanity defense based on proof of "conditions that grossly and demonstrably impair a person's perception or understanding of reality." Neither the federal statute nor the APA recognizes a volitional impairment defense. But if their approach to the mental disease or defect predicate were applied in the volitional context, would persons with impulse disorders (e.g., the kleptomaniac) and personality disorders (e.g., Murdock) have a defense under a control test? Would Pollard? Would the volitional prong have any significance independently of the cognitive prong?

Tightening the Definition of Volitional Impairment. A final reform, more widely espoused when the volitional prong was first adopted than presently, is to require that the impulsive act be truly "irresistible." This concept is colloquially captured by the "policeman at the elbow" inquiry: would the accused have committed the act had a policeman been present at the time? Even kleptomaniacs try to elude detection, and thus would probably not have a defense under a tightened volitional prong. However, determining whether the impulse was irresistible or merely not resisted will still be difficult for some cases. For instance, Hinckley committed his assassination attempt in the midst of several policemen and Secret Service agents. But was his attempt "irresistible"?

Other ways of conceptualizing volitional impairment that might have the effect of limiting its scope have been proposed. Professor Morse has suggested two. At one time, he proposed that a person might be excused for the criminal act if "the desire or craving was so intense that fear of the pain of not satisfying it was the true motive for offending." Stephen Morse, *Excusing the Crazy: The Insanity Defense Reconsidered*, 58 S.Cal. L. Rev. 777, 815 (1985). More recently, he borrowed from the law of duress (which excuses those who commit crime because of unbearable *external* pressures), to derive three criteria for determining when internal coercion should excuse:

> *First*, the person is subjected to an unjustifiable threat, that is a set of circumstances that will make the person worse off compared with some baseline if she doesn't perform the wrongful act.

Second, performing the wrongful act and suffering the threatened consequences for failing to perform it are both aversive choices, but doing the wrongful act is an excusable alternative because it is unfair to require the agent to refrain under the circumstances.

Third, the person is not responsible either for placing herself in or for failing to avoid the circumstances that produced the hard choice.

Stephen Morse, *Culpability and Control*, 142 U.Pa.L.Rev. 1587, 1613–14 (1994). Would Pollard have been "worse off" if he hadn't committed the burglaries? Would it be "unfair" to require him to refrain from the crimes? In connection with the third inquiry listed by Morse, was Pollard in any way "responsible" for placing himself in the position of committing crime?

Morse also argues, however, that most cases of internal coercion are better analyzed as cases involving lack of rationality—that is, these really are manifestations of a *cognitive* impairment. For instance, he contends, "the 'policeman at the elbow' test, which is usually understood as a volitional standard, is . . . better interpreted as a rationality test. Those who offend in the face of certain capture have either rationally decided for political or other reasons that the offense is worth the punishment, as in cases of civil disobedience, or they are irrational." Stephen Morse, *Causation, Compulsion and Involuntariness*, 22 Bull. Am. Acad. Psych & L. 159, 179 (1994). In this regard, see also Robert Schopp, Automatism, Insanity and the Psychology of Criminal Responsibility (1991), who argues that current control tests are "unnecessary and irrelevant or they are vacuous," id. at 174, and that "severe cognitive psychopathology" should be the sole basis for a volitional impairment excuse. Id. at 202–03. These suggestions may have the same effect as the limitations on the mental disease or defect threshold described above.

3.   *Research on the volitional prong.* Empirical evidence suggests that the concern over mistake or abuse that underlies at least some of the foregoing proposals may be unwarranted. Relying on results obtained by trained mental health professionals using a structured interview format, one study found that, while neither determination is likely to lead to highly reliable results, inter-rater agreement on the volitional and cognitive prongs was virtually identical. Richard Rogers, *Empiricism v. Emotionalism*, 42 Am.Psychol. 840, 841–42 (1987). Using the same interview format, a second study found that reliance on the volitional prong resulted in 23.5% fewer insanity recommendations from mental health professionals than did use of the cognitive prong. Richard Rogers & Charles Clark, *Diogenes Revisited: Another Search for the Ultimate NGRI Standard*, Paper presented at American Academy of Psychiatry and Law meeting, Albuquerque (October, 1985). Assume that research substantiates that psychiatric assessment of volitional impairment is at least as reliable as assessment of cognitive impairment, as well as less likely to result in acquittal. How would these findings affect your attitude toward eliminating the volitional prong or, if that prong is retained, narrowing the definition of mental disease or defect or increasing the level of control required?

4. *The Supreme Court and the volitional prong.* Although the Supreme Court has made clear that an insanity defense without a volitional prong is constitutional (see discussion of *Clark v. Arizona* on pp. 634–636), in *Robinson v. California*, 370 U.S. 660, 82 S.Ct. 1417, 8 L.Ed.2d 758 (1962) and *Powell v. Texas*, 392 U.S. 514, 88 S.Ct. 2145, 20 L.Ed.2d 1254 (1968), the Court suggested that some aspects of volition must be considered in gauging criminal liability. *Robinson* held that the Eighth Amendment's prohibition against cruel and unusual punishment bars punishing someone merely for being addicted to heroin. In *Powell* five justices interpreted this holding as a ban on convicting a person for an "irresistible urge," at least under certain circumstances. While the majority in *Powell* decided that an alcoholic could constitutionally be convicted for being drunk *in public*, Justice White wrote a concurring opinion in which he stated that, after *Robinson*, "the chronic alcoholic with an irresistible urge to consume alcohol should not be punishable [merely] for drinking or for being drunk", a statement with which the four dissenters agreed. Does this language, if it reflects the position of a majority of the Court, impose any limitations on the extent to which the state may punish someone who is mentally ill?

5. *Other cases involving volitional impairment.* Consider whether the individuals in the following cases should be found insane.

Case A. Foreman, age 18, is charged with six counts of arson and, in connection with one of the fires, three counts of murder. His earliest childhood memory was watching a neighbor burn trash in the backyard, and he was setting fires around his home at the age of eight. He also set fires on four separate occasions at his high school. At 16 he began calling for emergency assistance from the rescue squad by pretending to be suffocating. He felt a great sense of satisfaction from being cared for by the emergency crews on these occasions. Soon he joined the local squad and became especially close to James, an older member of the squad. Foreman had fantasies of being rescued from a fire by James, and reported sexual arousal in seeing firemen, particularly James, in their rubberized firefighting clothes. He soon began setting fires, hoping that James would arrive. An expert testified that Foreman was suffering from pyromania and that his "need to start the fire [that led to the deaths] in order to bring himself and Carson together was so strong that he unconsciously was able to keep from his awareness the possibility that others might be hurt or that extensive property damages might occur." (In a similar case, the defendant was convicted of arson. Did Foreman have the mens rea for murder, which requires either a purpose to kill or extreme recklessness with respect to the deaths?).

Case B. Tally, a 22 year-old college student, is charged with several counts of attempted rape. Immediately prior to each of his offenses, he experienced a powerful impulse to have forcible intercourse with a woman. As he put it, "There was a feeling of real power and hate and anger . . . I was really excited sexually. You, I just felt . . . there is a word, I can't think of it . . . " When he was overcome by these strong urges, Tally would become "panicky". He felt he had to have a woman or he would "go crazy." At times he could stifle the urge by shutting himself up in his room and listening to music, thinking about his girlfriend, or masturbating. At other times, usually after drinking or doing drugs, he would succumb. None of his victims was an acquaintance. He says he always became "scared" after entering the homes of his victims, but could not force himself to leave. He would be "horrified" at what he was doing but could not do anything about it. "I would watch myself doing this stuff and I couldn't believe it. One part of me was observing and didn't want to go through it, but I couldn't stop." Other than the intercourse itself, he never physically harmed the victims and he never penetrated the victim's vagina (either because he was unable to obtain an erection or he masturbated). Once through he would apologize, and become depressed at what he had done, but his panicky feeling was gone. (In a similar case, the defendant was convicted of the lesser crime of assault.)

Case C. Gorshen, a person who suffered from chronic schizophrenia, killed his employer. For twenty years he had periods where he hallucinated, seeing and hearing devils committing abnormal sexual acts, sometimes upon Gorshen himself. The hallucinations had increased of late. He had been drinking at work, and when his employer sent him home, a fight ensued. Gorshen went home, got a gun, and shot his employer. Expert testimony claimed that Gorshen's rage was a desperate attempt to ward off the imminent and total disintegration of his personality that would occur through regression into a schizophrenic relapse. (Based on *People v. Gorshen*, 51 Cal.2d 716, 336 P.2d 492 (1959), see pp. 534–536).

B. THE AUTOMATISM DEFENSE

NOTE ON AUTOMATISM

Except for strict liability offenses, which are not relevant to the topic of this chapter, every crime is comprised of at least two elements: (1) the physical conduct associated with the crime (known as the "actus reus"); and (2) the mental state, or level of intent, associated with the crime (known as the "mens rea"). To convict an individual of a particular crime, the state must prove beyond a reasonable doubt that the defendant committed the actus reus with the requisite mens rea for that crime.

The automatism defense developed out of the law's attempt to define the actus reus concept. The actus reus contemplates a voluntary physical act. For instance, if A pushes B's arm into C, B cannot be convicted of assault even though B's arm committed the actual touching, because B's touching was not voluntary. It could also be said that B did not intend to commit the assault, and thus did not have the mens rea for the crime. But a distinction is usually made between an act over which there is no conscious control and a conscious action with unintended consequences. The assault above is an example of the first type of act and has traditionally been analyzed under the voluntariness requirement of the actus reus. An example of the latter situation would be if B, in tapping C, meant only to frighten him but instead killed him; B's act would be voluntary, but he would not have the mens rea for murder.

The automatism (or "unconsciousness") defense recognizes that some criminal acts may be committed "involuntarily," even though no third party (like A in the example above) is involved. The classic example of the "automaton" is the person who commits an offense while sleep-walking; courts have held that such an individual does not have conscious control of his or her physical actions and therefore acts involuntarily. See, e.g., *Fain v. Commonwealth*, 78 Ky. 183 (1879). Other situations in which the defense might be implicated arise when a crime occurs during a state of unconsciousness induced by concussion following a head injury; by shock created by bullet wounds; or by metabolic disorders such as anoxia, hypoglycemia, or the involuntary ingestion of alcohol or drugs. Events caused by epilepsy are probably best placed in this category as well.

Several courts have limited the automatism defense by holding that a person claiming to have been affected by one of the above-named conditions at the time of the offense cannot prevail with the defense if the person had experienced the disability on previous occasions and could have taken reasonable steps to prevent the criminal occurrence. Thus, if a man knows he is subject to epileptic seizures, loses control of a car because of a seizure, and kills someone in the process, he may not be able to take advantage of the defense. See, e.g., *People v. Decina*, 2 N.Y.2d 133, 157 N.Y.S.2d 558, 138 N.E.2d 799 (1956).

Conceptually, the automatism defense differs from the insanity defense in three ways. First, insane persons, unlike "automatons," are generally conscious of their acts but either do not understand the true nature of the acts or cannot stop themselves from performing them. Second, while there is some dispute over whether sanity is an element that must be proven for each offense, the prosecution clearly bears the burden of establishing the actus reus and thus bears the burden of negating an automatism claim beyond a reasonable doubt. Finally, to prevail, a person alleging insanity must be found to have a mental disease or defect; there is no such requirement when automatism is involved.

QUESTIONS AND COMMENTS

1. *Application*. As indicated above, the automatism defense contemplates a loss of conscious control over one's bodily movements. Does either Heads or Pollard have a viable automatism claim? In *People v. Lisnow*, 88 Cal.App.3d Supp. 21, 26–27, 151 Cal.Rptr. 621, 623 (1978), the court held that a Vietnam veteran who struck a maitre d' in a restaurant for "no apparent reason" and then went into the parking lot and engaged in other "acts of violence" while in a "dreamlike" state was entitled to an instruction on the automatism defense. See also, Donald Apostle, *The Unconsciousness*

Defense as Applied to Post Traumatic Stress Disorder in a Vietnam Veteran, 8 Bull.Am.Acad.Psychiat. & L. 426 (1980). In a jurisdiction where the volitional prong of the insanity test is eliminated, would the automatism defense take up the slack? Why or why not?

Consider also cases involving a condition that was formerly called multiple personality disorder and is now called dissociative identity disorder. According to DSM–5, this diagnosis requires a "[d]isruption of identity characterized by two or more distinct personality states [that] involves marked discontinuity in sense of self and sense of agency [and] recurrent gaps in the recall of everyday events, important personal information, and/or traumatic events that are inconsistent with ordinary forgetting." In *United States v. Denny–Shaffer*, 2 F.3d 999 (10th Cir.1993), the defendant kidnapped an infant while impersonating a medical student; she was later found by her former boyfriend with the child in his bed, blood on the sheets, a human placenta in a bag, and claiming to have just given birth to the child. Defense and prosecution experts agreed that she had a "host," or dominant, personality and several different "alter" personalities, that the host did not control the alters, and that none of the personalities were necessarily aware of the others' actions. Both experts also agreed that two alters were in control during the planning of the abduction, the act itself, and the ensuing travel, but they could not agree on what role, if any, the host personality may have played. Neither expert was willing to testify that the alters, by themselves, met the test for insanity. Based on the experts' ambivalence about the latter issue, the trial court held that there was insufficient evidence to support an insanity verdict, but the Tenth Circuit reversed, holding that the issue should have been whether the dominant personality was unaware of the offense, or not in control when it took place.

Consider also *Washington v. Wheaton*, 121 Wash.2d 347, 850 P.2d 507 (1993), where the parties agreed that the defendant, charged with first-degree theft, had multiple personalities, and also agreed that the host personality was "not conscious or in executive control of the physical body and ha[d] no independent knowledge of the acts constituting the offense." The trial court nonetheless rejected the defendant's insanity claim, on the ground that the alter in control at the time of the offense was not insane. On appeal, the Washington Supreme Court admitted that multiple personality disorder was recognized in the then current DSM–III–R, but held that not enough was known about the nature of the disorder to decide whether the insanity assessment should be based on the sanity of the alter or instead on the extent to which the host was aware of the alter's actions; it then affirmed the conviction. In light of the automatism analysis described above, is the insanity defense the proper rubric for analyzing multiple personality cases?

Professor Saks argues that people with multiple personalities should be presumed to be *not* responsible for crimes they commit, either because they do not know the nature of their act, could not control it, or do not deserve punishment on characterological grounds. However, she would allow the presumption of nonresponsibility to be rebutted in those "rare" situations when: (1) "all of a multiple's alters know about and acquiesce in the crime;" (2) "the host personality commits the crime and the appearance of other alters is so extremely limited that punishing the person/body does not seem problematic;" and (3) a multiple "has a ringleader alter in addition to well-established lines of responsibility for different tasks [such that] each alter has sufficient knowledge and control over the others that group liability makes sense." Elyn Saks, *Multiple Personality Disorder and Criminal Responsibility*, 25 U.C. Davis L. Rev. 383, 452–54 (1992). She also argues that self-knowledge that one is a multiple should *not* lead to rebuttal of the presumption, because, in contrast to the person who knows he or she suffers from epilepsy, the multiple would have to take drastic steps (i.e., commit oneself) in order to avoid possible harm: "we simply cannot penalize people for failing to do what only the most saintly would do." Id. at 454–57.

2. *Incapacitation concerns.* Most commentators agree that an epileptic seizure is best characterized as an involuntary act rather than an "irresistible impulse," because the movements that occur during a seizure are not related to the individual's conscious, or even unconscious, processes. Yet courts in Britain, where the law of automatism is well developed, have rejected automatism defenses based on epilepsy and instead have permitted only claims of insanity in such cases, on the explicit ground that to do otherwise would result in immediate release of dangerous individuals. See, e.g., *Bratty v. Attorney–General for Northern Ireland,* 3 All E.R. 523 (1961). Why might commitment statutes for insanity acquittees not apply to those acquitted on an automatism defense? Is there any way to avoid distorting the insanity doctrine while at the same time protecting the public in the latter type of case?

C. EXPERT TESTIMONY ON MENS REA (THE DIMINISHED CAPACITY DOCTRINE)

NOTE ON MENS REA

The principal way the law grades the culpability of sane individuals is mental state. A person who deliberately plans a crime is more culpable than one who accidentally commits one. Under the common law, courts developed literally scores of "mens rea" terms to describe various levels of culpability. Unfortunately, these terms—"willful and wanton," "with a depraved heart," and so on—were more colorful than descriptive. Over the years, two generic categories were created to help categorize these diverse mental states, although they were only partially successful in doing so. "Specific intent" was meant to designate the mens rea for those crimes that require a further intention beyond that identified with the physical act connected with the offense (e.g., "premeditated" murder, "aggravated" assault, assault "with intent to rape"). "General intent" crimes, on the other hand, were those that merely required proof that the defendant was aware or should have been aware of his or her physical actions at the time of the offense (e.g., manslaughter, assault, rape).

Because neither the original mens rea terms nor the concepts of specific and general intent were necessarily self-defining, modern statutory codes have attempted to be more precise on issues relating to mental state. Most influential in this regard has been the ALI's Model Penal Code formulation, which attempts to simplify the mens rea inquiry by specifying a total of four levels of mens rea. In descending order of culpability, they are (1) "purpose," requiring proof that the offender intended the relevant conduct or result; (2) "knowledge," requiring proof that the offender was aware of the conduct or result; (3) "recklessness," requiring proof that the offender consciously disregarded "a substantial and unjustifiable risk" that he or she was engaging in the conduct or causing a result; and (4) "negligence," requiring proof that the offender should have been aware of "a substantial and unjustifiable risk" that he or she was engaging in the conduct or causing a result. The first two mental states clearly focus on subjective mental state, "negligence" is commonly said to be objectively defined, and "recklessness" falls somewhere in between. Although the common-law terms are so amorphous that equating them with Model Penal Code mental states is a somewhat risky venture, it is probably fair to say that "specific intent" most closely coincides with "purpose" and "knowledge," while "general intent" can be analogized to "recklessness" and "negligence."

As will become clear below, distinguishing between subjective mental states (purpose, knowledge, and specific intent) and objectively defined mental states (negligence, general intent) is important in understanding the courts' approach to clinical input on mens rea. It is also important to recognize that the mens rea inquiry described above is quite distinct from the insanity inquiry. While a few persons meet the *M'Naghten* test because they were incapable of forming the requisite intent for an offense, most insane persons have the appropriate mens rea for the crime they are alleged to have committed; they are acquitted not because they did not intend the results of their conduct but because their reasons for the conduct are considered "crazy." To use two well-known cases as examples, both Daniel M'Naghten and John Hinckley probably met the mens rea requirements for the crime charged (i.e., knowingly shooting at another with the purpose of killing him), but they were nonetheless found insane.

Out of this distinction has developed the so-called "diminished capacity" concept. In its broadest sense, the diminished capacity doctrine permits the accused to introduce clinical testimony focusing directly on the mens rea for the crime charged, without having to assert an insanity defense.[k] If the testimony negates the requisite mens rea for a particular

---

[k]   As the American Bar Association has pointed out, the phrase "diminished capacity" can be misleading since it implies a "quasi-insanity defense" that the defendant must prove, when in fact the underlying notion is merely a recognition that clinical testimony may be just as relevant to the mens rea inquiry as evidence of mistake or intoxication. See commentary to ABA Criminal Justice Mental Health Standard 7–6.2. This book will nonetheless use the phrase "diminished capacity doctrine" because, as subsequent materials make clear, most jurisdictions have

offense, the defendant cannot be guilty of that charge, though he may still be guilty of a lesser included offense. Thus, a person charged with first degree murder might be able to escape conviction on that charge if clinical testimony shows that he or she did not kill purposely or knowingly (or with specific intent). However, conviction may still occur on a lesser charge requiring a lesser intent (e.g. manslaughter or assault). The following materials evaluate the ramifications of this idea.

CLARK V. ARIZONA

Supreme Court of the United States, 2007.
548 U.S. 735, 126 S.Ct. 2709, 165 L.Ed.2d 842.

JUSTICE SOUTER delivered the opinion of the Court.

*   *   *

In the early hours of June 21, 2000, Officer Jeffrey Moritz of the Flagstaff Police responded in uniform to complaints that a pickup truck with loud music blaring was circling a residential block. When he located the truck, the officer turned on the emergency lights and siren of his marked patrol car, which prompted petitioner Eric Clark, the truck's driver (then 17), to pull over. Officer Moritz got out of the patrol car and told Clark to stay where he was. Less than a minute later, Clark shot the officer, who died soon after but not before calling the police dispatcher for help. Clark ran away on foot but was arrested later that day with gunpowder residue on his hands; the gun that killed the officer was found nearby, stuffed into a knit cap.

Clark was charged with first-degree murder under Ariz.Rev.Stat. Ann. 13–1105(A)(3) for intentionally or knowingly killing a law enforcement officer in the line of duty.[1] In March 2001, Clark was found incompetent to stand trial and was committed to a state hospital for treatment, but two years later the same trial court found his competence restored and ordered him to be tried. Clark waived his right to a jury, and the case was heard by the court. At trial, Clark did not contest the shooting and death, but relied on his undisputed paranoid schizophrenia at the time of the incident in denying that he had the specific intent to shoot a law enforcement officer or knowledge that he was doing so, as required by the statute. Accordingly, the prosecutor offered circumstantial evidence that Clark knew Officer Moritz was a law enforcement officer. The evidence showed that the officer was in uniform

developed special rules with respect to clinical mens rea testimony that go far beyond the simple relevance notion that usually applies to other mens rea testimony. At the same time, in recognition of the fact that the prosecution bears the burden of proving beyond a reasonable doubt that the defendant had the requisite mens rea, this book avoids calling the diminished capacity notion a "defense."

[1]   Section 13–1105(A)(3) provides that "[a] person commits first degree murder if . . . [i]ntending or knowing that the person's conduct will cause death to a law enforcement officer, the person causes the death of a law enforcement officer who is in the line of duty."

at the time, that he caught up with Clark in a marked police car with emergency lights and siren going, and that Clark acknowledged the symbols of police authority and stopped. The testimony for the prosecution indicated that Clark had intentionally lured an officer to the scene to kill him, having told some people a few weeks before the incident that he wanted to shoot police officers. At the close of the State's evidence, the trial court denied Clark's motion for judgment of acquittal for failure to prove intent to kill a law enforcement officer or knowledge that Officer Moritz was a law enforcement officer.

In presenting the defense case, Clark claimed mental illness, which he sought to introduce for two purposes. First, he raised the affirmative defense of insanity, putting the burden on himself to prove by clear and convincing evidence that "at the time of the commission of the criminal act [he] was afflicted with a mental disease or defect of such severity that [he] did not know the criminal act was wrong". Second, he aimed to rebut the prosecution's evidence of the requisite *mens rea*, that he had acted intentionally or knowingly to kill a law enforcement officer.

The trial court ruled that Clark could not rely on evidence bearing on insanity to dispute the *mens rea*. The court cited *State v. Mott*, 187 Ariz. 536, 931 P.2d 1046 (en banc), cert. denied, 520 U.S. 1234 (1997), which "refused to allow psychiatric testimony to negate specific intent," and held that "Arizona does not allow evidence of a defendant's mental disorder short of insanity . . . to negate the *mens rea* element of a crime." As to his insanity, then, Clark presented testimony from classmates, school officials, and his family describing his increasingly bizarre behavior over the year before the shooting. Witnesses testified, for example, that paranoid delusions led Clark to rig a fishing line with beads and wind chimes at home to alert him to intrusion by invaders, and to keep a bird in his automobile to warn of airborne poison. There was lay and expert testimony that Clark thought Flagstaff was populated with "aliens" (some impersonating government agents), the "aliens" were trying to kill him, and bullets were the only way to stop them. A psychiatrist testified that Clark was suffering from paranoid schizophrenia with delusions about "aliens" when he killed Officer Moritz, and he concluded that Clark was incapable of luring the officer or understanding right from wrong and that he was thus insane at the time of the killing. In rebuttal, a psychiatrist for the State gave his opinion that Clark's paranoid schizophrenia did not keep him from appreciating the wrongfulness of his conduct, as shown by his actions before and after the shooting (such as circling the residential block with music blaring as if to lure the police to intervene, evading the police after the shooting, and hiding the gun).

At the close of the defense case consisting of this evidence bearing on mental illness, the trial court denied Clark's renewed motion for a directed verdict grounded on failure of the prosecution to show that Clark knew the victim was a police officer. The judge then issued a special verdict of first-degree murder, expressly finding that Clark shot and caused the death of Officer Moritz beyond a reasonable doubt and that Clark had not shown that he was insane at the time. The judge noted that though Clark was indisputably afflicted with paranoid schizophrenia at the time of the shooting, the mental illness "did not . . . distort his perception of reality so severely that he did not know his actions were wrong." For this conclusion, the judge expressly relied on "the facts of the crime, the evaluations of the experts, [Clark's] actions and behavior both before and after the shooting, and the observations of those that knew [Clark]." The sentence was life imprisonment without the possibility of release for 25 years.

Clark moved to vacate the judgment and sentence, arguing, among other things, that Arizona's insanity test and its *Mott* rule each violate due process. . . . The court denied the motion.

The Court of Appeals of Arizona affirmed Clark's conviction, treating the conclusion on sanity as supported by enough evidence to withstand review for abuse of discretion, and holding the State's insanity scheme consistent with due process. . . . Beyond that, the appellate court followed *Mott*, reading it as barring the trial court's consideration of evidence of Clark's mental illness and capacity directly on the element of *mens rea*. The Supreme Court of Arizona denied further review.

We granted certiorari to decide whether due process prohibits Arizona from thus narrowing its insanity test or from excluding evidence of mental illness and incapacity due to mental illness to rebut evidence of the requisite criminal intent. We now affirm.

* * *

[The Court's analysis of why Arizona's insanity test does not violate due process is found on pp. 634–636]

* * *

Clark's second claim of a due process violation challenges the rule adopted by the Supreme Court of Arizona in *State v. Mott* This case ruled on the admissibility of testimony from a psychologist offered to show that the defendant suffered from battered women's syndrome and therefore lacked the capacity to form the *mens rea* of the crime charged against her. The opinion variously referred to the testimony in issue as "psychological testimony," and "expert testimony," and implicitly equated it with "expert psychiatric evidence" and "psychiatric testimony". The state court held that testimony of a professional psychologist or psychiatrist about a defendant's mental incapacity owing to mental disease or defect was admissible, and could be considered, only for its bearing on an insanity defense; such evidence could not be considered on the element of *mens*

[handwritten margin note: — testimony that lacked proper mens rea]

rea, that is, what the State must show about a defendant's mental state (such as intent or understanding) when he performed the act charged against him.

Understanding Clark's claim requires attention to the categories of evidence with a potential bearing on *mens rea.* First, there is "observation evidence" in the everyday sense, testimony from those who observed what Clark did and heard what he said; this category would also include testimony that an expert witness might give about Clark's tendency to think in a certain way and his behavioral characteristics. This evidence may support a professional diagnosis of mental disease and in any event is the kind of evidence that can be relevant to show what in fact was on Clark's mind when he fired the gun. Observation evidence in the record covers Clark's behavior at home and with friends, his expressions of belief around the time of the killing that "aliens" were inhabiting the bodies of local people (including government agents),[27] his driving around the neighborhood before the police arrived, and so on. Contrary to the dissent's characterization, observation evidence can be presented by either lay or expert witnesses.

Second, there is "mental-disease evidence" in the form of opinion testimony that Clark suffered from a mental disease with features described by the witness. As was true here, this evidence characteristically but not always comes from professional psychologists or psychiatrists who testify as expert witnesses and base their opinions in part on examination of a defendant, usually conducted after the events in question. The thrust of this evidence was that, based on factual reports, professional observations, and tests, Clark was psychotic at the time in question, with a condition that fell within the category of schizophrenia.

Third, there is evidence we will refer to as "capacity evidence" about a defendant's capacity for cognition and moral judgment (and ultimately also his capacity to form *mens rea*). This, too, is opinion evidence. Here, as it usually does, this testimony came from the same experts and concentrated on those specific details of the mental condition that make the difference between sanity and insanity under the Arizona definition. In their respective testimony on these details the experts disagreed: the defense expert gave his opinion that the symptoms or effects of the disease in Clark's case included inability to appreciate the nature of his action and to tell that it was wrong, whereas the State's psychiatrist was of the view that Clark was a schizophrenic who was still sufficiently able

---

[27] Clark's parents testified that, in the months before the shooting and even days beforehand, Clark called them "aliens" and thought that "aliens" were out to get him. One night before the shooting, according to Clark's mother, Clark repeatedly viewed a popular film characterized by her as telling a story about "aliens" masquerading as government agents, a story Clark insisted was real despite his mother's protestations to the contrary. And two months after the shooting, Clark purportedly told his parents that his hometown, Flagstaff, was inhabited principally by "aliens," who had to be stopped, and that the only way to stop them was with bullets.

[handwritten margin note at top: protection → schzo but knew what he was doing]

to appreciate the reality of shooting the officer and to know that it was wrong to do that. . . .

It is clear that *Mott* itself imposed no restriction on considering evidence of the first sort, the observation evidence. We read the *Mott* restriction to apply, rather, to evidence addressing the two issues in testimony that characteristically comes only from psychologists or psychiatrists qualified to give opinions as expert witnesses: mental-disease evidence (whether at the time of the crime a defendant suffered from a mental disease or defect, such as schizophrenia) and capacity evidence (whether the disease or defect left him incapable of performing or experiencing a mental process defined as necessary for sanity such as appreciating the nature and quality of his act and knowing that it was wrong).

* * *

Clark's argument that the *Mott* rule violates the Fourteenth Amendment guarantee of due process turns on the application of the . . . principle that a criminal defendant is entitled to present relevant and favorable evidence on an element of the offense charged against him. . . . [39] As already noted, evidence tending to show that a defendant suffers from mental disease and lacks capacity to form *mens rea* is relevant to rebut evidence that he did in fact form the required *mens rea* at the time in question; this is the reason that Clark claims a right to require the factfinder in this case to consider testimony about his mental illness and his incapacity directly, when weighing the persuasiveness of other evidence tending to show *mens rea,* which the prosecution has the burden to prove.

[handwritten margin note: right Clark claims to ha—]

As Clark recognizes, however, the right to introduce relevant evidence can be curtailed if there is a good reason for doing that. "While the Constitution . . . prohibits the exclusion of defense evidence under rules that serve no legitimate purpose or that are disproportionate to the ends that they are asserted to promote, well-established rules of evidence permit trial judges to exclude evidence if its probative value is outweighed by certain other factors such as unfair prejudice, confusion of the issues, or potential to mislead the jury." And if evidence may be kept out entirely, its consideration may be subject to limitation, which Arizona claims the power to impose here. State law says that evidence of mental disease and incapacity may be introduced and considered, and if sufficiently forceful to satisfy the defendant's burden of proof under the insanity rule it will displace the presumption of sanity and excuse from

---

[39] Clark's argument assumes that Arizona's rule is a rule of evidence, rather than a redefinition of *mens rea,* see *Montana v. Egelhoff,* 518 U.S. 37, 58–59, 116 S.Ct. 2013, 135 L.Ed.2d 361 (1996) (GINSBURG, J., concurring in judgment); *id.,* at 71, 116 S.Ct. 2013 (O'Connor, J., dissenting). We have no reason to view the rule otherwise, and on this assumption, it does not violate due process.

criminal responsibility. But mental-disease and capacity evidence may be considered only for its bearing on the insanity defense, and it will avail a defendant only if it is persuasive enough to satisfy the defendant's burden as defined by the terms of that defense. The mental-disease and capacity evidence is thus being channeled or restricted to one issue and given effect only if the defendant carries the burden to convince the factfinder of insanity; the evidence is not being excluded entirely, and the question is whether reasons for requiring it to be channeled and restricted are good enough to satisfy the standard of fundamental fairness that due process requires. We think they are.

The first reason supporting the *Mott* rule is Arizona's authority to define its presumption of sanity (or capacity or responsibility) by choosing an insanity definition, . . . and by placing the burden of persuasion on defendants who claim incapacity as an excuse from customary criminal responsibility. No one, certainly not Clark here, denies that a State may place a burden of persuasion on a defendant claiming insanity. And Clark presses no objection to Arizona's decision to require persuasion to a clear and convincing degree before the presumption of sanity and normal responsibility is overcome.

But if a State is to have this authority in practice as well as in theory, it must be able to deny a defendant the opportunity to displace the presumption of sanity more easily when addressing a different issue in the course of the criminal trial. Yet . . . just such an opportunity would be available if expert testimony of mental disease and incapacity could be considered for whatever a factfinder might think it was worth on the issue of *mens rea*. [T]he presumption of sanity would then be only as strong as the evidence a factfinder would accept as enough to raise a reasonable doubt about *mens rea* for the crime charged; once reasonable doubt was found, acquittal would be required, and the standards established for the defense of insanity would go by the boards.

Now, a State is of course free to accept such a possibility in its law. After all, it is free to define the insanity defense by treating the presumption of sanity as a bursting bubble, whose disappearance shifts the burden to the prosecution to prove sanity whenever a defendant presents any credible evidence of mental disease or incapacity. In States with this kind of insanity rule, the legislature may well be willing to allow such evidence to be considered on the *mens rea* element for whatever the factfinder thinks it is worth. What counts for due process, however, is simply that a State that wishes to avoid a second avenue for exploring capacity, less stringent for a defendant, has a good reason for confining the consideration of evidence of mental disease and incapacity to the insanity defense.

It is obvious that Arizona's *Mott* rule reflects such a choice. The State Supreme Court pointed out that the State had declined to adopt a defense of diminished capacity (allowing a jury to decide when to excuse a defendant because of greater than normal difficulty in conforming to the law). The court reasoned that the State's choice would be undercut if evidence of incapacity could be considered for whatever a jury might think sufficient to raise a reasonable doubt about *mens rea,* even if it did not show insanity. In other words, if a jury were free to decide how much evidence of mental disease and incapacity was enough to counter evidence of *mens rea* to the point of creating a reasonable doubt, that would in functional terms be analogous to allowing jurors to decide upon some degree of diminished capacity to obey the law, a degree set by them, that would prevail as a stand-alone defense.[42]

A State's insistence on preserving its chosen standard of legal insanity cannot be the sole reason for a rule like *Mott,* however, for it fails to answer an objection the dissent makes in this case. An insanity rule gives a defendant already found guilty the opportunity to excuse his conduct by showing he was insane when he acted, that is, that he did not have the mental capacity for conventional guilt and criminal responsibility. But, as the dissent argues, if the same evidence that affirmatively shows he was not guilty by reason of insanity (or "guilty except insane" under Arizona law) also shows it was at least doubtful that he could form *mens rea,* then he should not be found guilty in the first place; it thus violates due process when the State impedes him from using mental-disease and capacity evidence directly to rebut the prosecution's evidence that he did form *mens rea.*

Are there, then, characteristics of mental-disease and capacity evidence giving rise to risks that may reasonably be hedged by channeling the consideration of such evidence to the insanity issue on which, in States like Arizona, a defendant has the burden of persuasion? We think there are: in the controversial character of some categories of mental disease, in the potential of mental-disease evidence to mislead, and in the danger of according greater certainty to capacity evidence than experts claim for it.

To begin with, the diagnosis may mask vigorous debate within the profession about the very contours of the mental disease itself. And Members of this Court have previously recognized that the end of such debate is not imminent. Though we certainly do not "condem[n mental-

---

[42] It is beyond question that Arizona may preclude such a defense, see *Fisher v. United States,* 328 U.S. 463, 466–476, 66 S.Ct. 1318, 90 L.Ed. 1382 (1946), and there is no doubt that the Arizona Legislature meant to do so, see Ariz.Rev.Stat. Ann. § 13–502(A) (West 2001) ("Mental disease or defect does not include disorders that result from acute voluntary intoxication or withdrawal from alcohol or drugs, character defects, psychosexual disorders or impulse control disorders. Conditions that do not constitute legal insanity include but are not limited to momentary, temporary conditions arising from the pressure of the circumstances, moral decadence, depravity or passion growing out of anger, jealousy, revenge, hatred or other motives in a person who does not suffer from a mental disease or defect or an abnormality that is manifested only by criminal conduct").

disease evidence] wholesale," the consequence of this professional ferment is a general caution in treating psychological classifications as predicates for excusing otherwise criminal conduct.

Next, there is the potential of mental-disease evidence to mislead jurors (when they are the factfinders) through the power of this kind of evidence to suggest that a defendant suffering from a recognized mental disease lacks cognitive, moral, volitional, or other capacity, when that may not be a sound conclusion at all. Even when a category of mental disease is broadly accepted and the assignment of a defendant's behavior to that category is uncontroversial, the classification may suggest something very significant about a defendant's capacity, when in fact the classification tells us little or nothing about the ability of the defendant to form *mens rea* or to exercise the cognitive, moral, or volitional capacities that define legal sanity. The limits of the utility of a professional disease diagnosis are evident in the dispute between the two testifying experts in this case; they agree that Clark was schizophrenic, but they come to opposite conclusions on whether the mental disease in his particular case left him bereft of cognitive or moral capacity. Evidence of mental disease, then, can easily mislead; it is very easy to slide from evidence that an individual with a professionally recognized mental disease is very different, into doubting that he has the capacity to form *mens rea,* whereas that doubt may not be justified. And of course, in the cases mentioned before, in which the categorization is doubtful or the category of mental disease is itself subject to controversy, the risks are even greater that opinions about mental disease may confuse a jury into thinking the opinions show more than they do. Because allowing mental-disease evidence on *mens rea* can thus easily mislead, it is not unreasonable to address that tendency by confining consideration of this kind of evidence to insanity, on which a defendant may be assigned the burden of persuasion.

There are, finally, particular risks inherent in the opinions of the experts who supplement the mental-disease classifications with opinions on incapacity: on whether the mental disease rendered a particular defendant incapable of the cognition necessary for moral judgment or *mens rea* or otherwise incapable of understanding the wrongfulness of the conduct charged. Unlike observational evidence bearing on *mens rea,* capacity evidence consists of judgment, and judgment fraught with multiple perils: a defendant's state of mind at the crucial moment can be elusive no matter how conscientious the enquiry, and the law's categories that set the terms of the capacity judgment are not the categories of psychology that govern the expert's professional thinking. Although such capacity judgments may be given in the utmost good faith, their potentially tenuous character is indicated by the candor of the defense expert in this very case. Contrary to the State's expert, he testified that Clark lacked the capacity to appreciate the circumstances realistically and to understand the wrongfulness of what he was doing, but he said that "no one knows exactly what was on [his] mind" at the time of the shooting. And even when an expert is confident that his understanding of the mind is reliable, judgment addressing the basic categories of capacity requires a leap from the concepts of psychology, which are devised for thinking about treatment, to the concepts of legal sanity, which are devised for thinking about criminal responsibility. See . . . P. Giannelli & E. Imwinkelried, Scientific Evidence § 9–3(B), p. 286 (1986) ("[N]o matter how the test for insanity is phrased, a psychiatrist or psychologist is no more qualified than any other person to give an opinion about whether a particular defendant's mental condition satisfies the legal test for insanity"); cf. R. Slovenko, Psychiatry and Criminal Culpability 55 (1995) ("The scope of the DSM is wide-ranging and includes 'conduct disorders' but 'evil' is not mentioned"). In sum, these empirical and conceptual problems add up to a real risk that an expert's judgment in giving capacity evidence will come with an apparent authority that psychologists and psychiatrists do not claim to have. We think that this risk, like the difficulty in assessing the significance of mental-disease evidence, supports the State's decision to channel such expert testimony to consideration on the insanity defense, on which the party seeking the benefit of this evidence has the burden of persuasion.

It bears repeating that not every State will find it worthwhile to make the judgment Arizona has made, and the choices the States do make about dealing with the risks posed by mental-disease and capacity evidence will reflect their varying assessments about the presumption of sanity as expressed in choices of insanity rules. The point here simply is that Arizona has sensible reasons to assign the risks as it has done by channeling the evidence.[45]

* * *

The judgment of the Court of Appeals of Arizona is, accordingly, affirmed.

It is so ordered.

JUSTICE BREYER, concurring in part and dissenting in part [deleted].

---

[45] Arizona's rule is supported by a further practical reason, though not as weighty as those just considered. As mentioned before, if substantial mental-disease and capacity evidence is accepted as rebutting *mens rea* in a given case, the affirmative defense of insanity will probably not be reached or ruled upon; the defendant will simply be acquitted (or perhaps convicted of a lesser included offense). If an acquitted defendant suffers from a mental disease or defect that makes him dangerous, he will neither be confined nor treated psychiatrically unless a judge so orders after some independent commitment proceeding. But if a defendant succeeds in showing himself insane, Arizona law (and presumably that of every other State with an insanity rule) will require commitment and treatment as a consequence of that finding without more. It makes sense, then, to channel capacity evidence to the issue structured to deal with mental incapacity when such a claim is raised successfully. . . .

JUSTICE KENNEDY, with whom JUSTICE STEVENS and JUSTICE GINSBURG join, dissenting.

In my submission the Court is incorrect in holding that Arizona may convict petitioner Eric Clark of first-degree murder for the intentional or knowing killing of a police officer when Clark was not permitted to introduce critical and reliable evidence showing he did not have that intent or knowledge. . . .

The Court . . . adopts an evidentiary framework that, in my view, will be unworkable in many cases. The Court classifies Clark's behavior and expressed beliefs as observation evidence but insists that its description by experts must be mental-disease evidence or capacity evidence. These categories break down quickly when it is understood how the testimony would apply to the question of intent and knowledge at issue here. The most common type of schizophrenia, and the one Clark suffered from, is paranoid schizophrenia. The existence of this functional psychosis is beyond dispute, but that does not mean the lay witness understands it or that a disputed issue of fact concerning its effect in a particular instance is not something for the expert to address. Common symptoms of the condition are delusions accompanied by hallucinations, often of the auditory type, which can cause disturbances of perception. Clark's expert testified that people with schizophrenia often play radios loudly to drown out the voices in their heads. Clark's attorney argued to the trial court that this, rather than a desire to lure a policeman to the scene, explained Clark's behavior just before the killing. The observation that schizophrenics play radios loudly is a fact regarding behavior, but it is only a relevant fact if Clark has schizophrenia.

Even if this evidence were, to use the Court's term, mental-disease evidence, because it relies on an expert opinion, what would happen if the expert simply were to testify, without mentioning schizophrenia, that people with Clark's symptoms often play the radio loudly? This seems to be factual evidence, as the term is defined by the Court, yet it differs from mental-disease evidence only in forcing the witness to pretend that no one has yet come up with a way to classify the set of symptoms being described. More generally, the opinion that Clark had paranoid schizophrenia-an opinion shared by experts for both the prosecution and defense-bears on efforts to determine, as a factual matter, whether he knew he was killing a police officer. The psychiatrist's explanation of Clark's condition was essential to understanding how he processes sensory data and therefore to deciding what information was in his mind at the time of the shooting. Simply put, knowledge relies on cognition, and cognition can be affected by schizophrenia. The mental-disease evidence at trial was also intertwined with the observation evidence because it lent needed credibility. Clark's parents and friends testified Clark thought the people in his town were aliens trying to kill him. These claims might not be believable without a psychiatrist confirming the story based on his experience with people who have exhibited similar behaviors. It makes little sense to divorce the observation evidence from the explanation that makes it comprehensible.

* * *

The central theory of Clark's defense was that his schizophrenia made him delusional. He lived in a universe where the delusions were so dominant, the theory was, that he had no intent to shoot a police officer or knowledge he was doing so. It is one thing to say he acted with intent or knowledge to pull the trigger. It is quite another to say he pulled the trigger to kill someone he knew to be a human being and a police officer. If the trier of fact were to find Clark's evidence sufficient to discount the case made by the State, which has the burden to prove knowledge or intent as an element of the offense, Clark would not be guilty of first-degree murder under Arizona law.

The Court attempts to diminish Clark's interest by treating mental-illness evidence as concerning only "judgment," rather than fact. This view appears to derive from the Court's characterization of Clark's claim as raising only general incapacity. This is wrong for the reasons already discussed. It fails to recognize, moreover, the meaning of the offense element in question here. The *mens rea* element of intent or knowledge may, at some level, comprise certain moral choices, but it rests in the first instance on a factual determination. That is the fact Clark sought to put in issue. Either Clark knew he was killing a police officer or he did not.

real issue

The issue is not, as the Court insists, whether Clark's mental illness acts as an "excuse from customary criminal responsibility," but whether his mental illness, as a factual matter, made him unaware that he was shooting a police officer. If it did, Clark needs no excuse, as then he did not commit the crime as Arizona defines it. For the elements of first-degree murder, where the question is knowledge of particular facts-that one is killing a police officer-the determination depends not on moral responsibility but on empirical fact. Clark's evidence of mental illness had a direct and substantial bearing upon what he knew, or thought he knew, to be the facts when he pulled the trigger; this lay at the heart of the matter.

The trial court's exclusion was all the more severe because it barred from consideration on the issue of *mens rea* all this evidence, from any source, thus preventing Clark from showing he did not commit the crime as defined by Arizona law. Quite apart from due process principles, we have held that a bar of this sort can be inconsistent with the Confrontation Clause. See *Delaware v. Van Arsdall,* 475 U.S. 673, 106 S.Ct. 1431, 89 L.Ed.2d 674 (1986). In *Van Arsdall* the Court held a state court erred in making a ruling that "prohibited *all* inquiry into" an event.

At issue was a line of defense questioning designed to show the bias of a prosecution witness. In the instant case the ruling in question bars from consideration all testimony from all witnesses necessary to present the argument that was central to the whole case for the defense: a challenge to the State's own proof on an element of the crime. The Due Process and Compulsory Process Clauses, and not the Confrontation Clause, may be the controlling standard; but the disability imposed on the accused is every bit as substantial and pervasive here as it was in *Van Arsdall*.

Arizona's rule is problematic because it excludes evidence no matter how credible and material it may be in disproving an element of the offense. The Court's cases have noted the potential arbitrariness of *per se* exclusions and, on this rationale, have invalidated various state prohibitions. . . . This is not to suggest all general rules on the exclusion of certain types of evidence are invalid. If the rule does not substantially burden the defense, then it is likely permissible. Where, however, the burden is substantial, the State must present a valid reason for its *per se* evidentiary rule.

In the instant case Arizona's proposed reasons are insufficient to support its categorical exclusion. While the State contends that testimony regarding mental illness may be too incredible or speculative for the jury to consider, this does not explain why the exclusion applies in all cases to all evidence of mental illness. "A State's legitimate interest in barring unreliable evidence does not extend to *per se* exclusions that may be reliable in an individual case." *Rock v. Arkansas,* 483 U.S., at 61, 107 S.Ct. 2704 [striking down statute that categorically prohibited defense use of hypnotically-induced statements]. States have certain discretion to bar unreliable or speculative testimony and to adopt rules to ensure the reliability of expert testimony. Arizona has done so, and there is no reason to believe its rules are insufficient to avoid speculative evidence of mental illness. This is particularly true because Arizona applies its usual case-by-case approach to permit admission of evidence of mental illness for a variety of other purposes. See, *e.g., State v. Lindsey,* 149 Ariz. 472, 474–475, 720 P.2d 73, 74–75 (1986) (en banc) (psychological characteristics of molestation victims); *State v. Hamilton,* 177 Ariz. 403, 408–410, 868 P.2d 986, 991–993 (App.1993) (psychological evidence of child abuse accommodation syndrome); *Horan v. Indus. Comm'n,* 167 Ariz. 322, 325–326, 806 P.2d 911, 914–915 (App.1991) (psychiatric testimony regarding neurological deficits).

The risk of jury confusion also fails to justify the rule. The State defends its rule as a means to avoid the complexities of determining how and to what degree a mental illness affects a person's mental state. The difficulty of resolving a factual issue, though, does not present a sufficient reason to take evidence away from the jury even when it is crucial for the defense. "We have always trusted juries to sort through complex facts in various areas of law." Even were the risk of jury confusion real enough to justify excluding evidence in most cases, this would provide little basis for prohibiting all evidence of mental illness without any inquiry into its likely effect on the jury or its role in deciding the linchpin issue of knowledge and intent. Indeed, Arizona has a rule in place to serve this very purpose.

Even assuming the reliability and jury-confusion justifications were persuasive in some cases, they would not suffice here. It does not overcome the constitutional objection to say that an evidentiary rule that is reasonable on its face can be applied as well to bar significant defense evidence without any rational basis for doing so. In *Van Arsdall,* for example, the Court rejected the application of Delaware Rule of Evidence 403, which allows relevant evidence to be excluded where its probative value is substantially outweighed by the risk of unfair prejudice or other harms to the trial process. While the Rule is well established and designed for a legitimate function, the Constitution prevented an application that deprived the defendant of all inquiry into an important issue. Other cases have applied this same case-specific analysis in deciding the legitimacy of an exclusion. See, *e.g., Rock, supra,* at 62, 107 S.Ct. 2704 (the "circumstances present an argument for admissibility of petitioner's testimony in this particular case, an argument that must be considered by the trial court").

The Court undertakes little analysis of the interests particular to this case. By proceeding in this way it devalues Clark's constitutional rights. The reliability rationale has minimal applicability here. The Court is correct that many mental diseases are difficult to define and the subject of great debate. Schizophrenia, however, is a well-documented mental illness, and no one seriously disputes either its definition or its most prominent clinical manifestations. The State's own expert conceded that Clark had paranoid schizophrenia and was actively psychotic at the time of the killing. The jury-confusion rationale, if it is at all applicable here, is the result of the Court's own insistence on conflating the insanity defense and the question of intent. Considered on its own terms, the issue of intent and knowledge is a straightforward factual question. A trier of fact is quite capable of weighing defense testimony and then determining whether the accused did or did not intend to kill or knowingly kill a human being who was a police officer. True, the issue can be difficult to decide in particular instances, but no more so than many matters juries must confront.

The Court says mental-illness evidence "can easily mislead," and may "tel[l] us little or nothing about the ability of the defendant to form *mens rea.*" These generalities do not, however, show how relevant or misleading the evidence in this case would be (or explain why Arizona Rule of Evidence 403 is insufficient for weighing these factors). As explained above, the evidence of Clark's mental illness bears directly on *mens rea,* for it suggests Clark may not have known he was killing a human being. It is striking that while the Court discusses at length the likelihood of misjudgment from placing too much emphasis on evidence of mental illness, it ignores the risk of misjudging an innocent man guilty from refusing to consider this highly relevant evidence at all. Clark's expert, it is true, said no one could know exactly what was on Clark's mind at the time of the shooting. The expert testified extensively, however, about the effect of Clark's delusions on his perceptions of the world around him, and about whether Clark's behavior around the time of the shooting was consistent with delusional thinking. This testimony was relevant to determining whether Clark knew he was killing a human being. It also bolstered the testimony of lay witnesses, none of which was deemed unreliable or misleading by the state courts.

APA

For the same reasons, the Court errs in seeking support from the American Psychiatric Association's statement that a psychiatrist may be justifiably reluctant to reach legal conclusions regarding the defendant's mental state. In this very case, the American Psychiatric Association made clear that psychiatric evidence plays a crucial role regardless of whether the psychiatrist testifies on the ultimate issue: "Expert evidence of mental disorders, presented by qualified professionals and subject to adversarial testing, is both relevant to the mental-state issues raised by *mens rea* requirements and reliable. . . . Such evidence could not be condemned wholesale without unsettling the legal system's central reliance on such evidence."

Contrary to the Court's suggestion, the fact that the state and defense experts drew different conclusions about the effect of Clark's mental illness on his mental state only made Clark's evidence contested; it did not make the evidence irrelevant or misleading. The trial court was capable of evaluating the competing conclusions, as factfinders do in countless cases where there is a dispute among witnesses. In fact, the potential to mislead will be far greater under the Court's new evidentiary system, where jurors will receive observation evidence without the necessary explanation from experts.

The fact that mental-illness evidence may be considered in deciding criminal responsibility does not compensate for its exclusion from consideration on the *mens rea* elements of the crime. The evidence addresses different issues in the two instances. Criminal responsibility involves an inquiry into whether the defendant knew right from wrong, not whether he had the *mens rea* elements of the offense. While there may be overlap between the two issues, "the existence or nonexistence of legal insanity bears no necessary relationship to the existence or nonexistence of the required mental elements of the crime." *Mullaney v.*

Wilbur, 421 U.S. 684, 706, 95 S.Ct. 1881, 44 L.Ed.2d 508 (1975) (Rehnquist, J., concurring).

Even if the analyses were equivalent, there is a different burden of proof for insanity than there is for *mens rea.* Arizona requires the defendant to prove his insanity by clear and convincing evidence. The prosecution, however, must prove all elements of the offense beyond a reasonable doubt. See *Mullaney, supra,* at 703–704, 95 S.Ct. 1881; *In re Winship,* 397 U.S. 358, 364, 90 S.Ct. 1068, 25 L.Ed.2d 368 (1970). The shift in the burden on the criminal responsibility issue, while permissible under our precedent, cannot be applied to the question of intent or knowledge without relieving the State of its responsibility to establish this element of the offense. While evidentiary rules do not generally shift the burden impermissibly, where there is a right to have evidence considered on an element of the offense, the right is not respected by allowing the evidence to come in only on an issue for which the defendant bears the burden of proof. By viewing the Arizona rule as creating merely a "presumption of sanity (or capacity or responsibility)," rather than a presumption that the *mens rea* elements were not affected by mental illness, the Court fails to appreciate the implications for *Winship.*

The State attempts to sidestep the evidentiary issue entirely by claiming that its mental-illness exclusion simply alters one element of the crime. The evidentiary rule at issue here, however, cannot be considered a valid redefinition of the offense. Under the State's logic, a person would be guilty of first-degree murder if he knowingly or intentionally killed a police officer or committed the killing under circumstances that would show knowledge or intent but for the defendant's mental illness. To begin with, Arizona law does not say this. And if it did, it would be impermissible. States have substantial discretion in defining criminal offenses. In some instances they may provide that the accused has the burden of persuasion with respect to affirmative defenses. See *Patterson v. New York,* 432 U.S. 197, 210, 97 S.Ct. 2319, 53 L.Ed.2d 281 (1977). "But there are obviously constitutional limits beyond which the States may not go in this regard." If it were otherwise, States could label all evidentiary exclusions as redefinitions and so evade constitutional requirements. There is no rational basis, furthermore, for criminally punishing a person who commits a killing without knowledge or intent only if that person has a mental illness. Cf. *Robinson v. California,* 370 U.S. 660, 666, 82 S.Ct. 1417, 8 L.Ed.2d 758 (1962). The State attempts to bring the instant case within the ambit of *Montana v. Egelhoff,* 518 U.S. 37, 116 S.Ct. 2013, 135 L.Ed.2d 361 (1996); but in *Egelhoff* the excluded evidence concerned voluntary intoxication, for which a person can be held responsible. Viewed either as an evidentiary rule or a redefinition of the offense, it was upheld because it "comports with and implements society's moral perception that one who has voluntarily impaired his own faculties should be responsible for the consequences." An involuntary mental illness does not implicate this justification.

Future dangerousness is not, as the Court appears to conclude, see *ante* n. 45, a rational basis for convicting mentally ill individuals of crimes they did not commit. Civil commitment proceedings can ensure that individuals who present a danger to themselves or others receive proper treatment without unfairly treating them as criminals. The State presents no evidence to the contrary, and the Court ought not to imply otherwise.

* * *

While Arizona's rule is not unique, either historically or in contemporary practice, this fact does not dispose of Clark's constitutional argument. . . . While 13 States still impose significant restrictions on the use of mental-illness evidence to negate *mens rea,* a substantial majority of the States currently allow it. The fact that a reasonable number of States restrict this evidence weighs into the analysis, but applying the rule as a *per se* bar, as Arizona does, is so plainly unreasonable that it cannot be sustained. . . .

These are the reasons for my respectful dissent.

QUESTIONS AND COMMENTS

1.   *Rationales for Clark.* The Court holds that expert testimony that provides evidence of "mental disease" or "capacity" evidence, as opposed to "observation" evidence, may constitutionally be excluded. One rationale the Court gives for this holding is that the former types of testimony are too speculative and misleading. Do you agree (consider the materials on admissibility of expert testimony in Part II.B. of Chapter Six as well as the dissent's points)? In any event, is the speculative nature of psychiatric testimony a justifiable ground for exclusion in *all* mens rea cases, as the majority states? If so, then may the state also exclude such testimony when presented to bolster an insanity defense? If not, why not? Because insanity is a more fundamental issue than mens rea? Because the defense bears the burden of proof on insanity, but the prosecution bears the burden of proof on mens rea? (What if, as in true in some states, the prosecution bears the burden on both issues?) Because the result of a successful insanity defense is usually long-term or at least indeterminate incapacitation, but the result of a successful diminished capacity defense is release or a significantly shortened sentence? See note 45 of the majority opinion.

A second rationale the Court gives for its holding is that allowing the defendant to present expert mental disease and capacity testimony would "undercut" the state's entitlements to the presumption of sanity and to place the burden of proving insanity on the defendant, because it would enable a defendant raising an impaired mental state claim to obtain acquittal simply by creating a reasonable doubt (a far cry from the proof of insanity by clear and convincing demanded under Arizona's insanity statute). Justice Kennedy's dissent dismisses this point on the ground that due process, the Compulsory Process Clause and the Confrontation Clause prevent the state from categorically prohibiting testimony that negates an essential element of the crime. In rebuttal, the majority cites *Fisher v. United States*, 328 U.S. 463, 466–476, 66 S.Ct. 1318, 90 L.Ed. 1382 (1946), which held that states may deny defendants a diminished capacity defense. See note 42. But that case was decided long before the Court decided *In re Winship*, 397 U.S. 358, 90 S.Ct. 1068, 25 L.Ed.2d 368 (1970), which made clear that the prosecution must prove every element of the crime, including mens rea, beyond a reasonable doubt. More relevant is the holding in *Montana v. Egelhoff*, 518 U.S. 37, 116 S.Ct. 2013, 135 L.Ed.2d 361 (1996), mentioned by both the majority, see note 28, and the dissent. There the Court held that prohibiting voluntary intoxication to be taken into consideration in determining the presence of the requisite mental state does not violate due process. One rationale for this holding, endorsed by the four-member plurality in *Egelhoff*, was that the voluntary intoxication defense was of "recent vintage" and thus not a fundamental aspect of fair process. A second rationale, proffered by Justice Ginsburg in concurrence, was that Montana's intoxication statute had redefined the mens rea for first degree murder to include "intoxication-related automatism" to reflect the judgment that such a condition, which is often self-induced, entails sufficient culpability for murder; thus, she argued, Egelhoff's proffer of evidence about intoxication was irrelevant. Does either rationale in *Egelhoff* answer the dissent's concern?

2. *Legal status of diminished capacity doctrine.* As Justice Kennedy's dissent notes, more than half the states disagree with the result in *Mott* and permit clinical opinion testimony relevant to mens rea, at least under certain circumstances. About 40% of the states allow evidence of mental disability when relevant to negate any mental state, 30% limit such evidence to specific intent or homicide prosecutions, and 30% bar it altogether. Paul H. Robinson, *Abnormal Mental State Mitigations of Murder—the U.S. Perspective*, in Loss of Control and Diminished Responsibility: Domestic, Comparative and International Perspectives 291 (A. Reed & M. Bohlander eds., 2011). Federal courts have also permitted such testimony. See, e.g., *U.S. v. Cohen*, 510 F.3d 1114 (9th Cir. 2007). Some courts have held, consistent with the position endorsed by the dissent in *Clark*, that this position is constitutionally mandated. In *Commonwealth v. Walzack,* 468 Pa. 210, 360 A.2d 914, 920 (1976), for instance, the Pennsylvania Supreme Court held that, under the Pennsylvania constitution, due process requires the admission of psychiatric testimony that is relevant to the mens rea issue. The court stated: "It is inconsistent with fundamental principles of American jurisprudence to preclude an accused from offering relevant and competent evidence to dispute the charge against him." See also, *Hendershott v. People,* 653 P.2d 385, 394 (Colo.1982).

The drafters of the Model Penal Code came to the same conclusion on policy grounds. Section 4.02(1) of the Code provides: "Evidence that the defendant suffered from a mental disease or defect is admissible whenever it is relevant to prove that the defendant did not have a state of mind that is an element of the crime." In support of this provision, the drafters stated: "If states of mind such as deliberation or premeditation are accorded legal significance, psychiatric evidence should be admissible when relevant to prove or disprove their existence to the same extent as any other evidence." Model Penal Code, Comments to § 4.02, 193 (Tent.Draft No. 4, 1955). More recently, the American Bar Association, finding that "logical relevance" so requires, has recommended an identical rule. American Bar Association Criminal Justice Mental Health Standard 7–6.2 (1987).

Similarly, while the federal Insanity Defense Reform Act of 1984 states that, other than in insanity cases, "mental disease or defect does not . . . constitute a defense," most federal courts have found that this language was meant only to bar "affirmative" psychiatric defenses which the defendant seeks to raise (e.g., self-defense), not evidence that negates intent, an element of the crime. See 118 ALR Fed 281–85 (1993). In *Metrish v. Lancaster*, 133 S.Ct. 1781 (2013), the Supreme Court refused to find that the Michigan Supreme Court violated the due process clause when it retroactively applied a decision eliminating the diminished capacity defense. But since that case arrived at the Court via a habeas claim, the Court did not reach the issue directly, only deciding that the Michigan Court's action was not "unreasonable" in light of U.S. Supreme Court caselaw on retroactivity doctrine.

3. *Diminished capacity v. diminished responsibility.* To be distinguished from the diminished capacity idea, which focuses on the defendant's mens rea, is what is sometimes called the "partial" or "diminished responsibility" defense, which permits the factfinder to consider mitigating evidence of cognitive or volitional impairment that neither constitutes insanity nor negates mens rea. Until 2010 in Great Britain, for instance, a sane defendant for whom the actus reus and mens rea of murder have been proven could nonetheless be convicted only of manslaughter if the defense showed that at the time of the killing the defendant "was suffering from such abnormality of mind . . . as substantially impaired his mental responsibility for acts and omissions in . . . the killing." English Homicide Act, 5 & 6 Eliz. II, ch. 11, § 2(1) (1957). In 2010, this language was modified to permit a reduction from murder to manslaughter if the defendant "was suffering from an abnormality of mental functioning which arose from a recognised mental condition [and] substantially impaired [the actor's] ability to do one or more of the [following]: (a) to understand the nature of [actor's] conduct; (b) to form a rational judgment; (c) to exercise self-control." Coroners and Justice Act 2009 c. 25 Pt 2 c.1 s. 52. A somewhat less broad formulation of this idea is found in the Model Penal Code, in language followed by many American jurisdictions, which provides that a person who intentionally kills another may nonetheless be convicted only of manslaughter if, at the time of the killing, the person was "under the influence of extreme mental or emotional disturbance for which there is reasonable explanation or excuse" (see p. 702 for more elaborate discussion of this provision). If the diminished responsibility doctrine were recognized and made applicable to *all* crimes

(rather than just homicide, as in Great Britain), how would one gauge its mitigating impact? Morse has suggested that, if such a defense were permitted, it should lead to a sentence one-half the length normally received for the crime. Stephen Morse, *Diminished Capacity: A Moral and Legal Conundrum*, 2 Int'l J.Psychiat. 271 (1979). Consider, however, that people with "diminished responsibility" due to mental disorder may be more dangerous than the average offender. If so, shouldn't that lead to an *enhanced* sentence?

One criticism of the diminished capacity doctrine is that, while it is theoretically distinguishable from diminished responsibility, in practice it will open the door wide to undifferentiated psychiatric testimony similar to that contemplated by the latter doctrine. In perhaps the leading case supporting this position, *Bethea v. United States*, 365 A.2d 64 (D.C.App.1976), the District of Columbia Court of Appeals stated:

> The concept of mens rea involves what is ultimately the fiction of determining the actual thoughts or mental processes of the accused. It is obvious that a certain resolution of this issue is beyond the ken of scientist and laymen alike. Only by inference can the existence of intent—or the differentiation between its forms, such as general or specific—be determined. The law presumes that all individuals are capable of the mental processes which bear the jurisprudential label "mens rea"; that is, the law presumes sanity . . . The concept of insanity is simply a device the law employs to define the outer limits of that segment of the general population to whom these presumptions concerning the capacity for criminal intent shall not be applied. The line between the sane and the insane for the purposes of criminal adjudication is not drawn because for one group the actual existence of the necessary mental state (or lack thereof) can be determined with any greater certainty, but rather because those whom the law declares insane are demonstrably so aberrational in their psychiatric characteristics that they are incapable of possessing the specified state of mind. Within the range of individuals who are not "insane", the law does not recognize the readily demonstrable fact that as between individual criminal defendants the nature and development of their mental capabilities may vary greatly. . . . By contradicting the presumptions inherent in the doctrine of mens rea, the theory of diminished capacity inevitably opens the door to variable or sliding scales of criminal responsibility. We should not lightly undertake such a revolutionary change in our criminal justice system.

Id. at 88–89.

Consider expert evidence presented in the prosecution of Damian Williams on twelve charges, including attempted murder (a specific intent crime) and mayhem (a general intent crime). The charges arose out of an assault on Reginald Denny and seven others during the 1992 Los Angeles riots that followed the acquittal of the white police officers who beat Rodney King, an African–American, after stopping him on the highway. The lawyers in the Williams case used a social scientist to support the (successful) argument that the defendant, an African–American, was caught up in the "group contagion" of anger and frustration following the King verdict, so much so that he did not possess the mens rea for attempted murder. See George P. Fletcher, With Justice for Some: Victims' Rights in Criminal Trials 38, 234 (1995). In other words, the testimony was that the defendants were "out of control" at the time of the offense. Is such testimony evidence of diminished capacity, or instead only evidence of diminished responsibility? If the latter, is it admissible? Does it depend on whether the offense was attempted murder or mayhem? A jury acquitted Williams on both charges.

4.   *Limitations on clinical mens rea testimony.* Although many states permit clinical testimony that is relevant to mens rea (as opposed to diminished responsibility), they have done so cautiously. Most have placed limitations on such testimony beyond those constraints that are imposed by the rules of evidence on all expert opinion evidence.[1] The principal limitations are of three types: a requirement that the lack of mens rea be due to a significant mental disorder; a requirement that the testimony only address whether the defendant had the capacity to formulate the requisite mens rea; and a prohibition on mens rea testimony for certain types of crimes.

The Mental Disease or Defect Limitation. The first limitation is a requirement, imposed explicitly in several states and implicitly in any state that adopts the Model Penal Code language, that the diminished capacity be associated with a "mental disease or defect" similar to that required for the insanity defense. See, e.g., *State v. Humanik,* 199 N.J.Super. 283, 489 A.2d 691 (A.D.1985). Is such a requirement justifiable? Are the reasons for the mental disease or defect predicate in the insanity context applicable when the issue is whether the defendant had the requisite mental state at the time of the offense?

In *United States v. Bright,* 517 F.2d 584 (2d Cir.1975), the defendant was charged with three counts of violating a statute which penalizes anyone who knowingly possesses stolen mail. It was undisputed that Bright had had in her possession nine welfare checks that had been stolen from the mail and that she had cashed at least three of them. Her defense was that she had not known they were stolen. She had been given the checks by one Fred Scott, an acquaintance of her boyfriend Leslie; Scott gave Bright the checks to cash for him on the pretense that he had no bank account of his own. She testified that, although the checks were clearly made out to someone other than Scott, she had believed everything Scott had told her about the checks and had not suspected their source. In addition to her own testimony, she proffered the testimony of a psychiatrist, Dr. Weiss, who stated in part:

> [T]hough I do not consider Mrs. Bright to have been suffering mental illness, I believe that her dependent, childlike character structure unconsciously "needed" to believe that these men would never involve

---

[1]   See Chapter Six, particularly Parts II.B and III.D, for a thorough treatment of the constraints on expert testimony.

her in illegal activities and that Leslie could do no wrong. I believe that at the time of the alleged crime, because of this unconscious 'need', she did not think that the checks had been stolen. . . . I do not believe that she knew that the checks that she allegedly possessed were stolen as a result of her need to deny the possibility that the men involved would in any way take advantage of her. This passive-dependent personality disorder rendered her incapable of understanding this [see Appendix A for a description of the Dependent Personality Disorder].

Although the court appeared to be unwilling to foreclose a diminished capacity argument under all circumstances, it upheld the exclusion of the expert testimony, primarily because no mental disease analogous to that required for the insanity defense was found to be present:

> Couched in simpler language [the psychiatrist] was prepared to testify that [Bright] was a gullible person but a person unaffected either by psychosis or neurosis. . . .

> The mind and motivation of an accused who is not on the other side of the line [drawn by the insanity defense] is, by the judgment of experience, left to the jury to probe. The complexity of the fears and long-suppressed traumatic experiences of a lifetime is in the personality of all of us. All humankind is heir to defects of personality.

> To transmute the effect of instability, of undue reliance on another, of unrequited love, of sudden anger, of the host of attitudes and syndromes that are a part of daily living, into opinion evidence to the jury for exculpation or condemnation is to go beyond the boundaries of current knowledge. The shallower the conception the deeper runs the danger that the jury may be misled. . . .

> In short, [Bright] asks us to go beyond the boundaries of conventional psychiatric opinion testimony. We think the testimony offered was not sufficiently grounded in scientific support to make us reach or, indeed, cross the present frontier of admissibility. On the instant appeal we need decide no more than that [the trial judge] did not abuse her discretion in rejecting the opinion evidence.

Is it true, as suggested by the *Bright* court, that clinical testimony is less reliable if it is not based on a finding of significant mental disorder? Is such testimony any more suspect than the testimony offered in *Heads* or *Pollard*, excerpted earlier in this chapter? If it is, why not let the rules of evidence governing the admission of expert testimony take care of the problem rather than resorting to a mental disease limitation? Perhaps the rules of evidence are insufficient protection against testimony on the "outer boundaries?" Or is there another concern—similar to that evinced by the Supreme Court in *Clark*—underlying the court's position?

Because the psychiatric testimony was excluded, the sole basis for Bright's assertion—that she did not know the checks were stolen because she was abnormally willing to believe those upon whom she depended emotionally—was her own testimony. Consider the following comment about the *Bright* case.

> [E]xclusion [of the psychiatric testimony] compromises [Bright's] ability to persuade the factfinder not to draw inferences about her beliefs on the basis of what a normal person would have believed under the circumstances. Because [Bright] carries a de-facto burden of proof on this issue, the exclusion of expert testimony in effect holds her to the standards of a normally suspicious person, selectively redefining the offense to apply objective standards to her and subjective standards to everyone else.

Richard Bonnie & Christopher Slobogin, *The Role of Mental Health Professionals in the Criminal Process: The Case for Informed Speculation*, 66 Va.L.Rev. 427, 480–81 (1980). Is this concern, assuming it exists, sufficiently significant to outweigh the concerns identified by the *Bright* court?

The Capacity Limitation; Character Testimony. A second reason given by the *Bright* court for excluding the psychiatric testimony in that case centered on the form in which the testimony was offered. The court noted that the psychiatrist went beyond stating that Bright "did not have the capacity to form a specific intent to commit the crime" and instead directly asserted that Bright did not believe the checks were stolen. The court suggested that diminished capacity testimony should address *only* the capacity of the defendant to harbor the required mental state, not whether the defendant actually had that mental state. Several other courts have explicitly required that psychiatric testimony on mens rea be couched in terms of the defendant's "capacity." See, e.g., *Simpson v. State,* 269 Ind. 495, 381 N.E.2d 1229 (1978); *State v. Craig,* 82 Wash.2d 777, 514 P.2d 151 (1973). Most formulations of the diminished capacity doctrine do not limit clinical testimony in this way. See Model Penal Code § 4.01(1). What is the purpose of the limitation?

For one possible answer to this question, consider *Waine v. State,* 37 Md.App. 222, 377 A.2d 509 (1977). There the defendant was charged with two counts of first degree murder. In his defense, he called a psychiatrist who testified off the record that the defendant was a passive person and that, in his opinion, violence on the part of the defendant would be very unlikely. The psychiatrist also stated, again off the record, that there "is no way in the world I can say he didn't commit these [homicides] but I can say according to his lifestyle, this would be totally out of character." After hearing the proffer of the psychiatrist, the trial court allowed the psychiatrist to testify as to the "psychiatric makeup" of the defendant—to the effect that he was a "passivist"—but did not allow him to testify as to "whether or not this person might possibly be able to commit an act of violence . . . , or did in fact commit, possibly or not possibly, an act of violence . . . at the time these people were killed." The Maryland Court of Special Appeals upheld this ruling. Apparently, it was willing to allow this and like testimony, short of the "ultimate conclusion" as to whether the defendant committed the murders, because of a perceived analogy to evidentiary rules permitting criminal defendants to present "character evidence."[m]

How similar is the evidence in *Waine* to the evidence in *Bright*? In the former case the defendant's expert testimony aimed at proving the defendant did not have the capacity to commit the criminal act. In the latter case, the defendant admitted the actus reus but used expert testimony to support the argument that the defendant did not have the capacity to form the requisite mens rea. The Maryland Supreme Court upheld *Waine* in *Kanaras v. State*, 54 Md.App. 568, 460 A.2d 61, 73 (1983), one year after it held that diminished capacity testimony is *not* admissible. *Johnson v. State*, 292 Md. 405, 439 A.2d 542 (1982). Can *Kanaras* and *Johnson* be reconciled?

On the general issue of whether *any* psychiatric evidence on "character" short of insanity is material to criminal responsibility issues, consider the analysis of Professor Andrew Taslitz, in *Myself Alone: Individualizing Justice Through Psychological Character Evidence*, 52 Md. L.Rev. 1, 95–95 (1993). He argues that such evidence is important in a criminal system like ours, which recognizes a need for "individualized justice."

> Individualized justice requires consideration of a defendant's unique traits and circumstances to determine what that individual did or thought, not only what she should have done or thought. Yet our assembly-line justice system and common myths, prejudices, and misconceptions combine to lead to "normalized justice," to the trial of defendants for whom they are assumed to be and what they are assumed, therefore, to have done and thought. Such assumptions are largely based on what most people would do, clearly the opposite of individualized treatment. [P]sychological character evidence [is] a way to move judges and juries back toward an individualized assessment of the particular defendant before them. Psychological character testimony, because it focuses in part on a defendant's history, on special traits and their consequences, and on the interaction between those traits and situational factors, offers the prospect of leading juries to think of defendants as special human beings, rather than as stereotypes.

Id. at 120. In light of the above, Taslitz would allow not only expert testimony about character that tends to negate mens rea (as in the *Bright* case), but also character testimony that suggests the defendant did not commit the criminal act (as in *Waine*).

Should a concern for individualized justice lead to admission of any credible psychiatric evidence on character, as Taslitz proposes? Taslitz admits that "[p]sychological research supports the notion that behavior may often be controlled as much by situational factors as by one's essential

---

[m]   Cf. Fed.R.Evid., Rule 404(a)(1) ("Evidence of a person's character or a trait of character is not admissible for the purpose of proving action in conformity therewith on a particular occasion, except [when it is] evidence of a pertinent trait of character offered by an accused, or by the prosecution to rebut the same."); Fed.R.Evid., Rule 405(a) ("In all cases in which evidence of character or a trait of character of a person is admissible, proof may be made by testimony as to reputation or by testimony in the form of an opinion. . . . ")

'nature' or one's thoughts and feelings." Id. at 57. He also notes "the well-documented 'fundamental attribution error': the tendency of people to inflate the importance of personality traits while failing to recognize the importance of situational factors in prompting behavior." Id. at 110. Given these observations, one might argue that testimony about a defendant's dependent or passive nature is not of much value in a criminal case (which presumably centers around abnormal "situational factors"), and is also likely to be given too much weight by the factfinder. On the other hand, as noted above, the rules of evidence allow the defendant to present lay evidence of character in criminal cases (and permit the prosecution to present rebuttal evidence as well, once the defendant raises the character issue).

Would you allow expert testimony that a defendant charged with rape, who admittedly had intercourse with the victim, did not have the psychological traits of a rapist and therefore probably could not have forced intercourse on the victim? Cf. *New Jersey v. Cavallo*, 88 N.J. 508, 443 A.2d 1020 (1982) (finding the testimony relevant but not admissible under *Frye*). Testimony by a prosecution expert witness that a rape defendant, who had testified that the intercourse was consensual, *did* fit the profile of an aggressive rapist? Cf. *State v. Hickman*, 337 N.W.2d 512 (Iowa 1983) (permitting the testimony as rebuttal evidence).

Crime Limitation. Finally, most states restrict the admissibility of clinical mens rea evidence to certain types of crimes. This third limitation comes in two forms. One approach permits clinical testimony only in cases where defendants are charged with some type of intentional homicide. For instance, although the Pennsylvania Supreme Court has held that competent evidence of diminished capacity cannot constitutionally be prohibited, *Walzack,* supra, it has nonetheless limited such evidence to murder cases. *Commonwealth v. Garcia,* 505 Pa. 304, 479 A.2d 473, 477 (1984). A second approach admits clinical testimony on mens rea for any crime involving specific intent, but does not admit such evidence for crimes involving general intent. In "Model Penal Code" jurisdictions, an analogous result is achieved by permitting expert evidence for any element requiring purpose or knowledge, but barring such evidence when the mens rea is recklessness or negligence. See cases cited in *State v. Thompson,* 695 S.W.2d 154, 159 (Mo.App.1985).

The murder-only rule plainly violates the premise of the diminished capacity doctrine, since mental abnormality can lead to the absence of mens rea for other crimes as well. Expanding the doctrine's applicability to all specific intent crimes does not necessarily solve this problem. If the mens rea for general intent crimes (or recklessness and negligence) were truly "objectively" defined, then diminished capacity evidence would indeed be irrelevant in such cases. But such is not always the case.

Looking first at the Model Penal Code approach to mens rea, it is clear that even negligence contemplates some degree of investigation into the defendant's actual mental state. Section 2.02(2)d of the Model Penal Code states:

> A person acts negligently with respect to a material element of an offense when he should be aware of a substantial and unjustifiable risk that the material element exists or will result from his conduct. The risk must be of such a nature and degree that the actor's failure to perceive it, *considering the nature and purpose of his conduct and the circumstances known to him*, involves a gross deviation from the standard of care that a reasonable person would observe *in the actor's situation.*

(Emphasis supplied). Under § 213.4 of the Code, the crime of sexual assault is defined as, *inter alia*, "sexual contact with another . . . [when] (6) the other person is less than 16 years old and the actor is at least four years older than the other person." It is a defense to this crime if the victim was between 10 and 16 and the actor had a non-negligent belief that the victim was older than 16. See §§ 213.6; 1.13(16). Suppose a defendant wants to submit expert testimony that, due to mental illness or mental retardation, he thought a person with whom he admittedly had sexual contact was over 16 (even though a "normal" person should have known otherwise). Under the above definition of negligence, could not one make a plausible argument that such testimony should be admissible on diminished capacity grounds? The commentary to the Model Penal Code suggests a negative answer to this question:

> The standard for ultimate judgement [in negligence cases] invites consideration of the "care that a reasonable person would observe in the actor's situation." There is an inevitable ambiguity in "situation." If the actor were blind or if he had just suffered a blow or experienced a heart attack, these would certainly be facts to be considered in a judgement involving criminal liability, as they would be under traditional law. But the heredity, intelligence or temperament of the actor would not be held material in judging negligence, and could not be without depriving the criterion of all its objectivity. The Code is not intended to displace discriminations of this kind, but rather to leave the issue to the courts.

Model Penal Code § 2.02 comment 4, at 242 (1985). Doesn't the language "considering . . . the circumstances known to him" in the MPC's definition of negligence undercut the comment's statement that heredity, intelligence or tempe[...]are not "material"? In any event, the comment ends by saying "di[...]" between physical-external and psychological-internal [...]uation" should be left to the courts. What would you do?

[...]of problem occurs under the common law in [...]nd general intent crimes, primarily because the [...]in defining these terms. In *State v. McVey,* 376 [...]instance, the defendant was charged under a [...]eft for a person to "[exercise] control over stolen [...]n property to have been stolen, or having reasonable [...]at such property has been stolen, unless the person's pu[...] promptly restore it to the owner or to deliver it to an appr[...]public officer." West's Ann.Iowa Code 714.1(4). According to prior case law, the Iowa Supreme Court noted, "the mens rea of this offense requires proof that the accused actually believe the property is stolen." But case law had also established that the offense did not require proof of "specific intent." Rather "[t]he offense is a general intent crime because it is complete without intent to do a further act or achieve a further consequence." Id. at 586. The court then upheld the trial court's exclusion of psychiatric evidence proffered to show that the defendant did not know that an automobile in which he was apprehended was stolen. The court noted that, although Iowa courts had long recognized that a diminished capacity defense "is available to any crime in which specific intent is an element," expanding it to general intent crimes would be unsound:

> In practical terms a court's refusal to recognize the relevancy of evidence of mental impairment short of legal insanity results from the court's understanding of the legislative intention concerning the blameworthiness of the defendant's conduct. To the extent evidence of mental impairment that does not meet the legal insanity standard permits an accused to avoid responsibility for otherwise culpable conduct, the policy inherent in the insanity defense is undermined.

If the defendant's evidence proves that he did not know the car was stolen, is he blameworthy? Is this case any different from *Bright*?

Even in cases that clearly involve general intent crimes, psychiatric evidence might be considered relevant. Consider *New York v. Wilcox*, 194 A.D.2d 820, 599 N.Y.S.2d 131 (N.Y.App.Div.1993), in which a New York appeals court reversed a manslaughter conviction because the trial court failed to instruct the jury to consider whether the defendant's diminished mental capacity limited his ability to form the requisite mental state. The psychiatric expert had testified that the defendant had an IQ of 69 and a mental age of 10, and consequently could not perceive any danger to the victim (his 12–week old son) when he threw him on a chair. Presumably, in other words, the expert believed that while the defendant "intended" to throw the child, he did not intend to hurt him, much less kill him. Should the latter fact, if true, matter? Is there a difference between *Bright* and *McVey*, on the one hand, and *Wilcox* on the other, in terms of what the defendants were aware of?

The usual justification given for limiting diminished capacity evidence to certain types of mens rea is not the one advanced by the Iowa Supreme Court in *McVey* but rather stems from a utilitarian rationale: if no such limitation were imposed, some defendants with mental illness (including those who ordinarily would have pleaded insanity and thus been committed) would be able to use clinical evidence to elude confinement completely (cf. note 45 in *Clark v. Arizona*). The public is protected in states limiting clinical testimony on mens rea to murder cases because a defendant who escapes a murder conviction through using diminished capacity evidence can still be convicted of manslaughter. Similarly, in those states that have adopted the specific intent limitation, the defendant who successfully argues diminished capacity can still usually be convicted of a lesser included offense requiring only general intent.

In *People v. Wetmore,* 22 Cal.3d 318, 149 Cal.Rptr. 265, 583 P.2d 1308 (1978), the defendant was charged with burglary after being discovered in another person's apartment wearing that person's clothes and cooking his food. The defendant credibly showed that as a result of mental illness he had come to believe that he owned the apartment. He had lived in the apartment for three days prior to his arrest and been shocked and embarrassed when the police arrived and informed him that the apartment was not his. In overturning his conviction for burglary (for which there was no lesser included offense), the California Supreme Court stated:

> We reject the suggestion that we sustain the trial court by holding that a defense of diminished capacity cannot be raised whenever, owing to the lack of a lesser included offense, it might result in the defendant's acquittal. A defendant who, because of diminished capacity, does not entertain the specific intent required for a particular crime is entitled to be acquitted of that crime. If he cannot be convicted of a lesser offense and cannot safely be released, the state's remedy is to institute civil commitment proceedings, not to convict him of a specific-intent crime which he did not commit.

In California, the relevant civil commitment statute permits confinement of any person who "as a result of mental disorder [is] a danger to others, or to himself, or gravely disabled." Confinement under the first two criteria may last only 90 days unless the person "has threatened, attempted, or actually inflicted physical harm to another during his period of post-certification treatment." Is the court's solution sufficiently protective of the public? Would it be wise to amend the civil commitment statute to permit longer confinement of those acquitted on diminished capacity grounds? Or should we condone conviction of *some* offense, even one for which the defendant did not have the required mental state, as a compromise between retributive and utilitarian notions?

D. OTHER DEFENSES

NOTE ON SELF–DEFENSE, PROVOCATION AND DURESS

In adjudicating guilt, evidence of mental abnormality is most likely to be considered relevant to insanity, automatism or diminished capacity. Increasingly, however, psychiatric and psychological testimony has been proffered in support of other claims. This development is a direct outgrowth of the criminal law's movement toward a subjective definition of culpability. To illustrate this development and its ramifications, this section looks briefly at three criminal law doctrines: self-defense, provocation, and duress.

The traditional approach to self-defense is summarized by Professor LaFave as follows: "One who is not the aggressor in an encounter is justified in using a reasonable amount of force against his adversary when he reasonably believes that he is in immediate danger of unlawful bodily harm from his adversary and that the use of such force is necessary to avoid this danger." Wayne LaFave, Criminal Law, at 569 (5th ed. 2010). In a majority of jurisdictions a person may use deadly force to repel an attack that is reasonably believed to be deadly even if he or she could safely retreat from the attack; however, in a "strong minority" of jurisdictions, one must retreat before using deadly force, if the retreat can be accomplished safely. Even in the minority jurisdictions, one need not retreat if the attack takes place in the defendant's house, on the theory that one is entitled to stand firm in one's home. See id., at 578–79. A valid self-defense claim leads to acquittal on any charge.

The provocation "defense," on the other hand, is available only in homicide cases and, rather than acquittal, leads to reduction of the charge from murder to voluntary manslaughter. In most jurisdictions, this reduction occurs when the defendant can show that (1) the killing was in reaction to provocation that, while insufficient to justify the killing, would cause the "reasonable" person to lose control; (2) this provocation in fact provoked the defendant; (3) a "reasonable" person so provoked would not have cooled off in the interval of time between the provocation and the delivery of the final blow; and (4) the defendant did not in fact cool off. LaFave, supra, at 820–21. The provocation defense sometimes overlaps with a doctrine known as imperfect self-defense because it recognizes that some types of provocation, although they do not justify the use of deadly force in return, might make a "reasonable" person impulsively kill someone, and thus should be given mitigating (but not exculpatory) effect. The common law identified a number of situations in which such provocation might occur, e.g., serious battery not rising to deadly force, serious assault (i.e., attempted battery), mutual combat not involving deadly force, and discovery of adultery by the offended spouse. See id., at 821–23.

Finally, the defense of duress is recognized under the common law when a person's unlawful threat causes the defendant reasonably to believe that the only way to avoid imminent death or serious bodily injury to him or herself or to another is to engage in conduct which violates the criminal law, and the defendant acts on that belief. LaFave, supra, at 519. Duress is not normally a defense, however, to intentional homicide, since the rationale for the defense is generally thought to be that acquittal should be permitted only when the defendant, faced with a choice of evils, chooses to do the lesser evil.

It should be clear even from this brief description that, under the common law, "reasonableness" language dominates the definition of these defenses. Use of such language presumably renders mental abnormality irrelevant, because a person who is mentally disordered at the time of the offense never acts "reasonably". The reasonable person is the "normal" person as defined by the judge or members of the jury. Thus, for instance, with respect to provocation, in most jurisdictions "the defendant's special mental qualities . . . are not to be considered." LaFave, supra, at 827.

Modern developments in these three areas demonstrate an increasing willingness to consider the personal characteristics of the accused in deciding whether a defense is available. The Model Penal Code is representative. The Code permits "the use of force upon or toward another person . . . when the actor believes that such force is immediately necessary for the purpose of protecting himself against the use of unlawful force by such person on the present occasion." Model Penal Code § 3.04. This formulation makes the actor's beliefs relevant to a self-defense claim regardless of how "unreasonable" they are except, perhaps, in those cases in which negligence is the mens rea. The provision of the Code that is analogous to the common law provocation doctrine is somewhat more objectively defined but still incorporates subjective elements. It states that a homicide that would otherwise be murder is manslaughter if it "is committed under the influence of extreme mental or emotional disturbance for which there is reasonable explanation or excuse[,] . . . the reasonableness of such explanation or excuse [to] be determined *from the viewpoint of a person in the actor's situation under the circumstances as he believes them to be*." Model Penal Code § 210.3 (emphasis added). Similarly, with respect to duress, the Code provides for an affirmative defense when a person commits a crime "because he was coerced to do so by the use of, or a threat to use, unlawful force against his person or the person of another, which a person of reasonable firmness *in his situation* would have been unable to resist." Model Penal Code § 2.09(1)(emphasis added). The commentary to this provision states that its intent "is to give effect to the defense when an actor mistakenly believes that a threat to use unlawful force has been made." Id. § 2.09, comment 3, at 380 (1985). But the defense is not available when the "actor recklessly placed himself in a situation in which it was probable that he would be subjected to duress." Id. § 2.09(2).

According to LaFave, a "few" states have adopted the Model Penal Code's subjectified version of self-defense, a "substantial minority" have adopted its provocation formulation, and "a very distinct majority" have adopted its duress provision. As the following materials make clear, behavioral science testimony is often admitted on these types of issues. That is true even in federal courts, where the Insanity Defense Reform Act limits the admissibility of testimony about mental disease or defect to insanity and lack of mens rea issues. *United States v. Brown*, 891 F.Supp. 1501 (D. Kan. 1995) (duress).

JAHNKE V. STATE

Supreme Court of Wyoming, 1984.
682 P.2d 991.

THOMAS, JUSTICE.

The essential questions presented in this case arise out of a notion that a victim of abuse has some special justification for patricide.

* * *

The appellant's father, Richard Chester Jahnke, died on November 16, 1982, as a result of gunshot wounds. Those gunshot wounds were inflicted by the appellant, and that fact has never been an issue in this case.

* * *

The material facts relating to the death of the appellant's father can be briefly stated. On the night of his death the father took the mother out to dinner, apparently to celebrate the anniversary of their meeting. Earlier the appellant had been involved in a violent altercation with his father, and he had been warned not to be at the home when the father and mother returned. During the absence of his parents the appellant made elaborate preparation for the final confrontation with his father. He changed into dark clothing and prepared a number of weapons which he positioned at various places throughout the family home that he selected to serve as "backup" positions in case he was not successful in his first effort to kill his father. These weapons included two shotguns, three rifles, a .38 caliber pistol and a Marine knife. In addition, he armed his sister, Deborah, with a .30 caliber M–1 carbine which he taught her how to operate so that she could protect herself in the event that he failed in his efforts. The appellant removed the family pets from the garage to the basement to protect them from injury in a potential exchange of gunfire between him and his father, and he closed the garage door. He then waited inside the darkened garage in a position where he could not be seen but which permitted him to view the lighted driveway on the other side of the garage door. Shortly before 6:30 p.m. the parents returned, and the appellant's father got out of the vehicle and came to the garage door. The appellant was armed with a 12–gauge shotgun loaded with slugs, and when he could see the head and shoulders of his father through the spacing of the slats of the shade covering the windows of the garage door, he blew his R.O.T.C. command-sergeant-major's whistle for courage, and he opened fire. All six cartridges in the shotgun were expended, and four of them in one way or another struck the father.

* * *

After the shooting, and while the mother still was screaming in the driveway, the appellant and his sister exited the family home through a window in the mother's bedroom, which was at the far end of the house from the garage. The appellant and his sister then went separate ways, and the appellant was arrested at the home of his girl friend. Prior to the arrival of authorities the appellant told his girl friend's father that he had shot his dad for revenge. Subsequently, after being advised of his constitutional rights, the appellant made a statement in which he explained he had shot his father "for past things."

[Jahnke was convicted of voluntary manslaughter and sentenced to 5 to 15 years. On appeal he argued that the trial court erroneously excluded expert testimony describing him as a victim of the "battered person syndrome" who was in constant fear of serious bodily harm from his father but at the same time unable to leave the site of the battering.]

It is clear that self-defense is circumscribed by circumstances involving a confrontation, usually encompassing some overt act or acts by the deceased, which would induce a reasonable person to fear that his life was in danger or that at least he was threatened with great bodily harm.

* * *

Although many people, and the public media, seem to be prepared to espouse the notion that a victim of abuse is entitled to kill the abuser that special justification defense is antithetical to the mores of modern civilized society. It is difficult enough to justify capital punishment as an appropriate response of society to criminal acts even after the circumstances have been carefully evaluated by a number of people. To permit capital punishment to be imposed upon the subjective conclusion of the individual that prior acts and conduct of the deceased justified the killing would amount to a leap into the abyss of anarchy.

* * *

This record contained no evidence that the appellant was under either actual or threatened assault by his father at the time of the shooting. Reliance upon the justification of self-defense requires a showing of an actual or threatened imminent attack by the deceased.

Absent [such] a showing, the reasonableness of appellant's conduct at the time was not an issue in the case, and the trial court, at the time it made its ruling, properly excluded the hearsay testimony sought to be elicited from the forensic psychiatrist.

* * *

ROSE, JUSTICE, dissenting, with whom CARDINE, JUSTICE, joins

* * *

This case concerns itself with what happens—or can happen—and did happen when a cruel, ill-tempered, insensitive man roams, gun in hand, through his years of family life as a battering bully—a bully who, since his two children were babies, beat both of them and his wife regularly and unmercifully. Particularly, this appeal has to do with a 16–year–old boy who could stand his father's abuse no longer—who could not find solace or friendship in the public services which had been established for the purpose of providing aid, comfort and advice to abused family members—and who had no place to go or friends to help either him or his sister for whose protection he felt responsible and so—in fear and fright, and with fragmented emotion, Richard Jahnke shot and killed his father one night in November of 1982.

* * *

The Reasonableness of Self–Defense

* * *

In contemplating the overall problem which brings on my dissent, it is initially necessary to be aware of at least these following facts:

Richard Jahnke, a sensitive boy who had never been in any sort of trouble in his life, had been beaten regularly and unmercifully by his father since he was two years old. On the night of the homicide he had received a severe beating, and when his father and mother left the house to go to dinner that night, his father said:

"I'm disgusted with the shit you turned out to be. I don't want you to be here when I get back."

The father also said:

"I don't care what I have to do, I'm going to get rid of you. I don't know how but I'm going to get rid of you, you bastard."

The boy felt he had to protect his sister who was hysterical when the mother and father left for dinner. He did not believe that there was any place or anyone where or to whom they could go for safety. The mother testified that the elder Jahnke always carried a gun, and Richard believed he had one with him that night. Mrs. Jahnke said that when the father said to Richard, "I'm going to get rid of you"—

"He was trying to frighten him and maybe do something else besides just throwing him out of the house."

When Richard was in the garage after having stationed his father's guns around the house for "backup," he reflected upon past confrontations with his father and he was afraid the father would kill him when he returned and found what Richard had done with the guns. Even as he contemplated these things, the father drove the car into the driveway. Richard said he wanted to go and hug him and tell him he loved him, but he remembered when he had done this before, he had received a beating for his efforts. He knew from past experience that when his father "stomped" after him that he was in for a beating. He testified about how his father approached the garage door that night:

> "A. Yes. I remember he was stomping. When he stomped down the hall when he was really mad and really prepared to beat someone up, beat on one of us. I remember being a little kid, just sitting in my room. My dad stomping after me to hit me, that I could never stop him. This time I stopped him."

*   *   *

[In] the *ordinary* self-defense situation where there are no psychiatric implications and where the jury is permitted to know what the accused knew about the violent character of his victim, there need be no expert testimony touching upon the reasonableness of the defendant's behavior. In normal circumstances, these are things that jurors can fathom for themselves. However, when the beatings of 14 years have—or may have—caused the accused to harbor types of fear, anxiety and apprehension with which the nonbrutalized juror is unfamiliar and which result in the taking of unusual defensive measures which, in the ordinary circumstances, might be thought about as premature, excessive or lacking in escape efforts by those who are uninformed about the fear and anxiety that permeate the world of the brutalized—[then expert testimony is necessary to explain the battered-person syndrome and the way these people respond to what they understand to be the imminence of danger and to explain their propensity to employ deadly force in their self-defensive conduct.] Given this information, the jury is then qualified to decide the reasonableness of a self-defense defendant's acts at the time and place in question.

The Proffered Testimony of the Forensic Psychiatrist

Dr. McDonald, a forensic psychiatrist, was offered by the defendant for the purpose of testifying about the behavior of battered children—that Richard was a battered child—all as an aid to the triers of fact with respect to their obligation to decide whether or not this defendant—as a battered person—behaved reasonably on the night of November 16, 1982, but the court would not permit the jury to hear the testimony.

The defendant suggests that his offer of proof represented that Dr. McDonald would testify that:

1.   The doctor had diagnosed Richard Jahnke as a battered child, based on interviews with him and upon other information.

2.   Battered children behave differently from other children, and perceive things differently from other children.

3.   Because he was a battered child, Jahnke reasonably believed himself to be in immediate danger on the night he shot his father, and perceived himself as acting in self-defense.

*   *   *

The doctor described an extensive background of Richard receiving physical abuse from his father. His earliest memory was of his father beating him, his mother and his sister. Between the ages of four and 12, there was seldom a day without some sort of punishment by his father. The punishment became less frequent between 12 and 15—more like every other day, but there were more beatings when his father used his fists on him. He was beaten with his father's fists every couple of weeks between 15 and 16. He would be beaten for such things as not cleaning the basement the right way—for walking along with his mouth open—for spending too much time polishing his ROTC uniform. At one juncture, the doctor testified that the children were forced to eat with plastic spoons and forks because their father did not like the noise they made while eating with ordinary utensils. Dr. McDonald testified that Richard related that he would be beaten for things like defending his sister. If Richard would react to verbal abuse by changing facial expression, the father would physically abuse him. When Richard and his mother had an argument, she would call him a "bastard" and report him to his father who would beat him.

On May 2, 1982, after a severe beating by his father, he ran out of the house in his bare feet, then put his sneakers on and ran five miles to his ROTC instructor's home. He sat outside the instructor's house, afraid to go in, and was finally discovered there by the instructor. The doctor explained that children who are victims of abuse are often reluctant to report their problems to others. In Richard's case, he believed for many years that child beatings were the normal behavior for a father. He was humiliated by the abuse and even had trouble reporting it to the ROTC instructor with whom he had a close relationship. On this occasion, however, the instructor and Richard went to the sheriff to report the abuse. The family was then interviewed together, and Richard chose to return home rather than go to a foster home, principally because he saw himself as the protector of his mother and sister.

Richard believed the May visit to the sheriff's office was useless even though his father did not beat him for a week or more. When he returned from reporting his beating to the sheriff, he put a chair against his door every night so his father could not get in. A week and a half after the sheriff's incident, the father exclaimed, "That bastard reported me to the Sheriff," and would say things like

"I'll give him something that he can really complain about, that is if he can talk," the implication being that he would be in a condition that would prevent him from talking about anything.

*   *   *

[T]he doctor took other factors into account to reach his evaluation conclusion. For example, the beatings and verbal abuse had an adverse effect on Richard's psychological development. He testified that the boy does not have the ability to handle stress that other young people of his age have and any ability he does have in this regard has come about as a developed defensive mechanism against the brutality of his father. That was the problem on November 16, 1982—that is, when his mother turned on him, blaming him for all the trouble with her marriage and in the home generally, and when she kept calling him a bastard and throwing things at him it was too much for him to stand. He felt victimized when his mother reported him to his father that night because she reported things that he had never said about her. This series of events and its repercussions, together with his father's beating him that night and the father's threat that he should leave home, was more than Richard Jahnke could handle. In addition, according to Dr. McDonald, he was afraid of another beating when his father and mother returned from dinner. Therefore, taking all of these things into account, he was under unusual and, for him, unbearable pressure on the evening of November 16, 1982.

*   *   *

The Insanity Misconception

Both the State and the trial court believed the defendant was urging an insanity or diminished-capacity defense and thus were of the opinion that the proffered testimony was irrelevant.

The theory of Richard Jahnke's defense was misunderstood by the prosecuting attorney, the trial court and now, I submit, this court.

*   *   *

In these proceedings, the mental state of Richard Jahnke was not offered as a defense as would be the case with an insanity plea. Neither his mental capacity nor his intent to commit the crime was in issue. Rather, the specific defense is self-defense, which requires a showing that Jahnke reasonably believed it was necessary to use deadly force to prevent imminent death or great bodily harm to himself. In this situation, the expert testimony is offered, when the battered defendant pleads self-defense, as an aid to the jury in interpreting the surrounding circumstances as they affected the reasonableness of his belief. The expert testimony offered was secondary to the defense asserted. Given the opportunity, the defendant would not seek to show through the expert testimony that the mental and physical mistreatment which he suffered affected his mental state so that he *could not be responsible* for his actions; rather, the testimony was offered to show that, because he suffered from 14 years of brutalizing, *it was reasonable* for him to have remained in the home—to have prepared to respond to the beating that he had been promised would surely come and to have believed at that time and place that he was in imminent danger.

* * *

It is because a jury would not understand and would not be expected to understand why Richard Jahnke would remain in that environment and believe that he was in imminent danger that the expert testimony is critical to aid and assist them in evaluating these conditions, circumstances and behavior patterns.

* * *

QUESTIONS AND COMMENTS

1.   *Analyzing* Jahnke. Assuming that it otherwise met the criteria for expert testimony,[n] should the psychiatric opinion and associated factual evidence in *Jahnke* have been admitted under the traditional definition of self-defense? Provocation? Under the Model Penal Code's definitions of self-defense and provocation? Is the expert's testimony relevant to mens rea or insanity issues (is there a mental illness)? Or is it irrelevant to criminal liability? Note that one week after the court's decision, the governor commuted Jahnke's sentence to three years.

If, instead of killing his father, the defendant had stolen something from a store to prove that he was "tough" rather than "sensitive" so as to avoid further beatings, should he have a duress defense to a charge of theft?

2.   *The battered woman syndrome.* The issues raised in *Jahnke* were presaged in a number of cases involving women charged with killing their husbands after suffering through years of abuse. According to Dr. Lenore Walker (whose book, The Battered Woman Syndrome, was originally published in 1979 and is now in its third edition) some women who are subjected to abuse by their husbands develop what has come to be called "learned helplessness". Because of low self-esteem, passivity, an inability to express terror and anger, and inculcation of traditional societal attitudes toward females, these women believe that the batterer is all-powerful, that they are to blame for the battering, and that no one can help them. Emotionally and financially dependent upon the battering husband, and perhaps fearful of being stigmatized as failures, they develop "coping" responses rather than "escape" responses as a method of surviving the relationship. In other words, rather than leaving the batterer, they remain with him and put up with the beatings. The battering cycle usually proceeds

---

[n]   In a part of the opinion not reprinted, the majority suggested that the "battered-child syndrome" was not a "generally accepted diagnosis". See discussion of the general acceptance doctrine at pp. 527–530.

through three stages. The first phase—the "tension-building" stage—involves minor battering incidents and verbal abuse, during which the woman tries to placate the man and be as passive as possible to stave off further violence. Phase two is the "acute battering incident", usually precipitated by some event in the man's life outside the relationship, but sometimes triggered by the woman when she can no longer tolerate or control her reaction to the man's phase one actions. Phase three is characterized by contrition and reconciliation on the part of the man; he often promises to seek professional help, stop drinking and refrain from further violence. Sometimes, however, the normal cycle is disrupted during phase one or two. The woman either precipitates an incident or fights back and the husband is killed or badly hurt. See Lenore Walker, The Battered Woman (1979).

A number of researchers have challenged both the notion that domestic violence is cyclical and the claim that women who are battered always or usually experience "learned helplessness." Their conclusion is that there is no "single profile" of the battered woman. See Regina Schuller & Sara Rzepa, *The Scientific Status of Research on Domestic Violence Against Women*, in David Faigman et al., Science in the Law: Social and Behavioral Science Issues 206, 237 (2002). Nonetheless, the term "battered woman syndrome" now pervades the literature and court decisions. Evidence of the syndrome is introduced to support a number of legal theories, including insanity and diminished capacity, but it is most often offered to support a self-defense claim. The courts are split as to whether evidence of the syndrome is relevant to such a claim. For example, in *State v. Kelly*, 97 N.J. 178, 478 A.2d 364 (1984), the court permitted evidence about the syndrome in a homicide case:

> At the heart of the claim of self-defense was defendant's story that she had been repeatedly subjected to "beatings" over the course of her marriage. . . . The crucial issue of fact on which this expert's testimony would bear is why, given such allegedly severe and constant beatings, combined with threats to kill, defendant had not long ago left decedent. Whether raised by the prosecutor as a factual issue or not, our own common knowledge tells us that most of us, including the ordinary juror, would ask himself or herself just such a question. And our knowledge is bolstered by the experts' knowledge, for the experts point out that one of the common myths, apparently believed by most people, is that battered wives are free to leave. To some, this misconception is followed by the observation that the battered wife is masochistic, proven by her refusal to leave despite the severe beatings; to others, however, the fact that the battered wife stays on unquestionably suggests that the "beatings" could not have been too bad for if they had been, she certainly would have left. The expert could clear up these myths, by explaining that one of the common characteristics of a battered wife is her inability to leave despite such constant beatings; her "learned helplessness"; her lack of anywhere to go; her feeling that if she tried to leave, she would be subjected to even more merciless treatment; her belief in the omnipotence of her battering husband; and sometimes her hope that her husband will change his ways.

Consider whether *Kelly's* rationale supports a self-defense claim on the facts of *State v. Norman*, 89 N.C.App. 384, 366 S.E.2d 586 (1988), rev'd, 324 N.C. 253, 378 S.E.2d 8 (1989). Norman was beaten by her husband for years. He would demand that she bark like a dog, eat dog or cat food, and sleep on the cold concrete floor. If she refused he would hit her with whatever was handy: his fist, a flyswatter, a baseball bat, a shoe, an ashtray, all of which left scars. Two days before the killing, he took her to a truck stop and forced her to prostitute herself, something he had done on numerous other occasions. He also assaulted her, for which he was arrested. Upon returning from jail the next day, he beat her continuously, and Norman, apparently in distress, took an overdose of nerve pills. When emergency personnel arrived to treat her, the husband tried to interfere, stating, "Let the bitch die. . . . She ain't nothing but a dog. She don't deserve to live." Then next day, the day of the shooting, the husband again beat Norman all day, kicking her in the head, smashing food in her face, and putting a cigarette out on her chest. When he decided to take a nap, Norman took her daughter's baby, whom she had been babysitting, to her mother's house so her husband would not wake up from the crying. At her mother's, Norman picked up a gun, returned home, and killed her husband while he lay sleeping. Norman's self-defense claim failed.

Are claims such as those made in *Kelly* and *Norman* better characterized as claims of insanity or diminished responsibility that focus on inner "disease" states (i.e., an "excuse") rather than on the manner in which the woman's relationship with the batterer makes her actions reasonable (a self-defense "justification") or partially reasonable (a provocation or imperfect self-defense defense)? Compare *State v. Necaise*, 466 So.2d 660 (La.Ct.App. 1985) (concluding that syndrome testimony is meant to support a "partial responsibility" defense, and rejecting it as such) with *People v. Torres*, 128 Misc.2d 129, 488 N.Y.S.2d 358, 361–62 (Sup.Ct. 1985) (observing that the syndrome is not "intended to establish . . . a mental disease or defense relieving defendant of criminal responsibility" but rather "is best understood as being descriptive of an identifiable group of symptoms that characterize the behavior and state of mind of abused women rather than being disease-like in character"). Some writers have resisted the excuse characterization as demeaning to women. Elizabeth M. Schneider, *Describing and Changing Women's Self–Defense Work and the Problem of Expert Testimony*, 9 Women's Rights Law Reporter 195 (1986). Other writers, however, hold that the excuse characterization is appropriate because BWS focuses attention on the actor's condition rather than features of the situation (as is traditionally the case with justification defenses). Joshua Dressler, *Battered Women and Sleeping Abusers: Some Reflections*, 3 Ohio St. J. Crim. L. 457, 463 (2006).

3. *Other cases that might raise "other defense" issues.* Consider what defenses, if any, should be available in the following cases:

Case A. According to Parisie, charged with murder, on the night of the crime he was walking on 5th Street in Springfield when the decedent pulled up next to him in his car and offered him a lift. Parisie accepted, and they drove out of Springfield, turned down a gravel road and parked. After turning off the lights and sliding back the seat, the decedent made a homosexual advance, smiled and said if the defendant refused he would have to walk. Parisie just 'blew up, went crazy,' and vaguely remembered struggling with the decedent and hearing a noise that he assumed to be gunshots. The next thing he remembered clearly was being in the deceased's car in a Springfield parking lot. At trial, Parisie called a clinical psychologist who testified that Parisie suffered from paranoid schizophrenia, was a loner with a basic distrust of people, and was a highly latent homosexual with strong feelings of inferiority. Parisie then called a psychiatrist who testified that "homosexual panic" is a severe panic or fear reaction that is provoked by extreme anxiety connected with admitting homosexual tendencies or experiences, and that this panic often takes the form of a state of amnesia, in which the person sets aside or forgets unconsciously something that his conscious mind cannot tolerate. The psychiatrist also stated that a person suffering from this type of reaction, although not mentally ill, could act purely instinctively. See *People v. Parisie*, 5 Ill.App.3d 1009, 287 N.E.2d 310 (1972) (finding evidence insufficient for insanity, but not addressing other defensive issues).

Case B. "The defendant, charged with assaulting a jail guard, had been raped a year earlier in a small motel room by a man who had torn off her clothing. When she was arrested a year later on a charge of domestic violence, she was placed in a small holding room and approached by one of the guards, who forced her to stand up by grabbing her sweatpants in a way that resembled the actions of the rapist. She reacted by hitting the guard with a food tray. A psychologist testified that a post-traumatic stress disorder [stemming from the rape] caused her to be more fearful in that situation than a normal person would have been under the same circumstances." The defendant did not receive any mitigation. See Brett C. Trowbridge, *Self Defense as a Mental Defense*, 19 Am. J. Forensic Psychology 63, 67 (2001).

Case C. Cabarga grew up with his parents and two older brothers in an "experimental community" located in a vacant warehouse. When he was five years old, he and his brothers were befriended by a 33 year-old member of the community nicknamed Tree Frog. Cabarga's parents did not like Tree Frog but permitted him access to their children consistent with their open-minded lifestyle. Two years later Cabarga's parents broke up and the mother took custody. Tree Frog lived nearby and began having sex with Cabarga. Although the mother suspected as much she handed over parental custody to Tree Frog when Cabarga was nine, explaining she was tired of being a parent. After he gained custody, Tree Frog's physical and sexual abuse of Cabarga became routine; for instance, he would deny Cabarga food if he resisted having sex or otherwise disobeyed. Tree Frog believed that adults and children should have open sexual relationships, and eventually decided to kidnap a little girl, conceive a child with her, and raise the child. Cabarga, now seventeen, helped Tree Frog kidnap a 2 1/2 year-old girl. Tree Frog denied her food unless she had sex with Tree Frog and Cabarga. About ten months later police found Cabarga and the girl in a van under blankets, both naked from the waist down. When the girl was reunited with her parents, they did not recognize her. She had an extensive vocabulary of vulgar words and a therapist later concluded that her ordeal had scarred her for life. Cabarga received a 25 year sentence, Tree Frog a 527–year sentence. Cabarga was paroled after 11 years. Paul H. Robinson, Would You Convict? Seventeen Cases that Challenged the Law 199 (1999). Is there a legally relevant difference between Cabarga and someone like Murdock (see p. 664)?

4.   *The outer boundary of exculpation.* In contrast to the court in *Kelly*, the majority in *Jahnke* asserts that allowing self-defense in such abuse cases would be "antithetical to the mores of modern civilized society." Consider, in support of this position, the arguments of Justice Oliver Wendell Holmes in The Common Law (1881) to the effect that the deterrent purpose of the criminal law must take precedence over the retributive goal. Holmes began by asserting that "prevention" of criminal conduct is "the chief and only universal purpose of punishment." To accomplish the prevention goal, the criminal law must inflict pain on individuals who commit crime, thus using them as a "tools" to ensure the general welfare. Furthermore, the primacy of the prevention goal means that the purpose of the criminal law is only to induce "external conformity to rule;" the precise reasons why people obey the law are not important. Because the law uses people as tools to achieve this "external" result, "the actual degree of personal guilt involved in any particular transgression cannot be the only element . . . in the liability incurred."

To Holmes this conclusion did not mean that blameworthiness is irrelevant to criminal liability. But it did mean that blameworthiness should be defined in terms of the "average member of the community." He continued:

> [W]hen we are dealing with that part of the law which aims more directly than any other at establishing standards of conduct, we should expect there more than elsewhere to find that the tests of liability are external, and independent of the degree of evil in the particular person's motives or intentions. The conclusion follows directly from the nature of the standards to which conformity is required. These are not only external, as was shown above, but they are of general application. They do not merely require that every man should get as near as he can to the best conduct possible for him. They require him at his own peril to come up to a certain height. They take no account of incapacities, unless the weakness is so marked as to fall into well-known exceptions, such as infancy or madness. They assume that every man is as able as every other to behave as they command. If they fall on any one class harder than on another, it is on the weakest. For it is precisely to those who are most likely to err by temperament, ignorance, or folly, that the threats of the law are the most dangerous.

The reconciliation of the doctrine that liability is founded on blameworthiness with the existence of liability where the party is not to blame . . . is founded in the conception of the average man, the man of ordinary intelligence and reasonable prudence. Liability is said to arise out of such conduct as would be blameworthy in him. But he is an ideal being, represented by the jury when they are appealed to, and his conduct is an external or objective standard when applied to any given individual. That individual may be morally without stain, because he has less than ordinary intelligence or prudence. But he is required to have those qualities at his peril. If he has them, he will not, as a general rule, incur liability without blameworthiness.

How does Holmes's "average man" focus apply in Jahnke's case? The other cases described above? Should the test be adjusted in the relevant cases to focus on the "average child" or the "average woman"? The "average battered child or woman," the "average latent homosexual," or the "average" person in Cabarga's situation? On what grounds?

E. ABOLITION OF THE INSANITY DEFENSE

This topic has been reserved until now because proposals to abolish the insanity defense cannot properly be evaluated until one has some grasp of the framework of the criminal law. For instance, one could conclude that eliminating the insanity defense would change little if the automatism, diminished capacity, self-defense, and duress doctrines were given their full potential scope. See Christopher Slobogin, *An End to Insanity: Recasting the Role of Mental Disability in Criminal Cases*, 86 Va. L. Rev. 1199 (2000) (making this argument).

A more draconian way of limiting the exculpatory scope of the insanity defense has been termed the "mens rea" alternative. Although most jurisdictions retain the insanity defense, at least four states (Kansas, Idaho, Montana, and Utah) have replaced the defense with a provision allowing acquittal if the accused, as a result of mental disability, lacked the mens rea for the crime charged. In Montana, for instance, the defendant is to be acquitted if the jury finds that "due to a mental disease or defect he could not have had a particular state of mind that is an essential element of the offense charged." Other evidence of cognitive or volitional impairment due to mental disability is admissible only at sentencing; if the sentencing court finds that the offender "was suffering from a mental disease or defect which rendered him unable to appreciate the criminality of his conduct or to conform his conduct to the requirements of law," it may "sentence him to be committed to the custody of the director of the department of institutions to be placed in an appropriate institution for custody, care, and treatment for a definite time not to exceed the maximum term of imprisonment that could be imposed." Mont.Code Ann. 46–14–201(2), 46–14–311, 46–14–312. The provisions relating to the disposition of those who are acquitted by reason of mental disease or defect are similar to typical commitment statutes for insanity acquittees. Id.

The American Medical Association, in a report released shortly after the Hinckley verdict, supported this approach. See "Insanity Defense in Criminal Trials and Limitations of Psychiatric Testimony: Report of the Board of Trustees," 251 J.Am.Medical Ass. 2967 (1984). The Association's report stated in part:

> The essential goal of an exculpatory test for insanity is to identify the point at which a defendant's mental condition has become so impaired that society may confidently conclude that he has lost his free will. Psychiatric concepts of mental illness are ill-suited to this task. . . . Because free will is an article of faith, rather than a concept that can be explained in medical terms, it is impossible for psychiatrists to determine whether a mental impairment has affected the defendant's capacity for voluntary choice, or caused him to commit the particular act in question.

> * * *

> Even under a truncated test of insanity limited to cognitive impairments, the inscrutable cause-and-effect relationship between mental illness and free will remains the central question. . . . Meaningful reform can be achieved only if the focus of the inquiry is shifted away from the elusive notion of free will, and its relationship to mental disease, and back to the relatively objective standards of *mens rea* where it fell traditionally.

The AMA also asserted that several practical problems associated with the insanity defense would be solved by its approach.

> Most significantly, perhaps, abandonment of the moral pretense of the insanity defense in favor of a *mens rea* concept may lead to a more realistic appreciation of the relationship between mental impairment and criminal behavior. Some observers of the criminal justice system maintain that this relationship extends far beyond its manifestations in the case of those few offenders acquitted on claims of insanity; recognition of a special defense applicable to these few detracts from the legitimate treatment needs of the many. *Mens rea* proposals seek to correct this myopic focus of the insanity defense by emphasizing considerations of mercy and appropriate treatment for all mentally disordered offenders.

Additionally, according to the AMA, the mens rea approach would make expert testimony on volitional impairment irrelevant, and "diminish the scope and importance of psychiatric testimony relating to cognitive impairment in the vast majority of cases." Thus, for example, "psychiatric testimony would not be permitted to establish that a defendant's conscious premeditation or deliberation was the consequence of a mental disorder or that his intent to kill was motivated by unconscious aberrational influences."

QUESTIONS AND COMMENTS

1. *Constitutional status of the insanity defense.* In *State v. Korell,* 213 Mont. 316, 690 P.2d 992 (1984), the Montana Supreme Court upheld the constitutionality of the statute described above. Abolishing the insanity defense, the court concluded, does not violate the federal constitution as long as mental impairment is taken into account at sentencing. In modern times, most courts have followed *Korell's* lead.° In contrast, in 1910 the Washington Supreme Court declared unconstitutional a scheme that reserved the insanity issue until the sentencing stage. It stated that preventing the accused from offering evidence tending to prove that "he was insane at the time to the extent that he could not comprehend the nature and quality of the act—in other words, if he had no will to control the physical act of his physical body— . . . is in our opinion as much a violation of his constitutional right to trial by jury as to take from him the right to offer evidence before the jury tending to show that he did not physically commit the act or physically set in motion a train of events resulting in the act." *State v. Strasburg,* 60 Wash. 106, 110 P. 1020 (1910). See also, *State v. Lange,* 168 La. 958, 123 So. 639 (1929); *Sinclair v. State,* 161 Miss. 142, 132 So. 581 (1931).

The Supreme Court's position on the issue is unclear. In *Clark v. Arizona,* 548 U.S. 735, 126 S.Ct. 2709, 165 L.Ed.2d 842 (2006), it held that virtually any insanity formulation is permissible, but did not directly address the predicate issue of whether an insanity defense is constitutionally mandated. Possibly relevant is the Supreme Court's decision in *Montana v. Egelhoff,* 518 U.S. 37, 116 S.Ct. 2013, 135 L.Ed.2d 361 (1996). There, as recounted in the materials on diminished capacity, the Court held that Montana's statute eliminating the "voluntary intoxication defense" does not violate the Due Process Clause. The Montana Supreme Court had found that, since evidence of intoxication was "clearly relevant" to whether the defendant had the mens rea for murder ("purposely or knowingly" causing another's death), the statute was unconstitutional. But a four-member plurality of the Supreme Court held that the voluntary intoxication defense is not a "fundamental principle of justice." Their primary justification for this view was the fact that voluntary intoxication had not been an excuse in colonial times and that, although the defense had gained considerable acceptance since the nineteenth century, it was "of too recent vintage, and has not received sufficiently uniform and permanent allegiance to qualify as fundamental."

In *Finger v. State,* 117 Nev. 548, 27 P.3d 66 (2001), the Nevada Supreme Court relied on *Egelhoff,* as well as *Strasburg* and *Sinclair,* in holding that a state statute abolishing the insanity defense violated due process under both

---

°   See *State v. Searcy,* 118 Idaho 632, 798 P.2d 914 (Idaho 1990); *State v. Herrera,* 895 P.2d 359 (Utah 1995); *State v. Bethel,* 275 Kan. 456, 66 P.3d 840 (2003). But see *Finger v. State,* 117 Nev. 548, 27 P.3d 66 (2001), discussed below.

the state and federal constitutions. However, the court's explicit holding was that the insanity defense must be available when "a statute requires something more than the intent to commit a particular act." In *Finger*, that test was met because Finger's alleged crime was murder, which requires proof of malice aforethought. The court stated that when, as Finger alleged, a person "delusionally believes he was shooting enemy soldiers in a war, he cannot be said to kill with malice aforethought" and was entitled to raise the insanity defense. What other types of crimes require more than "the intent to commit a particular act"? Is this aspect of *Finger* a justification for reinstating the insanity defense or is it merely reinforcing the mens rea alternative to it?

Even if there are no constitutional problems with eliminating the insanity defense, the mens rea alternative may run afoul of the due process clause if it is meant to bar the automatism defense as well. Like mens rea, the actus reus is a fundamental element of each offense. Thus, analogous to those cases finding that the admission of diminished capacity evidence is constitutionally mandated, the due process clause might prohibit exclusion of evidence relevant to the "involuntariness" of the accused's act.

2. *Evaluating the theory behind the mens rea alternative.* Constitutional concerns aside, does limiting evidence concerning mental disease or defect to the mens rea issue capture the universe of mental disabled people who should have their disability accorded exculpatory effect? The American Bar Association rejected the mens rea alternative, noting that it would permit conviction of any defendants who "knew what they were doing at the time of an offense and possessed the intent to commit it." According to the ABA:

> The issue of criminal blameworthiness merits deeper inquiry because it implies a certain *quality* of knowledge and intent transcending a minimal awareness and purposefulness. Otherwise, for example, a defendant who knowingly and intentionally killed his son under the psychotic delusion that he was the biblical Abraham, and his son the biblical Isaac, could be held criminally responsible.

In response, consider this argument from Morris, a vigorous advocate of the mens rea approach:

> It too often is overlooked that one group's exculpation from criminal responsibility confirms the inculpation of other groups. Why not permit the defense of dwelling in a Negro ghetto? Such a defense would not be morally indefensible. Adverse social and subcultural background is statistically more criminogenic than is psychosis; like insanity, it also severely circumscribes the freedom of choice which a non-deterministic criminal law . . . attributes to accused persons. True, a defense of social adversity would politically be intolerable; but that does not vitiate the analogy for my purposes. [Some might argue] that insanity destroys, undermines, diminishes man's capacity to reject what is wrong and to adhere to what is right. So does the ghetto—more so. But surely, [it will

be replied,] I would not have us punish the sick. Indeed I would, if [one insists] on punishing the grossly deprived. To the extent that criminal sanctions serve punitive purposes, I fail to see the difference between these two defenses. To the extent that they serve rehabilitative, treatment, and curative purposes I fail to see the need for the difference.

. . . It seems clear that there are different degrees of moral turpitude in criminal conduct and that the mental health or illness of an actor is relevant to an assessment of that degree—as are many other factors in a crime's social setting and historical antecedents. This does not mean, however, that we are obliged to quantify these pressures for purposes of a moral assessment . . . leading to conclusions as to criminal responsibility.

Norval Morris, *Psychiatry and the Dangerous Criminal*, 41 S.Cal.L.Rev. 514, 520–21 (1968). Is Morris' equation of poverty and mental illness for purposes of determining criminal responsibility persuasive? See Stephen Morse, *Excusing the Crazy: The Insanity Defense Reconsidered*, 58 S.Cal.L.Rev. 779, 788–90, 793–95 (1985). If it is, why isn't it an argument for *expanding* the insanity defense rather than for its abolition?

3. *Evaluating the practical impact of the mens rea alternative.* Is the AMA correct in asserting that the mens rea alternative would reduce psychiatric testimony and acquittals based on mental disability? Professor Dershowitz has argued that it will not:

The clash of experts testifying about the defendant's state of mind will continue, as it has for more than a century. The battlefield may shift from the issue of right versus wrong to the equally troublesome issue of intent, but the jurors will hear testimony not substantially different—or more informative—from what they hear today.

In the last analysis, it is the jury that decides whether an accused is to be convicted or acquitted. No matter how the law reads, it is a deeply entrenched human feeling that those who are grossly disturbed—whether they are called "madmen," "lunatics," "insane," or "mentally ill"—should not be punished like ordinary criminals. This feeling, which is as old as recorded history, is unlikely to be rooted out by new legislation.

Alan Dershowitz, *Abolishing the Insanity Defense*, 9 Crim.L.Bull. 434, 438–39 (1973). Current empirical evidence on the impact of the mens rea alternative is inconclusive on this point. In a study of the impact of Montana's legislative changes in 1979 abolishing the insanity defense and limiting the mental disability defense to mens rea, researchers looked at various factors for the three years prior to and the three years after the reform. They found that the proportion of defendants who claimed a defense based on mental disease or defect was virtually unchanged between the pre and post periods. However, of those who claimed a psychiatric defense, 22.7% were successful and 49.3% were found guilty in the pre-reform period, while 2.3% were successful and 60.9% were found guilty in the post-reform period. At the same time, the number of psychiatric cases which were dismissed rose from 17.3% to 29.9% between the two periods, suggesting to the researchers that, after the reform, many of those who would have been found not guilty by reason of insanity were found incompetent to stand trial instead. They also found that, after the reform, a smaller percentage of those who raised a defense were imprisoned (35.4 to 29.1) or hospitalized (30.0 to 16.3) and a greater percentage were put on probation, conditional release or released altogether (25.7 to 46.5). Lisa Callahan, et al., *The Impact of Montana's Insanity Defense Abolition*, paper published by Policy Research Associates, Inc. (July, 1988). See also, H. Steadman, et al., Before and After Hinckley: Evaluating Insanity Defense Reform 136 (1994) (in Montana after the reform "if a person's mental status was seen as sufficient to warrant reduced criminal responsibility, they were found [incompetent to stand trial], and committed to the same hospital and the same wards where they would have been confined if they had been found NGRI.").

    4.   *Bifurcation.* An alternative that is functionally similar to the mens rea approach is to "bifurcate" the trial, adjudicating the issue of "factual guilt" at the first stage and leaving the insanity issue to the second stage. Bifurcation was first proposed as a method of (1) alleviating jury confusion by avoiding complex psychiatric testimony about insanity until after the defendant had been found "guilty" of the crime; (2) eliminating the risk of the jury returning a verdict of insanity out of sympathy for a mentally ill, but guilty, defendant; and (3) conserving judicial resources where the defendant was acquitted at the first stage.[p] The difference between the bifurcation and mens rea approaches is that in the former the insanity issue is still litigated at trial (albeit at the second stage), while in the latter any psychiatric information not relevant to mens rea is considered only at sentencing.

    As originally conceived, bifurcation was different from the mens rea alternative in an additional way: psychiatric testimony was to be excluded entirely from the first stage. But, as discussed previously, most courts found this scheme unconstitutional on the ground that such evidence could not be excluded if it was relevant to mens rea. See, e.g., *Sanchez v. State,* 567 P.2d 270 (Wyo.1977); but see, *Steele v. State,* 97 Wis.2d 72, 294 N.W.2d 2 (1980). According to the American Bar Association, once this position is accepted, "mandatory bifurcation loses its allure" because "relevant evidence of mental abnormality must be allowed at the first stage as well as the second, which uselessly duplicates evidence and nullifies many of the supposed advantages of bifurcation." ABA Criminal Justice Mental Health Standards, commentary to Standard 7–6.7, p. 341 (1987). Can the same type of claim be leveled at the mens rea approach? Colorado reverses the bifurcation process, adjudicating

---

[p]   Bifurcation was also supported by a fourth reason—protecting the fifth amendment right of a defendant who wanted to assert both a not guilty plea and a plea of not guilty by reason of insanity, without having to present possibly damaging psychiatric testimony during the adjudication of the first plea. Bifurcation allows adjudication of the factual defense at the first stage while adjudication of the second plea, if necessary, is reserved for the second stage. See p. 604.

the insanity issue before the guilt issue. C.R.S. 16–8–105. Would this approach alleviate the problems discussed above?

5.   *Abolition of insanity and mens rea defenses.* A final approach has been most forcefully presented by Lady Wootton in her book Crime and the Criminal Law (1963). She too suggests a bifurcated approach to determining the appropriate punishment, but with a significant difference. The first stage would consider only whether the defendant committed an antisocial act. *No* consideration of mental state, psychiatric or otherwise, would take place at this stage. At the second stage, the appropriate disposition of the defendant would be decided, based on expert opinion if deemed necessary or desirable. Lady Wootton defended her proposal as follows:

> The law, of course, always requires clear-cut distinctions. The responsible and sane stand on one side of the line, the irresponsible or insane on the other: every single defendant must be appropriately classified. Yet natura non facit saltum: in reality we are all strung out along a continuum which reaches from the most responsible to the most hopelessly weak-willed and weak-minded; and in many cases the degree of our responsibility almost certainly varies from time to time in accordance with our circumstances or physiological condition. In short, the "vital distinction between illness and evil" is anything but clear-cut. Indeed the worst feature of all the formulae that have been tried— McNaghten, Durham, British Homicide Act, or what have you—is their insistence on a hard and fast and totally unrealistic line between the sheep and the goats. Anyone who has followed trials in which this issue has been raised will be well aware of the sophisticated forensic subtleties for which it offers opportunity. Is careful planning of a crime consistent with diminished responsibility? Is it possible that a man should be fully responsible when he seizes a stick in the entrance to a house, but only partially so when he uses it to beat an old gentleman in bed upstairs? In these and the many similar examples which can be culled from trials in which the defendant's mens rea is in issue, all contact with reality seems to have been lost.

> Clearly the only way to avoid getting entangled in these niceties and absurdities is to demote the concept of blame from its dominant position in the criminal process. If we could emancipate ourselves from the deep-rooted tradition that the basic function of the criminal law is to identify and punish wickedness, all this farcical hairsplitting about the limits of mental abnormality could be done away with. Questions of the accused's mental condition could be ignored in the actual trial, the purpose of which would be to establish responsibility in a purely physical sense for the actus reus without reference to the presence, or absence, of malicious intent. Mens rea would thus no longer be written into the definition of every crime. Only after the accused's physical responsibility for a forbidden action had been proved would it be permissible to inquire into his mental condition, in order to determine how best he could be dealt with. In other words an offender's state of mind would be regarded as

relevant, not to the measure of his guilt, or to the crime of which he should be convicted, but to the choice of the treatment most appropriate to his case.

* * *

Hitherto, of course, strict liability has generally been restricted to such statutory offenses as are generally regarded as of minor importance. In such cases disregard of mens rea is defended on the dual ground, first, that the number of these offenses is so enormous that life is simply not long enough to inquire in every case into the accused's motivation or mental state (imagine what would happen, for example, in a busy city court which disposes of some 300 parking offenses in a morning if proof of mens rea were required in every case!); and, second, that in any case these offenses are not "truly criminal" and do not involve any serious "moral turpitude."

Yet could not an equally compelling argument be made the other way round; i.e., in favor of eliminating the requirement of mens rea from particularly grave offenses such as homicide or rape? Crimes such as these are just as damaging to their victims whether they are the result of calculated wickedness or of insane delusions. Is it not, therefore, proper that anyone who is suspected of having committed such an actus reus should be liable to answer for it in a criminal court, whatever the state of his mind—so long, that is, as he is not too ill to be able to instruct counsel or to understand court proceedings?

* * *

Obviously, if the essential purpose of a criminal court is to punish the blameworthy as they deserve, the compassionworthy must be rescued from its clutches. But, were this obsession with the punitive once dispelled, the courts could be free to deal with every lawbreaker in whatever way, consonant with the moral standards of the community, seemed best calculated to discourage future lawbreaking. Their eyes would be on the future, not on the past. Nor need they be bound by rigid diagnostic categories.

* * *

It follows logically that, once the practice of classifying offenders into the wicked and the weak-minded is abandoned, the similar distinction between prisons and hospitals becomes equally inappropriate. Already hybrid institutions, such as Grendon Underwood in Britain and similar establishments in the United States, are beginning to make their appearance; and suggestions that the courts should simply pass "custodial" sentences without specifying under what conditions, penal or medical, this sentence is to be served are much in the air, and much to be commended. Obviously, in the case of sentences of any considerable duration, the court is in no position to forecast what kind of regime will be best suited to an offender several years ahead. Hence the need for a variety of institutions and for easy transfer from one to another without inhibiting labels, at the discretion of those who are in continuous touch with persons under detention. Nor must this be read as merely a plea for the "soft" treatment of offenders. If the weaker vessels need the protection of a kindly environment, there are others for whom a more demanding regime is certainly indicated; and the response of a single individual to different types of treatment is not necessarily constant throughout his history.

Barbara Wootton, *Book Review of A. Goldstein, The Insanity Defense*, 77 Yale L.J. 1019, 1028–1032 (1968).

Is Wootton's proposal coherent? Can it be seen as the logical extension of Holmes' arguments described at pp. 714–715, or does it stray too far from Holmes' premise? Under her proposal, what happens to the person who wants to plead self-defense or duress? To what extent does her proposal undercut what was described in the introduction to this chapter as the central assumption of our criminal justice system—that we have "free will"? Consider the following from Donald Hermann, The Insanity Defense, 91–93 (1983):

An influential critique of the concept of responsibility has come from behaviorists who maintain that the determination of responsibility, in a moral or traditional legal sense, with elements of culpability and blameworthiness, is meaningless and reflects a fallacious understanding of human behavior. At the same time, it is argued that there should be a reformulation of the utilitarian objectives of the criminal law into one that can be stated succinctly as crime-preventive. Such a view [has been] urged quite eloquently by Lady Wooton. . . .

* * *

Even assuming the soundness of the determinism of the behaviorist view, there is a fundamental mistake in supposing that law is unrealistic in retaining the concepts of responsibility and punishment. This mistake stems from the assumption that ethics and law have the same point of view with regard to responsibility as does science. Unlike science, the ethical and legal systems are moral enterprises. The ascription of responsibility promotes ethical and legal values. Thus, even if it were true that a person cannot control the determinants of his conduct, and therefore is not free and responsible in some ultimate libertarian sense, the interest of law and ethics in minimizing socially harmful conduct is promoted by fostering feelings of responsibility in society. This need not be regarded as some "noble lie" but, rather, should be viewed in terms of an "as if" constituting an example of a pragmatic sense of truth. Ethical prohibitions and criminal law sanctions can themselves act as a determinant of choices, thereby assuring that actors will avoid condemnation and sanction. The influence of attribution of responsibility has been suggested by one commentator who observed: "[T]he individual who perceives himself as free and responsible behaves very differently than the individual who believes that he lacks choice and responsibility.

In general, the direction of this difference is toward a higher level of awareness, initiative, achievement, independence and complexity for those who perceive themselves as freely choosing to behave in certain ways and as responsible for the behavior." Moreover, the criminal sanction with its corollary of blameworthiness strengthens the resolve of persons to obey the law.

Another significant legal purpose is served by treating persons as responsible and blameworthy when they violate the law. By requiring guilt before criminal sanctions can be applied, the law-abiding person is protected from governmental interference. As one commentator succinctly stated: "The rule of law now guards the innocent, but its protective wall would not survive the dissolution of criminal responsibility." Elimination of the principle of responsibility would result in every attitude, disposition, or accidental movement seen by the state as undesirable, becoming a potential source of coercive intervention in the life of any and every citizen no matter how well intentioned he might be.

Would Hermann's criticism of Wooton's proposal disappear if intervention were limited to those situations where the individual commits a criminal act with at least a negligence *mens rea*? See Christopher Slobogin, *Prevention as the Primary Goal of Sentencing: The Modern Case for Indeterminate Dispositions in Criminal Cases*, 48 San Diego L. Rev. 1127 (2011).

6. *Tort liability.* By way of comparison to the foregoing materials, note that traditionally an "insane" person could not escape tort liability by reason of mental disability, at least in a negligence action. See Prosser & Keeton, Torts 1072–1075 (5th ed. 1984). California is among the jurisdictions that have codified this rule: "A person of unsound mind, of whatever degree, is civilly liable for a wrong done by the person, but is not liable in exemplary damages unless at the time of the act the person was capable of knowing that the act was wrongful." Cal Civ, Code § 41. The rationale for this rule, as described by the court in *Jolley v. Powell,* 299 So.2d 647 (Fla.App.1974), is as follows:

> [L]iability without subjective fault, under some circumstances, is one price men pay for membership in society. The sane and the insane, the awkward and the coordinated are equally liable for their acts or omissions. In such cases, we do not decide fault, rather we determine upon whom our society imposes the burden of redress for a given injury. As Holmes implied in his "awkward man" parable, a principle at least co-equal with that of the fault principle in the law of torts is that the innocent victim should have redress.

* * *

We therefore reiterate, when the predicate for a wrongful death action is unintentional tort the standard against which such tort is measured is the objective, "reasonable man standard" and the subjective state of mind of the tortfeasor is irrelevant.

Other reasons that have been given for the rule that people with mental disability are liable in tort regardless of their impairment are that imposing such liability will encourage those responsible for such people to prevent them from doing harm, discourage malingering, and avoid the problems the criminal justice system has confronted in determining insanity. See James Ellis, *Tort Responsibility of the Mentally Disabled*, 1981 Am. Bar Found. Res. J. 1079.

What are the differences and similarities between Lady Wootton's approach to criminal liability and the tort law's traditional approach to negligence liability? Are the justifications for the two approaches similar? Note that, as *Jolley* implies, mental disability is often considered a defense in intentional tort and punitive damage actions on grounds of lack of intent. See, e.g., *State Farm Fire & Casualty Co. v. James C. Wicka*, 474 N.W.2d 324 (Minn. 1991) (holding that an intentional act exclusion in an insurance policy does not apply to an insured whose act "is the product of a failure of . . . volitional or cognitive capacities" even though it was clear the insured, suffering from schizophrenia, "intended" to kill his victim). What are the implications of that fact for the tort-crime analogy?

F. THE "GUILTY BUT MENTALLY ILL" PLEA

A final reform aims not at abolishing the insanity defense, but at reducing the number of insanity pleas and acquittals by offering an alternative to the insanity verdict. Since 1975, at least 20 states have passed statutes authorizing the factfinder to return a verdict of "guilty but mentally ill" (GBMI). Although there are many different versions of the GBMI concept, most proposals work basically as follows: A defendant who pleads not guilty by reason of insanity may be found not guilty, guilty, not guilty by reason of insanity, or guilty but mentally ill at the time of the offense. If the jury makes the last mentioned finding, the *[sentencing]* defendant may be sentenced to any term appropriate for the offense, with the opportunity for treatment in a mental hospital during that period. Thus, jurors in insanity cases are given three sets of instructions with respect to the ultimate verdict they may reach: One explains under what circumstances a defendant may be found guilty of the crime charged; one describes the state's test for insanity; and one informs the jury when a defendant who is guilty beyond a reasonable doubt but not insane may be found GBMI. See, e.g., Mich.Comp.Laws Ann. § 768.36; Ill.—S.H.A. ch. 38, ¶ 115–2(b); Ky.Rev.Stat. 504.120. The definition of mental illness found in the last of these instructions varies from state to state, but usually borrows heavily from the definition of mental illness in the state's civil commitment statute. In Michigan, for instance, the definition is taken directly from the mental health code and states that mental illness is "[a] substantial disorder of thought or mood which significantly impairs judgment, behavior, capacity to recognize reality, or ability to cope with the ordinary demands of life." Mich.Comp.Laws Ann. § 330.1400a.

As the following case illustrates, a person who is found guilty but mentally ill is subject to the same dispositions as a person found guilty.

PEOPLE V. CREWS
Supreme Court of Illinois, 1988.
122 Ill.2d 266, 119 Ill.Dec. 308, 522 N.E.2d 1167.

* * *

JUSTICE MILLER delivered the opinion of the court:

The defendant, William Crews, pleaded guilty but mentally ill to one count each of murder and attempted murder in the circuit court of Randolph County. The trial judge sentenced the defendant to death for the murder conviction and imposed a 30–year prison term for the conviction for attempted murder. The defendant's execution was stayed pending direct review by this court.

The defendant's convictions stem from his attack on two correctional officers at Menard Correctional Center on November 30, 1984. The defendant was an inmate of Menard at the time of the offenses and was serving a 20–to–60–year term for an earlier murder conviction. The attack occurred on the gallery outside the defendant's cell. The defendant stabbed correctional officer Cecil Harbison to death with a shank and wounded another guard, Lamont Gilbert. The defendant then fled from the gallery, and he was captured moments later on the ground floor of the cellhouse.

The defendant initially pleaded not guilty to the charges here, but he later asked to change his plea to guilty but mentally ill (GBMI). As required by statute (see Ill.Rev.Stat.1983, ch. 38, pars. 113–4(d), 115–2(b)), the trial judge ordered the defendant to undergo a psychological examination, and a hearing was held in August 1985 on the defendant's mental condition. At the hearing, defense counsel presented the testimony of three psychiatrists—Drs. Pichardo, Vallabhaneni, and Parwatikar—who had treated the defendant at Menard Correctional Center or Menard Psychiatric Center. Dr. Pichardo first saw the defendant in February 1980 and last saw him in the middle of September 1984, a little more than two months before the defendant's attack on the two guards. Dr. Pichardo believed that the defendant was suffering from a mental illness during that period, but he could not say whether the defendant had a judgment-impairing, substantial disorder of thought, mood, or behavior. According to Dr. Pichardo, the defendant had attempted to commit suicide in April 1980.

Dr. Vallabhaneni saw the defendant several days after his attack on the guards and believed that at the time of the offenses the defendant was suffering from a mental illness and that his judgment was impaired, but he did not have a specific diagnosis for the defendant's condition.

Dr. Parwatikar believed that at the time of the offenses the defendant was mentally ill, in that he had a substantial disorder of mood, thought, or behavior. Dr. Parwatikar saw the defendant on December 2, 1984, two days after the offenses here, and his diagnosis then was of an intermittent explosive disorder.

The State disputed the defendant's contention that he was mentally ill at the time of the offenses. Dr. Daniel Cuneo, a clinical psychologist, testified in the State's behalf at the hearing. Dr. Cuneo had interviewed the defendant on two occasions—in March 1985 and in August 1985—and, based on those examinations, as well as on his review of the defendant's records, Dr. Cuneo concluded that the defendant was malingering and that he had an antisocial personality disorder. Dr. Cuneo believed that the defendant was only feigning mental illness.

The State also introduced into evidence statements the defendant made to authorities concerning the offenses here. In an initial statement given on the night of his attack on the two guards, the defendant said simply that he had gone berserk, and he did not provide a motive for his acts. In a statement given the next day, however, the defendant explained that he attacked the officers because he resented an order Harbison had given him shortly before that. The State also presented testimony from two inmates who spoke with the defendant in the period following his attack on the two guards. They testified that the defendant told them that he was trying to convince psychiatrists that he was crazy. Also, one of the inmates recalled that on the day of the occurrence here the defendant mentioned the name of a friend who had been killed earlier that year and made a comment suggesting that the friend's death should be avenged. Finally, the State presented evidence of the defendant's extensive history of disciplinary violations since 1974, when he began serving the prison sentence for his earlier murder conviction. These disciplinary tickets included 16 violations of rules, 10 assaults, 5 instances of damaging property, 19 instances of disobeying orders, and 11 instances of possession of contraband or dangerous weapons.

The trial judge accepted the defendant's GBMI plea, finding that there was a factual basis that the defendant was mentally ill when he committed the offenses here. The State then requested a death penalty hearing, and the defendant waived his right to a jury for that purpose. The defendant, who was born in 1952 and therefore 18 or older at the time of the offenses, was eligible for the death penalty because the murder victim was a correctional officer.

[Under the Illinois death penalty statute, the sentencing authority is to consider both aggravating and mitigating circumstances in deciding between life imprisonment and death. The prosecution must prove the existence of one aggravating circumstance (such as a significant history of criminal conduct); if it does so, the death penalty may be imposed unless the defense can convince the factfinder that mitigating factors outweigh the aggravating factor or factors. One of the mitigating factors listed in the Illinois statute is proof that the defendant "was under the influence of extreme mental or emotional disturbance" at the time of the offense.]

Dr. Cuneo testified in the State's behalf at the sentencing hearing, and he repeated his earlier diagnosis that the defendant had an antisocial personality disorder. Dr. Cuneo did not believe that the defendant was functioning under an extreme mental or emotional disturbance at the time of the offenses. Dr. Cuneo also said that he was familiar with capital sentencing in Illinois and that he did not know of any case in which a defendant received the death sentence after being found guilty but mentally ill.

* * *

The defendant did not present any testimony at the sentencing hearing. Included in a presentence investigation report, however, was a report dated August 5, 1985, by a psychiatrist, Dr. Moisy Shopper, who had examined the defendant and reviewed his prison file. Dr. Shopper described the defendant's suicide attempt in April 1980 and noted parallels between that event and the defendant's later attack on the two guards. Also, Dr. Shopper described the defendant's condition at the time of the offense as "an acute paranoid psychotic state with marked depressive features."

The trial judge sentenced the defendant to death for the murder conviction. The trial judge did not believe that imposition of the death penalty was precluded by the defendant's GBMI plea. The trial judge found that the defendant had a significant history of criminal conduct, and he did not believe that the defendant was acting under the influence of an extreme mental or emotional disturbance sufficient to preclude imposition of the death penalty.

* * *

The defendant . . . argues that the legislature did not intend the death penalty to be available as a possible punishment for GBMI offenders.

* * *

In support of this argument, the defendant relies on section 5–2–6 of the Unified Code of Corrections (Ill.Rev.Stat.1983, ch. 38, par. 1005–2–6).

Section 5–2–6 bears the heading "Sentencing and Treatment of Defendant Found Guilty but Mentally Ill," and the defendant contends that certain provisions in the statute signify the legislature's intent to preclude the death penalty as a possible punishment for GBMI offenders.

*   *   *

Although we agree with the defendant that section 5–2–6 of the Unified Code of Corrections is applicable to GBMI offenders, we do not believe that the statute may be understood as precluding the imposition of the death penalty. To the contrary, the plain language of the statute indicates otherwise. Section 5–2–6(a) provides, "The court may impose any sentence upon the defendant which could be imposed pursuant to law upon a defendant who had been convicted of the same offense without a finding of mental illness." Clearly, that language leaves available for GBMI offenders the full range of sentences—including the death penalty—that may be imposed on persons who are guilty of offenses and who are not mentally ill. This is entirely consistent with the legislature's definition of the term "mental illness" as a condition distinct from insanity. Section 6–2(c) of the Criminal Code of 1961 provides, "A person who, at the time of the commission of a criminal offense, was not insane but was suffering from a mental illness, is not relieved of criminal responsibility for his conduct and may be found guilty but mentally ill." (Ill.Rev.Stat.1983, ch. 38, par. 6–2(c).) Section 6–2(d) of the Criminal Code of 1961 provides, "For purposes of this Section, 'mental illness' or 'mentally ill' means a substantial disorder of thought, mood, or behavior which afflicted a person at the time of the commission of the offense and which impaired that person's judgment, but not to the extent that he is unable to appreciate the wrongfulness of his behavior or is unable to conform his conduct to the requirements of law." (Ill.Rev.Stat.1983, ch. 38, par. 6–2(d).) A GBMI offender is no less guilty than one who is guilty and not mentally ill; unlike insanity, a GBMI finding or plea does not relieve an offender of criminal responsibility for his conduct. By its plain terms, section 5–2–6(a) authorizes imposition on a GBMI offender of any sentence that could be imposed on one convicted of the same offense without the additional finding of mental illness; the death penalty therefore is available as a sentence for GBMI offenders who have been convicted of murder (see Ill.Rev.Stat.1983, ch. 38, par. 1005–5–3(c)(1)).

*   *   *

Opposing that interpretation of section 5–2–6 of the Unified Code of Corrections, the defendant argues that sentencing a GBMI offender to death would be inconsistent with the treatment alternatives prescribed for GBMI offenders in section 5–2–6 of the Unified Code of Corrections. The provisions concerning treatment do not pertain to defendants sentenced to death, however. Rather, they apply to persons sentenced to terms of imprisonment (see Ill.Rev.Stat.1983, ch. 38, pars. 1005–2–6(b), (c), (d)) and to those placed on probation or sentenced to a term of periodic imprisonment or a period of conditional discharge (see Ill.Rev.Stat.1983, ch. 38, par. 1005–2–6(e)). The statute thus does not mandate what is referred to in the dissent as the "meaningless" requirement of treatment for one awaiting execution. Having rejected the defendant's interpretation of section 5–2–6, we conclude that the statute does not preclude imposition of the death penalty on GBMI offenders.

* * *

The defendant also contends that the trial judge's stated reasons for imposing the death penalty in this case were inconsistent with his earlier finding of a factual basis for the defendant's GBMI plea. . . . The defendant contends that the trial judge's decision to accept the GBMI plea cannot be reconciled with his later statement, made at the sentencing hearing, that the defendant "may not have been under an extreme mental or emotional disturbance."

The defendant's argument assumes that mental illness, as that term is applied to GBMI offenders, is more serious than the mitigating circumstance of extreme mental or emotional disturbance, as that term is used in the death penalty statute. . . . We have already concluded that the legislature authorized imposition of the death penalty on GBMI offenders, and, consistent with that holding, we do not believe that a finding of mental illness necessarily establishes the mitigating circumstance of extreme mental or emotional disturbance. It is important to note here that the distinction between mental illness and the statutory mitigating circumstance of extreme mental or emotional disturbance does not mean that a GBMI plea or finding is irrelevant in a capital case. Because mitigating circumstances are not limited to those specifically enumerated in section 9–1(c) of the Criminal Code of 1961 (Ill.Rev.Stat.1983, ch. 38, par. 9–1(c)), evidence of a defendant's mental illness is admissible at a capital sentencing hearing regardless of the relationship between the GBMI provisions and the statutory mitigating circumstance of extreme mental or emotional disturbance. The trial judge's decision here to sentence the defendant to death was not contrary to the findings he made in accepting the defendant's GBMI plea. In accordance with the provisions of section 9–1(h) of the Criminal Code of 1961 (Ill.Rev.Stat.1983, ch. 38, par. 9–1(h)), the trial judge balanced the conflicting evidence and found that any mental or emotional disturbance of the defendant was not sufficient to preclude imposition of the death penalty.

* * *

JUSTICE SIMON, dissenting.

* * *

A sentence of death is completely inconsistent with the goals of the GBMI statutory provisions—providing treatment for the mentally ill as well as punishing them for the crimes they committed. During a reading of the GBMI bill on the Senate floor, the bill's co-sponsor, Senator Adeline J. Geo–Karis, emphasized this goal of treatment, stating that a "guilty but mentally ill defendant, for example, can be . . . sentenced exactly as a healthy defendant charged with the same crime, except that his sentence, either to probation, periodic imprisonment, or to the penitentiary, must include psychiatric and psychological treatment or counseling." The bill as enacted includes this requirement of treatment for the offender's mental illness. The statute also requires the Department of Corrections to make periodic inquiry and examination "concerning the nature, extent, continuance, and treatment of the defendant's mental illness" for those GBMI offenders who are imprisoned. The Department of Corrections is also to provide psychological, psychiatric and other counseling and treatment to the defendant and may transfer the inmate to the Department of Mental Health if necessary. This treatment requirement, however, would be meaningless for someone who is going to be put to death. "In view of the statutory treatment rights that underlie a GBMI verdict, to order death as a GBMI's treatment would not only be contrary to the legislature's objectives, but also would be morally reprehensible." Note, "Disposition of the Mentally Ill Offender in Illinois—'Guilty But Mentally Ill,'" 31 DePaul L.Rev. 869, 889–90 (1982).

*   *   *

[T]he majority [also] concludes that a finding of mental illness does not necessarily establish the mitigating circumstance of mental or emotional disturbance. On the contrary, a finding of mental illness is a recognition of the likelihood of a more serious disorder than the mental state of an extreme emotional disturbance.

Under Illinois law, a finding of mental illness is a recognition that the defendant's judgment at the time of the offense was seriously impaired, a mental state exceeded only by insanity, a complete defense. The legislature has provided for a special verdict form for GBMI defendants. Thus mental illness is unique among mitigating factors because it is the only one that can be incorporated into the judgment at trial. Finally, in order for a GBMI plea to be accepted, the defendant must be examined by a clinical psychologist or psychiatrist, the judge must examine the psychiatric or psychological report or reports and conduct a hearing on the issue of the defendant's mental health.

A finding of extreme mental or emotional disturbance requires none of the above procedures, indicating that the standard for this mitigating factor is much less stringent than that for mental illness. The failure to require a psychological or psychiatric examination to establish an extreme mental or emotional disturbance indicates that it can be established without a finding of mental illness, thus making it a much broader, less serious condition than mental illness. This is evidenced by cases where an extreme mental or emotional disturbance has been found without a finding that the defendant was mentally ill at the time of the offense. Moreover, a finding of extreme mental or emotional disturbance does not necessitate treatment for the offender, and there is no special verdict form for this type of disturbance.

The conclusion of the trial court and the majority that a finding of mental illness does not necessarily establish the mitigating factor of extreme mental or emotional disturbance is therefore clearly in error. By failing to recognize that mental illness is a more serious condition than extreme mental or emotional disturbance, the sentencing court did not give proper weight to the defendant's illness as a mitigating factor, and, a new sentencing hearing is required.

* * *

QUESTIONS AND COMMENTS

1.   *The GBMI verdict as a finding of diminished responsibility.* The court states that a person who is found guilty but mentally ill "is no less guilty than one who is guilty and not mentally ill." Clearly, as the court points out, the Illinois legislature did not want the verdict to be a finding of diminished responsibility that would reduce the degree of crime for which the defendant is convicted. But a GBMI verdict could still function as a determination of diminished responsibility that is implemented at *sentencing;* under this interpretation, the defendant found guilty but mentally ill would be convicted of the crime charged but would be entitled to greater mitigation at sentencing than someone found merely guilty of the same charge. Such an approach might seem particularly appealing in the capital sentencing context.[q] Does the majority in *Crews* hold that the evidence of mental illness associated with the GBMI verdict is irrelevant to the extreme mental or emotional distress issue in capital sentencing, relevant but not dispositive, or dispositive on that issue but not dispositive of the ultimate decision with respect to the death penalty? Of these three positions and the dissent's position that the verdict precludes imposition of the death penalty, which is the correct reading of legislative intent?

If one agrees with the majority's position, is there any point in having a distinct verdict indicating that the defendant is guilty of the offense and was also mentally ill (but not insane) during its commission? Or is it accurate to say, as Slovenko has asserted, that one might as well have a verdict called "guilty but flat feet"? Ralph Slovenko, *The Insanity Defense in the Wake of the Hinckley Trial*, 14 Rutgers L.J. 373, 393 (1983). Data from Georgia suggest

---

[q]   The role of mental abnormality in capital sentencing proceedings is discussed in greater detail in the next section, where the *Crews* case will be revisited.

that the GBMI verdict may actually be a prelude to *enhancement* of sentence. Steadman and his colleagues found that:

> GBMIs were more likely than [those who pleaded insanity and were found guilty] to go to prison or jail and to receive a life sentence. Further, those [GBMI] not receiving a life sentence were given longer sentences than their guilty counterparts. They were also confined for much longer periods of time than those found NGRI [and those found guilty].

Henry Steadman, et al., Before and After Hinckley: Evaluating Insanity Defense Reform 119 (1993). According to Steadman and his colleagues, no persons found GBMI in Georgia received the death penalty. Id. at 117. However, death sentences imposed on offenders found GBMI have been affirmed in Kentucky, South Carolina, and Indiana. See *Comm. v. Ryan*, 5 S.W.3d 113 (Ky. Sup. Ct. 1999); *State v. Wilson*, 413 S.E.2d 19 (S.C. 1992); *Harris v. State*, 499 N.E. 2d 723 (Ind. 1986).

2.   *The GBMI verdict and treatment.* Some have contended that, whatever the impact of the GBMI verdict in assessing the degree of culpability or punishment, it does afford better *conditions* of punishment. Mickenberg has argued that "although . . . GBMI does not reduce the degree of crime for which defendants are responsible, it does provide necessary and acceptable mitigation in the form of psychiatric assistance for the convicts while they serve their sentences." Ira Mickenberg, *A Pleasant Surprise: The Guilty But Mentally Ill Verdict Has Both Succeeded in Its Own Right and Successfully Preserved the Traditional Role of the Insanity Defense*, 55 Cinn.L.Rev. 943, 990 (1987). Isn't the holding in *Crews* inconsistent with this position?

Arguably, if the point of the GBMI scheme is to facilitate treatment for offenders with mental illness, it is both inefficient and unnecessary. A finding by a judge or jury that an offender was mentally ill *at the time of the offense* is not likely to be very useful in determining the offender's treatment needs (a fact which is recognized by provisions in most GBMI legislation—like Illinois'—requiring a post-conviction treatment assessment by mental health professionals). Moreover, adequate medical treatment—which includes psychiatric treatment—is constitutionally mandated under *Estelle v. Gamble*, 429 U.S. 97, 97 S.Ct. 285, 50 L.Ed.2d 251 (1976), every state makes provisions for prisoners with mental illness to be treated, and mental health programs are a requirement for prison accreditation by the American Correctional Association. American Correctional Association, Standards for Adult Correctional Institutions 108 (2003). In Illinois, for instance, well before passage of the state's guilty but mentally ill statute, the legislature required the Department of Corrections to ascertain whether *any* person committed to it needed psychiatric treatment, and authorized transfer of prisoners requiring such treatment to special facilities within the Department or to mental hospitals. Ill.—S.H.A. ch. 28, ¶ 1003–8–5. Research indicates that although GBMI legislation has focused attention on the paucity of treatment resources available to prisoners generally, it has not meant that those who are found guilty but mentally ill are more likely to receive treatment than those who are simply convicted and sentenced and are subsequently found to need treatment. Gary Smith & James Hall, *Evaluating Michigan's Guilty But Mentally Ill Verdict: An Empirical Study*, 16 Mich.J.Law Ref. 77, 104–106 (1982). Nor are most courts, whatever the original intent of the GBMI legislation, willing to redress this situation by according those found guilty but mentally ill special treatment status. See, e.g., *Neely v. Newton*, 149 F.3d 1074 (19th Cir. 1998) (Constitution not violated by statute preventing those found GBMI from being sentenced to a treatment facility); *People v. Marshall,* 114 Ill.App.3d 217, 70 Ill.Dec. 91, 102, 448 N.E.2d 969, 980 (1983); *People v. Sharif,* 87 Mich.App. 196, 200–01, 274 N.W.2d 17, 19–20 (1978). Is this stance wrong? If not, how does the verdict provide "mitigation," as that word is used by Mickenberg, that would not ordinarily be available without the verdict? See *Illinois v. Manning*, 883 N.E. 492 (Ill. Sup. Ct. 2008) (holding that a defense attorney's failure to advise the defendant of the GBMI option was not ineffective assistance of counsel since that plea would not have altered the sentencing range that could have been imposed and would not have ensured access to treatment that would have otherwise been unavailable).

3.   *The GBMI verdict as a device for easing the factfinder's burden.* Questions about its conceptual underpinnings aside, might the GBMI verdict be sanctioned on the ground that it makes the difficult choice about criminal responsibility easier? In her study of jury reaction to the insanity defense, Simon found:

> Many of the jurors felt constrained by the verdict limitations placed upon them by the court. They would like to have a way of easing the choice between acquitting the defendant on grounds of insanity and finding him guilty. The former designation goes further than they want to go in distinguishing the defendant from the ordinary criminal, and the latter allows for no distinction. In many instances, the jury would have liked to declare the defendant guilty, but insane. That kind of verdict would permit the jurors to condemn the defendant's behavior . . . [and fulfill] their desire to commit the defendant to an institution that both punished and treated.

Rita Simon, The Jury and the Defense of Insanity 178 (1967).

Presumably, if the verdict were functioning in the way described by Simon, it would occasion a reduction in insanity acquittals. Certainly this was the hope of many who advocated adoption of the GBMI scheme. Yet a study of Michigan's GBMI reform found that the acquittal rate remained the same after passage of the statute. Smith & Hall, supra, at 100–102. In a mammoth multi-state study, the National Center for State Courts provided data from other states that suggested the same conclusion. See Christopher Slobogin, *The Guilty But Mentally Ill Verdict: An Idea Whose Time Should Not Have Come*, 53 Geo.Wash.L.Rev. 494, 507–08 (1985). There is some indication that the verdict reduced the acquittal rate marginally in one or two states. In particular, in Georgia a significant decrease in the success rate of insanity pleas for violent crime occurred after introduction of the GBMI verdict in 1982. But since Georgia law also halted automatic commitment of insanity acquittees at about the same time, the success rate may have been affected by a fear that acquittees would be let loose sooner. Steadman, et. al., supra, at 108–11.

To what extent does any reduction in the insanity acquittal rate caused by the verdict result from "improper" conviction of the insane, rather than prevention of "inappropriate" insanity acquittals? Although such things are obviously difficult to measure, it appears that most persons found guilty but mentally ill are more likely to have characteristics normally associated with guilt, rather than with insanity. Smith & Hall, supra, at 95–100; Criss & Racine, *Impact of Change in Legal Standard for Those Adjudicated Not Guilty By Reason of Insanity*, 8 Bull.Am.Acad. Psychiat. & L. 261 (1980). But see, *People v. Murphy,* 416 Mich. 453, 331 N.W.2d 152 (1982), in which the Michigan Supreme Court struck down a verdict of guilty but mentally ill and directed an insanity acquittal, noting that even the prosecution's expert agreed that the defendant was out of touch with reality and unable to control his behavior or appreciate the wrongfulness of his acts at the time of the offense. See also, *Michigan v. Fultz,* 111 Mich.App. 587, 314 N.W.2d 702 (1981). In one particularly interesting case, a defendant was found insane on murder with malice charges but found guilty but mentally ill of felony murder for the same crime because, despite his mental illness, he had realized that when he purchased the gun he used in the killing he was a convicted felon, and thus was committing a felony at the time of the killing. *Shepherd v. Georgia*, 626 S.E.2d 96 (Ga. 2006). Does *Shepherd* make sense?

> A sophisticated study of the GBMI verdict reported in 1991 found that:
>
> the field and laboratory studies offer substantial evidence that GBMI . . . does not make juries' decisions easier; it does not decrease their attention to extraneous issues (indeed, it serves as a distractor); . . . it does offer a compromise verdict that permits avoidance of hard questions of criminal responsibility. . . . In view of the fact that juries in the GBMI conditions in our studies still focused most of their attention on relevant variables, though, the question of whether the confusion experienced by such juries is sufficient on average to constitute a violation of defendants' rights to due process, a fair trial, and a jury trial remains an open question of law.

Gary Melton, et. al., *The Effects of the Addition of a GBMI Verdict*, National Institute of Mental Health, Grant No. RO1MH39243, p. 28 (1991).

III. SENTENCING

Once convicted, an offender is subjected to the sentencing process. Evidence of mental disorder could have a significantly greater impact here than at trial, for at least two reasons. First, many of the concerns that underlie proposals to restrict the role of mental disability in adjudicating guilt—i.e., the antipathy toward broad psychiatric defenses, the threat to public safety if acquittal occurs, the specter of confusing battles of the experts—are likely to lessen appreciably once the accused is convicted and decisionmaking takes place in the relatively informal sentencing atmosphere. Indeed, as previous material has suggested, one frequently suggested alternative to considering mental abnormality at trial is to shift most or all psychiatric inquiries to the sentencing stage, a practice that now occurs in other countries, including Great Britain. A second reason mental disorder is likely to play a greater role at sentencing was noted in the introduction to this chapter: once the question shifts from identifying who should be punished to determining what kind of punishment should be imposed, attention is more likely to focus on concerns connected with individual prevention, such as dangerousness, reducing recidivism, and rehabilitative potential. Addressing these issues opens up the inquiry beyond the backward-looking culpability assessments required at trial and toward probabilistic judgments about the future behavior of individuals with mental disorder.

This section will look at the role evidence of mental disability plays in two different sentencing contexts: capital sentencing and special track sentencing, in particular sentencing of those identified as "mentally disordered sex offenders." These two settings raise most starkly the tensions created by consideration of mental disability at the sentencing phase.

A. CAPITAL SENTENCING

NOTE ON SUPREME COURT CASES

Because "death is different," the constitutionality of the death penalty and the procedures for imposing it have been subjected to intense judicial scrutiny, primarily under the Eighth Amendment's ban on cruel and unusual punishment and the Fourteenth Amendment's due process clause. As a result, sentencing criteria in death penalty cases are far more developed than in other cases; most pertinent to our purposes, death penalty litigation has provided the most explicit consideration of the relationship between mental disability and criminal punishment. There follows a brief summary of the Supreme Court's pronouncements concerning the death penalty and the state statutes which attempt to implement those decisions, focusing in particular on material that bears on this relationship.

In 1972, the Supreme Court decided *Furman v. Georgia,* 408 U.S. 238, 92 S.Ct. 2726, 33 L.Ed.2d 346 (1972), which overturned the death sentences in four cases, by a vote of 5–4. In addition to a brief per curiam opinion announcing the court's decision, each of the nine justices wrote an opinion. Although there was no clear majority rationale, *Furman* was widely understood, under either an Eighth Amendment or due process rationale, to prohibit death penalty statutes that left the sentencing decision to the unguided discretion of the jury. For instance, in voting to overturn the death sentences, Justice Douglas spoke of the discriminatory impact of the death penalty on poor, black defendants. Justice Stewart asserted that the death penalty was "wantonly and freakishly imposed" and that death sentences were "cruel and unusual in the same way that being struck by lightning is cruel and unusual." Justice White believed that there was "no meaningful basis for distinguishing the few cases in which [the death penalty] is imposed from the many cases in which it is not." In addition to these three justices, two justices, Brennan and Marshall, concluded that the death penalty is unconstitutional under all circumstances.

Thirty-five states rewrote their statutes in response to *Furman.* Roughly half of these states removed jury discretion by making the death penalty mandatory in certain situations. The other half left the jury considerable decisionmaking latitude but attempted to set clearer guidelines as to how to exercise the sentencing power, usually by instructing the jury to weigh specified aggravating and mitigating circumstances. In five cases decided together in 1976, the Court found the former type of statute unconstitutional, but upheld the second type of statute.

One of the statutes that withstood constitutional scrutiny was Georgia's. See *Gregg v. Georgia,* 428 U.S. 153, 96 S.Ct. 2909, 49 L.Ed.2d 859 (1976). A later decision of the Court, *Zant v. Stephens,* 462 U.S. 862, 103 S.Ct. 2733, 77 L.Ed.2d 235 (1983), summarized why the statute was upheld:

> [Our] approval of Georgia's capital sentencing procedure in [*Gregg*] rested primarily on two features of the scheme: that the jury was required to find at least one valid statutory aggravating circumstance and to identify it in writing, and that the state supreme court reviewed the record of every death penalty proceeding to determine whether the sentence was arbitrary or disproportionate. These elements, the opinion concluded, adequately protected against the wanton and freakish imposition of the death penalty. This conclusion rested . . . on the fundamental requirement that . . . an aggravating circumstance must genuinely narrow the class of persons eligible for the death penalty and must reasonably justify the imposition of a more severe sentence on the defendant compared to others found guilty of murder.

North Carolina's mandatory execution statute, on the other hand, was found unconstitutional. See *Woodson v. North Carolina*, 428 U.S. 280, 96 S.Ct. 2978, 49 L.Ed.2d 944 (1976). Although the Court gave several reasons for this holding, the following language has assumed the most significance in later cases:

> A third constitutional shortcoming of the North Carolina statute is its failure to allow the particularized consideration of relevant

aspects of the character and record of each convicted defendant before the imposition upon him of a sentence of death. . . . A process that accords no significance to relevant facets of the character and record of the individual offender or the circumstances of the particular offense excludes from consideration in fixing the ultimate punishment of death the possibility of compassionate or mitigating factors stemming from the diverse frailties of humankind. . . .

. . . Consideration of both offender and the offense in order to arrive at a just and appropriate sentence has been viewed as a progressive and humanizing development. While the prevailing practice of individualizing sentencing determinations generally reflects simply enlightened policy rather than a constitutional imperative, we believe that in capital cases the fundamental respect for humanity underlying the eighth amendment requires consideration of the character and record of the individual offender and the circumstances of the particular offense as a constitutionally indispensable part of the process of inflicting the penalty of death.

This conclusion rests squarely on the predicate that the penalty of death is qualitatively different from a sentence of imprisonment, however long. Death, in its finality, differs more from life imprisonment than a 100–year prison term differs from one of only a year or two. Because of that qualitative difference, there is a corresponding difference in the need for reliability in the determination that death is the appropriate punishment in a specific case.

The central message of the 1976 cases appeared to be that while the jury may not be given unlimited discretion, neither may it be prevented from considering information relevant to the offender's characteristics. In two subsequent cases, the Supreme Court reinforced the latter notion. In *Lockett v. Ohio*, 438 U.S. 586, 98 S.Ct. 2954, 57 L.Ed.2d 973 (1978), seven members of the Court struck down a death penalty statute requiring the judge to impose the death penalty unless the defendant proved one of three mitigating circumstances—that the victim had induced or facilitated the offense; that the defendant was "under duress, coercion or strong provocation"; or that the offense was "primarily the product of psychosis or mental deficiency." In an opinion joined by four justices,[r] the Court stated that this statute improperly prevented individualization of the sentencing decision: "The eighth and 14th amendments require that the sentencer, in all but the rarest kind of capital case, not be precluded

---

[r]   Two other members of the Court, Justices Blackmun and White, concurred in the result because the defendant, who had waited in the "getaway car" during the commission of the robbery murder, may not have been sufficiently involved in the crime. Justice Marshall also joined the result, adhering to his opinion in *Furman* that the death penalty is unconstitutional under all circumstances. Justice Brennan, who had indicated in several opinions that he shared this view, did not participate. Only Justice Rehnquist dissented.

from considering, *as a mitigating factor,* any aspect of a defendant's character or record and any of the circumstances of the offense that the defendant proffers as a basis for a sentence less than death." (emphasis in original). In *Eddings v. Oklahoma,* 455 U.S. 104, 102 S.Ct. 869, 71 L.Ed.2d 1 (1982), the Court reversed, 5–4, the death sentence of a 16 year-old because the sentencing judge had failed to consider evidence of the defendant's "turbulent family history, of beatings by a harsh father and of severe emotional disturbance." Again, the Court made clear that relevant mitigating evidence should not be excluded, although the factfinder has discretion to give it little or no weight.

As a result of these developments, modern death penalty schemes provide that before a person convicted of capital murder[s] can be sentenced to death the factfinder must find at least one aggravating circumstance and find further that any mitigating circumstances that exist do not make imposition of the death penalty inappropriate. As the Court stated in *Zant,* to be sufficiently "aggravating" to justify the death penalty, a circumstance "must genuinely narrow the class of persons eligible for the death penalty and must reasonably justify the imposition of a more severe sentence on the defendant compared to others found guilty of murder." Typical aggravating factors found in state statutes (many of them copied from the Model Penal Code's death penalty provisions) include murders that are committed: (1) against certain types of persons (e.g., a police officer, a correctional officer, or a judge); (2) while the defendant is under sentence of imprisonment; (3) for "pecuniary gain"; (4) in the course of certain felonies, such as rape, robbery, arson and kidnapping; (5) for the purpose of avoiding arrest; and (6) in a particularly heinous, cruel or vile manner. Other aggravating circumstances focus on the defendant rather than the circumstances of the murder, e.g., murder committed by (7) someone who has been convicted of prior violent felonies; and (8) someone considered likely to commit violent acts in the future (the "dangerousness" criterion). In most states, the listed factors are exclusive. In some, so long as a statutory predicate for the death penalty has been established, consideration of non-statutory aggravating factors is permissible.

In addition to listing aggravating circumstances, which is apparently required under the Court's cases, most state statutes also list mitigating factors that must be considered by the jury. Again borrowing from the Model Penal Code, most states recognize mitigation for any person who (1) was only a "minor" participant in the murder; or (2) has no significant prior criminal history. A good number of state statutes also copy verbatim

---

[s] The Court's cases appear to hold that the death penalty may be imposed only on defendants who "intended that a killing take place or that lethal force be used." *Kennedy v. Louisiana,* 554 U.S. 407, 128 S.Ct. 2641, 171 L.Ed.2d 525 (2008) (death sentence not permissible for rape of a child); see also *Enmund v. Florida,* 458 U.S. 782, 102 S.Ct. 3368, 73 L.Ed.2d 1140 (1982); *Coker v. Georgia,* 433 U.S. 584, 97 S.Ct. 2861, 53 L.Ed.2d 982 (1977).

or with slight variation three other mitigation provisions found in the Model Penal Code: (3) "the defendant acted under duress or under the domination of another person;" (4) "the murder was committed while the defendant was under the influence of extreme mental or emotional disturbance;" and (5) "at the time of the murder, the capacity of the defendant to appreciate the criminality [wrongfulness] of his conduct or to conform his conduct to the requirements of the law was impaired as a result of mental disease or defect."[t] Model Penal Code § 210.6(4)(b), (f), (g). A few states also include as mitigating factors: (6) that the defendant believed the murder to be morally justified or committed under extenuating circumstances; and (7) that the defendant is not dangerous. Note that, after *Lockett,* statutory mitigating factors are not to be considered exclusive. They are meant to focus the factfinder's attention on those circumstances most likely to have mitigating impact.

A final question is how aggravating and mitigating circumstances are to be balanced against one another. Under the Model Penal Code's provisions, the factfinder may consider a death sentence only if it finds that "there are no mitigating circumstances sufficiently substantial to call for leniency." Model Penal Code § 210.6(2). Before it abolished the death penalty entirely, Connecticut made the death penalty even harder to obtain, by prohibiting its imposition if *any* statutory mitigating criterion is found. On the other hand, most state statutes are similar to Alabama's law, which provides that "the trial court shall determine whether the aggravating circumstances it finds to exist outweigh the mitigating circumstances it finds to exist." Ala.Code 1975, § 13A–5–47(e).

QUESTIONS AND COMMENTS

1. *Mental disability and aggravating circumstances.* The dangerousness criterion, an explicit aggravating factor only in a handful of state statutes but considered a legally relevant consideration in most death penalty states,[u] is the aggravating circumstance most likely to occasion expert testimony on the impact of mental disorder. In *Barefoot v. Estelle,* reprinted at p. 542, the Supreme Court specifically upheld the admissibility of psychiatric testimony on "future dangerousness." The predicate for *Barefoot* was *Jurek v. Texas,* 428 U.S. 262, 96 S.Ct. 2950, 49 L.Ed.2d 929 (1976), one of the five 1976 death penalty cases. There, the Supreme Court upheld a Texas statute that included as an aggravating factor proof that "there is a probability that the defendant would commit criminal acts of

---

[t]   Note that, since *Atkins v. Virginia,* reprinted in Part III.A of this chapter, people with mental retardation are exempt from the death penalty.

[u]   At least six states explicitly make dangerousness an aggravating circumstance (Idaho, Oklahoma, South Carolina, Texas, Virginia, and Washington) and 28 of the remaining death penalty states make it a nonstatutory aggravator (which means that once the prosecutor proves a statutory aggravator the jury may consider dangerousness when determining whether to sentence the offender to death). Mitzi Dorland & Daniel Krauss, *The Danger of Dangerousness in Capital Sentencing: Exacerbating the Problem of Arbitrary and Capricious Decision Making,* 29 L. & Psychol. Rev. 63, 64 nn.5, 12 (2005).

violence that would constitute a continuing threat to society." To the petitioner's argument that it is impossible to predict future behavior and that the statutory language is so vague as to be meaningless, the Court responded:

> It is, of course, not easy to predict future behavior. The fact that such a determination is difficult, however, does not mean that it cannot be made. Indeed, prediction of future criminal conduct is an essential element in many of the decisions rendered throughout our criminal justice system. The decision whether to admit a defendant to bail, for instance, must often turn on a judge's prediction of the defendant's future conduct. And any sentencing authority must predict a convicted person's probable future conduct when it engages in the process of determining what punishment to impose. For those sentenced to prison, these same predictions must be made by parole authorities. The task that a Texas jury must perform in answering the statutory question in issue is thus basically no different from the task performed countless times each day throughout the American system of criminal justice. What is essential is that the jury have before it all possible relevant information about the individual defendant whose fate it must determine. Texas law clearly assures that all such evidence will be adduced.

Although only three justices joined this language, the other opinions in *Jurek* made it clear that, as *Barefoot* later put it, "seven Justices rejected the claim that it was impossible to predict future behavior and that dangerousness was therefore an invalid consideration in imposing the death penalty."

Strong evidence exists from non-death-penalty contexts that if mental health professionals or laypersons try to make yes-or-no predictions about whether someone will cause harm to others, those predictions are wrong as often as they are right.[v] Does dangerousness—defined as a "probability" that the defendant will commit "criminal acts of violence"—"genuinely narrow the class of persons eligible for the death penalty" as reliably as do other aggravating circumstances? Assuming so, is there any other reason "proof" of dangerousness should be considered insufficient, by itself, to impose the death sentence on a person convicted of capital murder? In answering this question, is it relevant that, in all but one death penalty state, life without parole is the only alternative to a death sentence, or that the assault rate by those on death row and in the life-without-parole population is considerably lower than it is in the general prison population? See Mark Cunningham, *Dangerousness and Death: A Nexus in Search of Science and Reason*, American Psychologist 828, 832–33 (Nov. 2006).

2. *Mental disability and mitigating circumstances.* Of the mitigating circumstances typically listed in state death penalty statutes, four focus on the defendant's mental state at the time of the offense. Using the Model Penal Code language, they are: (a) whether the defendant was "under duress

---

[v]   See pp. 552–557.

or under the domination of another person;" (b) whether the defendant was suffering from "extreme mental or emotional disturbance"; (c) whether "the capacity of the defendant to appreciate the criminality [wrongfulness] of his conduct or to conform his conduct to the requirements of law was impaired as a result of mental disease or defect or intoxication"; and (d) whether "the murder was committed under circumstances which the defendant believed to provide a moral justification or extenuation for his conduct." All of these mitigating criteria have obvious analogues to defenses that are usually available at trial. The first is similar to the duress defense,[w] the second to the provocation defense, the third to the insanity defense, and the fourth to the self-defense doctrine. How does the language used to define the mitigating factors differ from the usual formulations of the defenses? Some state statutes use even broader language. For instance, with respect to the second mental state factor, some states omit the word "extreme." With respect to the third factor, some states omit the words "mental disease or defect."

Permissible Limitations. The essential preliminary question in determining the proper mitigating circumstances is whether courts should place *any* limitation on the type of mental state evidence that can be presented in mitigation at a death penalty proceeding. Arguably, given the gravity of the penalty, the usual concerns about wide-open consideration of a defendant's psychology should be suspended. In *Lockett,* the Court stated that restricting mitigating claims is impermissible because it "creates the risk that the death penalty will be imposed in spite of factors which may call for a less severe penalty." However, in a footnote, it also cautioned that "nothing in this opinion limits the traditional authority of a court to exclude, as irrelevant, evidence not bearing on the defendant's character, prior record, or the circumstances of his offense." Does this footnote limit mental state evidence in any way?

Consider *North Carolina v. Boyd,* 311 N.C. 408, 319 S.E.2d 189 (1984), cert. denied, 471 U.S. 1030, 105 S.Ct. 2052, 85 L.Ed.2d 324 (1985). In that case, Boyd was convicted of murdering a former girlfriend who had recently left him. At his sentencing hearing, he presented the following evidence: (1) his father had been an alcoholic who had abandoned his family when Boyd was young; (2) his grandfather—whom he had come to view as a father—had then died; (3) he had a history of losing jobs and repeated imprisonment; and (4) his life since adolescence had been characterized by drug and alcohol abuse. He also proffered testimony by a sociologist to the effect that his crime and life history conformed to a common pattern that distinguishes those who kill intimates from those who kill others. In particular, according to the sociologist, those who, like Boyd, suffer repeated deep personal losses often develop strong feelings of self-destructiveness that may cause them to kill a loved one as a way of destroying part of themselves. Thus, the sociologist testified, the defendant's crime could be seen "primarily as a depression-caused self-destructive act, closely related to the impulse of suicide, resulting

---

[w] Note that although the "duress" factor appears to be identical to the duress defense, it provides meaningful mitigation because the duress defense is usually unavailable in homicide cases.

from a life history of an inordinate number of losses beginning with the abandonment by the defendant's father and the death of his grandfather and culminating with the threatened loss of [the victim]." The expert also testified that Boyd told him during an interview that he so feared the end of his relationship with the girlfriend that he had contemplated suicide shortly before the murder. The defense attorney explained that the testimony was designed to "link together all of the defendant's mitigating evidence into a unified whole which explained the apparent contradiction of killing the person the defendant loved the most." The trial court excluded the sociologist's testimony. In a somewhat ambiguous opinion, the North Carolina Supreme Court upheld this ruling, either on the ground that the testimony was irrelevant or that it was relevant but was of so little weight that its exclusion was not a proper ground for vacating the death sentence. The United States Supreme Court denied certiorari, over a vigorous dissent by Justice Marshall, which Justice Brennan joined. Should the expert testimony have been admitted? Should it make a difference that the North Carolina statute did not include as an aggravating factor the dangerousness criterion?

Applying the Statutory Factors. A separate question is whether particular evidence, assuming it is admissible, meets the relevant statutory mitigating criteria. Because these criteria are not exclusive, one might conclude that the answer to this question doesn't matter; even if a court or jury determines that the defendant's evidence does not meet a particular criterion, the defendant can still argue it has mitigating value. But if a jurisdiction chose to follow the approach Connecticut took when it had the death penalty, which provide that proof of any statutory mitigating factor precluded a death sentence, the definition of a particular factor can assume extreme importance. Even in those states where the aggravating and mitigating circumstances are balanced against one another, the definition may be significant, since proof of statutory mitigating factors is likely to carry more weight than proof of nonstatutory factors.

Many courts have demonstrated a reluctance to define the statutory factors broadly. For instance, in *People v. Crews,* reprinted at p. 726, the Illinois Supreme Court refused to equate a guilty but mentally ill ruling with extreme mental or emotional distress; more significantly, it was unwilling to overturn the trial judge's ruling in the case that the defendant's evidence of mental illness, which was not insignificant, did not meet this or any other statutory factor. Was it right? Assuming so, should it have ruled differently had the Illinois statutory language, as is true with other statutes, not included the word "extreme"?

Consider also the case of *Johnson v. State,* 292 Md. 405, 439 A.2d 542 (1982), where the defendant was convicted of capital murder. The following testimony, introduced to bolster the argument that the killing was not committed willfully and with premeditation, was excluded at trial on the ground that expert testimony on mental state is relevant only on insanity (which the defendant conceded could not be proven). At the capital sentencing proceeding, should the testimony nonetheless be deemed sufficient to support a finding of extreme mental or emotional stress or impairment in ability to appreciate the wrongfulness of the act? To which MPC statutory mitigator, if any, is the evidence relevant?

> The patient [sic] is a 19–year old youth of medium height and build who presented a neat and clean appearance. He was extremely sullen and hostile, and his cooperation for interview and test was poor. In view of this test results have to be considered tentative.

TEST RESULTS:

> *On the WAIS he earned a Verbal I.Q. of 78, a Performance I.Q. of 68, and a Full Scale I.Q. of 72 which places him within the borderline range of intelligence.* His potential, as gauged by his abstract reasoning, is at least within the low average range. Intellectual efficiency is decreased by a combination of educational deprivation and negativism. There are some signs which point in the direction of bizarre thinking and a tenuous hold on reality. E.G. on Card 22 of the Holtzman he saw "the devil," and on Card 27 he saw "God over water." But these should be interpreted with caution, as they may also be attempts to embarrass and express contempt for the examiner by giving nonsensical answers.

> The personality picture is that of an extremely deprived individual who does not expect any affection and emotional support from either parental figure. He perceives the mother figure as domineering, but distant and devoid of warmth and understanding and the father figure as hostile and threatening. Yet he has conjured up the image of an idealized, all wise and all loving father surrogate with whom he will compare any male elder. Since such a person is bound to fall short of his ideal he is apt to equate this person with the real father figure whom he sees in negative terms and reject him. As a result he not only has trouble with authority figures, but perceives the world about him as a cold inhospitable place where he does not have a chance.

CONCLUSION:

> *The patient [sic] functions at the borderline intellectual level (I.Q. 72), but his potential is at least within the low average range. He can be described as a severely deprived individual with a hostile and negative orientation and an* [sic.] *severe authority problem.* Contact with reality is difficult to evaluate on account of his poor productivity resulting from extreme negativism.

3. *Mental disability as both an aggravating and a mitigating circumstance.* As the testimony in the *Johnson* case suggests, in many cases evidence of mental disability is relevant both to aggravating and mitigating circumstances. In *Miller v. State,* 373 So.2d 882 (Fla.1979), the facts adduced at trial were as follows. Miller was released from county jail on the morning of the murder, where he had been incarcerated for possession of a concealed weapon (a fishing knife). He wandered around Ft. Myers and bought a fishing knife similar to the one which had been taken from him by the police. An

employee in the store where the weapon was purchased stated that Miller was "wild looking" and was mumbling angrily to himself. This employee called the police and followed Miller to two nearby bars. Finally the employee saw Miller leaving in a taxi cab with a woman driver and contacted the taxi company to inform it of the apparent danger. The woman taxi driver was found murdered a short while later, having been stabbed nine times. Miller had apparently raped her when she was dead or dying. When Miller was arrested at the bus station that evening, his pants were still covered with blood. Blood-soaked money, some of which had been taken from the taxi driver, was found in his pockets.

After Miller was charged with this crime, he was found incompetent to stand trial and was committed to a state mental hospital. Two and a half years later, after being heavily medicated, he was found to be competent to stand trial and convicted of capital murder. At the sentencing hearing psychiatric testimony suggested that Miller was suffering from paranoid schizophrenia and hallucinations. He had been committed to mental hospitals on several previous occasions, and had a long history of drug abuse. Testimony also indicated that Miller had a severe hatred of his mother, and had planned to kill her after his release from the Lee County Jail, just prior to this murder. Apparently this hatred arose in part from the fact that his mother, who had been married four times, had refused any contact with her son for several years. On several previous occasions, Miller suffered hallucinations in which he saw his mother in other persons, in a "yellow haze." On at least one previous occasion, he had senselessly assaulted another woman during such hallucinations. Miller testified that at the time of the capital murder, he saw his mother's face on the 56 year-old woman taxi driver, in a "yellow haze," and proceeded to stab her to death.

The jury recommended a death sentence. In Florida, as in most states, the trial judge must decide if this penalty is appropriate. The relevant portions of the Florida Supreme Court's description of the judge's deliberations and its analysis of the judge's conclusions follows:

> The trial court found that the evidence introduced at the sentencing hearing proved beyond a reasonable doubt three statutory aggravating circumstances: (1) the defendant was previously convicted of a felony involving the threat of violence to another person; (2) the murder was committed while the defendant was engaged in the commission of or attempt to commit robbery, and was thus committed for pecuniary gain; and (3) the murder was especially heinous, atrocious, and cruel.

> In addition, the trial court found several mitigating circumstances to exist: (1) the murder was committed while the defendant was under the influence of extreme mental disturbance; (2) the defendant acted under mental duress; (3) due to mental sickness, the defendant's capacity and ability to conform his conduct to the requirements of law were substantially impaired. In addition, the trial court specifically found from the evidence presented at the sentencing hearing that the

defendant was suffering from mental illness at the time the murder was committed.

Based upon these factual findings, the trial judge explained the reasoning which led him to conclude that the death penalty was appropriate:

> [I]n weighing the aggravating and mitigating factors, I have to conclude that the aggravating factors are such that the reality of Florida law wherein life imprisonment is not, in fact, life imprisonment; and, in fact, the defendant would be subject to be released into society—In other words, it doesn't mean life imprisonment and there is a substantial chance he could be released into society. And the testimony overwhelmingly establishes that the mental sickness or illness that he suffers from is such that he will never recover from it, it will only be repressed by the use of drugs.

> Thus, in light of that fact, in light of the aggravating factors here, I have to conclude the only certain punishment and the only assurance society can receive that this man never again commits to another human being what he did to that lady, is that the ultimate sentence of death is imposed.

> If the law in Florida were such that life imprisonment meant the ability to live in a prison environment for the entire, remainder of one's life, I would have the conclusion that there would be sufficient mitigating factors to offset the aggravating factors, and allow him to live in prison.

> But since that is not the case, the reality is that life imprisonment does not mean that, I conclude in this case that the aggravating factors heavily outweigh the mitigating factors.

> The heinousness of the crime, the way in which it was committed speaks for itself. Now I, as the Judge, must therefore impose the sentence of death and do so.

It is clear from the trial judge's sentencing order that he considered as an aggravating factor the defendant's allegedly incurable and dangerous mental illness. The use of this nonstatutory aggravating factor as a controlling circumstance tipping the balance in favor of the death penalty was improper. The aggravating circumstances specified in the statute are exclusive, and no others may be used for that purpose. This court [has] stated: "We must guard against any unauthorized aggravating factor going into the equation which might tip the scales of the weighing process in favor of death."

Strict application of the sentencing statute is necessary because the sentencing authority's discretion must be "guided and channeled" by requiring an examination of specific factors that argue in favor of or against imposition of the death penalty, thus eliminating total arbitrariness and capriciousness in its imposition. The trial judge's use of the defendant's mental illness, and his resulting propensity to commit violent acts, as an aggravating factor favoring the imposition of the death penalty appears contrary to the legislative intent as set forth in the statute. The legislature has not authorized consideration of the probability of recurring violent acts by the defendant if he is released on parole in the distant future. To the contrary, a large number of the statutory mitigating factors reflect a legislative determination to mitigate the death penalty in favor of a life sentence for those persons whose responsibility for their violent actions has been substantially diminished as a result of a mental illness, uncontrolled emotional state of mind, or drug abuse.

If dangerousness *had* been an aggravating circumstance under the Florida death penalty scheme (or if Florida were one of the states in which non-statutory aggravating factors may be considered once at least one statutory factor is proven), would the trial judge's ruling have been appropriate? Consider another Florida case, *Huckaby v. State,* 343 So.2d 29 (Fla.1977). There the Florida Supreme Court held that, although there was insufficient proof of insanity, the evidence showed Huckaby's mental illness motivated his murder of members of his family. The court reversed the trial court's imposition of the death penalty and held that the mitigating circumstances outweighed the aggravating circumstances. It explained:

> Our decision here is based on the causal relationship between the mitigating and aggravating circumstances. The heinous and atrocious manner in which this crime was perpetrated, and the harm to which the members of Huckaby's family were exposed, were the direct consequence of his mental illness, so far as the record reveals.

Note that one of the aggravating factors found by the trial judge in *Miller* was the heinousness of the crime. In light of *Huckaby,* was that finding permissible? How do you think the Florida Supreme Court would answer the question at the beginning of this paragraph?

More generally, in cases such as *Miller* and *Huckaby,* how should one balance the desire to accord mitigating impact to mental disability on the one hand and, on the other, the two goals of incapacitating the very dangerous (who may be mentally ill) and punishing severely those who commit particularly heinous crimes (perhaps because of mental illness)? Should the conclusion as to when the mitigating impact of mental disability "trumps" its aggravating aspects differ depending upon whether the aggravating aspect is dangerousness or vileness of the crime?

Of what relevance is research showing that unsuccessfully raising an insanity defense (a scenario that describes a significant portion of those defendants who use mental illness as a mitigator at the sentencing phase) correlates *positively* with a death sentence, ahead of such variables as prior record and commission of another crime at the time of the homicide? David Baldus et al., Equal Justice and the Death Penalty 644, 645 (1999). See also David Baldus et al., *Racial Discrimination and the Death Penalty in the Post–*

Furman Era: An Empirical and Legal Overview, with Recent Findings from Philadelphia, 83 Cornell L. Rev. 1638, 1688–89 (1998) (Table 6) (evidence of "extreme mental or emotional disturbance" correlates *positively* with death sentences); Julie Goetz & Gordon P. Waldo, *Why Jurors in Florida Vote for Life or Death: The Florida Component of the Capital Jury Project* 34 (presented at the conference on Life Over Death XV, Ft. Lauderdale, Fl., Sept. 27, 1996) ("[a] defendant's odds of receiving a death sentence increased significantly when the defendant had a history of childhood abuse, drug abuse and/or addiction, and mental and/or emotional disturbance"); Phoebe C. Ellsworth et al., *The Death–Qualified Jury and the Defense of Insanity*, 8 Law & Hum Behav. 81 (1984) (finding that mock jurors are much more hostile to defendants with schizophrenia than to defendants with mental retardation and other types of defendants). Are death sentences received under such circumstances a violation of due process of law? Note that in *Zant* the Supreme Court stated that "it would be constitutionally impermissible to give aggravating effect to . . . conduct that actually should militate in favor of a lesser penalty, such as perhaps the defendant's mental illness." 462 U.S. 862, 885, 462 U.S. 862, 103 S.Ct. 2733, 2747, 77 L.Ed.2d 235, 238 (1983). Do the findings in the above studies prove that mental illness is being given aggravating effect or can they be explained in some other way?

ATKINS V. VIRGINIA

Supreme Court of the United States, 2002.
536 U.S. 304, 122 S.Ct. 2242, 153 L.Ed.2d 335.

JUSTICE STEVENS delivered the opinion of the Court.

Those mentally retarded persons who meet the law's requirements for criminal responsibility should be tried and punished when they commit crimes. Because of their disabilities in areas of reasoning, judgment, and control of their impulses, however, they do not act with the level of moral culpability that characterizes the most serious adult criminal conduct. Moreover, their impairments can jeopardize the reliability and fairness of capital proceedings against mentally retarded defendants. Presumably for these reasons, in the 13 years since we decided *Penry v. Lynaugh*, 492 U.S. 302, 109 S.Ct. 2934, 106 L.Ed.2d 256 (1989), the American public, legislators, scholars, and judges have deliberated over the question whether the death penalty should ever be imposed on a mentally retarded criminal. The consensus reflected in those deliberations informs our answer to the question presented by this case: whether such executions are "cruel and unusual punishments" prohibited by the Eighth Amendment to the Federal Constitution.

I

Petitioner, Daryl Renard Atkins, was convicted of abduction, armed robbery, and capital murder, and sentenced to death. At approximately midnight on August 16, 1996, Atkins and William Jones, armed with a semiautomatic handgun, abducted Eric Nesbitt, robbed him of the money on his person, drove him to an automated teller machine in his pickup truck where cameras recorded their withdrawal of additional cash, then took him to an isolated location where he was shot eight times and killed. Jones and Atkins both testified in the guilt phase of Atkins' trial.[1] Each confirmed most of the details in the other's account of the incident, with the important exception that each stated that the other had actually shot and killed Nesbitt. Jones' testimony, which was both more coherent and credible than Atkins', was obviously credited by the jury and was sufficient to establish Atkins' guilt. At the penalty phase of the trial, the State introduced victim impact evidence and proved two aggravating circumstances: future dangerousness and "vileness of the offense." To prove future dangerousness, the State relied on Atkins' prior felony convictions as well as the testimony of four victims of earlier robberies and assaults. To prove the second aggravator, the prosecution relied upon the trial record, including pictures of the deceased's body and the autopsy report.

In the penalty phase, the defense relied on one witness, Dr. Evan Nelson, a forensic psychologist who had evaluated Atkins before trial and concluded that he was "mildly mentally retarded."[3] His conclusion was based on interviews with people who knew Atkins, a review of school and court records, and the administration of a standard intelligence test which indicated that Atkins had a full scale IQ of 59.[5]

---

[1] Initially, both Jones and Atkins were indicted for capital murder. The prosecution ultimately permitted Jones to plead guilty to first-degree murder in exchange for his testimony against Atkins. As a result of the plea, Jones became ineligible to receive the death penalty.

[3] The American Association of Mental Retardation (AAMR) defines mental retardation as follows: "Mental retardation refers to substantial limitations in present functioning. It is characterized by significantly subaverage intellectual functioning, existing concurrently with related limitations in two or more of the following applicable adaptive skill areas: communication, self-care, home living, social skills, community use, self-direction, health and safety, functional academics, leisure, and work. Mental retardation manifests before age 18." Mental Retardation: Definition, Classification, and Systems of Supports 5 (9th ed.1992). The American Psychiatric Association's definition is similar: "The essential feature of Mental Retardation is significantly subaverage general intellectual functioning (Criterion A) that is accompanied by significant limitations in adaptive functioning in at least two of the following skill areas: communication, self-care, home living, social/interpersonal skills, use of community resources, self-direction, functional academic skills, work, leisure, health, and safety (Criterion B). The onset must occur before age 18 years (Criterion C). Mental Retardation has many different etiologies and may be seen as a final common pathway of various pathological processes that affect the functioning of the central nervous system." American Psychiatric Association, Diagnostic and Statistical Manual of Mental Disorders 41 (4th ed.2000). "Mild" mental retardation is typically used to describe people with an IQ level of 50–55 to approximately 70.

[5] Dr. Nelson administered the Wechsler Adult Intelligence Scales test (WAIS–III), the standard instrument in the United States for assessing intellectual functioning. AAMR, Mental Retardation, supra. The WAIS–III is scored by adding together the number of points earned on different subtests, and using a mathematical formula to convert this raw score into a scaled score. The test measures an intelligence range from 45 to 155. The mean score of the test is 100, which means that a person receiving a score of 100 is considered to have an average level of cognitive functioning. A. Kaufman & E. Lichtenberger, Essentials of WAIS–III Assessment 60 (1999). It is estimated that between 1 and 3 percent of the population has an IQ between 70 and 75 or lower, which is typically considered the cutoff IQ score for the intellectual function prong of

The jury sentenced Atkins to death, but the Virginia Supreme Court ordered a second sentencing hearing because the trial court had used a misleading verdict form. At the resentencing, Dr. Nelson again testified. The State presented an expert rebuttal witness, Dr. Stanton Samenow, who expressed the opinion that Atkins was not mentally retarded, but rather was of "average intelligence, at least," and diagnosable as having antisocial personality disorder.[6] The jury again sentenced Atkins to death.

The Supreme Court of Virginia affirmed the imposition of the death penalty. . . . Because of the gravity of the concerns expressed by the dissenters [in that decision], and in light of the dramatic shift in the state legislative landscape that has occurred in the past 13 years, we granted certiorari to revisit the issue that we first addressed in the *Penry* case.

II

The Eighth Amendment succinctly prohibits "excessive" sanctions. It provides: "Excessive bail shall not be required, nor excessive fines imposed, nor cruel and unusual punishments inflicted." In *Weems v. United States*, 217 U.S. 349, 30 S.Ct. 544, 54 L.Ed. 793 (1910), we held that a punishment of 12 years jailed in irons at hard and painful labor for the crime of falsifying records was excessive. We explained "that it is a precept of justice that punishment for crime should be graduated and proportioned to the offense." We have repeatedly applied this proportionality precept in later cases interpreting the Eighth Amendment. Thus, even though "imprisonment for ninety days is not, in the abstract, a punishment which is either cruel or unusual," it may not be imposed as a penalty for "the 'status' of narcotic addiction," *Robinson v. California*, 370 U.S. 660, 666–667, 82 S.Ct. 1417, 8 L.Ed.2d 758 (1962), because such a sanction would be excessive. As Justice Stewart explained in Robinson: "Even one day in prison would be a cruel and unusual punishment for the 'crime' of having a common cold."

---

the mental retardation definition. 2 B. Sadock & V. Sadock, Comprehensive Textbook of Psychiatry 2952 (7th ed.2000).

At the sentencing phase, Dr. Nelson testified: "[Atkins'] full scale IQ is 59. Compared to the population at large, that means less than one percentile. . . . Mental retardation is a relatively rare thing. It's about one percent of the population." According to Dr. Nelson, Atkins' IQ score "would automatically qualify for Social Security disability income." Dr. Nelson also indicated that of the over 40 capital defendants that he had evaluated, Atkins was only the second individual who met the criteria for mental retardation. He testified that, in his opinion, Atkins' limited intellect had been a consistent feature throughout his life, and that his IQ score of 59 is not an "aberration, malingered result, or invalid test score."

6   Samenow's testimony was based upon two interviews with Atkins, a review of his school records, and interviews with correctional staff. He did not administer an intelligence test, but did ask Atkins questions taken from the 1972 version of the Wechsler Memory Scale. Dr. Samenow attributed Atkins' "academic performance [that was] by and large terrible" to the fact that he "is a person who chose to pay attention sometimes, not to pay attention others, and did poorly because he did not want to do what he was required to do."

A claim that punishment is excessive is judged not by the standards that prevailed in 1685 when Lord Jeffreys presided over the "Bloody Assizes" or when the Bill of Rights was adopted, but rather by those that currently prevail. As Chief Justice Warren explained in his opinion in *Trop v. Dulles*, 356 U.S. 86, 78 S.Ct. 590, 2 L.Ed.2d 630 (1958): "The basic concept underlying the Eighth Amendment is nothing less than the dignity of man. . . . The Amendment must draw its meaning from the evolving standards of decency that mark the progress of a maturing society." Proportionality review under those evolving standards should be informed by " 'objective factors to the maximum possible extent.' " We have pinpointed that the "clearest and most reliable objective evidence of contemporary values is the legislation enacted by the country's legislatures." *Penry*.

Relying in part on such legislative evidence, we have held that death is an impermissibly excessive punishment for the rape of an adult woman, *Coker v. Georgia*, 433 U.S. 584, 593–596, 97 S.Ct. 2861, 53 L.Ed.2d 982 (1977), or for a defendant who neither took life, attempted to take life, nor intended to take life, *Enmund v. Florida*, 458 U.S. 782, 789–793, 102 S.Ct. 3368, 73 L.Ed.2d 1140 (1982). In *Coker*, we focused primarily on the then-recent legislation that had been enacted in response to our decision 10 years earlier in *Furman v. Georgia*, 408 U.S. 238, 92 S.Ct. 2726, 33 L.Ed.2d 346 (1972) (per curiam), to support the conclusion that the "current judgment," though "not wholly unanimous," weighed very heavily on the side of rejecting capital punishment as a "suitable penalty for raping an adult woman." The "current legislative judgment" relevant to our decision in *Enmund* was less clear than in *Coker* but "nevertheless weigh[ed] on the side of rejecting capital punishment for the crime at issue."

We also acknowledged in *Coker* that the objective evidence, though of great importance, did not "wholly determine" the controversy, "for the Constitution contemplates that in the end our own judgment will be brought to bear on the question of the acceptability of the death penalty under the Eighth Amendment." For example, in *Enmund*, we concluded by expressing our own judgment about the issue: "For purposes of imposing the death penalty, Enmund's criminal culpability must be limited to his participation in the robbery, and his punishment must be tailored to his personal responsibility and moral guilt. Putting Enmund to death to avenge two killings that he did not commit and had no intention of committing or causing does not measurably contribute to the retributive end of ensuring that the criminal gets his just deserts. This is the judgment of most of the legislatures that have recently addressed the matter, and *we have no reason to disagree* with that judgment for purposes of construing and applying the Eighth Amendment." (emphasis added). Thus, in cases involving a consensus, our own judgment is "brought to bear," by asking whether there is reason to disagree with the judgment reached by the citizenry and its legislators. Guided by our approach in these cases, we shall first review the judgment of legislatures that have addressed the suitability of imposing the death penalty on the mentally retarded and then consider reasons for agreeing or disagreeing with their judgment.

III

The parties have not called our attention to any state legislative consideration of the suitability of imposing the death penalty on mentally retarded offenders prior to 1986. In that year, the public reaction to the execution of a mentally retarded murderer in Georgia apparently led to the enactment of the first state statute prohibiting such executions. In 1988, when Congress enacted legislation reinstating the federal death penalty, it expressly provided that a "sentence of death shall not be carried out upon a person who is mentally retarded." In 1989, Maryland enacted a similar prohibition. It was in that year that we decided *Penry*, and concluded that those two state enactments, "even when added to the 14 States that have rejected capital punishment completely, do not provide sufficient evidence at present of a national consensus."

Much has changed since then. Responding to the national attention received by the Bowden execution and our decision in *Penry*, state legislatures across the country began to address the issue. In 1990 Kentucky and Tennessee enacted statutes similar to those in Georgia and Maryland, as did New Mexico in 1991, and Arkansas, Colorado, Washington, Indiana, and Kansas in 1993 and 1994. In 1995, when New York reinstated its death penalty, it emulated the Federal Government by expressly exempting the mentally retarded. Nebraska followed suit in 1998. There appear to have been no similar enactments during the next two years, but in 2000 and 2001 six more States—South Dakota, Arizona, Connecticut, Florida, Missouri, and North Carolina—joined the procession. The Texas Legislature unanimously adopted a similar bill, and bills have passed at least one house in other States, including Virginia and Nevada.

. . . Given the well-known fact that anticrime legislation is far more popular than legislation providing protections for persons guilty of violent crime, the large number of States prohibiting the execution of mentally retarded persons (and the complete absence of States passing legislation reinstating the power to conduct such executions) provides powerful evidence that today our society views mentally retarded offenders as categorically less culpable than the average criminal. The evidence carries even greater force when it is noted that the legislatures that have addressed the issue have voted overwhelmingly in favor of the prohibition. Moreover, even in those States that allow the execution of mentally retarded offenders, the practice is uncommon. Some States, for example New Hampshire and New Jersey, continue to authorize executions, but none have been carried out in decades. Thus there is little need to pursue legislation barring the execution of the mentally retarded in those States. And it appears that even among those States that regularly execute offenders and that have no prohibition with regard to the mentally retarded, only five have executed offenders possessing a known IQ less than 70 since we decided *Penry*. The practice, therefore, has become truly unusual, and it is fair to say that a national consensus has developed against it.[21]

To the extent there is serious disagreement about the execution of mentally retarded offenders, it is in determining which offenders are in fact retarded. In this case, for instance, the Commonwealth of Virginia disputes that Atkins suffers from mental retardation. Not all people who claim to be mentally retarded will be so impaired as to fall within the range of mentally retarded offenders about whom there is a national consensus. As was our approach in *Ford v. Wainwright,* with regard to insanity, "we leave to the State[s] the task of developing appropriate ways to enforce the constitutional restriction upon its execution of sentences." 477 U.S. 399, 405, 416–417, 106 S.Ct. 2595, 91 L.Ed.2d 335 (1986).[22]

IV

This consensus unquestionably reflects widespread judgment about the relative culpability of mentally retarded offenders, and the relationship between mental retardation and the penological purposes served by the death penalty. Additionally, it suggests that some characteristics of mental retardation undermine the strength of the procedural protections that our capital jurisprudence steadfastly guards.

---

[21] Additional evidence makes it clear that this legislative judgment reflects a much broader social and professional consensus. For example, several organizations with germane expertise have adopted official positions opposing the imposition of the death penalty upon a mentally retarded offender. See Brief for American Psychological Association et al. as Amici Curiae; Brief for AAMR et al. as Amici Curiae. In addition, representatives of widely diverse religious communities in the United States, reflecting Christian, Jewish, Muslim, and Buddhist traditions, have filed an amicus curiae brief explaining that even though their views about the death penalty differ, they all "share a conviction that the execution of persons with mental retardation cannot be morally justified." See Brief for United States Catholic Conference et al. as Amici Curiae in *McCarver v. North Carolina*, O.T.2001, No. 00–8727, p. 2. Moreover, within the world community, the imposition of the death penalty for crimes committed by mentally retarded offenders is overwhelmingly disapproved. Brief for The European Union as Amicus Curiae in *McCarver v. North Carolina*, O.T.2001, No. 00–8727, p. 4. Finally, polling data shows a widespread consensus among Americans, even those who support the death penalty, that executing the mentally retarded is wrong. R. Bonner & S. Rimer, Executing the Mentally Retarded Even as Laws Begin to Shift, N.Y. Times, Aug. 7, 2000, p. A1; App. B to Brief for AAMR as Amicus Curiae in *McCarver v. North Carolina*, O.T.2001, No. 00–8727 (appending approximately 20 state and national polls on the issue). Although these factors are by no means dispositive, their consistency with the legislative evidence lends further support to our conclusion that there is a consensus among those who have addressed the issue. See *Thompson v. Oklahoma*, 487 U.S. 815, 830, 831, n. 31, 108 S.Ct. 2687, 101 L.Ed.2d 702 (1988) (considering the views of "respected professional organizations, by other nations that share our Anglo–American heritage, and by the leading members of the Western European community").

[22] The statutory definitions of mental retardation are not identical, but generally conform to the clinical definitions set forth in n. 3, supra.

As discussed above, clinical definitions of mental retardation require not only subaverage intellectual functioning, but also significant limitations in adaptive skills such as communication, self-care, and self-direction that became manifest before age 18. Mentally retarded persons frequently know the difference between right and wrong and are competent to stand trial. Because of their impairments, however, by definition they have diminished capacities to understand and process information, to communicate, to abstract from mistakes and learn from experience, to engage in logical reasoning, to control impulses, and to understand the reactions of others. There is no evidence that they are more likely to engage in criminal conduct than others, but there is abundant evidence that they often act on impulse rather than pursuant to a premeditated plan, and that in group settings they are followers rather than leaders. Their deficiencies do not warrant an exemption from criminal sanctions, but they do diminish their personal culpability.

In light of these deficiencies, our death penalty jurisprudence provides two reasons consistent with the legislative consensus that the mentally retarded should be categorically excluded from execution. First, there is a serious question as to whether either justification that we have recognized as a basis for the death penalty applies to mentally retarded offenders. *Gregg v. Georgia*, 428 U.S. 153, 183, 96 S.Ct. 2909, 49 L.Ed.2d 859 (1976), identified "retribution and deterrence of capital crimes by prospective offenders" as the social purposes served by the death penalty. Unless the imposition of the death penalty on a mentally retarded person "measurably contributes to one or both of these goals, it 'is nothing more than the purposeless and needless imposition of pain and suffering,' and hence an unconstitutional punishment." *Enmund*. With respect to retribution—the interest in seeing that the offender gets his "just deserts"—the severity of the appropriate punishment necessarily depends on the culpability of the offender. Since *Gregg*, our jurisprudence has consistently confined the imposition of the death penalty to a narrow category of the most serious crimes. For example, in *Godfrey v. Georgia*, 446 U.S. 420, 100 S.Ct. 1759, 64 L.Ed.2d 398 (1980), we set aside a death sentence because the petitioner's crimes did not reflect "a consciousness materially more 'depraved' than that of any person guilty of murder."

If the culpability of the average murderer is insufficient to justify the most extreme sanction available to the State, the lesser culpability of the mentally retarded offender surely does not merit that form of retribution. Thus, pursuant to our narrowing jurisprudence, which seeks to ensure that only the most deserving of execution are put to death, an exclusion for the mentally retarded is appropriate. With respect to deterrence—the interest in preventing capital crimes by prospective offenders—"it seems likely that 'capital punishment can serve as a deterrent only when murder is the result of premeditation and deliberation.'" *Enmund*. Exempting the mentally retarded from that punishment will not affect the "cold calculus that precedes the decision" of other potential murderers. *Gregg.* Indeed, that sort of calculus is at the opposite end of the spectrum from behavior of mentally retarded offenders. The theory of deterrence in capital sentencing is predicated upon the notion that the increased severity of the punishment will inhibit criminal actors from carrying out murderous conduct. Yet it is the same cognitive and behavioral impairments that make these defendants less morally culpable—for example, the diminished ability to understand and process information, to learn from experience, to engage in logical reasoning, or to control impulses—that also make it less likely that they can process the information of the possibility of execution as a penalty and, as a result, control their conduct based upon that information. Nor will exempting the mentally retarded from execution lessen the deterrent effect of the death penalty with respect to offenders who are not mentally retarded. Such individuals are unprotected by the exemption and will continue to face the threat of execution. Thus, executing the mentally retarded will not measurably further the goal of deterrence.

The reduced capacity of mentally retarded offenders provides a second justification for a categorical rule making such offenders ineligible for the death penalty. The risk "that the death penalty will be imposed in spite of factors which may call for a less severe penalty," *Lockett v. Ohio,* 438 U.S. 586, 605, 98 S.Ct. 2954, 57 L.Ed.2d 973 (1978), is enhanced, not only by the possibility of false confessions,[25] but also by the lesser ability of mentally retarded defendants to make a persuasive showing of mitigation in the face of prosecutorial evidence of one or more aggravating factors. Mentally retarded defendants may be less able to give meaningful assistance to their counsel and are typically poor witnesses, and their demeanor may create an unwarranted impression of lack of remorse for their crimes. As *Penry* demonstrated, moreover, reliance on mental retardation as a mitigating factor can be a two-edged sword that may enhance the likelihood that the aggravating factor of future dangerousness will be found by the jury. Mentally retarded defendants in the aggregate face a special risk of wrongful execution.

Our independent evaluation of the issue reveals no reason to disagree with the judgment of "the legislatures that have recently addressed the matter" and concluded that death is not a suitable punishment for a mentally retarded criminal. We are not persuaded that the execution of mentally retarded criminals will measurably advance the deterrent or the retributive purpose of the death penalty. Construing and applying the

---

[25] Despite the heavy burden that the prosecution must shoulder in capital cases, we cannot ignore the fact that in recent years a disturbing number of inmates on death row have been exonerated. As two recent high-profile cases demonstrate, these exonerations include mentally retarded persons who unwittingly confessed to crimes that they did not commit. See Baker, Death–Row Inmate Gets Clemency; Agreement Ends Days of Suspense, Washington Post, Jan. 15, 1994, p. A1; Holt & McRoberts, Porter Fully Savors First Taste of Freedom; Judge Releases Man Once Set for Execution, Chicago Tribune, Feb. 6, 1999, p. n1.

Eighth Amendment in the light of our "evolving standards of decency," we therefore conclude that such punishment is excessive and that the Constitution "places a substantive restriction on the State's power to take the life" of a mentally retarded offender. *Ford.* The judgment of the Virginia Supreme Court is reversed and the case is remanded for further proceedings not inconsistent with this opinion.

It is so ordered.

[The dissenting opinion of CHIEF JUSTICE REHNQUIST, with whom JUSTICE SCALIA and JUSTICE THOMAS join, is deleted.].

JUSTICE SCALIA, with whom THE CHIEF JUSTICE and JUSTICE THOMAS join, dissenting.

. . .

II

. . .

The Court makes no pretense that execution of the mildly mentally retarded would have been considered "cruel and unusual" in 1791. Only the severely or profoundly mentally retarded, commonly known as "idiots," enjoyed any special status under the law at that time. . . . The Court is left to argue, therefore, that execution of the mildly retarded is inconsistent with the "evolving standards of decency that mark the progress of a maturing society." Before today, our opinions consistently emphasized that Eighth Amendment judgments regarding the existence of social "standards" "should be informed by objective factors to the maximum possible extent" and "should not be, or appear to be, merely the subjective views of individual Justices." "First" among these objective factors are the "statutes passed by society's elected representatives," *Stanford v. Kentucky;* because it "will rarely if ever be the case that the Members of this Court will have a better sense of the evolution in views of the American people than do their elected representatives," *Thompson v. Oklahoma* (SCALIA, J., dissenting).

The Court pays lipservice to these precedents as it miraculously extracts a "national consensus" forbidding execution of the mentally retarded, from the fact that 18 States—less than half (47%) of the 38 States that permit capital punishment (for whom the issue exists)—have very recently enacted legislation barring execution of the mentally retarded. . . . That bare number of States alone—18—should be enough to convince any reasonable person that no "national consensus" exists. How is it possible that agreement among 47% of the death penalty jurisdictions amounts to "consensus"? Our prior cases have generally required a much higher degree of agreement before finding a punishment cruel and unusual on "evolving standards" grounds. In *Coker,* we proscribed the death penalty for rape of an adult woman after finding that only one jurisdiction, Georgia, authorized such a punishment. In *Enmund*, we invalidated the death penalty for mere participation in a robbery in which an accomplice took a life, a punishment not permitted in 28 of the death penalty States (78%). In *Ford*, we supported the common-law prohibition of execution of the insane with the observation that "[t]his ancestral legacy has not outlived its time," since not a single State authorizes such punishment. In *Solem v. Helm*, 463 U.S. 277, 300, 103 S.Ct. 3001, 77 L.Ed.2d 637 (1983), we invalidated a life sentence without parole under a recidivist statute by which the criminal "was treated more severely than he would have been in any other State." What the Court calls evidence of "consensus" in the present case (a fudged 47%) more closely resembles evidence that we found inadequate to establish consensus in earlier cases. *Tison v. Arizona*, 481 U.S. 137, 154, 158, 107 S.Ct. 1676, 95 L.Ed.2d 127 (1987), upheld a state law authorizing capital punishment for major participation in a felony with reckless indifference to life where only 11 of the 37 death penalty States (30%) prohibited such punishment. *Stanford* upheld a state law permitting execution of defendants who committed a capital crime at age 16 where only 15 of the 36 death penalty States (42%) prohibited death for such offenders.

. . .

Even less compelling (if possible) is the Court's argument that evidence of "national consensus" is to be found in the infrequency with which retarded persons are executed in States that do not bar their execution. To begin with, what the Court takes as true is in fact quite doubtful. It is not at all clear that execution of the mentally retarded is "uncommon," as even the sources cited by the Court suggest. See also Bonner & Rimer, Executing the Mentally Retarded Even as Laws Begin to Shift, N.Y. Times, Aug. 7, 2000 p. A1 (reporting that 10% of death row inmates are retarded). If, however, execution of the mentally retarded is "uncommon"; and if it is not a sufficient explanation of this that the retarded comprise a tiny fraction of society (1% to 3%), Brief for American Psychological Association et al. as Amici Curiae 7; then surely the explanation is that mental retardation is a constitutionally mandated mitigating factor at sentencing. *Penry*. For that reason, even if there were uniform national sentiment in favor of executing the retarded in appropriate cases, one would still expect execution of the mentally retarded to be "uncommon." To adapt to the present case what the Court itself said in *Stanford*: "[I]t is not only possible, but overwhelmingly probable, that the very considerations which induce [today's majority] to believe that death should never be imposed on [mentally retarded] offenders . . . cause prosecutors and juries to believe that it should rarely be imposed."

But the Prize for the Court's Most Feeble Effort to fabricate "national consensus" must go to its appeal (deservedly relegated to a footnote) to the views of assorted professional and religious organizations, members of the so-called "world community," and respondents to opinion polls. I agree with the Chief Justice that the views of professional and religious organizations and the results of opinion polls are irrelevant. Equally irrelevant are the practices of the "world community," whose notions of justice are (thankfully) not always those of our people. "We must never forget that it is a Constitution for the United States of America that we are expounding. . . . [W]here there is not first a settled consensus among our own people, the views of other nations, however enlightened the Justices of this Court may think them to be, cannot be imposed upon Americans through the Constitution." *Thompson* (SCALIA, J., dissenting).

III

. . .

The genuinely operative portion of the opinion, then, is the Court's statement of the reasons why it agrees with the contrived consensus it has found, that the "diminished capacities" of the mentally retarded render the death penalty excessive. The . . . Court gives two reasons why the death penalty is an excessive punishment for all mentally retarded offenders. First, the "diminished capacities" of the mentally retarded raise a "serious question" whether their execution contributes to the "social purposes" of the death penalty, viz., retribution and deterrence. (The Court conveniently ignores a third "social purpose" of the death penalty—"incapacitation of dangerous criminals and the consequent prevention of crimes that they may otherwise commit in the future," *Gregg* (joint opinion of STEWART, POWELL, STEVENS). But never mind; its discussion of even the other two does not bear analysis.) Retribution is not advanced, the argument goes, because the mentally retarded are no more culpable than the average murderer, whom we have already held lacks sufficient culpability to warrant the death penalty, see *Godfrey v. Georgia* (plurality opinion). Who says so? Is there an established correlation between mental acuity and the ability to conform one's conduct to the law in such a rudimentary matter as murder? Are the mentally retarded really more disposed (and hence more likely) to commit willfully cruel and serious crime than others? In my experience, the opposite is true: being childlike generally suggests innocence rather than brutality.

Assuming, however, that there is a direct connection between diminished intelligence and the inability to refrain from murder, what scientific analysis can possibly show that a mildly retarded individual who commits an exquisite torture-killing is "no more culpable" than the "average" murderer in a holdup-gone-wrong or a domestic dispute? Or a moderately retarded individual who commits a series of 20 exquisite torture-killings? Surely culpability, and deservedness of the most severe retribution, depends not merely (if at all) upon the mental capacity of the criminal (above the level where he is able to distinguish right from wrong) but also upon the depravity of the crime—which is precisely why this sort of question has traditionally been thought answerable not by a categorical rule of the sort the Court today imposes upon all trials, but rather by the sentencer's weighing of the circumstances (both degree of retardation and depravity of crime) in the particular case. The fact that juries continue to sentence mentally retarded offenders to death for extreme crimes shows that society's moral outrage sometimes demands execution of retarded offenders. By what principle of law, science, or logic can the Court pronounce that this is wrong? There is none. Once the Court admits (as it does) that mental retardation does not render the offender morally blameless, there is no basis for saying that the death penalty is never appropriate retribution, no matter how heinous the crime. As long as a mentally retarded offender knows "the difference between right and wrong," only the sentencer can assess whether his retardation reduces his culpability enough to exempt him from the death penalty for the particular murder in question.

As for the other social purpose of the death penalty that the Court discusses, deterrence: That is not advanced, the Court tells us, because the mentally retarded are "less likely" than their non-retarded counterparts to "process the information of the possibility of execution as a penalty and . . . control their conduct based upon that information." Of course this leads to the same conclusion discussed earlier—that the mentally retarded (because they are less deterred) are more likely to kill—which neither I nor the society at large believes. In any event, even the Court does not say that all mentally retarded individuals cannot "process the information of the possibility of execution as a penalty and . . . control their conduct based upon that information"; it merely asserts that they are "less likely" to be able to do so. But surely the deterrent effect of a penalty is adequately vindicated if it successfully deters many, but not all, of the target class. Virginia's death penalty, for example, does not fail of its deterrent effect simply because some criminals are unaware that Virginia has the death penalty. In other words, the supposed fact that some retarded criminals cannot fully appreciate the death penalty has nothing to do with the deterrence rationale, but is simply an echo of the arguments denying a retribution rationale, discussed and rejected above. I am not sure that a murderer is somehow less blameworthy if (though he knew his act was wrong) he did not fully appreciate that he could die for it; but if so, we should treat a mentally retarded murderer the way we treat an offender who may be "less likely" to respond to the death penalty because he was abused as a child. We do not hold him immune from capital punishment, but require his background to be considered by the sentencer as a mitigating factor.

The Court throws one last factor into its grab bag of reasons why execution of the retarded is "excessive" in all cases: Mentally retarded offenders "face a special risk of wrongful execution" because they are less able "to make a persuasive showing of mitigation," "to give meaningful assistance to their counsel," and to be effective witnesses. "Special risk" is pretty flabby language (even flabbier than "less likely")—and I suppose a similar "special risk" could be said to exist for just plain stupid people, inarticulate people, even ugly people. If this unsupported claim has any substance to it (which I doubt) it might support a due process claim in all criminal prosecutions of the mentally retarded; but it is hard to see how it has anything to do with an Eighth Amendment claim that execution of the mentally retarded is cruel and unusual. We have never before held it to be cruel and unusual punishment to impose a sentence in violation of some other constitutional imperative.

IV

. . . There is something to be said for popular abolition of the death penalty; there is nothing to be said for its incremental abolition by this Court.

. . .

I respectfully dissent.

QUESTIONS AND COMMENTS

1. *Implementation of* Atkins. *Atkins* left the definition of mental retardation for purposes of administering the death penalty up to the states. Arkansas defines retardation as an IQ below 65 and "significant" impairment in adaptive behavior. Several other states set the minimum IQ at 70 or 75, but also require an additional showing of impairment in adaptive functioning. Finally a number of states do not use IQ scores to define retardation, but rather require a showing of "significantly subaverage intelligence" that exists concurrently with deficits in adaptive functioning. Subaverage intelligence is variously defined as "an intelligence quotient more than two stand deviations below the mean for the test" (i.e., a score below 70 on the most commonly used intelligence measures) (Maryland), impairment that is manifested by "limitations in two or more adaptive behaviors" (such as communication, self-care, social skills, work) (Missouri), or a condition "which substantially impairs one's capacity to appreciate the criminality of one's conduct or to conform one's conduct to the requirements of law" (Kansas). See David DeMatteo, Geoffrey Marczyk & Michel Pich, *A National Survey of State Legislation Defining Mental Retardation: Implications for Policy and Practice* Atkins, 25 Beh. Sci. & L. 781 (2007).

Both IQ and adaptive functioning can be hard to measure precisely. Consider these observations from psychiatrist Douglas Mossman:

The availability of IQ test scores suggests that mental health professionals can offer courts objective, precise methods for deciding who is, or is not, impaired enough to receive the death penalty. Yet the numbers that IQ tests generate are far from being perfectly reliable measurements of a person's cognitive ability. Under the best conditions, IQ tests have a "measurement error" of about five points. An individual who scores, say, 68 on one administration has a ninety-five percent chance of scoring between 63 and 73 on subsequent administrations. More than half of those persons whose IQ results fall in the mildly retarded range receive scores of 65 to 70, that is, their scores' margin of error will include 70.

Another source of uncertainty stems from the fact that, for many items, the test administrator has to decide how many points a subject's response deserves. In normal clinical use, these imperfections do not matter a great deal. When testing a defendant for whom a one-or two-point change in IQ score has life-and-death implications, however, clinicians may have a hard time being dispassionately "objective" about how they interpret a response. The net result of all these imperfections is that judges, or juries, will often have a hard time deciding on which side of the arbitrary line between mentally retarded and merely "dull" a defendant falls.

If IQ testing generates nettlesome problems with imprecision and measurement error, measuring adaptive functioning—a key feature defining mental retardation [under psychiatric diagnostic criteria]—is even trickier. As one leading text on behavioral assessment points out, several features of adaptive behavior make it "difficult to define." Adaptive behavior is really not separable from intelligence; individuals use both cognitive and behavioral abilities to master social problems and function in their environment. What counts as adaptive behavior changes as one grows older: during school years, academic performance is crucial, but in adulthood, living independently and ability to earn a living are paramount. Adaptive behavior is also a function of a person's living situation and the demands of his unique social environment. Some people can function adequately in a close-knit rural town but cannot cope with demands of life in an urban metropolis. Far more than is the case with measuring intelligence, "adaptive behavior represents the interaction of personal, cognitive, social, and situational variables." Finally, the various available instruments for measuring adaptive behavior may give different results. This may be a consequence of differences in the instruments' content, the type of responses the instruments require, the times at which the instruments were created, the types of persons used to develop the instruments, or simply the persons who do the ratings.

Douglas Mossman, *Beyond* Atkins: *A Psychiatric Can of Worms*, 33 N.Mex. L. Rev. 255, 269–71 (2003).

IQ scores can also be affected by the "Flynn Effect," which posits that if IQ tests are not recalibrated periodically, they will overstate an individual's IQ vis-a-vis the rest of the population by about three points per decade. See *Walker v. True*, 399 F.3d 315 (4th Cir. 2005) (holding that testimony about the Flynn Effect is admissible to determine whether an offender is mentally retarded under *Atkins*). Also noteworthy is the fact that the DSM–5 no longer includes IQ scores as part of the official diagnosis, but rather merely requires "deficits in intellectual functions . . . confirmed by both clinical assessment and individualized, standardized intelligence testing," although commentary indicates that a score two standard deviations below the mean (typically a score below 75, given standard measure error) on a standard IQ test is typical for people with intellectual disability, the term the DSM now uses for what was formerly called mental retardation). (See Appendix A for the full diagnostic criteria). Courts are not always sensitive to the measurement errors noted by Mossman, *Walker*, and the DSM–5. In *Cherry v. State*, 959 So.2d 702 (Fla. 2007), for instance, the offender's full IQ score was 72, but experts testified that, given measurement error, his actual IQ could range between 67 and 77. The Supreme Court of Florida, citing the 70 IQ cutoff in the statute, rejected the *Atkins* claim. Is *Cherry* correctly decided? Alternatively, given the measurement error, should courts in states that set the IQ level for *Atkins* purposes at 70 recognize an *Atkins* claim when the offender's IQ tests at 75?

Courts have also had difficulty with the adaptive functioning criterion. The point that they sometimes miss is that a person who has an adaptive deficit in one area—and meets the subaverage intelligence and onset criteria as well—is intellectually disabled even if there is little or no evidence of adaptive deficits in other areas. For example, courts will point to an individual's ability to operate heavy machinery, hold two jobs, buy a car, or wash clothes as dispositive evidence of adaptive functioning, in the face of clear evidence that in other aspects of daily life the individual has serious deficits. See, e.g., *Williams v. Quarterman*, 293 Fed.Appx. 298 (5th Cir. 2008). Even more commonly, courts will closely evaluate the individual's capital offense and, if it appears to be complex enough, will declare that the individual is not intellectually disabled regardless of other evidence of adaptive deficits. See, e.g., *Ex Parte Smith*, 2010 WL 4148528, *7 (Ala. Sup. Ct. 2010); *Van Tran v. State* 2006 WL 3327828, *24–25 (Tenn. Crim. Ct. App. 2006). As the Court of Criminal Appeals of Oklahoma recognized, if evidence of particular competencies or actions at the time of the crime do not rebut the individual's specific claims of adaptive limitations, it is not "relevant" under the official definition of intellectual disability. *Lambert v. State*, 71 P.3d 30, 31 (Okla. Crim. Ct. App. 2003). What can be said about Daryl Atkins in this regard (see in particular note 4 in the opinion)?

In addition to IQ score and adaptive functioning, a third criterion found in mental health professionals' definitions of intellectual disability is age of onset. The usual requirement here is that the relevant impairments manifest themselves before age 18, the point being that a decrement in intelligence that occurs later—say, as a result of head trauma—should be classified as something other than an intellectual disability. In a few cases, courts have rejected an *Atkins* claim because, even though the offender was able to prove the first two elements, he did not present strong enough proof that these factors existed before 18. See *Stallings v. Bagley*, 561 F.Supp.2d 821, 881–86 (N.D. Ohio 2008); *State v. Strode*, 232 S.W. 3d 1, 16–17 (Tenn. 2007). Why should the point at which impairment occurs be relevant to whether a person is exempt from the death penalty? Is the issue merely one of credibility? Or is there some normative reason why exemption is barred if onset occurs after age 18 (say due to head trauma)?

Procedural issues left undiscussed in *Atkins* include the burden of proof, whether a judge or jury should make the decision about intellectual disability, and whether the decision should be made before or during the capital sentencing decision. Most states require the defendant to show intellectual disability by a preponderance of the evidence, but six states require clear and convincing evidence and one, Georgia, requires proof beyond a reasonable double. *Hill v. Humphrey*, 662 F.3d 1335, 1365 (11th Cir. 2011) (collecting cases). Most states allow the capital sentencing jury to decide whether the defendant meets the burden. See, e.g., *Murphy v. State*, 54 P.3d 556 (Okla.Crim.App. 2002). Before it eliminated the death penalty, New Jersey followed a different procedure. It required the judge to make a pretrial assessment of retardation in those cases "where reasonable minds cannot differ" about the issue. If the judge rejected the *Atkins* claim, a jury considered the issue post-conviction, but prior to sentencing, and the vote in favor of finding the offender intellectually disabled did not need to be unanimous. *State v. Jiminez*, 908 A.2d 181, 191–92 (N.J. 2006). Which approach is preferable?

Despite these various conundra, *Atkins* claims often prevail. One review of 234 cases adjudicating the substance of *Atkins* claims found that about 40% were successful, a rate substantially higher than that associated with most other claims in capital cases. John H. Blume, Sheri Lynn Johnson & Christopher Seeds, *An Empirical Look at* Atkins v. Virginia *and Its Application in Capital Cases*, 76 Tenn. L. Rev. 625, 628 (2009). About half of the unsuccessful claims failed on both of the first two prongs, with most of the remainder failing on one of the first two prongs. Id. at 630.

2.   *Intellectual deficiency and the purposes of punishment.* As Justice Scalia points out, the majority's evidence of "national consensus" was weaker in *Atkins* that it had been in any other case in which the Court found the eighth amendment to be violated. (Although three years later, in *Roper v. Simmons*, 543 U.S. 551, 125 S.Ct. 1183, 161 L.Ed.2d 1 (2005), the Court exempted offenders under the age of 18 from the death penalty on slightlty weaker state legislative evidence of a national consensus.) The majority's conclusion thus also rests heavily on its assumption that people with mental retardation are relatively less culpable and deterrable than others. With respect to the culpability issue, of what relevance is the fact, cited by Scalia, that perhaps 10% of those on death row are suffering from mental retardation? With respect to the deterrability issue, of what relevance is the

fact that people with mental retardation are not disproportionately likely to commit crime? James Ellis & Ruth Luckasson, *Mentally Retarded Criminal Defendants*, 53 Geo. Wash. L.Rev. 414, 426 (1985) ("The best modern evidence suggests that the incidence of criminal behavior among people with mental retardation does not greatly exceed the incidence of criminal behavior among the population as a whole."). Scalia also points out that the majority does not mention incapacitation as a goal of capital punishment. If people with mental retardation are more impulsive, as the majority indicates, doesn't that make them more dangerous? Atkins had 16 prior felony convictions for robbery, attempted robbery, abduction, use of a firearm, and maiming.

Consider also this comment about the relationship between mental retardation and culpability.

> The tests that are typically used to measure "mental retardation" have been used in educational contexts (e.g., to address questions about the student's academic strengths and limitations and what types of special educational services must be provided) and eligibility for services and benefits (e.g., to address whether the individual qualifies for a vocational training or sheltered-living program, or for social security disability benefits). These tests were not developed for the purpose of distinguishing between capital offenders whose deficits in intellectual functioning render them are ineligible for the death penalty from those capital offenders without such deficits.

Lois A. Weithorn, *Conceptual Hurdles in the Application of* Atkins v. Virginia, 59 Hastings L. J. 1203, 1223 (2008).

3. *Categorical exemptions from the death penalty.* In *Atkins*, Justice Scalia objected to the categorical nature of the majority's exemption, noting that it is antithetical to Supreme Court death penalty jurisprudence which, since *Woodson* and *Lockett*, has called for individualization of punishment, and asking "what scientific analysis can possibly show that a mildly retarded individual who commits an exquisite torture-killing is 'no more culpable' than the 'average' murderer in a holdup-gone-wrong or a domestic dispute?" Disability rights advocates have levied a similar criticism at *Atkins*. Donald Bersoff has argued that *Atkins* mischaracterizes the capacities of people with mental retardation. Noting that people with mental retardation can act with "intent and foresight," he states: "As important as it is to protect those who cannot protect themselves, it is equally important to promote the right of all persons to make their own choices, and, as a corollary, to be accountable for those choices." Donald N. Bersoff, Some Contrarian Concerns about Law, Psychology, and Public Policy, 26 L. & Hum. Beh. 565, 568–69 (2002). Bersoff also suggests that *Atkins* may lead to a retraction of the rights and privileges that people with disability currently possess. He asserts, "[i]f we accept the concept of blanket incapacity, we relegate people with retardation to second-class citizenship, potentially permitting the State to abrogate the exercise of such fundamental interests as the right to marry, to have and rear one's children, to vote, or such everyday entitlements as entering into contracts or making a will." Id.

Consider as a partial response to these points the following comments:

According to the DSM–IV–TR, even people with "mild" retardation at most can develop academic skills up to the sixth-grade level, amounting to the maturity of a twelve-year-old. By exempting this whole category of people from its purview, *Atkins* constitutionalized the idea that the death penalty may be imposed only on people who are particularly culpable. . . . More important for present purposes, its holding (as distinguished, perhaps, from some of its language about the average murderer) does not mischaracterize the capacities of people with disability in the way Bersoff suggests. *Atkins* does not say that people with retardation are incapable of committing crime with intent or foresight. Nor, of course, does it say that murderers with serious disability should not be held accountable for their choices, as they still can be given life sentences. All *Atkins* says is that people with retardation, even those who commit a "horrible" murder, can never be as evil as the most evil murderers in our society, and thus that the ultimate punishment may not be imposed on them.

For related reasons, . . . Bersoff's claim that *Atkins* will encourage use of categorical disability-based exemptions in the civil rights setting [is overstating the dangers of the decision]. . . . The inquiry in the civil setting is not whether the disabled person is "average," but whether the person meets a minimum level of competence. In other words, even a person whose capacities are "below average" can, under the law, contract, marry, vote, and so on. Thus, neither the holding nor the unnecessarily broad language of *Atkins* sabotages these types of laws.

Christopher Slobogin, Minding Justice: Laws that Deprive People with Disability of Life and Liberty 85–86 (2006).

4. *Mental retardation and competency.* In addition to the state-consensus and lesser-blameworthiness rationales, the *Atkins* Court gave a third reason for exempting people with intellectual disability from the death penalty: the greater likelihood they will have difficulty communicating with their attorneys and their tendency, due to their suggestibility and desire to please those in authority, to confess to acts they did not commit. The competency and confession issues are covered in detail in Part V of Chapter Nine. But it is worth noting here the possible impact of Daryl Atkins' impairment on the accuracy of his conviction for capital murder. Even after *Atkins*, Virginia continued to push for Atkins' execution. In 2005 the state convinced a jury that Atkins' was not intellectually disabled, in part based on a recent IQ test of 76 and in part because, the state asserted, some of his previous IQ scores had been affected by drug and alcohol use. Three years later, however, a trial judge commuted Atkins' new death sentence, after the lawyer for Atkins' co-defendant revealed (subsequent to the co-defendant's death) that the co-defendant had pulled the trigger, a fact which, under Virginia law, precluded the death penalty for Atkins. Adam Liptak, *Lawyer Reveals Secret, Toppling Death Sentence*, N.Y. Times, Jan. 19, 2008. It turns out that, given where Atkins had been seated at the time of the crime and the

fact that the door on his side of the truck did not open, the physical evidence was inconsistent with the prosecution's case. One wonders whether Atkins' attorney could have done a better job proving this fact at the initial trial had Atkins been less impaired. On a different point raised by the facts recounted above, should an IQ score obtained *after* the offense be relevant to the *Atkins* issue?

5. *Mental illness as a bar to the death penalty*. Like people with intellectual disabilities who kill, people who commit capital murder while experiencing psychosis are, as a class, less blameworthy and less deterrable than the average murderer. Yet they are frequently convicted and sentenced to death. See Dorothy Otnow Lewis et al., *Psychiatric, Neurological, and Psychoeducational Characteristics of 15 Death Row Inmates in the United States*, 143 Am. J. Psychiatry 838 (1986) (six of 15 randomly selected death row inmates "had schizophrenia psychosis antedating incarceration and two others were manic-depressive"). Should such death sentences be prohibited in light of *Atkins*? As noted in previous materials, a number of states have upheld death sentences imposed on those found "guilty but mentally ill." Thus, there is nothing close to the "consensus" that the majority found in *Atkins* against execution of people with retardation, and an eighth amendment argument would presumably be unavailing. But can one make an equal protection argument, to the effect that, now that people with mental retardation may not be executed, allowing the capital punishment of offenders who were experiencing psychosis at the time of the offense is irrational? In equal protection terms, what are the justifications for continuing to permit, post-*Atkins*, execution of people with severe mental illness at the time of their crime? Are people with mental illness more "at fault" for their condition than those with mental retardation? Do they have greater opportunities or capacities to learn right from wrong and correct bad behavior? Are they more dangerous than people with mental retardation?

If the answer to these questions is no (consider previous materials), then is there any other rational basis for distinguishing the two groups? Is mental illness more difficult to diagnose than mental retardation? (In this regard, do you think Atkins is "mentally retarded" for purposes of the death penalty bar? Someone with an IQ of 72, like Johnson in *Johnson v. State*, excerpted at pp. 743–744? Someone like Shawn Grell, who scored 72, 67, 69, 70, 57, 65 and 74 on IQ tests administered at various times, as described in *Arizona v. Grell*, 205 Ariz. 57, 66 P.3d 1234 (2003)? See note 1 above and notes 3, 5 & 22 of the majority opinion in *Atkins*). If mental illness is more difficult to diagnose, is that a reason to reject extension of *Atkins* to people with mental illness, or instead merely a reason to require strong proof of mental illness? See Christopher Slobogin, *What* Atkins *Could Mean for People with Mental Illness*, 33 N.M. L. Rev. 293 (2003).

In 2007, the American Bar Association, the American Psychiatric Association and the American Psychological Association jointly endorsed a resolution which reads as follows:

Defendants shall not be executed or sentenced to death if, at the time of the offense, they had a severe mental disorder or disability that significantly impaired their capacity (1) to appreciate the nature, consequences, or wrongfulness of their conduct, (2) to exercise rational judgment in relation to the conduct, or (3) to conform their conduct to the requirements of the law. A disorder manifested primarily by repeated criminal conduct or attributable solely to the acute effects of voluntary use of alcohol or other drugs does not, standing alone, constitute a mental disorder or disability for purposes of this provision.

The ABA's commentary to the Resolution notes that, although this language is similar to the ALI insanity test, most states have more restrictive insanity tests or no insanity defense at all, and thus this language would have an impact at the sentencing stage in most jurisdictions. The Resolution and commentary is available at www.abanet.org/crimjust/policy/am06122a.pdf.

B. NON–CAPITAL SENTENCING

1. History: Retribution v. Incapacitation/Rehabilitation

The history of sentencing outside the capital punishment context reflects the tension between two different models: the retribution/deterrence model and the incapacitation/rehabilitation model. Under the first model, the type and duration of punishment is determined by assessing the offender's blameworthiness (as indicated by the offense committed and perhaps the offender's other criminal behavior as well) and the message punishment will send to others. Under the second model, the type and duration of punishment is dependent upon the offender's perceived dangerousness and the extent to which those criminal propensities can be reduced through treatment. Because information about blameworthiness of the offender and the deterrent value of particular punishments is usually known at the time of sentencing, the first model is more likely to result in determinate sentences, or at least sentences with a relatively narrow range. Conversely, the second model is more likely to produce indeterminate sentences with no specific termination point because, at the time of sentencing, it is not known how long a person will have to be incapacitated and treated before he or she is considered nondangerous. It is sometimes suggested that under the first model the effort is to fit the punishment to the crime, while under the second, punishment is designed to fit the criminal. This statement is somewhat misleading, because the blameworthiness assessment called for by the first model may consider individual traits (such as mental state at the time of the offense), while the dangerousness assessment mandated by the second model may in practice focus on the type of crime committed by the offender more than any other single factor. But it is fair to say that, as a general matter, the second model places more emphasis on individualization of punishment than does the first.

In the United States, the retribution/deterrence model dominated sentencing practices until the mid–19th century. Sentences tended to be uniform for each type of crime or at least defined by narrow ranges; an offender's rehabilitative potential was usually ignored. After the Civil War, concurrent with optimism that the causes of crime could be identified and treated, movement toward the incapacitation/rehabilitation approach gained momentum. By 1922, 37 states had enacted indeterminate sentencing statutes, and several others had parole systems functionally similar to the indeterminate sentence. The remaining states set maximum sentences for each crime, but allowed the judge and parole board to determine when within that time limit release would occur. In 1949, the United States Supreme Court seemed to approve of this trend when it described as the "prevalent modern philosophy of penology" the idea that "the punishment should fit the offender and not merely the crime. . . . Retribution is no longer the dominant objective of the criminal law. Reformation and rehabilitation of offenders have become important goals of criminal jurisprudence." *Williams v. New York*, 337 U.S. 241, 69 S.Ct. 1079, 93 L.Ed. 1337 (1949).

However, in the mid–1970's a countertrend emerged, often labeled the "just deserts" movement. Advocates of this approach believed that "those whose criminal actions are equally reprehensible deserve like amounts of punishment." Andrew VonHirsch & Kathleen Hanrahan, *Determinate Penalty Systems in America: An Overview*, 27 Crime & Delinq. 289, 294 (1981). In the next three decades, perhaps twenty jurisdictions, including the federal government, developed "guidelines" imposing "fixed" or "presumptive" sentences, or permitting sentences only within a very narrow range, unless a showing is made that the offender should be treated differently. Under most of these schemes, variance from the legislated sentence is usually permissible only on culpability grounds (such as whether the defendant chose a vulnerable victim, was a leader or follower, accepted responsibility or obstructed justice, and is a career or first-time offender); concerns about dangerousness or rehabilitation are not supposed to influence the sentencing authority or are only secondary considerations. For instance, under the federal Sentencing Reform Act of 1984 the court is generally limited to imposing a sentence within a small range, the maximum of which may not exceed the minimum by more than the greater of 25% or six months. 28 U.S.C. § 994(a). Parole is abolished, 18 U.S.C. § 3624(a)(b), and rehabilitation rejected as a purpose of punishment. 28 U.S.C. § 994(k). While a number of states with guidelines systems emphasize prior record as one of the sentencing factors (which suggests that dangerousness is at least a background consideration), and virtually all guidelines states permit judges to impose probation conditions for certain crimes when an offender is "amenable" to probation, retributive considerations govern the sentence maxima and minima in virtually all of these states. Richard Frase, *State Sentencing Guidelines:*

Diversity, Consensus and Unresolved Policy Issues, 105 Colum. L. Rev. 1190, 1202–03 (2005). See also *Tapia v. United States*, ___ U.S. ___, 131 S.Ct. 2382, 180 L.Ed.2d 357 (2011) (prohibiting enhancement of a federal sentence "to promote rehabilitation").

Recent Supreme Court decisions have loosened some of the restrictions imposed on judges in guidelines regimes. See *United States v. Booker*, 543 U.S. 220, 125 S.Ct. 738, 160 L.Ed.2d 621 (2005) (federal sentencing guidelines are not mandatory); *Gall v. United States*, 552 U.S. 38, 128 S.Ct. 586, 169 L.Ed.2d 445 (2007) (sentences that depart from guidelines must be reviewed under a deferential abuse-of-discretion standard). Once departures for cooperation with the government are eliminated, however, the vast majority of sentences in guidelines regimes fall within the guidelines, at least within the federal system. In 2011, for instance, 54.5% of federal sentences were within the guidelines; 26.3% were government-sponsored downward departures for cooperation with the government; 17.4% were non-government sponsored downward departures; 1.8% were upward departures. U.S. Sentencing Commission, Annual Report, ch. 5, at 36 (2012).

These vacillations in sentencing policy reflect several different influences. The just deserts variant of the retribution/deterrence model is founded on the belief that culpability is the touchstone of punishment: while incapacitation and rehabilitation goals may be achieved through punishment indirectly, they should not determine its scope; indeed, even the deterrence objective is deemphasized. The movement also seems to be a product of disenchantment with prison rehabilitation efforts, a belief that neither dangerousness nor treatability predictions are very accurate, and a desire to reduce sentencing disparity and indeterminacy, which are believed to be inequitable and have harmful psychological effects on inmates. See generally, Andrew VonHirsch, Doing Justice (1976). See also Kevin R. Reitz, *Demographic Impact Statements, O'Connor's Warning, and the Mysteries of Prison Release: Topics from a Sentencing Reform Agenda*, 61 Fla. L. Rev. 683, 699–700 (2009) ("Presumptive guidelines are more often respected by judges, produce more consistency of thought and transparency in sentencing decisions, are more effective in reducing racial disparities in sentencing decisions, are more reliable in introducing systemic controls on prison population growth . . . , are superior at implementing line-by-line policy priorities in how bed spaces should be filled, and have proven essential in state systems to the inculcation of meaningful appellate review of trial court sentences.").

The incapacitation/rehabilitation model still has many adherents, however. For instance, noted criminologist Joan Petersilia notes that under California's determinate sentencing regime, "a large percentage of Californians who are nonviolent criminals are accumulating very extensive criminal records . . . [yet] may not be any more dangerous than offenders in other states who are left 'on the street' and successfully handled through an array of community-based intermediate sanctions. [At the same time], California's sentencing system also releases violent offenders who amass lengthy criminal records—individuals who in a system more carefully tailored to protect public safety, probably should not have been released in the first place."). Joan Petersilia, *California's Correction Paradox of Excess and Deprivation*, in 37 Crime and Justice 207, 252–53 (Michael Tonry ed. 2008). See also, Douglas A. Berman, *The Enduring (and Again Timely) Wisdom of the Original MPC Sentencing Provisions*, 61 Fla. L. Rev. 709, 721 (2009) (describing "the real possibility that, despite the very best of intentions, the theoretical underpinnings, legal structures, social policies, and political rhetoric of modern sentencing reforms [based on retributive principles] have contributed to the growth in prison populations and the extreme liberty deprivations that have now become so common in American criminal justice systems.").

The two models differ significantly in their treatment of evidence concerning psychological makeup. Theoretically, under the incapacitation/rehabilitation approach to sentencing, all aspects of an individual's personality are relevant, including every shade of mental disability. Sentencing under this model

> is premised on the assumption that a sentencing judge, armed with an intimate knowledge of the offender's character and background and aided by scientific and clinical evaluations, can determine an appropriate sentence and treatment program that will rehabilitate the offender. Under this model, the sentencing judge seeks to define the offender's exact personality and social situations, and then prescribes an "individualized" sentence and treatment program.

Alan Dershowitz, *The Role of Psychiatry in the Sentencing Process*, 1 Int'l J.L.Psychiat. 63, 66 (1978). In those states that follow this approach or variations on it, sentencing criteria are rarely specified because the information that may be considered by the judge is so wide-ranging.

Under the retributive/deterrence model, on the other hand, only those aspects of mental disability relevant to blameworthiness may be considered and, in most state statutes that reflect the influence of this model, these features are specifically identified as aggravating and mitigating factors. For instance, under the Minnesota sentencing scheme, the judge must normally impose a sentence based on the crime committed and the offender's previous criminal history unless specified aggravating or mitigating circumstances are shown. Included in the statute as mitigating factors are the following:

> (1) the offender played a minor or passive role in the crime or participated under circumstances of coercion or duress.

(2) the offender, because of physical or mental impairment, lacked substantial capacity for judgment when the offense was committed. The voluntary use of intoxicants (drugs or alcohol) does not fall within the purview of this factor.

(3) other substantial grounds exist which tend to excuse or mitigate the offender's culpability, although not amounting to a defense.

Minn. Stat. Ann., Sentencing Guidelines, Guideline 2, subd. D, ch. 44 Appendix (2013). In some states, proof of an aggravating or mitigating factor can result in a substantial variance from the presumptive sentence. For instance, in Arizona the judge may increase the sentence by up to 25% if an aggravating factor is shown and reduce the sentence by up to 50% if a mitigating circumstance is proven. Arizona R.S. §§ 13–502, 13–7–1, 13–7–2. See also, *United States v. Chambers*, 885 F.Supp. 12 (D.D.C.1995) (reducing sentence of person with mental retardation from federal guideline minimum of 188 months to 21 months); cf. *United States v. Lewinson*, 988 F.2d 1005 (9th Cir. 1993) (holding that mental disorder need not be "severe" to warrant downward departure, as long as it resulted in "significant impairment" that affects "behavior and decision-making during the offense period").

One pre-*Booker* review of federal caselaw found, however, that downward departures on grounds of mental disability (e.g., depression, manic psychosis, severe emotional stress, psychosis) are usually "summarily rejected" and also noted that in some cases evidence of past insanity acquittals has been viewed as an aggravating circumstance. Michael L. Perlin & Keri K. Gould, *Rashomon and the Criminal Law: Mental Disability and the Federal Sentencing Guidelines*, 22 Am. J. Crim. L. 431, 448–49 (1995). That finding is not surprising, since under the Federal Guidelines a downward departure for diminished capacity should generally occur only if the individual shows that he had a "significantly impaired ability to (A) understand the wrongfulness of the behavior comprising the offense or to exercise the power to reason; or (B) control behavior that the defendant knows is wrongful." U.S. Sentencing Guidelines Manual § 5K2.13. Further, the downward departure is not permitted if the diminished capacity was the result of voluntary drug use, the offense involved the use of violence or the threat of violence, or the defendant had a dangerous criminal history. Id. Mere mental or emotional "conditions" are "not . . . relevant in determining whether a departure is warranted," but "may be relevant in determining the conditions of probation or supervised release." Id. at § 5H1.3. Prior to *Booker*, downward departures on the basis of "diminished capacity" occurred in about 2.6% of cases. Alan Ellis, *Federal Sentencing*, 21 Crim. Justice 36, 37 (2007). Although judges' adherence to the Guidelines is now voluntary, see *Booker*, supra, such downward departures continue to be rare. U.S. Sentencing Commission, Annual Report, ch. 5, at 35 (2011) (noting that the percentage of cases in which a non-government-sponsored downward departure occurred on *any* specified ground was 3.4%).

Various compromises between the retribution/deterrence and incapacitation/rehabilitation approaches have been proposed. A recent development along these lines is the ongoing revision of the Model Penal Code's sentencing provisions, which endorses the concept of "limiting retributivism." Under this approach, the relative gravity of the offense, the harm to the victim, and the "blameworthiness" of the offender dictate the potential range of the sentence. However, within this range, considerations relating to the offender's dangerousness and treatability may influence the sentencing decision if achieving these preventive goals is "reasonably feasible." While the range dictated by retributive principles is supposed to be relatively narrow, the new provisions also permit non-prison terms for low-risk felons and sentence enhancements for high-risk felons, assuming such a disposition is not too lenient or harsh under desert principles. Model Penal Code: Sentencing §§ 1.02(2); 6B.09 (2011).

To the extent the retribution/deterrence model of sentencing is concerned with mental disability, this book's materials on capital sentencing discuss many of the pertinent issues;[x] little further discussion is warranted. The legal issues connected with the incapacitation/rehabilitation model are worth delving into in more detail. Examples of statutes that adopt this approach are numerous. At the federal level, for instance, they range from the Narcotic Addict Rehabilitation Act, 18 U.S.C. §§ 4251 et seq., which permits the addicted person with charges pending to elect treatment for a specified period of time, to the Youth Correction Act, 18 U.S.C. §§ 5005 et seq., which, before its repeal in 1986, granted the courts authority to sentence persons between 21 and 26 to indeterminate confinement not to exceed four years for "corrective and preventive guidance and training designed to protect the public by correcting the antisocial tendencies of youth offenders." Id. § 5006(f). Probably the purest expression of the incapacitation/rehabilitation model, however, is found in statutes providing for the indeterminate confinement of those found to be "mentally disordered sex offenders." We now turn to an examination of these statutes.

---

[x] Although they usually do not include predictive criteria such as dangerousness and treatability, determinate sentencing statutes are otherwise similar to capital sentencing statutes in structure; thus, many of the same legal issues may arise (e.g., when is a particular mitigating factor proven, how does the court "count" mental disability which is both mitigating and aggravating).

2. Mentally Disordered Sex Offender Statutes[y]

In the early part of the twentieth century, a number of states passed legislation aimed at diverting into special indeterminate treatment programs a category of offenders who came to be known as "defective delinquents." Many of these states had already adopted an indeterminate sentencing system. Thus, the apparent impetus for these special sentencing programs was to remove from the regular prison system particularly disruptive and hard to treat offenders. Although some states still have such statutes, they have rarely been enthusiastically implemented.[z]

Much more popular were statutes aimed at diverting those charged with sex offenses, the first of which was passed by Michigan in 1937. At one time, more than 25 states had such statutes, which have come to be called mentally disordered sex offender (MDSO) statutes. Samuel Brakel & Richard Rock, The Mentally Disabled and the Law 341 (1971). Programs singling out sex offenders succeeded where the defective delinquent statutes did not because sex offenders were believed to be particularly likely to recidivate if not treated and at the same time particularly amenable to treatment. Additionally, sex offenders, especially pedophiles, tend to be mistreated by other prisoners and are often segregated from the rest of the prison population in any event.

MDSO statutes vary both substantively and procedurally. A MDSO "commitment proceeding" usually can only be triggered by conviction for a sex offense. However, several states permit such a proceeding upon indictment for a sex offense, and at least one state—Illinois—authorizes initiation of MDSO proceedings after an individual is charged with *any* offense. In the earliest statutes, commitment as a MDSO usually requires a showing that the person is predisposed to commit sexual offenses as a result of "mental disease or defect." A few statutes also require a separate showing of repeated sexual misconduct (in Illinois, because the proceeding is initiated by indictment, the subject must have "demonstrated propensities towards acts of sexual assault or acts of sexual molestation of children"); a few other states require a showing of treatability. Under most of the original statutes, commitment as a MDSO resulted in indeterminate confinement, with release dependent upon initiation of discharge proceedings by the superintendent of the treating facility and approval by the committing court. Later statutes limited the

---

[y] Most of this introduction is taken from George Dix, *Special Dispositional Alternatives for Abnormal Offenders*, in John Monahan & Henry Steadman, Mentally Disordered Offenders: Perspectives from Law and Social Science 133, 134–145 (1983).

[z] An exception was the Maryland Defective Delinquent Act, Art. 31B (1964), which was frequently used to confine defective delinquents indeterminately until 1978, when the duration of confinement was limited to the maximum sentence that would have been received. See Louis Kohlmeyer, *The First Year of Operation Under the New Patuxent Laws*, 7 Bull. Amer. Acad. Psychiat. & L. 95 (1979). The Act was repealed in 1989.

time of confinement to the maximum term that could have been imposed for the crime committed by the offender, although in some of these states commitment may be renewed if a new commitment proceeding is held at which more stringent criteria are met.

MDSO statutes waned in popularity in the 1970's and 1980's for a number of reasons, including the feminist movement's opposition to the medicalization of rape, the belief among many psychiatrists that sex offenders are not particularly risky or treatable, and a general distaste for rehabilitation-oriented programs. Eric S. Janus & Robert A. Prentky, *Sexual Predator Laws: A Two Decade Retrospective*, 21 Fed. Sent. Rep. 90, 91 (2008). But in the 1990's a new version of these statutes, dubbed "sexual predator" laws, revived the concept; by 2006, twenty states and the federal government had such laws and over 4500 individuals had been committed under them. Washington State Institute for Public Policy, Comparison of State Law Authorizing Involuntary Commitment of Sexually Violent Predators: 2006 Update (2007). The current sexual predator laws permit confinement not only of persons who are charged or convicted but also of persons who have completed their sentences for a sex offense. The following U.S. Supreme Court decision upheld one of these laws against several constitutional challenges and, in so doing, raised fundamental questions not just about the scope of MDSO statutes but also about the scope of civil commitment, the subject of the next chapter.

KANSAS V. HENDRICKS

Supreme Court of the United States, 1997.
521 U.S. 346, 117 S.Ct. 2072, 138 L.Ed.2d 501.

JUSTICE THOMAS delivered the opinion of the Court.

In 1994, Kansas enacted the Sexually Violent Predator Act, which established procedures for the civil commitment of persons who, due to a "mental abnormality" or a "personality disorder," are likely to engage in "predatory acts of sexual violence." Kan. Stat. Ann. § 59–29a–1 et seq. (1994). The State invoked the Act for the first time to commit Leroy Hendricks, an inmate who had a long history of sexually molesting children, and who was scheduled for release from prison shortly after the Act became law. Hendricks challenged his commitment on, inter alia, "substantive" due process, double jeopardy, and ex post facto grounds. The Kansas Supreme Court invalidated the Act, holding that its pre-commitment condition of a "mental abnormality" did not satisfy what the court perceived to be the "substantive" due process requirement that involuntary civil commitment must be predicated on a finding of "mental illness." The State of Kansas petitioned for certiorari. Hendricks subsequently filed a cross-petition in which he reasserted his federal double jeopardy and post facto claims. We granted certiorari on both the petition and the cross-petition, and now reverse the judgment below.

I

A

The Kansas Legislature enacted the Sexually Violent Predator Act (Act) in 1994 to grapple with the problem of managing repeat sexual offenders. Although Kansas already had a statute addressing the involuntary commitment of those defined as "mentally ill," the legislature determined that existing civil commitment procedures were inadequate to confront the risks presented by "sexually violent predators." In the Act's preamble, the legislature explained:

> "[A] small but extremely dangerous group of sexually violent predators exist who do not have a mental disease or defect that renders them appropriate for involuntary treatment pursuant to the [general involuntary civil commitment statute]. . . . In contrast to persons appropriate for civil commitment under the [general involuntary civil commitment statute], sexually violent predators generally have anti-social personality features which are unamenable to existing mental illness treatment modalities and those features render them likely to engage in sexually violent behavior. The legislature further finds that sexually violent predators' likelihood of engaging in repeat acts of predatory sexual violence is high. The existing involuntary commitment procedure . . . is inadequate to address the risk these sexually violent predators pose society. The legislature further finds that the prognosis for rehabilitating sexually violent predators in a prison setting is poor, the treatment needs of this population are very long term and the treatment modalities for this population are very different than the traditional treatment modalities for people appropriate for commitment under the [general involuntary civil commitment statute]."

As a result, the Legislature found it necessary to establish "a civil commitment procedure for the long-term care and treatment of the ,definition sexually violent predator." The Act defined a "sexually violent predator" as:

> "any person who has been convicted of or charged with a sexually violent offense" and who suffers from a mental abnormality or personality disorder which makes the person "likely to engage in the predatory acts of sexual violence."

A "mental abnormality" was defined, in turn, as a "congenital or acquired condition affecting the emotional or volitional capacity which predisposes the person to commit sexually violent offenses in a degree constituting such person a menace to the health and safety of others."

As originally structured, the Act's civil commitment procedures pertained to (1) a presently confined person who, like Hendricks, "has been convicted of a sexually violent offense" and is scheduled for release;

(2) a person who has been "charged with a sexually violent offense" but has been found incompetent to stand trial; (3) a person who has been found "not guilty by reason of insanity of a sexually violent offense"; and (4) a person found "not guilty" of a sexually violent offense because of a mental disease or defect.

The initial version of the Act [which has since been amended in ways irrelevant to the current decision], as applied to a currently confined person such as Hendricks, was designed to initiate a specific series of procedures. The custodial agency was required to notify the local prosecutor 60 days before the anticipated release of a person who might have met the Act's criteria. The prosecutor was then obligated, within 45 days, to decide whether to file a petition in state court seeking the person's involuntary commitment. If such a petition were filed, the court was to determine whether "probable cause" existed to support a finding that the person was a "sexually violent predator" and thus eligible for civil commitment. Upon such a determination, transfer of the individual to a secure facility for professional evaluation would occur. After that evaluation, a trial would be held to determine beyond a reasonable doubt whether the individual was a sexually violent predator. If that determination were made, the person would then be transferred to the custody of the Secretary of Social and Rehabilitation Services (Secretary) for "control, care and treatment until such time as the person's mental abnormality or personality disorder has so changed that the person is safe to be at large."

In addition to placing the burden of proof upon the State, the Act afforded the individual a number of other procedural safeguards. In the case of an indigent person, the State was required to provide, at public expense, the assistance of counsel and an examination by mental health care professionals. The individual also received the right to present and cross-examine witnesses, and the opportunity to review documentary evidence presented by the State.

Once an individual was confined, the Act required that "the involuntary detention or commitment . . . shall conform to constitutional requirements for care and treatment." Confined persons were afforded three different avenues of review: First, the committing court was obligated to conduct an annual review to determine whether continued detention was warranted. Second, the Secretary was permitted, at any time, to decide that the confined individual's condition had so changed that release was appropriate, and could then authorize the person to petition for release. Finally, even without the Secretary's permission, the confined person could at any time file a release petition. If the court found that the State could no longer satisfy its burden under the initial commitment standard, the individual would be freed from confinement.

B

In 1984, Hendricks was convicted of taking "indecent liberties" with two 13 year-old boys. After serving nearly 10 years of his sentence, he was slated for release to a halfway house. Shortly before his scheduled release, however, the State filed a petition in state court seeking Hendricks' civil confinement as a sexually violent predator. On August 19, 1994, Hendricks appeared before the court with counsel and moved to dismiss the petition on the grounds that the Act violated various federal constitutional provisions. Although the court reserved ruling on the Act's constitutionality, it concluded that there was probable cause to support a finding that Hendricks was a sexually violent predator, and therefore ordered that he be evaluated at the Larned State Security Hospital.

Hendricks subsequently requested a jury trial to determine whether he qualified as a sexually violent predator. During that trial, Hendricks' own testimony revealed a chilling history of repeated child sexual molestation and abuse, beginning in 1955 when he exposed his genitals to two young girls. At that time, he pleaded guilty to indecent exposure. Then, in 1957, he was convicted of lewdness involving a young girl and received a brief jail sentence. In 1960, he molested two young boys while he worked for a carnival. After serving two years in prison for that offense, he was paroled, only to be rearrested for molesting a 7 year-old girl. Attempts were made to treat him for his sexual deviance, and in 1965 he was considered "safe to be at large," and was discharged from a state psychiatric hospital.

Shortly thereafter, however, Hendricks sexually assaulted another young boy and girl—he performed oral sex on the 8 year-old girl and fondled the 11 year-old boy. He was again imprisoned in 1967, but refused to participate in a sex offender treatment program, and thus remained incarcerated until his parole in 1972. Diagnosed as a pedophile, Hendricks entered into, but then abandoned, a treatment program. He testified that despite having received professional help for his pedophilia, he continued to harbor sexual desires for children. Indeed, soon after his 1972 parole, Hendricks began to abuse his own stepdaughter and stepson. He forced the children to engage in sexual activity with him over a period of approximately four years. Then, as noted above, Hendricks was convicted of "taking indecent liberties" with two adolescent boys after he attempted to fondle them. As a result of that conviction he was once again imprisoned, and was serving that sentence when he reached his conditional release date in September 1994.

Hendricks admitted that he had repeatedly abused children whenever he was not confined. He explained that when he "gets stressed out," he "can't control the urge" to molest children. Although Hendricks recognized that his behavior harms children, and he hoped he would not sexually molest children again, he stated that the only sure way he could keep from sexually abusing children in the future was "to die." Hendricks readily agreed with the state physician's diagnosis that he suffers from pedophilia and that he is not cured of the condition; indeed, he told the physician that "treatment is bull."[2] The jury unanimously found beyond a reasonable doubt that Hendricks was a sexually violent predator. The trial court subsequently determined, as a matter of state law, that pedophilia qualifies as a "mental abnormality" as defined by the Act, and thus ordered Hendricks committed to the Secretary's custody.

Hendricks appealed, claiming, among other things, that application of the Act to him violated the Federal Constitution's Due Process, Double Jeopardy, Ex Post Facto Clauses. The Kansas Supreme Court accepted Hendricks' due process claim. The court declared that in order to commit a person involuntarily in a civil proceeding, the State is required by "substantive" due process to prove by clear and convincing evidence that the person is both (1) mentally ill, and (2) a danger to himself or to others. The court then determined that the Act's definition of "mental abnormality" did not satisfy what it perceived to be this Court's "mental illness" requirement in the civil commitment context. As a result, the court held that "the Act violates Hendricks' substantive due process rights."

* * *

II

A

Kansas argues that the Act's definition of "mental abnormality" satisfies "substantive" due process requirements. We agree. Although freedom from physical restraint "has always been at the core of the liberty protected by the Due Process Clause from arbitrary governmental action," *Foucha v. Louisiana* [see pp. 987–990], that liberty interest is not absolute. The Court has recognized that an individual's constitutionally protected interest in avoiding physical restraint may be overridden even in the civil context: "The liberty secured by the Constitution of the United States to every person within its jurisdiction does not import an absolute right in each person to be, at all times and in all circumstances, wholly free from restraint. There are manifold restraints to which every person

---

[2]   In addition to Hendricks' own testimony, the jury heard from Hendricks' stepdaughter and stepson, who recounted the events surrounding their repeated sexual abuse at Hendricks' hands. One of the girls to whom Hendricks exposed himself in 1955 testified as well. The State also presented testimony from Lester Lee, a licensed clinical social worker who specialized in treating male sexual offenders, and Dr. Charles Befort, the chief psychologist at Larned State Hospital. Lee testified that Hendricks had a diagnosis of personality trait disturbance, passive-aggressive personality, and pedophilia. Dr. Befort testified that Hendricks suffered from pedophilia and is likely to commit sexual offenses against children in the future if not confined. He further opined that pedophilia qualifies as a "mental abnormality" within the Act's definition of that term. Finally, Hendricks offered testimony from Dr. William S. Logan, a forensic psychiatrist, who stated that it was not possible to predict with any degree of accuracy the future dangerousness of a sex offender.

is necessarily subject for the common good. On any other basis organized society could not exist with safety to its members." *Jacobson v. Massachusetts*. Accordingly, States have in certain narrow circumstances provided for the forcible civil detainment of people who are unable to control their behavior and who thereby pose a danger to the public health and safety. We have consistently upheld such involuntary commitment statutes provided the confinement takes place pursuant to proper procedures and evidentiary standards. *Foucha*; *Addington v. Texas* [holding that commitment upon proof of clear and convincing evidence of dangerousness is permissible, see p. 922]. It thus cannot be said that the involuntary civil confinement of a limited subclass of dangerous persons is contrary to our understanding of ordered liberty.

The challenged Act unambiguously requires a finding of dangerousness either to one's self or to others as a prerequisite to involuntary confinement. Commitment proceedings can be initiated only when a person "has been convicted of or charged with a sexually violent offense," and "suffers from a mental abnormality or personality disorder which makes the person likely to engage in the predatory acts of sexual violence." The statute thus requires proof of more than a mere predisposition to violence; rather, it requires evidence of past sexually violent behavior and a present mental condition that creates a likelihood of such conduct in the future if the person is not incapacitated. As we have recognized, "previous instances of violent behavior are an important indicator of future violent tendencies." *Schall v. Martin*, 467 U.S. 253, 104 S.Ct. 2403 (1984) (explaining that "from a legal point of view there is nothing inherently unattainable about a prediction of future criminal conduct"). A finding of dangerousness, standing alone, is ordinarily not a sufficient ground upon which to justify indefinite involuntary commitment. We have sustained civil commitment statutes when they have coupled proof of dangerousness with the proof of some additional factor, such as a "mental illness" or "mental abnormality." See, e.g., *Heller v. Doe* [p. 1007] (Kentucky statute permitting commitment of "mentally retarded" or "mentally ill" and dangerous individual); *Allen v. Illinois* [see p. 951]; *Minnesota ex rel. Pearson v. Probate Court*. These added statutory requirements serve to limit involuntary civil confinement to those who suffer from a volitional impairment rendering them dangerous beyond their control. The Kansas Act is plainly of a kind with these other civil commitment statutes: It requires a finding of future dangerousness, and then links that finding to the existence of a "mental abnormality" or "personality disorder" that makes it difficult, if not impossible, for the person to control his dangerous behavior. The precommitment requirement of a "mental abnormality" or "personality disorder" is consistent with the requirements of these other statutes that we have upheld in that it narrows the class of person eligible for confinement to those who are unable to control their dangerousness.

Hendricks nonetheless argues that our earlier cases dictate a finding of "mental illness" as a prerequisite for civil commitment, citing *Foucha* and *Addington*. He then asserts that a "mental abnormality" is not equivalent to a "mental illness" because it is a term coined by the Kansas Legislature, rather than by the psychiatric community. Contrary to Hendricks' assertion, the term "mental illness" is devoid of any talismanic significance. Not only do "psychiatrists disagree widely and frequently on what constitutes mental illness," but the Court itself has used a variety of expressions to describe the mental condition of those properly subject to civil confinement. See, e.g., *Addington*, (using the terms "emotionally disturbed" and "mentally ill"); *Jackson v. Indiana*, 406 U. S., at 732, 737 (using the terms "incompetency" and "insanity"); cf. *Foucha*, 504 U.S., at 88 (O'CONNOR, J., concurring in part and concurring in judgment) (acknowledging State's authority to commit a person when there is "some medical justification for doing so"). Indeed, we have never required State legislatures to adopt any particular nomenclature in drafting civil commitment statutes. Rather, we have traditionally left to legislators the task of defining terms of a medical nature that have legal significance. As a consequence, the States have, over the years, developed numerous specialized terms to define mental health concepts. Often, those definitions do not fit precisely with the definitions employed by the medical community. The legal definitions of "insanity" and "competency," for example, vary substantially from their psychiatric counterparts. Legal definitions, however, which must "take into account such issues as individual responsibility . . . and competency," need not mirror those advanced by the medical profession. American Psychiatric Association, Diagnostic and Statistical Manual of Mental Disorders xxiii, xxvii (4th ed. 1994).

To the extent that the civil commitment statutes we have considered set forth criteria relating to an individual's inability to control his dangerousness, the Kansas Act sets forth comparable criteria and Hendricks' condition doubtless satisfies those criteria. The mental health professionals who evaluated Hendricks diagnosed him as suffering from pedophilia, a condition the psychiatric profession itself classifies as a serious mental disorder. See *id.*; American Psychiatric Association, Treatments of Psychiatric Disorders, 617–633 (1989).[3] Hendricks even conceded that, when he becomes "stressed out," he cannot "control the

---

[3] We recognize, of course, that psychiatric professionals are not in complete harmony in casting pedophilia, or paraphilias in general, as "mental illnesses." Compare Brief for American Psychiatric Association as Amicus Curiae 26 with Brief for Menninger Foundation et al. as Amici Curiae 22–25. These disagreements, however, do not tie the State's hands in setting the bounds of its civil commitment laws. In fact, it is precisely where such disagreement exists that legislatures have been afforded the widest latitude in drafting such statutes. Cf. *Jones v. United States* [see pp. 978–984]. As we have explained regarding congressional enactments, when a legislature "undertakes to act in areas fraught with medical and scientific uncertainties, legislative options must be especially broad and courts should be cautious not to rewrite legislation."

urge" to molest children. This admitted lack of volitional control, coupled with a prediction of future dangerousness, adequately distinguishes Hendricks from other dangerous persons who are perhaps more properly dealt with exclusively through criminal proceedings. Hendricks' diagnosis as a pedophile, which qualifies as a "mental abnormality" under the Act, thus plainly suffices for due process purposes.

DP
satisfied

B

We granted Hendricks' cross-petition to determine whether the Act violates the Constitution's double jeopardy prohibition or its ban on ex post facto lawmaking. The thrust of Hendricks' argument is that the Act establishes criminal proceedings; hence confinement under it necessarily constitutes punishment. He contends that where, as here, newly enacted "punishment" is predicated upon past conduct for which he has already been convicted and forced to serve a prison sentence, the Constitution's Double Jeopardy and Ex Post Facto Clauses are violated. We are unpersuaded by Hendricks' argument that Kansas has established criminal proceedings.

The categorization of a particular proceeding as civil or criminal "is first of all a question of statutory construction." *Allen*. We must initially ascertain whether the legislature meant the statute to establish "civil" proceedings. If so, we ordinarily defer to the legislature's stated intent. Here, Kansas' objective to create a civil proceeding is evidenced by its placement of the Sexually Violent Predator Act within the Kansas probate code, instead of the criminal code, as well as its description of the Act as creating a "civil commitment procedure." Nothing on the face of the statute suggests that the legislature sought to create anything other than a civil commitment scheme designed to protect the public from harm. Although we recognize that a "civil label is not always dispositive," *Allen*, we will reject the legislature's manifest intent only where a party challenging the statute provides "the clearest proof" that "the statutory scheme [is] so punitive either in purpose or effect as to negate [the State's] intention" to deem it "civil." In those limited circumstances, we will consider the statute to have established criminal proceedings for constitutional purposes. Hendricks, however, has failed to satisfy this heavy burden.

As a threshold matter, commitment under the Act does not implicate either of the two primary objectives of criminal punishment: retribution or deterrence. The Act's purpose is not retributive because it does not affix culpability for prior criminal conduct. Instead, such conduct is used solely for evidentiary purposes, either to demonstrate that a "mental abnormality" exists or to support a finding of future dangerousness. We have previously concluded that an Illinois statute was nonpunitive even though it was triggered by the commission of a sexual assault, explaining that evidence of the prior criminal conduct was "received not to punish past misdeeds, but primarily to show the accused's mental condition and to predict future behavior." *Allen*. In addition, the Kansas Act does not make a criminal conviction a prerequisite for commitment—persons absolved of criminal responsibility may nonetheless be subject to confinement under the Act. An absence of the necessary criminal responsibility suggest that the State is not seeking retribution for a past misdeed. Thus, the fact that the Act may be "tied to criminal activity" is "insufficient to render the statute punitive." Moreover, unlike a criminal statute, no finding of scienter is required to commit an individual who is found to be a sexually violent predator; instead, the commitment determination is made based on a "mental abnormality" or "personality disorder" rather than on one's criminal intent. The existence of a scienter requirement is customarily an important element in distinguishing criminal from civil statutes. The absence of such a requirement here is evidence that confinement under the statute is not intended to be retributive.

Nor can it be said that the legislature intended the Act to function as a deterrent. Those persons committed under the Act are, by definition, suffering from a "mental abnormality" or a "personality disorder" that prevents them from exercising adequate control over their behavior. Such persons are therefore unlikely to be deterred by the threat of confinement. And the conditions surrounding that confinement do not suggest a punitive purpose on the State's part. The State has represented that an individual confined under the Act is not subject to the more restrictive conditions placed on state prisoners, but instead experiences essentially the same conditions as any involuntarily committed patient in the state mental institution. Because none of the parties argues that people institutionalized under the Kansas general civil commitment statute are subject to punitive conditions, even though they may be involuntarily confined, it is difficult to conclude that persons confined under this Act are being "punished."

Although the civil commitment scheme at issue here does involve an affirmative restraint, "the mere fact that a person is detained does not inexorably lead to the conclusion that the government has imposed punishment." *United States v. Salerno* [upholding pretrial detention of dangerous individuals]. The State may take measures to restrict the freedom of the dangerously mentally ill. This is a legitimate non-punitive governmental objective and has been historically so regarded. The Court has, in fact, cited the confinement of "mentally unstable individuals who present a danger to the public" as one classic example of nonpunitive detention. *Id.* If detention for the purpose of protecting the community from harm necessarily constituted punishment, then all involuntary civil commitments would have to be considered punishment. But we have never so held.

Hendricks focuses on his confinement's potentially indefinite duration as evidence of the State's punitive intent. That focus, however, is misplaced. Far from any punitive objective, the confinement's duration is instead linked to the stated purposes of the commitment, namely, to hold the person until his mental abnormality no longer causes him to be a threat to others. If, at any time, the confined person is adjudged "safe to be at large," he is statutorily entitled to immediate release. Furthermore, commitment under the Act is only potentially indefinite. The maximum amount of time an individual can be incapacitated pursuant to a single judicial proceeding is one year. If Kansas seeks to continue the detention beyond that year, a court must once again determine beyond a reasonable doubt that the detainee satisfies the same standards as required for the initial confinement. This requirement again demonstrates that Kansas does not intend an individual committed pursuant to the Act to remain confined any longer than he suffers from a mental abnormality rendering him unable to control his dangerousness.

Hendricks next contends that the State's use of procedural safeguards traditionally found in criminal trials makes the proceedings here criminal rather than civil. In *Allen*, we confronted a similar argument. There, the petitioner "placed great reliance on the fact that proceedings under the Act are accompanied by procedural safeguards usually found in criminal trials" to argue that the proceedings were civil in name only. We rejected that argument, however, explaining that the State's decision "to provide some of the safeguards applicable in criminal trials cannot itself turn these proceedings into criminal prosecutions." The numerous procedural and evidentiary protections afforded here demonstrate that the Kansas Legislature has taken great care to confine only a narrow class of particularly dangerous individuals, and then only after meeting the strictest procedural standards. That Kansas chose to afford such procedural protections does not transform a civil commitment proceeding into a criminal prosecution.

Finally, Hendricks argues that the Act is necessarily punitive because it fails to offer any legitimate "treatment." Without such treatment, Hendricks asserts, confinement under the Act amounts to little more than disguised punishment. Hendricks' argument assumes that treatment for his condition is available, but that the State has failed (or refused) to provide it. The Kansas Supreme Court, however, apparently rejected this assumption, explaining:

> "It is clear that the overriding concern of the legislature is to continue the segregation of sexually violent offenders from the public. Treatment with the goal of reintegrating them into society is incidental, at best. The record reflects that treatment for sexually violent predators is all but nonexistent. The legislature concedes that sexually violent predators are not amenable to treatment under [the

existing Kansas involuntary commitment statute]. If there is nothing to treat under [that statute], then there is no mental illness. In that light, the provisions of the Act for treatment appear somewhat disingenuous."

It is possible to read this passage as a determination that Hendricks' condition was untreatable under the existing Kansas civil commitment statute, and thus the Act's sole purpose was incapacitation. Absent a treatable mental illness, the Kansas court concluded, Hendricks could not be detained against his will.

Accepting the Kansas court's apparent determination that treatment is not possible for this category of individuals does not obligate us to adopt its legal conclusions. We have already observed that, under the appropriate circumstances and when accompanied by proper procedures, incapacitation may be legitimate end of the civil law. *Allen*; *Salerno*. Accordingly, the Kansas court's determination that the Act's "overriding concern" was the continued "segregation of sexually violent offenders" is consistent with our conclusion that the Act establishes civil proceedings, especially when that concern is coupled with the State's ancillary goal of providing treatment to those offenders, if such is possible. While we have upheld state civil commitment statutes that aim both to incapacitate and to treat, see *Allen*, we have never held that the Constitution prevents a State from civilly detaining those for whom no treatment is available, but who nevertheless pose a danger to others. A State could hardly be seen as furthering a "punitive" purpose by involuntarily confining persons afflicted with an untreatable, highly, contagious disease. Accord *Compagnie Francaise de Navigation a Vapeur v. Louisiana Bd. of Health*, 186 U.S. 380 (1902) (permitting involuntary quarantine of persons suffering from communicable diseases). Similarly, it would be of little value to require treatment as a precondition for civil confinement of the dangerously insane when no acceptable treatment existed. To conclude otherwise would obligate a State to release certain confined individuals who were both mentally ill and dangerous simply because they could not be successfully treated for their afflictions.

Alternatively, the Kansas Supreme Court's opinion can be read to conclude that Hendricks' condition is treatable, but that treatment was not the State's "overriding concern," and that no treatment was being provided (at least at the time Hendricks was committed). Even if we accept this determination that the provision of treatment was not the Kansas Legislature's "overriding" or "primary" purpose in passing the Act, this does not rule out the possibility that an ancillary purpose of the Act was to provide treatment, and it does not require us to conclude that the Act is punitive. Indeed, critical language in the Act itself demonstrates that the Secretary of Social and Rehabilitation Services, under whose custody sexually violent predators are committed, has an obligation to provide treatment to individuals like Hendricks. ("If the court or jury determines that the person is a sexually violent predator, the person shall be committed to the custody of the secretary of social and rehabilitation services for control, care and treatment until such time as the person's mental abnormality or personality disorder has so changed that the person is safe to be at large"). Other of the Act's sections echo this obligation to provide treatment for committed persons. Thus, as in *Allen*, "the State has a statutory obligation to provide 'care and treatment for [persons adjudged sexually dangerous] designed to effect recovery,'" and we may therefore conclude that "the State has . . . provided for the treatment of those it commits."

Although the treatment program initially offered Hendricks may have seemed somewhat meager, it must be remembered that he was the first person committed under the Act. That the State did not have all of its treatment procedures in place is thus not surprising. What is significant, however, is that Hendricks was placed under the supervision of the Kansas Department of Health and Social and Rehabilitative Services, housed in a unit segregated from the general prison population and operated not by employees of the Department of Corrections, but by other trained individuals. And, before this Court, Kansas declared "absolutely" that persons committed under the Act are now receiving in the neighborhood of "31.5 hours of treatment per week."[5]

Where the State has "disavowed any punitive intent"; limited confinement to a small segment of particularly dangerous individuals; provided strict procedural safeguards; directed that confined persons be segregated from the general prison population and afforded the same status as others who have been civilly committed; recommended treatment if such is possible; and permitted immediate release upon a showing that the individual is no longer dangerous or mentally impaired, we cannot say that it acted with punitive intent. We therefore hold that the Act does not establish criminal proceedings and that involuntary confinement pursuant to the Act is not punitive. Our conclusion that the Act is nonpunitive thus removes an essential prerequisite for both Hendricks' double jeopardy and ex post facto claims.

*   *   *

---

[5] Indeed, we have been informed that an August 28, 1995, hearing on Hendricks' petition for state habeas corpus relief, the trial court, over admittedly conflicting testimony, ruled that: "The allegation that no treatment is being provided to any of the petitioners or other persons committed to the program designated as a sexual predator treatment program is not true. I find that they are receiving treatment." Thus, to the extent that treatment is available for Hendricks' condition, the State now appears to be providing it. By furnishing such treatment, the Kansas Legislature has indicated that treatment, if possible, is at least an ancillary goal of the Act, which easily satisfies any test for determining that the Act is not punitive.

The concurring opinion of JUSTICE KENNEDY and the dissenting opinion of JUSTICE BREYER, joined by JUSTICES STEVENS, SOUTER and GINSBURG, are omitted.

QUESTIONS AND COMMENTS

1. *The definition of punishment.* The Kansas Sexually Violent Predator Act permits long-term confinement in a maximum security institution. Why is this confinement not criminal punishment (and thus barred under the double jeopardy clause when imposed on a person who has already served a sentence)? The Court's principal answer to this question is that the confinement "does not implicate either of the two primary objectives of criminal punishment: retribution or deterrence." Do you agree?

Even if the only purposes behind the statute are public protection through incapacitation and rehabilitation, does it follow that the confinement it authorizes is not punishment? Recall from the introduction of this chapter that, although retributive and deterrence considerations do control the scope of criminal liability, the individual prevention goals such as incapacitation and rehabilitation can play a significant role at sentencing. Cf. Frank Zimring & Gordon Hawkins, Incapacitation 3 (1995) ("Incapacitation now serves as the principal justification for imprisonment in American criminal justice: offenders are imprisoned in the United States to restrain them from offending again while they are confined. . . ."). Should the state at least have to provide treatment that is likely to be effective or, as the Court seems to say, is pure incapacitation (without any retributive, deterrent or rehabilitative purpose) also outside the punishment category? The four dissenters in *Hendricks* argued that the statute was punitive in intent because Hendricks's treatment needs had been ignored for the 10 years he was in prison and were likely to be ignored under the new regime as well; "when a State decides offenders can be treated and confines an offender to provide that treatment, but then refuses to provide it, the refusal to treat while a person is fully incapacitated begins to look punitive." 521 U.S. at 381, 117 S.Ct. at 2091–92 (Breyer, J., dissenting).

In *Seling v. Young,* 531 U.S. 250, 121 S.Ct. 727, 148 L.Ed.2d 734 (2001), the Court again rejected the argument that failure to provide treatment to a specific individual committed as a sexual predator can result in punishment of that individual. It concluded that permitting such claims would permit an "end-run" around the determination that sex offender commitment programs are "civil" in nature. However, the Court intimated that committed individuals might be able to bring a due process challenge to confinement conditions. After noting that state law provided that sexual predator commitment is for the purpose of incapacitation and *treatment*, the Court stated that "due process requires that the conditions and duration of confinement under the Act bear some reasonable relation to the purpose for which persons are committed." 531 U.S. at 265, 121 S.Ct. at 736 (see Chapter Ten for further discussion of the right to treatment and remedies for its violation).

2.   *The criteria for confinement.* As the introduction to this chapter indicated, because of its retributive and deterrent underpinnings, criminal liability traditionally has been predicated on proof of a criminal act and may not be based on speculation about future criminality. However, if, as the Court held with respect to the Kansas Sexual Predator Act, criminal punishment is not involved, then state deprivation of liberty based on a prediction of bad behavior might be permissible. Under what circumstances?

Sexually violent predator (SVP) statutes require proof of: (1) the commission of a "sexually violent act; (2) a propensity to commit sexually violent acts; and (3) some sort of psychological abnormality. The statutes usually define "sexually violent act" as any violent act that is "sexually motivated"; the offense need not be against children, constitute sexual battery or attempted sexual battery, or be recent. See, e.g., Ariz. Stat. § 13–118; Fla. Stat. § 394.912(9)(h). The definition of dangerousness ranges from "more likely than not," Mo.Stat. § 632.480(5), to "substantially probable," Ill. Stat. 207/5(f), to "a propensity to commit acts of sexual violence . . . of such as degree as to pose a menace to the health and safety of others." Kan. § 59–29a02(c). Why require a past illegal act if the requisite degree of risk is shown? What degree of risk should have to be shown? Assuming the first two predicates are met, why is the third criterion required?

With respect to the last question, *Hendricks* stated that "[a] finding of dangerousness, standing alone, is ordinarily not a sufficient ground upon which to justify indefinite involuntary commitment"; "some additional factor, such as a 'mental illness' or 'mental abnormality' " is required. If a person is shown by clear evidence to be a threat to the community, why should we require something more? And why should that additional factor be some sort of mental disability?

Some commentators have argued that preventive detention of dangerous people with serious mental disability is justified as a "gap-filler." While most dangerous people can be criminally punished, those who are not guilty by reason of insanity cannot be; therefore, society needs some other means of protecting itself from the latter group. Stephen J. Schulhofer, *Two Systems of Social Protection: Comments on the Civil–Criminal Distinction, with Particular Reference to Sexually Violent Predator Laws*, 7 J. Contemp. Legal Issues 69, 85 (1996) (" 'civil' deprivation of liberty is permissible only as a gap-filler, to solve problems the criminal process cannot address"). On the other hand, it is asserted, preventive detention of those who are not insane would not be justified by this gap-filling rationale. Is that true? What if a clearly dangerous person has just been released from prison but has not yet committed another offense? Doesn't society need some "gap-filling" means to protect itself from such an individual?

Other commentators have argued that preventive detention of people with serious mental disability is permissible because they are lacking in autonomy. These scholars begin with the premise that preventive detention generally is impermissible because it treats people as "automatons" or "non-persons" who cannot control their behavior. Conversely, however, people with serious mental disability can be singled out for preventive detention because they are non-responsible, and thus their incarceration for acts they have yet to commit does not violate notions of autonomy. See, e.g., Eric S. Janus, Hendricks *and the Moral Terrain of Police Power Civil commitment*, 4 Psychol. Pub. Pol'y & L. 297, 298 (1998) ("Properly understood, the *Hendricks* decision will limit civil commitment to those who are 'too sick to deserve punishment.'"); Stephen Morse, *Uncontrollable Urges and Irrational People*, 88 Va. L. Rev. 1025, 1025–27 (2002) (arguing that sexual predator commitment should be limited to those who are "nonresponsible").

A third rationale for preventive detention of people with serious mental disorder, as well as other narrow categories of people who are not mentally disordered, is based on a notion of "undeterrability." On this view, the state may resort to a system other than the criminal justice process to prevent harm to others "when, and only when (1) the criteria for criminal punishment do not apply and (2) the individual is unlikely to be affected by a significant prospect of serious criminal punishment because he or she either cannot or will not choose the right course." Christopher Slobogin, *Prevention Detention in the United States and Europe*, in Preventing Danger 137, 149 (Michael Ciananello & Michael Corrado, eds. 2013). Those considered undeterrable in this sense would include not only those who are seriously mentally ill but also people with severe impulse disorders, enemy combatants who are under orders to kill, and people with communicable diseases who, when in public, have no control over the harm they can cause. Id. at 151–52 (describing why the criminal law "cannot works as a preventive mechanism" in these situations).

The Kansas statute permits commitment of any sex offender "who suffers from a mental abnormality . . . which . . . predisposes the person to commit sexually violent offenses in a degree constituting such person a menace to the health and safety of others." Does this language adequately define the class of sex offenders who may be committed? Does it require proof of anything other than dangerousness? The *Hendricks* Court construes the Kansas statute to permit confinement only of those "who suffer from a volitional impairment rendering them dangerous beyond their control." Is that construction necessary to save the statute? Sufficient? How is it different from a finding of insanity under the volitional prong? Put differently, should the state be able to secure a conviction of a sex offender at trial based on the argument that he is sane and then, once he has served his sentence, argue that he should be committed as a sexual predator?

The Supreme Court partially answered these questions in *Kansas v. Crane*, 534 U.S. 407, 122 S.Ct. 867, 151 L.Ed.2d 856 (2002). Consider this excerpt from Justice Breyer's opinion for seven members of the Court:

> . . . *Hendricks* set forth no requirement of total or complete lack of control. *Hendricks referred to the Kansas* Act as requiring a "mental abnormality" or "personality disorder" that makes it "*difficult*, if not impossible, for the [dangerous] person to control his dangerous behavior." The word "difficult" indicates that the lack of control to which

this Court referred was not absolute. Indeed, as different amici on opposite sides of this case agree, an absolutist approach is unworkable. Brief for Association for the Treatment of Sexual Abusers as Amicus Curiae 3; cf. Brief for American Psychiatric Association et al. as Amici Curiae 10; cf. also American Psychiatric Association, Statement on the Insanity Defense 11 (1982), reprinted in G. Melton, J. Petrila, N. Poythress, & C. Slobogin, Psychological Evaluations for the Courts 200 (2d ed. 1997) (" 'The line between an irresistible impulse and an impulse not resisted is probably no sharper than that between twilight and dusk' "). Moreover, most severely ill people—even those commonly termed "psychopaths"—retain some ability to control their behavior. Insistence upon absolute lack of control would risk barring the civil commitment of highly dangerous persons suffering severe mental abnormalities.

We do not agree with the State, however, insofar as it seeks to claim that the Constitution permits commitment of the type of dangerous sexual offender considered in *Hendricks* without any lack-of-control determination. *Hendricks* underscored the constitutional importance of distinguishing a dangerous sexual offender subject to civil commitment "from other dangerous persons who are perhaps more properly dealt with exclusively through criminal proceedings." That distinction is necessary lest "civil commitment" become a "mechanism for retribution or general deterrence"—functions properly those of criminal law, not civil commitment. Id. (KENNEDY, J., concurring); cf. also Moran, The Epidemiology of Antisocial Personality Disorder, 34 Social Psychiatry & Psychiatric Epidemiology 231, 234 (1999) (noting that 40%–60% of the male prison population is diagnosable with Antisocial Personality Disorder). The presence of what the "psychiatric profession itself classifie[d] . . . as a serious mental disorder" helped to make that distinction in *Hendricks*. And a critical distinguishing feature of that "serious . . . disorder" there consisted of a special and serious lack of ability to control behavior.

In recognizing that fact, we did not give to the phrase "lack of control" a particularly narrow or technical meaning. And we recognize that in cases where lack of control is at issue, "inability to control behavior" will not be demonstrable with mathematical precision. It is enough to say that there must be proof of serious difficulty in controlling behavior. And this, when viewed in light of such features of the case as the nature of the psychiatric diagnosis, and the severity of the mental abnormality itself, must be sufficient to distinguish the dangerous sexual offender whose serious mental illness, abnormality, or disorder subjects him to civil commitment from the dangerous but typical recidivist convicted in an ordinary criminal case. *Foucha v. Louisiana*, 504 U.S. 71, 82–83, 112 S.Ct. 1780, 118 L.Ed.2d 437 (1992) (rejecting an approach to civil commitment that would permit the indefinite confinement "of any convicted criminal" after completion of a prison term).

We recognize that *Hendricks* as so read provides a less precise constitutional standard than would those more definite rules for which the parties have argued. But the Constitution's safeguards of human liberty in the area of mental illness and the law are not always best enforced through precise bright-line rules. For one thing, the States retain considerable leeway in defining the mental abnormalities and personality disorders that make an individual eligible for commitment. For another, the science of psychiatry, which informs but does not control ultimate legal determinations, is an ever-advancing science, whose distinctions do not seek precisely to mirror those of the law. Consequently, we have sought to provide constitutional guidance in this area by proceeding deliberately and contextually, elaborating generally stated constitutional standards and objectives as specific circumstances require. *Hendricks* embodied that approach.

. . .

The State also questions how often a volitional problem lies at the heart of a dangerous sexual offender's serious mental abnormality or disorder. It points out that the Kansas Supreme Court characterized its state statute as permitting commitment of dangerous sexual offenders who (1) suffered from a mental abnormality properly characterized by an "emotional" impairment and (2) suffered no "volitional" impairment. It adds that, in the Kansas court's view, *Hendricks* absolutely forbids the commitment of any such person. And the State argues that it was wrong to read *Hendricks* in this way. We agree that *Hendricks* limited its discussion to volitional disabilities. And that fact is not surprising. The case involved an individual suffering from pedophilia—a mental abnormality that critically involves what a lay person might describe as a lack of control. DSM–IV 571–572 (listing as a diagnostic criterion for pedophilia that an individual have acted on, or been affected by, "sexual urges" toward children). Hendricks himself stated that he could not "'control the urge'" to molest children. In addition, our cases suggest that civil commitment of dangerous sexual offenders will normally involve individuals who find it particularly difficult to control their behavior—in the general sense described above. Cf. *Seling v. Young*; cf. also Abel & Rouleau, Male Sex Offenders, in Handbook of Outpatient Treatment of Adults: Nonpsychotic Mental Disorders 271 (M. Thase, B. Edelstein, & M. Hersen eds.1990) (sex offenders' "compulsive, repetitive, driven behavior . . . appears to fit the criteria of an emotional or psychiatric illness"). And it is often appropriate to say of such individuals, in ordinary English, that they are "unable to control their dangerousness." *Hendricks*.

Regardless, *Hendricks* must be read in context. The Court did not draw a clear distinction between the purely "emotional" sexually related mental abnormality and the "volitional." Here, as in other areas of psychiatry, there may be "considerable overlap between a . . . defective understanding or appreciation and . . . [an] ability to control . . .

behavior." American Psychiatric Association Statement on the Insanity Defense, 140 Am. J. Psychiatry 681, 685 (1983) (discussing "psychotic" individuals). Nor, when considering civil commitment, have we ordinarily distinguished for constitutional purposes among volitional, emotional, and cognitive impairments. The Court in *Hendricks* had no occasion to consider whether confinement based solely on "emotional" abnormality would be constitutional, and we likewise have no occasion to do so in the present case.

A number of jurisdictions have construed *Crane* to require volitional impairment and a few courts have reversed commitments lacking such proof. See, e.g., *Thomas v. Missouri*, 74 S.W.3d 789 (Mo. 2002), *In re W.Z.*, 173 N.J. 109, 801 A.2d 205 (2002). Yet in many states juries are not even given instructions requiring a finding of "difficulty-in-control." Kenneth W. Gaines, *The Jury:* Crane's *'Serious Difficulty' Requirement and Due Process*, 56 S.C. L. Rev. 291 (2004). Moreover, the last two paragraphs excerpted above suggest that the Court would permit indeterminate long-term commitment of people who are dangerous because of cognitive impairments as well as volitional impairments. Should the former category include only those who are insane under one of the cognitive insanity tests, such as M'Naghten? Or, since the Court is willing to permit commitment of those whose volitional impairments would not amount to insanity under volitional insanity tests, does (should) that category encompass a more broadly defined group? Nationally, only 12% of those committed as sexual predators are diagnosed with a "serious mental illness;" the rest have disorders characterized primarily by antisocial behavior, like paraphilia and antisocial personality disorder. W. Lawrence Fitch, *Sex Offender Commitment in the United States: Legislative and Policy Concerns*, in Sexually Coercive Behavior: Understanding and Management 489, 492 (Robert Prentky et al., eds., 2003) (Table I).

3.   *Other constitutional challenges to sex offender statutes.* Hendricks raised substantive due process, double jeopardy and ex post facto challenges to the Kansas statute. MDSO statutes have also been challenged on equal protection and eighth amendment grounds. In *State ex rel. Pearson v. Probate Court*, 309 U.S. 270, 60 S.Ct. 523, 84 L.Ed. 744 (1940), briefly mentioned in *Hendricks*, the defendant argued that an indeterminate sentence enhancement scheme that focused solely on sex offenders violates the equal protection guarantee. In rejecting that claim, the Supreme Court stated:

> [T]he legislature is free to recognize degrees of harm, and it may confine its restrictions to those classes of cases where the need is deemed to be clearest. If the law "presumably hits the evil where it is most felt, it is not to be overthrown because there are other instances to which it might have been applied."

309 U.S. at 275, 60 S.Ct. at 526. Some classes of offenders might be considered at least as "dangerous" as sex offenders. Consider, for instance, the fact that people who commit property crime are much more likely to recidivate than sex offenders, and that about three-fifths of all rapes in the

home, three-fifths of all home robberies, and about a third of home aggravated and simple assaults are committed by burglars. Bureau of Justice Stats., Home Burglary 1 (Jan. 1985). Of course, another response to such an equal protection challenge is to expand those subject to commitment. California has for some time committed "mentally disordered offenders" after completion of sentence if (1) the original offense used violence or caused serious bodily injury; (2) the offender's mental disorder is severe and not in remission or cannot be kept in remission without treatment; and (3) as a result the person represents a substantial danger of physical harm to others. Cal. Penal Code §§ 2960–2981 (1999). However, offenders committed under this law seem to have more serious disorders than the average sexual predator; further, the average length of commitment is less than two years. Jon Fetterly, Commitment Under California's Mentally Disordered Offender Law (2003).

cruel punishment

State v. Little, 199 Neb. 772, 261 N.W.2d 847 (1978), analyzed two eighth amendment challenges to an MDSO statute. The first was based on *Robinson v. California*, 370 U.S. 660, 82 S.Ct. 1417, 8 L.Ed.2d 758 (1962). The *Little* court's description and application of *Robinson* follows:

> In *Robinson*, the defendant had been arrested after a police officer had observed needle marks on his arm. The defendant was convicted under a statute that made it an offense to use or be addicted to narcotics despite the fact that it was never proven the defendant had used drugs while in the jurisdiction. According to the Supreme Court, the effect of the statute was to allow a conviction for the mere status of addiction rather than from the actual use of drugs. It was suggested that punishment for the status of being addicted to drugs is just as repugnant to traditional ideas of fairness and justice as punishment for a physical illness such as leprosy or venereal disease or a mental illness. The Court held that a status offense was one where there is no actus reus present and the imposition of any punishment for such an offense violates the cruel and unusual punishment prohibition of the Eighth Amendment.

> We do not find *Robinson* controlling on the issue of the constitutionality of confinement under Nebraska's Sexual Sociopath Act. [The statute] provides that a proceeding under the act may only be instituted following a criminal conviction. The conviction is the actus reus that was absent in *Robinson* and distinguishes it from that case.

How would the Kansas statute at issue in *Hendricks* fare under a *Robinson*-type challenge? Is the eighth amendment even applicable, given *Hendrick's* holding that the Kansas statute does not involve punishment?

Below is the *Little* court's treatment of the second eighth amendment challenge raised in that case:

> Defendant's major argument that the confinement of untreatable sexual sociopaths dictated by statute constitutes cruel and unusual punishment rests on the premise that the sentence is disproportionate to the nature of the offense. [Under the statute, a sexual sociopath who is designated

"untreatable" is confined to a ward within the Nebraska Penal and Correctional Complex; release from this confinement may be sought at one-year intervals on a motion by or on behalf of the defendant].

We cannot ignore the reality that, even with this procedure for discharge, the indefinite term of confinement may easily become a life sentence. Once the designation of untreatability is made, the statute places the sexual sociopath in legal limbo. The defendant is sent to a segregated portion of the penal complex with no evidence that he is given other than custodial care. By the terms of the statute, he is given no treatment. He is expected to bear the burden of proving he has somehow recovered in the vacuum situation in which the statute places him. . . . Despite the labeling of the initial commitment as civil, the statute's provision for possible life confinement, without any provisions for treatability or review of treatability, make[s] the statute penal in nature.

* * *

[W]e agree with [the defendant] that treatment is a necessary part of a statutory scheme involving sexual sociopaths. The Nebraska statute has no provision for even review of treatability once the initial determination of untreatability is made. As defendant points out, under the terms of the Sexual Sociopath Act: "For appellant and other untreatable sexual sociopaths, even the milieu of hope and opportunity of a treatment facility is foreclosed." Thus, without more, the untreatable sexual sociopath faces a probable life sentence. As such, the statute is penal in nature and the sentence under it is so disproportionate to the offense committed in this case as to constitute cruel and unusual punishment.

The *Little* court did not strike down the statute, however. Instead, it upheld the statute on condition that "an annual evaluation by qualified professional personnel . . . be made of each sexual sociopath [an old term for MDSO] housed in the penal complex and an annual review of treatability be made by the District Court from which such individual was originally committed." With that requirement added, commitment under the statute no longer constituted punishment for eighth amendment purposes.

In contrast to the Nebraska law at issue in *Little*, the statute at issue in *Hendricks* requires annual review. Is that enough? Since 1939, Minnesota has had a statute similar to Kansas', including an annual review provision. Based on a review of records beginning, of 75 individuals committed under the statute, "[n]ot one person committed since 1975 has been discharged from a final sex offender commitment," although one was provisionally discharged and five others were put in state nursing homes. Eric S. Janus, *Preventing Sexual Violence: Setting Principled Constitutional Boundaries on Sex Offender Commitments*, 72 Ind. L. J. 157, 206 (1996). Washington, which pioneered sex predator legislation in 1990, had released two individuals committed under that law as of mid–1998. Rael Jean Isaac, *Put Sex Predators Behind Bars, Not on the Couch*, Wall St. Journal, May 8, 1998. None of the more than 400 individuals committed under California's law since it was enacted in 1995 had been released by 2002. Grant Morris, *Punishing the Unpunishable—The Abuse of Psychiatry to Confine Those We Love to Hate*, 30 J. Am. Acad. Psychiatry & L. 556, 561 (2002).

One final constitutional challenge to post-sentence commitment laws was raised in *United States v. Comstock*, 560 U.S. 126, 130 S.Ct. 1949, 176 L.Ed.2d 878 (2010). There the petitioner, a federal prisoner, argued that the Adam Walsh Child Protection and Safety Act, which *inter alia* permits post-sentence commitment of sexually dangerous offenders (modeled on the Kansas statute in *Hendricks*), was unconstitutional, because regulating dangerous individuals is not within Congress's enumerated powers under the Constitution. The Court rejected the claim, reasoning that the Congress had the authority to pass such legislation under the Necessary and Proper Clause in Article I of the Constitution, which has long been construed to permit federal criminalization of conduct and enactment of laws governing federal prisons, despite the fact that authority to do so is not explicitly provided for in the Constitution.

4.   *Treatment considerations.* Perhaps relevant to these constitutional issues is research on the treatability of those who are committed to sex offender programs. Whereas traditional psychotherapy appears to be ineffective with sex offenders, several studies report some success with comprehensive cognitive-behavioral programs, at least among child molesters and exhibitionists (recidivism among rapists is not reduced as significantly). See R. Karl Hanson et al., *The Principles of Effective Correctional Treatment Also Apply To Sexual Offenders: A Meta–Analysis*, 26 Crim. Just. Behav. 865 (2009); Marnie Rice & Grant Harris, *The Treatment of Mentally Disordered Offenders*, 3 Psychol., Pub. Pol. & L. 126, 154–56 (1997); John Kip Cornwell, *Protection and Treatment: The Permissible Civil Detention of Sexual Predators*, 54 Wash. & Lee L. Rev. 1293, 1330 (1996). Such a program might involve a three-tier system: (1) initial placement in a maximum security institution for six months with three hours of daily group therapy and individual therapy for one or two hours, aimed at reducing inappropriate attitudes and addressing issues relating to sexuality, social competence, lifestyle, and relapse prevention; (2) transfer to a minimum security facility where the focus is on developing a relapse prevention plan and continuing to eliminate "inappropriate cognitive processes"; (3) reentry into the community with periodic re-evaluations and outpatient treatment. W.L. Marshall et al., *A Three–Tiered Approach to the Rehabilitation of Incarcerated Sex Offenders*, 11 Behav. Sci. & L. 441 (1993). Recent evidence suggests that the most effective psychotherapeutic interventions maximize offenders' ability to learn by providing cognitive-behavioral treatment and matching interventions to offenders' learning styles, motivations, and abilities. Hanson et al., supra, 884–86; R. Hanson et al., *First Report of the Collaborative Outcome Data Project on the Effectiveness of Psychological Treatment for Sex Offenders*, 14 Sexual Abuse 169, 183, 185 (2002) (based on a meta-review of programs, such treatment reduces sexual recidivsm almost by half, from 17% to 10%, and general recidivism by more than a third, from 51% to 32%).

Over the past three decades, psychiatrists have created a huge research literature showing that drugs that reduce testosterone levels reduce the deviant thinking associated with commission of many sex offenses and reduce likelihood of recidivism. These drugs include the hormonal therapies cyproterone acetate (CPA; available in Canada, but not in the U.S.), medroxyprogesterone acetate (MPA) (the hormonal agent most frequently used in the U.S.), luteinizing hormone-releasing hormone (LHRH) agonists such as luprolide, as well as SSRIs, which appear to achieve their effects through actions on serotonin as well as on testosterone. Many offenders see these drugs as desirable therapies because they reduce sometimes-obsessive preoccupations with and urges to commit deviant sexual behavior. But taking MPA regularly commonly causes side effects, including weight gain, decreased sperm production, fatigue, headaches, reduced body hair, depression, and gastrointestinal problems. Furthermore, the effectiveness of the drugs is limited because their physiological effects completely (and sometimes quickly) reverse upon drug withdrawal. Rice & Harris, supra, at 154. Nonetheless, at least one state permits "chemical castration" with MPA after a first sex offense and *requires* such castration after a second sex offense, if a doctor indicates the defendant is an appropriate candidate for the treatment. Fl. Stat. § 794.0235. The statute also provides that the drug treatment is not to be in lieu of any other punishment provided by statute. Defendants may, however, instead elect to undergo "physical castration" (surgical removal of testicles) if they provide the court with "intelligent, knowing, and voluntary consent to physical castration as an alternative penalty." Id.

5.   *Prediction accuracy.* A final challenge to sex offender statutes is that we lack sufficient knowledge to identify who will commit another sex offense. The Supreme Court rejected an identical argument in connection with capital sentencing in *Jurek v. Texas,* described on p. 565, and is likely to do so in this context as well when directly confronted with the issue. Furthermore, courts have not been very demanding with respect to proof of dangerousness. For instance, the California Supreme Court ruled that the language in the state's sexual predator statute requiring that the person be "likely to engage in acts of sexual violence without appropriate treatment and custody" does not require proof that violence is "better than even" but only proof of "substantial danger—that is, a serious and well-founded risk of criminal sexual violence." *People v. Superior Court (Ghilotti)*, 27 Cal.4th 888, 119 Cal.Rptr.2d 1, 44 P.3d 949, 954 (2002). For an argument that such a standard is unconstitutional in light of the Supreme Court's decision in *Addington* requiring proof of dangerousness by clear and convincing evidence, see Fredrick E. Vars, *Delineating Sexual Dangerousness*, 50 Houston L. Rev. 855 (2013) (equating the clear and convincing evidence standard with a 75% level of certainty)

Nonetheless, it is worth considering how dangerousness is to be proven. Previous materials have looked at the difference between clinical and actuarial prediction methods, including those that might be used in predicting sex offenses (see Chapter Six, Part II.C). Most knowledgeable mental health professionals now agree that the actuarial approaches to ranking sex offenders' risk are superior to unstructured clinical judgment. But actuarial approaches are far from perfect. Mossman provides an example, assuming use of an actuarial risk assessment instrument of typical accuracy to evaluate a group of sex offenders with a 15% overall five-year recidivism rate (assumptions that are typical of recent findings). Using the two highest scores on the instrument as a cut-off would identify a small subpopulation in which the rate of recidivism was 48%, a fairly good "hit rate." But use of that cut-off score would also misidentify 85% of the recidivists (because they scored below the cut-off) and 3% of the non-recidivists (who scored above the cut-off). Douglas Mossman, *Analyzing the Performance of Risk Assessment Instruments: A Response to Vrieze and Grove*, 32 Law Hum. Behav. 279, 287 (2008).

In evaluating these numbers, which may well represent the best we can do with current methodologies, consider this assessment of the inaccuracy associated with the criminal justice system:

> Every criminal law professor knows the difficulty of differentiating premeditation from ordinary intent, recklessness from negligence. Even if agreement can be reached as to the precise definition of these concepts, independent judges and juries applying such definitions are bound to arrive at different results on the same facts; for instance, disagreement is highly likely in deciding between first and second degree murder, unprovoked and provoked killing, and voluntary and involuntary manslaughter. These disparities are an inevitable aspect of a system that relies on moral judgments about invisible internal mental states. In social science terms, this high degree of inter-rater inconsistency (or unreliability) cannot help but indicate a high degree of inaccuracy (or invalidity) as well. The assertion that we can know, beyond a reasonable doubt, that a person "deserves" a particular verdict and punishment expresses a hope rather than a reality. And the costs of this inaccuracy are huge—a finding of premeditation can result in the death penalty rather than a 20–year sentence, a conclusion that a defendant's belief was "unreasonable" can mean the difference between conviction and acquittal. If we are willing to countenance a criminal system based on this degree of uncertainty, we may be hard pressed to criticize a preventive detention regime on unreliability grounds.

Christopher Slobogin, *A Jurisprudence of Dangerousness*, 98 Nw. L. Rev. 1, 7–8 (2003).

6.   *Political/moral considerations.* Compare these two comments:

Let us make the reasonable assumption that the risk of a false positive in predicting future sexual violence is approximately 50%. Let us further suppose that we are deciding the disposition of two already convicted sex offenders, now about to be released from prison, one of whom will and one of whom will not commit a violent sexual crime in the future. These two offenders have similar records and psychological profiles. We do not know which of the two will offend if both are not confined.

We have only two options: to release both or confine both.

* * *

A mistaken decision to confine, however painful to the offender involved, is, in my view, simply not morally equivalent to a mistaken decision to release. There is a significant difference between the two. One is much less harmful than the other.

Libertarians who focus exclusively, or heavily, on the injustice being done to a mistakenly confined offender tend to place less significance on the harms caused by the alternative decision, to the extent that they consider them at all. We have been socialized to emphasize injustices to offenders. We have not been sufficiently sensitive to the harm inflicted by sex offenders, especially violent rapists and violent child abusers.

Alexander Brooks, *The Constitutionality and Morality of Civilly Committing Violent Sexual Predators*, 15 U. Puget Sound L. Rev. 709, 753 (1992).

[Sexual predator laws] permit a legislature to use lifetime preventive detention on any group of offenders who have served their prison terms and have been, or will be, released. All that is required to accomplish such a goal is a statute that labels criminals who have committed a single criminal act as suffering from a "mental abnormality" that makes them "likely to reoffend" and authorizes their lifetime confinement for "treatment." Simply put, the predator commitment law has detached involuntary commitment from the medical model of mental illness and *bona fide* treatment.

Once detached, literally no stopping point exists. The logic of the predator commitment law can be applied to people who drive while under the influence of alcohol, who assault their domestic partners or children, who use crack cocaine, or who commit whatever the new "crime-of-the-month" happens to be. Indeed, if mental abnormality, future recidivism, and the need for treatment can be deduced by the commission of a single past crime, the legislature is totally free to create what Justice Stevens aptly called a "shadow . . . criminal code." Such a code can be invoked, not only as an alternative to crime and punishment, but as a way of extending punishment indefinitely.

John LaFond, *Washington's Sexually Violent Predator Law: A Deliberate Misuse of the Therapeutic State for Social Control*, 15 U. Puget Sound L. Rev. 655, 698–99 (1992).

7. *International perspectives.* A number of European countries authorize post-sentence commitment, either indeterminately or for a set time such as ten years. Since 2010, these regimes have been the focus of several decisions by the European Court of Human Rights interpreting the European Convention on Human Rights. In *M. v. Germany*, Application No. 19359/04

(Oct. 5, 2010), the Court held, in contrast to *Hendricks*, that post-sentence confinement is a "penalty," because (1) it is "severe" compared to the typical criminal sentence, (2) it prolongs confinement of people who have repeatedly been found guilty of criminal offenses, which suggests that the detention is really additional punishment, and (3) it takes place in "ordinary prisons, albeit in separate wings," with only "minor" privileges that failed to differentiate it from actual prison. While the European Court noted that the facilities in which people like M. were housed were of "a good or even very good standard," the vast majority of inmates "were completely demotivated" and their "psychological care appeared to be seriously inadequate." The Court indicated that, to avoid the penalty label, such facilities must provide "a high level of care involving a team of multi-disciplinary staff, intensive work with inmates on an individual basis, within a coherent framework for progression toward release, which should be a real option." Since M.'s post-sentence commitment did not meet this requirement it was a "penalty" that could only be imposed pursuant to a conviction for an offense, as required by article 5, § 1 of the European Convention of Human Rights; M.'s detention after he completed his sentence was therefore illegitimate. In a later decision, the European Court suggested that unless an offender has a very serious mental disorder requiring treatment in a mental hospital, post-sentence commitment is not permissible. *Haidn v. Germany*, Application No. 6587/04 (Jan. 13, 2011). Germany significantly revamped its preventive detention schemes as a result of these decisions. Michael Bohlander, Principles of German Criminal Procedure 235 (2012).

A separate international development is the ratification by many countries (but not the United States) of the Convention on the Rights of Persons with Disabilities, which is available at http://www.un.org/disabilities/convention/conventionfull.shtml. Article 14 of the Convention provides in part that "States Parties shall ensure that persons with disabilities, on an equal basis with others: a. Enjoy the right to liberty and security of person; b. Are not deprived of their liberty unlawfully or arbitrarily, and that any deprivation of liberty is in conformity with the law, and that *the existence of a disability shall in no case justify a deprivation of liberty*." (emphasis added). It has been argued that

> [n]o mental health law, no matter how narrowly framed, can ever meet the [italicized] requirements of Article 14, so long as it contains any provision whatsoever that allows involuntary confinement of people with psychosocial disabilities for purposes of treatment or preventive detention, or for any other reason linked in legislation to the existence of the disability. . . . If a state designs a law for preventive detention, or one for detention of people deemed in need of care and treatment, that is aimed at continuing the confinement of people with psychosocial disabilities in institutions against their will, or that has a disproportionate effect of confining people with psychosocial disabilities because of hidden bias in its standards or enforcement, such a law would not be in fact disability-neutral and would need to be repealed."

Tina Minkowitz, *Why Mental Health Laws Contravene the CRPD—An Application of Article 14 with Implications for the Obligations of States Parties*, available at ssrn.com/abstract–19286800 (2012); see also Office of the High Commissioner for Human Rights Thematic Study on Legal Measures for Ratification and Implementation of CRPD, A/HRC/10/48, paras. 48–49. Does this interpretation of Article 14 prohibit statutes like those in *Hendricks* and *M.* even if excellent treatment is provided to those confined and release is a realistic option? Does it prohibit the insanity defense and other defenses based on mental disability? Does it prohibit civil commitment (the subject of the next chapter)?

8. *Alternatives to sex predator laws.* As the previous comment suggests, the sexual predator statute could be described as a "hybrid" law that incorporates aspects of both the criminal law and civil commitment. There are at least four alternatives to such laws that are based more firmly on one of these two traditional paradigms: (1) indeterminate sentencing; (2) sentence enhancement; (3) community notification and residential restriction laws; and (4) traditional civil commitment. How are these alternatives different from the sexual predator statute at issue in *Hendricks*? Which approach is preferable in dealing with violent sex offenders?

The typical indeterminate sentencing scheme was described at the beginning of this section. In *Specht v. Patterson*, 386 U.S. 605, 87 S.Ct. 1209, 18 L.Ed.2d 326 (1967), the Supreme Court held that, to the extent an indeterminate sentence imposed on a sex offender is based on a finding of dangerousness, it must be preceded by a formal hearing (with the right to counsel, cross-examine witnesses, etc.). But the Court also appeared to affirm that, if such process is provided, the state may confine a sex offender for as long as he or she remains dangerous (which the Court recognized might amount to lifetime confinement). In what practical sense is a sexual predator statute different? One difference is that a sexual predator program costs almost $100,000 per person per year, while the per capital annual cost of prison may come closer to $20,000, presumably in part because of lower treatment costs. Eric S. Janus & Robert A. Prentky, *Sexual Predator Laws: A Two–Decade Retrospective*, 21 Fed. Sent. Rep. 90, 91 (2008).

A sentence enhancement scheme (sometimes called a three-strikes statute or habitual offender law) authorizes an extended sentence after a third (or second) conviction for a particular type of offense. For instance, a person convicted of a third sexual battery (for which the usual sentence is, say, 10 years) could have 30 years added to his sentence for the third offense. Though such sentence enhancement schemes achieve a forward-looking incapacitation goal, some would justify them using retributive and deterrent rationales—i.e., that a three-time offender is more blameworthy than one who has offended fewer times, and that maximum deterrence is necessary to forestall those most prone to recidivism. The Supreme Court has upheld against eighth amendment challenges a number of extremely long sentences that seemed out of proportion to the final offense. See, e.g., *Ewing v. California*, 538 U.S. 11, 123 S.Ct. 1179, 155 L.Ed.2d 108 (2003) (25 year sentence for a fourth offense involving theft of $1200 of golf equipment); *Rummel v. Estelle*, 445 U.S. 263, 100 S.Ct. 1133, 63 L.Ed.2d 382 (1980) (life sentence for a third minor felony); cf. *Solem v. Helm*, 463 U.S. 277, 103 S.Ct. 3001, 77 L.Ed.2d 637 (1983) (hinting the eighth amendment might be violated on *Rummel*-type facts if there were no right to parole). From a civil libertarian view, which is preferable, the "selective" incapacitation represented by sexual predator statutes, based on dangerousness, or the "general" incapacitation represented by enhancement laws, based on prior offenses?

The third alternative relies on community-based interventions, and can consist of at least two options. The first—known as "Megan's Law"—requires released sex offenders to register with the state, which then provides their identity and location to the public. In *Connecticut Dep't of Public Safety v. Doe*, 538 U.S. 1, 123 S.Ct. 1160, 155 L.Ed.2d 98 (2003), the Supreme Court held that sex offenders have no procedural due process right to a pre-registration hearing on whether they are currently dangerous, because the Connecticut law is based solely on the fact of previous conviction, for which adequate process had occurred. In *Smith v. Doe*, 538 U.S. 84, 123 S.Ct. 1140, 155 L.Ed.2d 164 (2003), the Court upheld a notification law against an ex post facto attack, relying heavily on *Hendricks* in concluding that such laws are not punishment. The Court left open whether such laws might be infirm on substantive due process grounds because they infringe a liberty interest. This "alternative" could of course instead serve as a supplement to indeterminate or enhanced sentencing laws, as well as to sexual predator laws. A number of released sex offenders have been killed or assaulted, allegedly by individuals who discovered their identities from Internet sex offender registries. David Crary, *Rethinking Sex Offender Laws a Tough Sell*, Associated Press, April 19, 2006 (describing murder of two men listed on Maine's Internet registry and noting "many cases of vigilantism in the past").

Another type of community-based restriction on released sex offenders is a prohibition on living within "buffer zones" around areas in which children congregate. Perhaps 20 states have passed such laws. See Susan Broderick, *Innovative Legislative Strategies for Dealing with Sexual Offenders*, 18(1) Update 1 (American Prosecutor's Research Institute, 2006), http://www.ndaa.org/pdf/update_vol_18_number_10_2006.pdf. For instance, Iowa has enacted a law that prohibits persons convicted of certain sex offenses against minors from living within 2000 feet of a school or a child care facility. As a result, in one county 77% of the residential units were unavailable to sex offenders and cities like Des Moines were virtually off-limits. Nonetheless, citing the two *Doe* cases from the Supreme Court, the Eighth Circuit upheld the statute, finding it did not amount to banishment, and that it was a rational response to the fact that convicted sex offenders are more likely to commit sex offenses against minors than the general population and are tempted to reoffend when around children. *Doe v. Miller*, 405 F.3d 700 (8th Cir. 2005). A subsequent report found that many Iowa towns had further restricted residential options by adding parks, swimming pools, libraries, and bus stops to the locations that sex offenders may not live near. Thus, some sex offenders were sleeping in cars or trucks or clustering in trailer parks, far from potential support networks, and the number who failed to register increased substantially compared to the period before enactment of the laws. Monica Davey, Iowa's Residency Rules Drive Sex Offenders Underground, N.Y. Times, Mar. 15, 2006. In recent years, several research reports have found that residency restrictions have no effect on recidivism and may increase risk of recidivism by making it difficult for released sex offenders to find housing and work—two known stabilizing factors. See, e.g., Paul A. Zandbergen et al., *Residential Proximity to Schools and Daycares: An Empirical Analysis of Sex Offense Recidivism*, 37 Crim. Just. Behav. 482 (2010). Should such findings undercut "rational basis" arguments supporting residency restriction laws? Are the residential restrictions different enough from notification laws to require, contrary to the *Miller* holding, a hearing before it is imposed? See *State v. Samples*, 198 P.3d 803 (Mont. 2008) (hearing required before corrections department may assign a risk level for released offender); *State v. Briggs*, 199 P.3d 935 (Utah 2008) (hearing required before state may publish information about an offender's typical "primary" and "secondary" targets, because such designation implies the offender is currently dangerous); *State v. Dykes*, 728 S.E.2d 455 (S.C. 2012) (hearing required before mandatory lifetime satellite monitoring of sex offender is permitted).

The final alternative to the sexual predator law—civil commitment—is the subject of the next chapter. Note the reasons the Kansas legislature gives (described in the beginning of *Hendricks*) in explaining why "general involuntary commitment" was inadequate for its needs. Consider the validity of these reasons as you read the next chapter.

CHAPTER 8

CIVIL COMMITMENT

■ ■ ■

Table of Sections

————————

I.   INTRODUCTION

History.[a] Involuntary treatment or care of people with mental disorder, outside the criminal setting, is usually called civil commitment. For many years, the United States did not have a "commitment system" as such. Once a method for committing people with mental disorder did develop, the dominant approach varied considerably over time, tending toward either a purely "libertarian" model—which is aimed at limiting the impact of commitment to those who will otherwise harm society—or a purely "paternalistic" model—which seeks to commit anyone who may benefit from state intervention.

In colonial America, people with mental disorder were the responsibility of their family or friends. For those unfortunate persons who lacked such support, the town sometimes would provide money to a designated individual for their care, but more frequently would banish them; thus they would often end up in bands of "drifters" that roamed the countryside. If a "madd" person became violent, he or she might be punished as a criminal. If not, the person was subjected to restraint and perhaps whipping; no treatment was provided, since none existed. In most locales, it is doubtful any explicit legal authority existed for such non-criminal detention. One exception was Massachusetts which, in 1676, enacted a statute ordering the selectmen of towns which had "dangerously distracted persons" to restrain them "that they do not damify others."

During the last half of the eighteenth century, some communities became considerably more involved in dealing with people who had mental problems. In 1752, the Pennsylvania Assembly, in response to a petition drawn by Benjamin Franklin, authorized establishment of the first hospital to receive the sick poor, including people with mental illness who were poverty-stricken. The first hospital devoted exclusively to the latter group was constructed at Williamsburg, Virginia in 1773. Also during this period, state legislatures began enacting statutes that provided express authority for confining people with mental disability in community institutions. For instance, in 1788, the New York legislature passed a statute that permitted constables, after procuring a warrant from two or more justices, to apprehend and lock up the "furiously madd" or those "so far disordered in their senses that they may be dangerous to be permitted to go abroad." Confinement was permitted for the duration of the individual's dangerous condition, although the statute also provided that it should not be construed to prevent friends or relatives from assuming custody of the individual. Thus, this statute appeared to be aimed primarily at people who were violent and who could not be cared

---

[a]   The following historical account through the 1960's is taken from Samuel Brakel et al., The Mentally Disabled and the Law 12–15 (1986); Albert Deutsch, The Mentally Ill in America: A History of the Their Care and Treatment from Colonial Times (2d ed. 1949).

for privately; those disordered individuals who were non-threatening or who could be controlled by private citizens were not the principal targets of the law.

Some evidence suggests that, by the middle of the nineteenth century, detention of these latter two groups of individuals may have become more commonplace. For example, a 1842 New York statute *required* the confinement of *all* "lunatics," not just dangerous ones who were at large. It commissioned "assessors" to search for such people and allowed commitment, upon the authority of two assessors, for a *minimum* of six months. Another example of broadening hospitalization standards was the case of Josiah Oakes. In 1845, Oakes was detained in a hospital, not because he was violent, but on the ground that he suffered from hallucinations and had mismanaged his business affairs, as evidenced by the fact that he became engaged to a young woman of "unsavory" character a few days after the death of his wife. Oakes sought release via a writ of habeas corpus, alleging he had been illegally committed. In rejecting this claim, the Massachusetts Supreme Court stated:

> The right to restrain an insane person of his liberty is found in that great law of humanity, which makes it necessary to confine those whose going at large would be dangerous to themselves or others. . . . And the necessity which creates the law, creates the limitation of the law. The question must then arise in each particular case, whether a patient's own safety, or that of others, requires that he should be restrained for a certain time, and whether restraint is necessary for his restoration, or will be conducive thereto. The restraint can continue as long as the necessity continues.

Although the court recognized that limitations should be placed on the state's authority, it explicitly permitted indeterminate detention not only for those who demonstrated a proneness to harm others but also for those who might harm themselves.

The reasons for this "expansion"[b] of commitment authority are undoubtedly complex, but two explanations stand out. First, as society became more interdependent and government more pervasive, the traditional view that the family was obligated to take care of its own became outmoded. Second, a perception developed that techniques for caring for people with disability had improved. What ultimately became the American Psychiatric Association was founded in 1844. Many of its members, including Benjamin Rush and Isaac Ray, advocated and tried to

---

[b] Some authors, see, e.g., John Myers, *Involuntary Civil Commitment of the Mentally Ill: A System in Need of Change*, 29 Vill.L.Rev. 367, 380 n. 62, 386 n. 102 (1983), have suggested that *Oakes* was merely a restatement of law that had existed for centuries, permitting the state to intervene when a person's mental disability might lead to dissipation of his or her estate. (For a description of this law, see the introduction to guardianship in Chapter Nine). Assuming this is so, *Oakes* still marks one of the first times a court explicitly permitted involuntary *commitment* of a nondangerous person.

develop a scientific approach to the treatment of people with mental illnesses. These apparent advances in medicine meant that commitment could be characterized not merely as detention but as a means of providing treatment, or "restoration", as the *Oakes* court put it.

Nonetheless, for a time after the Civil War, a movement aimed at curtailing the reach of commitment law flourished, motivated in large part by a former mental hospital patient named Mrs. Packard. Packard was committed in 1860 under the following statute: "Married women and infants, who in the judgment of the medical superintendent are evidently insane or distracted, may be received and detained in the hospital at the request of the husband, . . . or [the] guardian of the infants, without the evidence of insanity or distraction required in other cases." Apparently, the primary evidence supporting Packard's commitment under this statute was provided by two doctors, one of whom stated she was rational but was a "religious bigot like Henry Ward Beecher and Horace Greeley," and the second of whom opined that her ideas were "novel." After her release three years later, Packard campaigned against laws and practices that permitted hospitalization solely on the basis of a person's opinions, with no attempt to gauge moral accountability. Her efforts were aided by the publication of "muckraking" books describing pitiful hospital conditions. By the 1890's, many states had adopted statutes that required a jury determination of the commitment issue, authorized the presence of counsel at the hearing, and penalized criminally anyone who knowingly sought the illegal commitment of another.

The movement toward a more legalized commitment process was relatively short-lived, however. From the "Packard era" until the 1970's (with the exception of a period during the 1930's), most changes in civil commitment law aimed at making commitment easier rather than more difficult, again in large part due to medical advances that increased optimism about treatment efficacy. By the early years of the twentieth century, in response to the ceaseless efforts of Dorothea Dix and others, at least 20 states established mental hospitals or enlarged or improved those in existence. Through the middle of the twentieth century, the construction of mental hospitals continued apace, and medical science developed several new treatment modalities, including modern psychotherapy, electro-convulsive therapy, psychosurgery and, probably most importantly, pharmacologial therapies. Concurrent with these developments, many states "medicalized" the procedural requirements associated with commitment. Judges and juries were replaced by physicians or "lunacy commissions" and dangerousness almost disappeared as a criterion for commitment. By 1970, 31 states provided for hospitalization based simply on the certification of one or more physicians that the individual suffered from mental illness and needed treatment.

In the early 1970's, the pendulum swung back toward libertarianism once again. Influenced by the civil rights movement of the 1960's, by exposés of poor hospital conditions and commitment abuses, and by a distrust of psychiatric expertise and the medical model of mental illness upon which it is based, groups of lawyers, mental health professionals and patients successfully exerted pressure for legal reform. The leading statutory indication of the shift was the Lanterman–Petris–Short Act (LPS) in California. Passed in 1969, this statute made dangerousness to self or others the core criterion for commitment, defined this criterion relatively narrowly, and provided extensive procedural protections for respondents (the persons who responded to the allegation they were mentally ill). The LPS provided a model for many other state statutes. On the judicial front, the most important decision was handed down in 1973 by the federal district court for the Eastern District of Wisconsin. In *Lessard v. Schmidt*, excerpted later in this chapter, that court found the Wisconsin civil commitment statute unconstitutional "insofar as it . . . permits commitment without proof . . . that the patient is both 'mentally ill' and dangerous." *Lessard* also mandated procedural changes similar to those available in the criminal context. Several other federal and state courts followed *Lessard's* lead.

More recent decades have seen signs of retrenchment. In 1979, the United States Supreme Court refused to hold that the criminal reasonable doubt standard is constitutionally required in the civil commitment context. *Addington v. Texas,* infra. The same year, it also found that the right to counsel and a judicial tribunal were not necessary attributes of a system for hospitalizing minors. *Parham v. J.R.* infra. In 1997, the Court upheld a statute that permitted sex offender commitments upon proof of dangerousness and "mental abnormality," suggesting that the (more severe) "mental illness" required by *Lessard* may not be constitutionally necessary under some circumstances. *Kansas v. Hendricks* (see p. 774). The appearance of more homeless persons on America's streets in the 1980s, the rise in the number and proportion of persons with mental illness in prisons and jails, and several highly publicized criminal acts by these people have led to calls for liberalizing commitment criteria, calls that several state legislatures have heeded. Whether the pendulum will continue to swing toward a more paternalistic and protectionist model or will instead move back to more stringent libertarianism remains to be seen.

Modern Commitment Statutes. Three general diagnostic populations are subject to today's civil commitment laws: people with mental illnesses, people with developmental disabilities (including people with intellectual disabilities, still referred to in statutes and case law as persons with mental retardation), and persons who are addicted to drugs and alcohol. Many states have separate commitment laws for each. Commitment statutes may also vary depending upon the legal context.

For instance, most states distinguish between adults and minors in establishing criteria and procedures for commitment. Most states also have separate statutes for commitment of those persons acquitted by reason of insanity and prisoners transferred to mental hospitals for treatment. The first four sections of this chapter examine the laws dealing with commitment of the adults with mental illness who have not been processed by the criminal system, because these laws have served as the model for other commitment laws. The final section examines commitment of insanity acquittees, prisoners, people with intellectual disabilities, people with substance abuse disorders, and minors.

Modern statutes governing the commitment of adults with mental illness are relatively uniform. No state still adheres solely to the "mental illness plus need for treatment" standard of commitment; typically a person may not be involuntarily hospitalized unless the government can show that, as a result of mental illness, the person poses a risk of harm to others or to self. Almost all states also permit commitment of a person who is shown to be, as a result of mental illness, "unable to provide for his or her basic needs," "gravely disabled" or "likely to deteriorate." Even if the proper criteria are met, virtually all statutes prohibit institutionalization unless no less restrictive alternative is available in the community. Every state also provides for a commitment hearing, with notice and counsel, and requires periodic reviews of the legal status of committed persons. Additionally, most states have enacted statutes that provide those who have been hospitalized with various rights, including the right to a treatment plan, the right to a safe, clean environment, and the right to communicate with the outside world. The various issues raised by these statutes will be treated in this and subsequent chapters.

The Context of Civil Commitment Law: Deinstitutionalization, Reinstitutionalization, and Privatization. In evaluating and interpreting civil commitment laws, it is important to have some sense of the context in which they operate—the public mental health system. Though we do not provide a full description of this context here, the following remarks should be sufficient to set the stage for an intelligent assessment of civil commitment law.

Probably the most significant historical fact connected with the public mental health system is that the census of public mental hospitals has dropped dramatically since the mid–1950's. In 1956, the number of patients in such institutions on an average day was 551,390 (out of a total U.S. population of 169 million). By 1980, one estimate indicated that the average daily population had dropped to 132,000. During the same time period, however, the annual admission rate for public mental hospitals doubled, from 185,597 to 390,000. Samuel Brakel et al., The Mentally Disabled and the Law 47 (1986). By 2004, the number of involuntarily committed patients at any given time had fallen to 55,000 (out of a population of 275 million), but because of the "revolving door" phenomenon, involving repeat hospitalizations, as many as 660,000 commitments could occur each year. Bruce J. Winick, Civil Commitment: A Therapeutic Justice Model 3 (2004). This number does not include people hospitalized (mostly voluntarily) for treatment of substance use disorders (involving alcohol, cocaine, opiates, methamphetamine, and marijuana), which amounts to about 1.8 million per year. Substance Abuse and Mental Health Services Administration, State Admissions to Substance Abuse Treatment Services 1 (2010).

Several phenomena help to account for this process of "deinstitutionalization," as it has come to be called, and the accompanying surge in admissions rates. The legal reforms of the 1960's and 70's may have had some effect. In a number of states, narrowed commitment criteria, the least restrictive alternative doctrine, and additional procedural protections helped reduce the number of people sent to hospitals, at the same time shortened commitment terms made possible recommitments within the same year and thus increased the annual admission rate.[c] However, a number of studies also concluded that the "libertarian" reforms of the 1970's had only a minimal impact on the number or type of people hospitalized, largely because the new statutory language is still broad enough to be flexibly applied.[d] This research suggests that factors other than legal reform were responsible for much of the changing patterns in the hospital population and in admission rates.

One factor was the advent of psychotropic medication, first introduced as a treatment option in the mid–1950's and described in detail in Chapter One. The growing availability of medications that alleviate the symptoms of persons with schizophrenia, manic-depressive psychosis, depression and other major illnesses[e] offered, for the first time, inexpensive and relatively quick treatments for many people with mental illness. Hospital beds could be emptied much faster, allowing more admissions but also, in the long run, reducing the overall population.

Working in tandem with the medication revolution was the community treatment movement. In 1963, Congress passed the Community Mental Health Centers Act, which provided funding for the

---

[c] See Roger Peters, et al., *The Effects of Statutory Change on the Civil Commitment of the Mentally Ill*, 11 Law & Hum.Beh. 73 (1987) for a survey of the research.

[d] James Luckey & John Berman, *Effects of a New Commitment Law on Involuntary Admissions and Service Utilization Patterns*, 3 Law & Hum.Behav. 149 (1979) (Nebraska); Serena Stier & Kurt Stoebe, Involuntary Hospitalization of the Mentally Ill in Iowa: The Failure of the 1975 Legislation, 64 Iowa L.Rev. 1284, 1371–90 (1979); Larry Faulkner, et al., *Effects of a New Involuntary Commitment Law: Expectations and Reality*, 10 Bull.Am.Acad. Psychiat. & L. 249 (1982); Sara Cleveland, et al., *Do Dangerousness–Oriented Commitment Laws Restrict Hospitalization of Patients Who Need Treatment? A Test*, 40 Hosp. & Comm.Psychiat. 266 (1989) (Pennsylvania).

[e] The treatment of choice for manic-depressive psychosis is lithium, which is not technically an anti-psychotic drug. For further discussion of these medications, see Chapter One, Part III.

establishment of outpatient treatment centers. The CMHC Act was representative of a widespread effort to move the locus of treatment from isolated hospitals to the community, where patients could be closer to support groups and employment opportunities. It reflected a perception that community treatment is at least as effective as confinement in a hospital, which many patient advocates thought aggravated rather than ameliorated patients' problems. The Act and related federal laws also allowed state legislatures to reduce funding by closing state hospitals and shifting much of the financial burden to federal programs. Indeed, convincing arguments have been made that fiscal considerations were the *primary* motivation behind states' actions that resulted in deinstitutionalization. See Carol Warren, The Court of Last Resort: Mental Illness and the Law 21–24 (1982); Ann Braden Johnson, Out of Bedlam: The Truth about Deinstitutionalization (1990). The community mental health centers and other community treatment programs, both outpatient and inpatient, which came into being as a result of this effort to offer an alternative to the traditional public mental hospital undoubtedly contributed to the reduction in the hospital population.

Over the last three decades, numerous studies have examined causes of readmission and the increases in admission rates. Though these studies have yielded sometimes-conflicting results, a multitude of factors play interacting roles: shorter (and possible inadequate) lengths of inpatient stays generally; a view that short-term but frequent acute-care hospitalizations are an acceptable approach to managing persons with persistent and severe psychiatric illness; patient characteristics (e.g., diagnoses of severe mental illness, substance abuse problems, medication noncompliance, violent or criminal behavior); and service delivery factors such as limited access to aftercare and other outpatient services to support community living. Jill B. Romansky et al., *Factors Related to Psychiatric Hospital Readmission Among Children and Adolescents in State Custody*, 54 Psychiatric Serv. 356 (2003).

Other factors that have influenced the public hospital census are the increased use of private and veterans' hospitals as a result of improved insurance coverage, and the advent of Medicaid and Medicare funding, which made possible largescale release of chronic patients to community nursing homes. As Part V.A of Chapter One indicated, the latter development may be the single largest contributing factor to deinstitutionalization. Additionally, hospital population was reduced significantly by the death of elderly patients, a factor which accounted for 20 to 40 percent of all "releases" until the early 1960's, when community placement became available. See Howard Goldman et al., *Deinstitutionalization: The Data Demythologized*, 34 Hosp. & Comm.Psych. 129 (1983).

Despite the many forces pushing for deinstitutionalization, a process of "reinstitutionalization" is taking place in some locales. Again, changes in the law may be partially responsible for this trend. As recounted later in this chapter, for instance, a number of states have broadened their commitment criteria. Another form of re-institutionalization involves the imprisonment of people with mental illness. Some individuals who in the past would have been psychiatrically hospitalized are now processed through the criminal justice system—often on misdemeanor charges akin to "vagrancy" violations—in an effort to remove them from the community. As a result, "we incarcerate, for lack of any alternatives, hundreds of thousands of persons with serious mental health problems." David Cole, *A Closing Keynote: A Comment on Mass Incarceration in the United States*, 11 U. Pa. J. Const. L. 207, 210 (Dec. 2008).

For decades, a debate has raged over whether this development represents the "criminalization of mentally disordered behavior," the "psychiatrization of criminal behavior," or a process of "transinstitutionalization," in which "the mentally ill are alternately and repeatedly routed between the mental health and criminal justice systems." Ralph Slovenko, *The Transinstitutionalization of the Mentally Ill*, 29 Ohio N.U.L. Rev. 641 (2003). On the one hand, some researchers and policymakers have attributed a causal connection between deinstitutionalization and increased numbers of mentally ill persons in jails and prisons, and they conclude that greater access to public sector psychiatric hospitals might restore a more sensible balance. Countering this position is the view that blaming deinstitutionalization alone is too simple; imprisonment rates generally have increased in the United States over the past three decades, and sentencing schemes and parole policies tend to disfavor individuals with severe mental illnesses. These kinds of considerations have motivated recent efforts to divert persons with severe mental illness who are charged with minor crimes into community treatment settings often supervised by mental health courts. Seth J. Prins, *Does Transinstitutionalization Explain the Overrepresentation of People with Serious Mental Illnesses in the Criminal Justice System?* 47 Community Ment. Health J. 716 (2011).

A final development that is likely to have significant impact on the civil commitment process is the trend toward government contracts with private companies, often associated with managed care regimes, to administer publicly financed human service programs. In many jurisdictions, people who are involuntarily committed are hospitalized in a state hospital only after assessment and treatment in a private or quasi-private setting. In Florida, for instance, the 60,000 or so people subject to commitment each year are assessed and initially treated in a community hospital or similar setting. Whether or not they stay in the community or are instead committed to a state hospital may depend upon whether they are enrolled in a managed care program and whether that program will pay for the community treatment. In such cases the ultimate commitment decision "is influenced by external factors having little to do with the statutory terms of the civil commitment law." John Petrila, *Ethics, Money, and the Problem of Coercion in Managed Behavioral Health Care*, 40 St. Louis Univ. L. J. 359, 397 (1996). Another conflict between public and private goals might arise when a managed care company, concerned about costs, disagrees with a commitment court's exercise of "clinical" judgment and refuses to pay for or provide the ordered treatment. Although such an occurrence may seem unlikely, if the company is the payor, as opposed to the provider of the service, it may not be directly subject to a contempt citation from the court; further its liability for any consequences of a failure to treat may be significantly limited by the Employee Retirement Income Security Act (ERISA) (see pp. 277–278). See also John Petrila, *Courts as Gatekeepers in Managed Care Settings*, Mental Health Care 109, 113–14 (Mar.–Apr. 1998); Paul Appelbaum, *A History of Civil Commitment and Related Reforms*, 25 Dev. Mental Health L. 13, 20 (2006) (noting that "managed care organizations . . . have adopted a de facto admission standard of dangerous to self or others . . . , whether it be voluntary or involuntary" and that "[w]ith an increasingly smaller number of publicly-funded beds available, if managed care does not sign-off on admission, admission does not occur, regardless of the existing criteria for civil commitment.").

In short, although the theoretical underpinnings of commitment and commitment standards and procedures should matter to clinicians and their patients, as well as to courts and lawyers, the formulation of commitment law is just one of many variables affecting the numbers and types of individuals who are subject to involuntary commitment. How the legal doctrines discussed in this chapter actually get implemented depends in major part on factors only tangentially related to the language found in civil commitment statutes.

II.   THE BASIS FOR STATE INTERVENTION

A. INTRODUCTION

CASE ILLUSTRATIONS

The following descriptions of twelve individuals who were hospitalized in a psychiatric facility are taken from 45 cases reported in George Dix, *Acute Psychiatric Hospitalization of The Mentally Ill in the Metropolis: An Empirical Study*, 1968 Wash.U.L.Q. 485, 504–47. Each of these individuals was admitted to the St. Louis Acute Facility, as either a voluntary or involuntary patient. In about one-fifth of the 45 cases the patient "presented" him or herself, that is, came on his or her own to the hospital to get help. In another fifth the police brought the patient. In the rest of the cases, family members, relatives or members of the community were responsible for bringing the individual to the attention of the facility. Id. at 503.

Illustration 2. The patient was observed by police wandering on the street wearing hospital pajamas and a surgical cap. He did not respond to attempts to elicit information from him. Several hospitals in the vicinity were contacted but reported that they were not missing any patients. The patient was then taken to the Acute Facility.

Illustration 5. The patient believed that he was an F.B.I. agent, and he carried at least one weapon. He had accused his wife of being a "spy" and his mother-in-law of poisoning him. Three weeks before presentation he had been arrested for carrying a concealed weapon. Although it is extremely likely that he was exhibiting these symptoms at that time, he was not presented until several days before his preliminary hearing, when his wife called police and asked that they assist in presentation.

Illustration 6. The patient reportedly drank one pint of whiskey and, becoming irritated at a group of children, shook one of them. Police were called and the child was taken to a hospital where it was determined that she had suffered no significant harm. The officers then took the patient to the Acute Facility and told the resident that if the patient were not admitted he would be released, as there were no charges against him. The patient exhibited no symptoms of present mental illness. When the decision to admit was made, one officer called his superior and reported in a relieved tone, "They'll take him."

Illustration 7. The family reported that for the last two months the patient had been sleeping poorly and his general level of activity had increased. He spent money freely and the family was consequently forced into debt. Recently he had attempted to open several new charge accounts. The family also complained of the patient's argumentativeness and "resentfulness" at home and repeated complaints of his irritability at work.

Illustration 10. The patient had been depressed for a period of time and had considered attempting suicide for two weeks. He had specifically threatened to kill himself, but no attempt was made to present him to the Acute Facility until his wife happened to notice an apparatus apparently designed by the patient to hang himself.

Illustration 15. The patient, a 44 year-old woman, was brought to the Acute Facility by her husband who was 85 years old. He reported that she suffered from insomnia and sometimes locked herself in the bathroom. During the interview with the resident, the patient talked to the empty emergency room. Among the factors influencing the decision to admit her on an involuntary basis was the resident's observation that in her neighborhood "people were robbing and raping all the time" and that she would be particularly subject to such attacks.

Illustration 17. The patient had been given a ride by a truck driver who found him hitchhiking along a highway. When the truck driver noticed that the patient had a gun, he took him to the police station. The police brought him to the Acute Facility where he refused to divulge anything other than the pronunciation of his name. He was admitted on a nonvoluntary basis.

Illustration 19. A 26 year-old woman had reportedly been "imagining things" since her marriage six months before presentation. She had accused her husband of spying on other men in public washrooms and believed that he had holes in the wall of their home through which he spied on her. She was presented at the facility by her husband and police officers after she called police and reported that her husband, in an attempt to kill her, had filled the apartment with gas. When police arrived they observed no gas and found the husband asleep. When the patient returned to her home, she was taken to the Acute Facility. In explaining her nonvoluntary admission, the resident emphasized her symptoms of psychosis.

Illustration 20. A medical report submitted to the probate court contained the following assertion offered to support the conclusion that the patient's judgment and insight were "poor": "He still sees no harm in the fact that he lived with a sixteen year old girl as husband and wife . . . [H]is reasoning at the present time is that his wife was not satisfactory at that time so why not have the girl . . . "

Illustration 22. An 18 year-old youth was admitted after being in an auto accident while under the influence of a drug. He denied taking amphetamines in addition to the drug which he had taken prior to the accident, but the staff psychiatrist indicated that he would be retained, involuntarily if necessary, for a week, because it was believed that he was in fact taking amphetamines and the psychiatrist expected withdrawal symptoms to develop.

Illustration 24. The patient, a 61 year old woman, lived alone. She had a history of persecutory delusions extending back over fifteen years. On a number of previous occasions, she had screamed at the neighbors; they finally responded by calling the police. On the occasion preceding her presentation, the neighbors specifically demanded that the police secure the patient's hospitalization. When examined at the Acute Facility, the patient indicated that she believed spirits came to her home and attempted to have "spiritual sex" with her. The resident, who admitted her on a nonvoluntary basis, indicated that a major factor in his decision was that he was not certain "how much the neighbors could take."

Illustration 29. The patient, who lived with her sister's family, reportedly threatened the members of the family. On the morning of her presentation to the Acute Facility, she threw a cup of hot coffee on her sister; this stimulated her presentation.

NOTE: GOVERNMENT AND INDIVIDUAL INTERESTS

Whether in its libertarian or paternalistic guise, civil commitment law is usefully contrasted to the criminal law. Theoretically, the primary purpose of the criminal law is to punish; entry into the criminal justice system depends upon whether a person has engaged in behavior that is considered blameworthy enough, and sufficiently costly to society, that harsh sanctions are deserved, as well as necessary to deter others from engaging in similar behavior. The primary purpose of civil commitment, on the other hand, is not to punish for past acts but to avert future ones: the impetus for a civil commitment system does not stem from retributive or deterrence concerns but rather from a perceived need for incapacitation or treatment, or both. This is not to say that civil commitment has never been used as a sanctioning device, or that the criminal law does not perform a control function. But, in theory at least, punishment is the preserve of the criminal system, while civil commitment is reserved for those who the state cannot, or will not, punish but who nonetheless need to be controlled for their own good or the good of others. As a result, the criminal law focuses on already committed conduct, while the civil commitment system relies on predictions of conduct.

The criminal justice system is justified as an exercise of the state's "police power," the power to act in furtherance of the general welfare and public safety. In *Jacobson v. Massachusetts*, 197 U.S. 11, 25 S.Ct. 358, 49 L.Ed. 643 (1905), the Supreme Court upheld a Massachusetts provision that permitted fines or imprisonment to be imposed on those who refused or neglected to be vaccinated for smallpox. In support of this decision, the Court described as a "fundamental principle" the idea that

> persons and property [can be] subjected to all kinds of restraints and burdens, in order to secure the general comfort, health, and prosperity of the State[.] . . . The possession and enjoyment of all rights are subject to such reasonable conditions as may be deemed by the governing authority of the country essential to the safety, health, peace, good order and morals of the community. Even liberty itself, the greatest of all rights, is not unrestricted license to act according to one's will.

Clearly, when someone has committed a crime the state has the authority to deprive that person of liberty under the police power described in *Jacobson*.

The justification advanced for civil commitment depends upon the reason for commitment. When the government commits a person with mental disability on the ground that he or she is "dangerous to others," the usual justification advanced for this deprivation of liberty is, as with criminal punishment, the police power. Confining a dangerous person is permissible to protect the public. On the other hand, when a person is committed for reasons other than potential harmfulness to others, the government's action is usually justified on a different ground: the *parens patriae*, or "parental," authority of the state. With respect to this second governmental power, the Supreme Court has stated:

The concept of *parens patriae* is derived from the English constitutional system. As the system developed from its feudal beginnings, the King retained certain duties and powers, which were referred to as the "royal prerogative." . . . These powers and duties were said to be exercised by the King in his capacity as guardian of persons under legal disabilities to act for themselves. For example, Blackstone refers to the sovereign or his representative as "the general guardian of all infants, idiots and lunatics," and as the superintendent of all "charitable uses in the kingdom." In the United States, the "royal prerogative" and the "*parens patriae*" function of the King passed to the States.

Hawaii v. Standard Oil, 405 U.S. 251, 92 S.Ct. 885, 31 L.Ed.2d 184 (1972).

Accepting that both the police power and the *parens patriae* power are inherent attributes of sovereignty does not necessarily justify civil commitment, however. As the Supreme Court has recognized (in dicta), civil commitment results in a "massive deprivation of liberty." *Humphrey v. Cady*, 405 U.S. 504, 509, 92 S.Ct. 1048, 1052, 31 L.Ed.2d 394 (1972). One commentary described the impact of commitment as follows:

The most basic deprivation caused by civil commitment is the restriction of liberty—the interest of "transcending value"—for a possibly indefinite period. When a patient is hospitalized, not only are his movements restricted to the confines of the institution, but his freedom to move about within the institution itself may also be regulated or completely deprived for safety or disciplinary reasons. Even if the individual is committed to a community mental health center, he will probably be required to report to the center periodically. . . .

Equally important, although a physically ill individual is ordinarily permitted to choose whether to seek medical attention and is protected in this right by common law tort doctrines, an involuntarily committed patient may not have the right to refuse treatment. This refusal to allow a committed individual to decline unwanted medical examination and treatment might, in the absence of a compelling state interest, infringe a constitutional right to bodily privacy which has been adumbrated in various judicial statements. Moreover, hospitalization itself interferes with privacy, since the patient cannot shield himself from constant observation by both his fellow patients and the staff of the institution. Furthermore, patients in hospitals risk brutality at the hands of their fellow residents and even their attendants, and may be subjected to life in an institution which is overcrowded, inadequately staffed, poorly maintained, and unsanitary.

Compounding all of these deprivations is the fact that most persons are currently committed for an indefinite period of time. While statistics reveal that the average length of stay in mental institutions is relatively short, in most states an individual facing civil commitment is potentially exposed to lifelong deprivation of many of his most basic civil rights.

Individuals face further legal and social deprivations as a result of commitment. . . . Law enforcement officials might view a prior commitment as reason for viewing otherwise innocuous behavior with suspicion, and the entry of the patient's fingerprints and photographs in official records might have an impact similar to that of a criminal record. [Although commitment no longer leads to automatic loss of the right to vote, serve on a jury, have a driver's license, and similar rights and privileges,] a patient whose release from commitment is conditional may be subject to summary recommitment, mandatory psychiatric tests, prior approval of his choice of home or job, and other deprivations of his civil rights. . . . Along with these official deprivations, a former mental patient may suffer from the social opprobrium which attaches to treatment for mental illness and which may have more severe consequences than do the formally imposed disabilities. Many people have an "irrational fear of the mentally ill." The former mental patient is likely to be treated with distrust and even loathing; he may be socially ostracized and victimized by employment and educational discrimination. Finally, the individual's hospitalization and posthospitalization experience may cause him to lose self-confidence and self-esteem.

Note, *Developments in the Law—Civil Commitment of the Mentally Ill*, 87 Harv.L.Rev. 1190, 1193–1201 (1974). Given the impact of involuntary commitment on a person's liberty, privacy, freedom of association and freedom of movement, it remains a matter of some controversy whether the state should be able to exercise its police and *parens patriae* powers through civil commitment and, if so, under what limitations.

B. POLICE POWER COMMITMENT

1. Rationale

condemned

Preventive detention—confinement based on a prediction of antisocial behavior rather than on conviction of crime—has been condemned primarily on two grounds. The first is that predicting behavior is much more difficult than ascertaining whether certain behavior has occurred and therefore should not normally form the basis for state intervention. As John Stuart Mill stated:

hard to predict behavior

The preventive function of government . . . is far more liable to be abused, to the prejudice of liberty, than the punitory function, for there is hardly any part of the legitimate freedom of action of a human being which would not admit of being represented, and fairly too, as increasing the facilities for some form or other of delinquency. [I]f a public authority, or even a private person, sees any one evidently preparing to commit a crime, they are not bound to look on inactive. . . . Nevertheless, when there is not a certainty, but only a danger of mischief, no one but the person himself can judge of the sufficiency of the motive which may prompt him to incur the risk. . . .

John Stuart Mill, *On Liberty*, in The Philosophy of John Stuart Mill 197, 196 (1961).

Even if the requisite certainty of harm to society is present, preventive detention may be repugnant for a second reason. In describing why the criminal law requires proof of an act prior to criminal conviction, Professor Packer wrote:

> It is important, especially in a society that likes to describe itself as "free" and "open," that a government should be empowered to coerce people only for what they do and not for what they are. . . . Now, this self-denying ordinance can be and often is attacked as being inconsistent with the facts of human nature. People may in fact have little if any greater capacity to control their conduct . . . than their emotions or their thoughts. It is therefore unrealistic or hypocritical, so the argument runs, to deal with conduct as willed or to treat it differently from personality and character. This attack is, however, misconceived. . . . The idea of free will in relation to conduct is not, in the legal system, a statement of fact, but rather a value preference having very little to do with the metaphysics of determinism and free will. . . .

Herbert Packer, The Limits of the Criminal Sanction 74–75 (1968).

For these reasons, imposing *criminal liability* in anticipation of harm (as opposed to a past act) probably violates the eighth amendment's prohibition against cruel and unusual punishment. In *Robinson v. California,* 370 U.S. 660, 82 S.Ct. 1417, 8 L.Ed.2d 758 (1962), the Supreme Court held that the eighth amendment was violated by a statute which criminalized narcotics addiction, as opposed to possession or sale of narcotics. In *Powell v. Texas,* 392 U.S. 514, 532, 88 S.Ct. 2145, 2154, 20 L.Ed.2d 1254 (1968), four members of the Supreme Court explained this holding in the following words:

> Evidence of propensity can be considered relatively unreliable and more difficult for a defendant to rebut; the requirement of a specific act thus provides some protection against false charges. . . . Perhaps more fundamental is the difficulty of distinguishing, in the absence of any conduct, between desires of the day-dream variety and fixed intentions that may pose a real threat to society; extending the criminal law to cover both types of desire would be unthinkable, since "[t]here can hardly be anyone who has never thought evil." When a desire is inhibited it may find expression in fantasy; but it would be absurd to condemn this natural psychological mechanism as illegal.

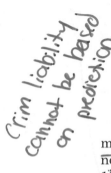
Crim liability cannot be based on prediction

While the Supreme Court has thus signaled that criminal liability may not be based solely on a prediction, it has also held that "regulatory," nonpunitive confinement may be. *United States v. Salerno,* 481 U.S. 739, 107 S.Ct. 2095, 95 L.Ed.2d 697 (1987). In particular, the Court made

[handwritten margin note: cannot predict mental disability]

clear that civil commitment of people with mental disability may be predicated on speculation about future behavior. See *Addington v. Texas*, 441 U.S. 418, 99 S.Ct. 1804, 60 L.Ed.2d 323 (1979); *Heller v. Doe*, 509 U.S. 312, 113 S.Ct. 2637, 125 L.Ed.2d 257 (1993); *Kansas v. Hendricks*, 521 U.S. 346, 117 S.Ct. 2072, 138 L.Ed.2d 501 (1997). It has also authorized preventive detention of other populations. See *Salerno* (upholding a pretrial detention statute that authorized incarceration of people charged with serious offenses if necessary to "reasonably assure . . . the safety of any other person or the community."); *Pennsylvania ex rel. Sullivan v. Ashe*, 302 U.S. 51, 61, 58 S.Ct. 59, 82 L.Ed. 43 (1937) (recognizing that a sentence *after* conviction for an act can be based in whole or part on a desire to "deter or to reform the offender"). But no one other than a person with mental disability may be subject to longterm preventive detention of the type associated with civil commitment. In *Salerno*, for instance, the Court emphasized the fact that pretrial preventive detention is strictly limited in duration (e.g., by speedy trial requirements), and a sentence requires a conviction. In contrast, civil commitment may last many years (although this is unusual nowadays, and is subject to periodic review) and does not require commission of a crime. Why are people with mental disability singled out in this way? Consider the following excerpts.

[handwritten margin note: long term civil commitment = mental disability only]

NOTE, CIVIL COMMITMENT OF THE MENTALLY ILL: DEVELOPMENTS IN THE LAW

87 Harvard Law Rev. 1190, 1230 (1974).

. . . One potential justification for the restriction of preventive detention to the mentally ill might be that the mentally ill, solely by reason of their condition, are substantially more dangerous than other groups. Although there is evidence that this belief is commonly held, studies indicate that the mentally ill as a class are at most slightly more dangerous, and quite possibly less dangerous, than their fellow citizens. Society would therefore obtain roughly similar protection against antisocial conduct if involuntary commitment were limited to the mentally healthy or were employed randomly. Since the vast majority of mentally ill individuals will not engage in dangerous behavior if they are permitted to retain their freedom, preventive detention based solely on mental illness would not appear to be even rationally related to the state's police power interest in protecting society. . . .

A second possible rationale for limiting preventive detention of the dangerous to the mentally ill is premised on the ability of society to provide treatment which benefits them. However, to the extent that the state relies on the benefit which the individual will derive from treatment to support his commitment, it confuses the *parens patriae* and police power justifications for commitment. Requiring a competent individual to accept treatment for his own benefit should be viewed as an additional deprivation of liberty rather than as a benefit which justifies confinement for the protection of others.

Nevertheless, the state might argue that only the dangerous mentally ill are preventively detained because the ability to cure their illness enables the state to safeguard society's interests without indefinite deprivation of their liberty. However, since some mental illnesses are presently untreatable and others cannot be readily cured, many of the dangerous mentally ill face indefinite institutionalization as a result of commitment. Moreover, dangerousness, the link between preventive detention and the police power, may be treated through behavior conditioning which is applicable to the mentally ill and nonmentally ill alike.

A final justification for limiting involuntary police power commitments to the mentally ill can be derived from the reasons apparently underlying the decision not to authorize preventive detention of other dangerous individuals. By requiring a conviction before depriving persons who are not mentally ill of their liberty, the criminal law system relies on deterrence to reduce antisocial behavior. A state could argue that this punishment-deterrence approach fosters personal autonomy by allowing its citizens to choose whether to obey the law. The state's interest in employing a deterrence system that recognizes individual autonomy furnishes a rationale for excluding criminally responsible individuals—those able to appreciate the sanctions imposed for criminal activity and capable of conforming their actions to the dictates of the criminal law—from a prediction-prevention approach to harmful conduct. This justification would seem to provide a distinction between equally dangerous groups of mentally healthy and criminally insane individuals sufficient to satisfy the demands of equal protection. The latter group contains individuals whose mental condition excludes them from the operation of the traditional punishment-deterrence system, because they are both unable to make autonomous decisions about their antisocial behavior and unaffected by the prospect of punishment. . . .

STEPHEN MORSE, A PREFERENCE FOR LIBERTY: THE CASE AGAINST INVOLUNTARY COMMITMENT OF THE MENTALLY DISORDERED

70 Cal.L.R. 54, 59–65 (1982).

The belief that disordered persons particularly lack competence or behavioral control is a strongly ingrained social dogma that underlies the special legal treatment accorded mentally disordered persons.

*   *   *

But the assertion that the crazy behavior of mentally disordered persons is compelled, in contrast to the freely chosen behavior of normal persons, is a belief that rests on commonsense intuitions and not on scientific evidence. Indeed, the degree of lack of behavioral control necessary to justify involuntary commitment is fundamentally a moral, social, and legal question—not a scientific one. Social and behavioral scientists can only provide information about the pressures affecting an actor's freedom of choice. The law must determine for itself when the actor is no longer to be treated as autonomous.

In fact, empirical evidence bearing on the question of the control capacity of mentally disordered persons would seem to indicate that mentally disordered persons have a great deal of control over their crazy behavior and legally relevant behavior related to it; indeed, often they may have as much control over their behavior as normal persons do.

* * *

For comparison, imagine the case of a habitually hot-tempered person who takes offense at something his doctor says and threatens to harm the doctor. Is this person more in control or rational than the delusional person? Or, consider the case of a severely ill cardiac patient who refuses to modify dietary, exercise, or smoking habits because the person prefers his or her habitually unhealthy lifestyle. The person's behavior can disrupt the well-being of the family, help drive up health care and insurance costs, and, if the result is an untimely death, impoverish the family. Is this person more in control or rational than the delusional person, and if so, in what sense? Of course, we all "understand" the behavior of the hot-tempered person and the cardiac patient, while the behavior of the delusional person makes no sense whatsoever. Still, there is no conclusive means to prove that any of these persons has greater or lesser control than any of the others.

QUESTIONS AND COMMENTS

1. *Dangerousness and people with mental illness.* Based on research conducted before the mid–1970s, the Developments piece asserts that people with mental illness are no more dangerous as a class than the general population. This view changed in the 1990s as researchers availed themselves of new databases and computerized versions of statistical techniques. Professor Monahan, summarizing research through the early 1990s, stated:

> The data that have recently become available, fairly read, suggest the one conclusion I did not want to reach: whether the measure is the prevalence of violence among the disordered or the prevalence of disorder among the violent, whether the sample is people who are selected for treatment as inmates or patients in institutions or people randomly chosen from the open community, and no matter how many

social and demographic factors are statistically taken into account, there appears to be a relationship between mental disorder and violent behavior. Mental disorder may be a robust and significant risk factor for the occurrence of violence. . . .

John Monahan, *Mental Disorder and Violent Behavior: Perceptions and Evidence*, 47 Am.Psychol. 511, 519 (1992).

Subsequent studies have shown that this conclusion, though true, requires an interpretation more nuanced than simply saying, "Mental illness is associated with an increased risk of violence." A mammoth study funded by the MacArthur Foundation in the mid–1990s, involving more than a thousand patients released from Pittsburgh hospitals and a comparison group of more than 500 people living in the neighborhoods in which the patients resided after discharge, found that persons with severe mental illnesses had higher rates of violence than the community sample. Yet it also found that these differences were statistically attributable not to the patients' major mental illnesses, but to their problems with substance abuse. As the researchers explain:

> the prevalence of violence among patients without symptoms of substance abuse is statistically indistinguishable from the prevalence of violence among others in their neighborhoods without symptoms of substance abuse. Substance abuse significantly raised the prevalence of violence in both patient and community samples. Among those who reported symptoms of substance abuse, the prevalence of violence among patients was significantly higher than the prevalence of violence among others in their neighborhoods during the first follow-up. The patient sample also was significantly more likely to report such symptoms of substance abuse than was the community sample.

Henry Steadman, et al., *Violence by People Discharged from Acute Psychiatric Inpatient Facilities and by Others in the Same Neighborhoods*, 55 Arch. Gen Psychiatry 393, 400 (1998). A more recent evaluation of epidemiological data showed—consistent with the findings reported by Steadman and colleagues—that the higher incidence of violence among people with severe mental illnesses was attributable to their substance use problems, as well as to historical, clinical, dispositional, and contextual factors that are reported more often by people with mental illness. Eric B. Elbogen & Sally C. Johnson, *The Intricate Link Between Violence and Mental Disorder: Results From the National Epidemiologic Survey on Alcohol and Related Conditions*, 66 Arch. Gen. Psychiatry 152 (2009).

A number of other studies have suggested that *certain types* of psychotic symptoms are associated with violence. In particular, some studies suggest that "threat/control-override" (TCO) symptoms—delusional beliefs that others are threatening you or controlling and overriding your thoughts—do increase the risk of violence. Dale E. McNiel, *The Relationship between Aggressive Attributional Style and Violence by Psychiatric Patients*, 71 J. Consulting & Clin. Psychology 404, 405 (2003); Sven Bjorkly, *Psychotic*

Symptoms and Violence Toward Others—A Literature Review of Some Preliminary Findings, 7 Aggression and Violent Behavior 605–631 (2002); Bruce Link et al., *Real in Their Consequences: A Sociological Approach to Understanding the Association between Psychotic Symptoms and Violence*, 64 Am. Sociological Rev. 316 (1999). Not all studies have found support for the salience of TCO delusions, however. A subsequent summary of the MacArthur study's findings with respect to violence and serious mental illness describes the data somewhat differently:

> The MacArthur data suggest that the presence of delusions does not predict higher rates of violence among recently discharged psychiatric patients. This conclusion remains accurate even when the type of delusions and their content (including violent content) is taken into account. In particular, the much-discussed findings of a relationship between threat/control-override delusions were not confirmed in the MacArthur study. On the other hand, non-delusional suspiciousness—perhaps involving a tendency toward misperception of other's behavior as indicating hostile intent—does appear to be linked with subsequent violence, and may account for the findings of previous studies. Although command hallucinations [e.g., a belief that God is commanding violence] per se did not elevate violence risk, if the voices commanded violent acts, the likelihood of their occurrence over the subsequent year was significantly increased.

John Monahan, *Violence Risk Assessment*, in Comprehensive Handbook of Psychology (Alan Goldstein ed., 2003). Nonetheless, most U.S. studies of the relationship between mental illness and violence suggest that the statistical association between increased violence and having severe mental illnesses such as schizophrenia and manic-depressive psychosis accrues primarily from those times when persons are suffering from severe symptoms of their illness, and is not attributable to just having the diagnosis itself.

Notwithstanding the statistical link between violence and mental illness, many segments of the population are more dangerous than people with mental illness. As Ennis & Emery point out:

> Probably 50 to 80 percent of all ex-felons will commit crimes after release from prison. But when their sentences expire, we let them go, and do not "civilly commit" them as dangerous. Ghetto residents and teenage males are also much more likely to commit dangerous acts than the "average" citizen, but we do not confine them.

Bruce Ennis & Richard Emery, The Rights of Mental Patients 45 (1978). In contrast, the base rate for violence among people with serious mental illness, even those with acute symptoms, is probably much lower, around 10% if substance abuse and psychopathy are controlled for. Sheilagh Hodgins et al., *The Antecedents of Aggressive Behavior Among Men with Schizophrenia: A Prospective Investigation of Patients in Community Treatment*, 21 Beh. Sci. & L. 523, 540 (Table 4) (2003)(finding recidivism rates among people who experience TCO symptoms to be between 5.5% and 10.6%).

What implications does this information have for police power civil commitment of people with mental disability? Should it be abolished? Limited to those with severe mental illness? Those with only persecutory delusions (threat/control override symptoms)? Expanded to include those with mental conditions associated with a relatively high recidivism rate? In connection with this last question, note that certain non-psychotic "mental disorders," in particular antisocial personality disorder, are highly correlated with violence-proneness (see pp. 556–557) and Seena Fazel and John Danesh, *Serious Mental Disorder in 23,000 Prisoners: A Systematic Review of 62 Surveys*, 359 Lancet 545 (2002) (rate of antisocial personality disorder among prisoners was about ten times that seen in the general population).

2. *Treatability and people with mental illness.* The Development authors' assertion that some mental disorders are difficult to treat also retains validity. However, as noted in the introduction to this chapter and in Chapter One, many of the psychoses (e.g., schizophrenia, manic-depressive psychosis) and depression are responsive to medication. Thus, a person whose dangerousness stems from one of these mental disorders *may* be more "treatable" (with respect both to efficacy and to necessary duration of confinement) than a person whose dangerousness can only be treated through the behavioral therapy mentioned in the excerpt. Does this possibility justify treating people with mental illness differently?

Conversely, if the person who is dangerous to others is not treatable or no treatment is available should commitment be barred? Consider the following excerpt from *Lynch v. Baxley,* 386 F.Supp. 378, 391–2 (M.D.Ala.1974):

> An exception to this general requirement of due process [that commitment occur only when treatment is available] is recognized in the case of a presently and seriously dangerous person for whose illness there is no known cure or treatment. In such instances, the state may well have an obligation under the police power to restrain the liberty of the threatening individual, even though his condition is not amenable to any currently available treatment. Since the involuntary commitment of an untreatable person is an exception to the general due process requirement that treatment be available and afforded, the committing court must make a finding, based upon clear and convincing evidence, that confinement even without a proposed treatment program is necessary for the safety and well-being of the community and of the person to be committed. Such orders of commitment, when granted, shall provide that, should treatment for the patient's illness become available at any time during the period of his confinement, such treatment shall be made available to him immediately.

In thinking about this question, consider that several states have and commonly use statutes authorizing the in-hospital detention of individuals with tuberculosis when (among other possible reasons) a person is contagious and carries a bacillus that is resistant to available antibiotics (and is therefore untreatable). See, e.g., Fla. Stat. Ann. § 392.56 (2009), New York Health Code § 11.21 (2009), Wis. Stat. Ann. § 252.07 (2009).

3.   *Rational control and people with mental illness.* The Developments article suggests that the best explanation for allowing long-term preventive detention of people with mental illness is that they lack autonomy and therefore cannot be deterred by the dictates of the criminal law. In other words, even if they are no more dangerous or treatable than other identifiable groups, people who are mentally ill can justifiably be singled out for preventive detention because of their relative undeterrability. Assuming people with mental illness are less autonomous, does this rationale make sense? Are there not other groups of individuals (pedophiles, recidivist burglars, repeat drunk drivers) who are not deterred by the threat of punishment? Is their undeterrability different from the undeterrability of people with mental illness?

As to the assertion made by Morse that people with mental disability "often . . . have as much control over their behavior as normal persons do," considerable research supports his conclusion. For instance, several studies (as will even a short visit to any inpatient psychiatric unit) show that most people with mental disorder who are hospitalized respond to rewards and disincentives in a way that is consistent with rationally controlled behavior. William Fisher, et. al. *Implications for Concepts of Psychopathology of Studies of Economic Principles in Behavior Therapy*, 166 J. Nervous & Mental Disease 187, 191–93 (1978). However, none of these studies permit the conclusion that all people with mental illness behave as rationally as others. As Morse stated in another article:

> Again, I do not mean to make an absurd claim. A chronically disabled, hallucinating, and delusional person who wanders the streets in rags speaking gibberish is not "like" normal persons, and the law should probably treat this person specially. Nevertheless, the law should be far more cautious before concluding that large numbers of crazy people are so incapable of responsible behavior that deprivation of liberty is justified.

Stephen Morse, *Treating Crazy People Less Specially*, 90 W.Va.L.Rev. 353, 370 (1988).

4.   *Ease of prediction and people with mental illness.* A final possible justification for permitting at least certain types of preventive detention of those with mental illness, not mentioned in either excerpt, is that their dangerousness might be easier to predict. As explained in Chapter Six, many studies of risk assessment instruments allow the conclusion that, by selecting stringent cut-offs, mental health professionals can identify small subgroups of patients whose risk of violence is 50% or higher. Of course, even if predictive accuracy is 50 or 75%, one might object to a process that erroneously subjects 1 out of every 2 to 4 people to the "massive deprivation of liberty" associated with commitment. The following materials flesh out the meaning of dangerousness to others in the civil commitment context.

2. Implementing the Police Power

a. *Defining Mental Illness*

DODD V. HUGHES

Supreme Court of Nevada, 1965.
81 Nev. 43, 398 P.2d 540.

THOMPSON, JUSTICE.

By a habeas corpus application addressed to the Second Judicial District Court, Dodd sought his release from the Nevada State Hospital (NRS 433.040). He had been committed to that institution as a mentally ill person by order of the Fourth Judicial District Court. At the habeas hearing, the Superintendent of the Nevada State Hospital gave his opinion that Dodd, though a sociopath, was not psychotic, and therefore not "mentally ill" within the meaning of NRS 433.200. He suggested that Dodd be released from his confinement. Another doctor was of a different view. Though he agreed that Dodd was not psychotic, he believed that a sociopathic personality may be considered "mentally ill" as that term is used in the state. Additionally, he stressed Dodd's high potential for homicidal activity. At the conclusion of the hearing, the court directed the superintendent to apply to the board of the state prison commissioners for that board's consent to confine Dodd at the Nevada State Prison. The superintendent did as directed. The prison commissioners consented, and Dodd was delivered to the Nevada State Prison for confinement until further order of the court (NRS 433.310).[2]

The legislature did not define "mentally ill" when it passed the law governing the Nevada State Hospital (NRS 433.010–433.640). Its failure to do so supplies the basis for Dodd's appeal. It is his position that a person must exhibit one of the psychotic reactions as classified by the American Psychiatric Association before he may be considered mentally ill. Absent a classified psychosis, one may not be committed and confined. A sociopath (defined in the testimony as a disorder of personality affecting the ethical and moral senses) like Dodd, (and all the evidence is in accord that Dodd is, indeed, a sociopath), does not fall within any of the classified psychotic reactions and, therefore, may not be institutionalized. So it is that we are urged to fashion a definition for the words "mentally ill" and thereby fill the void in the statutory hospital law. It is suggested

---

[2] NRS 433.310 provides:

"1. Whenever a person legally adjudged to be mentally ill is deemed by the court or the superintendent to be a menace to public safety, and the court is satisfied that the facilities at the hospital are inadequate to keep such mentally ill person safely confined, the court may, upon application of the superintendent, commit such person to the Nevada state prison. The person shall be confined in the Nevada state prison until the further order of the committing court either transferring him to the hospital or declaring him to be no longer mentally ill."

that we confine mental illness to the psychotic reactions as classified by the American Psychiatric Association. We are wholly unable to follow that suggestion. The record before us shows that the psychiatrists who testified do not agree on the statutory meaning of "mentally ill." Further, the record reflects that psychiatrists in general are at war over the propriety of the classifications of psychosis as specified by the American Psychiatric Association. We seriously doubt that the legislature ever intended medical classifications to be the sole guide for judicial commitment. The judicial inquiry is not to be limited so as to exclude the totality of circumstances involved in the particular case before the court. Recidivism, repeated acts of violence, the failure to respond to conventional penal and rehabilitative measures, and public safety, are additional and relevant considerations for the court in deciding whether a person is mentally ill. The assistance of medical examination and opinion is a necessary concomitant of the court hearing, but the court alone is invested with the power of decision. That power is to be exercised within the permissible limits of judicial discretion.

Here the record demonstrates a combination of things which should, and did, unquestionably, influence the lower court to enter the order it did. Dodd, an 18 year-old, was shown, by testing, to have the intelligence quotient of a high grade moron. All agree that he is a sociopath almost devoid of moral sense. He has been proven, at least to date, wholly unresponsive to either penal or rehabilitative measures,[3] nor does he give promise of response to available probation services or psychiatric treatment. He possesses homicidal tendencies, and is dangerous. Finally, one of the testifying psychiatrists stated that Dodd is mentally ill within the intendment of the statute. In these circumstances the lower court did not abuse its discretion in denying habeas relief and ordering that Dodd be transferred to the Nevada State Prison for confinement.

Affirmed.

QUESTIONS AND COMMENTS

1.   *State statutes.* Every state requires proof of mental illness or mental disorder as a predicate for police power commitment. At one time, most commitment statutes, like the Nebraska statute at issue in *Dodd*, did not define mental illness or defined it tautologically. See, e.g., Vernon's Ann. Texas Civ.Stat. § 5547–4(k)(1982)(defining a mentally ill person as "a person whose mental health is substantially impaired"). Some states still do so. See, e.g., Or. Stat. § 426.005(1)(d)("Mentally ill person" means a person who, because of a mental disorder, is one or more of the following: (A) Dangerous

---

[3]   He experienced trouble with the police when eight years old. He was placed in the Elko Boys School from 1960–1962. While there he fought frequently. He escaped. While loose he hit an elderly man on the head with a crowbar, covered him with kerosene or gas, and set him on fire. He was then sent to Preston, California, a prison for hardcore youth criminals. In 1963 he was committed to the Nevada State Hospital, from which he "eloped" on four separate occasions.

to self or others. (B) Unable to provide for basic personal needs and is not receiving such care as is necessary for health or safety."). Most state laws today, however, contain language similar to that found in Ohio's statute: "'Mental illness' means a substantial disorder of thought, mood, perception, orientation, or memory that grossly impairs judgment, behavior, capacity to recognize reality, or ability to meet the ordinary demands of life." Ohio Rev. Code Ann. § 5122.01(A) (2008). Usually this definition applies both to police power and *parens patriae* commitment.

2. *Antisocial personality disorder.* Probably the most controversial issue connected with the definition of mental illness in police power commitment is that posed in *Dodd*—whether the definition should include sociopathy (a condition that today might be labeled as antisocial personality disorder). What are the implications of the holding in *Dodd*? Why do you think the superintendent of the Nevada State Hospital was arguing that Dodd was *not* mentally ill? Assuming Dodd was mentally ill, should it be permissible to transfer him from the hospital to the state prison, as provided by NRS 433.310?

The Supreme Court of Minnesota has held that an antisocial personality is not within the definition of mental illness unless the individual has "lost the ability to control his actions." *Johnson v. Noot,* 323 N.W.2d 724, 727 (Minn.1982). Arizona's statute excludes from the definition of mental disorder "[c]haracter and personality disorders characterized by lifelong and deeply ingrained anti-social behavior patterns, including sexual behaviors which are abnormal and prohibited by statute unless the behavior results from a mental disorder." Ariz.Rev.Stat. § 36–501(1)(c). Is either of these a better approach than *Dodd's*? Would Dodd be committable under the New Mexico statute quote in Note 1? Look at the definition of antisocial personality disorder in Appendix A before answering.

3. *The Supreme Court and police power commitment.* In *Foucha v. Louisiana,* 504 U.S. 71, 112 S.Ct. 1780, 118 L.Ed.2d 437 (1992), the defendant sought release from the hospital four years after his acquittal by reason of insanity on charges of aggravated burglary and unlawful discharge of a firearm. At the release hearing, experts stated that Foucha no longer suffered from "mental illness," but further noted that, because of his untreatable "antisocial personality disorder," Foucha might still be a danger to others. On the basis of this testimony, the Louisiana trial judge refused release. In an opinion for five members of the Court, Justice White *assumed* (but did not *hold*) that Foucha was no longer mentally ill, and concluded that, as a result, under the due process clause "the basis for holding Foucha as an insanity acquittee has disappeared, and the State is no longer entitled to hold him on that basis." In a part of the opinion in which only three other members of the Court joined, White also argued that continued confinement of Foucha would violate the equal protection clause:

> The State . . . insists on holding [Foucha] indefinitely because he at one time committed a criminal act and does not now prove he is not dangerous. Louisiana law, however, does not provide for similar

confinement of other classes of persons who have committed criminal acts and who cannot later prove they would not be dangerous. Criminals who have completed their prison terms, or are about to do so, are an obvious and large category of such persons. Many of them will likely suffer from the same sort of personality disorder that Foucha exhibits. However, state law does not allow for their continuing confinement based merely on dangerousness. Instead, the State controls the behavior of these similarly situated citizens by relying on other means, such as punishment, deterrence, and supervised release. Freedom from physical restraint being a fundamental right, the State must have a particularly convincing reason, which it has not put forward, for such discrimination against insanity acquittees who are no longer mentally ill.

Foucha is excerpted more fully in the materials on commitment of insanity acquittees (pp. 987–990).

Compare the above language in *Foucha* to *Kansas v. Hendricks*, 521 U.S. 346, 117 S.Ct. 2072, 138 L.Ed.2d 501 (1997), reprinted at p. 774. *Hendricks*, the Court considered the constitutionality of Kansas' Sexually Violent Predator Act, which authorizes longterm commitment of a prisoner who has completed his sentence for a serious sex offense if the person is found to be dangerous due to a "mental abnormality" or "personality disorder." Hendricks argued that, as a matter of substantive due process, only a finding of "mental illness" may serve as the predicate for civil commitment. The Court, in a 5–4 opinion, rejected this argument:

> Contrary to Hendricks' assertion, the term "mental illness" is devoid of any talismanic significance. "[P]sychiatrists disagree widely and frequently on what constitutes mental illness. . . ." [W]e have never required State legislatures to adopt any particular nomenclature in drafting civil commitment statutes. Rather we have traditionally left to legislators the task of defining terms of a medical nature that have legal significance. . . .

> To the extent that the civil commitment statutes we have considered set forth criteria relating to an individual's inability to control his dangerousness, the Kansas Act sets forth comparable criteria and Hendricks' condition doubtless satisfies those criteria. The mental health professionals who evaluated Hendricks diagnosed him as suffering from pedophilia, a condition the psychiatric profession itself classifies as a serious mental disorder. Hendricks even conceded that, when he becomes "stressed out," he cannot "control the urge" to molest children. This admitted lack of volitional control, coupled with a prediction of future dangerousness, adequately distinguished Hendricks from other dangerous persons who are perhaps more properly dealt with exclusively through criminal proceedings. Hendricks' diagnosis as a pedophile, which qualifies as a "mental abnormality" under the Act, thus plainly suffices for due process purposes.

In *Kansas v. Crane*, 534 U.S. 407, 122 S.Ct. 867, 151 L.Ed.2d 856 (2002), the Court further construed the definition of mental illness for purposes of committing people likely to commit sex offenses, in response to the argument that emotional or cognitive impairment, as well as volitional impairment, can form the predicate for such commitment.

> *Hendricks* must be read in context. The Court did not draw a clear distinction between the purely "emotional" sexually related mental abnormality and the "volitional." Here, as in other areas of psychiatry, there may be "considerable overlap between a . . . defective understanding or appreciation and . . . [an] ability to control . . . behavior." American Psychiatric Association Statement on the Insanity Defense, 140 Am. J. Psychiatry 681, 685 (1983) (discussing "psychotic" individuals). Nor, when considering civil commitment, have we ordinarily distinguished for constitutional purposes among volitional, emotional, and cognitive impairments. The Court in *Hendricks* had no occasion to consider whether confinement based solely on "emotional" abnormality would be constitutional, and we likewise have no occasion to do so in the present case.

With respect to the mental disorder predicate for civil commitment, what are the implications of the opinions in *Foucha* and the majority opinions in *Hendricks* and *Crane*? May a person who has "only" an antisocial personality disorder be committed? If so, does that disorder have to cause a "lack of volitional control" or can a disorder that leads to a lack of "moral sense" (the language used by the court to describe Dodd) also be the basis of commitment? Is there a difference between the two?

4. *Incompetency and police power commitment.* The American Psychiatric Association's Model Law for civil commitment permits involuntary hospitalization of a person who is mentally ill and dangerous but only upon a showing that the person lacks "capacity to make an informed decision concerning treatment." Clifford Stromberg & Alan Stone, *A Model State Law on Civil Commitment of the Mentally Ill*, 20 Harv.J.Leg. 275, 301 (1982). A few states appear to have adopted such a requirement. See, e.g., Kan. Stat. Ann. § 59–2946(f)(1). Apparently, the fact that its general commitment statute only permitted confinement of those who lack "capacity to make an informed decision concerning treatment" led the state of Kansas to conclude that it could not confine sexual predators under that law and that the special commitment law at issue in *Hendricks* was needed. 521 U.S., at 377, 117 S.Ct. at 2089 (Breyer, J., dissenting). Is this capacity restriction on the effect of mental illness required in the context of police power commitments? Advisable?

5. *Causation.* Most state statutes require proof that the person's dangerousness is "caused by" or is "the result of" mental illness before commitment may occur. Does this requirement follow from the purported rationales of police power commitment? If so, is the Nevada statute under which Dodd was committed invalid on its face? Assuming sociopathy is a

mental illness for purposes of civil commitment, was Dodd's dangerousness "caused" by his mental disorder?

b.   Defining Danger to Others

LESSARD V. SCHMIDT

United States District Court, E.D. Wisconsin, 1972.
349 F.Supp. 1078.

SPRECHER, CIRCUIT JUDGE.

*   *   *

Wisconsin defines "mental illness" as "mental disease to such extent that a person so afflicted requires care and treatment for his own welfare, or the welfare of others, or of the community." Wis.Stat.Ann. § 51.75, Art. II(f) (1971 Supp.). Interpreting § 51.02(5) in the light of this provision in Humphrey v. Cady, 405 U.S. 504, 509, 92 S.Ct. 1048, 1052, 31 L.Ed.2d 394 (1972), the Supreme Court noted (in dicta) that implicit in this definition is the requirement that a person's "potential for doing harm, to himself or to others, is great enough to justify such a massive curtailment of liberty." In other words, the statute itself requires a finding of "dangerousness" to self or others in order to deprive an individual of his or her freedom. The Court did not directly address itself to the degree of dangerousness that is constitutionally required before a person may be involuntarily deprived of liberty. However, its approval of a requirement that the potential for doing harm be "*great enough* to justify such a *massive curtailment* of liberty" implies a balancing test in which the state must bear the burden of proving that there is an extreme likelihood that if the person is not confined he will do immediate harm to himself or others. Although attempts to predict future conduct are always difficult, and confinement based upon such a prediction must always be viewed with suspicion, we believe civil confinement can be justified in some cases if the proper burden of proof is satisfied and dangerousness is based upon a finding of a recent overt act, attempt or threat to do substantial harm to oneself or another.

*   *   *

ALEXANDER BROOKS, DANGEROUSNESS DEFINED IN LAW, PSYCHIATRY & MENTAL HEALTH SYSTEMS 680

(1974).

*   *   *

Definitions of what is "dangerous" tend to be as diverse as the views of individual judges, courts, and jurisdictions. It may be that persons committed on the basis that they are "dangerous" need not be, and would not be, if the term were more carefully defined and its component elements identified, even if those elements could not be evaluated with a high degree of accuracy or quantification. A more rigorous analysis, if not too cumbersome, might well result in more sophisticated judicial decision-making.

The term "dangerous" can be broken down into at least four component elements: (1) magnitude of harm; (2) probability that the harm will occur; (3) frequency with which the harm will occur; (4) imminence of the harm.

To call a person "dangerous" is to express a judgment in the form of a prediction about his potential behavior. A person can be characterized as "dangerous" or not, depending on a balancing of these four components. For example, a harm which is not likely to occur, but which is very serious, may add up to "dangerousness." By the same token, a relatively trivial harm which is highly likely to occur with great frequency might also add up to dangerousness. On the other hand, a trivial harm, even though it is likely to occur, might not add up to dangerousness.

* * *

MATTER OF GREGOROVICH

Appellate Court of Illinois, First District, 1980.
89 Ill.App.3d 528, 44 Ill.Dec. 615, 411 N.E.2d 981.

LORENZ, JUSTICE:

This is an appeal by respondent from an order entered in the circuit court of Cook County, finding her to be a person subject to involuntary admission under the provisions of the Mental Health and Developmental Disabilities Code. (Ill.Rev.Stat.1979, ch. 91 1/2, pars. 1–100 et seq., 1–119.) * * *

On May 9, 1979, respondent's mother, Celia Gregorovich filed a petition for involuntary judicial admission, alleging that respondent was reasonably expected to inflict serious physical harm upon herself or another in the near future and was unable to provide for her basic physical needs so as to guard herself from serious harm and that she was in need of immediate admission for the prevention of such harm. The petition alleged that respondent had threatened to harm herself and her mother after she had cut all the cords to the electrical lamps and television.

The following pertinent evidence was adduced at the hearing on May 9, 1979.

Celia Gregorovich

Her husband, respondent's father, had been sick for 7 years with Parkinson's Disease and had been hospitalized since January 1979. Respondent, who was 21 years of age, blamed her mother for her father's illness, started talking to herself and would not eat. About a month earlier, when respondent cursed her, she struck respondent with a broom, and respondent then scratched her hand with her nails. The scratch marks took 3 weeks to heal. When she asked respondent to lower the television volume, respondent cut the television wires with scissors. Respondent then held the scissors in her fist, with the point sticking out, and pointed them at her mother, who was about 2 or 3 feet away. When respondent put down the scissors, Mrs. Gregorovich called the police. On cross-examination, she testified she did not have to seek medical attention when respondent scratched her hands, and respondent had never physically harmed her before this or tried to hurt herself. She further indicated respondent took care of herself at home and was very clean and neat about herself.

Gregory Nooney, mental health worker at Northwestern Hospital

Respondent, who was hospitalized at Northwestern, said she would not change her clothes until she went to court because that would prove she was not crazy; she slept in her clothes and had not bathed although she was eating. Respondent told him she knew that mental patients often had symptoms similar to ESP and she wanted to prove that she had ESP and that she was not crazy. On cross-examination, he testified respondent had never attacked any other patient on the hospital unit or caused any physical harm to anyone.

Dr. David Altman, a Board Certified Psychiatrist

He examined respondent on May 4, 1979. Respondent was sitting on the couch, moving her mouth and gesturing toward the television set which was turned on. When he was introduced to her, respondent yelled at him, then turned back toward the television set and continued to gesture toward it. When he attempted to engage her in a conversation, she moved to another part of the room and continued to face the television and gesture toward it. When he saw that respondent was becoming more upset, he told her he would stop, and respondent became calm and laughed in the direction of the television set. This process was repeated during the day on May 4. He also observed respondent in front of the television on other occasions when she would at times be watching the television with other patients, moving her mouth and occasionally making gestures. He spoke to her again the morning of the hearing, May 9, when respondent was again in front of the television set. She told him she did not want to talk to him, and the only information he was able to obtain from the interview was that respondent believed that it was dangerous for her to be in the hospital and that she would gain more ESP power from other patients and this would be dangerous. When he asked her to elaborate, respondent said that she would explain it to the judge.

In his opinion, based on information he received from other members of the staff and based on his contact with respondent, she was suffering from an acute schizophrenic episode, a mental illness involving auditory and visual hallucinations. He believed she was under a delusion, a fixed false belief, since she thought she had the power to control peoples' minds and read other persons' minds. He concluded that respondent would be unable to take care of her basic physical needs and protect herself against physical injury based on the fact that she cut the electrical wires prior to admission, that she was quite hostile, that she refused a physical examination and routine laboratory work upon admission because it would somehow prejudice her case, that she thinks she has extra sensory powers rather than having a mental illness, and that she had not bathed and was "essentially not caring for herself in a manner which she would need to do in order to be released." He recommended that she continue to be hospitalized although she had not inflicted injury on herself or anyone else in the hospital.

*   *   *

Dr. Sydney Wright, licensed Physician and Psychiatric Resident at Northwestern Memorial Hospital

He examined respondent on May 3, 1979. Respondent told him she felt she was being brought into the hospital against her will. In an effort to demonstrate her dissatisfaction about being brought to the hospital, she kicked a police officer when she was being escorted to Northwestern Hospital. Respondent told this doctor that she had received ESP powers, but that people doubted that she had these powers. She said she had been involved in a power struggle with another person called Jeffery who had ESP and lived in Philadelphia and who had sent her ESP messages that he loved her; but she subsequently became aware of the fact that he wished to harm her and became involved in an ESP power struggle with him in which he attempted to kill her. She believed her ESP powers may have killed Jeffery since she had not recently heard from him.

Respondent also told him she had cut the television cord because God had told her to do so, and she became convinced that a university was "bugging" her house and was receiving information about her activities which would end if she cut the cord. She also stated that she was going to kill her mother.

In his opinion, respondent was suffering from a mental illness and would be unable to take care of her basic physical needs or protect herself against physical injury. Dr. Wright also noted that respondent showed gross disorganization of her thought processes characterized by concrete thinking, a looseness of association, and a marked pressure of speech.

When asked if she might intentionally or unintentionally harm others, he answered, "I believe that is a possibility based on her statements to me." When asked if she was more likely than not to harm herself or others without further treatment, he related another episode which occurred the day following hospitalization. When the nurse assigned to work with respondent approached respondent, she told her she was a whore and would have nothing to do with her.

When he was again asked if it was more likely than not without further treatment that respondent might intentionally or unintentionally harm someone within a reasonable time, Dr. Wright responded: "Well, it is very difficult for me to predict the future. I would say there is a possibility she could harm someone." He recommended that respondent remain in the hospital for continued treatment. This course of action was based on respondent's statements to him that she believed her powers were sufficient to kill another individual, that she wanted to kill her mother and that she had an "aggressive and hostile stance toward specific staff members." He concluded, "I would say there is a possibility she could injure someone."

Respondent, on her own Behalf

She would get out-patient treatment if she were discharged. On cross-examination, when asked why she would not accept out-patient treatment at Northwestern Hospital, respondent explained that she was not told why she was there and that she was taken there forcibly even though she did not do anything violent. When asked if she needed any help from a mental point of view, she answered, "Possible, but I don't think so, I just need someone to talk to." She admitted she had "mental problems" in the past but had "got over it." When asked if there was anything currently wrong, she mentioned her mother saying, "but, if you knew my mother you would understand."

Opinion

Section 1–119 of the Mental Health and Developmental Disabilities Code (Ill.Rev.Stat.1979, ch. 91 1/2, par. 1–119) defines persons subject to involuntary admission as:

> "(1) A person who is mentally ill and who because of his illness is reasonably expected to inflict serious physical harm upon himself or another in the near future; or

> (2) . . . who because of his illness is unable to provide for his basic physical needs so as to guard himself from serious harm."

The State is required to prove that respondent is a person subject to involuntary admission by clear and convincing evidence. Respondent argues she was not proven to be a person subject to involuntary commitment in that it was not established that she was unable to provide for her basic physical needs so as to guard herself from serious harm. The State does not address this argument in its brief; however, we do not consider the evidence establishes respondent was unable to take care of her basic physical needs so as to guard herself from physical harm.

Respondent also argues there was insufficient evidence that she was reasonably expected in the near future to inflict serious physical harm upon herself or another. For reasons set forth below we conclude that the evidence presented in this case was clear and convincing that respondent was mentally ill and because of this was reasonably expected to inflict serious physical harm upon another person in the near future.[1]

* * *

We first conclude that the uncontradicted expert medical evidence, which was supported by the lay testimony, clearly and convincingly established respondent was "mentally ill." Respondent's assertion that she merely had powers of extra sensory perception, given evidence to the contrary, is unconvincing.

In *People v. Sansone* (1974), 18 Ill.App.3d 315, 326, 309 N.E.2d 733, this court held that the State must prove the person is in need of mental treatment by means of a medical opinion which is clear and convincing and which is based upon facts which are established by clear and convincing evidence. Thus, we held both (1) that the facts upon which the medical opinion was based must be established by clear and convincing evidence, and (2) that the medical opinion, itself, must be clear and convincing. * * *

 State must prove

In this case, we find Dr. Wright's testimony, when considered along with the evidence of previous dangerous conduct, was sufficiently clear and convincing evidence that respondent was reasonably expected to inflict serious physical harm upon another in the near future. Respondent's actions including scratching her mother on the hand during an altercation and holding a pair of scissors a few feet from her mother on the occasion which led to her emergency hospitalization are supportive of this conclusion. The latter conduct was a serious threat which (apart from the issue of criminal intent), could constitute an aggravated assault.

Obviously, her mother felt threatened, since she immediately called police. Respondent, in cross-examining her mother through her attorney, attempted to show that although respondent at this time had the opportunity to harm her mother, she did not do so, and she repeats this argument here. However, the statute [does] not require the infliction of actual harm before commitment was authorized. Other evidence, including respondent's admissions and her own testimony, established respondent's continuing hostility, particularly toward her mother.

---

[1] We do not therefore, find it necessary to consider whether the evidence was sufficient to show she was likely to harm herself[.]

Respondent in fact threatened to kill her mother following her hospitalization on an emergency basis, and it is apparent that respondent's hostility toward her mother increased following her hospitalization. Respondent in her testimony blamed her present difficulties on her mother. Respondent had the opportunity, when she testified, to explain the incident with the scissors, but she failed to do so.

* * *

Respondent would have us focus narrowly on Dr. Wright's use of the term "possibly" in evaluating his testimony, to show it was of an equivocal nature. A similar opinion was found not to be a clear and convincing medical opinion of the type required in *Sansone. People v. Bradley*. In *Bradley*, the expert witness phrased his opinion in terms of "conceivably," rather than "possibly." However, this requirement has been somewhat relaxed in subsequent cases especially when there is clear evidence of prior dangerous conduct or strong lay evidence. This court has upheld commitment orders under resembling circumstances in which there was no explicit medical opinion regarding the patient's future dangerous conduct, but where there was evidence of actual prior dangerous conduct and other evidence such as lay opinion. After considering the doctor's entire testimony together with the other evidence presented, we conclude that there was sufficient evidence in the present case to show respondent's dangerous propensities.

IN INTEREST OF NYFLOT
Supreme Court of North Dakota, 1983.
340 N.W.2d 178.

GIERKE, JUSTICE.

This is an appeal by the respondent, Cynthia Jewel Nyflot, from an Order for Hospitalization and Treatment Following Treatment Hearing entered in the County Court of Cass County on September 14, 1983. We affirm.

* * *

The respondent's fourth contention is that the facts do not support the conclusion that the respondent is a person requiring treatment because she did not present a serious risk of harm, as defined by § 25–03.1–02(11), N.D.C.C.

The court found as a fact that:

". . . on August 29 and September 2, 1983, the respondent started two separate fires in the women's bathroom at the dormitory and that on one of those occasions a great amount of smoke escaped from the bathroom causing personnel to check into the bathroom where the respondent was found by herself in her pajamas; . . . "

respondent argues no danger

Respondent contends that because these fires amounted to little property damage, due to the fact that the bathrooms where the fires were started were virtually inflammable, there was no substantial likelihood that significant property damage or bodily harm could have resulted to the respondent or others as a result of the fires. The statute, however, is not concerned with harm which occurred in the past except as it establishes a potential for serious harm by future behavior of the respondent acting in conformity with previous conduct. The respondent testified that she started the fires to gain attention and to dramatize the fact that she did not want to be in the institution. She also testified that it was not her intent to harm anyone, including herself, and that she felt that there was no likelihood of such harm under the circumstances. Her subjective intentions and assessment of the likelihood of harm, however, do not alter the fact that she was willing to start fires to attract attention to herself. Absent compelling evidence to the contrary, it is a mere fortuity that more damage was not done or that the respondent suffered no ill effects from the smoke produced.

Other undisputed facts further support the conclusion that the respondent presented a serious risk of harm. She rolled lit cigarettes under the door of another patient's room. When the attendants attempted to take her cigarette lighter away from her, she concealed it in her vagina. She cut the screen on a window, using wire cutters which had been smuggled into the institution to her by a friend and, when discovered, she hid the wire cutters in her panties. We believe that these facts clearly support the court's determination that the respondent presented a serious risk of harm to herself, to others, and to property.

Concludes she was a danger

For the reasons stated in the opinion, the order of the county court is affirmed.

ERICKSTAD, C.J., and PEDERSON, VANDEWALLE and SAND, JJ., concur.

WHALEY V. JANSEN

District Court of Appeal, Fourth District, California, 1962.
208 Cal.App.2d 222, 25 Cal.Rptr. 184.

[Whaley brought a civil action against the city of San Diego, the police of that city, and two psychiatrists, among others, alleging false arrest and false imprisonment. According to the court]:

Plaintiff alleges generally that on May 29, 1959, while he was going from house to house in San Diego "exposing wrong-doers in government," he carried with him a letter entitled, "A MOST APPALLING CONDITION," which letter outlined his grievances and requested the use of the home to call in the neighbors and friends so he could deliver a lecture and obtain voluntary contributions from them to carry on his work; that about noon he was walking on the sidewalk in a residential district when defendant Officer Ludvigson stopped him and questioned him; that plaintiff told Officer Ludvigson what he had been doing and the officer asked him to get into the patrol car and talk and that plaintiff walked away; that the officer told him that if he walked away he would place him under arrest; that plaintiff continued walking away from the officer and the officer stated, "You're under arrest for vagrancy"; that plaintiff was forced into the car and literature was removed from his pocket with such titles as "A MOST APPALLING CONDITION, KIDNAPPED AND RAILROADED TO THE BUG HOUSE," and "Earl Warren a Travesty of Equal Justice Under the Law"; that after reading the articles and talking to plaintiff, Officer Ludvigson transported plaintiff to the police station and plaintiff remained in the car while the officer went to the office; that Officer Ludvigson returned and asked plaintiff if he had a permit to solicit and plaintiff answered that he had none because he was not soliciting money; that the officer then went back and in a few minutes returned with another officer and they took plaintiff to the county psychiatric unit; that plaintiff told them that they had no right to do this and attempted to walk away from them and Officer Drake took him into the psychiatric unit; that he was there interviewed by Dr. Reed and plaintiff demanded of the doctor that he be released; that the doctor replied that he had no authority to do so and that plaintiff's release would have to be effected through defendants Dr. Wiend or Dr. Lengyel; that on June 1, 1959, these two doctors interviewed plaintiff and on June 3, 1959, without being formally charged with a crime or mental illness, he was released.

* * *

Sufficient facts are recited in the complaint to justify the officer's belief that plaintiff was so mentally ill as to be likely to cause injury to himself or others and to require medical care or restraint.

[handwritten: facts support to show mental illness]

QUESTIONS AND COMMENTS

1. *Typical state statutes; vagueness doctrine.* Some state statutes, like *Lessard* and the California statute at issue in *Whaley*, still do not identify the type of danger to others that must be manifested in order to justify commitment. For instance, Alabama defines the danger that justifies commitment as a "real and present threat of substantial harm to self and/or others." Ala. Stat. 22–52–10.4(a). California's Lanterman–Petris–Short Act, enacted seven years after the *Whaley* decision, merely requires proof of a "demonstrated danger of inflicting substantial physical harm upon others." Cal.Welf. & Inst.Code § 5300(a). Even the most elaborate statutes provide little more by way of definition. For example, in Massachusetts the relevant criterion permits commitment upon a showing of "a substantial risk of

[handwritten: no specification of type of danger]

physical harm to other persons as manifested by evidence of homicidal or other violent behavior or evidence that others are placed in reasonable fear of violent behavior and serious physical harm to them." Mass.St., c. 123, § 1.

Consider this criticism of commitment statutes from Professor Dershowitz:

> Imagine . . . a penal code which simply made it an imprisonable crime to cause injury to self or others, without defining injury. . . . To be sure there are differences between the criminal and the civil commitment processes: the criminal law is supposed to punish people for having committed harmful acts in the past; whereas civil commitment is supposed to prevent people from committing harmful acts in the future. While this difference may have important implications in some contexts, it would seem entirely irrelevant in deciding which acts are sufficiently harmful to justify incarceration either as an after-the-fact punitive sanction or as a before-the-fact preventive sanction. The considerations which require clear definition of such harms in the criminal process would seem to be fully applicable to the civil commitment process.

Alan Dershowitz, *Dangerousness as a Criterion for Confinement*, 2 Bull.Amer.Acad.Psychiat. & Law 172 (1974).

Should commitment statutes be more specific, as is usually the case with the criminal law? To answer this question, some understanding of the void-for-vagueness doctrine might be useful. The doctrine developed in the nineteenth century as a means of judicially monitoring the precision of the criminal law. Two rationales are advanced to support it. The first is that ambiguous language fails to give potential violators fair warning of the conduct that is criminal. The second, more important, rationale is that ambiguous language allows law enforcement officials, the jury and the courts, rather than duly elected legislators, to decide at their whim the type of conduct that will be defined as criminal.

Although the doctrine is potentially quite broad in its reach given the imprecision found in many statutes, it has been applied sparingly. Most of the laws that the Supreme Court has found unconstitutional on vagueness grounds impinged upon "fundamental" interests, such as freedom of expression, or were perceived to be vehicles for harassment of minority groups or the poor. See, e.g., *F.C.C. v. Fox Television Stations, Inc.*, 132 S.Ct. 2307 (2012); *Kolender v. Lawson*, 461 U.S. 352, 103 S.Ct. 1855, 75 L.Ed.2d 903 (1983). In *Papachristou v. City of Jacksonville*, 405 U.S. 156, 92 S.Ct. 839, 31 L.Ed.2d 110 (1972), for instance, the Supreme Court considered a municipal ordinance which classified as "vagrants," among others, "rogues and vagabonds, or dissolute persons who go about begging . . . common drunkards, . . . lewd, wanton and lascivious persons, . . . persons wandering or strolling around from place to place without any lawful purpose or object, habitual loafers, disorderly persons, [and] . . . persons able to work but habitually living upon the earnings of their wives or minor children. . . ." In striking down this statute on vagueness grounds, and reversing the convictions of two white women and two black men found driving on the main thoroughfare of Jacksonville, the Court stated:

> Those generally implicated by the imprecise terms of the ordinance— poor people, non-conformists, dissenters, idlers—may be required to comport themselves according to the lifestyle deemed appropriate by the Jacksonville police and the courts. Where, as here, there are no standards governing the exercise of the discretion granted by the ordinance, the scheme permits and encourages an arbitrary and discriminatory enforcement of the law. . . . It results in a regime in which the poor and the unpopular are permitted to "stand on a public sidewalk . . . only at the whim of any police officer." . . . Under this ordinance, "[I]f some carefree type of fellow is satisfied to work just so much, and no more, as will pay for one square meal, some wine, and a flophouse daily, but a court thinks this kind of living subhuman, the fellow can be forced to raise his sights or go to jail as a vagrant."

> . . . Of course, vagrancy statutes are useful to the police. Of course, they are nets making easy the roundup of so-called undesirables. But the rule of law implies equality and justice in its application. Vagrancy laws of the Jacksonville type teach that the scales of justice are so tipped that even-handed administration of the law is not possible. The rule of law, evenly applied to minorities as well as majorities, to the poor as well as the rich, is the great mucilage that holds society together.

When a statute does not "chill" fundamental rights or create the type of problem described in *Papachristou,* it is less likely to be found vague, even if the language is very ambiguous. See, e.g., *Nash v. United States*, 229 U.S. 373, 33 S.Ct. 780, 57 L.Ed. 1232 (1913) (upholding a provision in the Sherman Antitrust Act which makes illegal "[e]very contract, combination in the form of trust or otherwise, or conspiracy in restraint of trade or commerce," so long as it is interpreted to prohibit only "undue" restraints of trade). Moreover, the Supreme Court has indicated that a statute is less likely to be declared void for vagueness if more precise language would be difficult to produce. *United States v. Petrillo*, 332 U.S. 1, 67 S.Ct. 1538, 91 L.Ed. 1877 (1947).

The following notes explore whether more precision is possible in drafting police power commitment laws. Brooks' four-factor analysis of dangerousness (excerpted above) will be used as an organizing device, beginning with the first factor, magnitude of harm.

2. *Magnitude of harm.* Assuming the validity of police power commitment, homicide or serious bodily injury would presumably be a harm the state may act to prevent. For what other types of predicted harms may the state deprive one of liberty?

Minor physical injury and threatening behavior. Should the type of injury suffered by the mother of Gregorovich be sufficient to justify commitment, if we could predict accurately that it would occur again? Note that the assault statutes in most states require "bodily injury" for the result element of that crime. See, e.g., Model Penal Code § 211.1. Under the Model Penal Code, this term is defined as "physical pain, illness, or any impairment of physical condition." Model Penal Code § 210.0(2).

Consider also *In re Mental Commitment of Cheri V.*, 2012 WL 6571724 (Wisc. App. 2012). In that case Ms. V. voluntarily went to a county mental health facility because, she said, she was "being followed by people on Facebook" and the facility "would probably be the safest place . . . to get away from people trying to run me over." Once at the facility, however, she felt she was being harassed "because some of the people who were trying to hurt me out there are checking themselves in here." At that point she said that because she was a veteran (although "not a war veteran") she'd rather go to outpatient treatment at the Veteran's Administration Hospital. The registered nurse who admitted Mrs. V. stated that when Ms. V. arrived at the facility she was "very upset, very angry." During the initial assessment, Ms. V. was "real agitated, highly suspicious." At one point, the nurse testified, Ms. V. began pointing at a male nurse, moving near him, and shouting that he was harassing her. Other patients were nearby. Ms. V. was put in restraints for "the patients' sake" and, after a psychiatrist diagnosed her as having "a psychotic disorder and/or borderline personality disorder" with "some paranoid delusions," she was committed. The appellate court nullified the commitment, stating that "*there is absolutely no evidence that any of the statutory prerequisites are met*—yelling at and pointing a finger at another person [unless meant to goad the other person], is not such evidence." (emphasis in original). Do you agree with the appellate court's decision?

Non-physical danger to others. A few states explicitly permit commitment if the court finds that a person may cause "emotional" or "psychic" harm to others. For instance, Iowa law authorizes commitment of a person with mental illness who is "likely to inflict serious emotional injury on members of his or her family or others who lack reasonable opportunity to avoid contact with the afflicted person if the afflicted person is allowed to remain at liberty without treatment." Iowa Code Ann. § 229.1(16)(b). "Serious emotional injury" is defined as "[i]njury which does not necessarily exhibit any physical characteristics, but which can be recognized and diagnosed by a licensed physician or other qualified mental health professional and which can be causally connected with the act or omission of a person who is, or is alleged to be, mentally ill." § 229.1(15). In *State v. Hungerford*, 84 Wis.2d 236, 267 N.W.2d 258 (1978), the Wisconsin Supreme Court held that, in connection with commitment as a mentally disordered sex offender, a prediction of physical harm is not required and that "moral" harm alone might be sufficient.

The criminal law contains provisions that are analogous. For instance, the Model Penal Code includes a crime called "harassment" which is defined as follows:

A person commits a petty misdemeanor if, with purpose to harass another, he: (a) makes a telephone call without purpose of legitimate communication; or (b) insults, taunts or challenges another in a manner likely to provoke violent or disorderly response; or (c) makes repeated communications anonymously or at extremely inconvenient hours, or in offensively coarse language; or (d) engages in any other course of harmful conduct serving no legitimate purpose of the actor.

Model Penal Code § 250.4. Professor Feinberg argued that such criminal law provisions are justified based on what he calls the "offense" principle, which he distinguishes from the "harm" principle, the latter being the primary justification for criminalizing behavior. In Feinberg's view, the state may penalize seriously offensive behavior, even though it does not cause physical harm. Borrowing from nuisance theory in tort, he attempts to provide some guidelines for evaluating the offensiveness of behavior:

> The seriousness of the offensiveness would be determined by (1) the intensity and durability of the repugnance produced, and the extent to which repugnance could be anticipated to be the general reaction of strangers to the conduct displayed or represented (conduct offensive only to persons with an abnormal susceptibility to offense would not count as *very* offensive); (2) the ease with which unwilling witnesses can avoid the offensive displays; and (3) whether or not the witnesses have willingly assumed the risk of being offended either through curiosity or the anticipation of pleasure. . . .

> These factors would be weighed as a group against the reasonableness of the offending party's conduct as determined by (1) its personal importance to the actors themselves and its social value generally, remembering always the enormous social utility of unhampered expression (in those cases where expression is involved); (2) the availability of alternative times and places where the conduct in question would cause less offense; (3) the extent, if any, to which the offense is caused with spiteful motives.

Joel Feinberg, Offense to Others 26 (1985). Should this type of analysis be applied to the civil commitment context? How would you apply it to *Whaley*? To Case 24 on p. 814?

In answering these questions, should it matter what the alternative to hospitalization is? Consider these comments:

> [F]ailure to commit those with grave mental disorders in treatment facilities paradoxically results in involuntary confinement of a different sort. A consequence of this failure is that they are frequently incarcerated for minor crimes. In fact, in the first year following the enactment of the [Lanterman–Petris–Short] Act, the number of mentally ill people in the prisons rose dramatically. Most of these arrests were for misdemeanors and were highly correlated with the offender's mental illness and corresponding behavior. Police often use catch-all charges to sweep mentally ill people off the street. These charges may include petty theft, assault, trespassing, and disorderly conduct. "Mercy-bookings" by policemen are also common as a way to protect people the police feel are easily victimized.

The consequences of this situation are drastic. One article in the Los Angeles Times described the prison system as "the world's largest mental institution." . . . Depending on the study, researchers investigating the records of prison inmates have found that between six to eight percent suffer from a serious psychiatric illness. Research based on inmate interviews shows that the number of prisoners with a psychiatric disorder jumps to ten to fifteen percent . . .

. . . Moreover, the incarceration of people who are gravely disabled by mental illness can lead to tragic results. Prison is designed for criminals and operates by rigid rules that the mentally ill might find difficult to follow. The bizarre behavior that mentally ill people display is often met with a lack of understanding and violence by guards and inmates. Suicide is also common for mentally ill inmates, and about half of prison suicides are committed by people who were previously hospitalized for mental illness. Furthermore, incarcerating a mentally ill person is likely to exacerbate their symptoms, often resulting in solitary confinement sometimes without any medical treatment.

Meredith Karasch, *Where Involuntary Commitment, Civil Liberties, and the Right to Mental Health Care Collide: An Overview of California's Mental Illness System*, 54 Hastings L.J. 493, 520–21 (2003).

Danger to property. Some states also include harm to "property" as a commitment criterion. See, e.g., Alaska Stat. § 47.30.915(10)(A–B); Wash. Rev. Code Ann. § 71.05.020(23)(a)(iii). In *Suzuki v. Yuen*, 617 F.2d 173 (9th Cir.1980), the Ninth Circuit Court of Appeals found such a provision in Hawaii's statute unconstitutionally broad. It stated:

We need not decide whether a state may ever commit one who is dangerous to property. This statute would allow commitment for danger to any property regardless of value or significance. . . . Under the current Hawaii definition of "danger to property," a person could be committed if he threatened to shoot a trespassing dog. The state's interest in protecting animals must be outweighed by the individual's interest in personal liberty.

Do you agree? How can the state legislature retain danger to property as a criterion for commitment while avoiding the court's prohibition? Could Nyflot be committed under a standard consistent with *Yuen*? Consider also Case 7 on p. 813. Such a person risks certain losses—money, job, friends, embarrassment. But he is not risking serious physical harm to himself or others. Should he therefore not be committable?

3.   *Frequency of harm.* No state statute makes explicit a requirement that the factfinder assess the frequency of the anticipated harm, perhaps because, as the excerpt from Feinberg illustrates, frequency is an integral part of the magnitude-of-harm analysis. Consider, however, *Millard v. Harris*, 406 F.2d 964 (D.C.Cir.1968), where the court reversed the recommitment of an exhibitionist, who conceded he was receiving treatment at the government hospital. Writing for the court, Judge Bazelon stated:

The unanimous testimony of all the expert witnesses that serious psychological harm would result from public exposure only to unusually sensitive adult women and small children leads us to conclude that the future sexual misconduct of the appellant, if any, is not sufficiently likely to cause the sort of harm required by the statute to justify further commitment. The appellant did not, it is true, prove that no such "potential viewers" would view him in the course of any future exhibitionism. But having shown that he was unlikely to commit such acts with great or uncontrollable frequency, and that in the event of such misconduct harm would be produced in only a small proportion of the population, the appellant could fairly demand of the Government that it show that the members of these restricted classes were not merely "potential viewers," but likely viewers. This the Government wholly failed to do. And without the assistance of any evidence adduced on this score, we cannot conclude that supersensitive women and small children are likely to suffer serious harm from isolated instances of exhibitionism. "Very seclusive, withdrawn, shy, sensitive" women are a minority. While the law must and does protect them like other citizens, there are limits on the extent to which the law can sweep the streets clear of all possible sources of occasional distress to such women. Small children present a different problem. But the expert testimony was not that the typical small child would be injured by witnessing an isolated act of exposure on the part of a stranger, but rather that psychological danger to their development was likely from repeated exposure to such abnormal adult sexual behavior. We therefore conclude that the likelihood of serious injury to a child happening to see the appellant expose himself in public is too remote to justify commitment. As for harm to the appellant's own children, we have already adverted in passing to the questionable nature of the sole evidence that the appellant ever did expose himself in his home before them. Even if we accept this evidence, however, and assume that the appellant might expose himself in his home if released, his children can be protected from the harm which might follow from repeated exposure by other means than his involuntary hospitalization. His wife need not permit the appellant to so abuse his children, and other legal remedies are available to her to insure that he does not inflict such harm on his children.

4.   *Probability of harm.* As noted earlier, the Supreme Court has held that, under the due process clause of the federal constitution, the criteria for civil commitment must be proven by clear and convincing evidence, a standard of proof below the criminal reasonable doubt standard and above the preponderance of the evidence standard used in most civil trials. A few states have opted for the higher reasonable doubt standard. See Superintendent of Worcester State Hospital v. Hagberg, 374 Mass. 271, 372 N.E.2d 242 (1978); see also, Hawaii Rev.Stat. § 334–60.5(i); Lausche v. Commissioner of Public Welfare, 302 Minn. 65, 225 N.W.2d 366 (1974), cert. denied 420 U.S. 993, 95 S.Ct. 1430, 43 L.Ed.2d 674 (1975).

Given the research finding that attempts to make yes-or-no predictions that someone will act violently in the future will often be wrong, is it possible to prove dangerousness beyond a reasonable doubt, or even by clear and convincing evidence? Litwack and Schlesinger think so. After a meticulous review of the then-existing literature, they noted that few studies on risk assessment had tested the accuracy of explicit predictions of dangerousness for people who were subsequently released in the community rather than confined and treated.[f] Thus, they "suggest":

clear and convincing evidence exists whenever any of the following indicia of future violence are evident: (1) a recent history of repeated violence (absent treatment or evidence of significant changes in the circumstances or attitudes that led to violence in the past); (2) a more distant history of violence together with clear and convincing evidence that the complex of attitudes and personality traits (and physical abilities) that led to violence in the past still exist and that there is a likelihood that the circumstances (or like circumstances) that led to violence in the past will recur in the foreseeable future (or, in any event, before the individual's violence-tending attitudes are likely to change); (3) unequivocal threats or other like evidence of serious intentions to commit violence, especially when based on delusional thinking; and (4) other clear and convincing evidence that the individual whose violence is being predicted is on the brink of violence. One example of this latter criterion would be that of a man who sat incessantly at the edge of his bed with a loaded rifle vigilantly waiting, because of his paranoid delusions, for his home to be attacked. Other examples would include individuals with a history of violence who express paniclike fears of losing control over violent impulses or who feel driven toward violence (e.g., by command hallucinations).

[W]e note again that while research has yet to establish the predictive power of these indices—and because of the practical and ethical problems involved may never do so—neither (to our knowledge) is there any evidence that refutes the legitimacy of relying on these indices to establish "clear and convincing" evidence of "dangerousness". On the other hand, we question, again, whether "clear and convincing" evidence of dangerousness can be had without any of these or similar indicia.

Thomas Litwack & Louis Schlesinger, *Assessing and Predicting Violence: Research, Law, and Applications*, in Handbook of Forensic Psychology 205, 224 (Weiner & Hess, eds., 1987).

At least one court has required that certain factors be considered before a clear and convincing finding of dangerousness can be made. In *In re Linehan*, 518 N.W.2d 609 (Minn.1994), the Minnesota Supreme Court held that, in determining the likelihood of violent behavior, courts should consider: (1) the person's demographic traits (e.g., age and education); (2) the person's history of violent behavior (paying particular attention to recency, severity,

---

[f]   See Chapter Six, Part II.C for a more detailed treatment of this research.

and frequency of violent acts); (3) base rate statistics for violent behavior among individuals of this person's background; (4) the sources of stress in the environment (cognitive and affective factors which indicate that the person may be predisposed to cope with stress in a violent or nonviolent manner); (5) the similarity of the present or future context to those contexts in which the person has used violence in the past; and (6) the person's record with respect to therapy programs. To the extent information exists, how do the factors identified in *Linehan* and by Litwack and Schlesinger apply in *Gregorovich* and *Nyflot*?

For base rate information, consider the materials in Note 1 on pp. 821–824 and the materials on actuarial prediction on pp. 557–564. Consider also the variables listed in the HCR–20, one of the most heavily researched structured clinical prediction devices. The HCR–20 consists of 20 items relating to historical, clinical and risk factors. The historical factors are previous violence; young age at first violent incident; relationship instability; employment problems; substance use problems; major mental illness; psychopathy; early maladjustment; personality disorder; prior supervision failure. The clinical factors are lack of insight; negative attitudes; active symptoms of major mental illness; impulsivity; unresponsiveness to treatment. The risk management factors are: plans lack feasibility; exposure to destabilizers; lack of personal support; noncompliance with remediation attempts; and stress. The evaluator scores the individual on a scale of 0 to 2 for each factor, with a score of 40 indicating a maximum degree of risk. See Christopher D. Webster et al., The HCR–20 Scheme: The Assessment of Dangerousness and Risk (1995).

The first peer-reviewed study of the HCR–20 looked at the instrument's performance in former civilly commitment patients after their release from the hospital. The patients who scored in the highest range (27 and over) were 17 times as likely to commit criminal violence within 2 years after release as those who scored below 19. Yet only 35% of those in the 27–plus range were found to have committed criminal violence during the follow-up period, and "criminal violence" included minor physical harm. K. Douglas et al., "Assessing Risk for Violence Among Psychiatric Patients: The HCR–20 Violence Risk Assessment Scheme and the Psychopathy Checklist: Screening Version," 67 J. Consulting & Clinical Psychology 917 (1999). Assume Gregorovich scores a 27 on the HCR–20. What are the implications of this finding?

Mossman, Schwartz, and Elam argue that, given the statutory language in most states' civil commitment laws focusing on "dangerousness" rather than "probability" or "likelihood" of violence, the focus of inquiry should have nothing to do with predictions. These authors explain that the connotation of "risk" has changed since the 1960s and 1970s, when most legislatures formulated their current civil commitment laws. As the statutes are written, "risk" refers not to what might happen, but what respondents *have already done* that indicates a danger is still present. That is, proof of dangerousness involves a showing that the individual remains mentally ill and that the mental illness has led to some overt act—a threat or an action that implied a risk of harm to self or others.

> When people make credible threats to do harm or engage in potentially or actually harmful behavior, they make a feature of themselves—their dangerousness—manifest. Through their action, the danger that they represent to themselves or others becomes a presence in the environment, in the same way that reckless driving is a presence for other persons on or near the road, and in the same way that toxic waste may be a presence in the lives of persons who live near a dumpsite. Overt behavior establishes that a risk is present, though actual future harm remains a less-than-certain probability.

> . . . [T]he probabilistic evidence established by mental health professionals' [actuarial risk assessment instruments] may have, at most, ancillary significance for civil commitment proceedings in jurisdictions that require behavioral proof of danger . . .

Douglas Mossman, Allison Schwartz & Elise R. Elam, *Risky Business Versus Overt Acts: What Relevance Do "Actuarial," Probabilistic Risk Assessments Have for Judicial Decisions on Involuntary Psychiatric Hospitalization?* 11 Hous. J. Health L. & Pol'y 365, 450 (2011).

Sex offender commitment statutes are worded differently from the mental health commitments laws described by Mossman and colleagues, in that the former laws seek to identify and detain persons who are, as the Kansas statutes puts it, "likely to engage in repeat acts of sexual violence." Kan. Stat. § 59–29a02(a). In this regard, consider *In re M.B.K.*, 639 N.W.2d 473 (N.D. 2002), where the state sought to commit, under a sexually violent predator law, a person who had pleaded guilty to a Class B felony sex offense and was nearing the end of his three-year sentence. The Supreme Court of North Dakota held that the state need merely prove that the individual posed "a threat to society" and further held that statistical proof that the individual had (depending on the actuarial device used) a 37 to 45% chance of "reoffending" within ten years was "clear and convincing" proof under this standard. The court justified its definition of dangerousness on two grounds: (1) other states had adopted the same standard, and (2) the standard "prevents a contest over percentage points and the results of other actuarial tools, and allows experts to use the fullness of their education, experience and resources available to them in order to determine if an individual poses a threat to society."

Is the court correct in stating that commitment may be based on a 37 to 45% chance of reoffending, given the clear and convincing evidence standard of proof? Monahan and Wexler argue that the answer to this question might be yes, depending on the typical definition of dangerousness. Many statutes require only that the state prove the person is "likely" or "probable" or "more likely than not" harmful to others. Quantifying the matter, these statutes could be said to define "dangerousness" as a 51% chance that the person will harm someone in the future. Assuming that proof by clear and convincing evidence correlates with a 75% degree of certainty, these states only require a showing of something like a 38% (75% × 51%) chance that the person will harm others in the future. John Monahan & David Wexler, *A Definite Maybe: Proof and Probability in Civil Commitment*, 2 Law & Hum.Beh. 37 (1978). In those jurisdictions that use the "more-likely-than-not" standard, is commitment of a person based on a 38% chance of harmful behavior justifiable?

5. *Imminence requirement. Lessard* and the statutes of a small and dwindling number of states prohibit commitment as dangerous to others unless the danger is "imminent." Alison Pfeffer, *"Imminent Danger" Standard for Involuntary Civil Commitment in the Wake of the Virginia Tech Tragedy*, 30 Cardozo L. Rev. 277, 289–90 (2008). Should this be a requirement in all statutes? If so, should it be made more specific (e.g., within the next two weeks, within the next two days) or should its definition depend upon the other factors discussed above?

c.   *The Overt Act Requirement*

PEOPLE V. SANSONE
Appellate Court of Illinois, 1974.
18 Ill.App.3d 315, 309 N.E.2d 733.

STAMOS, JUSTICE.

*   *   *

Initially, respondent argues that to sustain a finding of likelihood of injury to respondent or others, proof of prior dangerous conduct must be adduced, and in the absence of such proof, civil commitment is preventive detention. Respondent asserts that, pursuant to the theory of Robinson v. California, 370 U.S. 660, 82 S.Ct. 1417, 8 L.Ed.2d 758, confinement based upon a prediction of future dangerous conduct is confinement based upon status. Respondent relies upon Cross v. Harris, 135 U.S.App.D.C. 259, 418 F.2d 1095 and Lessard v. Schmidt, 349 F.Supp. 1078 (E.D.Wis.) for the proposition that a prediction of future dangerousness must be based upon documented prior overt acts or threats.

*   *   *

In the area of mental health law, the State must balance the curtailment of liberty against the danger of harm to the individual or others. The paramount factor is the interest of society which naturally includes the interest of the patient in not being subjected to unjustified confinement. We agree with respondent that the "science" of predicting future dangerous behavior is inexact, and certainly is not infallible. We also agree that the mere establishment of a mental problem is not an adequate basis upon which to confine a person who has never harmed or attempted to harm either himself or another. However, we are of the opinion that a decision to commit based upon a medical opinion which clearly states that a person is reasonably expected to engage in dangerous conduct, and which is based upon the experience and studies of qualified psychiatrists, is a determination which properly can be made by the State.

Moreover, we cannot agree that commitment in the absence of evidence of prior harmful conduct is preventive detention based upon the patient's status as a mentally ill person. Again, we reiterate that a finding must be based upon an explicit medical opinion regarding the patient's future conduct, and cannot be based upon a mere finding of mental illness. Secondly, the purpose of the Mental Health Code is to provide treatment, and in fact, the Code affords every patient the right to treatment. This is a very different situation from that in Robinson v. California, supra, wherein the Court held that a law which imprisons a person afflicted with a disease inflicts cruel and unusual punishment. The Court in *Robinson* distinguished criminal punishment and detention from detention based upon laws which require medical treatment. 370 U.S. 660, 666, 82 S.Ct. 1417, 8 L.Ed.2d 758. Therefore, we hold that a finding of "in need of mental treatment," absent evidence of prior harmful conduct, is not *per se* violative of due process.

* * *

In the instant case, respondent's delusions regarding law enforcement and law enforcement officers were established without contradiction by the testimony of the psychiatrist and the social worker, both of whom interviewed respondent on two different occasions. The medical opinion was that respondent believed that persons were "after him," and that respondent could be dangerous to others. The psychiatrist testified that persons he had known with the same type of delusions had injured or attempted to injure others. Therefore, although the psychiatrist could not give any degree of probability of dangerousness, and although there was no evidence of prior dangerous conduct, the uncontradicted testimony established by clear and convincing evidence that respondent was in need of mental treatment.

IN MATTER OF MENTAL HEALTH OF D.R.S.

Supreme Court of Montana, 1986.
221 Mont. 245, 718 P.2d 335.

[D.R.S. was committed under a statute which required the state to show that he was "suffering from a mental disorder which has resulted in . . . injury to others or the imminent threat thereof. . . ." The statute defined injury to mean "physical injury," Mont.Code Ann. 53–21–102(14), and provided that imminent threat of injury to others "shall be evidenced by overt acts, sufficiently recent in time as to be material and relevant as to the respondent's present condition." Mont.Code Ann. 53–21–126(2). The sole overt act proven by the state was an armed robbery for which D.R.S. was not convicted. As described by the Montana Supreme Court, D.R.S. and another person "committed the robbery" on November 5, 1982. In the course of the robbery, they took the store clerk behind a woodpile by the store, taped him up, covered him with wood and left him in the cold. The clerk identified D.R.S. as the person who taped him and stated that the other person threatened to shoot him if he didn't tell them the combination to the safe. The clerk testified that both robbers frightened him and that he feared for his life.

D.R.S. was found incompetent to stand trial on the robbery charge and hospitalized for the purpose of restoration to competency. After almost two years in the hospital, he was found competent, but charges against him were dismissed on speedy trial grounds on January 8, 1985. On February 14, 1985, he was civilly committed. The Montana Supreme Court upheld the commitment against a challenge that the robbery was insufficiently recent. The court justified this decision as follows]:

The circumstances in the case at bar are such that a lapse of time between the overt act and the commitment proceedings do not preclude relying on the overt act [the robbery] as evidence of D.R.S.' mental condition.

Dr. James Deming, the psychologist who treated D.R.S. for the two-year period at Montana State Hospital testified that D.R.S.' condition was essentially unchanged from that in 1982. He testified that:

[D.R.S.] continued to exhibit symptoms of a significant mental illness, continued to be confused, continued to develop neologisms or new words, continued to be convinced of specific bizarre ideations, as an example, [D.R.S.] was convinced that his lawyer was my brother. On the basis of the information that both of us wore mustaches. He continued to have—to exhibit a significant thought disorder which renders him unpredictable, and in my judgment, imminently dangerous.

Dr. Deming relied on several factors in concluding that D.R.S. is dangerous. In addition to the primary element of the charges against D.R.S., Dr. Deming considered his statements of unwillingness to accept supervision in a community setting for his disorder, D.R.S.' stated intent to use alcohol when he leaves the hospital, and the deterioration of his condition while in the county jail. Dr. Deming explained that a small amount of alcohol would render D.R.S. confused and disoriented, resulting in dangerous behavior, and that he had not received medication during his stay in jail. The fact that D.R.S. had not exhibited dangerous or "acting-out" behavior in the hospital was due to the supervised environment and the control of his medication. If taken out of this supervised setting, Dr. Deming said that D.R.S. would become imminently dangerous within two months. Finally, the doctor expressed his opinion that D.R.S. is seriously mentally ill and imminently dangerous to himself and others due to his mental disease of paranoid schizophrenia.

D.R.S.' conduct during the robbery, under the circumstances presented here, is "sufficiently recent in time as to be material and relevant" to his present condition. The time lapse between the overt act and his commitment hearing was due to his serious mental illness. The evidence showed his condition remained as it was at the time of the overt act. In addition, the psychiatric evaluation stated that D.R.S. would be imminently dangerous within two months of leaving the supervised hospital setting. We hold that the District Court had sufficient evidence to find D.R.S. is seriously mentally ill.

QUESTIONS AND COMMENTS

1. *The need for an overt act requirement.* The *Lessard* decision prohibited commitment unless the person is found to be dangerous "based upon a finding of a recent overt act, attempt or threat to do substantial harm." Thirty-seven state statutes include a similar provision or a provision like Montana's. See Douglas Mossman, Allison Schwartz & Elise R. Elam, *Risky Business v. Overt Acts: What Relevance Do "Actuarial" Risk Assessments Have for Judicial Decisions on Involuntary Psychiatric Hospitalization?* 11 Hous. J. Health L. & Pol'y 365, 447 (2012) (Table 2) The rest do not require proof of an overt act.

What is the argument that the Constitution mandates such a showing? Cf. *Robinson v. California,* supra. Are there other, "pragmatic," reasons for such a requirement? Under California's LPS Act, those considered dangerous to others are potentially subject to three "stages" of commitment: a 72–hour emergency detention, a 14–day short-term detention, and a 180–day commitment. Proof of an overt act is required for the third-stage 180–day commitment, but not for the first and second stages of the commitment process. Cal.Code §§ 5150, 5200, 5250, 5300. Can you think of a rationale for this approach?

2. *The content of the overt act requirement.* If proof of an overt act is required, how should it be defined? Is a threat to harm another enough? Statements like those in *Sansone* that "people are out to get me?" Purchase of a weapon?

The criminal law has dealt with an analogous issue through definition of the actus reus for attempt crimes. Typically, "mere preparation" for a crime is considered insufficient conduct to impose liability for attempt. Various tests developed to capture this notion. For instance, one such test asked whether the person had committed the "last proximate act" of the offense in question. Thus, if a person fires a gun at the intended victim and misses, he can be found guilty of attempted murder. If he merely lies in wait for the victim but does not fire the gun, he cannot be. A second, less restrictive test, developed by Justice Holmes, focused on whether the person was in "dangerous proximity to success." See generally, Wayne R. LaFave, Criminal Law 623–626 (5th ed. 2010). Should civil commitment statutes require something beyond mere preparation? What effect would an overt act requirement have in Case 5 on p. 813? Case 17 on p. 814? Regarding the sufficiency of threats, consider further that some states make menacing a crime. See, e.g., Ohio Rev. Code § 2903.22(A) (defining "menacing" as "knowingly caus[ing] another to believe that the offender will cause physical harm to the person or property of the other person . . . "). If a state does not have such a provision, should threats be a sufficient overt act?

3.   *Recency of the overt act.* The *Lessard* court also requires that the overt act be "recent," as does the Montana statute in *D.R.S.* Other states (e.g., California) do not explicitly include a recency requirement. What is the purpose of this requirement? Does it link with the imminence requirement? Do you agree with the holding in *D.R.S.* on this issue? How do you evaluate the statute below (which at one time was the law in Arizona)?

> § 36–501(3). "Danger to others" means behavior which constitutes a danger of inflicting substantial bodily harm upon another person based upon a history of having inflicted or having attempted to inflict substantial bodily harm upon another person within twelve months preceding the hearing on court ordered treatment, except that:

> (a) If the proposed patient has existed under conditions of being restrained by physical or pharmacological means, or of being confined, or of being supervised, which have deterred or tended to deter him from carrying out acts of inflicting or attempting to inflict bodily harm upon another person, the time limit of within twelve months preceding the hearing may be extended to a time longer than twelve months as consideration of the evidence indicates; or,

> (b) If the bodily harm inflicted upon or attempted to be inflicted upon another person was grievous or horrendous, the time limit of within twelve months preceding the hearing may be extended to a time longer than twelve months as consideration of the evidence indicates.

4.   *Standard of proof.* Although proof of dangerousness need only be by clear and convincing evidence, can an argument be made that proof of the overt act must be beyond a reasonable doubt? Montana's statute, at issue in *D.R.S.*, is unique among the states, in that it requires proof beyond a reasonable doubt of any "physical facts or evidence" and clear and convincing proof "as to all other matters [except that] mental disorders must be proved to a reasonable medical certainty." Mont.Code Ann. § 53–21–126(2). Is the Montana approach coherent? As applied to the criteria necessary to commit D.R.S., is the standard met?

C. *PARENS PATRIAE* COMMITMENTS

1. Rationale

The *parens patriae* authority is premised on the power of government to act as "parent" toward its citizens. The United States has a strong anti-paternalistic tradition, based on strains of individualism dating back to the colonization of the eastern seaboard by dissidents and outcasts. John Stuart Mill provided one of the earliest and most incisive defenses of the anti-paternalism position.

> The only purpose for which power can be rightfully exercised over any member of a civilized community against his will, is to prevent harm to others. His own good, either physical or moral, is not a sufficient warrant. He cannot rightfully be compelled to do or forbear because it will be better for him to do so, because it will make him happier, because in the opinion of others to do so would be wise, or even right. These are reasons for remonstrating with him, or reasoning with him, or persuading him, or entreating him, but not for compelling him, or visiting him with any evil in case he do otherwise.

J.S. Mill, *On Liberty*, in The Philosophy of John Stuart Mill 197 (1961).

Yet, as Professor Shapiro has pointed out, "if antipaternalism is the dominant strain, it has surely not won the day:"

> Defenders of paternalism, or at least of a more neutral stance, have argued forcefully for their position on both descriptive and normative grounds. Paternalist motives, they suggest, help to account for a vast range of present-day legislation and judicial doctrine (not to speak of the actions of individuals toward one another); failure to recognize these motives can only lead to confusion and hypocrisy. Moreover, paternalism has a legitimate place among human motivations— perhaps more legitimate than other, more selfish, reasons for action—since its regard for others is rooted in "empathy or love."

David Shapiro, *Courts, Legislatures, and Paternalism*, 74 Va.L.Rev. 519, 519–20 (1988). As Shapiro notes, paternalistic legislation has become an accepted feature of modern life. Laws regulating food quality and the environment, employment conditions (e.g., minimum wage and maximum hour laws), and transportation (e.g., seat-belt and motorcycle helmet statutes) are just a few examples of legislation that might be characterized as paternalistic in motivation.

Civil commitment remains the most dramatic example of state paternalism. Every state permits involuntary, prolonged hospitalization of persons, who because of mental illness, are "dangerous to self," "unable to care" for themselves, "gravely disabled" or some combination thereof. The usual justification advanced for these provisions is that people with mental illness lack the capacity to make decisions about treatment and hospitalization; thus, the state has the authority to make those decisions for them. Note, *Civil Commitment of the Mentally Ill: Developments in the Law*, 87 Harv.L.Rev. 1190, 1212 (1974). John Rawls, whose political philosophy famously makes liberty a principle of highest priority, recognized that rational individuals nonetheless should adopt "principles stipulating when others are authorized to act in their behalf and to override their present wishes if necessary . . . recognizing that sometimes their capacity to act rationally for their good may fail, or be lacking altogether." John Rawls, A Theory of Justice 249 (1971). Even Mill recognized an exception to his general rule for those who are "incompetent," including youth and people with mental disability, on the ground that one cannot exercise one's political rights unless one has the capacity to do so. See Mary Ellen Waithe, *Why Mill Was For Paternalism*, 6 Int'l J.L. & Psychiat. 101 (1983).

Several arguments against this use of state power can be advanced. The first, analogous to the argument against police power commitment of people with mental illness, is that people with mental illness as a class are no more incompetent than others and therefore should not be singled out for special treatment. Professor Morse makes the argument most directly:

> Are the mentally disordered particularly incompetent? The question is crucial because involuntary commitment substitutes the state's judgment about the necessity for hospitalization (and often for treatment as well) for the judgment of the individual. Although commitment rarely includes a formal finding of legal incompetence at present, it at least implies the judgment that in some cases the person cannot cope or make decisions in his or her own best interest. * * *

> There is however, little empirical or theoretical justification for the belief that the mentally disordered as a class are especially incapable of managing their lives or deciding for themselves what is in their own best interests. Available empirical evidence demonstrates that the mentally disordered as a class are probably not more incompetent than normal persons as a class. Indeed, there is no necessary relationship between mental disorder and legal incompetence.

> . . . While some disordered persons are clearly incompetent according to any reasonable criteria, the social goal of reducing the consequences of incompetence is not well served by allowing involuntary hospitalization, guardianship, or treatment of only the mentally disordered.

Stephen Morse, *A Preference for Liberty: The Case Against Involuntary Commitment of the Mentally Disordered*, 70 Cal.L.Rev. 54, 63–64 (1982).

Subsequent research appears to undercut this conclusion, however. In a MacArthur Foundation study comparing the competency of large groups of patients with schizophrenia, patients with depression, patients with heart disease, and persons in the community, the patients with schizophrenia were found to be significantly more impaired.

> Nearly one half of the schizophrenia group and 76% of the depression group performed in the "adequate" range (according to *ad hoc* definitions of adequacy used in this study) across all decision-making measures, and a significant portion performed at or above the mean for persons without mental illness. . . . On the other hand, the data confirm that significant differences exist in decision-making abilities between persons with and without mental illness, especially when the comparisons focus on patients with schizophrenia. For any given measure, approximately 25% of the schizophrenic group scored in the "impaired" range, compared with 5–7% of angina patients and only 2% of community controls. . . . When all measures are combined, 52% of patients with schizophrenia showed impairment on at least one measure, in contrast to 12% of angina patients and 4% of community controls.

Thomas Grisso & Paul Appelbaum, *Abilities of Patients to Consent to Psychiatric and Medical Treatments*, 19 L. & Hum. Beh. 149, 171 (1995). It may also be relevant that major psychiatric illness is implicated in no less than 93% of suicides, with the diagnoses most often assigned being major depression (40–60%), chronic alcoholism (20%) and schizophrenia (10%). David Clark & Jan Fawcet, *Review of Empirical Risk Factors for Evaluation of the Suicidal Patient*, in Suicide: Guidelines for Assessment, Management and Treatment 18–19 (Bruce Bongar ed. 1992).

The second argument against *parens patriae* commitment assumes the theoretical validity of committing people with mental illness who are incompetent (at least when incompetency causes serious dysfunction), but questions whether "reasonable criteria" for judging who is incompetent can be developed and applied. Dr. Szasz is particularly vigorous in advancing this view. In one of his later works, for instance, he stated:

> [W]henever one person, A, claims that another person, B, is incompetent, we are confronted with a situation from which we can draw two quite different inferences, one more probable than the other. The less probable inference is that A's assertion is true: in other words, that B is indeed incompetent. The more probable inference is that A's assertion is untrue: in other words, that A wants to paternistically control or coerce B.

Thomas Szasz, Insanity: The Idea and Its Consequences 249–50 (1987). A more detailed investigation of this difficult issue is left until Chapter Nine, which deals with the question of competency generally. For now, the following definition of competency is offered:

Since the purpose of the incapacity standard is to distinguish persons whose decisions to refuse treatment must be accepted as final from those whose choices may be validly overridden through *parens patriae* commitments, the standard should focus on the ability to engage in a decision-making process rather than the resulting decision. . . . [C]ommentary accompanying the National Institute of Mental Health's 1952 Draft Act Governing Hospitalization of the Mentally Ill appears to provide a workable definition of incapacity[:] an individual lacks capacity if, as a result of a mental disease or disorder, he has lost the "power to make choices or become so confused . . . [that he cannot] make a decision having any relation to the factors bearing on his hospitalization."

Developments, supra at 1217.

Even if one accepts that *parens patriae* commitment is theoretically justified and that the incompetent mentally ill can be accurately identified, the following question must also be answered: who among the incompetent mentally ill may be involuntarily hospitalized? This section addresses this question.

NOTE, CIVIL COMMITMENT OF THE MENTALLY ILL: DEVELOPMENTS IN THE LAW
87 Harvard L.R. 1190, 1218–19 (1974).

* * *

Best Interest of the Individual: A Balancing Requirement.—After the threshold requirement of incapacity has been met, the state may act as *parens patriae* for the individual. Although the state ideally should attempt to duplicate the decision which its ward would have made, the need to ascertain each ward's value structure would make such a process highly impractical. Consequently, the state as substitute decision-maker should objectively evaluate alternatives and select the one which best serves the ward's interest. The propriety of a decision to require psychiatric treatment or to compel hospitalization will thus depend on whether either action constitutes the most desirable response to the individual's condition. The advisability of ordering commitment will naturally vary depending on such individual factors as the debilitating effect of the mental disorder, the prognosis with and without treatment, the expected duration of treatment, the need for and length of institutionalization, the institutional conditions, the legal disabilities resulting from commitment, and the disruptive effect on preexisting lifestyle.

Although the "best interest" test entails a flexible balancing of costs and benefits, the serious stigma and the interference with physical freedom produced by even short term commitment to a mental institution suggest that a substantial expected benefit should be required for involuntary commitment. Consequently, a mental disorder which does not pose a danger to the individual's physical health or substantially impair his ability to function in society should rarely result in forced institutional care. State commitment statutes which require that the individual be dangerous to himself or that his condition create a substantial risk of his physical injury can be viewed as expressing a legislative judgment that the likelihood that individuals who do not meet those standards would not benefit sufficiently to justify their confinement outweighs the possibility that commitment would sometimes be appropriate in such cases.

The potential of beneficial treatment is another possible limitation on *parens patriae* commitments derived from the best interest requirement. In *In re Ballay,* the District of Columbia Circuit contended in dictum that "[w]ithout some form of treatment the state justification for acting as *parens patriae* becomes a nullity." However, the court's belief that custodial care is an impermissible use of the *parens patriae* power seems unwarranted. As with other relevant factors, the untreatable patient's potential need for indefinite confinement for his own protection should be considered in balancing the costs and benefits of imposing various types of care. The danger of substantial physical harm created when an untreatable mental disorder impairs the individual's ability to provide for his basic needs might well be sufficient to justify action under the *parens patriae* power, although there are alternative modes of providing protective care which may be preferable to hospitalization of the untreatable. . . .

O'CONNOR V. DONALDSON

Supreme Court of the United States, 1975.
422 U.S. 563, 95 S.Ct. 2486, 45 L.Ed.2d 396.

*   *   *

MR. JUSTICE STEWART delivered the opinion of the Court.

The respondent, Kenneth Donaldson, was civilly committed to confinement as a mental patient in the Florida State Hospital at Chattahoochee in January 1957. He was kept in custody there against his will for nearly 15 years. The petitioner, Dr. J.B. O'Connor, was the hospital's superintendent during most of this period. Throughout his confinement Donaldson repeatedly, but unsuccessfully, demanded his release, claiming that he was dangerous to no one, that he was not mentally ill, and that, at any rate, the hospital was not providing treatment for his supposed illness. Finally, in February 1971, Donaldson brought this lawsuit under 42 U.S.C. § 1983, in the United States District Court for the Northern District of Florida, alleging that O'Connor, and other members of the hospital staff named as defendants, had intentionally and maliciously deprived him of his constitutional right to liberty. After a four-day trial, the jury returned a verdict assessing both compensatory and punitive damages against O'Connor and a codefendant. The Court of Appeals for the Fifth Circuit affirmed the judgment. We granted O'Connor's petition for certiorari, because of the important constitutional questions seemingly presented.

I

Donaldson's commitment was initiated by his father, who thought that his son was suffering from "delusions." After hearings before a county judge of Pinellas County, Fla., Donaldson was found to be suffering from "paranoid schizophrenia" and was committed for "care, maintenance, and treatment" pursuant to Florida statutory provisions that have since been repealed.[2] The state law was less than clear in specifying the grounds necessary for commitment, and the record is scanty as to Donaldson's condition at the time of the judicial hearing. These matters are, however, irrelevant, for this case involves no challenge to the initial commitment, but is focused, instead, upon the nearly 15 years of confinement that followed.

The evidence at the trial showed that the hospital staff had the power to release a patient, not dangerous to himself or others, even if he remained mentally ill and had been lawfully committed. Despite many requests, O'Connor refused to allow that power to be exercised in Donaldson's case. At the trial, O'Connor indicated that he had believed that Donaldson would have been unable to make a "successful adjustment outside the institution," but could not recall the basis for that conclusion. O'Connor retired as superintendent shortly before this suit was filed. A few months thereafter, and before the trial, Donaldson secured his release and a judicial restoration of competency, with the support of the hospital staff.

The testimony at the trial demonstrated, without contradiction, that Donaldson had posed no danger to others during his long confinement, or indeed at any point in his life. O'Connor himself conceded that he had no

---

2   The judicial commitment proceedings were pursuant to § 394.22(11) of the State Public Health Code, which provided:

"Whenever any person who has been adjudged mentally incompetent requires confinement or restraint to prevent self-injury or violence to others, the said judge shall direct that such person be forthwith delivered to a superintendent of a Florida state hospital, for the mentally ill, after admission has been authorized under regulations approved by the board of commissioners of state institutions, for care, maintenance, and treatment, . . . "

* * *

Donaldson had been adjudged "incompetent" several days earlier under § 394.22(1), which provided for such a finding as to any person who was "incompetent by reason of mental illness, sickness, drunkenness, excessive use of drugs, insanity, or other mental or physical condition, so that he is incapable of caring for himself or managing his property, or is likely to dissipate or lose his property or become the victim of designing persons, or inflict harm on himself or others. . . . " Fla.Gen.Laws 1955, c. 29909, § 3, p. 831.

personal or secondhand knowledge that Donaldson had ever committed a dangerous act. There was no evidence that Donaldson had ever been suicidal or been thought likely to inflict injury upon himself. One of O'Connor's codefendants acknowledged that Donaldson could have earned his own living outside the hospital. He had done so for some 14 years before his commitment, and immediately upon his release he secured a responsible job in hotel administration.

Furthermore, Donaldson's frequent requests for release had been supported by responsible persons willing to provide him any care he might need on release. In 1963, for example, a representative of Helping Hands, Inc., a halfway house for mental patients, wrote O'Connor asking him to release Donaldson to its care. The request was accompanied by a supporting letter from the Minneapolis Clinic of Psychiatry and Neurology, which a codefendant conceded was a "good clinic." O'Connor rejected the offer, replying that Donaldson could be released only to his parents. That rule was apparently of O'Connor's own making. At the time, Donaldson was 55 years old, and, as O'Connor knew, Donaldson's parents were too elderly and infirm to take responsibility for him. Moreover, in his continuing correspondence with Donaldson's parents, O'Connor never informed them of the Helping Hands offer. In addition, on four separate occasions between 1964 and 1968, John Lembcke, a college classmate of Donaldson's and a longtime family friend, asked O'Connor to release Donaldson to his care. On each occasion O'Connor refused. The record shows that Lembcke was a serious and responsible person, who was willing and able to assume responsibility for Donaldson's welfare.

The evidence showed that Donaldson's confinement was a simple regime of enforced custodial care, not a program designed to alleviate or cure his supposed illness. Numerous witnesses, including one of O'Connor's codefendants, testified that Donaldson had received nothing but custodial care while at the hospital. O'Connor described Donaldson's treatment as "milieu therapy." But witnesses from the hospital staff conceded that, in the context of this case, "milieu therapy" was a euphemism for confinement in the "milieu" of a mental hospital.[4] For substantial periods, Donaldson was simply kept in a large room that housed 60 patients, many of whom were under criminal commitment. Donaldson's requests for ground privileges, occupational training, and an opportunity to discuss his case with O'Connor or other staff members were repeatedly denied.

At the trial, O'Connor's principal defense was that he had acted in good faith and was therefore immune from any liability for monetary damages. His position, in short, was that state law, which he had believed

---

[4] There was some evidence that Donaldson, who is a Christian Scientist, on occasion refused to take medication. The trial judge instructed the jury not to award damages for any period of confinement during which Donaldson had declined treatment.

valid, had authorized indefinite custodial confinement of the "sick," even if they were not given treatment and their release could harm no one.

The trial judge instructed the members of the jury that they should find that O'Connor had violated Donaldson's constitutional right to liberty if they found that he had

> "confined [Donaldson] against his will, knowing that he was not mentally ill or dangerous or knowing that if mentally ill he was not receiving treatment for his alleged mental illness.

* * *

> "Now, the purpose of involuntary hospitalization is treatment and not mere custodial care or punishment if a patient is not a danger to himself or others. Without such treatment there is no justification from a constitutional stand-point for continued confinement unless you should also find that [Donaldson] was dangerous to either himself or others."[6]

The trial judge further instructed the jury that O'Connor was immune from damages if he

> "reasonably believed in good faith that detention of [Donaldson] was proper for the length of time he was so confined. . . .

> "However, mere good intentions which do not give rise to a reasonable belief that detention is lawfully required cannot justify [Donaldson's] confinement in the Florida State Hospital."

The jury returned a verdict for Donaldson against O'Connor and a codefendant, and awarded damages of $38,500, including $10,000 in punitive damages.

The Court of Appeals affirmed the judgment of the District Court in a broad opinion dealing with "the far-reaching question whether the Fourteenth Amendment guarantees a right to treatment to persons involuntarily civilly committed to state mental hospitals." The appellate court held that when, as in Donaldson's case, the rationale for confinement is that the patient is in need of treatment, the Constitution

---

6   The District Court defined treatment as follows:

"You are instructed that a person who is involuntarily civilly committed to a mental hospital does have a *constitutional right to receive such treatment as will give him a realistic opportunity to be cured or to improve his mental condition*." (Emphasis added.) O'Connor argues that this statement suggests that a mental patient has a right to treatment even if confined by reason of dangerousness to himself or others. But this is to take the above paragraph out of context, for it is bracketed by paragraphs making clear the trial judge's theory that treatment is constitutionally required only if mental illness alone, rather than danger to self or others, is the reason for confinement. If O'Connor had thought the instructions ambiguous on this point, he could have objected to them and requested a clarification. He did not do so. We accordingly have no occasion here to decide whether persons committed on grounds of dangerousness enjoy a "right to treatment."

* * *

requires that minimally adequate treatment in fact be provided. The court further expressed the view that, regardless of the grounds for involuntary civil commitment, a person confined against his will at a state mental institution has "a constitutional right to receive such individual treatment as will give him a reasonable opportunity to be cured or to improve his mental condition." Conversely, the court's opinion implied that it is constitutionally permissible for a State to confine a mentally ill person against his will in order to treat his illness, regardless of whether his illness renders him dangerous to himself or others.

II

We have concluded that the difficult issues of constitutional law dealt with by the Court of Appeals are not presented by this case in its present posture. Specifically, there is no reason now to decide whether mentally ill persons dangerous to themselves or to others have a right to treatment upon compulsory confinement by the State, or whether the State may compulsorily confine a non-dangerous, mentally ill individual for the purpose of treatment. As we view it, this case raises a single, relatively simple, but nonetheless important question concerning every man's constitutional right to liberty.

The jury found that Donaldson was neither dangerous to himself nor dangerous to others, and also found that, if mentally ill, Donaldson had not received treatment. That verdict, based on abundant evidence, makes the issue before the Court a narrow one. We need not decide whether, when, or by what procedures, a mentally ill person may be confined by the State on any of the grounds which, under contemporary statutes, are generally advanced to justify involuntary confinement of such a person— to prevent injury to the public, to ensure his own survival or safety, or to alleviate or cure his illness. For the jury found that none of the above grounds for continued confinement was present in Donaldson's case.[10]

Given the jury's findings, what was left as justification for keeping Donaldson in continued confinement? The fact that state law may have authorized confinement of the harmless mentally ill does not itself establish a constitutionally adequate purpose for the confinement. Nor is it enough that Donaldson's original confinement was founded upon a constitutionally adequate basis, if in fact it was, because even if his

---

[10] O'Connor argues that, despite the jury's verdict, the Court must assume that Donaldson was receiving treatment sufficient to justify his confinement, because the adequacy of treatment is a "nonjusticiable" question that must be left to the discretion of the psychiatric profession. That argument is unpersuasive. Where "treatment" is the sole asserted ground for depriving a person of liberty, it is plainly unacceptable to suggest that the courts are powerless to determine whether the asserted ground is present. See *Jackson v. Indiana*, 406 U.S. 715, 92 S.Ct. 1845, 32 L.Ed.2d 435. Neither party objected to the jury instruction defining treatment. There is, accordingly, no occasion in this case to decide whether the provision of treatment, standing alone, can ever constitutionally justify involuntary confinement or, if it can, how much or what kind of treatment would suffice for that purpose. In its present posture this case involves not involuntary treatment but simply involuntary custodial confinement.

involuntary confinement was initially permissible, it could not constitutionally continue after that basis no longer existed.

A finding of "mental illness" alone cannot justify a State's locking a person up against his will and keeping him indefinitely in simple custodial confinement. Assuming that that term can be given a reasonably precise content and that the "mentally ill" can be identified with reasonable accuracy, there is still no constitutional basis for confining such persons involuntarily if they are dangerous to no one and can live safely in freedom.

May the State confine the mentally ill merely to ensure them a living standard superior to that they enjoy in the private community? That the State has a proper interest in providing care and assistance to the unfortunate goes without saying. But the mere presence of mental illness does not disqualify a person from preferring his home to the comforts of an institution. Moreover, while the State may arguably confine a person to save him from harm, incarceration is rarely if ever a necessary condition for raising the living standards of those capable of surviving safely in freedom, on their own or with the help of family or friends. See *Shelton v. Tucker,* 364 U.S. 479, 488–490, 81 S.Ct. 247, 252–253, 5 L.Ed.2d 231.

May the State fence in the harmless mentally ill solely to save its citizens from exposure to those whose ways are different? One might as well ask if the State, to avoid public unease, could incarcerate all who are physically unattractive or socially eccentric. Mere public intolerance or animosity cannot constitutionally justify the deprivation of a person's physical liberty.

In short, a State cannot constitutionally confine without more a nondangerous individual who is capable of surviving safely in freedom by himself or with the help of willing and responsible family members or friends. Since the jury found, upon ample evidence, that O'Connor, as an agent of the State, knowingly did so confine Donaldson, it properly concluded that O'Connor violated Donaldson's constitutional right to freedom.

MR. CHIEF JUSTICE BURGER, concurring.

Although I join the Court's opinion and judgment in this case, it seems to me that several factors merit more emphasis than it gives them. I therefore add the following remarks. * * *

There can be no doubt that involuntary commitment to a mental hospital, like involuntary confinement of an individual for any reason, is a deprivation of liberty which the State cannot accomplish without due process of law. Commitment must be justified on the basis of a legitimate state interest, and the reasons for committing a particular individual must be established in an appropriate proceeding. Equally important, confinement must cease when those reasons no longer exist.

The Court of Appeals purported to be applying these principles in developing the first of its theories supporting a constitutional right to treatment. It first identified what it perceived to be the traditional bases for civil commitment—physical dangerousness to oneself or others, or a need for treatment—and stated:

> "[W]here, as in Donaldson's case, the rationale for confinement is the *'parens patriae'* rationale that the patient is in need of treatment, the due process clause requires that minimally adequate treatment be in fact provided. . . . 'To deprive any citizen of his or her liberty upon the altruistic theory that the confinement is for humane therapeutic reasons and then fail to provide adequate treatment violates the very fundamentals of due process.'"

The Court of Appeals did not explain its conclusion that the rationale for respondent's commitment was that he needed treatment. The Florida statutes in effect during the period of his confinement did not require that a person who had been adjudicated incompetent and ordered committed either be provided with psychiatric treatment or released, and there was no such condition in respondent's order of commitment. More important, the instructions which the Court of Appeals read as establishing an absolute constitutional right to treatment did not require the jury to make any findings regarding the specific reasons for respondent's confinement or to focus upon any rights he may have had under state law. Thus, the premise of the Court of Appeals' first theory must have been that, at least with respect to persons who are not physically dangerous, a State has no power to confine the mentally ill except for the purpose of providing them with treatment.

That proposition is surely not descriptive of the power traditionally exercised by the States in this area. Historically, and for a considerable period of time, subsidized custodial care in private foster homes or boarding houses was the most benign form of care provided incompetent or mentally ill persons for whom the States assumed responsibility. Until well into the 19th century the vast majority of such persons were simply restrained in poorhouses, almshouses, or jails. The few States that established institutions for the mentally ill during this early period were concerned primarily with providing a more humane place of confinement and only secondarily with "curing" the persons sent there.

As the trend toward state care of the mentally ill expanded, eventually leading to the present statutory schemes for protecting such persons, the dual functions of institutionalization continued to be recognized. While one of the goals of this movement was to provide medical treatment to those who could benefit from it, it was acknowledged that this could not be done in all cases and that there was a large range of mental illness for which no known "cure" existed. In time, providing places for the custodial confinement of the so-called "dependent insane" again emerged as the major goal of the States' programs in this area and remained so well into this century.

In short, the idea that States may not confine the mentally ill except for the purpose of providing them with treatment is of very recent origin, and there is no historical basis for imposing such a limitation on state power. Analysis of the sources of the civil commitment power likewise lends no support to that notion. There can be little doubt that in the exercise of its police power a State may confine individuals solely to protect society from the dangers of significant antisocial acts or communicable disease. *Jacobson v. Massachusetts,* 197 U.S. 11, 25–29, 25 S.Ct. 358, 360–362, 49 L.Ed. 643 (1905). Additionally, the States are vested with the historic *parens patriae* power, including the duty to protect "persons under legal disabilities to act for themselves." The classic example of this role is when a State undertakes to act as " 'the general guardian of all infants, idiots, and lunatics.' "

Of course, an inevitable consequence of exercising the *parens patriae* power is that the ward's personal freedom will be substantially restrained, whether a guardian is appointed to control his property, he is placed in the custody of a private third party, or committed to an institution. Thus, however the power is implemented, due process requires that it not be invoked indiscriminately. At a minimum, a particular scheme for protection of the mentally ill must rest upon a legislative determination that it is compatible with the best interests of the affected class and that its members are unable to act for themselves. Moreover, the use of alternative forms of protection may be motivated by different considerations, and the justifications for one may not be invoked to rationalize another.

However, the existence of some due process limitations on the *parens patriae* power does not justify the further conclusion that it may be exercised to confine a mentally ill person only if the purpose of the confinement is treatment. Despite many recent advances in medical knowledge, it remains a stubborn fact that there are many forms of mental illness which are not understood, some which are untreatable in the sense that no effective therapy has yet been discovered for them, and that rates of "cure" are generally low. There can be little responsible debate regarding "the uncertainty of diagnosis in this field and the tentativeness of professional judgment." Similarly, as previously observed, it is universally recognized as fundamental to effective therapy that the patient acknowledge his illness and cooperate with those attempting to give treatment; yet the failure of a large proportion of mentally ill persons to do so is a common phenomenon. It may be that some persons in either of these categories,[6] and there may be others, are unable to function in society and will suffer real harm to themselves unless provided with care in a sheltered environment. At the very least, I am not able to say that a state legislature is powerless to make that kind of judgment.

* * *

STATE EX REL. HAWKS V. LAZARO

Supreme Court of West Virginia, 1974.
157 W.Va. 417, 202 S.E.2d 109.

* * *

[W]e hold unconstitutional the standard enunciated in Code, 27–5–4(2), as amended, which permits involuntary hospitalization if the individual:

> "(2) Is in need of custody, care or treatment in a hospital and, because of his illness or retardation lacks sufficient insight or capacity to make responsible decisions with respect to his hospitalization. . . . "

* * *

Society abounds with persons who should be hospitalized, either for gallbladder surgery, back operations, corrective orthopedic surgery, or other reasons; yet, in these areas society would not contemplate involuntary hospitalization for treatment. As Code, 27–5–4, as amended, permits incarceration, due process as developed with regard to criminal statutes mandates that the grounds for incarceration be stated with specificity. The standard of hospitalization for the benefit of the individual leaves an entirely subjective determination for the committing authority which violates due process because it forecloses a meaningful appeal and places the individual in jeopardy of losing his freedom without providing an objective standard against which the committing authority's determination can be measured.

* * *

Modern welfare programs, community mental health facilities and private social service agencies have eliminated the problems of actual starvation and persecution of the mentally disturbed which were prevalent in the latter half of the Nineteenth Century. Accordingly, it is

---

[6] Indeed, respondent may have shared both of these characteristics. His illness, paranoid schizophrenia, is notoriously unsusceptible to treatment, see Livermore, Malmquist, & Meehl, On the Justifications for Civil Commitment, 117 U.Pa.L.Rev. 75, 93, and n. 52 (1968), and the reports of the Florida State Hospital staff which were introduced into evidence expressed the view that he was unwilling to acknowledge his illness and was generally uncooperative.

possible for many nonviolent people, even those who suffer from a mental disease or retardation to such an extent that they are unable to earn a living, to live outside of an institution, and when these people prefer to do so, regardless of the wisdom of their decision, or the strength of their reasoning powers, the constitution guarantees them the right to follow their own desires.

Notwithstanding the invalidity of Code, 27–5–4(2), as amended, we hold that Code, 27–5–4(1), as amended, does establish reasonable and definite criteria for involuntary hospitalization when it permits the State to hospitalize an individual if:

> "(1) Because of his illness or retardation [he] is likely to injure himself or others if allowed to remain at liberty. . . ."

Society is entitled to protect itself against predatory acts on the part of anti-social people, regardless of the cause of their anti-social actions. Therefore, if the State can prove that an individual is likely to injure others if left at liberty, it may hospitalize him. The State is also entitled to prevent a person from injuring himself in the very specific sense of doing physical damage to himself, either actively or passively. Therefore, when it can be demonstrated that an individual has a self-destructive urge and will be violent towards himself, or alternatively that he is so mentally retarded or mentally ill that by sheer inactivity he will permit himself to die either of starvation or lack of care, then the State is entitled to hospitalize him. The State would also be permitted, under the Constitution, to hospitalize a person who suffers from a mental illness or retardation which is likely to produce some form of injury other than direct physical injury, if the type of injury were definitely ascertainable, and if the State had a treatment program which it could be demonstrated offered a reasonable likelihood of ameliorating the illness or condition.

QUESTIONS AND COMMENTS

1. *The meaning of* Donaldson. As presented to the Supreme Court, *Donaldson* was in part a "right to treatment" case. The Fifth Circuit Court of Appeals had decided that all civilly committed patients are entitled to treatment. Clearly, the Supreme Court avoided deciding this issue; what is not clear is what the Court did establish. The key sentence in *Donaldson* is usually thought to be the following: "In short, a State cannot constitutionally confine without more a nondangerous individual who is capable of surviving safely in freedom by himself or with the help of willing and responsible family members or friends." From the rest of the opinion, are you able to discern the conditions under which a person might be considered incapable "of surviving safely"? Does the incapacity have to be the result of mental illness, or can it merely result from physical, financial or motivational limitations? Does use of the phrase "surviving *safely*" mean that people who can "survive" outside the hospital may nonetheless be committable under certain circumstances? What circumstances? Even if a person is shown to be nondangerous and capable of

surviving safely without hospitalization, the Court apparently would permit confinement if "more" than mere confinement is provided. Is the "more" to which the Court refers treatment or, as Chief Justice Burger's concurring opinion contends, is "custodial care" sufficient under some circumstances? If treatment is required, precisely what must the treatment accomplish? Do you agree with the answers to these questions provided by the West Virginia Supreme Court's opinion in *Lazaro?*

2. *Treatment efficacy.* As the preceding material makes clear, crucial to an assessment of the validity of *parens patriae* commitment is a showing that commitment will confer some benefit on, or at least not harm, the potential patient. The primary treatment modalities for people with serious mental illness are hospitalization and drugs. Both have benefits and drawbacks.

Research and practice suggest that to the extent suicide or self-neglect is caused by psychosis or depression, brief hospitalizations that include use of various types of drugs, a supportive environment, and provision of assistance in arranging after-discharge follow-up reduce the likelihood that a severely ill person will come to harm (see Part III.B in Chapter One). No data support any benefit from longer (as opposed to shorter) hospitalizations. Nisreen Alwan, Paul Johnstone, & Gabriella Zolese, *Length of Hospitalization for People with Severe Mental Illness*, Cochrane Database Syst. Rev. 2008 Jan 23;(1):CD000384. Other studies (mainly from outside the U.S.) suggest that provision of appropriate community care allows even individuals with severe mental illnesses to manage adequately outside hospitals. See, e.g., Coletta Hobbs et al., *Deinstitutionalization for Long–Term Mental Illness: A 6–Year Evaluation*, 36 Aust. New Z. J. Psychiatry 60 (2002). See also, Thomas W. Kallert et al., *Are Day Hospitals Effective for Acutely Ill Psychiatric Patients? A European Multicenter Randomized Controlled Trial*, 68 J. Clin. Psychiatry 278 (2007) ("day hospital care is as effective on clinical outcomes as conventional inpatient care and more effective on social outcomes.)"

In any event, long-term hospitalization is rare now unless patients have previously been involved with the criminal justice system (e.g., insanity acquittees). In 2009, the average length of hospitalization for people with mental disability was 7.5 days; for the subgroup with schizophrenia and related conditions, the average was 11.2 days. Center for Disease Control, National Hospital Discharge Survey: 2009 (table). In public healthcare systems, powerful financial incentives motivate service providers to avoid hospitalization whenever possible, and the third-party payors who finance private-sector psychiatric hospitalization keep a tight leash on length of stay. Most psychiatrists now view hospitalization only as a short-term, temporary intervention for protective and stabilizing purposes—not as a *treatment* that confers long-lasting benefits.

With respect to drug therapy, Chapter One described evidence that psychotropic medications are not helpful for all patients who take them. Yet as a group, patients who take medications—particularly the antipsychotic medications used to treatment schizophrenia—are better off than patients who do not. A huge 2012 meta-analysis of high-quality, placebo-controlled trials showed that 64% of patients with schizophrenia who took placebo relapsed within seven to twelve months and that taking antipsychotic drugs reduced the relapse rate 27%. Moreover, 10% of patients who took medication were readmitted to hospital, compared to 25% of the patients who took placebo. The study also yielded some evidence that patients given antipsychotic drugs enjoyed a better quality of life and engaged in fewer aggressive acts after release. Weighed against these outcomes, however, were side effects and adverse events such as movement disorders (e.g., tardive dyskinesia), restlessness, dystonia, sedation, and weight gain. Though antipsychotic drugs reduce rates of relapsing to psychosis, no evidence suggests that these drugs affect the often-more-disabling problems suffered by people with schizophrenia, such as their cognitive limitations and impaired motivation. Stefan Leucht et al., *Antipsychotic Drugs versus Placebo for Relapse Prevention in Schizophrenia: A Systematic Review and Meta–Analysis*, 379 Lancet 2063 (2012).

3.   *The harm of no treatment.* Assuming that hospitalization may actually cause some harm to a patient, should it nonetheless be allowed if that harm is less than the harm that would occur if the person were allowed to remain at liberty? Many commentators believe that involuntary treatment, despite its problems, is preferable to no treatment. Dr. Torrey asserts: "A tragic consequence of the efforts of mental health lawyers to make it difficult to hospitalize and treat the mentally ill is that the person's symptoms may irreversibly worsen." E. Fuller Torrey, M.D., Out of the Shadows: Confronting America's Mental Illness Crisis 152 (1997). Stavis states that "[c]ourt attitudes [that are] based on an archaic view of civil commitment as a life long imprisonment . . . ignore[] the current reality that government no longer is motivated to hospitalize patients, if at all, for any longer than is absolutely necessary. Indeed, the contemporary problem is obtaining treatment, not refusing its imposition." Paul Stavis, *Foreword: First Annual Symposium on Mental Illness and the Law*, 11 Geo. Mason U. Civ. Rts. L. J. 1, 7 (2000). Recall also that people with mental illness who are not hospitalized are often jailed, even when they are not dangerous to others, a process police call "mercy-booking." Finally, consider these comments by Klein, who describes the kind of people who may be neither hospitalized nor jailed:

> For example, some depressed people believe they are unworthy of help. There are also paranoids who reject treatment on such grounds as that the psychiatrist 'is a CIA agent who will plant a tape recorder in my head.' And, perhaps most significantly, there are numerous extremely passive people, including many elderly, who simply will not seek treatment on their own. If they are not treated involuntarily—and here I think the concept of "involuntariness" is largely metaphysical—we know by recent experience that many of them will wander aimlessly through our blighted inner cities, subject to a host of dangers.

Joel Klein, *Legal Doctrine at the Crossroads*, Mental Health Law Project Summary of Activities 7, 8 (Mar. 1976) (quoted in Hermann, *Barriers to*

Providing Effective Treatment: A Critique of Revisions in Procedural, Substantive, and Dispositional Criteria in Involuntary Civil Commitment, 39 Vand.L.Rev. 83, 95 n. 63 (1986)).

4. *Predictions of self-harming behavior.* As with police power commitments, *parens patriae* commitments usually require a prediction of harm—that the person will commit suicide, starve, or otherwise fare poorly without state intervention. Research on our ability to make predictions of suicidal behavior is voluminous; in general the accuracy rate seems to be quite low. What the research shows, in general, is that while psychiatrists can point to symptoms and conditions that greatly increase the risk of suicide, the base rate of actual suicide (as opposed to suicidal thinking or unsuccessful attempts) is so low that even most patients predicted to be "high-risk" patients do not kill themselves. Matthew Large et al., *Systematic Review and Meta–Analysis of the Clinical Factors Associated with the Suicide of Psychiatric In–Patients*, 124 Acta Psychiatr. Scand. 18 (2011)("Despite the apparently strong association between high-risk categorization and subsequent suicide, the low base rate of in-patient suicide means that predictive value of a high-risk categorization is below 2%."). However, as with violence-proneness prediction research, studies of predictive validity in this area are usually compromised by the fact that once such a prediction is made, intervention takes place, thereby presumably reducing the potential for harm.

5. *Revisiting the incapacity-as-threshold requirement.* Assume that the state can establish by clear and convincing evidence that a particular individual is more likely than not unable to survive "safely" outside the hospital and that short-term treatment or custodial care in a hospital would enable him to do so. Should it also have to show—as traditional theory has posited and we have assumed up to now—that the person is "incompetent" to make a decision about the advisability of hospitalization in order to justify involuntary commitment under the *parens patriae* authority? This type of issue is most starkly raised when the state seeks commitment of a person who has tried to commit suicide for reasons that cannot clearly be labelled "irrational." Consider the following excerpt:

> Obviously, paternalistic measures taken on behalf of a person *with* his or her consent are ordinarily unobjectionable. Furthermore, as the contemporary philosopher Gerald Dworkin has demonstrated in his essay "Paternalism", there are instances where paternalistic interference can be justified by the doctrine of consent even though, at the precise time of the paternalistic intervention, the affected individual might object to the action[.] . . . Dworkin . . . gives an example:
>
> > [I]t is very difficult for a child to defer gratification for any considerable period of time. . . . [G]iven the very real and permanent dangers that may befall the child it becomes not only permissible but even a duty of the parent to restrict the child's freedom in various ways. There is however an important moral limitation on the exercise of such parental power which is provided by the notion

of the child eventually coming to see the correctness of his parent's interventions. Parental paternalism may be thought of as a wager by the parent on the child's subsequent recognition of the wisdom of the restrictions. There is an emphasis on what could be called future-oriented consent—on what the child will come to welcome, rather than on what he does welcome.

"Future-oriented" consent, while used in the above example to justify interference with a legally incompetent subject, need not necessarily be restricted to instances of incompetency. Persons who attempt suicide are by no means always mentally incompetent at the time of the attempt. Of the competent ones, some may have rationally wanted to die, while others, though perhaps sincere in their desire to die, may have been 'wrong.' If all persons who attempted suicide were somehow saved by society's suicide prevention efforts, the saved persons would presumably have differing reactions concerning society's paternalistic efforts. The incompetent ones, if and when they regained competency, might well appreciate society's efforts, as might those who were competent but "wrong" about their decision to die. Only those who were competent and arguably rational about their attempted suicide (for instance, terminally ill persons, etc.) might strongly object to society's "benevolent" action in saving them.

If we wanted to be philosophically pure in our paternalistic suicide prevention efforts—and if we were practically equipped to make the necessary subtle distinctions—we might well let the competent but 'correct' persons die, but might save the others in the expectation of receiving their future consent. Surely, if future consent were to be actually given, we would doubtless feel justified in our earlier paternalistic invasions. And because we cannot in practice determine at the critical time of rescue which persons would give future consent to the rescue efforts and which would not, we feel justified in saving them all, presumably on the assumption—and this is an empirical matter—that not an insubstantial number would be belatedly appreciative.

David Wexler, Mental Health Law: Major Issues 45–7 (1981). Cf. Mel Blaustein and Anne Fleming, *Suicide From the Golden Gate Bridge*, 166 Am. J. Psychiatry 1111, 1115 (2009) (arguing for preventive measures and citing a followup study of 515 people whom police or workers had stopped from jumping off the bridge; "94% either were still alive or had died of natural causes, and only 6% had committed suicide or died in accidents suggestive of suicide").

Do you agree with Wexler's suggestion that the degree of incompetency is irrelevant when deciding whether to commit potential suicides? Should this reasoning be extended to those who are not suicidal but merely have trouble subsisting? Cf. William Gardner et al., *Patients' Revisions of Their Beliefs About the Need for Hospitalization*, 156 Am. J. Psychiatry 1385 (1999)("[m]ore than 50 percent of the reinterviewed patients who had initially said they did not need to be hospitalized said that now, in retrospect, they believed that they did need hospitalization when they were interviewed at follow-up").

Perhaps of relevance is language from the U.S. Supreme Court's decision in *Cruzan v. Director, Missouri Dept. of Health*, 497 U.S. 261, 110 S.Ct. 2841, 111 L.Ed.2d 224 (1990), which held that a state may require "clear and convincing evidence" that a person who is now in a "persistent vegetative state" had previously expressed a wish, while competent, to have life-sustaining treatment withdrawn. In the course of reaching this conclusion, the Court stated:

> Missouri relies on its interest in the protection and preservation of human life, and there can be no gainsaying this interest. As a general matter, the States—indeed, all civilized nations—demonstrate their commitment to life by treating homicide as serious crime. Moreover, the majority of States in this country have laws imposing criminal penalties on one who assists another to commit suicide. We do not think a State is required to remain neutral [even] in the face of an informed and voluntary decision by a physically-able adult to starve to death.

See also, *Washington v. Glucksberg*, 521 U.S. 702, 117 S.Ct. 2258, 2269, 2271, 138 L.Ed.2d 772 (1997) (considering "whether the 'liberty' specially protected by the Due Process Clause includes a right to commit suicide which itself includes a right to assistance in doing so," and finding that the latter is not a "fundamental right").

Elyn Saks (a law professor who suffers from schizophrenia) has proposed a "one free shot" commitment regime that would permit commitment over objection, even in the absence of dangerousness or incompetence, for people who are "psychotic, suffering, impaired, not themse[lf], and likely to benefit from treatment." However, after this initial commitment, commitment could occur on an involuntary basis only if the persons "self-bind to future such treatment in like circumstances." Elyn R. Saks, Refusing Care: Forced Treatment and the Rights of the Mentally Ill 201 (2002). Is this proposal a useful revision of Wexler's future-oriented consent idea? The one-shot idea and advanced directives of the type Saks proposes are discussed further in Chapter Nine.

2.   Implementing the *Parens Patriae* Authority

MAYOCK V. MARTIN

Supreme Court of Connecticut, 1968.
157 Conn. 56, 245 A.2d 574, cert. denied 393 U.S. 1111, 89 S.Ct. 924, 21 L.Ed.2d 808 (1969).

RYAN, ASSOCIATE JUSTICE. In this application for a writ of habeas corpus, the plaintiff claims that his confinement in the Norwich State Hospital is illegal because his present mental condition does not require, nor does it legally justify, his involuntary confinement or custodial care. From the judgment dismissing the writ, the plaintiff has appealed.

The few corrections to which the plaintiff has shown himself entitled are incorporated in the following statement of facts found by the trial court: The plaintiff was first confined to the Norwich State Hospital in October, 1943, and was released in January, 1944. On July 23, 1944, the plaintiff removed his right eye and was recommitted but was released subsequently for a probationary period. On July 20, 1947, the last day of the probationary period, the plaintiff, after examination by a staff physician, was unconditionally discharged from the hospital. Three days later, on July 23, 1947, the plaintiff removed his right hand. Shortly thereafter, he was again committed to the state hospital, where he is still confined. The plaintiff runs the newsstand in the hospital's administration building, where he sells newspapers and magazines to employees and to patients of the hospital. In this operation, he has been entrusted with the handling of financial matters. He has been placed in charge of a recreation center for parole-privileged patients which is operated by a committee of patients for group-recreational activity on weekends and which also serves coffee and performs other functions for patients. He believes sincerely that he is a prophet or revelator with a divine message. He believes in God and in doing what God wants us to do on earth. He also believes that society is trying to establish world peace by force but that God's way is by a brotherhood which seeks through the commandment of God to make people love one another; that world peace and brotherhood will be established by a certain church of God which the Old Testament refers to as being established by God in the latter days in the Holy Mountain; that, if the world continues in the present direction, many lives will be lost and that he has a responsibility in this matter; that he has a key role to fulfil in establishing world peace through the revelation and disclosure of the divine message; that he was not born into the country without a reason and that he was not born left-handed without a reason; that God has intended that one man shall be called to make a peace offering to God; that it is far better for one man to believe and accept an appropriate message from God to sacrifice an eye or a hand according to the sacred scriptures rather than for the present course of the world to cause even greater loss of human life; that the removal of his eye in July, 1944, was an offer of thanks to God for a revelation which he received and that it was God's command that he remove it; that the removal of his right hand in July, 1947, was an offering to God as a covenant between God and him as the person selected; that in each of these acts he has complied properly with sacred scripture; and that he is the one man called upon by God to make such spiritual sacrifices. The plaintiff has a strong belief in the Bible. Although he does not plan to cut off either of his feet or any other part of his body, he admits that he would cut off his foot either as a freewill offering or in response to a revelation from the Lord. The plaintiff wants to be released from the hospital so that he can better express his divine message to our people and our policy makers.

The court also found as facts the following: When the plaintiff first entered the state hospital on October 2, 1943, his mental condition was diagnosed as dementia praecox [an old term for schizophrenia], paranoid type, and this continued to be the diagnosis to the time of trial. This condition is manifested by what psychiatrists term the plaintiff's false beliefs regarding his role as a prophet, his divine message and the meaning of sacred scripture. These beliefs and the fact that he acted upon them by the removal of his eye and the amputation of his hand are the only factors which entered into the diagnosis that the plaintiff is mentally ill. Such beliefs were held by the plaintiff not only before these incidents but ever since then. Because of his persistent false beliefs without any observable improvement, it is expected that these beliefs will remain for a foreseeable period of time, and the possibility of a further self-injurious act cannot be ruled out. Although the possibility of suicide is ruled out, there is a possibility that the plaintiff might receive further communications from God and might respond by removing a foot. The mere medical diagnosis of dementia praecox, paranoid type, would not in itself require the plaintiff's confinement in a hospital for the mentally ill. In the opinion of the psychiatrist from the staff of the state hospital, the plaintiff is not dangerous to anyone other than himself. He has not done any self-injurious act in twenty years. The plaintiff's mental condition has remained about the same since 1947, but there is no evidence of gross worsening of this condition. The fact that the plaintiff currently needs further confinement in a hospital for the mentally ill is based on the opinion of the psychiatrist that there is a possibility that the plaintiff might cut off his right foot. The plaintiff's religious beliefs are considered by the psychiatrist as "grandiose" and "grossly false" and represent a fantasy which is one of the primary symptoms of schizophrenic reaction, paranoid type. The plaintiff's removal of his right eye in 1944 and his right hand in 1947 were not the manifestations of a religious belief but indications of a mental illness. The mental illness from which the plaintiff suffered in 1947 still persists, and he is currently in need of further confinement in a hospital for the mentally ill.

* * *

The plaintiff's basic claim is that he is being illegally confined because of his religious beliefs in violation of the first and fourteenth amendments to the United States constitution and of article first, §§ 3 and 20, of the Connecticut constitution. He urges that he is not likely to injure any other person; that, at the very worst, the state is concerned with a mere possibility that he will remove a foot; and that even if he did remove a foot, there is no evidence that the removal would prevent him from leading a useful and productive life. * * * A "mentally ill person" includes "each person afflicted by mental disease to such extent that he requires care and treatment for his own welfare or the welfare of others or of the community." General Statutes § 17–176. The claim of the plaintiff that he is being confined solely because of his religious beliefs is not supported by the finding. It is common knowledge that the mental illness of many persons is associated with apparently fervent religious beliefs. The court found, on the basis of expert psychiatric evaluation, that the incidents wherein the plaintiff removed his eye and his hand were not manifestations of a religious belief but were symptoms of mental illness which continued to exist to the date of trial.

* * *

Although the psychiatrist who examined the plaintiff had never heard of anyone else having a religious belief which caused the believer to do this kind of damage to himself, and the trial court so found, the plaintiff insists that his confinement discriminates against him because of his religious belief. "The First Amendment declares that Congress shall make no law respecting an establishment of religion or prohibiting the free exercise thereof. * * * No one would contest the proposition that a State may not, by statute, wholly deny the right to preach or to disseminate religious views. Plainly such a previous and absolute restraint would violate the terms of the guarantee. It is equally clear that a State may * * * safeguard the peace, good order and comfort of the community, without unconstitutionally invading the liberties protected by the Fourteenth Amendment." Cantwell v. State of Connecticut, 310 U.S. 296, 303, 60 S.Ct. 900, 903, 84 L.Ed. 1213.

The conclusions of the trial court that the continued confinement for treatment of the plaintiff in accordance with statute is not illegal and that there has been no infringement of the rights accorded him by the constitution of the United States and the constitution of Connecticut cannot be disturbed.

There is no error.

SHEA, ACTING JUSTICE (dissenting).

The opinion of the psychiatrist that there is a possibility that the plaintiff might cut off his right foot is the sole basis for the conclusion that further confinement of the plaintiff is needed. The finding states also that "the plaintiff is not dangerous to anyone other than himself, and the latter danger is not a definite thing, in that it is only a possibility in the plaintiff's mind." . . .

To warrant a conclusion under the statute that the welfare of the plaintiff requires continued treatment in a mental institution, the risk of self-inflicted mayhem on his part ought to be substantially greater than for normal citizens engaged in the many hazardous pursuits of modern life. Perhaps the subordinate facts found, relating to acts performed by the plaintiff twenty years ago, would support such an inference, if it had been drawn by the trial court. A court of review, however, is limited to the finding, and here it is explicitly stated that the need for confinement is based solely on the possibility that the plaintiff may harm himself upon release.

As between the possibility that the plaintiff may amputate his foot and the certainty that, under this judgment, he must remain incarcerated against his will indefinitely, I choose the former.[g]

Accordingly, I dissent.

BOGGS V. N.Y. CITY HEALTH & HOSP. CORP.

Supreme Court, Appellate Division, First Department, 1987.
132 A.D.2d 340, 523 N.Y.S.2d 71.

* * *

Ms. Billie Boggs (Ms. Boggs) is a forty-year old woman, whose real name is Ms. Joyce Brown. She chooses to use the name Ms. Billie Boggs, since she admires a television personality of that name, and she desires to thwart her family's efforts to locate her. For the past year, Ms. Boggs has lived on the public sidewalk in front of a restaurant, located on 65th Street and Second Avenue, in New York County, and she has used this location as her bedroom, toilet and living room.

Over the course of the subject year, Ms. Boggs has been observed on an almost daily basis by persons affiliated with Project Help, which is an emergency psychiatric service for allegedly mentally ill homeless persons, who live on the streets in New York City. The personnel of this organization are comprised of a clinical team of psychiatrists, nurses and social workers, who travel around New York City, for the purpose of identifying persons, who live in the street, and who appear to be particularly in need of immediate psychiatric hospital treatment, due to the fact that those persons appear to be in danger of doing serious harm to themselves or others.

On October 28, 1987, Dr. Lincoln Robert Asher Hess, who is a psychiatrist with Project Help, determined, after a number of observations of Ms. Boggs, at her location on the pavement, that Ms. Boggs was severely mentally ill, and that she needed *immediate hospitalization,* since she posed a danger of serious harm to herself. Thereafter, Project Help arranged for Ms. Boggs' transportation, against her will, to Bellevue Hospital (Bellevue), pursuant to § 9.39 of the Mental Hygiene Law (MHL). In pertinent part, subdivision (a) of § 9.39 of the MHL authorizes a hospital to receive and retain as a patient, for a period of fifteen days, any person "alleged to have a mental illness for which

---

[g]   A recent book states, "[S]elf-injurers do not want to die but rather to live free from troublesome emotions, thoughts, and behaviors. People who really want to die commit suicide . . . , but self-injury is a morbid act of regeneration, a return to a state of normalcy, and a seeking to feel better." Armando R. Favazza, Bodies under Siege: Self-mutilation, Nonsuicidal Self-injury, and Body Modification, in Culture and Psychiatry 198 (3rd ed., 2011). [Footnote by eds.]

immediate observation, care, and treatment in a hospital is appropriate and which is likely to result in serious harm to . . . [herself] or others . . . " [material in brackets added].

* * *

On October 30, 1987, a hearing was conducted, and both the petitioner and respondents presented evidence.

* * *

The respondents presented their case first, in opposition to Ms. Boggs' release.

* * *

On direct examination, Dr. Hess, after his qualification as an expert by the Court, testified, that he works as a psychiatrist with Project Help three days a week; in the course of his duties with Project Help, he first saw Ms. Boggs in the street on July 23, 1987; on that occasion, he approached her, with the knowledge that Ms. Boggs had exhibited hostility to Project Help's staff in the past; he observed that Ms. Boggs was dressed in disheveled clothing; although, it was not raining, Ms. Boggs was twirling an open umbrella to avoid eye contact with him and the persons passing by; at that time, Dr. Hess heard Ms. Boggs speaking in rhymes, and, according to the witness, the content of these rhymes was sexual, and related to Dr. Hess' and Ms. Boggs' genitals; in the witness' professional opinion this type of verbalization is referred to as "Clanging", and is indicative of a thought disorder, in which a person transfers their thinking from one thought to another without any logical sequence.

The second time Dr. Hess observed Ms. Boggs in the street was five days later, on July 28, 1987. Since the first time that he had seen her, Dr. Hess testified, in substance, that Ms. Boggs' clothing had become more disheveled, dirty and torn, and she was barefoot. When Dr. Hess attempted to speak to Ms. Boggs, she cursed him, flipped open her skirt and exposed her nude buttocks, and made references to his genitals. In Dr. Hess' professional opinion, on July 28th, Ms. Boggs appeared to be flat and disordered, which he testified is characteristic of schizophrenia.

Dr. Hess made his third street observation of Ms. Boggs on September 22, 1987. As before, Dr. Hess found Ms. Boggs at the same location, which was the sidewalk at Second Avenue near 65th Street. In pertinent part, Dr. Hess testified that Ms. Boggs' clothes were even dirtier than before, and torn to the point that large portions of her torso were exposed, and her clothing was inadequate for the weather; her hair was matted; he noticed the smell of urine and feces emanating from her; he saw pieces of United States currency, which had been torn up in neat pieces stuck to the sidewalk near Ms. Boggs, upon which she appeared to have urinated; Ms. Boggs cursed and shouted obscenities at him; nevertheless, Ms. Boggs did accept food from him, after first refusing it, but, after accepting same, she then threw the contents of this lunch at Dr. Hess, and chased him around the corner. On this occasion of September 22nd, Dr. Hess evaluated Ms. Boggs as having angry, threatening, and intensely hostile feelings, and "again there was a sign of throatiness in the sense there was no modulation . . . ".

In evaluating Ms. Boggs, Dr. Hess considered his personal observations, her history, and information he received from other Project Help members, such as psychiatrists, nurses and social workers. As a result of this data, Dr. Hess was of the opinion that Ms. Boggs exhibited a deteriorating psychosis and a deteriorating ability to care for herself. For example, he had received information that Ms. Boggs had run out into the traffic to throw away warm clothing that she had received from personnel representing Project Help.

Finally, on October 28th, Dr. Hess observed Ms. Boggs lying at her location with her head resting on a cardboard box. She smelled strongly of feces, and Dr. Hess again saw torn currency stuck to the pavement and stained by urine. The currency was very neatly torn and urinated upon, and Dr. Hess testified that this was a ritualistic tearing, which suggested magical thinking or delusion. She said repeatedly to Dr. Hess, "What is my name?", which is also indicative of a thought disorder.

* * *

Ms. Putnam was a psychiatric social worker, who had been the coordinator of Project Help for five years and she was qualified by the Court as an expert psychiatric social worker. [A]ccording to Ms. Putnam, as Project Help observed Ms. Boggs, over the course of the year, her behavior changed for the worse. In the winter of 1986–87, Ms. Boggs appeared to be passive, but by the Spring, Ms. Boggs became more aggressive.

On May 8th, 1987, Ms. Putnam personally observed an incident, involving Ms. Boggs' hostile reaction to some delivery men, who were across the street from her location. These men were gathered outside a restaurant, apparently making a delivery. Suddenly, according to Ms. Putnam, Ms. Boggs began screaming racial epithets at these men, calling them f . . . . . . n . . . . . . , b . . . . . . s . . . . . . "shouting at them to get away from her, and cursing at them. As a result of this incident, Ms. Putnam became concerned that Ms. Boggs might be assaulted, due to her provocative behavior, and Ms. Putnam perceived that Ms. Boggs might have delusions regarding black men, whom she believed treated her as a prostitute. Also, Ms. Putnam reported her May 8th, 1987 observation about Ms. Boggs' reaction to the delivery men, to Project Help psychiatrists."

* * *

The next witness, for the respondents, was Dr. Mahon, who was Ms. Boggs' treating psychiatrist at respondent Bellevue. Before testifying, Dr. Mahon was qualified by the Court as an expert in psychiatry.

* * *

Dr. Mahon, . . . first saw Ms. Boggs on October 29th; at that time, Dr. Mahon did not speak with Ms. Boggs, since Ms. Boggs' was hostile, angry, and used threatening gestures; verbally, Ms. Boggs was obscene and loud. Thereafter, Dr. Mahon, saw Ms. Boggs on October 30th; and, on that date, Ms. Boggs appeared to be less angry and Dr. Mahon spent about 30 minutes with her. [T]he third time Dr. Mahon saw Ms. Boggs was on October 31st. Dr. Mahon noted that on each encounter, Ms. Boggs and Dr. Mahon established more of a relationship.

Finally, on November 2nd, the morning of the Hearing, Dr. Mahon saw Ms. Boggs again, and found her to be bright, verbal and oriented, as to time and place. Furthermore, that morning, Ms. Boggs was more cooperative than ever, even allowing Dr. Mahon to ask her to interpret certain proverbs.

In her diagnosis, Dr. Mahon found Ms. Boggs to be a chronic schizophrenic, axis one, paranoid type. Moreover, Dr. Mahon stated that Ms. Boggs' mental condition had improved during her hospitalization at Bellevue, and that it was very common for a patient like Ms. Boggs to stabilize in a structured setting. Furthermore, Dr. Mahon thought that some of Ms. Boggs' improvement may have been due to a dose of medication, "Heloperidol", which she received when she was first admitted to the hospital.

* * *

[T]he Court asked if Ms. Boggs' mental status could change markedly in three weeks, from the time Ms. Boggs was seen at Metropolitan Hospital, until she was admitted to Bellevue. Dr. Mahon answered that question, in substance, as follows:

"I think Miss Boggs shows remarkable ability, as is not uncommon with some psychiatric patients, to adapt and to regroup and organize herself temporarily in settings such [as] psychiatric emergency rooms, such as the inpatient service here at Bellevue and appear to be very rational and appear not to have any severe psychosis.

"However, as a psychiatrist what I have to do is make sure I evaluate not only what I am seeing now and on a daily basis with Miss Boggs, but look at the history, and running in front of traffic and saying she has a right to endanger her life is suicidal and as a psychiatrist, I have to call that suicidal behavior and I have to treat it as a clinician . . .". [material in brackets added]

*   *   *

Ms. Boggs, the petitioner, then presented her case.

*   *   *

One psychiatrist who testified for Ms. Boggs was Dr. Gould, who was a professor of psychiatry at New York Medical College, and an attending psychiatrist at Metropolitan Hospital. Respondents stipulated that he is an expert in psychiatry.

In substance, on direct examination, Dr. Gould testified, as follows: four days after Ms. Boggs was admitted to Bellevue, on November 1st, 1987, he first examined Ms. Boggs, and found her to be "warm and open, spoke without any pressure spontaneously, coherently, logically, without any tangential thinking, . . ."; he had never seen Ms. Boggs on the street; he found no suicidal or homicidal ideation and no delusions or hallucinations concerning Ms. Boggs; and, upon this basis he concluded that Ms. Boggs was not psychotic.

Furthermore, Dr. Gould noted that Ms. Boggs' judgment "was the only thing that was slightly impaired in a sense that she was not aware socially of the kind of troubles ensue from her behavior. [Her] insight was somewhat impaired along the same lines, but by no means nil . . ." In the witness' professional opinion, Ms. Boggs is not schizophrenic; he discussed with Ms. Boggs the incidents reported by other doctors, and, that she explained her reasons for her actions; he indicated that Ms. Boggs has no delusions about money, rather, he explained, that when someone threw paper money at Ms. Boggs and she found it insulting or degrading, she would destroy it; with respect to her urinating and defecating on the street, the witness thought that it was not delusional because Ms. Boggs, according to him, had no alternative; he did not believe Ms. Boggs was either suicidal or dangerous to herself; when Ms. Boggs ran in front of traffic, the witness testified "there was no indication, in my questioning her about this, that she was interested in having herself killed . . ."; he further noted "the fact that she has never been hurt and she's never hurt herself is strong indication that she has very good survival skills"; he believed Ms. Boggs' verbal abuse of others presented no danger, since he explained that Ms. Boggs simply did not wish to be disturbed by some individuals who invaded her privacy and she cursed at them to go away; he stated that Ms. Boggs was congenial to those people she liked, even though he had never observed her in the street; when asked if her verbal response to those she disliked presented a danger, the witness responded "I think that comes under the old cliche of sticks and stones may break my bones, but words can never hurt me. That is all she's ever done, being verbally abusive . . ."; he rejected the testimony of respondents' experts that a paranoid schizophrenic could stabilize within a few days of an involuntary admission to a hospital; in fact, in his opinion, rather than stabilized, he believed that Ms. Boggs would become more angry; he indicated that, in his opinion, the small amount of medication Ms. Boggs had been given could not account for the change in her behavior following her admission to Bellevue; with respect to predictions of future dangerousness, he found them suspect, in view of the fact that to diagnose someone who is suicidal, there must be a history of severe depression and usually suicide attempts; with respect to violent behavior towards others, it would be necessary, in his opinion, to show violence in the past, "that she may have been carrying weapons or using weapons at times . . ."; he found no evidence of deterioration in Ms. Boggs mental or physical condition; he believed she provided for herself quite well, by eating every day from a nearby deli; and he found that her only deterioration was in the state of her clothing.

*   *   *

Ms. Boggs testified in her own behalf. She lives next to a restaurant on Second Avenue, between 65th and 66th Streets and she stays at that location, since there is a hot air vent, although she lived on the streets during the winter of 1986, she indicated that she had never been cold; she panhandles money for food, and, in that fashion, she makes between eight and ten dollars a day; she needs allegedly about seven dollars a day to buy her food; she admitted to urinating and defecating on the street, she denied defecating on herself or in her clothes; . . . she admitted . . . that she did defecate and urinate in her clothes; she claims she has adequate clothes, and that when she needed more she had "friends" who would supply them to her; she used profanity in order to make the staff of Project Help go away; she claims that her umbrella serves the purpose of protecting her from the sun; she claimed that she had never run in traffic, but, on one occasion, when Project Help tried to offer her a pair of slacks, she stepped between two cars and threw the slacks into the street; she destroys paper money, if it is thrown at her or given to her in an allegedly offensive manner; she has no delusions about black persons giving her money for sex; and, she never hurt anyone on the street or threatened anyone, and no one ever threatened her for using profanity.

Furthermore, Ms. Boggs testified that she would go back to the streets, if released.

*   *   *

It is well-established in this State that a person may be involuntarily confined for care and treatment, where his or her mental illness manifests itself in neglect or refusal to care for themselves to such an extent that there is presented "serious harm" to their own well-being. . . .

*   *   *

We find that the Hearing Court erred in placing "great weight on the demeanor, behavior and testimony" of Ms. Boggs, since the Hearing Court does not claim that the demeanor and behavior of Ms. Boggs, when she appeared before it, remotely resembled the demeanor and behavior she exhibited when she lived on the streets, and was involuntarily committed to Bellevue on October 28, 1987.

It is hardly surprising that the Hearing Court stated, "Throughout her testimony, . . . [Ms. Boggs] was rational, logical, coherent. Her use of English, both in syntox (sic) and vocabulary, is very good and bespeaks an educated, intelligent person. She displayed a sense of humor, pride, a fierce independence of spirit, quick mental reflexes . . .", in view of the fact that, when Ms. Boggs was in the courtroom, she had recently been bathed, was dressed in clean clothes, and had just received approximately a week of hospital treatment.

* * *

We reject, as against the weight of the evidence, the Hearing court's conclusion that, in substance, Ms. Boggs' homelessness is not a result of serious mental illness, but, rather, is the result of New York's lack of housing for the poor.

* * *

Accordingly, order, Supreme Court, New York County (Robert D. Lippmann, J.), entered November 12, 1987, which granted the petition of Ms. Billie Boggs, and directed her release from respondent Bellevue Hospital by 6:00 P.M. on November 12, 1987, is reversed, on the law and on the facts, petition is denied and the proceeding is dismissed, without costs.

* * *

MILONAS, JUSTICE (dissenting).

* * *

All of respondents' psychiatrists specifically deny that Brown has suicidal ideation. She has certainly never physically harmed herself, and respondents do not really advance the proposition that she is apt to do so in the future. The record does not show a single instance in which petitioner has ever hurt herself.

* * *

In the end, respondents' effort to institutionalize petitioner can be narrowed down to one claim: she is dangerous to herself because, as a result of her abusive and obscene speech and generally obnoxious behavior, she is likely to provoke others to do injury to her. Respondents contend that Brown has been living on the streets for some time, cursing

provoke others

and shouting and engaging in various bizarre behavior. Yet no one has assaulted her.

*   *   *

Petitioner's conduct on the street is understandable if we appreciate her obvious pride in her independence and in her ability to survive on her own. She derives a <u>unique sense of success</u> and <u>accomplishment</u> in her street life. In petitioner's words, when poignantly describing her ability to endure on the streets, she has called herself a "professional". Now in the face of petitioner's assessment of herself, and in her own view, Project HELP has been endeavoring to compel her to accept assistance and be dependent. Moreover, on at least five occasions, Project HELP forced her, while handcuffed, to be transported to Metropolitan Hospital, where various physicians always refused to admit her since she was deemed to be not dangerous. In fact, she was taken to Metropolitan Hospital under restraint shortly after both incidents considered significant by respondents—her running into the street and her shouting at the delivery men. Both times she was observed by different doctors while she was at her worst and still determined not to be dangerous to herself or others. Petitioner's explanation for her street conduct is that she has learned that by employing her "profanity" and assorted bag of obnoxious tricks, she was always able to induce Project HELP to retreat.

*   *   *

It is a tragedy that in our wealthy society so many people have been driven to homelessness, and those of us who are more fortunate must helplessly witness and feel their misery on a daily basis. Regrettably, our affluent, sophisticated and medically advanced society has not developed a more rational, effective and humane way of dealing with the mentally disturbed homeless than in a manner other than what appears to be revolving door mental health—that is, forcibly institutionalize, forcibly medicate, stabilize, discharge back into the same environment, and then repeat the cycle. These ill and unfortunate citizens especially deserve our sympathy since they are not only homeless, but hopeless. Yet, they have shown extraordinary courage, strength and resourcefulness in their ability to survive in conditions where the "normal" person would be unable to endure.

QUESTIONS AND COMMENTS

1. *Mental illness and parens patriae commitment.* Although incapacity to make treatment decisions has traditionally been thought to be the necessary predicate for *parens patriae* commitment, only a few states specifically require such a finding; most merely require proof that "mental illness" is causing the self-harming condition. As suggested in the previous materials, there may be theoretical justification for the latter approach. In

light of *Mayock* and *Boggs,* do you think an incapacity requirement would make a difference in practice?

2.   *Defining the bases for intervention.* A perusal of judicial decisions reveals several separate grounds for intervention under the *parens patriae* authority. They might be classified generally under two categories: actions intended to do direct physical harm to oneself and self-neglecting behavior. Under the first category would fall (1) suicide; (2) "self-mutilation", as illustrated by *Mayock;* and (3) harm to oneself caused by provocation of others (as argued by the state in *Boggs*). Self-neglect might be subdivided into (4) an inability to provide for one's survival needs; (5) a present ability to survive, but an inattention to deteriorating mental and physical health; or, most broadly, (6) a need for treatment.

[margin note: intervention under parens patriae]

Most state statutes do not explicitly differentiate between these various bases for commitment. In several states the only *parens patriae* ground for commitment is "danger to self." This language clearly encompasses suicidal behavior but is also, as *Boggs* illustrates, often interpreted to include other self-harming conduct as well, including at least some versions of self-neglectful behavior. Cf. *Lazaro, supra.* Most other statutes divide *parens patriae* commitment into two categories: danger to self and inability to care for self. The latter standard is framed in a number of different ways. Many states just use inability to care language. California permits commitment when a person is "gravely disabled," which is defined as "[a] condition in which a person, as a result of a mental disorder, is unable to provide for his basic personal needs for food, clothing, or shelter." Cal.Code § 5008(h)(1). Michigan's statute is more specific, requiring proof that the person "is unable to attend to those of his basic physical needs such as food, clothing, or shelter that must be attended to in order for him to avoid serious harm in the near future, and who has demonstrated that inability by failing to attend to those basic physical needs." Mich.Comp.Laws Ann. § 330.1401(1)(b).

A few states explicitly permit commitment on "potential-for-deterioration" grounds (number (5) above), a standard that has been forcefully recommended by the American Psychiatric Association. The APA's Model Act would permit commitment when the person "will if not treated suffer or continue to suffer severe and abnormal mental, emotional, or physical distress, and this distress is associated with significant impairment of judgement, reason or behavior causing a substantial deterioration of his previous ability to function on his own." Clifford Stromberg & Alan Stone, *A Model State Law on Civil Commitment of the Mentally Ill,* 20 Harv.J.Legis. 275, 330 (1983). The APA states that this provision is meant to permit commitment "of severely mentally ill individuals who are moving toward sudden collapse," id. at 305, and that it applies to a group of people "commonly excluded from the mental health system by current legal standards [such as grave disability]." Id. at 304, 335.

[margin note: PFD Standard]

Research seems to bear this latter assertion out. In 1979, Washington amended its definition of grave disability to include not only a person with mental illness who "is in danger of harm resulting from a failure to provide for essential human needs of health or safety," but also someone who "manifests severe deterioration in routine functioning evidenced by repeated and escalating loss of cognitive or volitional control over his or her actions and [who] is not receiving such care as is essential for his or her health or safety." West's Rev.Code Wash.Ann. 71.05.020(1). A study comparing commitment records for the two years prior to passage of this amendment to the two years after passage found that the amendment had a significant impact on the hospital population. Among its findings were the following:

> 2) the number of patients committed involuntarily increased significantly, and many patients who had had no previous contact with state hospitals were committed to psychiatric facilities; 3) these new patients stayed in hospitals longer than other patients and became chronic users of the state mental hospitals; 4) the major state mental hospital became extremely overcrowded and tried unsuccessfully to put a limit on new admissions; 5) voluntary patients were virtually excluded from state hospitals . . .

Mary Durham & John LaFond, *The Empirical Consequences and Policy Implications of Broadening the Statutory Criteria for Civil Commitment*, 3 Yale Law & Policy Review, 395, 401 (1985); see also, Tad Hasebe & John McRae, *A Ten–Year Study of Civil Commitments in Washington State*, 38 Hosp. & Comm.Psychiat. 983 (1987).

Whether the prevention-of-deterioration standard vastly increases the number hospitalized is open to some dispute, however. Professor Miller's study of eight states, each of which adopted the prevention-of-deterioration standard or in some other way broadened their commitment criteria, found a *decrease* in admissions in at least five of the states after the change. Robert Miller, *"Need-for-Treatment" Criteria for Involuntary Civil Commitment: Impact in Practice*, 149 Am. J.Psych. 1380 (1992). Miller does not conclude, of course, that the broadening of criteria caused the decrease in admissions but rather notes that "[c]hanges in admission and census rates are multidetermined and cannot be simplistically attributed to a single cause, such as changes in commitment criteria." Id. at 1383. The prevention-of-deterioration standard is used most often in connection with *outpatient* commitment, and is discussed in more detail in the materials relating to that issue (see pp. 897–902).

The final variation of *parens patriae* commitment (number (6) above) is simply a standard that permits involuntary hospitalization if a person needs treatment as a result of mental illness. Although prior to 1970 many statutes used this language, today only one or two do so. See, e.g., N.Y. Men. Hyg. Laws § 9.27(a)(authorizing commitment of a person who is "mentally ill and in need of involuntary care and treatment"). Some commentators advocate for rejuvenation of this standard, particularly now that hospitals have shrunk and outpatient civil commitment has become more common. E. Fuller Torrey and Mary Zdanowicz, *Outpatient Commitment: What, Why, and for Whom*, 52 Psychiatric Serv. 337 (2001) (arguing that "outpatient commitment is needed because many individuals with severe psychiatric illnesses lack awareness of their illness").

Under which of these formulations, if any, would Mayock or Brown be committable? The persons described in Cases 2, 19 and 22, on pp. 813–814? Relevant to *Boggs*, consider research which found that the vast majority of the homeless people studied in Los Angeles "would rather live in filth and be subjected to beatings and violence than to be institutionalized, even in our finest mental hospitals." Robert Farr, *A Mental Health Treatment Program for the Mentally Ill in the Los Angeles Skid Row Area*, in B. E. Jones, Treating the Homeless 64, 71 (1986).

3. *Vagueness doctrine.* Some courts have held that particular language implementing the *parens patriae* authority is so vague that it violates the due process clause of the United States Constitution.[h] *Lazaro*, supra, is one example. Another is *Commonwealth ex rel. Finken v. Roop*, 234 Pa.Super. 155, 339 A.2d 764 (1975), in which the court struck down a Pennsylvania statute that permitted commitment of any person who "is believed to be mentally disabled and in need of care or treatment of such mental disability." The court stated: " 'In need of care' is so broad as to be virtually meaningless. Furthermore, once a finding of mental illness is made, it would be impossible not to find that the individual is in need of care." Is the vagueness doctrine the appropriate vehicle for such a decision? See pp. 840–841. If so, might it not also be used to strike down statutes that permit commitment of those who are "dangerous to self"?

4. *Parens patriae and guardianship.* In several states, procedures exist for appointing a guardian for individuals who are committed for self-neglecting behavior. For instance, in California, a "conservator" may be appointed to make decisions about treatment and other personal matters for anyone who is found to be gravely disabled (but not for those who are committed as suicidal). Cal.Code § 5350. In many jurisdictions, the process may be reversed; that is, a person may be adjudicated incompetent to handle his or her affairs and thus in need of a guardian, who might then seek court authorized institutionalization. Guardianship will be discussed in more detail in Chapter Nine. For present purposes, the following questions about guardianship and its relationship to commitment can be posed. If commitment is under the *parens patriae* authority, is there some value in having a guardian make the ultimate decisions about treatment or care, rather than the patient or the treatment staff? If so, should a guardian be appointed for every person committed under the *parens patriae* authority? Or, as is true in California, should a guardian be appointed only for those who fall under certain categories of *parens patriae* commitment?

5. *Comparing parens patriae and police power commitment.* Setting aside the obvious differences concerning the harms focused upon, provisions

---

h   Statutory language authorizing state intervention on dangerousness to others grounds has also been challenged on vagueness grounds, see, e.g., Jurek v. Texas, 428 U.S. 262, 96 S.Ct. 2950, 49 L.Ed.2d 929 (1976), but most, if not all, *successful* vagueness challenges of civil commitment statutes have focused on *parens patriae* provisions.

implementing the *parens patriae* and police power authority tend to be consistent. For instance, as already noted, the same definition of mental illness is used in both contexts. Other aspects of the *parens patriae* and police power perspectives worth comparing are considered below.

The Overt Act and Imminence Requirements. Typically, a state statute that requires a recent overt act and a prediction of imminent danger when defining the police power also does so when defining danger to self; likewise, if these requirements are not present in the definition of danger to others, they are absent when defining danger to self as well. Douglas Mossman, Allison Schwartz & Elise R. Elam, *Risky Business v. Overt Acts: What Relevance Do "Actuarial" Risk Assessments Have for Judicial Decisions on Involuntary Psychiatric Hospitalization?* 11 Hous. J. Health L. & Pol'y 365, 447 (2012) (Table 2). Are the theoretical and practical justifications for the overt act and imminence requirements in police power commitment present when committing someone whom doctors believe is suicidal? In this regard, consider that only "one quarter to one half of all completed suicides have a history of prior suicide attempts" and that "the majority of patients who attempt suicide do not go on to commit suicide." Robert Hirschfeld & Lucy Davidson, *Clinical Risk Factors for Suicide*, 18 Psychiatric Annals 628, 632 (1988).

In connection with the inability-to-care-for-self criterion, most state statutes do not require an overt act in so many words but, as the examples given above illustrate, they do require a showing that the person is unable to provide for basic needs, which may be equivalent. Mossman et al., supra. On the other hand, some versions of the deterioration standard (see language from APA Act, supra) do not seem to contemplate any explicit overt act requirement. Professor Wexler argued that this extension of the commitment criterion might actually be countertherapeutic. He speculated that "the very process of gathering evidence of a person's committability under a [law that requires specific indicia of inability to care] may operate therapeutically to render commitment unnecessary." In contrast, laws that do not require such indicia may encourage a failure to assert oneself and test one's abilities, thus ultimately creating a dependence upon state institutions. David Wexler, *Grave Disability and Family Therapy: The Therapeutic Potential of Civil Libertarian Commitment Codes*, 9 Int'l. J.L. & Psychiat. 39, 54 (1986).

Parens patriae provisions often do not include an imminence requirement either. Is this appropriate? Consider this example from Darold Treffert, *The Practical Limits of Patients' Rights*, 5 Psychiat. Annals 4 (1975).

no imminence

A 49 year-old woman with anorexia nervosa, admitted to a medical unit in a general hospital because of profound weight loss, steadfastly refused to eat. She presented a life-threatening situation, albeit not an imminent one. This was her response to a family struggle in which she was deeply enmeshed, but she was in good general contact with reality and was not flagrantly psychotic. She refused voluntary psychiatric intervention and, in spite of her frail and deteriorating condition, insisted on leaving the hospital. Her family and physician petitioned the court for psychiatric observation of the patient. The judge believed, however, that the situation lacked dangerousness in an *immediate or imminent sense,* and the patient therefore failed to qualify for involuntary commitment. She was sent home, as she desired, and three weeks later she died from inanition.

[Emphasis in original].

Durational Limitations. Most states also do not differentiate between the length of commitment authorized for police power and *parens patriae* commitment. California's statute, on the other hand, provides several different durational limits. All patients are subject to an initial 72–hour emergency detention period and a 14 day "intensive treatment" period. But if further commitment is necessary the statute distinguishes between categories. It limits confinement of suicidal individuals to 14 additional days, while authorizing confinement of those considered dangerous to others for up to 180 days (with additional 180–day extensions, if an overt act occurs during confinement). For those who are found to be gravely disabled, after a 30 day investigation period commitment is authorized for up to one year (with continuous one-year extensions permitted). Cal.Code §§ 5260, 5300, 5361.

Overlap. Ultimately, how meaningful is the distinction between the two grounds for intervention when applied to individual cases? Cannot an argument be made that both Mayock and Brown are dangerous to others, at least under the broader definitions of that term? Cannot one say that Nyflot, Sansone and D.R.S. acted in "self-harming" ways? Is there a reason for avoiding such characterizations (perhaps by saying we're only interested in the behavior that is "proximately caused" by mental illness), or should we be willing to classify individuals under both categories if we can possibly do so?

III.   THE LEAST RESTRICTIVE ALTERNATIVE DOCTRINE

Whether the basis of state intervention is the police power or *parens patriae,* almost all state statutes require the committing authority to consider dispositions other than hospitalization. This requirement has come to be known as the least restrictive alternative doctrine. Least restrictive alternative analysis has also played a significant role in two other contexts associated with mental disability law. First it has been used as a device for regulating treatment imposed on persons *after* they have been committed or otherwise subjected to state intervention. Second, it has been relied upon in asserting that the government has an *obligation to create* community-based services. These second and third variants of the doctrine are considered in Chapter Ten. Here the focus will be on how the least restrictive alternative doctrine regulates the "front-end" dispositional decision made by the committing authority.

consider everything but hospitalization

LAKE V. CAMERON

United States Court of Appeals, District of Columbia Circuit, 1966.
364 F.2d 657.

BAZELON, CHIEF JUDGE:

Appellant is confined in Saint Elizabeths Hospital as an insane person and appeals from denial of release in habeas corpus. On September 29, 1962, when she was sixty years old, a policeman found her wandering about and took her to the D.C. General Hospital. On October 11, 1962, she filed in the District Court a petition for a writ of habeas corpus. The court transferred her to St. Elizabeths Hospital for observation in connection with pending commitment proceedings, allowed her to amend her petition by naming the Superintendent of Saint Elizabeths as defendant, and on November 2, 1962, dismissed her petition without holding a hearing or requiring a return.

After she filed her appeal from denial of habeas corpus, she was adjudged "of unsound mind" and committed to Saint Elizabeths. At the commitment hearing two psychiatrists testified that she was mentally ill and one of them that she was suffering from a "chronic brain syndrome" associated with aging and "demonstrated very frequently difficulty with her memory * * *. Occasionally, she was unable to tell me where she was or what the date was." Both psychiatrists testified to the effect that she could not care for herself adequately. She did not take a timely appeal from the commitment order. We heard her appeal from the summary dismissal of her petition for habeas corpus and remanded the case to the District Court with directions to require a return and hold a hearing.

At the hearing on remand, the sole psychiatric witness testified that appellant was suffering from a senile brain disease, "chronic brain syndrome, with arteriosclerosis with reaction." The psychiatrist said she was not dangerous to others and would not intentionally harm herself, but was prone to "wandering away and being out exposed at night or any time that she is out." This witness also related that on one occasion she wandered away from the Hospital, was missing for about thirty-two hours, and was brought back after midnight by a police officer who found her wandering in the streets. She had suffered a minor injury which she attributed to being chased by boys. She thought she had been away only a few hours and could not tell where she had been. The psychiatrist also testified that she was "confused and agitated" when first admitted to the Hospital but became "comfortable" after "treatment and medication."

At both the commitment hearing and the habeas corpus hearing on remand, appellant testified that she felt able to be at liberty. At the habeas corpus hearing her husband, who had recently reappeared after a long absence, and her sister said they were eager for her release and would try to provide a home for her. The District Court found that she "is suffering from a mental illness with the diagnosis of chronic brain syndrome associated with cerebral arteriosclerosis"; that she "is in need of care and supervision, and that there is no member of the family able to give the petitioner the necessary care and supervision; and that the family is without sufficient funds to employ a competent person to do so"; that she "is a danger to herself in that she has a tendency to wander about the streets, and is not competent to care for herself." The District Court again denied relief in habeas corpus, but noted appellant's right "to make further application in the event that the patient is in a position to show that there would be some facilities available for her provision." The court thus recognized that she might be entitled to release from Saint Elizabeths if other facilities were available, but required her to carry the burden of showing their availability.

Appellant contends in written and oral argument that remand to the District Court is required for a consideration of suitable alternatives to confinement in Saint Elizabeths Hospital in light of the new District of Columbia Hospitalization of the Mentally Ill Act, which came into effect after the hearing in the District Court. Indeed, her counsel appointed by this court, who had interviewed appellant, made clear in answer to a question from the bench on oral argument that although appellant's formal pro se pleading requests outright release, her real complaint is total confinement in a mental institution; that she would rather be in another institution or hospital, if available, or at home, even though under some form of restraint.

* .* *

We are not called upon to consider what action we would have taken in the absence of the new Act, because we think the interest of justice and furtherance of the congressional objective require the application to the pending proceeding of the principles adopted in that Act. It provides that if the court or jury finds that a "person is mentally ill and, because of that illness, is likely to injure himself or other persons if allowed to remain at liberty, the court may order his hospitalization for an indeterminate period, or order any other alternative course of treatment which the court believes will be in the best interests of the person or of the public." D.C.Code § 21–545(b) (Supp. V, 1966). This confirms the view of the Department of Health, Education and Welfare that "the entire spectrum of services should be made available, including outpatient treatment, foster care, halfway houses, day hospitals, nursing homes, etc." The alternative course of treatment or care should be fashioned as the interests of the person and of the public require in the particular case. Deprivations of liberty solely because of dangers to the ill persons themselves should not go beyond what is necessary for their protection.

The court's duty to explore alternatives in such a case as this is related also to the obligation of the state to bear the burden of exploration of possible alternatives an indigent cannot bear. This appellant, as appears from the record, would not be confined in Saint Elizabeths if her family were able to care for her or pay for the care she needs. Though she cannot be given such care as only the wealthy can afford, an earnest effort should be made to review and exhaust available resources of the community in order to provide care reasonably suited to her needs.

At the habeas corpus hearing, the psychiatrist testified that appellant did not need "constant medical supervision," but only "attention"; that the psychiatrist would have no objection if appellant "were in a nursing home, or a place where there would be supervision." At the commitment hearing one psychiatrist testified that "Mrs. Lake needs care, whether it be in the hospital or out of the hospital," and did not specify what, if any, *psychiatric* care she needs. The second psychiatrist testified that she "needs close watching. She could wander off. She could get hurt and she certainly needs someone to see that her body is adequately cared for * * *. [She] needs care and kindness * * *." It does not appear from this testimony that appellant's illness required the complete deprivation of liberty that results from commitment to Saint Elizabeths as a person of "unsound mind."

*   *   *

We remand the case to the District Court for an inquiry into "other alternative courses of treatment." The court may consider, *e.g.,* whether the appellant and the public would be sufficiently protected if she were required to carry an identification card on her person so that the police or others could take her home if she should wander, or whether she should be required to accept public health nursing care, community mental health and day care services, foster care, home health aide services, or whether available welfare payments might finance adequate private care. Every effort should be made to find a course of treatment which appellant might be willing to accept.

*   *   *

We express no opinion on questions that would arise if on remand the court should find no available alternative to confinement in Saint Elizabeths.

*   *   *

Remanded for further proceedings in accordance with this opinion.

[The concurring opinion of J. SKELLY WRIGHT is omitted.]

BURGER, CIRCUIT JUDGE, with whom DANAHER and TAMM, CIRCUIT JUDGES, join dissenting.

We disagree with remanding the case to require the District Court to carry out an investigation of alternatives for which Appellant has never indicated any desire. The only issue before us is the legality of Mrs.

Lake's confinement in Saint Elizabeths Hospital and the only relief she herself has requested is immediate unconditional release. The majority does not intimate that Appellant's present confinement as a patient at Saint Elizabeths Hospital is illegal, or that there is anything wrong with it except that she does not like it and wishes to get out of any confinement. Nevertheless, this Court now orders the District Court to perform functions normally reserved to social agencies by commanding search for a judicially approved course of treatment or custodial care for this mentally ill person who is plainly unable to care for herself. Neither this Court nor the District Court is equipped to carry out the broad geriatric inquiry proposed or to resolve the social and economic issues involved.

* * *

If Appellant were to receive precisely the same care she is presently receiving in the geriatrics ward of St. Elizabeths at an institution elsewhere with a name like Columbia Rest Haven, it does not appear that there would be much disagreement over the propriety of her confinement. However, a person's freedom is no less arrested, nor is the effect on him significantly different, if he is confined in a rest home with a euphemistic name rather than at St. Elizabeths Hospital.

* * *

We can all agree in principle that a series of graded institutions with various kinds of homes for the aged and infirm would be a happier solution to the problem than confining harmless senile ladies in St. Elizabeths Hospital with approximately 8000 patients, maintained at a great public expense. But it would be a piece of unmitigated folly to turn this appellant loose on the streets with or without an identity tag; and I am sure for my part that no District Judge will order such a solution. This city is hardly a safe place for able-bodied men, to say nothing of an infirm, senile, and disoriented woman to wander about with no protection except an identity tag advising police where to take her. The record shows that in her past wanderings she has been molested, and should she be allowed to wander again all of her problems might well be rendered moot either by natural causes or violence. . . .

QUESTIONS AND COMMENTS

1.   *The constitutional status of the least restrictive alternative doctrine.* The court in *Lake* based its holding on an interpretation of the District of Columbia's commitment statute. Yet the United States Supreme Court has never ruled that placement in the least restrictive setting is a constitutional right. As a theoretical matter, limiting state intervention to that necessary to achieve the government's objective might seem an important goal; indeed, the Supreme Court has applied this idea in a number of individual cases, most

notably those involving the first amendment. In *Shelton v. Tucker*, 364 U.S. 479, 81 S.Ct. 247, 5 L.Ed.2d 231 (1960), the most widely cited case of this type, the Court stated:

> In a series of decisions this Court has held that, even though the governmental purpose be legitimate and substantial, that purpose cannot be pursued by means that broadly stifle fundamental personal liberties when the end can be more narrowly achieved. The breadth of legislative abridgement must be viewed in light of less drastic means for achieving the same basic purpose.

Id. at 488, 81 S.Ct. at 252. But the Court has been unwilling to adopt the "least drastic means" principle as a mandatory aspect of judicial review in any area of the law.

This ambivalence toward less drastic means analysis has carried over into civil commitment. In *Sanchez v. New Mexico*, 396 U.S. 276, 90 S.Ct. 588, 24 L.Ed.2d 469 (1970), the Supreme Court dismissed "for want of a substantial federal question" a New Mexico supreme court decision rejecting the argument that *Shelton* and other cases required the committing authority to consider alternatives to hospitalization. However, in *O'Connor v. Donaldson*, supra, the Court cited *Shelton* in support of the following statement: "[W]hile the State may arguably confine a person to save him from harm, incarceration is rarely if ever a necessary condition for raising the living standards of those capable of surviving safely in freedom, on their own or with the help of family or friends." In a more recent case, *Youngberg v. Romeo*, 457 U.S. 307, 321, 102 S.Ct. 2452, 2461, 73 L.Ed.2d 28 (1982), the Supreme Court considered the minimal conditions that the due process clause requires the state to provide to hospitalized mental patients. There it expressly adopted the following statement made by a judge in the lower court:

> [T]he Constitution only requires that the courts make certain that professional judgment in fact was exercised. It is not appropriate for the courts to specify which of several professionally acceptable choices should have been made.

Additionally, in *Heller v. Doe*, 509 U.S. 312, 330, 113 S.Ct. 2637, 2648, 125 L.Ed.2d 257 (1993), the Court held, in connection with commitment *procedures*, that "as long as [the state] 'rationally advances a reasonable and identifiable governmental objective, we must disregard' the existence of alternative methods of furthering the objectives 'that we, as individuals, might have preferred.'"

For the purpose at issue here—that is, evaluating the impact of the doctrine on the dispositional decision made by the committing authority—the constitutional status of the doctrine may not be an important issue. At least forty-seven states require that involuntary patients be committed to treatment in the least restrictive setting. Ilissa L. Watnik, *A Constitutional Analysis of Kendra's Law: New York's Solution for Treatment of the Chronically Mentally Ill*, 149 U. Pa. L. Rev. 1181, 1203 (2001).

2. *The meaning of the doctrine.* As Hoffman and Foust pointed out many decades ago, neither the purpose of the least restrictive alternative doctrine nor the manner in which it is supposed to operate are clear.

The [least restrictive alternative] doctrine's current conceptualization and application to the involuntary treatment of the mentally ill . . . raises serious questions about its implementation, definition and fundamental purpose. As applied at the outset of the commitment process, for example, the least restrictive alternative concept makes little practical sense. Virtually all jurisdictions relying upon mandatory application of the doctrine prior to court-ordered hospitalization foresee this application as an additional safeguard to prevent unnecessarily coercive treatment. It is as if no one prior to the commitment hearing had examined or even entertained the possibility of alternatives to hospitalization. But in the majority of cases this is patently absurd. Civil commitment proceedings more often *follow* trials of less restrictive alternatives than trigger them. The competent clinician treating a patient as an outpatient, for example, tries to avoid hospitalization until virtually no other alternative offers sufficient therapeutic promise or safety for the patient and others. Family members and friends of the patient also seek alternatives to involuntary hospitalization even if for no other reason than to avoid the personal discomfort and stigma of formal commitment proceedings. The unworkability of less restrictive alternatives, and not the failure to consider them, ultimately leads to most commitment proceedings. It is little wonder, therefore, that many judges . . . believe the requirement to find less restrictive alternatives inappropriate before ordering involuntary hospitalization to be a mere formality.

Even assuming a serious judicial interest in less restrictive alternatives, current statutory construction of the doctrine does not designate who will search for or assess the relative merits of less restrictive treatment alternatives. Moreover, the judiciary's attempts to assign these responsibilities to itself, the state, the clinician, or the patient have failed to achieve meaningful results because these parties have been incapable or unwilling to assume the tasks. . . .

The confusion apparent in the administration of the doctrine is compounded by current legislative and judicial constructions which rely upon simple definitions of its critical elements. . . . [T]he doctrine's exclusive reliance upon physical restrictiveness is untenable on its face. The psychic intrusiveness of chemical or biological treatments, for instance, which are administered in a variety of therapies may be no less important than the physical aspects of the treatment facility. In addition to the nature of treatment and the setting in which it occurs, the duration of coerced treatment may be relevant to considerations of its restrictiveness.

However slippery its definition of restrictiveness, the doctrine's conceptualization of effectiveness seems even more elusive. Presumably the doctrine contemplates a consensus—medical, legal, and preferably both—about how treatment effectiveness will be measured, and what should be the minimum goals attained by the patient before the state's interest in coerced treatment will no longer prevail. Yet historically, the absence of consensus about the goals of treatment has characterized the endless debates over involuntary treatment of the mentally ill. [Moreover], the clinician is often unable to predict the outcome of a treatment alternative without an adequate trial of that therapeutic option and an empirical assessment of its results.

If there can be no immediate agreement about the goals of treatment, or even about the threshold below which the state will not coerce treatment, perhaps the doctrine would at least presume some relationship between the variables of restrictiveness and treatment effectiveness. Of course, there may be no relationship between these variables, but restrictiveness might vary inversely with effectiveness so that least restrictive treatment provides the least effective care. Finally, a third relationship might exist in which the variables are directly related, rather than inversely, and the most effective treatment is unfortunately also the most restrictive. . . .

This problem arises frequently in decisions to commit patients to the hospital for acute and intensive care in lieu of providing treatment within the community. The acutely psychotic patient, for example, who is out of touch with reality, suffers generally from severe environmental over-stimulation.[118] Literally flooded with confusing sensations and thoughts, these patients frequently benefit from and even request physical isolation or seclusion from other persons to better organize their thoughts and perceptions.[119] Indeed, for these patients, institutions during the pre-phenothiazine era functioned as true "asylums" for the insane. In the alternative, certain adolescent patients locked in destructive conflicts with their parents or other authorities may consciously or unconsciously seek restrictions on their behavior. A consistent, fair, and even restrictive parent (or parent-substitute) may provide the adolescent with an essential model of human behavior to emulate in later years. To the extent that such goals are thought to be desirable, appropriate treatment may be more restrictive. . . .

Obviously, when effective treatment is also the most restrictive, a balance must be struck between the interests of liberty on the one hand and therapy on the other. Moreover, the balance will be different for individual patients according to their idiosyncrasies. Yet even as a normative statement, the doctrine does not establish a sufficiently precise theoretical basis for making these difficult clinical judgments.

---

[118] So desperate may be the need of such patients for less, rather than more stimulation, that some authors question whether the normal hospital environment is sufficiently tranquil. See Van Putten, *Milieu Therapy: Contraindications?*, 130 Arch. Gen. Psych. 52 (1973).

[119] Not only do certain patients seek isolation from others, but they improve with such "treatment." See Goldberg & Rubin, *Recovery of Patients During Periods of Supposed Neglect*, 37 Brit. J. Med. Psychiat. 265 (1964).

Instead, all too often it finds expression in inarticulate statutory construction and simple judicial notions of "need for treatment," and "restrictiveness.". . . .

Browning Hoffman & Lawrence Foust, *Least Restrictive Treatment of the Mentally Ill: A Doctrine in Search of Its Senses*, 14 San Diego L.Rev. 1100, 1139–43 (1977)

Hoffman and Foust suggest that, at the initial commitment proceeding, the most effective treatment should be sought; the physical restrictiveness of the therapy should be a secondary concern. Only after "the maximum benefits of care have already accrued, or the patient has not responded to the institution and is untreatable in that setting" should "the importance of patient treatability diminish . . . [and] that of treatment restrictiveness emerge. . . . " Id. at 1146. Is the approach suggested by Hoffman and Foust consistent with the premise of the least restrictive alternative doctrine? Does their approach mean that Lake should be hospitalized? How would it apply to Brown in the *Boggs* case?

3.   *Effectiveness of community treatment.* As Hoffman and Foust note, whether or not it is the primary consideration, treatment effectiveness should presumably at least be considered in deciding between hospitalization and some community alternative, such as a nursing home, a halfway house, or outpatient treatment. Even before the advent of more innovative community treatment programs, a survey of studies comparing hospital and community treatment found the latter programs to be at least as efficacious. Charles Kiesler & Amy Sibulkin, Mental Hospitalization 152–180 (1987). After looking at all the available studies involving random assignment of patients to either hospital or alternative care, these authors concluded that "the most general conclusion one can draw . . . is that alternative care is more effective and less costly than mental hospitalization." Id. at 179. In another summary of basically the same data, Kiesler stated:

> It seems quite clear from these studies that for the vast majority of patients now being assigned to inpatient units in mental institutions, care of at least equal impact could be otherwise provided. There is not an instance in this array of studies in which hospitalization had any positive impact on the average patient care investigated in this study. In almost every case, alternative care had more positive outcomes. There were significant and powerful effects on such life-related variables as employment, school attendance, and the like. There were significant and important effects on the probability of subsequent readmission. Not only did the patients in the alternative care not undergo the initial hospitalization but they were less likely to undergo hospitalization later, as well.

Charles   Kiesler,   *Mental   Hospitals   and   Alternative   Care: Noninstitutionalization as Potential Public Policy for Mental Patients*, 37 Am.Psychol. 349, 350 (1982). As this chapter has already noted, subsequent studies have only confirmed these conclusions from the 1980s.

However, as Kiesler and Sibulkin admitted, the research consensus that alternative care is at least as effective as hospital treatment may not apply to *all* potential patients. While they note that most of the studies involved treatment of people with severe disability, they also state that their generalization about the superior quality of community care "may not be true for all disorders, age groups, etc. Insufficient detail is provided in these studies to assess such questions even preliminarily." Id. at 177. Indeed, none of the studies reviewed by Kiesler and Sibulkin appear to involve patients considered imminently dangerous to self or others. Given current perceptions about people with mental disability, it would be difficult, if not impossible, to arrange or ethically justify a study that randomly assigned (as all Kiesler's studies did and as subsequent studies have done) half the subjects to community treatment if the subjects were people who were eligible for civil commitment and thought to be on the verge of harming themselves or others. Assuming that alternative care would be more effective for a particular patient, a second problem with generalizing the research is that many communities still lack the types of innovative programs reported in the reviews mentioned above. Often, the only option available for very ill patients is treatment in an inpatient facility.

4. *Outpatient commitment.* One method of implementing the least restrictive alternative doctrine might be provision for commitment on an outpatient basis. A typical outpatient commitment might require the patient to report to a community clinic on a weekly basis for medication, therapy or both. In theory, outpatient commitment might also curtail the "revolving door" situation, in which patients are discharged into the community, go off medication, and are recommitted.

Statutes that explicitly authorize outpatient commitment differ significantly, but three general models can be posited. The first—conditional release—permits outpatient commitment only after some form of inpatient commitment, either in a hospital or in the community. Under this model, which is authorized in virtually every state, outpatient commitment functions somewhat like parole: the patient is permitted to remain outside the hospital so long as he or she continues to follow a certain outpatient treatment regimen. This approach might be especially useful for those patients who tend to stop their medication, quickly deteriorate, and return to the hospital. This type of outpatient commitment is discussed more fully at pp. 964–967 in connection with release procedures.

The second model of outpatient commitment, more relevant to the present discussion, authorizes outpatient commitment to a community facility at the "front end" of the commitment process if the traditional commitment criteria are met, without any preliminary requirement of inpatient treatment. This model is an explicit statutory effort to implement the least restrictive alternative doctrine. At least thirty-seven states have enacted statutes authorizing this type of commitment. Amy Allbright et al., *Outpatient Civil Commitment Laws: An Overview*, 26 Men. & Phys. Dis. L. Rep. 179 (2002).

preventive commitment

The third model—sometimes called preventive commitment—also permits outpatient commitment at the front end, but under commitment standards that are significantly different from typical "libertarian" commitment standards: they require only a showing that the individual will *soon meet* the traditional standards for institutionalization (and thus are very similar if not identical to the "deterioration" standard described in the previous section). Apparently this type of outpatient commitment is a response to a number of factors, including "concerns about . . . a growing number of mentally disordered people in shelters and on the streets, resistant to treatment and in various stages of decompensation, who cannot be hospitalized under the strict commitment criteria; a backlash among psychiatrists and mental health professionals to what is perceived as over-legalization of the mental health system; and advocacy by increasingly vocal parents' groups, particularly the National Alliance for the Mentally Ill, who are demanding treatment for their family members and increasingly allying themselves with mental health professionals to press for the easing of commitment standards." Susan Stefan, *Preventive Commitment: The Concept and Its Pitfalls*, 11 Men.Dis.L.Rep. 288 (1987). Perhaps ten states have enacted preventive outpatient commitment statutes. Mark Moran, *Coercion or Caring?*, Am Med. News (Apr. 17, 2000).

The implementation of any of these models can present significant obstacles. Professors Schwartz and Costanzo state:

> While outpatient commitment has been an available option in most jurisdictions for many years, several factors have precluded states from relying extensively on what is arguably a more desirable alternative. These operational barriers include: (1) the lack of appropriate community mental health programs; (2) the difficulty of compelling committed individuals to comply with treatment plans; (3) the probability that few persons would comply with court-ordered treatment and yet be unwilling to voluntarily participate in a community program; (4) the reluctance of mental health providers to treat their clients involuntarily and subject themselves to judicial supervision; (5) the absence of judicial mechanisms and personnel to adequately supervise outpatient care; (6) the resistance of neighbors and public officials to accept committed persons in their community; (7) the fears of professionals concerning liability for inadequate treatment or foreseeable harm; and (8) the potential creation of a governmental obligation to fund a comprehensive system of community services for individuals subject to outpatient commitment.

Steven Schwartz & Cathy Costanzo, *Compelling Treatment in the Community: Distorted Doctrines and Violated Values*, 20 Loyola L.A.L.Rev. 1329, 1377 (1987). Consistent with Schwartz and Costanzo's premise that outpatient commitment is rarely used, one survey found that "[t]he available research strongly suggests that the number of individuals likely to be subject to [involuntary outpatient commitment] is relatively small," perhaps 5–10% of those for whom involuntary commitment is considered. Ingo Keilitz,

Empirical Studies of Involuntary Outpatient Civil Commitment: Is It Working?, 14 Men. & Phys. Dis. L. Rep. 368, 370 (1990). Also consistent with their assertions are findings that approximately 50% of those patients who are treated on an outpatient basis stop taking their medication against medical advice. Gerald Kelly, et al., *Utility of the Health Model in Examining Medication Compliance Among Psychiatric Outpatients*, 25 Soc. Sci. Med. 1205 (1987); Allen Frances & Peter Weiden, *Promoting Compliance With Outpatient Drug Treatment*, 38 Hosp. & Comm. Psych. 1158, 1159 (1987); Stephen Kane, *Prevention and Treatment of Neuroleptic Noncompliance*, 16 Psych. Annals 576 (1986).

However, a number of studies also suggest that *intense* outpatient commitment approaches can reduce hospital readmission rates and lengths of stay. The best studies of outpatient commitment found that, for psychotic individuals, if outpatient commitment is prolonged (180 days or more) and if the level of outpatient services is "high" (with more than 7 encounters a month), readmission rates can be affected significantly. Marvin S. Swartz & Jeffrey Swanson, *Outpatient Commitment: When It Improves Patient Outcomes*, 7 Current Psychiatry 25 (2008); Marvin Swartz et al., *Can Involuntary Outpatient Commitment Reduce Hospital Recidivism?: Findings from a Randomized Trial with Severely Mentally Ill Individuals*, 156 Am. J. Psychiatry 1968 (1999). Extended outpatient commitment has also been found to increase use of case management services and social functioning and reduce rates of relapse, hospitalizations, criminal victimization and arrest in North Carolina. Marvin Swartz et al., *Randomized Controlled Trial of Outpatient Commitment in North Carolina*, 52 Psychiatric Services 325 (2001). Less clear is whether involuntary outpatient commitment is *needed* to treat the people it targets. See Virginia A. Hiday, *Outpatient Commitment: The State of Empirical Research on Outcomes*, 9 Psychol. Pub. Pol'y & L. 8, 23 (2003)("Opponents of outpatient commitment argue that some programs that are designed to be aggressive, comprehensive, and intensive, such as Assertive Community Treatment (ACT) expend mental health resources in manner that works with resistant, severely mentally ill persons and can produce the same positive outcomes without a court order as those seen under outpatient commitment.").

The legal issues associated with outpatient commitment center around the fact that the patient most likely to be subjected to it is one "who can be maintained in remission with medication but who does not take it voluntarily or consistently." Robert Miller and Paul Fiddleman, *Outpatient Commitment: Treatment in the Least Restrictive Environment?*, 35 Hosp. & Comm. Psychiat. 147, 149 (1984). At the time such a person is committed as an outpatient, he or she is not imminently dangerous; the commitment is based on the prediction that the person will deteriorate into dangerousness if medication is not maintained. Under these circumstances, is the second model of outpatient commitment, based on the traditional requirement of imminent dangerousness, workable? And given the lack of imminent danger (and the likely absence of an overt act) in such situations, is commitment on prevention-of-deterioration grounds (the third model) constitutional? Is a less stringent commitment standard justifiable when the "deprivation of liberty" that occurs is less significant than occurs with full hospitalization? What is the relevance of the finding described above that outpatient commitment generally only "works" if it lasts for more than 180 days and involves multiple contacts? Cf. W. Wood & D. Swanson, *Use of Outpatient Treatment during Civil Commitment: Law and Practice in Nebraska*, 41 J. Clinical Psychology 723 (1985)(finding that outpatient commitment in Nebraska lasted an *average* of three years).

In answering these questions, consider *In re Commitment of Dennis H.*, 255 Wis.2d 359, 647 N.W.2d 851 (2002), where the Wisconsin Supreme Court confronted a commitment standard that permitted outpatient *and* inpatient commitment if the state can show that the person is incompetent to make treatment decisions, refuses treatment, and "evidences a substantial probability, as demonstrated by both the individual's treatment history and his or her recent acts or omissions, [of a need for] care or treatment to prevent further disability or deterioration and a substantial probability that he or she will, if left untreated, lack services necessary for his or her health or safety and suffer severe mental, emotional or physical harm that will result in the loss of the individual's ability to function independently in the community or the loss of cognitive or volitional control over his or her thoughts or actions." In upholding this standard, the court declared:

> By permitting intervention before a mentally ill person's condition becomes critical, the legislature has enabled the mental health treatment community to break the cycle associated with incapacity to choose medication or treatment, restore the person to a relatively even keel, prevent serious and potentially catastrophic harm, and ultimately reduce the amount of time spent in an institutional setting. This type of "prophylactic intervention" does not violate substantive due process.

It has also been argued that individuals can be committed on an outpatient basis on a lesser showing than is required for inpatient treatment because, given the fact they will be on the streets rather than in a hospital, those committed on an outpatient basis pose a "higher risk." Rachel A. Scherer, *Toward a Twenty–First Century Civil Commitment Statute: A Legal, Medical, and Policy Analysis of Preventive Outpatient Treatment*, 4 Ind. Health L. Rev. 361, 405 (2007). Consider the applicability of outpatient commitment, both preventive and traditional, to Lake, Gregorovich and Brown in previous materials in this chapter.

5. *Kendra's law and assisted outpatient treatment.* In 1999, Andrew Goldstein, a person suffering from schizophrenia, pushed Kendra Webdale in front of a subway, killing her. Partly in response to this event, the New York legislature passed "Kendra's Law," which appears to extend the scope of outpatient commitment further than the laws described above. The law authorizes "assisted outpatient treatment" (AOT), a program designed to keep people with mental illness who are in the community in contact with treatment and support services through a comprehensive "case management" system that operates on an indeterminate basis. The law permits

intervention for up to six months if, *inter alia*, the person: is (1) 18 years-old or older; (2) "is in need of assisted outpatient treatment in order to prevent a relapse or deterioration which would be likely to result in serious harm to the patient or others;" and (3) has a "history" of non-compliance with treatment, as a result of which hospitalization has occurred twice within the last 36 months or violence has occurred within the last 48 months. N.Y. Men. Hyg. Laws § 9.60(c). In contrast to previously described statutes, failure to accept treatment may lead to 72 hours of hospitalization (although further hospitalization requires that the traditional commitment criteria be met). Id. at § 9.60(n).

In *In re K.L.*,1 N.Y.3d 362, 774 N.Y.S.2d 472, 806 N.E.2d 480 (2004), the New York Supreme Court upheld the constitutionality of Kendra's law against substantive and procedural due process challenges. Among other findings it rejected the argument that the law's failure to require proof that the patient lacked capacity to make treatment decisions (which the Wisconsin law described in note 4 above requires) made it unconstitutional:

> Since Mental Hygiene Law § 9.60 does not permit forced medical treatment, a showing of incapacity is not required. . . . The [72–hour] restriction on a patient's freedom effected by a court order authorizing assisted outpatient treatment is minimal, inasmuch as the coercive force of the order lies solely in the compulsion generally felt by law-abiding citizens to comply with court directives. For although the Legislature has determined that the existence of such an order and its attendant supervision increases the likelihood of voluntary compliance with necessary treatment, a violation of the order, standing alone, ultimately carries no sanction. Rather, the violation, when coupled with a failure of efforts to solicit the assisted outpatient's compliance, simply triggers heightened scrutiny on the part of the physician, who must then determine whether the patient may be in need of involuntary hospitalization.

> Of course, whenever a physician determines that a patient is in need of involuntary commitment—whether such a determination came to be made after an assisted outpatient failed to comply with treatment or was reached in the absence of any AOT order at all—the patient may be hospitalized [after the 72–hour hold period] only if the standards for such commitment contained in the Mental Hygiene Law are satisfied. These standards themselves satisfy due process. If, however, the noncompliant patient is not found to be in need of hospitalization, the inquiry will be at an end and the patient will suffer no adverse consequence. For as the statute explicitly provides, "Failure to comply with an order of assisted outpatient treatment shall not be grounds for involuntary civil commitment or a finding of contempt of court". Moreover, any restriction on an assisted outpatient's liberty interest felt as a result of the legal obligation to comply with an AOT order is far less onerous than the complete deprivation of freedom that might have been

necessary if the patient were to be or remain involuntarily committed in lieu of being released on condition of compliance with treatment.

Id. at 484–86. For different views on AOT laws, which now exist in several states, compare Scherer, supra, to Erin O'Connor, *Is Kendra's Law a Keeper? How Kendra's Law Erodes Fundamental Rights of the Mentally Ill*, 11 J. Law & Policy 321, 361–62 (2002).

Considerable data have been collected on the operation of Kendra's law. Between 1999 and 2008, 13,260 individuals were referred for evaluation under the law, but only 6,666 AOT orders were issued. Data collected in 2012–13 showed that roughly one-quarter of the individuals under such orders were treated for six months, while the rest had their orders renewed beyond six months and over 45% were treated for more than 3 years. Among those committed there was a 32% reduction in the incidence of harmful behaviors, a 60% reduction in emergency room visits, a 63% reduction in hospitalization rates, and a 37% reduction in the incidence of homelessness. The harmful-act recidivism rate of those who graduated from the AOT program was reduced by 23%. N.Y. State Office of Mental Health, Kendra's Law: Report on the Status of Assisted Outpatient Treatment (2013), available at http://bi.omh.state.ny.us/act/outcomes. See also Jeffrey W. Swanson et al., *The Cost of Assisted Outpatient Treatment: Can It Save States Money*, Am. J. Psychiatry (2013), available at http://ajp.psychiatryonline.org/Article.aspx? ArticleID=1722044 (finding that net costs declined over 50% in the first year of AOT and from 13 to 27% in the second year, while voluntary treatment did not save as much money, but was also less costly than inpatient treatment).

Interestingly, because Kendra's law focuses on people who are non-compliant, it probably would not have applied to Goldstein, who had sought treatment for some time prior to the subway incident. In 2001, another person with mental illness pushed an individual in front of a New York City subway; this person too claimed he was "desperate" for treatment, and in any event had not been identified for AOT. In 2002 Peter Troy, while suffering from paranoid schizophrenia, shot and killed a priest and a parishioner in the middle of mass on Long Island. His case had been referred for AOT but was never investigated; officials admitted he had "fallen through the cracks." Id. at 365–66.

6. *The Virginia Tech incident.* Another well-known case to consider in this context is that of Sueng–Hui Cho, who killed 32 people and wounded many more at Virginia Tech in April, 2007 in the deadliest school shooting in U.S. history. As recounted in Chapter Three (see pp. 281–289), Cho had been diagnosed with and was treated for a severe anxiety disorder in middle school, and he continued receiving therapy and special education support until his junior year of high school. However, his records were not transferred to Virginia Tech. While in college in 2005, Cho had been accused of stalking two female students and occasionally expressed a desire to kill himself. After a complaint from a female student that Cho had stabbed a carpet with a knife during a party, Cho was subjected to a screening process by a local Community Services Board (CSB) facility. A social worker found him

dangerous to *himself* and suffering from a "mood disorder," but an attending physician, who interviewed him for 15 minutes, did not think he was imminently dangerous. Nonetheless, at a hearing a Virginia special justice found him mentally ill and an "imminent danger to self" and ordered unspecified outpatient treatment. After the hearing, the CSB contacted Virginia Tech's counseling service to set up treatment for Cho, but because that service only treats voluntary patients it was up to Cho to decide whether to show up for treatment sessions, which he did not do. Virginia Tech's service did not report Cho's failure to show up for treatment to either the court or the CSB, perhaps because of the Family Educational Rights and Privacy Act, 20 U.S.C. § 1232g (see pp. 387–389), which only permits disclosure of health records held by an educational institution when there is a specific court order (which arguably did not exist in this case, given the ambiguity of the outpatient commitment order). In the ensuing two years, at least one professor asked Cho to seek counseling and several professors and students noted his reclusiveness and expressions of anger. However, nothing suggested that Cho was incompetent to make treatment decisions, and he had never been hospitalized prior to the shootings. Report on the Virginia Tech Incident to the Governor, Chap IV (Mental Health History of Sueng Hui–Cho) 31–52 (2007).

At the time of the Virginia Tech incident, federal law banned sale of guns to people who had been institutionalized in mental hospitals or declared "mentally defective" (defined as people who have been found mentally ill and dangerous to self or others or incompetent), but the record of Cho's emergency detention had never been communicated to federal authorities. As a result of Cho's rampage, Congress provided funding to the states for the purpose of ensuring that all people who are the subject of the federal ban are entered into the National Instant Criminal Background Check System. However, as of this writing, federal law still does not require background checks for people buying guns at gun shows. Would Cho have been committable under an AOT law? Can AOT laws or gun laws be reformed to try to prevent these types of occurrences consistent with due process, equal protection, and second amendment principles? Cf. *District of Columbia v. Heller*, 554 U.S. 570, 128 S.Ct. 2783, 2817, 171 L.Ed.2d 637 (2008) (holding that the second amendment guarantees citizens as well as militia a right to bear arms but "should not be taken to cast doubt on longstanding prohibitions on the possession of firearms by felons and the mentally ill."). For an argument that denying people with mental illness the right to bear arms based on "[a]n undifferentiated . . . determination that all persons with mental illness pose a grave threat to others" is probably impermissible, but that a denial of such a right based on the goal of preventing suicide is justifiable, see Fredrick E. Vars & Amanda Adcock Young, *Do the Mentally Ill Have a Right to Bear Arms?*, 48 Wake Forest L. Rev. 1 (2013).

IV.   PROCEDURES

A. GENERAL CONSIDERATIONS

As recounted at the beginning of this chapter, the civil commitment proceedings of many states were extremely informal prior to statutory changes in the 1970s. Because they were perceived to be medical rather than legal, commitment decisions were often made by mental health professionals, with little or no input by lawyers and few procedural rules. Today, however, all states grant civil commitment respondents procedural rights that, at least on paper, appear to provide the kinds of protections afforded to criminal defendants: the right to a public trial in front of a judge and/or jury, the right to notice of the charges, the rights to an opportunity to confront accusers and subpoena witnesses, the right to the assistance of counsel and the right to remain silent in response to government questions. This section examines the extent to which the criminal process model is an appropriate one for civil commitment; it begins with the first decision to so hold.

LESSARD V. SCHMIDT
United States District Court, E.D.Wisconsin, 1972.
349 F.Supp. 1078.

*   *   *

[T]he lifting of procedural safeguards in [civil commitment proceedings] appears to rest in part on the realities of better treatment for the person subjected to incarceration in a civil proceeding. In Kent v. United States, the Supreme Court, discussing the issue in the context of juvenile courts, observed:

> "The objectives are to provide measures of guidance and rehabilitation for the child and protection for society, not to fix criminal responsibility, guilt and punishment. The State is *parens patriae* rather than prosecuting attorney and judge. But the admonition to function in a 'parental' relationship is not an invitation to procedural arbitrariness.

> "2. Because the State is supposed to proceed in respect of the child as *parens patriae* and not as adversary, courts have relied on the premise that the proceedings are 'civil' in nature and not criminal, and have asserted that the child cannot complain of the deprivation of important rights available in criminal cases. It has been asserted that he can claim only the fundamental due process right to fair treatment. . . .

> "While there can be no doubt of the original laudable purpose of juvenile courts, studies and critiques in recent years raise serious

questions as to *whether actual performance measures well enough against theoretical purpose to make tolerable the immunity of the process from the reach of constitutional guaranties applicable to adults.* There is much evidence that some juvenile courts, . . . lack the personnel, facilities and techniques to perform adequately as representatives of the State in a *parens patriae* capacity, at least with respect to children charged with law violation. There is evidence, in fact, that there may be grounds for concern that the child receives the worst of both worlds: that he gets neither the protections accorded to adults nor the solicitous care and regenerative treatment postulated for children."

(Emphasis added). Few persons familiar with the mental health field will question the applicability of much of the above to persons subjected to involuntary commitment in state institutions.

In any event, the argument in favor of relaxed procedures on the basis of a subsequent right to treatment ignores the fact that unless constitutionally prescribed procedural due process requirements for involuntary commitment are met, no person should be subjected to "treatment" against his will. The argument also ignores the fact that many mental illnesses are untreatable, and the substantial evidence that any lengthy hospitalization, particularly where it is involuntary, may greatly increase the symptoms of mental illness and make adjustment to society more difficult.

* * *

A second justification for less stringent safeguards in civil commitment proceedings is simply that the proceedings are "civil" and not "criminal." That argument should have been laid to rest following the Supreme Court's decision in In re Gault, in which the Court found the distinction unpersuasive as an excuse for providing lesser safeguards for juveniles in delinquency proceedings than were given adults charged with violations of the criminal law.

* * *

Even a brief examination of the effects of civil commitment upon those adjudged mentally ill shows the importance of strict adherence to stringent procedural requirements and the necessity for narrow, precise standards.

An individual committed to a mental institution loses numerous civil rights. In Wisconsin, hospitalization for mental illness, whether by voluntary admission or involuntary commitment, raises a rebuttable presumption of incompetency. The presumption continues as long as the patient is under the jurisdiction of hospital authorities. An individual adjudged mentally ill in Wisconsin also faces restrictions on making contracts and limitations on the right to sue and be sued. Restrictions on licenses required to engage in certain professions also accompany an adjudication of mental illness in Wisconsin. Wis.Stat.Ann. § 441.07 (1972 Supp.) (registered and practical nurses), § 447.07(7) (1972 Supp.) (dentists and dental hygienists), § 256.286 (attorneys). Persons found mentally ill in Wisconsin are, like felons, unable to vote. The mentally ill are also prohibited from driving a car and serving on juries. No person found to be "insane, imbecile, or feeble-minded" may participate in a marriage contract.

It is obvious that the commitment adjudication carries with it an enormous and devastating effect on an individual's civil rights. In some respects, such as the limitation on holding a driver's license, the civil deprivations which follow civil commitment are more serious than the deprivations which accompany a criminal conviction.

In addition to the statutory disabilities associated with an adjudication of mental illness, and just as serious, are the difficulties that the committed individual will face in attempting to adjust to life outside the institution following release. Evidence is plentiful that a former mental patient will encounter serious obstacles in attempting to find a job, sign a lease or buy a house. One commentator, noting that "former mental patients do not get jobs," has insisted that, "[i]n the job market, it is better to be an ex-felon than ex-patient."

In summary, an adjudication of mental illness in Wisconsin carries with it loss of basic civil rights and loss of future opportunities. The damage done is not confined to a small number among the population. * * * It would thus appear that the interests in avoiding civil commitment are at least as high as those of persons accused of criminal offenses. The resulting burden on the state to justify civil commitment must be correspondingly high.

QUESTIONS AND COMMENTS

1.   *Procedural due process analysis.* Two years after *Lessard* the United States Supreme Court formulated what has become the standard analysis for determining how much process is due when a particular government action is contemplated. In *Mathews v. Eldridge*, 424 U.S. 319, 335, 96 S.Ct. 893, 903, 47 L.Ed.2d 18 (1976), involving the administration of social security benefits, the Court outlined three basic factors that must be considered: (1) the private interest that will be affected by the official action; (2) the risk of an erroneous deprivation of such interest through the procedures used, and the probable value, if any, of additional or substitute procedural safeguards; and (3) the government's interest, including the function involved and the fiscal and administrative burdens that the additional or substitute requirements would entail. *Mathews* is usually cited by courts considering the process due in civil commitment cases.

2. *Changes since* Lessard. Although true at the time of *Lessard,* few states today link involuntary hospitalization with incompetency to exercise the prerogatives of citizenship. Most jurisdictions have adopted (either by statute or through case law) the holding in *Wyatt v. Stickney,* 344 F.Supp. 373 (M.D.Ala.1972), that "[n]o person shall be deemed incompetent to manage his affairs, to contract, to hold professional or occupational or vehicle operator's licenses, to marry and obtain a divorce, to register and vote, or to make a will *solely* by reason of his admission or commitment to the hospital." Id. at 379. (Emphasis in original). Thus, until the person is adjudicated incompetent and has a guardian appointed, these privileges are not forfeited.[i] In many states, however, the hospitalized person in effect loses the right to refuse treatment; control over personal funds may also be circumscribed to some extent. How do these developments affect the analysis in *Lessard*?

3. *Juvenile justice analogy.* As *Lessard* indicates, changes in the juvenile justice system presaged reforms of civil commitment processes. Before the mid–1960's, hearings to determine whether a child was "delinquent" (i.e., had committed an act that would be a crime if the child were an adult) were very informal, often presided over by "judges" who were not legally trained; lawyers were either not present or acted perfunctorily. As with civil commitment, the premise of this system was paternalistic. Intervention by the state was for the purpose of setting the child on the right track, not to punish. If the outcome of a delinquency hearing is simply to implement treatment, proponents of the system argued, the trappings and procedural protections of the adult criminal system are inapposite.

In a series of decisions between 1966 and 1975, the Supreme Court seriously undermined this position. It revamped procedures for transferring children to adult court in *Kent v. United States,* 383 U.S. 541, 86 S.Ct. 1045, 16 L.Ed.2d 84 (1966), mandated that notice, counsel, confrontation rights and the right to remain silent be provided children alleged to be delinquent in *In re Gault,* 387 U.S. 1, 87 S.Ct. 1428, 18 L.Ed.2d 527 (1967) and, in *In re Winship,* 397 U.S. 358, 90 S.Ct. 1068, 25 L.Ed.2d 368 (1970), held that the reasonable doubt standard of proof applied in such proceedings. The chief rationale of these decisions was that delinquency findings often had consequences—such as curtailment of freedom for long periods—that were more like punishment than treatment, so that the differences between criminal proceedings against adults and delinquency proceedings against children were minimal. By 1975, Chief Justice Burger was able to state, in the course of holding that the double jeopardy clause applies to delinquency proceedings, that "it is simply too late in the day to conclude . . . that a juvenile is not put in jeopardy at a proceeding whose object is to determine whether he has committed acts that violate a criminal law and whose potential consequences include both the stigma inherent in such a determination and the deprivation of liberty for many years." *Breed v. Jones,* 421 U.S. 519, 95 S.Ct. 1779, 44 L.Ed.2d 346 (1975).

---

[i]   These issues are addressed further in Chapter Nine.

As *Lessard* illustrates, these cases were viewed as precedent for reform-minded courts deliberating on the proper procedures for civil commitment. In particular, note the court's use of *Kent* and *Gault* to rebut the two arguments usually advanced for relaxing procedures in the civil commitment context: the therapeutic goals of civil commitment and its "civil" label. But the comparison between the juvenile system and civil commitment is not necessarily as compelling as *Lessard* suggests. While rehabilitation remains an important goal of juvenile justice, dispositions in juvenile delinquency cases have a significant punitive element—even more so today than when the *Kent* and *Gault* were issued. See Richard E. Redding, *Adult Punishment for Juvenile Offenders: Does It Reduce Crime?*, in Handbook of Children, Culture and Violence 375, (Nancy E. Dowd et al. eds, 2006). Many states have moved away from indeterminate sentences—designed to provide flexibility for juvenile treatment authorities—toward strictly limited dispositions based on culpability and toward mandatory transfer of jurisdiction to adult court under various circumstances. See e.g., Redding, supra. The explicitly punitive orientation of the "new" juvenile court obviously distinguishes it from civil commitment. Should this difference matter when comparing procedures used in the two systems? Might the answer to this question depend upon whether the basis for commitment is the police power or *parens patriae*?

A second point worth considering when comparing delinquency and commitment is that, despite the new punishment orientation of the juvenile system, many policymakers remain ambivalent about imposing adult procedures in their entirety. This ambivalence was evident in the Supreme Court's decision in *McKeiver v. Pennsylvania*, 403 U.S. 528, 91 S.Ct. 1976, 29 L.Ed.2d 647 (1971), which refused to apply the right to jury trial in the juvenile delinquency context. In justifying this decision, the Court stated that applying the right to jury trial would "remake the juvenile proceeding into a fully adversary process and . . . put an effective end to what has been the idealistic prospect of an intimate, informal protective proceeding." The jury trial right would not necessarily lead to more accurate factfinding, while it "would tend once again to place the juvenile squarely in the routine of the criminal process" with the attendant "traditional delay, the formality, and the clamor of the adversary system." Imposing the right would also forbid the states "to experiment further and to seek in new and different ways the elusive answers to the problems of the young." The notions suggested by this language in *McKeiver* are worth noting because they resurface in some of the Court's later civil commitment cases.

4. *The impact of reform.* Do criminal-type procedural rules have any effect on outcome? Empirical research on the issue is ambiguous. Some studies show that reforms of both the substantive criteria and procedural rules have reduced hospital admissions. But a number of studies indicate little change in outcome. See e.g., Michael R. Bagby & Leslie Atkinson, *The Effects of Legislative Reform on Civil Commitment Admission Rates: A Critical Analysis*, 6 Behav. Sci. & L. 45 (1988)(decline in admissions resulting from reform is short-lived; admission rates reach pre-reform level within a two-year period). Most importantly for purposes of the topic at hand, the

research indicates that commitment hearings are usually adversarial in name only even in the most legalistic states.[j]

Representative are the findings of Serena Stier & Kurt Stoebe, in *Involuntary Hospitalization of the Mentally Ill in Iowa: The Failure of the 1975 Legislation*, 64 Iowa L.Rev. 1284 (1979). They concluded that, despite being highly "legalized" on paper, the Iowa commitment process was in fact very informal. They found that three-fourths of the referees (judges) and clerks of court admitted that commitment hearings were usually not conducted in an adversary manner. Defense attorneys requested an independent mental health evaluation (available by right under the statute) in fewer than 1% of cases, and they rarely called more than two witnesses (often none). The majority of attorneys failed to put the respondents on the stand. One attorney even reasoned that to do so would risk the respondents persuading the referee that they were not mentally ill. Consistent with their lack of active participation in the hearings, the attorneys uniformly spent less than two hours in preparation of these cases.

For their part, the referees encouraged passivity on the part of defense attorneys. Some referees expressly discouraged cross-examination of witnesses; if questions were to be asked, the referees themselves would ask them. The result was that commitment hearings were little more than a stamp of approval for the attending physician's opinion. In fact, a change in treatment plan from that which the hospital physician had recommended was observed in fewer than 1% of cases. Referees and attorneys generally agreed that clinicians should decide whether the elements of the standard for civil commitment had been met, and, if so, what the conditions of treatment should be.

Recent writings suggest that little has changed. Psychiatrists Pinals and Mossman note that in their experiences viewing hundreds of hearings in Massachusetts and Ohio:

> civil commitment hearings . . . are often quick and perfunctory, with little attention paid to the legal, clinical, and forensic issues at stake. In many settings, treating clinicians participate in civil commitment processes as part of their daily work routine, and evaluations do not involve assessments by experts with special forensic expertise.

> In most civil commitment proceedings, fundamental liberty issues and the moral significance of involuntary commitment are not foremost in the minds of the participants. In part, this may reflect the fact that civil commitment offers an opportunity for treatment intended to avert harm and limit the impact of a serious psychiatric illness. Also, desire for efficiency can affect how legal procedures intended to protect patients' rights are actually carried out. Prolonged adversarial proceedings would both delay treatment and extend a respondent's confinement.

---

[j]   See articles cited in footnotes c and d of this chapter.

Debra A. Pinals & Douglas Mossman, Evaluation for Civil Commitment 97 (2012). A study of 285 conservatorship hearings in California arrived at similar results. According to the author, the attorneys' performance during the hearings was "abysmal." Grant H. Morris, *"Let's Do the Time Warp Again": Assessing the Competence of Counsel in Mental Health Conservatorship Proceedings*, 46 San Diego L. Rev. 283, 285, 340–41 (2009) (counsel typically did not conduct cross-examinations, introduce the testimony of a psychiatrist, a family member, or a friend to counter that of the psychiatrist who testified in favor of the conservatorship).

Finally, with respect to the meaningfulness of reform, consider the following excerpt from Samuel Brakel et al., The Mentally Disabled and the Law 27–28 (1985):

> The erection of . . . legal safeguards [in civil commitment] is based on at least two basic assumptions about "involuntary" commitment: (1) that without the safeguards people who do not belong in mental institutions will be railroaded there and (2) that involuntary commitment is a real contest between parties with opposite interests—the party who applies for institutionalization (the state, the institution, or the family) versus the individual who does not want to be institutionalized. It is the wholesale unreality of these assumptions that threatens to make their implements, the procedural safeguards, inapposite or worse. And once the procedures are enacted, their effects are difficult to avoid: the prospect of being able to apply them with proper selectivity only to those relatively few cases in which they are useful is dim, and the price of such selectivity, as mentioned, is high.

5. *The therapeutic effect of adversarial procedures.* A common argument against adversarial procedures, alluded to in the foregoing passage, is that, if they *are* effectively implemented they will be antitherapeutic. A recent survey found that psychiatrists tended "to support relatively limited grounds for commitment," and were "more likely to agree than disagree [that] 'use of involuntary commitment against a patient damages the psychiatrist/patient relationship.'" Robert A. Brooks, *Psychiatrists' Opinions About Involuntary Civil Commitment: Results of a National Survey*, 35 J. Am. Acad. Psychiatry Law 219, 225 (2007). Claims have also been made that hearings can have a traumatic effect on the patient and family members. Other authors have argued that surfacing patient symptoms and family dynamics and forcing mental health professionals to state their views can provide better documentation and treatment of the patient's problems and avoid feelings of betrayal by the patient, who may otherwise believe the family and doctors are working behind their back. John Ensminger & Thomas Liguori, in *The Therapeutic Significance of the Civil Commitment Hearing: An Unexplored Potential*, 6 J. Psychiat. & L. 5 (1978).

Also relevant to the extent to which procedures are "therapeutic" is research on "procedural justice" which compares two procedural paradigms: the adversarial model (i.e., evidence presentation by openly biased parties) and the inquisitorial model (i.e., evidence investigation by an expert decisionmaker). The classic research on this issue was conducted by John Thibaut and Laurens Walker, reported in Procedural Justice: A Psychological Analysis (1975). Although this research and its progeny have been ambiguous as to which procedural approach produces the most accurate outcomes, it has consistently found that the adversarial process is perceived as more fair than a process in which the litigants do not have a formal ability to present their side of the case, because the disputants feel they have more control over the outcome of the dispute and because giving them "voice" in the process accords them status as full-fledged members of society. As a result, it is alleged, disputants in the adversarial mode have greater satisfaction with the outcome and more acceptance of the verdict, even if they lose. See generally Tom R. Tyler, *Procedural Justice, Legitimacy and the Effective Rule of Law*, 30 Crime & Just. 283 (2003).

Research on the related concept of "coercion" in the civil commitment context has arrived at somewhat more nuanced results. First, whether a person feels coerced is not necessarily linked to the type of procedure (adversarial or inquisitorial) but may depend primarily on the behavior of the participants in the process. As summarized in John Monahan et al., *Coercion in the Provision of Mental Health Services: The MacArthur Studies*, 10 Research in Community & Mental Health 13, 26–27 (1999):

> [T]he amount of coercion experienced [by people subjected to civil commitment] is strongly related to a patient's belief about the justice of the process by which he or she was admitted. That is, a patient's beliefs that others acted out of genuine concern, treated the patient respectfully and in good faith, and afforded the patient a chance to tell his or her side of the story, are associated with low levels of experienced coercion. This is true for both voluntary and involuntary patients. Patients report that the hospital admission process was characterized by less of this "procedural justice" than their family members or admitting clinicians report.

Second, patients who perceived their admission to be coercive are significantly more likely to react to the admission with sadness, confusion, fright and, in particular, anger, and are significantly less likely to respond with pleasure or relief. Henry Steadman et al., *Violence by People Discharged from Acute Psychiatric Inpatient Facilities and by Others in the Same Neighborhoods*, 55 Arch. Gen Psych. 1 (1998).

6. *Procedure as surrogate.* In thinking about how much procedure is due in civil commitment proceedings, the following questions, paraphrased from Robert Cover et al., Procedure 133–134 (1988), might be usefully kept in mind. Are your views on the proper level of procedural formality "outcome-driven?" In other words, are you an advocate for more procedural formality because you hope that, under such a regime, fewer people will be committed? Or an opponent because you believe that too many will not be? At a more general level, are you concerned about restraining government power because you have concerns about the likelihood it will be abused? In what sense other than these general outcome measures might increased procedural formality

improve the commitment decision? Do you believe it will improve the "accuracy" of the results reached in commitment hearings? Or, believing "accuracy" to be a loaded term, are you more influenced by the degree of participation or "sense of fairness" that various types of procedures produce?

B. EMERGENCY DETENTION AND SCREENING MECHANISMS

The focus of most litigation concerning the process of commitment has been on the procedural accoutrements of the "adjudicatory" commitment hearing, at which a determination is made about long-term commitment. These procedures are examined in the next section. Perhaps more important, however, are the procedures connected with emergency admission, which is the mechanism by which most individuals enter the civil commitment system. According to the National Center for State Courts in *Guidelines for Involuntary Civil Commitment*, 10 Men.Dis. Law Rep. 409, 427 (1986):

> The greatest activity in involuntary civil commitment proceedings occurs not in the court hearing—inaccurately considered by many to be the centerpiece of involuntary civil commitment—but rather during events before any formal judicial involvement. A person initially may become subject to involuntary civil commitment by one of several ways: by being apprehended by police; by being brought to a hospital by relatives or friends; by being converted from a voluntary patient to an involuntary patient when, after entering a mental health facility voluntarily, the person attempts to leave against the advice of the facility staff; or, finally, by being taken into custody as a result of a legal petition submitted to and validated by a court.[k] . . . For the most part, [these] persons become involuntary patients by means of "emergency" commitments resulting from apprehension by police or by simply appearing on the doorstep of a mental health facility [not as a result of formal involuntary commitment proceedings].

All states permit, under appropriate circumstances, the emergency admission of an individual without any prior formal legal hearing. In California, for instance, either a police officer or a clinician may authorize emergency admission. Cal.Code § 5150. In New York, the decision is made by a clinician at the admitting facility or by the county director of mental health. N.Y. Men. Hyg. Law §§ 9.37, 9.39. In Virginia a judge or magistrate makes the emergency detention decision, but he or she need not actually see the patient and in fact may make the decision based on information received over the phone. Va.Code § 37.1–67.1. The standard of proof to be applied by these decisionmakers is either not stated or

---

k   This last method of initiating the commitment process is analogous to an arrest warrant. [Eds.]

minimal. Neither New York nor Virginia require any particular standard of proof, California requires that the decisionmaker find that "probable cause" exists to believe that the person is mentally disordered and, as a result, gravely disabled or a danger to self or others. Cal.Code § 5150.

The lack of process associated with the initial emergency admission has rarely been challenged, since most agree that a more formal process would be counterproductive.[1] A more difficult question has been whether a subsequent "detention" hearing, separate from and prior to the ultimate "adjudicatory" hearing at which committability is decided, should be held to determine whether the initial admission was appropriate and, if so, how soon and with what procedural requirements. As the next case indicates, such a preliminary hearing is required in the criminal process under certain circumstances.

GERSTEIN V. PUGH
Supreme Court of the United States, 1975.
420 U.S. 103, 95 S.Ct. 854, 43 L.Ed.2d 54.

* * *

II

As framed by the proceedings below, this case presents two issues: whether a person arrested and held for trial on an information is entitled to a judicial determination of probable cause for detention, and if so, whether the adversary hearing ordered by the District Court and approved by the Court of Appeals is required by the Constitution.

A

Both the standards and procedures for arrest and detention have been derived from the Fourth Amendment and its common-law antecedents. . . . The standard for arrest is probable cause, defined in terms of facts and circumstances "sufficient to warrant a prudent man in believing that the [suspect] had committed or was committing an offense." Beck v. Ohio, 379 U.S. 89, 91, 85 S.Ct. 223, 225, 13 L.Ed.2d 142 (1964). . . . This standard, like those for searches and seizures, represents a necessary accommodation between the individual's right to liberty and the State's duty to control crime. . . .

To implement the Fourth Amendment's protection against unfounded invasions of liberty and privacy, the Court has required that the existence of probable cause be decided by a neutral and detached magistrate

---

[1]   One corollary issue that has been raised has to do with police authority to arrest people with a mental disorder. Under the common law, the traditional rule was that a police officer could not, absent a warrant, arrest someone for a misdemeanor (as opposed to a felony) unless the officer witnessed the misdemeanor occurring. However, at least one court has held that, if the consequence of the arrest is commitment, this rule need not be followed. *McKinney v. George,* 556 F.Supp. 645 (N.D.Ill.1983).

whenever possible. The classic statement of this principle appears in Johnson v. United States, 333 U.S. 10, 13–14, 68 S.Ct. 367, 369, 92 L.Ed. 436 (1948):

> "The point of the Fourth Amendment, which often is not grasped by zealous officers, is not that it denies law enforcement the support of the usual inferences which reasonable men draw from evidence. Its protection consists in requiring that those inferences be drawn by a neutral and detached magistrate instead of being judged by the officer engaged in the often competitive enterprise of ferreting out crime."

* * *

Maximum protection of individual rights could be assured by requiring a magistrate's review of the factual justification prior to any arrest, but such a requirement would constitute an intolerable handicap for legitimate law enforcement. Thus, while the Court has expressed a preference for the use of arrest warrants when feasible, . . . it has never invalidated an arrest supported by probable cause solely because the officers failed to secure a warrant. . . .

Under this practical compromise, a policeman's on-the-scene assessment of probable cause provides legal justification for arresting a person suspected of crime, and for a brief period of detention to take the administrative steps incident to arrest. Once the suspect is in custody, however, the reasons that justify dispensing with the magistrate's neutral judgment evaporate. There no longer is any danger that the suspect will escape or commit further crimes while the police submit their evidence to a magistrate. And, while the State's reasons for taking summary action subside, the suspect's need for a neutral determination of probable cause increases significantly. The consequences of prolonged detention may be more serious than the interference occasioned by arrest. Pretrial confinement may imperil the suspect's job, interrupt his source of income, and impair his family relationships. . . . Even pretrial release may be accompanied by burdensome conditions that effect a significant restraint of liberty. See, e.g., 18 U.S.C. §§ 3146(a)(2), (5). When the stakes are this high, the detached judgment of a neutral magistrate is essential if the Fourth Amendment is to furnish meaningful protection from unfounded interference with liberty. Accordingly, we hold that the Fourth Amendment requires a judicial determination of probable cause as a prerequisite to extended restraint of liberty following arrest.

* * *

B

Under the Florida procedures challenged here, a person arrested without a warrant and charged by information may be jailed or subjected to other restraints pending trial without any opportunity for a probable cause determination. Petitioner defends this practice on the ground that the prosecutor's decision to file an information is itself a determination of probable cause that furnishes sufficient reason to detain a defendant pending trial. Although a conscientious decision that the evidence warrants prosecution affords a measure of protection against unfounded detention, we do not think prosecutorial judgment standing alone meets the requirements of the Fourth Amendment.

*   *   *

III

Both the District Court and the Court of Appeals held that the determination of probable cause must be accompanied by the full panoply of adversary safeguards—counsel, confrontation, cross-examination, and compulsory process for witnesses.

These adversary safeguards are not essential for the probable cause determination required by the Fourth Amendment. The sole issue is whether there is probable cause for detaining the arrested person pending further proceedings. This issue can be determined reliably without an adversary hearing. The standard is the same as that for arrest. That standard—probable cause to believe the suspect has committed a crime—traditionally has been decided by a magistrate in a nonadversary proceeding on hearsay and written testimony, and the Court has approved these informal modes of proof.

The use of an informal procedure is justified not only by the lesser consequences of a probable cause determination but also by the nature of the determination itself. It does not require the fine resolution of conflicting evidence that a reasonable-doubt or even a preponderance standard demands, and credibility determinations are seldom crucial in deciding whether the evidence supports a reasonable belief in guilt. . . . This is not to say that confrontation and cross-examination might not enhance the reliability of probable cause determinations in some cases. In most cases, however, their value would be too slight to justify holding, as a matter of constitutional principle, that these formalities and safeguards designed for trial must also be employed in making the Fourth Amendment determination of probable cause.

*   *   *

Although we conclude that the Constitution does not require an adversary determination of probable cause, we recognize that state systems of criminal procedure vary widely. . . . Whatever procedure a State may adopt, it must provide a fair and reliable determination of probable cause as a condition for any significant pretrial restraint of liberty,[26] and this determination must be made by a judicial officer either before or promptly after arrest.

*   *   *

QUESTIONS AND COMMENTS

1. *Applicability of* Gerstein *to commitment.* What implications, if any, does *Gerstein* have for the emergency admission process? Is emergency admission a "seizure" as that word is used in the Fourth Amendment? Should there be a hearing, presided over by a judicial officer, to check the emergency admission decision? Should a showing of probable cause be required? How formal should such a proceeding be in other respects? Should there be a right to be present? The right to an attorney?

Most states require some kind of post-admission check after emergency admission of a person thought to be mentally disabled, but the procedures vary widely. In Virginia, for instance, a hearing presided over by a judge, with the respondent and an attorney for the respondent present, must take place within 48 hours of admission (usually the full-fledged adjudicatory hearing takes place at this time as well). Va.Code § 37.2–814. In California, "certification" must take place within 72 hours, but requires only that two professionals, one of them a physician, sign a notice of certification finding that the person meets the commitment criteria. Once certified, a person may be detained for up to 14 days before a full judicial hearing. Moreover, the patient may be detained for a further 14 days without such a hearing if two professionals find that the patient "threatened or attempted to take his own life or . . . was detained for evaluation and treatment because he threatened or attempted to take his own life and . . . continues to present an imminent threat of taking his own life." Cal.Code §§ 5250, 5251, 5260, 5261. In New York, the individual may be detained up to 15 days if a mental health professional other than the admitting clinician has examined the person within 48 hours of admission and finds that the individual is mentally ill and dangerous to self or others. N.Y. Men. Hyg. Law § 9.39(a). Confinement for a further *60* days is permitted if two physicians certify that the individual meets the commitment standards and a third physician, at the admitting institution, agrees after examining the patient and considering alternatives. N.Y. Men. Hyg. Law §§ 9.33(a). In all states, judicial review (via habeas corpus) is available during the initial detention period, but only upon the patient's request and usually only after some delay (in New York, for instance, review need not take place until five days from the request date). Additionally, in New York, the Mental Hygiene Legal Service, a legal advocacy organization, is located on the grounds of most facilities and monitors the patients who are admitted. N.Y.Men. Hyg. Law § 9.39(a).

---

[26] Because the probable cause determination is not a constitutional prerequisite to the charging decision, it is required only for those suspects who suffer restraints on liberty other than the condition that they appear for trial. There are many kinds of pretrial release and many degrees of conditional liberty. . . . We cannot define specifically those that would require a prior probable cause determination, but the key factor is significant restraint on liberty.

2. *Procedural timeframes. Gerstein* does not set any time limits for the criminal probable cause hearing, merely stating that it should be soon after arrest and prior to subjecting the accused to release conditions such as bail. In *Riverside County v. McLaughlin,* 500 U.S. 44, 111 S.Ct. 1661, 114 L.Ed.2d 49 (1991), however, the Supreme Court held that the "*Gerstein* hearing" should normally take place within 48 hours of a warrantless arrest. The time period between the *Gerstein* hearing and trial can vary immensely, limited only by statutory speedy trial provisions (rarely requiring trial less than 100 days from arrest) and the guarantee of a speedy trial in the Sixth Amendment.

In civil commitment, as the foregoing statutory illustrations indicate, the analogous time periods between detention and the detention hearing (if there is one), and between the latter hearing and the adjudicatory hearing also vary significantly, although the latter hearing always occurs much earlier, relatively speaking, than the typical criminal trial. What considerations should govern the duration of these timeframes? In *Lynch v. Baxley,* 386 F.Supp. 378, 388 (M.D.Ala.1974), the court stated:

> Just as emergency detention is justified only until a probable cause hearing can be conducted, temporary detention following a finding of probable cause to believe that confinement is necessary can be justified only for the length of time required to arrange a full hearing on the need for commitment. Due process requires that such hearing be held within a reasonable time following initial detention, but in no event sooner than will permit adequate preparation of the case by counsel or later than thirty (30) days from the date of the initial detention.

The United States Supreme Court is perhaps willing to stretch the pre-hearing periods considerably further. In the 1970's, it summarily affirmed[m] both *French v. Blackburn,* 428 F.Supp. 1351 (M.D.N.C.1977), affirmed 443 U.S. 901, 99 S.Ct. 3091, 61 L.Ed.2d 869 (1979), and *Logan v. Arafeh,* 346 F.Supp. 1265 (D.Conn.1972), affirmed sub nom., *Briggs v. Arafeh,* 411 U.S. 911, 93 S.Ct. 1556, 36 L.Ed.2d 304 (1973). The three-judge district court in *Blackburn* had found a statute permitting a ten-day period between detention and the "probable cause" hearing constitutional. In *Arafeh,* a three-judge court had upheld a statute under which a hearing could be delayed for up to 45 days, so long as a physician certified that the person met the commitment criteria and a "complaint" was filed within fifteen days. Although the Supreme Court did not issue an opinion in connection with its affirmance of these decisions, both lower court opinions relied on the same two grounds, which are concisely summarized by this language from *Blackburn:* "During [the pre-hearing] period the respondent is receiving treatment which may not only aid his health, but which also may be

---

[m] A summary affirmance is considered binding precedent. *Hicks v. Miranda,* 422 U.S. 332, 95 S.Ct. 2281, 45 L.Ed.2d 223 (1975). However, "finding the precise limits of a summary affirmance has proven to be no easy task." *Hardwick v. Bowers,* 760 F.2d 1202, 1207 (11th Cir.1985). Without analyzing the ultimate precedential significance of *Blackburn* and *Arafeh,* it is important to note that their weight as precedent is somewhat suspect.

necessary to an adequate and informed hearing on the necessity of his commitment." 428 F.Supp. at 1355. See also, *Arafeh,* 346 F.Supp. at 1268–69.

Are the courts' assumptions accurate about how much time is needed for lawyers and clinicians to develop information relevant to commitment issues? Good clinical practice dictates that decisions about treatment be predicated on careful observation and a trial of treatment. Recall, however, that the average hospital stay, even for people with schizophrenia, is under 12 days.

3.   *Justice Brennan's* Parham *dissent.* In *Parham v. J.R. et al.,* 442 U.S. 584, 99 S.Ct. 2493, 61 L.Ed.2d 101 (1979), the Supreme Court deliberated upon the proper procedural protections for the commitment of juveniles. This decision, reprinted in Part V.E. of this chapter, has several possible implications for adult commitment procedures as well, all of which will be explored in this section. Of concern here is Justice Brennan's opinion in *Parham,* concurring in part and dissenting in part, because it suggests still other considerations in deciding whether and when to hold a formal legal hearing. The majority in *Parham* held that juveniles could be admitted initially to a mental institution based on the authority of their parents and the treating professionals, without benefit of legal counsel; it did not directly address whether the Constitution requires, at some later point in time, more formal procedures to determine whether continuing commitment is justified (although it suggested strongly that it did not). Brennan argued that procedures akin to those provided adults should be required before long-term detention. However, he also stated the following:

> . . . While as a general rule due process requires that commitment hearings precede involuntary hospitalization, when parents seek to hospitalize their children special considerations militate in favor of postponement of formal commitment proceedings and against mandatory adversarial preconfinement commitment hearings.

> First, the prospect of an adversarial hearing prior to admission might deter parents from seeking needed medical attention for their children. Second, the hearings themselves might delay treatment of children whose home life has become impossible and who require some form of immediate state care. Furthermore, because adversarial hearings at this juncture would necessarily involve direct challenges to parental authority, judgment or veracity, preadmission hearings may well result in pitting the child and his advocate against the parents. This, in turn, might traumatize both parent and child and make the child's eventual return to his family more difficult.

> Because of these special considerations I believe that States may legitimately postpone formal commitment proceedings when parents seek in-patient psychiatric treatment for their children. Such children may be admitted, for a limited period, without prior hearing, so long as the admitting psychiatrist first interviews parent and child and concludes that short term in-patient treatment would be appropriate.

442 U.S. at 632–633, 99 S.Ct. at 2519–2520. To what extent is this passage applicable to adult commitment?

4. *Pre-hearing screening.* Beginning in the 1980's, a number of states established, by statute, "screening" organizations at the community level that are charged with referring people with mental disability to the most effective treatment program available. National Center for State Courts, *Guidelines for Involuntary Civil Commitment*, 10 Men.Dis.Law Rep. 409, 429–433 (1986). A number of other jurisdictions have set up equivalent systems through local custom. Id. at 429.

In jurisdictions that have developed such programs, the number of people subjected to the involuntary commitment process—including the emergency detention hearing—may be reduced considerably. According to one report, in these localities, "the great majority of persons entering the mental health-judicial system never see the inside of a courthouse, and many persons are screened and diverted to more suitable alternatives, many elect to enter mental health treatment and care programs voluntarily, and some are discharged shortly after arrival at a mental health facility." Id. at 427. For instance, Arizona requires that screening agencies—usually the local community mental health center—complete a "pre-petition screening" within forty-eight hours of initial contact with an individual alleged to be disordered, designed to determine the best possible disposition. Ariz.Stat. § 36–529. Although "emergency" cases are specifically exempted from this procedure, it nonetheless appears to have enabled a significant number of individuals who would have been "emergency admissions" under the old system to avoid the involuntary commitment process altogether. A 1980s study of such a program in Tucson showed that about three times as many individuals are diverted through screening—to voluntary care, to halfway houses, and to other social agencies—than proceed through the involuntary petition process. Institute on Mental Disability and the Law, National Center for State Courts, "A Model for the Application of the Least Restrictive Alternative Doctrine in Involuntary Civil Commitment" 291–323 (1984).

Many commentators argue that such pre-hearing diversion is highly beneficial and should be encouraged. For instance, the National Task Force on Guidelines for Involuntary Civil Commitment asserted the following:

> Screening should begin as early as possible in the involuntary civil commitment process in order to avoid unnecessary infringement of liberty, to ensure that persons are guided quickly and effectively toward the placement and treatment indicated by their presenting problems, and to minimize needless waste of limited resources. Initial processing decisions are based not merely on whether the legal criteria for involuntary civil commitment are met. The threshold question may be whether the person who is considered a candidate for involuntary civil commitment is indeed mentally disordered. If so, are there alternative forms of treatment and care, other than involuntary civil commitment? Even if the person is not considered to be mentally disordered, he or she may require social services of some type. Is mandatory hospitalization

necessary? Will the person consider seeking mental health treatment voluntarily? Answers to these questions require intervention and decisions long before a candidate for involuntary civil commitment has a judicial hearing.

Such early intervention may entail no more than a mental health worker answering a telephone call from a distraught individual who is seeking help for a family member. Referral to a community mental health center or a family support group may divert a person who may otherwise become subject to formal involuntary civil commitment proceedings. These early interventions should be based on knowledge of the mental health services delivery in the area and should take into account such factors as the range of treatment and services available, the criteria for admission to various facilities, the security of particular mental health facilities, and the conditions within facilities. Good initial processing decisions also require an understanding of the linkages between the agencies.

Id. at 428.

As this excerpt suggests, in a sense the pre-hearing screening programs function as the procedural facet of the least restrictive alternative doctrine. One possible problem with such programs is that they encourage "voluntary" dispositions that are in fact not voluntary at all. This issue is addressed in detail in the materials on voluntary treatment, at pp. 967–978.

5. *Police use of excessive force.* As noted above, police are often involved in bringing people with mental illness to the attention of the mental health system. A number of lawsuits have been filed against the police for injuring such people in the course of taking them into custody. For instance, in *Drummond v. City of Anaheim*, 343 F.3d 1052 (9th Cir. 2003), cert. denied, 542 U.S. 918, 124 S.Ct. 2871, 159 L.Ed.2d 775 (2004), police responded to calls on two separate days that a man with a history of mental illness had run out of medication and was hallucinating and paranoid. On the first day they concluded he was not a danger to himself or others, but on the second day they decided to take him into custody "for his own safety." When he became agitated, they forced him on the ground, handcuffed him and then placed their knees on his back and neck, even though he told the officers he could not breathe. After 20 minutes he lost consciousness, sustained brain damage, and declined into a permanent vegetative state. In *Champion v. Dickhaus*, 380 F.3d 893 (6th Cir. 2004), cert. denied, 544 U.S. 975, 125 S.Ct. 1837, 161 L.Ed.2d 725 (2005), a 32 year-old man with autism brought to a store by his caregiver began to hit himself in the face and bite his hand. The police officer who responded to a 911 call was told he was mentally ill but was not told the man was nonverbal and nonresponsive. When the officer asked the man's name he began hitting and biting himself and approached the officer. When he grabbed her shirt, she sprayed pepper spray on his face. Two other newly arrived officers, both of whom were told the man was mentally ill, then wrestled him to the ground, applied handcuffs and a hobble device that bound his ankles together, then applied pressure to his back and

continued to use pepper spray. After several minutes on the ground, the man began to vomit, went into cardiac arrest, and subsequently died. In both cases claims of excessive force were upheld. Recent years have witnessed numerous cases in which families of mentally ill individuals have sued police agencies after their relatives died following use of Tasers.

Consider the following passages, taken from Int'l Ass. Chiefs of Police, Building Safer Communities: Improving Police Response to Persons with Mental Illness (2010):

> A number of studies . . . document that persons with mental illness are more likely than those without mental illness to come into contact with police as suspected offenders, most often for relatively minor offenses, and to be re-arrested more frequently. . . . CIT [Crisis Intervention Team] is a pre-booking jail diversion program intended to "improve the outcomes of police interactions with people with mental illnesses" by de-escalating crisis situations, decreasing the use of force by officers and increasing mental health consumers' access to community treatment options. . . . In jurisdictions that have implemented CIT, its central feature is a 40–hour training program for law enforcement officers that includes information on how to recognize the behavioral characteristics of persons with mental illness; local mental health system characteristics; and methods of de-escalating crisis situations. In most communities, some of the training is planned and delivered by mental health consumers and family members. . . . A number of law enforcement agencies around the country have not only implemented CIT but also have augmented that approach with mental health professionals hired as staff members to provide on-site and telephone consultations to officers in the field. In a few communities, mental health agencies have located some of their staff members in law enforcement facilities to provide these services. . . . A number of communities have designated specific mental health facilities as 24/7 "drop-off" sites that guarantee there will be space for people with mental illness transported there by law enforcement.

If a community does not develop a CIT-type program, should liability for law enforcement be automatic in situations like those described above? Cf. *City of Canton v. Harris*, 489 U.S. 378, 390k, 109 S.Ct. 1197, 103 L.Ed.2d 412 (1989) ("The need to train officers in the constitutional limitations on the use of deadly force . . . can be said to be 'so obvious,' that failure to do so could properly be characterized as 'deliberate indifference' to constitutional rights.").

C. ADJUDICATORY HEARING PROCEDURES

1. Standard of Proof

ADDINGTON V. TEXAS
Supreme Court of the United States, 1979.
441 U.S. 418, 99 S.Ct. 1804, 60 L.Ed.2d 323.

MR. CHIEF JUSTICE BURGER delivered the opinion of the Court.

The question in this case is what standard of proof is required by the Fourteenth Amendment to the Constitution in a civil proceeding brought under state law to commit an individual involuntarily for an indefinite period to a state mental hospital.

* * *

II

The function of a standard of proof, as that concept is embodied in the Due Process Clause and in the realm of factfinding, is to "instruct the factfinder concerning the degree of confidence our society thinks he should have in the correctness of factual conclusions for a particular type of adjudication." The standard serves to allocate the risk of error between the litigants and to indicate the relative importance attached to the ultimate decision.

Generally speaking, the evolution of this area of the law has produced across a continuum three standards or levels of proof for different types of cases. At one end of the spectrum is the typical civil case involving a monetary dispute between private parties. Since society has a minimal concern with the outcome of such private suits, plaintiff's burden of proof is a mere preponderance of the evidence. The litigants thus share the risk of error in roughly equal fashion.

In a criminal case, on the other hand, the interests of the defendant are of such magnitude that historically and without any explicit constitutional requirement they have been protected by standards of proof designed to exclude as nearly as possible the likelihood of an erroneous judgment. In the administration of criminal justice, our society imposes almost the entire risk of error upon itself. This is accomplished by requiring under the Due Process Clause that the state prove the guilt of an accused beyond a reasonable doubt.

The intermediate standard, which usually employs some combination of the words "clear," "cogent," "unequivocal," and "convincing," is less commonly used, but nonetheless "is no stranger to the civil law." One typical use of the standard is in civil cases involving allegations of fraud or some other quasi-criminal wrongdoing by the defendant. The interests at stake in those cases are deemed to be more substantial than mere loss of money and some jurisdictions accordingly reduce the risk to the defendant of having his reputation tarnished erroneously by increasing the plaintiff's burden of proof. Similarly, this Court has used the "clear, unequivocal and convincing" standard of proof to protect particularly important individual interests in various civil cases [*i.e., deportation and denaturalization*].

Candor suggests that, to a degree, efforts to analyze what lay jurors understand concerning the differences among these three tests on the nuances of a judge's instructions on the law may well be largely an academic exercise; there are no directly relevant empirical studies. Indeed, the ultimate truth as to how the standards of proof affect decisionmaking may well be unknowable, given that factfinding is a process shared by countless thousands of individuals throughout the country. We probably can assume no more than that the difference between a preponderance of the evidence and proof beyond a reasonable doubt probably is better understood than either of them in relation to the intermediate standard of clear and convincing evidence. Nonetheless, even if the particular standard-of-proof catchwords do not always make a great difference in a particular case, adopting a "standard of proof is more than an empty semantic exercise."

III

In considering what standard should govern in a civil commitment proceeding, we must assess both the extent of the individual's interest in not being involuntarily confined indefinitely and the state's interest in committing the emotionally disturbed under a particular standard of proof. Moreover, we must be mindful that the function of legal process is to minimize the risk of erroneous decisions.

A

This Court repeatedly has recognized that civil commitment for any purpose constitutes a significant deprivation of liberty that requires due process protection. Moreover, it is indisputable that involuntary commitment to a mental hospital after a finding of probable dangerousness to self or others can engender adverse social consequences to the individual. Whether we label this phenomena "stigma" or choose to call it something else is less important than that we recognize that it can occur and that it can have a very significant impact on the individual.

The state has a legitimate interest under its *parens patriae* powers in providing care to its citizens who are unable because of emotional disorders to care for themselves; the state also has authority under its police power to protect the community from the dangerous tendencies of some who are mentally ill. Under the Texas Mental Health Code, however, the State has no interest in confining individuals involuntarily if they are not mentally ill or if they do not pose some danger to themselves or others. Since the preponderance standard creates the risk of increasing the number of individuals erroneously committed, it is at least unclear to what extent, if any, the state's interests are furthered by using a preponderance standard in such commitment proceedings.

The expanding concern of society with problems of mental disorders is reflected in the fact that in recent years many states have enacted statutes designed to protect the rights of the mentally ill. However, only one state by statute permits involuntary commitment by a mere preponderance of the evidence, Miss.Code Ann. § 41–21–75 (1978 Supp.), and Texas is the only state where a court has concluded that the preponderance-of-the-evidence standard satisfies due process. We attribute this not to any lack of concern in those states, but rather to a belief that the varying standards tend to produce comparable results. As we noted earlier, however, standards of proof are important for their symbolic meaning as well as for their practical effect.

At one time or another every person exhibits some abnormal behavior which might be perceived by some as symptomatic of a mental or emotional disorder, but which is in fact within a range of conduct that is generally acceptable. Obviously, such behavior is no basis for compelled treatment and surely none for confinement. However, there is the possible risk that a factfinder might decide to commit an individual based solely on a few isolated instances of unusual conduct. Loss of liberty calls for a showing that the individual suffers from something more serious than is demonstrated by idiosyncratic behavior. Increasing the burden of proof is one way to impress the factfinder with the importance of the decision and thereby perhaps to reduce the chances that inappropriate commitments will be ordered.

The individual should not be asked to share equally with society the risk of error when the possible injury to the individual is significantly greater than any possible harm to the state. We conclude that the individual's interest in the outcome of a civil commitment proceeding is of such weight and gravity that due process requires the state to justify confinement by proof more substantial than a mere preponderance of the evidence.

B

Appellant urges the Court to hold that due process requires use of the criminal law's standard of proof—"beyond a reasonable doubt."

* * *

There are significant reasons why different standards of proof are called for in civil commitment proceedings as opposed to criminal prosecutions. In a civil commitment state power is not exercised in a punitive sense. Unlike the delinquency proceeding in *Winship,* a civil

Policy

commitment proceeding can in no sense be equated to a criminal prosecution.

In addition, the "beyond a reasonable doubt" standard historically has been reserved for criminal cases. This unique standard of proof, not prescribed or defined in the Constitution, is regarded as a critical part of the "moral force of the criminal law," and we should hesitate to apply it too broadly or casually in noncriminal cases.

The heavy standard applied in criminal cases manifests our concern that the risk of error to the individual must be minimized even at the risk that some who are guilty might go free. The full force of that idea does not apply to a civil commitment. It may be true that an erroneous commitment is sometimes as undesirable as an erroneous conviction * * *. However, even though an erroneous confinement should be avoided in the first instance, the layers of professional review and observation of the patient's condition, and the concern of family and friends generally will provide continuous opportunities for an erroneous commitment to be corrected. Moreover, it is not true that the release of a genuinely mentally ill person is no worse for the individual than the failure to convict the guilty. One who is suffering from a debilitating mental illness and in need of treatment is neither wholly at liberty nor free of stigma. It cannot be said, therefore, that it is much better for a mentally ill person to "go free" than for a mentally normal person to be committed.

Finally, the initial inquiry in a civil commitment proceeding is very different from the central issue in either a delinquency proceeding or a criminal prosecution. In the latter cases the basic issue is a straightforward factual question—did the accused commit the act alleged? There may be factual issues to resolve in a commitment proceeding, but the factual aspects represent only the beginning of the inquiry. Whether the individual is mentally ill and dangerous to either himself or others and is in need of confined therapy turns on the *meaning* of the facts which must be interpreted by expert psychiatrists and psychologists. Given the lack of certainty and the fallibility of psychiatric diagnosis, there is a serious question as to whether a state could ever prove beyond a reasonable doubt that an individual is both mentally ill and likely to be dangerous.

The subtleties and nuances of psychiatric diagnosis render certainties virtually beyond reach in most situations. The reasonable-doubt standard of criminal law functions in its realm because there the standard is addressed to specific, knowable facts. Psychiatric diagnosis, in contrast, is to a large extent based on medical "impressions" drawn from subjective analysis and filtered through the experience of the diagnostician. This process often makes it very difficult for the expert physician to offer definite conclusions about any particular patient. Within the medical discipline, the traditional standard for "factfinding" is a "reasonable medical certainty." If a trained psychiatrist has difficulty with the categorical "beyond a reasonable doubt" standard, the untrained lay juror—or indeed even a trained judge—who is required to rely upon expert opinion could be forced by the criminal law standard of proof to reject commitment for many patients desperately in need of institutionalized psychiatric care. Such "freedom" for a mentally ill person would be purchased at a high price.

* * *

That some states have chosen—either legislatively or judicially—to adopt the criminal law standard gives no assurance that the more stringent standard of proof is needed or is even adaptable to the needs of all states. The essence of federalism is that states must be free to develop a variety of solutions to problems and not be forced into a common, uniform mold. As the substantive standards for civil commitment may vary from state to state, procedures must be allowed to vary so long as they meet the constitutional minimum. We conclude that it is unnecessary to require states to apply the strict, criminal standard.

C

Having concluded that the preponderance standard falls short of meeting the demands of due process and that the reasonable-doubt standard is not required, we turn to a middle level of burden of proof that strikes a fair balance between the rights of the individual and the legitimate concerns of the state. We note that 20 states, most by statute, employ the standard of "clear and convincing" evidence; 3 states use "clear, *cogent,* and convincing" evidence; and 2 states require "clear, *unequivocal* and convincing" evidence.

We have concluded that the reasonable-doubt standard is inappropriate in civil commitment proceedings because, given the uncertainties of psychiatric diagnosis, it may impose a burden the state cannot meet and thereby erect an unreasonable barrier to needed medical treatment. Similarly, we conclude that use of the term "unequivocal" is not constitutionally required, although the states are free to use that standard. To meet due process demands, the standard has to inform the factfinder that the proof must be greater than the preponderance-of-the-evidence standard applicable to other categories of civil cases. * * *

Vacated and remanded.

MR. JUSTICE POWELL took no part in the consideration or decision of this case.

QUESTIONS AND COMMENTS

1. *Implications of* Addington. The selection of the proper standard of proof is really a "substantive" issue, not a "procedural" one. See John Jeffries

& Paul Stephan, *Defenses, Presumptions, and Burden of Proof in the Criminal Law*, 88 Yale L.J. 1325 (1979). In civil commitment, as previous sections made clear, whether someone is committed should depend upon whether the state can establish by a given *probability,* designated by the standard of proof, that he or she will commit a harmful act or that he or she is gravely disabled.[n] But *Addington* is usefully considered in a discussion of procedural issues as well because of the insight it gives into the Court's general perception of the competing interests involved in civil commitment. In this regard, several aspects of the Court's justification for adopting the clear and convincing standard rather than the reasonable doubt standard are worth noting: (1) the Court's insistence that the decisions made at a civil commitment hearing are primarily "medical" in nature; (2) its implicit conclusion that civil commitment is unlike juvenile delinquency proceedings, as evidenced by its refusal to follow *Winship,* the decision that imposed the reasonable doubt standard in such proceedings; and (3) its statement that "[i]t cannot be said . . . that it is much better for a mentally ill person to 'go free' than for a mentally normal person to be committed." Do you agree with these perceptions?

2.   *The basis of intervention.* Should the Court have considered whether the standard of proof should vary depending upon whether the basis for intervention is the police power or the *parens patriae* authority?

2.   The Decisionmaker

In criminal proceedings, the accused is guaranteed a right to a jury trial by the Sixth Amendment. This right may be waived, in which case the trial is presided over by a judge. At the adjudicatory hearing stage of civil commitment, at least four different types of ultimate decisionmakers have been authorized by state statutes: (1) a judicial officer (very often a "special judge" or a probate judge); (2) a jury (usually six strong); (3) an administrative board that does not include a judicial officer; and (4) a psychiatric board. Today almost every state relies upon a legally trained judicial officer to make the long-term commitment decision. However, several provide the respondent with the right to jury trial, if a jury is requested. A small number permit commitment based on the decision of an administrative board. See, e.g., Neb.Rev.Stat. § 71–915 (establishing a "mental health board" consisting of a lawyer, a mental health professional and a third person who is either a mental health professional or a layperson). None currently authorize the fourth option, although it was the dominant method of decisionmaking prior to 1970. The closest any state comes to a psychiatric board is New York, which permits involuntary hospitalization based on the authority of three mental health

---

[n] It should be remembered that the standard of proof may interact with the statutory definition of the criteria to produce a lower burden of proof overall. Thus, if the state defines "danger to others" as a likelihood that a person will harm others, and this likelihood is to be proven by clear and convincing evidence, the state can argue it need only show something like a 38% chance of harm to others. See discussion on pp. 848–849.

professionals for up to 60 days, after which time a judicial hearing must take place. N.Y.Code §§ 9.31, 9.33.

QUESTIONS AND COMMENTS

1. *Jury trial.* As noted earlier, the United States Supreme Court held in *McKeiver v. Pennsylvania,* 403 U.S. 528, 91 S.Ct. 1976, 29 L.Ed.2d 647 (1971), that there is no right to jury trial in juvenile delinquency proceedings, citing in particular the need to maintain the "intimacy" of the proceeding and to avoid the "clamor" of the adversary process. Most courts have relied on *McKeiver* in deciding that the right is not required at commitment proceedings either. See, e.g., *Lynch v. Baxley,* 386 F.Supp. 378 (M.D.Ala.1974); *Markey v. Wachtel,* 164 W.Va. 45, 264 S.E.2d 437 (1979). In the latter case the court stated:

> The heart of the adversarial issue is the mental condition of the individual which, as *Addington* recognizes, is a technically complex question based on the testimony of experts which a lay jury has difficulty understanding. We are unwilling to hold as a constitutional principle that the resolution of this issue can only be accomplished by a jury. Neither historical precedent nor the requisite due process procedural balance mandates such a conclusion.

Id. at 443.

Duncan v. Louisiana, 391 U.S. 145, 88 S.Ct. 1444, 20 L.Ed.2d 491 (1968), is the Supreme Court decision which held that the right to jury trial is a fundamental right guaranteed to state criminal defendants through the fourteenth amendment. *Duncan* stressed that the jury trial tradition resulted from "a reluctance to entrust plenary powers over the life and liberty of the citizen to one judge or a group of judges" and that the jury "in serious criminal cases is a defense against arbitrary law enforcement." *Duncan* also pointed to the role of the jury as a means of providing decisionmaking by representatives of the community and promoting a sense of citizen participation. The Court rejected the argument that juries cannot be trusted to reach accurate conclusions. It stated that if juries occasionally reach a different decision than a judge in a particular case, "it is usually because they are serving some of the very purposes for which they were created and for which they are now employed."

Are these same points as valid when applied to civil commitment? To what extent does the jury's traditional role as a group of "peers" affect its usefulness in civil commitment? To what extent, independent of its "accuracy" as a decisionmaker, would the presence of a jury as the decisionmaker affect the "image" of civil commitment? How would it affect the mental state of the respondent? How might empirical research comparing the civil commitment decisionmaking of jurors and judges be helpful to you in answering these questions? What kinds of questions would you like social scientists to answer? Note that the Supreme Court later limited the jury trial right in criminal proceedings to those cases involving a crime carrying a sentence of more than six months, on the ground that the "disadvantages, onerous though they may be," of imprisonment for six months or less are "outweighed by the benefits that result from speedy and inexpensive nonjury adjudication." Baldwin v. New York, 399 U.S. 66, 90 S.Ct. 1886, 26 L.Ed.2d 437 (1970). Consider also these comments from C. Peter Erlinder, *Of Rights Lost and Rights Found: The Coming Restoration of the Right to a Jury Trial in Minnesota Civil Commitment Proceedings*, 29 Wm. Mitchell L. Rev. 1269, 1284 (2003):

> Jury trials in both the criminal and civil context usually require commitment of greater resources for all parties than those generally associated with bench trials. The decision to seek indefinite commitment will be far more costly and complicated for all parties concerned. In addition, the impaneling of a jury adds an element of unpredictability into the decision-making process that gives defense counsel a means to encourage opposing counsel to resolve contested matters to avoid an unexpected jury verdict. Perhaps most importantly, all parties will likely benefit from a more careful preparation and presentation of the evidence and judicial rulings in the conduct of the proceedings and opportunities to exercise unreviewable discretion will be reduced.

2. *Administrative boards.* In *Doremus v. Farrell*, 407 F.Supp. 509, 516 (D.Neb.1975), a federal district court held that the Nebraska administrative board (at that time composed of a lawyer, a psychiatrist and the clerk of the court) did not violate the constitution:

> Although a judicial determination would be desirable, since courts can more effectively preserve procedural due process and constitutional rights, as well as rule more proficiently on evidentiary questions, we do not believe that due process or equal protection mandates a judicial hearing. The Supreme Court has recognized the power of administrative boards to revoke parole and probation. *Gagnon v. Scarpelli*, 411 U.S. 778, 93 S.Ct. 1756, 36 L.Ed.2d 656 (1973); *Morrissey v. Brewer*, 408 U.S. 471, 92 S.Ct. 2593, 33 L.Ed.2d 484 (1972). The deportation of aliens has long been considered a proper function for executive commissions. The procedural safeguards guaranteed by due process, the standards for commitment and the availability of prompt de novo review by the district court after the finding of mental illness by the county board, convinces the Court that an administrative determination is not constitutionally objectionable.

Whether the court would have arrived at the same conclusion had there been no provision for de novo review by a court is unclear. The court also found that using the board did violate the constitution if—as was apparently quite frequently the case in Nebraska—the psychiatrist who examined the respondent for purposes of the commitment proceeding also sat on the board. The court stated that "combin[ing] the investigative, prosecutorial and adjudicative functions in one authority . . . denies the subject due process of law." Id. at 516.

While the Supreme Court has not directly addressed the decisionmaker issue, at least two of its opinions are relevant. The first is *Vitek v. Jones,* 445 U.S. 480, 100 S.Ct. 1254, 63 L.Ed.2d 552 (1980), in which the Court considered the proper procedures for transferring prisoners alleged to need psychiatric care from correctional facilities to psychiatric facilities. Despite the fact that such prisoners are already confined at the time of transfer, the Court found that some process is due prior to such transfers because they occasion "adverse social consequences," including the stigma of being labelled mentally ill, and may involve exposure to mandatory behavior modification. But the Court was unwilling to require that a judicial officer preside over such hearings; rather it mandated only that an "independent decisionmaker" fulfill this role. Moreover, the independent decisionmaker need not come from outside the prison or hospital administration; to hold otherwise would cause "unnecessary intrusion into either medical or correctional judgments."

The second relevant Supreme Court decision is *Parham v. J.R.,* 442 U.S. 584, 99 S.Ct. 2493, 61 L.Ed.2d 101 (1979), in which the Court held that the decision to admit a child to a mental facility may be made by a mental health professional, even, apparently, if that professional is the evaluating clinician. In justifying this decision, the Court stated:

> Due process has never been thought to require that the neutral and detached trier of fact be law-trained or a judicial or administrative officer. Surely, this is the case as to medical decisions for "neither judges nor administrative hearing officers are better qualified than psychiatrists to render psychiatric judgments." Thus, a staff physician will suffice, so long as he or she is free to evaluate independently the child's mental and emotional condition and need for treatment.

* * *

> What process is constitutionally due cannot be divorced from the nature of the ultimate decision that is being made. . . . Here, the questions are essentially medical in character: whether the child is mentally or emotionally ill and whether he can benefit from the treatment that is provided by the state. While facts are plainly necessary for a proper resolution of those questions, they are only a first step in the process. In an opinion for a unanimous Court, we recently stated in *Addington v. Texas* that the determination of 'whether [a person] is mentally ill turns on the *meaning* of the facts which must be interpreted by expert psychiatrists and psychologists.'

> Although we acknowledge the fallibility of medical and psychiatric diagnosis, we do not accept the notion that the shortcomings of specialists can always be avoided by shifting the decision from a trained specialist using the traditional tools of medical science to an untrained judge or administrative hearing officer after a judicial-type hearing. Even after a hearing, the nonspecialist decisionmaker must make a medical-psychiatric decision. Common human experience and scholarly opinions suggest that the supposed protections of an adversary

proceeding to determine the appropriateness of medical decisions for the commitment and treatment of mental and emotional illness may well be more illusory than real. [Here the Court cited studies showing the informality of supposedly "legalized" proceedings].

Id. at 606–09, 99 S.Ct. at 2506–07. The primary state interests the Court identified in support of this decision were "a significant interest in not imposing unnecessary procedural obstacles that may discourage the mentally ill or their families from seeking needed psychiatric assistance" and a "genuine interest in allocating priority to the diagnosis and treatment of patients as soon as they are admitted to a hospital rather than to time-consuming procedural minuets before the admission." Id. at 605, 99 S.Ct. at 2505. Although, as noted earlier, the Court's decision focused on the process for reviewing the initial admission decision rather than on periodic review procedures, it also stated, in dictum, that the "child's continuing need for commitment" need only be reviewed "by a similarly independent procedure." Id. at 607, 99 S.Ct. at 2506.

Do you think the Court would uphold Nebraska's administrative board as a decisionmaking body for civil commitment of adults? A psychiatric board? Should it? With respect to the last question, consider the following excerpt from David Bazelon, *Institutionalization, Deinstitutionalization and the Adversary Process*, 75 Colum.L.Rev. 897, 910–911 (1975).

There is a central but limited role for courts in [the system for involuntarily hospitalizing disturbed or disturbing individuals]—that role is to guide professional decisionmaking, and may be best described by the familiar model of judicial review of administrative decisionmaking. Courts must determine whether there has been a full exploration of all relevant facts, opposing views and possible alternatives, whether the results of the exploration relate rationally to the ultimate decision, and whether constitutional and statutory procedural safeguards have been faithfully observed. Our function is thus not to determine whether the decisions taken by those charged with handling disturbed or disturbing individuals are correct or wise—but whether they are rational in the manner I have just described.

There are some who still say that we should leave these delicate questions of state intervention to the behavioral experts. But I would remind those who suggest this—both outside and within the legal profession—that state intervention involves a serious compromise of individual rights and hence a difficult balancing of power between the state and the individual, where the stakes are highest for human and personal rights. Courts have traditionally been the protector of individual rights against state power, and there is no reason why the particularly difficult problems in the area of state intervention are any different. We cannot delegate this responsibility to the medical professions. Those disciplines are, naturally enough, oriented toward helping people by treating them. Their value system assumes that disturbed and disturbing individuals need treatment, that medical disciplines can provide it, and that attempts to resist it are misguided or delusionary. The medical disciplines can no more judge the legitimacy of state intervention into the lives of disturbed or disturbing individuals than a prosecutor can judge the guilt of a person he has accused.

Finally, it is interesting to note that some research indicates that judges usually defer to the experts and may even be more likely than psychiatrists to believe that commitment is required. Christyne E. Ferris, *The Search for Due Process in Civil Commitment Hearings: How Procedural Realities Have Altered Substantive Standards*, 61 Vand. L.Rev. 959, 971–2 (2008) (citing studies that describe "Realities in the Courtroom"); Robert Simon & William Cockerham, *Civil Commitment, Burden of Proof, and Dangerous Acts: A Comparison of the Perspectives of Judges and Psychiatrists*, 5 J. Psychiat. & L. 571, 590 (1977).

3. The Adversary Process: Notice, Public Trial and Confrontation Rights

The notion of an "adversary process" is relatively easy to visualize: the relevant parties confront each other with their version of the facts, after which an impartial decisionmaker decides who wins. The specific means by which this process is implemented in criminal trials in the United States derive primarily from the Sixth Amendment, which states in pertinent part:

> In all criminal prosecutions, the accused shall enjoy the right to a . . . public trial . . . and to be informed of the nature and cause of the accusation; to be confronted with the witnesses against him; to have compulsory process for obtaining witnesses in his favor, and to have the Assistance of Counsel for his defence.

The right to notice of one's charges is essential as a means of initiating the adversary process. As Justice Frankfurter stated in *Joint Anti–Fascist Refugee Committee v. McGrath,* 341 U.S. 123, 171–72, 71 S.Ct. 624, 648–49, 95 L.Ed. 817 (1951), "No better instrument has been devised for arriving at truth than to give a person in jeopardy of serious loss notice of the case against him and opportunity to meet it." Notice is considered so important that, as a matter of due process, it has been required prior to virtually all proceedings in which the government is a party, not just prior to the "criminal prosecutions" to which the Sixth Amendment refers. See, e.g., *Vitek v. Jones,* 445 U.S. 480, 100 S.Ct. 1254, 63 L.Ed.2d 552 (1980); *In re Gault,* 387 U.S. 1, 87 S.Ct. 1428, 18 L.Ed.2d 527 (1967).

Although perhaps not theoretically necessary to a well-functioning adversary process, ensuring that the public can observe that process at work has always been considered a second important attribute of the system. The Sixth Amendment's public trial provision was meant to deter the government from engaging in "Star Chamber" proceedings that ignore or merely mimic procedural formality; it thus encourages proceedings that are truly adversarial. In *In re Oliver,* 333 U.S. 257, 68 S.Ct. 499, 92 L.Ed. 682 (1948), the Supreme Court stated that the right "has always been recognized as a safeguard against any attempt to employ our courts as instruments of persecution. The knowledge that every criminal trial is subject to contemporaneous review in the forum of public opinion is an effective restraint on possible abuse of judicial power." Id. at 270. The Court explained further that "the presence of interested spectators may keep [the accused's] triers keenly alive to a sense of their responsibility and to the importance of their functions." Id. at 270 n. 25.

The third and most obviously "adversarial" attribute of the adversary process is the right to confront one's accusers and the associated right to subpoena witnesses to rebut one's accusers (the right to "compulsory process"). For reasons that should be apparent, the right to confrontation incorporates the right to be present at trial and the right to cross-examine one's accusers. The Supreme Court has termed the right to be present "one of the most basic of the rights guaranteed by the Confrontation Clause . . ." *Illinois v. Allen,* 397 U.S. 337, 90 S.Ct. 1057, 25 L.Ed.2d 353 (1970). And in *Pointer v. Texas,* 380 U.S. 400, 85 S.Ct. 1065, 13 L.Ed.2d 923 (1965), the decision that applied the confrontation clause to the states, the Court stated "probably no one, certainly no one with experience in the trial of lawsuits, would deny the value of cross-examination in exposing falsehood and bringing out the truth in the trial of a criminal case."

The following notes discuss application of these rights to civil commitment. Discussion of the right to counsel, probably the most important method of ensuring a truly adversary process, is deferred until the next subsection.

QUESTIONS AND COMMENTS

1. *Notice.* The most fundamental issue connected with the right to notice in civil commitment is whether the state can forego such notice to protect the putative patient or a third party (such as the person who brought the petition). This topic is closely connected with the right to be present, discussed below. For now, it should be noted that some states provide for special methods of giving notice to individuals who are allegedly mentally disabled. For instance, Vermont's statute states: "If the court has reason to believe that notice to the proposed patient will be likely to cause injury to the proposed patient or others, it shall direct the proposed patient's counsel to give the proposed patient oral notice prior to written notice under circumstances most likely to reduce likelihood of injury." Vt.Stat.Ann. tit. 18, § 7613(c).

A second issue raised by the cases has to do with the type of information that must be included in the notice. The Supreme Court has held that constitutional requirements are satisfied if the notice "is reasonably calculated to inform the person to whom it is directed of the nature of the proceeding." *Mullane v. Central Hanover Bank & Trust Co.,* 339 U.S. 306, 70 S.Ct. 652, 94 L.Ed. 865 (1950). In *Doremus v. Farrell,* 407 F.Supp. 509 (D.Neb.1975), the court explained that this rule, when applied to civil commitment, meant the following:

> The notice prior to the preliminary inquiry for the emergency detention must inform the person of the nature of grounds, reasons and necessity for the emergency detention, in addition to notice of the time and location of the hearing. The notice should also inform the subject of his right to counsel. The notice prior to the formal hearing must include, in addition to notice of the time and location of the hearing, notice to the individual of the reasons for his detention, the standards for commitment, and the petition itself . . .

In *French v. Blackburn,* 428 F.Supp. 1351 (M.D.N.C.1977), affirmed 443 U.S. 901, 99 S.Ct. 3091, 61 L.Ed.2d 869 (1979), however, the court held that notice need not include the reasons for detention, the standards for commitment, nor the petition itself. The court found that the statute before it, which provided for notice of the purpose of the hearing, the right to counsel, the right to present evidence, and the possible consequences of the hearing, was sufficient. It further stated:

> At first blush it would appear that it might be better to serve the respondent with a copy of the petition or affidavit forming the basis of his custody. This would parallel the service of a copy of the complaint in a traditional civil action and a copy of the indictment or information in a criminal proceeding. However, . . . [a]s was the case here, the petitions may have been filed by members of the respondent's family and service of such might possibly cause more harm to such a respondent than nonservice.

Id. at 1357 n. 10.

A third issue associated with notice is when it should be given. The general rule is that it be given "sufficiently in advance of the proceeding to afford one a reasonable opportunity to prepare." *In re Gault,* 387 U.S. 1, 33, 87 S.Ct. 1428, 1446, 18 L.Ed.2d 527 (1967). In *Blackburn,* the court held that 48 hour notice is sufficient. 428 F.Supp. at 1357. In many states, given the time between initial admission and the detention hearing, this approximates the maximum time available (though under the statute at issue in *Blackburn* the hearing did not take place until ten days after admission). Of course, if a detention hearing is held, notice of the adjudicatory hearing can be, and often is, given at that time.

A final issue that may arise is whether notice should be given to anyone other than the respondent and the attorney. Many states also provide for notice to the parents, guardian, spouse or next-of-kin of the patient. See, e.g., Tenn.Code § 33–3–605. Do these latter parties have a *right* to notice?

2.   *Public trial.* Commitment hearings are likely to canvass very intimate, personal information. Thus, even assuming that respondents have

a right to a public hearing, they may often want to waive the right. The state may also want to exclude the public, to protect "confidential" information and to expedite the process. Most state statutes that address the issue express a preference for private proceedings. Some simply close all hearings to the public, permitting only those who have "a legitimate interest in the hearing" to attend. N.D. Stat. § 25–03.1–19; Iowa Code § 229.12(2). Ohio is representative of many states in keeping the hearing closed unless the patient and counsel request it to be open. § 5122.15–(a)(5). Finally, a number of states leave the question to the court's discretion. See, e.g., Kansas Stat. § 59–2959 ("all persons not necessary for the conduct of the proceedings may be excluded").

If the general public or the press want to witness a particular proceeding, should the respondent be able to keep it closed? May the *state*, by statute, keep the public from attending commitment proceedings? These issues have seldom been raised, probably because most commitment hearings are of little interest to the public and are not widely publicized.

However, there has been considerable litigation over analogous issues in the criminal and juvenile delinquency contexts. While the Supreme Court has made it clear that a criminal defendant can waive his Sixth Amendment right to a public proceeding, *Gannett Co., Inc. v. DePasquale,* 443 U.S. 368, 99 S.Ct. 2898, 61 L.Ed.2d 608 (1979), it has also vigorously upheld, even over the defendant's objection, the *public's* right of access to trial, based on the First Amendment. In *Richmond Newspapers, Inc. v. Virginia,* 448 U.S. 555, 100 S.Ct. 2814, 65 L.Ed.2d 973 (1980), the Court held that the right of the public and the press to attend criminal trials, which it called "implicit in the guarantees of the First Amendment" rights to free speech and press, would normally outweigh any interest the defendant might have in closing the trial. Only if making the trial public creates problems "beyond the realm of the manageable"—by which the Court seemed to mean problems having to do with maintaining court decorum—can the trial be closed. Id. at 581. See also *Press–Enterprise Co. v. Superior Court,* 478 U.S. 1, 106 S.Ct. 2735, 92 L.Ed.2d 1 (1986).

In contrast, at least until the 1990s the clear tendency in the juvenile delinquency context was to allow closure. See Patrick McNulty, *First Amendment Versus Sixth Amendment: A Constitutional Battle in the Juvenile Courts,* 10 N.M.L.Rev. 311 (1980). In *In re J.S.,* 140 Vt. 458, 438 A.2d 1125 (1981), the Vermont Supreme Court held that *Richmond Newspapers* does not apply to juvenile proceedings. In the course of its opinion, it quoted from Justice Rehnquist's opinion in *Smith v. Daily Mail Publishing Co.,* 443 U.S. 97, 107, 99 S.Ct. 2667, 2673, 61 L.Ed.2d 399 (1979):

> It is a hallmark of our juvenile justice system in the United States that virtually from its inception at the end of the last century its proceedings have been conducted outside of the public's full gaze and the youths brought before our juvenile courts have been shielded from publicity. This insistence on confidentiality is born of a tender concern for the welfare of the child, to hide his youthful errors and "bury them in the

graveyard of the forgotten past." The prohibition of publication of a juvenile's name is designed to protect the young person from the stigma of his misconduct and is rooted in the principle that a court concerned with juvenile affairs serves as a rehabilitative and protective agency of the State.

In the 1990s, as juvenile courts became more punitive and the push for public accountability became more intense, many states reversed course. Kristin Henning, *Eroding Confidentiality in Delinquency Proceedings: Should Schools and Public Housing Authorities Be Notified*, 79 N.Y.U. L. Rev. 520, 536–37 (2004) "(As the rehabilitative philosophy of juvenile court falls away, confidentiality loses its place. While almost every state still has some statutory provision for the confidentiality of juvenile hearings and records, the majority of states now grant multiple exceptions to the general rule."). Even before this movement, courts were willing to open juvenile proceedings upon the motion of the juvenile. In *RLR v. State,* 487 P.2d 27 (Alaska 1971), for instance, the court stated:

> Delinquency proceedings as much as adult criminal prosecutions can be used as instruments of persecution, and may be subject to judicial abuse. The appellate process is not a sufficient check on juvenile courts, for problems of mootness and the cost of prosecuting an appeal screen most of what goes on from appellate court scrutiny. We cannot help but notice that children's cases appealed to this court have often shown much more extensive and fundamental error than is generally found in adult criminal cases, and wonder whether secrecy is not fostering a judicial attitude of casualness toward the law in children's proceedings. . . . Therefore, we hold that children are guaranteed the right to a public trial by the Alaska Constitution.

> . . . It is an abuse of discretion for the court to refuse admittance to individuals whose presence is favored by the child, except in special circumstances such as the unavailability of a courtroom sufficiently large to hold all the individuals whose presence is sought. If a child or his guardian ad litem wants the press, friends, or others to be free to attend, then the hearing must be open to them. The area of discretion in the rule, where the court may refuse to open the hearing, involves persons whose presence is not desired by the child.

Courts have reached widely disparate results on the public access issue in the civil commitment context. Compare *Matter of Belk*, 107 N.C.App. 448, 420 S.E.2d 682 (1992) (rejecting a First Amendment challenge to state statute closing commitment hearings, on the ground that such a holding was necessary to afford respondents "a measure of dignity") with *Kirk v. Comm.*, 459 Mass. 67, 944 N.E.2d 235 (2011) (rejecting the *respondent's* motion for a closed hearing on the ground that "[p]ublic access to the commitment proceedings underscores the seriousness of a potential deprivation of liberty and combats tendencies toward informality that may threaten an individual's due process rights"; the court also found unpersuasive the respondent's vague claim that an open hearing would have a "devastating impact" on the her treatment). Might civil commitment respondents *benefit* from public exposure of their hearings? See Mia Fontaine, *Learning from Britney's Troubles*, New York Times (Feb. 10, 2008) (arguing that "the paparazzi" may have helped Ms. Spears because "they provided ample documentation to support the doctors' decision to" extend her involuntary hospitalization).

3.   *Presence of respondent.* The right to be present at one's criminal trial can be abridged if the defendant is so disruptive that an orderly proceeding cannot take place. *Illinois v. Allen,* 397 U.S. 337, 90 S.Ct. 1057, 25 L.Ed.2d 353 (1970). The right may also be waived, if the waiver is "knowing and intelligent." *Tacon v. Arizona,* 410 U.S. 351, 93 S.Ct. 998, 35 L.Ed.2d 346 (1973). Otherwise, the criminal accused's right to be present at trial is sacrosanct. In contrast, a large number of state commitment statutes permit the court to exclude the respondent if, in the court's opinion, presence would be harmful to the respondent. See, e.g., Alas.Stat. § 47.30.735(b)(1) (permitting exclusion if the respondent lacks capacity to decide about presence and there is a "substantial likelihood" that presence would be "seriously injurious" to the person's mental health).

In *Stamus v. Leonhardt,* 414 F.Supp. 439 (S.D.Iowa 1976), the court found such a provision in the Iowa commitment statute unconstitutional.

> Section 229.4 of the Code accorded the subject the right to be present at hearings unless the hospitalization commission found that the subject's presence would "probably be injurious" to the subject "or attended with no advantage." Pursuant to this provision, Dorothy Stamus was taken before the hospitalization commission during her hearing and questioned. However, as was the general practice in Polk County, she was excluded from the hearing room preceding and after the questioning period. This restriction on the plaintiff's right to be present was an unconstitutional deprivation of her right to due process.

* * *

> . . . The same purposes for requiring the person's presence exist in both the civil and criminal context: to allow the individual to assure that his or her interests are being protected and to give the fact-finder an opportunity to speak with the person and observe his or her demeanor. The results of the hearings, confinement in an institution and a loss of personal liberty, are often the same in the civil commitment and criminal context. Thus, there must be a right for the individual under discussion to be present at all proceedings for civil commitment. . . .

What is the impact of an adversary hearing on the typical person alleged to be mentally disabled? Recall the assertion by Ensminger and Liguori in the introduction to this section that confronting one's family and the treating professionals can often be "therapeutic." Consider also, however, the following passage:

> The patient who has his "day in court" may be subjected to anguish, humiliation, suspicion, alienation from family, self-depreciation, and

anxiety. Consider patient A, a paranoid person who thinks people are against him; patient B, a manic who has all kinds of funny, grandiose ideas; patient C, a depressed person who feels nobody loves him or wants him. Suppose each of these patients were to insist on his day in court. Patient A would hear neighbors say why he ought to be hospitalized. What would that do to his paranoid ideas? Patient B would provide an uproariously good time for spectators as he made a clown of himself. What would that do to his loved ones? Patient C would hear his nearest and dearest swear that he ought to be hospitalized. What would this do to his self-evaluation?

Henry Davidson, *Mental Hospitals and the Civil Liberties Dilemma*, 51 Mental Hygiene 371, 374 (1967). Finally, compare this passage to the more recent, research-based findings from the MacArthur studies, previously noted, that the amount of coercion that patients experience is strongly related to their belief about the justice of the process that led to hospitalization.

According to the Supreme Court, the right to be present in criminal proceedings incorporates not only the right to be physically present but the right to be "mentally present," i.e., competent to stand trial. *Pate v. Robinson*, 383 U.S. 375, 86 S.Ct. 836, 15 L.Ed.2d 815 (1966). Defendants must have a minimal understanding of the proceedings against them and be able to assist the attorney in confronting their accusers, or the state may not try them. Should the right to avoid trial while incompetent be extended to civil commitment respondents? In answering this question, consider that delaying the hearing until competency is restored (through involuntary treatment) might significantly prolong hospitalization. Consider also that, in the criminal system, defendants found incompetent to stand trial are allowed to attend hearings about their competency provided that they behave satisfactorily.

4. *Cross-examination and hearsay.* The principal issue connected with the right to cross-examine accusers at civil commitment proceedings is the extent to which hearsay is admissible. Since hearsay, by definition, involves out-of-court statements by persons who are not present in the courtroom, the Confrontation Clause could be construed to exclude all hearsay, or at least all hearsay statements made to a government official. Cf. *Crawford v. Washington*, 541 U.S. 36, 124 S.Ct. 1354, 158 L.Ed.2d 177 (2004), discussed on p. 614. However, the Confrontation Clause only applies in "criminal prosecutions." In civil cases, there are many exceptions to the hearsay rule. These exceptions include the party admission rule, which would permit description by the person who heard them of the respondent's out-of-court statements about his or her mental state or intended actions, and the "business records" exception, which would admit virtually all observations of the respondent's mental state made by clinicians and recorded as a routine matter in medical and psychiatric records. See Fed.R.Evid. 801(d)(2); 803(6).

An example of testimony that would not fit any well-accepted hearsay exception would be a witness' description of an out-of-court declaration by a third-party about what the respondent did or said on a particular day (so-called "double hearsay" because the person who observed or heard the respondent is not in court). For instance, the hearsay rule would probably bar a mental health professional's testimony that, two days before the hearing, a family member told him that the respondent had threatened to hurt the family member.[o] Similarly, the rule would prohibit the respondent's mother from testifying that the respondent's friend had told her the respondent had attempted suicide on several occasions.

Should such testimony be admissible in any event? Or should the state be required to present the people who heard the respondent's statements first-hand, if they are available? Several courts have held that the rules of evidence, including the hearsay rule, should apply in commitment proceedings. See, e.g., *Mental Health of D.L.T.*, 314 Mont. 297, 67 P.3d 189, ¶¶ 10, 11, 18 (2003) (citing statute with approval); *State ex rel. Hawks v. Lazaro*, 157 W.Va. 417, 202 S.E.2d 109, 125 (W.Va.1974); *Lessard v. Schmidt*, 349 F.Supp. 1078 (E.D.Wis.1972). Some state statutes take this stance as well. Many others are simply silent about the issue, and some provide, as Utah does, that the hearing "shall be conducted in as informal a manner as may be consistent with orderly procedure." Utah Stat. § 62A–15–631(9)(d). The American Psychiatric Association's Model Law provides that "[h]earsay evidence may be received, and experts and other witnesses may, consistent with law, testify to any relevant and probative facts at the discretion of the court." Clifford Stromberg & Alan Stone, *A Model State Law on Civil Commitment of the Mentally Ill*, 20 Harv.J.Legis. 275, 340 (1983). In support of this position, the commentary states, id. at 340–41:

> [H]earsay evidence may be especially necessary in some civil commitment cases because the facts sought to be established include the elusive datum of mental status, not just physical events as in most criminal trials. Especially where the issues are tried before a judge, who can weigh the probative value of the evidence, such hearsay need not be excluded. It also may be proper to afford a broader ambit to psychiatric opinion evidence. Similarly, the interests that underlie the privilege against spousal testimony in criminal cases may not be served by invoking such a privilege in civil commitment. There may be proper exceptions to other privileges as well, such as the psychotherapist-patient privilege.

5. *Compulsory process.* Of course, if the respondent in a civil commitment proceeding has a wide-open right to subpoena witnesses, then he or she can circumvent any attempt by the state to rely on hearsay by serving process on the relevant out-of-court declarants. Some state statutes explicitly grant the respondent subpoena authority for persons and documents, but whether such a right is constitutionally required and the

---

[o] Note, however, that under Federal Rule of Evidence 703 and equivalent state rules such testimony, although hearsay, would still be admissible if of the type "reasonably relied upon" by experts in the field. Information from outside sources that might be considered hearsay in court is often crucial, in practice, to mental health professionals' judgments—indeed, *not* obtaining and considering such information might be malpractice.

extent to which it can be exercised as a discovery mechanism is unclear. Perhaps of relevance here is *Vitek v. Jones,* 445 U.S. 480, 100 S.Ct. 1254, 63 L.Ed.2d 552 (1980), the case involving the process due prisoners who are transferred to psychiatric facilities. In *Vitek,* the Supreme Court held that the state must give the prisoner the "opportunity . . . to present testimony of witnesses . . . and to confront and cross-examine witnesses called by the state, *except* upon a finding, not arbitrarily made, of good cause for not permitting such presentation, confrontation or cross-examination." [emphasis added] The Court held that such a limitation was permissible because it recognized "[t]he interests of the State in avoiding disruption." Id. at 495–96.

Another limitation on the respondent's compulsory process right may arise from the by-now familiar concern that the information thereby obtained will harm either the respondent or third parties who have revealed information about the respondent. Although virtually every state and federal HIPAA regulations allow patients to see their medical records, disclosure is not required of certain types of information, such as information from third parties disclosed in confidence, information that would be "injurious" to the patient or the patient's relationships with others, and the therapist's impressions (as opposed to official diagnostic information). See Chapter 5, Part II. Also of possible relevance here is the Supreme Court's decision in *Pennsylvania v. Ritchie,* 480 U.S. 39, 107 S.Ct. 989 94 L.Ed.2d 40 (1987), in which the Court held that even a criminal defendant's "right to discover exculpatory evidence does not include the unsupervised authority to search through the Commonwealth's files." At most, the Court held, the defense may ask the trial court to review the files *in camera* to determine what information, if any, is material to the defendant's case; even this limited right is conditioned upon the defendant "first establishing a basis for his claim that it contains material evidence." Thus, the state may be able to stymie a respondent's attempt, prior to a civil commitment hearing, to subpoena evidence possessed by the state (e.g., in hospital records) by requiring a showing of materiality and a judicial determination that the records should be disclosed.

4. The Right to Counsel

The Supreme Court has clearly established a right to counsel at trial—and a concomitant duty on the part of the state to provide counsel to indigents who cannot afford one—for both the criminal accused, *Gideon v. Wainwright,* 372 U.S. 335, 83 S.Ct. 792, 9 L.Ed.2d 799 (1963); *Argersinger v. Hamlin,* 407 U.S. 25, 92 S.Ct. 2006, 32 L.Ed.2d 530 (1972), and juveniles alleged to be delinquent, *In re Gault,* 387 U.S. 1, 87 S.Ct. 1428, 18 L.Ed.2d 527 (1967), at least when imprisonment is imposed. Endorsement of a right to counsel in civil commitment proceedings has been less firm. While virtually every state provides for counsel at commitment and every modern court that has considered the issue has held that the due process clause requires counsel at the commitment hearing, the Supreme Court has not been as clear on the matter. In both

Parham v. J.R. (dealing with commitment of children) and *Vitek v. Jones* (dealing with the transfer of prisoners to mental health facilities) the Court refused to find a right to legally trained counsel for persons subjected to a proceeding to determine the existence and extent of their mental disability. The language of Justice Powell's concurring opinion in *Vitek,* which controlled the disposition of the right to counsel issue in that case, is worth looking at in full:

VITEK V. JONES
Supreme Court of the United States, 1980.
445 U.S. 480, 100 S.Ct. 1254, 63 L.Ed.2d 552.

MR. JUSTICE POWELL, concurring in part.

*   *   *

I

In *Gagnon v. Scarpelli,* 411 U.S. 778, 93 S.Ct. 1756, 36 L.Ed.2d 656 (1973), my opinion for the Court held that counsel is not necessarily required at a probation revocation hearing. In reaching this decision the Court recognized both the effects of providing counsel to each probationer and the likely benefits to be derived from the assistance of counsel. "The introduction of counsel into a revocation proceeding [would] alter significantly the nature of the proceeding," because the hearing would inevitably become more adversarial. We noted that probationers would not always need counsel because in most hearings the essential facts are undisputed. In lieu of a *per se* rule we held that the necessity of providing counsel should be determined on a case-by-case basis. In particular, we stressed that factors governing the decision to provide counsel include (i) the existence of factual disputes or issues which are "complex or otherwise difficult to develop or present," and (ii) "whether the probationer appears to be capable of speaking effectively for himself."

Consideration of these factors, and particularly the capability of the inmate, persuades me that the Court is correct that independent assistance must be provided to an inmate before he may be transferred involuntarily to a mental hospital. The essence of the issue in an involuntary commitment proceeding will be the mental health of the inmate. The resolution of factual disputes will be less important than the ability to understand and analyze expert psychiatric testimony that is often expressed in language relatively incomprehensible to laymen. It is unlikely that an inmate threatened with involuntary transfer to mental hospitals will possess the competence or training to protect adequately his own interest in these state-initiated proceedings. And the circumstances of being imprisoned without normal access to others who may assist him places an additional handicap upon an inmate's ability to represent himself. I therefore agree that due process requires the provision of assistance to an inmate threatened with involuntary transfer to a mental hospital.

II

I do not believe, however, that an inmate must always be supplied with a licensed attorney. "[D]ue Process is flexible and calls for such procedural protections as the particular situation demands." *Morrissey v. Brewer,* 408 U.S. 471, 481, 92 S.Ct. 2593, 2600, 33 L.Ed.2d 484 (1972). Our decisions defining the necessary qualifications for an impartial decisionmaker demonstrate that the requirements of due process turn on the nature of the determination which must be made. "Due Process has never been thought to require that the neutral and detached trier of fact be law-trained or a judicial or administrative officer." *Parham v. J.R.,* 442 U.S. 584, 607, 99 S.Ct. 2493, 2506, 61 L.Ed.2d 101 (1979). In that case, we held that due process is satisfied when a staff physician determines whether a child may be voluntarily committed to a state mental institution by his parents. That holding was based upon recognition that the issues of civil commitment "are essentially medical in nature," and that " 'neither judges nor administrative hearing officers are better qualified than psychiatrists to render psychiatric judgments.' "

In my view, the principle that due process does not always require a law-trained decisionmaker supports the ancillary conclusion that due process may be satisfied by the provision of a qualified and independent advisor who is not a lawyer. As in *Parham v. J.L.,* the issue here is essentially medical. Under state law, a prisoner may be transferred only if he "suffers from a mental disease or defect" and "cannot be given proper treatment" in the prison complex. Neb.Rev.Stat. § 83–180(1). The opinion of the Court allows a non-lawyer to act as the impartial decisionmaker in the transfer proceeding.

The essence of procedural due process is a fair hearing. I do not think that the fairness of an informal hearing designed to determine a medical issue requires participation by lawyers. Due process merely requires that the State provide an inmate with qualified and independent assistance. Such assistance may be provided by a licensed psychiatrist or other mental health professional. Indeed, in view of the nature of the issue involved in the transfer hearing, a person possessing such professional qualifications normally would be preferred. As the Court notes, "[t]he question whether an individual is mentally ill and cannot be treated in prison 'turns on the meaning of the facts which must be interpreted by expert psychiatrists and psychologists.' " *Ante,* at 1265, quoting *Addington v. Texas.* I would not exclude, however, the possibility that the required assistance may be rendered by competent laymen in some cases. The essential requirements are that the person provided by the State be competent and independent, and that he be free to act solely in the inmate's best interest.

In sum, although the State is free to appoint a licensed attorney to represent an inmate, it is not constitutionally required to do so. Due process will be satisfied so long as an inmate facing involuntary transfer to a mental hospital is provided qualified and independent assistance.

QUESTIONS AND COMMENTS

1. *Implications of the Court's cases.* What are the implications of *Vitek* and *Parham* for the civil commitment process? Note that Justice Powell relied heavily on *Gagnon v. Scarpelli* and *Morrissey v. Brewer* in reaching his conclusions. Consider this fuller excerpt from *Scarpelli:*

> The introduction of counsel into a revocation proceeding will alter significantly the nature of the proceeding. If counsel is provided for the probationer or parolee, the State in turn will normally provide its own counsel; lawyers, by training and disposition, are advocates and bound by professional duty to present all available evidence and arguments in support of their clients' positions and to contest with vigor all adverse evidence and views. The role of the hearing body itself, aptly described in *Morrissey* as being "predictive and discretionary" as well as fact finding, may become more akin to that of a judge at a trial, and less attuned to the rehabilitative needs of the individual probationer or parolee. In the greater self-consciousness of its quasi-judicial role, the hearing body may be less tolerant of marginal deviant behavior and feel more pressure to reincarcerate than to continue nonpunitive rehabilitation. Certainly, the decisionmaking process will be prolonged, and the financial cost to the State—for appointed counsel, counsel for the State, a longer record and the possibility of judicial review—will not be insubstantial.

> In some cases, these modifications in the nature of the revocation hearing must be endured and the costs borne because, as we have indicated above, the probationer's or parolee's version of a disputed issue can fairly be represented only by a trained advocate. But due process is not so rigid as to require that the significant interests in informality, flexibility, and economy must always be sacrificed.

Is *Scarpelli* authority for or against a right to counsel at civil commitment?

2. *The role of counsel.* Assuming the person subjected to commitment proceedings has an advocate, should the advocate take an *adversarial* role and strive to prevent commitment? Or, as suggested by Justice Powell's reasoning in *Scarpelli,* might the nature of the commitment process justify a different, less adversarial approach? At least three possible advocacy roles can be envisioned in the commitment context. The first is the adversarial role traditionally taken by lawyers in criminal and civil cases, in which it is assumed that the client knows best and the advocate makes the most persuasive arguments available in support of the client's wishes. The second role might be called the "guardian ad litem" stance, in which the advocate acts in the "best interests" of the client, after assessing all the circumstances. Although the client's wishes are taken into account, they are not dispositive;

lawyer knows best
doctor knows best
client knows best

thus, under this model, it is assumed that the lawyer, rather than the client, knows best. Finally, there is a cooperative role in which the advocate assumes that the "doctor knows best." Under this model, the advocate makes sure the state proves its case and elicits facts for the expert's consideration, but does not dispute the expert's final decision.

The Model Code of Professional Responsibility is not particularly helpful in deciding, from a professional ethics standpoint, which role may or should be followed. Canon 7 of the Code states: "A lawyer should represent a client zealously within the bounds of the law." Consider the following "Ethical Considerations" (EC) designed to flesh out this Canon:

EC 7–7 In certain areas of legal representation not affecting the merits of the cause or substantially prejudicing the rights of a client, a lawyer is entitled to make decisions on his own. But otherwise the authority to make decisions is exclusively that of the client and, if made within the framework of the law, such decisions are binding on his lawyer. As typical examples in civil cases, it is for the client to decide whether he will accept a settlement offer or whether he will waive his right to plead an affirmative defense. A defense lawyer in a criminal case has the duty to advise his client fully on whether a particular plea to a charge appears to be desirable and as to the prospects of success on appeal, but it is for the client to decide what plea should be entered and whether an appeal should be taken.

* * *

EC 7–12 Any mental or physical condition of a client that renders him incapable of making a considered judgment on his own behalf casts additional responsibilities upon his lawyer. Where an incompetent is acting through a guardian or other legal representative, a lawyer must look to such representative for those decisions which are normally the prerogative of the client to make. If a client under disability has no legal representative, his lawyer may be compelled in court proceedings to make decisions on behalf of the client. If the client is capable of understanding the matter in question or of contributing to the advancement of his interests, regardless of whether he is legally disqualified from performing certain acts, the lawyer should obtain from him all possible aid. If the disability of a client and the lack of a legal representative compel the lawyer to make decisions for his client, *the lawyer should consider all circumstances then prevailing and act with care to safeguard and advance the interests of his client* (emphasis added). But obviously a lawyer cannot perform any act or make any decision which the law requires his client to perform or make, either acting for himself if competent, or by a duly constituted representative if legally incompetent.

The ABA's Model Rules of Professional Conduct are not much more helpful. Model Rule 1.14 states: "(a) When a client's ability to make adequately considered decisions in connection with the representation is impaired, whether because of minority, mental disability or for some other reason, the lawyer shall, as far as reasonably possible, maintain a normal client-lawyer relationship with the client; (b) A lawyer may seek the appointment of a guardian or take other protective action with respect to a client, only when the lawyer reasonably believes that the client cannot adequately act in the client's own interests." An earlier, rejected draft of subsection (b) stated: "A lawyer shall secure the appointment of a guardian or other legal representative, or seek a protective order with respect to a client, when doing so is necessary *in the client's best interests*" (emphasis added). Compare the Restatement of the Law Governing Lawyers § 35(2), which states: "A lawyer representing [an impaired client] for whom no guardian or other representative is available to act, must, with respect to a matter within the scope of the representation, pursue the lawyer's reasonable view of the client's objectives or interests as the client would define them if able to make adequately considered decisions on the matter, *even if the client expresses no wishes or gives contrary instructions*" (emphasis added).

Assume that you are representing a client who appears to be imminently suicidal and treatable, but who adamantly refuses to consent to any type of treatment or hospitalization because "the hospital is Hell and if I kill myself I'll go to Heaven." Alternatively, assume your client is extremely malnourished and disheveled, murmuring incoherently, smearing feces on the wall, and able only to nod negatively when asked if he is willing to go to the hospital. Under the Model Code, the Model Rules or the Restatement, what options are available to you? Should you follow the clients' direction? Seek appointment of a guardian? Withdraw? Disregard the clients' wishes because you believe that treatment would be in the client's best interests? The last sentence of the Model Code excerpt prohibits attorneys from performing any act or making any decision "which the law requires his client to perform or make." In the hypothesized situations, what does "the law" leave up to the client? Would your approach to these situations be different if, as is true in many states, the government is "represented" solely by a mental health professional because no provision is made for state attorneys to appear in commitment hearings?

Even before the due process revolution in the 1970s, commentators emphasized that, whatever role the advocate assumes—adversarial, guardian ad litem, or cooperative—the advocate should at least perform an investigative function.

> Prior to the hearing the attorney must make a thorough study of all the records that are available to him through the court, the hospital, and, at times, social agencies. He must always communicate with the proposed patient and, where possible, family and friends. The attorney should work toward an understanding of the events that led up to and contributed to the filing of the petition. Only in this way can he attempt to develop possible alternatives to hospitalization.

Fred Cohen, *The Function of the Attorney and the Commitment of the Mentally Ill*, 44 Tex.L.Rev. 424, 452 (1966). Armed with this knowledge, the advocate may be able to bargain for a less restrictive disposition and will be able to conduct more effective questioning of witnesses. The advocate can also make sure the proper procedures are followed at the hearing, both through objections and through appealing various rulings, if appeal is available. See also, *Preparation and Trial of a Civil Commitment Case*, 5 Men.Dis.L.Rep. 201, 281 (1981); *National Center for State Courts' Guidelines for Involuntary Civil Commitment*, 10 Men. & Phys. Dis. L. Rep. 409 (1986).

The role of counsel is made more difficult by the possibility that the client does not express, or perhaps even know, what he or she "really" wants. For instance, Miller and colleagues assert that patients sometimes make complaints to protect themselves "from having to deal with painful intrapsychic conflicts unrelated to the subjects of the actual grievances." They also contend that attorneys may reinforce the resistance of these patients to treatment by taking the complaints at face value. As an example of this process and what might be done about it, they provided the following description of a case:

> Mr. A [a 29 year-old state hospital resident with diagnoses of pedophilia, borderline personality and antisocial personality, among others] frequently stated his intent to sue everyone who could not "cure" these various problems . . . In individual psychotherapy, he began to focus on intrapsychic problems such as his extremely negative self-image and his difficulty with intimacy and rejection . . . [In therapy with two different therapists,] a pattern began to emerge. He would begin to deal with a significant internal conflict, and then would switch to talking almost exclusively about a grievance or lawsuit. . . . While the litigious behavior served to help him feel in control, and to project his negative feelings onto the staff, it also provided protection against the pain associated with dealing with powerful internal conflicts. As soon as this pattern was discovered, it was interpreted to Mr. A. by both therapists; after each interpretation, he returned to dealing with his deeper conflicts. He accepted the interpretations, and the frequency of complaints decreased significantly . . . Most staff came to accept his changes as genuine; their responses then also reinforced Mr. A.'s behavior.

> Mr. A.'s litigious behavior was initially reinforced by responses of some patient advocates and attorneys. . . . At first, the supervising attorneys in the state patient's rights office, who had no clinical experience and a significant libertarian orientation, did not recognize the hidden agendas behind many of Mr. A's charges, and unwittingly contributed to his therapeutic resistance by supporting his overt grievances. After considerable effort at education by clinical staff about borderline psychodynamics, however, the attorneys realized how they had been furthering their client's resistance (and thus hindering his treatment) by accepting his grievances at face value. Once they understood the nature of his resistance, they often reinforced the therapy through clinically insightful responses to his grievances, while still maintaining their concern for his rights. Their opinions were initially received by Mr. A.

differently from clinical staff's opinions, and helped to set effective limits to his acting-out behavior before the clinical staff's reaction to Mr. A. had changed significantly.

Mr. A. was told of the therapists' contacts with the advocates, and offered the opportunity for joint sessions with both clinicians and advocates. While he declined the sessions, he accepted the reasons for the collaboration and offered no objections to its continuing.

Robert Miller, et. al., *Litigiousness as a Resistance to Therapy*, in David Wexler, ed., Therapeutic Jurisprudence: The Law as Therapeutic Agent, 332–35 (1991). This example involved representing a person with mental illness who is already in the hospital. Are the ethical issues different when the same type of dynamic occurs at the commitment hearing?

3. *Ineffective assistance of counsel.* Most commitment attorneys apparently do not undertake even the modest tasks described in the previous note. As indicated earlier, numerous studies have documented that attorneys rarely spend more than a few minutes preparing for the hearing, seldom call witnesses, and usually fail to engage in vigorous cross-examination of the experts. To some extent, this state of affairs may be due to their unfamiliarity with psychiatric issues or the low fees provided by the state for defending commitment respondents. But one study suggests that, even when these factors are not present, many attorneys continue to be passive. Poythress found that even after lawyers were specifically trained to adopt a more adversarial stance and were provided with information about the inadequacies of testimony by mental health professionals, they persisted in avoiding careful cross-examination of expert witnesses, apparently because of a belief that to do so was in the best interests of their clients. Norman Poythress, *Psychiatric Expertise in Civil Commitment: Training Attorneys to Cope with Expert Testimony*, 2 Law Hum.Behav. 1 (1978).

One possible remedy for this situation, if a remedy is thought to be worthwhile, is to require legislatively that the attorneys perform certain duties. For instance, Arizona has granted the commitment court the power to hold attorneys in contempt unless they perform several listed tasks prior the hearing. Ariz.Stat. § 36–537(B)(requiring the attorney, *inter alia*, to interview the client, obtain records, and seek a screening evaluation at least 24 hours before hearing, with failure to perform punishable by contempt of court). If localities refuse to pay attorneys decently, might such requirements dissuade all but the least capable attorneys from representing respondents in commitment hearings?

A second possible approach is to import Sixth Amendment ineffective assistance of counsel analysis into the commitment context. In *Strickland v. Washington*, 466 U.S. 668, 104 S.Ct. 2052, 80 L.Ed.2d 674 (1984), the Supreme Court established a two-prong test for determining whether defense counsel was ineffective under the Sixth Amendment. The defendant must show both that "counsel's performance was deficient" and that "the deficient performance prejudiced the defense." Performance is "deficient" if the attorney fails "to advocate the defendant's cause[,] . . . consult with the defendant on important decisions, [or] . . . keep the defendant informed of important developments." The attorney must also "bring to bear such skill and knowledge as will render the trial a reliable adversarial testing process" and "make reasonable investigations or . . . make a reasonable decision that makes particular investigations unnecessary." Proof of "prejudice" exists if "there is a reasonable probability that, but for counsel's unprofessional errors, the result of the proceeding would have been different." If both prongs are met, the defendant's conviction must be reversed. Would application of *Strickland's* standards to civil commitment (through the due process clause, since the sixth amendment applies only to "criminal prosecutions") provide a realistic remedy for attorney passivity? How often would a former respondent undertake the necessary appeal and have the resources to carry it out?

In *In the Matter of the Mental Health of K.G.F.*, 306 Mont. 1, 29 P.3d 485 (2001), the Montana Supreme Court stated:

> Although in numerous respects the procedural due process rights of an involuntary commitment patient-respondent are identical to those afforded an accused criminal defendant, we . . . conclude that the standard under *Strickland* simply does not go far enough to protect the liberty interests of individuals such as K.G.F., who may or may not have broken any law, but who, upon the expiration of a 90–day commitment, must indefinitely bear the badge of inferiority of a once "involuntarily committed" person with a proven mental disorder. The *Strickland* decision, for example, provides that a court "must indulge a strong presumption that counsel's conduct falls within the wide range of reasonable professional assistance;" that is, the defendant must overcome the presumption that, under the circumstances, the challenged action might be considered sound trial strategy. Even a cursory review of legal commentary reveals the flawed reasoning of applying the foregoing *Strickland* standard to involuntary civil commitment proceedings. Namely, "reasonable professional assistance" cannot be presumed in a proceeding that routinely accepts—and even requires—an unreasonably low standard of legal assistance and generally disdains zealous, adversarial confrontation. . . . We also agree with Amicus that the *Strickland* burden of proving that counsel's "deficient performance prejudiced the defense so as to deny the defendant a fair trial," is contrary to our prior case law that mandates that unless civil commitment laws are strictly followed, a commitment order must be reversed. . . .

> [B]ecause the fundamental rights attached to decisions within the "provider-patient relationship" may be overridden by the State's *parens patriae* duties and police power authority, the role of counsel is all the more critical where a patient may be involuntarily committed. The threats to individual liberty posed by involuntary commitment . . . arise at a time "when the individual with a mental illness is least able to defend against them—during a time of crisis, confusion, fatigue." *See*

also Bruce J. Winick, *Therapeutic Jurisprudence and the Civil Commitment Hearing,* 10 J. Contemp. Legal Issues 37, 44–45 (1999) (observing that "[p]erhaps nothing can threaten a person's belief that he or she is an equal member of society as much as being subjected to a civil commitment hearing" and when "legal proceedings do not treat people with dignity, they feel devalued as members of society"). . . .

Relying in part on the National Center for State Courts' Guidelines for Involuntary Civil Commitment cited above in note 2, the court then established a number of rules governing attorneys involved in the commitment process regarding investigation, communication with the client, and advocacy of the client's wishes. The court ended with the following language:

> As the Commentary to the *Guidelines* states: "[w]hen an attorney fails to act as an advocate and assumes a paternalistic or passive stance, the balance of the system is upset, the defense attorney usurps the judicial role, and the defendant's position goes unheard." Accordingly, we agree with the *Guidelines* . . . that the proper role of the attorney is to "represent the perspective of the respondent and to serve as a vigorous advocate for the respondent's wishes." . . . The foregoing guidelines create the presumption that a client wishes to not be involuntarily committed. . . . *Thus, we conclude that pursuant to the foregoing guidelines, evidence that counsel independently advocated or otherwise acquiesced to an involuntary commitment—in the absence of any evidence of a voluntary and knowing consent by the patient-respondent—will establish the presumption that counsel was ineffective.* . . . Upon a substantial showing of evidence . . . that counsel did not effectively represent the patient-respondent's interests pursuant to the foregoing standards, an order of involuntary commitment should be vacated.

Id. at 500–01 (emphasis added). In the two hypotheticals described in note 2 involving the suicidal and malnourished individuals, should a failure on the part of the attorney to argue vigorously against hospitalization vacate commitment and lead to a finding of ineffective assistance under *K.G.F.*? Two other state appellate courts have refused to adopt *K.G.F.*'s expansion of *Strickland* in the civil commitment context. *In re L.G.* 2006 WL 2780157, at *8 (Ohio Ct. App., Sept. 28, 2006); *In re T.A.H.–L.,* 97 P.3d 767, 771 (Wash. Ct. App. 2004).

4.   *The right to an independent expert evaluation.* To what extent does the effective assistance of counsel notion require that the advocate seek consultation with a mental health professional? For the wealthy respondent such consultation is easily arranged, but for the indigent (and typical) person subjected to civil commitment, the only expertise available in most jurisdictions is provided by those mental health professionals who testify for the government. Only a few states have authorized the appointment of an independent expert if the defendant so requests. See, e.g., Fl. Stat. § 394.4655(6)(a)2. Some courts have held that the latter type of provision is

constitutionally required. In *In re Gannon,* 123 N.J.Super. 104, 301 A.2d 493, 494 (1973), the court stated:

> Commitment to a psychiatric hospital obviously entails a significant loss of liberty which, as in a criminal proceeding, must be under due process of law. It is the opinion of this court that in a commitment proceeding due process of law includes the right to an independent psychiatric examination.
>
> The right of an indigent to have counsel appointed has already been established, but the presence of a lawyer at the commitment hearing is not a sufficient safeguard for the patient's rights. No matter how brilliant the lawyer may be, he is in no position to effectively contest the commitment proceedings because he has no way to rebut the testimony of the psychiatrist from the institution who has already certified to the patient's insanity. . . .
>
> This court has had enough experience to know that psychiatrists differ very definitely in their evaluations and diagnoses of mental illness. In a commitment proceeding where the court is in effect bound by the expertise of the psychiatrist, the right to counsel is of little value without a concurrent right to an independent psychiatric examination.

However, the court limited the right to an independent evaluation in the following manner:

> The right to counsel has not been construed to allow an indigent to choose his own lawyer. Similarly, an indigent in a commitment proceeding should not have the right to "shop around" for a psychiatrist who agrees with him. The independent psychiatrist is to assist the court, not the patient; all he need do is render his best judgment and make all relevant information available both to the court and to the defense.

Id. at 494.

Does the court's conclusion follow from its analogy between choosing a lawyer and choosing an expert? Note that in *Ake v. Oklahoma,* 470 U.S. 68, 105 S.Ct. 1087, 84 L.Ed.2d 53 (1985), reprinted at pp. 580–586, the Supreme Court held, using reasoning similar to that used by the *Gannon* court, that the due process clause entitles the indigent criminal defendant to a psychiatric consultant when sanity at the time of the offense is "a significant factor at trial" and, in capital cases, when dangerousness is a factor to be considered at sentencing. More specifically, on the insanity expert issue, the Court held:

> We therefore hold that when a defendant demonstrates to the trial judge that his sanity at the time of the offense is to be a significant factor at trial, the State must, at a minimum, assure the defendant access to a competent psychiatrist who will conduct an appropriate examination and assist in evaluation, preparation, and presentation of the defense. This is not to say, of course, that the indigent defendant has a constitutional right to choose a psychiatrist of his personal liking or to receive funds to

hire his own. Our concern is that the indigent defendant have access to a competent psychiatrist for the purpose we have discussed, and as in the case of the provision of counsel we leave to the State the decision on how to implement this right.

470 U.S. at 83, 105 S.Ct. at 1096. To what extent does *Ake* support the result in *Gannon*? At least one court has held that an evaluation is "independent" for purposes of civil commitment even when conducted by a state-employed doctor. *In re Barnard*, 247 Ill.App.3d 234, 186 Ill.Dec. 524, 616 N.E.2d 714 (1993).

5.   The Privilege against Self–Incrimination

ALLEN V. ILLINOIS

Supreme Court of the United States, 1986.
478 U.S. 364, 106 S.Ct. 2988, 92 L.Ed.2d 296.

JUSTICE REHNQUIST delivered the opinion of the Court.

The question presented by this case is whether the proceedings under the Illinois Sexually Dangerous Persons Act (Act), Ill.Rev.Stat., ch. 38, ¶ 105–1.01 *et seq.* (1985),[p] are "criminal" within the meaning of the Fifth Amendment's guarantee against compulsory self-incrimination.

*   *   *

The Self–Incrimination Clause of the Fifth Amendment, which applies to the States through the Fourteenth Amendment, *Malloy v. Hogan,* 378 U.S. 1, 84 S.Ct. 1489, 12 L.Ed.2d 653 (1964), provides that no person "shall be compelled in any criminal case to be a witness against himself." This Court has long held that the privilege against self-incrimination "not only permits a person to refuse to testify against himself at a criminal trial in which he is a defendant, but also 'privileges him not to answer official questions put to him in any other proceeding, civil or criminal, formal or informal, where the answers might incriminate him in future criminal proceedings.' " In this case the Illinois Supreme Court ruled that a person whom the State attempts to commit under the Act is protected from use of his compelled answers in any subsequent criminal case in which he is the defendant. What we have here, then, is not a claim that petitioner's statements to the psychiatrists might be used to incriminate him in some future criminal proceeding, but instead his claim that because the sexually dangerous person proceeding is itself "criminal," he was entitled to refuse to answer any questions at all.

The question whether a particular proceeding is criminal for the purposes of the Self–Incrimination Clause is first of all a question of

---

p   For a full discussion of sex offender statutes, see Chapter Seven, Part III.B.

statutory construction. Here, Illinois has expressly provided that proceedings under the Act "shall be civil in nature," ¶ 105–3.01, indicating that when it files a petition against a person under the Act it intends to proceed in a nonpunitive, noncriminal manner, "without regard to the procedural protections and restrictions available in criminal prosecutions." As petitioner correctly points out, however, the civil label is not always dispositive. Where a defendant has provided "the clearest proof" that "the statutory scheme [is] so punitive either in purpose or effect as to negate [the State's] intention" that the proceeding be civil, it must be considered criminal and the privilege against self-incrimination must be applied. We think that petitioner has failed to provide such proof in this case.

The Illinois Supreme Court reviewed the Act and its own case law and concluded that these proceedings, while similar to criminal proceedings in that they are accompanied by strict procedural safeguards, are essentially civil in nature. We are unpersuaded by petitioner's efforts to challenge this conclusion. Under the Act, the State has a statutory obligation to provide "care and treatment for [persons adjudged sexually dangerous] designed to effect recovery," ¶ 105–8, in a facility set aside to provide psychiatric care, *ibid.* And "[i]f the patient is found to be no longer dangerous, the court shall order that he be discharged." ¶ 105–9. While the committed person has the burden of showing that he is no longer dangerous, he may apply for release at any time. *Ibid.* In short, the State has disavowed any interest in punishment, provided for the treatment of those it commits, and established a system under which committed persons may be released after the briefest time in confinement. The Act thus does not appear to promote either of "the traditional aims of punishment—retribution and deterrence." Cf. *Addington v. Texas,* 441 U.S. 418, 428, 99 S.Ct. 1804, 1810, 60 L.Ed.2d 323 (1979) (in Texas "civil commitment state power is not exercised in a punitive sense"); *French v. Blackburn,* 428 F.Supp. 1351, 1358–1359 (M.D.N.C. (1977)), summarily aff'd, 443 U.S. 901, 99 S.Ct. 3091, 61 L.Ed.2d 869 (1979) (state need not accord privilege against self-incrimination in civil commitment proceeding).

Petitioner offers several arguments in support of his claim that despite the apparently nonpunitive purposes of the Act, it should be considered criminal as far as the privilege against self-incrimination is concerned. He first notes that the State cannot file a sexually-dangerous-person petition unless it has already brought criminal charges against the person in question. ¶ 105–3. In addition, the State must prove that the person it seeks to commit perpetrated "at least one act of or attempt at sexual assault or sexual molestation." 107 Ill.2d, at 105, 89 Ill.Dec., at 854, 481 N.E.2d, at 697. To petitioner, these factors serve to distinguish the Act from other civil commitment, which typically is not tied to any criminal charge and which petitioner apparently concedes is not "criminal" under the Self–Incrimination Clause. We disagree. That the State has chosen not to apply the Act to the larger class of mentally ill persons who might be found sexually dangerous docs not somehow transform a civil proceeding into a criminal one. And as the State points out, it must prove more than just the commission of a sexual assault: the Illinois Supreme Court, as we noted above, has construed the Act to require proof of the existence of a mental disorder for more than one year and a propensity to commit sexual assaults, in addition to demonstration of that propensity through sexual assault.

The discussion of civil commitment in *Addington, supra,* in which this Court concluded that the Texas involuntary-commitment scheme is not criminal insofar as the requirement of proof beyond a reasonable doubt is concerned, fully supports our conclusion here:

> "[T]he initial inquiry in a civil commitment proceeding is very different from the central issue in either a delinquency proceeding or a criminal prosecution. In the latter cases the basic issue is a straight-forward factual question—did the accused commit the act alleged? There may be factual issues to resolve in a commitment proceeding, but the factual aspects represent only the beginning of the inquiry. Whether the individual is mentally ill and dangerous to either himself or others and is in need of confined therapy turns on the *meaning* of the facts which must be interpreted by expert psychiatrists and psychologists." 441 U.S., at 429, 99 S.Ct., at 1811 (emphasis in original).

While here the State must prove at least one act of sexual assault, that antecedent conduct is received not to punish past misdeeds, but primarily to show the accused's mental condition and to predict future behavior.

In his attempt to distinguish this case from other civil commitment, petitioner places great reliance on the fact that proceedings under the Act are accompanied by procedural safeguards usually found in criminal trials. In particular, he observes that the Act provides an accused with the right to counsel, ¶ 105–5, the right to demand a jury trial, *ibid.,* and the right to confront and cross-examine witnesses. At the conclusion of the hearing, the trier of fact must determine whether the prosecution has proved the person's sexual dangerousness beyond a reasonable doubt. ¶ 105–3.01. But as we noted above, the State has indicated quite clearly its intent that these commitment proceedings be civil in nature; its decision nevertheless to provide some of the safeguards applicable in criminal trials cannot itself turn these proceedings into criminal prosecutions requiring the full panoply of rights applicable there.

Relying chiefly on *In re Gault,* 387 U.S. 1, 87 S.Ct. 1428, 18 L.Ed.2d 527 (1967), petitioner also urges that the proceedings in question are "criminal" because a person adjudged sexually dangerous under the Act is committed for an indeterminate period to the Menard Psychiatric Center, a maximum security institution that is run by the Illinois Department of Corrections and that houses convicts needing psychiatric care as well as sexually dangerous persons. Whatever its label and whatever the State's alleged purpose, petitioner argues, such commitment is the sort of punishment—total deprivation of liberty in a criminal setting—that *Gault* teaches cannot be imposed absent application of the privilege against self-incrimination. We believe that *Gault* is readily distinguishable.

First, *Gault's* sweeping statement that "our Constitution guarantees that no person shall be 'compelled' to be a witness against himself when he is threatened with deprivation of his liberty" is plainly not good law. Although the fact that incarceration may result is relevant to the question whether the privilege against self-incrimination applies, *Addington* demonstrates that involuntary commitment does not itself trigger the entire range of criminal procedural protections. Indeed, petitioner apparently concedes that traditional civil commitment does not require application of the privilege. * * *

The Court in *Gault* was obviously persuaded that the State intended to punish its juvenile offenders, observing that in many States juveniles may be placed in "adult penal institutions" for conduct that if committed by an adult would be a crime. Here, by contrast, the State serves its purpose of *treating* rather than punishing sexually dangerous persons by committing them to an institution expressly designed to provide psychiatric care and treatment. That the Menard Psychiatric Center houses not only sexually dangerous persons but also prisoners from other institutions who are in need of psychiatric treatment does not transform the State's intent to treat into an intent to punish. Nor does the fact that Menard is apparently a maximum security facility affect our analysis:

> "The state has a legitimate interest under its *parens patriae* powers in providing care to its citizens who are unable because of emotional disorders to care for themselves; the state also has authority under its police power to protect the community from the dangerous tendencies of some who are mentally ill." *Addington,* 441 U.S., at 426, 99 S.Ct., at 1809.

Illinois' decision to supplement its *parens patriae* concerns with measures to protect the welfare and safety of other citizens does not render the Act punitive.

Petitioner has not demonstrated, and the record does not suggest, that "sexually dangerous persons" in Illinois are confined under conditions incompatible with the State's asserted interest in treatment. Had petitioner shown, for example, that the confinement of such persons imposes on them a regimen which is essentially identical to that imposed upon felons with no need for psychiatric care, this might well be a different case. But the record here tells us little or nothing about the regimen at the psychiatric center, and it certainly does not show that there are no relevant differences between confinement there and confinement in the other parts of the maximum-security prison complex. Indeed, counsel for the State assures us that under Illinois law sexually dangerous persons must not be treated like ordinary prisoners. We therefore cannot say that the conditions of petitioner's confinement themselves amount to "punishment" and thus render "criminal" the proceedings which led to confinement.

Our conclusion that proceedings under the Act are not "criminal" within the meaning of the Fifth Amendment's guarantee against compulsory self-incrimination does not completely dispose of this case. Petitioner rather obliquely suggests that even if his commitment proceeding was not criminal, the Fourteenth Amendment's guarantee of due process nonetheless required application of the privilege. In particular, petitioner contends that the Illinois Supreme Court "grossly miscalculated" in weighing the interests set out in *Mathews v. Eldridge,* 424 U.S. 319, 96 S.Ct. 893, 47 L.Ed.2d 18 (1976). This Court has never held that the Due Process Clause of its own force requires application of the privilege against self-incrimination in a noncriminal proceeding, where the privilege claimant is protected against his compelled answers in any subsequent criminal case. We decline to do so today.

We think that the parties have in their reliance on *Mathews v. Eldridge* misconceived that decision. *Mathews* dealt with the procedural safeguards required by the Due Process Clause of the Fifth Amendment before a person might be deprived of property, and its focus was on such safeguards as were necessary to guard against the risk of erroneous deprivation. As the Supreme Court of Illinois and the State have both pointed out, it is difficult, if not impossible, to see how requiring the privilege against self-incrimination in these proceedings would in any way advance reliability. Indeed, the State takes the quite plausible view that denying the evaluating psychiatrist the opportunity to question persons alleged to be sexually dangerous would *decrease* the reliability of a finding of sexual dangerousness. As in *Addington,* "to adopt the criminal law standard gives no assurance" that States will reach a "better" result.

The privilege against self-incrimination enjoined by the Fifth Amendment is not designed to enhance the reliability of the fact-finding determination; it stands in the Constitution for entirely independent reasons. Just as in a "criminal case" it would be no argument against a claim of the privilege to say that granting the claim would decrease the reliability of the fact-finding process, the privilege has no place among the procedural safeguards discussed in *Mathews v. Eldridge,* which are designed to enhance the reliability of that process.

For the reasons stated, we conclude that the Illinois proceedings here considered were not "criminal" within the meaning of the Fifth Amendment to the United States Constitution, and that due process does not independently require application of the privilege. * * * The judgment of the Supreme Court of Illinois is therefore

Affirmed.

QUESTIONS AND COMMENTS

1. *The right to remain silent and civil commitment.* Because it limits application of the right to remain silent to criminal proceedings, *Allen* presumably forecloses a court from finding, under the federal constitution, that the right applies in civil commitment proceedings. See also, *French v. Blackburn,* 428 F.Supp. 1351, 1358–9 (M.D.N.C.1977), affirmed mem. 443 U.S. 901, 99 S.Ct. 3091, 61 L.Ed.2d 869 (1979). In fact, prior to *Allen,* only a few courts had so held. See, e.g., *Lessard v. Schmidt,* 349 F.Supp. 1078 (E.D.Wis.1972). Most decisions, even those that were otherwise sympathetic to constitutional claims in the civil commitment context, presaged *Allen* and found no right to remain silent at any point in the commitment process. See, e.g., *State ex rel. Hawks v. Lazaro,* 157 W.Va. 417, 202 S.E.2d 109, 126 (1974); *Suzuki v. Yuen,* 617 F.2d 173, 177–78 (9th Cir.1980); *Tippett v. Maryland,* 436 F.2d 1153 (4th Cir.1971).

However, some states, including Illinois, require that persons who are the subject of civil commitment proceedings be advised that they may refuse to talk to examining experts. See 405 Ill.Stat. 5/3–208. Moreover, statements that are "compelled" by the state during the commitment process are probably not admissible in a subsequent criminal proceeding; at least, *Allen* strongly implied as much with respect to statements made in the course of sex offender proceedings.

2. *Evaluating* Allen. In deciding that the privilege against self-incrimination does not apply to sex offender proceedings, the Court rejected a "deprivation of liberty" analysis and focused instead on whether the objective of such proceedings is punishment or treatment. Accepting this change in analysis, is the aim of civil commitment *always* treatment?

Perhaps, as its rejection of the petitioner's due process claim suggests, the Court was also concerned about the practical consequences of a contrary decision. Consider the commentary to the American Psychiatric Association's "model" provision recommending that the respondent in civil commitment proceedings not be accorded a right to remain silent:

> Many cases that discuss whether the privilege should apply focus on the metaphysical issue of whether commitment is "essentially" a civil or criminal proceeding. This analysis misses the point. Advising a patient— who may well have an emergency psychiatric condition—at the beginning of an interview about his right to remain silent would be fundamentally inconsistent with the therapeutic purposes of the process. It might bewilder and alarm the patient. It might make it impossible to

ascertain the patient's mental state, thereby preventing the assessment both of his need for treatment and his potential dangerousness.

Commitment decisions would be transformed into judgments based solely on overt acts, becoming virtually indistinguishable from decisions made in the criminal process. Granting the Fifth Amendment privilege would establish a bootless procedural right—in some cases forcing the state to instigate criminal proceedings and in many cases depriving seriously mentally ill persons of needed treatment.

Clifford Stromberg & Alan Stone, *A Model State Law on Civil Commitment of the Mentally Ill*, 20 Harv.J.Legis. 274, 342–43 (1983).

Would the right to remain silent make it "impossible," as the excerpt suggests, to garner evidence about the mental state of a person undergoing emergency involuntary hospitalization? Note that even in criminal cases, only about 20% of the defendants who are told they have a right to remain silent assert that right. See Richard A. Leo, *Inside the Interrogation Room*, 86 J. Crim. L. & Criminol. 266, 276 (1996) (78% waiver rate). Similarly, Miller and his colleagues found that few persons subjected to commitment refuse to talk as a result of warnings. They speculate, based on other studies of the admission process, that this is because "most patients understand and recall little of what they are told on admission," that "many patients tend to perceive clinicians as helpers no matter what the situation," and that "warnings may actually seduce some patients into feeling secure enough to reveal more information than they otherwise would have done. . . . " Robert Miller et al., *The Right to Remain Silent During Psychiatric Examination in Civil and Criminal Cases—A National Survey and an Analysis*, 9 Int'l J. L. & Psychiat. 77, 91–92 (1986). In any event, how important is it to have access to the subject of the proceeding when the issue is dangerousness or treatability (as compared, for instance, to sanity at the time of the offense)? Would it not be useful, through recognition of the right to remain silent, to encourage the state to develop alternative sources of information? Consider also that in most physician-patient encounters (not just psychiatry), the most important information that the physician obtains comes from speaking with the patient. In the context of an emergency hospitalization, which is more important: protecting the rights of someone suffering from a severe mental illness, or facilitating accurate information-gathering and diagnosis?

3. *Consequences of* Allen. If there is no right to remain silent in civil commitment proceedings, then the state may not only compel the respondent to answer questions during a psychiatric examination (as was the case in *Allen*), but may also compel testimony in court. What sanction may be imposed on the person who refuses to speak to the examiner or in court? In the analogous situations in criminal proceedings, the court has several options: (1) a contempt citation; (2) an instruction that the jury may infer guilt from the defendant's silence; and (3) prohibition of the defendant's expert testimony, at least in cases where the defendant has refused to talk to the state's expert. Will any of these sanctions "work" in the civil commitment context? With respect to the first sanction, what "punishment" should be

imposed once the respondent is found in contempt? In regard to the second sanction, what inferences can be drawn from the respondent's silence? As to the third sanction, is it fair if the respondent is willing to talk in court?

Another issue associated with the right to remain silent is whether the respondent's attorney may observe the pre-hearing examination process. If the fifth amendment applied, then by analogy to the Supreme Court's opinion in *Miranda v. Arizona*, 384 U.S. 436, 86 S.Ct. 1602, 16 L.Ed.2d 694 (1966), the respondent should be told not only of the right to remain silent but also of the right to have counsel present during the examination. Is this a good idea? Even if there is no fifth amendment right to have counsel present during the evaluation, can one construct a sixth amendment argument in support of that right? What if waiting for the attorney delays urgently needed care?

4. *Conditioning treatment on surrendering silence.* The Supreme Court has also held, in *McKune v. Lile*, 536 U.S. 24, 122 S.Ct. 2017, 153 L.Ed.2d 47 (2002), that the state may require sex offenders who want to participate in sex abuse treatment programs to reveal incriminating information about their previous offenses, both charged and uncharged. Under the Kansas program at issue in *Lile*, those offenders who choose not to reveal this information not only are denied access to the treatment program but also have various privileges curtailed, such as visitation from anyone other than lawyers, family or clergy; work opportunities; the ability to send money to family and make canteen expenditures; and access to personal television. Additionally, those who refuse to participate are likely to be transferred to more dangerous maximum security units to make room for those in the program. Five members of the Court found these consequences of refusal too "minimal" to constitute fifth amendment compulsion. Providing the fifth vote for the result was Justice O'Connor, who concluded that none of these consequences was "likely" to compel incrimination. In particular, she noted that prisoners who refused to talk still kept some visitation rights, and did not require most of the other lost privileges, given the prison's provision of basic needs. With respect to the potential for transfer to a more dangerous prison setting, O'Connor stated that "it may be assumed that the prison is capable of controlling its inmates so that respondent's personal safety is not jeopardized by being placed in maximum security, at least in the absence of proof to the contrary." In light of *Lile*, any program of treatment in the traditional civil commitment setting that is conditioned on surrendering one's right to silence is unlikely to be unconstitutional.

D. RELEASE PROCEDURES

FASULO V. ARAFEH

Supreme Court of Connecticut, 1977.
173 Conn. 473, 378 A.2d 553.

LONGO, ASSOCIATE JUSTICE.

Ann Fasulo was civilly committed to Connecticut Valley Hospital in 1951, as was Marie Barbieri in 1964. * * * They claim that because their commitments are of indefinite duration and there is no procedure for periodic court review of the necessity for their confinement, their confinement is in violation of the due process guarantee of article first, § 8, of the Connecticut constitution.

*   *   *

As the United States Supreme Court has recognized, "At the least, due process requires that the nature and duration of commitment bear some reasonable relation to the purpose for which an individual is committed." *Jackson v. Indiana,* 406 U.S. 715, 738. Once the purpose of the commitment no longer exists, there is no constitutional basis for the state to continue to deprive the individual of his liberty. To satisfy due process, the procedure for releasing a civilly committed patient must be adequate to assure release of those who may no longer constitutionally be confined.

These plaintiffs have been deprived of their liberty. Their loss is already great, but can be initially justified as a result of the legitimate exercise of the *parens patriae* power of the state. The plaintiffs, however, have been committed indefinitely and confined for periods of twenty-six and thirteen years respectively, thus requiring us to heed the warning of the United States Supreme Court that the longer the commitment, the greater the safeguards which are required to ensure that no one is deprived of liberty without due process. We must, therefore, review the plaintiffs' claims in light of the important interest at stake—liberty—and the great loss which its extended deprivation constitutes.

Any procedure to allow the release of involuntarily confined civilly committed individuals must take account of the controlled and often isolated environment of the mental hospital from which the confined individuals will seek release. It must calculate the possible incompetence of those confined, their limited knowledge of release procedures, the cost of pursuing review and the amount of effort necessary to pursue review. Further, the procedure must be adapted to the possible effect of drugs or other treatment on the patient's capacity and must be formulated with consideration of institutional pressures to rely on the *medical* judgments of the hospital staff rather than to pursue extrainstitutional *legal* remedies. See Note, "Civil Commitment of the Mentally Ill," 87 Harv.L.Rev. 1190, 1398.

At present, Connecticut provides several routes by which a mental patient can challenge his confinement. General Statutes § 17–192 allows for release (1) by order of the Probate Court "upon application and satisfactory proof that such person has been restored to reason," or (2) "[i]f the officers, directors or trustees of a state hospital for mental illness are notified by the superintendent or other person in a managerial capacity of such institution that he has reason to believe that any person committed thereto by order of a probate court is not mentally ill or a suitable subject to be confined in such institution, such officers, directors or trustees may discharge such person." Under the second method the patient runs the risk of having his release prevented by a superintendent whose determination may later be found by a court to have been erroneous. Furthermore, the second procedure disregards the fundamental fact that the state's power legitimately to confine an individual is based on a legal determination under General Statutes § 17–178 "that the person complained of is mentally ill and dangerous to himself or herself or others or gravely disabled" and that the commitment shall only continue "for the period of the duration of such mental illness or until he or she is discharged in due course of law." The state's power to confine terminates when the patient's condition no longer meets the legal standard for commitment. Since the state's power to confine is measured by a legal standard, the expiration of the state's power can only be determined in a judicial proceeding which tests the patient's present mental status against the legal standard for confinement. That adjudication cannot be made by medical personnel unguided by the procedural safeguards which cushion the individual from an overzealous exercise of state power when the individual is first threatened with the deprivation of his liberty.

* * *

We also find the first method of release provided for in General Statutes § 17–192 constitutionally deficient. The method allows release of a patient after he has applied to the Probate Court for discharge and has proved that he has been "restored to reason." We find this procedure inadequate on two grounds. First, it places the burden of initiating review of his status on the patient, a requirement which suffers from conceptual as well as serious practical deficiencies. As we stated previously, since the state's power to confine is premised on the individual's present mental status, the original involuntary commitment proceeding can only establish that the state may confine the individual at the time of the hearing and for the foreseeable period during which that status is unlikely to change. Upon the expiration of that period, the state's power to deprive the patient of his liberty lapses and any further confinement must be justified anew. The state, therefore, must bear the burden of initiating recommitment proceedings.

This same reasoning applies to the burden of proof at the recommitment hearing. The burden should not be placed on the civilly committed patient to justify his right to liberty. Freedom from involuntary confinement for those who have committed no crime is the natural state of individuals in this country. The burden must be placed on the state to prove the necessity of stripping the citizen of one of his most fundamental rights, and the risk of error must rest on the state.

*   *   *

Furthermore, to require a patient to initiate judicial review of his confinement and to bear the burden of proving the nonexistence of the necessity for that confinement ignores the practical considerations discussed above which are inherent in the mental patient's situation. Briefly, these include the difficulties of overcoming an isolated environment to initiate and coordinate a challenge to one's confinement. For instance, we cannot assume that friends and allies will always be available to secure counsel and marshal evidence on the patient's behalf. Nor can we assume that even if a patient is notified of his right to pursue any of the available remedies, he will be adequately protected. [Merely giving the patient notice] ignores the practical difficulties of requiring a mental patient to overcome the effects of his confinement, his closed environment, his possible incompetence and the debilitating effects of drugs or other treatment on his ability to make a decision which may amount to the waiver of his constitutional right to a review of his status.

*   *   *

We, therefore, hold that these plaintiffs have been denied their due process rights under the Connecticut constitution by the state's failure to provide them with periodic judicial review of their commitments in the form of state-initiated recommitment hearings replete with the safeguards of the initial commitment hearings at which the state bears the burden of proving the necessity for their continued confinement.

*   *   *

[The dissenting opinion of JUSTICE LOISELLE in which CHIEF JUSTICE HOUSE concurred is omitted.]

QUESTIONS AND COMMENTS

1. *Current status of periodic review.* Although at one time commitment in many states was truly indeterminate, virtually every state now requires, in line with the holding in *Fasulo,* that a review hearing be held after a certain period of involuntary treatment. Typically, a hearing similar in kind to the initial adjudicatory hearing must be held within six months of the

previous commitment; other fairly common review periods are three months and a year.

Of course, judicial review through a writ of habeas corpus is always available if the patient requests it. Moreover, most patients are released prior to the first review hearing. The length of hospital stay for the majority of patients was under 90 days even in the 1970's when *Fasulo* was decided. See Walter Gove & Terry Fain, *A Comparison of Voluntary and Committed Mental Patients*, 34 Arch.Gen.Psychiat. 669, 673 (1977) (67% of involuntary patients discharged within 38 days); Carlos Tomelieri et al., *Who are the Committed?*, 165 J. Nervous & Mental Dis. 288, 291 (1977) (63% of committed patients discharged within 90 days). As we noted earlier in this chapter, the average duration of psychiatric hospitalization today is less than two weeks. For some patients, however, lengths of stay in state hospitals (which now serve only the most severely ill patients) can be much longer. Frederick Holt et al., *The Length of Psychiatric Hospital Stays and Community Stays*, published by Va. Dept. Men. Health & Men. Retardation (2001) (41.7 days is the average length of stay in Virginia state psychiatric hospitals); Idaho Department of Health and Welfare, About Idaho's State Hospitals, http://www.healthandwelfare.idaho.gov/Medical/MentalHealth/StateHospital s/tabid/495/Default.aspx (accessed March 3, 2013) (average is 70 days); Pennsylvania Department of Public Welfare, Pennsylvania State Hospital System Length–Of–Stay, Demographics & Diagnoses Report for June 30, 2012 (Table 6) (27% of civil patients discharged in FY2012 had stays longer than two years). And relief via habeas corpus is hampered not only by the requirement that the patient initiate such proceedings but also because the petitioner bears the burden of proving the challenged detention is illegal.

2.   *Timing of review. Fasulo* does not indicate when the judicial review it mandates must take place. However, it does quote the Supreme Court's statement in *Jackson v. Indiana,* 406 U.S. 715, 92 S.Ct. 1845, 32 L.Ed.2d 435 (1972), that "due process requires that the nature and duration of commitment bear some reasonable relation to the purpose for which the individual is committed."[q] With this language in mind, assume, as research has long shown, that the vast majority of civilly committed patients can be treated effectively within 100 days. Gerald Klerman, *National Trends in Hospitalization*, 30 Hosp. & Comm. Psychiat. 110 (1979). On this assumption, should a hearing be constitutionally mandated at the end of this period? Alternatively, given the possibility that no further treatment will be effective, should all patients simply be released at the expiration of 100 days? In arguing in favor of such a rule, Stromberg and Stone cite the above-mentioned research and state:

> We believe that after a certain period of treatment and involuntary confinement, society must give patients a chance on their own. We might agree that this should not apply to an imminently suicidal person if it

---

[q]   *Jackson* held that hospitalization of those found incompetent to stand trial may last only so long as there is a substantial probability that the patient will attain competency in the foreseeable future. See pp. 1151–1158.

would be predicted that some finite further period of treatment would likely end the person's suicidal impulses. Unfortunately, this is rarely possible.

Clifford Stromberg & Alan Stone, *A Model State Law on Civil Commitment of the Mentally Ill*, 20 Harv.J.Leg. 275, 380 (1983). Might agreement with the Stromberg and Stone proposal depend upon whether the commitment is for *parens patriae* or police power purposes? Does it matter that patients might take longer than 100 days to recover?

3. *Formality of review.* Are there any differences between the initial commitment and the review process that merit additional (or fewer) procedural protections at the latter proceeding? Should the state have to meet a heavier burden if it seeks continued commitment? Might a public jury decision be more useful in the review process than at the initial commitment?

4. *Waiver of review hearing.* The *Fasulo* court suggested that allowing the patient to decide whether a hearing should take place is unconstitutional. Does this mean that the majority would reject a provision allowing a waiver of the right to a hearing? Consider the following, from David Wexler, *The Waivability of Recommitment Hearings*, 20 Ariz.L.Rev. 175, 184–86 (1978).

> Clearly, if mechanisms could be devised to eliminate the need for those, and only those, recommitment hearings that are truly unnecessary and truly unwanted by the patients, a host of considerations would favor a rule of waivability. A number of such considerations come quickly to mind.
>
> There is, of course, the sheer economic consideration involving the depletion of judicial, mental health, and related resources. Courts sitting in the vicinity of state hospitals have terribly heavy commitment calendars. They assuredly would wish to be spared the time and expense of conducting unnecessary and unwanted recommitment hearings.
>
> The judicial time-and-cost saving interest would be particularly evident, of course, if an appreciable number of patients wished to waive such hearings. At the moment, the percent of patients desiring waiver is an empirical unknown. It would not be at all surprising, however, for a rather large number of patients to desire waiver. The depressed and suicidal might well constitute one such patient category. So too, many elderly, "gravely disabled" patients might opt for waiver, were it available, rather than attend hearings only to learn what they already know: that their clinical and family situation is unchanged or has worsened, and that no facilities less restrictive than full-time hospitalization can yet be found for their placement.
>
> Needless to say, physicians, nurses, and ward attendants would also prefer to treat than to testify. To the extent that they are called upon to testify in unnecessary and unwanted hearings, the patients and the public would be best served by those mental health witnesses playing instead a therapeutic role.

* * *

The interests of psychotherapists and of certain patients converge in their concern over the possible traumatic and anti-therapeutic effects of recommitment hearings. Unlike initial hearings, where the possible trauma to the patient is probably outweighed by the feedback to him of the impropriety of his behavior and by the presentation of convincing evidence that commitment is called for, the interests deserve to be balanced differently in the framework of recommitment.

By the time of recommitment, a patient may well be quite aware of what is objectionable about his behavior or of why alternative placement seems unsuitable. Moreover, whether hearing adverse testimony will prove traumatic or anti-therapeutic is no longer a matter of enormous abstract speculation: the patient will have already experienced one commitment hearing and may now be in a fairly good position to assess the relative costs and benefits of contesting recommitment. If recommitment is in any event likely, a number of patients may wish to avoid hearings at which testimony will be given regarding, for example, the persistence of their depressed and suicidal state, or the continuing unwillingness of families or of nursing homes to accept patients who act out conflicts or who are sometimes assaultive.

* * *

. . . Waivability—consent to recommitment for up to a specified period— should probably be authorized if a lawyer playing an adversary role certifies to the court that he has investigated the case and has consulted with his client, that he has explained to the client the options and the right to consent recommitment, and that he has concluded that the client desires to consent to recommitment.

5. *Conditional release and outpatient commitment after hospitalization.* Economic pressures have shortened hospitalization for all patients over the past two decades. In response, many states use various forms of conditional release (often, an outpatient commitment) after hospitalization, hoping to keep formerly hospitalized patients in treatment to continue their recovery. Theoretically, these programs function somewhat like parole. A patient is released on "conditional," "convalescent" or outpatient commitment status to a community mental health center, halfway house, or other community service in an effort to ease the transition to normal life, on the condition that the patient adheres to a particular treatment regimen (e.g., periodic medication, attendance at group therapy sessions) and remains stable. Immediate rehospitalization is permissible, however, if the patient is shown to require it.

A preliminary question with respect to conditional release is whether such programs are permissible exercises of state power. Most statutes imply, if they do not state explicitly, that those patients who are conditionally released no longer meet inpatient commitment standards. See *True v. State*

Department of Health and Welfare, 103 Idaho 151, 645 P.2d 891, 898 (1982). If so, under what authority may the state continue to maintain *any* control over the patient? Perhaps, as discussed in the materials on the least restrictive alternative doctrine, the justification for such continued interference is that it contemplates a lesser deprivation of liberty and thus is permissible on a lesser showing than that demanded by the inpatient commitment standards. There may be other justifications as well. Cf. American Bar Association Criminal Justice Mental Health Standard 7–7.4 (permitting continued confinement of an insanity acquittee who no longer meets the commitment criteria if the state can show that the only reason the criteria are not met is that the patient is undergoing treatment that is likely to end unless commitment continues).

In any event, the most significant litigation with respect to conditional release programs has assumed their constitutionality and focused instead on procedural questions. In particular, courts have been concerned with provisions that permit conditional release to be revoked on the authority of the hospital director, with no requirement of judicial supervision other than, in some states, an ex parte order. Not surprisingly, given the similarity between conditional release and parole, these courts have focused on the Supreme Court's decision in *Morrissey v. Brewer,* 408 U.S. 471, 92 S.Ct. 2593, 33 L.Ed.2d 484 (1972), which held that the "conditional liberty" of paroled criminals entitles them to preliminary and final parole revocation hearings, notice and confrontation rights and, in "complex" revocation proceedings, the right to counsel as well.

In *Dietrich v. Brooks,* 27 Or.App. 821, 558 P.2d 357 (1976), the court found that there are "profound differences of nature, degree and function" between conditional hospital release and parole. Specifically, the court noted three distinctions: (1) the underlying nature of imprisonment and parole is penal, while conditional release is a therapeutic device; (2) the length of the deprivation of liberty differs; and (3) there is a closer relationship between the conditional liberty and the institutional program with conditional release than with parole. Thus, the court held, summary revocation of conditional release is adequate under the due process clause.

Other courts have decided that more process is due patients whose conditional release is revoked. For instance, in *True v. State Department of Health and Welfare,* 103 Idaho 151, 645 P.2d 891 (1982), the court considered the constitutionality of a statute that permitted immediate revocation of conditional release status when (1) the "director of the [mental health] department or his designated representative" believed that the patient had failed to meet the conditions of his release and that "conditions justifying hospitalization continue[d] to exist;" or when (2) the director or his designate had reason to believe that the patient had "relapsed" and was "again in need of hospitalization," based on the report of two persons "who are either licensed physicians, health officers, designated examiners or peace officers, the prosecuting attorney or a judge of a court." The court rejected the state's argument that the patient's ability to appeal any hospitalization decision within 30 days and the additional right to habeas relief adequately protected the patient's due process interests, for the same types of reasons given by the court in *Fasulo* in explaining its requirement of periodic review. It then required: "(1) prompt written notice to the patient of the reasons for and evidence relied on justifying rehospitalization as well as notice of the right to challenge the allegations and (2) a hearing before a neutral hearing body to be held as soon as is reasonably possible following the patient's rehospitalization, at which time the patient is to be afforded the right to counsel, the right to present evidence and examine witnesses, and upon a decision sustaining the order of rehospitalization, the right to a written statement by the fact-finding body as to the reasons for revocation of the patient's conditional release status." The court did not require an immediate revocation proceeding, distinguishing *Morrissey* on the following grounds:

> [T]iming becomes more critical in the instant case than it is in the parole setting. In the parole situation a delay in the revocation of an individual's parolee status, while highly undesirable in cases where revocation is found to be justified, does not present a serious threat to the degree of rehabilitation achieved prior to the violation. In contrast, in cases where a mental health patient is suspected of remission, the Department's interest in rehospitalization for immediate treatment is paramount, as the progress towards recovery which had been achieved is seriously jeopardized by a remission which is left untreated.

* * *

> The great weight we accord the Department's need for immediate rehospitalization of a conditionally released mental health patient suspected of remission is such that the general rule that an individual be given an opportunity for a hearing before he is deprived of a protectible interest is inapplicable. The situation present when a decision is made to revoke the conditional release status of the patient is extraordinary: the patient because of a suspected remission in his mental condition possibly poses a danger to others and/or to himself.

Most statutes are unclear as to whether revocation of conditional release begins an entirely new commitment period or instead only authorizes hospitalization for the remainder of the original commitment. Should this matter? Note that parole revocation, at issue in *Morrissey*, only permits the state to force completion of the sentence already imposed by the sentencing court.

A final issue connected with conditional release that has yet to be extensively litigated concerns the types of limitations the Constitution places on the conditions that may be imposed as part of such a program. For instance, in a jurisdiction that recognizes a right to refuse medication, may release be conditioned upon the patient's agreement to accept medication? In the sentencing context, probationary conditions that are "reasonably related" to the probationer's rehabilitation and protection of the public are virtually always upheld. But conditions that unreasonably trench on first amendment, fourth amendment or foundational privacy rights (e.g., a sterilization requirement or a requirement that the defendant not fraternize with users of narcotics or ex-felons) have been declared unconstitutional. See *People v. Garcia*, 12 Cal.Rptr.2d 341 (1993).

E. VOLUNTARY ADMISSION PROCEDURES

Involuntary civil commitment is no longer the primary means by which people with mental problems receive inpatient psychiatric treatment. Every state allows people to admit themselves for psychiatric treatment. Nationally, such admissions probably comprise over 50% of the mental hospital population and about 85% of the population in psychiatric units of general hospitals. Susan C. Reed and Dan A. Lewis, in *The Negotiation of Voluntary Admission in Chicago's State Mental Hospitals*, 18 J. Psychiatry & L. 137 (1990)(roughly 75% admitted voluntarily at intake and roughly 80% of those remaining admitted voluntarily within 10 days). One early explanation of why voluntary status has been so favored asserted:

> [Voluntary admission] enjoys the unique position of being favored by all of the groups concerned with influencing legislation in this field. The medical profession endorses this procedure because of its simplicity and the complete lack of any court action. The patient who can recognize his illness and seek hospitalization on his own volition is the one who will actively participate in his treatment, cooperate with his doctor, and benefit the most from the treatment. As a result the voluntary patient will be discharged more rapidly, thereby alleviating the generally crowded conditions that exist in most mental facilities. Those who are concerned with civil liberties of mental patients are reassured, since the dangers of wrongful detention exist only in involuntary hospitalization procedures.

Comment, *Hospitalization of the Mentally Disabled in Pennsylvania: The Mental Health–Mental Retardation Act of 1966*, 71 Dick.L.Rev. 307, 308–09 (1967); see also Group for the Advancement of Psychiatry, Forced into Treatment: The Role of Coercion in Clinical Practice (1994). This section examines the procedures associated with hospitalizing a person whom the state is willing to admit as a "voluntary" patient.

JANET SCHMIDT & JOHN GILBOY "VOLUNTARY" HOSPITALIZATION OF THE MENTALLY ILL
66 N.W.L.Rev. 429 (1971).

Both the medical and legal proponents of voluntary care share a conception of voluntary admission as an individual decision to accept mental treatment, made entirely apart from involuntary commitment procedures, thereby avoiding the therapeutic and legal problems of coercion. We have recently studied the use of voluntary admission procedures in Illinois, a state in which a substantial majority of persons hospitalized in mental institutions are now admitted under voluntary procedures. The results of our study indicate that the foregoing conception is wrong.

In a majority of cases voluntary admission is utilized to hospitalize persons who are already in some form of official custody. Voluntary admission avoids procedural complexity and the need for officials to assume responsibility, both inherent drawbacks to compulsory commitment from the officials' point of view. Individuals are therefore induced to voluntarily commit themselves with the threat of involuntary commitment as the principal means of persuasion, and with little concern for the adequacy of the information on which the individual's decision is based or whether it is "voluntary" at all.

*   *   *

Although our study was limited to analysis of relevant statistical data and direct personal observation of commitment procedures in Illinois, that state's procedures for commitment of the mentally ill are similar to those of many other states.

Definition of Voluntary Admission

Under Illinois law there are two different procedures for voluntary admission to mental hospitals. Under the first procedure, known as "informal admission," an individual is admitted to a mental hospital without formal application and is free to leave at any time during normal day-shift hours. Under the second procedure, known as "voluntary admission," an individual is admitted to a mental hospital upon formal application and is free to leave "within 5 days, excluding Saturdays, Sundays and holidays, after he gives any professional staff person notice of his desire to leave, ..." However, during that 5-day notice period, the hospital officials may ask a court to hold an involuntary commitment hearing, which must be set within 5 days after such petition. The patient continues to be hospitalized pending a final order of the court at the hearing. Thus, informal admission may be described as an entirely voluntary process. Voluntary admission, in contrast, requires an initial voluntary decision on the part of the patient, but, once that decision is made, the patient is subject to restraint on his right to leave the hospital, and may be required to remain a week or more after he expresses a desire to leave.

A striking preliminary fact which our study disclosed is that informal admission is almost never utilized. In fact, in only about one percent of the cases admitted to mental institutions in Illinois is "informal admission" utilized. In contrast, voluntary admission is used in about 68% of all cases. The reason for the greater use of voluntary admission appears to be the additional restraining power the procedure gives the hospital over the patient. "With 'informal admission' the units just do not feel enough control over the patient," one hospital admissions officer remarked. Another hospital official described informal admission as an "inconvenience" to hospital staff personnel and an unnecessary "allowance" to patients. In one case described to us by an admissions officer, informal admission was used to house overnight an individual admittedly not in need of hospitalization, but for whom no other immediate shelter could be found.

The almost total refusal to use the entirely voluntary informal admission procedure is suggestive at the outset of the general attitude of officials toward voluntary admission procedures. The value of such procedures to officials, as will be more evident below, is not primarily in allowing individuals to remain in control of their own circumstances, but rather in hospitalizing individuals with a minimum of official responsibility and difficulty.

Police Custody Cases

The case which proponents of voluntary admission almost always have in mind is that of an individual who arrives at a mental institution by himself, or accompanied by a physician, family, relatives or friends, and asks to be admitted for treatment. We call these "non-custody cases" to denote the absence of any official custody prior to the individual's decision to commit himself.

* * *

Our study disclosed that about 40% of all voluntarily admitted patients are brought to the mental hospital by the police and in about 55% of the cases where individuals are brought to the hospital by the police, voluntary admission results. While some studies of civil commitment have recognized that a significant number of persons are brought to mental institutions by the police, there has been little recognition that such cases often result in voluntary rather than involuntary commitment.

* * *

It is important to understand the difference between these police custody cases and the non-custody cases which proponents of voluntary care have usually assumed. In non-custody cases, the individual is making a choice between voluntarily committing himself or remaining outside the hospital, which is a fairly simple choice. The application form for voluntary admission discloses the restrictions on the right to leave the hospital which that status will impose.

In police custody cases, on the other hand, the alternatives as they appear to the individual are voluntary admission versus involuntary commitment. This is a much more difficult decision. In these cases, to make a reasonable choice, the individual must be informed about the nature of the involuntary commitment process since that is the major alternative before him. [M]ost persons unquestionably have only the vaguest idea, if any at all, about the nature of the involuntary commitment procedure. Indeed, most persons probably have only a vague idea of the substantive legal standard to be applied at such a hearing.

The typical practice in cases, however, is to explain voluntary admission to the patient in a very cursory manner, describing it as a desirable alternative to involuntary commitment. The explanation "If you sign a voluntary admission it will only be between you and the doctor and not the judge," is typical. To regard the uninformed decision to accept hospitalization as "voluntary" is highly artificial.

Court Cases

Our study disclosed that approximately 10–11% of voluntary admissions to mental hospitals result from decisions made, or announced, in court at the time of an involuntary commitment hearing. Voluntary admission occurs in approximately 35% of the cases which come to court for involuntary commitment hearings. The court hearing may be the result of initial involuntary commitment on the basis of an emergency petition or physician's certificate as described earlier. However, in about 60% of cases the court hearing follows an initial criminal arrest.

* * *

A decision to accept voluntary admission by a defendant at a court hearing raises the same issue of adequate disclosure discussed earlier in connection with voluntary admission of persons brought by the police to the hospital admissions office. It might be expected that the involvement of the public defender and the judge at the time of a court hearing would insure that any decision on admission would be fully informed. However, the judges involved appear to give no consideration to the defendant's awareness of his situation. Any indication that the public defender and state's attorney are agreeable to voluntary admission and that the patient will agree is sufficient to dispose of the case. There is no inquiry to ascertain whether the defendant understands the choices before him and the decision he is making. The public defender, because of the time pressures to which he is subject and the non-adversary conception of his job, does not seek to advise patients of their rights so that they can make an informed judgment. Rather, the public defender makes his own judgment as to whether voluntary admission is appropriate and, if so, then urges the defendant to accept such hospitalization in a manner not unlike that of admissions officers in cases discussed earlier.

Where persons come to civil commitment hearings after having initially been arrested on criminal charges (a majority of the cases in Chicago), a further legal issue is raised. In these cases the individuals are under an added pressure: the threat of criminal prosecution if they should successfully resist civil commitment. If the individual is committed, voluntarily or involuntarily, the criminal charge against him is usually dropped.

* * *

Our study disclosed that in a majority of the cases in which voluntary admission procedures were used, the individuals were already under some form of official custody and were faced with the threat of involuntary commitment proceedings as the principal alternative to voluntary admission.

QUESTIONS AND COMMENTS

1. *The informed consent model of voluntary admission.* Gilboy and Schmidt suggest that many voluntary admissions in Illinois were not really voluntary because of the implicit and explicit pressures exerted on those who agree to such admissions and because of the failure to explain to them the nature and consequence of such admissions. Would their concerns be addressed by imposing an informed consent requirement on the voluntary admission process? As discussed in Chapter Four, the informed consent doctrine requires that, before treatment is administered, the potential patient must (1) be told of its risks and benefits; (2) be able to competently assess them; and (3) make a voluntary decision to undergo the treatment based on this assessment. The three aspects of the doctrine as they might apply in the voluntary admission context are discussed below.

Disclosure of Information. Gilboy and Schmidt's research indicates that persons who are admitted as voluntary patients rarely have their options fully explained to them and as a result have only vague notions about them. Presumably, all potential patients should be told about the alternatives open to them, the nature and consequences of involuntary commitment (and of the criminal process, if this is a disposition being considered) and the nature and consequences of voluntary commitment. Is this enough?

A study conducted of voluntary admission practices in Chicago conducted almost twenty years after the study reported above found many of the same practices that Gilboy & Schmidt did. Susan Reed & Dan Lewis, *The Negotiation of Voluntary Admission in Chicago State Mental Hospitals*, 18 J. Psychiatry & L. 137 (1990). The authors report that in order to get a voluntary admission, hospital staff would often hide the fact that those who are involuntarily committed do not necessarily stay in the hospital any longer than those who are admitted voluntarily. According to one coordinator:

> I tell the person that I will do everything possible to get them out of the hospital as soon as possible, but that if they get committed they'll stay for 60 days. I don't tell them that I would discharge them just as soon whether they sign a voluntary or they go to court. That's true, but you just don't bother to tell them that part of the truth.

Id. at 144. Is this a violation of the disclosure principle?

Competency. As developed in Chapter Nine, determining whether the information that is imparted is competently assessed is problematic, given the difficulty of defining competency. But every study of the issue has concluded that most voluntary patients have significant difficulty understanding their situation. One study, which involved interviews of 50 voluntary patients within two days of their admission, found that "a large percentage of the patients who voluntarily entered [the] hospital were not competent to consent to their own admission." Paul Appelbaum et al., *Empirical Assessment of Competency to Consent to Psychiatric Hospitalization*, 138 Am.J.Psych. 1170, 1174 (1981). This finding held "whether competency was defined on narrow clinical grounds, with a broader clinically oriented focus, in terms that measure understanding of legal rights, or by means of criteria that combined all of these definitions." Id. Interestingly, the study also found that "50% of the patients did not acknowledge their need to be in a psychiatric hospital; the vast majority of these denied it outright." Id. at 1173.

A more recent study—also coauthored by Dr. Appelbaum—evaluated how well 100 voluntarily hospitalized psychiatric patients comprehended two brief paragraphs (written at an eighth grade level) that were read to them within two days of their acceptance of voluntary status. One paragraph explained the purposes of psychiatric hospitalization, the second explained policies for discharge. After hearing each paragraph, patients heard two sets of questions, one set testing their recall of the information and the second set that used true-or-false questions to test patients' recognition of the information. The study concluded that "[t]he vast majority of patients were able to comprehend the information that the [American Psychiatric Association] task force suggested was relevant to their decision," though the "patients who were initially admitted involuntarily" and later agreed to remain voluntarily "had significantly poorer performance and may constitute a group who need special educational efforts focused on the consequences of voluntary admission." Binyamin C. Appelbaum, Paul S. Appelbaum, & Thomas Grisso, *Competence to Consent to Voluntary Psychiatric Hospitalization: A Test of a Standard Proposed by APA*, 49 Psychiatr. Serv. 1193 (1998).

Voluntariness. The claim that many voluntary admissions are not truly voluntary, put forth in the Gilboy and Schmidt article, is also made by Reed and Lewis, supra:

> For the treatment coordinator the most desirable resolution of the problem of the patient's legal status is the patient's signature on a voluntary admission form. As soon as the patient signs that form, the treatment coordinator can send it onto the court and avoid any further negotiations with the court and its personnel. . . . One treatment coordinator said, "I never go to court. I've been here 18 years. If the court depended on me, it would close down."

* * *

The most common strategy [to get the signature on the voluntary form], and usually the first, is a combination of *persuasion and coercion.* The treatment coordinator points out to the patient the advantages of voluntary admission over involuntary commitment in order to convince him/her to sign. . . . Most suggest to patients that they are likely to be involuntarily committed if they refuse to sign a voluntary. For example, one treatment coordinator says, "If they don't sign, I say to them, 'You look committable to me.' They go for that. I tell them to put themselves in the judge's shoes. What would they do? They usually sign."

* * *

If this combination of persuasion and coercion does not break down the patients' resistance to voluntary admission, the treatment coordinator may try *bartering.* This strategy involves the exchange of hospital privileges for the patient's signature on a voluntary admission form . . . However, patients sometimes complain that the deals they negotiate with their treatment coordinators fall through. As one patient said of his therapist, "He promised me a grounds pass if I signed a voluntary, but he never delivered. I should never should have signed." Staff, of course, have the option of withholding privileges once the form has been signed.

* * *

Stalling can [also] be a strategy. . . . In some few cases emergency certified patients continue to refuse to sign a voluntary admission form despite this massive institutional effort to get them to do so. The hospital staff can solve their legal dilemma by getting additional continuances from the court until the patient is ready for discharge. Only four continuances are allowed per case, but two continuances are usually enough to get a patient ready for discharge. [Lewis and his coauthors] found that continuances kept patients in the hospital an average of just under 10 days.

Id. at 144–152.

Are any of the strategies described by this study impermissible as a legal matter? Consider the law on plea bargaining, the process by which criminal defendants agree to plead guilty in exchange for a reduced charge or sentence. The Supreme Court has held that a guilty plea produced by this process may be rendered involuntary by "coercion, terror, inducements, [and] subtle or blatant threats." *Boykin v. Alabama,* 395 U.S. 238, 89 S.Ct. 1709, 23 L.Ed.2d 274 (1969). At the same time, the Court has refused to invalidate guilty pleas simply because the defendant's situation is an unpleasant one. So long as a guilty plea represents a reasoned choice from among alternatives that are legitimately offered by the prosecution, it is not "involuntary." *Bordenkircher v. Hayes,* 434 U.S. 357, 98 S.Ct. 663, 54 L.Ed.2d 604 (1978); *Brady v. United States,* 397 U.S. 742, 90 S.Ct. 1463, 25 L.Ed.2d 747 (1970). If a staff member or treating psychiatrist tells a patient truthfully that he meets commitment criteria and the court is very likely to order involuntary hospitalization, would the patient's decision to sign in "voluntarily" really be "involuntary"? If not, is there still a reason for withholding the voluntary label from such a person?

2. *Alternatives to the informed consent model.* In light of the difficulties with the informed consent model of voluntary admission, particularly with respect to ensuring competent decisionmaking, various alternatives have been proposed. The first alternative is to allow voluntary admission of anyone who is "suitable" for such admission and fails to object to it. Several states appear to permit so-called "non-protesting" admissions. See, e.g., Mass Gen.Laws Ann. ch. 111, § 63(a); D.C.Stat. § 21–513.

> Although such [provisions] slight the value of individual autonomy that the informed consent is designed to foster, it would be no worse than the present system and would have the additional virtue of avoiding pretense. This system could, in addition, be augmented with the kind of internal review procedures (e.g. utilization review, staff conferences) that the Supreme Court indicated were adequate to protect the rights of minors admitted by their parents [in *Parham v. J.R.*]. Such a change would maximize therapeutic interests, while relegating more formal, legalistic proceedings to the background.

Appelbaum et al. (1981), supra at 1175. Are provisions that permit admission of non-protesting persons an end-run around the procedural requirements of involuntary commitment? Or are they justified by the "need for a simple, non-traumatic admission process for those individuals who either do not recognize their need for hospitalization or are unwilling to seek admission, but nevertheless do not object when others initiate the admission process?" Note, *District of Columbia Hospitalization of the Mentally Ill Act*, 65 Colum.L.Rev. 1062, 1065 (1965). In the past, many of the admissions under such statutes have been of senile persons who make no objection to psychiatric hospitalization. See *Application for Certification of William R*, 9 Misc.2d 1084, 172 N.Y.S.2d 869 (1958).

The second alternative to an informed consent model of voluntary admission is to appoint a guardian for all persons who assent to or do not protest hospitalization. The guardian's function would be to decide whether hospitalization is in the person's best interests, considering all relevant factors, including the person's wishes. This substituted judgment model is widely used as a method of institutionalizing minors and people with developmental disabilities. Very often the guardian is one of the patient's relatives, but it could be a judge or a public guardian. Does this approach provide any better protection against the practices observed by Gilboy and Schmidt?

A third alternative, of course, is to prohibit admission into a public psychiatric facility unless the person meets the criteria for involuntary commitment. Presumably, this option would bar some people who want or need treatment from obtaining it. Some commentators argue against *any* procedure which has this effect:

> In the vast majority of involuntary *and* voluntary cases, it is the family or relatives who move toward, pressure for, or insist on commitment. If state law enforcement personnel are involved, it is as often as not at the request of the family or relatives. In many instances where it orders commitment, the state's judicial machinery merely formalizes and sanctions a decision arrived at by the family and the family doctor. In admitting a mentally disabled person to one of its institutions, the state often does no more than facilitate the provision of wanted treatment that is difficult or too costly to obtain otherwise. With respect to the commitment process, the patient himself . . . may be confused or indifferent, generally agitated, unable to understand its necessity, or simply unable to comprehend. The phenomenon of a freely derived, fully conscious, voluntary decision to enter a mental facility (particularly a public facility) is as rare as knowing, overt resistance to involuntary commitment. In short, the voluntary-involuntary dichotomy of mental institutionalization, the traditional roles that are assigned to the participants in this dichotomized process, and many of the laws and procedures enacted to regulate it suffer from their irrelevance to practical situations.

Brakel et al., supra, at 32.

3. *The Supreme Court and voluntary commitment.* In *Zinermon v. Burch*, 494 U.S. 113, 110 S.Ct. 975, 108 L.Ed.2d 100 (1990), the plaintiff was asked to sign forms giving his consent to admission and treatment, even though staff evaluation showed that, upon his arrival at the evaluating facility, he was "hallucinating, confused, psychotic, and believed he was 'in heaven.'" Within the next three days, he signed voluntary admission forms on two other occasions. He subsequently brought a § 1983 action against the state of Florida, alleging that his due process rights were violated by the staff when they admitted him as a voluntary patient knowing he was incompetent, rather than affording him the procedural protections granted those subjected to involuntary commitment. Although the U.S. Supreme Court did not address the merits, it held that this claim was justiciable in federal court under § 1983. Portions of the Court's opinion may be of interest in deciding between the informed consent model and one of the alternative approaches:

> The Florida statutes, of course, do not allow incompetent persons to be admitted as "voluntary" patients. . . . A patient who is willing to sign forms but incapable of informed consent certainly cannot be relied on to protest his "voluntary" admission and demand that the involuntary placement procedure be followed. The staff are the only persons in a position to take notice of any misuse of the voluntary admission process, and to ensure that the proper procedure is followed.

> Florida chose to delegate to petitioners a broad power to admit patients to FSH, i.e., to effect what, in the absence of informed consent, is a

substantial deprivation of liberty. Because petitioners had state authority to deprive persons of liberty, the Constitution imposed on them the State's concomitant duty to see that no deprivation occurs without adequate procedural protections.

It may be permissible constitutionally for a State to have a statutory scheme like Florida's, which gives state officials broad power and little guidance in admitting mental patients. But when those officials fail to provide constitutionally required procedural safeguards to a person whom they deprive of liberty, the state officials cannot then escape liability. . . . It is immaterial whether the due process violation Burch alleges is best described as arising from petitioners' failure to comply with state procedures for admitting involuntary patients, or from the absence of a specific requirement that petitioners determine whether a patient is competent to consent to voluntary admission.

Professor Winick argued that *Zinermon* is misguided to the extent it suggests that a patient seeking voluntary treatment is required to understand the clinical and legal risks and benefits of hospitalization and its alternatives. He contends that such a rule would "relegate many to the burdens and stigma of involuntary commitment." Instead,

> a low standard of competency is all that should be required. As long as the patient understands that the facility he is seeking admission to is a psychiatric hospital, that he will receive care and treatment there, and that release is not automatic, but can occur if he should change his mind and that in such an event he can obtain help from any staff member to gain his release, he should be deemed competent.

The primary justification for this approach, according to Winick, is the large body of cognitive and social psychology literature (to date not adequately tested in the commitment context) which suggests that people who "feel personally committed" to a goal are more likely to achieve it. The literature also suggests that, "[e]xcept for young children, and sometimes even including them, the more choice we give individuals, the more they will act as mature, self-determining adults." Coercion, on the other hand, "may backfire, producing a negative 'psychological reactance' that sets up failure." Bruce Winick, *Competency to Consent to Voluntary Hospitalization: A Therapeutic Jurisprudence Analysis of* Zinermon v. Burch, 14 Int'l J.L. & Psych. 169, 191–98 (1991).

The American Psychiatric Association has essentially endorsed this approach, although its proposal also has elements of the non-protesting admission scheme described earlier. Francine Cournos, et al., *Report on the Task Force on Consent to Voluntary Hospitalization*, 21 Bull. Am.Acad.Psychiatry & L. 392 (1993). The APA recommends that voluntary hospitalization should continue even if the capacity of an assenting patient is in doubt, so long as an "independent psychiatrist" confirms that hospitalization is "appropriate and that the patient is continuing to assent to hospitalization." Id. at 304.

4. *Release of voluntary patients.* The procedure for releasing voluntary patients under the Illinois statute described by Gilboy and Schmidt is similar to that found in most states. Typically, a voluntary patient who wants to leave the hospital may not do so immediately but must give notice, ranging from three to ten days, during which time the hospital may initiate commitment proceedings if it feels involuntary commitment is warranted. See, e.g., Ohio Rev. Code § 5122.03. This restraint on release has been justified by Manfred Guttmacher and Henry Weihofen, Psychiatry and the Law 306 (1952), as follows:

> With regard to provisions for release, two opposing considerations must be weighed. On the one hand, complete freedom to leave the hospital at any time will almost certainly lead a number of patients to leave a few days after being admitted, for restlessness and dissatisfaction with the restraints of hospitalization are common and natural, especially during the first period of adjustment. This makes the admission a complete waste of time and money. On the other hand, refusal to release a voluntary patient on demand would not only be difficult to justify legally but would be highly undesirable, because resort to voluntary admission will be discouraged unless it is made quite clear that a patient may change his mind and leave. Most voluntary admission statutes meet the problem by providing that a voluntary patient shall be released within a specified number of days after he gives written notice of his desire to leave, unless in the meanwhile the hospital authorities start proceedings to have his status changed to that of involuntary patient.

If the patient is not told of such a notice-and-detention scheme, is *Zinermon* violated? Even if it is, would invalidating the notice-and-detention provision make any practical difference? Couldn't the patient who demands release be discharged and then immediately detained and subjected to involuntary commitment proceedings?

5. *Review of voluntary patients; conversion to voluntary status.* Many patients who are admitted voluntarily never request release, especially those who are admitted under the non-protesting admissions statutes described earlier. Are voluntary patients entitled to periodic review, as is true with involuntary patients? As the next section indicates, there has been considerable litigation on this issue in connection with specific types of "voluntary" patients, i.e., people with developmental disabilities and children. As a general matter, these cases mandate some type of review, although not necessarily judicial. Compare *Fasulo*, in the previous section.

Some courts have considered the review issue in the context of conversion of involuntary patients to voluntary status. Many states authorize this conversion whenever the hospital staff believes the change is indicated, in the belief that a voluntary relationship enhances therapy. See, e.g., Ark.Stats. § 20–47–224; N.Y.Code § 9.23(a). One court has found that the patient subject to such conversion in status is entitled to a judicial hearing reviewing the change as well as the same sort of periodic review provided involuntary patients. *Matter of Buttonow*, 23 N.Y.2d 385, 297 N.Y.S.2d 97,

244 N.E.2d 677 (1968). The dissenting opinion in *Buttonow* stated, in part: "[T]he salutary effect of voluntary status may be impaired by repeated judicial proceedings, or worse, remove the incentive of the institutions to arrange for conversions of status." Id. at 684 (Breitel, J., dissenting).

V.   COMMITMENT OF OTHER POPULATIONS

As noted at the outset of this chapter, most states have enacted separate commitment statutes for certain groups of people with mental disabilities. The most prominent such groups are insanity acquittees, prison and jail inmates requiring psychiatric treatment, people who abuse psychoactive substances, people who are developmentally disabled, and children with mental disabilities. This section examines the special considerations involved in commitment of these groups, with frequent comparison to the preceding materials.

A. INSANITY ACQUITTEES

Every state permits immediate commitment of persons who have been found not guilty by reason of insanity. Some states require a hearing before such commitment, but most states allow the acquittee to be committed "automatically" for a short time, after which a hearing is held to determine whether further commitment is proper. Almost all states also provide for later periodic judicial review, although in a few jurisdictions release is left up to the initiation of the hospital or the acquittee. One might argue that because insanity acquittees have by definition eluded conviction, they are similarly situated to persons subject to regular civil commitment and thus should be processed according to the same standards and procedures. But the Supreme Court has indicated that the Constitution does not require such an equation.

JONES V. UNITED STATES
Supreme Court of the United States, 1983.
463 U.S. 354, 103 S.Ct. 3043, 77 L.Ed.2d 694.

JUSTICE POWELL delivered the opinion of the Court.

The question presented is whether petitioner, who was committed to a mental hospital upon being acquitted of a criminal offense by reason of insanity, must be released because he has been hospitalized for a period longer than he might have served in prison had he been convicted.

I

In the District of Columbia a criminal defendant may be acquitted by reason of insanity if his insanity is "affirmatively established by a preponderance of the evidence." D.C.Code § 24–301(j) (1981). If he successfully invokes the insanity defense, he is committed to a mental hospital. § 24–301(d)(1). The statute provides several ways of obtaining release. Within 50 days of commitment the acquittee is entitled to a judicial hearing to determine his eligibility for release, at which he has the burden of proving by a preponderance of the evidence that he is no longer mentally ill or dangerous. § 24–301(d)(2).[3] If he fails to meet this burden at the 50–day hearing, the committed acquittee subsequently may be released, with court approval, upon certification of his recovery by the hospital chief of service. § 24–301(e). Alternatively, the acquittee is entitled to a judicial hearing every six months at which he may establish by a preponderance of the evidence that he is entitled to release. § 24–301(k).

Independent of its provision for the commitment of insanity acquittees, the District of Columbia also has adopted a civil-commitment procedure, under which an individual may be committed upon clear and convincing proof by the Government that he is mentally ill and likely to injure himself or others. § 21–545(b). The individual may demand a jury in the civil-commitment proceeding. § 21–544. Once committed, a patient may be released at any time upon certification of recovery by the hospital chief of service. §§ 21–546, 21–548. Alternatively, the patient is entitled after the first 90 days, and subsequently at 6–month intervals, to request a judicial hearing at which he may gain his release by proving by a preponderance of the evidence that he is no longer mentally ill or dangerous. §§ 21–546, 21–547.

II

On September 19, 1975, petitioner was arrested for attempting to steal a jacket from a department store. The next day he was arraigned in the District of Columbia Superior Court on a charge of attempted petit larceny, a misdemeanor punishable by a maximum prison sentence of one year. The court ordered petitioner committed to St. Elizabeths, a public hospital for the mentally ill, for a determination of his competency to stand trial. On March 1, 1976, a hospital psychologist submitted a report to the court stating that petitioner was competent to stand trial, that petitioner suffered from "Schizophrenia, paranoid type," and that petitioner's alleged offense was "the product of his mental disease." The court ruled that petitioner was competent to stand trial. Petitioner subsequently decided to plead not guilty by reason of insanity. The Government did not contest the plea, and it entered into a stipulation of facts with petitioner. On March 12, 1976, the Superior Court found petitioner not guilty by reason of insanity and committed him to St. Elizabeths pursuant to § 24–301(d)(1).

---

[3] The statute does not specify the standard for determining release, but the District of Columbia Court of Appeals held in this case that, as in release proceedings under § 24–301(e) and § 21–545(b), the confined person must show that he is either no longer mentally ill or no longer dangerous to himself or others. See 432 A.2d 364, 372, and n. 16 (1981) (en banc).

On May 25, 1976, the court held the 50–day hearing required by § 24–301(d)(2)(A). A psychologist from St. Elizabeths testified on behalf of the Government that, in the opinion of the staff, petitioner continued to suffer from paranoid schizophrenia and that "because his illness is still quite active, he is still a danger to himself and to others." Petitioner's counsel conducted a brief cross-examination, and presented no evidence.[8] The court then found that "the defendant-patient is mentally ill and as a result of his mental illness, at this time, he constitutes a danger to himself or others." Petitioner was returned to St. Elizabeths. Petitioner obtained new counsel and, following some procedural confusion, a second release hearing was held on February 22, 1977. By that date petitioner had been hospitalized for more than one year, the maximum period he could have spent in prison if he had been convicted. On that basis he demanded that he be released unconditionally or recommitted pursuant to the civil-commitment standards in § 21–545(b), including a jury trial and proof by clear and convincing evidence of his mental illness and dangerousness.

III

It is clear that "commitment for any purpose constitutes a significant deprivation of liberty that requires due process protection." *Addington v. Texas,* 441 U.S. 418, 425, 99 S.Ct. 1804, 1809, 60 L.Ed.2d 323 (1979). Therefore, a State must have "a constitutionally adequate purpose for the confinement." *O'Connor v. Donaldson,* 422 U.S. 563, 574, 95 S.Ct. 2486, 2493, 45 L.Ed.2d 396 (1975). Congress has determined that a criminal defendant found not guilty by reason of insanity in the District of Columbia should be committed indefinitely to a mental institution for treatment and the protection of society. Petitioner does not contest the Government's authority to commit a mentally ill and dangerous person indefinitely to a mental institution, but rather contends that "the petitioner's trial was not a constitutionally adequate hearing to justify an indefinite commitment."

Petitioner's argument rests principally on *Addington v. Texas, supra,* in which the Court held that the Due Process Clause requires the Government in a civil-commitment proceeding to demonstrate by clear and convincing evidence that the individual is mentally ill and dangerous. Petitioner contends that these due process standards were not met in his case because the judgment of not guilty by reason of insanity did not constitute a finding of present mental illness and dangerousness and because it was established only by a preponderance of the evidence. Petitioner then concludes that the Government's only conceivably legitimate justification for automatic commitment is to ensure that insanity acquittees do not escape confinement entirely, and that this

---

8   Petitioner's counsel seemed concerned primarily about obtaining a transfer for petitioner to a less restrictive wing of the hospital. See Tr. 11–12.

interest can justify commitment at most for a period equal to the maximum prison sentence the acquittee could have received if convicted. Because petitioner has been hospitalized for longer than the one year he might have served in prison, he asserts that he should be released unconditionally or recommitted under the District's civil-commitment procedures.

A

We turn first to the question whether the finding of insanity at the criminal trial is sufficiently probative of mental illness and dangerousness to justify commitment. A verdict of not guilty by reason of insanity establishes two facts: (i) the defendant committed an act that constitutes a criminal offense, and (ii) he committed the act because of mental illness. Congress has determined that these findings constitute an adequate basis for hospitalizing the acquittee as a dangerous and mentally ill person. See H.R.Rep. No. 91–907, *supra,* at 74 (expressing fear that "dangerous criminals, particularly psychopaths, [may] win acquittals of serious criminal charges on grounds of insanity" and yet "escape hospital commitment"); S.Rep. No. 1170, 84th Cong., 1st Sess., 13 (1955) ("Where [the] accused has pleaded insanity as a defense to a crime, and the jury has found that the defendant was, in fact, insane at the time the crime was committed, it is just and reasonable in the Committee's opinion that the insanity, once established, should be presumed to continue and that the accused should automatically be confined for treatment until it can be shown that he has recovered"). We cannot say that it was unreasonable and therefore unconstitutional for Congress to make this determination.

The fact that a person has been found, beyond a reasonable doubt, to have committed a criminal act certainly indicates dangerousness. Indeed, this concrete evidence generally may be at least as persuasive as any predictions about dangerousness that might be made in a civil-commitment proceeding.[13] We do not agree with petitioner's suggestion that the requisite dangerousness is not established by proof that a person committed a non-violent crime against property. This Court never has

---

[13] In attacking the predictive value of the insanity acquittal, petitioner complains that "[w]hen Congress enacted the present statutory scheme, it did not cite any empirical evidence indicating that mentally ill persons who have committed a criminal act are likely to commit additional dangerous acts in the future." He further argues that the available research fails to support the predictive value of prior dangerous acts. We do not agree with the suggestion that Congress' power to legislate in this area depends on the research conducted by the psychiatric community. We have recognized repeatedly the "uncertainty of diagnosis in this field and the tentativeness of professional judgment. The only certain thing that can be said about the present state of knowledge and therapy regarding mental disease is that science has not reached finality of judgment. . . . " The lesson we have drawn is not that government may not act in the face of this uncertainty, but rather that courts should pay particular deference to reasonable legislative judgments.

held that "violence," however that term might be defined, is a prerequisite for a constitutional commitment.[14]

Nor can we say that it was unreasonable for Congress to determine that the insanity acquittal supports an inference of continuing mental illness. It comports with common sense to conclude that someone whose mental illness was sufficient to lead him to commit a criminal act is likely to remain ill and in need of treatment. The precise evidentiary force of the insanity acquittal, of course, may vary from case to case, but the Due Process Clause does not require Congress to make classifications that fit every individual with the same degree of relevance. Because a hearing is provided within 50 days of the commitment, there is assurance that every acquittee has prompt opportunity to obtain release if he has recovered.

Petitioner also argues that, whatever the evidentiary value of the insanity acquittal, the Government lacks a legitimate reason for committing insanity acquittees automatically because it can introduce the insanity acquittal as evidence in a subsequent civil proceeding. This argument fails to consider the Government's strong interest in avoiding the need to conduct a *de novo* commitment hearing following every insanity acquittal—a hearing at which a jury trial may be demanded, § 21–544, and at which the Government bears the burden of proof by clear and convincing evidence. Instead of focusing on the critical question whether the acquittee has recovered, the new proceeding likely would have to relitigate much of the criminal trial. These problems accent the Government's important interest in automatic commitment. See *Mathews v. Eldridge,* 424 U.S. 319, 348, 96 S.Ct. 893, 909, 47 L.Ed.2d 18 (1976). We therefore conclude that a finding of not guilty by reason of insanity is a sufficient foundation for commitment of an insanity acquittee for the purposes of treatment and the protection of society.

B

Petitioner next contends that his indefinite commitment is unconstitutional because the proof of his insanity was based only on a preponderance of the evidence, as compared to *Addington's* civil-commitment requirement of proof by clear and convincing evidence. In equating these situations, petitioner ignores important differences between the class of potential civil-commitment candidates and the class of insanity acquittees that justify differing standards of proof. The *Addington* Court expressed particular concern that members of the public could be confined on the basis of "some abnormal behavior which might be perceived by some as symptomatic of a mental or emotional disorder, but

---

[14] See *Overholser v. O'Beirne,* 112 U.S.App.D.C. 267, 276, 302 F.2d 852, 861 (1961) (Burger, J.) ("[T]o describe the theft of watches and jewelry as 'non-dangerous' is to confuse danger with violence. Larceny is usually less violent than murder or assault, but in terms of public policy the purpose of the statute is the same as to both") (footnote omitted). It also may be noted that crimes of theft frequently may result in violence from the efforts of the criminal to escape or the victim to protect property or the police to apprehend the fleeing criminal.

which is in fact within a range of conduct that is generally acceptable." In view of this concern, the Court deemed it inappropriate to ask the individual "to share equally with society the risk of error." But since automatic commitment under § 24–301(d)(1) follows only if the *acquittee himself* advances insanity as a defense and proves that his criminal act was a product of his mental illness, there is good reason for diminished concern as to the risk of error. More important, the proof that he committed a criminal act as a result of mental illness eliminates the risk that he is being committed for mere "idiosyncratic behavior." A criminal act by definition is not "within a range of conduct that is generally acceptable."

We therefore conclude that concerns critical to our decision in *Addington* are diminished or absent in the case of insanity acquittees. Accordingly, there is no reason for adopting the same standard of proof in both cases. "[D]ue process is flexible and calls for such procedural protections as the particular situation demands." The preponderance of the evidence standard comports with due process for commitment of insanity acquittees.[17]

C

The remaining question is whether petitioner nonetheless is entitled to his release because he has been hospitalized for a period longer than he could have been incarcerated if convicted. The Due Process Clause "requires that the nature and duration of commitment bear some reasonable relation to the purpose for which the individual is committed." *Jackson v. Indiana,* 406 U.S. 715, 738, 92 S.Ct. 1845, 1858, 32 L.Ed.2d 435 (1972). The purpose of commitment following an insanity acquittal, like that of civil commitment, is to treat the individual's mental illness and protect him and society from his potential dangerousness. The committed acquittee is entitled to release when he has recovered his sanity or is no longer dangerous. And because it is impossible to predict how long it will take for any given individual to recover—or indeed whether he ever will recover—Congress has chosen, as it has with respect to civil commitment, to leave the length of commitment indeterminate, subject to periodic review of the patient's suitability for release.

In light of the congressional purposes underlying commitment of insanity acquittees, we think petitioner clearly errs in contending that an acquittee's hypothetical maximum sentence provides the constitutional limit for his commitment. A particular sentence of incarceration is chosen to reflect society's view of the proper response to commission of a

---

[17] A defendant could be required to prove his insanity by a higher standard than a preponderance of the evidence. See *Leland v. Oregon,* 343 U.S. 790, 799, 72 S.Ct. 1002, 1007, 96 L.Ed. 1302 (1952). Such an additional requirement hardly would benefit a criminal defendant who wants to raise the insanity defense, yet imposition of a higher standard would be a likely legislative response to a holding that an insanity acquittal could support automatic commitment only if the verdict were supported by clear and convincing evidence.

particular criminal offense, based on a variety of considerations such as retribution, deterrence, and rehabilitation. The State may punish a person convicted of a crime even if satisfied that he is unlikely to commit further crimes.

Different considerations underlie commitment of an insanity acquittee. As he was not convicted, he may not be punished. His confinement rests on his continuing illness and dangerousness. Thus, under the District of Columbia statute, no matter how serious the act committed by the acquittee, he may be released within 50 days of his acquittal if he has recovered. In contrast, one who committed a less serious act may be confined for a longer period if he remains ill and dangerous. There simply is no necessary correlation between severity of the offense and length of time necessary for recovery. The length of the acquittee's hypothetical criminal sentence therefore is irrelevant to the purposes of his commitment.

IV

We hold that when a criminal defendant establishes by a preponderance of the evidence that he is not guilty of a crime by reason of insanity, the Constitution permits the Government, on the basis of the insanity judgment, to confine him to a mental institution until such time as he has regained his sanity or is no longer a danger to himself or society. This holding accords with the widely and reasonably held view that insanity acquittees constitute a special class that should be treated differently from other candidates for commitment.

*   *   *

[The dissenting opinion of JUSTICE BRENNAN, with whom JUSTICE MARSHALL and JUSTICE BLACKMUN join, is omitted].

QUESTIONS AND COMMENTS

1.   *"Automatic" commitment.* In parts III(A) and III(B) of its opinion in *Jones,* the Supreme Court focused primarily on the constitutionality of "automatically" committing persons acquitted by reason of insanity. The Court sanctioned confinement without a hearing for at least 50 days when a criminal adjudication establishes beyond a reasonable doubt that the defendant has committed a criminal act and by a preponderance of the evidence that the defendant was insane at the time of the act. Does the Court's reasoning in Part III(B) of the opinion sanction automatic commitment in jurisdictions that allow an insanity verdict based on a reasonable doubt about sanity?[r] Even if it does not, could resort to automatic commitment in such jurisdictions be supported by analogizing to emergency

---

[r]   About 15 states require the state to prove sanity beyond a reasonable doubt. See pp. 636–638.

commitment in the civil commitment context, which is normally permitted on a showing well below the preponderance level?

Of course, even if only minimal proof of mental disability and dangerousness is sufficient for automatic commitment, one might question the Court's conclusion that the evidence adduced at a criminal trial (or, as in *Jones,* pursuant to a plea bargain) meets this standard. At most, all that is proven at such proceedings is that, at some time in the past, the defendant committed an antisocial act while insane. Do you agree with the Court's reasoning in Part III(A) that this finding is sufficient to support an "automatic" finding of present mental illness and dangerousness?

2. *Timing of hearing.* In holding that automatic commitment is permissible, *Jones* stated: "Because a hearing is provided within 50 days of the commitment, there is assurance that every acquittee has prompt opportunity to obtain release if he has recovered." Does the opinion *require* a "prompt" hearing (within 50 days) for the acquittee who has been automatically committed? In *Glatz v. Kort,* 807 F.2d 1514 (10th Cir. 1986), the Court held that hospitalization for 180 days before the "mandatory hearing" was not unconstitutional because (1) the acquittee could petition for earlier release; (2) doctors needed considerable time to treat the acquittee; and (3) acquittees are informed they will be automatically committed until they are eligible for release.

3. *Burden and standard of proof at the commitment hearing.* While *Jones* can be construed to require a hearing at some point after automatic commitment, it probably also sanctions the type of hearing authorized by the District of Columbia, which places the burden of proof on the acquittee by a preponderance of the evidence. See James Ellis, *The Consequences of the Insanity Defense: Proposals to Reform Post–Acquittal Commitment Law,* 35 Cath.U.L.Rev. 961, 972 (1986). Whether or not *Jones* so holds, a large number of states, as well as the District of Columbia, continue to place the burden of proof on the acquittee at the commitment hearing; some even require the acquittee to produce *clear and convincing* proof of noncommittability.[s] Of those that place the burden on the state, many require merely a preponderance of the evidence showing. See generally 53 Am. Jur. 2d § 59 (2013). Obviously, all of these statutes would be unconstitutional in the civil commitment context, given *Addington.* On what grounds might they be upheld in the post-insanity acquittal context? Several possibilities exist.

Risk of Error Analysis. First, consider again the reasoning in Part III(B) of *Jones* finding that such statutes are constitutional because there is "good reason for diminished concern as to the risk of error." By the time of the review hearing, is it still plausible to say that the risk of error on the issue of present mental disability and dangerousness is sufficiently diminished by proof at trial of insanity and a criminal act to differentiate this situation from

---

[s] The federal Insanity Defense Reform Act of 1984 requires those acquitted of "violent" crimes to prove noncommittability by clear and convincing evidence. 18 U.S.C. § 4243(d). This provision was upheld in *United States v. Wattleton,* 296 F.3d 1184, 1198 (11th Cir. 2002).

civil commitment? In *Ernst J. v. Stone,* 452 F.3d 186 (2d Cir. 2006), the court cited *Jones* in holding that, even at a *re*commitment hearing that takes place after the initial hearing, an insanity acquittee may be committed on a preponderance of the evidence "because having concededly once engaged in a criminal conduct as a result of mental illness, the insanity acquittee continues to present a serious risk of recurrence of dangerous behavior derived from mental illness."

The Public Safety Rationale. Most courts justify placing more of an evidentiary burden on insanity acquittees than on others subject to commitment on a different ground—that insanity acquittees, as a class, are more dangerous than other groups. See, e.g., *People v. Chavez,* 629 P.2d 1040, 1047–8 (Colo.1981). Insanity acquittees are likely to have committed acts more serious and more harmful than those committed by persons who are subjected to civil commitment. But one study has suggested that this fact does not correlate with a greater likelihood of recidivism. See Note, *Commitment and Release of Persons Found Not Guilty by Reason of Insanity: A Georgia Perspective,* 15 Ga.L.Rev. 1065, 1079 (1981). At the least, shouldn't those acquittees charged with "minor" crimes (akin to the type of act that might also trigger civil commitment) be treated the same as those subjected to civil commitment? See American Bar Association Criminal Justice Mental Health Standard 7–7.3(b). Or does the fact that acquittees have been charged with crime, albeit minor, make them different? Should the burden issue depend on whether a police officer decides to arrest someone like Jones (who attempted to steal a jacket) or instead decided to take him to the local crisis management unit?

The Lack of Autonomy Rationale. Another argument against applying *Addington* to commitment of insanity acquittees, at least those charged with violent crime, is advanced by Warren Ingber in *Rules for An Exceptional Class: The Commitment and Release of Persons Acquitted of Violent Offenses by Reason of Insanity,* 57 N.Y.U.L.Rev. 281, 301–02, 309 (1982). Ingber notes that one reason for limiting exercise of the police power in the civil commitment context is the societal interest in fostering autonomy. But, he contends, the insanity acquittee, unlike the person subjected to civil commitment, has been found deficient as an autonomous human being. Therefore the acquittee charged with a violent crime may be committed under a lower standard of proof.

> In a civil hearing, the state's interest in the safety of its citizens is partly offset by its interest in promoting autonomy; not so in a violent acquittee's commitment hearing. Thus, the state has a greater net interest in favor of a lower standard of proof in the latter hearing. In a word, it has no reason to be concerned about the effects such a standard will have on the autonomy of persons at large in society. The greater net state interest in a lower standard supports a reduction of the standard to a preponderance of the evidence.

Is this reasoning persuasive? Would it support not only reducing the standard of proof but shifting the burden of proof to the defendant?

The Clean-up Doctrine. Finally, consider the strength of what has been called the "clean-up doctrine," see Note, *Commitment Following an Insanity Acquittal*, 94 Harv.L.Rev. 605, 617 (1981), as support for placing a heavier burden on insanity acquittees than on those subjected to civil commitment.

> If an insanity acquittee is wrongly committed, so the argument goes, he was probably sane at trial and therefore wrongly acquitted of the crime in the first place. "While the acquittee therefore may be deprived erroneously of his liberty in the *commitment* process, the liberty he loses is likely to be liberty which society mistakenly had permitted him to retain in the *criminal* process."

Id. at 618 (emphasis in original).

4. *Commitment criteria.* A separate question from the burden and standard of proof issue is the extent to which the commitment criteria for insanity acquittees should track civil commitment criteria. This question can be broken down into several subparts.

Is dangerousness alone sufficient ground for commitment? In *Jones*, the Court stated that an acquittee who is found insane by a preponderance of the evidence may be confined to a mental institution "until such time as he has regained his sanity or is no longer a danger to himself or society." This language suggested that, as is true with a civil committee, an acquittee who is no longer mentally disordered must be released. In *Foucha v. Louisiana*, 504 U.S. 71, 112 S.Ct. 1780, 118 L.Ed.2d 437 (1992), the Supreme Court affirmed, as a matter of due process, that once an insanity acquittee is no longer "mentally ill," he or she must be released despite a finding of dangerousness. At a bench trial, Foucha had been acquitted by reason of insanity on charges of aggravated burglary and illegal discharge of a firearm, based on reports from two state-employed medical doctors. Four years later he sought release from the hospital. At the release hearing, the same two doctors who testified about his sanity at the time of the offense testified, in the Court's words, that "upon commitment Foucha probably suffered from a drug induced psychosis but that he had recovered from that temporary condition; that he evidenced no signs of psychosis or neurosis and was in 'good shape' mentally; that he has, however, an antisocial personality, a condition that is not a mental disease and that is untreatable." The doctors also testified that they could "not certify that he would not constitute a menace to himself or others if released." On these facts, the Supreme Court held, 5–4, that Foucha could no longer be confined in the hospital.

According to Justice White, who wrote the majority opinion:

> A State, pursuant to its police power, may of course imprison convicted criminals for the purposes of deterrence and retribution. But there are constitutional limitations on the conduct that a State may criminalize. See, e.g., *Robinson v. California*, 370 U.S. 660, 82 S.Ct. 1417, 8 L.Ed.2d 758 (1962). Here, the State has no such punitive interest. As Foucha was not convicted, he may not be punished. *Jones.* Here, Louisiana has by

reason of his acquittal exempted Foucha from criminal responsibility as La. Rev. Stat. Ann. § 14:14 (West 1986) requires.

The State may also confine a mentally ill person if it shows "by clear and convincing evidence that the individual is mentally ill and dangerous," *Jones*. Here, the State has not carried that burden; indeed, the State does not claim that Foucha is now mentally ill.

We have also held that in certain narrow circumstances persons who pose a danger to others or to the community may be subject to limited confinement and it is on these cases, particularly *United States v. Salerno* [upholding pretrial detention], that the State relies in this case.

Salerno does not save Louisiana's detention insanity acquittees who are no longer mentally ill. Unlike the sharply focused scheme at issue in *Salerno*, the Louisiana scheme of confinement is not carefully limited. . . . It was emphasized in *Salerno* that the detention we found constitutionally permissible was strictly limited in duration. Here, in contrast, the State asserts that because Foucha once committed a criminal act and now has an antisocial personality that sometimes leads to aggressive conduct, a disorder for which there is no effective treatment, he may be held indefinitely. This rationale would permit the State to hold indefinitely any other insanity acquittee not mentally ill who could be shown to have a personality disorder that may lead to criminal conduct. The same would be true of any convicted criminal, even though he has completed his prison term. It would also be only a step away from substituting confinements for dangerousness for our present system which, with only narrow exceptions and aside from permissible confinements for mental illness, incarcerates only those who are proved beyond reasonable doubt to have violated a criminal law.

Justice O'Connor, who was the fifth member of the majority for that part of the opinion excerpted above, wrote a concurring opinion suggesting that, because an insanity acquittee in Louisiana has been found, beyond a reasonable doubt, to have committed an offense "with the required level of criminal intent,"

[i]t might therefore be permissible for Louisiana to confine an insanity acquittee who has regained sanity if, unlike the situation in this case, the nature and duration of detention were tailored to reflect pressing public safety concerns related to the acquittee's continuing dangerousness.

[However,] acquittees could not be confined as mental patients absent some medical justification for doing so; in such a case the necessary connection between the nature and purposes of confinement would be absent. Nor would it be permissible to treat all acquittees alike, without regard for their particular crimes. For example, the strong interest in liberty of a person acquitted by reason of insanity but later found sane might well outweigh the governmental interest in detention where the only evidence of dangerousness is that the acquittee committed a non-violent or relatively minor crime.

The four dissenters argued that Louisiana should be able to confine Foucha. Justice Kennedy, joined by Chief Justice Rehnquist and Justice Scalia, and Justice Thomas, joined by Scalia, concluded that the fact that the state had established Foucha's commission of a criminal act beyond a reasonable doubt to be dispositive, and the Court's neglect of that fact to be an implicit overruling of *Jones*. According to Justice Kennedy:

> First, . . . the procedural protections afforded in a criminal [trial] surpass those in a civil commitment; indeed, these procedural protections are the most stringent known to our law. Second, proof of criminal conduct in accordance with *In re Winship* eliminates the risk of incarceration "for mere 'idiosyncratic behavior,' [because a] criminal act by definition is not 'within a range of conduct that is generally acceptable.' " *Jones*, quoting *Addington*. The criminal law defines a discrete category of conduct for which society has reserved its greatest opprobrium and strictest sanctions; past or future dangerousness, as ascertained or predicted in civil proceedings, is different in kind. Third, the State presents distinct rationales for these differing forms of commitment: In the civil context, the State acts in large part on the basis of its *parens patriae* power to protect and provide for an ill individual, while in the criminal context, the State acts to ensure the public safety.

* * *

Although Louisiana has chosen not to punish insanity acquittees, the State has not surrendered its interest in incapacitative incarceration. The Constitution does not require any particular model for criminal confinement, and upon compliance with *In re Winship*, the State may incarcerate on any reasonable basis. Incapacitation for the protection of society is not an unusual ground for incarceration. "[I]solation of the dangerous has always been considered an important function of the criminal law," *Powell v. Texas* (Blackmun, J., concurring), and insanity acquittees are a special class of offenders proved dangerous beyond their own ability to comprehend. The wisdom of incarceration under these circumstances is demonstrated by its high level of acceptance. Every State provides for discretionary or mandatory incarceration of insanity acquittees, and as JUSTICE THOMAS observes in his dissent, provisions like those in Louisiana, predicated on dangerousness alone, have been enforced by the Model Penal Code and adopted by the legislatures of no fewer than 11 other States.

It remains to be seen whether the majority, by questioning the legitimacy of incapacitative incarceration, puts in doubt the confinement of persons other than insanity acquittees. Parole release provisions often place the burden of proof on the prisoner to prove his lack of dangerousness. To use a familiar example, under the federal parole system in place until the enactment of the Sentencing Guidelines, an inmate could not be released on parole unless he established that his "release would not jeopardize the public welfare." This requirement reflected "the incapacitative aspect of the use of imprisonment which has the effect of denying the opportunity for future criminality, at least for a time." U.S. Dept. of Justice, United States Parole Commission Rules and Procedures Manual 69 (July 24, 1989). This purpose is consistent with the parole release provisions of Alabama, Colorado, Hawaii, Massachusetts, Michigan, New York, and the District of Columbia, to name just a few. It is difficult for me to reconcile the rationale of incapacitative incarceration, which underlies these regimes, with the opinion of the majority, which discounts its legitimacy.

Looking first at the majority's reasoning, is the distinction between *Foucha* and *Salerno* persuasive? If so, under what circumstances, if any, might detention of an insanity acquittee on dangerousness grounds alone be constitutional? How does Justice O'Connor answer this question? Would due process requirements be met if detention were limited to those acquitted on charges involving violence, the burden of proving dangerousness is placed on the state, review proceedings are frequent, and those found dangerous are not designated as mental patients but housed in prison settings? With respect to Justice Kennedy's dissent, note the reliance on *In re Winship* (which requires the prosecution to prove each essential element of the offense beyond a reasonable doubt). If sanity is not an "essential element" of the offense, then why shouldn't the state be able, as Kennedy suggests, to confine a dangerous person when it otherwise proves its case? If sanity *is* an element of each offense, does his argument make sense? With respect to the "pragmatic" aspect of his dissent, how might one distinguish the parolee and the insanity acquittee?

What is the definition of mental illness? A second issue connected with the commitment criteria for insanity acquittees has to do with the definition of mental illness. As previous materials explained,[t] the mental illness predicate for the insanity defense is generally thought to require severe mental disorder. Does the presence of severe mental disorder also have to be shown in order to meet the commitment criteria? In *Jones*, the Court refers to whether the acquittee has "regained sanity" in discussing when an acquittee must be released. In *Foucha*, the Court uses the arguably broader term "mental illness," but assumes that Foucha, who was diagnosed as an antisocial personality disorder "for which there is no effective treatment," was no longer "mentally ill." Yet just five years later, in *Kansas v. Hendricks*, 521 U.S. 346, 117 S.Ct. 2072, 138 L.Ed.2d 501 (1997), dealing with commitment of sexually violent predators, the Court authorized commitment predicated on "mental abnormality" and on a "personality disorder." See generally, Chapter Seven, Part III.B.

What is the definition of dangerousness? The statutes in both *Jones* and *Foucha* allow continued confinement upon proof of danger to self grounds, as

---

[t]   See pp. 646–648 for a discussion of the mental disease or defect requirement in insanity cases.

well as upon proof of danger to others. Should *parens patriae* commitment be permissible in this context?

Dangerousness to others may be defined more broadly in this context than in some civil commitment statutes. For instance, in *Jones* the Court asserts that crimes against property should be a legitimate basis for commitment. See n. 14 of the opinion. Lower courts have also held that a showing of imminent danger is not required to commit insanity acquittees. See, e.g., *Hill v. State*, 358 So.2d 190 (Fla.App.1978).

5.   *Procedures.* The only procedural aspect of the post-acquittal commitment hearing addressed by *Jones* was the right to jury trial. In a footnote, the Court stated:

> The District of Columbia provides for a jury at civil-commitment hearings, . . . and petitioner contends that equal protection requires that insanity acquittees also be permitted to demand a jury at the 50–day hearing. Because we determine that an acquittee's commitment is based on the judgment of insanity at the criminal trial, rather than solely on the findings at the 50–day hearing, . . . the relevant equal protection comparison concerns the procedures available at the criminal trial and at a civil-commitment hearing. We therefore agree with the Court of Appeals that the absence of a jury at the 50–day hearing 'is justified by the fact that the acquittee has had a right to a jury determination of his sanity at the time of the offense.'

463 U.S. at 362 n. 10, 103 S.Ct. at 3048 n. 10. Would the Court's analysis justify denying an acquittee counsel or other rights normally associated with civil commitment? Switching from equal protection analysis to a due process perspective, recall that two principal reasons given by the Supreme Court for relaxing procedures in the civil commitment context are the medical nature of the issues involved and the need to avoid procedures that will deter friends and families from seeking treatment. See *Addington,* supra; *Parham v. J.R.* Are these concerns present in the post-insanity acquittal context? What other state interests should be weighed in the balance in deciding how much process is due?

6.   *Duration of commitment.* Despite the Supreme Court's holding in *Jones,* several commentators have argued, and several state statutes provide, that commitment of acquittees be limited to the maximum sentence the acquittee would have received had he or she been found responsible for the crime charged. Cf. *Illinois v. Pastewski*, 251 Ill.App.3d 358, 190 Ill.Dec. 659, 622 N.E.2d 69 (1993) (maximum period of commitment of insanity acquittee cannot exceed the maximum sentence for crime with which he was charged, less good conduct credit, with the latter to be determined by the director of the Department of Mental Health). One rationale for such a rule is that commitment of insanity acquittees is, contrary to the Court's assertion, punitive and thus should be limited by the relevant criminal sentence. Three judges of the District of Columbia Court of Appeals panel in the *Jones* case reasoned as follows:

[A]cquittees are not confined to mental institutions for medical reasons alone. They are confined there in part because society is unwilling to allow those who have committed crimes to escape without paying for their crimes. The intent of the statute is partially punitive, and thus the [stricter procedures governing commitment and release of acquittees] reflect this added burden on the defendant. Because of this punitive purpose, the maximum statutory period of confinement becomes relevant, for at that point society no longer has a valid interest in continued confinement on the basis of a shortcut procedure.

Consider also this alternative critique of this aspect of *Jones*, from Ellis, supra at 981–82:

The majority's analysis attempts to answer the wrong question. The issue is not how long Jones could be lawfully committed, but rather how long he could be confined under procedures different from those employed for general commitment patients. The Court is correct in stating that treatment needs should be a determining factor in ascertaining the appropriate length of commitment. But the duration of the applicability of special commitment procedures should be set independently by principles of fairness and equality. Those principles require that special commitment be limited to the period of time during which the individual could have been confined had he been convicted.

* * *

. . . The state interest occasioned by attempted petit larceny is finite and measured by the maximum sentence; it does not increase when the offender proves to be mentally disabled. Any greater interest in confining the disabled offender must arise from his disability rather than his offense. Confining an acquittee for a longer period than the maximum sentence for his crime can only be justified by his continuing treatment or habilitation needs, and at that point, the fact of his offense becomes irrelevant. Therefore, there is no justification for treating him differently than general commitment patients who have a continuing treatment or habilitation need. Thus general commitment procedures should be the only means of extending such a commitment.

Cf. *Ernst J. v. Stone*, 452 F.3d 186, 201 (2d Cir. 2006) (expressing some doubt as to whether an acquittee subject to recommitment is distinguishable, for equal protection purposes, from a person subject to civil commitment, at least when the recommitment seeks institutionalization of an acquittee who has been released subject to conditions and is alleged to have violated the conditions).

In practice, insanity acquittees tend to spend about the same amount of time in the hospital as do convicted persons charged with similar crimes, although the time periods vary from state to state. Once released, insanity acquittees are no more likely to recidivate than released felons who were charged with similar offenses. Indeed, most research indicates a lower rate of recidivism for insanity acquittees. See, e.g., Stuart B. Silver et al., *Follow–Up after Release of Insanity Acquittees, Mentally Disordered Offenders and Convicted Felons*, 17 Bull. Am. Acad. Psychiatry & L. 387 (1989).

7.   *The Oregon review board.* As with civil commitment, perhaps more important than the various standards and procedures accompanying post-acquittal commitment are the systemic measures established for handling insanity acquittees who are determined to be mentally ill and dangerous. In 1977, the Oregon legislature enacted legislation setting up an innovative approach toward this problem. Or.Rev.Stat. §§ 161.327 to 161.336. Its most significant innovation was to shift responsibility for committed acquittees from the trial court to a Psychiatric Security Review Board (PSRB), on the theory that courts lack the staff, expertise and motivation to assure adequate treatment and monitoring of acquittees. The PSRB consists of five members, usually a psychiatrist, a psychologist, a person with expertise in parole and probation matters, a criminal trial lawyer, and a member of the general public. It has jurisdiction over all committed acquittees for the term of the maximum sentence they would have received had there been a conviction. It has authority to arrange treatment in many different types of programs, and leans heavily on conditional release arrangements. Any acquittee dissatisfied with the Board's disposition of his or her case may appeal to the courts. During the first five years of its operation, 6% of the 295 people conditionally released under the PSRB's authority were arrested for felony charges. Jeffrey Rogers et al., *After Oregon's Insanity Defense: A Comparison of Conditional Release and Hospitalization*, 5 Int'l J.L. & Psychiat. 391, 398 (1982).

B. PRISON AND JAIL INMATES

Of those individuals with a mental disorder who are processed through the criminal justice system, far fewer than one percent are acquitted by reason of insanity. Only a slightly larger proportion are sentenced under the types of special sentencing provisions discussed in Chapter Seven, such as those that establish indeterminate sentences and separate treatment facilities for persons found to be "mentally disordered sex offenders" or "sexually violent predators." The vast majority of persons with mental disorders who are charged with crime and not diverted out of the system prior to adjudication are convicted and sentenced to jail or prison. A large percentage of these individuals suffer from some type of mental disorder. According to the Bureau of Justice Statistics, 24% of state prisoners and 21% of jail inmates report a history of mental illness, and about 15% of state prisoners and 24% of jail inmates manifest psychotic symptoms. Doris James & Lauren Glaze, Mental Health Problems of Prison and Jail Inmates, U.S. Dep't of Justice Stats. (2006). Each year, jails book over two million people with serious mental illness. Henry J. Steadman et al., *Prevalence of Serious Mental Illness Among Jail Inmates*, 60 Psychiatric Serv. 761, 761 (2009). At some point during their sentence, many of these people need treatment that cannot be provided in jail or prison. Until 1980, in most states these people could be transferred to a mental health facility (either within the correctional system or within the mental health system) on the say-so of a mental health professional. That has now changed.

VITEK V. JONES

Supreme Court of the United States, 1980.
445 U.S. 480, 100 S.Ct. 1254, 63 L.Ed.2d 552.

MR. JUSTICE WHITE delivered the opinion of the Court, except as to Part IV–B.

The question in this case is whether the Due Process Clause of the Fourteenth Amendment entitles a prisoner convicted and incarcerated in the State of Nebraska to certain procedural protections, including notice, an adversary hearing, and provision of counsel, before he is transferred involuntarily to a state mental hospital for treatment of a mental disease or defect.

I

Nebraska Rev.Stat. § 83–176(2) (1976) authorizes the Director of Correctional Services to designate any available, suitable, and appropriate residence facility or institution as a place of confinement for any state prisoner and to transfer a prisoner from one place of confinement to another. Section 83–180(1), however, provides that when a designated physician or psychologist finds that a prisoner "suffers from a mental disease or defect" and "cannot be given proper treatment in that facility," the director may transfer him for examination, study, and treatment to another institution within or without the Department of Correctional Services. Any prisoner so transferred to a mental hospital is to be returned to the Department if, prior to the expiration of his sentence, treatment is no longer necessary. Upon expiration of sentence, if the State desires to retain the prisoner in a mental hospital, civil commitment proceedings must be promptly commenced. § 83–180(3).

On May 31, 1974, Jones was convicted of robbery and sentenced to a term of three to nine years in state prison. He was transferred to the penitentiary hospital in January 1975. Two days later he was placed in solitary confinement, where he set his mattress on fire, burning himself severely. He was treated in the burn unit of a private hospital. Upon his release and based on findings required by § 83–180 that he was suffering from a mental illness or defect and could not receive proper treatment in the penal complex, he was transferred to the security unit of the Lincoln Regional Center, a state mental hospital under the jurisdiction of the Department of Public Institutions.

Jones challeng[es] on procedural due process grounds the adequacy of the procedures by which the Nebraska statutes permit transfers from the prison complex to a mental hospital.

* * *

III

On the merits, the threshold question in this case is whether the involuntary transfer of a Nebraska state prisoner to a mental hospital implicates a liberty interest that is protected by the Due Process Clause.

* * *

Undoubtedly, a valid criminal conviction and prison sentence extinguish a defendant's right to freedom from confinement. Such a conviction and sentence sufficiently extinguish a defendant's liberty "to empower the State to confine him in any of its prisons." *Meachum v. Fano,* 427 U.S., at 224, 96 S.Ct., at 2538 (emphasis deleted). It is also true that changes in the conditions of confinement having a substantial adverse impact on the prisoner are not alone sufficient to invoke the protections of the Due Process Clause "[a]s long as the conditions or degree of confinement to which the prisoner is subjected is within the sentence imposed upon him."

Appellants maintain that the transfer of a prisoner to a mental hospital is within the range of confinement justified by imposition of a prison sentence, at least after certification by a qualified person that a prisoner suffers from a mental disease or defect. We cannot agree. None of our decisions holds that conviction for a crime entitles a State not only to confine the convicted person but also to determine that he has a mental illness and to subject him involuntarily to institutional care in a mental hospital. Such consequences visited on the prisoner are qualitatively different from the punishment characteristically suffered by a person convicted of crime. Our cases recognize as much and reflect an understanding that involuntary commitment to a mental hospital is not within the range of conditions of confinement to which a prison sentence subjects an individual. *Baxstrom v. Herold,* 383 U.S. 107, 86 S.Ct. 760, 15 L.Ed.2d 620 (1966); *Specht v. Patterson,* 386 U.S. 605, 87 S.Ct. 1209, 18 L.Ed.2d 326 (1967); *Humphrey v. Cady,* 405 U.S. 504, 92 S.Ct. 1048, 31 L.Ed.2d 394 (1972); *Jackson v. Indiana,* 406 U.S. 715, 724, 725, 92 S.Ct. 1845, 1851, 32 L.Ed.2d 435 (1972). A criminal conviction and sentence of imprisonment extinguish an individual's right to freedom from confinement for the term of his sentence, but they do not authorize the State to classify him as mentally ill and to subject him to involuntary psychiatric treatment without affording him additional due process protections.

In light of the findings made by the District Court, Jones' involuntary transfer to the Lincoln Regional Center pursuant to § 83–180, for the purpose of psychiatric treatment, implicated a liberty interest protected by the Due Process Clause. Many of the restrictions on the prisoner's freedom of action at the Lincoln Regional Center by themselves might not constitute the deprivation of a liberty interest retained by a prisoner. But here, the stigmatizing consequences of a transfer to a mental hospital for involuntary psychiatric treatment, coupled with the subjection of the prisoner to mandatory behavior modification as a treatment for mental illness, constitute the kind of deprivations of liberty that requires procedural protections.

IV

The District Court held that to afford sufficient protection to the liberty interest it had identified, the State was required to observe the following minimum procedures before transferring a prisoner to a mental hospital:

"A. Written notice to the prisoner that a transfer to a mental hospital is being considered;

"B. A hearing, sufficiently after the notice to permit the prisoner to prepare, at which disclosure to the prisoner is made of the evidence being relied upon for the transfer and at which an opportunity to be heard in person and to present documentary evidence is given;

"C. An opportunity at the hearing to present testimony of witnesses by the defense and to confront and cross-examine witnesses called by the state, except upon a finding, not arbitrarily made, of good cause for not permitting such presentation, confrontation, or cross-examination;

"D. An independent decisionmaker;

"E. A written statement by the fact-finder as to the evidence relied on and the reasons for transferring the inmate;

"F. Availability of legal counsel, furnished by the state, if the inmate is financially unable to furnish his own; and

"G. Effective and timely notice of all the foregoing rights."

A

We think the District Court properly identified and weighed the relevant factors in arriving at its judgment. Concededly the interest of the State in segregating and treating mentally ill patients is strong. The interest of the prisoner in not being arbitrarily classified as mentally ill and subjected to unwelcome treatment is also powerful, however; and as the District Court found, the risk of error in making the determinations required by § 83–180 is substantial enough to warrant appropriate procedural safeguards against error.

We recognize that the inquiry involved in determining whether or not to transfer an inmate to a mental hospital for treatment involves a question that is essentially medical. The question whether an individual is mentally ill and cannot be treated in prison "turns on the meaning of the facts which must be interpreted by expert psychiatrists and psychologists." *Addington v. Texas,* 441 U.S., at 429, 99 S.Ct., at 1811. The medical nature of the inquiry, however, does not justify dispensing with due process requirements. It is precisely "[t]he subtleties and nuances of psychiatric diagnoses" that justify the requirement of adversary hearings.

Because prisoners facing involuntary transfer to a mental hospital are threatened with immediate deprivation of liberty interests they are currently enjoying and because of the inherent risk of a mistaken transfer, the District Court properly determined that procedures similar to those required by the Court in *Morrissey v. Brewer,* 408 U.S. 471, 92 S.Ct. 2593, 33 L.Ed.2d 484 (1972), were appropriate in the circumstances present here.

The notice requirement imposed by the District Court no more than recognizes that notice is essential to afford the prisoner an opportunity to challenge the contemplated action and to understand the nature of what is happening to him. Furthermore, in view of the nature of the determinations that must accompany the transfer to a mental hospital, we think each of the elements of the hearing specified by the District Court was appropriate. The interests of the State in avoiding disruption was recognized by limiting in appropriate circumstances the prisoner's right to call witnesses, to confront and cross examine. The District Court also avoided unnecessary intrusion into either medical or correctional judgments by providing that the independent decisionmaker conducting the transfer hearing need not come from outside the prison or hospital administration.

B

The District Court did go beyond the requirements imposed by prior cases by holding that counsel must be made available to inmates facing transfer hearings if they are financially unable to furnish their own. We have not required the automatic appointment of counsel for indigent prisoners facing other deprivations of liberty, *Gagnon v. Scarpelli,* 411 U.S., at 790, 93 S.Ct., at 1763; but we have recognized that prisoners who are illiterate and uneducated have a greater need for assistance in exercising their rights. *Gagnon v. Scarpelli, supra,* at 786–787, 93 S.Ct., at 1761–1762. A prisoner thought to be suffering from a mental disease or defect requiring involuntary treatment probably has an even greater need for legal assistance, for such a prisoner is more likely to be unable to understand or exercise his rights. In these circumstances, it is appropriate that counsel be provided to indigent prisoners whom the State seeks to treat as mentally ill.

V

Because Mr. Justice Powell, while believing that Jones was entitled to competent help at the hearing, would not require the State to furnish a licensed attorney to aid him, the judgment below is affirmed as modified to conform with the separate opinion filed by Mr. Justice Powell.

So ordered.

[On the right to counsel issue, Mr. Justice Powell's concurring opinion, reprinted at pp. 941–943, found that due process requires only "a qualified and independent advisor" who "may be . . . a licensed psychiatrist or other mental health professional." The remaining four members of the Court dissented on the ground that the case was moot.]

QUESTIONS AND COMMENTS

1. *Comparison to civil commitment.* Although *Vitek* clearly held that something more than a diagnosis from a mental health professional is necessary before a prison-to-hospital transfer may take place, it just as clearly does not require procedural protections that are as extensive as the protections most states provide those subject to civil commitment.[u] Prior to *Vitek* some lower courts held that the equal protection clause required civil commitment procedures prior to such transfers. In *United States ex rel. Schuster v. Herold,* 410 F.2d 1071 (2d Cir.), cert. denied 396 U.S. 847, 90 S.Ct. 81, 24 L.Ed.2d 96 (1969), for instance, the court held that the prison inmate subjected to a transfer should be accorded "substantially the same procedures . . . as are granted to civilians when they are involuntarily committed to a mental hospital." Id. at 1084. Accord, *Matthews v. Hardy,* 420 F.2d 607 (D.C.Cir.1969), cert. denied 397 U.S. 1010, 90 S.Ct. 1231, 25 L.Ed.2d 423 (1970). The *Schuster* court based its decision primarily on the Supreme Court's decision in *Baxstrom v. Herold,* 383 U.S. 107, 86 S.Ct. 760, 15 L.Ed.2d 620 (1966). *Baxstrom* held unconstitutional, under the equal protection clause, a New York law providing a relatively informal commitment process for prisoners who were on the verge of completing their prison term; the Court reasoned that prisoners who have served their terms are similarly situated to persons subjected to civil commitment and therefore may only be committed pursuant to normal civil commitment procedures. If raised by the petitioner in *Vitek,* should *Baxstrom* and equal protection analysis have governed the decision, as *Schuster* suggests?

Instead of equal protection analysis, the Court relied on *Morrissey v. Brewer* and *Gagnon v. Scarpelli,* which dealt with the procedures necessary to revoke probation and parole under the due process clause. Recall that traditional due process analysis, under *Mathews v. Eldridge,* 424 U.S. 319, 96 S.Ct. 893, 47 L.Ed.2d 18 (1976), requires balancing (1) the significance of the private interest to be adjudicated under the procedures at issue; (2) the risk

---

    [u] Note that the Supreme Court has yet to indicate whether civil commitment requires anything more in the way of procedural formality than it provides prisoners subject to hospital transfers.

of an erroneous deprivation under the procedures; and (3) the government's interest in maintaining them. In *Vitek,* the Court identified two private interests affected by transfer: the stigma associated with being labelled mentally disordered and the possibility of compelled treatment. There are at least two other possible drawbacks to transfer: the "strong likelihood that an inmate transferred to a mental health facility will be paroled later than a like inmate who remained in the correctional facility" (given "that most parole authorities would be wary of releasing a person from a mental health facility directly to the community"), and the possibility that transferees will be denied good-time credits for the time they are in the hospital. Michael Churgin, *The Transfer of Inmates to Mental Health Facilities,* in John Monahan & Henry Steadman, eds., Mentally Disordered Offenders 220 (1983). Are these factors enough to make prison-to-hospital transfers equivalent to the deprivation of liberty associated with civil commitment? Are there any relevant differences between transfers and commitment with respect to the second and third prongs of the *Mathews v. Eldridge* analysis?

2. *Pre-trial detainees.* A separate transfer issue arises in the context of pretrial detention. As noted earlier, of the millions of individuals who pass through the jails each year, a substantial percentage are seriously mentally ill. Although some of these people have been convicted and sentenced to serve time in jail, most are there because they have been unable to make bail and thus are confined pending trial or some other proceeding. Of this latter group, many will eventually be evaluated and found incompetent to stand trial, a procedure explored in Chapter Nine. But a large number are not found incompetent, yet need treatment that cannot be provided in jail. See Henry Steadman et al., The Mentally Ill in Jail: Planning for Essential Services (1989). Should *Vitek* apply to these people? Or is civil commitment the proper route? If the latter, should commitment *criteria* as well as procedures be applicable?

3. *Hospital-to-prison transfers.* Usually a person transferred to a mental health facility will eventually be returned to the prison.[v] Sometimes, this retransfer may be premature (if, for example, the hospital believes the person is a "troublemaker"). Is such a person entitled to a hearing to review the hospital's decision? At least two courts have considered this issue; they reached opposite results. *Burchett v. Bower,* 355 F.Supp. 1278 (D.Ariz.1973) (yes); *Cruz v. Ward,* 558 F.2d 658 (2d Cir.1977) (no).

If such a hearing is held, what criteria should apply? Perhaps of relevance here is *Bowring v. Godwin,* 551 F.2d 44 (4th Cir.1977), which found a right to psychiatric treatment for prisoners, but only when that treatment is a "medical necessity":

> [A prisoner] is entitled to psychological or psychiatric treatment if a physician or other health care provider, exercising ordinary skill and care at the time of observation, concludes with reasonable medical

---

[v] Presumably, at the least, hospitalization is limited by the length of the sentence. Some sort of periodic review is probably also required, although it may be very informal. *Westerfer v. Neal,* 682 F.3d 679 (7th Cir. 2012).

certainty (1) that the prisoner's symptoms evidence a serious disease or injury; (2) that such disease or injury is curable or may be substantially alleviated; and (3) that the potential for harm to the prisoner by reason of delay or the denial of care would be substantial.

Cf. *Estelle v. Gamble,* 429 U.S. 97, 97 S.Ct. 285, 50 L.Ed.2d 251 (1976) (holding that the eighth amendment obligates the government to provide medical care for prisoners, but only to the extent necessary to avoid "deliberate indifference to serious medical needs of prisoners.")

4. *Mental health courts.* Reacting to failures in the mental health system that have led to incarceration of thousands of mentally ill persons in jails and prisons, the first mental health court began operating in Broward County, Florida in 1997; since then, some form of these courts has emerged in most states. As of 2009, more than 250 mental health courts were in operation in the U.S., and many additional courts were being planned. Lauren Almquist & Elizabeth Dodd, Mental Health Courts: A Guide to Research–Informed Policy and Practice 2 (Council of State Governments Justice Center, 2009). Rather than seeking conviction and imprisonment of criminals, these courts try to ensure that people with mental illness who become enmeshed in the criminal system obtain mental health treatment. In many programs, jurisdiction is limited to those who have committed misdemeanors, but almost half also accept those charged or convicted of non-violent felonies. Arthur J. Lurigio & Jessica Snowden, *Putting Therapeutic Jurisprudence into Practice: The Growth, Operations, and Effectiveness of Mental Health Court,* 36 Just. Sys. J. 196, 198 (2009). Incentives to engage in treatment range from simple praise at a weekly status hearing in front of a judge to having the initial charges dropped or the conviction vacated. Sanctions for non-compliance also vary, and include requiring more or different treatment, increased supervision, and expulsion from the program (resulting in placement in jail). Id. at 207. Virtually all of the programs require the consent of the defendant. Roughly 95% of those given the choice between mental health court and regular criminal court choose the former. John Petrila et al., *Preliminary Observations from an Evaluation of the Broward County Florida Mental Health Court,* 37 Court Review 14 (2001).

Such a choice may not always be a wise one. A Bazelon Center for Mental Health Law survey of 20 mental health courts found that roughly half required a guilty plea in order to trigger jurisdiction, and those that instead permitted dismissal of charges after "completion of treatment" did not define the term clearly. In at least 40% of the jurisdictions surveyed, length of court supervision significantly exceeded possible length of incarceration and probation for the offense; in most, "treatment" involved indeterminate supervision, and often required anti-psychotic medication. In 64% of the courts, the sanction for noncompliance was jail time (with the rest relying primarily on adjustment of services and increased judicial persuasion). Over half the jurisdictions surveyed did not allow the offender to withdraw from mental health court and seek traditional criminal court adjudication. These various aspects of the court's process were not necessarily explained to those who are deciding between mental health court and regular criminal court. Bazelon Center for Mental Health, *The Role of Mental Health Courts in System Reform*, available at http://www.bazelon.org/.

While cautiously supportive of the concept if various modifications are made, the Bazelon Center also expressed concern that mental health courts will divert resources from reform of mental health services generally, and tempt government officials and others to use the criminal system as a means of seeking help for those with mental illness, resulting in the criminalization of mental illness. Accordingly, it recommends, contrary to the mandate of most mental health court systems, that mental health courts focus on offenders who commit serious crimes and allow those charged with misdemeanors to be handled through pre-existing, non-judicial diversion programs of the type described on pp. 919–920. It also argues against requiring a guilty plea, which it asserts will "hinder reintegration [by leading] to denial of housing and employment." Id.

Other research looks at the efficacy of mental health courts (MHC) from a number of different perspectives. According to one summary, "[a]cross several studies, there is consistent, if not robust, evidence that MHC participants are better off than comparable non-MHC participants," in terms of booking rates, treatment referral, and overall functioning (although re-arrest rates within a 12–month period can still be as high as 47%). Allison D. Redlich, *Voluntary, But Knowing and Intelligent?: Comprehension in Mental Health Courts*, 4 Psychol., Pul. Po'y & L. 605, 613 (2005). At the same time, a substantial percentage of MHC participants may not fully understand their options, with upward of 25% not meeting competency to stand trial standards. Id. at 614–16.

Is the mental health court a good idea? Should it be "voluntary," or mandated for people with serious mental disorders? Should it be limited to people charged with misdemeanors, to those charged with felonies, or should it handle both groups? Why shouldn't the court have jurisdiction over *all* offenders with mental disorder, even those who are not seriously mentally ill? At least one mental health court does not require proof that the person has a mental disorder. Id. at n.11. Arguing against such an expansive view, one commentator notes the voluminous research, described at pp. 821–824, indicating that crimes committed by people with mental illness are usually caused by something other than mental illness (substance abuse, family problems, and antisocial tendencies). If that research is correct, she argues, the conceptual basis of mental health courts (which assumes a link between mental illness and crime) is suspect and the treatment aimed at alleviating the mental illness may be ineffective at reducing recidivism. Lea Johnston, *Theorizing Mental Health Courts*, 89 Wash. U. L. Rev. 519 (2012).

C. CHEMICALLY DEPENDENT PERSONS

According to the U.S. Dep't of Health and Human Services' National Household Survey on Drug Abuse, in 2010 an estimated 22.5 million Americans aged 12 or older, comprising 7.3% of the population, were dependent on or abused alcohol and 2.3%, or 8.6 million, were dependent on or abused illicit drugs (the two groups overlap to some extent). SAMHSA, Substance Abuse Disorders in Substate Regions, 2008–2010 (2012), available at http://www.samhsa.gov/data/2k12/NSDUH113/ SR113StateSubUseDisorder2012.htm. Most states have special statutes for the commitment of people perceived to be addicted to alcohol or drugs and who are dangerous to self or others as a result. Those states that do not have special statutes usually permit commitment of addicted individuals under general commitment statutes. See, e.g., Ind. Code § 12–7–2–130(1); Me. Rev. Stat. Tit. 34–B, § 3801(5). Many of the special commitment statutes define the predicate for commitment as use of alcohol or drugs that causes a "habitual lack of self-control," unconsciousness, or an inability to make "a rational decision with respect to . . . need for treatment [or] basic personal needs or safety." See, e.g., Colo. §§ 25–1–302(1)(9); 25–1–1101(11). Others are more behaviorally oriented. See, e.g., Fla. Stat. § 397.311(13)(defining an "habitual user" as someone "brought to the attention of law enforcement for being substance impaired . . . and who has been taken into custody for such impairment three or more times during the preceding 12 months"). Finally, some laws are more conclusory. See, e.g., Tex. Health & Safety Code § 461.002(1)(defining "chemical dependency" as "abuse of alcohol or a controlled substance, psychological or physical dependence on alcohol or a controlled substance or addiction to alcohol or a controlled substance"). Many states require that the commitment take place at specialized facilities, but many do not, and some permit commitment to jail if special facilities are not available. See, e.g., Mass. St. ch.123 § 35. In a number of states, commitment periods for those who abuse substances are shorter than for general commitment. See, e.g., N.D. Cent Code § 25–03.1–17 (14 days); Colo. Stat. § 25–1–311(5)(30 days); Haw. Rev. Stat. § 334–60.5(i)(90 days).

QUESTIONS AND COMMENTS

1. *The definition of disorder.* Should addiction be grounds for commitment? Several years ago, Professor Fingarette argued that there is no empirical support for the view that alcoholism is a disease. Herbert Fingarette, Heavy Drinking: The Myth of Alcoholism as a Disease (1988). He noted that most substance abusers never develop serious dependency problems. He also noted that, in contrast to those with mental illness, many who suffer addiction rehabilitate themselves (noting, for instance, that many veterans returning from Vietnam abandoned their heroin addictions upon return to civilian life). Nonetheless, the American Psychiatric Association's Diagnostic and Statistical Manual includes a category for substance abuse disorder. In connection with alcohol, for instance, it defines the disorder as "[a] problematic pattern of alcohol use . . . as manifested by at least two of the following, occurring within a 12–month period" [listing, inter alia]: (1) "alcohol is often taken in larger amounts or over a longer period than was

intended;" (2) "a great deal of time is spent in activities necessary to obtain alcohol, use alcohol, or recover from its effects;" (3) "a failure to fulfill major role obligations at work, school, or home;" (4) "recurrent alcohol use in situations in which it is physically hazardous;" (5) "a need for markedly increased amounts of alcohol to achieve intoxication or desired effect;" (6) "alcohol . . . is taken to relieve or avoid withdrawal symptoms." DSM–5, at 490–91. Is this a sufficient predicate for commitment, assuming the requisite danger is also shown? If not, are the Colorado, Florida or Texas definitions given above any better?

2. *Police power commitment.* In *Robinson v. California*, 370 U.S. 660, 82 S.Ct. 1417, 8 L.Ed.2d 758 (1962), the Supreme Court held that drug and alcohol addiction per se may not be punished criminally because, among other things, addiction is not a voluntary act. But in *Powell v. Texas*, 392 U.S. 514, 88 S.Ct. 2145, 20 L.Ed.2d 1254 (1968), it made clear that if an addict commits any type of crime, even if it is being drunk in public, then he or she may be punished. Thus criminal sanctions continue to be society's primary response to addicted individuals who commit antisocial acts.

Recall that the standard justifications for police power commitment of people with mental illness are that they are either more dangerous, more treatable or less deterrable than the general population. Do people with addictions fit into any of these categories?

3. *Drug courts.* Many jurisdictions permit commitment of drug addicts who are charged with crime as an alternative to criminal sentence. One of the first efforts in this regard was the National Addict Rehabilitation Act of 1966, 42 U.S.C. 3401 et seq. A more recent development in this regard is the "drug court." Analogous to the mental health courts discussed in the previous section, drug courts differ from earlier court diversion programs in that

> the court rather than a treatment center is the focal point of the treatment process . . . The judge engages the clients directly, asks personal questions, and encourages them in the treatment process. Judges interact with clients in a manner more like proactive therapists than dispassionate judicial officers. The role of attorneys is also substantially different in the drug court than in a traditional court. Not only is the relationship between public defender and prosecutor no longer adversarial, but lawyers generally play a less prominent role. In many drug courts the lawyers do not even show up for the regular drug court sessions, and even when they do, it is often difficult to determine just which persons in the courtroom are the attorneys. . . . As Judge Jeff Rosnik of the Miami drug court put it, in drug court "the players' roles are altered, modified, inextricably changed. . . . Legal Justice becomes therapeutic jurisprudence. And crime and punishment becomes holistic justice."

James L. Nolan, Reinventing Justice: The American Drug Court Movement 40, 42 (2001). The heavy involvement of judges in treatment supervision is thought to enhance treatment compliance. The de-emphasis of traditional lawyering stems from the courts' focus on treatment rather than adjudication of guilt and punishment.

The evidence suggests that drug courts are superior to criminal justice prosecutions at reducing crime, because they "quickly identify substance abusing offenders and place them under ongoing judicial monitoring and community supervision, coupled with effective, long-term treatment services." C. West Huddleston III, Doulgas B. Marlowe & Rachel Casebolt, Nat'l Drug Court Inst., Painting the Current Picture: A National Report Card on Drug Courst and Other Problem–Solving Court Programs in the United States 2 (2008). A 2005 GAO study of drug courts came to a number of conclusions, summarized below:

> The authors of the GAO study reached a series of conclusions about the effectiveness of adult drug treatment courts, based upon a systematic collection of information from the twenty-seven selected evaluations (which studied thirty-nine distinct courts). Their analysis showed that most, although not all, of the programs that had collected data on criminal reoffending produced a reduction in the rate of participants' recidivism, relative to the comparison groups, "during periods of time that generally corresponded to the length of the drug court program— that is, within-program." These reductions tended to hold in terms of the number of participants who were rearrested for new offenses during the program and in terms of the percentage of drug court participants who had "recidivism events." . . . With respect to clinical outcomes, the GAO authors examined whether drug courts generally are successful in reducing substance use relapse. They concluded that the evidence was "limited and mixed." . . . The authors of the GAO study also examined the rates at which participants completed, or "graduated from," the drug court programs under review, as well as the factors associated with successful program completion. They found a wide variation among the jurisdictions, ranging from a low of twenty-seven percent program completion to a high of sixty-six percent . . . Not surprisingly, the factor most closely associated with program completion was the participants' compliance with drug court procedures and requirements. "No other program factor, such as the severity of the sanction that would be imposed if participants failed to complete the program or the manner in which judges conducted status hearings, predicted participants' program completion." In light of the claim that criminal system coercion is an important therapeutic lever in successful drug courts, it is significant that the GAO evaluators were unable to confirm that program completion rates were associated with the "legal consequences of program failure. . . . In essence, the findings of the GAO study suggest that drug courts succeed in retaining participants in treatment (to the extent that they do so) not so much because of the particular elements or design features of a given program, but rather because of the characteristics of individual participants, including those characteristics that make substance users "treatment ready." The authors' conclusion, "that drug court programs can be an effective means to deal with some

offenders," recognizes this fundamental fact about the importance of tailoring therapeutic interventions to the individual needs of those with substance use disorders.

Richard C. Bolt, *The "Tomahawk" and the "Healing Balm": Drug Treatment Courts in Theory and Practice*, 10 U. Md. L.J. Race, Religion, Gender & Class 45, 50–58 (2010).

How similar are drug courts to traditional civil commitment? Are they a model worth emulating throughout the criminal justice system?

4.   *Parens patriae commitment.* Professor Wexler doubts the propriety of committing narcotics addicts under the *parens patriae* power.

> Drug addicts . . . are seldom classified as psychotic, and they ordinarily retain contact with reality. If addicts are to be considered incompetent, then, it must be because their overpowering compulsion to consume drugs prevents them from reaching a rational decision regarding treatment. . . . But it is true, of course, that some addicts *do* decide to enter treatment, and that cuts against a blanket notion equating addiction with incompetence. One commentator has argued rather persuasively that addiction should not in itself establish incompetency.
>
> > But if addicts have lost their powers of self-control, so have all chain smokers and compulsive gamblers. They have all lost control over a partial and clearly limited area of conduct, but not over conduct or decision-making capacity generally. They are unable to decide not to smoke or gamble, but they are as competent to decide to attempt a cure of their habit as to decide whether to undergo an operation or to come in out of the rain. Addiction, as a shorthand expression for compulsive psychological dependence, makes no man a ward of the state unless his weakness has some additional effects on his mental processes generally.

David Wexler, Mental Health Law 42–44 (1981).

Wexler points out that the benefit the addict receives from commitment is also unclear. First, the addict may prefer his addicted state to confinement and indefinite supervision or even to his or her previous life prior to addiction. Second, Wexler questions the efficacy of addiction treatment, although on this point more recent research suggests that he was too pessimistic. D. Dwayne Simpson, George W. Joe, & Kirk M. Broome, *A National 5–Year Follow–Up of Treatment Outcomes for Cocaine Dependence*, 59 Arch. Gen. Psychiatry 538 (2002) (only a quarter of patients interviewed 5 years after discharge from a national sample of treatment programs still used cocaine weekly); Robert Hubbard, et al., Drug Abuse Treatment: A National Study of Effectiveness 125 (1989) (less than 20% of participants in any treatment modality were regular users of opiates or heroin three to five years after entering treatment).

How do you respond to this analysis? Does it have relevance for those addicted to alcohol?

D. PEOPLE WITH DEVELOPMENTAL DISABILITIES

The term "developmental disability" was not widely used until the 1970's. It is meant to designate a large group of individuals with mental disorder who are distinguished from both persons with mental illness and persons addicted to alcohol and drugs. Under the federal Developmentally Disabled Assistance and Bill of Rights Act, 42 U.S.C. §§ 6000, 6001(7), the term is defined to include:

> a severe, chronic disability of a person which (A) is attributable to a mental or physical impairment or combination of mental and physical impairments; (B) is manifested before the person attains age twenty-two; (C) is likely to continue indefinitely; (D) results in substantial functional limitations in three or more of the following areas of major life activity: (i) self-care, (ii) receptive and expressive language, (iii) learning, (iv) mobility, (v) capacity for independent living, and (vi) economic self-sufficiency; and (E) reflects the person's need for a combination and sequence of special, interdisciplinary, or generic care, treatment or other services which are of lifelong or extended duration and are individually planned and coordinated.

The group of individuals most commonly categorized as developmentally disabled are people with mental retardation—in current psychiatric terminology, persons with intellectual disabilities. But also included are people who suffer from learning disabilities, epilepsy, cerebral palsy and autism.

Almost every state has a special commitment statute for people with developmental disabilities. Many use this term specifically, while others refer to people with mental retardation (as do most of the court cases that follow, which is why in the material below we frequently use the term as well). In many states, the differences between this statute and the commitment statute for people with mental illness are insignificant. In a number of states, however, the commitment criteria for people with developmental disabilities are both broader and narrower: they permit commitment based on a finding of a need for treatment or inability to care, at the same time dangerousness is removed as a criterion. Ark. Stat. § 20–48–404(1); Del.Code tit. 16, § 5504; Mont.Stat. § 53–20–125. Several statutes also appear to contemplate only "voluntary" admissions, initiated either by the person or the person's relatives of guardian. Ga.Stat. § 37–4–40. Finally, a few states do not contemplate any type of commitment for people with developmental disabilities, see, e.g., Alaska Stat. § 47.30.700; Va. Code Ann. § 37.2, and at least ten jurisdictions have eliminated institutions for this group. David Braddock et al., State of the States in Developmental Disabilities 50 (2008). As the following case makes clear, in some states there are other differences as well.

HELLER V. DOE

Supreme Court of the United States, 1993.
509 U.S. 312, 113 S.Ct. 2637, 125 L.Ed.2d 257.

JUSTICE KENNEDY delivered the opinion of the Court.

In the Commonwealth of Kentucky, involuntary civil commitments of those alleged to be mentally retarded and of those alleged to be mentally ill are governed by separate statutory procedures. Two differences between these commitment proceedings are at issue in this case. First, at a final commitment hearing, the applicable burden of proof for involuntary commitment based on mental retardation is clear and convincing evidence, while the standard for involuntary commitment based on mental illness is beyond a reasonable doubt. Second, in commitment proceedings for mental retardation, unlike for mental illness, "[g]uardians and immediate family members" of the subject of the proceedings "may participate . . . as if a party to the proceedings," with all attendant rights, including the right to present evidence and to appeal. Respondents are a class of mentally retarded persons committed involuntarily to Kentucky institutions. They argue that these distinctions are irrational and violate the Equal Protection Clause of the Fourteenth Amendment. . . . We reject these contentions and hold the Kentucky statutes constitutional.

* * *

II

Respondents contend that, in evaluating the constitutionality of the distinctions drawn by Kentucky's statutes, we should apply not rational-basis review, but some form of heightened scrutiny. This claim is not properly presented. Respondents argued before the District Court and the Court of Appeals only that Kentucky's statutory scheme was subject to rational-basis review, and the courts below ruled on that ground. . . . We therefore decide this case as it has been presented to the courts whose judgments are being reviewed.

III

We many times have said, and but weeks ago repeated, that rational-basis review in equal protection analysis "is not a license for courts to judge the wisdom, fairness, or logic of legislative choices." Nor does it authorize "the judiciary [to] sit as a superlegislature to judge the wisdom or desirability of legislative policy determinations made in areas that neither affect fundamental rights nor proceed along suspect lines." For these reasons, a classification neither involving fundamental rights nor proceeding along suspect lines is accorded a strong presumption of validity. . . . A State, moreover, has no obligation to produce evidence to sustain the rationality of a statutory classification. "[A] legislative choice is not subject to courtroom factfinding and may be based on rational speculation unsupported by evidence or empirical data." A statute is presumed constitutional, and "[t]he burden is on the one attacking the legislative arrangement to negative every conceivable basis which might support it," whether or not the basis has a foundation in the record. Finally, courts are compelled under rational-basis review to accept a legislature's generalizations even when there is an imperfect fit between means and ends. A classification does not fail rational-basis review because it "is not made with mathematical nicety or because in practice it results in some inequality." . . . We have applied rational-basis review in previous cases involving the mentally retarded and the mentally ill. See *Cleburne v. Cleburne Living Center, Inc.*, 473 U.S. 432, 105 S.Ct. 3249, 87 L.Ed.2d 313 (1985); *Schweiker v. Wilson*, 450 U.S. 221, 101 S.Ct. 1074, 67 L.Ed.2d 186 (1981). In neither case did we purport to apply a different standard of rational-basis review from that just described. True, even the standard of rationality as we so often have defined it must find some footing in the realities of the subject addressed by the legislation. That requirement is satisfied here. Kentucky has proffered more than adequate justifications for the differences in treatment between the mentally retarded and the mentally ill.

A

Kentucky argues that a lower standard of proof in commitments for mental retardation follows from the fact that mental retardation is easier to diagnose than is mental illness. That general proposition should cause little surprise, for mental retardation is a developmental disability that becomes apparent before adulthood. See American Psychiatric Assn., Diagnostic and Statistical Manual of Mental Disorders 29 (3d rev. ed. 1987) (hereinafter Manual of Mental Disorders); American Assn. on Mental Retardation, Mental Retardation: Definition, Classification, and Systems of Support 5, 16–18 (9th ed. 1992) (hereinafter Mental Retardation). By the time the person reaches 18 years of age the documentation and other evidence of the condition have been accumulated for years. Mental illness, on the other hand, may be sudden and may not occur, or at least manifest itself, until adulthood. See, *e.g.*, Manual of Mental Disorders 190 (onset of schizophrenia may occur any time during adulthood); *id.*, at 220, 229 (onset of depression usually is during adulthood). Furthermore, as we recognized in an earlier case, diagnosis of mental illness is difficult. See *Addington v. Texas*. Kentucky's basic premise that mental retardation is easier to diagnose than is mental illness has a sufficient basis in fact.

This difference between the two conditions justifies Kentucky's decision to assign a lower standard of proof in commitment proceedings involving the mentally retarded. In assigning the burden of proof, Kentucky was determining the "risk of error" faced by the subject of the proceedings. *Addington*. If diagnosis is more difficult in cases of mental illness than in instances of mental retardation, a higher burden of proof for the former tends to equalize the risks of an erroneous determination that the subject of a commitment proceeding has the condition in question. From the diagnostic standpoint alone, Kentucky's differential burdens of proof (as well as the other statutory distinction at issue), are rational.

There is, moreover, a "reasonably conceivable state of facts" from which Kentucky could conclude that the second prerequisite to commitment—that "[t]he person presents a danger or a threat of danger to self, family, or others," Ky. Rev.Stat.Ann. § 202B.040 (Michie 1991)—is established more easily, as a general rule, in the case of the mentally retarded. Previous instances of violent behavior are an important indicator of future violent tendencies. Mental retardation is a permanent, relatively static condition, so a determination of dangerousness may be made with some accuracy based on previous behavior. We deal here with adults only, so almost by definition in the case of the retarded there is an 18–year record upon which to rely.

This is not so with the mentally ill. Manifestations of mental illness may be sudden, and past behavior may not be an adequate predictor of future actions. Prediction of future behavior is complicated as well by the difficulties inherent in diagnosis of mental illness. It is thus no surprise that many psychiatric predictions of future violent behavior by the mentally ill are inaccurate. For these reasons, it would have been plausible for Kentucky to conclude that the dangerousness determination was more accurate as to the mentally retarded than the mentally ill.

A statutory classification fails rational-basis review only when it " 'rests on grounds wholly irrelevant to the achievement of the State's objective.' " Because ease of diagnosis is relevant to two of the four inquiries, it is not "wholly irrelevant" to the achievement of Kentucky's objective, and thus the statutory difference in the applicable burden of proof survives rational-basis review. In any event, it is plausible for Kentucky to have found that, for purposes of determining the acceptable risk of error, diagnosis and dangerousness are the most critical factors in the commitment decision, so the appropriate burden of proof should be tied to them.

There is a further, more far-reaching rationale justifying the different burdens of proof: The prevailing methods of treatment for the mentally retarded, as a general rule, are much less invasive than are those given the mentally ill. The mentally ill are subjected to medical and psychiatric treatment which may involve intrusive inquiries into the patient's innermost thoughts, and use of psychotropic drugs. By contrast, the mentally retarded in general are not subjected to these medical treatments. Rather, " 'because mental retardation is . . . a learning disability and training impairment rather than an illness,' the mentally retarded are provided "habilitation," which consists of education and training aimed at improving self-care and self-sufficiency skills. It is true that the loss of liberty following commitment for mental illness and mental retardation may be similar in many respects; but the different treatment to which a committed individual is subjected provides a rational basis for Kentucky to decide that a greater burden of proof is needed before a person may be committed for mental illness. . . . It may also be true that some persons committed for mental retardation are subjected to more intrusive treatments while confined. Nonetheless, it would have been plausible for the Kentucky Legislature to believe that most mentally retarded individuals who are committed receive treatment that is different from, and less invasive than, that to which the mentally ill are subjected. "States are not required to convince the courts of the correctness of their legislative judgments." Thus, since " 'the question is at least debatable,' " rational-basis review permits a legislature to use just this sort of generalization.

. . . Kentucky's burden of proof scheme, then, can be explained by differences in the ease of diagnosis and the accuracy of the prediction of future dangerousness and by the nature of the treatment received after commitment. Each of these rationales, standing on its own, would suffice to establish a rational basis for the distinction in question.

B

There is a rational basis also for the other distinction challenged by respondents: that Kentucky allows close relatives and guardians to participate as parties in proceedings to commit the mentally retarded but not the mentally ill. As we have noted, by definition, mental retardation has its onset during a person's developmental period. Mental retardation, furthermore, results in "deficits or impairments in adaptive functioning," that is to say, "the person's effectiveness in areas such as social skills, communication, and daily living skills, and how well the person meets the standards of personal independence and social responsibility expected of his or her age by his or her cultural group." Manual of Mental Disorders 28–29. See also Mental Retardation 5–6, 15–16, 38–41. Based on these facts, Kentucky may have concluded that close relatives and guardians, both of whom likely have intimate knowledge of a mentally retarded person's abilities and experiences, have valuable insights that should be considered during the involuntary commitment process.

Mental illness, by contrast, may arise or manifest itself with suddenness only after minority, when the afflicted person's immediate family members have no knowledge of the medical condition and have long ceased to provide care and support. Further, determining the proper course of treatment may be far less dependent upon observations made in a household setting. Indeed, we have noted the severe difficulties inherent in psychiatric diagnosis conducted by experts in the field. *Addington*. In addition, adults previously of sound mental health who are diagnosed as mentally ill may have a need for privacy that justifies the State in confining a commitment proceeding to the smallest group compatible with due process. Based on these facts, Kentucky may have concluded that participation as parties by relatives and guardians of the mentally ill would not in most cases have been of sufficient help to the trier of fact to justify the additional burden and complications of granting party status. To be sure, Kentucky could have provided relatives and guardians of the mentally retarded some participation in commitment proceedings by methods short of providing them status as parties. That, however, is irrelevant in rational-basis review. We do not require Kentucky to have chosen the least restrictive means of achieving its legislative end. As long as Kentucky "rationally advances a reasonable and identifiable governmental objective, we must disregard" the existence of alternative methods of furthering the objective "that we, as individuals, perhaps would have preferred." *Schweiker*.

*   *   *

JUSTICE SOUTER, with whom JUSTICE BLACKMUN and JUSTICE STEVENS join, and with whom JUSTICE O'CONNOR joins as to Part II, dissenting.

*   *   *

II

Obviously there are differences between mental retardation and mental illness. They are distinct conditions, they have different manifestations, they require different forms of care or treatment, and the course of each differs. It is without doubt permissible for the State to treat those who are mentally retarded differently in some respects from those who are mentally ill. The question here, however, is whether some difference between the two conditions rationally can justify the particular disparate treatment accorded under this Kentucky statute.

The first distinction wrought by the statute is the imposition of a lesser standard of proof for involuntary institutionalization where the alleged basis of a need for confinement is mental retardation rather than mental illness. . . . In upholding this disparate treatment, the Court relies first on the State's assertion that mental retardation is easier to diagnose than mental illness. . . . [But] the question whether a lower burden of proof is rationally justified . . . turns not only on whether ease of diagnosis and proof of dangerousness differ as between cases of illness and retardation, but also on whether there are differences in the respective interests of the public and the subjects of the commitment proceedings, such that the two groups subject to commitment can rationally be treated differently by imposing a lower standard of proof for commitment of the retarded. The answer is clearly that they can not. While difficulty of proof, and of interpretation of evidence, could legitimately counsel against setting the standard so high that the State may be unable to satisfy it (thereby effectively thwarting efforts to satisfy legitimate interests in protection, care, and treatment), that would at most justify a lower standard in the allegedly more difficult cases of illness, not in the easier cases of retardation. We do not lower burdens of proof merely because it is easy to prove the proposition at issue, nor do we raise them merely because it is difficult.[5] Nor do any other reasonably conceivable facts cut in favor of the distinction in treatment drawn by the Kentucky statute. Both the ill and the retarded may be dangerous, each may require care, and the State's interest is seemingly of equal strength in each category of cases. No one has or would argue that the value of liberty varies somehow depending on whether one is alleged to be ill or retarded, and a mentally retarded person has as much to lose by civil commitment to an institution as a mentally ill counterpart, including loss of liberty to "choos[e] his own friends and companions, selec[t] daily activities, decid[e] what to eat, and retai[n] a level of personal privacy," among other things. . . .

The Court also rests its conclusion on the view that "it would have been plausible for the Kentucky Legislature to believe that most mentally retarded individuals who are committed receive treatment that is . . . less invasive tha[n] that to which the mentally ill are subjected." Nothing cited by the Court, however, demonstrates that such a belief would have been plausible for the Kentucky Legislature, nor does the Court's discussion render it plausible now. One example of the invasiveness to which the Court refers is the use of (and the results of the administration of) psychotropic drugs. [A]ny apparent plausibility in the Court's suggestion that "the mentally retarded in general are not subjected to th[is] medical treatmen[t]," dissipates the moment we examine readily available material on the subject, including studies of institutional practices affecting the retarded comparable to those studies concerning the treatment of mental illness cited by the Court. One recent examination of institutions for the mentally retarded in Kentucky's neighboring State of Missouri, for example, found that 76% of the institutionalized retarded receive some type of psychoactive drug and that fully 54% receive psychotropic drugs.

. . . The Court also suggests that medical treatment for the mentally retarded is less invasive than in the case of the mentally ill because the

---

[5]   And indeed, to the extent *Addington v. Texas* does discuss the difficulty of diagnosing mental illness, it supports use only of a *lesser* standard of proof because of the practical problems created by a supposed "serious question as to whether a state could ever prove beyond a reasonable doubt that an individual is both mentally ill and likely to be dangerous." Of course, in this case Kentucky has determined that the liberty of those alleged to be mentally ill is sufficiently precious that the State should assume the risk inherent in use of that higher standard.

mentally ill are subjected to psychiatric treatment that may involve intrusive enquiries into the patient's innermost thoughts. Again, I do not disagree that the mentally ill are often subject to intrusive psychiatric therapy. But the mentally retarded too are subject to intrusive therapy, as the available material on the medical treatment of the mentally retarded demonstrates. The mentally retarded are often subjected to behavior modification therapy to correct, among other things, anxiety disorders, phobias, hyperactivity, and antisocial behavior, therapy that may include aversive conditioning as well as forced exposure to objects that trigger severe anxiety reactions. . . .

III

With respect to the involvement of family members and guardians in the commitment proceeding, the Court holds it to be justified by the fact that mental retardation "has its onset during a person's developmental period," while mental illness "may arise or manifest itself with suddenness only after minority." [A]lthough these differences might justify a scheme in which immediate relatives and guardians were automatically called as witnesses in cases seeking institutionalization on the basis of mental retardation, they are completely unrelated to those aspects of the statute to which Doe objects: permitting these immediate relatives and guardians to be involved "as parties" so as to give them, among other things, the right to appeal as "adverse" a decision not to institutionalize the individual who is subject to the proceedings. Where the third party supports commitment, someone who is alleged to be retarded is faced not only with a second advocate for institutionalization, but with a second prosecutor with the capacity to call and cross-examine witnesses, to obtain expert testimony and to raise an appeal that might not otherwise be taken, whereas a person said to require commitment on the basis of mental illness is not. This is no mere theoretical difference, and my suggestion that relatives or guardians may support curtailment of liberty finds support in the record in this case. It indicates that of the 431 commitments to Kentucky's state-run institutions for the mentally retarded during a period between 1982 and the middle of 1985, all but one were achieved through the application or consent of family members or guardians.

. . .

Without plausible justification, Kentucky is being allowed to draw a distinction that is difficult to see as resting on anything other than the stereotypical assumption that the retarded are "perpetual children," an assumption that has historically been taken to justify the disrespect and "grotesque mistreatment" to which the retarded have been subjected. As we said in *Cleburne*, the mentally retarded are not "all cut from the same pattern: . . . they range from those whose disability is not immediately evident to those who must be constantly cared for." In recent times, at least when imposing the responsibilities of citizenship, our jurisprudence has seemed to reject the analogy between mentally retarded adults and nondisabled children. See, e.g., *Penry v. Lynaugh*, 492 U.S. 302, 338, 109 S.Ct. 2934, 2957, 106 L.Ed.2d 256 (1989) (controlling opinion of O'CONNOR, J.) (not "all mentally retarded people . . . —by virtue of their mental retardation alone, and apart from any individualized consideration of their personal responsibility—inevitably lack the cognitive, volitional, and moral capacity to act with the degree of culpability associated with the death penalty"); see also id. at 340 ("reliance on mental age to measure the capabilities of a retarded person for purposes of the Eighth Amendment could have a disempowering effect if applied in other areas of the law"). When the State of Kentucky sets up respective schemes for institutionalization on the basis of mental illness and mental retardation, it too is obliged to reject that analogy, and to rest any difference in standards for involuntary commitment as between the ill and the retarded on some plausible reason.

QUESTIONS AND COMMENTS

1. *Equal protection and people with development disabilities.* The majority opinion emphasizes that Kentucky needed only a "rational basis," as opposed to a substantial or compelling reason, for its differential treatment of people with mental illness and people with retardation. Thus, the Court suggested, without directly holding, that persons with intellectual disabilities do not comprise a "suspect class" for equal protection purposes. Eight years earlier, the Court had supposedly explicitly held that mental disability is not a suspect class in *Cleburne v. Cleburne Living Center, Inc.*, 473 U.S. 432, 105 S.Ct. 3249, 87 L.Ed.2d 313 (1985), a decision briefly mentioned by both the majority and dissenting opinions in *Heller*. Yet, contrary to the usual outcome in a rational-basis review case, in *Cleburne* the government lost; the Supreme Court struck down a zoning ordinance that required group homes for people with retardation to obtain permits that medical hospitals, nursing homes, apartment houses, and fraternities and sororities did not need to obtain. That fact led some commentators to suggest that *Cleburne* actually applied a heightened "rational-basis-with-bite" test to cases involving mental disability. See, e.g., Gayle Lynn Pettinga, *Rational Basis with Bite: Intermediate Scrutiny by Any Other Name*, 62 Ind. L.J. 779, 793–99 (1987). *Heller* did not entirely settle this issue, given its curiously indirect manner of deciding that rational basis review was the appropriate analysis in that case. The implications of *Cleburne*, *Heller* and other cases addressing equal protection for people with mental disability are discussed further in Chapter Twelve.

2. *Analysis of* Heller. Assuming rational-basis review is the correct analysis, is there a rational basis for Kentucky's commitment law? Couldn't the differing burdens of proof be seen as an attempt to provide extra protection for people with mental illness rather than as discrimination against people with mental retardation (who, after all, are still accorded the constitutionally required clear-and-convincing standard of proof)? Is that type

of question irrelevant if, as Justice Souter suggests, both groups are subjected to the same degree of liberty deprivation? On the latter score, note that, although Justice Souter's data suggest that the practice is different, in theory only people with mental illness or people who are dually diagnosed (i.e., who are suffering from both mental retardation *and* mental illness) should receive psychotropic medication. On the other hand, as detailed below, people with retardation usually end up hospitalized for much longer periods of time than people with mental illness, and in many states are not accorded as much periodic review. As to the provision that makes relatives and guardians parties to the case, is it accurate to characterize these individuals as "prosecutors," as Justice Souter does? If, as the notes below suggest, the main issue in such commitment hearings is placement, might it not make sense to make relatives parties who have concomitantly greater say as to where their loved ones go? As a counter, consider the trial court's findings in *Secretary of Public Welfare of Penn. v. Institutionalized Juveniles,* 442 U.S. 640, 99 S.Ct. 2523, 61 L.Ed.2d 142 (1979), that parents' decision to hospitalize a child with mental retardation may be the result of community pressure, emotional difficulties in dealing with the child, or financial problems connected with providing necessary care. Finally, does *Atkins v. Virginia,* the case which prohibited execution of people with mental retardation, support the majority or the dissent?

3.   *Voluntary admission and periodic review.* As mentioned at the beginning of this section, one frequent difference between commitment statutes for people with retardation and people with mental illness is that the former are often admitted by their relatives or guardians as "voluntary" patients.[w] See James W. Ellis, *Decisions by and for People with Mental Retardation: Balancing Considerations of Autonomy and Protection,* 37 Villanova L. Rev. 1779, 1809 (1992)("a majority of persons with mental retardation who are confined to large residential institutions are there as 'voluntary patients,' [y]et . . . [i]t is certain that a large percentage of these individuals have not validly 'consented' to their placement by any process that will bear inspection."). That practice probably results from the fact that many retarded persons are not considered capable of communicating their desires. In *In re Hop,* 29 Cal.3d 82, 171 Cal.Rptr. 721, 623 P.2d 282 (1981), the California Supreme Court found that such "voluntary" admissions violated the equal protection clause. Stated the court, "No other class of adults similarly situated and in need of protective custody may lawfully be placed in a state hospital without a knowing and intelligent waiver of rights, or a request, or a judicial determination that placement is appropriate." It thus required a judicial hearing to determine whether a person with developmental disability is gravely disabled or a danger to self or others, and whether placement in a state hospital is warranted. Would the Supreme Court agree with this analysis?

The *Hop* court did not directly address whether and when periodic review should take place once a person with developmental disability is

---

[w]   See discussion of non-protesting admissions of people with mental illness, pp. 974–976.

committed. In *Matter of Harhut,* 385 N.W.2d 305 (Minn.1986), the court was confronted with a statutory scheme for commitment of people with retardation that, unlike the statute at issue in *Hop,* required an initial judicial determination of committability but, like that statute, did not establish periodic judicial review procedures. Lawyers for the petitioner, a 35–year–old man who was blind, mildly mentally retarded, and autistic "at times," argued there was no rational or compelling basis for requiring individuals with mental retardation (or their relatives or guardians) to request judicial review when the state mandated such review for people with mental illness and for chemically dependent persons. Citing *Cleburne,* the court rejected this argument:

> [T]he distinction between the commitment periods . . . is based on a legislative judgment that mental retardation is, unlike chemical dependency or mental illness, a condition not usually susceptible of great or rapid improvement. The legislature decided that indeterminate commitment subject to judicial review on the motion of the patient was the more effective and efficient way to deal with the state's responsibility to treat retarded persons. This is a legitimate public purpose, and it is not clear beyond a reasonable doubt that indeterminate commitment is an unreasonable means of assuring the state's interest.

Although the court found no equal protection violation, it did find that, under the due process clause, every person with mental retardation who is committed to an institution is entitled to have counsel receive the results of staff medical reviews; according to the statute, these reviews were to occur "as frequently as necessary but not less than annually." It further held that some type of judicial review—not necessarily rising to the level of a hearing— must occur once every three years (the review period for people with mental illness and people deemed chemically dependent was one year). In Arkansas, no periodic review is required; rather commitment ends only in the "sole judgment" of the state agency's board of directors. Ark. Code Ann. § 20–48– 412. This statute was upheld, on condition that an annual internal review of all indefinitely committed individuals take place. *Porter v. Knickrehm,* 457 F.3d 7794 (8th Cir. 2006).

Is relative incapacity to communicate one's desires a "rational basis" for permitting "non-protesting admission" of people with retardation when it is prohibited for others? Is their relative stability a "rational basis" for relying on patient-initiated review (or no review at all) for people with developmental disabilities in those jurisdictions that require periodic review for people with mental illness? If they are unable to communicate their desires, how can they initiate review?

4. *Commitment criteria.* As noted in the introduction to this subsection, many statutes governing commitment of people with developmentally disability allow confinement based merely on a finding of disability and a "need for treatment"—or, to use more modern terminology, "habilitation" or "training in survival skills." At least one court has found such statutes unconstitutional. See, e.g., *Kinner v. State,* 382 So.2d 756

(Fla.App.1980) (the statute must include "criteria limiting persons who may be involuntarily committed to those who lack the capacity to weigh for themselves the risks of freedom and the benefits of hospitalization and/or to those who are dangerous to themselves or others."). See also, *People v. Reliford,* 65 Ill.App.3d 177, 21 Ill.Dec. 778, 382 N.E.2d 72 (1978). In contrast, one court has upheld against a vagueness challenge a statute that permitted commitment if the court certifies simply that the person is "mentally deficient." *Matter of Vandenberg,* 48 Or.App. 609, 617 P.2d 675 (1980). The court found that, unlike the criteria for commitment of people with mental illness, "the standard for commitment [under this statute] is set by scientific tests monitoring levels of intellectual functioning and adaptive behavior." The statute and accompanying regulations permitted court certification only if the examining institution found (a) that the person met the definition of mental retardation found in the then-current Manual of the American Association of Mental Deficiency (which now calls itself the "American Association on Intellectual and Developmental Disabilities") and (b) that "admission to a state institution for the mentally retarded [is] the optimal available plan and is in the best interest of the person and the community." The definition of mental retardation in the Manual did not require consideration of the person's ability to understand or consent to treatment.

Is there a rational basis for establishing broader commitment criteria for people with developmental disabilities? How do you think the Supreme Court would answer this question?

5. *Alternatives to institutionalization.* Given the obvious impairment of many people with developmental disabilities, until recently the major problem connected with their commitment was not that it frequently coerced people who did not want or need state-provided habilitation but that it usually meant long-term institutionalization in mega-facilities that were inadequate at providing training and even tended to accentuate dependency and deterioration. See David Ferleger, *Anti–Institutionalization: The Promise of the Pennhurst Case,* 31 Stanford L.Rev. 717, 720–724 (1979). The least restrictive alternative doctrine has particular applicability here. Dybwad and Herr have suggested that, once it is determined that a person with developmental disability is incapable of giving meaningful consent and requires close supervision due to a lack of survival skills, the relevant placement criteria should be "whether any in-home supportive services or respite care services could be provided as an alternative to removal from home surroundings; factually-grounded expectations of effective treatment in other settings; and a realistic assessment of whether the benefits to the resident of removal from community surroundings outweigh the harms." Gunnar Dybwad & Stanley Herr, *Unnecessary Coercion: An End to Involuntary Civil Commitment of Retarded Persons,* 31 Stanford L.Rev. 753, 764 (1979).

Fortunately the trend has been toward de-institutionalization; while in 1982 only about one-fifth of people with developmental disabilities were housed in community-based settings, by 2006 over 90% were in such settings.

See Braddock, supra, at 19, and, as noted earlier, ten states have done away with institutions for people with developmental disability. Id. at 50. Unfortunately, many localities still lack either home or community services for people with developmental disabilities. Indeed, most of the litigation that attempts to force states to create alternatives to institutions has been brought on behalf of this group. These efforts, and the legislation they have spawned, are discussed in Chapters Ten, Eleven and Twelve.

E. CHILDREN

Until the 1950's, the procedures for committing children were usually similar, if not identical, to those governing commitment of adults. But since that time, in conjunction with the general trend toward voluntary hospitalization, most states have enacted special statutes allowing "voluntary" admission of children on the petition of their parents or guardians. By the mid–1970's, three-quarters of the states had special statutory provisions allowing parents to commit their children to mental institutions without a court hearing or any lesser form of judicial oversight and leaving release up to the hospital and the parents. Toward the end of the 1970's, motivated by the reforms of adult commitment, some of these states had revised their statutes to require adult-type hearings, at least when the child objected to commitment or requested release. S. Brakel, J. Parry & B. Weiner, The Mentally Disabled and the Law 43–44 (1985). It was in this context that the Supreme Court decided *Parham v. J.R.*

PARHAM v. J.R. ET AL.
Supreme Court of the United States, 1979.
442 U.S. 584, 99 S.Ct. 2493, 61 L.Ed.2d 101.

[The plaintiffs in this class action were two minors who had been institutionalized in a psychiatric facility operated by the state of Georgia at the initiation of their guardians. One of the plaintiffs, J.L., was initially admitted into Central State Hospital at the age of six. At the time of his admission he had been expelled from school for "uncontrollable behavior" and had manifested "extremely aggressive" behavior at home. For a period of time J.L. was permitted to go home, but his behavior during these visits was "erratic," and the parents asked for discontinuance of the home visits. Two years later a new program was implemented that permitted J.L. to live at home and attend school in the hospital. However, when the parents found they were unable to control J.L.'s behavior, they requested his readmission into Central State Hospital.

The second plaintiff, J.R., was declared a neglected child and removed from his natural parents when he was three months old. He lived in a succession of foster homes until he reached the age of seven, when his disruptive and "incorrigible" behavior both at home and school led his seventh set of foster parents to request his removal. J.R. was thereafter institutionalized in Central State Hospital at the initiative of the Georgia Department of Family and Student Services. At the time of his admission, he was diagnosed as "borderline retarded" and suffering from "unsocialized aggressive reaction."]

MR. CHIEF JUSTICE BURGER delivered the opinion of the Court.

The question presented in this appeal is what process is constitutionally due a minor child whose parents or guardian seek state administered institutional mental health care for the child and specifically whether an adversary proceeding is required prior to or after the commitment.

* * *

A three-judge District Court was convened pursuant to 28 U.S.C. §§ 2281 and 2284. After considering expert and lay testimony and extensive exhibits and after visiting two of the State's regional mental health hospitals, the District Court held that Georgia's statutory scheme was unconstitutional because it failed to protect adequately the appellees' due process rights.

To remedy this violation the court enjoined future commitments based on the procedures in the Georgia statute. It also commanded Georgia to appropriate and expend whatever amount was "reasonably necessary" to provide nonhospital facilities deemed by the appellant state officials to be the most appropriate for the treatment of those members of plaintiffs' class, who could be treated in a less drastic, nonhospital environment.

Appellants challenged all aspects of the District Court's judgment.

* * *

Georgia Code, § 88–503.1 provides for the voluntary admission to a state regional hospital of children such as J.L. and J.R. Under that provision admission begins with an application for hospitalization signed by a "parent or guardian." Upon application the superintendent of each hospital is given the power to admit temporarily any child for "observation and diagnosis." If, after observation, the superintendent finds "evidence of mental illness" and that the child is "suitable for treatment" in the hospital, then the child may be admitted "for such period and under such conditions as may be authorized by law."

Georgia's mental health statute also provides for the discharge of voluntary patients. Any child who has been hospitalized for more than five days may be discharged at the request of a parent or guardian. Even without a request for discharge, however, the superintendent of each regional hospital has an affirmative duty to release any child "who has recovered from his mental illness or who has sufficiently improved that the superintendent determines that hospitalization of the patient is no longer desirable."

Georgia's Mental Health Director has not published any statewide regulations defining what specific procedures each superintendent must employ when admitting a child under 18. Instead, each regional hospital's superintendent is responsible for the procedures in his or her facility. There is substantial variation among the institutions with regard to their admission procedures and their procedures for review of patients after they have been admitted.

*   *   *

[At Southwestern Hospital, after] a child is admitted, the hospital has weekly reviews of his condition performed by its internal medical and professional staff. There also are monthly reviews of each child by a group composed of hospital staff not involved in the weekly reviews and by community clinic staff people. The average stay for each child who was being treated at Southwestern in 1975 was 100 days.

*   *   *

[At Atlanta Regional Hospital, after] admission the staff reviews the condition of each child every week. In addition, there are monthly utilization reviews by nonstaff mental health professionals; this review considers a random sample of children's cases. The average length of each child's stay in 1975 was 161 days.

*   *   *

[The Court described similar procedures at three other facilities].

*   *   *

III

*   *   *

The parties agree that our prior holdings have set out a general approach for testing challenged state procedures under a due process claim. Assuming the existence of a protectible property or liberty interest, the Court has required a balancing of a number of factors:

"First, the private interest that will be affected by the official action; second, the risk of an erroneous deprivation of such interest through the procedures used, and the probable value, if any, of additional or substitute procedural safeguards; and finally, the Government's interest, including the function involved and the fiscal and administrative burdens that the additional or substitute procedural requirement would entail."

Mathews v. Eldridge, 424 U.S. 319, 335, 96 S.Ct. 893, 903, 47 L.Ed.2d 18 (1976).

In applying these criteria, we must consider first the child's interest in not being committed. Normally, however, since this interest is inextricably linked with the parents' interest in and obligation for the welfare and health of the child, the private interest at stake is a combination of the child's and parents' concerns. Next we must examine the State's interest in the procedures it has adopted for commitment and treatment of children. Finally, we must consider how well Georgia's procedures protect against arbitrariness in the decision to commit a child to a state mental hospital.

(a) It is not disputed that a child, in common with adults, has a substantial liberty interest in not being confined unnecessarily for medical treatment and that the State's involvement in the commitment decision constitutes state action under the Fourteenth Amendment.

We also recognize that commitment sometimes produces adverse social consequences for the child because of the reaction of some to the discovery that the child has received psychiatric care. This reaction, however, need not be equated with the community response resulting from being labeled by the state as delinquent, criminal, or mentally ill and possibly dangerous. The state through its voluntary commitment procedures does not "label" the child; it provides a diagnosis and treatment that medical specialists conclude the child requires. In terms of public reaction, the child who exhibits abnormal behavior may be seriously injured by an erroneous decision not to commit. Appellees overlook a significant source of the public reaction to the mentally ill, for what is truly "stigmatizing" is the symptomatology of a mental or emotional illness. The pattern of untreated, abnormal behavior—even if nondangerous—arouses at least as much negative reaction as treatment that becomes public knowledge. A person needing, but not receiving, appropriate medical care may well face even greater social ostracism resulting from the observable symptoms of an untreated disorder.

However, we need not decide what effect these factors might have in a different case. For purposes of this decision, we assume that a child has a protectible interest not only in being free of unnecessary bodily restraints but also in not being labeled erroneously by some because of an improper decision by the state hospital superintendent.

(b) We next deal with the interests of the parents who have decided, on the basis of their observations and independent professional recommendations, that their child needs institutional care. Appellees argue that the constitutional rights of the child are of such magnitude and the likelihood of parental abuse is so great that the parents' traditional interests in and responsibility for the upbringing of their child must be subordinated at least to the extent of providing a formal adversary hearing prior to a voluntary commitment.

Our jurisprudence historically has reflected Western Civilization concepts of the family as a unit with broad parental authority over minor children. Our cases have consistently followed that course; our constitutional system long ago rejected any notion that a child is "the mere creature of the State" and, on the contrary, asserted that parents generally "have the right, coupled with the high duty, to recognize and prepare [their children] for additional obligations."

Surely, this includes a "high duty" to recognize symptoms of illness and to seek and follow medical advice. The law's concept of the family rests on a presumption that parents possess what a child lacks in maturity, experience, and capacity for judgment required for making life's difficult decisions. More important, historically it has recognized that natural bonds of affection lead parents to act in the best interests of their children.

As with so many other legal presumptions, experience and reality may rebut what the law accepts as a starting point; the incidence of child neglect and abuse cases attests to this. That some parents "may at times be acting against the interests of their child" creates a basis for caution, but is hardly a reason to discard wholesale those pages of human experience that teach that parents generally do act in the child's best interests. The statist notion that governmental power should supersede parental authority in *all* cases because *some* parents abuse and neglect children is repugnant to American tradition.

Nonetheless, we have recognized that a state is not without constitutional control over parental discretion in dealing with children when their physical or mental health is jeopardized. Moreover, the Court recently declared unconstitutional a state statute that granted parents an absolute veto over a minor child's decision to have an abortion. *Planned Parenthood of Missouri v. Danforth*, 428 U.S. 52, 96 S.Ct. 2831, 49 L.Ed.2d 788 (1976). Appellees urge that these precedents limiting the traditional rights of parents, if viewed in the context of the liberty interest of the child and the likelihood of parental abuse, require us to hold that the parents' decision to have a child admitted to a mental hospital must be subjected to an exacting constitutional scrutiny, including a formal, adversary preadmission hearing.

Appellees' argument, however, sweeps too broadly. Simply because the decision of a parent is not agreeable to a child or because it involves risks does not automatically transfer the power to make that decision from the parents to some agency or officer of the state. The same characterizations can be made for a tonsillectomy, appendectomy or other medical procedure. Most children, even in adolescence, simply are not able to make sound judgments concerning many decisions, including their need for medical care or treatment. Parents can and must make those judgments. * * * The fact that a child may balk at hospitalization or complain about a parental refusal to provide cosmetic surgery does not diminish the parents' authority to decide what is best for the child.

* * *

Appellees place particular reliance on *Planned Parenthood,* arguing that its holding indicates how little deference to parents is appropriate when the child is exercising a constitutional right. The basic situation in that case, however, was very different; *Planned Parenthood* involved an absolute parental veto over the child's ability to obtain an abortion. Parents in Georgia in no sense have an absolute right to commit their children to state mental hospitals; the statute requires the superintendent of each regional hospital to exercise independent judgment as to the child's need for confinement.

In defining the respective rights and prerogatives of the child and parent in the voluntary commitment setting, we conclude that our precedents permit the parents to retain a substantial, if not the dominant, role in the decision, absent a finding of neglect or abuse, and that the traditional presumption that the parents act in the best interests of their child should apply. We also conclude, however, that the child's rights and the nature of the commitment decision are such that parents cannot always have absolute and unreviewable discretion to decide whether to have a child institutionalized. They, of course, retain plenary authority to seek such care for their children, subject to a physician's independent examination and medical judgment.

(c) The State obviously has a significant interest in confining the use of its costly mental health facilities to cases of genuine need. The Georgia program seeks first to determine whether the patient seeking admission has an illness that calls for in-patient treatment. To accomplish this purpose, the State has charged the superintendents of each regional hospital with the responsibility for determining, before authorizing an admission, whether a prospective patient is mentally ill and whether the patient will likely benefit from hospital care. In addition, the State has imposed a continuing duty on hospital superintendents to release any patient who has recovered to the point where hospitalization is no longer needed.

* * *

The State also has a genuine interest in allocating priority to the diagnosis and treatment of patients as soon as they are admitted to a hospital rather than to time-consuming procedural minuets before the admission. One factor that must be considered is the utilization of the time of psychiatrists, psychologists and other behavioral specialists in preparing for and participating in hearings rather than performing the task for which their special training has fitted them. Behavioral experts in courtrooms and hearings are of little help to patients.

The *amicus* brief of the American Psychiatric Association points out at page 20 that the average staff psychiatrist in a hospital presently is able to devote only 47% of his time to direct patient care. One consequence of increasing the procedures the state must provide prior to a child's voluntary admission will be that mental health professionals will be diverted even more from the treatment of patients in order to travel to and participate in—and wait for—what could be hundreds—or even thousands—of hearings each year. Obviously the cost of these procedures would come from the public monies the legislature intended for mental health care.

(d) We now turn to consideration of what process protects adequately the child's constitutional rights by reducing risks of error without unduly trenching on traditional parental authority and without undercutting "efforts to further the legitimate interests of both the state and the patient that are served by" voluntary commitments. We conclude that the risk of error inherent in the parental decision to have a child institutionalized for mental health care is sufficiently great that some kind of inquiry should be made by a "neutral factfinder" to determine whether the statutory requirements for admission are satisfied. That inquiry must carefully probe the child's background using all available sources, including, but not limited to, parents, schools and other social agencies. Of course, the review must also include an interview with the child. It is necessary that the decisionmaker have the authority to refuse to admit any child who does not satisfy the medical standards for admission. Finally, it is necessary that the child's continuing need for commitment be reviewed periodically by a similarly independent procedure.[15]

We are satisfied that such procedures will protect the child from an erroneous admission decision in a way that neither unduly burdens the states nor inhibits parental decisions to seek state help.

Due process has never been thought to require that the neutral and detached trier of fact be law-trained or a judicial or administrative officer. Surely, this is the case as to medical decisions for "neither judges nor administrative hearing officers are better qualified than psychiatrists to render psychiatric judgments." Thus, a staff physician will suffice, so long

---

[15] As we discuss more fully later, the District Court did not decide and we therefore have no reason to consider at this time what procedures for review are independently necessary to justify continuing a child's confinement. We merely hold that a subsequent, independent review of the patient's condition provides a necessary check against possible arbitrariness in the *initial* admission decision.

as he or she is free to evaluate independently the child's mental and emotional condition and need for treatment.

It is not necessary that the deciding physician conduct a formal or quasi-formal hearing. A state is free to require such a hearing, but due process is not violated by use of informal traditional medical investigative techniques. Since well-established medical procedures already exist, we do not undertake to outline with specificity precisely what this investigation must involve. The mode and procedure of medical diagnostic procedures is not the business of judges. What is best for a child is an individual medical decision that must be left to the judgment of physicians in each case. We do no more than emphasize that the decision should represent an independent judgment of what the child requires and that all sources of information that are traditionally relied on by physicians and behavioral specialists should be consulted. * * * [One of the] problem(s) with requiring a formalized, factfinding hearing lies in the danger it poses for significant intrusion into the parent-child relationship. Pitting the parents and child as adversaries often will be at odds with the presumption that parents act in the best interests of their child. It is one thing to require a neutral physician to make a careful review of the parents' decision in order to make sure it is proper from a medical standpoint; it is a wholly different matter to employ an adversary contest to ascertain whether the parents' motivation is consistent with the child's interests.

Moreover, it is appropriate to inquire into how such a hearing would contribute to the long range successful treatment of the patient. Surely, there is a risk that it would exacerbate whatever tensions already existed between the child and the parents. Since the parents can and usually do play a significant role in the treatment while the child is hospitalized and even more so after release, there is a serious risk that an adversary confrontation will adversely affect the ability of the parents to assist the child while in the hospital. Moreover, it will make his subsequent return home more difficult. These unfortunate results are especially critical with an emotionally disturbed child; they seem likely to occur in the context of an adversary hearing in which the parents testify. A confrontation over such intimate family relationships would distress the normal adult parents and the impact on a disturbed child almost certainly would be significantly greater.

* * *

By expressing some confidence in the medical decisionmaking process, we are by no means suggesting it is error free. On occasion parents may initially mislead an admitting physician or a physician may erroneously diagnose the child as needing institutional care either because of negligence or an overabundance of caution. That there may be risks of error in the process affords no rational predicate for holding unconstitutional an entire statutory and administrative scheme that is generally followed in more than 30 states. "[P]rocedural due process rules are shaped by the risk of error inherent in the truthfinding process as applied to the generality of cases, not the rare exceptions." In general, we are satisfied that an independent medical decisionmaking process, which includes the thorough psychiatric investigation described earlier followed by additional periodic review of a child's condition, will protect children who should not be admitted; we do not believe the risks of error in that process would be significantly reduced by a more formal, judicial-type hearing.

* * *

IV

(a) Our discussion in Part III was directed at the situation where a child's natural parents request his admission to a state mental hospital. Some members of appellees' class, including J.R., were wards of the State of Georgia at the time of their admission. Obviously their situation differs from those members of the class who have natural parents. While the determination of what process is due varies somewhat when the state, rather than a natural parent, makes the request for commitment, we conclude that the differences in the two situations do not justify requiring different procedures at the time of the child's initial admission to the hospital.

For a ward of the State, there may well be no adult who knows him thoroughly and who cares for him deeply. * * * Contrary to the suggestion of the dissent, however, we cannot assume that when the State of Georgia has custody of a child it acts so differently from a natural parent in seeking medical assistance for the child. [T]here is no evidence that the State, acting as guardian, attempted to admit any child for reasons unrelated to the child's need for treatment. Indeed, neither the District Court nor the appellees have suggested that wards of the State should receive any constitutional treatment different from children with natural parents.

* * *

Once we accept that the State's application of a child for admission to a hospital is made in good faith, then the question is whether the medical decisionmaking approach of the admitting physician is adequate to satisfy due process. We have already recognized that an independent medical judgment made from the perspective of the best interests of the child after a careful investigation is an acceptable means of justifying a voluntary commitment. We do not believe that the soundness of this decisionmaking is any the less reasonable in this setting.

Indeed, if anything, the decision with regard to wards of the State may well be even more reasonable in light of the extensive written records that are compiled about each child while in the State's custody.

* * *

Since the state agency having custody and control of the child *in loco parentis* has a duty to consider the best interests of the child with respect to a decision on commitment to a mental hospital, the State may constitutionally allow that custodial agency to speak for the child, subject, of course, to the restrictions governing natural parents.

* * *

(b) It is possible that the procedures required in reviewing a ward's need for continuing care should be different from those used to review a child with natural parents. As we have suggested earlier, the issue of what process is due to justify continuing a voluntary commitment must be considered by the District Court on remand. In making that inquiry the District Court might well consider whether wards of the State should be treated with respect to continuing therapy differently from children with natural parents.

The absence of an adult who cares deeply for a child has little effect on the reliability of the initial admission decision, but it may have some effect on how long a child will remain in the hospital. We noted in *Addington v. Texas, supra,* "the concern of family and friends generally will provide continuous opportunities for an erroneous commitment to be corrected." For a child without natural parents, we must acknowledge the risk of being "lost in the shuffle."

* * *

Whether wards of the State generally have received less protection than children with natural parents, and, if so, what should be done about it, however, are matters that must be decided in the first instance by the District Court on remand, if the Court concludes the issue is still alive. * * * [W]e are satisfied that Georgia's medical factfinding processes are reasonable and consistent with constitutional guarantees. Accordingly, it was error to hold unconstitutional the State's procedures for admitting a child for treatment to a state mental hospital. The judgment is therefore reversed and the case is remanded to the District Court for further proceedings consistent with this opinion.

Reversed and remanded.

* * *

MR. JUSTICE BRENNAN, with whom MR. JUSTICE MARSHALL and MR. JUSTICE STEVENS join, concurring in part and dissenting in part.

*   *   *

I

Rights of Children Committed to Mental Institutions

It may well be argued that children are entitled to more protection than are adults. The consequences of an erroneous commitment decision are more tragic where children are involved. Children, on the average, are confined for longer periods than are adults. Moreover, childhood is a particularly vulnerable time of life and children erroneously institutionalized during their formative years may bear the scars for the rest of their lives. Furthermore, the provision of satisfactory institutionalized mental care for children generally requires a substantial financial commitment that too often has not been forthcoming.

*   *   *

In addition, the chances of an erroneous commitment decision are particularly great where children are involved. Even under the best of circumstances psychiatric diagnosis and therapy decisions are fraught with uncertainties. These uncertainties are aggravated when, as under the Georgia practice, the psychiatrist interviews the child during a period of abnormal stress in connection with the commitment, and without adequate time or opportunity to become acquainted with the patient. These uncertainties may be further aggravated when economic and social class separate doctor and child, thereby frustrating the accurate diagnosis of pathology.

These compounded uncertainties often lead to erroneous commitments since psychiatrists tend to err on the side of medical caution and therefore hospitalize patients for whom other dispositions would be more beneficial. The National Institute of Mental Health recently found that only 36% of patients below age 20 who were confined at St. Elizabeths Hospital actually required such hospitalization. Of particular relevance to this case, a Georgia study Commission on Mental Health Services for Children and Youth concluded that more than half of the State's institutionalized children were not in need of confinement if other forms of care were made available or used.

*   *   *

II

Rights of Children Committed by Their Parents

*   *   *

I believe that States may legitimately postpone formal commitment proceedings when parents seek in-patient psychiatric treatment for their children. Such children may be admitted, for a limited period, without prior hearing, so long as the admitting psychiatrist first interviews parent and child and concludes that short term in-patient treatment would be appropriate.

I do not believe, however, that the present Georgia juvenile commitment scheme is constitutional in its entirety. Although Georgia may postpone formal commitment hearings, when parents seek to commit their children, the State cannot dispense with such hearings altogether.

* * *

The informal postadmission procedures that Georgia now follows are simply not enough to qualify as hearings—let alone reasonably prompt hearings. The procedures lack all the traditional due process safeguards. Commitment decisions are made *ex parte*. Georgia's institutionalized juveniles are not informed of the reasons for their commitment; nor do they enjoy the right to be present at the commitment determination, nor the right to representation, the right to be heard, the right to be confronted with adverse witnesses, the right to cross-examine, or the right to offer evidence of their own. By any standard of due process, these procedures are deficient.

The special considerations that militate against preadmission commitment hearings when parents seek to hospitalize their children do not militate against reasonably prompt postadmission commitment hearings. In the first place, postadmission hearings would not delay the commencement of needed treatment. Children could be cared for by the State pending the disposition decision.

Second, the interest in avoiding family discord would be less significant at this stage since the family autonomy already will have been fractured by the institutionalization of the child. In any event, postadmission hearings are unlikely to disrupt family relationships. At later hearings the case for and against commitment would be based upon the observations of the hospital staff and the judgments of the staff psychiatrists, rather than upon parental observations and recommendations. The doctors urging commitment, and not the parents, would stand as the child's adversaries. As a consequence, postadmission commitment hearings are unlikely to involve direct challenges to parental authority, judgment or veracity. To defend the child, the child's advocate need not dispute the parents' original decision to seek medical treatment for their child, or even, for that matter, their observations concerning the child's behavior. The advocate need only argue, for example, that the child had sufficiently improved during his hospital stay to warrant out-patient treatment or outright discharge. Conflict between doctor and advocate on this question is unlikely to lead to family discord.

As a consequence, the prospect of a postadmission hearing is unlikely to deter parents from seeking medical attention for their children and the hearing itself is unlikely to so traumatize parent and child as to make the child's eventual return to the family impracticable.

* * *

III

Rights of Children Committed by Their State Guardians

Georgia does not accord prior hearings to juvenile wards of the State of Georgia committed by state social workers acting *in loco parentis.* The Court dismisses a challenge to this practice on the grounds that state social workers are obliged by statute to act in the children's best interest.

* * *

To my mind, there is no justification for denying children committed by their social workers the prior hearings that the Constitution typically requires. * * * [First, the] rule that parents speak for their children, even if it were applicable in the commitment context, cannot be transmuted into a rule that state social workers speak for their minor clients. The rule in favor of deference to parental authority is designed to shield parental control of childrearing from state interference. * * * The social worker-child relationship is not deserving of the special protection and deference accorded to the parent-child relationship and state officials acting *in loco parentis* cannot be equated with parents.

Second, the special considerations that justify postponement of formal commitment proceedings whenever parents seek to hospitalize their children are absent when the children are wards of the State and are being committed upon the recommendations of their social workers. The prospect of preadmission hearings is not likely to deter state social workers from discharging their duties and securing psychiatric attention for their disturbed clients. Moreover, since the children will already be in some form of state custody as wards of the State, prehospitalization hearings will not prevent needy children from receiving state care during the pendency of the commitment proceedings. Finally, hearings in which the decisions of state social workers are reviewed by other state officials are not likely to traumatize the children or to hinder their eventual recovery.

For these reasons I believe that, in the absence of exigent circumstances, juveniles committed upon the recommendation of their social workers are entitled to preadmission commitment hearings. As a consequence, I would hold Georgia's present practice of denying these juveniles prior hearings unconstitutional.

QUESTIONS AND COMMENTS

1. Institutionalized Juveniles. In a companion case to *Parham, Secretary of Public Welfare of Penn. v. Institutionalized Juveniles,* 442 U.S. 640, 99 S.Ct. 2523, 61 L.Ed.2d 142 (1979), the Court upheld Pennsylvania's system for committing children with mental illness and mental retardation on the petition of their parents or guardian. As it had in *Parham,* the Court stressed the thoroughness of the preadmission procedure.

> No child is admitted without at least one and often more psychiatric examinations by an independent team of mental health professionals whose sole concern under the statute is whether the child needs and can benefit from institutional care. The treatment team not only interviews the child and parents but also compiles a full background history from all available sources. If the treatment team concludes that institutional care is not in the child's best interest, it must refuse the child's admission. Finally, every child's condition is reviewed at least every 30 days.

Also as in *Parham,* the Court declined to decide what, if any, judicial postadmission procedures are required.

2. *Children's competence.* The majority opinion in *Parham* states that "[m]ost children, even in adolescence, simply are not able to make sound judgments concerning many decisions, including their need for medical care or treatment." Studies available at the time of *Parham* indicated, to the contrary, that by age 14 minors are typically as competent as adults in making treatment decisions and that some children under that age are equally competent. See, e.g., Lois Weithorn & Susan Campbell, *The Competency of Children and Adolescents to Make Informed Treatment Decisions,* 53 Child Dev. 1589 (1982). Most of this research involved "nonclinical" (i.e., non-mentally ill) populations, however. Further, more recent research suggests there might be significant differences between adolescents 17 and older and those who are younger in terms of "maturity" of judgment (as defined by degree of self-reliance, clarity of identity, and ability to limit impulsivity, avoid extremes, evaluate situations, and acknowledge the complexity of situations). See Laurence Steinberg & Elizabeth Cauffman, *Maturity of Judgment in Adolescence: Psychosocial Factors in Adolescent Decision Making,* 20 L. & Hum. Beh. 249 (1996). Kathryn Lynn Modeck', *"It's a Rush": Psychosocial Content of Antisocial Decision Making,* 33 Law & Hum Beh. 183 (2009) (finding that adolescents tended to underestimate actual legal consequences more than did college-age students and adults).What impact, if any, should these findings have on the due process analysis of commitment of minors?

3. *Parental and governmental good faith.* In holding that children subject to commitment are not entitled to the procedural protections afforded adults, the Court's decisions in *Parham* and *Institutionalized Juveniles* rely in part on the assumption that most parents seeking such commitment act in

the "best interest" of their children. In this regard, consider the following passage:

> The dangers inherent in "voluntary" psychiatric commitment of adolescents are well illustrated by *R.J.D. v. Vaughan Clinic, P.C.* In this case, seventeen-year-old R.J.D.'s mother committed her to a private psychiatric hospital because the mother disapproved of R.J.D.'s relationship with a man seven years her senior. R.J.D.'s objections to her hospitalization landed her in a secure ward where she was denied access to telephones. This situation occurred despite an earlier evaluation at a different facility conducted during the same week which resulted in a recommendation of "no medication and no follow-up," a finding endorsed by a family court referee following yet another evaluation. A guard informed the girl that she would stay in the hospital " 'as long as someone was footing the bill.' "

> Perhaps the case of fifteen-year-old Sheila (a pseudonym) is more typical if less theatrical. Sheila's divorced mother despaired of disciplining her after Sheila began experimenting with drugs, became sexually active, and dropped out of school. The mother sent Sheila to live with her father. When Sheila arrived at the airport in the city where her father lived, he refused to pick her up because he thought her presence would upset his new family. Sheila spent five weeks in state detention and shelter facilities, after which her father committed her to an adolescent treatment facility for a "conduct disorder." After exhausting Sheila's insurance coverage, the father agreed to pay $50,000 a year to keep Sheila institutionalized until she turned eighteen. The institution did not develop any rehabilitation plan for Sheila. Its treatment of its residents, including the use of tiny isolation cells, was virtually unregulated by the state.

> Unfortunately, these stories are not anomalies. Although no precise statistics are available concerning adolescent psychiatric hospitalization, experts estimate recent admissions of adolescents to private psychiatric hospitals—free of even the token procedural precautions imposed on public facilities under *Parham*—to be as high as between 150,000 and 250,000 each year. Indeed, children under the age of eighteen comprise over forty percent of the patients in private psychiatric facilities. Many of these children, admitted as "voluntary" patients at their parents' request, exhibit behaviors that would not normally lead to hospitalization of an adult, including "conduct disorders" manifested by behavior such as "chronic violation of a variety of important rules . . . at home . . . or at school . . . [and] persistent lying." A substantial percentage of youngsters doubtless exhibit these behaviors at some point during adolescence.

Catherine J. Ross, *From Vulnerability to Voice: Appointing Counsel for Children in Civil Litigation*, 64 Fordham L. Rev. 1571, 1581–82 (1996).

Parental temptation to abuse civil commitment may be exacerbated by the deinstitutionalization of the juvenile justice system (in particular, its divestment of status offenses such as "children in need of supervision" jurisdiction) and "the proliferation of investor-owned, for-profit psychiatric hospitals [that are] often affordable due to insurance policies which fully reimburse for inpatient treatment but which restrict coverage for outpatient services." See Dennis E. Cichon, *Developing a Mental Health Code For Minors*, 13 Thomas M. Cooley L. Rev. 529, 530 (1996).[x] A GAO Report found that, in 2001, parents "were forced to place more than 12,700 children in the child welfare or juvenile justice systems as a last resort for those children who needed mental health care treatment." President's New Freedom Commission on Mental Health 33–34 (May, 2003)(also noting that five of the largest states did not submit data for the report).

On the other hand, the social worker in charge of a child who is a ward of the state is presumably not affected by such considerations when making placement decisions. Are there other reasons for suspecting the sincerity of a social worker's decision to seek institutionalization of such a child? At one time, the guardianship statutes of several states barred state social service officials from serving as guardians out of a fear of conflict of interest. Legal Counsel for the Elderly, Decisionmaking, Incapacity and the Elderly 75 (1987).

4. *The independent decisionmaker.* The *Parham* Court placed considerable faith in the psychiatric interview as a means of ferreting out inappropriate petitions, whether they are brought by parents or state guardians. James Ellis, in *Volunteering Children: Parental Commitment of Minors to Mental Institutions*, 62 Cal.L.Rev. 840, 864 (1974) has questioned the efficacy of this type of review:

> Experience shows that in the most blatant cases of parental error psychiatrists do screen out admissions which are not warranted by apparent pathology in the child. In less obvious cases, however, psychiatrists may fail to perform an effective screening function. There are three reasons for this failure: (1) The performance of psychiatrists in precommitment interviews and examinations is often perfunctory and tends toward overdiagnosis; (2) Psychiatrists may be insensitive to legally important commitment issues; (3) The effectiveness of the psychiatrist in the admitting process is weakened by uncertainty over whose agent he or she is in such circumstances—the parent's or the child's.

On the latter point, Ellis notes: "While the goal of the psychiatrist will be expressed—and perceived—as the best welfare of the child-patient, it is the parent who has come to seek help, whose situation seems most desperate,

---

[x] Financially strapped parents of children with mental and physical handicaps have received a significant boost with the Individuals with Disabilities Education Children Act, 20 U.S.C. §§ 1400–1461, which provides federal and state funding for "mainstreaming" handicapped children in the public school system. This Act, which is discussed in detail in Chapter Eleven, may have taken some pressure off the commitment system.

who seems the most reliable source of information about what is wrong, who is closest to the psychiatrist in age and social outlook, and who is paying the psychiatrist's fee." Id. at 866.

There is little information bearing on the number of "inappropriate" admissions of children under procedures like those in use in Georgia. The figures provided by Justice Brennan in dissent suggesting that a large number of children are improperly hospitalized were probably as much a function of the unavailability of community resources as an indication of the accuracy of decisions made by admitting clinicians. However, it is worth noting that the amicus brief submitted by the American Psychiatric Association, upon which the majority heavily relies, questioned the wisdom of leaving the hospitalization decision to a psychiatrist in all circumstances.

> While Amici agree with appellant that psychiatric diagnosis—i.e., identification of specific mental illnesses—are medically reliable, we recognize that this fact is not dispositive of the issue of when a hearing is constitutionally required. Even if a child is properly diagnosed, it does not follow that hospitalization is necessary or desirable. Rather, Amici believe that in appropriate circumstances a due process hearing may provide a reasonable forum for deciding what care should be provided to a properly diagnosed child.

Amicus Brief for the American Psychiatric Association, et. al., at 24. Specifically, the APA advocated following the Georgia procedure only when (a) parents in an intact family wish to admit (b) a preadolescent child (c) to an accredited institution (d) for a short-term period (e.g., less than 45 days). In all other circumstances, concluded the APA, the danger of inappropriate placement merits affording the child more formal due process protections.

5.   *Postadmission review*. In *Parham* the Court required some sort of "independent review of the patient's condition" but then remanded to the district court for a determination as to the precise postadmission procedure mandated by the constitution. Several states provide for automatic judicial review procedures akin to those provided in adult commitment. Many, however, provide such review only at the child's request. In other states, because they are "voluntary" patients, children are not entitled to either periodic review or habeas review. At the same time, because they are children, they cannot give notice of an intention to leave, as can adult voluntary patients, unless they obtain approval of their parents or guardian. Ellis, supra at 847.

Although the postadmission issue is at least as important as the issues addressed by the Court, the only guidance the Court provided on remand was to indicate that children confined pursuant to a petition by the state may be entitled to more procedural oversight than children whose confinement was sought by their parents. This was because parents are more likely to make sure their children do not get "lost in the shuffle." Are parents any more likely to seek release of their children than the state is of its wards? Consider

Allen Shoenberger, *"Voluntary" Commitment of Mentally Ill or Retarded Children: Child Abuse by the Supreme Court*, 7 U.Dayton L.Rev. 1, 30 (1981):

> Once a family decides to institutionalize a mentally retarded child . . . reopening that emotionally charged decision is very difficult, even in the context of available supportive social services for in-home care that, if previously available, might have prevented institutionalization. Indeed, every time a family member visits the retarded individual, "all the old guilt feelings and indecisiveness surge up about whether or not they made the right decision."

6. *Criteria.* Do the differences between adults and children permit different *standards* of commitment as well as different procedures? As with some of the statutes governing commitment of people with developmental disabilities, the Georgia statute at issue in *Parham* permits admission of the child solely upon a finding by the admitting psychiatrist that the child is mentally disordered and suitable for treatment. Had the Supreme Court been asked to address the constitutionality of these criteria, how should it have held? Would a decision upholding the statute be consistent with *O'Connor v. Donaldson?*

7. *Implications of* Parham *for adults.* Should the reasoning found in *Parham* be extended to *adult* civil commitment, thus permitting commitment of adults under a need for treatment criterion as interpreted by a "neutral physician?" How much of the Court's rationale for its decision in *Parham* is dependent upon some special characteristic of children and their situation? At the least, could *Parham's* reasoning be applied to commitment of the adults who are developmentally disabled, given the fact that they are often wards of their relatives or the state?

CHAPTER 9

COMPETENCY DETERMINATIONS

■ ■ ■

Table of Sections

I.   INTRODUCTION

The issue of competency—the capacity to decide or to perform certain functions—permeates both the criminal and civil justice systems, although the precise decisions to be made and functions to be carried out vary from context to context. In civil cases, for instance, competency may refer to a capacity to understand and approve the terms of a contract or a will, to manage financial affairs, or to make treatment decisions. In criminal cases, it may designate the capacity to comprehend legal proceedings and assist one's attorney, or to understand and waive certain rights, such as the right to remain silent.

In all of these situations, the state may intervene to ensure that a person is capable of performing the required tasks. More significantly, if the state determines the person is incompetent, it may deprive him or her of liberty, property or the option to act. In the civil contexts noted above, an incompetent person may be prohibited from making a contract or will or having it implemented, required to surrender control of financial or personal affairs to a guardian, or forced to undergo unwanted treatment. In the criminal-law context, the person found incompetent may be forcibly treated, in a hospital or elsewhere, for the purpose of "restoring" competency to undergo legal proceedings and make waiver decisions; in the meantime the defendant will be prevented from obtaining adjudication of the pending charges.

The primary justification for these types of interventions stems from society's preference for autonomy—the freedom to make and act upon one's decisions. We value autonomy because we assume people are ordinarily the best judges of their own interests and because, even if they are not, taking away their opportunity to decide would show insufficient respect for the person. Because of this preference for autonomy, we generally allow individuals considerable latitude when engaging in behavior that is not directly harmful to others. But when a person appears to lack autonomy, either because of externally imposed coercion or—more relevant to this book—"internal" causes, we are less likely to respect his or her choices, even if they affect no one else. Because these people are not deemed to be able to function or to make decisions in their own best interests, we are more willing to override their decisions even if doing so will make them feel devalued or minimized. At the least, many would argue, the state's *parens patriae* power—its power to act as parent for disabled citizens—authorizes interfering with an incompetent person when harm to self would otherwise result and the intervention will not itself cause harm.[a] Beyond this, there may even be an affirmative *duty* to intervene under such circumstances.

To take an extreme example, suppose a man is unable to control his bodily movements or speak. When asked a question, his head might nod "yes" or "no" completely randomly. Most would agree that taking some important action—say, giving or withholding experimental but potentially life-saving treatment—based on such a nod would be improper. There is no necessary correlation between the nod and the person's "true" desires. Indeed, the nod is not really a "choice" in any sense of the word; acting on it could be viewed as an insult to him. Therefore, consistent with the autonomy preference, the state is justified in attempting to enable him to respond in a meaningful fashion and, if that fails, in making the decision for him if a decision is necessary.

A second possible justification for refusing to honor the man's "decision" and allowing government intervention under these circumstances is more general in nature. Not only would acting on a random nod be callous and insulting; it would also make a mockery of the concept of autonomy itself. It would suggest that society sanctions random decisionmaking. Thus, the competency requirement protects not only the interests of individuals but those of society at large.

---

     a   See discussion of the *parens patriae* power in Chapter Eight, Part II.C.

The central issue addressed in this chapter is the extent to which the state may intervene to further these interests when a person who is allegedly mentally disabled wants to, is asked to, or is required to perform a particular task. Although this chapter will allude to a number of such tasks, it will focus on management of essential survival chores, making treatment decisions, assisting counsel at trial, and waiving constitutional rights. First, we will look more closely at the competency notion.

II.   GENERAL CONSIDERATIONS

TEST CASES

In the following four cases, the subjects were found incompetent. Reflect on whether you agree as you read the following materials.

Case 1. Mr. B, a 43 year-old man, has long-standing glaucoma in both eyes. In one eye, vision remains only for motion. In the other eye, vision is better, but his internal eye pressure is only poorly controlled by medication. Mr. B's ophthalmologist has proposed a drainage procedure for the second eye that has a high chance of improving his vision for several months (at which time it could be undertaken again) and a negligible chance of damaging the eye. Although Mr. B expresses concern about the pressure in his eye and is fearful of going blind, he refuses the drainage procedure, explaining that his "voices" would be "angry with him" if he underwent the procedure. When his reasons for refusal are explored further, he notes that his mother had a similar drainage procedure which had not been helpful. He then discusses his attachment to his mother, stating that he feels that whatever happened to his mother will also happen to him.[b]

Case 2. Ms. N. is 72 years old and is presently in the intensive care unit of General Hospital in Nashville, Tenn., because of gangrene in both her feet. Doctors estimate that the probability of her surviving without amputation of the feet is 5 to 10% and the probability of survival after amputation is about 50%. Ms. N. refuses to consent to the amputation or consider the possibility that it is necessary to save her life. She feels very strongly that her physical condition is improving and that she will recover without the necessity of surgery. When asked if she would prefer to die rather than lose her feet, she answered "Possibly." The flesh on her feet is black, shriveled, rotting, and stinking; she believes their appearance is a result of soot or dirt.[c]

---

[b] This case is adapted from Paul Appelbaum & Loren Roth, *Clinical Issues in the Assessment of Competency*, 138 Am.J.Psychiat. 1462, 1464 (1981). The authors conclude that the patient was "apparently incompetent", thus permitting doctors to override the refusal.

[c] These facts are taken from State Dept. of Human Services v. Northern, 563 S.W.2d 197 (Tenn.App.1978), where the court authorized amputation of Ms. Northern's foot if her condition "has developed to such a critical stage as to demand immediate amputation to save her life." Doctors later decided the surgery was too dangerous, and Ms. Northern died of a gangrenous clot in 1978.

Case 3. Ms. K. dies, leaving only $1.00 of a sizeable estate to her only child, Ms. R., with the rest going to a church. Testimony at a will contest proceeding reveals that, when asked why she wanted to distribute her estate in this way, Ms. K. stated that she had not gotten along well with Ms. R., that while living with the R.s she had been required to do things which she did not want to do, that Mr. R. had made a derogatory remark concerning Germans (K. was of German descent), that the R.s were lacking in religious spirit, and that Ms. R. had tried to kill her by putting glass in her pudding. She also stated that she (Ms. K.) had failed to contribute enough in support of the church. Independent evidence disclosed that the daughter had prepared the pudding with the glass in it but that the glass was there accidentally. Furthermore, Ms. K. had been assured by many people that such was the case, but she persisted in believing that her daughter had wanted to harm her.[d]

Case 4. Mr. F., diagnosed as suffering from manic-depressive psychosis, began to emerge from the depressed phase in August. Previously frugal and cautious, he began to drive at high speeds, to be sexually more active with his wife and to discuss the purchase of land for development. In September, against the advice of his lawyer, he contracted for land in the Catskills and talked about erecting a 400-room hotel with a marina and golf course. On September 23, he signed another contract—after his lawyer counseled against it and withdrew from negotiations—to buy more property, on which he planned to erect a drug store and merchandise mart. Under this contract, title was not to change hands until October 20. Within two weeks of signing the contract, he arranged for a title search, giving correct details concerning the property and price, and also asked that the search be completed within a week. He also persuaded a former employee to join in the enterprise (promising him a salary and a Lincoln Continental when the project was complete), had a sign erected on the premises stating that F. Drug Company and merchandise mart were coming soon, hired an architect, initiated a mortgage application, hired laborers to begin digging, filed plans with city officials, and went to Albany to obtain the necessary approval for building. He also went to a psychiatrist to get help for his wife, who he stated was trying to stop his activities. This psychiatrist saw him on three subsequent occasions. On October 8th Mr. F. was hospitalized after purchasing a hunting gun, with all doctors agreeing on a diagnosis of manic-depressive psychosis.[e]

---

[d]   The case is based on In re Klein's Estate, 28 Wash.2d 456, 183 P.2d 518 (1947), in which the court declared Ms. Klein's will void.

[e]   This case is based on Faber v. Sweet Style Mfg. Corp., 40 Misc.2d 212, 242 N.Y.S.2d 763 (1963), in which the court voided Faber's second contract on the ground of incompetency.

PAUL APPELBAUM & LOREN ROTH, COMPETENCY TO CONSENT TO RESEARCH: A PSYCHIATRIC OVERVIEW

39 Arch.Gen.Psychiat. 951, 952–56 1982).

* * *

Evidencing a Choice

The least rigorous standard for competency . . . is the subject's actual communication of a decision as to his participation in the proposed project. This requirement has been phrased as demanding that the subject "manifest his consent" or "express a positive interest in taking part".

To the uninitiated, operationalizing the requirement that the subject evidence a choice may seem a trivial exercise; in most instances one need only ask the subject whether or not he desires to participate. There are occasions, however, in which the communication from the subject will be so ambiguous as to raise serious questions about whether or not consent has occurred. These include cases in which the subject's verbal and behavioral responses diverge (for example, when a subject declines to participate in a study requiring venipuncture, then rolls up his sleeve and holds out his arm to the experimenter).

* * *

Factual Understanding of the Issues

standard of competency

The subject's understanding of the issues relevant to participation is the single factor that has been most widely accepted as a standard for competency. A typical formulation requires that the subject have "the cognitive capacity to consider the relevant issues". Those areas that have been considered to be crucial for the subject to understand include "the nature of the procedure, its risks, and other relevant information," "the nature and likelihood of success of the proposed treatment and . . . of its risks and side-effects," "the available options, their advantages and disadvantages," "the knowledge that he has a choice to make," "who he is, where he is, what he is reading and what he is doing in signing the paper," and "the consequences of participation or non-participation."

* * *

The rigor of the requirement of understanding obviously increases with the amount and complexity of material that is required to be understood. Some writers make understanding the sine qua non of their standard of competency, and it has long been the primary element of legal tests of contractual and testamentary capacity.

"Factual understanding" actually encompasses two different standards: one can require, as many writers do, that the subject have the "ability to understand," or more strictly, one can insist that the subject manifest "actual understanding" of the material.

* * *

Means of demonstrating a subject's actual understanding of issues related to his decision include, in increasing order of difficulty, asking him to repeat the information provided, asking him to paraphrase it in his own words, and requiring that he display an ability to put some or all of the information to practical use. One difficulty in testing understanding of the consequences of a decision (often conceptualized as the risks and benefits) is the possibility of divergence between what the investigator perceives as a benefit or a risk and the subject's view of the matter. Consequences of participation, such as prolonged hospitalization, which are often thought of as a disadvantage, might seem quite desirable to a socially isolated or otherwise impoverished subject.

Rational Manipulation of Information

One step beyond measuring factual understanding is determining how the information that the subject assimilates is utilized in the decision-making process. The rubrics by which this standard is discussed include judgment, rationality, rational weighing of risks and benefits, reality testing, and decision-making capacity. Legal rules concerning contractual and testimonial capacity traditionally have recognized at least one defect of rationality, the presence of "insane delusions," as grounds for invalidating a person's acts.

* * *

The subjective nature of any assessment of rationality frequently has been pointed to as a major obstacle to the successful use of such a test. But an even greater problem may lie in the consensus of most experts today that an impairment of rationality does not necessarily affect global decision-making ability, that is, that the impact of delusions, for example, may be limited to a discrete area of mental functioning. Although this belief awaits definitive empirical verification, it indicates the possible utility of a test of rationality directed to the specific decision at hand rather than to the person's general functioning.

* * *

Appreciation of the Nature of the Situation

The strictest standard for competency requires that, once understanding has been attained, the rational manipulation of information take place in the context of the subject's appreciation of the nature of his situation.

Appreciation is distinct from factual understanding in that it requires the subject to consider the relevance to his immediate situation of those facts he has understood previously in the abstract. It differs from the rational manipulation of information by requiring that the subject take certain crucial data into consideration, rather than merely asking him to manipulate rationally whatever information is already at hand. This has been phrased in a variety of ways, asking that the subject "appreciate the consequences of giving or withholding consent," have "a sense of who he is and why he is agreeing," recognize, "in a mature fashion, the implications of alternative courses of action and appreciate both cognitively and affectively the nature of the thing to be decided," or "appreciate what is relevant to forming a judgment of the issue in question—i.e., . . . consider relevant evidence."

* * *

Whether the extent of the subject's appreciation needs to coincide precisely with the investigator's is a controversial topic. Some commentators have suggested that, in a therapeutic setting, the patient need only "understand the nature of the mental condition which the psychiatrist believes him to have," without necessarily agreeing with that judgment. Such a standard, however, more closely resembles a factual-understanding test than a genuine test of appreciation. Although some people may be uncomfortable with such a criterion, of necessity the subject's views (e.g., on the presence or absence of illness or the results of accepting or refusing participation) ultimately must be measured by their correspondence with the consensus of knowledgeable (usually professional) opinion on those issues.

Choosing the Standard

Despite wide variation in the wording of many attempts to define the standards for competency, they appear, as was just shown, to be classifiable into four general categories. Rather than deriving a single standard for competency from this discussion of the relevant mental functions and the psychopathologic states that may impair them, one is left with a range of testable functions that, depending on where the line is drawn, can yield multiple standards for competency of varying stringency. Furthermore, it is clear from this approach that any of the four resulting standards, or some combination of them, are "legitimate" as long as they can be justified from some reasonable policy perspective.

DUNCAN KENNEDY, DISTRIBUTIVE AND PATERNALISTIC MOTIVES IN CONTRACT AND TORT LAW, WITH SPECIAL REFERENCE TO COMPULSORY TERMS AND UNEQUAL BARGAINING POWER

41 Md.L.Rev., 563, 642–646 (1982).

The principled anti-paternalist admits readily that one sometimes has to overrule another's choice in his best interest, but argues that those

cases are explained by incapacity, or perhaps by another similar principled exception to the general idea that people are autonomous. (Likewise, the principled paternalist will argue that there are some cases in which people should be allowed to choose on their own—the two positions are indistinguishable for the purposes of my argument here.)
. . .

The idea of incapacity will *sometimes* help in explaining the actor's decision to intervene. Sometimes one feels that the other has really and truly lost selfhood, become a walking automaton or disintegrated, so that someone has simply to take care of them, make decisions for them, control their lives. As the actor, you have to worry that you will make bad custodial decisions, but not that you will be criticized for intervening at all. But those are extreme cases, and the difficulties with paternalism arise in situations where you have occasion to act without being able to appeal to any such blanket permission as is afforded by the other being just crazy.

*   *   *

The problem with the notion of capacity in [the more typical] setting is not that it's positively wrong—just that it doesn't help. The strategy is to divide the decision into two parts, hoping that will make it easier than if the question whether to act is treated as a single whole. First, we try to decide whether the other possesses a trait or quality called "ability to determine her own best interests." If she does, we accede to her wishes even if in that particular case we are convinced that her action is not in her best interests. If it were truly easier to decide the presence or absence of the quality of capacity than to decide on balance whether we should intervene, treating that question all together, then capacity would be useful. But the question of capacity is hopelessly intertwined with the question of what the other wants to do in this particular case.

First, there is no such "thing" as capacity, and there can be no such thing as its "absence" either. We ask the question of capacity already oriented to the further question whether we will have to let the person do something injurious to herself. There is no other reason to ask the question. Now if you ask me to *answer* the question without knowing what the potentially injurious thing is, it seems to me I should refuse. I don't believe that capacity exists except as capacity-to-make-this-decision. But as soon as I am deciding the issue of capacity-to-make-this decision, I find myself considering all the factors, testing my intuition of the other's false consciousness, the severity of the consequences, the possibility that I want to render the other dependent through paternalism, just as I would if I frankly admitted at the beginning that it's just a big mess, with no principled way to find your way through.

I come back to ad hoc paternalism, by which I mean that in fear and trembling you approach each case determined to act if that's the best thing to do, recognizing that influencing another's choice—another's life— in the wrong direction, or so as to reinforce their condition of dependence, is a crime against them. Of course, I haven't proved the impossibility of a principled anti-paternalist stance. I think I've undermined the idea that we can decide when to act and when not to act through a notion like: "Do not overrule the choice of a person who has the capacity to choose on their own". . . .

* * *

. . . Principled anti-paternalism is a defense mechanism. One way to deal with the pain and fear of having to make an ad hoc paternalist decision—one way to deny the pain and fear—is to claim that you "had" to do what you did because principle (say, the principle of incapacity) required it. That the principle doesn't really work is less important than that it anesthetizes. . . .

BRUCE WINICK, THE SIDE EFFECTS OF INCOMPETENCY LABELING AND THE IMPLICATIONS FOR MENTAL HEALTH LAW

1 Psychology, Public Policy & Law 6, 41 (1995).

Incompetency labeling can produce serious adverse consequences for those labeled. They are stigmatized in the eyes of the community in a manner that influences the way others perceive and treat them. Moreover, they may come to view themselves in ways that can reinforce and even worsen their impairment. Labeling them incompetent may cause them to inhibit performance or to avoid it altogether in the area in which they previously have performed poorly. Their motivation to attempt future behavior in the area in question may be altered in ways that prevent future success, and they may experience serious depression and a damaged sense of psychological well-being. Their sense of self-esteem and self-efficacy may be impaired in ways that are debilitating. They may experience learned helplessness, becoming withdrawn, unresponsive, passive, submissive, helpless, and hopeless. In summary, incompetency labeling may itself be psychologically damaging and even disabling. It may set up a self-fulfilling prophecy that serves to increase and perpetuate the individual's social and mental health problems.

An understanding of the serious adverse consequences of incompetency labeling should sensitize legal decision makers to redesign legal standards, procedures, and the roles of counsel, judges, and other legal actors in ways that are calculated to avoid or minimize these damaging effects. The law should rely less on compulsion and paternalism. Instead, it should encourage voluntariness, providing incentives for individuals to act in desired ways rather than requiring them to do so. In some cases it may be preferable to allow individuals to make their own choices, even if unwise.

Incompetency should be narrowly defined, and competency should be presumed. An inquiry into competency should be required only when specific behavior calls an individual's behavior into question. Mental illness alone should not justify such an inquiry, and when a determination of competency is required, the burden of proof should be on the party asserting that individuals are incompetent.

QUESTIONS AND COMMENTS

1. *Levels of competency.* Appelbaum and Roth appear to rank the four categories of competency tests, from the least demanding to the most demanding, in the following order: evidencing a choice, understanding material information, rational manipulation and appreciation. In more recent work, Appelbaum and Grisso treat these categories as different *aspects* of decision-making capacities, rather than as a hierarchy. For instance, they state that "[e]ven in the presence of good understanding and appreciation, decision making still might be impaired if patients fail to process information logically. Conversely, the rational manipulation standard might be met even by patients who have impaired understanding or defective appreciation if the reasoning processes are intact." Paul Appelbaum & Thomas Grisso, *Mental Illness and Competence to Consent to Treatment*, 19 Law & Hum. Beh. 105, 110 (1995). Nonetheless, the hierarchy they present is a useful starting point.

A fifth competency standard, which will often be more demanding than any of the four identified by Appelbaum and Roth, is the "reasonable outcome" standard suggested by Kennedy's excerpt. This standard looks not at the reasoning process of the individual, but rather at the reasonableness of the decision according to some "objective" observer. A sixth and final competency standard, one that seems to be more stringent than the understanding standard but not as demanding as the rational manipulation, appreciation and reasonable outcome tests, has been called the "understanding and belief" test. See Elyn Saks, *Competency to Refuse Treatment*, 69 N.C. L. Rev. 945 (1991). This standard requires understanding of material information, but does not require an ability to rationally manipulate or fully appreciate it. Rather it merely requires that the individual have no "patently false beliefs" about the information (e.g., a belief that medication will make one's head explode). Saks believes that this standard makes the most sense as a normative matter:

> A competency standard [should] designate a reasonably small class of individuals as incompetent in the face of the pervasive influence of the irrational and the unconscious. Indeed, if any person whose decisionmaking showed irrationality were deemed incompetent, then there would be virtually NO competent decisionmakers to be found; psychiatrists and psychologists have convincingly demonstrated the

everpresent influence of primitive hopes, wishes, and fears on the mental lives of us all. . . . An apparently intact reasoner, for example, may choose a treatment because of [unconscious] fantasies of merger with the doctor/patient, or, less fancifully perhaps, because he overvalues a vivid memory.

Id. at 950. Thus, Saks argues, only a person who does not understand the relevant facts, or who understands them but holds a belief about them which is patently false is incompetent.

    2.   *Varying competency with the choice to be made.* Many commentators have argued that differing levels of competency should be required depending upon the nature of the decision being made. For instance, Appelbaum and Roth, at the end of the above excerpt, state that "any of the four categories of [standards], or some combination of them, are 'legitimate' as long as they can be justified from some reasonable policy perspective." This idea is expanded upon in Loren Roth et al., *Tests of Competency to Consent to Treatment,* 134 Am.J. Psychiat. 279, 283 (1977):

> When there is a favorable risk/benefit ratio to the proposed treatment in the opinion of the person determining competency and the patient consents to the treatment, there does not seem to be any reason to stand in the way of administering treatment. To accomplish this, a test employing a low threshold of competency may be applied to find even a marginal patient competent so that his or her decision may be honored. This is what happens daily when uncomprehending patients are permitted to sign themselves into the hospital. Similarly, when the risk/benefit ratio is favorable and the patient refuses treatment, a test employing a higher threshold of competency may be applied. Under such a test even a somewhat knowledgeable patient may be found incompetent so that consent may be sought from a substitute decision maker and treatment administered despite the patient's refusal. An example would be the patient withdrawing from alcohol who, although intermittently resistive, is nevertheless administered sedative medication. In both of these cases, in which the risk/benefit ratio is favorable, the bias of physicians, other health professionals, and judges is usually skewed toward providing treatment. Therefore, a test of competency is applied that will permit the treatment to be administered irrespective of the patient's actual or potential understanding.
>
> However, there is a growing reluctance on the part of our society to permit patients to undergo treatments that are extremely risky or for which the benefits are highly speculative. Thus if the risk/benefit ratio is unfavorable or questionable and the patient refuses treatment, a test employing a low threshold of competency may be selected so that the patient will be found competent and his or her refusal honored. This is what happens in the area of sterilization of mentally retarded people, in which at least from the perspective of the retarded individual, the risk/benefit ratio is questionable. On the other hand, when the risk/benefit ratio is unfavorable or questionable and the patient consents

to treatment, a test using a higher threshold of competency may be applied preventing even some fairly knowledgeable patients from undergoing treatment. The judicial opinion in the well-known Kaimowitz psychosurgery case delineated a high test of competency to be employed in that experimental setting.

While these comments pertain to competency to make treatment decisions, similar contentions have been made about other contexts. For instance, some courts have said that the level of competency necessary to enter into a contract is greater than the level needed to make a will, see, e.g., *McPheters v. Hapke,* 94 Idaho 744, 497 P.2d 1045 (1972), and that pleading guilty requires more capacity than does going to trial. See, e.g., *Sieling v. Eyman,* 478 F.2d 211 (9th Cir.1973). These statements could be interpreted to mean merely that making a contract or pleading guilty requires understanding more facts, or facts that are more complicated, than does making a will or going to trial (where most decisions will be made by a lawyer). But in context the courts that make these statements appear to be recognizing different *levels* of competency for different types of decisions. Thus, if one followed the courts' suggestion, factual understanding might be sufficient to be competent to stand trial or write a valid will, while full "appreciation" of the situation might be required to plead guilty or make a contract.

Professor Saks disagrees with the "different levels" thesis. She argues that one standard—the understanding and belief standard—should apply to all situations.

> All competency areas encompass decisions ranging from very important to trivial, so that ranking competency areas as generally more or less consequential is extremely difficult. For example, a medical decision may prevent the immediate death of a young, otherwise healthy person, or it may provide relief from a minor headache. A will may dispose of the vast estate of a person whose family is in dire need, or the small estate of a person who has one wealthy, remote relative. And a trial decision may lead to either the death penalty or a day in jail. Because of this, to say that will-making as an area is less important than other competency areas—in particular, than the area of treatment choice—is impermissible, even though will-making involves interests of people other than the testator (he may care for them more than for himself, as it were), and even though it involves only property. The plain fact is that we cannot decide whether liberty, health, or property is more important without knowing how much of each, and with what further consequences: an abstract ranking is simply not possible.

* * *

Indeed, if varying the level of competency based on the importance of decisions made sense, a competency theorist might urge us to *lower* the level of competency for potentially consequential decisions. Because people care more about more consequential decisions, we should arguably permit them to choose what they will have to live with. Moreover, taking away consequential decisions may entail a greater assault on individual dignity. For example, telling a person that he can decide what kind of ice cream to have, but not where to live, may more seriously injure his self-esteem. Such a theory, indeed, seems already to inform some areas of the law. For example, some states permit minors to accept or to reject psychiatric treatment without regard to their competency, presumably because the decision is so important. In short, if varying levels of competency is acceptable at all, *lowering* the level of competency for crucial decisions would be most in the spirit of competency doctrine.

Id. at 992–998.

With whom do you agree? Under Saks's approach, could we allow voluntary admissions of non-protesting persons (discussed at pp. 974–978)? Should a person be able to consent to extremely experimental and life-threatening treatment if he or she is only able to meet Saks' understanding and belief test? Under the approach advocated by Roth, Meisel and Lidz, who should make the decision as to whether a treatment is "favorable," "questionable" or "dangerous"? Once that decision is made, should the competency level for a "dangerous" treatment be higher or lower than the competency level for a favorable or questionable treatment? Should the answer to that question depend upon whether the person is refusing or consenting to the treatment, as Roth, Meisel and Lidz suggest?

3.   *Other possible competency tests.* All of the tests discussed above are essentially cognitive in orientation. Traditionally, competency has been conceptualized as a matter of awareness, understanding, and reasoning ability. But competency can be viewed from other perspectives as well. Two other approaches are worth mentioning.

Volitional Test. Analogous to some versions of the insanity defense, one could require not only a minimal level of cognitive functioning but also a demonstration that the choice being made is "voluntary." Although assessing whether a choice is or is not an exercise of "free will" is problematic conceptually,[f] the rationale for requiring a volitional inquiry is straightforward: a person is not acting autonomously if his or her choices are "compelled." For instance, a severely depressed, suicidal person confronted with various treatment options may understand all of them but find it very difficult to resist choosing the most dangerous treatment, even though the remaining treatments are just as effective. Roth, Meisel and Lidz report the following case: "A 49 year-old woman whose understanding of treatment was otherwise intact, when informed that there was a 1 in 3,000 chance of dying from ECT, replied, 'I hope I am the one.'" Roth, Meisel & Lidz, supra at 282. Should such a person be considered competent to make this treatment decision? Whether you answer "yes" or "no," is it appropriate to consider her decision "compelled," or does it reflect some other kind of impediment?

is this compelled decision?

---

f   See Chapter Six, Part II.A.3 for discussion of this issue in the insanity defense context.

Professor Garrison has expanded on the idea of incompetency as a lack of volition, through a focus on "the coercive influence of depression and disordered insight." Marsha Garrison, *The Empire of Illness: Competence and Coercion in Health–Care Decision Making*, 49 Wm. & Mary L. Rev. 781 (2007). People with depression and people with disordered insight can usually understand relevant information about a decision. But Professor Garrison argues that people with these conditions should nonetheless often be found incompetent. With respect to depression, she points to research which indicates that, "for some patients [depression's effects] appear to overcome the desire for life and health and to coerce decisions against the patient's medical interests." Thus, she concludes, "untreated major depression poses a very high risk of unduly influencing treatment preferences and rendering them inauthentic." Id. at 834. Similarly, with respect to disordered insight, she states that "there are six million individuals with serious mental illnesses, half of whom do not believe they are ill . . . " As an example, she quotes a patient who could understand the supposed benefits of treatment but would always eventually be non-compliant because "[d]elusions and hallucinations support you in the belief that you are very special, and that powerful forces know you are very special, and even on medication individuals will be very reluctant to give that up." Accordingly, "if the patient has been medically assessed and found to be afflicted with severely disordered insight, then it is reasonable to assume that it is the coercive influence of illness, and not the patients authentic goals and values, that lead the patient to favor continuation of her disease over her life and health." Id. at 823. In short, she argues, knowledge of risks and benefits alone is insufficient to make one competent; one must also be free of "undue influence" stemming from mental disability. Does this formulation add anything to the competency tests already discussed?

Different Person Test. A final approach to competency is described and critiqued by Saks, supra.

> The "different person" theory rationalizes our intuition that mentally ill choices are incompetent by focusing on the change in personality that mental illness brings about, and the effects of that change on decisional capacity. The theory holds that a person is incompetent, not if what appear to be her values and beliefs are unacceptable according to some external standard, but rather if they are not *her* values and beliefs, because she has been transformed by mental illness into a "different person." The idea is that the person has lost touch with her own values and ways of looking at the world: she is simply not *herself*. The testamentary capacity cases, with their symbolic notion of testation as representative of the testator's psychic will, at times use language suggestive of this theory, as when they say that a will is not truly the "testator's." The "different person" theory deftly sidesteps the "irrationality" and "unconventionality" criteria; the decisionmaker's irrationality is irrelevant, and her thinking and feeling are not forced into a conventional mold. All that the "different person" theory requires is that the decisionmaker be true to herself. . . .

Mental illness is often described in a way that lends itself to the "different person" theory. For example, a mentally ill person is said to suffer "ego alien" impulses and thoughts, and, on recovery, to return to his "premorbid personality." Sometimes he does not even remember his experiences and, when he does, he may not recognize himself in them: he *feels* as if he was then a different person. The "different person" theory predicts that the recovered psychiatric patient will repudiate the choices and actions of his mentally ill self, and will thank the treatment provider for overriding his refusal and requiring treatment.

On examination, however, this theory is not as compelling as it seems. The problem is that the classic model does not fit all, or even most, mental illness—still less the choices made by its sufferers. Most obviously, some patients never return to their "premorbid" personalities, and so their mentally ill choices *become* authentic. Yet even when their illness is temporary, recovered patients may well not repudiate their past choices and thank their caregivers. Of course, all such patients might be unduly grudging. But it seems far more plausible to suppose that many of their choices are *misidentified* as "mentally ill" choices, or—even though truly "mentally ill"—are not experienced as the choices of a different person.

The essential problem is that determining reliably which choices are "mentally ill" and will later be repudiated is very difficult. . . .

See also, Ruth Faden & Tom Beauchamp, A History of Informed Consent 262–269 (1986).

4. *The* Katz *Case.* A case that might help flesh out some of the concepts discussed above is *Katz v. Superior Court,* 73 Cal.App.3d 952, 141 Cal.Rptr. 234 (1977), which involved a guardianship proceeding. The proposed wards were young adults (over the age of majority) who had become members of the Unification Church, headed by Reverend Moon. The parents of these individuals claimed that psychological pressure exerted by the church had impaired the physical and mental health of their children; specifically, it was alleged that the children had experienced "abrupt personality changes," and were the victims "of mind control through hypnosis, mesmerism, and/or brainwashing." 141 Cal.Rptr. at 239 n. 7. The father of one of the children testified that while his daughter was in the church "she became somewhat child-like in her belief and acceptance of this unitary system of beliefs, and her interests were almost totally devoted to that system of beliefs, to the exclusion of virtually all else." He noted that her voice had changed from being hoarse to high-pitched. He also believed she was being "imposed upon" because she received no compensation outside of minimal food and a place to sleep for her constant work for the church. On cross-examination, he acknowledged that she had looked healthy. Id. at 246.

One of the experts for the parents testified as follows:

It is my opinion that all five of these well-meaning, well-intentioned young people—Jan Kaplan, Leslie Brown, John Hovard, Jacqueline Katz and Barbara Underwood—have several symptoms which are not present in the average individual of their ages and background.

During my interviews with them, it was as though these individuals responded to a pre-set (i.e., there was an effort made to answer all questions out of a limited set of answers). This limited set of answers appeared to be alien or inconsistent with those of their non-cult peers.

They all suffered from gross lack of information regarding current events; they all seemed to be preoccupied with a concern about their selfishness, but all reported that they worked as much as twenty hours a day.

They all showed a moderate degree of memory impairment, especially about their childhoods; their functional vocabulary in terms of the words that they used during the interview was limited and constricted.

Their affects were blunted, emotionality frozen in a child-like inappropriate smile to all input, whether it be hostile or otherwise.

They were all wide-eyed, had short attention spans and a decreased ability towards abstractions; they were full of inconsistencies, contradictions and confabulations when pressured.

They uniformly held that the Unification Church was not responsible for anything unless it was positive.

They had very little concern for previous and future personal goals; they were paranoid about previous relationships, and had defensive attitudes toward id urges.

Their inner sense of authority was lost, and all responded as if they were influenced by an outside authority.

They all showed various degrees of regression and child-like attitudes, especially when stressed.

In general, they did not respond as one would expect from their background and personality types.

The expert did not diagnose any of the young adults as psychotic nor did he give them any other standard psychiatric diagnosis, but he did predict that staying in the church environment for the next six months would not be in the best interests of their health. Id. at 248–49.

The children testified at trial, and described their beliefs. They stated that their mode of living was one they had chosen to follow. They denied any coercive persuasion and pointed out that there was no physical restraint involved. One member of the group had left the church, but returned after four days of reflection. The young adults "insisted on their competency." Id. at 250. They also introduced expert testimony which asserted that "the experiences relied upon by the parents' experts were no more than usually accompany devotion to a religious belief." Id. at 250.

Assume the issue is whether the children's decision to stay with the Unification Church was a competent one.[g] What if Saks' "understanding and belief" test were applied to the *Katz* facts? The different person theory? A competency test that recognized a volitional component? One of the standards described by Roth, et al.? Should the fact that religious preferences are involved raise the level of incompetency required before state intervention may take place? Should the fact that the parents only wanted the children to go through a "deprogramming" session after which they would be free to return to the church lower the level of incompetency required for intervention? How do the observations of Professors Kennedy and Winick affect your analysis?

III. GUARDIANSHIP

A. HISTORY AND DEVELOPMENT

GARY MELTON, JOHN PETRILA, NORMAN POYTHRESS & CHRISTOPHER SLOBOGIN, PSYCHOLOGICAL EVALUATIONS FOR THE COURTS: A HANDBOOK FOR MENTAL HEALTH PROFESSIONALS AND LAWYERS

(New York: Guilford Press, 3d. ed., 2007), pp. 370–371.

Guardianship is the legal mechanism by which the state delegates authority over an individual's person or estate to another party. It is probably the most ancient aspect of mental health law. In both Roman and English common law, the sovereign possessed the power and duty to "guard" the estate of incompetent persons. This power, which emanated from the state's interest in the preservation of its wealth, is the historic basis of the *parens patriae* authority, which has since been applied broadly—and perhaps illogically—to the regulation by the state of many other aspects of decisionmaking by children and people with mental disability. In any event, it was this power that the state delegated to third parties (usually family members or members of the government) through the guardianship process.

Today guardianship comes in many forms. In some jurisdictions, there are separate provisions for appointment of a guardian of one's person (e.g., with authority over health care decisions) and a guardian of one's estate (e.g., with authority over contracts to sell one's property). The latter type of guardian is often called a "conservator" or "committee," although this nomenclature is not consistent across jurisdictions (with some, like California, using the former term to cover both person and

---

[g] The court did not frame the issue this way, but rather held that guardianship could be imposed only if the children were "gravely disabled," as defined by California's commitment law. Since there was "no real showing . . . that the [proposed wards] are physically unhealthy, or actually deprived of, or unable to secure food, clothing and shelter," the court denied the petition for guardianship. The standards for guardianship are discussed further in the next section of this chapter.

property). In addition to, or instead of this distinction, some jurisdictions also distinguish between "general" ("plenary") and "specific" guardianship. As the name implies, in the latter form of guardianship, the guardian's powers are restricted to particular types of decisions. Thus, with respect to guardianship of the person, the guardian may have authority only to make a specific treatment decision (e.g., consent to a specific course of treatment that has been proposed) or "nonroutine" treatment decisions (e.g., consent to any major surgery); the ward would remain free to make other health care decisions. Similarly, a person with mental disorder under limited guardianship of the estate might be able to make decisions about the property, except with respect to a particular complicated business deal that has been proposed, or any purchase over $100. On the other hand, under general guardianship, the guardian has total control of the individual's person, estate, or both.

* * *

Beyond these distinctions about the *scope* of guardianship, it is also important to recognize disparate *bases* of guardianship. In most instances, individuals are found, on the basis of particularized evidence, to lack specific or general capacities. They are actually (or *de facto*) incompetent and in need of a guardian to make decisions for them. On the other hand, some people are *presumed* to require a guardian. Regardless of their *de facto* level of competency, they are incompetent in law (*de jure*).

For example, even though older minors are often as competent as adults to make decisions of various types, they are *de jure* incompetent for most purposes and, as a result, lack legal authority to act on their own behalf. Even in those instances in which the law permits some minors to make decisions independently, they generally are presumed incompetent until they are able to rebut this presumption. Because there is such a strong legal presumption of minors' incompetency, there usually is no need to adjudicate their need for guardianship. . . . In most cases, there also is no need to determine who the guardian will be. Children are generally subject to the wishes of their "natural" guardians—their parents—who are presumed, in the absence of strong evidence to the contrary, to act in their best interests.

Civilly committed adults may also find themselves presumed incompetent to make many decisions. At one time, civil commitment often carried with it collateral loss of rights to marry, possess a driver's license, refuse intrusive treatments, manage one's property, and so forth. Although most states now provide that commitment does not automatically render a person incompetent to perform such functions, vestiges of these practices remain, especially with respect to treatment refusal and management of one's property. In such instances, there often is no need to appoint a guardian, in that state statutes provide authority to particular individuals (often state officials) to make decisions on behalf of the committed person. . . .

B. THE BASIS FOR INTERVENTION

ESTATE OF GALVIN v. GALVIN

Appellate Court of Illinois, First District, First Division, 1983.
112 Ill.App.3d 677, 68 Ill.Dec. 370, 445 N.E.2d 1223.

GOLDBERG, JUSTICE:

After a hearing, the trial court denied the petition of Mildred Tobias (petitioner) to be appointed guardian of the estate and person of Harold Galvin (respondent). Petitioner appeals.

Petitioner called Dr. William Reotutar, a qualified physician, to testify. The doctor testified he first treated respondent in October of 1980, after respondent had been admitted to St. Anne's Hospital. Respondent was suffering from "advanced multiple arthritis." Also, the respondent had a "cerebral vascular accident" or stroke.

* * *

Respondent was readmitted to the hospital in the fall of 1981 for treatment of his heart, cerebral, and arthritic conditions. The witness diagnosed another stroke and noted that respondent was "a little bit confused at times and was a little bit agitated at times." A psychiatric consultant observed that respondent experienced "some delusions" and "hallucinations." Dr. Reotutar diagnosed the respondent as having "organic brain syndrome" which describes "behavioral disorder due to some degeneration or atrophy of the brain cells." Respondent remained in the hospital for about two months. Respondent is currently under medication for his heart condition. Failure to take the medication as prescribed could endanger his life. While his heart condition is currently stable, the condition is irreversible. Similarly organic brain syndrome is irreversible and progressive. Although the doctor did not know how respondent handled his financial affairs, he believed respondent was disabled and unable to manage his affairs. On cross-examination the doctor testified that the respondent had made some recent improvement. He stated the respondent was "more oriented and more realistic."

Under questioning by the trial judge, respondent testified he owns the three-flat building in which he lives. He occupies the basement apartment with two men, John and Mike. They do not pay rent but respondent does collect rent from the other two apartments. Respondent handles his own financial affairs and has a checking account which currently has a balance of $350. Respondent receives social security of about $550 per month. Respondent did not believe he had a heart condition but he continues to take the medication prescribed by the doctor.

Under adverse examination by counsel for petitioner, the respondent testified he never had a checking account, he invented the snowmobile, at one time he had a pet black widow spider, and he could produce fire by pointing his finger. He also testified that John and Mike sometimes prepare his meals but he can and sometimes does prepare his own meals. He stated he could shop by himself and go to the laundromat with use of his walker and pulling a shopping cart. He testified he was able to take care of himself and did not want a guardian.

During the examination of respondent, the trial judge interrupted the proceedings and stated, "There is no way in God's world that I am going to adjudicate him a disabled person. He is physically suffering from some disability. . . . He is eccentric . . . but there is no way I am going to adjudicate him in need of a guardian. . . . He lives a bizarre, strange life. I might not want to do it, but unless you can make an offer of proof that is going to show me that he does not understand the things he's doing—. He understands."

Thereafter, counsel for petitioner made an oral offer of proof that John and Mike would testify respondent had no concept of time relationship, believed he had been a co-worker with the Shah of Iran, and the men plan to move out of respondent's apartment so that respondent would be left alone. In addition, petitioner's attorney offered to call Lorraine Polinski, cousin of the respondent, for examination. . . . The attorney stated this witness would testify that she had hired an attorney and that "She insisted a will be drawn, naming her as executor of this estate." The witness has recommended to respondent that he go to Oak Forest [Hospital]. Also, the respondent is "constantly" at petitioner's home where she and her mother "take care of" the respondent. In addition . . . the respondent [went] outside without shoes or stockings and wearing only slippers during sub-zero weather. Also, "another neighbor" would testify that when respondent went to the hospital his shopping and other needs were provided by the petitioner. The trial judge refused the offer of proof and denied the petition.

In this court, petitioner contends the decision of the trial court was against the manifest weight of the evidence and petitioner was denied due process because the trial judge abused his discretion and did not allow her to a full opportunity to present her case. We disagree.

A trial court is mandated to adjudicate a person incompetent and appoint a guardian only when the alleged incompetent is "not fully able to manage his person or estate. . . ." (Ill.Rev.Stat.1981, ch. 110½, pars. 11a–2, 11a–3.) The pertinent statute applicable to the case before us was amended effective as of September 16, 1979.

* * *

" 'Disabled person' defined. 'Disabled person' means a person 18 years or older who (a) because of mental deterioration or physical incapacity is not fully able to manage his person or estate, or (b) is mentally ill or developmentally disabled and who because of his mental illness or developmental disability is not fully able to manage his person or estate, or (c) because of gambling, idleness, debauchery or excessive use of intoxicants or drugs, so spends or wastes his estate as to expose himself or his family to want or suffering.

"Adjudication of disability—Power to appoint guardian. (a) Upon the filing of a petition by a reputable person or by the alleged disabled person himself or on its own motion, the court may adjudge a person to be a disabled person and may appoint (1) a guardian of his person, if because of his disability he lacks sufficient understanding or capacity to make or communicate responsible decisions concerning the care of his person, or (2) a guardian of his estate, if because of his disability he is unable to manage his estate or financial affairs or (3) a guardian of his person and of his estate.

"Guardianship shall be utilized only as is necessary to promote the well-being of the disabled person, to protect him from neglect, exploitation, or abuse, and to encourage development of his maximum self-reliance and independence. Guardianship shall be ordered only to the extent necessitated by the individual's actual mental, physical and adaptive limitations."

In commenting specifically upon these portions of the pertinent statute, this court stated that the legislature made these amendments "an express part of the statutory scheme for appointed guardians for disabled adults."

* * *

"Under the new sections, the legislature has made it clear that although a person may be a disabled person, in the statutory sense of not being fully able to manage his person, a guardian is not therefore permissible or appropriate, if that person is capable of making and communicating responsible decisions concerning the care of his person. Thus, a person who was physically unable to care for himself, but who could direct others in such activity, would not necessarily need a guardian over his person. Similarly, a person might be a 'disabled person' but nevertheless not be in need of a guardian over his estate, because with help from others he is able to direct and manage his affairs and estate."

* * *

In the case at bar, it is clear the respondent suffers from some physical disability and has some mental peculiarities. Nevertheless, with particular reference to the above citation, we cannot say the determination of the trial judge that respondent was not unable to manage his person and estate is contrary to the manifest weight of the evidence.

IN THE MATTER OF THE GUARDIANSHIP OF MARY LOU RENZ, AN INCAPACITATED PERSON

Supreme Court of North Dakota, 1993.
507 N.W.2d 76.

LEVINE, JUSTICE.

Mary Lou Renz appeals from an order denying her petition to terminate her guardianship and granting her guardian and conservator's petition for authority to sell Renz's home and automobile. As we are satisfied with the trial court's prudent approach to guardianship in this case and we find no clear error in the trial court's findings on guardianship or abuse of discretion in its order authorizing the sale of Renz's home and automobile, we affirm.

Renz has a long history of alcohol abuse and is an admitted alcoholic. She began drinking following the death of her husband in 1973 and since that time, she has undergone inpatient treatment for alcoholism at the North Dakota State Hospital fourteen times and at the Heartview Foundation seven times. Following each course of treatment, she eventually returned to her home. After a particularly serious incident of alcohol abuse in December 1991, the Heartview Foundation refused to admit Renz again unless a guardian was appointed for her.

Subsequently, in late 1991, William Chaussee, the Burleigh County Public Administrator, petitioned the trial court for guardianship. In February 1992, the trial court, finding that Renz was unable to provide for her personal care or perform necessary daily activities due to chronic alcoholism, granted limited guardianship over Renz's legal and financial affairs and full guardianship over her living arrangements.

The next month, after Renz was admitted to the North Dakota State Hospital following another incident of alcohol abuse, Chaussee petitioned the court for modification of the guardianship. The trial court then issued an amended order granting Chaussee authority to place Renz in a structured care facility as recommended by the State Hospital and control over Renz's assets to pay for such care (the court required its approval prior to the sale of Renz's home or automobile).

In June 1992, the court again modified Chaussee's guardianship to include conservatorship and full authority over Renz's place of residence, financial matters, and medical treatment, and limited authority over

Renz's legal matters, vocation, and education. Renz did not appeal this order or any of the court's prior orders.

In September 1992, Chaussee petitioned the trial court for authority to sell Renz's home and automobile. Renz then petitioned the court for termination of the guardianship, based on her recent sobriety. The trial court denied Renz's petition for termination and granted Chaussee's petition for authority to sell. Renz appealed.

Renz first argues that although she is an alcoholic with a long history of unsuccessful treatment for alcoholism, she presently is sober and thus, no longer is an incapacitated person. Therefore, she argues, the trial court "abused its discretion" by finding her incapacitated. Renz misstates the appropriate standard of review. We examine the trial court's findings on guardianship under a clearly erroneous standard. NDRCivP 52(a); In re Braaten, 502 N.W.2d 512 (N.D.1993). A finding of fact is clearly erroneous "if it is induced by an erroneous view of the law, if there is no evidence to support it, or if, although there is some evidence to support it, the reviewing court, on the entire evidence, is left with a definite and firm conviction that a mistake has been made." Swanston v. Swanston, 502 N.W.2d 506, 508 (N.D.1993). Renz's argument is twofold: that she presently is capable and that a court may not base a finding of incapacity on the perceived likelihood of a future relapse. We examine each aspect in turn.

The trial court found that Renz is "a chronic, relapse-prone, alcoholic" and "requires a great deal of support and structure to maintain sobriety[, which] will continue to be a struggle for her." The court found that since she has lived at the Chateau, a structured care facility, Renz has remained sober and regularly attends Alcoholics Anonymous meetings. We agree with the trial court that the fact that Renz has maintained sobriety while in a structured setting does not in itself imply that she no longer is an incapacitated person. Renz's argument makes an unfounded leap from the fact that she may be sober while she is in a structured facility and under a guardian's care to the assertion that she is capable of maintaining her sobriety without the structure and support furnished under a guardianship. We conclude that the trial court's finding that Renz remains incapacitated is supported by the evidence, and we are not convinced that the court made a mistake in its finding.

Renz also argues that the trial court incorrectly based its finding of incapacity on the likelihood that Renz would relapse into alcohol abuse. Renz cites several cases in support of this contention, only two of which we find arguably applicable to the case at hand. In Estate of Murphy, 134 Cal.App.3d 15, 184 Cal.Rptr. 363 (1982), the court held that a trial court may not find an alcoholic residing in a care facility and currently able to manage his own affairs "gravely disabled" based only on the likelihood that, were the court to terminate the conservatorship, he would begin drinking again. *Murphy* is distinguishable from the case at hand in two respects. First, as discussed above, we do not believe Renz presently is capable. Second, there is no indication in *Murphy*, as there is here, that the conservatee's sobriety was dependent on his placement in a care facility. In In re Benevenuto, 180 Cal.App.3d 1030, 226 Cal.Rptr. 33 (1986), the court applied *Murphy* to hold that a schizophrenic was not gravely disabled where he currently was able to manage his own affairs, despite evidence that if released from the mental health facility where he resided, he would stop taking his medication and become gravely disabled. Again, *Benevenuto* is distinguishable because Renz presently remains incapacitated. In addition, we note that the California courts may be moving away from *Benevenuto* and *Murphy*. See In re Walker, 206 Cal.App.3d 1572, 254 Cal.Rptr. 552 (1989) [affirming trial court's finding that delusional conservatee presently was gravely disabled based not on future likelihood that conservatee would stop taking medication but on conservatee's present incomprehension of his mental illness]. We also note that none of the cases cited by Renz involves a ward with an extensive history of unsuccessful alcoholism treatment, as does the case before us. Finally, we consider prognostic evidence in other proceedings which bear on an individual's rights. See, e.g., Steckler v. Steckler, 492 N.W.2d 76, 81 (N.D.1992) [stating in a termination of parental rights case that where "there exists a history of visitation violations and allegations of abuse, the court may consider what happened [in the past] as relevant evidence of what might occur in the future. It need not await a more tragic event to take action"]. Accordingly, we pay no heed to the California precedents because they pay no heed to either historical or prognostic evidence. We conclude that the trial court's findings on Renz's proclivity for alcoholism and her need for structure and support are not mistaken.

Renz's second argument is that the trial court "abused its discretion" in finding that no less restrictive form of intervention or alternative resource plan was available to allow Renz to return to her home. Implicit in this argument is that the trial court abused its discretion in authorizing the sale of Renz's home and automobile. Again, we examine the trial court's findings on guardianship under a clearly erroneous standard. In Braaten, supra at 517, we discussed North Dakota's "legislative mandate to maximize the autonomy of an incapacitated person by the least restrictive appointment of limited guardians." We believe the trial court's initial order of a limited guardianship and later orders incrementally broadening the guardian's authority as proved necessary conform to the circumspect approach required by North Dakota law. Here, the trial court found that "[i]t is not reasonable to assume that Mary Lou Renz will be able to live independently again" and that "there is no combination of services available to her [in her home] which would provide the required level of structure for her." The evidence shows that

Renz was unable to care for her personal cleanliness or that of her home, even with support services, when she lived independently. Several witnesses testified as to the unsanitary condition of Renz's home and her failure to attend to her incontinence. We believe the court's findings are supported by the record and we are not left with a definite and firm conviction that a mistake has been made. Therefore, we conclude that the findings are not clearly erroneous.

*   *   *

The portion of the trial court's order denying Renz's petition for termination of the guardianship is not clearly erroneous and the portion authorizing the sale of Renz's home and automobile is not an abuse of discretion. Accordingly, we affirm.

QUESTIONS AND COMMENTS

1. *Typical criteria for guardianship.* There are at least three approaches to determining whether a person should be subject to guardianship. See Phillip Tor, *Finding Incompetency in Guardianship: Standardizing the Process*, 35 Ariz. L. Rev. 739, 743–44 (1993). The first approach, which has parallels to the reasonable outcome competency test discussed at p. 1046, focuses on whether the person is capable of taking "proper" care of self or property. Statutes in this vein also often add inquiries into whether the person can "provide for his family", avoid the "dissipation of his property" or resist "artful and designing persons."

The second approach, which could be called the "process" approach, is reflected in an early version of the Uniform Probate Code, which defined an incapacitated person as "any person who is impaired by reason of mental illness, mental deficiency, physical illness or disability, advanced age . . . or other cause (except minority) to the extent that he lacks sufficient understanding or capacity to make or communicate responsible decisions concerning his person." National Conference of Commissioners on Uniform State Law, Uniform Probate Code § 5 (4th ed. 1975). Consistent with the rational manipulation standard discussed at p. 1042, this approach reflects a movement toward "criteria that minimize the importance of the results of an individual's decision and instead examine the ability of the individual to go through the cognitive process of making rational decisions." Samuel Brakel et al., The Mentally Disabled and the Law 371 (1985).

The third approach, sometimes called the "functional" approach, permits guardianship only if specific dysfunctions exist. For instance, under New Hampshire's statute the term "incapacity"

> means a legal, not a medical, disability and shall be measured by functional limitations. It shall be construed to mean or refer to any person who has suffered, is suffering or is likely to suffer substantial harm due to an inability to provide for his personal needs for food, clothing, shelter, health care or safety or an inability to manage his or

her property or financial affairs. Inability to provide for personal needs or to manage property shall be evidenced by acts or occurrences, or statements which strongly indicate imminent acts or occurrences. All evidence of inability must have occurred within 6 months prior to the filing of the petition and at least one incidence of such behavior must have occurred within 20 days of the filing of the petition for guardianship.

N.H. § 464 A:2. The functional approach grew out of concern that the Uniform Probate Code's approach was insufficiently objective and therefore subject to abuse. Illustrative of this concern is *In re Boyer,* 636 P.2d 1085 (Utah 1981), where the Utah Supreme Court construed a statute patterned on the Uniform Probate Code. The law was challenged on the ground that the words "capacity to make or communicate responsible decisions concerning his person" would allow appointment of a guardian for a person "who makes decisions regarded by some as irresponsible, even though he has sufficient capacity to make personal management decisions which allow him to function in a manner acceptable to himself and without any threat of injury to himself." The court agreed, but avoided declaring the statute unconstitutionally vague by construing it to require an impairment which renders the person "unable to care for his or her personal safety or attend to or provide for such necessities as food, shelter, clothing, and medical care, without which physical injury or illness may occur."

Recall that the Uniform Probate Code provision was meant to focus the inquiry more on the quality of the person's thought process—"the ability of the individual to go through the cognitive process of making rational decisions"—than on the "results of the individual's decision." Don't *Boyer* and the functional approach return the law of guardianship to a consideration of the results of the individual's decision, albeit one associated with more precise standards? Is there any way out of this circle? Consider a fourth approach, followed by roughly 18 states today and adopted in the newest version of the Uniform Probate Code and the Uniform Guardianship and Protective Proceedings Act (UGPPA), which defines an incapacitated person as someone who cannot "receive and evaluate information or make or communicate decisions to such an extent that the individual lacks the ability to meet essential requirements for physical health, safety or self-care even with appropriate technological assistance" (National Conference of Commissioners on Uniform State Laws, 1997, § 102(5)). Does this standard adequately reconcile the previous approaches? Consider also the material in section II of this chapter. For instance, if Saks' understanding-and-belief competency standard were adopted, the question would not be whether the person was unable to provide for basic necessities, nor would it be whether the person's thought process was "rational" or "responsible." Rather it would be whether the person understood the consequences of his or her decisions and had no patently false beliefs about the material aspects of his or her situation. Is this a better standard for deciding whether a guardian should be appointed?

Which of these various standards is reflected in the Illinois statute at issue in *Galvin*? How do the standards apply to Galvin? Is he able to care for himself? Does he make "responsible" decisions? Are any of his delusions patently false beliefs about his situation?

In contrast to Galvin, Renz appears to have had no significant mental problems at the time of the guardianship proceeding. Instead the court seems to be basing its decision on a "potential for deterioration" standard of the type that some states have adopted in the outpatient civil commitment context. See pp. 884–885. Should the state be able to force a guardian on a competent person when it predicts the person will be incompetent sometime in the future? Is the court's analogy to civil commitment, which is explicitly based on prediction of future behavior, appropriate? Conversely, should the state have to wait until Renz decompensates before it can sell the house and car? Is it relevant that a committed patient can be forced to reimburse the state for its treatment expenses (see pp. 1304–1306)? Isn't it possible Renz will ultimately cost the state more money if the house is sold?

Not clear is whether courts attend to these various nuances in the definition of capacity. What is clear is that most (more than 90%) of guardianship petitions are granted. See Jennifer L. Wright, *Guardianship for Your Own Good: Improving the Well–Being of Respondents and Wards in the USA*, 33 Int'l J. L. & Psychiatry 350, 359 (2010).

2. *Guardianship and civil commitment.* The preceding discussion makes clear that the standards for guardianship bear a close relationship to the standards for *parens patriae* commitment. Until the 1970's, most states equated the two, a correlation which was symbolized by the practice in many states of delegating commitment authority to probate courts. In these states, institutionalized persons were presumed incompetent at least until their release and perhaps until a court "restored" them to competency. Thus, as the Melton et al. excerpt noted, these people not only lost the authority to make their own treatment decisions but also were automatically deprived, without further judicial proceeding, of the right to vote, possess a driver's license, manage property or marry. Today most states specifically eliminate the presumption of incompetency for institutionalized persons and require a separate incompetency adjudication. No state allows the mere fact of commitment to substitute for a general incompetency determination. Brakel et al., supra, at 509.

If their standards are the same, why *shouldn't* guardianship and commitment be dealt with in the same proceeding? In California, for instance, a person who is found to be gravely disabled has a "conservator" appointed who then decides whether to commit the ward. Cal.Code § 5350. In thinking about this issue, consider the materials in the following note.

3. *Guardianship and the least restrictive alternative.* As noted previously, while guardians traditionally exerted complete power over the ward, in more recent times a distinction has developed between guardianships of the estate and guardianships of the person. In practice, does

this distinction make sense? Both *Galvin* and *Renz* appear to involve both a guardian of the estate and of the person. Should they have?

Also noted in the introductory materials is the movement away from "general" guardianship toward "specific" or "limited" guardianship, whether the guardianship is of the person or of the estate. Ideally, perhaps, general guardianships should be rare. That is, the court should allow the guardian to control only those areas where the ward has demonstrated incompetence. Thus, a court should gauge a person's ability to vote, to handle varying levels of financial transactions, to make decisions about food and shelter, to choose from among various types of treatment and so on, and shape the guardianship accordingly. Virtually all states today attempt to implement this idea statutorily. See, e.g., Idaho Code § 15–5–420 (authorizing limited conservatorships); Me.Rev.Stat.Ann., tit. 18–A, § 5–304(a)(court shall "make appointive and other orders only to the extent necessitated by the incapacitated person's actual mental and adaptive limitations or other conditions warranting the procedure"); Fla. Stat. § 744.344(1)(2) (authorizing limited guardianships and stating that the order "must be the least restrictive appropriate alternative, and must reserve to the incapacitated person the right to make decisions in all matters commensurate with the person's ability to do so.").

Most research indicates that these changes have had limited impact. See, e.g., Jennifer Moye et al., *Clinical Evidence in Guardianship of Older Adults Is Inadequate: Findings from a Tri–State Study*, 47 Gerontologist, 604, 611 (2007) (reporting an examination of nearly 300 guardianship cases adjudicated in Colorado (major reform), Pennsylvania (intermediate reform), and Massachusetts (limited reform) in 2002–05 that found that limited guardianship orders were issued in a third of Colorado cases, but only rarely in Massachusetts and Pennsylvania cases). Even in those states, like Colorado, that have enacted "major reform," most of the "limited" guardianship orders actually are "plenary orders with some specific limitations on the guardians' powers added in." Wright, supra, at 367 n.144. See also Pat M. Keith & Robbyn R. Wacker, Older Wards and Their Guardians 177, 180 (1994)(after reforms, requests for limited guardianship increased from zero to one percent, with most denied); Lawrence Friedman & Mark Savage, *Taking Care: The Law of Conservatorship in California*, 61 S. Cal. L. Rev. 278, 283 (1988). Accordingly, some authors have called for abolition of general guardianship, to encourage narrower grants of power to the guardian. Lawrence A. Frolik, *Promoting Judicial Acceptance and Use of Limited Guardianship*, 31 Stetson L. Rev. 735 (2002) (noting that advocates for people with mental disability often see plenary guardianship "as completely at odds with integrating the disabled individuals into the community" because "individuals [under a plenary guardianship cannot] handle their financial affairs, make a valid contract, control their medical care, or even decide where to live."). Is there any downside to the limited guardianship idea? Might it encourage overuse of guardianship, in the same way outpatient commitment might encourage overuse of commitment?[h] Because the capacities of wards tend to decline, won't a preference for limited guardianships require considerably more judicial resources, as guardians seek to expand their powers? Should a limited guardianship have been used in *Galvin*? Was its use in *Renz* appropriate?

Even a clear finding of incompetency may not warrant guardianship or commitment. A number of other "less restrictive" protective arrangements are available. These include "protective services" (in which case workers are appointed to supervise the person and ensure that he or she receives community services, voluntarily or involuntarily), powers of attorney, "living wills" or advanced directives (by which a person authorizes certain actions contingent upon certain conditions developing), court authorizations of single transactions (e.g., kidney transplants), representative payee arrangements (used for receipt of welfare entitlements), trusts, joint tenancies, and transfers of property. See N.Y. Mental Hyg. Law § 81.03(e). But see John Petrila & Jeffrey Swanson, Mental Illness, Law, and a Public Health Law Research Agenda 34–35 (2010) (noting that the incapacity and resources of the ward limit the use of many of these alternatives). Would any of these alternatives have been useful in *Galvin* or *Renz*?

4. *Supportive decision-making.* A version of the least restrictive alternative idea that has gained traction since the mid–2000s is known as "supportive decision-making." Under this approach, which some see as a replacement for guardianship, a support relationship is established only if the "principal" (a word used in place of "ward") freely enters into it. Further, the relationship can be terminated at any time, mandates that the principal be allowed to participate actively in decisions, and time limits the surrogate decision-maker's power. See Leslie Salzman, *Guardianship for Persons with Mental Illness—A Legal and Appropriate Alternative?*, 4 St. Louis U. J. Health L. & Pol'y 279, 306–07 (2011). In British Columbia, such an arrangement is called a "super power of attorney," but in contrast to the typical power of attorney, it "seeks to maximize the on-going and active involvement of the principal in the decision-making process" and can be established even if the individual "would not be deemed to have the generally accepted level of legal capacity to enter into a general or health care power of attorney." Id. at 308. Rather the goal is "to assess the nature and amount of support needed by the individual to exercise his or her legal capacity as autonomously as possible." Id. at 313.

In no jurisdiction that has authorized supportive decision-making has guardianship been abolished; rather it is considered a "last resort." Id. at 311. But Professor Salzman has argued that, given the supportive decision-making option, guardianship violates both the Americans with Disabilities Act (which prohibits discrimination based on mental disability and has been held, in *Olmstead v. L.C.*, 527 U.S. 581, 119 S.Ct. 2176, 144 L.Ed.2d 540 (1991) to require community-based services for people with mental disability under some circumstances), and the 2006 United Nations Convention on the

---

[h] See pp. 899–902.

Right of Persons with Disabilities (which provides that any measures that limit an individual's exercise of legal capacity must "respect the rights, will and preferences of the person, [be] free of conflict of interest and undue influence, [be] proportional and tailored to the person's circumstances, apply for the shortest time possible and [be] subject to regular review by a competent, independent and impartial authority or judicial body." CRPD, Article 12). Professor Salzman asserts that "by removing the individual's right to make decisions, guardianship not only perpetuates stereotypes that wards are incapable or unworthy of participating in community life, but because of the constructive isolation of guardianship, also diminishes the ward's opportunities to participate in the host of every day social, economic, civil, and cultural activities cited by the *Olmstead* court." Id. at 314. The ADA and *Olmstead* are discussed further in Chapter Ten, Part IV. For now, consider whether and how supportive decision-making would work in *Galvin* and *Renz*. Are the guardianship orders imposed in those cases discriminatory in the sense suggested by Salzman?

5. *Procedures.* Every state provides for a hearing to determine the need for guardianship. Concerns connected with notice, the right to be present, the right to a public jury trial, application of the rules of evidence and most other aspects of the hearing are similar to those that arise in the civil commitment context, discussed in Chapter Eight. As a result, the procedures tend to be similar in many jurisdictions. Below is a description of the process afforded people subjected to guardianship.

> [A study of practices in ten states] revealed that of 566 cases, twenty-five percent lasted less than five minutes, and fifty-eight percent lasted less than fifteen minutes. Despite a statutory requirement that the respondent attend absent a specific finding by the court, seventy-five percent of guardian ad litem reports specified that the proposed ward should not be required to attend. At least sixty-six percent of respondents were in fact absent, regardless of the statutory language. Despite the reform emphasis on professional testimony, the record clearly indicated that a physician was present at only eight percent of hearings. Further, many physician reports lack detailed information about the respondent's decision-making capacities. A 2001 task force in Illinois found that courts often are not provided with sufficient detailed information about respondents' decision-making capacities, instead receiving information about physical or other impairments.

> Most states do not require the court to appoint counsel for the respondent. Perhaps more significant, where counsel was required, a review of the record showed that respondent's counsel might not speak at all at the hearing, which suggests an unusually passive role. All guardian reports in one county were fully missing from half of the case files reviewed; the inventory of assets by the guardian after appointment was absent in thirty percent of reviewed case files.

Alison Barnes, *The Liberty and Property of Elders: Guardianship and Will Contests as the Same Claim*, 11 Elder L. J. 1 (2003); see also, Associated

Press Special Report, *Guardians of the Elderly: An Ailing System*, L.A. Times, Sept. 27, 1987, at 2, 20, 28.

Some courts have upheld these practices. For instance, in *Rud v. Dahl*, 578 F.2d 674, 679 (7th Cir.1978), the court held that counsel for the prospective ward is not "an essential element of due process" at guardianship proceedings:

> First of all, the nature of the intrusion on liberty interests from an adjudication of incompetency is far less than the intrusion resulting from other types of proceedings in which the presence of counsel has been mandated. Involuntary incarceration, for example, does not result from an incompetency proceeding. Moreover, the technical skills of an attorney are less important, as the procedural and evidentiary rules of an incompetency proceeding are considerably less strict than those applicable in other types of civil and criminal proceedings. Finally, the costs associated with the mandatory appointment of counsel will undermine one of the essential purposes of the proceeding itself— protection of the limited resources of the incompetent's estate from dissipation—for few alleged incompetents will be able to effect a 'knowing and intelligent' waiver of undesired counsel.

In many jurisdictions, representation of the ward is required but only by a guardian ad litem, who functions not as an advocate for the client's views but rather acts according to what he or she feels is in the best interests of the proposed ward. Many guardians ad litem are not performing this function. See Winsor Schmidt et al., *Developments and Trends in the Status of Public Guardianship: Highlights of the 2007 National Guardianship Survey*, 33 Men. & Phys. Dis. L. Rep. 728, 730 (2009) (reporting that guardians ad litem often had "little training or experience and abysmal pay, . . . never visited the alleged incapacitated person . . . failed to investigate the appropriateness of the guardianship, . . . provided the court with incomplete information, [did not reveal] conflict[s] of interest . . . and . . . were unclear regarding whether their appropriate role was working as an investigator, a best interests advocate, or a zealous advocate.").

For reasons similar to those described in *Rud*, many courts have upheld application of the preponderance of the evidence standard at guardianship proceedings despite the Supreme Court's ruling in *Addington v. Texas*, 441 U.S. 418, 99 S.Ct. 1804, 60 L.Ed.2d 323 (1979), requiring the clear and convincing standard at civil commitment proceedings. As explained by one court:

> We do not feel that more harm will befall an individual who is erroneously subjected to guardianship than to an individual who is in need of a guardian but is erroneously denied one. If an individual is erroneously subjected to a guardianship, then [state law] allows such a ward to file a petition for the removal of his guardian.

Guardianship of Roe, 383 Mass. 415, 421 N.E.2d 40 (1981).

6.   *Who may serve as guardian.* The filing of a petition for guardianship is generally considered "jurisdictional"; that is, the court may appoint anyone guardian, not just the petitioner. Most state statutes establish priorities for deciding who should be guardian, with family members and relatives occupying the foremost positions. See, e.g., Uniform Guardian and Protective Proceeding Act §§ 2–205, 2–309. However, nonfamily members may be appointed in lieu of available and willing family members when "(1) the family member has an adverse interest to that of the ward; (2) there is dissension within the family; (3) the family member lacks business ability; or (4) some other substantial reason for disqualification exists." Legal Counsel for the Elderly, Decisionmaking, Incapacity and the Elderly 75 (1987). An increasing number of states also require that guardians meet certain qualifications and even undergo training programs. See, e.g., Fla.Stat.Ann. § 744.3145 (requiring 8 hours of instruction on the duties of the guardian, the rights of the ward, the availability of local resources, and the preparation of treatment plans and reports, in a course approved by the court within one year of appointment as guardian). Despite these steps, the petitioner is almost always appointed guardian. Lawrence A. Frolik, *Guardianship Reform: When the Best is the Enemy of the Good*, 9 Stan. L. & Pol'y Rev. 347,351 (1998).

At least 44 states provide for public guardians, like the one appointed in *Renz*. Schmidt et al., supra, at 728. Intended primarily for those with no relatives or relatives who are unsuitable as guardians, the public guardian device appears to fill a significant need. A study of institutionalized individuals in Florida in the 1980s found that over 11,000 people were probably legally incompetent and in need of either a guardianship of the person, guardianship of the estate, or both; since then, the need for public guardianships has "escalated." Id. The identity of the public guardian varies widely among jurisdictions. For instance, the "clear majority" of states specifically authorize departments of mental health or social services to serve as public guardians. Others specifically prohibit these entities from serving, because they often provide the treatment or services about which the guardian must decide, thus creating a possible conflict of interest. Id. supra, at 729. What are the potential conflicts in *Renz*?

Other studies of public guardianship have found that, even if the conflict of interest problem is solved, the responsible agencies are often overburdened and impersonal in nature, thus resulting in a tendency to institutionalize their wards. Id. at 729–30. In one study of 200 wards with public guardians, competency was restored to only four, "possibly because the files for these cases were the few with up-to-date status reports." Phillip B. Tor & Bruce D. Sales, *A Social Science Perspective on the Law of Guardianship: Directions for Improving the Process and Practice*, 18 Psychol. & L. Rev. 1, 25 (1994). At the same time, in theory at least, public guardians should offer greater sophistication and expertise and should be more in tune with available services than are private guardians. One possible method of reducing the negative and accentuating the positive aspects of public guardianship is to create a nonprofit corporation using concerned citizens as guardians, as New

York has done with the Association for Retarded Citizens. Based on the available information, who would have been the best guardian in *Galvin* and *Renz*?

    7.   *Restoration of competency.* The general practice with respect to terminating a guardianship is described by Brakel et al., supra at 392–93:

> Restoration is a legal determination that individuals who have been adjudged incompetent are now able to manage their business and personal affairs adequately. The law presumes that persons who are adjudicated incompetent remain so. In order for wards to regain their competent status they normally must vindicate themselves in a separate judicial proceeding or, in a few states, be discharged from a mental institution. This second method is a holdover from the time when it was common to merge commitment and competency hearings. It avoids the need to prevail in a hearing that may be even more difficult than challenging an assertion of incompetency in the first instance.

Should the fact that Renz was applying for termination of a guardianship rather than trying to avoid imposition of one in the first instance make a difference in her case, given the presumption of incompetency described by Brakel, et al.?

    A few states, including California, provide for automatic restoration of competency after one year unless the conservator applies for reappointment. In virtually every state, the ward can initiate restoration proceedings, as can a "next friend," and most also have a periodic review process. Are the state statutory schemes that do not provide such review constitutional, in light of the Supreme Court's decision in *Parham v. J.R.,* discussed in Chapter Eight, PartV.E.? What is the relevance of the fact that "[p]sychosocial conditions are often temporary or episodic, and the individual may experience significant improvement in decisionmaking capabilities, or even full recovery, within a reasonably short time period"? Salzman, supra, at 305.

C. POWERS AND DUTIES OF THE GUARDIAN

    Whatever kind of guardianship is established (i.e. of the person or of the estate, general or limited), the guardian has authority to make decisions concerning the ward. However, there are two further types of limitations on this authority. First, the guardian is supposed to take only those actions that will be in the "best interests" of the ward; that is, the guardian is in a fiduciary relationship with the ward. In some jurisdictions, the best interest test has been modified to require the guardian to make the decision that the ward would have made had he or she been competent. Both the best interest and substituted judgment standards are discussed further below.

    The second type of limitation on the guardian's authority bars unmonitored surrogate decisions in certain instances. For instance, a guardian of the estate, even one with general powers, is often prohibited by statute from executing a will for the ward, and usually must obtain a court order before selling real property or revoking certain types of trusts. Similarly, a guardian of the person, although authorized to make most medical decisions for the ward, must usually seek court approval before consenting to certain types of procedures viewed as "extraordinary", such as abortion, psychosurgery, organ transplants, or sterilization. The following materials focus on sterilization as paradigmatic of the situations in which guardians must make difficult choices, although several other situations are discussed as well.

MATTER OF GUARDIANSHIP OF HAYES
Supreme Court of Washington, 1980.
93 Wash.2d 228, 608 P.2d 635.

*   *   *

HOROWITZ, JUSTICE.

*   *   *

Petitioner Sharon Hayes is the mother of Edith Melissa Maria Hayes, who was born severely mentally retarded on December 17, 1963. She petitioned the Superior Court for an order appointing her as the guardian of Edith's person and specifically authorizing a sterilization procedure on Edith. The court dismissed the petition on a motion for summary judgment on the ground it had no authority to issue an order for sterilization of a retarded person.

*   *   *

Edith Hayes is severely mentally retarded as a result of a birth defect. Now 16 years old, she functions at the level of a four to five year old. Her physical development, though, has been commensurate with her age. She is thus capable of conceiving and bearing children, while being unable at present to understand her own reproductive functions or exercise independent judgment in her relationship with males. Her mother and doctors believe she is sexually active and quite likely to become pregnant. Her parents are understandably concerned that Edith is engaging in these sexual activities. Furthermore, her parents and doctors feel the long term effects of conventional birth control methods are potentially harmful, and that sterilization is the most desirable method to ensure that Edith does not conceive an unwanted child.

Edith's parents are sensitive to her special needs and concerned about her physical and emotional health, both now and in the future. They have sought appropriate medical care and education for her, and provided her with responsible and adequate supervision. During the year or so that Edith has been capable of becoming pregnant, though, they have become frustrated, depressed and emotionally drained by the stress of seeking an effective and safe method of contraception. They believe it is impossible to supervise her activities closely enough to prevent her from becoming involved in sexual relations. Thus, with the consent of Edith's father, Sharon Hayes petitioned for an order appointing her guardian and authorizing a sterilization procedure for Edith.

I

Jurisdiction

Edith's court appointed guardian ad litem contended below, and now maintains on appeal, that a superior court has no power to authorize a sterilization absent specific statutory authority. He cites in support of that view cases from other jurisdictions in which courts have concurred that specific statutory authority is required.

* * *

The courts of this state have long recognized the inherent power of the superior court "to hear *and determine* all matters legal and equitable in all proceedings known to the common law." Original jurisdiction is granted to superior courts over all cases and proceedings in which jurisdiction is not vested exclusively in some other court by Washington Const. art. 4, § 6.

* * *

We therefore hold that Washington Const. art. 4, § 6 gives the superior courts of this state the jurisdiction to entertain and act upon a request for an order authorizing sterilization of a mentally incompetent person.

II

Standards for Sterilization

Our conclusion that superior courts have the power to grant a petition for sterilization does not mean that power must be exercised. Sterilization touches upon the individual's right of privacy and the fundamental right to procreate. It is an unalterable procedure with serious effects on the lives of the mentally retarded person and those upon whom he or she may depend. Therefore, it should be undertaken only after careful consideration of all relevant factors. We conclude this opinion with a set of guidelines setting out of the questions which must be asked and answered before an order authorizing sterilization of a mentally incompetent person could be issued. First, however, the consideration which are important to this determination can be best illuminated by discussing briefly the historical context from which they arise.

Sterilization of the mentally ill, mentally retarded, criminals, and sufferers from certain debilitating diseases became popular in this country in the early 20th century. The theory of "eugenic sterilization" was that the above-named traits and diseases, widely believed at that time to be hereditary, could be eliminated to the benefit of all society by simply preventing procreation.

More than 20 states passed statutes authorizing eugenic sterilizations. Washington passed a punitive sterilization law aimed at habitual criminals and certain sex offenders in 1909. The law exists today as RCW 9.92.100. Another statute, also enacted early in the century, denied certain persons, including the mentally retarded, the right to marry unless it is established that procreation by the couple is impossible. RCW 26.04.030, repealed by Laws of 1979, 1st Ex.Sess., ch. 128, § 4. While this statute did not authorize sterilizations, it was clearly based on eugenic principles.

In 1921 the Washington legislature enacted a law providing for sterilization of certain mentally retarded, mentally ill and habitually criminal persons restrained in a state institution. Laws of 1921, ch. 53, p. 162. This statute was held unconstitutional because of its failure to provide adequate procedural safeguards in *In re Hendrickson,* 12 Wash.2d 600, 123 P.2d 322 (1942).

The United States Supreme Court upheld the constitutionality of a eugenic sterilization law which provided adequate procedural safeguards, however, in *Buck v. Bell,* 274 U.S. 200, 47 S.Ct. 584, 71 L.Ed. 1000 (1927). Since that time it has generally been believed that eugenic sterilization statutes are constitutional although, as noted above, more recent Supreme Court decisions suggest the importance of respecting the individual's constitutional rights of privacy and procreation.

More recently scientific evidence has demonstrated little or no relationship between genetic inheritance and such conditions as mental retardation, criminal behavior, and diseases such as epilepsy. Geneticists have discovered, for example, that some forms of mental retardation appear to have no hereditary component at all, while in some others the element of heredity is only one of a number of factors which may contribute to the condition. In short the theoretical foundation for eugenic sterilization as a method of improving society has been disproved.

At the same time other previously unchallenged assumptions about mentally retarded persons have been shown to be unreliable. It has been found, for example, that far from being an insignificant event for the retarded person, sterilization can have longlasting detrimental emotional effects. Furthermore, while retarded persons, especially children, are often highly suggestible, there is evidence they are also capable of learning and adhering to strict rules of social behavior. Many retarded persons are capable of having normal children and being good parents.

Of great significance for the problem faced here is the fact that, unlike the situation of a normal and necessary medical procedure, in the question of sterilization the interests of the parents of a retarded person cannot be presumed to be identical to those of the child. The problem of parental consent to sterilization is of great concern to professionals in the field of mental health, and the overwhelming weight of opinion of those who have studied the problem appears to be that consent of a parent or guardian is a questionable or inadequate basis for sterilization. It is thus clear that in any proceedings to determine whether an order for sterilization should issue, the retarded person must be represented, as here, by a disinterested guardian ad litem.

Despite all that has been said thus far, in the rare case sterilization may indeed be in the best interests of the retarded person. However, the court must exercise care to protect the individual's right of privacy, and thereby not unnecessarily invade that right. Substantial medical evidence must be adduced, and the burden on the proponent of sterilization will be to show by clear, cogent and convincing evidence that such a procedure is in the best interest of the retarded person.

Among the factors to be considered are the age and educability of the individual. For example, a child in her early teens may be incapable at present of understanding the consequences of sexual activity, or exercising judgment in relations with the opposite sex, but may also have the potential to develop the required understanding and judgment through continued education and developmental programs.

A related consideration is the potential of the individual as a parent. As noted above, many retarded persons are capable of becoming good parents, and in only a fraction of cases is it likely that offspring would inherit a genetic form of mental retardation that would make parenting more difficult.

Another group of relevant factors involve the degree to which sterilization is medically indicated as the last and best resort for the individual. Can it be shown by clear, cogent and convincing evidence, for example, that other methods of birth control are inapplicable or unworkable?

In considering these factors, several courts have developed sterilization guidelines. With the assistance of the brief of Amicus Mental Health Law Project, a careful review of these considerations allows us to provide the superior court with standards to be followed in exercising its jurisdiction to issue an order authorizing sterilization of a mentally incompetent individual.

The decision can only be made in a superior court proceeding in which (1) the incompetent individual is represented by a disinterested guardian ad litem, (2) the court has received independent advice based upon a comprehensive medical, psychological, and social evaluation of the individual, and (3) to the greatest extent possible, the court has elicited and taken into account the view of the incompetent individual.

Within this framework, the judge must first find by clear, cogent and convincing evidence that the individual is (1) incapable of making his or her own decision about sterilization, and (2) unlikely to develop sufficiently to make an informed judgment about sterilization in the foreseeable future.

Next, it must be proved by clear, cogent and convincing evidence that there is a need for contraception. The judge must find that the individual is (1) physically capable of procreation, and (2) likely to engage in sexual activity at the present or in the near future under circumstances likely to result in pregnancy, and must find in addition that (3) the nature and extent of the individual's disability, as determined by empirical evidence and not solely on the basis of standardized tests, renders him or her permanently incapable of caring for a child, even with reasonable assistance.

Finally, there must be no alternatives to sterilization. The judge must find that by clear, cogent and convincing evidence (1) all less drastic contraceptive methods, including supervision, education and training, have been proved unworkable or inapplicable, and (2) the proposed method of sterilization entails the least invasion of the body of the individual. In addition, it must be shown by clear, cogent and convincing evidence that (3) the current state of scientific and medical knowledge does not suggest either (a) that a reversible sterilization procedure or other less drastic contraceptive method will shortly be available, or (b) that science is on the threshold of an advance in the treatment of the individual's disability.

There is a heavy presumption against sterilization of an individual incapable of informed consent that must be overcome by the person or entity requesting sterilization. This burden will be even harder to overcome in the case of a minor incompetent, whose youth may make it difficult or impossible to prove by clear, cogent and convincing evidence that he or she will never be capable of making an informed judgment about sterilization or of caring for a child.

Review of the facts in this case in light of these standards make it clear that the burden has not yet been met. It cannot be said that Edith Hayes will be unable to understand sexual activity or control her behavior in the future. The medical testimony and report of the mental health board are not detailed enough to provide clear, cogent and convincing evidence in this regard. Edith's youth is of particular concern, since she has many years of education before her. Furthermore, although there is evidence that some methods of birth control have already been tried, there is insufficient proof that no conventional form of contraception is a reasonable and medically acceptable alternative to sterilization. Nor is there any evidence such a procedure would not have detrimental effects on Edith's future emotional or physical health. Finally, there is no evidence that a pregnancy would be physically or emotionally hazardous to Edith, and insufficient evidence that she would never be capable of being a good parent.

Additional factfinding at the trial level will help the superior court judge answer the questions set out in this opinion. Therefore, the case is reversed and remanded for further proceedings consistent with this opinion.

* * *

QUESTIONS AND COMMENTS

1. *The competency standard for sterilization.* Assuming the requisite statutory or judicial authority, when may a court authorize or undertake a surrogate decision concerning sterilization? The formulation found in *Hayes* is widely followed. Looking closely at the guidelines of that case, the court appears to state that if a person is competent to understand the sterilization process and its consequences but refuses the procedure, the state may take no further action. Conversely, if the person cannot understand the procedure and its consequences, *Hayes* appears to hold that he or she is incompetent for purposes of making the sterilization decision and that a surrogate decision (taking into account such factors as the likelihood of sexual activity and the person's parenting ability) is permitted.

Is this the correct competency test? Or should the test instead be whether the person is "competent" to be a parent? Consider this excerpt from Elizabeth Scott, *Sterilization of Mentally Retarded Persons: Reproductive Rights and Family Privacy*, 1986 Duke L.J. 806, 837–38 (1986):

> [C]ompetency to make a meaningful choice to procreate rests on the individual's ability to fulfill the basic responsibilities of parenthood. A mildly impaired person may have this ability regardless of whether she is legally competent to make medical decisions regarding sterilization. Her interest in making her own reproductive decisions should be legally protected. On the other hand, a severely disabled person's childlike wish for a baby does not signify a meaningful choice. A decision to have a child is, most importantly, a decision to become a parent—to assume a role that requires a minimal level of competency. If the individual lacks this capability and the state would predictably intervene to remove any child produced in order to protect it, then the choice to have a child is not a legally protectable exercise in personal autonomy. Thus, the interest in autonomy is derivative of the underlying interest in having children. If the retarded individual lacks the ability to exercise the substantive interest, she lacks the interest in making the choice.

Under Scott's approach, what should be the competency standard for decisionmaking about abortion?

2. *Best interests analysis.* Assuming a person is found incompetent to make the sterilization decision under the appropriate standard, what factors will justify making a surrogate decision in favor of the procedure? In other words, when is sterilization in an incompetent person's best interests? *Hayes* lists several factors. Note that the court seems to consider sterilization the option of last resort, because it requires that all "less drastic" contraceptive measures "have been proved unworkable." Other courts are even more restrictive. For instance, one court allowed sterilization of an incompetent person only upon a finding that the procedure is medically essential "to preserve the life or physical or mental health of the incompetent person." In the *Matter of A.W., 637 P.2d 366, 375 (Colo.1981).*

Are these types of "least restrictive alternative" rules sensible? If the person is not competent to make a decision about having children, why should we prefer a nonpermanent procedure such as contraceptive pills or an intrauterine device? If sterilization is not performed, but because of the increased risks of pregnancy and increased burden on the family, the person is eventually institutionalized, has the "least drastic" method been pursued?

3. *The substituted judgment standard.* Some courts eschew a "best interests" analysis in favor of a substituted judgment test. This approach was described in *Matter of Moe,* 385 Mass. 555, 432 N.E.2d 712 (1982), which also involved a sterilization decision:

> In utilizing the doctrine of substituted judgment, this court seeks to maintain the integrity of the incompetent person by giving the individual a forum in which his or her rights may be exercised. The court dons 'the mental mantle of the incompetent' and substitutes itself as nearly as possible for the individual in the decision making process. In utilizing the doctrine the court does not decide what is necessarily the best decision but rather what decision would be made by the incompetent person if he or she were competent.

The factors the court then listed as considerations in making the substituted judgment decision are virtually identical to those listed in *Hayes,* except that the court added that the individual's religious beliefs, if any, must be ascertained. Would a substituted judgment analysis be any different than a best interests analysis on the *Hayes* facts? Does application of the substituted judgment test make sense in such a situation?

4. *Relevance of the ward's desires; advanced directives.* Under both the best interest and substituted judgment tests, at least as described by *Hayes* and *Moe,* the decisionmaker is to inquire into and take into account the ward's desires. Does this requirement ever make sense when the individual has been found incompetent?

For instance, should any weight be given to a previous statement made while the person is *competent?* Suppose that a woman of 20 suffers an incapacitating head injury which leaves her sexually active but so cognitively impaired that she can neither understand the sterilization procedure nor make a decision concerning having a child. One year before the accident, she had indicated that she would never want to be sterilized or otherwise give up her capacity to have children. Should this fact bar a court under either test from authorizing sterilization? Would it make any difference if the reason given for not wanting sterilization was based on religious preferences? In the alternative, what if, a year before the accident, she had indicated she never wanted to have children?

Consider *Cruzan v. Director, Missouri Dept. of Health*, 497 U.S. 261, 110 S.Ct. 2841, 111 L.Ed.2d 224 (1990). There, the parents and co-guardians of Nancy Cruzan requested the termination of procedures which were sustaining the life of their daughter, a 26 year old woman who was left in a permanent vegetative state following an automobile accident. The trial court found that, before the accident, Nancy had been a "vivacious, active, outgoing, independent person who preferred to do for herself." It also found that about a year prior to her accident, she had "discussions with her then housemate, friend and co-worker," during which "she expressed the feeling that she would not wish to continue living if she couldn't be at least halfway normal." The court characterized these conversations as "somewhat serious." The finding that Nancy's "lifestyle and other statements to family and friends suggest that she would not wish to continue her present existence without hope as it is" heavily influenced the trial court in ordering the state of Missouri to honor the co-guardians' request.

The Missouri Supreme Court reversed, calling the evidence about Nancy's wishes "inherently unreliable and thus insufficient to support the co-guardians' claim to exercise substituted judgment on Nancy's behalf." *Cruzan by Cruzan v. Harmon,* 760 S.W.2d 408, 426 (Mo.1988) The court concluded: "The State's interest is in preservation of life, not only Nancy's life, but also the lives of persons similarly situated yet without the support of a loving family. This interest outweighs any rights invoked on Nancy's behalf to terminate treatment in the face of the uncertainty of Nancy's wishes and her own right to life." Id. The U.S. Supreme Court affirmed the Missouri Supreme Court's decision. Specifically, it held that the state may require a "clear and convincing" showing that Cruzan expressed a desire to withdraw life-sustaining treatment prior to her accident before withdrawal is permitted. At least when the treatment refusal will result in death, the Court strongly suggested that when stopping treatment will result in death, only a formal written statement of intent, or so-called "living will," would suffice for constitutional purposes, given the state's interest in preserving life. In support of this decision, the Court stated:

> An erroneous decision not to terminate results in a maintenance of the status quo; the possibility of subsequent developments such as advancements in medical science, the discovery of new evidence regarding the patient's intent, changes in the law, or simply the unexpected death of the patient despite the administration of life-sustaining treatment, at least create the potential that a wrong decision

will eventually be corrected or its impact mitigated. An erroneous decision to withdraw life-sustaining treatment, however, is not susceptible of correction.

The *Cruzan* Court also rejected the argument that, because of the Court's decision in *Parham v. J.R.*, reprinted in Chapter Eight, Part V.E., permitting parents to make the hospitalization decision for their children, Ms. Cruzan's parents could be authorized to terminate life-sustaining treatment. The Court stated that "petitioners would seek to turn a decision which allowed a State to rely on family decisionmaking into a constitutional requirement that the State recognize such decisionmaking." It continued:

> [W]e do not think the Due Process Clause requires the State to repose judgment on these matters with anyone but the patient herself. Close family members may have a strong feeling—a feeling not at all ignoble or unworthy, but not entirely disinterested, either—that they do not wish to witness the continuation of the life of a loved one which they regard as hopeless, meaningless, and even degrading. But there is no automatic assurance that the view of close family members will necessarily be the same as the patient's would have been had she been confronted with the prospect of her situation while competent.

Cruzan hastened the development of statutory authorization for "advanced directives" in a number of states. An advanced directive is an instruction from a competent individual that directs or authorizes certain action in the event the individual becomes unable to make a decision about the action. Such directives, if valid, are binding on the guardian; indeed, they are usually meant to eliminate the need for a court-appointed guardian in the specified situation. In Florida, for example, a person (the "principal") can designate a "health care surrogate" through a simple, one-page advanced directive document. The document must be witnessed by two persons, neither of whom is the designated surrogate. Subsequently if two doctors certify that the principal has become incapacitated (meaning "physically or mentally unable to communicate a willful and knowing health care decision"), the surrogate is to make the necessary health care decision in accordance with the principal's instructions in the advanced directive. Although these decisions may be challenged judicially by the attending physicians, the health care facility, the patient's family, or "any other interested person," they are presumptively valid. Fl.Stat.§ 765.101 et. seq. More will be said about advanced directives in connection with mental health care in Part IV of this chapter at pp. 1102–1104.

5. *Intervention for the benefit of third parties.* Many courts that have sanctioned surrogate decisionmaking in the sterilization context have emphasized that the decision should take into account only the interests of the ward. For instance, in *Moe*, supra, the court stated: "No sterilization is to be compelled on the basis of any State or parental interest." 432 N.E.2d at 721. Does the *Hayes* court take a position on this issue? *Should* third party interests be taken into account?

In answering this last question, consider a case involving a decision other than sterilization. *In re Guardianship of Pescinski*, 67 Wis.2d 4, 226 N.W.2d 180 (1975) addressed whether a court may order an operation to transplant the kidney of an incompetent person to save the life of a relative. Tests showed that Richard Pescinski, who suffered from schizophrenia and had a mental capacity consistent with age twelve, was a suitable kidney donor for his sister, who would die without a transplant. While removal of a kidney is not a particularly risky operation, it causes some discomfort and of course leaves the donor with no backup kidney; for this reason, Richard and Elaine's parents, age 70 and 67, Elaine's six minor children, their older sister (who had diabetes) and their older brother (who had nine minor children, needed a special diet and had a rupture on his left side), either were not suitable donors or refused to donate. Applying the best interest test, the court upheld the guardian's decision not to order the kidney removal from Richard: "In the absence of real consent on his part, and in a situation where no benefit to him has been established, we fail to find any authority for the county court, or this court, to approve this operation."

In his dissent, Justice Day argued in favor of the substituted judgment test:

> I think the court as a court of equity does have authority to permit the kidney transplant operation requested in the petition of the guardian of Richard Pescinski. I agree with the reasoning of the Court of Appeals of the state of Kentucky in Strunk v. Strunk, 445 S.W.2d 145 (Ky.1969). That case involved the authorization of a transplant from a 27–year–old incompetent to his 28–year–old brother. The court in that case did find, based on the testimony of a psychiatrist, that while the incompetent had the mental age of six, it would be of benefit to him to keep his brother alive so that his brother could visit him on occasion[.] . . . In the case before us, if the incompetent brother should happily recover from his mental illness, he would undoubtedly be happy to learn that the transplant of one of his kidneys to his sister saved her life. This at least would be a normal response and hence the transplant is not without benefit to him.

> The majority opinion would forever condemn the incompetent to be always a receiver, a taker, but never a giver. For in holding that only those things which financially or physically benefit the incompetent may be done by the court, he is forever excluded from doing the decent thing, the charitable thing. The [substituted judgement] approach gives the incompetent the benefit of the doubt, endows him with the finest qualities of his humanity, assumes the goodness of his nature instead of assuming the opposite.

6. *Procedure. Hayes* is typical in its requirement that a court be involved in the sterilization decision. For instance, in *Moe,* 432 N.E.2d at 716–17, the court stated:

Since sterilization is an extraordinary and highly intrusive form of medical treatment that irreversibly extinguishes the ward's fundamental right of procreative choice, we conclude that a guardian must obtain a proper judicial order for the procedure before he or she can validly consent to it. Guardians and parents, therefore, absent statutory or judicial authorization, cannot consent to the sterilization of a ward in their care or custody.

What makes sterilization "extraordinary" and "intrusive," compared for instance to a decision regarding financial affairs? In another Massachusetts case, the court identified several factors to be considered in determining whether a court order must authorize medical intervention:

[T]he extent of impairment of the patient's mental faculties, whether the patient is in custody of a State institution, the prognosis without the proposed treatment, the prognosis with the proposed treatment, the complexity, risk and novelty of the proposed treatment, its possible side effects, the patient's level of understanding and probable reaction, the urgency of decision, the consent of the patient, spouse or guardian, the good faith of those who participate in the decision, the clarity of professional opinion as to what is good medical practice, the interests of third persons, and the administrative requirements of any institution involved.

Matter of Spring, 380 Mass. 629, 405 N.E.2d 115 (1980).

Scott, supra at 859–863, disagrees with the requirement that a judicial hearing be held in all sterilization cases, relying in part on *Parham v. J.R.* (*Parham* permitted parents to commit their children if an independent assessment by a mental health professional concurs.) Scott argues that in some cases a *Parham*-type arrangement is sufficient to authorize the sterilization decision, at least when the ward's parents are the surrogate decisionmakers:

[If a "reliable clinical evaluation" finds that] the child is not potentially capable of reproductive choice, she is less at risk than the child for whom hospitalization is sought. Parents seeking sterilization are not trying to "dump" their retarded child. Their initiative may well be an effort to facilitate her continued care at home. Thus, potential conflicts of interest would seem less probable in this situation than when psychiatric hospitalization is proposed.

* * *

If the disability is less severe, the possibility of underestimating the interest in reproductive choice becomes greater, and the costs of procedural protection become more acceptable. Thus, if the findings of the expert raise any ambiguity about the individual's potential interest in reproductive choice, judicial review is warranted.

7. *Hospitalizing the ward.* Similar issues arise in the context of making decisions about psychiatric treatment. Is a decision to hospitalize the

ward in a mental institution "extraordinary," so that hospitalization may not take place unless procedures for involuntary commitment are followed? Or may a guardian avoid court disposition by admitting the ward as a "voluntary" patient? In most states today, a guardian may not follow the latter course, at least if the ward objects to hospitalization. See ABA Comm'n on Law & Aging, *Guardian Authority for Residential Decisions: State Statutory Provisions* (as of August 2010), available at http://new.abanet. org/aging/PublicDocuments (noting, however, that several states still allow a guardian to consent to involuntary commitment, at least for limited time periods). In the words of one court:

> If we were not to require at least substantial compliance with the [involuntary commitment] law to fully protect the rights of incompetents it would be possible for an unscrupulous person to have himself appointed guardian and then lock his ward in a mental institution and proceed to waste the ward's estate. If a state and the judiciary are not vigilant in the protection of the rights of incompetents it is likely to lead to the abuse of the person and estate of such incompetents. The mentally ill are unable to think and care for themselves in a normal manner and of necessity depend upon the state and the courts for protection. . . . We . . . must hold in this case that the ward was not afforded either procedural or substantive due process. . . .

Von Luce v. Rankin, 267 Ark. 34, 588 S.W.2d 445 (1979). In *Von Luce* the ward protested the hospitalization. Should involuntary proceedings be required if the ward does not protest? To what extent does *Parham* undercut *Von Luce* and permit a guardian to "voluntary in" his or her ward if a mental health professional employed by the hospital sanctions the decision?

An even more controversial issue has been the guardian's authority to consent to various types of psychiatric treatments, ranging from drug therapy to psychosurgery. That issue is addressed in the next section, as part of a discussion on the larger issue of when persons with mental disability have the right to refuse or consent to psychiatric treatment.

IV.   THE RIGHT TO REFUSE AND CONSENT TO PSYCHIATRIC TREATMENT

In Chapter Four, we discussed the informed consent doctrine, which is normally thought to require professionals who are engaged in treating patients to honor an informed, voluntary decision by a competent individual. This common law doctrine regulates the relationship between doctor and patient by imposing liability on doctors who do not obtain informed consent for nonemergency treatment. However, when the treatment at issue is psychiatric in nature and the patient is thought to be seriously mentally ill (as opposed to anguished or very troubled), the informed consent doctrine has not found uniform acceptance. For instance, until the 1970's people who were civilly committed or hospitalized as incompetent to stand trial or criminally insane could be

[handwritten margin note: no informed consent for mentally ill]

forcibly medicated regardless of their competency to make treatment decisions. Apparently, the assumption was that since these people were subject to involuntary hospitalization, they were not competent to veto a particular treatment decision. At the same time, they were considered incompetent to insist on certain types of treatment. Similarly, uninstitutionalized persons who were supervised by guardians (of the person) had little or no control over their treatment.

These practices continue today in a number of jurisdictions. However, virtually every court that has considered the matter now recognizes a "right to refuse" psychotropic medication for people who are hospitalized, in the process constitutionalizing a version of the informed consent doctrine in that context. The precise scope of this right is still being fleshed out, at least at the Supreme Court level; its application to other types of psychiatric treatment is also unclear. This section first examines the right to refuse antipsychotic medication. It then addresses consent and refusal with respect to three other psychiatric treatment techniques: electro-convulsive therapy, psychosurgery, and behavior modification. Before reading the following materials, review the materials in Chapter One on the efficacy and side effects of medication and the other treatments discussed below.

A. PSYCHOTROPIC MEDICATION

WASHINGTON V. HARPER

Supreme Court of the United States, 1990.
494 U.S. 210, 110 S.Ct. 1028, 108 L.Ed.2d 178.

JUSTICE KENNEDY delivered the opinion of the Court.

The central question before us is whether a judicial hearing is required before the State may treat a mentally ill prisoner with antipsychotic drugs against his will. Resolution of the case requires us to discuss the protections afforded the prisoner under the Due Process Clause of the Fourteenth Amendment.

I

Respondent Walter Harper was sentenced to prison in 1976 for robbery. From 1976 to 1980, he was incarcerated at the Washington State Penitentiary. Most of that time, respondent was housed in the prison's mental health unit, where he consented to the administration of antipsychotic drugs. Antipsychotic drugs, sometimes called "neuroleptic" or "psychotropic drugs," are medications commonly used in treating mental disorders such as schizophrenia. As found by the trial court, the effect of these and similar drugs is to alter the chemical balance in the brain, the desired result being that the medication will assist the patient in organizing his or her thought processes and regaining a rational state of mind.

Respondent was paroled in 1980 on the condition that he participate in psychiatric treatment. While on parole, he continued to receive treatment at the psychiatric ward at Harborview Medical Center in Seattle, and was later sent to Western State hospital pursuant to a civil commitment order. In December 1981, the State revoked respondent's parole after he assaulted two nurses at a hospital in Seattle.

Upon his return to prison, respondent was sent to the Special Offender Center (SOC or Center), a 144–bed correctional institute established by the Washington Department of Corrections to diagnose and treat convicted felons with serious mental disorders. At the Center, psychiatrists first diagnosed respondent as suffering from a manic-depressive disorder. At first, respondent gave voluntary consent to treatment, including the administration of antipsychotic medications. In November 1982, he refused to continue taking the prescribed medications. The treating physician then sought to medicate respondent over his objections, pursuant to SOC Policy 600.30.

Policy 600.30 was developed in partial response to this Court's decision in *Vitek v. Jones*, 445 U.S. 480, 100 S.Ct. 1254, 63 L.Ed.2d 552 (1980).[i] The Policy has several substantive and procedural components. First, if a psychiatrist determines that an inmate should be treated with antipsychotic drugs but the inmate does not consent, the inmate may be subjected to involuntary treatment with the drugs only if he (1) suffers from a "mental disorder" and (2) is "gravely disabled" or poses a "likelihood of serious harm" to himself, others, or their property.[3] Only a psychiatrist may order or approve the medication. Second, an inmate who refuses to take the medication voluntarily is entitled to a hearing before a special committee consisting of a psychiatrist, psychologist, and the Associate Superintendent of the Center, none of whom may be, at the

---

[i] *Vitek* is reprinted at pp. 994–998.

[3] The Policy's definitions of the terms "mental disorder," "gravely disabled," and "likelihood of serious harm" are identical to the definitions of the terms as they are used in the state involuntary commitment statute. "Mental disorder" means "any organic, mental, or emotional impairment which has substantial adverse effects on an individual's cognitive or volitional functions." Wash.Rev.Code § 71.05.020(2) (1987). "Gravely disabled" means "a condition in which a person, as a result of a mental disorder: (a) [i]s in danger of serious physical harm resulting from a failure to provide for his essential human needs of health or safety, or (b) manifests severe deterioration in routine functioning evidenced by repeated and escalating loss of cognitive or volitional control over his or her actions and is not receiving such care as is essential for his or her health or safety." § 71.05.020(1). "Likelihood of serious harm" means "either: (a) [a] substantial risk that physical harm will be inflicted by an individual upon his own person, as evidenced by threats or attempts to commit suicide or inflict physical harm on one's self, (b) a substantial risk that physical harm will be inflicted by an individual upon another, as evidenced by behavior which has caused such harm or which places another person or persons in reasonable fear of sustaining such harm, or (c) a substantial risk that physical harm will be inflicted by an individual upon the property of others, as evidenced by behavior which has caused substantial loss or damage to the property of others." § 71.05.020(3).

time of the hearing, involved in the inmate's treatment or diagnosis. If the committee determines by a majority vote that the inmate suffers from a mental disorder and is gravely disabled or dangerous, the inmate may be medicated against his will, provided the psychiatrist is in the majority.

Third, the inmate has certain procedural rights before, during, and after the hearing. He must be given at least 24 hours' notice of the Center's intent to convene an involuntary medication hearing, during which time he may not be medicated. In addition, he must receive notice of the tentative diagnosis, the factual basis for the diagnosis, and why the staff believes medication is necessary. At the hearing, the inmate has the right to attend; to present evidence, including witnesses; to cross-examine staff witnesses; and to the assistance of a lay advisor who has not been involved in his case and who understands the psychiatric issues involved. Minutes of the hearing must be kept, and a copy provided to the inmate. The inmate has the right to appeal the committee's decision to the Superintendent of the Center within 24 hours, and the Superintendent must decide the appeal within 24 hours after its receipt. The inmate may seek judicial review of a committee decision in state court by means of a personal restraint petition or extraordinary writ.

Fourth, after the initial hearing, involuntary medication can continue only with periodic review. When respondent first refused medication, a committee, again composed of a non-treating psychiatrist, a psychologist, and the Center's Associate Superintendent was required to review an inmate's case after the first seven days of treatment. If the committee reapproved the treatment, the treating psychiatrist was required to review the case and prepare a report for the Department of Corrections medical director every 14 days while treatment continued.

In this case, respondent was absent when members of the Center staff met with the committee before the hearing. The committee then conducted the hearing in accordance with the Policy, with respondent being present and assisted by a nurse practitioner from another institution. The committee found that respondent was a danger to others as a result of a mental disease or disorder, and approved the involuntary administration of antipsychotic drugs. On appeal, the Superintendent upheld the committee's findings. Beginning on November 23, 1982, respondent was involuntarily medicated for about one year. Periodic review occurred in accordance with the Policy.

In November 1983, respondent was transferred from the Center to the Washington State Reformatory. While there, he took no medication, and as a result, his condition deteriorated. He was retransferred to the Center after only one month. Respondent was the subject of another committee hearing in accordance with Policy 600.30, and the committee again approved medication against his will. Respondent continued to receive antipsychotic drugs, subject to the required periodic reviews, until he was transferred to the Washington State Penitentiary in June 1986.

In February 1985, respondent filed suit in state court under 42 U.S.C. § 1983 against various individual defendants and the State, claiming that the failure to provide a judicial hearing before the involuntary administration of antipsychotic medication violated the Due Process, Equal Protection, and Free Speech clauses of both the federal and state constitutions, as well as state tort law. He sought both damages and declaratory and injunctive relief. After a bench trial in March 1987, the court held that, although respondent had a liberty interest in not being subjected to the involuntary administration of antipsychotic medication, the procedures contained in the Policy met the requirements of due process as stated in *Vitek*.

On appeal, the Washington Supreme Court reversed and remanded the case to the trial court. Agreeing with the trial court that respondent had a liberty interest in refusing antipsychotic medications, the Court concluded that the "highly intrusive nature", of treatment with antipsychotic medications warranted greater procedural protections than those necessary to protect the liberty interest at stake in *Vitek*. It held that, under the Due Process Clause, the State could administer antipsychotic medication to a competent, nonconsenting inmate only if, in a judicial hearing at which the inmate had the full panoply of adversarial procedural protections, the State proved by "clear, cogent, and convincing" evidence that the administration of antipsychotic medication was both necessary and effective for furthering a compelling state interest.

We granted certiorari, and we reverse.

* * *

III

* * *

Restated in the terms of this case, the substantive issue is what factual circumstances must exist before the State may administer antipsychotic drugs to the prisoner against his will; the procedural issue is whether the State's nonjudicial mechanisms used to determine the facts in a particular case are sufficient. The Washington Supreme Court in effect ruled upon the substance of the inmate's right, as well as the procedural guarantees, and both are encompassed by our grant of certiorari. We address these questions beginning with the substantive one.

* * *

We have no doubt that respondent possesses a significant liberty interest in avoiding the unwanted administration of antipsychotic drugs under the Due Process Clause of the Fourteenth Amendment. *Vitek.* Upon full consideration of the state administrative scheme, however, we find that the Due Process Clause confers upon respondent no greater right than that recognized under state law.

Respondent contends that the State, under the mandate of the Due Process Clause, may not override his choice to refuse antipsychotic drugs unless he has been found to be incompetent, and then only if the factfinder makes a substituted judgment that he, if competent, would consent to drug treatment. We disagree. The extent of a prisoner's right under the Clause to avoid the unwanted administration of antipsychotic drugs must be defined in the context of the inmate's confinement. The Policy under review requires the State to establish, by a medical finding, that a mental disorder exists which is likely to cause harm if not treated. Moreover, the fact that the medication must first be prescribed by a psychiatrist, and then approved by a reviewing psychiatrist, ensures that the treatment in question will be ordered only if it is in the prisoner's medical interests, given the legitimate needs of his institutional confinement.[8] These standards, which recognize both the prisoner's medical interests and the State's interests, meet the demands of the Due Process Clause.

* * *

There can be little doubt as to both the legitimacy and the importance of the governmental interest presented here. There are few cases in which the State's interest in combating the danger posed by a person to both himself and others is greater than in a prison environment, which, "by definition," is made up of persons with "a demonstrated proclivity for antisocial criminal, and often violent, conduct." We confront here the State's obligations, not just its interests. The State has undertaken the obligation to provide prisoners with medical treatment consistent not only with their own medical interests,

---

8. The dissent contends that the SOC Policy permits respondent's doctors to treat him with antipsychotic medications against his will without reference to whether the treatment is medically appropriate. For various reasons, we disagree. That an inmate is mentally ill and dangerous is a necessary condition to medication, but not a sufficient condition; before the hearing committee determines whether these requirements are met, the inmate's treating physician must first make the decision that medication is appropriate. The SOC is a facility whose purpose is not to warehouse the mentally ill, but to diagnose and treat convicted felons, with the desired goal being that they will recover to the point where they can function in a normal prison environment. In keeping with this purpose, an SOC psychiatrist must first prescribe the antipsychotic medication for the inmate, and the inmate must refuse it, before the Policy is invoked. Unlike the dissent, we will not assume that physicians will prescribe these drugs for reasons unrelated to the medical needs of the patients; indeed, the ethics of the medical profession are to the contrary. See Hippocratic Oath; American Psychiatric Association, *Principles of Medical Ethics With Annotations Especially Applicable to Psychiatry*, in Codes of Professional Responsibility 129–135 (R. Gorlin ed. 1986). . . .

not only prisoners interest

but also with the needs of the institution. Prison administrators have not only an interest in ensuring the safety of prison staffs and administrative personnel, but the duty to take reasonable measures for the prisoners' own safety. These concerns have added weight when a penal institution, like the Special Offender Center, is restricted to inmates with mental illnesses. Where an inmate's mental disability is the root cause of the threat he poses to the inmate population, the State's interest in decreasing the danger to others necessarily encompasses an interest in providing him with medical treatment for his illness.

Special Offender Center Policy 600.30 is a rational means of furthering the State's legitimate objectives. Its exclusive application is to inmates who are mentally ill and who, as a result of their illness, are gravely disabled or represent a significant danger to themselves or others. The drugs may be administered for no purpose other than treatment, and only under the direction of a licensed psychiatrist. There is considerable debate over the potential side effects of antipsychotic medications, but there is little dispute in the psychiatric profession that proper use of the drugs is one of the most effective means of treating and controlling a mental illness likely to cause violent behavior.

The alternative means proffered by respondent for accommodating his interest in rejecting the forced administration of antipsychotic drugs do not demonstrate the invalidity of the State's policy. Respondent's main contention is that, as a precondition to antipsychotic drug treatment, the State must find him incompetent, and then obtain court approval of the treatment using a "substituted judgment" standard. The suggested rule takes no account of the legitimate governmental interest in treating him where medically appropriate for the purpose of reducing the danger he poses. A rule that is in no way responsive to the State's legitimate interests is not a proper accommodation, and can be rejected out of hand. Nor are physical restraints or seclusion "alternative[s] that fully accommodat[e] the prisoner's rights at de minimis cost to valid penological interests." Physical restraints are effective only in the short term, and can have serious physical side effects when used on a resisting inmate, as well as leaving the staff at risk of injury while putting the restraints on or tending to the inmate who is in them. Furthermore, respondent has failed to demonstrate that physical restraints or seclusion are acceptable substitutes for antipsychotic drugs, in terms of either their medical effectiveness or their toll on limited prison resources.

We hold that, given the requirements of the prison environment, the Due Process Clause permits the State to treat a prison inmate who has a serious mental illness with antipsychotic drugs against his will, if the inmate is dangerous to himself or others and the treatment is in the inmate's medical interest. Policy 600.30 comports with these requirements; we therefore reject respondent's contention that its substantive standards are deficient under the Constitution.

IV

Having determined that state law recognizes a liberty interest . . . protected by the Due Process Clause, which permits refusal of antipsychotic drugs unless certain preconditions are met, we address next what procedural protections are necessary to ensure that the decision to medicate an inmate against his will is neither arbitrary nor erroneous under the standards we have discussed above. The Washington Supreme Court held that a full judicial hearing, with the inmate being represented by counsel, was required by the Due Process Clause before the State could administer antipsychotic drugs to him against his will. In addition, the court held that the State must justify the authorization of involuntary administration of antipsychotic drugs by "clear, cogent, and convincing" evidence. We hold that the administrative hearing procedures set by the SOC Policy do comport with procedural due process, and conclude that the Washington Supreme Court erred in requiring a judicial hearing as a prerequisite for the involuntary treatment of prison inmates.

A

The primary point of disagreement between the parties is whether due process requires a judicial decisionmaker. As written, the Policy requires that the decision whether to medicate an inmate against his will be made by a hearing committee composed of a psychiatrist, psychologist, and the Center's Associate Superintendent. None of the committee members may be involved, at the time of the hearing, in the inmate's treatment or diagnosis; members are not disqualified from sitting on the committee, however, if they have treated or diagnosed the inmate in the past. The committee's decision is subject to review by the Superintendent; if the inmate so desires, he may seek judicial review of the decision in a state court. Respondent contends that only a court should make the decision to medicate an inmate against his will.

Respondent's interest in avoiding the unwarranted administration of antipsychotic drugs is not insubstantial. The forcible injection of medication into a nonconsenting person's body represents a substantial interference with that person's liberty. The purpose of the drugs is to alter the chemical balance in a patient's brain, leading to changes, intended to be beneficial, in his or her cognitive processes. While the therapeutic benefits of antipsychotic drugs are well documented, it is also true that the drugs can have serious, even fatal, side effects. One such side effect identified by the trial court is acute dystonia, a severe involuntary spasm of the upper body, tongue, throat, or eyes. The trial court found that it may be treated and reversed within a few minutes through use of the medication Cogentin. Other side effects include akathesia (motor restlessness, often characterized by an inability to sit still); neuroleptic malignant syndrome (a relatively rare condition which can lead to death from cardiac dysfunction); and tardive dyskinesia, perhaps the most discussed side effect of antipsychotic drugs. Tardive dyskinesia is a neurological disorder, irreversible in some cases, that is characterized by involuntary, uncontrollable movements of various muscles, especially around the face. The State, respondent, and amici sharply disagree about the frequency with which tardive dyskinesia occurs, its severity, and the medical profession's ability to treat, arrest, or reverse the condition. A fair reading of the evidence, however, suggests that the proportion of patients treated with antipsychotic drugs who exhibit the symptoms of tardive dyskinesia ranges from 10% to 25%. According to the American Psychiatric Association, studies of the condition indicate that 60% of tardive dyskinesia is mild or minimal in effect, and about 10% may be characterized as severe.

Notwithstanding the risks that are involved, we conclude that an inmate's interests are adequately protected, and perhaps better served, by allowing the decision to medicate to be made by medical professionals rather than a judge. The Due Process Clause "has never been thought to require that the neutral and detached trier of fact be law trained or a judicial or administrative officer." *Parham v. J.R.* Though it cannot be doubted that the decision to medicate has societal and legal implications, the Constitution does not prohibit the State from permitting medical personnel to make the decision under fair procedural mechanisms. Particularly where the patient is mentally disturbed, his own intentions will be difficult to assess, and will be changeable in any event. Respondent's own history of accepting and then refusing drug treatment illustrates the point. We cannot make the facile assumption that the patient's intentions, or a substituted judgment approximating those intentions, can be determined in a single judicial hearing apart from the realities of frequent and ongoing clinical observation by medical professionals. Our holding in *Parham* that a judicial hearing was not required prior to the voluntary commitment of a child to a mental hospital was based on similar observations:

> ". . . [D]ue process is not violated by use of informal, traditional medical investigative techniques. . . . The mode and procedure of medical diagnostic procedures is not the business of judges. . . . Although we acknowledge the fallibility of medical and psychiatric diagnosis, we do not accept the notion that the shortcomings of specialists can always be avoided by shifting the decision from a trained specialist using the traditional tools of medical science to an untrained judge or administrative hearing officer after a judicial-type hearing. Even after a hearing, the nonspecialist decisionmaker must make a medical-psychiatric decision. Common human experience and scholarly opinions suggest that the supposed protections of an adversary proceeding to determine the appropriateness of medical

[handwritten marginalia: doctors judgement better than judge]

decisions for the commitment and treatment of mental and emotional illness may well be more illusory than real."

Nor can we ignore the fact that requiring judicial hearings will divert scarce prison resources, both money and the staff's time, from the care and treatment of mentally ill inmates.

* * *

[A]dequate procedures exist here. In particular, independence of the decisionmaker is addressed to our satisfaction by these procedures. None of the hearing committee members may be involved in the inmate's current treatment or diagnosis. . . . In the absence of record evidence to the contrary, we are not willing to presume that members of the staff lack the necessary independence to provide an inmate with a full and fair hearing in accordance with the Policy. In previous cases involving medical decisions implicating similar liberty interests, we have approved use of similar internal decisionmakers. See *Vitek*; *Parham*.[13] As we reasoned in *Vitek*, it is only by permitting persons connected with the institution to make these decisions that courts are able to avoid "unnecessary intrusion into either medical or correctional judgments." *Vitek*.

B

The procedures established by the Center are sufficient to meet the requirements of due process in all other respects, and we reject

---

[13] In an attempt to prove that internal decisionmakers lack the independence necessary to render impartial decisions, respondent and various amici refer us to other cases in which it is alleged that antipsychotic drugs were prescribed not for medical purposes, but to control or discipline mentally ill patients. We rejected a similar claim in *Parham*, and do so again here, using much the same reasoning. "That such a practice may take place in some institutions in some places affords no basis for a finding as to [Washington's] program," *Parham*, particularly in light of the trial court's finding here that the administration of antipsychotic drugs to respondent was consistent with good medical practice. Moreover, the practical effect of mandating an outside decisionmaker such as an "independent psychiatrist" or judge in these circumstances may be chimerical. Review of the literature indicates that outside decisionmakers concur with the treating physician's decision to treat a patient involuntarily in most, if not all, cases. See Bloom, Faulkner, Holm, & Rawlinson, *An Empirical View of Patients Exercising Their Right to Refuse Treatment*, 7 Int'l J. Law & Psychiatry 315, 325 (1984) (independent examining physician used in Oregon psychiatric hospital concurred in decision to involuntarily medicate patients in 95% of cases); Hickman, Resnick, & Olson, *Right to Refuse Psychotropic Medication: An Interdisciplinary Proposal*, 6 Mental Disability Law Reporter 122, 130 (1982) (independent reviewing psychiatrist used in Ohio affirmed the recommendation of internal reviewer in 100% of cases). Review by judges of decisions to override a patient's objections to medication yields similar results. Appelbaum, *The Right to Refuse Treatment With Antipsychotic Medications: Retrospect and Prospect*, 145 Am. J. Psychiatry 413, 417–418 (1988). In comparison, other studies reveal that review by internal decisionmakers is hardly as lackluster as the dissent suggests. See Hickman, Resnick, & Olson, *supra*, at 130 (internal reviewer approved of involuntary treatment in 75% of cases); Zito, Lentz, Routt, & Olson, *The Treatment Review Panel: A Solution to Treatment Refusal?*, 12 Bull.Am.Acad.Psychiatry Law 349 (1984) (internal review panel used in Minnesota mental hospital approved of involuntary medication in 67% of cases). See generally Appelbaum & Hoge, *The Right to Refuse Treatment: What the Research Reveals*, 4 Behavioral Sciences & the Law 279, 288–290 (1986) (summarizing results of studies on how various institutions review patients' decisions to refuse antipsychotic medications and noting "the infrequency with which refusals are allowed, regardless of the system or the decisionmaker").

respondent's arguments to the contrary. The Policy provides for notice, the right to be present at an adversary hearing, and the right to present and cross-examine witnesses. See *Vitek*. The procedural protections are not vitiated by meetings between the committee members and staff before the hearing. Absent evidence of resulting bias, or evidence that the actual decision is made before the hearing, allowing respondent to contest the staff's position at the hearing satisfies the requirement that the opportunity to be heard "must be granted at a meaningful time and in a meaningful manner." We reject also respondent's contention that the hearing must be conducted in accordance with the rules of evidence or that a "clear, cogent, and convincing" standard of proof is necessary. This standard is neither required nor helpful when medical personnel are making the judgment required by the regulations here. See *Vitek*. Finally, we note that under state law an inmate may obtain judicial review of the hearing committee's decision by way of a personal restraint petition or petition for an extraordinary writ, and that the trial court found that the record compiled under the Policy was adequate to allow such review.

Respondent contends that the Policy is nonetheless deficient because it does not allow him to be represented by counsel. We disagree. "[I]t is less than crystal clear why lawyers must be available to identify possible errors in medical judgment." Given the nature of the decision to be made, we conclude that the provision of an independent lay advisor who understands the psychiatric issues involved is sufficient protection. See *Vitek* (Powell, J., concurring).

V

In sum, we hold that the regulation before us is permissible under the Constitution. It is an accommodation between an inmate's liberty interest in avoiding the forced administration of antipsychotic drugs and the State's interests in providing appropriate medical treatment to reduce the danger that an inmate suffering from a serious mental disorder represents to himself or others. The Due Process Clause does require certain essential procedural protections, all of which are provided by the regulation before us. The judgment of the Washington Supreme Court is reversed and the case remanded for further proceedings.

It is so ordered.

JUSTICE STEVENS, with whom JUSTICE BRENNAN and JUSTICE MARSHALL join, concurring in part and dissenting in part.

* * *

I

The Court acknowledges that under the Fourteenth Amendment "respondent possesses a significant liberty interest in avoiding the unwanted administration of antipsychotic drugs," but then virtually ignores the several dimensions of that liberty. They are both physical and intellectual. Every violation of a person's bodily integrity is an invasion of his or her liberty. The invasion is particularly intrusive if it creates a substantial risk of permanent injury and premature death. Moreover, any such action is degrading if it overrides a competent person's choice to reject a specific form of medical treatment. And when the purpose or effect of forced drugging is to alter the will and the mind of the subject, it constitutes a deprivation of liberty in the most literal and fundamental sense.

> "The makers of our Constitution undertook to secure conditions favorable to the pursuit of happiness. They recognized the significance of man's spiritual nature, of his feelings and of his intellect. They knew that only a part of the pain, pleasure and satisfactions of life are to be found in material things. They sought to protect Americans in their beliefs, their thoughts, their emotions and their sensations. They conferred, as against the Government, the right to be let alone—the most comprehensive of rights and the right most valued by civilized men." Olmstead v. United States, 277 U.S. 438, 478, 48 S.Ct. 564, 572, 72 L.Ed. 944 (1928) (Brandeis, J., dissenting).

The liberty of citizens to resist the administration of mind altering drugs arises from our Nation's most basic values.

The record of one of Walter Harper's involuntary medication hearings at the Special Offense Center (SOC) notes: "Inmate Harper stated he would rather die th[a]n take medication." That Harper would be so opposed to taking psychotropic drugs is not surprising: as the Court acknowledges, these drugs both "alter the chemical balance in a patient's brain" and can cause irreversible and fatal side effects.[5] The Prolixin injections that Harper was receiving at the time of his statement exemplify the intrusiveness of psychotropic drugs on a person's body and mind. Prolixin acts "at all levels of the central nervous system as well as on multiple organ systems." It can induce catatonic-like states, alter electroencephalographic tracings, and cause swelling of the brain.

---

[5] The Court relies heavily on the brief filed by the American Psychiatric Association and the Washington State Psychiatric Association as Amici Curiae (Psychiatrists' Brief), to discount the severity of these drugs. However, medical findings discussed in other briefs support the conclusions of the Washington Supreme Court and challenge the reliability of the Psychiatrists' Brief. For example, the Brief for American Psychological Association as Amicus Curiae (Psychologists' Brief) points out that the observation of tardive dyskinesia has been increasing "at an alarming rate" since the 1950–1970 data relied on by the Psychiatrists' Brief, and that "the chance of suffering this potentially devastating disorder is greater than one in four." See also Brief for Coalition for the Fundamental Rights and Equality of Ex–Patients as Amicus Curiae 16–18 (court findings and recent literature on side effects); Brief for National Association of Protection and Advocacy Systems et al. Amici Curiae 7–16 (same). Psychiatrists also may not be entirely disinterested experts. The psychologists charge: "As a psychiatrist has written, '[l]itigation from patients suffering from TD [tardive dyskinesia] is expected to explode within the next five years. Some psychiatrists and other physicians continue to minimize the seriousness of TD . . . [despite] continual warnings.' "

Adverse reactions include drowsiness, excitement, restlessness, bizarre dreams, hypertension, nausea, vomiting, loss of appetite, salivation, dry mouth, perspiration, headache, constipation, blurred vision, impotency, eczema, jaundice, tremors, and muscle spasms. As with all psychotropic drugs, prolixin may cause tardive dyskinesia, an often irreversible syndrome of uncontrollable movements that can prevent a person from exercising basic functions such as driving an automobile, and neuroleptic malignant syndrome, which is 30% fatal for those who suffer from it. The risk of side effects increases over time.

The Washington Supreme Court properly equated the intrusiveness of this mind altering drug treatment with electroconvulsive therapy or psychosurgery. It agreed with the Supreme Judicial Court of Massachusetts' determination that the drugs have a " 'profound effect' " on a person's " 'thought processes' " and a " 'well-established likelihood of severe and irreversible adverse side effects,' " and that they therefore should be treated " 'in the same manner we would treat psychosurgery or electroconvulsive therapy.' " There is no doubt, as the State Supreme Court and other courts that have analyzed the issue have concluded, that a competent individual's right to refuse such medication is a fundamental liberty interest deserving the highest order of protection.

II

Arguably, any of three quite different state interests might be advanced to justify a deprivation of this liberty interest. The State might seek to compel Harper to submit to a mind altering drug treatment program as punishment for the crime he committed in 1976, as a "cure" for his mental illness, or as a mechanism to maintain order in the prison. The Court today recognizes Harper's liberty interest only as against the first justification.

Forced administration of antipsychotic medication may not be used as a form of punishment. This conclusion follows inexorably from our holding in *Vitek v. Jones* that the Constitution provides convicted felon the protection of due process against an involuntary transfer from the prison population to a mental hospital for psychiatric treatment.

* * *

The Court does not suggest that psychotropic drugs, any more than transfer for medical treatment, may be forced on prisoners as a necessary condition of their incarceration or as a disciplinary measure. Rather, it holds:

> "[G]iven the requirements of the prison environment, the Due Process Clause permits the State to treat a prison inmate who has a serious mental illness with antipsychotic drugs against his will, if the inmate is dangerous to himself or others and the treatment is in the inmate's medical interest. Policy 600.30 comports with these

[handwritten margin note: -danger to himself or others can be forcibly given drugs + medical interest]

requirements; we therefore reject respondent's contention that its substantive standards are deficient under the Constitution."

Crucial to the Court's exposition of this substantive due process standard is the condition that these drugs "may be administered for no purpose other than treatment," and that "the treatment in question will be ordered only if it is in the prisoner's medical interests, given the legitimate needs of his institutional confinement." Thus, although the Court does not find, as Harper urges, an absolute liberty interest of a competent person to refuse psychotropic drugs, it does recognize that the substantive protections of the Due Process Clause limit the forced administration of psychotropic drugs to all but those inmates whose medical interests would be advanced by such treatment.

[W]hether or not the State's alleged interest in providing medically beneficial treatment to those in its custody who are mentally ill may alone override the refusal of psychotropic drugs by a presumptively competent person, a plain reading of Policy 600.30 reveals that it does not meet the substantive standard set forth by the Court. Even on the Court's terms, the Policy is constitutionally insufficient.

Policy 600.30 permits forced administration of psychotropic drugs on a mentally ill inmate based purely on the impact that his disorder has on the security of the prison environment. The provisions of the Policy make no reference to any expected benefit to the inmate's medical condition. . . . Although any application of Policy 600.30 requires a medical judgment as to a prisoner's mental condition and the cause of his behavior, the Policy does not require a determination that forced medication would advance his medical interest. Use of psychotropic drugs, the State readily admits, serves to ease the institutional and administrative burdens of maintaining prison security and provides a means of managing an unruly prison population and preventing property damage. By focusing on the risk that the inmate's mental condition poses to other people and property, the Policy allows the State to exercise either parens patriae authority or police authority to override a prisoner's liberty interest in refusing psychotropic drugs. Thus, most unfortunately, there is simply no basis for the Court's assertion that medication under the Policy must be to advance the prisoner's medical interest.

*   *   *

The State advances security concerns as a justification for forced medication in two distinct circumstances. A SOC Policy provision not at issue in this case permits 72 hours of involuntary medication on an emergency basis when "an inmate is suffering from a mental disorder and as a result of that disorder presents an imminent likelihood of serious harm to himself or others." In contrast to the imminent danger of injury that triggers the emergency medication provisions, a general risk of illness-induced injury or property damage—evidenced by no more than past behavior—allows long-term, involuntary medication of an inmate with psychotropic drugs under Policy 600.30. This ongoing interest in security and management is a penological concern of a constitutionally distinct magnitude from the necessity of responding to emergencies. It is difficult to imagine what, if any, limits would restrain such a general concern of prison administrators who believe that prison environments are, " 'by definition,' . . . made up of persons with 'a demonstrated proclivity for antisocial criminal, and often violent, conduct.' " A rule that allows prison administrators to address potential security risks by forcing psychotropic drugs on mentally ill inmates for prolonged periods is unquestionably an "exaggerated response" to that concern.

[T]he record before us does not establish that a more narrowly drawn policy withdrawing psychotropics from only those inmates who actually refuse consent[15] and who do not pose an imminent threat of serious harm[16] would increase the marginal costs of SOC administration. Harper's own record reveals that administrative segregation and standard disciplinary sanctions were frequently imposed on him over and above forced medication and thus would add no new costs. Similarly, intramuscular injections of psychotropics, such as those frequently forced on Harper, entail no greater risk than administration of less dangerous

---

[15] There is no evidence that more than a small fraction of inmates would refuse drugs under a voluntary policy. Harper himself voluntarily took psychotropics for six years, and intermittently consented to them after 1982. See e.g., *Rogers v. Okin*, 478 F.Supp. 1342, 1369 (D.Mass.1979) (only 12 of 1,000 institutionalized patients refused psychotropic drugs for prolonged periods during the two years that judicial restraining order was in effect), modified, 634 F.2d 650 (C.A.1 1980), vacated and remanded, sub nom. *Mills v. Rogers*, 457 U.S. 291, 102 S.Ct. 2442, 73 L.Ed.2d 16 (1982). The efficacy of forced drugging is also marginal; involuntary patients have a poorer prognosis than cooperative patients. See Rogers & Webster, *Assessing Treatability in Mentally Disordered Offenders*, 13 Law and Human Behavior 19, 20–21 (1989).

[16] As the Court notes, properly used, these drugs are "one of the most effective means of treating and controlling" certain incurable mental illnesses, but they are not a panacea for long-term care of all patients.

"[T]he maintenance treatment literature . . . shows that many patients (approximately 30%) relapse despite receiving neuroleptic medication, while neuroleptics can be withdrawn from other patients for many months and in some cases for years without relapse. Standard maintenance medication treatment strategies, though they are indisputably effective in group comparisons, may be quite inefficient in addressing the treatment requirements of the individual patient."

Lieberman et al., *Reply to Ethics of Drug Discontinuation Studies in Schizophrenia*, 46 Archives of General Psychiatry 387, 387 (1989) (footnotes omitted).

Indeed, the drugs appear to have produced at most minor "savings" in Harper's case. Dr. Petrich reported that "medications are not satisfactory in containing the worst excesses of his labile and irritable behavior. He is uncooperative when on medication." [A] therapy supervisor reported before Harper's involuntary medication began: "during the time in which he assaulted the nurse at Cabrini he was on neuroleptic medication yet there is indication that he was psychotic. However, during his stay at SOC he has been off of all neuroleptic medications and at times has shown some preoccupation and appearance of psychosis but has not become assaultive. His problems on medication, such as the paradoxical effect from the neuroleptic medications, may be precipitated by increased doses of neuroleptic medications and may cause an exacerbation of his psychosis. Though Mr. Harper is focused on psychosomatic problems from neuroleptic medications as per the side effects, the real problem may be that the psychosis is exacerbated by neuroleptic medications."

drugs such as tranquilizers. Use of psychotropic drugs simply to suppress an inmate's potential violence, rather than to achieve therapeutic results, may also undermine the efficacy of other available treatment programs that would better address his illness.

[T]he flaw in Washington's Policy 600.30—and the basic error in the Court's opinion today—is the failure to divorce from each other the two justifications for forced medication [i.e., security and rehabilitation] and to consider the extent to which the Policy is reasonably related to either interest. The State, and arguably the Court, allows the SOC to blend the state interests in responding to emergencies and in convenient prison administration with the individual's interest in receiving beneficial medical treatment. The result is a muddled rationale that allows the "exaggerated response" of forced psychotropic medication on the basis of purely institutional concerns. So serving institutional convenience eviscerates the inmate's substantive liberty interest in the integrity of his body and mind.

III

The procedures of Policy 600.30 are also constitutionally deficient. Whether or not the State ever may order involuntary administration of psychotropic drugs to a mentally ill person who has been committed to its custody but has not been declared incompetent, it is at least clear that any decision approving such drugs must be made by an impartial professional concerned not with institutional interests, but only with the individual's best interests. The critical defect in Policy 600.30 is the failure to have the treatment decision made or reviewed by an impartial person or tribunal.[20]

* * *

The decisionmakers [under Policy 600.30] have two disqualifying conflicts of interest. First, the panel members must review the work of treating physicians who are their colleagues and who, in turn, regularly review their decisions. Such an in-house system pits the interests of an inmate who objects to forced medication against the judgment not only of his doctor, but often his doctor's colleagues.[22] Furthermore, the Court's

---

[20] It is not necessary to reach the question whether the decision to force psychotropic drugs on a competent person against his will must be approved by a judge, or by an administrative tribunal of professionals who are not members of the prison staff, in order to conclude that the mechanism of Policy 600.30 violates procedural due process. The choice is not between medical experts on the one hand and judges on the other; the choice is between decisionmakers who are biased and those who are not.

[22] As regular SOC staff, 600.30 committee members are: "susceptible to implicit or explicit pressure for cooperation ('If you support my orders, I'll support yours'). It is instructive that month after month, year after year, this 'review' panel always voted for more medication—despite the scientific literature showing that periodic respites from drugs are advisable and that prolonged use of antipsychotic drugs is proper only when the medical need is clear and compelling." Psychologists' Brief 26–27 (footnote omitted).

conclusion that "[n]one of the hearing committee members may be involved in the inmate's current treatment or diagnosis" overlooks the fact that Policy 600.30 allows a treating psychiatrist to participate in all but the initial seven-day medication approval. This revolving door operated in Harper's case. Dr. Petrich treated Harper through 1982 and recommended involuntary medication on October 27, 1982. Dr. Loeken, staff psychologist Giles, and Assistant Superintendent Stark authorized medication for seven days after a 600.30 hearing on November 23, 1982. Dr. Petrich then replaced Dr. Loeken on the committee, and with Giles and Stark approved long-term involuntary medication on December 8, 1982. Solely under this authority, Dr. Petrich prescribed more psychotropic medication for Harper on December 8, 1982 and throughout the following year.

Second, the panel members, as regular staff of the Center, must be concerned not only with the inmate's best medical interests, but also with the most convenient means of controlling the mentally disturbed inmate. The mere fact that a decision is made by a doctor does not make it "certain that professional judgment in fact was exercised." The structure of the SOC committee virtually insures that it will not be. While the initial inquiry into the mental bases for an inmate's behavior is medical, the ultimate medication decision under Policy 600.30 turns on an assessment of the risk that an inmate's condition imposes on the institution. The prescribing physician and each member of the review committee must therefore wear two hats. This hybrid function disables the independent exercise of each decisionmaker's professional judgment. The structure of the review committee further confuses the objective of the inquiry; two of the committee members are not trained or licensed to prescribe psychotropic drugs, and one has no medical expertise at all. The trump by institutional interests is dramatized by the fact that appeals of committee decisions under the Policy are made solely to the SOC Superintendent.

* * *

The institutional bias that is inherent in the identity of the decisionmakers is unchecked by other aspects of Policy 600.30. The committee need not consider whether less intrusive procedures would be effective, or even if the prescribed medication would be beneficial to the prisoner, before approving involuntary medication. Findings regarding

---

Rates of approval by different review bodies are of limited value, of course, because institutions will presumably adjust their medication practices over time to obtain approval under different standards or by different reviewing bodies. However, New Jersey's review of involuntary psychotropic medication in mental institutions is instructive. In 1980 external review by an "independent psychiatrist" who was not otherwise employed by the Department of Human Services resulted in discontinuation or reduction of 59% of dosages. After the Department moved to an internal peer review system, that percentage dropped to 2.5% of cases. Brief for New Jersey Department of Public Advocate as Amicus Curiae 38–54.

the severity or the probability of potential side effects of drugs and dosages are not required. And, although the Policy does not prescribe a standard of proof necessary for any factual determination upon which a medication decision rests, the Court gratuitously advises that the "clear, cogent, and convincing" standard adopted by the State Supreme Court would be unnecessary.

Nor is the 600.30 hearing likely to raise these issues fairly and completely. An inmate recommended for involuntary medication is no more capable of " 'speaking effectively for himself' " on these "issues which are 'complex or otherwise difficult to develop or present' " than an inmate recommended for transfer to a mental hospital. *Vitek* (Powell, J., concurring in part). Although single doses of some psychotropic drugs are designed to be effective for a full month, the inmate may not refuse the very medication he is contesting until 24 hours before his hearing. Policy 600.30 also does not allow the inmate to be represented by counsel at hearings, but only to have present an advisor, who is appointed by the SOC. These advisors, of questionable loyalties and efficacy, cannot provide the "independent assistance" required for an inmate fairly to understand and participate in the hearing process.[30] In addition, although the Policy gives the inmate a "limitable right to present testimony through his own witnesses and to confront and cross-examine witnesses," in the next paragraph it takes that right away for reasons that "include, but are not limited to such things as irrelevance, lack of necessity, redundancy, possible reprisals, or other reasons relating to institutional interests of security, order, and rehabilitation." Finally, because Policy 600.30 provides a hearing only for the seven-day committee, and just a paper record for the long-term committee, the inmate has no opportunity at all to present his objections to the more crucial decision to medicate him on a long-term basis.

In sum, it is difficult to imagine how a committee convened under Policy 600.30 could conceivably discover, much less be persuaded to overrule, an erroneous or arbitrary decision to medicate or to maintain a specific dosage or type of drug. Institutional control infects the decisionmakers and the entire procedure. . . .

I continue to believe that "even the inmate retains an unalienable interest in liberty—at the very minimum the right to be treated with dignity—which the Constitution may never ignore." A competent individual's right to refuse psychotropic medication is an aspect of liberty

---

[30] The prisoner is introduced to, and may consult with, his appointed advisor at the commencement of the hearing. Harper's advisor on November 23, 1982, a nurse practitioner from Washington State Reformatory, asked Harper three questions in the hearing. The other five advisors appointed for Harper never spoke in the hearings. All five were apparently staff at the SOC: SOC Psychiatric Social Worker Hyden (who sat for the SOC Assistant Superintendent on the next 180–day committee that reapproved Harper's medication), a prison chaplain, two registered nurses, and a correctional officer.

requiring the highest order of protection under the Fourteenth Amendment. Accordingly, ... I respectfully dissent from the Court's opinion and judgment.

QUESTIONS AND COMMENTS

1. *The rationale for a right to refuse.* The majority opinion in *Harper* relies on the due process clause in holding that a prisoner has a "right" to refuse unwanted antipsychotic drugs. Other possible bases for a right to refuse that have been advanced by various courts and commentators include: (1) the first amendment's protection of thought and expression; (2) the eighth amendment's prohibition against cruel and unusual punishment; (3) the equal protection clause's requirement that like classes be treated alike (here the comparable class is the non-mentally ill, who are protected by the informed consent doctrine); and (4) the "penumbral" right to privacy's protection of bodily integrity. See 2 Men.Dis.L.Rep. 43, 46 (1977) (discussing these and other bases for the right). Among the lower court decisions that have found a constitutional right to refuse medication, most have relied on the last theory. See, e.g., *United States v. Charters*, 863 F.2d 302 (4th Cir.1988) (dealing with patients found incompetent to stand trial); *Rogers v. Okin*, 634 F.2d 650 (1st Cir.1980) (civilly committed patients); *Rennie v. Klein*, 653 F.2d 836 (3d Cir.1981) (civilly committed patients). Is the right to privacy approach significantly different from the Supreme Court's approach in *Harper*? Of the various approaches, which is the most persuasive? How would the choice of a particular constitutional basis affect the scope of the right (e.g., under what circumstances, if any, would danger to self or others be an exception to the right to refuse)?

2. *The substantive scope of the right.* Focusing solely on the scope of the right, rather than the procedures for implementing it, what are the implications of *Harper* for persons who are civilly committed? For those who are committed after acquittal by reason of insanity? If prison confinement is indistinguishable from commitment in this regard, does *any* involuntarily committed person have a federal constitutional right to refuse medication after *Harper*? See *Hightower by Dahler v. Olmstead*, 959 F.Supp. 1549 (N.D. Ga. 1996) (holding that the state's interest in cases involving refusal by civilly committed patients are "similar" to the interests of prisoners and upholding a policy allowing forcible medication when forgoing medication would be "unsafe to patient or others").

In *Riggins v. Nevada*, 504 U.S. 127, 112 S.Ct. 1810, 118 L.Ed.2d 479 (1992), the Supreme Court dealt with forcible medication of a person during his trial on capital charges. In the course of deciding to remand the case for further deliberations the Court stated:

> Nevada certainly would have satisfied due process if the prosecution had demonstrated and the District Court had found that treatment with antipsychotic medications was medically appropriate and, considering less intrusive alternatives, essential for the sake of Riggins' own safety or the safety of others. Similarly, the State might have been able to

justify medically appropriate, involuntary treatment with the drug by establishing that it could not obtain an adjudication of Riggins' guilt or innocence by using less intrusive means.

Riggins is described in more detail in the materials concerning forcible medication of those found incompetent to stand trial. For present purposes, does the above language broaden the scope of the right to refuse medication announced in *Harper*, at least for populations other than convicted prisoners?

Some state court decisions focusing on the civil commitment context have arrived at standards that appear to establish a stronger right to refuse than the policy upheld in *Harper*. In *Rogers v. Commissioner*, 390 Mass. 489, 458 N.E.2d 308 (1983), the Supreme Judicial Court of Massachusetts developed standards under Massachusetts law that can be summarized as follows:

(1) Administration of antipsychotic medication over a competent patient's objection is permissible if the patient "poses an imminent threat of harm to himself or others, and . . . if there is no less intrusive alternative to antipsychotic drugs." Id. at 321.

(2) Otherwise, forcible medication is permissible only if the patient is incompetent to made a treatment decision. A *doctor's* determination of incompetency will justify forcible medication only if the medication is necessary "to prevent the 'immediate, substantial, and irreversible deterioration of a serious mental illness,' in cases in which 'even the smallest of avoidable delays would be intolerable.'" Id. at 322.

(3) If medication is necessary beyond this emergency period, and in all other circumstances, incompetence must be determined by a judge, at a hearing with notice and a guardian ad litem appointed to assist the court in the treatment decision. Id. at 322–23.

(4) If the judge finds the patient incompetent, he or she must make a substituted judgment decision and approve a treatment plan. Either the judge or a court-appointed guardian must monitor the subsequent treatment process. Id. at 318.

Similar state court holdings came in *Rivers v. Katz*, 67 N.Y.2d 485, 495 N.E.2d 337, 504 N.Y.S.2d 74 (1986) and *Riese v. St. Mary's Hospital and Medical Center*, 209 Cal.App.3d 1303, 271 Cal.Rptr. 199 (1st Dist. 1988).

In contrast is *Rennie v. Klein*, 653 F.2d 836 (3d Cir.1981). There, as in *Rogers*, the Third Circuit permitted forcible medication of those who are imminently dangerous to self or others, and of those for whom "there is a significant possibility" of harm to self, provided medication is the least intrusive means of accomplishing the state's goals of treatment and security. But *Rennie* also denied a right to refuse to competent, nondangerous patients, if the medication "would probably improve the patient's condition within a significantly shorter time period" than alternative treatment plans. Id. at 852. Other courts have reduced the right even further, holding that the patient's competency "is properly treated as simply another factor in the ultimate medical decision to administer the medication involuntarily." *United States v. Charters*, 863 F.2d 302 (4th Cir.1988). See also *In re Commitment of G.M.*, 743 N.E.2d 1148, 1152–53 (Ind.Ct.App. 2001).

3. *Defining incompetency*. Under any of these formulations, dangerousness and incompetency diminish or eliminate the right to refuse medication. Dangerousness has already been explored fully in Chapter Eight. How should incompetency be defined in this context? Assume in the following hypotheticals that the person understands the risks and benefits of the medication in the abstract. Is the reason for refusing the medication a "competent" one?

a.   "I've had treatment for so many years and nothing has changed."

b.   "I don't really need the medication. Many people get better without it."

c.   "How could the medication help if nothing else in my life changes?"

d.   "It's in the hands of God. Who knows?"

e.   "The only thing that will work is if you just convince yourself that you are going to get better."

f.   "Those medications just make you feel worse."

g.   "I just think it won't help."

h.   "That medication is poison."

i.   "That medication will harm my baby" (the person is not pregnant).

j.   "Large dosages of that medication hurt my stomach, so I'm not taking small dosages."

k.   "I don't want the medication because you doctors are psychotic."

l.   "You doctors are practicing witchcraft."

m.   "I'm not mentally ill."

n.   "I'm not hearing voices; they're really there."

See Christopher Slobogin, *"Appreciation" as a Measure of Competency: Some Thoughts about the MacArthur Group's Approach*, 2 Psychol. Pub. Pol'y & L. 18, 25–27 (1996)(arguing that reasons a through g do not demonstrate incompetence under Saks' understanding-and-belief test); Grant Morris, *Judging Judgment: Assessing the Competence of Mental Patients to Refuse Treatment*, 22 San Diego L. Rev. 343, 408–22 (1995)(describing cases in which reasons h through l were found to demonstrate incompetence).

Many people with schizophrenia suffer from "anosognosia"—an organic condition associated with a dysfunction in the right hemisphere of the brain—that renders individuals unable to recognize their symptoms and much less likely to comply with treatment recommendations. For instance, one study found that 63% of psychiatric patients with anosognosia were noncompliant with medications compared to a 24% noncompliance rate for patients who were aware of their illness. H. Rittmannsberger et al., *Medication Adherence among Psychotic Patients before Admission to Inpatient Treatment*, 55 Psychiat. Serv. 174 (2004). See also Jonathan P. Lacro et al., *Prevalence of and Risk Factors for Medication Nonadherence in Patients with Schizophrenia: A Comprehensive Review of Recent Literature*, 63 J. Clin. Psychiat. 892 (2002). People with severe anosognosia do not recognize that they are having delusions or hallucinations or that they are experiencing abnormal bodily movements, such as those associated with tardive dyskinesia, and are usually unconcerned about their situation. Should such people be considered incompetent to make treatment decisions? Or, as some have claimed, is the notion of anosognosia, which has yet to be correlated with a specific neurological deficit, simply a "Catch–22" for patients: either they admit they are mentally ill or they are labeled mentally ill because of their failure to admit it? Cf. Stephen Morse, *Steel Traps and Unattainable Aspirations: A Comment on Kress*, 24 Beh. Sci. & L. 599, 606 (2006) ("In many cases, I suggest, it will be difficult to distinguish lack of insight from disagreement with the doctor.").

4. *Substituted judgment and advanced directives.* A finding of incompetency does not mean treatment is automatic. As discussed in the previous section, surrogate decisionmaking can be based on a "best interest" or a "substituted judgment" test. To the extent courts have considered the matter in the medication context, they have usually adopted the best interest approach, which means in effect that the doctor's recommendation—imposition of medication—is followed. In contrast, *Rogers*, described in note 2, requires a "substitute judgment decision," which makes dispositive the outcome the incompetent person would have wanted, regardless of its benefit. In *Cruzan v. Director, Missouri Dep't of Health*, 497 U.S. 261, 110 S.Ct. 2841, 111 L.Ed.2d 224 (1990), described at pp. 1077–1078, the Supreme Court appeared to subscribe to this approach, at least when the incompetent person is in a vegetative coma, although it required such strong proof of the person's desires that in practice the test might reduce to the best interest formulation.

Assuming *Cruzan* requires the substituted judgment test in the vegetative coma situation, to which other situations should its reasoning apply? Consider *In re Jeffers*, 239 Ill.App.3d 29, 179 Ill.Dec. 895, 606 N.E.2d 727 (1992), in which a patient argued that her forcible medication, upon her guardian's consent, was inappropriate under *Cruzan* because the trial court did not determine whether the guardian's decision "would reflect respondent's decision if she were competent." The appeals court refused to apply *Cruzan's* standard in this context (and opted for the best interest test instead) for three reasons: (1) "the incompetency of an incompetent person in a vegetative state does not lead him to pose a danger to himself or others while the incompetency of the mental health incompetent does," thus permitting the state to ignore what the patient would have wanted if competent; (2) "the choices involved in the present case hold far less drastic consequences than the choices of a guardian on behalf of a person in a vegetative state"; (3) "a person who suffers from mental incompetency might *never* have had the competency to make a reasoned decision regarding medication, as opposed to a person who lives in a vegetative coma."

If the incompetent person *has* previously been competent and, while in that state, clearly indicates a desire to avoid medication in the future, should that desire be honored? In other words, should we recognize the force of advanced directives in this context? Professor Winick thinks we should, at least in *parens patriae* cases (when the person is dangerous to others, he believes the state's interest trumps the individual's desires). Bruce Winick, *Advanced Directive Instruments for Those with Mental Illness*, 51 U. Miami L. Rev. 57 (1996). Winick argues that this approach is not only more respectful of autonomy, but it also has a beneficial therapeutic effect because "the ability to be self-determining—to plan for the future, to envision future contingencies and bring about those that are desired and avoid those that are undesired, to set goals and see them achieved—is an important aspect of mental health and self-esteem." Id. at 84.

Should we respect an advanced directive that explicitly prohibits medication "even if I become suicidal [or homeless and jobless]"? Should the answer to this question depend upon whether the person has been suicidal or homeless or jobless in the past? What if the advanced directive prohibits medication but circumstances change (e.g., a new drug with fewer side effects—see note 7 below—is developed)? What if the person's advanced directive *opts* for medication but then, as the person begins to decompensate but before he or she becomes completely incompetent, refusal occurs?

In the changed circumstances scenario, Winick suggests an analogy to the *cy pres* doctrine in probate law. That doctrine allows a court to modify a will provision that, in light of unanticipated circumstances, seems inconsistent with the testator's intentions (e.g., a bequest to the League of Nations will be changed to a bequest to the United Nations). Winick concludes, "[a]pplying a form of the *cy pres* doctrine, courts and administrative bodies can modify advance directive health-care instruments in a similar way." Id. at 91. In the change-of-circumstances scenario (involving new medication), Winick argues that a person of uncertain competency should be able to change an advanced directive only if the decision comports with medical advice; if, on the other hand, the person refuses medication against medical advice, the advanced directive stands. Id. at 91–92. Compare this proposal to Roth et al.'s on p. 1047.

The potential risks of psychotropic medication figure strongly in both the *Harper* dissent and Winick's analyses. But what about the risks of going without treatment? Psychiatrists who prescribe psychotropic medication for severely ill hospitalized persons undertake their efforts in the belief that, without such treatment, their patients have a high likelihood of languishing in the hospital for months or years. Very long hospitalizations were commonplace before psychotropic medications became available in the mid–20th century. Psychiatrists also have accumulated evidence that untreated psychosis may be neurotoxic—that it increases the death rate of brain cells. Nancy C. Andreasen et al., *Relapse Duration, Treatment Intensity, and Brain*

Tissue Loss in Schizophrenia: A Prospective Longitudinal MRI Study, 170 Am. J. Psychiatry 609, 613 (2013) (finding "that duration of relapse is closely related to loss of brain tissue over time in multiple brain regions . . . particularly the frontal lobes," but recommending that "clinicians should strive to use the lowest possible dosage to control symptoms" because antipsychotic drugs may also cause tissue loss). Should a patient's advance directive refusing medication be considered competently executed if the document lacks evidence that the patient knew about these risks and consequences of not taking medication?

5.   *Procedures.* What are the procedural implications of *Harper* for civilly committed patients? The majority relies heavily not only on *Vitek v. Jones*, which involved the due process rights of prisoners transferred to mental hospitals, but also on *Parham v. J.R.*, which involved the civil commitment of children. Given the liberty interests at stake in those cases, are the citations to either *Vitek* or *Parham* apposite in deciding upon the proper procedures for implementing the right to refuse in the adult civil commitment context?

Consider the following methods of implementing the right in non-emergency situations: (1) judicial determination and monitoring (see *Rogers*, described in note 2); (2) judicial appointment of a guardian who makes all treatment decisions (an option permitted by *Rogers* after the initial judicial intervention, see note 2); (3) review by professionals from outside the institution (required by the trial court in *Rennie v. Klein*, 462 F.Supp. 1131, 1147 (D.N.J.1978)); (4) review by professionals from the same institution (as permitted in *Harper*); (5) a judicial determination at the commitment hearing, with no further review (see Clifford Stromberg & Alan Stone, *A Model State Law on Civil Commitment of the Mentally Ill*, 20 Harv.J.Legis. 265, 356–57 (1983)); (6) no review of the professional's decision (see e.g., *Dautremont v. Broadlawns Hosp.*, 827 F.2d 291 (8th Cir.1987)). In light of the realities described in *Harper*, which option do you prefer? If some type of hearing is appropriate, what standard of proof should apply? Should the patient be entitled to an advocate? Relevant to this last question and option (2) above, a number of studies indicate that surrogates, in particular family members, are better than doctors at predicting a patient's treatment preferences. David I. Shalowitz et al., *The Accuracy of Surrogate Decision Makers: A Systematic Review*, 116 Arch. Internal Med. 493 (2006).

People with mental disability or their guardians may be required to consent to treatment to obtain disability benefits (social security, housing, etc.). See John Monahan et al., *Use of Leverage to Improve Adherence to Psychiatric Treatment in the Community*, 56 Psychiatric Serv. 37, 37–44 (2005). Should the government be able to condition disability payments on compliance with treatment? How is such an arrangement different from a probation condition requiring medication or drug court (see pp. 1003–1005)?

6.   *Benefits and costs of the right to refuse.* Some research on the impact of the right to refuse litigation is reported in the following excerpt from

Alexander Brooks, *The Right to Refuse Antipsychotic Medication: Law and Policy*, 39 Rutgers L.Rev. 339, 367–374 (1987).

Benefits

* * *

Decreasing the amount of medication used was an objective of refusal litigation. . . . Studies show that there has been a substantial lowering of individual dosages in a number of hospitals. . . .

Another aspect of "too much drugs" is "too many different drugs." The practice of polypharmacy, though widely disapproved, was widespread in pre-litigation years. Current data from Napa State indicate that polypharmacy has been virtually eliminated. In 1974 a mean of 2.3 drugs were used for a single patient in the first eight weeks of confinement, with a range up to five different drugs. In 1983 [after a consent decree required review of refusals by outside psychiatrists] the mean during the same period of time was only 1.1. . . .

A third benefit would result from changing types of medications to see whether patients respond less dysphorically and with fewer side effects to a medication different from one originally prescribed. There is no hard data on this important change, so we can only speculate about it, but there is anecdotal data that this now occurs more frequently than before.

A fourth benefit would be reducing the incidence of inappropriate delegation by physicians to other staff prescribing medication. This was once a major problem. . . . In *Davis v. Hubbard,* the court found that, at Lima State Hospital in Ohio, PRN orders were being written that permitted attendants to decide when medication should be administered. These PRN orders often had no termination or review date. It was further reported that attendants could obtain medication from the pharmacy by submitting appropriate forms "without a physician's signature." In Ohio hospitals such PRN orders have been eliminated. Inappropriate delegations have been terminated.

A fifth benefit has been the encouragement of processes of negotiation and participation by patients in their own treatment programs, a process that is initiated when a patient refuses medication. . . . The process of negotiation is not only responsive to patient needs, but also encourages patient autonomy and enhances patient dignity. [Moreover], research has indicated that negative reaction to medication is a powerful predictor of noncompliance and poor outcome.

* * *

Patient Costs

What are the costs to the patient? One is delay in treatment. In states like Massachusetts, the procedure requires a judicial hearing to determine whether the patient is competent to refuse. Veliz and James show that there are long delays between the refusal, the petition to compel medication, and the hearing, on average four and one-half months, and ranging from two to seven months. But . . . [i]t is not obvious that patients actually suffer from such delays, nor do Veliz and James present any data to that effect. Put otherwise, there is no evidence that the delays cause patients to "rot."

It has been argued that a significant cost to refusing patients would be longer stays in the hospital. Do refusers, in fact, spend more time in the hospital than consenters? Evidence suggests that refusers are discharged at approximately the same rate as consenters. Refusal seems not to prolong hospitalization.

Do refusers deteriorate, remain the same, or improve? . . . Hargreaves and associates studied forty-seven cases (out of 2,700 reviews) in which refusals were upheld. Deterioration occurred in twenty-five patients of whom twenty were remedicated. No adverse consequences were seen in eight patients. The outcome was "unclear" for the rest. There was thus no harm to the patient in approximately 50 percent of these refusals, and presumably little harm to the twenty who were remedicated.

Have a larger number of antisocial incidents occurred because refusing patients went untreated? Psychiatrists had predicted outbreaks of violence and disruption by non-medicated refusers. Have there been transfers to locked wards, self-injurious behaviors, property destruction, suicide attempts, verbal threats, assaults, AWOLs, escapes, or displays of non-cooperation? Were seclusion and restraint used more extensively? A Minnesota study shows no statistical difference in these areas between refusers and consenters.

Costs to Staff and State

* * *

It is to be expected that many staff members, though not all, would find refusals a burden. . . . Hargreaves and associates asked doctors and nurses for their views about refusal at Napa State. Eighty-five percent of the doctors thought the refusal consent decree made their work more difficult. Nurses were more negative than doctors, saying that the decree went "too far." Twenty-five percent of nurses thought that the consent decree was "absurd." Ninety percent of nurses said that the consent decree made their jobs more difficult. Many felt that the decree was a waste of money, that it impaired treatment quality and made their work more dangerous. . . . It is difficult to evaluate such reactions since they are subjective and unsupported by specific illustrations of ways in which work has been made "more difficult." Some increases in difficulty surely result from an increase in the complexity of the caring task in response to legitimate patient needs. But are there inappropriate burdens unrelated to providing care? . . . A crucial aspect of the problem is that there is a long history of neglect of public sector patients. Any legal requirement that strikes at this neglect increases a burden. It is not clear how this particular "cost" should be weighed as against the benefits described.

Finally, we reach a twofold cost to the state. The first is the cost of hearings, which requires paying outside reviewers, lawyers, and others. The second is the cost involved in diverting personnel from other functions to the job of preparing for and appearing at hearings.

Hargreaves and associates have calculated that salary costs for outside psychiatric reviewers, patient advocates, hospital support staff, departmental staff, and the like, came to over $300,000 in the first year of the consent decree at Napa State Hospital. A "hidden" cost included the diversion of clinicians from other duties to the preparation of paper work for reviews. Since there were 2,800 reviews, each single review cost approximately $100. Hargreaves estimates that at this rate it would cost approximately $1–$1.5 million per year for reviews in all five major mental hospitals in California.

* * *

[I]s the cost too high because relatively few patients refuse and even fewer refusals are upheld? . . . The first data available from the Boston State Hospital, involved in the *Rogers* case, showed an incidence of about 9 percent refusals for 1,400 patients. Later data shows a proportion of refusals in a variety of hospitals ranging from 2.4 and 5 percent to 15 percent.

The data on refusal overrides shows proportions ranging from 100 percent of overrides in a study of nine patients to only 67 percent of overrides in a study of 19 Minnesota patients. In other words, in Minnesota, one-third of refusals were upheld, a much larger proportion than anywhere else. It has been suggested that the greater deference in Minnesota to refusals is a result of the fact that only one member of the five-member Anoka Treatment Review Panel was a physician.

It has been argued that the significance to the patient of a right to refuse has been exaggerated and should be abandoned. It has also been argued that even such a small incidence as 5% refusals interferes with the treatment of more than 15,000 patients a year, assuming an annual commitment rate of 300,000.

What would happen if people with psychosis were not treated, but simply institutionalized? Consider this excerpt from Douglas Mossman, *Unbuckling the 'Chemical Straitjacket': The Legal Significance of Recent Advances in the Pharmacological Treatment of Psychosis*, 39 San Diego L. Rev. 1033, 1063–64 (2002):

Because appellate court decisions and other legal publications often emphasize the adverse effects of older antipsychotic drugs, it is worth pausing to consider what life for psychotic patients was like before the advent of chlorpromazine and other antipsychotic drugs. "Before the introduction of chlorpromazine in 1953, most individuals with schizophrenia were destined to spend their entire adult lives within large, often remote psychiatric hospitals." By 1955, U.S. state mental hospitals housed more than one-half million persons, many of whom suffered from psychotic disorders; patients often spent years and decades living in horrifying, wretched conditions. Writes Ann Braden Johnson:

> If you have ever spent time with a floridly psychotic person who is expressing himself in behavior that was supposed to have been extinguished in childhood, you will never forget how terrifying it is to see someone so utterly out of control. But now imagine yourself in a huge, old building that is visibly falling apart, in charge of sixty to eighty adults, all acting like one-, two-, and three-year-olds in mid-tantrum—such were the patients that the state hospitals, alone and unaided, kept in their wards for over a hundred years [from the mid–19th to the mid–20th centuries]. A doctor from that era described a women's ward at New York's Pilgrim State Hospital before the introduction of phenothiazines:
>
>> [They were] so wild I couldn't keep them decent. They'd soil themselves, tear their clothes off, smash the windows, and gouge the plaster out of the walls. One of them would even rip radiators right off the wall. We'd sometimes have to surround them with mattresses in order to give them sedative injections, and these would help for a while, but then they'd get addicted to the sedative and we'd have to take them off it.
>
> [T]he new drugs made the wholesale removal of patients from hospitals imaginable and then possible, which in the end became one of the most effective selling points of the new medications.

7. *Uninstitutionalized persons' right to refuse.* The case law described above concerns the right of persons who are hospitalized to refuse medication. In contrast to the narrowed right accorded this population, the non-mentally ill individual is, as noted at the beginning of this section, normally entitled to the protections of the informed consent doctrine, which provides a relatively robust right to refuse. What is the scope of the right for persons with mental illness who are not hospitalized?

In re Guardianship of Roe, 383 Mass. 415, 421 N.E.2d 40 (1981), involved the right of a 21 year-old ward to refuse medication after his release from the hospital. The Massachusetts Supreme Court held that the ward's guardian, his father, could not unilaterally make the treatment decision for the ward unless an "emergency" existed. Otherwise, a court must make the treatment decision. Further the court could authorize forcible medication only if one of two circumstances were met:

> (1) where a judicial substituted judgment determination indicates that the incompetent individual would, if competent, accept antipsychotic drugs, or (2) where there exists a State interest of sufficient magnitude to override the individual's right to refuse. If the asserted State interest is the prevention of violent conduct by non-institutionalized mentally ill

individuals, then, upon a showing equivalent to that necessary to commit an individual against his will, the State is entitled to force the individual to choose, by way of substituted judgment, either involuntary commitment or medication with antipsychotic drugs.

Id. at 61.

Roe raises three issues. The first has to do with the role of the court vis-a-vis the role of the guardian. Do you agree with *Roe's* requirement that a court order be obtained prior to forcibly medicating a ward whose validly appointed guardian has consented to the treatment?[j] The second issue concerns the consequences of a refusal by an uninstitutionalized person. As indicated above, under *Roe*, if a dangerous person chooses hospitalization over medication, then the state must acquiesce in that choice. May the person continue to refuse medication once in the hospital? In a footnote, the *Roe* court stated: "We do not address the question of whether and to what extent the State interest in *institutional* order and safety may be capable of overwhelming the right of an involuntarily committed individual to refuse medical treatment. . . . " Id. at 61 n. 23 (emphasis in original).

Finally, *Roe* seems to hold that if a person does *not* meet the criteria for involuntary hospitalization, forcible medication is impermissible. Doesn't that position make impossible forcible medication in the outpatient setting when outpatient commitment is based on the predicted deterioration standard (see pp. 884–885)? See generally, John Kip Cornwell & Raymond Deeney, *Exposing the Myths Surrounding Preventive Outpatient Commitment for Individuals with Chronic Mental Illness*, 9 Psychol. Pub. Pol'y & L. 209, 224 (2003)("Were psychiatric medication to be administered forcibly in a state with a lower threshold for outpatient commitment [than for inpatient commitment], its constitutionality would be more open to question; however, because the [preventive commitment] standards typically require a documented history of violence or prior inpatient hospitalization to justify commitment, the practice would likely satisfy substantive due process.").

8. *New and better drugs.* As described in Chapter One, "atypical" or "second-generation" antipsychotic medications (SGAs) cause fewer neuromotor side effects than the antipsychotic drugs that were available when *Harper* and the others cases described above were decided. How, if at all, should the advent of these new drugs change the right to refuse debate? Consider this excerpt from Douglas Mossman (a psychiatrist), in *Unbuckling the "Chemical Straightjacket,"* supra at 1048–49:

> For several reasons, it seems very unlikely that courts will undo the cautions and procedural protections embodied in litigation that addressed involuntary treatment with older, more noxious antipsychotic drugs. First, [many of] the newer drugs, though much more tolerable,

---

[j] The answer to this question may depend upon whether one views antipsychotic medication as an "extraordinary treatment" (see pp. 1079–1080). Most, but not all, states require some sort of adversarial hearing. See ABA Comm'n on Law & Aging, Guardian Authority for Residential Decisions: State Statutory Provisions (as of August 2010), available at http://news.abanet.org/aging/PublicDocuments.

still carry some risk of the neurological side effects that alarmed courts in the 1970s and 1980s. Second, the newer drugs appear to place patients at more risk than neuroleptics of developing troublesome metabolic conditions, including obesity, alterations in lipid metabolism, and diabetes mellitus. Though these conditions are not as uncomfortable as the acute neurological side effects induced by [older, first-generation] neuroleptics, they are sources of concern for doctors and patients and should receive courts' consideration as well. Third, when the new drugs serve their intended purpose, they lead to changes in the way patients think. Almost any reasonable observer would characterize quelling psychosis as a desirable outcome of medical treatment. Yet this means that [SGAs] are indeed "mind altering," and their unwanted administration therefore should raise legally significant questions about intrusions into a person's privacy. Finally, current legal rules and procedures concerning involuntary drug therapy may, and probably should, be preserved because they serve a valuable ethical purpose beyond protecting patients from side effects. Even if legal barriers to automatic administration of unwanted medication were initially justified in consequentialist terms, these protections also serve the nonconsequentialist purpose of respecting the personhood of patients. This is especially true in those states that require a judicial finding of incompetence before authorization of involuntary medication.

Though courts can be expected to preserve currently existing legal barriers against automatic treatment of drug refusing psychotic patients, [some recent] decisions may show us how future courts will evaluate and make decisions about involuntary administration of antipsychotic drugs. In these cases . . . the flaws of antipsychotic medications are often noted, but so are their benefits. Gone are extensive judicial diatribes about horrible side effects that all but ignore the benefits of medication and the horror of being psychotic. In some cases, courts have even endorsed the values of antipsychotic therapy, and because such treatment can be delivered with less risk to a patient's nervous system, judges have seemed more willing to approve of its involuntary administration.

Professor Mossman notes the "changes" that can result from the new drugs. Assuming the people described in the following excerpt pose no danger to others but require medication of some type to provide for their basic necessities, consider whether they should be allowed to refuse the new drugs for the reasons suggested in their accounts.

We interviewed 15 long-term outpatients with schizophrenia or schizoaffective disorder who were living in the community and who had shown significant clinical improvement on these new compounds. . . . We found that, because of the extent and longevity of their psychotic symptoms, many awakened patients have experienced a process of psychological redefinition and have confronted developmental tasks that were dormant prior to their improvement.

One 32 year-old man who was diagnosed with schizoaffective disorder 15 years ago told us ... "My brain was preoccupied with discovering whether this is real or this is not real. What clozapine has done is break up this pattern of thought process. I had certain behaviors that I had adopted in dealing with being an inpatient. With clozapine it as ... sort of like waking up. In a lot of ways, the psychosis acted as my defense and was my way of relating to the world for so long. It was a relief initially not to be crazy. But it is also painful ... like being crazy kept me innocent in a way. Sometimes I can't bear the weight of my own grief."

... [A] young woman who repeatedly starts and stops her atypical antipsychotic treatment explains that the weight gain she experiences on clozapine is sufficiently unpleasant to her that she takes breaks from it. Her mental state is strikingly different on clozapine, and she is able to avoid using drugs when she takes it. "It seems I can only have a mind or a body," she reports.

... A 52 year-old man with paranoid schizophrenia, who had been hospitalized more than 20 times, had been living a profoundly isolated life while conventional antipsychotics poorly controlled his positive and negative symptoms. He lived marginally in his own apartment and refused offers of group living or day programs. Following a 14–month trial on olanzapine his grooming improved, as did his ability to describe his affective experiences, and he became romantically involved with a woman at a day treatment center. After living 20 years without an intimate relationship, he felt overwhelmed with the newfound stresses of this connection. He discussed the pressures of being in this relationship and twice switched back between his old medication and the newer medications.

Kenneth Duckworth, *Awakenings with the New Antipsychotics*, Psychiatric Times, May, 1998. Over the long-term people who take SGAs are just as likely to discontinue the treatment as those taking older drugs. See Jeffrey A. Lieberman et al., Effectiveness of Antipsychotic Drugs in Patients with Chronic Schizophrenia, 353 N.Eng. J. Med. 1209 (2005) (finding that a "majority of patients" in each medication group—consisting of three groups on SGAs and one group on an older agent—discontinued the drug within 6 months "owing to inefficacy or intolerable side effects or for other reasons," except for the group taking the SGA drug olanzapine, which discontinued at an average of a little over 9 months).

9. *The one-free shot proposal.* Some authors have proposed that the government be authorized to medicate forcibly even competent individuals, if they are experiencing their first psychotic break. Professor Saks argues that this one shot at forced treatment would allow the individual to experience the benefits of medication and thus more fully understand the consequences of a subsequent medication refusal. Elyn Saks, Refusing Care: Forced Treatment and the Rights of the Mentally Ill 90 (2002). Adam Gerhardstein makes a similar proposal because: "(1) it would soften the trauma of a first episode, assisting families in their attempts to intervene before their loved ones' lives

are in complete disarray and their episodes escalate to the point of violence; (2) it would expand access to early, effective treatment, which gives individuals experiencing their first major episodes the best chance for a healthy long-term prognosis; and (3) it would cut down health care costs paid by government programs." Adam G. Gerhardstein, *A First Episode Standard for Involuntary Treatment*, available at http://papers.ssrn.com/sol3/papers.cfm?abstract_id=2155246. Finally, Professor Bennion proposes that "(1) if a person is suffering from a severe psychotic episode, (2) earnest efforts have been made to convince the patient to voluntarily take medication—including discussion regarding why the patient objects and possible alternatives that could meet those concerns, (3) and medication is in their best medical interest, then (4) involuntary treatment should be allowed at least during the first two years of the illness (measured from the first date of treatment following a severe psychotic break) or age 27, whichever is later." She continues:

> The rationale for 27 years is that psychotic breaks for a disease like schizophrenia peak from 18 to 25—when the brain is still maturing. This period seems to be a crucial one in brain development and manifestation of the disease. Putting the age at 27 would ensure both that patients can be medicated during the crucial period of brain maturation and that all who have their first psychotic break within the peak period will have at least two years of leeway for getting needed treatment when their symptoms become severe. Because treatment in the initial years of illness is so critical to long term prognosis and prevention of irreversible injury—I would allow the 2 years from whenever a patient first begins being treated for severe psychosis—even if it is after age 27.

Elizabeth Bennion, *A Right to Remain Psychotic?* ___ Loyola L.A. L. Rev. ___ (2014).

B. ELECTROCONVULSIVE THERAPY AND PSYCHOSURGERY

ADEN V. YOUNGER

Court of Appeal, Fourth District, Division 1, 1976.
57 Cal.App.3d 662, 129 Cal.Rptr. 535.

GERALD BROWN, PRESIDING JUSTICE.

Petitioners Jane Doe and Betty Roe are mentally ill. Doe has had electro-convulsive therapy (ECT) and may need further voluntary treatments. Roe wants a surgical "Multiple target procedure," or psychosurgery. . . .

* * *

The Attorney General, the Director of Health, and the Board of Medical Examiners are respondents.

The law involved in this petition is part of the Lanterman–Petris–Short Act (Welf. & Inst.Code §§ 5000–5404.1). The law changes conditions under which psychosurgery and shock treatment can be performed. The changes applicable to persons involuntarily detained and persons voluntarily admitted to state hospitals, private mental institutions, county psychiatric hospitals and certain mentally retarded persons, are:

Psychosurgery: (§§ 5325, 5326, 5326.3.)

Patients have the right to refuse psychosurgery and the professional person in charge of the facility may not deny them that right. If a patient refuses consent, it must be entered on the record.

If a patient wants psychosurgery, then the conditions for performing such surgery include:

(a) The patient must give written informed consent, dated, witnessed and entered in his record. The consent may be withdrawn at any time. An oral explanation by the doctor is necessary.

(b) The patient must have capacity to consent.

(c) An oral explanation must be given to a responsible relative, guardian or conservator.

(d) The reasons for surgery must be in the patient's treatment record, other treatments must be exhausted and surgery must be critically needed.

(e) Three appointed physicians (two board-certified psychiatrists or neurosurgeons), must examine the patient and unanimously agree with the treating physician's determinations and that the patient has capacity to consent. There must be a 72–hour wait after the patient's written consent before surgery.

Shock Treatment: (§ 5326.4.)

If the treating physician feels shock treatments are necessary, he must give an extensive oral explanation to the patient and his relative, guardian, or conservator.

Shock treatments shall be performed only after:

(a) The patient gives written informed consent.

(b) The patient has capacity to consent.

(c) A relative, guardian or conservator has been given a thorough oral explanation.

(d) "Adequate documentation" has been entered in the patient's record. All other treatments have been exhausted and the treatment is critically needed.

(e) There has been a review by three appointed physicians (two board-certified) who agree with the treating physician that the patient has capacity to consent.

If the patient does not have the capacity to consent, shock treatments can be given if conditions (c), (d) and (e) are met.

No shock treatments may be given if the patient is able to give informed consent and refuses.

*   *   *

The petitioners, and amici curiae in support of the petition for writ of mandate, rest their attack on the amended and added Welfare & Institutions Code sections on several asserted constitutional infirmities:

*   *   *

A. Equal Protection

Petitioners' equal protection arguments [i.e., that they should be able to obtain psychosurgery or ECT treatment as easily as non-mental patients] are without merit.

*   *   *

Mental patients are distinct from other ill patients in two special circumstances. First, their competence to accede to treatment is more questionable than that of other patients. Mental patients' incompetence may not be presumed solely by their hospitalization (§ 5331), but it is common knowledge mentally-ill persons are more likely to lack the ability to understand the nature of a medical procedure and appreciate its risks. Second, their ability to voluntarily accept treatment is questionable. The impossibility of an involuntarily detained person voluntarily giving informed consent to these medical procedures is fully treated in *Kaimowitz v. Department of Mental Health for the State of Michigan.* "Voluntary" patients, newly included within the protection of the "Patients' Bill of Rights" (§ 5325) are susceptible to many of the pressures placed on involuntary patients. The Legislature's inclusion of these "voluntary" patients recognizes the fact the "voluntary" label is a creation of the Legislature, and often only means the patient did not formally protest hospitalization. These circumstances make the separate treatment of mental patients clearly rationally related to the objective of insuring their rights to refuse treatment. The special regulation of psychosurgery and ECT is also a reasonable classification because these procedures, associated with *mental* illness, present a great danger of violating the patient's rights.

B. Vagueness

[The court found that the provisions in both the psychosurgery and ECT statute requiring that the treatment be "critically needed" were unconstitutionally vague because they provided "no guide to the degree of need required".]

*　*　*

A patient with acute depression and suicidal tendencies would come within the standard if the form of treatment were essential to protect his life. But what of the patient who does not have self-destructive tendencies and is completely dysfunctional psychologically? Does an inability to remain employed or married qualify as a "critical" condition? Must there be a danger of deterioration, or is a stable condition of severe psychosis critical? If all other forms of appropriate therapies have been attempted, has a "critical" need for ECT or psychosurgery been established?

It seems probable the legislative intent was to require a compelling need for these forms of treatment beyond the mere existence of a behavioral or mental disorder. There seems to be a tacit assumption by the Legislature the cure is sometimes more harmful than the disease, and only the most dangerous and harmful conditions should be so treated. Some persons of "common intelligence" may agree an assessment of impending injury, absent prompt treatment, gives rise to a critical need. Others of like intelligence may demand considerably more, or somewhat less. We conclude on its face the "critically needed" criterion is impermissibly vague.

C. Due Process

The regulation of ECT and psychosurgery is a legitimate exercise of the state's inherent police power. The state has an interest in seeing that these procedures, like other medical procedures, are performed under circumstances insuring maximum safety for the patient. Arrayed against these legitimate state interests are equally valid considerations of rights of privacy, freedom of speech and thought, and the right to medical treatment.

[The court found that the first two rights—the right to privacy and the right to freedom of speech and thought—could be treated together as aspects of the right to "privacy of the mind" or "freedom of thought".]

*　*　*

Freedom of thought is intimately touched upon by any regulation of procedures affecting thought and feelings. In an effort to protect freedom of thought, the state has put procedural and substantive obstacles in the path of those who both need and desire certain forms of treatment, and in that way their freedom of thought remains impaired because they cannot get treatment. Psychosurgery and ECT are viewed, rightly or wrongly, as drastic, radical forms of treatment compared to psychotherapy or drug therapy, and indicative of more severe illness. Public exposure, or even disclosure to limited numbers of government representatives, may have a chilling effect on patients' efforts to undergo these treatments, thereby restricting their freedom of thought. Some patients will be denied treatment as a natural and intended result of this legislation. Although the reasons for such denials may be the patients' own best interests, such regulation must be justified by a compelling state interest.

* * *

[T]he state's interests, as expressed in the challenged law, may be summarized as the protection of the right to refuse treatment and the prevention of unnecessary administration of hazardous and intrusive treatments. The test of the constitutionality of these provisions will be whether each of them furthers a compelling state interest and is necessary to accomplish the purpose.

* * *

[A]n analysis of the review procedures involved in each form of treatment will be considered separately.

Consent to psychosurgery is regulated and applied differently to three groups of patients: incompetent, involuntary, and all others. The state's interest in protecting patients from unconsented-to and unnecessary administrations of psychosurgery clearly justifies a review procedure which insures the competence of the patient and the truly voluntary nature of his consent. The incompetent patient is incapable of consenting to such a procedure, and the state's interest in protecting him from such procedures fully justifies the attendant invasion of privacy. Although there are substantial problems of procedural due process involved, a review of a patient's competence by a review committee is constitutional where, as here, there is reason to suspect incompetence.

The involuntary patient presents the dilemma of either prohibiting the administration of psychosurgery to such patients (see *Kaimowitz v. Department of Mental Health for the State of Michigan, supra*, 2 Prison L.Rptr. 433), or providing for a substitute decision-making process. Because the voluntariness of such a patient's consent can never be adequately confirmed, the establishment of a review committee to make the treatment decision for the patient is justified by the state's compelling interest in preventing involuntary administration of psychosurgery.

The substantive review of proposed treatments for competent and voluntary patients is a different problem. Once the competency of the patient and voluntariness of the consent is confirmed, what interest of the state can justify the substitution of the review committee's decision for that of the patient and his physician?

The hazardous, experimental nature of psychosurgery is a legitimate reason for the state to regulate its use as a treatment of last resort. Requiring unanimity by the review committee insures each approved treatment is an appropriate use of an experimental procedure. The importance of assuring that consents to psychosurgery be voluntarily given by informed, competent mental patients, plus the need to regulate an experimental procedure, justify the Legislature's decision to remove these considerations from the sole discretion of the treating physician. There are sound reasons why the treating physician's assessment of his patient's competency and voluntariness may not always be objective, and he may not necessarily be the best or most objective judge of how appropriate an experimental procedure would be. Because the consequences to the patient of such a procedure are so serious, and the effects he may suffer are so intrusive and irreversible, tort damages are totally inadequate. The need for some form of restraint is a sufficiently compelling state interest to justify the attendant invasion of the patient's right to privacy. That right to privacy is not absolute and must give way to appropriate regulation.

The new regulatory scheme as it applies to "shock treatment" is almost identical to the regulatory system for psychosurgery. The review procedures of section 5326.3, as applied to involuntary or incompetent patients, function the same as those under section 5326.4, and the review is also constitutional. These procedures for involuntary patients provide for a substitute decision-making process because of the difficulty of acquiring a truly voluntary consent to such a procedure. In the case of incompetent patients, the substitute decision-making process permits the use of this form of treatment for patients who cannot consent for themselves. These applications of section 5326.4 are constitutional for the reasons previously discussed.

The thorny question in section 5326.4 concerns the application of the review system to voluntary competent patients. As already noted, the state has a compelling interest in assuring the competency and voluntariness of patients who undergo this form of treatment. To this end, the review system is compatible with due process. However, once the competency of a voluntary patient has been confirmed, and the truly voluntary nature of his consent is determined, the state has little excuse to invoke the substitute decision-making process. "Shock treatment," or more precisely ECT, is not an experimental procedure, nor are its hazards as serious as those of psychosurgery. . . . Where informed consent is adequately insured, there is no justification for infringing upon the patient's right to privacy in selecting and consenting to the treatment. The state has varied interests which are served by the regulation of ECT, but these interests are not served where the patient and his physician are the best judges of the patient's health, safety and welfare.

Therefore, insofar as section 5326.4 applies to competent and voluntary patients who have given competent, voluntary and informed consent, it is unconstitutional. Substantive review is proper for involuntary or incompetent patients because there is a need for a substitute decision-maker. Any possible need which exists for the voluntary and competent patient cannot prevail in the face of the serious infringement to the patient's right to privacy as guaranteed by *Roe v. Wade,* 410 U.S. 113, 93 S.Ct. 705, 35 L.Ed.2d 147.

*   *   *

Relying upon *Jacobson v. Massachusetts,* 197 U.S. 11, 25 S.Ct. 358, 49 L.Ed. 643, petitioners also assert a constitutional right to care for one's own health is unconstitutionally invaded by the new procedure. We reject the notion the case recognizes any such fundamental right. The court deciding *Jacobson* held the vaccination of citizens against smallpox is a valid exercise of the state's police power. Petitioners also unmeritoriously assert a constitutional right to medical treatment. Where this right is concerned, due process requires only that the state, once it has institutionalized a person for the purpose of treatment, provide reasonable treatment or release the person. In the present case, any denial of treatment is tantamount to a finding that that particular form of treatment is not reasonable. It is not a denial of any or all treatment.

QUESTIONS AND COMMENTS

1.   *Consent to treatment. Aden* represents a case in which patients sought treatment rather than refused it. The extent to which persons with mental disability have a right to *some* type of therapy is addressed in subsequent chapters. Here the issue is not whether individuals with disabilities have a general entitlement to psychiatric treatment but whether a person who wants a particular treatment (or at least does not refuse it) may be forced to undergo scrutiny and jump procedural hurdles that are not ordinarily required when treatment is sought.

Assume that a person (1) wants psychosurgery or ECT; (2) asserts he or she is competent to consent to such treatment; and (3) is considered competent by the treating physician. May the state require this person to show that the treatment is "critically needed" (as defined in *Aden*) and to convince a review board that he or she is competent before the treatment may occur? *Aden* holds that if the patient is "voluntary" and wants ECT, the answer to this question is no. But if the patient wants psychosurgery, or is an involuntary patient and wants ECT, the answer is yes. Is *Aden's* differentiation between ECT and psychosurgery, involuntary and voluntary patients defensible? How should persons who are not hospitalized and who want psychosurgery or ECT be handled? Do improvements in these two treatment modalities (see pp. 33–34 and 41–42) change the calculus?

2.   *Kaimowitz.* Another court has also stressed differences between hospitalized patients and other patients in determining the scope of the "right to consent" to intrusive psychiatric treatment. *Aden* relies on *Kaimowitz v. Department of Mental Health,* No. 73–19434–AW (Cir.Ct. of Wayne Cty., Mich., July 10, 1973), *abstracted* in 13 Crim.L.Rep. 2452 (1974), which provides the best-known analysis of the legal issues that arise when institutionalized individuals are asked to consent to psychosurgery. The case arose when one "John Doe," who was in a state hospital after being committed under Michigan's sex psychopath statute, signed an "informed consent" form and obtained signatures from his parents authorizing doctors to implant depth electrodes in him. The treatment was part of an experimental program designed to determine whether psychosurgery would reduce aggression. Attorney Kaimowitz became aware of the planned operation and petitioned the court for a restraining order. The court granted relief, concluding that, when the person who consents is involuntarily detained by the state, "the three basic elements of informed consent— competency, knowledge, and voluntariness—cannot be ascertained with a degree of reliability warranting resort to use of such an invasive procedure."

With respect to competency, the court found that

> [i]nstitutionalization tends to strip the individual of the support which permits him to maintain his sense of self-worth and the value of his own physical and mental integrity. An involuntarily confined mental patient clearly has diminished capacity for making a decision about irreversible experimental psychosurgery.

On the knowledge prong, the court held that, from the record developed in the case, "the facts surrounding experimental brain surgery are profoundly uncertain, and the lack of knowledge on the subject makes a knowledgeable consent to psychosurgery literally impossible." Finally, concerning the voluntariness issue, the court stated:

> Involuntarily confined mental patients live in an inherently coercive institutional environment. Indirect and subtle psychological coercion has profound effect upon the patient population. Involuntarily confined patients cannot reason as equals with the doctors and administrators over whether they should undergo psychosurgery. They are not able to voluntarily give informed consent because of the inherent inequality in their position.[23]

---

[23] It should be emphasized that once John Doe was released in this case and returned to the community he withdrew all consent to the performance of the proposed experiment. His withdrawal of consent under these circumstances should be compared with his response . . . to questions placed to him [while he was] waiting the implantation of depth electrodes. The significant questions and answers are as follows:

"1. Would you seek psychosurgery if you were not confined to an institution?

A. Yes, if after testing this showed it would be of help.

2. Do you believe that psychosurgery is a way to obtain your release from the institution?

What are the implications of the court's reasoning for involuntarily committed patients who consent to *other* types of treatment? For nonhospitalized persons who want to consent to psychosurgery? At the end of its opinion, the court stated: "When the state of medical knowledge develops to the extent that the type of psychosurgical intervention proposed here becomes an accepted neurosurgical procedure and is no longer experimental, it is possible, with appropriate review mechanisms, that involuntarily detained mental patients could consent to such an operation." Doesn't this language undercut the reasoning in the rest of the opinion?

3. *Ranking treatments.* Assuming the state may legally make more difficult the ability to consent to certain types of treatment, how does one decide which treatments to put in this category? This question is of course related to the previous discussion concerning when a guardian's or clinician's decision about treatment for a refusing or nonprotesting patient must be subject to further monitoring, judicial or otherwise. But the issues are not necessarily identical. In addition to reviewing the previous materials on the subject, consider Professor Michael Shapiro's attempt, in *Legislating the Control of Behavior Control: Autonomy and the Coercive Use of Organic Therapies*, 47 S.Cal.L.Rev. 237, 256 n. 51 (1974), to identify factors relevant to determining when judicial or administrative oversight of a treatment decision might be most useful:

> (1) the extent to which the effects of the therapy upon mentation are reversible;
>
> (2) the extent to which the resulting psychic state is "foreign," "abnormal," or "unnatural" for the person in question, rather than simply a restoration of his prior psychic state (this is closely related to the "magnitude" or "intensity" of the change);
>
> (3) the rapidity with which the effects occur;
>
> (4) the scope of the change in the total "ecology" of the mind's functions;
>
> (5) the extent to which one can resist acting in ways impelled by the psychic effects of the therapy; and
>
> (6) the duration of the change.

Is this list comprehensive enough? Should the extent to which the treatment is considered "experimental" be added as a criterion?

It may also be useful at this point to revisit an issue alluded to at the beginning of this chapter. If a treatment is considered so extraordinary that special procedural precautions are mandated before a consenting person is permitted to undergo the treatment, should we, for the same reason, raise the level of competency required to make the decision (perhaps requiring "full

---

A. No, but it would be a step in obtaining my release. It is like any other therapy or program to help persons to function again.

3. Would you seek psychosurgery if there were other ways to obtain your release?

A. Yes. If psychosurgery were the only means of helping my physical problem after a period of testing."

appreciation" of the treatment and its consequences)? Should we also make it particularly easy to refuse the treatment (perhaps by honoring any indication of refusal, regardless of the person's mental capacity)? Conversely, if a treatment is not extraordinary, should we facilitate consent (perhaps by allowing it upon mere assent of the patient) and make refusal more difficult?

C. BEHAVIOR MODIFICATION TECHNIQUES

KNECHT v. GILLMAN
United States Court of Appeals, Eighth Circuit, 1973.
488 F.2d 1136.

ROSS, CIRCUIT JUDGE.

This is an action by Gary Knecht and Ronald Stevenson, both in the custody of the State of Iowa, against officials of that state, under 42 U.S.C. § 1983. Their complaint alleged that they had been subjected to injections of the drug apomorphine at the Iowa Security Medical Facility (ISMF) without their consent and that the use of said drug by the defendants constituted cruel and unusual punishment in violation of the eighth amendment. The trial court dismissed their complaint for injunctive relief. We reverse with directions to enjoin the defendants from further use of the drug except pursuant to specific guidelines hereinafter set forth.

* * * [T]he evidence contained in the report of the magistrate showed that apomorphine had been administered at ISMF for some time prior to the hearing as "aversive stimuli" in the treatment of inmates with behavior problems. The drug was administered by intra-muscular injection by a nurse after an inmate had violated the behavior protocol established for him by the staff. Dr. Loeffelholz testified that the drug could be injected for such pieces of behavior as not getting up, for giving cigarettes against orders, for talking, for swearing, or for lying. Other inmates or members of the staff would report on these violations of the protocol and the injection would be given by the nurse without the nurse or any doctor having personally observed the violation and without specific authorization of the doctor.

When it was determined to administer the drug, the inmate was taken to a room near the nurses' station which contained only a water closet and there given the injection. He was then exercised and within about fifteen minutes he began vomiting. The vomiting lasted from fifteen minutes to an hour. There is also a temporary cardiovascular effect which involves some change in blood pressure and "in the heart." This aversion type "therapy" is based on "Pavlovian conditioning."

The record is not clear as to whether or not the drug was always used with the initial consent of the inmate. It has apparently been administered in a few instances in the past without obtaining written consent of the inmate and once the consent is given, withdrawal thereof was not permitted. Apparently, at the time of trial apomorphine was not being used unless the inmate signed an initial consent, but there is no indication that the authorities now permit an inmate to withdraw his consent once it is given. Neither is there any indication in the record that the procedure has been changed to require the prior approval of a physician each time the drug is administered. Likewise there is no indication that there has been any change in the procedure which permits the administration of the drug upon reports of fellow inmates despite a recommendation by the magistrate that this practice should be avoided.

The testimony relating to the medical acceptability of this treatment is not conclusive. Dr. Steven Fox of the University of Iowa testified that behavior modification by aversive stimuli is a "highly questionable technique" and that only a 20% to 50% success is claimed. He stated that it is not being used elsewhere to his knowledge and that its use is really punishment worse than a controlled beating since the one administering the drug can't control it after it is administered.

On the other hand, Dr. Loeffelholz of the ISMF staff testified that there had been a 50% to 60% effect in modifying behavior by the use of apomorphine at ISMF. There is no evidence that the drug is used at any other inmate medical facility in any other state.

The Iowa Security Medical Facility is established by Section 223.1, Code of Iowa, 1973. It is an institution for persons displaying evidence of mental illness or psychological disorders and requiring diagnostic services and treatment in a security setting.

*   *   *

* * * [T]he purpose of confinement at ISMF is not penal in nature, but rather one of examination, diagnosis and treatment. Naturally, examination and diagnosis, by their very definition, do not encompass the administration of drugs. Thus, when that course of conduct is taken with respect to any particular patient, he is the recipient of treatment.

The use of apomorphine, then, can be justified only if it can be said to be treatment. Based upon the testimony adduced at the hearing and the findings made by the magistrate and adopted by the trial court, it is not possible to say that the use of apomorphine is a recognized and acceptable medical practice in institutions such as ISMF. Neither can we say, however, that its use on inmates who knowingly and intelligently consent to the treatment, should be prohibited on a medical or a legal basis. The authorities who testified at the evidentiary hearing indicate that some form of consent is now obtained prior to this treatment. The only question then is whether, under the eighth amendment, its use should be prohibited absent such consent; and if so what procedure must be followed to prevent abuses in the treatment procedures and to make certain the consent is knowingly and intelligently made.

At the outset we note that the mere characterization of an act as "treatment" does not insulate it from eighth amendment scrutiny.

* * *

Here we have a situation in which an inmate may be subjected to a morphine base drug which induces vomiting for an extended period of time. Whether it is called "aversive stimuli" or punishment, the act of forcing someone to vomit for a fifteen minute period for committing some minor breach of the rules can only be regarded as cruel and unusual unless the treatment is being administered to a patient who knowingly and intelligently has consented to it. To hold otherwise would be to ignore what each of us has learned from sad experience—that vomiting (especially in the presence of others) is a painful and debilitating experience. The use of this unproven drug for this purpose on an involuntary basis, is, in our opinion, cruel and unusual punishment prohibited by the eighth amendment.

We turn then to the question of how best to prevent abuse in the treatment procedures of consenting participants and how to make certain that the consent is knowingly and intelligently given.

* * *

In this case the trial court should enjoin the use of apomorphine in the treatment of inmates at the ISMF except when the following conditions are complied with:

1. A written consent must be obtained from the inmate specifying the nature of the treatment, a written description of the purpose, risks and effects of treatment, and advising the inmate of his right to terminate the consent at any time. This consent must include a certification by a physician that the patient has read and understands all of the terms of the consent and that the inmate is mentally competent to understand fully all of the provisions thereof and give his consent thereto.

2. The consent may be revoked at any time after it is given and if an inmate orally expresses an intention to revoke it to any member of the staff, a revocation form shall be provided for his signature at once.

3. Each apomorphine injection shall be individually authorized by a doctor and be administered by a doctor, or by a nurse. It shall be authorized in each instance only upon information based on the personal observation of a member of the professional staff.

Information from inmates or inmate aides of the observation of behavior in violation of an inmate's protocol shall not be sufficient to warrant such authorization.

The judgment of the district court is reversed with directions to grant the injunction under the terms hereinbefore set forth.

*   *   *

QUESTIONS AND COMMENTS

1.   *The definition of punishment.* Although the regimen followed in *Knecht* may seem particularly prone to abuse, conceivably any modality used in psychiatric treatment—be it psychotherapy, medication or psychosurgery—could be used as punishment, depending upon how that concept is defined and how the "treatment" was administered. Eighth amendment cases hold that the prohibition against cruel and unusual punishment "must draw its meaning from the evolving standards of decency that mark the progress of a maturing society." *Trop v. Dulles*, 356 U.S. 86, 101, 78 S.Ct. 590, 598, 2 L.Ed.2d 630 (1958). Prisoners have successfully used the clause to obtain court censure of corporal punishment, inadequate medical care, solitary confinement, assaults by guards, and generally abysmal conditions. But in reaching these results, the courts have usually required proof of egregious behavior that prison officials recognize is harmful. See *Rhodes v. Chapman*, 452 U.S. 337, 347, 101 S.Ct. 2392, 2399, 69 L.Ed.2d 59 (1981) (indicating that the Eighth Amendment is not violated if the prison provides "a minimal civilized measure of life's necessities"); Sharon Dolovich, *Cruelty, Prison Conditions and the Eighth Amendment*, 84 NYU L. Rev. 881 (2009) (criticizing Supreme Court jurisprudence holding that prison officials violate the Eighth Amendment only when they are aware of and disregard a substantial risk of harm). The Supreme Court has also been called upon to define punishment in *due process* cases alleging that certain conditions imposed on pretrial detainees constitute punishment prior to a determination of guilt. In *Bell v. Wolfish*, 441 U.S. 520, 99 S.Ct. 1861, 60 L.Ed.2d 447 (1979), the Court stated:

> If a particular condition or restriction of pretrial detention is reasonably related to a legitimate governmental objective, it does not, without more, amount to "punishment." Conversely, if a restriction or condition is not reasonably related to a legitimate goal—if it is arbitrary or purposeless—a court permissibly may infer that the purpose of the governmental action is punishment that may not constitutionally be inflicted upon detainees qua detainees.

The Court went on to permit a number of practices—such as limits on mail privileges, unannounced searches of detainees' living areas, and visual body cavity inspections—that it felt were related to legitimate security needs.

A number of other factors might be relevant to determining whether a particular treatment is punishment. Consider this excerpt from Paul

Friedman, *Legal Regulation of Applied Behavior Analysis in Mental Institutions and Prisons*, 17 Ariz.L.Rev. 39, 70–71 (1975):

> . . . The intent of the person applying the procedure is certainly one factor [in determining whether the procedure is punishment], though probably not a sufficient factor. Physical offensiveness or deprivation of things desired would probably be a second criterion. Even a combination of an actual intent to punish and an offensive procedure, however, would not necessarily define the procedure as punishment. Consider, for example, a normal appendectomy performed in the case of acute appendicitis by a sadistic surgeon who actually intends to punish his patient. In this case, the law would probably deem the procedure treatment rather than punishment despite the painful impact of the procedures and the surgeon's punitive intent. Thus the recognized therapeutic nature of a procedure would be another criterion. On the other hand, where a hazardous or intrusive procedure of recognized therapeutic value is utilized against a patient's will, it might be deemed punishment, despite its recognized therapeutic value, depending on the surgeon's punitive intent. Thus, the lack of consent of the patient to a procedure would be another criterion of punishment.
>
> The upshot of this discussion is that for a procedure to be considered punishment for eighth amendment purposes, it must first be physically offensive or depriving of things desired and imposed with an intent to punish. In addition, it must be either without recognized therapeutic value or with recognized therapeutic value but imposed without the patient's consent. In this latter instance, the patient's consent would remove the procedure from the category of punishment, making it unnecessary to say that he has waived his protection against cruel and unusual punishment. In the former instance, consent would not be permitted for the same reason one would not be permitted to consent to mayhem; consent would not serve any legitimate interest of either the subject or society.

What procedures should be considered "physically offensive" or "depriving of things desired"? Should antipsychotic medication be included in the first category? Freedom to leave the hospital ward in the second? With respect to the therapeutic value of a procedure, could not any procedure be characterized as "therapeutic" in the abstract? In *Knecht*, for instance, cannot one make a reasonable argument for the therapeutic value of apomorphine? Should therapeutic value also depend upon the type of symptom or event meant to be extinguished by use of the procedure? (Consider, for instance, the reasons clinicians gave for using apomorphine in *Knecht*.)

2.   *The role of consent.* Finally, what role should the patient's consent play in deciding whether a procedure is punishment? In *Knecht* Dr. Fox testified that the use of apomorphine was "punishment worse than a controlled beating." Would an inmate's consent to a beating make it treatment? Do the considerations discussed in the materials on consent to psychosurgery apply to the *Knecht* facts as well?

3. *Operant conditioning.* Unlike the aversive conditioning at issue in *Knecht,* a number of "behavior modification" programs rely on positive reinforcement, i.e., rewards for sought-after behavior. See, e.g., Michael G. McDonell et al., *Randomized Controlled Trial of Contingency Management for Stimulant Use in Community Mental Health Patients With Serious Mental Illness,* 170 Am. J. Psychiatry 94 (2013) (in an outpatient treatment program for mentally ill persons with stimulant dependence, reinforcement ["contingency management"] was associated with marked reduction in illicit drug use). Hospital units and courts apply implicit operant conditioning procedures when they grant hospital amenities (e.g., off-ward activities) or grounds privileges when unwanted behaviors (e.g., threats or aggressive acts) cease.

When long-term hospitalization was common, numerous studies documented the use and effectiveness of operant and social learning techniques. Steven M. Silverstein et al., *Behavioral Rehabilitation of the 'Treatment–Refractory' Schizophrenia Patient: Conceptual Foundations, Interventions, and Outcome Data,* 3 Psychol. Serv. 145, 146–47 (2006) (citing studies). More recent literature demonstrates the helpfulness of token economy programs in improving the behavior and readiness for discharge of chronically ill inpatients who benefit only modestly from medication. Id., at 161–64 (describing improved behavior and reduction in use of seclusion). Silverstein et al. explain, "Incentive systems, such as token economies and privileging systems, are designed to reward individuals for performing adaptive skills both while in groups and while in the treatment environment." Id. at 147. But might one also characterize these "incentive systems" as punishment programs? Mental health professionals believe that their patients' informed consent makes such program a form of treatment. But for involuntary patients, is that really true?

Assuming consent of the patient is required before a token economy program may be instituted, should such consent be revocable, as *Knecht* holds? Can "behavior modification" techniques work if consent is revocable?

V.   COMPETENCY IN THE CRIMINAL PROCESS

At several points in the criminal process, the law requires that the criminal accused demonstrate "competency" of some sort. For instance, the Supreme Court has held that, under the fifth amendment, a person may not be subjected to custodial interrogation unless he or she understands and voluntarily waives the right to remain silent and the right to have an attorney present during interrogation. *Miranda v. Arizona,* 384 U.S. 436, 86 S.Ct. 1602, 16 L.Ed.2d 694 (1966). The Court has also held, under the due process clause, that a guilty plea is not valid unless the accused understands the nature and consequences of the plea and enters the plea voluntarily. *Boykin v. Alabama,* 395 U.S. 238, 89 S.Ct. 1709, 23 L.Ed.2d 274 (1969). Similarly, an accused may not undergo trial unless he or she understands the trial process and can communicate.

with the attorney. *Drope v. Missouri,* 420 U.S. 162, 95 S.Ct. 896, 43 L.Ed.2d 103 (1975). After conviction, most states require that the defendant be competent to participate in the sentencing proceeding, a rule the Court may constitutionalize when given the opportunity to do so. Cf. *Green v. United States,* 365 U.S. 301, 304, 81 S.Ct. 653, 655, 5 L.Ed.2d 670 (1961) ("The most persuasive counsel may not be able to speak for a defendant [at sentencing] as the defendant might, with halting eloquence, speak for himself."). Finally, the Court has held that persons convicted of capital murder and sentenced to death may not be executed unless competent to understand what is happening to them. *Ford v. Wainwright,* 477 U.S. 399, 106 S.Ct. 2595, 91 L.Ed.2d 335 (1986).

Thus, a finding of incompetency could stall the criminal process at a number of different points. One can imagine a quite different system. Analogous to the plenary power given a guardian of the person, the lawyer for a criminal defendant found incompetent could be empowered to act and make decisions for the defendant. But, in contrast to most areas of the civil law, the criminal law has made incompetency an absolute bar to action under a wide variety of circumstances. The wisdom of this distinction should be considered throughout this section.

The first topic discussed is "competency to proceed" with a given proceeding, which includes competency to stand trial and competency to be sentenced. Then "decisional competency" is examined, in particular competency to plead guilty, waive counsel, waive the insanity defense, and waive rights associated with interrogation. As developed below, these competencies differ from the first type in that they involve the defendant's ability to make particular kinds of decisions. Finally, the chapter closes with materials concerning competency to be executed, which fits neither of the first two categories and which has only an attenuated connection to the autonomy interests that underlie the competency notion.

A. COMPETENCY TO PROCEED

1. Criteria

GARY MELTON, JOHN PETRILA, NORMAN POYTHRESS AND CHRISTOPHER SLOBOGIN, PSYCHOLOGICAL EVALUATIONS FOR THE COURTS

(New York: Guilford Press) 126–127 (3d ed. 2007).

(A) Historic Antecedents

The rule that an individual must be competent in order to undergo the criminal process originated in the common law and has been traced at least to the 17th century. In those days, as is true today, the defendant was required to plead to the charge prior to trial. Some commentators believe that the concept of competency first arose as a reaction by the English courts to defendants who, rather than making the required plea, stood mute. In such a case, the court would then seek to ascertain whether the defendant was "mute of malice" or "mute by visitation of God." If the individual fell into the first category, the court sought to force a plea by ordering increasingly heavier weights to be placed upon the individual's chest. If the individual fell into the latter category, he or she was spared this ordeal. The category "mute by visitation from God" initially included the literally deaf and mute, but over time was expanded to include the "lunatic."

Although the requirement that the defendant be competent may have developed as a practical response to a practical problem, it also seems to have its roots in a more general concern that subjecting certain types of individuals to trial was simply unfair. Thus, in the 18th century Blackstone observed that a defendant who "becomes mad . . . ought not to be arraigned for it; because he is not able to plead . . . with that advice and caution that he ought. And if, after he has pleaded, the prisoner becomes mad, he shall not be tried: for how can he make his defense?" This idea was also reflected in early English court decisions. For example, in *Frith's Case,* the court found that trial must be postponed until the defendant "by collecting together his intellects, and having them entire, he shall be able so to model his defense and to ward off the punishment of the law."

Early American courts, which relied heavily upon English common law, also recognized the incompetency plea. In 1835, for instance, the man who attempted to assassinate President Andrew Jackson was declared unfit to stand trial. In 1899, a federal court of appeals gave the doctrine constitutional status; the court held it to be "fundamental that an insane person can neither plead to an arraignment, be subjected to a trial, or, after trial, receive judgment, or, after judgment, undergo punishment; to the same effect are all the common-law authorities. . . . It is not 'due process of law' to subject an insane person to trial upon an indictment involving liberty or life." Since that time, the United States Supreme Court has on several occasions stated that the right of an incompetent defendant to avoid trial is "fundamental to an adversary system of justice." [See, e.g., *Drope v. Missouri,* 420 U.S. 162, 172, 95 S.Ct. 896, 43 L.Ed.2d 103 (1975)].

These holdings have been based on the due process clause but are probably best thought of as attempts to implement the Sixth Amendment, which guarantees criminal defendants the rights to effective counsel, confront one's accusers, and present evidence. Exercise of these rights requires more than physical presence; defendants who are not present mentally cannot help their attorneys rebut the state's case or discover helpful evidence. Put another way, in an ideal world the criminal process should provide a trial between evenly matched adversaries. This process posits defendants able to participate in their own defense. Without the competency doctrine, the rights afforded by the Sixth Amendment would be empty for many individuals.

A second rationale for the competency requirement focuses not on the individual's rights but on society's interests. The defendant must be competent not only to ensure fair results but also to guarantee a dignified criminal process. As one commentator has observed, "The adversary form of the criminal proceeding necessarily rests on the assumption that defendant will be a conscious and intelligent participant; the trial of a defendant who cannot fulfill this expectation appears inappropriate and irrational". Even a proceeding that produces an accurate guilty verdict would be repugnant to our moral sense if the convicted individual were unaware of what was happening or why. [T]his latter rationale for the competency requirement is important, as it seems to underlie many of the substantive and procedural aspects of competency doctrine.

(B) The Competency Test

In *Dusky v. United States* [362 U.S. 402, 80 S.Ct. 788, 4 L.Ed.2d 824 (1960)], the United States Supreme Court set forth a definition of competency to stand trial that has since come to be the standard in federal court and most state jurisdictions. The Court stated that "the test must be whether he [the defendant] has sufficient present ability to consult with his attorney with a reasonable degree of rational understanding and a rational as well as factual understanding of proceedings against him." Although actually only a repetition of a test put forth by the Solicitor General in the case, this formulation is now viewed as having constitutional status, with the result that many state statutes and courts follow it verbatim and most others track its basic components.

These components are several in number. First, the Court's test delineates two prongs to the competency test: the defendant's capacity to understand the criminal process, including the role of the participants in that process, and the defendant's ability to function in that process primarily through consulting with counsel in the preparation of a defense. Legal efforts to define competency further have consistently focused on these two prongs.

Second, *Dusky* makes clear competency focuses on the defendant's *present* ability to consult with counsel and to understand the proceedings. It therefore differs fundamentally from the test for criminal responsibility, which is a retrospective inquiry focusing on the defendant's state of mind at the time of the offense. It also differs from the predictive inquiry required for civil commitment although, as will be noted below, a degree of prediction may be necessary to determine competency in some instances.

③   Third, the test emphasizes the defendant's capacity as opposed to willingness, to relate to counsel and understand the proceedings. The defendant who refuses to talk to the attorney even though capable of doing so is making a rational choice knowing the consequences. Unless the lack of motivation is based on irrational factors, thereby calling into question one's capacity to assist in one's defense, it is not ground for an incompetency finding. Similarly when a suspect's inability to state the precise charge or describe the role of the judge results from failure to be apprised of the relevant information rather than a cognitive deficiency, a finding of incompetency is unwarranted.

④   Fourth, the requirement that the defendant possess a reasonable degree of understanding suggests that the test as applied to a particular case is a flexible one. "Perfect" or complete understanding on the part of the defendant will not be required—in fact, most observers agree that the threshold for a finding of competency is not particularly high. At the same time, that threshold may vary according to context. With respect to the first prong of the competency test, for instance, a level of capacity sufficient to understand simple charges (e.g., driving without a license) may be grossly insufficient when a complicated offense is involved. Similarly, the defendant's capacity to communicate with counsel may depend as much on the attorney's personality and the facts of the case as one any aspect of the defendant's mental condition. Relevant in the latter regard, however, is the Supreme Court's decision in Morris v. Slappy [461 U.S. 1, 103 S.Ct. 1610, 75 L.Ed.2d 610 (1983)], which held that the Constitution does not guarantee a "meaningful relationship" between a defendant and his or her attorney (primarily because, according to the Court, such a guarantee is impossible). Although this decision was in the context of claims that counsel's assistance was ineffective, it suggests that the Court will not require a particularly high-quality attorney-client relationship in the competency context.

⑤   A fifth and final component of the *Dusky* standard is its emphasis on the presence or absence of "rational" and "factual" understanding, which suggests an emphasis on cognitive *functioning*. As many courts have held, the mere fact that a defendant has psychotic symptoms or has a particular IQ does not mean that the defendant is incompetent to stand trial. Neither mental illness nor the defendant's need for treatment is sufficient for an incompetency finding. The presence of mental illness is relevant only insofar as that illness affects one's "rational understanding" as one consults with counsel and undergoes criminal trial. At the same time, note that understanding must be factual and rational; factual understanding alone is not enough. A defendant who understands that a particular prison term is associated with his charges but believes for irrational reasons that he will never serve any time in prison may be incompetent. . . .

There have been a number of efforts by legislators, courts, and clinicians to add content to the rather sparsely worded standard enunciated by the Supreme Court. For example, the Florida Rules of Criminal Procedure provide that "the following factors and any others deemed relevant" should be assessed during a competency evaluation:

The defendant's capacity to:

1.   Appreciate the charges or allegations against him;

2.   Appreciate the range and nature of possible penalties, if applicable, which may be imposed in the proceedings against him;

3.   Understand the adversary nature of the legal process;

4.   Disclose to his attorney facts pertinent to the proceedings at issue;

5.   Manifest appropriate courtroom behavior;

6.   Testify relevantly.

These criteria operationalize both prongs of *Dusky*. The first three criteria relate to the defendant's ability to understand the legal process. Defendants who cannot grasp the charges or possible penalties, or who cannot understand that trial involves an attempt by the prosecutor to obtain a conviction from a jury or judge, are unlikely to be able to confront their accusers or have the motivation to defend themselves. The last three criteria concern defendants' ability to function in the process. The fourth criterion focuses on the ability to communicate facts about the alleged crime to the attorney, obviously an important aspect of confronting accusers and assuring a fair trial. . . . The fifth and sixth criteria relate to the defendant's ability to function in the courtroom.

Note further that the latter two criteria call for predictions as to how the defendant will fare in the courtroom. Competency to stand trial assessments focus primarily on present mental status. These factors are nonetheless important because a defendant who will disrupt and distract the factfinding process may prejudice the factfinder and make defense counsel's job difficult, and a defendant who is incapable of testifying, even though able to talk to the attorney in private, may be deprived of a fair trial.

QUESTIONS AND COMMENTS

1.   *Competency to proceed.* Competency to stand trial is not the only "competency to proceed" issue that might arise. For instance, cases have dealt with a defendant's capacity to understand and assist counsel with sentencing and probation revocation proceedings. See, e.g., *Saddler v. United States*, 531 F.2d 83 (2d Cir.1976).

2.   *The first prong: understanding.* Under any competency to proceed standard, the criminal defendant must have some understanding of the proceedings to which he or she will be subjected. Typically, as the above material suggests, it is thought the defendant should grasp the roles of the judge, prosecutor and defense attorney and the general nature of the adversary process. One issue that has arisen in this regard is the extent to which cynical but plausible, views of the process suggest incompetency. For instance, an early competency interview "protocol" directed mental health professionals to give a high score (meaning a score suggesting competency) to a statement that the judge is "fair," and a low score to a statement that the judge is "unjust," "too harsh," or "wrong." The same protocol gives low scores for the statement that a defendant's biggest concern with his lawyer is "tardiness" and for a statement that, in disagreeing with his attorney, the defendant might feel there is "no sense arguing." See description of the Competency Screening Test, in Ronald Roesch & Stephen Golding, Competency to Stand Trial 60–61 (1980). Are these ratings valid?

The defendant should also be able to understand the *specific* case against him or her. As the above material suggests, this requirement is generally thought to include knowing the charges or issues to be resolved, the consequences of an adverse decision, and the crucial arguments for and against the defense.

3.   *The second prong: providing information.* Whether seen as a due process or effective assistance of counsel concern, a key reason underlying the competency to proceed requirement is the belief that defendants should be able to tell their attorneys their side of the story. Thus, it is important that the defendant be able to recall and describe the time period surrounding the alleged offense. Yet many defendants have or claim to have amnesia for this period. Genuine amnesia can result from physical events (e.g., a blow to the head suffered at the time of the offense or by excessive ingestion of intoxicants prior to the offense) and from psychological processes (e.g., defense mechanisms such as repression that result in forgetting traumatic events). Many defendants also claim—falsely—that they cannot remember events because they are ashamed, because they are malingering memory problems, or because they believe that their statements about what they remember will be used to prosecute them. When, if ever, should amnesia require a finding of incompetency?

Most courts hold that amnesia per se is not a bar to a finding of competency. Probably the leading case in this area is *Wilson v. United States,* 391 F.2d 460 (D.C.Cir.1968). Expert testimony established that the defendant in *Wilson* had no memory of the time period before, during, and immediately after the armed robbery with which he was charged because he suffered a fractured skull during the car chase leading to his arrest. The D.C. Circuit nonetheless held that Wilson was not necessarily incompetent to stand trial, because he understood the charges against him and could otherwise communicate with his attorney. However, the court also cautioned that on remand the trial court should, before imposing sentence, evaluate the effects of the amnesia on the trial, including:

(1) The extent to which the amnesia affected the defendant's ability to consult with and assist his lawyer.

(2) The extent to which the amnesia affected the defendant's ability to testify in his own behalf.

(3) The extent to which the evidence in suit could be extrinsically reconstructed in view of the defendant's amnesia. Such evidence would include evidence relating to the crime itself as well as any reasonably possible alibi.

(4) The extent to which the Government assisted the defendant and his counsel in that reconstruction.

(5) The strength of the prosecution's case. Most important here will be whether the Government's case is such as to negate all reasonable hypothesis of innocence. If there is any substantial possibility that the accused could, but for his amnesia, establish an alibi or other defense, it should be presumed that he would have been able to do so.

(6) Any other facts and circumstances which would indicate whether or not the defendant had a fair trial.

The court then stated, "After finding all the facts relevant to the fairness of the trial, considering the amnesia, the court will then make a judgment whether, under applicable principles of due process, the conviction should stand.[4]"

Judge Fahy argued in dissent that the indictment against the defendant should have been dismissed:

Appellant by reason of physical brain injury has not simply been completely and permanently deprived of all knowledge of the robbery itself but of all knowledge of anything covering the entire period surrounding it. To try him for crimes which occurred during this period is thus to try him for something about which he is mentally absent altogether, and this for a cause not attributable to his voluntary conduct. The effect is very much as though he were tried in absentia notwithstanding his physical presence at the time of trial.

---

[4] It would of course be desirable that defendants not only be competent to stand trial, but also have present awareness of their whereabouts and activities at the time of the crime of which they are accused. But courts have not considered such awareness as an essential ingredient of competence itself. As Judge Leventhal [in concurrence] points out, the man accused of committing a crime while drunk may have no recollection concerning the alleged events. And in the so-called "delayed arrest" narcotics cases, while the guilty man may remember his crime, the innocent accused may remember nothing at all about his activities at the critical time. Yet this court, while acknowledging that a delayed arrest may entail loss of memory, has never considered such lack of memory as going directly to competence to stand trial. Instead, it has required that where there has been substantial delay in arrest there can be a conviction only if the Government's case has strong corroboration. This approach . . . makes the probability of prejudice, not lack of memory per se, controlling.

* * *

The remand proceedings required by the court cannot solve the problem presented by this case. Appellant will no more be able to assist his counsel, and his counsel will no more be able effectively to assist him, at the remand hearing than at the trial itself. The terms of the remand in substance required a hearing on the issue of prejudice. To try separately this issue would leave us where we are now, with the added difficulty that at the remand hearing it appears appellant would be required to testify whether or not he wished to do so, raising another Fifth Amendment problem. If the case is to turn on the issue of prejudice we should determine now that prejudice is inherent in the situation. . . .

Is the majority's approach fair? Wilson and another man (who died in the crash) were believed to have robbed a pharmacy of money and the drug Desputal, as well as stolen a car; Wilson was found in the stolen car, as was some money, a gun and Desputal, and the pharmacy clerk positively identified him as one of the robbers. What possible defenses might Wilson have been able to raise based on memory of the time surrounding the alleged offense? Are the intoxication and delayed arrest cases referred to by the majority good precedent? Under Judge Fahy's approach, would it matter whether the amnesia was caused by organic dysfunction, psychogenic or feigned? In terms of providing assistance to counsel, isn't the result the same, regardless of the reason for the amnesia?

What if instead of claiming amnesia, Wilson had described the offense as an attempt to deprive aliens of material needed to make a bomb to blow up the world (and he honestly believed his story)? Should that fact alone lead to a finding of incompetency? ___yes

Competency Problem I

Decide whether the individual interviewed below, whose psychological tests indicate an IQ of 52, is competent to proceed on a charge of attempted rape. The interview is transcribed verbatim to give the flavor of a typical competency examination.

Q: Hello. This is Dr. Smith and I'm Dr. Falkin. Are you Phil Jones?

A: Yeah.

Q: We would like to talk to you briefly about the criminal case against you. Do you know where you are?

A: Some hospital.

Q: Do you know the name of the hospital?

A: Uh-uh [meaning no].

Q: Do you know what time it is?

A: I really don't know. I can't tell time too good.

Q: Do you have a watch?

A: Uh-uh.

Q: You talked to someone here last week didn't you?

A: Yes sir.

Q: Do you remember the name of that person?

A: I think her name was Sally [real name was Shelley].

Q: Sally?

A: Yeah.

Q: Do you remember what she told you about what was going to happen today?

A: No.

Q: Do you have any idea what is happening today? What we're here for? Why we're asking you questions?

A: Uh-uh.

Q: Can you guess?

A: Something 'bout going to court.

Q: Can you go any further than that?

A: That's all I know.

Q: Did your lawyer talk to you about this at all?

A: Uh-uh.

Q: He didn't say anything about it?

A: He didn't say nothing.

Q: Okay. Can you tell me your attorney's name? Your lawyer's name?

A: I don't know his name neither.

Q: Do you get along with your attorney?

A: He don't care about the case.

Q: How do you know?

A: I just know.

Q: Can you talk to him?

A: He don't talk much.

Q: How many times have you seen him?

A: One time [this turns out to be true].

Q: Just one?

A: Uh-huh [meaning yes].

Q: Do you ever talk to him on the phone?

A: No.

Q: Do you know what he looks like?

A: He's tall and uh, uh, tall and skinny [this is accurate].

Q: The one time you saw him where did you see him?

A: Uh—the courthouse. And he's supposed to let me know when I'm supposed to go back to court, but I ain't heard nothing yet.

Q: Why were you at the courthouse?

A: Uh—something about, something about a girl.

Q: Did you see a judge there?

A: Yeah—the only thing he told me, to stay out of trouble and don't go over there where she's at and he told me to stay out of Greenbrier [the area where the alleged incident occurred].

Q: Did he say anything else?

A: That's all.

Q: You're sure?

A: Yeah, that's all he said.

Q: Did he say anything about why you were in court?

A: Yeah, uh, he asked me that and he said something like—uh you know it's a—uh bad charge against me.

Q: A what?

A: That it's a bad charge against me.

Q: What was it?

A: 'Tempted rape, that's all. The only thing I done—I didn't try to rape her or nothing like that—the only thing I done was pushed her down in the bushes and that's all I did. I don't 'member doing anything else.

Q: The police report says you waited for her and tried to take off her clothes. Is that right?

A: I don't know 'bout that.

Q: After you pushed her in the bushes what happened?

A: She said she was taking medicine, so I jumped on my bike and went to the Seven–Day Junior [a convenience store next to his brother's gas station].

Q: You don't remember anything else?

A: Nope. [The victim claimed that Jones had pushed her and tried to take off her belt. When she screamed, he got on his bike and left. She mentioned nothing about medicine.]

Q: Do you know what an insanity defense is?

A: No.

Q: An insanity defense is—your lawyer might tell the judge or the jury that you were having emotional or mental problems when you pushed the girl.

A: I didn't do nothing wrong.

Q: Would you let your lawyer argue that—the insanity defense?

A: All I done was pushed her in the bushes.

Q: So you are saying you would not be willing to plead guilty to your charges? You would not want to tell the judge that you did something bad?

A: I never done nothing bad.

Q: Let's assume that you had done something bad. Would you be willing to tell the judge that if you could get a good deal?

A: I never done nothing bad.

* * *

Q: What is it—what does the word attempt mean to you?

A: Umm—taking something that belongs to somebody else.

Q: Attempt means that?

A: Yeah.

Q: Do you know the difference between rape and attempted rape?

A: No.

Q: Will you try to think about it and tell me? The difference between rape and attempted rape?

A: (Long pause). That's all I know.

Q: Do you think you're going to go to court?

A: Huh?

Q: Is this, are you going to—are you going to have a trial?

A: Yeah, I hope so.

Q: You hope so. What happens in a trial in a courtroom?

A: I really don't know.

Q: What's your idea of what happens in a trial?

A: Sometimes they throw it out of court.

Q: Throw it out of court. Throw what out of court?

A: Uh, if you, if you, if ah, if ah, if you done it or didn't do it.

Q: And what happens if you throw it out of court—which way does it go?

A: (Pause). I don't know which way it goes.

Q: If you go to court will you see a prosecutor?

A: The prosecutor, yeah.

Q: What does he do?

A: He's . . . ah, I don't know.

Q: He brings the case against you for the state. He tries to convict you.

A: Yeah, he's wants to, uh, get me (laughs).

Q: What could he do to you if he got you?

A: Uh, he'd send me to the state farm [apparently referring to a mental hospital, where Mr. Jones had been briefly confined once before ten years earlier].

Q: The state farm?

A: Yeah, I'd have to stay at the state farm for a long time.

Q: What if the judge said you had to go to jail instead of the state farm?

A: Jail.

Q: Do you understand what a jail is?

A: It's got bars.

Q: If you had to choose between jail and the state farm, where would you like to go?

A: I don't know.

Q: Can you think about it and tell me?

A: Uh . . . The people at the state farm make fun.

Q: They make fun of you?

A: Yeah.

* * *

Q: What temperature do you think it is outside?

A: (Pause). Four o'clock.

Q: No, temperature.

A: (Pause). I don't know.

Q: Do you know what temperature means?

A: No.

Q: How hot or cold do you think it is?

A: I don't know.

Q: Weren't you outside today?

A: Yeah. I never did get cold much.

Q: You were outside today, right?

A: Uh-huh.

Q: I thought it was pretty cold, I thought it was really cold, I thought it was almost freezing. It was like almost about to snow [in fact the day was quite warm].

A: Felt like it.

Q: Do you know the month and the day and the year?

A: I don't know the date.

Q: Do you have any idea what month it is?

A: Um . . . no.

Q: What season of the year is it?

A: I don't know that either.

Q: You don't?

A: No.

Q: How about the year. Do you keep up with the years at all?

A: No.

Q: Okay, if I'd say it's either March or November or August, which month seems most right [it was November]?

A: August.

Q: Seems like August to you?

A: Yeah.

Q: What is August like? When we talk about the month of August what do you think about? Or what makes right now seem like August?

A: Cold weather.

Q: Cold weather?

A: Cold weather.

Q: Okay, what months make you think about warm weather? Can you name some months?

A: I don't know the months. I ain't gone through school.

Q: Do you know how many months there are in a year?

A: (Pause). Seven.

Q: Seven? Can you count to seven?

A: No.

Q: How far can you count?

A: Um, not too far.

* * *

Q: You say you got a divorce. What happens when you get a divorce and what is a divorce?

A: Just me and her just separated. She got her divorce and I got mine.

Q: If you found a stamped letter laying on the walk somewhere and you were walking along and it was just laying there like somebody just dropped it, what would you do with it?

A: Um, turn it into the postman.

Q: You'd turn it into the postman? Can you count money?

A: Um, not too good.

Q: If I gave you a ten dollar bill and asked for half of it back how much of it would you give me back?

A: (Pause). Five.

Q: Okay. Then you gave me the five dollars back and I said you can have half of that back, I'll give half of it back to you. Then how much would I be giving you back?

A: (Long pause). Four.

Q: Four? If your little girl would start crying what would you think would be wrong with her, what would be the—just crying—what would be some of the things that that could mean?

A: She be crying for something.

Q: Like what maybe?

A: Um, like uh, candy bar or something.

Q: Could there be other reasons?

A: Sometimes she cries and she gets a high fever and she gets sick sometimes.

Q: So she cries sometimes when she's sick? And any other things that you can think about that would make a little child that age cry?

A: Uh uh.

Q: A couple more questions and then we're going to stop I think. But I'm gonna list several things and you try to pick out the thing in the list of three or four things that I say that might be different. Okay? Orange, apple, a pear, baby rattle.

A: Um, baby rattle.

Q: Baby rattle. You picked that out because of what?

A: I don't know why I picked it out, it was a baby rattle.

Q: Okay, let's try it again. Hammer, saw, a square, and an ice cream cone.

A: (Pause). Ice cream cone.

Q: Okay, why did you say an ice cream cone?

A: You can eat an ice cream cone.

not competent

Mr. Jones chopped wood for a living. If you were the judge who had to make the decision about whether Mr. Jones was competent to proceed with adjudication, what additional information would you want?[k] If you think that the defendant is not at present competent to proceed, do you think he is "restorable" to competency? If so, should he be hospitalized for this purpose? Or can steps short of that be taken?

law CP doesn't mean you need to be hospitalized

Competency Problem II

A 42 year-old male defendant is charged with stalking a famous movie actor. He tells the forensic examiner that he will plead "not guilty" as he was acting in "self defense". The defendant completely understands the nature of the criminal proceedings. Regarding his defensive strategy, he explains that the actor implanted microchips into his brain and was controlling his behavior through these microchips by administering painful electric shocks to him each time the defendant behaved in a way that the actor did not like. Apart from the alleged stalking, the defendant's behavior and speech was and remains normal.

depends on trial → insanity

Competency Problem III

A 23 year-old female defendant is charged with murdering her husband after learning that he was having an affair with her sister. Upon being arrested, she became belligerent with the sheriff, leading to her being "hog tied". Once in jail, she was "pepper sprayed" by the jail staff after she refused to comply with directions. The jail psychiatrist diagnoses the defendant with impulse control disorder not otherwise specified (NOS) and offers her medication, which she refuses. In court, she screams profanities at the judge, spits at the bailiff, and turns over the defense table. She is selectively mute with the forensic examiner but knows why she is in jail and argues: "the dirty bum deserved what he got."

competent

The final two competency problems are taken from Grant H. Morris, Ansar M. Haroun & David Naimark, *Competency to Stand Trial on Trial*, 4 Houston J. Health L. & Pol'y 193, 213 (2004). Of 196 psychiatrists and psychologists presented with Competency Problem II, 44.4% found the defendant competent to proceed and 55.6% found the defendant incompetent. Out of 185 psychiatrists and psychologists presented with Competency Problem III, 70.3% found the defendant competent and 29.7% found her incompetent. Id. at 214.

---

[k] When shown the videotape from which this interview was transcribed, approximately half of a group of state court judges stated they would have found the defendant competent to stand trial; the other half found him incompetent. Before his case was resolved, Mr. Jones died from exposure.

2. Procedures for Assessing Competency to Proceed

In *Pate* v. *Robinson*, 383 U.S. 375, 86 S.Ct. 836, 15 L.Ed.2d 815 (1966), the Supreme Court held that the due process clause requires the trial court to order an inquiry into competency to stand trial whenever a "bona fide doubt" on the issue exists. The one case in which it has applied the standard was *Drope v. Missouri,* 420 U.S. 162, 95 S.Ct. 896, 43 L.Ed.2d 103 (1975), in which the defendant was charged, along with two others, with the forcible rape of his wife. At the time of trial, Drope had been found competent, based largely on a report submitted by a psychiatrist. The report stated that the defendant had no "delusions, illusions, hallucinations," was "well-oriented in all spheres," and "was able, without trouble to answer questions testing judgement." The report also noted, however, that the defendant "had difficulty in participating well," "had a difficult time relating," and was "markedly circumstantial and irrelevant in his speech." Furthermore, the defendant's wife testified at trial that the defendant was sick, that he would roll down the stairs when he did not "get his way or [was] worried about something," and that he had choked her the Sunday evening before trial (an event that removed her initial reluctance about pursuing the prosecution). On the second day of trial, the defendant shot himself, apparently in a suicide attempt. The Missouri Court of Appeals found that neither the psychiatric report nor the suicide attempt created a reasonable doubt as to the defendant's competence. The Supreme Court reversed. While the Court noted that neither the report nor the defense attorney's motion for a continuance after the suicide attempt provided facts "bearing specifically on the issue of petitioner's competence to stand trial," it found that "the record reveals a failure to give proper weight to the information suggesting incompetence which came to light during trial." Thus, a competency evaluation should have been ordered on the second day of the trial. The Court also stated:

> [E]vidence of defendant's irrational behavior, his demeanor at trial, and any prior medical opinion on competence to stand trial are all relevant in determining whether further inquiry is required, but even one of these factors standing alone may, in some circumstances, be sufficient. There are, of course, no fixed or immutable signs which invariably indicate the need for further inquiry to determine fitness to proceed; the question is often a difficult one in which a wide range of manifestations and subtle nuances are implicated. That they are difficult to evaluate is suggested by the varying opinions trained psychiatrists can entertain on the same facts.

Id. at 180, 95 S.Ct. at 908.

In most jurisdictions, any party—the defense attorney, the prosecutor, or the trial judge sua sponte—may raise the competency issue. If the court finds that a bona fide doubt about competency exists, and if the incompetency appears related to mental disability (which is almost always the case), the court orders one or more mental health professionals to perform an evaluation. For many years, this assessment was performed in a hospital, where the defendant was "evaluated" for several weeks or even months. Since the 1970's many states have shortened the duration of hospital evaluations; many have also moved toward providing outpatient evaluations either in the jail or, if the defendant has obtained pretrial release, in a local clinic. Patricia A. Zapf & Virginia G. Cooper, *Competency to Stand Trial*, in Encyclopedia of Psychology and Law 120 (Brian Cutler, 2008),

Very often, the report that results from the evaluation is the only information available to the court. Twenty-four states explicitly allow the competency decision to be based solely on the expert's report, unless one of the parties disagrees with its conclusions. Id. A late 1970s survey of 55 North Carolina judges found that 59% of them virtually never held a formal hearing to assess evidence of the defendant's competency. Ronald Roesch & Stephen Golding, Competency to Stand Trial 193 (1980). If a hearing does take place, it is usually informal and perfunctory. In the survey noted above, 35% of the judges said they never disagreed with the clinical report and the remaining 65% stated that disagreement was rare. Id. More recent research suggests that similar practices still prevail. See Patricia A. Zapf, *Have the Courts Abdicated Their Responsibility for Determination of Competency to Stand Trial to Clinicians?*, 4 J. Forensic Psychol. Prac. 27, 34 (2004) (finding that courts agreed with the forensic evaluator's judgment in 327 out of 328 cases, or 99.7% of the time). States vary as to which party bears the burden of proof, with the tendency being to put the burden on the party alleging incompetency. Most states also adopt the preponderance of the evidence standard of proof. Wayne LaFave, Criminal Law 8.1(a)(2d ed. 2003).

If the defendant is found competent to stand proceed, then, of course, the prosecution resumes. If the defendant is found incompetent and the court determines competency can be restored, the trial court will order him or her to undergo treatment. This treatment usually takes place in a hospital, though courts occasionally permit restoration to take place in outpatient treatment settings or in jails. In *Jackson v. Indiana,* 406 U.S. 715, 92 S.Ct. 1845, 32 L.Ed.2d 435 (1972), the Supreme Court imposed limitations on the duration of treatment to restore competency:

> A person charged by a State with a criminal offense who is committed solely on account of his incapacity to proceed to trial cannot be held more than a reasonable period of time necessary to determine whether there is a substantial probability that he will attain the capacity in the foreseeable future. If it is determined that this is not the case, then the State must either institute the

customary civil commitment proceedings that would be required to commit indefinitely another citizen or release the defendant.

Id. at 737–38, 92 S.Ct. at 1858. *Jackson* is discussed in more detail after the following notes on procedural issues.

QUESTIONS AND COMMENTS

1. *The bona fide doubt standard*. In *Drope* the Supreme Court listed three factors—evidence of defendant's irrational behavior, his demeanor at trial and any prior medical opinion on competence to stand trial—and then stated that "even one of these factors standing alone may, in some circumstances, be sufficient." Is this standard too low? Studies conducted in recent years have reported that only 13 to 46% (average = 26%) of defendants referred for competency evaluations were judged incompetent by clinicians. Gary B. Melton et al., supra, at 141 (citing studies covering seven jurisdictions published in 1997–2004). Moreover, this figure probably overstates the proportion of defendants who were actually incompetent because mental health professionals tend to err on the side of an incompetency finding, especially when charges are serious. Alec Buchanan, *Competency to Stand Trial and the Seriousness of the Charge*, 34 J. Am. Acad. Psychiatry Law 458, 459–62 (2006)(explaining the rationale for doing so). Thus, it appears that a significant number of referrals for competency evaluation should not have occurred.

Over-referral may result from abuses of the competency system. As described in Melton, et al., supra, at 127–128, these abuses could include: (1) referral for a competency examination when the real purpose is to obtain evaluations about criminal responsibility or disposition, the procedures for which are more cumbersome; (2) incompetency referrals "used as a ruse to force treatment of persons who do not meet dangerousness requirements for civil commitment and who may be acting bizarrely;" given the low threshold of the bona fide doubt standard, "a defendant [who] acts bizarrely or presents management problems in jail . . . is most readily placed in the mental health system through such a referral than through a commitment petition requiring a full hearing with counsel," particularly since the court itself or the prosecution may raise the question; (3) finally,

> [C]ompetency referrals may be for purely strategic reasons unrelated to any concern with defendants' mental status. Perhaps foremost among these purposes is simply delay. In a case where the alleged offense has created public uproar, defense counsel may succeed in bringing about the defendant's removal from the community until public emotions have calmed by having him or her hospitalized for a competency evaluation. Similarly, if the evidence is weak but the public sentiment for prosecution is strong, prosecutors may have the defendant "put away" for a period through a competency evaluation. The result may be pretrial detention without the opportunity for bail.

The survey of North Carolina judges described above found that judges suspect abuses of the competency referral process, especially by defense attorneys who misunderstand the concept or who merely seek delay. Nonetheless, the majority of judges reported that they routinely grant motions for competency evaluations without requiring evidence that there is cause to raise the issue. Roesch & Golding, supra at 192.

Before concluding that over-referrals are necessarily the result of abuse, however, consider some analogous situations in medicine. Physicians recommend that individuals above a certain age periodically undergo several cancer screening tests—such as colonoscopies and mammograms—that usually turn up no malignancy and in which ambiguous results lead to further "false positive" studies. Though these practices sometimes generate disagreement and controversy, doctors do not conclude that a large fraction of no-malignancy outcomes is necessarily bad. Rather, they try to figure out whether, considering the consequences of false positives and false negatives, the balance of errors seems correct. In a similar vein, attorneys and courts may well conclude that "over-diagnosing" incompetence is a "good" mistake in that it leads to treatment for someone who needs it anyway and it minimizes the chances of a far more grievous error—trying and convicting someone who actually is incompetent.

2.   *Community evaluations.* An indirect way to discourage abuse of the competency system is the development of a community evaluation system. If an order authorizing a competency evaluation results only in a brief evaluation either in jail or in the local clinic, defense attorneys or prosecutors who seek a competency evaluation to delay trial or remove the defendant from the community will achieve less from an illegitimate referral. Roesch and Golding demonstrated that a relatively brief interview in the community can arrive at results on the competency issue that are at least as reliable as those reached by hospital clinicians after prolonged observation of the defendant in the hospital. Roesch & Golding, supra at 188–191. Given this finding, one could argue that outpatient evaluations are required under least restrictive alternative analysis. The right to pretrial release and the right to speedy trial may also be infringed by prolonged pretrial hospitalization.[1]

In light of these considerations, should hospitalization for the purpose of evaluating the competency of an individual be prohibited? Would a time-limited evaluation period be satisfactory protection? Cf. Ohio Rev. Code § 2945.371(C) ("defendant may be held [in a hospital] for evaluation for a reasonable period of time not to exceed twenty days"). Alternatively, in addition to a showing that there is a bona fide doubt about competency, should statutes require a showing that the evaluation could not be achieved outside a hospital setting or that the criteria for civil commitment are met? If the latter route is appropriate, and the defense attorney is the one who raised

---

[1]   Note, however, that the state may deny pretrial release for a legitimate "regulatory" reason, *United States v. Salerno,* 481 U.S. 739, 107 S.Ct. 2095, 95 L.Ed.2d 697 (1987), and that statutes which implement the speedy trial right usually exempt time spent performing a competency evaluation or undergoing treatment to restore competency from the time period relevant to determining whether the right is violated. See, e.g., 18 U.S.C. § 3161(h)(4).

the competency issue, what role should he or she play at the commitment hearing, if any? Might a conflict of interest arise in this situation? At the time of his evaluation, Jones, the subject of Problem I above, was in jail. Was there potential for the types of abuses described above in his case? If so, what can be done to prevent them?

3. *Parties who may raise the issue.* Another means of limiting abuse of the competency evaluation process is to prohibit the judge or the prosecution, or both, from raising the issue. See, e.g., Stuart Eizenstat, *Mental Competency to Stand Trial*, 4 Harv.Civ.Rts. Civ.Lib.L.Rev. 379, 384–85 (1969). Is such a prohibition justifiable?

Given the possibly adverse consequences of a competency evaluation, should the *defense attorney* be barred from raising the issue when the client does not want it raised? The American Bar Association Criminal Justice Mental Health Standards require the defense attorney to move for an evaluation of competency whenever he or she "has a good faith doubt as to the defendant's competence," even over the client's objection. Standard 7–4.2. The commentary to the standard justifies this approach as follows:

> Because the trial of an incompetent defendant necessarily is invalid as a violation of due process, a defense lawyer's duty to maintain the integrity of judicial proceedings requires that the trial court be advised of the defendant's possible incompetence.[16] Ultimately, this requirement provides protections for criminal defendants. In addition, to permit defense counsel to proceed to trial with incompetent clients deprives defendants of their personal right to participate in and to control the thrust of their defense. It further assumes that defense attorneys properly determine the best interests of their clients. Criminal defendants, even though represented by trial counsel, have the exclusive right to make certain critical decisions, e.g., to waive or demand jury trial, to decide whether or not to testify in personal defense, and to decide the plea to be entered. Obviously, incompetent defendants cannot make these decisions and they may not be made by their attorneys.
>
> Standard 7–4.2(c) recommends a clear requirement that defense counsel raise the issue of a defendant's present mental incompetence whenever counsel has a good faith doubt about competence. It resolves the difficult conflict of concerns inherent in such circumstances . . . in favor of counsel's obligation to the court. The conflict, if it exists, arises from a perceived pragmatic failure of the criminal justice system to live up to its promise, in that the deficiencies in the system of incompetence evaluation and treatment implicitly threaten excessive or inappropriate sanctions against defendants. The standard takes the position that, if such problems exist, the thrust should be to correct the problems, not to permit a pragmatic but philosophically unsound mechanism to avoid them. If elements of unfairness are eliminated from the system,

---

[16] See Model Rules of Professional Conduct 3.3(a)(1) ("A lawyer shall not knowingly . . . make a false statement of material fact or law to a tribunal").

defendants will have little reason to prefer a pragmatic avoidance of the competence issue in favor of trial on the merits.

Rodney Uphoff, in *The Role of the Criminal Defense Lawyer in Representing the Mentally Impaired Defendant: Zealous Advocate or Officer of the Court?*, 1988 Wisc.L.Rev. 65, 89–96, criticizes the ABA approach:

> Although truth, and efficient, fair results are important systemic goals, the lawyer's role in the adversary system generally permits her to represent her client zealously even at the expense of these systemic goals. It is not enough to state in conclusory fashion that requiring defense counsel to assume an officer-of-the-court role serves these systemic goals. Rather, if defense counsel for a mentally impaired defendant is to play a different, lesser role than zealous advocate, it should be incumbent on those who wish to change counsel's role to provide the authority or to explain the policy warranting such a change.

> The commentary to ABA Standard 7–4.2, however, offers little authority for its restricted view of defense counsel's role. It suggests that defense counsel's failure to disclose a doubt about her client's competency constitutes a false statement of material fact. Certainly counsel, as an officer of the court, has a duty to avoid perpetrating a fraud on the court. Yet, the ethics codes, acclaiming the virtues of the adversary system and the principle of zealous partisanship, generally permit a criminal defense lawyer to withhold information or even create a misleading impression. The controversy surrounding the lawyer's duty to divulge a client's perjury reflects the limited scope of the criminal defense lawyer's obligation to disclose a client's fraud and the importance of the value of confidentiality. While the Model Rules now require disclosure of a client's intention to commit perjury, it is a major leap to equate nondisclosure of defense counsel's doubts about a client's competence with fraud. . . .

> . . . A number of courts have held that a lawyer can be compelled to testify regarding counsel's opinion of a client's competency even though the lawyer's observations would involve privileged client communications, but the better reasoned position is that a lawyer's opinion about a client's competence or state of mind is inextricably mixed with the client's private communications. Accordingly, the lawyer should not be forced to raise competency and thereby disclose privileged matters unless that disclosure is consistent with the client's interests or wishes.

* * *

> . . . If a lawyer does not adequately investigate the [competency] issue or fails to raise competency without a legitimate reason, that lawyer's representation should be deemed inadequate. Yet it is neither unduly burdensome nor difficult to scrutinize trial counsel's reasons for not acting.

lawyer must investigate competency

Appellate review of the limited instances in which counsel decides for strategic reasons not to raise competency is less costly overall to the criminal justice system than obligating defense counsel to act whenever she has a reasonable doubt. If defense lawyers strictly adhere to this duty, they will be raising competency in many cases in which the client ultimately will be found competent. This will mean additional court hearings, unnecessary hospitalization, and increased costs for all of the major participants in the criminal justice system.

Moreover, even if counsel raises competency, the defendant still has a right to challenge the doctor's opinion. At this hearing, the defense lawyer, whose request triggered the evaluation in the first place, will be representing the defendant. The defendant may be understandably reluctant to trust defense counsel in view of counsel's previous actions. Furthermore, defense counsel's role at this hearing will be impossibly complicated. She cannot act as an advocate while at the same time offering testimony, based in part on confidential communications, that is adverse to her client.

* * *

. . . If the prosecutor or the trial court feels that the judicial process is being demeaned by proceeding against an incompetent defendant, either can raise competency. Similarly, either can raise the issue if defense counsel appears to be inadequately protecting a mentally ill client.

Which stance is more persuasive? What if the defense attorney *knows* that the mental condition of his evaluation-refusing client prevents the client from understanding proceedings, providing adequate assistance, or considering options rationally? If you were the attorney for Jones in Problem I would you press for a competency evaluation if he insisted he did not want to go to the "state farm" (hospital) again?

4.   *Hearing procedures.* A final method of discouraging abuse of the system is to formalize the competency determination process. If the parties know that the results of an evaluation (and thus its necessity) will be closely scrutinized by a court, they may be less willing to initiate the process in the first place. Independent of this practical concern is whether the constitution *requires* more formal proceedings than presently occur. In particular: (1) is the present tendency to allow the competency decision to be made by stipulation of the parties proper? (2) when a hearing does take place, is the preponderance of the evidence standard high enough and who should bear the burden of proof? In the Jones case, would the defense argue for competency or incompetency? Which party should bear the burden of proof?

On the latter issue, the U.S. Supreme Court has handed down two decisions. In *Medina v. California*, 505 U.S. 437, 112 S.Ct. 2572, 120 L.Ed.2d 353 (1992), it upheld against a due process challenge a state statute that: (1) put the burden of proving incompetency on the party asserting it; and (2) established a presumption of competency. In *Cooper v. Oklahoma*, 517 U.S. 348, 116 S.Ct. 1373, 134 L.Ed.2d 498 (1996), it held unconstitutional a statute that placed the burden on the defendant to show incompetency by clear and convincing evidence (a standard of proof more onerous than the preponderance standard).

Medina is worth looking at in more detail. Medina, charged with capital murder, was found competent by a jury during a pretrial hearing; he was subsequently tried, convicted, and sentenced to death. After finding "no historical basis for concluding that the allocation of the burden of proving competence to the defendant violates due process," Justice Kennedy's majority opinion turned "to consider whether [California's] rule transgresses any recognized principle of 'fundamental fairness' in operation."

> Petitioner relies upon federal and state-court decisions which have said that the allocation of the burden of proof to the defendant in these circumstances is inconsistent with the rule of *Pate v. Robinson*, where we held that a defendant whose competence is in doubt cannot be deemed to have waived his right to a competency hearing. Because " 'it is contradictory to argue that a defendant may be incompetent, and yet knowingly or intelligently "waive" his right to have the court determine his capacity to stand trial,' " it has been said that it is also "contradictory to argue that a defendant who may be incompetent should be presumed to possess sufficient intelligence that he will be able to adduce evidence of his incompetency which might otherwise be within his grasp."

> In our view, the question whether a defendant whose competence is in doubt may waive his right to a competency hearing is quite different from the question whether the burden of proof may be placed on the defendant once a hearing is held. The rule announced in *Pate* was driven by our concern that it is impossible to say whether a defendant whose competence is in doubt has made a knowing and intelligent waiver of his right to a competency hearing. Once a competency hearing is held, however, the defendant is entitled to the assistance of counsel, e.g., *Estelle v. Smith*, and psychiatric evidence is brought to bear on the question of the defendant's mental condition. Although an impaired defendant might be limited in his ability to assist counsel in demonstrating incompetence, the defendant's inability to assist counsel can, in and of itself, constitute probative evidence of incompetence, and defense counsel will often have the best-informed view of the defendant's ability to participate in his defense. While reasonable minds may differ as to the wisdom of placing the burden of proof on the defendant in these circumstances, we believe that a State may take such factors into account in making judgments as to the allocation of the burden of proof, and we see no basis for concluding that placing the burden on the defendant violates the principle approved in *Pate*.

In dissent, Justice Blackmun, joined by Justice Stevens, stated in part:

> The Court suggests that "defense counsel will often have the best-informed view of the defendant's ability to participate in his defense." There are at least three good reasons, however, to doubt the Court's

confidence. First, while the defendant is in custody, the State itself obviously has the most direct, unfettered access to him and is in the best position to observe his behavior. In the present case, Medina was held before trial in the Orange county jail system for more than a year and a half prior to his competency hearing. During the months immediately preceding the competency hearing, he was placed several times for extended periods in a padded cell for treatment and observation by prison psychiatric personnel. While Medina was in the padded cell, prison personnel observed his behavior every 15 minutes.

Second, a competency determination is primarily a medical and psychiatric determination. Competency determinations by and large turn on the testimony of psychiatric experts, not lawyers. "Although competency is a legal issue ultimately determined by the courts, recommendations by mental health professionals exert tremendous influence on judicial determinations, with rates of agreement typically exceeding 90%." Nicholson & Johnson, Prediction of Competency to Stand Trial: Contribution of Demographics, Type of Offense, Clinical Characteristics, and Psycholegal Ability, 14 Int'l J. Law and Psych. 287, 287 (1991). While the testimony of psychiatric experts may be far from infallible, it is the experts and not the lawyers who are credited as the "best-informed," and most able to gauge a defendant's ability to understand and participate in the legal proceedings affecting him.

Third, even assuming that defense counsel has the "best-informed view" of the defendant's competency, the lawyer's view will likely have no outlet in, or effect on, the competency determination. Unlike the testimony of medical specialists or lay witnesses, the testimony of defense counsel is far more likely to be discounted by the factfinder as self-interested and biased. Defense counsel may also be discouraged in the first place from testifying for fear of abrogating an ethical responsibility or the attorney-client privilege. By way of example from the case at hand, it should come as little surprise that neither of Medina's two attorneys was among the dozens of persons testifying during the six days of competency proceedings in this case.

* * *

The allocation of the burden of proof reflects a societal judgment about how the risk of error should be distributed between litigants. This Court has said it well before: "The individual should not be asked to share equally with society the risk of error when the possible injury to the individual is significantly greater than any possible harm to the state." *Addington v. Texas.*

Professor Winick questions the majority's reasoning in *Medina*, but applauds its conclusion that the defendant be presumed competent. Recognizing that this rule might lead to trial of "marginally incompetent" defendants, he nonetheless defends it on three grounds: (1) it can reduce the "burdens and costs imposed by the incompetency doctrine" by helping to "minimize the inappropriate use of the incompetency doctrine for defendants who are not . . . severely impaired;" (2) it will also speed the disposition of criminal charges for these defendants, who in minor cases might otherwise spend a longer time confined (in the hospital) than they would have had they been tried immediately and convicted; (3) it will have a therapeutic effect on the marginally competent, especially when the prosecution rather than the defendant alleges incompetence, because it will tend to avoid both stigmatizing them with the incompetency label and creating an incentive to resist treatment. Bruce Winick, *Presumptions and Burdens of Proof in Determining Competency to Stand Trial: An Analysis of* Medina v. California *and the Supreme Court's New Due Process Methodology in Criminal Cases*, 47 Miami L. Rev. 817, 849–58 (1993). Do any of these reasons apply in *Medina*?

Note that California is in a distinct minority in affording a jury trial on the competency issue to any defendant who requests one. Indeed, one court has held that a jury trial is not required in competency proceedings even when it is required in civil commitment proceedings, because the consequences of the former are "temporary" rather than "permanent." *State ex rel. Matalik v. Schubert*, 57 Wis.2d 315, 204 N.W.2d 13 (1973). Might the Supreme Court's opinion in *Medina* been influenced by a similar perception about the consequences of an incompetency finding? Consider the materials below.

3. Disposition

JACKSON V. INDIANA
Supreme Court of the United States, 1972.
406 U.S. 715, 92 S.Ct. 1845, 32 L.Ed.2d 435.

MR. JUSTICE BLACKMUN delivered the opinion of the Court.

We are here concerned with the constitutionality of certain aspects of Indiana's system for pretrial commitment of one accused of crime.

Petitioner, Theon Jackson, is a mentally defective deaf mute with a mental level of a pre-school child. He cannot read, write, or otherwise communicate except through limited sign language. In May 1968, at age 27, he was charged in the Criminal Court of Marion County, Indiana, with separate robberies of two women. The offenses were alleged to have occurred the preceding July. The first involved property (a purse and its contents) of the value of four dollars. The second concerned five dollars in money. The record sheds no light on these charges since, upon receipt of not-guilty pleas from Jackson, the trial court set in motion the Indiana procedures for determining his competency to stand trial. Ind.Ann.Stat. § 9–1706a (Supp.1971), now Ind.Code 35–5–3–2 (1971).

As the statute requires, the court appointed two psychiatrists to examine Jackson. A competency hearing was subsequently held at which petitioner was represented by counsel. The court received the examining doctors' joint written report and oral testimony from them and from a deaf-school interpreter through whom they had attempted to communicate with petitioner. The report concluded that Jackson's almost non-existent communication skill, together with his lack of hearing and his mental deficiency, left him unable to understand the nature of the charges against him or to participate in his defense. One doctor testified that it was extremely unlikely that petitioner could ever learn to read or write and questioned whether petitioner even had the ability to develop any proficiency in sign language. He believed that the interpreter had not been able to communicate with petitioner to any great extent and testified that petitioner's "prognosis appears rather dim." The other doctor testified that even if Jackson were not a deaf mute, he would be incompetent to stand trial, and doubted whether petitioner had sufficient intelligence ever to develop the necessary communication skills. The interpreter testified that Indiana had no facilities that could help someone as badly off as Jackson to learn minimal communication skills.

On this evidence, the trial court found that Jackson "lack[ed] comprehension sufficient to make his defense," § 9–1706a, and ordered him committed to the Indiana Department of Mental Health until such time as that Department should certify to the court that "the defendant is sane."

* * *

For the reasons set forth below, we conclude that, on the record before us, Indiana cannot constitutionally commit the petitioner for an indefinite period simply on account of his incompetency to stand trial on the charges filed against him. Accordingly, we reverse.

* * *

Equal Protection

Because the evidence established little likelihood of improvement in petitioner's condition, he argues that commitment under § 9–1706a in his case amounted to a commitment for life. This deprived him of equal protection, he contends, because, absent the criminal charges pending against him, the State would have had to proceed under other statutes generally applicable to all other citizens: either the commitment procedures for feeble-minded persons, or those for mentally ill persons. He argues that under these other statutes (1) the decision whether to commit would have been made according to a different standard, (2) if commitment were warranted, applicable standards for release would have been more lenient, (3) . . . he could have been assigned to a special institution affording appropriate care, and (4) he would then have been entitled to certain privileges not now available to him.

In *Baxstrom v. Herold*, 383 U.S. 107, 86 S.Ct. 760, 15 L.Ed.2d 620 (1966), the Court held that a state prisoner civilly committed at the end of his prison sentence on the finding of a surrogate was denied equal protection when he was deprived of a jury trial that the State made generally available to all other persons civilly committed. Rejecting the State's argument that Baxstrom's conviction and sentence constituted adequate justification for the difference in procedures, the Court said that "there is no conceivable basis for distinguishing the commitment of a person who is nearing the end of a penal term from all other civil commitments." . . . The Court also held that Baxstrom was denied equal protection by commitment to an institution maintained by the state corrections department for "dangerously mentally ill" persons, without a judicial determination of his "dangerous propensities" afforded all others so committed.

If criminal conviction and imposition of sentence are insufficient to justify less procedural and substantive protection against indefinite commitment than that generally available to all others, the mere filing of criminal charges surely cannot suffice. . . .

*   *   *

Consequently, we hold that by subjecting Jackson to a more lenient commitment standard and to a more stringent standard of release than those generally applicable to all others not charged with offenses, and by thus condemning him in effect to permanent institutionalization without the showing required for commitment or the opportunity for release afforded by [the commitment statutes for those with mental illness and those with mental retardation], Indiana deprived petitioner of equal protection of the laws under the Fourteenth Amendment.

Due Process

For reasons closely related to those discussed in Part II above, we also hold that Indiana's indefinite commitment of a criminal defendant solely on account of his incompetency to stand trial does not square with the Fourteenth Amendment's guarantee of due process.

*   *   *

The States have traditionally exercised broad power to commit persons found to be mentally ill. The substantive limitations on the exercise of this power and the procedures for invoking it vary drastically among the States. The particular fashion in which the power is exercised—for instance, through various forms of civil commitment, defective delinquency laws, sexual psychopath laws, commitment of persons acquitted by reason of insanity—reflects different combinations of distinct bases for commitment sought to be vindicated. The bases that have been articulated include dangerousness to self, dangerousness to others, and the need for care or treatment or training. Considering the number of persons affected, it is perhaps remarkable that the substantive constitutional limitations on this power have not been more frequently litigated.

We need not address these broad questions here. It is clear that Jackson's commitment rests on proceedings that did not purport to bring into play, indeed did not even consider relevant, *any* of the articulated bases for exercise of Indiana's power of indefinite commitment. The state statutes contain at least two alternative methods for invoking this power. But Jackson was not afforded any "formal commitment proceedings addressed to [his] ability to function in society," or to society's interest in his restraint, or to the State's ability to aid him in attaining competency through custodial care or compulsory treatment, the ostensible purpose of the commitment. At the least, due process requires that the nature and duration of commitment bear some reasonable relation to the purpose for which the individual is committed.

We hold, consequently, that a person charged by a State with a criminal offense who is committed solely on account of his incapacity to proceed to trial cannot be held more than the reasonable period of time necessary to determine whether there is a substantial probability that he will attain that capacity in the foreseeable future. If it is determined that this is not the case, then the State must either institute the customary civil commitment proceeding that would be required to commit indefinitely any other citizen, or release the defendant. Furthermore, even if it is determined that the defendant probably soon will be able to stand trial, his continued commitment must be justified by progress toward that goal. In light of differing state facilities and procedures and a lack of evidence in this record, we do not think it appropriate for us to attempt to prescribe arbitrary time limits. We note, however, that petitioner Jackson has now been confined for three and one-half years on a record that sufficiently establishes the lack of a substantial probability that he will ever be able to participate fully in a trial.

* * *

IV

Disposition of the Charges

Petitioner also urges that fundamental fairness requires that the charges against him now be dismissed. The thrust of his argument is that the record amply establishes his lack of criminal responsibility at the time the crimes are alleged to have been committed. . . .

Both courts and commentators have noted the desirability of permitting some proceedings to go forward despite the defendant's incompetency. For instance, § 4.06(3) of the Model Penal Code would permit an incompetent accused's attorney to contest any issue "susceptible of fair determination prior to trial and without the personal participation of the defendant." An alternative draft of § 4.06(4) of the Model Penal Code would also permit an evidentiary hearing at which certain defenses, not including lack of criminal responsibility, could be raised by defense counsel on the basis of which the court might quash the indictment. Some States have statutory provisions permitting pretrial motions to be made or even allowing the incompetent defendant a trial at which to establish his innocence, without permitting a conviction. We do not read this Court's previous decisions to preclude the States from allowing, at a minimum, an incompetent defendant to raise certain defenses such as insufficiency of the indictment, or make certain pretrial motions through counsel. Of course, if the Indiana courts conclude that Jackson was almost certainly not capable of criminal responsibility when the offenses were committed, dismissal of the charges might be warranted. But even if this is not the case, Jackson may have other good defenses that could sustain dismissal or acquittal and that might now be asserted. We do not know if Indiana would approve procedures such as those mentioned here, but these possibilities will be open on remand.

Reversed and remanded.

QUESTIONS AND COMMENTS

1.   *Analyzing* Jackson. With respect to the equal protection basis for *Jackson,* is the Court correct when it concludes that persons found incompetent to stand trial are similarly situated to civil committees or to prisoners who have served their sentences? Is the Court's finding in this regard consistent with its decision in *Jones v. United States*, reprinted in Chapter Eight, Part V.A, which held that persons acquitted by reason of insanity and civil committees are not similarly situated? With respect to the due process basis of *Jackson,* would the Court's holding authorize hospitalization of an incompetent individual beyond the maximum sentence permitted for the alleged crime?

2.   *State implementation of* Jackson. Reaction to *Jackson* has been diverse. As of 2012, 11 states place a specific time limit on restoration commitment (ranging from six months to five years, with most limiting the period to nine months), 11 states do not place any upper limit on the duration of commitment for restoration of competency purposes, and 20 states tie the duration of confinement to the sentence connected with the charge, with the result that the cap in some states can be as long as twenty years or, in Pennsylvania for a murder charge, life. In the remaining states, commitment is based on a finding of dangerousness, and thus technically avoids the *Jackson* limitation. Nicolas Rosinia, *How "Reasonable" Has Become Unreasonable: A Proposal for Rewriting the Lasting Legacy of* Jackson v. Indiana, 89 Wash. U. L. Rev. 673, 689–90 (2012). Also of note are court rulings that a *mandatory* period of hospitalization, of up to six months, is permissible for *anyone* found incompetent to stand trial. See, e.g., *United*

States v. Ferro, 321 F.3d 756 (8th Cir. 2003), cert. denied, 540 U.S. 878, 124 S.Ct. 296, 157 L.Ed.2d 142 (2003) (upholding an automatic four-month detention even when evaluators conclude restoration is not possible, because that period allowed a more careful and accurate diagnosis and was limited in length, and because "the miracles of science suggest that few conditions are truly without the possibility of improvement.").

A separate but analogous question is when the state must dismiss charges against an incompetent defendant. The Supreme Court in *Jackson* avoided deciding this issue. As a result, even if the state is required to release or civilly commit an incompetent person under *Jackson,* it is not required to dismiss the charge. Many states link dismissal with the end of the "*Jackson* treatment period," others do not provide for dismissal until after release from civil commitment, and several make no explicit provision for dismissal or dismiss "without prejudice" to the state's ability to recharge. See Grant H. Morris & J. Reid Meloy, *Out of Mind? Out of Sight: The Uncivil Commitment of Permanently Incompetent Criminal Defendants,* 27 U. C. Davis L.Rev. 1, 22 n.106 (1993). For instance, Florida requires dismissal of charges against an incompetent defendant charged with a felony after 5 years, but the dismissal may be without prejudice. Fla.Stat. § 916.145.

3.   *The clinical perspective.* How sensible are the various approaches adopted by the states in response to *Jackson?* Shortly after that decision, Alan Stone, at one time president of the American Psychiatric Association, asserted that, six months should be the outer limit for hospitalization of defendants found incompetent in most cases:

> Six months is a period much longer than that shown to be necessary to treat most civilly committed patients, particularly since the advent of drug therapy. It is my belief that after 6 months, the vast majority of the alleged incompetents will be in one of two categories: those who are competent to stand trial, and those who are suffering from mental disabilities, such as mental retardation, brain damage, or chronic deteriorated states such that restoration to competency, ever, is unlikely. The first group should be brought to trial, and charges against the second group should be dropped. A small residual category of persons not clearly in either group could, under carefully reviewed procedures, be confined for another 6 months and then disposed of as previously indicated. In the case of those charged with minor offenses, the time should be even shorter and the reviewing court should promptly consider alternatives to prolonged incarceration such as probation, outpatient care, or dismissal of the charges. Courts should, of course, be attentive to any tendency to subvert the previously discussed limits by periodic recommitments on dubious minor charges.

Alan Stone, Mental Health and Law: A System in Transition 212–13 (1975); see also Rosinia, supra, at 694–95 (collecting several studies conducted between 1978 and 2008 indicating that all or almost all individuals in the samples studied were restored to competence in well under six months). Note, however, that these studies and Dr. Stone's comments do not take into account delays in getting effective treatment that occur when patients refuse competency-restoring medication. When this occurs, it may take several months before the judicial process allows clinicians to proceed with appropriate psychiatric care.

4.   *Reform proposals. Jackson's* ruling that a person charged with a criminal offense who is not restorable to competency must either be released or civilly committed has been attacked from two directions. From the state's point of view, *Jackson* is problematic because it results in release (or relatively insecure civil confinement) of dangerous, mentally unstable individuals. From the defendant's perspective, *Jackson* as implemented results in prolonged confinement of those who have not been found guilty of any crime; indeed, as noted above, many states still permit periods of hospitalization ranging well beyond six months. These two strains of thought have coalesced into a suggestion that, after reasonable attempts at restoration have been made, defendants who remain incompetent should be tried.

The proposal that unrestorably incompetent defendants be tried comes in several forms: (1) At the end of trial but before a verdict is reached, the court determines—along the lines suggested by *Wilson* when dealing with amnesic defendants (see pp. 1132–1133)—whether the defendant's participation was necessary and lacking. If so, no verdict is reached; if not, the factfinder reaches a verdict and it stands; (2) The defendant is tried through to verdict at an "innocent only" trial, which results in release of the defendant if acquittal results, and a vacation of the verdict and a "*Jackson* disposition" if conviction occurs. Donal Paull, *S.B. 133: The Near Resolution of a Major Problem: Fitness in the Criminal Law*, 56 Chi–Kent L.Rev. 1107, 1118–19 (1980); (3) The defendant is tried through to verdict at a "super-fair" trial (at which a particularly high burden is placed on the prosecution and restrictions on discovery are loosened) whose verdict—whether acquittal or conviction—is final. See Robert Burt & Norval Morris, *A Proposal for the Abolition of the Incompetency Plea*, 40 U.Chi.L.Rev. 66, 77 (1972). Combining various aspects of these proposals, the American Bar Association has recommended still another approach for handling those it calls the "permanently incompetent" (i.e., those who are still incompetent after 12 to 18 months of treatment). Under the ABA proposal, permanently incompetent individuals who are charged with minor crimes are released or civilly committed. Those charged with serious felonies are tried; however, if conviction results the defendant is *committed* under the procedures and criteria applicable to those found not guilty by reason of insanity. ABA Criminal Justice Mental Health Standards, Standard 7–4.13 (1989).

Which of these procedures, if any, is constitutional under current law? Does the last paragraph of *Jackson* sanction any of these approaches? Several commentators have argued that language in *Pate* to the effect that convicting an incompetent person violates due process is dictum, since that case (as well as *Drope*) focused on the procedural issue of when a hearing to determine competency must be held, rather than on the substantive issue of when if ever a person may be tried despite incompetency. See, e.g., Burt & Morris, supra at 75–76. Moreover, in *Drope* the Court stated that deferring the competency hearing until after trial "may have advantages." 420 U.S. at 182, 95 S.Ct. at 909. If all of these options are constitutional, are any preferable to *Jackson's* approach?

5. *Incompetent defendants' right to refuse.* For most defendants found incompetent, the appropriate medical treatment is psychotropic medication— usually antipsychotic drugs, mood stabilizers, or both. At one time, many courts adhered to an "automatic bar" rule, prohibiting trial of those defendants who were restored to competency solely through medication. Bruce Winick, *Psychotropic Medication and Competence to Stand Trial*, 3 Am.Bar Found. Research J. 769, 775 (1968). The automatic bar rule prohibited trial of medicated defendants whether or not they refused the medication. The result was a revolving door effect: defendants who were rendered competent through medication and sent back for trial were returned to the hospital untried because the trial judge ordered them taken off medication, thus allowing deterioration into incompetency. Id. at 773.

Partly because of this problem, by 1990 most jurisdictions permitted forcible medication of criminal defendants found incompetent to stand trial. See *United States v. Charters*, 863 F.2d 302 (4th Cir.1988). Three U.S. Supreme Court decisions, however, have changed the legal landscape in this area. In *Washington v. Harper*, 494 U.S. 210, 110 S.Ct. 1028, 108 L.Ed.2d 178 (1990), discussed earlier in this chapter, the Court upheld a prison treatment policy that permitted forcible medication for prisoners who were dangerous to self or others. Although this decision did not change the lower courts' approach to medication in incompetency cases when the defendant was dangerous to self or others, it did lead to a more cautious attitude in some courts when the incompetent defendant was *not* dangerous but rather needed medication solely to restore him to competency. See Dora W. Klein, *Trial Rights and Psychotropic Drugs: The Case Against Administering Involuntary Medications to a Defendant During Trial*, 55 Vanderbilt L. Rev. 165, 180–84 (2002).

The second case was *Riggins v. Nevada*, 504 U.S. 127, 112 S.Ct. 1810, 118 L.Ed.2d 479 (1992), in which the Supreme Court focused on the effect of *over*medication on a defendant's ability to assist at trial. During his trial on capital charges, Riggins had been involuntarily medicated with 800 milligrams of Mellaril a day (the maximum recommended adult dose). Although he had previously agreed to take the drug, as trial approached he asked for permission to discontinue its use, arguing that it would infringe on his freedom, affect his demeanor and mental state during trial, and deny him the right to show the jury his true mental state when he offered his insanity defense. The trial court, after hearing testimony from four doctors (at least two of whom concluded that the defendant would remain competent if taken off Mellaril) denied Riggins permission to go off the medication, without stating a rationale. Riggins presented his insanity defense and testified, and was permitted to offer expert testimony describing his demeanor while unmedicated. He was convicted and sentenced to death.

Justice O'Connor, writing for the seven member majority, stated the Court was only deciding whether the medication prevented "a full and fair trial." She began by noting that, under *Washington v. Harper*, forcible medication "is impermissible absent a finding of overriding justification and a determination of medical appropriateness." Whereas in *Harper* the state had shown that medication was necessary to curtail dangerous behavior, the record in *Riggins* reflected no equivalent showing that "treatment with antipsychotic medication was medically appropriate and, considering less intrusive alternatives, essential for the sake of Riggins' own safety or the safety of others." Nor had the government shown that it "could not obtain an adjudication of Riggins' guilt or innocence by using less intrusive means." Rather, the majority found, the record suggested that the medication may have diminished the fairness of the defendant's trial: "We . . . are persuaded that allowing Riggins to present expert testimony about the effect of Mellaril on his demeanor did nothing to cure the possibility that the substance of his own testimony, his interaction with counsel, or his comprehension at trial were compromised by forced administration of Mellaril." Because the trial court had not developed the effect of the medicine in these respects, the Court remanded the case for a determination of whether Riggins suffered actual prejudice.

Justice Kennedy, in a concurring opinion not joined by any member of the Court, contended that "[i]f the State cannot render the defendant competent without involuntary medication, then it must resort to civil commitment, if appropriate;" prosecution of an involuntarily medicated defendant should be permitted only upon an "extraordinary showing." But the majority made clear that, at most, it was deciding that a competent person cannot be medicated to the extent it impairs the ability to assist counsel. The Court emphasized that "[t]he question whether a competent criminal defendant may refuse antipsychotic medication if cessation of medication would render him incompetent at trial is not before us." In the following case, it finally did confront that issue.

SELL v. UNITED STATES

Supreme Court of the United States, 2003.
539 U.S. 166, 123 S.Ct. 2174, 156 L.Ed.2d 197.

BREYER, J., delivered the opinion of the Court, in which RENHQUIST C.J., and STEVENS, KENNEDY, SOUTERS, and GINSBURG, JJ., joined.

The question presented is whether the Constitution permits the Government to administer antipsychotic drugs involuntarily to a mentally ill criminal defendant—in order to render that defendant competent to stand trial for serious, but nonviolent, crimes. We conclude that the Constitution allows the Government to administer those drugs, even against the defendant's will, in limited circumstances, i.e., upon satisfaction of conditions that we shall describe. Because the Court of Appeals did not find that the requisite circumstances existed in this case, we vacate its judgment.

I

A

Petitioner Charles Sell, once a practicing dentist, has a long and unfortunate history of mental illness. In September 1982, after telling doctors that the gold he used for fillings had been contaminated by communists, Sell was hospitalized, treated with antipsychotic medication, and subsequently discharged. In June 1984, Sell called the police to say that a leopard was outside his office boarding a bus, and he then asked the police to shoot him. Sell was again hospitalized and subsequently released. On various occasions, he complained that public officials, for example, a State Governor and a police chief, were trying to kill him. In April 1997, he told law enforcement personnel that he "spoke to God last night," and that "God told me every [Federal Bureau of Investigation] person I kill, a soul will be saved."

In May 1997, the Government charged Sell with submitting fictitious insurance claims for payment. A Federal Magistrate Judge (Magistrate), after ordering a psychiatric examination, found Sell "currently competent," but noted that Sell might experience "a psychotic episode" in the future. The judge released Sell on bail. A grand jury later produced a superseding indictment charging Sell and his wife with 56 counts of mail fraud, 6 counts of Medicaid fraud, and 1 count of money laundering.

In early 1998, the Government claimed that Sell had sought to intimidate a witness. The Magistrate held a bail revocation hearing. Sell's behavior at his initial appearance was, in the judge's words, " 'totally out of control,' " involving "screaming and shouting," the use of "personal insults" and "racial epithets," and spitting "in the judge's face." A psychiatrist reported that Sell could not sleep because he expected the FBI to " 'come busting through the door,' " and concluded that Sell's condition had worsened. After considering that report and other testimony, the Magistrate revoked Sell's bail.

In April 1998, the grand jury issued a new indictment charging Sell with attempting to murder the FBI agent who had arrested him and a former employee who planned to testify against him in the fraud case. The attempted murder and fraud cases were joined for trial.

In early 1999, Sell asked the Magistrate to reconsider his competence to stand trial. The Magistrate sent Sell to the United States Medical Center for Federal Prisoners at Springfield, Missouri, for examination. Subsequently the Magistrate found that Sell was "mentally incompetent to stand trial." He ordered Sell to "be hospitalized for treatment" at the Medical Center for up to four months, "to determine whether there was a substantial probability that [Sell] would attain the capacity to allow his trial to proceed."

Two months later, Medical Center staff recommended that Sell take antipsychotic medication. Sell refused to do so. The staff sought permission to administer the medication against Sell's will. That effort is the subject of the present proceedings.

B

We here review the last of five hierarchically ordered lower court and Medical Center determinations. First, in June 1999, Medical Center staff sought permission from institutional authorities to administer antipsychotic drugs to Sell involuntarily. A reviewing psychiatrist held a hearing and considered Sell's prior history; Sell's current persecutional beliefs (for example, that Government officials were trying to suppress his knowledge about events in Waco, Texas, and had sent him to Alaska to silence him); staff medical opinions (for example, that "Sell's symptoms point to a diagnosis of Delusional Disorder but . . . there well may be an underlying Schizophrenic Process"); staff medical concerns (for example, about "the persistence of Dr. Sell's belief that the Courts, FBI, and federal government in general are against him"); an outside medical expert's opinion (that Sell suffered only from delusional disorder, which, in that expert's view, "medication rarely helps"); and Sell's own views, as well as those of other laypersons who know him (to the effect that he did not suffer from a serious mental illness).

The reviewing psychiatrist then authorized involuntary administration of the drugs, both (1) because Sell was "mentally ill and dangerous, and medication is necessary to treat the mental illness," and (2) so that Sell would "become competent for trial." The reviewing psychiatrist added that he considered Sell "dangerous based on threats and delusions if outside, but not necessarily in[side] prison" and that Sell was "[a]ble to function" in prison in the "open population."

Second, the Medical Center administratively reviewed the determination of its reviewing psychiatrist. A Bureau of Prisons official considered the evidence that had been presented at the initial hearing, referred to Sell's delusions, noted differences of professional opinion as to proper classification and treatment, and concluded that antipsychotic medication represents the medical intervention "most likely" to "ameliorate" Sell's symptoms; that other "less restrictive interventions" are "unlikely" to work; and that Sell's "pervasive belief" that he was "being targeted for nefarious actions by various governmental . . . parties," along with the "current charges of conspiracy to commit murder," made Sell "a potential risk to the safety of one or more others in the community." The reviewing official "upheld" the "hearing officer's decision that [Sell] would benefit from the utilization of anti-psychotic medication."

Third, in July 1999, Sell filed a court motion contesting the Medical Center's right involuntarily to administer antipsychotic drugs. In September 1999, the Federal Magistrate who had ordered Sell sent to the Medical Center held a hearing. The evidence introduced at the hearing for the most part replicated the evidence introduced at the administrative hearing, with two exceptions. First, the witnesses explored the question of the medication's effectiveness more thoroughly. Second, Medical Center doctors testified about an incident that took place at the Medical Center *after* the administrative proceedings were completed. In July 1999, Sell had approached one of the Medical Center's nurses, suggested that he was in love with her, criticized her for having nothing to do with him, and, when told that his behavior was inappropriate, added " 'I can't help it.' " He subsequently made remarks or acted in ways indicating that this kind of conduct would continue. The Medical Center doctors testified that, given Sell's prior behavior, diagnosis, and current beliefs, boundary-breaching incidents of this sort were not harmless and, when coupled with Sell's inability or unwillingness to desist, indicated that he was a safety risk even within the institution. They added that he had been moved to a locked cell.

In August 2000, the Magistrate found that "the government has made a substantial and very strong showing that Dr. Sell is a danger to himself and others at the institution in which he is currently incarcerated"; that "the government has shown that anti-psychotic medication is the only way to render him less dangerous"; that newer drugs and/or changing drugs will "ameliorat[e]" any "serious side effects"; that "the benefits to Dr. Sell . . . far outweigh any risks"; and that "there is a substantial probability that" the drugs will "retur[n]" Sell "to competency." The Magistrate concluded that "the government has shown in as strong a manner as possible, that anti-psychotic medications are the only way to render the defendant not dangerous and competent to stand trial." The Magistrate issued an order authorizing the involuntary administration of antipsychotic drugs to Sell, but stayed that order to allow Sell to appeal the matter to the Federal District Court.

Fourth, the District Court reviewed the record and, in April 2001, issued an opinion. The court addressed the Magistrate's finding "that defendant presents a danger to himself or others sufficient" to warrant involuntary administration of antipsychotic drugs. After noting that Sell subsequently had "been returned to an open ward," the District Court held the Magistrate's "dangerousness" finding "clearly erroneous." The court limited its determination to Sell's "dangerousness *at this time* to himself and to those around him *in his institutional context*" (emphasis added).

Nonetheless, the District Court affirmed the Magistrate's order permitting Sell's involuntary medication. The court wrote that "antipsychotic drugs are medically appropriate," that "they represent the only viable hope of rendering defendant competent to stand trial," and that "administration of such drugs appears necessary to serve the government's compelling interest in obtaining an adjudication of defendant's guilt or innocence of numerous and serious charges" (including fraud and attempted murder). The court added that it was "premature" to consider whether "the effects of medication might prejudice [Sell's] defense at trial." The Government and Sell both appealed.

Fifth, in March 2002, a divided panel of the Court of Appeals affirmed the District Court's judgment. The majority affirmed the District Court's determination that Sell was not dangerous. The majority noted that, according to the District Court, Sell's behavior at the Medical Center "amounted at most to an 'inappropriate familiarity and even infatuation' with a nurse." The Court of Appeals agreed, "[u]pon review," that "the evidence does not support a finding that Sell posed a danger to himself or others at the Medical Center."

The Court of Appeals also affirmed the District Court's order requiring medication in order to render Sell competent to stand trial. Focusing solely on the serious fraud charges, the panel majority concluded that the "government has an essential interest in bringing a defendant to trial." It added that the District Court "correctly concluded that there were no less intrusive means." After reviewing the conflicting views of the experts, the panel majority found antipsychotic drug treatment "medically appropriate" for Sell. It added that the "medical evidence presented indicated a reasonable probability that Sell will fairly be able to participate in his trial." One member of the panel dissented primarily on the ground that the fraud and money laundering charges were "not serious enough to warrant the forced medication of the defendant."

We granted certiorari to determine whether the Eighth Circuit "erred in rejecting" Sell's argument that "allowing the government to administer antipsychotic medication against his will solely to render him competent to stand trial for non-violent offenses," violated the Constitution—in effect by improperly depriving Sell of an important "liberty" that the Constitution guarantees.

* * *

III

We turn now to the basic question presented: Does forced administration of antipsychotic drugs to render Sell competent to stand trial unconstitutionally deprive him of his "liberty" to reject medical treatment? Two prior precedents, *Harper* and *Riggins*, set forth the framework for determining the legal answer. . . . These two cases . . . indicate that the Constitution permits the Government involuntarily to administer antipsychotic drugs to a mentally ill defendant facing serious criminal charges in order to render that defendant competent to stand trial, but only if the treatment is medically appropriate, is substantially unlikely to have side effects that may undermine the fairness of the trial, and, taking account of less intrusive alternatives, is necessary significantly to further important governmental trial-related interests.

This standard will permit involuntary administration of drugs solely for trial competence purposes in certain instances. But those instances may be rare. That is because the standard says or fairly implies the following:

First, a court must find that *important* governmental interests are at stake. The Government's interest in bringing to trial an individual accused of a serious crime is important. That is so whether the offense is a serious crime against the person or a serious crime against property. In both instances the Government seeks to protect through application of the criminal law the basic human need for security. See *Riggins* (" '[P]ower to bring an accused to trial is fundamental to a scheme of "ordered liberty" and prerequisite to social justice and peace' ").

Courts, however, must consider the facts of the individual case in evaluating the Government's interest in prosecution. Special circumstances may lessen the importance of that interest. The defendant's failure to take drugs voluntarily, for example, may mean lengthy confinement in an institution for the mentally ill—and that would diminish the risks that ordinarily attach to freeing without punishment one who has committed a serious crime. We do not mean to suggest that civil commitment is a substitute for a criminal trial. The Government has a substantial interest in timely prosecution. And it may be difficult or impossible to try a defendant who regains competence after years of commitment during which memories may fade and evidence may be lost. The potential for future confinement affects, but does not totally undermine, the strength of the need for prosecution. The same is true of the possibility that the defendant has already been confined for a significant amount of time (for which he would receive credit toward any sentence ultimately imposed, see 18 U.S.C. § 3585(b)). Moreover, the Government has a concomitant, constitutionally essential interest in assuring that the defendant's trial is a fair one.

Second, the court must conclude that involuntary medication will *significantly further* those concomitant state interests. It must find that administration of the drugs is substantially likely to render the defendant competent to stand trial. At the same time, it must find that administration of the drugs is substantially unlikely to have side effects that will interfere significantly with the defendant's ability to assist counsel in conducting a trial defense, thereby rendering the trial unfair. See *Riggins* (KENNEDY, J., concurring in judgment).

Third, the court must conclude that involuntary medication is *necessary* to further those interests. The court must find that any alternative, less intrusive treatments are unlikely to achieve substantially the same results. Cf. Brief for American Psychological Association as Amicus Curiae 10–14 (nondrug therapies may be effective in restoring psychotic defendants to competence); but cf. Brief for American Psychiatric Association et al. as Amici Curiae 13–22 (alternative treatments for psychosis commonly not as effective as medication). And the court must consider less intrusive means for administering the drugs, e.g., a court order to the defendant backed by the contempt power, before considering more intrusive methods.

Fourth, as we have said, the court must conclude that administration of the drugs is *medically appropriate*, i.e., in the patient's best medical interest in light of his medical condition. The specific kinds of drugs at issue may matter here as elsewhere. Different kinds of antipsychotic drugs may produce different side effects and enjoy different levels of success.

We emphasize that the court applying these standards is seeking to determine whether involuntary administration of drugs is necessary significantly to further a particular governmental interest, namely, the interest in rendering the defendant *competent to stand trial*. A court need not consider whether to allow forced medication for that kind of purpose, if forced medication is warranted for a *different* purpose, such as the purposes set out in *Harper* related to the individual's dangerousness, or purposes related to the individual's own interests where refusal to take drugs puts his health gravely at risk. There are often strong reasons for a court to determine whether forced administration of drugs can be justified on these alternative grounds *before* turning to the trial competence question.

For one thing, the inquiry into whether medication is permissible, say, to render an individual nondangerous is usually more "objective and manageable" than the inquiry into whether medication is permissible to render a defendant competent. *Riggins* (KENNEDY, J., concurring in judgment). The medical experts may find it easier to provide an informed opinion about whether, given the risk of side effects, particular drugs are medically appropriate and necessary to control a patient's potentially dangerous behavior (or to avoid serious harm to the patient himself) than to try to balance harms and benefits related to the more quintessentially legal questions of trial fairness and competence.

For another thing, courts typically address involuntary medical treatment as a civil matter, and justify it on these alternative, *Harper*-type grounds. Every State provides avenues through which, for example, a doctor or institution can seek appointment of a guardian with the power to make a decision authorizing medication—when in the best interests of a patient who lacks the mental competence to make such a decision. And courts, in civil proceedings, may authorize involuntary medication where the patient's failure to accept treatment threatens injury to the patient or others.

If a court authorizes medication on these alternative grounds, the need to consider authorization on trial competence grounds will likely disappear. Even if a court decides medication cannot be authorized on the alternative grounds, the findings underlying such a decision will help to inform expert opinion and judicial decisionmaking in respect to a request to administer drugs for trial competence purposes. At the least, they will facilitate direct medical and legal focus upon such questions as: Why is it medically appropriate forcibly to administer antipsychotic drugs to an individual who (1) is *not* dangerous *and* (2) *is* competent to make up his own mind about treatment? Can bringing such an individual to trial *alone* justify in whole (or at least in significant part) administration of a drug that may have adverse side effects, including side effects that may to some extent impair a defense at trial? We consequently believe that a court, asked to approve forced administration of drugs for purposes of rendering a defendant competent to stand trial, should ordinarily determine whether the Government seeks, or has first sought, permission for forced administration of drugs on these other *Harper*-type grounds; and, if not, why not.

When a court must nonetheless reach the trial competence question, the factors discussed above should help it make the ultimate constitutionally required judgment. Has the Government, in light of the efficacy, the side effects, the possible alternatives, and the medical appropriateness of a particular course of antipsychotic drug treatment, shown a need for that treatment sufficiently important to overcome the individual's protected interest in refusing it?

IV

The Medical Center and the Magistrate in this case, applying standards roughly comparable to those set forth here and in *Harper*, approved forced medication substantially, if not primarily, upon grounds of Sell's dangerousness to others. But the District Court and the Eighth Circuit took a different approach. The District Court found "clearly erroneous" the Magistrate's conclusion regarding dangerousness, and the Court of Appeals agreed. Both courts approved forced medication solely in order to render Sell competent to stand trial.

We shall assume that the Court of Appeals' conclusion about Sell's dangerousness was correct. But we make that assumption *only* because the Government did not contest, and the parties have not argued, that particular matter. If anything, the record before us, described in Part I, suggests the contrary.

The Court of Appeals apparently agreed with the District Court that "Sell's inappropriate behavior . . . amounted at most to an 'inappropriate familiarity and even infatuation' with a nurse." That being so, it also agreed that "the evidence does not support a finding that Sell posed a danger to himself or others at the Medical Center." The Court of Appeals, however, did not discuss the potential differences (described by a psychiatrist testifying before the Magistrate) between ordinary "over-familiarity" and the same conduct engaged in persistently by a patient with Sell's behavioral history and mental illness. Nor did it explain why those differences should be minimized in light of the fact that the testifying psychiatrists concluded that Sell was dangerous, while Sell's own expert denied, not Sell's dangerousness, but the efficacy of the drugs proposed for treatment.

The District Court's opinion, while more thorough, places weight upon the Medical Center's decision, taken after the Magistrate's hearing, to return Sell to the general prison population. It does not explain whether that return reflected an improvement in Sell's condition or whether the Medical Center saw it as permanent rather than temporary. Cf. *Harper* (indicating that physical restraints and seclusion often not acceptable substitutes for medication).

Regardless, as we have said, we must assume that Sell was not dangerous. And on that hypothetical assumption, we find that the Court of Appeals was wrong to approve forced medication solely to render Sell competent to stand trial. For one thing, the Magistrate's opinion makes clear that he did not find forced medication legally justified on trial competence grounds alone. Rather, the Magistrate concluded that Sell was dangerous, and he wrote that forced medication was "the only way to render the defendant *not dangerous and* competent to stand trial" (emphasis added).

Moreover, the record of the hearing before the Magistrate shows that the experts themselves focused mainly upon the dangerousness issue. Consequently the experts did not pose important questions—questions, for example, about trial-related side effects and risks—the answers to which could have helped determine whether forced medication was warranted on trial competence grounds alone. Rather, the Medical Center's experts conceded that their proposed medications had "significant" side effects and that "there has to be a cost benefit analysis." And in making their "cost-benefit" judgments, they primarily took into account Sell's dangerousness, not the need to bring him to trial.

The failure to focus upon trial competence could well have mattered. Whether a particular drug will tend to sedate a defendant, interfere with communication with counsel, prevent rapid reaction to trial developments, or diminish the ability to express emotions are matters important in determining the permissibility of medication to restore competence, *Riggins* (KENNEDY, J., concurring in judgment), but not necessarily relevant when dangerousness is primarily at issue. We cannot tell whether the side effects of antipsychotic medication were likely to undermine the fairness of a trial in Sell's case.

Finally, the lower courts did not consider that Sell has already been confined at the Medical Center for a long period of time, and that his refusal to take antipsychotic drugs might result in further lengthy confinement. Those factors, the first because a defendant ordinarily receives credit toward a sentence for time served, 18 U.S.C. § 3585(b), and the second because it reduces the likelihood of the defendant's committing future crimes, moderate—though they do not eliminate—the importance of the governmental interest in prosecution.

V

For these reasons, we believe that the present orders authorizing forced administration of antipsychotic drugs cannot stand. The Government may pursue its request for forced medication on the grounds discussed in this opinion, including grounds related to the danger Sell poses to himself or others. Since Sell's medical condition may have changed over time, the Government should do so on the basis of current circumstances. The judgment of the Eighth Circuit is vacated, and the case is remanded for further proceedings consistent with this opinion. It is so ordered.

QUESTIONS AND COMMENTS

1. *Alternative grounds for forcible medication. Sell* states that forcible medication "solely for trial competency purposes . . . may be rare." But it also indicates that forcible medication that restores competency may be justifiable on alternative grounds, such as a finding that the defendant is dangerousness to self or others, assuming the medication is "medically appropriate" (as per *Harper*) and would not affect trial rights (as per *Riggins*). Was Sell dangerous? What was the Supreme Court's view on this issue?

Some caselaw suggests that dangerousness is defined somewhat differently in this setting than in other settings. Consider *United States v. Weston*, 255 F.3d 873 (D.C.Cir.2001), decided before *Sell*. On July 24, 1998 Russell Weston, apparently believing that an evil machine was housed inside the United States Capitol building, allegedly forced his way past security checkpoints at the Capitol, shooting and killing two officers of the Capitol Police and seriously wounding a third officer. He was found incompetent to stand trial due to schizophrenia, but refused antipsychotic medication. A panel of the D.C. Circuit had concluded that antipsychotic medication was not needed to contain his dangerousness. As later described by the full court, the panel held that:

> Weston's situation in confinement—total seclusion and constant observation—obviated any significant danger he might pose to himself or others. There appears no basis to believe that Weston's worsening condition renders him more dangerous given his near-total incapacitation. Weston remains in seclusion under constant observation. Absent a showing that Weston's condition now exceeds the institution's ability to contain it through his present state of confinement, the prior decision appears to preclude a finding of dangerousness. . . . Accordingly, to medicate Weston, the government must prove that restoring his competence to stand trial is necessary to accomplish an essential state policy.

For a similar holding, post-*Sell*, see *United States v. Grape*, 509 F.Supp.2d 484, 494 (W.D. Pa. 2007) (defendant not a danger in confinement).

Consider also the case of Jared Loughner. On March 3, 2011, a federal grand jury in Arizona indicted Loughner on multiple charges, including the murder of a federal judge and several other federal employees and the attempted assassination of a member of Congress (Gabrielle Giffords). Found incompetent to stand trial two months later, Loughner was sent to the Federal Medical Center in Springfield, Missouri. When he refused medication, the staff declared him a danger to others, based on evidence that he had thrown a plastic chair at a staff member, spat at his attorney, and thrown a wet roll of toilet paper at a camera. A three-judge panel of the Ninth Circuit found that Loughner's interest in avoiding the possible side effects of the medication was more "immediate" than the government interest in preventing harm to others, noting that the government "has managed to keep Loughner in custody for over six months without injury to anyone." However, six days after this opinion was handed down, the staff at Springfield concluded that Loughner was very depressed and "an immediate threat to himself" and still needed medication, based on evidence that he would often cry for hours at a time, engaged in so much pacing that he began limping, and refused to eat many of his meals and stayed awake for twenty-four hours at a time. Additionally, on at least one occasion he stated "I want to die. Give me the injection, kill me now." The defense argued that these symptoms could be handled through use of minor tranquilizers, but the same three-judge panel denied Loughner's request for an injunction. Another three-judge panel affirmed this decision four months later. See Christopher Slobogin, Sell's *Conundrums: The Right of Incompetent Defendants to Refuse Anti–Psychotic Medication*, 89 Wash. U. L. Rev. 1523, 1528–29 (2012). If a defendant assaults someone on a hospital ward, does this indicate a risk of further aggression that is sufficient to justify forcible medication? Is months or years of confinement in an isolation room (the primary alternative for both Weston and Loughner) "less intrusive" than medication? Is the answer to this question the same if the danger is to self rather than to others?

Are there other alternative justifications for forcibly medicating a defendant found incompetent to stand trial? What if the person is not only incompetent to stand trial but also incompetent to make treatment decisions? If the latter type of incompetency permits forcible medication, doesn't *Sell* become virtually moot? See Robert Schopp, *Involuntary Treatment and Competence to Proceed in the Criminal Process*, 24 Beh. Sci. & L. 495, 502–10 (2006) (arguing that virtually every person who is incompetent to stand trial is incompetent to make treatment decisions and thus should not have a right to refuse). Does Justice Breyer recognize this point, reject it, or ignore it? Look at the penultimate paragraph in Part III of the *Sell* opinion.

A separate question has to do with the defense attorney's role in these cases. Is it ethical for a defense attorney to argue that his or her client is not dangerous or is not incompetent to make treatment decisions, knowing that winning the argument will mean no effective treatment will occur? As noted earlier, the longer the duration between the onset of serious psychosis and treatment, the more likely long-term disability will result, Max Marshall et al., *Association Between Duration of Untreated Psychosis and Outcome in the Cohorts of 'First Episode' Patients: A Systematic Review*, 62 Arch. Gen. Psychiatry 975 (2005), and quick withdrawal from treatment, sought by the defense in *Loughner*, is likely to be more damaging than slow withdrawal. See J. Moncreiff, *Does Antipsychotic Withdrawal Provoke Psychosis? Review of the Literature on Rapid Onset Psychosis (Supersenstivity Psychosis) and Withdrawal–Related Relapse*, 114 Acta Psychiatria Scandinavica 3 (2006). See also Thomas H. McGlashan, *Schizophrenia in Translation: Is Active Psychosis Neurotoxic?*, 32 Schizophrenia Bull. 609, 613 (2006) (discussing evidence that the longer one is psychotic the less likely remission will occur and the more damage, usually irreversible, is done to one's brain).

2. *Important government interest.* Assuming an alternative justification is not available, *Sell* permits forcible medication for the sole purpose of restoring a defendant to competency only if: (1) an important government interest is at stake; (2) the medication is substantially likely to achieve restoration and substantially unlikely to have side effects that will infringe trial rights; (3) the medication is the least intrusive means of achieving the government's aim; and (4) the medication is medically appropriate. The following notes address these four issues.

The first criterion—the importance of the government interest—itself involves consideration of two issues: which types of prosecutions are so serious that they presumptively trump a medication refusal and when is that presumption overcome because the government interest in protecting society can be met without forcibly medicating a defendant? In analyzing offense seriousness, some federal courts have looked at the relevant statutory maximum, while others have looked at the (usually much lower) federal guidelines maximum (see pp. 767–772 for a discussion of sentencing under guidelines systems). Compare *United States v. Evans*, 404 F.3d 227, 237–38 (4th Cir. 2005) (holding that the statutory maximum is the appropriate benchmark because it determines the right to jury trial and because guidelines sentences cannot be predicted pre-trial) with *United States v. Hernandez–Vasquez*, 506 F.3d 811 (9th Cir.2007) (noting that while the guidelines "no longer are mandatory, they are the best available predictor of the length of a defendant's incarceration [and] any difficulty in estimating the likely guideline range exactly is an insufficient reason to ignore *Sell's* direction that courts should consider the specific circumstances of individual defendants in determining the seriousness of a crime."). Some state courts are even more generous in defining when a crime is serious for purposes of *Sell*. See State v. Fairley, 2012 WL 2464869 (Del. 2012) (charges arising out of threatening neighbors with a hammer); State v. Seekins, 299 Conn. 141, 8 A.3d 491 (2010) (possession of marijuana). Courts have also been influenced by other factors in determining the importance of the government's prosecution. See, e.g., *Hernandez–Vasquez*, supra (92–115 month potential guidelines sentence, together with prior convictions for molesting child under 15 and assaulting a corrections officer, is sufficiently serious); *United States v. Dumeny*, 295 F.Supp.2d 131, 132 (D. Me. 2004) (maximum 10–year sentence for possession of firearm by person previously committed to a mental health institute not sufficiently serious); *United States v. Valenzuela–Puentes*, 479 F.3d 1220, 1225 (10th Cir. 2007) (6–to–8–year maximum guidelines sentence for illegally entering the United States sufficiently serious, given defendant's long criminal history); *United States v. Lindauer*, 448 F.Supp.2d 558, 562 (S.D.N.Y. 2006) (10–year maximum sentence for failing to register as an Iraqi agent and engaging in financial transactions with Iraqi agents was insufficiently serious where defendant was alleged only to have met with Iraqi agents and to have delivered a letter pleading Iraq's case to the home of a government official). What are the possible problems with considering the defendant's prior record or alleged actions at the time of the crime in determining offense seriousness?

More complicated still is calibrating the impact of pre-trial and post-release detention on the determination of whether the government's interest in forcible medication is "important" under *Sell*. In *United States v. Evans*, supra, the court held that pre-trial confinement of two years did not outweigh the fact that the defendant still faced eight years in prison if convicted (at least under the statutory maximum; the guidelines sentence in this case was 14–20 months). In *Grape*, supra, the court was willing to consider the likelihood that, if released, Grape would be civilly committed and thus society protected, but ultimately decided that the seriousness of Grape's charges (which upon conviction would bring minimum sentences of 10 and 15 years) outweighed this consideration. In *United States v. Rodman*, 446 F.Supp.2d 487, 496–97 (D.S.C. 2006), the court noted that Rodman had already been held for almost the entire duration of time he'd have been imprisoned if convicted, and also noted that, if tried, Rodman would probably be found not guilty by reason of insanity; thus, the court held, rather than forcibly medicate Rodman and trying him, the state should simply commit him.

Should pre-trial and potential future confinement be relevant in determining the importance of the government's interest under *Sell*? Consider this statement in *Weston*:

We . . . do not believe that the "governmental interest in medicating a defendant in order to try him is diminished . . . by the option of civil commitment." The civil commitment argument assumes that the government's essential penological interests lie only in incapacitating dangerous offenders. It ignores the retributive, deterrent, communicative, and investigative functions of the criminal justice system, which serve to ensure that offenders receive their just deserts, to make clear that offenses entail consequences, and to discover what happened through the public mechanism of trial. Civil commitment addresses none of these interests.

More fundamentally, is the Court in *Sell* correct when it states that "[t]he defendant's failure to take drugs voluntarily . . . may mean lengthy confinement in an institution for the mentally ill . . . "? On what ground could such commitment take place? If the defendant is dangerous, then isn't forcible medication permissible under *Harper*, treatment that might end up restoring the competency of the defendant? If the defendant is not dangerous, is the Court stating that, nonetheless, he or she may continue to be confined, albeit "in an institution for the mentally ill"? What are the arguments that such a detention would be unconstitutional?

If detention is permissible and occurs, should the defendant have a right to refuse medication while committed? Recall that all states allow forced medication of civilly committed persons if they are imminently dangerous and/or incompetent to make treatment decisions. If the committed defendant does not have a right to refuse, and the medication works, can the defendant then be tried? If the committed defendant continues to have a right to refuse and exercises that right, then, analogous to disposition under *Jackson v. Indiana*, should charges be dismissed? Alternatively, should proposals to permit trial of incompetent defendants, described in note 4 on pp. 1157–1158, be adapted to permit trial of defendants who are unrestorably incompetent simply because they refuse medication? *Sell* does not answer any of these questions.

3.   *Effects of medication.* A good example of a court struggling with the second *Sell* criterion—which involves gauging the likelihood medication will restore competency without infringing trial rights—is found in *Weston*, supra:

[Weston] claims that the fit between involuntary medication and the government's interest is not sufficiently tight in two respects. First, he argues that the medication will not restore his competence to stand trial because he is not likely to respond to it. Second, he contends that the medication's mind-altering properties and likely side effects will prejudice his right to a fair trial such that the government could not lawfully try him even if his competence were restored. Either way, the argument goes, there is an insufficient probability that forcible medication will satisfy the government's interest.

That antipsychotic medication must be necessary to restore Weston's competence to stand trial does not mean there must be a 100%

probability that it will produce this result.... As the Court has recognized, "necessity" may mean "absolute physical necessity or inevitability" or "that which is only convenient, useful, appropriate, suitable, proper, or conducive to the end sought." Even narrow tailoring in strict scrutiny analysis does not contemplate a perfect correspondence between the means chosen to accomplish a compelling governmental interest. The government has established a sufficient likelihood that antipsychotic medication will restore Weston's competence while preserving his right to a fair trial. The district court acknowledged that "it is not certain that the medication will restore Weston's competency," but "credit[ed] the ... testimony of the mental health experts that this outcome is likely." The government presented evidence that antipsychotic medication mitigated symptoms for at least 70 percent of patients. Dr. Johnson testified that the response rate is probably higher with the atypicals. The government also provided reason to believe that the probability of restoring competence might be higher in Weston's case because of Weston's "relatively little exposure to antipsychotic medication" and his generally positive response to the limited medication he received in 1996.

. . .

Weston points out that there is also a possibility that antipsychotic medication could prejudice his right to a fair trial by, for instance, altering his courtroom demeanor, interfering with his recollection and ability to testify, and obstructing his right to present an insanity defense. We agree with the district court that "[t]here is no reason to conclude, at this time, that involuntary medication would preclude Weston from receiving a fair trial." The general right to a fair trial includes several specific rights such as the right to be tried only while competent, that is, while able to understand the proceedings, consult with counsel, and assist in the defense. As we determined, there is a sufficiently high probability that antipsychotic medication will restore Weston's competence to stand trial. The district court found and the evidence indicates that "a strong likelihood exists that medication will *enhance* some of Weston's trial rights, particularly his right to consult with counsel and to assist in his defense."[6]

Another aspect of the right to a fair trial is Weston's right to testify and "to present his own version of events in his own words." The defense is

---

[6] See also Tr. at 8 (Dr. Johnson's testimony that "I would really expect him, from a mental status standpoint, to be functioning in a much enhanced manner over his current psychotic state to the point where I believe his competence could be restored"); id. at 9 (Dr. Johnson stating that "I actually firmly believe that treatment with the medication will enhance his ability to follow the issues at the trial"); Tr. at 24 (Dr. Johnson's testimony that "successful treatment would result in a decrease in his delusional thinking, hopefully a resolution of that, an increase in his attention, ability to concentrate, and a change in his affect, or the way his mood appears to someone who is looking onto the situation. His preoccupation with his delusional system has led me to believe at various points that he has also experienced some hallucinatory phenomena, and I would expect that to resolve.").

concerned that the medication might affect Weston's memory and his capacity to relate his delusions and other aspects of his mental state at the time of the crime, which in turn "may impair his ability to mount an effective insanity defense." But the record contains no basis to suppose that antipsychotic drugs will prevent Weston from testifying in a meaningful way. Rather, it indicates that medication will more likely improve Weston's ability to relate his belief system to the jury. The benefits of antipsychotic medication in terms of Weston's ability to understand the proceedings and communicate with his attorneys presumably will also translate into an improved capacity to communicate from the witness stand. And although memory loss is a potential side effect, Dr. Johnson testified that she thought "he'd be able to remember his belief system." Tr. at 50 (also stating that "I don't think the treatment would impact his memory"); see also Tr. at 4–5 (Dr. Johnson's testimony that "I don't expect him to lose the memory of his delusional beliefs as a result of treatment").

There is a possibility that the medication could affect Weston's behavior and demeanor on the witness stand such that the jury might regard his "synthetically sane" testimony as inconsistent with a claim of insanity. As Justice Kennedy put it in *Riggins*, "[i]f the defendant takes the stand . . . his demeanor can have a great bearing on his credibility and persuasiveness, and on the degree to which he evokes sympathy." We recognize this small risk, but we see little basis to suppose that the jury will take Weston's testimony (if he decides to testify) as an indication that he must have been sane at the time of the crime, or that he is making it up, or that he deserves no sympathy. There is ample evidence of Weston's history of mental illness and bizarre behavior; the jury's overall impression of Weston will depend as much on this evidence as his testimony.

The district court also correctly held that a defendant does not have an absolute right to replicate on the witness stand his mental state at the time of the crime. A defendant asserting a heat-of-passion defense to a charge of first degree murder does not have the right to whip up a frenzy in court to show his capacity for rage, nor does a defendant claiming intoxication have the right to testify under the influence. There is little meaningful distinction between these cases and medication-induced competence to stand trial. Either way, the defendant's mental state on the stand is different from the mental state he claims to have operated under at the time of the crime. The tolerable level of difference no doubt increases in a case like this where there is substantial evidence of mental state other than the defendant's present appearance.

Weston will not have to rely solely on his own testimony to show his state of mind on July 24, 1998. Involuntary medication therefore stands little chance of impairing his right to present an insanity defense. There is extensive documentation and testimony concerning Weston's delusional system, his history of mental illness, and his "behavior, appearance, speech, actions, and extraordinary or bizarre acts . . . over a significant period." Multiple experts have examined Weston and presumably may testify. Many of these examinations no doubt related to his trial competence, but "[t]he tapes and psychiatric reports . . . document Weston's delusional state over several years." There is also a taped interview in which Weston discussed his delusional beliefs with the Central Intelligence Agency. Given the wealth of expert and lay testimony and other documentation the district court described, Weston's insanity defense does not stand or fall on his testimony alone.

A third trial right that could be implicated by antipsychotic medication is Weston's right to be present at trial in a state that does not prejudice the factfinder against him. To the extent the medication alters Weston's demeanor, courtroom behavior, or reactions to events in the courtroom, it may cause the jury to see Weston in a state that might seem inconsistent with a claim of insanity. It could also produce a flattened emotional affect that could convey to the jury a lack of remorse, a critical consideration if this case proceeded to sentencing.

Here again the record indicates that medication will likely enhance rather than impair Weston's right to a fair trial. Dr. Johnson stated that medication "will alter [Weston's demeanor] to the extent that it will be more a return to his baseline non-psychotic state. I would anticipate he would have less blunting or flattening of his affect. He would be able to respond more appropriately from an emotional standpoint with his facial expression than he is now." See also Tr. at 22–24 (Dr. Johnson agreeing with the proposition that, with medication, Weston's "expressions potentially could be more appropriate to the context of what's occurring in the courtroom"; also, her testimony that "[i]t is the patient who is over-medicated or whose side effects are not managed who would demonstrate an increased lack of responsiveness").

The possibility of side effects from antipsychotic medication is undeniable, but the ability of Weston's treating physicians and the district court to respond to them substantially reduces the risk they pose to trial fairness. The district court found that Weston's doctors can manage side effects in a number of ways: "the Court credits the testimony of the government experts and Dr. Daniel, the independent expert, that the side effects of medication are manageable through adjustments in the timing and amount of the doses, and through supplementary medications." See also Tr. at 125 (Dr. Daniel's testimony that antipsychotic medications have side effects but "[g]enerally they can be treated or an adjustment made in the medication, or the medication replaced with a different one. There's generally a way to deal with the side effects."); 4 Joint Appendix 102 (Statement in Dr. Daniel's report to the district court that "the side effects can most often be managed or an alternative course of treatment provided to the benefit of the patient. General experience with antipsychotics, particularly the newer medications, indicates that given their benefits they are reasonably safe and well-tolerated.''). As the Court wrote in *Harper*, the "risks associated with antipsychotic drugs are for the most part medical ones, best assessed by medical professionals."[7]

The district court also has measures at its disposal: "If Weston is medicated and his competency is restored, the Court is willing to take whatever reasonable measures are necessary to ensure that his rights are protected. This may include informing the jurors that Weston is being administered mind-altering medication, that his behavior in their presence is conditioned on drugs being administered to him at the request of the government, and allowing experts and others to testify regarding Weston's unmedicated condition, the effects of the medication on Weston, and the necessity of medication to render Weston competent to stand trial." Weston is free to propose other options.

255 F.3d at 882–86.

The *Weston* court emphasizes several times that medication will improve Weston's ability to exercise his trial rights (see in particular note 6). Should that be the standard for determining whether medication can be imposed to restore competency? Whatever the standard for competency, is a 70% chance that medication will restore competency sufficient? Cf. *United States v. Rivera–Morales*, 160 Fed. Appx. 648 (9th Cir. 2005) ("although the court declines to determine the exact percentage of success that equates with a substantial likelihood that a defendant's competency is restored, it is clear that a chance of success that is simply more than a 50% chance of success does not suffice to meet this standard"); *Grape*, supra, at 489 (citing a study of federal defendants showing that 23.7% of those who were involuntarily medicated could not be restored).

If Weston were medicated for trial, how is the court to discover whether the medication is negatively affecting his demeanor, memory, ability to testify, or ability to consult with counsel? Should the court hold a hearing, with defense counsel as a witness? Is another evaluation necessary? If the side effects are considered serious, should the court then postpone trial while the medication is more carefully titrated (a process that could take several days or weeks)? In the alternative, should the court seek certification from defense counsel that the side effects are not serious *before* trial begins?

---

[7]   Antipsychotic drugs have progressed since Justice Kennedy discussed their side effects in *Riggins*. There is a new generation of medications having better side effect profiles. See Paul A. Nidich & Jacqueline Collins, *Involuntary Administration of Psychotropic Medication: A Federal Court Update*, 11 No. 4 Health Lawyer 12, 13 (May 1999) ("[I]n light of the progress made in the development of new antipsychotic medications since the Supreme Court's Riggins decision in 1992, the courts should revisit this issue with an open mind. . . . [Because of new atypicals,] the fear of side effects should not weigh heavily in the decision whether to treat pretrial detainees or civilly committed persons with antipsychotic medication against their will when that treatment is medically appropriate."). Although the government presently plans to medicate Weston with the older generation of typicals, it could switch to the newer atypicals if side effects from the typicals threaten to impair his right to a fair trial. The district court analyzed the side effects of both. Dr. Johnson testified that Weston cannot be treated with atypicals unless he agrees to take them orally. The parties dispute whether Weston would so agree. When Weston originally withheld consent to antipsychotic medication, he indicated that he would comply with court-ordered medication.

Finally, how is the court to analyze the effects of the medication on the defendant's ability to present an effective defense? Will expert and documentary descriptions of Weston come close to giving the jury as accurate an idea of Weston's mental problems as viewing Weston in an unmedicated state would? On this score, how can the defense desire to show the jury the defendant's unmedicated state be reconciled with the prohibition against trying incompetent defendants? One solution was proposed by the New Hampshire Supreme Court in *State v. Hayes*, 118 N.H. 458, 389 A.2d 1379 (1978). *Hayes* permits the state to compel medication of an incompetent defendant initially, but

> [i]f the defendant by his own voluntary choice, made while competent, becomes incompetent to stand trial because he withdraws from the medication, he may be deemed to have waived his right to be tried while competent. The trial court should however carefully examine the defendant on the record, while competent, to establish the following: that the defendant understands that if he is taken off the psychotropic medication he may become legally incompetent to stand trial; that he understands that he has a constitutional right not to be tried while legally incompetent; that the defendant voluntarily gives up this right by requesting that he be taken off the psychotropic medication; and that he understands that the trial will continue whatever his condition may be.

The court also held that, in the event an effective waiver is made, the defendant may still be kept on medication until the point prior to trial when withdrawing medication would reproduce most nearly the defendant's mental state at the time of the offense. Leave aside, for the moment, that doctors have no way of knowing how to do this; patterns of relapse are not consistent. For present purposes, suppose that a defendant had previously been on medication, but stopped taking it two weeks prior to the offense. *Hayes* suggests that the state should be able to forcibly medicate until two weeks prior to trial and in essence proposes an advanced directive approach in the competency to stand trial context. Does it make sense, legally, to try to replicate past mental states in this manner? Would it be medically ethical to do so? If the defendant had been off medication for six months before the alleged offense, should his trial be delayed for six months after achieving competency? Can a defendant "waive" the right to be tried while competent (an issue discussed further on p. 1197)?

4. *Least intrusive means.* The evidence adduced in *Grape*, supra, on this third *Sell* criterion and the court's analysis of it is typical:

> Both doctors agreed that treatment other than medication may be helpful but only if such treatment was administered after, or in conjunction with, the administration of antipsychotic medication. Given Mr. Grape's unwillingness to cooperate with virtually everyone and his refusal to believe that he is suffering from any problems, an Order from this Court directing him to take his medications would be futile. If he disobeyed such an Order, which all parties expect that he would, we do not have any practical punishment option to coerce him to obey an

Order, as he is already confined in a single cell in a lock down unit at a medical prison. In addition, Mr. Grape's counsel conceded that less intrusive means of treating Mr. Grape are not available. We therefore find that less intrusive means are not available to the Court. We expect that the medical staff will continue to try to persuade Mr. Grape to take his medications. As noted, Dr. Sarrazin's plan clearly contemplates as one of its goals the voluntary participation of Mr. Grape with any medication treatment.

509 F.Supp.2d at 499.

One possible alternative to medication is cognitive behavioral therapy (CBT), described in more detail at pp. 12–14. CBT has been described as "a promising intervention for recovery and improved long-term outcome in individuals with early psychosis." Young–Chul Chung, et al., *Group Cognitive–Behavioral Therapy for Early Psychosis*, 27 Cognitive Therapy & Research 2, 403, 404 (2013). However, CBT is not very effective during an acute phase of psychosis, unless accompanied by medication. Nicholas Tarrier and Til Wykes, *Is There Evidence that Cognitive Behavior Therapy is an Effective Treatment for Schizophrenia? A Cautious or Cautionary Tale?* 42 Behavior Research & Therapy 1379 (2004). Additionally, many people found incompetent may not believe they are ill and thus might resist any type of talking therapy. See *United States v. Ruiz–Gaxiola*, 623 F.3d. 684, 702–703 (9th Cir. 2010) (stating that if the defendant "does not believe he is mentally ill and does not believe he needs treatment of any kind," he will not "participate voluntarily in therapy," rendering the possibility of alternative treatments moot).

5. *Medically appropriate*. Since *Sell* reiterated *Riggins'* requirements, a number of courts have become quite strict in monitoring this fourth *Sell* criterion. For instance, in *United States v. Hernandez–Vasquez*, 506 F.3d 811, 819 (9th Cir. 2007), the court held that:

Sell does not identify a requisite degree of specificity concerning the drugs to be used for involuntary medication. However, it does imply that a court should consider these issues at a detailed level: "The specific kinds of drugs at issue may matter here as elsewhere. Different kinds of antipsychotic drugs may produce different side effects and enjoy different levels of success." . . . Accordingly, we hold that a *Sell* order must provide some limitations on the specific medications that may be administered and the maximum dosages and duration of treatment. At a minimum, to pass muster under Sell, the district court's order must identify: (1) the specific medication or range of medications that the treating physicians are permitted to use in their treatment of the defendant, (2) the maximum dosages that may be administered, and (3) the duration of time that involuntary treatment of the defendant may continue before the treating physicians must report back to the court on the defendant's mental condition and progress. By setting such parameters within which physicians must operate, district courts will leave physicians enough discretion to act quickly to respond to changes in the defendant's condition. Moreover, the Government or the defendant may move to alter the court's order as the circumstances change and more becomes known about the defendant's response to the medication.

Some courts have also required use of atypical medications as opposed to older medications, as a means of minimizing side effects. See, e.g., *United States v. Gomes*, 387 F.3d 157, 162 (2d Cir. 2004).

6. *The impact of* Sell. It has been estimated that up to 75% of criminal defendants who are found incompetent to stand trial refuse medication. Robert Miller et al., *The Right to Refuse Treatment in a Forensic Patient Population: Six–Month Review*, 17 Bull. Amer.Acad. Psychiatry & L. 107 (1989). See also Howard Zonana, *Conundrums and Controversies in Mental Health and Illness: Physicians Must Honor Refusal of Treatment to Restore Competency by Non–Dangerous Inmates on Death Row*, 38 J. Law., Med. & Ethics 764, 765 (Winter 2010) (stating that refusal rates among all people with schizophrenia are between 40 and 50%). If the right to refuse in this context depended primarily on the nature of the crime charged and were relegated to misdemeanor cases, then *Sell* might have the salutary effect of promoting diversion of mentally ill people charged with minor crimes out of the criminal justice system, if prosecutors are willing to dismiss their charges.

But consider also this description of *Sell's* possible systemic impact:

Now that the circumstances under which forcible medication solely for the purpose of competency restoration "may be rare," defense lawyers and defendants are more likely to claim incompetency, and defendants are more likely to refuse treatment. In response, courts, prosecutors, and forensic clinicians are more likely to take advantage of the *Harper/Riggins* exception to the right to refuse and find that "dangerousness" exists in a greater number of cases, and prosecutors are more likely to bring the highest possible charge to ensure it is considered "serious." In short, all parties are more likely to act pretextually, with no deserved gain for anyone, since refusing defendants either will still be detained (illegitimately) or will be released without adjudication merely because they have refused treatment.

Christopher Slobogin, *The Supreme Court's Recent Criminal Mental Health Cases: Rulings of Questionable Competence*, ABA Crim. Just. Mag. 8, 10 (Fall, 2007).

B. DECISIONAL COMPETENCY

GODINEZ v. MORAN

Supreme Court of the United States, 1993.
509 U.S. 389, 113 S.Ct. 2680, 125 L.Ed.2d 321.

JUSTICE THOMAS delivered the opinion of the Court.

This case presents the question whether the competency standard for pleading guilty or waiving the right to counsel is higher than the competency standard for standing trial. We hold that it is not.

I

On August 2, 1984, in the early hours of the morning, respondent entered the Red Pearl Saloon in Carson City, Nevada, and shot the bartender and a patron four times each with an automatic pistol. He then walked behind the bar and removed the cash register. Nine days later, respondent arrived at the apartment of his former wife and opened fire on her; five of his seven shots hit their target. Respondent then shot himself in the abdomen and attempted, without success, to slit his wrists. Of the four victims of respondent's gunshots, only respondent himself survived. On August 13, respondent summoned police to his hospital bed and confessed to the killings.

After respondent pleaded not guilty to three counts of first-degree murder, the trial court ordered that he be examined by a pair of psychiatrists, both of whom concluded that he was competent to stand trial.[1] The State thereafter announced its intention to seek the death penalty. On November 28, 1984, two and a half months after the psychiatric evaluations, respondent again appeared before the trial court. At this time respondent informed the court that he wished to discharge his attorneys and change his pleas to guilty. The reason for the request, according to respondent, was to prevent the presentation of mitigating evidence at his sentencing.

On the basis of the psychiatric reports, the trial court found that respondent

> "is competent in that he knew the nature and quality of his acts, had the capacity to determine right from wrong; that he understands the nature of the criminal charges against him and is able to assist in his defense of such charges, or against the pronouncement of the judgment thereafter; that he knows the consequences of entering a

---

[1] One of the psychiatrists stated that there was "not the slightest doubt" that respondent was "in full control of his faculties" insofar as he had the "ability to aid counsel, assist in his own defense, recall evidence and . . . give testimony if called upon to do so." The other psychiatrist believed that respondent was "knowledgeable of the charges being made against him"; that he had the ability to "assist this attorney, in his own defense, if he so desire[d]"; and that he was "fully cognizant of the penalties if convicted."

plea of guilty to the charges; and that he can intelligently and knowingly waive his constitutional right to assistance of an attorney."

The court advised respondent that he had a right both to counsel and to self-representation, warned him of the "dangers and disadvantages" of self-representation, inquired into his understanding and his awareness of his rights, and asked why he had chosen to represent himself. It then accepted respondent's waiver of counsel. The court also accepted respondent's guilty pleas, but not before it had determined that respondent was not pleading guilty in response to threats or promises, that he understood the nature of the charges against him and the consequences of pleading guilty, that he was aware of his rights he was giving up, and that there was a factual basis for the pleas. The trial court explicitly found that respondent was "knowingly and intelligently" waiving his right to the assistance of counsel, and that his guilty pleas were "freely and voluntarily" given.

On January 21, 1985, a three-judge court sentenced respondent to death for each of the murders. The Supreme Court of Nevada affirmed respondent's sentences for the Pearl Saloon murders, but reversed his sentence for the murder of his ex-wife and remanded for imposition of a life sentence without the possibility of parole.

On July 30, 1987, respondent filed a petition for post-conviction relief in state court. Following an evidentiary hearing, the trial court rejected respondent's claim that he was "mentally incompetent to represent himself," concluding that "the record clearly shows that he was examined by two psychiatrists both of whom declared [him] competent." The Supreme Court of Nevada dismissed respondent's appeal, and we denied certiorari.

Respondent then filed a habeas petition in the United States District Court for the District of Nevada. The District Court denied the petition, but the Ninth Circuit reversed. The Court of Appeals concluded that the "record in this case" should have led the trial court to "entertai[n] a good faith doubt about [respondent's] competency to make a voluntary, knowing, and intelligent waiver of constitutional rights," and that the Due Process Clause therefore "required the court to hold a hearing to evaluate and determine [respondent's] competency . . . before it accepted his decision to discharge counsel and change his pleas." [Further], the Court of Appeals held that "the state court's post-conviction ruling was premised on the wrong legal standard of competency." "Competency to waive constitutional rights," according to the Court of Appeals, "requires a higher level of mental functioning than that required to stand trial"; while a defendant is competent to stand trial if he has "a rational and factual understanding of the proceedings and is capable of assisting his counsel," a defendant is competent to waive counsel or plead guilty only if he has "the capacity for 'reasoned choice' among the alternatives available to him." The Court of Appeals determined that the trial court had "erroneously applied the standard for evaluating competency to stand trial, instead of the correct 'reasoned choice' standard," and further concluded that when examined "in light of the correct legal standard," the record did not support a finding that respondent was "mentally capable of the reasoned choice required for a valid waiver of constitutional rights."[4] The Court of Appeals accordingly instructed the District Court to issue the writ of habeas corpus within 60 days, "unless the state court allows [respondent] to withdraw his guilty pleas, enter new pleas, and proceed to trial with the assistance of counsel."

Whether the competency standard for pleading guilty or waiving the right to counsel is higher than the competency standard for standing trial is a question that has divided the federal courts of appeals[5] and state courts of last resort. We granted certiorari to resolve the conflict.

II

A criminal defendant may not be tried unless he is competent, Pate v. Robinson, and he may not waive his right to counsel or plead guilty unless he does so "competently and intelligently," Johnson v. Zerbst, 304 U.S. 458, 468 (1938). In Dusky v. United States, we held that the standard for competence to stand trial is whether the defendant has "sufficient present ability to consult with his lawyer with a reasonable degree of rational understanding" and has "a rational as well as factual understanding of the proceedings against him." While we have described the standard for competence to stand trial, however, we have never expressly articulated a standard for competence to plead guilty or to waive the right to the assistance of counsel.

Relying in large part upon our decision in Westbrook v. Arizona, 384 U.S. 150 (1966) (per curiam), the Ninth Circuit adheres to the view that the competency standard for pleading guilty or waiving the right to counsel is higher than the competency standard for standing trial. See Sieling v. Eyman, 478 F. 2d 211 (9th Cir.1973). In *Westbrook*, a two-paragraph per curiam opinion, we vacated the lower court's judgment affirming the petitioner's conviction, because there had been "a hearing on the issue of [the petitioner's] competence to stand trial," but "no hearing or inquiry into the issue of his competence to waive his constitutional right to the assistance of counsel." The Ninth Circuit has

---

[4] In holding that respondent was not competent to waive his constitutional rights, the court placed heavy emphasis on the fact that respondent was on medication at the time he sought to discharge his attorneys and plead guilty.

[5] While the Ninth Circuit and the District of Columbia Circuit, see United States v. Masthers, 176 U.S.App.D.C. 242, 247, 539 F. 2d 721, 726 (1976), have employed the "reasoned choice" standard for guilty pleas, every other circuit that has considered the issue has determined that the competency standard for pleading guilty is identical to the competency standard for standing trial. . . .

reasoned that the "clear implication" of *Westbrook* is that the *Dusky* formulation is not "a high enough standard" for determining whether a defendant is competent to waive a constitutional right. We think the Ninth Circuit has read too much into *Westbrook*, and we think it errs in applying two different competency standards.

A

The standard adopted by the Ninth Circuit is whether a defendant who seeks to plead guilty or waive counsel has the capacity for "reasoned choice" among the alternatives available to him. How this standard is different from (much less higher than) the *Dusky* standard—whether the defendant has a "rational understanding" of the proceedings—is not readily apparent to us. In fact respondent himself opposed certiorari on the ground that the difference between the two standards is merely one of "terminology," and he devotes little space in his brief on the merits to a defense of the Ninth Circuit's standard. But even assuming that there is some meaningful distinction between the "capacity for reasoned choice" and a "rational understanding" of the proceedings, we reject the notion that competence to plead guilty or to waive the right to counsel must be measured by a standard that is higher than (or even different from) the *Dusky* standard.

We begin with the guilty plea. A defendant who stands trial is likely to be presented with choices that entail relinquishment of the same rights that are relinquished by a defendant who pleads guilty: He will ordinarily have to decide whether to waive his "privilege against compulsory self-incrimination," Boykin v. Alabama, 395 U.S. 238, 243 (1969), by taking the witness stand; if the option is available, he may have to decide whether to waive his "right to trial by jury," and, in consultation with counsel, he may have to decide whether to waive his "right to confront [his] accusers," by declining to cross-examine witnesses for the prosecution. A defendant who pleads not guilty, moreover, faces still other strategic choices: In consultation with his attorney, he may be called upon to decide, among other things, whether (and how) to put on a defense and whether to raise one or more affirmative defenses. In sum, criminal defendants—not merely those who plead guilty—may be required to make important decisions once criminal proceedings have been initiated. And while the decision to plead guilty is undeniably a profound one, it is no more complicated than the sum total of decisions that a defendant may be called upon to make during the course of a trial. (The decision to plead guilty is also made over a shorter period of time, without the distraction and burden of a trial.) This being so, we can conceive of no basis for demanding a higher level of competence for those defendants who choose to plead guilty. If the *Dusky* standard is adequate for defendants who plead not guilty, it is necessarily adequate for those who plead guilty.

Nor do we think that a defendant who waives his right to the assistance of counsel must be more competent than a defendant who does not, since there is no reason to believe that the decision to waive counsel requires an appreciably higher level of mental functioning than the decision to waive other constitutional rights. Respondent suggests that a higher competency standard is necessary because a defendant who represents himself " 'must have greater powers of comprehension, judgment, and reason than would be necessary to stand trial with the aid of an attorney.' " But this has a flawed premise; the competence that is required of a defendant seeking to waive his right to counsel is the competence to waive the right, not the competence to represent himself. In Faretta v. California, 422 U.S. 806 (1975), we held that a defendant choosing self-representation must do so "competently and intelligently," but we made it clear that the defendant's "technical legal knowledge" is "not relevant" to the determination whether he is competent waive his right to counsel, and we emphasized that although the defendant "may conduct his own defense ultimately to his own detriment, his choice must be honored." Thus, while "[i]t is undeniable that in most criminal prosecutions defendants could better defend with counsel's guidance than by their own unskilled efforts," a criminal defendant's ability to represent himself has no bearing upon his competence to *choose* self-representation.

B

A finding that a defendant is competent to stand trial, however, is not all that is necessary before he may be permitted to plead guilty or waive his right to counsel. In addition to determining that a defendant who seeks to plead guilty or waive counsel is competent, a trial court must satisfy itself that the waiver of his constitutional rights is knowing and voluntary. In this sense there is a "heightened" standard for pleading guilty and for waiving the right to counsel, but it is not a heightened standard of competence.[12]

This two-part inquiry is what we had in mind in *Westbrook*. When we distinguished between "competence to stand trial" and "competence to waive [the] constitutional right to the assistance of counsel," we were using "competence to waive" as a shorthand for the "intelligent and competent waiver" requirement of Johnson v. Zerbst. This much is clear from the fact that we quoted that very language from *Zerbst* immediately after noting that the trial court had not determined whether the petitioner was competent to waive his right to counsel. (" 'This protecting

---

[12] The focus of a competency inquiry is the defendant's mental capacity; the question is whether he has the ability to understand the proceedings. The purpose of the "knowing and voluntary" inquiry, by contrast, is to determine whether the defendant actually does understand the significance and consequences of a particular decision and whether the decision is uncoerced. See *Faretta*, supra (defendant waiving counsel must be "made aware of the dangers and disadvantages of self-representation, so that the record will establish that 'he knows what he is doing and his choice is made with eyes open' "); *Boykin*, supra (defendant pleading guilty must have "a full understanding of what the plea connotes and of its consequence").

duty imposes the serious and weighty responsibility upon the trial judge of determining whether there is an intelligent and competent waiver by the accused'"). Thus, *Westbrook* stands only for the unremarkable proposition that when a defendant seeks to waive his right to counsel, a determination that he is competent to stand trial is not enough; the waiver must also be intelligent and voluntary before it can be accepted.

III

Requiring that a criminal defendant be competent has a modest aim: It seeks to ensure that he has the capacity to understand the proceedings and to assist counsel. While psychiatrists and scholars may find it useful to classify the various kinds and degrees of competence, and while States are free to adopt competency standards that are more elaborate than the *Dusky* formulation, the Due Process Clause does not impose these additional requirements. The judgment of the Court of Appeals is reversed, and the case is remanded for further proceedings consistent with this opinion.

So ordered.

The opinion of JUSTICE KENNEDY, with whom JUSTICE SCALIA joins, concurring in part and concurring in the judgment, is deleted.

JUSTICE BLACKMUN, with whom JUSTICE STEVENS joins, dissenting.

I

*   *   *

In August 1984, after killing three people and wounding himself in an attempt to commit suicide, Moran was charged in a Nevada state court with three counts of capital murder. He pleaded not guilty to all charges, and the trial court ordered a psychiatric evaluation. At this stage, Moran's competence to represent himself was not at issue.

The two psychiatrists who examined him therefore focused solely upon his capacity to stand trial with the assistance of counsel. Dr. Jack A. Jurasky found Moran to be "in full control of his faculties insofar as his ability to aid counsel, assist in his own defense, recall evidence and to give testimony if called upon to do so." Dr. Jurasky, however, did express some reservations, observing: "Psychologically, and perhaps legally speaking, this man, because he is expressing and feeling considerable remorse and guilt, may be inclined to exert less effort towards his own defense." Nevertheless, under the circumstances, Dr. Jurasky felt that Moran's depressed state of mind was not "necessarily a major consideration." Dr. William D. O'Gorman also characterized Moran as "very depressed," remarking that he "showed much tearing in talking about the episodes that led up to his present incarceration, particularly in talking about his exwife." But Dr. O'Gorman ultimately concluded that

Moran "is knowledgeable of the charges being made against him" and "can assist his attorney, in his own defense, if he so desires."

In November 1984, just three months after his suicide attempt, Moran appeared in court seeking to discharge his public defender, waive his right to counsel, and plead guilty to all three charges of capital murder. When asked to explain the dramatic change in his chosen course of action, Moran responded that he wished to represent himself because he opposed all efforts to mount a defense. His purpose, specifically, was to prevent the presentation of any mitigating evidence on his behalf at the sentencing phase of the proceeding. The trial judge inquired whether Moran was "presently under the influence of any drug or alcohol," and Moran replied: "Just what they give me in, you know, medications." Despite Moran's affirmative answer, the trial judge failed to question him further regarding the type, dosage, or effect of the "medications" to which he referred. Had the trial judge done so, he would have discovered that Moran was being administered simultaneously four different prescription drugs—phenobarbital, dilantin, inderal, and vistaril. Moran later testified to the numbing effect of these drugs, stating: "I guess I really didn't care about anything. I wasn't very concerned about anything that was going on far as the proceedings and everything were going."[1]

Disregarding the mounting evidence of Moran's disturbed mental state, the trial judge accepted Moran's waiver of counsel and guilty pleas after posing a series of routine questions regarding his understanding of his legal rights and the offenses, to which Moran gave largely monosyllabic answers. In a string of affirmative responses, Moran purported to acknowledge that he knew the import of waiving his constitutional rights, that he understood the charges against him, and that he was, in fact, guilty of those charges. One part of this exchange, however, highlights the mechanical character of Moran's answers to the questions. When the trial judge asked him whether he killed his ex-wife "deliberately, with premeditation and malice aforethought," Moran unexpectedly responded: "No. I didn't do it—I mean, I wasn't looking to kill her, but she ended up dead." Instead of probing further, the trial judge simply repeated the question, inquiring again whether Moran had acted deliberately. Once again, Moran replied: "I don't know. I mean, I don't know what you mean by deliberately. I mean, I pulled the trigger on purpose, but I didn't plan on doing it; you know what I mean?" Ignoring the ambiguity of Moran's responses, the trial judge reframed the question to elicit an affirmative answer, stating: "Well, I've previously explained to you what is meant by deliberation and premeditation. Deliberate means

---

[1] Moran's medical records, read in conjunction with the Physician's Desk Reference (46th ed. 1992), corroborate his testimony concerning the medications he received and their impact upon him. The records show that Moran was administered dilantin, an anti-epileptic medication that may cause confusion; inderal, a beta-blocker anti-arrhythmic that may cause light-headedness, mental depression, hallucinations, disorientation, and short-term memory loss; and vistaril, a depressant that may cause drowsiness, tremors, and convulsions.

that you arrived at or determined as a result of careful thought and weighing the consideration for and against the proposed action. Did you do that?" This time, Moran responded: "Yes."

It was only after prodding Moran through the plea colloquy in this manner that the trial judge concluded that he was competent to stand trial and that he voluntarily and intelligently had waived his right to counsel. Accordingly, Moran was allowed to plead guilty and appear without counsel at his sentencing hearing. Moran presented no defense, called no witness, and offered no mitigating evidence on his own behalf. Not surprisingly, he was sentenced to death.

II

[A] finding that a defendant is competent to stand trial establishes only that he is capable of aiding his attorney in making critical decisions required at trial or in plea negotiations. The reliability or even relevance of such a finding vanishes when its basic premise—that counsel will be present—ceases to exist. The question is no longer whether the defendant can proceed with an attorney, but whether he can proceed alone and uncounselled. I do not believe we place an excessive burden upon a trial court by requiring it to conduct a specific inquiry into that question at the juncture when a defendant whose competency already has been questioned seeks to waive counsel and represent himself.

The majority concludes that there is no need for such a hearing because a defendant who is found competent to stand trial with the assistance of counsel is, *ipso facto*, competent to discharge counsel and represent himself. But the majority cannot isolate the term "competent" and apply it in a vacuum, divorced from its specific context. A person who is "competent" to play basketball is not thereby "competent" to play the violin. The majority's monolithic approach to competency is true to neither life nor the law. Competency for one purpose does not necessarily translate to competency for another purpose. See Bonnie, The Competence of Criminal Defendants: A Theoretical Reformulation, 10 Behav. Sci. & L. 291, 299 (1992); R. Roesch & S. Golding, Competency to Stand Trial 10–13 (1980). [I]n Westbrook v. Arizona, 384 U. S. 150 (1966), the Court reiterated the requirement that the determination of a defendant's competency be tailored to the particular capacity in question, observing: "Although petitioner received a hearing on the issue of his competence to stand trial, there appears to have been no hearing or inquiry into the issue of his competence to waive his constitutional right to the assistance of counsel and to proceed, as he did, to conduct his own defense."

*   *   *

The majority asserts that "the competence that is required of a defendant seeking to waive his right to counsel is the competence to waive the right, not the competence to represent himself." But this assertion is simply incorrect. The majority's attempt to extricate the competence to waive the right to counsel from the competence to represent oneself is unavailing, because the former decision necessarily entails the latter. It is obvious that a defendant who waives counsel must represent himself. Even Moran, who pleaded guilty, was required to defend himself during the penalty phase of the proceedings. And a defendant who is utterly incapable of conducting his own defense cannot be considered "competent" to make such a decision, any more than a person who chooses to leap out of a window in the belief that he can fly can be considered "competent" to make such a choice.

The record in this case gives rise to grave doubts regarding respondent Moran's ability to discharge counsel and represent himself. Just a few months after he attempted to commit suicide, Moran essentially volunteered himself for execution: he sought to waive the right to counsel, to plead guilty to capital murder, and to prevent the presentation of any mitigating evidence on his behalf. The psychiatrists' reports supplied one explanation for Moran's self-destructive behavior: his deep depression. And Moran's own testimony suggested another: the fact that he was being administered simultaneously four different prescription medications. It has been recognized that such drugs often possess side effects that may "compromise the right of a medicated criminal defendant to receive a fair trial . . . by rendering him unable or unwilling to assist counsel." Moran's plea colloquy only augments the manifold causes for concern by suggesting that his waivers and his assent to the charges against him were not rendered in a truly voluntary and intelligent fashion. Upon this evidence, there can be no doubt that the trial judge should have conducted another competency evaluation to determine Moran's capacity to waive the right to counsel and represent himself, instead of relying upon the psychiatrists' reports that he was able to stand trial with the assistance of counsel.

QUESTIONS AND COMMENTS

1.   *Competency to plead guilty.* Roughly 90% of all criminal cases are resolved through pleas of guilty. Thus it would seem—contrary to the impression one gets from case law and commentary—that a criminal defendant's competency to plead guilty and participate in plea negotiations, rather than his or her competency to stand trial, should be the primary focus of the parties in most cases (as it was in earlier times—see p. 1128). Many authorities suggest that this oversight is of little practical import. For instance, the American Bar Association has stated: "Ordinarily, absent additional information bearing on defendant's competence, a finding made that the defendant is competent to stand trial should be sufficient to establish the defendant's competence to plead guilty." Criminal Justice

Mental Health Standard 7–5.1(a)(i). As the majority in *Godinez* points out, most federal courts have found that *Dusky's* language suffices in this context.

However, some differences between the two situations are worth noting. On the one hand, the person pleading guilty will not have to undergo the stress of trial. On the other, unlike the person going to trial, the person who pleads guilty necessarily waives the rights to jury trial and trial counsel, the right to confront one's accusers, and the privilege against self-incrimination. While, as *Godinez* points out, the person who is going to trial is faced with the same issues, in most cases the default is to assert rather than waive all of these rights, and counsel, rather than the defendant, is the one who decides whether to do so. This difference may explain why the Ninth Circuit rejected *Dusky's* "rational understanding" language in favor of a "rational choice" standard for determining competency to plead guilty.

In practice, would requiring "more" competency to plead guilty than to stand trial be likely to "create a class of semi-competent defendants who are not protected from prosecution because they have been found competent to stand trial, but who are denied the leniency of the plea bargaining process because they are not competent to plead guilty?" Note, *Competence to Plead Guilty: A New Standard*, 1974 Duke Law Journal 149, 170. On the other hand, does equation of the standards lead to inappropriate guilty pleas? Assume, for instance, that Jones, subject of Problem I on pp. 1134–1141, is competent to stand trial, but cannot meet the Ninth Circuit's reasoned choice test. Should he be barred from pleading guilty?

2.   *Distinguishing adjudicative competency and decisional competency.* Professor Bonnie has suggested a different way of looking at these issues that may help explain why most courts have not followed the Ninth Circuit. Richard Bonnie, *The Competence of Criminal Defendants: A Theoretical Reformulation*, 10 Behav. Sci. & L. 291 (1992). He first makes the distinction, alluded to above, between adjudicative competency and decisional competency. The adjudicative competencies, like competency to stand trial and other competency to proceed standards, focus on generalized capacities— a capacity to understand the proceedings and an ability to relate to one's attorney—and are required to protect the reliability and dignity of the criminal process. Decisional competencies, like competency to plead guilty or competency to waive an attorney, differ from adjudicative competencies because they assess the capacity to make a specified decision and are required as a means of protecting autonomy. Bonnie then analogizes pleading guilty to treatment decisionmaking, which also involves making a specific decision. This analogy enables him to make use of the notion, developed by those who have analyzed treatment decisionmaking, that the level of competency required to consent to a recommended treatment should be lower than the level of competency required for a refusal of a recommended treatment (an idea discussed at pp. 1047–1049). Applied to guilty pleas, this framework would require greater competency to make a plea that is inconsistent with advice of counsel.

In a later article developing his thesis, Professor Bonnie differentiated between the "basic understanding" test, the "basic rationality" test, the "appreciation" test, and the "reasoned choice" test (which correspond to the understanding, understanding-and-belief, appreciation, and rational manipulation tests described earlier in this chapter). Richard Bonnie, *The Competence of Criminal Defendants: Beyond* Dusky *and* Drope, 47 U. Miami L. Rev. 539 (1993). According to Bonnie, a waiver of rights consistent with counsel's advice should require only basic understanding (for waiver of most rights) or basic rationality (for pleading guilty). In contrast, a waiver *against* the advice of counsel should normally be considered valid only if the person can pass the appreciation test (for most rights) or the reasoned choice test (for pleading guilty). Id. at 577–580. Can you see how this analysis might explain why, in cases where client and attorney agree about the plea, courts are willing to equate competency to stand trial and competency to plead guilty? How would Bonnie analyze Moran's competency to plead guilty?

Consider now the following facts, taken from *United States v. Timmins*, 301 F.3d 974 (9th Cir.2002):

> The defendant, indicted on five counts of bank robbery and one count of using and carrying a firearm during a crime of violence, was offered a plea bargain of 12½ years. Though faced with overwhelming evidence against him and a possible 30–year sentence if he was convicted, he refused the plea, rejecting his counsel's strong recommendation to accept it. Because of this disagreement and further disagreement about his mental condition, Timmins requested new counsel. The new attorney stated that, although he also recommended that the defendant accept the plea agreement, the defendant would be able to aid and assist in his defense at a trial, and specifically noted that Timmins was able to discuss the strengths and weaknesses of the case and possible witnesses and strategy. He also noted that the defendant understood that his defenses were "somewhat uphill." At a hearing to determine his competency, one expert likewise concluded Timmins was able to aid and assist his attorney, while the second expert disagreed with this assessment, in large part because Timmins described his charges as "trivial." Both experts agreed, however, that Timmins was delusional and paranoid. Specifically, they noted that he had a fixed delusional belief that he was being harassed by the police and "the system" because of envy and resentment about his athletic ability and his intellect. One expert reported that Timmins was convinced he would be acquitted and the other noted that he would likely "make ineffectual arguments against the apparently strong evidence that exists against him [which] would seem to be the same as allowing any 'obviously' guilty party to proceed to trial with no defense except a denial of guilt." The judge permitted trial to proceed and the defendant was convicted. [The Ninth Circuit reversed the conviction on the ground Timmins was incompetent].

How would the Supreme Court analyze this case? Bonnie? If Timmins had instead agreed to the plea, should that fact alone change the analysis of whether he is competent, as Bonnie implies? Compare *Timmins* to *United States v. Damon*, 191 F.3d 561 (4th Cir. 1999), where the defendant pleaded guilty to capital charges with the *concurrence* of his attorneys. As the dissenting opinion described the facts:

> [T]he district court, after learning that Damon had taken medication during his stay at the hospital, asked Damon whether he understood (1) the charges against him, (2) the constitutional rights he was waiving by pleading guilty, (3) the terms of his Plea Agreement, and (4) the consequences of his guilty plea. Damon answered each question in the affirmative and in a coherent fashion. Damon also told the district court that he was satisfied with his attorneys and that he was in fact guilty of the offense to which he pled guilty. The district court also asked Damon's lawyers whether they had any reason to question Damon's competence to plead guilty. Although aware that Damon had taken some medication earlier, his lawyers, both of whom were highly experienced due to the fact that Damon was subject to the death penalty, answered no.

Id. at 567 (Williams, J., dissenting). Nonetheless the majority held that Damon's guilty plea must be overturned because the district court failed to inquire further into the effects of the anti-depressant medication Damon was taking. Id. at 565. Is this result consistent with *Godinez*?

3. *Competency to waive an attorney. Godinez* also equated competency to waive one's attorney with competency to stand trial. Would Bonnie agree with the Court's analysis on this point? Does the Court's additional requirement that waivers of counsel be "voluntary and intelligent" in effect demand a higher level of competency, or is this requirement aimed merely at ensuring the defendant "understands" the consequences of proceeding *pro se*, i.e., the fact that the defendant will be responsible for tactical, evidentiary and procedural decisions? See note 12 of the majority opinion. Should Moran have been permitted to waive his attorney? Note that even if a defendant is permitted to proceed *pro se*, the court may appoint "standby counsel" who may give the defendant legal advice so long as the defendant retains actual control over the case presented to the jury and the jury retains the perception that the defendant represents him or herself. *McKaskle v. Wiggins*, 465 U.S. 168, 104 S.Ct. 944, 79 L.Ed.2d 122 (1984).

In *Indiana v. Edwards*, 554 U.S. 164, 128 S.Ct. 2379, 171 L.Ed.2d 345 (2008), the Court revisited the waiver-of-counsel issue and concluded that a state may force counsel on a defendant who is competent to stand trial if the trial judge does not believe the defendant is "mentally competent" to represent him or herself. Justice Breyer wrote the majority opinion. He began by distinguishing *Edwards* from *Godinez*:

> We . . . conclude that *Godinez* does not answer the question before us now. . . . [T]he *Godinez* defendant sought only to change his pleas to guilty, he did not seek to conduct trial proceedings, and his ability to

conduct a defense at trial was expressly not at issue. Thus we emphasized in *Godinez* that we needed to consider only the defendant's "competence to *waive the right*." And we further emphasized that we need *not* consider the defendant's "technical legal knowledge" about how to proceed at trial. [Further], *Godinez* involved a State that sought to *permit* a gray-area defendant to represent himself. *Godinez*'s constitutional holding is that a State may do so. But that holding simply does not tell a State whether it may *deny* a gray-area defendant the right to represent himself—the matter at issue here. One might argue that *Godinez*'s grant (to a State) of permission to allow a gray-area defendant self-representation must implicitly include permission to deny self-representation. Cf. 509 U.S., at 402 ("States are free to adopt competency standards that are more elaborate than the *Dusky* formulation"). Yet one could more forcefully argue that *Godinez* simply did not consider whether the Constitution *requires* self-representation by gray-area defendants even in circumstances where the State seeks to disallow it (the question here). The upshot is that, in our view, the question before us is an open one.

Are you convinced that *Godinez* did not settle the question in *Edwards*? (Note that the Indiana Supreme Court and the dissent in *Edwards* believed that *Godinez* had settled the question.) In any event, Breyer went on to explain why a person who is competent to stand trial under *Dusky*'s standard might nonetheless be denied the right to self-representation.

[F]irst, . . . the Court's "mental competency" cases set forth a standard that focuses directly upon a defendant's "present ability to consult with his lawyer" [*Dusky*; *Drope*]. These standards assume representation by counsel and emphasize the importance of counsel. They thus suggest (though do not hold) that an instance in which a defendant who would choose to forgo counsel at trial presents a very different set of circumstances, which in our view, calls for a different standard.

. . .

Second, the nature of the problem before us cautions against the use of a single mental competency standard for deciding both (1) whether a defendant who is represented by counsel can proceed to trial and (2) whether a defendant who goes to trial must be permitted to represent himself. Mental illness itself is not a unitary concept. It varies in degree. It can vary over time. It interferes with an individual's functioning at different times in different ways. . . . In certain instances an individual may well be able to satisfy *Dusky*'s mental competence standard, for he will be able to work with counsel at trial, yet at the same time he may be unable to carry out the basic tasks needed to present his own defense without the help of counsel. The American Psychiatric Association (APA) tells us (without dispute) in its *amicus* brief filed in support of neither party that "[d]isorganized thinking, deficits in sustaining attention and concentration, impaired expressive abilities, anxiety, and other common symptoms of severe mental illnesses can impair the defendant's ability to play the significantly expanded role required for self-representation even if he can play the lesser role of represented defendant." . . .

Third, in our view, a right of self-representation at trial will not "affirm the dignity" of a defendant who lacks the mental capacity to conduct his defense without the assistance of counsel. To the contrary, given that defendant's uncertain mental state, the spectacle that could well result from his self-representation at trial is at least as likely to prove humiliating as ennobling. Moreover, insofar as a defendant's lack of capacity threatens an improper conviction or sentence, self-representation in that exceptional context undercuts the most basic of the Constitution's criminal law objectives, providing a fair trial. As Justice Brennan put it, "[t]he Constitution would protect none of us if it prevented the courts from acting to preserve the very processes that the Constitution itself prescribes."

Further, proceedings must not only be fair, they must "appear fair to all who observe them." An *amicus* brief reports one psychiatrist's reaction to having observed a patient (a patient who had satisfied *Dusky*) try to conduct his own defense: "[H]ow in the world can our legal system allow an insane man to defend himself?" The application of *Dusky*'s basic mental competence standard can help in part to avoid this result. But given the different capacities needed to proceed to trial without counsel, there is little reason to believe that *Dusky* alone is sufficient. At the same time, the trial judge, particularly one such as the trial judge in this case, who presided over one of Edwards' competency hearings and his two trials, will often prove best able to make more fine-tuned mental capacity decisions, tailored to the individualized circumstances of a particular defendant.

We consequently conclude that the Constitution permits judges to take realistic account of the particular defendant's mental capacities by asking whether a defendant who seeks to conduct his own defense at trial is mentally competent to do so. That is to say, the Constitution permits States to insist upon representation by counsel for those competent enough to stand trial under *Dusky* but who still suffer from severe mental illness to the point where they are not competent to conduct trial proceedings by themselves.

Indiana has also asked us to adopt, as a measure of a defendant's ability to conduct a trial, a more specific standard that would "deny a criminal defendant the right to represent himself at trial where the defendant cannot communicate coherently with the court or a jury." We are sufficiently uncertain, however, as to how that particular standard would work in practice to refrain from endorsing it as a federal constitutional standard here. We need not now, and we do not, adopt it.

Indiana has also asked us to overrule *Faretta*. We decline to do so. We recognize that judges have sometimes expressed concern that *Faretta*, contrary to its intent, has led to trials that are unfair. But recent empirical research suggests that such instances are not common. See, *e.g.*, Hashimoto, *Defending the Right of Self–Representation: An Empirical Look at the Pro Se Felony Defendant*, 85 N. C. L. Rev. 423, 427, 447, 428 (2007) (noting that of the small number of defendants who chose to proceed *pro se*—"roughly 0.3% to 0.5%" of the total, state felony defendants in particular "appear to have achieved higher felony acquittal rates than their represented counterparts in that they were less likely to have been convicted of felonies"). At the same time, instances in which the trial's fairness is in doubt may well be concentrated in the 20 percent or so of self-representation cases where the mental competence of the defendant is also at issue. See *id.*, at 428 (about 20 percent of federal *pro se* felony defendants ordered to undergo competency evaluations). If so, today's opinion, assuring trial judges the authority to deal appropriately with cases in the latter category, may well alleviate those fair trial concerns.

JUSTICE SCALIA, joined by JUSTICE THOMAS, author of *Godinez*, dissented:

[U]ntil today, the right of self-representation has been accorded the same respect as other constitutional guarantees. The only circumstance in which we have permitted the State to deprive a defendant of this trial right is the one under which we have allowed the State to deny *other* such rights: when it is necessary to enable the trial to proceed in an orderly fashion. That overriding necessity, we have said, justifies forfeiture of even the Sixth Amendment right to be present at trial—if, after being threatened with removal, a defendant "insists on conducting himself in a manner so disorderly, disruptive, and disrespectful of the court that his trial cannot be carried on with him in the courtroom." *Illinois* v. *Allen*, 397 U.S. 337, 343 (1970). A *pro se* defendant may not "abuse the dignity of the courtroom," nor may he fail to "comply with relevant rules of procedural and substantive law," and a court may "terminate" the self-representation of a defendant who "deliberately engages in serious and obstructionist misconduct." This ground for terminating self-representation is unavailable here, however, because Edwards was not even allowed to begin to represent himself, and because he was respectful and compliant and did not provide a basis to conclude a trial could not have gone forward had he been allowed to press his own claims.

Beyond this circumstance, we have never constrained the ability of a defendant to retain "actual control over the case he chooses to present to the jury"—what we have termed "the core of the *Faretta* right." Thus, while *Faretta* recognized that the right of self-representation does not bar the court from appointing standby counsel, we explained in *Wiggins* that "[t]he *pro se* defendant must be allowed to control the organization and content of his own defense, to make motions, to argue points of law, to participate in *voir dire*, to question witnesses, and to address the court and the jury at appropriate points in the trial." Furthermore, because "multiple voices 'for the defense'" could "confuse the message the defendant wishes to convey," a standby attorney's participation would be barred when it would "destroy the jury's perception that the defendant is representing himself."

. . . I would not adopt an approach to the right of self-representation that we have squarely rejected for other rights—allowing courts to disregard the right when doing so serves the purposes for which the right was intended. But if I were to adopt such an approach, I would remain in dissent, because I believe the Court's assessment of the purposes of the right of self-representation is inaccurate to boot. While there is little doubt that preserving individual " 'dignity' " (to which the Court refers), is paramount among those purposes, there is equally little doubt that the loss of "dignity" the right is designed to prevent is *not* the defendant's making a fool of himself by presenting an amateurish or even incoherent defense. Rather, the dignity at issue is the supreme human dignity of being master of one's fate rather than a ward of the State—the dignity of individual choice. *Faretta* explained that the Sixth Amendment's counsel clause should not be invoked to impair " 'the exercise of [the defendant's] free choice' " to dispense with the right, for "whatever else may be said of those who wrote the Bill of Rights, surely there can be no doubt that they understood the inestimable worth of free choice." Nine years later, when we wrote in *Wiggins* that the self-representation right served the "dignity and autonomy of the accused," we explained in no uncertain terms that this meant according every defendant the right to his say in court. In particular, we said that individual dignity and autonomy barred standby counsel from participating in a manner that would to "destroy the jury's perception that the defendant is representing himself," and meant that "the *pro se* defendant is entitled to preserve actual control over the case he chooses to present to the jury." In sum, if the Court is to honor the particular conception of "dignity" that underlies the self-representation right, it should respect the autonomy of the individual by honoring his choices knowingly and voluntarily made.

A further purpose that the Court finds is advanced by denial of the right of self-representation is the purpose of assuring that trials "appear fair to all who observe them." To my knowledge we have never denied a defendant a right simply on the ground that it would make his trial appear less "fair" to outside observers, and I would not inaugurate that principle here. But were I to do so, I would not apply it to deny a defendant the right to represent himself when he knowingly and voluntarily waives counsel. When Edwards stood to say that "I have a defense that I would like to represent or present to the Judge," it seems to me the epitome of both actual and apparent unfairness for the judge to say, I have heard "your desire to proceed by yourself and I've denied your request, so your attorney will speak for you from now on."

. . .

. . . [T]o hold that a defendant may be deprived of the right to make legal arguments for acquittal simply because a state-selected agent has made different arguments on his behalf is, as Justice Frankfurter wrote in *Adams*, to "imprison a man in his privileges and call it the Constitution." In singling out mentally ill defendants for this treatment, the Court's opinion does not even have the questionable virtue of being politically correct. At a time when all society is trying to mainstream the mentally impaired, the Court permits them to be deprived of a basic constitutional right—for their own good.

Today's holding is extraordinarily vague. The Court does not accept Indiana's position that self-representation can be denied " 'where the defendant cannot communicate coherently with the court or a jury.' " It does not even hold that Edwards was properly denied his right to represent himself. It holds only that lack of mental competence can under some circumstances form a basis for denying the right to proceed *pro se*. We will presumably give some meaning to this holding in the future, but the indeterminacy makes a bad holding worse. Once the right of self-representation for the mentally ill is a sometime thing, trial judges will have every incentive to make their lives easier—to avoid the painful necessity of deciphering occasional pleadings of the sort contained in the Appendix to today's opinion—by appointing knowledgeable and literate counsel.

The majority opinion described in detail Edwards's lengthy history of psychiatric hospitalizations and his struggle to maintain competence, as well as the fact that he still had some symptoms of schizophrenia at the time of his second trial. In the appendix referred to by the dissent the majority also included one of his motions, which included sentences such as: "The appointed motion of permissive intervention filed therein the court superior on, 6–26–01 caused a stay of action and apon [sic] it's [sic] expiration or thereafter three years the plan to establish a youth program to and for the coordination of aspects of law enforcement to prevent and reduce crime amoung [sic] young people in Indiana became a diplomatic act as under the Safe Streets Act of 1967, 'A omnibuc [sic] considerate agent: I membered [sic] clients within the public and others that at/production of the courts actions showcased causes.' " However, the trial judge had found Edwards competent based on numerous psychiatric reports, and the dissent noted the following facts:

> Edwards made arguments in the courtroom that were more coherent than his written pleadings. In seeking to represent himself at his first trial, Edwards complained in detail that the attorney representing him had not spent adequate time preparing and was not sharing legal materials for use in his defense. The trial judge concluded that Edwards had knowingly and voluntarily waived his right to counsel and proceeded to quiz Edwards about matters of state law. Edwards correctly answered questions about the meaning of *voir dire* and how it operated, and described the basic framework for admitting videotape evidence to trial, though he was unable to answer other questions, including questions about the topics covered by state evidentiary rules that the judge

identified only by number. He persisted in his request to represent himself, but the judge denied the request because Edwards acknowledged he would need a continuance. Represented by counsel, he was convicted of criminal recklessness and theft, but the jury deadlocked on charges of attempted murder and battery.

At his second trial, Edwards again asked the judge to be allowed to proceed *pro se.* He explained that he and his attorney disagreed about which defense to present to the attempted murder charge. Edwards' counsel favored lack of intent to kill; Edwards, self-defense. As the defendant put it: "My objection is me and my attorney actually had discussed a defense, I think prosecution had mentioned that, and we are in disagreement with it. He has a defense and I have a defense that I would like to represent or present to the Judge."

128 S.Ct. at 2390. If these were the only reasons Edwards gave for wanting to represent himself (if, in other words, he did not give other, clearly "crazy" reasons), would you as a trial judge force an attorney on him? What else would you like to know?

4. *Competency to waive the right to tried while competent.* Earlier this chapter (see pp. 1146–1148) examined the issue of whether counsel should be able to override a client's objection to a competency evaluation. Reconsider that issue now in light of the present material. What level of competency would Bonnie require of a defendant who wants to proceed to trial despite counsel's concern about competency to stand trial? Is *Edwards* relevant here as well?

5. *Competency to waive an insanity defense.* A number of other situations arise in which "decisional" competency could be implicated. According to the American Bar Association's Model Rules of Professional Conduct, for instance, the client, not the lawyer, should be the ultimate authority for all "fundamental decisions" in the criminal process. In addition to deciding whether or not to plead guilty, the rule lists as "fundamental" the decisions to waive the right to jury trial, testify, and forego an appeal. Proposed Rule 1.2(a) (Final Draft 1982). Left unclear by the ABA Rule is how much control the defendant should have over the legal strategy of the case (outside of the decision to testify).

One issue that arises occasionally in this regard is whether an insanity defense may be raised over the defendant's objection. Several courts have required a separate hearing to determine whether an objecting defendant is voluntarily and intelligently waiving the defense; if so, the defendant's wishes are honored. See, e.g., *Frendak v. United States,* 408 A.2d 364 (D.C.App.1979). In contrast, for some time the District of Columbia Circuit Court of Appeals permitted assertion of the defense over the defendant's objection, even if the defendant was *competent* to make such a decision, on the ground that convicting a person who was insane at the time of the offense would be morally repugnant. *Whalem v. United States,* 346 F.2d 812 (D.C.Cir.1965). However in *United States v. Marble,* 940 F.2d 1543

(D.C.Cir.1991), the D.C. Circuit overturned *Whalem*, primarily because Congress had since made clear, via the Insanity Defense Reform Act of 1984, that insanity is an affirmative defense in federal court, thus making its assertion the prerogative of the defense.

Under the *Whalem* approach, the defendant's wishes are to be taken into account but are not dispositive. Is this justifiable? Judge Bazelon, who wrote *Whalem,* undoubtedly would support a competent nondangerous person's right to refuse psychiatric treatment. Cf. David Bazelon, *Implementing the Right to Treatment*, 36 Chicago L.Rev. 742 (1969). How, if at all, is compelling the assertion of an insanity defense different from compelling treatment over a competent person's objection?

Under the *Frendak* approach, note that a finding of competency to stand trial does not necessarily mean the person is competent to make a decision about the insanity defense; a separate hearing is required in *all* cases. How does this result comport with *Godinez's* analysis? Bonnie's?

Consider in this regard the case of Theodore Kaczynski, a.k.a. the Unabomber. Kaczynski was charged with several capital crimes arising from deaths caused by bombs that he sent through the mail. Most mental health professionals who evaluated Kaczynski thought he was suffering from schizophrenia, in large part because of his delusion that he was being "maligned and harassed by family members and modern society." See William Glaberson, *Kaczynski's Lawyers Now Say He is Competent*, N.Y. Times, Jan. 21, 1998. Yet Kaczynski was adamant that evidence of mental aberration not be presented either at trial, in connection with an insanity or diminished capacity defense, or at sentencing in mitigation. According to his attorneys, he had a "deep and abiding fear" that he would be perceived as mentally ill, a fear he had possessed his entire life. In his famous Manifesto he had suggested that he would rather die than be subjected to the indignity of being called mentally ill. See generally, Stephen J. Dubner, *I Don't Want to Live Long*, Time, Oct. 18, 1999, at 44, 46. Either by himself or with the help of lawyers, he apparently planned instead to assert what amounted to a "necessity" defense—an argument that the letter bombs, most of which were sent to people who had some connection with technology, were a "necessary" way of alerting the world to the deaths and widespread destruction of civilization that technological "progress" will cause. William Glaberson, *Kaczynski Tries Unsuccessfully to Dismiss His Lawyers*, N.Y. Times, Jan. 8, 1998. Although the court found Kaczynski competent to stand trial, it never had to decide whether he could forego the insanity defense against his lawyers' wishes because he pleaded guilty to the charges in exchange for four life sentences (a decision he made, he later claimed, because he wanted to avoid his lawyers labeling him paranoid schizophrenic). Dubner, supra.

Was Kaczynski "competent" to waive the insanity defense? How would the Supreme Court analyze this issue? Bonnie? Would it make any difference if Kaczynski clearly acknowledged that he was mentally ill but said he could not tolerate the stigma of being so labeled? What if the reason Kaczynski gave for wanting to avoid the defense was that testimony bolstering such a defense might reveal that he had wanted a sex-change operation in 1966 and that at one time he had fantasized about mutilating his girl friend (both facts revealed in the psychiatric reports)? What if his denial that he was mentally ill stemmed from mental illness (the anosognosia condition referred to at pp. 1102–1103)? Would such a denial of a fact about himself that was highly relevant to his defense render him incompetent to stand trial? Doctor Amador, a psychologist involved in the case, wrote the following:

> In most cases involving people with schizophrenia, severe deficits in illness-awareness and the irrational compulsion to prove one's "sanity" despite life threatening consequences, are a consequence of brain dysfunction rather than manipulation or defensiveness. It was anosognosia, a neurological condition that results in the type of unawareness just described, that kept [Kaczynski] from complying with the court order to be examined by experts, as opposed to manipulation or a willful violation of the judge's decree. . . . The high prevalence of unawareness of illness in schizophrenia has been replicated in several studies. . . . Research indicates that anosognosia typically does not improve when individuals with schizophrenia are treated with antipsychotic medications. Thus, the patient with anosognosia who is treated successfully, who is less delusional, is still likely to believe he is not ill and feel the compulsion to prove this belief to be true at all costs. . . . In other words, if [a person like Kaczynski]'s anosognosia persists after treatment with antipsychotic medication and he continues to prohibit his attorneys to mount a mental illness defense, an argument once again can be made that he is incompetent to stand trial.

Xavier F. Amador & Andrew A. Shiva, *Insight into Schizophrenia: Anosognosia, Competency, and Civil Liberties*, 11 Geo. Mason Civ. Rts. L. J. 25, 26–39 (2000).

Assume that Kaczynski had not pleaded guilty and had continued to insist that mental state issues not be raised at his trial. What should the lawyers have done? Followed his wishes? Presented the defense over his objection? Withdrawn? (Under the ABA's Model Code of Professional Conduct Rule 1.16(b)(3), the lawyer may withdraw if "a client insists upon pursuing an objective that the lawyer considers repugnant or imprudent.") See generally, Christopher Slobogin & Amy Mashburn, *The Criminal Defense Lawyer's Fiduciary Duty to Clients with Mental Disability*, 68 Fordham L. Rev. 1581 (2000)(analyzing the lawyer's ethical duty in Kaczynski case and similar cases).

6. *Competency to waive presentation of mitigating evidence in capital cases.* In *Schriro v. Landrigan*, 550 U.S. 465, 127 S.Ct. 1933, 167 L.Ed.2d 836 (2007), the Supreme Court held that an attorney's failure to fully investigate mitigating evidence in a capital case is not ineffective assistance of counsel when the defendant refuses to permit any mitigating evidence to be presented, even if the defendant's demand may not be good strategy. Presumably, however, the defendant who makes such a decision must be competent to do so, and waiver must be knowing and voluntary, per *Godinez*

v. Moran and *Edwards v. Arizona.* Recall Professor Garrison's argument, at p. 1050, that for some individuals the effects of depression "appear to overcome the desire for life and health and to coerce decisions against the patient's medical interests." If the reason for prohibiting the presentation of mitigating evidence is depression, should the individual be considered competent? Was Moran competent in this respect?

Some commentators and a few courts have taken the position that even if the objecting offender is competent, the state's interest in a just outcome under the Eighth Amendment *requires* the presentation of mitigating evidence. See Linda E. Carter, *Maintaining Systemic Integrity in Capital Cases: The Use of Court–Appointed Counsel to Present Mitigating Evidence When the Defendant Advocates Death*, 55 Tenn. L.Rev. 95, 140–44 (1987); Anthony J. Casey, *Maintaining the Integrity of Death: An Argument for Restricting a Defendant's Right to Volunteer for Execution at Certain Stages in Capital Proceedings*, 30 Am. J. Crim. L. 75 (2002). How is presenting psychiatric evidence over a competent defendant's objection at a capital sentencing proceeding different from presenting evidence of insanity at trial over a competent defendant's objection (which, as the previous note indicates, few jurisdictions officially permit today)?

In light of the foregoing material, consider whether the court in *Smith v. State*, 686 N.E.2d 1264 (Ind. 1997), was correct when it affirmed Smith's plea to a capital charge and his refusal to present mitigating evidence. In his testimony at the competency hearing, Smith stated:

> I don't feel I'm incompetent, you know. I don't think my attorneys feel I'm incompetent. You know, I feel [my attorneys actions are] more of a humanitarian act now, you know, and-you know, I'm through pissing around with it. I mean, you know, I come here today to get sentenced, you know. I mean, that's what I want. You know, my attitude has not changed, you know. You probably could hire 50 psychiatrists and have my attorneys pay half of them and the prosecutor pay half of them and they would come up with 50 different evaluations, you know.
>
> . . . .
>
> . . . I know what I'm doing, you know. I'm fully aware, you know. This is one of the tests they gave me here. I want to read it to the court here, some of the questions on here, and this is how they say I'm extremely depressed, you know. I mean, I'm in prison. Everybody in prison is depressed, you know. I mean, if I was happy, I mean, . . . I wouldn't want to die if I was happy where I was at. I mean, it's no secret, you know. Prison isn't a nice place, you know. I've been in prison for the last 13 years, you know. I'm tired of being in prison, you know, and I'm at the point now where life doesn't have a whole lot of meaning for me and-you know, these are some of the questions that they-Question One, ["]I feel downhearted, blue, and sad.["] It says ["]none or little of the time, some of the time, a good part of the time, more or all of the time.["] I mean, how would anybody in prison answer that question? All of the time. I

mean, you know, I'm not living at the Hilton Hotel, you know. The second question is, ["]Morning is when I feel the best.["] You know, I don't feel good any of the time, you know. I'm miserable. You know, my life is miserable. It's a miserable existence. I don't blame anybody for it, you know. I put myself in prison, you know, and I'm dealing with what I've got to do, you know. . . . Any normal man that's in prison, you know, is, you know, going to feel downhearted, blue, or sad, you know. I mean, I don't see anybody running around the prison smiling and laughing, you know. I mean, it don't happen. . . . ["]My mind is as clear as it used to be.["] My mind is probably more clear now than its ever been. . . . ["]I feel hopeful about the future.["] I don't have a future, you know. I mean, if I don't get the death sentence, I still don't have a future. What I've got is a slow death. I'm asking the court to give me justice, give me-let me die, you know. I mean, I've got a slow death right now, you know. I'm never getting out of prison. You know, I killed somebody. You know, I'm asking the court to give me what I've got coming, you know. . . .

I'm asking the court to get it on. Let's do it and get it over with because you're wasting my time and the court's time, you know. I'm not going to participate in any more psychiatrists or therapists or any of that there, you know. I'm no more incompetent now than I was June 30th when the crime was committed and I will not participate. I mean, if you want to drop the charges on me, go ahead and drop them. If you don't want to drop the charges, then give me what I've got coming and let's get it over with because I'm through pissing around. . . . I'm not going to sit here and have this guy's family sit in here and look at me.

Id. at 1268. One of Smith's lawyers, who had talked to Smith some time earlier, testified: "If he was out of the [solitary housing unit] and in a different living situation, he has told me point-blank on two occasions that he would probably change his mind about the death penalty." Id. at 1267. In response to this latter testimony, a doctor agreed that solitary confinement could be affecting Smith's decision, but that "[i]f he can make his own decision depending upon those circumstances and [it] varies as a consequence, that would indicate his ability to assess and make judgments about his environment and his future actions on the basis of that environment and that he is not inflexibly, as a consequence of mental disorder or disease, unable to exercise that judgment. That led to my conclusion that he was competent." Id. at 1269.

7. *Waiving the right to remain silent; voluntariness.* Under the constitution, most waiver decisions in the criminal context must not only be "knowing and intelligent" but also "voluntary."[m] As *Godinez* indicates, for instance, guilty pleas and waivers of counsel must be knowing, intelligent and voluntary. Voluntariness is usually not a significant issue in connection with these latter issues because counsel is intimately involved in the

---

[m] Note the analogy here to the informed consent doctrine, which requires not only a competent decision based on full disclosure of relevant information, but also that the decision be voluntary. See Chapter Four.

decisionmaking process and can protect against coercion. Consider, however, the Jones case (Problem I on pp. 1134–1141). If you were the judge in that case, would you accept a plea of guilty from the defendant, knowing that his attorney had suggested that he plead guilty?

It is in connection with police interrogation, where counsel is often not present, that the voluntariness concept has received the most attention. The law of confessions is governed by two separate constitutional provisions. As with guilty pleas, a confession is invalid under the due process clause if, in the totality of the circumstances, it is involuntarily made. *Brown v. Mississippi,* 297 U.S. 278, 56 S.Ct. 461, 80 L.Ed. 682 (1936). Additionally, a confession may be considered inadmissible by virtue of the fifth amendment's privilege against self-incrimination, as interpreted by *Miranda v. Arizona,* 384 U.S. 436, 86 S.Ct. 1602, 16 L.Ed.2d 694 (1966). *Miranda* requires that, before every "custodial interrogation", the police must inform the defendant of the right to remain silent and the right to an attorney during the interrogation; if these warnings are not given, any admissions obtained during the interrogation are not admissible (even though, in fact, the admissions may not be "coerced"; thus, this part of *Miranda* devised a prophylactic rule designed to provide defendants with information concerning their right to remain silent). If the warnings are given, subsequent admissions may still be inadmissible if the state is unable to show by a preponderance of the evidence that they were given after a knowing, intelligent and voluntary waiver of the right to remain silent and the right to counsel. On the other hand, if the admissions are voluntarily made before custodial interrogation begins or are the product of a valid post-warning waiver, then they are admissible. The following materials further explore, in the interrogation context, the problematic "voluntariness" issue.

COLORADO V. CONNELLY

Supreme Court of the United States, 1986.
479 U.S. 157, 107 S.Ct. 515, 93 L.Ed.2d 473.

* * *

CHIEF JUSTICE REHNQUIST delivered the opinion of the Court.

* * *

I

On August 18, 1983, Officer Patrick Anderson of the Denver Police Department was in uniform, working in an off-duty capacity in downtown Denver. Respondent Francis Connelly approached Officer Anderson and, without any prompting, stated that he had murdered someone and wanted to talk about it. Anderson immediately advised respondent that he had the right to remain silent, that anything he said could be used against him in court, and that he had the right to an attorney prior to any police questioning. See *Miranda v. Arizona,* 384 U.S. 436, 86 S.Ct. 1602,

16 L.Ed.2d 694 (1966). Respondent stated that he understood these rights but he still wanted to talk about the murder. Understandably bewildered by this confession, Officer Anderson asked respondent several questions. Connelly denied that he had been drinking, denied that he had been taking any drugs, and stated that, in the past, he had been a patient in several mental hospitals. Officer Anderson again told Connelly that he was under no obligation to say anything. Connelly replied that it was "all right," and that he would talk to Officer Anderson because his conscience had been bothering him. To Officer Anderson, respondent appeared to understand fully the nature of his acts.

Shortly thereafter, Homicide Detective Stephen Antuna arrived. Respondent was again advised of his rights, and Detective Antuna asked him "what he had on his mind." Respondent answered that he had come all the way from Boston to confess to the murder of Mary Ann Junta, a young girl whom he had killed in Denver sometime during November 1982. Respondent was taken to police headquarters, and a search of police records revealed that the body of an unidentified female had been found in April 1983. Respondent openly detailed his story to Detective Antuna and Sergeant Thomas Haney, and readily agreed to take the officers to the scene of the killing. Under Connelly's sole direction, the two officers and respondent proceeded in a police vehicle to the location of the crime. Respondent pointed out the exact location of the murder. Throughout this episode, Detective Antuna perceived no indication whatsoever that respondent was suffering from any kind of mental illness.

Respondent was held overnight. During an interview with the public defender's office the following morning, he became visibly disoriented. He began giving confused answers to questions, and for the first time, stated that "voices" had told him to come to Denver and that he had followed the directions of these voices in confessing. Respondent was sent to a state hospital for evaluation. He was initially found incompetent to assist in his own defense. By March 1984, however, the doctors evaluating respondent determined that he was competent to proceed to trial.

At a preliminary hearing, respondent moved to suppress all of his statements. Doctor Jeffrey Metzner, a psychiatrist employed by the state hospital, testified that respondent was suffering from chronic schizophrenia and was in a psychotic state at least as of August 17, 1983, the day before he confessed. Metzner's interviews with respondent revealed that respondent was following the "voice of God." This voice instructed respondent to withdraw money from the bank, to buy an airplane ticket, and to fly from Boston to Denver. When respondent arrived from Boston, God's voice became stronger and told respondent either to confess to the killing or to commit suicide. Reluctantly following the command of the voices, respondent approached Officer Anderson and confessed.

Dr. Metzner testified that, in his expert opinion, respondent was experiencing "command hallucinations." This condition interfered with respondent's "volitional abilities; that is, his ability to make free and rational choices." Dr. Metzner further testified that Connelly's illness did not significantly impair his cognitive abilities. Thus, respondent understood the rights he had when Officer Anderson and Detective Antuna advised him that he need not speak. Dr. Metzner admitted that the "voices" could in reality be Connelly's interpretation of his own guilt, but explained that in his opinion, Connelly's psychosis motivated his confession.

On the basis of this evidence the Colorado trial court decided that respondent's statements must be suppressed because they were "involuntary." [T]he court ruled that a confession is admissible only if it is a product of the defendant's rational intellect and "free will." Although the court found that the police had done nothing wrong or coercive in securing respondent's confession, Connelly's illness destroyed his volition and compelled him to confess. The trial court also found that Connelly's mental state vitiated his attempted waiver of the right to counsel and the privilege against compulsory self-incrimination. Accordingly, respondent's initial statements and his custodial confession were suppressed.

The Colorado Supreme Court affirmed. In that court's view, the proper test for admissibility is whether the statements are "the product of a rational intellect and a free will." Indeed, "the absence of police coercion or duress does not foreclose a finding of involuntariness. One's capacity for rational judgment and free choice may be overborne as much by certain forms of severe mental illness as by external pressure." The court found that the very admission of the evidence in a court of law was sufficient state action to implicate the Due Process Clause of the Fourteenth Amendment to the United States Constitution. The evidence fully supported the conclusion that respondent's initial statement was not the product of a rational intellect and a free will. The court then considered respondent's attempted waiver of his constitutional rights and found that respondent's mental condition precluded his ability to make a valid waiver. The Colorado Supreme Court thus affirmed the trial court's decision to suppress all of Connelly's statements.

II

The Due Process Clause of the Fourteenth Amendment provides that no State shall "deprive any person of life, liberty, or property, without due process of law." Just last Term, in *Miller v. Fenton*, we held that by virtue of the Due Process Clause "certain interrogation techniques, either in isolation or as applied to the unique characteristics of a particular suspect, are so offensive to a civilized system of justice that they must be condemned."

Indeed, coercive government misconduct was the catalyst for this Court's seminal confession case, *Brown v. Mississippi,* 297 U.S. 278, 56 S.Ct. 461, 80 L.Ed. 682 (1936). In that case, police officers extracted confessions from the accused through brutal torture. The Court had little difficulty concluding that even though the Fifth Amendment did not at that time apply to the States, the actions of the police were "revolting to the sense of justice." The Court has retained this due process focus, even after holding, in *Malloy v. Hogan,* 378 U.S. 1, 84 S.Ct. 1489, 12 L.Ed.2d 653 (1964), that the Fifth Amendment privilege against compulsory self-incrimination applies to the States.

Thus the cases considered by this Court over the 50 years since *Brown v. Mississippi* have focused upon the crucial element of police overreaching. While each confession case has turned on its own set of factors justifying the conclusion that police conduct was oppressive, all have contained a substantial element of coercive police conduct. Absent police conduct causally related to the confession, there is simply no basis for concluding that any state actor has deprived a criminal defendant of due process of law. Respondent correctly notes that as interrogators have turned to more subtle forms of psychological persuasion, courts have found the mental condition of the defendant a more significant factor in the "voluntariness" calculus. But this fact does not justify a conclusion that a defendant's mental condition, by itself and apart from its relation to official coercion, should ever dispose of the inquiry into constitutional "voluntariness."

Respondent relies on *Blackburn v. Alabama,* 361 U.S. 199, 80 S.Ct. 274, 4 L.Ed.2d 242 (1960), and *Townsend v. Sain,* 372 U.S. 293, 83 S.Ct. 745, 9 L.Ed.2d 770 (1963), for the proposition that the "deficient mental condition of the defendants in those cases was sufficient to render their confessions involuntary." But respondent's reading of *Blackburn* and *Townsend* ignores the integral element of police overreaching present in both cases. In *Blackburn,* the Court found that the petitioner was probably insane at the time of his confession and the police learned during the interrogation that Blackburn had a history of mental problems. The police exploited this weakness with coercive tactics: "The eight-to nine-hour sustained interrogation in a tiny room which was upon occasion literally filled with police officers; the absence of Blackburn's friends, relatives, or legal counsel; [and] the composition of the confession by the Deputy Sheriff rather than by Blackburn." These tactics supported a finding that the confession was involuntary. Indeed, the Court specifically condemned police activity that "wrings a confession out of an accused against his will." *Townsend* presented a similar instance of police wrongdoing. In that case, a police physician had given Townsend a drug with truth-serum properties. The subsequent confession, obtained by officers who knew that Townsend had been given drugs, was held involuntary. These two cases demonstrate that while mental condition is surely relevant to an individual's susceptibility to police coercion, mere examination of the confessant's state of mind can never conclude the due process inquiry.

* * *

"[T]he central purpose of a criminal trial is to decide the factual question of the defendant's guilt or innocence" and while we have previously held that exclusion of evidence may be necessary to protect constitutional guarantees, both the necessity for the collateral inquiry and the exclusion of evidence deflect a criminal trial from its basic purpose. Respondent would now have us require sweeping inquiries into the state of mind of a criminal defendant who has confessed, inquiries quite divorced from any coercion brought to bear on the defendant by the State. We think the Constitution rightly leaves this sort of inquiry to be resolved by state laws governing the admission of evidence and erects no standard of its own in this area. A statement rendered by one in the condition of respondent might be proved to be quite unreliable, but this is a matter to be governed by the evidentiary laws of the forum, see, *e.g.,* Fed.Rule Evid. 601, and not by the Due Process Clause of the Fourteenth Amendment. "The aim of the requirement of due process is not to exclude presumptively false evidence, but to prevent fundamental unfairness in the use of evidence, whether true or false." . . .

We hold that coercive police activity is a necessary predicate to the finding that a confession is not "voluntary" within the meaning of the Due Process Clause of the Fourteenth Amendment. We also conclude that the taking of respondent's statements, and their admission into evidence, constitute no violation of that Clause.

III

* * *

We also think that the Supreme Court of Colorado was mistaken in its analysis of the question of whether respondent had waived his *Miranda* rights in this case.[3] Of course, a waiver must at a minimum be "voluntary" to be effective against an accused. The Supreme Court of Colorado in addressing this question relied on the testimony of the court-appointed psychiatrist to the effect that respondent was not capable of making a "free decision with respect to his constitutional right of silence . . . and his constitutional right to confer with a lawyer before talking to the police."

---

[3] Petitioner conceded at oral argument that when Officer Anderson handcuffed respondent, the custody requirement of *Miranda* was satisfied. For purposes of our decision we accept that concession, and we similarly assume that the police officers "interrogated" respondent within the meaning of *Miranda.*

We think that the Supreme Court of Colorado erred in importing into this area of constitutional law notions of "free will" that have no place there. There is obviously no reason to require more in the way of a "voluntariness" inquiry in the *Miranda* waiver context than in the Fourteenth Amendment confession context. The sole concern of the Fifth Amendment, on which *Miranda* was based, is governmental coercion.

* * *

IV

The judgment of the Supreme Court of Colorado is accordingly reversed, and the cause remanded for further proceedings not inconsistent with this opinion.

* * *

JUSTICE STEVENS, concurring in the judgment in part and dissenting in part.

* * *

When the officer whom respondent approached elected to handcuff him and to take him into custody, the police assumed a fundamentally different relationship with him. Prior to that moment, the police had no duty to give respondent *Miranda* warnings and had every right to continue their exploratory conversation with him. Once the custodial relationship was established, however, the questioning assumed a presumptively coercive character. In my opinion the questioning could not thereafter go forward in the absence of a valid waiver of respondent's constitutional rights unless he was provided with counsel. Since it is undisputed that respondent was not then competent to stand trial, I would also conclude that he was not competent to waive his constitutional right to remain silent.

The Court seems to believe that a waiver can be voluntary even if it is not the product of an exercise of the defendant's " 'free will.' " The Court's position is not only incomprehensible to me; it is also foreclosed by the Court's recent pronouncement in *Moran v. Burbine* that "the relinquishment of the right must have been voluntary in the sense that it was the product of a free and deliberate choice . . . ". Because respondent's waiver was not voluntary in that sense, his custodial interrogation was presumptively coercive. The Colorado Supreme Court was unquestionably correct in concluding that his post-custodial incriminatory statements were inadmissible.

Accordingly, I concur in the judgment insofar as it applies to respondent's precustodial statements but respectfully dissent from the Court's disposition of the question that was not presented by the certiorari petition.

J USTICE B RENNAN, with whom J USTICE M ARSHALL joins, dissenting.

*   *   *

I

The respondent's seriously impaired mental condition is clear on the record of this case. At the time of his confession, Mr. Connelly suffered from a "longstanding severe mental disorder," diagnosed as chronic paranoid schizophrenia. He had been hospitalized for psychiatric reasons five times prior to his confession; his longest hospitalization lasted for seven months. Mr. Connelly heard imaginary voices and saw nonexistent objects. He believed that his father was God, and that he was a reincarnation of Jesus.

At the time of his confession, Mr. Connelly's mental problems included "grandiose and delusional thinking." He had a known history of "thought withdrawal and insertion." Although physicians had treated Mr. Connelly "with a wide variety of medications in the past including antipsychotic medications," he had not taken any antipsychotic medications for at least six months prior to his confession. Following his arrest, Mr. Connelly initially was found incompetent to stand trial because the court-appointed psychiatrist, Dr. Metzner, "wasn't very confident that he could consistently relate accurate information." Dr. Metzner testified that Mr. Connelly was unable "to make free and rational choices" due to auditory hallucinations: "[W]hen he was read his *Miranda* rights, he probably had the capacity to know that he was being read his *Miranda* rights [but] he wasn't able to use that information because of the command hallucinations that he had experienced." He achieved competency to stand trial only after six months of hospitalization and treatment with antipsychotic and sedative medications.

*   *   *

II

*   *   *

A

*   *   *

While it is true that police overreaching has been an element of every confession case to date, it is also true that in every case the Court has made clear that ensuring that a confession is a product of free will is an independent concern. The fact that involuntary confessions have always been excluded in part because of police overreaching signifies only that this is a case of first impression. Until today, we have never upheld the admission of a confession that does not reflect the exercise of free will.

* * *

B

Since the Court redefines voluntary confessions to include confessions by mentally ill individuals, the reliability of these confessions becomes a central concern. [W]e have to date not required a finding of reliability for involuntary confessions only because *all* such confessions have been excluded upon a finding of involuntariness, regardless of reliability. The Court's adoption today of a restrictive definition of an "involuntary" confession will require heightened scrutiny of a confession's reliability.

The instant case starkly highlights the danger of admitting a confession by a person with a severe mental illness. The trial court made no findings concerning the reliability of Mr. Connelly's involuntary confession, since it believed that the confession was excludable on the basis of involuntariness. However, the overwhelming evidence in the record points to the unreliability of Mr. Connelly's delusional mind. Mr. Connelly was found incompetent to stand trial because he was unable to relate accurate information, and the court-appointed psychiatrist indicated that Mr. Connelly was actively hallucinating and exhibited delusional thinking at the time of his confession. The Court, in fact, concedes that "[a] statement rendered by one in the condition of respondent might be proved to be quite unreliable. . . ."

Moreover, the record is barren of any corroboration of the mentally ill defendant's confession. No physical evidence links the defendant to the alleged crime. Police did not identify the alleged victim's body as the woman named by the defendant. Mr. Connelly identified the alleged scene of the crime, but it has not been verified that the unidentified body was found there or that a crime actually occurred there. There is not a shred of competent evidence in this record linking the defendant to the charged homicide. There is only Mr. Connelly's confession.

Minimum standards of due process should require that the trial court find substantial indicia of reliability, on the basis of evidence extrinsic to the confession itself, before admitting the confession of a mentally ill person into evidence. I would require the trial court to make such a finding on remand. To hold otherwise allows the State to imprison and possibly to execute a mentally ill defendant based solely upon an inherently unreliable confession.

III

* * *

B

The Court imports its voluntariness analysis, which makes police coercion a requirement for a finding of involuntariness, into its evaluation of the waiver of *Miranda* rights. My reasoning in Part II, applies *a fortiori* to involuntary confessions made in custody involving the waiver of constitutional rights. I will not repeat here what I said there.

I turn then to the second requirement, apart from the voluntariness requirement, that the State must satisfy to establish a waiver of *Miranda* rights. Besides being voluntary, the waiver must be knowing and intelligent. We recently noted that "the waiver must have been made with a full awareness both of the nature of the right being abandoned and the consequences of the decision to abandon it." The two requirements are independent: "Only if the 'totality of the circumstances surrounding the interrogation' reveal *both* an uncoerced choice *and* the requisite level of comprehension may a court properly conclude that the *Miranda* rights have been waived."

*   *   *

Since the Colorado Supreme Court found that Mr. Connelly was "clearly" unable to make an "intelligent" decision, clearly its judgment should be affirmed. The Court reverses the entire judgment, however, without explaining how a "mistaken view of voluntariness" could "taint" this independent justification for suppressing the custodial confession, but leaving the Supreme Court of Colorado free on remand to reconsider other issues, not inconsistent with the Court's opinion. Such would include, in my view, whether the requirement of a knowing and intelligent waiver was satisfied.

I dissent.

QUESTIONS AND COMMENTS

1. *Evaluating the voluntariness of confessions.* The majority in *Connelly* holds that "absent police conduct causally related to the confession," a confession is "voluntary" under the due process clause. When it as statement "caused" by police? Consider this comment from Joseph Grano, *Voluntariness, Free Will, and the Law of Confessions*, 65 Va.L.Rev. 859, 886–87 (1979):

> Causal language . . . is not helpful in solving concrete cases. Philosophical attempts to explain causation usually focus on the realm of physical impacts and motion, as the example of one billiard ball striking another classically illustrates. When one billiard ball strikes another, it may be appropriate to view the first ball as both a necessary and sufficient cause of the second ball's motion. To say, however, that one individual "caused" another to do something is to use the notion of causation in quite a different sense. With respect to confessions, the

conduct of the police, proper or improper, never can be considered a sufficient cause of a resulting confession; the defendant's choice to confess always will be a necessary cause, except in those few cases where hypnosis, a drug, or some other procedure negates the defendant's consciousness. [On the other hand, l]ike the billiard ball, the police conduct can [always] be considered a necessary cause of a resulting confession, except perhaps when a suspect comes to the station desiring to confess. Were admissibility of confessions thus to turn on the sufficiency of the police interrogation process as a cause, few confessions would be suppressed; were it to turn on the necessity of the process as a causal factor, few confessions would be admitted. Neither extreme, of course, describes the law of confessions.

Even if the statements that Connelly made in response to police questions were "caused" by the police, neither a due process nor a *Miranda* violation necessarily occurred. The majority in *Connelly* requires not only police "causation" but also police "coercion" for a constitutional violation. What are the differences between the majority's and Justice Stevens's definition of "coercion"? More generally, assuming police causation, how much additional pressure by the police is necessary before a confession becomes "coerced" and "involuntary"? Again, an excerpt from Grano, discussing "the extent to which the state may impair the mental freedom of suspects to secure confessions," might be useful:

> A subjective standard of voluntariness, taking into account all the defendant's weakness and infirmities, would make it exceedingly difficult to procure admissible confessions. The vast majority of defendants, weak or strong, initially are disinclined to provide the police self-incriminating statements. The objective of the interrogation session is to overcome this initial unwillingness without creating a risk that an innocent person will falsely confess. To take into account the peculiar weaknesses of each defendant would frustrate this objective, for the permissible level of police pressure would then decrease in direct proportion to the weakness of the suspect, thus leaving room for little more than volunteered statements.

* * *

Nevertheless, we cannot ignore the Court's numerous references to defendants' subjective characteristics. In Haley v. Ohio, for example, a fifteen-year-old boy arrested for murder confessed after continuous interrogation between midnight and five o'clock in the morning. In finding the confession involuntary, the Court reasoned that a fifteen-year-old cannot be judged by the more exacting standards of maturity. Similarly, the Court consistently has held that a defendant's physical or mental condition is a relevant factor [citing, inter alia, *Blackburn*]. The Court thus recently held involuntary a confession obtained from a wounded defendant in a hospital intensive care unit.

Cases such as these reflect society's basic sense of justice. Indeed, it would seem inconceivable to hold a child or a gravely ill person to the same powers of resistance as the normal adult. Thus, the mental freedom test cannot remain true to our fundamental normative judgments unless we incorporate some of the defendant's individual characteristics. . . .

. . . Characteristics that are feigned easily and difficult to verify properly may be excluded, much as they are in everyday discourse and in the substantive criminal law. We generally do not excuse conduct because of social adversity, peculiar personality traits, abnormal temperament, or low intelligence; rather, we expect an individual to overcome these conditions or characteristics. We do, however, morally empathize with the physically or mentally ill, the feeble, the very young, and the very old. These, moreover, are stark characteristics that an interrogating officer can be expected to recognize.

* * *

Thus, the mental freedom component of the due process voluntariness test should ask whether a person of ordinary firmness, innocent or guilty, having the defendant's age, physical condition, and relevant mental abnormalities (but not otherwise having the defendant's personality traits, temperament, intelligence, or social background), and strongly preferring not to confess, would find the interrogation pressures overbearing. Although primarily objective, this test takes sufficient account of the defendant's individual capacities to satisfy our fundamental moral concerns about impairment of mental freedom.

Id. at 900–906. Was Connelly's confession voluntary under this test?

2. *The cognitive aspect of voluntariness.* In addition to considering a person's capacity to withstand police pressure, should we evaluate the person's cognitive capacity when determining voluntariness? Assuming that the police action is insufficient for "coercion," is the resulting confession always "voluntary," even if the confessor does not grasp its significance for the prosecution's case? How does the majority answer this question? Justice Stevens and Justice Brennan? Is it relevant, as both Stevens and Brennan seem to think, that Connelly may have been incompetent to stand trial when he made the statements? Finally, note the majority's holding that, even if the statements were voluntarily obtained, state evidentiary law might bar their admission on remand. How do you evaluate Connelly's chances for success on this score?

One study found that only 10% of people with mental disability who were tested on the *Miranda* warnings had a good understanding of them. Richard Rogers et. al., *Knowing and Intelligent: A Study of* Miranda *Warnings in Mentally Disordered Defendants*, 31 L. & Hum. Behav. 401, 408 (2007). This level of understanding is significantly below the level evidenced by people who do not have mental disorder—which itself is not very good. Richard Rogers et al., *"Everyone Knows Their* Miranda *Rights": Implicit*

Assumptions and Countervailing Evidence, 16 Psychol., Public Pol'y & L. 300, 307–11 (2010) (finding misunderstanding of various components of *Miranda* in from 13% to 52% of a college-age sample, depending on the issue). Yet, a 2012 survey of the 42 Circuit Courts of Appeals decisions since 2000 that have addressed the validity of a *Miranda* waiver by a person with mental disability found that the waiver was upheld in every case. Russell E. Yates, *Waiving Goodbye to* Miranda: *Better Protection for Mentally Ill and Mentally Retarded People is Better for Us All*, (forthcoming, 2013), available at http://papers.ssrn.com/sol3/papers.cfm?abstract_id=2080313.

3.   *Interrogation and people with mental retardation.* People with intellectual disabilities (formerly mental retardation) are particularly at risk in the interrogation context. Researchers have documented a number of cases in which people with such disabilities confessed to crimes they did not commit. See Richard A. Leo & Richard J. Ofshe, *The Consequences of False Confessions: Deprivations of Liberty and Miscarriages of Justice in the Age of Psychological Interrogation*, 88 J. Crim. L. & Criminology 429, 452–90 (1998). One possible reason for this result is that people with intellectual disabilities tend to answer questions they do not understand (including leading questions) affirmatively, and they are particularly "suggestible," i.e., they are more likely to answer leading questions affirmatively, and are more easily manipulated. See Solomon M. Fulero & Carolina Everington, *Assessing the Capacity of Persons with Retardation to Waive Miranda Rights: A Jurisprudent Therapy Perspective*, 28 L. & Psychol. Rev. 53, 56–58 (2004) (describing research indicating that such people usually have "a strong desire to please others, especially those in authority" and often manifest "acquiescence," a tendency to answer "yes" even to absurd questions). Among the reasons for this suggestibility is a desire to appear normal and to hide their impairment. Id. at 57.

People with intellectual disabilities may also have great trouble understanding the socially complex context that constitutes an interrogation. Consider these findings about the ability of such individuals to understand the *Miranda* warnings:

> The empirical research conducted in this study shows that contrary to *Miranda's* core assumption, retarded people simply do not understand their *Miranda* rights. They do not understand the words comprising the warnings. They do not understand the rights themselves. They do not understand the legal context in which the rights arise. *Miranda* fails to protect the rights of mentally retarded people, and it may fail for others as well. The results of our study suggest that people who are not classified as retarded, but who have low IQs, also may not understand the warnings.

> Finally, the empirical results demonstrate that the totality-of-the-circumstances analysis courts typically use to determine whether mentally retarded suspects could understand the *Miranda* warnings also does not work. Factors including the degree of retardation, the mentally retarded suspect's age, education level, experience with the criminal

justice system, and history of being *"Mirandized"* fail as indicators of a mentally retarded person's competence to understand the warnings and to execute a valid waiver. The results of the empirical analysis indicate that for this population the factor that matters is the presence of retardation, even mild retardation. If mental retardation is present, the existence of the other factors does not overcome the disabled person's inability to understand the warnings.

. . .

Searching for solutions to this problem only accentuates the difficulty of identifying a set of rules or procedures that will protect the rights of these individuals while permitting law enforcers to carry on legitimate investigations. In the end, it may be that this accommodation is not possible. It may be that the only way to ensure the constitutional rights of mentally retarded suspects is to adopt a per se rule excluding their confessions. The cost of this approach is obvious: if the confession is true, then law enforcers and prosecutors are deprived of probative evidence. The cost of not adopting such a per se rule is just as obvious: confessions pried from the most vulnerable of our people may be false, and those false words may help send them to prison, or even to death row. In the end, we may be forced to decide if we can stomach that cost.

Morgan Cloud et al., *Words Without Meaning: The Constitution, Confessions, and Mentally Retarded Suspects*, 69 U. Chi. L. Rev. 495, 590–91 (2002).

Do you agree that confessions from people with retardation should be inadmissible? If so, would this be on the ground of incompetency or some other ground? Should it matter whether the interrogating officer knew the individual had mental retardation?

C. DIGNITARIAN COMPETENCY

FORD V. WAINWRIGHT

Supreme Court of the United States, 1986.
477 U.S. 399, 106 S.Ct. 2595, 91 L.Ed.2d 335.

*   *   *

JUSTICE MARSHALL announced the judgment of the Court and delivered the opinion of the Court with respect to Parts I and II . . .

For centuries no jurisdiction has countenanced the execution of the insane, yet this Court has never decided whether the Constitution forbids the practice. Today we keep faith with our common-law heritage in holding that it does.

I

Alvin Bernard Ford was convicted of murder in 1974 and sentenced to death. There is no suggestion that he was incompetent at the time of his offense, at trial, or at sentencing. In early 1982, however, Ford began to manifest gradual changes in behavior. They began as an occasional peculiar idea or confused perception, but became more serious over time. After reading in the newspaper that the Ku Klux Klan had held a rally in nearby Jacksonville, Florida, Ford developed an obsession focused upon the Klan. His letters to various people reveal endless brooding about his "Klan work," and an increasingly pervasive delusion that he had become the target of a complex conspiracy, involving the Klan and assorted others, designed to force him to commit suicide. He believed that the prison guards, part of the conspiracy, had been killing people and putting the bodies in the concrete enclosures used for beds. Later, he began to believe that his women relatives were being tortured and sexually abused somewhere in the prison. This notion developed into a delusion that the people who were tormenting him at the prison had taken members of Ford's family hostage. The hostage delusion took firm hold and expanded, until Ford was reporting that 135 of his friends and family were being held hostage in the prison, and that only he could help them. By "day 287" of the "hostage crisis," the list of hostages had expanded to include "senators, Senator Kennedy, and many other leaders." In a letter to the Attorney General of Florida, written in 1983, Ford appeared to assume authority for ending the "crisis," claiming to have fired a number of prison officials. He began to refer to himself as "Pope John Paul, III," and reported having appointed nine new justices to the Florida Supreme Court.

Counsel for Ford asked a psychiatrist who had examined Ford earlier, Dr. Jamal Amin, to continue seeing him and to recommend appropriate treatment. On the basis of roughly 14 months of evaluation, taped conversations between Ford and his attorneys, letters written by Ford, interviews with Ford's acquaintances, and various medical records, Dr. Amin concluded in 1983 that Ford suffered from "a severe, uncontrollable, mental disease which closely resembles 'Paranoid Schizophrenia With Suicide Potential'"—a "major mental disorder . . . severe enough to substantially affect Mr. Ford's present ability to assist in the defense of his life."

Ford subsequently refused to see Dr. Amin again, believing him to have joined the conspiracy against him, and Ford's counsel sought assistance from Dr. Harold Kaufman, who interviewed Ford in November 1983. Ford told Dr. Kaufman that "I know there is some sort of death penalty, but I'm free to go whenever I want because it would be illegal and the executioner would be executed." When asked if he would be executed, Ford replied: "I can't be executed because of the landmark case. I won. Ford v. State will prevent executions all over." These statements appeared amidst long streams of seemingly unrelated thoughts in rapid succession. Dr. Kaufman concluded that Ford had no understanding of why he was being executed, made no connection between the homicide of which he had been convicted and the death penalty, and indeed sincerely believed that he would not be executed because he owned the prisons and could control the Governor through mind waves. Dr. Kaufman found that there was "no reasonable possibility that Mr. Ford was dissembling, malingering or otherwise putting on a performance. . . . " The following month, in an interview with his attorneys, Ford regressed further into nearly complete incomprehensibility, speaking only in a code characterized by intermittent use of the word "one," making statements such as "Hands one, face one. Mafia one. God one, father one, Pope one. Pope one. Leader one."

Counsel for Ford invoked the procedures of Florida law governing the determination of competency of a condemned inmate, Fla.Stat. § 922.07 (1985). Following the procedures set forth in the statute, the Governor of Florida appointed a panel of three psychiatrists to evaluate whether, under § 922.07(2), Ford had "the mental capacity to understand the nature of the death penalty and the reasons why it was imposed upon him." At a single meeting, the three psychiatrists together interviewed Ford for approximately 30 minutes. Each doctor then filed a separate two- or three-page report with the Governor, to whom the statute delegates the final decision. One doctor concluded that Ford suffered from "psychosis with paranoia" but had "enough cognitive functioning to understand the nature and the effects of the death penalty, and why it is to be imposed on him." Another found that, although Ford was "psychotic," he did "know fully what can happen to him." The third concluded that Ford had a "severe adaptational disorder," but did "comprehend his total situation including being sentenced to death, and all of the implications of that penalty." He believed that Ford's disorder, "although severe, seem[ed] contrived and recently learned." Thus, the interview produced three different diagnoses, but accord on the question of sanity as defined by state law.

The Governor's decision was announced on April 30, 1984, when, without explanation or statement, he signed a death warrant for Ford's execution.

II

*   *   *

There is now little room for doubt that the Eighth Amendment's ban on cruel and unusual punishment embraces, at a minimum, those modes or acts of punishment that had been considered cruel and unusual at the time that the Bill of Rights was adopted. "Although the Framers may have intended the Eighth Amendment to go beyond the scope of its English counterpart, their use of the language of the English Bill of Rights is convincing proof that they intended to provide at least the same protection. . . . "

Moreover, the Eighth Amendment's proscriptions are not limited to those practices condemned by the common law in 1789. Not bound by the sparing humanitarian concessions of our forebears, the Amendment also recognizes the "evolving standards of decency that mark the progress of a maturing society." *Trop v. Dulles*, 356 U.S. 86, 101, 78 S.Ct. 590, 598, 2 L.Ed.2d 630 (1958) (plurality opinion). In addition to considering the barbarous methods generally outlawed in the 18th century, therefore, this Court takes into account objective evidence of contemporary values before determining whether a particular punishment comports with the fundamental human dignity that the Amendment protects.

A

We begin, then, with the common law. The bar against executing a prisoner who has lost his sanity bears impressive historical credentials; the practice consistently has been branded "savage and inhuman." 4 W. Blackstone, Commentaries * 24–* 25 (hereinafter Blackstone). Blackstone explained:

> "[I]diots and lunatics are not chargeable for their own acts, if committed when under these incapacities: no, not even for treason itself. Also, if a man in his sound memory commits a capital offence, and before arraignment for it, he becomes mad, he ought not to be arraigned for it: because he is not able to plead to it with that advice and caution that he ought. And if, after he has pleaded, the prisoner becomes mad, he shall not be tried: for how can he make his defence? If, after he be tried and found guilty, he loses his senses before judgment, judgment shall not be pronounced; and if, after judgment, he becomes of nonsane memory, execution shall be stayed: for peradventure, says the humanity of the English law, had the prisoner been of sound memory, he might have alleged something in stay of judgment or execution." *Ibid.* (footnotes omitted).

Sir Edward Coke had earlier expressed the same view of the common law of England: "[B]y intendment of Law the execution of the offender is for example, . . . but so it is not when a mad man is executed, but should be a miserable spectacle, both against Law, and of extream inhumanity and cruelty, and can be no example to others."

As is often true of common-law principles, the reasons for the rule are less sure and less uniform than the rule itself. One explanation is that the execution of an insane person simply offends humanity, another, that it provides no example to others and thus contributes nothing to whatever deterrence value is intended to be served by capital punishment. Other commentators postulate religious underpinnings: that it is uncharitable to dispatch an offender "into another world, when he is not of a capacity to fit himself for it." It is also said that execution serves no purpose in these cases because madness is its own punishment: *furiosus solo furore punitur.* More recent commentators opine that the community's quest for "retribution"—the need to offset a criminal act by a punishment of equivalent "moral quality"—is not served by execution of an insane person, which has a "lesser value" than that of the crime for which he is to be punished. Unanimity of rationale, therefore, we do not find. "But whatever the reason of the law is, it is plain the law is so." We know of virtually no authority condoning the execution of the insane at English common law.

Further indications suggest that this solid proscription was carried to America, where it was early observed that "the judge is bound" to stay the execution upon insanity of the prisoner. . . .

B

This ancestral legacy has not outlived its time. Today, no State in the Union permits the execution of the insane. It is clear that the ancient and humane limitation upon the State's ability to execute its sentences has a firm a hold upon the jurisprudence of today as it had centuries ago in England. The various reasons put forth in support of the common-law restriction have no less logical, moral, and practical force than they did when first voiced. For today, no less than before, we may seriously question the retributive value of executing a person who has no comprehension of why he has been singled out and stripped of his fundamental right to life. Similarly, the natural abhorrence civilized societies feel at killing one who has no capacity to come to grips with his own conscience or deity is still vivid today. And the intuition that such an execution simply offends humanity is evidently shared across this Nation. Faced with such widespread evidence of a restriction upon sovereign power, this Court is compelled to conclude that the Eighth Amendment prohibits a State from carrying out a sentence of death upon a prisoner who is insane. Whether its aim be to protect the condemned from fear and pain without comfort of understanding, or to protect the dignity of society itself from the barbarity of exacting mindless vengeance, the restriction finds enforcement in the Eighth Amendment.

* * *

JUSTICE POWELL, concurring in part and concurring in the judgment.

* * *

A

As the Court recognizes, the ancient prohibition on execution of the insane rested on differing theories. . . .

[The contention that prohibiting execution of the insane is justified as a way of preserving the defendant's ability to make arguments on his own behalf] has slight merit today. Modern practice provides far more extensive review of convictions and sentences than did the common law, including not only direct appeal but ordinarily both state and federal collateral review. Throughout this process, the defendant has access to counsel, by constitutional right at trial, and by employment or appointment at other stages of the process whenever the defendant raises substantial claims. Nor does the defendant merely have the right to counsel's assistance; he also has the right to the *effective* assistance of counsel at trial and on appeal. These guarantees are far broader than those enjoyed by criminal defendants at common law. It is thus unlikely indeed that a defendant today could go to his death with knowledge of undiscovered trial error that might set him free.

In addition, in cases tried at common law execution often followed fairly quickly after trial, so that incompetence at the time of execution was linked as a practical matter with incompetence at the trial itself. Our decisions already recognize, however, that a defendant must be competent to stand trial, and thus the notion that a defendant must be able to assist in his defense is largely provided for. . . .

B

The more general concern of the common law—that executions of the insane are simply cruel—retains its vitality. It is as true today as when Coke lived that most men and women value the opportunity to prepare, mentally and spiritually, for their death. Moreover, today as at common law, one of the death penalty's critical justifications, its retributive force, depends on the defendant's awareness of the penalty's existence and purpose. Thus, it remains true that executions of the insane both impose a uniquely cruel penalty and are inconsistent with one of the chief purposes of executions generally. For precisely these reasons, Florida requires the Governor to stay executions of those who "d[o] not have the mental capacity to understand the nature of the death penalty and why it was imposed" on them. A number of States have more rigorous standards, but none disputes the need to require that those who are executed know the fact of their impending execution and the reason for it.

Such a standard appropriately defines the kind of mental deficiency that should trigger the Eighth Amendment prohibition. If the defendant perceives the connection between his crime and his punishment, the retributive goal of the criminal law is satisfied. And only if the defendant is aware that his death is approaching can he prepare himself for his passing. Accordingly, I would hold that the Eighth Amendment forbids the execution only of those who are unaware of the punishment they are about to suffer and why they are to suffer it.

Petitioner's claim of insanity plainly fits within this standard. According to petitioner's proffered psychiatric examination, petitioner does not know that he is to be executed, but rather believes that the death penalty has been invalidated. If this assessment is correct, petitioner cannot connect his execution to the crime for which he was convicted.

*   *   *

[The opinion of JUSTICE O'CONNOR, concurring in part and dissenting in part, in which JUSTICE WHITE joined, and the dissenting opinion of JUSTICE REHNQUIST, in which CHIEF JUSTICE BURGER joined, are deleted.]

QUESTIONS AND COMMENTS

1.   *The rationale for the competency requirement in death penalty cases.* The Court in *Ford* notes at least six rationales that might justify its rule that a person be competent prior to execution: (1) an incompetent person might be unable to provide counsel with last minute information leading to vacation of the sentence; (2) madness is punishment enough in itself; (3) an incompetent person cannot make peace with God; (4) execution of an incompetent person has no deterrent effect on the population; (5) such execution "is a miserable spectacle . . . of extream inhumanity and cruelty"; (6) the retribution or vengeance meant to be realized by execution cannot be exacted from an incompetent person. Do any of these rationales distinguish the incompetent from the competent sufficiently to justify a prohibition against execution only of the incompetent? Might it not be more "cruel" to execute a fully aware individual than one who is not? Many years ago psychiatrists thought that, for some individuals, psychosis was a defense mechanism against the horrors of the death penalty. Harvey Bluestone & Carl McGahee, *Reaction to Extreme Stress: Impending Death by Execution*, 119 Am.J.Psychiat. 392 (1962). Other legal traditions take a different view of the condemned man's awareness of his fate. For example, the Jewish Talmud requires that a condemned man be given wine prior to execution to "benumb his senses," Mishne Torah, Sanhedrin 13:2, cited in Fred Rosner, Encyclopedia of Medicine in the Bible and the Talmud 19 (2000).

For a view that, of the rationales advanced by the Court, only the retributive one is supportable, see Barbara Ward, *Competency for Execution: Problems in Law and Psychiatry*, 14 Fla.St.U.L.Rev. 35, 49–56 (1986).[n] As described by Ward:

> The retributive theory of competency for execution is predicated upon an assumption that every wrong act must be avenged by a punitive act of equal quality. Presumably, killing an insane person does not satisfy the societal interest in reprisal for the previous wrong as well as does killing a sane person. Therefore, imposing the death penalty on incompetent prisoners exacts a punishment less valuable than the crime itself.

Id. at 54. See also, Geoffrey Hazard & David Louisell, *Death, the State, and the Insane: Stay of Execution*, 9 UCLA L.Rev. 381 (1962).

---

[n]   Ward also argues, however, that the rule could be supported on the additional ground that society is ambivalent about the death penalty and thus "the number of death penalties imposed should be decreased in various ways," including the incompetency bar. Id. at 56.

In *Panetti v. Quarterman*, 551 U.S. 930, 127 S.Ct. 2842, 168 L.Ed.2d 662 (2007), the Court appeared to agree with this analysis.

> [I]t might be said that capital punishment is imposed because it has the potential to make the offender recognize at last the gravity of his crime and to allow the community as a whole, including the surviving family and friends of the victim, to affirm its own judgment that the culpability of the prisoner is so serious that the ultimate penalty must be sought and imposed. The potential for a prisoner's recognition of the severity of the offense and the objective of community vindication are called in question, however, if the prisoner's mental state is so distorted by a mental illness that his awareness of the crime and punishment has little or no relation to the understanding of those concepts shared by the community as a whole.

Id. at 958–59; 127 S.Ct. at 2861.

Professor Bonnie offers a different rationale for the competency requirement—the dignity of the offender:

> Whose interests are protected by the bar against executing the incompetent? . . . Consider, by way of analogy, the trend toward supposedly more "humane" methods of execution, such as lethal injection. It is conceivable that a prisoner may find death by this method to be offensive to his own sense of dignity because it treats him as an object, like a dog being put to sleep: he may prefer to die by firing squad or on the gallows. When we sterilize the act of execution, do we do it for ourselves or for the prisoner? . . . If [the prohibition on executing offenders who are incompetent] has any continuing justification in the contemporary context, I believe it must be found in respect for the dignity of the condemned. The prisoner has a right, even under imminent sentence of death, to be treated as a person worthy of respect, not as an object of the State's effort to carry out its promises. As Justice Powell suggested, a person under the shadow of death should have the opportunity to make the few choices that remain available to him. He should have the opportunity to decide who should be present at his execution, what he will eat for his last meal, what, if anything, he will utter for his last words, and whether he will repent or go defiantly to this grave. A prisoner who does not understand the nature and purpose of the execution is not able to exercise the choices that remain to him. To execute him in this condition is an affront to his dignity as a person and to the "dignity of man," the core value of the Eighth Amendment.

Richard Bonnie, Panetti v. Quarterman: *Mental Illness, the Death Penalty, and Human Dignity*, 5 Ohio St. J. Crim. L. 257, 276–77 (2007). How do you answer the question posed by Professor Bonnie at the beginning of this excerpt?

2. *The competency standard.* After *Ford*, most jurisdictions defined competency to be executed using Justice Powell's language: Offenders must know that they are being executed and why. Applying the retributive

rationale, which it said *Ford* adopted, the Supreme Court in *Panetti* rejected a narrow interpretation of this language. Its description of the expert testimony in that case and its analysis of the competency issue follows:

> Four expert witnesses testified on petitioner's behalf in the District Court proceedings. One explained that petitioner's mental problems are indicative of "schizo-affective disorder," resulting in a "genuine delusion" involving his understanding of the reason for his execution. According to the expert, this delusion has recast petitioner's execution as "part of spiritual warfare . . . between the demons and the forces of the darkness and God and the angels and the forces of light." As a result, the expert explained, although petitioner claims to understand "that the state is saying that [it wishes] to execute him for [his] murder[s]," he believes in earnest that the stated reason is a "sham" and the State in truth wants to execute him "to stop him from preaching." Petitioner's other expert witnesses reached similar conclusions concerning the strength and sincerity of this "fixed delusion."

> While the State's expert witnesses resisted the conclusion that petitioner's stated beliefs were necessarily indicative of incompetency, particularly in light of his perceived ability to understand certain concepts and, at times, to be "clear and lucid," they acknowledged evidence of mental problems. Petitioner's rebuttal witness attempted to reconcile the experts' testimony:

>> "Well, first, you have to understand that when somebody is schizophrenic, it doesn't diminish their cognitive ability. . . . Instead, you have a situation where—and why we call schizophrenia thought disorder[—]the logical integration and reality connection of their thoughts are disrupted, so the stimulus comes in, and instead of being analyzed and processed in a rational, logical, linear sort of way, it gets scrambled up and it comes out in a tangential, circumstantial, symbolic . . . not really relevant kind of way. That's the essence of somebody being schizophrenic. . . . Now, it may be that if they're dealing with someone who's more familiar . . . [in] what may feel like a safer, more enclosed environment . . . those sorts of interactions may be reasonably lucid whereas a more extended conversation about more loaded material would reflect the severity of his mental illness."

> See also [Record] (suggesting that an unmedicated individual suffering from schizophrenia can "at times" hold an ordinary conversation and that "it depends [whether the discussion concerns the individual's] fixed delusional system"). There is, in short, much in the record to support the conclusion that petitioner suffers from severe delusions.

> The Court of Appeals concluded that its standard foreclosed petitioner from establishing incompetency by the means he now seeks to employ: a showing that his mental illness obstructs a rational understanding of the State's reason for his execution. As the court explained, "[b]ecause we

hold that 'awareness,' as that term is used in *Ford*, is not necessarily synonymous with 'rational understanding,' as argued by [petitioner,] we conclude that the district court's findings are sufficient to establish that [petitioner] is competent to be executed."

In our view the Court of Appeals' standard is too restrictive to afford a prisoner the protections granted by the Eighth Amendment. . . . The Court of Appeals' standard treats a prisoner's delusional belief system as irrelevant if the prisoner knows that the State has identified his crimes as the reason for his execution. See 401 F.Supp.2d., at 712 (indicating that under Circuit precedent "a petitioner's delusional beliefs—even those which may result in a fundamental failure to appreciate the connection between the petitioner's crime and his execution—do not bear on the question of whether the petitioner 'knows the reason for his execution' for the purposes of the Eighth Amendment").Yet the *Ford* opinions nowhere indicate that delusions are irrelevant to "comprehen[sion]" or "aware [ness]" if they so impair the prisoner's concept of reality that he cannot reach a rational understanding of the reason for the execution. If anything, the *Ford* majority suggests the opposite.

* * *

The principles set forth in *Ford* are put at risk by a rule that deems delusions relevant only with respect to the State's announced reason for a punishment or the fact of an imminent execution, as opposed to the real interests the State seeks to vindicate. We likewise find no support elsewhere in *Ford*, including in its discussions of the common law and the state standards, for the proposition that a prisoner is automatically foreclosed from demonstrating incompetency once a court has found he can identify the stated reason for his execution. A prisoner's awareness of the State's rationale for an execution is not the same as a rational understanding of it. *Ford* does not foreclose inquiry into the latter.

This is not to deny the fact that a concept like rational understanding is difficult to define. And we must not ignore the concern that some prisoners, whose cases are not implicated by this decision, will fail to understand why they are to be punished on account of reasons other than those stemming from a severe mental illness. The mental state requisite for competence to suffer capital punishment neither presumes nor requires a person who would be considered "normal," or even "rational," in a layperson's understanding of those terms. Someone who is condemned to death for an atrocious murder may be so callous as to be unrepentant; so self-centered and devoid of compassion as to lack all sense of guilt; so adept in transferring blame to others as to be considered, at least in the colloquial sense, to be out of touch with reality. Those states of mind, even if extreme compared to the criminal population at large, are not what petitioner contends lie at the threshold of a competence inquiry. The beginning of doubt about competence in a case like petitioner's is not a misanthropic personality or an amoral character. It is a psychotic disorder.

Petitioner's submission is that he suffers from a severe, documented mental illness that is the source of gross delusions preventing him from comprehending the meaning and purpose of the punishment to which he has been sentenced. This argument, we hold, should have been considered.

The flaws of the Court of Appeals' test are pronounced in petitioner's case. Circuit precedent required the District Court to disregard evidence of psychological dysfunction that, in the words of the judge, may have resulted in petitioner's "fundamental failure to appreciate the connection between the petitioner's crime and his execution." To refuse to consider evidence of this nature is to mistake *Ford*'s holding and its logic. Gross delusions stemming from a severe mental disorder may put an awareness of a link between a crime and its punishment in a context so far removed from reality that the punishment can serve no proper purpose. It is therefore error to derive from *Ford*, and the substantive standard for incompetency its opinions broadly identify, a strict test for competency that treats delusional beliefs as irrelevant once the prisoner is aware the State has identified the link between his crime and the punishment to be inflicted.

Id. at 954–60; 127 S.Ct. at 2859–62.

In light of *Panetti*, decide whether the offenders in the following cases, handed down prior to *Panetti*, were competent to be executed. Would the result be different under Professor Bonnie's rationale?

The inmate believed that his dead aunt would protect him from the sedative and toxic effects of the drugs used to execute him. *Garrett v. Collins*, 951 F.2d 57 (5th Cir. 1992) (holding the inmate was competent).

The inmate believed he was God, that his sentence had been overturned, that the State was holding him illegally, and that there was a conspiracy to execute him. He also believed that he had been set free in August 1997. *Singleton v. Norris*, 267 F.3d 859 (8th Cir. 2001) (holding the inmate was incompetent, and granting a permanent stay of execution; but see note 4 in these materials).

The inmate had what doctors called a "delusional hope" that he would not be executed. He was convinced that his death penalty would be overturned and he would be spared execution. *State v. Harris, III*, 114 Wash.2d 419, 789 P.2d 60 (1990) (competent).

The inmate believed he was an angel and that he had received absolution for his crime, which meant the state would not be able to execute him. *Billiot v. State*, 655 So.2d 1 (Miss 1995) (competent).

The inmate believed that death was not real, but only inflicted pleasure and pain. As a result, he was not concerned about his execution. *Calambro v. State*, 114 Nev. 961, 964 P.2d 794 (1998) (competent).

Finally, consider *Ferguson v. Sect'y, Florida Dep't Corrections*, 716 F.3d 1513 (11th Cir. 2013), decided after *Panetti*. Ferguson, diagnosed with schizophrenia, believed that he was the "Prince of God" and would be resurrected after his death to sit at the right hand of God. The Eleventh Circuit upheld the Florida Supreme Court's conclusion that Ferguson was competent to be executed, stating that "while Ferguson's thoughts about what happens after death may seem extreme to many people, nearly every major world religion—from Christianity to Zoroastrianism—envisions some kind of continuation of life after death, often including resurrection."

Panetti states that a condemned psychopath who knows he has murdered someone but sees nothing wrong with his action should be found competent to be executed. Should a crucial legal distinction rest on the type of psychiatric symptoms that are the source of the individual's beliefs about execution?

3.   *Procedures.* The second issue the Court addressed in *Ford* was the proper procedure for determining competency to be executed. As recounted above, Florida allowed the governor to make the final decision on competency, based on reports from three psychiatrists. Three members of the Court joined Justice Marshall in deciding that the due process clause required more: specifically, a hearing on the competency issue, presided over by a judicial officer, at which the prisoner would have the right to be present with counsel and confront the experts. Justice O'Connor, joined by Justice White, also concluded that due process was violated by the Florida procedure, but indicated that all the state was constitutionally required to provide was some procedure for receiving the written submissions of the prisoner. Justice Rehnquist, joined by Chief Justice Burger, voted to uphold the Florida procedure.

As a result of this lineup, Justice Powell's opinion was controlling on the procedural issue. He agreed with Marshall that the Florida procedures were inadequate, but stated: "I would not require the kind of full-scale 'sanity trial' that Justice Marshall appears to find necessary." In explaining this stance, he stated:

> First, the Eighth Amendment claim at issue can arise only after the prisoner has been validly convicted of a capital crime and sentenced to death. Thus, in this case the State has a substantial and legitimate interest in taking petitioner's life as punishment for his crime. That interest is not called into question by petitioner's claim. Rather, the only question raised is not whether, but when, his execution may take place. This question is important, but it is not comparable to the antecedent question whether petitioner should be executed at all. It follows that this Court's decisions imposing heightened procedural requirements on capital trials and sentencing proceedings do not apply in this context.

> Second, petitioner does not make his claim of insanity against a neutral background. On the contrary, in order to have been convicted and sentenced, petitioner must have been judged competent to stand trial, or

his competency must have been sufficiently clear as not to raise a serious question for the trial court. The State therefore may properly presume that petitioner remains sane at the time sentence is to be carried out, and may require a substantial threshold showing of insanity merely to trigger the hearing process.

Finally, the sanity issue in this type of case does not resemble the basic issues at trial or sentencing. Unlike issues of historical fact, the question of petitioner's sanity calls for a basically subjective judgment. And unlike the determination of whether the death penalty is appropriate in a particular case, the competency determination depends substantially on expert analysis in a discipline fraught with "subtleties and nuances." This combination of factors means that ordinary adversarial procedures—complete with live testimony, cross-examination, and oral argument by counsel—are not necessarily the best means of arriving at sound, consistent judgments as to a defendant's sanity. Cf. *Parham v. J.R.*

477 U.S. at 425–26, 106 S.Ct. at 2609–10. In light of this reasoning, Justice Powell concluded that the state needed only to provide an "impartial officer or board that can receive evidence and argument from the prisoner's counsel, including psychiatric evidence that may differ from the State's own psychiatric examination." Id. at 427, 106 S.Ct. at 2610.

If the rationale for the prohibition on executing incompetent prisoners is retributive (see note 1), does the individual have *any* interest in making sure the conclusion about competency is accurate? Should the individual even have "standing" to raise the issue? In *Panetti*, the Court seemed to answer this latter question in the affirmative, although it refrained from holding that the Constitution requires a hearing, instead merely reiterating that the offender is entitled to respond to the state's evidence with experts of his own. *Panetti*, 127 S.Ct. at 2856–57.

4. *Treating the offender found incompetent.* If a person is found incompetent to be executed, does he or she have the right to refuse treatment that would restore and maintain competency to be executed? Are the reasons given by Justice Powell in justifying minimal procedures at the competency determination relevant here as well? In *Perry v. Louisiana*, 498 U.S. 1075, 111 S.Ct. 804, 112 L.Ed.2d 865 (1991), the Supreme Court granted certiorari in a case involving forcible medication of a person found incompetent to be executed, but then remanded the case in light of its intervening decision in *Washington v. Harper*, supra. On remand, the Louisiana Supreme Court concluded that forcibly medicating individuals to render them competent to be executed is impermissible. *State v. Perry*, 610 So.2d 746 (La.1992). It distinguished *Harper* by concluding that forcing drugs merely "to facilitate . . . execution does not constitute medical treatment but is antithetical to the basic principles of the healing arts." Id. at 751. It also found, as a matter of state law, that medicating an objecting individual to facilitate execution constitutes cruel and unusual punishment because it "fails to measurably contribute to the social goals of capital punishment," "would add severity and

indignity to the prisoner's punishment beyond that required for the mere extinguishment of life," and "is apt to be administered erroneously, arbitrarily or capriciously." Id. at 747–48. In at least one state, an official finding of incompetence requires commutation of the death sentence to a life sentence without parole, even if the individual can be or is subsequently rendered competent through medication. Md. Ann. Code § 3–904 (2012).

In *Singleton v. Norris*, 319 F.3d 1018 (8th Cir.2003), the Eighth Circuit reached a different conclusion than the Louisiana Supreme Court. There the court relied on *Harper v. Washington*, *Riggins v. Nevada* and its own opinion in *Sell v. United States* (see pp. 1159–1179 for discussion of these cases) in holding that a person who is incompetent to be executed may be forcibly medicated under certain circumstances. Specifically,

> the government must (1) "present an essential state interest that outweighs the individual's interest in remaining free from medication," (2) "prove that there is no less intrusive way of fulfilling its essential interest," and (3) "prove by clear and convincing evidence that the medication is medically appropriate." "Medication is medically appropriate if: (1) it is likely to render the patient competent; (2) the likelihood and gravity of side effects do not overwhelm its benefits; and, (3) it is in the best medical interests of the patient."

As to the first requirement, the court stated "[w]e need not decide under what circumstances carrying out a particular sentence is not 'essential.' Society's interest in punishing offenders is at its greatest in the narrow class of capital murder cases in which aggravating factors justify imposition of the death penalty." After finding that medication was necessary to restore Singleton to competency (the second factor), the court addressed the third issue of whether the medication was medically appropriate:

> Central to Singleton's argument is his contention that medication "obviously is not in the prisoner's ultimate best medical interest" where one effect of the medication is rendering the patient competent for execution. Singleton does not dispute that the antipsychotic medication is in his medical interest during the pendency of a stay of execution. He has stated he takes it voluntarily because he does not like the symptoms he experiences without it. He also does not dispute the lack of serious side effects. . . . Singleton's argument regarding his long-term medical interest boils down to an assertion that execution is not in his medical interest. Eligibility for execution is the only unwanted consequence of the medication. The due process interests in life and liberty that Singleton asserts have been foreclosed by the lawfully imposed sentence of execution and the *Harper* procedure. In the circumstances presented in this case, the best medical interests of the prisoner must be determined without regard to whether there is a pending date of execution.

Judge Heaney, who had ordered a permanent stay of execution in Singleton's case two years earlier (see note 2) was joined by three others in dissent.

Once an execution date was set, I believe that the justification for medicating Singleton under *Harper* evaporated. An inquiry into the State's motivation is unhelpful, for it presupposes a single, directed motivation, which is not the case here. In fact, the evidence suggests two competing interests: the welfare of the prison, and the execution of the prisoner's sentence. At the very least, the setting of an execution date calls into question the State's true motivation for administering the medication in the first instance. The circumstances of Singleton's case changed once the execution date was set, and changed in such a way that *Harper* no longer supports the prison forcing him to take medication.

Singleton was decided by the same court that was reversed by the U.S. Supreme Court in *Sell v. United States*, which significantly limited the government's ability to use medication to restore competency to stand trial over the defendant's objection. Are the state and individual interests stronger or weaker in the competency to be executed context? If Singleton had refused medication because of its side effects should the outcome have been different? In *Sell*, the Supreme Court stated that, while the permissible circumstances under which forcible medication administered solely for the purpose of restoring competency "may be rare," forcible medication will always be permissible to reduce dangerousness (if medically appropriate and necessary to that purpose). Should the same rule apply here? If so, is Judge Heaney's argument in dissent irrelevant? Finally, what is the disposition if a right to refuse is recognized? Commutation of sentence? Singleton argued that he could be executed only if and when he became competent naturally, without psychotropic intervention.

As the Louisiana Supreme Court decision in *Perry* indicates, one problem created by forcible restoration of a person's competence to be executed is ethical rather than legal. It involves the role of the mental health professional in restoring competency. As noted in Note, *Medical Ethics and Competency to be Executed*, 96 Yale L.J. 167, 178–79 (1986),

> the express purpose of competency treatment is to guarantee that the patient will be killed. Each treatment strategy to heal the inmate is in fact another strategy to ensure his death. No intervening acts save the minuscule likelihood that, once sane, the inmate will articulate a heretofore unknown reason for a stay of execution, will prevent the execution that the physician has made possible.

Is this passage correct in equating the provision of standard medical treatment to a psychotic individual with participation in an execution? The American Medical Association appears to think so. It has adopted the following position: "The physician, as a member of a profession dedicated to the preserving of life when there is hope of doing so, should not be a participant in a legally authorized execution." Is this stance ethical in view of the suffering an untreated person might experience? Consider the fact that many persons on death row decide they would rather be executed than continue living in prison. See Welsh White, *Defendants Who Elect Execution*,

48 U.Pitt.L.Rev. 853, 854–55 (1987). Consider also the argument that the treatment needs of an offender are not linked to his or her sentence as an ethical matter. See Robert Schopp, *Involuntary Treatment and Competence to Proceed in the Criminal Process: Capital and Noncapital Cases*, 24 Beh. Sci. & L. 1, 40 (2006) (arguing that an interpretation of doctors' "obligation to promote their clients' well-being [to include] an obligation to assist their clients in avoiding legally imposed criminal sentences would undermine the justification for granting legal weight to professional ethics because it would render those ethical standards inconsistent with the broader set of societal values embodied in law.").

5.   *Decisional competency and the death penalty.* In this regard, how competent must a person on death row be before he or she can abort collateral proceedings and demand that the state carry out the death sentence? Cf. *Gilmore v. Utah,* 429 U.S. 1012, 1013, 97 S.Ct. 436, 437, 50 L.Ed.2d 632 (1976) (in which the Supreme Court held that Gilmore could waive further judicial review of his case and proceed to execution because he "made a knowing and intelligent waiver of any and all federal rights he might have asserted . . . ".). Several courts have required a relatively high level of competency in this situation (i.e., higher than what is required for competency to proceed), given the irreversibility of the decision. See e.g., *Franz v. State,* 296 Ark. 181, 188–89, 754 S.W.2d 839, 843 (1988). Is this stance required after *Godinez v. Moran* or *Edwards v. Arizona*?

In 2007, the American Bar Association, the American Psychiatric Association, and the American Psychological Association endorsed a resolution that provides: "If a court finds that a prisoner under sentence of death who wishes to forgo or terminate post-conviction proceedings has a mental disorder or disability that significantly impairs his or her capacity to make a rational decision, the court should permit a next friend acting on the prisoner's behalf to initiate or pursue available remedies to set aside the conviction or death sentence." See ABA Resolution on Mental Disability and the Death Penalty, www.abanet.org/crimjust/policy/am06122a.pdf. When is a decision to waive appeals rational? In particular, if an offender waives appeals because he or she is depressed, is the decision irrational? Note 6 following the materials on *Godinez* discussed when a capital defendant who is suffering from depression may waive the right to present mitigating evidence at the capital sentencing proceeding (see pp. 741–744). Should the same analysis, whatever it may be, also apply to the decision by a depressed offender to waive collateral proceedings?

Professor John Blume calculates that approximately 13% of all executions have been of "volunteers" (i.e., individuals who have waived their collateral appeals), and that roughly 77% of these individuals were suffering from mental illness at the time of their waiver. John Blume, *Killing the Willing: "Volunteers," Suicide and Competency*, 103 Mich. L. Rev. 939, 962–63 (2005). Professor Blume concludes: "When a volunteer is both competent to make legal choices and motivated to accept the justness of his punishment, then he should be permitted to waive his further appeals. There are some such defendants, and their decisions should, in fact must, be respected, at least so long as other litigants have the power to override their attorney's recommendations. On the other hand, even if the volunteer is competent, when suicidal desires represent the dominant motivation, courts should not permit waiver." In the latter situation, Professor Blume argues, execution would amount to state-assisted suicide, which is banned in all but a few states (and in the latter states it is permitted only when the person is terminally ill). Id. at 984–85. Do you agree?

If an offender is found incompetent to waive appeals under the appropriate standard and can be restored through medication, is it permissible to medicate the individual over his or her objection? How is this scenario different from forcibly medicating an individual to restore competency to be executed?

6.   *Adjudicative competence and the death penalty.* The period between a sentence of execution and the execution itself averages more than a decade, in part because of collateral proceedings in state and federal courts. See Death Penalty Information Center, Time on Death Row, available at http://www.deathpenaltyinfo.org/time-death-row. Should these collateral proceedings (e.g. coram nobis or habeas petitions) be suspended if the offender becomes incompetent to assist counsel? The joint ABA/APA/APA resolution cited above provides that "[i]f a court finds at any time that a prisoner under sentence of death has a mental disorder or disability that significantly impairs his or her capacity to understand or communicate pertinent information or otherwise to assist counsel in connection with post-conviction proceedings, and that the prisoner's participation is necessary for a fair resolution of specific claims bearing on the validity of the conviction or death sentence, the court should suspend the proceedings. If the court finds that there is no significant likelihood of restoring the prisoner's capacity to participate in post-conviction proceedings in the foreseeable future, it should reduce the prisoner's sentence to the sentence imposed in capital cases when execution is not an option."

However, in *Ryan v. Gonzales*, ___ U.S. ___, 133 S.Ct. 696, 184 L.Ed.2d 528 (2013), the Supreme Court held, in a unanimous opinion written by Justice Thomas, that the Constitution does not require that an offender be competent during post-conviction proceedings. It reasoned that, "[g]iven the backward-looking, record-based nature of most federal habeas proceedings, counsel can generally provide effective representation to a habeas petitioner regardless of the petitioner's competence. . . . Attorneys are quite capable of reviewing the state-court record, identifying legal errors, and marshaling relevant arguments, even without their clients' assistance." By entertaining (albeit ultimately rejecting) the petitioners' claims that their incompetence could affect the fairness of habeas review in their cases, the Court signaled that it might be willing to recognize an exception to its holding if the habeas petitioner's assistance turned out to be necessary. But the Court concluded its opinion by stating: "If a district court concludes that the petitioner's claim could substantially benefit from the petitioner's assistance, the district court should take into account the likelihood that the petitioner will regain competence in the foreseeable future. Where there is no reasonable hope of competence, a stay is inappropriate and merely frustrates the State's attempts to defend its presumptively valid judgment." How does this last sentence square with the ABA's position? Is it consistent with the Court's own reasoning? Is it consistent with *Jackson v. Indiana* (discussed on pp. 1151–1159).

CHAPTER 10

POST–COMMITMENT ISSUES

■ ■ ■

Table of Sections

I.   INTRODUCTION

The Supreme Court has made clear that "a state is under no constitutional duty to provide substantive services for those within its borders." *Youngberg v. Romeo,* 457 U.S. 307, 316, 102 S.Ct. 2452, 2458, 73 L.Ed.2d 28 (1982). But after the state intervenes in a person's life, it must obey constitutional dictates. This chapter focuses on the states' constitutional obligations toward persons who are involuntarily committed through civil or criminal processes. It also examines the constitutional prerogatives of various groups of "voluntary" patients (e.g., nonprotesting admittees, children committed by their parents, individuals committed by their guardians). The various *statutory* enactments that may require the state to provide services for certain populations (e.g., the Americans with Disabilities Act and the Individuals with Disabilities Education Act) are touched upon as well, although the primary discussion of these provisions is found in Part III of this book.

Determining the extent to which the state is constitutionally obligated to provide for the needs and demands of those whom it has deprived of liberty is a complex matter. For instance, if the state provides decent living quarters for those who are involuntarily hospitalized, has it met its constitutional duty? If it must provide more, is mere prevention of deterioration enough? Or must the state afford committed individuals treatment or habilitation[a] that will improve their condition? Assuming a duty to provide something more than food and shelter for those it deprives of liberty, is the state also obligated to create community resources if community treatment or habilitation appears more effective and appropriate than a hospital placement? Within an institutional

---

[a] Habilitation is the term used to refer to treatment and education of the developmentally disabled.

environment (whether inpatient or outpatient) to what extent may the state limit access to mail and phone service, sexual contact, exercise and so on? When, if ever, must the state pay a patient for work performed at the institution?

Assessing the scope of the constitutional right to treatment and habilitation raises systemic concerns more dramatically than other issues addressed in this book. Do courts have the expertise to assess the effectiveness of treatment? Do they have the authority to force states to create new treatment facilities and programs? If so, how is this authority to be enforced?

These are the primary issues examined in this chapter. To provide a realistic backdrop to this discussion, we offer the following excerpt describing the experiences of several patients in the Texas mental health system. The excerpt below does not necessarily reflect reality in other states (which vary immensely in their approach to mental health care) and is outdated in some respects (especially in terms of the medications provided the patients). But it still captures the atmosphere of many mental health systems today, and it also reflects the type of system that courts confronted in much of the litigation described in the rest of this chapter. The two shorter excerpts that follow provide more recent perspectives on the mental health system.

JOSEPH NOCERA, THE LONG, LONESOME ROAD
Texas Monthly 43–49 (1986).

*   *   *

A real mental health system does not exist in Texas. Instead, a group of independent fiefdoms and power bases all operate under the loose rubric of the Texas Department of Mental Health and Mental Retardation (MHMR). State hospitals are one power base, and local mental health authorities are another. Probate judges try to get mentally ill people into state hospitals, while hospital social workers try just as hard to get them out. There is even a federal judge involved in running the state hospital. As a result of a class-action suit brought a dozen years ago on the behalf of patients, federal district judge Barefoot Sanders is immersed in every aspect of hospital life, and although his intimidating presence has made the hospitals marginally better, the improvements have come at the expense of the local authorities. Part of the reason that everyone seems to be working at cross-purposes is that there is honest disagreement about how best to treat the mentally ill. But the chaos that reigns in the Texas mental health system also results from some of the worst reasons imaginable: bureaucratic infighting and turf battles, and a preference for the status quo over innovation or change.

Fred Thomas is in many ways typical of the people who populate that system. He is black. He is poor. He is unquestionably a tough case, partly because of the severity of his illness, but also because, as I discovered in the five months I spent with him a year ago, he lacks the motivation to try to make something of his life. Though instilling such motivation is perhaps the most fundamental goal of the modern mental health movement, the Texas system has seemed utterly helpless to change Fred. Instead, the system has been content to process him into the state hospital and process him out—always sending him back to his mother's house, where inevitably and tragically he would revert to his old ways. Although Texas' mental health hospitals are no longer hellholes, they are still little more than benign jails. One former social worker used to tell patients about to be released: "If you can survive in this place, you can survive anything." When I first met Fred Thomas, he had learned to survive in the hospital. The question confronting him was whether he could survive beyond its walls.

* * *

On a bright April day, in a large outdoor area of the Austin State Hospital, Fred Thomas sat down across from me at a picnic table. In hospital jargon, he was in the Harris K patio—the Harris K unit being the drab, one-story, pentagon shaped building that surrounds the patio. The men on Fred's ward were outdoors for an hour of "exercise"—thus satisfying one of Judge Sanders' requirements for structured daily activities. As far as I could see, only two men were actually exercising: a member of the ward staff and a patient were shooting baskets through a worn, bent rim. A few other patients were walking, somewhat frantically, along a cement pathway. The rest were either sitting in chairs or sprawling out under one of the pecan trees, fast asleep. . . . Most of them looked harmless enough, except for one, a black, middle-aged schizophrenic with a Fu Manchu moustache who was standing in the center of the patio screaming about the CIA and the KGB. I would later learn that he was Donald Peterson.

Fred . . . was wearing a grimy sweatshirt, slightly tattered green jogging pants, and old-fashioned high-top sneakers without socks. Upon reaching the table, Fred sat down across from me, but at first he ignored me. [Eventually, however,] he looked up and began talking.

Fred's speech was characterized by what psychiatrists call "loose association" or "tangential thought"—that is, skipping rapidly from one topic to the next, usually with a tenuous thread linking each new thought to the one before it. When I introduced myself, he said, "Joe. Where you gonna go, Joe? Joe Willie Namath." And that led him to a brief discussion of Namath's bad knees, and on to trees and bees, and then to the birds and the bees, and then to honey, which led to girls, and finally to a recently released patient whom he claimed had been his girlfriend.

[T]hat April marked the beginning of Fred's fifth stay at the Austin State Hospital. After his initial admission in 1979, he had managed to stay out of the hospital for four years. But between March 1984 and March 1985, he had been in three times.

*   *   *

It's 8 a.m. on a Thursday in early May: time for the "morning meds" in Ward B, one of the four male wards in the Harris K unit (there are two female wards). Ward B has been Fred Thomas' home for more than a month.

The heart of an Austin State Hospital ward is the central dayroom, no larger than a bank president's office; it is filled with beat-up chairs, a few card tables, and a television set that is constantly on. Plexiglass windows and locked doors separate the dayroom and a nurse's station, from which the ward staff keeps watch over its charges. There are some 25 men in the Ward B dayroom this morning, at least 7 more than the ward was intended to hold. During the time I spent at Harris K, the dayroom was constantly overcrowded, which greatly increased the level of agitation and even danger. Fred, however, does not seem agitated. He is wearing a clean pair of short pants, a new T-shirt, and his ever-present basketball sneakers, unlaced. He is standing in front of a full-length mirror, mumbling to himself. No one seems to notice.

[T]he two mental health workers sitting in the nurse's station don't notice Fred because, by their lights, he is being good. To such nonprofessionals, who make less than a good grocery clerk, a patient's goodness is measured entirely on the basis of how little trouble he causes. Fred may be incoherent, but at least he's not starting a fight. Besides, they are busy with their morning ration of paperwork, which is voluminous, as usual.

The other patients don't take any special note of Fred because most of them are equally absorbed in their own private worlds. . . . Three or four men are sitting stonily in chairs, grumbling angrily at the walls. Another man erupts into loud, incomprehensible laughter. A new patient tries to flick something off his shoulder, a motion he repeats again and again; there is nothing there. In the bathroom an extremely delusional, muscular man stuffs magazines down a toilet. The man's parents conceived him (so the story goes) while both were patients at Rusk State Hospital. He has been flushing magazines down the toilet every morning for over a week, ever since someone sent dozens of old copies of the New Yorker to Ward B.

Although all the patients were roused out of bed two hours ago, the only things they have been required to do so far are brush their teeth, comb their hair, and make their beds, activities that exhaust no more than five minutes apiece. Thus the rest of their time has been spent doing what they're doing now—milling about. When you're confined to a state hospital ward, you're forced to spend a lot of time with your thoughts, however terrifying they might be. This cruel fact cannot possibly help anyone get better, but that's the way it is. Other than the television, there are very few distractions. Milling about is the basic activity in the ward.

In the middle of the low-level chaos, a nurse holding a carton containing the morning medication walks into the nurse's station. Her name is Sue Dennison. "Okay," she announces in a tone that is both firm and pleasant, "get in line for your morning meds." The two mental health workers go into the dayroom to help the patients form a scraggly line. One by one the patients step up to the nurse's station to receive their medication. The psychotropic drugs they take—with names like Thorazine, Navane, Prolixin, Mellaril, and Haldol—are the primary, indeed, the only, form of real treatment they will receive in the hospital. And while there is no doubt that most of the people in this dayroom need the drugs desperately, there is considerable doubt as to whether some of them might not also benefit from other forms of help—from therapy, for instance. The issue of alternative treatments, which is the subject of a fierce national debate, does not get addressed in Austin. It is drugs that can prop people up the fastest, and get them out the quickest, and soak up the least amount of money. So drugs are what is used.

The first person Sue Dennison sees on this Thursday morning is a short, shy, soft-spoken man who looks about fifty years old. He is a murderer. In June 1980, six weeks after being released from the state hospital, he shot his next-door neighbor. He had heard voices telling him the neighbor was about to shoot him. Every time the doctors think he is well enough to stand trial, he is sent to prison. But as soon as he gets to prison, he regresses and has to be returned to the state hospital.

"How are you feeling today?" Dennison asks him. A few days before, the man had asked a ward staffer if the attendant was going to kill him soon. "Oh, just fine," he says meekly.

Next, a young black man steps up to the window. He has a little goatee and wears a baseball cap turned backward. When he sees Dennison, he puts his chin on the window ledge and stares at her salaciously. "Come on Michael," she says. "I can't give you your medicine if you're doing that." He keeps staring.

Michael is retarded. He was committed by a probate judge in Harris County, thus making him Austin's problem instead of Houston's. Harris County washed its hands of him not long after he arrived by sending a letter to the hospital stating that Michael could not be returned to Houston because the city lacked an "appropriate placement." But Austin doesn't have any place for him either. He belongs in a state school for the mentally retarded, but he can't get into one; the waiting period is about two years. Judge Sanders' monitors have raised the issue of retarded people languishing in the state hospitals. But what can the staff on Ward B do? All they can do is wait.

[B]ringing up the end of the line is Donald Peterson (not his real name). He is the toughest patient on the ward; he has lived at least half of his adult life in an institution—either a mental hospital or Huntsville State Prison (for armed robbery). The other patients are afraid of him. The staff prefers to keeps its distance too. Peterson, who looks old beyond his 44 years, hasn't shaved or bathed in days. He smells of stale cigarettes and rancid sweat, and the other patients have been complaining about him. Eventually, staff will have to force Peterson to take a shower, but they're not in any hurry. The last time they tried to make Peterson clean up—it happened about a week ago—one of the mental health workers wound up with torn ligaments in his thumb.

Don Peterson seems quite comfortable living in Ward B. And why not? His life on the outside is unrelievedly sad. His elderly father refuses to have anything to do with him. The mental health system barely knows he exists. He sleeps in a sickeningly ramshackle house in a Houston ghetto with a dozen other mentally ill people. For human companionship, he hangs out at the Star of Hope Mission in downtown Houston, where he is prey for thugs.

In the hospital, on the other hand, his living conditions are dramatically improved, he knows the ropes, and he can play the hunter instead of the prey. Soon after [one patient] arrived, for instance, Peterson sidled up to him on a bench with a can of Coke in his hand and asked with a smirk, "Do you think I can kill you with this?" Peterson also, from time to time, initiates sex with other men in the ward. This is not uncommon among the patients; even Fred was once caught trading a sexual act for cigarettes.

. . . After Sue Dennison gives Peterson his medicine, he quickly walks away—a little too quickly, in Dennison's opinion. She believes Peterson has been "cheeking his meds" lately—that is, only pretending to take his medication until he can get to the bathroom and spit it out. She thinks this because he has begun talking about how John Kennedy and Martin Luther King have deputized him "to be with white women." The mental health workers stop Peterson before he can get to the bathroom. He glares at them for a few seconds, but finally he swallows.

After Fred takes his morning medication and has breakfast in the ward cafeteria, he gets his two-cigarette allotment from the ward's "point store" (patients trade "points" they have earned in return for cigarettes or candy or coffee).

*   *   *

What happened to Fred in the past month offers a short course in the vagaries of patient care at the state hospital. His commitment began on

March 26, when he was admitted to Ward B as an "acute" patient, a status that legally limits his stay to a maximum of ninety days. He told the admissions staff glumly, "This is where I belong."

The doctor for Wards A and B (A is one of the female wards) was a kindly, Egyptian-born psychiatrist whose command of English was tentative at best, and who had a reputation for being cautious—too cautious, in fact, for the bureaucracy, which felt that he was gumming up the works by not releasing patients quickly enough. After about twenty minutes with Fred, the doctor diagnosed his illness as "Schizophrenia undifferentiated chronic"—very much in line with previous diagnoses—and prescribed Prolixin, a safe choice that also reflected Fred's history.

A month later Fred's first doctor left the hospital; he was replaced by a Cuban-born psychiatrist named Heriberto Cabada. Brusque and garrulous, Cabada was almost the complete opposite in temperament from his predecessor, with whom he shares only one apparent trait: heavily accented English. (Like most state hospitals, Austin is full of foreign-born and trained psychiatrists.) A large man with a pronounced girth who favored guayabera shirts and a three-day growth of beard, Cabada was the shortest of the short-timers. In little more than a month he would finish and move to Miami to begin what he hoped to be a lucrative private practice. Wards A and B were about the last place on earth he wanted to be. "This is a first-year resident's rotation," he groused to anyone within earshot. But he knew why he had been brought in.

In his three years at the hospital, Cabada had learned how to play the game, and he had become fairly cynical about it. He knew how to keep his head down whenever there was trouble; he had learned that lesson when one of his patients committed suicide while he was on vacation, and he nearly lost his residency as a result. Although he bridled at the paperwork ("It's a wonder we have time to see any patients at all"), he knew the importance of leaving a paper trail to keep the court and the bureaucracy satisfied. He knew he was there to prescribe drugs and not to administer psychotherapy. "This is a place to stabilize people and to get them out," he said bluntly. And when he got to Wards A and B, he immediately understood what was expected of him. Within a week, Cabada has released enough patients that the census on Ward B had dropped from 24 to 18. "I love that Cabada," said one of the workers on the ward.

And when Cabada saw Fred Thomas for the first time—fifteen minutes on the morning of May 2—he knew what was expected of him there too. Prolixin, which the previous doctor had prescribed, was popular in community outpatient clinics because it was the only drug at the time that could be given by injection with long-lasting (up to two weeks) effect. But the imperative at the state hospital makes Prolixin much less ideal because it is so slow-acting compared with most other psychotropic drugs.

As Cabada noted in Fred's chart, the patient "is progressing slowly, although he is not at the point where he should be." To speed things along, Cabada decided to switch Fred to Haldol, a potent, fast-acting . . . drug. Haldol is as popular inside the hospital as Prolixin is outside. At an initial dose of thirty milligrams a day, Fred was more drugged, and more sedated, and feeling more side effects than he had in his life.

Late one afternoon, a few days after the change, I got an inkling of how Haldol was affecting Fred. The patients were out on the patio; Fred was sitting in a chair he had pulled out from the ward. He was in a bad way. His lips were tight and trembled slightly, and he constantly touched them. He scratched his legs until they were white with scratch marks, and he was very groggy. Peterson came up to Fred and started screaming at him; Fred barely noticed. Instead he began talking to himself softly; "Rolling bowling green."

*   *   *

[While Dr. Cabada was on vacation, Fred was seen by a Dr. Kerr. According to Kerr, "When I was in medical school, we were always taught that a psychotic person was schizophrenic until proven otherwise." But after working in state hospitals, Kerr came to believe that many of the delusional patients he saw were not afflicted solely with schizophrenia or solely with manic depression, but rather with some combination of the two. Kerr rediagnosed Fred as suffering from a "schizoaffective disorder" and put him on Tegretol, 200 milligram three times a day, stating "There is nothing empirical about this. All you can do is bring your experience and your training." On this drug, Fred improved to the point where the hospital staff considered releasing him to a community facility].

MY WEEK IN THE PSYCH WARD
Laurie Kramer (2012).

[*The following excerpt is taken from a blog and provides a description of a hospital experience from the perspective of a patient who is more well-to-do than those patients described in the previous excerpt*]

I went to my current psychiatrist after suffering a high blood pressure episode brought on by eating aged cheese, a dangerous combination with my anti-depressant. I wanted to change my medication and although he recommended against it, he agreed to help me. After tapering down and then stopping the Nardil [an anti-depressant], depression hit within two days. By day five it was so bad that there seemed no choice but to go back on it, which I did and was better within a few days. I assumed everything would be like it had been before, but was wrong. The next month, in the space of only a few hours, I became close to catatonic. I could barely speak or walk, but I could understand and interestingly, I wasn't terribly depressed. I didn't even have the energy for that. This event lasted for a day and a half then disappeared almost as quickly as it had arrived, which it continued to do every few weeks over the following months.

The sudden onset and rapid cessation of these episodes, along with some other symptoms led my psychiatrist to diagnosis me with Bipolar II disorder. Unlike Bipolar I (what most people think of as "manic depression") which is notable for its extreme mania, Bipolar II has what is called hypomania, often characterized by elation or hyperactivity. Anger is another way hypomania is expressed and unfortunately this is usually what happens to me. I go into a rage, screaming and throwing things. Once I broke a kitchen cabinet.

That fateful Monday followed a horrible weekend where I was consumed by depression and fixated on suicide. For the first time I not only wished for death but planned how to do it. When I told my psychiatrist, he asked me whether I really meant it. I couldn't say no. He asked if I would agree to go to the hospital. I didn't know what to say but somehow I finally said yes. I know now that I had no choice and that my psychiatrist let me decide on my own before he made the decision for me. I'm grateful for that. He called Phillip who came with clothes, toiletries and a look that combined fear, worry and caring. As we drove out of the parking lot my psychiatrist walked outside to his car, and all I could think was that he was going home and I was going to a psychiatric ward.

Aside from a half-hour with a crisis counselor and a couple of chaperoned trips to the bathroom, I spent six hours on that gurney in the hallway of the emergency room (except for the single psych ward, this was a medical hospital). Phillip and I talked during this time, and he gently and carefully explained how bereft he would be if I were to take my own life. His feelings reached and I started to believe that I had to stay, for him, and for the other people I loved. I sent him home at midnight, after they told us it wouldn't be too much longer. A woman in hospital scrubs took his place and sat with me for the next two hours while I continued to wait. She never said a word except to scold me when I threw my pillow down the hall.

They took me upstairs at 2am. The quiet after the emergency room hallway was a relief. The nurses asked me some questions, they weighed and measured me, and they calmed and reassured me. When we were done, they took me to my room and gave me a sleeping pill and a mild tranquilizer. I got into my dormitory-style bed, missing my husband, missing my dogs, wondering who the woman in the other bed was. I was depressed, anxious, but mostly stunned. I slept most of the entire next day.

The very unusual thing about the psych ward is that they lock up your dental floss and hair dryer but allow you to keep sneakers in your room. Certainly sneaker laces could inflict just as much harm as dental floss or a hair dryer cord? Not only do they lock up your possessions, but they go through the drawers in your room each day. They examine the contents of your visitors' bags but not always that well because one day Phillip managed to sneak in my laptop. The utensils are plastic and the pictures are caulked onto the wall to prevent, I guess, suicide by art.

I woke up most days in a panic about being there. My depression eased over the week, but the confinement had caused a whole new agony. Almost every day I played a game in my head, imagining that I could convince them to let me go home early, but knowing that it wouldn't happen. When the game was over, I went to my room in frustration where I would close the door and cry. My roommate asked what was wrong to which I could only say, over and over, "I want to go home."

We had two group sessions each day. They were optional but strongly encouraged. Most revolved around the stress in our lives and how we could reduce it. I don't remember much of what we discussed, but it wasn't very helpful for me. I wanted and needed to talk about how horrible it had been to plan my own death. Instead I got the Bob Newhart show. We had an hour of recreation in the afternoon where we could use one of three exercise bikes or glue shells to pieces of wood (I chose the former.)

I made several friends by the second day, joining a group of four other women at meals. Our moods varied from day to day, sometimes from meal to meal, but there were always a couple of us doing well and we'd support the others. Two had been there before after suffering post-partum depression. Both were back because they decided they no longer needed anti-depressants. Let that be a lesson. I also got to know a funny and thoughtful man who had also contemplated suicide but was now more concerned about how he would tell his 13–year old son why Dad had been in the hospital.

Visiting hours were from 6 to 8pm on weekdays and 2 to 8pm on the weekend. Phillip spent every minute with me. Without this precious time together, I don't know how I could have made it through the week. Nothing was scheduled for us on weekends so those six hours really meant a lot. On Sunday the husband of one of my friends there brought a cake for Phillip. It was his 50th birthday.

By far the strangest and most ironic thing about the psych ward is the fact that no one asks for help or reports anything wrong to the staff. The only goal is to get out, and to mention side effects or unhappiness is to risk being given extra days by the psychiatrists and nurses who control your fate. We imagined a point system where you needed a certain number of points to get out. Points were gained for going to group therapy, chatting with the nurses, laughing. You lost points for crying, being angry, sleeping too much, or being negative. Hence the goal was to tell and show them what they wanted to hear. One day I started to hear an echo that no one else did, and noticed during the group meeting that everyone's voices were out of synch with their mouths, like a soundtrack that's a few seconds behind the movie. I thought it was pretty weird but figured it was just a temporary side effect of the new drug I was taking. In any case, I had absolutely no intention of telling anyone about it.

Each day we saw a psychiatrist who was assigned to us. Mine had the reputation as a superb psychopharmacologist, and although he was a pleasant man, his bedside manner left a bit to be desired. He met with his patients on one of the couches in the hall, where anyone could (and did) listen to the conversation. As my only goal was to be released, I was a fountain of good news everytime we talked. I missed my own psychiatrist but their involvement is limited to speaking with the hospital psychiatrist.

Most of my fellow patients were ordinary people, with a few exceptions of course. They ranged in age from 19 to over 70. The youngest, a petite girl who changed her clothes several times a day, had a temper tantrum her first evening. We all watched nervously as they led her into the "quiet" room, then listened to her scream and throw herself against the padded wall. They called in the cavalry, three burly security guards who accompanied a nurse with a syringe to sedate her. Another woman on the ward told us that she didn't work and did nothing day at home but watch TV and play on the computer. Her arms were covered with scars and healing wounds which looked like cigarette burns. Ironically, despite my earlier plan to commit suicide, I couldn't imagine how anyone could hurt themselves like she had. Another woman who was ate with us was in the hospital for ECT. No medication had significantly helped her depression and this was her last shot at health. When they wheeled her back to the ward after her fourth treatment, she had a big smile on her face. It was a thrilling sight.

The phone was our link to the outside world. There were two pay phones, located right next to each other in the hall where a TV blared most of the day. Phillip brought me a phone card with 900 minutes on it. I used over 300 during that week, five hours hunched in the corner, a finger in one ear to block the TV noise, talking to Phillip, to my sister, and to my friend Rita, a nurse trained in psychiatry who understood what I was going through. And each night I called my 88–year old father on Phillip's cell phone (also illegal), who lived in a nursing on the west coast. The fact of my hospitalization could have done him in, so I never told him where I was, and tried to sound happy as we talked each evening. "What did you do today?" he'd ask. "Not much," I'd reply, truthfully.

One week after that fateful Monday I met with my psychiatrist on the couch in the hallway. He had been away for four days and I felt a lot better. I didn't think he would let me leave that day, but I was determined to make my best effort. So I told him how well I felt, how free of side effects I had been (putting aside that little matter of the echo, which, by the way, was short-lived) and why I should go home that day. Amazingly he agreed. Freedom was mine. I gave a thumbs up to my friends, then felt a huge surge of guilt for abandoning them.

Did my week in the psych ward help me? It did relieve my depression and allowed me to get to a therapeutic level of lithium quickly instead of having to build up to it. My suicidal thoughts dissipated in the emergency room as I revealed them to my husband. Phillip and I became closer than ever. He was my rock and I couldn't have made it through without him. I met some wonderful people and learned that I was not alone in my illness. The comfort we gave each other by our mere presence was more effective than all the pills we swallowed. My family rallied around me and provided nothing but support. But I am still reeling from the experience. The isolation and removal from the "real world" certainly contributed to my recovery, but that and the loss of control were terribly difficult to bear. It was an experience I hope never to relive. Given the nature of this illness, however, I can't be sure of it.

WILLIAM FISHER, JEFFREY L. GELLER & JOHN A. PANDINI, THE CHANGING ROLE OF THE STATE PSYCHIATRIC HOSPITAL

(2012).

State hospitals were once the most prominent components of U.S. public mental health systems. But a major focus of mental health policy over the past fifty years has been to close these facilities. These efforts led to a 95 percent reduction in the country's state hospital population. However, more than 200 state hospitals remain open, serving a declining but challenging patient population. . . . ; indeed, across the United States, the decline in the state hospital population has stalled and for the first time in more than fifty years has shown an uptick in some states. . . . Several patient populations have gained prominence in recent years and likely will define the state hospital's mission for the foreseeable future. Among these are people with past criminal justice involvement, a growing "forensic" population, sexually dangerous persons, and, finally, what has been termed a "difficult-to-discharge" population. . . .

People with criminal justice histories. . . . A recent Massachusetts study of the arrest patterns of the SMHA's [state mental health agency's] clientele found that nearly 30 percent of a cohort of nearly 14,000 people experienced at least one arrest over a ten-year period. Many also experienced state hospital stays, and their previous charges, including drug and violent offenses, may have complicated their housing arrangements, employment, and other aspects of successful hospital discharge and community integration. Other studies have shown that arrests and state hospital admissions often coincide within a narrow time frame, which suggests that the challenge of managing hospital discharges for people with recent arrest histories may be quite common.

Forensic patients. . . . Since the increased admission rate of this patient group was first noted at the end of the 1970s, the percentage of people committed via this route, rather than through civil commitment, has continued to grow. For example, between 1988 and 2008, the proportion of Vermont state hospital admissions accounted for by forensic patients increased 50 percent; in Massachusetts, 281 percent; in New York, 309 percent; and in Pennsylvania, 379 percent. This trend has major implications for state hospital operations and financing, in that the criminal courts, not SMHAs, control forensic patients' admissions and discharges, but SMHAs nonetheless are liable for the costs of their hospitalization. . . . .

Sexually dangerous persons. Correctional officials in many states have long recognized that even after completing lengthy prison sentences for sexual assault and related offenses, many people remain, in some cases by their own admission, "sexually dangerous." . . . Risk management protocol dictates that releasing them could pose a major threat to public safety. But even if a person has responded to treatment and is deemed unlikely to pose such a threat, community placement remains a daunting task, given prevailing public attitudes toward sex offenders. Many such people will thus experience lengthy stays, and, as new cases are admitted, sexually dangerous persons will become a part of new long-stay population—one that, again, will be the financial responsibility of the SMHA.

Difficult-to-discharge patients. Despite the widespread expansion of community services, many state hospitals retain groups of difficult-to-discharge patients. A Massachusetts study, using detailed treatment team assessments of all patients residing in state hospitals for more than three years, identified many residents who presented one or more so-called barriers to discharge. These included combinations of complex medical conditions, "inappropriate behaviors"—some directly attributable to patients' psychiatric illnesses, others not—and potentially problematic sexual or other behaviors that would complicate their outplacement and could present risks to themselves or others. In addition to these barriers, a major challenge to discharge is some people's reluctance to leave the hospital and confront the challenges of life in a new setting. This reluctance has required development of new approaches to improving people's "readiness for change" in addition to addressing other identified barriers to discharge.

Impact of economic climate. The deteriorating economic climate of the early twenty-first century compounds some of these challenges. Efforts to outplace the difficult-to-discharge patients can go forward only if appropriate community services exist to accommodate them and hospital staff are available to prepare them for discharge. If new settings or intensified staffing levels are required for these efforts, this process will likely be put on hold, leaving these patients in the care of the state hospital, even if community placement would ultimately be less costly.

Shifting demographics of state hospitals. Not surprisingly, perhaps, the increased presence of people with histories of arrest or incarceration and those who have been eschewed by other settings has over time altered the demographics of state hospital populations. This change is reflected in data provided to us by the Organization of Northeast Mental Health Statistics Improvement Programs, which has monitored state hospital use since the 1980s. These data reveal the growth of two demographic populations that also predominate in the criminal justice environment: males and nonwhites. The proportion of males increased an average of 20 percent between 1991 and 2007 in the eleven states monitored for both years, while that of nonwhites increased an average of 48 percent between 1991 and 2007 in seven reporting states, ranging from 53 percent in Delaware to 158 percent in Massachusetts.

II. THEORETICAL UNDERPINNINGS OF THE RIGHT TO TREATMENT AND HABILITATION

DONALDSON V. O'CONNOR

United States Court of Appeals, Fifth Circuit, 1974.
493 F.2d 507, 519–531.

* * *

The question for decision, whether patients involuntarily civilly committed in state mental hospitals have a constitutional right to treatment, has never been addressed by any of the federal courts of appeals. Four district courts, however, have decided the question within the last three years, three of which held that there is a constitutional right to treatment. The Court of Appeals for the District of Columbia Circuit, in a landmark case decided eight years ago, took note in dictum of the existence and seriousness of the question, although in the same case the court held that the Hospitalization of the Mentally Ill Act of 1964 creates a *statutory* right to treatment on the part of mental patients in the District of Columbia.[11] The idea of a constitutional right to treatment has received an unusual amount of scholarly discussion and support, and there is now an enormous range of precedent relevant to, although not squarely in point with, the issue. The idea has been current at least since 1960, since the publication in the May 1960 issue of the American Bar Association Journal of an article by Dr. Morton Birnbaum, a forensic medical doctor now generally credited with being the father of the idea of

---

[11] Rouse v. Cameron, 1966, 125 U.S.App.D.C. 366, 373 F.2d 451.

a right to treatment. The A.B.A. Journal editorially endorsed the idea shortly after the publication of Dr. Birnbaum's article.

We hold that a person involuntarily civilly committed to a state mental hospital has a constitutional right to receive such individual treatment as will give him a reasonable opportunity to be cured or to improve his mental condition.

In reaching this result, we begin by noting the indisputable fact that civil commitment entails a "massive curtailment of liberty" in the constitutional sense. [B]eyond this, the conclusion that the due process clause guarantees a right to treatment rests upon a two-part theory. The first part begins with the fundamental, and all but universally accepted, proposition that "any nontrivial governmental abridgement of [any] freedom [which is part of the 'liberty' the Fourteenth Amendment says shall not be denied without due process of law] must be justified in terms of some 'permissible governmental goal.'" Once this "fairly sweeping concept of substantive due process" is assumed, the next step is to ask precisely what government interests justify the massive abridgement of liberty civil commitment entails.

* * *

The key point of the first part of the theory of a due process right to treatment is that where, as in Donaldson's case, the rationale for confinement is the "*parens patriae*" rationale that the patient is in need of treatment, the due process clause requires that minimally adequate treatment be in fact provided. This in turn requires that, at least for the nondangerous patient, constitutionally minimum standards of treatment be established and enforced. As Judge Johnson expressed it in the *Wyatt* case: "To deprive any citizen of his or her liberty upon the altruistic theory that the confinement is for humane therapeutic reasons and then fail to provide adequate treatment violates the very fundamentals of due process." Wyatt v. Stickney, 325 F.Supp. at 785. This key step in the theory also draws considerable support from, if indeed it is not compelled by, the Supreme Court's recent decision in *Jackson v. Indiana,* 1972, 406 U.S. 715, 92 S.Ct. 1845, 32 L.Ed.2d 435. In *Jackson,* the Supreme Court established the rule that "[a]t the least, due process requires that the nature and duration of commitment bear some reasonable relation to the purposes for which the individual is committed". If the "purpose" of commitment is treatment, and treatment is not provided, then the "nature" of the commitment bears no "reasonable relation" to its "purpose," and the constitutional rule of *Jackson* is violated.

This much represents the first part of the theory of a due process right to treatment; persons committed under what we have termed a *parens patriae* ground for commitment must be given treatment lest the involuntary commitment amount to an arbitrary exercise of government power proscribed by the due process clause. The second part of the theory draws no distinctions between persons committed under "*parens patriae*" rationales and those committed under "police power" rationales. This part begins with the recognition that, under our system of justice, long-term detention is, as a matter of due process, generally permitted only when an individual is (1) proved, in a proceeding subject to the rigorous constitutional limitations of the due process clause of the fourteenth amendment and the Bill of Rights, (2) to have committed a *specific act* defined as an offense against the state. Moreover, detention, under the criminal process, is usually allowed only for a period of time explicitly fixed by the prisoner's sentence. The second part of the theory of a due process right to treatment is based on the principle that when the three central limitations on the government's power to detain—that detention be in retribution for a specific offense; that it be limited to a fixed term; and that it be permitted after a proceeding where fundamental procedural safeguards are observed—are absent, there must be a *quid pro quo* extended by the government to justify confinement.[21] And the *quid pro quo* most commonly recognized is the provision of rehabilitative treatment, or, where rehabilitation is impossible, minimally adequate habilitation and care, beyond the subsistence level custodial care that would be provided in a penitentiary.

* * *

The appellants argue strenuously that a right to constitutionally adequate treatment should not be recognized, because such a right cannot be governed by judicially manageable or ascertainable standards. In making the argument, they rely heavily upon the Northern District of Georgia's decision in *Burnham v. Department of Public Health,* 1972, 349 F.Supp. 1335, 1341–1343. In *Burnham,* the district judge held that a class action seeking declaratory and injunctive relief requiring the Georgia Department of Public Health to provide treatment at Georgia mental hospitals presented a nonjusticiable controversy. He quoted *Baker v. Carr,* 1962, 369 U.S. 186, 198, 82 S.Ct. 691, 700, 7 L.Ed.2d 663, for the proposition that determining whether a suit was justiciable requires determining whether "the duty asserted can be judicially identified and its breach judicially determined, and whether protection for the right asserted can be judicially molded". He then cited the ambiguity of the dictionary definition of treatment, a passage from a law review article

---

[21] In *Welsch v. Likins,* 1974, 373 F.Supp. 487, the District of Minnesota described, and rejected, a different *quid pro quo* rationale for a right to treatment. We also reject the rationale described by the *Welsch* court, and the rationale we embrace should be carefully contrasted with it:

> One theory is that commitment pursuant to civil statutes generally lacks the procedural safeguards afforded those charged with criminal offense. The constitutional justification for this abridgment of *procedural rights* is that the purpose of commitment is treatment. (Emphasis supplied).

Welsch v. Likins, 373 F.Supp. at 496.

noting the fact that there are as many as forty different methods of psychotherapy, and a passage from the Supreme Court's decision in *Greenwood v. United States*, 1956, 350 U.S. 366, 76 S.Ct. 410, 100 L.Ed. 412, concerning the "tentativeness" and "uncertainty" of "professional judgment" in the mental health field. He concluded: "[T]he claimed duty (i.e. to 'adequately' or 'constitutionally treat') defies judicial identity and therefore prohibits its breach from being judicially defined."

The defendants' argument can be answered on two levels. First, we doubt whether, even if we were to concede that courts are incapable of formulating standards of adequate treatment in the abstract, we could or should for that reason alone hold that no right to treatment can be recognized or enforced. There will be cases—and the case at bar is one—where it will be possible to make determination whether a given individual has been denied his right to treatment without formulating in the abstract what constitutes "adequate" treatment.

* * *

We do not, however, concede that determining what constitutes adequate treatment is beyond the competence of the judiciary. In deciding in individual cases whether treatment is adequate, there are a number of devices open to the courts, as Judge Bazelon noted in discussing the implementation of the statutory right to treatment in the landmark case of Rouse v. Cameron:

> But lack of finality [of professional judgment] cannot relieve the court of its duty to render an informed decision. Counsel for the patient and the government can be helpful in presenting pertinent data concerning standards for mental care, and, particularly when the patient is indigent and cannot present experts of his own, the court may appoint independent experts. Assistance might be obtained from such sources as the American Psychiatric Association, which has published standards and is continually engaged in studying the problems of mental care. The court could also consider inviting the psychiatric and legal communities to establish procedures by which expert assistance can be best provided.

* * *

In summary, we hold that where a nondangerous patient is involuntarily civilly committed to a state mental hospital, the only constitutionally permissible purpose of confinement is to provide treatment, and that such a patient has a constitutional right to such treatment as will help him to be cured or to improve his mental condition. . . .

O'CONNOR V. DONALDSON

Supreme Court of the United States, 1975.
422 U.S. 563, 95 S.Ct. 2486, 45 L.Ed.2d 396.

JUSTICE BURGER, concurring.

A

[The Supreme Court's majority opinion in this case, reprinted at pp. 858–863, avoided the right to treatment issue. However, Chief Justice Burger, in a concurring opinion, directly addressed it, arguing that no such right should be recognized. In the first part of his concurrence, also reprinted at pp. 863–866, he responded to the Fifth Circuit's "first theory" justifying the right to treatment by disputing that court's apparent conclusion that "with respect to persons who are not physically dangerous, a State has no power to confine the mentally ill except for the purpose of providing them with treatment." Burger contended that, historically, parens patriae commitment had been primarily for custodial care, not treatment. Even today, "it remains a stubborn fact that there are many forms of mental illness which are not understood, some of which are untreatable in the sense that no effective therapy has yet been discovered for them, and that rates of 'cure' are generally low." Burger also noted the uncertainty of psychiatric diagnosis and the difficulty of treating mentally ill individuals who are unwilling to recognize they are ill. He concluded: "It may be that some persons in . . . these categories, and there may be others, are unable to function in society and will suffer real harm to themselves unless provided with care in a sheltered environment." Burger then addressed the Fifth Circuit's "second theory" justifying a constitutional right to treatment.]

B

Alternatively, it has been argued that a Fourteenth Amendment right to treatment for involuntarily confined mental patients derives from the fact that many of the safeguards of the criminal process are not present in civil commitment. The Court of Appeals described this theory as follows:

> "[A] due process right to treatment is based on the principle that when the three central limitations on the government's power to detain—that detention be in retribution for a specific offense; that it be limited to a fixed term; and that it be permitted after a proceeding where the fundamental procedural safeguards are observed—are absent, there must be a *quid pro quo* extended by the government to justify confinement. And the *quid pro quo* most commonly recognized is the provision of rehabilitative treatment." 493 F.2d, at 522.

To the extent that this theory may be read to permit a State to confine an individual simply because it is willing to provide treatment, regardless of the subject's ability to function in society, it raises the gravest of constitutional problems, and I have no doubt the Court of Appeals would agree on this score. As a justification for a constitutional right to such treatment, the *quid pro quo* theory suffers from equally serious defects.

It is too well established to require extended discussion that due process is not an inflexible concept. Rather, its requirements are determined in particular instances by identifying and accommodating the interests of the individual and society. Where claims that the State is acting in the best interests of an individual are said to justify reduced procedural and substantive safeguards, this Court's decisions require that they be "candidly appraised." However, in so doing judges are not free to read their private notions of public policy or public health into the Constitution.

The *quid pro quo* theory is a sharp departure from, and cannot coexist with, due process principles. As an initial matter, the theory presupposes that essentially the same interests are involved in every situation where a State seeks to confine an individual; that assumption, however, is incorrect. It is elementary that the justification for the criminal process and the unique deprivation of liberty which it can impose requires that it be invoked only for commission of a specific offense prohibited by legislative enactment.[7] But it would be incongruous, for example, to apply the same limitation when quarantine is imposed by the State to protect the public from a highly communicable disease.

A more troublesome feature of the *quid pro quo* theory is that it would elevate a concern for essentially procedural safeguards into a new substantive constitutional right. Rather than inquiring whether strict standards of proof or periodic redetermination of a patient's condition are required in civil confinement, the theory accepts the absence of such safeguards but insists that the State provide benefits which, in the view of a court, are adequate "compensation" for confinement. In light of the wide divergence of medical opinion regarding the diagnosis of and proper therapy for mental abnormalities, that prospect is especially troubling in this area and cannot be squared with the principle that "courts may not substitute for the judgments of legislators their own understanding of the public welfare, but must instead concern themselves with the validity under the Constitution of the methods which the legislature has selected." Of course, questions regarding the adequacy of procedure and the power of a State to continue particular confinements are ultimately for the courts, aided by expert opinion to the extent that is found helpful. But I am not persuaded that we should abandon the traditional limitations on the scope of judicial review.

---

[7] This is not to imply that I accept all of the Court of Appeals' conclusions regarding the limitations upon the States' power to detain persons who commit crimes. For example, the notion that confinement must be "for a fixed term" is difficult to square with the widespread practice of indeterminate sentencing, at least where the upper limit is a life sentence.

YOUNGBERG V. ROMEO

Supreme Court of the United States, 1982.
457 U.S. 307, 102 S.Ct. 2452, 73 L.Ed.2d 28.

JUSTICE POWELL delivered the opinion of the Court.

The question presented is whether respondent, involuntarily committed to a state institution for the mentally retarded, has substantive rights under the Due Process Clause of the Fourteenth Amendment to (i) safe conditions of confinement; (ii) freedom from bodily restraints; and (iii) training or "habilitation." Respondent sued under 42 U.S.C. § 1983 three administrators of the institution, claiming damages for the alleged breach of his constitutional rights.

I

Respondent Nicholas Romeo is profoundly retarded. Although 33 years old, he has the mental capacity of an 18–month–old child, with an I.Q. between 8 and 10. He cannot talk and lacks the most basic self-care skills. Until he was 26, respondent lived with his parents in Philadelphia. But after the death of his father in May 1974, his mother was unable to care for him. Within two weeks of the father's death, respondent's mother sought his temporary admission to a nearby Pennsylvania hospital.

Shortly thereafter, she asked the Philadelphia County Court of Common Pleas to admit Romeo to a state facility on a permanent basis. Her petition to the court explained that she was unable to care for Romeo or control his violence.[2] As part of the commitment process, Romeo was examined by a physician and a psychologist. They both certified that respondent was severely retarded and unable to care for himself. On June 11, 1974, the Court of Common Pleas committed respondent to the Pennhurst State School and Hospital, pursuant to the applicable involuntary commitment provision of the Pennsylvania Mental Health and Mental Retardation Act.

At Pennhurst, Romeo was injured on numerous occasions, both by his own violence and by the reactions of other residents to him. Respondent's mother became concerned about these injuries. After objecting to respondent's treatment several times, she filed this complaint on November 4, 1976, in the United States District Court for the Eastern District of Pennsylvania as his next friend. The complaint alleged that "[d]uring the period July, 1974 to the present, plaintiff has suffered injuries on at least sixty-three occasions." The complaint originally sought damages and injunctive relief from Pennhurst's director and two supervisors; it alleged that these officials knew, or should have known,

---

2   Mrs. Romeo's petition to the Court of Common Pleas stated: "Since my husband's death I am unable to handle him. He becomes violent—kicks, punches, breaks glass; He can't speak— wants to express himself but can't. He is [a] constant 24 hr. care. [W]ithout my husband I am unable to care for him."

that Romeo was suffering injuries and that they failed to institute appropriate preventive procedures, thus violating his rights under the Eighth and Fourteenth Amendments.

Thereafter, in late 1976, Romeo was transferred from his ward to the hospital for treatment of a broken arm. While in the infirmary, and by order of a doctor, he was physically restrained during portions of each day. These restraints were ordered by Dr. Gabroy, not a defendant here, to protect Romeo and others in the hospital, some of whom were in traction or were being treated intravenously. Although respondent normally would have returned to his ward when his arm healed, the parties to this litigation agreed that he should remain in the hospital due to the pending lawsuit. Nevertheless, in December 1977, a second amended complaint was filed alleging that the defendants were restraining respondent for prolonged periods on a routine basis. The second amended complaint also added a claim for damages to compensate Romeo for the defendants' failure to provide him with appropriate "treatment or programs for his mental retardation." All claims for injunctive relief were dropped prior to trial because respondent is a member of the class seeking such relief in another action.[6]

An 8–day jury trial was held in April 1978. Petitioners introduced evidence that respondent participated in several programs teaching basic self-care skills.[7] A comprehensive behavior-modification program was designed by staff members to reduce Romeo's aggressive behavior,[8] but that program was never implemented because of his mother's objections. Respondent introduced evidence of his injuries and of conditions in his unit.

At the close of the trial, the court instructed the jury that "if any or all of the defendants were aware of and failed to take all reasonable steps to prevent repeated attacks upon Nicholas Romeo," such failure deprived him of constitutional rights. The jury also was instructed that if the defendants shackled Romeo or denied him treatment "as a punishment for filing this lawsuit," his constitutional rights were violated under the Eighth Amendment. Finally, the jury was instructed that only if they found the defendants "deliberate[ly] indifferen[t] to the serious medical [and psychological] needs" of Romeo could they find that his Eighth and Fourteenth Amendment rights had been violated. The jury returned a verdict for the defendants, on which judgment was entered.

---

[6] *Pennhurst State School and Hospital v. Halderman,* 451 U.S. 1, 101 S.Ct. 1531, 67 L.Ed.2d 694 (1981) (remanded for further proceedings).

[7] Prior to his transfer to Pennhurst's hospital ward, Romeo participated in programs dealing with feeding, showering, drying, dressing, self-control, and toilet training, as well as a program providing interaction with staff members. Some programs continued while respondent was in the hospital, and they reduced respondent's aggressive behavior to some extent.

[8] The program called for short periods of separation from other residents and for use of "muffs" on plaintiff's hands for short periods of time, *i.e.,* five minutes, to prevent him from harming himself or others.

The Court of Appeals for the Third Circuit, sitting en banc, reversed and remanded for a new trial. The court held that the Eighth Amendment, prohibiting cruel and unusual punishment of those convicted of crimes, was not an appropriate source for determining the rights of the involuntarily committed. Rather, the Fourteenth Amendment and the liberty interest protected by that Amendment provided the proper constitutional basis for these rights. In applying the Fourteenth Amendment, the court found that the involuntarily committed retain liberty interests in freedom of movement and in personal security. These were "fundamental liberties" that can be limited only by an "overriding, non-punitive" state interest. It further found that the involuntarily committed have a liberty interest in habilitation designed to "treat" their mental retardation.

The en banc court did not, however, agree on the relevant standard to be used in determining whether Romeo's rights had been violated. Because physical restraint "raises a presumption of a punitive sanction," the majority of the Court of Appeals concluded that it can be justified only by "compelling necessity." A somewhat different standard was appropriate for the failure to provide for a resident's safety. The majority considered that such a failure must be justified by a showing of "substantial necessity." Finally, the majority held that when treatment has been administered, those responsible are liable only if the treatment is not "acceptable in the light of present medical or other scientific knowledge."[14]

Chief Judge Seitz, concurring in the judgment, considered the standards articulated by the majority as indistinguishable from those applicable to medical malpractice claims. In Chief Judge Seitz' view, the Constitution "only requires that the courts make certain that professional judgment in fact was exercised." He concluded that the appropriate standard was whether the defendants' conduct was "such a substantial departure from accepted professional judgment, practice, or standards in the care and treatment of this plaintiff as to demonstrate that the defendants did not base their conduct on a professional judgment."

We granted the petition for certiorari because of the importance of the question presented to the administration of state institutions for the mentally retarded.

---

[14] Actually, the court divided the right-to-treatment claim into three categories and adopted three standards, but only the standard described in text is at issue before this Court. The Court of Appeals also stated that if a jury finds that *no* treatment has been administered, it may hold the institution's administrators liable unless they can provide a compelling explanation for the lack of treatment, but respondent does not discuss this precise standard in his brief and it does not appear to be relevant to the facts of this case. In addition, the court considered "least intrusive" analysis appropriate to justify severe intrusions on individual dignity such as permanent physical alteration or surgical intervention, but respondent concedes that this issue is not present in this case.

II

We consider here for the first time the substantive rights of involuntarily committed mentally retarded persons under the Fourteenth Amendment to the Constitution. In this case, respondent has been committed under the laws of Pennsylvania, and he does not challenge the commitment. Rather, he argues that he has a constitutionally protected liberty interest in safety, freedom of movement, and training within the institution; and that petitioners infringed these rights by failing to provide constitutionally required conditions of confinement.

The mere fact that Romeo has been committed under proper procedures does not deprive him of all substantive liberty interests under the Fourteenth Amendment. See, *e.g., Vitek v. Jones,* 445 U.S. 480, 491–494, 100 S.Ct. 1254, 1262–1264, 63 L.Ed.2d 552 (1980). Indeed, the state concedes that respondent has a right to adequate food, shelter, clothing, and medical care. We must decide whether liberty interests also exist in safety, freedom of movement, and training. If such interests do exist, we must further decide whether they have been infringed in this case.

A

Respondent's first two claims involve liberty interests recognized by prior decisions of this Court, interests that involuntary commitment proceedings do not extinguish. The first is a claim to safe conditions. In the past, this Court has noted that the right to personal security constitutes a "historic liberty interest" protected substantively by the Due Process Clause. And that right is not extinguished by lawful confinement, even for penal purposes. If it is cruel and unusual punishment to hold convicted criminals in unsafe conditions, it must be unconstitutional to confine the involuntarily committed—who may not be punished at all—in unsafe conditions.

Next, respondent claims a right to freedom from bodily restraint. In other contexts, the existence of such an interest is clear in the prior decisions of this Court. Indeed, "[l]iberty from bodily restraint always has been recognized as the core of the liberty protected by the Due Process Clause from arbitrary governmental action." This interest survives criminal conviction and incarceration. Similarly, it must also survive involuntary commitment.

B

Respondent's remaining claim is more troubling. In his words, he asserts a "constitutional right to minimally adequate habilitation." This is a substantive due process claim that is said to be grounded in the liberty component of the Due Process Clause of the Fourteenth Amendment.[19]

---

[19] Respondent also argues that because he was committed for care and treatment under state law he has a state substantive right to habilitation, which is entitled to substantive, not procedural, protection under the Due Process Clause of the Fourteenth Amendment. But this

The term "habilitation," used in psychiatry, is not defined precisely or consistently in the opinions below or in the briefs of the parties or the *amici*.[20] [T]he term refers to "training and development of needed skills." Respondent emphasizes that the right he asserts is for "minimal" training, and he would leave the type and extent of training to be determined on a case-by-case basis "in light of present medical or other scientific knowledge."

In addressing the asserted right to training, we start from established principles. As a general matter, a State is under no constitutional duty to provide substantive services for those within its border. See *Harris v. McRae,* 448 U.S. 297, 318, 100 S.Ct. 2671, 2689, 65 L.Ed.2d 784 (1980) (publicly funded abortions); *Maher v. Roe,* 432 U.S. 464, 469, 97 S.Ct. 2376, 2380, 53 L.Ed.2d 484 (1977) (medical treatment). When a person is institutionalized—and wholly dependent on the State— it is conceded by petitioners that a duty to provide certain services and care does exist, although even then a State necessarily has considerable discretion in determining the nature and scope of its responsibilities. Nor must a State "choose between attacking every aspect of a problem or not attacking the problem at all."

Respondent, in light of the severe character of his retardation, concedes that no amount of training will make possible his release. And he does not argue that if he were still at home, the State would have an obligation to provide training at its expense. The record reveals that respondent's primary needs are bodily safety and a minimum of physical restraint, and respondent clearly claims training related to these needs. As we have recognized that there is a constitutionally protected liberty interest in safety and freedom from restraint, training may be necessary to avoid unconstitutional infringement of those rights. On the basis of the record before us, it is quite uncertain whether respondent seeks any "habilitation" or training unrelated to safety and freedom from bodily restraints. In his brief to this Court, Romeo indicates that even the self-care programs he seeks are needed to reduce his aggressive behavior. And in his offer of proof to the trial court, respondent repeatedly indicated that, if allowed to testify, his experts would show that additional training programs, including self-care programs, were needed to reduce his aggressive behavior. If, as seems the case, respondent seeks only training related to safety and freedom from restraints, this case does not present the difficult question whether a mentally retarded person, involuntarily committed to a state institution, has some general constitutional right to

---

argument is made for the first time in respondent's brief to this Court. It was not advanced in the courts below, and was not argued to the Court of Appeals as a ground for reversing the trial court. Given the uncertainty of Pennsylvania law and the lack of any guidance on this issue from the lower federal courts, we decline to consider it now.

[20] Professionals in the habilitation of the mentally retarded disagree strongly on the question whether effective training of all severely or profoundly retarded individuals is even possible.

training *per se,* even when no type or amount of training would lead to freedom.[23]

Chief Judge Seitz, in language apparently adopted by respondent, observed:

> "I believe that the plaintiff has a constitutional right to minimally adequate care and treatment. The existence of a constitutional right to care and treatment is no longer a novel legal proposition."

Chief Judge Seitz did not identify or otherwise define—beyond the right to reasonable safety and freedom from physical restraint—the "minimally adequate care and treatment" that appropriately may be required for this respondent. In the circumstances presented by this case, and on the basis of the record developed to date, we agree with his view and conclude that respondent's liberty interests require the State to provide minimally adequate or reasonable training to ensure safety and freedom from undue restraint. In view of the kinds of treatment sought by respondent and the evidence of record, we need go no further in this case.

III

A

We have established that Romeo retains liberty interests in safety and freedom from bodily restraint. Yet these interests are not absolute; indeed to some extent they are in conflict. In operating an institution such as Pennhurst, there are occasions in which it is necessary for the State to restrain the movement of residents—for example, to protect them as well as others from violence. Similar restraints may also be appropriate in a training program. And an institution cannot protect its residents from all danger of violence if it is to permit them to have any freedom of movement. The question then is not simply whether a liberty interest has been infringed but whether the extent or nature of the restraint or lack of absolute safety is such as to violate due process.

Accordingly, whether respondent's constitutional rights have been violated must be determined by balancing his liberty interests against the relevant state interests. If there is to be any uniformity in protecting these interests, this balancing cannot be left to the unguided discretion of a judge or jury. We therefore turn to consider the proper standard for determining whether a State adequately has protected the rights of the involuntarily committed mentally retarded.

---

[23] In the trial court, respondent asserted that "state officials at a state mental hospital have a duty to provide residents . . . with such treatment as will afford them a reasonable opportunity to acquire and maintain those life skills necessary to cope as effectively as their capacities permit." But this claim to a sweeping *per se* right was dropped thereafter. In his brief to this Court, respondent does not repeat it and, at oral argument, respondent's counsel explicitly disavowed any claim that respondent is constitutionally entitled to such treatment as would enable him "to achieve his maximum potential."

B

We think the standard articulated by Chief Judge Seitz affords the necessary guidance and reflects the proper balance between the legitimate interests of the State and the rights of the involuntarily committed to reasonable conditions of safety and freedom from unreasonable restraints. He would have held that "the Constitution only requires that the courts make certain that professional judgment in fact was exercised. It is not appropriate for the courts to specify which of several professionally acceptable choices should have been made." Persons who have been involuntarily committed are entitled to more considerate treatment and conditions of confinement than criminals whose conditions of confinement are designed to punish. At the same time, this standard is lower than the "compelling" or "substantial" necessity tests the Court of Appeals would require a State to meet to justify use of restraints or conditions of less than absolute safety. We think this requirement would place an undue burden on the administration of institutions such as Pennhurst and also would restrict unnecessarily the exercise of professional judgment as to the needs of residents.

Moreover, we agree that respondent is entitled to minimally adequate training. In this case, the minimally adequate training required by the Constitution is such training as may be reasonable in light of respondent's liberty interests in safety and freedom from unreasonable restraints. In determining what is "reasonable"—in this and in any case presenting a claim for training by a State—we emphasize that courts must show deference to the judgment exercised by a qualified professional. By so limiting judicial review of challenges to conditions in state institutions, interference by the federal judiciary with the internal operations of these institutions should be minimized. Moreover, there certainly is no reason to think judges or juries are better qualified than appropriate professionals in making such decisions. For these reasons, the decision, if made by a professional,[30] is presumptively valid; liability may be imposed only when the decision by the professional is such a substantial departure from accepted professional judgment, practice, or standards as to demonstrate that the person responsible actually did not base the decision on such a judgment. In an action for damages against a professional in his individual capacity, however, the professional will not be liable if he was unable to satisfy his normal professional standards

---

[30] By "professional" decisionmaker, we mean a person competent, whether by education, training or experience, to make the particular decision at issue. Long-term treatment decisions normally should be made by persons with degrees in medicine or nursing, or with appropriate training in areas such as psychology, physical therapy, or the care and training of the retarded. Of course, day-to-day decisions regarding care—including decisions that must be made without delay—necessarily will be made in many instances by employees without formal training but who are subject to the supervision of qualified persons.

because of budgetary constraints; in such a situation, good-faith immunity would bar liability.

IV

In deciding this case, we have weighed those postcommitment interests cognizable as liberty interests under the Due Process Clause of the Fourteenth Amendment against legitimate state interests and in light of the constraints under which most state institutions necessarily operate. We repeat that the State concedes a duty to provide adequate food, shelter, clothing, and medical care. These are the essentials of the care that the State must provide. The State also has the unquestioned duty to provide reasonable safety for all residents and personnel within the institution. And it may not restrain residents except when and to the extent professional judgment deems this necessary to assure such safety or to provide needed training. In this case, therefore, the State is under a duty to provide respondent with such training as an appropriate professional would consider reasonable to ensure his safety and to facilitate his ability to function free from bodily restraints. It may well be unreasonable not to provide training when training could significantly reduce the need for restraints or the likelihood of violence.

Respondent thus enjoys constitutionally protected interests in conditions of reasonable care and safety, reasonably nonrestrictive confinement conditions, and such training as may be required by these interests. Such conditions of confinement would comport fully with the purpose of respondent's commitment. Cf. *Jackson v. Indiana,* 406 U.S. 715, 738, 92 S.Ct. 1845, 1858, 32 L.Ed.2d 435 (1972) [reprinted at p. 1151]. In determining whether the State has met its obligations in these respects, decisions made by the appropriate professional are entitled to a presumption of correctness. Such a presumption is necessary to enable institutions of this type—often, unfortunately, overcrowded and understaffed—to continue to function. A single professional may have to make decisions with respect to a number of residents with widely varying needs and problems in the course of a normal day. The administrators, and particularly professional personnel, should not be required to make each decision in the shadow of an action for damages.

In this case, we conclude that the jury was erroneously instructed on the assumption that the proper standard of liability was that of the Eighth Amendment. We vacate the decision of the Court of Appeals and remand for further proceedings consistent with this decision.

So ordered.

JUSTICE BLACKMUN, with whom JUSTICE BRENNAN and JUSTICE O'CONNOR join, concurring.

I join the Court's opinion. I write separately, however, to make clear why I believe that opinion properly leaves unresolved two difficult and important issues.

The first is whether the Commonwealth of Pennsylvania could accept respondent for "care and treatment," as it did under the Pennsylvania Mental Health and Mental Retardation Act of 1966, and then constitutionally refuse to provide him any "treatment," as that term is defined by state law. Were that question properly before us, in my view there would be a serious issue whether, as a matter of due process, the State could so refuse. I therefore do not find that issue to be a "frivolous" one, as the Chief Justice does.

In *Jackson v. Indiana,* 406 U.S. 715, 92 S.Ct. 1845, 32 L.Ed.2d 435 (1972), this Court, by a unanimous vote of all participating Justices, suggested a constitutional standard for evaluating the conditions of a civilly committed person's confinement: "At the least, due process requires that the nature and duration of commitment bear some reasonable relation to the purpose for which the individual is committed."

*   *   *

In respondent's case, the majority and principal concurring opinions in the Court of Appeals agreed that "[b]y basing [respondent's] deprivation of liberty at least partially upon a promise of treatment, the state ineluctably has committed the community's resources to providing minimal treatment." Neither opinion clarified, however, whether respondent in fact had been totally denied "treatment," as that term is defined under Pennsylvania law. To the extent that the majority addressed the question, it found that "the evidence in the record, although somewhat contradictory, suggests not so much a total failure to treat as an inadequacy of treatment."

This Court's reading of the record supports that conclusion. Moreover, the Court today finds that respondent's entitlement to "treatment" under Pennsylvania law was not properly raised below. Given this uncertainty in the record, I am in accord with the Court's decision not to address the constitutionality of a State's total failure to provide "treatment" to an individual committed under state law for "care and treatment."

The second difficult question left open today is whether respondent has an independent constitutional claim, grounded in the Due Process Clause of the Fourteenth Amendment, to that "habilitation" or training necessary to *preserve* those basic self-care skills he possessed when he first entered Pennhurst—for example, the ability to dress himself and care for his personal hygiene. In my view, it would be consistent with the Court's reasoning today to include within the "minimally adequate training required by the Constitution," such training as is reasonably necessary to prevent a person's pre-existing self-care skills from *deteriorating* because of his commitment.

The Court makes clear that even after a person is committed to a state institution, he is entitled to such training as is necessary to prevent unreasonable losses of additional liberty as a result of his confinement— for example, unreasonable bodily restraints or unsafe institutional conditions. If a person could demonstrate that he entered a state institution with minimal self-care skills, but lost those skills after commitment because of the State's unreasonable refusal to provide him training, then, it seems to me, he has alleged a loss of liberty quite distinct from—and as serious as—the loss of safety and freedom from unreasonable restraints. For many mentally retarded people, the difference between the capacity to do things for themselves within an institution and total dependence on the institution for all of their needs is as much liberty as they ever will know.

Although respondent asserts a claim of this kind, I agree with the Court that "[o]n the basis of the record before us, it is quite uncertain whether respondent [in fact] seeks any 'habilitation' or training unrelated to safety and freedom from bodily restraints." Since the Court finds respondent constitutionally entitled at least to "such training as may be reasonable in light of [his] liberty interests in safety and freedom from unreasonable restraints," I accept its decision not to address respondent's additional claim.

If respondent actually seeks habilitation in self-care skills not merely to reduce his aggressive tendencies, but also to maintain those basic self-care skills necessary to his personal autonomy within Pennhurst, I believe he is free on remand to assert that claim.

* * *

The Court finds it premature to resolve this constitutional question on this less than fully developed record. Because I agree with that conclusion, I concur in the Court's opinion.

CHIEF JUSTICE BURGER, concurring in the judgment.

I agree with much of the Court's opinion. However, I would hold flatly that respondent has no constitutional right to training, or "habilitation," *per se*. The parties, and the Court, acknowledge that respondent cannot function outside the state institution, even with the assistance of relatives. Indeed, even now neither respondent nor his family seeks his discharge from state care. Under these circumstances, the State's provision of food, shelter, medical care, and living conditions as safe as the inherent nature of the institutional environment reasonably allows, serves to justify the State's custody of respondent. The State did not seek custody of respondent; his family understandably sought the State's aid to meet a serious need.

I agree with the Court that some amount of self-care instruction may be necessary to avoid unreasonable infringement of a mentally retarded person's interests in safety and freedom from restraint; but it seems clear to me that the Constitution does not otherwise place an affirmative duty on the State to provide any particular kind of training or habilitation—even such as might be encompassed under the essentially standardless rubric "minimally adequate training," to which the Court refers. Since respondent asserts a right to "minimally adequate" habilitation "[q]uite apart from its relationship to decent care," unlike the Court I see no way to avoid the issue.*

I also point out that, under the Court's own standards, it is largely irrelevant whether respondent's experts were of the opinion that "additional training programs, including self-care programs, were needed to reduce [respondent's] aggressive behavior,"—a prescription far easier for "spectators" to give than for an institution to implement. The training program devised for respondent by petitioners and other professionals at Pennhurst was, according to the Court's opinion, "presumptively valid"; and "liability may be imposed only when the decision by the professional is such a substantial departure from accepted professional judgment, practice, or standards as to demonstrate that the person responsible actually did not base the decision on such a judgment." Thus, even if respondent could demonstrate that the training programs at Pennhurst were inconsistent with generally accepted or prevailing professional practice—if indeed there be such—this would not avail him so long as his training regimen was actually prescribed by the institution's professional staff.

QUESTIONS AND COMMENTS

1. *Choosing a rationale.* Of the various constitutional theories described in the preceding opinions, which is the most convincing? The first rationale advanced by the Fifth Circuit (discussed also by Justice Blackmun in *Youngberg*) is premised on *Jackson v. Indiana's* notion that the nature of confinement must bear a reasonable relationship to its purpose. Does a right to treatment for civilly committed patients necessarily flow from this premise, in light of the points made by Chief Justice Burger in his concurring opinion in *Donaldson?* In *Jackson* itself, the Court required that all persons committed for restoration of competency to stand trial receive treatment to effect that restoration unless they are unrestorable, in which case they

---

* Indeed, in the trial court respondent asserted a broad claim to such "treatment as [would] afford [him] a reasonable opportunity to acquire and maintain those life skills necessary to cope as effectively as [his] capacities permit."

Respondent also maintains that, because state law purportedly creates a right to "care and treatment," he has a *federal substantive* right under the Due Process Clause to enforcement of this state right. This contention is obviously frivolous; were every substantive right created by state law enforceable under the Due Process Clause, the distinction between state and federal law would quickly be obliterated.

should be released *or* civilly committed. Does not this holding support Burger's assertions about the possible purposes of civil (as opposed to criminal) commitment?

In response, consider this excerpt from *Wyatt v. Aderholt,* 503 F.2d 1305, 1313 (5th Cir.1974), in which the Fifth Circuit addressed a contention similar to Burger's:

> [W]e find it impossible to accept the [state's] underlying premise that the "need for care" for the mentally ill—and to relieve their families, friends, or guardians of the burden of doing so—can supply a constitutional justification for civil commitment . . . The state interest thus asserted may be, strictly speaking, a "rational" state interest. But we find it so trivial beside the major personal interests against which it is to be weighed that we cannot possibly accept it as a justification for the deprivations of liberty involved.

Note also that a majority of states today recognize by statute a right to treatment (as opposed to "care") for every committed patient, whether committed under *parens patriae* or police power authority (although some states make the provision of treatment contingent on funding). Samuel Brakel et al., The Mentally Disabled and the Law 337 (1985). Of what significance is this fact in evaluating the importance of *Jackson* in establishing a constitutional right to treatment? In his *Youngberg* concurrence, how does Burger amend his *Donaldson* argument to take into account this modern statutory development (see his footnote)? Does Justice Powell's *Youngberg* opinion foreclose a right to treatment based on the "*Jackson*" rationale?

With respect to the Fifth Circuit's second rationale for a constitutional right to treatment (the "quid pro quo" theory), does not the court's reasoning imply that provision of treatment is the only justification for affording civil committees fewer procedural and substantive protections than criminal defendants? To what extent *are* the differences between civil commitment and the criminal process justified by an assumed treatment orientation of the former (cf. *Addington, Parham, Allen v. Illinois*)?

Turning to the Supreme Court's reasoning in *Youngberg,* note that it avoided reliance on the eighth amendment's cruel and unusual punishment clause. Some lower courts have based a right to treatment on this provision in light of the Supreme Court's opinion in *Robinson v. California,* 370 U.S. 660, 82 S.Ct. 1417, 8 L.Ed.2d 758 (1962), which held that the clause prohibits criminal punishment of a person for the status of being an addict. In *Welsch v. Likins,* 373 F.Supp. 487, 496–7 (D.Minn.1974), for instance, the court held that confining someone who is mentally ill and dangerous without treatment is like punishing someone for being an addict, and thus is a violation of the eighth amendment. One reason for rejecting this approach to the right to treatment is that the cruel and unusual punishment clause has normally been applied only to criminal punishment. See *Bell v. Wolfish,* 441 U.S. 520, 99 S.Ct. 1861, 60 L.Ed.2d 447 (1979) (claims brought by pretrial detainees about conditions imposed on them prior to trial not actionable under the eighth amendment); see also *Kansas v. Hendricks*, 521 U.S. 346, 117 S.Ct. 2072, 138 L.Ed.2d 501 (1997) (holding that incapacitation without treatment under a sexual predator act is not punishment for double jeopardy and ex post facto purposes). Assuming this problem is overcome, is *Robinson* good precedent for establishing a right to treatment?

In *Youngberg*, the Court focused instead on the liberty interests of committed patients under the due process clause. Relying on this clause, the majority clearly established a right to "minimally adequate treatment" which, "in this case," consisted of a right to safe conditions and freedom from bodily restraint. At first glance, this formulation may seem narrow. But consider the following excerpt from Note, *The Supreme Court: 1981 Term*, 96 Harv.L.Rev. 77, 82–84 (1982):

> Although the Court [in *Youngberg*] sidestepped a direct affirmation of broad rights to habilitation, Justice Powell's liberty-based rationale for a constitutional right to training may lead to a comparable result by any of three avenues. First, although Justice Powell failed to define the scope of "training related to safety and freedom from restraints," he explicitly included training necessary to prevent the violence of self-destructive behavior that creates both a more dangerous institutional environment and a heightened need for bodily restraint. Moreover, the right must encompass training based upon individualized evaluations of patients; only such training can reasonably ensure effective protection of a given patient's liberty interest. Most significantly, Justice Powell's formulation may itself imply a right to habilitative treatment. Training in basic self-care skills—such as dressing oneself and reading—fits within his formulation, because substantial psychiatric study shows that such training reduces violent and self-destructive behavior.

> Second, if logically extended, Justice Powell's liberty-based rationale would justify even broad constitutional rights to treatment. As Justice Blackmum observed in his concurrence, a constitutional right to "such training as is reasonably necessary to prevent a person's pre-existing self-care skills from deteriorating" is "consistent" with the majority's opinion. The deterioration of basic skills, Justice Blackmum noted, presents 'a loss of liberty quite distinct from—and as serious as—the loss of safety and freedom from unreasonable restraints.'

> Third, the Court's reasoning implies the existence of expansive rights that protect the patient's principal liberty interest—the interest in release from involuntary confinement. Psychiatrists have observed that the absence of the training necessary to improve a person's basic skills can unduly prolong confinement. Thus, the majority's liberty-based rationale suggests that mental patients have a constitutional right to habilitative rather than merely protective treatment.

A variant of this last possible interpretation of *Youngberg* was proposed in Roy Spece, *Preserving the Right to Treatment: A Critical Assessment and*

Constructive Development of Constitutional Right to Treatment Theories, 20 Ariz.L.Rev. 1, 33–46 (1978). Relying on least restrictive alternative theory, Spece argued that "virtually all patients are entitled to superior, individual treatment . . . unless the state can meet the heavy burden of demonstrating either that treatment would neither hasten release nor enhance freedom within the institution or that confinement with treatment would be less effective than confinement simpliciter in achieving the state's commitment goals." Id. at 34–35. According to Spece, this theory "comfortably accommodates the confinement of those who are untreatable but otherwise committable." Id. at 44. At the same time, Spece asserts, it requires the state to provide treatment for virtually every patient who is treatable. To what extent does *Youngberg* endorse this theory? In the majority opinion, look at both the penultimate paragraph and footnote 14.

2.   *The professional judgment standard.* Whatever the ultimate scope of the right to treatment, the question as to whether that right has been infringed may well depend upon how courts construe *Youngberg's* professional judgment standard. For instance, even if patients had a right to treatment or habilitation that will enable them to leave the hospital as soon as possible, deciding whether a particular treatment program implements that right would probably depend solely upon whether "professional judgment was exercised" in deciding upon the program. Note also that *Youngberg* stated that if the reason professional judgment is not exercised or implemented is budgetary, then damages cannot be awarded against an individual professional (the "good faith" defense). However, the Court made no comment on the viability of a "budgetary defense" in an individual or class action suit seeking to enjoin the state to provide treatment.

3.   *Aftermath of* Youngberg. Courts have diverged sharply on the proper formulation of the right to care under *Youngberg* and the Due Process Clause. For instance, *Sharp v. Weston,* 233 F.3d 1166, 1172 (9th Cir.2000), held that civilly committed persons must be provided "a realistic opportunity to be cured or improve the mental condition for which they were confined." In contrast, another federal circuit court of appeals concluded that "[w]here the state does not provide treatment designed to improve a mentally retarded individual's condition, it deprives the individual of nothing guaranteed by the Constitution; it simply fails to grant a benefit of optimal treatment that it is under no obligation to grant." *Feagley v. Waddill,* 868 F.2d 1437, 1440 (5th Cir.1989). See also, *Allison v. Snyder,* 332 F.3d 1076, 1081 (7th Cir.2003) (holding that committed individuals are entitled to some treatment, but that what that treatment entails must be decided by mental health professionals). In-between is a third approach, represented by the Second Circuit's decision in *Society for Good Will to Retarded Children, Inc. v. Cuomo,* 737 F.2d 1239 (2d Cir.1984) (hereafter *SGW v. Cuomo*). Although it held that after *Youngberg* the Constitution does not require the state to provide treatment designed to improve the condition of a person with mental retardation, the court endorsed Justice Blackmun's right-to-avoid-deterioration standard. See also, *Frederick L. v. Department of Public Welfare,* 157 F.Supp.2d 509, 524–

25 (E.D.Pa.2001); *Assoc. for Retarded Citizens of North Dakota v. Olson,* 561 F.Supp. 473, 487 (D.N.D.1982), affirmed 713 F.2d 1384 (8th Cir.1983).

Courts have expanded upon *Youngberg* in other ways as well. First, some courts have broadly defined the professional judgment rule. While Chief Justice Burger's concurrence asserted that *Youngberg* would require only that the challenged decision be made by a professional, as of 1993 "[n]one of the courts deciding professional judgment cases ha[d] followed Justice Burger's interpretation." Susan Stefan, *What Constitutes Departure from Professional Judgment?*, 17 Men. & Phys. Dis. L. Rep. 207, 209 (1993). More recent decisions continue this tendency. In *Johnson v. State*, 289 Kan. 642, 215 P.3d 575, 584 (2009), the Court applied (although it did not officially adopt) a formulation that asks "whether the treatment fell within the range of treatment recognized by reasonable professionals." Probably the most expansive interpretation of the professional judgment rule that a court has adopted came in *Thomas S. v. Morrow,* 601 F.Supp. 1055 (W.D.N.C.1984), which held that professional judgment is not exercised when "the professional's stated judgment was modified to conform to the *available* treatment, rather than the *appropriate* treatment, for the plaintiff's condition." Id. at 1059 (emphasis in original). Judgments that appear to have been made for administrative or staff convenience or that depart from institutional or state guidelines or regulations have also been found to violate the professional judgment rule. For instance, in a later version of the *Thomas S.* case, the Fourth Circuit held that the state should be liable under *Youngberg* because of "substantial" departures from professional standards involving: confinement of people with retardation in psychiatric hospitals; the use of seclusion and mechanical restraints without employing behavioral treatment programs; the overuse of antispsychotic mediation; and insufficient consideration of treating professionals' recommendations on community placement. *Thomas S. v. Flaherty*, 902 F.2d 250 (4th Cir. 1990). See also *Evans v. Fenty*, 701 F.Supp.2d 126, 163 (2010) (citing *Thomas S.* approvingly); *Gary H. v. Hegstrom*, 831 F.2d 1430, 1439 (9th Cir. 1987). On the other hand, mere expert disagreement with the state's experts is very unlikely to rebut the professional judgment presumption. See, e.g., *SGW v. Cuomo*, supra, at 1249.

A second manifestation of judicial resistance to a narrow reading of *Youngberg* is the rejection of the "budgetary defense" in cases seeking injunctions. For instance, in *Clark v. Cohen*, 613 F.Supp. 684, 704 (E.D.Pa.1985), the court compelled community placement of a patient with intellectual disabilities despite financially-based objections by the state, emphasizing that professional judgment, to be entitled to judicial deference, "has to be based on medical or psychological criteria and not on exigency, administrative convenience, or other non-medical criteria." See also, *Thomas S. v. Morrow*, 781 F.2d 367, 375 (4th Cir.1986) (*Youngberg* did not apply the budgetary defense to "prospective injunctive relief").

4. Youngberg *and voluntary patients.* Although *Youngberg* involved an involuntarily committed individual, some courts initially refused to

distinguish between involuntary and voluntary hospital patients in applying its ruling. See, e.g., *SGW v. Cuomo,* supra at 1245–46 ("[O]nce [the state] chose to house . . . voluntary patients, thus making them dependent on the state, it was required to do so in a manner that would not deprive them of constitutional rights"). That position was called into doubt seven years after *Youngberg,* when the Supreme Court decided *DeShaney v. Winnebago County Dept. of Social Servs.,* 489 U.S. 189, 109 S.Ct. 998, 103 L.Ed.2d 249 (1989), which emphasized *Youngberg's* statement that the state has no constitutional duty to ensure an individual's care and safety when it has not affirmatively acted to deprive an individual of liberty. The plaintiff in *DeShaney* was the mother of a boy named Joshua, who was in a life-threatening coma as a result of a beating by his father that occurred when Joshua was in his father's custody. Over one year before the beating, the state child protection agency had received complaints suggesting that the father was abusing Joshua; although the state decided it lacked sufficient evidence to remove custody from the father, it did take several other steps, including enrolling Joshua in a pre-school program, providing the father with counselling services and encouraging the girlfriend to move out of the home; in addition a caseworker made monthly visits. During several of these visits, the caseworker noted evidence of abuse and was told during the two visits previous to the coma-inducing beating that Joshua was too ill to be seen, but no further official action was taken until that beating had occurred. The Supreme Court held that a due process claim against the state would not lie on these facts. Citing *Youngberg,* it stated: "[I]t is the State's affirmative act of restraining the individual's freedom to act on his own behalf—through incarceration, institutionalization, or other similar restraint of personal liberty—which is the 'deprivation of liberty' triggering the protections of the Due Process Clause, not its failure to act to protect his liberty interests against harms inflicted by other means." Id. at 1006.

Given what you know about voluntary commitment (see pp. 967–978), after *DeShaney* should there be a constitutional right to treatment for voluntary patients who are institutionalized? Most courts today hold that *Youngberg* does not apply to voluntary patients, but require a close examination of whether a "voluntary" patient is in fact voluntary. See, e.g., *Doe ex rel. Tarlow v. Dist. Columbia,* 2013 WL 394051 (D.D.C.) ("Most circuits regard the voluntary or involuntary nature of confinement as a question of fact rather than formality, determined by whether a patient is actually free to leave."); *Torisky v. Schweiker,* 446 F.3d 438, 446–47 (3d Cir. 2006). Other courts do not think the distinction is relevant. *Lanman v. Hinson,* 529 F.3d 673, 688–89 (6th Cir. 2008) ("the voluntary/involuntary distinction, while perhaps relevant to whether the state has the duty to protect patients from third-party harm, is irrelevant to the right of individuals, whatever their status, to be free from physical abuse at the hands of the State.").

5.   *Other bases for a right to treatment.* Some state courts have relied on state statutory language rather than the federal constitution to justify wide-ranging treatment obligations on the government. See, e.g., *Arnold v.*

Sarn, No. C–432355 (Ariz.Super.Ct., Maricopa Cty., May 29, 1985). Similarly, a number of federal statutes enacted since *Youngberg* have provided more attractive bases for suit than the holding in *Youngberg* which, despite the above-described interpretations, remains a narrow holding. These statutory-based developments are discussed further in Section IV of this chapter.

III. IMPLEMENTING THE RIGHT: WYATT V. STICKNEY

The following section examines various aspects of one "right to treatment" case, originally styled as *Wyatt v. Stickney.* Although filed over a decade before *Youngberg* and based on a theory of the right to treatment that was not endorsed by that decision, the *Wyatt* litigation is a useful focal point for further study of post-commitment treatment issues for a number of reasons. First, as the first major class action brought to enforce a systemwide right to treatment and habilitation, the case has had a significant impact on judicial and legislative decisions around the country that are still in force today. Second, *Wyatt's* long procedural history provides a particularly good illustration of the vagaries of attempting to implement judicially the right to treatment and habilitation. Third, even assuming *Youngberg* effectively narrows the scope of the right to treatment, *Wyatt* has many lessons to offer future litigators. As the previous notes indicate, *Youngberg* has not deterred courts from using constitutional or state or federal statutory language as a basis for reviewing decisions by state hospital employees and administrators. Moreover, most of these more recent cases are, like *Wyatt* (and unlike *Youngberg*), class action suits that involve requests for injunctive relief. In *Wyatt v. Aderholt,* 503 F.2d 1305, 1316 (5th Cir.1974), the court explained why this kind of suit is likely to be preferred over individual actions:

> . . . In the first place, habeas corpus relief and tort damages are available only after the fact of a failure to provide individual treatment. Here the plaintiffs seek preventive relief, to assure in advance that mental patients will at least have the *chance* to receive adequate treatment by proscribing the maintenance of conditions that foredoom *all* mental patients *inevitably* to inadequate mental treatment. Moreover, there are special reasons why reliance upon individual suits by mental patients would be especially inappropriate. Mental patients are particularly unlikely to be aware of their legal rights. They are likely to have especially limited access to legal assistance. Individual suits may be protracted and expensive, and individual mental patients may therefore be deterred from bringing them. And individual suits may produce distortive therapeutic effects within an institution, since a staff may tend to give especially good—or especially harsh—treatment to patients the staff expects or knows to be litigious.

(Emphasis in original). Given the likelihood of injunctive actions, the tactical lessons derived from the *Wyatt* litigation will continue to be useful, regardless of the theoretical underpinnings of the right to treatment ultimately settled upon.

Ironically, as initially conceived *Wyatt v. Stickney* was not a right to treatment suit. Filed in October, 1970, ostensibly on behalf of patients at Bryce Hospital in Tuscaloosa, Alabama, the suit asked for an injunction prohibiting anticipated layoffs of hospital personnel (which were to occur because a cut in the Alabama cigarette tax had reduced the money available to the state hospital system). Although Ricky Wyatt, a patient, was the named plaintiff, in fact "a fairly small number of staff, not a group of indignant patients or their relatives" was the "motivating power behind the suit." Stonewall Stickney, "*Wyatt v. Stickney:* The Right to Treatment," in Bonnie, ed., Psychiatrists and the Legal Process: Diagnosis and Debate 274, 278 (1977). Under the auspices of federal district court judge Frank Johnson, however, the suit triggered a wide-ranging investigation of the deplorable conditions at Bryce and other institutions in Alabama[b] and resulted in substantial changes in the system. In the original *Wyatt* decision, Judge Johnson, relying on a "*Jackson*" theory of the right to treatment, held that every civilly committed patient possesses "a constitutional right to receive such individual treatment as will give them a realistic opportunity to be cured or to improve his or her mental condition." 325 F.Supp. 781, 784 (M.D.Ala.1971). The decision set out below is his enforcement decree. Note that it contains standards for virtually every aspect of hospital operation, ranging from the proper temperature of hot water, to the number of social workers and clerk typists per unit, to the types of documents which must be included in each patient's files. The materials following the decision use *Wyatt* and its progeny to provide a flavor of right to treatment litigation and its consequences.

---

[b] The *Wyatt* record is replete with accounts of patients who died or were seriously harmed as a result of inattention by staff, as well descriptions of patient abuse, of filthy conditions, and of general neglect. For instance, the record disclosed that, at one of the institutions involved in the *Wyatt* litigation, four patients had died "due to understaffing, lack of supervision, and brutality."

> One of the four died after a garden hose had been inserted into his rectum for five minutes by a working patient who was cleaning him; one died when a fellow patient hosed him with scalding water; another died when soapy water was forced into his mouth; and a fourth died from a self-administered overdose of drugs which had been inadequately secured.

Wyatt v. Aderholt, 503 F.2d 1305, 1311 n. 6. (5th Cir.1974).

WYATT V. STICKNEY

United States District Court, Middle District Alabama, 1972.
344 F.Supp. 373.

Order and Decree

JOHNSON, CHIEF JUDGE.

This class action originally was filed on October 23, 1970, in behalf of patients involuntarily confined for mental treatment purposes at Bryce Hospital, Tuscaloosa, Alabama. On March 12, 1971, in a formal opinion and decree, this Court held that these involuntarily committed patients "unquestionably have a constitutional right to receive such individual treatment as will give each of them a realistic opportunity to be cured or to improve his or her mental condition." The Court further held that patients at Bryce were being denied their right to treatment and that defendants, per their request, would be allowed six months in which to raise the level of care at Bryce to the constitutionally required minimum. Wyatt v. Stickney, 325 F.Supp. 781 (M.D.Ala.1971). In this decree, the Court ordered defendants to file reports defining the mission and functions of Bryce Hospital, specifying the objective and subjective standards required to furnish adequate care to the treatable mentally ill and detailing the hospital's progress toward the implementation of minimum constitutional standards. Subsequent to this order, plaintiffs, by motion to amend granted August 12, 1971, enlarged their class to include patients involuntarily confined for mental treatment at Searcy Hospital and at Partlow State School and Hospital for the mentally retarded.

On September 23, 1971, defendants filed their final report, from which this Court concluded on December 10, 1971, that defendants had failed to promulgate and implement a treatment program satisfying minimum medical and constitutional requisites. Generally, the Court found that defendants' treatment program was deficient in three fundamental areas. It failed to provide: (1) a humane psychological and physical environment, (2) qualified staff in numbers sufficient to administer adequate treatment and (3) individualized treatment plans. More specifically, the Court found that many conditions, such as nontherapeutic, uncompensated work assignments, and the absence of any semblance of privacy, constituted dehumanizing factors contributing to the degeneration of the patients' self-esteem. The physical facilities at Bryce were overcrowded and plagued by fire and other emergency hazards. The Court found also that most staff members were poorly trained and that staffing ratios were so inadequate as to render the administration of effective treatment impossible. The Court concluded, therefore, that whatever treatment was provided at Bryce was grossly deficient and failed to satisfy minimum medical and constitutional standards. Based upon this conclusion, the Court ordered that a formal hearing be held at which the parties and amici[3] would have the opportunity to submit proposed standards for constitutionally adequate treatment and to present expert testimony in support of their proposals.

Pursuant to this order, a hearing was held at which the foremost authorities on mental health in the United States appeared and testified as to the minimum medical and constitutional requisites for public institutions, such as Bryce and Searcy, designed to treat the mentally ill. At this hearing, the parties and amici submitted their proposed standards, and now have filed briefs in support of them. Moreover, the parties and amici have stipulated to a broad spectrum of conditions they feel are mandatory for a constitutionally acceptable minimum treatment program. This Court, having considered the evidence in the case, as well as the briefs, proposed standards and stipulations of the parties, has concluded that the standards set out in Appendix A to this decree are medical and constitutional minimums. Consequently, the Court will order their implementation. In so ordering, however, the Court emphasizes that these standards are, indeed, both medical and constitutional minimums and should be viewed as such. The Court urges that once this order is effectuated, defendants not become complacent and self-satisfied. Rather, they should dedicate themselves to providing physical conditions and treatment programs at Alabama's mental institutions that substantially exceed medical and constitutional minimums.

In addition to asking that their proposed standards be effectuated, plaintiffs and amici have requested other relief designed to guarantee the provision of constitutional and humane treatment. Pursuant to one such request for relief, this Court has determined that it is appropriate to order the initiation of human rights committees to function as standing committees of the Bryce and Searcy facilities. The Court will appoint the members of these committees who shall have review of all research proposals and all rehabilitation programs, to ensure that the dignity and the human rights of patients are preserved. The committees also shall advise and assist patients who allege that their legal rights have been infringed or that the Mental Health Board has failed to comply with judicially ordered guidelines. At their discretion, the committees may consult appropriate, independent specialists who shall be compensated by the defendant Board. Seven members shall comprise the human rights committee for each institution. . . .

This Court will reserve ruling upon other forms of relief advocated by plaintiffs and amici, including their prayer for the appointment of a

---

[3] The amici in this case, including the United States of America, the American Orthopsychiatric Association, the American Psychological Association, the American Civil Liberties Union, and the American Association on Mental Deficiency, have performed exemplary service for which this Court is indeed grateful.

[Note the absence of the American Psychiatric Association, which declined Judge Johnson's offer to participate. Eds.]

master and a professional advisory committee to oversee the implementation of the court-ordered minimum constitutional standards.[6] Federal courts are reluctant to assume control of any organization, but especially one operated by a state. This reluctance, combined with defendants' expressed intent that this order will be implemented forthwith and in good faith, causes the Court to withhold its decision on these appointments. Nevertheless, defendants, as well as the other parties and amici in this case, are placed on notice that unless defendants do comply satisfactorily with this order, the Court will be obligated to appoint a master.

Because the availability of financing may bear upon the implementation of this order, the Court is constrained to emphasize at this juncture that a failure by defendants to comply with this decree cannot be justified by a lack of operating funds. As previously established by this Court:

> "There can be no legal (or moral) justification for the State of Alabama's failing to afford treatment—and adequate treatment from a medical standpoint—to the several thousand patients who have been civilly committed to Bryce's for treatment purposes. To deprive any citizen of his or her liberty upon the altruistic theory that the confinement is for humane therapeutic reasons and then fail to provide adequate treatment violates the very fundamentals of due process."

From the above, it follows consistently, of course, that the unavailability of neither funds, nor staff and facilities, will justify a default by defendants in the provision of suitable treatment for the mentally ill.

Despite the possibility that defendants will encounter financial difficulties in the implementation of this order, this Court has decided to reserve ruling also upon plaintiffs' motion that defendant Mental Health Board be directed to sell or encumber portions of its land holdings in order to raise funds. Similarly, this Court will reserve ruling on plaintiffs' motion seeking an injunction against the treasurer and the comptroller of the State authorizing expenditures for nonessential State functions, and on other aspects of plaintiffs' requested relief designed to ameliorate the financial problems incident to the implementation of this order. The Court stresses, however, the extreme importance and the grave immediacy of the need for proper funding of the State's public mental

---

[6] The Court's decision to reserve its ruling on the appointment of a master necessitates the reservation also of the Court's appointing a professional advisory committee to aid the master. Nevertheless, the Court notes that the professional mental health community in the United States has responded with enthusiasm to the proposed initiation of such a committee to assist in the upgrading of Alabama's mental health facilities. Consequently, this Court strongly recommends to defendants that they develop a professional advisory committee comprised of amenable professionals from throughout the country who are able to provide the expertise the evidence reflects is important to the successful implementation of this order.

health facilities. The responsibility for appropriate funding ultimately must fall, of course, upon the State Legislature and, to a lesser degree, upon the defendant Mental Health Board of Alabama. For the present time, the Court will defer to those bodies in hopes that they will proceed with the realization and understanding that what is involved in this case is not representative of ordinary governmental functions such as paving roads and maintaining buildings. Rather, what is so inextricably intertwined with how the Legislature and Mental Health Board respond to the revelations of this litigation is the very preservation of human life and dignity. Not only are the lives of the patients currently confined at Bryce and Searcy at stake, but also at issue are the well-being and security of every citizen of Alabama. As is true in the case of any disease, no one is immune from the peril of mental illness. The problem, therefore, cannot be overemphasized and a prompt response from the Legislature, the Mental Health Board and other responsible State officials, is imperative.

In the event, though, that the Legislature fails to satisfy its well-defined constitutional obligation, and the Mental Health Board, because of lack of funding or any other legally insufficient reason, fails to implement fully the standards herein ordered, it will be necessary for the Court to take affirmative steps, including appointing a master, to ensure that proper funding is realized[8] and that adequate treatment is available for the mentally ill of Alabama.

This Court now must consider that aspect of plaintiffs' motion of March 15, 1972, seeking an injunction against further commitments to Bryce and Searcy until such time as adequate treatment is supplied in those hospitals. Indisputably, the evidence in this case reflects that no treatment program at the Bryce–Searcy facilities approaches constitutional standards. Nevertheless, because of the alternatives to commitment commonly utilized in Alabama, as well as in other states, the Court is fearful that granting plaintiffs' request at the present time would serve only to punish and further deprive Alabama's mentally ill.

* * *

---

[8] The Court understands and appreciates that the Legislature is not due back in regular session until May, 1973. Nevertheless, special sessions of the Legislature are frequent occurrences in Alabama, and there has never been a time when such a session was more urgently required. If the Legislature does not act promptly to appropriate the necessary funding for mental health, the Court will be compelled to grant plaintiffs' motion to add various State officials and agencies as additional parties to this litigation, and to utilize other avenues of fund raising.

Appendix A

MINIMUM Constitutional STANDARDS for Adequate
Treatment of The Mentally Ill.

I.   *Definitions:*

   a.   "Hospital"—Bryce and Searcy Hospitals.

   b.   "Patients"—all persons who are now confined and all persons who may in the future be confined at Bryce and Searcy Hospitals pursuant to an involuntary civil commitment procedure.

   c.   "Qualified Mental Health Professional"—

   (1) a psychiatrist with three years of residency training in psychiatry;

   (2) a psychologist with a doctoral degree from an accredited program;

   (3) a social worker with a master's degree from an accredited program and two years of clinical experience under the supervision of a Qualified Mental Health Professional;

   (4) a registered nurse with a graduate degree in psychiatric nursing and two years of clinical experience under the supervision of a Qualified Mental Health Professional.

   d.   "Non–Professional Staff Member"—an employee of the hospital, other than a Qualified Mental Health Professional, whose duties require contact with or supervision of patients.

II. *Humane Psychological and Physical Environment*

   1.   Patients have a right to privacy and dignity.

   2.   Patients have a right to the least restrictive conditions necessary to achieve the purposes of commitment.

   3.   No person shall be deemed incompetent to manage his affairs, to contract, to hold professional or occupational or vehicle operator's licenses, to marry and obtain a divorce, to register and vote, or to make a will *solely* by reason of his admission or commitment to the hospital.

   4.   Patients shall have the same rights to visitation and telephone communications as patients at other public hospitals, except to the extent that the Qualified Mental Health Professional responsible for formulation of a particular patient's treatment plan writes an order imposing special restrictions. The written order must be renewed after each periodic review of the treatment plan if any restrictions are to be continued. Patients shall have an unrestricted right to visitation with attorneys and with private physicians and other health professionals.

5.   Patients shall have an unrestricted right to send sealed mail. Patients shall have an unrestricted right to receive sealed mail from their attorneys, private physicians, and other mental health professionals, from courts, and government officials. Patients shall have a right to receive sealed mail from others, except to the extent that the Qualified Mental Health Professional responsible for formulation of a particular patient's treatment plan writes an order imposing special restrictions on receipt of sealed mail. The written order must be renewed after each periodic review of the treatment plan if any restrictions are to be continued.

6.   Patients have a right to be free from unnecessary or excessive medication. No medication shall be administered unless at the written order of a physician. The superintendent of the hospital and the attending physician shall be responsible for all medication given or administered to a patient. The use of medication shall not exceed standards of use that are advocated by the United States Food and Drug Administration. Notation of each individual's medication shall be kept in his medical records. At least weekly the attending physician shall review the drug regimen of each patient under his care. All prescriptions shall be written with a termination date, which shall not exceed 30 days. Medication shall not be used as punishment, for the convenience of staff, as a substitute for program, or in quantities that interfere with the patient's treatment program.

7.   Patients have a right to be free from physical restraint and isolation. Except for emergency situations, in which it is likely that patients could harm themselves or others and in which less restrictive means of restraint are not feasible, patients may be physically restrained or placed in isolation only on a Qualified Mental Health Professional's written order which explains the rationale for such action. The written order may be entered only after the Qualified Mental Health Professional has personally seen the patient concerned and evaluated whatever episode or situation is said to call for restraint or isolation. Emergency use of restraints or isolation shall be for no more than one hour, by which time a Qualified Mental Health Professional shall have been consulted and shall have entered an appropriate order in writing. Such written order shall be effective for no more than 24 hours and must be renewed if restraint and isolation are to be continued. While in restraint or isolation the patient must be seen by qualified ward personnel who will chart the patient's physical condition (if it is compromised) and psychiatric condition every hour. The patient must have bathroom privileges every hour and must be bathed every 12 hours.

8.   Patients shall have a right not to be subjected to experimental research without the express and informed consent of the patient, if the patient is able to give such consent, and of his guardian or next of kin, after opportunities for consultation with independent specialists and with

legal counsel. Such proposed research shall first have been reviewed and approved by the institution's Human Rights Committee before such consent shall be sought. Prior to such approval the Committee shall determine that such research complies with the principles of the Statement on the Use of Human Subjects for Research of the American Association on Mental Deficiency and with the principles for research involving human subjects required by the United States Department of Health, Education and Welfare for projects supported by that agency.

9. Patients have a right not to be subjected to treatment procedures such as lobotomy, electro-convulsive treatment, aversive reinforcement conditioning or other unusual or hazardous treatment procedures without their express and informed consent after consultation with counsel or interested party of the patient's choice.

10. Patients have a right to receive prompt and adequate medical treatment for any physical ailments.

11. Patients have a right to wear their own clothes and to keep and use their own personal possessions except insofar as such clothes or personal possessions may be determined by a Qualified Mental Health Professional to be dangerous or otherwise inappropriate to the treatment regimen.

12. The hospital has an obligation to supply an adequate allowance of clothing to any patients who do not have suitable clothing of their own. Patients shall have the opportunity to select from various types of neat, clean, and seasonable clothing. Such clothing shall be considered the patient's throughout his stay in the hospital.

13. The hospital shall make provision for the laundering of patient clothing.

14. Patients have a right to regular physical exercise several times a week. Moreover, it shall be the duty of the hospital to provide facilities and equipment for such exercise.

15. Patients have a right to be outdoors at regular and frequent intervals, in the absence of medical considerations.

16. The right to religious worship shall be accorded to each patient who desires such opportunities. Provisions for such worship shall be made available to all patients on a nondiscriminatory basis. No individual shall be coerced into engaging in any religious activities.

17. The institution shall provide, with adequate supervision, suitable opportunities for the patient's interaction with members of the opposite sex.

18. The following rules shall govern patient labor:

A. *Hospital Maintenance* No patient shall be required to perform labor which involves the operation and maintenance of the hospital or for which the hospital is under contract with an outside organization. Privileges or release from the hospital shall not be conditioned upon the performance of labor covered by this provision. Patients may voluntarily engage in such labor if the labor is compensated in accordance with the minimum wage laws of the Fair Labor Standards Act, 29 U.S.C. § 206 as amended, 1966.

B. *Therapeutic Tasks and Therapeutic Labor*

(1) Patients may be required to perform therapeutic tasks which do not involve the operation and maintenance of the hospital, provided the specific task or any change in assignment is:

a. An integrated part of the patient's treatment plan and approved as a therapeutic activity by a Qualified Mental Health Professional responsible for supervising the patient's treatment; and

b. Supervised by a staff member to oversee the therapeutic aspects of the activity.

(2) Patients may voluntarily engage in therapeutic labor for which the hospital would otherwise have to pay an employee, provided the specific labor or any change in labor assignment is:

a. An integrated part of the patient's treatment plan and approved as a therapeutic activity by a Qualified Mental Health Professional responsible for supervising the patient's treatment; and

b. Supervised by a staff member to oversee the therapeutic aspects of the activity; and

c. Compensated in accordance with the minimum wage laws of the Fair Labor Standards Act, 29 U.S.C. § 206 as amended, 1966.

C. *Personal Housekeeping* Patients may be required to perform tasks of a personal housekeeping nature such as the making of one's own bed.

D. Payment to patients pursuant to these paragraphs shall not be applied to the costs of hospitalization.

19. *Physical Facilities*

A patient has a right to a humane psychological and physical environment within the hospital facilities. These facilities shall be designed to afford patients with comfort and safety, promote dignity, and ensure privacy. The facilities shall be designed to make a positive contribution to the efficient attainment of the treatment goals of the hospital.

A. *Resident Unit*

The number of patients in a multi-patient room shall not exceed six persons. There shall be allocated a minimum of 80 square feet of floor space per patient in a multi-patient room. Screens or curtains shall be provided to ensure privacy within the resident unit. Single rooms shall have a minimum of 100 square feet of floor space. Each patient will be furnished with a comfortable bed with adequate changes of linen, a closet or locker for his personal belongings, a chair, and a bedside table.

B. *Toilets and Lavatories*

There will be one toilet provided for each eight patients and one lavatory for each six patients. A lavatory will be provided with each toilet facility. The toilets will be installed in separate stalls to ensure privacy, will be clean and free of odor, and will be equipped with appropriate safety devices for the physically handicapped.

C. *Showers*

There will be one tub or shower for each 15 patients. If a central bathing area is provided, each shower area will be divided by curtains to ensure privacy. Showers and tubs will be equipped with adequate safety accessories.

D. *Day Room*

The minimum day room area shall be 40 square feet per patient. Day rooms will be attractive and adequately furnished with reading lamps, tables, chairs, television and other recreational facilities. They will be conveniently located to patients' bedrooms and shall have outside windows. There shall be at least one day room area on each bedroom floor in a multi-story hospital. Areas used for corridor traffic cannot be counted as day room space; nor can a chapel with fixed pews be counted as a day room area.

E. *Dining Facilities*

The minimum dining room area shall be ten square feet per patient. The dining room shall be separate from the kitchen and will be furnished with comfortable chairs and tables with hard, washable surfaces.

F. *Linen Servicing and Handling*

The hospital shall provide adequate facilities and equipment for handling clean and soiled bedding and other linen. There must be frequent changes of bedding and other linen, no less than every seven days to assure patient comfort.

G. *Housekeeping*

Regular housekeeping and maintenance procedures which will ensure that the hospital is maintained in a safe, clean, and attractive condition will be developed and implemented.

H. *Geriatric and Other Nonambulatory Mental Patients*

There must be special facilities for geriatric and other nonambulatory patients to assure their safety and comfort, including special fittings on toilets and wheelchairs. Appropriate provision shall be made to permit nonambulatory patients to communicate their needs to staff.

I. *Physical Plant*

(1) Pursuant to an established routine maintenance and repair program, the physical plant shall be kept in a continuous state of good repair and operation in accordance with the needs of the health, comfort, safety and well-being of the patients.

(2) Adequate heating, air conditioning and ventilation systems and equipment shall be afforded to maintain temperatures and air changes which are required for the comfort of patients at all times and the removal of undesired heat, steam and offensive odors. Such facilities shall ensure that the temperature in the hospital shall not exceed 83° F nor fall below 68° F.

(3) Thermostatically controlled hot water shall be provided in adequate quantities and maintained at the required temperature for patient or resident use (110° F at the fixture) and for mechanical dishwashing and laundry use (180° F at the equipment).

(4) Adequate refuse facilities will be provided so that solid waste, rubbish and other refuse will be collected and disposed of in a manner which will prohibit transmission of disease and not create a nuisance or fire hazard or provide a breeding place for rodents and insects.

(5) The physical facilities must meet all fire and safety standards established by the state and locality. In addition, the hospital shall meet such provisions of the Life Safety Code of the National Fire Protection Association (21st edition, 1967) as are applicable to hospitals.

19A.   The hospital shall meet all standards established by the state for general hospitals, insofar as they are relevant to psychiatric facilities.

20. *Nutritional Standards*

Patients, except for the non-mobile, shall eat or be fed in dining rooms. The diet for patients will provide at a minimum the Recommended Daily Dietary Allowances as developed by the National Academy of Sciences. Menus shall be satisfying and nutritionally adequate to provide the Recommended Daily Dietary Allowances. In developing such menus, the hospital will utilize the Low Cost Food Plan of the Department of Agriculture. The hospital will not spend less per patient for raw food, including the value of donated food, than the most recent per person costs of the Low Cost Food Plan for the Southern Region of the United States, as compiled by the United States Department of Agriculture, for appropriate groupings of patients, discounted for any savings which might result from institutional procurement of such food. Provisions shall be made for special therapeutic diets and for substitutes at the request of the patient, or his guardian or next of kin, in accordance with the religious requirements of any patient's faith. Denial of a nutritionally adequate diet shall not be used as punishment.

III. *Qualified Staff in Numbers Sufficient to Administer Adequate Treatment*

21. Each Qualified Mental Health Professional shall meet all licensing and certification requirements promulgated by the State of Alabama for persons engaged in private practice of the same profession elsewhere in Alabama. Other staff members shall meet the same licensing and certification requirements as persons who engage in private practice of their specialty elsewhere in Alabama.

22. a. All Non–Professional Staff Members who have not had prior clinical experience in a mental institution shall have a substantial orientation training.

b. Staff members on all levels shall have regularly scheduled in-service training.

23. Each Non–Professional Staff Member shall be under the direct supervision of a Qualified Mental Health Professional.

24. *Staffing Ratios*

The hospital shall have the following minimum numbers of treatment personnel per 250 patients. Qualified Mental Health Professionals trained in particular disciplines may in appropriate situations perform services or functions traditionally performed by members of other disciplines. Changes in staff deployment may be made with prior approval of this Court upon a clear and convincing demonstration that the proposed deviation from this staffing structure will enhance the treatment of the patients.

Classification	Number of Employees
Unit Director	1
Psychiatrist (3 years' residency training in psychiatry)	2
MD (Registered physicians)	4
Nurses (RN)	12

Classification	Number of Employees
Licensed Practical Nurses	6
Aide III	6
Aide II	16
Aide I	70
Hospital Orderly	10
Clerk Stenographer II	3
Clerk Typist II	3
Unit Administrator	1
Administrative Clerk	1
Psychologist (Ph.D.) (doctoral degree from accredited program)	1
Psychologist (M.A.)	1
Psychologist (B.S.)	2
Social Worker (MSW) (from accredited program)	2
Social Worker (B.A.)	5
Patient Activity Therapist (M.S.)	1
Patient Activity Aide	10
Mental Health Technician	10
Dental Hygienist	1
Chaplain	5
Vocational Rehabilitation Counselor	1
Volunteer Services Worker	1
Mental Health Field Representative	1
Dietitian	1
Food Service Supervisor	1
Cook II	2
Cook I	3
Food Service Worker	15
Vehicle Driver	1
Housekeeper	10
Messenger	1
Maintenance Repairman	2

IV. *Individualized Treatment Plans*

25. Each patient shall have a comprehensive physical and mental examination and review of behavioral status within 48 hours after admission to the hospital.

26. Each patient shall have an individualized treatment plan. This plan shall be developed by appropriate Qualified Mental Health Professionals, including a psychiatrist, and implemented as soon as possible—in any event no later than five days after the patient's admission. Each individualized treatment plan shall contain:

a.   a statement of the nature of the specific problems and specific needs of the patient;

b.   a statement of the least restrictive treatment conditions necessary to achieve the purposes of commitment;

c.   a description of intermediate and long-range treatment goals, with a projected timetable for their attainment;

d.   a statement and rationale for the plan of treatment for achieving these intermediate and long-range goals;

e.   a specification of staff responsibility and a description of proposed staff involvement with the patient in order to attain these treatment goals;

f.   criteria for release to less restrictive treatment conditions, and criteria for discharge;

g.   a notation of any therapeutic tasks and labor to be performed by the patient in accordance with Standard 18.

27. As part of his treatment plan, each patient shall have an individualized post-hospitalization plan. This plan shall be developed by a Qualified Mental Health Professional as soon as practicable after the patient's admission to the hospital.

28. In the interests of continuity of care, whenever possible, one Qualified Mental Health Professional (who need not have been involved with the development of the treatment plan) shall be responsible for supervising the implementation of the treatment plan, integrating the various aspects of the treatment program and recording the patient's progress. This Qualified Mental Health Professional shall also be responsible for ensuring that the patient is released, where appropriate, into a less restrictive form of treatment.

29. The treatment plan shall be continuously reviewed by the Qualified Mental Health Professional responsible for supervising the implementation of the plan and shall be modified if necessary. Moreover, at least every 90 days, each patient shall receive a mental examination from, and his treatment plan shall be reviewed by, a Qualified Mental Health Professional other than the professional responsible for supervising the implementation of the plan.

30. In addition to treatment for mental disorders, patients confined at mental health institutions also are entitled to and shall receive appropriate treatment for physical illnesses such as tuberculosis. In providing medical care, the State Board of Mental Health shall take advantage of whatever community-based facilities are appropriate and available and shall coordinate the patient's treatment for mental illness with his medical treatment.

31. Complete patient records shall be kept on the ward in which the patient is placed and shall be available to anyone properly authorized in writing by the patient. These records shall include:

a.   Identification data, including the patient's legal status;

b.   A patient history, including but not limited to:

(1) family data, educational background, and employment record;

(2) prior medical history, both physical and mental, including prior hospitalization;

c.   The chief complaints of the patient and the chief complaints of others regarding the patient;

d.   An evaluation which notes the onset of illness, the circumstances leading to admission, attitudes, behavior, estimate of intellectual functioning, memory functioning, orientation, and an inventory of the patient's assets in descriptive, not interpretative, fashion;

e.   A summary of each physical examination which describes the results of the examination;

f.   A copy of the individual treatment plan and any modifications thereto;

g.   A detailed summary of the findings made by the reviewing Qualified Mental Health Professional after each periodic review of the treatment plan which analyzes the successes and failures of the treatment program and directs whatever modifications are necessary;

h.   A copy of the individualized post-hospitalization plan and any modifications thereto, and a summary of the steps that have been taken to implement that plan;

i.   A medication history and status, which includes the signed orders of the prescribing physician. Nurses shall indicate by signature that orders have been carried out;

j.   A detailed summary of each significant contact by a Qualified Mental Health Professional with the patient;

k.   A detailed summary on at least a weekly basis by a Qualified Mental Health Professional involved in the patient's treatment of the patient's progress along the treatment plan;

l.   A weekly summary of the extent and nature of the patient's work activities described in Standard 18, *supra,* and the effect of such activity upon the patient's progress along the treatment plan;

m.   A signed order by a Qualified Mental Health Professional for any restrictions on visitations and communication, as provided in Standards 4 and 5, *supra;*

n.   A signed order by a Qualified Mental Health Professional for any physical restraints and isolation, as provided in Standard 7, *supra*;

o.   A detailed summary of any extraordinary incident in the hospital involving the patient to be entered by a staff member noting that he has personal knowledge of the incident or specifying his other source of information, and initialed within 24 hours by a Qualified Mental Health Professional;

p.   A summary by the superintendent of the hospital or his appointed agent of his findings after the 15–day review provided for in Standard 33 *infra*.

32.   In addition to complying with all the other standards herein, a hospital shall make special provisions for the treatment of patients who are children and young adults. These provisions shall include but are not limited to:

a.   Opportunities for publicly supported education suitable to the educational needs of the patient. This program of education must, in the opinion of the attending Qualified Mental Health Professional, be compatible with the patient's mental condition and his treatment program, and otherwise be in the patient's best interest.

b.   A treatment plan which considers the chronological, maturational, and developmental level of the patient;

c.   Sufficient Qualified Mental Health Professionals, teachers, and staff members with specialized skills in the care and treatment of children and young adults;

d.   Recreation and play opportunities in the open air where possible and appropriate residential facilities;

e.   Arrangements for contact between the hospital and the family of the patient.

33.   No later than 15 days after a patient is committed to the hospital, the superintendent of the hospital or his appointed, professionally qualified agent shall examine the committed patient and shall determine whether the patient continues to require hospitalization and whether a treatment plan complying with Standard 26 has been implemented. If the patient no longer requires hospitalization in accordance with the standards for commitment, or if a treatment plan has not been implemented, he must be released immediately unless he agrees to continue with treatment on a voluntary basis.

34.   The Mental Health Board and its agents have an affirmative duty to provide adequate transitional treatment and care for all patients released after a period of involuntary confinement. Transitional care and treatment possibilities include, but are not limited to, psychiatric day care, treatment in the home by a visiting therapist, nursing home or

extended care, out-patient treatment, and treatment in the psychiatric ward of a general hospital.

V.   *Miscellaneous*

35. Each patient and his family, guardian, or next friend shall promptly upon the patient's admission receive written notice, in language he understands, of all the above standards for adequate treatment. In addition a copy of all the above standards shall be posted in each ward.

QUESTIONS AND COMMENTS

1.   *The Partlow order.* As the court noted, a second filing in the *Wyatt* case dealt with conditions in Partlow State School and Hospital, an institution for people with intellectual disabilities. Judge Johnson's order concerning Partlow was similar to the order governing Bryce and Searcy, except that it was even more extensive. See *Wyatt v. Stickney,* 344 F.Supp. 387 (M.D.Ala.1972). For instance, in defining the meaning of "adequate habilitation" for residents of Partlow, the order specified the class size, length of school year and minimum length of school day. The guidelines for the first two areas varied depending upon the patient's degree of intellectual impairment, while the length of the school day was fixed at 6 hours for all groups. Id. at 397.

2.   *Subsequent history and impact of* Wyatt *litigation.* Both of Judge Johnson's orders were substantially affirmed in *Wyatt v. Aderholt,* 503 F.2d 1305 (5th Cir.1974). Between 1970 and 1975, the population at Bryce Hospital was reduced by 61.3%. Although this reduction was due to a number of factors (e.g., the creation of community mental health centers and the initiation of federal welfare programs subsidizing nursing home care), it was,

> in significant part, . . . attributable to specific aspects of the *Wyatt* litigation. The ban on nontherapeutic patient labor "made it undesirable to have a large number of productive individuals in the hospital"; pressure to comply with patient-staff ratios "tended to create a climate in which discharge of patients was seen as beneficial;" and the publicity spawned by the suit "probably created more favorable public attitudes toward return of patients to the community than had existed previously."

2 Michael Perlin, Mental Disability Law: Civil and Criminal 52 (1999). Between 1970 and 1975, expenditures of the Alabama Department of Health increased by over 327%. During this time, the state significantly improved its psychologist-patient and social worker-patient ratios. However, it hired only a small number of additional psychiatrists, which meant that the few who were on staff did not have the time to oversee some of the activities the court had ordered them to monitor (such as development and implementation of individualized treatment and post-hospitalization plans). As a "direct result" of the suit, the state installed air conditioning, shower and toilet partitions and pay phones, and patients began to receive uncensored mail. Patient abuse declined significantly, primarily due to the reduction in patients, the

increased number of supervisory personnel and the presence of human rights committees brought about by *Wyatt*. At the same time, staff became fearful of giving patients any "negative feedback" lest it be construed as abuse. Id. at 52–53. These changes probably improved the quality of care, though no data directly addressed individual therapeutic success rates. L. Ralph Jones & Richard Parlour, *Wyatt v. Stickney:* Retrospect and Prospect xi, xii (1981).

Believing that insufficient progress was made in this regard and in many other areas, the plaintiffs asked the court in 1977 to appoint a receiver who would supervise the functions of the Alabama mental health bureaucracy. Judge Johnson agreed that there had been "substantial noncompliance" in a number of areas. He granted the plaintiffs' motion, giving them three weeks to nominate a receiver. However, because the governor had also asked to be appointed as receiver, the court gave the governor ten weeks to file "specific proposals as to the remedial steps [he] will take if appointed receiver." *Wyatt v. Ireland,* 515 F.Supp. 888 (M.D.Ala.1981). The governor was eventually appointed as the receiver.

Soon thereafter, the defendants asked for a modification of the 1972 orders, which they claimed were too rigid. They charged that the court's overall approach "seriously detracted from resident care, treatment and training" because of its inordinate recordkeeping requirements, its imposition of "ritualistic and meaningless" procedures, and its failure to stop the "harassment" of the human rights committees demoralized the staff. See Perlin, supra, at 49. The defendants also asked for certain specific relief. They contended, for example, that requiring 6 hours of training per day, as the Partlow order did, was not always in the best interests of the residents, especially those who were profoundly or severely retarded. Continuing a routine training regimen for patients who did not show substantial improvement could be "pejorative and demeaning" and might even constitute "cruel and inhuman treatment." Instead, the defendants argued, residents who failed to improve with extensive education and training should be switched to "a full program of enriching activities, work activities, sheltered employment, physical exercise and therapies, and such other programs that tend to give meaning and dignity to their lives." The court rejected this request, stating that, if granted, it would "threaten [the] constitutional right [of each resident] . . . to a habilitation program which will maximize his human abilities and enhance his ability to cope with his environment." Id. at 47–49. How does this holding compare to *Youngberg's*? See footnote 23 of that opinion.

In September, 1986, sixteen years after the initial complaint was filed, the *Wyatt* suit was officially settled. As part of the settlement agreement, the state of Alabama agreed to make "reasonable efforts" to achieve full accreditation by the relevant accrediting authorities. The agreement also required the state to make "substantial progress" toward establishing needed community facilities. Further, the agreement established patient advocacy and quality assurance programs. An advisory committee, which included the plaintiffs' attorney, also informally monitored hospital compliance. Finally, both parties agreed that the original standards set out in *Wyatt v. Stickney* still applied. *Wyatt v. Wallis*, 1986 WL 69194 (M.D.Ala.1986). Thus, the suit seemed to be largely ended at this point.

However, in 1991, when the state moved for a finding that their obligations had been met, the plaintiffs moved for further enforcement of the decree and for further relief. Six years later, the court found that the defendants should be released from the consent decree with respect to 17 of the mental-illness standards and 35 of the mental-retardation standards, but that several standards still needed to be met. *Wyatt v. Rogers*, 985 F.Supp. 1356 (M.D.Ala.1997). In the course of doing so, the court made some interesting comments about the relevance of *Youngberg* to the *Wyatt* litigation:

> [T]he responsibility of this court is to secure the defendants' swift and full compliance with the 1986 consent decree. Nevertheless, as would be the case with a court seeking to vindicate the liberty interests identified in *Youngberg*, the court is still an interloper, for the ultimate responsibility for the operation of the Alabama Mental Health and Mental Retardation System still lies with the State of Alabama. Therefore, interference by this court "with the internal operations of [the Alabama Department of Mental Health and Mental Retardation] should be minimized," to that necessary to vindicate compliance with the decree. Similarly, because "there certainly is no reason to think [this] judge[ ] . . . [is] better qualified than appropriate professionals in making . . . decisions" in the Alabama system calling for professional judgment, a "decision, if made by a professional, [should be] presumptively valid."

> [However,] a decision is entitled to such deference only if it is one that calls for professional judgment. For example, whether a patient should be placed in a community setting would be a decision that would call for professional judgment, and the court should not second guess such a decision as long as it was based on acceptable professional judgment. However, whether the Department of Mental Health and Mental Retardation has met its obligation to create community facilities would not turn exclusively on professional judgment. The bottom line is that, in those instances where professionals have determined that a patient could or should be in a community setting, the decree requires that, within practical administrative and budgetary limits, the department have such settings available, and the court's limited role under the consent decree is to make sure that this is so. The force of the 1986 consent decree is that, if a state professional finds that a patient could or should be in a local community facility, the patient should not he hospitalized far away from home, from family, and from local community simply because an appropriate local community facility is not, within practical limits, available.

> Moreover, it is the court's responsibility to ensure that a judgment is made by a competent professional based on professional standards and practices, appropriate medical and psychological criteria, and not on

administrative convenience or nonmedical criteria . . . Thus, the court has a responsibility to assess a professional's expert opinion, by assessing the expert's credibility and the reliability of the information on which the expert bases his or her opinion. The court has assessed the credibility of each witness and the weight to be given each witness's testimony. In assessing the credibility of the experts, the court took into account the sources of the expert's opinions. Some of the experts' selection of data was decidedly unprofessional. Where the expert's data were not random, but selected by the party he or she represented, where the expert relied on the representations of the parties instead of making an independent determination, and where the expert deliberately attempted to mislead the court, the court has taken all these into account in its assessment.

Id. at 1386–87.

From 1998 to 2000 the parties worked to resolve disputes with respect to the remaining mental illness and mental retardation standards. They reached a second settlement agreement in 2000, which the trial court accepted. *Wyatt ex rel. Rawlins v. Sawyer*, 105 F.Supp.2d 1234 (M.D.Ala. 2000). The court found that all facilities under court order had been accredited; that at least 26 full-time advocates for the patients were in those facilities; that Alabama was committed to reducing the census by 300 patients at Bryce Hospital and related entities and also by 300 at Partlow and related entities; that Alabama would develop a plan for community placement; and that the state would remained committed to meeting the "minimum constitutional standards" set out in the 1986 consent decree. The court retained jurisdiction over the case for the limited purpose of enforcing the settlement agreement until September, 2003. Id. at 1238–39. At the end of 2003, the case was dismissed at the request of both sides. 219 F.R.D. 529 (2004). So the *Wyatt* litigation lasted thirty-one years. When it ended, 1,500 patients were housed in Alabama state institutions and roughly 100,000 people were receiving community-based services, compared to 15,000 hospitalized patients and no community-based mental health system when the suit started. Phillip Rawls, The Associated Press, Dec. 6, 2003.

But is the case really over? Consider the last paragraph of *Wyatt ex rel. Rawlins v. Sawyer*, 219 F.R.D. 529, 536 (2004):

It is appropriate to conclude this opinion with the comments of Governor Riley at the December 5 fairness hearing, comments which aptly summarize the import of the dismissal of this lawsuit: "We do not look at the end of this case as a diminishment of our responsibilities, but as more of a responsibility we have to shoulder ourselves." Indeed, if the State fails to shoulder its responsibility, it will find itself back in court as sure as the night follows the day, albeit a defendant in a new and separate lawsuit seeking enforcement of the now well-established principles of this litigation. In this sense, this litigation, the *Wyatt* case, has not ended; its principles (now codified in statutes and regulations) of humane treatment for people with mental illness and mental retardation remain, ever present and hovering over the State.

3. *The national impact of* Wyatt. *Wyatt* has had a huge influence on state hospital care throughout the U.S. Less than a decade after Judge Johnson's first ruling, one commentator concluded that, because of *Wyatt,* thirty-five departments of mental health had instituted changes in regulations governing treatment of patients. Harry Schnibbe, *Changes in State Mental Health Service Systems Since* Wyatt, in Jones & Parlour, supra at 173, 174. Many states passed "Patients Bill of Rights" legislation that replicated to a greater or lesser extent the *Wyatt* order. *The* Wyatt *Standards: An Influential Force in State and Federal Rules*, 28 Hosp. & Comm. Psychiat. 374 (1977). *Wyatt* also influenced the Task Force Panel on Legal and Ethical Issues of the President's Commission on Mental Health, which in turn motivated Congress' passage of the Bill of Rights section of the Mental Health Systems Act. 2 Perlin, supra at 54. This Act, passed in 1983, requested the states to revise their laws taking into account the recommendations of the President's Commission. 42 U.S.C. § 9501.

Finally, *Wyatt* influenced several courts, which issued *Wyatt*-type orders. For instance, Judge Sanders, described in the excerpt at the beginning of this chapter, patterned his monitoring of the Texas mental health system on Judge Johnson's. See also *Welsch v. Likins,* 373 F.Supp. 487 (D.Minn.1974); *Gary W. v. Louisiana,* 437 F.Supp. 1209 (E.D.La.1976). Most of these decisions were narrower in scope than *Wyatt* but, in the areas they dealt with, the relief they granted was at least as extensive as that granted in *Wyatt.* The following notes examine more closely some of the issues addressed by the *Wyatt* litigation and subsequent cases, and the extent to which *Youngberg* has changed the legal landscape. As Professor Perlin notes, although there have been fewer "institutional rights" cases brought since *Youngberg,* "*Youngberg* should emphatically not be read as a bar to further developments in this area." 2 Perlin, supra at 393. In particular, the lessons of *Wyatt* might fruitfully be applied in connection with litigation seeking to improve the treatment of persons committed under sexually violent predator statutes, which typically authorize long-term, indeterminate confinement, ostensibly aimed at treatment. See generally, Douglas G. Smith, *The Constitutionality of Civil Commitment and the Requirement of Adequate Treatment*, 49 B.C. L. Rev. 1383, 1425 (2008) (describing institutional litigation in Washington state attempting to obtain treatment for committed sex offenders and concluding that "[s]tates may be able to enact statutes that declare treatment as a goal, but in practice, that goal may prove to be a sham.").

4. *Individualized treatment plans.* A widely emulated aspect of the *Wyatt* order is the detailed blueprint it established for preparing individualized treatment plans for each patient. See Appendix, paras. 25–29. The individualized plan has become a standard feature of hospital administration in every state (in part because of state hospitals' efforts to achieve accreditation through the Joint Commission). How "individualized"

do these plans have to be? If they are not prepared or adhered to, what should the patient's remedy be? See Appendix, para. 33. May the patient force a change in the plan by refusing the treatment indicated?[c] Perhaps most importantly, after *Youngberg,* to what extent is a patient entitled, under the federal constitution, to internal or judicial review of the adequacy of the treatment plan and its implementation? See Appendix, paras. 28, 29, 33. Consider also this excerpt from *United States v. Charters,* 863 F.2d 302, 312–13 (4th Cir.1988), construing *Youngberg's* professional judgment rule.

> Making an acceptable professional judgment [in the treatment context] does not require any internal adversarial hearing. The decision may be based upon accepted medical practices in diagnosis, treatment and prognosis, with the aid of such technical tools and consultative techniques as are appropriate in the profession. . . . [T]he basis for the decision should be supported by adequate documentation, not only because of normal professional requirements, but as a potential aid to judicial review. One could of course imagine any number of special internal review and consultative practices specifically designed to ensure confidence in the professional basis of specific medical decisions, and medical professionals, aware of the constitutional standard under which they are operating, are of course free to employ any that seem appropriate.

Compare this holding to the thesis of Professor Susan Stefan, in *Leaving Civil Rights to the 'Experts': From Defense to Abdication Under the Professional Judgment Standard*, 102 Yale L.J. 639 (1992). Relying on the standard distinction between positive rights (where the claimant is asking the state for a benefit) and negative rights (where the claimant is attempting to avoid state intervention), Stefan concludes the following about *Youngberg's* professional judgment standard:

> The professional judgement standard comes into play at significantly different stages in these two kinds of decisions, with very different effects. In claims for constitutionally adequate government services, the court applies a constitutional analysis to determine whether the plaintiff is entitled to state services and the general contours of the services to which she is entitled, and only then relies on professional judgment to determine how, specifically, these services should be provided. This approach defers to professionals in decisions they are competent to make. Such deference is appropriate here because the plaintiff is affirmatively seeking to compel state actors to exercise professional judgment on her behalf.

> In negative rights claims, however, the plaintiff seeks protection against the exercise of professional judgment by the state. In this context, professional judgment inappropriately displaces the protection of rights from governmental intrusion. If a court applies the professional

---

[c]   As developed Chapter Nine, Part IV, civilly committed patients may not have a right to refuse medication. But if such a right exists, it may be in tension with the right to treatment.

judgment standard in negative rights cases, professional judgment as to appropriate services or treatment supersedes any judicial analysis regarding the plaintiff's constitutional rights or liberties. The professional effectively exercises his judgement to choose between a patient's rights to family visitation, speech, or freedom from restraint on the one hand, and treatments that may preclude these on the other, without mediation or review by the court.

This approach thus severely curtails constitutional protection of civil rights. . . . [V]alues of autonomy, self-determination or freedom from intrusion will probably receive little attention in the medical professional's decision. Indeed, in these cases the very exercise of professional judgment constitutes the alleged abuse of power. This is particularly true in institutional settings, where all aspects of an individual's life are subject to professional oversight: from hygiene to letter writing to marriage. To assert that constitutional rights in these areas are not violated as long as a professional exercises judgment in limiting or eliminating them substitutes professional values for constitutional values and thereby constitutes an abdication by the courts of their critical obligation to protect individual rights. The Due Process Clause, intended to "prevent government 'from abusing [its] power, or employing it as an instrument of oppression' " is virtually erased by such an approach.

Id. at 668–69. Distinguishing between a positive and a negative right can be a difficult task. For instance, suppose Fred, in the excerpt at the beginning of this chapter, demanded a second-generation antipsychotic medication, one that had fewer neuromotor side effects than the medications the hospital staff was giving him, but which was much more expensive. Is this request (and concomitant refusal to take other drugs) an attempt to obtain professional services (i.e., an assertion of a positive right) or an attempt to avoid state intervention (an assertion of a negative right)?

Professor Stefan's analysis focuses on the substantive standard to be applied in treatment cases. Does it have implications for the procedural issue addressed in *Charters*? The issues raised in the following notes?

5. *Treatment in the least restrictive conditions.* Another innovation in *Wyatt* was its application of the least restrictive alternative idea to treatment *within* the institution. See Appendix, para. 2. Although the language in the Bryce order is quite general, the Partlow order provided more detail as to how this aspect of the right to treatment was to be implemented.

[T]he institution shall make every attempt to move residents from (1) more to less structured living; (2) larger to smaller facilities; (3) larger to smaller living units; (4) group to individual residences; (5) segregated from the community to integrated into the community living; (6) dependent to independent living.

344 F.Supp. 373, 386 (M.D.Ala.1972).

Some courts have been even more precise. In *Goodwin v. Shapiro,* 545 F.Supp. 826 (D.N.J.1982), the court created three levels of supervision designed to enforce the "presumption" that "all patients shall be restricted only to the extent which shall be clinically necessary or necessary to the Hospital's internal order and security, but not for administrative convenience." Id. at 847. Supervisory Level A, which allows the patient "maximum institutional flexibility subject only to curfews and the patient's individual responsibility for meeting treatment or obligations" applies to all patients who do not meet Level B or Level C criteria. Level B applies when "[t]here is a reasonable basis to believe that the patient could be a danger to him/herself, or to others, or might cause significant damage to the property of others" or when "[t]here is a reasonable basis to believe that the patient is an elopement risk." This level of restriction allows grounds privileges "for a reasonable period of time every day without supervision" and "additional on-ground activity, off-ground activity, weekend passes and other such unsupervised activities as the treatment team deems appropriate." Level C, which applies to those who are *clearly* dangerous to self, others or property, or who are clearly an elopement risk, contemplates "complete and constant" supervision.

The Third Circuit's decision in *Youngberg* held that the plaintiff had a right to treatment in the least intrusive manner, and devised a three-tier framework for review similar to that set out in *Goodwin. Romeo v. Youngberg,* 644 F.2d 147, 164–170 (3d Cir.1980). Although the Supreme Court's decision in *Youngberg* did not explicitly address the least intrusive means issue, in its conclusion it included in the list of rights the plaintiff enjoyed the right to "reasonably nonrestrictive confinement conditions." 457 U.S. at 324. However, the Court also rejected the contention that physical restrictions on liberty should only be imposed in the face of a "compelling" or "substantial necessity;" instead the professional judgment rule applies. Can *Youngberg* be construed to require a system similar to that ordered in *Goodwin?* Is such a system a good idea? Recall Hoffman and Foust's argument that effectiveness of treatment must be taken into account if the least restrictive idea is to make sense (see pp. 894–896).

6. *Restraints and seclusion.* One concrete application of the least restrictive idea arises when hospital staff members decide to use physical restraints or seclusion. As indicated in *Youngberg,* restraints are any means of restricting a patient's ability to react physically, usually involving the use of devices such as cuffs, straps, mittens, or braces. "Seclusion . . . involves placing the patient in one of the individual sleeping rooms in the ward, usually furnished with only a bed, and locking the door." *Eckerhart v. Hensley,* 475 F.Supp. 908, 926 (W.D.Mo.1979). Note *Wyatt's* regulation of these two modalities. Appendix, para. 7. Compare these rules to federal law, most recently revised in 2007, which regulates the use of seclusion and restraints in all institutions receiving federal payments:

> Unless superseded by State law that is more restrictive (i) Each order for restraint or seclusion used for the management of violent or self-

destructive behavior that jeopardizes the immediate physical safety of the patient, a staff member, or others may only be renewed in accordance with the following limits for up to a total of 24 hours: (A) 4 hours for adults 18 years of age or older; (B) 2 hours for children and adolescents 9 to 17 years of age; or (C) 1 hour for children under 9 years of age; and (ii) After 24 hours, before writing a new order for the use of restraint or seclusion for the management of violent or self-destructive behavior, a physician or other licensed independent practitioner who is responsible for the care of the patient as specified under § 482.12(c) of this part and authorized to order restraint or seclusion by hospital policy in accordance with State law must see and assess the patient. (iii) Each order for restraint used to ensure the physical safety of the non-violent or non-self-destructive patient may be renewed as authorized by hospital policy. . . . When restraint or seclusion is used for the management of violent or self-destructive behavior that jeopardizes the immediate physical safety of the patient, a staff member, or others, the patient must be seen face-to-face within 1 hour after the initiation of the intervention [by a designated caregiver] to evaluate (A) The patient's immediate situation; (B) The patient's reaction to the intervention; (C) The patient's medical and behavioral condition; and (D) The need to continue or terminate the restraint or seclusion.

42 C.F.R. § 482.13(e)(8)(12). Are such rules constitutionally required by *Youngberg*? Recall that the plaintiff in that case was subjected to "soft restraints," allegedly as part of a training regimen.

Some states prohibit all seclusion and restraint. Stacey A. Tovino, *Psychiatric Restraint and Seclusion: Resisting Legislative Solution*, 47 Santa Clara L. Rev. 511, 551 (2007). In part, this move may be motivated by fear of liability and in part by reports from former patients consistently describing the seclusion and restraint experience in negative terms. Id. at 531–32. For instance, one ex-patient stated: "I can't bring myself to describe the moment-by-moment struggles and shear gut-wrenching terror of being put into five-point restraint. . . . I don't feel comfortable wearing watches anymore and for a long time belts were out of the question. . . . The terror of confinement, the pain of the restraint, and the wound to my soul made me want to stay as far away from the mental health system as possible." Id. Recall also Laurie Kramer's account, in the second excerpt at the beginning of this chapter, of the young woman put in a "padded cell." However, Professor Tovino argues that "When a physician or other licensed independent practitioner reasonably believes that a patient's behavior poses an imminent threat to the life or health of the patient or a third party and all less restrictive measures have proven ineffective, the option to use restraint or seclusion should be preserved." Id at 566.

7.   *Privacy and communication.* The *Wyatt* order provided that patients "shall have an unrestricted right to send sealed mail" and conditioned access to the phone. See Appendix, paras. 5, 4. Two years later in *Procunier v. Martinez*, 416 U.S. 396, 94 S.Ct. 1800, 40 L.Ed.2d 224 (1974), the Supreme

Court articulated the following test to be applied to regulation of prison inmate correspondence:

> First the regulation or practice in question must further an important or substantial government interest unrelated to the suppression of expression. Prison officials may not censor inmate correspondence simply to eliminate unflattering or unwelcome opinions or factually inaccurate statements. Rather they must show that a regulation authorizing mail censorship furthers one or more of the substantial governmental interests of security, order and habilation. Second, the limitation on First Amendment freedoms must be no greater than is necessary or essential to the protection of the particular governmental interest involved. Thus a restriction on inmate correspondence that furthers an important or substantial interest in penal administration will nevertheless be invalid if its sweep is unnecessarily broad.

In *Davis v. Balson*, 461 F.Supp. 842 (N.D.Ohio 1978), the court relied on *Martinez* in holding that interdicting letters from mental patients addressed to the Pope and the Queen of England was not permissible.

In light of this caselaw, consider the examples of actual or contemplated censorship provided in Henry Davidson, "Mental Hospitals and the Civil Liberties Dilemma," 31 Mental Hygiene 371, 374–76 (1967):

> A letter from a patient, addressed to a 12–year–old child, was in an envelope that was bordered by a bizarre design. The child's mother opened it and found a letter containing imaginative sexual proposals, all profusely illustrated by the patient with fine artistic skill. The father called the hospital in understandable indignation.

> A high school team played baseball on the grounds of our hospital. A male patient fell in love with one of the boys—from a distance—and sent him a homosexual love letter.

> A 70–year–old patient, whose 40–year–old daughter had applied for her commitment, sent a letter to her 10–year–old granddaughter, addressing it to her at school. She wrote: "Your mother is a whore. She sent me away to get rid of me so she could entertain men at home. She will do the same to you unless you send her away." The child read this letter, and was brutally shocked. The mother felt that the child was entitled to some protection from communications like this.

* * *

> ... In the last three years we have had to impose restrictions on the outgoing mail of 11 patients. Since we have 3,800 patients, that is not a bad ratio. ... The telephone has been a more troublesome instrument and, in three years we have had to put some restrictions on use of the phone by 26 patients, because the recipients of obscene, threatening, or other painful calls made protests to us.

* * *

Most acutely mental ill patients recover; and they would then be embarrassed by the delusional ideas expressed in their own handwriting. It may sound sanctimonious to say that we are censoring mail for the patient's own good; but, in truth, that *does* happen. I recall a lawyer who came to us in a manic attack. He sent out some very silly letters to his valued clients, overflowing with reckless and grandiose ideas. When he recovered, he found that they would never trust him again. He upbraided us for not stopping those foolish letters.

Statutes protect the privacy of patients by restricting any general revelation of their identities. Thus, we may not permit "pen pals" to fish for names of patients, no matter how worthy their project may be. Sometimes we get into trouble because a patient has written home identifying another patient as being in the same ward, thus violating that other patient's right of privacy. The only way we could plug that leak would be to censor the first patient's mail—but this is where we came in in the first place. As you see, it is not as simple as it sounds.

How should a hospital handle such situations? Is it permissible to indicate on the outside of the envelope that the sender is a mental patient? Consider also the result in *Martyr v. Mazur–Hart*, 789 F.Supp. 1081 (D.Or. 1992). There the court permitted restrictions on the patient's outgoing mail that were rationally related to treatment—e.g., restrictions on sending letters to general members of the community expressing anger at his commitment that, the court concluded, should have been expressed to treatment staff. But it granted a permanent injunction prohibiting hospital officials from censoring or delaying mail addressed to public officials, advocacy groups, attorneys, or journalists.

Other censorship issues arose in connection with John Hinckley, who was hospitalized after his acquittal by reason of insanity on charges of shooting President Reagan and three others. Hospital officials routinely intercepted his outgoing mail. One letter they found requested aid in killing actress Jodie Foster, the actress about whom Hinckley fantasized as he plotted to assassinate President Reagan. The letter was turned over to the F.B.I. Hinckley was also denied interviews with the media pursuant to the following policy:

> The purpose of this policy is to prohibit personal interviews of patients on the maximum security wards ... by representatives of the media. This policy is being enacted based upon a concern that such interviews and publicity could adversely affect the clinical well-being and treatment progress of such patients. These maximum security patients ... may be unable to understand the implications of their own statements to the media. It is felt that this policy is necessary in order to preserve the integrity of patients' treatment and to prevent a disruption of the therapeutic milieu of these wards.

The policy applied to all personal interviews, face-to-face and over the phone, but not to communication with the media by mail. In a suit brought in federal court, Hinckley alleged the policy violated his first amendment right. The court rejected Hinckley's claim, finding that the policy, as applied to Hinckley "is reasonably related to legitimate therapeutic and institutional interests." *U.S. v. Hinckley,* Criminal No. 81–0306, Nov. 28, 1989.

Note that *Wyatt* allowed restrictions on incoming mail, if a "Qualified Mental Health Professional" so orders (see Appendix, para. 5). More recent decisions are consistent with this rule. For instance, in *Belton v. Singer et al.,* 2011 WL 2690595 (D.N.J. 2011), the court permitted staff "to open packages not marked as 'legal mail' to assure that the packages do not contain contraband (*i.e.,* items either harmful to staff and residents, or detrimental to rehabilitation)." Id. at *11. The court explained, "[t]he staff clearly must determine if any items coming through the mail pose a threat to the safety of the staff or the other residents. They also must decide if any of the materials passing through the mail could be detrimental to a resident's therapy." Id. How are officials to determine whether mailed items "pose a threat to the safety of the staff or other residents"? *Belton* involved mail sent to a committed sex offender. Should a different test apply to unconvicted civil committees? Cf. *Serna v. Goodno,* 567 F.3d 944, 948 (8th Cir.2009) (claims by civil committed individuals "should be evaluated under the . . . standard usually applied to . . . pretrial detainees" not the standard applied to prisoners). Is censoring mail because it might be "detrimental to a resident's therapy" permissible? If incoming mail is opened by staff, should the patient have the right to be present?

8.   *Payment for maintenance labor. Wyatt* included relatively detailed rules concerning patient labor. See Appendix, para. 18. Particularly important are its provisions governing labor involving the operation and maintenance of the hospital or for which the hospital would otherwise have to pay an employee. See Appendix, paras. 18A and 18B(2). These provisions were thought necessary to prevent exploitation of patients. Until the mid–1970's hospitals routinely required patients to perform, without pay, housekeeping in the wards, grounds maintenance, laundry duty, cooking and farming. For instance, in *Weidenfeller v. Kidulis,* 380 F.Supp. 445 (E.D.Wis.1974) the court described a 44 year-old intellectually disabled man who "mowed the grass, cleaned patients' rooms, and washed dishes in the kitchen," and a 31 year-old male with intellectual disability whose "tasks included such endeavors as unloading various materials, cleaning toilets and sinks, and scrubbing the kitchen floor," neither of whom were paid. In a study of 154 institutions conducted in 1972, approximately 30% of the patient workers (out of a total of 32,180) were not paid at all, and 50% received less than $10.00 a week. Paul Friedman, *The Mentally Handicapped Citizen and Institutional Labor,* 87 Harv.L.Rev. 567, 568 (1974). Another study indicated that patient labor saved the state of Pennsylvania roughly $10 million a year. See Samuel Brakel et al., The Mentally Disabled and the Law 280 (1985).

Properly administered, however, compensated labor confers psychological benefits for persons with severe mental illness. As a 2002 review explained:

> Research on the relationship between work and symptom level or
> symptom changes in [persons with severe mental illness] ... has
> revealed that participation in vocational programs is correlated with
> decreases in symptoms, but researchers are not sure which symptoms.
> For instance, [a 1996 study] found that weeks of participation in a work
> therapy program was related to decreases in symptoms of emotional
> discomfort (depression and anxiety), positive symptoms, and hostility
> symptoms but not to decreases in negative or cognitive disorganization
> symptoms. [A 1997 study] found that work participation was related to
> decreases in thought disorder, whereas [a 1991 study] found that
> quantity of work was related to improvements in both positive and
> negative symptoms.

Gary Bryson, Paul Lysaker & Morris Bell, *Quality of Life Benefits of Paid
Work Activity in Schizophrenia*, 28 Schizophrenia Bull. 249, 249 (2002)
(citations omitted). The inverse is also true. Ample evidence suggests that
unemployment is harmful to mental health:

> Unemployed individuals suffer from an increase in the release of stress
> hormones, a deterioration of health behaviour, and an increased
> mortality rate ... [A]lthough mental distress may cause unemployment
> in some cases and keep mentally distressed people out of work in other
> cases, the most significant correlation between unemployment and
> mental health is that of causation: unemployment causes mental
> distress ... through financial deprivation, loss of control, stress, loss of
> social support, and other latent functions associated with employment.

Mikael Skärlund, Annika Ahs & Ragnar Westerling, *Health–Related and
Social Factors Predicting Non–Reemployment Amongst Newly Unemployed*,
12 BMC Public Health 893, 893 (2012) (citations omitted).

These types of concerns led Judge Johnson to modify, six months after
the *Wyatt* decree was issued, paragraph 18A requiring compensation for
institution-maintaining labor. As described in Note, *The Wyatt Case:
Implementation of a Judicial Decree Ordering Institutional Change*, 84 Yale
L.J. 1338, 1376 (1975):

> Shortly after the decree was entered, the Partlow Human Rights
> committee began to note numerous complaints from patients who had
> been working without compensation before the issuance of the decree but
> who, after the issuance of the decree, were no longer allowed to work
> because the administration allegedly lacked the resources to pay them.
> "These residents are now bored and anxious to be doing something," the
> PHRC noted. This problem had not been foreseen by the court. It was
> eventually corrected by clarifying the decree to allow patients to perform
> uncompensated labor for therapeutic purposes.

Nonetheless, the courts have generally held that, with the exception of
personal chores, maintenance labor must be compensated. Most commonly,
these decisions rely on the provisions of the Fair Labor Standards Act.
Plaintiffs have also argued, however, that the thirteenth amendment and the

right to treatment require the same result. These three legal avenues are examined below.

The Thirteenth Amendment. The thirteenth amendment prohibits "slavery" and "involuntary servitude." Courts have held that a valid thirteenth amendment claim requires proof (1) that the work was done involuntarily and (2) that there is no compelling governmental interest justifying the involuntary labor. *Butler v. Perry*, 240 U.S. 328, 36 S.Ct. 258, 60 L.Ed. 672 (1916). With respect to the involuntariness requirement, the Supreme Court has held, in the context of a criminal action against state officials based on an alleged violation of the thirteenth amendment, that unpaid labor is not involuntary unless it is produced by "the use or threat of physical restraint or physical injury" or "the use or threat of coercion through law or the legal process." *United States v. Kozminski*, 487 U.S. 931, 108 S.Ct. 2751, 101 L.Ed.2d 788 (1988). The Court went on to state:

> Our holding does not imply that evidence of other means of coercion, or of poor working conditions, or of the victim's special vulnerabilities is irrelevant in a prosecution under these statutes. [T]he vulnerabilities of the victim are relevant in determining whether the physical or legal coercion or threat thereof could plausibly have compelled the victim to serve. In addition, a trial court could properly find that evidence of other means of coercion or of extremely poor working conditions is relevant to corroborate disputed evidence regarding the use or threatened use of physical or legal coercion, the defendant's intention in using such means, or the causal effect of such conduct. We hold only that the jury must be instructed that compulsion of services by the use or threatened use of physical or legal coercion is a necessary incident of a condition of involuntary servitude.

One earlier case dealing with the application of the thirteenth amendment to patient labor stated that the "source of coercion" could be "said to be the boredom of institutional life and the belief of patients that it will be advantageous to them to appear to cooperate with the institution." Moreover, "coercion results from deprivation of the right to leave the ward on 'grounds' privileges or being otherwise restricted." *Downs v. Department of Public Welfare*, 368 F.Supp. 454, 458–59 (E.D.Pa.1973). Would any of these "sources of coercion" be found to implicate the thirteenth amendment today? Are there any other sources of coercion?

With respect to the second aspect of thirteenth amendment analysis, all courts agree that the government interest in requiring uncompensated patient labor is "compelling" if the labor can be characterized as "therapeutic." Most courts have placed a "heavy burden" on the plaintiff to demonstrate that a particular task is not therapeutic. *Weidenfuller v. Kidulis, supra* at 451. Thus, one court found that over 6,000 hours of work "at several different jobs, varying from food preparation and service to . . . cleaning and maintenance of the physical plant of the hospital" were "related to a therapeutic program of rehabilitation." *Estate of Buzzelle v. Colorado State Hospital*, 176 Colo. 554, 556, 491 P.2d 1369, 1370–71 (1971). Moreover, many courts have held that, under some circumstances, involuntary work that is admittedly *non*therapeutic fails to implicate the thirteenth amendment. In *Jobson v. Henne,* 355 F.2d 129 (2d Cir.1966), still the leading case in this regard, the court held that "the states are not . . . foreclosed [by the thirteenth amendment] from requiring that a lawfully committed inmate perform without compensation certain chores designed to reduce the financial burden placed on a state by its program of treatment for people with mental retardation, if the chores are reasonably related to a therapeutic program, or if not directly so related, chores of a normal house keeping type and kind." Id. at 132. See also, *Channer v. Hall,* 112 F.3d 214, 218 (5th Cir.1997), citing *Bayh v. Sonnenburg,* 573 N.E.2d 398, 412 (Ind.1991) (labor performed by mental hospital patients who performed a variety of work duties while hospitalized such as fixing meals, scrubbing dishes, doing the laundry and cleaning the building, fit within the Thirteenth Amendment's "civic duty" exception).

Fair Labor Standards Act. Until they were significantly limited by the Supreme Court (see below), patient claims for compensation under the Fair Labor Standards Act, 29 U.S.C. §§ 201–219, were much more successful. In 1966, the Act, which establishes minimum wage and maximum hour levels, was amended to apply to state hospitals and institutions for people with mental disability, with provision for payment below the minimum wage to workers unable to work at a normal level because of mental or physical handicap. In *Wyatt,* Judge Johnson ordered that, in those circumstances when payment was due (recall the modification to the order discussed earlier), it had to be in accordance with the FLSA. See Appendix, paras. 18A, 18B(2)(c). Other courts went further. In *Souder v. Brennan,* 367 F.Supp. 808 (D.D.C.1973), the court held that the Act applied to virtually all work performed by patients at state institutions.

> Economic reality is the test of employment and the reality is that many patient-workers perform work for which they are in no way handicapped and from which the institution derives full economic benefit. So long as the institution derives any consequential economic benefit the economic reality test would indicate an employment relationship rather than mere therapeutic exercise. To hold otherwise would make therapy the sole justification for thousands of positions as dishwashers, kitchen helpers, messengers, and the like.

Id. at 813. The U.S. Department of Labor has adopted *Souder's* definition of therapeutic work in the following regulation:

> With respect to patient workers . . . a major factor in determining if an employment relationship exists is whether the work performed is of any consequential economic benefit to the institution. Generally, work shall be considered to be of consequential economic benefit if it is of the type that workers without disabilities normally perform, in whole or in part in the institution or elsewhere. However, a patient does not become an employee if he or she merely performs personal housekeeping chores, such as maintaining his or her own quarters, or receives a token

remuneration in connection with such services. It may also be possible for patients in family-like settings such as group homes to rotate or share household tasks or chores without becoming employees.

29 CFR § 525.4 (2006). Obviously, this definition of therapeutic work under the FLSA is quite different from the typical definition of therapeutic work under the thirteenth amendment. Are there reasons for this distinction? In any event, is it correct to assume, as the *Souder* court seems to, that a particular job's economic benefit to the state is inversely related to its "therapeutic value"? Is there a better way to define the term?

Souder had a dampening effect on patient work programs. As one comment noted, "Thanks to *Souder*, enforced idleness has become one of the worst features of mental hospitals and a standard complaint of commissions investigating state hospitals has been (in the words of a New York commission) 'the total lack of occupation' on the wards." Treatment Advocacy Center, available at http://www.treatmentadvocacycenter.org/index.php?option=com_content&task=view&id=347 (last accessed May 7, 2013). While *Souder* continues to control the FLSA's application to most civilly committed hospitals, it does not apply to persons committed under sexually violent predator laws. *Gonzalez v. Mayberg*, 2008 WL 6632574 (C.D. Cal. 2008); *Miller v. Dukakis*, 961 F.2d 7, 9 (1st Cir. 1992). Is this distinction justified?

The Right to Treatment. Plaintiffs have also argued that the constitutional right to treatment requires the state to make paid work programs available to patients. Such an argument was made, for instance, in *Schindenwolf v. Klein,* reported in 5 MDLR 60 (N.J.Super.Ct., Mercer Cty.1980); the result was a consent decree in which New Jersey agreed to employ or provide vocational rehabilitation for 25% of the patients in five state facilities. Under the decree, this group of patients would be given institutional work assignments that do "not impede the residents' movement towards discharge" and that are neither "created nor maintained for the sole purpose of providing residents with activity." Id. at 63. The decree required that this work be compensated; personal housekeeping chores required of the patients need not be. See also, *Davis v. Balson*, 461 F.Supp. 842, 852–53 (D.C. Ohio 1978).

Of the arguments that can be advanced in support of the result in *Schindenwolf* the strongest derives from the least restrictive alternative rationale for the right to treatment. As described by Perlin, the plaintiffs' attorney in *Schindenwolf* litigation, the least restrictive alternative doctrine "mandates that infringement of individual interests and liberties go no further than that which is absolutely necessary for the achievement of the state's interest. Since the state's interest in confinement is treatment coupled with security, the right to work, especially in light of the demonstrated viability and success of therapeutic work programs, must be preserved." Michael Perlin, *The Right to Voluntary, Compensated, Therapeutic Work as Part of the Right to Treatment: A New Theory in the Aftermath of* Souder, 7 Seton Hall L.Rev. 298, 332–33 (1976). Does this argument survive

Youngberg? If it does, does it also require that work programs be either voluntary or compensated?

In light of the foregoing, consider the work required of Fred Thomas at the hospital (pp. 1236–1237 & 1308–1309, infra). What is your analysis of the work arrangement? Should basic privileges such as access to one's own money be contingent on the performance of routine chores?

9. *Enforcing the right to treatment and habilitation.* In light of *Youngberg's* definition of treatment and its adoption of the professional judgment rule, individual damages actions are not likely to be a useful enforcement mechanism for many of the entitlements dealt with in *Wyatt.* In any event, systemic reform is likely to bring more benefit to more people.

In this regard, *Wyatt* is again instructive. Throughout the *Wyatt* litigation, Judge Johnson attempted to avoid dramatic confrontation with the state. His handling of the state's "budgetary defense" is one example. In *Wyatt v. Stickney,* he clearly stated that the state of Alabama would not be able to avoid constitutional dictates through pleading insolvency. As the decision indicates, he even contemplated ordering the state to sell land in order to provide funding for the hospital system. But the order was never issued. The Fifth Circuit was equally circumspect in this regard. In *Wyatt v. Aderholt,* 503 F.2d 1305, 1318 (5th Cir.1974), it stated that "[t]he serious constitutional questions presented by federal judicial action ordering the sale of state land, or altering the state budget, or which may otherwise arise in the problem of financing, in the event the governing authorities fail to move in good faith to ensure what all parties agree are minimal requirements, should not be adjudicated unnecessarily and prematurely." As this passage indicates, the court's caution resulted both from concern over the scope of federal judicial authority over state legislatures and from a perception that the state had been relatively cooperative up to that point.

When the state is *not* cooperative, what options short of the rather dubious step of ordering the state legislature to appropriate money are available to a federal court? One option is to close down the institutions. This approach has been taken in prison cases. See, e.g., *Ramos v. Lamm,* 485 F.Supp. 122, 169–70 (D.Colo.1979). A second option for the court is use of its contempt authority to force the relevant officials to act in accordance with the court order. On one occasion, for instance, the *Wyatt* plaintiffs moved to cite several Bryce staff members for violating paragraph 9 of the order concerning electroshock therapy. Although the citation was not granted, no further violations of this part of the order occurred. See Jack Drake, *Judicial Implementation and* Wyatt v. Stickney, 32 Ala.L.Rev. 299, 308 (1981).

Also illustrated by *Wyatt* is the use of masters and receivers. The receiver appointed in *Wyatt v. Ireland* was responsible for overseeing the operation of the Alabama hospitals and reporting to the court. Court-appointed officials can also perform more limited functions. As an example of the latter role, in *Lynch v. Baxley,* 386 F.Supp. 378 (M.D.Ala.1974), the court ordered special judges to preside over discharge hearings at Bryce and

Searcy; over 3,100 patients were evaluated, and of that number 1,287 were discharged, 888 were committed, 777 were held pending placement, and 167 were voluntarily committed. Drake, supra at 309. Another potentially powerful enforcement mechanism is economic sanction. The court can assess damages for constitutional violations on a per patient, per day basis. Id. at 309–310.

A final enforcement mechanism, perhaps the most important, is a reliable information-gathering and advocacy system. Judge Johnson appointed human rights committees and monitors who were charged with reporting to the court about compliance with the order. His order also provided that "[p]atients shall have an unrestricted right to visitation with attorneys." Appendix, para. 4. Other approaches are legion. The Developmentally Disabled Assistance and Bill of Rights Act of 1975, 42 U.S.C. § 6012, provided funding for advocates for people with developmental disability. Eleven years later Congress passed the Protection and Advocacy for Mentally Ill Persons Act of 1986, 42 U.S.C. § 10801 et. seq., which is meant "to protect and advocate the rights" of people with mental illness and "investigate incidents of abuse and neglect of individuals with mental illness." Id. These Acts make receipt of federal funding contingent on establishing protection and advocacy systems (P & A's). See *Michigan Protection & Advocacy Serv. v. Miller*, 849 F.Supp. 1202 (W.D.Mich.1994). Many hospitals also have legal aid services, funded by a number of different mechanisms, which provide legal representation on discharge, "institutional" and civil legal issues.

If a lawyer is involved in monitoring the rights of institutionalized persons, what should his or her role be? At least one commentator has suggested that the traditional adversarial stance is not appropriate in most situations:

> For the in-hospital lawyer to act in [an adversarial] fashion routinely, for him to take seriously and pursue uncompromisingly the bulk of patient complaints and grievances or to generally set himself up as a force hostile to the institution only spells disaster. It bogs the lawyer down in controversies of little merit whose ultimate outcome is often not in the best interests of either the individual patient or the general patient population. It causes him to lose the cooperation of the institutional staff without which—given the knowledge of and control over patients possessed by the staff—it is difficult to do the patients' interests justice. Carried far enough, this approach could also seriously hamper the institution's capacity to work to the benefit of the patients. The achievement of success in institutionally treating mental patients is already difficult enough—the illnesses may not be curable, the staff may be overworked and insufficiently expert, and the prospects upon discharge, even after improvement, may be dismal because the underlying or contributing conditions (problems of family, money, employment) remain unchanged. For a legal project to further reduce the chances of success by creating needless antagonisms between patients

and staff and by intimidating medical or supervisory personnel and inhibiting them in carrying out their functions is irresponsible.

Samuel Brakel, *Legal Aid in Mental Hospitals*, 1981 Am.Bar. Found.Res. Journ. 23.

10.   *The right to treatment in private institutions.* A number of states are now encouraging private operators to establish facilities for treatment and habilitation of people with mental disability. See, e.g., Leonard Gilroy, *Privatization Can Transform the Delivery of State Psychiatric Services*, Reason Foundation, Dec. 29, 2008 (describing privatization of mental health services in Virginia, Florida, Georgia and the District of Columbia), available at http://reason.org/news/printer/privatization-can-transform-th. Are such facilities governed by the constitutional rulings described above? In other words, is there "state action" in such situations?

In *Blum v. Yaretsky*, 457 U.S. 991, 102 S.Ct. 2777, 73 L.Ed.2d 534 (1982), the Supreme Court held that residents of a private nursing home had failed to establish that a decision by the home to transfer them to a lower-level facility constituted state action. Neither the fact that state funds paid for more than 90 percent of the cost of the patients' care nor the fact that the facility was extensively regulated by state agencies was deemed sufficient to establish state action. However, the Court also noted that the home was not performing "a function that has traditionally been the exclusive prerogative of the State."

In *West v. Atkins*, 487 U.S. 42, 108 S.Ct. 2250, 101 L.Ed.2d 40 (1988), the Court indicated that this latter caveat may cover state-retained private caretakers. In *Atkins*, the Court held that Dr. Atkins, a private doctor hired by the state prison to operate two clinics each week at the prison, was a "state official acting under color of state law" for purposes of a civil rights action against the state:

> . . . It is the physician's function within the state system, not the precise terms of his employment, that determines whether his actions can fairly be attributed to the State. Whether a physician is on the state payroll or is paid by contract, the dispositive issue concerns the relationship among the State, the physician, and the prisoner. Contracting out prison medical care does not relieve the State of its constitutional duty to provide adequate medical treatment to those in its custody[.] . . . The State bore an affirmative obligation to provide adequate medical care to West; the State delegated that function to respondent Atkins; and respondent voluntarily assumed that obligation by contract.

Most courts have read *West* restrictively. As one court has summarized matters:

> Under the public function test, a private party is a state actor if he exercises powers "traditionally reserved exclusively to the state." The public function test has been interpreted narrowly. Only functions like holding elections, exercising eminent domain, and operating a company-owned town, fall under this category of state action. Thus, courts have

concluded that actions like performing forensic interviews and providing court-ordered counseling services do not meet the standard.

Kolley v. Adult Protective Services, 786 F.Supp.2d 1277, 1312 (2011). Under the Court's decisions would a privately-run halfway house or outpatient clinic be governed by the Constitution?

11.   *The right to treatment in prisons.* In *Brown v. Plata*, ___ U.S. ___, 131 S.Ct. 1910, 179 L.Ed.2d 969 (2011), the Supreme Court held that failure to provide adequate mental health care to prisoners is a violation of the Eighth Amendment. The decision was based on a district court finding that the state of California had failed to provide "minimal, adequate care" to prisoners with serious mental illness, and a subsequent order by a three-judge panel requiring the state to reduce its prison population to 137.5% of its design capacity within two years. The evidence showed that California prisons had high vacancy rates for medical and mental health staff (e.g., 54.1% for psychiatrists) and that even if vacant positions were budgeted for and filled, the state did not have sufficient space for the additional professionals. The Supreme Court concluded that this shortfall contributed to "significant delays" in treating mentally ill prisoners, who had to be housed in administrative segregation for extended periods while awaiting transfer to scarce mental health treatment beds. The Court also concluded that these conditions created unsanitary and dangerous conditions, promoted unrest and violence, and caused prisoners with mental illness to worsen and develop overt symptoms. Accordingly, the Court held that the three-judge panel's disposition of the case was appropriate, rejecting the state's claim that it could deal with the problem through additional hiring or transfer of prisoners. The Eighth Amendment prohibits cruel and unusual "punishment." Could it nonetheless be the basis for a right to treatment suit aimed at state forensic hospitals that house defendants found incompetent to stand trial or not guilty by reason of insanity, which are often short of beds?

As to whether treatment in prison does any good, several meta-reviews have concluded that certain types of interventions (e.g., cognitive behavior therapy, assertive community treatment) can have some effect on recidivism by offenders with mental disorders, although the effect is only weak to moderate. See, e.g., Michael Martin et al., *Stopping the Revolving Door: A Meta–Analysis on the Effectiveness of Interventions for Criminally Involved Individuals with Major Mental Disorders*, 36 L. & Hum Beh. 1 (2012); Joshua J. Knabb et al., *Treatment Alternatives for Mentally Disordered Offenders: A Literature Review*, 2 Psychology 122 (2011).

12.   *Reimbursement for treatment.* Every state has enacted legislation making voluntary *and* involuntary patients liable for the cost of their treatment. Forty-seven states extend this liability to the patient's relatives, usually including at least the patient's spouse, parents and adult children. Brakel et al., supra, Table 2.17. At least one court has held that since prisoners do not have to pay for the cost of their imprisonment, such statutes are unconstitutional. In *Department of Mental Hygiene v. Kirchner,* 60 Cal.2d

716, 36 Cal.Rptr. 488, 388 P.2d 720 (1964), the California Supreme Court declared:

> Whether the commitment is incidental to an alleged violation of a penal statute . . . or is essentially a civil commitment as in the instant case, the purposes of confinement and treatment or care in either case encompass the protection of society from the confined person, and his own protection and possible reclamation as a productive member of the body politic. Hence the cost of maintaining the state institution, including provision of adequate care for its inmates, cannot be arbitrarily charged to one class in the society; such assessment violates the equal protection clause.[d]

Most courts, contrary to *Kirchner*, have upheld state reimbursement statutes against such equal protection challenges. See generally, Reimbursement of Costs; Validity of Recoupment Statutes, 52 Am.Jur.2d § 153 (2013)., Is there a rational basis for distinguishing between prisoners and patients in this regard? Might the state have to show *more* than a rational basis?

Consider in this regard *Chill v. Mississippi Hospital Reimbursement Commission*, 429 So.2d 574 (Miss.1983), in which the court held that, given a state statute which prohibited the state from seeking reimbursement "beyond ability to pay," "the legitimate needs and comforts of the patient and his or her dependents or surviving relatives" had an "absolute priority" over state claims. Id. 586–87. In *In re Guardianship of Nelson*, 98 Wis.2d 261, 296 N.W.2d 736 (1980), by contrast, the trial court's order granting the state all but $1,500 of the patient's $27,000 estate was affirmed. Might not the *Nelson* holding deter persons with mental disability and their relatives from seeking treatment?

A final question is whether the state may levy on funds the patients earn at the hospital. At the end of its provisions concerning patient labor, the *Wyatt* order states that "[p]ayment to patients pursuant to these paragraphs shall not be applied to the costs of hospitalization." See Appendix, para. 18D. What is the rationale for this rule? Consider the arguments in favor of allowing patient wages to setoff part of the costs of hospitalization in Marshall Kapp, *Residents of State Mental Institutions and Their Money (or, the State Giveth and the State Taketh Away)*, 6 J.Psychiat. & Law 287, 304–05 (1979):

> [S]et-offs could provide a fair way to balance the resident's fundamental need to work (and to do so without exploitation), against the legitimate interest of the state mental health official in averting bankruptcy. The resident could be protected by a regulation limiting the percentage of his wages that could be set-off against his institutional charges, so that he would be assured of actually pocketing some of his earnings. Payment of

---

[d] On remand from the U.S. Supreme Court, the California Supreme Court held that *Kirchner* was based on an interpretation of the equal protection clause in the California constitution. 62 Cal.2d 586, 43 Cal.Rptr. 329, 400 P.2d 321 (1965). *Kirchner's* reach has since been significantly curtailed. See, e.g., *Swoap v. Superior Court*, 10 Cal.3d 490, 111 Cal.Rptr. 136, 516 P.2d 840 (1973).

wages, even if immediately recouped by the state, would give the resident knowledge that he or she is earning his or her room and board, and is not a mere ward of the state, knowledge which carries a sense of accomplishment, self-respect, and dignity of considerable therapeutic worth. Finally, permitting a resident to work and earn wages, even if they are subject to a set-off, could potentially provide him or her with certain tangible benefits including social security, state retirement payments, and workmen's compensation.

IV.   THE RIGHT TO COMMUNITY SERVICES

In paragraph 34 of the order in *Wyatt v. Stickney,* the court decreed that the Alabama Mental Health Board and its agents had "an affirmative duty to provide adequate transitional treatment and care for all patients released after a period of involuntary confinement." A similar provision appeared in the Partlow order. 344 F.Supp. at 397, 407. Yet subsequently the court substantially undercut these provisions, holding that the Partlow Human Rights Committee's jurisdiction was limited to the institution. Note, *The* Wyatt *Case: Implementation of a Judicial Decree Ordering Institutional Change*, 84 Yale L.J. 1339, 1374–75 (1975). As one commentator stated:

> Because the PHRC was the only method the court had to supervise the decree, this restriction effectively limited the scope of the decree to the institution's walls. Yet it was clear that problems existed with residents released from the institution. Storekeepers in local communities complained of former residents engaging in such conduct as urinating on the floors, opening up and using packages of make-up, and bouncing on beds in furniture stores. Discharged residents allegedly engaged in improper sexual behavior, leading to complaints and criminal charges. Citizens of one town in Alabama applied for and were granted a state court injunction to close a halfway house for residents discharged from one of the *Wyatt* institutions, alleging that the house was so badly supervised that it constituted a nuisance which devalued local property. The lack of adequate post-institutional placement and followup was also evidenced by complaints received by the Alabama Mental Health Board from local mental health organizations, which stated that Partlow residents had been inappropriately placed under their care in facilities that were not suited to meet those persons' needs.

> The district court's decision to limit the PHRC's jurisdiction to the institution was probably founded on well-intentioned beliefs that the problems should be attacked one at a time. However, the court apparently failed to anticipate that the decree itself would create problems outside the institution, through the discharge of residents, and thus did not take sufficient measures to minimize these effects.

Id. As this passage illustrates, for most patients a right to treatment is not particularly effective unless it also applies outside the institution. The following materials explore the right to treatment in the community. They begin with the continuing saga of Fred and his experiences in the Texas mental health system after he was discharged from the hospital.

JOSEPH NOCERA, THE LONG, LONESOME ROAD
Texas Monthly 49–53 (1986).

* * *

No one can doubt that deinstitutionalization has done a lot of good. Many who didn't need to be there were languishing in mental hospitals; their lives have been immeasurably improved. In 1970 alone, the Austin State Hospital's population dropped from 3400 to 1800, and almost all releases were easy cases. But if deinstitutionalization has done some unquestioned good, it has also had its share of unintended consequences. Look around downtown Houston, where as many as 2000 mentally ill people, "freed" from the state hospital, wander the streets like modern-day paupers, and you quickly realize how far the promise of deinstitutionalization is from the reality. The miracle drugs that were going to "cure" the mentally ill have turned out to be not so miraculous after all—helpful, yes, but not miraculous. The extensive network of community programs and halfway houses that were expected to absorb the thousands of mentally ill streaming out of state hospitals never developed—especially not in Texas, where the state hospitals still pull in nearly 80 per cent of all the mental health money even as their populations have been reduced by more than two thirds. A patient's right under the law to be released from a state hospital commitment after ninety days has been largely responsible for the so-called revolving door syndrome, in which patients spend their lives shuttling back and forth from the hospital to the community. The right to live in the least restrictive environment has meant that thousands of mentally ill people, not sick enough to be confined to a hospital ward but still desperately in need of care, live in the least restrictive environment imaginable: the streets.

And yet the pressure on the state hospitals to "get the census down" remains as inexorable as ever. It comes from state and federal law and from a society still unwilling to admit that deinstitutionalization has not worked the way it was supposed to. And it also comes from Judge Sanders. The judge's mental health monitors—the people overseeing the hospital system on his behalf—deny that depopulation is their intent, but they cannot deny the result. Their goal is purely to improve conditions at the state hospital, with little thought given to how the judge's orders will affect the rest of the system. Several years ago, when Judge Sanders, acting on the masters' recommendations, ordered that the staff-to-patient ratio be significantly lowered, his aim was to make each ward a less dangerous place. But since the hospitals didn't have the money to hire the hundreds of staff members needed to comply with the order, they reacted—predictably—not by adding staff but by increasing medication dosages for the patients, to get them out more quickly. The hospitals can say—and do say, all the time—that they are only doing their job while complying with a court order. The judge can say that he is doing his job. (The population in Austin today is around 550.) And meanwhile, a few thousand more mentally ill people are released to the streets, where they find . . . nothing.

Well, not exactly nothing. Houston, for example, does have some outpatient clinics, some apartments for mentally ill people, and one small halfway house to serve the thousands of mentally ill people who live in the city. The halfway house is Tarry Hall, on a residential street in Montrose. It has 27 beds. It is the reality of deinstitutionalization in Houston. . . .

*   *   *

"Hygiene and room check are now beginning."

It was 9:15 a.m. . . . , and the voice booming over the intercom belonged to Dennis Milam, a bearded, sandaled social worker who is third in command at Tarry Hall. By this time, the residents (as Tarry Hall calls its clientele) had been awake for nearly three hours, and theoretically they should have finished their hygiene and room chores. Instead, most were in the same position as Fred. They hadn't even started.

Tarry Hall is a deceptively large house built in the shape of a square doughnut. Its central feature is an outdoor courtyard surrounded by four wide corridors. In the front of the building is a pool room, and in the back, a den. Because it has a TV and a stereo, the den serves much the same function as the dayroom in Austin; it is where the residents can usually be found when they have nothing else to do. It was where Talvin Paul—a 25–year–old graduate of Grambling who was Fred's caseworker—now found his new charge.

"Have you taken a shower yet, Fred?" asked Talvin.

"Too early for that, man." Fred stared straight ahead while Talvin spoke. "One of the expectations around here is that everybody takes a shower," Talvin said. Still, Fred didn't move. It was 9:25. Over the intercom Dennis said, "Fred Thomas, you are needed in your room." Fred crushed his cigarette butt into the floor—ignoring Talvin's admonition to put it in an ashtray—and shuffled off to his room.

The purpose of the hygiene and room chores is to instill a sense of responsibility in the residents, and those who accomplish their daily tasks are rewarded with access to their money and cigarettes and with the accumulation of free time—time they can spend away from the halfway house. Fred and his new roommate, another recent arrival from Austin, listened impassively as Dennis explained what was expected of them each morning: besides making their beds and putting their clothes away, they were supposed to sweep, mop, and dust their rooms. In addition, each would soon be given a household chore (Fred was eventually assigned a bathroom to keep clean). "Do you understand?" asked Dennis. Fred nodded and began picking up his sheets. But as soon as Dennis left, Fred dropped the sheets, wandered back into the den, and turned on the stereo. It was 9:35.

Fifteen minutes later, Dennis found him. "In the morning," he said, "we don't have the stereo or TV on." He flicked the music off. "Your roommate is sweeping the room right now, so why don't you get the mop?" Annoyed by that, Fred nonetheless got a mop and dragged it behind him toward his bedroom. When he got there he gave the floor a few halfhearted passes. But as soon as the coast was clear, Fred started to walk back to the den. Talvin spotted him. "Fred," he shouted, "you need to be in your room!"

That was more than Fred could bear. He stalked past Talvin into the den and again turned on the stereo. When Talvin caught up with him, Fred glared. "Why are you trying to punish me, man?" he asked. It was 10:15.

Today hygiene and room check took nearly two hours. Up until a few months ago, it had taken a half-hour. Back then, the staff had encouraged residents to look for work, and the residents themselves had run a meeting every Friday to decide how much free time each person had earned. Now the staff was spending its time encouraging residents to comb their hair, and the Friday meeting was run by staff members, who had already decided how much time each resident had earned. Things were different because the residents were different; the mentally ill people whom Tarry Hall once treated had been much less sick than the ones it treated now.

That era had only recently ended, yet it was already viewed nostalgically by the Tarry Hall staff. It had been more fun to work with higher functioning residents: they were more motivated to succeed and easier to reach, and the psychic rewards for the staff were much more immediate. Tarry Hall had enjoyed a great deal of independence in the old days. Stripped of that independence, Tarry Hall was bitter.

For most of its eight-year existence, the halfway house had successfully resisted efforts to make it a port of entry for released state hospital patients. Never mind that Tarry Hall was the only county-funded halfway house in the city and that there were mentally ill people in the streets of Houston who needed the kind of help Tarry Hall could offer. For years Tarry Hall administrators refused to admit that those two facts were connected.

Early in 1985, however, in its never-ending effort to reduce hospital populations, MHMR began dangling money in front of local mental health agencies as an inducement to treat more mentally ill people. Each agency would receive $35.50 per patient per day that the census was reduced in Austin. Gradually, the Harris County mental health authorities began making changes aimed at keeping more people out of the hospital. For instance, they assigned caseworkers to monitor the progress of recently released state hospital patients. They also began scrambling for more placement possibilities: inevitably, they saw Tarry Hall as a luxury they could no longer afford. In late March 1985 Tarry Hall had begun accepting its first handful of residents from Austin.

The change from without imposed on Tarry Hall also brought changes from within. Tarry Hall used to have a library: now the library was being converted to a point store. The former clientele had attended current-events classes; the new clientele took walks in the neighborhood. In general sights were lowered. Among the staff members, who had agreed to the changes only because they had no other choice, morale was very weak.

The question that remained unanswered was whether the new Tarry Hall was equipped to help its new residents. For years the staff had done a good job with the people it chose to work with. Now, though the residents were different, the staff was the same. Could the staff teach residents to comb their hair and take a shower as well as they had once taught current events? Could Tarry Hall motivate the truly unmotivated? As Fred had shown, it would be no easy trick.

* * *

One morning in early July I decided to see how the other half lived— the mentally ill people in Houston who do not have one of the 27 beds in Tarry Hall or access to the other facilities available to the lucky few. I went looking for Don Peterson [who had been released unconditionally at about the same time Fred was released].

I started at the [Reverend] Armstrong house where Peterson lived and talked my way inside for a quick glance around. I didn't find Peterson, but what I did find left me reeling. Peterson's tiny bedroom, which he shared with two other people, was particularly gruesome. A spoon on his bureau had been there for so long that whatever food it once held had turned moldy and black and so hard that it appeared glued to the surface. I saw a black woman walking around naked. I tried to talk to her, but two young white "attendants" shooed me away. The attendants would be fired a few weeks later when Armstrong found them "misusing one of the girls," as he phrased it, though not sexually, he quickly added.

Before I left, one of the tenants told me that Peterson usually hung out at the Star of Hope Mission during the day.

That's where I found Peterson, sitting in a lower downtown parking lot across the street from the mission, a large, two-story building that can accommodate as many as five hundred homeless every night. Next to him was a white teenager, a runaway. Despite the heat, Peterson wore his usual four shirts, a vest, a jacket, and a pair of new tan cowboy boots. Sweat was dripping from the end of his moustache, and a dirty winger coat lay on the sidewalk next to him. He held a Burger King bag that contained a bottle of Thunderbird wine, which he had bought from someone at the mission for 13 cents.

Every day Peterson got up before dawn and took a bus downtown in order to be at the mission in time for breakfast, which began at 5 a.m. He usually stayed through the dinner hour. I thought at first that he came because the food was better, but he quickly disabused me. "Rev's [Reverend Armstrong's] food's about the same." So why did he do it? "Dunno," he said. "Guess it's cause this is where all my friends are." He pointed in the direction of the runaway. I asked him what his friend's name was. He didn't know.

The real reason for Peterson's routine was that the Star of Hope Mission came the closest to approximating life in an institution. He was used to the barter economy of the state hospital; that also existed among the transient population. He was even used to the danger. The runaway told me, somewhat nervously, that in the last week there had been four stabbings outside the mission. From reading the newspaper you can get the impression that mentally ill people commit an inordinate number of violent crimes. At a place like the Star of Hope Mission, you quickly see that the opposite is true: their sickness makes them easy targets.

*   *   *

You didn't have to spend much time in Houston mental health circles to hear the allegations about the Reverend Alvin Armstrong. They were rampant. There were allegations of sexual abuse at his house, of serious untreated illness, and more. From time to time, someone in the bureaucracy would poke around, but the investigations were always halfhearted at best. The system's dirty little secret is that it needs Armstrong, desperately, to provide his wretched shelter. However many mentally ill people are wandering the streets of Houston, there would be hundreds more without the Alvin Armstrongs of the world. Mentally ill street people shame the society that lets them live as they do. In Armstrong's house, tucked away in the ghetto, they are out of sight and out of mind.

Everyone in the system knew how bad this house was; everyone felt helpless to do anything. The existence of places like Armstrong's was seen as a fact of life in the mental health business—one of the awful, unintended consequences of deinstitutionalization. A social worker who refers patients to Armstrong told me that she couldn't bring herself to visit the house. "I don't want to see it," she said. "I don't want to know where I'm sending them."

* * *

QUESTIONS AND COMMENTS

1. *The nature and scope of community treatment.* Since *Wyatt*, the objective of most right-to-treatment litigation has been obtaining treatment in the community. Sometimes the community treatment sought is outpatient, but often the need is for inpatient treatment or a local living arrangement that affords easy access to treatment. In many states, financial incentives from the federal government and fiscal pressures were the primary forces behind deinstitutionalization—not litigation (see Chapter One, pp. 70–72).

Whether in response to litigation or something else, many states have made efforts to create community resources. As previous materials have indicated, a number of community-based programs are highly effective at ameliorating many types of mental disabilities. Unfortunately, as the above excerpt suggests, other community programs simply replicate the problems found in mental hospitals. A particularly problematic type of community service is the "group home" for adults with mental disorder. Created for the purpose of caring for the thousands of patients released from closed or restructured mental hospitals, group homes are state licensed entities that provide room-and-board, case management, and assistance with medication and personal care. One multi-state congressional survey of these residences in the late 1990s concluded they were "a national tragedy." Adena Genn, *For the Mentally Ill, A Long Search for a Bed*, N.Y. Times, Jan. 26, 2003, at 1, col. 3 (Long Island). More recently, a series of articles in the New York Times described the horrible conditions in many of the group homes in New York. According to the Times, even the well-run homes were plagued by "untrained staff and gaps in supervision." Id. Many of the homes were run-down, filthy, and neglectful. Drug-dealing, prostitution and violence were common. Residents were sometimes beaten, and premature deaths from lack of medical or personal care are frequent. Clifford J. Levy, *For Mentally Ill, Death and Misery*, N.Y. Times, April 28, 2002, at 1, col. 3. Treatment at one of the homes, dubbed "The New Warehouse for the Insane" by the state inspection agency, was described as follows:

> The home itself does not provide psychiatric services, but it is expected to ensure that residents obtain them, either from the Kingsboro clinic at the home or from other psychiatrists who periodically visit. But the clinic, staffed by a psychiatrist and a few other trained workers, writes prescriptions that go unfilled. It asks that fragile residents be closely watched, and they are not, according to interviews with clinic workers

and their records. The home's administrators, meanwhile, have long accused clinic workers of not doing their jobs.

At nights and on weekends, the residents are largely on their own. The clinic is closed, and the home has almost no one on duty. "Nobody wanted to take responsibility for patients who went berserk at night," said Louis Rossetti, who worked as a nurse at the clinic from 1980 until 1996 and then as a volunteer. "We would come in the morning and have to go upstairs and calm them down. It just over all got worse and worse."

Clifford J. Levy, *Here, Life is Squalor and Chaos*, N.Y. Times, April 29, 2002, at A–1, col. 2.

In 2002, operation New York's group homes cost about $600 million a year. Most of this money came from federal sources, which mandate that the homes be maintained as residences rather than as hospitals. As a result, treatment must primarily come from off-site services. In the 2000s, the typical adult home might cost each patient $3000 a month, while "community residences" (which do not provide as much case management or treatment) cost $2,000 to $2,500 a month, and supported apartments (which do not provide meals) cost around $800 a month. Yet the typical disability check is about $600 a month, meaning that residents without outside assistance must be subsidized or double or triple-up in the rooms. Genn, supra; Clifford J. Levy, *Ingredients of a Failing System: A Lack of State Money, A Group Without a Voice*, N.Y. Times, April 28, 2002, at 32, col. 1.

Despite their uneven quality, community-based programs continue to be attractive for both fiscal and therapeutic reasons. Based on 2009 estimates, the average annual cost of community-based programs for people with developmental and intellectual disabilities ranged from $26,086 per person for supportive services in the home to $191,118 per person for institutional care. David Braddock et al., The State of the States in Developmental Disabilities 64 (2011). Almost a quarter of a million people with these disabilities who were eligible for home and community-based services were on waitlists. Id. at 18.

    2.   *The federal constitutional basis for a right to community treatment.* Today the most fertile basis for establishing some "right" to treatment in the community is the Americans with Disabilities Act, a development discussed below. For a number of years, however, most plaintiffs seeking state-provided community treatment usually based their arguments on the federal Constitution. Most of these cases had limited success. For instance, in *Lelsz v. Kavanaugh*, 807 F.2d 1243 (5th Cir. 1987), the plaintiffs sought to enforce, in federal court, the following provision of a consent decree earlier agreed upon by the Texas Department of Mental Health and Retardation:

> Defendants will provide each member of the plaintiff class with the least restrictive alternative living conditions possible consistent with the person's particular circumstances, including age, degree of retardation and handicapping conditions. Consistent with the person's capacities, each member of the plaintiff class will be taught adequate skills to help

the person progress within the environment and to live as independently as possible. Services will be offered with utmost regard for the class member's dignity and personal autonomy.

The plaintiffs argued that this provision was constitutionally-based because the Supreme Court had established, in *Youngberg* and *Jackson*, "rights to enjoy safe conditions and to be free from harm, the right to be free from unnecessary institutionalization, and to have commitment bear some reasonable relation to its purpose." But the court concluded, to the contrary, that *Youngberg* had specifically refused to establish "a constitutionally-founded right to receive treatment in the least restrictive alternative setting." The court continued:

> *Youngberg* also held that in determining whether the state has met its obligations in these respects, decisions made by the appropriate professional are entitled to a presumption of correctness. "[L]iability may be imposed only when the decision by the professional is such a substantial departure from accepted professional judgment, practice, or standards as to demonstrate that the person responsible actually did not base the decision on such a judgment." The constitutional minimum standard of habilitation thus relates, not to the qualitative betterment of a retarded person's life, but only to the training necessary to afford him safety and freedom from bodily restraint. Whether that training is adequate must be determined in light of expert testimony; no constitutional violation exists unless the level of training is such a substantial departure from accepted professional judgment or standards as to demonstrate that the person responsible actually did not base the decision on such a judgment. . . .

It is also worthwhile to observe that should the optimum standard of habilitation ... become coextensive with federal constitutional requirements, the emphasis of *Youngberg* on the judgment of the State's professionals will be thoroughly undermined. The constitutional standard in that instance would be determined by the views of expert witnesses, and outside consultants could effectively overrule state programs, contrary to *Youngberg*. While *Youngberg* may eventually have to be squared with the duty of a state to prevent deterioration of skills of the retarded committed to its institutions (*see Youngberg,* 457 U.S. at 327–29, 102 S.Ct. at 2464–65 (Blackmun, J. concurring)) this is by no means the same as requiring the State to provide the best care possible or the optimum location to improve the client's physical, mental and emotional conditions. [T]he due process clause only forbids *deprivations* of liberty without due process of law. "Where the state does not provide treatment designed to improve a mentally retarded individual's condition, it deprives the individual of nothing guaranteed by the Constitution; it simply fails to grant a benefit of optimal treatment that it is under no constitutional obligation to grant."

Id. at 1250–51.

Lelsz represents the predominant judicial response to claims that the Constitution requires the state to transfer institutionalized patients who can be treated outside the hospital to community facilities and to create such facilities if they do not already exist. See *Evans v. Fenty*, 701 F.Supp.2d 126, 152–156 (D.D.C. 2010) (collecting cases). In line with *Lelsz*, most courts hold that *Youngberg's* professional judgment rule is the dispositive test in this context: so long as such judgment is exercised, the resulting placement, whether it is an institution or a community facility, is constitutional. See e.g., *S.H. v. Edwards*, 886 F.2d 292 (11th Cir. 1989); *Rennie v. Klein,* 720 F.2d 266 (3d Cir.1983); *Phillips v. Thompson,* 715 F.2d 365, 368 (7th Cir.1983).

A few courts have rejected this interpretation of *Youngberg,* however, at least under certain circumstances. In *Association for Retarded Citizens v. Olson,* 561 F.Supp. 473, 486 (D.N.D.1982), affirmed 713 F.2d 1384 (8th Cir.1983), the court construed *Youngberg* to mean "that a constitutional right to the least restrictive method of care or treatment exists . . . insofar as professional judgment determines that such alternatives would measurably enhance the resident's enjoyment of basic liberty interests." In *Thomas S. v. Morrow,* 601 F.Supp. 1055 (W.D.N.C.1984), affirmed 781 F.2d 367 (4th Cir.1986), the court applied this reasoning in finding that the plaintiff was entitled to "a non-institutional specialized adult foster care situation" or "a group home with adults of average intelligence." The state had presented affidavits by state officials contending that the plaintiff's past treatment (which had consisted of placement in over 40 facilities, including mental hospitals) had been "minimally adequate." But the district court rejected this evidence as immaterial "because the professional's stated judgment was modified to conform to the *available* treatment, rather than to the *appropriate* treatment, for the plaintiff's condition." 601 F.Supp. at 1059. Instead the court relied on evidence the plaintiff presented, as well as evidence presented by other state-employed mental health professionals, in finding that "professional consensus" favored the ordered placement. See also *Thomas S. v. Flaherty,* 699 F.Supp. 1178, 1184 (W.D.N.C. 1988), aff'd 902 F.2d 250 (4th Cir. 1990).

Another important aspect of *Thomas S.* relates to how both the district court and the circuit court of appeals dealt with the fact that, when the district court issued its final order, the plaintiff had been out of the hospital for about five months and was residing in a "detoxification and night care facility." The defendants argued that under such conditions—not involving commitment to an institution—the state is not infringing any liberty interests, and thus *Youngberg* did not apply. But both the district court and the Fourth Circuit held that the plaintiff's interest in liberty was implicated in this situation. As the Fourth Circuit put it:

> Although during the course of this litigation Thomas's lodging has changed from a state hospital to a night care unit at a detoxification center, his status has not changed. He remains a legally incompetent adult who is a ward of a guardian appointed by the state. He did not choose to live at the detoxification center, and he is neither an alcoholic

nor a drug addict. *Youngberg* does not suggest that an incompetent person sheds the basic liberty interests that the Court identified when state officials and his guardian move him from one facility to another.

See also, *Clark v. Cohen*, 794 F.2d 79 (3d Cir.), cert. denied 479 U.S. 962, 107 S.Ct. 459, 93 L.Ed.2d 404 (1986). Can this analysis be reconciled with *Youngberg's* statement that "a State is under no constitutional duty to provide substantive services for those within its borders"? With the statement in *DeShaney v. Winnebago Cty. Dep't of Social Services*, 489 U.S. 189, 109 S.Ct. 998, 103 L.Ed.2d 249 (1989) that "it is the State's affirmative act of restraining the individual's freedom to act on his own behalf—through incarceration, institutionalization, or other similar restraint of personal liberty—which is the 'deprivation of liberty' triggering the protections of the Due Process Clause, not its failure to act to protect his liberty interests against harms inflicted by other means"? What if Thomas had not been a ward of the state?

Consider *Philadelphia Police & Fire Ass'n v. Philadelphia*, 874 F.2d 156 (3d Cir.1989). Pennsylvania, like many states, provides habilitation services for people with mental disability in a variety of settings, ranging from state institutions to the disabled person's home. The plaintiff class in *Police and Fire Ass'n* received their habilitation at their homes, financed primarily by the city of Philadelphia. When the city cut support for these home habilitation programs (as a result of a cutback in state funding), the class sued under *Youngberg*. The members of the class claimed that because they had to be accepted by the habilitation program, which determines their placement, and because without state services they might end up in an institution, the cutbacks were unconstitutional. The Third Circuit disagreed, citing *DeShaney* for the proposition that "the State does not become the permanent guarantor of an individual's safety by having once offered him shelter." Id. at 168. To the argument that people with intellectual disabilities are uniquely dependent on the state, the court noted that, in *DeShaney*, "the state of Wisconsin had acted in such a way as to make Joshua particularly dependent upon it for protection from abuse, but the majority found no substantive due process violation." Id.

Compare this decision to the arguments of Professors Jan Costello and James Preis in *Beyond Least Restrictive Alternative Doctrine: A Constitutional Right to Treatment for Mentally Disabled Persons in the Community*, 20 Loyola L.A.L.Rev. 1527 (1987). They conclude that when professional consensus indicates that a particular institutionalized individual or group of institutionalized individuals is "capable of functioning outside an institution with assistance, institutional care *cannot be* 'minimally adequate' treatment." Id. at 1552 (emphasis in original). They go on to argue that this reasoning should apply *whenever* a person or group of people can show that they require community treatment to avoid institutionalization, even if they are not hospitalized at the time they make the claim.

A "minimally adequate" system of community-based programs and services, by increasing mentally disabled persons' ability to function in the community, will reduce the risk of state restriction on their liberty through the criminal justice or the civil mental health systems. Thus, the right to "minimally adequate" treatment in the community may be asserted for mentally disabled persons who are now inappropriately hospitalized, who have been institutionalized and are trapped in the "revolving door," or for those who, although never hospitalized, are dependent upon the state for assistance and thus subject to state restrictions on their liberty.

Id. at 1523. Do you agree? If the courts adopted the stance advocated by Costello and Preis, how would they enforce it?

3.   *State law bases for a right to community treatment.* Like *Lelsz, Dixon v. Weinberger,* 405 F.Supp. 974 (D.D.C.1975), was a class action brought in federal court alleging that hospitalized patients should be transferred to the community. The plaintiffs alleged that, due to a deficiency in outpatient facilities, 43 percent of the patients in St. Elizabeths Hospital in Washington, D.C. were improperly institutionalized (based on an assessment by the hospital staff itself). However, the district court in *Dixon,* unlike the district court in *Lelsz,* relied exclusively on *state statutory* grounds in ordering the federal and District of Columbia governments to reallocate funds to create community facilities. The court found that the purpose of the District of Columbia's Hospitalization of the Mentally Ill Act was to return patients to a full and productive life in the community through care and treatment. It held further that patients were entitled to placement in the most appropriate setting, including non-hospital settings, and that the government had the primary responsibility for creating alternative settings.

Some *state* courts have also flexed their muscle in this area. For instance, in *Arnold v. Sarn,* No. C 432455 (Ariz.Super.Ct. Maricopa Cty. Mar. 15, 1985), the court found a right to community-based treatment for persons with chronic mental illnesses based on statutory provisions that required the state mental health director to implement "unified" mental health programs (including "the functions of state hospital and community mental health"), and to take "appropriate steps to provide health care services to the medically dependent citizens of this state." See also, *State ex rel. Cottrill v. Meigs Cty. Bd. of Mental Retardation & Dev. Disabilities,* 86 Ohio App.3d 596, 601, 621 N.E.2d 728 (1993). State constitutions are another source for a right to community-based treatment. Most state constitutions contain provisions protecting liberty and privacy rights, as well as a provision guaranteeing due process of law, and several state constitutions explicitly recognize treatment rights for people with mental illness. See Antony B. Klapper, *Finding a Right in State Constitutions for Community Treatment of the Mentally Ill,* 142 U. Pa. L. Rev. 739, 819 (1993) (listing six states with constitutional provisions recognizing affirmative rights of the mentally ill).

4.   *Federal statutory grounds for a right to community treatment.* Federal statutes provide a final basis for a right to community-based treatment. For instance, the Developmentally Disabled Assistance and Bill of Rights Act, 42 U.S.C. §§ 6000–6081, which provides federal funds to those

states willing to develop habilitation programs for the developmentally disabled, provides that this group has "a right to appropriate treatment, services, and habilitation" in the "setting that is least restrictive of . . . personal liberty." Id. § 6010. The American with Disabilities Act, 42 U.S.C. §§ 12101 et. seq., which prohibits discrimination "by reason of . . . disability" when "reasonable accommodations" for the disability are possible, might also form the basis for a right to community treatment claim. Finally, the Individuals with Disabilities Education Act, 20 U.S.C. §§ 1411–1420, establishes an entitlement to education in the public school system for disabled children who qualify.

The DD Act is, on its face, potentially the most useful federal statute for those seeking a right to treatment in the community, since it clearly announces a right to treatment in a less restrictive setting, at least for all developmentally disabled individuals. However, in *Pennhurst State School & Hospital v. Halderman,* 451 U.S. 1, 101 S.Ct. 1531, 67 L.Ed.2d 694 (1981) (*Pennhurst I*), the Supreme Court significantly undermined any hope that this provision could be used to pressure states into creating community facilities. *Pennhurst* was the culmination of lengthy *Wyatt*-like litigation challenging the conditions of confinement at the Pennhurst institution for people with mental retardation in Pennsylvania. The Third Circuit had held that § 6010 of the DD Act created a substantive right in favor of the retarded, and that the conditions at Pennhurst violated those rights. 612 F.2d 84 (3d Cir.1979). The Supreme Court held, however, that § 6010 merely expresses a preference for treatment services in the least restrictive setting. The Court emphasized that courts should be cautious in attributing to Congress an intent to create rights when those rights impose affirmative obligations on the states to fund certain services. According to the Court, unless Congress unambiguously declares its intent in such situations, no substantive right exists. The Court found "nothing" in the Act or its legislative history "to suggest that Congress intended to require the States to assume the high cost of providing 'appropriate treatment' in the 'least restrictive environment' to their mentally retarded citizens."

Although its language does not in so many words endorse the least restrictive alternative idea, the Americans with Disabilities Act may turn out to be a much more fruitful source of support for community services than the DD Act, as the following case suggests.

OLMSTEAD V. L.C. EX REL. ZIMRING

Supreme Court of the United States, 1999.
527 U.S. 581, 119 S.Ct. 2176, 144 L.Ed.2d 540.

JUSTICE GINSBURG announced the judgment of the Court and delivered the opinion of the Court with respect to Parts I, II, and III–A, and an opinion with respect to Part III–B, in which JUSTICE O'CONNOR, JUSTICE SOUTER, and JUSTICE BREYER join.

This case concerns the proper construction of the anti-discrimination provision contained in the public services portion (Title II) of the Americans with Disabilities Act of 1990 (ADA), 104 Stat. 337, 42 U.S.C. § 12132. Specifically, we confront the question whether the proscription of discrimination may require placement of persons with mental disabilities in community settings rather than in institutions. The answer, we hold, is a qualified yes. Such action is in order when the State's treatment professionals have determined that community placement is appropriate, the transfer from institutional care to a less restrictive setting is not opposed by the affected individual, and the placement can be reasonably accommodated, taking into account the resources available to the State and the needs of others with mental disabilities. In so ruling, we affirm the decision of the Eleventh Circuit in substantial part. We remand the case, however, for further consideration of the appropriate relief, given the range of facilities the State maintains for the care and treatment of persons with diverse mental disabilities, and its obligation to administer services with an even hand.

I

. . . Mindful that it is a statute we are construing, we set out first the legislative and regulatory prescriptions on which the case turns. In the opening provisions of the ADA, Congress stated findings applicable to the statute in all its parts. Most relevant to this case, Congress determined that "(2) historically, society has tended to isolate and segregate individuals with disabilities, and, despite some improvements, such forms of discrimination against individuals with disabilities continue to be a serious and pervasive social problem; (3) discrimination against individuals with disabilities persists in such critical areas as . . . institutionalization . . . ; . . . (5) individuals with disabilities continually encounter various forms of discrimination, including outright intentional exclusion, . . . failure to make modifications to existing facilities and practices, . . . [and] segregation. . . ." Congress then set forth prohibitions against discrimination in employment (Title I), public services furnished by governmental entities (Title II), and public accommodations provided by private entities (Title III). The statute as a whole is intended "to provide a clear and comprehensive national mandate for the elimination of discrimination against individuals with disabilities."[2] There is no dispute that L.C. and E.W. [the respondents in the case] are disabled within the meaning of the ADA.

This case concerns Title II, the public services portion of the ADA. The provision of Title II centrally at issue reads: "Subject to the provisions of this subchapter, no qualified individual with a disability

---

[2]   The ADA defines "disability," "with respect to an individual," as "(A) a physical or mental impairment that substantially limits one or more of the major life activities of such individual;" (B) a record of such an impairment; or "(C) being regarded as having such an impairment."

shall, by reason of such disability, be excluded from participation in or be denied the benefits of the services, programs, or activities of a public entity, or be subjected to discrimination by any such entity." 42 U.S.C. § 12132. Title II's definition section states that "public entity" includes "any State or local government," and "any department, agency, [or] special purpose district." The same section defines "qualified individual with a disability" as "an individual with a disability who, with or without reasonable modifications to rules, policies, or practices, the removal of architectural, communication, or transportation barriers, or the provision of auxiliary aids and services, meets the essential eligibility requirements for the receipt of services or the participation in programs or activities provided by a public entity." . . .

Congress instructed the Attorney General to issue regulations implementing provisions of Title II, including § 12132's discrimination proscription. The Attorney General's regulations, Congress further directed, "shall be consistent with this chapter and with the coordination regulations . . . applicable to recipients of Federal financial assistance under [§ 504 of the Rehabilitation Act]." One of the § 504 regulations requires recipients of federal funds to "administer programs and activities in the most integrated setting appropriate to the needs of qualified handicapped persons."

As Congress instructed, the Attorney General issued Title II regulations, see 28 CFR pt. 35 (1998), including one modeled on the § 504 regulation just quoted; called the "integration regulation," it reads: "A public entity shall administer services, programs, and activities in the most integrated setting appropriate to the needs of qualified individuals with disabilities." 28 CFR § 35.130(d) (1998). The preamble to the Attorney General's Title II regulations defines "the most integrated setting appropriate to the needs of qualified individuals with disabilities" to mean "a setting that enables individuals with disabilities to interact with non-disabled persons to the fullest extent possible." Another regulation requires public entities to "make reasonable modifications" to avoid "discrimination on the basis of disability," unless those modifications would entail a "fundamenta[l] alter[ation]"; called here the "reasonable-modifications regulation," it provides: "A public entity shall make reasonable modifications in policies, practices, or procedures when the modifications are necessary to avoid discrimination on the basis of disability, unless the public entity can demonstrate that making the modifications would fundamentally alter the nature of the service, program, or activity." 28 CFR § 35.130(b)(7) (1998).

*   *   *

III

Endeavoring to carry out Congress' instruction to issue regulations implementing Title II, the Attorney General, in the integration and reasonable-modifications regulations made two key determinations. The first concerned the scope of the ADA's discrimination proscription, 42 U.S.C. § 12132; the second concerned the obligation of the States to counter discrimination. As to the first, the Attorney General concluded that unjustified placement or retention of persons in institutions, severely limiting their exposure to the outside community, constitutes a form of discrimination based on disability prohibited by Title II. See 28 CFR § 35.130(d) (1998) ("A public entity shall administer services . . . in the most integrated setting appropriate to the needs of qualified individuals with disabilities."). Regarding the States' obligation to avoid unjustified isolation of individuals with disabilities, the Attorney General provided that States could resist modifications that "would fundamentally alter the nature of the service, program, or activity." 28 CFR § 35.130(b)(7) (1998). The Court of Appeals essentially upheld the Attorney General's construction of the ADA. [T]he appeals court ruled that the unjustified institutionalization of persons with mental disabilities violated Title II; the court then remanded with instructions to measure the cost of caring for L.C. and E.W. in a community-based facility against the State's mental health budget.

We affirm the Court of Appeals' decision in substantial part. Unjustified isolation, we hold, is properly regarded as discrimination based on disability. But we recognize, as well, the States' need to maintain a range of facilities for the care and treatment of persons with diverse mental disabilities, and the States' obligation to administer services with an even hand. Accordingly, we further hold that the Court of Appeals' remand instruction was unduly restrictive. In evaluating a State's fundamental-alteration defense, the District Court must consider, in view of the resources available to the State, not only the cost of providing community-based care to the litigants, but also the range of services the State provides others with mental disabilities, and the State's obligation to mete out those services equitably.

A

We examine first whether, as the Eleventh Circuit held, undue institutionalization qualifies as discrimination "by reason of . . . disability." The Department of Justice has consistently advocated that it does. Because the Department is the agency directed by Congress to issue regulations implementing Title II, its views warrant respect. . . . The State argues that L.C. and E.W. encountered no discrimination "by reason of" their disabilities because they were not denied community placement on account of those disabilities. Nor were they subjected to "discrimination," the State contends, because " 'discrimination' necessarily requires uneven treatment of similarly situated individuals," and L.C. and E.W. had identified no comparison class, i.e., no similarly situated individuals given preferential treatment. We are satisfied that Congress had a more comprehensive view of the concept of discrimination advanced in the ADA.[10]

The ADA stepped up earlier measures to secure opportunities for people with developmental disabilities to enjoy the benefits of community living. The Developmentally Disabled Assistance and Bill of Rights Act, a 1975 measure, stated in aspirational terms that "[t]he treatment, services, and habilitation for a person with developmental disabilities . . . should be provided in the setting that is least restrictive of the person's personal liberty." In a related legislative endeavor, the Rehabilitation Act of 1973, Congress used mandatory language to proscribe discrimination against persons with disabilities. Ultimately, in the ADA, enacted in 1990, Congress not only required all public entities to refrain from discrimination; additionally, in findings applicable to the entire statute, Congress explicitly identified unjustified "segregation" of persons with disabilities as a "for[m] of discrimination." See § 12101(a)(2) ("historically, society has tended to isolate and segregate individuals with disabilities, and, despite some improvements, such forms of discrimination against individuals with disabilities continue to be a serious and pervasive social problem"); § 12101(a)(5) ("individuals with disabilities continually encounter various forms of discrimination, including . . . segregation").

Recognition that unjustified institutional isolation of persons with disabilities is a form of discrimination reflects two evident judgments. First, institutional placement of persons who can handle and benefit from community settings perpetuates unwarranted assumptions that persons so isolated are incapable or unworthy of participating in community life. Second, confinement in an institution severely diminishes the everyday life activities of individuals, including family relations, social contacts, work options, economic independence, educational advancement, and

---

[10] The dissent is driven by the notion that "this Court has never endorsed an interpretation of the term 'discrimination' that encompassed disparate treatment among members of the same protected class" (opinion of THOMAS, J.), that "[o]ur decisions construing various statutory prohibitions against 'discrimination' have not wavered from this path," and that "a plaintiff cannot prove 'discrimination' by demonstrating that one member of a particular protected group has been favored over another member of that same group." The dissent is incorrect as a matter of precedent and logic. See O'Connor v. Consolidated Coin Caterers Corp., 517 U.S. 308, 312, 116 S.Ct. 1307, 134 L.Ed.2d 433 (1996) (The Age Discrimination in Employment Act of 1967 "does not ban discrimination against employees because they are aged 40 or older; it bans discrimination against employees because of their age, but limits the protected class to those who are 40 or older. The fact that one person in the protected class has lost out to another person in the protected class is thus irrelevant, so long as he has lost out because of his age."); cf. Oncale v. Sundowner Offshore Services, Inc., 523 U.S. 75, 76, 118 S.Ct. 998, 140 L.Ed.2d 201 (1998) ("[W]orkplace harassment can violate Title VII's prohibition against 'discriminat[ion] . . . because of . . . sex' when the harasser and the harassed employee are of the same sex."); Jefferies v. Harris County Community Action Assn., 615 F.2d 1025, 1032 (C.A.5 1980) ("[D]iscrimination against black females can exist even in the absence of discrimination against black men or white women.").

cultural enrichment. Dissimilar treatment correspondingly exists in this key respect: In order to receive needed medical services, persons with mental disabilities must, because of those disabilities, relinquish participation in community life they could enjoy given reasonable accommodations, while persons without mental disabilities can receive the medical services they need without similar sacrifice. The State urges that, whatever Congress may have stated as its findings in the ADA, the Medicaid statute "reflected a congressional policy preference for treatment in the institution over treatment in the community." The State correctly used the past tense. Since 1981, Medicaid has provided funding for state-run home and community-based care through a waiver program. Indeed, the United States points out that the Department of Health and Human Services (HHS) "has a policy of encouraging States to take advantage of the waiver program, and often approves more waiver slots than a State ultimately uses."

We emphasize that nothing in the ADA or its implementing regulations condones termination of institutional settings for persons unable to handle or benefit from community settings. Title II provides only that "qualified individual[s] with a disability" may not "be subjected to discrimination." 42 U.S.C. § 12132. "Qualified individuals," the ADA further explains, are persons with disabilities who, "with or without reasonable modifications to rules, policies, or practices, . . . mee[t] the essential eligibility requirements for the receipt of services or the participation in programs or activities provided by a public entity." § 12131(2). Consistent with these provisions, the State generally may rely on the reasonable assessments of its own professionals in determining whether an individual "meets the essential eligibility requirements" for habilitation in a community-based program. Absent such qualification, it would be inappropriate to remove a patient from the more restrictive setting. Nor is there any federal requirement that community-based treatment be imposed on patients who do not desire it. See 28 CFR § 35.130(e)(1) (1998) ("Nothing in this part shall be construed to require an individual with a disability to accept an accommodation . . . which such individual chooses not to accept."). In this case, however, there is no genuine dispute concerning the status of L.C. and E.W. as individuals "qualified" for noninstitutional care: The State's own professionals determined that community-based treatment would be appropriate for L.C. and E.W., and neither woman opposed such treatment.

B

The State's responsibility, once it provides community-based treatment to qualified persons with disabilities, is not boundless. The reasonable-modifications regulation speaks of "reasonable modifications" to avoid discrimination, and allows States to resist modifications that entail a "fundamenta[l] alter[ation]" of the States' services and programs.

28 CFR § 35.130(b)(7) (1998). The Court of Appeals construed this regulation to permit a cost-based defense "only in the most limited of circumstances," and remanded to the District Court to consider, among other things, "whether the additional expenditures necessary to treat L.C. and E.W. in community-based care would be unreasonable given the demands of the State's mental health budget."

The Court of Appeals' construction of the reasonable-modifications regulation is unacceptable for it would leave the State virtually defenseless once it is shown that the plaintiff is qualified for the service or program she seeks. If the expense entailed in placing one or two people in a community-based treatment program is properly measured for reasonableness against the State's entire mental health budget, it is unlikely that a State, relying on the fundamental-alteration defense, could ever prevail. Sensibly construed, the fundamental-alteration component of the reasonable-modifications regulation would allow the State to show that, in the allocation of available resources, immediate relief for the plaintiffs would be inequitable, given the responsibility the State has undertaken for the care and treatment of a large and diverse population of persons with mental disabilities.

When it granted summary judgment for plaintiffs in this case, the District Court compared the cost of caring for the plaintiffs in a community-based setting with the cost of caring for them in an institution. That simple comparison showed that community placements cost less than institutional confinements. As the United States recognizes, however, a comparison so simple overlooks costs the State cannot avoid; most notably, a "State . . . may experience increased overall expenses by funding community placements without being able to take advantage of the savings associated with the closure of institutions."

As already observed, the ADA is not reasonably read to impel States to phase out institutions, placing patients in need of close care at risk. Nor is it the ADA's mission to drive States to move institutionalized patients into an inappropriate setting, such as a homeless shelter, a placement the State proposed, then retracted, for E.W. Some individuals, like L.C. and E.W. in prior years, may need institutional care from time to time "to stabilize acute psychiatric symptoms." For other individuals, no placement outside the institution may ever be appropriate. See Brief for American Psychiatric Association et al. as Amici Curiae 22–23 ("Some individuals, whether mentally retarded or mentally ill, are not prepared at particular times—perhaps in the short run, perhaps in the long run— for the risks and exposure of the less protective environment of community settings"; for these persons, "institutional settings are needed and must remain available."); Brief for Voice of the Retarded et al. as Amici Curiae 11 ("Each disabled person is entitled to treatment in the most integrated setting possible for that person—recognizing that, on a case-by-case basis, that setting may be in an institution.")

To maintain a range of facilities and to administer services with an even hand, the State must have more leeway than the courts below understood the fundamental-alteration defense to allow. If, for example, the State were to demonstrate that it had a comprehensive, effectively working plan for placing qualified persons with mental disabilities in less restrictive settings, and a waiting list that moved at a reasonable pace not controlled by the State's endeavors to keep its institutions fully populated, the reasonable-modifications standard would be met. See Tr. of Oral Arg. 5 (State's attorney urges that, "by asking [a] person to wait a short time until a community bed is available, Georgia does not exclude [that] person by reason of disability, neither does Georgia discriminate against her by reason of disability"); see also id., at 25 ("[I]t is reasonable for the State to ask someone to wait until a community placement is available."). In such circumstances, a court would have no warrant effectively to order displacement of persons at the top of the community-based treatment waiting list by individuals lower down who commenced civil actions.

For the reasons stated, we conclude that, under Title II of the ADA, States are required to provide community-based treatment for persons with mental disabilities when the State's treatment professionals determine that such placement is appropriate, the affected persons do not oppose such treatment, and the placement can be reasonably accommodated, taking into account the resources available to the State and the needs of others with mental disabilities. The judgment of the Eleventh Circuit is therefore affirmed in part and vacated in part, and the case is remanded for further proceedings. It is so ordered.

JUSTICE KENNEDY, concurring in the judgment.

. . . Putting aside issues of animus or unfair stereotype, I agree with Justice THOMAS [in dissent] that on the ordinary interpretation and meaning of the term, one who alleges discrimination must show that she received differential treatment vis-à-vis members of a different group on the basis of a statutorily described characteristic. In my view, however, discrimination so defined might be shown here. . . . [I]f respondents could show that Georgia (i) provides treatment to individuals suffering from medical problems of comparable seriousness, (ii) as a general matter, does so in the most integrated setting appropriate for the treatment of those problems (taking medical and other practical considerations into account), but (iii) without adequate justification, fails to do so for a group of mentally disabled persons (treating them instead in separate, locked institutional facilities), I believe it would demonstrate discrimination on the basis of mental disability. . . .

. . . This inquiry would not be simple. Comparisons of different medical conditions and the corresponding treatment regimens might be difficult, as would be assessments of the degree of integration of various settings in which medical treatment is offered. For example, the evidence might show that, apart from services for the mentally disabled, medical treatment is rarely offered in a community setting but also is rarely offered in facilities comparable to state mental hospitals. Determining the relevance of that type of evidence would require considerable judgment and analysis. However, as petitioners observe, "[i]n this case, no class of similarly situated individuals was even identified, let alone shown to be given preferential treatment." Without additional information regarding the details of state-provided medical services in Georgia, we cannot address the issue in the way the statute demands. As a consequence, the judgment of the courts below, granting partial summary judgment to respondents, ought not to be sustained. . . .

[Justice Kennedy did not join Part IIIB of Justice Ginsburg's opinion because he believed the case should be remanded to determine whether there was a statutory violation of the type described above. Justice STEVENS did not join Part IIIB because he believed the fundamental alteration issue was not ripe].

[The dissenting opinion of JUSTICE THOMAS, joined by CHIEF JUSTICE REHNQUIST and JUSTICE SCALIA, is omitted.]

QUESTIONS AND COMMENTS

1.   *Impact of* Olmstead. Writing soon after *Olmstead*, Professor Perlin wrote that the decision was potentially "the most important civil mental disability law case since the Supreme Court decided *Youngberg v. Romeo* in 1982. . . . [If] taken seriously, it may change the debate on [mental health issues], . . . and perhaps most importantly, on how we feel about persons with [mental] disabilities." Michael L. Perlin, *Institutional Segregation, Community Treatment, the ADA, and the Promise of* Olmstead v. L.C., 17 Cooley L. Rev. 53, 56 (2000). In 2001, the White House ordered that *Olmstead* be implemented vigorously, stating "[t]he Federal Government must assist States and localities to implement swiftly the *Olmstead* decision, so as to help ensure that all Americans have the opportunity to live close to their families and friends, to live more independently, to engage in productive employment, and to participate in community life." Exec. Order No. 13217 (1)(e)(June 18, 2001). A number of suits have been brought on *Olmstead* grounds, including one (the *Paterson* case described in the notes below) attacking the New York system of group homes that was described in Note 1 on pp. 1312–1313. See Clifford Levy, *Suit Says State is Segregating Mentally Ill*, N.Y. Times, July 1, 2003, B1, col. 5. But several developments, explored in the following notes, may curb *Olmstead's* potential.

2.   *Limitations on the ADA*. As recounted in more detail in Chapter Twelve, the Supreme Court has significantly limited the remedial potential of

the ADA since *Olmstead*. In *Board of Trustees of Univ. of Alabama v. Garrett*, 531 U.S. 356, 121 S.Ct. 955, 148 L.Ed.2d 866 (2001), the Court held that private damages claims under Title I of the ADA are barred by the Eleventh Amendment, which has been construed to immunize states from damages suits under certain circumstances. *Garrett* did not specifically address the Eleventh Amendment's application to Title II, the section of the ADA at issue in *Olmstead*. See *Hason v. Medical Bd. of Calif.*, 279 F.3d 1167, 1171 (9th Cir.2002) (continuing to permit damages actions under Title II). Moreover, *Garrett* only limited damages claims; injunctive actions under the ADA, of the type brought in *Olmstead*, are probably unaffected by its holding. Id. However, these matters are not completely settled. See, e.g., Erwin Chemerinsky, Federal Jurisdiction 453–462 (4th ed. 2003); *Thompson v. Colorado*, 258 F.3d 1241, 1245–46 n.2 (10th Cir.2001) (holding that Title II cannot be used to sue state officials for damages, and noting the possibility that injunctive relief against individual state officers may not be available either, if the ADA is not a valid exercise of congressional power).

3. *The meaning of discrimination.* Assuming Title II of the ADA is available as a basis for injunctive action against the states, how is its prohibition of "discrimination" against people with mental disability violated by treating people with mental disability in an institution rather than in a community setting? According to Justice Thomas in his *Olmstead* dissent, "the type of claim approved of by the majority does not concern a prohibition against certain conduct (the traditional understanding of discrimination), but rather concerns imposition of a standard of care. As such, the majority can offer no principle limiting this new species of 'discrimination' claim apart from an affirmative defense [of fundamental alteration] because it looks merely to an individual in isolation, without comparing him to otherwise similarly situated persons, and determines that discrimination occurs merely because that individual does not receive the treatment he wishes to receive." 527 U.S. at 623–24, 119 S.Ct. at 2198 (Thomas, J., dissenting).

What is Justice Kennedy's answer to this complaint? Consider, as an alternative, this answer:

> The difference between Justice Ginsburg's and Justice Thomas's versions of the ADA is crucial to the goal of integration. The dissenters' view of the ADA adopts a "traditional" view of discrimination law. That "traditional" view is purely and formally equalitarian. It takes current social structures as given and simply mandates precisely equal treatment: no person may be treated differently on the basis of, for example, their race, ethnic group, religion, or gender than a similarly-situated person of another race, ethnic group, religion, or gender except in narrow situations, to remedy past unequal treatment. Viewed from the disability rights perspective, this interpretation of the ADA simply blinks at reality. The lower-caste treatment of people with disabilities is due in part to invidious, irrational treatment at the hands of those who dislike or fear them. But it also derives from the social structures and practices that are designed for the benefit of the able-bodied and that

inhibit people with disabilities from participating fully in society. Correcting inequality requires more than raising the consciousness of bigots. It requires affirmative changes in the social context that render and support the disparate treatment of people with disabilities.

. . . As the *Olmstead* majority recognized, the harm suffered by L.C. and E.W. was traceable directly to their isolation, without any therapeutic justification, in a locked ward in a psychiatric hospital, and not to the disparate treatment vis-á-vis some other group under traditional discrimination law. Failure to recognize this integrationist aspect of the ADA would deprive people with severe psychiatric and cognitive disabilities of any benefit. Disparate treatment is often rational in the strict sense, and is therefore untouched by equalitarian norms. The opportunity for "[l]ife, [l]iberty and the pursuit of [h]appiness" for *Olmstead* plaintiffs depends almost entirely on the integration mandate.

John V. Jacobi, *Federal Power, Segregation, and Mental Disability*, 39 Hous. L. Rev. 1231, 1246–48 (2003). Is Professor Jacobi providing a definition of "discrimination" or instead is he defining, in Justice Thomas' words, a "standard of care"? Does it matter, under the ADA and its implementing regulations?

4. *Defining the standard of care.* In *Olmstead*, the Court stated that "the State generally may rely on the reasonable assessments of its own professionals in determining whether an individual meets the essential eligibility requirements for habilitation in a community-based program." Is this a "perpetuation of *Youngberg v. Romeo's* 'substantial professional judgment' standard"? Michael L. Perlin, The Hidden Prejudice: Mental Disability on Trial 199 (2000). Some courts appear to think otherwise, because they have permitted plaintiffs to rely on their own experts and other sources in showing they can be treated in community settings. See, e.g., *Disability Advocates, Inc. v. Paterson*, 653 F.Supp.2d 184, 258–59 (E.D.N.Y. 2009) (relying largely on the plaintiff's experts in holding that the conditions in New York City's adult homes "do not represent current practice in the mental health field."); *Joseph S. v. Hogan*, 561 F.Supp.2d 280, 291 (E.D.N.Y. 2008); *Frederick L. v. Dep't of Pub. Welfare*, 157 F.Supp.2d 509, 540 (E.D.Pa. 2001).

In addition to the standard of care issue, Professor Bagenstos has identified two other ambiguities in *Olmstead's* holding:

Olmstead explains that there is no "federal requirement that community-based treatment be imposed on patients who do not desire it." But relying on the principle of choice in this context presents two distinct problems. First, particularly for people with mental disabilities, a large proportion of the people whose living situation will be determined by *Olmstead* litigation have been placed under guardianship. . . . Much may depend on whose choice *Olmstead* is interpreted as implementing: the choice of the individual with a disability herself, or the choice her guardian makes on her behalf. . . . The courts have not definitively resolved this question, though a number have suggested that it is the guardian's choice that matters.

Second, where resources are limited it may be impossible to satisfy the preferences of all individuals with disabilities (or their guardians). If some want to remain in institutions while others want supports in the community, the state will have a choice of how to allocate its limited finds. . . . The tradeoff has led to intense conflict over *Olmstead* settlements between, on the one hand, the plaintiffs (who want to leave institutions) and the state (which wants to provide them with community services), and, on the other hand, intervening guardians who want to retain the option of institutional placement for their wards.

Samuel R. Bagenstos, *The Past and Future of Deinsitutionalization Litigation*, 34 Cardozo L. Rev. 1, 38–39 (2012). How should these two ambiguities in *Olmstead* be resolved? Both issues came to the fore in *United States v. Arkansas*, 2911 U.S.Dist. LEXIS 61347 (2011). In holding that the Department of Justice did not meet its burden of proving an ADA violation, the court noted that "[m]ost of the parents or residents were fully satisfied with the services provided and opposed the DOJ claims." It also concluded that the institutional staff "made professional judgments in determining the least restrictive placement appropriate for each resident, even though staff and families agreed that the professionals often did not recommend placement [in the community] unless requested to do so by the parents or guardians."

    5.   *The fundamental alteration defense.* Even if a state is found to have discriminated against institutionalized people with mental disabilities, *Olmstead* held that relief may be granted under the ADA only if it would not require the state to alter its programs "fundamentally." Does the fundamental alteration defense prevent L.C. and E.W. from obtaining relief under the ADA if the state does not already have an outpatient program for them in their respective communities? Consider this excerpt from the Eleventh Circuit's opinion in *Olmstead*:

    There is evidence in the record that suggests that, because of fixed overhead costs associated with providing institutional care, the State will be able to save money by moving patients from institutionalized care to community-based care only when it shuts down entire hospitals or hospital wings, but not when it moves one or two patients from a hospital into the community. Thus, it may be that requiring the State to treat L.C. and E.W. in a community-based program will require additional expenditure of state funds.

    Nonetheless, the ADA may still require the State to expend additional funds in order to provide L.C. and E.W. with integrated services. Unless the State can prove that requiring it to make these additional expenditures would be so unreasonable given the demands of the State's mental health budget that it would fundamentally alter the service it provides, the ADA requires the State to make these additional expenditures . . . [10]

L.C. by Zimring v. Olmstead, 138 F.3d 893, 905 (1998). Consider in contrast this assessment of the fundamental alteration defense:

> . . . No bright line has been identified to separate states that can rely on the fundamental-alteration defense from those that cannot. The reluctance of the courts to trample on executive branch prerogatives has always been the bugaboo of the least restrictive alternative doctrine. Whatever else it may accomplish, the decision in *Olmstead v. L.C.* is unlikely to precipitate the widespread creation of community-based services for persons with mental disabilities.

Paul S. Appelbaum, *Least Restrictive Alternative Revisited:* Olmstead's *Uncertain Mandate for Community–Based Care*, 50 Psychiatric Serv. 1271, 1272 (1999).

Developments since *Olmstead* send mixed signals about the impact of the fundamental alteration defense. Most courts have held that any temporary increase in statewide mental health care costs that might occur as a result of deinstitutionalization is not a fundamental alteration, and that, before the defense can be claimed, the state must demonstrate continued progress toward community-based programs through an *"Olmstead* plan" that specifies how patients will be moved into integrated settings. See *Fisher v. Oklahoma Health Care Authority*, 335 F.3d 1175, 1183 (10th Cir. 2003) (holding that allowing substantial initial costs to constitute a fundamental alteration would make "the ADA's integration mandate . . . hollow indeed."); *Frederick L. v. Dep't of Publ. Welfare*, 364 F.3d 487 (3d Cir. 2004); *Arc of Washington State v. Braddock*, 427 F.3d 615 (9th Cir. 2005). ADA-based litigation, much of it initiated by the Department of Justice, has frequently resulted in detailed settlement agreements that involve reallocation of funds, harkening back to *Wyatt*-type regulation. For example, in *United States v. Delaware*, the state agreed to: (1) a full range of crisis services, with the goal of reducing hospitalization by fifty percent; (2) intensive case supports and community supports; (3) integrated supported housing; and (4) a "rebalancing of Delaware's mental health system from one reliant on state-funded institutional care to one focused on Medicaid-reimbursable community-based services." See Sharaya L. Cabansaq, *Defending Access to Community–Based Services for Individuals with Developmental Disabilities in the Wake of the "Great Recession,"* 55 Howard L. J. 1025, 1049, 1050 (2012).

However, commentators who have analyzed the lawsuits brought under the ADA have generally been critical of the results. John F. Muller, Olmstead v. L.C. *and the Voluntary Cessation Doctrine: Toward a More Holistic Analysis of the "Effectively Working Plan,"* 118 Yale L.J. 1013, 1013 (2009) ("Ten years after the Court's decision, comparisons with *Brown* [*v. Board of*

---

[10] We note that this case is not a class action, but a challenge brought on behalf of two individual plaintiffs. Our holding is not meant to resolve the more difficult questions of fundamental alteration that might be present in a class action suit seeking deinstitutionalization of a state hospital.

Education] have proved apt if inauspicious."). See also Cabansaq, *supra*, at 1050–51. Muller notes that some courts look to see whether the state's *Olmstead* plan ends existing segregation and other courts look at whether the state can be expected to follow its plan, and that, under either approach, courts tend to find for the state. Id. at 1020.

6.   *Community treatment.* Could the reasoning in *Olmstead* be construed to grant an entitlement to treatment under the ADA to those who are *not* hospitalized? Building on the analysis excerpted above, Professor Jacobi answers this question in the affirmative:

> Just as the failure to provide appropriate community placements causes isolation by locking people into unwarranted institutionalization, so too the lack of a sound system of services for the mentally disabled risks the institutionalization of people with mental illness that could be treated in the community. Social supports comprising therapeutic resources, social services, and housing and employment assistance are necessary to enable the mentally disabled not only to avoid unnecessary institutionalization, but also to avoid inpatient care in the first instance. The integrationist focus, then, should be on both the person in an institution who can be returned to the community with proper services, as well as the person in the community who can remain there—avoiding institutional care, with appropriate service support.

Jacobi, *supra*, at 1251–52. In *Paterson*, *supra*, the court found that New York's "Adults Homes . . . had the look and feel of 'back wards' State hospitals and . . . bear little resemblance to the homes in which people without disabilities normally live." It ordered that 4300 people with mental illness who were living in the homes be afforded "supported housing . . . where they would live independently while also receiving assistance like case-management services and visits from psychiatrists and nurses." A subsequent ruling appointed a magistrate to oversee the integration process. *Disability Advocates, Inc. v. Paterson*, 2010 WL 786657 (E.D.N.Y. 2010).

Of course, even if one agrees with this interpretation of the ADA, the fundamental alteration defense might pose a significant obstacle to its implementation. In contrast, the Individuals with Disabilities Education Act (IDEA), the third federal statute mentioned earlier, clearly provides an entitlement to "community treatment" for people (specifically, children) who are not institutionalized, and does not explicitly contain a fundamental alteration defense. The IDEA, as well as the ADA and similar federal statutes, are examined further in Part III of this book.

PART 3

BENEFITS ELIGIBILITY AND LEGAL PROTECTION AGAINST DISCRIMINATION

■ ■ ■

CHAPTER 11

ENTITLEMENTS FOR PEOPLE WITH
MENTAL DISABILITIES

■ ■ ■

Table of Sections

I.   SPECIAL EDUCATIONAL BENEFITS

Originally called the Education of All Handicapped Children Act when it was passed in 1975, the Individuals with Disabilities Education Act (IDEA), 20 U.S.C. § 1401 et seq., seeks to provide a "free appropriate public education" in the "least restrictive environment" for all children with disabilities. The 1975 preamble to the IDEA stated that more than eight million children in the United States were disabled, that more than half of these children were not receiving an appropriate education, and that more than one million of them were excluded from the public school system entirely. 20 U.S.C. § 1400(b). In passing the Act, Congress appeared to be motivated by findings that many children with disabilities were educable, yet were housed in abominable institutions, often unconnected with the school system or with the communities from which they came.

The Act aims to benefit persons up to the age of 21 who have mental or physical disabilities. As amended in 2004, the Act covers children who require "special education and related services" because of any of the following disabilities: intellectual disability, "serious emotional disturbance," "traumatic brain injury," "other health impairments," and "specific learning disabilities". At the same time, learning problems that result from "conduct disorders," family dysfunction, psychosocial stressors, "lack of appropriate instruction in reading [or] math," or "limited English proficiency" do not come within the coverage of the Act. 20 U.S.C. § 1414(b)(5).

Despite the last three limitations (which were largely designed to avoid misdiagnosis of disadvantaged children who are not disabled), the potential scope of IDEA is quite broad. Thus, the IDEA can be viewed as a government-subsidized regime for community-based treatment and habilitation of young people with mental illnesses or cognitive disabilities to the extent such treatment or habilitation can be categorized as "educational." As such, the IDEA could potentially provide a significant alternative to the mental health system discussed in Part II of this book. Whether it does so depends primarily on how one defines "free appropriate education" for children "with disabilities" and how one interprets the provision that such education take place in the "least restrictive environment" (the latter a requirement that the Act also refers to as "mainstreaming"). These two topics are examined below.

A. SCOPE OF GUARANTEED BENEFITS

BOARD OF EDUCATION V. ROWLEY
Supreme Court of the United States, 1982.
458 U.S. 176, 102 S.Ct. 3034, 73 L.Ed.2d 690.

JUSTICE REHNQUIST delivered the opinion of the Court.

This case presents a question of statutory interpretation. Petitioners contend that the Court of Appeals and the District Court misconstrued the requirements imposed by Congress upon States which receive federal funds under the Education of the Handicapped Act. We agree and reverse the judgment of the Court of Appeals.

I

The Education of the Handicapped Act (Act), 84 Stat. 175, as amended, 20 U.S.C. § 1401 *et seq.* (1976 ed. and Supp. IV), provides federal money to assist state and local agencies in educating handicapped children, and conditions such funding upon a State's compliance with extensive goals and procedures. The Act represents an ambitious federal effort to promote the education of handicapped children, and was passed in response to Congress' perception that a majority of handicapped children in the United States "were either totally excluded from schools or [were] sitting idly in regular classrooms awaiting the time when they were old enough to 'drop out.'" H.R.Rep. No. 94–332, p. 2 (1975).

* * *

In order to qualify for federal financial assistance under the Act, a State must demonstrate that it "has in effect a policy that assures all handicapped children the right to a free appropriate public education." 20 U.S.C. § 1412(1). That policy must be reflected in a state plan submitted to and approved by the Secretary of Education, § 1413, which describes in detail the goals, programs, and timetables under which the State intends to educate handicapped children within its borders. §§ 1412, 1413. States receiving money under the Act must provide education to the handicapped by priority, first "to handicapped children who are not receiving an education" and second "to handicapped children . . . with the most severe handicaps who are receiving an inadequate education," § 1412(3), and "to the maximum extent appropriate" must educate handicapped children "with children who are not handicapped." § 1412(5).[4] The Act broadly defines "handicapped children" to include "mentally retarded, hard of hearing, deaf, speech impaired, visually handicapped, seriously emotionally disturbed, orthopedically impaired, [and] other health impaired children, [and] children with specific learning disabilities." § 1401(1).

The "free appropriate public education" required by the Act is tailored to the unique needs of the handicapped child by means of an "individualized educational program" (IEP). § 1401(18). The IEP, which is prepared at a meeting between a qualified representative of the local educational agency, the child's teacher, the child's parents or guardian, and, where appropriate, the child, consists of a written document containing

> "(A) a statement of the present levels of educational performance of such child, (B) a statement of annual goals, including short-term instructional objectives, (C) a statement of the specific educational services to be provided to such child, and the extent to which such child will be able to participate in regular educational programs, (D) the projected date for initiation and anticipated duration of such services, and (E) appropriate objective criteria and evaluation procedures and schedules for determining, on at least an annual basis, whether instructional objectives are being achieved." § 1401(19).

Local or regional educational agencies must review, and where appropriate revise, each child's IEP at least annually. § 1414(a)(5). See also § 1413(a)(11).

In addition to the state plan and the IEP already described, the Act imposes extensive procedural requirements upon States receiving federal funds under its provisions. Parents or guardians of handicapped children must be notified of any proposed change in "the identification, evaluation, or educational placement of the child or the provision of a free appropriate public education to such child," and must be permitted to bring a complaint about "any matter relating to" such evaluation and education. §§ 1415(b)(1)(D) and (E).

---

4   Despite this preference for "mainstreaming" handicapped children—educating them with nonhandicapped children—Congress recognized that regular classrooms simply would not be a suitable setting for the education of many handicapped children. The Act expressly acknowledges that "the nature or severity of the handicap [may be] such that education in regular classes with the use of supplementary aids and services cannot be achieved satisfactorily." § 1412(5). The Act thus provides for the education of some handicapped children in separate classes or institutional settings. See *ibid.;* § 1413(a)(4).

Complaints brought by parents or guardians must be resolved at "an impartial due process hearing," and appeal to the state educational agency must be provided if the initial hearing is held at the local or regional level. §§ 1415(b)(2) and (c). Thereafter, "[a]ny party aggrieved by the findings and decision" of the state administrative hearing has "the right to bring a civil action with respect to the complaint . . . in any State court of competent jurisdiction or in a district court of the United States without regard to the amount in controversy." § 1415(e)(2).

Thus, although the Act leaves to the States the primary responsibility for developing and executing educational programs for handicapped children, it imposes significant requirements to be followed in the discharge of that responsibility. Compliance is assured by provisions permitting the withholding of federal funds upon determination that a participating state or local agency has failed to satisfy the requirements of the Act, §§ 1414(b)(2)(A), 1416, and by the provision for judicial review. At present, all States except New Mexico receive federal funds under the portions of the Act at issue today.

II

This case arose in connection with the education of Amy Rowley, a deaf student at the Furnace Woods School in the Hendrick Hudson Central School District, Peekskill, N.Y. Amy has minimal residual hearing and is an excellent lipreader. During the year before she began attending Furnace Woods, a meeting between her parents and school administrators resulted in a decision to place her in a regular kindergarten class in order to determine what supplemental services would be necessary to her education. Several members of the school administration prepared for Amy's arrival by attending a course in sign-language interpretation, and a teletype machine was installed in the principal's office to facilitate communication with her parents who are also deaf. At the end of the trial period it was determined that Amy should remain in the kindergarten class, but that she should be provided with an FM hearing aid which would amplify words spoken into a wireless receiver by the teacher or fellow students during certain classroom activities. Amy successfully completed her kindergarten year.

As required by the Act, an IEP was prepared for Amy during the fall of her first-grade year. The IEP provided that Amy should be educated in a regular classroom at Furnace Woods, should continue to use the FM hearing aid, and should receive instruction from a tutor for the deaf for one hour each day and from a speech therapist for three hours each week. The Rowleys agreed with parts of the IEP, but insisted that Amy also be provided a qualified sign-language interpreter in all her academic classes in lieu of the assistance proposed in other parts of the IEP. Such an interpreter had been placed in Amy's kindergarten class for a 2–week experimental period, but the interpreter had reported that Amy did not need his services at that time. The school administrators likewise concluded that Amy did not need such an interpreter in her first-grade classroom. They reached this conclusion after consulting the school district's Committee on the Handicapped, which had received expert evidence from Amy's parents on the importance of a sign-language interpreter, received testimony from Amy's teacher and other persons familiar with her academic and social progress, and visited a class for the deaf.

When their request for an interpreter was denied, the Rowleys demanded and received a hearing before an independent examiner. After receiving evidence from both sides, the examiner agreed with the administrators' determination that an interpreter was not necessary because "Amy was achieving educationally, academically, and socially" without such assistance. The examiner's decision was affirmed on appeal by the New York Commissioner of Education on the basis of substantial evidence in the record. Pursuant to the Act's provision for judicial review, the Rowleys then brought an action in the United States District Court for the Southern District of New York, claiming that the administrators' denial of the sign-language interpreter constituted a denial of the "free appropriate public education" guaranteed by the Act.

The District Court found that Amy "is a remarkably well-adjusted child" who interacts and communicates well with her classmates and has "developed an extraordinary rapport" with her teachers. It also found that "she performs better than the average child in her class and is advancing easily from grade to grade," but "that she understands considerably less of what goes on in class than she could if she were not deaf" and thus "is not learning as much, or performing as well academically, as she would without her handicap." This disparity between Amy's achievement and her potential led the court to decide that she was not receiving a "free appropriate public education," which the court defined as "an opportunity to achieve [her] full potential commensurate with the opportunity provided to other children." According to the District Court, such a standard "requires that the potential of the handicapped child be measured and compared to his or her performance, and that the resulting differential or 'shortfall' be compared to the shortfall experienced by nonhandicapped children." The District Court's definition arose from its assumption that the responsibility for "giv[ing] content to the requirement of an 'appropriate education'" had "been left entirely to the [federal] courts and the hearing officers."

A divided panel of the United States Court of Appeals for the Second Circuit affirmed. The Court of Appeals "agree[d] with the [D]istrict [C]ourt's conclusions of law," and held that its "findings of fact [were] not clearly erroneous." 632 F.2d 945, 947 (1980).

We granted certiorari to review the lower courts' interpretation of the Act. Such review requires us to consider two questions: What is meant by the Act's requirement of a "free appropriate public education"? And what is the role of state and federal courts in exercising the review granted by 20 U.S.C. § 1415? We consider these questions separately.

III

A

This is the first case in which this Court has been called upon to interpret any provision of the Act. As noted previously, the District Court and the Court of Appeals concluded that "[t]he Act itself does not define 'appropriate education,'" 483 F.Supp., at 533, but leaves "to the courts and the hearing officers" the responsibility of "giv[ing] content to the requirement of an 'appropriate education.'" See also 632 F.2d, at 947. Petitioners contend that the definition of the phrase "free appropriate public education" used by the courts below overlooks the definition of that phrase actually found in the Act. Respondents agree that the Act defines "free appropriate public education," but contend that the statutory definition is not "functional" and thus "offers judges no guidance in their consideration of controversies involving 'the identification, evaluation, or educational placement of the child or the provision of a free appropriate public education.'" The United States, appearing as *amicus curiae* on behalf of respondents, states that "[a]lthough the Act includes definitions of a 'free appropriate public education' and other related terms, the statutory definitions do not adequately explain what is meant by 'appropriate.'"

We are loath to conclude that Congress failed to offer any assistance in defining the meaning of the principal substantive phrase used in the Act. It is beyond dispute that, contrary to the conclusions of the courts below, the Act does expressly define "free appropriate public education":

> "The term 'free appropriate public education' means *special education* and *related services* which (A) have been provided at public expense, under public supervision and direction, and without charge, (B) meet the standards of the State educational agency, (C) include an appropriate preschool, elementary, or secondary school education in the State involved, and (D) are provided in conformity with the individualized education program required under section 1414(a)(5) of this title." § 1401(18) (emphasis added).

"Special education," as referred to in this definition, means "specially designed instruction, at no cost to parents or guardians, to meet the unique needs of a handicapped child, including classroom instruction, instruction in physical education, home instruction, and instruction in hospitals and institutions." § 1401(16). "Related services" are defined as "transportation, and such developmental, corrective, and other supportive services . . . as may be required to assist a handicapped child to benefit from special education." § 1401(17).

Like many statutory definitions, this one tends toward the cryptic rather than the comprehensive, but that is scarcely a reason for abandoning the quest for legislative intent.

* * *

According to the definitions contained in the Act, a "free appropriate public education" consists of educational instruction specially designed to meet the unique needs of the handicapped child, supported by such services as are necessary to permit the child "to benefit" from the instruction. Almost as a checklist for adequacy under the Act, the definition also requires that such instruction and services be provided at public expense and under public supervision, meet the State's educational standards, approximate the grade levels used in the State's regular education, and comport with the child's IEP. Thus, if personalized instruction is being provided with sufficient supportive services to permit the child to benefit from the instruction, and the other items on the definitional checklist are satisfied, the child is receiving a "free appropriate public education" as defined by the Act.

* * *

Noticeably absent from the language of the statute is any substantive standard prescribing the level of education to be accorded handicapped children. Certainly the language of the statute contains no requirement like the one imposed by the lower courts—that States maximize the potential of handicapped children "commensurate with the opportunity provided to other children." That standard was expounded by the District Court without reference to the statutory definitions or even to the legislative history of the Act.

* * *

B

* * *

(ii)

Respondents contend that "the goal of the Act is to provide each handicapped child with an equal educational opportunity." We think, however, that the requirement that a State provide specialized educational services to handicapped children generates no additional requirement that the services so provided be sufficient to maximize each child's potential "commensurate with the opportunity provided other children."

* * *

(iii)

Implicit in the congressional purpose of providing access to a "free appropriate public education" is the requirement that the education to which access is provided be sufficient to confer some educational benefit upon the handicapped child. It would do little good for Congress to spend millions of dollars in providing access to a public education only to have the handicapped child receive no benefit from that education. The statutory definition of "free appropriate public education," in addition to requiring that States provide each child with "specially designed instruction," expressly requires the provision of "such . . . supportive services . . . as may be required to assist a handicapped child *to benefit* from special education." § 1401(17) (emphasis added). We therefore conclude that the "basic floor of opportunity" provided by the Act consists of access to specialized instruction and related services which are individually designed to provide educational benefit to the handicapped child.

The determination of when handicapped children are receiving sufficient educational benefits to satisfy the requirements of the Act presents a more difficult problem. The Act requires participating States to educate a wide spectrum of handicapped children, from the marginally hearing-impaired to the profoundly retarded and palsied. It is clear that the benefits obtainable by children at one end of the spectrum will differ dramatically from those obtainable by children at the other end, with infinite variations in between. One child may have little difficulty competing successfully in an academic setting with non-handicapped children while another child may encounter great difficulty in acquiring even the most basic of self-maintenance skills. We do not attempt today to establish any one test for determining the adequacy of educational benefits conferred upon all children covered by the Act. Because in this case we are presented with a handicapped child who is receiving substantial specialized instruction and related services, and who is performing above average in the regular classrooms of a public school system, we confine our analysis to that situation.

* * *

C

When the language of the Act and its legislative history are considered together, the requirements imposed by Congress become tolerably clear. Insofar as a State is required to provide a handicapped child with a "free appropriate public education," we hold that it satisfies this requirement by providing personalized instruction with sufficient support services to permit the child to benefit educationally from that instruction.

* * *

IV

A

As mentioned in Part I, the Act permits "[a]ny party aggrieved by the findings and decision" of the state administrative hearings "to bring a civil action" in "any State court of competent jurisdiction or in a district court of the United States without regard to the amount in controversy." § 1415(e)(2). The complaint, and therefore the civil action, may concern "any matter relating to the identification, evaluation, or educational placement of the child, or the provision of a free appropriate public education to such child." § 1415(b)(1)(E). In reviewing the complaint, the Act provides that a court "shall receive the record of the [state] administrative proceedings, shall hear additional evidence at the request of a party, and, basing its decision on the preponderance of the evidence, shall grant such relief as the court determines is appropriate." § 1415(e)(2).

The parties disagree sharply over the meaning of these provisions, petitioners contending that courts are given only limited authority to review for state compliance with the Act's procedural requirements and no power to review the substance of the state program, and respondents contending that the Act requires courts to exercise *de novo* review over state educational decisions and policies. We find petitioners' contention unpersuasive, for Congress expressly rejected provisions that would have so severely restricted the role of reviewing courts. In substituting the current language of the statute for language that would have made state administrative findings conclusive if supported by substantial evidence, the Conference Committee explained that courts were to make "independent decision[s] based on a preponderance of the evidence."

But although we find that this grant of authority is broader than claimed by petitioners, we think the fact that it is found in § 1415, which is entitled "Procedural safeguards," is not without significance. When the elaborate and highly specific procedural safeguards embodied in § 1415 are contrasted with the general and somewhat imprecise substantive admonitions contained in the Act, we think that the importance Congress attached to these procedural safeguards cannot be gainsaid. It seems to us no exaggeration to say that Congress placed every bit as much emphasis upon compliance with procedures giving parents and guardians a large measure of participation at every stage of the administrative process, see, *e.g.,* §§ 1415(a)–(d), as it did upon the measurement of the resulting IEP against a substantive standard. We think that the congressional emphasis upon full participation of concerned parties throughout the development of the IEP, as well as the requirements that state and local plans be submitted to the Secretary for approval, demonstrates the legislative conviction that adequate compliance with the procedures prescribed would in most cases assure much if not all of what Congress wished in the way of substantive content in an IEP.

Thus the provision that a reviewing court base its decision on the "preponderance of the evidence" is by no means an invitation to the courts to substitute their own notions of sound educational policy for those of the school authorities which they review. The very importance which Congress has attached to compliance with certain procedures in the preparation of an IEP would be frustrated if a court were permitted simply to set state decisions at nought. The fact that § 1415(e) requires that the reviewing court "receive the records of the [state] administrative proceedings" carries with it the implied requirement that due weight shall be given to these proceedings.

*   *   *

Therefore, a court's inquiry in suits brought under § 1415(e)(2) is twofold. First, has the State complied with the procedures set forth in the Act? And second, is the individualized educational program developed through the Act's procedures reasonably calculated to enable the child to receive educational benefits? If these requirements are met, the State has complied with the obligations imposed by Congress and the courts can require no more.

B

In assuring that the requirements of the Act have been met, courts must be careful to avoid imposing their view of preferable educational methods upon the States. The primary responsibility for formulating the education to be accorded a handicapped child, and for choosing the educational method most suitable to the child's needs, was left by the Act to state and local educational agencies in cooperation with the parents or guardian of the child.

We previously have cautioned that courts lack the "specialized knowledge and experience" necessary to resolve "persistent and difficult questions of educational policy." *San Antonio Independent School Dist. v. Rodriguez,* 411 U.S., at 42, 93 S.Ct., at 1301. We think that Congress shared that view when it passed the Act. As already demonstrated, Congress' intention was not that the Act displace the primacy of States in the field of education, but that States receive funds to assist them in extending their educational systems to the handicapped. Therefore, once a court determines that the requirements of the Act have been met, questions of methodology are for resolution by the States.

*   *   *

VI

Applying these principles to the facts of this case, we conclude that the Court of Appeals erred in affirming the decision of the District Court. Neither the District Court nor the Court of Appeals found that petitioners had failed to comply with the procedures of the Act, and the findings of neither court would support a conclusion that Amy's educational program failed to comply with the substantive requirements of the Act. On the contrary, the District Court found that the "evidence firmly establishes that Amy is receiving an 'adequate' education, since she performs better than the average child in her class and is advancing easily from grade to grade." 483 F.Supp., at 534. In light of this finding, and of the fact that Amy was receiving personalized instruction and related services calculated by the Furnace Woods school administrators to meet her educational needs, the lower courts should not have concluded that the Act requires the provision of a sign-language interpreter. Accordingly, the decision of the Court of Appeals is reversed, and the case is remanded for further proceedings consistent with this opinion.

So ordered.

* * *

[The concurring opinion of MR. JUSTICE BLACKMUN is omitted].

JUSTICE WHITE, with whom JUSTICE BRENNAN and JUSTICE MARSHALL join, dissenting.

In order to reach its result in this case, the majority opinion contradicts itself, the language of the statute, and the legislative history. Both the majority's standard for a "free appropriate education" and its standard for judicial review disregard congressional intent.

* * *

I

I agree that the language of the Act does not contain a substantive standard beyond requiring that the education offered must be "appropriate." However, if there are limits not evident from the face of the statute on what may be considered an "appropriate education," they must be found in the purpose of the statute or its legislative history.

* * *

The majority opinion announces a different substantive standard, that "Congress did not impose upon the States any greater substantive educational standard than would be necessary to make such access meaningful." *Ante,* at 3043. While "meaningful" is no more enlightening than "appropriate," the Court purports to clarify itself. Because Amy was provided with *some* specialized instruction from which she obtained *some* benefit and because she passed from grade to grade, she was receiving a meaningful and therefore appropriate education.

This falls far short of what the Act intended. * * * The basic floor of opportunity is as the courts below recognized, intended to eliminate the effects of the handicap, at least to the extent that the child will be given an equal opportunity to learn if that is reasonably possible. Amy Rowley, without a sign-language interpreter, comprehends less than half of what is said in the classroom—less than half of what normal children comprehend. This is hardly an equal opportunity to learn, even if Amy makes passing grades.

* * *

The issue before us is what standard the word "appropriate" incorporates when it is used to modify "education." The answer given by the Court is not a satisfactory one.

II

The Court's discussion of the standard for judicial review is as flawed as its discussion of a "free appropriate public education." According to the Court, a court can ask only whether the State has "complied with the procedures set forth in the Act" and whether the individualized education program is "reasonably calculated to enable the child to receive educational benefits." *Ante,* at 3051. Both the language of the Act and the legislative history, however, demonstrate that Congress intended the courts to conduct a far more searching inquiry.

* * *

There is no doubt that the state agency itself must make substantive decisions. The legislative history reveals that the courts are to consider, *de novo,* the same issues.

* * *

Thus, the Court's limitations on judicial review have no support in either the language of the Act or the legislative history. * * * I respectfully dissent.

DEAL V. HAMILTON COUNTY BD. OF EDUCATION

United States Court of Appeals, Sixth Circuit, 2004.
392 F.3d 840, cert. denied, 546 U.S. 936.

MARBLEY, DISTRICT JUDGE.

This case arises under the Individuals with Disabilities Education Act, 20 U.S.C. §§ 1400 et seq. ("IDEA"), and corresponding Tennessee laws and rules. Plaintiffs–Appellants, Maureen and Phillip Deal (the "Deals"), bring this action for and on behalf of their autistic son, Zachary.

Defendant–Appellee is the Board of Education of Hamilton County, Tennessee (the "School System"). Plaintiffs–Appellants appeal the decision of the district court reversing in part and affirming in part the decision of the administrative law judge ("ALJ") who presided over the administrative hearing. Plaintiffs–Appellants assert that the School System failed to provide Zachary with a "free and appropriate public education" ("FAPE") in Zachary's "least restrictive environment" ("LRE") and that they therefore are entitled to reimbursement from the School System for the education that they provided Zachary at their own expense. The ALJ found several procedural and substantive violations of the IDEA and ordered the School System to pay some of the reimbursement sought by the Deals. The district court found no IDEA violations and reversed the reimbursement ordered by the ALJ. Based on the following analysis, the Court AFFIRMS in part and REVERSES in part.

I.   BACKGROUND

A.   Factual Background

In 1997, when Zachary was three years old, the School System and the Deals developed Zachary's first "individualized education program" ("IEP").[1] Pursuant to the terms of the IEP, Zachary attended a preschool comprehensive development class ("CDC") at Ooltewah Elementary School. While Zachary was assigned to Ooltewah, his parents, in September 1997, began to teach Zachary outside of school using a program developed by the Center for Autism and Related Disorders ("CARD"). According to the ALJ, this program is patterned after a methodology for treating autistic children developed by Dr. Ivar Lovaas at the University of California at Los Angeles.[2] The CARD program consists of one-on-one applied behavioral analysis ("ABA") that relies heavily on extremely structured teaching and comprehensive data collection and analysis.

On May 11, 1998, an IEP team met to consider extended school year ("ESY") services for Zachary. The Deals, convinced that Zachary was

---

[1]   Zachary has been diagnosed with autism spectrum disorder, hereinafter referred to as "autism":

"Autism" means a developmental disability, which significantly affects verbal and nonverbal communication and social interaction, generally evident before age three (3), that adversely affects a child's educational performance. Other characteristics often associated with autism are engagement in repetitive activities and stereotyped movements, resistance to environmental change or change in daily routines, and unusual responses to sensory experiences.

[2]   Dr. Lovaas, in his seminal research conducted in the 1980s on methodologies for teaching autistic children, achieved extraordinary results. Virtually all students in his study group showed significant improvement, and his best outcome students exhibited dramatic gains in IQ and in their ability to function within a regular educational setting. A follow up study published in 1993 found that 47% of the students who had received Dr. Lovaas's intervention went on to become "indistinguishable" in their regular education classrooms. The ALJ found that Lovaas style interventions of ten hours per week or less have no effect.

making exceptional progress because of the one-on-one ABA program they were funding in their home, requested that the School System fund a 40–hour per week home based ABA program for the summer, as well as provide for year-round speech therapy. The School System refused to fund the parents' program and likewise refused to provide the Deals with data regarding the efficacy of the School System's approach to teaching autistic children. Instead, the agreed upon IEP provided for ESY services consisting of three 45 minute speech therapy sessions per week.

On October 9, 1998, an IEP meeting was held to develop Zachary's 1998–1999 IEP. The 95–page IEP, dated October 15, 1998, provided, among other things, for 35 hours per week of special education instruction, with many explicit goals. Zachary also was to receive related services, including physical therapy and speech therapy. The Deals filed a "minority report" requesting that the School System fund their private ABA program in the home. The School System convened additional IEP meetings that were attended by the Deals in November 1998, December 1998, February 1999, and March 1999 to discuss Zachary's progress and the Deals' concerns. During the 1998–1999 school year, Zachary attended the School System's program only 16% of the time.

At a May 24, 1999, IEP meeting, the Deals requested an ESY program of 43 hours per week of one-on-one ABA therapy and 5 hours per week of speech therapy. The IEP team determined that it could not document any regression Zachary would suffer without ESY services due to his lack of attendance at the School System's program, so the School System declined to offer any ESY services.

On August 20 and again on August 25, 1999, an IEP team met to develop an IEP for Zachary for the 1999–2000 school year. The School System proposed that Zachary would, in addition to his CDC classes, attend a regular kindergarten classroom three times per week for 15 minutes each. He would also have lunch with a regular kindergarten class. The time spent with the regular class would increase as Zachary was able to tolerate it. Zachary would have with him a classroom assistant familiar with and trained to meet his needs. The proposal included specific goals and objectives. Teaching methods would include one-on-one discrete trial teaching; the use of picture cues; incidental teaching to provide an opportunity for carry over and application of learned skills; continual use of functional communication techniques; activity-based instruction; the use of music, story telling, and reading; and other techniques. The proposal also provided for speech and language therapy for 30 minutes five times per week, occupational therapy two times per month, and physical therapy for 30 minutes once a week.

On September 2, 1999, Zachary began attending a private preschool, the Primrose School, at which his parents had enrolled him. Zachary attended a regular pre-K class at the Primrose School for 3 hours per day,

2 days per week, with a personal aide paid for by the Deals. On September 7, 1999, the Deals informed the School System of their rejection of the IEP in favor of the private program. The Deals' disagreement with the IEP stemmed from their belief that Zachary should spend more time in a regular education classroom, as well as their desire to have the School System pay for the CARD program or offer similar ABA therapy. On September 16, 1999, the Deals requested a due process hearing under the provisions of the IDEA. Zachary did not attend public school at all during the 1999–2000 school year.

On August 11, 2000, an IEP meeting was held to develop an IEP for Zachary for the 2000–2001 school year. The proposed IEP called for Zachary to be placed primarily in a regular education kindergarten class at Westview Elementary School. The IEP included specific goals and objectives and provided for various support services, including pre-teaching and re-teaching sessions. The full school day and week program included related services of speech therapy and occupational therapy. The Deals rejected the IEP and continued to insist that the School System pay for their private ABA program for Zachary. Zachary did attend Westview that year, but only part time.

B.   Procedural History

The administrative hearing requested by the Deals on September 16, 1999, began on March 15, 2000, and concluded on February 13, 2001. The hearing encompassed 27 full days of testimony from 20 fact and expert witnesses. The ALJ also reviewed tens of thousands of pages of exhibits, viewed several video tapes, and personally observed Zachary in a number of settings.

In an opinion and order dated August 20, 2001, the ALJ made explicit credibility findings as to all 20 witnesses and provided 191 findings of fact. He also announced the following legal conclusions:

> (1) The School System violated the procedural requirements of the IDEA by predetermining, pursuant to an unofficial policy of refusing to consider "Lovaas style ABA," that the School System's extant program was appropriate for Zachary.[4]

---

[4]   The ALJ concluded that the School System's refusal to offer Lovaas style ABA was based largely on cost considerations. Indeed, the School System had never funded an intensive Lovaas style ABA program, despite the dramatic difference in results between such a program and the standard School System program: under the strongest evidence offered by the School System, only 14% of autistic children receiving only the School System program went on to become "indistinguishable" from the children in regular education classrooms. School System representatives even acknowledged the effectiveness of Zachary's ABA program: one representative told the Deals that there were things she wished she could recommend for Zachary but then she would have to give them to everyone. The ALJ found that the School System should, at the very least, have informed the Deals about the Lovaas style of ABA and explained why it would recommend against such a program.

(2) The School System's failure to have regular education teachers attend the IEP team meetings also constituted a procedural violation.

(3) These procedural violations themselves amounted to denial of a FAPE.

(4) The School System had substantively violated the IDEA by failing to provide a proven or even describable methodology for educating autistic children.[5]

(5) An additional substantive violation resulted from the School System's failure to provide Zachary with 30 hours per week of the intensive Lovaas style ABA that had been proven to be effective for him.[6]

(6) The School System also substantively violated the IDEA by failing to provide Zachary with ESY services in 1999.

(7) The Deals were not entitled to reimbursement for private evaluations of Zachary.

(8) The Deals were entitled to reimbursement for up to 30 hours per week of the home based ABA services they had provided to Zachary, and the School System was to continue to reimburse the Deals for such services until a properly constituted IEP team, which must include at least one expert in and advocate for Lovaas style ABA, had developed an IEP for Zachary that included at least 30 hours per week of Lovaas style ABA.

(9) The School System did not sufficiently consider the LRE requirement of the IDEA in developing Zachary's 1999–2000 IEP, but the Deals nonetheless were not entitled to reimbursement for Zachary's tuition at the Primrose School because they failed to provide the School System with the required statutory notice.

(10) The School System had mishandled its obligation to provide the related services of physical therapy, occupational therapy, and speech therapy to Zachary and therefore was required to reimburse

---

[5] The School System methodology, described as an "eclectic" approach, involved the use of various components from other methodologies, primarily Treatment and Education of Autistic and Related Communication Handicapped Children ("TEACCH"). In his factual findings, the ALJ found TEACCH to be "a cradle to grave support system based on the assumption that the core clinical problems in autism are lifelong." The ALJ found TEACCH, a less expensive program than Lovaas style ABA, to be "a humane and effective methodology for addressing the needs of older autistic children and younger autistic children who have not shown or who are incapable of making the progress and IQ gains demonstrated by Lovaas style ABA." The ALJ credited the expert testimony of Dr. James A. Mulick, who stated that, out of almost 2,000 autistic children he had evaluated, the only ones he had seen who had become "indistinguishable" in a regular education setting were those who received intensive Lovaas style ABA.

[6] The ALJ described the "remarkable" progress that Zachary had achieved through the Lovaas style ABA and found that the continuation of such a program was appropriate because any other methodology would actually retard his education or development.

the Deals for any out of pocket costs they had incurred in providing such related services to Zachary.

(11) The Deals have no right to veto competent providers of services called for in a properly constituted IEP.

(12) Zachary Deal was the prevailing party.

On October 1, 2001, the Deals initiated review of portions of the ALJ's decision in the district court. They sought reimbursement of certain expenses that the ALJ had declined to award, as well as attorney's fees for the administrative hearing. The School System filed a counterclaim seeking reversal of the ALJ's determinations that the failure to offer Zachary a "Lovaas style" program violated Zachary's right to a FAPE and that the Deals were entitled to reimbursement for privately obtained related services.

On May 30, 2002, the School System requested that the district court hear additional evidence pursuant to the IDEA's "additional evidence" provision, 20 U.S.C. § 1415(i)(2)(B)(ii). . . . After a series of nationwide depositions and substantial additional document discovery conducted by the School System, the "additional evidence" trial was held on January 23 and 24, 2003. The district court heard testimony from two School System lay witnesses and four expert witnesses and received 24 exhibits into evidence. The Deals did not offer any additional evidence, despite the district court having indicated that they would be permitted to do so.

In an opinion and order dated March 4, 2003, the district court reversed in part and affirmed in part the ALJ's decision. The court ruled that there had been no procedural or substantive violations of the IDEA and that the Deals were not entitled to any reimbursement relief. The district court held that the ALJ had erred in exalting the Deals' preferred educational methodology above other appropriate methods. This appeal followed. . . .

II. STANDARD OF REVIEW

. . . "[A] district court is required to make findings of fact based on a preponderance of the evidence contained in the complete record, while giving some deference to the fact findings of the administrative proceedings." This Court, in turn, applies a clearly erroneous standard of review to the district court's findings of fact and a de novo standard of review to its conclusions of law. Mixed questions of law and fact, including the question of whether a child was denied a FAPE, are reviewed de novo. This Court also must accord due deference to the state administrative hearing officer's decision. . . .

III. DISCUSSION

*   *   *

C.   Violations of the IDEA

1.   Standards Under the IDEA

. . . There are two parts to a court's inquiry in suits brought pursuant to the IDEA. First, the court must determine whether the school system has complied with the procedures set forth in the IDEA. Second, the court must assess whether the IEP developed through those procedures was reasonably calculated to enable the child to receive educational benefits. *Rowley*, 458 U.S. at 206–07, 102 S.Ct. 3034. "If these requirements are met, the State has complied with the obligations imposed by Congress and the courts can require no more." Id. Parties challenging an IEP have the burden of proving by a preponderance of the evidence that the IEP devised by the school district is inappropriate. . . .

2.   Procedural Violations

a.   Predetermination

This Court's review of the predetermination decision is de novo, since it is a mixed question of law and fact. . . . [The IDEA prohibits a school from predetermining the child's educational program before the IEP process has taken place.]

The facts of this case strongly suggest that the School System had an unofficial policy of refusing to provide one-on-one ABA programs and that School System personnel thus did not have open minds and were not willing to consider the provision of such a program. [T]he School System steadfastly refused even to discuss the possibility of providing an ABA program, even in the face of impressive results. Indeed, School System personnel openly admired and were impressed with Zachary's performance (presumably attained through the ABA program), until the Deals asked the School System to pay for the ABA program. Several comments made by School System personnel suggested that they would like to provide Zachary with ABA services, i.e., they recognized the efficacy of such a program, but they were prevented from doing so, i.e., by the School System policy. The clear implication is that no matter how strong the evidence presented by the Deals, the School System still would have refused to provide the services. This is predetermination. . . .

The School System seemed to suggest, at oral argument, that it is entitled to invest in a program such as TEACCH and then capitalize on that investment by using the TEACCH program exclusively. But this is precisely what it is not permitted to do, at least without fully considering the individual needs of each child. A school district unquestionably may consider cost in determining appropriate services for a child. The school district is required, however, to base its placement decision on the child's IEP, 34 C.F.R. § 300.552, rather than on the mere fact of a pre-existing investment. In other words, the school district may not, as it appears happened here, decide that because it has spent a lot of money on a program, that program is always going to be appropriate for educating children with a specific disability, regardless of any evidence to the contrary of the individualized needs of a particular child. A placement decision may only be considered to have been based on the child's IEP when the child's individual characteristics, including demonstrated response to particular types of educational programs, are taken into account. A "one size fits all" approach to special education will not be countenanced by the IDEA.

A procedural violation can cause substantive harm when it seriously infringes upon the parents' opportunity to participate in the IEP process. Because the School System deprived the Deals of a meaningful opportunity to participate, the predetermination amounts to denial of a FAPE for Zachary. The Court accordingly REVERSES the district court's decision on this basis.

b.   Presence of Regular Education Teachers at IEP Meetings

. . . A school district is required to "ensure that the IEP team for each child with a disability includes . . . [a]t least one regular education teacher of the child (if the child is, or may be, participating in the regular education environment)." 34 C.F.R. § 300.344(a). There appears to be no dispute that the School System technically violated the IDEA by failing to include regular education teachers at certain IEP meetings. The question is whether these violations caused substantive harm to either Zachary or his parents. . . .

. . . The rationale for requiring the attendance of a regular education teacher is closely tied to Congress's "least restrictive environment" mandate. The input provided by a regular education teacher is vitally important in considering the extent to which a disabled student may be integrated into a regular education classroom and how the student's individual needs might be met within that classroom. One of the Deals' main objections to the 1999–2000 IEP developed for Zachary is that it did not provide for sufficient integration. The absence of the unique perspective that could have been provided by a regular education teacher therefore had a real impact on the decision-making process.[15] The Court therefore REVERSES the district court's decision based on this procedural violation, as well.

3.   Substantive Violations

. . . This Court and others faced with essentially the same question have decided that school systems are not required to provide autistic children with the sort of intensive (and expensive) educational program

---

[15] Defendant–Appellant's argument that the school principal and others familiar with the regular education program were present at these meetings misses the mark. The regulation explicitly requires the attendance of a "regular education teacher of the child." 34 C.F.R. § 300.344(a). The regulation does not state an exception where other knowledgeable people are present.

pioneered by Dr. Lovaas. . . . At some point, however, this facile answer becomes insufficient. Indeed, there is a point at which the difference in outcomes between two methods can be so great that provision of the lesser program could amount to denial of a FAPE. A school district clearly is not required to "maximize each child's potential commensurate with the opportunity provided other children," *Rowley*, i.e., to provide all children with equal educational opportunity. The Third Circuit, however, has held that an IEP must confer a "meaningful educational benefit." *Polk v. Cent. Susquehanna Intermediate Unit 16*, 853 F.2d 171, 182 (3d Cir.1988). Further, that benefit "must be gauged in relation to a child's potential." Based on the analysis set forth below, we agree that the IDEA requires an IEP to confer a "meaningful educational benefit" gauged in relation to the potential of the child at issue.

In *Polk*, the issue was the provision of physical therapy as a "related service." Rather than providing direct physical therapy from a licensed physical therapist, the school district shifted to a "consultative" model whereby a physical therapist did not provide any therapy directly, but instead trained the classroom teacher to integrate physical therapy with the disabled student's education. The parents alleged that the failure to provide direct physical therapy at least once a week had hindered their child's progress in meeting his educational goals. The Third Circuit first held that there was a genuine issue of material fact regarding whether the defendants had failed to provide individualized educational programs due to their refusal, as a blanket rule, even to consider providing handicapped students with direct physical therapy from a licensed therapist. The court next concluded that the lower court had erred in evaluating the disabled child's educational program by a standard under which even trivial educational advancement could satisfy the substantive requirements of the statute.

The court held that a FAPE must provide "more than a trivial educational benefit." Noting that *Rowley* was a narrow decision and that the precise issue of how much educational benefit must be provided had not been squarely before the Court in that case, the *Polk* court relied on *Rowley's* use of the word "meaningful," as well as legislative history emphasizing the importance of self-sufficiency, to find that the educational benefit must be more than de minimis. . . . At the very least, the intent of Congress appears to have been to require a program providing a meaningful educational benefit towards the goal of self-sufficiency, especially where self-sufficiency is a realistic goal for a particular child.[17] Indeed, states providing no more than some educational benefit could not possibly hope to attain the lofty goals proclaimed by Congress. In evaluating whether an educational benefit is

---

[17] The implication from these manifestations of congressional intent might be that, where self-sufficiency is a realistic goal for a child, a program that maximizes the possibility of self-sufficiency could be required.

meaningful, logic dictates that the benefit "must be gauged in relation to a child's potential." *Polk*, 853 F.2d at 185. Only by considering an individual child's capabilities and potentialities may a court determine whether an educational benefit provided to that child allows for meaningful advancement. In conducting this inquiry, courts should heed the congressional admonishment not to set unduly low expectations for disabled children.

The obvious objection to the meaningful benefit standard is the expense involved. As the Supreme Court has noted, however, "There is no doubt that Congress imposed a significant financial burden on States and school districts that participate in the IDEA." *Florence County Sch. Dist. Four v. Carter ex rel. Carter*, 510 U.S. 7, 15, 114 S.Ct. 361, 126 L.Ed.2d 284 (1993). School districts are permitted to consider cost in devising an appropriate educational program. A case such as Zachary Deal's, however, is precisely the sort of situation where judicial intervention is necessary to fulfill congressional intent and serve the public interest. Left to its own devices, a school system is likely to choose the educational option that will help it balance its budget, even if the end result of the system's indifference to a child's individual potential is a greater expense to society as a whole.

. . . On remand, the district court must carefully consider all of the evidence in this case, giving due deference to the ALJ's findings, in determining whether a substantive IDEA violation occurred under the meaningful benefit standard. In conducting this inquiry, the court should "carefully consider[ ] the student's individual abilities." The district court's decision regarding substantive violations is REVERSED, and this case is REMANDED to allow the court to determine whether the School System provided Zachary with a meaningful educational benefit.

4.   Reimbursement

. . . Once an IDEA violation is found, the court is authorized to "grant such relief as the court determines is appropriate." 20 U.S.C. § 1415(i)(2)(B)(iii). Parents are entitled to retroactive reimbursement if the school district failed to provide the student with a FAPE and if the private placement chosen by the parents was reasonably calculated to enable the child to receive educational benefits. *Florence County.* Here, the Deals are entitled to reimbursement. The School System deprived Zachary of a FAPE by predetermining his placement and by failing to ensure the attendance of regular education teachers at certain IEP meetings. Furthermore, the district court has the opportunity, on remand, to find an additional, substantive, IDEA violation by the School System. The private educational services provided by the Deals clearly were proper under the IDEA. The district court's task on remand thus is to determine the level of reimbursement that is "appropriate" in light of the IDEA's purpose. For the reasons previously stated, the district court's reimbursement decision is REVERSED, and the case is REMANDED for the court to weigh the equities and determine the appropriate level of reimbursement.

QUESTIONS AND COMMENTS

1. *The "some benefit" standard.* The courts have interpreted the substantive standard under the IDEA in a number of ways. In *Rowley* the Supreme Court held that, to meet the requirements of the IDEA, education need only be of "some benefit" to the child, and strongly suggested that Amy Rowley's schooling met that standard. The Third Circuit opinion in *Polk*, which is described in *Deal*, subsequently held that *Rowley's* "some benefit" standard demands that the child receive more than a "trivial benefit"; it then construed that standard to require, despite the parents' admission that their son was receiving "some" benefit from his current schooling, that Polk should receive additional physical therapy services. More demanding than the some-benefit standard, whatever it may entail, is the test devised by the district court in *Rowley* and rejected by the Supreme Court in that case, which required that the child be provided "an opportunity to achieve [his or her] full potential commensurate with the opportunity provided to other children." See also *In re Conklin*, 946 F.2d 306, 320–21 (4th Cir.1991) (summarizing state statutes, some of which adopt this standard). Perhaps most demanding is the test announced in *B.G. v. Cranford Board of Education*, 702 F.Supp. 1140 (D.N.J.1988), which explicitly adopted, as a matter of state law, a higher standard than required by *Rowley*. There, the court noted that New Jersey law requires school boards "to provide educational services according to how the student can *best* achieve success in learning." Id. at 1148 (emphasis in original). The court found that this standard required a residential placement of an emotionally disturbed child. The school district's day school placement of the child "though perhaps sufficient to satisfy the minimum federal standards under *Rowley*, is insufficient and inconsistent with New Jersey's requirements that B.G. be afforded a program that assures him the fullest opportunity to develop his intellectual capacities." Id. at 1157 How do these various IDEA standards compare to *Youngberg v. Romeo* and other caselaw dealing with the right to treatment for those who are institutionalized (see Chapter Ten, Part II?

Which standard does the Sixth Circuit apply in *Deal*? Given the one-on-one teaching and various other activities the school provided Zachary before his parents removed him from the regular school setting, wasn't Zachary receiving more than a trivial benefit from the program the school was offering? The ALJ was impressed by the statistics indicating that the CARD program developed by Dr. Lovass was more successful than the school's TEACCH program at making autistic children "indistinguishable" from other students (see notes 2 and 4 of the decision). Does or should the IDEA obligate schools to provide disabled children with the services that are best at making them indistinguishable from non-disabled students? Is this standard different from an obligation to provide students with disabilities the services that are most likely to make them "self-sufficient"? (See note 17). In light of *Deal*, will the school system (or all school systems) have to provide the CARD program or something like it to all students with autism (see the comments from one of the school representatives in note 4)? If so, what if Dr. Lovass and his associates cannot accommodate all of the new students?

What if the child is so impaired he or she cannot significantly benefit from any education? In *Timothy W. v. Rochester, New Hampshire School Dist.*, 975 F.2d 954 (1st Cir. 1989), the court held that, even though the plaintiff-child had multiple disabilities, including profound intellectual disabilities, spastic quadriplegia, cerebral palsy, seizure disorder, and cortical blindness, the Education Act was meant to cover all children and that this particular child could respond to tactile stimulation, his mother's voice and touch, and familiar voices. Special education, the court stated, includes instruction in hospitals and institutions, and can focus on functional as well as cognitive skills.

2.   *Related services.* The IDEA obligates the state to provide not only a free appropriate education but also "related services." In *Polk*, for instance, the physical therapy sought by Polk's parents was a related service. According to the statute, related services are programs and treatments that are "required to assist a child with a disability to benefit from special education," including "developmental, corrective, and other supportive services . . . psychological services . . . therapeutic recreation, social work services, counselling services [and] rehabilitation counselling and medical services [the latter to be provided 'for diagnostic and evaluation purposes only].'" 20 U.S.C. § 1401(17). In *Irving Independent School District v. Tatro*, 468 U.S. 883, 104 S.Ct. 3371, 82 L.Ed.2d 664 (1984), the Supreme Court interpreted this provision to require, consistent with *Rowley*, "only those services necessary to aid a handicapped child to benefit from a special education."

In determining what "necessary" might mean in this context, consider *T.G. v. Board of Education of Piscataway*, 576 F.Supp. 420 (D.N.J.1983), where parents of an emotionally disturbed child placed him in a residential facility "to provide him with the controls and attention necessary for social and environmental development" and then requested reimbursement for the cost of the placement. The school board denied the claim on the grounds that " 'psychotherapy' other than that necessary for diagnostic or evaluative purposes was not a 'related service' for which a local school district would be responsible under the mandate of the Act." Id. at 422. In granting summary judgment for the parent-claimant the court held that psychotherapy provided to an emotionally disturbed child is a related service under the Act because "the therapy was designed as an essential service to allow [the child] to simply benefit from the educational program planned for him." Id. at 424. See also, *Kruelle v. New Castle County School District*, 642 F.2d 687 (3d Cir.1981) (holding that 24–hour care in a residential setting was necessary to allow a child with profound mental retardation to learn). But see *Field v. Haddonfield Bd. of Educ.*, 769 F.Supp. 1313, 1326–27 (D.N.J. 1991), which held that a substance abuse program is not a related service even though "successful completion of a substance abuse program can be expected to increase the effectiveness of the child's education program," and the school in this case required the plaintiff to undergo such a program before he could return to school.

Note that, while the IDEA clearly includes "psychological services" in the related services category, it also states that medical services need be provided at state expense only for "diagnostic and evaluation purposes." In *Tatro*, the Supreme Court appeared to interpret the latter language to mean that if the medical services could readily be performed by a school nurse they would generally be related services for purposes of the Act, whereas if they could only be provided by a licensed physician they would usually not be. See also, *Cedar Rapids Comm. School Dist. v. Garret F.*, 526 U.S. 66, 119 S.Ct. 992, 143 L.Ed.2d 154 (1999) (affirming *Tatro's* "bright-line test" between physician-provided and non-physician-provided medical services). The *Tatro* Court concluded that it was reasonable to believe that Congress included the exception in connection with medical services to "spare schools from an obligation to provide a service that might well prove unduly expensive and beyond the range of their competence." Id. at 892. Lower courts have also indicated that, in considering the scope of medical services exception, "it is appropriate to take into account the risk involved [in the medical procedure] and the liability factor of the school district inherent in providing a service of a medical nature." See *Neely v. Rutherford County School*, 68 F.3d 965, 971 (6th Cir.1995).

Does this reasoning exclude the administration of psychotropic medication from the IDEA's related services requirement? Should it matter that, once prescribed by a licensed psychiatrist, a nurse or nurse's aide can administer the drug? Therapy of the type provided in *T.G.* or *Kruelle*? Substance abuse treatment of the type sought in *Field*? Should the answers to these questions depend, as it apparently does after *Tatro* and *Garret F.*, upon whether the service must be provided by a psychiatrist as opposed to a non-physician? At the school or somewhere else? Compare *Babb v. Knox Cty. School System*, 965 F.2d 104 (6th Cir.1992) (school district must pay for all institutional services provided a teenager who, since at least the age of 13, "was suffering from a fairly severe degree of psychopathology.... [and] exhibit[ed] a highly ideational/schizoid personality style that is marked by underlying rage, paranoid misinterpretation of interpersonal situations, hyper-vigilance, affective reactivity, impulsive acting out of unconscious issues, intense splitting, suspiciousness, and withdrawal into fantasy") with *Tice v. Botetourt Cty. School Bd.*, 908 F.2d 1200 (4th Cir.1990) (differentiating between institutional medical services and institutional psychological and counseling services that are "educational") and *Clovis Unified School Dist. v. California Office of Admin. Hearings*, 903 F.2d 635 (9th Cir.1990) (child hospitalized primarily for "medical, psychiatric" reasons and therefore school not liable). If these types of services are *not* excluded medical services, does the IDEA in essence provide a right to state-paid psychiatric treatment for all disabled children up to age 21 (the point at which IDEA benefits cease)?

In *Bryant v. New York State Education Department*, 692 F.3d 202 (2d Cir. 2012), a group of parents claimed that the state's prohibition on aversive interventions, including electric skin shock therapy, violated the IDEA because, with respect to their children, the interventions were "necessary to control the severe behavioral disorders that undermine the children's education." According to proponents of electric skin shock, the therapy feels like a "hard pinch" but is otherwise harmless and can help minimize self-destructive behavior such as mutilation, pulling out teeth, butting one's head against the wall, and other violent actions; according to the state, in contrast, the therapy is not accepted practice and can cause extreme pain. See Anna Stolley Persky, *A Question of Education*, ABA Journal 13–15 (Jan. 2013). The court upheld the state's prohibition of electric skin therapy on both procedural and substantive grounds. Procedurally, the regulation "prohibits only consideration of a single method of treatment without foreclosing other options. Nothing in the regulation prevents individualized assessment, predetermines the children's course of education, or precludes educators from considering a wide range of possible treatments." Substantively, while "[a]versive interventions may help maximize the children's potential, . . . the IDEA does not require such measures." 692 F.3d. at 214. Assuming electric skin shock therapy does cause some pain, should parents and students who want the therapy nonetheless be able to obtain it as a "related service" if they can show it is necessary to help the students learn?

3.   *Definition of disability.* Rowley and Deal were clearly seriously disabled. But most of the resources currently expended under the IDEA are for children who are only moderately impaired. Under the Act, the disability must be (1) an enumerated impairment which (2) adversely affects educational performance and (3) creates a need for special education and related services. The enumerated mental impairments most likely to cause controversy are "learning disabilities" and "emotional disturbance." Proof of a learning disability can consist of a discrepancy between IQ and achievement, but may also rely on a finding that the child does not make sufficient progress when provided with research-based educational interventions. 20 U.S.C. § 1414(b)(6). "Emotional disturbance" for purposes of the IDEA is defined in the relevant regulations as a condition persisting "over a long period of time and to a marked degree that adversely affects a child's educational performance" which is characterized by: (1) an inability to learn that cannot be explained by intellectual, sensory, or health factors; (2) an inability to build or maintain satisfactory interpersonal relationships with peers and teachers; (3) inappropriate types of behavior or feelings under normal circumstances; (4) a general pervasive mood of unhappiness or depression; or (5) a tendency to develop physical symptoms or fears associated with personal or school problems. 34 C.F.R. § 300.8(C)(4)(i)(A). Although Congress resisted including attention deficit/ hyperactivity disorder (ADHD) in the statute, the Department of Education's regulations list both conditions as examples of chronic or acute conditions that might cause "other

health impairments," a catchall disability listed under the statute which the regulation defines as an impairment that limits "strength, vitality, or alertness, including a heightened alertness to environmental stimuli that results in limited alertness with respect to the educational environment." 34 C.F.R. § 300.8(c)(9) (2006).

Some courts have equated the term "educational performance" under the Act with "academic performance;" thus, if a student is able to achieve satisfactory grades, perform the required classroom work, or demonstrate the ability to learn in any respect, he or she does not possess a qualifying impairment regardless of other performance difficulties in school. See, e.g., *Doe ex rel. Doe v. Bd. of Educ.*, 753 F.Supp. 65, 70 (D. Conn. 1990) (finding student who was hospitalized for depression and aggression ineligible where grades were satisfactory before and after hospitalization). Others have required that the adverse impact be substantial. See, e.g., *Ashli C. ex rel. Sidney C. v. State of Hawaii*, 2007 WL 247761, at *9 (D. Haw., 2007) (holding that "adverse effect" language requires evidence of more than a "minimal" impact on education). Several courts have taken a contrary position, however. See *Mr. & Mrs. I. v. Maine Sch. Admin. Dist. 55*, 2007 U.S. App. LEXIS 5128 (1st Cir., 2007) (finding IDEA eligibility even though child's performance was above average levels); *Westchester Area Sch. Dist. V. Bruce C.*, 194 F.Supp.2d 417 (E.D. Pa. 2002) (upholding IDEA eligibility of child with ADHD despite child's satisfactory grades).

If a student is able to obtain A's and B's despite an "emotional disturbance" or a "learning disability," why should special accommodations be made? Consider these comments:

> Children with less severe impairments are likely to have the best opportunity for meaningful integration into mainstream classrooms. Many children with learning disabilities, for example, can succeed in general education when provided with additional individualized instruction or alternative methods of delivery that often enhance the learning opportunities of other children in the classroom. Limiting the reach of the IDEA to only those with serious impairments threatens to transform special education into a place rather than a set of services. Because children with more significant impairments may be less likely to secure an appropriate education in an integrated setting, the severity-linked identification of disability becomes irretrievably associated with a self-contained classroom separate and apart from the general school population.

* * *

> Tying assistance to academic failure and impaired functioning creates perverse incentives to emphasize the significance of a child's impairment in his life. Because eligibility is all or nothing, parents and students are encouraged to characterize a child's functioning as negatively as possible to the eligibility team. They may be reluctant to share a child's strengths and abilities with educators out of fear that the same will result in a

refusal of services. This characterization is damaging both to a parent's perception of his child and the child's perception of himself to the extent that he is involved in the evaluation process. Children with disabilities will increasingly be viewed as a bundle of problems to solve rather than as individuals with strengths and weaknesses in need of educational redress. The moral foundation of supporting these children is no longer the educational system's failure to meet their needs, but instead the extent of the children's internal impairments. The resources and educational services schools allocated to this population look more like benevolent charity and less like the equitable distribution of resources to all children in society. The medical model of disability, eroded by the passage of EAHCA, is resurrected as the dominant paradigm in American special education.

* * *

It is important to recognize that the advancement of people with disabilities will not be achieved by conceding that the stigma attached to this status is so great that any reasonable person would do anything to avoid such a label, including foregoing services designed to foster educational success. It is in such concessions that the imagery of disability as an unnatural and pathetic state is reinforced and entrenched. It is only by normalizing the concept of impairment, rather than restricting disability status to the most severely impaired, that the stigma of disability will be reduced. If students capable of even modest academic success are deemed insufficiently "special" to qualify for assistance, this will not occur. It is not the legal identification process itself that harms the student, but rather the negative imagery of disability that is communicated by teachers, administrators and fellow students in the wake of labeling.

Wendy F. Hensel, *Sharing the Short Bus: Eligibility and Identity under the IDEA*, 58 Hastings L.J. 1147, 1181–82, 1187, 1196 (2007).

4.   *Costs*. One's perspective on the scope of the "appropriate education," "related services" and "disabled" requirements might depend upon the financial burdens these requirements place on school districts. Because of medical advances that allow more severely impaired children to survive the neonatal period and because of newer diagnostic procedures that allow better discernment of children's disabilities, by 2010 the number of "special education" students had skyrocketed to 1 out of 7 children, or 6.5 million. Sharon Otterman, *A Struggle to Educate the Severely Disabled*, N.Y. Times at A1 (June 19, 2010). Spending on special education quadrupled between 1970 and 2010 to $74 billion. Id. The IDEA was meant to cover 40% of these costs, but today federal spending on special education is closer to 20%. Mark Weber, Understanding Disability Law 100 (2007). Although every state now has its own version of the IDEA, most do not pick up much more of the cost, which means that localities may have to foot as much as 75% of the special education bill. As far back as 1991, for instance, a quarter of one South Dakota school district's 80% increase in budget for 1992 (roughly $125,000)

was due to costs associated with one autistic student. Sam Allis, *The Struggle to Pay for Special Ed.*, TIME, November 4, 1996, at 82–83.

Can parents be asked to defray at least part of the costs? Given IDEA's stipulation that education of eligible children be "free," the short answer is no. In fact, as *Deal* indicates, school districts must reimburse parents for reasonable costs incurred as a result of the school district's failure to abide by the IDEA. In *School Comm. of Town of Burlington v. Department of Educ. of Mass.*, 471 U.S. 359, 105 S.Ct. 1996, 85 L.Ed.2d 385 (1985), the Supreme Court held that the school district even has to reimburse parents for the costs of *private* placement subsequently found to be more appropriate than the public school placement advocated by the school district. In *Florence County Sch. Dist. Four v. Carter ex rel. Carter*, 510 U.S. 7, 15, 114 S.Ct. 361, 126 L.Ed.2d 284 (1993), the Court extended *Burlington* in requiring reimbursement for placements in schools that are *not approved* by the state educational authority. Accord, *Forest Grove School Dist. v. T.A.*, 557 U.S. 230, 129 S.Ct. 2484, 174 L.Ed.2d 168 (2009). However, if the parents place their child in a private facility unilaterally, without working with the state to produce an IEP, reimbursement may not be required. See, e.g., *Tucker v. Calloway County Bd. of Educ.*, 136 F.3d 495 (6th Cir.1998).

As a counter to concerns about costs, consider this language from the sponsors of the original Education Act:

> [P]ublic agencies and taxpayers will spend billions of dollars over the lifetimes of [children covered by the Act] to maintain such persons as dependents and in a minimally acceptable lifestyle. With proper education services, many would be able to become productive citizens, contributing to society instead of being forced to remain burdens. Others, through such services, would increase their independence, thus reducing their dependence on society.

S.Rep. No. 94–168, at 9 (1975). More is said about the relevance of costs to coverage under the IDEA in the next section.

5.   *Procedures.* As *Rowley* and *Deal* note, the primary mechanism for implementing the IDEA is the Individualized Education Plan (IEP). The IEP is supposed to be the product of a multidisciplinary team composed of a professional who is knowledgeable about the child's suspected disability (e.g., an occupational or physical therapist or school psychologist), as well as the child's teacher and parents and, "whenever appropriate," the child. In *Deal*, the court finds that Zachary's education was "predetermined" because the parents were denied "meaningful" participation in the IEP process. Given the fact that the parents were involved in that process, how could the court arrive at that conclusion? According to the court, the absence of Deal's regular education teacher from the IEP procedure was also a non-technical violation of the IDEA, despite the presence of the principal and others familiar with the regular education process (see note 15). Why?

Under the IDEA, the team must rely on multiple sources. The IDEA specifically provides that "intelligence tests may not form the only basis for an evaluation," nor should placement decisions "be based on tests alone, but should include at least one other evaluation source, such as a teacher's observation of the child's classroom performance." 20 U.S.C. § 1412(a)(6)(B). Assume that a child scores in the intellectual disability range on an intelligence test. Can a court nonetheless find that the child is not eligible for IDEA benefits based on good evidence from the school that the child's "classroom performance" is satisfactory?

The 2004 reauthorization of the Act made clear that the IEP need only be revised once a year, unless the parties agree otherwise, and must provide annual goals that are "measurable" (consistent with the results-oriented provisions of the No Child Left Behind Act of 2001). Thus the IEP must include sections on (1) the child's present level of educational performance; (2) measurable annual goals; (3) the special education and related services to be provided to the child; (4) the extent, if any, to which the child will not participate with nondisabled children in the regular classroom; (5) any individual modifications in the administration of assessments that are needed for the child to participate in an assessment; (6) the projected dates for the beginning and duration of services; (7) needed transition services at applicable ages; and (8) how the child's progress toward the annual goals will be measured. See Gary Melton et al., Psychological Evaluations for the Courts: A Handbook for Mental Health Professionals and Lawyers 569 (3d ed. 2007).

If the parents are dissatisfied with the IEP process they can ask for an independent evaluation at school expense or go directly to a hearing; even if the parents lose at this hearing, they may request an independent evaluation. If the parents lose in the administrative process, they can take the issue to the courts. 20 U.S.C. §§ 1414(e)(f); 1414(a)(2). As *Deal* demonstrates, these proceedings can be prolonged and expensive. The Supreme Court has held that the parents bear the burden of proof in such proceedings, *Schaffer ex rel. Schaffer v. Weast*, 546 U.S. 49, 126 S.Ct. 528, 163 L.Ed.2d 387 (2005), and must bear the cost of non-attorney expert fees, *Arlington Cent. Sch. Dist. v. Murphy*, 548 U.S. 291, 126 S.Ct. 2455, 165 L.Ed.2d 526 (2006). If the parents prevail, the state must pay the parents' attorney's fees; if the parents lose, they must pay the state's attorney's fees if their suit is determined to have been frivolous or brought for an improper purpose. 20 U.S.C. § 1415(i)(3)(B). In *Dellmuth v. Muth*, 491 U.S. 223, 242, 109 S.Ct. 2397, 2402, 105 L.Ed.2d 181 (1989), the Court also limited, on Eleventh Amendment grounds, the ability of private litigants to obtain money damages from the state. Some lower courts have held that even injunctive relief from the state is not available under the IDEA. See *Pace v. Bogalusa City Sch. Bd.*, 325 F.3d 609 (5th Cir. 2003). Of course, school districts, which are not agencies of the state, may still be enjoined and sued for damages under the IDEA. Chapter Twelve (pp. 1446–1447) describes the eleventh amendment defense in more detail.

6.   *IDEA's interaction with other sources of law.* Before the IDEA was enacted, a few courts had held that the Due Process and Equal Protection

clauses of the U.S. Constitution entitled people with disabilities to free and appropriate public-funded education and training. See, e.g., *Pennsylvania Ass'n for Retarded Citizens v. Pennsylvania*, 343 F.Supp. 279, 313 (E.D. Pa. 1972); *Mills v. Board of Education*, 348 F.Supp. 866 (D.D.C. 1972). Statutes other than the IDEA might also provide a basis for obtaining special educational services. In 1973 Congress passed the Rehabilitation Act which, in section 504, prohibits discrimination on the basis of disability in providing federally-funded public education. In *Smith v. Robinson*, 468 U.S. 992, 104 S.Ct. 3457, 82 L.Ed.2d 746 (1984), the Supreme Court held that the Education Act, enacted after these developments, was meant to be the exclusive avenue for claims of disability discrimination in public education. But Congress superseded that decision by passing the Handicapped Children Protection Act of 1986, which provides, subject to an exhaustion requirement, that rights, procedures and remedies available under the Constitution, section 504, and other federal laws are not restricted by the IDEA. 20 U.S.C.A. § 1414(l). That provision was subsequently also extended to the Americans with Disabilities Act, passed in 1990, which like section 504 of the Rehabilitation Act, prohibits discrimination in the education context (both statutes are discussed in detail in Chapter Twelve).

Section 504 and the ADA apply to post-secondary education as well as pre-school, elementary and high school education, and both statutes prohibit discrimination against all school-age children with disabilties, even those who do not require special education programs. Both statutes can therefore provide remedies (including a "reasonable accommodation" of the disability) in contexts or situations where the IDEA does not. From age 9 onward, Section 504 and the ADA cover a wider array of disabilities than the IDEA, including: children with alcohol and drug addiction, children with ADHD, children with AIDs, and children who have no present symptoms but have a history of disorder, are regarded as having a disorder, or are asymptomatic because of treatment. The 2008 amendments to the ADA expand the definition of disability in other ways. See Chapter Twelve. However, the anti-discrimination statutes also allow school systems to argue against proposed interventions on grounds that they would constitute a fundamental alteration or create undue hardship, defenses which are not available under the IDEA.

Despite this last limitation, Section 504 and the ADA could become the primary vehicle for ensuring that children with disabilities receive a free, appropriate education. See Mark Weber, *Procedures and Remedies Under Section 504 and the ADA for Public School Children with Disabilities*, 32–2 J. Nat' Assoc. Administrative Law Judiciary 611, 615 (2012) (making this assertion). Section 504 regulations define appropriate education as "the provision of regular or special education and related aids and services that are designed to meet the individual educational needs of handicapped persons as adequately as the needs of non-handicapped person are met." 34 C.F.R. § 104.33(b)(1). At least one case has suggested that the "as-adequately-met" standard requires that the depth and quality of services provided children with disabilities be comparable to those provided children without disabilities, and that this standard is higher than *Rowley's* "some benefit" standard. *Mark H. v. Lemahieu*, 620 F.3d 1090 (9th Cir. 2010). A Department of Education opinion also indicates that Section 504 recognizes no cost-limit in the elementary and high school contexts. See Weber, supra, at 622. However, the Department's regulations also state that "[i]mplementation of an [IEP] developed in accordance with [the IDEA] is one means of meeting the [as-adequately-met] standard." 34 C.F.R. § 104.33(b)(2) (2012). Does it make sense to have different definitions of disability for the IDEA and anti-discrimination law? If the definitions of disability and the age-coverage were the same, would or should anti-discrimination law add anything to the protections already provided by the IDEA? Would the Deals have an even stronger case?

B. MAINSTREAMING

In enacting the predecessor to the IDEA in 1975, Congress signaled a clear preference for the educational "mainstreaming" of handicapped children. The statute barred placement in a special class or school unless the nature or severity of the handicap was such that regular classroom education could not be achieved satisfactorily. 20 U.S.C. § 1412(5)(B). Although this language was relatively strong, the 1990 amendments to the Act again emphasized that "mainstreaming" is a priority.

The original preference for "mainstreaming" was a response to the previously common practice of segregating handicapped children in often-ill-equipped special classrooms or schools, without considering whether they might attend and even flourish at regular schools. Congress's 1990 reiteration of mainstreaming's priority was probably a reaction to research showing that, even after passage of the IDEA, most children covered by the Act were still being educated in separate classes (albeit usually on a regular school campus). For instance, one study found that 74% of all eligible children received their education in "pull-out" classes. See, e.g., Alan Gartner & Dorothy Lipsky, *Beyond Special Education: Toward a Quality System for All Students*, 57 Harv. Educ. Rev. 367 (1987). In another district, only three to seven percent of the students with disability were assigned to regular academic classes, with mainstreaming occurring only in such subjects as art, music, and physical education. Janet Sansone & Naomi Zigmond, *Evaluating Mainstreaming through an Analysis of Students' Schedules*, 52(5) Exceptional Children 452 (1986).

BOARD OF EDUC., SACRAMENTO CITY UNIFIED SCHOOL DIST. V. HOLLAND

Eastern District, California, 1992.
786 F.Supp. 874.

LEVI, DISTRICT JUDGE

[I]

. . . Rachel Holland is a nine year old girl who is moderately mentally retarded. She has an I.Q. of 44 and on academic testing functions at about the level of a four year old child. . . . Rachel attended a variety of special education programs provided by the District from 1985 until 1989. While Rachel was in special education classes provided by the District, she spent a small part of each day with nonhandicapped children. For the period from 1987 through 1989, Rachel received no more than approximately one hour per day of integration with a regular class. Her parents repeatedly sought, with little success, to increase the amount of time Rachel spent in regular classrooms. In the fall of 1989, the Hollands requested that Rachel be placed full-time in a regular classroom for the 1989–90 school year. The District rejected this request and offered only special education placements for Rachel. Later, after mediation, the District proposed a placement for Rachel that included some integration into a regular classroom. The proposed placement would have divided Rachel's time between a regular class for nonacademic activities—such as art, music, lunch, and recess—and a special education class of handicapped children for all academic subjects. This would have required moving Rachel at least six times each day between the two classes. The Hollands rejected the District's proposals and entered Rachel in a regular kindergarten class at the Shalom School, a private school. Rachel has remained at the Shalom School in regular classes and is now in second grade. She is assisted by a part-time aide who sits by her in the classroom.

Although unable to agree on a placement for Rachel, the District and the Hollands, through mediation, agreed on an Individualized Education Program for Rachel. The IDEA requires such a program, known as an IEP, for each handicapped child and requires that it be reviewed at least annually. See 20 U.S.C. § 1401(19). Because of the dispute between the District and the Hollands, Rachel's IEP has not been revised since January 1990. Rachel's 1990 IEP stresses language and communication goals. The agreed objectives include: speaking in four or five word sentences; repeating instructions of complex tasks; initiating and terminating conversations; verbally stating her name, address, and telephone number; participating in a personal safety program with classmates; developing a 24–word sight vocabulary; counting to 25; printing her first and last name and the alphabet; playing cooperatively; participating in lunch without teacher supervision; identifying upper and lower case letters and sounds associated with them; and following her schedule of daily activities.

The Hollands appealed the District's placement decision to a state hearing officer, as provided by the IDEA. See 20 U.S.C. § 1415(b)(2). The District's position at the hearing, as here, was that Rachel is too severely handicapped to benefit from a full time placement in a regular class.

* * *

II

The Individuals with Disabilities Education Act, which governs this lawsuit, provides federal funds to states for the education of handicapped children. *Board of Educ. v. Rowley*, 458 U.S. 176, 179, 102 S.Ct. 3034, 3037, 73 L.Ed.2d 690 (1982). If a state elects to receive these funds, the Act requires that the state adopt certain procedures and practices in the education of the handicapped. The IDEA requires that each handicapped child be provided a free appropriate education, and be educated "to the maximum extent appropriate" with children who are not handicapped. 20 U.S.C. 1412(1) and (5); see 20 U.S.C. 1401(a)(1) (broadly defining "handicapped"). The free appropriate education requirement is satisfied if "personalized instruction is being provided with sufficient support services to permit the child to benefit from the instruction, and other items of the definitional checklist are satisfied." Rowley, 458 U.S. at 189, 102 S.Ct. at 3042.

The second requirement, that each child be educated with non-handicapped children to the maximum extent appropriate, is the basis of the dispute in this case. The Act requires each state receiving federal funds to establish

> procedures to assure that, to the maximum extent appropriate, handicapped children . . . are educated with children who are not handicapped and that special classes, separate schooling, or other removal of handicapped children from the regular educational environment occurs only when the nature or severity of the handicap is such that education in regular classes with the use of supplementary aids and services cannot be achieved satisfactorily.

20 U.S.C. § 1412(5)(B). The placement of handicapped children in regular classrooms "to the maximum extent appropriate" is sometimes referred to as "mainstreaming" or as placement in the "least restrictive environment." See 34 C.F.R. § 300.550. The Act "has a strong preference for mainstreaming" which rises to the level of a rebuttable presumption. *Daniel R.R. v. State Bd. of Educ.*, 874 F.2d 1036, 1044–45 (5th Cir.1989). The Act also views each handicapped child as having unique needs entitled to individualized consideration. See 20 U.S.C. § 1400(c), 1401(a)(16) & (19). Thus, the decision as to whether any particular child should be educated in a regular classroom setting, all of the time, part of

the time, or none of the time, is necessarily an inquiry into the needs and abilities of one child, and does not extend to a group or category of handicapped children, as the District suggests. See *Daniel R.R.*, 874 F.2d at 1048 ("our analysis is an individualized, fact-specific inquiry").

III

In considering whether the District has proposed a placement for Rachel that complies with the Act, the court must determine what is meant by the requirement that handicapped children be mainstreamed "to the maximum extent appropriate." Because the Act does not define this requirement, cases interpreting the Act guide the court's analysis. The federal appellate courts have recognized the following factors as relevant to determining if a placement is appropriate: (1) the educational benefits available to the child in a regular classroom, supplemented with appropriate aids and services, as compared to the educational benefits of a special education classroom; (2) the non-academic benefits to the handicapped child of interaction with nonhandicapped children; (3) the effect of the presence of the handicapped child on the teacher and other children in the regular classroom; and (4) the costs of supplementary aids and services necessary to mainstream the handicapped child in a regular classroom setting. *Greer v. Rome City Sch. Dist.*, 950 F.2d 688, 697 (11th Cir.1991); *Barnett v. Fairfax County Sch. Bd.*, 927 F.2d 146, 153–54 (4th Cir.), cert. denied, 502 U.S. 859, 112 S.Ct. 175, 116 L.Ed.2d 138 (1991); *Daniel R.R.*, 874 F.2d at 1048–50; *Roncker v. Walter*, 700 F.2d 1058 (6th Cir.), cert. denied, 464 U.S. 864, 104 S.Ct. 196, 78 L.Ed.2d 171 (1983).

As to the first factor, if the child's disabilities are so severe that he or she will receive little or no academic benefit from placement in a regular education class, then mainstreaming may not be appropriate. *DeVries v. Fairfax County Sch. Bd.*, 882 F.2d 876, 879 (4th Cir.1989) (disparity between cognitive levels of handicapped 17–year old and non-handicapped peers so great that 17–year old would be simply "monitoring" regular classes). However, the Act's requirement of integration, based on recognition of the non-academic value of such integration, is not overcome by a showing that a special education placement may be academically superior to placement in a regular classroom. *Roland v. Concord School Comm.*, 910 F.2d 983, 993 (1st Cir.1990), cert. denied, 499 U.S. 912, 111 S.Ct. 1122, 113 L.Ed.2d 230 (1991) (citing *Roncker*, 700 F.2d at 1063); *Norton Sch. Comm. v. Massachusetts Dept. of Educ.*, 768 F.Supp. 900, 910 (D.Mass.1991). The Act's presumption in favor of mainstreaming requires that a handicapped child be educated in a regular classroom if the child can receive a satisfactory education there, even if it is not the best academic setting for that child. Further, in considering the relative educational benefits available in integrated and non-integrated settings, the school district must demonstrate that it has considered "whether supplemental aids and services would permit satisfactory education in the regular classroom." *Greer*, 950 F.2d at 696. Only if the child cannot receive a satisfactory education in a regular education class, even if appropriate support services are offered, should the child be placed in a special education class. See *Roncker*, 700 F.2d at 1063.

The second factor addresses the significant non-academic benefits a handicapped child may receive from exposure to nonhandicapped peers. This factor reflects the fundamental purpose of the IDEA's mainstreaming requirement. A handicapped child may benefit from language and behavior models provided by nonhandicapped children. See *Daniel R.R.*, 874 F.2d at 1049 ("[T]he language and behavior models available from nonhandicapped children may be essential or helpful to the handicapped child's development. In other words, although a handicapped child may not be able to absorb all of the regular education curriculum, he may benefit from nonacademic experiences in the regular education environment."); accord, *Greer*, 950 F.2d at 697; *Liscio v. Woodland Hills Sch. Dist.*, 734 F.Supp. 689, 702 (W.D.Pa.), aff'd w/o op., 902 F.2d 1561 (3d Cir.1990) (partial integration appropriate where child "benefits from his interaction with non-handicapped peers . . . and enjoys such interaction"). Moreover, the non-academic benefits of mainstreaming a child are closely related to the academic benefits. See *Greer*, 950 F.2d at 697. For example, a child may be better able to learn academic subjects because of improved self-esteem and increased motivation due to placement in regular education.

The third factor addresses the possible negative effects of placing a handicapped child in a regular classroom. The child may be disruptive to other children or may unreasonably occupy the teacher's time to the detriment of other students. *Daniel R.R.*, 874 F.2d at 1049. If other children are disadvantaged by the presence of the handicapped child, mainstreaming is not appropriate. Id. When evaluating the burden that would be created by placing a handicapped child in a regular education class, the school district must consider all reasonable means to minimize the demands on the teacher:

> A handicapped child who merely requires more teacher attention than most other children is not likely to be so disruptive as to significantly impair the education of other children. In weighing this factor, the school district must keep in mind its obligation to consider supplemental aids and services that could accommodate a handicapped child's need for additional attention.

Greer, 950 F.2d at 688. A teacher's aide can minimize the burden on the teacher if the handicapped child is not disruptive but needs special assistance. This factor weighs against placing a handicapped child in regular education only if, after taking all reasonable steps to reduce the burden to the teacher, the other children in the class will still be deprived of their share of the teacher's attention.

Finally, a school district may properly consider cost as a factor in making placement decisions.

> The school district must balance the needs of each handicapped child against the needs of other children in the district. If the cost of educating a handicapped child in a regular classroom is so great that it would significantly impact upon the education of other children in the district, then education in a regular classroom is not appropriate.

Greer, 950 F.2d at 697; see *Barnett*, 927 F.2d at 154; *Roncker*, 700 F.2d at 1063 (cost a factor because excessive spending on one handicapped child may deprive other handicapped children). Only where the cost of placing a handicapped child in regular education will significantly affect other children in the district will this factor weigh against placement in a regular classroom.

In addition to the four factors discussed above, the District urges the court to consider the extent of curriculum modification as a distinct factor. But modification of the curriculum for a handicapped child, even dramatic modification, has no significance in and of itself. The IDEA, in its provision for the IEP process, contemplates that the academic curriculum may be modified to accommodate the individual needs of handicapped children. Curriculum modification becomes significant only if it bears upon the factors already noted. For example, modification of the curriculum may place undue burdens on the teacher both because to modify the curriculum is time consuming and to teach, in effect, two classes in one room could prove impossible. Also, a drastically modified curriculum could deprive the handicapped child of that sense of belonging to a regular class that is important to the achievement of nonacademic benefit.

IV

The District has the burden of demonstrating that its proposed placement of Rachel in a regular classroom for slightly less than half of the day provides mainstreaming to "the maximum extent appropriate" for Rachel.[7] As discussed below, three of the four factors favor

---

[7] The statutory presumption in favor of mainstreaming has been construed as imposing a burden on the school district to prove that a child cannot be mainstreamed. Davis v. District of Columbia Bd. of Educ., 530 F.Supp. 1209, 1211 (D.D.C.1982) (school district has burden of proving that placement is appropriate).

This burden is explicit in 45 C.F.R. § 84.34, a regulation which implements the Rehabilitation Act of 1973, designed to prevent discrimination against people with handicaps in any program receiving federal funding. "A recipient [of federal funds] shall place a handicapped person in the regular educational environment . . . unless it is demonstrated by the recipient that the education of the person in the regular environment with the use of supplementary aids and services cannot be achieved satisfactorily." Although this regulation is not promulgated under the IDEA, it reflects the same strong preference for mainstreaming. Moreover, the District also bears the burden of proof because it seeks to overturn the decision of the hearing officer.

mainstreaming, and on the fourth, cost, the District has not met its burden.

A.   *Educational Benefits to Rachel.*

The first factor, the comparative educational benefits to placement in regular or special education classes, weighs in favor of placing Rachel in a regular classroom. The Holland witnesses credibly testified that all of Rachel's goals and objectives could be achieved either in the regular class with some curriculum modification, or through supplementary aids and services. Most of Rachel's IEP goals relate to communication, which the Holland witnesses testified could best be taught by exposure to other children. The District's proffered testimony was focussed primarily on Rachel's educational limitations, but did not establish that the educational opportunities available through special education were superior or equal to those available in a regular education setting.

The bulk of the evidence presented by the District related to Rachel's performance on achievement and aptitude testing conducted by the California Diagnostic Center, and observation of Rachel at school by members of the Diagnostic Center team that tested Rachel. According to the Diagnostic Center witnesses, Rachel has made no progress toward her 1990 IEP goals and derives little academic benefit from regular class placement. These witnesses further suggest that supplemental aids and services are ineffective. By contrast, the Hollands' witnesses testified that Rachel had made significant academic strides at the Shalom School. They suggest that her motivation to learn stems from the regular classroom placement and that she is learning language and other skills from modelling the behavior of her non-handicapped peers. The California Department of Education agrees with the Hollands that Rachel benefits academically from placement in a regular education class.

It is evident that the contrary assessments of Rachel's academic progress are founded in conflicting educational philosophies. The Diagnostic Center witnesses do not believe that a child with Rachel's I.Q. can be effectively educated in a regular classroom.[8] They believe that Rachel's education at this point should focus on functional skills, such as handling money, doing laundry, and using public transportation. Conversely, the Holland experts believe that all handicapped children, even children with much greater handicaps than Rachel, are best educated in regular classrooms. They believe that it is a mistake to limit Rachel's learning opportunities to functional skills.

These sharply different points of view have led the experts to different evaluations of the progress Rachel has made since placement in

---

[8]   "The perception that a segregated institution is academically superior for a handicapped child may reflect no more than a basic disagreement with the mainstreaming concept. Such a disagreement is not, of course, any basis for not following the Act's mandate." *Roncker*, 700 F.2d at 1063 (citing *Campbell v. Talladega City Bd. of Educ.*, 518 F.Supp. 47, 55 (N.D.Ala.1981)).

a regular class at the Shalom School in 1989. One example illustrates how differing educational philosophies may color perceptions. During the November 1991 assessment, one of the Diagnostic Center witnesses observed Rachel in Hebrew class. She was holding the book upside down. The witness drew the conclusion that Rachel was deriving no benefit from inclusion in the class. One of the Holland witnesses observed the same incident. This witness saw that another child helped Rachel right the book and find her place. From this incident, the witness concluded that Rachel had positive interaction with her peers that would be important to her future ability to live in society.

The court suggests no criticism of these witnesses. But because of the radically different points of view from which they start, their observations on Rachel's academic progress are by no means objective. Nonetheless, the court finds more credible the Holland witnesses' testimony concerning Rachel's academic progress. First, these witnesses have more background in evaluating handicapped children placed in regular classrooms, and they had greater opportunity to observe Rachel over an extended period of time in normal circumstances. Moreover, it appears that for much of the formalized testing by the Diagnostic Center, Rachel was uncomfortable and unhappy. Finally, to the extent that the Holland witnesses have a preference for mainstreaming, it is a preference shared by Congress and embodied in the IDEA.

Because of the conflict among the experts as to Rachel's academic progress, the testimony of her current teacher is all the more important. The District concedes that Nina Crone, Rachel's second grade teacher, is an experienced, skillful teacher. She has no partisan involvement in this controversy. Crone testified that Rachel is a full member of the second grade class. She participates in all activities. For the class as a whole, Crone's major areas of emphasis are socialization, behavior and communication. These are the same areas of emphasis in Rachel's IEP. Crone testified that Rachel was making progress on her IEP goals. For example, Crone noted that Rachel is learning one-to-one correspondence in counting. She can recite the English and Hebrew alphabets, and her communication abilities and sentence length are also improving. Crone testified that Rachel is in many ways a typical second grader. She is eager to participate in class activities and is very motivated. She has become more self-confident and independent. Crone's testimony is consistent with the testimony of Rachel's kindergarten teacher at the Shalom School. See hearing officer's op. at 5–6.

The District offered no persuasive evidence that Rachel would receive educational benefits in special education classes that are equal to or greater than those available in special education classes. Although the District's witnesses testified that many of Rachel's IEP goals could best be implemented in a special education setting, there is no empirical evidence to support this assertion. Rachel made very little progress while in special education in kindergarten. Her special education teacher testified that Rachel had an extremely slow rate of learning, poor social skills, and interacted better with adults than children. When Rachel was shuttled into a regular education class for an informal mainstreaming program, she was treated as an outsider by the non-handicapped children and derived little benefit from her short exposure to these children. The program currently proposed by the District mirrors in part the deficiencies of the previous program. The proposed program would move Rachel out of the regular class whenever academic subjects were being taught. Rachel would be moved in and out of class at least six times per day. Such a program would mark Rachel as an outsider, depriving her of the primary benefit of mainstreaming.

In short, the District has failed to meet its burden of establishing that Rachel would not receive academic benefits in regular classes and has failed to demonstrate that placement in special classes will provide equal or greater educational benefit to Rachel. Based on the record below and the supplemental evidence presented at the hearing, the court finds that Rachel receives substantial academic benefits in regular education. The court finds that all of Rachel's IEP goals could be implemented in a regular education setting with some modification to the curriculum and with the assistance of a part-time aide.

B. Non-academic Benefits to Rachel.

As discussed above, a handicapped child may derive significant non-academic benefits from education with nonhandicapped peers. The District's evidence tended to show that Rachel is not learning from exposure to other children and that she is isolated from her classmates. The Hollands' evidence supported the conclusion that Rachel has developed her social and communication skills as well as her self-confidence from her placement in regular education. As before, these differing evaluations in large part reflect the predisposition of the evaluators. The court finds the testimony by Rachel's current teacher and Rachel's mother the most credible as to the non-academic benefits Rachel derives from her placement in a regular classroom. Perhaps the strongest evidence that Rachel is gaining incidental benefits from being mainstreamed is her excitement about school and her improved self-confidence. The two witnesses who testified to Rachel's positive attitude, her mother and her teacher, are in a far better position to know and understand Rachel's emotional well-being and social development than the District's witnesses, who evaluated Rachel primarily by using standardized testing techniques. Although Rachel's mother cannot be considered an objective observer, she has had the opportunity to compare Rachel's attitude toward school when she was in special education and since she has been in regular education. She testified that since Rachel was placed in a regular class, she has been excited and enthusiastic about learning. Rachel relishes the new friendships that she has developed at the Shalom School. Because of the evidence that Rachel is developing socially from her full-time placement in a regular education class, this factor weighs in favor of placing Rachel in a regular class.[10]

C. Effect on the Teacher and Other Children.

The third factor—effect on others in the class—has two aspects. The first is whether there is detriment to the other students because the handicapped child is disruptive, distracting, or unruly. There has been no evidence presented to this court that Rachel is a discipline problem at school or distracts other children. The witnesses, including the District's, were in agreement that Rachel is an agreeable child who follows directions and is well-behaved. When Rachel works separately with her aide, it is not a distraction for the other children. The second consideration is whether the handicapped child would take up so much of the teacher's time that the other students would suffer from lack of attention. The most germane evidence on this point comes from Rachel's second grade teacher, who testified that she does not find that Rachel's presence interferes with her ability to teach the other children. Rachel's teacher testified that she was initially apprehensive about her ability to teach Rachel and the rest of the class. Now that she has had experience with Rachel, she finds that Rachel's assignment to her class is not burdensome.

Because there is no evidence of detriment to other children in Rachel's regular education classroom, this factor also weighs in favor of placing Rachel in a regular education program.

D. Cost

The question of how much it would cost to place Rachel in a regular education class with the necessary support services was vigorously contested by the District on one hand and by the California Department of Education and the Hollands on the other. According to the District witnesses, the placement that the Hollands are requesting for Rachel would cost $109,000 per year. This cost estimate is based on a full-time aide for Rachel, and also attributes to Rachel alone the cost of school-wide training programs that would benefit other students.

The District has painted an exaggerated, hyperbolic picture of what it would cost to educate Rachel in a regular classroom with appropriate support services. For example, the District claims that it would cost over

---

[10] Rachel is currently in second grade. The District asserts that Rachel should be placed in fourth grade next year so she can model age appropriate behavior. However, Dr. Sailor testified that although Rachel should be educated with children near her age, it is not necessary that there be an exact match. Rachel is no more than two years older than the children with whom she is now placed. This age difference is not so pronounced that she is learning inappropriate behavior, or is not perceived as part of the class.

$80,000 to provide school-wide sensitivity training. Yet the District does not establish that such training is necessary. And even if it is, the California Department of Education provided evidence that such training may be had for free. Nor is it appropriate to assign the total cost to Rachel when other handicapped children will benefit. Similarly, the evidence does not suggest that Rachel requires a full-time aide.[11]

In reality the cost comparison is between placing Rachel in a special class with a full-time special education teacher and two full-time aides, with approximately 11 other children, with placing her in a regular class with a part-time aide. The District has provided no evidence of this cost comparison, presumably because the difference is modest. To the extent that the special class has fewer than 12 children, and that the cost of a special education teacher exceeds that of an aide, the difference in cost will be reduced. Moreover, the California Department of Education provides free in-service training programs to assist schools that wish to fully integrate handicapped students.

The District also argues that it will lose significant funding from the state if Rachel does not spend at least 51% of her time in special education classes. Ordinarily, state funding is allocated according to a formula that is based in part on how much time a child spends in a special education class. If Rachel were moved out of special education class, the District claims it would lose funding equivalent to one teacher and three aides. However, the California Department of Education witness testified that waivers are available from the state if a school district seeks to adopt a program that does not fit neatly with funding guidelines. If a school district receives a waiver, it will not lose any funding because it places handicapped students in regular classes. The District has not applied for such a waiver. According to the California Department of Education's evidence, the District will incur little additional cost by providing full-time placement in regular education classes among the continuum of options offered to handicapped children.

Furthermore, the IDEA provides funding for the specific purpose of educating handicapped children, and envisions that those monies will be used in part to provide the supplemental aids and services that make

---

[11] The District asserts that the Hearing Officer's proposed placement in a regular second grade class with a part-time aide violates California law requiring that handicapped children receive instruction on their IEP goals from specially credentialed teachers. This argument misconceives California's credentialing requirements. Although Rachel's educational program must be supervised by an appropriately credentialed professional, there is no requirement that she learn academic subjects only from a special education credentialed teacher. Furthermore, even if California did require that handicapped children be taught only by specially credentialed teachers, it would conflict with the IDEA's mainstreaming requirement favoring education by regular teachers. Where federal law conflicts with state law, federal law prevails.

Furthermore, Cal.Educ.Code § 56101 provides that a school district can request a waiver of any provision of the Education Code necessary to implement a student's IEP. The District could apply for a waiver of the credentialing requirement, if there were one, in order to educate Rachel in a regular class.

mainstreaming possible. The funding provisions suggest that the IDEA foresees some possible increased costs due to mainstreaming. Those increased costs are permissible so long as they are not of a magnitude that will affect other programs or other handicapped children

In short, the court concludes that the cost of placing Rachel full-time in a regular class, as opposed to placing her in a special class for handicapped children, is modest if there is any additional cost at all. By inflating the costs, and failing to address the true comparison, the District does not meet its burden of proving that regular placement would burden the District funds or adversely affect services available to other children. Because the District has offered no persuasive or credible evidence in support of its claim that educating Rachel in a regular education classroom with appropriate services would be significantly more expensive than educating her in the District's proposed setting, this factor does not weigh against mainstreaming Rachel.

V

For the reasons discussed, the court finds that the appropriate placement for Rachel Holland, under the Individuals with Disabilities Education Act, is in a regular second grade classroom, with some supplemental services, as a full-time member of that class.

Children change, the educational demands on them change, and Rachel may change.[12] If Rachel does not flourish under this placement in the future, then adjustments should be made. The IDEA foresees such adjustments at the annual IEP review. But the weight of the evidence suggest that this is the appropriate placement now for Rachel Holland.

The decision of the hearing officer is affirmed.

IT IS SO ORDERED.

QUESTIONS AND COMMENTS

1.   *The definition of "mainstreaming".* Mainstreaming can be a relative term. Practically speaking, a variety of possible placements for children with disabilities are possible: state institutions; county "center" schools which are fully segregated; "self-contained" classrooms located at certain regular schools but which keep the disabled children largely segregated and apart from the general school population; self-contained classrooms located in the child's neighborhood school; splitting the child's day between placements in special classes and regular classrooms (with certain classes like art and music usually taking place in the latter); and regular classrooms. Some courts reserve the term "mainstreaming" only for the final option. See, e.g.,

---

[12] See [Lou] Brown, *How Much Time Should Students with Severe Intellectual Disabilities Spend in Regular Education Classrooms and Elsewhere?*, TASH, 1991 Vol. 16, No. 1, at 46 ("How much time should be spent in regular classes? Enough to ensure that the student is a member, not a visitor. A lot, if the student is engaged in meaningful activities. Quite a lot if she is young, but less as she approaches 21. There is still a lot we do not know.").

Thomas v. Cincinnati Bd. of Educ., 918 F.2d 618, 627 (6th Cir.1990). Most courts, however, consider any movement from the beginning of the list toward the end as a move toward "mainstreaming." Further, the regulations implementing the IDEA require states to provide a continuum of placement options, which implies that placement in a regular class is not the only conceivably acceptable option. See 34 C.F.R. § 300.551.

2. *Determining when mainstreaming should occur.* The courts have developed several methods of operationalizing the mainstreaming inquiry. Compare *Roncker v. Walter*, 700 F.2d 1058 (6th Cir.1983) to *Daniel R.R. v. State Bd. of Educ.*, 874 F.2d 1036 (5th Cir.1989). See generally, *Stacey Gordon, Making Sense of the Inclusion Debate Under IDEA*, 2006 B.Y.U. Educ. L.J. 189. The four-factor test developed in *Holland*, which was affirmed and adopted by the Ninth Circuit in *Sacramento City Unified School Dist. v. Rachel H.*, 14 F.3d 1398 (9th Cir.1994), purports to combine the factors found in the other tests. Because the *Holland* test represents a composite of the thinking of several circuits, it will be used as an organizing framework for these notes, beginning with the "educational benefit" factor.

3. *Educational benefit.* How do you evaluate the educational (as opposed to non-academic) benefits of Rachel's mainstream placement? Assume that, although both placements would meet *Rowley's* "some benefit" test, the school district is correct in its argument that Rachel would do better academically in a special education class where one-to-one and small-group instruction is more likely to occur than in a regular school placement. Does this fact matter, in light of the IDEA's preference for mainstreaming? See note 8 in *Holland*. See also *Roncker*, supra, at 1063 (where the court, stating that the student's "progress, or lack thereof . . . is not dispositive," held that the mainstreaming presumption applied to a child with intellectual disability even though he appeared to be regressing in the integrated environment).

Consider in this regard the fact that, in many cases involving the mainstreaming issue, the role of the parties is reversed: School districts prefer mainstreaming as a cost-saving measure, while parents want segregated placement in the belief that special classes will confer superior services. For instance, *Kerkam v. McKenzie*, 862 F.2d 884, 889 (D.C.Cir.1988), the parents of a child with a severe mental disability wanted to place him in a residential facility in a different state, while the school district determined that a day placement at a local school would be appropriate. While admitting that there was "little doubt" that the child would make "less progress" in the school district's program, the D.C. Circuit stated that *"Rowley* precludes our taking that factor into account so long as the public-school alternative confers some educational benefit." In *Swift II v. Rapides Parish Public School System*, 812 F.Supp. 666 (W.D.La.1993), the parents of a child with several behavioral disorders who had been hospitalized three times following altercations at school were denied a nearby residential placement on the ground that the school's program could still provide some benefit. On similar facts the court in *Hall v. Shawnee Mission School Dist.*, 856 F.Supp. 1521 (D.Kan.1994), concluded that "such a [residential] placement is not mandated by IDEA, and in fact may have been more than the district could legally choose in light of IDEA's mainstreaming goal." In all of these cases, the school preferred placement in a segregated classroom. Is there an argument that this placement is not really "less restrictive" than a residential placement?

4.   *Non-academic benefit.* In *Daniel R.R.*, supra, the court stated that "[a]cademic achievement is not the only purpose of mainstreaming. Integrating a handicapped child into a nonhandicapped environment may be beneficial in and of itself." 874 F.2d at 1049. *Holland* alludes to several specific "non-academic benefits" that might come from mainstreaming; in particular, increased self-confidence and other psychosocial skills can result from interacting with those who do not have disability. Other such benefits might be closer proximity to family (compared to placement in a residential facility) and facilitation of the child's transition to his or her community once school ends. These benefits have been compared to the benefits often ascribed to *Brown v. Board of Education*, where one rationale for barring *de jure* segregation was the belief that attending integrated schools would enhance the status and acceptance of African–Americans. Analogously, the argument goes, people with mental disability should attend school with the rest of the populace, or prejudice against them will be perpetuated and their position in society will remain precarious.

Does the analogy work? Professor Minow has argued that discrimination based on perceived differences usually does not depend upon the extent to which those who are different are physically integrated with the rest of the population. Martha Minow, *Learning to Live with the Dilemma of Difference: Bilingual and Special Education*, 48 Law & Contemp. Probs. 157 (1985). Just as segregation can stigmatize people with mental disability by marking them as different, incautious integration might stigmatize them by making their difficulties painfully obvious. Minow suggests this "dilemma of difference" can be overcome through integration, but only if differences are treated as aspects of the community's identity rather than as evidence of inequality or lower status. For example, rather than singling out the deaf child who has been mainstreamed by providing her an interpreter or requiring her to attend special classes after regular hours, the entire class could be taught sign language. This approach, Minow asserts, would be effective in "making the hearing-impaired child's difference no longer signify stigma or isolation while still responding to that difference as an issue for the entire community." Id. at 208. As another example, Minow suggests that all students, not just those who are handicapped, spend different days or portions of different days in different settings, with different mixes of children and teachers. As she states, "a real mix of special classes could modulate the implicit hierarchy of such extra classes, and diminish the implication that difference resides in the unusual student rather than in all the students." Id. at 209.

Is Minow's proposal realistic when applied to children who are emotionally disturbed or have intellectual disabilities? If her proposal cannot be implemented effectively, should the "dilemma of difference" lead to a more cautious approach to mainstreaming? Consider this comment:

> Children only qualify for assistance under the IDEA if they are not able to attain adequate educational success under the regular education program. Each child needs an IEP because a regular program does not meet their educational needs. Why, then, would we presume that the regular classroom is the best program for them? If anything, we might presume that the regular classroom poses problems for these children such that a school district should have to demonstrate that it has made significant and effective changes to the regular classroom before placing a child with a disability in that environment. [In fact,] the empirical literature regarding children with mental retardation, emotional impairments, or learning impairments does not support an integration presumption. Instead, these studies suggest that such children often benefit from education by special education teachers for at least some of the day and often attain more educational benefits when not in a fully inclusive environment.

Ruth Colker, *The Disability Integration Presumption: Thirty Years Later*, 154 U. Pa. L. Rev. 789, 796–97, 835 (2006). Compare Wayne Sailor & Blair Roger, *Rethinking Inclusion: Schoolwide Applications*, 86 Phi Delta Kappan 503 (2005) (outlining improvements in integrative services and describing potential benefits to students with disabilities).

In this regard, how much weight should be given to the extent to which a placement provides an opportunity for interaction with non-handicapped children? In *School District of Kettle Moraine v. Grover*, 755 F.Supp. 243 (E.D.Wis. 1990) the parents wanted their 16–year–old child with "Downs Syndrome" (trisomy 21) to be placed in a segregated school for those with intellectual disabilities rather than in a special education class. They asserted that most of the child's disabled friends from her previous school would be matriculating at the segregated school, that the integrated environment at the regular school might be hostile and insensitive to their daughter and thus interfere with her education, and that the Special Olympics program at the segregated school would be superior to what the integrated school would offer. They also noted that integration at the regular school would only occur in art, physical education, chorus, and marketing and that education at the regular school was more regimented that its segregated counterpart. The court denied their request, leaning heavily on the school district's experts, who testified that the child's "socialization needs could be met only at [the integrated school] because only that school would provide [her] with any opportunities to interact with age-appropriate non-handicapped peers," opportunities which were "essential for her social development." Id. at 247. If mainstreaming is the only way to satisfy a particular child's socialization needs should a disabled child who has been mainstreamed in a regular classroom be automatically promoted through each grade so as to enable continued interaction with children of the same age? See, e.g., *Mavis v. Sobol*, 839 F.Supp. 968, 974 (N.D.N.Y. 1993) (child with moderate retardation advanced through sixth grade so as not to be "too far removed from her chronological peers").

If placement outside the regular school system is the only means of meeting the some benefit test, does the "non-academic benefit" of being close to one's original community and family dictate that placement be in one's own community? In *Todd D. v. Andrews*, 933 F.2d 1576 (11th Cir.1991), the district court upheld a decision by the local school district and the state to place the child in an out-of-state psychiatric facility, given the lack of such a facility in Georgia; the court opined that failing to do so would place on the state "the obligation to establish facilities in every community of Georgia in which a handicapped child preparing for discharge resides." Id. at 1581. The Eleventh Circuit reversed the district court's holding, which it characterized as a conclusion that Todd "need not be placed in a facility in proximity to his home community." Id. at 1584. It pointed to federal regulations providing that when determining the least restrictive educational environment the agency is required to consider the proximity of the facility to the child's home. 34 C.F.R. § 300.552 (1989). The Eleventh Circuit also noted that Todd's IEP specifically called for "transition" into the Georgia community in the county in which he lived. Id. at 1582. Thus, the district court's holding was "clearly not in line with [the Act's] requirement that each handicapped child's IEP be crafted to meet that child's individual needs. . . . Todd must . . . be placed at a facility close enough to his home community to allow implementation of his transition goals." Id. The Eleventh Circuit went on to hold that if the county did not have such facilities, the state was ultimately obligated under the statute to provide them. Id. at 1582–83.

Does *Todd D.* create a statutory right to force creation of community services for children covered by the IDEA? Compare this case to *Lelsz v. Kavanagh's* treatment of the argument that the Constitution requires creation of less restrictive alternatives for institutionalized persons and to *Olmstead v. L.C.'s* treatment of a similar argument under the Americans with Disabilities Act (see pp. 1313–1316 & 1318–1326).

5.   *Effects on the class.* The district court in *Holland* found that neither Rachel's presence nor the presence of an aide had an adverse effect on the class. Given the fact that Rachel could not learn the same material as the rest of the class, at least as readily, wouldn't the teacher have to spend more time with her, to the detriment of the other students? Or if an aide picks up the slack, wouldn't that conflict with the IDEA's requirement that instruction be by regular teachers (see note 11 of the opinion)?

In some cases involving assaultive behavior and the like, the child with disability is clearly disruptive and the school may seek to have the student suspended (temporarily) or expelled (permanently). Under Supreme Court case law construing the due process clause, the typical disruptive student may be suspended for ten days after being allowed to tell his or her side of the story; if expulsion is sought, more process, including counsel and an impartial hearing officer, is required, although the suspension may continue pending the proceeding. *Goss v. Lopez*, 419 U.S. 565, 95 S.Ct. 729, 42 L.Ed.2d

725 (1975). In *Kaelin v. Grubbs,* 682 F.2d 595 (6th Cir.1982), the court held that this procedure would be inadequate where disabled students are concerned. According to the court, "one of the principal features of the [IDEA] is the concept of individualized educational planning for handicapped children. This concept would be eviscerated if school officials could expel handicapped children using traditional expulsion procedures." Id. at 602. Thus, it held that any change in placement must take place through the IEP process, which is considerably more elaborate than the usual expulsion process. In *Honig v. Doe,* 484 U.S. 305, 108 S.Ct. 592, 98 L.Ed.2d 686 (1988), the Supreme Court appeared to concur with the position adopted in *Kaelin* with respect to expulsions (although it held that suspensions did not require special process). The Court added that, in view of the IDEA's "stay put" provision, 20 U.S.C. § 1415(e)(3), which requires keeping the child in his or her current placement pending review of changes in placement, the typical practice of barring school access to suspended students pending the outcome of the expulsion proceeding was also inappropriate, unless the child's parents consented or the school could show that keeping the child in school "is substantially likely to result in injury either to himself or herself, or to others." Id. at 327. The 2004 amendments to the IDEA allow a ten-day suspension for children with disabilities (during which time alternative services must be provided) if the school treats non-disabled children the same way. But before imposing any discipline lasting longer than ten days, the school must carry out a "manifestation determination" IEP review to determine whether the behavior was caused by the child's disability. 20 U.S.C.A. § 1415(k)(1).

The differential treatment between disabled and non-disabled children considered for expulsion occasioned the following comment, which may be generally applicable to administration of the IDEA:

> By training and inclination, the administrator views rules as tautological, gaining their meaning from their mere existence and the need for order. To create multiple exceptions to these rules for handicapped students is to challenge the entire structure within which rules operate. He is forced to operate two systems within the same school: one based on rules and structure, the other on standards and flexibility. Faced with [this situation], he may attempt to resolve the problem by asserting the norms of the dominant system over those of the subordinate system. When he does, he conflicts with the statute and litigation results.

Kevin Hill, *Legal Conflicts in Special Education: How Competing Paradigms in the Education for All Handicapped Children Act Create Litigation,* 64 Det. C.L.Rev. 129, 153 (1986). Perhaps partly for this reason, the 2004 amendments to the IDEA narrowed the scope of the stay-put provision by giving the local education agency the authority to immediately remove a child who has inflicted "serious bodily injury" or possessed a weapon or illegal drugs to an interim placement for not more than 45 days. 20 U.S.C. § 1415(k)(1)(G).

One possible broader benefit of mainstreaming—analogous again to the perceived benefit of racial integration—is that it can undermine prejudice that results from ignorance. Whether this actually happens is an empirical matter, however, and where disability is involved older studies indicated that it does not. See, e.g., W. N. Bender, *The Case Against Mainstreaming: Empirical Support for the Political Backlash*, 105 Educ. 279 (1985) (discussing negative attitudes expressed by teachers and peers involved in mainstreaming); Marty Abramson, *Implications of Mainstreaming: A Challenge for Special Education*, in The Fourth Review of Special Education 315, 325 (Lester Mann & David A. Sabatino, eds., 1980) (indicating that children with disabilities prefer special education classes because integration and social acceptance are not linked). A 2007 review of studies evaluating mainstreaming concludes:

> Overall, the weight of evidence reviewed in this paper cannot be said to provide a clear endorsement for the positive effects of inclusion [the author's more formal term for mainstreaming] . . . Taken as a whole, and with the pre–2000 evidence, which presents a similar picture, there is a lack of a firm research base for inclusive education to support either whether this is a preferable approach in terms of outcomes, or how inclusion should be implemented. This amounts to a clear indication of the power of policies argued to be supporting children's rights (to be included) rather than of evidence of optimal practice.

Geoff Lindsay, *Educational Psychology and the Effectiveness of Inclusive Education/Mainstreaming*, 77 Brit. J. Educational Psychology 1, 16 (2007).

6.   *Costs.* The district court in *Holland* states that "only where the cost of placing a handicapped child in regular education will significantly affect other children in the district will this factor weigh against placement in a regular classroom." Is it fair to say that mainstreaming Rachel will not have a significant effect on the resources available to other children? Whatever the answer to this question, much of the foregoing material—dealing with matters ranging from the need to provide (and create) residential treatments to the need for special hearings—suggests that the IDEA as a whole is a very expensive proposition. Thus, there is a real tension between the goals of the IDEA, which is based on the premise that expenditure of resources should be individualized, and the goals of the traditional school system, which generally allocate expenditures by category.

Professor Bartlett suggests that these competing concerns can be reconciled (albeit while still spending considerably more for children with disabilities than other children) through following the "program parity" concept in allocating resources:

> Program parity requires that educational needs be identified for every child and programs hypothesized to satisfy those needs. Resource availability would then determine what portion of a child's needs could be met, and schools would adjust programs so that each child would be afforded the same portion (or relative deprivation) as others. The

purpose of this standard is to ensure that in allocating scarce resources, some students are not favored over others. More precisely, the standard ensures that decisionmakers do not disfavor members of certain targeted groups and make them absorb more than their fair share of the effects of resource scarcity.

The concept of program parity begins with the identification of 'first-rate' educational programs. A first-rate educational program is not one for which improvements cannot be imagined, but rather one that is reasonably comprehensive and which adopts the highest standards of practice among professionals in the field. There is reason to believe that such programs can be identified, at least in general categories. Theoretically, one could begin this process by defining an optimal program, and work down from there in parallel fashion for all educational programs. [The concept would then require that children with disabilities receive the same level of program within their hierarchy of programs that children without disabilities receive].

* * *

The program parity model ... mediates the tension between the need-based framework for determining educational services for the handicapped and the merit-based framework of public education. Program parity recognizes that there are differences in need and ability that will justify different treatment, but compels evenhanded consideration of the interests of both. Differences in ability between the handicapped and nonhandicapped justify neither a lower level of attention, because of the inability of the handicapped to demonstrate the same levels of "innate" ability, nor compensation for the handicapped so extensive as to eliminate as far as educationally possible the effects of that handicap without regard to resource limitations. Instead, it requires school districts to offer services based on need to the handicapped on a par with services to others whose positions in the system will still be based on merit. Merit thus retains its established place in the public education system without compromising the need-based rationale for allocating resources to the handicapped.

Katharine T. Bartlett, *The Role of Cost in Educational Decisionmaking for the Handicapped Child*, 48(2) L. & Contemp. Probs. 7, 38–43 (1985). Is the program parity concept consistent with *Rowley*?

II. SOCIAL SECURITY DISABILITY BENEFITS

A number of public programs and many private insurance plans provide compensation to persons who become disabled. Eligibility for the benefits provided by these programs is likely to turn on a determination that a disabling physical or mental impairment exists. The determination process can be complex to administer, especially in cases of psychiatric disabilities. In these cases, the determination of disability will in large part rest on individuals' reports of symptoms that can be difficult to verify objectively and that have inconsistent effects on individuals' social, academic, and vocational functioning.

This section focuses on two disability benefits programs, Social Security Disability Insurance ("SSDI") and Supplemental Security Income ("SSI"). Both of these programs were created by the federal Social Security Act and are administered by the Social Security Administration ("SSA"). SSDI and SSI provide valuable financial benefits on their own terms. SSDI and SSI are also important because, as discussed further in Section IV of Chapter One, they are respectively linked to Medicare and Medicaid eligibility.

Social Security Disability Insurance ("SSDI") is available for disabled persons who have been employed and have therefore made tax payments to the Social Security system. Eligibility for SSDI (and the amount of an SSDI payment) is therefore based on the claimant's work and earnings history. In contrast, the Supplement Security Income Program ("SSI") program is a benefit available to "aged, blind, and disabled individuals" whose income and resources fall below a certain level. Eligibility is based not on work history but on present level of financial need. The procedures and criteria used to determine whether an individual is disabled are the same under both SSI and SSDI, however. According to the Social Security Administration the number of people who sought Social Security benefits on the basis of mental disability rose from 1,346,310 in 1996 to 2,469,423 in 2008, an 80% increase. As of 2008, 3.3 million people were receiving Social Security payments for mental disabilities. Oren R. Griffin, *Social Security Disability Law and the Obstacles Facing Claimants with Mental Disabilities*, 36 Law & Psychol. Rev. 147, 186 (2012).

KOHLER V. ASTRUE

United States Court of Appeals, Second Circuit, 2008.
546 F.3d 260.

SOTOMAYOR, CIRCUIT JUDGE:

Plaintiff Kathy Kohler appeals from a decision of the United States District Court for the Northern District of New York (Sharpe, J.), dated November 3, 2006, granting the motion for judgment on the pleadings by defendant Commissioner of the Social Security Administration ("Commissioner") and affirming the Commissioner's denial of her application for Social Security Disability Insurance ("SSDI") and Supplemental Security Income ("SSI") benefits. We hold that the Administrative Law Judge ("ALJ") erred by not following the mandatory "special technique" set forth in 20 C.F.R. § 404.1520a for evaluating the severity of a mental impairment, and we cannot conclude from the current record that this error was harmless. Accordingly, we VACATE the judgment of the district court insofar as it upheld the Commissioner's decision to deny Kohler benefits and we REMAND to the district court with instructions to remand the matter to the Commissioner for further proceedings consistent with this opinion.

BACKGROUND

Kathy Kohler, who is now 51 years old, was diagnosed with bipolar disorder in 1992. She applied for SSDI and SSI benefits on March 25, 2002, asserting that her mental impairment constituted a disability preventing her from engaging in substantial gainful employment. Her application was initially denied, but that decision was vacated and remanded by the United States District Court for the Northern District of New York on October 5, 2004 because of an inaudible tape of the hearing. A second hearing on Kohler's application was held by ALJ Carl Stephan on February 15, 2005. Kohler appeals from the ALJ's decision denying benefits following this hearing.

Medical History

In 1992, Kohler was hospitalized twice within about a month. On the first occasion, she was brought to the hospital by police after she broke down the door of an acquaintance's house. Initially observed to be agitated and confused, her demeanor improved with medication and she was released after two weeks. She was returned to the hospital ten days later by her husband, who reported that she was "out of control." She again was treated with medication and was discharged after approximately two weeks.

In 1996, Kohler moved from Buffalo, N.Y. to the North Country near Plattsburgh, NY, and began receiving medical services from North Star Behavioral Health Services ("North Star"). Her treating physician at North Star at all relevant times has been Naveen Achar. In addition, she was treated at North Star (and later in private practice) by Lorna Jewell, a nurse practitioner. At Kohler's initial screening exam in 1996, Achar noted that Kohler was not in distress, appeared to have a calm mood and bright affect, and was alert and oriented, with good memory, concentration, and judgment. He observed that Kohler's lithium prescription for the prior 4 years "seems to have controlled her mania and depressive symptoms." His notes indicate that Kohler's "global assessment of functioning (GAF)" was 60, and that its highest value during the preceding year was 75.[1]

---

[1]   The GAF is a scale promulgated by the American Psychiatric Association to assist "in tracking the clinical progress of individuals [with psychological problems] in global terms." Am. Psychiatric Ass'n, Diagnostic and Statistical Manual of Mental Disorders 32 (4th ed.2000). [Note from eds.: DSM–5 no longer recommends use of the GAF, reasoning that psychiatrists should distinguish clearly between mental disorders themselves and any disabilities that result from a particular disorder.] A GAF between 51 and 60 indicates "[m]oderate symptoms (e.g., flat affect and circumstantial speech, occasional panic attacks) OR moderate difficulty in social, occupational or school functioning (e.g., few friends, conflicts with peers or co-workers)." Id. at 34. A GAF between 71 and 80 indicates that "[i]f symptoms are present, they are transient and

In April 1998, Kohler was again hospitalized, for just over a week, after the staff of a hospital at which her boyfriend was being treated for injuries from a serious head-on collision found her wandering the hallways, talking to herself and acting bizarrely. She was diagnosed with mild lithium toxicity and showed improvement within 24 hours after her dosage was reduced. She was discharged with a GAF score of 65, which reflects "[s]ome mild symptoms (e.g. depressed mood or mild insomnia) OR some difficulty in social, occupational, or school functioning ... but generally functioning pretty well, has some meaningful interpersonal relationships." Am. Psychiatric Ass'n, Diagnostic and Statistical Manual of Mental Disorders 34 (4th ed.2000).

Jewell's notes from appointments with Kohler in 2000 indicate that Kohler continued to take her medications with good effect, was stable, and generally able to manage the stresses of her daily life, including stresses associated with ending a relationship of six years. After an appointment on January 3, 2001, Jewell similarly noted that Kohler was taking her medication with good effect, "appear[ed] to be stable," and was enjoying her independence.

Two weeks later, however, Kohler's condition deteriorated. On January 16, 2001, she was brought to the emergency room at the direction of Jewell, after Kohler's family reported that her behavior had become increasingly bizarre over the prior two days, and that she was agitated, talking rapidly, and unable to stop running around the house. Kohler reported that she had not been sleeping well, had missed two days of her lithium, and was experiencing symptoms such as extreme irritability and obsessive cleaning. She was given the medication Haldol to help her sleep and was sent home with her brother.

Kohler's family remained concerned about her "changed and still unstable behavior" throughout the following two weeks, leading to a telephone conference with Jewell on January 23, 2001 and an in-person appointment on January 30, 2001. At the appointment, Kohler acknowledged that she was "not doing her best and that an adjustment in medication might be called for." Jewell's notes indicate that Kohler was "not manic, but [was] perhaps approaching hypomania as indicated by her unpatterned sleeping and eating." Jewell hypothesized that the episode had been triggered by emotional stress, and suggested that Kohler might need the assistance of an "intensive case manager" ("ICM") to help organize her affairs. Kohler evidently agreed, and met with an ICM regularly for at least the next year.

---

expectable reactions to psycho-social stressors (e.g. difficulty concentrating after family argument); no more than slight impairment in social, occupational, or school functioning." Id.

Medical Evaluations

Achar, Kohler's treating physician, filled out an evaluation regarding Kohler's ability to do work-related activities on October 21, 2003. He indicated that she had only slight restriction in her ability to understand, remember, and carry out detailed instructions, and to maintain socially appropriate behavior. He further indicated that Kohler had no restriction in her ability to (a) understand, remember, and carry out short, simple instructions; (b) make judgments on simple work-related decisions; and (c) adhere to basic standards of cleanliness. Achar also reported that Kohler had no more than slight restrictions in various work-related social functions, such as interacting appropriately with the public or supervisors.

Kohler was independently evaluated by Brett T. Hartman, a psychologist, on October 9, 2003. He concluded that her prognosis was "fair, given her current stabilization of symptoms." He noted that Kohler reported a history of insomnia, but not in the previous year, and that she experienced a "variety of depressive symptoms at this time." He also noted that Kohler had reported that she "has a history of manic episodes, as recently as 1 1/2 years ago, . . . but she has not had such episodes since that time." With respect to Kohler's vocational and functional capacities, Hartman concluded:

> [I]t appears that Ms. Kohler is able to follow and understand simple directions and instructions. She is also able to perform a variety of simple and rote tasks. She has fair attention and concentration skills and a fair ability to learn new information. She also has a fair ability to make appropriate decisions at this time. Claimant may have mild difficulty performing tasks on a consistent basis. She also would appear to have mild to moderate problems performing a variety of complex tasks independently, given her mild intellectual deficits. It would also appear that she would have mild problems relating adequately to others and dealing appropriately with the normal stressors of life.

In addition, Terri Linden Bruni, a state agency psychological consultant, evaluated the record evidence and completed a psychiatric review of Kohler's condition on June 3, 2002. She concluded that Kohler had "bipolar syndrome with a history of episodic periods manifested by full symptomatic picture of both manic and depressive symptoms." She rated Kohler's degree of functional limitation as "slight" for restriction of daily activities and deficiencies maintaining concentration, persistence or pace; as "moderate" for difficulties in maintaining social functioning; and "never" for repeated episodes of deterioration, each of extended duration. Bruni evaluated Kohler to be "not significantly limited" for all indicators except three, in which she found Kohler "moderately limited": (1) ability to maintain attention and concentration for extended periods, (2) ability to complete a normal workday and work week without interruptions from psychologically-based symptoms and to perform at a consistent pace without an unreasonable number and length of rest periods, and (3) ability to interact appropriately with the general public. Bruni concluded that Kohler had good results controlling her manic symptoms with medication and that her recent mental status exams "ha[d] essentially been within normal limits on all parameters."

Employment

From approximately 1982 to 1991, Kohler worked as a housecleaner for about 30 hours per week. She has not since held steady, long-term employment.[2]

At the time of the hearing in 2005, Kohler's only employment was babysitting a child with Down syndrome once a week for approximately five hours, which she has been doing since 1996. Her two previous jobs (other than babysitting) were in the fall of 2000, when she worked as a cashier at a Citgo gas station and at an Alaskan Oil gas station, in each case for only two to three weeks. Kohler testified that she quit the Citgo job because the company wanted her to make bank deposits late at night and it made her too nervous, and that she left Alaskan Oil because she was nervous around customers and had difficulty concentrating. Kohler also worked as a baker at a supermarket for approximately three weeks in 1998, but she left that job because she "just couldn't handle it any longer."

ALJ Decision

The ALJ found that, as a result of her bipolar disorder, Kohler suffers from a "severe impairment" that limits her capacity to work. He then determined, however, that her impairment "fails to meet or equal the level of severity of any disabling condition contained in Appendix 1, Subpart P of the Social Security Regulations." The ALJ provided little analysis for this conclusion, and instead moved on to evaluate Kohler's residual functional capacity ("RFC"). The ALJ examined Kohler's medical reports, including evaluations by Achar and treatment notes by Jewell, and concluded that Kohler generally "displayed mild symptoms" that "appear well controlled" when properly medicated. Based on these medical reports, the ALJ could "identify no more than occasional problems with the claimant's capacity to understand and execute detailed instructions, her capacity to handle work stressors, and her ability to deal with others." He also found "no treating reports which would suggest that the claimant experiences more than occasional problems in social and occupational functioning." He concluded that Kohler had the RFC to

---

[2] The record indicates that Kohler also worked as a cleaner in an ice-cream and cake shop for approximately 7 months, but does not clarify when she held this job.

perform her past relevant work as a housekeeper/cleaner, and that a finding of "not disabled" was therefore required.

Kohler timely sought review of the ALJ's final determination in the district court pursuant to 42 U.S.C. § 405(g). On November 3, 2006, the district court entered judgment upholding the denial of benefits and granting the Commissioner's motion for judgment on the pleadings. Kohler timely appealed to this Court.

DISCUSSION

"When deciding an appeal from a denial of disability benefits, we focus on the administrative ruling rather than the district court's opinion." "On appeal, we conduct a plenary review of the administrative record to determine if there is substantial evidence, considering the record as a whole, to support the Commissioner's decision and if the correct legal standards have been applied." Failure to apply the correct legal standard constitutes reversible error, including, in certain circumstances, failure to adhere to the applicable regulations.

To be eligible to receive benefits, "an applicant must be 'insured for disability insurance benefits.'" Here, the parties do not contest that Kohler last met the requirements for "insured status" on March 31, 2001. Thus, Kohler must prove that she was disabled within the meaning of the Social Security Act on or before that date.

"Disability" is statutorily defined as the "inability to engage in any substantial gainful activity by reason of any medically determinable physical or mental impairment . . . which has lasted or can be expected to last for a continuous period of not less than 12 months." 42 U.S.C. § 423(d)(1)(A).[3] The Commissioner of Social Security has adopted regulations that provide a five-step framework for evaluating disability claims. They are as follows:

> The first step of this process requires the Secretary to determine whether the claimant is presently employed. If the claimant is not employed, the Secretary then determines whether the claimant has a "severe impairment" that limits her capacity to work. If the claimant has such an impairment, the Secretary next considers whether the claimant has an impairment that is listed in Appendix 1 of the regulations. When the claimant has such an impairment, the Secretary will find the claimant disabled. However, if the claimant does not have a listed impairment, the Secretary must determine, under the fourth step, whether the claimant possesses the residual functional capacity to perform her past relevant work. Finally, if the claimant is unable to perform her past relevant work, the Secretary determines whether the claimant is capable of performing any other

---

[3] The definition of "disability" is the same for SSDI and SSI benefits. *Perez v. Chater*, 77 F.3d 41, 46 (2d Cir.1996).

work. If the claimant satisfies her burden of proving the requirements in the first four steps, the burden then shifts to the Secretary to prove in the fifth step that the claimant is capable of working.

Perez, 77 F.3d at 46; see also 20 C.F.R. §§ 404.1520(a)(4), 416.920(a)(4).

In addition to the five-step analysis outlined in 20 C.F.R. § 404.1520, the Commissioner has promulgated additional regulations governing evaluations of the severity of mental impairments. 20 C.F.R. § 404.1520a. These regulations require application of a "special technique" at the second and third steps of the five-step framework, and at each level of administrative review. This technique requires the reviewing authority to determine first whether the claimant has a "medically determinable mental impairment." If the claimant is found to have such an impairment, the reviewing authority must "rate the degree of functional limitation resulting from the impairment(s) in accordance with paragraph (c)," which specifies four broad functional areas: (1) activities of daily living; (2) social functioning; (3) concentration, persistence, or pace; and (4) episodes of decompensation.[5] According to the regulations, if the degree of limitation in each of the first three areas is rated "mild" or better, and no episodes of decompensation are identified, then the reviewing authority generally will conclude that the claimant's mental impairment is not "severe" and will deny benefits. If the claimant's mental impairment is severe, the reviewing authority will first compare the relevant medical findings and the functional limitation ratings to the criteria of listed mental disorders in order to determine whether the impairment meets or is equivalent in severity to any listed mental disorder. If so, the claimant will be found to be disabled. If not, the reviewing authority will then assess the claimant's residual functional capacity.

Importantly, the regulations require application of this process to be documented. At the initial and reconsideration levels of administrative review, a medical or psychological consultant generally will complete a standard document, known as a Psychiatric Review Technique Form ("PRTF"). Until 2000, the regulations also required the ALJ to complete a PRTF and attach it to his decision. While the regulations no longer require the ALJ to complete that standard form, they do require the ALJ's written decision to reflect application of the technique, and explicitly provide that the decision "*must* include a specific finding as to

---

[5] "Episodes of decompensation are exacerbations or temporary increases in symptoms or signs accompanied by a loss of adaptive functioning, as manifested by difficulties in performing activities of daily living, maintaining social relationships, or maintaining concentration, persistence, or pace." United States Social Security Administration, Disability Evaluation Under Social Security § 12.00 (June 2006) available at http://www.ssa.gov/disability/professionals/bluebook/12.00-MentalDisorders-Adult.htm.

the degree of limitation in each of the functional areas described in paragraph (c) of this section." (emphasis added).

The foregoing regulations apply to the evaluation of Kohler's application, and neither party disputes that Kohler's bipolar disorder constitutes a "medically determinable mental impairment." The ALJ therefore was required to evaluate the severity of Kohler's impairment per the procedure set forth in the regulations and summarized above, and to include the necessary findings in his written decision. But the ALJ failed to adhere to the regulations, as his written decision does not reflect application of the special technique and, in particular, lacks specific findings with respect to each of the four functional areas described in § 404.1520a(c).

The consequence of noncompliance with 20 C.F.R. § 404.1520a is a matter of first impression in this Circuit. Other courts of appeals have not hesitated to remand where an ALJ's noncompliance with § 404.1520a results in an inadequately developed record with respect to the four functional categories. For example, in *Moore v. Barnhart*, 405 F.3d 1208 (11th Cir.2005) (per curiam), the Commissioner conceded that the ALJ erred by not completing a PRTF or complying with the mode of analysis set forth in 20 C.F.R. § 404.1520a, but argued that remand was inappropriate because the error was harmless. The Eleventh Circuit rejected that argument, observing that "[t]he ALJ failed to even analyze or document Moore['s] condition in two of the . . . functional areas: social functioning and prior episodes of decompensation. Because the ALJ's decision lacks consideration of these factors and their impact on his ultimate conclusion as to Moore's RFC, we cannot even evaluate the Commissioner's contention that the error was harmless."

Under the previous regulations that required the ALJ to append a PRTF to its written decision, the Ninth Circuit held that failure to follow § 404.1520a requires remand "where there is a colorable claim of mental impairment." *Gutierrez v. Apfel*, 199 F.3d 1048, 1051 (9th Cir.2000). In doing so, it joined several other circuits that have remanded based on noncompliance with § 404.1520a, either under a harmless error analysis or something akin to it.

In this case, the ALJ does not appear to have evaluated each of the four functional areas, and did not record specific findings as to Kohler's degree of limitation in any of the areas. Nor did he conduct a distinct analysis that would permit adequate review on appeal even without the requisite findings. The bulk of the ALJ's decision focused on Kohler's ability to maintain concentration, persistence or pace and her periods of decompensation (or lack thereof). It addressed how Kohler's bipolar disorder restricts her daily activities or social functioning only in general terms, despite some evidence in the record that these limitations were more than mild.[7] It did not make the findings required by the regulations, but nevertheless concluded that Kohler suffered a severe impairment prior to the date she was last insured, and that this impairment "fail[ed] to meet or equal the level of severity of any disabling condition" listed in the regulations.

Effective review by this Court is frustrated by the decision's failure to adhere to the regulations. First, because the decision contains no specific findings regarding Kohler's degree of limitation in the four functional areas by which disabling conditions are rated, the Court cannot determine whether there is substantial evidence for the ALJ's conclusion that Kohler's impairment, while severe, was not as severe as any listed disabling condition. Second, the ALJ's decision discusses much of the relevant evidence primarily in the context of Kohler's residual functional capacity to perform work and not in the context of the four functional areas identified by the regulations. Thus, it is not clear whether the ALJ adequately considered the entire record when determining the severity of Kohler's impairment, or whether he might have found it to equal the severity of a listed condition had he followed the regulations and made specific findings regarding Kohler's degree of limitation in each functional area. It also is not clear whether the ALJ would have arrived at the same conclusion regarding Kohler's residual functional capacity to perform work had he adhered to the regulations.

These deficiencies are compounded by the ALJ's tendency to overlook or mischaracterize relevant evidence, often to Kohler's disadvantage. Four examples illustrate that the effects may have been material. First, the ALJ's decision does not mention the PRTF completed by Bruni in 2002. Bruni, who based her evaluation on a review of Kohler's records, rated the limitations on Kohler's social functioning as "moderate." That suggests a more negative assessment than was reached by the ALJ, who could find "no treating reports which would suggest that the claimant experiences more than occasional problems in social and occupational functioning."[8] Second, the ALJ's decision twice emphasizes that nurse practitioner Jewell wrote in February 2002 that Kohler "had been stable for several years with but one episode of mania." Jewell's notes in fact state (as the decision elsewhere acknowledges in passing) that Kohler "has been stable for the past several years with one episode of mania requir[ing] hospitalization in 1997." That modifier is important because

---

[7] For example, the PRTF completed in 2002 by Bruni reports that Kohler suffered "moderate" limitations on her social functioning.

[8] Because Bruni completed the PRTF in 2002, it evaluated Kohler's condition more than a year after she was last insured. Nevertheless, if considered appropriately and with other evidence in the record, the PRTF might have assisted the ALJ in supporting his decision because it was completed specifically to assist evaluations of Kohler's mental condition and rates her degree of limitation in the four functional areas specified by the regulations. Only the limitations on Kohler's social functioning are rated as "moderate" (or equivalent severity), and Bruni concluded that an RFC assessment was necessary.

Kohler also experienced a significant episode of mania in mid-January 2001, but that episode did not lead to overnight hospitalization. It also is important, and not mentioned by the ALJ, that the notes from Jewell's next meeting with Kohler are significantly less enthusiastic, reporting that Kohler "has been stable for the last year or so with some hypomania presentation." Third, the ALJ consistently interprets reports that Kohler's condition has been "stable" to mean that Kohler's condition has been good, when the term could mean only that her condition has not changed, and she could be stable at a low functional level. Finally, and most notably, the ALJ's decision never mentions Jewell's opinion that "if Ms. Kohler were capable of working in a sustainable manner in a fulltime position, she would have and maintain such a job." Although the ALJ was not required to give controlling weight to Jewell's opinion, because she is not a "treating source" under 20 C.F.R. § 404.1502, he should have given her opinion some consideration, particularly because Jewell was the only medical professional available to Kohler for long stretches of time in the very rural "North Country" of New York State. . . .

While we leave open the possibility that an ALJ's failure to adhere to the regulations' special technique might under other facts be harmless, the record in this case does not allow us to say that the ALJ's failure here was harmless. We can neither identify findings regarding the degree of Kohler's limitations in each of the four functional areas nor discern whether the ALJ properly considered all evidence relevant to those areas. We therefore cannot determine whether the ALJ's decision regarding Kohler's claim is supported by substantial evidence and reflects application of the correct legal standards.

CONCLUSION

For the reasons discussed, we VACATE the judgment of the district court insofar as it upheld the Commissioner's decision to deny Kohler benefits and we REMAND to the district court with instructions to remand the matter to the Commissioner for further proceedings consistent with this opinion.

QUESTIONS AND COMMENTS

1. *The five-step process.* The five-step process described in *Kohler* must be followed in every case involving a claim for Social Security benefits based on disability. On remand, how should the ALJ decide the case? The first step is to determine whether the claimant is engaged in "substantial gainful activity." Why isn't Ms. Kohler's baby-sitting job sufficient to disqualify her at this stage? Assuming she is not gainfully employed, Ms. Kohler must then demonstrate that her condition is so "severe" that it significantly limits her physical or mental ability to do basic work activities (stage two) and, if successful on that score, that the impairment is found in the SSA's "Listed Impairments" Appendix (stage three). The Appendix contains detailed

definitions of the following mental disability categories: "organic mental disorders," "schizophrenic, delusional (paranoid), schizoaffective, and other psychotic disorders," "mood disorders," "mental retardation," "anxiety disorders," "somatoform, eating, and tic disorders," "personality disorders," "psychoactive substance dependence disorders," "autistic disorder and other pervasive developmental disorders," and "attention deficit hyperactivity disorder." How would Ms. Kohler fare with respect to the second and third stages of the analysis, taking into account the four functional inquiries that are required in evaluating cases involving mental disability? Isn't the issue settled by the expert opinions that Ms. Kohler's impairment was at worst "moderate" (see, for instance, notes 7 and 8 of the opinion)? If the claimant's disorder is not severe, the fourth stage involves inquiring into the claimant's "residual functional capacity" (RFC) to perform the claimant's prior work. What was Ms. Kohler's prior work, and is she capable of performing it (see in particular note 2 of the opinion)? If the claimant is not capable of performing his or her prior work, the inquiry moves to the fifth step, where a decision is made as to whether the claimant, in light of RFC, age, education, and work experience, has the capacity to perform other work in the national economy. Here the burden shifts from Ms. Kohler to the SSA. What result if the analysis gets to this fifth stage?

As *Kohler* demonstrates, courts have resisted attempts by the SSA or ALJs to circumvent this individualized, multi-step process. In *City of New York v. Heckler*, 742 F.2d 729 (2d Cir.1984), aff'd *Bowen v. City of New York*, 476 U.S. 467, 106 S.Ct. 2022, 90 L.Ed.2d 462 (1986), the Second Circuit rejected an informal SSA policy which presumed that those whose mental impairments were not as severe as the Listed Impairments retained an RFC sufficient to perform at least unskilled work. The practical effect of the presumption had been to end the five-step process for most claimants at step three. However, the balance has not always been struck in favor of individualization. In *Bowen v. Yuckert*, 482 U.S. 137, 107 S.Ct. 2287, 96 L.Ed.2d 119 (1987), the claimant challenged step two of the five-step review procedure, arguing that, under the language of the Social Security Act, a determination of severity could not be made without consideration of the claimant's age, education, or work experience. The Court upheld the challenged regulation, noting that it increased "the efficiency and reliability of the evaluation process by identifying at an early stage those claimants whose medical impairments are so slight that it is unlikely they would be found to be disabled even if their age, education, and experience were taken into account."

2.   *The treating physician rule.* ALJs are supposed to give more weight to opinions from treating sources than from other examiners, such as consultative examiners. 20 C.F.R. § 404.1527(d)(2). The regulations note that the treating physician is "most able to provide a detailed, longitudinal picture" of the medical impairment. Id. Does Judge Sotomayor (yes, that Judge Sotomayor) pay sufficient attention to this rule?

3. *The "objective medical evidence" requirement.* The language in § 423(d) of the Social Security Act governing evidence of disability reads as follows:

> (3) For purposes of this subsection, a "physical or mental impairment" is an impairment that results from anatomical, physiological, or psychological abnormalities which are demonstrable by medically acceptable clinical and laboratory diagnostic techniques.

* * *

> (5)(A) An individual shall not be considered to be under a disability unless he furnishes such medical and other evidence of the existence thereof as the Secretary may require. An individual's statement as to pain or other symptoms shall not alone be conclusive evidence of disability as defined in this section; there must be medical signs and findings, established by medically acceptable clinical or laboratory diagnostic techniques, which show the existence of a medical impairment that results from anatomical, physiological, or psychological abnormalities which could reasonably be expected to produce the pain or other symptoms alleged and which, when considered with all evidence required to be furnished under this paragraph (including statements of the individual or his physician as to the intensity and persistence of such pain or other symptoms which may reasonably be accepted as consistent with the medical signs and findings), would lead to a conclusion that the individual is under a disability. Objective medical evidence of pain or other symptoms established by medically acceptable clinical or laboratory techniques (for example, deteriorating nerve or muscle tissue) must be considered in reaching a conclusion as to whether the individual is under a disability. . . .

How does this language apply in mental disability cases? Does the *Kohler* decision reveal whether "medically acceptable clinical or laboratory diagnostic techniques" were used in that case? Did the experts and the courts consider "[o]bjective medical evidence of . . . symptoms . . . in reaching a conclusion as to whether the individual is under a disability"? What if—as is true for most serious psychiatric disorders—no laboratory techniques exist? Are the claimant's reports and the clinician's observations (which usually constitute the full basis for making psychiatric diagnoses) sufficient? Or would a thorough record review and a detailed, structured diagnostic interview (which yield more reliable diagnostic conclusions, but which take a lot of time to do well) be required?

4. *Procedural foreclosure and the claimant with mental disability.* Claimants are supposed to file their claims within 12 months of experiencing their disability. 42 U.S.C. § 423(b). In *Tusson v. Bowen,* 675 F.Supp. 1032 (E.D.La.1987), aff'd 847 F.2d 284 (5th Cir.1988), the claimant argued that the 12–month limitation violates the Due Process Clause and the Equal Protection Clause when, because of severe mental illness, a claimant is not

capable of bringing the claim within that period. The Court rejected both arguments:

> [T]he twelve-month limitation does not violate due process principles. . . . Ordinarily, a mentally impaired person will have a caretaker of some kind but, of course, that will not always be true. Indeed, in the case at bar, Tusson was not in the care of a guardian or some other person. He was capable of taking care of most of his needs, but relied on family members for special needs. [However,] the fact that *some* mentally impaired persons cannot rely on others to file their application does not render the twelve-month limitation fundamentally unfair, arbitrary, or unreasonable. . . . Particularly when we deal with a withholding of a noncontractual benefit under a social welfare program such as this, we must recognize that the Due Process Clause can be thought to interpose a bar only if the statute manifests a patently arbitrary classification, utterly lacking in rational justification. . . . Congress' decision that the grace period should terminate at twelve months is not so arbitrary or irrational as to violate due process.

> With respect to Tusson's equal protection claim, a challenged statutory classification is presumed valid if it serves a rational means of furthering a legitimate legislative end. The Court notes that the twelve-month limit applies evenhandedly to all claimants; mentally incompetent claimants are not treated differently from other claimants. The legislative purpose for not creating an exception for the mentally impaired is clear. Application of the twelve-month period to all claimants helps to preserve the fiscal integrity of the social security trust fund. Even if the volume of such claims as Tusson's were low enough to allay concerns for financial integrity, an ever-growing corpus of government funds would need to be set aside for late-filers to insure that ample funds would be available when claimed. The Court realizes that some mentally impaired people, who are entitled to disability benefits but who cannot file for themselves or rely on others to do so, may not receive benefits to which they would be entitled upon a timely filing. However, as the Supreme Court has recognized, legislation "does not offend the Constitution simply because [it] 'is not made with mathematical nicety or because in practice it results in some inequality.'"

As discussed further in Chapter Twelve, the district court's conclusion that legislation affecting people with mental disability need only have a rational basis is in accord with more recent Supreme Court pronouncements on the constitutional status of individuals with disabilities. But does the 12–month rule have even a rational basis?

5. *Eligibility of people with addictions.* Spurred by reports that benefits recipients with substance abuse problems were using the benefits to buy drugs and alcohol, in 1994 Congress set a 36–month limit to payments for individuals with addictions and required that payments be sent to a representative payee rather than directly to the claimant. 42 U.S.C. § 423(d)(1)(A) (1994). Two years later, Congress went further, barring

eligibility of persons whose alcoholism or drug addiction is "a contributing factor material to the Commissioner's determination that the individual is disabled." 42 U.S.C. § 423(D)(2)(C). As a consequence of the amendment, an estimated 200,000 individuals lost cash and associated medical benefits. See Andrew Shaner et al., *Disability Income, Cocaine Use, and Repeated Hospitalization among Schizophrenic Cocaine Abusers: A Government– Sponsored Revolving Door?* 333 New Eng. J. Med 777 (1995).

Despite the statutory exclusion, several courts have held that addicted individuals can still receive payments if the substance abuse is caused by a covered disability. See, e.g., *Nieves v. Astrue*, 2008 WL 4277995, at *3 (D.Colo. 2008) (ALJ erred in finding that plaintiff's drug and alcohol addiction was a contributing factor to the disability determination, because the record lacked longitudinal medical or psychological evidence on the plaintiff's impairments if the substance abuse stopped). The SSA's regulation is consistent with this holding, providing that whether a person's "drug addiction or alcoholism is a contributing factor material to the determination of disability" depends on "whether we would still find you disabled if you stopped using drugs or alcohol . . . If we determine that your remaining limitations are disabling, you are disabled independent of your drug addiction or alcoholism and we will find that your drug addiction or alcoholism is not a contributing factor material to the determination of disability." 20 CFR 404.1535. Finally, some have proposed that benefits be conditioned on undergoing, and continued participation in, treatment programs. Warnecke Miller & Rebecca Griffin, *Adjudicating Addicts: Social Security Disability, The Failure to Adequately Address Substance Abuse, and Proposals for Change*, 64 Admin. L. Rev. 967 (2012). Of these four approaches to substance abuse and social security (the 1994 amendments, the 1996 amendments, *Nieves*, or Miller & Griffin's proposal), which do you prefer?

6.   *Children and social security.* The SSI program also assists disabled low-income children. Prior to 1990, the procedure for determining the eligibility of children was terminated at the third step of the five stage process: a child qualified for benefits if he or she was "not doing any substantial gainful activity" and his or her impairment matched or was medically equal to one of the specific "Listed Impairments." In *Sullivan v. Zebley*, 493 U.S. 521, 110 S.Ct. 885, 107 L.Ed.2d 967 (1990), the Supreme Court struck down this procedure. The Court emphasized that the statute granted eligibility to any child who "suffer[ed] from 'any . . . impairment of comparable severity' to one that would render an adult 'unable to engage in any substantial activity.'" Id. at 529 (citing 42 U.S.C. § 1382c(a)(3)(A) (1982 ed.)). Because the method for determining a child's disability did not include any individualized inquiry similar to the inquiry for adults, it did not meet the statutory standard that required child claimants "to receive benefits whenever their impairments were of 'comparable severity' to ones that would qualify an adult for benefits under the individualized, functional analysis contemplated by the statute and provided to adults. . . . " Id. at 539.

The SSA responded to *Zebley* by issuing regulations calling for an "individualized functional assessment" ("IFA") of each child claimant's disability. Under these regulations, if the child was not engaged in any substantial gainful activity and also had a severe impairment, the decisionmaker had to determine whether the impairment met or equaled one of the "Listed Impairments." 20 C.F.R. § 416.924(e). If one of the Listed Impairments was met or equaled, the child was deemed disabled. Id. If none of the Listed Impairments was met or equaled, the evaluation would determine whether the claimant had an impairment or impairments of comparable severity to those that would prevent any adult from engaging in substantial gainful activity. See id. § 416.924(f).

After the IFA requirement was put into place, the number of children who qualified as disabled increased substantially: while only 296,300 children received SSI disability payments in 1989, by 1995 the number had increased to almost 1 million, with children who had intellectual disabilities making up approximately 42% of those covered and children with other mental disorders 25%. Influenced by critics who alleged that parents were coaching their children to fake mental disorders, Congress reinstated, in 1996, the three-step procedure that had existed prior to *Zebley*. The new regulations provide that a child is not disabled unless the child's impairments meet, are medically equal to, or are functionally equal in severity to a "Listed Impairment." 20 C.F.R. § 416.924(d)(2) (1997). The functional equivalence standard looks at six areas of functioning in children: acquiring and using information; attending and completing tasks; interacting and relating with others; moving about and manipulating objects; caring for oneself; and health and physical being. It then asks whether the child suffers from "extreme" limitations in one area or "marked" limitation in two areas. As a consequence of this legislation, about 42% of children lost their benefits. Bazelon Center for Mental Health Law, *The Impact of Children's SSI Program Changes in Welfare Reform*, 1, 2 (Aug. 7, 1997). What is the justification for treating children differently than adults? Does the IDEA pick up the slack for those children who do not have a listed impairment or its functional equivalent?

7. *Disability determination review.* The SSA requires determinations of disability for both adults and children to be reviewed by the state agency every three years, with two exceptions. First, where a disability has been found to be permanent, that determination may be reviewed "at such times as the Secretary determines to be appropriate." Second, the Secretary may waive the three-year review requirement for a particular state and instead require the state to review an "appropriate number" of cases. Determinations of the appropriate number of cases depend upon the state's backlog of pending reviews, projected number of new applications, and staffing levels. *See* 42 U.S.C. § 421(I). Significantly, the disability review is not a de novo determination of disability. Rather, Congress has specified that the Social Security Administration be prohibited from redetermining claims in the absence of an initial finding that the recipient's medical condition has improved. 42 U.S.C § 423(f).

8.   *The interaction of disability benefits programs with the ADA.* As discussed further in Chapter Twelve, the Americans with Disabilities Act of 1990 ("ADA") seeks to integrate individuals with disabilities into the workforce by requiring employers to provide disabled individuals with "reasonable accommodations" that will enable these individuals to discharge the essential responsibilities of the jobs they seek. May people who receive Social Security benefits because they cannot work bring a claim under the ADA that an employer's refusal to accommodate their disability is discriminatory? In *Cleveland v. Policy Management Systems Corp.*, 526 U.S. 795, 119 S.Ct. 1597, 143 L.Ed.2d 966 (1999), the Supreme Court held that an ADA claim is not necessarily foreclosed in such a situation. The Court noted that since the SSA does not consider possible "reasonable accommodations" in determining SSDI eligibility, an ADA plaintiff's claim that she can perform her job *with* reasonable accommodation may well prove consistent with an SSDI claim that she cannot perform her own job (or other jobs) *without* it. Additionally, an individual might qualify for SSDI under the SSA's Listed Impairments and yet, due to special individual circumstances, be capable of performing the essential functions of her job. Or her condition might have changed over time, so that a statement about her disability made at the time of her application for SSDI benefits does not reflect her capacities at the time of the relevant employment decision.

Some commentators have nonetheless suggested that the disability benefits programs, which tend to segregate individuals with disabilities from the workforce, are at odds with the philosophy of the ADA. See, e.g., Matthew Diller, *Dissonant Disability Policies: The Tensions between the Americans with Disabilities Act and Federal Disability Benefit Programs*, 76 Tex. L. Rev. 1003 (1998). Furthermore, *Cleveland* leaves unanswered how to draw the line between an individual who is so impaired he or she cannot work at all and an individual who could work with sufficient "reasonable accommodations." Consider, for instance, whether Ms. Kohler could work if she were afforded a "reasonable accommodation" for her disability (e.g., flexible hours for counseling; shorter working hours; work breaks during depressed periods).

Some people who receive Social Security benefits or are applying for them do not want to work even if reasonable accommodations for their disability were possible and are offered. Proposals for encouraging SSI and SSDI recipients to enter or return to the workforce employ both carrots and sticks, ranging from rehabilitation and counseling services for those who seek to return to work to time limits on disability benefits for those who do not. Additionally, people with disabilities need to be assured they will not lose Medicare or Medicaid healthcare coverage if they return to work. Under the SSDI work incentive program, benefits recipients can work for a trial period of up to nine months. The Social Security Administration continues to pay benefits during this time and does not view work done during this time as evidence of a lack of disability. 20 C.F.R. § 404.1592(a) (2006). The SSI program includes a complicated scheme under which recipients can continue to qualify for "special" SSI benefits even when they have earnings above the threshold that would otherwise lead to termination from the program. See 20

C.F.R. § 416.260 et. seq. Consider how these programs interact with the ADA's provisions, examined in the next chapter.

CHAPTER 12

PROTECTION AGAINST DISCRIMINATION

■ ■ ■

Table of Sections

I.   ANTI–DISCRIMINATION LAW: AN OVERVIEW

A number of laws protect people with mental (and physical) disabilities from certain types of discrimination. The two most important of these laws are the Rehabilitation Act of 1973 and the Americans with Disabilities Act of 1990 ("ADA"). Section 504 of the Rehabilitation Act covers programs that are operated or funded by the federal government. It bars employment and other types of discrimination against a person "by reason of his or her disability," when that person is "otherwise qualified" to engage in the job or activity. 29 U.S.C. § 794(a). The ADA, amended most recently in 2008, uses similar language but is much broader in scope. It applies to non-federal employers that have more than 15 employees (Title I), public services and programs provided by state and local governments (Title II), and "public accommodations" (Title III), a broadly defined category that includes everything from private educational institutions to insurance offices and the "professional office of a health care provider." 42 U.S.C. § 12181(7)(F). Congress has granted the Equal Employment Opportunity Commission (EEOC) authority to issue interpretive regulations covering employment under Title I of the ADA, 42 U.S.C. § 12116, while the Justice Department is charged with promulgating regulations that implement Titles II and III of the ADA. 42 U.S.C. § 12134(a); id. § 12186(b).

Both the Rehabilitation Act and the ADA cover individuals who either: (1) have "a physical or mental impairment which substantially

1401

limits one or more . . . major life activities," (2) have "a record of such impairment," or (3) are "regarded as having such an impairment." 29 U.S.C. § 706(8)(B) (Rehabilitation Act); 42 U.S.C. § 12102(2) (ADA). The last two provisions "are intended to protect people who may be victimized by myths, fears, and stereotypes about certain mental or physical conditions," misperceptions that "are especially common with mental disabilities." John Parry, Mental Disabilities and the Americans with Disabilities Act: A Practitioner's Guide to Employment, Insurance Treatment, Public Access, and Housing, American Bar Association 12 (1994). Neither the Rehabilitation Act nor the 1990 version of the ADA defined "major life activity," but the EEOC regulations promulgated under the original ADA stated that major life activities included "functions such as caring for oneself, performing manual tasks, walking, seeing, hearing, speaking, breathing, learning, and working," 29 C.F.R. § 1630.2(i), and the 2008 amendments to the Act now incorporate similar language in the statute itself. 42 U.S.C. § 12101(2). If the person alleging discrimination has a disability, so defined, the court must then inquire into whether, despite the disability, the individual meets the "essential eligibility requirements" of the job or program, either without help or with a "reasonable" accommodation or modification of the job or program. Reasonable accommodations or modifications are those that can be undertaken without causing "undue burden" to the program or activity in question.

As this brief description indicates, these two anti-discrimination laws differ from other civil rights laws in three important respects. First, in contrast to people of color or women seeking relief under Title VII or the Equal Protection Clause, a claimant under the ADA or the Rehabilitation Act must prove he or she is a member of the protected group.[a] Second, while discrimination on the basis of characteristics such as race is presumptively illegal, disability-based discrimination is only illegal if the individual targeted is "otherwise qualified" to perform the job sought or participate in the desired program. Third, unlike members of other protected minority groups, individuals with disabilities can, through the reasonable accommodation requirement, demand that resources be directed toward them. Cf. Christine Jolls, *Anti-discrimination and Accommodation*, 114 Harv. L. Rev. 642 (2001) (recognizing this point, but arguing that the disparate impact strand of traditional anti-discrimination liability can resemble the reasonable accommodation requirement). Under both the ADA and the Rehabilitation Act, the

---

[a] Because only people with disabilities are protected by the statutes, so-called "reverse-discrimination" claims are not possible under the ADA. Compare 42 U.S.C. § 12201(g) ("Nothing in this act shall provide the basis for a claim by an individual without a disability that the individual was subject to discrimination because of the individual's lack of disability") to *Regents of the University of California v. Bakke*, 438 U.S. 265, 98 S.Ct. 2733 (1978) (granting relief to a white applicant who claimed he was denied admission to college because of an affirmative action program).

challenged program or activity must bear the cost of the reasonable accommodation.

During a three-year period near the turn of the century, the Supreme Court decided a number of cases that significantly limited the scope of the 1990 version of the ADA (and, given its parallel language, the Rehabilitation Act as well). In *Sutton* v. *United Air Lines*, 527 U.S. 471, 119 S.Ct. 2139, 144 L.Ed.2d 450 (1999), two severely myopic sisters claimed they were denied jobs as international pilots because of their disability despite being "otherwise qualified" given their corrected vision of 20/20. The Court held that the sisters did not have a disability for purposes of the ADA because, while seeing is a "major life activity," their vision was not impaired in its "mitigated" state. The Court emphasized that a contrary holding would be inconsistent with the congressional finding, incorporated in the ADA, that 43 million people in the United States had disabilities, after noting that, by itself, visual impairment afflicts upwards of 100 million people. The petitioners also argued that they should be covered by the ADA because they were "regarded as" having an impairment in the major life activity of working. The Court rejected this argument as well, on the ground that the airline only regarded them as unqualified to hold the single position of global airline pilot, not the entire class of related jobs that utilized their skills, such as regional pilot or pilot instructor. The same day *Sutton* was decided, the Court handed down two other decisions that came to similar conclusions. *Murphy* v. *United Parcel Service*, 527 U.S. 516, 119 S.Ct. 2133, 144 L.Ed.2d 484 (1999) (holding that a person with high blood pressure that is treatable with medication is neither impaired nor regarded as impaired); *Albertsons, Inc.* v. *Kirkingburg*, 527 U.S. 555, 119 S.Ct. 2162, 144 L.Ed.2d 518 (1999) (suggesting that a person who can compensate for his serious vision problems is not disabled under the ADA).

Three years later the Court decided *Toyota Motor Manufacturing* v. *Williams*, 534 U.S. 184, 122 S.Ct. 681, 151 L.Ed2d (2002), which further limited the scope of the ADA. Williams claimed that her carpal tunnel syndrome and other orthopedic difficulties prevented her from lifting more than 20 pounds or frequently lifting or carrying objects up to 10 pounds, and also prevented her for repetitively extending or flexing her wrists or elbows or doing overhead work. Rather than granting her an accommodation that avoided this type of work, Toyota fired her. The Supreme Court reversed the lower court's holding that Williams was disabled under the ADA. Citing the same 43 million figure it had in *Sutton*, the Supreme Court stated that the term "major life activity" and other definitions in the ADA "need to be interpreted strictly to create a demanding standard for qualifying as disabled." Thus, the proper focus in this case was not whether Williams could perform the specific manual tasks involved in her job, but whether she could perform household chores and tend to her own hygiene, because "household chores, bathing, and brushing one's teeth are among the types of manual tasks of central importance to people's daily lives." Id. at 202. In two other decisions handed down in 2002 (discussed further below), the Court granted employers greater discretion in determining whether an individual is qualified, *Chevron U.S.A. Inc. v. Echazabal*, 536 U.S. 73, 122 S.Ct. 2045, 153 L.Ed.2d 82 (2002) and limited the scope of the reasonable accommodation requirement. *US Airways, Inc. v. Barnett*, 535 U.S. 391, 122 S.Ct. 1516, 152 L.Ed.2d 589 (2002).

These decisions—in particular the "*Sutton* trilogy" and *Toyota*—met with Congressional disfavor. In 2008, Congress passed the ADA Amendments Act (ADAAA) expressly to overturn aspects of those decisions. The ADAAA removes the ADA's reference to 43 million people with disabilities as well as language in the ADA stating that people with disabilities are a "discrete and insular minority," and instead states that its aim is to "carry out the ADA's objectives . . . by reinstating a broad scope of protection." 42 U.S.C. § 12101(b)(1). Thus, the ADAAA explicitly rejects the "demanding standard" language in *Toyota*. Id. § 12010(4). It also provides that disability is to be determined without regard to the ameliorating effects of mitigating measures, other than ordinary eye glasses or contact lenses. Id. The ADAAA contains for the first time a statutory definition of the term "major life activity" and broadens its scope; of particular relevance to this chapter, the statute includes "concentrating," "thinking" and "communicating" in the list. Id. § 12012(2)(A). Finally, the ADAAA states that a person making a claim under the "regarded as" prong of disability does not need to show, as *Sutton* seemed to require, that the perceived impairment limit a major life activity. Rather, as long as the perceived impairment is not "minor or transitory (i.e. one that last less than six months)" it can form the basis for an ADA claim. Id. § 12101(3)(A). However, the ADAAA also states that a person who is disabled only under the "regarded as" prong need not be accommodated. Id. § 12201(h). It also continues to recognize that persons with disabilities who constitute a "direct threat" to others are not entitled to relief under the Act, unless a reasonable accommodation can eliminate the threat. Id. § 12113(b).

Prior to the ADAAA, ADA plaintiffs were among the least successful classes of federal litigants. See Sharona Hoffman, *Settling the Matter: Does Title I of the ADA Work?* 59 Ala. L.Rev. 305 (2008) (finding that 97% of ADA plaintiffs lose their cases). A perusal of more recent cases indicates that since passage of the ADAAA, the success rate of discrimination claims brought by people with disability has not appreciably increased, although the rationale for rejecting the claims now differs. Stephen F. Befort, *An Empirical Analysis of Case Outcomes under the ADA Amendments Act*, 70 Wash. & Lee L. Rev. ___ (2014) (finding that employers are winning fewer summary judgment motions on the disability issue and winning more often on the "qualified individual" issue). Some commentators have argued that this poor track record in the courts indicates that the ADA may have been "enacted ahead of its time, in that much of the country is not yet ready to embrace the precepts on which the ADA is premised." Bonnie P. Tucker, *The ADA's Revolving Door: Inherent Flaws in the Civil Rights Paradigm*, 62 Ohio St.L.J. 335, 337 (2001). Empirical studies of cases litigated to a final outcome suffer from selection bias, however. The evidence indicates that parties claiming ADA violations in employment cases are sometimes able to secure significant settlements, either during the EEOC's administrative proceedings (which are required under the ADA's and Rehabilitation Act's exhaustion rules, 42 U.S.C. § 12117) or at the subsequent litigation stage in federal court. See Hoffman, supra.

This chapter discusses three areas in which the ADA and the Rehabilitation Act may affect the lives of individuals with mental disabilities: employment, postsecondary education, and the licensing activities of state government agencies. (Previous chapters have discussed the ADA in connection with mental health treatment, see pp. 1318–1331, elementary and high school education, see pp. 1363–1365, and social security, see pp. 1399–1400, and Chapter One discussed anti-discrimination issues related to insurance for mental health care, see pp. 88–90). This chapter also discusses discrimination against people with mental disabilities in connection with housing. Here the most important statute is the Fair Housing Act (FHA), although Titles II and III of the ADA also cover limited classes of housing and the legal analysis under the FHA is quite similar to that under the ADA and the Rehabilitation Act. Before examining these statutes, this chapter briefly surveys the Supreme Court's equal protection jurisprudence as it applies to people with mental disabilities, which provides a constitutional backdrop for the statutory protections now available.

II. THE CONSTITUTION AND DISCRIMINATION ON THE BASIS OF MENTAL DISABILITY

CITY OF CLEBURNE, TEXAS V. CLEBURNE LIVING CENTER

Supreme Court of the United States, 1985.
473 U.S. 432, 105 S.Ct. 3249, 87 L.Ed.2d 313.

JUSTICE WHITE delivered the opinion of the Court.

A Texas city denied a special use permit for the operation of a group home for the mentally retarded [until recently, the term used to designate persons with intellectual disabilities], acting pursuant to a municipal zoning ordinance requiring permits for such homes. The Court of Appeals for the Fifth Circuit held that mental retardation is a "quasi-suspect" classification and that the ordinance violated the Equal Protection Clause because it did not substantially further an important governmental purpose. We hold that a lesser standard of scrutiny is appropriate, but conclude that under that standard the ordinance is invalid as applied in this case.

I

In July 1980, respondent Jan Hannah purchased a building at 201 Featherston Street in the city of Cleburne, Texas, with the intention of leasing it to Cleburne Living Center, Inc. (CLC), for the operation of a group home for the mentally retarded. It was anticipated that the home would house 13 retarded men and women, who would be under the constant supervision of CLC staff members. The house had four bedrooms and two baths, with a half bath to be added. CLC planned to comply with all applicable state and federal regulations.

The city informed CLC that a special use permit would be required for the operation of a group home at the site, and CLC accordingly submitted a permit application. In response to a subsequent inquiry from CLC, the city explained that under the zoning regulations applicable to the site, a special use permit, renewable annually, was required for the construction of "[h]ospitals for the insane or feeble-minded, or alcoholic [*sic*] or drug addicts, or penal or correctional institutions."[3] The city had determined that the proposed group home should be classified as a "hospital for the feeble-minded." After holding a public hearing on CLC's application, the City Council voted 3 to 1 to deny a special use permit.

CLC then filed suit in Federal District Court against the city and a number of its officials, alleging, *inter alia,* that the zoning ordinance was invalid on its face and as applied because it discriminated against the mentally retarded in violation of the equal protection rights of CLC and its potential residents. The District Court found that "[i]f the potential residents of the Featherston Street home were not mentally retarded, but the home was the same in all other respects, its use would be permitted under the city's zoning ordinance," and that the City Counsel's decision "was motivated primarily by the fact that the residents of the home would

---

[3]   The site of the home is in an area zoned "R–3," an "Apartment House District." App. 51. Section 8 of the Cleburne zoning ordinance, in pertinent part, allows the following uses in an R–3 district:

> "1. Any use permitted in District R–2.
>
> "2. Apartment houses, or multiple dwellings.
>
> "3. Boarding and lodging houses.
>
> "4. Fraternity or sorority houses and dormitories.
>
> "5. Apartment hotels.
>
> "6. Hospitals, sanitariums, nursing homes or homes for convalescents or aged, *other than for the* insane or *feeble-minded* or alcoholics or drug addicts."
>
> "7. Private clubs or fraternal orders, except those whose chief activity is carried on as a business.
>
> "8. Philanthropic or eleemosynary institutions, other than penal institutions.
>
> "9. Accessory uses customarily incident to any of the above uses. . . . " *Id.,* at 60–61 (emphasis added).

be persons who are mentally retarded." Even so, the District Court held the ordinance and its application constitutional. Concluding that no fundamental right was implicated and that mental retardation was neither a suspect nor a quasi-suspect classification, the court employed the minimum level of judicial scrutiny applicable to equal protection claims. The court deemed the ordinance, as written and applied, to be rationally related to the city's legitimate interests in "the legal responsibility of CLC and its residents, . . . the safety and fears of residents in the adjoining neighborhood," and the number of people to be housed in the home.

The Court of Appeals for the Fifth Circuit reversed, determining that mental retardation was a quasi-suspect classification and that it should assess the validity of the ordinance under intermediate-level scrutiny. Because mental retardation was in fact relevant to many legislative actions, strict scrutiny was not appropriate. But in light of the history of "unfair and often grotesque mistreatment" of the retarded, discrimination against them was "likely to reflect deep-seated prejudice." In addition, the mentally retarded lacked political power, and their condition was immutable. The court considered heightened scrutiny to be particularly appropriate in this case, because the city's ordinance withheld a benefit which, although not fundamental, was very important to the mentally retarded. Without group homes, the court stated, the retarded could never hope to integrate themselves into the community. Applying the test that it considered appropriate, the court held that the ordinance was invalid on its face because it did not substantially further any important governmental interests. The Court of Appeals went on to hold that the ordinance was also invalid as applied.

* * *

II

The Equal Protection Clause of the Fourteenth Amendment commands that no State shall "deny to any person within its jurisdiction the equal protection of the laws," which is essentially a direction that all persons similarly situated should be treated alike. *Plyler v. Doe,* 457 U.S. 202, 216, 102 S.Ct. 2382, 2394, 72 L.Ed.2d 786 (1982). Section 5 of the Amendment empowers Congress to enforce this mandate, but absent controlling congressional direction, the courts have themselves devised standards for determining the validity of state legislation or other official action that is challenged as denying equal protection. The general rule is that legislation is presumed to be valid and will be sustained if the classification drawn by the statute is rationally related to a legitimate state interest.

* * *

The general rule gives way, however, when a statute classifies by race, alienage, or national origin. These factors are so seldom relevant to the achievement of any legitimate state interest that laws grounded in such considerations are deemed to reflect prejudice and antipathy—a view that those in the burdened class are not as worthy or deserving as others. For these reasons and because such discrimination is unlikely to be soon rectified by legislative means, these laws are subjected to strict scrutiny and will be sustained only if they are suitably tailored to serve a compelling state interest. Similar oversight by the courts is due when state laws impinge on personal rights protected by the Constitution.

Legislative classifications based on gender also call for a heightened standard of review. That factor generally provides no sensible ground for differential treatment. "[W]hat differentiates sex from such nonsuspect statuses as intelligence or physical disability . . . is that the sex characteristic frequently bears no relation to ability to perform or contribute to society." Rather than resting on meaningful considerations, statutes distributing benefits and burdens between the sexes in different ways very likely reflect outmoded notions of the relative capabilities of men and women. A gender classification fails unless it is substantially related to a sufficiently important governmental interest. Because illegitimacy is beyond the individual's control and bears "no relation to the individual's ability to participate in and contribute to society," official discriminations resting on that characteristic are also subject to somewhat heightened review.

* * *

We have declined, however, to extend heightened review to differential treatment based on age. . . .

* * *

III

Against this background, we conclude for several reasons that the Court of Appeals erred in holding mental retardation a quasi-suspect classification calling for a more exacting standard of judicial review than is normally accorded economic and social legislation. First, it is undeniable, and it is not argued otherwise here, that those who are mentally retarded have a reduced ability to cope with and function in the everyday world. Nor are they all cut from the same pattern: as the testimony in this record indicates, they range from those whose disability is not immediately evident to those who must be constantly cared for. They are thus different, immutably so, in relevant respects, and the States' interest in dealing with and providing for them is plainly a legitimate one. How this large and diversified group is to be treated under the law is a difficult and often a technical matter, very much a task for legislators guided by qualified professionals and not by the perhaps ill-informed opinions of the judiciary. Heightened scrutiny inevitably involves substantive judgments about legislative decisions, and we doubt that the predicate for such judicial oversight is present where the classification deals with mental retardation.

Second, the distinctive legislative response, both national and state, to the plight of those who are mentally retarded demonstrates not only that they have unique problems, but also that the lawmakers have been addressing their difficulties in a manner that belies a continuing antipathy or prejudice and a corresponding need for more intrusive oversight by the judiciary.

* * *

Third, the legislative response, which could hardly have occurred and survived without public support, negates any claim that the mentally retarded are politically powerless in the sense that they have no ability to attract the attention of the lawmakers. Any minority can be said to be powerless to assert direct control over the legislature, but if that were a criterion for higher level scrutiny by the courts, much economic and social legislation would now be suspect.

Fourth, if the large and amorphous class of the mentally retarded were deemed quasi-suspect for the reasons given by the Court of Appeals, it would be difficult to find a principled way to distinguish a variety of other groups who have perhaps immutable disabilities setting them off from others, who cannot themselves mandate the desired legislative responses, and who can claim some degree of prejudice from at least part of the public at large. One need mention in this respect only the aging, the disabled, the mentally ill, and the infirm. We are reluctant to set out on that course, and we decline to do so.

Doubtless, there have been and there will continue to be instances of discrimination against the retarded that are in fact invidious, and that are properly subject to judicial correction under constitutional norms. But the appropriate method of reaching such instances is not to create a new quasi-suspect classification and subject all governmental action based on that classification to more searching evaluation. Rather, we should look to the likelihood that governmental action premised on a particular classification is valid as a general matter, not merely to the specifics of the case before us. Because mental retardation is a characteristic that the government may legitimately take into account in a wide range of decisions, and because both State and Federal Governments have recently committed themselves to assisting the retarded, we will not presume that any given legislative action, even one that disadvantages retarded individuals, is rooted in considerations that the Constitution will not tolerate.

Our refusal to recognize the retarded as a quasi-suspect class does not leave them entirely unprotected from invidious discrimination. To withstand equal protection review, legislation that distinguishes between the mentally retarded and others must be rationally related to a legitimate governmental purpose. This standard, we believe, affords government the latitude necessary both to pursue policies designed to assist the retarded in realizing their full potential, and to freely and efficiently engage in activities that burden the retarded in what is essentially an incidental manner. The State may not rely on a classification whose relationship to an asserted goal is so attenuated as to render the distinction arbitrary or irrational.

* * *

IV

We turn to the issue of the validity of the zoning ordinance insofar as it requires a special use permit for homes for the mentally retarded. We inquire first whether requiring a special use permit for the Featherston home in the circumstances here deprives respondents of the equal protection of the laws. If it does, there will be no occasion to decide whether the special use permit provision is facially invalid where the mentally retarded are involved, or to put it another way, whether the city may never insist on a special use permit for a home for the mentally retarded in an R–3 zone. This is the preferred course of adjudication since it enables courts to avoid making unnecessarily broad constitutional judgments.

The constitutional issue is clearly posed. The city does not require a special use permit in an R–3 zone for apartment houses, multiple dwellings, boarding and lodging houses, fraternity or sorority houses, dormitories, apartment hotels, hospitals, sanitariums, nursing homes for convalescents or the aged (other than for the insane or feebleminded or alcoholics or drug addicts), private clubs or fraternal orders, and other specified uses. It does, however, insist on a special permit for the Featherston home, and it does so, as the District Court found, because it would be a facility for the mentally retarded. May the city require the permit for this facility when other care and multiple-dwelling facilities are freely permitted?

It is true, as already pointed out, that the mentally retarded as a group are indeed different from others not sharing their misfortune, and in this respect they may be different from those who would occupy other facilities that would be permitted in an R–3 zone without a special permit. But this difference is largely irrelevant unless the Featherston home and those who would occupy it would threaten legitimate interests of the city in a way that other permitted uses such as boarding houses and hospitals would not. Because in our view the record does not reveal any rational basis for believing that the Featherston home would pose any special threat to the city's legitimate interests, we affirm the judgment below insofar as it holds the ordinance invalid as applied in this case.

The District Court found that the City Council's insistence on the permit rested on several factors. First, the Council was concerned with the negative attitude of the majority of property owners located within 200 feet of the Featherston facility, as well as with the fears of elderly residents of the neighborhood. But mere negative attitudes, or fear, unsubstantiated by factors which are properly cognizable in a zoning proceeding, are not permissible bases for treating a home for the mentally retarded differently from apartment houses, multiple dwellings, and the like.

*   *   *

Second, the Council had two objections to the location of the facility. It was concerned that the facility was across the street from a junior high school, and it feared that the students might harass the occupants of the Featherston home. But the school itself is attended by about 30 mentally retarded students, and denying a permit based on such vague, undifferentiated fears is again permitting some portion of the community to validate what would otherwise be an equal protection violation. The other objection to the home's location was that it was located on "a five hundred year flood plain." This concern with the possibility of a flood, however, can hardly be based on a distinction between the Featherston home and, for example, nursing homes, homes for convalescents or the aged, or sanitariums or hospitals, any of which could be located on the Featherston site without obtaining a special use permit. The same may be said of another concern of the Council—doubts about the legal responsibility for actions which the mentally retarded might take. If there is no concern about legal responsibility with respect to other uses that would be permitted in the area, such as boarding and fraternity houses, it is difficult to believe that the groups of mildly or moderately mentally retarded individuals who would live at 201 Featherston would present any different or special hazard.

Fourth, the Council was concerned with the size of the home and the number of people that would occupy it. The District Court found, and the Court of Appeals repeated, that "[i]f the potential residents of the Featherston Street home were not mentally retarded, but the home was the same in all other respects, its use would be permitted under the city's zoning ordinance." Given this finding, there would be no restrictions on the number of people who could occupy this home as a boarding house, nursing home, family dwelling, fraternity house, or dormitory. The question is whether it is rational to treat the mentally retarded differently. It is true that they suffer disability not shared by others; but why this difference warrants a density regulation that others need not observe is not at all apparent. At least this record does not clarify how, in this connection, the characteristics of the intended occupants of the Featherston home rationally justify denying to those occupants what would be permitted to groups occupying the same site for different purposes. Those who would live in the Featherston home are the type of individuals who, with supporting staff, satisfy federal and state standards for group housing in the community; and there is no dispute that the home would meet the federal square-footage-per-resident requirement for facilities of this type. In the words of the Court of Appeals, "[t]he City never justifies its apparent view that other people can live under such 'crowded' conditions when mentally retarded persons cannot."

In the courts below the city also urged that the ordinance is aimed at avoiding concentration of population and at lessening congestion of the streets. These concerns obviously fail to explain why apartment houses, fraternity and sorority houses, hospitals and the like, may freely locate in the area without a permit. So, too, the expressed worry about fire hazards, the serenity of the neighborhood, and the avoidance of danger to other residents fail rationally to justify singling out a home such as 201 Featherston for the special use permit, yet imposing no such restrictions on the many other uses freely permitted in the neighborhood.

The short of it is that requiring the permit in this case appears to us to rest on an irrational prejudice against the mentally retarded, including those who would occupy the Featherston facility and who would live under the closely supervised and highly regulated conditions expressly provided for by state and federal law.

The judgment of the Court of Appeals is affirmed insofar as it invalidates the zoning ordinance as applied to the Featherston home. The judgment is otherwise vacated, and the case is remanded.

It is so ordered.

JUSTICE STEVENS, with whom THE CHIEF JUSTICE joins, concurring.

* * *

Every law that places the mentally retarded in a special class is not presumptively irrational. The differences between mentally retarded persons and those with greater mental capacity are obviously relevant to certain legislative decisions. An impartial lawmaker—indeed, even a member of a class of persons defined as mentally retarded—could rationally vote in favor of a law providing funds for special education and special treatment for the mentally retarded. A mentally retarded person could also recognize that he is a member of a class that might need special supervision in some situations, both to protect himself and to protect others. Restrictions on his right to drive cars or to operate hazardous equipment might well seem rational even though they deprived him of employment opportunities and the kind of freedom of travel enjoyed by other citizens. "That a civilized and decent society expects and approves such legislation indicates that governmental consideration of those differences in the vast majority of situations is not only legitimate but also desirable."

Even so, the Court of Appeals correctly observed that through ignorance and prejudice the mentally retarded "have been subjected to a history of unfair and often grotesque mistreatment." 726 F.2d 191, 197 (C.A.5 1984). The discrimination against the mentally retarded that is at issue in this case is the city's decision to require an annual special use permit before property in an apartment house district may be used as a group home for persons who are mildly retarded. The record convinces me that this permit was required because of the irrational fears of neighboring property owners, rather than for the protection of the mentally retarded persons who would reside in respondent's home.

Although the city argued in the Court of Appeals that legitimate interests of the neighbors justified the restriction, the court unambiguously rejected that argument. *Id.,* at 201. In this Court, the city has argued that the discrimination was really motivated by a desire to protect the mentally retarded from the hazards presented by the neighborhood. Zoning ordinances are not usually justified on any such basis, and in this case, for the reasons explained by the Court, I find that justification wholly unconvincing. I cannot believe that a rational member of this disadvantaged class could ever approve of the discriminatory application of the city's ordinance in this case.

Accordingly, I join the opinion of the Court.

JUSTICE MARSHALL, with whom JUSTICE BRENNAN and JUSTICE BLACKMUN join, concurring in the judgment in part and dissenting in part.

*   *   *

I share the Court's criticisms of the overly broad lines that Cleburne's zoning ordinance has drawn. But if the ordinance is to be invalidated for its imprecise classifications, it must be pursuant to more powerful scrutiny than the minimal rational-basis test used to review classifications affecting only economic and commercial matters.

*   *   *

In light of the importance of the interest at stake and the history of discrimination the retarded have suffered, the Equal Protection Clause requires us to do more than review the distinctions drawn by Cleburne's zoning ordinance as if they appeared in a taxing statute or in economic or commercial legislation. The searching scrutiny I would give to restrictions on the ability of the retarded to establish community group homes leads me to conclude that Cleburne's vague generalizations for classifying the "feeble-minded" with drug addicts, alcoholics, and the insane, and excluding them where the elderly, the ill, the boarder, and the transient are allowed, are not substantial or important enough to overcome the suspicion that the ordinance rests on impermissible assumptions or outmoded and perhaps invidious stereotypes.

*   *   *

In light of the scrutiny that should be applied here, Cleburne's ordinance sweeps too broadly to dispel the suspicion that it rests on a bare desire to treat the retarded as outsiders, pariahs who do not belong in the community. The Court, while disclaiming that special scrutiny is necessary or warranted, reaches the same conclusion. Rather than striking the ordinance down, however, the Court invalidates it merely as applied to respondents. I must dissent from the novel proposition that "the preferred course of adjudication" is to leave standing a legislative Act resting on "irrational prejudice", thereby forcing individuals in the group discriminated against to continue to run the Act's gauntlet.

The Court appears to act out of a belief that the ordinance might be "rational" as applied to some subgroup of the retarded under some circumstances, such as those utterly without the capacity to live in a community, and that the ordinance should not be invalidated *in toto* if it is capable of ever being validly applied. But the issue is not "whether the city may never insist on a special use permit for the mentally retarded in an R–3 zone." The issue is whether the city may require a permit pursuant to a blunderbuss ordinance drafted many years ago to exclude all the "feeble-minded," or whether the city must enact a new ordinance carefully tailored to the exclusion of some well-defined subgroup of retarded people in circumstances in which exclusion might reasonably further legitimate city purposes.

*   *   *

Invalidating on its face the ordinance's special treatment of the "feebleminded," in contrast, would place the responsibility for tailoring and updating Cleburne's unconstitutional ordinance where it belongs: with the legislative arm of the City of Cleburne. If Cleburne perceives a legitimate need for requiring a certain well-defined subgroup of the retarded to obtain special permits before establishing group homes, Cleburne will, after studying the problem and making the appropriate policy decisions, enact a new, more narrowly tailored ordinance. That ordinance might well look very different from the current one; it might separate group homes (presently treated nowhere in the ordinance) from hospitals, and it might define a narrow subclass of the retarded for whom even group homes could legitimately be excluded. Special treatment of the retarded might be ended altogether. But whatever the contours such an ordinance might take, the city should not be allowed to keep its ordinance on the books intact and thereby shift to the courts the responsibility to confront the complex empirical and policy questions involved in updating statutes affecting the mentally retarded. A legislative solution would yield standards and provide the sort of certainty to retarded applicants and administrative officials that case-by-case judicial rulings cannot provide. Retarded applicants should not have to continue to attempt to surmount Cleburne's vastly overbroad ordinance.

QUESTIONS AND COMMENTS

1. *Impact of an "invalid as applied" holding.* What is the practical significance of a holding that invalidates the city of Cleburne's ordinance "as applied" to the Cleburne Living Center but leaves the regulatory scheme in place? Are there any circumstances under which the city of Cleburne might now constitutionally deny a permit to applicants seeking to establish a group home for people with intellectual disabilities? Put another way, how would the "more narrowly tailored statute" desired by the dissent differ from the current ordinance? Finally, do you think the outcome in *Cleburne* would have been different had the group home been for people with mental illness?

2. *People with mental disability as a quasi-suspect class.* Because rational basis review is rarely used to strike down legislative enactments and because *Cleburne* in effect did so, commentators writing immediately following the *Cleburne* decision suggested that the Court was really applying a heightened form of scrutiny—dubbed "rational-basis-with-bite" by some. See, e.g., Laurence H. Tribe, American Constitutional Law (2nd ed. 1988), § 16–3, at 1444–46. However, in *Heller v. Doe*, 509 U.S. 312, 113 S.Ct. 2637, 125 L.Ed.2d 257 (1993), a majority of the Court applied ordinary rational-basis analysis in upholding civil commitment provisions that tended to make commitment of people with intellectual disabilities easier than commitment of people with mental illness, albeit only after noting the parties had not argued for a heightened standard of review. (*Heller* is discussed further at pp. 1107–1117). And in *Board of Trustees of the University of Alabama v. Garrett*, 531 U.S. 356, 121 S.Ct. 955, 148 L.Ed.2d 866 (2001), a five-member majority flatly stated that "states are not required by the Fourteenth Amendment to make special accommodations for the disabled, so long as their actions toward such individuals are rational."

However, *Garrett* did not apply the rational-basis test to any particular factual situation, so whether that test will turn into "rational-basis-with-bite" when applied to an actual case, as it did in *Cleburne*, remains to be seen. Furthermore, two members of the five-member majority in *Garrett* wrote a concurring opinion that emphasized the absence of proof that state entities (as opposed to local ones) had engaged in a "pattern or practice" that was "designed" to discriminate against people with disabilities. When the views of these two justices are combined with the views of the four-member dissent, which expressed a more expansive view of *Cleburne* than the majority, the equal protection status of mental disability remains in some doubt, at least where the state intentionally discriminates based on that classification. See generally, Mark C. Weber, *Disability Harassment in the Public Schools*, 43 Wm. & Mary L. Rev. 1079, 1128 (2002) (asserting, after canvassing how the Court eventually adopted the intermediate standard of review in gender cases, that "[h]istory suggests that an erratic pattern of decision, combined with protests by the Court that it is applying a rational-basis test, may lead to an eventual use of intermediate scrutiny.").

3. *Anti-discrimination legislation.* In 1988, amendments to the Fair Housing Act made it "unlawful to discriminate in the sale or rental or otherwise make unavailable or deny a dwelling to any buyer or renter because of a handicap." 42 U.S.C. § 3604(f)(1). As discussed in the final section of this chapter, zoning ordinances of the type adopted by the city of *Cleburne* are now frequently challenged under that Act. Similarly, in the employment, education and licensing contexts covered in the next three sections of this chapter, federal and state statutes have largely mooted the issue of whether *Cleburne* endorsed more than a rational-basis test.

III. EMPLOYMENT OPPORTUNITIES

Employment discrimination claims brought under the ADA and Rehabilitation Act often allege discrimination on the basis of emotional or psychiatric impairment. In 2012, for example, approximately 20% of claims brought to the EEOC under the ADA involved some sort of mental disorder: 6.8% involved depression, 5.1% anxiety disorders, 3.3% bipolar disorder, 2.4% post-traumatic stress disorder, .8% intellectual disability, .6% alcoholism, .5% drug addiction, and 1.4% other mental disorders. EEOC, ADA Charge Data by Impairments/Bases, available at http://www.eeoc.gov/eeoc/statistics/enforcement/ada-merit.cfm. Under-scoring the significance of these percentages are data suggesting that people with mental impairments have much lower employment rates than the general population and also have lower employment rates than people with physical disabilities. See, for example, Jane K. Burke–Miller et al., *Demographic Characteristics and Employment Among People with Severe Mental Illness in a Multisite Study*, 42 Community Ment. Health J. 143 (2006).

A. CONDITIONS GIVING RISE TO COVERAGE

Before the ADAAA, most employment-related ADA litigation focused on whether the claimant had a mental impairment that was covered by the ADA. As the following case illustrates, the ADAAA has reduced controversy about this issue, but has raised other issues. As is true in any discrimination case, the plaintiff claiming disability discrimination can proceed on either a "disparate treatment" theory, which usually requires proof of discriminatory intent as evidenced on the face of a rule or by the actions of the defendant, or through a "disparate impact theory," which requires proof that legal criteria or actions that appear neutral actually have an adverse impact on one or more members of a protected group. The following case illustrates the typical disparate impact analysis in ADA cases.

- appear neutral, but have adverse impact

MURRAY ET AL. v. UHS OF FAIRMOUNT, INC.
United States District Court, E.D. Pennsylvania, 2011.
2011 WL 5449364.

MCLAUGHLIN, DISTRICT JUDGE.

This lawsuit arises from the termination of Nancy Murray's employment as a staff nurse for the defendant, UHS of Fairmount ("UHS"). . . . The defendant, UHS, moves for summary judgment under Rule 56 of the Federal Rules of Civil Procedure. The Court will grant the defendant's motion.

I.   Factual Background

. . .

A.   Nancy Murray's Mental Health Issues and Leaves of Absence

Nancy Murray worked as a staff nurse in the mental health unit at UHS's Fairmount Hospital from June 25, 2007 until her termination on May 15, 2009. Her boyfriend, Ira Newman, also worked at UHS until March 2009.

Murray began suffering from depression in 2003. Her mental health issues subsided briefly in 2007 when Murray procured employment at UHS. At some point, although the record is unclear on when, Murray began suffering from depression again. As a result, Murray was forced to take leave from work.

Murray took two leaves of absence from UHS: the first from December 24, 2008 to January 7, 2009, and the second from April 27, 2009 to May 4, 2009. She took these leaves because of her depression. Murray supplied a doctor's note upon returning from leave, but the doctor's note did not specify that mental illness was the reason for her absence.

B.   UHS's Awareness of Murray's Mental Health Issues

After returning from leave, Murray told the charge nurse, Beth Ann Watson, in confidence that her anxiety and depression necessitated the absence. Beth Ann Watson forwarded Murray's doctor's note to the UHS human resources ("HR") department, but testified that she did not discuss Murray's mental condition with anyone else at UHS.

Theresa Mahoney, the HR director, was aware of Murray's medical absences in late 2008 and in 2009. However, she testified that she did not recall the reasons for the absences. In addition, Theresa Mahoney was not aware that Murray had any medical issues other than an infection and a dental issue; no one had ever told her Murray was suffering from anxiety or depression.

A few weeks before Ira Newman left UHS in March 2009, Jack Plotkin, the Chief Nursing Officer and Watson's supervisor, pulled Newman into his office to inquire about Murray's mental health issues. In particular, Plotkin asked Newman how Murray was feeling and what medications she was taking. Murray herself also received inquiries about her mental health from both Beth Ann Watson and Jack Plotkin when she returned to work after her second leave of absence in May 2009. Jack Plotkin asked Murray how she was doing several times between her return to work on May 4, 2009 and her termination from UHS on May 15, 2009.

C. UHS Narcotics Distribution and Administration Procedure

UHS has specific guidelines regarding the distribution of narcotics.[b] Before being put in a position to distribute narcotics, UHS employees receive training regarding the distribution, accounting, and storage of narcotics.

The UHS pharmacy delivers medication when needed to a locked med room near the nurse's station for which only a nurse has the key. UHS tracks narcotics distribution via two documents: (1) the Pharmacy Controlled Drug Unit Supply Record (the "Pharmacy Record") and (2) the Schedule II Controlled Substance sheet (the "Schedule II").[c] First, the nurse that receives narcotics from the pharmacy counts and signs for the amount received on the Pharmacy Record. Second, that same nurse enters the corresponding amount received from the pharmacy on the Schedule II, which is also kept in the locked med room.

The medication administration record ("MAR") contains the doctor's orders regarding how much medication each patient on the unit is supposed to receive, and when. Every administration of narcotics to a patient is recorded on the Schedule II to keep a constant count of how many narcotics are in the medication drawer.

Occasionally, nurses have to "waste," or dispose of narcotic medications—for example, if a patient refuses to take them or a nurse pours out too many pills. UHS's wasting procedure requires that another nurse "witness" the disposal of the drugs-usually down the sink drain. The witness must then sign the Schedule II to confirm the waste.

---

[b] Here, "narcotics" refers to drugs deemed to have addictive potential. 21 U.S.C. § 812(b).

[c] Schedule II drugs have accepted medical uses but a high potential for abuse and dependence.

 Examples include opioid pain killers such as hydromorphone (Dilaudid®) and morphine, and stimulants such as amphetamine (Adderall® and others) and methylphenidate (Ritalin®) used to treat attention-deficit/ hyperactivity disorder. 21 C.F.R. § 1308.12.

At the end of every shift, the leaving and oncoming nurse count the narcotics in the medication drawer to make sure there are no discrepancies between the count and the amount listed on the Schedule II. If there is a discrepancy in the narcotics count, the nurses must call the nursing management or supervisor about the problem.

D.   The May 14, 2009 Narcotics Mistakes

The record reflects that Nancy Murray made two narcotics-related mistakes on May 14, 2009, shortly after she returned from her second leave of absence: (1) Murray did not secure a witness's signature for narcotics that she wasted; and (2) Murray mistakenly signed for 25 doses of Adderall from the pharmacy when only 23 doses were provided. Although the first error occurred before the second, the Court recites the facts here in reverse.

1.   Discrepancy Between the Pharmacy Record and the Schedule II

On May 14, 2009, the Schedule II reflected that the medication cart contained five 10 mg pills of Adderall at the beginning of the Nancy Murray's 7:00 a.m. shift. That day, Murray signed out two 20 mg doses (4 pills total) of Adderall for a patient named "A.M." and one 10 mg dose (1 pill) of Adderall for a different patient. With the Adderall count down to zero, Murray ordered more Adderall from the pharmacy.

When the pharmacy technician arrived, Murray signed the Pharmacy Record, mistakenly acknowledging that 25 doses (10 mg) of Adderall were provided to her. In fact, the pharmacy provided only 23 doses to Murray. When she signed the Adderall into the Schedule II, Murray recorded only 23 doses (10 mg) of Adderall.

2.   Lack of a Wasting Signature

According to Murray, patient "A.M." refused to take some of her Adderall on May 14, 2009. Another nurse, Elizabeth Rody, watched Murray waste some Adderall down the sink. However, Nurse Rody was called away on a psychological emergency before she could sign the Schedule II as a witness to wasting, as required by UHS narcotics procedures. Although Murray admitted that she should have done so, Murray did not otherwise indicate on the Schedule II that any of the Adderall she signed out for "A.M." had been wasted. After Murray's shift, the oncoming nurse, Debbie Stabler, signed off on the Schedule II despite the absence of a wasting signature.

Murray did not report to her supervisors either the mistake she made in signing out 25 doses of Adderall from the pharmacy or her inability to secure a witness's signature for wasted medication.

E. Investigation of the Narcotics Mistakes and Murray's Termination on May 15, 2009

The following day, a different nurse on the unit contacted Jack Plotkin, the Chief Nursing Officer, with concerns about the administration of medication to patient "A.M." on May 14, 2009. The nurse informed Plotkin that she could not find a doctor's order that justified the amount of Adderall administered to patient "A.M." the day before, as indicated on the Schedule II.

Plotkin investigated by examining the Schedule II as well as the medication administration record ("MAR") for patient "A.M." Plotkin understood the MAR to order one 10 mg dose of Adderall for "A.M." at 9:00 a.m. on May 14, 2009. After bringing the issue to the attention of Theresa Mahoney in the HR department, Plotkin probed further and noticed the discrepancy between the 25 doses of Adderall signed out from the Pharmacy Record by Murray and the 23 doses signed into the Schedule II.

. . .

Plotkin also spoke to Nurse Elizabeth Rody as part of his investigation. In that conversation, Rody told Plotkin that she did not recall witnessing Nancy Murray waste medication on May 14, 2009. After Plotkin spoke with Rody, he and Theresa Mahoney decided to terminate Murray's employment with UHS.

It is disputed whether Murray was asked for an explanation for her narcotics mistakes on May 14, 2009, but according to Murray, she was never given a chance to explain what happened. Murray was terminated on May 15, 2009, eleven days after returning from her second leave of absence.

II. Analysis

A. Legal Standard

Summary judgment is appropriate if there is "no genuine dispute as to any material fact and the movant is entitled to judgment as a matter of law." Fed.R.Civ.P. 56(a). . . . Once a party files a properly supported motion for summary judgment, the burden shifts to the nonmoving party, who must set forth specific facts showing that there is a genuine issue of material fact for trial. . . . A fact is "material" if it might affect the outcome of the suit under the governing law. A dispute is genuine if the evidence is such that a reasonable jury could return a verdict for the nonmoving party. The court must view the facts in the light most favorable to the nonmoving party.

[handwritten margin notes: 1) plaintiff prima facie case 2) Defendent says nondiscrim reason for termination 3) Plaintiff must prove Defendent lying]

B.   Legal Framework

Where there is no direct evidence of discrimination, [courts analyze] ADA disparate treatment and retaliation claims . . . under the burden-shifting framework announced in *McDonnell Douglas Corp. v. Green*, 411 U.S. 792, 802–04, 93 S.Ct. 1817, 36 L.Ed.2d 668 (1973). Under that framework, the plaintiff must first establish a prima facie case of discrimination. If the plaintiff succeeds in doing so, the burden of production shifts to the defendant "to articulate some legitimate, nondiscriminatory reason for the employee's rejection." Finally, if the defendant carries its burden, the plaintiff must have the opportunity to prove that the reasons offered by the defendant were not its true reasons, but rather a pretext for discrimination.

C.   Prima Facie Case: ADA Claims

The ADA makes it unlawful for an employer to discriminate against an employee on the basis of her disability. On behalf of Nancy Murray, the plaintiff brings actual and perceived disability discrimination as well as retaliation claims under the ADA.

1.   Disability Discrimination

In order to make out a prima facie case of discrimination under the ADA, the plaintiff must establish that Murray (1) has a disability, (2) is a qualified individual, and (3) has suffered an adverse employment action because of that disability. Here, UHS disputes only that Murray has a disability as defined by the ADA.

The ADA defines "disability" as "a physical or mental impairment that substantially limits one or more major life activities of such individual," "a record of such an impairment," or "being regarded as having such an impairment." As a preliminary matter, the ADA Amendments Act of 2008 ("ADAAA" or the "Act") made it easier for plaintiffs to prove that they are "disabled" within the meaning of the ADA.[10] Section 2(b)(5) of the Act provides that "the question of whether an individual's impairment is a disability under the ADA should not demand extensive analysis." Similarly, section 4(a) of the Act provides that the definition of "disability" under the ADA "shall be construed in favor of broad coverage of individuals." In doing so, the ADAAA specifically overrules the Supreme Court's definition of "substantially limit" as requiring significant restriction compared to the general population. See id. § 2(b)(4)–(5) (superseding *Toyota Motor Mfg. v. Williams*, 534 U.S. 184, 198, 122 S.Ct. 681, 151 L.Ed.2d 615 (2002)).

[handwritten margin note: ADAAA → easier to prove disability]

Murray raises claims of actual disability as well as "regarded as" or perceived disability. The Court addresses these claims in order.

---

[10] The amendments took effect on January 1, 2009, and are thus applicable to the conduct in this case.

a.   Actual Disability: Impairment That Substantially Limits One or More Major Life Activities.

UHS does not dispute that depression qualifies as an impairment under the ADA. Rather, UHS makes three arguments: (1) first, UHS challenges the sufficiency of the plaintiff's evidence of depression; (2) second, UHS argues that the plaintiff has not demonstrated impairment of a "major life activity"; (3) third, UHS challenges whether any such impairment has been "substantial."

— *(1) Medical Evidence of Depression*

UHS complains that the plaintiff has not submitted medical evidence of Nancy Murray's depression. Murray testified in her deposition that she suffered from anxiety and depression and received a diagnosis from a doctor regarding the same. UHS has not offered evidence to the contrary, medical or otherwise. Nor has UHS cited any case law that requires medical evidence of an impairment. Indeed, the Third Circuit has stated that "the necessity of medical testimony turns on the extent to which the alleged impairment is within the comprehension of a jury that does not possess a command of medical or otherwise scientific knowledge." *Marinelli v. City of Erie*, 216 F.3d 354, 360 (3d Cir.2000).

In *Marinelli*, the Third Circuit found that arm and back pain were not technical in nature and were thus amenable to comprehension by a lay jury. Thus, the court found that the plaintiff's failure to present medical evidence did not warrant judgment as a matter of law in favor of the defendant. Similarly, here, depression is also amenable to comprehension by a lay jury. A reasonable jury could conclude on the basis of Murray's deposition testimony that she was, in fact, depressed. Thus, the plaintiff's failure to produce medical evidence regarding Murray's depression is not, by itself, fatal to her claim.

(2) "Major Life Activity"

Being diagnosed with depression, by itself, does not make an employee "disabled" under the ADA; the plaintiff must show with medical evidence that the depression substantially limits a major life activity. See *Toyota Motor Mfg. v. Williams*, 534 U.S. 184, 198, 122 S.Ct. 681, 151 L.Ed.2d 615 (2002), superseded by statute on other grounds. Here, UHS argues that Murray has not identified any major life activities impaired by her depression.

The record reflects otherwise. Murray testified in her deposition that she experienced symptoms such as "[n]ot eating, not sleeping, having racing thoughts . . . [and] just feeling hopeless, helpless, sad." UHS has not offered evidence to the contrary. Thinking, eating, and sleeping are specifically listed in the ADA as major life activities.

(3) Sufficiency of Evidence That the Limitation Is "Substantial"

Finally, UHS argues that the plaintiff has adduced no evidence of substantial limitation on Murray's major life activities. UHS makes both a temporal argument and a challenge to the sufficiency of the evidence presented.

UHS first makes a temporal argument that transitory, temporary, or impermanent impairments do not "substantially limit" as a legal matter. UHS is correct that prior to the ADAAA, among the factors the Third Circuit examined to determine whether a plaintiff was substantially limited were: (1) the nature and severity of the impairment; (2) the duration or expected duration of the impairment; and (3) the permanent or long term impact, or the expected permanent or long term impact of or resulting from the impairment.

However, since the passage of the ADAAA, the EEOC has adopted regulations interpreting the statute. The EEOC regulations provide that "effects of an impairment lasting or expected to last fewer than six months can be substantially limiting." 29 C.F.R. § 1630.2(j)(1)(ix). Furthermore, "[a]n impairment that is episodic or in remission is a disability if it would substantially limit a major life activity when active." The post-ADAAA EEOC regulations also caution that "substantially limits" is "not meant to be a demanding standard" and shall be construed broadly in favor of expansive coverage, to the "maximum extent permitted by the ADA." These updated regulations bring into question the continuing vitality of the "permanent or long term impact" factor laid out by the Third Circuit.

In this case, Murray testified that she has suffered from depression and anxiety since 2003. She also testified that in 2007, when she applied and got a job at UHS, she was happy and not suffering from the illnesses. The record is unclear about when Murray's illness returned, but Murray testified that her leaves of absences in 2008 and 2009 were due to her depression and anxiety. Murray also testified that she was taking three medications to treat her depression.

Although the record in this case is sparse, there is evidence to support the inference that Murray's depression has been of significant duration and chronic in nature, even if it has occasionally subsided. In light of the purpose of the ADAAA and the EEOC regulations interpreting the statute, the Court agrees with the plaintiff that the nature of Murray's depression, by itself, does not preclude a finding that her depression "substantially limits" major life activities.

Next, UHS generally argues that Murray has not proffered sufficient evidence of substantial limitation. Here, the only evidence that Murray has produced to show that her depression has limited her eating, sleeping, and thinking is her deposition testimony that she experienced symptoms such as "[n]ot eating, not sleeping, having racing thoughts . . . [and] just feeling hopeless, helpless, sad." She did not testify as to the severity, duration, or frequency of these symptoms and has submitted no other evidence to indicate that the impact on these major life activities has been substantial.

Under pre-ADAAA case law, Murray's evidence would almost certainly have failed to demonstrate substantial limitation. But post-ADAAA, the result is more uncertain given the statute's command that "substantially limits" is not meant to be a demanding standard.

The post-ADAAA EEOC regulations provide some guidance, but do not clearly dictate a result. On the one hand, the regulations provide that an impairment "need not prevent, or significantly or severely restrict, the individual from performing a major life activity in order to be considered substantially limiting." The inquiry into substantial limitation "should not demand extensive analysis." Furthermore, section (j)(3)(iii) specifically states that "it should easily be concluded" that "major depressive order . . . substantially limit[s] brain function."[17]

Nevertheless, the regulations also caution that "not every impairment will constitute a disability within the meaning of [the ADA]," so a line must be drawn somewhere. In addition, an impairment is a disability within the meaning of the ADA only if it *substantially* limits the ability of an individual to perform a major life activity "as compared to most people in the general population." (emphasis added). Although the comparison of an individual's performance of a major life activity "usually will not require scientific, medical, or statistical analysis," Murray has not produced a modicum of evidence in this case that would allow the Court to even engage in a comparison of her symptoms with those of others.

There is also relatively little case law applying the more relaxed post-ADAAA standard for substantial limitation. The Court is aware of one case directly on point. See *Naber v. Dover Healthcare Assoc., Inc.*, 765 F.Supp.2d 622 (D.Del.2011). In *Naber*, the court noted that the ADAAA did not relieve the plaintiff of her burden to prove that her impairment substantially limits her ability to sleep. The court found that there was a question of fact as to whether the plaintiff's depression was the cause of her inability to sleep and whether the sleeplessness was substantially limiting as compared to the average person in the general population. Thus, the court stated that it could not grant summary judgment for failure to set forth a prima facie case (but granted summary judgment on other grounds).

---

[17] Nothing in the record suggests an answer as to whether Murray's depression is equivalent to "major depressive order." The Court expresses no view on the question.

The record in this case is less robust than that in *Naber*. In *Naber*, the plaintiff testified that prior to her termination, she was unable to sleep at all one or two nights a week because of her depression, and that the condition had persisted through the time of her deposition. Thus, the *Naber* court had a few data points with which it could draw comparisons to the general population. By contrast, Murray's evidence boils down to a brief mention in her deposition of not eating, not sleeping, and having racing thoughts without any details as to duration, frequency, or severity.

The Court recognizes that the record as to whether Murray's depression substantially limits her major life activities is incredibly sparse. Nevertheless, given the stated intent of the ADAAA, the statute's command to construe "disability" broadly, and the dearth of post-ADAAA case law opining on the issue, the Court declines to grant summary judgment on the basis of failing to make out a prima facie case of "disability" under the ADA. Rather, the Court grants summary judgment because the plaintiff has failed to raise a genuine issue of material fact regarding pretext, as discussed below.

b. Perceived Disability

"Regarded as" disability does not depend on the plaintiff having any impairment. The question is not the plaintiff's actual condition, but rather her condition as perceived by her employer, including the "reactions and perceptions of the persons interacting or working with [her]."

The ADAAA clarified two points about "regarded as" disability. First, a plaintiff meets the requirement of being "regarded as" disabled if she establishes discrimination "because of an actual or perceived physical or mental impairment *whether or not the impairment limits or is perceived to limit a major life activity.*" (emphasis added). Second, a plaintiff cannot be "regarded as" disabled if the actual or perceived impairment is "transitory and minor," which is defined as one "with an actual or expected duration of 6 months or less."

The record in this case shows that Beth Ann Watson, the charge nurse who supervises Murray, knew that Murray suffered from depression and anxiety. Construed in the light most favorable to the plaintiff, the facts as set forth above also show that Jack Plotkin, the Chief Nursing Officer, was aware of Murray's mental health issues. As discussed previously, the record is spotty on the issue of duration, but there is at least some evidence to support a jury finding that Murray's depression was chronic and recurring and, hence, not transitory. Because the ADAAA no longer requires a showing that Murray's impairment was perceived to substantially limit a life activity, the plaintiff has raised a genuine issue of material fact as to whether Murray was regarded as disabled by UHS under the ADAAA.

Nevertheless, as discussed below, the Court grants summary judgment on other grounds.

2. Retaliation for Requesting an Accommodation under the ADA

In order to establish a prima facie case of illegal retaliation under the ADA, a plaintiff must show (1) protected employee activity; (2) adverse action by the employer either after or contemporaneous with the employee's protected activity; and (3) a causal connection between the employee's protected activity and the employer's adverse action. Unlike a claim for discrimination, an ADA retaliation claim does not require that the plaintiff show that she is "disabled" as defined by the ADA. A plaintiff alleging retaliation need only show that she had a "reasonable, good faith belief that she was entitled to request the reasonable accommodation she requested."

Murray argues that she requested accommodation for her depression in the form of two leaves of absence from work, and that UHS retaliated by firing her. UHS argues that Murray did not request an accommodation and that, in any case, UHS allowed Murray to be absent from work. UHS's counter is neither here nor there, however, as it does not address Murray's claim that she was terminated for taking her leaves of absence.

* * *

E. Defendant's Burden: Legitimate Non–Discriminatory Reason for Termination

[T]he defendant UHS has met its burden of showing that there was a legitimate, nondiscriminatory reason for Murray's termination. UHS provides ample evidence of Murray's narcotics errors and subsequent failure to report the errors. In particular, UHS's narcotics distribution and accounting procedures at the hospital are uncontested. Murray also admitted that she made mistakes on the Pharmacy Record and Schedule II. UHS has provided testimony that Murray was terminated because of her errors, her failure to report the errors, and her inability to explain the errors, and not because of her mental health issues.

F. Plaintiff's Burden: Pretext

UHS argues that even if the plaintiff has presented a prima facie case of discrimination and retaliation under the ADA . . . , she has not offered evidence raising a genuine factual dispute as to whether UHS's proffered non-discriminatory reason for terminating Nancy Murray was pretextual. The Court agrees.

To defeat a motion for summary judgment where a defendant has offered a legitimate, non-discriminatory reason for an adverse employment action, "the plaintiff must point to some evidence, direct or circumstantial, from which a factfinder could reasonably either (1) disbelieve the employer's articulated legitimate reasons; or (2) believe that an invidious discriminatory reason was more likely than not a motivating or determinative cause of the employer's action." These are two ways by which the plaintiff can prove that the defendant's reasons was pretextual.

1.   First Pretext Test: Discrediting the Employer's Reason

To discredit the employer's articulated reasons, "the plaintiff cannot simply show that the employer's decision was wrong or mistaken." "Rather, the non-moving plaintiff must demonstrate such weaknesses, implausibilities, inconsistencies, incoherencies, or contradictions in the employer's proffered legitimate reasons for its action that a reasonable factfinder could rationally find them 'unworthy of credence. . . .'" The plaintiff must show by a preponderance of the evidence "not merely that the employer's proffered reason was wrong, but that it was so plainly wrong that it cannot have been the employer's real reason."

Although the plaintiff points out one inconsistency in the record, she has not met her burden here. UHS's proffered reason for termination was not only the narcotics errors and the failure to report the errors, but also Murray's inability to explain her errors when confronted with them. As the plaintiff points out, however, Murray testified—and this Court must accept as true—that she was never even given a chance to explain the errors.

Although this factual inconsistency does raise some questions as to whether the failure to explain was truly a reason for termination, it does not make termination for the narcotics errors themselves and for failure to report them implausible or so plainly wrong that they could not have been the real reasons for termination.

2.   Second Pretext Test: An Invidious Discriminatory Reason Was More Likely Than Not a Motivating Factor

The plaintiff must "point to evidence with sufficient probative force for a factfinder" to make the conclusion that an invidious discriminatory reason was more likely than not a motivating factor for the termination. One example of such evidence is more favorable treatment of other employees not exercising the same right.

The plaintiff argues that other employees who also made narcotics errors were not similarly disciplined. UHS argues that the other employees who erred are not comparable because Murray is the only one who did not report her errors. The Court concurs with UHS.

The *Naber* case provides a useful comparison. In that case, the court found that an employee who incorrectly recorded the date of an activity that she provided to a nursing home resident was not comparable to the plaintiff's error of falsifying a treatment record of a resident who was not in the nursing home. The employee's behavior after making the error distinguished the plaintiff from the alleged comparator.

Such is the case here. For example, Jack Plotkin testified that one of the alleged comparators, Joe Wall, reported his narcotics recording error to his supervisor. Similarly, Murray admitted that another alleged comparator, Jennifer O'Donnell, reported her error to management. And former charge nurse Linda Brem certified that nurses who had made multiple mistakes with narcotics filled out forms after each incident and reported the mistakes to management. Although Murray testified that Beth Ann Watson made up an incident report regarding a missing narcotic and did not notify management, there is no evidence in the record that management was aware of the narcotics error (and, hence, that management had the opportunity to discipline Beth Ann Watson for the error).

Murray is the only instance of a nurse who made not one, but two narcotics errors and failed to report those errors to her superiors. Although Murray testified that she was unaware of her mistake regarding the 25 doses signed out of the Pharmacy Record, she admitted that she should have secured a wasting signature for the medications that she allegedly wasted. The other alleged comparators proffered by Murray are not comparable.

Therefore, drawing all factual inferences in favor of the plaintiff, the Court grants summary judgment on all claims because the plaintiff has failed to raise a genuine issue of material fact as to whether UHS's proffered reasons for Murray's termination were pretextual.

* * *

QUESTIONS AND COMMENTS

1. *Disability under the ADAAA.* As the preceding materials make clear, the ADAAA was aimed at expanding the definition of disability under the ADA. Focusing first on Murray's claim of actual disability, can an argument be made that, even under the ADAAA, a claimant's mere allegation that she is "[n]ot eating, not sleeping, having racing thoughts . . . [and] just feeling hopeless, helpless, sad" is insufficient to establish a disability? Does Murray offer any other evidence on this issue? Recall from Chapter Eleven that, to prove disability under the Social Security laws, "objective medical evidence" is required. See p. 1395. Why does the ADAAA not impose the same requirement? Assuming Murray's evidence is credible, does it show that she has a substantial limitation "as compared to most people in the general population" (a phrase still found in the regulations)? See 27 C.F.R. § 1630.2(j)(1)(ii). Alternatively, Murray argued that she was regarded as having a disability. Is there proof that UHS employees thought she had a disability that was not minor or transitory? Of course, in a motion for summary judgment such as was involved in this case, the court is not

resolving these questions, but merely determining whether a genuine issue of fact exists.

The third basis for a finding of disability under the ADA is that the claimant has a record of disability. Might Murray have a stronger claim under this prong (see the third paragraph of the opinion)? Some courts have concluded that this prong is not met unless the employer's perception is based on an actual tangible record indicating the existence of disability. Alex B. Long, *Introducing the New and Improved Americans with Disabilities Act: Assessing the ADA Amendments Act of 2008*, 103 Nw. U. L. Rev. Coll. 217, 227 (2008). Does that make sense?

2. *Retaliation claims.* The court in *Murray* states: "[A]n ADA retaliation claim does not require that the plaintiff show that she is 'disabled' as defined by the ADA. A plaintiff alleging retaliation need only show that she had a reasonable, good faith belief that she was entitled to request the reasonable accommodation she requested." Recall, however, that a claimant who proceeds under the regarded-as prong is not entitled to accommodation. If the regarded-as prong were Murray's only disability theory, could she bring a retaliation claim? In other words, would she be able to argue that UHS retaliated against her because she requested an accommodation, when her belief that she was entitled to such an accommodation was objectively wrong?

UHS responds to the retaliation claim by stating that it had a non-pretextual reason for Murray's dismissal. Yet, according to Murray, she was never allowed to explain her error and at least one other nurse also failed to report a recording error, yet was not dismissed. Furthermore, the only "comparators" UHS produced were cases where the employee was not dismissed, not cases where the employee was, like Murray, dismissed. Why aren't these facts enough to get past a summary judgment motion on the retaliation claim? Do Murray's errors strike you as intentional or in bad faith? Is *Murray* evidence of the finding, noted in the introduction to this chapter, that the ADAAA's changes will simply lead courts to construe other parts of the ADA narrowly?

3. *Major life activities.* Under either the actual disability or record of disability prong, a claimant must show a significant limitation in a major life activity. Work is a major life activity. However, in *Sutton*, the Court held that merely showing that one cannot perform the specific job at issue is insufficient proof of a disability under the ADA; rather the claimant must show an inability to perform in a class of jobs. The ADAAA did not eliminate this aspect of *Sutton*, but was meant to reduce its impact. Thus, the EEOC's commentary states:

> In the rare cases where an individual has a need to demonstrate that an impairment substantially limits him or her in working, the individual can do so by showing that the impairment substantially limits his or her ability to perform a class of jobs or broad range of jobs in various classes as compared to most people having comparable training, skills, and abilities. In keeping with the findings and purposes of the Amendments

Act, the determination of coverage under the law should not require extensive and elaborate assessment, and the EEOC and the courts are to apply a lower standard in determining when an impairment substantially limits a major life activity, including the major life activity of working, than they applied prior to the Amendments Act. . . . For example, if a person whose job requires heavy lifting develops a disability that prevents him or her from lifting more than fifty pounds and, consequently, from performing not only his or her existing job but also other jobs that would similarly require heavy lifting, that person would be substantially limited in working because he or she is substantially limited in performing the class of jobs that require heavy lifting.

29 C.F.R. § 1630 App. *Murray* demonstrates why reliance on work as a major life activity may be, as the above comment suggests, "rare"; usually some other major life activity can be the basis of a disability claim.

Another life activity that is often at issue in cases involving people who claim mental disability is interacting or socializing with others. Prior to the ADAAA, courts split on whether this function was a major life activity. The First, Fourth, and Eighth Circuits questioned whether the "ability to get along with others" is a major life activity, see *Soileau v. Guilford of Me., Inc.*, 105 F.3d 12, 15 (1st Cir. 1997); *Davis v. Univ. of N.C.*, 263 F.3d 95 (4th Cir. 2001); *Amir v. St. Louis Univ.*, 184 F.3d 1017 (8th Cir. 1999), while the Ninth Circuit held that it was, *McAlindin v. County of San Diego*, 192 F.3d 1226 (9th Cir. 1999), and the Second Circuit grudgingly said so as well. *Jacques v. DiMarzio, Inc.*, 386 F.3d 192 (2d Cir. 2004). The ADAAA does not include this function in its list of major life activities, but that list is not meant to be exclusive; furthermore, the current list does include "communicating."

In connection with this discussion of the definition of major life activity, consider *Robinson v. Purcell Construction Company*, 859 F.Supp.2d 245 (N.D.N.Y. 2012), where the plaintiff claimed that, because of her anxiety, depression, and post-traumatic stress disorder, she was perceived as being unable to get along with others, and thus was regarded as substantially limited in this "necessary work skill." Is getting along with others a "necessary work skill" among the general population? If not, should Purcell nonetheless be able to proceed under the ADAAA on the theory that she was "regarded as" unable to get along with others? In the actual case, which arose under the pre-ADAAA statute, the court dismissed the ADA claim because Purcell could not show she was either limited in the "work skill" of working well with others or regarded as being so limited. Had Purcell's case come under the ADAAA, would it have mattered that she was not actually limited in this work skill?

4.   *The interaction of the ADAAA and DSM–5.* As indicated in Chapter One, DSM–5 has expanded the categories of conditions or behaviors that are subject to psychiatric diagnoses. For instance, DSM–5 lists the diagnosis of "mild neurocognitive disorder," which is based on:

evidence of modest cognitive decline from a previous level of performance in one or more cognitive domains [as corroborated by] concern of the individual, a knowledgeable informant, or the clinician that there has been a mild decline in cognitive function and a modest impairment in cognitive performance, preferably documented by standardized neuropsychological testing or, in its absence, another quantified clinical assessment.

These cognitive deficits must "interfere with capacity for independent everyday activities" such as "paying bills or managing medications" in the sense that they might require "greater effort, compensatory strategies, or accommodation." American Psychiatric Association, Diagnostic and Statistical Manual 605 (5th ed., 2013). "Social (pragmatic) communication disorder" exists if the person experiences "persistent difficulties in social use of verbal and nonverbal communication as manifested by all of the following: (1) deficits in using communication for social purposes, such as greeting and sharing information, in a manner that is appropriate for the social context; (2) impairment of the ability to change communication to match context or the needs of the listener; . . . (3) difficulties following rules for conversation and storytelling; . . . and (4) difficulties in understanding what is not explicitly stated (e.g., making inferences) and nonliteral or ambiguous meanings of language (e.g., idioms, humor, metaphors, multiple meanings that depend on the context for interpretation)." Id. at 47–48. These and other changes in the DSM represent a move toward the "spectrum model" of mental disorder. Consider the following comments:

> The threshold coverage issue of "disability" has been defined into virtual irrelevance under the ADAAA, the EEOC's regulations, and recent case law. As individuals learn more about the new DSM–5 mental disorders and the ADAAA's relaxed definition of "disability," more individuals will request accommodation. While the wider DSM–5 net will undoubtedly catch individuals unfairly excluded from the interactive process under the DSM–IV and pre-ADAAA regimes, it will also attract others who want to game the system. The regulatory impact analysis that accompanied the proposed regulations recited that as many as one million additional individuals may consistently meet the ADAAA's definition of "disability," costing employers as much as $235 million per year over five years for additional accommodations. With the relaxation of the DSM–5's standards, one million presumably unfairly excluded individuals may pale in comparison to the total number of newly "disabled" individuals under the DSM–5.

> Although the ADAAA, combined with the release of the DSM–5, may create significant uncertainty, the legal community can take steps to limit this dangerous interaction. Regardless of the relative wisdom of the DSM–5 approach for the medical community, the "spectralization" of mental illness means that legal practitioners, including courts and government agencies, must . . . remove the DSM from its lofty pedestal of authority.

Douglas A Hass, *Could the American Psychiatric Association Cause You Headaches? The Dangerous Interaction Between the DSM–5 and Employment Law*, 44 Loy. U. Chi. L.J. 683, 713–14 (2013). Do you agree?

5. *Normative approaches to defining disability.* The interpretation of disability under the ADA might be informed by theories of disability. For example, disability could be defined to encompass only the most disadvantaged. This approach could be seen as implementing John Rawls's principle of preferential treatment of those individuals who are worst off. See Chapter One, Section V. According to some disability rights scholars, the Supreme Court's parsimonious approach to defining disability in the *Sutton* trilogy is a reflection of a belief that only this "truly disabled" group deserves to be protected. Bonnie P. Tucker, *The Supreme Court's Definition of Disability Under the ADA: A Return to the Dark Ages*, 52 Ala.L.Rev. 321 (2000). The disability scholar Samuel Bagenstos has articulated an alternate normative principle that would include the "truly disabled" but also encompass those individuals who are systematically subject to stigma on the basis of their impairment. According to Bagenstos, while a stigma-based approach is arguably in accord with the outcomes (if not the reasoning) in cases like *Sutton* and *Murphy* (because few individuals with myopia or elevated blood pressure are stigmatized), it is more expansive because it implements an alternative component of John Rawls's model of distributive justice—the idea that all individuals should be given fair equality of opportunity. See generally Samuel R. Bagenstos, *Subordination, Stigma, and "Disability*," 86 Va.L.Rev. 397 (2000). A third suggested normative approach would reject the ADA model of attempting to define a limited class subject to its protection: on this view, anyone who has a mental or physical impairment of any sort (or was seen as having such an impairment) would be protected from irrational discrimination. See Robert L. Burgdorf, Jr., *Substantially Limited Protection from Disability Discrimination: The Special Treatment Model and Misconstructions of the Definition of Disability*, 42 Vill.L.Rev. 409 (1997) (advocating this approach).

Which, if any, of these normative approaches is adopted by the ADAAA? Which is applied in *Murray* and *Purcell*? Which do you find most appealing?

6. *Pre-employment inquiries as to disability.* Under the ADA, an employer may not ask a job applicant questions about whether the applicant has a disability and/or about the nature or severity of the disability. Rather, at the pre-employment stage, the employer is restricted to inquiries into the ability of an applicant to perform job-related functions. 42 U.S.C. § 12112(d)(2)(A,B). Similarly, under a regulation promulgated pursuant to the Rehabilitation Act, employers that receive federal funds "may not make pre-employment inquiry of an applicant as to whether the applicant is a handicapped person or as to the nature or severity of a handicap"; employers may inquire only "into an applicant's ability to perform job related functions." 45 C.F.R. § 84.14(a). A similar prohibition applicable to federal employers appears in 29 C.F.R. § 1613.706. For a strong critique of the prohibition on pre-employment inquiries, see Richard Epstein, *The Legal Regulation of*

Genetic Discrimination: Old Responses to New Technologies, 74 B.U. L. Rev. 1 (1994).

Why shouldn't entities like UHS be able to ask prospective employees like Murray whether they suffer from depression, in order, for instance, to find out if some accommodation is necessary? Wouldn't the ADA still protect Murray from a refusal to hire her on the basis of a disability or record thereof if she was otherwise qualified? Or, as the ADA provides, should the *applicant* control whether accommodation becomes an issue? On this point, why did Murray try to hide her depression from most of her colleagues and (apparently) request a doctor's note that did not mention it? See Cressida Manning & Peter D. White, *Attitudes of Employers to the Mentally Ill,* 19 Psychiatr. Bull. 541 (1995) (employer survey study finding, *inter alia*, that "[o]ver half of employers would never/occasionally employ someone who was currently depressed").For consideration of these issues in the context of professional licensing and certification, *see* Section IV, *infra*.

B. QUALIFICATION AND REASONABLE ACCOMMODATION

Once a claimant has proved that he or she is "disabled" within the meaning of the anti-discrimination laws, the claimant must show he or she is also a "qualified individual with a disability"—that is, someone who, "with or without reasonable accommodation, can perform the essential functions of the employment position that such individual holds or desires." 42 U.S.C. § 12111(8) (ADA); 29 C.F.R. § 1613.702(f); 45 C.F.R. § 84.3K If the plaintiff can prove these claims, the burden then shifts to the defendant to either rebut those claims or establish that any reasonable accommodation of the disability would create an undue hardship. In determining whether an accommodation would create an undue hardship, courts may consider "the nature and cost of the accommodation," "the overall financial resources of the covered entity," "the composition, structure and functions of the workforce," and whether the accommodation can "eliminate" any "direct threat"—defined in the statute as "a significant risk to the health or safety of others." 42 U.S. C. § 12111(4)(1). As the following case illustrates, key terms such "disability", "essential functions," "reasonable accommodation," and "direct threat" can all be in some tension with one another.

HOBACK v. CHATTANOOGA

United States District Court, E.D. Tennessee, 2012.
2012 WL 3834828.

CURTIS L. COLLIER, CHIEF JUDGE.

I. BACKGROUND

Plaintiff was hired as a police officer by the Chattanooga Police Department ("CPD") on July 21, 2000. In 2002, Plaintiff took a brief leave from the CPD to enter basic training for the United States Army. Following basic training, Plaintiff returned to the CPD until June 22, 2004, when his National Guard unit was activated and deployed to Iraq. Plaintiff served in Iraq until being honorably discharged on November 27, 2005. In February, 2006 Plaintiff resumed his duties as a CPD police officer.

At some point after returning from Iraq, Plaintiff was diagnosed with Post–Traumatic Stress Disorder ("PTSD"). Plaintiff received counseling and treatment, including psychotropic medication, from the Veterans Administration ("VA"). On April 13, 2009, Plaintiff met with Dr. Estella Acosta of the VA. During the course of the meeting, Dr. Acosta became concerned that Plaintiff was suicidal and dangerous. She filled out a Certificate of Need for Involuntary Commitment, which stated Plaintiff was "depressed and despondent and states that he is feeling suicidal," and further said "[Plaintiff] indicated using a gun although he stated he does not own a gun." Plaintiff was not involuntarily committed, however; apparently he slipped out the back door of the clinic while Dr. Acosta was making arrangements for his committal.

After leaving the VA clinic, Plaintiff drove himself to the VA hospital in Murfreesboro, Tennessee and checked himself in [where his counselor was Mr. Bearden, whose notes were to be important evidence at trial]. Plaintiff was kept overnight, and released the next day. The CPD became aware of the attempted involuntary commitment of Plaintiff on April 14, 2009. On that date, the Bradley County Sheriff's Department called CPD to inform CPD it was attempting to serve emergency committal papers on Plaintiff, and to ask CPD's help in locating Plaintiff. After some investigation, CPD discovered Plaintiff had already checked himself into the VA hospital. Also on April 14, 2009, Freeman Cooper, CPD Chief of Police, wrote a letter relieving Plaintiff from duty, and placing him on administrative leave. The letter further stated Plaintiff would be required to complete a "fitness for duty" psychological examination.

In April and May, 2009, Donald L. Brookshire, Psy.D., met with Plaintiff several times to conduct the fitness for duty psychological examination. In a seven-page, single-spaced report, Dr. Brookshire concluded Plaintiff was "not psychologically fit to safely perform the duties as a police officer." Following this evaluation, Plaintiff was told he needed to either apply for another position with the City, or file for Family Medical Leave Act ("FMLA") benefits. Plaintiff did neither. Subsequently, Plaintiff requested a second evaluation be performed by another psychologist. In June and July, 2009, Plaintiff was evaluated by Terrell M. McDaniel, Ph.D. Dr. McDaniel's report, while acknowledging Dr. Brookshire's conclusion may have been justified at the time, concluded Plaintiff was now fit for duty as a police officer. However, the report advised that "adequately monitoring Mr. Hoback's behavior and mental health status will be essential but difficult," and recommended he be placed in "a position that provides acceptable levels of monitoring at the beginning of his re-engagement," and continue receiving intensive counseling and psychological monitoring for at least 90 days.

On July 21, 2009, after Plaintiff had exhausted all his personal leave time, Chief Cooper terminated Plaintiff's employment with the CPD based on Dr. Brookshire's determination Plaintiff was not fit for duty. Chief Cooper did not significantly rely upon Dr. McDaniel's report, because he viewed its conditions regarding the need to continue actively monitoring Plaintiff as belying the formal conclusion that Plaintiff was now fit for duty. He was, however, made aware of its contents. Following his termination, Plaintiff exercised his right to appeal to a panel of the Chattanooga City Council. After a hearing on November 9, 2009, his termination was upheld by a 2–1 vote.

On April 12, 2010, Plaintiff filed suit in this court alleging claims under the Americans with Disabilities Act [and] the Rehabilitation Act of 1973. . . . The jury returned a verdict in favor of Plaintiff on September 15, 2011, awarding him $130,000 in back pay, $300,000 in front pay, and $250,000 for emotional distress for a total award of $680,000. The City filed this motion for judgment as a matter of law or for a new trial on October 13, 2011, objecting to the verdict and the computation of damages.

II. LEGAL STANDARDS

[To obtain a judgment notwithstanding the verdict under Federal Rule of Civil Procedure 50, the City] must show "no reasonable juror could have found for the nonmoving party." . . . [Under Rule 59, a court] should not grant a new trial on the grounds the verdict is against the weight of the evidence "unless the verdict was unreasonable"; that is, "if a reasonable juror could reach the challenged verdict, a new trial is improper." Although both standards discuss the reasonableness of a jury verdict, the standard for granting a new trial is less stringent than the standard for granting a judgment as a matter of law. . . .

III. DISCUSSION

The City argues the evidence at trial demonstrates no reasonable jury could have determined (1) the City regarded Plaintiff as disabled and discriminated against him; or (2) Plaintiff was a qualified individual who could perform the essential functions of a police officer. While the Court finds the City's arguments to be nonfrivolous, the Court concludes a reasonable jury could have reached the verdict reached, and therefore the City's motion for judgment as a matter of law and for a new trial must be denied.

A. ADA Claim

Under the ADA, an employer may not "discriminate against a qualified individual with a disability." Plaintiff had the burden at trial to prove he was disabled and he was a qualified individual. An individual is "disabled" under the ADA if he has "(A) a physical or mental impairment that substantially limits one or more major life activities of such individual; (B) a record of such an impairment; or (C) [is] regarded as having such an impairment." Under the "regarded as" prong in (C), an individual must only show he was regarded as having a perceived impairment, and does not need to prove his perceived impairment would substantially limit a major life activity. A "qualified individual" is "an individual with a disability who, with or without reasonable accommodation, can perform the essential functions of [the] employment position." Such reasonable accommodations include "job restructuring, part-time or modified work schedules, reassignment to a vacant position, . . . and other similar accommodations.". However, an individual who is only "regarded as" disabled must be able to perform the essential functions of the job without reasonable accommodation. 42 U.S.C. § 12201(h).

1. Disability

The City argues the evidence presented at trial was insufficient for a reasonable jury to conclude the City regarded Plaintiff as disabled and discriminated against him. Specifically, the City argues it only regarded Plaintiff as incapable of performing the functions of a police officer, and did not regard Plaintiff's condition as substantially limiting any major life activity. . . . This argument would have been convincing, and perhaps determinative, if the relevant events in this case occurred before January 1, 2009. However, because the events occurred after January 1, 2009, the ADAAA applies to the City's conduct. To be liable under the "regarded as" prong as amended by the ADAAA, a defendant need not regard an individual as substantially limited in a major life activity. A plaintiff must only show that he was "subjected to an action prohibited under [the ADA] because of an actual or perceived physical or mental impairment whether or not the impairment limits a major life activity." Therefore, if a reasonable jury could have concluded the City terminated Plaintiff because of an actual or perceived physical or mental impairment—in this case, PTSD—then this ground is insufficient to grant the City's motion.

A reasonable jury could have concluded, based on the evidence submitted at trial, the City terminated Plaintiff because of the reports submitted to CPD management regarding Plaintiff's PTSD. In fact, in its motion for judgment as a matter of law, the City admits Plaintiff's termination was based on Chief Cooper's belief that Plaintiff's PTSD disqualified him to perform the essential functions of a police officer ("Dr. Brookshire provided a medical report to Chief Cooper that informed the

Chief that Hoback was not fit for duty in May 2009 and Chief Cooper informed Hoback that he could not continue as a police officer due to that medical determination.") ("I terminated Mickel Hoback, after he exhausted all of his leave and personal time, based on the fact that he was deemed to be unfit by Dr. Brookshire and not free of any and all mental disorders."). Based on the evidence submitted at trial, a reasonable jury could conclude the City regarded Plaintiff as disabled, and terminated him on the basis of an actual or perceived mental impairment. The City's argument as to that issue fails.

2.   Qualified Individual

The more difficult question is whether Plaintiff is a qualified individual who could perform the essential functions of the job. Where, as here, a plaintiff brings a "regarded as" claim, he must show he is a qualified individual without the benefit of any reasonable accommodation; that is, he must show he can perform the essential functions of the job as it is normally performed. [Further,] the ADA limits its scope of protection and excludes otherwise qualified individuals who pose "a 'direct threat' to the health or safety of others that cannot be eliminated by a reasonable accommodation." A plaintiff in a "regarded as" claim is also not entitled to reasonable accommodation in the direct threat determination.

The City's argument necessarily blends the essential functions and direct threat analyses, and indeed in this case these analyses go hand-in-hand. In fact, some courts have considered the burden to be on plaintiff in cases where the essential functions of the job implicate the safety of others. Others treat it as a defense with the burden on the defendant. However, the Sixth Circuit has yet to rule on this matter. Because the Sixth Circuit has referred to the direct threat inquiry as a "defense," the Court treats it as such, as have other district courts in the Sixth Circuit. The Court, then, will consider the essential functions analysis and the direct threat defense separately.

a.   Essential Functions

. . . Plaintiff here is only incapable of performing the essential functions of his job to the extent his supervisors believed he posed a danger to himself and others while employed. For the purposes of this motion, the Court will assume the jury concluded the essential functions of the position of police officer were those described by Chief Cooper in his testimony, and relied on by the City in its motion:

> Police officers are individuals that are not just working a 9:00–to–5:00 job. They're people that are distinguished by a uniform. They wear a badge and a gun. They expose themselves to danger. They carry assault weapons. They have to be able to make split-second decisions, life-and-death decisions that may take someone's life or

take someone's freedom away. They have to be of sound mind, clear-thinking, able-bodied people in good physical health and mental health. And they have to be able to control themselves in very, very high situations at some times without losing control themselves, being able to maintain calmness and to restore calm and peace in these situations. And they have to be able, counted on, relied upon by myself and the citizens that they serve, to use only the amount of force necessary when dealing with situations and citizens that's deemed necessary to control that situation, up to and including taking someone's life.

In support of its argument [that] Plaintiff was not qualified to perform the essential functions of the position, the City notes Plaintiff's diagnosis with severe PTSD by the VA, involuntary commitment by a VA psychiatrist, Plaintiff's medication, and Plaintiff's VA Counselor's notes detailing Plaintiff's descriptions of various violent thoughts and acts. The evidence the City relies on was presented at trial and the jury was in a position to consider it with the testimony of Plaintiff himself and Chief Cooper who terminated Plaintiff. Most notably, on direct examination, Plaintiff detailed his version of multiple events mentioned in Counselor Bearden's notes [described in more detail below] and relied on by Dr. Brookshire in his report, which convinced Chief Cooper to terminate Plaintiff's employment. Included in Plaintiff's testimony was discussion of embellishments he made to Counselor Bearden in order to receive larger benefits from the VA. He also noted the only side effects from his medication were headaches and nausea. Further, Plaintiff detailed some of his experiences in the military, on which a reasonable jury could rely to conclude he was capable of withstanding the types of stresses Chief Cooper acknowledged in his essential functions discussion. . . .

The events as relayed to Counselor Bearden would concern any supervisor, particularly a supervisor of a police officer. But the question presented to the jury was whether Plaintiff could perform the essential functions of the position. A reasonable jury could have heard all the evidence and placed significant weight on Plaintiff's explanation of Counselor Bearden's notes, discounted his embellishments to his VA Counselor, weighed the credibility of the testifying mental health professionals, and concluded the evidence presented was sufficient to show Plaintiff could perform the essential functions of the position.

b.   Direct Threat

The City argues Plaintiff was a "direct threat" to the health and safety of others in his workplace. In a direct threat defense, a defendant must show its determination the plaintiff posed a direct threat was premised on "an individualized inquiry into the individual's actual medical condition, and the impact, if any, the condition might have on that individual's ability to perform the job in question. . . . This assessment shall be based on a reasonable medical judgment that relies on the most current medical knowledge and/or on the best available objective evidence." 29 C.F.R. § 1630.2(r). The decision of the employer or its medical professionals who made the decision must also be "objective[ly] reasonable[ ]" in light of available medical evidence. *Bragdon v. Abbott*, 524 U.S. 624, 650, 118 S.Ct. 2196, 141 L.Ed.2d 540 (1998).

After determining the sufficiency of an employer's termination procedures, the next step is determining whether the plaintiff "meets the standard for posing a direct threat." This analysis is rooted in a consideration of four factors provided by 29 C.F.R. § 1620.29(r): "(i) [T]he duration of the risk [posed by plaintiff], (ii) the nature and severity of the potential harm, (iii) the likelihood that the potential harm will occur, and (iv) the imminence of the potential harm." The risk must be significant; it cannot be speculative or remote.

First, the City argues its procedures were adequate. It points to the fitness determination performed by Dr. Brookshire, which was based on the notes taken by VA Counselor Bearden and Dr. Brookshire's own in-person evaluation. It also points to Plaintiff's testimony at trial admitting to the embellishments and falsehoods he related to Counselor Bearden. In these sources, the City highlights Plaintiff's diagnosis with severe PTSD by the VA and involuntary commitment by a VA psychiatrist. It also emphasizes Plaintiff's VA Counselor's notes detailing Plaintiff's descriptions of various violent thoughts and acts ("[Plaintiff] described nightmares, intrusive thoughts, and loss of control of his anger. He stated on several occasions he has 'choked' or hit people he is interacting with when he has gotten mad (including fellow police officers . . . ")." The City argues, considering Plaintiff's claims to his VA Counselor about violent episodes, a judgment in his favor puts the City in the impossible position of choosing between retaining high-risk employees and subjecting itself to possible § 1983 claims, or dismissing high-risk employees and subjecting itself to ADA claims.

Although the Court is sensitive to the City's dilemma, the Court may not "set aside the verdict [even if] it believes [ ] another outcome is more justified." There was sufficient evidence for a reasonable jury to conclude the City's evaluation of Plaintiff was not based on the best objective medical evidence. For instance, prior to firing Plaintiff, Chief Cooper was aware of a determination by Dr. McDaniel finding Plaintiff fit for duty, although he also recommended certain actions on the part of the police department. When asked if that decision affected his opinion regarding Plaintiff's qualification, Chief Cooper responded, "Absolutely not. He was either fit for duty or not fit for duty. And if he was only fit for duty based on a number of conditions, then that was not fit for duty."[2]

A reasonable jury could have concluded Dr. McDaniel's findings reflected poorly on the soundness of Dr. Brookshire's conclusions and should have been considered by Chief Cooper before termination. . . . For example, Dr. Brookshire failed to consider Plaintiff's explanations for events from Counselor Bearden's notes,[3] whereas [Dr. McDaniel] either discounted the events for lack of corroborating information, or heavily considered those explanations. Dr. Brookshire also failed to consider the circumstances of Plaintiff's commitment, including that it occurred under some controversy and he was immediately discharged the following day. [Dr. McDaniel] discounted the commitment after investigating the circumstances surrounding it.

Based on these discrepancies, a reasonable jury could have considered Dr. Brookshire's report to lack the type of individualized inquiry or reasonable medical judgment required by the ADA. The jury could have determined Chief Cooper's nearly sole reliance on Dr. Brookshire's report, and failure to consider Dr. McDaniel's conclusions, to indicate his determination was not based on "the best available objective evidence."

Second, the jury could have determined Plaintiff was not a direct threat under the four-factor test provided by C.F.R. § 1620.29(r). First, the jury could have determined duration of the risk was too short, or even nonexistent, to pose a significant threat of harm given the testimony of [Dr. McDaniel] agreeing Plaintiff was relatively asymptomatic. . . . Further, the violent episodes detailed in Dr. Brookshire's report were uncorroborated and Plaintiff testified extensively and provided explanations for their presence in Counselor Bearden's notes. The jury could have concluded Plaintiff had performed his duties without significant incident and relied on that determination to find he did not pose a significant threat of harm in the future. Second, the jury could have concluded the nature and severity of the potential harm was low, as the jury could have considered Plaintiff's explanations of his symptoms

---

[2] Because Plaintiff proceeded on a "regarded as" theory, Chief Cooper was correct that he was not required to provide any accommodations recommended by Dr. McDaniel. However, a reasonable jury could have concluded Dr. McDaniel's determination cast doubt on the reliability of Dr. Brookshire's report, and therefore Chief Cooper did not rely on the best available medical evidence.

[3] Hoback: "More or less we covered some things in [Counselor Bearden's] notes. . . . One of them was, I guess, about a lawyer that I had got in an argument with. . . . And as I tried to explain them to him, he didn't want to hear anything. He said I was minimizing everything in the notes."

Attorney: "Did you ask him anything about verifying with your fellow workers information?"

Hoback: "There was an incident which will come up where it says I choked or punched fellow officers. I advised him what had happened with me and this other officer, 'That's not actually what happened.' I said, 'You can call him and check.' And he said, 'I'm sure he would lie for you. He's your buddy.'"

and [Dr. McDaniel's] analyses more credible than Dr. Brookshire's. Third, the jury could have similarly concluded the likelihood the potential harm will occur was low after considering the testimony of the doctors and Plaintiff. Finally, the jury could have found the potential harm lacked imminence by relying on testimony stating Plaintiff's symptoms had dissipated and his condition was in remission.

. . . Because the evidence was sufficient for a reasonable jury to conclude Plaintiff was a qualified individual capable of performing the essential functions of a police officer and did not pose a direct threat to himself or others in his workplace, the City's motion must be DENIED. Because the Court finds there was sufficient evidence to sustain the jury's verdict under the ADA, discussion of Plaintiff's Rehabilitation Act claim is unnecessary.

B.   Damages

The jury awarded Plaintiff $130,000 in back pay, $300,000 in front pay, and $250,000 for emotional distress for a total award of $680,000. [The Court reduced the back pay award by $9,700, and upheld both the front pay award and the award for emotional distress.]

QUESTIONS AND COMMENTS

1.   *The interaction of disability analysis and qualifications analysis.* Under the ADA, a claimant must submit proof of a disability and yet also demonstrate an ability to meet the essential qualifications for the job, with or without reasonable accommodation. If the claimant is proceeding under the record-of or regarded-as prongs of disability, the tension between these two proof requirements is not significant. But, as noted in the previous section, if the claimant is asserting he or she has an "actual disability," proof of a "substantial limitation" on a major life activity, such as work, is necessary, although the implementing regulations also state that this threshold "should not demand extensive analysis." 29 C.F.R. § 1630.2(j)(1)(iii). Did Hoback have sufficient proof of an actual disability? If so, was he nonetheless qualified to carry out the essential aspects of his job with CPD without any accommodation (see, in particular, Dr. McDaniel's report)? If some sort of accommodation was necessary, what would it have been and would it have been "reasonable" or instead unduly burdensome on the CPD to institute it? Should a person with a mental disorder like PTSD ever be allowed to be a police officer on the beat? How does the ADA's definition of "direct threat" answer this question? Another way to get at the accommodation point: Why wasn't reinstatement rather than damages the remedy at issue in *Hoback*?

If instead, Hoback was not actually impaired, but rather regarded as impaired, then, as noted earlier, he is not entitled to accommodation. So again, was he qualified for the job without an accommodation? Does the prohibition on accommodation for people in the regarded-as category make sense? Might there not be people who do not meet the actual disability standard but still require some accommodation? Does Hoback fit in that category?

2. *Danger to health or safety of person with disability.* In light of Hoback's suicidal behavior, could the CPD have asserted a "threat to self" defense? The language of the ADA only authorizes a threat to others exception. But in *Chevron U.S.A. Inc. v. Echazabal*, 536 U.S. 73, 122 S.Ct. 2045, 153 L.Ed.2d 82 (2002), the Supreme Court upheld an EEOC regulation that permits a danger-to-self defense (now codified at 29 C.F.R. § 1630.2(r)). The Court concluded that the broad language of the ADA's affirmative defense provision (Section 12113), which allows employers to set qualification standards that are "job-related and consistent with business necessity," coupled with the authority Congress specifically delegated to the EEOC to interpret Title I of the ADA, gave the agency significant discretion in specifying such standards. In addition, according to the Court, the EEOC regulation did not promote the "kind of workplace paternalism the ADA was meant to outlaw." In the Court's view, what Congress meant to prohibit was blanket refusal to give opportunities to individuals with disabilities based on "untested and pretextual stereotypes." Congress did not mean to outlaw the "particularized inquiry into the harms the employee would probably face" required by the EEOC regulation.

3. *Medication and disability.* Although the *Sutton* trilogy suggested that a person whose mental problems are controlled by medication would not have a disability under the ADA, the ADAAA has made clear that any serious mental illness meets that threshold, regardless of whether it can be "mitigated" with medication. Assume Hoback's anxiety and Murray's depression could have been substantially alleviated with medication, but that they refused to take it. Must an employer try to accommodate such a person? Consider the following comment about how various commentators and courts have tried to resolve this issue:

> One theory called for a balancing of the burdens of accommodation versus mitigation between the employer and the plaintiff; another theory would allow the employer, after the plaintiff has made his prima facie case, to show that mitigating measures are more reasonable than an accommodation by the employer; and yet another theory would compare the plaintiff's decision not to mitigate to what a "reasonable person" would do in the same situation. These proposals claim to be consistent with public policy in requiring that the plaintiffs help themselves to some degree before turning to their employers or the courts for accommodation. All of these proposals, however, run counter to the spirit of the ADA, especially in light of the passage of the ADAAA. In the ADAAA, Congress specifically stated its intent that a "broad scope of protection . . . be available under the ADA" and further stated that the "primary object of attention" in ADA cases is whether covered entities "complied with their obligations." Thus, it is logical to assume that Congress intended for courts to consider the employer's actions in offering reasonable accommodations, rather than whether the plaintiff's

decision to mitigate was reasonable. Additionally, some argue that the term "reasonable" modifies the term "accommodation" and has nothing to do with an evaluation of the employee's actions.

Jennifer M. Jackson, *The Americans with Disabilities Act, Mental Illness, and Medication: A Historical and Hope for the Future*, 12 Marq. Elder's Advisor 219, 243–44 (2010).

4.   *Reasonable accommodation and undue hardship.* To get a better idea of what an employment accommodation for a person with a serious mental disability might look like, consider this hypothetical accommodation plan, created in a case involving an individual with bipolar disorder (Johnson) employed as a sales agent by a technology company (Perfect):

Reasonable Accommodation: The following steps might assist in improving Mr. Johnson's performance at Perfect:

1.   The company could, consistent with confidentiality concerns, provide to Ms. Coltrane (Mr. Johnson's supervisor) and others who work closely with Mr. Johnson a description of bipolar disorder written in lay terms, to dispel common myths associated with the illness. This description should include the facts that people with bipolar disorder experience periods of mania and depression; that symptoms of mania include abundant energy, an unrealistic belief in one's abilities, increased risk taking, and irritability or distractibility; and that symptoms of depression include pessimism, sleep problems, decreased energy, social withdrawal, and difficulty making decision. It should also make clear that treatment for bipolar disorder is generally effective and that persons with this condition function for long periods free of debilitating symptoms.

2.   Probably no new staff support position is needed to accommodate Mr. Johnson's disability. In other words, Mr. Johnson does not need a full-time assistant to "shadow" him as he performs his duties. However, Mr. Johnson could benefit from peer support, because he travels for prolonged periods and could suffer a relapse while on the road caused by failing to eat or sleep regularly and by the increased stress of traveling. One possible approach would be for Perfect, during a six-week transitional period, to send a coworker— preferably one of Mr. Johnson's choice—to accompany Mr. Johnson on extended national sales campaigns. This coworker would ensure that Mr. Johnson eats and sleeps and does not become overanxious due to stressful traveling. An assessment should be made at the end of this six-week period as to whether the coworker is needed further; if so, appropriate arrangements should be made.

3.   To the extent possible, the high performance periods required of Mr. Johnson should be correlated with periods during which his bipolar illness is at its lowest ebb. The latter periods can be ascertained by conferring with Mr. Johnson and Dr. Jones [the consulting psychiatrist]. To facilitate this inquiry, Mr. Johnson and Ms.

Coltrane should meet weekly at an established time to discuss matters including sales calls, sales proposals, Mr. Johnson's new initiatives, and other essential tasks Mr. Johnson performs. The goal of these meetings, to which Ms. Coltrane appears amenable, is to permit the two to make adjustments to the accommodation plan when necessary.

4. In addition, flexible scheduling should be permitted, to enable Mr. Johnson to obtain appropriate medical care and attend group therapy sessions.

5. Finally, Mr. Johnson should have a private office, to minimize interruptions during his periods of stress.

Before the company decides to implement these accommodations, Ms. Coltrane should of course be consulted. As noted earlier, when asked whether she would mind meeting with Mr. Johnson on a weekly or more frequent basis, she stated that she would not mind doing so if the meetings were not long and if they would guarantee high-quality work from Mr. Johnson. However, if friction does develop between the two, Mr. Johnson's stress could be exacerbated. Thus ensuring that Ms. Coltrane agrees with the preceding suggestions is important.

Threats to Others: At the present time, Mr. Johnson appears to pose absolutely no threat to others in the physical sense. . . .

Adapted from Peter David Blanck et al., *Implementing Reasonable Accommodations Using ADR Under the ADA: The Case of a White-collar Employee with Bipolar Mental Illness*, 18 Men. & Phys. Dis. L. Rep. 458 (1994).

Do these accommodations seem "reasonable"? Under Title I of the ADA, private employers bear the cost of reasonable accommodation. Was the decision to place these costs on private employers a good idea? One study found a decrease in employment rates among people with disabilities after enactment of the ADA, and suggested that the decrease was directly attributable to the law's accommodation requirement. Christine Jolls & J.J. Prescott, *Disaggregating Employment Discrimination: The Case of Disability Discrimination*, Harvard Public Law Working Paper No. 106 (2005), available at http://papers.ssrn.com/sol3/papers.cfm?abstract_id=580741. In contrast, a study conducted at Sears, Roebuck, & Co. between 1993 and 1995 indicated that workers with mental and behavioral disorders represented only 7% of the population requesting accommodation and that the average cost of accommodation was negligible. See Terry Carter, *Unhappy to Oblige*, ABA Journal 36 (July, 1997) (summarizing study results). Similarly, according to one commentator, the majority of workplace disability cases involve stress-related disabilities triggered by aspects of the workplace environment that can readily be remedied. See Susan Stefan, *"You'd Have to Be Crazy To Work Here": Worker Stress, the Abusive Workplace, and Title I of the ADA*, 31 Loy. L.A.L. Rev. 795 (1998). For an argument that reasonable accommodations should nonetheless be funded through general taxation rather than private employers, see Scott A. Moss and Daniel A. Malin, Note, *Public Funding for Disability Accommodations: A Rational Solution to Rational Discrimination*, 33 Harv. C.R.–C.L. L. Rev. 197 (1998). For an argument that the reasonable accommodation requirement, and the ADA more generally, may increase efficiency, see J.H. Verkerke, *Is the ADA Efficient?*, 50 U.C.L.A. Rev. 903 (2003) (arguing that disability discrimination law can combat problems of incomplete and asymmetric information that would otherwise arise when individuals with disabilities are in the labor market but hide their disabilities).

In *U.S. Airways v. Barnett*, 535 U.S. 391, 122 S.Ct. 1516, 152 L.Ed.2d 589 (2002) the Supreme Court suggested that it may take a conservative view of the reasonable accommodation requirement. In that case, the Court held that proof that a requested accommodation conflicts with seniority rules is ordinarily sufficient to show, as a matter of law, that the accommodation is not reasonable. Lower courts have also taken a parsimonious view of the reasonable accommodation requirement, suggesting that only those accommodations that yield benefits in excess of their costs should be considered reasonable. See, e.g., *Vande Zande v. Wisconsin Dep't of Administration*, 44 F.3d 538 (7th Cir.1995). According to *Vande Zande*, a focus on cost-benefit analysis is consistent with the ADA's purpose of saving society the costs of welfare dependency by individuals with disabilities: "The savings will be illusory if employers are required to expend many more billions in accommodation than will be saved by enabling disabled people to work." Id. at 543. On that premise, the court held that the employer did not have to allow telecommuting to accommodate an employee with pressure ulcers. See also *Mason v. Avaya Communications*, 357 F.3d 1114 (10th Cir. 2004) (rejecting a requirement of telecommuting for an employee with posttraumatic stress disorder). Would the *Vande Zande* court find the accommodations recommended in the Johnson case above reasonable?

The ADAAA may not have changed much on this score. Consider these comments from Long, supra, at 228–29:

> One of the more persuasive explanations as to why the federal courts initially made it so difficult for ADA plaintiffs to qualify as having a disability is that the courts sought to avoid having to deal with complex and messy reasonable accommodation issues. By adopting a strict definition of disability, courts were able to avoid dealing with accommodation issues that, due to their fact-specific nature, were not easily decided on a motion for summary judgment and that had the potential to place significant burdens on employers. Regardless of the reason, the end result has been a marked lack of clear rules on the subject of reasonable accommodation. The new amendments do virtually nothing to assist courts and potential litigants in this regard. The amendments leave a host of reasonable accommodation issues unresolved, such as whether an employer must, as part of its duty of reasonable accommodation, reassign an individual with a disability to a vacant position when there is another, more qualified applicant and

whether there should be a presumption that allowing an employee to work from home is not a reasonable accommodation. Instead of taking the opportunity to resolve the conflicting standards on these points, by relaxing the standard for qualifying as having a disability, Congress may have actually made the job of courts tougher.

5.   *Damages and the ADA.* Title I of the ADA specifically incorporates by reference the procedural and remedial requirements set forth in Title VII of the Civil Rights Act of 1964. See 42 U.S.C. § 12117. Pursuant to the subsequent Civil Rights Act of 1991, employees bringing Title I claims may seek not only reinstatement and back pay but also compensatory and punitive damages. 42 U.S.C. § 1981a. Compensatory damages are only recoverable, however, in cases involving intentional discrimination or discrimination that demonstrates gross misjudgment, bad faith, or deliberate indifference. See, e.g., *M.P. v. Indep. School Dist. No. 721*, 326 F.3d 975 (8th Cir.2003). To recover punitive damages, the claimant must prove that the employer "engaged in a discriminatory practice with malice or with reckless indifference to the federally protected rights of an aggrieved individual." 29 U.S.C. § 1981a(b)(1). Are the damages in *Hoback* warranted under these provisions?

The damages suit in *Hoback* was brought against the police department in Chattanooga, a municipality. Had it been brought against a state entity, it would probably have been barred by the Supreme Court's decision in *Board of Trustees of the University of Alabama v. Garrett*, 531 U.S. 356, 121 S.Ct. 955, 148 L.Ed.2d 866 (2001). Under *Garrett* and the line of cases it followed, the Eleventh Amendment prohibits Congress from abrogating state sovereign immunity when it acts pursuant to its powers under Section 5 of the Fourteenth Amendment (which allows Congress to pass legislation implementing the Equal Protection Clause), unless the legislation exhibits "congruence and proportionality between the injury to be prevented or remedied and the means adopted to that end." Id. at 365 (citing *City of Boerne v. Flores*, 521 U.S. 507, 520, 117 S.Ct. 2157, 138 L.Ed.2d 624 (1997)). According to the Court in *Garrett*, the ADA does not meet this test. As noted in Part I of this chapter, the primary basis for the latter conclusion was the Court's belief that Congress had not provided sufficient evidence that state governments (as opposed to local governments) had engaged in a pattern of irrational discrimination against people with disabilities. Moreover, the Court held, even if Congress had found such a pattern of disability-based discrimination, the rights and remedies created by the ADA, particularly the affirmative requirement of reasonable accommodation, raised questions of "congruence and proportionality" when applied to state employers. The four-member dissent pointed out that the majority's rational basis analysis originated as a mechanism for limiting judicial power vis-à-vis legislatures, and was never meant to control congressional authority to enforce civil rights.

Garrett does not mean the ADA cannot be enforced against state entities. The United States government can sue state entities for damages, and private individuals can still sue individual state officials (as contrasted with state institutions) for prospective injunctive relief. Id. at 374 n.9. Furthermore, to the extent that the state government employer receives federal government funding, it may be vulnerable to suits for monetary damages under the Rehabilitation Act. See *College Savings Bank v. Florida Prepaid Postsecondary Education Expense Board, et al.*, 527 U.S. 666, 686, 119 S.Ct. 2219, 144 L.Ed.2d 605 (1999) (recognizing that Congress may "condition its grant of funds to States upon their taking certain actions that Congress could not require them to take," including a waiver of sovereign immunity); see also *Lane v. Pena*, 518 U.S. 187, 116 S.Ct. 2092, 135 L.Ed.2d 486 (1996); *Duncan v. Washington Metropolitan Area Transit Authority*, 214 F.R.D. 43, 47 (2003) (holding that Section 2000d–7 of the Rehabilitation Act is a "valid and unambiguous waiver" of sovereign immunity and citing various decisions by Ninth, Sixth, Eighth, Fourth, and Fifth Circuits that have relied on *Lane* or Section 2000d–7 to reach the same holding).

C. AFFIRMATIVE ACTION PROGRAMS

Section 501 of the Rehabilitation Act of 1973 requires each federal agency to promulgate "an affirmative action program plan for the hiring, placement, and advancement of individuals with handicaps. . . ." 29 U.S.C. § 791(b). The agency is to include within the plan "a description of the extent to which and methods whereby the special needs of employees with handicaps are being met." Id. However, this affirmative action requirement is fairly narrow: it extends only to federal agencies and not to entities receiving federal funds. (Nor does the ADA pick up the slack, since it does not adopt an affirmative action requirement.) As is clear from the case that follows, the Rehabilitation Act allows private causes of action for alleged violations of Section 501.

ALLEN V. HECKLER

United States Court of Appeals, District of Columbia Circuit, 1985.
780 F.2d 64.

MIKVA, CIRCUIT JUDGE:

This appeal involves a claim under the Rehabilitation Act of 1973. 29 U.S.C. § 701 *et seq.* (1982) ("the Act"). Section 501 of the Act, 29 U.S.C. § 791 (1982), requires each federal executive department to formulate an affirmative action plan that provides adequate career opportunities for handicapped people. The plaintiffs, a class of former patients at St. Elizabeth's, a federal mental hospital, were hired by the Hospital pursuant to one such plan. They now claim that this plan is inadequate because it allows St. Elizabeth's to discriminate against them on the basis of their previous institutionalization.

The district court agreed and granted summary judgment in favor of the plaintiffs. We now affirm the court's finding of discrimination, but vacate and remand for reconsideration of the remedy.

I.

Eleon Allen, the named plaintiff, is a former patient at St. Elizabeth's Hospital, a federal mental institution in Washington, D.C. After his discharge as a patient in 1978, Allen was hired by St. Elizabeth's as a housekeeping aide pursuant to 5 C.F.R. § 213.3102(h) (1984) ("subsection (h)"). Subsection (h) provides that patients who have been discharged from federal mental hospitals may be given special hiring consideration at the institution where they previously received treatment. The key to subsection (h) is that ex-patients are excused from the usual competitive process for obtaining federal employment, and thus are considered "excepted" service employees. Although the former patients must have the necessary skills for the jobs they seek, it is considered "not practical" to subject them to the competitive civil service examination.

Excepted employees, such as the ex-patients here, perform exactly the same work as their "competitive" service counterparts. Their duties and responsibilities are the same, their work is judged by the same standards, and their pay is the same. The excepted workers, however, are given fewer job benefits than competitive employees. Subsection (h) workers may not participate in the civil service retirement program. If they are disciplined or discharged, they do not have the right to an evidentiary hearing before an independent decisionmaker, or the right to appeal to the Merit Systems Protection Board. Excepted workers also have fewer job protections and no "bumping" rights (*i.e.,* no right to take jobs from employees with less seniority) when there is a reduction in work force.

An excepted worker under subsection (h) is free to enter the competitive service at any time by taking the regular civil service exam; the drawback is that the excepted worker must start on the same footing as a first-time applicant. The former patient enjoys no advantage because of his on-the-job experience, nor does he get seniority or other credit for the time spent before conversion toward permanent career status, the federal equivalent of tenure.

Allen and fifty-two other former patients ("plaintiffs") working at St. Elizabeth's sued the Director of the Department of Health and Human Services and the Director of the Office of Personnel Management ("the government") under the Rehabilitation Act. Section 501 of the Act requires that each executive department and agency promulgate an affirmative action plan that provides adequate "hiring, placement, and advancement" opportunities for handicapped people. The plaintiffs contend, and the government does not contest, that they are "handicapped" within the meaning of the Act. Although plaintiffs are no longer institutionalized, the Act recognizes that discrimination also occurs against those who at one time had a disabling condition. The handicap that these people face is the continuing stigma of being a former psychiatric patient; this disability did not disappear upon discharge from the hospital, as the dissent apparently believes. The regulations thus define a handicapped person as, *inter alia,* one who "has a *history* of . . . a mental or physical impairment that substantially limits one or more major life activities."

Plaintiffs claim that granting excepted workers fewer benefits for the same work is discrimination based on their previous medical condition. They argue that subsection (h) violates the Act's affirmative action requirement because it does not provide "adequate" advancement opportunities. The district court (per Judge June Green) agreed and granted summary judgment in favor of the plaintiff class. As a remedy, Judge Green ordered that all subsection (h) employees who had completed two years of satisfactory service must be allowed to convert to competitive status, with full benefits and credits.

The government makes two claims on appeal: first, that subsection (h) does not violate the Act because it does not distinguish among workers on the basis of handicap; second, that the district court's remedy was improper in these circumstances.

II.

There is clearly tension, if not conflict, between the two well-meaning attempts to assist the handicapped at issue in this case. The subsection (h) excepted service program was created by St. Elizabeth's in the 1950s to help recently discharged mental patients return to the work force. Doctors at the Hospital believed that without some special assistance, former patients might be unable to find jobs because of the stigma that follows people who have been institutionalized. By excusing ex-patients from the civil service exam and employing them in familiar surroundings, it was hoped that they would build a good employment record to help them return to the work force when they left the Hospital.

The Rehabilitation Act of 1973 was a more sweeping, statutory attempt to combat all forms of discrimination against the handicapped. Congress made it clear in both the Act and its 1978 amendments, that it viewed discrimination against the handicapped as an evil on a par with racial, sexual, and ethnic discrimination. The Act is a command to remove artificial barriers that prevent handicapped citizens from reaching their full potential. Recognizing the federal government's obligation to be an equal opportunity employer, the Act requires each department and agency to take affirmative steps to hire and promote handicapped workers.

Given this statutory command, subsection (h) clearly falls short of the Act's affirmative action requirement. Giving unequal benefits for equal work is precisely the type of treatment the Act was designed to eliminate. Hiring the excepted workers under a special provision does not justify giving them second-class status once they are on the job.

*   *   *

Subsection (h) would be less problematic if there were a fair way for former patients to convert from the excepted to the competitive service. But as the trial court found, there is no way for the patients to convert; their only option is to apply, along with all other applicants, for a position as a first-time federal worker. This arrangement gives the workers no seniority credit for time spent in the excepted service. So before a worker can take a step forward to enjoy equal pay for equal work, he must first step back to an entry-level position. Surely the protections of the Rehabilitation Act are not this illusory.

These considerations and the case law reinforce our conclusion that the government may not justify disparate treatment of the handicapped simply because they were beneficiaries of the excepted hiring process. The Act requires that unless there is a legitimate government interest to the contrary, handicapped employees must be treated the same as other workers. We therefore affirm the district court's decision that subsection (h) does not provide adequate opportunities to former mental patients, in violation of § 501 of the Act. Fashioning a remedy for such unequal treatment, however, is more complicated.

III.

The trial court recognized the difficulties in devising a remedy. The relief order has to end the discrimination, and at the same time respect the government's interest in assisting the handicapped. Judge Green's order allowed all subsection (h) employees who have completed two or more years of satisfactory service to convert to career or career-conditional status, which would automatically grant all the benefits and protections of the competitive service. Newly converted workers also would receive seniority credit for their time in the excepted service.

This remedy is modeled after the revised subsections (t) [pertaining to persons with intellectual disabilities] and (u), [pertaining to persons with severe physical disability] which were amended by Executive Order in 1979. The regulations now allow both physically handicapped and mentally retarded workers with two years of excepted-service experience to convert to competitive status without taking an exam. For some reason, subsection (h) was not amended at the same time.

Although it might seem logical to make subsection (h) conform to the requirements of closely parallel provisions, we have determined that this symmetrical approach is flawed. Such a remedy would impermissibly interfere with a legitimate government interest because it fails to account for work-related differences between former mental patients and other handicapped workers. We therefore remand to the district court for a reconsideration of the remedy.

There is obviously some government interest in distinguishing between handicapped and non-handicapped employees. The existence of the excepted service confirms this: if handicapped employees did not require special consideration, affirmative action goals could be best met by immediately placing excepted workers in the competitive service, with full benefits and protections. But when subsections (t) and (u) were amended, mentally retarded and physically handicapped people were not given full rights instantly; instead they were given a two year "trial" period. If after two years the employee's handicap proves not to be an impediment to satisfactory performance, the government's interest in treating the excepted class differently disappears.

The problem in the current case is that there are continuing differences between former mental patients and other excepted employees. While a mentally retarded or physically handicapped person's condition usually remains constant or changes gradually, a former mental patient's status is more prone to rapid change. A subsection (h) employee may perform perfectly well for several years, and then have recurring problems that require prompt attention, for the sake of both the worker and the employer.

The possibility of recurring problems was recognized by the Second Circuit in *Doe v. New York University*, 666 F.2d 761 (2d Cir.1981), where a former mental patient brought suit under § 504 of the Act, 29 U.S.C. § 794 (1982), to compel her admission to medical school. After her initial hospitalization, plaintiff's symptoms of mental illness lay dormant for almost seven years before reemerging. She was then re-hospitalized periodically for several years, but at the time of her suit had gone more than four years without apparent problems. Although there was testimony that plaintiff was cured, the court held that the medical school was entitled to consider the likelihood of a reoccurrence of the illness when evaluating her application.

The government and St. Elizabeth's have a strong interest in maintaining the flexibility to handle these situations as they arise. . . . But as anyone familiar with the civil service knows, removing a competitive status employee from his job is a slow and painstaking process. A former patient who is insulated by the competitive-service job protections may experience continuing mental problems, yet the Hospital would be powerless to respond immediately to correct the situation. The ultimate result might well be contrary to the purpose of the Act: St. Elizabeth's might hire only those with a low risk of recurring problems (those least in need of the excepted service program), while those with uncertain diagnoses would be denied the benefits of subsection (h).

On remand, the district court should fashion a remedy that takes account of this interest. Benefits concerning tenure of employment protections should not diminish St. Elizabeth's flexibility to set reasonable rules for granting or denying job tenure to excepted workers, as their condition dictates. We hasten to add, however, that any benefits or protections *un*related to this interest must be granted in full. It is impermissible, for example, to deny subsection (h) workers full pension rights and other financial benefits, since the government has no interest in treating former patients differently in these respects. Even protections against reductions in force should be given without distinction, since they do not affect the Hospital's ability to treat workers according to their individual needs. While the district court is still free to require a two-year delay before granting excepted workers benefits unrelated to the government interest, a *permanent* denial violates the Act; these non work-related benefits must be given to all employees within a reasonable time.

* * *

Conclusion

We emphasize the narrowness of our disagreement with the district court. We affirm the finding below that subsection (h) violates § 501 of the Rehabilitation Act. We also agree that at some point excepted workers are entitled to most of the benefits enjoyed by their competitive counterparts. Commendable as the government's initiative in hiring these workers may be, it defeats the clear command of statute and fairness to treat them as inferior employees in benefits and protections afforded to others. Any distinctive treatment must be related to legitimate work-place needs that the government may have.

We therefore vacate the remedy and remand only for a reconsideration of the handicapped workers' entitlement to those benefits relating to job tenure, in light of the government's legitimate interest in preserving flexibility. In all other respects we affirm.

It is so ordered.

FRIEDMAN, CIRCUIT JUDGE, dissenting:

I would reverse the district court's grant of summary judgment in favor of the appellees and direct that court to dismiss their complaint. In my view, St. Elizabeth's Hospital's practice of hiring its former mental patients by appointing them under 5 C.F.R. § 213.3102(h) (1984) (subchapter (h)) to positions in the excepted service without requiring them to meet the standards necessary for appointment in the competitive service, and without their obtaining all the benefits of the competitive service, is consistent with the Rehabilitation Act of 1973, 29 U.S.C. § 701 *et seq.* (1982), and does not improperly discriminate against those employees on the basis of their former institutionalization in the Hospital.

Ordinarily, an individual obtains an executive branch position in the federal civil service by passing a competitive examination that establishes his or her qualifications for the position sought. After completing a probationary period, an employee thus appointed becomes entitled to the rights and benefits that the civil service system provides. Congress has recognized, however, that there are certain categories of federal positions that should not be subject to the competitive appointment requirements of civil service and therefore has provided for the "excepted service" to cover those positions. 5 U.S.C. § 2107 (1982). Persons appointed to the excepted service do not receive the same rights and benefits as the employees in the competitive service.

In its governing regulations, the Office of Personnel Management has specified a number of positions that are in the excepted service, which may be filled without following the regular procedures for appointment in the classified service. Two of these categories cover individuals who, because of their handicaps, would not be qualified for initial appointment in the competitive service. These provisions are 5 C.F.R. §§ 213.3102(t) and (u), which respectively cover "mentally retarded persons" and "severely physically handicapped persons." Employees in either of these two categories may be converted to competitive status "[u]pon completion of 2 years of satisfactory service under this authority. . . ."

The present case involves subsection (h) of the regulation, which authorizes the appointment at federal mental institutions of former patients of those institutions, who have been discharged and have been certified by medical authority "as recovered sufficiently to be regularly employed but it is believed desirable and in the interest of the persons and the institution that they be employed at the institution." All of the appellees in this case are in that category. They were appointed to positions at St. Elizabeth's Hospital without having to meet the competitive civil service requirements that other persons seeking the same position would have had to satisfy.

*   *   *

The differences between subsection (h) and subsections (t) and (u) are substantial. The latter two subsections deal with persons who are disabled at the time of their appointment and therefore would not qualify for the job under the usual competitive examination procedures. Those individuals are given temporary appointments but, if after two years they have demonstrated their ability to perform the job, they are converted to the competitive status and have the rights and benefits they would have obtained initially had they not been disabled from passing the competitive examination.

Persons given indefinite appointments under subsection (h), on the other hand, are former patients of the mental institution who no longer are disabled at the time of their appointment, but whose well-being favors their employment at the institution with which they are familiar. Some of those individuals might have qualified initially for appointment in the competitive service by taking and passing the usual examination, and any of them could have obtained such competitive permanent positions after appointment by following that course. Indeed, a number of former patients of St. Elizabeth's, originally appointed under subsection (h), have done precisely that and now hold permanent appointments in the classified service with the accompanying rights and benefits. Although the appellees might have obtained a classified position after their appointment by taking and passing the same competitive examination that other nondisqualified persons routinely take, they have not attempted to do so.

The appellees' position is that because they perform the same work as other employees who occupy identical positions in the competitive service, they are entitled to the same benefits the other employees have, and that the denial of those benefits illegally discriminates against them on the basis of their former mental disability. The different treatment of the appellees from the other employees performing the same work, however, results not from the former mental disability of the appellees but from the fact that they were appointed without having to comply with the requirements for the competitive service. In order to achieve the benefits from employment in an environment with which they had become familiar and in which they were comfortable, the government permitted the appellees to obtain their positions without taking and passing the competitive examination that other employees were required to take to obtain the same jobs.

In my view, the government justifiably treated these two categories of employees differently in not giving to the appellees all the civil service protections and benefits of the employees who obtained their positions through the competitive examination process. The difference in the nature of their appointments warranted the different rights and benefits given to each category.

*   *   *

As a policy matter, the result reached in the present case is commendable. My difficulty with that result is that I do not think it reflects a proper use of judicial power. Congress has given the President broad discretion by regulation to administer the laws regulating government employment and therefore to determine the bases for appointments to positions in the executive branch and to define the rights and benefits of employees so appointed. 5 U.S.C. § 3301 (1982). The President in turn has delegated this authority to the Office of Personnel Management. * * * If the type of appointment under subsection (h) and the rights and benefits of employees appointed under that subsection are to be changed, I think such changes must come from the Office of Personnel Management and not from the courts.

QUESTIONS AND COMMENTS

1.   *The scope of the affirmative action requirement.* Neither Section 501 nor the implementing regulations prescribes how agencies should design affirmative action plans. Given this textual ambiguity, did the majority have the authority to find a Section 501 violation? What are the likely long term effects of decisions such as *Allen v. Heckler*?

2.   *Disabled v. "recovered" employees.* The dissent states that while persons covered by subsections (t) and (u) of the regulations concerning excepted positions are disabled at the time they are hired, persons covered by subsection (h) are not disabled at the time they are hired. Given the definition of disability under the Rehabilitation Act (which is identical to the definition of disability under the ADA), is this assertion accurate? The majority, in contrast, states that people with mental illness may be treated differently than people with intellectual or physical disabilities in affirmative action programs because their condition is more likely to change. Had *Allen* been decided today, would this position be consistent with the ADAAA, the regulations for which, it will be recalled, state that episodic conditions can nonetheless be disabilities under the ADA?

3.   *Remedies for Section 501 violations.* The Rehabilitation Act gives courts broad power to remedy Section 501 violations. It provides that courts should "take into account the reasonableness of any necessary workplace accommodation, and the availability of alternatives therefor or other appropriate relief in order to achieve an equitable and appropriate remedy." 29 U.S.C. § 794a(a)(1). In *Allen*, what remedy besides the one rejected by the D.C. Circuit Court of Appeals can the district fashion that will be consistent with the D.C. Circuit's reasoning?

IV.   POSTSECONDARY EDUCATION

The Individuals with Disabilities Education Act ("IDEA"), discussed in Chapter Eleven provides special educational benefits at the elementary and secondary school level for people with disabilities. No comparable statute applies to the postsecondary level. However, the ADA and the Rehabilitation Act require postsecondary educational institutions to make accommodations for students with disabilities. Moreover, the IDEA has had a significant effect on postsecondary education, because it has led to improved education for many more children with disabilities, who in turn have increasingly applied to colleges and universities. See Melana Zyla

Vickers, *Accommodating College Students with Learning Disabilities: ADD, ADHD and Dyslexia*, The John Williams Pope Center for Education Policy 2, 5 (2010), available at http://www.popecenter.org/acrobat/vickers-mar2010.pdf (stating that, in the ten years up to 2010, the number of college students with ADHD, ADD, and learning disabilities had more than doubled to 2%, and attributing the rise to the IDEA and the ADA); *More Youths with Disabilities Going to College*, USA Today, Oct. 17, 2010 (stating that college programs for people with intellectual disabilities increased from 8 to 250 in the previous four years, and attributing this growth to the IDEA and increased federal funding for such programs); John Guthman et al., College Students Exhibiting More Serious Mental Illness, APA Proceedings (August 12, 2010), available at http://www.apa.org/news/press/releases/2010/08/students-mental-illness.aspx (reporting study finding that, from 1998 to 2009, the percentage of college students with moderate or severe depression had increased from 34% to 41% and the percentage of students taking psychiatric medication increased from 11% to 24%).

As noted earlier, depending on how the postsecondary educational institution is funded, one or more of the following anti-discrimination provisions may be applicable: Section 504 of the Rehabilitation Act, Title II of the ADA, or Title III of the ADA. Each statutory provision prohibits the educational institution from denying services or programs to qualified disabled students or from adopting program eligibility criteria that tend to screen out qualified disabled students. The Supreme Court has interpreted this language strictly, stating that "[a]n otherwise qualified person is one who is able to meet all of a program's requirements in spite of his handicap," with or without reasonable accommodation. *Southeastern Community College v. Davis*, 442 U.S. 397, 99 S.Ct. 2361, 60 L.Ed.2d 980 (1979) (construing the Rehabilitation Act).

Probably the most important issue in the application of anti-discrimination law to educational institutions is the scope of the reasonable accommodation requirement. Under Titles II and III of the ADA, for example, an accommodation is not reasonable under two circumstances: (1) if it would cause undue hardship (the same limitation as in Title I); or (2) if it would cause a "fundamental alteration" of the service or program in question. *See* 28 C.F.R. §§ 35.130(b)(7), 35.164 (regulations interpreting Title II); 28 C.F.R. §§ 36.302(a), 36.303(a) (regulations interpreting Title III). The case below is one of the leading decisions on this issue. As it illustrates, courts often defer to the professional judgment of educators in determining whether a requested accommodation is "unreasonable."

WYNNE V. TUFTS UNIVERSITY SCHOOL OF MEDICINE

United States Court of Appeals, First Circuit, 1992.
976 F.2d 791.

SELYA, CIRCUIT JUDGE.

This appeal requires us to revisit a longstanding dispute between Tufts University School of Medicine and Steven Wynne, a former student. On a previous occasion, we vacated the district court's entry of summary judgment in Tufts' favor. *See Wynne v. Tufts Univ. School of Medicine,* 932 F.2d 19 (1st Cir.1991) (en banc). After further proceedings, the district court again entered summary judgment for the defendant. This time around, on an augmented record, we affirm.

Background

The facts pertinent to Wynne's banishment from the groves of academe are chronicled in our earlier opinion and need not be fully rehearsed. A succinct summary suffices.

Wynne matriculated at Tufts in 1983. He failed eight of fifteen first-year courses. Although academic guidelines provided for dismissal after five course failures, the dean granted Wynne a special dispensation and allowed him to repeat the first year of medical school. Over the summer of 1984, Wynne underwent neuropsychological testing at Tufts' instance and expense. The results, described in detail in our earlier opinion, showed cognitive deficits and weaknesses in processing discrete units of information. However, no differential diagnosis of dyslexia or any other particularized learning disability was made at this time.

During Wynne's second tour of the first-year curriculum, Tufts arranged to supply him with tutors, counsellors, note-takers, and other aids. This time, he passed all but two courses: pharmacology and biochemistry. Tufts still did not expel Wynne. Instead, it permitted him to take make-up examinations in these two subjects. He passed pharmacology but failed biochemistry. That ended the matter. Wynne was dismissed in September, 1985.

Prior Proceedings

In his court case, Wynne alleged that he was learning-disabled and that Tufts had discriminated against him on the basis of his handicap. In short order, Wynne refined his claim to allege that his disability placed him at an unfair disadvantage in taking written multiple-choice examinations and that Tufts, for no good reason, had stubbornly refused to test his proficiency in biochemistry by some other means. Eventually, the district court granted summary judgment in Tufts' favor on the ground that Wynne, because of his inability to pass biochemistry, was not an "otherwise qualified" handicapped person within the meaning of section 504 of the Rehabilitation Act of 1973, 29 U.S.C. § 794 (1988), as explicated by the relevant caselaw.

On appeal, a panel of this court reversed. That opinion was withdrawn, however, and the full court reheard Wynne's appeal. We concluded that, in determining whether an aspiring medical student meets section 504's "otherwise qualified" prong, it is necessary to take into account the extent to which reasonable accommodations that will satisfy the legitimate interests of both the school and the student are (or are not) available and, if such accommodations exist, the extent to which the institution explored those alternatives. *See Wynne*, 932 F.2d at 24–26 (citing, *inter alia*, *School Bd. of Nassau County v. Arline*, 480 U.S. 273, 107 S.Ct. 1123, 94 L.Ed.2d 307 (1987)). Recognizing the unique considerations that come into play when the parties to a Rehabilitation Act case are a student and an academic institution, particularly a medical school training apprentice physicians, we formulated a test for determining whether the academic institution adequately explored the availability of reasonable accommodations:

> If the institution submits undisputed facts demonstrating that the relevant officials within the institution considered alternative means, their feasibility, cost and effect on the academic program, and came to a rationally justifiable conclusion that the available alternatives would result either in lowering academic standards or requiring substantial program alteration, the court could rule as a matter of law that the institution had met its duty of seeking reasonable accommodation. In most cases, we believe that, as in the qualified immunity context, the issue of whether the facts alleged by a university support its claim that it has met its duty of reasonable accommodation will be a purely legal one. Only if essential facts were genuinely disputed or if there were significantly probative evidence of bad faith or pretext would further fact finding be necessary.

Id. at 26 (citation and internal quotation marks omitted). Because the summary judgment record did not satisfactorily address this issue,[1] we vacated the judgment and remanded for further proceedings, leaving the district court "free to consider other submissions [and] to enter summary judgment."

Following remand, Tufts filed a renewed motion for summary judgment accompanied by six new affidavits. The plaintiff filed a

---

[1] Tufts had filed only a single affidavit touching upon this issue. Scrutiny of that affidavit, signed by the dean, revealed the following shortcomings: "There is no mention [in the dean's affidavit] of any consideration of possible alternatives, nor reference to any discussion of the unique qualities of multiple choice examinations. There is no indication of who took part in the decision [not to deviate from multiple choice examinations] or when it was made." *Wynne*, 932 F.2d at 28. Because we thought that a party seeking summary judgment should proffer more than "the simple conclusory averment of the head of an institution," we declined to accept the dean's affidavit as a sufficient basis for shortstopping the litigation thereon "if [an expanded record] meet[s] the standard we have set forth". *Id.* at 28.

comprehensive opposition supported, inter alia, by his own supplemental affidavit. The court below read the briefs, heard oral argument, reviewed the parties' updated submissions, and determined that Tufts had met its burden under Wynne. In the lower court's view, the expanded record clearly showed that Tufts had evaluated the available alternatives to its current testing format and had reasonably concluded that it was not practicable in this instance to depart from the standard multiple-choice format. Accordingly, the court again entered summary judgment in Tufts' favor. This appeal ensued.

Issues

The principal issue on appeal is whether, given those facts not genuinely in dispute, Tufts can be said, as a matter of law, either to have provided reasonable accommodations for plaintiff's handicapping condition or to have demonstrated that it reached a rationally justifiable conclusion that accommodating plaintiff would lower academic standards or otherwise unduly affect its program. There is also a secondary issue: whether plaintiff has advanced significantly probative evidence sufficient to ground a finding that Tufts' reasons for not making further accommodations were pretextual or asserted in bad faith.

*   *   *

Discussion

We have carefully reviewed the amplitudinous record and are fully satisfied that the district court did not err in granting summary judgment. Fairly read, the record presents no genuine issue as to any material fact. Because this case has consumed so many hours of judicial time, we resist the temptation to wax longiloquent. Instead, we add only a few decurtate observations embellishing what the en banc court previously wrote and remarking the significance of the new materials adduced below.

First: Following remand, Tufts satisfactorily filled the gaps that wrecked its initial effort at summary judgment. The expanded record contains undisputed facts demonstrating, in considerable detail, that Tufts' hierarchy "considered alternative means" and "came to a rationally justifiable conclusion" regarding the adverse effects of such putative accommodations. *Wynne*, 932 F.2d at 26. Tufts not only documented the importance of biochemistry in a medical school curriculum, but explained why, in the departmental chair's words, "the multiple choice format provides the fairest way to test the students' mastery of the subject matter of biochemistry." Tufts likewise explained what thought it had given to different methods of testing proficiency in biochemistry and why it eschewed alternatives to multiple-choice testing, particularly with respect to make-up examinations. In so doing, Tufts elaborated upon the unique qualities of multiple-choice examinations as they apply to biochemistry and offered an exposition of the historical record to show the background against which such tests were administered to Wynne. In short, Tufts demythologized the institutional thought processes leading to its determination that it could not deviate from its wonted format to accommodate Wynne's professed disability. It concluded that to do so would require substantial program alterations, result in lowering academic standards, and devalue Tufts' end product—highly trained physicians carrying the prized credential of a Tufts degree.

To be sure, Tufts' explanations, though plausible, are not necessarily ironclad. For instance, Wynne has offered evidence that at least one other medical school and a national testing service occasionally allow oral renderings of multiple-choice examinations in respect to dyslexic students. But, the point is not whether a medical school is "right" or "wrong" in making program-related decisions. Such absolutes rarely apply in the context of subjective decisionmaking, particularly in a scholastic setting. The point is that Tufts, after undertaking a diligent assessment of the available options, felt itself obliged to make "a professional, academic judgment that [a] reasonable accommodation [was] simply not available." *Wynne*, 932 F.2d at 27–28. Phrased another way, Tufts decided, rationally if not inevitably, that no further accommodation could be made without imposing an undue (and injurious) hardship on the academic program. With the diligence of its assessment and the justification for its judgment clearly shown in the augmented record, and with the fact of the judgment uncontroverted, the deficiency that spoiled Tufts' original effort at brevis disposition has been cured.

Second: The undisputed facts show that Tufts neither ignored Wynne nor turned a deaf ear to his plight. To the contrary, the defendant (a) warned Wynne in 1983 that he was failing biochemistry and suggested he defer his examination (a suggestion that Wynne scotched); (b) arranged for a complete battery of neuropsychological tests after Wynne failed eight courses in his freshman year; (c) waived the rules and permitted Wynne to repeat the first-year curriculum; (d) furnished Wynne access to tutoring, taped lectures, and the like; (e) allowed him to take untimed examinations; and (f) gave him make-up examinations in pharmacology and biochemistry after he again failed both courses. Given the other circumstances extant in this case, we do not think that a reasonable factfinder could conclude that Tufts, having volunteered such an array of remedial measures, was guilty of failing to make a reasonable accommodation merely because it did not also offer Wynne, unsolicited, an oral rendering of the biochemistry examination.

Third: Reasonableness is not a constant. To the contrary, what is reasonable in a particular situation may not be reasonable in a different situation—even if the situational differences are relatively slight. *Cf., e.g., United States v. Rodriguez–Morales*, 929 F.2d 780, 785 (1st Cir.1991) (concluding that "reasonableness has a protean quality"), *cert. denied*, 502 U.S. 1030, 112 S.Ct. 868, 116 L.Ed.2d 774 (1992); *Sierra Club v. Secretary of the Army*, 820 F.2d 513, 517 (1st Cir.1987) (paraphrasing Emerson and observing that "reasonableness 'is a mutable cloud, which is always and never the same.'"). Ultimately, what is reasonable depends on a variable mix of factors.

In the section 504 milieu, an academic institution can be expected to respond only to what it knows (or is chargeable with knowing). This means, as the Third Circuit has recently observed, that for a medical school "to be liable under the Rehabilitation Act, [it] must know or be reasonably expected to know of [a student's] handicap." *Nathanson v. Medical College of Pa.*, 926 F.2d 1368, 1381 (3d Cir.1991). A relevant aspect of this inquiry is whether the student ever put the medical school on notice of his handicap by making "a sufficiently direct and specific request for special accommodations." *Id.* at 1386. Thus, we must view the reasonableness of Tufts' accommodations against the backdrop of what Tufts knew about Wynne's needs while he was enrolled there.

Several factors are entitled to weight in this equation, including the following: (a) Wynne was never diagnosed as dyslexic while enrolled at Tufts; (b) the school gave him a number of special dispensations and "second chances"—including virtually every accommodation that he seasonably suggested; (c) Wynne had taken, and passed, multiple-choice examinations in several courses; and (d) he never requested, at any time prior to taking and failing the third biochemistry exam, that an oral rendering be substituted for the standard version of the multiple-choice test. Under these circumstances, we do not believe a rational factfinder could conclude that Tufts' efforts at accommodation fell short of the reasonableness standard.

Fourth: Wynne's allegations of pretext do not raise prohibitory doubts about the reasonableness of Tufts' attempted accommodations or about the honesty of its assessment of alternatives to multiple-choice examinations vis-a-vis the school's educational plan. When pretext is at issue in a discrimination case, it is a plaintiff's duty to produce specific facts which, reasonably viewed, tend logically to undercut the defendant's position. The plaintiff may neither "rest[ ] merely upon conclusory allegations, improbable inferences, and unsupported speculation," nor measurably bolster his cause by hurling rancorous epithets and espousing tenuous insinuations.

Here, Wynne's charges comprise more cry than wool. They consist of unsubstantiated conclusions, backed only by a few uncoordinated evidentiary fragments. More is required to forestall summary judgment.

Conclusion

We need go no further. In our earlier opinion, we recognized the existence of a statutory obligation on the part of an academic institution such as Tufts to consider available ways of accommodating a handicapped student and, when seeking summary judgment, to produce a factual record documenting its scrupulous attention to this obligation. Of course, the effort requires more than lip service; it must be sincerely conceived and conscientiously implemented. We think that Tufts, the second time around, has cleared the hurdle that we envisioned: the undisputed facts contained in the expanded record, when considered in the deferential light that academic decisionmaking deserves, meet the required standard.

We add a final note of caution. Although both parties to this litigation invite us to paint with a broad brush, we decline their joint invitation. The issue before us is not whether a medical student, authoritatively diagnosed as a dyslexic and known to the school to be so afflicted, is ever entitled, upon timely request, to an opportunity to take an examination orally. Rather, we are limited to the idiosyncratic facts of Wynne's case. The resulting record presents a narrower, easier issue— and we believe that the district court resolved that issue correctly.

Affirmed.

QUESTIONS AND COMMENTS

1. *Deference to academics and educators.* Deference to the decisionmaking of academics and educators is a longstanding judicial principle. The Supreme Court has noted that "[w]hen judges are asked to review the substance of a genuinely academic decision . . . they should show great respect for the faculty's professional judgment." *Regents of Univ. of Mich. v. Ewing*, 474 U.S. 214, 227, 106 S.Ct. 507, 88 L.Ed.2d 523 (1985). Like *Wynne*, most courts interpreting the ADA follow this precept. See *Zukle v. Regents of the University of California*, 166 F.3d 1041 (9th Cir. 1999) (granting summary judgment against a medical student with learning disabilities who had been dismissed from medical school after receiving poor grades despite various accommodations); *Halasz v. University of New England*, 1992 WL 404581 (D.Me.1992) (deferring to university decision to mandate a *higher* GPA for students in school's special learning disability program than for other students); *Doe v. New York University*, 666 F.2d 761 (2d Cir.1981) (deferring to medical school decision that applicant with history of mental illness and antisocial behavior was not qualified to reenter medical school). Arguably, however, blind deference can mean that the court is abdicating the responsibility it has to enforce anti-discrimination law. Do you think that the *Wynne* court's refusal to look into whether what Tufts had done was "right" or "wrong" constituted an abdication of its responsibility? Should the court have inquired further into the effectiveness and feasibility of oral examinations, given the fact that at least one other school permits

such examinations? Or had Tufts already provided enough accommodations to Wynne?

How specific must the showings in these cases be? For instance, should the court have required Tufts to show that the specific knowledge areas it was testing were relevant to achieving its curricular goal of creating competent physicians? Suppose that Wynne had provided evidence that five years after graduation from medical school, almost all physicians would fail the biochemistry exams that he could not pass. Should such evidence have affected the court's judgment about what would constitute a reasonable accommodation for his disability? In contrast, if Tufts had shown that Wynne would have to know how to answer minutia-laden multiple-choice questions if he wanted to pass his national medical licensure examinations upon graduation from Tufts, would this have supported Tufts's argument against the type of accommodation that Wynne was requesting?

Some commentators have argued that courts are more willing to defer to academic decisionmaking in cases involving students with mental disabilities than in cases involving students with physical disabilities. See Bonnie Poitras Tucker, *Application of the Americans with Disabilities Act (ADA) and Section 504 to Colleges and Universities*, 23 J.C. & U.L. 1, 39 (1996). Can you think of any reasons why this might be the case? One possibility is cost. Inexpensive accommodations for students with learning and other disabilities include additional time for examinations, changes in examination format, reduced course loads, and course substitutions. More expensive accommodations include the provision of taped texts, notetakers, and readers for course materials and exams. See Tucker, supra, at 16–25 (summarizing accommodations considered by courts and suggested by applicable regulations). Postsecondary educational institutions are required to pay for all reasonable accommodations. They may not impose a surcharge on disabled students or require such students to demonstrate a lack of ability to pay. See *United States v. Board of Trustees for University of Alabama*, 908 F.2d 740 (11th Cir.1990).

2. *Admissions testing.* Entities that give standardized examinations for admission to postsecondary institutions are governed by Title III of the ADA and are thus subject to anti-discrimination requirements. *See* 42 U.S.C. § 12189 ("Any person that offers examinations or courses related to applications, licensing, certification, or credentialing for secondary or post-secondary education, professional, or trade purposes shall offer such examinations or courses in a place and manner accessible to persons with disabilities . . . "). Regulations expand the type of modifications that are required. 28 C.F.R. § 36.309(b)(2) (2011) ("Required modifications to an examination may include changes in the length of time permitted for completion of the examination and adaptation of the manner in which the examination is given."), Thus, virtually without exception, standardized testing programs provide accommodations for students with learning disabilities. Because testing programs provide this accommodation, educational institutions can use standardized test scores as a criterion for

admission without running afoul of the anti-discrimination laws. In addition, the Department of Education's Office of Civil Rights ("OCR"), which has responsibility for investigating complaints of discrimination brought under the Rehabilitation Act and Title II, has taken the position that educational institutions are not required to lower their admissions standards in order to accommodate applicants with disabilities. See Laura Rothstein, *Higher Education and Disabilities: Trends and Developments*, 27 Stetson L.Rev. 119, 122 (1997) (collecting cases).

One controversy that remains concerns the practice of "flagging" the scores of those who take standardized tests under nonstandard conditions. In the case of the Scholastic Aptitude Test ("SAT"), the scores of all test-takers who receive any sort of accommodation are flagged. In the case of the Law School Admission Test ("LSAT"), only the scores of those who receive extended time are flagged. Most courts have held that these procedures do not deny applicants "access" to educational testing services or programs, on the ground that experts have yet to determine how to compare scores taken under nonstandard conditions with other scores. See, e.g., *Doe v. National Board of Medical Examiners*, 199 F.3d 146, 157 (3d. Cir. 1999) (holding that the plaintiff states a claim against flagging only if he shows that "his scores are psychometrically comparable to the scores of candidates who take the test under standard time conditions or that his [flagged] scores will be ignored by the programs to which they are reported."). However, other courts have essentially shifted the burden to test providers to show equalizing test conditions are not possible. For instance, in *Dep't Fair Employment & Housing v. Law School Admission Council (LSAC)*, 896 F.Supp.2d 849 (N.D. Cal., 2012), the court refused to dismiss a complaint against the LSAC's flagging practices because § 36.309(b) "imposes a *duty on test providers* to best ensure that their tests are selected and administered to equally measure the abilities of disabled and nondisabled test takers. . . . [If] *test providers* meet this burden, then there would be no reason to flag the test results of disabled test takers who receive accommodations." Only if "there is no way to ensure that the test results are precisely equivalent" might flagging be appropriate. Id. at 868–69 (emphasis in original). The court also refused to dismiss a claim that flagging discourages potential test-takers from seeking accommodations and punishes those who do. Id. at 870. If the equivalency of test results under different conditions cannot be assured, how does flagging solve the problem? Won't flagging create a temptation to discount the flagged results, without knowing whether, or how much, to do so? For an argument that the practice of flagging scores violates the ADA and the Rehabilitation Act, see Kristan S. Mayer, Note, *Flagging Nonstandard Test Scores in Admissions to Institutions of Higher Education*, 59 Stan. L. Rev. 469 (1998).

3. *Definition of disability.* Prior to passage of the ADAAA, courts in education cases often defined "disability" narrowly, just as they did in employment cases. For instance, in *Betts v. Rector and Visitors of the University of Virginia*, 18 Fed.Appx. 114, 118 (4th Cir. 2001), the court agreed that Betts had a learning impairment. However, given his superior IQ and the coping mechanisms he had developed to mitigate his learning

impairment, he was not substantially limited in his ability to learn in comparison with the general population. See also *Price v. National Board of Medical Examiners*, 966 F.Supp. 419 (S.D.W.Va. 1997) (noting that a student with average intellectual ability and an impairment such as dyslexia that allowed him to learn only at the tenth percentile of the general population would be considered disabled under the ADA, but that a student with a superior IQ whose dyslexia caused her to learn only as well as the average person would not be considered disabled).

The ADAAA has clearly changed the analysis to the extent courts determine disability in its mitigated state. It may have changed the analysis in other ways as well. *Jenkins v. National Bd. of Medical Examiners*, 2009 WL 331638 (6th Cir. 2009), involved a person with a reading disorder who wanted extra time to take the medical licensing examination. The lower court decision, applying pre-ADAAA standards and in particular the holding in *Toyota Motor Manufacturing v. Williams*, denied relief on the ground the plaintiff did not have a disability protected by the ADA. It first noted that courts had determined that test-taking is not a "major life activity" (citing, e.g., *Singh v. Geo. Wash. Univ. Sch. of Med. & Health,* 508 F.3d 1097 (D.C.Cir.2007) and *Wong v. Regents of the Univ. of California,* 410 F.3d 1052 (9th Cir.2005)). While acknowledging that reading could be a major life activity, it then emphasized *Toyota's* requirement that the impairment be in an activity that is "central to most people's daily lives." With respect to reading, the court stated, such activities could include reading the newspaper, reading a label on a food container, or reading a menu in a restaurant, all of which Jenkins indicated that he was capable of doing, albeit perhaps 50% more slowly than others. But the fact that reading medical texts was even more difficult for Jenkins, given the unfamiliar words he encountered, was "entirely a function of his choice to pursue a higher education, not a function of the demands of the daily life of most people." The Sixth Circuit disagreed with this reasoning. In remanding the case, that court first found that since Jenkins was seeking prospective relief, the ADAAA applied. It then stated that reconsideration was necessary because "the district court relied on the very language from *Toyota* that Congress repudiated in the ADA Amendments Act." Id. at *4.

Even in cases where the court rejects the contention that the plaintiff's learning impairment substantially limits a major life activity, it may find that the plaintiff is protected by the ADA because it concludes that the defendant regarded the plaintiff as having such an impairment. For example, in the *Betts* case described above, the court ultimately determined that because the defendant had provided Betts with a large variety of accommodations, it regarded Betts as having a disability. What sorts of incentives does this line of reasoning create for educational institutions?

More fundamentally, how do you respond to these various definitions of disability as they apply in the postsecondary education context? The increasing number of students claiming mental disabilities has generated much controversy. Critics have charged that institutions of higher education are succumbing to pressures to grant accommodations to students who are not entitled to receive them. Suzanne Wilhelm, *Accommodating Mental Disabilities in Higher Education: A Practical Guide to ADA Requirements*, 32 J.L & Educ.217 (2003) (discussing case of *Guckenberger v. Boston University*, 957 F.Supp. 306 (D.Mass.1997), in which the court found that several students who had received accommodations lacked sufficient documentation). Critics also claim that the ADA, together with the DSM's broader definitions of disorders, has created an unfair system in which certain students improperly receive advantages and thus have a greater likelihood of success. Mark Kelman & Gillian Lester, Jumping the Queue: An Inquiry into the Legal Treatment of Students With Learning Disabilities (1997). Consider in this regard, note a on p. 1402 of this chapter.

4. *Remedies.* Depending on the type of educational institution involved, a challenge to its practices may be brought under Title II of the ADA, Title III of the ADA, or the Rehabilitation Act. As discussed in the previous section, damages under Title II, which can be invoked against state universities, may be limited by the Supreme Court's decision in *Board of Trustees of Univ. of Ala. v. Garrett*, 531 U.S. 356, 121 S.Ct. 955, 148 L.Ed.2d 866 (2001). See, e.g., *Garcia v. S.U.N.Y. Health Sciences Center of Brooklyn*, 280 F.3d 98 (2d Cir.2001). Furthermore, Title III of the ADA, which can be invoked against any private university, incorporates the public accommodations provisions of the Civil Rights Act of 1964 and hence does not include monetary damages among the available remedies. However, many universities, both public and private, receive federal funding under the Rehabilitation Act, and most courts have held that acceptance of Rehabilitation Act funds constitutes a waiver of sovereign immunity, with the result that damages actions are permissible. See *Nieves–Marquez v. Puerto Rico*, 353 F.3d 108, 129–30 (1st Cir. 2003).

V.   LICENSING AND CERTIFICATION PROGRAMS

Regulations promulgated under Title II of the ADA extend its anti-discrimination requirements to the licensing activities of state agencies. See 28 C.F.R. § 35.130(b)(6). Traditionally, state agencies with authority over medical licensing or bar admission have, as part of the admissions process, inquired into the applicant's mental health history, purportedly in an effort to protect the public from practitioners whose mental condition might impair their ability to provide competent services. With the enactment of the ADA, these types of inquiries have been the subject of numerous court challenges. The case below provides a comprehensive overview of this area.

CLARK V. VIRGINIA BOARD OF BAR EXAMINERS

United States District Court, E.D. Virginia, 1995.
880 F.Supp. 430.

Memorandum Opinion

CACHERIS, CHIEF JUDGE.

The issue before the Court is whether a question appearing on the Virginia Board of Bar Examiners' "Applicant's Character and Fitness Questionnaire" addressing an applicant's history of mental or emotional disorders violates the Americans with Disabilities Act, 42 U.S.C. §§ 12101 et seq. (1994). Following a preamble explaining that the Virginia Board of Bar Examiners is concerned only with "severe forms of mental or emotional problems," Question 20(b) asks: "Have you within the past five (5) years been treated or counselled for any mental, emotional or nervous disorders?" If Question 20(b) is answered affirmatively, applicants must then give specific treatment information pursuant to Question 21.

For the reasons set forth below, the Court finds that Question 20(b) is framed too broadly and violates the Plaintiff's rights under the Americans with Disabilities Act. Accordingly, judgment is entered in favor of the Plaintiff and the Virginia Board of Bar Examiners is enjoined from requiring that future applicants answer Question 20(b).

I.   Findings of Fact

Plaintiff Julie Ann Clark brings this action against the Virginia Board of Bar Examiners (the "Board") to have Question 20(b) stricken from the Board's "Applicant's Character and Fitness Questionnaire" (the "Questionnaire") because it violates the Americans with Disabilities Act (the "ADA"). The Board maintains that Question 20(b) is posed appropriately and is necessary to identify applicants with mental disabilities that would seriously impair their ability to practice law and protect their clients' interests. The Court, after reviewing the evidence, authorities and arguments of counsel, makes the following findings of fact.

A.   The Parties to the Case

Plaintiff Julie Ann Clark, a resident of Virginia, graduated from George Mason University Law School in June of 1993. She is currently employed as a children's program specialist at the Bazelon Center for Mental Health Law. * * * Ms. Clark suffers from a condition previously diagnosed as "major depression, recurrent". Plaintiff's Exhibit 68(a). * * * This condition, which occurred a few years ago, affected her for thirteen months.

The Virginia Board of Bar Examiners, an entity created under the authority of Virginia Code § 54.1–3919 (1994), is responsible for the examination of applicants for licenses to practice law in Virginia. Under

Va.Code § 54.1–3925.1(A), the Board must determine, prior to licensing, that each applicant is a "person of honest demeanor and good moral character, is over the age of eighteen and possesses the requisite fitness to perform the obligations and responsibilities of a practicing attorney at law." The Board makes this determination "from satisfactory evidence produced by the applicant in such form as the board may require." *Id.* As a precondition to licensure, the Board requires that applicants answer all of the questions contained in its Questionnaire, including Question 20(b).

* * *

B.   *Application for Admission to the Virginia State Bar*

On or about December 13, 1993, Plaintiff completed the Questionnaire and filed it with the Board. Plaintiff declined to answer Questions 20(b) and 21 of the Questionnaire on the grounds that they violated Title II of the ADA. Question 20(b) and 21, and the preamble introducing these questions, read as follows:

> The Board is required to assess effectively the fitness of each applicant to perform the obligations and responsibilities of a practicing attorney at law. In this regard, a lawyer's chemical dependency or untreated or uncontrolled mental or emotional disorders may result in injury to the public. Questions 20 and 21 request information essential to the Board's assessment. The members of the Board recognize that stress of law school, as well as other life factors, frequently result in applicants seeking psychiatric or psychological counseling. The Board encourages you to obtain counseling or treatment if you believe that you may benefit from it. Because generally only severe forms of mental or emotional problems will trigger an investigation or impact on bar admission decisions, your decision to seek counseling should not be colored by your bar application. . . .

* * *

Question

20. (b) Have you within the past five (5) years, been treated or counselled for a mental, emotional or nervous disorders?

* * *

21. If your answer to question 20(a), (b) or (c) is yes, complete the following that apply:

(a) Dates of treatment or counseling;

(b) Name, address and telephone number of attending physician or counselor or other health care provider;

(c) Name, address and telephone number of hospital or institution;

(d) Describe completely the diagnosis and treatment and the prognosis and provide any other relevant facts. You may attach letters from your treating health professionals if you believe this would be helpful.

See Pl.Ex. 1 (emphasis in original).

On February 8, 1994, the Board advised Ms. Clark that her refusal to provide relevant information would prevent her from taking the bar examination. Pursuant to agreement of counsel, the Board subsequently agreed to allow Ms. Clark to sit for the February bar examination without answering Questions 20(b) and 21 of the Questionnaire. However, the Board indicated that it would not grant her a license until she completed the Questionnaire.

Ms. Clark took the Virginia bar examination on February 22 and 23, 1994 and passed it. She completed all of the application procedures with the exception of answering Questions 20(b) and 21. The Board concedes that, but for her refusal to answer Questions 20(b), it has no reason to believe that Ms. Clark lacks the requisite character and fitness to practice law in Virginia. Pl.Ex. 6. As the only thing preventing Ms. Clark's licensure is her refusal to answer Question 20(b), the issue of whether Question 20(b) violates the ADA is properly framed for the Court.

* * *

D.   Battle of the Experts

Plaintiff maintains that Question 20(b) must be rejected because it is overbroad and is ineffectual in identifying those applicants unfit to practice law. Plaintiff offered the testimony of Dr. Howard V. Zonana, Director of the Law and Psychiatric Division and Professor of Clinical Psychology at the Yale University School of Medicine, to support its contention that there is no correlation between past mental health counseling and fitness to practice law. Dr. Zonana testified that Question 20(b) elicits information that, unlike evidence of past behavior, is unrelated to applicants' present ability to practice law and has little or no predictive value. According to Dr. Zonana, there is little evidence to support the ability of bar examiners, or even mental health professionals, to predict inappropriate or irresponsible future behavior based on a person's history of mental health treatment. Dr. Zonana believes that evidence of past behavior, as elicited by the Board's other "characterological" questions, provides the best indicator of an applicant's present ability to function and work.

The credibility of Dr. Zonana's position is supported by its consistency with the position of the American Psychiatric Association (the "APA"). According to the APA, psychiatric history should not be the subject of applicant inquiry because it is not an accurate predictor of fitness.

In support of maintaining Question 20(b), the Board offered the testimony of Dr. Charles B. Mutter, a psychiatrist, assistant professor of Psychiatry and Family Medicine at the University of Miami School of Medicine, and member of the Florida Board of Bar Examiners from 1989 to 1993. Dr. Mutter, drafter of a question similar to Question 20(b) included in Florida's bar application, testified that Question 20(b) is appropriate as posed. He stated that attorneys, as protectors of clients' rights and assets, hold a special position of trust with the public which must be safeguarded with mental health pre-screening. Further, Dr. Mutter insisted that broad mental health questions are essential for collecting complete information regarding applicants' fitness to practice law. Narrower mental health questions, in Dr. Mutter's view, are inadequate because they allow applicants to filter their responses and provide self-promoting answers.

Dr. Mutter's immoderate position, however, is unsupported by objective evidence and is discordant with a contemporary understanding of mental health questions under the ADA. For one, Dr. Mutter was unable point to any evidence proving a correlation between mental health questions and an inability to practice law. * * * Accordingly, the Court finds that, although both doctors have impressive curricula vitarum, Dr. Zonana's position is more credible and persuasive than that of Dr. Mutter.

E.   Need for Inquiry into Mental Health

The Court accepts that an attorney's uncontrolled and untreated mental or emotional illness may result in injury to clients and the public. This conclusion is supported by the recent cases of acute mental disability among lawyers which have resulted in license suspensions by the Virginia State Bar. Dr. Zonana acknowledged that there are many mental illnesses which may adversely affect, or even preclude, a person's ability to practice law. See He also indicated that, while responses to behavioral questions are better indicators of mental health, inquiry into an applicant's mental health is necessary for a complete evaluation of their fitness to practice law. Thus, it is clear from the facts before the Court that, at some stage in the application proceeding, some form of mental health inquiry is appropriate.

F.   Efficiency of Question 20(b)

Assuming that a mental health question is allowed under the ADA, the Court must determine whether Question 20(b) is a permissible mental health inquiry. Although characterological questions elicit useful information about past behaviors likely to shed light on applicants' fitness, the Board insists that it is necessary to probe applicants' mental health with Question 20(b). Conversely, Ms. Clark maintains that the question is objectionable because it is intrusive without being effective.

According to testimony presented by both Plaintiff and Defendant, approximately twenty percent of the population suffers from some form of mental or emotional disorder at any given time. However, despite reviewing some 2000 applications per year, the Board has received only forty-seven affirmative answers to its mental health questions in the past five years. This affirmative response rate, or "hit" rate, of less than one percent is far below the expected rate of twenty percent. The Board has presented no evidence to suggest, nor is there any reason to believe, that bar applicants are not reflective of the general population. Thus, the great discrepancy between the Board's hit rate and the reported percentage of persons suffering from mental impairment indicates that Question 20(b) is ineffective in identifying applicants suffering from mental illness.

Notwithstanding its receipt of forty-seven affirmative responses, the Board has never denied a license on the basis of prior mental health counseling. Although the Virginia State Bar has suspended attorneys for mental disability, the Board is unable to point to a single instance where an affirmative answer to Question 20(b) has prevented licensure. Thus, based on the Board's own experience, Question 20(b) has failed to serve its purpose of preventing the licensure of applicants lacking the fitness to practice law.

G.   Deterrent Effect

In addition to being ineffectual, Plaintiff argues that Question 20(b) has a deterrent effect which inhibits applicants from getting necessary mental health counseling or treatment. Plaintiff presented the deposition testimony of Dean Paul M. Marcus, Acting Dean and Professor of Law at the Marshall–Wythe School of Law at the College of William and Mary, and Philip P. Frickey, Professor of Law at the University of Minnesota Law School, on the deterrent effect of broad mental health questions, like Question 20(b). Drawing on his experience counseling law students as both a teacher and administrator, Dean Marcus concluded that questions such as Question 20(b) deter law students from seeking counseling or treatment from which they might otherwise benefit. Similarly, Professor Frickey stated that broad mental health questions like Question 20(b) have a strong negative effect upon many law students, often discouraging them from seeking beneficial mental health counseling.

* * *

H.   Data from other Jurisdictions and Authorities

* * *

In the wake of the passage of the ADA, which became effective for public entities in January 1992, the inclusion of mental health questions on bar applications has gained new significance. At least eight states, including Connecticut, Florida, Maine, Minnesota, New York, Pennsylvania, Rhode Island and Texas, have recently altered their mental health questions in light of potential or actual litigation under the ADA.

The changes in these states are reflected in similar adjustments in the policies of the American Bar Association ("ABA") and the NCBE [National Commission of Bar Examiners], two leading national legal organizations. In August 1994, the House of Delegates of the American Bar Association ("ABA") adopted a recommendation that:

> when making character and fitness determinations for the purpose of bar admission, state and territorial bar examiners, in carrying out their responsibilities to the public to admit only qualified applicants worthy of the public trust, should consider the privacy concerns of bar admission applicants, tailor questions concerning mental health and treatment narrowly in order to elicit information about current fitness to practice law, and take steps to ensure that their processes do not discourage those who would benefit from seeking professional assistance with personal problems and issues of mental health from doing so.

Proposal 110, A.B.A. House of Delegates (August 9, 1994). While not the most strongly worded admonition, the resolution represents an acknowledgement of the changing atmosphere under the ADA.

Recently, the NCBE has acted to change the mental health questions on its character and fitness questionnaire. Formerly, questions 28 and 29 of the NCBE's character and fitness application asked, respectively: "Have you ever been treated or counseled for any mental, emotional or nervous disorder or condition?" and "Have you ever voluntarily entered or been involuntarily admitted to an institution for treatment of a mental, emotional or nervous disorder or condition?" These questions formed the basis for many states' mental health questions, including Virginia. As of February 17, 1995, the NCBE altered its mental health questions to limit their scope and to more sharply focus on chronic mental conditions which affect the ability to practice law. While the actions of the NCBE and ABA are not binding on the states, they signify the substantial impact the ADA is having on the formulation of mental health inquiries.

II.   Conclusions of Law

Title II of the Americans with Disabilities Act prohibits discrimination against disabled persons by public entities. It provides that "no qualified individual with a disability shall, by reason of such disability, be excluded from participation in or be denied the benefits of the services, programs, or activities of a public entity, or be subject to discrimination by such entity." A "public entity" is defined as "any department, agency . . . or other instrumentality of a State . . . government." 42 U.S.C. § 12131(1)(B). The Virginia Board of Bar Examiners concedes that it is a public agency within this definition.

A "qualified individual with a disability" is defined as "[a]n individual with a disability who, with or without reasonable modification to rules, policies, or practices . . . meets the essential eligibility requirements for the receipt of services or participation in programs or activities provided by the public entity." Under regulations promulgated by the Department of Justice, "disability" is further defined as "a physical or mental impairment that substantially limits one or more of the major life activities of such individual; a record of such impairment; or being regarded as having such an impairment." 28 C.F.R. § 35.104. "Major life activities" include "functions such as caring for one's self, performing manual tasks, walking, seeing, hearing, speaking, breathing, learning, and working." *Id.*

The Court finds, based on the affidavit Plaintiff filed under seal, that Ms. Clark is a person with a disability or, alternatively, a person with a past record of impairment within the meaning of the ADA. Further, Ms. Clark has shown that she can meet the essential eligibility requirements of practicing law and is "a qualified person with a disability" under the ADA. While Defendant argues that Ms. Clark is not an "otherwise qualified individual" because she failed to answer Question 20(b), this argument begs the question of whether Question 20(b) must be answered at all.

An applicant may not meet the essential eligibility requirements, however, where they "pose[ ] a direct threat to the health or safety of others." A determination that a person poses a "direct threat" must be based not on generalizations or stereotypes, but on:

> an individualized assessment, based on reasonable judgment that relies on current medical evidence or on the best available objective evidence to determine: the nature, duration, and severity of the risk; the probability that potential injury will actually occur; and whether reasonable modification of policies, practices and procedures will mitigate the risk.

The Board has presented no evidence to suggest that all or most of the applicants answering Question 20(b) affirmatively threaten the health or safety of the public. Nor is there any evidence that the Board engaged in any individualized assessment in formulating Question 20(b) as called for by 28 C.F.R. pt. 35, app. A at 446. Absent a showing that Ms. Clark would pose a direct threat to the health or safety of others, the Court finds that Ms. Clark meets all of the "essential eligibility requirements" for admission to the bar of the Commonwealth of Virginia.

In addition to the general provisions of Title II, public entities are specifically prohibited from acting discriminatorily in administering licensing programs. 28 C.F.R. § 35.130(b)(6). This regulation provides:

> A public entity may not administer a licensing or certification program in a manner that subjects qualified individuals with disabilities to discrimination on the basis of disability, nor may a public entity establish requirements for the programs or activities of licensees or certified entities that subject qualified individuals with disabilities to discrimination on the basis of disability. . . .

28 C.F.R. § 35.130(b)(6). Further, 28 C.F.R. § 35.130(b)(8) forbids a public entity from:

> impos[ing] or apply[ing] eligibility criteria that screen out or tend to screen out any individual with a disability or any class of individuals with disabilities from fully and equally enjoying any service, program, or activity, unless such criteria can be shown to be necessary for the provision of the service, program or activity being offered.

Id. As a public licensing agency, the Board must comply with the strict requirements of 28 C.F.R. §§ 35.130(b)(6) and (8) in probing applicants' mental health histories.

In assessing the propriety of Question 20(b), the Court is faced with two issues: (1) whether the Board has established requirements or imposed eligibility criteria that subject qualified individuals to discrimination on the basis of their disability, and (2) whether such requirements or criteria are necessary to the Board's licensing function.

A.   Question 20(b) Subjects Qualified Individuals with a Disability to Discrimination on the Basis of that Disability

To find a violation of the ADA, the Court first must determine whether the Board, in posing Question 20(b), subjects persons with disabilities to discrimination on the basis of their disability. While it is not clear that Question 20(b) "screens out" potential applicants, it is clear that Question 20(b) imposes an additional burden on applicants with disabilities to satisfy additional eligibility criteria. . . .

Unlike other applicants, those with mental disabilities are required to subject themselves to further inquiry and scrutiny. The Court finds that this additional burden discriminates against those with mental disabilities. Thus, to avoid violating the ADA, the Board must show that Question 20(b) is necessary to the performance of its licensing function.

B.   Necessity of Imposing Question 20(b)

"The practice of law is not a matter of grace, but of right for one who is qualified by his learning and his moral character." *Baird v. State Bar of Arizona*, 401 U.S. 1, 8, 91 S.Ct. 702, 707, 27 L.Ed.2d 639 (1971). It is generally accepted that a state can set high standards of qualification and, to this end, may investigate an applicant's character and fitness to practice law. *See Schware v. Board of Bar Examiners of New Mexico*, 353

U.S. 232, 239, 77 S.Ct. 752, 756, 1 L.Ed.2d 796 (1957). It is equally clear that all states have set qualifications of moral character as preconditions for admission to the practice of law, with the burden of demonstrating good character borne by the applicant. *See Konigsberg v. State Bar of California*, 366 U.S. 36, 41 n. 4, 81 S.Ct. 997, 1002 n. 4, 6 L.Ed.2d 105 (1961). While the Board's broad authority to set licensing qualifications is well established, such authority is subject to the requirements of the ADA.

1.   Duty to assess the character and fitness of applicants

The Board is charged with a statutory duty to find, prior to licensure, that each applicant has the "requisite fitness to perform the obligations and responsibilities of a practicing attorney at law." Va.Code § 54.1–3925.1. As part of this duty, the Board must identify those people who suffer from mental conditions which would severely affect or impair their ability to practice law.

The Board contends that, in fulfilling this duty, it is necessary to ask Question 20(b) to uncover all of the skeletons hidden in each applicant's psychological closet. Further, the Board opines that its ability to investigate applicants' character and fitness is limited by inadequate resources and time constraints. According to the Board, Question 20(b) is necessary because it enables the Board to identify potentially unfit applicants with the limited resources and time available to it. While the Court recognizes that the Board has limited resources with which to discharge its duty under Va.Code § 54.1–3925.1, the Court finds such limitations do not make Question 20(b) "necessary" under the ADA.

2.   Decisions in other jurisdictions

Other courts, considering broad mental health questions similar to Question 20(b), have concluded that such inquiries would violate Title II of the ADA. . . . While not binding authority, these cases offer persuasive guidance in the evaluation of Question 20(b) under the ADA.

In support of maintaining Question 20(b), the Board relies on *Applicants v. Texas State Board of Bar Examiners*, No. 93 CA 740SS, 1994 WL 776693 (W.D.Tex.1994), which upheld the right of the Texas Board of Bar Examiners to inquire into an applicant's mental history. Unlike Question 20(b), however, the questions considered in *Texas State Board of Bar Examiners* were addressed only to specific behavioral disorders found relevant to the practice of law.[24] Further, the *Texas State*

---

[24] The *Texas State Board of Bar Examiners* court reviewed question 11 of the bar application which asked:

(a) Within the last ten years, have you been diagnosed with or have you been treated [for] bipolar disorder, schizophrenia, paranoia, or any other psychotic disorder?

(b) Have you, since attaining the age or eighteen or within the last ten years, whichever is shorter, been admitted to a hospital or other facility for the treatment of bipolar disorder, schizophrenia, paranoia, or any other psychotic disorder?

Board of Bar Examiners court noted that the mental health question used by the Texas Board of Bar Examiners before 1992, which asked "[h]ave you within the last ten (10) years . . . [b]een examined or treated for any mental, emotional or nervous conditions," was "revised . . . to comply with the ADA." Id. at 4. Hence, the *Texas State Board of Bar Examiners* decision has limited application and does not support the breadth of inquiry posed by the Board.

* * *

III. CONCLUSION * * *

As the Court's job in this case is to decide whether 20(b) complies with the ADA, not to draft a question that would comply with the ADA, the Court will refrain from offering any dictum guidance. The imposition of Question 20(b) by the Board violates the ADA. While the licensure of attorneys implicates issues of public safety, the Board has failed to show that Question 20(b), as posed, is necessary to the Board's performance of its licensing function. Accordingly, judgment is entered for the Plaintiff and the Virginia Board of Bar Examiners is enjoined from requiring that future applicants answer Question 20(b) of the Questionnaire.

* * *

QUESTIONS AND COMMENTS

1. *State bar inquiry into mental health.* Most state bar examiners either: 1) ask no mental health questions; 2) ask only about hospitalization or institutionalization; 3) ask only about specific diagnoses; or 4) ask applicants if they have any mental disorder that they believe will affect their ability to practice law. In 2011 the Indiana State Bar asked the following questions of all applicants to the bar:

> 22. Have you been diagnosed with or have you been treated for bi-polar disorder, schizophrenia, paranoia, or any other psychotic disorder?

> 23. From the age of 16 years to the present, have you been diagnosed with or treated for any mental, emotional or nervous disorders?

> 24. Do you have any condition or impairment (including, but not limited to, substance abuse, alcohol abuse, or a mental, emotional, or nervous disorder or condition) which in any way currently affects, or if untreated could affect, your ability to practice law in a competent and professional manner?

> 25. IF YOUR ANSWER TO QUESTION 24 IS AFFIRMATIVE, are the limitations or impairments caused by your mental health condition or substance abuse problem reduced or ameliorated because you receive

---

The *Texas State Board of Bar Examiners* court concluded that these inquiries did not violate the ADA because they narrowly addressed only those disorders relevant to the practice of law. *Id.* at 24.

ongoing treatment (with or without medication) or because you participate in a monitoring program?

In *ACLU of Indiana v. Individual Members of the Indiana State Bd. of Law Examiners*, 2011 WL 4387470 (S.D. Ind. 2011), the court concluded that question 23 violated the ADA, for reasons similar to those given in *Clark*. However, it upheld the other three questions. With respect to question 22, which is similar but not identical to the Texas bar examiner question quoted in note 3 of *Clark* (it leaves out the ten-year limitation), the court stated: "The fact that a person may have experienced an episode of one of these mental illnesses in the past but is not currently experiencing symptoms does not mean that the person will not experience another episode in the future or that the person is currently fit to practice law." With respect to questions 24 and 25, which the ACLU argued captured people who were not "direct threats," the court stated:

> the Board's evidence shows that even if the applicant is seeking treatment, "all available treatments have their limitations and there are few [mental] disorders where it is possible to be cured." [Further] if the Court adopted Plaintiffs' position, then the Board would be required to jettison the portion of the inquiry related to treatment. However, this is an important part of the question. Without it, the question is reduced to a mere subjective inquiry into the applicant's belief about his or her own current ability to practice law. But this isn't much of an inquiry. Obviously, the vast majority of, if not all, bar applicants believe they are fit to practice law. In sum, because Questions 24 and 25 appropriately bear on the applicant's *current* ability to practice law, they are permissible under the ADA.

Id. at *10. Do you agree?

2. *American Psychiatric Association ("APA") guidelines for medical licensing.* In summarizing Dr. Zonana's testimony, *Clark* quoted from the APA's recommendation that medical licensing boards and regulatory agencies adhere to the APA's guidelines for mental health inquiry. In full, these guidelines provide:

> 1) Prior psychiatric treatment is, per se, not relevant to the question of current impairment. It is not appropriate or informative to ask about past psychiatric treatment in the context of understanding current functioning. A past history of work impairment, but not simply of past treatment or leaves of absence, may be gathered.

> 2) The salient concern is always the individual's current capacity to function and/or current impairment. Only information about current impairing disorder affecting the capacity to function as a physician, and which is relevant to present practice, should be disclosed on application forms. Types of impairment may include emotional or mental difficulties, physical illness, or dependency upon alcohol or other drugs.

> 3) Applicants must be informed of the potential for public disclosure of any information they provide on applications.

Clark, 880 F. Supp. at 435. Do these rules make sense in the legal profession context?

3.   *Licensing examinations and the determination of disability.* Courts have held that the requirements of the ADA also extend to professional licensing examinations. Thus, in administering such examinations, state agencies must reasonably accommodate test takers who can prove that they are disabled within the meaning of the ADA. Under both the relevant Department of Justice regulations and most courts decisions, including those interpreting the ADAAA, the reference population against whom the plaintiff should be compared is the general population. See, e.g., *Healy v. National Bd. Osteopathic Medical Examiners, Inc.* 870 F.Supp.2d 607 (S.D.Ind., 2012) (noting that while the plaintiff's reading ability was slow for someone of his IQ it was average compared to the general population, and thus plaintiff was not disabled under the ADAAA). At the same time, the ADAAA has made clear that the impairment need not be "central" to a major life activity. See *Jenkins v. National Bd. of Medical Examiners*, 2009 WL 331638 (6th Cir. 2009) (remanding because the district court had not considered plaintiff's difficulty in reading medical texts but only his ability to read newspapers, menus and food labels, on the inappropriate pre-ADAAA ground that only impairments "central to daily life" were relevant). Should licensing examiners have to accommodate these less "central" impairments if they are "central" to the jobs test-takers are trying to obtain? In other words, if examiners can anticipate that accommodating a person's disability once they are licensed would be unreasonable, should they be able to avoid making an accommodation during test-taking, even if it is reasonable?

4.   *Remedies Available Against State Licensing Agencies.* Given the Supreme Court's recent decisions on sovereign immunity, discussed at length in Sections III and IV, it is likely that only injunctive relief will be available against state licensing board defendants.

VI.   HOUSING

The principal anti-discrimination statute in the housing context is the Fair Housing Act (FHA). As passed in 1968 the FHA prohibited housing discrimination only on the basis of race, color, religion or national origin. But in 1988, Congress enacted the Fair Housing Amendments Act (FHAA), which also prohibits discrimination on the basis of mental or physical disability. 42 U.S.C. §§ 3601–3614. The ADA, specifically Titles II and III, also prohibits discrimination in housing, but the FHAA is more comprehensive and is the principal focus here.

Under the FHA and FHAA, private parties may bring judicial actions seeking damages or injunctive relief. 42 U.S.C. § 3613. Private parties may also file complaints with the Secretary of Housing and Urban Development. The Secretary is responsible for investigating the allegedly discriminatory practice. If the Secretary finds evidence of illegal discrimination, the complainant then has the option of proceeding either administratively or judicially. *See* 42 U.S.C. §§ 3610, 3612. If the illegality involves a state or local zoning or land use regulation, however, the Secretary is required by the FHA to refer the matter to the Attorney General. 42 U.S.C. § 3610(g)(2)(C).

The FHAA bans both disparate-treatment and disparate-impact discrimination based on mental or physical disability in all sales and rentals of multi-family housing; only transactions between private persons involving single-family units are not covered. The definition of disability and the scope of coverage under the FHAA largely parallels that of the ADA and Rehabilitation Act. Under the FHAA, "handicapped" persons are: 1) those who have physical or mental impairments that substantially limit their major life activities; 2) those who have a record of such impairments; or 3) those who are regarded as having such impairments. 42 U.S.C. § 3602(h). The FHAA also requires those "reasonable modifications" or "reasonable accommodations" that are necessary to provide persons with disabilities equal access to housing, 42 U.S.C. § 3604(f)(3)(A),(B), although it recognizes that accommodations may be more difficult for those who are "a direct threat to the health and safety of other individuals or whose tendency would result in substantial physical damage to the property of others." 42 U.S.C. § 3604(f)(9). The following case demonstrates these parallels between the FHAA and other anti-discrimination statutes.

SINISGALLO v. TOWN OF ISLIP HOUSING AUTHORITY

United States District Court, E.D. New York, 2012.
865 F.Supp.2d 307.

SPATT, DISTRICT JUDGE.

* * *

I.   BACKGROUND

The defendant Town of Islip Housing Authority is a municipal housing authority, created in accordance with the provisions of the New York State Public Housing Law. The IHA is categorized as a public housing authority ("PHA") under the United States Department of Housing and Urban Development ("HUD") regulations. Pursuant to HUD regulations, the IHA maintains a public housing program ("the Program"), through which it provides housing for eligible families, including low income families and families with elderly and disabled individuals. The defendant Richard Wankel is the Executive Director in charge of the Program for the IHA.

On June 10, 2010, the plaintiffs, Kathie Sinisgallo and Steve Tsilimparis, entered into a lease for public housing provided by the IHA located at 81 Mill Pond Lane, Bay Shore, New York. On the lease, Sinisgallo is identified as the "tenant" and Tsilimparis is identified as a "co-tenant". Both Sinisgallo and Tsilimparis assert that they are mentally disabled individuals. Sinisgallo contends that she suffers from paranoid schizophrenia; receives psychiatric treatment for her illness from the Hands Across Long Island Personal Recovery Program; and that her income consists of Social Security Disability Insurance ("SSDI") payments because she is permanently disabled. According to Tsilimparis, he suffers from bipolar disorder; receives psychiatric care for his illness from the Family Service League's South Shore Family Center Clinic; and his income consists of Supplemental Security Income ("SSI") payments because he is permanently disabled. Although not married, the Plaintiffs have been engaged in a romantic relationship for more than thirty years and have lived together continuously for that period. The Plaintiffs described their relationship as one that is "[s]imilar to a spousal relationship". On or about May 23, 2011, Sinisgallo submitted a complaint to defendant Richard Wankel's office, stating that her neighboring tenant, Michael Collins, shot the Plaintiffs' pet cat with his BB gun and injured the cat superficially. Subsequently, on May 26, 2011, Tsilimparis confronted Collins while Collins was spraying the grass in front of the Plaintiffs' apartment. The culmination of this interaction resulted in Tsilimparis physically striking Collins.

On July 13, 2011, Collins filed a complaint with the Suffolk County Police Department regarding the May 26, 2011 altercation. The criminal violation was Adjourned in Contemplation of Dismissal, pursuant to New York Criminal Procedure Law § 170.55.

On May 27, 2011, Sinisgallo received a notice from the IHA terminating her tenancy and participation in the Program. On June 15, 2011, Sinisgallo requested an informal settlement telephone conference to review the determination to terminate her residency. This conference was held between Sinisgallo and Wankel. In this informal hearing, Sinisgallo was not represented by counsel, and argued that her tenancy should not be terminated because Tsilimparis struck Collins in self-defense. On August 1, 2011, Sinisgallo received a Summary Decision and termination notice, which stated that the IHA had determined to continue the eviction process. Consistent with IHA procedures, Sinisgallo made a written request for a formal administrative hearing, which was granted.

The administrative hearing to review the termination of the Plaintiff's tenancy was held over two sessions on December 20, 2011 and January 9, 2012. These proceedings were presided over by defendant Paul E. Levitt, a private attorney who was acting in his capacity as a the Hearing Officer.

At the hearing, Levitt heard the testimony of Collins, Wankel, Sinisgallo, Tsilimparis, and Lillian Barnes, a neighbor who witnessed the altercation. The Plaintiffs were represented by counsel and had an opportunity to cross-examine witnesses, present evidence, and submit post-hearing written briefs. At the hearing, the Plaintiffs argued that they were disabled individuals and that Tsilimparis's conduct was caused by his disability. In support of this contention, the Plaintiffs submitted a letter dated September 26, 2011 from Meredith Braddock, Licensed Master Social Worker ("LMSW") to the Nassau Suffolk Law Services, stating as follows:

> Mr. Tsilimparis has been a client at our South Shore Family Center Clinic since 9/08. Mr. Tsilimparis is being treated for Bipolar Disorder. On 5/27/11 Mr. Tsilimparis' medication was adjusted and therapy was intensified due to present symptoms. He is now being seen for weekly individual therapy with Licensed Master Social Worker and monthly medication management with our Psychiatrist. He is being treated with Symbyax, Tegretol and Clonazepam . . . . .

According to the Plaintiffs, during the hearing, they requested a reasonable accommodation based on their various disabilities, which they contend would have permitted them to continue to participate in the Program. In particular, they sought a probationary period during which a further determination could be made that the change to Tsilimparis's medical treatment would continue to prevent a recurrence of his violent behavior towards Collins or other tenants.

Following the hearing, counsel for both sides submitted written memoranda. The Plaintiffs' submission primarily argued that the IHA's decision to terminate their tenancy violated the FHA because they were disabled individuals and therefore entitled to a reasonable accommodation. . . . For its part, the IHA argued that it was not required to offer a reasonable accommodation to a tenant that engages in illegal behavior, or, in the alternative, that no reasonable accommodation existed that would eliminate the threat posed by Tsilimparis to the other tenants. Finally, the Plaintiffs submitted a supplemental letter on January 27, 2012, arguing that the empirical evidence indicated that the attack was an isolated incident insofar as, since the changes to Tsilimparis's medication, no further incident had occurred despite continued provocation by Collins. In this letter submission, the Plaintiffs reiterated their request for a reasonable accommodation and that the termination of their tenancy be rescinded pursuant to the FHA.

On March 1, 2012, Levitt issued a decision finding that Sinisgallo had violated lease provision paragraphs XIV(a)(7) and IX(k)(L)(1) ("the Decision"). In the Decision, after summarizing the testimony, Levitt stated that, based on "the evidence presented at the hearing and the post-hearing arguments", he found that "Steven Tsilimparis did strike Michael Collins with his fist causing injury and bleeding to Collins' left eye on or about May 26, 2011." As a result, Levitt held:

> I find that since Sinisgallo violated lease provision paragraph XIV(a)(7) which provides that a lease may be terminated for serious

or repeated violations such as criminal activity by tenant, household member, guest or other person under tenant's control. Tsilimparis struck Michael Collins with his fist causing injury and bleeding to Collins' left eye and nose. This was unprovoked activity and was not in self-defense. Tsilimparis threatened the health, safety, and right to peaceful enjoyment of the public housing premises by Collins, a resident of the same project. I also find that Sinisgallo and Tsilimparis violated the "Tenant's Obligations", more specifically, paragraph IX(k)(L)(1).

Although Levitt discussed the credibility of the various witnesses with respect to the incident, absent from the Decision was any reference to the Plaintiffs' request for a reasonable accommodation or the allegation that the termination of their tenancy violated the FHA. In addition, while Levitt referenced the existence of the letter from Social Worker Braddock regarding Tsilimparis's disability and treatment, he did not explain whether or to what extent it affected his decision.

Thereafter, the IHA commenced a summary holdover proceeding in the Fifth District Court of Suffolk County, to enforce the eviction of the Plaintiffs ("the eviction proceedings" or the "summary holdover proceeding").

On April 4, 2012, the Plaintiffs commenced the present lawsuit asserting five causes of action as against all of the Defendants, alleging that: (1) the Defendants' policies and practices of denying requests for reasonable accommodations made by persons with disabilities constitutes discrimination against persons with disabilities in violation of the ADA, FHA, and Rehabilitation Act, and (2) by failing to provide a reasonable accommodation for Tsilimparis's disability, the Defendants' termination of their participation in the Program violated the FHA, ADA, and Rehabilitation Act. . . .

Because the Plaintiffs seek to have this Court enjoin a state court proceeding, the Court directed the parties to submit supplemental briefing addressing whether: (1) the Anti–Injunction Act precluded the Court from enjoining the eviction proceeding, and (2) *Younger* abstention warranted the dismissal of the complaint. [The Court proceeded to find that neither the Anti–Injunction Act nor Younger prevented the Court from enjoining the eviction proceeding, and then analyzed each element of the FHA claim].

*   *   *

Whether the Plaintiff was Disabled

A person is considered a "qualified individual" with a disability under the FHA, ADA, and Rehabilitation Acts if that individual (1) has "a physical or mental impairment that substantially limits one or more of the major life activities of such individual;" (2) has "a record of such an impairment;" or (3) is a person "regarded as having such an impairment."

The IHA contends that the Plaintiffs are unlikely to succeed on the merits of their claims because there is insufficient evidence that Tsilimparis suffers from a handicap because "[t]he only allegations made of such a condition are the self serving claims by the plaintiff's [sic] themselves". The Court finds this argument unpersuasive.

Here, the Plaintiffs have submitted affidavits attesting to the nature of their mental disabilities. While this alone would be insufficient, the Plaintiffs also allege that Sinisgallo is a recipient of SSDI based on her status as a permanently disabled paranoid schizophrenic, and Tsilimparis is a recipient of SSI because his bipolar disorder renders him permanently disabled.

[handwritten margin note: receives benefits, proves they are disabled]

The IHA does not dispute that the Plaintiffs receive SSDI and SSI. As a general matter, in most cases, individuals who meet the definition of disability for purposes of receiving SSI or SSDI benefits also qualify as disabled under the federal disability statutes. . . . Furthermore, the Plaintiffs presented a letter from Braddock, a Licensed Master Social Worker, attesting to the fact that Tsilimparis suffers from bipolar disorder and has been treated for his disorder at the South Shore Family Center Clinic since September of 2008. . . . The Court finds that the fact that the Plaintiffs receive SSDI and SSI based on their mental disabilities; the letter from the social worker attesting to Tsilimparis's bipolar disorder and treatment history; and the Plaintiffs' affidavits attesting to their mental disabilities, constitute sufficient proof of qualifying disabilities under the federal disability statutes for the purposes of this motion. Thus, the Court finds that the Plaintiffs are likely to prevail on their claim that they are disabled with the meaning of the federal disability statutes.

Whether the IHA was Aware of the Plaintiffs' Disabilities

Relevant to the Plaintiffs' FHA claim is not only the existence of a disability, but whether the IHA was aware of the disability when making the decision to terminate the tenancy. The relevant date for the purpose of establishing the IHA's knowledge is not when the IHA sent the initial eviction notice, but when the Plaintiffs are actually evicted. . . .

The record reflects that the IHA had knowledge of the Plaintiffs' disabilities prior to commencing the summary holdover proceeding. First, courts have held that, because a housing authority is aware of the source of a public housing tenant's income, a housing authority is on notice of a tenant's disability when they are recipients of SSI or SSDI. *See Boston Hous. Auth. v. Bridgewaters,* 452 Mass. 833, 845, 898 N.E.2d 848, 857–58 (Mass.2009). However, even if the IHA was not aware of the Plaintiffs' disabilities prior to the hearing, the Plaintiffs informed the hearing officer

[handwritten margin note: housing knew of income + why they had benefits]

of the existence of their disabilities and their request for a reasonable accommodation during the hearing and in their post-hearing submissions. The IHA is charged with that same knowledge because it has the power to overturn a hearing officer's decision if it is contrary to HUD regulations or "applicable Federal, State or local law". 24 C.F.R. § 966.57(b)(2).

Thus, the Plaintiffs are likely to prevail on their claim that the IHA was aware of the Plaintiffs purported disabilities prior to the commencement of the eviction proceeding.

Whether there is a Causal Connection Between Tsilimparis's Disability and the Attack on Collins

In addition to being classified as "disabled" under the statutes, the FHA, ADA, and Rehabilitation Act all require a causal nexus between the plaintiff's disability and the underlying basis for terminating the tenancy before the duty to consider a reasonable accommodation arises. Thus, for the Plaintiffs to prevail, they must establish that the attack on Collins is traceable to the alleged handicap of Tsilimparis. . . . The IHA contends that the Plaintiffs' tenancy was "not terminated because of any alleged disability", but rather because Tsilimparis "in an unprovoked attack, struck a neighbor . . . ".

Nevertheless, the Plaintiffs do not now—and did not at the administrative hearing—solely rely on the question of whether the attack was provoked to support a causal link. Rather, the Plaintiffs also rely on an inference created by the letter from Braddock stating that Tsilimparis's medication was adjusted the day after the attack on Collins. They also rely on the fact that, from the date that his medication was readjusted, until the date of the hearing—more than six months—and even until the present—more than one year later—no further incidents have occurred. . . .

no new incidents since adjustment of meds

Although it is a close question, the Court finds that, for the purposes of this motion, the Plaintiffs have shown a causal connection between Tsilimparis's disability and the attack on Collins so that the IHA was required to attempt to reasonably accommodate the Plaintiffs prior to commencing the summary holdover proceeding.

Whether the Plaintiffs Proposed, and the IHA Considered, a "Reasonable Accommodation"

Assuming the Plaintiffs are able to show that they are disabled within the meaning of the statutes, and that the attack on Collins was caused by Tsilimparis's disability, the Plaintiffs must also show that the IHA failed to provide or consider a reasonable accommodation in order to demonstrate a likelihood of success on the merits of their claims under the federal disability statutes. Here, the Plaintiffs assert that the IHA's failure or refusal to accommodate Tsilimparis's disability by providing a probationary period, which the Plaintiffs believe would be a reasonable accommodation, violates the FHA, ADA and the Rehabilitation Act.

The Second Circuit has defined a "reasonable accommodation" as "one that gives the otherwise qualified plaintiff with disabilities 'meaningful access' to the program or services sought." *Henrietta D.,* 331 F.3d at 282 (quoting *Alexander v. Choate,* 469 U.S. 287, 301, 105 S.Ct. 712, 83 L.Ed.2d 661 (1985)). "A defendant must incur reasonable costs and take modest, affirmative steps to accommodate the handicapped as long as the accommodations sought do not pose an undue hardship or a substantial burden."

Where, as here, the disabled plaintiff committed an act of violence in the housing project, the plaintiff "faces a more difficult burden of establishing that [the] request is reasonable" . . . "[S]uch adjustments are ordinarily not *reasonable* accommodations, and therefore are required only in unusual circumstances." Congress did not "intend[ ] accommodations to be attempted or implemented if there is no reasonable expectation that the accommodation will protect the other tenants". However, in order to comply with the relevant statutes "if a handicapped tenant is a direct threat to the health and safety of other tenants, the landlord is obligated to either reasonably accommodate the tenant's handicap or show that no reasonable accommodation will eliminate or acceptably minimize the risk posed by the handicapped tenant". "When the landlord shows that no reasonable accommodation will curtail the risk, its duty to accommodate ceases." Whether a requested accommodation is required by law is "highly fact-specific, requiring case-by-case determination."

Here, the Plaintiffs' proposed accommodation is that the IHA grant them a probationary period to show that the adjustments to Tsilimparis's medication and treatment would prevent him from constituting a direct threat to the safety of his neighbors. . . . This type of "second chance" accommodation . . . has been adopted as a reasonable accommodation by a number of courts. *Super,* 2010 WL 3926887, at *6 ("Courts have accepted a second chance—that is, a tenant's opportunity to remain in her dwelling notwithstanding the landlord's disability-neutral justification for eviction—as an accommodation, provided that it is coupled with the tenant seeking assistance for her disability."). It is undisputed that the IHA has offered no accommodation to the Plaintiffs, nor explained why the proposed accommodation is not reasonable under the circumstances of this case.

However, there is some evidence that the IHA undertook the requisite analysis for determining whether a reasonable accommodation was possible so that Tsilimparis would not constitute a "direct threat". In particular, in its submission at the administrative hearing, the IHA, although predominantly arguing it was not required to provide or consider any reasonable accommodation, set forth its individualized assessment as follows:

> (1) the nature, duration and severity of the risk of injury is great—as stated above it can not be disputed that Mr. Tsilimparis struck Mr. Collins three times with sufficient force to be heard within a nearby apartment. (2) the probability that injury will actually occur is 100%—injury has already occurred; (3) there are no reasonable accommodation that will eliminate the direct threat—short of assigning twenty four security to stand guard over Mr. Tsilimparis there is no manner in which the Housing Authority can prevent another attack.

Although the IHA undertook an assessment, it is unclear whether this assessment satisfies the HUD regulations or sufficiently alleviates its duty to accommodate the Plaintiffs under the federal disability statutes. Absent from the record is the IHA's basis for concluding that the only possible accommodation would be a twenty-four hour security guard, or whether this determination was made in reliance "on current medical knowledge or on the best available objective evidence". 24 C.F.R. § 9.131(c). By contrast, the Plaintiffs have submitted evidence that the proposed accommodation has been found to be reasonable by HUD, the Department of Justice, and other courts; that the medication and treatment of Tsilimparis were adjusted the day after the assault; and that Tsilimparis has not engaged in any further acts of violence since the adjustment to his medication. Thus, for the purposes of this motion, the Plaintiffs have satisfied their burden of showing that they proposed a reasonable accommodation, and the IHA has failed to sufficiently show why the proposed accommodation, or any other accommodation, would not have been reasonable under the circumstances of this case.

Accordingly, the Court finds that the Plaintiffs' have shown a likelihood of success on the merits of their claims under the FHA, ADA, and Rehabilitation Act for the purposes of obtaining preliminary injunctive relief.

Balance of the Equities

. . . Ultimately, the Plaintiffs have sufficiently shown a likelihood of success on the merits of their federal disability claims to warrant injunctive relief. Federal law allows for reasonable accommodations of individuals with mental disabilities and has set forth procedures and guidance to assist housing authorities such as the IHA with determining whether and to what extent an existing tenant is entitled to such an accommodation. The IHA cannot disregard or pay lip-service to federal law before terminating the tenancy of a mentally disabled individual, and the IHA has failed to show that it gave any serious consideration to the Plaintiffs' rights under the federal disability statutes before initiating the summary holdover proceeding.

The Court understands that the IHA is required to consider the safety of all its public housing tenants, and that, if the Plaintiffs ultimately do not prevail, there is a concern that the safety of those tenants will be comprised if the Court does not allow it to proceed with the eviction action. However, the IHA does not dispute that, in the one year after the attack on Collins, neither plaintiff has acted in a violent manner towards any of the tenants. Thus, in this case, the Court finds that the likelihood that the Plaintiffs will prevail on their federal disability claims, and the threat of irreparable injury to the Plaintiffs, outweighs the IHA's concern. Accordingly, the Court finds that a balance of the equities favors granting the Plaintiffs' motion for preliminary injunctive relief.

[handwritten margin note: Plaintiff > IHA's concern]

CONCLUSION

For the foregoing reasons, it is hereby:

ORDERED, the Plaintiffs' motion for a preliminary injunction is granted, and it is further,

ORDERED, that the IHA is enjoined from proceeding with the state court summary holdover action pending the outcome of the instant case.

QUESTIONS AND COMMENTS

1. *The structure of an FHAA argument.* As this case illustrates, the analysis under the FHAA tracks the analysis under the ADA. On the disability issue in *Sinisagallo*, did the plaintiffs provide enough proof of a disability that limited a major life activity? Should receipt of Social Security benefits suffice? When, if ever, should the testimony of a non-medically trained social worker be relevant on the disability issue? If, as the court intimates, IHA was not aware of the disability until the hearing, should a discrimination claim lie? On the qualification/accommodation issue, is the plaintiff a "direct threat"? (Consider the research on the violent tendencies of people with serious mental illness and the tendency of people on anti-psychotic medication to stop their medication, on pp. 821–824). Should the fact that Tsilimparis was not involuntarily committed be dispositive on this issue? If he was a threat, can the threat be accommodated in a way that does not impose an undue hardship on IHA, given its concern about harm to other tenants? How many chances should a tenant like Tsilimparis get as an accommodation? Should the answer to that question depend on the type of mental problem that underlies the threat? Cf. *Stout v. Kokomo Manor Apartments*, 677 N.E.2d 1060 (Ind.Ct.App. 1997) (holding that the defendant need not provide housing for a person convicted of child molestation because he posed a "direct threat to the health or safety of other individuals").

2. *Other accommodations.* Courts routinely consider requests under the FHAA for accommodations that violate the typical rental agreement. See, e.g., *Association of Apartment Owners of Liluokalani Gardens at Waikiki v. Taylor*, 892 F.Supp.2d 1268 (D. Hawai'i, 2012) (denying summary judgment

for defendant, who claimed that disabled plaintiff's "companion animal" was an unreasonable accommodation in light of apartment's no-pet policy); *Douglas v. Kriegsfeld Corp.*, 884 A.2d 1109 (D.C. Oct 13, 2005) (overturning jury verdict for defendant, who had claimed that plaintiff's accommodation request that she be allowed to stay in a filthy apartment if the city helped clean it was unreasonable, over a dissent noting that the plaintiff had persistently failed to take her medication and clean her apartment, resulting in prolonged "unsanitary, unhealthy, and unlawful conditions"); *United States v. California Mobile Home Park Management Co.*, 29 F.3d 1413 (9th Cir. 1994) (reversing dismissal of a case brought by a plaintiff who argued that the defendant should lower the usual parking fee for long-term guests in her case because of her need for a home health aide).

3.   *Alternative housing.* If people like Tsilimparis and Sinisgallo are evicted, where could they go? One goal of the FHAA is to provide alternatives to institutions and group homes which, as previous materials suggested, are not always ideal living arrangements for people with mental disabilities (see pp. 1312–1313). If people with mental disability do end up in a group home, the FHAA has something to say about that as well, as the next case illustrates.

OXFORD HOUSE, INC. v. TOWN OF BABYLON

United States District Court, E.D. New York, 1993.
819 F.Supp. 1179.

Amended Order

WEXLER, DISTRICT JUDGE.

Pursuant to the Fair Housing Act, 42 U.S.C. § 3601 et seq. ("FHA"), Oxford House, Inc. ("Oxford House") and Gary and Geri Erichson ("the Erichsons"), plaintiffs in the above referenced action, seek to enjoin the Town of Babylon ("Town" or "defendant") from evicting persons with handicaps (also referred to as "plaintiffs") from their residence at 73 East Walnut Avenue, East Farmingdale, New York. Now before the Court is plaintiffs' motion for partial summary judgment pursuant to Rule 56 of the Federal Rules of Civil Procedure on the ground that the Town violated the Fair Housing Act because its proposed eviction of plaintiffs has a disparate impact on persons with handicaps; or, in the alternative, because the Town failed to make reasonable accommodations in its zoning ordinances as may have been necessary to afford plaintiffs an equal opportunity to enjoy housing in the Town. For the reasons discussed below, plaintiffs' motion for partial summary judgment is granted.

I.   BACKGROUND

Oxford House was founded in 1975 by a group of men who were recovering from drug and/or alcohol addiction. Today there are 375 individual "Oxford Houses" which are operated on the same premise as the original. * * * [The court then describes how the Oxford House at issue in this case was set up.] The house is owned by the Erichsons, and is located in a residential district in the Town, which is zoned for single family dwellings only.

Shortly after the lease was signed, neighbors complained to Town officials that recovering alcoholics were living in their community. On September 3, 1991, a Town meeting was held to discuss the new residents. This was followed by a letter from the Town Attorney to the representatives of Oxford House, alleging that the house in East Farmingdale was in violation of the Multiple Dwelling Code because the residents were not a family.[3] On or about September 6, 1991, Oxford House requested that the Town make a reasonable accommodation in the application of its zoning ordinance so that the residents could continue living there. The Town has never responded.

On or about September 17, 1991, the Town Board authorized the Town attorney to commence appropriate litigation, including injunctive relief and contempt proceedings, to evict the residents of the East Farmingdale Oxford House. That same day, plaintiffs filed this action to enjoin the Town from carrying out its resolution.

* * *

II.   DISCUSSION

* * *

B.   Overview of the Fair Housing Act

Under the FHA, it is unlawful to discriminate in the sale or rental, or to otherwise make unavailable or deny a dwelling to any buyer or renter because of a handicap. 42 U.S.C. § 3604(f)(1). A person is handicapped if he or she has a mental or physical impairment. 42 U.S.C. § 3602(h). It is well established that individuals recovering from drug or alcohol addiction are handicapped under the FHA. * * * A plaintiff can establish a violation under the FHA by proving the disparate impact of a practice or policy on a particular group, *Huntington Branch, NAACP v. Town of Huntington*, 844 F.2d 926, 933 (2d Cir.), *aff'd*, 488 U.S. 15, 109 S.Ct. 276, 102 L.Ed.2d 180 (1988), or by showing that the defendant failed to make reasonable accommodations in rules, policies, or practices so as to afford people with disabilities an equal opportunity to live in a dwelling. 42 U.S.C. § 3604(f)(3)(B). Once an FHA violation is established, the plaintiff is entitled to injunctive relief.

[handwritten margin notes: "Addiction = handicap" and "test"]

---

[3] The Town of Babylon Multiple Dwelling Code § 153–13 states that a family is one or more persons related by blood, marriage, or adoption. It may also be a number of unrelated persons, not exceeding four, who are not related by blood, marriage or adoption. The East Farmingdale Oxford House accommodates from five to eight individuals.

C.   Plaintiff's Claim that the Town's Zoning Ordinance Has a Disparate Impact on People with Handicaps

To establish a prima facie case under the disparate impact analysis, a plaintiff must prove that the challenged practice "actually or predictably" results in discrimination. Once the plaintiff establishes a prima facie case, the burden shifts to the defendant to prove that "its actions furthered, in theory and in practice, a legitimate, bona fide governmental interest and that no alternative would serve the interest with less discriminatory effect."

In the end, the court must balance the plaintiff's showing of discriminatory impact against the defendant's justifications for its conduct. When conducting this balance, two factors weigh heavily in the plaintiffs' favor: (1) evidence of discriminatory intent on the part of the defendant; and (2) evidence that the plaintiff is seeking only to require a municipal defendant to eliminate an obstacle to housing rather than suing to compel it to build.

Plaintiffs in the present case have set forth evidence to establish that the Town's proposed eviction actually or predictably results in discrimination. The Town asserts that the Oxford House facility is not permitted at 73 East Walnut Avenue because the residents are not a "family" or the "functional and factual equivalent of a natural family." Under § 213–1 of the Town Code, a "family" is a group of persons related by "kinship, adoption, blood or marriage." The "functional and factual equivalent of a natural family" is defined as a "single housekeeping unit" bearing the same characteristics as a biological family, including a stable non-transient existence. The Town maintains that because plaintiffs are transients, they do not function as a family unit, and can therefore be evicted pursuant to the Town Code.

Applying § 213–1 of the Town Code to evict plaintiffs would discriminate against them because of their handicap. Recovering alcoholics or drug addicts require a group living arrangement in a residential neighborhood for psychological and emotional support during the recovery process. As a result, residents of an Oxford House are more likely than those without handicaps to live with unrelated individuals. Moreover, because residents of an Oxford House may leave at any time due to relapse or any other reason, they cannot predict the length of their stay. Therefore, a finding of a violation of the Town Code leading to the town's eviction of plaintiffs from a dwelling due to the size or transient nature of plaintiffs' group living arrangement actually or predictably results in discrimination.

Once the plaintiff establishes a prima facie case, the burden shifts to the defendant to prove that its actions furthered a legitimate governmental interest and that there were no less discriminatory alternatives . . . Defendant in the present case asserts that the ordinance is designed to keep boarding houses, rooming houses, multiple family dwellings, and other similar arrangements out of residential neighborhoods. The Town contends that it enforces the ordinance against all violators; the enforcement of the ordinance furthers a legitimate governmental interest in maintaining the residential character of the areas zoned for single family dwellings; and any discriminatory effect it may have on plaintiffs is due to plaintiffs' transiency and failure to live as a family, not because of their handicap.

Although a town's interest in zoning requirements is substantial, *see Village of Belle Terre v. Boraas*, 416 U.S. 1, 94 S.Ct. 1536, 39 L.Ed.2d 797 (1974), the Court finds that evicting plaintiffs from the East Farmingdale Oxford House is not in furtherance of that interest. Five Town officials testified that the Town has received no substantial complaints from plaintiffs' neighbors within the past year. Furthermore, the house is well maintained and does not in any way burden the Town or alter the residential character of the neighborhood. The presence of the East Farmingdale Oxford House in a single family, residential district does not undermine the purpose of the Town's zoning ordinance. Therefore, defendant cannot justify evicting plaintiffs as being in furtherance of its asserted governmental interest.

Even if the Town's proposed enforcement of its zoning ordinance advances a legitimate governmental interest, the Court nevertheless finds that plaintiffs' showing of discriminatory effect far outweighs the Town's weak justifications. Although the plaintiff is not required to prove discriminatory intent in order to show discriminatory effect, in balancing disparate impact against a governmental interest, evidence of such intent weighs heavily in the plaintiff's favor . . . Plaintiffs in the present case have set forth substantial evidence to indicate that the Town had the intent to evict them because they were recovering alcoholics.

On September 3, 1991, a public meeting was held to discuss the East Farmingdale Oxford House. So many neighbors came to the meeting that Supervisor Pitts suspended the normal rules. These neighbors were "hostile" to it, expressing their fears regarding the safety of children and senior citizens. No one from the community or the Town Board spoke in favor of the East Farmingdale Oxford House.

*   *   *

After the Town meeting, the Town attorney sent a letter to Oxford House asserting that plaintiffs did not comport with the definition of a "family" in the Multiple Dwelling Code. Next, the Town alleged that the East Farmingdale Oxford House violated the Town Code because it was a "boarding house or the house of transients." The Town presently contends that plaintiffs are in violation of the Town Code because they are not a "family" or the "functional and factual equivalent of a natural family."

The statements made at the Town Board meeting, in conjunction with the shifting bases for eviction asserted by the Town, indicates that the Town wants to evict plaintiffs because they are recovering alcoholics.

Furthermore, in *Huntington Branch, NAACP*, the court held that where the plaintiff was not suing to require the municipal defendant to build housing, but rather to remove an obstacle to housing, the defendant needs to establish a more substantial justification for its conduct. *Huntington Branch, NAACP*, 844 F.2d at 936. Plaintiffs in the present case merely seek to require the Town to permit them to continue to use housing which already exists. This is another factor which weighs heavily in plaintiffs' favor. Accordingly, because there is no genuine issue of material fact as to whether the Town's conduct actually or predictably has a discriminatory effect on plaintiffs due to their handicap, and the showing of discriminatory effect far outweighs defendant's justifications for its predisposition, plaintiffs' motion for partial summary judgment is granted.

D.   Plaintiffs' Claim that the Town Failed to Make Reasonable Accommodations Necessary to Permit Handicapped Persons to Use and Enjoy a Dwelling

Even if the Town's proposed eviction of plaintiffs does not have a disparate impact on handicapped persons, the Court nevertheless finds that defendant's conduct constituted discrimination as it is defined in 42 U.S.C. § 3604(f)(3)(B). Under the FHA, it is a discriminatory practice to refuse to make "a reasonable accommodation in rules, policies, practices, or services when such accommodation may be necessary to afford [a handicapped] person equal opportunity to use and enjoy a dwelling." 42 U.S.C. § 3604(f)(3)(B). Courts have unanimously applied the reasonable accommodations requirement to zoning ordinances and other land use regulations and practices.

In the present case, plaintiffs requested that the Town modify the definition of a "family" as it was applied to them. Plaintiffs have demonstrated that as recovering alcoholics and drug addicts, they must live in a residential neighborhood because an Oxford House "seeks to provide a stable, affordable, and drug-free living situation so as to increase the likelihood that a person will stay sober." In *Township of Cherry Hill*, the court held that the location of the houses in a drug-free, single family neighborhood played a crucial role in an individual's recovery by "promoting self-esteem, helping to create an incentive not to relapse, and avoiding the temptations that the presence of drug trafficking can create." *Township of Cherry Hill*, 799 F.Supp. at 450. This Court finds that reasoning persuasive. Because an Oxford House cannot exist in a single family, residential district under the Town Code, a modification of the definition of a "family" in plaintiffs' situation is warranted so that they may have the same opportunity to rent a house as do persons without handicaps.

Plaintiffs have also established that the requested accommodation was reasonable. An accommodation is reasonable under the FHA if it does not cause any undue hardship or fiscal or administrative burdens on the municipality, or does not undermine the basic purpose that the zoning ordinance seeks to achieve. Because one of the purposes of the reasonable accommodations provision is to address individual needs and respond to individual circumstances, courts have held that municipalities must change, waive, or make exceptions in their zoning rules to afford people with disabilities the same access to housing as those who are without disabilities.

[handwritten margin note: Accomodation/Reasonableness test]

As discussed above, the East Farmingdale Oxford House has no adverse effect on the residential character of the neighborhood that the Town Code seeks to preserve. Moreover, neither the operation of the house nor the residents themselves have caused any financial or administrative burdens on the Town. Consequently, the Court finds that the requested accommodation was reasonable and defendant's failure to make such accommodation was discriminatory conduct. Accordingly, even if the Court did not find that defendant's conduct had a disparate impact on plaintiffs, there is nevertheless no genuine issue of material fact with regard to defendant's violation of 42 U.S.C. § 3604(f)(3)(B), and plaintiffs' motion for partial summary judgment would be granted on this ground as well.

III. CONCLUSION

Accordingly, for the foregoing reasons, plaintiffs' motion for partial summary judgment pursuant to Rule 56 of the Federal Rules of Civil Procedure is granted and defendant is enjoined from taking any further steps to evict plaintiffs from the East Farmingdale Oxford House.

SO ORDERED.

QUESTIONS AND COMMENTS

1. *The relevance of community opposition to group homes for people with mental disability.* The community reaction encountered by Oxford House in the above case is typical.

> Residents regularly oppose the establishment of group homes in residential neighborhoods. One study found that group home providers experience at least some initial neighborhood opposition in seventy-two percent of selected locations. Frequent concerns include fear of decreased real estate values, poorly maintained property, and criminal behavior. However, studies suggest that group homes do not negatively affect property values. In fact, one recent study actually found that the development of group homes in Denver had a positive effect on the

values of nearby single-family homes. Other studies indicate that group homes do not tend to generate undue increases in traffic or noise, and that residents of group homes demonstrate lower crime rates than the general population.

Even when confronted with information suggesting that group homes do not exhibit significant negative externalities, skeptical neighbors often claim their neighborhood is different. In part, this response is attributable to a preference to avoid interactions with disabled people, based on stereotypes, fear, and stigma. These reactions are buttressed by broadly held public perceptions that people with mental disabilities are dangerous, and the best treatment for them is large-scale institutionalization.

Stephen F. Hayes, *The 'Usual Incidents of Citizenship': Rethinking When People with Disabilities Must Participate in Public Variance Proceedings*, 109 Colum. L. Rev. 2044, 2064–65 (2009). Is this type of reaction "irrational," in the constitutional sense (see *City of Cleburne v. Cleburne Living Center*, discussed in Part I of this Chapter). If the town had been able to show that a violent incident had been perpetrated by a member of the home or that group homes are not as therapeutic as single-family residences, should that change the equal protection analysis? To what extent should reasoning in FHAA cases like *Sinisgallo* affect this analysis?

2.   *Drug and alcohol addiction.* Similar types of questions can be asked under the FHAA itself. For instance, as *Town of Babylon* indicates, persons undergoing treatment for drug or alcohol abuse are covered by the FHAA. However, the FHAA excludes from coverage those who are "actively using illegal drugs." 42 U.S.C. § 3604(f)(9) Does that mean as soon as one member of the group home uses illegal drugs, the town can ban the group home?

3.   *Disparate treatment v. disparate impact.* If the claim under the FHAA is a disparate treatment challenge, the burden on the plaintiff may be identical to the burden in constitutional cases—that is, the plaintiff may have to show the defendant is irrationally biased against people with disability. *See, e.g., Oxford House–C v. City of St. Louis*, 77 F.3d 249, 252 (8th Cir.1996); but see *Bangerter v. Orem City Corporation*, 46 F.3d 1491 (10th Cir.1995) (facially discriminatory treatment of people with mental disability is justified only if (1) it was based on specific concerns about safety or (2) it actually benefitted the disabled). However, most FHAA cases involving zoning laws are disparate impact cases; that is, as in *Town of Babylon*, the challenged ordinance is neutral on its face but the plaintiff argues that it has an adverse impact on people with disability. In disparate impact cases, the plaintiff need merely make out a prima facie case of adverse impact, at which point the burden shifts to the defendant to show, as the *Babylon Town* court states, that "its actions further, in theory and in practice, a legitimate, bona fide governmental interest and that no alternative would serve the interest with less discriminatory effect." Yet the FHAA also lightens the government's burden in this regard by exempting from its coverage "reasonable local, State, or Federal restrictions regarding the maximum number of occupants

permitted to occupy a dwelling." 42 U.S.C. § 3607(b)(1). Does that exemption apply in *Town of Babylon* (see note 5 of the opinion)?

In *City Of Edmonds v. Oxford House, Inc.*, 514 U.S. 725, 115 S.Ct. 1776, 131 L.Ed.2d 801 (1995), another case involving a group home for people recovering from substance abuse, the Supreme Court may have answered that question. There the Court stated that "rules that cap the total number of occupants in order to prevent overcrowding of a dwelling 'plainly and unmistakably' fall within [the FHA exemption]; rules designed to preserve the family character of a neighborhood, fastening on the composition of households rather than on the total number of occupants living quarters can contain, do not." It then held that the city's ordinance limiting the number of unrelated individuals living in a house to five fit in the latter category (without deciding whether the group home, which housed 10–12 unrelated people, could ultimately be banned under the FHAA). What type of ordinance is involved in *Town of Babylon*?

4.   *Spacing requirements.* Ordinances that require facilities for people with mental disability to be located a minimum distance apart from one another have also been the subject of FHAA-based challenges. These disparate treatment challenges have had mixed success. In *Familystyle of St. Paul v. City of St. Paul*, 923 F.2d 91 (8th Cir.1991), the Eighth Circuit held that a state statute and local zoning ordinance which required that homes for people with mental disability be located at least a quarter of a mile apart did not violate the FHAA. According to the court, the ordinance furthered Minnesota's deinstitutionalization policy, which called for all persons with mental illness to live in settings that "maximize community integration and opportunities for acceptance." *Id.* at 93. By contrast, in *Larkin v. State of Michigan Department of Social Services*, 89 F.3d 285 (6th Cir.1996), the court struck down a 1500–foot spacing requirement. The court reasoned that "integration is not a sufficient justification for maintaining permanent quotas under the FHA . . . " *Id.* at 291. While the *Familystyle* court applied a rational basis test to evaluate the defendant's justifications for its discriminatory treatment, the *Larkin* looked at whether the defendant could demonstrate that its discriminatory treatment was " 'warranted by the unique and specific needs and abilities of those handicapped persons' to whom the regulations apply." *Id.* at 290 (citation omitted). Is there any rational basis for concluding that locating homes for people with mental disability a quarter mile apart "maximizes community integration," as the *St. Paul* case holds?

APPENDIX A

EXCERPTS FROM CRITERIA FOR SELECTED DIAGNOSES IN DSM-5[1]

■ ■ ■

NEURODEVELOPMENTAL DISORDERS

Intellectual Disability[2]

A. Deficits in intellectual functions (e.g., reasoning, problem solving, abstract thinking, or learning) observed in clinical assessment and formal intelligence testing.[3]

B. Deficits in adaptive functioning: the person does not meet age-appropriate developmental and sociocultural standards for personal independence and responsibility. Without others' help, deficits limit functioning in one or more activities of daily life (e.g., communication, social participation, independent living) across several settings (home, school, work).

C. Onset during the developmental period.[4]

In DSM-5, severity of an intellectual disability is coded by considering the individual's deficits in conceptualization, socialization, and practical functioning.[5] The following chart gives examples from severity levels in adults:

---

[1] Because most cases excepted in this book refer to diagnoses and criteria used in older DSMs, comments about major changes from DSM-IV-TR appear in footnotes.

[2] Replaces "Mental Retardation"

[3] Previously, this criterion was defined in terms of an IQ below 70 on standardized testing.

[4] Previously, onset was specified as before age 18 years.

[5] Previously, the severity or level of mental retardation was coded based on IQ test scores: mild (scores of 50–55 to approximately 70); moderate (scores of 35–40 to 50–55); severe (scores of 20–25 to 35–40); profound (scores 20 or 25).

Severity	Conceptual	Social	Practical
Mild	Limited memory and strategic ability; concrete thinking	Limited and concrete communication; immature social judgment	May work in jobs that do not require conceptual skills; needs help with major decisions
Moderate	Needs daily assistance with conceptual tasks in everyday life	Problems perceiving social cues; needs help with many choices; needs social and communicative support in work settings	Needs much support to manage work tasks, transportation, scheduling, money, and for adult-level participation in household
Severe	Throughout life, caretakers provide extensive support for problem solving	Understands simple speech and gestures; communication focuses on here-and-now events	Needs ongoing assistance in home, recreation, and work; skills are learned after long-term teaching
Profound	May use objects for self-care; sensorimotor impairments may limit functioning	Very limited speech; enjoys well-known family; uses gestural and emotional cues	Relies on others for daily physical care; may assist with simple tasks; enjoys outings with support

Attention-Deficit/Hyperactivity Disorder

A. The diagnosis requires: having six or more symptoms from categories 1 and/or 2 below; these symptoms have lasted for at least 6 months; the symptoms are present to a degree that is inconsistent with the person's developmental level and adversely affect social or occupational activities; the symptoms do not stem from oppositional behavior, defiance, hostility, or failure to understand instructions.

    1. **Inattention:** Six or more of the following:

        a. often fails to give close attention to details or makes careless mistakes in schoolwork, work, or other activities.

        b. often has difficulty sustaining attention in tasks or play activities.

    c. often does not seem to listen when spoken to directly.

    d. often does not follow through on instructions and fails to finish schoolwork, chores, or workplace duties.

    e. often has difficulty organizing tasks and activities.

    f. often avoids, dislikes, or is reluctant to engage in tasks that require sustained mental effort (schoolwork, preparing reports, reading lengthy documents).

    g. often loses things necessary for tasks or activities (e.g., school assignments, pencils, books, paperwork, tools, or telephones).

    h. is often easily distracted by extraneous stimuli.

    i. is often forgetful in daily activities (e.g., chores, errands, appointments).

2. **Hyperactivity and impulsiveness:** Six or more of the following:

    a. often fidgets with hands or feet or squirms in seat.

    b. often leaves seat in situations (e.g., classroom, workplace, office) where remaining seated is expected.

    c. often runs about or climbs excessively in situations where this is inappropriate (in adolescents or adults, may be limited to subjective feeling of restlessness).

    d. often cannot play or engage in leisure activities quietly.

    e. is often "on the go" or acts as if "driven by a motor" (may be experienced by others as restless or hard to keep up with).

    f. often talks excessively.

    g. often blurts out answers before questions have been completed (e.g., completes others' sentence; cannot take turns in conversation).

    h. often has difficulty waiting his or her turn (e.g., in line).

    i. often interrupts or intrudes on others (e.g., butts into conversations or games).

B. Several hyperactive-impulsive or inattentive symptoms were present before age 12 years.

C. Several symptoms are evident in two or more settings (e.g., at school [or work], with friends, and at home).

D. The symptoms clearly interfere with or reduce the qualities of social, academic, or occupational functioning.

E. The symptoms do not occur exclusively during the course of a psychotic disorder and are not better accounted for by another mental order (e.g., a mood disorder, anxiety disorder, dissociative disorder, intoxication, or personality disorder).

SCHIZOPHRENIA SPECTRUM AND OTHER PSYCHOTIC DISORDERS

SCHIZOPHRENIA[6]

A. Two or more of the following signs or symptoms; each is present for a significant portion of time during a one-month period (or less if successfully treated); at least one of the symptoms must be 1, 2, or 3:

1. delusions.

2. hallucinations.

3. disorganized speech (e.g., frequent derailment or incoherence).

4. grossly disorganized or catatonic behavior.

5. negative symptoms, i.e., diminished emotional expression or avolition.

Schizoaffective Disorder

A. An uninterrupted period of illness during which there is a major mood (manic or depressive) episode [see below for criteria for these diagnoses], concurrent with symptoms that meet Criterion A for schizophrenia.

B. At some point during the illness, delusions lasting for at least 2 weeks in the absence of symptoms of a major mood episode.

C. Symptoms that meet criteria for a major mood episode are present during most of the active and residual portions of the illness.

Delusional Disorder

A. Delusion for at least one month.[7]

---

[6] DSM-5 does away with subtypes of schizophrenia that appeared in previous DSM editions, but which ultimately proved to have low diagnostic reliability and validity. These subtypes were:

Paranoid: Preoccupation with delusions or frequent auditory hallucinations, without much disorganization in speech or thought, and without flattened or inappropriate affect.

Disorganized: disorganized speech and behavior; flat or inappropriate affect.

Catatonic: motoric immobility or excessive motor activity (that is apparently purposeless); extreme negativism (motiveless resistance to instructions, maintenance of a rigid posture) or mutism; posturing, stereotyped movements, prominent mannerisms, or prominent grimacing; echolalia or echopraxia.

Undifferentiated: symptoms that meet Criterion A are present, but the criteria for the above three subtypes are not satisfied.

[7] Criterion A no longer states (as did DSM-IV) that the delusions must be "nonbizarre," that is, something that is physically possible or involves situations that could occur in real life, such as being followed, poisoned, infected, loved at a distance, deceived by spouse or lover, or having a disease.

B. Criterion A for schizophrenia has never been met. Note: hallucinations, if present, are not prominent and are related to the delusional theme.

C. The person's functioning and behavior are not markedly impaired apart from the direct influence of the delusion.

The type of delusional disorder is based on the predominant delusional theme:

Erotomanic: that another person (often of higher status) is in love with the individual.

Grandiose: having great (but unrecognized) talent or insight, or having make some important discovery.

Jealous: that the individual's spouse or lover is unfaithful.

Persecutory: that the person is being conspired against, harassed, obstructed, followed, or malevolently treated in some way.

Somatic: the delusion involves body functions or sensations.

Mixed: no single theme predominates.

Unspecified Type: the dominant delusional theme cannot be clearly determined or is not included among the specific subtypes above.

Brief Psychotic Disorder

A. Presence of one (or more) of the following symptoms; 1, 2, or 3 must be present:

1. delusions.

2. hallucinations.

3. disorganized speech (e.g., frequent derailment or incoherence).

4. grossly disorganized or catatonic behavior.

Note: Do not include a symptom if it is a culturally sanctioned response pattern.

B. Duration of an episode of the disturbance is at least 1 day but less than 1 month, with eventual full return to one's premorbid level of functioning.

BIPOLAR AND RELATED DISORDERS[8]

Bipolar I Disorder

Making this diagnosis requires that, at some point during the course of illness (which may include periods of depression), the individual's symptoms have met the criteria for a **manic episode**, which is:

---

[8] Previously, bipolar disorders appeared in a broad category of "mood disorders" along with syndromes characterized only of depressive symptoms.

A. A distinct period of abnormally and persistently elevated, expansive, or irritable mood and abnormally and persistently increased energy or activity, lasting at least 1 week (or any duration if hospitalization is necessary).

B. During the period of mood disturbance and increased energy/activity, three or more of the following symptoms (four or more if the mood is only irritable) have been present to a significant degree and represent a noticeable change from usual behavior:

   1. inflated self-esteem or grandiosity.

   2. decreased need for sleep (e.g., feels rested after only 3 hours of sleep).

   3. more talkative than usual or pressure to keep talking.

   4. flight of ideas or subjective experience that thoughts are racing.

   5. distractibility (i.e., attention is drawn too easily to unimportant or irrelevant stimuli).

   6. increase in goal-directed activity (either socially, at work or school, or sexually) or psychomotor agitation (purpose, non-directed activity).

   7. excessive involvement in activities that have a high potential for painful consequences (e.g., unrestrained buying sprees, sexual indiscretions, or foolish business investments).

C. The mood disturbance is severe enough to cause marked impairment in functioning or to necessitate hospitalization, or the episode includes having psychotic symptoms (e.g., delusional thinking and/or hallucinations).

Bipolar II Disorder

To receive this diagnosis, an individual's symptoms must have met criteria for a previous or current episode of depression (explained below, in the section on depressive disorders) and a previous or current episode of hypomania. The criteria for a **hypomanic episode** are the same as those for a manic episode, except that a hypomanic need last only 4 days and does not lead to severe impairment in functioning or hospitalization.

DEPRESSIVE DISORDERS

Disruptive Mood Dysregulation Disorder[9]

A. Recurrent, severe temper outbursts (e.g., verbal rages or physical aggression toward people or objects) that are grossly out of proportion to the provocation or circumstances.

B. The outbursts are not consistent with the developmental level.

C. The outbursts occur, on average, at least three times a week.

D. Between outbursts, the individual's mood is irritable or angry most of the day, every day.

E. Criteria A–D have been met for at least a 12-month period during which the individual had no period longer than 3 months in which all the criteria were not satisfied.

F. Criteria A and D are met in a least two settings (home, school, and with peers) and are severe in at least one setting.

G. The diagnosis should not be made for the first time in children less than 6 years old nor after a person has reached age 18 years.

H. The onset of symptoms satisfying Criteria A–E occurred before age 10 years.

I. The person has never had a period of more than one day during which criteria for mania or hypomanic were satisfied.

Major Depressive Disorder

A. Five (or more) of the following symptoms have been present during the same 2-week period and represent a change from previous functioning; at least one of the symptoms is either (1) depressed mood or (2) loss of interest or pleasure. Note: Do not include symptoms that are clearly due to a general medical condition.

　1. depressed mood most of the day, nearly every day, as indicated by either subjective report (e.g., feels sad, empty, or hopeless) or others' observations (e.g., appears tearful). **Note:** In children and adolescents, can be irritable mood.

　2. markedly diminished interest or pleasure in all, or almost all, activities most of the day, nearly every day (as indicated by either subjective account or others' observations.

　3. significant weight loss when not dieting or weight gain (e.g., a change of more than 5% of body weight in a month), or decrease or

---

[9] This is a new diagnosis, added to address widespread concerns that under previous diagnostic schemes, children and adolescents with persistent irritability and frequent, severe problems with self-control were being incorrectly diagnosed as having—and were incorrectly being treated for—bipolar disorder.

increase in appetite nearly every day. Note: In children, consider failure to make expected weight gains.

4. trouble sleeping or sleeping too much nearly every day.

5. psychomotor agitation or retardation nearly every day (observable by others, not merely subjective feelings of restlessness or being slowed down).

6. fatigue or loss of energy nearly every day.

7. feeling worthless, or feeling excessive or inappropriate guilt (which may be delusional) nearly every day (not merely self-reproach or guilt about being sick).

8. diminished ability to think or concentrate, or indecisiveness, nearly every day (either by subjective account or as observed by others).

9. recurrent thoughts of death (not just fear of dying), recurrent suicidal ideation without a specific plan, or a suicide attempt or a specific plan for committing suicide.

Persistent Depressive Disorder[10]

A. Depressed mood for most of the day, for more days than not, as indicated either by subjective account or others' observations, for at least 2 years. Note: In children and adolescents, mood can be irritable and duration must be at least 1 year.

B. Presence, while depressed, of two (or more) of the following:

1. poor appetite or overeating.

2. insomnia or hypersomnia.

3. low energy or fatigue.

4. low self-esteem.

5. poor concentration or difficulty making decisions.

6. feelings of hopelessness.

C. During the 2-year period (1 year for children), the person has never been without the symptoms in Criteria A and B for more than two months at a time.

---

[10] What DSM-IV called "dysthymia" now falls under this category, which includes both chronic depression and the previous dysthymic disorder. The scientific rationale for this combination was an inability to find meaningful differences between these two conditions.

ANXIETY DISORDERS

Panic Disorder

A. Recurrent, unexpected panic attacks. A panic attack is an abrupt surge of intense fear or discomfort that reaches a peak within minutes and in which four or more of the following symptoms occur:

1. palpitations, pounding heart, or accelerated heart rate.

2. sweating.

3. trembling or shaking.

4. sensations of being short of breath or smothering.

5. feelings of choking.

6. chest pain or discomfort.

7. nausea or abdominal distress.

8. feeling dizzy, unsteadly, lightheaded, or faint.

9. chills or heat sensations.

10. paresthesias (numbness or tingling sensations).

11. derealization (feelings of unreality) or depersonalization (being detached from oneself).

12. fear of losing control or "going crazy."

13. fear of dying.

B. At least one of the attacks was followed by a period of a month or more in which the person had one of both of these symptoms:

1. Persistent concern or worry about additional panic attacks or their consequences (e.g., fear of having a heart attack)

2. A significant, maladaptive change in behavior related to the attacks (e.g., avoiding situations or types of activities to avoid having another attack)

Social Anxiety Disorder (Social Phobia)

A. Marked fear or anxiety about one or more social situations in which the person is exposed to possible scrutiny by others. Examples: having a conversation, meeting unfamiliar people, being observed eating, or giving a speech. Note: In children, the anxiety must occur in peer settings, not just in interactions with adults.

B. The individual fears that he or she will act in a way or show anxiety symptoms that will be evaluated negatively (i.e., will be humiliating or embarrassing, will lead to rejection, or will offend others).

C. The socials situation almost always provoke fear or anxiety. Note: In children, the fear or anxiety may be expressed by crying, tantrums, freezing, clinging, shrinking, or failing to speak.

D. The social situations are avoided or else are endured with intense fear or anxiety.

E. The fear or anxiety is out of proportion to the sociocultural context and to any actual threat posed by the social situation.

F. The fear, anxiety, or avoidance is persistent (typically lasting 6 months or more).

G. The fear, anxiety, or avoidance causes clinical significant distress or impairment in social, occupational, or other important areas of functioning.

TRAUMA- AND STRESSOR-RELATED DISORDERS[11]

Posttraumatic Stress Disorder[12]

Criteria for persons older than age six years:[13]

A. Exposure to actual or threatened death, serious injury, or sexual violence in one of more of the following ways:

  1. Directly experiencing the traumatic event(s).

  2. Witness the event(s) in person, as it occurred to others.

  3. Learning that a violent or accidental traumatic event(s) occurred to a close family member or close friend.

  4. Experiencing repeated or extreme exposure to aversive details of the traumatic event(s) (e.g., first responders collecting human remains).

B. One of more of the following intrusion symptoms associated with the traumatic event(s):

  1. Recurrent, involuntary, and intrusive distressing memories of the event(s).

  2. Recurrent, distressing dreams of which the content of or feelings in the dream are related to the event(s).

---

[11] A new subsection in DSM-5, this grouping includes some conditions that previously were listed as anxiety disorders.

[12] PTSD criteria in DSM-5 criteria differ substantially from the DSM-IV criteria. How the person experience the trauma is spelled out in more detail, and the person's subjective reaction was eliminated. Two symptom clusters in DSM-IV—reexperiencing and arousal—are retained in DSM-5, but the previous avoidance/numbing cluster is split into avoidance symptoms and persistent negative alterations in cognitions and mood. The "negative alterations" category includes most of the numbing symptoms in DSM-IV but adds new or reconceptualized emotional states. Irritable or aggressive behavior and reckless or self-destructive behavior are now included as possible evidence of altered emotional arousal and reactivity.

[13] Younger children have separate criteria not reprinted here.

3. Dissociative reactions (e.g., flashbacks) in which the individual feels or acts as if the event(s) were recurring.

4. Intense or prolonged distress at exposure to cues that symbolize or resemble an aspect of the event(s).

5. Marked emotional reactions to cues that resemble or symbolize an aspect of the event(s).

C. Persistent avoidance of stimuli associated with the traumatic event(s), evidence by either of the following:

1. Avoidance or efforts to avoid distressing memories, thoughts, or feelings related to the event(s).

2. Avoidance or efforts to avoid reminders (people, places, things, situations, activities) of the event(s).

D. Negative alterations or cognitions and mood associated with the traumatic event(s), evidenced by two or more of the following:

1. Inability to remember an important aspect of the traumatic event(s).

2. Persistent and exaggerated negative beliefs or expectations about oneself, others, or the world (e.g., "my whole nervous system is ruined," "the world is dangerous").

3. Persistent, distorted cognitions about the cause or consequences of the event(s) that lead to self-blame.

4. Persistent negative emotional state (e.g., fear, horror, anger, guilt)

5. Markedly diminished interest or participation in activities.

6. Estrangement or detachment from others.

7. Persistent inability to experience positive emotions (e.g., happiness, satisfaction, affection).

E. Marked alterations in arousal and reactivity associated with the traumatic event(s), evidenced by two or more of the following:

1. Irritability and angry outbursts.

2. Reckless or self-destructive behavior.

3. Hypervigilance.

4. Exaggerated startle response.

5. Problems with concentration.

6. Problems with sleeping (e.g., difficulty falling or staying asleep).

DISSOCIATIVE DISORDERS

Dissociative Identity Disorder

A. Experiencing two or more distinct personality states, described in some cultures as an experience of being possessed. This disruption in identity involves marked discontinuity in one's sense of self and agency, and is accompanied by related alterations in affect, behavior, consciousness, memory, perception, thinking, or sensorimotor functioning. These phenomena may be observed by others or reported by the individual.

B. Recurrent gaps in recall of everyday events, important personal information, or traumatic events that go beyond ordinary forgetfulness.

C. The symptoms cause distress or impairment in functioning.

D. The disturbance is not a normal part of a broadly accepted cultural practice.

E. The disturbance is caused by the physiological effects of a substance (e.g., blackouts or chaotic behavior during alcohol intoxication) or another medical condition (e.g., complex partial seizures).

DISRUPTIVE, IMPULSE–CONTROL, AND CONDUCT DISORDERS

Intermittent Explosive Disorder

A. Recurrent behavioral outbursts, manifested in either of the following ways:

   1. Verbal aggression (e.g., temper tantrums, tirades, arguments) or physical aggression toward property, animals, or other persons, occurring twice a week on average, for a period of 3 months. The physical aggression does not damage property or physically injure other persons.

   2. Within a 12-month period, three behavioral outbursts involving damage or destruction of property and/or physical assault involving physical injury to animals or other persons.

B. The magnitude of the aggressiveness during the outbursts is grossly out of proportion to the provocation or precipitating incident.

C. The aggression is not premeditated, but is impulsive or anger-based, and it is not committed to achieve some tangible result (e.g., money, power, intimidation).

D. The outbursts are not better explained as symptoms of another mental disorder (e.g., bipolar disorder), another medical condition (e.g., Alzheimer's disease), or an intoxicant (e.g., alcohol). Note: the diagnosis may be rendered despite the presence of ADHD, conduct disorder, oppositional defiant disorder, or autism when the outbursts are in excess of those usually associated with these conditions and warrant separate clinical attention.

Kleptomania

A. Recurrent failure to resist urges to steal objects that are not needed for personal use or for their monetary value.

B. Increasing sense of tension immediately before the theft.

C. Pleasure, gratification, or relief at the time of the theft.

D. The stealing is not committed to express anger or vengeance and is not a response to a delusion or a hallucination.

SUBSTANCE-RELATED AND ADDICTIVE DISORDERS

Gambling Disorder[14]

A. Persistent, recurrent, problematic gambling that leads to significant impairment or distress. At least four of the following characteristics are present in a 12-month period:

1. Need to gamble with increasing amounts of money to achieve a desired level of excitement.

2. Restlessness or irritability when trying to limit or stop gambling.

3. Repeated, unsuccessful attempts to limit, control, or stop gambling.

4. Preoccupation with gambling (e.g., thoughts of reliving past gambling experiences, planning the next venture, thinking of ways to get money to gamble).

5. Often gambling when distressed (e.g., when feeling helpless, guilty, or depressed).

6. After losing money gambling, often returns another day to get even ("chasing" losses).

7. Lying to conceal extent of gambling.

8. Has jeopardized or lost a significant relationship, job, or educational or career opportunity because of gambling.

9. Relying on others for money to get out of desperate financial situations caused by gambling.

B. The gambling behavior is not better explained as part of a manic episode.

---

[14] DSM-IV listed the diagnosis of "pathological gambling" in the section on disorders of impulse control. In DSM-5, gambling disorder appears in the section on substance-related and addictive disorders, a change that reflects evidence that gambling and drugs of abuse activate the brain reward system in similar ways and that symptoms of gambling disorder to some extent resemble symptoms of substance use disorders.

PERSONALITY DISORDERS

A personality disorder is an enduring pattern of inner experience and behavior that deviates markedly from the expectations of the individual's culture, is pervasive and inflexible, has an onset in adolescence or early adulthood, is stable over time, and leads to distress or impairment.

The following personality disorders are included in the chapter. [Full criteria are provided only for a few disorders.]

- **Paranoid personality disorder** is a pattern of distrust and suspiciousness such that others' motives are interpreted as malevolent.

- **Schizoid personality disorder** is a pattern of detachment from social relationships and a restricted range of emotional expression.

- **Schizotypal personality disorder** is a pattern of acute discomfort in close relationships, cognitive or perceptual distortions, and eccentricities of behavior.

- **Antisocial personality disorder** is a pattern of disregard for, and violation of, the rights of others.

- **Borderline personality disorder** is a pattern of instability in interpersonal relationships, self-image, and affects, and marked impulsivity.

- **Histrionic personality disorder** is a pattern of excessive emotionality and attention seeking.

- **Narcissistic personality disorder** is a pattern of grandiosity, need for admiration, and lack of empathy.

- **Avoidant personality disorder** is a pattern of social inhibition, feelings of inadequacy, and hypersensitivity to negative evaluation.

- **Dependent personality disorder** is a pattern of submissive and clinging behavior related to an excessive need to be taken care of.

- **Obsessive-compulsive personality disorder** is a pattern of preoccupation with orderliness, perfectionism, and control.

- **Personality change due to another medical condition** is a persistent personality disturbance that has resulted from the direct effects of a medical condition (e.g., frontal lobe damage).

- **Other specified personality disorder and unspecified personality disorder** is a category reserved for situations in which the individual's personality pattern meets the general criteria for a personality disorder and:

1) exhibits traits of several different personality disorders but the pattern does not satisfy criteria for any specific personality disorder; or

2) the individual displays characteristics of a personality disorder that is not listed in DSM-5 (e.g., passive-aggressive personality disorder).

Schizoid Personality Disorder

A. A pervasive pattern of detachment from social relationships and a restricted range of expression of emotions in interpersonal settings, as indicated by four or more of the following traits:

1. neither desires nor enjoys close relationships, including being part of a family.

2. almost always chooses solitary activities.

3. has little, if any, interest in having sexual experiences with another person.

4. takes pleasure in few, if any, activities.

5. lacks close friends or confidants other than first-degree relatives.

6. appears indifferent to the praise or criticism of others.

7. shows emotional coldness, detachment, or flattened affectivity.

B. These characteristics do not occur exclusively during the course of schizophrenia, a mood disorder with psychotic features, another psychotic disorder, or autism spectrum disorder, they do not stem from the direct physiological effects of another medical condition.

Schizotypal Personality Disorder

A. A pervasive pattern of social and interpersonal deficits marked by acute discomfort with, and reduced capacity for, close relationships as well as by cognitive or perceptual distortions and eccentricities of behavior, as indicated by five or more of the following:

1. ideas of reference (excluding delusions of reference).

2. odd beliefs or magical thinking that influences behavior and is inconsistent with subcultural norms (e.g., superstitiousness, belief in clairvoyance, telepathy, or "sixth sense"; in children and adolescents, bizarre fantasies or preoccupations).

3. unusual perceptual experiences, including bodily illusions.

4. odd thinking and speech (e.g., vague, , metaphorical, overelaborate, or stereotyped).

5. suspiciousness or paranoid thinking.

6. inappropriate or constricted affect.

7. behavior or appearance that is odd, eccentric, or peculiar.

8. lack of close friends or confidants other than first-degree relatives.

9. excessive social anxiety that does not diminish with familiarity and tends to be associated with paranoid fears rather than negative judgments about self.

B. Does not occur exclusively during the course of schizophrenia, a mood disorder with psychotic features, another psychotic disorder, or an autism spectrum disorder.

Antisocial Personality Disorder

A pervasive pattern of disregard for and violation of the rights of others, occurring since age 15 years, as indicated by three or more of the following:

1. failure to conform to social norms with respect to lawful behavior, as indicated by repeatedly performing acts that are grounds for arrest.

2. deceitfulness: repeated lying, use of aliases, or conning others for personal profit or pleasure.

3. impulsiveness or failure to plan ahead.

4. irritability and aggressiveness: repeated physical fights or assaults.

5. reckless disregard for safety of self or others.

6. consistent irresponsibility: repeated failure to sustain consistent work behavior or honor financial obligations.

7. lack of remorse: indifferent to or rationalizing having hurt, mistreated, or stolen from another.

Other diagnostic requirements: the individual must be at least 18 years old, the individual met diagnostic criteria for conduct disorder by the age of 15 years, and the antisocial behavior has not occurred only while the individual suffered from schizophrenia or was experiencing a manic episode.

Borderline Personality Disorder

A pervasive pattern of unstable interpersonal relationships, self-image, and emotions, plus marked impulsiveness, as indicated by five or more of the following:

1. frantic efforts to avoid real or imagined abandonment. Note: Do not include suicidal or self-mutilating behavior covered in Criterion 5.

2. unstable and intense interpersonal relationships that alternate between extremes of idealization and devaluation.

3. identity disturbance: markedly and persistently unstable self-image or sense of self.

4. Impulsiveness of at least two types that is potentially self-damaging (e.g., spending, sex, substance abuse, reckless driving, binge eating). Note: Do not include suicidal or self-mutilating behavior covered in Criterion 5.

5. recurrent suicidal behavior, gestures, or threats, or self-mutilating behavior.

6. affective instability due to a marked reactivity of mood (e.g., intense episodic dysphoria, irritability, or anxiety usually lasting a few hours and only rarely more than a few days).

7. chronic feelings of emptiness.

8. inappropriate, intense anger or difficulty controlling anger (e.g., frequent displays of temper, constant anger, recurrent physical fights).

9. transient, stress-related paranoid ideation or dissociation.

Narcissistic Personality Disorder

A pervasive pattern of grandiose fantasies or behavior, need for admiration, and lack of empathy, as indicated by five or more of the following:

1. a grandiose sense of self-importance (e.g., exaggerates achievements and talents, expects to be recognized as superior without commensurate achievements).

2. preoccupation with fantasies of unlimited success, power, brilliance, beauty, or ideal love.

3. believing that one is "special" and unique and can only be understood by, or should associate with, other special or high-status people (or institutions).

4. needs excessive admiration.

5. feels entitled, i.e., anticipates getting especially favorable treatment or automatic compliance with his or her expectations.

6. is interpersonally exploitative, i.e., takes advantage of others to achieve his or own ends.

7. lacks empathy: is unwilling to recognize or identify with the feelings and needs of others.

8. envy of beliefs that others are envious.

9. arrogant, haughty behaviors or attitudes.

Dependent Personality Disorder

A pervasive and excessive need to be cared for that leads to submissive, clinging behavior and fear of separation, indicated by five or more of the following:

1. difficulty making everyday decisions without an excessive amount of advice and reassurance from others.

2. needing others to assume responsibility for most major areas of his or her life.

3. difficulty expressing disagreement with others because of fear of loss of support or approval. Note: Do not include realistic fears of retribution.

4. difficulty initiating things on his or her own because of a lack of self-confidence in judgment or abilities, rather than a lack of motivation or energy.

5. going to excessive lengths to obtain nurturance and support from others, to the point of volunteering to do things that are unpleasant.

6. feeling uncomfortable or helpless when alone because of exaggerated fears of being unable to care for himself or herself.

7. urgently seeking another relationship as a source of care and support when a close relationship ends.

8. unrealistically preoccupation with fears of being left to take care of oneself.

INDEX

References are to Pages